Project Manager: Ruston Anne Drach
Senior Acquisitions Editor: Jonathan Joyce
Acquisitions Editor: Jay Campbell
Custom Product Development Editor: Salimah Perkins
Manager of Health Professions Marketing: Shauna Kelley
Senior Marketing Manager: Leah Thomson
Manufacturing Coordinator: Margie Orzech
Design Coordinator: Stephen Druding

<u>Content Source Titles for CSK 100 – Study Skills & CAT 150 – Anatomy, Physiology, and Terminology:</u>

Published by Wolters Kluwer
Philadelphia, PA 19103
Copyrights by Lippincott Williams & Wilkins, a business of Wolters Kluwer

<u>Content Source Title for CMF 95 – Math Fundamentals:</u>

2nd Custom Edition ISBN: 978-1-4963-7379-3

Printed in China

<u>Disclaimer:</u>

Wolters Kluwer

When you have to be right

Career Prep

2nd Custom Edition

CSK 100 – Study Skills

CMF 95 – Math Fundemantals

CAT 150 – Anatomy, Physiology, and Terminology

PIMA MEDICAL INSTITUTE®

Trusted. Respected. Preferred.

<u>Content Source Titles:</u>

LWW's Student Success for Health Professionals Made Incredibly Easy, Second Edition
Tom Lochhaas, Contributing Writer

Introduction to Health Care & Careers
by Roxann DeLaet, RN, MS

Introductory Mathematics: Concepts with Applications
by Charles P. McKeague, BA, MS

Medical Terminology: An Illustrated Guide, Eighth Edition
by Barbara Janson Cohen, MEd & Ann DePetris, RN, MSA, CCRP

Reviewers

Gloria Chatfield, BS, LMT
Pima Medical Institute
Career Prep Instructor
Colorado Springs, CO Campus

Nelsy Chavoya
Pima Medical Institute
Career Prep Instructor
Chula Vista, CA Campus

Carri Enright
Pima Medical Institute
Lead Career Prep Instructor
Renton, WA Campus

Dr. Natalia Kakorina, MD
Pima Medical Institute
Career Prep Instructor
Albuquerque, NM Campus

Holly Lough
Pima Medical Institute
Career Prep Instructor
Chula Vista, CA Campus

Dan McCants
Pima Medical Institute
Medical Assistant Instructor
Seattle, WA Campus

Veronica Perez, RMA, AHI
Pima Medical Institute
Lead Career Prep Instructor
Albuquerque West, NM Campus

Bianca Servin, BS, MA
Pima Medical Institute
Lead Career Prep Instructor
Mesa, AZ Campus

Gulzar Siddiqui
Pima Medical Institute
Lead Career Prep Instructor
Denver, CO Campus

Jen Spurlin
Pima Medical Institute
Corporate Education Department
Regulatory Affairs Coordinator
Tucson, AZ

Dr. Mark Woolley
Pima Medical Institute
Lead Career Prep Instructor
Las Vegas, NV Campus

Contents

NOTE: Some chapters are intentionally missing, as their content was not applicable to the course objectives. This will also affect the ordering of some part and page numbers.

CSK 100 - Study Skills

LWW's Student Success for Health Professionals Made Incredibly Easy
Second Edition

Introduction to Health Care & Careers
by Roxann DeLaet

CMF 95 - Math Fundamentals

Introductory Mathematics: Concepts with Applications
by Charles P. McKeague

CAT 150 – Anatomy, Physiology & Terminology

Medical Terminology: An Illustrated Guide, Eighth Edition by
Barbara Janson Cohen & Ann DePetris

Contents
User's Guide

CAT 150 – Anatomy, Physiology & Terminology

Introduction to Health Care & Careers
by Roxann DeLaet
Contents
User's Guide
Part V - Essentials of Human Anatomy and Physiology

CSK 100
Study Skills

Content Source Titles:

LWW's Student Success for Health Professionals Made Incredibly Easy, Second Edition
Tom Lochhaas, Contributing Writer

and

Introduction to Health Care & Careers
by Roxann DeLaet, RN, MS

LWW's
STUDENT SUCCESS FOR
HEALTH PROFESSIONALS
Made Incredibly Easy

Second Edition

TOM LOCHHAAS
Contributing Writer

 Wolters Kluwer

Contents

PART TWO
SHARPENING YOUR SKILLS

User's Guide

To reach their career goals, health professions students will travel through an obstacle course of classes, skills practice labs, and clinical rotations or externships. *Student Success for Health Professionals Made Incredibly Easy* is designed to help students through this process with practical study tips that will make them confident and successful students—as well as valuable members of the health professions team—by helping them understand the rules of the game and the skills and strategies they need to win it.

Student Success for Health Professionals Made Incredibly Easy uses the popular "Incredibly Easy" style to make learning enjoyable with a light hearted, humorous approach to presenting information. Hope, a health professions instructor, guides students through the book, offering helpful tips and insights. Along the way, she gets help from three health professions students: Amy, Anthony, and Leslie. Even when the tone is light, however, the concepts and tips are quite serious!

Hi, my name is Hope, and I'm your guide to success as a health professions student.

HOW THIS BOOK IS ORGANIZED

Student Success for Health Professionals Made Incredibly Easy is designed to be enjoyable to read, as well as highly informative. The book is divided into three parts:

- Part One presents basic principles for student success. Chapter 1 helps students get focused on academic success by setting their goals and anticipating obstacles. Chapter 2 focuses on managing one's time as a student—a skill that is increasingly important in today's hectic world. Chapter 3 covers basic issues related to health and well-being as a student, including how to prevent stress from hindering academic success. Chapter 4 then discusses the all-important world of interacting with others as a student, including getting to know instructors, networking with other students, and celebrating diversity.

- Part Two helps students sharpen their skills through several chapters focused on learning style and critical thinking (Chapter 5); improving listening, note-taking, and reading skills (Chapter 6); strengthening one's communication skills, including speaking and writing (Chapter 7); mastering effective

Congratulations on choosing the health professions for your career! I'm Amy.

study skills (Chapter 8); and conquering tests (Chapter 7). All these chapters contain practical guidelines and tips for sharpening skills that will serve students well both in school and in their careers thereafter.

- In Part Three, Chapter 12 explores how students can build on all their student success skills in the workplace—and the job application skills needed to get there.

Welcome, I'm Anthony. Glad you're joining the health professions team!

SPECIAL FEATURES

Each chapter of *Student Success for Health Professionals Made Incredibly Easy* includes special features designed to engage students with the topics and guide them in their study. Each can be identified by its unique icon:

Winning Strategy–kicks off each chapter with a list of objectives.

 **Playing for Real**–lets health professions students discuss how they put success tips into practice.

 **Tips from the Pros**–highlights important tips for student success.

 **The Finish Line**–wraps up each chapter with a summary of the key points.

 Keeping Score–presents review and critical thinking questions, along with chapter activities.

In addition to these features, *Student Success for Health Professionals Made Incredibly Easy* includes both useful and practical illustrations and fun cartoons. The appendix contains answers to review and critical thinking questions.

Hi, I'm Leslie. You're off to a great start by using this book!

ADDITIONAL RESOURCES

In addition to the text, the following resources are available for students:

- A **Student's Resource Website** with printable note-taking guides for each chapter, printable calendar pages for effective time management, sample health professions cover letters and résumés, and other student activities including a self-paced online course with quizzes and a final exam!

All resources are available on the following companion website: http://thepoint.lww.com/StudentSuccess2e

PRINCIPLES OF STUDENT SUCCESS

CHAPTER 1

Focusing on Success

WINNING STRATEGY

On completion of this chapter and the learning activities you will be able to:

- List your reasons for wanting to continue your education

- Describe some obstacles that might limit your success as a student

- Understand why a positive attitude matters for success

- Practice staying motivated and focused on your studies

- Know the importance of goals

- Differentiate between short-term and long-term goals

- Set goals for yourself and make a plan of action to accomplish them

- Describe the three traits of good academic character

Way to go! By opening the pages of this book, you've taken a big first step toward your goal of continuing your education. In fact, you've already shown that you're motivated to succeed as a student!

The decision to continue your education may not have been an easy one to make. Maybe you haven't always had positive experiences with school. Or maybe you're worried about whether you'll have the time, energy, or money to stick with it. These concerns are normal—they're also shared by many of your classmates. By using the strategies explained in this chapter, you can gain confidence and sharpen your focus. Zeroing in on what you really want to get out of school will help you stay in the race and cross the finish line.

In this chapter, you'll take the first steps toward becoming a successful student. You'll think about why you're here—your dreams, the courage you've shown, the choices you've made, and the obstacles you've faced so far. You'll learn about what motivates you and about how to keep a positive attitude and stay motivated and focused. Most importantly, you'll learn how to set and achieve your goals while following other tips that will help you succeed in school. As a key part of success, you'll also learn the importance of maintaining a good academic character.

WHY YOU'RE HERE

You may have just graduated from high school or perhaps you're returning to school after several years to start a new career. But, regardless of your age or experience, why is it important to think about your reasons for going to school? Because these reasons are where you'll find your motivation during those late night study sessions if you become tired and discouraged. Yes, even the best of students get tired and discouraged sometimes! And those are the times when it is most important to remember why you wanted to do this in the first place.

Taking a few minutes to be totally honest with yourself and really think about why you're here will give you a sense of purpose. A purpose that's personal and important to you will help you set goals for yourself. With real and reachable goals, you'll be more likely to succeed.

Student success means more than just passing your classes and earning your degree or program certificate. "Success," as it will be discussed throughout this book, also includes developing all the characteristics of a professional ready to practice in your chosen field. If that sounds like a lot, don't worry! This book will help you every step of the way.

Thinking about why you're here gives you reasons to go after your dreams.

Dreams

What kinds of dreams have led you to this point? Maybe you're interested in finding a career you truly enjoy. Or maybe, you'd simply like to learn more about a subject that appeals to you. There are several reasons why people choose to continue their education. Do you have dreams of:

- improving your lifestyle? You may be the first in your family to attend college. If so, congratulations! The knowledge and skills you'll learn in school will give you more career choices.

- supporting your family? You may come from a single-parent home or you may be a single parent yourself. The ability to provide for your loved ones is an important dream to pursue.

- gaining self-respect? You may wish to continue your education to feel accomplished. Careers in health care provide both dignity and respect and are fulfilling work.

Whatever your dreams may be, they have brought you this far. Hold onto them and help yourself reach them by creating a plan for success!

Courage

It takes courage to pursue your dreams. You've already shown courage just by being here! Stepping into the unknown is never easy, but you have taken the first step. Right now, school may seem full of unknowns. If so, know that you're not alone. Many students feel this way at first.

The best way to overcome a fear of the unknown is to become familiar with it. This book will answer questions you may have about school. You also will learn simple strategies to help you succeed as a student.

Remember that it takes courage to do something you've never done before. Taking this leap to continue your education will fully prepare you for other exciting things in your future.

Choices

By choosing to continue your schooling, you are making your own path in life. It takes strength to make your own life choices and to work hard for what you want. Just as you've made a decision to continue your education, you can choose to have a positive attitude and be a successful student as well.

OBSTACLES YOU MAY FACE

It becomes easier to overcome obstacles when you're able to recognize them. You may have overcome obstacles in getting this far. Let's explore this.

- What kinds of things have discouraged you in the past?
- How have people in your life helped or hurt your dream of going to school?
- What life experiences have influenced the way you see yourself?
- Do you foresee any obstacles in completing your education now?
- Do you feel confident you will be able to continue overcoming obstacles?
- Have you made a plan to overcome the obstacles you may face?

Recognizing the obstacles you've faced in the past will give you confidence to face future difficulties. You're probably stronger than you think! Although it may not be fun to face challenges, you can benefit from your experiences. If athletes never challenged themselves, there would be no championship games or world record holders. Overcoming obstacles helps you see your true potential.

Starting with this chapter, this book will help you develop student success skills to overcome both personal and academic obstacles that may arise between now and graduation.

INGREDIENTS FOR SUCCESS: ATTITUDE AND MOTIVATION

Self-image affects your attitude and motivation. These two things are very important to your success as a student. If you feel good about yourself and have confidence, it is easier to develop a positive attitude and the motivation to learn.

Liking Yourself as a Student

Of all of the factors that affect how well one does educationally, attitude is probably the single most important. A positive attitude leads to motivation and someone who is strongly motivated to succeed can overcome obstacles and succeed when others might give up or accept doing lower quality work. Your attitude toward education begins with your attitude toward yourself as a student. You may not have realized it yet, but you have become a new person. You're not just the same old person who happens now to be taking courses.

What do you think of this new person? Do you like him or her?

If you're feeling excited and enthusiastic, capable and confident in your new life, great! But if you are feeling any doubts, take comfort in knowing that you're not alone. A lot of new students worry, "I'm not a good enough student" or "I can't keep up with all this." Some may become fearful or apathetic.

An attitude that is less than positive, however, can hinder your motivation and ability to succeed. If you think you can't make it, that might become true. This is called a "self-fulfilling prophecy," and psychologists have shown it happens often. For example, if you do not do well on a particular test, you might start thinking you're not very good with that class. Once you feel that way, your studying will be less productive, your attitude will be less positive and enthusiastic, and you'll set lower expectations for yourself. All these factors, then may lead to your not doing well on the next test; also, you will have made your own prophecy come true. But, on the other hand, if you tell yourself that you just weren't fully prepared for that first test but will do very well on the next, then your attitude and enthusiasm will contribute to more productive studying and you'll very likely do quite well. In the same way, you'll have made your positive prophecy come true!

If you sometimes have negative thoughts about being a student, think about why that is. Are you just reacting to getting a low grade on some test? Are you just feeling this way because you see other students who look like they know what they're doing and you're feeling out of place?

Some students also fall into a "victim mentality"—blaming their circumstances or other people if they are not successful. This is a kind of negative attitude that sets one up for failure. After all, if it's someone else's fault that things are difficult, then you can't expect to do well. Watch out for this kind of psychological trap! Now that you're in school pursuing your education, you have the same opportunities as others and can succeed on your own abilities once you know how.

The main reason why some students find it hard to succeed in their studies is that they haven't fully developed the right skills for succeeding in their education. So cheer up! You're on the right track right now to learn everything you need to succeed. This book will help you learn these skills—everything from how to study effectively, how to do better on tests, even how to read your textbooks more effectively.

Just remember that it all begins with a good attitude about yourself as a student. Remember your purpose—why you enrolled in your school or program to begin with—and stay enthusiastic.

Does Your Attitude Need a Boost?

Your attitude often determines your performance in school. It's reflected in how much interest you take in your studies or how meaningful your work is to you. If you have a positive attitude about school, you will be better able to:

- figure out your responsibilities in the learning process
- set learning goals for yourself
- study for your classes in a more effective way
- improve your grades and performance as a student

What attitude do you currently have about learning? Find out by looking at some positive and negative examples of feelings about school. (See *Attitude Check*.)

Motivation is related to attitude and just as important. It's what makes you want to accomplish a task. As a student, the right motivation can help you:

- get started on projects and assignments
- meet deadlines without last minute stress

The secrets to becoming a successful student are having a positive attitude and staying motivated.

- move closer to your goals
- keep working on tasks until you succeed

Throughout this book, you'll learn how to motivate yourself to be a successful student, starting with the next section.

Attitude Check

Is your learning attitude positive or negative?

Positive	*Negative*
• I'm good at studying. I focus well.	• It's hard for me to study. I get distracted easily.
• I enjoy learning new things no matter what the subject may be.	• I enjoy learning only about subjects that interest me.
• It's easy for me to learn new information.	• It's hard for me to process new information.
• If the instructor doesn't tell me what to study, I'll develop my own studying strategy.	• If the instructor doesn't tell me what to study, I'm often lost.
• I'm confident that I can learn and succeed.	• I'm doubtful about my ability to learn and succeed.
• I have a support system of family, friends, and coworkers—and I rely on them often!	• I don't like to ask people for help and I don't have a good support system.
• I exercise my mind, as well as my body, on a regular basis.	• I don't have time to exercise and I'd rather watch TV than read a book.
• I consider myself an optimist.	• I consider myself a pessimist.

If you have more negative traits than positive, don't be discouraged! Recognizing a negative attitude is the first step toward changing it.

ATTITUDE READJUSTMENT

If you find it difficult sometimes to maintain a positive attitude, there are many things you can do to help get back on track. Here are just a few that have proven to work:

- *Talk positively to yourself.* We all have conversations with ourselves. You might not have been successful on a test and start saying to yourself, "I'm just not smart enough" or "That teacher is so hard, no one could pass that test." The problem when we talk to ourselves this way is that we listen—and we start believing what we're hearing. Then our attitude becomes negative. Instead, have upbeat conversations with yourself. Say, "I've been paying attention in class and doing my homework and I just know I'm going to ace that test!"

- *Spend time with positive people.* If you notice that the people you're hanging out with tend to complain a lot and blame others for their problems, it's time for a change. Spend some time with other students who are happy with themselves as students. A positive attitude is contagious! It's also more fun to be with people who are upbeat and enjoying life.

- *Overcome resistance to change.* You're no doubt very busy in your new life and probably many things have changed for you. Sometimes we're slow to accept change and our attitude can become negative if we're always looking back. Consider instead your positive changes: the exciting and interesting people you're meeting, the education you're getting that will lead to a bright future, and the challenges and stimulation you're feeling every day. The first step in overcoming resistance to change may be simply to see yourself succeeding in your new life. Visualize yourself as a student taking control, enjoying classes, studying effectively, and getting good grades.

- *Overcome fears.* One of the most common fears students have is a fear of failure—of not making the grade. Life is not all roses and we all know we won't succeed at everything we try—and everyone has fears. The question is what one does about it. If you worry about not succeeding, turn that fear around and use it in a positive way. If you're afraid you may not do well on an upcoming exam, don't mope around. Instead, sit down and schedule your studying well ahead of time. Think of all the times you've been successful and tell yourself you'll do it again now. With that attitude adjustment, you'll more easily find you can!

Hey! It's still half full!

You're more successful when you're upbeat about things.

Your Cheering Section

As a student beginning a new education, it's important to surround yourself with people who love and support you. A strong support system helps you maintain a winning attitude. And a winning attitude will put you ahead of the game in school!

To become a successful student, seek out support from people and resources such as:

- friends and family
- coworkers
- other students
- campus discussion groups
- instructors and tutors
- academic advisors
- student support services
- campus resources (libraries, computer labs, writing centers, etc.)

To maintain good relationships, be sure to discuss with your family and friends how things are changing while you're in school. Because of your new schedule, you may find that you need extra help with household chores or running errands. If you have young children, be sure to explain your schedule changes to them as well. Let your family and friends know that these demands on your time aren't permanent and that you're going to need their help while you're in school. Make these discussions positive and upbeat so that your family and friends feel good about how they're supporting your success as a student!

Working hard is easier when you have people to cheer you on!

Uncertainty, Fear, Discouragement— Stop the Cycle!

If you feel uncertain or fearful about school, you won't perform as well and then you'll feel even more discouraged. This becomes a self-reinforcing cycle that can spiral further downward. By developing a positive attitude about learning, however, you can replace this with a cycle of self confidence, strong performance, and success. Here's how:

- Take responsibility for your education. Don't simply rely on others to teach you. If a class becomes difficult, ask for help! Your instructor, a tutor, or a classmate may be able to explain difficult concepts.

- Be an active learner. Ask questions about things that interest you. Look for ways to expand your education beyond time spent in the classroom.

- Decide what you want to learn from each course. Evaluate what courses you are enjoying most and, if you identify an area of difficulty, you may want to think about whether a particular degree or certificate plan is right for you. (In Chapter 10, you'll learn how to match your interests and abilities with the right health care career.)

Stress can be another cause of discouragement. When it seems like you have too much work to do and not enough time, stress can be overwhelming. Everyone experiences stress at one point or another. The good news is that there are many different ways of handling stress. Choose a method that works best for you. How well you manage stress will determine how much it affects your performance as a student. When stress is managed well overall, small amounts of stress actually help you stay focused and complete tasks. Don't let stress control you. Instead, take control of stress! (Chapter 3 provides some tips for managing stress.)

You Can Do It!

To avoid discouragement, stay motivated. Use whatever motivates you to stay focused on succeeding in school. Your motivation may come from within yourself (intrinsic) or from outside benefits (extrinsic). Although intrinsic motivation generally can be more powerful and longer lasting (because *you* really want to accomplish the task), extrinsic motivation is also a powerful force. Take the Motivation Quiz to find out what motivates you to learn. (See *Motivation Quiz.*)

Motivation Quiz

1. I spend time studying for my courses because . . .
   a. I truly enjoy learning new information.
   b. I want to improve my grades and test scores.
2. I've chosen to go to school because . . .
   a. I want to excel at something.
   b. it will help me get a better job and a higher salary.
3. Going to school demonstrates to others that . . .
   a. I'm willing to take risks.
   b. I have an impressive résumé.
4. Learning new things . . .
   a. satisfies my curiosity.
   b. shows others I can get the job done.
5. I'm continuing my education because . . .
   a. I'm very interested in the subjects I'm studying.
   b. I'm looking forward to future promotions in my career.

If you answered mostly a's, then you're intrinsically motivated. If you answered mostly b's, then you're extrinsically motivated. If you answered a combination of a's and b's, then you're motivated in many different ways!

THE FUN PART: CHOOSING YOUR MOTIVATORS

Once you know how you are motivated, you can choose your motivators. A motivator is a reward you promise yourself for completing a task. Choose one and then reward yourself for your hard work.

When choosing which motivators to use for school, think about the tasks you accomplish outside school. Where does your motivation come from? For example, if you volunteer at a homeless shelter once a month, what motivates you? Do you help out because it makes you feel good about yourself? Do you like to talk with the people you meet there? Do you enjoy helping others?

Understanding where your motivation comes from will help you choose effective motivators for school. If you are intrinsically motivated, it may be enough to know that you accomplished a task—and that you're moving steadily toward your long-term goal. If you are extrinsically motivated, you may want to promise yourself a more concrete reward. This can be as simple as having a nice snack after studying, enjoying a movie on the weekend, or buying a new laptop after successfully completing the academic term.

My motivation for working out is the reward of something sweet every once in a while!

HOW TO STAY MOTIVATED

Okay, you've got a positive attitude. You're psyched! But you've got a lot of reading to do for classes to do tonight, a test tomorrow, and a paper due the next day. Maybe you're a little bored with one of your reading assignments. Maybe you'd rather play a computer game. Uh oh—now what? One of the interesting things about attitude is that it can change at almost any moment.

One of the characteristics of people who are successful is that they accept that interruptions will happen and plan ahead. Staying focused does not mean you become a boring person who does nothing but go to class and study all the time. You just need to make a plan.

Planning ahead is the single best way to stay focused and motivated. Don't wait until the night before an exam, for example. If you know you have a major exam in 5 days, start by reviewing the material and deciding how many hours of study are needed. Then schedule those hours spread over the next few days at times when you are most alert and least likely to be distracted. You also allow for time to see friends, see a movie, or surf the Web for a while to relax, rewarding yourself for your successful studying.

When the exam comes, you're relaxed, you know the material, you're in a good mood and confident, and you do well. You stayed focused and planned well and you had some fun along the way. Most important, you're maintaining a cycle of positive attitude and successful performance!

Planning is mostly a matter of managing your time well. We'll look at specific ways to do that in the next chapter. Here are some other tips for staying focused and motivated:

- If you're not feeling motivated, remind yourself why you're taking these classes. Remember the exciting career you're preparing for.

- Say it aloud—to yourself or a friend—with a positive attitude: "I'm going to study now for another hour before I take a break—and I'm getting an A on that test tomorrow!" It's amazing how saying something aloud helps you feel committed.

- Remember your successes, even small successes. As you begin a project or start studying for a test, think about your past success on a different project or test. Remember how good it feels to succeed.

- Focus on the here and now. For some people, looking ahead to goals, or to anything else, may lead to daydreaming that keeps them from focusing on what they need to do right now. Don't be too concerned about what you're doing tomorrow or next week or month.

- If you just can't focus in on what you know you should be doing because the task seems too big and daunting (like sitting down to study for a final exam), break the task into smaller, manageable pieces. Don't start out thinking, "I need to study for the next 4 hours" (a plan that might feel depressing to many students), but think, "I'll spend the next 30 minutes going through my class notes from the last 3 weeks and figure out what topics I need to spend more time on." It's a lot easier to stay focused when you're sitting down for 30 minutes at a time.

- Never, ever try to multitask while studying! You may think that you can monitor email and send text messages while studying, but in reality, these other activities lower the quality of your studying and lower your motivation.

It's easier to stay focused if you avoid distractions. Get away from your computer and phone—try the library!

- Imitate successful people. Does a friend always seem better able to stick with studying or work until they get it done? What are they doing that you're not? *Visualize yourself* studying in the same way and getting that same high grade on the test or paper.

- Give yourself a reward when you complete a significant task—but only when you are done. Some people stay focused better when there's a reward waiting.

- Get the important things done first. When you're not feeling motivated, it's easy to decide you need to do your laundry instead of studying. Although cleanliness is important, this is a form of procrastinating and trying to fool yourself into feeling you're accomplishing something by doing laundry. Stay focused!

Tips for Staying Motivated

- Keep your eye on your long-term goals to stay motivated with immediate tasks.
- Keep your priorities straight—but also save some time for fun.
- Keep the company of positive people; imitate successful people.
- Don't let past negative or less effective habits drag you down.
- Plan well ahead to avoid last minute pressures.
- Focus on your successes.
- Break large projects down into smaller tasks or stages.
- Reward yourself for completing significant tasks.
- Avoid multitasking.
- Network with other students; form a study group.

BONUS BENEFITS

While motivating yourself to do well in school, you'll be accomplishing other things along the way. These long-term rewards may include:

- the ability to apply your study skills to other areas of your life
- a greater understanding of the course material
- confidence and an improved self-image
- better grades and test scores
- stronger performance in classes in the future
- better options in terms of salary and career

Motivating yourself as a student is a win–win situation. Not only will you be successful in school, but you'll be collecting short-term and long-term rewards along the way.

The Balancing Act

You need to focus on your studies to do well in school. Worrying about money, your job, or other distractions can hurt your progress as a student. It can be difficult trying to balance all aspects of your life.

If you need to balance going to school with working full- or part-time, have patience with yourself. You can take courses at a pace that fits with your work schedule. You can learn time management strategies to create a manageable daily schedule that helps you maintain a good attitude and stay motivated. You'll learn about time management in the next chapter.

Distractions and other responsibilities also can be obstacles to developing a good attitude. Remember, you have to take care of yourself, too! Getting enough rest, eating healthy food, and exercising regularly will help you keep a good attitude. The better care you take of yourself, the better you'll be able to focus on reaching your goals.

Another way to avoid distractions is to set goals for yourself. By focusing on your goals, you will be less likely to become distracted.

SETTING GOALS

Start with smaller goals and move on to larger ones. If you wanted to become a mountain climber, you wouldn't start with Mount Everest!

Setting goals for yourself is very important. It does, however, take a little practice. Some people are natural planners and can't help looking far ahead and, if you're like that, you may already feel comfortable setting goals and writing them down. But for those who like to dive right in and start "doing," goal-writing may feel frustrating and dull (at first!). But goal setting doesn't have to be complicated. Starting small will help you see how easy it is to write goals.

Begin by choosing goals that are simple and practical. By setting goals that are easily accomplished, you will pave the way for tackling larger goals in your future.

- An example of a good goal for right now might be to become familiar with your school's resources for helping students study. This goal is both simple and practical.

- An example of a bad goal would be promising to read your entire textbook before the first day of class. This is an unrealistic goal.

You should give yourself time by starting with smaller, more manageable goals. Once you have accomplished those, your goals can become more complex.

Why Goals Are Important

Having goals helps you avoid distractions. Goals keep you from procrastinating, losing your concentration, and losing your motivation in school. In this way, goals are similar to the lanes on a racetrack. They help you stay on track as you run toward the finish line.

Goals come in many shapes and sizes. They can be small or large, easy or hard, immediate or future. Reaching your smaller goals will motivate you to keep reaching for your larger ones. Even completing a small task can give you a feeling of accomplishment. Overall, the more desirable a goal is, the more you'll want to reach it.

Goals should have three major characteristics. When setting goals for yourself, make sure they are:

- *Measurable.* All goals need a starting point and an ending point. Be specific. A goal such as "I want to complete all the assigned reading before each class this week" is more easily measured than "I want to be a good student."

- *Reachable.* Make sure your goals are realistic. Unrealistic goals can lead to discouragement. Remember, don't start with Mount Everest!

- *Desirable.* These are *your* goals. Make sure your goals reflect things you want for yourself. Also, make sure your goals are rewarding. Will reaching a particular goal give you a feeling of accomplishment?

Long-Term Goals, Short-Term Goals, and Everything in Between

Goals can be divided into four main categories:

- long-term (5 to 10 years away)
- intermediate (3 to 5 years away)
- short-term (6 months to 2 years away)
- immediate (1 day, 1 week, or 1 month away)

LONG-TERM GOALS

Long-term goals are often career or educational goals. These are things you hope to accomplish in the next 5 to 10 years. Consider your long-term goals as your finish line. Any other goals you accomplish along the way should help you make it to the end of the race.

INTERMEDIATE GOALS

Intermediate goals are the next step below long-term goals. These goals are things you would like to accomplish in the next 3 to 5 years. If one of your long-term goals is to become a practicing medical assistant, your intermediate goals may include completing your education.

SHORT-TERM GOALS

Short-term goals will help you reach your intermediate goals. Short-term goals are usually 6 months to 2 years in the future. If your intermediate goals include obtaining a degree or certificate, it may be helpful to have several short-term goals each semester or term, such as to excel in certain courses of particular importance to your program.

IMMEDIATE GOALS

Immediate goals are things you plan to accomplish today, this week, or this month. These goals are small tasks that can usually be completed in an hour or less. Your immediate goals should help you reach a short-term goal. For example, suppose one of your short-term goals is to complete a lengthy research paper by the end of the semester. You can start by dividing the work into several smaller tasks that can be completed in an hour or less. These tasks could include choosing a topic, doing the research, making an outline, and writing a paragraph or two at a time. By completing these smaller tasks (your immediate goals), you will accomplish your short-term goal.

At 3 to 5 years away, your intermediate goals may seem distant. Don't lose sight of them!

Goal-Writing Exercise

Writing down your goals will help you stay committed and focused on reaching them. On the next page is a format for writing out your goals. Keep in mind that writing down your goals doesn't make them permanent. You'll be able to evaluate your progress and change your goals if necessary.

In addition, your long-term, intermediate, short-term, and immediate goals should all be linked together. For example, reading 20 pages of course material today (your immediate goal) leads to getting a good grade in the course (short-term goal), which contributes to earning your degree or certificate (intermediate goal), which in turn leads to the opportunity to become a practicing health care professional (long-term goal).

Long-Term Goal (to be accomplished in the next 5 to 10 years):

_____

_____

_____

_____

Intermediate Goals (to be accomplished in the next 3 to 5 years):

1. _____

2. _____

Short-Term Goals (to be accomplished in the next 6 months to 2 years):

1. _____

2. _____

3. _____

Immediate Goals (to be accomplished today, this week, or this month):

1. _____

2. _____

3. _____

Is each of your goals:

✓ Measurable?

✓ Reachable?

✓ Desirable?

Reaching Your Short-Term Goals

Short-term goals are things you would like to accomplish over the next 6 months to 2 years. Follow these steps to reach a short-term goal:

1. Write down your goal—the more specific you are, the better!

2. Set a reasonable deadline for your goal.

3. Think about possible obstacles to achieving your goal and how to avoid them.

4. Write down a step-by-step process to help you reach your goal—a plan of action.

5. Set reasonable deadlines for completing each step in the process.

If at First You Don't Succeed, Revise and Try Again

Throughout the learning process, you may need to adjust your goals. Don't be afraid to make changes! Your goals are meant to serve *you*, not the other way around. They are not set in stone.

You may discover better ways of working toward your long-term goals. You may have to find creative ways of working around obstacles. Short-term goals can and should be changed to help you achieve success.

Along the way, you may decide to work toward an entirely different long-term goal. You may even be attending school without a clear long-term goal in mind. Once you decide to pursue a particular career path, you may reevaluate and possibly change your previous goals. If you find something you're passionate about, go for it! But don't be afraid to go back to the drawing board and change direction. Being excited about a long-term goal can be a great motivator.

If you miss a goal, don't punish yourself. Adjust your time line and keep going!

New Goals, New Future

When I first started taking courses, my long-term goal was to become a radiologic technologist. Then I started working as a part-time administrative assistant in a dental office. I really liked getting to know the patients and seeing them every 6 months. The dental assistants in the office all seemed to enjoy their work. After one semester of school, I decided to change my long-term goal. My intermediate, short-term, and immediate goals all had to be adjusted. But I went back and revised my goals. Now I'm a certified dental assistant and I love my job!

REWARD YOURSELF!

Rewards will keep you motivated as you work toward your goals. Rewards can be large or small, as long as they are appropriate for the tasks completed. For example, if you do well on an exam for which you've been studying for the past 2 weeks, it may be appropriate to reward yourself with a nice dinner out with friends. A large task deserves a large reward. However, it probably wouldn't be appropriate to reward yourself with dinner out every time you complete a 20-minute assignment! Maybe taking 5 minutes to listen to a favorite song would be more appropriate. In other words, smaller tasks deserve rewards as well, provided that the rewards are smaller.

PEER PRESSURE AND PENALTIES

Another way to stay motivated is to tell a friend about your goals. Having another person to hold you accountable will put more pressure on you to keep working hard. In this respect, peer pressure can be healthy. Just be sure to tell someone who supports your goals. Encouragement from others can be an excellent motivator.

An unproductive form of motivation is punishing yourself for not completing tasks. Punishment often has the opposite effect of motivation. It can discourage you and affect your attitude in a negative way. If you miss a goal by failing to complete a task, try adjusting your time line instead. (See *If at First You Don't Succeed, Revise and Try Again.*) It's better to accomplish a goal a bit behind schedule than to become discouraged and give up on the goal altogether.

Obstacles should make you adjust your game plan, not give up on your goals!

Will This Be On the Test?

Grades help students measure their progress toward meeting their goals. However, a word to the wise: don't put too much emphasis on grades. Although that's easier said than done, in the long run, learning should be the true goal. Focusing on learning will help you grasp new information and then correctly apply it to situations in the future. After all, you won't be a very effective health professional if you don't learn the material in your courses!

Although grades should not be the entire focus of your learning experience, they can, of course, be great motivators. Achieving the grade you wanted on a big test that you studied hard for can help motivate you to study just as hard for the next one. Grades can also help you gauge your progress. You'll feel great when you see yourself doing better and better. On the other hand, if you're not getting the grades you want, you'll know you have to make some adjustments in your approach to your coursework.

To achieve your long-term goals, you may occasionally have to complete some school work that you don't enjoy very much. Maybe something that doesn't seem relevant. But stay positive even when you don't feel like completing these assignments. Although some tasks may seem dreary at times, you will always have the motivation if your main goal is to learn. Remember, if learning is itself a goal, you can more easily stay motivated to succeed.

ACADEMIC CHARACTER

There's one more important topic for this first chapter, something you should be thinking about from your first day at school. What kind of person are you as a student? What kind of character will you have in your future career?

The character you have as a student is the character you'll have as a health care professional. You're facing the challenges of your new career today—learning new information, dealing with associates (the classmates of today are the coworkers of tomorrow), and taking responsibility for your work and your decisions.

Working in health care is different from working in most other careers. You are entrusted with patients' personal information on a daily basis. One day, you might listen to very private concerns, examine people's bodies, or handle their financial information. You must take these responsibilities seriously. People share information in a health care setting that they would never share anywhere else. You may learn things about patients that their own families don't know. The trust your patients put in you is critically important and sacred.

In school, you should develop the characteristics you'll need to become a trusted health care professional. Here are some main characteristics to work on:

> Your personal character matters when it comes to being a health care professional.

- *Honesty.* Be someone your instructors, patients, and colleagues can trust.
- *Avoiding gossip.* Don't talk about other students, patients, or professional colleagues.
- *Accountability.* Be accountable for what you do at school and work all day, every day.
- *Responsibility.* Be someone who never tries to get out of doing work.

Honesty

You should be familiar with academic honesty. It boils down to doing your own work: no plagiarism from books or articles, no copying a classmate's work, and no cheating on tests or assignments.

Honesty and ethical behavior have critical importance in health care. How would you feel if your doctor or nurse had passed a final by cheating? Or plagiarized their final paper? Or had a lab partner who did all the work for them? You would think that particular doctor or nurse was not qualified to answer your health questions or treat you. You would be right. Doing your own work is never more important than when you're learning to care for someone's health. You *must* know the material—you won't be able to fake it in a professional setting.

Make a concrete commitment to honesty.

- Do your own work.
- Avoid plagiarizing. Make sure you understand ideas well enough to put them in your own words.
- Own up to work you haven't done. If you're not prepared for a class or lab, admit it. Promise to make it up and that you won't let it happen again—and don't let it happen again!

Even though you are honest, you may find that some of your classmates are not. Take a stand here, too.

- Expect the members of your study group to do their own work.
- Don't let anyone copy your work. Sharing notes is not the same as letting someone copy an assignment you completed. Notes are raw material, not finished work that uses ideas and analysis.
- Don't let classmates force you to cover for them if they haven't done their work. You don't have to be confrontational, just firm.

Whenever you're in doubt about whether something you're doing is honest, think about it this way: would you want your doctor or nurse to do what you're thinking of doing? If the answer is no, don't do it. Period.

Don't Gossip!

One of the biggest mistakes people working in a health care facility can make is gossiping about patient information. For example, suppose a coworker asks you a casual question about a patient. Even though it may seem like a harmless question, keep your lips sealed. Not only does sharing patient information violate the patient's privacy and the health care facilities policies, it can get you fired. (All health care workers must follow the privacy regulations of the Health Insurance Portability and Accountability Act [HIPAA], about which you'll learn more later.) You never know who is listening or where else that information might travel. Only share confidential information when it is required for providing care of the patient.

Even as a student, get in the habit of avoiding gossiping with other students. Even though it may seem harmless to chat about other students, gossiping can be habit forming, and talking about others now will make it more difficult to avoid later on in a professional environment. In addition to violating the privacy of others, gossip distracts people from focusing on the work at hand and can lead to conflict among health care staff.

Note that gossip and idle conversation about others extends also to your online presence in email and on websites like Facebook. Some students forget that even if they attempt to keep their personal information and image private when online, this information can be shared or become public in other ways. Make it your goal to present only a very professional image from this day forward!

No Bending of the Rules

I work at a local hospital on Tuesdays and Thursdays and the staff there know I'm a health care student. One day, a nurse's assistant was telling me about a patient of his. He likes to quiz me, so he gave me the patient's chart and asked me what I thought. It was tempting to show off what I've learned. But I gave the chart right back without looking at it. I reminded him of HIPAA regulations and told him I couldn't look at a patient's private information.

Accountability

Being accountable means you have to be able to explain your actions. You are held to certain standards. An employee, for instance, is accountable to a supervisor. As a student, you are accountable to:

- your instructor
- your classmates
- yourself

You have to be able to explain to your instructor the quality of your work, your attendance, and your attitude. This means things like owning up to whether or not you studied and explaining why you turned in an assignment late.

How do classmates come into play? If you're working on a group project, you need to be able to tell the other group members about the work you've done toward the group goal—or why you didn't complete that work. You also need to be able to help everyone learn by participating in group discussions.

Be a team player! Stay accountable to your classmates during group projects.

You're accountable to yourself in that you're working toward your own goals. If you're letting yourself down, you have to be able to admit it and then ask yourself why. You need to be honest in assessing your personal performance and behavior.

As a health care professional, you'll be accountable to:

- patients
- your supervisor
- your workplace

Helping patients is the reason why everyone at a clinic, doctor's office, or hospital is there. You are accountable to your patients.

When it comes to your supervisor, you'll have to answer questions about the work you've done. For example, a medical assistant might have to answer questions such as:

- Did you file all the paperwork?
- Did you check every vital sign?
- Did you label all specimens?
- Did you write down symptoms correctly and pass them on to the nurse or doctor?

And, more importantly, did you do all this correctly and on time?

Finally, you are accountable to your workplace—the health care facility where you work. Always work and act as though you might be called upon to explain your actions.

The way to make accountability easy is to toe the line. Do what you're supposed to do when you're supposed to do it. Be focused on your work when you're at work. If you form that habit now while in school, all the tips you learn about prioritizing and scheduling will come to your rescue after you graduate.

Responsibility

Personal responsibility is key in school, work, and life. At school, you need to be responsible for managing your time, completing your work, and doing your best. As a health care professional, you will be responsible for all of those things and more—you'll be responsible for caring for patients, too.

Here are some things to keep in mind about your responsibilities at school and later in your career:

- You are responsible for your job—and only *your* job. It's great to help others when you can—you'll need the return favor some hectic day—but if others try to talk you into doing their work for them, politely refuse. Avoid adding tasks to your own. You may not be qualified to do them or they may be someone else's responsibility.

- You are responsible for your time—manage it well. Be able to account for it.

- You are responsible for your property—make sure you have the materials and supplies you need to do your job. Make sure everything is where you need it and clean up equipment and restock supplies after completing procedures.

- You are responsible for security and privacy. File sensitive patient information immediately and only share it with your supervisor.

- You are responsible for being educated and informed—keep brushing up on your job skills. Read professional journals, talk with colleagues, and ask questions. Ask to sit in on specific procedures if you need improvement. Review your old textbooks and make sure you know what you're doing. Participate in continuing education activities such as professional presentations.

- You are responsible for your actions—avoid the urge to blame someone else in a situation where your actions are being examined. Take responsibility for your mistakes. It's much better than trying to lie or shift the blame. Your instructors, colleagues, and supervisors will respect you for being honest.

All of these characteristics are being honed now while you're in school. Honesty, accountability, and responsibility are also the traits of a good student.

CHAPTER SUMMARY

- One of the first steps toward student success is thinking about why you're interested in continuing your education. Your dreams are important in determining your goals.

- Learning to recognize and overcome obstacles will help you become a better student.

- A positive attitude and staying motivated are critical for achieving academic success. Work to develop a positive cycle of self-confidence and successful performance.

- Goals keep you from procrastinating, losing your concentration, or losing your motivation in school. Set goals for yourself so you can stay focused and organized.

- Short-term goals are usually set 6 months to 2 years in the future. These goals should help you reach your long-term goals, or career goals. Your long-term goals represent the things you'd like to accomplish in the next 5 to 10 years.

- When setting goals for yourself, make sure each goal is measurable, reachable, and desirable.

- Develop a good academic character as a student that will serve you well also in your future career. Be honest, accountable, and responsible.

REVIEW QUESTIONS

1. What are some common reasons why people choose to continue their education?
2. Write three to five sentences about how people in your life have helped or hurt your dream of going to school.
3. Name several groups of people or resources you could look to for support in your effort to be a successful student.
4. Explain the importance of a positive attitude for success in school.
5. List techniques you can use to stay motivated.
6. What three characteristics should each of your goals have?
7. Give three examples of problems that can occur in health care if professionals were not honest, accountable, and responsible on the job.

CHAPTER ACTIVITIES

1. Get together with another student in one of your classes and talk about what you anticipate will be the most difficult assignment or project in that course. Discuss ways you work on it to ensure you are successful. Be sure to end on a positive, upbeat note showing your confidence in your ability to do it well.
2. Ask someone who has been out of school for years what they remember as the most discouraging experience they had as a student. Talk about how they might have prevented that negative experience with a more positive attitude, more motivated studying, and the use of motivational strategies discussed in this chapter.

CHAPTER 2

Getting Organized and Managing Your Time

WINNING STRATEGY

On completion of this chapter and the learning activities you will be able to:

- Know why it's important to attend all classes

- Use all the class materials you receive

- Pay close attention to your syllabus

- Find and use campus resources that can help you succeed

- Develop effective time management strategies

- Get organized with a calendar, weekly planner, and to-do list

- Schedule and use your time effectively

- Recognize the symptoms of procrastination and take steps to keep on track

Attending classes is what school is all about, but being organized is also a large part of being successful in school. For example, your course documents will let you know ahead of time what each course will cover and exactly which assignments or activities your instructor considers most important. How you manage your time will also determine your success as a student. In this chapter, you'll learn how to use your course documents and campus resources to your advantage. You'll also learn how to organize your schedule and use your time efficiently. All these skills also help you stay focused on what really matters for success.

ORGANIZING FOR CLASSES

Ultimately, attending your classes is most important for success. This starts with attending all classes, all the time, but also includes being organized with class materials and schedules.

Being There

One of the most important steps in your student success game plan is to be there. This means attending all your classes, every day, beginning with the very first class. You have enrolled in your courses for a purpose. Missing a class here and there will make it harder to achieve your goals. Attending every class should be a top priority.

There are several reasons why attendance from the first day is essential. You will:

- get to know your instructors and other students
- take notes if your instructors lecture on the first day of class
- find out about helpful campus resources
- receive important handouts so you'll know what to expect during the semester

Being there puts you in the winner's circle!

Although some students think that nothing important happens in the first class and may be tempted to skip, that's a dangerous way to start the term! It's true that some instructors use that first day to introduce students to the course and then let class out a few minutes early. But many other instructors use the entire class time and start their lectures right away. They'll expect students to start taking notes on the first day. Missing the first class would put you behind in more ways than one.

Some students are also tempted to skip classes at the end of a term in order to spend extra time studying for final exams. But going to class should take priority. Instructors often provide their own review of the course and tell you which items or ideas will be covered on the final exam. If you schedule your study time well and stick with your daily and weekly schedules, you'll have plenty of time to study *and* go to class.

WHY ATTENDANCE ALWAYS MATTERS

Class time is important because it gives you a chance to see the material you're studying through the eyes of an expert—your instructor. The instructor goes over key points, provides analysis, and brings ideas to life in real-world applications. In class, you learn what is most important for succeeding in the course and for entering your new career. Attending class needs to be one of your top priorities if your goal is to be a successful student!

Attending class means arriving on time (or even a few minutes early) and staying until your instructor has concluded the class and dismissed everyone. The first 5 minutes of class are just as important as the middle of the lecture. During this time, your instructor might make important announcements. The last 5 minutes of class are equally critical because your instructor might take this time to summarize important information or answer questions about an assignment. If you have an instructor who is occasionally late, don't use this as an excuse to skip the first few minutes of class. Instead, make use of the extra time by bringing other assignments or notes to review until your instructor arrives.

In school, showing up for practice means attending every class. If you practice enough, you'll be ready for game day!

Really, think twice before you miss a class. You joined the team— now you need to show up for practice. Each time you miss class, you fall behind. Even if you keep up with your reading and other assignments, when you skip a lecture or class discussion, you're missing out on an important part of the learning process. In class, the information from your assigned reading is analyzed and used as a building block for other, new information you won't get from a book.

Class time offers information you won't get any- where else. It offers the instructor's own experiences and opinions on what you read in your textbook. During class, the instructor may share journal articles that discuss what you've read and take it further. Even if the instructor sticks to the textbook, you never know where in class discussion will take that information. You may hear a new idea during discussion that you never would have thought of on your own. Although some students think they can gain everything they need from borrowing another student's notes if they miss class, they will still miss the value of class discussion and interaction with the instructor. More real learning goes on during this time than can ever be captured in notes on the page.

Another important reason to make it a priority to attend every class: your instructor will notice if you skip a class or two. Instruc- tors quickly memorize faces, even in large survey courses. They know when you're absent. And even if they don't pick up on your absence at first, if you go to office hours with a lot of basic questions, the instructor will inevitably take out the attendance log to see if you've been missing class. Even if attendance doesn't count in your course grade (it often does!), missing classes will affect your grade and make a poor impression on your instructors. It's a statement of how seri- ously you take your education and a measure of your desire to start a new career. If you take your classes seriously, your instructors will take you seriously.

If You *Must* Miss a Class . . .

- If you know you will miss a class, take steps in advance. Ask your instructor if he or she teaches another section of the course that you might attend instead. Ask about any handouts or announcements.

- Ask another student whose judgment you trust if you can copy their notes. Also ask if you can spend a few minutes with them after you've read their notes to go over things that may be unclear to you.

- You may not need to see your instructor after missing a lecture class and no instructor wants to give you 50 minutes of office time to repeat the lecture for you. But, if you are having difficulty after the next class because of something you missed, stop in and see your instructor and ask what you can do to get caught up.

- Remember the worst thing you can say to an instructor: "I missed class—did you talk about anything important?" This statement tells the instructor that you don't consider class time important—a major insult to the instructor!—and that you're not taking responsibility for your own learning.

Using Class Materials

Attending every class is an excellent beginning, but being organized also means making effective use of course materials. Starting the first day of class, your instructors will give you various handouts and tell you about other materials you may need to access. These documents are critical for charting your path to success throughout the term.

WHY ALL THE PAPER?

There's a reason instructors hand out so much paper at the beginning of the semester. They've spent the weeks before the first class planning every class session during the semester. They create a game plan of the material they're going to teach, the order in which it will be taught, and what you'll need to learn. Then they hand that game plan to you, in the form of course documents. Course documents help you get in the game quickly and easily.

Your course documents may include:

- a syllabus
- a class schedule
- a course materials list
- study guides or lecture outlines
- practice exercises
- assignment instructions

Course documents make life easier for you and your instructor. These documents help ensure that you're both headed in the same direction. This is very important for your game plan.

Download This! Online Documents

Many instructors make their course materials available online after having spent a great deal of time developing their websites to help students get the most from their studies. Be sure to get all the information you need to access the instructor's site. This usually includes:

- the URL (web address)
- your user name
- your password

Once you have your password, keep it in a safe place. You never know when you'll need to go to the course website to review a course document. Also, if you happen to lose any of this material, you can print out a copy from the website.

COURSE DOCUMENTS—GAME PLAN FOR YOUR CLASSES

For the most effective learning, you need to come to class prepared. You can find out exactly what's coming next by reading—and using—your course documents. In fact, reviewing course documents right away, at the beginning of the course, can sometimes help you decide whether or not to stay in a particular class. Look over the books and articles you'll be required to read. Consider how much time you'll have to spend in the lab. See how many exams you'll be taking and how much time you'll be expected to spend on homework. You may find that you've signed up for too many demanding classes during the same term. In that case, you might want to talk to your advisor about your course load and see if you should consider rescheduling one of your courses for another semester.

SYLLABUS

The course syllabus includes key information about your class, just like a coach's playbook. Most instructors hand out a syllabus for their courses. The syllabus tells you almost everything you need to know about the course and what the instructor expects of you. A typical syllabus includes:

- the instructor's name and contact information
- the course name, catalog number, and credit hours
- when and where the class meets
- the goals your instructor has for you (what you will learn)
- the grading policy—how much tests, papers, daily participation, group work, and/or attendance contribute to your final grade

- information about whether the instructor will accept late assignments

- any special classroom rules

Most instructors will read through the syllabus in class on the first day and explain key points. Be prepared to highlight or mark these key points. This is an essential part of your first day, because you will learn about what each instructor considers most important. Some instructors place heavy emphasis on tests and papers, whereas others place a greater value on participation in class. As your instructor reviews the syllabus, you'll get an idea of what it will take to succeed in the course. Listen carefully to the instructor and be sure to ask questions about anything you don't understand. And, as with all handouts you receive, file your syllabus in a safe place right away.

Your instructor gives you a game plan in the form of course documents. Review these handouts so you know what to expect!

Staying Organized

TIPS from THE PROS

All that paper you receive from instructors is important! Look through it all carefully, organize it, and don't lose any of it. Set up a binder or folder for each of your classes. Place your syllabus at the front of the binder or folder because you'll need to refer to it often. Then continue to file all the papers the instructor hands out in class. You don't want to misplace any of your course documents or leave them behind in class!

The Game Plan for Grades

Successful students have a game plan. They think through what they have to do to do well in their classes. They calculate what it's going to take to get the grade they want. This calculation often involves points or percentages. Unfortunately, many students find grades a source of confusion and frustration. They get their graded tests and assignments back, but aren't sure what the numbers really mean in terms of their overall grade.

This is another time when the course syllabus is very important: it will help you know how to figure out where you stand grade-wise at any time during the semester. But it may take some deciphering! For now, keep in mind that the syllabus has the information you need to figure your to-the-minute grade. In Chapter 9, we'll take a closer look at how to calculate grades.

CLASS SCHEDULE

Usually, a class schedule is included with the syllabus and contains information about:

- what topics will be covered each day in class
- assignment due dates
- test and quiz dates

If the instructor has already organized the class schedule in calendar form, keep it in your binder for easy reference. If the class schedule is just a list of dates, get out your calendar (which you'll learn to make later in this chapter) and carefully write in the important dates. You might try using different colors, such as red for tests and blue for homework.

COURSE MATERIALS LIST

The course materials list includes everything you'll need to participate in each class. This might include the following:

- *Textbooks.* If your school bookstore offers used textbooks for sale, this can save you a lot of money; just make sure you buy the right edition. Unless you must buy your books on campus, you may also find less expensive copies online—just be sure to order early enough that you have the book before class starts! Some textbooks come with CDs or an online component that your instructor may require you to use. Be sure if you buy a used textbook that it has the CD or online code with it. If you purchase your books before the first day of class, you will have a better idea of the material that will be covered in each course.

- Some schools offer used textbooks for sale at reduced prices. Because these books usually are sold on a first-come, first-served basis, it pays to purchase your books early.

- *Workbooks.* These may come with your textbook as a set or you may have to buy the workbook separately.

- *Photocopied readings.* Sometimes, an instructor makes handouts that he or she gives out in class. Other times, you'll need to retrieve handouts from the course website, the campus library, or the resource center. Be sure you have the course materials list with you so you get the correct handouts.

- *Uniforms, stethoscopes, etc.* The course materials list or your instructor will specify where to purchase these items. Ask if there are stores that offer special student discounts.

Sometimes an item on the list is recommended rather than required. Ask your instructor how important it is that you buy recommended items.

GETTING ORGANIZED ON CAMPUS

Being organized and prepared doesn't end with attending class and organizing your course materials. Your success as a student is also enhanced by knowing about and using other resources on campus.

Speaking the Language

Becoming familiar with your school and the resources it offers to students can be like learning a different language. Don't worry! There are people there to help you learn about things like course catalogs and financial aid. If you have questions but don't know who to ask, a good place to start is your school's information office. Look around at the more experienced students who seem like they have all the answers and remember that each of them had to start at the beginning, just like you! Trust that, in no time at all, you'll know your way around and be speaking the language like a pro.

Using Campus Resources

Hi, my name is André. I started taking classes a few months ago to become a physical therapy assistant. Going to school and working at a local restaurant keeps me pretty busy. I even thought about skipping the first day of class because I assumed it would be a waste of time. The instructors usually just talk about unimportant stuff and let everyone out early, right?

I ended up going anyway and I'm glad I did. My instructor talked about a lot of campus resources I didn't even know existed. He even gave us user names and passwords so we could access a free online tutoring system. It's been great! When I have to work an extra shift and don't have time to meet with my study group, I can log on and talk to a tutor. I never would've known about it if I hadn't gone to that first class. Being there on the first day has saved me a lot of time this semester!

Course Catalogs, Credits, and Confusion

The college catalog or course catalog is one of the most important documents you'll use in school. It describes all of the classes offered in your program. It tells you about the requirements for your degree or certificate plan. And, it also helps you figure out when you will complete your education!

Your school may update the course catalog every year or every term. You should be able to get a printed copy or access the catalog online. Be sure to have an up-to-date version handy when planning your class schedule.

TIPS FOR SCHEDULING SUCCESS

If you're attending a career or technical school, your course scheduling may be done for you. In other schools though, you may be responsible for registering for courses and organizing your own schedule. The way you organize your class schedule can affect your success as a student. A well-organized schedule ensures that you will be able to devote enough time to each course. There are a few tricks to organizing a schedule that works for you.

- Schedule your classes evenly throughout the week. You can accomplish this by scheduling classes every day. Overloading your schedule to have class every other day can lead to unnecessary stress. Distributing your classes evenly throughout the week will keep you from becoming burned out.

- Make allowances for tough courses. You can do this by scheduling tough courses when you are fresh. For example, schedule challenging classes in the mornings if you are a morning person. Another way to get through difficult courses is to balance your schedule for the term. Try to balance every difficult course with an easier one, if possible, so your schedule doesn't become overwhelming.

- Keep personal commitments in mind when scheduling classes. You may have to schedule your classes around work, family, and other obligations.

- Make informed decisions when choosing your instructors. Certain courses may be offered by several different instructors. When you have a choice, check with other students or your student government association for information on each instructor's teaching style.

DON'T GET LOST—GET A MAP!

The first step toward becoming familiar with your campus is to locate a campus map. Maps may be found in the course catalog, on the school's website, or posted at different locations on campus. The school's information office can be helpful in answering questions about student parking and parking permits, if needed.

Knowing your way around campus can help you avoid unnecessary stress on the first day of class.

Each academic term, when you're taking new classes in perhaps new locations, plan to arrive a few minutes early the first week. Or, if possible, scout your classroom locations before the term starts so you know the route from the parking lot or bus stop and from class to class. It can be difficult getting used to a new routine and remembering where to go. Prevent unnecessary stress by giving yourself extra time to make it to your classes. It's better to be early and calm than harried, late, and out of breath!

Campus Resources

There are a lot of resources available on most campuses that you may not yet have heard about. Most schools provide a variety of free services to any student who seeks them out, although it can take some hunting to find all of them. There are so many bulletin boards crammed with flyers advertising services and events that they can all merge into a senseless blur.

The fact that you also have to use your own initiative to find many free resources can be daunting. Who has the time and energy to track these things down? But, as usual, making the effort is worth it. Because so few students take the time to find all the resources available to them, there usually is an abundance of resources waiting for the person who does make the effort.

These resources and services can make a big difference in your student experience. Most are free for students or are already included in your tuition. Some of these services include:

- tutoring
- learning labs
- writing centers
- computer labs
- libraries
- fitness centers
- career placement services
- counseling

Need help revising a paper? Visit the writing center! Need access to a computer to do research or work on a report? Visit the computer lab! The people working in these labs and resource centers are often more than willing to help. Take advantage of their advice and expertise.

Make the most of the resources your school has to offer.

Searching for Resources: The Starting Line

If you're having trouble finding out about the resources offered by your school, you probably just need to know where to look. Here are some tips to get you started on your search.

- Visit your school's information office and ask where you can find out about things like free seminars and learning labs.
- Ask your academic advisor to point you in the right direction. If you're struggling with a certain course, for example, your advisor may be able to suggest a possible tutor.
- Visit your school's website. You may find a "Student Services" section or a link to the Office of Special Services at your school and its list of offerings.
- Ask a librarian about resources available to students in the campus library. As a student, you may have access to special computer search engines, videos, and professional journal articles.

THE CAMPUS LIBRARY

Although you probably know where the library is located, you may need to learn how to use the unique services available there. Your campus library has a wealth of resources: videos, books, articles, and other supplemental materials. Find out if there's a free orientation tour on how to use the library so you know how to find everything you need. Knowing how to use the reference area of a library is invaluable, but you may need to ask for help to use it effectively.

LEARNING LABS

Libraries and learning labs are important campus resources. Most people know what a library is, but what's a learning lab? A learning lab is a place where students can go to meet with tutors or study groups, use campus computers, or use extra learning resources. These labs usually have very specialized learning material in them. For example, there may be life-size plastic anatomical models to help you learn anatomy. Some will have computers to aid you in learning how to use certain software programs. Knowledgeable people who can help you make the most of these specialized resources usually staff learning labs.

Find out if your school has a learning lab and, if so, find out where it's located before you need it. Remember, your goal is to be prepared. This saves you the stress of hunting for these resources later when you may be pressed for time.

CAMPUS COUNSELING CENTER

The campus counseling center is also a good place to investigate. These centers often sponsor free seminars on studying, how to stay healthy, and how to manage stress. These can be great places to pick up information to share with your network.

HUMAN RESOURCES

Don't think of resources only as offices and special rooms or buildings. The most valuable resources for heightening your learning are the people you see in your classrooms: your instructor and other students. Don't forget them!

In later chapters we'll talk about networking with students and forming study groups. Study groups can be among the most enjoyable—as well as most effective—ways to learn. You'll also be learning more about how to successfully interact with your instructors. But, from this point on, start thinking of your instructors as your most valuable resources.

Help From Your Instructor

In addition to being available by phone or email, almost all instructors have regular office hours when they are available to meet with students one-on-one. You can go to your instructor's office and talk over anything you need help with. It's like having the instructor as your private tutor—for free! Find out when the office hours are (often on the syllabus) and write them in your schedule.

Check your class syllabus to see if you need to make an appointment for one-on-one time with your instructor. Also, keep in mind that office hours are for everyone in the class. Your instructor will have limited time to help you during office hours. If you feel like you need more help, such as weekly extended one-on-one tutoring, ask your instructor to recommend a personal tutor.

There are other options aside from meeting your instructor in his or her office. Some instructors offer help over the phone or by email. Some even set up online discussion boards. Remember not to assume that you can call your instructor at any time or that you can call as often as you want. Your instructor's time should be respected and shared equally with other members of the class. Be sure to call only during the appointed times.

If you send an email, you may not get an answer immediately. Most instructors will tell you what their response time is for email. Ask your instructor if he or she doesn't include this information in the syllabus.

Find out whether your campus counseling center offers free seminars. There might be one that captures your interest!

Special Services for Special Needs

Some students have special physical, mental, and learning needs. Special needs can include:

- physical disabilities
- mental disabilities
- learning disabilities

Most schools have resources to help meet these additional needs. For students with particular needs or disabilities, specially trained staff at the school can arrange for individual accommodations in the classroom. For example, students with hearing impairments may be able to apply for sign language interpreters to assist them. Students who have learning disabilities, such as dyslexia, can work with their academic counselors to find extra teaching and learning aids.

If you feel you need special assistance in school, you may need to seek out services yourself. Your school most likely has an office dedicated to helping students with special needs. Find that office to learn more about the resources available on your campus. If you aren't sure, set up a meeting with your advisor right away to find out what assistance is available for you. Although students are sometimes required to help pay for some of these resources, other times they are free.

ORGANIZING YOUR TIME

A full-time student spends about 15 hours a week in the classroom and 2 hours of time preparing for each hour of class work. That's about 45 hours a week either spent in class or preparing for class. On top of these responsibilities, many students also devote time to their jobs, families, and other activities, along with time for exercise, socializing with friends, and all the other things you like to do. That's a full plate!

This is one of the things virtually all students agree on: there's not enough time for everything you want to do. But you can't "make" time, nor can you "save" it up for use later on. We only have so much time, so we have to learn to use it as well as possible. We need to be organized in our approach to time—this is called time management.

Time management is actually a set of skills. They are well worth learning because you can use them in your future career and through-out life. The better you manage your time, the less stress you'll feel, the more you'll get done, and the more time you'll feel like you have for doing those things you enjoy.

Here are some of the things involved in successful time management:

- knowing how much time you should spend studying
- knowing how to increase your studying time if needed
- knowing the times of day you are at your best and most focused
- using effective study strategies
- scheduling study activities in realistic segments
- using calendars to plan ahead and set priorities
- staying motivated to follow your plan and avoiding procrastination

Making Time Work for Me

My name is Angel. I'm 37 and I have two children. I work 30 hours a week at a bank and I go to school every day. My goal is to eventually become a certified nurse assistant. In a typical week, I spend 30 hours at the bank, 45 hours doing school-related work, and who knows how many uncounted, unaccounted-for hours making dinner, helping with homework, and doing laundry. I don't have a lot of wiggle room in my life. With so many responsibilities, I'm a typical student. Managing time efficiently is the key to my success.

Where Does the Time Go?

We all have the same 24 hours a day, but some people just seem to have "more" time than others. How does that happen? Two different students might have identical amounts of homework in the same classes, work the same number of hours a week, and sleep and exercise in identical amounts, but one feels rushed and always behind in studying whereas the other feels calm and always has enough time to do a good job. What's the difference between them? Which type are you?

> *I had no idea how much time I was spending just hanging out with friends!*

Chances are, these two students have different attitudes toward time. One may be more aware of time than the other—and therefore may be better able to manage it. Time management starts with being aware of where the time goes. Most people in fact often cannot account for how they spend all their time.

Accounting for and learning to manage time is so important for success as a student that it's worth spending some time learning to better understand time. Doing the following exercises and activities will give you a clearer idea where your own time goes. Step 1 is to see if you know how you actually spend your time day after day.

Where Does Your Time Go?

See if you can account for a week of your time. For each of the categories listed, make your best estimate of how many hours you spend. (For categories that are about the same every day, just estimate for one day and multiply by 7 for that line.)

Category of Activity	Number of Hours per Week
Sleeping	_____
Eating and preparing food	_____
Bathing, personal hygiene, etc.	_____
Working, volunteer service, internship	_____
Chores, cleaning, errands, shopping, etc.	_____
Attending class	_____
Studying, reading textbooks, researching (outside class)	_____
Transportation to work and/or school	_____
Organized activities: clubs, church services, etc.	_____
Casual time with friends (include TV, video games, etc.)	_____
Attending entertainments (movies, parties, etc.)	_____
Time alone with TV, video games, surfing the Web, etc.	_____
Exercise, sports activities	_____
Reading for fun, other interests done alone	_____
Talking on phone, email, Facebook, etc.	_____
Other—specify: _____	_____
Other—specify: _____	_____

Now get out your calculator and total up all your estimated hours. Is your number larger or smaller than 168, the number of actual hours in a week? If your estimate is higher, go back through your list and adjust your numbers to be more realistic. If your estimated hours total to less than 168, do not make any changes. Instead, ask yourself this question: *Where does the time go?* We'll analyze it to find out!

Step 2 in your time analysis is to actually track your time for a few days and see where you *really* spend your time. This may seem like a lot of work, but it really only takes a minute or two a day. The self-knowledge most people gain from this activity is well worth it and can pay off through all your time in school.

Make copies of the "Daily Time Log" (page 43). Carry it with you and every so often fill in what you have been doing (in 15-minute increments). Do this for several days and then add up the times for the different categories of activities in the earlier exercise on page 41. How does your actual time use compare with your earlier estimates? What have you learned about yourself?

Many students are surprised that they spend a lot more time than they thought just hanging out with friends—or surfing the Web, or playing around with Facebook, or any of the many other things people do. You can learn to use some of this time to your advantage! When you begin using a calendar or planner to schedule your study time the same way you plan ahead to attend class, you'll be on your way to efficient time management.

Time Management Strategies That Work

Because you don't have all the time in the world, you want to use well the time that you do have for your studies. This approach promotes academic success while still providing enough time to enjoy life with friends, family, and other activities. Try these strategies:

- *Prepare to be successful.* While you are planning ahead for studying, think yourself into the right mood as well. Fight off any negative thoughts by focusing on the positive. "When I get these chapters read tonight, I'll be ahead in studying for the next test, and I'll also have plenty of time tomorrow to do X." *Visualize* yourself studying well!

- *Use your best time of day.* Different tasks require different mental skills. Maybe you can focus best on reading later in the day after you've burned off restless energy with some exercise. Maybe you can write a class paper more successfully earlier in the day when you still have a lot of energy. Some kinds of studying you may be able to start first thing in the morning as you wake, whereas others need your most alert moments at another time.

- *Break up large projects into small pieces.* Whether it's writing a paper for class, studying for a final exam, or reading a long assignment or full book, students often feel daunted at the beginning of a large project. That leads to a tendency to put it off. It's usually easier to get going if you break it up into stages that you schedule at separate times—and then begin with the first section that requires only an hour or two.

- *Do most important studying first.* When two or more separate things require your attention, do the more crucial one first. If something interrupts your work and you don't complete everything you planned to do, you'll suffer less if the most crucial work has been done.

- *If you have trouble getting started, do an easier task first.* Like large tasks, complex or difficult ones can be daunting. If you really

Daily Time Log

AM		PM	
5:00	_____	5:00	_____
5:15	_____	5:15	_____
5:30	_____	5:30	_____
5:45	_____	5:45	_____
6:00	_____	6:00	_____
6:15	_____	6:15	_____
6:30	_____	6:30	_____
6:45	_____	6:45	_____
7:00	_____	7:00	_____
7:15	_____	7:15	_____
7:30	_____	7:30	_____
7:45	_____	7:45	_____
8:00	_____	8:00	_____
8:15	_____	8:15	_____
8:30	_____	8:30	_____
8:45	_____	8:45	_____
9:00	_____	9:00	_____
9:15	_____	9:15	_____
9:30	_____	9:30	_____
9:45	_____	9:45	_____
10:00	_____	10:00	_____
10:15	_____	10:15	_____
10:30	_____	10:30	_____
10:45	_____	10:45	_____
11:00	_____	11:00	_____
11:15	_____	11:15	_____
11:30	_____	11:30	_____
11:45	_____	11:45	_____

PM		AM	
12:00	_____	12:00	_____
12:15	_____	12:15	_____
12:30	_____	12:30	_____
12:45	_____	12:45	_____
1:00	_____	1:00	_____
1:15	_____	1:15	_____
1:30	_____	1:30	_____
1:45	_____	1:45	_____
2:00	_____	2:00	_____
2:15	_____	2:15	_____
2:30	_____	2:30	_____
2:45	_____	2:45	_____
3:00	_____	3:00	_____
3:15	_____	3:15	_____
3:30	_____	3:30	_____
3:45	_____	3:45	_____
4:00	_____	4:00	_____
4:15	_____	4:15	_____
4:30	_____	4:30	_____
4:45	_____	4:45	_____

can't get going, switch to an easier task you can accomplish quickly. That will give you momentum, and often, you feel more confident tackling the difficult task after being successful in the first one.

- *If you're really floundering, talk to someone.* A problem getting going on a project or large assignment may be the result of not really understanding what you should be doing. Talk with your instructor or another student in the class. Usually this will help you get back on track.

- *Take a break.* We all need breaks to help us concentrate without becoming fatigued and burned out. As a general rule, a short break every hour or so is effective in helping recharge your study energy. Get up and move around to get your blood flowing, clear your thoughts, and work off any stress that's building up.

- *Use unscheduled times to work ahead.* If you have a few minutes waiting for the bus, start a reading assignment now, or flip through the chapter to get a sense of what you'll be reading later. Either way, you'll be better prepared when you reach your scheduled reading time and will likely need less time. Use other down times during the day and you may be amazed how much studying you can get done in casual times.

- *Keep your momentum.* Remember to prevent distractions that will only slow you down. Save checking for messages, for example, until your scheduled break time.

- *Reward yourself.* Let's be honest; it's not easy to sit still for hours of studying or work on a special project. When you successfully complete the task, you should feel good about yourself and the reward of a (healthy) snack or a quick video game or social activity—whatever you enjoy doing—can help you feel even better about your successful use of time.

- *Just say no.* Tell others nearby when you're studying to reduce the chances of being interrupted. If an interruption happens, it helps to have your "no" prepared in advance: "No, I *really* have to be ready for this test" or "That's a great idea, but let's do it tomorrow—I *just can't* today."

- *Have a life.* Never schedule your day or week so full of work and study that you have no time at all for yourself, your family and friends, your larger life. Without a personal life, even the most dedicated student will suffer in a way that can negatively impact studies.

- *Use a calendar planner and daily to-do list.* We'll look at these time management tools in the next section.

Calendars

People who manage their time well aren't just successful students—they're successful people. They take all areas of their busy lives into account and give each task the right amount of time and attention. The one tool successful people swear by is their personal calendar or schedule.

Calendars help keep you working right on schedule!

Using a calendar seems like a negative thing to some people. When they see those days fill up on the page, they feel trapped and overwhelmed. How will they get it all done? A calendar is powerful; it shows you exactly what you're doing each day and how busy you really are. But this is a good thing. Being able to see each week or month at a glance will show you days where you're trying to do too many things at once. A calendar shows you places where your time stretches too thin and emptier places where you can move some of those tasks.

Most importantly, a calendar helps you to be prepared. If something unexpected comes up, you can consult your calendar and immediately determine how that emergency is going to affect you. A calendar will keep you on track and help you remember important dates. Developing a personal schedule goes a long way toward fulfilling your time management goals.

As a student, you need to do both short-range and long-range planning. You'll need certain items to make this possible.

- a yearly calendar that you keep at home. This can be a paper calendar or an electronic version.

- a small weekly planner that you carry with you, adding new items as you hear about them. You can add the new information to your yearly calendar and check for any conflicts.

- a daily to-do list. You'll fill this list with items from your yearly calendar and/or your weekly planner.

You might choose to use an all-in-one organizer. Electronic organizers can store large amounts of information, yet they're small enough to carry with you wherever you go. Just be careful about keeping all your information in one place. If you lose it, you won't know your own schedule. It's always a good idea to have a backup, such as a yearly calendar at home that holds all your information. You can also find printable weekly and daily planner pages on the student website that comes with this book! See the inside front cover for access information.

WHAT TO SCHEDULE ON YOUR CALENDAR—AND WHY

Don't think of your calendar or planner as only an academic planner. It is that and it has to include everything important in your life in order to work well, but you also have a life outside school. You need to include many important things to keep your schedule organized and avoid time conflicts. The calendar won't do its job for you if you mark next Tuesday's test but not your doctor's appointment scheduled for the same time. Put your whole life—work, school, home—on your calendar.

Due Dates and Deadlines

Due dates and deadlines are usually stated in each course syllabus. These are very important! Turning in work on time helps you stay on schedule and keep up with the rest of the class. Although some instructors have special policies allowing for work to be turned in late, make a habit of turning things in when work is due.

Tests and Quizzes

Test and quiz dates should also be marked on your calendar. Carve out blocks of time beginning several days before each test for studying. If you don't reserve time for studying, it could slip away from you. Prioritize your study time by scheduling it during a time of day when your mind is sharp.

Of course, you also have to prioritize attendance on test days. These are the "big game" days. If there is absolutely no way you can be in class on a test day (due to a family emergency, illness, or other circumstance beyond your control), let your instructor know as soon as possible and ask if the exam can be made up. Many instructors will not allow this, so if yours will, do whatever you can to make it up on the day provided.

Projects and Group Work

When it comes to projects and group work, the scheduling isn't only up to you. As soon as you're assigned to a group, get together with your group members and block out times to work on the project. Start with the project due date and your instructor's recommendations of how much time you'll need to complete the work. Set aside times to work individually and times to get together.

It's tempting to leave this until later—why schedule time weeks in advance? But it's very hard to find one time when three or more people can get together. You and your classmates all have busy schedules. You'll have to prioritize your group work by getting out your calendars and determining a work/study schedule. That way, if someone tries to cancel, you can all remind that person that the date was agreed upon long ago and should be honored.

You'll also have more team spirit if you're working together according to a reasonable plan, rather than trying to cram in meetings with each other at the last minute or to assign work via email.

Homework

Homework usually includes writing or reading assignments. Some students don't take homework seriously enough to include it in their calendar planner—they may think they'll "just get to it" eventually. But homework is actually a very important part of student success.

Written assignments show your instructor how well you understand the material. They show how much work you've finished and whether you know exactly what you're doing. Reading assignments don't give the instructor immediate feedback on your performance, but most instructors consider reading to be just as important as written work. You might see questions about reading assignments on quizzes or tests. Your instructor may base class discussions on the assigned readings. If your instructor relies on class discussions, be sure to complete the reading so you'll be prepared to participate!

When planning your weekly schedule, try to estimate how long it will take you to complete each homework assignment. This will be easier to do as you become more familiar with your instructors and your coursework. But at first, it's probably a good idea to add 30 minutes to your estimate. For example, if you think it should take you an hour to complete a homework assignment, schedule an hour and a half, just in case it takes longer. If you find it really does take you just an hour, you'll have 30 minutes to review, get started on something else, or just take a well deserved break!

Often, you will have homework based on an assigned reading or lab work. Try to get into the habit of doing the homework soon after the reading or lab work is done, when it's still fresh in your mind. The old saying, "Don't put off until tomorrow what you can do today," is never truer than in the context of homework.

Field Trips

Field trips are invaluable opportunities to visit your future workplace. But they also can wreak havoc on your schedule. Do everything you can to make these trips. Your instructor probably will make clear to you how important it is to be there. Put field trip dates into your calendar so you can prepare for them in advance. You might need to:

- arrange childcare if you have young children
- take the necessary time off work
- ask your spouse or a friend to pitch in and help with any other responsibilities you may have on those days

Also, be aware that you may run late getting back from the field trip, so try to schedule some extra time for delays.

Study Days

If your school schedules "study days" into each semester or term, plan to make use of these. Add these dates to your calendar well in advance. This will help you keep the days free as you schedule your other events and commitments. Try to avoid the urge to use your study days for any purpose other than studying!

Other Responsibilities

Like most students, you probably have family, work, or other responsibilities outside of school. Sometimes, you might have to put off doing homework because of a more pressing obligation. This is understandable and, when this happens, it's okay to adjust your schedule. The key is to stay balanced. When you postpone working on a homework assignment because of another responsibility, be sure to make time in your schedule to complete the assignment before it's due.

Time-out!

Whenever you can, try to create free time for yourself. You have to plan breaks if you want to avoid burnout—the fatigue, boredom, and stress that can make life miserable. A break can mean many things: switching from one task to another, getting together with classmates to discuss a group project, or moving from one subject to another.

You can also avoid burnout by keeping your daily schedule flexible. Be realistic when you're planning. If your calendar shows you have 3 days to complete an assignment, avoid trying to cram it all into 1 day. If you schedule commitments too tightly, you might not complete them on time (or at all), which can leave you feeling discouraged.

> Holidays are for relaxing and spending time with the people you care about. Try to complete your coursework before the holiday begins.

Holidays

Holidays are times to relax and have fun. So make sure you do just that. It's tempting to put off coursework when you're busy, thinking, "I'll do that during vacation week." But vacation week often means your family is home, you're traveling, you're working so you can make some extra money, or you're getting together with friends. You won't want to spend that time trying to get work done— or failing to get it done. Block off holiday time and keep it free of any school obligations. You'll need that time to rest so you can come back refreshed and ready to get back to your schoolwork.

Add/Drop Dates

You can avoid having to add or drop courses after the start of a semester by preparing properly before registration. Before you register for a particular course, gather as much information as you can. Meet with your academic advisor to determine the appropriateness of each course you plan to take. This way, you can avoid registering for courses you don't need. You'll also want to make sure you won't be taking several very demanding courses at the same time.

But even if you do everything right, you can occasionally run into snags after the semester begins. Maybe after attending your first few math classes, you find that it takes you a lot longer than you thought to complete the homework. It becomes clear that you won't have enough time this semester to devote to the class. For this type of situation, there is a solution—the drop/add period. During specific drop/add dates at the beginning of each semester or term, you can drop or add a course from your schedule without being penalized for it. Mark these dates on your calendar just in case this happens.

Keep in mind, however, that you need to be considerate of your fellow students. Often, there are students on waiting lists who need to take certain courses for their degree or certificate programs. Avoid using the drop/add period as a time to "test drive" courses. You may be taking a spot that someone else desperately needs! Instead, plan ahead before you register and avoid the stressful drop/add shuffle altogether.

Last Day of Class

The last day of class is another important date to mark on your calendar. This date usually occurs several days before the start of exams. Although it's important to attend each class period, being there on the last day before exams is particularly important. Often, instructors review material that will appear on the exams and answer questions during this last class.

Registration Dates for Next Semester

Approaching the end of one semester or term means it's time to prepare for the next! Mark registration dates on your calendar and give yourself enough time to prepare before registration begins. You might need to research certain courses or set up an appointment with your academic advisor to make sure you're on track for your degree or certificate plan. Remember, if you prepare properly before registration, you can avoid the drop/add hassle after the next semester or term begins!

It's also important to be prepared so you can register as early as possible. Required courses often fill up quickly. If you wait too long, you might not get into a course you need. Stay ahead of the game by going in on the first day of registration and getting it done.

Finally, don't forget about your finances. If you need to save money for the registration fee, you won't be caught unaware if you keep the date in mind.

Managing Time by the Year

As mentioned earlier, you should keep a long-range yearly calendar as well as a weekly planner. You can use a traditional paper calendar or an online scheduling resource, such as the electronic calendars offered by free email providers. Use this calendar to record:

- class times
- midterm and final exam dates
- due dates for papers and other projects
- deadlines for completing each phase of lengthy projects
- test dates
- your instructors' office hours
- important extracurricular and recreational events
- deadlines for drop/add
- holidays, school vacations, and social commitments

OFF TO A GOOD START

You'll probably notice right away that the beginning of each school term is a very busy and important time. During the first few weeks of a term, the instructor forms an opinion about what kind of student you are. Are you organized? Do you ask good questions? Do you know what you're supposed to do? Do you complete your work on time? Is your work done correctly? This kind of informal evaluation can help or hurt you. You'll want to be very organized from the start so you get a good reputation as a student.

Think of the beginning of each semester or term as a fresh start, or a new season. Just as athletes have the chance to prove themselves with the start of each new season, you can prove yourself a good student with each new semester. So start strong!

A STRONG FINISH

A team that does well in the beginning of the season but loses steam before the championship game is soon forgotten. In school, you need to start *and* finish each semester with the same amount of hard work and dedication. The end of the term is important because you'll be running out of time to catch up if you've fallen behind in your work. Avoid letting your strong start from the beginning of the semester go to waste! Look at your calendar well ahead of time and try to clear less important events from the last few weeks of class so you can focus on a strong finish.

Clear your schedule at the end of each semester so you'll have time to study hard and finish strong!

MANAGING TIME BY THE WEEK

Keeping a weekly planner helps you tackle the things listed on your long-term calendar, one week at a time. At the beginning of each week, you can plan for the tasks that are scheduled for that week. Here are some guidelines to follow as you create your weekly calendar.

- List regularly scheduled events and tasks first (such as class times, meal times, and the time you'll spend at work).

- Try to schedule time before each class for a brief review of your notes and to prepare for that day's lecture.

- When possible, allow yourself a few minutes after each class to review and organize your notes. Summarizing is a great (and quick!) way to review the material you just covered.

- Use your time efficiently by grouping similar activities together.

- Make it a habit to complete assignments before they're due. This way, you'll be able to turn in your work on time even if you come across snags in your schedule.

- Plan to study for 50 to 90 minutes at a stretch and be sure to allow yourself 15-minute breaks between study sessions.

- Base your study time on how many hours of class time you have each week. It's safe to estimate 2 hours of study time for every hour you spend in class.

- If possible, study at the same time every day. Choose a time when you're awake and alert.

- Use "gaps" in your schedule (such as time between classes) as study time. This way, you'll get more work done during the day and you'll have time to relax or do other things in the evenings.

- Schedule at least 1 hour per week to review how you will need to prepare for each class period.

- Be flexible by leaving some time unscheduled.

Different Forms for Different Folks

A wide variety of planners and calendars are available for purchase or downloading from the Internet if you want to make your own. Is it better to have a separate page for every day—or a week spread over a two-page spread?

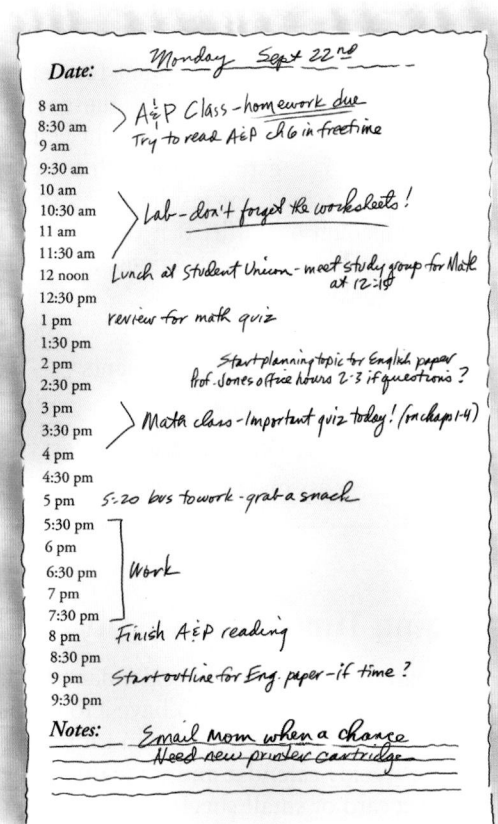

Sample planner page.

How should the time slots be broken down? This is all up to you. You'll soon find out what system works best for you.

It's usually best, however, to start out having *more* room on the page per day rather than less. If you don't have room enough to write down everything and to cross out items and add new ones when things change, then the planner can't do its job well and you may forget something important. The sample daily calendar page shown on p. 51 is just one student's preferred way of doing it, but it works well for this student. See what works best for you!

Pregame Planning

TIPS from THE PROS

It's best to create your weekly calendar on Sunday, before the week begins. Consider it your pregame planning session. Looking at the week ahead will help you spot any conflicts before they occur, so you can reschedule tasks as necessary. And being able to view the coming week at a glance will give you a chance to see how busy each day will be. Try to spread out your activities so each day is just as manageable as the next. You won't want to overload your schedule on Monday only to become burned out by Tuesday!

As you plan out your week, be realistic about the amount of time you estimate for each activity. In scheduling time for your commute to and from school, for instance, you should consider things such as the time of day and amount of traffic. If it takes longer to get to school in the mornings than it does to get home in the evenings, be sure to allow yourself enough time as you create your weekly schedule.

Other activities you should include in your weekly schedule are:

- homework assignments
- papers due
- upcoming quizzes and tests
- assigned readings

Managing Time with a Daily To-Do List

Even though you have a weekly calendar with key information for each day, it's still a good idea to have a to-do list for the next day's activities. This gives you a game plan for the new day. Every night, check your weekly calendar and write down the next day's activities on an index card or small sheet of paper. If you use an electronic organizer, such as a personal data assistant (PDA), enter these activities into the next day's to-do list. Include things such as homework, study time, errands, and other tasks that are specific to that day—all the personal and academic tasks you need to accomplish that day. The tasks on your list should be specific and you should be able to accomplish them in the time you have. Include on your to-do list those little things not on your calendar that you still need to do, such as to buy a new cartridge for your printer, pay a bill before it becomes overdue, ask a friend to borrow a book—whatever you don't want to forget.

Keep in mind that you can switch certain items around as the day goes on if it will make your day more efficient. The point is to get everything done, regardless of the order in which you wrote the items down. Allowing yourself some flexibility will keep you from becoming stressed.

It's also important to reward yourself for accomplishing everything on your to-do list. Cross off each item after you've completed it. This will give you a visual record of your success. Giving yourself 5 minutes of free time for each large task you finish is another good way to reward yourself—and to make sure you don't overdo it.

Or try this: each day you complete everything on your to-do list, put a certain amount of money into a jar. At the end of the month, use the money to treat yourself. This works better than setting up punishments. Recognize achievement and use days you don't get everything done as opportunities to look at your schedule and to see what changes might make your days more efficient.

I reward myself with some much-deserved free time after finishing everything on my to-do list!

PRIORITIES

A big part of keeping a schedule involves managing priorities. Should you read an assigned chapter in your history textbook tonight or study for the anatomy test tomorrow? Both are important—both need to be done. But which is the priority right now? Setting priorities is important to your success as a student. You'll need to set priorities for tasks, class attendance, and homework.

As you'll learn in coming chapters, it's better to start early on big projects (studying for an exam, writing a paper, etc.) and spread out the work over time. Use your weekly calendar to schedule things well ahead of due dates to ensure you have plenty of less stressful time to work ahead. So even though you may have that anatomy test tomorrow,

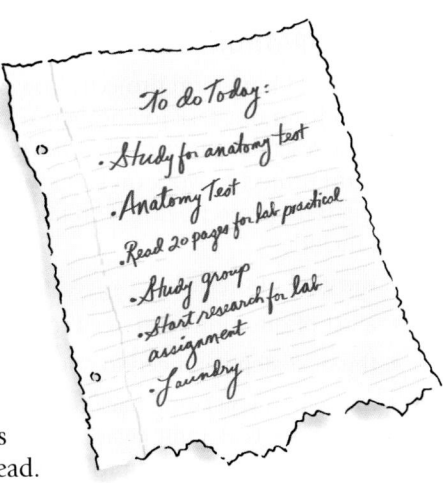

To do Today:
- Study for anatomy test
- Anatomy Test
- Read 20 pages for lab practical
- Study group
- Start research for lab assignment
- Laundry

Sample planner page.

you ideally might have already studied enough for it and, instead of trying to "cram" tonight, you can do your history reading more leisurely and get to bed early!

It's all a matter of setting priorities and planning ahead.

Making Progress

When you have several tasks with the same deadline, it's tempting to switch back and forth from one task to another. This feels like progress on all the tasks—they're all moving ahead. However, you're probably losing valuable time. When you switch from one task to another, you lose momentum. Your brain has to switch gears and begin thinking about a new project. Then, when you return to the first task, you often have to backtrack by finding out where you left off and what other steps need to be completed to finish the task.

IN AN HOUR OR LESS

If you have an hour or less to work, your priority should be completing a single task as opposed to inching forward on several tasks. Here are a couple reasons why it's better to focus on completing one task when you're short on time.

- Completing an activity on your daily to-do list will give you a sense of satisfaction. Once you've crossed an item off your list, you'll have one less task to worry about completing!

- Completing a task moves you closer toward your goals. Think about it this way: Your instructors won't give you credit for simply working on a homework assignment, but they *will* give you credit if you complete the assignment correctly and on time.

THOSE MARATHON PROJECTS

In the case of long-term projects, however, it's sometimes necessary to switch from one task to another. You can't expect to complete a 10-page research paper in one sitting! If you interrupt work on a long-term project to work on something else, write a few notes on the long-term project before you take a break from it. Your notes could include:

- the goal of the task
- a list of questions you need to answer
- the next step you need to complete

This way, when you come back to the long-term project, you'll be ready to get to work right away. Also, remember to keep all the materials you need for that project in one place so you don't have to spend time looking for them.

PROCRASTINATION PITFALLS

Procrastination is the enemy of time management. Procrastination is so common that we tend to fall into its trap easily, thinking it's not so bad to put things off. But procrastination is just a fancy word for wasting time. And you know that wasting time harms your success as a student. It leads to missed opportunities, poor performance, low self-esteem, and heavy stress.

When you procrastinate, you spend your time worrying instead of working. The task you postponed starts to weigh heavily on your mind. You imagine how hard it will be and you start to dread it. But this doesn't have to be the case! There are several steps you can take to recognize procrastination and put a stop to it.

> *Getting work done on time means having less stress to deal with later.*

PRIORITIZE, PRIORITIZE, PRIORITIZE

One habit that leads to procrastination is failing to prioritize your tasks correctly. Putting low-priority (nonurgent) tasks ahead of high-priority (urgent) tasks is all too common. There are many familiar excuses for avoiding important work, such as:

- I'm not in the mood. I have to wait until I'm in the mood or I won't do well.

- I feel like taking a break to celebrate finishing one chapter. I'll read the second chapter after that.

- I'll do it tomorrow.

- I've got plenty of time—there's no rush.

- I don't know where to start.

- I like working under pressure.

- I need to do other things first or I won't be able to concentrate.

What's the thinking behind all these excuses? Often it's a lack of confidence. You might think the task is going to be too hard. You worry about being able to do it right. You fear it will take forever. You read every bit of material you can to "prepare" for the project—buying time before you have to begin. When you're worried about the outcome of a project, it's hard to find the motivation to get started.

Now's the time to shake off the lack of confidence that wastes your valuable time. First, remember who you are—a motivated, efficient student dedicated to your education and your future career. Then, remember why you're doing the project—to get the information and experience you'll need in your new career. Last, remember that nothing is as hard as it seems. You just have to start. The sooner you start, the sooner you'll be done!

Here are some ways to get started on that big project right away.

- Do a little bit at a time.
- Juggle your deadlines.
- Set realistic goals.
- Stay focused.
- Be confident about your decisions.
- Keep your goals in mind.

A LITTLE AT A TIME

Try spending just 5 minutes on the project you've been dreading and putting off. Once you start, you'll probably find that you can keep working beyond 5 minutes.

JUGGLING DEADLINES

Occasionally, the problem is having several deadlines in the same week. It's tempting to do the easier projects first, "leaving time" for the hardest one at the end of the week. But it would be wise to clear the most difficult project out of the way first. With the pressure off, you'll be able to relax a bit and work on the smaller projects.

If the projects are equally large, try parceling out the work. Set apart small tasks that can be done quickly for each project. Once you have those small tasks out of the way, you can focus all your energy on one project first, then the other. Completing several small tasks gives you confidence and gets you closer to being done.

When juggling deadlines, divide your work into smaller tasks to make it more manageable.

KEEP IT REAL

What if the problem is unrealistic goals? Some students don't start projects in time because they set standards that are too high (by accepting nothing less than 100% or vowing to do something better and faster than everyone else in the class). Then they're afraid they won't live up to those high standards. Or they won't stop working until they feel the project is perfect, which causes them to miss the deadline.

What is the solution? Weigh the consequences of handing in what you think is an imperfect project against the consequences of handing it in late or not at all. A passing grade for an imperfect assignment is better than a zero for not handing it in at all.

BE CONFIDENT ABOUT YOUR DECISIONS

Uncertainty leads to indecisiveness, which usually ends in procrastination. For example, if you're not sure which topic to choose for a project, it becomes easier to put off starting the project. When this happens, remind yourself that you have to be decisive to become a successful student. Have confidence in yourself! The next time you're feeling lost and having a hard time choosing a topic, use these tips to help you get started.

- Brainstorm for ideas with other students.
- Ask your instructor for suggestions.
- Research several topics that might interest you.

KEEP YOUR EYES ON THE PRIZE

Remember the long-term and short-term goals you wrote down in Chapter 1? By keeping these goals in mind, you'll have an easier time staying on track and avoiding procrastination. When you're thinking about your goals, an assignment becomes more than just another task that has to be gotten through. It becomes your ticket to reaching your short-term goal of passing the course. And passing the course moves you closer toward your long-term goal of eventually becoming a licensed professional.

By focusing on your goals, you can give yourself the motivation you need to complete assignments that you might otherwise put off. Review your goals whenever you feel the urge to procrastinate. Also, looking at your goals is a good way to get back on track if you notice that you're putting too much energy into one assignment at the expense of other projects and commitments. Your goals will help you stay balanced and moving forward to greater success.

STAY FOCUSED

Where there's distraction, there's procrastination. Your mind will seek out distractions to avoid starting a project. You have to fight it. Get your game face on! Work on the project in a quiet area that is free from distractions. If you're in the kitchen, you might eat or do dishes as opposed to working. If you're in the living room, you might be distracted by the TV.

Another good way to avoid distractions is to make sure you have all the materials you need before sitting down to begin a project. It can be disruptive to your train of thought if you're constantly getting up to find another resource. Even small interruptions can cause you to lose momentum. Instead, gather your materials before you get started and then prepare to focus!

CHAPTER SUMMARY

- Make it a habit to attend all your classes. You'll be a much better student.

- Use the course documents provided by your instructor to find out what to expect in each course you take.

- Investigate what campus resources are available to you, including your instructors and other students, to help you achieve success.

- Organize your time by creating yearly, weekly, and daily schedules.

- Schedule your time well for efficient and effective studying.

- Avoid procrastination by dividing large projects into several smaller tasks and setting realistic goals to focus on. Focus isn't something you have, it's something you do. In other words, you can *learn* to stay focused.

REVIEW QUESTIONS

1. What can happen if you get in the habit of skipping classes?
2. How can your syllabus help you be successful in a course?
3. What items do you need to put into your yearly schedule?
4. Name several techniques for controlling your procrastination tendencies.

CHAPTER ACTIVITIES

Planning Exercise: Work as a group to create a long-term calendar for a student taking the course for which you are now reading this text. Plan out the entire school term by referring to the syllabus or class schedule for information on:

- class times
- midterm and final exam dates
- due dates for papers and other projects
- deadlines for completing each phase of lengthy projects
- test dates
- the instructor's office hours
- deadlines for drop/add
- holidays and school vacations

Maintaining Your Health and Well-Being

On completion of this chapter and the learning activities you will be able to:

- Understand how your health and well-being contribute to your success as a student

- Recognize the symptoms of stress and know how to manage it

- Stay healthy with exercise, good nutrition, and sufficient rest

- Know how to stay safe and avoid harmful substances

- Make and use a budget for financial well-being

When you're in school, you don't put life on hold. You still feel stress, or not, and you're healthy and happy—or not. If anything, health and well-being are even more important in school than at other times. You're likely to be stressed by a complicated life with many pressures. But you're also forming habits that you may carry forward into the rest of your life.

For all these reasons, it's critical to pay attention to your own health and well-being while a student. Stress can make you unhealthy, but good physical and mental health can reduce stress. Your overall well-being involves not only managing stress but also exercise, nutrition, and rest—the keys to good physical health—as well as maintaining personal safety and controlling your finances. Paying attention to all these dimensions of your life will contribute much to your success as a student.

STRESSED?! WHO'S STRESSED?!?

The word *stress* usually carries a negative connotation. The dictionary defines it as "a physical, chemical, or emotional factor that causes bodily or mental tension and may be a factor in disease causation."

As you have probably experienced, stress can cause physical and emotional tension. It also has been linked to illness. These are all very negative effects. However, there are different types of stress and different reactions to stress. How you choose to manage stress can determine whether you have positive or negative reactions to it.

I Stress, Eustress, Distress, We All Stress!

The two main types of stress are:

When managed correctly, eustress keeps me alert and focused. It helps me complete projects and meet deadlines.

- *Eustress.* This type of stress causes positive reactions. Low levels of stress often motivate people to complete tasks, meet deadlines, and solve problems. You may encounter this type of stress every day. Eustress can be helpful. It can stimulate you to accomplish your day-to-day tasks.

- *Distress.* This type of stress causes negative reactions. High levels of stress often cause people to overreact. Distress can cause you to feel nervous and unfocused. It can hurt your ability to participate in and enjoy normal activities.

SYMPTOMS OF STRESS

Identifying the symptoms of stress can help you manage it more easily. Recognizing stress at an early stage can help you keep short-term symptoms from becoming prolonged symptoms.

Some of these short-term symptoms of stress may seem familiar:

- You begin to take faster, shallow breaths.

- Your heart begins to beat faster.

- The muscles in your shoulders, forehead, and the back of your neck begin to tighten.

- Your hands and feet start to feel cold and clammy.

- You have a feeling of "butterflies" in your stomach.

- You feel physically ill, experiencing diarrhea, vomiting, or frequent urination.

- Your mouth becomes dry.

- Your hands and knees begin to shake or become unsteady.

These short-term symptoms of stress are fairly similar for most people. They are also easily recognizable. Short-term symptoms stop occurring once you remove yourself from the stressful situation. For example, you may experience short-term symptoms of stress immediately before giving a speech in class. After your speech, however, your heart rate will return to normal and your palms will no longer feel sweaty.

Prolonged stress can have more damaging effects over time:

- Your immune system begins to break down as a result of lost white blood cells. You become sick more easily and more often.
- Free fatty acids are released into your bloodstream, which can clog arteries and eventually lead to a heart attack or stroke.
- Your risk for developing many different diseases increases.

The symptoms of stress are not always physical. Stress also can affect your mental and emotional well-being. Psychological symptoms of stress include:

- losing your ability to think clearly or remember things
- having difficulty solving problems
- experiencing anxiety or fear
- losing your ability to sleep through the night
- changing your eating habits—either eating significantly less or more than usual
- worrying
- becoming exhausted

With all these effects, it should be clear that stress can really get in the way of academic success. Fortunately, you can learn to take control of stress before it begins to affect you seriously.

Taking Control of Stress

Just as there are different types of stress, there are different ways of dealing with stress. Several healthy ways of managing stress include:

- setting priorities
- simplifying your life
- learning to relax
- thinking positively
- gaining the support of others
- maintaining a healthy body

SETTING PRIORITIES

Setting priorities means determining which commitments are necessary and which commitments or tasks aren't. Priorities help you manage your time wisely. By determining which activities are most important, you can avoid the stress that comes with trying to do everything. On a given day, your schedule may include attending class, studying, working, spending time with family or friends, and exercising or enjoying other hobbies. As you look at each task on your to-do list, ask yourself, "Is it absolutely necessary to get this task done today, or would it just be nice to get it done today?" Move the absolutely necessary tasks to the top of your list. After—and only after—those tasks have been accomplished, consider tackling the other items. If you're unable to complete all the tasks on your list, don't stress. Instead, feel good about everything you did manage to accomplish that day.

Prioritizing your activities allows you to feel satisfied with your accomplishments each day. If you find that some activities regularly fall toward the bottom of your list, you might need to cut those activities out of your schedule entirely. You may not have time for everything, but you can make time for the most important things.

URGENCY OR EMERGENCY?

Another way to reduce stress is to adjust your schedule to fit your needs. If you have too many responsibilities that you aren't able to manage, try to give yourself more time. You may be surprised to see how many false deadlines you impose on yourself.

For example, if your coursework becomes overwhelming, consider taking fewer courses during the next term. It would be better to graduate several months later than to become overly stressed, break down, and wind up, unable to finish your degree or certification.

You can also avoid unnecessary stress by being able to tell the difference between an urgency and an emergency. When you feel stressed, divide your tasks into three separate groups:

- *Emergencies.* A task is an emergency if it absolutely has to be done immediately. For example, taking an injured pet to the veterinarian is an emergency.

- *Urgencies.* A task is urgent if it is important, but does not need to be dealt with immediately. For example, taking a pet in for its shots is urgent and should be done as soon as you have time.

- *Nonurgencies.* If a task is neither urgent nor an emergency, it is nonurgent. For example, whereas it is important to care for your pet, giving your healthy dog a bath is nonurgent.

If you have tasks that don't fit into any of the three groups, remove them from your list. They are not important and should be accomplished only if and when you have extra time.

Don't let your daily "To-Do" list get out of control. Less important activities can wait.

SIMPLIFY, SIMPLIFY, SIMPLIFY!

Because time is often short and most students have complex lives, simplifying your daily life can be another good strategy for avoiding stress. The following tips can help you simplify.

- Try to do all your errands in one place at one time. Going to several different locations may help you save money, but getting everything done at the same location saves you valuable time and energy.
- Don't watch TV every day.
- Let your voice mail take messages for you.
- Don't worry about sending greeting cards during the holidays.
- Stop attending functions you don't enjoy if they are not required.
- Avoid optional activities if they take up valuable time, such as chatting with your coworkers after work.
- Learn to say "no" when you have too much to do. Practice saying *no* to at least one request or invitation every week.
- Take time for relaxing when the job's done!

Keep It Simple

As a massage therapy student with a part-time job, I find some weeks are more stressful than others. When school gets busy, I try to keep everything else as simple as possible. I do my grocery shopping and run errands before the week starts. After getting home in the evenings, instead of turning on the TV, I sit down, close my eyes, and relax. Even if it's just for a few minutes, it helps me feel less rushed. I also find that I get a lot more done on the nights I don't watch TV!

RELAX INSIDE AND OUT

When you're stressed, your body reacts as if it's being attacked. Both your brain and the rest of your nervous system tense up. You can help back off from this "red alert" and reduce the stress you feel by learning to relax your body and your mind.

Try relaxation and stress management techniques such as massage, yoga, and meditation. Exercise is another relaxation technique. When you're sweating on a treadmill or pushing up a hill on your bike, exercise may not seem so relaxing. But after you finish your exercise session, you'll feel stronger, calmer, and more positive.

Don't Forget to Breathe

The next time you feel tense, try following this simple relaxation exercise.

1. Relax the muscles in your neck and shoulders.
2. Slowly lower your head forward.
3. Gently roll your head to the right and pause for 3 seconds.
4. Gently roll your head to the left and pause for 3 seconds.
5. Slowly roll your head down toward the center of your chest and pause for 3 seconds.
6. Switch sides and repeat, moving from left to right this time.

MIND OVER MATTER

Stress can be caused or intensified by negative thoughts, such as worrying about school work or personal issues. To combat this stress, train your mind to focus on the positive. Try not to dwell on the stress you're facing. Acknowledge it and then move on to a solution. Focus on the goals you want to achieve and imagine how you will be successful. For example, you could start by acknowledging to yourself or a close friend that you're stressed about an upcoming test or the piles of paper-work waiting for you at work. Then, you could move on to a solution by making time to study thoroughly or by setting aside lower-priority tasks.

Remember that imagining worst-case scenarios can lead to anxiety and stress. Worrying is rarely productive. On the other hand, if you spend your time thinking about success, you will stay motivated to achieve it.

It's also important to spend time with people who can help reinforce your positive thinking. Family, friends, classmates, and others can help you stay positive and remind you that people care about you no matter what. Other positive coworkers can remind you that you're all in this together.

If you are unable to ignore your negative thoughts, try this meditation exercise:

1. Find a quiet place and sit or lie down comfortably with your eyes closed.
2. Begin to inhale slowly and exhale fully.
3. As you exhale, imagine that you are expelling the stress and negative thoughts from your body.
4. As you inhale, imagine that you are replacing the negative thoughts with encouraging, positive thoughts.
5. Slowly inhale and exhale until you feel the tension and stress fading away.

Yoga relaxes my body and clears my mind.

Think Positively!

If you want to succeed, you should think like a person who expects success. Some ways to train your mind to think positively are:

- Say something positive every time you have a negative thought. You may want to repeat an inspiring quote or song every time your mind strays toward the negative. Little by little, you will overcome your anxiety.

- Get excited about upcoming projects and events. Imagine being successful in specific situations.

- Repeat positive mantras: "I *can* do this. I can *do* this."

- Be prepared. Have a "plan B" in case obstacles arise.

- Think of events that cause you to worry as learning experiences. You don't have to do everything perfectly as long as you learn something from your mistakes.

- Think of tests and exams as ways to demonstrate what you've learned. Don't get discouraged for not remembering everything. Completing an exam should make you feel proud and accomplished, not worried and inadequate.

I'm trying to be positive. I'm positive I have too much work to do!

NO MAN (OR WOMAN) IS AN ISLAND

The poet John Donne wrote, "No man is an island." There will be times when you'll need to depend on others for support. Having a network of supportive friends or family members will help you deal with stress. People in your network of support may include:

Rely on others for support when you're stressed.

- family members
- friends
- coworkers
- other students and classmates
- members of religious groups
- people who share your interests in sports or hobbies

Discussing your problems or frustrations with others can help alleviate stress. People in your support system may be able to give advice or offer new perspectives. Surrounding yourself with people who care about you will keep you encouraged to reach your goals.

A HEALTHY BODY MEANS A HAPPIER YOU

As you are entering a health care career, you probably already know much about why good health is important. Taking good care of your body helps prevent many serious illnesses—and it also helps you handle stress more easily. Not least among the many reasons why good health is important is the fact that you'll be able to succeed in school more readily if you're healthy!

Four keys to good health are:

- Regular exercise
- A healthful diet
- Sufficient sleep and rest
- Avoidance of harmful substances

Ready, Set, Exercise!

Exercising is an important way to keep your energy level up and help you feel good about yourself. Aerobic activities, such as running, swimming, or cycling, strengthen your heart and offer many other benefits as well. People who exercise aerobically:

- are less likely to get sick
- have more energy and mental alertness
- are less stressed and tense
- sleep better
- maintain an appropriate weight more easily
- improve their self-esteem

Choose an activity you truly enjoy. If you try to force yourself to do something you dislike, you won't be motivated to exercise on a regular basis. Another way to stay motivated is to exercise with a friend or in a group. Check around your campus for organized activities such as intramural sports, bicycle rides, a hiking club, etc.

If your daily schedule is busy, you may have to find time for regular exercise—add it to your weekly planner! Many working people, for example, exercise during their lunch break. Exercise may seem like a luxury, but it's a necessity for fighting stress and maintaining good health. If you take good care of your body, you'll be better able to keep up with your busy schedule.

For your body to receive the full benefits of exercise, you should work out at least three times a week for 20 to 30 minutes at a time.

For even greater improvement, work your way up to exercising four to six times per week. Just remember to give yourself at least 1 day of rest each week.

Food = Fuel

Think of food as fuel. Eating breakfast every morning will prepare your body for the busy day ahead. You can give your body the energy it needs by eating healthy foods. This will prepare your body to deal with stress as well.

FOOD FOR STRESS CONTROL

Vitamin B, vitamin C, and folic acid all help your body handle stress. These nutrients can be found in citrus fruits and leafy green vegetables, among other foods. And, the next time you find yourself reaching for something sweet to lift your mood, try eating foods that contain tryptophan instead, such as:

- milk
- eggs
- poultry
- legumes
- nuts
- cereal

Exercise with a friend and motivate each other to keep going!

Along with avoiding too much sugar, try to reduce your caffeine intake. Caffeine can cause tension and anxiety. Coffee, tea, and certain soft drinks contain caffeine and should be consumed in moderation.

FOOD FOR THOUGHT

Your brain needs nutrition to function properly. Eating right can give you the strength you need and help you stay alert throughout the day.

Part of healthy eating also means having a balanced diet of vegetables, fruits, grains, and low-fat proteins. It's important to cut back on things like sugar, salt, saturated fat, and caffeine. Several cups of coffee each morning may seem like the best way to wake up and get moving, but caffeine can cause tension and anxiety. As a result, you may find it harder to deal with stress. If you're looking for an energy boost, it's best to rely on healthier options, such as eating nutritious foods, exercising regularly, and getting enough rest.

The key to keeping your body and mind in top working condition is to have a well-balanced diet. Electrolytes, such as potassium, calcium, and magnesium improve your physical and mental performance. Consider incorporating foods that contain these nutrients into your healthy eating plan.

Good sources of potassium include:

- fish, such as salmon, cod, flounder, and sardines
- vegetables, such as broccoli, peas, lima beans, tomatoes, and potatoes (with their skins)
- leafy green vegetables, such as spinach and parsley
- citrus fruits
- other fruits, such as bananas, apples, and dried apricots

Good sources of calcium include:

- milk
- yogurt
- cheese
- soybeans
- some vegetables, such as collard greens and spinach

Good sources of magnesium include:

- some fish, such as halibut
- dry roasted nuts, such as almonds, cashews, and peanuts
- soybeans
- spinach
- whole grains
- potatoes (with their skins)

Today's specials are a treat for the brain as well as the palate— a well-balanced diet with a side of electrolytes!

EATING FOR HEALTH

Eating right can be fairly simple. Just remember these basic guidelines.

- Make sure you include different types of food in your diet each day, such as vegetables, fruit, grains, and low-fat proteins.
- Check nutrition labels and look for foods low in saturated fat and cholesterol.
- Try to limit your intake of sugar, salt, and oils.
- Eat or drink caffeinated food or beverages in moderation.

- Drink plenty of water and avoid drinking too much alcohol.
- Balance the number of calories you eat each day with the amount of physical activity you do.

Getting Enough Rest

Rest is also an important key to maintaining a healthy body. When you are well rested, you're able to complete tasks more efficiently. In contrast, feeling tired can increase the amount of stress you feel, which can wear your body down even more. Take cues from your body—when you feel tired, make sure you give yourself enough time to rest.

According to the National Institutes of Health, most adults need 8 hours of sleep each night. But, what if you're still unable to get a good night's rest even when you go to bed at a reasonable hour? Other things may be affecting your sleep.

- *Caffeine.* Do you often drink caffeinated beverages in the afternoons or evenings? Depending on how much caffeine you consume on a regular basis, it may be affecting your body's ability to rest at the end of the day. Caffeine is a stimulant that can stay in your system for 6, or even up to 12, hours. Your body may not be able to wind down properly in the evenings if caffeine is still affecting your system.

- *Nicotine.* Nicotine is a stimulant as well. If you're a heavy smoker, you may experience nicotine withdrawal during the night. Waking up multiple times can affect the quality of your sleep.

- *Alcohol.* Although having a glass or two of wine with dinner may make you feel drowsy, it can disturb your sleep later on. Alcohol can cause you to wake up during the night. As a result of drinking alcohol before going to sleep, you may wake up the next morning not feeling rested.

- *Food.* Eating foods that cause heartburn can affect your sleep. Not only does heartburn become worse after you lie down, it can interrupt your sleep during the night. Also, the amount of food you eat before falling asleep may affect the quality of your rest. Eating a large meal may make you uncomfortable and unable to sleep well. However, eating too little before bed also can make it hard to get a good night's rest.

On a positive note, a healthy diet and regular exercise can improve your ability to sleep. Making changes in those two areas may be all that's needed for you to start getting enough rest.

However, if you still have trouble sleeping, you may want to discuss it with your doctor. Getting good rest not only helps you manage stress, it's extremely important to your physical, emotional, and mental health as well.

Sleep: How Much Is Enough?

When you're tired, you're more likely to feel helpless, incapable, and defeated. Nothing sabotages a positive attitude like fatigue. Make sure you get 8 hours of sleep each night. That may seem like a lot—another luxury—but it's necessary for your emotional, mental, and physical health. Sleep is key to good performance in school, at work, and in life in general. By taking courses, you've been asking yourself to do more each day, so it's a good idea to give your body the rest it needs. And getting enough rest will also help you do more in your job and make more of your career.

Avoid Harmful Substances

"Substance" is the word health professionals use for many things people take into their bodies besides food. Although water and nutrients are needed by the body, these "substances" are not. When people talk about substances, they often mean drugs—but alcohol and nicotine are also drugs and considered substances the same as other drugs.

Why would you want to put something in your body that will only slow you down and maybe lead to a real problem?

Substances—any kind of drug—have effects on the body and mind. People use these substances for their effects. Some people use substances to try to alleviate stress. But many substances have negative effects, including being physically or psychologically addictive, and over time they actually increase one's stress. What is important with any substance is to be aware of its effects on your health and on your life as a student and to make smart choices. Use of any substance to the extent that it has negative effects is substance abuse.

The most commonly abused substances are tobacco, alcohol, and prescription and illegal drugs.

- If you don't use tobacco now, good!—but don't make the mistake some people make with "social smoking" with a friend, thinking there is plenty of time to quit later. Nicotine is one of the most addictive drugs in our society today—it will never be easy to quit. If you use tobacco now, start planning to quit by getting help. You might begin by downloading the booklet "Clearing the Air: Quit Smoking Today" at www.smokefree.gov.

- Alcohol is the most commonly used drug on most campuses. Drinking causes injuries to about 600,000 college students each year, resulting in 1,700 deaths. Almost 100,000 alcohol-related sexual assaults occur to college students. And about a fourth of all students report academic problems resulting from alcohol, resulting in lower grades. If you choose to drink at all, moderation is essential to avoid becoming a statistic yourself! Don't fall for the common myths about drinking not being all that dangerous. Learn more at www.collegedrinkingprevention .gov/CollegeStudents/alcoholMyths.

- People use prescription and illegal drugs for the same reasons people use alcohol. They say they enjoy getting high. They may say a drug helps them relax or unwind, have fun, enjoy the company of others, or escape the pressures of being a student. Like other substances, drugs have harmful effects on the body, affect one's judgment in ways that increase the risks for injury, and involve serious legal consequences if the user is caught. Why would any thinking student risk everything for a momentary high? If you have a problem using drugs, see a counselor at your campus health clinic for confidential help.

HAVE A LIFE!

Don't let your busy life as a student prevent you from having a social life. People are social creatures and friendships and interactions with others help us all control stress—and just have fun! But sometimes students feel they are so busy with their studies and work that they should never take time out to enjoy the company of others.

School also offers the opportunity to meet many people you would likely not meet otherwise in life. Make the most of this opportunity! From social interactions you can gain a number of benefits:

- The emotional comfort of friendships with people who understand you and with whom you can talk about your problems, joys, hopes, fears—everything you feel—without worrying how they may react

- A growing understanding of diverse other people, how they think and what they feel, that will serve you well throughout your life and in your future career

- A heightened sense of your own identity, especially as you interact with others with different personalities and from different backgrounds

When you join study groups with other students, you get the best of both worlds: while enjoying the social interaction, you're also learning more and in more ways than when you study alone.

> Studying together is a great way to get some work done while still having some fun!

STAYING SAFE

Your health and well-being as a student involves one more thing: personal safety and security. Although most campuses are very safe places, our world as a whole, sadly, is not always safe. Safety issues include preventing assault, date rape, and other violent crimes. By following a few common sense guidelines, you can stay safe both on and off campus:

- It's unwise to meet off-campus with people you don't know very well, especially after dark. Go to parties with friends—and stay with them to avoid becoming separated. Because date rape drugs are often added to drinks at parties, do not drink anything unless you know for certain it has not been tampered with.

- Don't give out your personal contact information (phone number, email address, etc.) until you have gotten to know a person well.

- Be careful if your date is drinking heavily or using drugs.

- Stay in public places where there are other people. Do not invite a date to your home before your relationship is well established.

- If you are sexually active, be sure to practice safe sex. Remember that most birth control methods do not protect against sexually transmitted diseases.

FINANCIAL WELL-BEING

One of the most common reasons for students to drop out of school before completing their program is financial: taking on too much debt. This happens because some students simply spend too much and fail to keep a budget until it's too late, often taking on too much debt through credit cards and loans. True, school is expensive. But, by learning to budget and control your spending, you can avoid any more debt than is necessary to complete your education.

Get a Job!

Most students these days work at least part-time. If you practice good time management (Chapter 2), you should have enough time for both work and school. Some students with greater financial responsibilities are able to work full-time while taking part-time classes.

Your school likely has a job office that will help you find a job if needed. The best jobs are those on or near campus, so you don't lose commute time, and those involving the school community rather than the general public. Working around other students and professors helps you feel connected to your school work and provides more satisfaction.

Spending Less

Remember the exercise in Chapter 2 where you estimated how you spend your time—but when you actually monitored your time, you may have been surprised where much of it goes? The same is true of money: most people really don't know where it all goes. See how much you know about your own spending habits with the activity "Where Does the Money Go?"

Where Does the Money Go?

Do your best to remember how much you have spent in the last 30 days in each of the following categories:

1. Coffee, soft drinks, bottled water $ _____
2. Fast food lunches, snacks, gum, candy, cookies, etc. $ _____
3. Social dining out with friends (lunch, dinner) $ _____
4. Movies, music concerts, sports events, night life $ _____
5. Cigarettes, smokeless tobacco $ _____
6. Beer, wine, liquor (stores, bars) $ _____
7. Lottery tickets $ _____
8. Music, DVDs, other personal entertainment $ _____
9. Ring tones, mobile phone applications $ _____
10. Fun techno-gadgets, video or computer games, etc. $ _____
11. Gifts $ _____
12. Hobbies $ _____
13. Newspapers, magazines $ _____
14. Travel, day trips $ _____
15. Bank account fees, ATM withdrawal fees $ _____
16. Credit card finance charges $ _____

Now, add it all up: _____

Be honest with yourself: is this *really* all you spent on these items? Most of us tend to forget small, daily kinds of purchases or underestimate how much we spend on them. Notice that this list does not include essential spending for things like room and board or an apartment and groceries, utilities, tuition and books, and so on. The greatest potential for cutting back on spending is to look as the optional things you spend your money on.

Because most students can't simply work more hours to provide a greater income, the better solution to avoiding debt is to learn to spend less. Follow these tips:

- Be aware of what you're spending. Write down everything you spend for a month to discover your habits.

- Use cash instead of a credit card for most purchases—you'll pay more attention.

- Look for alternatives. Buying bottled water, for example, can costs hundreds of dollars a year! Carry your own refillable water bottle and save the money.

- Plan ahead to avoid impulse spending. If you have a healthy snack in your backpack, it's easier to avoid the vending machines when you're hungry on the way to class.

- Shop around, compare prices online, buy in bulk. Buy generic products instead of name brands. Shop at thrift stores and yard sales.

- Stop to think a minute before spending. Often this is all it takes to avoid budget-busting purchases. With larger purchases, postpone buying for a couple days (you may find you don't "need" it after all).

- Make and take along your own lunches instead of eating out on campus.

- Read newspapers and magazines online or in the library.

- Cancel cable TV and watch programs online for free.

- Use free campus and local Wi-Fi spots and cancel your home high-speed connection.

- Cancel your health club membership and use a free facility on campus or in the community.

- Avoid ATM fees by finding a machine on your card's network (or change banks); avoid checking account monthly fees by finding a bank with free checking.

- Get cash from an ATM only in small amounts so you never feel "rich."

- Look for free fun instead of movies and concerts—most schools have frequent free events.

- If you pay your own utility bills, make it a habit to conserve: don't leave lights burning or your computer on all night.

- Use your study skills to avoid any risk of failing a class—paying to retake a course is one of the quickest ways to get in financial trouble!

Managing a Budget

Most people don't use a budget to help manage their money—and most people in our society admit to frequent financial troubles. Could those two facts be related?

How can you know if you can afford to buy a new laptop or cell phone right now? Can you afford to eat out tonight or should you go home and cook dinner? Should you take that weekend trip? Will you be tempted to spend the money because it's there in your checking account? Or because your credit card hasn't hit its limit yet? But then, what about those textbooks you need to buy, or those groceries, or the utility bill that arrives tomorrow—will you have money for those things too?

Unless you keep a budget, you really can't know for sure. That seems so simple—but then again, *not* keeping a budget is why so many people have so many money problems. Using a budget is just like using a calendar to schedule your time: it keeps you on track. Managing a budget involves three steps:

1. Calculating all your monthly sources of income.

2. Calculating and analyzing all your monthly expenditures.

3. Making adjustments in your budget (and lifestyle, if needed) to ensure the money isn't going out faster than it's coming in.

This may seem time-consuming the first time you create and use a budget, but this is time very well spent—literally! Soon it becomes an automatic, easy process.

STEP 1: CALCULATE YOUR INCOME

Use Table 3.1 to account for all funds available to you on a monthly basis.

Table 3.1 Monthly Income and Funds

Source of Income/Funds	Amount in Dollars
Job income/salary (take-home amount)	_____
Funds from parents/family/others	_____
Monthly draw from savings	_____
Monthly draw from financial aid	_____
Monthly draw from student/other loans	_____
Other income source: _____	_____
Other income source: _____	_____
Other income source: _____	_____
Total Monthly Incoming	_____

STEP 2: TRACK YOUR EXPENSES

Tracking expenditures is more difficult than tracking income. Some fixed expenses (tuition, rent, etc.) you should already know, but until you've actually added up everything you spend money on for a typical month, it's hard to estimate how much you're really spending on cups of coffee or snacks between class, groceries, entertainment, etc. You can start with the numbers you estimated earlier in "Where Does the Money Go?" Put these into the spaces in Table 3.2.

Note that there are *lots* of spending categories in Table 3.2. This is important—because, if you find you need to cut back your spending to stay on budget, you need to know *specifically* where you can make the cuts.

STEP 3: BALANCE YOUR BUDGET

Now compare your total monthly incoming with your total monthly outgoing. How balanced does your budget look at this point? Remember that you probably had to estimate several of your expenditures. You can't know for sure until you actually track your expenses for at least a month and have real numbers to work with.

What if your expense total is significantly higher than your income total? First, you need to make your budget work on paper. Go back through your expenditure list and see where you can cut. Students shouldn't try to live like working professionals. There are many dozens of ways to spend less so that you can live within your budget.

It's normal to have to make adjustments at first. Just make sure to keep the overall budget balanced as you make adjustments. For example, if you discover that you have to increase what you spend for textbooks, you may choose to spend less on eating out—and subtract the amount from that category that you add to the textbook category. Get in the habit of thinking this way instead of reaching for a credit card when you don't have enough in your budget for something you want or need. That's your long-term plan for controlling your financial life.

If you want to get fancy and *really* take control, you can use a computer spreadsheet or financial program to track all your expenditures and manage your budget.

Now I've saved enough for a new lab coat without having to go without eating for a week!

Table 3.2 Monthly Expenditures

Expenditures	Amount in Dollars
Tuition and fees (1/12 of annual)	_____
Textbooks and supplies (1/12 of annual)	_____
Housing: monthly mortgage, rent, or room and board	_____
Home repairs (estimated)	_____
Renter's insurance (1/12 of annual)	_____
Property tax (1/12 of annual)	_____
Average monthly utilities (electricity, water, gas, oil)	_____
Optional utilities (cell phone, Internet service, cable TV)	_____
Dependent care, babysitting	_____
Child support, alimony	_____
Groceries	_____
Meals and snacks out (including coffee, water, etc.)	_____
Personal expenses (toiletries, cosmetics, haircuts, etc.)	_____
Auto expenses (payments, gas, tolls) plus 1/12 of annual insurance premium—or public transportation costs	_____
Loan repayments, credit card pay-off payments	_____
Health insurance (1/12 of annual)	_____
Prescriptions, medical expenses	_____
Entertainment (movies, concerts, nightlife, sporting events, purchases of CDs, DVDs, video games, etc.)	_____
Bank account fees, ATM withdrawal fees, credit card finance charges	_____
Newspaper, magazine subscriptions	_____
Travel, day trips	_____
Cigarettes, smokeless tobacco	_____
Beer, wine, liquor	_____
Gifts	_____
Hobbies	_____
Major purchases (computer, home furnishings) (1/12 of annual)	_____
Clothing, dry cleaning	_____
Memberships (health clubs, etc.)	_____
Pet food, veterinary bills, etc.	_____
Other expenditure: _____	_____
Other expenditure: _____	_____
Other expenditure: _____	_____
Other expenditure: _____	_____
Other expenditure: _____	_____
Total Monthly Outgoing	_____

School Loans, Grants, and More

Most schools offer financial aid. The federal government also offers several different types of aid. According to the U.S. Department of Education, more than nine million students receive some form of financial aid every year. This may include:

- *Flexible payment plans.* Some schools allow students to make several smaller payments throughout the semester instead of paying one lump sum for tuition expenses.

- *Loans.* A loan is an amount of money given by a lender. Loans must be repaid within a certain period of time, usually with interest. The federal government, as well as private lenders (banks), offer several different types of student loans.

- *Grants and scholarships.* Unlike loans, grants and scholarships do not have to be paid back. The qualifications are often highly specific. There may be a grant or scholarship out there just for you.

- *Work-study programs.* Some schools participate in work-study programs by arranging part-time jobs for students with financial need. Students are paid an hourly rate to earn money for tuition.

Financial aid is available to most students—take advantage of it! Make an appointment with one of your school's financial aid advisors. An advisor can help determine which type of aid will work best for you. But note: never take out more loans than you really need for your education. You don't want to spend the first 10 years of your new career struggling to pay them off!

Questions about financial aid? Your financial aid advisor has answers!

CHAPTER SUMMARY

- Control stress by setting priorities, simplifying your life, learning to relax, thinking positively, and maintaining social supports.

- Regular exercise, good nutrition for physical and mental health, and plenty of sleep every night promote good health, reduce the risks of disease, and make it easier to succeed in school.

- Balance your school life with a social life that can contribute much to your well-being.

- Ensure you take steps to maintain your personal safety on and off campus.

- Use your personal budget to keep control over your finances and prevent debt that could stall your academic progress.

REVIEW QUESTIONS

1. List three specific stress reduction techniques that work for you as an individual.

2. Name four foods you will try to eat more of to improve your health and three dietary substances you will try to minimize in your meals.

3. Describe the benefits of regular exercise.

4. What kinds of unnecessary expenditures do you sometimes make that negatively affect your budget?

CHAPTER ACTIVITIES

1. Go to www.mypyramid.gov and read about how to stay within your daily calorie needs in order to maintain an appropriate weight.

2. For further information on types of financial aid, visit the U.S. Department of Education website: www2.ed.gov/fund/grants-college.html

3. First complete the "Where Does the Money Go?" exercise in this chapter. Then get together with a friend and compare notes. Brainstorm together how you might change your habits to cut back in some areas to help minimize your debt.

CHAPTER 4

Interacting with Others

WINNING STRATEGY

On completion of this chapter and the learning activities you will be able to:

- Know why it's important to get to know your instructors

- Describe how participating in class contributes to your success as a student

- List the benefits of networking with other students

- Participate in campus life

- Understand and celebrate diversity

Succeeding in school involves so much more than simply sitting in classes, reading textbooks and doing homework, and completing assignments and tests. Education is an active learning process and students learn best through interacting with their instructors and other students. This experience includes individual interactions with your instructor, participating in classes by engaging in discussions with the instructor and other students, and networking with other students outside class. This chapter explains how to create a network that can benefit your studies while helping you share what you've learned with others. People in your network can be great resources of information, advice, and support. As you meet more and more people through all your educational experiences, you are also learning more about cultural diversity and gaining skills that will also serve you well in your future health care career.

GETTING TO KNOW YOUR INSTRUCTORS

From the first day of class on, you are getting to know your instructors. At the start you may have wondered what your instructors will be like. Will they be nice? Are they going to be fair? Will they present things so you can understand them? Are you going to like and respect them? Are they going to like and respect you? As you listen and observe in class from the first day, you will begin to pick up on the instructor's personality, communication style, and perception of students.

Getting to know your instructors helps put you ahead of the game because you'll feel comfortable in the classroom more quickly. In turn, you will be able to concentrate on your studies sooner and more effectively.

Teaching Styles

Some instructors like to share their philosophies about teaching. They'll also let you know how they prefer to run their classes.

- Some instructors like a formal atmosphere where they lecture and students raise their hands during a specified question and answer period.
- Others prefer a more informal environment where there's open classroom discussion and students can interrupt at any time to ask questions.

Knowing your instructor's teaching style gives you an advantage in the classroom. You'll learn to anticipate your instructor's next moves. This will help you study for exams, take effective notes, and participate in class. The sooner you can do these things, the easier it will be to do well in the course.

Making a Good Impression

Getting to know your instructors involves more than simply observing them. Keep in mind that they are observing you too! You are making an impression whether you want to or not. It's worthwhile to make a good impression from the start by being attentive in class, participating in class discussions, and not hesitating to interact with the instructor.

An important first step is to introduce yourself to the instructor early in the term, even on the first day of class. Although it may seem intimidating, this is a very important step toward becoming a successful student.

Be reassured—most instructors welcome opportunities to meet their students. They enjoy teaching and they like to get to know their students. As soon as the instructor learns your name and knows that you're serious about being successful, then you're one step ahead of hundreds of other students. This isn't brownnosing. It's just good strategy.

YOU DON'T KNOW ME, BUT . . .

"You don't know me, but . . ." may be the first words that come to mind. But that phrase sounds self-doubting. Instead, practice an introduction that conveys confidence. Try saying something such as, "Hi, my name is Melody Harris. I'm taking this course as a prerequisite for my Radiology Technician Certification. I'm really looking forward to a great semester. I'll see you at the next class." It's as simple as that.

It's a good idea to plan ahead and practice what you're going to say. If you're especially anxious about this introduction, you might want to write down what you'd like to say and memorize it beforehand. When you approach the instructor, relax by taking a slow, deep breath. Then, put on a friendly smile, make eye contact, and make your introduction. If you're comfortable offering a handshake, that would be appropriate, too.

Be confident when introducing yourself to your instructor.

If your instructor didn't cover it in the class introduction in the first class, now is an ideal time to ask about the best way to contact him or her when needed. Should you have any questions over the course of the semester, you'll need to know how to get in touch with your instructor. Some instructors prefer email. Others prefer a visit during their office hours or a phone call. Be sure to make a note of this information.

CLOSE ENCOUNTERS

There are places, such as large lecture halls that hold hundreds of students, where it may not be possible to introduce yourself after class. In these cases, consider seeking out the instructor during office hours to make your introduction. Your instructor certainly will remember and be impressed with you. And, in this more relaxed setting, the instructor may engage you in conversation for a few minutes about your career plans or the class. You may walk away with some interesting insights and valuable information.

Instructor Conferences

It's a good idea to have an individual conference with every instructor at least once during the semester or term. A student-teacher conference gives you the opportunity to ask questions about lecture content, learn about your instructor's expectations of students, or discuss any other important issues related to the course.

Here are a few tips to consider when scheduling a conference:

- Decide on a specific topic to discuss, such as your first test or a confusing concept from a recent lecture.
- Write down any questions you'd like to ask about that topic, putting your most important questions at the top of the list. Your instructor may have a limited amount of time to meet with you.

Schedule a student–teacher conference to learn more about what your instructor expects of students.

If you're organized and prepared for the meeting, you'll have a better chance of getting the information you need in that short period of time. Also, if the idea of a student–teacher conference makes you nervous, having questions already written out will put your mind at ease and help you stay focused.

By taking initiative and meeting with your instructor one-on-one, you'll demonstrate that you're concerned about your success as a student. You'll also gain a better understanding of your instructor. This will help you make sure you're on the same wavelength—it's always better to be aware of your instructor's expectations than to blindly assume you're doing well in a course.

PARTICIPATING IN CLASS

Participating in class, interacting with the instructor and other students as part of the group, is also essential for being actively engaged in learning. Those who fail to participate, who sit passively in the classroom listening to others, are not fully engaged. They simply will not learn as well as those who make the effort to speak up. This principle applies both in lecture and discussion classes as well as laboratory classes.

A Winning Game Plan

How can you pave the way for success in the classroom? There are several tactics you can use to join in and participate:

- Sit in the front of the room.
- Make sure you can see projection screens and in-class demonstrations.
- Make sure you can hear your instructor clearly.

- Ask questions to the instructor when appropriate.
- Answer questions the instructor asks the class.
- Respond to the comments of other students when invited by the instructor.

But Why Participate?

Remember that education is an *active* experience. You don't just passively receive knowledge and skills by sitting there like a stone. Participating in class is the best way to actively engage. Here are some of the benefits of participating:

- Studies show that students actively engaged by participating in class learn more—and thus get better grades. One reason is that when you speak out in class and answer instructors' questions, you are more likely to remember the discussion than if you were passively listening to others speak.

- Paying close attention, thinking critically about what an instructor is saying, and making an effort to relate what is being said in a lecture can dramatically improve your enjoyment of the class and your impression of the instructor. You'll notice things you'll miss if you're feeling bored. You also may discover your instructor is much more interesting than you first thought.

- Asking the instructor questions, answering the instructor's questions posed to the class, and responding to other students' comments is a good way to make a good impression on your instructor. Then, in office hour visits and other interactions, the instructor will remember you as an engaged student. This helps you form an effective relationship with the instructor if you later need extra help or maybe even a mentor.

- Participating in class discussions is also a good way to start meeting other students. You may meet others with whom you can form a study group, borrow class notes if you miss a class, or team up with in a group project. Other students are often happy when you ask a question that was in their mind too and you'll gain their respect and find it easier to talk with them outside class.

Take a step toward success by being a front-runner. Sit in the front row on the first day of class!

The Front-Runner

Most of us have been to school assemblies or conferences where there are rows of seats. The front of the room is where the speaker's chair or podium is placed. As everyone files in to choose their seats, not many people go straight to the front row to sit. Even when there is "standing room only," seats in the front row often stay empty. We could spend a lot of time analyzing this scenario, but let's cut to the chase: sitting up front in the classroom is actually a very good thing.

Often students would rather blend into the background. They don't want to be noticed by the instructor or other students. Although you may have serious reservations about sitting in the front of the classroom, you'll find that it's in your best interest. Just remember—you're the student with the winning game plan. You're the one who's going to slide into home plate with room to spare.

If you think only the "A" students sit up front, you may be right. But they probably became "A" students by choosing to sit up front, in addition to employing other strategies. It takes effort to achieve success in the classroom. Sitting in the front row is one way to demonstrate that you're willing to make the effort. It also makes it easier to interact with the instructor during the class.

TURN UP THE VOLUME

When choosing a seat up front, be sure to find one that lets you hear the instructor well. If you miss hearing important information in any class, it can have a negative effect on your overall performance in the course.

THE ROAR OF THE CROWD

Classrooms tend to get noisy. One example is when the instructor discusses clinical rotation assignments. This is a very exciting time in health professions classes. Often, before the instructor can finish explaining all the details, students start talking back and forth. Some students begin asking the instructor questions while other students continue talking among themselves. The noise level rises. Unfortunately, this is when students either completely miss what the instructor is saying or hear it incorrectly. Misinformation then gets passed from student to student.

By sitting near the instructor, however, you'll be more likely to hear over the noise. When you're able to hear clearly, you can be one of the informed students who leaves class knowing exactly when and where you are supposed to go for your clinical assignment.

"How Do I Do It?"

If you're one of those students who has always sat quietly in class, you may have to take active steps to start participating. Following are some pointers to get going.

When your instructor asks a question to the class:

- Raise your hand and make eye contact, but don't wave your hand all around trying to catch attention or call out. This isn't a game where the first, wildest, or loudest one wins!

- Be sure you have something to say before speaking. Take a moment to gather your thoughts and take a deep breath. Don't just blurt it out, but speak calmly and clearly.

When you want to ask the instructor a question:

- Don't ever feel your question is "stupid." If you have been paying attention in class and have done the reading and you still don't understand something, you have every right to ask. Many others in the class are probably wondering the same thing too!

- Ask at the appropriate time. Even if the instructor has said you can ask a question at any time, don't try to interrupt the instructor mid-sentence. Wait for a natural pause and a good moment to ask. But, unless the instructor asks students to hold all questions until the end of class, don't let too much time go by or you may forget your question.

- Be sure it's a real question, not an admission that you weren't paying attention. If you drifted off during the first half of class, don't ask a question about something that was already covered.

- Be open minded and show you really do want to learn. Don't let your question sound like a complaint or disagreement. You may be thinking: "Why would so-and-so believe that? That's just crazy!" But take a moment to think about what you're feeling. It's much better to say, "I don't understand what so-and-so is saying here. What evidence did he/she use to argue for that position?"

- Be sensitive to the needs of other students and avoid dominating a discussion.

Remember, there's no such thing as a "stupid" question. But it can be "dumb" not to ask if you don't understand something!

When your instructor asks you a question directly:

- Be honest and admit it if you don't know the answer or are not sure. Don't try to fake it or make excuses. With a question that asks for an opinion, feel free to express your ideas openly. It's also fine to explain why you haven't decided yet.

- Organize your thoughts before answering. Instructors seldom want just a yes-or-no answer. Give your answer and then provide reasons for your position.

Participation Helps Your Instructor Too

By staying engaged and asking questions about the lecture, you'll also help your instructor clear up any misunderstandings about the material. Other students might be confused about the same concepts that are confusing to you. The instructor's answers to your questions may be helpful to your classmates as well.

Also, by speaking up in class, you'll let your instructors know how well you're grasping the material they're presenting. When instructors feel that students are keeping up with the pace of the class, they know their teaching is being successful. If students are not keeping up, they can make adjustments or present the material in a different way.

Your network is your home team—it's easier to succeed when you work together!

NETWORKING WITH OTHER STUDENTS

Networking with other students is another key way to actively participate in your education. Networking should be an integral part of your winning strategy—not only while you're in school, but later on in your health care career. In school, your network is an informal academic support system that you develop with some of your classmates.

So what exactly is networking? How does it differ from simply having friends?

The Home Team

You've heard of television networks and computer networks. A network is an interconnected group or system. A television network is a group of local stations that share the same programming. A computer network is a group of computers that share information. A network can be big or small.

A network also can be a group of people who choose to share information and expertise with one another. Usually, people "network" with others who share their interests or occupation. A network has several key features:

- It is voluntary—you choose to join and participate in a network.
- It is focused—information and expertise on a specific topic are shared.
- It is respectful—members all treat each other with respect, sharing ideas and asking questions freely.

Sometimes, a network forms naturally. For example, your instructor might put you into a group in class. You might find this group stays together even after the course is over. But usually, networks have to be purposely created.

Why Network?

Networking is valuable for many reasons. Having a study group you can count on, getting tips for succeeding in a certain instructor's course, and being able to borrow notes from someone when you can't make it to class are all good reasons to network. As a student, networking gives you advantages you wouldn't have if you choose to keep to yourself.

Perhaps the most important reason to network is to give and receive support. Your peers at school probably understand better than anyone else the challenges you're facing. Members of your network can offer support by

- listening to your ideas
- sharing ideas with you
- making study time more relaxing
- helping you in tough times

Networks provide support by bringing people with the same goals together to help each other. The more you give, the more you get, and the better you feel.

> You're in the same boat as many of your classmates. Share what you know and learn from others by networking.

Unexpected Benefits of Networking

Hi, my name is Roman and I'm training to become a medical coding specialist. I didn't like the idea of networking when I first started taking courses. It's hard for me to meet new people and I usually prefer to work on my own anyway.

But when I started having trouble in my medical terminology course, I had to ask for help. My academic advisor suggested that I talk to some of my classmates and try to form a study group. It wasn't easy, but I introduced myself to a couple of guys in my class and we started meeting regularly every week. Not only did my grades improve, but I ended up gaining two friends—something I wasn't expecting at all!

Casting Your Net for an Informal Network

Even if you're shy or not very good at meeting new people, you'll find that informal networking is fairly simple and painless. Begin by introducing yourself to students sitting near you in class. If a conversation ensues, great! If not, you can speak to them again at the next class.

After you've spoken to another student a few times, bring up the idea that the two of you could make a deal. Propose that the two of you periodically share or compare lecture notes. Mention that you think it might help both of you understand the material better if you go over your notes together. You also can offer to share your notes if your classmate ever has to miss a lecture. If you're willing to help someone else, that person may be willing to share information with you when you need it.

Because everyone's schedules are already full, it may be difficult to arrange a time to meet. You might suggest meeting in the campus library or student study lounge a few minutes before class once a week. Your new acquaintances might not take you up on your offer right away. If they don't like the idea of networking, they may not realize they're turning down an excellent opportunity. If the first student you talk to is not interested, don't take it personally. Just move on, meet other classmates, and try again.

Creating a More Formal Network

Creating a more formal network requires three things:

- You have a reason for forming the network. That way, you can keep the network focused. The reason may be to form a study group, for example. This study technique is discussed in more detail in Chapter 8.

- You add value to the network. You can contribute information as well as consume it.
- You have ground rules for participation.

Creating a network takes time, but it's worth it. If you develop a network of people you know and like, who can help you *and* learn from you, then you'll get the full benefit of this kind of interaction. Learning how to network successfully is very important for your future career, when you'll need to keep up on the latest information and techniques.

FIRST-ROUND DRAFT PICKS

Begin by making a list of some classmates you'd like to include in your network. Choose two or three people from that list. Your network can grow over time, but it's best to start small. You'll find it's easier with a small group to get to know everyone and to arrange times to meet.

To narrow your list, think about the people on it:

- How much time does each person have to spend?
- How might each person contribute?
- What are people's strengths and weaknesses?
- Have you ever worked together before?

Weaknesses don't necessarily disqualify someone—we all have them. But think about how that person will fit into the group.

SETTING UP THE RULES

Once you have your list, approach the people on it and suggest networking. The key here is to be clear about what you're proposing and to be respectful. If you want to have an informal network, where members email when they have a question or something to contribute, explain that. If you want a formal network, where members meet regularly in addition to emailing and having one-on-one conversations, make that clear.

Remember to be open to the suggestions and constraints of others. If someone can't meet when you'd like but is very valuable to the network, be flexible so you can include them. If someone doesn't have the time or simply doesn't want to be part of a formal network, graciously thank them and let them off the hook. That student can still be a personal, one-on-one source of information and sharing for you.

Using Your Network

Remember, networking means interaction. Everyone in the network contributes information *and* consumes it. That's what makes the network valuable; everyone benefits from everyone else's knowledge and different ways of looking at things. When you network, you share what you know with others who do the same, creating something new in the combination of ideas. It's the sharing of ideas, or the dialogue, that makes a network successful.

GIVE CREDIT WHERE CREDIT IS DUE

Information shared in a network is free. If something is shared in a network, all the members of the network should be allowed to use the information. But that doesn't mean you write down what someone else says and pass it off as your own opinion or knowledge. Always acknowledge your network. Be honest by saying your idea was inspired by someone in your network.

STAY SAFE

Once your networking group is established, you're likely to have people's phone numbers and other personal information, like email addresses or home addresses. Guard these carefully and don't share them with anyone without asking first. And remember not to wear out your network with constant contact, especially with network members who are busy with their home lives and jobs.

Be safe! Only give out your email address and phone number to people you trust. And **never** share other people's contact information without asking first!

When to Network

Informal networking goes on all the time—between classes, over lunch, and on the phone. Activate your formal network at specific times:

- *At the beginning of the semester.* Find out which students in your class have had this instructor before and what you should expect. Ask them for tips and advice about being successful in this class, but *never* ask for old tests and quizzes.

- *After class or lab sessions.* Strike while the iron is hot. Talk about the ideas you had during class, find out what your classmates thought, and then debate and expand the conversation. Take notes of your conversations next to your lecture notes.

- *After a missed class.* Call on your network to fill you in, but remember not to lean on your network to do your work for you.

Network Online

You also can network online. This works well for a network that is spread out. For instance, if your cousin is a health professional in another state, you can include him or her in an online network. Just remember to be careful online. All the rules for face-to-face networks apply here. Only talk online with people you trust and don't invite strangers in without talking with the whole group first. Avoid giving out network members' email addresses. You should only share information online with people you know and trust.

ACADEMIC ADVISORS AND COUNSELORS

So far in this chapter, we've discussed the many benefits of interacting with both instructors and other students—and the value this has for your academic success and future career. But there are others, too, on campus with whom your interaction is very important, including those in administrative and counseling offices. Among these, the most important for students are academic advisors.

They're Here to Help

A school's academic counselors are there to advise students. Counselors work with course catalogs and student problems every day. If you have a question about your requirements, or if you just need advice, your school's academic counselors are great resources. They can often provide you with information you won't find in the course catalog.

It's also important to establish a relationship with your academic counselors for the future. Some schools offer job placement services as well. Your school's academic counselors may be important contacts to have in your network once you begin looking for a full-time position in your field.

CAMPUS LIFE

The social world of your school is an important part of the total experience. Social relationships help make you feel more at home on campus and also contribute to your happiness and success as a student. Take advantage of opportunities to meet new people and become involved in campus life.

- Keep the door open for meeting new people. For example, don't follow the same routine with your meals on campus, but try to sit with different people so you can get to know them in a relaxed setting. Study in a common area or lounge where others may happen upon you when you need to take a break or study with someone else.

- Stay open in your interests. Don't limit yourself just to past interests, or you'll miss many opportunities to make friendships that may start based on some other activity.

- On the other hand, don't try to get involved in everything going on around you. Overcommitting yourself to too many activities or trying to join too many social groups will spread yourself too thin. Remember: it's the quality, not the quantity, of your social interactions that matters.

- Let others see who you really are. How can someone want to spend time interacting with you if they don't know who you are?

- While letting others get to know you, make an effort to get to know them, too. Show some interest. Don't talk just about your interests—ask them about theirs. Show others that you're interested, that you think they're worth spending time with, that you really do want to get to know them. It's easy enough to show your feelings with casual comments like, "It was really fun studying together—I think we should do it again!"

- Once a friendship has started, be a good friend. Respect your friend for what he or she is and don't criticize them or talk about them behind their back. Take the time to understand your friend when they're feeling sad or frustrated or just "need a friend." Give emotional support when your friend needs it and accept their support as well when you need it.

Clubs and Organizations

Organized groups and activities offer a great way to enrich your social interactions on campus. But participating in organized activities requires some initiative—you can't be passive and expect these opportunities to come knocking on your door. A stimulating life on campus offers many benefits, including these:

- Organized groups and activities speed your transition into your new life as a student.

- Organized groups and activities help you experience a much greater variety of social life. If you interact only with other students your own age with similar backgrounds, you'll miss out on the broader campus diversity: students who are older and may have a perspective you may otherwise miss, upperclass students who can share much from their experience, and students of diverse heritage or culture whom you might not meet otherwise.

- Organized groups and activities help you gain new skills, whether technical, physical, intellectual, or social. Such skills may find their way into your résumé when you next seek a job or your application for a scholarship or other future educational opportunity. Employers like to see well-rounded students with a range of proficiencies and experiences.

- Organized groups and activities are fun and a great way to relieve to stay healthy and stress. As discussed in Chapter 2, exercise and physical activity are essential for health and well-being and many organized activities offer a good way to keep moving.

FINDING ACTIVITIES YOU LIKE

There are many ways to learn about groups on your campus and opportunities for various activities. Start by browsing the school's website, where you're likely to find links to student clubs and organizations. Watch for club fairs, open houses, and similar activities on campus. Especially near the beginning of the year, an activity fair may include tables set up by many groups to provide students with information. Look for notices on bulletin boards around campus. Stop by the appropriate school office, such as the student affairs or student activities office or cultural center. Most schools make an attempt to provide information about all clubs and groups on campus.

DIVERSITY

Ours is a very diverse society—and increasingly so. Already in many parts of the country, non-Hispanic whites comprise more than 50% of the population and, by 2020, one in three Americans, and about half of all college students, will be a person of color. But "diversity" means much more than racial and ethnic differences. Diversity refers to the great variety of human characteristics—ways that we are different even as we are all human and share more similarities than differences. These differences enrich humanity and all of us as individuals.

Experiencing diversity while in school brings many benefits both in the present and for the future:

- Experiencing diversity in school prepares students for the diversity they will encounter the rest of their lives. Those who work in health care careers will work with other professionals and patients who may be very different from themselves. Success in your future career will require being able to understand people in new ways and interacting with new skills. Experiencing diversity in school assists in this process.

- Students learn better in a diverse educational setting. Encountering new concepts, values, and behaviors leads to thinking in deeper, more complex, more creative ways. Studies have shown, for example, that students who experience racial and ethnic diversity in their classes are more engaged in active thinking processes and develop more intellectual and academic skills than others with limited experience of diversity.

- Experiencing diversity on campus is beneficial for both minority and majority students. All students have more fulfilling social relationships and report more satisfaction and involvement with their academic experience.

- Diversity experiences help break patterns of segregation and prejudice that have characterized American history. Discrimination against others—whether by race, gender, age, sexual orientation, or anything else—is rooted in ignorance and sometimes fear of people who are different. Getting to know people who are different is the first step in accepting those differences, furthering the goal of our society becoming free of all forms of prejudice and unfair treatment of people.

- Experiencing diversity makes us all better citizens in our democracy. When we can better understand and consider the ideas and perspectives of others, we are better equipped to participate meaningfully in our society. This is especially important for those in health care careers.

- Diversity enhances self-awareness. We gain insights into our own thought processes, life experiences, and values as we learn from people whose backgrounds and experiences are different from our own.

What Is Cultural Diversity?

When people talk about cultural diversity, they are referring to the ways in which all people are similar to and different from each other. Racial classifications, ethnicity, gender, sexual orientation, religious affiliation, socioeconomic status, and age are all elements of cultural diversity.

It's natural to note differences between yourself and those around you. As you enter the world of health care, it is important to understand that, regardless of differences, you must treat everyone with equal care and respect. This means refusing to allow any preconceived notions about others to affect the quality of your work. By openly accepting diversity, we can move closer toward appreciating the things that make people different and treating everyone with the same care and respect.

Part of being a professional means treating everyone you encounter—patients, supervisors, and coworkers—with equal care and respect.

Cultural diversity is an especially important part of health care because of the genetic characteristics, cultural values, and belief systems that affect people's health. By knowing and understanding these cultural differences, you'll be able to provide better care.

RACE AND ETHNICITY

The term *race* is typically based on a person's physical characteristics, such as skin color, facial features, hair texture, and body stature. *Ethnicity* is the concept of identifying with the traditions and values of a particular cultural group. Although the terms ethnicity and race are often used interchangeably, they refer to different aspects of a person's identity. An individual can be of one race, yet identify with a different ethnicity.

In health care, race is sometimes a factor in diagnosis and treatment because genetic traits are often more common in certain racial groups than in others. Likewise, ethnic values and traditions also can have an effect on a patient's health and well-being.

GENDER ROLES

It's important to consider gender roles when interacting with others of a different background. In some cultures, for example, the male is considered the head of the household. In these cases, a male family member might speak for his female family members. In other cultures, women are the dominant family members. It's important that health care professionals consider this when providing care. Gender roles may influence the way in which a patient prefers to be treated. Every patient has a different role in the family and it's important to be sensitive to the different needs and priorities of each.

SEXUAL ORIENTATION

A person's sexual orientation is a personal matter—true for both your fellow students and patients and coworkers with whom you will interact in the future. Again, it is important not to prejudge another person but to accept all forms of diversity. In health care, there are times when sexual orientation may be an important issue, such as when addressing sexually transmitted diseases. Regardless of what information patients choose to reveal, it's important to avoid making judgments or assumptions about a patient's sexual orientation or lifestyle choices.

RELIGION

Everyone has freedom of religion in our society and all people's religious choices should be respected. In health care, patients' religious beliefs and values may affect how they wish to be treated by health care professionals. For example, a person's religious affiliation can influence decisions about diet and nutrition, sexual lifestyle, and other health matters. As a health care professional, you'll need to be sensitive to each patient's values and beliefs when providing care. You can do this by respecting the personal choices made by patients and adapting care to suit each patient's needs.

Keeping an Open Mind

My name is Ling and I'm a medical assistant. There was one patient I came across during my clinical experience who I thought had something against women. He wouldn't let me take his blood pressure—he always asked for a man to do it. I thought he was prejudiced against me and, I admit, I felt angry. So I talked to my mentor. She told me that I shouldn't make assumptions or take his actions personally. She said that part of providing the best care meant doing what I could to accommodate different patients' needs, whether they make sense to me or not.

Later, I found out that the patient was an Orthodox Jew and it was against his religion to be touched by a woman not in his family. I was embarrassed about my assumptions. After that, I made sure a male medical assistant was around to take the patient's blood pressure and other vital signs during his office visits.

SOCIOECONOMIC STATUS

Socioeconomic status is yet another way in which people are different and no one should be judged or discriminated against based on such differences. A person's socioeconomic status should not affect the kind of care and treatment that a health care professional provides. Every patient, regardless of financial situation, should be given the best possible care and attention. Avoid stereotyping patients according to their level of education or how much money they make. Instead, focus on each patient as an individual worthy of your attention, respect, and sensitivity.

AGE

Age is another of the many ways in which individuals differ. In health care, age is often important because the aging process affects the health of patients in different ways. Younger patients often have health care needs different from those of older patients. You'll need to be sensitive to patients' changing physical and emotional needs as they grow older. It's also essential that you avoid making assumptions about a patient based on age. It is important to remember that physical fitness and health can vary for different people at every age and stage in their lives.

Celebrate Diversity!

Diversity is not something just to know in your head like a concept you've learned in school. Diversity is an essential part of the rich experience of humanity—it is something to be celebrated and embraced as part of being human! Don't think of diversity as something to be aware of just in your future health care profession as you work with patients. You'll grow as a person as you seek out diverse experiences now as a student and actively promote understanding of the many differences among us all.

Here are things you can do to celebrate diversity, challenge old stereotypes, and promote a healthy multiculturalism on your campus and in your community:

- Acknowledge your own uniqueness, for you too are diverse.
- Consider your own (possibly unconscious) stereotypes so you can work to eliminate them.
- Do not try to ignore differences among people.
- Do not expect all individuals within any group to be alike.
- Don't apply any group generalizations to individuals.
- Take advantage of campus opportunities to increase your cultural awareness, such as cultural fairs and celebrations, concerts, and other programs.
- Take the initiative in social interactions with diverse others.
- Work through any conflicts as in any other social interaction.
- Take a stand against prejudice and hate when you see it.

CHAPTER SUMMARY

- Make a good first impression on your instructors. Introduce yourself and plan a visit for an individual conference during office hours.
- Sit in the front of the room. Have a great seat with the best view and best sound. This sets you up for successful participation in class.
- Ask questions in class and answer those posed by your instructors. Active engagement in the process is the most effective way to learn.
- Network with other students to get ahead. Develop good study networks that will help you learn and support your academic goals. Remember to play it safe.
- Networking is important because it allows you to share your ideas and learn from others. Networks also can be a source of support during the challenges you face as a student.

- Investigate campus organizations and activities to become part of the wider academic community while having fun and maintaining your health.
- Challenge yourself to better understand and celebrate the diverse differences among people. Never prejudge others who are different from you in any way.

REVIEW QUESTIONS

1. Why is it important to sit in the front of the classroom?

2. What is an example of a time when health professions classrooms become particularly noisy? Why is it essential to be able to hear your instructor at a time like this?

3. Give an example of how you might be making an impression on your instructors even when you may not be aware of it.

4. How would introducing yourself to your instructor help prepare you for future clinical experience?

5. List several benefits of developing both an informal and formal network with other students.

6. What are several challenges you might face when creating a network?

7. List at least six ways in which people may be different from each other.

8. Why should diversity be celebrated?

CHAPTER ACTIVITIES

1. Networking Exercise: Talk with at least two friends at school about creating a network. Each of you will then come up with one other person you know and trust from one of your classes. Give yourselves a week to contact the other people. Then, meet as a group to see how you all get along. If everyone seems like compatible network members, decide on a place and time to meet regularly.

2. Campus Life Activity: Using the tips presented in this chapter to learn about campus organizations and activities at your school, find at least three you might be interested in participating in. Using the school's website or other resources, investigate these three to learn more about what goes on in each.

SHARPENING YOUR SKILLS

Making the Most of Your Learning Style

On completion of this chapter and the learning activities you will be able to:

- Describe the brain's role in learning

- Identify your learning style and know how to make the most of it

- Explain how critical thinking applies in health care settings

- Describe Benjamin Bloom's six levels of cognitive learning

Do you know there are different styles of learning? For example, you might absorb information better when you see it (as in a chart) than when you hear it (as in a lecture). Some people learn better when they can "do" the material, as in a lab experiment. Most classes are made up of students who have a variety of different learning styles. What works for one student might not work as well for the next.

This chapter discusses several major learning styles and how you can use your individual learning style, as well as other methods, to become a successful student. We'll also talk about the importance of critical thinking and how it relates to both learning and your future career.

LEARNING STYLES

Your brain, and how it functions, is a contributing factor to the way you learn. By understanding how your brain works, you'll be on your way to understanding your particular learning style. And, by being aware of your learning style, you'll discover ways you can learn more efficiently.

The Brain and Learning

The human brain weighs about three pounds. Although small, this organ functions as the control center for the entire body. It determines how a person thinks, feels, and acts. The brain is where all learning takes place.

YOUR HARDWORKING BRAIN

It's true that people use only a percentage of the brain's full capability. Even so, the human brain is responsible for an amazing number of functions, including:

- breathing, circulation, temperature regulation, and other involuntary functions
- balance and equilibrium
- voluntary actions
- emotional reactions
- reasoning and thinking
- the ability to convert things you experience with your senses into recognizable images, sounds, feelings, smells, or tastes

BRAIN ZONES

The three main areas of the brain include:

- the brain stem
- the cerebellum
- the cerebrum (see *The Human Brain*)

> The way your brain works has an effect on how you learn.

The Human Brain

The three main areas of the brain all have different roles in the learning process:

- Brain stem: connects the brain to the spinal cord and controls basic functions
- Cerebellum: controls basic functions such as balance and coordination
- Cerebral cortex: controls high-level functions and voluntary muscle movements

cerebral cortex
cerebellum
brain stem

Star Players: The Brain Stem and Cerebellum

The different areas of the brain all work together. However, each area is responsible for controlling certain functions. For example, the brain stem and cerebellum, located nearest the spinal cord, control basic functions. These areas of your brain determine your body's ability to maintain muscle tone. They also regulate involuntary actions, such as your heartbeat and breathing.

Team Captain: The Cerebrum

The cerebrum, the largest portion of the brain, contains the cerebral cortex. The cerebral cortex is very complex. It controls many high-level functions of the mind, such as sight and conscious thought. It also controls the body's voluntary muscle movements.

The brain's cortex is divided into two hemispheres. Different types of thought processes begin in each hemisphere:

- The left hemisphere is responsible for controlling language and logical thinking. In terms of physical movement, the left hemisphere controls the right side of the body.

- The right hemisphere controls nonverbal processes, such as intuitive thinking and imagination. It manages movement of the left side of the body.

You may have heard the expressions "left-brained" and "right-brained." A person who is an artistic daydreamer may be considered "right-brained." A mathematician, on the other hand, may be considered "left-brained." One hemisphere of their brains may be more dominant, making certain tasks easier than others. This doesn't mean those individuals only use a single hemisphere of their brains. On the contrary, the left and right hemispheres of the brain are always active in everyone. Whether your personality is more logical or creative, you can use both sides of your brain. When it comes to learning, knowing your brain's strengths and weaknesses is helpful.

Left Brain vs. Right Brain

You may be a musician with an ear for rhythm or a math whiz with an eye for sequential order. In either case, both hemispheres of your brain are available to help you learn. By recognizing which hemisphere of your brain is stronger, you'll become aware of the kinds of tasks that require your brain to work slightly harder. The illustration on the right lists the major "left-brain" and "right-brain" reasoning tasks.

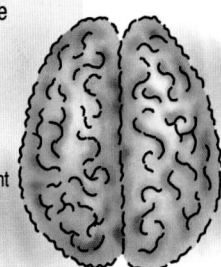

Left Hemisphere
- language and word use
- logic, reason, and analysis
- numbers and math
- rational thought
- sequence and order

Right Hemisphere
- artistic perception
- creativity
- intuitive thought
- music and rhythm
- imagination and abstract thought
- daydreaming and reflection
- random thought

ON A CELLULAR LEVEL

There are two main types of brain cells:

- *glial cells.* These cells are the brain's supporting structures.

- *neurons.* These cells receive and send messages to one another in the form of electrochemical nerve impulses. Neurons play a role in complex functions of the mind and body, such as learning, motion, and sensations.

Good News Travels Fast!

News travels fast in the human brain. For example, an electrical signal travels from one neuron to the next at a rate of 200 miles per hour (100 meters per second)! These electric signals move from one neuron to another through a network of dendrites and axons.

The following steps trace the path of an electrical signal from one neuron to the next:

1. The electrical signal travels down the axon.

2. The axon releases neurotransmitters (chemicals).

3. The neurotransmitters travel across the synaptic gap and are received by the dendrites of the next neuron.

4. The next neuron absorbs the neurotransmitters.

5. The neurotransmitters change the second neuron's electrical state.

6. A new electrical pulse is produced by the second neuron.

Making Connections

Each infant is born with a complete set of neurons. As a child learns, those neurons develop connections between themselves. Every time sensory cells are stimulated by outside forces, nerve impulses travel from one neuron to the next.

Every time you learn something new, the neurons in your brain begin sending messages in a certain pattern. If stimulation is repeated, it becomes easier for the same nerve impulses to travel from one neuron to the next. This is because patterns begin to form and the neurons involved gain better connections between themselves. Your neurons "learn" these patterns and develop faster ways of communicating with each other.

Losing Ground

Learning new information causes the number of connections between your neurons to increase. Unfortunately, it's a two-way street. As soon as you stop learning new things, some of those connections begin to disappear. The solution to the problem is continued learning. You can rebuild those lost connections by relearning things you've forgotten.

Learning new things, such as how to ride a bike, develops connections between your neurons. The more you practice something, the stronger those connections become.

Keeping Your Brain Healthy

A healthy body translates to a healthy mind. By taking care of your body, you'll be taking care of your brain, too. And, if you treat your brain right, you'll become a better learner.

You're probably aware that your diet has an impact on your physical performance. A doughnut in the morning won't give you lasting energy. But a healthy breakfast, such as a bowl of oatmeal and a cup of yogurt, will give you energy. Believe it or not, the food you eat and the fluids you drink affect how you learn as well. Diet has been linked to mood, behavior, and mental performance. For example, substances called electrolytes actually speed your thought processes. These substances work as conductors in the brain. Electrolytes help conduct the electrical currents that travel from one neuron to the next. Put simply, they help your brain think faster and work more efficiently.

Chapter 3 discusses healthy eating as a way to help your body cope with stress. Another reason to have a well-balanced diet is that it can enhance your ability to learn.

WHAT'S YOUR STYLE?

Now that we have looked at how the brain functions, let's focus on learning styles. A learning style is an individual's preferred way to receive and process information during the learning process. One student may learn better by reading about a topic, for example, whereas another student learns better by hearing the instructor talk about the topic.

Three major learning styles are:

- visual
- auditory
- kinesthetic

What's my learning style?

Just as one hemisphere of your brain might be more dominant than the other, it's likely that you prefer one particular learning style to the rest. There is no right or wrong style, no best or worst style—people simply learn in different ways. The key is to identify your own style and then use this knowledge to your advantage. Being aware of your learning strengths can help you improve your studying and test-taking skills. You'll also be better equipped to compensate for your weaknesses. By making your learning style work for you, you'll get more out of your courses. You'll have improved interaction with your instructors and other students. As an added benefit, you'll also more fully enjoy the learning process.

The Eyes Have It

Visual learners prefer to read about things or watch demonstrations. They like looking at charts, diagrams, and images. They like it quiet when they study. They may use arrows and circles when taking notes to visually show relationships of ideas or their importance.

If you're a visual learner, seek out all kinds of visual materials. These include:

- textbooks
- demonstrations (in class or on video)
- handouts from your instructors
- information on the Internet
- lecture notes
- articles in magazines, newspapers, and professional journals

Here are some study tips for visual learners:

- Pay close attention to visual presentations.
- Take notes using visual cues (circles, arrows, color highlighting, concept maps).
- Highlight in your textbook and jot margin notes.
- Make flashcards that include visual cues to help you remember key concepts.
- When studying, visualize things the instructor wrote on the board or included in a PowerPoint presentation.

Sounds Good to Me

Auditory learners gain the most information when they hear about things. This includes listening to your instructor and other students, as well as recorded presentations. If you learn best by listening, think of where you can find auditory information. Resources that may be helpful to you include:

- class discussions
- class lectures
- question-and-answer sessions
- giving speeches
- reading aloud
- recorded lectures or speeches (video or online)

Here are some study tips for auditory learners:

- Choose a class seat where you can hear well without noisy distractions.
- Form a study group with others who prefer to talk over course topics.

- Read your notes aloud when studying. Record your readings and replay.
- Record key class lectures (with instructor's permission) and review later as needed.
- Be sure to participate in class.

Jump Right In

Kinesthetic learners prefer to learn by doing. They like to move around and may have difficulty sitting still for long periods. They prefer a hands-on approach to learning. If it's easier for you to grasp information after putting it to use by actively doing something, you're a kinesthetic learner. To enhance your learning opportunities:

- Seek out workshops and skills labs.
- Volunteer to perform in-class demonstrations.
- Attend field trips.
- Help out with group projects.
- Seek out internships or volunteer work in your field.
- Offer to tutor a classmate.

Here are some study tips for kinesthetic learners:

- Use interactive computer learning aids to engage with the subject.
- Study while physically moving; take frequent breaks to walk around; read assignments on a treadmill or exercise bike.
- Make flashcards frequently and sort them as you review.

Being a Kinesthetic Learner

Hi, my name is Marcela and I'm training to become a surgical technician. I used to have a hard time learning new information. I'd read something and it wouldn't sink in. Or I'd sit and listen to a lecture only to feel like I wasn't getting it. I thought maybe I wasn't cut out for school.

That all changed when I took my first skills lab. All of a sudden, it's like a lightbulb went on in my head! When I had a chance to demonstrate my skills, I actually understood and remembered the procedures.

Now that I know I'm a kinesthetic learner, I look for other ways to help me learn, in addition to reading my textbooks and going to classes. I attend workshops, go on field trips, and get plenty of hands-on experience volunteering at a local hospital.

- If having difficulty sitting still, chew gum or repetitively tense and relax body muscles.
- Talk to a study partner while walking or jogging.

Discovering Your Own Learning Style

From the preceding discussion, you probably already have a good idea about your own style. In reality, however, few people have purely only one learning style. You may favor one dominant approach, but likely you still learn through other styles also. To discover more exactly your preferences and receive tips to help you learn as fully as possible, take a few minutes to check out the learning styles assessment from MyPower Learning. You can access this by first visiting thePoint website that comes along with this text (http://thePoint.lww.com/StudentSuccess2e). See the inside front cover for login information. You can also visit the MyPower Learning website at www.mypowerlearning.com.

This learning style assessment asks you questions that relate to how you interact with and process new information. The questions are simple and easy to answer. Following the questions, you receive a custom report that evaluates your learning style preferences with comparative scores in the three styles described earlier: visual, auditory, and kinesthetic. Your scores identify your strongest style, your second strongest, and your least favored style.

Be sure to click on the "Detailed Report" option at the end of your score report and print it out for the list of tips for maximizing your learning in these three areas:

- Participating in class
- Doing homework assignments
- Preparing for class and exams

Students with different learning styles, or mixes of styles, will gain from different study and preparation techniques. It pays to find out what works best for you!

How Large Do You Think?

Another difference in how people learn and think involves the scope of thought. Some people just naturally think in large, abstract terms—thinking globally. Others naturally think more in terms of the details. As with the previous learning styles, understanding your own thinking and learning preferences can help maximize your learning in classes.

GOING GLOBAL

Global learners excel when they think about the "big picture." If you're a global learner, you may find that you enjoy learning how concepts are related to one another. Your favorite instructor may be one who gives plenty of analogies to show how the information is connected. Or you may prefer a class where the instructor lays out certain facts and helps students make conclusions about the material. If this is the case, try using the following tips to get the most out of your courses:

What do you usually see, the tree or the forest?

- Summarize your lecture notes and draw conclusions about the material.
- Sketch diagrams to show how different ideas come together to form the "big picture."
- Come up with questions about the topics covered in class.

IT'S ALL IN THE DETAILS

Detail learners prefer to learn new information in a logical pattern. For example, many people have had the experience of purchasing items labeled "some assembly required." If you're prone to looking at instruction manuals and following directions closely—as opposed to jumping right in and randomly trying to fit pieces together—you're probably a detail learner.

If you're a detail learner, you may do best in a class where the instructor follows a strict outline. But regardless of your instructor's teaching style, there are ways you can use your strengths to your advantage:

- Summarize your lecture notes with bulleted points.
- Draw diagrams to relate small pieces of information (details) to larger themes or ideas.
- Create a to-do list for yourself before you sit down to study.

- Write down questions as they come to mind during lectures or while reading.
- Think of examples you can use to illustrate particular details.

CRITICAL THINKING AND LEARNING

Closely related to learning skills are critical thinking skills. It's especially important for health care professionals to have solid critical thinking skills. When you think critically, you analyze information to form judgments about it. The information may be gathered from your observations, personal experience, reasoning, or communication. In your profession, you may be required to gather and analyze information and evaluate results on a daily basis. If you're able to think critically and make good judgments based on the information you can gather, you'll have a positive impact on your patients' health.

Critical Thinking Skills in the Workplace

My name is Derek. I've been working as a certified medical assistant for about a year now and I've definitely had to put my critical thinking skills to the test! I work in a family practice office, so our patients are all ages and they come in for a lot of different reasons.

Last week, one of our patients made an appointment because he was experiencing abdominal pain. He arrived early for his appointment and said he was still experiencing pain and was feeling nauseous, too. I could tell he was in obvious distress—his skin was pale and he was holding his stomach in pain. Even though his appointment time wasn't for another 20 minutes, I decided to take him back to wait in an empty exam room. Then I gave the physician a heads-up about his symptoms, in case he needed to be examined right away. It's a good thing I did, because as it turned out, the patient had appendicitis!

Direct Yourself to Learning

Individuals who are successful in both school and the workplace have achieved their success by becoming self-directed learners. Being a self-directed learner means that you take responsibility for your own education, regardless of your preferred learning style. In the coming chapters, you'll learn more about different ways to accomplish this.

For example, if you're having a hard time understanding a particular concept in class, you can find other resources, ask your instructor for clarification, or meet with your study group. Although test scores are important, your main goal in school should be to learn the material. Being a self-directed learner means not only studying in order to do well on tests and quizzes, but also studying in order to store information in your long-term memory. It also means being able to apply that information to new situations once you become a practicing health care professional.

Likewise, successful professionals must be self-directed learners. Once you are no longer a student, you'll have to take even more responsibility for your own learning. This may mean keeping yourself up-to-date on the latest research by reading articles related to your field. Or it may mean requesting to observe a procedure you've been struggling to learn. In these cases, you should be aware of what you need to learn and how you can go about increasing your knowledge and improving your skills.

Regardless of your past experience as a student, you can achieve success now by becoming a self-directed learner. You have chosen to further your education because of your motivation toward a particular career goal. Contrary to how you may feel at first, you *can* control a great deal of what you learn and how your educational experience will unfold.

Learning is a process. By understanding how the process works, you can begin to develop the learning skills you'll use as a student and later in your professional career.

Bloom's Learning Levels

Cognitive learning, closely related to critical thinking, occurs in several stages. Benjamin Bloom, a noted neuropsychologist, assigned the following names to these stages in the 1950s:

- knowledge
- comprehension
- application
- analysis
- synthesis
- evaluation

Although other psychologists have developed new theories about thinking since the 1950s, most theories are similar to Bloom's. In other theories, the stages may be named or ordered differently, but their descriptions remain relatively the same.

Learning is a process. You have to start at the bottom and work your way up to the next level.

KNOWLEDGE

During the knowledge stage, you memorize information and repeat it word for word. At this point, you don't necessarily have to understand the information to memorize it. Some examples of things you may need to memorize are:

- formulas in a math class
- people's names, addresses, and phone numbers
- simple instructions, such as steps in a skill

COMPREHENSION

In the comprehension stage, you understand information enough to be able to restate it in your own words. If you take effective notes during class, your notes should reflect your comprehension. You can accomplish this by:

- drawing charts and diagrams
- summarizing and paraphrasing information
- describing how concepts are related
- explaining the material to someone else

APPLICATION

During this stage, you use the information you've memorized and comprehended to accomplish a task. Examples of application include:

- using a mathematical formula to solve a problem
- using a rule or principle to classify information
- successfully completing a project after receiving and following directions

ANALYSIS

Analysis involves breaking information into parts to understand how those parts are organized and related to one another. For example, when you read an article in a magazine, you first look at the different pieces of information presented. An author may provide several anecdotes to illustrate a single main point. Then, you analyze the different pieces of information by thinking about how they are related. How does each anecdote relate to the author's theme or main point? What message is the author communicating?

SYNTHESIS

In the synthesis stage, you put your analysis to use by developing a new idea. In a sense, you take parts of information and put them together in a different way to form a new concept. This stage of learning and thinking is more creative than the others. It includes:

- building on the pieces of information contained in your notes and writing a paper or presentation
- forming a plan for conducting a lab experiment
- writing a poem or short story

Remember, critical thinking is a tool used not just by students, but by health care professionals as well.

EVALUATION

During the last stage in critical thinking, you evaluate information. This means you use other methods, such as comprehension and analysis, to determine whether or not information has value or relevance. Evaluation can include:

- determining which conclusions are actually supported by facts and research
- judging the value of a work of art or a piece of writing based on specific standards
- determining the value and relevance of information presented in a textbook, lecture, or class discussion

Be Critical

When reading your textbooks or other material, you shouldn't just passively receive the information but rather be an active reader. During active reading, it's important to be a critical reader. Now is the time to analyze the text and question the author. By asking questions about the text, you'll begin to think critically about the material. As a result, you'll improve your comprehension and remember more. You'll be better able to apply, analyze, and evaluate the information. Ask yourself:

- How would I apply this information if I were caring for a patient?
- How is this material related to what I've studied in the past?
- How does this information measure up to the information in other sources I've read? Does it support or contradict what I already know about the topic?
- Are there any inconsistencies?
- Does the author present an objective view of the material? Is the information based on assumptions, facts, experiences, or opinions?
- Do I agree with the author? Why or why not?
- On which topic would I like more information?

CHAPTER SUMMARY

- Your brain plays a role in determining your particular learning style.

- Play to your strengths by identifying your learning style and being aware of how to enhance it.

- Enhance your learning and prepare for your future career by thinking critically about what you are learning.

REVIEW QUESTIONS

1. Describe the benefits of knowing your own learning style preferences.

2. What types of resources or activities would be helpful to someone who is an auditory learner?

3. Write a definition for critical thinking in your own words.

4. Why do synthesis and evaluation learning skills come after knowledge and comprehension skills?

CHAPTER ACTIVITIES

1. Discovering Your Learning Style: Take the learning styles assessment by My Power Learning by first visiting thePoint website (http://thePoint/lww.com/Student Success2e). Use the access code in the front cover of this textbook. After you take the assessment, print your Learning Style Index and specialized report.

2. Working Together: Divide into three groups based on your learning style assessment results (visual, auditory, or kinesthetic). In your group, come up with an idea for an activity or project that would help students with your learning style understand the information in this chapter. Then, write three to five sentences explaining how and why the activity or project would accommodate your particular learning style. Present your ideas to the other two groups in the class.

3. Critical Thinking Exercise: Review *Bloom's Learning Levels*. Draw a pyramid, set of stairs, skyscraper, or another image to illustrate Bloom's six levels of learning. Label each level and provide a practical example. For instance, a practical example for the lowest level of learning, knowledge, could be memorizing the definition of a key term and repeating it word for word.

Listening, Taking Notes, and Reading

WINNING STRATEGY

On completion of this chapter and the learning activities you will be able to:

- Use active listening techniques in the classroom
- Adjust to different lecture styles
- Maximize your learning in the classroom
- Take effective notes in class
- Develop a strategy for reading actively
- Create a note-taking outline

Listening, taking notes, and reading skills are all necessary if you want to succeed as a student. During lectures, it may seem like your only responsibility is to sit quietly while your instructor speaks. This method might even have served you well in high school. But now you have the opportunity to do much more! By using the strategies discussed in this chapter, you'll be able to take charge of your own learning process. And, when you're in control, nothing can stand in your way of learning new things and accomplishing your long-term goals. You'll be able to round the bases and slide safely into home!

LISTENING SKILLS

The importance of listening carefully is discussed throughout this book. Good listening skills should be cultivated during your time in school. These skills will play a big role in your success not only as a student, but also as a health care professional. When miscommunication occurs in health care, the results can have negative consequences for patients.

Not hearing about assignments in school can, at the very least, result in frustration and grades that don't reflect your true ability.

A lot of valuable information is given out in class from the first day forward. Because most of it is verbal, it's worthwhile to start sharpening your listening skills. Make it a point to listen closely instead of jumping to conclusions. Watch and listen for essential clues in the classroom. Ask questions if you don't hear something and write down as much as you can to help you remember what was said.

Active Listening

To become an active participant in your own learning process, try to keep your mind engaged instead of sitting back and relaxing while your instructor lectures. Make an effort to listen actively. To better understand the material, think of questions to ask the instructor. You can write your questions in your notes and refer back to them at the end of the lecture. If your instructor offers to answer questions toward the end of class, ask then. If not, look up the answers on your own after class.

There may be times, however, when you'll have a question that can't wait until the end of the lecture. If you feel that your instructor is moving too quickly, politely raise your hand and ask him or her to repeat or clarify a specific point. But keep in mind that you should do so only when you have prepared for the class properly beforehand—don't embarrass yourself by asking something you should already have known from doing assigned reading!

Give yourself a head start—practice good listening habits from day one in the classroom.

Stop, Look, and Listen

Active listening involves thinking about how you are listening and continually working to improve your listening skills. When you are listening actively in the classroom, you're doing more than simply hearing words. You're also deciphering main ideas, deciding what information is most important, and making adjustments in how you listen according to your instructor's teaching style.

In the game of school, an active listener is participating in the game, not just standing on the sidelines. Whether you need to become an active listener or merely improve your active listening skills, all students can follow these guidelines:

- Avoid doing things that can distract you from listening.
- Identify main ideas.
- Pay attention to the speaker's transition cues.
- Mentally organize information as you hear it and devote your attention to material that seems more important.
- Take effective notes.

INTERFERENCE!

There are several behaviors that could be sabotaging your active listening game. Make an effort to avoid:

- letting distractions interrupt your train of thought
- tuning out difficult material
- allowing your emotions to cloud your thinking
- assuming the material is boring
- concentrating on the speaker's quirks
- letting your mind wander
- pretending to listen
- listening only for facts and not ideas
- trying to write down every word in your notes

IDENTIFY MAIN IDEAS

Identifying main ideas is a key element of active listening. Each lecture you hear will include main ideas even though they may be presented in different ways. Some of the approaches your instructor may take are:

- introducing new topics
- summarizing main points
- listing or discussing a main idea's supporting details
- showing two sides of the same issue
- discussing causes and effects related to a main idea
- identifying a main idea's problems and solutions

Avoid behaviors that could be hurting your active listening game. Keep your eye on the ball and stay focused!

WAIT FOR A SIGNAL

Listening for signal words is another way to guide yourself through a lecture. These words are like play-by-play commentary in the classroom. They let you know which direction your instructor is headed.

Signal words can indicate transitions in a lecture. By paying attention to transitions, you'll be able to organize your thoughts and your notes as you listen actively. A few examples of signal words and phrases are:

- *Likewise.* This word indicates that the speaker is about to show how two concepts or examples are similar.
- *On the other hand.* When you hear this phrase or something similar, you know that the speaker is about to begin discussing an opposing fact or opinion.
- *Therefore.* This word usually indicates that the speaker is about to present an effect in a cause-and-effect relationship or a logical conclusion.

- *Finally.* This word lets you know that the speaker is arriving at the end of a point or the end of the lecture.
- *To sum up.* This phrase indicates the preceding points are about to be pulled together for the main idea. Be sure to get this in your notes!

WHAT IS MOST IMPORTANT?

Being able to separate more important information from less important information is a skill all active listeners need. Instructors often have similar ways of communicating important information. Some write key terms and concepts on the board as they lecture. Some use a PowerPoint presentation with key points bulleted. Others distribute copies of lecture outlines at the beginning of class. By picking up on these clues, you'll have an easier time determining what information your instructor considers most important.

The following behaviors also can draw your attention to important material. Your instructor may:

- pause to allow students to write down information in their notes
- repeat facts or definitions
- emphasize certain information with tone of voice
- directly tell students what information is important (e.g., "Remember this for next Tuesday's test.")
- use gestures and facial expressions to draw attention to key information
- use visual aids, such as films, television segments, life-size plastic models, and information or images on projector screens
- have students turn to certain pages in the textbook

Your instructors might not say, "This information is important." It's more likely that their behavior will give you the clues you'll need to figure out if it's important on your own. One way to pick up on these clues is to listen closely. Pay attention not only to your instructor's words but to the tone and volume of their voice as well. Another way to notice clues about important material is to observe. Even if you are listening closely to every word your instructor says, if your head is buried in your notebook the whole time, you might miss certain clues. Instead, look up from your notes from time to time to observe your instructor's actions. Hand gestures and facial expressions can indicate important information almost as clearly as words.

If your instructor repeats something, it's probably important information to remember.

LISAN AND LEARN

One of the benefits of active listening is that it helps you take more effective class notes. You'll learn about different note-taking methods later in this chapter. When deciding what format to use when you take notes, make sure your note-taking method encourages active listening. The LISAN method of note taking focuses on the following:

L *Lead instead of follow.* Think about what your instructor might say next.

I *Ideas.* What are the main ideas?

S *Signal words.* Listen for signal words that indicate transitions in the lecture. In which direction is the lecture headed?

A *Actively listen.* Make sure your mind stays engaged. Ask questions or make a note to yourself to seek clarification for difficult concepts later.

N *Notes.* Write down main ideas, key terms, and all other important information. Be selective.

Listening Levels

Listening has to reach a certain level before it is considered active. Consider the chart to see how well you listen in class. What level are you?

Level	Explanation
Reception	hearing words without thinking about them
Attention	passive listening; not making an effort to understand the information
Definition	entering into active listening; attaching meaning to certain facts and details but not yet organizing the material in your head
Integration	relating new information to your background knowledge and knowledge from previous classes
Interpretation	putting information into your own words; paraphrasing
Implication	thinking about how different pieces of information fit together; drawing conclusions
Application	considering how the information applies to you personally; using it in new situations
Evaluation	making judgments about the accuracy and relevance of the information

Remember that active listening is a learned skill. By following the tips in this chapter, you can learn to listen at a higher level. And once you know how to apply and evaluate information as you listen, you'll be that much further on your way to becoming a successful student!

Potential Listening Problems

With so much learning taking place by listening to the instructor speak in the classroom, a problem may occur if you can't follow the instructor well because he or she is speaking too fast or so slowly that your mind wanders. Either way, you can make the effort to gain the most from the class.

AT BREAKNECK SPEEDS

What happens if the instructor is moving too quickly? If you're prepared for class and keeping up with your reading and still can't keep up with the lecture, you should speak up! When doing this, be specific. Avoid interrupting with a vague statement such as, "I don't understand." This kind of statement implies that you didn't prepare for class. Also, it may be frustrating to your instructor because it doesn't indicate what information you need explained more fully. Instead, show your instructor what part of the material you *did* understand by summarizing it in your own words. Then, ask a specific question. For example, you could say, "I understand that sterile technique means doing things to prevent contamination, like wearing sterile gloves and using sterile instruments. But could you explain the difference between sterile technique and aseptic technique? Are they the same?"

Occasionally, you may feel like the only student in the class who isn't keeping up. You're not alone—many students have felt this way at one point or another. If this is the case, it's probably because the other students in the class already have a greater foundation of knowledge. They may have taken prerequisite courses that you haven't. If this happens, try not to get discouraged or give up following along with the lecture. Instead, make an effort to listen more closely and continue taking notes, being careful to write down confusing terms or concepts. After class, look in your textbook or ask your instructor for clarification. This practice of writing down what you don't understand is also helpful if you meet regularly with a tutor. It gives you specific pieces of information to review.

AT A SNAIL'S PACE

Alternatively, you may encounter instructors who present material at a much slower pace. If you allow yourself to become bored during these classes, your mind will begin to wander. To stay focused on the material, there are several tricks you can use:

- Practice summarizing information in your head. By forcing your brain to think about putting ideas into your own words, you'll stay alert.
- Try to memorize definitions of key terms as your instructor goes over them. Instead of simply reading the definitions or hearing

about them, you'll be committing them to memory for future reference.

- Predict what information your instructor will cover next. This causes you to consider how your instructor thinks. You will gain a better understanding of what your instructor expects students to know.

When an Instructor Moves Too Slowly

My name is Sean. I'm going to school to become a dental assistant. For the most part, I've liked my classes, but I've had to take a few boring ones, too. I had this one instructor who talked *so slowly* that I could hardly stay awake during class. Even when I brought a cup of coffee with me, I still found myself nodding off by the end of the lecture.

Then I discovered a solution. I realized it was a lot easier to stay awake if I had to think about the information and put it in my own words. So I'd just summarize in my head what my instructor was saying. It worked a lot better than caffeine!

MAKE ADJUSTMENTS

Occasionally, you'll have to make your own adjustments for an instructor who doesn't present information clearly. In such cases, you may have to think of examples, draw conclusions, or apply new information on your own. To do these things, you'll need to maintain active listening.

Here are several tips you can use to make sure you keep listening actively:

- Remember your purpose for listening.
- Pay special attention to the beginning and end of the lecture, when your instructor might introduce and summarize key points.
- Take effective notes.
- Sit up straight to avoid feeling sleepy and to show your interest in the lecture.
- Make sure your eyes stay focused on the instructor.
- Ignore external and internal distractions by concentrating on the instructor's words.
- Analyze the material.
- Listen for main points.
- Make a note of words or concepts you don't understand so you can look them up after class.
- Adjust to the pace of the lecture.

Trying to learn new material from a poor speaker might feel like you're climbing uphill. Show that you're up for the challenge by being an active listener!

LEARNING IN THE CLASSROOM

So far, we've discussed how to listen actively in the classroom. But much more goes on in the classroom than just the instructor's spoken words. To be an active learner, you'll also use observational skills, your own thinking skills, note-taking skills, and much more—often all at the same time!

Different Teaching Styles

During your time in school, you will come across many different types of instructors. One instructor may seem disorganized and another doesn't seem to cover the material in your textbook. Some instructors might not tell you exactly what you'll need to know for tests and quizzes. Although these situations may seem frustrating at first, you shouldn't use them as excuses to give up. To become a successful student, you'll need to learn to roll with the punches!

When faced with these difficult situations, use them as opportunities to engage in your own learning process. When you're an active participant, you can achieve goals other than simply learning the required material. You can accomplish things such as:

Jab, feint, weave, and watch your footwork! As a student, sometimes you have to roll with the punches.

- *Improving your learning skills.* You'll use these skills not only in school but in your future career as well. Remember, learning is a lifelong process!

- *Recognizing how lecture content is organized.* Whether your instructor follows the textbook, lectures independently of the text, or uses other media should help shape your learning focus for a particular class.

- *Discovering how to measure up to your instructor's expectations.* This is also a useful skill for when you become a practicing health care professional. In the future, you may not have to answer to an instructor, but you will want to know if you're meeting your supervisor's expectations.

Improve Your Learning Skills

Improving your learning skills also helps you succeed in the classroom. Learning skills include:

- memorization
- the ability to apply new knowledge
- interpretation of difficult material
- the ability to identify different teaching styles

It may be that an instructor is not an ineffective or bad lecturer, but one who presents material in a different way from your other instructors. Or it may be that the material in a particular class requires a different style of teaching than you're used to. When this happens, look for clues to discover your instructor's teaching style. Then use your different learning skills to help you adapt to the class.

MEMORIZE IT!

You'll probably find that a lot of memorization is required in your introductory courses. However, your instructors may not always tell you which specific information to memorize. In these cases, look for clues to identify important information and commit it to memory.

For example, if your instructor writes a new concept or a definition on the board, you should make an effort to memorize it. Likewise, if your instructor distributes a handout depicting a diagram or a list of facts, it would be wise to remember that information as well. By learning early on to pay attention to your instructor's cues, you'll know what material to memorize before the first quiz or test.

APPLY IT!

Some instructors focus on getting students to consider how the course material will apply to their future careers. If this is your instructor's goal, you'll do well in the course by showing that you can apply new knowledge. There are several ways in which your instructor might encourage you to do this:

- If your instructor gives many written assignments, be prepared to give examples of real-life applications in writing.
- If your instructor has students work through case studies during class, expect to see similar case studies on tests.
- If your instructor often calls students to the board to solve problems, be prepared to explain to the rest of the class how you would apply your new knowledge.

INTERPRET IT!

In advanced science and health classes, instructors may ask students to interpret new information. This means you'll be expected to put ideas into your own words to show how well you understand the material. You'll recognize instructors who focus on interpretation by the fact that they often use class periods to ask questions and provide guidance on student responses. If your instructor uses this particular method, be sure to complete all assigned readings before class. Being prepared will allow you to participate in class discussions.

Don't sit on the bench during class discussions. Be prepared so you can participate!

KNOW WHEN TO SHIFT GEARS

Being watchful to identify shifts in your instructor's teaching style keeps you alert and helps you follow along with the lecture. For example, the notes you take during a class discussion are different from the notes you take when your instructor gives you key terms and definitions to memorize. During a group discussion, you're focused more on ideas and the relationships between them. You won't be writing down everything said in class. In contrast, when your instructor gives you a definition to memorize, you'll need to either highlight the definition in your textbook or copy it word for word into your notes.

So, the next time your instructor interrupts a class discussion to write an important date or key term on the board, you'll identify the switch from an interpretive style of teaching to a memorization mode. You'll be able to adapt to this shift in teaching style by switching gears and recording the information from the board into your notes.

By listening actively, you'll soon become more familiar with your instructors' behavior. Pay attention to patterns in the way your instructors teach. One may tell students directly that a particular concept is important. But another may give less obvious clues, such as becoming animated or using gestures when explaining important points. Once you can recognize shifts in an instructor's teaching style, you'll begin to get more out of each lecture.

DISCOVER HOW LECTURE CONTENT IS ORGANIZED

The content in lectures can be organized in one of two ways:

1. *Text-dependent.* In lectures where the content is text-dependent, the material is presented very similarly to how it's presented in your textbook.

2. *Text-independent.* In these lectures, instructors cite resources other than the textbook when presenting the information they consider most important.

Regardless of how closely their lectures follow the text, many instructors use media as well to help them present lecture content.

A Textbook Case

If an instructor often conducts text-dependent lectures, it's especially important that you complete the assigned reading before class. If you're familiar with the material already, you'll have an easier time following along.

It's also important to bring your textbook to each class. As your instructor talks about sections in the text, note important ideas in the margins of your book. Highlight any passages or definitions your instructor reads aloud. If your instructor mentions that a particular section is unimportant or that you don't need to know the information it contains, cross it out.

Some students don't like to mark up their books by writing in the margins or highlighting sections of text. This is because, if you plan to sell the book back to the bookstore after the term, the bookstore will pay more for books that haven't been marked up. At first, this may sound like a good plan for the budget-conscious student. However, carefully consider whether it's really worth it. Being able to highlight and quickly refer back to important lecture points is likely well worth the few dollars difference. Actually, it's better not to sell them back at all but to keep your textbooks to build a reference library to use later on in your professional career.

Beyond the Text

For lectures in which the content is text-independent, the focus shifts from your textbook to your notes. It's important to take effective notes during these lectures because you won't be able to refer back to your textbook for information you missed. After class, review or outline your notes to make sure you understand the key points. To gain a better understanding of the information, you may want to discuss each lecture with a classmate—you could take turns "teaching" each other the material, which will help cement it in your brain. You can also use supplementary material, such as computer software or online articles, to review concepts presented by your instructor.

Before you sit down to study any material, set study goals to remind yourself what information you need to learn. This is essential when dealing with content that doesn't appear in your textbook. You'll need to create your own learning objectives for the information in your lecture notes because the chapter objectives from your textbook may not apply.

A Media Frenzy

A third element that affects lecture content is the use of media. Handouts, films, slide or PowerPoint presentations, plastic models, and other media give students new ways of learning material. For example, a movie might cause you to have an emotional response to a certain topic, whereas a plastic model might give you an opportunity to practice your clinical skills. With each form of media, you connect to the material in a different way. Often, this allows you to learn and understand more information than you would by simply hearing your instructor discuss it.

When dealing with media in the classroom, focus on two key questions. Ask yourself:

- Why is the instructor using this particular medium?
- How does this medium meet my learning needs?

For instance, suppose your instructor plays a television segment during class. If the segment is about a topic you've already covered, it can help you review necessary information. But if the segment introduces a new topic, it can meet your learning needs by providing you with background knowledge.

Taking Up the Slack

If a speaker is hard to follow, pick up the slack in the lecture by using the strategies listed in the chart.

If your instructor doesn't . . .	You should . . .
explain goals for the day's lecture	set goals yourself by referring to your textbook or syllabus
go over information covered in the previous lecture	review your lecture notes for a few minutes before each class
provide an introduction or summary at the beginning and end of a lecture	write a brief summary of each lecture after class
supply an outline of each lecture	review the assigned reading before class or outline your notes after the day's lecture
give students enough time to write notes before moving on to the next topic	politely ask your instructor to repeat or clarify information
speak in a clear, loud tone of voice	politely ask your instructor to speak louder, or move to a closer seat, as long as you don't disrupt the class
answer students' questions without being sarcastic or discouraging	avoid taking your instructor's remarks personally
stay on topic and instead begins talking about personal experiences	think about how the instructor's stories relate to the topic
explain the chapter and instead reads directly from the textbook	follow along by highlighting the text your instructor reads; outline or summarize the text in your notes
provide the main points of the lecture	reread your textbook after class and locate main points
clarify confusing information or provide examples	ask your instructor to provide an example or come up with an example on your own
write key terms and definitions on the chalkboard	look up key terms in a dictionary or in the glossary of your textbook

PARTICIPATE IN CLASS

Active learning includes fully engaging with the learning process while in the classroom. Participating in class by asking the instructor questions, answering questions the instructor poses to the class, and responding to the comments of other students all help you engage more fully in the process. Be sure to try the participation techniques you learned in Chapter 4 to stay actively involved in all your classes rather than a passive student.

Seeing Is Believing

It may seem obvious, but being able to see in the classroom is critical to your success in the course. Make sure you have a clear view of the instructor and the front of the room. Pay special attention to where visual aids, such as projector screens, are located. Be sure to choose a seat with an unobstructed view of boards and screens. The instructor may write key terms or main ideas on the board during a lecture. Being able to see this information will be helpful as you take notes.

CHARTS AND MODELS

Instructors often use anatomical charts and plastic lifelike models, particularly in health science classes. For example, when you are learning about the human skeletal system, a full skeleton model may be used in class. Seeing the model up close will help you learn and remember the names of the bones more easily.

SKILLS DEMONSTRATIONS

Skills demonstrations are common in many health professions classrooms. In fact, many health science classrooms are designed specifically for demonstrations and student practice sessions. It's especially important to scope out such a room and choose a seat nearest where the demonstrations are going to be given. This way, you'll be able to see everything being demonstrated.

In skills labs, students learn and practice new clinical skills, such as how to take a patient's blood pressure or count a pulse. During labs, you'll be asked to perform the skills your instructor has demonstrated. Having a clear view of in-class demonstrations will make it easier for you to learn new skills and perform them correctly.

In class, make sure you have a clear view of the action!

Getting the Most out of Class

Listening in class, watching presentations, participating in discussions and asking questions, and taking notes are key ways to increase learning in the classroom, but they're not everything. To increase your learning potential, also pay close attention to:

- information presented in handouts
- key terms or ideas the instructor writes on the chalkboard
- any questions raised by classmates and your instructor's responses to those questions
- your own opinions and thoughts about material presented by your instructor
- material that isn't covered in the textbook
- your instructor's introductory and summary statements (given at the beginning and end of each lecture)

Remember that using your personal learning style can give you an advantage in the classroom, as discussed in Chapter 5. Being aware of *how* you learn can help you increase the amount of information you understand and remember. Try to use a variety of learning techniques both to accommodate your own learning style and to increase your skills with other styles as well. Follow the tips for your own style presented in Chapter 5. Not only will you begin to perform better academically, but you'll have better communication with your instructors.

If the instructor writes it on the board, it's important enough for you to remember!

EFFECTIVE NOTE TAKING

Another way to get the most out of your classes is to take good notes. This is a good habit to develop from the first day of class and use during the rest of the course. One of the immediate benefits of note taking is that it familiarizes you with your instructor's teaching style. Another benefit is that you are more likely to remember information after writing it down. Studies have shown that when students take notes, they remember the information included in their notes 34% of the time. Without taking notes, however, the average student remembers the same information only 5% of the time.

Note taking often involves listing main ideas and summarizing information in your own words. It keeps your brain engaged and helps you analyze information while your instructor is speaking. There are several other good reasons to take notes during lectures.

- Notes provide you with memory cues to help you review and study the information covered during class. This can be critical when the time comes to prepare for tests and quizzes.
- Lecture notes show you what material the instructor considers important. The notes can help you gauge what information will appear on tests and quizzes.
- Taking notes helps you stay more focused during the lecture. You'll more easily become familiar with and better understand new material.

This section discusses several methods all students can use to take effective notes.

Take Notes in Class

It may seem as if some students were born with the ability to take good notes. But note taking is a learned skill! You can learn how to take effective notes by using the following tips.

- Use your own shorthand.
- Make sure your notes contain personal applications.
- Use a note-taking strategy that fits your style of learning and your instructor's style of teaching.
- Organize your notes while taking them.
- Review your notes after class, correct any unclear writing, and write a summary of the class.

SHORTHAND HELPS YOU KEEP UP THE PACE

Develop your own shorthand for taking notes. By abbreviating words and using symbols, you'll be able to keep up with a fast-paced lecture. To improve your speed in taking notes:

- Abbreviate commonly used words. For example, the abbreviation pt. can be used for the word *patient*. You can make up your own abbreviations. Just remember to use them consistently.
- Develop shorthand symbols for other common words. For example, the symbol → means "leads to" or "causes." The symbol > means "greater than."
- Leave out conjunctions (*or, and, but*) and prepositions (*of, in, for, on, to, with*, etc.) if they aren't needed to understand the idea.
- Take a moment to think before you jot down a note. This helps you focus on one thought and write it down quickly and concisely.

- Don't try to write down the instructor's exact words except with definitions or other precise wordings.
- Don't copy text directly out of the textbook. Instead, highlight the text in your book and refer to the appropriate page number in your notes.

Use Symbols + Abbr.

The chart lists some common note-taking abbreviations and symbols. Speed your note taking by using these shortcuts or coming up with your own.

Abbreviations		Symbols	
Abt	about ~ ✗	®	right
b/c	because 2°	Ⓛ	left
Dx	diagnose or diagnosis	↑	increase, increased, or increasing
e.g.	for example	↓	decrease, decreased, or decreasing
h/a	headache HA	→	leads to or causes
Hx	history	>	more than
Imp	important Impt ✳	<	less than
Incl.	including	Δ	change
Pt	patient Pt	~	about, approximately
Px	~~physical~~ Prognosis	+	and, in addition
Rx	treat or treatment Rx	#	pounds or number
s/e	side effects	*	important or stressed by instructor
s/s	signs and symptoms	p̄	after
w/	with c̄	ā	before
w/o	without s̄	—	negative
PE Physical exam		c̄	with
		s̄	without

> Be sure to keep a copy of your shorthand key handy when taking notes.

APPLY IT!

Be sure to include personal applications in your notes. Write down cues to help you link new information to your previous knowledge. This not only helps you maintain active listening but will also help you study the material later.

Using someone else's lecture notes should be a last resort. Copying notes doesn't allow you to analyze the material. For this reason, borrow notes only on the rare occasions when you are unable to attend a class. You'll have an easier time learning the information if you're present for each lecture and take notes yourself.

PEN AND PAPER ARE BETTER

Although it may seem like a wise idea, tape-recording lectures isn't the most efficient way to learn or study new material. Some of the problems with recording are:

- It increases your review/study time. It only takes a few minutes to read through your lecture notes for the day. However, listening to the entire lecture all over again takes much longer.

- A tape recording doesn't include diagrams or other important information the instructor writes on the chalkboard during a lecture.

- Even your best intentions can be thwarted by technical difficulties. Dead batteries or a poor quality recording can cause you to miss out on important information from the lecture.

- Not all instructors allow students to record their lectures. If you must use a tape recorder, ask your instructor before class.

There is one instance when tape recording might be your best option. If you ever have to miss a class, it may be helpful to have a classmate tape the lecture. In this case, listening to the lecture on tape and taking your own notes might be more beneficial than simply copying someone else's notes.

NOTE TAKING—WHAT'S YOUR STYLE?

Develop a note-taking style that works best for you. Following are some suggestions for personalizing your method of taking notes:

- Remember how to read your own shorthand by creating a key to keep in your notebook.

- Copy down information and diagrams that your instructor writes on the chalkboard.

- Write neatly so you can use your notes when studying for quizzes and tests.

- Leave space in your notes that you can fill in later with information from your textbook.

- Read over your notes after class and make any necessary corrections.

- Separate groups of ideas by skipping a line in your notes.

- Use a color-coding system to mark groups of ideas or to emphasize important terms and concepts.

Your note-taking style also should work well with how your instructor lectures. Your notes can be formatted in several different ways. Keep your instructor's teaching style in mind when choosing the best format for your notes:

- *Outline.* This format works well with instructors who follow strict outlines and give very organized lectures.

- *Asymmetrical columns.* If your instructor frequently gives reminders ("Remember this for the test on Tuesday") or refers to your textbook during lectures ("Let's look at page 52"), this format may work best for you. See the following section "The Cornell Method of Note Taking."

- *Compare/contrast.* This format works well with an instructor who often discusses two separate topics at the same time to show how the topics are alike and different.

- *Concept map.* This format works well with instructors who provide many anecdotes or examples of a single main idea, but who don't necessarily follow a strict outline.

Another formatting tip is to leave space (2 inches or so) at the bottom of each page for a brief summary. Reviewing your notes and summarizing each page after class helps you process the information.

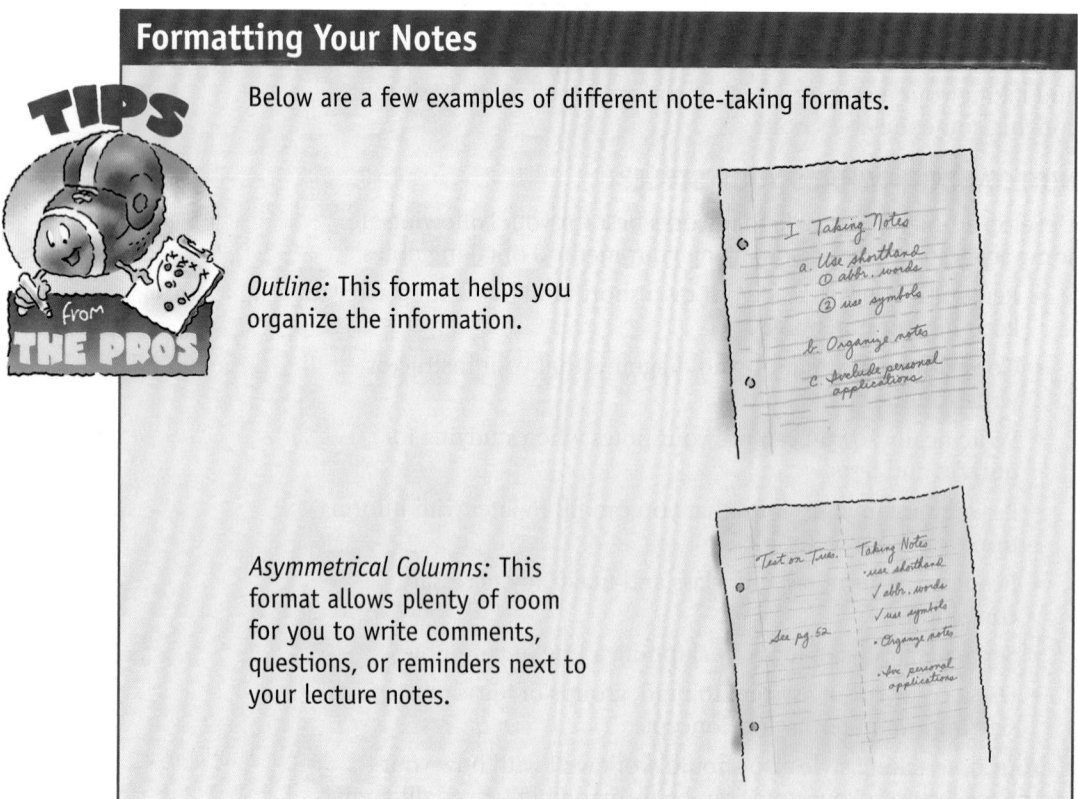

Formatting Your Notes

Below are a few examples of different note-taking formats.

Outline: This format helps you organize the information.

Asymmetrical Columns: This format allows plenty of room for you to write comments, questions, or reminders next to your lecture notes.

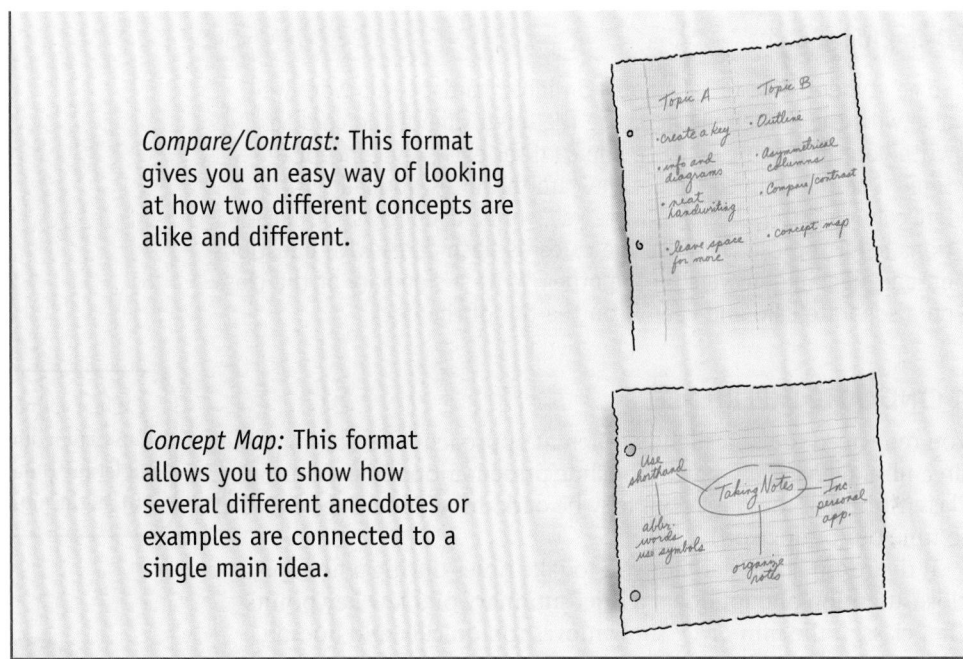

Compare/Contrast: This format gives you an easy way of looking at how two different concepts are alike and different.

Concept Map: This format allows you to show how several different anecdotes or examples are connected to a single main idea.

The Cornell Method of Note Taking

The Cornell method was developed in the 1950s at Cornell University and is still recommended by many schools because of its usefulness and flexibility. It works well for taking notes, defining priorities, and studying.

The Cornell method uses four boxes: a header, two columns, and a footer. The header is a small box across the top of the page where you write the course name, the date of the class, and other identifying information. Beneath are two columns: a narrow one on the left and a wide notes column on the right. The wide column is used for notes in an outline, list, or concepts map format. The left column is used for main ideas, key words, questions, and clarifications. Use the right column during class and the left both during the class and when reviewing your notes later. Use the box at the foot of the page to write a summary of the class. This helps you make sense of your notes during future studying. An example is shown in the illustration.

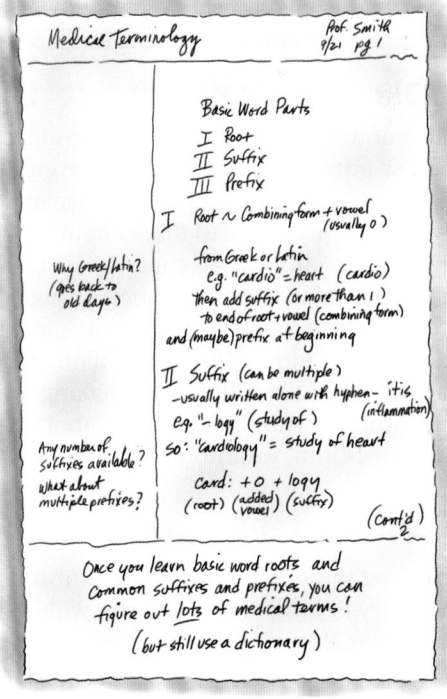

Using Index Cards

Some students like to take notes on index cards. Cards work well also with the Cornell method. Use the lined side of the card to write your notes in class. Use one card for each key concept or topic. Use the unlined side of the card for notes normally in the left column; after class you write key words, comments, or questions here. You can then use the cards as flash cards with questions on one side and answers on the other. Write a summary of the class on a separate card and keep it on the top of the deck.

A CINEMATIC EXPERIENCE

You may need to use a slightly different approach when taking notes on a film, television segment, or slide presentation shown during class. Although the classroom may be dark, these are not good times to tune out or doze off!

In the room is too dark for you to take notes during a film, pay close attention and jot down a brief summary or a few key points after class. If the film or TV show moves too quickly and doesn't allow you enough time to take effective notes, consider watching it again. Often, instructors place these types of presentations on reserve in the campus library. Watching the film or looking at the slides a second time will give you a chance to write down any important information you missed during class.

FINDING A HAPPY MEDIUM

The amount of notes you take determines their effectiveness. Taking too few notes means you won't have enough material to jog your memory later. However, taking too many notes during class won't give you enough time to think about and process the information. So how do you know when enough is enough?

If your notes resemble a brief, disorganized list of facts, you're probably taking too few. In this case, focus on noting how those facts relate to one another. On the other hand, if your pen never leaves the page during class, you might be taking too many notes. Instead, work on writing down only the most important information. By finding a happy medium, your notes will become more effective.

A Note After Class

The most important thing to remember about your notes is to review them. Try to look over your notes within 24 hours after class. It's easier to make corrections and add to your notes while the lecture is still fresh in your mind. Reviewing your notes soon after you take them also helps you commit the information to memory.

When your instructor shows a film during class, it's not leisure time! Take notes to get the most out of it.

Getting Organized

As discussed in Chapter 2, organization is critical to your success as a student. It also makes a difference in the effectiveness of your notes. Your lecture notes can be an excellent study tool, but not if they're in a disorganized jumble of papers. Take the time, either during or after class, to organize your notes. You'll thank yourself later!

ACADEMIC READING

Do you like to read? Maybe you've been out of school for a few years but you still read newspapers, magazines, or novels? If you have been away from school for some time, it's likely that your reading has been fairly casual. The sort of concentrated reading you will do in your textbooks is very different from that casual reading. For each hour in the classroom, you may spend 2 to 3 hours studying between classes and most of that will be reading. Reading assignments are much longer than in high school and much more difficult. Textbook authors often use many technical terms and cover complex material. Some textbooks are written in a style that may be much dryer than what you're used to.

For all these reasons, it's a good idea to think about *how* to read and develop habits to remember more about what you read. Even if you don't like to read, you can develop these skills, which will pay off in a big way.

Preparing for Class—The Need to Read

The relationship between a class of students and their instructor is comparable to the relationship between a team of athletes and their coach. Athletes must train on their own to master the basics of their sport. That way, they're prepared to refine their skills and learn about the nuances of the game when they meet with their coach. Similarly, when students work on their own to prepare for class, they become better equipped to understand and remember information from their instructor's lectures.

Even if you attend every lecture and participate in all classroom activities, you still need to prepare for class and read your course material. Reading is assigned by your instructor to help you understand concepts more fully.

Visual learners are in luck. In most courses, over 75% of the information you receive will be in the form of printed materials. This means reading is an important part of preparing for class. If you learn best by reading, here's your opportunity to take advantage of your learning strengths and put them to good use.

If you don't happen to be a visual learner, be encouraged! Regardless of your particular learning style, all students can use the same methods to develop better reading skills and improve comprehension. Ways you can get more out of reading include:

- skimming for main ideas
- using active reading techniques
- reading chapter summaries to check your comprehension

The information in the following sections will show you how to become a more successful reader. If you aren't a visual learner, you may have avoided reading in the past whenever possible. Being aware of this weakness, however, is the first step toward improving upon it. If you *are* a visual learner and you enjoy reading, the tips in this section will help you hone your preferred method of learning.

If you use these methods often enough, they'll become routine. Soon, you'll be able to read a chapter without consciously thinking about the different tasks involved in reading.

The Anatomy and Physiology of a Textbook

First, take out one of your textbooks and give it a good looking over. Textbooks generally have a number of elements, and considering these will help prepare you for getting the most out of your reading. Here are key elements in most textbooks:

- *Preface, Introduction, Foreword.* This gives you perspective about the author's point of view. This section may also guide you on how to use the textbook and its features. It may provide hints as to why your instructor selected the book for your course.

- *Author Profile or Biography.* This helps you understand what the author considers important.

- *Table of Contents.* This is an outline of the entire book. It is very helpful in making links between the text and your course's objectives and syllabus.

- *Chapter Preview, Learning Objectives.* These sections indicate what you should pay special attention to. Compare these objectives with the course objectives stated in the syllabus.

- *Chapter Introduction.* Introductions are "must reads" because they give you a road map to the material you are about to read, directing you to notice what is truly important in the chapter or section.

- *Exercises, Activities.* These features give you a great way to confirm your understanding of the material. If you have trouble with them, you should go back and reread the section. They have the added benefit of improving your recall of the material.

- *Chapter Summary, Highlights, or Review.* It is a good idea to read this section before reading the body of the chapter. It will help you strategize about where you should invest your reading effort. Answer review questions after reading the chapter to confirm your understanding of the material.

- *Photos, Illustrations, Graphics.* Many students are tempted to skip over graphic material. Don't! Take the time to read and understand all graphics. They increase your understanding and, because they engage different learning styles, they create different memory links to help you remember the material. Use your critical thinking skills to understand why each illustration is present and what it means.

Paying attention to these textbook elements before you begin a reading assignment helps set you up for a successful experience. Now you can begin the actual reading process.

The Steps of Effective Reading

With a newspaper or magazine, you probably just start reading from the top. Maybe you look over at a photo or illustration first, but generally you just read from the start to the end. You could do it this way with a textbook too, but you'd not learn nearly as well as you can using a more structured approach. Try using the following steps.

START BY SKIMMING

Before you begin reading a chapter, flip though the pages and skim the material first. Doing this will give you a chance to look at the general organization of the chapter and identify key points. The purpose of skimming is to get your brain in gear so you'll absorb more information during active reading. By taking the time to skim over the chapter first, you'll give your brain the time it needs to begin organizing information in your head. This means you'll be able to mentally file information as soon as you begin reading. Not only does skimming allow you to understand the material more quickly, it also helps you to remember more of what you read.

When skimming a chapter, follow these guidelines:

1. Look at the illustrations, graphs, charts, and tables. Read any captions.

2. Read the chapter introduction (usually located in the first paragraph).

3. Read the section headings throughout the chapter.

4. Take note of emphasized words in bold or italics as you flip through the pages.

5. Read the chapter summary (usually located in the closing paragraph).

Graphic elements, such as charts and tables, illustrate important concepts covered in the chapter. Often, graphics provide snapshot views of the same information it may take several pages of text to explain. If you glance at each graphic element while skimming a chapter, you'll give yourself a quick preview of the material.

> Skimming a chapter before reading it is like stretching your muscles before running a race. You need to make sure your brain is prepared to learn new information!

Build a Solid Foundation

When preparing to read a difficult chapter, make sure you first have some background knowledge of the topics covered. When you have a good foundation of knowledge on which to build, you'll have an easier time understanding complex new ideas.

For example, suppose a dental assistant and an experienced radiology technician both read a section in a textbook on using contrast media in certain x-ray procedures. Which individual would be able to comprehend the material more quickly and easily? Although both people may have had some experience taking x-rays, the radiology technician is likely to have a better foundation of knowledge in this particular area. The technician's background and experience would give him or her an advantage over the dental assistant, who has not had the opportunity of working with contrast media. Even the technician's familiarity with the vocabulary used to describe such procedures would make it easier for him or her to read and understand the text.

As a student, how can you expand your foundation of knowledge? One way to give yourself some background information is to read an online or magazine article on the topic. Another way to prepare for reading a difficult chapter is to attend a lecture or seminar on a related topic. At the very least, you'd become familiar with the vocabulary used in the chapter. By the time you sat down to read your textbook, you would be able to focus your energy on trying to understand the concepts presented, rather than having to try to figure out what specific words mean.

Take a Look at the Structure

Another tactic to use when skimming text is looking at how the chapter is organized. The chapter may be structured in several different ways:

- *Subject development or definition structure.* These paragraphs present a single concept and then list supporting details. Introductory paragraphs usually are structured this way.
- *Sequence structure.* These paragraphs usually include signal words, such as *first, second, next, then,* and *finally.* The information in these paragraphs is presented in sequential order. Numbered lists also fall into this category.

- *Compare and contrast structure.* These paragraphs discuss how two or more concepts are alike and different. Words that signal comparisons include *both, similarly, too,* and *also.* Contrasting statements may include the signal words *yet, but, however,* or *on the other hand.*

- *Cause-and-effect structure.* These paragraphs often include signal words or phrases, such as *cause, effect, due to, in order to, resulting from,* and *therefore.* These paragraphs explain how one idea or event results from another idea or event.

Once you identify how the chapter is organized, you'll be on your way to pinpointing the most important information. This will help you focus when the time comes to read the full chapter.

READY, SET, READ!

After you've skimmed the chapter, you can begin reading actively. But note that active reading goes beyond simply recognizing the words on each page. It includes using other tactics to aid your comprehension. In order to make sure you're reading actively, try putting some of the following tips into practice.

- Read aloud.

- Take notes or draw graphics as you read. (The Cornell note-taking method works well for reading also.)

- Write down any questions you have about confusing concepts or ideas.

- Think about how information in the chapter relates to important points outlined in the table of contents (or outlined at the beginning of the chapter).

- Make a note of any difficult sections you'd like to read a second time.

Stay Focused

Active reading requires concentration. Here are some basic guidelines to help you stay focused. (Chapter 8 provides additional study tips.)

- Read during the time of day you are most alert.

- Avoid trying to read too much at one time. When you start to feel your mind wandering, take a 5-minute break.

- Find a quiet place to read. Avoid distractions, such as watching TV or listening to loud music.

- Sit in a comfortable (but not too comfortable!) chair in order to stay awake and alert while reading.

- Supply yourself with a healthy snack and water to avoid getting distracted by being hungry or thirsty.

Help yourself avoid distractions by finding a quiet place to read.

Postgame Highlights

As you actively read each chapter, highlight important ideas or mark them with sticky notes. You can also make notes right in the margins. Just be careful not to mark too much text. If 90% of the material on every page is highlighted, it doesn't truly show which ideas are most important. But a chapter that is highlighted correctly is an excellent study tool. Being able to locate key ideas quickly will help you study more efficiently.

When deciding which text to highlight, think about what should be considered truly "important" material. Here are some hints:

- Highlight any information your instructor emphasizes in class. If your instructor considers a particular topic important, chances are that topic may appear on a test or quiz.

- Highlight portions of text that answer any questions you came up with while skimming the chapter.

- Look for and highlight topic sentences. These sentences generally include the main idea(s) in each paragraph.

Highlighting can help you find important information later, but keep in mind that it doesn't actually help you learn the material. To learn the information, spend a few extra minutes summarizing the text you highlighted in your own words. If you prefer, create a chart or diagram instead to illustrate key points. This helps you process the information and commit it to memory.

Bright Idea: Highlighting Text

By highlighting text and making notes in the margins of your textbook, you'll remember more of what you read. You'll also be able to locate key ideas later when studying for the next test or quiz. Keep these tips in mind as you read.

- Read the entire paragraph or section before highlighting any of it.
- Highlight portions of text that answer any questions you thought of while skimming the chapter.
- Look for items presented in sequential order and number them accordingly.
- Highlight key terms, names, dates, and places.
- Summarize main ideas in the margins.
- Insert a question mark next to confusing paragraphs or sentences. Write any questions or comments you may have in the margins.
- Mark any information your instructor considers important with a star or exclamation point.
- Highlight important information in the table of contents or create a list of the most important topics.

Make It Personal

Another way to make sure you're reading actively is to connect with the material on a personal level. By making the information more personal, you'll have an easier time remembering it. You can do this by:

- *Making associations.* For example, you might be able to remember an important date by associating it with the birthday of someone you know. (Chapter 8 discusses associations in more detail.)
- *Having an emotional response to the material.* Reacting to the information you read will make it more memorable.
- *Drawing pictures to illustrate different concepts.* A picture might be easier to remember than a paragraph of text.

Know the Lingo

Reading actively also involves making sure you understand the vocabulary used to describe new concepts. You should always determine the meaning of an unfamiliar word before continuing your reading. In scientific texts especially, it's important to know the meaning of the technical terms used. Knowing the vocabulary makes your job of understanding the material much easier. For example, suppose you are reading a passage discussing what happens to the body during a myocardial infarction. Knowing that *myocardial infarction* is the medical term for "heart attack" would help you understand the passage more readily.

A baseball game makes a lot more sense if you're familiar with the lingo. The same is true for reading scientific texts. If you don't know a word, look it up!

When you notice an unfamiliar word, first try to figure out its meaning from context clues. Context clues can include other words or sentences that provide hints about the word's meaning. They also can include root words, prefixes, and suffixes. If you're unable to determine the word's meaning from the context, look it up in a dictionary or glossary. Saying it aloud will help you remember it. Then make a note of the definition and pronunciation in the margin of your textbook or in your notes. If the word appears once in the chapter, it may appear again.

When skimming a chapter, you may notice many unfamiliar words. It may be helpful to look up all the definitions before you begin actively reading the text.

Read Chapter Summaries

In most textbooks, all chapters are formatted similarly. The chapter summary usually appears toward the end of the chapter in the form of a summary paragraph, bulleted statements, or review questions.

One of the last steps in active reading is reviewing the chapter summary. Read the chapter summary and refer back to the table of contents to make sure you understood the key points of the chapter. If there are sections you didn't understand, reread them or make a note to ask your instructor for clarification.

When rereading, try using a different method from what you used during your first active reading of the chapter. You can adjust the speed of your reading by reading a particular section more slowly, for example. Reading aloud is another method. When rereading text, make an effort to understand each sentence before continuing. Think about how each new concept you encounter relates to other information in the chapter.

Game Plan for Reading

- *Pace yourself.* Unless it is very short, divide the assignment into smaller blocks rather than trying to read it all at once. If you have a week to do the assignment, for example, divide the work into five daily blocks, leaving an extra day for review.

- *Schedule your reading.* Try to read at the time of day when you are most alert.

- *Choose the right space.* Read in a quiet, well-lit space. Sit in a comfortable chair with good support. The library is an excellent option. Don't read in bed because that space is associated with sleeping.

- *Avoid distractions.* Active reading takes place in short-term memory. With every distraction, you lose continuity and have to restart. Multitasking—listening to music or texting while you read—makes for poor reading comprehension and makes the reading take much longer.

- *Prevent reading fatigue.* Give yourself a 5- to 10-minute break every hour. Put down the book, walk around, have a healthy snack, stretch, or do deep knee bends. You'll feel refreshed and be better able to stay focused.

- *Read more difficult assignments early* in your scheduled reading time when you are freshest.

- *Stay interested.* Actively go looking for answers that pop up in your mind as you read. Carry on a mental conversation with the author.

Use Your Reading Notes Before Class

Review your textbook and create a note-taking outline before each lecture. This familiarizes you with the material and helps to organize your notes. By locating key terms and main ideas beforehand, you'll provide yourself with a basic outline to follow and fill in during the lecture. In essence, your note-taking outline is your "road map" for the lecture. By using it, there's less chance of getting lost!

To determine which terms and concepts to include in your outline, follow these steps:

1. Look at the general layout of the chapter. Make a mental note of each section's length—longer sections will need more space in your outline.

2. Read the introductory paragraph. The first paragraph in a chapter often lists main ideas.

3. Review any graphs, charts, or diagrams.

4. Search for any bold or italic words. If a word or phrase is emphasized in the chapter, it should be included in your outline.

5. Look over passages you highlighted while reading, including margin notes, questions, and other notes.

6. Read the closing paragraph. The last paragraph in a chapter usually summarizes important information and draws conclusions.

During the lecture, fill in any gaps left in your outline. Add to it by including information from the lecture that is not provided by your textbook.

Taking notes without a basic outline is like driving without directions. It's easy to get lost!

CHAPTER SUMMARY

- Develop your active listening skills to get the most out of every class.
- Avoid behaviors that can interfere with active listening.
- When listening actively, identify main ideas and pay attention to signal words.
- Use techniques to compensate for different lecture styles and become an active participant in your own learning process.
- Learning involves several skills, including memorizing, applying, and interpreting new information.

- Develop a note-taking style that works for you. Keep your instructor's lecturing style in mind when deciding how to format your notes.
- Reading is a multipart process that includes skimming, active reading, and later reviewing and rereading.
- Give yourself a road map to follow during class by creating a note-taking outline.

REVIEW QUESTIONS

1. List at least five behaviors that could be interfering with your ability to listen actively in class.

2. How would you cope with an instructor who moves too slowly?

3. Which note-taking format would work best in a class where the instructor routinely gives a lot of anecdotes and examples to illustrate a single main idea?

4. What should you do with your class notes after you've written them in class?

5. What are at least three things you can do to make sure you're reading actively?

CHAPTER ACTIVITIES

1. Group Exercise: Using a highlighter, read the first five pages of this chapter and highlight important passages following the guidelines given in this chapter. Then go back through these pages, looking only at what you have highlighted, and mark with a large penciled asterisk one key concept that would most likely be on a quiz covering this chapter. Finally, get together in groups of three or four students and compare what you have highlighted and marked with the asterisk. Talk about how you know what is most important here.

2. Analysis Exercise: Select a few pages of notes you took in one class session of a different course at any time *before* reading this chapter. Examine these notes to see how well they follow the guidelines suggested in the "Take Notes in Class" section of this chapter. What could you have done differently to improve the process of taking notes in class and the resulting notes?

Communication Skills

On completion of this chapter and the learning activities you will be able to:

- Know why it's important for health care professionals to have good communication skills

- Be comfortable speaking informally in class and in formal presentations

- Describe the structural parts of an academic writing assignment

- Successfully use the steps of the writing process

- Effectively research information using the library and the Internet

- Participate with others in group projects

- Communicate successfully via a computer

To succeed as a student, you'll need to learn how to express yourself both through speaking and writing. This involves developing and using good communication skills both as a student and in your future career as a health professional. In this chapter, we'll discuss how to enhance your learning by speaking out in class and giving successful class presentations, whether individually or as part of a group project. You'll also learn about academic writing and how to use the writing process to ensure you do your best. Finally, we'll examine the role of computers in communication, from best email practices to online courses. All these topics involve core principles of communication. Effective communication skills are essential in all health careers. Develop yours now as a student and you'll thank yourself in the future!

SPEAKING

During your time as a student, you may be required to give a few speeches or oral presentations. Much of your speaking in public, however, will be more informal. Whether you're asking a question during a lecture or participating in a group discussion, you should use good public speaking skills. When you're able to express yourself, you'll receive better answers to your questions and you'll also get more out of group discussions.

I used to be so afraid to speak in front of others! Now, I'm over it.

Me? Speak in Public?

If speaking to a group of people makes you feel nervous, nauseous, or as if you'd rather stay in bed and avoid the situation altogether, know that you're not alone. *Glossophobia*, the fear of public speaking, is considered by some to be the most common phobia.

Researchers aren't sure exactly what causes this fear. However, most agree that having a bad or embarrassing experience with public speaking is usually a major contributor. There's nothing like the embarrassment of getting up in front of a group of people and stumbling over your words (or forgetting them altogether) to make you want to avoid doing so ever again. Fortunately, there are tips you can use to improve your ability to speak up in a group setting.

Learning to Speak Up

TIPS from THE PROS

Follow this step-by-step process to relax yourself before speaking up in class.

- Acknowledge your fear and admit to yourself that you're nervous about public speaking. It's very difficult to overcome a fear that "doesn't exist." Remember that stage fright is completely normal.

- Understand that your instructor and other students are not looking for faults. They likely don't even know that you're nervous and won't see your anxiety.

- Reassure yourself that you have something important to say and that your instructor and your classmates are interested in hearing it.

- Think about what you are going to say. This will give you a chance to calm your nerves. When you speak, stay focused on *what* you're saying, not *how* others are viewing you.

- Be confident. This will command everyone's interest. It may help you feel self-assured if you jot your question or comment in your notes before raising your hand to speak.

- Speak loudly and clearly. If everyone hears you the first time, you will avoid having to repeat yourself.

Speaking Informally in Class

As mentioned previously, most of your "public" speaking will occur informally when you speak in the classroom. You might be asking a question, answering a question, or giving your perspective about someone else's comment. We call this informal speaking because the situation does not involve planning ahead to deliver a more formal presentation—a situation we'll look at later in this chapter.

Even though participating in class discussions is less formal, it still helps to be prepared and follow some basic guidelines. Start with the general principles for class participation described in Chapter 4.

FIRST, ORGANIZE YOUR THOUGHTS

The first thing to remember is to organize your thoughts. Make sure you have read assigned material before class so that you have good background information for the lecture. During the lecture, pay attention and listen closely to make sure your instructor hasn't already addressed the question you're about to ask. Then, ask directly. There is no need to beat around the bush. Go ahead and ask for clarification of an idea or challenge a statement that seems contradictory. In most classrooms, students are encouraged to participate in this way.

Don't ever feel your question is "stupid." If you have paid attention in class and did assigned reading but you still don't understand something, you have every right to ask. Many other students in the class are probably wondering the same thing—and they'll be happy you took the initiative to ask!

Before speaking up in class, take a moment to organize your thoughts.

COME TO THE POINT

As described in Chapter 4, there's a right way and a wrong way to go about seeking clarification during a lecture. First, choose carefully your moment to speak. How the instructor moves and gestures, and the looks on his or her face, not only adds meaning to the words but also cues you when it's a good time to ask a question or stay silent.

Then think about what you will say. The wrong way is to interrupt class with a vague statement such as, "I don't get it." Instead, it's better to state briefly and in your own words what you *do* understand and then ask your question.

For example, suppose your radiology instructor is explaining how to position patients for different types of x-rays. If you need clarification, you could say, "I understand that in both the recumbent and supine positions, the patient should be lying down. But what is the difference between the two positions?" This statement clearly shows that you understand at least part of the information. It's an effective question because it comes to the point and tells your instructor exactly which part of the material you don't understand.

On the other hand, suppose you encounter a situation where you want to challenge a statement that seems to contradict your background knowledge of a particular topic. Let's say your class is having a discussion about patient privacy rights. Your instructor says, "State law requires that if a patient is diagnosed with a sexually transmitted disease, that information must be reported to the local health department." In a previous course, however, you learned that a patient's diagnosis is confidential. Your instructor's statement seems to contradict what you've already learned about patient confidentiality. How would you form a respectful question to challenge your instructor's statement?

Speaking Up

Hi, my name is Suki. I'm studying to become a lab technician. In one of the first courses I took, it was really hard to keep up with the instructor. But I was afraid to ask questions in front of everyone else in class. The few times I tried, I was so nervous that I raised my hand and then completely forgot what I was going to say.

But then I started writing down my questions so I could read them after the instructor called on me. It was so much easier! Writing down what I wanted to say gave me the time I needed to organize my thoughts. It also kept me from being too nervous and having my mind go blank.

PARTICIPATE—GROUP DISCUSSIONS

A good way to practice speaking up in class is to participate in group discussions with your classmates. These situations provide you with low-stress opportunities to express your thoughts and ask questions. Once you become comfortable with speaking to a group of your peers, you'll gain confidence to speak up in other situations, such as asking your instructor for clarification.

Once you are comfortable speaking in class, be sure not to overdo it or dominate a discussion. Be sensitive to the needs of other students and give them the chance to ask their questions, too.

For Future Use

The speaking skills you develop as a student will be useful throughout your career. You can bet that at some point, a situation will arise where you need to clarify a physician's instructions. You'll be thankful for all the practice you had in class communicating with your instructors! As a health care professional, you can apply the same principles you used in class when asking your supervisors for clarification.

1. First, organize your thoughts in order to ask a direct question.

2. Then, come to the point while remembering to be respectful and to use your critical thinking skills.

You'll also need to have good speaking skills when you communicate with patients. For example, when gathering a patient's medical history, you'll be required to ask direct questions and clarify the patient's responses. In this case, you'll need to be able to form clear, easily understandable questions to obtain the information you need. It also will be important to make sure you understand the patient's responses correctly before recording the information in a medical chart.

Good speaking skills, and good communication skills in general, are very important in the health care professions. Eventually, you'll be required to use your skills on a daily basis. Just remember that the best way to develop good skills is to practice!

Speaking well helps communicate that you're a professional!

Giving Presentations

A formal presentation, another form of public speaking, involves preparation outside of class and sometimes significant research and planning. That part of the process is actually similar to writing a paper for a class or even studying for an exam. What's different is this preparation leads to a presentation given in class, in front of other students and the instructor—a situation that usually makes students *very* nervous. But relax—with good planning and communication skills, you can develop the ability to give good presentations and you may even become a classroom star!

Begin by making sure you understand the exact requirements of the assignment. What's the topic and how long should it be? Then you can begin planning. Class presentations are not difficult if you follow these six basic steps:

1. Analyze your audience and goals.

2. Plan, research, and organize your content.

3. Draft and revise the presentation.

4. Prepare visual aids.

5. Practice the presentation.

6. Deliver the presentation.

WHO'S YOUR AUDIENCE? WHAT'S YOUR POINT?

In most class presentations, the first question seems
obvious: other students and the instructor. Check the
assignment, however—maybe you're supposed to address
the class as if they were patients in a health care setting?
Even if the audience is your class, you still need to think
about what they already know and don't know about your
topic. How much background information do they already
have based on previous lectures and reading? Be careful
not to give a boring recap of things they already know. But it may be
important to show how your specific topic fits in with subjects that
have been discussed already in class.

> In a presentation, it's better to cover a smaller topic well and meet your goal than to try too much with a larger topic and not cover it fully.

Think also about your goal for the presentation. The assignment instructions from your instructor may provide the goal,
but you may need to adjust it to what you can cover well in the
time you're given for the presentation.

PLAN, PLAN, PLAN

Start by brainstorming about your topic. You may also
need do some more reading or research. Don't worry
at first about how much material you're gathering.
It's much better to know too much and then pick
out the most important things to say in your allotted time than to rush ahead and then realize you
don't have enough material.

Organizing a presentation or speech is similar to organizing
topics in a paper for class (see *Structurally Speaking* in the Writing
for Classes section). Introduce your topic and state your main
idea, go into more detail about specific ideas in the body of the
presentation, and conclude. Look for a logical order for the body of
the presentation. Some topics might be covered in a chronological
(time) order, whereas others are best developed through a compare-
and-contrast organization. If your goal is to persuade, sort out your
separate arguments and build to the strongest or most important. Put
similar ideas together and think about how you'll need to transition
between very different ideas.

While researching your topic and outlining your main points, also
start thinking about visual aids for the presentation.

DRAFT AND REVISE

You don't need to actually write out the presentation in full sentences and paragraphs because you shouldn't read it aloud—that
makes for a dull presentation. Some students speak well from
brief phrases written on note cards, whereas others prefer a more
detailed outline.

You can't know for sure how long your presentation will last until you rehearse it, but try to estimate the time while drafting it. Figure that it takes 2 to 3 minutes to speak the amount of writing on a standard double-spaced page—but with visual aids, pauses, and audience interaction, it may take longer. This is only a rough guide, but you might start out thinking of a 10-minute presentation as the equivalent of a 3- to 4-page paper.

As you draft your speaking notes, consider questions like these:

- Am I going on too long about minor points?

- Do I have good explanations and reasons for my main points? Do I need more data or better examples? Where would visual aids be most effective?

- Am I using the best words for this topic and this audience? Should I be more or less informal in the way I talk about my topic?

- Does it all hold together and flow well from one point to the next? Do I need a transition when I shift from one idea to another?

PREPARE VISUAL AIDS

Most presentations gain from visuals and, with visual technology used in many classrooms, visual aids are often expected. Consider all possibilities when choosing appropriate visuals:

- charts, graphs
- maps
- photos, other images
- video clips
- handouts (only when necessary—otherwise may be distracting)

PRACTICE, PRACTICE, PRACTICE

Practice is the most important step in preparing. It also helps you get over stage fright and gain the confidence that you'll do a good job.

Practice first alone, either to a mirror or in an empty room where you imagine people sitting (so that you can move your eyes around the room to this "audience"). Do not read your notes aloud but speak in sentences natural for you. Glance down at your notes only briefly, then look up immediately to the mirror or around the room. Time yourself but don't obsess about using precisely the exact number of minutes your instructor requested. If your presentation is way off, however, adjust your outlined notes.

Once you feel good about delivering your content from your notes, practice some more to work on your delivery. You might want to record or videotape your presentation or ask a friend or roommate to watch your presentation.

Using Visual Aids

Use the available technology, whether an overhead projector or PowerPoint screen, or a flip chart or posters. Always check the assignment to confirm your instructor's expectations for your use of visual aids. You might also talk to your instructor about resources and software for designing your visuals. Follow these guidelines:

- Design your visuals carefully. Use a simple, neutral background. Minimize the amount of text in visuals. Don't simply present word outlines of what you are saying.

- Don't use more than two pictures in a slide and use two only to make a direct comparison. Image montages are hard to focus on and distracting.

- Don't put a table of numbers in a visual aid. If you need to illustrate numerical data, use a graph. Don't use too many visuals or move through them so quickly that the audience gives all its attention to them rather than to you.

- Practice your presentation using your visual aids, because they will affect your timing.

- Explain visuals when needed but not when they're obvious.

- Keep your eyes on your audience, only briefly glancing at visuals to stay in synch with them.

- Practice a good opening to capture the audience's attention. Start with a striking fact or example (illustrating an issue, a problem), a brief interesting or humorous anecdote (historical, personal, current event), a question to the audience, or an interesting quotation. Then relate the opening to your topic and your main point and move into the body of the presentation.

- Try to speak in your natural voice, not a monotone as if you were just reading aloud.

- Practice making changes in your delivery speed and intensity to emphasize key points in your presentation.

- Don't keep looking at your notes. It's fine if you use words that are different from those you wrote down—the more you rehearse without looking at your notes, the more natural you will sound.

- Be sure you can pronounce all new words and technical terms correctly. Practice saying them slowly and clearly to yourself until you can say them naturally.

- Don't forget transitions. A reader notices it when a writer moves on to a new point (with a heading in the text, a paragraph break, or a transitional phrase), and listeners also need a cue that you're moving to a new idea. Practice phrases such as "Another important reason for this is . . ." or "Now let's move on to why this is so. . . ."

- Watch out for all those little "filler" words people so often use in conversation, such as *like, you know, well,* and *uh.*

- Pay attention to your body language when practicing. Stand up straight and tall in every practice session so that you become used to it. Unless you have to use a fixed microphone in your presentation, practice moving around while you speak. Make natural gestures. Keep your eyes moving and making eye contact with the audience when you present. Practice smiling and occasionally pausing at key points.

I practice in front of a mirror to feel someone's eyes watching me as I present. It actually helps!

DELIVER THE PRESENTATION

On presentation day, get plenty of sleep and eat a healthy breakfast. Don't drink too many caffeinated drinks because that may make you hyper and nervous. Wear comfortable shoes and appropriate professional clothing that won't restrict you or make you self-conscious as you move around before the audience.

Remember: the audience is on your side! If you're still nervous before your presentation, take a few deep breaths. Rehearse your opening lines in your mind so that you don't have to look at your notes immediately when starting. Instead, look out and around your audience. Smile as you move to the front of the room. You'll see some friendly faces smiling back encouragingly.

WRITING FOR CLASSES

Writing, like speaking, is an important communication skill. As a student, you'll most likely be required to write essays, reports, and research papers. The writing skills you develop in school will carry over into your professional career as well. As an allied health professional, you'll need solid writing skills for recording accurate and concise information in patient charts and medical records.

Writing skills can be helpful for a number of other reasons, one of which is securing your first job. A well-written résumé and cover letter can help you get your foot in the door and get an interview, as discussed in Chapter 12. Even in email messages, being able to express yourself well shows that you are intelligent and competent. It also effectively gets your message across to the person with whom you are communicating. Good writing skills help you avoid misunderstandings that can result from poor communication.

Structurally Speaking

Whether you're writing a 15-page paper or a brief essay, your writing assignments should be structured in roughly the same way. Like an oral presentation, formal writing includes an introduction, a body, and a conclusion.

Spice up your introduction by beginning with a brief story, asking a question, or presenting an interesting fact.

INTRODUCTION

Always begin your written assignments with an introduction. The introduction should interest the reader in the topic you're about to discuss. Your introduction can be structured in a number of different ways. It can:

- be centered on a thesis statement (a thesis statement is a statement of the opinion or idea to be discussed in your paper)
- present a problem or ask a question that you intend to answer
- describe a dramatic event or incident
- provide interesting statistics
- set a scene
- relate a short story

For example, in a persuasive essay, your introduction could begin by presenting a topic. Then, your thesis statement could include the main point you intend to prove about that topic.

Keep in mind that your introduction doesn't have to be the first thing you write. Even if you start with a basic outline and have a general idea of how you'd like to approach your topic, it's easy to get stuck on the introduction. If this happens, try working on other portions of the paper for a while and come back to it. Your introduction will be easier to write once you have a clear purpose in mind.

The introduction should be roughly 5% to 15% of the length of your entire paper. It needs to be informative but to the point. It should be interesting without giving away too much detail. For these reasons, it takes time and effort to write a good introduction. You may want to revise it again after you've completed your paper.

BODY

You do most of your writing in the body, which makes up about 70% to 90% of a paper's total length. The body of a paper presents details that support your thesis. This may include:

- background information about your topic
- facts and supporting research
- explanations of key terms or phrases used throughout the paper
- quotes from other credible sources
- different arguments against your thesis and your responses to those arguments

CONCLUSION

A strong conclusion ends the discussion presented in the paper and makes the reader think. To accomplish this, the conclusion needs to do more than blandly summarize main points. To write a strong conclusion, consider including:

- a quotation that relates to or sums up your thesis
- a question for the reader to consider
- encouragement for the reader to act in support of your idea
- one last example or story to reiterate your point

BIBLIOGRAPHY AND REFERENCES

The bibliography is a list of the sources you used to write your paper. It's important because it helps you back up the information included in your paper and gives credit to your sources of research. Whether you gathered information from a book, a website, a television program, or a magazine article, each source must be included in your bibliography. A bibliography only shows the general sources, however. For quotations, specific statistics, and the theories and opinions of others, you'll need to include specific references, either as footnotes or numbered endnotes. Your instructor will tell you the specific reference format to use.

APPENDIX

You probably won't need to include an appendix with each formal writing assignment you complete. An appendix is only necessary when you need to include other supportive materials that do not belong or cannot fit in the body of your paper. A few examples of such materials are:

- a list of key terms and definitions
- photos, illustrations, or figures
- tables, charts, maps, and other graphic elements

The Writing Process

So you've decided on the type of paper you're going to write. You know it needs to have an introduction, a body, and a conclusion. What next? First, carefully reread the assignment to make sure you fully understand it. Is your topic appropriate? Are you expected to do research? How long should the final result be? When you are clear about all aspects of the assignment, you're ready to start the process.

Writing a paper involves several steps in a process. The writing process is a time-tested method to ensure you do your best on the paper.

1. Set your schedule.
2. Select a topic.
3. Collect information.
4. Organize the information.
5. Evaluate the information.
6. Create an outline.
7. Write a first draft.
8. Revise the first draft.
9. Finalize the paper.

SCHEDULING

A good way to set up a schedule for writing a paper is to work backward from the due date listed in your syllabus. Then, mark the following on your calendar and weekly planner:

- due date for the paper
- amount of time you need to revise the paper
- amount of time you need to write the first draft
- date you should complete your research
- date you need to begin research

When scheduling your time, be generous! Unexpected problems can arise, making some steps take longer than you anticipated. For example, you may go to the library to find that a book you need has already been checked out. Or you may find that you need extra time to evaluate and organize the materials you gathered. Whatever delays may occur, you can avoid stress by building in extra time for the full process.

Another aspect that may affect your writing schedule is the paper's length. Sometimes it's hard to predict how much work you'll need to do to complete the assignment. When considering how much time to allow yourself to write the paper, keep the following in mind:

- the required length of the paper
- the amount of time you have before the due date
- the amount of research you're expected to do
- the number of references your instructor requires you to have

SELECTING A TOPIC

If your instructor assigns a specific topic, you won't have to worry about this stage of the writing process. If not, your instructor may give you a list of acceptable topics or guidelines for creating your own topic. When thinking about possible topics, select one that captures your interest. When you write about a subject that interests you, you'll be better motivated to work on the paper. Also, be sure to select a topic that you'll be able to research adequately. You'll have a hard time completing an assignment that requires a lot of research on an obscure topic.

Good places to search for topic ideas include:

- the table of contents in your textbook
- your lecture notes
- brainstorming sessions with your study group
- magazines, journals
- websites

Just remember to keep your topic fairly narrow. A more focused topic means a more focused writing process and a better paper. When looking for a topic, try to find a balance. Your topic should provide you with enough material to complete the assignment, but it should be focused enough so that you can explain it fully in your paper.

One way to see if a topic is well defined or focused enough is to think about your thesis statement and the title of the paper. A good title is clear and appealing. The reader should know what the paper is about just by reading the title. However, if you come up with a title before writing the paper, keep in mind that the title isn't permanent and may need to be changed after the paper has been completed. Sometimes, it's simply a good exercise to think about the main point you'd like to communicate in your paper. Doing so may help you decide on a particular topic.

COLLECTING INFORMATION

When gathering information for your paper, it's probably wise to begin at the library. Start by looking up your topic in the library's computer system or reference books for the subject. (See the later section *Library Research*.)

Use the required page length to help you figure out how long it will take you to write the paper.

Other Sources of Information

In addition to the library, other excellent sources of information include:

- *Interviews with professors or experts in the field.* Conducting interviews will prepare you for future clinical work, when you may have to conduct information-gathering interviews with patients. In both cases, the process is similar.

  1. Be prepared. Make a list of the questions you'd like to ask. Make sure the most important questions are at the top of your list.

  2. During the interview, keep the conversation focused. If you only have a limited amount of time, try to avoid talking about things unrelated to your questions.

  3. Finally, when gathering information for a paper, you may wish to audiotape the interview in addition to taking notes. This can help you remember quotes accurately. It also gives you a way to review any information you may have missed. Just remember to ask permission first. You can do this when scheduling the interview to avoid putting your interviewee on the spot when you meet; not everyone is comfortable with being recorded.

- *Surveys and statistics.* The results of professional surveys may add to the information for your paper. But you can conduct your own surveys as well. Statistics can be calculated after you receive responses to your survey. For example, suppose you surveyed 50 subjects and 15 of those individuals answered *yes* to a particular question. The other 35 subjects answered *no.* Your statistics for that question would be 30% answering *yes* and 70% answering *no.* These results could then be used in your paper to support or argue against a particular point.

- *Resources on the Internet.* When searching for information online, there are two very important guidelines to keep in mind.

  1. Make sure the material you find is reliable. (See the *Websites* section later in this chapter.)

  2. Remember to cite any online information you use in your paper. Your instructor will be able to tell you which reference format to use when citing information. You'll most likely need to include the Web address, site owner, date the site was last updated (if available), and the date you accessed the information.

- *Unbiased observations.* Your own unbiased observations can be used as a source of information for your paper. However, the key word here is *unbiased.* There are several methods you can use to avoid allowing your own opinions to cloud your observations. For example, you could create a checklist of things to look for as you observe a certain situation. During your observation, use the checklist to guide your note taking. The checklist and thorough notes add reliability to your observations.

- *Personal experiences.* Some assignments allow you to use information gathered from your own experiences. Just be sure the experiences you draw from are directly related to the topic of your paper. Also, back up your experiences with more objective information from sources you trust, such as reference books or articles in academic journals.

ORGANIZING YOUR INFORMATION

Index cards are an excellent way to begin organizing your information. Fill out one index card per source, including main ideas and references to page numbers. (You'll need to know page numbers for the bibliography or references part of your paper.)

Start by creating cards for your general sources and then move to more specific sources. This is a good time to take notes on each source and look for quotes as well. Be sure to copy down quotes word for word and cite them accurately on your index cards. In the sources themselves, use sticky notes to mark relevant chapters or sections. For photocopied pages, you can use colorful highlighters to mark important information.

Next, sort your index cards according to topic. If you have several sources that provide the same information, discard the ones you won't need. Begin thinking about the basic layout of your paper at this point. Separate your cards into three stacks:

Try using a color-coding system or symbols to keep your index cards organized. Just be creative and use a method that works easily for you.

- The first stack is for information that belongs toward the beginning of your paper.
- The second stack is for material you plan to use toward the middle of your paper.
- The third stack holds the cards you'll need to consult when writing the end of your paper.

EVALUATING YOUR INFORMATION

After you've organized your sources, you'll need to check each one for relevance to your topic:

- Check the publication date (if possible, try to avoid using sources published more than 5 years ago).
- Make sure each source contains supporting information.

If you find a source that argues against your thesis, it may still be relevant to your paper. You can write a stronger paper by including differing points of view and defending your thesis. Sources that contain counterpoint material also help you determine how well your thesis holds up against arguments. If you find that your thesis is too weak, this is a good point in the writing process to rethink the focus of your paper. It would be much easier to rewrite your thesis than it would be to try to write an entire paper about an idea you're unable to support.

Once you've sorted relevant sources, make sure the information they contain is reliable. As you review each source, ask yourself:

- *Is the author biased?* Does the author merely present personal opinions without backing up statements with facts or research? Does the author criticize certain ideas without giving solid reasons why those ideas are faulty? Have statistics been presented in a misleading way to further the author's opinion?

- *Is the source primary or secondary?* A primary source contains firsthand information. A secondary source restates material from a primary source. Occasionally, secondary sources reproduce quotes made in primary sources. Out of context, those quotes may take on different meanings, which affect their reliability. Whenever possible, use primary sources.

Remember that statistics can be manipulated. Even if information is presented as fact, you still need to evaluate it!

After evaluating your sources, keep only those that contain reliable information important to your topic. Then, set aside those index cards for sources you've decided not to use. Later, when you're sure you're not going to need those sources, you can discard them.

CREATING AN OUTLINE

The next stage in the writing process is creating an outline. Your thesis statement can serve as the outline's introduction. This will help you stay focused on your main point as you write the rest of the outline. Another way to stay focused is to write a brief conclusion. You can expand this conclusion later when you write the first draft of your paper.

Next, refer to your index card notes as you map out the body of the outline. If you're required to submit a title page, table of contents, appendix, or bibliography with your final paper, use simple one-line entries to note these items on your outline as well.

When deciding how to organize the body of your outline, think about your three stacks of index cards for the beginning, middle, and end.

As you write your outline, and even as you write your paper, you're free to move sections around and reorganize information. The purpose of having an outline is to give yourself a guide. But it isn't set in stone. An outline allows you to see the organization of your paper at a glance and make necessary changes before you begin writing your first draft.

Anatomy of an Outline

Follow these tips when creating an outline for your paper.
I. Creating an outline
  A. Sections
    1. Introduction (use thesis statement)
    2. Body (consult index cards)
    3. Conclusion
    4. Other items (one-line entries)
      a. title page
      b. table of contents
      c. appendix
      d. bibliography
  B. Organization
    1. Use index cards to organize info in the body
      a. beginning of paper (first stack of cards)
      b. middle of paper (second stack of cards)
      c. end of paper (third stack of cards)
    2. Move sections around as necessary

WRITING A FIRST DRAFT

The first draft of your paper is just that—a draft. Don't worry about editing and polishing your writing at this point. There will be plenty of time for that later. The most important thing is to put your ideas into sentences and paragraphs.

While writing the first draft, you'll develop the introduction and body of your paper. You'll need to begin keeping track of references (using footnotes or the system required by your instructor) and bibliography sources. You'll also expand on the brief conclusion you wrote for your outline.

Another important part of writing a first draft involves developing the tone you'll use throughout your paper. To do this, think about your audience:

- Is this paper intended for your instructor?

- Will you be presenting it to the rest of the class?

To have a consistent tone in all sections of your paper, keep your audience in mind as you write.

Your outline should guide the process of writing the first draft. As you begin writing, however, feel free to make changes if the organization of your outline isn't working. Using a word processing program makes it easy to move sections of text. Just remember to save your work often! It's also a good idea to back up your writing on disk or by some other method.

The last step in writing your first draft is to put it away for a while. Depending on your schedule, this may mean 24 hours or several days. This gives your brain time to process what you've written. During the time you spend away from writing, you may think of ways to improve your paper. Whether you come up with the perfect introduction or a better way to state your conclusion, these ideas are valuable. Write them down so you can incorporate them later as you make revisions to your first draft.

> The wheels in your head will keep turning even after you take a break from your paper. After you finish the first draft, put it away for a while and let your brain keep working.

REVISING THE FIRST DRAFT

After you've been away from your paper for some time, you can begin revising for the second draft. By this time, you should have a better idea of how the overall organization of your paper is working. If any big organizational changes need to be made, such as moving one whole section closer to the beginning or the end of the paper, now is the time to make them.

Again, if you're working on a computer, remember to save often! Another helpful tip for computer users is to rename each draft (e.g., Draft 1, Draft 2, Draft 3). That way, you can always refer to a previous version of your paper if you delete a section by mistake or if you decide to go back to your original organization.

With each draft, your paper should resemble more closely how it will look in its final stage. But how many drafts are needed? Reading your entire paper aloud is one way to help you notice parts that may need improvement. As you read, consider the following:

- *Organization.* Does the overall organization make sense? Does the paper move forward in a logical and clear way?

- *Paragraph structure.* Does each paragraph have a main idea and supporting details? Does the paper include transitions from one paragraph to the next?

- *Sentence flow.* Do the sentences flow smoothly from one to the next?

As you revise your paper, also keep the due date in mind. Be sure to allow yourself enough time for editing the final draft.

Once you're satisfied with the body of your paper, it's time to create the title page, table of contents (page numbers can be inserted after your final edit), bibliography and references, appendix, and any other items required by your instructor. Then, have someone else read the paper—it's always a good idea to have a fresh pair of eyes look for anything you may have missed. (Your school may also have a writing center staffed with people who can fill this role.) Your reviewer can look at things such as spelling, grammar, organization, logic, and any other elements your instructor may use to grade the paper. But keep in mind that any suggestions made by your reviewer are merely suggestions. In the end, you must decide yourself what changes to make.

Well, I'm satisfied with this paper. Now I just need someone else to review it.

FINALIZING THE PAPER

The final stage in the writing process involves editing, formatting, and proofreading your paper.

1. During editing, it's helpful to consult other resources, such as a dictionary, thesaurus, and an English grammar and usage guide. These resources should be available in the reference section of the library. As you edit your work, follow these guidelines.

   - Check the paper's tone to make sure it remains consistent.

   - Make sure terms are used consistently throughout the paper. For example, if you used *congestive heart failure* in one paragraph, avoid changing it to *heart failure* in another paragraph if it refers to the same condition.

   - Spell check your paper. Check any words the spell-checker doesn't recognize (such as scientific terms). Remember that the spell-checker doesn't know the difference between "your" and "you're"—and can leave you with many confusing errors.

   - Check your grammar. For example, make sure all singular subjects have singular verbs and all plural subjects have plural verbs. ("He walks," not "He walk.")

   - Check your punctuation. All sentences should end with a period or other punctuation mark. All text in quotes should have both opening and closing quotation marks.

   - Check the spacing between lines of text. Most instructors require students to use double spacing to allow plenty of room for marks and comments.

   - Make sure the font size is appropriate (12-pt. font is standard).

2. The next step in finalizing your paper is formatting. Use the following tips as you format your paper:

- Follow your instructor's formatting guidelines. If specific guidelines aren't provided, your instructor may require you to adhere to a particular style manual instead (such as the *Publication Manual of the American Psychological Association*). Style manuals can answer questions you may have about specialized terms and industry style and formatting standards. The manual will likely also include information on how to format your references and bibliography. These resources also can be found in the reference section of the library.

- Print a hard copy of your paper. Reviewing a hard copy is easier than looking at your paper on a computer screen and formatting errors are much more visible.

3. Take a short break before you begin the last step—proofreading. If you're too familiar with the text of your paper, your eyes might begin to skip over errors. By waiting a bit, you'll come back refreshed and ready to read your paper closely. Here are some proofreading tips:

- Read your entire paper aloud (if possible).

- Remember your spell-checker will miss common errors and may actually create errors—you need to check every word yourself.

- Be on the lookout for any errors in punctuation or capitalization.

- When you come across an unfamiliar word, look it up in the dictionary to check its spelling and meaning.

- Read your paper from end to beginning. It sounds strange, but this will interrupt the rhythm you've developed from reading your paper many times and will help you see errors you might otherwise miss.

After completing this last step, you can hand in your final paper feeling confident about your work!

RESEARCHING FOR WRITING OR PRESENTATIONS

As mentioned previously, you'll likely need to do some research for writing a paper or preparing a class presentation. Your best methods of research are your school's library and the Internet.

Library Research

Many younger students have grown up with computers and the Internet and seldom use libraries. Don't fall into this trap! Libraries continue to provide a wide range of valuable information, much of which cannot be found online. Get to know your school's library. It likely has an online catalog that makes it easy to search for the information you need. Specific library resources typically include:

- Books and journals stored in the library stacks, reference room, and other reading rooms. Especially important are the journals of the professional associations in your chosen health career.

- Reference manuals, indexes of articles sorted by subject and title, and other specialized works kept in the reference department.

- Librarians—yes, people! Librarians are highly trained experts on research techniques, as well as the information that can be found in the library. They will be happy to give you personal assistance if you experience any difficulty finding material on your topic.

Internet Research

When you sit down at a computer, you literally have access to a world of resources. The material you can find online far outweighs the volume of material stored in any library. The key is determining which sources on the Web are reliable and which are not.

WEBSITES

Websites consist of one or more Web pages. When you are "surfing the Web," it means you are moving from one Web page to another. You do this by clicking on hyperlinks, which usually look like graphics, buttons, or underlined words onscreen.

It's a good thing surfing the Web is a lot easier than this!

All websites have a "home page." This is the main page for the site. A home page usually includes text or graphics as well as links to additional pages within the site. Because there are billions of websites on the Internet, it's helpful to have an idea of how to search for particular information and which websites to trust. By following some simple guidelines, your online research will go more smoothly.

On the Corner of http:// and www

Each Web page has an address, otherwise known as a URL (universal resource locator). If you know a site's URL, you'll have no trouble locating it among the many other sites on the Web.

Web addresses, especially lengthy ones, might look confusing. But each address is made up of the same basic components. Below is an explanation of each component, based on the fictional Web address http://www.acmesportsequipment.com.

- *http://* These letters stand for hypertext transfer protocol. Most Web addresses start out this way.
- *www.* This acronym for World Wide Web appears in many, but not all, URLs.
- *acmesportsequipment* This portion of the Web address indicates the name of the site. In this example, the site is named for the Acme Sports Equipment Company.
- *.com* This portion of the URL is called the suffix. The suffix provides additional information about the site.

What's in a Name?

Usually, you can gather certain information about a website just by looking at the suffix of its URL. Here's a list of common suffixes:

- *.com* This suffix usually indicates that a particular site is intended for commercial use. Most sites ending in .com are owned by businesses or individuals.
- *.edu* Web addresses ending in .edu indicate educational institutions (colleges and universities). If your school has a website, its URL probably ends in .edu.
- *.gov* This suffix indicates that a particular site is owned and operated by a government institution or agency.
- *.net* Web addresses ending in .net usually indicate Internet service providers (ISPs).
- *.org* This suffix indicates a nonprofit organization.

THE SEARCH IS ON!

What happens if you don't know the URL of the site you're looking for? Or what if you prefer to search for several different websites that deal with a specific topic? This is where search engines come in.

For example, suppose you needed to locate information on how to perform cardiopulmonary resuscitation (CPR). You use a search engine such as Google and enter keywords into the search box. For this particular search, *CPR* would be an appropriate keyword. The search engine then compiles a list of websites that may be relevant to your search. You view the results of your search and click on the links to websites that seemed applicable.

Most Web browsers now have one or more search engines, such as Google or Yahoo, built in on a toolbar for easy searching. Or you can go directly to a search engine's site, such as www.google.com or www.yahoo.com

Improve Your Searching Skills

With so much information on the Web, it's sometimes tricky trying to locate the information you need. The following tips will help you perform better Internet searches.

Starting Your Search

- Avoid using words such as *a, an,* and *the* when entering keywords into a search bar. Most search engines ignore these words anyway.

- If you are looking for a specific phrase, enclose it in quotation marks. Most search engines recognize text contained within quotes as a single item. For example, if you needed to find information on heart disease in children, you would enter *"heart disease in children"* in the search bar.

- Be specific. Entering *diabetes education* in the search bar would give you more specific results to sort through than the more general search term *diabetes*.

- Avoid being overly specific. If your search returns very few results, broaden your search terms.

Keeping At It

- If your first search is unsuccessful, try rephrasing your keyword(s). You may find what you need by looking up a related word.

- If you still can't find what you're looking for, try using a different search engine.

- For complicated searches, look for an "advanced search" button in the search engine. Advanced search features include the ability to exclude results with a certain key term and to search for synonyms in addition to an exact phrase.

Again, don't forget the librarians! If you still have trouble with your searches after trying these techniques, a librarian may be able to help you find what you're looking for.

THE RELIABILITY TEST

Just because information has been posted on the Internet doesn't make it trustworthy. When performing research online, remember to be wary of unreliable websites. Use these tips when trying to spot the difference between reliable and unreliable sites:

- Compare sources to verify information. If a statement posted on a website seems too outrageous to be true, check it against a source you trust.

- Beware of sites that seem biased or push a specific agenda. These sites may skew facts or give blatant misinformation.

- Pay attention to URL suffixes. Usually, you can assume that sites ending in .gov or .edu contain reliable information. However, be wary of .edu sites that are owned by individual students at a university. These sites generally are not regulated for accuracy.

- As a general rule, the sites of well-known associations or agencies tend to post reliable information.
- Be especially critical of information posted on sites owned by individuals or small, unknown organizations. The owners of these sites do not have the same accountability as reputable businesses or organizations.

When conducting online research, only use information from sites you can trust.

Reliable Websites

Your instructor may be able to provide you with a more complete listing of reliable health professions websites related to your specific career area. Check the chart for a list to get you started.

Site Name	Address	Brief Summary
American Association of Medical Assistants	www.aama-ntl.org	Offers information for students and employers
American Dental Assistants Association	www.dentalassistant.org	Includes information on membership in the association, education, and employment
American Heart Association	www.americanheart.org	Includes information on continuing education and resources for professionals
American Red Cross	www.redcross.org	Offers health and safety information
American Society of Radiologic Technologists	www.asrt.org	Includes information on continuing education; provides links to online publications and an on-line learning center
HealthAnswers Education	www.healthanswers.com	Offers interactive training for individuals in the pharmaceutical and biotechnology industries
Lippincott Williams & Wilkins	www.lww.com	Publisher of allied health texts; provides health care news, continuing education information, and other resources
Massage Therapy Foundation	www.massagetherapy foundation.org	Provides resources for students, including a massage therapy research database

Site Name	Address	Brief Summary
Mayo Clinic	www.mayoclinic.com	Provides health information from the scientists and doctors at the Mayo Clinic
National Institutes of Health (NIH)	www.nih.gov	Government-sponsored site; functions as the home page for all other NIH sites, such as the National Cancer Institute, National Institute on Aging, and others
PubMed	http://www.ncbi.nlm.nih.gov/pubmed	A medical information search engine from the National Library of Medicine, useful for professional medical material
WebMD	www.webmd.com	Offers health information and links to articles on health-related issues; provides online discussion boards

GROUP PROJECTS

When group-writing projects or presentations are assigned, your main focus should be on acting as a dependable teammate. Not only will you need to contribute quality material, but you'll need to offer your input to the rest of the group and complete your work on time.

As described in Chapter 8, study group members need to be *committed contributors* who are *compatible* with one another and *considerate* of each other. The same is true when working with a group of your classmates on a writing assignment or class presentation.

- First and foremost, everyone in the group needs to be committed to the project.
- Each person is responsible for bringing something to the table, such as supplying ideas and written or graphical material.
- Even if your instructor assigned you to work with a group of people you don't get along with, you should find a way to overlook your differences and focus on the project.
- If everyone in the group makes an effort to speak politely and be considerate of each other's time, the project will go more smoothly.

Be a Team Player

When working in a group on a writing assignment or class presentation, the group uses the same process as described earlier for preparing a presentation or the writing process. Group dynamics, however, often require call for additional planning and shared responsibilities. Keep these guidelines in mind:

Be a team player when helping out with group projects!

1. Schedule a group meeting as soon as possible to get started. Don't let anyone put things off. Explain that you're too busy and won't have time at the last minute to do your share.

2. Begin your first meeting by brainstorming together about the written assignment's topic or the presentation's audience and goals. Make sure everyone understands the assignment and is on the same wavelength. Then discuss who should do what. One or more students may begin research and gathering information, another may do the initial drafting, others may develop visual aids, and so on. You also need a team leader—someone to keep everyone on schedule, organize meetings, etc. The team leader needs good social skills and the ability to motivate cooperation among everyone in the group.

3. Assigned tasks can then be carried out individually, but everyone should stay in touch. For example, a student developing visual aids should be talking to those doing the researching and drafting to see what visuals will be needed or useful.

4. Before writing the first draft or outlining the presentation, the group should meet again to go over the work in process. Everyone should be comfortable with the plan as it has emerged so far. At this time, make final decisions about who will complete the next stages, such as who will do the presenting or final editing. With a presentation involving multiple speakers, plan for the student with the strongest speaking skills to open and/or close the presentation, with others doing specific parts in the middle.

5. The whole group should work together during the presentation practice or revising of the paper. Everyone should have the opportunity to comment on polishing the final work.

6. With a presentation, especially if technology is used for visual aids, one student should manage the visuals while one or more others do the presenting. If several students present different segments, plan transitions so that the presentation flows without pauses or delays.

COMPUTER COMMUNICATION

Two common forms of computerized communication use the Internet and email. All the same principles of communication generally apply the same as with written and spoken communication, with a few additional considerations.

On the Web

Because the Internet connects computers around the world, it is easily used by many as a communication tool. Here are few examples:

- The Web allows businesses to communicate with each other and with consumers.
- Health care providers use the Internet to communicate with each other and patients or the general public.
- Students can use the Internet to communicate with classmates and instructors.

A traditional method of online communication uses online message boards, or discussion boards, where you can post questions or comments to your classmates and instructors. Some message boards are set up so students and instructors from different schools anywhere in the world can communicate with each other. Because their format encourages discussion, message boards can be a great source of supplemental material.

Technology keeps getting easier and more available, but common courtesy never goes out of style!

Nowadays, it is very easy to access the Internet through wired or wireless connections available at school, in public "hot spots," in many homes, and on many mobile phones. Most computers already include the appropriate hardware and software. Through programs such as Skype, you can also have direct video conferencing between two computers equipped with Web cams, speakers, and microphones. Other online meeting services allow video to be sent out from a presenter and multiple viewers to connect back with the full group through audio or text messages.

New applications for online communication are being implemented almost every day, and the specific forms you may use now as a student and in your future health career may vary. The use of these programs is increasingly simple—and now can usually be learned in a few minutes.

More important, however, is recognizing that even these forms of communication, which may seem as casual as a telephone call between friends, require professionalism. Always assume that what you say or write online might be captured or saved and then viewed later by someone else. Speak or write in respectful tones and maintain the privacy and confidentiality of others.

Email

Email is now a preferred form of communication in education, business, and many health care practices. In addition to messages, you can send documents and digital images to anyone with Internet access. If you have a free email account through your school or place of employment, it's a good idea to keep it separate from your personal account. This will help keep you and your school materials organized!

Email Best Practices

Email communication with an instructor or business associate is a professional form of communication and shouldn't look like the sort of messages frequently sent between friends. For example, rather than using abbreviations and shorthand, most instructors expect email messages to be in full sentences with correctly spelled words and reasonable grammar. Follow these guidelines:

- Use a professional email name, not a casual or humorous name you might use with friends. For example, JohnSmith@gmail.com is better than SuperGuy@gmail.com.

- In the subject line, label your message so the reader knows at a glance what the message concerns. "May I make an appointment?" is clear, but "In your office now?" isn't.

- Address email messages as you would a letter, such as "Dear Professor Jones." Be sure to sign with your full name.

- Get to your point quickly and concisely. Don't force the reader to scroll ahead down a long email to see what you want to say.

- Avoid any temptations to be funny, ironic, sarcastic, etc. Write as you would in a paper for class. In a large lecture class or an online course, your email voice may be the primary way your instructor knows you, and emotionally charged messages can be confusing or give a poor impression.

- Don't use capital letters to emphasize. All caps look like SHOUTING.

- Avoid abbreviations, nonstandard spelling, slang, and emoticons like smiley faces. These are not professional.

- When replying to a message, leave the original message within yours (typically below your new message). Your reader may need to recall what he or she said in the original message.

- Be polite. End the message with a "Thank you" or something similar.

- Check the subject line and text of your message for correct spelling and punctuation. Many email programs include a spell-check feature—use it!

- Review your message for content as well as correctness before clicking to send it. You may have expressed an emotion or thought that you will think better about later.

Communicating in Online Courses

Many schools now offer online courses you can take from the comfort of your own home. Such courses can include most of the elements from traditional classes, such as instructor-led presentations, question-and-answer sessions, assignments, and tests. Online courses are especially convenient for working students who have limited time to come to campus. However, online courses require high levels of commitment and self-discipline. Students take more responsibility for their own learning.

Before deciding to take an online course, think about your individual strengths and weaknesses as well as your personal learning style:

- Are you self-disciplined?
- Do you enjoy being able to complete tasks according to your own schedule?
- Do you need the structure of a traditional classroom course?
- Online courses typically require a lot of reading and independent study—does that match your learning style?

I never thought I'd take an online course, but I've found it plays to my strengths!

An additional consideration with online courses involves communication with the instructor and sometimes with other students. Unlike regular classes where you hear others speak and can talk directly to your instructor and ask questions or meet during office hours, your communication in an online course will be mostly, or entirely, written. Are you comfortable with written communication and confident of your ability to express yourself well in writing? If you feel you need more experience with academic writing, you might choose to put off taking any online courses until you've done more writing assignments in regular courses and have gained that confidence.

A final word: because most or all of the communication with an online instructor will occur through email, be sure to follow the guidelines listed in *Best Email Practices*. Your instructor may never even see your face—the impression you make will come entirely from your words!

CHAPTER SUMMARY

- Improve your ability to express yourself by speaking up during class and participating in discussions.
- Develop good writing skills now for your future use in health care settings, such as writing accurate and concise reports in patient charts.
- Use the library, Internet, and other resources to research information for written assignments and class presentations.

- Be a dependable team player in group-writing projects or class presentations. Participate by giving your input, completing your work on time, and being sure to contribute quality material.

- Use effective techniques in all forms of academic and professional communication, including online and email practices.

REVIEW QUESTIONS

1. What specific things can you do to overcome stage fright when preparing to give a presentation to a class?

2. When gathering material for a paper, what are several sources where you can look to find information?

3. Why is it important to follow the full process steps for a writing assignment or presentation?

4. Name three important things to remember when working on a team project.

5. Describe the appearance of a professional email.

CHAPTER ACTIVITIES

1. Group Discussion: Begin with a warm-up exercise to get everyone participating. Think of something, aside from family and friends, that you value (such as a painting, CD collection, book, etc.). Then, in 1 to 2 minutes, share with the rest of the class what that object is and why it's important to you. After everyone has had a chance to participate in the warm-up exercise, discuss as a group several reasons why people may have a fear of public speaking. Why is the ability to speak up particularly important in a health care setting?

2. Online Investigation: Visit your school's website to learn whether you may include online courses as part of your academic program. (If not, for this exercise, go to the website of a nearby community college or state university.) Choose a course you might find interesting and learn as much about it as you can. How is information presented (videos, textbook, online instruction)? What are the major kinds of assignments? Is there an opportunity to meet online with other students? What kinds of communications with the instructor are expected? Finally, based on what you learn about this course, decide whether you are prepared with the right skills at present for succeeding in this course.

Study Skills

On completion of this chapter and the learning activities you will be able to:

- Use course materials to focus on your study goals
- Select and prepare a study space
- Improve your concentration and memorization skills
- Explore different study strategies to improve your efficiency
- Build and use a study group effectively
- Make use of supplemental study materials
- Improve your study skills for math and science

Much of your time as a student will be spent studying. If that thought makes you groan, don't despair! There are many simple strategies you can use to make the most of your study time and the resources available to you. In this chapter, you'll learn how to study effectively, starting with how to select a study space and how to prepare yourself for studying. You'll learn tips for improving your concentration and long-term memory as well. Study strategies can help you make the most of your time to help ensure your success as a student. In addition, you'll learn how to form and work with a study group and how to use textbook and other resources as you study. Finally, you'll learn some special study skills for math and science.

WHAT ARE YOU GOING TO STUDY?

Although it may seem obvious, you need a focus before starting to study. Are you studying a chapter to prepare for class? Studying for an upcoming test? Studying how to perform a certain health care procedure before you do it in the lab tomorrow? Start by considering your reasons for studying and setting your goals.

This step begins with materials your instructor has provided you, including:

- the syllabus
- study guides and lecture outlines
- practice exercises
- assignment instructions

Start with the Syllabus

Chapter 2 points out the importance of the syllabus for each class and how to use it. The syllabus gives you key information such as reading assignments, exam dates, and due dates for papers and other out-of-class work. Chapter 2 also discusses how to manage your time well by scheduling study periods well ahead of time to avoid last-minute "cramming," which is the least effective way to study. Your syllabus is your road map for starting to get organized for studying, but it's not your only resource.

Study Guides and Lecture Outlines

Many instructors not only tell you what general topic you'll cover each day of class, but they may also provide an outline of each day's lecture for you. You can use this outline as you prepare for class. It allows you to focus your reading and studying on the points listed in the outline. Keep these main ideas in mind as you read to help you prepare well for class.

An added benefit is that you will not have to take as many notes during class because the outline is already provided for you! And don't forget to put the study guide or outline in your notebook under a tab where you can find it later. You'll also find it very helpful when studying for tests.

Practice Exercises

Some instructors also provide practice exercises for you. These may be on a handout or on the course website. Practice exercises are a great way to drill. If your instructor goes to the trouble of giving you practice exercises for a chapter or section, you should assume that the material is particularly important to know and that it may be on a test. File these exercises in a safe place so you can use them later as you study. Save any completed exercises so you can check your work when you get graded tests back.

Doing drills and practice exercises is a great way to prepare for upcoming tests!

Assignment Instructions

Your instructor may also give you a handout that tells you exactly how certain assignments are to be done. These instructions can include things such as:

- style guides for papers—details on how papers should be typed, how to format your citations and bibliography, what margins to use, etc.
- step-by-step walkthroughs—such as for clinical procedures; sometimes, many different procedures start with the same basic steps
- research tips—resources for finding information on the Internet or in the library

Remember to file your assignment instructions in your notebook under the correct tab.

GETTING ORGANIZED TO STUDY

Studying is much more efficient when you're organized. Organization is a key to your success not only as a health professions student, but also as a health care professional. Being organized for studying simply makes the most efficient use of your time.

If you're already a very organized person, you may not need to make any changes in your system for keeping track of things. On the other hand, if you consider yourself less than organized or even hopelessly disorganized, take heart! The following tips and suggestions are simple and easy to implement.

Organization is a key to your success both as a student and as a future health care professional.

Location, Location, Location

The first step to getting organized is finding or making a place for everything. This means you'll need to find a place to keep the materials and supplies for each class you're taking. Most students find that the best organizational system uses three-ring binders (or twin-pocket folders with notebook fasteners) with tabbed dividers.

Dedicate one binder for each class. Keep all handouts, notes, charts—everything related to that class—together in that binder.

Divide and Conquer

Next, decide how you want to organize the material in each binder, using labeled tabbed dividers or a similar system. You may find it helpful to use the same set of divider names in each binder. This will minimize the time it takes to find things. Use a pen or colored permanent marker to label the tabs on the dividers. You can purchase tabbed dividers or make your own from card-stock paper. The following is an example of a typical set of divider names:

- schedule
- syllabus
- handouts
- assignments
- notes

In this system, your class schedule is at the front. This helps you see at a glance what's going to be covered in the next class period. The syllabus needs to be accessible, too, because it contains other critical information. Every time you receive a new handout, place it behind the "Handouts" tab; do the same with assignments. The last section is for taking notes in class and during your reading. Keep a supply of new notebook paper behind this tab.

Organizing Your Notes

You may prefer to use a spiral notebook instead of loose-leaf paper for taking notes. Just be sure to keep the notebook with the appropriate binder for each class. To avoid confusion, use a separate notebook for each class. Mixing notes from several classes will disrupt your organization and derail your game plan.

Chapter 6 describes how to take good notes in class. After class, take a few minutes to organize your notes by following these simple steps.

- Record the date of the lecture.
- Number your pages.
- Write down reminders about upcoming assignments and due dates. Make sure the dates are written in your weekly planner.

The Backpack Black Hole

One final note about organization: Beware the backpack black hole. If you are in a rush after class, it may be tempting to gather your papers, shove them into your backpack, and forget about them. The only problem with this method is that when you need to review one of those papers several days or weeks later, you might not be able to find it. A lack of organization makes it easy for important papers to get lost. The backpack black hole occurs when things go in and are never to be seen again.

Stay organized to avoid the backpack black hole!

STUDYING 101

Studying seems simple: Get out your books and notes and study them. But what does it really mean to study? Studying involves:

- refreshing your memory
- taking in new information
- organizing and memorizing data

That's a lot! It's no surprise that many students sit down to study and find themselves feeling overwhelmed. And then any little distraction can throw a wrench in the works, keeping you from studying efficiently. That's why it's important to study the right way.

Scope out a Study Area

First, find a good place to study. Look for a location that is free of distractions. (See *How to Find a Distraction-Free Study Zone*.) Make sure the area is large enough for you to arrange all your study materials. Think about any furniture you might need, such as a desk or large table.

Many students prefer to sit at a table when they study. This arrangement keeps them alert and focused while helping them keep their materials organized. They can put the study materials they're using on the table and keep materials they'll need later underneath it. Other students feel more comfortable sitting on a sofa, with their study materials on a coffee table or spread out on the floor below. One place you may want to avoid studying is your bed, which may tempt you to take a nap!

> When it comes to studying, think **location, location, location!** Finding a good place to study is just as important as the study methods you use.

How to Find a Distraction-Free Study Zone

Think about two or three areas that might make good study spaces. Then choose the place that best addresses these questions:

- Are there a lot of other people in the same space who could interrupt me?
- Are there things in the space that will distract me from studying?
- Is there a TV or radio in the space that might be turned on?
- Is there a phone that might ring too often?
- Is this space easy for me to get to on a regular basis?
- Is the temperature comfortable? If it isn't, can I change it?
- Will cooking odors come into this space, making me feel hungry and distracted?
- Is this space big enough so it won't get cluttered when I spread out all my materials?
- Is there enough light so I can read without straining my eyes?

LIGHTING

Make sure your study space has good lighting you can control. Light is very important. Too much will make your eyes hurt, whereas too little will make your eyes strain. The light should shine evenly over all your work and not directly into your eyes.

TEMPERATURE

You'll want to be comfortable when you study. Being too cold will distract you; it's difficult to take notes with cold fingers. Being too warm also can hurt your accuracy, speed, and mental sharpness—plus it makes you sleepy! For good studying, the best temperature is between 65° and 70° F (18° to 21° C).

To make sure your study space is a comfortable temperature, test out a few spaces. Sit down and read or study for a half hour. Are you under an air-conditioning or heating vent that will make you too cold or too hot? Are you near a door that causes a draft whenever it's opened? These factors are out of your control and should disqualify a potential study space.

SURROUNDINGS

Your study space should be inviting. You should feel good about yourself when you're there. A pleasant space can make you more alert. Here are some tips for improving your study surroundings:

- The right kind of background music can promote relaxed alertness, which stimulates learning. It also may improve your recall. In theory, if you always study biology with Bach in the background, you'll remember biology facts when you hear Bach. But be careful with music that is too loud or that will tempt you to sing along.

- Let the answering machine or voice mail pick up your calls, ideally in another room.

- Turn off the TV (or better yet, study in a room without a TV).

- Some people like white noise: a bubbling aquarium, quiet instrumental music, or even an electric fan. White noise blocks out other sounds without creating a distraction.

Pregame Stretch

Your brain is part of your body. If your body is uncomfortable, your brain has a harder time doing its work. When you're studying, you need your brain to focus on your work, not your aching back. You can stay comfortable by having good posture, avoiding eyestrain, moving around, and eating healthy snacks during long study sessions. (See *Fit for Studying*.)

Get your body in the game by warming up for study time!

Fit For Studying

Here are some ways to stay alert and be comfortable as you study.

- Sit up straight to keep your back and neck from getting stiff. It's worth the effort and it can become a habit if you stick with it. Sitting up straight also keeps you alert and helps you concentrate.

- Position your reading material at a 45-degree angle from your work surface at least 15 inches away from your eyes. If you're too close, your eyes can't focus properly. If you're too far away, you'll strain forward.

- Don't be afraid to get up and walk around every so often when you're studying. Stay in your study area, but try pacing around, doing jumping jacks, or performing simple stretching exercises. When you stand, 5% to 15% more blood flows to your brain. This means your brain gets more oxygen and is more stimulated!

- What about food? If you're going to study for more than an hour at a time, bring a healthy and easy snack, like grapes, so you can eat without mess or distraction.

The Whistle: Getting Started

Sometimes, it's easier to find a good study space than to actually sit down in that space and study! Getting started can be a big challenge.

The first step in meeting that challenge is planning ahead. Decide which tasks you want to accomplish before you sit down to study and develop a plan for accomplishing those tasks. As mentioned previously, start with your syllabus and other course materials to get focused. The next step is breaking your big tasks down into smaller tasks. Several small tasks will be easier to accomplish than one big task. With each accomplishment, you'll become more confident, which will motivate you to keep going!

HAVE A GAME PLAN

Before you start a study session, plan it out. Have a goal for each session and a game plan for achieving that goal. Ask yourself the following questions.

- What do I want to get out of this study time?

- What do I need to learn from the material?

Skim the material you need to study and decide how much of it you'll really need to dive deep into and how much you can cover with just a few notes. Not everything needs detailed attention. That way, you'll spend your time wisely and get more out of studying.

TIMING IS EVERYTHING

Choose your study time carefully. Try not to set aside time you usually spend eating or socializing for studying; you'll only think about what you're missing. This can be hard to do when you're a busy working student with a family. You might feel that you don't have any time when nothing else important is going on! But there probably are adjustments you can make to your daily routine. For example, if you usually spend 2 hours watching TV after dinner, try spending just 1 hour watching TV and use that other hour for studying.

Also, you should try to study when you are naturally more productive and awake. Some of us are morning people; others are night owls. If you tend to feel fresh and alert in the mornings, consider planning some of your study time then. If you're groggy and tired in the morning, but come alive when the sun goes down, evenings are probably the best time for you to study. Use your planner, as described in Chapter 2, to plan out your study sessions at your best times throughout the week.

SET ATTAINABLE GOALS

Breaking up big tasks is part of setting attainable goals. When you set realistic goals, you set yourself up for success. By taking small steps toward your ultimate goal, you get moving, which is the most important thing.

For example, suppose you have a reading assignment that you don't feel like starting. Begin by telling yourself that you'll read for just 5 minutes, so at least you can get some of the assignment done. After the first 5 minutes, tell yourself that you'll keep reading for a few more minutes and keep repeating this cycle. Before you know it, you'll have read for a half hour or more and maybe even completed a good portion of the assignment.

GET YOUR BRAIN IN STUDY MODE

Here are some more questions to ask yourself before and during study time to get your brain into study mode. These questions will help enhance your study time retention and later recall.

- Why is this information important?
- What does this information tell me about other topics?
- Is this information fact or opinion?

- What if I looked at this material in a different way?
- How can I compare and contrast different information?
- Does this material remind me of something else I've learned?

> Learning to tune out distractions helps your concentration. Think of a basketball player tuning out a stadium full of people to make a foul shot!

Improve Your Concentration

We've already talked a little about the distractions that can interfere with your study time. External distractions, like smells or noises, can cause you to lose your concentration. There are internal distractions as well, like hunger or anxiety, that can make studying difficult.

You can learn to improve your concentration skills so you can overcome those distractions. But it takes motivation to improve your concentration. You must want to learn the material in front of you. You have to know why it's important to your future career. Your desire to learn will help you stay focused on studying. Also, you need to be awake, alert, and prepared to learn. Being alert the first time you study helps you avoid multiple review sessions.

As an added bonus, improving your concentration during study time also helps you remember more material. This means you'll get better scores on tests, quizzes, and assignments.

Do You Have a Wandering Mind?

Some people seem to remember everything they see or hear. Other people forget their own phone numbers. Does your mind wander? To find out how well you pay attention, ask yourself the following questions. If you answer *yes* often, you may have a wandering mind that could use some concentration strategies.

- Do you forget the names of people you just met?
- Do you ask people to repeat themselves?
- Do you lose track of what's going on around you?
- Do you sometimes stare blankly at a page?
- Do you sometimes feel like you don't remember information you just read?

It's normal for your mind to wander occasionally. But the most important thing is being aware of when it happens, so you can get back on track.

READY YOUR MIND AND BODY

First, you'll need to prepare your mind and body to concentrate. The following strategies will help you find your focus before you begin studying:

- Take a walk for 5 to 10 minutes to clear your head and relax your body.
- Meditate for about 5 minutes. Sit quietly, perhaps in your study area with the lights off. Sit up straight and picture something still and peaceful. Breathe deeply and slowly.
- Try to avoid caffeine. Too much can cause you to become jumpy and make it harder to concentrate.

CONCENTRATE!

Next, work on improving your concentration as you study. You can do this by using some of the strategies discussed earlier in this chapter, such as avoiding distractions and setting realistic goals. Here are some other good ways to improve your concentration:

- Study during a time of day when you're awake and alert.
- Focus on one topic at a time.
- Keep your brain active by engaging in different activities, such as reading, taking notes, and spending time thinking.
- Take a short break every 45 minutes to 1 hour.

As with so many things, practice makes perfect when it comes to concentration. It might seem discouraging if you get distracted easily the first few times you study. But keep at it and you'll train your brain to stay focused.

Improve Your Memory Skills

Information is stored in different ways in your brain. That's why it's easy to remember some events or people and harder to remember others. Memory isn't a sense; it's a skill you can develop and improve. By understanding how memory works, you can learn ways to improve it.

THE MEMORIZATION PROCESS

Why is it that you remember some things but forget others? It depends in large part on how the brain processes memories. The three stages of information processing are:

1. registration
2. short-term memory
3. long-term memory

As you learn new material in school, your goal is to get the most important information into your long-term memory—and then to keep it there. That way, you'll be able to recall what you learned during tests and put your knowledge to use later when you're on the job. Let's take a look at how memories move through the three stages.

As a student, one of your main goals is to store important information in your long-term memory.

Registration

During registration, the brain receives information. That information eventually may be understood and selected for remembering. Registration is a three-part process: reception, perception, and selection.

1. In the *reception* phase, you automatically take in information, even when not knowing what it means. For instance, you might listen to a patient's bowels and hear whooshing sounds, without knowing what the sounds mean or what condition they represent.

2. During *perception*, you recognize what you've experienced and give it a meaning. Suppose you remember from class that whooshing sounds might mean the bowel is obstructed. You've attached a meaning to the sound—that's perception.

3. Finally, during *selection*, your brain chooses which pieces of information to remember. The information it selects depends on:

   - the information available at the moment
   - your reason for remembering it
   - your background knowledge of the topic
   - the content and how difficult it is
   - the way in which the information is organized

Your brain recognizes information as important or unimportant. If you perceive or decide something is important, like the fact that whooshing sounds could mean an obstructed bowel, then that fact is processed for remembering. If you perceive or decide it's unimportant, the information is forgotten. Processed information is then sent to short-term memory.

Short-Term Memory

Short-term memory can last as little as 15 seconds—that's short! Short-term memory can't hold very much information and what it can hold doesn't stay there for long. Research has shown that short-term memory can hold five to nine chunks of information, depending on how the information is grouped.

For example, you can remember the numbers 1-9-2-9-0-0-7 by grouping them: 1929 and 007. 1929 is easy to remember because it's a date, and 007 is famous from James Bond movies. This way, instead of trying to remember seven different numbers, you only have to recall two groups of information. Grouping makes space for more data in your short-term memory.

> **Break It Up**
>
> When you first learn something new, it's hard for your brain to group the information when it's not sure of relationships among the bits of material. You can make things easier on your brain by learning small chunks of information at a time, instead of trying for one large chunk all at once. Your brain can organize small amounts of information more easily.

Long-Term Memory

After information has entered short-term memory, your brain either soon forgets it or moves it to long-term memory where it is organized and stored for long periods. How long depends on how completely the information is processed and how often you recall and use it. (See *Making Memories for the Long Haul.*) There are many ways to help move information from short- to long-term memory, but the best way is to recall and use information immediately and often.

GETTING THINGS INTO YOUR BRAIN: WORKING MEMORY

The term *working memory* describes how your brain stores and retrieves information from short-term and long-term memory. Improving your working memory is critical to remembering what you study. You can use four strategies to improve your working memory:

MEMORY AT WORK

- selection
- association
- organization
- rehearsal

Selection

During selection, you single out the information you want to remember and start to select ways to process that information. For example, say you need to learn the steps involved in CPR. Because you know you'll need to demonstrate these steps in class, you immediately decide that all the steps are important to remember.

We make more conscious decisions about what is important all the time. For instance, a parent might know the phone number for her child's school or doctor by heart because she made a conscious effort to learn it. Why? Because she decided the number was very important and trained herself to remember it. She selected the number as information important enough to go into long-term memory. Learning new material begins with making a conscious decision to remember it.

Making Memories for the Long Haul

There are many ways to make sure important information gets into your long-term memory. Use the following tips while you're studying to help you identify and sort long-term memory information.

When working alone:

- Attach strong emotions to the material you're studying.
- Rewrite the material in your own words.
- Build a working model of the material you're studying; create an image of it that you can remember.
- Create a song about the material or put definitions to a familiar tune.
- Draw a picture or create a poster using intense colors.
- Repeat and review the material 10 minutes after you read it, 48 hours afterward, and 7 days afterward.
- Summarize the material in your own words in your notes.
- Immediately apply what you've learned to activities in your daily life.
- Use mnemonics and acronyms to organize the material.
- Write about the material in a journal.
- State key information out loud, as though you were lecturing to a group of people.

When working with others:

- Act out the material or role-play a situation related to the material being studied.
- Join a study group or other support group.
- Discuss the information with a peer to gain an additional perspective and solidify the material in your mind.
- Make a videotape or audiotape related to the material being studied.
- Make up and tell a story about the material.

Remember: the more often you think about or repeat a piece of information, the stronger it will be in your short-term memory. Many people use this technique, for example, to remember the name of someone they've just met. For example, if you've been introduced to Bob Hall at a social function, you'll likely still remember his name a week from now if you use it now in conversation with him, saying things like "That's an interesting idea, Bob." You can also strengthen the memory by associating his name with something else, such as by thinking, "I just met Bob Hall while standing in the hall." It may sound silly, but it works!

Association

Association is a very powerful way of committing something to memory. It involves making an association between something you already know and the thing you're trying to learn.

For example, to remember information about a particular disease, try associating that information with someone you know who has the disease. This will provide a memory cue that helps you recall the information later.

Organization

During organization, you memorize information in an ordered way. For example, if it seems there are many steps involved in CPR, break the process down into smaller chunks made up of a few steps each. With repetition, you can push each chunk or group of steps into your long-term memory. Rewrite the steps, recite them out loud, or act them out. This will help you remember the steps more efficiently, move them into long-term memory, and clear your working memory for the next piece of new information.

When it comes to rehearsing information, think of a tennis player practicing their serve over and over. With frequent rehearsal, the information you're trying to remember will become second nature!

Rehearsal

An athlete may practice a certain skill over and over to perfect their technique. Think of a tennis player serving the ball again and again, going through the same motions each time. You can use a similar method to improve your memory skills. Rehearsal involves repeatedly reviewing information you've learned over short periods of time.

Several short bursts of rehearsal are better than one long cram session. For instance, rehearse the steps for CPR for 5 minutes four times a day over 3 days rather than once for an hour. Challenge yourself to rehearse the steps at different times during the day, such as while on the bus ride home, while you're making dinner, or while you're in the shower. Rehearsing information moves it into your long-term memory.

MEMORY RETRIEVAL: USE IT OR LOSE IT

As you have seen, information you process might not stay in your long-term memory if you don't use it regularly. It also can be forgotten if you're not interested in the information, if your purpose for learning is not strong, or if you have few or no connections between the memory and other pieces of information.

Hunting Down a Memory

The next time you have trouble remembering something important, try these strategies to search for your lost memory.

1. Say or write down everything you can remember about the information you're seeking.
2. Try to recall events or information in a different order.
3. Re-create the learning environment or relive the event. Include sounds, smells, and details about the weather, objects, or people who were there. Try to recapture what you said, thought, or felt at the time.

Show Your Interest

In general, the more you care about a topic, the stronger your memory of it will be. For example, if you know you have a quiz next week on a particular topic in anatomy class, you'll store information about that topic more successfully in your long-term memory.

Understand It

It is possible to memorize information without understanding it. Most of us know the words to the Pledge of Allegiance or the national anthem, even if we might not have thought about what those words really mean. But you have to understand a concept to be able to remember and apply it. Try putting new concepts into your own words and explaining them to someone else. If you can make a layperson understand it, you've got it.

Go Deep!

The more deeply your brain processes a topic, the more solid your long-term memory of that topic becomes. Processing depth depends on how you process the information, as well as your:

- background knowledge
- desire for learning
- intended use of the information
- level of concentration
- interest in the topic
- overall attitude

> It's easy to remember facts about your favorite sports team. The more interested you are in a topic, the better your retention of it will be.

Use Study Strategies

There are many study strategies that can help you recall information later during tests and clinical exercises. You've already read about a few of these strategies. Using a variety of study methods helps your brain take in and store the same information in different ways. This creates multiple pathways for your brain to use when you're trying to recall the information later. So give your brain a boost and see which study strategies work best for you!

PRACTICE, PRACTICE, PRACTICE!

Practice and repetition are very similar to rehearsal. Practice not only helps you store information in your long-term memory, it also helps you retrieve that information from your memory when you need it. Here's how you can apply the strategy of practice and repetition as you study:

- Repeat information out loud or in a group discussion.
- Write or diagram the same material several times.
- Read and then reread information silently.

TAKE BREAKS

Spaced study is a method that allows you to alternate short study sessions with breaks. Study goals are set by time or task. For example, you could read for at least 15 minutes or read at least 10 pages at a time. After meeting your goal, you would take a short break and then move on to the next goal.

Spaced study works for several reasons:

- It gives immediate rewards for your hard work.
- It helps you complete manageable amounts of work.
- It helps you set deadlines so you can make efficient use of your study time.
- It keeps information moving from your working memory to your long-term memory. (See *Getting Things Into Your Brain: Working Memory.*)
- It gives you study breaks to keep you sharp when you're studying complex subjects.

MAKE ASSOCIATIONS

Always try to make links between familiar items and new information you want to remember. Once you establish them, these links become automatic. Each time you recall a familiar item, you also remember the information you associated with it.

Follow these steps to form associations as you study:

1. Select the information you want to remember. For example, suppose you want to remember information about osteoporosis, a condition that causes a person's bones to become brittle.

2. Next, create an association to the information. To remember facts about osteoporosis, you might associate that information with a person you know who has the condition. (Osteoporosis reminds me of Mary, who broke her hip. Osteoporosis → Mary → brittle bones.)

The strongest associations are personal, such as associating a song, a person, or a scent with the item you're trying to commit to memory. You probably know certain songs that take you right back to where you were when the song was popular. Associate information to that song and your memory of the information will be just as sharp.

ACRONYMS AND ACROSTICS

Acronyms and acrostics are handy for recalling information, too. Acronyms are created from the first letter of each item on a list. *ASAP* is an acronym for the phrase "as soon as possible." The acronym *HOMES* helps people remember the Great Lakes:

H Huron

O Ontario

M Michigan

E Erie

S Superior

Have fun with it! Use acronyms and acrostics to enhance your long-term memory.

Acrostics are phrases or sentences that are created from the first letter of each item in a list. In health care, a well-known acrostic is one about the 12 cranial nerves: *On Old Olympus' Towering Tops, A Finn and a Swedish Girl Viewed Some Hops.* This stands for the olfactory, optic, oculomotor, trochlear, trigeminal, abduscens, facial, sensorimotor, glossopharyngeal, vagus, spinal accessory, and hypoglossal nerves.

Acronyms and acrostics work in situations where it's hard to find a personal association for a piece of data. (For example, it's difficult to feel personal about the 12 cranial nerves!) Acronyms and acrostics associate key information to a new but easily remembered word or phrase, improving your memory of the information.

PUT INFORMATION IN ITS PLACE

You can understand a piece of information more easily once you put it in a larger framework of understanding. For example, a small area on a street map makes more sense when you view the map in its entirety. Sometimes, it helps to see how the information you're studying fits into the bigger picture.

You can apply this practice to studying by learning more about a topic in general before focusing on a particular assignment. General magazine articles or Internet encyclopedias are good places to look for general information. After you've gained some background knowledge of a certain topic, you'll be able to associate new information about that topic with what you already know. Your brain can then find a place for the new information in your memory.

REDUCE INTERFERENCE

Interference sometimes occurs when you're trying to remember two very similar pieces of information. It's like what happens when you tune in one radio station and another station's signal causes static, interfering with your reception. Your brain has to work harder to recognize the differences between the two pieces of information before you can commit both to memory.

Interference! Two similar pieces of information may interfere with your brain's ability to remember either of them. Focus on what makes each item different.

For example, if you're trying to learn a lot of new terms and two of them are similar, you might have trouble remembering either of them. To reduce interference, try to relate each new term to information you already know. Your background knowledge will help you recognize the differences between the two terms, allowing you to store each as a separate memory.

If you need to study similar subjects one after the other, take a break between study sessions. Moving to a different study space or changing positions will reinforce the difference between the two subjects. It will associate one subject with one location and the next subject with the next location. This way, your brain can better organize the new information in your memory.

CREATE LISTS

Lists are another well-known study aid. You can organize ideas by categories that they have in common. The point is that you create a classification system of some kind. Because items relate to each other within the system, you can rearrange and reorganize that information as needed to help your recall.

For example, suppose you're learning about different types of drugs in a pharmacology course. To help you study the material, you create lists of drugs according to what they're used for. Drugs used to treat diabetes are placed in one list, with drugs used to treat heart conditions in another, and so on.

USE IMAGERY

People often think visually—in images instead of words. Visual aids can help you recall familiar and unfamiliar information when you're studying. This is because images are stored differently than words in the brain.

Adding meaningful doodles, colors, or symbols to your notes allows you to organize them visually by topic. When you use visual representations effectively, you'll remember more information with less effort.

Visualize It!

I'm Chantal. I used to have a real mental block when it came to the forearm bones. I just couldn't remember which is the radius and which is the ulna. Then, I figured out how I could use imagery to help me remember. I pictured myself taking a patient's radial pulse—the end of the radius is located right beneath that pulse! Now, when I have to know the forearm bones, I just picture taking a pulse. The image in my head helps me remember which bone is the radius.

Think in Pictures

Imagery helps you link concrete objects with images, like a picture of a tree with the word *tree*. It also links abstract concepts with symbols, like a heart shape for *love*. As you study, draw pictures or symbols to illustrate important concepts. These visual cues will give your brain yet another way to remember the information.

Use Color Coding

Colors can give meaning to the information you're studying as well. For example, you could use a variety of highlighters to color-code your lecture notes according to topic. You also could use color to indicate key points or to mark two or more related concepts in your textbook. Using color gives you a way to visually organize the material you're trying to learn and remember.

Improve Your Efficiency of Studying

There are many ways to improve your efficiency as you study. Most of these techniques focus on helping you restate material in your own words. Here, we'll look at *reciprocal teaching* and *metalearning*.

RECIPROCAL TEACHING

Reciprocal teaching is a method that will help you:

- summarize the content of a passage
- ask one good question about the main point of a passage
- clarify difficult parts of a passage
- predict what information will come in the next passage

Reciprocal teaching starts when you and the instructor read a short passage silently. Then the instructor summarizes, questions, clarifies, and predicts based on the passage. Next, you read another passage, but this time you do the summarizing, questioning, clarifying, and predicting. The instructor may give you clues, guidance, and other encouragement to help you master this method.

You can use the reciprocal teaching method in your individual study time after you've learned to use it. Read a passage or section, then summarize, question, clarify, and predict based on the passage. When you're done, you'll know the material inside and out.

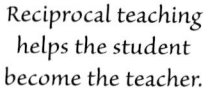

Reciprocal teaching helps the student become the teacher.

METALEARNING

The prefix *meta-* means something that is aware of itself and refers to itself. Metalearning is a process where you ask yourself questions to become aware of your own motives, understanding, challenges, and goals.

In metalearning, you ask yourself a series of questions:

- *Why am I reading or listening to this?* In the metalearning process, you briefly state your purpose for studying certain material. Your purpose and goals set the stage for your study time.

- *What's the basic content of this material?* Preview material before you read. For long or complex material, translate your preview into a chapter map or outline. You also might want to write what you know about the topic and what you'd like to know or think you will know once you're done studying.

- *What are the orientation questions?* Orientation questions give background information on a topic or concept by asking about definitions, examples, types, relationships, or comparisons. The purpose of using orientation questions is to see how many questions you can ask about the material and how many answers you can find.

- *What's really important in this material?* Identify information you should focus on, ignore, or just skim. As in planning ahead, this helps you figure out where to spend your time. If you can't decide whether something is important or whether it should be skimmed or ignored, assume it's important.

- *How would I put this information in my own words?* Putting things in your own words is called paraphrasing. Paraphrasing helps you understand concepts better and identify gaps in your learning right away. Make sure you can put unique terminology for each subject into your own words.

- *How can I draw the information?* Visual learners can get a lot out of drawing the information they're studying. Representing information in pictures is very useful for building understanding.
- *How does the information fit with what I already know?* If you already have a solid foundation of knowledge about a topic, you can learn new things about that topic more easily.

Rest, Relax, and Eat Right

As you study, your brain needs time to sort information and store it in your memory. To do that, your brain needs rest. Have you ever had a busy day at work and then dreamt about doing the same tasks? That's no accident. During deep sleep, the brain keeps right on sorting and storing information, saving important information, and forgetting unimportant details. By getting enough rest and relaxation, your brain can take a break from processing information, allowing it to catch up.

As Chapter 3 explains, what you eat also affects how your brain functions. A healthy, balanced diet gives you the energy and nutrition you need for studying.

Reward Yourself

After studying, reward yourself for a successful study session. The reward can be something small, such as allowing yourself to watch a television show in the evening. What the reward itself isn't as important as getting a good feeling about the work you've done. And a positive attitude toward studying, as you learned earlier in this chapter, will motivate you to keep at it!

STUDY GROUPS

Most of the study techniques we've been discussing so far in this chapter are things you can use on your own to learn and remember information, but they also work well when you study with others in a group. Study groups also allow for additional ways of learning and can be one of the best ways for students to master their course material.

Study groups may be informal, as simple as talking with a friend in the same class about an upcoming test of project due. More formal groups involving two or three others can be organized and scheduled for regular time. Both types of study groups can be very effective.

Study Groups—Informal or Formal?

Being a part of a study group can help you learn and study course material. Even if your study group is not always able to answer your questions, teaching others can be a good way to learn. Explaining difficult concepts to someone else will help you review the information and get a firm grasp of important points. Going over course material with other students is an excellent way to help you understand it better and move it firmly into your long-term memory. This process can work in both informal and formal study groups.

INFORMAL STUDY GROUPS

Students often get together before or after class to go over the material. These are informal groups where you are under no obligation to attend. When joining with others even in an informal group, however, you are expected to contribute to the discussion.

If you notice students gathering after class, hang around and see what they're talking about. If they're going over class material, introduce yourself and see if you can participate, too. Remember the discussion of networking in Chapter 4—studying with others is a great way also to build your network. Once you've discovered others in your class with whom you study well, consider making a more formal study group with them.

FORMAL STUDY GROUPS

A formal study group is more organized. Students in the same class purposefully decide to get together to study, usually periodically during the school term. It usually helps to have a scheduled time to study together in a formal group rather than having to depend on casually finding someone in the class to talk with.

Review the section in Chapter 4 on networking with other students for suggestions on how to form a formal study group.

Building a Study Group

A formal study group doesn't just happen—you and other students have to put in a little effort to get it started and keep it on track. You'll need to consider a few issues to build an effective group:

- How many students in the group?
- How and when to schedule meetings?
- Where to meet?
- How to ensure everyone participates fairly?

IF THREE'S A CROWD . . .

It's easier to stay on task when everyone in the group is interested in the same thing—studying. If the group becomes too large (more than four or five members), it can be broken down into smaller groups. Meeting with a smaller number of people makes it easier to review all the necessary material and answer each other's questions.

SCHEDULING MEETINGS BY THE BOOK

It's great to have a regularly scheduled time for a study group—a time when everyone comes prepared to discuss a certain topic. Meeting regularly to go over material helps you all come up with new ideas and approaches.

When participating in an online discussion, only talk to people you know and trust.

It can be hard to find a time when busy people can meet. Do the best you can to come up with a regular meeting time, such as every week or every 2 weeks. If evenings are best, go with that. If two half-hour meetings a week are better for everyone's schedule than one hour-long meeting per week, go with two half-hour meetings.

When You Can't Find a Scheduling Solution

If you are unable to find a time to meet in person, you create an online group site or message board. Everyone can visit the group site and contribute to it whenever they're free. You can create a group on websites like Yahoo Groups where members log in and talk via instant message boards. But be vigilant about keeping passwords strictly within the network, for safety's sake. You'll want to avoid having strangers posting on your site.

Where to Meet

There are many places for a study group to meet. Finding the one that is right for you can take a little trial and error—what seems perfect at first may not actually work out later. Keep at it until you get to the right place.

Many students find it easiest to meet on campus in a common area or in a library discussion room (just make sure you're not out in the middle of the library disrupting others). If your regular meeting time falls during the school day, this may be the best option for you.

Meeting off campus may work better if your meeting time falls after classes have ended for the day. It also may work better for members who are not on campus (professionals in the workplace or students at another campus). In this case, meet at a centrally located coffee shop or take turns hosting the group at your homes.

Just remember—safety first! Make sure you know everyone in your group well before you agree to meet them somewhere or invite them to your home.

Keeping the Group Focused

When it comes to study groups, remember the four Cs. A successful study group will have members who are:

- committed—interested in learning the material
- contributors—willing to share their knowledge
- compatible—able to overlook differences and focus on studying together
- considerate—willing to arrive at meetings on time

When forming a study group, remember the four Cs. All group members should be Committed Contributors who are Compatible and Considerate.

To have productive meetings, your group might choose to designate a "timekeeper." This person keeps everyone moving along at a good pace. That way, your group will be sure to cover the necessary material during each session.

You might also need to designate a "gatekeeper." This person makes sure the group stays focused on appropriate topics. When people start to discuss things unrelated to the course material, that person can remind everyone to stay focused.

It's everyone's responsibility to prepare before meeting with the group. You should be familiar with the material you'll be studying together, even if you have questions about it. Your questions may be helpful to the rest of the group. Make sure you can explain other concepts in your own words. Successful study groups have a give-and-take. If the group answers your questions about one concept, you may be able to return the favor by explaining another idea to the rest of the group.

Giving Your Two Cents

Students in an effective study group listen to every member because every member has something valuable to say. Even though not everyone is an expert or has 20 years' experience, all students should be studying hard, make the most of what they do know, and want to learn more.

In an effective study group, all members share their ideas and information. No one should be worried that what they say will be taken out of context or used to try to gain an unfair advantage. No one tries to gain from other people's experience without sharing their own. In a good group, everyone contributes fairly and benefits equally.

THE HUDDLE

A study group should be made up of people you like and respect. A study session should be stress-free and it's OK if it sometimes includes informal conversation. You should be able to laugh, share funny stories, and confide your doubts and worries without being concerned that the whole school will find out about it later.

For example, a football player wouldn't leave the huddle and then tell the other team what the next play is going to be. That would be disloyal to teammates. Be sure to have the same respect for the other members of your network. If someone mentions any personal matter in the group, avoid the urge to gossip. Keep personal information private.

Teammates trust each other—be the kind of person your study group can trust. If another member mentions something in confidence, avoid the urge to gossip.

MORE RESOURCES FOR STUDYING

We've been looking at how you and your study group can use your textbook, class notes, and materials from your instructor when studying. In addition to all this, there's another whole world of supplemental materials out there to help you learn. Never discount the value of using additional materials when studying, even when not assigned or required by the instructor.

Using Supplemental Materials

Using supplemental material is another way to accommodate your personal learning style. If you have a hard time learning information from a lecture or a textbook, it's especially helpful to supplement your education. When the same information is presented to you in a variety of ways, you'll learn more and have better recall of important points. You may also use supplemental material as a way of finding out more about an interesting topic covered in one of your classes. Whatever your reason may be, making use of supplemental material gives you an advantage as a student.

Your textbook may include a toll-free phone number that you can call for help with finding supplemental materials. Browse the text materials near the front of the book for information about resources available for students.

TEXTBOOK CDS

Textbooks often come with CDs or workbooks that are loaded with practice quizzes, sample test questions, games, and other learning tools designed to increase learning. Often, these involve the same information as the textbook but in a different format. For example, some CDs may include interactive exercises. This can be helpful to students who have a difficult time understanding the material as it's presented in the textbook. CDs also can be helpful to students looking for ways to improve their recall of information in the textbook.

SOFTWARE AND ONLINE RESOURCES

There are many different kinds of educational software that you may find helpful. Such software may be available on a student disk with a textbook, at a computer lab at your school or library, online, or elsewhere. Types of software that are particularly beneficial to students include:

- practice exercises
- tutorials
- simulations
- assessments
- video and audio podcasts

Software such as this may be included on a CD or DVD accompanying your textbook. Some commercially available software may also be helpful, depending on your particular field of study. Finally, the same sorts of materials are often available at websites—like the student resources on this book's companion website! Aside from requiring an Internet connection, supplementary material on the Web is often, in practical terms, indistinguishable from software running on your own computer.

Practice Makes Perfect

Some website software provides practice exercises. These may be in the form of quizzes you can take or problems you can solve. Their purpose is to help students learn and remember facts and vocabulary. They can also aid in your understanding of how different concepts are related. The more you practice, the more you'll be required to use your new knowledge. This increases your ability to remember and comprehend the material in your textbook.

Your Own Private Tutor

If you find yourself lost even after attending lectures and getting clarification from your instructor, tutorial software or websites can help. These are designed to teach concepts. Although they may include brief quizzes to assess your level

Students with full-time jobs or families may prefer to use tutorial software instead of taking extra time to meet with a tutor.

of knowledge, the main focus is instruction. The material may be presented in several different formats, making use of text, images, audio, and video. They may also be interactive, with content covered depending on student responses.

Is This for Real?

Simulations are another type of educational software or Web application. Simulations are computerized versions of real-life experiences. They are interactive and often require decision making on the part of the student. Health profession students can use these programs to learn or hone their clinical skills. The beauty of simulations is that they are forgiving of mistakes made during the learning process. After all, it's better to make a mistake while caring for a simulated patient than to make one while caring for an actual patient!

How Am I Doing?

Assessment software and websites can be beneficial to students and instructors alike. On one hand, computerized testing helps students determine their level of knowledge. As a student, being aware of how much you know can help you set goals for yourself. It allows you to focus on what you have yet to learn. On the other hand, assessments can also be helpful to instructors. Once they are able to determine their students' progress, they can adjust the curriculum appropriately.

Podcasts

Instructors at some schools video or audio tape their lectures and make these available for students as podcasts that can be played on a computer or an mp3/mp4 device. If your school produces podcasts, your instructor will tell you about this. Because a recording cannot capture the full experience of attending class, don't consider a podcast a replacement for attending class—but it can be a helpful review when needed.

In addition, educational podcasts are available online or through "iTunes U." You do not need an iPod to view these videos or listen to audios; programs on many subjects are available to everyone through the free iTunes program or the websites of individual schools. For example, if you are having difficulty understanding the anatomy of a particular organ or body system, dozens of video podcasts are available to help walk you through this information. Podcasts from other schools do not replace your textbook, of course, and may contain more or less detail than you need to understand for your course, but when used as supplementary material, they can enrich your understanding.

The Wonderful World Wide Web

As described in Chapter 7, you can find a wealth of supplemental material online for any course you're taking. Just remember to stay safe when on the Internet.

- Make sure websites are trustworthy. Websites that end in .gov or .edu generally contain reliable information.
- Make sure any website you use is accurate (up-to-date and unbiased). Personal websites, like blogs, may have a lot of information, but there is no guarantee that the information is accurate.
- Only use websites that are free. And never give out your own personal information to use a website.
- If possible, get a list of reliable websites from your instructor.
- Textbook publishers also often have websites where you can find lots of resources to help you study.

STUDY SKILLS FOR MATH AND SCIENCE

Many people have something we call "math anxiety" or feel apprehensive about taking science courses. Perhaps the world of numbers or science seems strange and alien to them. Or maybe they had a bad experience with a math or science class when they were younger. It can be hard to overcome this anxiety, especially in a society where this anxiety is accepted as normal and understandable.

But overcoming this anxiety is important. Math is used in daily life and math classes are unavoidable when you're in school. Most health care careers also require some familiarity with the sciences, particularly those involving the human body. You'll want to be able to approach these classes with confidence and a fresh attitude. You may need to pay special attention to math and science, then, in your studies.

Why Is Math So Important?

Many people struggle through high school math, hoping or assuming they'll never need to deal with it later in life. But math is all around you. Health care professionals need to be competent in math to perform many tasks:

- measuring solutions
- figuring dosages
- converting pounds to kilograms for weights

- creating department budgets
- scheduling staff assignments
- handling patients' claims and bills

No matter where you go in your health career, you'll need good math skills. Take the time to hone them now!

Math Myths

One of the reasons it's hard to overcome math anxiety is that people believe things about math that just aren't true. Let's look at some of the most common math myths and how to shake them.

"I'M JUST NOT GOOD AT MATH"

People think of math as much harder than other topics, a kind of mystery where numbers are a foreign language. Sometimes, students are told they just can't do math and should leave it alone.

Are you a problem-solver? Are you driven to succeed? If your answer is yes, then you probably have greater math aptitude than you think. Math is all about solving problems. All you have to learn is the language of math—numbers—and you can start solving math problems.

"MY CALCULATOR DOES THE MATH FOR ME"

A calculator is just a tool to do math problems faster. A calculator might be able to multiply more easily than you can. But it can't tell you what the x stands for in an algebra equation or why an x is used in that problem in the first place. It can't explain what a square root is or how it's used in real life.

Think of your calculator as a tool to help you perform basics like addition, subtraction, multiplication, and division faster and with fewer errors. But be sure to learn how math really works. Your calculator can only take you so far.

"I DON'T USE MATH IN MY LIFE—WHY LEARN IT?"

In fact, math is used in everyday life, even though you may not always see it or realize it. For instance, learning how to make conversions between different systems of measurement will help you calculate proper medication dosages for patients. Learning about other math concepts will allow you to create budgets at work and at home and complete many other vital tasks. Basic math is needed to balance your checkbook, understand a mortgage payment or interest on a car loan, and cope with many day-to-day aspects of life.

Success in Math Class

Some students dread math class. Somehow, they have the feeling they're supposed to know the material already. They're embarrassed to admit they don't understand a problem or a concept. But a math class is where you *learn math*. If there's any place in the world where you can put your math fears on the table and conquer them, it's math class. Here are some resources to use that will make math class a success for you.

A math tutor can give you the encouragement you need to keep working at it!

TALK TO YOUR INSTRUCTOR

Many students are embarrassed to tell their instructor they don't understand something. But your instructor is there to help you. If you hide the fact that you don't understand something, your instructor can't help you. But if you let your instructor know, you can get the help you need.

USE YOUR TEXTBOOK

Most math textbooks have plenty of practice questions, either at the end of each chapter or grouped together in the back of the book. Use these practice questions. Working through them helps you see some of the underlying patterns of a concept or technique and helps get you in the swing of using certain functions or solutions. Never skip over math questions or problems, because it's likely the next material you'll need to understand will build on what you're reading and doing now. If you skip over something that doesn't seem clear, the problem will only grow worse.

Personal Trainer

There are people other than your instructor who can help you with math. You can find mentors at school or in your own family. And tutors are usually available—just ask your instructor or the secretary in the math department. Check bulletin boards in the math department and student centers, too; you'll probably find many ads posted that offer tutoring services. Some may even be free. There are also interactive online tutoring sites. Finally, a math study group can be a huge help. So get off the bench and get some help tackling your toughest math problems!

WRITE IT ALL DOWN

Do each step of a math problem on paper, not in your head. Even if you know the formula well, write down each step. It helps you focus and gets your mind in the problem-solving groove. Just like a great musician still practices scales each day, you should write down even basic steps. It can also help you find careless errors in your work.

READ CAREFULLY

Get in the habit of reading very carefully when you go through a math problem. Most errors occur when you misread a problem. Read through each problem out loud so that each part of it makes sense to you. Sometimes, you might think you see "add" when the symbol actually says "divide"; talking through the problem helps eliminate these kinds of errors.

SEE WHAT'S NOT THERE

If you don't understand the solution to a problem, there might be something missing from the problem itself. People do make mistakes! Prepare a list of problems you are unable to work out and discuss each one with your instructor. This way, you'll learn to see what you're missing.

DO THE MATH!

Students sometimes think that the assigned materials are the only ones they should use. But supplementary materials can give you fresh examples and practice problems. It's worth it to get these extra materials. Before you invest in one, make sure it has a lot of examples and step-by-step instructions. It should include proofs or derivations for the formulas it uses. Remember, different authors might use different notation systems, so be sure to familiarize yourself with them.

Preparing for Math Class

Math is sequential—every concept builds on a previous concept. If you miss one step, the next one won't make sense to you. That's why it's important to go to every class and set aside time each day to go over what you've learned. Here are the basics to review daily:

- vocabulary
- basic formulas
- working cooperatively
- testing yourself

TALK THE TALK

Like many subjects, math has a specialized vocabulary. If you don't know the most common math terms, you'll have trouble with problems you could otherwise solve. Make a list of key words and study them. This list can include words emphasized by your instructor or your textbook, as well as words you find you have trouble remembering.

Treat math like a foreign language; you learn a language by picking out vocabulary words and memorizing them. You have to know how to pronounce vocabulary words, what they mean, and when they are used.

KNOW THE FORMULAS

Like vocabulary, math formulas form the basis for solving math problems. It's valuable to understand why a formula works the way it does. It's especially important to memorize basic formulas, as these are the formulas you'll use most often.

TEAMWORK

Usually, math isn't taught collaboratively. Students are rarely broken into groups to work something out. That's one of the reasons many students fear math: they are on their own, left to sink or swim.

But many instructors have come to realize the benefits of letting students work with a partner. Once you find a good partner, you can help each other solve problems. A partner can bring you:

- *Another point of view.* This helps you see more possibilities, thus improving your learning.

- *Increased personal accountability.* If someone is depending on you to help them study and learn, you will take that responsibility seriously.

- *An audience.* If you can explain a concept to your partner, you can explain it to the instructor on a test.

- *Praise and encouragement.* You and your partner will root for each other and provide positive feedback, helping create confidence.

Even if your instructor does not pair you with a partner, remember that you can set up your own study group to go over the math you're learning in class. Often, it's easiest to learn how to apply formulas when talking them through with other students. Just make sure you really understand it! If you let others do your thinking for you, you'll have trouble with future math problems that build on the understanding of these formulas.

Working as a team can help you tackle the toughest math problems.

Studying Science

Much of the preceding discussion of math and studying math is also true of the sciences and studying science. In fact, many people have the same anxiety or apprehensions about science as they do about math, and understanding many of the sciences requires understanding mathematical formulas.

Try to apply all the same principles when studying for your science courses. Most important, don't be afraid to ask your instructor questions.

If you feel frustrated reading scientific information or texts, take a moment and remind yourself that health care is largely based on science. To understand how illness can be prevented or treated, we need to understand how the body works, beginning with basic biology. To understand how to take x-ray exposures and process images, we need to understand the basic physics of x-ray beams and their interaction with matter. Even to understand medical terminology, we need to feel comfortable with scientific language. Although you may not immediately see the value of something scientific you are studying, rest assured that later on, as you enter your chosen health care career, that knowledge will have a big payoff because you better understand the reasons for actions you take on the job. The more you understand of the scientific side of health care, the more deeply involved you'll feel in your work—and the happier you'll be with your career choice.

CHAPTER SUMMARY

- Set goals for each study session to give yourself a game plan to follow and to make the most efficient use of your study time.

- Get organized. Organize your school papers (notes, syllabi, schedule, etc.) for quick and easy access.

- Consider a space's lighting, temperature, and surroundings when choosing a study space.

- Get more out of studying by using strategies to improve your concentration and memory.

- Use different study methods, such as repeating information, taking short breaks, and using acronyms or acrostics.

- Rest, exercise, and proper nutrition will give you the energy you need to stay alert and focused as you study.

- Develop good study groups that will help you learn and support your academic goals.

- Use supplemental material to increase your learning. Resources, such as textbook CDs, educational software, the Internet, and online instruction, can provide benefits beyond the classroom.

REVIEW QUESTIONS

1. What are at least two tips for getting organized?
2. Name at least three different study strategies.
3. What are four characteristics that members of a successful study group should have? (Hint: Remember the four Cs.)
4. How does assessment software benefit students and instructors?
5. Explain why it's not a good idea to expect a calculator to do all of your math for you.

CHAPTER ACTIVITIES

1. Study Space Checklist: Review *Scope out a Study Area* and make a list of the characteristics you find most important for a study space. Then locate at least two places that meet your criteria—your principal study area and a backup when the first is not available for any reason.

2. Getting Organized Checklist: Review *Getting Organized* and compose a checklist of things to do in order to organize your paperwork for each class.

3. Study Group Planning: Choose one of your classes and look around at the other students in the room. Based on what you have observed about them from how they interact in the classroom, select three students you'd ideally like to have in your study group. (If you haven't already formed a group for that class, talk to these students soon to see if they're interested.)

CHAPTER 9

Test-Taking Skills

WINNING STRATEGY

On completion of this chapter and the learning activities you will be able to:

- Understand and fight test anxiety

- Prepare and study for tests

- Use different strategies to do well on objective, subjective, and other tests

- Succeed on math tests

- Know how to calculate grades

- Prepare for a certification or licensure exam

Does anyone you know *love* taking tests? Probably not! Tests are something all students face and tests cause almost everyone anxiety. In this chapter, you'll find out how to plan and prepare for tests so you can improve your test-taking abilities and feel more confident. You'll also learn about special skills for managing test anxiety. Tips and guidelines will be presented for math tests and special exams such as those required for certification or licensure in many health care careers.

HEALTH AND STRESS MANAGEMENT

Doing well on a test starts long before you take out your pencil on the big day. It starts with how well you take care of your mind and your body. Yes, studying is certainly key to your success, but how you care for your health and how you manage stress are very important, too.

Here's a quick review of what Chapter 3 describes about caring for your body for maximum functioning and low stress.

- Regular exercise can lower stress, keep you fit and looking good, and make you feel better mentally and physically.
- Sometimes rest is more important than completing every task on your daily to-do list.
- A balanced and nutritious diet is important for your health and managing stress.
- Breathing and relaxation techniques or yoga can help release tension.

Chapter 3 also explains that your mind needs recharging. Here's a review of some of the techniques you can use:

- *Keep negative thoughts under control.* Use positive imagery to move your mind toward your goals and away from your fears.
- *Calm your body to calm your mind.* When you have negative thoughts, use body-calming techniques (such as those discussed in Chapter 3) to enter a more calm and relaxed state of mind.
- *Visualize yourself achieving your goals and overcoming obstacles.* Think about how you feel when you visualize these things and remember that feeling when negativity rears its head.
- *Build a social support network.* Family, friends, classmates, coworkers, and people who share your interests are all good choices for a social support network. They give you an outlet for discussing your problems with people who care for you and want to help.

Running makes me feel tired right now, but later it will give me the energy I need!

TEST ANXIETY

Remember what *eustress* means? That's right—good healthy, levels of stress. But most of us are more familiar with *distress*—high, unhealthy levels of stress. Most students experience some stress at test time, but for some, increased stress at test time interferes with their ability to think. They know the material. They've studied hard and effectively. But they just get so tense at test time that they can't put down the right answers. The way to beat test anxiety is to first recognize it and then prepare to fight it!

My friends help me see my problems in perspective and find solutions to them.

Are You an Anxious Student?

Part of recognizing test anxiety is figuring out whether you're an anxious student. The following sections describe several different characteristics of anxious students.

FEELINGS, TOO MANY FEELINGS . . .

Really anxious students go back and forth between focusing on new material and thinking about how nervous they are. They find it difficult to maintain their concentration during a lecture or a reading session. They keep noticing their discomfort and think, "I'm so tense—I just can't do this!" Because very anxious students' attention is focused on worrying about doing a bad job, being criticized, or feeling embarrassed, they may miss the information they need to learn.

LOST IN THE DETAILS

Anxious students often have poor study habits. It's hard for them to learn if the material is:

- disorganized
- broken down in many parts
- difficult to understand
- focused on memorization

Avoid the Big Freeze-Up

The most common test anxiety experience is a mental block or "freeze-up." Although many students experience some level of this, students with severe test anxiety might read a test question over and over and never take in its meaning. Other symptoms of severe mental block include:

- doing poorly on a test after proving you know the material during class and in study groups
- feeling sweaty, shaky, or physically ill before and during a test
- obsessing over how well you're doing compared with other students
- thinking about how to get out of finishing the test, such as by faking an illness

If you're so overwhelmed with test anxiety that you can't do well on tests—even when you've attended every class, studied hard, and proven that you know the material—talk to your instructor about it. Your instructor might have another solution you haven't thought of. Alternately, ask a peer tutor or friend to "test" you with questions you haven't seen and a set time limit for completing the work. Taking practice tests beforehand can help you ease into the real thing.

In these situations, anxious students are very easily distracted by irrelevant or minor details of the tasks at hand. They can't see the forest for the trees, which means they focus on details and miss the main point.

Recognize Test Anxiety

You've read about what goes wrong for very anxious students. But a little anxiety can be a good thing. Slight anxiety can improve your focus and mental sharpness. It keeps you from feeling complacent and helps you stay motivated to study. But if you consistently feel nervous and distracted, test anxiety is probably taking over.

Test anxiety may produce many effects before and during a test. Here are some common effects of test anxiety:

- freezing up, when your brain doesn't take in the meaning of questions or you have to read questions over and over to understand them

- panicking about tough questions or about time running out before you're done

- worrying about the grade you'll receive

- becoming easily distracted, daydreaming, or thinking about how you could escape taking the test

- feeling nervous about your ability to do well or about how you'll do compared to others

- having physical symptoms of stress, such as sweating, nausea, muscle tension, and headaches

- feeling like you're not interested in the topic or like you don't care how well you do on the test

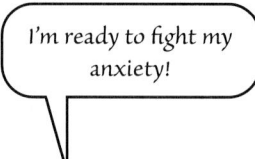

I'm ready to fight my anxiety!

Prepare to Fight Anxiety

The key to staying on top of anxiety for most successful students is using a combination of techniques to prepare for tests. This section discusses tips and guidelines all students can use. Remember that you need to prepare your mind and body. Keeping this balance will help you overcome your test anxiety and do your best.

STUDY WELL

Studying well is the best preparation for a test—and the best cure for test anxiety. Studying can give you a sense of accomplishment that boosts your self-confidence. When you know the material backward and forward, you won't feel as nervous going into the test.

RELAX YOUR MIND

Relaxation, along with other stress-reduction techniques, can help lessen test anxiety. When your body is relaxed, your mind is free to absorb new information. Try using breathing exercises or meditation to clear your mind.

THINK POSITIVELY

Test anxiety can result from low self-esteem. Focus on being positive about tests. Say to yourself, "I've studied hard and I know this material. I can do this!" Being prepared and having a positive attitude often lead to success.

GIVE YOURSELF A BREAK

If you start to feel anxious during a test, consider doing something to break the tension, such as putting down your pencil, closing your eyes, and taking a few slow deep breaths. If your shoulders are hunched, make a conscious effort to lower them and relax. If the instructor allows, you might even get up and sharpen your pencil or ask a question. Sometimes you can feel anxiety because you're physically tired and need a break.

GET YOUR ZZZs

Rest and relaxation are great fatigue-fighters. You can do more when you feel rested and relaxed than when you're tired. Try using these tips before your next test.

Make sure you eat breakfast on the day of a test!

- Get enough sleep—at least 7 to 8 hours at a time.
- Change activities from time to time.
- Exercise on a regular basis.
- Relax by allowing yourself breaks for TV, music, friends, or light reading.

SIT UP STRAIGHT

Your posture matters when you're studying or taking a test. If you're sitting in an uncomfortable position, it stresses your muscles. This stress is communicated to your brain, which in turn creates anxiety. Slouching can hurt your back and make you feel tired. Sit up straight and allow your concentration to return.

EAT WELL, TEST WELL

Good nutrition keeps you healthy. It also can improve your study habits and test-taking skills. Class time, work time, and study time often conflict with meal times. To counter this, avoid skipping meals and eat nutritious snacks between sessions.

If You Get Sick . . .

Even the healthiest person can get sick. When you're ill, you can't perform well on a test. So, if you feel very ill as a test approaches, contact the instructor. This shows you care about your performance and about missing the test. You may be able to work out an arrangement with the instructor and this will help you avoid anxiety about

Defeat Test Anxiety!

Here's a checklist of things to do the next time you're feeling nervous about a test.

Before the test:

- Talk to your instructor and classmates about what the test will cover.
- Use the study skills you learned in Chapter 8. Develop a method that works for you!
- Divide your study time over several days instead of trying to review everything the night before the test. Use the time management skills you learned in Chapter 2.
- When studying, use all your resources, including your textbook, lecture notes, and completed homework assignments.
- Create 3 × 5 cards for all key concepts or formulas that might appear on the test. Use the flash cards to practice and test your memory.
- Take a practice test. Find a room that's free of distractions and give yourself a specific amount of time to complete the test.
- Try to avoid studying right before taking the test. Put those notes away and take some time to relax!
- Arrive 5 minutes early so you'll be ready when the instructor begins the test. Just don't arrive too early—sitting in an empty classroom or listening to other students' nervous chattering might make you feel anxious.

During the test:

- Break the tension. If your instructor allows it, get up to ask a question, sharpen your pencil, or get a drink.
- Focus on tensing and relaxing muscles in different parts of your body, such as your neck and shoulders. Then close your eyes and take a few deep breaths.
- Calm your nerves by putting the test into perspective. Life will go on after the test is over. Remember that doing your best is sufficient.
- Think of something calm and soothing when you feel test anxiety is getting the best of you.

postponing the test. Be sure to follow all your doctor's instructions so you can get well as soon as possible. Avoid using sick time as study time and get the rest you need.

Stay on Schedule

When a test approaches, keep things as normal as possible. If you normally take a walk before dinner, keep up with your routine instead of skipping your walk to study. If you usually sleep 8 hours a night, avoid the urge to cram until 2:00 AM. Breaking good habits will only contribute to your mental and physical stress.

PREPARING AND PLANNING AHEAD

When it comes to test taking, preparation is important. Knowing *what* you need to do *before* you have to do it gives you time to work out the best *way* to do it.

Know What Will Be Covered

You can't study well for a test if you don't know what kind of test it will be. If you know what kind of test to expect, you can put your study time to good use. Objective tests, such as short answer, sentence completion, multiple choice, matching, and true/false, require you to remember facts and details and to recognize related material. Essay and oral tests require you to make good arguments about general topics and to support your arguments with critical details.

SIZE IT UP

You should always attend class, but it's especially important leading up to a test. Your instructor will probably explain the format of the test during class time. If not, visit your instructor during office hours and ask these questions:

- Will the test be comprehensive or will it cover select material only (like a few chapters)?
- Approximately how many questions will there be?
- How will the questions be weighted? For example, will multiple choice questions be worth 5 points each, whereas essays will be worth 20 points?
- How much will this test count toward my final grade?
- What materials will I need? A calculator? Scrap paper?

LEARN FROM THE PAST

If you've already taken tests in the course or attended another course given by the same instructor, you probably have some idea of what the upcoming test will be like. For example, you might know that the instructor focuses on details rather than principles or that sometimes uses trick questions.

But if it's your first test for a particular course or instructor, you can still do a little extra preparation. Ask your instructor if practice tests or exams from the past are available for students to study. But remember, although past tests can give you an idea of what the test may be like, you won't see the same questions on your upcoming test.

LEARN FROM THE CLASS

Think about how you've learned things in class so far. Which topics has the instructor spent the most time discussing? Have you focused on details or large concepts in class discussions? Some instructors offer review sessions before the test. If your instructor does this, be there and be prepared. Plan ahead of time for the review session by writing down the questions you'd like to ask.

Get Ready, Get Set...

Give yourself a head start before you begin studying for an upcoming test. Thorough preparation short-circuits anxiety. The class schedule likely lists test dates and other deadlines. Put those test dates in your planning calendar. If your instructor didn't provide a class schedule at the beginning of the term, ask about approximate dates of tests.

CREATE A GAME PLAN

First, create an organized study plan. For example, you could set aside some time to study each day for a week before the test. Studying every day keeps the material fresh in your mind. Give yourself enough time to review your lecture notes, study materials, and old tests (if possible) several times. Choose a good place to study. Consider your study group; you can ask each other questions of the sort likely to appear on the test. Commit to studying and you'll be as prepared as possible for the test.

You might already review your notes after each class, which is good practice. But remember that it's not enough before a test. You'll need more intense review. In some classes, you may even have unannounced pop quizzes before a test. In those cases, you'll be glad you spent extra time studying!

The Trouble with Cramming

The trouble with cramming is that it doesn't work. You simply can't cram data into the brain and have it stick. Most of the information disappears in a few hours. And, by the time you're sitting down to the test, your brain is so tired that it can't retrieve most of the data it did manage to retain. As a result, you "blank out" and are unable to answer questions you might otherwise have easily answered.

Trying to Beat the Clock

When you have a test coming up and you feel unprepared for it, the best thing to do is stay calm and focused. Double-check with your instructor or a classmate about the format of the test. Use your textbook to create a master study outline. Focus on chapter headings, summaries, highlighted words, formulas, definitions, and the first and last sentences of every paragraph. Write key points and an outline of each chapter on notebook paper.

> I can't cram in any more information—my brain is too full of fatigue!

When you're done outlining in this way, review your class notes and handouts. Make some "must-know" flash cards for what you feel is the most important information. Flip through the flash cards until you're too tired to continue. Make sure to wake up at least 1 hour before the test to review your outline and flip through the flash cards again.

BRING THE RIGHT EQUIPMENT

Remember to bring the right "equipment" to your study session. A student trying to study without a textbook is like a football player showing up to practice without a helmet! So, before you begin studying, gather all your review materials, textbooks, and notes. Look for information about the main terms, facts, concepts, themes, problems, questions, and issues that were covered in those materials. It's especially handy to compare the way your textbook covers an idea or concept with how your instructor covered it in class.

When you're studying for a test, it's not a good use of time to try to reread entire chapters of your textbook. Instead, armed with your knowledge about what kinds of questions will be asked and which topics will be covered, use your textbook's index and glossary to look up just those topics. Find definitions of key terms in the glossary and look for important details in handouts and other supplementary material. Make lists of definitions and rehearse them.

MAKE A STUDY SHEET

Summarize your notes on one piece of paper. Review this study sheet, then place it face down and try to re-create your notes from memory. Think about where each topic was placed on the page. That way, when you encounter a certain topic on the test, you can flash back to your notes page and actually "see" the information.

Equations and Graphs

For math or science tests, practice your skills by rewriting equations and graphs. Solve sample problems and write out formulas. If you have trouble with certain formulas or graphs, make a separate sheet for those troublemakers and review it during gaps in your schedule throughout the day.

Main Terms

For short-answer tests, go through your textbook or lecture notes and make a list of important terms. Then add the definitions and think of an example of each term that you could use in a short answer.

Practice Run

For an essay test, prepare by doing a practice run. First, look at previous assignments and tests to see how essay questions are worded. Then, choose a topic from the material you're studying now and develop an essay question. Finally, write an answer for your essay question, giving yourself as much time as you'll have during your upcoming test. (See *Subjective Tests* for tips on how to develop a good essay.)

My Study Strategy

My name is Sujala. I'm studying to become a pharmacy technician. When I have a big test coming up, I do a couple of things to prepare. First, I talk with the instructor and find out what kinds of questions the test will have—multiple choice, short answer, or other kinds. Then I go through my notes and make practice questions out of them. For instance, I put my notes into multiple choice format. That way, I can see how the information looks in test form. I make up a study sheet, too. The night before the test, I get a babysitter to watch my kids so I can review the study sheet and get it down pat.

BE YOUR OWN COACH

Giving yourself a practice test allows you to be your own coach. Practice tests help you recognize the topics you struggle with most, which focuses your studying. To make a practice test, look at your study sheet and turn it into a series of questions. Then, answer the questions as if you are really taking a test. Sit in a quiet room and give yourself a certain amount of time to work. You may feel less anxiety when you take the real test if it feels familiar.

Be your own coach when it comes to studying! Give yourself a practice test to figure out how well you know the material.

After you complete the practice test, use your study resources to check your answers. Spend extra time studying the questions you answered incorrectly.

GAME DAY

On the day of the test, there are several things you can do to make sure you're in top condition.

- *Rest.* You need at least 7 to 8 hours of sleep the night before a test.

- *Eat small meals.* Breakfast is the most important. Just avoid eating too much or you'll feel sleepy.

- *Avoid caffeine.* You don't want to be jittery.

- *Exercise.* Even a short exercise session will help you feel mentally and physically invigorated.

- *Have your test materials ready to go.* Do this the night before so you won't waste time frantically searching for something on test day. Include all written materials, notes, pens, erasers, pencils, calculators, and whatever else is allowed or required.

- *Arrive on time.* Make sure you wear a watch. Not only will this help you avoid being late or having to rush to be on time, but during the test you can track how much time is left. It's best to arrive 5 minutes early so you can be seated and ready by the time the test begins.

- *Pay attention to the test instructions.* Do this before you rush right to the questions. Read or listen to directions, such as "copy the question" or "show your work." Then, skim the test. Jot a few notes that bring bits of information to mind. By reviewing questions quickly in advance, your brain can work on answers to longer questions while you complete shorter questions.

- *Budget test time efficiently.* After you skim the test, think about how to budget your time. Think about how much time you have to finish the test, the total number of questions, the type and difficulty of each question, and the point value of each. If you start to lag during the test, don't stress. You can rebound by adjusting your schedule.

TEST-TAKING STRATEGIES

You'll take many different kinds of tests during your student career, each of which requires unique strategies. There are objective tests, such as multiple choice and true/false, and subjective tests, such as essays. There are vocabulary, reading comprehension, open-book, take-home, oral, and standardized tests as well.

You've probably seen some of these test types before. You might even have an idea of which kinds of tests you find easier or more difficult. But no matter where your strengths or weaknesses lie, all students can use the same basic tips to improve their test-taking skills. And once you can conquer any test, you'll be well on your way to success!

Bloom's Taxonomy and Question Types

Before we look at different types of test questions commonly used, it's helpful to understand how instructors think about tests—and what it is they're actually testing. The system developed by Benjamin Bloom to explain different cognitive levels or ways of thinking has shaped how many educators think about what and how they want their students to learn. This is called Bloom's Taxonomy of the Cognitive Domain or sometimes Bloom's learning levels. The six learning levels are described in Chapter 5:

- knowledge
- comprehension
- application
- analysis
- synthesis
- evaluation

As you prepare for a test in any course, it helps to think also about these levels. Your primary consideration involves what learning activities your course focuses on and what kinds of test questions may be used to assess your mastery of that learning.

For example, let's say you have been learning how to take patients' vital signs—to take a temperature, measure blood pressure, and so on. Your instructor has emphasized that accuracy is the most important aspect of performing these skills. You need to perform each step in each procedure correctly. As described in Chapter 5, this learning is primarily in the first two levels of Bloom's Taxonomy: knowledge and comprehension. You have to remember exactly what steps to use, for example, in using blood pressure equipment. You also need to understand what you are doing—the comprehension level—in order to do your job well. You can expect, therefore, that a test that includes this topic will likely include knowledge and comprehension types of questions. As noted in Chapter 5, this means not only recalling pertinent information and facts but also being able to describe in your own words information such as how to take a blood pressure.

Although knowledge and comprehension may be most important for this learning, the next level in the taxonomy is likely also important: application. That is so because as you learned the steps for how to take a blood pressure, you also learned you may need to vary the equipment or process in different situations. Can you explain *why* to use a different blood pressure cuff for a child or an adult with a large arm—and how the readings you obtain may be inaccurate if you do not? Because the application learning level is also important for this topic, it's likely the test may include questions such as this also.

Remember that the three highest learning levels—analysis, synthesis, and evaluation—are involved in critical thinking. In these levels, it's not enough just to remember how to do something, why, and how to apply it in a new situation. Instead, you're expected to think more deeply about the issues involved. For example, you take a patient's temperature and find it normal, but an hour later, it is 3° F higher. Do you evaluate that fact as meaningful? Do you just record the information as you've been taught to and go on about your work, or do you decide this is a significant change you should report immediately to a physician or nurse in case the patient's condition is rapidly declining? Why, or why not?

As you begin to prepare for any test, review in your memory how your instructor talked about the information you have been learning. This will help you determine whether the test may focus more or less on memory and comprehension or on higher-level thinking such as application, analysis, and evaluation—or perhaps both. This will also help you know what kinds of test questions to expect.

For example, for memory and comprehension, usually objective test questions are used. These include multiple choice, true/false, and similar question types. Test questions focusing on higher-level understanding may also include objective questions but also likely include short-answer and essay questions. We'll look at all these types of questions in the next sections.

Objective Tests

There is only one right answer for each question on an objective test. The point is to test your recall of facts. Most standardized tests are objective with one or more of these types of questions:

- multiple choice
- true or false

- short answer
- sentence completion
- problem solving

When taking an objective test, first look over the entire test to see how many questions there are. Try to answer them in order, but if you hit a difficult one, move on to the next. Just make sure you mark the tough question so you remember to come back to it. You can go back to the hard questions you marked when you've reached the end of the test and have extra time. Working on the easier questions first may help you answer the hard ones. Information from other questions might spark memories and prompt you to remember the answers.

HOW TO DECIPHER MULTIPLE CHOICE QUESTIONS

There are certain guidelines to follow on a multiple choice test.

- Read each question carefully. Phrases like *except, not,* and *all of the following* provide important clues to the correct answer.

- Try to answer each question before you look at the answer choices. Then, try to match your answer to one of the choices. Even if you feel you have a match at choice one, read the rest of the choices to see if there's an even closer match.

- Use a process of elimination to narrow your answer choices. Some answers are clearly wrong. Cross them out and focus on the ones that might be correct.

- Work quickly! You won't have time to go back and answer truly hard questions if you take too long checking and double-checking the ones you think you answered correctly.

My "objective" is to succeed on any and every test!

Who Decides What's *Best*?

You do! Sometimes, test instructions tell you to choose the "best" answer. That means more than one answer choice may technically be correct, but only one choice fully answers the question. You have to prioritize the answers to determine which best answers the question.

When you're prioritizing answer choices, use well-known theories or principles. For a question that asks what you would do first, for example, think of Maslow's hierarchy of needs. This theory basically says that although all needs seem important, they can be ranked. Needs at the bottom of the rankings can be dropped. In a well-written test, all answer choices seem plausible. No single choice stands out as obviously wrong. To apply Maslow's hierarchy to tests, you have to try and rank the choices. Look for a clue in the question that makes one answer better than the others. Sometimes, questions and answers are taken word for word from your textbook or lecture notes. If you recognize familiar words or phrases in only one of the options, that option is probably the right answer.

Be alert for "attractive distracters," or words that look like the correct answer but aren't. For instance, if *ileum* is the correct answer on an anatomy test, *ilium* might be included as another answer choice.

TRUE OR FALSE?

In general, true/false questions are meant to see if you recognize when simple facts and details are misrepresented. Most true/false statements are straightforward and are based on key words or phrases from your textbook or lectures. Always decide whether the statement is completely true before you mark it as true. If it is only partly true, then the statement should be marked false. Statements containing extreme words can be tricky. Watch out for words such as the following:

- all
- always
- never
- none
- only

any exception = false

> **Always** watch out for statements with extreme words.

SHORT ANSWER

Short-answer questions are like the 100-meter dash of test items. These types of questions usually ask for one or two specific sentences, such as writing a definition or giving a formula. When you're taking a short-answer test, quickly scan the test items to organize them in three categories:

- answers I know without hesitation
- answers I can get if I think for a moment
- answers I really don't know

Answer the questions you know first and then move on to the questions that need a little thought. Once you're rolling and feeling confident, go for the tougher questions.

Note: most short-answer questions are objective questions, with only one correct answer. In some cases, however, a short-answer question may be subjective, allowing you to demonstrate your understanding through a variety of possible answers. Either way, just make sure your answer is clearly and concisely stated.

FILLING IN THE BLANKS

Sentence completion or fill-in-the-blank questions usually ask you to supply an exact word or phrase from memory. Sometimes, you can use the length and number of blanks as a clue to the best answer. Many instructors will indicate whether they expect one word, two, or a phrase by using longer and shorter blanks. Also, make sure your answer is consistent with the grammar of the sentence. For example, if the question reads, "The medical term for heart muscle is _____ muscle," the answer should be *cardiac*, not *cardio* or *cardium*.

If you're really in doubt, go ahead and guess—you may receive partial credit.

Many times, the question itself will give clues to the right answer. For instance, a date may help you narrow the scope of answers by providing a historical point of reference. Suppose you think a scientific discovery might have been made by either Anton van Leeuwenhoek or Louis Pasteur and the date given is 1870. The right answer would have to be Pasteur because van Leeuwenhoek died in 1723.

THE SOLUTION TO YOUR PROBLEMS

Problem-solving tests are most often found in subjects dealing with numbers and equations, such as math and science. With a problem-solving test, first read through all the problems before answering any of them. Underline key words in the directions and important data in the questions. Make notes next to any questions that bring thoughts or data points to mind. Then, go back and begin to fully answer the questions.

What to Tackle First

Students often think they should start with the hardest problems so they can be sure those problems will be completed. They believe they can rush through the easy questions at the end. But it's actually better to start with the easy questions. They warm up your brain and build your confidence. Additionally, rushing to complete easy questions at the end can lead to careless mistakes and omissions.

Moving On

If you have trouble solving a problem, move on. When you come back to that problem, take advantage of the fact that you've been working on

Start with easy problems to warm yourself up for the big ones.

something different and look at the old problem in a new way. Will any of the strategies or formulas you used on the other problems work? There's usually more than one way to solve a problem. If the strategy you started with isn't working, try something else.

Get It All Down

Show your work! If you make a mistake, the instructor will be able to see where you got off track and may give you partial credit. Also, when you write down all your work, you can check it yourself before you turn in the test. Checking your work helps you make sure you haven't made any careless errors or forgotten anything.

Subjective Tests

In a subjective test, there's no single right answer. Instead, you're graded on how well you demonstrate your understanding of the material. Follow these steps for successfully completing essay tests.

- Read all the directions, underlining important words and phrases.
- Read all the questions, even if you're not required to answer them all. Jot down facts and thoughts for each question.
- Estimate how long you think you'll need to answer each question.
- Choose the questions you want to answer, when given a choice.
- Outline each answer.
- Write the answers.
- Review and proofread your answers. Then, reread the directions, making sure you followed them correctly.

Think about essays as endurance races. If completing a short-answer question is like running the 100-meter dash, then writing an essay is like running a 5-kilometer race. It just takes a little more thought and planning.

LOOK BEFORE YOU LEAP

When you read all the directions in a test first, you reduce your chances of losing points by not following the directions. For example, the directions may ask you to provide three supporting facts for your statement. If you skip over that part of the directions, you might provide only one or two facts. When you're reading through the directions, underline the key points so you can refer to them with a glance as you write.

Preview the Questions

Next, read through each question and make notes about any ideas or facts that come to mind. You can include things like formulas, names, dates, and your impressions. You'll need this information later as you create an outline. This step also helps you choose which questions to answer because it gives you an idea of how much you know about each topic.

It's Just a Matter of Time

The next step is estimating how long it will take to answer each question. Consider things like the number of questions and how many points each question is worth. If one question is worth half the test grade, for example, plan to spend half your time answering it. Factor in things like the time you'll need to organize an outline, write the essay, and proofread your work.

ORGANIZE AN OUTLINE

When you begin making an outline, start with your thesis statement. Choose a title that reflects your thesis and write it at the top of your paper. That way, you can use your title and thesis statement to guide your writing and keep it on track.

Content and organization typically count for most of the points on an essay test. The five-paragraph format is a good way to organize your information. (See *Five-Paragraph Format*.) If you run out of time and can't finish your essay, you can at least turn in your outline to let your instructor know that time was the problem, not comprehension.

Five-Paragraph Format

The five-paragraph format is an easy-to-follow structure for stating and supporting an opinion. It's a great way to get started on your essay, and it also helps you finish writing by taking the guesswork out of where to go next.

1. *Introduction.* Briefly outline your opinion and the facts you will use to support it.

2. *First point.* State your first point and include one to two supporting facts.

3. *Second point.* State your second point and include one to two supporting facts.

4. *Third point.* State your third point and include one to two supporting facts.

5. *Conclusion.* Pull together the three main points in a summary.

Note, however, that there's nothing magic about the number *three* for your key points! If you have only two main points to make, don't trump up some third thing just to have three in the body of your essay—that would just weaken your essay overall. Similarly, if you have a fourth key point to make, don't leave it out just because you think you *must* have five paragraphs. In other words, your essay should reflect what you actually have to say on the subject.

FOLLOW YOUR GAME PLAN

When you're writing, stick to your outline to avoid wasting time. Your thesis statement should be a clear, but brief, answer to the essay question. In your introduction, explain what the remaining paragraphs in your essay will discuss. The essay question may ask you to "explain a cause-and-effect relationship" or "summarize key ideas." Be sure to follow directions here.

Using an outline helps you stay on track and prove your point in an essay.

Each paragraph in the body of the essay should make one point and support it with facts. This will help you be clear in your writing. There's no need to develop long, winding arguments. Go straight from point A to point B and give the facts that led you there. Avoid making several points in one paragraph or bringing in facts that don't really apply to your point or that you'll use later. Each paragraph should have a topic sentence that flows from your thesis statement. Write simple, direct sentences that follow one another logically.

In the conclusion, restate your thesis, then refer to the points you've made that prove it. Use the conclusion to draw your ideas together.

Essay Tests Made Easy

Hi, I'm Owen. I used to be very anxious about essay tests. I felt like I couldn't remember the main point I was trying to make—I got lost in the details. Now what I do is write my outline on a separate sheet of paper and I leave a lot of space between sections. Then I write one sentence that gives a fact to back up my point under each section in the outline. After that, I go back and write one more sentence with a fact under each section. I do this until I have four sentences under each section. Then I copy what I've written onto my test paper, adding any more details I can think of. This way, I know my essay won't be top-heavy at the start and rushed at the end and I stay on track with my main point.

INSTANT REPLAY

When you're done writing, go back and read the question you've answered and the directions again. Make sure you've answered the question fully. Then review your essay for grammar errors and make sure your handwriting is legible. Make corrections where necessary.

Essay Quick-Check

After completing an essay, check your work. Ask yourself these questions regarding the following three elements of your essay:

Content:

- Did I stick to my thesis statement?

- Did I prove each point I made?

- Did I use examples?

- Did I distinguish fact from opinion?

- Did I mention any exceptions to my general statements?

Organization:

- Did I open with my thesis statement?

- Does the thesis statement answer the question?

- Did I follow my outline?

- Does my conclusion pull together all my points?

Writing mechanics:

- Does every sentence make a clear point?

- Did I use all words correctly?

- Are spelling, grammar, punctuation, and sentence structure all correct?

- Is my work neat and my handwriting legible?

Other Types of Tests

Other types of tests include:

- *Vocabulary.* These tests assess your ability to remember the meaning of a word and to use it correctly. They're used in foreign language courses or fields with specialized terminology.

- *Reading comprehension.* These tests require you to read a passage and answer questions about its content.

- *Open-book and take-home.* You're usually allowed to use any and all materials you want when taking these kinds of tests. Critical thinking is more important than a good memory here. However, there's less slack given for making factual errors.

- *Oral.* Speaking clearly and fluently is key here. If you can choose your topic in advance, do so and prepare like you were going to write an essay, with a thesis statement and outline. Try to make three points supported by facts.
- *Standardized.* The Graduate Record Examination (GRE) and Scholastic Assessment Test (SAT) are two examples of standardized tests. They are used for placement and admissions. Most tests required for certification or licensure in a health care career (discussed later in this chapter) are also standardized tests.

VOCABULARY TESTS

Vocabulary tests call for some special strategies:

- Avoid decoy answer choices that look correct but aren't.
- Try to figure out if the word is a noun, verb, adjective, etc., and choose grammatically correct answers only.
- If you don't know the meaning of a word, try to remember where you've heard it and how it was used in the sentence. Select the answer that seems closest in meaning.
- Apply your knowledge of other languages. Prefixes, suffixes, and root words can offer clues about meaning.

READING COMPREHENSION TESTS

These types of tests will go more smoothly if you read the questions first. Then, as you read the passage, you can focus on finding the information you need. Use only facts found in the passage! This is one case where applying outside knowledge is not helpful.

OPEN-BOOK TESTS

Open-book tests also require special strategies:

- Use the index and table of contents to locate information.
- Avoid copying directly from your materials! Use as many resources as are allowed, but put ideas into your own words.
- Check your answers to make sure you didn't insert any incorrect information or unsupported arguments by mistake.
- As always, proofread your work!

ORAL TESTS

Oral tests should be prepared for like written tests, with one twist: you should rehearse your answers out loud. Here are more strategies:

- Dress well and look neat. Stand up straight and look your listener(s) in the eye.
- Speak clearly and speak up. Don't go too fast or too slowly (rehearsal will help you with this).

- If you're giving a speech, prepare notes and rehearse speaking with only a few glances at your notes. Never read directly from your notes—your voice will be muffled and you won't make eye contact.

- Use your everyday language (except for slang) as much as possible. Using big or unfamiliar words will cause you to hesitate—and make mistakes.

- If you don't understand a question you get during or after your speech, ask for clarification. If you're still unsure, rephrase the question yourself.

- If you don't know the answer to a question, explain why. Perhaps it is outside your realm of expertise.

- When the test is over, gather your papers together and thank your audience for their attention.

Oral tests are much like presentations and public speaking. See the tips in Chapter 7.

STANDARDIZED TESTS

Prepare for standardized tests by taking a practice test in similar testing conditions. Find a room that's free of distractions and allow yourself the same amount of time you'll have for the real test. The company that publishes the test likely provides practice questions or other study materials. If not, there are often published guides, like books and software, for each test. These guides contain practice exercises and self-tests.

These guidelines are true also for certification and licensure exams in many health care professions.

Postgame Commentary

Reviewing your test after it has been graded can help you learn where you got off track and what you need to go over before the next test. When you get a corrected test back, ask yourself:

- Was there one concept or problem that tripped me up?

- How would I sum up the instructor's comments?

- Did I prepare adequately? How should I prepare differently next time?

- Did I make any careless mistakes? How can I avoid them next time?

- What can I learn from my mistakes?

One Final Strategy

Tests give you an opportunity to evaluate how well you're doing in a course. Many instructors review tests with the entire class. One final test-taking strategy is to review your own test when it's given back to you. (See *Postgame Commentary*.) Try to learn from the comments your instructor made. If you have questions, make an appointment to see the instructor during office hours.

Remember, it's never good to argue with an instructor about your grade in class. But if you have questions or believe the instructor made an error in grading, approach the instructor privately—outside of class. Be sure to present your concerns in a respectful way.

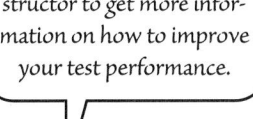

Try talking with your instructor to get more information on how to improve your test performance.

SUCCEEDING ON MATH TESTS

Many students are especially anxious about math tests. But with good study habits and advance preparation, math tests should not be any more difficult than other types of tests.

Math questions generally fall into one of two categories: number questions and word problems. Both types involve solving problems and using math principles. Several strategies can be used to approach either type of test.

Practice Tests

Take some practice tests to prepare for test day. Many textbooks include practice questions. You also can find many websites that offer practice tests—some created by instructors for their students using old tests! Take the test without looking at the answers and then grade yourself. You'll be glad you took practice tests when you sit down for your actual exam—they build your confidence and get you used to performing under test conditions.

Number Problems

Here are a few simple steps that can help you increase your likelihood of success when taking a number-problem test:

- *Work carefully and deliberately.* You can really sabotage yourself by being careless or working too fast. Thorough work is required.

Write carefully, perform the calculations in reverse to check your answer, keep numbers in straight columns, and copy accurately.

- *Write out all steps.* Sometimes, students feel that showing all their work is childish. But it's a good practice at any age. If you write out your work, you can catch errors in it more easily.

- *Estimate first.* Try to estimate the answer to a problem before you start working. Then, solve the problem without referring to the estimate. When you finish your calculations, compare your answer with the estimate to see how close they are. If they're not close, you may have made a mistake in your calculations—a decimal point in the wrong place, an extra zero, etc.

- *Make sure your calculations use all the information given in the problem.* There's rarely unnecessary data given in a math problem. Most of the time, each piece of data is essential to solving the problem.

- *Read each question twice.* After you think you have the right answer, read the question again. Use a mental checklist. Did you show your work? Did you answer in the correct units? Did you answer all parts of the question? Does your answer make sense? If your answers are yes, you're on the right track.

- *Be persistent.* Everyone gets stuck sometimes. There are ways you can get yourself moving again. Round fractions up to whole numbers to put a problem into simpler form. Try to figure out what information you think you're missing. What doesn't make sense? Where do you lose track? If all else fails, move on to other questions and come back to the tougher ones later.

Avoiding Careless Mistakes

Careless mistakes result when students speed through problems. To avoid these mistakes and increase your accuracy, follow these tips:

- Write your numbers carefully so your sevens don't look like ones or fours and your eights don't look like sixes or zeroes.

- Whether you're doing simple or elaborate calculations, keep your digits in straight columns. You don't want numbers in the tens column being counted in the hundreds column.

- If you copy a problem onto another page, double-check to make sure you copied it accurately. You'd be surprised how often you can overlook a silly mistake—like writing a subtraction sign instead of a division sign—and not even realize it.

Word Problems

Word problems have a bad reputation for being difficult. But word problems simply put numbers in a nonnumber context. There are some things you can do to make word problems more approachable:

- Look at the big picture.
- Plan well.
- Use strategies for dealing with difficult word problems.
- Learn from past mistakes with similar problems.

THE BIG PICTURE

When you're facing a test that includes word problems, look over the whole test first. As you read each problem, jot down notes in the margin about how you might solve it.

Work on the easiest problems first. Those are the problems where the solutions you should use are easy to identify. Solving easy problems first warms up your brain and builds confidence.

SET THE CLOCK

Consider planning for the test as you would plan time for a study session. Allow more time for problems worth more points. Budget time at the end of the test to review and to go back to difficult problems.

Those tough problems can derail your planning, but it doesn't have to be that way. Stay calm. Try not to give in to panic or feeling overwhelmed. There are several strategies you can use to solve tough problems:

- Mark key words and numbers, which can narrow the problem down to its essential elements.
- Sketch a diagram of the problem to make it more comprehensible.
- List all the formulas you think are relevant and decide which to use first.
- Think about similar practice problems and how you solved them.
- Guess at a reasonable answer if other strategies fail, then check it. If you can't work out the problem to get to your answer, you may think of another solution.

LEARN FROM YOUR MISTAKES

After the test is over and you get it back from the instructor, read through the comments and suggestions. Try to avoid making assumptions about why you missed certain problems. Assumptions

like "I just can't do math" or "It's just too hard" are unhelpful and counterproductive. Instead, ask yourself these questions:

- Did I make careless mistakes?
- Did I misread questions?
- Did I miss the same kind of problem over and over?
- Did I remember formulas incorrectly or incompletely?
- Did I run out of time?
- Did I practice enough or did I skimp on practice problems?
- Did I let my anxiety get the best of me, making me miss problems I really know how to solve?

Based on your answers to these questions, you can identify ways to improve your performance on future tests.

CALCULATING GRADES

One of the reasons many students are anxious about tests is that they generally contribute heavily to the grade for the whole course. It's important, therefore, to understand how much any given quiz or test counts toward your grade and to be able to calculate your current grade status regardless of which of varying systems your instructor may use. Calculating your grade involves looking at what activities—tests, quizzes, homework, papers, etc.—earn points and how much each counts toward your final grade. Your syllabus usually provides this information.

In this section we'll describe how to calculate grades for point systems, averages, and weighted grade systems.

Understanding Grades

Your instructor might assign a number of points or percentage values to each activity on the syllabus. If your instructor uses a point-based system, the easiest way to determine your grade is to convert the points to percentages. For example, if you take a test and receive a score of 40 out of 50 possible points (40/50), you can convert this score to a percentage to figure out your grade on the test. When figuring out percentages, remember to divide the number of points you received by the total number of possible points. A score of 40/50 equals 80%.

At any point during a semester or term, you also should be able to figure out your overall grade in a course. Let's say your syllabus lists the following information:

- Five quizzes—worth 40 points each
- Test 1—worth 100 points
- Test 2—worth 200 points

So far, the class has taken one quiz and Test 1, for a total of 140 possible points (40 + 100 = 140). After adding up the points you received on the quiz and test, you find that you have a total of 120 out of 140 possible points (120/140). Based on this information, you can figure out your overall percentage grade.

$$120 \div 140 = 85.7\%$$

If you keep track of your quiz and test scores (as well as any other graded activities) throughout the term, you'll be able to determine your overall grade in a course at any time. Knowing your grade in each course can help you gauge whether or not you're on target to meet your goals. Also, by keeping tabs on your grades, you can react early if they begin to slip. You may realize that you need to put in more study time, meet with your instructor, or visit the tutoring center. But if you wait until the end of the semester to figure out your overall grade in a course, it may be too late to improve it!

To find your "batting average" in a course, just add up your scores and divide by the number of activities that have been assigned so far.

Batting Averages

Now let's look at a grading system based on *averages*. Suppose your instructor says that the average of six test grades will be your final grade in the course. By the middle of the term, the class has taken three tests. For example, if your test grades were 78%, 91%, and 95%, what would your overall grade be so far? Follow these simple steps to determine your average grade.

1. First, add your three test scores (78 + 91 + 95 = 264).
2. Then, divide the total by the number of tests you've taken so far (264 ÷ 3 = 88).

This means your grade in the course would be 88%.

Weighting

In some cases, each activity listed on a syllabus is *weighted*, or assigned a certain percentage of the final grade. This means some activities will affect your final grade more than others, as shown below.

- Five quizzes—each is worth 10% of your final grade
- Test 1—worth 20% of your final grade
- Test 2—worth 30% of your final grade

Let's analyze these percentages. At first glance, it looks like the quizzes are not worth as much as Test 1 or Test 2. But look more closely; the syllabus says that *each* quiz is worth 10% of your final grade, which means:

$$5 \text{ quizzes} \times 10\% = 50\%$$

Therefore, the quizzes will make up 50% or half of your final grade. That's a big difference from 10%!

When Projects, Papers, and Homework Are in Play

Many instructors also include activities such as projects, papers, homework, and participation in a student's final grade. Let's look at a scenario with several weighted activities.

- Four quizzes—each is worth 5% of your final grade
- Test 1—worth 10% of your final grade
- Test 2—worth 20% of your final grade
- Group project—worth 5% of your final grade
- Homework—worth 5% of your final grade
- Attendance and participation make up the rest of your grade

Now, which is most important? You might think the quizzes or tests are more important to your final grade than your attendance and participation. Look more closely.

- Quizzes are 20% of your final grade (4 quizzes × 5% = 20%).
- The tests together equal 30% of your grade (10% + 20% = 30%).
- The group project plus homework equal 10% of your grade (5% + 5% = 10%).

That leaves 40% for your attendance and participation—the largest percentage of all!

Calculating Your Stats

So how do you figure out your grade in a course where the activities are weighted? Let's determine a student's grade based on the following syllabus information.

- Quizzes—average of six quizzes is worth 15% of your final grade
- Test 1—worth 25% of your final grade
- Test 2—worth 60% of your final grade

Suppose a student averaged all of her quizzes for a score of 70%. On Test 1, her grade was 80% and on Test 2, she received a score of 90%. How can we determine her final grade in the course if the activities are all weighted differently?

1. First, take all three scores and multiply each by the appropriate percentage, as listed on the syllabus. This will give each score the correct weight.

   Quizzes—70(.15) = 10.5

   Test 1—80(.25) = 20

   Test 2—90(.60) = 54

2. Next, add the three products you came up with in step 1.

   10.5 + 20 + 54 = 84.5

3. The sum is the student's overall grade in the course: 84.5%.

Grading Scales

It's no use knowing how many points you earned or what your grade averages were if you're unable to translate that information into a letter grade. Here's a sample grading scale from a syllabus:

97 − 100 = A+

94 − 96 = A

90 − 93 = A−

86 − 89 = B+

83 − 85 = B

80 − 82 = B−

76 − 79 = C+

73 − 75 = C

70 − 72 = C−

66 − 69 = D+

63 − 65 = D

60 − 62 = D−

59 and under = F

For example, if a student received an overall grade of 84.5% in a course, that would translate to a B.

Keep track of your stats in each course by recording your scores when your instructor hands back graded assignments.

Many schools use the 4.0 system to calculate student grade point averages (GPAs). To do this, they assign point values to each student's letter grades. Here's a sample list based on the 4.0 system:

A+ = 4.3

A = 4.0

A− = 3.7

B+ = 3.3

B = 3.0

B− = 2.7

C+ = 2.3

C = 2.0

C− = 1.7

D+ = 1.3

D = 1.0

D− = 0.7

F = 0.0

Let's calculate the GPA of a student who has completed one semester. Suppose this student took four three-credit courses during his first semester. His overall grades were A, B+, A+, and C−. What would his GPA be?

1. First, list the point values assigned to each of the letter grades the student received.

   A   = 4.0

   B+ = 3.3

   A+ = 4.3

   C− = 1.7

2. Next, find the average of the four point values.

   4.0 + 3.3 + 4.3 + 1.7 = 13.3

   13.3 ÷ 4 = 3.325

3. The average is the student's GPA: 3.325 (which, rounded to the nearest decimal point, comes to 3.3).

Keep in mind that the 4.0 system varies from school to school. For example, certain courses may be weighted more than others. You can talk to your academic advisor if you have questions about the system your school uses.

The Home Stretch

Suppose you're in the home stretch—the term is almost over and you just have one more biology test to take. You'd really like to reach your goal of getting a B in the course, but you're not sure if that's possible. What grade would you have to get on the last test in order to get a B in the course?

1. First, look at the syllabus to see how much each graded activity is worth. For example, suppose your syllabus lists this information:
   - Five quizzes—average of 5 quizzes is worth 20% of your final grade
   - Test 1—worth 30% of your final grade
   - Test 2—worth 50% of your final grade

2. Next, list your scores for each activity. Let x stand for the score of your last test, since you haven't taken it yet. For the sake of this example, we'll use the following scores:

   Quizzes—70%

   Test 1—75%

   Test 2—x

3. Then, take all three scores and multiply each by the appropriate percentage, as listed on the syllabus. This will give each score the correct weight.

   Quizzes—70(.20) = 14

   Test 1—75(.30) = 22.5

   Test 2—x(.50) = .5x

> A simple equation can help you figure out how to achieve your goal grade in a course.

4. Now, add the three products you came up with and make the sum equal to 80, as below. (This will be a basic algebraic equation used to find the value of x.) The value of x is the percent grade you will need to get on the test in order to receive a B (or at least 80%) in the course.

   $14 + 22.5 + .5x = 80$

   $36.5 + .5x = 80$

   $36.5 + .5x - 36.5 = 80 - 36.5$

   $.5x = 43.5$

   $.5x \div .5 = 43.5 \div .5$

   $x = 87$

5. And you have your answer! In order to receive a B in the course, you'd have to score at least 87% on the last test.

Grade Calculation Practice

At the midpoint in a semester, suppose a student has received the following scores:

- Quizzes—8/10, 6/10, 9/10, 10/10
- Homework assignments—5/5, 4/5, 3/5, 5/5
- Research paper—139/150
- Midterm exam—184/200

Based on the information above, calculate the following percentages (check your answers in the Appendix):

1. Assuming that each activity is weighted equally, what is the student's overall grade in the course so far?

2. What is the student's average quiz grade?

3. What is the student's average homework grade?

4. What percentage grade did the student receive on the research paper?

5. What percentage grade did the student receive on the midterm exam?

CERTIFICATION AND LICENSURE EXAMS

> If you have the option, becoming certified in your field is one of the best ways to get your new career off to a great start.

After you complete your educational program, to enter many health care careers, you may be required to take a licensure examination. This is a test mandated by state law to ensure you are prepared to practice in your field. Such a licensure examination is used in most professions, the same as a law school graduate having to pass the bar exam before practicing law.

Certification may also be required or may be an option for you, depending on your chosen health career and your state. In most health care careers in which certification is available but is voluntary, it is still a good idea to become certified because this usually makes it easier to find the kind of job you want and to advance within your career. Certification, like licensure, requires an examination after completing your educational program. Certification is usually controlled by a professional association.

Because there are literally hundreds of specific health careers with their own legal requirements for licensure (which may vary by state) and different associations controlling certification, it is impossible to tell you *exactly* what to expect from these exams in your specific field. But you can easily find out yourself, and we can generalize about most licensure and certification exams. Follow these guidelines:

- Don't wait until you're almost finished with school before thinking about an upcoming licensure or certification exam. You should find out at the start of your program what the certification requirements are for your profession. Start by asking an instructor about what exam(s) you will need or want to take.

- Visit the website of your state's licensing agency and the professional association that administers the certification exam. Print out the basic information and highlight things like when the exam is given, when and how to register for the exam, what the exam covers, and the type of questions on the exam.

- Pay special attention to the test itself and the testing situation. Most such exams are multiple choice and some are given only on computers at the test site.

- Plan a study schedule well in advance of the exam, reviewing your educational materials related to topics you can expect on the exam. Use the study strategies described earlier in this chapter and in Chapter 8.

- Prepare for the type of test as described earlier in this chapter, such as how to perform best on multiple choice tests.

- Practice exams (and often review books with practice exams) are available in almost all health care fields where licensure or certification requires an exam. Taking one or more practice exams well before the test date will help you see if you need to study certain areas more and will give you confidence for the actual exam.

- Keep the exam in mind throughout your school program. Hang on to materials that you think will help you study for the exam when the time comes.

CHAPTER SUMMARY

- Help reduce test stress by taking care of your body by exercising, eating right, and getting enough rest.

- Meet stress head-on with relaxation techniques, positive thinking, and by relying on your support network.

- Give yourself time to prepare and plan for tests. Talk with your instructor about what to expect, create a study plan, and take practice tests.

- With all kinds of tests, always read the directions and skim through the questions before you begin.

- When taking objective tests, work on the easier questions first to warm up your brain and jog your memory.
- For subjective tests, create an outline to help you get started on your essay.
- Review all graded tests to see where you can make improvements.
- Begin preparing well ahead for a licensure or certification exam, and take a practice test or two to ensure you've mastered the material and are confident for test day.

REVIEW QUESTIONS

1. Short Essay: Write three to five sentences describing how to fight test anxiety.

2. How can you find out more about an upcoming test?

3. Short Essay: Write three to five sentences describing how to write an outline for an essay and why doing so is important.

4. List some tips for doing well on multiple choice questions, whether on a class test or licensure exam.

CHAPTER ACTIVITIES

1. Exercise Checklist: Review *Health and Stress Management.* Choose the types of exercise and/or relaxation techniques you wish to do on a regular basis to minimize your stress and test anxiety and make a note of what you'll have to do to get started.

2. Test-Taking Exercise: Divide into groups of three. Each group member will come up with a five-question test for this course. The questions can be multiple choice, sentence completion, true/false, etc., or a mixture of question styles. Arrange a time to meet for 1 hour. Each of you will take a test you didn't write and complete it in 20 minutes. For the rest of the hour, go over the tests as a group, helping each other see where you made mistakes or did well. Discuss the strategies you used to answer the different types of test questions.

3. Looking Ahead Activity: Find out whether you will be taking a licensure exam after finishing your education and visit the website of the licensing agency to learn about the exam.

ENTERING A HEALTH PROFESSION

Chapter 12 • Succeeding in Your Future

Succeeding in Your Future

WINNING STRATEGY

On completion of this chapter and the learning activities you will be able to:

- See your dreams becoming reality

- Understand the positive choices you make each day

- Explain how to carry your new skills and knowledge into the future

- Know what's involved in the job application process and how to find and get the position you've been dreaming of

You're likely finishing reading this book while still near the beginning of your academic program, but it's still worthwhile to take a look at where you're headed in the future. This chapter will help you connect what you are learning now, and what you have learned in this book, with your future career in health care. You'll also get a head start with information about the job application process you'll be going through as you enter your career. Though this may seem off in the future, understanding the process has great value in the here and now.

BUILDING ON YOUR ACCOMPLISHMENTS

Now that you're nearing the end of this book, it's a good time to look back on what brought you to this point. Are you closer to fulfilling your original dreams? What obstacles have you overcome along the way? What goals have you accomplished? And most important for this chapter, what skills and knowledge will you be able to use in the future?

You've come a long way since you first opened this book. You've learned how to:

- set and meet goals
- plan ahead and be prepared
- schedule multiple activities and meet deadlines
- identify and deal with stress and anxiety
- listen effectively and apply your critical thinking skills
- meet the challenges of learning and take responsibility for the results
- network and contribute in group activities
- explore optional resources to help you get ahead
- meet standards of professionalism and uphold patients' rights

Now imagine yourself 5 or 10 years down the road, working in your chosen career. Look back at the list above of all of the things that you have already learned. You can apply every one of these new skills to help you succeed in all of your future career and education goals. Ask any health care professional and they'll readily agree, for example, that being able to schedule multiple activities and plan ahead are critical to their job success.

Now it's time to look back on just how far you've come.

Make Your Dream a Reality

Even if you're still a year or more away from starting your career in health care, you have done the hardest, most important part: taking action. You tackled the sometimes difficult and complicated task of applying to school and enrolling in courses. You shuffled your work and other responsibilities to make time for class. You studied hard and completed your coursework. All these things have brought you closer to making your dream a reality.

It's important to recognize and take pride in your accomplishments, no matter how small they may seem at the time. Celebrate each success now, whether it's doing well on a test, completing a research project, or forming a study group with a few fellow students. Remember, it's the small steps that move you toward accomplishing big things!

I **can** do this and it **is** worth it!

Courage

You've also shown to yourself and proved to those around you that you have the courage and fortitude to stick with it and meet your goals. It takes courage to believe in yourself and to believe that you can make changes in terms of your education and future career. It takes courage to say, "I *can* do this and it *is* worth it." Carry that attitude through your transition into the professional world of work.

Having the Courage to Succeed

My name is Leila. When I first thought about starting school, I was intimidated. It was a big financial and emotional investment for my family and me. What if I couldn't handle it and had to drop out after one semester? I was worried about what people would think. But then I remembered how my uncle always used to say, "Nothing ventured, nothing gained." If I never took a chance, I'd never achieve anything. I decided it was better to take a chance than to tell myself I couldn't do it.

Choices

To make it this far, you had to have faith in your choices. You've had to make many decisions about your education, your courses, and your career goals. In so doing, you've improved your decision-making skills, which will remain important as you move into your career.

As you approach the end of your educational program, you'll face many new decisions as you look for the career position that best meets your needs and desires. You'll have to decide where to look for a job, perhaps what specific kind of job to pursue, and how to apply and interview most successfully. This chapter introduces that process and will help you get started.

Touchdown! Every time you overcome an obstacle to your success, take time to celebrate!

MEETING CHALLENGES

You know it hasn't been easy to arrive at where you are today. By the time you complete your educational program, you will have overcome many obstacles, likely including financing your education, finding time for studying and the rest of your life, and managing relationships and family life through a long, stressful period.

How have you overcome these obstacles to your success? You've learned may techniques in this book already, including ways to cope with stress, build confidence, and accept the support of others.

In your future career, you similarly will face new challenges. Things change fast in health care and your job undoubtedly will also change. You will be given new responsibilities and you'll be asked to do more. As technology advances, you'll need to learn new knowledge and skills. But your experience now as a student will have prepared you well to meet those challenges, too.

GO-O-O-AL!

When you think of your main goal as a student, you probably see yourself working in your new health care career. But you also have many smaller goals between now and that future:

- doing well in your courses
- learning new skills
- finding the right job

These are big picture goals you'll reach by achieving smaller goals, such as keeping your study schedule, attending class, balancing work and school, and registering for the right courses—all the things we've been talking about throughout this book.

Adjust your short-term goals to make sure you reach your long-term go-o-o-al!

Your Goals and You: A Long-Term Relationship

As you look ahead to the future, review the goals you were asked to think about at the beginning of this book. Remember there are four categories of goals:

- *Long-term.* These are things you hope to accomplish in the next 5 to 10 years.
- *Intermediate.* These are things you would like to accomplish in the next 3 to 5 years.
- *Short-term.* These goals are 6 months to 2 years into the future.
- *Immediate.* These are things you hope to accomplish today, this week, or this month.

Remember too that your goals need to be realistic, measurable, and reachable.

Change Can Be Good

Students adjust their goals for many reasons. Maybe they found their original goals to be unrealistic once they actually started school. Maybe as they began taking courses, they became interested in a different career. These are good reasons to adjust your goals. As you review your goals, ask yourself the following questions:

- Have any of my goals changed since I started school? If so, how and why have they changed?

How Are You Doing?

Take some time to evaluate your progress so far by writing your goals here.

Long-Term Goal:

1. _____

Intermediate Goals:

1. _____
2. _____

Short-Term Goals:

1. _____
2. _____
3. _____

Immediate Goals:

1. _____
2. _____
3. _____

Now, ask yourself these questions:

1. When I started reading this book, what immediate or short-term goals had I hoped to accomplish by now? Have I accomplished these goals?

2. If there are goals I have not accomplished, what stopped me?

3. How did I accomplish my other goals?

4. What can I do differently next term to make sure I meet all my immediate or short-term goals?

5. What are two or three new immediate goals I can accomplish today, this week, or this month?

- How do I feel when I make adjustments to my goals? Is it discouraging (I feel like I failed to meet my original goals) or empowering (I know I can adjust my goals without giving up on them)?

Remember, it's always better to modify your goals or your time line than to give up!

When you choose to adjust your goals, avoid seeing changes as a failure of any sort. Instead, be happy with your new goals and focus on finding creative ways to keep moving forward. Being flexible is critical to your success.

Adjusting Your Goals

If you feel uncomfortable about changing your goals, talk to an academic advisor or someone else you trust.

1. Tell your advisor what adjustments you're considering.
2. Give your reasons for considering the adjustments.
3. Ask your advisor if your adjustments seem positive or whether there may be a way to continue working toward your original goals.

If you talk to someone who is encouraging and supportive, you can feel at ease listening to that person's advice. But in the end, only you can decide if you really need to change your goals.

A Rewarding Experience

To many students, graduation day is when you're rewarded for all your hard work. Others may see the first day of their new career as the big reward. But those long-term benefits may still be far away in the future.

That's why you should give yourself small rewards along the way. If you do well on a big test, for example, maybe you could go out with friends to celebrate. If you finish a big project you've been working on for weeks, consider taking a Saturday off to do something fun. The kinds of rewards are up to you. The point is to reward yourself for all of your achievements, big and small, so you can stay motivated to keep going!

CARRYING YOUR NEW SKILLS INTO THE FUTURE

You're on the track to success as a student and in your career. You've learned a lot about what it takes to do well in school. Five or 10 years from now, these things will be just as important. Here are just a few of the characteristics and skills you've been developing that will continue to be important in your future career:

- *Motivation.* Whether motivated by an intrinsic desire to succeed or a curiosity to learn new things, or extrinsic motivators such as good grades or a higher paying job down the road, your motivation to complete your education should carry over into your career. In the same way, you will be motivated to do your job well, and in the same way you will find success! Motivation is the key to overcome obstacles both in school and on the job.

- *Positive attitude.* If you believe you can do something, you'll find a way to do it. Believing in yourself—having a positive attitude—is the first step toward accomplishing your goals. A positive attitude helps you identify and accept your responsibilities in the learning process and on the job. This has already helped you study effectively and continually improve your grades. In the future, your positive attitude will continue to help you advance in your career. In addition, everyone enjoys working with a person who is a pleasure to be around!

- *Persistence.* Doing your best even during difficult times is a very important life skill. In all health care settings, there are difficult times. For example, during cold and flu season demands on your time may be greater and your work days more hectic. Everyone has tough times; it's how you respond to them that matters.

- *Learning abilities.* Learning how to study well for your courses will likely be more valuable than you can guess once you are in your new career—and not just because you will continue to learn new things on the job. You're also learning now how to stay focused. Working through distractions is a critical skill, whether you're in class or in the middle of a task at work. Health care is a very busy business! Your ability to focus and stay on task will be put to the test daily.

Once you've found your motivation, those obstacles don't stand a chance!

- *Managing stress and taking care of yourself.* You've come to realize stress is a part of life and especially life as a student. It would be nice to think you'll never feel stressed again after graduation, but that's just a pleasant day dream! Remember to keep practicing ways to reduce the stress you feel, including maintaining your physical and mental health, and these good habits will carry into your future job as well. Although there will always be stressful situations, you don't have to feel stressed out when you've developed ways to cope and succeed!

- *Managing your time and resources.* In school, you have to plan for study time, class time, tests, and so much more to accomplish everything. You've already learned a lot about time management and these skills will carry over into work as well. For example, you'll need to create a schedule that allows you to get everything done efficiently and accurately. You'll likely also have to manage resources in the same way you're now managing your financial life as a student.

- *Interacting with others.* You've already learned much about how to interact successfully with your instructors and other students and you will continue to refine these networking and communication skills. At school, other students can be valuable sources of information and support. Your network will also be valuable when you are conducting your first job search. Then, at work, coworkers can offer the same benefits.

- *Speaking the language.* You may feel like a rookie in your first semester or term at school, but you already know much more than you did before. You've begun to "speak the language" by picking up new knowledge and skills related to your future career. As a professional, you'll continue to gain more knowledge and learn new techniques. In addition, you've learned much about the career you've chosen. Knowing what to expect helps you make informed decisions for your future. Keep reminding yourself that you've come a long way so far; you owe it to yourself to keep going!

Stretch yourself to become an even more active learner!

- *Knowing your way around.* In school, you're doing more than simply reading textbooks and going to class. You might be networking with classmates, learning to manage a busy schedule, and using available campus resources. These accomplishments can increase your confidence, which will help you get the job done in your future career. Becoming an expert at school will make it easier to become an expert in the work-place. You'll be ahead of the game when it's easy for you to learn where everything is kept, who can help you solve problems, and how to get information quickly.

Shake It Off!

When you get nervous about the obstacles you face, you can become fearful of them. This leads you to doubt your ability to overcome those obstacles, which might make you discouraged. Taking small steps can help you shake off those feelings of fear, doubt, and discouragement.

For example, one of the biggest challenges you may have faced is learning how to be an active learner. When you're working and going to class, as well as fulfilling other responsibilities, you may not have a lot of energy left to ask questions in class, visit your instructor during office hours, join a study group, take on an internship, or go the extra mile to get your education.

But as you took each of these small steps, it probably became easier to extend yourself. Now that you're in the habit of being an active learner, it's become second nature. And there are other things you can do to become an even more active learner. If you joined a study group, why not lead one? If you know what field you want to enter, why not set up some informational interviews with professionals working in that field? It's just a matter of taking what you're already doing one step further.

And being an active learner now is good practice for being a go-getter on the job. Everyone knows that the go-getters do better in their chosen careers. Think about it. If you had to hire someone to get things done, would you choose the applicant who waited to be told what to do?

You're not a rookie anymore—even if you've just started school, you've already learned a lot!

Getting Comfortable With People

I'm Thomas. I've always been a quiet person and when I first started college, I was kind of shy. I didn't go out of my way to meet new people or strike up conversations. But I was invited to join a study group with other students I didn't know and gradually I opened up more. It took a while, but by the end of my program I'd gotten comfortable introducing myself to strangers and talking with new people. And when I started my first job as a medical assistant, was I ever happy I'd developed some skills interacting with others. In our clinic, I greet the patients, bring them back to the exam room, and ask questions about their health issues. If I'd started this job being as shy as I was when I started college, I might have disappeared at lunch time and never gone back! But, instead, I've learned how to interact comfortably with all kinds of people and I really enjoy my work at the clinic.

GETTING YOUR FIRST PROFESSIONAL JOB

Soon you'll be looking for your first full-time job in health care or a part-time or summer job for experience. You'll need a well-written résumé, an eye-catching cover letter, and polished interviewing skills. But where do you begin? Just as when you started school, the first step is the hardest. Here are some pointers to get you to the next step.

Learning the Ropes

I'm Charles. When I first started school, I was really lost. The campus seemed huge. Every time I needed to do something, like sign up for courses or ask about my financial aid, I was told to go to some building I'd never heard of. My instructors all had materials on reserve at the library and I wasn't sure how to get them. And I was embarrassed to ask questions all the time. I thought it made me look dumb.

But there was no way around it, so I had to swallow my pride and ask. And you know what? I found out that people were happy to help me. No one thought I was dumb. After a few weeks, I didn't have the same problems any more—I knew where things were. Then *I* could be the one to help other students, which made me feel confident—like a leader. I realized that finding my way around campus wasn't an impossible challenge; it was just part of the learning process.

Writing Your Résumé

Students often seek the "perfect" résumé format to guarantee they'll get the job they want, but in reality there is no one correct or best way to write a résumé. You can spend some time on websites that present a variety of résumé formats, to get ideas about what organization and appearance best fits your own experience, background, and personality.

One more word about résumé appearance. Increasingly, job applications are being submitted online. The facility's website, for example, may ask you to submit your résumé by copying it into an online form. Often, this means that special formatting you may have worked on so hard to make your résumé look great on paper is lost when you cut and paste into their form. It can be reduced to a "plain text" version without boldface, italics, large fonts, bullet points, etc. What this really means is that they're much more interested in the substance of the résumé than what it looks like. What does it actually say about you?

Remember also that a résumé doesn't actually get you the job—its goal is to get you an interview. An employer who posts a job opening may receive dozens of résumés. You can't guess all the precise characteristics the employer is looking for, but your résumé can show what you yourself are like. If you are a match, then you're more likely to reach the interview stage.

New graduates often worry that they have less chance of being the one an employer is interested in and this lack of confidence can lead to an uninspiring résumé. But that's not how you should be thinking! For example, if like most new graduates you haven't yet worked in the career position you're seeking, you may worry that the job will go to someone with more experience. Actually, however, if it is an entry-level position, the employer may specifically be seeking someone without direct experience—and someone who has already worked for years in the field can be at a disadvantage for that job. The employer may want you to be open and flexible and willing to learn how things are done at

> Learning the ropes will help you become more confident. And when you're working in health care, it's very important to be confident in your abilities!

their particular health care facility and, as a new graduate, you may be perfect. You might land a job because in the past, even as a part-time student job, you developed certain skills—such as working with a variety of people, or handling money, or working on a computer, or working with math, or anything else you may have done—that the employer is seeking for this specific position. You really can't know *exactly* what they want, but you can honestly present your strengths, whatever they are, so that the employer can see how you may be right for the job. So don't worry about competing for jobs with others who have more experience, or different experience. You'll get the job where they want *you*—they just need to see who you are! That's what your résumé will do for you in this process.

Regardless of format, every résumé is built on the same basics:

- contact information—your name, phone number(s), address, and email address

- education—relevant courses you've completed, diplomas, certifications, or degrees you've earned, along with educational honors and achievements

- work experience—relevant positions you have held, along with your responsibilities and achievements in them, and the names and addresses of your past employers and the dates you worked for them

In addition, you should consider including:

- your objective—the title of the job position you want or one or two sentences about what you want to do

- skills, traits, and achievements relevant to the job—for example, computer skills, language skills, people skills, technical skills (be specific! Don't just say "proficient with computers" but list types of programs you're good at)

- references—contact information for former employers who have been impressed with your work (only if there is room without your résumé becoming too long)

If you don't put references on your résumé, have a separate list available for any interviewer who requests it.

In general, a good résumé is easy to read and neat (no coffee stains!), has no typos or spelling errors (proofread twice!), and shows a potential employer why you are the person for the job without exaggerating your abilities. See *Characteristics of a Good Résumé*.

I want my résumé to get me the interview for that special job!

Characteristics of a Good Résumé

- A short résumé is better than a long one. One page is enough unless if you have a lot of relevant experience.

- Focus on what you've actually done, not just position titles. Use strong verbs (e.g., *analyzed, chaired, created, developed, implemented, managed, organized, performed, planned, researched, wrote,* etc.).

- Use specific numbers when appropriate to describe what you accomplished at work and in school. If you're proud of your GPA, for example, include it.

- Use keywords related to the specific job or career. Some hiring managers review submitted résumés with software that looks for keywords.

- Be sure information is easy to find. Use the standard convention of using a reverse chronological listing of experience, starting with your current or most recent job and moving backward in time, unless you have a good reason for using a different format.

- Unless the position you are applying for is almost always identical in all health care facilities, customize your résumé for the specific application rather than sending one "generic" résumé everywhere. For example, if an advertised position mentions they're looking for applicants with "people skills," make sure the résumé you submit has some specifics about working with people—not just a listing of your technical skills.

- With paper résumés, follow conventional appearance. Do not use a font size smaller than 11 points. Use 1-inch margins all the way around. Print your résumé on a quality bright white paper.

Finding Openings

As you're working on your résumé, you should also be starting your search for job openings for which you may apply. There are many different ways you can find out about open positions. If you look only in the want ads, you'd likely not discover many positions for which you are qualified. Successful job applicants consider every possible avenue in their job search:

- Listings in your school's placement or career office
- Online listings on job bulletin boards (do an Internet search for *"career title* jobs")

- Listings with professional associations or in professional journals or websites
- Classified ads (newspapers, Craigslist.com)
- Word of mouth (check with everyone in your network)
- Websites of health care facilities

Composing a Cover Letter

You should always include a cover letter with every résumé you send out. This will improve the odds that your résumé will get the attention it deserves. In fact, the whole purpose of a cover letter is to motivate the reader to look carefully at your résumé.

A good cover letter is not, however, your résumé in paragraph form. Instead, use the cover letter to tell more about yourself and why you want that particular job—and most important, why you would be good at it. Write a separate, individualized cover letter for each employer to whom you are sending your résumé. Carefully study the job description and analyze what they're looking for. What are the key words they use in the description? Talk to friends or others knowledgeable about the type of work or the specific facility, if possible, and ask what kind of people work there and what the "climate" is like. Then review your own interests and background for specifics that will suggest how you'll fit in perfectly.

Be sure to address the cover letter to the specific person or company to which you are applying. Keep in mind also that your cover letter shows how well you communicate, which is important in many careers. Write clearly—and carefully! You're making a first impression with your cover letter and you won't get a second chance if you misspell the name of the facility or use sloppy grammar and punctuation. After you polish the letter to your best, ask someone to read it, whose judgment you trust and who won't just automatically tell you it's great.

As with your résumé, keep the formatting simple because you may have to cut and paste it into an online form.

Finally, don't be discouraged if you never hear back after making an application or receive only a form letter response. Long gone are the days when companies used to respond individually to every job applicant; many companies no longer respond at all to applicants who are not invited to an interview. Remember that there may have been many, many applicants—and that they are not rejecting you personally. It just means they aren't perfect match for you. Don't let it affect your self-confidence. After all, now you're free to find and accept a job that *is* a perfect match with your interests and skills!

Acing the Interview

Your résumé and cover letter get you the interview, but they don't get you the job. For many students, this is where the real stress of the job application process sets in. Remember to use the stress reduction techniques described in earlier chapters!

Think of your interview as your first day on the job. But it is also like the first day of your clinical rotation and you will have already been through that. So you should have the confidence you need to give a good interview even if you're nervous. Remember: *all* job applicants are nervous and the person interviewing you knows and accepts that.

Here are some guidelines for the interview:

Do:

- Be on time! Check the address and directions ahead of time, know where to park if you're driving, know how long it will take to get to the building at that time of day, and give yourself a little extra time to collect your thoughts as you walk to the office.

- Wear serious, modest clothing and look professional and competent.

- Bring a notebook and pen, in addition to extra copies of your résumé and list of references.

- Make pleasant eye contact, shake hands with confidence, and remember your interviewer's name.

- Ask questions. After all, you're trying to decide whether to work for them as much as they're trying to decide whether to hire you. Questions also demonstrate your interest and motivation.

Did you notice that everything in this list sounds familiar? That's because you've learned about all of these things in previous chapters on being a successful student. Now you're simply applying them in another setting!

Don't:

- Eat, drink, chew gum, wear headphones, or let your cell phone ring.

- Flirt or promise anything you can't deliver.

- Exaggerate (or lie!) about anything in your background. Anything later discovered or perceived to be a falsehood is grounds for immediate dismissal.

Although you can't exactly practice an interview with someone you already know, you can rehearse what you will say to certain kinds of questions you should expect in an interview. Think about what you will say to questions such as these:

- Tell me about yourself.
- Why did you choose to enter this career field?
- Why do you want to work here more than somewhere else?
- Why should we hire you?
- Where do you see yourself in 5 years? In 10 years?
- What are your primary strengths?
- What are your weaknesses?

New applicants can be thrown off by that last question—after all, you're ready to talk about your experiences and skills and suddenly they're asking what you are *not* good at! In part, this question is designed to test your honesty. Everyone has some weakness and a job applicant who brags that there's really nothing he or she isn't good at will seem arrogant and not make a very good impression. The key here is to turn a negative into a positive. For example, if you feel your math skills are weak, you could admit that (especially if math is not a big part of the job you're applying for), and then go on to say that because you never felt strong in math, you've learned to work hard at it and now you always check your work twice to guard against mistakes. You've turned a weakness into a strength!

The bottom line is that your résumé, cover letter, and interview should be honest and confident. Don't oversell yourself, but don't sell yourself short either.

Following Up the Interview

Immediately after the interview, write some notes for yourself about what you learned in the interview. You may have new questions now about the job or the work environment, which you'll want to ask if you are invited back. In some cases, employers have a second interview in more depth; if invited back for a second interview, you'll want to be ready to discuss things the first interviewer indicated are important or emphasized in their questions.

Within a day after the interview, send a short thank you note to each person you interviewed with. Try to make this message significant by referring to something in the interview that made an impression on you. You might say, for example, how much you enjoyed learning about the facility and that now you are even more interested in working there because of . . . . You can send your thank you note by email if you have the interviewer's email address, especially if your communication with the employer has been online.

Then there's nothing you can do but wait for a response. In the meantime, continue to look for other openings and make additional applications. And, more than anything, don't get discouraged if you don't get the job. As with your original application, this only means that you and the employer aren't a perfect match—not that they found anything wrong with you personally. So keep looking until you find that perfect match where the best career position awaits!

A PARTING WORD

You've reached the end of this book and, although you're likely to still have some time from reaching the end of your academic program, you're better prepared now for the rest of your education and entry into your career thereafter. Congratulations! You have much to feel good about and much to look forward to in your future! Just keep applying the skills you've developed here and, soon, these habits for success will become part of who you are, and something you don't even have to think about.

Embrace your future!

We'd also like to plant a seed for a future thought once you've established yourself in your health care career. Remember the help you received from instructors, your network, and maybe a special mentor along the way and consider ways you can give back to the profession and its educational process. Perhaps you'll become a mentor yourself for the next generation of students coming along. While the profession will gain, you'll also feel good about yourself for participating!

CHAPTER SUMMARY

- Looking at how far you've come can be an encouragement to keep pursuing your dreams.
- It's important to celebrate every accomplishment, no matter how small.
- By thinking about the obstacles you've overcome so far, you can find ways to face future challenges.

- Evaluate how well you met your goals this semester or term and make plans to avoid problems in the future.
- The knowledge and skills you're learning now will be important in your future career in health care.
- Carefully crafting your résumé and cover letter, and preparing for interviews, helps you land the job you're seeking.

REVIEW QUESTIONS

1. Short Essay: Write three to five sentences describing the dreams that brought you to where you are now.
2. What is the biggest obstacle you've overcome so far in your quest for a new career?
3. What goal are you most proud of accomplishing so far?
4. Short Essay: Write three to five sentences about the career knowledge you've gained since beginning school.
5. List skills you have developed in the last 3 years that may be relevant to a future health care career.

CHAPTER ACTIVITIES

1. Assess Your Success: Make a time line starting from when you first decided you wanted to pursue a health care career and ending with your long-term goal. First, mark the steps you've taken so far, such as narrowing down your career choices, choosing a school, enrolling, registering for courses, adjusting your work schedule, etc. Then, add your intermediate and short-term goals to the timeline. Finally, look at how far you've come and how much farther you need to go.
2. Share the Wealth: Divide into groups of three to five students. Ask each member of the group to talk about the fears he or she had when they first started school and how they found the courage to overcome those fears. Use a chalkboard or poster paper to make a list of fears and how each was overcome so everyone can take notes.
3. Job Search Preparation: Write a résumé based on your work and experience to date, taking note of any areas in which you can become stronger in the period before you actually start making job applications.

Index

INTRODUCTION TO HEALTH CARE & CAREERS

Roxann DeLaet, RN, MS

Professor of Nursing
Sinclair Community College
Dayton, Ohio

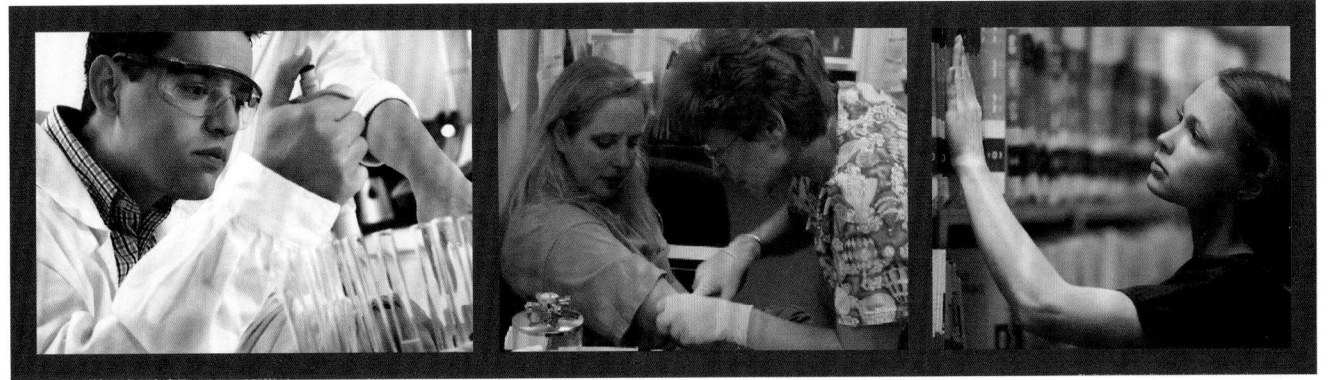

. Wolters Kluwer

Philadelphia • Baltimore • New York • London
Buenos Aires • Hong Kong • Sydney • Tokyo

Contents

NOTE: Some chapters are intentionally missing, as their content was not applicable to the course objectives. This will also affect the ordering of some part and page numbers.

User's Guide

Chapter Opening Features

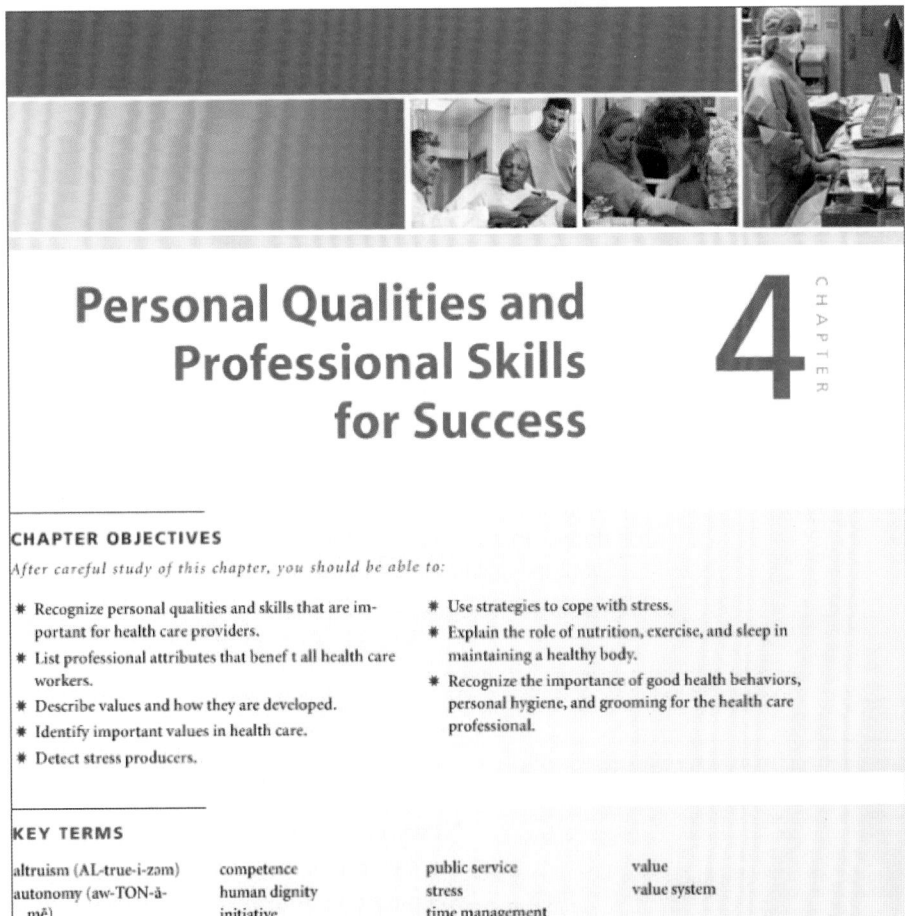

CHAPTER 4

Personal Qualities and Professional Skills for Success

CHAPTER OBJECTIVES

After careful study of this chapter, you should be able to:

* Recognize personal qualities and skills that are important for health care providers.
* List professional attributes that benefit all health care workers.
* Describe values and how they are developed.
* Identify important values in health care.
* Detect stress producers.

* Use strategies to cope with stress.
* Explain the role of nutrition, exercise, and sleep in maintaining a healthy body.
* Recognize the importance of good health behaviors, personal hygiene, and grooming for the health care professional.

KEY TERMS

altruism (AL-true-i-zəm)	competence	public service	value
autonomy (aw-TON-ă-mē)	human dignity	stress	value system
	initiative	time management	

The opening page of each chapter offers multiple entry points into the material ahead and a variety of effective methods for review of that information. For example, Chapter Overviews briefly introduce the chapter to come and provide a synopsis of its contents. These jumping-off points are opportunities to spark lively and provocative classroom discussion as well as individual deliberation. Also kicking off each chapter are the following features:

* **Chapter Objectives** list key learning goals for the chapter. This useful feature has a triple function: First, review these objectives at the beginning of the chapter to familiarize yourself with what you need to take away from the chapter. Second, when you have finished the chapter and its accompanying exercises, revisit the objectives to assess your level of mastery. Third, refer back to objectives lists to provide an effective framework for test prep.

* **Key Terms** alphabetized lists present need-to-know terms for the specific chapter content covered. Alerting readers to important concepts that will be defined within the chapter and in the end-of-book Glossary, this feature also includes pronunciations for the most challenging words. For your convenience, each term appears in boldface at its first use in the chapter. These lists structure each chapter and offer an alternate means of chapter review and study.

Intrachapter Features

> ### ✓ CHECK POINT
>
> **1** List major factors causing a rise in health care costs.
>
> **2** What are some major differences among the three types of health care institutions (voluntary nonprofit, proprietary, and government) found in the U.S.?

Each chapter offers a variety of fun features to complement and enliven the narrative text. Immerse yourself in these features to savor each chapter to the fullest.

CheckPoints interspersed throughout chapters pose 1 or 2 short-answer, recall questions for you to answer based on what you have read so far. They also provide interludes for you to pause and reflect on what you have learned. Complete each CheckPoint to steadily build your knowledge and reinforce learning before continuing on to the next section. Answers to CheckPoints are found with your bonus material located at thePoint.

On Location boxes depict brief scenarios involving patient interactions or other health care tasks that a health care worker might actually encounter. Each scene is followed by open-ended questions that ask you to think critically about how you might act or what you might suggest in such a circumstance based on what you are learning. Enjoy this advance opportunity to walk in a health care professional's shoes for a while and visualize yourself in your future career!

> ## ON LOCATION
>
> ### Ethical Dilemma
>
> *How would you handle the following hypothetical situation?*
>
> You are a certified nursing assistant in a hospital, and one of the physicians with whom you work has diagnosed a female patient on your floor with cancer. The physician informs the patient's husband of the diagnosis, but does not plan to tell the patient that she has cancer or that she has six months to live. The husband agrees with the doctor's decision not to tell the patient because he believes his wife will become depressed or hysterical. Do you think the doctor acted ethically? How do the doctor's actions affect your and other health care workers' abilities to care for the patient?

> ### NEWSREEL
>
> #### Oral Pathology
>
> Every dental checkup includes a thorough examination of the mouth for evidence of disease. Dentists and dental hygienists are trained to detect not just common problems like tooth decay or gum disease, but a wide range of diseases that affect the mouth and other parts of the body. The first signs of some medical problems—osteoporosis or AIDS, for example—can appear in the mouth.
>
> In oral pathology classes, dental professionals learn to identify diseases, or narrow the possibilities, from signs such as the appearance of a lesion or ulcer or a characteristic swelling or inflammation. General dentists treat some diseases themselves; for others, they refer the patient to a specialist. Diseases that affect the teeth,
>
> tongue, gums, jaw, and lining of the mouth may be referred to an oral and maxillofacial pathologist for final diagnosis and treatment.
>
> Examples of oral diseases include stomatitis, a viral illness; burning mouth or burning tongue syndrome; a yeast infection known as oral candidiasis; recurrent canker sores; and various bone diseases.
>
> The ADA recently concluded a three-year public awareness program on oral cancer. Although the number of new cases and deaths among the general public has been falling slowly for many years, the number of new cases among adults under age 40 has been rising significantly. The goals of the campaign were to boost public awareness of oral cancer and to highlight the dentist's role in identifying the disease.

Newsreel features brief "articles" on current trends and research information. Keeping you informed in the constantly growing and developing field of health care, this feature is your very own medical "journal," conveniently located right inside your textbook!

ZOOM IN

The Computer Explosion

Just a few decades ago, computers were the size of a large room. These early computers were costly to build, difficult to run, and expensive to maintain. As a result, the use of computers was limited to universities, large corporations, and governments.

In the 1980s, however, personal computers became affordable and popular. Now computers touch nearly every facet of life. While processing power and complexity increased, size and cost significantly decreased. Today, smart phones, roughly the size of a credit card, have thousands times more computing power than the machines that helped put the first man on the moon.

The use of computers in health care has paralleled the use of computers in the world in general. Initially, computers were used only in large research hospitals or institutions with vast amounts of funding. Today, however, even a small doctor's office likely maintains patient records electronically. Many health care professionals use tablet PCs as they examine patients to record temperature and other vital statistics directly into patient medical records.

Zoom In features offer useful facts and tips about patient care and other on-the-job practices. Get an inside look into working in health care with these snapshots of key day-to-day aspects of the job. Use this sneak peek to help you make the jump from classroom to job.

End-of-Chapter Features

Chapter Wrap-Up

Don't forget to visit thePoint companion website for additional study resources!

CHAPTER HIGHLIGHTS

- Personal qualities and skills that are important for any successful health care professional include enthusiasm, optimism, self-esteem, honesty, patience, cooperation, organization, responsibility, flexibility, and sociability.

REVIEW QUESTIONS

Matching

1. _____ A belief about the worth or importance of something that acts as a standard to guide one's behavior.
2. _____ Ability to act and make decisions without the help or advice of others.

Multiple Choice

6. Important personal skills for those entering a health care profession include
   - a. organization
   - b. flexibility
   - c. sociability
   - d. all of the above

Completion

11. _____ may be caused by any number of physical, chemical, or emotional factors and can produce both physical and emotional tension.
12. A common stimulant that can stay in a person's system from 6–12 hours is _____.

Short Answer

16. Why are enthusiasm and optimism important qualities for health care workers?

_____

_____

INVESTIGATE IT

1. What are your strongest personal qualities? Which qualities do you feel are your weakest? Use the Internet to search for information on personality assessment resources, such as the Myers-Briggs Type Indicator and StrengthsFinder. In addition, you can also assess your learning style (visual, auditory, or kinesthetic) by using the *MyPowerLearning* diagnostic tool provided with this text. See the inside front cover for details on how to access all the student resources that accompany this text.

RECOMMENDED READING

Eade, Diane M. *Motivational Management; Developing Leadership Skills.* Available at: http://www.adv-leadership-grp.com/Motivational_Article.html.

Heroux, Neomi. *Nutrition and Diet; Clean Living Could Reduce Your Cancer Risk.* Available at: http://www.healthnews.com/nutrition-diet/clean-living-could-reduce-your-cancer-risk-2706.html.

Chapter Wrap-Ups end each chapter on a high note. Providing the triple benefit of review, self-assessment, and suggestions for further exploration, these features are your chapter support network, assuring that you have mastered the chapter content. Well-placed, timely suggestions to visit thePoint are also included here to alert you to even more available resources relevant to the chapter you just finished. In Chapter Wrap-Ups you will find:

- **Chapter Highlights** that provide you with a summary of the chapter in easy-to-skim and remember bullet points. Make sure you take away the chapter's most significant concepts by reviewing this list. Also use Chapter Highlights to study for tests and quizzes.
- **Review Questions** help you check your learning and prepare for exams. A variety of the most effective question formats are given at the end of each chapter to keep you on your toes and engaged. They are organized into groups by type:
  - *Matching, Multiple Choice, and True/False* questions check your retention of the facts you learned in the chapter.
  - *Short Answer and Open-Ended* questions require you to apply your learning of facts and concepts to show that you have not only remembered information but also have a good grasp of its significance for health care.

Answers to the Review Questions are available on the text's companion website http://thePoint.lww.com/DeLaet so that you can check your progress and understanding.

- **Investigate It** activities invite you to take your health care knowledge outside of the classroom into the world at large to develop a fuller understanding of your chosen career. Complete these active learning exercises to connect your education with your future and begin to explore the professional sphere.
- **Recommended Reading** lists offer you suggestions for independent exploration of key chapter topics. Use these well-researched resources to learn more about the aspects of health care that intrigue and excite *you*.
- **Websites for Selected Professional Organizations** lists are your very own library of resources in a convenient and easy-to-locate spot. Visit these websites to obtain additional information about topics covered in the particular chapter,

Electronic Student Resources

Carefully designed online ancillaries available at www.thepoint.lww.com/DeLaet will offer still more opportunity to reinforce and retain skills and concepts learned from the text. In this blockbuster package, students are given free access to a host of captivating tools and exercises. Get a learning advantage with these exciting ***Bonus Features:***

- Interactive question bank
- Skills assessment worksheets
- Spanish English audio glossary
- Heart and breath audio sounds
- Online activities
- Videos and animations
- Free study guide
- Answers to the Checkpoint and Chapter Wrap-Up questions

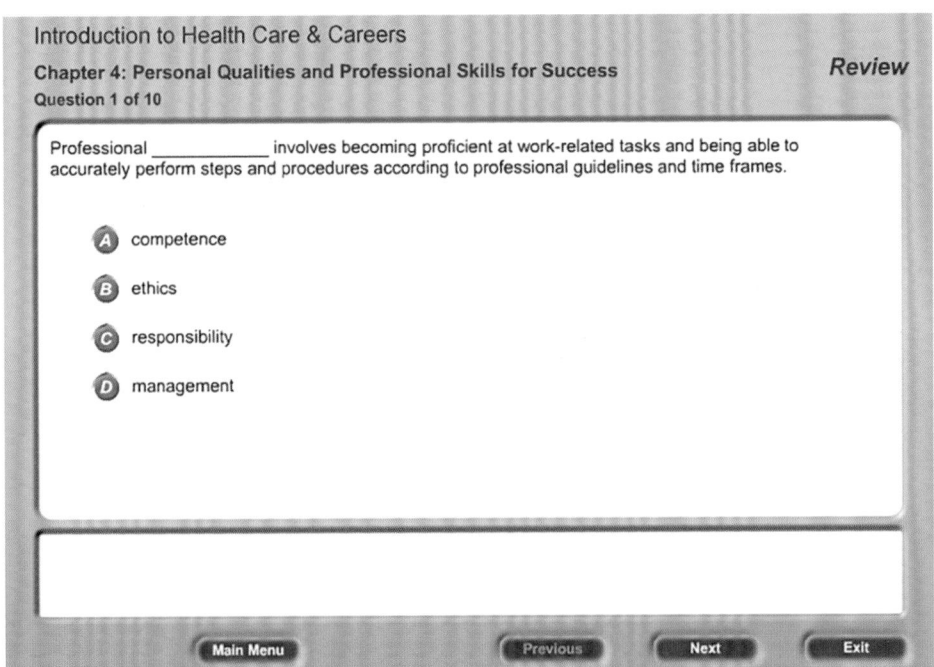

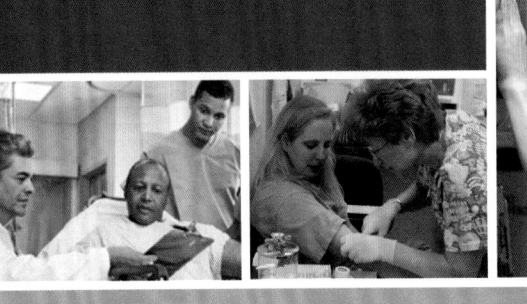

PROFESSIONAL SKILLS

PART

II

This section of the book helps students develop the personal qualities and "soft skills" they'll need in order to become successful health professionals.

CHAPTER 4 outlines the personal and professional attributes and values essential to successful health professionals, as well as tips on stress management and personal health.

CHAPTER 5 discusses communication processes and modes in the health care workplace, as well as communication challenges, recording and reporting, and manners.

CHAPTER 6 covers the issues surrounding cultural and ethnic differences and diversity in health care practice.

CHAPTER 7 focuses on two essential professional skills in health care – critical thinking and problem solving – as well as study skills.

CHAPTER 8 discusses teamwork and leadership and explains why they are important.

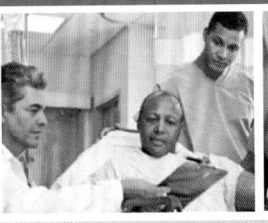
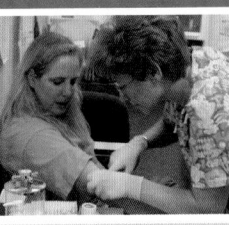
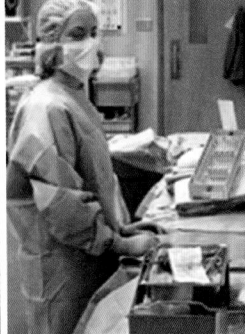

Personal Qualities and Professional Skills for Success

CHAPTER OBJECTIVES

After careful study of this chapter, you should be able to:

* Recognize personal qualities and skills that are important for health care providers.
* List professional attributes that benefit all health care workers.
* Describe values and how they are developed.
* Identify important values in health care.
* Detect stress producers.

* Use strategies to cope with stress.
* Explain the role of nutrition, exercise, and sleep in maintaining a healthy body.
* Recognize the importance of good health behaviors, personal hygiene, and grooming for the health care professional.

KEY TERMS

altruism (AL-true-i-zəm)
autonomy (aw-TON-ă-mē)

competence
human dignity
initiative

public service
stress
time management

value
value system

To find success in any given career, you must possess the qualities essential to your chosen vocation. Professions in health care demand a unique combination of personal and professional qualities. Your attitude and integrity directly affect your ability to perform your work. And while medical skills are central to a majority of health-related jobs, other skills, like time management, are often just as important. Health care professionals should possess certain values, such as a respect for human dignity. They also need to take care of their own health and learn effective ways to cope with stress.

PERSONAL ATTRIBUTES

Most people begin to develop their personality early in life. This includes their interests, behavioral patterns, emotional responses, and attitudes. People's personalities affect how they cope with different situations, both at home and at work. Personal qualities and skills that are important for any successful health care professional include:

- **Enthusiasm.** When you're enthusiastic about your career, it shows in everything that you do. Professionals who are passionate about their work take an active interest in their duties and strive to do the best job possible. Enthusiasm for the care of others is essential in any health care career. Health care professionals with enthusiasm are more likely to do a better job.

student are predictors of those you will project as a health care professional. You can make a commitment to honesty by always doing your own work, avoiding plagiarism, and owning up when you're unprepared or your work isn't completed.

- **Patience.** Another fundamental trait for any health care professional is the ability to remain calm in the midst of difficulties. Complex and stressful situations are a normal part of the health care professional's day. Providers need to demonstrate patience when interacting with both patients and coworkers. Regardless of the circumstances, care workers need to take the time necessary to understand all aspects of a patient's situation. This will help patients feel that their well-being is a top priority.

Enthusiasm is one of many important personal attributes for health care workers.

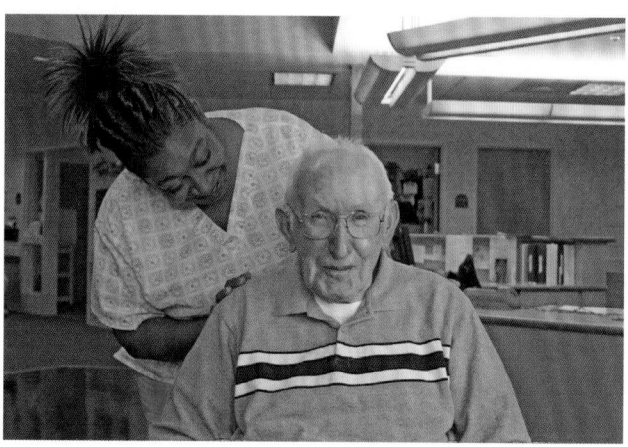

As a health care professional, it's important to be patient and sociable.

- **Optimism.** A positive attitude shapes a person's outlook on different situations and affects job performance. When your attitude remains bright, cheerful, and hopeful, you're more likely to focus on the positive aspects of a given situation. And a positive attitude is contagious: It can help encourage patients to remain focused on the positive aspects of their conditions.
- **Self-esteem.** High self-esteem leads to confidence in one's skills. Health care professionals who project confidence in their own abilities help their patients feel more secure. Coworkers generally develop a greater respect for individuals who are confident in their own abilities. A provider who is self-assured wins the confidence of patients and associates more easily than someone who is insecure and indecisive.
- **Honesty.** Health care professionals must earn the trust of those they serve and those they work with. Providers should always be truthful. This establishes trust in any relationship. The characteristics you display as a

- **Cooperation.** An important personal skill for any health care professional is the ability to interact well with other health care team members. A patient's well-being and care are the most important objective, and all team members should work together toward this same goal. Through teamwork and cooperation, professionals can promote more effective and efficient methods of health care. When it comes to a health care team, all of the team members are important—from the professional handling the medical billing to the member providing direct patient care. To provide the best overall care, workers should show sensitivity to the needs, feelings, and ideas of other team members.
- **Organization.** Being organized is a key to success in almost any career. As a student, you learn early on that organization involves making a place for everything so that items can be easily accessed. The organizational skills you learn as a student and bring to your health care career will be a major professional asset. Materials, supplies, notes, charts, reports, schedules, and

contacts are just some of the many items health care workers reference and work with on a regular basis. Since time is valuable for you, your coworkers, and your patients, the more emphasis you place on getting and staying organized, the more effective you will be in your job and your interactions with others.

- **Responsibility.** Personal responsibility is important in school, work, and life. While in school, you know that you need to complete assignments and turn them in on time, without having to be reminded. This same sense of responsibility should carry over into your health care career. A person's willingness to fulfill obligations and accept responsibility for his or her own actions is extremely important in any health care career. Professionals must be counted on to complete their work in a timely, correct manner, always doing their best.

- **Flexibility.** Most health care positions require workers who are flexible with both their time and talent. Illnesses, emergencies, and other health-related issues don't keep to a regular 9-to-5 work schedule, and neither do those who deal with them. Laboratory and diagnostic tests can vary greatly in the amount of time they require to complete, and workers are often expected to run tests or perform procedures with very little advance notice. New and improved methods of care bring about frequent changes in health-related procedures, and professionals must be willing to acquire and perfect new skills as needed.

- **Sociability.** Since health care professionals interact with a wide range of people every day, sociability is an important interpersonal skill for those in health care professions. Whether providing care to a patient, overseeing office administrative tasks, or assisting a colleague, health care workers should be personable and at ease in work-related social situations. As a health care professional, your ability to interact well with others on a daily basis will directly impact your work, your patients, and other professionals working around you.

✔ **CHECK POINT**

1 Why is a health care worker's personality important?

2 What are some personal attributes a health care professional should possess?

PROFESSIONAL ATTRIBUTES

Professionals are expected to behave in a manner consistent with the standards, views, and behaviors of their profession. Students often begin developing professional

qualities and skills while interacting with faculty members, administrators, and other students. These attributes continue to develop as students begin their health care careers and interact with patients, health care team members, and others in a professional environment.

Your professional qualities will be critical beginning in school and carrying through to your first job interview and throughout your career.

Professional Qualities and Skills

For those who wish to become competent health care professionals, the right personal and professional characteristics are crucial. Like other professionals, health care workers must balance their personal and professional lives. Their personality traits don't affect just one aspect of their lives, but serve them on both a personal and a professional level.

Several qualities and skills are both personal and professional. For example, compassion, empathy, sympathy, honesty, integrity, and accountability are all traits that most people (including health care professionals) use in their personal lives. However, for health care professionals, these traits are also important career tools. Several of these characteristics were described as personal attributes earlier in the chapter, but they also affect a person's professional behavior.

Although different positions demand different qualities and skills, some professional attributes benefit all health care workers. These include:

- **Dedication to public service.** Health care professionals perform a type of **public service**, contributing to the good of society through their work with others. Those professionals who recognize and believe in the value of their work to society likely view their occupations as a calling, or their "life's work." They're attracted to their career because of the importance of the work itself, rather than what they stand to gain personally from the career.

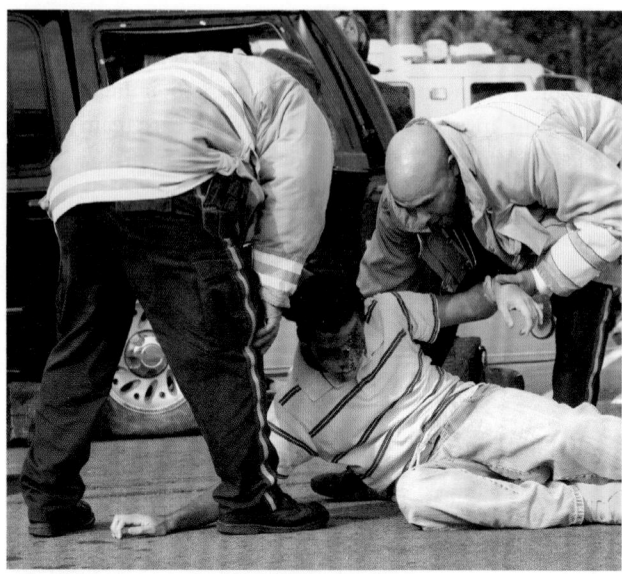

Motivation to help others and dedication to public service can offer health care workers true professional fulfillment.

A person's ability to act selflessly for the well-being of others is an essential attribute for health care workers. Professionals who are dedicated to public service consistently demonstrate attitudes of service to others; perform the duties of their work out of a desire to help, rather than merely an obligation; reap satisfaction from their work; and support and participate in professionally-related activities and groups, such as professional organizations.

- **Being motivated by job fulfillment.** A health care career provides many different rewards. Independence, continuing professional development, and economic security are attractive personal benefits for those in health-related careers. Professionals who choose this type of work because they enjoy it, however, gain a sense of satisfaction and contentment that can't be gained through an attractive salary alone. Those with a true passion, enthusiasm, and strong personal desire to help others are more likely to find fulfillment in a health-related career.

- **Trustworthiness.** Patients, coworkers, and supervisors need to know that they can trust a health care professional. Patients place their most precious possession, their lives, in the hands of their caregivers. Building trust requires dependability. This means that others can count on the person to follow through on promises, live up to agreements, and always be honest. Trustworthiness and dependability begin with regularly attending and being on time for school. Your attendance record is an important reflection of your dependability.

- **Competence.** People exhibit **competence** when they're proficient in what they've learned and are capable of performing related tasks. Competent people are able to follow steps and procedures accurately and in a timely manner. Competence involves a willingness to:

  - *Learn.* To be competent in any health care profession, you must be self-motivated and have a desire to learn. Because new techniques and health care technologies are developed frequently, a commitment to continuing education is necessary in order to maintain your competency.

  - *Change.* New technologies and innovations bring constant change to the field of health care. For the good of patients, health care professionals must be willing to change the way they perform their duties or administer treatments. Professionals shouldn't be resistant to change but should have a desire and enthusiasm for learning new techniques and better ways of doing their jobs.

  - *Admit mistakes.* Competent people willingly accept evaluation of their performance from managers, colleagues, and other professionals. They know that they need to keep the lines of communication open, even if at first they may not like what they hear. Whether in school, at home, or in the workplace, everyone makes mistakes. Mistakes aren't necessarily failures, so accepting and learning from those mistakes is an important trait.

  - *Accept criticism.* Constructive criticism from coworkers, teachers, friends, or patients can help a health care professional improve and become more successful on the job. Professionals should avoid negative reactions to criticism. Anger, excuses, laying the blame elsewhere, or walking away aren't acceptable, or professional, reactions to criticism.

- **Good time management.** People who are able to complete their work in a timely manner, while skillfully handling any tasks, concerns, or issues that arise, are using **time management** skills. A familiar saying in the business world is "time is money." In a health care setting, time may be even more valuable, because a patient's health and well-being may be at risk. Most health care professionals find themselves working on multiple issues at the same time, and these may involve numerous patients, tests, and documents. As you prepare for a health care career, it's imperative that you learn to deal with more than one task at a given time by setting priorities, staying focused on the task at hand, and avoiding procrastination. You can work to improve your time management skills while you are still a student by learning to balance your many different responsibilities.

● **Initiative, problem solving, and critical thinking.** Health care professionals often find themselves in situations that call for quick and decisive action. They need confidence in their own ability to make important decisions, because input from others isn't always immediately available. The ability to act and make decisions without the help or advice of others is known as **initiative**. For example, a care worker takes the initiative when realizing that a patient will need something even before the patient asks. Health care professionals also use initiative when they employ problem solving and critical thinking skills, both of which require independent and logical reasoning. Common sense and sound judgment gained through experience are also valuable assets for health care professionals.

● **Good communication skills.** As an allied health professional, you will frequently interact with other members of the health care team and—depending on the health care profession you choose—you may also interact with patients. Clearly and accurately conveying information in both verbal and written forms will be crucial to your professional success. Communication skills are discussed more fully in Chapter 5, "Health Care Communication."

Professional Attitude and Behavior

Your attitude and behavior in the workplace—with patients, coworkers, and administrators—are the outward display of your personal and professional qualities and skills. Whether treating a patient or consulting with another health professional, it is important to look and behave professionally.

Professional behavior involves not only appropriate use of language, manners, and dress, but also the outward expression of qualities and skills, such as integrity, honesty, and dependability. For example, how you handle mistakes is a reflection of your integrity. The mark of a true professional is the ability to admit mistakes and take full responsibility for all actions. Otherwise, patients and colleagues are likely to lose confidence in your abilities and judgment.

How and what you communicate with your patients and coworkers is a reflection of your honesty. Always present facts in a straightforward manner. It is never acceptable to mislead patients or health care associates.

Being dependable is another outward sign of your personal and professional qualities and skills. In most health care settings, you will work and interact with other members of a health care team, and your colleagues need to be able to depend on you to fulfill your duties and obligations and follow through in a timely manner.

✔ **CHECK POINT**

3 What are some professional attributes that benefit all health care workers?

4 How are professional behavior and personal qualities and skills related?

VALUES

Personal qualities and professional behavior are often a reflection of a person's values. A **value** is a belief about the worth or importance of something that acts as a standard to guide one's behavior. The amount of time and money you devote to relationships, work, study, fitness, leisure, and other activities reveals something about the importance, or value, you attach to them.

Value System

A **value system** is a person's ranked personal principles, which often lead to a personal code of conduct. Your values influence your beliefs about human needs, health, and illness. They also impact how you practice health care and respond to illness. For example, individuals who place a high value on health and personal responsibility often work hard to reach their fitness goals. Individuals who value high-risk leisure activities may attach less value to life and health. Certain values, such as a concern for others and respect for human dignity, are essential for health care workers.

Development of Values

An individual isn't born with values. They're formed throughout one's lifetime from experiences combined with family, cultural, and environmental influences. Values are often formed by observing and modeling the behavior of parents, peers, colleagues, or others. They also may be acquired through instruction from parents or an institution, such as a church or school.

Important Values in Health Care

Values shape decisions in everyday life and are often echoed in one's behavior. These values are also the foundation for personal and professional qualities and skills.

Values supply a framework for a health care professional's career. Examine your personal values to ensure that they match up with the values regarded as essential by others in the profession. For example, health care workers should display tactfulness and discretion when dealing with patients' private medical information and should always value their patients' right to confidentiality. Sensitivity to a patient's situation, condition, and needs is another important value, and this extends to a patient's family as well. Other values that are essential in health care careers are:

- altruism
- respect for patient autonomy
- respect for human dignity

Altruism

A concern for the welfare and well-being of others is known as **altruism**. In health care, altruism is reflected in the provider's concern for the welfare of patients and other health care providers. Professional behaviors that display altruism include:

- demonstrating an understanding of the cultures, beliefs, and perspectives of others
- advocating for patients, particularly the most vulnerable
- taking risks on behalf of patients and colleagues
- mentoring other professionals

Respect for Patient Autonomy

Respect for the right to self-determination, or **autonomy**, is another important value in health care. Providers who value patient autonomy respect patients' rights to make decisions about their health care. Professional behaviors that display respect for patient autonomy include:

- planning a patient's care in partnership with the patient
- honoring the right of patients and their families to make decisions about health care
- providing information so patients can make informed choices

Respect for Human Dignity

To value **human dignity** is to respect the inherent worth and uniqueness of all individuals. Professional behaviors that demonstrate respect for human dignity include:

- providing culturally sensitive care
- protecting the patient's privacy
- preserving the confidentiality of patient and health care provider information
- designing care with sensitivity to individual patient needs

✓ CHECK POINT

5 What is a value system, and how does it impact a person's life?

6 What are some values that are essential in health care careers?

STRESS MANAGEMENT

Everyone feels stress, but professionals must manage it so that it doesn't affect their work. This is especially true for health care professionals. **Stress** is brought on by any number of physical, chemical, or emotional factors. It can produce both physical and emotional tension and has been linked to illnesses and disease. There are different types of stress and different reactions to stress.

◉ ZOOM IN

CPR: A Stress Inducer

Performing cardiopulmonary resuscitation (CPR) on a real person for the first time can be a very stressful situation for any health care provider. Just knowing that a person's life is in your hands is enough to raise your stress level. Health care professionals, however, must find ways to cope with this stress while still functioning, because others count on their skills and professionalism in the most difficult of situations.

When performing CPR, several different actions must be coordinated and recalled in an instant. Emergency situations often can be complicated by additional factors, such as:

- panicky family members
- language barriers
- unknown health conditions

The most important thing to remember when preparing to perform CPR is to stay calm, no matter what happens. This helps reduce any stressful feelings, which will allow you to focus on the patient. With proper training and practice, CPR skills can become almost second nature. In emergency situations, trained health professionals should be able to rely on that training to take over.

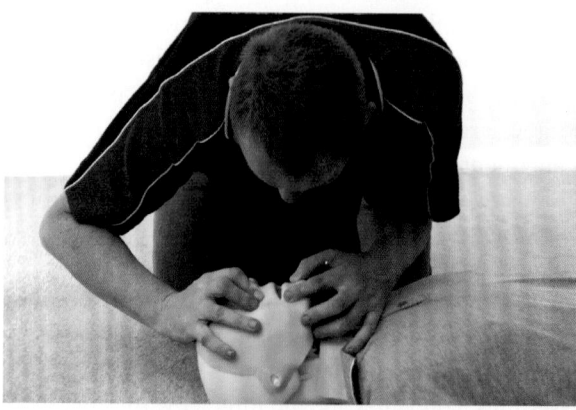

If you are called upon to perform CPR in a real emergency, stay calm and remember your training.

How people manage stress determines whether they react positively or negatively in stressful situations.

Types of Stress

There are two main types of stress—"good" stress and 'bad' stress. "Good" stress, called eustress (yōō-stres), leads to positive reactions. Low levels of stress often motivate people to complete tasks, meet deadlines, and solve problems. Many people experience this type of stress every day. Eustress can be helpful when it motivates a person to accomplish necessary tasks. "Bad" stress, also known as distress, causes negative reactions. High levels of stress often cause people to feel nervous and unfocused or to overeat or not be able to eat at all. Distress can hinder a person's ability to participate in and enjoy normal activities.

Stress Producers

Causes of stress typically depend on each individual's personality. What may be an extremely stressful situation for one person may produce little or no stress for someone else. However, there are some common stress producers that people struggle with every day:
- living a chaotic or disorderly lifestyle
- lacking the ability to say "no"

Even the best health care providers can begin to feel the strain when dealing with life and death situations on a regular basis.

- taking problems and criticism personally
- maintaining unrealistic expectations
- dealing with excessive demands
- remaining inflexible
- suffering self-doubt

For health care workers, excessive demands on their time and talent are often the rule rather than the exception. For some health care workers, handling emergencies is a normal occurrence. However, dealing with life and death situations on a regular basis puts strains and pressures on even the best providers. All of these factors are significant producers of stress.

A person feeling stress generally shows physical signs, such as increased anxiety, agitation, or depression. These signs often are easily detected by others. When a health care worker's attitude turns negative due to stress, it has a harmful effect on both the worker and his or her coworkers.

Strategies for Coping with Stress

Health care providers who are dealing with stress can have a difficult time focusing on the needs of others. It is vital that they develop methods and strategies for coping with stress before it has a chance to get in the way of the main goal—providing the best possible care for each patient.

Stress should be dealt with before it has a chance to lead to overload or burnout. Since stress producers vary from one person to another, individuals must first identify the specific situations, activities, and relationships that bring about stress in their lives. Only they can determine how they will respond to or manage their stress. Some people try to handle their stress by overeating, drinking, or using drugs. However, these strategies eventually produce more stress. Positive strategies that health care professionals can use to handle stress include the following:
- set priorities
- keep life and work simple
- identify and reduce stress producers
- shift thinking
- enlist social support
- relax and renew

Set Priorities

Oftentimes you can become stressed because you feel overwhelmed—too much to do and not enough time to do it. One way to reduce this stress is to set priorities and stick with them; as discussed earlier, this is a key aspect of time management. As you look at each task or commitment on your daily to-do list, determine which are necessary and which are not. Ask yourself, "Is it absolutely necessary that I get this task done today, or would it just be nice to get it done today?" Then move the absolutely necessary tasks to the top of the list. After—and only after—the most important tasks have been accomplished should you consider tackling the other items on the list.

Keep Life and Work Simple

A complicated schedule often produces stress. This is true in personal life, as well as professional life. Basic time management practices can help health care providers avoid this common stress producer. Once you've set priorities, avoid procrastination. Errands and tasks should be combined whenever possible. This not only saves time, it also reduces stress.

You shouldn't feel obligated to participate in optional activities that don't hold any professional or personal value to you. These activities consume time that could be used to complete necessary tasks. Also, remember that it's okay to say "no" to additional projects, responsibilities, or demands when accepting them would over-commit your time. Complaining, though, isn't the same as saying "no." Complaining doesn't relieve stress—it simply reinforces it.

Identify and Reduce Stress Producers

Once you have identified the main stressors in your life, you can stop them from getting out of control. A simple yet effective method anyone can employ is to write down tasks or situations that produce stress. Doing this often leads to new ideas for eliminating the stress. For example, suppose weekday morning activities—getting ready for school or work (showering, dressing, eating breakfast, packing a lunch, driving in rush-hour traffic, and so forth) causes stress for you each day. Writing down each of those stressors may help you think of ways to eliminate some or all of the stress, such as laying out your clothes the night before or beginning your morning routine 15 minutes earlier so that you beat the rush-hour traffic. Keep in mind, however, that there will always be new and changing situations that might cause stress.

Shift Thinking

Health care providers can cope with stress by changing how they think about stressful circumstances, activities, or relationships. They can greatly reduce stress by learning to look at problems or stressful situations as opportunities. Accepting a difficult task as a normal part of the job, rather than complaining about it, can reduce stress.

Enlist Social Support

The poet John Donne wrote, "No man is an island." There are times when everyone needs to depend on others for support. Having a network of supportive friends, family members, or colleagues helps individuals deal with stress. People in your support network may include:

- family members
- friends
- coworkers
- students or classmates
- members of religious groups
- people who share common interests or hobbies

When you discuss your problems or frustrations with others, this can help alleviate stress. And the people in your support network may be able to give advice or offer new perspectives.

Relax and Renew

When stress threatens to get the better of you, it's time to take a break and relax. By pausing the daily routine and engaging in enjoyable activities, you can reduce stress and help yourself cope with the stressful situations in your life.

One way to cope with work stress is spending time with your family.

There are a number of ways to relax, but not everyone finds the same activities relaxing. For some, listening to relaxing music brings relief in a stressful situation. The aroma of a scented candle might bring relief to others. Time spent with family or friends can also help alleviate stress—as long as there are no ongoing conflicts that may surface and bring on additional stress.

A good laugh is a sure way to relieve any stressful situation. Professionals should ensure that they're sensitive to the opinions and feelings of others, however. What is funny to one person may be offensive to another.

✓ CHECK POINT

7 What is the difference between eustress and distress?

8 Why is it important for health care workers to develop methods and strategies for dealing with stress?

PERSONAL HEALTH

Since stress can take a physical toll on your body, taking proper care of your health helps prepare you to manage stressful situations. As a health care professional, you must take good care of yourself so that you will be able to provide proper care to others. You also need to be a good role model for others, including patients, friends, and family. With proper nutrition, exercise, and sleep, you stay on a healthy path to success.

Nutrition

Food can be thought of as fuel for the body. A proper breakfast prepares a person's body for the day ahead. You can give your body the energy it needs by eating healthy food. This also helps your body deal with stress, helps maintain a healthy body weight, and promotes good health generally. A wealth of information about nutrition and healthy eating can be found at MyPyramid.gov, a web site of the U.S. Department of Agriculture.

Exercise

Exercising is an important way to keep your energy level up, and it can help you feel good about yourself. Aerobic activities, such as running, swimming, or cycling, strengthen your heart and offer other benefits as well. People who exercise aerobically:

- have more energy.
- are less stressed and tense.

NEWSREEL

Disease Prevention through Diet and Exercise

Using data collected in Brazil, China, Britain, and the U.S., researchers have found that healthy living brings about a reduction in cancer rates. Findings suggest that a healthier diet, regular exercise, and maintaining a healthy weight could prevent nearly 34 percent of all cancer cases in the U.S. alone.

In the study, conducted by the American Institute for Cancer Research (AICR), along with the U.K.-based World Cancer Research Fund (WCRF), 12 common types of cancers were assessed against diet, exercise, and weight. Researchers wanted to find out how these factors contribute to the different types of cancer. Their conclusion is that, generally, cancer is preventable.

In their report, researchers recommend the development of a public health policy aimed at preventing, not just treating, cancer. They believe that this strategy would be a better way of treating cancer and that it also would reduce the amount of public health funds spent annually. Nutrition experts agreed that prevention is the clear winner in the contest of treatment versus prevention. In addition to cancer, nutrition and exercise also help prevent cardiovascular and other diseases, such as diabetes.

A healthy diet is important for cancer prevention.

World Cancer Research Fund. *Policy and Action for Cancer Prevention.* Available at http://www.dietandcancer report.org/?p=home.

Walking with a friend is one way to relieve stress and preserve your own health.

- maintain an appropriate weight more easily.
- have improved self-esteem.

Choose an activity you truly enjoy. If you try to force yourself to do something you dislike, you won't be motivated to exercise on a regular basis. Another way to stay motivated is to exercise with a friend or in a group.

To receive the full benefits of exercise, work out at least three times a week for 20 to 30 minutes at a time. For even greater health, you can work your way up to exercising four to six times per week. However, it is important to allow at least one day of rest each week.

Sleep

Rest is also important for maintaining a healthy body. When you're well rested, you're able to complete tasks more efficiently. In contrast, feeling tired can increase the amount of stress you feel, which can wear you down even more. Take cues from your body: When you feel tired, give yourself time to rest.

According to the National Institutes of Health, most adults need eight hours of sleep each night. Going to bed at a reasonable hour aids in getting a good night's sleep. However, some people are unable to get a good night's rest, even after going to bed at a reasonable hour. Possible factors that can interfere with a good night's rest include:

- **Caffeine.** Drinking caffeinated beverages in the afternoon or evening can affect your ability to rest at the end of the day. Caffeine is a stimulant that can stay in your system for 6–12 hours. You may not be able to wind down properly in the evenings if caffeine is still affecting your system.
- **Nicotine.** Nicotine is another stimulant. Heavy smokers may experience nicotine withdrawal during the night, which can disrupt their sleep. Waking up multiple times can affect the quality of a person's sleep.
- **Alcohol.** While having a glass of wine or two with dinner makes some people feel drowsy, it can lead to sleep disruptions later on in the night. As a result, individuals may wake up the next morning feeling like they didn't get enough rest.
- **Food.** Eating foods that cause heartburn can interfere with sleep. Heartburn becomes worse after lying down. The amount of food you eat before falling asleep also may affect the quality of your rest.

On a positive note, a healthy diet and regular exercise can greatly improve one's ability to get a good night's sleep. Making changes in those two areas alone may be enough to promote quality sleep. However, when people still have trouble sleeping, they should discuss the problem with their physician. Good rest not only helps a person manage stress, it is also extremely important to physical, emotional, and mental health.

Personal Hygiene and Grooming

First impressions are often based on the image a person projects. As a health care professional, personal hygiene and grooming can set the tone for a patient visit or a meeting with colleagues. Your attire is also important. When your wardrobe consists of appropriate and professional attire, you're perceived as qualified and capable. Most workplaces have some form of a dress code, but general guidelines for professional dress include wearing:

- clean, pressed, and tear-free clothing
- polished, unsoiled, and professionally appropriate shoes
- plain and simple jewelry

This pharmacy worker's hair is neat, her clothing is appropriate, and her make-up and jewelry are unobtrusive.

CHECK POINT

9 Why is it important to eat a healthy diet?

10 What influence does a healthy diet and regular exercise have on sleep?

 ZOOM IN

Hygiene and Grooming

Health care professionals should pay particular attention to their personal hygiene and grooming. People who are ill are often sensitive to odors and extremely susceptible to germs. Keep these things in mind if you come into regular contact with others:

- Daily showers or baths are important.
- Use unscented deodorant.
- Avoid perfume, cologne, fragrant lotion, and scented hair spray.
- Avoid foods that produce offensive odors, such as garlic or onions.
- Hair should be clean and pulled back.
- Fingernails should be trimmed and clean.
- Makeup should be natural, unscented, and lightly applied.

Chapter Wrap-Up

Don't forget to visit the Point companion website for additional study resources!

CHAPTER HIGHLIGHTS

- Personal qualities and skills that are important for any successful health care professional include enthusiasm, optimism, self-esteem, honesty, patience, cooperation, organization, responsibility, flexibility, and sociability.
- A number of qualities and skills are both personal and professional, such as compassion, empathy, sympathy, honesty, integrity, and accountability.
- Professional attributes that benefit all health care workers include dedication to public service; being motivated by job fulfillment; trustworthiness; competence; good time management; initiative, problem solving, and critical thinking; and good communication skills.
- Your values influence your beliefs about human needs, health, and illness, and they impact how you practice health care and respond to illness.
- Stress can result from physical, chemical, and emotional factors. It can produce both physical and emotional tension and has been linked to illnesses and disease.
- Stress can be minimized by setting priorities; keeping life and work simple; identifying and reducing stress producers; shifting thinking; enlisting social support; and taking time to relax and renew.
- Proper nutrition, exercise, and sleep help health care professionals reduce stress and provide better patient care.
- Health care professionals should pay particular attention to personal hygiene and grooming, because people who are ill are often sensitive to odors and susceptible to germs.

REVIEW QUESTIONS

Matching

1. _____ A belief about the worth or importance of something that acts as a standard to guide one's behavior.

2. _____ Ability to act and make decisions without the help or advice of others.

3. _____ The right to self-determination, including the right to make decisions about one's own health care.

4. _____ Contributing to the good of society through one's work with others.

5. _____ Ability to set priorities and complete work in a timely manner.

   a. autonomy   **b.** public service   **c.** initiative   **d.** time management   **e.** value

Multiple Choice

6. Important personal skills for those entering a health care profession include
   - **a.** organization
   - **b.** flexibility
   - **c.** sociability
   - **d.** all of the above

7. One personal quality that is NOT important for health care professionals is
   - **a.** enthusiasm
   - **b.** self-esteem
   - **c.** honesty
   - **d.** none of the above

8. Health care professionals should possess a desire for
   a. recognition
   b. a regular work schedule
   c. public service
   d. all of the above

9. A person's ranking of personal principles, which often lead to a personal code of conduct, is known as
   a. altruism
   b. a value system
   c. human dignity
   d. initiative

10. A concern for the welfare and well-being of others is known as
    a. optimism
    b. altruism
    c. autonomy
    d. human dignity

Completion

11. _____ may be caused by any number of physical, chemical, or emotional factors and can produce both physical and emotional tension.

12. A common stimulant that can stay in a person's system from 6–12 hours is _____.

13. _____ involves a willingness to learn, change, admit mistakes, and accept criticism.

14. Health care professionals value _____ when they respect the inherent worth and uniqueness of all individuals and protect patients' privacy and confidentiality.

15. The two main types of stress are eustress and _____.

Short Answer

16. Why are enthusiasm and optimism important qualities for health care workers?

   _____

   _____

17. What are some ways health care workers can show patience and demonstrate that a patient's well-being is the top priority?

   _____

   _____

18. How do a person's values develop?

   _____

   _____

19. Briefly describe five common stress producers.

   _____

   _____

   _____

   _____

   _____

20. What are some positive strategies that health care professionals can use to handle stress?

   _____

   _____

INVESTIGATE IT

1. What are your strongest personal qualities? Which qualities do you feel are your weakest? Use the Internet to search for information on personality assessment resources, such as the Myers-Briggs Type Indicator and StrengthsFinder. In addition, you can also assess your learning style (visual, auditory, or kinesthetic) by using the *MyPowerLearning* diagnostic tool provided with this text. See the inside front cover for details on how to access all the student resources that accompany this text.

2. Playing games can actually be a great way to manage stress. Search the Internet and other available resources to locate stress management games. Use the search phrase *stress management games* to begin your Internet search.

RECOMMENDED READING

Eade, Diane M. *Motivational Management; Developing Leadership Skills*. Available at: http://www. adv-leadership-grp.com/Motivational_Article.html.

Heroux, Neomi. *Nutrition and Diet; Clean Living Could Reduce Your Cancer Risk*. Available at: http://www.healthnews.com/nutrition-diet/clean-living-could-reduce-your-cancer-risk-2706. html.

Medical Library Association. *Competencies for Lifelong Learning and Professional Success: The Educational Policy Statement of the Medical Library Association. Personal Attributes That Contribute to Success*. Available at http://www.mlanet.org/education/policy/success.html.

Quan, Kathy. *Skills for Health Care Workers; Beyond a Desire to Help is a Need for Talents and Abilities*. Available at http://healthfieldmedicare.suite101.com/article.cfm/skills_for_health_care_ workers.

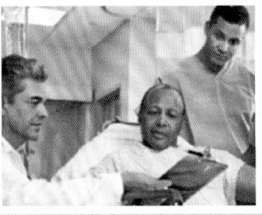
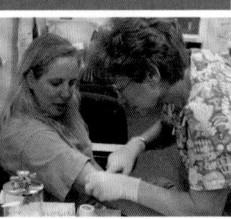
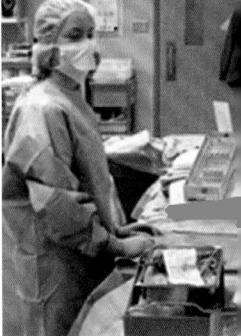

Health Care Communication

CHAPTER OBJECTIVES

After careful study of this chapter, you should be able to:

✳ Explain how the communication process is important in health care.

✳ Differentiate among the three most common modes of communication and how they are used in health care.

✳ Describe the different methods and types of patient communication.

✳ Communicate successfully with patients.

✳ Explain the importance of accuracy and security in health care recording and reporting.

✳ Identify the most common communication challenges in health care and know how to overcome them.

✳ Use good telephone manners in communication.

KEY TERMS

body language
channel of communication
chronological organization
clarification
communication

comparison organization
feedback
kinesics (ki-NĒ-siks)
message

non-language sounds
paraphrasing
problem-oriented organization

proxemics (präk-SĒ-miks)
reflecting
source

ommunication, defined as an exchange of information, is important throughout the health care system. Whether your communication involves assessment, diagnosis, treatment, or documentation, you regularly share information about a patient's health or other information. Therefore, precision and confidentiality are imperative in all aspects of health care communications.

Excellent communication skills are crucial for all health care professionals. The clear and accurate transfer of information ensures that every person involved with a patient's care is using the same information. Breakdowns in communication in the form of incomplete patient histories, test inaccuracies, billing miscalculations, or treatment oversights can have devastating consequences. Prescription errors, misdiagnoses, or even death can result from communication failures.

COMMUNICATION PROCESS

The communication process involves the sending and receiving of information between two or more individuals It is the foundation of society and the most primary aspect of the patient-provider relationship. Without communication, it would be impossible to share experiences, gain knowledge, arrange treatments, or establish and maintain records. By nature, humans are social beings, and human needs are met through association with other humans. The ability to communicate is basic to human functioning and well-being.

In health care, the communication process often begins with a patient need that must be addressed. Three central elements are present within any communication process (Figure 5-1):

• sender—the person who transmits the message
• message—the information the sender conveys
• receiver—the person who gets the message

There is also a fourth, optional, element within the communication process:

• feedback—evaluation by the receiver and sender to verify that both understand the message that was sent

The communication process begins with a message. The sender, or **source**, of the message is the person or group that begins the communication process. The **message** comes from the source. It may be spoken words from a patient describing a symptom, information obtained during a consultation or telephone conversation, data entered in a patient's chart, written correspondence, or even a gesture.

Once a message is sent, the receiver interprets it. In most conversations, people shift back and forth

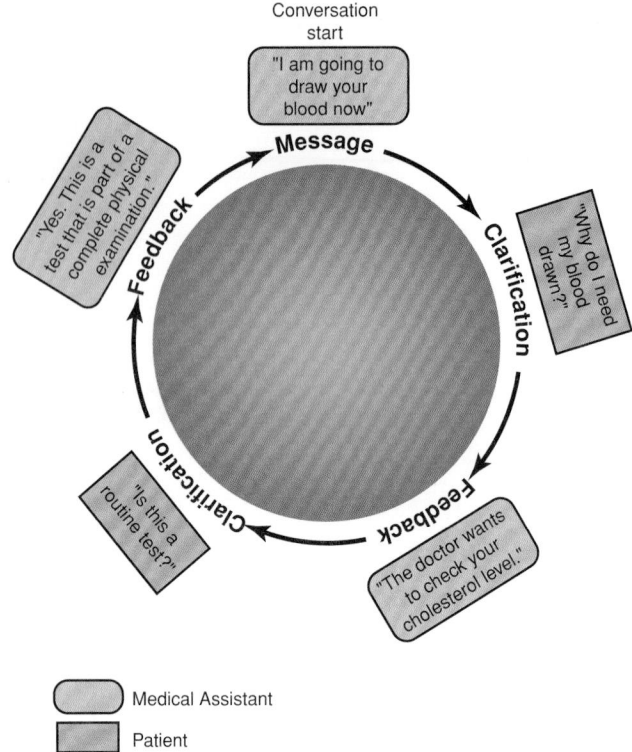

Figure 5-2 Example of flow of communication between a medical assistant and a patient.

between the roles of sender and receiver. Once you, as the receiver, understand the message, you decide how to respond. When you require **clarification**, or a better understanding of a message, your response is sent back to the sender. This is called **feedback**. For example, you might give a patient instructions about how to care for an incision at home—in which case you're the sender. The patient then asks a question that shows that he or she has not fully understood your instructions. This feedback from the patient gives you an opportunity to clarify your instructions. Figure 5-2 illustrates the flow of communication.

The **channel of communication** is the medium by which a message is sent. The most common channel is speaking. However, messages can also be sent and received through sight and touch. As a health care professional, you will use all three of these channels to communicate with patients and colleagues alike.

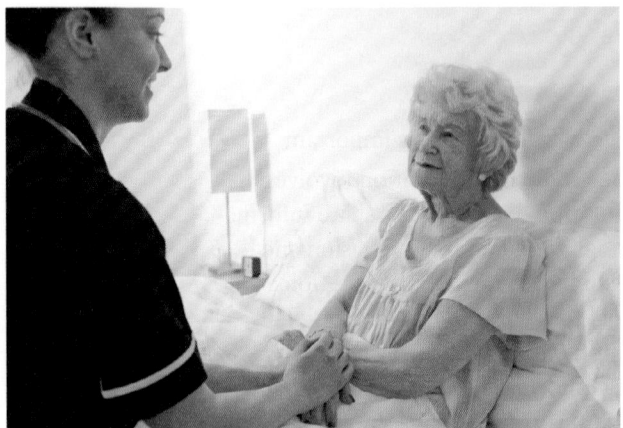

Figure 5-1 Communication in health care revolves around addressing patient needs.

> **✔ CHECK POINT**
>
> **1** What three elements are present in all forms of communication?
>
> **2** What is the optional fourth element of communication?

ZOOM IN

Clear Communication

Anyone who has visited a physician is probably familiar with a standard physical exam. Although the steps in this exam are routine for many patients, you should not assume that all patients understand exactly what they're expected to do. Directions should be given clearly to patients throughout the exam.

For example, one procedure involves a nurse or doctor listening to a patient's lungs with a stethoscope, while instructing the patient to breathe deeply in and out. This procedure verifies that the lungs are clear, healthy, and functioning well. The practitioner also directs the patient to hold his or her breath for a moment.

Next, the patient is instructed to breathe out again. At this point in the exam, one might say to the patient, "I want you to expire now." Although this phrase is technically correct, the word *expire* has different meanings and may not be interpreted correctly by the patient. It would be much better to say, "You can breathe out now," or "I need you to exhale."

COMMUNICATION MODES

Information can be exchanged by different methods. The three most common modes of communication are:

- verbal communication
- nonverbal communication
- written communication

A sender's words (either verbal or written) and body language (nonverbal) often vary depending on the sender's socioeconomic background, culture, age, and education. For example, if you say, "I want you to expire now," some patients might think you mean "I want you to die," rather than "I want you to exhale"—the medical meaning of "expire" means something totally different from its other meaning, as understood by someone with a different background and education.

Verbal and nonverbal communication often happen at the same time.

Verbal Communication

In verbal communication, spoken words are used to exchange information. Because you choose the words you want to communicate, this is a deliberate form of communication. It is also the most common form of communication.

Good verbal communication skills are an important and necessary tool for all health care professionals. Whether scheduling appointments, providing patient education, arranging referrals, or sharing information with a colleague, you should follow a few simple verbal communication guidelines:

- Always use a polite tone. A pleasant manner of speaking helps put people at ease.
- Always use proper English. Using bad grammar or slang expressions implies that you are uneducated and unprofessional.
- Speak respectfully to colleagues and patients. Never "talk down" to someone.
- Avoid using an overly technical vocabulary. Many patients are unfamiliar with lengthy medical terms.

Tips for Successful Verbal Communication

Several factors are involved in successful communication between health care professionals and their patients and colleagues.

Language. The language a person uses often contributes to the first impression the person makes. Speaking clearly and concisely and using terms that patients can understand helps convey that you are competent, intelligent, and caring. For the most part, avoid medical terminology when speaking to patients. Instead, use normal, everyday language. For example, instead of saying, "The nurse will be catheterizing you tomorrow for a urinalysis," you might say, "Tomorrow the nurse will get a sample of your urine by putting a small tube into your bladder." As you speak, watch the other person to see whether your message is making the desired impression. If not, you should reword the message and try again.

Manner and Tone. The volume and tone of your voice can convey many things, including anger, caring, happiness, excitement, and much more. You can calm or agitate a patient with your tone of voice. If you drop a pile of paperwork into a patient's lap and say, "Fill this out; it's self explanatory," while using a hurried manner and tone, the patient hears, "I do not have time to deal with you right now, so do not ask any questions."

Competence. It is important for patients to trust your abilities as a health care professional, because they're putting their health and well-being into your care. You gain trust by being knowledgeable, honest, and dependable—in a word, competent. All information you give to patients should be up-to-date and accurate. You need to convey confidence and certainty in what you're saying, while still being able to acknowledge your limitations. When you say to a patient, "This is a new drug the doctor has ordered; let me tell you about it," you reassure the patient that you're not only knowledgeable, but very thorough in how you perform your job.

Verbal Encouragement. One easy way to make people feel good about a situation is through verbal encouragement. This is a great way to help patients feel like they're partners in health care communication. To encourage patients to speak openly, you should always appear receptive. Use verbal encouragement, such as saying "yes?" or "go on," to persuade patients to share all of their concerns before they begin patient treatment.

Humor. Mild and respectful humor can be an effective means of minimizing status differences between a patient and caregiver. You must be careful, however, and ensure that your comments are sensitive and respectful to all people. What one person may think is funny, another person may consider disrespectful or even hurtful.

Non-Language Sounds

Another form of communication, non-language sounds, may transmit messages unintentionally. **Non-language sounds** include sighs, sobs, laughs, grunts, and so on. These sounds can give spoken words very different meanings. For example, people who say, "Everything is fine," while sobbing, are sending a message that they may not feel fine at all.

Assertive Communication

When interacting with patients, family members, and colleagues, you should communicate in a way that demonstrates respect for all parties. Assertive behaviors,

ZOOM IN

Seeing Eye-To-Eye

Looking someone directly in the eyes has different meanings in different cultures. In the U.S., good eye contact usually implies that a person is honest and concerned. However, people from other cultures may feel differently about eye contact.

- In some cultures, including Asian and Native American cultures, direct eye contact is viewed as disrespectful. It may even seem sexually suggestive or aggressive.
- In other cultures, including Latino cultures, avoiding eye contact or casting the eyes downward is a sign of respect.

which are a hallmark of professional relationships, are different from aggressive behaviors, which are harsh and destructive.

The key to assertiveness is open, honest, and direct communication. "I" statements like "I feel . . ." and "I think . . ." play an important role in assertive statements. Table 5-1 gives examples of assertive and nonassertive speech.

The four basic components of an assertive response or approach are:
- having empathy
- describing feelings or the situation
- clarifying one's expectations
- anticipating consequences

For example, you might communicate in the following ways with your instructor:
- *Having empathy*: "I know you work hard each week to give us good clinical assignments."
- *Describing feelings*: "I want to share with you how the patient felt after I taught her to give her own insulin injection."
- *Clarifying expectations*: "I understand that each week I need to do teaching with my patients."
- *Anticipating consequences*: "Can we review the test together, as I did not do as well as I thought I would on it, and I'm afraid of not doing well in the course."

Characteristics of an assertive demeanor include having a confident, open body posture; making eye contact; using clear, concise "I" statements; and sharing thoughts, feelings, and emotions honestly.

An assertive work attitude is characterized by:
- a capacity to work with or without supervision
- the ability to remain calm under pressure
- a willingness to ask for help when necessary

Table 5-1 Examples of Assertive and Nonassertive Speech

	Assertive	Nonassertive
Health care worker to coworker	"I know we all lose track of time occasionally, but I'm finding it harder and harder to cover for you when you take extra time for lunch. I don't think it's fair for your patient and me to have to wait an extra 30 minutes every day for you to come back from lunch. Can we talk about this?"	"Huh? No, I didn't really mind. Luckily I wasn't too busy today." Thought: "What a sucker I am. Now I'll have to grab a quick bite so that I can get back on time."
Health care worker to another professional at a supervisory level	"I know we talked about this patient's condition before, but I've collected some new data. I believe a change in his treatment should be discussed."	"Um . . . yes I know you already changed the treatment. It's just that I thought it still wasn't working. Maybe I didn't give it enough time. Thanks for listening to me anyway. I'm sorry to bother you with this."
Student to Preceptor (Mentor/Trainer)	"Can you help me with this procedure? I reviewed the procedure steps, but I'd appreciate your talking me through this because I've never done it before."	"Uh . . . I'm sorry to be such a pain again. I have to do this procedure and don't know where to begin. I know you must be busy, but, uh, is there any way you might have time for me?"

- the ability to give and accept compliments
- honesty in admitting mistakes and taking personal responsibility for them

Active Listening

Active listening is necessary to ensure that messages are correctly received and interpreted. Failure to use active listening can result in poor patient care. By listening actively, you can help ensure that you understand completely what a patient or colleague is trying to communicate. As a result, you're more likely to gain valuable information.

Being an active listener helps you establish positive relationships with patients and other health care workers.

Being an active listener helps you establish positive relationships with patients and other health care workers. Although you listen with your ears, you can't truly understand what another person is saying unless you also use your brain. You must concentrate to absorb what another person is saying. To listen actively, follow these guidelines:

- Give your full attention to the person who is speaking.
- Don't interrupt.
- Pay attention to the speaker's body language and nonverbal cues.

ZOOM IN

Digital Communication

In today's high-tech, fast-paced world, many of the messages people send and receive are handled digitally. Email, texting, and instant messaging are all common methods. Educational materials, seminars, and even continuing education courses can be accessed online without leaving the comfort of home or office.

Although technology brings efficiency and convenience to the process of exchanging information, health care professionals must not overlook the human element in communication. When delivering information, such as a patient's diagnosis, test results, or prognosis, the value of face-to-face contact between a health care professional and patient cannot be overstated. At the very least, important or sensitive information should be relayed through a telephone call. While digital communication is a highly effective tool for some aspects of health care, it must be used responsibly so that it does not diminish a patient's overall health care experience.

Nonverbal Communication

Nonverbal communication, also known as **body language**, relays a message without speaking or writing a single word. Because nonverbal behavior is less consciously controlled than verbal behavior, it often tells others more about what you're feeling than your spoken words. It is estimated that between 60 percent and 90 percent of your true emotions are conveyed through body language. For example, you may say to a patient, "I would be happy to sit here and talk with you"; but if you glance nervously at your watch every few seconds, you convey a different message to the patient. You should also pay attention to the patient's body language. For example, a patient's body language can provide feedback that shows whether they understand what you're saying or not. Table 5-2 lists a few examples of body language and what each of them can mean.

There are several different forms of nonverbal communication, including kinesics, proxemics, and touch. Eye contact is another important element of nonverbal communication.

Eye Contact

Maintaining good eye contact shows that you're interested in other people and what they're saying. When you look away during a conversation, you may give the impression that you think the speaker's message isn't important enough for your full attention. Likewise, good eye contact when you're speaking adds a sense of truthfulness to your message. If you look away from a patient or colleague while delivering a message, you will seem uncomfortable with what you're saying, and the receiver will become uncomfortable as well.

Table 5-2 Nonverbal Communication/Body Language Chart	
Body Movements or Expressions	**Meanings**
Leaning back in a chair, yawning, looking at a clock, shifting, or shuffling feet	● Boredom ● Fatigue ● Disinterest ● Impatience
Smiling, nodding agreement, keeping eye contact, and leaning forward	● Interest ● Enthusiasm ● Agreement ● Humor
Avoiding eye contact, frowning, scratching head, and pursing lips	● Confusion ● Disagreement ● Suppressing thoughts or feelings ● Anger ● Suspicion

Kinesics or Body Movement

One of the most powerful ways for a human to communicate nonverbally is through **kinesics**, or body movement. Body movements include facial expressions, gestures such as shrugging, and eye movement. Portrayed moods and emotions may either emphasize or contradict what's being said. Patients' faces often reveal their true inner feelings, such as anger, despair, or fear, which otherwise may be concealed in a conversation.

Proxemics or Personal Space

Personal space, or **proxemics**, is like an invisible bubble that surrounds you. If others move inside this bubble while talking to you, it may make you feel uncomfortable. Everyone's personal space is somewhat different. How close you normally stand to another person during a conversation most likely depends on your relationship with that person. Here are some interesting facts about personal space:

● Personal space is larger when talking to a stranger. For example, most people in the U.S. like to be about four to seven feet away from each other when holding a conversation with a stranger.
● The better you know the person you're talking with, the smaller the personal space can be between the two of you.
● Personal space is typically larger between two men than between two women.
● Personal space differs from culture to culture. For example, many Europeans are comfortable with a personal space that is about half of what Americans prefer. As a result, some Americans feel uncomfortable when talking with someone from Europe who is standing closer.

When you provide care or perform tests on a patient, you will probably need to enter that person's personal space. It is important that you approach the patient in a professional manner and explain clearly what you intend to do. Your explanation and professionalism will help the patient feel more comfortable and less anxious about what will take place.

Touch

Touch is experienced in many ways. Handshakes, pats, and kisses are just a few of the ways people communicate through touch. Research shows that touching can create either positive or negative feelings. Feelings are positive when a touch is perceived to be natural. On the other hand, when a touch is perceived to be manipulative or insincere, negative feelings will result. For some patients, a gentle touch provides emotional support. For others, however, it may produce a negative response.

When touching a patient, watch for nonverbal cues, such as expressions and body language, to determine how the patient feels about being touched.

Here are some guidelines to help you effectively transmit and receive nonverbal communications.

1. Maintain proper personal space, position, and posture. Your nonverbal communication is sending messages to the patient too.
   - Always look the patient in the face and be at eye level. Be aware of cultural differences when it comes to eye contact.
   - If the patient is sitting, you should sit too (if possible).
   - Use proper gestures.
   - Use touch, if the situation is appropriate.
2. Observe the patient's facial expressions and posture. People's nonverbal messages can differ from their verbal ones.
   - If the patient's nonverbal cues differ from what he or she is saying, ask appropriate questions to clarify the mixed message.
   - If a patient's verbal response still doesn't match what you're seeing, tell your supervisor of your concerns.

When touching a patient, watch for nonverbal cues, such as expressions and body language, to determine how the patient feels about being touched.

Written Communication

Another means of communication in health care is written communication. The ability to write clearly and accurately is important in the health care profession. As a health care professional, you may be responsible for one or more different types of written communications, such as:

- agendas for meetings
- letters
- messages
- patient charts
- consultation reports
- patient instructions
- laboratory reports

Patient charts and other written communications are key elements of health care communication.

Your written communication should be concise and use language that all parties will understand. Proper grammar may be even more important in written communication than in verbal communication. People may eventually forget about an incorrectly spoken word or term, but a written mistake will often be read many times. Grammatical errors reflect badly on the writer, as well as the writer's practice or office.

Also take enough time to ensure that every word is spelled correctly. As explained in Chapter 10, "Medical Terminology Basics," just one incorrect letter in a word can completely change the meaning of a medical term. Because written communications, like patient charts and lab reports, are accessed often, incorrectly spelled words can have devastating consequences for both health care professionals and patients.

Preparation is important for any form of written communication. Plan the content of a document before you begin to write. Written information should be organized logically. The three basic ways of organizing information in written communications include:

- **Chronological organization.** When information is written using **chronological organization**, items are presented in sequence, from the earliest date to the most recent date. For example, this organization might be used when writing about a physician's background in a brochure for new patients.
- **Problem-oriented organization.** When information is written using **problem-oriented organization**, a problem is identified and explained, and then instructions are given for correcting the problem. For example, a letter written to a patient reporting abnormal blood

test results would first state the problem, such as a low potassium level, then explain the possible causes of the problem, and finally suggest treatments and follow-up procedures.

- **Comparison organization.** When two or more pieces of information are compared, this is known as **comparison organization.** For instance, when a health care administrator writes a report to the board of directors that describes the pros and cons of two different electronic health record systems, this approach is being used.

The organization of written information is discussed in more depth in Chapter 11, "Medical Documentation."

Interoffice communications, such as memos and meeting notes, are typically less formal than other forms of communication, because they're not usually seen by patients or other professionals outside the practice. Nonetheless, they require the same preparation, composition, and editing as other written communications. Most computer software programs contain templates for the most common forms of written correspondence. These programs usually have a basic spell-check feature. Although this feature is helpful, a basic spell-check program cannot handle all medical terminology. Specialized medical dictionary software can be used when editing health care documents. These programs are discussed in Chapter 9, "Computers and Other Technology."

Medical Writing

Medical writing requires even more accuracy and clarity than business or personal correspondence. You must pay very close attention to detail when writing medical letters, reports, and other documents. These items may be placed in a patient's permanent medical record. Mistakes in written medical communications could cause injury or death, lawsuits, or professional harm to you or your employer. Some important guidelines for medical writing include the following:

Spelling. Always proofread your written communications. While the spell-check features in word-processing programs can be a great help, they are not a substitute for proofreading. For example, the spell-check feature in a word-processing program cannot find mistakes when words are spelled correctly but misused. For example, the term *mucus* refers to a sticky secretion, while the term *mucous*, spelled with the letter *o*, refers to the membrane that secretes mucus. If the word *mucus* is accidentally misspelled as *mucous*, the spell-check feature would consider the word correct, even though it is actually incorrect.

Capitalization. Pay special attention to how words and abbreviations are capitalized. Although a word may appear to be incorrectly typed or written, take the time to verify the information with the attending physician or other professional before changing it. For example, *m-BACOD* is a very different treatment from *M-BACOD*. Medical terminology is discussed in more detail in Chapter 10.

Abbreviations and Symbols. Using abbreviations and symbols saves time when making hand-written notes. However, when you are typing medical information, words should be spelled out. For example, *PM* (time) is commonly understood, but *NPO* ("nothing by mouth") is not. Most offices keep a list of approved abbreviations and symbols commonly used at the office. You should be familiar with the list at your office. (See Appendix D for a list of abbreviations and symbols commonly used in health care.)

Numbers. The numbers one through ten are usually spelled out in medical writing. There are exceptions, however:

- Units of measurement should always be written as numbers, no matter how small (for example, 5 mg).
- Numbers referring to an obstetrical patient's condition are not spelled out. (For example, the numbers in "the patient is gravid 3, para 2" should not be converted to words.)

✔ **CHECK POINT**

3 What are the three most common modes of communication?

4 What are the four basic components of an assertive response or approach?

5 Why shouldn't you rely solely on a spell-checker to find spelling errors?

COMMUNICATION WITH PATIENTS

One of the most challenging aspects of working in any health care profession is communicating accurately and effectively with patients. Whether taking information from a new patient, discussing a course of treatment, or revealing test results, good communication between you and the patient is essential to the patient's care.

Patient Interviews

Many careers in health care require that you interview patients. You could be responsible for gathering initial information from a patient or for updating existing information. When conducting an interview, keep the following points in mind:

- Listen actively.
- Ask appropriate questions.
- Record information accurately.

A typical task in many health care careers is conducting patient interviews.

During a patient interview, you must demonstrate professionalism and concern for the patient's privacy. Conduct the interview in a private area, and begin by introducing yourself. Being organized is the key to good interviewing. Know the questions that you're going to ask and the order of the questions before the interview begins. Be prepared to record patient answers, either on paper or electronically. (Chapter 11 provides in-depth information on medical documentation). Do not answer phone calls or attend to other distractions until you have completed the interview. Finally, when leaving the room, let the patient know who will be in next to see him or her and approximately how long it will take. For example, you might say, "Dr. Bradshaw will be in to see you next. It should be just a few minutes."

Basic Interview Techniques

The methods and procedures used during patient interviews vary by provider. However, you should be familiar with six basic interviewing techniques:

- reflecting
- paraphrasing
- clarification
- open-ended questioning
- summarizing
- silences

Reflecting. When you use open-ended statements to repeat back what you have heard from a patient, you are **reflecting**. With this technique, you do not complete a sentence but leave it up to the patient to do so. For example, you might say, "Mrs. Gomez, you were saying that when your back hurts you . . ." Reflecting encourages the patient to make further comments and ensures that the patient's meaning is correctly understood. It also helps bring the patient back to the subject if the conversation begins to drift. Reflecting is a useful tool, but you should be careful not to overuse it, as some patients find it annoying to have their words constantly parroted back to them.

Paraphrasing. Restating or **paraphrasing** means using your own words or phrases to repeat what you have heard. Paraphrasing helps verify that you have understood correctly what has been said. It also allows patients the opportunity to clarify their thoughts or statements. A paraphrased statement typically begins with a phrase like "You're saying that . . ." or "It sounds as if . . . ," followed by the rephrased content.

Clarification. If you're confused about some of the information you've received from a patient, you need to ask the patient to give an example of the situation being described. For instance, you might ask, "Can you describe one of these dizzy spells?" The patient's example should help you better understand what the patient is saying. It also provides insight into how the patient perceives the situation.

Open-Ended Questioning. The best way for you to obtain information is by asking open-ended questions that require the patient to formulate an answer and provide details. Open-ended questions usually begin with the words *what*, *when*, or *how*. For example:

- "What medications did you take this morning?"
- "When did you stop taking your medication?"
- "How did you get that large bruise on your arm?"

Be careful about asking "why" questions, because they often sound judgmental or accusing. For example, asking "Why did you do that?" or "Why didn't you follow the directions?" may make patients feel that you are criticizing their behavior, and they may become defensive and uncooperative. Instead, you might ask, "What parts of the instructions were unclear?" or "How can we help you follow these instructions?"

Generally, avoid closed-ended questions that allow patients to give one-word answers like "Yes" or "No." For example, if you ask, "Are you taking your medication?" the patient may say "Yes" but may not be taking all of the medications that have been prescribed or may not be taking the proper dosage of each medication. However, by asking questions like "What medications do you take every day?" and "How many of those tablets do you take each day?" you will get answers from the patient that will give you a clearer understanding of whether the patient is taking the correct dosage.

However, keep in mind that sometimes closed-ended questions are necessary. For example, you might ask, "Are you still having pain?" after administering medication. Still, in many cases you might need to follow up with open-ended questions.

Summarizing. Use the summarizing technique to review the information that you have obtained and to give the patient another chance to clarify statements or correct misinformation. This method also helps you organize complex information or events in sequential order. For example, if a patient has been feeling dizzy and stumbling a lot, you might summarize by saying, "You told me that you have been feeling dizzy for the past three days and that you often stumble as you're walking. Is that correct?" The patient then has a chance to verify the information or correct something you may have misunderstood.

Silences. Periods of silence sometimes occur during an interview. Some people are uncomfortable with prolonged silences and feel a need to break the silence with words. However, silences can be beneficial. They are a natural part of conversation and can give patients time to formulate their thoughts, reconstruct events, evaluate their feelings, or assess what has already been said. During moments of silence, you can gather your own thoughts and formulate any additional questions you may have.

New Patient Interviews

New patient interviews cover several topics, and patient information is recorded in a patient medical record. (You will learn more about new patient interviews in Chapter 11.) Topics covered during a new patient interview include the patient's medical and family history, a brief review of body systems, the patient's social history, and medications the patient is taking. Important information that you need to obtain from a patient during a new patient interview is listed in Table 5-3.

Established Patient Interviews

An interview of an established patient, or a patient that you or your practice has seen before, is quite different. When interviewing an established patient, you will:
- Review the patient's chart for information about health problems.
- Make a list of questions to ask the patient in order to update health information, including current medical problems and any changes in health.
- Confirm that the patient is still on the medications and treatments listed in the chart.
- Ask about any known allergies.
- Record patient information.

Table 5-3 Key Subjects in a New Patient Interview	
Key Subjects	**What You Need to Know**
Medical History	Any hospitalizations and dates
	Any surgeries and dates
	Any chronic problems
Female Patients	Any pregnancies and complications
	Any miscarriages, stillbirths, or abortions
Family History	Age and health of parents (if deceased, cause and age at death)
	Age and health of brothers and sisters
	Any genetic problems in family
Body System Review	General questions about all body systems: cardiovascular, pulmonary, integumentary, musculoskeletal, sensory, neurological, gastrointestinal, immune, endocrine, urological, and reproductive
Social History	Alcohol use
	Tobacco use
	Any drug use
	Hobbies
	Education
	Employment
Medications	Any prescription medicines (when taken and how much)
	Any over-the-counter medicines (when taken and how much)
	Any vitamins and herbal supplements

Patient Education

Patient education is more than just telling a patient which medications to take or suggesting which lifestyle behaviors to change. Effective communication is the key component in educating patients and includes:
- helping the patient accept illness
- involving the patient in the knowledge-gaining process
- providing positive reinforcement

Both active listening and interviewing skills are central to the patient education process. You also need to be aware of current medical issues, discoveries, and trends, as well as useful community services that are available in your area (Table 5-4).

The patient education process includes these five steps:
1. **Assess.** Collect information about the patient's current health care needs and abilities.
2. **Plan.** Establish goals and objectives. These are more valuable and meaningful when patient input is included.

ON LOCATION

Handling Patients' Questions

Assume you are working in a physicians' office where you're one of the first contacts with patients. The next patient is a woman in her early 30s who recently gave birth. She has only lived in town for a few months, and this is her first visit to your office. Immediately after you introduce yourself, the patient begins telling you the reasons for her visit and asks a barrage of questions:

"I've been having pains in my neck, chest, abdomen, and legs off and on for the past six months. The pains seem to be worse at night. I've been so busy with our recent move and our two-month old baby that I really haven't had time to see a doctor about this before now. I'm very concerned it could be something serious. Do you think the pains are all related? Or could my chest pains be caused by a heart problem? My father suffered from heart disease. I wonder if the headaches are related to stress. But if they're stress related, would I also have pains in my chest, abdomen, and legs? Diabetes runs in my family. Could my symptoms be related to that?"

Because she is a new patient, you need to collect her complete medical history before the doctor performs an exam. Once the medical history is taken, how would you respond to the questions she's asked so far?

Remember that it is inappropriate for you to respond to most of her questions. You should explain that she will have an opportunity to ask the doctor her questions.

---

3. **Implement.** Begin the training process, ensuring that the lines of communication between you and the patient remain open.

4. **Evaluate.** Determine how well the patient is adapting to the course of action and whether or not the patient is applying the new information to daily life.

5. **Document.** All conversations, events, and results related to the patient education process should be accurately recorded.

If possible, find a quiet room where you can talk with the patient. Allow sufficient time so that the patient does not feel rushed or interrupted. Patients should feel that

---

Table 5-4 Guidelines for Identifying and Using Community Resources

Being aware of community resources is important to your role as a patient educator. Follow these guidelines to develop and use a list of community resources.

1. Determine what types of resources are most useful for the patients your employer sees. This often depends on your employer's medical specialty, but patients also may have needs that are not directly related to their medical problem. Services that might help with such needs are:
   - support groups and services for people with serious and potentially fatal diseases such as cancer or MS
   - support groups and services for people suffering from various types of abuse
   - services such as meals-on-wheels that help people who are ill or older
   - services for hearing- or sight-impaired people or those with mental disabilities.

2. Create a contact list of sources from which to create a list of community services. Such a contact list might include:
   - social services departments at local hospitals
   - the local public health department
   - nursing home associations
   - local charities and church organizations
   - community service numbers in the local phone book
   - the Internet

3. Contact these resources to create a list of community services complete with addresses, email addresses, and phone numbers. Keep this list on your computer so that it can be routinely updated. You can create a binder of this information or print it as needed.

4. Provide patients with a printed list of specific services from your general list, according to their needs. Answer any questions they may have.

5. Offer to make the first contact for the patient. Recognize, however, that patients may prefer to do this themselves.

6. Document in the patient's chart that the information was provided.

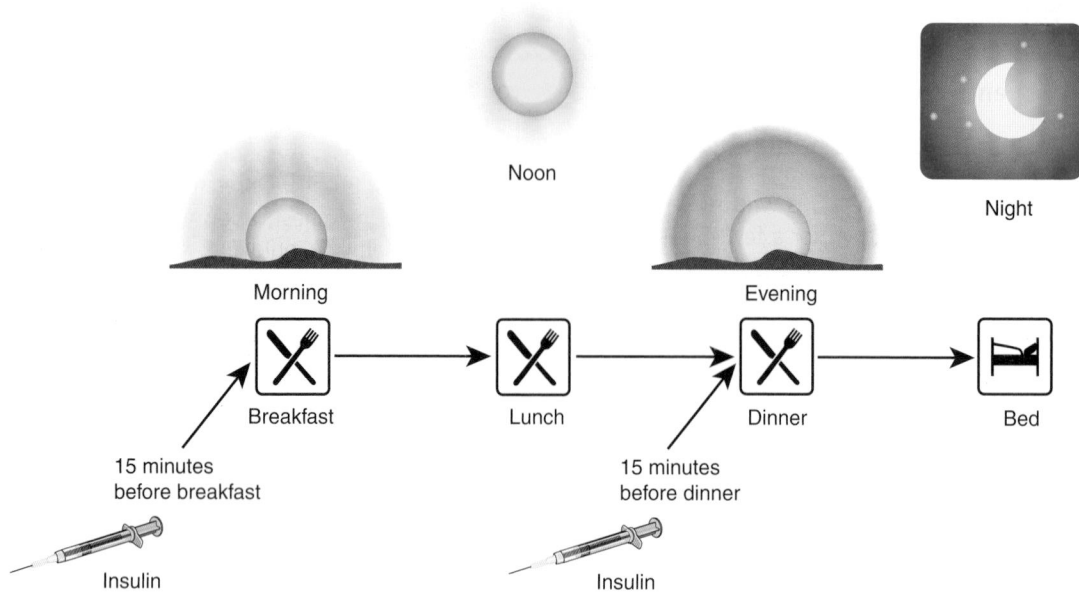

Example of a pictogram that might be given to patients to help them understand medication administration.

they can ask follow-up questions until they are comfortable with the information that they are learning.

Provide information in a clear, concise, and sequential manner. In addition to verbal instructions, give written instructions to help the patient remember the information after leaving the office. Keep informational handouts up to date and available for easy distribution. Information can also be posted on a practice's web site.

Once the educational materials have been reviewed, ensure that there is enough time for the patient to process the new information. Always encourage questions. Even if the patient has no questions, you should ask open-ended questions of your own. This helps ensure that the patient understands all of the information he or she has just received. Finally, make sure that the patient understands that it is okay to call the office with any additional questions that may arise later.

> ### ✔ CHECK POINT
>
> **6** When conducting an interview, what three points should the provider keep in mind?
>
> **7** What is the key component in educating patients, and what does it include?

RECORDING AND REPORTING

Assessment of a patient's needs and condition requires accurate documentation. Most patients receive care from more than one health care professional, so it is extremely important that patient information is passed on to others accurately. To ensure both consistent care and patient safety, patient information needs to be recorded completely and precisely, with no room for misinterpretation by other health care professionals. And because patient information is confidential, it is vital that you record this information only in secure and appropriate locations.

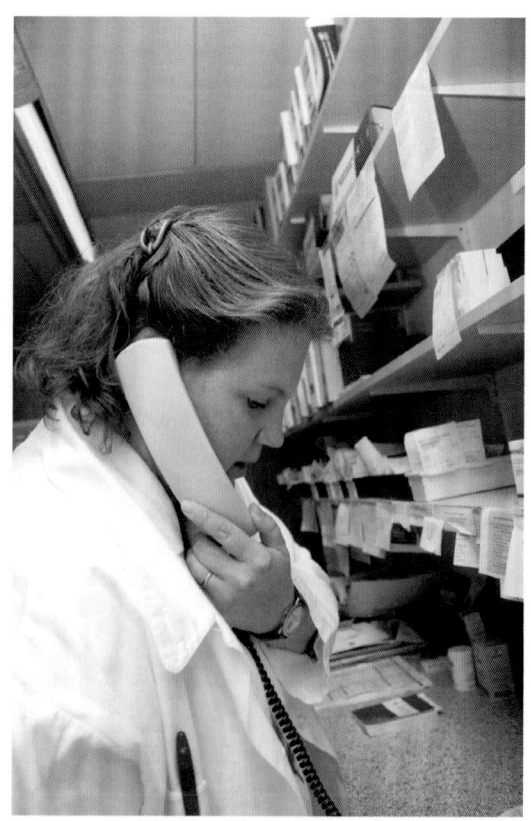

It's important to record accurately information received over the telephone.

ZOOM IN

Tips for Keeping Patient Communications Confidential

All patient communication is confidential. In fact, a patient's right to privacy and confidentiality is a basic civil right protected under the Health Insurance Portability and Accountability Act (HIPAA). HIPAA regulations are discussed in more detail in Chapter 3, "Law, Ethics, and Professionalism in Health Care."

Patient information is sometimes discussed unintentionally, however. To avoid breaching confidentiality unintentionally, follow these guidelines:

- Never discuss patient problems in public places, such as elevators or parking lots. A patient's friends or family members might overhear a conversation and misinterpret what is said.
- Close the glass window between the waiting room and the reception desk and keep it closed unless you are talking directly with a patient at the window.
- Keep your voice low and calm so that you will not be overheard by others.
- When calling coworkers over an office intercom, never use patients' names or reveal patient information. Avoid saying anything revealing, such as "Bob Smith is on the phone and wants to know if his strep throat culture came back." Instead, you should say simply, "There's a patient on line 1."
- Before going home, destroy any slips of paper in your pockets that may contain patient information, such as reminders or other notes.

Any actions you take concerning a patient should also be recorded. This information is often recorded in a narrative manner. When a patient calls or emails the office, the conversation should be immediately documented in the patient's chart. Documentation is discussed in detail in Chapter 11.

 CHECK POINT

8 Why does patient information need to be recorded completely and precisely?

COMMUNICATION CHALLENGES

There are many different barriers to good communication. No matter how hard you try, patients may not always receive your message the way you intended, and you may not always understand what patients are telling you.

Patients may misunderstand your message for any number of reasons. As mentioned earlier, many patients do not understand complex medical terms. Avoid using medical terminology when speaking with patients.

Distractions also can lead to misunderstanding. Both health care workers and patients can be easily distracted. When you become too busy and distracted, you are less likely to ensure that patients understand all of the information you've transmitted. Many factors, such as pain or hunger, cause patients to be distracted. When patients are distracted, they are less likely to focus on what you're saying.

Environmental noise often causes distractions. Health care facilities are full of sounds. Noise can come from many sources, including other patients, stations where health care workers interact, and cleaning services. When possible, speak with patients in quiet, private areas.

Language barriers also present communication challenges. When a patient does not speak or understand English well enough for effective communication, an interpreter may be necessary. Use caution when a family member is a patient's interpreter, however. Patients over 18 years of age must give written permission allowing the family member access to their medical history. Otherwise, the family member is prohibited by HIPAA from participating in any provider-patient conversations.

Hearing-impaired patients present a special communication challenge. Impairments range from partial to complete hearing loss and may prevent patients from being able to communicate with health care professionals. When communicating with a hearing-impaired patient, gently touch the patient to gain his or her attention if needed. Always talk directly in front of the patient so that he or she can read your lips. Short sentences, spoken clearly, and written words and picture boards can also be helpful.

People with brain injuries, Alzheimer's disease, strokes, or other diseases often have difficulty with normal thought processes. They also may have trouble speaking and may become disoriented. People with these and other cognitive difficulties should be accompanied by someone with an appointed power of attorney, so that you can speak with that person on their behalf.

Illnesses, financial matters, and time spent waiting are just a few of the issues that can make patients angry or upset. Never be defensive with a patient. Instead, let patients know how long they may have to wait for you or for the next health care professional that they will be seeing. Upfront information about the cost of the visit and payment options, when appropriate, can help combat the financial distress a patient may be experiencing.

Sometimes you will find yourself treating patients who are experiencing grief. Patients may be grieving the loss of a loved one, or they may be grieving their own personal health issues. You should allow grieving patients an opportunity to talk about their feelings. Terminally ill patients may want to discuss their fear of dying and their concern for surviving loved ones. Dying patients may choose to talk to you, because they may want to spare their families' feelings. You need to allow patients time to discuss their emotions and listen actively to what they have to say.

Remember that some patients may have difficulty understanding information or instructions.

CHECK POINT

9 What are some barriers to communication?

10 What factors can cause a patient to be distracted and less able to focus on what you're trying to communicate?

TELEPHONE MANNERS

The telephone is an important means of communication for many health care professionals. You must be able to communicate a positive image through the telephone.

📷 ZOOM IN

Triaging Incoming Calls

Assume you work as a medical assistant in a busy medical practice. The telephone has four incoming lines, which allow several patients to call at once. Suppose the following calls were on the lines at the same time:

- **Line 1:** The caller wants to make an appointment for her son, who has a 101.3° fever but no other serious symptoms.
- **Line 2:** The caller wants to see the physician this afternoon. He's having chest pains.
- **Line 3:** The caller is upset because she's been disconnected three times. She has a question about her bill.
- **Line 4:** The caller needs a prescription refill.

You must triage these calls—that is, you must sort them into order of importance. Which call should be handled first? Which second? Which last?

- Talk to the caller on line 2 first. Any possible life-threatening situation must have top priority. Follow your office policy for emergencies in handling this call. In some offices, you would transfer the call to a nurse, who would assess the situation. In others, you would advise the patient to call 911.
- Take caller 3 next. The longer she waits, the more upset she'll be. That will make her more difficult to please.
- Then make the appointment for caller 1, following your office policies on patient care issues.
- The caller on line 4 is last because he has the least urgent need.

One tip for triaging calls is to keep a notebook by the phone. You can use it to make notes about who is calling and why. This will help you remember the details and decide which call is most urgent.

This is sometimes more difficult than in face-to-face communication. You need excellent verbal skills to project a caring and professional attitude while talking on the telephone. Even though a patient can't see the person on the other end of the phone, if you're smiling, you're more likely to project a cheerful and professional image when you're talking on the phone.

The tone of your voice and the quality of your speech shapes the impression you send over the telephone. Follow these guidelines when answering the phone:

- Answer the phone promptly—by the second ring if possible.

- Identify yourself and your office to the caller. This lets the caller know that he or she has reached the correct number.
- Always speak politely, even if the call has interrupted work. Never allow your voice to show impatience or irritation.
- Never answer a phone call and immediately put the caller on hold. Instead, first ask the caller if he or she would mind holding. Both courtesy and the patient's well-being require waiting for an answer to ensure that there isn't an emergency before putting a caller on hold.

CHECK POINT

11 Why can communication by telephone be more challenging than face-to-face communication?

12 Why is it important for you to identify yourself and your office when answering the telephone?

Chapter Wrap-Up

Don't forget to visit thePoint companion website for additional study resources!

CHAPTER HIGHLIGHTS

- Communication is important throughout the health care system, and good communication between a provider and patient is essential to good patient care.
- The communication process involves the sending and receiving of information between two or more individuals. It consists of three central elements—the sender, the message, and the receiver—and often includes a fourth element, feedback.
- The three basic communication modes are verbal, nonverbal, and written.
- Verbal communication involves the use of spoken words.
- Assertive communication and active listening are important aspects of verbal communication.
- Nonverbal communication, also known as body language, relays a message without speaking or writing a single word. Three forms of nonverbal communication include kinesics (body movement), proxemics (personal space), and touch.
- Medical writing requires accuracy and clarity. Mistakes in written medical communications could cause injury or death, lawsuits, or professional harm to you or your employer.
- When conducting a patient interview, be an active listener, ask appropriate questions, and record answers accurately.
- The interview process for a new patient is quite different from that for an established patient.
- Effective communication is the key component in patient education.
- To ensure both consistent care and patient safety, patient information must be recorded completely and accurately.
- There are many barriers to good communication, including the use of medical terms, distractions, environmental noise, language barriers, hearing impairments, brain injuries and other cognitive difficulties, anger, and grief.
- The telephone is an important means of communication for many health care professionals, so they must be able to communicate a positive image through the telephone.

REVIEW QUESTIONS

Matching

1. _____ Body movement
2. _____ Both active listening and interviewing skills are central to this process.
3. _____ The person or group that begins the communication process
4. _____ Include sighs, sobs, laughs, grunts, and so on.
5. _____ Personal space

   a. non-language sounds   **b.** source   **c.** proxemics   **d.** kinesics   **e.** patient education

Multiple Choice

6. Health care workers regularly communicate with patients and other professionals regarding
   - **a.** assessment
   - **b.** diagnosis
   - **c.** treatment
   - **d.** all of the above

7. Which of the following elements is NOT present within *every* communication process?
   - **a.** message
   - **b.** feedback
   - **c.** receiver
   - **d.** sender

8. Using your own words or phrases to repeat what you have heard is called
   a. reflecting
   b. paraphrasing
   c. comparison organization
   d. problem-oriented organization

9. In health care, a message can be
   a. a patient describing a symptom
   b. information obtained during a telephone conversation
   c. a gesture
   d. all of the above

10. Using open-ended statements to repeat back what you have heard is called
    a. reflecting
    b. paraphrasing
    c. comparison organization
    d. problem-oriented organization

Completion

11. The three most common modes of communication are verbal, _____ and written communication.

12. _____ listening ensures that health care professionals understand completely what a patient or colleague is trying to communicate.

13. Maintaining good _____ shows that you're interested in what other people are saying and adds a sense of truthfulness to your message.

14. Nonverbal communication, also known as _____, relays a message without speaking or writing a single word.

15. Health care providers need excellent _____ skills to project a caring and professional attitude while talking on the telephone.

Short Answer

16. What are some of the possible consequences of communication failures?

   _____

   _____

17. Why does nonverbal behavior often reveal more than verbal behavior?

   _____

   _____

18. Why is proper grammar important in written communication?

   _____

   _____

19. What are some of the common communication barriers between a provider and patient?

   _____

   _____

20. How does the interview of an established patient differ from that of a new patient?

   _____

   _____

INVESTIGATE IT

1. Complete the following communication/interpersonal skill survey. How well do you really communicate with others? Do you communicate well at work? At home? Read each question below and then put a circle around the letter that best describes you. *Be honest with yourself.*

   A = Always/Usually   B = Sometimes   C = Seldom/Rarely

   1. I am not afraid to ask questions when I do not understand something.
      A   **B**   **C**

   2. I repeat what someone has said in my own words to check my understanding.
      A   **B**   **C**

   3. I notice people's body language.
      A   **B**   **C**

   4. I give clear, brief directions.
      A   **B**   **C**

   5. I listen carefully and speak clearly.
      A   **B**   **C**

   6. I ask questions in a way that is easy to understand.
      A   **B**   **C**

   7. I clearly state my opinions and give good reasons to back them up.
      A   **B**   **C**

   8. I respect other people's right to their opinions.
      A   **B**   **C**

   9. I listen carefully to others when they disagree with me.
      A   **B**   **C**

   10. I accept and think about constructive criticism.
       A   **B**   **C**

   Use what you have learned about your communication and interpersonal skills to help you improve in your weakest areas. Making changes in these areas will help you become a more effective health care professional.

RECOMMENDED READING

Bub B. The Lament, Hidden Key to Effective Listening. *Health Care Communication Review* [serial online]. Summer/Fall 2005;5(2):PS1-2. Available at http://www.healthcarecommunication. org/pro/hcrps/v5n2ps.pdf.

Kale-Smith G. *Medical Assisting Made Incredibly Easy: Administrative Competencies.* Baltimore: Lippincott, Williams, and Wilkins, 2008.

Kronenberger J. *Comprehensive Medical Assisting.* Baltimore: Lippincott, Williams, and Wilkins, 2008.

Smith M., Segal J. Supporting a Grieving Person: Helping Others Through Grief, Loss, and Bereavement. Available at http://www.helpguide.org/mental/helping_grieving.htm.

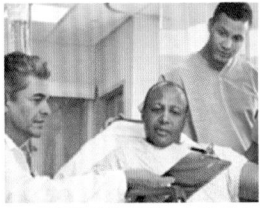
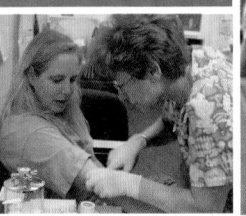

Diversity and Difference in Health Care

CHAPTER OBJECTIVES

After careful study of this chapter, you should be able to:

✳ Name cultural and ethnic differences that you may encounter in the workplace and explain how they may relate to health care.

✳ Describe how people of different races and cultures vary physically and psychologically.

✳ Give examples of cultural differences involving reactions to pain, gender roles, time orientation, and food and nutrition preferences.

✳ Identify differences among individuals based on socioeconomic factors, age, and religion.

✳ Describe examples of diverse health care practices, including natural remedies and complementary and alternative treatments.

KEY TERMS

acculturation
cultural assimilation
cultural diversity
culture

dominant group
ethnicity
ethnocentrism

folk medicine
hereditary
immigrate

minority group
race
subculture

Health care professionals interact with people from a variety of backgrounds and cultural origins. This is true of both the patients they care for and the people they work with. From genetic characteristics to cultural values and beliefs, diversity is evident throughout health care today.

In our society, **cultural diversity** is characterized by a wide range of distinctions, including:
- race
- national origin
- religion

- language
- physical size
- gender
- sexual orientation
- age

- disability
- socioeconomic status
- occupational status
- geographic location

Individual patients and providers both have their own beliefs and values, which give rise to personal principles. How a person perceives situations and other people is greatly influenced by their beliefs, including:

- cultural beliefs
- social beliefs
- religious beliefs
- personal convictions

As a rule, you should work to avoid **ethnocentrism**, the belief or assumption that a particular social or cultural group is superior in some way. Every person, whether an acquaintance, patient, or coworker, should be viewed as a unique, valuable individual. People shouldn't be judged based on cultural or societal differences. Such prejudging leads to—or results from—*stereotypes*, mistaken perceptions that are typically rooted in strong feelings and lack of knowledge. Instead, the differences among people should be appreciated and respected.

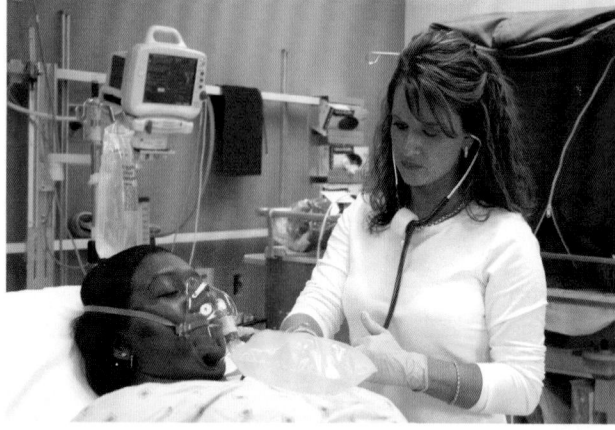

It is vital that you, as a health care professional, understand the different needs of a culturally diverse patient population.

Viewing and treating people as individuals is especially important for health care workers. Part of the health care provider's ethical code demands that everyone be treated with equal care and respect. This chapter focuses on diversity in patient care and the workplace.

CULTURAL AND ETHNIC DIFFERENCES

The U.S. is a multicultural, multiethnic, and multiracial country. **Culture** is a shared system of beliefs, values, and behavioral expectations that provide structure for daily living. Culture influences people's roles and interactions with others and is revealed in the attitudes, customs, and institutions unique to particular groups. Culture is influenced by, and rooted in, many aspects of human society, including:

- beliefs
- habits
- likes
- dislikes
- customs
- rituals

It is vital that you, as a health care professional, understand the different needs of a culturally diverse patient population. Following are some facts about culture:

- Culture is shared by, and helps provide an identity for, members of a cultural group. It guides group members into behaviors that are acceptable to the group.
- Culture influences the way people in a group view themselves, what expectations they have, and how they behave in response to certain situations.
- The practices of a particular culture often can be traced to the group's social and physical environment.
- Cultural practices and beliefs may evolve over time, but many traits remain constant.
- Each new generation learns the norms, or expected behaviors, of its culture through formal teaching and by watching the behavior of elders. Language is a primary means of transmitting culture.

Because a culture is made up of individuals, there are differences within each culture, as members reflect cultural attitudes or behaviors in varying ways. Therefore, you must be careful not to assume that every member of a particular culture or ethnic group is exactly the same.

While it is natural to note differences among individuals, you must never allow any preconceived notions about others to affect the quality of your work. By avoiding making judgments about others, you can learn to appreciate the things that make people different. This will help you treat everyone with the same care and respect. Health care professionals who are aware of, and understand, cultural differences provide better patient care.

Individuals may vary from their culture's norms. Within a given culture, smaller groups, or subcultures, also express cultural differences. A **subculture** is a group of people who are members of a larger cultural group, but whose attitudes and behaviors reflect different beliefs and values from those of the larger culture. A subculture might be based on occupational status or age. For example, nursing is a subculture of the larger health care system culture. In the U.S., teens and older adults are often regarded as subcultures of the general population. Subcultures can also be based on ethnicity or language.

Ethnicity involves a sense of identification with a group based on a common heritage. A person belongs to a specific ethnic group either through birth or through the adoption of that group's characteristics. People within an ethnic group generally share unique cultural and social characteristics, including:

- language and dialect
- religious practices
- literature
- folklore
- music
- political interests
- food preferences

The term *ethnicity* is often used interchangeably with the term *race*. However, these two terms do not mean the same thing. **Race** is normally based on specific physical characteristics, such as skin pigmentation, body stature, facial features, and hair texture. When people speak of racial groups in the U.S., they typically distinguish among whites, African Americans, American Indians and Alaska natives, Asian Americans, and native Hawaiians and other Pacific islanders (using Census Bureau categories). The U.S. government views Hispanics as an ethnic, rather than a racial, group.

Cultures include both dominant groups and minority groups. A **dominant group** is the group within a society that tends to control that society's values. Although the dominant group is usually the largest group in a society, it does not have to be. For example, from the time it was colonized until the early 1990s, South Africa's dominant group was made up of white people of European ancestry, despite the fact that this group accounted for only 13 percent of the country's population. The values of a dominant group strongly influence the value system of its society.

A **minority group** usually has some physical or cultural characteristics that identify the people within it as different from the dominant group, such as:

- race
- religion
- beliefs
- customs or practices

Some members of minority groups maintain their culture in the midst of the dominant culture. Others, however, lose the cultural characteristics that once made them different. This process is called **cultural assimilation or acculturation**. Assimilation occurs when an individual shifts his or her identity from the minority group

ZOOM IN

State Variations in Population Diversity

Cultural diversity varies greatly from state to state, and even from county to county within a state. While the range of patient diversity ultimately depends on the state or region in which a health care professional practices, all providers are likely to encounter a variety of different cultures and ethnicities in their health care careers.

According to U.S. Census Bureau statistics, white non-Hispanics make up approximately 79.6 percent of the population of the U.S. As indicated by the map below, Northern states have a higher than average percentage of white non-Hispanics, while Southern states have a lower than average percentage.

Percentages vary greatly from state to state. The smallest population of white, non-Hispanics is found in New Mexico (44.7 percent), California (46.7 percent), and Texas (52.4 percent). At the opposite end of the spectrum, the largest white, non-Hispanic populations are found in Maine (96.5 percent), Vermont (96.2 percent), and West Virginia (94.6 percent).

to the dominant group and adopts the values, attitudes, and behaviors of the dominant culture. When people **immigrate**, or settle in a new country, they may find that their values differ from those of the dominant culture. As immigrants go to work and to school and learn the dominant language, they often move closer to the dominant culture.

Living in a dominant culture that differs from one's own can produce feelings of psychological discomfort or disturbance called *culture shock*. The patterns of behavior that an individual learned were acceptable and effective in his or her native culture are often not suited to the new one. Culture shock often produces stress and may lead an individual to feel foolish, fearful, inadequate, embarrassed, humiliated, or inferior.

These feelings can lead to frustration, anxiety, and loss of self-esteem. These issues are intensified when the person is also trying to cope with a disease or illness. Health care professionals need to understand and appreciate the differences among cultural and ethnic groups. When put into practice, this understanding can help reduce a patient's stress and improve his or her care experience. Table 6-1 (following page) provides ten culturally sensitive questions health care professionals should consider when caring for patients from different cultural backgrounds.

Table 6-1 Questions about Health-Related Beliefs and Practices

1. To what cause(s) does the patient attribute illness and disease (e.g., divine wrath, imbalance in hot/cold or yin/yang, punishment for moral transgressions, hex, soul loss, pathogenic organism)?
2. What are the patient's cultural beliefs about the ideal body size and shape? What is the patient's self-image compared to the ideal?
3. What name does the patient give to his or her health-related condition?
4. What does the patient believe promotes health (eating certain foods; wearing amulets to bring good luck; sleep; rest; good nutrition; reducing stress; exercise; prayer; rituals to ancestors, saints, or intermediate deities)?
5. What is the patient's religious affiliation (e.g., Judaism, Islam, Pentacostalism, West African voodooism, Seventh-Day Adventism, Catholicism, Mormonism)? How actively involved in the practice of this religion is the patient?
6. Does the patient rely on cultural healers (e.g., curandero, shaman, spiritualist, priest, minister, monk)? Who determines when the patient is sick and when the patient is healthy? Who influences the choice/type of healer and treatment that should be sought?
7. In what types of cultural healing practices does the patient engage (use of herbal remedies, potions, or massage; wearing of talismans, copper bracelets, or charms to discourage evil spirits; healing rituals, incantations, or prayers)?
8. How do the patient and his or her family perceive health care providers? What type of care do they expect from health care professionals?
9. What comprises appropriate "sick role" behavior? Who determines what symptoms constitute disease/illness? Who decides when the patient is no longer sick? Who cares for the patient at home?
10. How does the patient's cultural group view mental disorders? Are there differences in acceptable behaviors for physical versus psychological illnesses?

From Andrews, M., & Boyle, J. (2002b). *Transcultural concepts in nursing care* (4th ed.). Philadelphia: Lippincott Williams & Wilkins.

Physical Characteristics

Human physical features have evolved over time as a response to environmental demands. Skin color is an example. Evidence suggests that humans first arose in Africa, and scientists believe that early humans had dark skin. Over time, however, some human populations have developed much lighter skin color. Scientists believe that this change was an adaptation to the environment. As populations moved to northern climates, they developed lighter skin to better synthesize vitamin D from sunlight. They needed this adaptation because northern climates have less sunlight throughout the year. Nose shape and size may also have evolved because of different climates in which human groups lived. These adaptations were natural changes that helped improve the lives and well-being of humans.

Studies have shown that certain racial or ethnic groups possess specific characteristics that make them more prone to developing particular diseases and conditions. Below are four examples of disorders that are, or may be, **hereditary**, or inherited genetically:

- *Tay-Sachs disease.* This condition is a rare genetic disorder that progressively destroys nerve cells in the brain and spinal cord. Infants born with this disease may develop normally for the first few months of their lives, but they later develop a growing inability to move and eventually die. The incidence of this disease has declined over the years due to genetic testing, but there is still no known treatment. Individuals of Eastern European Jewish descent are most likely to develop Tay-Sachs disease.
- *Keloids.* Keloids are an overgrowth of connective tissue that forms during healing from an injury to the skin. Rather than healing level with the surrounding skin tissue, the wound heals with a rough, lumpy, or elevated scar. People with dark skin are much more likely to develop keloids. The tendency towards keloids seems to run in families, suggesting a genetic cause. Scientists have not yet determined the genetic mechanism, however.
- *Lactase deficiency and lactose intolerance.* The milk of all mammals contains *lactose*, a sugar. The body needs the enzyme *lactase* to break down lactose during digestion. Without lactase, the lactose ferments in the intestines, resulting in gas, diarrhea, and bloating. Lactase deficiency and lactose intolerance are more common among certain groups, including Hispanic women and men and women of African, Chinese, and Thai descent. People with lactase deficiency can drink milk substitutes or dairy products that have been enriched with lactase.

- *Sickle cell anemia.* Sickle cell anemia is a hereditary disorder in which the body makes sickle-shaped, or c-shaped, red blood cells. These cells break down more rapidly than normal red blood cells. The sickle shape also prevents the red blood cells from moving easily through the smaller blood vessels in the body. This can cause blood vessels to be clogged by red blood cells, which can lead to many serious problems. Sickle cell anemia primarily affects people of African descent; Hispanics of Caribbean ancestry; and individuals with Middle Eastern, Indian, Latin American, Native American, or Mediterranean heritage.

Psychological Characteristics

In social interactions, people interpret the behaviors of others around them. This is true for both health care providers and patients. While you're assessing the attitude and behavior of a patient, the patient is probably evaluating your conduct as well.

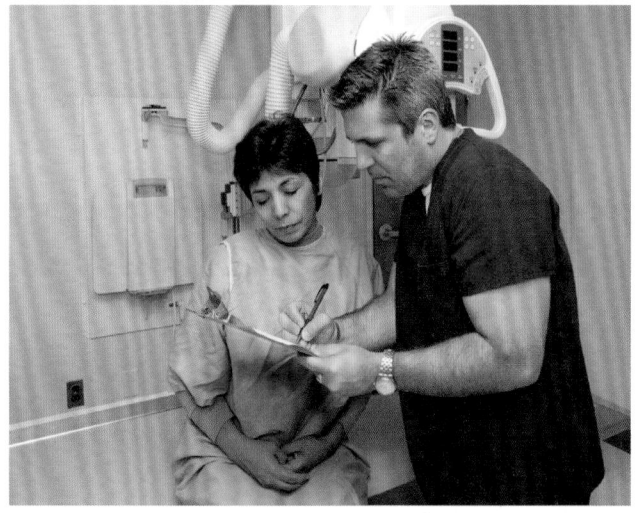

Health careers that involve patient care are rich with social interactions.

As a result, you need to remember that your view of the situation could differ from your patient's view. Even if a patient's concerns seem unreasonable or irrelevant, you must remember that these concerns are very real and important to the patient. In interactions with patients, then, you need to put aside your own opinions and try to look at the circumstances from the patient's point of view. Values and beliefs about health, illness, and treatments are shaped by cultural and ethnic influences.

You must not presume to know a person's true feelings or intentions based solely on gestures or body language. Your understanding of a patient's actions may be different from the patient's true intentions. Keep in mind that

people may interpret behaviors differently. One person may feel that standing close to another person is a sign of respect. The other person, however, may view this as aggressive behavior. Some individuals consider a casual touch or direct eye contact to be courteous, while others find this same conduct disrespectful.

Reactions to Pain

Researchers have discovered that many of the expressions and behaviors of people in pain are culturally influenced. Some cultures allow, and even encourage, the open expression of pain, while other cultures frown on such open display.

Health care providers may assume that a patient who does not complain of pain is not experiencing any pain. As a result, a patient who deals with pain quietly and stoically may have his or her need for pain treatment ignored. If you are providing direct patient care, you should be sensitive to signs that patients are in pain, even if they do not complain of pain. On the other hand, you shouldn't consider patients who freely express their discomfort to be constant complainers whose requests for pain relief are excessive. Pain is a warning from the body that something is wrong. Pain is what a person says it is, and every complaint of pain should be assessed carefully.

Health care providers can follow these guidelines to treat patients with cultural sensitivity:

- Recognize that culture is an important part of an individual's approach to the world and that each person holds (and has the right to hold) his or her own beliefs about health.

- Respect the patient's right to respond to health care issues in whatever manner he or she wishes.
- Never stereotype a patient's perceptions or responses based on his or her culture.

Gender Roles

In many cultures, males are dominant and generally make decisions for all family members. In some Muslim families, for example, if approval for medical care is needed, the male head of the family gives that approval regardless of which family member needs care. In male-dominant cultures, women are usually passive. However, in other cultures, women are dominant and make the decisions.

Knowing which member of the family is dominant is an important consideration when planning patient care. If the dominant member is ill and can no longer make decisions, the whole family may be anxious and confused. If a non-dominant family member is ill, he or she may need help verbalizing needs, particularly if those needs differ from what the dominant member perceives as important.

Time Orientation

Americans are very time oriented. Many people—and almost all institutions—in the U.S. value promptness and punctuality. Whether arriving for an appointment, doing a job, or even meeting for recreation, being on time and getting the job done promptly are viewed as important.

In other cultures, punctuality and completing tasks within an allotted amount of time may not be valued as highly. For example, in some South Asian cultures, being late is considered a sign of respect.

Another cultural difference related to time involves perceptions of past, present, and future. While the dominant American culture is future oriented, other cultures are more concerned with the present or the past.

These cultural differences in time orientation can affect patient care. For example, a patient raised in a culture that focuses primarily on the present may find it difficult to understand the importance of planning for long-term care. With such patients, health care professionals may need to take some extra time to explain the seriousness of a medical situation and then follow up to ensure that the patient fully understands all instructions. (Chapter 5, "Health Care Communication," provides more information about communicating with patients.)

Cultural differences related to time can also surface in interactions between coworkers. A colleague who is habitually late for work or meetings may be viewed by others as lazy or irresponsible. However, that individual may be an extremely hard-working, responsible professional who simply comes from a culture that does not emphasize punctuality. Avoid making assumptions about others based solely on your own beliefs or cultural norms. This can lead to tensions in the workplace that produce unhealthy working conditions and can lead to poor patient care.

Food and Nutrition

Culture strongly influences food preferences, including both ingredients and how foods are prepared. Most cultures consider certain foods to be dietary staples. For example, rice is a staple of many Asian cuisines, while pasta is a staple in southern Italy. Be careful not to make assumptions, however. While many Hispanic cultures favor beans, not all Hispanic cuisine is the same. Mexican cooking, for example, features chili peppers and tortillas, while Caribbean Hispanics often pair beans with rice.

Health care providers who teach about diet should take these cultural differences into account. Dietary advice should also recognize cultural attitudes about the social significance and sharing of food. Table 6-2 provides some

---

Table 6-2 Cultural Influences that Affect Diet and Nutrition

1. Which foods are considered edible and which are not?
   - In France, corn is considered an animal feed, whereas corn is a commonly eaten vegetable in the United States.
   - Religious beliefs prohibit some Jewish, Muslim, and Seventh-Day Adventist patients from eating pork.
   - Patients who follow a vegetarian diet do not eat pork, beef, or chicken

2. What times and types of food are considered meals?
   - Anglo-Americans typically eat three meals a day, with foods such as bacon and eggs or cereal for breakfast, sandwiches and soup for lunch, and meat with potatoes and vegetables for dinner.
   - Vietnamese may eat soup for every meal.
   - Beans are a staple for meals among Mexican people.
   - People from Middle Eastern countries often eat cheese and olives for breakfast.
   - Native American and Latin American people usually eat two meals a day.
   - Rural southern African Americans may eat large amounts of food on weekends and less food at meals during the week.
   - Holy days or religious holidays influence food choices for almost all cultures.

culturally sensitive questions and facts to consider regarding diet and nutrition.

OTHER DIFFERENCES AMONG INDIVIDUALS

In addition to cultural influences on beliefs about health, illness, and treatments, other factors play significant roles in shaping every individual's view of health care. Economics, age, and religion all shape how patients and health care providers view one another. These same factors can also impact patient care.

Socioeconomic Factors

Family income affects individual health and access to health care. While most middle-class families have the resources for health care when needed, many poorer Americans do not. Studies have shown that people in upper-income groups tend to live longer and experience less disability than those in lower-income groups. Although a number of programs help families with low incomes meet their health care needs (see Chapter 2, "Health Care Economics"), many poorer Americans still go without regular health care.

Poverty particularly affects older Americans and families headed by single mothers. It often leads to inadequate care of infants and children, poor preventive care, poor diet, and homelessness. In addition, many poor families cannot afford the transportation they need to get to a health care provider. All of these factors affect health care.

Many poor families lack affordable or adequate housing, which can also affect the health of family members. When low-income housing is available, it may lack necessities like running water, heat, and electricity. To stretch their money and to pool resources, many poor people live in crowded conditions, with multiple families joining together in one household. Research has shown that people living in crowded conditions have a diminished sense of individuality. Crowded living conditions have also been associated with higher crime rates and can contribute to psychological problems, such as schizophrenia, alienation, and feelings of worthlessness. Such living conditions can also contribute to the spread of disease.

ZOOM IN

Poverty by Ethnicity

According to the U.S. Census Bureau 2007 estimates, around 18 percent of Americans live in poverty. When broken down by race or ethnic group, poverty rates show stark differences:

- White, non-Hispanics: 10.1 percent
- Asian Americans: 12.5 percent
- Hispanic Americans: 28.6 percent
- African Americans: 34.5 percent

Source: U.S. Bureau of the Census. *Current Population Survey, Annual Social and Economic Supplements.*

Many poorer American must go without regular health care, which may lead to ER visit that might otherwise have been preventable.

Age

An individual's age affects his or her health in different ways. Younger people have different health care needs from older adults. Adults are better able to communicate their symptoms and responses to medication than children, although some older adults may also have communication problems. Health care providers need to be sensitive to patients' changing physical and emotional needs as they grow older.

However, it is essential to not make assumptions about a patient based solely on his or her age. Physical fitness and levels of health vary at every age. Sixty-year-olds who exercise regularly and have no chronic conditions or disease may be healthier than younger adults who are obese and suffering from related conditions. Age is just one of many different factors that affect health.

ZOOM IN

Religious Affiliation, Attendance at Religious Services, and Hospitalization

Researchers at the Duke University Medical Center examined a group of older patients to study the relationship between religious affiliation, attendance at religious services, and the use of acute hospital care. The study analyzed these variables for medical center patients aged 60 or older. Data on their use of acute hospital services during the prior year and the length of their stay at the medical center were also collected.

Findings showed that patients who attended religious services at least once a week were significantly less likely to have been admitted to the hospital in the previous year. They also had fewer overall hospital admissions and spent fewer total days in the hospital than those attending services less often.

Patients with no religious affiliation had significantly longer hospital stays—25 days, on average—than those with a religious affiliation, with stays averaging only 11 days. The correlation between religious affiliation and reduced hospitalization was even stronger when physical health and other variables were controlled. Among older adults in this study, at least, religious affiliation and practice was correlated with better health.

Religion

Patients' religious beliefs and values may affect how they wish to be treated by health care professionals. Health care providers must be sensitive to each patient's values and beliefs. For example, male Orthodox Jews may not be touched by women who are not members of their families. Because such patients would be uncomfortable interacting with a female care provider, it would be important to have a male health care professional attend to them.

> **✔ CHECK POINT**
>
> **3** What potential impact could socioeconomic factors, age, and religion have on a person's health or interaction with health care professionals?
>
> **4** How might lack of affordable and adequate housing affect a person's health?

DIVERSITY IN HEALTH CARE PRACTICES

There are countless ways to describe or label health care practices and systems: modern, conventional, traditional, complementary, alternative, allopathic, homeopathic, and folk, to name a few. While modern medical care is the norm for health care in the U.S., many patients prefer other kinds of health care. These preferences may be the result of poverty, language, availability of different kinds of care, lack of insurance, and preference for familiar and personal care.

Some providers choose to combine their medical training with nontraditional healing techniques. For example, some physicians learn the Chinese practice of acupuncture.

Regardless of your own treatment philosophy, you must be open and accepting of other professionals who use different methods in certain situations. You must also be conscious of your own perceptions of health, illness, and health care practices.

Folk Medicine

Folk medicine is widely practiced in the U.S. and throughout the world. In general, **folk medicine** is a form of prevention and treatment that uses old-fashioned remedies and household medicines handed down from generation to generation within a particular culture.

In some cultures, the power to heal is thought to be a gift from God bestowed on certain people. People in these cultures believe that healers know what's wrong with them through divine revelation. A patient accustomed to traditional healers may consider health care providers incompetent if they ask a list of questions before treating an illness. They also might not understand the need to undergo some laboratory tests. Traditional healers speak the patient's language, are often more accessible, and are usually more understanding of the patient's cultural and personal needs.

Nontraditional healing includes several different therapies, such as:
- *Cutaneous stimulation.* This technique involves stimulating the skin through massage, vibration, heat, or cold to reduce the intensity of pain.
- *Therapeutic touch.* In this therapy, the healer uses touch to transfer energy to the patient in order to stimulate the patient's healing potential.
- *Acupuncture.* A method that originated in China, this therapy prevents, diagnoses, and treats pain and disease

by inserting special needles into the body at specified locations.

- *Acupressure.* In acupressure, the provider performs deep pressure massage at certain points in the body.

Natural Remedies

Throughout history, herbs have been a common method of treatment in many cultures. In fact, many medications used today are based on these traditional substances. If a patient normally drinks an herbal tea to alleviate symptoms, there's no reason why both the herbal tea and prescribed medications can't be used together, as long as the tea is safe to drink and its ingredients don't interfere with, or exaggerate the action of, the medication.

You should be prepared to work with patients who prefer natural remedies over more conventional medications. You must keep your own personal opinions or biases from coloring your interactions with patients. If a patient feels that you're ridiculing his or her treatment choices, the patient will be less likely to talk to you about other treatments or remedies in the future. This could have devastating effects on the patient's health.

Complementary or Alternative Medicine

As you may recall from Chapter 1, "Today's Health Care System," complementary or alternative medicine typically promotes healing through nutrition, exercise, or relaxation. Many complementary therapies are culturally based, and some of today's modern healing practices have

Acupuncture is a healing practice that originated in China but has now been incorporated into nontraditional western medicine.

ON LOCATION

Jehovah Witnesses and Transfusions

Many practicing Jehovah Witnesses consider it a sin to receive the blood of another person in a transfusion. As a health care worker, how would you feel if a patient refused a blood transfusion following an automobile accident? Based on your medical training, you may feel strongly that the blood could save the patient's life, but you also know that each patient has the right to make his or her own medical decisions. (For more on this right, see Chapter 3, "Law, Ethics, and Professionalism in Health Care".)

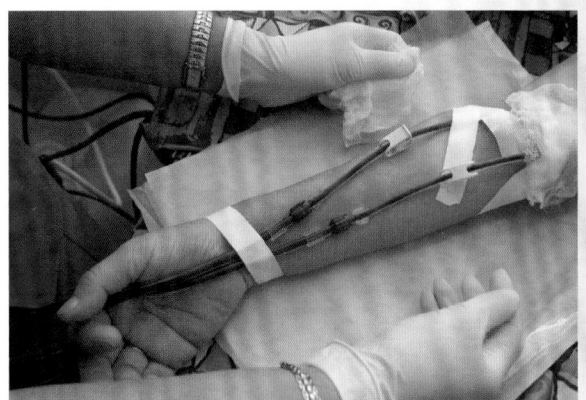

How would you react if a patient objected to a life-saving blood transfusion because of his religious beliefs?

historical roots in the complementary therapies of various cultural or ethnic groups. For example, Hawaiian medical practices have traditionally emphasized preventive medicine. An emphasis on preventive medicine is becoming more and more common in modern health care.

From African American faith healing to Asian Taoism, complementary and alternative medicine practices are as diverse as the cultures from which they originated. Table 6-3 (following page) lists some of the cultural factors that affect patient care, including both folk and traditional healing.

CHECK POINT

5 What are some of the reasons a person may prefer to use a health care provider outside the modern health care system?

6 Give four examples of traditional therapies classified as folk medicine.

Table 6-3 Cultural Factors that Influence Patient Care

Cultural Group	Family	Folk and Traditional Health Care	Values and Beliefs	Patient Care Considerations
White Non-Hispanic	• Nuclear family is highly valued • Older family members may live in a nursing home when they can no longer care for themselves.	• Self-diagnosis of illnesses • Use of over-the-counter drugs (especially vitamins and analgesics) • Dieting (especially fad diets) • Extensive use of exercise and exercise facilities	• Youth is valued over age • Cleanliness • Orderliness • Attractiveness • Individualism • Achievement • Punctuality	• Careful assessment of patient's use of over-the-counter medications • Nutritional assessments of dietary habits
African American	• Close and supportive extended-family relationships • Strong kinship ties with non-blood relatives from church or organizational and social groups • family unity, loyalty, and cooperation are important • Usually matriarchal	• Varies extensively and may include spiritualists, herb doctors, root doctors, conjurers, skilled elder family members, voodoo, faith healing	• Present oriented • Members of the African American clergy are highly respected in the black community • Frequently highly religious	• Many African American families may still use various folk healing practices and home remedies for treating particular illnesses. • Special care may be necessary for hair and skin. • Special consideration should be given to the sometimes extensive and frequently informal support networks of patients (i.e., religious and community group members who offer assistance in a time of need).
Asian (Beliefs and practices vary, but most Asian cultures share some characteristics.)	• Welfare of the family is valued above the person. • Extended families are common. • A person's lineage (ancestors) is respected. • Sharing among family members is expected.	• Theoretical basis is in Taoism, which seeks a balance in all things. • Good health is achieved through the proper balance of yin (feminine, negative, dark, cold) and yang (masculine, positive, light, warm). • An imbalance in energy is caused by an improper diet or strong emotions. • Diseases and foods are classified as hot or cold, and a proper balance between them will promote wellness (e.g., treat a cold disease with hot foods).	• Strong sense of self-respect and self-control • High respect for age • Respect for authority • Respect for hard work • Praise of self or others is considered poor manners • Strong emphasis on harmony and the avoidance of conflict	• Some members of the Asian culture may be upset by the drawing of blood for laboratory tests. They consider blood to be the body's life force, and some do not believe it can be regenerated. • Some members believe that it is best to die with the body intact, so they may refuse surgery except in dire circumstances. • Members of many Asian cultures seldom complain about what is bothering them. Therefore, the health professional must carefully assess the patient for pain or discomfort, such as facial grimacing or wincing and holding of the painful area.

- Some Asians consider it polite to give a person the responses the person is expecting. Therefore, some Asian patients may provide misinformation in an effort to be respectful.
- Some Asians refuse to have diagnostic studies done because they believe that a skilled and competent physician can diagnose an illness solely through a physical examination.
- Some Asians may have a difficult time understanding the importance of taking a regimen of medications because many of their fold treatments involve the ingestion of only one dose of herbal mixtures.
- Dietary counseling may be necessary if the patient is on a salt-restricted diet because many Asian foods have a high salt content related to the use of soy sauce.
- It may be difficult to convince an asymptomatic patient that he or she is ill.
- Special diet considerations are necessary if the patient believes in the hot/cold theory of treating illnesses.
- Diet counseling may be necessary at times because many members have a normal diet that is high in starch.

- Many Asian health care systems use herbs, diet, and the application of hot or cold therapy. Also many Asians believe that there are points on the body that are located on the meridians or energy pathways. If the energy flow is out of balance, treatment of the pathways may be necessary to restore the energy equilibrium.

- Respect is given according to age (older) and sex (male).
- Roman Catholic Church may be very influential.
- God gives health and allows illness for a reason; therefore, may perceive illness as a punishment from God. An illness of this type can be cured through atonement and forgiveness.

Hispanic

- Familial role is important.
- *Campadrazgo:* special bond between a child's parents and his or her grandparents
- Family is the primary unit of society.

- *Curanderas(os):* folk healers who base treatments on humoral pathology—basic functions of the body are controlled by four body fluids or "humors":
  (1) Blood—hot and wet
  (2) Yellow bile—hot and dry
  (3) Black bile—cold and dry
  (4) Phlegm—cold and wet
- The secret of good health is to balance hot and cold within the body; therefore, most foods, beverages, herbs, and medications are classified as hot (*caliente*) or cold (*fresco, frio*) (a cold disease will be cured with a hot treatment).

(continued)

Table 6-3 Cultural Factors that Influence Patient Care (continued)

Cultural Group	Family	Folk and Traditional Health Care	Values and Beliefs	Patient Care Considerations
Puerto Rican	• *Campadrazgo*—same as in Hispanic culture	• Similar to that of other Spanish-speaking cultures	• Place a high value on safeguarding against group pressure to violate a person's integrity (may be difficult for Puerto Ricans to accept teamwork) • Close-mouthed about personal and family affairs (psychotherapy may be difficult to achieve at times because of this belief) • Proper consideration should be given to cultural rituals such as shaking hands and standing up to greet and say goodbye to people. • Time is a relative phenomenon; little attention is given to the exact time of day. • *Ataques*—culturally acceptable reaction to situations of extreme stress, characterized by hyperkinetic seizure activity	• It may be difficult to teach Puerto Rican patients to follow time-oriented actions (e.g., taking medications, keeping appointments).
Native American (Each tribe's beliefs and practices vary to some degree.)	• Families are large and extended. • Grandparents are official and symbolic leaders and decision makers. • A child's namesake may become the same as another parent to the child.	• Medicine men (*shaman*) are heavily used. • Heavy use of herbs and psychological treatments, ceremonies, fasting, meditation, heat, and massages	• Present oriented. Taught to live in the present and not to be concerned about the future. This time consciousness emphasizes finishing current business before doing something else. • High respect for age • Great value is placed on working together and sharing resources. • Failure to achieve a personal goal frequently is believed to be the result of competition.	• The family is expected to be part of the care plan. • Note-taking often is taboo. It is considered an insult to the speaker because the listener is not paying full attention to the conversation. Good memory skills often are required by the caregiver. • Indirect eye contact is acceptable and sometimes preferred. • It often is considered rude or impolite to indicate that a conversation has not been heard.

		• High respect is given to a person who gives to others. The accumulation of money and goods often is frowned on. • Some Native Americans practice the Peyotist religion, in which the consumption of peyote, an intoxicating drug derived from mescal cacti, is part of the service. Peyote is legal if used for this purpose. It is classified as a hallucinogenic drug.		• A low tone of voice often is considered respectful. • A Native American patient may expect the caregiver to deduce the problem through instinct and not through asking many questions and history taking. If this is the case, it may help to use declarative sentences rather than direct questioning.
Hawaiian	• Familial role is important. • *Ohana*, or extended families, are jointly involved in childrearing. • Hierarchy of family structure, each gender and age have specific duties • Closely knit families in small, isolated communities	• *Kahuna La'au Lapa'nu* is the ancient Hawaiian medical practitioner. • View patient's illness as part of the whole. • Relationships among the physical, psychological, and spiritual • Emphasis on preventive medicine • Treatment uses more than 300 medicinal plants and minerals	• *Aloha:* a deep love, respect, and affection between people and the land • Respect given to people and land • Christian gods replaced the myriad of Hawaiian gods. • Lifestyle more revered than compliance with health care issues. • Present oriented, less initiative and drive rather than direction and achievement • Death seen as part of life and not feared.	• Many Hawaiians may still use folk healing practices and home remedies. • Special consideration given to the extensive family network during hospitalization • Acceptance from health care practitioners of current health practices and lifestyle
Appalachian	• Intense interpersonal relations • Family is cohesive, and several generations often live close to each other. • Older members are respected as providers. • Tend to live in rural, isolated areas	• "Granny" woman, or folk healer, provides care and may be consulted even if receiving traditional care. • Various herbs, such as foxglove and yellow root, are used for common illnesses, such as malaise, chest discomfort, heart problems, and upper respiratory infections. • Older members may have had only limited contact with health care providers and be skeptical of modern health care.	• Independence and self-determination • Isolation is accepted as a way of life. • Person-oriented • May be fatalistic about losses and death • Belief in a divine existence rather than attending a particular church	• Treat each person with regard for personal dignity. • Allow family members to remain with patient as support system. • Acceptance from health care providers of current health practices and lifestyle • Allow patients to make decisions about care.

Chapter Wrap-Up

Don't forget to visit thePoint companion website for additional study resources!

CHAPTER HIGHLIGHTS

- Culture affects roles and interactions with others and is apparent in the values, attitudes, and behaviors of particular groups.
- Cultures include both dominant groups and minority groups. A minority group usually has some physical or cultural characteristics that identify the people within it as different from the dominant group.
- Ethnicity involves a sense of identification with a group, largely based on the group's common heritage.
- Race, ethnicity, and culture can influence an individual's physical characteristics. Membership in a particular race might make an individual more likely to develop a genetic condition that can affect his or her health.
- Health care professionals must understand that their view of a given situation could differ from their patient's view.
- Attitudes toward time, including punctuality and orientation toward the past, present, or future, vary culturally.
- Family income affects individual health and access to health care.
- Health care professionals need to be sensitive to patients' changing physical and emotional needs as they grow older.
- Patients' religious beliefs and values may affect how they wish to be treated by health care professionals.
- Methods for treating various illnesses have been passed down from generation to generation within many cultures, and members of those cultures may prefer to rely on such methods or to supplement their medical care with those techniques.

REVIEW QUESTIONS

Matching

1. _____ The presence of people from a variety of ethnic backgrounds and cultural origins in the same society

2. _____ A group of people who are members of a larger cultural group, but whose attitudes and behaviors reflect different beliefs and values from those of the larger culture

3. _____ The group within a society that tends to control that society's values

4. _____ Involves a sense of identification with a group based on a common heritage

5. _____ Belief or assumption that a particular social or cultural group is superior in some way

    a. ethnocentrism **b.** cultural diversity **c.** ethnicity **d.** subculture **e.** dominant group

Multiple Choice

6. Which of the following is NOT a reason that poor families often have poorer health than middle-class or upper-income families?
    a. lack of income
    b. lack of transportation
    c. lack of intelligence
    d. lack of adequate housing

7. Which of the following is an example of a physical or cultural characteristic that may identify members of a minority group?
   - **a.** race
   - **b.** religion
   - **c.** customs and practices
   - **d.** all of the above

8. Which of the following treatments involves inserting needles at specified locations in the body?
   - **a.** acupressure
   - **b.** acupuncture
   - **c.** cutaneous stimulation
   - **d.** therapeutic touch

9. A form of prevention and treatment that uses old-fashioned remedies handed down from generation to generation is known as
   - **a.** conventional medicine
   - **b.** modern medicine
   - **c.** folk medicine
   - **d.** mainstream medicine

10. The feelings of discomfort, stress, and sometimes inferiority that a person experiences when placed in a different culture is known as
    - **a.** ethnic cleansing
    - **b.** culture shock
    - **c.** stereotyping
    - **d.** cultural assimilation

Completion

11. In many cultures, males are _____ and make decisions about health care for the entire family.

12. A shared system of beliefs, values, and behavioral expectations that provide structure for daily living is known as _____.

13. Cultural _____ occurs when an individual shifts his or her identity from the minority group to the dominant group.

14. The hereditary disorder known as _____ affects the shape of red blood cells and interferes with circulation.

15. _____ is different from ethnicity and is normally based on specific physical characteristics, such as skin pigmentation, body stature, facial features, and hair texture.

Short Answer

16. What are stereotypes, and how might they interfere with good patient care?

   _____

   _____

17. How are racial groups typically classified in the U.S.?

   _____

   _____

18. In addition to cultural influences, what other factors play a significant role in shaping a person's view of health care?

   _____

   _____

19. Why might a patient accustomed to folk healers consider modern health care providers incompetent?

   _____

   _____

20. How might religion affect a person's health and health care?

_____

_____

INVESTIGATE IT

1. Ethnic diversity varies widely from city to city, region to region, and state to state. Using the Internet and other available resources, find out which cultures have been most influential in your home state's history. Are those same cultures evident today? For your Internet search, use the words *cultures* and *history*, followed by the name of your state.

2. Folk and traditional health care remedies are often passed down from generation to generation. Ask your parents or other family members about folk remedies that have been passed down in your family. Using the Internet and other available resources, research some folk remedies for conditions that you are interested in. Use the search terms *home remedies* or *natural remedies* to start your search.

RECOMMENDED READING

Koenig HG, Larson DB. Use of hospital services, religious attendance, and religious affiliation [abstract]. *South Med J.* 1998 Oct; 91(10):925–932. Available at http://www.ncbi.nlm.nih.gov/pubmed/9786287.

Taylor C. *Fundamentals of Nursing: The Art and Science of Nursing Care.* Baltimore: Lippincott, Williams, and Wilkins, 2008.

U.S. Census Bureau. Population and Household Economic Topics. Available at http://www.census.gov/population/www/pubs.html.

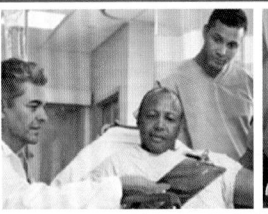
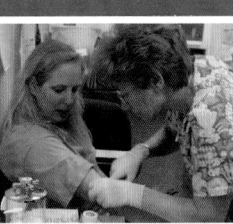

Critical Thinking and Problem Solving

7 C H A P T E R

CHAPTER OBJECTIVES

After careful study of this chapter, you should be able to:

* Define critical thinking.
* Discuss the importance of critical thinking in health care.
* Identify the characteristics of a critical thinker.
* Explain the basic problem-solving approach used in health care.
* Compare and contrast the basic problem-solving method with trial-and-error problem solving,

scientific problem solving, and intuitive problem solving.
* Explain the best way to study.
* Describe the features of a good study area.
* Outline the learning process and important strategies for learning.

KEY TERMS

acronym
acrostic
critical thinking

intuitive problem solving
perception phase
reception phase

scientific problem
 solving
selection phase

trial-and-error problem
 solving
working memory

Health care professionals work with patients whose health involves many different factors. They confront situations that require quick and clear-minded decision making. For these reasons, most health care professionals use critical-thinking and problem-solving skills every day.

Although critical thinking and problem solving are two separate skills, they're both useful tools for making good decisions and finding the best solution to a problem. Health care workers who can think critically and make good judgments based on the information at hand are better equipped to do their job well. This chapter discusses the use of critical thinking and problem solving in health care careers. It also describes study skills that will serve you now as a student and later in your career.

CRITICAL THINKING

As a health care professional, you should use critical thinking—continually and proactively *thinking* about the tasks at hand, applying your knowledge and skills in a thoughtful and "present" way—and not simply rely on rote actions and skills. **Critical thinking**, as defined by Dr. Richard Paul, Director of Research and Professional Development at the Center for Critical Thinking, is "a systematic way to form and shape one's thinking. It functions purposefully and exactingly. It is thought that is disciplined, comprehensive, based on intellectual standards, and, as a result, well-reasoned." Critical-thinking skills allow you to achieve results through focused thinking. Effective critical thinking in health care has four features:

● It is purposeful and results-oriented.
● It is based on principles of health care practice and the scientific method, which means that judgments are based on evidence rather than guesswork.
● It is guided by professional standards and ethics codes.
● It is self-correcting through constant reevaluation and reflects a desire to improve.

Critical thinking skills are crucial in emergencies and other high-pressure health care situations.

Analyzing and Evaluating Information

When you think critically, you analyze information objectively to form your own judgment about it. The information may come from your own observations, personal experience, and reasoning, or it may be data communicated to you by others. As a health care professional, you continually gather and analyze information and evaluate results on a daily basis. If you're able to think critically and make good judgments based on information you gather, you'll have a positive impact on patients' health.

Whether it involves a patient's medical history or an article to be read for class, the analysis process involves breaking information into parts that can be easily understood. For example, if you have been assigned to read articles on a topic and then give a class presentation, you must first ensure that you understand the information contained in each article. You can't talk about a subject if you don't fully understand it yourself. To do this, you must break the information into parts and ask a few basic questions:

● What is the main purpose of each article?
● What is the most important information in each article?
● What data support the main purpose of each article?
● What are the key concepts or most important ideas in each article? How do they relate to the article's main purpose?
● What message is the author trying to convey?

Health care professionals follow the same analytical process. When analyzing patient information, for example, you might ask these questions:

● What is the main purpose of this patient's visit?
● What is the most important information given by this patient?
● What data support the information presented by the patient?
● What are the key concepts or most important ideas learned from the information? How does each relate to the patient's purpose?
● What message is the patient trying to communicate?

To determine whether information you've gathered has value or relevance, you must evaluate it by assessing which conclusions are actually supported by facts and research.

Characteristics of a Critical Thinker

Critical thinkers have certain characteristics or qualities:
● fair-mindedness
● autonomy
● perseverance
● integrity
● creativity

- humility
- confidence

Fair-Mindedness versus Unfair-Mindedness

Critical thinking is not based on stereotypes or unreasoned opinions. Critical thinkers are open to all viewpoints and evaluate the viewpoints equally. This enables them to consider opposing points of view and understand new ideas fully before accepting or rejecting them. For example, a health care professional who thinks critically will listen to statements by the patient, members of the patient's family, and other health care professionals before reaching a conclusion.

Autonomy versus Conformity

In Chapter 4, "Personal Qualities and Professional Skills for Success," you learned about respecting patient autonomy—patients' rights to make decisions about their health care (even if you do not agree). Autonomy is also a component of critical thinking. To be a critical thinker, you must think for yourself and reach your own conclusions. Critical thinkers are committed to analyzing and evaluating beliefs and values; they do not simply accept established ways of doing things. Critical thinkers question when it's reasonable to question, believe when it's reasonable to believe, and conform when it's reasonable to conform. For a health care worker, thinking autonomously might mean, for example, being open to talking with a patient in a different manner in order to learn the patient's medical history. It may not be reasonable to always follow the same routine exactly the way you originally learned it.

Perseverance versus Laziness

Perseverance requires dedication and determination to find an effective solution to a problem. Important issues are often complex and confusing and require a great deal of thought and research in order to reach the best solution. It can be tempting to find the quickest, easiest answer when a situation becomes confusing or frustrating. However, the critical thinker will persevere to find the best solution. Suppose, for example, that an occupational therapist designs a set of exercises for a patient recovering from a stroke. If the therapist determines that the patient finds the exercises too difficult at this stage of recovery, he or she needs to persevere in developing a new set of steps.

Integrity versus Deceit

Integrity means that a person applies the same rigorous standards of proof to his or her own knowledge and beliefs as the person would apply to the knowledge and beliefs of others. Health care professionals who are critical thinkers question their own knowledge and beliefs as thoroughly as they challenge those of colleagues, patients, and others. For example, a dietetic technician believes that a certain type of low-fat diet is best for patients seeking to lose weight. However, reading an article about a new study comparing the varying effectiveness of different types of diets for different people may lead to reconsidering that belief.

Creativity versus Lack of Creativity

A critical thinker always questions the best way to accomplish any task. While critical thinkers value traditional solutions to problems, they also recognize that more creative solutions may be needed. For example, suppose a five-year-old boy has just had abdominal surgery. He needs to breathe deeply with an apparatus to help prevent pneumonia. He resists doing this, however, because it's painful and the apparatus upsets him. Rather than insisting that the boy use the apparatus, the respiratory therapist considers other, less intimidating methods that can help the boy breathe deeply. To solve the problem, the therapist obtains some bubble solutions and has the boy blow bubbles through a wand. Now the boy is breathing deeply while simultaneously having fun.

Humility versus Arrogance

People who are humble are aware of the limits of their own knowledge. Being willing to admit what you don't know is an important characteristic of a critical thinker. For example, Regina, a young woman right out of school, is hired as a radiologic technician at a local hospital. Recognizing that she is still learning, she doesn't simply forge ahead, assuming that she knows everything about her job. Instead, she asks her mentor for advice and guidance when she doesn't understand a directive or procedure.

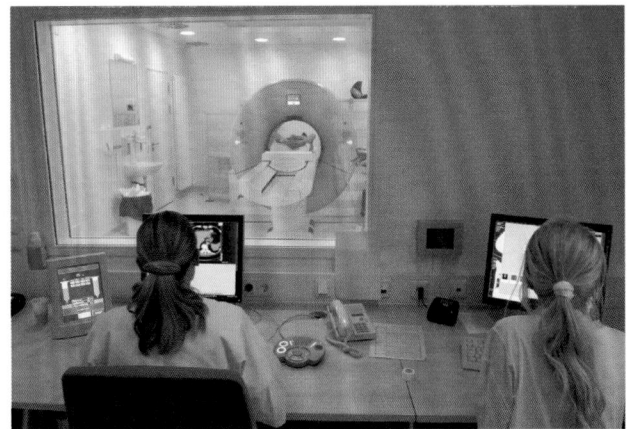

It is not a sign of weakness to ask a more experienced colleague or supervisor for help or guidance.

Confidence versus Distrust

Critical thinkers believe that well-reasoned thinking will lead to trustworthy conclusions, so they have confidence in the reasoning process. For example, Jeff, a dental hygienist who works with a dentist in private practice, sees a patient for prophylactic treatment while the dentist is out of the office and notes what may be an oral medical condition. Although not qualified to make a diagnosis, he takes the initiative to schedule the patient for another appointment with the dentist. With his 10 years of experience, he is confident in his ability to make this decision.

Improving Your Critical-Thinking Skills

How can you improve your critical-thinking skills? There's no one right answer to that question, but the first step is to be critical of your thinking—to think about how you think. Here are a few ideas to get you started thinking about your thinking:

- **Clarify your thinking.** What's the real meaning behind what people are saying in a conversation, a journal article, or a news story? What's the real meaning behind what you're saying? Summarize what you hear or read and ask for confirmation that you understood it correctly. Don't agree or disagree until you're sure that you understand what was said or what you've read. Conversely, when you are transmitting information, restate your point in different words or give examples to illustrate your point, and then ask those receiving the information to summarize or restate it.
- **Discipline your thinking.** Focus your thinking on what is relevant to the task at hand or the problem you're trying to solve. Be on the lookout for illogical leaps in thinking. Retain those thoughts that are logically

connected to the main task or problem, but don't allow your mind to wander to unrelated thoughts.
- **Ask meaningful questions.** What types of questions do you typically ask? Are they superficial questions whose answers don't really increase your understanding, or are they penetrating questions that, when answered, lead to deeper understanding of an issue or clarification of a problem? Become a skilled questioner so that you can clarify situations, problems, and solutions more effectively. Don't simply accept how others portray situations or problems.
- **Be willing to change your mind.** It is human nature to believe that your thoughts and views are sound and accurate—and they may be. But other people often have better thoughts and views. Are you willing to consider the views of others? Be open to changing your mind when presented with good reasons to change it.

✓ CHECK POINT

1 What are the seven characteristics of critical thinkers?

PROBLEM SOLVING

Everyone solves problems (either effectively or less so) in both their personal and professional lives. While there are different approaches to solving problems, most health care professionals use the general problem-solving technique illustrated in Figure 7-1.

Basic Problem-Solving Approach in Action

The basic problem-solving approach involves five steps: (1) identify the problem; (2) gather information and identify

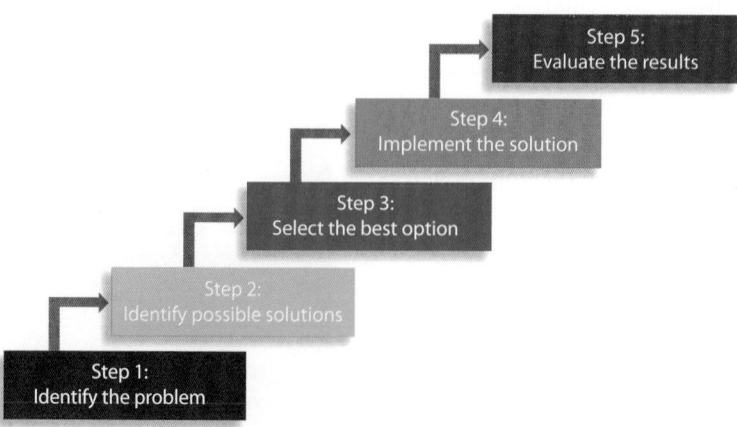

Figure 7-1 This basic problem-solving process is a logical, thorough method health care workers can use to analyze problems and identify the best solution.

possible solutions; (3) select the best option; (4) implement the solution; and (5) evaluate the results. To demonstrate the process, let's use an example to see it in action:

As a health care professional, you recommend that one of your patients attend a local support group that meets once a month. Your patient agrees, but he has no car, and the bus ride from his apartment to the meeting place is very long. The plan, then, seems unrealistic. This situation calls for problem solving.

- **Identify the Problem.** You begin by clearly defining the problem, so that you and the patient are focused on the same issue. In this example, the problem is the patient's lack of convenient transportation to the support group.
- **Gather Information and Identify Possible Solutions.** After identifying the problem, you need to gather all the pertinent data. Get all the facts that you can that relate to this situation. This step may take some time, but it will lay a solid foundation for your decision-making process. Collect data that can help you solve the problem. Ways to do this include:
  - Brainstorming in small groups
  - Collecting data from the patient through assessment
  - Conducting research
- Brainstorming encourages people to generate creative thoughts spontaneously, without stopping to analyze each idea. During brainstorming sessions, there should be no criticism of ideas. You are trying to open up possibilities and break down wrong assumptions about the limits of the problem. People may come up with ideas and thoughts that seem to be a bit shocking or crazy at first. Ideas should only be judged or analyzed at the end of the brainstorming session. At that point, you can change and improve them into possible solutions that are useful—and often quite original.
- Continuing with our example, you and the patient make a list of ways to solve the problem. These might include getting a ride from someone else attending the same meeting, getting a ride from a relative, taking the bus and bringing along a book to read during the trip, or finding a closer support group.
- **Select the Best Option.** From among the various ideas, choose the course of action that will provide the greatest chance for success. Consider the short- and long-term effects of each idea. In our example, you encourage the patient to decide which solution he thinks will work best. Because he enjoys reading, he decides that he can make good use of the time he spends riding the bus to and from meetings by reading.
- **Implement the Solution.** Some solutions provide immediate results, and some take a while to show results, so be sure to give the solution enough time to

work. In our example, you encourage the patient to put this solution into action, reminding him to remain open-minded about it. You explain that he may need to try riding the bus a few times, especially if the trip seems too long or unpleasant at first. You point out that he may get used to it over time.

- **Evaluate the Results.** After allowing time for the solution to work, reassess the situation. Has the problem been solved? To conclude our example, after a period of time, you meet again with the patient to determine whether the goal has been reached. If the patient regularly attends the group, the problem is solved. If not, you encourage the patient to try another solution, and then schedule a follow-up appointment to reevaluate his situation.

Trial-and-Error Problem Solving

Trial-and-error problem solving involves testing any number of solutions until one is found that solves a particular problem. While this method may be a useful problem-solving technique for some aspects of everyday life—such as solving the problem of a boring diet by experimenting with different new foods—it is not an effective problem-solving technique for health care professionals, and it could be dangerous to patients. For example, it would be dangerous if you used trial and error to determine the food to supply a dehydrated and malnourished patient. Instead, you need to know, based on clinical research, exactly what food and fluid supplements are most likely to reverse the patient's deficiencies.

Scientific Problem Solving

Scientific problem solving is a systematic problem-solving process that involves the following seven steps:

1. problem identification
2. data collection
3. hypothesis formulation
4. plan of action
5. hypothesis testing
6. interpretation of results
7. evaluation

Scientific problem solving is a more complex version of the basic problem-solving method. Because of the rigorous demands of scientific proof, it is used in controlled laboratory settings to carry out experiments. For example, a clinical laboratory technologist working at a pharmaceutical company would use a process similar to this one. (Health care occupations in laboratory services are detailed in Chapter 21, "Laboratory and Pharmacy Services.")

Because of the rigorous demands of scientific proof, scientific problem solving is used in controlled laboratory settings to carry out experiments.

Intuitive Problem Solving

While some health care theorists and educators argue that clinical judgments should be based on data alone, others acknowledge the role intuition plays in clinical decision making. Many health care professionals can describe situations in which an inner prompting led to a quick intervention that saved a patient's life.

When a person instinctively, without logical thinking, identifies a solution to a problem based on its similarity or dissimilarity to other problems, he or she is using **intuitive problem solving**. For example, a recovery room nurse who intervenes to help a postoperative patient whose condition is worsening, even before there are measurable signs of trouble, is using intuitive problem solving.

✓ CHECK POINT

2 What are the five steps of basic problem solving?

3 Where is the scientific problem-solving technique most often used?

STUDY SKILLS

Applying critical-thinking and problem-solving skills as you study will help you learn more successfully, both now and later in your chosen health care field. A career in health care involves life-long learning—and life-long studying—so it's important to learn effective study skills while you're still in school.

Many strategies can help both students and health care professionals make the most of their study time and resources. To some, studying is fairly straightforward. They simply gather their books and begin reading and taking notes. Others are less certain what it means to study. Studying involves four processes:

- refreshing one's memory
- taking in new information
- organizing and memorizing data
- making connections among information

Many individuals feel overwhelmed at the thought of studying an unfamiliar subject. Any little distraction can divert their attention and keep them from studying efficiently. To really learn and understand something, you first must learn the right way to study.

Study Area

You need a good place to study. Look for a location that is free of distractions. Ask yourself the following questions:

- Are there a lot of other people in the same area who could interrupt me?
- Are there things in the area that will distract me from studying?
- Is there a TV or radio in the area that might be turned on?
- Is there a phone that might ring too often?
- Is this area easy for me to get to regularly?
- Is the temperature comfortable? If it isn't, can I change it?
- Will cooking odors come into this area, making me feel hungry and distracted?
- Is this area big enough so that it won't get cluttered when I spread out all of my materials?
- Is there enough light so that I can read without straining my eyes?

The area should be large enough to arrange all study materials. For example, some students prefer to sit at a table when they study. This arrangement keeps them alert and focused, while helping them keep their materials organized. Other students, however, feel more comfortable sitting on a sofa, placing study materials on a coffee table or on the floor below. One place to avoid studying is in bed, where taking a nap may be too tempting.

To choose a good study area, you also need to think about the lighting, temperature, and surroundings.

Lighting

A good study area needs sufficient lighting that can be controlled. Light is very important. Too much will make your eyes hurt, while too little will force you to strain your eyes. The light should shine evenly over all your work and not directly into your eyes.

Temperature

Most people want to be comfortable when studying. Being too cold is distracting, and it is difficult to take notes with cold fingers. However, being too hot can cause heat stress, which impairs mental sharpness and can lead to drowsiness. For studying, the best temperature is between 65 and 70° F (18 to 21° C).

The best way to make sure that a study area is set to a comfortable temperature is to try it out yourself. A half-hour should be sufficient for you to judge whether the area's temperature is comfortable. Bear in mind that a nearby air conditioning or heating vent can make you too cold or too hot, or a nearby door may cause you to feel a draft.

Surroundings

A study area should be inviting. It should make you feel good and encourage you to want to spend time there. A pleasant space can make you more alert. The following tips will help you be more alert and avoid distractions while studying:

- Background music can promote relaxed alertness, which stimulates learning. It also may improve your recall. But avoid music that is too loud or that tempts you to sing along.
- Rather than music, some people like what is called white noise, such as a bubbling fountain or the hum of an electric fan. White noise blocks out other sounds without creating a distraction.
- To avoid the distraction of phone calls, leave your phone in another room, or turn it off and let an answering machine or voice mail take messages. Similarly, avoid reading or replying to text messages, sending emails, or engaging in other forms of social networking.
- Turn off the TV, or, better yet, study in a room without a TV.

Daily Preparation

Daily preparation helps you keep up with your coursework or job. To prepare for each day, make to-do lists and keep a daily planner. Then review all the resources related to the upcoming tasks, such as:

- reading texts
- reviewing notes
- studying patient files
- analyzing test results
- consulting fellow learners or colleagues
- examining additional resources

It is also wise to cover material in small amounts at a time. Information is more easily absorbed in chunks. Thus, reading short segments of a text or studying notes for brief periods of time is more effective than long cramming sessions. Studying in one-hour sessions, with breaks between sessions, is a productive study schedule.

In school as well as in your career, you'll be more productive and focused if you start each day with a solid "to do" list.

ZOOM IN

More Study Tips

From books to web sites, many resources provide tips and tricks for improving study habits. In addition to the skills already covered in this chapter, here are more techniques for making the most of your study time:

- Think of studying as practice, not work—practice makes perfect.
- Remember that the quality of study time is much more important than the quantity.
- Study every day—make it a habit.
- Determine your best study time, and plan on studying at the same time every day.
- Study with a friend, colleague, or study group; compare notes and ask each other questions.
- Start with the most difficult tasks or assignments, and then move on to the easier ones; this focuses maximum brain power on the hardest tasks.
- Spend more time, not less, on the subjects you find most difficult.
- Try to recall the main points and as many details as possible after every study session.
- Try relating new information to something you already know.
- Ask a teacher, parent, colleague, or friend for help when you're unsure of something—asking questions is one of the most effective ways to learn.
- Plan a fun activity as a reward for when you're done studying.

The Learning Process

Learning involves much more than short-term memorization or "just knowing it for the test." To truly learn something, you must understand the subject fully, so that you can recall it and apply it when necessary.

The learning process begins when the brain receives information. This information can be received through a variety of ways, but reading is a very common one for students. Reading is more than simply running your eyes over a page. As you read, you should be asking yourself questions about the material. This helps ensure that you understand what you're reading. Many textbooks include review questions at the end of each chapter. Check your comprehension by trying to answer these questions, even if they haven't been assigned. If you're able to answer these questions correctly, you likely understand the material.

When reading material, you should:

- Pay special attention to bold and italicized print.
- Write main paragraph points in page margins or a notebook.
- Read everything, including tables, graphs and illustrations.

Whether through reading, listening, or using some other means, the process of learning information has three parts: reception, perception, and selection. In the **reception phase**, you take in information without yet knowing what it means. For instance, you may read about a symptom in your anatomy and physiology textbook, such as a "whooshing" sound coming from the bowel. However, you don't know what the sound means or what condition it represents. During the **perception phase**, you give meaning to the information. For example, your instructor may say that whooshing sounds might mean that the bowel is obstructed. You can now attach a meaning to the sound, and you begin to understand the symptom you've been reading about in your A&P textbook. Finally, during the **selection phase**, your brain recognizes information as important or unimportant. If you decide something is important, like the fact that whooshing sounds could mean an obstructed bowel, then that fact is processed for remembering. If you decide the fact is unimportant, you may forget it.

To ensure you remember information you've received, you should review it—ideally immediately after receiving it. It is a mistake to wait until just before an examination to begin reviewing.

To review something that you've studied, you rely on your working memory. The term **working memory** describes how the brain stores and retrieves information from short-term and long-term memory. Short-term memory is limited. It lasts as little as 15 seconds and can't store a great deal of information. In fact, research has shown that short-term memory can hold only five to nine chunks of information, depending on how well the information is grouped. For example, the numbers 1-9-2-9-0-0-7 are more easily remembered through grouping: 1929 and 007. These two groups are much easier to remember than all seven individual numbers. Grouping makes space for more data in short-term memory.

After information has been grouped, the brain either forgets it or moves it to long-term memory, where it's organized and stored for longer periods. How long depends on how completely the information is processed and how often you recall and use it. There are many ways to help move information from short- to long-term memory, but the best way is to recall or review the information immediately and often.

Sometimes, though, despite our efforts, information is forgotten. However, it may still be possible to retrieve that information. The next time you have trouble remembering something important, try these techniques to help you remember:

1. Say or write down everything you can remember about the information you're seeking.

2. Try to recall events or information in a different order.

3. Recreate the learning environment or relive the event. Include sounds, smells, and details about the weather, objects, or people who were there. Try to recapture what you said, thought, or felt at the time.

Different Strategies for Learning

Once information has been received and reviewed, the problem most people face is making sure the information stays in their long-term memory. This can be difficult, especially if the information isn't used regularly. Information is more easily forgotten when you're not very interested in the subject, when you lack a real purpose for learning, or when you have few or no connections between the memory and other pieces of information. However, you can use several fun strategies to help you store information in your long-term memory.

Make Associations

Making links between familiar items and new information helps you remember the new information. Once established, these links become automatic. Each time you recall a familiar item, you also remember the information associated with it.

Follow these steps to form associations as you study:

1. First, select the information to be remembered. For example, suppose you want to remember that osteoporosis causes a person's bones to become brittle.

2. Next, create an association to the information. You might associate the details about osteoporosis with the name of a person you know who has the condition. (Osteoporosis reminds me of Mary, who broke her hip. Osteoporosis → Mary → brittle bones.)

The most effective associations are personal, such as associating a song, a person, or a scent with the item being remembered. For some people, a certain smell takes them right back to a specific time in their past. When such people associate information with that smell, the memory of the information will be just as sharp.

Acronyms and Acrostics

Acronyms and acrostics are handy ways of recalling information, too. **Acronyms** are words created from the first letter of each word in a phrase or each item on a list. For example, ASAP is an acronym for the phrase "as soon as possible." The acronym **_RICE_** helps people remember the treatment of some musculoskeletal injuries:

- **R**est
- **I**ce
- **C**ompression
- **E**levation

Acrostics are phrases or sentences created from the first letter of each item on a list. In health care, a well-known acrostic helps identify the 12 cranial nerves: **_O_**n **_O_**ld **_O_**lympus' **_T_**owering **_T_**ops, **_A_** **_F_**inn and a **_S_**wedish **_G_**irl **_V_**iewed **_S_**ome **_H_**ops. The initial letters stand for the nerves:

- **O**lfactory nerve
- **O**ptic nerve
- **O**culomotor nerve
- **T**rochlear nerve
- **T**rigeminal nerve
- **A**bduscens nerve
- **F**acial nerve
- **S**ensorimotor nerve
- **G**lossopharyngeal nerve
- **V**agus nerve
- **S**pinal accessory nerve
- **H**ypoglossal nerve

Acronyms and acrostics work especially well when it's hard to find a personal memory or other association for a piece of data. For example, it's probably difficult for someone to feel personal about the 12 cranial nerves. Acronyms and acrostics connect pieces of information to a new, but easily remembered, word or phrase, thus improving a person's ability to retain the information.

Flashcards

Flashcards are an effective study tool for learning new material or reviewing information. Write a term on one side of the card and the definition, formula, or other information about the term on the other side. When used with a partner, flashcards can be a fun review game. As a study partner holds up each card, attempt to recall the pertinent information. Mix up the cards to ensure that you understand each term separately, rather than as part of a certain sequence.

Music

Most people can still remember the lyrics of songs they heard years ago. Even if they haven't heard the song in years, hearing the first few notes may be enough to help them remember all of its lyrics. If they were asked to speak the lyrics, however, they might not be able to. The addition of a melody helps trigger memory. This principle can be applied to other information you need to learn. Making up a short jingle to go along with new material can make it much easier to recall the information later on.

Study Groups

Some people learn new information better by explaining it to someone else, like a classmate or coworker. By explaining it, they're actively processing the information, or thinking about it more clearly and deeply.

Studying in a small group can be helpful to all group members because everyone is "thinking out loud," sharing ideas, and learning from one another. Even if a study group is unable to answer everyone's questions, hearing others' thoughts on a subject is a good way to learn.

Studying in a small group can be helpful to all group members because interacting and sharing ideas can lead to participants learning from one another.

Getting the Group Together

A successful study group has members who reflect the four C's:

- Committed—truly interested in learning the material
- Contributing—willing to share their knowledge
- Compatible—able to overlook differences and focus on studying together
- Considerate—willing to arrive for studying on time

It is easier to stay on task when everyone in the group is interested in the same thing—studying. If the group becomes too large (more than four or five members), it should break into smaller groups. A smaller number makes it easier to review all the necessary material and answer each other's questions.

Making the Most of the Group Session

One of the greatest benefits of studying in a small group is the mutual support. Working in a group can also reinforce what you have learned and deepen your understanding of complex concepts. These tips will help you get the most out of study group sessions:

- **Determine objectives**. Group members need to know what they're going to achieve at each session. The group might want to pick a designated or rotating leader to set the objectives.
- **Prepare in advance**. Group members need to come to the study session prepared, by reading, reviewing notes, or doing whatever else needs to be done. This will help to make the most of everyone's time together.
- **Alternate instruction**. When group members take turns instructing the group, everyone in the group learns the material better.
- **Focus on the task**. The group needs to stay on the topic at hand. The group leader needs to steer the group back if it veers off that topic.

CHECK POINT

4 What are the important characteristics of a good study area?

5 List effective strategies for learning and retaining knowledge in long-term memory.

Don't forget to visit thePoint companion website for additional study resources!

CHAPTER HIGHLIGHTS

- Health care professionals should use critical thinking, a systematic way to form and shape one's thinking, and not simply rely on rote actions and skills.
- The characteristics of critical thinkers include fair-mindedness, autonomy, perseverance, integrity, creativity, humility, and confidence.
- The problem-solving technique used by most health care professionals involves five steps: (1) identifying the problem, (2) gathering information and identifying possible solutions, (3) selecting the best option, (4) implementing the solution, and (5) evaluating the results. Other problem-solving techniques include trial and error, scientific problem solving, and intuition.
- Studying involves four processes: (1) refreshing one's memory; (2) taking in new information; (3) organizing and memorizing data; and (4) making connections among information.
- A good place to study is free of distractions and has adequate space and lighting, a comfortable temperature, and pleasant surroundings.
- Learning involves much more than short-term memorization. When you truly learn something, you understand it fully, so that you can recall it and apply it when necessary.
- Strategies that can help you store information in long-term memory include making associations, using acronyms and acrostics, making flashcards, putting information to music, and studying in small groups.

REVIEW QUESTIONS

Matching

1. _____ Encourages people to generate creative thoughts spontaneously, without stopping to analyze each idea

2. _____ Being capable of thinking for oneself and reaching one's own conclusions

3. _____ Word created from the first letter of each word in a phrase or each item on a list

4. _____ Phrase or sentence created from the first letter of each item on a list

5. _____ Being open to all viewpoints and evaluating them equally

   a. fair-mindedness **b.** acrostic **c.** autonomy **d.** brainstorming **e.** acronym

Multiple Choice

6. Studying involves
   - **a.** refreshing one's memory
   - **b.** taking in new information
   - **c.** organizing and memorizing data
   - **d.** all of the above

7. When a person instinctively, without logical thinking, identifies a solution to a problem based on its similarity or dissimilarity to other problems, which type of problem solving is the person using?
   - **a.** trial-and-error
   - **b.** intuitive
   - **c.** scientific
   - **d.** brainstorming

8. Surveying material that has already been covered is called
   - **a.** reviewing
   - **b.** receiving
   - **c.** perception
   - **d.** selection

9. Where does the brain organize and store information for extended periods?
   a. long-term memory
   b. short-term memory
   c. working memory
   d. none of the above

10. Which type of memory can hold five to nine chunks of information, depending on how well the information is grouped?
   a. long-term memory
   b. short-term memory
   c. working memory
   d. none of the above

Completion

11. _____ thinking is a systematic way to form and shape one's thinking that functions purposefully and exactingly.

12. The basic problem-solving process includes identifying the problem; identifying possible _____; selecting the best option; implementing the solution; and evaluating the results.

13. _____ problem solving is a systematic problem-solving process used in controlled laboratory settings.

14. A good study area should be free of _____ and have adequate space and lighting, a comfortable temperature, and pleasant surroundings.

15. _____ memory describes how the brain stores and retrieves information from short-term and long-term memory.

Short Answer

16. Name at least five characteristics of critical thinkers.

   _____

   _____

17. What steps are involved in the scientific problem-solving process?

   _____

   _____

18. What are the four features of effective critical thinking in health care?

   _____

   _____

19. Briefly describe the three-part process of learning information.

   _____

   _____

20. What four elements should members of a successful study group possess?

   _____

   _____

Table 7-1 Characteristics of Critical Thinkers

Rating	Characteristic
	Fair-mindedness—is open to all viewpoints and evaluates them equally
	Autonomy—thinks for oneself and reaches one's own conclusions
	Perseverance—persists to find an effective solution to a problem
	Integrity—applies the same rigorous standards of proof to one's own knowledge and beliefs as to those of others
	Creativity—questions the best way to accomplish a task and devises new or different approaches to solve a problem
	Humility—is aware of the limits of one's own knowledge and is willing to admit a lack of knowledge
	Confidence—believes that well-reasoned thinking will lead to trustworthy conclusions

INVESTIGATE IT

1. Characteristics of critical thinkers are summarized in Table 7-1 above. Think about situations where you either demonstrated or failed to demonstrate these characteristics. Using a scale of 1 to 7, with 1 meaning "almost never" and 7 meaning "always," rate how well you think you demonstrate each of the characteristics in the table. Then invite others who know you well to rate you, too. Did you and the others who rated you reach the same conclusions?

2. Puzzles, logic problems, and riddles are all fun ways to sharpen one's critical-thinking skills. Using the Internet and other available resources, find some interesting "brain teaser" exercises and use critical-thinking skills to solve them. A variety of puzzles can be found at the following web sites:

   - http://www.mathsisfun.com/chicken_crossing.html
   - http://www.brainbashers.com

RECOMMENDED READING

Elder L. Are you a critical thinker? Available at: http://www.csmonitor.com/2009/0312/p09s01-coop.html.

Olrech N. *Student Success for Health Professionals Made Incredibly Easy*. Baltimore: Lippincott Williams & Wilkins, 2008

Paul R. *Critical Thinking: How to Prepare Students for a Rapidly Changing World*. Santa Rosa, CA: Foundation for Critical Thinking, 1995.

Taylor C. *Fundamentals of Nursing: The Art and Science of Nursing Care*. Baltimore: Lippincott Williams & Wilkins, 2008.

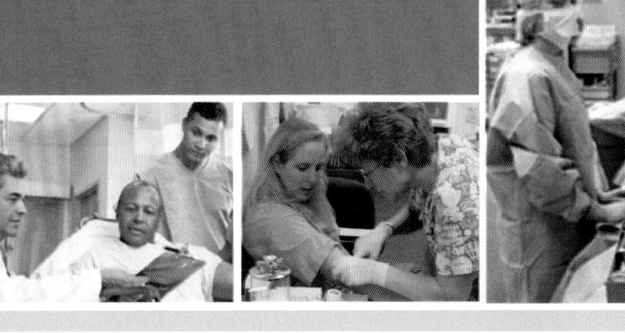

Teamwork and Leadership

CHAPTER OBJECTIVES

After careful study of this chapter, you should be able to:

✳ Explain the characteristics of effective teams.

✳ Give an example of how a health care team may be composed.

✳ Characterize the elements of team structure.

✳ List tips for effective teamwork.

✳ Explain how to manage conflict.

✳ Define leadership skills, styles, and responsibilities.

KEY TERMS

autocratic leadership

conflict

democratic leadership

directive leadership

group dynamics

health care team

laissez-faire leadership (le-sā-FAR)

leadership

multidisciplinary team

nondirective leadership

teamwork

When discussing teamwork, people often use sports examples. These examples are effective because the basic principles that make up a good sports team also apply to professional teams. Sports teams, military teams, academic competition teams, management teams, and health care teams all have one thing in common—they're made up of a group of individuals working cooperatively toward a common goal. In health care, teams can take various forms, including:

● administrative teams
● medical emergency teams
● hospital patient care teams
● physician's office teams
● dental office teams
● outpatient care teams

At the helm of any successful team is a good leader. Teamwork and leadership both play important roles in all health care careers.

DEFINITION OF A TEAM

The most basic definition of a team is two or more individuals organized to function cooperatively together. The way a team is organized depends on the purpose of the team.

Team Composition

Teams are composed of members who are focused on the same results. Whether the end result is a sports victory, a successful business project, or quality patient care, teams are organized to make the most of different members' strengths in order to achieve the team's goals.

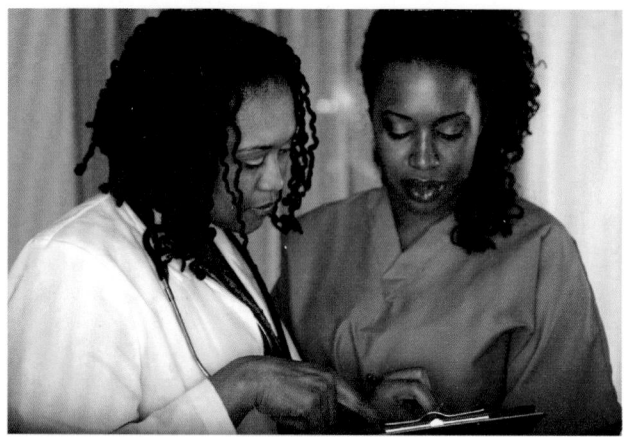

Teams are composed of members who are focused on the same results, even though their specific responsibilities may differ.

A **health care team** consists of health care professionals who often have a variety of health-related backgrounds, education, and experiences. The two main types of health care teams are those composed of individuals from the same profession and those that include individuals from more than one discipline.

One-Profession Team

A team consisting of professionals working within the same field is a one-profession team. A team leader or coordinator is responsible for organizing and overseeing a one-profession team. This person assigns tasks to individual members and serves as the central point of communication within the team.

A nursing team is a good example of a one-profession health care team. A nursing team may consist of a combination of nursing professionals:
- registered nurses (RNs)
- licensed practical nurses (LPNs)
- licensed vocational nurses (LVNs)
- certified nursing assistants (CNAs)

Each team member provides a different nursing-related service. These services are coordinated under the leadership of the RN, who outlines and implements patient care plans. This includes assigning team members tasks that utilize their individual abilities. Nursing team members all work toward the common goal of providing quality patient care.

Multidisciplinary Team

A **multidisciplinary team** is a cooperative group that includes professionals with different qualifications, skills, and areas of expertise. While each member has different capabilities, they generally complement each other. In health care, multidisciplinary teams provide comprehensive care. A cardiac rehabilitation team, for example, provides patients with physical, emotional, social, and occupational therapy after a heart attack. The common goal of this team is to restore the skills and abilities of the patient while providing care. This broad goal couldn't be achieved with members from only one health care area. Instead, a combination of specialists from a wide range of health care areas is needed. This team may consist of all or some of the members listed in Table 8-1.

Elements of Team Structure

The structure of a team, and how well the team members understand that structure, often determines whether or not a team is successful. Members are responsible for determining the team's purpose, specific goals, the roles of team members, and the functions of the team. It is very important for all team members to understand each element of a team's structure. If not, members risk wasting valuable time and resources working toward different objectives.

Team Purpose

A team's purpose needs to be defined. What is the reason for the team? What does it hope to accomplish? A team's purpose points all members in the right direction and determines how the team should develop and move forward. A health care team's general purpose is to provide or support patient care, although certain health care teams may have other specific purposes.

Team Goals

A properly functioning team requires all members to interact and coordinate their actions in order to achieve common goals or objectives. This means that decisions can't be made independently. Instead, decisions need to be made as a group, in the best interest of the team and its goals. To

Table 8-1 Potential Members of a Cardiac Rehabilitation Team and Their Responsibilities

Team Member	Responsibilities
Cardiologist	• Evaluate and treat patients with heart problems • Coordinate patient care services with other team members
Rehabilitation Nurse	• Specialize in rehabilitative care • Assist patients in achieving maximum independence • Provide patient and family education
Clinical Social Worker	• Professional counselor • Acts as liaison for the patient, family, and rehabilitation treatment team • Coordinates and provides support for discharge planning and referrals • Helps coordinate care with insurance companies
Physical Therapist and Physical Therapy Assistants	• Work to restore functions for patients with problems related to movement, muscle strength, exercise, and joint function
Occupational Therapist and Occupational Therapy Assistants	• Work to restore functions for patients with problems related to activities of daily living (ADLs) including work, school, family, and community and leisure activities
Registered Dietitian	• Evaluate and provide for the dietary needs of each patient based on the patient's particular medical and nutritional needs, eating abilities, and food preferences

accomplish the team's goals, all team members need to be willing to listen to the opinions of other team members.

Health care teams interact to make decisions and coordinate care as a group.

Team Members' Roles

Teams typically include individuals possessing unique and distinct skill sets. The most productive teams have members with a balanced combination of talents and abilities, with each member contributing to the overall purpose. Members have roles within the team based on their strengths. Each member is expected to perform all relevant tasks to the best of his or her ability. Some roles within a team might be assigned, while others might simply be assumed by the person best able to carry them out at the time. Individuals may also have different roles

in different situations. General roles found within any team are:

- *Team leader.* Defines issues, sets the agenda, and coordinates work of team members.
- *Recorder or secretary.* Records the ideas of all team members; may act as a timekeeper during meetings.
- *Spokesperson.* Maintains contact with others on behalf of the group.
- *Resource.* Provides unique knowledge or expertise on a particular issue.
- *Implementers.* Carry out the specific activities, such as patient care, determined by the team.

Members bring a variety of personalities to a team, each playing an important role. For example, a *reflector* observes the group process while participating in team activities. This team member can report the results of these observations, providing insight into the way team members are working together. Another important role is that of the *optimist.* This team member has a positive attitude that encourages others to find solutions and overcome challenges. Another team member may play the role of *skeptic*, reviewing ideas for potential problems.

Every team member and every role is just as valuable as another. Depending on the purpose and goals of a team, roles may be added, adjusted, or removed. Some members may also assume more than one role on a team. Once members assume specific roles on a team, they're responsible for fulfilling the tasks relating to those roles. When members attempt to perform duties outside their roles, they risk steering the team away from meeting its goals. For example, if the secretary of a team attempts to coordinate patient care, this interferes with the team leader's role and may leave the recording duties unfulfilled.

Team Functions

Team functions are the activities that the team members must carry out to meet the team's goals. Because a team may have many different specific goals, certain team members will accomplish some of the goals, while other members will work on other goals. When health care professionals work as a team, they can focus their time and attention on performing the functions appropriate to their individual skills and experience. For example, while a registered nurse may actively implement certain medical interventions, a nurse assistant may provide the patient with hygiene care. Or when a dentist is about to perform a restoration procedure, a dental assistant may prepare the patient and organize the equipment needed for the procedure.

How well team members perform their assigned duties has a direct impact on other members, the team's goals, and the patient's care. Given the rapid advances in all areas of health care, team members must keep their knowledge and skills up to date. Through continuing education, they can learn about new methods and procedures, treatment options, and other health care advances.

Tips for Effective Teamwork

Being *on* a team does not necessarily mean that you are working *as* a team. **Teamwork** involves cooperating with other team members to accomplish the task at hand. Effective teamwork depends on open and honest communication, sufficient organizational resources, and mutual support among team members. Most importantly, effective teamwork requires understanding and recognizing the role and function of each member. By identifying each member's responsibilities, the health care team is able to deliver more efficient and thorough health care.

Meetings to Share Information

To work as a team, all team members need access to the same information. The best way to ensure this is through regular team meetings. The team leader or spokesperson should follow these guidelines when preparing team meetings:

- Set the meeting time and place in advance.
- Choose a day and time when all team members are available.
- If the team meets on a regular basis, schedule the meetings for the same day and time so that they become a regular part of every member's schedule.

- Distribute an agenda prior to the meeting. Agendas list the topics to be covered in the order they will be discussed. They also stimulate ideas and thoughts and help keep the team focused.

Group Communication

Communication is vital to the success of a health care team. Poor communication can lead to mistakes—and when health care is involved, mistakes can have very serious consequences. Team members must communicate in order to achieve the team's goals. (Chapter 5, "Health Care Communication" has detailed information on effective verbal and nonverbal communication.)

The more people involved in the communication process, the more complex it becomes. The most effective groups have members who communicate openly and honestly with one another. Good communication also helps team members build trust and mutual respect for one another. To promote good communication within a group, every team member should:

- listen with full attention to other members
- express ideas as clearly as possible
- encourage feedback on all ideas
- avoid letting negative emotions cloud communications

Tips for Contributing to a Team

How individual group members relate to one another is known as **group dynamics**. Although effective leadership helps a group reach its goals, the group's success ultimately depends on contributions by all of its members. A group with positive group dynamics will foster an atmosphere in which that can take place.

In effective groups, no member should dominate the group process. Everyone in the group should respect the views of other group members and feel comfortable voicing their own opinions. Table 8-2 lists some characteristics of effective and ineffective groups.

Conflict

Conflict, or a disagreement between team members, often occurs when a variety of personalities are brought together on a team. But disputes within a team aren't always a bad thing. They often reflect the passion that members feel for their vocation or their team's purpose. When health care professionals strive to provide the best possible care for their patients, disagreements are likely to result. Therefore, conflict management is an essential skill for all team members to find the solution that will most benefit the patient.

Table 8-2 Characteristics of Effective and Ineffective Groups

Element	Effective Group	Ineffective Group
Group identity	Group members value and "own" the goals of the group; goals are clearly defined.	The group's goals are not of great importance to the group's members.
Cohesiveness	Group members generally trust and like one another and are loyal to the group; they have a high degree of commitment and a high degree of cooperation.	Group members often feel alienated from the group and from one another. There is a low degree of commitment to the group and members tend to work better alone than with the group.
Communication	Honest and direct communication flows freely. Group members support, praise, and critique one another.	Communication is limited; members rarely share information about themselves. Some group members may restrict communication flow by dominating group discussions or preventing others from participating.
Decision making	Problems are identified; an appropriate method of decision making is used; the decision is implemented, and there is follow-up. Group commitment to the decision is high.	Problems are allowed to build without resolution, and little responsibility is shown for problem solving. Group commitment to a decision is low.
Responsibility	Group members feel a strong sense of responsibility for group outcomes.	Little responsibility for the group is felt by the group members.
Leadership	An effective style of leadership is used to achieve the desired goals.	Leadership is ineffective.
Power	Sources of power among group members are recognized and used appropriately. The needs or interests of members with little power are considered.	Power is used and abused to "fix" immediate problems. Little attention is given to the needs or interests of members with little power.

Sources of Conflict

Conflict may result from either substance—such as disagreements over what caused a patient's problem or how to address the problem—or personality differences. When team members have different ideas, opinions, and perspectives, disputes are bound to arise. Substance conflicts can be minimized, however, when members remain open-minded and respectful of one another.

Despite the term "health care team," many health care professionals spend most of their time working independently. This leads to limited opportunities for group conversation, which can create an atmosphere of distrust and suspicion. Coupled with differences in training, knowledge, and experience, a competitive work environment can develop. The end result may be an inability for team members to work together productively.

Managing Conflict

Health care professionals frequently encounter conflict between colleagues, patients, and themselves. Unresolved conflict can lower morale and threaten quality care. Problem-solving skills help manage conflict. Steps in problem solving include:

- *Assessing.* Gather information about the conflict.
- *Diagnosing.* Analyze the details about the conflict and the attitudes of the members involved to determine the cause of the conflict.
- *Creating a plan.* Determine the best method for resolving the conflict.
- *Implementing the plan.*
- *Evaluating the plan.* Review the effects of the attempted solution. Has the conflict been resolved?
- *Modifying the plan (if necessary).* Based on the evaluation, make any modifications or develop a new plan.

Depending on the situation, health care professionals may choose to work through these steps independently or as a group. Even if a conflict arises between only two members, the situation affects other team members as well. Therefore, it is often beneficial to discuss areas of conflict openly within a team setting. This builds understanding within the entire group and allows those directly involved in the conflict to hear different viewpoints, which may help lead to a resolution.

To prevent conflict in team meetings, the leader needs to keep the meeting focused on the agenda. All members of the team should be encouraged to participate. This

ON LOCATION

The Difficulties of Group Dynamics

The St. Elizabeth Diabetic Education Team is made up of seven health care professionals, including a registered nurse, a dietician, a physician, an optometrist, an occupational therapist, a pharmacist, and a patient educator. The team has been charged with researching and approving the purchase of a new style of blood glucose meter to be used throughout the hospital.

For the past month, the team has been meeting twice a week to test, discuss, and debate the pros and cons of various meters. The pharmacist has arrived at least 10 minutes late for nearly every meeting. The dietician spends most of the meetings taking phone calls. The patient educator, who is the team leader, knows that these behaviors are disruptive to the meetings, but because she avoids confrontation, she has ignored both problems. She also ignored the fact that the registered nurse told an off-color joke during the first meeting, which offended the optometrist. Those two team members haven't spoken to one another since.

After testing twelve different meters, the team narrowed the choices to three models at the last meeting. Realizing that the purchase deadline was near, the patient educator emailed team members to schedule a final team meeting for early the next morning. Unfortunately, two members would not be in the office that morning and could not attend the last-minute meeting.

The dietician spent most of the meeting talking on the phone, and the pharmacist arrived a full half hour late. For most part of the meeting, the team members debated the merits of each meter, while the patient educator simply sat back and listened. When the registered nurse announced that there was only one meter that she approved, the optometrist immediately said that he would never accept that particular meter. By the end of the meeting, the team was reduced to arguing over the different meters and was unable to reach a consensus decision.

- How can the team identify and resolve the conflicts and move on to a solution?
- What factors do you think might be creating problems within the group process?
- Why do you think the team is unable to reach a consensus?
- Do you think the group members' behaviors are creating difficulties within the group?
- Is there anything the team leader can do to help resolve the conflict?

---

ensures that everyone's opinion is heard. It also helps avoid situations in which one member feels animosity toward the group if it seems that his or her opinion isn't valued. All members of the group should feel free to communicate their thoughts and opinions without censorship or anger.

CHECK POINT

1 What four basic elements make up a team's structure?

2 What should every member do to promote good communication within a team?

LEADERSHIP

Leadership is the ability to influence others while working toward a vision or goal. Successful leaders can direct or motivate those around them to work toward the same objective. Health care providers become successful leaders when they:

- understand the complexity of coordinated care
- remain open to different points of view
- understand the interdependency of the health care team

The power to influence a group or team depends on a person's leadership style and skills. Health care professionals can use leadership skills to make many kinds of change in how health care is provided.

Leadership Skills

Whether leadership is direct or implied, leaders have power. The most effective group leaders use this power to encourage members to cooperate. Health care leaders need four basic leadership skills: communication skills, problem-solving skills, management skills, and self-evaluation skills.

- *Communication skills.* Leaders use communication skills to form strong interpersonal relationships with patients, peers, and colleagues. These skills also help establish and reach goals and improve the leader's own personal and professional growth.
- *Problem-solving skills.* Problem-solving skills allow leaders to analyze all sides of a problem before making a decision.
- *Management skills.* Management skills help leaders recognize and foster unique talents and skills in other team members and direct others toward goals. These skills

ZOOM IN

Building Teamwork and Leadership Skills

Student organizations provide a wealth of opportunities for students to begin building teamwork and leadership skills. Whether holding an office or simply participating in meetings and activities, participation in a student organization provides students with a chance to learn, while interacting with others who share a similar interest. Possibilities include:

- social organizations
- sports teams
- academic clubs
- religious groups
- political societies
- service organizations
- cultural associations

After entering your career, you can continue building your teamwork and leadership skills through participation in a professional organization. Nearly every health care field offers a local, state, national, or international association, many of which are discussed in Part IV, "Career Profiles: The Most In-Demand Professions." A few examples include

- American Association of Healthcare Administrative Management
- American Society of Radiologic Technologists
- National Association of State EMS Officials
- Society of Diagnostic Medical Sonography
- American Academy of Physician Assistants
- American Association of Medical Assistants
- American Medical Technologists
- American Optometric Association
- Association of Surgical Technologists
- National Association of Emergency Medical Technicians

---

also help leaders to stay organized, control finances, and use resources wisely.

- *Self-evaluation skills.* Self-evaluation skills help leaders to assess their own effectiveness and to accept criticism, as well as praise.

Leadership Styles

The complexity of the modern health care system allows for many different styles of leadership. Leadership is a behavior—something that an individual does to influence others. This influence can take many forms and requires much creativity, intellect, and savvy to manage the influence in positive directions. Different leadership styles are used in different situations and at different levels.

Autocratic Leadership

In the **autocratic leadership** style, also known as **directive leadership**, the leader assumes complete control over the decisions and activities of the group. A health care professional with this type of leadership style may be described as firm, self-assured, or even dominating. For example, Brian is a recovery nurse with nearly 15 years of experience. He discovers that a patient is bleeding excessively from a surgical incision and realizes that the patient needs immediate attention. Brian calls the unit coordinator and asks her to notify the surgeon of the problem. He then contacts an on-duty licensed practical nurse and a nursing assistant. He asks the nursing assistant to gather

the necessary supplies needed to care for the patient and then directs the licensed practical nurse to assist in stabilizing the patient. In this situation, Brian has assumed the autocratic style of leadership so that all of the necessary tasks can be accomplished immediately.

Leadership styles vary depending on personality, situation, and professional environment.

Democratic Leadership

The **democratic leadership** style promotes a sense of equality between the leader and other participants by sharing decisions and activities among all members of the team. The group and the leader work together to accomplish goals and outcomes that have been mutually agreed upon. Kathy, for example, is a head respiratory therapist who realizes that respiratory treatments aren't being given on time. Although she's not exactly sure why the treatments aren't being provided according to the schedule, she knows that the issue needs to be addressed. Kathy calls together the rest of the staff and leads a discussion to discover possible causes and solutions. In this situation, Kathy has assumed the democratic style of leadership to help motivate the staff to make sure that the treatment schedule is followed more closely.

Laissez-Faire Leadership

In the laissez-faire leadership style, also known as non-directive leadership, the leader hands power over to the group members. This approach encourages independent activity by group members, and its success depends on team members being able to direct their own activities. This leadership style is more effective when all team members are clinical experts with a thorough understanding of both clinical and administrative processes. For example, Lamar is the head of an occupational therapy department and wants to promote the use of a new treatment for brain injury rehabilitation. He posts an article related to this new technique on the hospital's intranet site. He's confident that the other therapists are professionals who want to improve their care and that they will choose to read and follow the findings within this new article.

Leadership and Management

While leaders are not always managers, managers are always leaders. Many health care professionals serve in management roles, often in addition to their professional roles. Managers generally have four functions:

- *Planning.* Managers are skilled at identifying problems and developing long-term goals, short-term objectives that build toward those goals, and strategies to achieve those objectives and goals. The plans they develop must fit within financial and workforce constraints.

- *Organizing.* Managers acquire, mobilize, and manage resources to carry out the planned strategies.
- *Directing.* Managers direct the work of others, instructing them about when and how to carry out tasks.
- *Controlling.* Managers monitor the work of those for whom they are responsible, by creating and implementing a method for evaluating the group's work. Managers need to stay focused on clinical quality and financial accountability.

Preparing for a Leadership Role

All health care professionals, to the extent that they work with others, can become leaders. Even students can begin to assume leadership roles, such as in their study groups or on team projects. To prepare for a leadership role, take some time to reflect on the following:

- *Identify your strengths.* Continually improve the things that you do best. Work on acquiring the skills and knowledge you need to maximize your strengths and remedy your bad habits. Honestly assess your "intellectual arrogance." Realize that being bright is not a substitute for knowledge.
- *Evaluate how you accomplish work.* We all try to work in ways that yield the best results for us. Do you work more productively in teams or alone? Are you more productive as a decision maker or as an advisor?
- *Clarify your values.* Working in an organization or a group whose value system is unacceptable or incompatible with your own can lead to frustration and poor performance. Identify your values and seek a work environment that fits those values.
- *Assume responsibility for relationships.* Cultivate relationships, and analyze the differences you may have with others. Know and understand the strengths, values, and work styles of your coworkers and managers.

✔ **CHECK POINT**

3 What four basic skills are needed by health care leaders?

4 What are three types of leadership styles?

Don't forget to visit the Point companion website for additional study resources!

CHAPTER HIGHLIGHTS

- A health care team consists of members with a variety of health-related backgrounds, education, and experiences.
- The structure of a team, and how well the team members understand that structure, often determine whether a team is successful. The elements of team structure include the team's purpose, specific goals, the roles of team members, and the functions of the team.
- Effective teamwork requires open and honest communication, organizational resources, and mutual support among team members.
- Conflict management is an essential skill for health care professionals and involves finding the right solution for the situation.
- Leadership is the ability to influence others while working toward a vision or goal.
- The three main leadership styles are autocratic, democratic, and laissez-faire.
- Health care professionals who serve in managerial roles are responsible for planning, organizing, directing, and controlling.

REVIEW QUESTIONS

Matching

1. _____ Leadership style in which the leader assumes complete control over decisions and group activities

2. _____ Leadership style in which the leader and group work together to accomplish mutually agreed upon goals

3. _____ Two or more individuals organized to function cooperatively as a group

4. _____ Leadership style in which team members are allowed to act independently

5. _____ Depends on open and honest communication, sufficient organizational resources, and mutual support

    a. team **b.** laissez-faire **c.** autocratic **d.** democratic **e.** teamwork

Multiple Choice

6. A health care team consists of members with a variety of health-related
    a. backgrounds   **c.** experiences
    b. education   **d.** all of the above

7. This is to be expected when a variety of ideas and personalities are brought together on a team.
    a. teamwork   **c.** democracy
    b. conflict   **d.** all of the above

8. The ability to influence others while working toward a vision or goal is
    a. planning   **c.** leadership
    b. organization   **d.** all of the above

9. Which of the following is NOT an example of a team member role?
    a. patient   **c.** resource
    b. spokesperson   **d.** optimist

10. The most effective group leaders use power to encourage members to
    a. form similar opinions
    b. confront one another
    c. cooperate with one another
    d. define their own goals

Completion

11. A team's _____ points it in the right direction.

12. A team _____ defines issues, sets the agenda, and coordinates team members.

13. Team _____ are the activities that the team members must carry out to meet the team's goals.

14. A group of registered nurses working on a common problem is an example of a/an_____ team.

15. Teams made up of professionals with different qualifications, skills, and areas of expertise are _____ teams.

Short Answer

16. How could the fact that many health care professionals spend most of their time working independently of others create an atmosphere of distrust and suspicion?

    _____

    _____

17. Why is it useful to have regular meetings of a team occur on the same day and at the same time?

    _____

    _____

18. What role does the reflector play on a team?

    _____

    _____

19. What are the basic elements of team structure?

    _____

    _____

20. Why might a leader want to distribute an agenda to team members prior to a meeting?

    _____

    _____

INVESTIGATE IT

1. Self-evaluation is one means by which individuals can assess their leadership attitudes and skills. The following site provides four different questionnaires that can be used as self-evaluation tools: http://www.adv-leadership-grp.com/Self-Evaluations.html. Complete at least one self-evaluation questionnaire from this web site.

2. How good are you at managing and resolving conflict? Do you believe that in order for one person to "win," another person has to "lose"? Is conflict always a bad thing? Search the Internet and other available resources to find information about conflict management. Use the search terms *conflict management* or *conflict resolution* to begin your Internet search.

RECOMMENDED READING

Cook DJ, Griffith LE, Sackett DL. Importance of and Satisfaction with Work and Professional Interpersonal Issues: A Survey of Physicians Practicing General Internal Medicine in Ontario. *Can Med Assoc J* [serial online]. Sept. 15, 1995; 153(6):755–764. Available at http://www.pubmedcentral.nih.gov/picrender.fcgi?artid=1487276&blobtype=pdf.

Eade DM. Motivational Management: Developing Leadership Skills. Available at http://www.adv-leadership-grp.com/Motivational_Article.html.

Physical Medicine and Rehabilitation Team. [New York-Presbyterian Hospital web site]. Available at http://nyp.org/health/physical-medicine-rehabilitation-team.html.

Index

Note: Page numbers followed by *f* indicate figures; those followed by a *t* indicate tables and those followed by a *b* indicate a box.

CMF 95

Math Fundamentals

<u>Content Source Title:</u>

Introductory Mathematics: Concepts with Applications
by Charles P. McKeague, BA, MS

Quick Reference Conversions

Standard Time and Military Time

Content/Figures Source Title:
Clinical Calculations Made Easy: Solving Problems Using Dimensional Analysis, Fifth Edition

Standard Time	Military Time	Standard Time	Military Time
1:00 am	0100	1:00 pm	12+1 = 1300
1:05 am	0105	1:05 pm	1305
2:00 am	0200	2:00 pm	12+2 = 1400
2:10 am	0210	2:10 pm	1410
3:00 am	0300	3:00 pm	12+3 = 1500
3:15 am	0315	3:15 pm	1515
4:00 am	0400	4:00 pm	12+4 = 1600
4:20 am	0420	4:20 pm	1620
5:00 am	0500	5:00 pm	12+5 = 1700
5:25 am	0525	5:25 pm	1725
6:00 am	0600	6:00 pm	12+6 = 1800
6:30 am	0630	6:30 pm	1830
7:00 am	0700	7:00 pm	12+7 = 1900
7:35 am	0735	7:35 pm	1935
8:00 am	0800	8:00 pm	12+8 = 2000
8:40 am	0840	8:40 pm	2040
9:00 am	0900	9:00 pm	12+9 = 2100
9:45 am	0945	9:45 pm	2145
10:00 am	1000	10:00 pm	12+10 = 2200
10:50 am	1050	10:50 pm	2250
11:00 am	1100	11:00 pm	12+11 = 2300
11:55 am	1155	11:55 pm	2355
12:00 pm (noon)	1200	12:00 am	12+12 = 2400

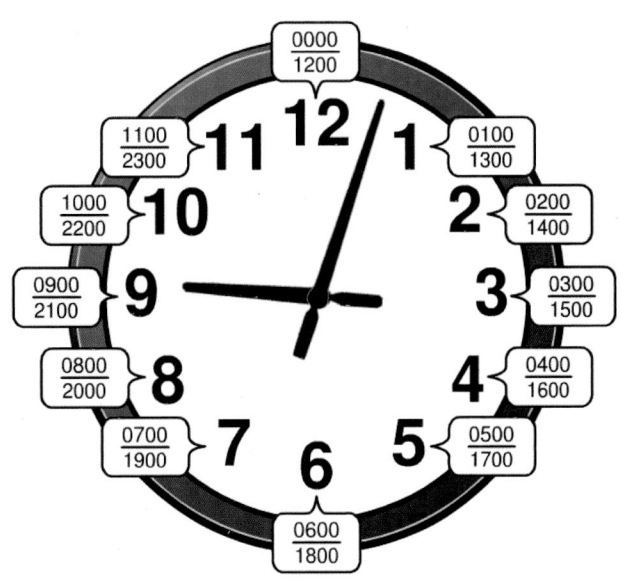

Standard Math Conversions

WEIGHT / MASS - kilogram (kg), gram (g), milligram (mg), microgram (mcg)

- 1 mg = 1,000 mcg
- 1 gr (grain) = 64.79 mg (round to 65 mg)
- 1 g = 1,000 mg
- 1 kg = 1,000 g
- 1 kg = 2.2 lbs. (pounds)
- 1 lb = 16 oz (ounces)
- 1 oz = 28.35 g (round to 30 g)

VOLUME / LIQUID MEASUREMENT – liter (L), milliliter (mL)

- 1 tsp (teaspoon) = 5 mL
- 1 Tbs (tablespoon) = 3 tsp = 15 mL
- 1 fl (fluid) oz = 29.5 mL (round up to 30 mL)
- 30 mL = 2 Tbs = 6 tsp
- 1 c (cup) = 8 fl oz = 240 mL
- 1 pt (pint) = 2 c = 16 fl oz = 480 mL
- 1 qt (quart) = 2 pt = 4 c = 32 fl oz = 960 mL
- 1 gal (gallon) = 4 qt = 8 pt = 128 fl oz = 3,840 mL
- 1 L = 1,000 mL

LENGTH / LINEAR MEASUREMENT – meter (m), centimeter (cm), millimeter (mm)

- 1 m = 100 cm = 39.4 in. (inches)
- 1 ft (foot) = 12 in.
- 1 in. = 2.54 cm
- 1 ft = 30 cm

TIME

- 1 minute = 60 seconds
- 1 day = 24 hours
- 1 week = 7 days
- 1 year = 12 months = 52 weeks = 365 days

HOUSEHOLD & METRIC EQUIVALENTS

- 1 gr (grain) = 64.79 mg (round to 65 mg)
- 1 tsp (teaspoon) = 5 Ml
- 1 Tbs (tablespoon) = 3 tsp
- 1 fluid dram = 5 mL
- 1 fl oz = 6 fl drams = 2 Tbs = 30 mL
- 1 c (cup) = 8 fl oz = 240 mL
- 1 pt (pint) = 2 c = 16 fl oz = 480 mL
- 1 qt (quart) = 32 fl oz
- 1 L = 1,000 mL
- 1 cc (cubic centimetre) = 1 mm

SOLUTION CONCENTRATIONS

- "X" gm per 100 mL of solution
  - Example: D5W 1 L = 5 g Dextrose per 100 mL solution (i.e. 50 g/L)

TEMPERATURE CONVERSIONS

- F (Fahrenheit) to C (Celsius) = (F - 32) / 1.8 = C
- C to F = (C x 1.8) + 32 = F

Introductory Mathematics

for Pima Medical Institute

Charles P. McKeague

*xyz*textbooks

*xyz*textbooks

For product information and technology assistance, contact us at
XYZ Textbooks, 1-877-745-3499

For permission to use material from this text or product,
e-mailed: **info@mathtv.com**

XYZ Textbooks
1339 Marsh St.
San Luis Obispo, CA 93401
USA

For your course and learning solutions, visit **www.xyztextbooks.com**

Contents

User's Guide

XYZ Textbooks is on a mission to improve the quality and affordability of course materials for mathematics. Our 2013 Concepts with Applications Series brings a new level of technology innovation, which is certain to improve student proficiency.

As you can see, these books are presented in a format in which each section is organized by easy to follow learning objectives. Each objective includes helpful example problems, as well as additional practice problems in the margins, and are referenced in each exercise set. To help students relate what they are studying to the real world, each chapter and section begin with a real-life application of key concepts. You and your students will encounter extensions of these opening applications in the exercise sets.

We have put features in place that help your students stay on the trail to success. With that perspective in mind, we have incorporated this navigational theme into the following new and exciting features.

QR Codes

Unique technology embedded in each exercise set allows students with a smart phone or other internet-connected mobile device to view our video tutorials without being tied to a computer.

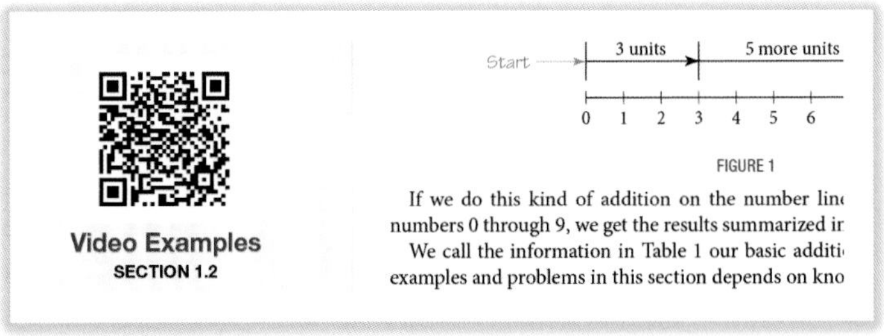

Video Examples
SECTION 1.2

Start ⟶ |← 3 units →|← 5 more units →|

0 1 2 3 4 5 6

FIGURE 1

If we do this kind of addition on the number line numbers 0 through 9, we get the results summarized in We call the information in Table 1 our basic additi examples and problems in this section depends on kno

Vocabulary Review

A list of fill-in-the-blank sentences appears at the beginning of each exercise set to help students better comprehend and verbalize concepts.

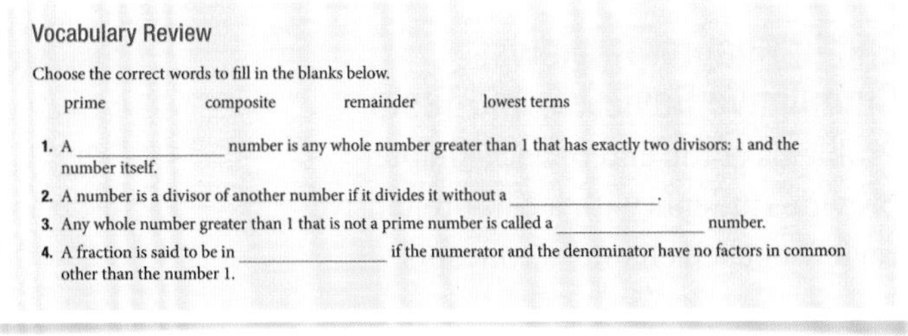

Vocabulary Review

Choose the correct words to fill in the blanks below.

prime   composite   remainder   lowest terms

1. A _____ number is any whole number greater than 1 that has exactly two divisors: 1 and the number itself.
2. A number is a divisor of another number if it divides it without a _____.
3. Any whole number greater than 1 that is not a prime number is called a _____ number.
4. A fraction is said to be in _____ if the numerator and the denominator have no factors in common other than the number 1.

Getting Ready For Class

Simple writing exercises for students to answer after reading each section increases their understanding of key concepts.

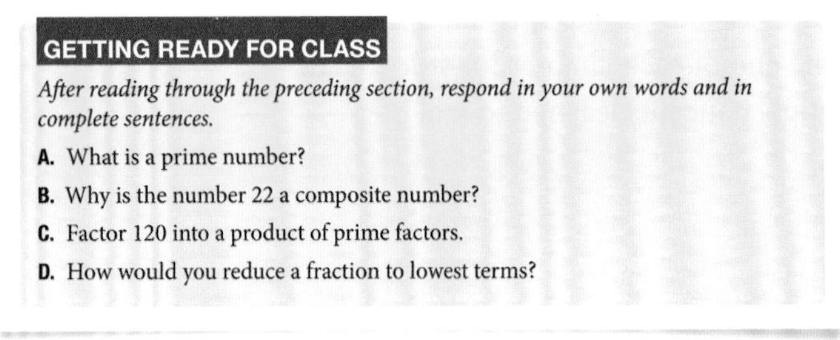

GETTING READY FOR CLASS

After reading through the preceding section, respond in your own words and in complete sentences.

A. What is a prime number?
B. Why is the number 22 a composite number?
C. Factor 120 into a product of prime factors.
D. How would you reduce a fraction to lowest terms?

User's Guide

Key words

A list of important vocabulary appears at the beginning of each section to help students prepare for new concepts.

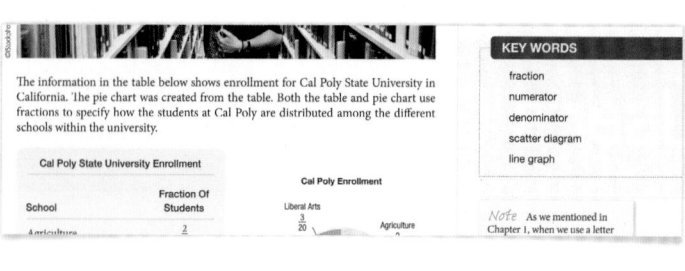

Navigation Skills

A discussion of important study skills appearing in each chapter anticipates students' needs as they progress through the course.

Find the Mistake

Complete sentences that include common mistakes appear in each exercise set to help students identify errors and aid their comprehension of the concepts presented in that section.

Landmark Review

A review appears in the middle of each chapter for students to practice key skills, check progress, and address difficulties.

End of Chapter Reviews, Cumulative Reviews, and Tests

Problems at the end of each chapter provide students with a comprehensive review of each chapter's concepts.

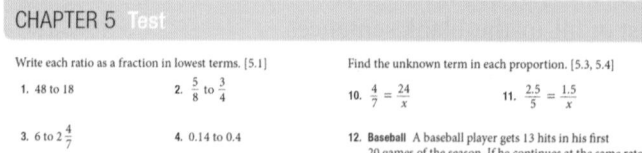

Trail Guide Projects

Individual or group projects appear at the end of each chapter for students to apply concepts learned to real life.

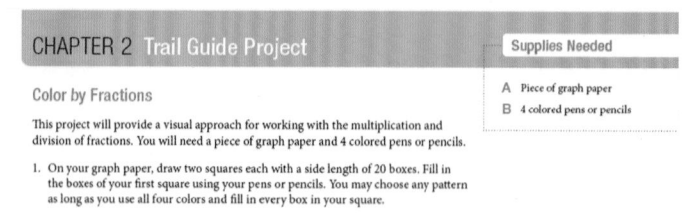

XYZ Textbooks is committed to helping students achieve their goals of success. This new series of highly-developed, innovative books will help students prepare for the course ahead and navigate their way to a successful course completion.

Whole Numbers

Washington D.C., USA
Gray Buildings © 2008 Sanborn
Gray Buildings © District of Columbia (DC GIS) & CyberCity
Gray Buildings © 2010 CyberCity
Google

Just before the beginning of the United States' involvement in World War II, our military was in great need of office space in and around Washington, DC. Coming up with a solution to this problem fell to Brigadier General Brehon B. Somervell who worked in the construction division. He summoned one of his subordinates and a civilian architect to his office on Thursday July 17, 1941, and informed them that he wanted plans for a structure to house 40,000 workers by Monday. After what was described as a "very busy weekend," the Monday deadline was met and the idea for the Pentagon was born. Construction began September 11, 1941 and was completed January 15, 1943 at a cost of $85 million. Still serving as headquarters of the Department of Defense, approximately 25,000 civilian and military employees report to work there each day. These workers use 131 stairways, 13 elevators, or 19 escalators to reach their offices on one of 7 floors. Despite its large size, the building is still regarded as one of the most efficient in the world. It takes no more than 7 minutes to walk between any two points.

921 feet

Suppose you wanted to know the length of the Pentagon's perimeter. After examining the illustration above, we can tell that the length of one outside wall of the Pentagon measures 921 feet. We can then use this measurement to calculate the total perimeter. In this chapter, we will work problems similar to this one.

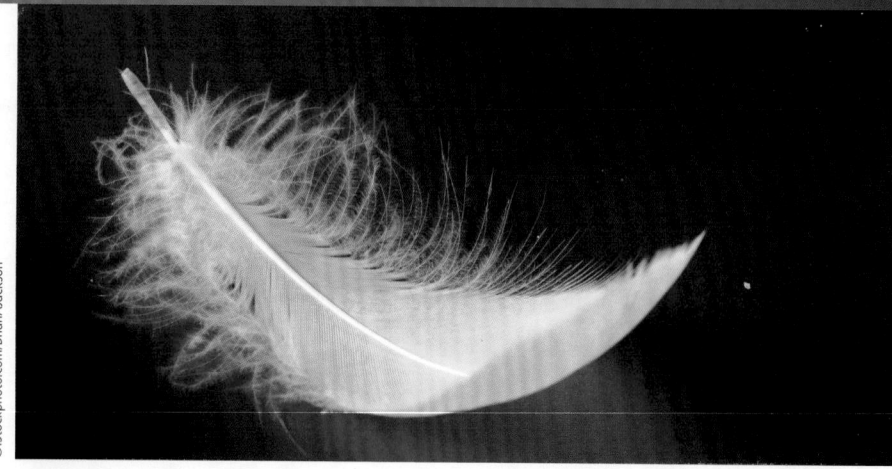

©iStockphoto.com/BrianAJackson

April 3rd is International Pillow Fight Day. In 2010, the 5th Pillow Fight NYC took place in Union Square, New York City. People from all over the city filled the square and wielded pillows. When the fight began, people swung their pillows from side to side, hoping it would land on the nearest victim before getting hit themselves. The city's inaugural pillow fight took place in 2006 and had 500 participants. By 2010, the event garnered at least 5000 people.

In this section, we will learn about place value and its relation to decimals. Comparing the number of participants in the 2006 pillow fight to the 2010 pillow fight, we can see that the 5 moves from the hundreds place value to the thousands place value.

A Place Value

Our number system is based on the number 10 and is therefore called a "base 10" number system. We write all numbers in our number system using the digits 0, 1, 2, 3, 4, 5, 6, 7, 8, and 9. The positions of the digits in a number determine the values of the digits. For example, the 5 in the number 251 has a different value from the 5 in the number 542.

The place values in our number system are as follows: The first digit on the right is in the ones column. The next digit to the left of the ones column is in the tens column. The next digit to the left is in the hundreds column. For a number like 542, the digit 5 is in the hundreds column, the 4 is in the tens column, and the 2 is in the ones column.

If we keep moving to the left, the columns increase in value. The following table shows the name and value of each of the first seven columns in our number system. Also, notice how the number 1 is located in the appropriate place value column.

Table 1

Millions Column	Hundred Thousands Column	Ten Thousands Column	Thousands Column	Hundreds Column	Tens Column	Ones Column
1,000,000	100,000	10,000	1,000	100	10	1

EXAMPLE 1 Give the place value of each digit in the number 305,964.

Solution Starting with the digit at the right, we have 4 in the ones column, 6 in the tens column, 9 in the hundreds column, 5 in the thousands column, 0 in the ten thousands column, and 3 in the hundred thousands column.

Practice Problems

1. Give the place value of each digit in the number 17,045.

Answers

1. 1 = ten thousands, 7 = thousands, 0 = hundreds, 4 = tens, 5 = ones

Large Numbers

The photograph shown here was taken by the Hubble telescope in April 2002. The object in the photograph is called the Cone Nebula. In astronomy, distances to objects like the Cone Nebula are given in light-years—the distance light travels in a year. If we assume light travels 186,000 miles in one second, then a light-year is 5,865,696,000,000 miles; that is,

5 trillion, 865 billion, 696 million miles

To find the place value of digits in large numbers, we can use Table 2. Note how the Ones, Thousands, Millions, Billions, and Trillions categories are each broken into Ones, Tens, and Hundreds. Note also that we have written the digits for our light-year in the last row of the table.

NASA

Table 2

Trillions			Billions			Millions			Thousands			Ones		
Hundreds	Tens	Ones	Hundreds	Tens	Ones	Hundreds	Tens	Ones	Hundreds	Tens	Ones	Hundreds	Tens	Ones
		5	8	6	5	6	9	6	0	0	0	0	0	0

Note When writing numbers with four or more digits, we use a comma to separate every three digits, starting from the ones column.

EXAMPLE 2   Give the place value of each digit in the number 73,890,672,540.

Solution   The following diagram shows the place value of each digit.

Ten Billions	*Billions*	*Hundred Millions*	*Ten Millions*	*Millions*	*Hundred Thousands*	*Ten Thousands*	*Thousands*	*Hundreds*	*Tens*	*Ones*
7	3,	8	9	0,	6	7	2,	5	4	0

2. Give the place value of each digit in the number 4,572,106,890.

B Expanded Form

We can use the idea of place value to write numbers in expanded form. For example, the number 542 is written in condensed (standard) form. We can also write it in expanded form as

$$542 = 500 + 40 + 2$$

because the 5 is in the hundreds column, the 4 is in the tens column, and the 2 is in the ones column.

Here are more examples of numbers written in expanded form:

EXAMPLE 3   Write 5,478 in expanded form.

Solution $5,478 = 5,000 + 400 + 70 + 8$

3. Write 23,187 in expanded form.

Answers

Billions	Hundred Millions	Ten Millions	Millions	Hundred Thousands	Ten Thousands	Thousands	Hundreds	Tens	Ones

2. 4, 5 7 2, 1 0 6, 8 9 0
3. 20,000 + 3,000 + 100 + 80 + 7

We can use money to make the results from Example 3 more intuitive. Suppose you have $5,478 in cash as follows:

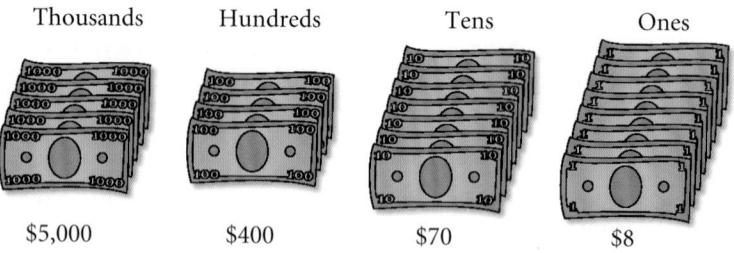

Thousands	Hundreds	Tens	Ones
$5,000	$400	$70	$8

Using this diagram as a guide, we can write

$$\$5,478 = \$5,000 + \$400 + \$70 + \$8$$

which shows us that our work writing numbers in expanded form is consistent with our intuitive understanding of the different denominations of money.

EXAMPLE 4   Write 56,094 in expanded form.

Solution   Notice that there is a 0 in the hundreds column. This means we have 0 hundreds. In expanded form, we have

$$56,094 = 50,000 + 6,000 + 90 + 4$$
↑
Note that we don't have
to include the 0 hundreds.

Now let's reverse the process. In the next two examples, we will take an expression in expanded form and condense it back to standard form.

EXAMPLE 5   Write $10,000 + 7,000 + 500 + 60 + 9$ in condensed (standard) form.

Solution $10,000 + 7,000 + 500 + 60 + 9 = 17,569$

EXAMPLE 6   Write $5,000,000 + 70,000 + 600 + 3$ in condensed (standard) form.

Solution   Note that the digit is 0 in the hundred thousands, thousands and tens place. The answer is

$$5,070,603$$

C Writing Numbers in Words

The idea of place value and expanded form can be used to help write the names for numbers. Naming numbers and writing them in words takes some practice. Let's begin by looking at the names of some two-digit numbers. Table 3 lists a few. Notice that the two-digit numbers that are greater than twenty and do not end in 0 have two parts. These parts are separated by a hyphen.

Table 3

Number	In English	Number	In English
25	*Twenty-five*	30	*Thirty*
47	*Forty-seven*	62	*Sixty-two*
93	*Ninety-three*	77	*Seventy-seven*
88	*Eighty-eight*	50	*Fifty*

4. Write 1,049,580 in expanded form.

5. Write $60,000 + 8,000 + 700 + 90 + 3$ in condensed (standard) form.

6. Write $4,000,000 + 200,000 + 6,000 + 40 + 5$ in condensed (standard) form.

Answers
4. $1,000,000 + 40,000 + 9,000 + 500 + 80$
5. 68,793
6. 4,206,045

The following examples give the names for some larger numbers. In each case, the names are written according to the place values given in Table 2.

EXAMPLE 7 Write each number in words.

a. 452   **b.** 397   **c.** 608

Solution

a. Four hundred fifty-two

b. Three hundred ninety-seven

c. Six hundred eight

EXAMPLE 8 Write each number in words.

a. 3,561   **b.** 53,662   **c.** 547,801

Solution

a. Three thousand, five hundred sixty-one

↑

Notice how the comma separates the thousands from the hundreds.

b. Fifty-three thousand, six hundred sixty-two

c. Five hundred forty-seven thousand, eight hundred one

EXAMPLE 9 Write each number in words.

a. 507,034,005   **b.** 739,600,075   **c.** 5,003,007,006

Solution

a. Five hundred seven million, thirty-four thousand, five

b. Seven hundred thirty-nine million, six hundred thousand, seventy-five

c. Five billion, three million, seven thousand, six

The next examples show how we write a number given in words as a number written with digits.

EXAMPLE 10 Write five thousand, six hundred forty-two, using digits instead of words.

Solution Five thousand, six hundred forty-two

| 5 | 6 | 42 | → | 5,642 |

EXAMPLE 11 Write each number using digits instead of words.

a. Three million, fifty-one thousand, seven hundred

b. Two billion, five

c. Seven million, seven hundred seven

Solution

a. 3,051,700

b. 2,000,000,005

c. 7,000,707

7. Write each number in words.
  a. 752
  b. 386
  c. 507

8. Write each number in words.
  a. 4,865
  b. 51,508
  c. 408,623

9. Write each number in words.
  a. 406,058,210
  b. 3,200,486,404

10. Write eight thousand, two hundred thirty-nine using digits instead of words.

11. Write each number using digits instead of words.
  a. Seven million, forty-two thousand, six hundred.
  b. Twelve million, four hundred.
  c. Six hundred thousand, eight.

Answers

7. a. Seven hundred fifty-two
   b. Three hundred eighty-six
   c. Five hundred seven
8. a. Four thousand, eight hundred sixty-five.
   b. Fifty-one thousand, five hundred eight.
   c. Four hundred eight thousand, six hundred twenty three.
9. a. Four hundred six million, fifty-eight thousand, two hundred ten.
   b. Three billion, two hundred million, four hundred eighty-six thousand, four hundred four.
10. 8,239
11. a. 7,042,600   **b.** 12,000,400
   c. 600,008

Sets and the Number Line

In mathematics, a collection of numbers is called a set. In this chapter, we have been working with the set of counting numbers (also called natural numbers) and the set of whole numbers, which are defined as follows:

$$\text{Counting numbers} = \{1, 2, 3, \ldots\}$$

$$\text{Whole numbers} = \{0, 1, 2, 3, \ldots\}$$

The dots mean "and so on," and the braces { } are used to group the numbers in the set together.

Another way to visualize the whole numbers is with a number line. To draw a number line, we simply draw a straight line and mark off equally spaced points along the line, as shown in Figure 1. We label the point at the left with 0 and the rest of the points, in order, with the numbers 1, 2, 3, 4, 5, and so on.

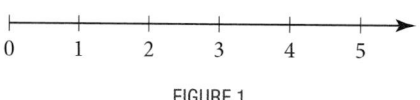

FIGURE 1

The arrow on the right indicates that the number line can continue in that direction forever.

GETTING READY FOR CLASS

Each section of the book will end with some problems and questions like the ones below. They are for you to answer after you have read through the section but before you go to class. All of them require that you give written responses in complete sentences. Writing about mathematics is a valuable exercise. As with all problems in this course, approach these writing exercises with a positive point of view. You will get better at giving written responses to questions as the course progresses. Even if you never feel comfortable writing about mathematics, just attempting the process will increase your understanding and ability in this course.

After reading through the preceding section, respond in your own words and in complete sentences.

A. Give the place value of the 9 in the number 305,964.

B. Write the number 742 in expanded form.

C. Place a comma and a hyphen in the appropriate place so that the number 2,345 is written correctly in words below:

Two thousand three hundred forty five

D. Is there a largest whole number?

Vocabulary Review

Choose the correct words to fill in the blanks below.

comma   set   expanded   hyphen   counting   condensed   whole   place value

1. _____ is the value of a digit in a number determined by its position.

2. The number 619 is written in _____ form, but is written in _____ form when it appears as 600 + 10 + 9.

3. The name of a two-digit number that is greater then twenty and does not end in 0 has two parts separated by a _____.

4. When writing a number with four or more digits, use a _____ to separate every three digits.

5. A collection of numbers is called a _____.

6. The set of _____ numbers is defined as {1, 2, 3,...}.

7. The set of _____ numbers is defined as {0, 1, 2, 3,...}.

Problems

A Give the place value of each digit in the following numbers.

1. 78   2. 93   3. 45   4. 79

5. 348   6. 789   7. 608   8. 450

9. 2,378   10. 6,481   11. 273,569   12. 768,253

Give the place value of the 5 in each of the following numbers.

13. 458,992   14. 75,003,782   15. 507,994,787   16. 320,906,050

17. 267,894,335   18. 234,345,678,789   19. 4,569,000   20. 50,000

B Write each of the following numbers in expanded form.

21. 658   22. 479   23. 68

24. 71   25. 4,587   26. 3,762

27. 32,674

28. 54,883

29. 3,462,577

30. 5,673,524

31. 407

32. 508

33. 30,068

34. 50,905

35. 3,004,008

36. 20,088,060

Write each of the following numbers in condensed (standard) form.

37. 500 + 40 + 7

38. 900 + 60 + 5

39. 6,000 + 300 + 20 + 3

40. 5,000 + 700 + 90 + 9

41. 20,000 + 7,000 + 30 + 5

42. 40,000 + 8,000 + 40 + 9

43. 70,000 + 900 + 7

44. 90,000 + 700 + 4

45. 100,000 + 80,000 + 600 + 40 +3

46. 700,000 + 40,000 + 7,000 + 50 + 7

47. 400,000 + 6,000 + 8

48. 700,000 + 40 + 5

C Write each of the following numbers in words.

49. 29

50. 75

51. 40

52. 90

53. 573

54. 895

55. 707

56. 405

57. 770

58. 450

59. 23,540

60. 56,708

61. 3,004

62. 5,008

63. 3,040

64. 5,080

65. 104,065,780

66. 637,008,500

67. 5,003,040,008

68. 7,050,800,001

69. 2,546,731

70. 6,998,454

71. 20,432,000

72. 300,508,100

Write each of the following numbers with digits instead of words.

73. Three hundred twenty-five

74. Forty-eight

75. Five thousand, four hundred thirty-two

76. One hundred twenty-three thousand, sixty-one

77. Eighty-six thousand, seven hundred sixty-two

78. One hundred million, two hundred thousand, three hundred

79. Two million, two hundred

80. Two million, two

81. Two million, two thousand, two hundred

82. Two billion, two hundred thousand, two hundred two

Applying the Concepts

83. Hot Air Balloon The first successful crossing of the Atlantic in a hot air balloon was made in August 1978 by Maxie Anderson, Ben Abruzzo, and Larry Newman of the United States. The 3,100-mile trip took approximately 140 hours. What is the place value of the 3 in the distance covered by the balloon?

84. Seating Arrangements The number of different ways in which 10 people can be seated at a table with 10 places is 3,628,800. What is the place value of the 3 in this number?

85. Seating Capacity The Rose Bowl, in Pasadena, CA, has a seating capacity of 106,721. Write this number in expanded form.

86. Astronomy The average distance from the sun to the earth is 92,897,416 miles. Write this number in expanded form.

87. Baseball Salaries Salary studies by mlbfanhouse.com show Major League Baseball's 2010 average player salary was $3,014,572, representing an increase of 0.6% from the previous season's average. Write 3,014,572 in words.

88. Top Disney Movies The illustration shows the average income for some of Disney's top grossing movies.

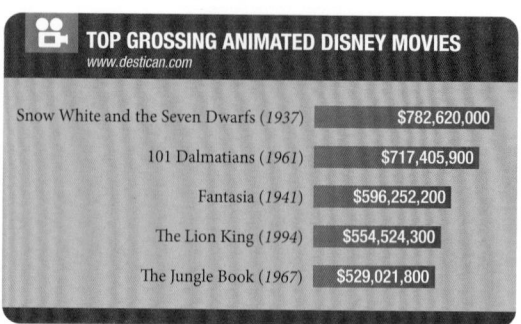

TOP GROSSING ANIMATED DISNEY MOVIES
www.destican.com

Snow White and the Seven Dwarfs (*1937*)	$782,620,000
101 Dalmatians (*1961*)	$717,405,900
Fantasia (*1941*)	$596,252,200
The Lion King (*1994*)	$554,524,300
The Jungle Book (*1967*)	$529,021,800

From the chart, write the following gross incomes in words.

a. Snow White and the Seven Dwarfs

b. The Jungle Book

Extending the Concepts

Many of the problem sets in this book will end with a few problems like the ones below. These problems challenge you to extend your knowledge of the material in the problem set. In most cases, there are no examples in the text similar to these problems. You should approach these problems with a positive point of view; even though you may not always work them correctly, just the process of attempting them will increase your knowledge and ability in mathematics.

The numbers on the number line below are each 1 inch apart. As with all number lines, the arrow indicates that the number line continues to the right indefinitely. Use this number line to answer Problems 91–100.

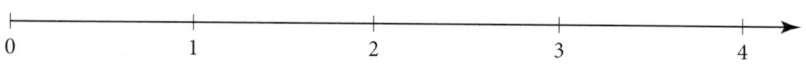

89. How far apart are the numbers 1 and 4?

90. How far apart are the numbers 2 and 5?

91. How far apart are the numbers 0 and 5?

92. How far apart are the numbers 0 and 10?

93. What number is 4 inches to the right of 2?

94. What number is 4 inches to the right of 3?

95. What number is 4 inches to the left of 7?

96. What number is 4 inches to the left of 12?

97. If 1 foot is 12 inches in length, what number is 1 foot from 0?

98. What number is 2 feet from 0?

Find the Mistake

Each sentence below contains a mistake. Circle the mistake and write the correct word(s) or number(s) on the line provided.

1. The place value of the 7 in the number 562,472 is hundreds. _____

2. The number 12,789 written in expanded form is $1,200 + 700 + 80 + 9$. _____

3. The number 9,023,627,003 written in words is nine and twenty-three million, six and twenty-seven thousand, three.

   _____

4. Writing forty million, three hundred forty-eight thousand, thirteen in digits gives 4,034,813. _____

Navigation Skills: Prepare, Study, Achieve

At the end of the first exercise set of each chapter, we provide an important discussion of study skills that will help you succeed in this course. Pay special attention to these skills. Ponder each one and apply it to your life. Your success is in your hands.

Studying is the key to success in this course. However, many students have never learned effective skills for studying. Study skills include but are not limited to the following:

- Work done on problems for practice and homework
- Amount of time spent studying
- Time of day and location for studying
- Management of distractions during study sessions
- Material chosen to review
- Order and process of review

Let's begin our discussion with the topic of homework. From the first day of class, we recommend you spend two hours on homework for every hour you are scheduled to attend class. Any less may drastically impact your success in this course. To help visualize this commitment, map out a weekly schedule that includes your classes, work shifts, extracurriculars, and any additional obligations. Fill in the hours you intend to devote to completing assignments and studying for this class. Post this schedule at home and keep a copy with your study materials to remind you of your commitment to success.

OBJECTIVES

A Solve addition problems without carrying.

B Solve addition problems involving carrying.

C Use the properties of addition.

KEY WORDS

carrying

sum

addition property of 0

commutative property of addition

associative property of addition

variable

solution

inspection

Video Examples
SECTION 1.2

Note Table 1 is a summary of the addition facts that you *must* know in order to make a successful start in your study of basic mathematics. You *must* know how to add any pair of numbers that come from the list. You *must* be fast and accurate. You don't want to have to think about the answer to 7 + 9. You should know it's 16. Memorize these facts now. Don't put it off until later.

When it comes to taking care of your houseplants, there is no more need to guess when they need water. A new device measures the water content of the plant's soil and sends a text message to the owner. The message can notify the owner of her thirsty plant, or even if she has overwatered her plant. Each device sells for $99. If we wanted to buy the device for two house plants, we would need to add 99 and 99 to find how much we will pay (before sales tax). In this section, we will learn how to do addition with whole numbers, such as adding 99 and 99. Let's begin by visualizing addition on the number line.

Facts of Addition

Using lengths to visualize addition can be very helpful. In mathematics, we generally do so by using the number line. For example, we add 3 and 5 on the number line like this: Start at 0 and move to 3, as shown in Figure 1. From 3, move 5 more units to the right. This brings us to 8. Therefore, $3 + 5 = 8$.

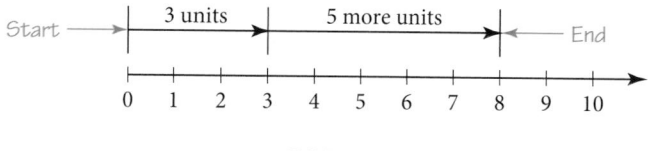

FIGURE 1

If we do this kind of addition on the number line with all combinations of the numbers 0 through 9, we get the results summarized in Table 1.

We call the information in Table 1 our basic addition facts. Your success with the examples and problems in this section depends on knowing the basic addition facts.

Table 1

Addition Table

	0	1	2	3	4	5	6	7	8	9
0	0	1	2	3	4	5	6	7	8	9
1	1	2	3	4	5	6	7	8	9	10
2	2	3	4	5	6	7	8	9	10	11
3	3	4	5	6	7	8	9	10	11	12
4	4	5	6	7	8	9	10	11	12	13
5	5	6	7	8	9	10	11	12	13	14
6	6	7	8	9	10	11	12	13	14	15
7	7	8	9	10	11	12	13	14	15	16
8	8	9	10	11	12	13	14	15	16	17
9	9	10	11	12	13	14	15	16	17	18

Suppose we want to use the Table 1 to find the answer to 3 + 5. We locate the 3 in the column on the left and the 5 in the row at the top. We read *across* from the 3 and *down* from the 5. The entry in the table that is across from 3 and below 5 is 8.

A Adding Whole Numbers

To add whole numbers, we add digits with the same place value. First we add the digits in the ones place, then the tens place, then the hundreds place, and so on.

EXAMPLE 1 Add: 43 + 52.

Solution This type of addition is best done vertically—aligning the digits with the same place value. First, we add the digits in the ones place.

$$\begin{array}{r} 43 \\ + 52 \\ \hline 5 \end{array}$$

Then we add the digits in the tens place.

$$\begin{array}{r} 43 \\ + 52 \\ \hline 95 \end{array}$$

EXAMPLE 2 Add: 165 + 801.

Solution Writing the sum vertically, we have

$$\begin{array}{r} 165 \\ + 801 \\ \hline 966 \end{array}$$ ← Add ones place.

Add tens place.

Add hundreds place.

B Addition with Carrying

In Examples 1 and 2, the sums of the digits with the same place value were always 9 or less. There are many times when the sum of the digits with the same place value will be a number larger than 9. In these cases, we have to do what is called *carrying* in addition. The following examples illustrate this process.

EXAMPLE 3 Add: 197 + 213 + 324.

Solution We write the sum vertically and add digits with the same place value.

$$\begin{array}{r} \overset{1}{1}97 \\ 213 \\ + 324 \\ \hline 4 \end{array}$$ When we add the ones, we get 7 + 3 + 4 = 14. We write the 4 and carry the 1 to the tens column.

$$\begin{array}{r} \overset{1\ 1}{1}97 \\ 213 \\ + 324 \\ \hline 34 \end{array}$$ We add the tens, including the 1 that was carried over from the last step. We get 13, so we write the 3 and carry the 1 to the hundreds column.

$$\begin{array}{r} \overset{1\ 1}{1}97 \\ 213 \\ + 324 \\ \hline 734 \end{array}$$ We add the hundreds, including the 1 that was carried over from the last step.

Practice Problems

1. Add: 23 + 45.

Note To show *why* we add digits with the same place value, we can write each number showing the place value of the digits:

$$\begin{array}{r} 43 = 4 \text{ tens} + 3 \text{ ones} \\ + 52 = 5 \text{ tens} + 2 \text{ ones} \\ \hline 9 \text{ tens} + 5 \text{ ones} \end{array}$$

2. Add: 243 + 526.

3. Add: 238 + 432 + 186.

Answers

1. 68
2. 769
3. 856

4. Add: $17,386 + 5,978 + 468$.

EXAMPLE 4   Add: $46,789 + 2,490 + 864$.

Solution   We write the sum vertically and then use the shorthand form of addition.

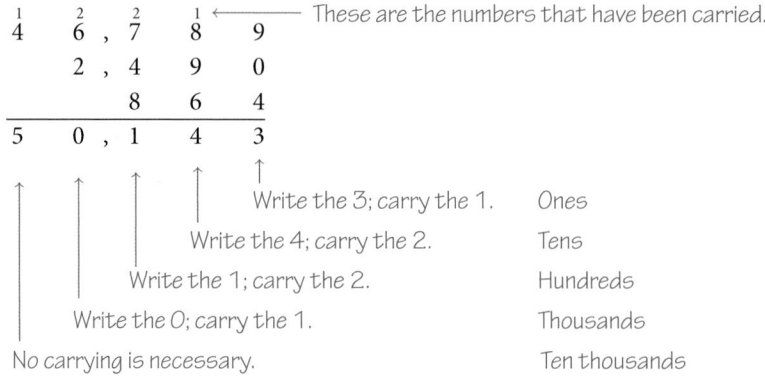

Adding numbers as we are doing here takes some practice. Most people don't make mistakes in carrying. Most mistakes in addition are made in adding the numbers in the columns. That is why it is so important that you maintain accuracy with the basic addition facts given in this chapter.

Vocabulary

The word we use to indicate addition is *sum*. If we say "the sum of 3 and 5 is 8," what we mean is $3 + 5 = 8$. The word sum always indicates addition. We can state this fact in symbols by using the letters *a* and *b* to represent numbers.

> **DEFINITION**   sum
>
> If *a* and *b* are any two numbers, then the **sum** of *a* and *b* is $a + b$. To find the sum of two numbers, we add them.

Note   When mathematics is used to solve everyday problems, the problems are almost always stated in words. The translation of English to symbols is a very important part of mathematics.

Table 2 gives some phrases and sentences in English and their mathematical equivalents written in symbols.

Table 2

In English	In Symbols
The sum of 4 and 1	$4 + 1$
4 added to 1	$1 + 4$
8 more than *m*	$m + 8$
x increased by 5	$x + 5$
The sum of *x* and *y*	$x + y$
The sum of 2 and 4 is 6.	$2 + 4 = 6$

C Properties of Addition

Once we become familiar with addition, we may notice some facts about addition that are true regardless of the numbers involved. The first of these facts involves the number 0 (zero).

Whenever we add 0 to a number, the result is the original number. For example,

$$7 + 0 = 7 \quad \text{and} \quad 0 + 3 = 3$$

Because this fact is true no matter what number we add to 0, we call it a property of 0

> **PROPERTY**   Addition Property of 0
>
> If we let a represent any number, then it is always true that
>
> $$a + 0 = a \quad \text{and} \quad 0 + a = a$$
>
> *In words*: Adding 0 to any number leaves that number unchanged.

A second property we notice by becoming familiar with addition is that the order of two numbers in a sum can be changed without changing the result.

$$3 + 5 = 8 \quad \text{and} \quad 5 + 3 = 8$$

$$4 + 9 = 13 \quad \text{and} \quad 9 + 4 = 13$$

This fact about addition is true for *all* numbers. The order in which you add two numbers doesn't affect the result. We call this fact the *commutative property of addition,* and we write it in symbols as follows:

> **PROPERTY**   Commutative Property of Addition
>
> If a and b are any two numbers, then it is always true that
>
> $$a + b = b + a$$
>
> *In words*: Changing the order of two numbers in a sum doesn't change the result.

EXAMPLE 5   Use the commutative property of addition to rewrite each sum.

a. $4 + 6$ **b.** $5 + 9$ **c.** $3 + 0$ **d.** $7 + n$

Solution   The commutative property of addition indicates that we can change the order of the numbers in a sum without changing the result. Applying this property we have

a. $4 + 6 = 6 + 4$

b. $5 + 9 = 9 + 5$

c. $3 + 0 = 0 + 3$

d. $7 + n = n + 7$

Notice that we did not actually add any of the numbers. The instructions were to use the commutative property, and the commutative property involves only the order of the numbers in a sum.

The last property of addition we will consider here has to do with sums of more than two numbers. Suppose we want to find the sum of 2, 3, and 4. We could add 2 and 3 first, and then add 4 to what we get.

$$(2 + 3) + 4 = 5 + 4 = 9$$

Or, we could add the 3 and 4 together first and then add the 2.

$$2 + (3 + 4) = 2 + 7 = 9$$

The result in both cases is the same. If we try this with any other numbers, the same thing happens.

We call this fact about addition the *associative property of addition,* and we write it in symbols as follows:

> **PROPERTY**   Associative Property of Addition
>
> If a, b, and c represent any three numbers, then
>
> $$(a + b) + c = a + (b + c)$$
>
> *In words*: Changing the grouping of three or more numbers in a sum doesn't change the result.

Note   When we use letters to represent numbers, as we do when we say, "If a and b are any two numbers," then a and b are called variables, because the values they take on vary. We use the variables a and b in the definitions and properties on this page because we want you to know that the definitions and properties are true for all numbers that you will encounter in this book.

5. Use the commutative property of addition to rewrite each sum.

   a. $5 + 9$

   b. $12 + 13$

   c. $17 + 0$

   d. $x + 3$

Note   This discussion is here to show why we write the next property the way we do. Sometimes it is helpful to look ahead to the property itself (in this case, the associative property of addition) to see what it is that is being justified.

Answers

5. a. $9 + 5$ **b.** $13 + 12$
    c. $0 + 17$ **d.** $3 + x$

6. Use the associative property of addition to rewrite each sum.
   a. $(2 + 5) + 6$
   b. $(x + 3) + 5$
   c. $5 + (4 + 7)$
   d. $11 + (8 + n)$

EXAMPLE 6   Use the associative property of addition to rewrite each sum.

a. $(5 + 6) + 7$ **b.** $(3 + 9) + 1$ **c.** $6 + (8 + 2)$

Solution   The associative property of addition indicates that we are free to regroup the numbers in a sum without changing the result.

a. $(5 + 6) + 7 = 5 + (6 + 7)$

b. $(3 + 9) + 1 = 3 + (9 + 1)$

c. $6 + (8 + 2) = (6 + 8) + 2$

The commutative and associative properties of addition tell us that when adding whole numbers, we can use any order and grouping. When adding several numbers, it is sometimes easier to look for pairs of numbers whose sums are 10, 20, and so on.

7. Add: $8 + 7 + 2 + 3 + 6$.

EXAMPLE 7   Add: $9 + 3 + 2 + 7 + 1$

Solution

$$9 + 3 + 2 + 7 + 1 = (9 + 1) + (3 + 7) + 2 \quad \text{Associative property of addition}$$
$$= 10 + 10 + 2$$
$$= 22$$

USING TECHNOLOGY   Calculators

From time to time we will include some notes like this one, which show how a calculator can be used to assist us with some of the calculations in the book. Most calculators on the market today fall into one of two categories: those with algebraic logic and those with function logic. Calculators with algebraic logic have a key with an equals sign on it. Calculators with function logic do not have an equals key. Instead they have a key labeled ENTER or EXE (for execute). Scientific calculators use algebraic logic, and graphing calculators, such as the TI-83/84, use function logic.

Here are the sequences of keystrokes to use to work the problem shown in Part c of Example 9.

Scientific Calculator: 36 $\boxed{+}$ 23 $\boxed{+}$ 24 $\boxed{+}$ 12 $\boxed{+}$ 24 $\boxed{=}$

Graphing Calculator: 36 $\boxed{+}$ 23 $\boxed{+}$ 24 $\boxed{+}$ 12 $\boxed{+}$ 24 $\boxed{\text{ENT}}$

GETTING READY FOR CLASS

After reading through the preceding section, respond in your own words and in complete sentences.

A. What number is the sum of 6 and 8?

B. Make up an addition problem using the number 456 that involves carrying from the ones column to the tens column only.

C. Explain the difference between the commutative property of addition and the associative property of addition.

D. What is the perimeter of a polygon?

Answers

6. a. $2 + (5 + 6)$
   b. $x + (3 + 5)$
   c. $(5 + 4) + 7$
   d. $(11 + 8) + n$
7. 26

Vocabulary Review

Choose the correct words to fill in the blanks below.

sum	associative	place value	carrying
commutative	addition	zero	

1. Learning the basic _____ facts is essential to your study of mathematics.

2. To add whole numbers, add digits of the same _____.

3. If the sum of the digits with the same place value is larger than 9, use the process called _____ to complete the problem.

4. The _____ of a and b is $a + b$ if a and b are any two numbers.

5. The addition property of _____ states that adding zero to any number leaves that number unchanged.

6. The _____ property of addition states that changing the order of two numbers in a sum doesn't change the result.

7. The _____ property of addition states that changing the grouping of three numbers in a sum doesn't change the result.

Problems

A Find each of the following sums. (Add.)

1. $3 + 5 + 7$ **2.** $2 + 8 + 6$ **3.** $1 + 4 + 9$ **4.** $2 + 8 + 3$

5. $5 + 9 + 4 + 6$ **6.** $8 + 1 + 6 + 2$ **7.** $1 + 2 + 3 + 4 + 5$ **8.** $5 + 6 + 7 + 8 + 9$

9. $9 + 1 + 8 + 2$ **10.** $7 + 3 + 6 + 4$

Add each of the following. (There is no carrying involved in these problems.)

11. $\begin{array}{r} 43 \\ +25 \\ \hline \end{array}$ **12.** $\begin{array}{r} 56 \\ +23 \\ \hline \end{array}$ **13.** $\begin{array}{r} 81 \\ +17 \\ \hline \end{array}$

14. $\begin{array}{r} 37 \\ +22 \\ \hline \end{array}$ **15.** $\begin{array}{r} 4,281 \\ +3,016 \\ \hline \end{array}$ **16.** $\begin{array}{r} 2,749 \\ +1,250 \\ \hline \end{array}$

17. 3,482
     + 3,005

18. 2,496
     +7,503

19. 32
     21
     +43

20. 521
     340
     +135

21. 6,245
     203
     + 1,001

22.   27
     4,510
     + 342

B Add each of the following. (All problems involve carrying in at least one column.)

23. 49
     +16

24. 85
     +29

25. 74
     +28

26. 36
     +46

27. 682
     +193

28. 439
     +270

29. 638
     +191

30. 444
     +595

31. 4,963
     +5,428

32. 8,291
     +7,489

33. 6,205
     +9,999

34. 8,888
     +9,999

35. 56,789
     +98,765

36. 45,678
     +87,654

37. 52,468
     +58,642

38. 13,579
     +97,531

39. 4,296
     8,720
     +4,375

40. 5,637
     481
     +7,899

41. 4,994
     449
     +9,449

42. 6,824
     371
     +4,857

43. 12
     34
     56
     +78

44. 21
     43
     65
     +87

45. 999
     444
     555
     +222

46. 646
     464
     525
     +252

47. 9,245
     672
     8,341
     +   27

48.   45
     9,876
     54
     + 6,789

49. 123
     469
     87
     + 95

50. 835
     84
     107
     + 98

51. 5,894
     256
     + 1,045

52. 8,265
     648
     + 2,384

Complete the following tables.

53.

First Number	Second Number	Their Sum
61	38	
63	36	
65	34	
67	32	

54.

First Number	Second Number	Their Sum
10	45	
20	35	
30	25	
40	15	

55.

First Number	Second Number	Their Sum
9	16	
36	64	
81	144	
144	256	

56.

First Number	Second Number	Their Sum
25	75	
24	76	
23	77	
22	78	

C Rewrite each of the following using the commutative property of addition.

57. $5 + 9$ **58.** $2 + 1$ **59.** $3 + 8$ **60.** $9 + 2$ **61.** $6 + 4$ **62.** $1 + 7$

Rewrite each of the following using the associative property of addition.

63. $(1 + 2) + 3$ **64.** $(4 + 5) + 9$ **65.** $(2 + 1) + 6$ **66.** $(2 + 3) + 8$

67. $1 + (9 + 1)$ **68.** $2 + (8 + 2)$ **69.** $(4 + n) + 1$ **70.** $(n + 8) + 1$

Applying the Concepts

The application problems that follow are related to addition of whole numbers. Read each problem carefully to determine exactly what you are being asked to find. Don't assume that just because a number appears in a problem you have to use it to solve the problem. Sometimes you do, and sometimes you don't.

71. Gallons of Gasoline Tim bought gas for his economy car twice last month. The first time he bought 18 gallons and the second time he bought 16 gallons. What was the total amount of gasoline Tim bought last month?

72. Tallest Mountain The world's tallest mountain is Mount Everest. On May 5, 1999, it was found to be 7 feet taller than it was previously thought to be. Before this date, Everest was thought to be 29,028 feet high. That height was determined by B. L. Gulatee in 1954. What is the current height of Mount Everest?

73. Checkbook Balance On Monday, Bob had a balance of $241 in his checkbook. On Tuesday, he made a deposit of $108, and on Thursday, he wrote a check for $24. What was the balance in his checkbook on Wednesday?

74. Number of Passengers A plane flying from Los Angeles to New York left Los Angeles with 67 passengers on board. The plane stopped in Bakersfield and picked up 28 passengers, and then it stopped again in Dallas where 57 more passengers came on board. How many passengers were on the plane when it landed in New York?

Check No.	Date	Description of Transaction	Payment/Debit (-)	Deposit/Credit (+)	Balance
					$241 00
	6/5	ATM Deposit		$108 00	?
1251	6/7	Electric Bill	$24 00		

Find the Mistake

Each sentence below contains a mistake. Circle the mistake and write the correct word(s) or number(s) on the line provided.

1. To find the sum of 786 and 49, add the ones place by writing the 1 and carrying the 5. _____

2. The problem (12 + 7) + 3 = 12 + (7 + 3) uses the commutative property of addition. _____

1.3 Subtraction with Whole Numbers

Image © sxc.hu, dafalias, 2005

The Excalibur Hotel and Casino in Las Vegas, Nevada has a new attraction called the Virtusphere. The plastic sphere is ten feet in diameter and spins on 45 small casters embedded in its frame. A person wearing knee and elbow pads and a virtual gaming headset encloses himself in the sphere. As a video game plays on the headset's screen, the person can interact with the game by walking, running, and rolling without leaving the safety of the sphere.

Let's say the person paid to play a video game inside the Virtusphere for 20 minutes. If the person played for 13 minutes, how many minutes does he have left? To answer this question, we need to understand a little more about subtraction.

Subtraction is the opposite operation of addition. If you understand addition and can work simple addition problems quickly and accurately, then subtraction shouldn't be difficult for you.

A Vocabulary

The word *difference* always indicates subtraction. We can state this in symbols by letting the letters a and b represent numbers.

DEFINITION difference

The **difference** of two numbers a and b is

$$a - b$$

Table 1 gives some word statements involving subtraction and their mathematical equivalents written in symbols.

Table 1

In English	In Symbols
The difference of 9 and 1	$9 - 1$
The difference of 1 and 9	$1 - 9$
The difference of m and 4	$m - 4$
The difference of x and y	$x - y$
3 subtracted from 8	$8 - 3$
2 subtracted from t	$t - 2$
The difference of 7 and 4 is 3.	$7 - 4 = 3$
The difference of 9 and 3 is 6.	$9 - 3 = 6$

B The Meaning of Subtraction

When we want to subtract 3 from 8, we write

$$8 - 3, \qquad 8 \text{ subtract } 3, \qquad \text{or} \qquad 8 \text{ minus } 3$$

The number we are looking for here is the difference between 8 and 3, or the number we add to 3 to get 8; that is,

$$8 - 3 = ? \qquad \text{is the same as} \qquad ? + 3 = 8$$

In both cases, we are looking for the number we add to 3 to get 8. The number we are looking for is 5. We have two ways to write the same statement:

$$\begin{array}{ccc} \textit{Subtraction} & & \textit{Addition} \\ 8 - 3 = 5 & \text{or} & 5 + 3 = 8 \end{array}$$

For every subtraction problem, there is an equivalent addition problem. Table 2 lists some examples.

Table 2

Subtraction		Addition
$7 - 3 = 4$	because	$4 + 3 = 7$
$9 - 7 = 2$	because	$2 + 7 = 9$
$10 - 4 = 6$	because	$6 + 4 = 10$
$15 - 8 = 7$	because	$7 + 8 = 15$

To subtract numbers with two or more digits, we align the numbers vertically and subtract in columns.

EXAMPLE 1   Subtract: $376 - 241$.

Solution   We write the problem vertically, aligning digits with the same place value. Then we subtract in columns.

$$
\begin{array}{r}
376 \\
-\ 241 \\
\hline
135
\end{array}
$$
← *Subtract the bottom number in each column from the number above it.*

We can visualize Example 1 using money.

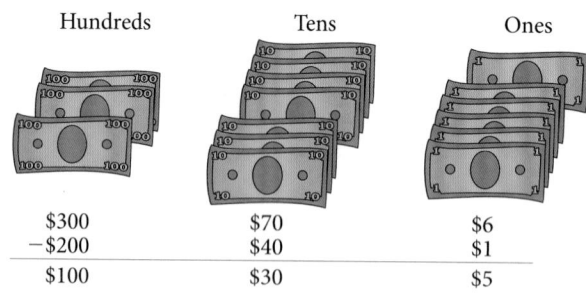

Hundreds	Tens	Ones
$300	$70	$6
−$200	$40	$1
$100	$30	$5

EXAMPLE 2   Subtract 503 from 7,835.

Solution   In symbols, this statement is equivalent to

$$7{,}835 - 503$$

To subtract, we write 503 below 7,835 and then subtract in columns.

$$
\begin{array}{r}
7\ ,\ 8\quad 3\quad 5 \\
-\ 5\quad 0\quad 3 \\
\hline
7\ ,\ 3\quad 3\quad 2
\end{array}
$$

$5 - 3 = 2$ *Ones*
$3 - 0 = 3$ *Tens*
$8 - 5 = 3$ *Hundreds*
$7 - 0 = 7$ *Thousands*

Practice Problems

1. Subtract: $485 - 123$.

2. Subtract 320 from 1,865.

Answers

1. 362
2. 1,545

As you can see, subtraction problems like the ones in Examples 1 and 2 are fairly simple. We write the problem vertically, lining up the digits with the same place value, and subtract in columns. We always subtract the bottom number from the top number.

C Subtraction with Borrowing

Subtraction must involve *borrowing* when the bottom digit in any column is larger than the digit above it. In one sense, borrowing is the reverse of the carrying we did in addition.

EXAMPLE 3   Subtract: $92 - 45$.

Solution   We write the problem vertically with the place values of the digits showing.

$$92 = 9 \text{ tens} + 2 \text{ ones}$$
$$- 45 = 4 \text{ tens} + 5 \text{ ones}$$

Look at the ones column. We cannot subtract immediately, because 5 is larger than 2. Instead, we borrow 1 ten from the 9 tens in the tens column. We can rewrite the number 92 as

$$9 \text{ tens} + 2 \text{ ones}$$
$$= 8 \text{ tens} + 1 \text{ ten} + 2 \text{ ones}$$
$$= 8 \text{ tens} + 12 \text{ ones}$$

Now we are in a position to subtract.

$$92 = 9 \text{ tens} + 2 \text{ ones} = 8 \text{ tens} + 12 \text{ ones}$$
$$- 45 = 4 \text{ tens} + 5 \text{ ones} = 4 \text{ tens} + 5 \text{ ones}$$
$$4 \text{ tens} + 7 \text{ ones}$$

The result is 4 tens + 7 ones, which can be written in standard form as 47.

Writing the problem out in this way is more trouble than is actually necessary. The shorthand form of the same problem looks like this:

$$\begin{array}{r} \overset{8}{\cancel{9}} \ \overset{12}{\cancel{2}} \\ - \ 4 \ 5 \\ \hline 4 \ 7 \end{array}$$

This shows we have borrowed 1 ten to go with the 2 ones.

$12 - 5 = 7$ *Ones*

$8 - 4 = 4$ *Tens*

This shortcut form shows all the necessary work involved in subtraction with borrowing. We will use it from now on.

The borrowing that changed 9 tens + 2 ones into 8 tens + 12 ones can be visualized with money.

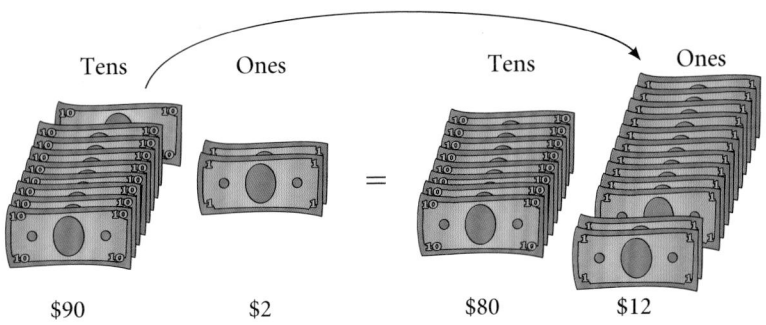

| Tens | Ones | | Tens | Ones |
| $90 | $2 | | $80 | $12 |

4. Find the difference of 268 and 179.

EXAMPLE 4   Find the difference of 549 and 187.

Solution   In symbols, the difference of 549 and 187 is written

$$549 - 187$$

Writing the problem vertically so that the digits with the same place value are aligned, we have

$$\begin{array}{r} 549 \\ -\,187 \end{array}$$

The top number in the tens column is smaller than the number below it. This means that we will have to borrow from the next larger column.

$$\begin{array}{r} \overset{4}{\cancel{5}}\ \overset{14}{\cancel{4}}\ 9 \\ -\,1\ 8\ 7 \\ \hline 3\ 6\ 2 \end{array}$$

— Borrow 1 hundred to go with the 4 tens.

$$9 - 7 = 2 \quad \text{Ones}$$
$$14 - 8 = 6 \quad \text{Tens}$$
$$4 - 1 = 3 \quad \text{Hundreds}$$

The actual work we did in borrowing looks like this:

$$5\text{ hundreds} + 4\text{ tens} + 9\text{ ones}$$
$$= 4\text{ hundreds} + 1\text{ hundred} + 4\text{ tens} + 9\text{ ones}$$
$$= 4\text{ hundreds} + 14\text{ tens} + 9\text{ ones}$$

5. Joshua has $615 in his checking account. If he writes a check for $289 to make his car payment, how much is left?

EXAMPLE 5   Jo Ann has $742 in her checking account. If she writes a check for $615 to pay the rent, how much is left in her checking account?

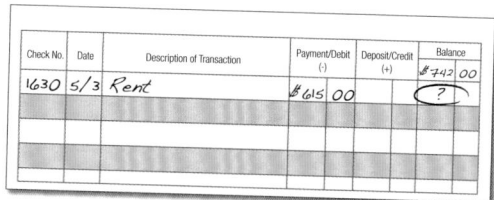

Solution   To find the amount left in the account after she has written the rent check, we subtract.

$$\begin{array}{r} \$7\ \overset{3}{\cancel{4}}\ \overset{12}{\cancel{2}} \\ -\ 6\ 1\ 5 \\ \hline \$1\ 2\ 7 \end{array}$$

She has $127 left in her account after writing a check for the rent.

USING TECHNOLOGY   Calculators

Here is how we would work the problem shown in Example 5 on a calculator:

Scientific Calculator: 742 $\boxed{-}$ 615 $\boxed{=}$

Graphing Calculator: 742 $\boxed{-}$ 615 $\boxed{\text{ENT}}$

Estimating

One way to estimate the answer to the problem shown in Example 5 is to round 742 to 700 and 615 to 600 and then subtract 600 from 700 to obtain 100, which is an estimate of the difference. Making a mental estimate in this manner will help you catch some of the errors that will occur if you press the wrong buttons on your calculator. We will cover estimating and rounding more thoroughly in the next section.

GETTING READY FOR CLASS

After reading through the preceding section, respond in your own words and in complete sentences.

A. Which sentence below describes the problem in Example 1?

    a. The difference of 241 and 376 is 135.

    b. The difference of 376 and 241 is 135.

B. Write a subtraction problem using the number 234 that involves borrowing from the tens column to the ones column.

C. Write a subtraction problem using the number 234 in which the answer is 111.

D. Describe how you would subtract the number 56 from the number 93.

Vocabulary Review

Choose the correct words to fill in the blanks below.

    columns   borrowing   difference   estimation

1. The _____ of two numbers a and b is $a - b$, and is the result of subtraction.

2. To subtract numbers with two or more digits, we align the number vertically and subtract in _____.

3. Subtraction involves _____ when the bottom digit in any column is larger than the digit above it.

4. _____ by rounding is a good way to catch errors.

Problems

A Perform the indicated operation.

1. Subtract 24 from 56.

2. Subtract 71 from 89.

3. Subtract 23 from 45.

4. Subtract 97 from 98.

5. Find the difference of 29 and 19.

6. Find the difference of 37 and 27.

7. Find the difference of 126 and 15.

8. Find the difference of 348 and 32.

Write each of the following expressions in words. Use the word *difference* in each case.

9. $10 - 2$

10. $9 - 5$

11. $a - 6$

12. $7 - x$

13. $8 - 2 = 6$

14. $m - 1 = 4$

Write each of the following expressions in symbols.

15. The difference of 8 and 3

16. The difference of x and 2

17. 9 subtracted from y

18. a subtracted from b

19. The difference of 3 and 2 is 1.

20. The difference of 10 and y is 5.

B Work each of the following subtraction problems.

21.
$$\begin{array}{r} 975 \\ -\ 663 \\ \hline \end{array}$$

22.
$$\begin{array}{r} 480 \\ -\ 260 \\ \hline \end{array}$$

23.
$$\begin{array}{r} 904 \\ -\ 501 \\ \hline \end{array}$$

24.
$$\begin{array}{r} 657 \\ -\ 507 \\ \hline \end{array}$$

25.
$$\begin{array}{r} 9,876 \\ -\ 8,765 \\ \hline \end{array}$$

26.
$$\begin{array}{r} 5,008 \\ -\ 3,002 \\ \hline \end{array}$$

27.
$$\begin{array}{r} 7,976 \\ -\ 3,432 \\ \hline \end{array}$$

28.
$$\begin{array}{r} 6,980 \\ -\ 470 \\ \hline \end{array}$$

C Find the difference in each case. (These problems all involve borrowing.)

29. $52 - 37$

30. $65 - 48$

31. $70 - 37$

32. $90 - 21$

33. $74 - 69$

34. $31 - 28$

35. $51 - 18$

36. $64 - 58$

37. $329 - 234$

38. $518 - 492$

39. $348 - 196$

40. $759 - 661$

41.
$$\begin{array}{r} 932 \\ -\ 658 \\ \hline \end{array}$$

42.
$$\begin{array}{r} 895 \\ -\ 597 \\ \hline \end{array}$$

43.
$$\begin{array}{r} 647 \\ -\ 159 \\ \hline \end{array}$$

44.
$$\begin{array}{r} 842 \\ -\ 199 \\ \hline \end{array}$$

45.
$$\begin{array}{r} 905 \\ -\ 367 \\ \hline \end{array}$$

46.
$$\begin{array}{r} 804 \\ -\ 238 \\ \hline \end{array}$$

47.
$$\begin{array}{r} 600 \\ -\ 437 \\ \hline \end{array}$$

48.
$$\begin{array}{r} 800 \\ -\ 342 \\ \hline \end{array}$$

49.
$$\begin{array}{r} 4,583 \\ -\ 2,973 \\ \hline \end{array}$$

50.
$$\begin{array}{r} 7,849 \\ -\ 2,957 \\ \hline \end{array}$$

51.
$$\begin{array}{r} 79,040 \\ -\ 32,957 \\ \hline \end{array}$$

52.
$$\begin{array}{r} 86,492 \\ -\ 78,506 \\ \hline \end{array}$$

Complete the following tables.

53.

First Number a	Second Number b	The Difference of a and b $a - b$
25	15	
24	16	
23	17	
22	18	

54.

First Number a	Second Number b	The Difference of a and b $a - b$
90	79	
80	69	
70	59	
60	49	

55.

First Number a	Second Number b	The Difference of a and b $a - b$
400	256	
400	144	
225	144	
225	81	

56.

First Number a	Second Number b	The Difference of a and b $a - b$
100	36	
100	64	
25	16	
25	9	

Applying the Concepts

Not all of the following application problems involve only subtraction. Some involve addition as well. Be sure to read each problem carefully.

57. Checkbook Balance Diane has $504 in her checking account. If she writes five checks for a total of $249, how much does she have left in her account?

58. Checkbook Balance Larry has $763 in his checking account. If he writes a check for each of the three bills listed, how much will he have left in his account?

Item	Amount
Rent	$418
Phone	$25
Car repair	$117

59. Tallest Mountain The world's tallest mountain is Mount Everest. On May 5, 1999, it was found to be 7 feet taller than it was previously thought to be. Before this date, Everest was thought to be 29,028 feet high. That height was determined by B. L. Gulatee in 1954. The first measurement of Everest was in 1856. At that time, the height was thought to be 29,002 feet. What is the difference between the current height of Everest and the height measured in 1856?

60. Home Prices In 1985, Mr. Hicks paid $137,500 for his home. He sold it in 2000 for $260,600. What is the difference between what he sold it for and what he bought it for?

61. Enrollment Six years ago, there were 567 students attending Smith Elementary School. Today the same school has an enrollment of 399 students. How much of a decrease in enrollment has there been in the last six years at Smith School?

62. Oil Spills In March 1977, an oil tanker hit a reef off Taiwan and spilled 3,134,500 gallons of oil. In March 1989, an oil tanker hit a reef off Alaska and spilled 10,080,000 gallons of oil. How much more oil was spilled in the 1989 disaster?

Checkbook Balance On Monday, Gil has a balance of $425 in his checkbook. On Tuesday, he deposits $149 into the account. On Wednesday, he writes a check for $37, and on Friday he writes a check for $188. Use this information to answer Problems 79–82.

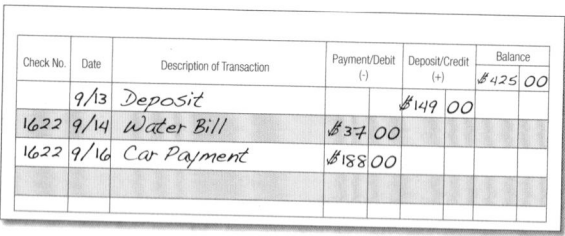

Check No.	Date	Description of Transaction	Payment/Debit (-)	Deposit/Credit (+)	Balance
					$425 00
	9/13	Deposit		$149 00	
1622	9/14	Water Bill	$37 00		
1622	9/16	Car Payment	$188 00		

63. Find Gil's balance after he makes the deposit on Tuesday.

64. What is his balance after he writes the check on Wednesday?

65. To the nearest ten dollars, what is his balance at the end of the week?

66. To the nearest ten dollars, what is his balance before he writes the check on Friday?

67. iPad Sales The bar chart shows the projected sales of iPads from 2010–2012.

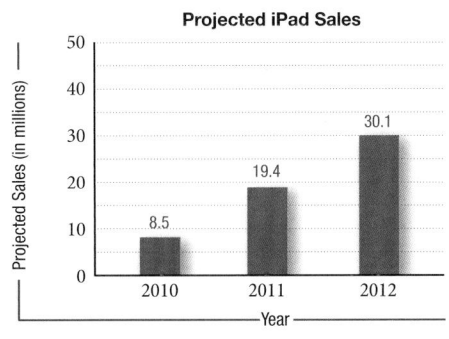

Source: Data from emarketer.com

Year	Projected Sales (Millions)
2010	
2011	
	30.1

a. Use the information in the bar chart to fill in the missing entries in the table.

b. What is the difference in projected iPad sales between 2012 and 2010?

68. U.S. Mobile Gaming Revenues The bar chart shows the projected revenue for paid mobile games.

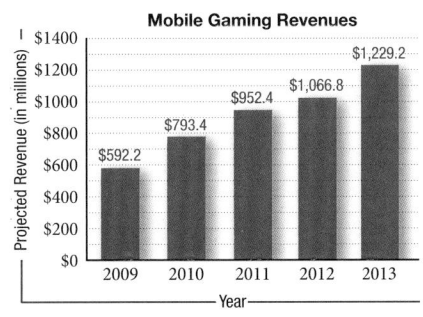

Source: emarketer.com

Year	Projected Revenue (Millions)
2009	
2010	
	$952.4
2012	
	$1,229.2

a. Use the chart to fill in the missing entries in the table.

b. What is the difference in projected revenue between 2012 and 2009?

Improving Your Quantitative Literacy

69. Beijing Olympic Venues The bar chart below shows the seating capacity for several Olympic venues in Beijing.

BEIJING OLYMPIC VENUE CAPACITY
en.beijing2008.cn

The National Stadium	91,000
The National Aquatics Center	17,000
The National Indoor Stadium	18,000
Beijing Olympic Green Tennis Courts	17,400
Olympic Sport Center Stadium	38,000

Venue	Capacity
National Stadium	
National Aquatic Center	
	18,000
Beijing Olympic Green Tennis Courts	
	38,000

a. Use the information in the bar chart to fill in the missing entries in the table.

b. How many more people can attend a competition in the National Stadium than in the National Aquatic Center?

Find the Mistake

Each sentence below contains a mistake. Circle the mistake and write the correct word(s) or number(s) on the line provided.

1. Translating "The difference of 22 and 3 is 19" into symbols gives us $3 - 22 = 19$. _____

2. To subtract 50 from 290, vertically align the tens column of the first number with the hundreds column of the second number. _____

3. To find the difference of 85 and 27, begin by subtracting 7 from 5. _____

Landmark Review: Checking Your Progress

This feature is intended as a review of key skills from the preceding sections in the chapter. Each review will give you the opportunity to utilize important concepts and check your progress as you practice problems of different types. Take note of any problems in this review that you find difficult. There is no better time than now to revisit and master those difficult concepts in preparation for any upcoming exams or subsequent chapters.

Write each of the following numbers in expanded form.

1. 549   **2.** 1,493   **3.** 60,243   **4.** 30,403,005

Perform the indicated operations.

5. $4 + 2 + 12$ **6.** $4 + 3 + 8 + 9 + 5 + 2$ **7.** $\begin{array}{r} 52 \\ + \ 65 \\ \hline \end{array}$

8. $\begin{array}{r} 2,435 \\ + \ 5,215 \\ \hline \end{array}$ **9.** $\begin{array}{r} 14,253 \\ 25,489 \\ 53,503 \\ + \ 10,456 \\ \hline \end{array}$ **10.** $\begin{array}{r} 145,358 \\ 256,789 \\ + \quad 15 \\ \hline \end{array}$

11. $\begin{array}{r} 957 \\ - \ 427 \\ \hline \end{array}$ **12.** $\begin{array}{r} 6,492 \\ - \ 5,257 \\ \hline \end{array}$ **13.** Subtract 15 from 32.

14. Subtract 5 from 27.   **15.** Find the difference of 37 and 25.   **16.** Find the difference of 142 and 40.

1.4 Rounding Numbers and Estimating Answers

OBJECTIVES

A Round numbers to specified place values.

B Estimate sums and differences.

KEY WORDS

rounding

estimate

Image © sxc.hu, romos, 2009

In Greece, millions of frogs decided to migrate all at once across a busy highway. Scientists believe the frogs left a nearby lake in search of food, but needless to say, the amphibian influx caused a major traffic jam. Greek officials shut down the highway for two hours out of concern for driver safety. Previously, three motorists had skidded off the road trying to avoid the frogs. It was nearly impossible to count all the frogs crossing the highway, so scientists relied on their estimation and rounding skills to come up with the quantity of millions.

In this section, we will learn how to round numbers to a specific place value and then apply that skill to estimating answers for math problems. First, let's consider another example that uses rounded numbers.

When we talk about numbers, it is sometimes helpful to use numbers that have been *rounded off*, rather than exact numbers. For example, the city where I live has a population of 45,119. But when I tell people how large the city is, I usually say, "The population is about 45,000." The number 45,000 is the original number rounded to the nearest thousand. The number 45,119 is closer to 45,000 than it is to 46,000, so it is rounded to 45,000. We can visualize this situation on the number line.

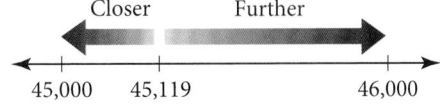

A Rounding Numbers

The steps used in rounding numbers are given below.

> **HOW TO** Steps for Rounding Whole Numbers
>
> 1. Locate the digit just to the right of the place you are to round to.
>
> 2. If that digit is less than 5, replace it and all digits to its right with zeros.
>
> 3. If that digit is 5 or more, replace it and all digits to its right with zeros, and add 1 to the digit to its left.

You can see from these steps that in order to round a number you must be told what column (or place value) to round to.

Video Examples
SECTION 1.4

Note After you have used the steps listed here to work a few problems, you will find that the procedure becomes almost automatic.

Practice Problems

1. Round 2,849 to the nearest hundred.

EXAMPLE 1   Round 5,382 to the nearest hundred.

Solution   The 3 is in the hundreds column. We look at the digit just to its right, which is 8. Because 8 is greater than 5, we add 1 to the 3, and we replace the 8 and 2 with zeros.

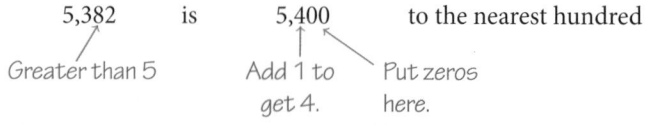

2. Round 1,427 to the nearest ten.

EXAMPLE 2   Round 94 to the nearest ten.

Solution   The 9 is in the tens column. To its right is 4. Because 4 is less than 5, we simply replace it with 0.

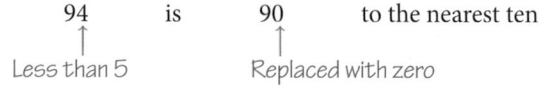

3. Round 955 to the nearest hundred.

EXAMPLE 3   Round 973 to the nearest hundred.

Solution   We have a 9 in the hundreds column. To its right is 7, which is greater than 5. We add 1 to 9 to get 10, and then replace the 7 and 3 with zeros.

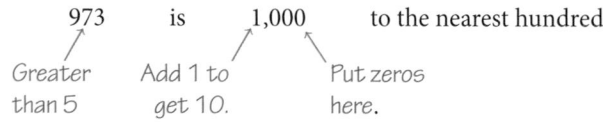

4. Round 479,580 to nearest thousand.

EXAMPLE 4   Round 47,256,344 to the nearest million.

Solution   We have 7 in the millions column. To its right is 2, which is less than 5. We simply replace all the digits to the right of 7 with zeros to get

$$47,256,344 \quad \text{is} \quad 47,000,000 \quad \text{to the nearest million}$$

Less than 5   Leave as is.   Replaced with zeros

Table 1 gives more examples of rounding.

Table 1

| | Rounded to the Nearest | | |
Original Number	Ten	Hundred	Thousand
6,914	6,910	6,900	7,000
8,485	8,490	8,500	8,000
5,555	5,560	5,600	6,000
1,234	1,230	1,200	1,000

RULE   Calculating and Rounding

If we are doing calculations and are asked to round our answer, we do all our arithmetic first and then round the result. That is, the last step is to round the answer; we don't round the numbers first and then do the arithmetic.

Answers

1. 2,800
2. 1,430
3. 1,000
4. 480,000

EXAMPLE 5   The pie chart below shows how a family earning $36,913 a year spends their money.

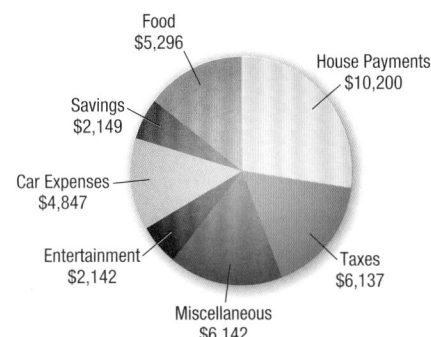

Food
$5,296

House Payments
$10,200

Savings
$2,149

Car Expenses
$4,847

Entertainment
$2,142

Taxes
$6,137

Miscellaneous
$6,142

a. To the nearest hundred dollars, what is the total amount spent on food and entertainment?

b. To the nearest thousand dollars, how much of their income is spent on items other than taxes and savings?

Solution   In each case, we add the numbers in question and then round the sum to the indicated place.

a. We add the amounts spent on food and entertainment and then round that result to the nearest hundred dollars.

Food	$5,296
Entertainment	+ 2,142
Total	$7,438 = $7,400 to the nearest hundred dollars

b. We add the numbers for all items except taxes and savings.

House payments	$10,200
Food	5,296
Car expenses	4,847
Entertainment	2,142
Miscellaneous	+ 6,142
Total	$28,627 = $29,000 to the nearest thousand dollars

B Estimating Sums and Differences

When we *estimate* the answer to a problem, we simplify the problem so that an approximate answer can be found quickly. There are a number of ways of doing this. One common method is to use rounded numbers to simplify the arithmetic necessary to arrive at an approximate answer, as our next example shows.

EXAMPLE 6   Estimate the answer to the following addition problem by rounding each number to the nearest thousand.

$$4,872$$
$$1,691$$
$$777$$
$$+ 6,124$$

Solution   We round each of the four numbers in the sum to the nearest thousand. Then we add the rounded numbers.

4,872	rounds to	5,000
1,691	rounds to	2,000
777	rounds to	1,000
+ 6,124	rounds to	+ 6,000
		14,000

We estimate the answer to this problem to be approximately 14,000. The actual answer, found by adding the original unrounded numbers, is 13,464.

5. Using the pie chart from Example 5, answer the following questions.
   a. To the nearest hundred dollars, what is the total amount spent on taxes and house payments?
   b. To the nearest thousand dollars, how much of their income is spent on items other than house payments?

6. Estimate the answer to the following addition problem by rounding each number to the nearest thousand.
$$15,465$$
$$1,564$$
$$893$$
$$+ 11,989$$

Answers
5. a. $16,300 **b.** $27,000
6. 30,000

7. Estimate the answer to the
following subtraction problem
by rounding each number to the
nearest hundred.

$$12,487 - 5,806$$

EXAMPLE 7   Estimate the answer to the following subtraction problem by rounding each number to the nearest hundred.

$$5,423 - 1,856$$

Solution   Round each number to the nearest hundred, then subtract.

5,432	rounds to	5,400
1,856	rounds to	− 1,900
		3,500

We estimate the answer to be approximately 3,500. The actual answer, found by subtracting the original numbers, is 3,567.

The method used in Examples 6 and 7 above does not conflict with the rule we stated before Example 5. In Examples 6 and 7, we are asked to *estimate* an answer, so it is okay to round the numbers in the problem before adding them. In Example 5, we are asked for a rounded answer, meaning that we are to find the exact answer to the problem and then round to the indicated place. In this case, we must not round the numbers in the problem before adding.

GETTING READY FOR CLASS

After reading through the preceding section, respond in your own words and in complete sentences.

A. Describe the process you would use to round 5,382 to the nearest thousand.

B. Describe the process you would use to round 47,256,344 to the nearest ten thousand.

C. Find a number not containing the digit 7 that will round to 700 when rounded to the nearest hundred.

D. When I ask a class of students to round the number 7,499 to the nearest thousand, a few students will give the answer as 8,000. In what way are these students using the rule for rounding numbers incorrectly?

Vocabulary Review

Choose the correct words to fill in the blanks below.

more   round   estimate   less

1. When asked to _____ your answer, do all calculations first then round the result.

2. When rounding numbers, if the digit to the right of the place you are to round to is _____ than 5, replace it and all digits to its right with zeros.

3. When rounding numbers, if the digit to the right of the place you are to round to is 5 or _____, replace it and all digits to its right with zeros, and add 1 to the digit to its left.

4. When asked to _____ your answer, use rounded numbers to arrive at an approximate answer.

Problems

A Round each of the numbers to the nearest ten.

1. 42	**2.** 44	**3.** 46	**4.** 48	**5.** 45	**6.** 73
7. 77	**8.** 75	**9.** 458	**10.** 455	**11.** 471	**12.** 680
13. 56,782	**14.** 32,807	**15.** 4,504	**16.** 3,897	**17.** 1,195	**18.** 10,998

Round each of the numbers to the nearest hundred.

19. 549	**20.** 954	**21.** 833	**22.** 604	**23.** 899	**24.** 988
25. 1090	**26.** 6,778	**27.** 5,044	**28.** 56,990	**29.** 39,603	**30.** 31,999

Round each of the numbers to the nearest thousand.

31. 4,670	**32.** 9,054	**33.** 9,760	**34.** 4,444
35. 978	**36.** 567	**37.** 657,892	**38.** 688,909
39. 608,433	**40.** 3,789,345	**41.** 5,744,500	**42.** 509,905

Complete the following table by rounding the numbers on the left as indicated by the headings in the table.

Original Number	Rounded to the Nearest		
	Ten	Hundred	Thousand
43. 7,821			
44. 5,945			
45. 5,999			
46. 4,353			
47. 10,985			
48. 11,108			
49. 99,999			
50. 95,505			

Applying the Concepts

51. Average Salary Salary studies by mlbfanhouse.com show that major league baseball's average player salary for the 2010 season was $3,014,572, representing an increase of 0.6% over the previous season's average. Round the 2010 average player salary to the nearest hundred thousand.

52. Tallest Mountain The world's tallest mountain is Mount Everest. On May 5, 1999, it was found to be 7 feet taller than it was previously thought to be. Before this date, Everest was thought to be 29,028 feet high. That height was determined by B. L. Gulatee in 1954. The first measurement of Everest was in 1856. At that time the height was given as 29,002 feet. Round the current height, the 1954 height, and the 1856 height of Mount Everest to the nearest thousand.

Fox Ratings The chart shows the number of viewers watching primetime shows on the Fox network in one week during 2009. Use the information to answer Problems 53-56.

53. What is the number of viewers watching these Fox shows during the week?

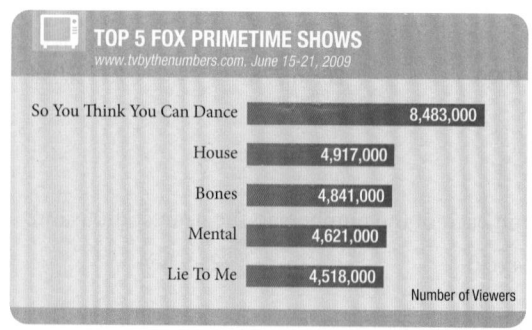

54. Using your answer from #53, is the statement "About 27 million viewers watched these shows" correct?

55. To the nearest hundred thousand, how many people watched "So You Think You Can Dance" during the week?

56. To the nearest ten thousand, how many people watched "Lie to Me" during the week?

Business Expenses The pie chart shows one year's worth of expenses for a small business. Use the chart to answer Problems 57–60.

57. To the nearest hundred dollars, how much was spent on postage and supplies?

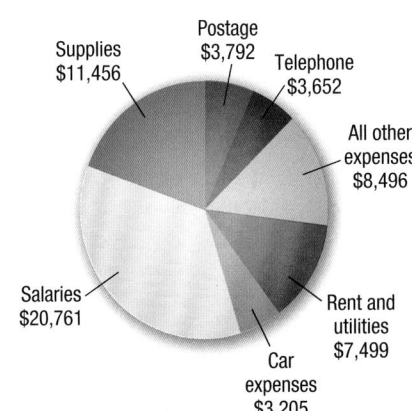

58. Find the total amount spent, to the nearest hundred dollars, on rent, utilities and car expenses.

59. To the nearest thousand dollars, how much was spent on items other than salaries, rent and utilities?

60. To the nearest thousand dollars, how much was spent on items other than postage, supplies, and car expenses?

B Estimating Estimate the answer to each of the following addition problems by rounding each number to the indicated place value and then adding.

61. Hundred
     750
     275
   + 120

62. Thousand
     1,891
     765
   + 3,223

63. Hundred
     472
     422
     536
   +511

64. Hundred
     399
     601
     744
   + 298

65. Thousand
     25,399
     7,601
     18,744
   + 6,298

66. Thousand
     9,999
     8,888
     7,777
   + 6,666

Estimate the answer to the following problems by rounding each number to the indicated place value and then subtracting.

67. Hundred
    17,487 − 5,640

68. Hundred
    986 − 249

69. Thousand
    8,946 − 3,815

70. Thousand
    18,955 − 12,049

71. Thousand
    204,489 − 107,815

72. Thousand
    49,899 − 29,846

Find the Mistake

Each sentence below contains a mistake. Circle the mistake and write the correct word(s) or number(s) on the line provided.

1. Rounding 12,456 to the nearest hundred gives us 12,400. _____

2. To round 102,673 to the nearest ten, replace the 3 with a zero and add 1 to the 7. _____

3. To estimate the sum of 14,256 and 2,789 by rounding to the nearest hundred, add 14,200 and 2,800. _____

A Multiply numbers by using repeated addition.

B Understand terminology and properties of multiplication.

C Multiply numbers involving carrying and place value.

KEY WORDS

repeated addition

product

factor

distributive property

multiplication properties

commutative property of multiplication

associative property of multiplication

applications

Practice Problems

1. Multiply 5 · 400 using repeated addition.

Video Examples
SECTION 1.5

Image © sxc.hu, bluehor, 2011

Engineers are working to perfect a new night vision system based on the amazing vision of a bee. The system will hopefully be used as a heads-up display to help drivers better navigate dark roads. A bee's eyes are called compound eyes because they are made up of 6000 tiny lenses. Each lens is attached to a tube containing 8 light receptors that help the bee see large range of colors and levels of light, even on the darkest nights.

Considering the information about a bee's eyes, how many total light receptors does he have? To answer this problem, we need to understand multiplication with whole numbers. Multiplication is what we will cover in this section.

A Multiplication as Repeated Addition

To begin, we can think of multiplication as shorthand for repeated addition. That is, multiplying 3 times 4 can be thought of this way:

$$3 \text{ times } 4 = 4 + 4 + 4 = 12$$

Multiplying 3 times 4 means to add three 4s. We can write 3 times 4 as 3×4, or $3 \cdot 4$.

EXAMPLE 1 Multiply $4 \cdot 400$ using repeated addition.

Solution Using the definition of multiplication as repeated addition, we have

$$4 \cdot 400 = 400 + 400 + 400 + 400$$

$$= 1{,}600$$

One way to visualize this process is to think about a 4 by 400 meter relay team.

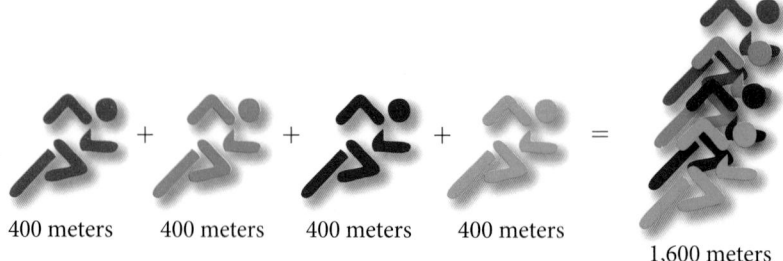

400 meters   400 meters   400 meters   400 meters   1,600 meters

Notice that if we had multiplied 4 and 4 to get 16 and then attached two zeros on the right, the result would have been the same.

Answer

1. 2,000

B Vocabulary and Properties

There are many ways to indicate multiplication. All the following statements are equivalent. They all indicate multiplication with the numbers 3 and 4.

$$3 \cdot 4, \quad 3 \times 4, \quad 3(4), \quad (3)4, \quad (3)(4), \quad \begin{array}{r} 4 \\ \underline{\times\, 3} \end{array}$$

If one or both of the numbers we are multiplying are represented by variables, we may also use the following notation:

$5n$ means 5 times n
ab means a times b

We use the word *product* to indicate multiplication. If we say, "The product of 3 and 4 is 12," then we mean

$$3 \cdot 4 = 12$$

Both $3 \cdot 4$ and 12 are called the product of 3 and 4. The 3 and 4 are called *factors*.

DEFINITION factors

Factors are numbers that when multiplied together give a product.

Table 1 gives some word statements involving multiplication and their mathematical equivalents written in symbols.

Table 1

In English	In Symbols
The product of 2 and 5	$2 \cdot 5$
The product of 5 and 2	$5 \cdot 2$
The product of 9 and 6 is 54.	$9 \cdot 6 = 54$
The product of 2 and 8 is 16.	$2 \cdot 8 = 16$

EXAMPLE 2 Identify the products and factors in the statement

$$9 \cdot 8 = 72$$

Solution The factors are 9 and 8, and the products are $9 \cdot 8$ and 72.

EXAMPLE 3 Identify the products and factors in the statement

$$30 = 2 \cdot 3 \cdot 5$$

Solution The factors are 2, 3, and 5. The products are $2 \cdot 3 \cdot 5$ and 30.

Distributive Property

To develop an efficient method of multiplication, we need to use what is called the *distributive property*. To begin, consider the following two problems:

Problem 1   Problem 2

$3(4 + 5)$ $3(4) + 3(5)$

$= 3(9)$ $= 12 + 15$

$= 27$ $= 27$

Note The kind of notation we will use to indicate multiplication will depend on the situation. For example, when we are solving equations that involve letters, it is not a good idea to indicate multiplication with the symbol $\times$, since it could be confused with the variable x. The symbol we will use to indicate multiplication most often in this book is the multiplication dot.

2. Identify the products and factors in the statement $5 \cdot 7 = 35$.

3. Identify the products and factors in the statement $2 \cdot 5 \cdot 11 = 110$.

Answers

2. Factors: 5, 7
   Products: $5 \cdot 7$, 35
3. Factors: 2, 5, 11
   Products: $2 \cdot 5 \cdot 11$, 110

The result in both cases is the same number, 27. This indicates that the original two expressions must have been equal also; that is,

$$3(4 + 5) = 3(4) + 3(5)$$

This is an example of the distributive property. We say that multiplication *distributes* over addition.

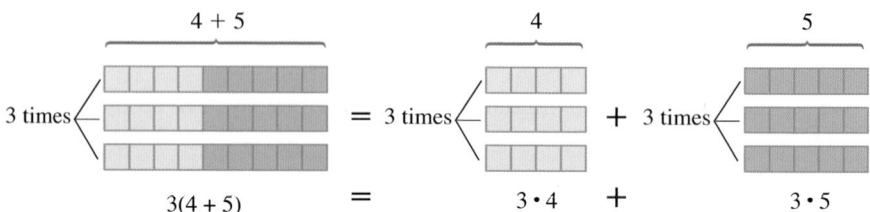

$$3(4 + 5) = 3(4) + 3(5)$$

We can write this property in symbols using the letters a, b, and c to represent any three numbers.

> **PROPERTY** **Distributive Property**
>
> If a, b, and c represent any three numbers, then
>
> $$a(b + c) = a(b) + a(c)$$

More Properties of Multiplication

> **PROPERTY** **Multiplication Property of 0**
>
> If a represents any number, then
>
> $$a \cdot 0 = 0 \quad \text{and} \quad 0 \cdot a = 0$$
>
> *In words:* Multiplication by 0 always results in 0.

> **PROPERTY** **Multiplication Property of 1**
>
> If a represents any number, then
>
> $$a \cdot 1 = a \quad \text{and} \quad 1 \cdot a = a$$
>
> *In words:* Multiplying any number by 1 leaves that number unchanged.

> **PROPERTY** **Commutative Property of Multiplication**
>
> If a and b are any two numbers, then
>
> $$ab = ba$$
>
> *In words:* The order of the numbers in a product doesn't affect the result.

> **PROPERTY** **Associative Property of Multiplication**
>
> If a, b, and c represent any three numbers, then
>
> $$(ab)c = a(bc)$$
>
> *In words:* We can change the grouping of the numbers in a product without changing the result.

To visualize the commutative property, we can think of a dining room with 8 guests.

4 tables with 2 people each   =   2 tables with 4 people each

EXAMPLE 4   Use the commutative property of multiplication to rewrite each of the following products.

a. $7 \cdot 9$ **b.** $4(6)$

Solution   Applying the commutative property to each expression, we have

a. $7 \cdot 9 = 9 \cdot 7$

b. $4(6) = 6(4)$

EXAMPLE 5   Use the associative property of multiplication to rewrite each of the following products.

a. $(2 \cdot 7) \cdot 9$ **b.** $3 \cdot (8 \cdot 2)$

Solution   Applying the associative property of multiplication, we regroup as follows:

a. $(2 \cdot 7) \cdot 9 = 2 \cdot (7 \cdot 9)$

b. $3 \cdot (8 \cdot 2) = (3 \cdot 8) \cdot 2$

C Multiplication with Whole Numbers

Suppose we want to find the product $7(65)$. By writing 65 as $60 + 5$ and applying the distributive property, we have

$$7(65) = 7(60 + 5) \qquad 65 = 60 + 5$$
$$= 7(60) + 7(5) \quad \text{Distributive property}$$
$$= 420 + 35 \quad \text{Multiply first, then add.}$$
$$= 455$$

We can write the same problem vertically like this:

$$
\begin{array}{r}
60 + 5 \\
\times \quad\quad 7 \\
\hline
35 \quad \leftarrow 7(5) = 35 \\
+ \quad 420 \quad \leftarrow 7(60) = 420 \\
\hline
455
\end{array}
$$

This saves some space in writing. But notice that we can cut down on the amount of writing even more if we write the problem this way:

Step 2: $7(6) = 42$; Add the → $\overset{3}{6}5$ Step 1: $7(5) = 35$; Write the 5
3 we carried to 42 to get 45. $\underline{\times\ 7}$ in the ones column, and then carry
455 ←   the 3 to the tens column.

This shortcut notation takes some practice.

EXAMPLE 6   Multiply: $9(43)$.

Solution

Step 2: $9(4) = 36$; Add the → $\overset{2}{4}3$ Step 1: $9(3) = 27$; Write the 7
2 we carried to 36 to get 38. $\underline{\times\ 9}$ in the ones column, and then carry
387 ←   the 2 to the tens column.

4. Use the commutative property of multiplication to rewrite each product.
   a. $5 \cdot 12$
   b. $6(x + y)$

5. Use the associative property of multiplication to rewrite each product.
   a. $(5 \cdot 8) \cdot 3$
   b. $3 \cdot (7 \cdot n)$

Note   When using the distributive property, we multiply $a(b)$ and $a(c)$ before adding their products together because of a rule called order of operations. Part of this rule states that once operations inside parentheses have been worked, then we multiply before we add. We will study this rule more later on in this chapter.

6. Multiply: $7(59)$.

Answers
4. a. $12 \cdot 5$ **b.** $(x + y)(6)$
5. a. $5 \cdot (8 \cdot 3)$ **b.** $(3 \cdot 7) \cdot n$
6. 413

7. Multiply: 67(45).

EXAMPLE 7   Multiply: 52(37).

Solution   This is the same as 52(30 + 7) or by the distributive property

$$52(30) + 52(7)$$

We can find each of these products by using the shortcut method.

$$
\begin{array}{r}
52 \\
\times\ 30 \\
\hline
1{,}560
\end{array}
\qquad
\begin{array}{r}
\overset{1}{5}2 \\
\times\ 7 \\
\hline
364
\end{array}
$$

The sum of these two numbers is $1{,}560 + 364 = 1{,}924$. Here is a summary of what we have so far:

$$
\begin{aligned}
52(37) &= 52(30 + 7) &&\quad 37 = 30 + 7 \\
&= 52(30) + 52(7) &&\quad \text{Distributive property} \\
&= 1{,}560 + 364 &&\quad \text{Multiply first, then add.} \\
&= 1{,}924
\end{aligned}
$$

The shortcut form for this problem is

$$
\begin{array}{r}
52 \\
\times\ 37 \\
\hline
364 \quad \longleftarrow\ 7(52) = 364 \\
+\ 1{,}560 \quad \longleftarrow\ 30(52) = 1{,}560 \\
\hline
1{,}924
\end{array}
$$

In this case, we have not shown any of the numbers we carried, simply because it becomes very messy.

8. Multiply: 124(375).

EXAMPLE 8   Multiply: 279(428).

Solution

$$
\begin{array}{r}
279 \\
\times\ 428 \\
\hline
2{,}232 \quad \longleftarrow\ 8(279) = 2{,}232 \\
5{,}580 \quad \longleftarrow\ 20(279) = 5{,}580 \\
+\ 111{,}600 \quad \longleftarrow\ 400(279) = 111{,}600 \\
\hline
119{,}412
\end{array}
$$

USING TECHNOLOGY   Calculator

Here is how we would work the problem shown in Example 8 on a calculator:

Scientific Calculator: 279 $\boxed{\times}$ 428 $\boxed{=}$

Graphing Calculator: 279 $\boxed{\times}$ 428 $\boxed{\text{ENT}}$

Estimating

One way to estimate the answer to the problem shown in Example 8 is to round each number to the nearest hundred and then multiply the rounded numbers. Doing so would give us this:

$$300(400) = 120{,}000$$

Our estimate of the answer is 120,000, which is close to the actual answer, 119,412. Making estimates is important when we are using calculators; having an estimate of the answer will keep us from making major errors in multiplication.

Answers

7. 3,015
8. 46,500

D Applications

EXAMPLE 9   A supermarket orders 35 cases of a certain soft drink. If each case contains 12 cans of the drink, then how many cans were ordered?

Solution   We have 35 cases and each case has 12 cans. The total number of cans is the product of 35 and 12, which is 35(12).

$$
\begin{array}{r}
12 \\
\times\ 35 \\
\hline
60 \\
+\ 360 \\
\hline
420
\end{array}
$$

$5(12) = 60$

$30(12) = 360$

There is a total of 420 cans of the soft drink.

EXAMPLE 10   Shirley earns \$12 an hour for the first 40 hours she works each week. If she has \$109 deducted from her weekly check for taxes and retirement, how much money will she take home if she works 38 hours this week?

Solution   To find the amount of money she earned for the week, we multiply 12 and 38. From that total we subtract 109. The result is her take-home pay. Without showing all the work involved in the calculations, here is the solution:

$$38(\$12) = \$456 \qquad \textit{Her total weekly earnings}$$

$$\$456 - \$109 = \$347 \qquad \textit{Her take-home pay}$$

EXAMPLE 11   In 1993, the government standardized the way in which nutrition information is presented on the labels of most packaged food products. Figure 1 shows one of these standardized food labels. It is from a box of original Cheez-It baked snack crackers. Approximately how many crackers are in the box, and what is the total number of calories consumed if all the crackers in the box are eaten?

Solution   Reading toward the top of the label, we see that there are about 27 crackers in one serving, and approximately 9 servings in the box. Therefore, the total number of crackers in the box is

$$9(27) = 243 \text{ crackers}$$

This is an approximate number, because each serving is approximately 27 crackers. Reading further we find that each serving contains 150 calories. Therefore, the total number of calories consumed by eating all the crackers in the box is

$$9(150) = 1{,}350 \text{ calories}$$

As we progress through the book, we will study more of the information in nutrition labels.

Nutrition Facts	
Serving Size 30 g. (About 27 crackers)	
Servings Per Container: 9	
Amount Per Serving	
Calories 150	Calories from fat 70
	% Daily Value*
Total Fat 8g	**12%**
Saturated Fat 2g	**10%**
Trans Fat 0g	
Cholesterol 0mg	**0%**
Sodium 230mg	**10%**
Total Carbohydrate 17g	**6%**
Sugars 0g	
Protein 3g	
Vitamin A 2% • Vitamin C 0%	
*Percent Daily Values are based on a 2,000 calorie diet	

FIGURE 1

9. A bar orders 45 cases of beer. If each case contains 24 bottles of beer, how many bottles were ordered?

10. Rodrigo earns \$9 per hour at his tutoring job. If he works 35 hours and has \$42 deducted for taxes, how much will his paycheck be for the week?

11. From Example 11, how many calories from fat will you consume if you eat the entire box of crackers?

Note   The letter g that is shown after some of the numbers in the nutrition label in Figure 1 stands for grams, a unit used to measure weight. The unit mg stands for milligrams, another smaller unit of weight. We will have more to say about these units later in the book.

Answers

9. 1,080 beers
10. \$273
11. 630 calories from fat

12. Using the chart from Example 12 suppose a 150-pound person bicycles for 3 hours and goes jogging for 2 hours in a week. How many calories did that person burn in a week?

EXAMPLE 12   The table below lists the number of calories burned in 1 hour of exercise by a person who weighs 150 pounds. Suppose a 150-pound person goes bowling for 2 hours after having eaten the box of crackers mentioned in Example 11. Will he or she burn all the calories consumed from the crackers?

Activity	Calories Burned in 1 Hour by a 150-Pound Person
Bicycling	374
Bowling	265
Handball	680
Jazzercize	340
Jogging	680
Skiing	544

Solution   Each hour of bowling burns 265 calories. If the person bowls for 2 hours, he or she will burn a total of

$$2(265) = 530 \text{ calories}$$

Because the box of crackers contained 1,350 calories, not all of them have been burned with 2 hours of bowling.

GETTING READY FOR CLASS

After reading through the preceding section, respond in your own words and in complete sentences.

A. Explain how multiplication is shorthand for repeated addition.

B. Use the variables a, b, and c to explain the distribution property.

D. What is the difference between the commutative property of multiplication and the associative property of multiplication?

Answer

12. 2,482 calories

Vocabulary Review

Choose the correct words to fill in the blanks below.

associative   distributive   addition   multiplication

unchanged   factors   commutative

1. Multiplication is repeated _____.

2. _____ are numbers that when multiplied together give a product.

3. The _____ property states that $a(b + c) = a(b) + a(c)$.

4. The _____ property of 0 states that multiplication by 0 always results in 0.

5. The multiplication property of 1 states that multiplying any number by 1 leaves that number _____.

6. The _____ property of multiplication states that the order of the numbers in a product doesn't affect the result.

7. The _____ property of multiplication states that $(ab)c = a(bc)$.

Problems

A Multiply each of the following using repeated addition.

1. $3 \cdot 100$ **2.** $7 \cdot 100$ **3.** $3 \cdot 200$ **4.** $4 \cdot 200$

5. $6 \cdot 500$ **6.** $8 \cdot 400$ **7.** $5 \cdot 1,000$ **8.** $8 \cdot 1,000$

9. $3 \cdot 7,000$ **10.** $6 \cdot 7,000$ **11.** $9 \cdot 9,000$ **12.** $7 \cdot 7,000$

B Write each of the following expressions in words, using the word *product*.

13. $6 \cdot 7$ **14.** $9(4)$ **15.** $2 \cdot n$

16. $5 \cdot x$ **17.** $9 \cdot 7 = 63$ **18.** $(5)(6) = 30$

Write each of the following in symbols.

19. The product of 7 and n **20.** The product of 9 and x **21.** The product of 6 and 7 is 42.

22. The product of 8 and 9 is 72.   **23.** The product of 0 and 6 is 0.   **24.** The product of 1 and 6 is 6.

Identify the products in each statement.

25. $9 \cdot 7 = 63$ **26.** $2(6) = 12$ **27.** $4(4) = 16$ **28.** $5 \cdot 5 = 25$

Identify the factors in each statement.

29. $2 \cdot 3 \cdot 4 = 24$ **30.** $6 \cdot 1 \cdot 5 = 30$ **31.** $12 = 2 \cdot 2 \cdot 3$ **32.** $42 = 2 \cdot 3 \cdot 7$

Rewrite each of the following using the commutative property of multiplication.

33. $5(9)$ **34.** $4(3)$ **35.** $6 \cdot 7$ **36.** $8 \cdot 3$

Rewrite each of the following using the associative property of multiplication.

37. $2 \cdot (7 \cdot 6)$ **38.** $4 \cdot (8 \cdot 5)$ **39.** $3 \times (9 \times 1)$ **40.** $5 \times (8 \times 2)$

Use the distributive property to rewrite each expression, then simplify.

41. $7(2 + 3)$ **42.** $4(5 + 8)$ **43.** $9(4 + 7)$ **44.** $6(9 + 5)$

45. $3(x + 1)$ **46.** $5(x + 8)$ **47.** $2(x + 5)$ **48.** $4(x + 3)$

C Find each of the following products (multiply). In each case, use the shortcut method.

49. $\begin{array}{r} 25 \\ \times\, 4 \\ \hline \end{array}$ **50.** $\begin{array}{r} 43 \\ \times\, 9 \\ \hline \end{array}$ **51.** $\begin{array}{r} 38 \\ \times\, 6 \\ \hline \end{array}$ **52.** $\begin{array}{r} 45 \\ \times\, 7 \\ \hline \end{array}$

53. $\begin{array}{r} 18 \\ \times\, 2 \\ \hline \end{array}$ **54.** $\begin{array}{r} 29 \\ \times\, 3 \\ \hline \end{array}$ **55.** $\begin{array}{r} 72 \\ \times\, 20 \\ \hline \end{array}$ **56.** $\begin{array}{r} 68 \\ \times\, 30 \\ \hline \end{array}$

57. $\begin{array}{r} 19 \\ \times\, 50 \\ \hline \end{array}$ **58.** $\begin{array}{r} 24 \\ \times\, 40 \\ \hline \end{array}$ **59.** $\begin{array}{r} 69 \\ \times\, 25 \\ \hline \end{array}$ **60.** $\begin{array}{r} 27 \\ \times\, 36 \\ \hline \end{array}$

61. $\begin{array}{r} 11 \\ \times\, 11 \\ \hline \end{array}$ **62.** $\begin{array}{r} 12 \\ \times\, 21 \\ \hline \end{array}$ **63.** $\begin{array}{r} 97 \\ \times\, 16 \\ \hline \end{array}$ **64.** $\begin{array}{r} 24 \\ \times\, 39 \\ \hline \end{array}$

65. 168
× 25

66. 452
× 34

67. 728
× 91

68. 680
× 76

69. 698
× 400

70. 879
× 600

71. 111
× 111

72. 123
× 321

73. 532
× 200

74. 277
× 900

75. 856
× 232

76. 455
× 248

77. 976
× 628

78. 432
× 555

79. 2,468
× 135

80. 2,725
× 324

81. 24,563
× 735

82. 56,728
× 852

83. 44,777
× 5,888

84. 33,999
× 2,555

Complete the following tables.

85.

First Number a	Second Number b	Their Product ab
11	11	
11	22	
22	22	
22	44	

86.

First Number a	Second Number b	Their Product ab
25	15	
25	30	
50	15	
50	30	

87.

First Number a	Second Number b	Their Product ab
25	10	
25	100	
25	1,000	
25	10,000	

88.

First Number a	Second Number b	Their Product ab
11	111	
11	222	
22	111	
22	222	

89.

First Number a	Second Number b	Their Product ab
12	20	
36	20	
12	40	
36	40	

90.

First Number a	Second Number b	Their Product ab
10	12	
100	12	
1,000	12	
10,000	12	

Exercise and Calories The table below is an extension of the table we used in Example 12 of this section. It gives the amount of energy expended during 1 hour of various activities for people of different weights. The accompanying figure is a nutrition label from a bag of cheddar Goldfish crackers. Use the information from the table and the nutrition label to answer Problems 113–118.

Calories Burned Through Exercise

Activity	Calories Per Hour 120 Pounds	Calories Per Hour 150 Pounds	Calories Per Hour 180 Pounds
Bicycling	299	374	449
Bowling	212	265	318
Handball	544	680	816
Jazzercise	272	340	408
Jogging	544	680	816
Skiing	435	544	653

Nutrition Facts

Serving Size 55 pieces
Servings Per Container About 4

Amount Per Serving

Calories 140   Calories from fat 45

	% Daily Value*
Total Fat 5g	8%
Saturated Fat 1g	5%
Cholesterol 5mg	2%
Sodium 250mg	10%
Total Carbohydrate 20g	7%
Dietary Fiber 1g	4%
Sugars 1g	
Protein 4g	

Vitamin A 0%	•	Vitamin C 0%
Calcium 4%	•	Iron 2%

*Percent Daily Values are based on a 2,000 calorie diet

91. Suppose you weigh 180 pounds. How many calories would you burn if you play handball for 2 hours and then ride your bicycle for 1 hour?

92. How many calories are burned by a 120-lb person who jogs for 1 hour and then goes bike riding for 2 hours?

93. How many calories would you consume if you ate the entire bag of crackers?

94. Approximately how many crackers are in the bag?

95. If you weigh 180 pounds, will you burn off the calories consumed by eating 3 servings of Goldfish crackers if you ride your bike 1 hour?

96. If you weigh 120 pounds, will you burn off the calories consumed by eating 3 servings of Goldfish crackers if you ride your bike for 1 hour?

Estimating

Mentally estimate the answer to each of the following problems by rounding each number to the indicated place and then multiplying.

97. 750 hundred
$\times$ 12 ten

98. 591 hundred
$\times$ 323 hundred

99. 3,472 thousand
$\times$ 511 hundred

100. 399 hundred
$\times$ 298 hundred

101. 2,399 thousand
$\times$ 698 hundred

102. 9,999 thousand
$\times$ 666 hundred

Find the Mistake

Each sentence below contains a mistake. Circle the mistake and write the correct word(s) or number(s) on the line provided.

1. Factors are numbers that when multiplied together give a sum. _____

2. The distributive property is used to show that $16(5 + 9) = 16(5) + 9$. _____

3. The first step when multiplying 73 and 4 is to multiply 4 and 3 by writing down the 1 and carrying the 2.

_____

1.6 Division with Whole Numbers

KEY WORDS

quotient

dividend

divisor

long division

remainder

In 2008, the *Alaska Ranger* crab-fishing ship sank leaving the 47-member crew floating in the near-freezing waters of the Bering Sea. The Coast Guard, 230 miles away, picked up the ship's mayday call before it sank and immediately set out to rescue the crew by helicopter. Other fishing vessels also picked up the ship's mayday and changed their courses toward the last known coordinates. One of the closest vessels was 250 miles away, and at top speed could travel at 35 miles per hour. How many hours did it take this vessel to reach the survivors? To answer this question, we need to divide 250 by 35. In this section, we will work with more division problems similar to this one.

A Notation

As was the case with multiplication, there are many ways to indicate division. All the following statements are equivalent. They all mean 10 divided by 5.

$$10 \div 5, \quad \frac{10}{5}, \quad 10/5, \quad 5\overline{)10}$$

The kind of notation we use to write division problems will depend on the situation. We will use the notation $5\overline{)10}$ mostly with the long division problems found in this chapter. The notation $\frac{10}{5}$ will be used in the chapter on fractions and in later chapters. The horizontal line used with the notation $\frac{10}{5}$ is called the fraction bar.

Vocabulary

The word *quotient* is used to indicate division. If we say, "The quotient of 10 and 5 is 2," then we mean

$$10 \div 5 = 2 \qquad \text{or} \qquad \frac{10}{5} = 2$$

The 10 is called the dividend, and the 5 is called the divisor. All the expressions, $10 \div 5$, $\frac{10}{5}$, and 2, are called the quotient of 10 and 5.

Table 1

In English	In Symbols
The quotient of 15 and 3	$15 \div 3$, or $\frac{15}{3}$, or 15/3
The quotient of 3 and 15	$3 \div 15$, or $\frac{3}{15}$, or 3/15
The quotient of 8 and n	$8 \div n$, or $\frac{8}{n}$, or 8/n
x divided by 2	$x \div 2$, or $\frac{x}{2}$, or x/2
The quotient of 21 and 3 is 7.	$21 \div 3 = 7$, or $\frac{21}{3} = 7$

The Meaning of Division

One way to arrive at an answer to a division problem is by thinking in terms of multiplication. For example, if we want to find the quotient of 32 and 8, we may ask, "What do we multiply by 8 to get 32?"

$$32 \div 8 = ? \qquad \text{means} \qquad 8 \cdot ? = 32$$

Because we know from our work with multiplication that $8 \cdot 4 = 32$, it must be true that

$$32 \div 8 = 4$$

Table 2 lists some additional examples.

Table 2		
Division		**Multiplication**
$18 \div 6 = 3$	because	$6 \cdot 3 = 18$
$32 \div 8 = 4$	because	$8 \cdot 4 = 32$
$10 \div 2 = 5$	because	$2 \cdot 5 = 10$
$72 \div 9 = 8$	because	$9 \cdot 8 = 72$

B Division by One-Digit Numbers

Consider the following division problem:

$$465 \div 5$$

We can think of this problem as asking the question, "How many fives can we subtract from 465?" To answer the question, we begin subtracting multiples of 5. One way to organize this process is shown below.

$$
\begin{array}{r}
90 \\
5\overline{)465} \\
-\,450 \\
\hline
15
\end{array}
$$

← We first guess that there are at least 90 fives in 465.
← $90(5) = 450$
← 15 is left after we subtract 90 fives from 465.

What we have done so far is subtract 90 fives from 465 and found that 15 is still left. Because there are 3 fives in 15, we continue the process.

$$
\begin{array}{r}
3 \\
90 \\
5\overline{)465} \\
-\,450 \\
\hline
15 \\
-\,15 \\
\hline
0
\end{array}
$$

← There are 3 fives in 15.

← $3 \cdot 5 = 15$
← The difference is 0.

The total number of fives we have subtracted from 465 is

$$90 + 3 = 93 \qquad \text{The number of fives subtracted from 465}$$

We now summarize the results of our work.

$$465 \div 5 = 93 \qquad \text{Which we check}$$

with multiplication →

$$
\begin{array}{r}
\overset{1}{9}3 \\
\times\ 5 \\
\hline
465
\end{array}
$$

Notation

The division problem just shown can be shortened by eliminating some of the information.

The shorthand form for this problem

$$
\begin{array}{r}
3 \\
90 \\
5\overline{)465} \\
-\ 450 \\
\hline
15 \\
-\ 15 \\
\hline
0
\end{array}
$$

looks like this.

$$
\begin{array}{r}
93 \\
5\overline{)465} \\
-\ 45\!\downarrow \\
\hline
15 \\
-\ 15 \\
\hline
0
\end{array}
$$

The arrow indicates that we bring down the 5 after we subtract.

The problem shown above on the right is the shortcut form of what is called *long division*. Here is an example showing this shortcut form of long division from start to finish.

EXAMPLE 1 Divide: $595 \div 7$.

Solution Because $7(8) = 56$, our first estimate of the number of sevens that can be subtracted from 595 is 80.

$$
\begin{array}{r}
8 \\
7\overline{)595} \\
-\ 56\!\downarrow \\
\hline
35
\end{array}
$$

← The 8 is placed above the tens column, so we know our first estimate is 80.
← $8(7) = 56$
← $59 - 56 = 3$; then bring down the 5.

Since $7(5) = 35$, we have

$$
\begin{array}{r}
85 \\
7\overline{)595} \\
-\ 56\!\downarrow \\
\hline
35 \\
-\ 35 \\
\hline
0
\end{array}
$$

← There are 5 sevens in 35.

← $5(7) = 35$
← $35 - 35 = 0$

Our result is $595 \div 7 = 85$, which we can check with multiplication.

$$
\begin{array}{r}
\overset{3}{85} \\
\times\ 7 \\
\hline
595
\end{array}
$$

Division by Two-Digit Numbers

EXAMPLE 2 Divide: $9,380 \div 35$.

Solution In this case our divisor, 35, is a two-digit number. The process of division is the same. We still want to find the number of thirty-fives we can subtract from 9,380.

$$
\begin{array}{r}
2 \\
35\overline{)9380} \\
-\ 70\!\downarrow \\
\hline
238
\end{array}
$$

← The 2 is placed above the hundreds column.
← $2(35) = 70$
← $93 - 70 = 23$; then bring down the 8.

We can make a few preliminary calculations to help estimate how many thirty-fives are in 238.

$$5 \times 35 = 175 \qquad 6 \times 35 = 210 \qquad 7 \times 35 = 245$$

Video Examples
SECTION 1.6

Because 210 is the closest to 238 without being larger than 238, we use 6 as our next estimate.

$$
\begin{array}{r}
26 \\
35\overline{)9380} \\
-70\downarrow| \\
\hline
238 \\
-210\downarrow \\
\hline
280
\end{array}
$$

← *6 in the tens column means this estimate is 60.*

← *6 (35) = 210*

← *238 − 210 = 28; bring down the 0.*

Because 35(8) = 280, we have

$$
\begin{array}{r}
268 \\
35\overline{)9380} \\
-70\downarrow| \\
\hline
238| \\
-210\downarrow \\
\hline
280 \\
-280 \\
\hline
0
\end{array}
$$

← *8(35) = 280*

← *280 − 280 = 0*

We can check our result with multiplication.

$$
\begin{array}{r}
268 \\
\times\ \ \ 35 \\
\hline
1,340 \\
+\ 8,040 \\
\hline
9,380
\end{array}
$$

3. Divide: 5,200 ÷ 16.

EXAMPLE 3   Divide: 1,872 by 18.

Solution   Here is the first step:

$$
\begin{array}{r}
1 \\
18\overline{)1872} \\
-18 \\
\hline
0
\end{array}
$$

← *1 is placed above hundreds column.*

← *Multiply 1(18) to get 18.*

← *Subtract to get 0.*

The next step is to bring down the 7 and divide again.

$$
\begin{array}{r}
10 \\
18\overline{)1872} \\
-18\downarrow \\
\hline
07 \\
-0 \\
\hline
7
\end{array}
$$

← *0 is placed above tens column. 0 is the largest number we can multiply by 18 and not go over 7.*

← *Multiply 0(18) to get 0.*

← *Subtract to get 7.*

Here is the complete problem:

$$
\begin{array}{r}
104 \\
18\overline{)1872} \\
-18\downarrow| \\
\hline
07| \\
-0\downarrow \\
\hline
72 \\
-72 \\
\hline
0
\end{array}
$$

To show our answer is correct, we multiply.

$$18(104) = 1,872$$

C Division with Remainders

Suppose Darlene is making bread using a five-pound (80 oz.) bag of flour. Her bread recipe calls for 30 ounces of flour for each loaf. To see how many ounces she could get from a 80-ounce bag, she would divide 80 by 30. If she did so, she would find that she could make two loaves, but she would have 20 ounces of flour left over. A diagram of this problem is shown in Figure 1.

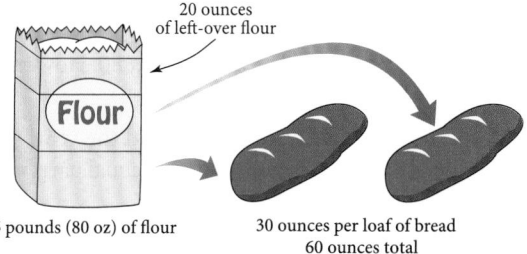

20 ounces of left-over flour

5 pounds (80 oz) of flour   30 ounces per loaf of bread
                                   60 ounces total

FIGURE 1

Writing the results in the diagram as a division problem looks like this:

$$
\begin{array}{r}
2 \quad \leftarrow \text{Quotient} \\
\text{Divisor} \rightarrow 30\overline{)80} \quad \leftarrow \text{Dividend} \\
-60 \\
\hline
20 \quad \leftarrow \text{Remainder}
\end{array}
$$

EXAMPLE 4   Divide: $1{,}690 \div 67$.

Solution   Dividing as we have previously, we get

$$
\begin{array}{r}
25 \\
67\overline{)1690} \\
-134\downarrow \\
\hline
350 \\
-335 \\
\hline
15 \quad \leftarrow \text{15 is left over.}
\end{array}
$$

We have 15 left, and because 15 is less than 67, no more sixty-sevens can be subtracted. In a situation like this, we call 15 the remainder and write

These indicate that the remainder is 15.

$$
\begin{array}{r}
25 \ \text{R} \ 15 \\
67\overline{)1690} \\
-134\downarrow \\
\hline
350 \\
-335 \\
\hline
15
\end{array}
\qquad \text{or} \qquad
\begin{array}{r}
25\,\tfrac{15}{67} \\
67\overline{)1690} \\
-134\downarrow \\
\hline
350 \\
-335 \\
\hline
15
\end{array}
$$

Both forms of notation shown above indicate that 15 is the remainder. The notation R 15 is the notation we will use in this chapter. The notation $\frac{15}{67}$ will be useful in the chapter on fractions.

To check a problem like this, we multiply the divisor and the quotient as usual, and then add the remainder to this result.

$$
\begin{array}{r}
67 \\
\times 25 \\
\hline
335 \\
+1{,}340 \\
\hline
1{,}675 \quad \leftarrow \text{Product of divisor and quotient}
\end{array}
$$

$$1{,}675 + 15 = 1{,}690$$

Remainder   Dividend

4. Divide: $1{,}572 \div 23$.

USING TECHNOLOGY   Calculators

Here is how we would work the problem shown in Example 4 on a calculator:

Graphing Calculator: 1690 $\div$ 67 $\boxed{\text{ENT}}$

Scientific Calculator: 1690 $\div$ 67 $\boxed{=}$

In both cases the calculator will display 25.223881 (give or take a few digits at the end), which gives the remainder in decimal form. We will discuss decimals later in the book.

EXAMPLE 5   A family has an annual income of $35,880. How much is their average monthly income?

Solution   Because there are 12 months in a year and the yearly (annual) income is $35,880, we want to know what $35,880 divided into 12 equal parts is. Therefore, we have

$$
\begin{array}{r}
2990 \\
12\overline{)35880} \\
-24 \\
\hline
118 \\
-108 \\
\hline
108 \\
-108 \\
\hline
00
\end{array}
$$

Because 35,880 $\div$ 12 = 2,990, the monthly income for this family is $2,990.

Division by Zero

We cannot divide by 0. That is, we cannot use 0 as a divisor in any division problem. Here's why:

Suppose there was an answer to the problem

$$\frac{8}{0} = ?$$

That would mean that $0 \cdot ? = 8$. But we already know that multiplication by 0 always produces 0. There is no number we can use for the ? to make a true statement out of $0 \cdot ? = 8$. Because this was equivalent to the original division problem

$$\frac{8}{0} = ?$$

we have no number to associate with the expression $\frac{8}{0}$. It is undefined.

RULE   Division by Zero

Division by 0 is undefined. Any expression with a divisor of 0 is undefined. We cannot divide by 0.

GETTING READY FOR CLASS

After reading through the preceding section, respond in your own words and in complete sentences.

A. Which sentence below describes the problem shown in Example 1?

   a. The quotient of 7 and 595 is 85.

   b. Seven divided by 595 is 85.

   c. The quotient of 595 and 7 is 85.

B. To find a solution to a division problem, how would you think in terms of multiplication?

C. Example 4 shows that 1,690 $\div$ 67 gives a quotient of 25 with a remainder of 15. If we were to divide 1,692 by 67, what would the remainder be?

D. Explain why division by 0 is undefined in mathematics.

---

5. A family has an annual income of $34,320. How much is their average monthly income?

Note   To estimate the answer to Example 5 quickly, we can replace 35,880 with 36,000 and mentally calculate

$$36,000 \div 12$$

which gives an estimate of 3,000. Our actual answer, 2,990, is close enough to our estimate to convince us that we have not made a major error in our calculation.

Answer

5. $2,860

Vocabulary Review

Choose the correct words to fill in the blanks below.

remainder   divisor   quotient   undefined

1. The word _____ is used to indicate division.

2. In the expression 12 ÷ 6, the 12 is called the _____, and the 6 is called the _____.

3. When a number does not divide evenly into another number, we are left with a _____.

4. An expression with a divisor of zero is _____.

Problems

A Write each of the following in symbols.

1. The quotient of 6 and 3

2. The quotient of 3 and 6

3. The quotient of 45 and 9

4. The quotient of 12 and 4

5. The quotient of r and s

6. The quotient of s and r

7. The quotient of 20 and 4 is 5.

8. The quotient of 20 and 5 is 4.

Write a multiplication statement that is equivalent to each of the following division statements.

9. $6 \div 2 = 3$

10. $6 \div 3 = 2$

11. $\dfrac{36}{9} = 4$

12. $\dfrac{36}{4} = 9$

13. $\dfrac{48}{6} = 8$

14. $\dfrac{35}{7} = 5$

15. $28 \div 7 = 4$

16. $81 \div 9 = 9$

B Find each of the following quotients. (Divide.)

17. $25 \div 5$

18. $72 \div 8$

19. $40 \div 5$

20. $12 \div 2$

21. $9 \div 0$

22. $7 \div 1$

23. $360 \div 8$

24. $285 \div 5$

25. $\dfrac{138}{6}$

26. $\dfrac{267}{3}$

27. $5\overline{)7,650}$

28. $5\overline{)5,670}$

29. $5\overline{)6,750}$ **30.** $5\overline{)6,570}$ **31.** $3\overline{)54,000}$ **32.** $3\overline{)50,400}$

33. $3\overline{)50,040}$ **34.** $3\overline{)50,004}$ **35.** $4\overline{)96,000}$ **36.** $5\overline{)25,450}$

Divide. You shouldn't have any wrong answers because you can always check your results with multiplication.

37. $1,440 \div 32$ **38.** $1,206 \div 67$ **39.** $\dfrac{2,401}{49}$ **40.** $\dfrac{4,606}{49}$

41. $28\overline{)12,096}$ **42.** $28\overline{)96,012}$ **43.** $63\overline{)90,594}$ **44.** $45\overline{)17,595}$

45. $87\overline{)61,335}$ **46.** $79\overline{)48,032}$ **47.** $45\overline{)135,900}$ **48.** $56\overline{)227,920}$

C Divide. The following division problems all have remainders.

49. $6\overline{)370}$ **50.** $8\overline{)390}$ **51.** $3\overline{)271}$ **52.** $3\overline{)172}$

53. $26\overline{)345}$ **54.** $26\overline{)543}$ **55.** $71\overline{)16,620}$ **56.** $71\overline{)33,240}$

57. $23\overline{)9,250}$ **58.** $23\overline{)20,800}$ **59.** $169\overline{)5,950}$ **60.** $391\overline{)34,450}$

Complete the following tables.

61.

First Number	Second Number	The Quotient of a and b
a	b	$\dfrac{a}{b}$
100	25	
100	26	
100	27	
100	28	

62.

First Number	Second Number	The Quotient of a and b
a	b	$\dfrac{a}{b}$
100	25	
101	25	
102	25	
103	25	

Estimating

Work these problems mentally, without using a calculator.

63. The quotient 845 ÷ 93 is closest to which of the following numbers?

    a. 10   **b.** 100   **c.** 1,000   **d.** 10,000

64. The quotient 762 ÷ 43 is closest to which of the following numbers?

    a. 2   **b.** 20   **c.** 200   **d.** 2,000

65. The quotient 15,208 ÷ 771 is closest to which of the following numbers?

    a. 2   **b.** 20   **c.** 200   **d.** 2,000

66. The quotient 24,471 ÷ 523 is closest to which of the following numbers?

    a. 5   **b.** 50   **c.** 500   **d.** 5,000

Without a calculator give a one-digit estimate for each of the following quotients. That is, for each quotient, mentally estimate the answer using one of the digits 1, 2, 3, 4, 5, 6, 7, 8, or 9.

67. 316 ÷ 289

68. 662 ÷ 289

69. 728 ÷ 355

70. 728 ÷ 177

71. 921 ÷ 243

72. 921 ÷ 442

73. 673 ÷ 109

74. 673 ÷ 218

Applying the Concepts

The application problems that follow may involve more than division. Some may require addition, subtraction, or multiplication, whereas others may use a combination of two or more operations.

75. Monthly Income A family has an annual income of $22,200. How much is their monthly income?

76. Hourly Wages If a man works an 8-hour shift and is paid $96, how much does he make for 1 hour?

77. Price per Pound If 6 pounds of a certain kind of fruit cost 96¢, how much does 1 pound cost?

78. Cost of a Dress A dress shop orders 45 dresses for a total of $675. If they paid the same amount for each dress, how much was each dress?

79. Fitness Walking The guidelines for fitness indicate that a person who walks 10,000 steps daily is physically fit. According to experts, it takes just over 2,000 steps to walk one mile. If that is the case, how many miles do you need to walk in order to take 10,000 steps?

80. Filling Glasses How many 8-ounce glasses can be filled from three 32-ounce bottles of soda?

81. Filling Glasses How many 5-ounce glasses can be filled from a 32-ounce bottle of milk? How many ounces of milk will be left in the bottle when all the glasses are full?

82. Filling Glasses How many 3-ounce glasses can be filled from a 28-ounce bottle of milk? How many ounces of milk will be left in the bottle when all the glasses are filled?

83. **Filling Glasses** How many 32-ounce bottles of Coke will be needed to fill sixteen 6-ounce glasses?

84. **Filling Glasses** How many 28-ounce bottles of 7-Up will be needed to fill fourteen 6-ounce glasses?

85. **Cost of Wine** If a person paid $192 for 16 bottles of wine, how much did each bottle cost?

86. **Miles per Gallon** A traveling salesman kept track of his mileage for 1 month. He found that he traveled 1,104 miles and used 48 gallons of gas. How many miles did he travel on each gallon of gas?

87. **Milligrams of Calcium** Suppose one egg contains 25 milligrams of calcium, a piece of toast contains 40 milligrams of calcium, and a glass of milk contains 215 milligrams of calcium. How many milligrams of calcium are contained in a breakfast that consists of three eggs, two glasses of milk, and four pieces of toast?

88. **Milligrams of Iron** Suppose a glass of juice contains 3 milligrams of iron and a piece of toast contains 2 milligrams of iron. If Diane drinks two glasses of juice and has three pieces of toast for breakfast, how much iron is contained in the meal?

Calculator Problems

Find each of the following quotients using a calculator.

89. $305,026 \div 698$

90. $771,537 \div 949$

91. 18,436,466 divided by 5,678

92. 2,492,735 divided by 2,345

93. The quotient of 603,955 and 695

94. The quotient of 875,124 and 876

95. $4{,}903\overline{)27{,}868{,}652}$

96. $3{,}090\overline{)2{,}308{,}230}$

97. **Gallons per Minute** If a 79,768-gallon tank can be filled in 472 minutes, how many gallons enter the tank each minute?

98. **Weight per Case** A truckload of 632 crates of motorcycle parts weighs 30,968 pounds. How much does each of the crates weigh, if they each weigh the same amount?

Find the Mistake

Each sentence below contains a mistake. Circle the mistake and write the correct word(s) or number(s) on the line provided.

1. The division notation $\frac{10}{5}$ is equivalent to $10\overline{)5}$. _____

2. The quotient of 198 and 11 is 11. _____

3. To divide 1,640 by 12, first subtract 12 from 40. _____

4. Dividing 2,380 by 13 gives a remainder of 13. _____

1.7 Order of Operations

Image © sxc.hu, Des1gn, 2005

In 1856, the steamboat *Arabia* got stuck in sunken woody debris in the Missouri River. One of the dead trees ripped a hole in the ship's hull, which subsequently filled with water and sank the ship. Over the years, the course of the river has shifted a half mile away, leaving the ship buried far below a Kansas City cornfield for more than a century.

In 1987, the local Hawley family set out to uncover the ship. After three weeks of digging using heavy equipment, the Hawleys finally reached the hull of the ship. The nutrient-rich mud had preserved much of the hull's cargo in pristine condition. The family uncovered artifacts such as elegant china, fancy clothes made of silk and beaver furs, medicines, perfumes, tools, weapons, eyeglasses, even jars of preserved food that are still edible nearly 150 years later!

The hole dug to find the Arabia was as large as a football field and was 45 feet deep. To calculate the volume of dirt excavated in order to unearth the Arabia, we need to multiply the square footage of a football field by the depth of the hole. A football field is 57,600 square feet (ft^2), therefore the hole's volume is 2,592,000 cubic feet (ft^3)!

A Order of Operations

The symbols we use to specify operations, $+$, $-$, $\cdot$, $\div$, along with the symbols we use for grouping, $(\ )$ and $[\ ]$, serve the same purpose in mathematics as punctuation marks in English. They may be called the punctuation marks of mathematics.

Consider the following sentence:

> Bob said John is tall.

It can have two different meanings, depending on how we punctuate it:

1. "Bob," said John, "is tall."
2. Bob said, "John is tall."

Without the punctuation marks we don't know which meaning the sentence has.

Now, consider the following mathematical expression:

$$4 + 5 \cdot 2$$

What should we do? Should we add 4 and 5 first, or should we multiply 5 and 2 first? There seem to be two different answers. In mathematics, we want to avoid situations in which two different results are possible. Therefore, we follow the rule for *order of operations*.

> **RULE** Order of Operations
>
> When evaluating mathematical expressions, we will perform the operations in the following order:
>
> 1. If the expression contains grouping symbols, such as parentheses ( ), brackets [ ], or a fraction bar, then we perform the operations inside the grouping symbols, or above and below the fraction bar, first.
> 2. Then we do all multiplications and divisions in order, starting at the left and moving right.
> 3. Finally, we do all additions and subtractions, from left to right.

According to our rule, the expression $4 + 5 \cdot 2$ would have to be evaluated by multiplying 5 and 2 first, and then adding 4. The correct answer—and the only answer—to this problem is 14.

$$4 + 5 \cdot 2 = 4 + 10 \qquad \text{Multiply first, then add.}$$
$$= 14$$

Here are some more examples that illustrate how we apply the rule for order of operations to simplify (or evaluate) expressions.

EXAMPLE 1   Simplify: $4 \cdot 8 - 2 \cdot 6$.

Solution   We multiply first and then subtract.

$$4 \cdot 8 - 2 \cdot 6 = 32 - 12 \qquad \text{Multiply first, then subtract.}$$
$$= 20$$

EXAMPLE 2   Simplify: $5 + 2(7 - 1)$.

Solution   According to the rule for the order of operations, we must do what is inside the parentheses first.

$$5 + 2(7 - 1) = 5 + 2(6) \qquad \text{Work inside parentheses first.}$$
$$= 5 + 12 \qquad \text{Then multiply.}$$
$$= 17 \qquad \text{Then add.}$$

EXAMPLE 3   Simplify: $9 \cdot 2 + 36 \div 3 - 8$.

Solution

$$9 \cdot 2 + 36 \div 3 - 8 = 18 + 12 - 8 \qquad \text{Multiply and divide, left to right.}$$
$$= 30 - 8$$
$$= 22 \qquad \left.\begin{array}{c}\\\end{array}\right\} \text{Add and subtract left to right,}$$

Video Examples
SECTION 1.7

1. Simplify: $5 \cdot 12 - 3 \cdot 7$.

2. Simplify: $3 + 7(8 - 3)$.

3. Simplify: $4 \cdot 9 + 24 \div 8 - 6$.

Answers
1. 39
2. 38
3. 33

Here is how we use a calculator to work the problem shown in Example 5:

Scientific Calculator: 5 $\boxed{+}$ 2 $\boxed{\times}$ $\boxed{(}$ $\boxed{(}$ 7 $\boxed{-}$ 1 $\boxed{)}$ $\boxed{=}$

Graphing Calculator: 5 $\boxed{+}$ 2 $\boxed{(}$ $\boxed{(}$ 7 $\boxed{-}$ 1 $\boxed{)}$ $\boxed{\text{ENT}}$

Example 6 on a calculator looks like this:

Scientific Calculator: 9 $\boxed{\times}$ 2 $\boxed{x^y}$ 3 $\boxed{+}$ 36 $\boxed{\div}$ 3 $\boxed{x^y}$ 2 $\boxed{-}$ 8 $\boxed{=}$

Graphing Calculator: 9 $\boxed{\times}$ 2 $\boxed{\wedge}$ 3 $\boxed{+}$ 36 $\boxed{\div}$ 3 $\boxed{\wedge}$ 2 $\boxed{-}$ 8 $\boxed{\text{ENT}}$

EXAMPLE 4   Simplify: $3 + 2[10 - 3(5 - 2)]$.

Solution   The brackets, [ ], are used in the same way as parentheses. In a case like this, we move to the innermost grouping symbols first and begin simplifying.

$$3 + 2[10 - 3(5 - 2)] = 3 + 2[10 - 3(3)]$$
$$= 3 + 2[10 - 9]$$
$$= 3 + 2[1]$$
$$= 3 + 2$$
$$= 5$$

4. Simplify: $4 + 2[12 - 2(6 - 3)]$.

Table 1 lists some English expressions and their corresponding mathematical expressions written in symbols.

Table 1

In English	Mathematical Equivalent
5 times the sum of 3 and 8	$5(3 + 8)$
Twice the difference of 4 and 3	$2(4 - 3)$
6 added to 7 times the sum of 5 and 6	$6 + 7(5 + 6)$
The sum of 4 times 5 and 8 times 9	$4 \cdot 5 + 8 \cdot 9$
3 subtracted from the quotient of 10 and 2	$10 \div 2 - 3$

GETTING READY FOR CLASS

After reading through the preceding section, respond in your own words and in complete sentences.

A. Give a written description of how you would use the order of operations to simplify the expression below.

$$3 + 4(5 + 6)$$

B. Name the three steps in the order of operations.

Answers

4. 16

EXERCISE SET 1.7

Vocabulary Review

Choose the correct words to fill in the blanks below.

left   right   grouping symbols
after   before

1. For the order of operations, we perform all operations inside the _____ before any other operations.
2. When performing operations, we always start at the _____ and move to the _____.
3. When following the order of operations, simplify any numbers with exponents _____ doing any multiplications or divisions.
4. When following the order of operations, we do all subtractions or additions _____ any multiplications or divisions.

Problems

A Use the rule for the order of operations to simplify each expression.

1. $16 - 8 + 4$

2. $16 - 4 + 8$

3. $20 \div 2 \cdot 10$

4. $40 \div 4 \cdot 5$

5. $20 - 4 \cdot 4$

6. $30 - 10 \cdot 2$

7. $3 + 5 \cdot 8$

8. $7 + 4 \cdot 9$

9. $3 \cdot 6 - 2$

10. $5 \cdot 1 + 6$

11. $6 \cdot 2 + 9 \cdot 8$

12. $4 \cdot 5 + 9 \cdot 7$

13. $4 \cdot 5 - 3 \cdot 2$

14. $5 \cdot 6 - 4 \cdot 3$

15. $9 - 2(4 - 3)$

16. $15 - 6(9 - 7)$

17. $4 \cdot 3 + 2(5 - 3)$

18. $6 \cdot 8 + 3(4 - 1)$

19. $4[2(3) + 3(5)]$

20. $3[2(5) + 3(4)]$

21. $(7 - 3)(8 + 2)$

22. $(9 - 5)(9 + 5)$

23. $3(9 - 2) + 4(7 - 2)$

24. $7(4 - 2) - 2(5 - 3)$

25. $18 + 12 \div 4 - 3$

26. $20 + 16 \div 2 - 5$

27. $5 + 2[9 - 2(4 - 1)]$

28. $6 + 3[8 - 3(1 + 1)]$

29. $3 + 4[6 + 8(2 - 0)]$

30. $2 + 5[9 + 3(4 - 1)]$

31. $\dfrac{15 + 5(4)}{17 - 12}$

32. $\dfrac{20 + 6(2)}{11 - 7}$

Translate each English expression into an equivalent mathematical expression written in symbols. Then simplify.

33. 8 times the sum of 4 and 2

34. 3 times the difference of 6 and 1

35. Twice the sum of 10 and 3

36. 5 times the difference of 12 and 6

37. 4 added to 3 times the sum of 3 and 4

38. 25 added to 4 times the difference of 7 and 5

39. 9 subtracted from the quotient of 20 and 2

40. 7 added to the quotient of 6 and 2

41. The sum of 8 times 5 and 5 times 4

42. The difference of 10 times 5 and 6 times 2

Applying the Concepts

Nutrition Labels Use the three nutrition labels below to work Problems 43-46.

Pizza Dough (Crust)

Nutrition Facts
Serving Size 1/6 of package (65g)
Servings Per Container: 6

Amount Per Serving

Calories 160   Calories from fat 18

% Daily Value*

Total Fat 2g	3%
Saturated Fat 0.5g	3%
Poly unsaturated Fat 0g	
Monounsaturated Fat 0g	
Cholesterol 0mg	0%
Sodium 470mg	20%
Total Carbohydrate 31g	10%
Dietary Fiber 1g	4%
Sugars 4g	
Protein 5g	

Vitamin A 0%   •   Vitamin C 0%

Calcium 0%   •   Iron 10%

*Percent Daily Values are based on a 2,000 calorie diet

Tomato Sauce

Nutrition Facts
Serving Size 1/4 cup (62g)
Servings Per Container: 5

Amount Per Serving

Calories 15   Calories from fat 0

% Daily Value*

Total Fat 0g	0%
Saturated Fat 0g	0%
Cholesterol 0mg	0%
Sodium 360mg	15%
Potassium 0mg	0%
Total Carbohydrate 3g	1%
Dietary Fiber 1g	4%
Sugars 2g	
Protein 1g	

Vitamin A 4%   •   Vitamin C 8%

Calcium 0%   •   Iron 0%

*Percent Daily Values are based on a 2,000 calorie diet. Your daily values may be higher or lower depending on your calorie needs.

Shredded Mozzarella Cheese

Nutrition Facts
Serving Size 1 oz (28.3g)
Servings Per Container: 12

Amount Per Serving

Calories 72   Calories from fat 41

% Daily Value*

Total Fat 4.5g	7%
Saturated Fat 2.9g	14%
Cholesterol 18mg	6%
Sodium 175mg	7%
Total Carbohydrate 0.8g	0%
Fiber 0g	0%
Sugars 0.3g	
Protein 6.9g	

Vitamin A 3%   •   Vitamin C 0%

Calcium 22%   •   Iron 0%

*Percent Daily Values (DV) are based on a 2,000 calorie diet

Find the total number of calories in each of the following meals.

43. Pizza Crust   1 serving
Tomato Sauce   1 serving
Cheese   1 serving

44. Pizza Crust   1 serving
Tomato Sauce   2 servings
Cheese   1 serving

45. Pizza Crust   2 servings
Tomato Sauce   1 serving
Cheese   1 serving

46. Pizza Crust   2 servings
Tomato Sauce   1 serving
Cheese   2 servings

The following table lists the number of calories consumed by eating some popular fast foods. Use the table to work Problems 47 and 48.

Calories in Food

Food	Calories
McDonald's hamburger	270
Burger King hamburger	260
Jack in the Box hamburger	280
McDonald's Big Mac	510
Burger King Whopper	630
Jack in the Box Colossus burger	940

47. Compare the total number of calories in the meal in Problem 43 with the number of calories in a McDonald's Big Mac.

48. Compare the total number of calories in the meal in Problem 46 with the number of calories in a Burger King hamburger.

Find the Mistake

The sentence below contains a mistake. Circle the mistake and write the correct word(s) or number(s) on the line provided.

1. Following the order of operations, work all additions and subtractions before evaluating anything inside parentheses.

_____

Fibonacci Sequence

Fibonacci was an Italian mathematician in the 12th and 13th centuries. He enjoyed investigating sequences of numbers and is credited with discovering the sequence of numbers written below.

$$1, 1, 2, 3, 5, 8, 13, 21, 34, 55...$$

1. If you were to describe the Fibonacci sequence in words, you would start this way: "The first two numbers are 1's. After that, each number is found by..." Finish the sentence so that someone reading it will know how to find members of the Fibonacci sequence.

2. On a sheet of graph paper, draw a 1 x 1 square and write the number 1 in the center. To the right of your first square, draw a second 1 x 1 square that shares a side with your first square. Write the number 1 in this second square as well. On top of the two 1 x 1 squares, draw a 2 x 2 square that shares the side length of the first two squares. Write the number 2 in this new square. To the left of the first three squares, draw a square with a side length of 3 that shares a side with the 2 x 2 square and the first 1 x 1 square. The fifth square you draw should be below the others, have a side length of 5, and share a side with the 3 x 3 square and both 1 x 1 squares (see illustration).

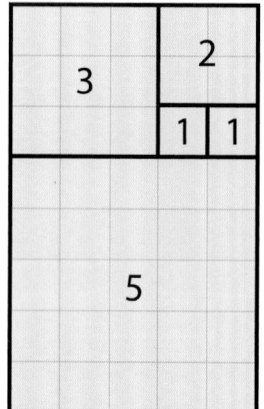

Continue drawing new squares in a spiral until you have drawn eight squares. Write the length of each new square's side in its center. Keep an ongoing list of each square's side length. Recognize the pattern?

If you draw a spiral curve that follows a diagonal in each square, beginning your curve at the upper left corner of the first 1 x 1 square, you will end up with what is known as the golden spiral. This spiral can be observed in nature, such as in the arrangement of artichoke leaves or pinecone scales.

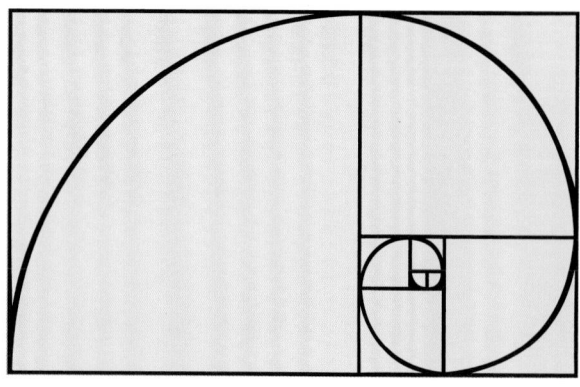

Chapter 1 Summary

The numbers in brackets indicate the sections in which the topics were discussed.

Place Values for Whole Numbers [1.1]

The place values for the digits of any base 10 number are as follows:

Table 1

Trillions			Billions			Millions			Thousands			Ones		
Hundreds	Tens	Ones	Hundreds	Tens	Ones	Hundreds	Tens	Ones	Hundreds	Tens	Ones	Hundreds	Tens	Ones

EXAMPLES

The margins of the chapter summaries will be used for examples of the topics being reviewed, whenever it is convenient.

1. The number 42,103,045 written in words is "forty-two million, one hundred three thousand, forty-five." The number 5,745 written in expanded form is $5,000 + 700 + 40 + 5$.

Vocabulary Associated with Addition, Subtraction, Multiplication, and Division [1.2, 1.3, 1.5, 1.6]

The word *sum* indicates addition.

The word *difference* indicates subtraction.

The word *product* indicates multiplication.

The word *quotient* indicates division.

2. The sum of 5 and 2 is $5 + 2$. The difference of 5 and 2 is $5 - 2$. The product of 5 and 2 is $5 \cdot 2$. The quotient of 10 and 2 is $10 \div 2$.

Properties of Addition and Multiplication [1.2, 1.5]

If a, b, and c represent any three numbers, then the properties of addition and multiplication used most often are

Commutative property of addition: $a + b = b + a$

Commutative property of multiplication: $a \cdot b = b \cdot a$

Associative property of addition: $(a + b) + c = a + (b + c)$

Associative property of multiplication: $(a \cdot b) \cdot c = a \cdot (b \cdot c)$

Distributive property: $a(b + c) = a(b) + a(c)$

3. a. $3 + 2 = 2 + 3$
b. $3 \cdot 2 = 2 \cdot 3$
c. $(x + 3) + 5 = x + (3 + 5)$
d. $(4 \cdot 5) \cdot 6 = 4 \cdot (5 \cdot 6)$
e. $3(4 + 7) = 3(4) + 3(7)$

Steps for Rounding Whole Numbers [1.4]

1. Locate the digit just to the right of the place you are to round to.

2. If that digit is less than 5, replace it and all digits to its right with zeros.

3. If that digit is 5 or more, replace it and all digits to its right with zeros, and add 1 to the digit to its left.

5. 5,482 to the nearest ten is 5,480. 5,482 to the nearest hundred is 5,500. 5,482 to the nearest thousand is 5,000.

6. Each of the expressions below are undefined.

$5 \div 0 \qquad \dfrac{7}{0} \qquad 4/0$

Division by 0 (Zero) [1.6]

Division by 0 is undefined. We cannot use 0 as a divisor in any division problem.

7. $4 + 6(8 - 2)$

$= 4 + 6(6)$ Work inside parentheses first,

$= 4 + 36$ Then multiply,

$= 40$ Then add.

Order of Operations [1.7]

To simplify a mathematical expression:

1. We simplify the expression inside the grouping symbols first. Grouping symbols are parentheses ( ), brackets [ ], or a fraction bar.

2. We then perform all multiplications and divisions in order, starting at the left and moving right.

3. Finally, we do all the additions and subtractions, from left to right.

At the end of each chapter, we will provide a review of problems similar to those you have seen in the chapter's previous sections. These problems are meant to supplement, not replace, a thorough review of the concepts, examples, and exercise sets presented in the chapter.

1. Write the number 50,631 in words. [1.1]

2. Write the number twelve million, seventy-two thousand, nine with digits instead of words. [1.1]

3. Write the number 123,321 in expanded form. [1.1]

Identify each of the statements in Problems 4–7 as an example of one of the following properties. [1.2, 1.5]

  a. Addition property of 0
  b. Multiplication property of 0
  c. Multiplication property of 1
  d. Commutative property of addition
  e. Commutative property of multiplication
  f. Associative property of addition
  g. Associative property of multiplication

4. $9 \cdot 1 = 9$

5. $4 + (7 + 2) = (4 + 7) + 2$

6. $9 \cdot 2 = 2 \cdot 9$

7. $5 + 0 = 5$

Find each of the following sums. (Add.) [1.2]

8. 128
  + 541

9. 5,213
    927
  + 10,182

Find each of the following differences. (Subtract.) [1.3]

10. 952
   − 141

11. 9,014
   − 6,528

12. Round the number 625,963 to the nearest ten thousand. [1.4]

Find each of the following products. (Multiply.) [1.5]

13. 8(137)

14. 71(238)

Find each of the following quotients. (Divide.) [1.6]

15. $1,235 \div 19$

16. $499\overline{)13,473}$

Write the following in numbers, then simplify as much as possible.

17. Three times the sum of 11 and 4. [1.2, 1.3, 1.5, 1.6]

18. The quotient of 30 and 5 decreased by 2. [1.2, 1.3, 1.5, 1.6]

Use the rule for the order of operations to simplify each expression as much as possible. [1.7]

19. $6 - 2(5 - 4)$

20. $5 + 4(57 - 7)$

21. $7(x - 2)$

The chart shows some of the most expensive cars in the world. Use the information to answer the following questions.

MOST EXPENSIVE CARS
www.thesupercars.org 2008

Bugatti Veyron	$1,700,000
Lamborghini Reventon	$1,600,000
McLaren F1	$970,000
Ferrari Enzo	$670,000
Pagani Zonda C12 F	$667,321

22. How much more does a Bugatti Veyron cost than a Ferrari Enzo? Write your answer in digits and words.

23. How much less does a McLaren F1 cost than a Lamborghini Reventon? Write your answer in digits and words.

CHAPTER 1 Test

At the end of each chapter, we will provide a test that you should use as a helpful study tool for a chapter exam. Remember, it is still important to study every aspect of the material presented in the chapter, and not rely solely on the Chapter Test to study for an exam.

1. Write the number 30,652 in words. [1.1]

2. Write the number six million, seven thousand, twenty-nine with digits instead of words. [1.1]

3. Write the number 285,634 in expanded form. [1.1]

Identify each of the statements in Problems 4–7 as an example of one of the following properties. [1.2, 1.5]

   a. Addition property of 0
   b. Multiplication property of 0
   c. Multiplication property of 1
   d. Commutative property of addition
   e. Commutative property of multiplication
   f. Associative property of addition
   g. Associative property of multiplication

4. $8 + 9 = 9 + 8$

5. $(5 \cdot 7) \cdot 8 = 5 \cdot (7 \cdot 8)$

6. $4 \cdot 1 = 4$

7. $8 \cdot 0 = 0$

Find each of the following sums. (Add.) [1.2]

8.
$$\begin{array}{r} 237 \\ + 461 \\ \hline \end{array}$$

9.
$$\begin{array}{r} 3,821 \\ 467 \\ + 20,315 \\ \hline \end{array}$$

Find each of the following differences. (Subtract.) [1.3]

10.
$$\begin{array}{r} 846 \\ - 325 \\ \hline \end{array}$$

11.
$$\begin{array}{r} 8,502 \\ - 3,715 \\ \hline \end{array}$$

12. Round the number 238,543 to the nearest ten thousand. [1.4]

Find each of the following products. (Multiply.) [1.5]

13. $5(162)$

14. $74(267)$

Find each of the following quotients. (Divide.) [1.6]

15. $1,224 \div 17$

16. $512\overline{)11,776}$

Write the following in numbers, then simplify as much as possible.

17. Twice the sum of 13 and 4. [1.2, 1.3, 1.5, 1.6]

18. The quotient of 18 and 6 increased by 12. [1.2, 1.3, 1.5, 1.6]

Use the rule for the order of operations to simplify each expression as much as possible. [1.7]

19. $9 - 3(7 - 5)$

20. $5 + 3(29 - 4)$

21. $5(x - 4)$

The chart shows how many Facebook fans each of these have. Use the information to answer the following questions.

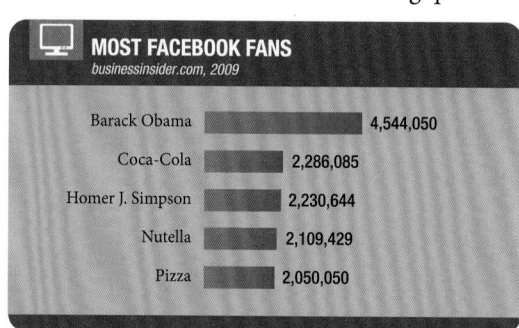

MOST FACEBOOK FANS
businessinsider.com, 2009

Barack Obama	4,544,050
Coca-Cola	2,286,085
Homer J. Simpson	2,230,644
Nutella	2,109,429
Pizza	2,050,050

22. How many more fans does Barack Obama have than Homer J. Simpson? Write your answer in digits and words.

23. How many fewer fans does Pizza have than Coca-Cola? Write your answer in digits and words.

Multiplication and Division of Fractions

2

The Roman Colosseum in Rome, Italy is a testament to the advancements made in engineering and architecture by the ancient Roman Empire. Initiated by the Roman Emperor Vespasianin in the year 70 AD, it was completed in 80 AD after his death. The next Emperor, Titus, opened the Colosseum to the public. It is said the inaugural ceremony lasted for more than 100 days. The Roman Colosseum is an amphitheater that had the capacity to hold 50,000 people, a huge number at that time in history.

For comparison, the table and bar chart below shows the seating capacity for other coliseums.

Seating Capacity	
Los Angeles Coliseum	134,254
Oakland Coliseum	55,528
Roman Colosseum	50,000
Nassau Veteran's Memorial Coliseum	15,000
The Coliseum at Caesars Palace	4,100
The Coliseum, St. Petersburg, FL	2,000

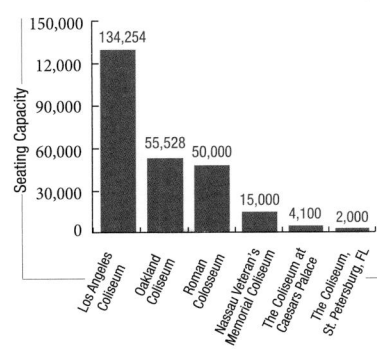

What fraction of the capacity of the Los Angeles Coliseum represents the capacity of the Roman Colosseum? Problems like this one require multiplying fractions, which is one of the topics of this chapter.

2.1 The Meaning and Properties of Fractions

©iStockphoto.com/urbancow

KEY WORDS

fraction

terms

numerator

denominator

proper

improper

equivalent

multiplication property for fractions

division property for fractions

scatter diagram

line graph

The information in the table below shows enrollment for Cal Poly State University in California. The pie chart was created from the table. Both the table and pie chart use fractions to specify how the students at Cal Poly are distributed among the different schools within the university.

Cal Poly State University Enrollment	
School	**Fraction Of Students**
Agriculture	$\frac{2}{9}$
Architecture and Environmental Design	$\frac{1}{9}$
Business	$\frac{1}{9}$
Engineering	$\frac{5}{18}$
Liberal Arts	$\frac{3}{20}$
Science and Mathematics	$\frac{3}{20}$

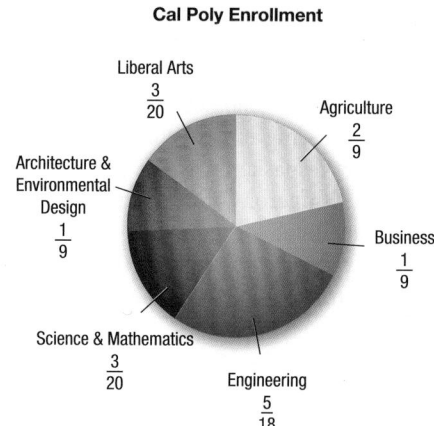

Cal Poly Enrollment

Liberal Arts $\frac{3}{20}$

Agriculture $\frac{2}{9}$

Architecture & Environmental Design $\frac{1}{9}$

Business $\frac{1}{9}$

Science & Mathematics $\frac{3}{20}$

Engineering $\frac{5}{18}$

Note As we mentioned in Chapter 1, when we use a letter to represent a number, or a group of numbers, that letter is called a variable. In the definition for a fraction, we are restricting the numbers that the variable *b* can represent to numbers other than 0. As you know we want to avoid writing an expression that would imply division by the number 0.

From the table, we see that $\frac{1}{9}$ (one-ninth) of the students are enrolled in the College of Business. This means one out of every nine students at Cal Poly is studying Business. The fraction $\frac{1}{9}$ tells us we have 1 part of 9 equal parts. That is, the students at Cal Poly could be divided into 9 equal groups, so that one of the groups contained all the business students and only business students.

Figure 1 shows a rectangle that has been divided into equal parts, four different ways. The shaded area for each rectangle is $\frac{1}{2}$ the total area.

Now that we have an intuitive idea of the meaning of fractions, here are the more formal definitions and vocabulary associated with fractions.

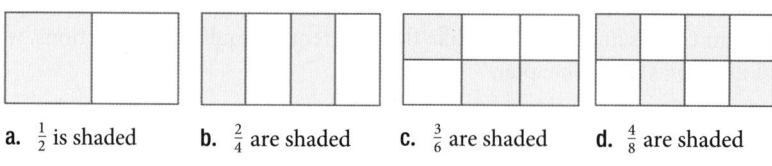

a. $\frac{1}{2}$ is shaded   **b.** $\frac{2}{4}$ are shaded   **c.** $\frac{3}{6}$ are shaded   **d.** $\frac{4}{8}$ are shaded

FIGURE 1

A Identifying Parts of a Fraction

> **DEFINITION** fraction
>
> A *fraction* is any number that can be put in the form $\frac{a}{b}$ (also sometimes written a/b), where a and b are numbers and b is not 0.

Some examples of fractions are

$\frac{1}{2}$	$\frac{3}{4}$	$\frac{7}{8}$	$\frac{9}{5}$
One-half	*Three-fourths*	*Seven-eighths*	*Nine-fifths*

> **DEFINITION** terms
>
> For the fraction $\frac{a}{b}$, a and b are called the *terms* of the fraction. More specifically, a is called the *numerator,* and b is called the *denominator.*

EXAMPLE 1 Name the numerator and denominator for each fraction.

a. $\frac{3}{4}$ **b.** $\frac{a}{5}$ **c.** 7

Solution

a. The terms of the fraction $\frac{3}{4}$ are 3 and 4. The 3 is called the numerator, and the 4 is called the denominator.

b. The numerator of the fraction $\frac{a}{5}$ is a. The denominator is 5. Both a and 5 are called terms.

c. The number 7 may also be put in fraction form, because it can be written as $\frac{7}{1}$. In this case, 7 is the numerator and 1 is the denominator.

> **DEFINITION** proper and improper fraction
>
> A *proper fraction* is a fraction in which the numerator is less than the denominator. If the numerator is greater than or equal to the denominator, the fraction is called an *improper fraction.*

CLARIFICATION 1: The fractions $\frac{3}{4}$, $\frac{1}{8}$, and $\frac{9}{10}$ are all proper fractions, because in each case the numerator is less than the denominator.

CLARIFICATION 2: The numbers $\frac{9}{5}$, $\frac{10}{10}$, and 6 are all improper fractions, because in each case the numerator is greater than or equal to the denominator. (As we have seen, 6 can be written as $\frac{6}{1}$, in which case 6 is the numerator and 1 is the denominator.)

B Fractions on the Number Line

We can give meaning to the fraction $\frac{2}{3}$ by using a number line. If we take that part of the number line from 0 to 1 and divide it into *three equal parts*, we say that we have divided it into *thirds* (see Figure 2). Each of the three segments is $\frac{1}{3}$ (one third) of the whole segment from 0 to 1.

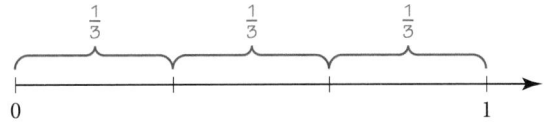

FIGURE 2

Video Examples
SECTION 2.1

Practice Problems

1. Name the numerator and denominator for each fraction.

   a. $\frac{5}{6}$

   b. $\frac{1}{8}$

   c. $\frac{x}{3}$

Note There are many ways to give meaning to fractions like $\frac{2}{3}$ other than by using the number line. One popular way is to think of cutting a pie into three equal pieces, as shown below. If you take two of the pieces, you have taken $\frac{2}{3}$ of the pie.

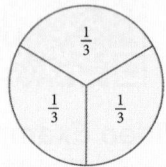

Two of these smaller segments together are $\frac{2}{3}$ (two thirds) of the whole segment. And three of them would be $\frac{3}{3}$ (three thirds), or the whole segment, as indicated in Figure 3.

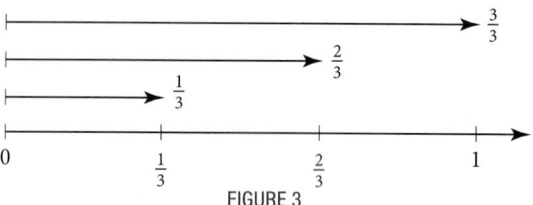

FIGURE 3

Let's do the same thing again with six and twelve equal divisions of the segment from 0 to 1 (see Figure 4).

The same point that we labeled with $\frac{1}{3}$ in Figure 3 is now labeled with $\frac{2}{6}$ and with $\frac{4}{12}$. It must be true then that

$$\frac{4}{12} = \frac{2}{6} = \frac{1}{3}$$

Although these three fractions look different, each names the same point on the number line, as shown in Figure 4. All three fractions have the same value, because they all represent the same number.

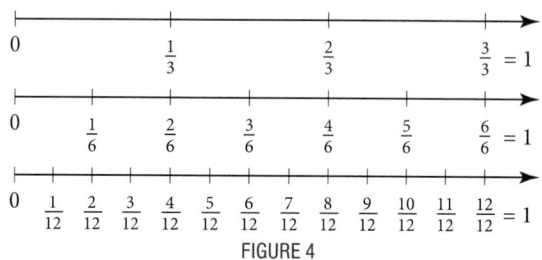

FIGURE 4

C Equivalent Fractions

> **DEFINITION** equivalent fractions
>
> Fractions that represent the same number are said to be *equivalent*. Equivalent fractions may look different, but they must have the same value.

It is apparent that every fraction has many different representations, each of which is equivalent to the original fraction. The next two properties give us a way of changing the terms of a fraction without changing its value.

> **PROPERTY** Multiplication Property for Fractions
>
> If a, b, and c are numbers and b and c are not 0, then it is always true that
>
> $$\frac{a}{b} = \frac{a \cdot c}{b \cdot c}$$
>
> *In words:* If the numerator and the denominator of a fraction are multiplied by the same nonzero number, the resulting fraction is equivalent to the original fraction.

2. Write $\frac{5}{6}$ as an equivalent fraction with a denominator of 30.

EXAMPLE 2 Write $\frac{3}{4}$ as an equivalent fraction with a denominator of 20.

Solution The denominator of the original fraction is 4. The fraction we are trying to find must have a denominator of 20. We know that if we multiply 4 by 5, we get 20. The multiplication property for fractions indicates that we are free to multiply the denominator by 5 so long as we do the same to the numerator.

$$\frac{3}{4} = \frac{3 \cdot 5}{4 \cdot 5} = \frac{15}{20}$$

The fraction $\frac{15}{20}$ is equivalent to the fraction $\frac{3}{4}$.

Answer

2. $\frac{25}{30}$

EXAMPLE 3 Write $\frac{3}{4}$ as an equivalent fraction with a denominator of $12x$.

Solution If we multiply 4 by $3x$, we will have $12x$.

$$\frac{3}{4} = \frac{3 \cdot 3x}{4 \cdot 3x} = \frac{9x}{12x}$$

3. Write $\frac{2}{3}$ as an equivalent fraction with a denominator of $15x$.

> **PROPERTY** Division Property for Fractions
>
> If a, b, and c are integers and b and c are not 0, then it is always true that
>
> $$\frac{a}{b} = \frac{a \div c}{b \div c}$$
>
> *In words:* If the numerator and the denominator of a fraction are divided by the same nonzero number, the resulting fraction is equivalent to the original fraction.

EXAMPLE 4 Write $\frac{10}{12}$ as an equivalent fraction with a denominator of 6.

Solution If we divide the original denominator 12 by 2, we obtain 6. The division property for fractions indicates that if we divide both the numerator and the denominator by 2, the resulting fraction will be equal to the original fraction.

$$\frac{10}{12} = \frac{10 \div 2}{12 \div 2} = \frac{5}{6}$$

4. Write $\frac{20}{25}$ as an equivalent fraction with a denominator of 5.

The Number 1 and Fractions

There are two situations involving fractions and the number 1 that occur frequently in mathematics. The first is when the denominator of a fraction is 1. In this case, if we let a represent any number, then

$$\frac{a}{1} = a$$

The second situation occurs when the numerator and the denominator of a fraction are the same nonzero number.

$$\frac{a}{a} = 1$$

EXAMPLE 5 Simplify each fraction.

a. $\frac{24}{1}$ **b.** $\frac{24}{24}$ **c.** $\frac{48}{24}$ **d.** $\frac{72}{24}$

Solution In each case, we divide the numerator by the denominator.

a. $\frac{24}{1} = 24$ **b.** $\frac{24}{24} = 1$ **c.** $\frac{48}{24} = 2$ **d.** $\frac{72}{24} = 3$

5. Simplify each fraction.

   a. $\frac{15}{1}$

   b. $\frac{15}{15}$

   c. $\frac{45}{15}$

   d. $\frac{150}{15}$

Comparing Fractions

We can compare fractions to see which is larger or smaller when they have the same denominator.

EXAMPLE 6 Write each fraction as an equivalent fraction with denominator 24. Then write them in order from smallest to largest.

$$\frac{5}{8} \qquad \frac{5}{6} \qquad \frac{3}{4} \qquad \frac{2}{3}$$

Solution We begin by writing each fraction as an equivalent fraction with denominator 24.

$$\frac{5}{8} = \frac{15}{24} \qquad \frac{5}{6} = \frac{20}{24} \qquad \frac{3}{4} = \frac{18}{24} \qquad \frac{2}{3} = \frac{16}{24}$$

6. Write each fraction as an equivalent fraction with denominator 36. Then write the original fractions in order from smallest to largest.
$$\frac{5}{9}, \frac{1}{3}, \frac{5}{6}, \frac{5}{12}$$

Answers

3. $\frac{10x}{15x}$

4. $\frac{4}{5}$

5. a. 15   **b.** 1   **c.** 3   **d.** 10

6. $\frac{1}{3} < \frac{5}{12} < \frac{5}{9} < \frac{5}{6}$

Now that they all have the same denominator, the smallest fraction is the one with the smallest numerator and the largest fraction is the one with the largest numerator. Writing them in order from smallest to largest we have

$$\frac{15}{24} < \frac{16}{24} < \frac{18}{24} < \frac{20}{24}$$

or

$$\frac{5}{8} < \frac{2}{3} < \frac{3}{4} < \frac{5}{6}$$

DESCRIPTIVE STATISTICS   Scatter Diagrams and Line Graphs

The table and bar chart give the daily gain in the price of Nintendo stock for one week in 2011. Figure 5 shows the same information in a bar chart.

Change in Stock Price	
Day	**Gain**
Monday	$\frac{7}{25}$
Tuesday	$\frac{1}{5}$
Wednesday	$\frac{9}{20}$
Thursday	$\frac{53}{100}$
Friday	$\frac{19}{100}$

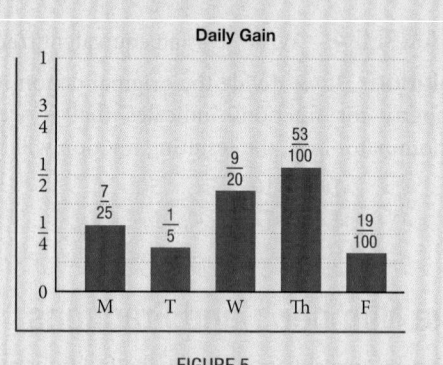

FIGURE 5

Figure 6 below shows another way to visualize the information in the table. It is called a scatter diagram. In the *scatter diagram*, dots are used instead of the bars shown in Figure 5 to represent the gain in stock price for each day of the week. If we connect the dots in Figure 6 with straight lines, we produce the diagram in Figure 7, which is known as a *line graph*.

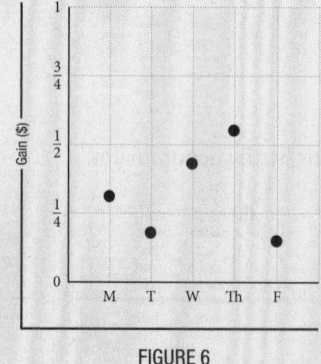

FIGURE 6

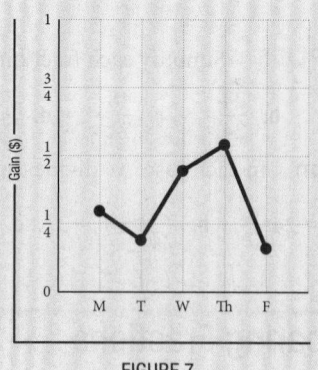

FIGURE 7

GETTING READY FOR CLASS

After reading through the preceding section, respond in your own words and in complete sentences.

A. What is a fraction?

B. Which term in the fraction $\frac{7}{8}$ is the numerator?

C. Is the fraction $\frac{3}{9}$ a proper fraction?

D. What word do we use to describe fractions such as $\frac{1}{5}$ and $\frac{4}{20}$, which look different, but have the same value?

Vocabulary Review

Choose the correct words to fill in the blanks below.

numerator   equivalent   proper   fraction   denominator   improper

1. A _____ is any number that can be put in the form $\frac{a}{b}$, where a and b are numbers and b is not zero.

2. For the fraction $\frac{a}{b}$, the term a is called the _____, and the term b is called the

_____.

3. A(n) _____ fraction is a fraction in which the numerator is less than the denominator.

4. A fraction is considered to be a(n) _____ fraction if the numerator is equal to or greater than the denominator.

5. _____ fractions are fractions that may look different but represent the same number.

Problems

A Name the numerator of each fraction.

1. $\frac{1}{3}$ **2.** $\frac{1}{4}$ **3.** $\frac{2}{3}$ **4.** $\frac{2}{4}$ **5.** $\frac{3}{8}$ **6.** $\frac{7}{10}$ **7.** $\frac{127}{256}$ **8.** $\frac{9}{14}$

Name the denominator of each fraction.

9. $\frac{2}{5}$ **10.** $\frac{3}{5}$ **11.** 6   **12.** 2   **13.** $\frac{11}{12}$ **14.** $\frac{9}{14}$

Complete the following tables.

15.

Numerator	Denominator	Fraction
3	5	
1		$\frac{1}{7}$
	8	$\frac{5}{8}$
7	9	

16.

Numerator	Denominator	Fraction
2	9	
	3	$\frac{4}{3}$
1		$\frac{1}{5}$
12		$\frac{12}{19}$

17. For the set of numbers $\left\{ \frac{3}{4}, \frac{6}{5}, \frac{12}{3}, \frac{1}{2}, \frac{9}{10}, \frac{20}{10} \right\}$, list all the proper fractions.

18. For the set of numbers $\left\{ \frac{1}{8}, \frac{7}{9}, \frac{6}{3}, \frac{18}{6}, \frac{3}{5}, \frac{9}{8} \right\}$, list all the improper fractions.

Indicate whether each of the following is *True* or *False*.

19. Every whole number greater than 1 can also be expressed as an improper fraction.

20. Some improper fractions are also proper fractions.

21. Adding the same number to the numerator and the denominator of a fraction will not change its value.

22. The fractions $\frac{3}{4}$ and $\frac{9}{16}$ are equivalent.

B The number line below extends from 0 to 2, with the segment from 0 to 1 and the segment from 1 to 2 each divided into 8 equal parts. Locate each of the following numbers on this number line.

23. $\frac{1}{4}$

24. $\frac{1}{8}$

25. $\frac{1}{16}$

26. $\frac{5}{8}$

27. $\frac{3}{4}$

28. $\frac{15}{16}$

29. $\frac{3}{2}$

30. $\frac{5}{4}$

31. $\frac{31}{16}$

32. $\frac{15}{8}$

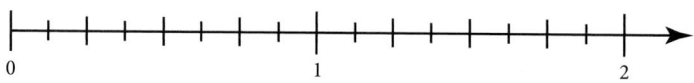

33. Write each fraction as an equivalent fraction with denominator 100. Then write the original fractions in order from smallest to largest.

$$\frac{3}{10} \qquad \frac{1}{20} \qquad \frac{4}{25} \qquad \frac{2}{5}$$

34. Write each fraction as an equivalent fraction with denominator 30. Then write the original fractions in order from smallest to largest.

$$\frac{1}{15} \qquad \frac{5}{6} \qquad \frac{7}{10} \qquad \frac{1}{2}$$

Write each of the following fractions as an equivalent fraction with a denominator of 6.

35. $\frac{2}{3}$

36. $\frac{1}{2}$

37. $\frac{55}{66}$

38. $\frac{65}{78}$

Write each of the following fractions as an equivalent fraction with a denominator of 12.

39. $\frac{2}{3}$

40. $\frac{5}{6}$

41. $\frac{56}{84}$

42. $\frac{143}{156}$

Write each fraction as an equivalent fraction with a denominator of 12.

43. $\dfrac{1}{6}$

44. $\dfrac{3}{4}$

45. $\dfrac{1}{2}$

46. $\dfrac{2}{3}$

Write each number as an equivalent fraction with a denominator of 8.

47. 2

48. 1

49. 5

50. 8

51. One-fourth of the first circle below is shaded. Use the other three circles to show three other ways to shade one-fourth of the circle.

52. The six-sided figures below are hexagons. One-third of the first hexagon is shaded. Shade the other three hexagons to show three other ways to represent one-third.

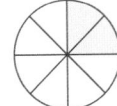 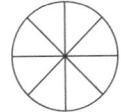  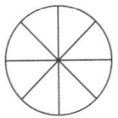   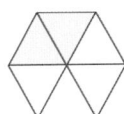   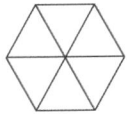

C Simplify by dividing the numerator by the denominator.

53. $\dfrac{3}{1}$

54. $\dfrac{3}{3}$

55. $\dfrac{6}{3}$

56. $\dfrac{12}{3}$

57. $\dfrac{37}{1}$

58. $\dfrac{37}{37}$

Divide the numerator and the denominator of each of the following fractions by 2.

59. $\dfrac{6}{8}$

60. $\dfrac{10}{12}$

61. $\dfrac{86}{94}$

62. $\dfrac{106}{142}$

Divide the numerator and the denominator of each of the following fractions by 3.

63. $\dfrac{12}{9}$

64. $\dfrac{33}{27}$

65. $\dfrac{39}{51}$

66. $\dfrac{57}{69}$

67. For each square below, what fraction of the area is given by the shaded region?

a.    b.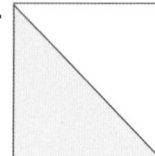

c.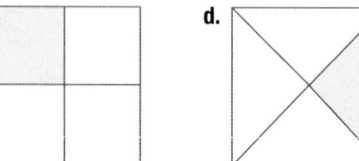

68. For each square below, what fraction of the area is given by the shaded region?

a. 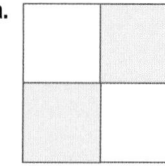   b.

c. 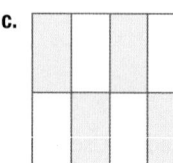   d.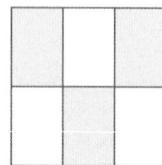

Applying the Concepts

69. Sending E-mail The pie chart below shows the fraction of workers who responded to a survey about sending non-work-related e-mail from the office. Use the pie chart to fill in the table.

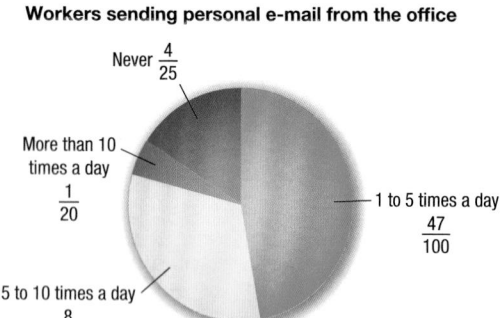

How often workers send non-work-related e-mail from the office	Fraction of respondents saying yes
Never	
1 to 5 times a day	
5 to 10 times a day	
More than 10 times a day	

70. Surfing the Internet The pie chart below shows the fraction of workers who responded to a survey about viewing non-work-related sites during working hours. Use the pie chart to fill in the table.

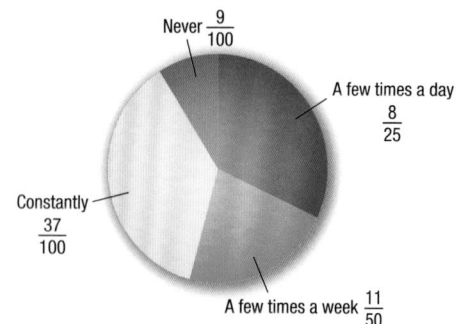

How often workers view non-work-related sites from the office	Fraction of respondents saying yes
Never	
A few times a week	
A few times a day	
Constantly	

71. **Number of Children** If there are 3 girls in a family with 5 children, then we say that $\frac{3}{5}$ of the children are girls. If there are 4 girls in a family with 5 children, what fraction of the children are girls?

72. **Medical School** If 3 out of every 7 people who apply to medical school actually get accepted, what fraction of the people who apply get accepted?

73. **Number of Students** Of the 43 people who started a math class meeting at 10:00 each morning, only 29 finished the class. What fraction of the people finished the class?

74. **Number of Students** In a class of 51 students, 23 are freshmen and 28 are juniors. What fraction of the students are freshmen?

75. **Expenses** If your monthly income is $1,791 and your house payment is $1,121, what fraction of your monthly income must go to pay your house payment?

76. **Expenses** If you spend $623 on food each month and your monthly income is $2,599, what fraction of your monthly income do you spend on food?

77. **Half-life of an Antidepressant** The half-life of a medication tells how quickly the medication is eliminated from a person's system. The line graph below shows the fraction of an antidepressant that remains in a patient's system once the patient stops taking the antidepressant. The half-life of the antidepressant is 5 days. Use the line graph to complete the table.

Concentration of Antidepressant

Days since discontinuing	Fraction remaining in patient's system
0	1
5	
	$\frac{1}{4}$
	$\frac{1}{16}$

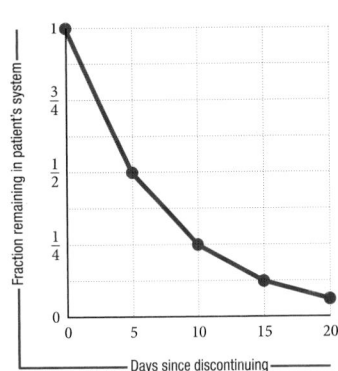

78. Carbon Dating All living things contain a small amount of carbon-14, which is radioactive and decays. The half-life of carbon-14 is 5,600 years. During the lifetime of an organism, the carbon-14 is replenished, but after its death the carbon-14 begins to disappear. By measuring the amount left, the age of the organism can be determined with surprising accuracy. The line graph below shows the fraction of carbon-14 remaining after the death of an organism. Use the line graph to complete the table.

Concentration of Carbon-14

Years since death of organism	Fraction of carbon-14 remaining
0	1
5,600	
	$\frac{1}{4}$
16,800	
	$\frac{1}{16}$

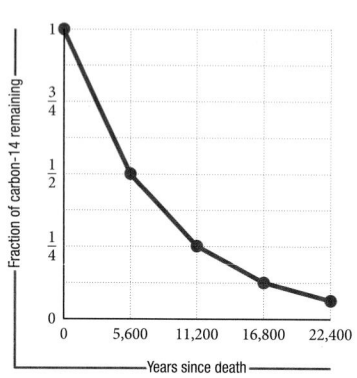

Estimating

79. Which of the following fractions is closest to the number 0?

  a. $\frac{1}{2}$ **b.** $\frac{1}{3}$ **c.** $\frac{1}{4}$ **d.** $\frac{1}{5}$

80. Which of the following fractions is closest to the number 1?

  a. $\frac{1}{2}$ **b.** $\frac{1}{3}$ **c.** $\frac{1}{4}$ **d.** $\frac{1}{5}$

81. Which of the following fractions is closest to the number 0?

  a. $\frac{1}{8}$ **b.** $\frac{3}{8}$ **c.** $\frac{5}{8}$ **d.** $\frac{7}{8}$

82. Which of the following fractions is closest to the number 1?

  a. $\frac{1}{8}$ **b.** $\frac{3}{8}$ **c.** $\frac{5}{8}$ **d.** $\frac{7}{8}$

Getting Ready for the Next Section

Multiply.

83. $2 \cdot 2 \cdot 3 \cdot 3 \cdot 3$ **84.** $2^2 \cdot 3^3$ **85.** $2^2 \cdot 3 \cdot 5$ **86.** $2 \cdot 3^2 \cdot 5$

Divide.

87. $12 \div 3$ **88.** $15 \div 3$ **89.** $20 \div 4$ **90.** $24 \div 4$

91. $42 \div 6$ **92.** $72 \div 8$ **93.** $102 \div 2$ **94.** $105 \div 7$

Improving Your Quantitative Literacy

95. True or False? If three positive fractions all have the same denominator, then the largest fraction has the largest numerator and the smallest fraction has the smallest numerator. Explain.

96. True of False? If three fractions all have the same numerator, then the largest fraction has the largest denominator and the smallest fraction has the smallest denominator. Explain.

97. iPhones The chart shows the distribution of iPhones around the world.

a. Write the number of iPhones in Western Europe as an equivalent fraction with denominator 50.

b. Write the number of iPhones in Oceania as an equivalent fraction with denominator 75.

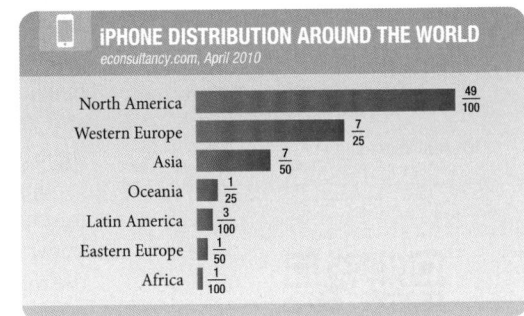

iPHONE DISTRIBUTION AROUND THE WORLD
econsultancy.com, April 2010

North America	$\frac{49}{100}$
Western Europe	$\frac{7}{25}$
Asia	$\frac{7}{50}$
Oceania	$\frac{1}{25}$
Latin America	$\frac{3}{100}$
Eastern Europe	$\frac{1}{50}$
Africa	$\frac{1}{100}$

Find the Mistake

Each sentence below contains a mistake. Circle the mistake and write the correct word(s) or number(s) on the line provided.

1. For the fraction $\frac{21}{7}$, the numerator is 7. _____

2. The fraction $\frac{90}{15}$ is considered a proper fraction. _____

3. The multiplication property for fractions states that if the numerator and the denominator of a fraction are multiplied by the same nonzero number, the resulting fraction is improper to the original fraction. _____

4. If we divide the numerator and denominator of the fraction $\frac{8}{12}$ by 4, then we get the equivalent fraction $\frac{4}{3}$. _____

Navigation Skills: Prepare, Study, Achieve

Your instructor is a vital resource for your success in this class. Make note of your instructor's office hours and utilize them regularly. Compile a resource list that you keep with your class materials. This list should contain your instructor's office hours and contact information (e.g., office phone number or e-mail), as well as classmates' contact information that you can utilize outside of class. Communicate often with your classmates about how the course is going for you and any questions you may have. Odds are that someone else has the same question and you may be able to work together to find the answer.

OBJECTIVES

A Identify prime factors of a composite number.

B Reduce fractions to lowest terms.

KEY WORDS

prime number

divisor

composite number

reduce

lowest terms

Video Examples
SECTION 2.2

Note You may have already noticed that the word *divisor* as we are using it here means the same as the word *factor*. A divisor and a factor of a number are the same thing. A number can't be a divisor of another number without also being a factor of it.

Practice Problems

1. Identify each number as either prime or composite. For those that are composite, give two divisors other than the number itself or 1.
  a. 61
  b. 33

In 2006, Christian Schou earned the world record title for highest slackline walk at a height of 3,280 feet across a Norwegian fjord. A slackline is made of flat nylon webbing and anchored between two points, similar to a tightrope. But in contrast to a taut tightrope, the slackline is strung to allow it to stretch and bounce under the walker's feet.

Suppose the length of a walker's slackline is 30 feet. If the walker walks 15 feet to the middle of the rope, we can say the the walker has walked $\frac{15}{30}$ of the rope's length. We know that he is also standing in the middle of the rope, therefore, he has walked $\frac{1}{2}$ of the rope's length. The fraction $\frac{15}{30}$ is equivalent to the fraction $\frac{1}{2}$; that is, they both have the same value. The mathematical process we use to rewrite $\frac{15}{30}$ as $\frac{1}{2}$ is called *reducing to lowest terms*. Before we look at that process, we need to define some new terms.

A Prime and Composite Numbers

> **DEFINITION** prime number
>
> A *prime number* is any whole number greater than 1 that has exactly two divisors—itself and 1. (A number is a divisor of another number if it divides it without a remainder.)
>
> Prime numbers = {2, 3, 5, 7, 11, 13, 17, 19, 23, 29, 31, 37, . . . }

> **DEFINITION** composite number
>
> Any whole number greater than 1 that is not a prime number is called a *composite number*. A composite number always has at least one divisor other than itself and 1.

EXAMPLE 1 Identify each of the numbers below as either a prime number or a composite number. For those that are composite, give two divisors other than the number itself or 1.

a. 43   **b.** 12

Solution

a. 43 is a prime number, because the only numbers that divide it without a remainder are 43 and 1.

b. 12 is a composite number, because it can be written as $12 = 4 \cdot 3$, which means that 4 and 3 are divisors of 12. (These are not the only divisors of 12; other divisors are 1, 2, 6, and 12.)

Answers

1. a. Prime   **b.** 3, 11

Every composite number can be written as the product of prime factors. Let's look at the composite number 108. We know we can write 108 as $2 \cdot 54$. The number 2 is a prime number, but 54 is not prime. Because 54 can be written as $2 \cdot 27$, we have

$$108 = 2 \cdot 54$$
$$= 2 \cdot 2 \cdot 27$$

Now the number 27 can be written as $3 \cdot 9$ or $3 \cdot 3 \cdot 3$ (because $9 = 3 \cdot 3$), so

$$108 = 2 \cdot 54$$
$$108 = 2 \cdot 2 \cdot 27$$
$$108 = 2 \cdot 2 \cdot 3 \cdot 9$$
$$108 = 2 \cdot 2 \cdot 3 \cdot 3 \cdot 3$$

This last line is the number 108 written as the product of prime factors. We can use exponents to rewrite the last line.

$$108 = 2^2 \cdot 3^3$$

EXAMPLE 2 Factor 60 into a product of prime factors.

Solution We begin by writing 60 as $6 \cdot 10$ and continue factoring until all factors are prime numbers.

$$60 = 6 \cdot 10$$
$$= 2 \cdot 3 \cdot 2 \cdot 5$$
$$= 2^2 \cdot 3 \cdot 5$$

Notice that if we had started by writing 60 as $3 \cdot 20$, we would have achieved the same result:

$$60 = 3 \cdot 20$$
$$= 3 \cdot 2 \cdot 10$$
$$= 3 \cdot 2 \cdot 2 \cdot 5$$
$$= 2^2 \cdot 3 \cdot 5$$

B Reducing Fractions

We can use the method of factoring numbers into prime factors to help reduce fractions to lowest terms. Here is the definition for lowest terms:

> **DEFINITION** lowest terms
>
> A fraction is said to be in *lowest terms* if the numerator and the denominator have no factors in common other than the number 1.

Clarification 1: The fractions $\frac{1}{2}$, $\frac{1}{3}$, $\frac{2}{3}$, $\frac{1}{4}$, $\frac{3}{4}$, $\frac{1}{5}$, $\frac{2}{5}$, $\frac{3}{5}$, and $\frac{4}{5}$ are all in lowest terms, because in each case the numerator and the denominator have no factors other than 1 in common. That is, in each fraction, no number other than 1 divides both the numerator and the denominator exactly (without a remainder).

Note This process works by writing the original composite number as the product of any two of its factors and then writing any factor that is not prime as the product of any two of its factors. The process is continued until all factors are prime numbers.

2. Factor 80 into a product of prime factors.

Note There are some "shortcuts" to finding the divisors of a number. For instance, if a number ends in 0 or 5, then it is divisible by 5. If a number ends in an even number (0, 2, 4, 6, or 8), then it is divisible by 2. A number is divisible by 3 if the sum of its digits is divisible by 3. For example, 921 is divisible by 3 because the sum of its digits is $9 + 2 + 1 = 12$, which is divisible by 3.

Answer

2. $2^4 \cdot 5$

Clarification 2: The fraction $\frac{6}{8}$ is not written in lowest terms, because the numerator and the denominator are both divisible by 2. To write $\frac{6}{8}$ in lowest terms, we apply the division property for fractions and divide both the numerator and the denominator by 2.

$$\frac{6}{8} = \frac{6 \div 2}{8 \div 2} = \frac{3}{4}$$

The fraction $\frac{3}{4}$ is in lowest terms, because 3 and 4 have no factors in common except the number 1.

Reducing a fraction to lowest terms is simply a matter of dividing the numerator and the denominator by all the factors they have in common. We know from the division property for fractions that this will produce an equivalent fraction.

3. Reduce the fraction $\frac{30}{45}$ to lowest terms by using prime factors.

EXAMPLE 3   Reduce the fraction $\frac{12}{15}$ to lowest terms by first factoring the numerator and the denominator into prime factors, and then dividing both the numerator and the denominator by the factor they have in common.

Solution   The numerator and the denominator factor as follows:

$$12 = 2 \cdot 2 \cdot 3 \quad \text{and} \quad 15 = 3 \cdot 5$$

The factor they have in common is 3. The division property for fractions tells us that we can divide both terms of a fraction by 3 to produce an equivalent fraction.

$$\frac{12}{15} = \frac{2 \cdot 2 \cdot 3}{3 \cdot 5} \qquad \textit{Factor the numerator and the denominator completely.}$$

$$= \frac{2 \cdot 2 \cdot 3 \div 3}{3 \cdot 5 \div 3} \qquad \textit{Divide by 3.}$$

$$= \frac{2 \cdot 2}{5} = \frac{4}{5}$$

The fraction $\frac{4}{5}$ is equivalent to $\frac{12}{15}$ and is in lowest terms, because the numerator and the denominator have no factors other than 1 in common.

> *Note*   The slashes in Example 4 indicate that we have divided both the numerator and the denominator by $2 \cdot 2$, which is equal to 4. With some fractions it is apparent at the start what number divides the numerator and the denominator. For instance, you may have recognized that both 20 and 24 in Example 4 are divisible by 4. We can divide both terms by 4 without factoring first. The division property for fractions guarantees that dividing both terms of a fraction by 4 will produce an equivalent fraction.
>
> $$\frac{20}{24} = \frac{20 \div 4}{24 \div 4} = \frac{5}{6}$$

We can shorten the work involved in reducing fractions to lowest terms by using a slash to indicate division. For example, we can write the above problem this way:

$$\frac{12}{15} = \frac{2 \cdot 2 \cdot \cancel{3}}{\cancel{3} \cdot 5} = \frac{4}{5}$$

So long as we understand that the slashes through the 3s indicate that we have divided both the numerator and the denominator by 3, we can use this notation.

4. Laura is baking cupcakes for her party. She bakes two dozen cupcakes, and six are eaten. What fraction of the cupcakes are left?

EXAMPLE 4   Laura is having a party. She puts 4 six-packs of diet soda in a cooler for her guests. At the end of the party, she finds that only 4 sodas have been consumed. What fraction of the sodas are left? Write your answer in lowest terms.

Solution   She had 4 six-packs of soda, which is $4(6) = 24$ sodas. Only 4 were consumed at the party, so 20 are left. The fraction of sodas left is

$$\frac{20}{24}$$

Factoring 20 and 24 completely and then dividing out both the factors they have in common gives us

$$\frac{20}{24} = \frac{\cancel{2} \cdot \cancel{2} \cdot 5}{\cancel{2} \cdot \cancel{2} \cdot 2 \cdot 3} = \frac{5}{6}$$

EXAMPLE 5 Reduce $\frac{6}{42}$ to lowest terms.

Solution We begin by factoring both terms. We then divide through by any factors common to both terms.

$$\frac{6}{42} = \frac{\cancel{2} \cdot \cancel{3}}{\cancel{2} \cdot \cancel{3} \cdot 7} = \frac{1}{7}$$

We must be careful in a problem like this to remember that the slashes indicate division. They are used to indicate that we have divided both the numerator and the denominator by $2 \cdot 3 = 6$. The result of dividing the numerator 6 by $2 \cdot 3$ is 1. It is a very common mistake to call the numerator 0 instead of 1 or to leave the numerator out of the answer.

5. Reduce $\frac{10}{35}$ to lowest terms.

EXAMPLE 6 Reduce $\frac{4}{40}$ to lowest terms.

$$\frac{4}{40} = \frac{\cancel{2} \cdot \cancel{2} \cdot 1}{\cancel{2} \cdot \cancel{2} \cdot 2 \cdot 5}$$

$$= \frac{1}{10}$$

6. Reduce $\frac{6}{30}$ to lowest terms.

EXAMPLE 7 Reduce $\frac{105}{30}$ to lowest terms.

$$\frac{105}{30} = \frac{\cancel{3} \cdot \cancel{5} \cdot 7}{2 \cdot \cancel{3} \cdot \cancel{5}}$$

$$= \frac{7}{2}$$

7. Reduce $\frac{140}{30}$ to lowest terms.

GETTING READY FOR CLASS

After reading through the preceding section, respond in your own words and in complete sentences.

A. What is a prime number?

B. Why is the number 22 a composite number?

C. Factor 120 into a product of prime factors.

D. How would you reduce a fraction to lowest terms?

Answers

5. $\frac{2}{7}$

6. $\frac{1}{5}$

7. $\frac{14}{3}$

Vocabulary Review

Choose the correct words to fill in the blanks below.

prime   composite   remainder   lowest terms

1. A _____ number is any whole number greater than 1 that has exactly two divisors: 1 and the number itself.

2. A number is a divisor of another number if it divides it without a _____.

3. Any whole number greater than 1 that is not a prime number is called a _____ number.

4. A fraction is said to be in _____ if the numerator and the denominator have no factors in common other than the number 1.

Problems

A Identify each of the numbers below as either a prime number or a composite number. For those that are composite, give at least one divisor (factor) other than the number itself or the number 1.

1. 11   **2.** 23   **3.** 105   **4.** 41

5. 81   **6.** 50   **7.** 13   **8.** 219

Factor each of the following into a product of prime factors.

9. 12   **10.** 8   **11.** 81   **12.** 210

13. 215   **14.** 75   **15.** 15   **16.** 42

B Reduce each fraction to lowest terms.

17. $\dfrac{5}{10}$ **18.** $\dfrac{3}{6}$ **19.** $\dfrac{4}{6}$ **20.** $\dfrac{4}{10}$ **21.** $\dfrac{8}{10}$ **22.** $\dfrac{6}{10}$

23. $\dfrac{36}{20}$ **24.** $\dfrac{32}{12}$ **25.** $\dfrac{42}{66}$ **26.** $\dfrac{36}{60}$ **27.** $\dfrac{24}{40}$ **28.** $\dfrac{50}{75}$

29. $\dfrac{14}{98}$ **30.** $\dfrac{12}{84}$ **31.** $\dfrac{70}{90}$ **32.** $\dfrac{80}{90}$ **33.** $\dfrac{42}{30}$ **34.** $\dfrac{18}{90}$

35. $\dfrac{150}{210}$ **36.** $\dfrac{110}{70}$ **37.** $\dfrac{45}{75}$ **38.** $\dfrac{180}{108}$ **39.** $\dfrac{60}{36}$ **40.** $\dfrac{105}{30}$

41. $\dfrac{96}{108}$ **42.** $\dfrac{66}{84}$ **43.** $\dfrac{126}{165}$ **44.** $\dfrac{102}{114}$ **45.** $\dfrac{102}{114}$ **46.** $\dfrac{255}{285}$

47. $\dfrac{294}{693}$ **48.** $\dfrac{273}{385}$

49. Reduce each fraction to lowest terms.

  a. $\dfrac{6}{51}$ **b.** $\dfrac{6}{52}$ **c.** $\dfrac{6}{54}$ **d.** $\dfrac{6}{56}$ **e.** $\dfrac{6}{57}$

50. Reduce each fraction to lowest terms.

  a. $\dfrac{6}{42}$ **b.** $\dfrac{6}{44}$ **c.** $\dfrac{6}{45}$ **d.** $\dfrac{6}{46}$ **e.** $\dfrac{6}{48}$

51. Reduce each fraction to lowest terms.

  a. $\dfrac{2}{90}$ **b.** $\dfrac{3}{90}$ **c.** $\dfrac{5}{90}$ **d.** $\dfrac{6}{90}$ **e.** $\dfrac{9}{90}$

52. Reduce each fraction to lowest terms.

  a. $\dfrac{3}{105}$ **b.** $\dfrac{5}{105}$ **c.** $\dfrac{7}{105}$ **d.** $\dfrac{15}{105}$ **e.** $\dfrac{21}{105}$

53. The answer to each problem below is wrong. Give the correct answer.

  a. $\dfrac{5}{15} = \dfrac{\cancel{5}}{3 \cdot \cancel{5}} = \dfrac{0}{3}$

  b. $\dfrac{5}{6} = \dfrac{3 + \cancel{2}}{4 + \cancel{2}} = \dfrac{0}{4}$

  c. $\dfrac{6}{30} = \dfrac{2 \cdot 3}{2 \cdot 3 \cdot 5} = 5$

54. The answer to each problem below is wrong. Give the correct answer.

  a. $\dfrac{10}{20} = \dfrac{7 + \cancel{3}}{17 + \cancel{3}} = \dfrac{7}{17}$

  b. $\dfrac{9}{36} = \dfrac{\cancel{3} \cdot \cancel{3}}{2 \cdot 2 \cdot \cancel{3} \cdot \cancel{3}} = \dfrac{0}{4}$

  c. $\dfrac{4}{12} = \dfrac{\cancel{2} \cdot \cancel{2}}{\cancel{2} \cdot \cancel{2} \cdot 3} = 3$

55. Which of the fractions $\frac{6}{8}$, $\frac{15}{20}$, $\frac{9}{16}$, and $\frac{21}{28}$ does not reduce to $\frac{3}{4}$?

56. Which of the fractions $\frac{4}{9}$, $\frac{10}{15}$, $\frac{8}{12}$, and $\frac{6}{12}$ do not reduce to $\frac{2}{3}$?

The number line below extends from 0 to 2, with the segment from 0 to 1 and the segment from 1 to 2 each divided into 8 equal parts. Locate each of the following numbers on this number line.

57. $\dfrac{1}{2}, \dfrac{2}{4}, \dfrac{4}{8}$, and $\dfrac{8}{16}$

58. $\dfrac{3}{2}, \dfrac{6}{4}, \dfrac{12}{8}$, and $\dfrac{24}{16}$

59. $\dfrac{5}{4}, \dfrac{10}{8}$, and $\dfrac{20}{16}$

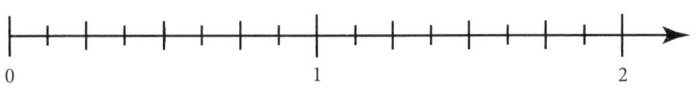

60. $\dfrac{1}{4}, \dfrac{2}{8}$, and $\dfrac{4}{16}$

Applying the Concepts

61. Income A family's monthly income is $2,400, and they spend $600 each month on food. Write the amount they spend on food as a fraction of their monthly income in lowest terms.

62. Hours and Minutes There are 60 minutes in 1 hour. What fraction of an hour is 20 minutes? Write your answer in lowest terms.

63. Final Exam Suppose 33 people took the final exam in a math class. If 11 people got an A on the final exam, what fraction of the students did not get an A on the exam? Write your answer in lowest terms.

64. Income Tax A person making $21,000 a year pays $3,000 in income tax. What fraction of the person's income is paid as income tax? Write your answer in lowest terms.

Nutrition The nutrition labels below are from two different snack crackers. Use them to work Problems 65–70.

Cheez-It Crackers

Nutrition Facts

Serving Size 30 g. (About 27 crackers)
Servings Per Container: 9

Amount Per Serving

Calories 150   Calories from fat 70

	% Daily Value*
Total Fat 8g	12%
Saturated Fat 2g	10%
Trans Fat 0g	
Polysaturated Fat 4g	
Monounsaturated Fat 2g	
Cholesterol 0mg	0%
Sodium 230mg	10%
Total Carbohydrate 17g	6%
Dietary Fiber less than 1g	3%
Sugars 0g	
Protein 3g	

Vitamin A 2%	•	Vitamin C 0%
Calcium 4%	•	Iron 6%

*Percent Daily Values are based on a 2,000 calorie diet

Goldfish Crackers

Nutrition Facts

Serving Size 55 pieces
Servings Per Container About 4

Amount Per Serving

Calories 140   Calories from fat 45

	% Daily Value*
Total Fat 5g	8%
Saturated Fat 1g	5%
Cholesterol 5mg	2%
Sodium 250mg	10%
Total Carbohydrate 20g	7%
Dietary Fiber 1g	4%
Sugars 1g	
Protein 4g	

Vitamin A 0%	•	Vitamin C 0%
Calcium 4%	•	Iron 2%

*Percent Daily Values are based on a 2,000 calorie diet

65. What fraction of the calories in Cheez-It crackers comes from fat?

66. What fraction of the calories in Goldfish crackers comes from fat?

67. For Cheez-It crackers, what fraction of the total fat is from saturated fat?

68. For Goldfish crackers, what fraction of the total fat is from saturated fat?

69. What fraction of the total carbohydrates in Cheez-It crackers is from sugar?

70. What fraction of the total carbohydrates in Goldfish crackers is from sugar?

Getting Ready for the Next Section

Multiply.

71. $1 \cdot 3 \cdot 1$

72. $2 \cdot 4 \cdot 5$

73. $3 \cdot 5 \cdot 3$

74. $1 \cdot 4 \cdot 1$

75. $5 \cdot 5 \cdot 1$

76. $6 \cdot 6 \cdot 2$

Factor into prime factors.

77. 60 **78.** 72 **79.** $15 \cdot 4$ **80.** $8 \cdot 9$

Expand and multiply.

81. 3^2 **82.** 4^2 **83.** 5^2 **84.** 6^2

Improving Your Quantitative Literacy

85. Wimbledon The graphic shown here gives the most Wimbledon Men's Champions by country. Which of the following is the closest to the fraction of champions from France as compared to Australia?

a. $\frac{1}{10}$ b. $\frac{1}{3}$ c. $\frac{3}{4}$ d. $\frac{1}{2}$

WIMBLEDON - MOST MEN'S SINGLES CHAMPS
wimbledon.org

United States	33
British Isles	32
Australia	21
France	7
Sweden	7
Switzerland	6

Find the Mistake

Each sentence below contains a mistake. Circle the mistake and write the correct word(s) or number(s) on the line provided.

1. The number 30 is a prime number because it has 10 as a divisor. _____

2. The number 70 factored into a product of primes is $7 \cdot 10$. _____

3. When reducing the fraction $\frac{32}{48}$ to lowest terms, we divide out the common factors 2 and 3 to get $\frac{2}{3}$.

_____

4. Reducing the fraction $\frac{112}{14}$ to lowest terms gives us $\frac{7}{2}$. _____

Landmark Review: Checking Your Progress

Name the numerator and denominator for each fraction.

1. $\frac{3}{5}$ **2.** $\frac{1}{3}$ **3.** $\frac{7}{15}$ **4.** $\frac{4}{x}$

Write each of the following fractions as an equivalent fraction with a denominator of $8x$.

5. $\frac{1}{2}$ **6.** $\frac{3}{4}$ **7.** $\frac{1}{8}$ **8.** $\frac{5}{2}$

Reduce each fraction to lowest terms.

9. $\frac{17}{34}$ **10.** $\frac{15}{25}$ **11.** $\frac{48}{80}$ **12.** $\frac{135}{216}$ **13.** $\frac{68}{72}$ **14.** $\frac{93}{126}$

2.3 Multiplication with Fractions

©iStockphoto.com/ Zinni-Online

Once a year on Christmas Island, in Australia, millions of bright red crabs migrate from the rain forest for several miles to the beach. They spawn in the sea, where the eggs hatch almost immediately upon contact with the salt water. For days, the crabs swarm train tracks, highways, and other busy thoroughfares on the island. They even take over golf courses, and according to a special rule, a golfer must play a ball where it lies even if a crab knocks it to another spot.

Let's suppose a group of crabs are crawling down a railroad track when they hear a train coming. $\frac{3}{4}$ of the crabs scurry into the bushes on either side of the track, $\frac{1}{2}$ of the $\frac{3}{4}$ going to the right and $\frac{1}{2}$ to the left. What fraction of the original group of crabs crawls to the right of the track? This question can be answered by multiplying $\frac{1}{2}$ and $\frac{3}{4}$. Here is the problem written in symbols:

$$\frac{1}{2} \cdot \frac{3}{4} = \frac{3}{8}$$

If you analyze this example, you will discover that to multiply two fractions, we multiply the numerators and then multiply the denominators. We begin this section with the rule for multiplication of fractions.

A Multiplication of Fractions

RULE Product of Two Fractions

The product of two fractions is a fraction whose numerator is the product of the two numerators, and whose denominator is the product of the two denominators. We can write this rule in symbols as follows:

If a, b, c, and d represent any numbers and b and d are not zero, then

$$\frac{a}{b} \cdot \frac{c}{d} = \frac{a \cdot c}{b \cdot d}$$

Video Examples
SECTION 2.3

Practice Problems

1. Multiply: $\frac{5}{6} \cdot \frac{7}{8}$.

EXAMPLE 1 Multiply: $\frac{3}{5} \cdot \frac{2}{7}$.

Solution Using our rule for multiplication, we multiply the numerators and multiply the denominators.

$$\frac{3}{5} \cdot \frac{2}{7} = \frac{3 \cdot 2}{5 \cdot 7} = \frac{6}{35}$$

The product of $\frac{3}{5}$ and $\frac{2}{7}$ is the fraction $\frac{6}{35}$. The numerator 6 is the product of 3 and 2, and the denominator 35 is the product of 5 and 7.

Answer

1. $\frac{35}{48}$

EXAMPLE 2 Multiply: $\frac{3}{8} \cdot 5$.

Solution The number 5 can be written as $\frac{5}{1}$. That is, 5 can be considered a fraction with numerator 5 and denominator 1. Writing 5 this way enables us to apply the rule for multiplying fractions.

$$\frac{3}{8} \cdot 5 = \frac{3}{8} \cdot \frac{5}{1}$$
$$= \frac{3 \cdot 5}{8 \cdot 1}$$
$$= \frac{15}{8}$$

EXAMPLE 3 Multiply: $\frac{1}{2}\left(\frac{3}{4} \cdot \frac{1}{5}\right)$.

Solution We find the product inside the parentheses first and then multiply the result by $\frac{1}{2}$.

$$\frac{1}{2}\left(\frac{3}{4} \cdot \frac{1}{5}\right) = \frac{1}{2}\left(\frac{3}{20}\right)$$
$$= \frac{1 \cdot 3}{2 \cdot 20}$$
$$= \frac{3}{40}$$

The properties of multiplication that we developed in Chapter 1 for whole numbers apply to fractions as well. That is, if a, b, and c are fractions, then

$$a \cdot b = b \cdot a \qquad \text{Multiplication with fractions is commutative.}$$

$$a \cdot (b \cdot c) = (a \cdot b) \cdot c \qquad \text{Multiplication with fractions is associative.}$$

To demonstrate the associative property for fractions, let's do Example 3 again, but this time we will apply the associative property first.

$$\frac{1}{2}\left(\frac{3}{4} \cdot \frac{1}{5}\right) = \left(\frac{1}{2} \cdot \frac{3}{4}\right) \cdot \frac{1}{5} \qquad \text{Associative property}$$
$$= \left(\frac{1 \cdot 3}{2 \cdot 4}\right) \cdot \frac{1}{5}$$
$$= \left(\frac{3}{8}\right) \cdot \frac{1}{5}$$
$$= \frac{3 \cdot 1}{8 \cdot 5}$$
$$= \frac{3}{40}$$

The result is identical to that of Example 3.

B Multiplying and Simplifying Fractions

The answers to all the examples so far in this section have been in lowest terms. Let's see what happens when we multiply two fractions to get a product that is not in lowest terms.

EXAMPLE 4 Multiply: $\frac{15}{8} \cdot \frac{4}{9}$.

Solution Multiplying the numerators and multiplying the denominators, we have

$$\frac{15}{8} \cdot \frac{4}{9} = \frac{15 \cdot 4}{8 \cdot 9}$$
$$= \frac{60}{72}$$

2. Multiply: $\frac{7}{12} \cdot 5$.

3. Multiply: $\frac{2}{3}\left(\frac{1}{3} \cdot \frac{5}{9}\right)$.

4. Multiply: $\frac{9}{16} \cdot \frac{4}{3}$.

Answers

2. $\frac{35}{12}$

3. $\frac{10}{81}$

4. $\frac{3}{4}$

The product is $\frac{60}{72}$, which can be reduced to lowest terms by factoring 60 and 72 and then dividing out any factors they have in common.

$$\frac{60}{72} = \frac{\cancel{2} \cdot \cancel{2} \cdot \cancel{3} \cdot 5}{\cancel{2} \cdot \cancel{2} \cdot 2 \cdot \cancel{3} \cdot 3}$$

$$= \frac{5}{6}$$

We can actually save ourselves some time by factoring before we multiply. Here's how it is done:

$$\frac{15}{8} \cdot \frac{4}{9} = \frac{15 \cdot 4}{8 \cdot 9}$$

$$= \frac{(3 \cdot 5) \cdot (2 \cdot 2)}{(2 \cdot 2 \cdot 2) \cdot (3 \cdot 3)}$$

$$= \frac{\cancel{3} \cdot 5 \cdot \cancel{2} \cdot \cancel{2}}{2 \cdot \cancel{2} \cdot \cancel{2} \cdot \cancel{3} \cdot 3}$$

$$= \frac{5}{6}$$

The result is the same in both cases. Reducing to lowest terms before we actually multiply takes less time. Here are some additional examples. Problems like these will be useful when we solve equations.

EXAMPLE 5
$$\frac{9}{2} \cdot \frac{8}{18} = \frac{9 \cdot 8}{2 \cdot 18}$$

$$= \frac{(3 \cdot 3) \cdot (2 \cdot 2 \cdot 2)}{2 \cdot (2 \cdot 3 \cdot 3)}$$

$$= \frac{\cancel{3} \cdot \cancel{3} \cdot \cancel{2} \cdot 2 \cdot 2}{\cancel{2} \cdot 2 \cdot \cancel{3} \cdot \cancel{3}}$$

$$= \frac{2}{1}$$

$$= 2$$

EXAMPLE 6
$$\frac{2}{3} \cdot \frac{6}{5} \cdot \frac{5}{8} = \frac{2 \cdot 6 \cdot 5}{3 \cdot 5 \cdot 8}$$

$$= \frac{2 \cdot (2 \cdot 3) \cdot 5}{3 \cdot 5 \cdot (2 \cdot 2 \cdot 2)}$$

$$= \frac{\cancel{2} \cdot \cancel{2} \cdot \cancel{3} \cdot \cancel{5}}{\cancel{3} \cdot \cancel{5} \cdot \cancel{2} \cdot \cancel{2} \cdot 2}$$

$$= \frac{1}{2}$$

The word *of* used in connection with fractions indicates multiplication. If we want to find $\frac{1}{2}$ of $\frac{2}{3}$, then what we do is multiply $\frac{1}{2}$ and $\frac{2}{3}$.

5. Multiply: $\frac{9}{5} \cdot \frac{10}{21}$.

Note Although $\frac{2}{1}$ is in lowest terms, it is still simpler to write the answer as just 2. We will always do this when the denominator is the number 1.

6. Multiply: $\frac{3}{4} \cdot \frac{4}{9} \cdot \frac{6}{7}$.

Answers

5. $\frac{6}{7}$

6. $\frac{2}{7}$

EXAMPLE 7 Find $\frac{1}{2}$ of $\frac{2}{3}$.

Solution Knowing the word *of*, as used here, indicates multiplication, we have

$$\frac{1}{2} \text{ of } \frac{2}{3} = \frac{1}{2} \cdot \frac{2}{3}$$

$$= \frac{1 \cdot 2}{2 \cdot 3} = \frac{1}{3}$$

This seems to make sense. Logically, $\frac{1}{2}$ of $\frac{2}{3}$ should be $\frac{1}{3}$, as Figure 1 shows.

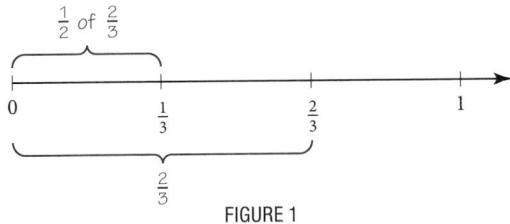

FIGURE 1

7. Find $\frac{3}{4}$ of $\frac{5}{6}$.

EXAMPLE 8 What is $\frac{3}{4}$ of 12?

Solution Again, the word *of* means multiply.

$$\frac{3}{4} \text{ of } 12 = \frac{3}{4}(12)$$

$$= \frac{3}{4}\left(\frac{12}{1}\right)$$

$$= \frac{3 \cdot 12}{4 \cdot 1}$$

$$= \frac{3 \cdot 2 \cdot 2 \cdot 3}{2 \cdot 2 \cdot 1}$$

$$= \frac{9}{1} = 9$$

8. What is $\frac{7}{8}$ of 24?

Note As you become familiar with multiplying fractions, you may notice shortcuts that reduce the number of steps in the problems. It's okay to use these shortcuts if you understand why they work and are consistently getting correct answers. If you are using shortcuts and not consistently getting correct answers, then go back to showing all the work until you completely understand the process.

GETTING READY FOR CLASS

After reading through the preceding section, respond in your own words and in complete sentences.

A. When we multiply the fractions $\frac{3}{5}$ and $\frac{2}{7}$, the numerator in the answer will be what number?

B. When we ask for $\frac{1}{2}$ of $\frac{2}{3}$, are we asking for an addition problem or a multiplication problem?

C. True or false? Reducing to lowest terms before you multiply two fractions will give the same answer as if you were to reduce after you multiply.

Answers

7. $\frac{5}{8}$

8. 21

EXERCISE SET 2.3

Vocabulary Review

Choose the correct words to fill in the blanks below.

    multiplication   fractions   product

1. The _____ of two fractions is a fraction whose numerator is the product of the two numerators, and whose denominator is the product of the two denominators.

2. In symbols, the multiplication of _____ is written as $\frac{a}{b} \cdot \frac{c}{d} = \frac{a \cdot c}{b \cdot d}$.

3. The word *of* used in connection with fractions indicates _____.

Problems

A Find each of the following products. (Multiply.)

1. $\frac{2}{3} \cdot \frac{4}{5}$

2. $\frac{5}{6} \cdot \frac{7}{4}$

3. $\frac{1}{2} \cdot \frac{7}{4}$

4. $\frac{3}{5} \cdot \frac{4}{7}$

5. $\frac{5}{3} \cdot \frac{3}{5}$

6. $\frac{4}{7} \cdot \frac{7}{4}$

7. $\frac{3}{4} \cdot 9$

8. $\frac{2}{3} \cdot 5$

9. $\frac{6}{7} \left(\frac{7}{6} \right)$

10. $\frac{2}{9} \left(\frac{9}{2} \right)$

11. $\frac{1}{2} \cdot \frac{1}{3} \cdot \frac{1}{4}$

12. $\frac{2}{3} \cdot \frac{4}{5} \cdot \frac{1}{3}$

13. $\frac{2}{5} \cdot \frac{3}{5} \cdot \frac{4}{5}$

14. $\frac{1}{4} \cdot \frac{3}{4} \cdot \frac{3}{4}$

15. $\frac{3}{2} \cdot \frac{5}{2} \cdot \frac{7}{2}$

16. $\frac{4}{3} \cdot \frac{5}{3} \cdot \frac{7}{3}$

Complete the following tables.

17.

First Number x	Second Number y	Their Product xy
$\frac{1}{2}$	$\frac{2}{3}$	
$\frac{2}{3}$	$\frac{3}{4}$	
$\frac{3}{4}$	$\frac{4}{5}$	
$\frac{5}{a}$	$\frac{a}{6}$	

18.

First Number x	Second Number y	Their Product xy
12	$\frac{1}{2}$	
12	$\frac{1}{3}$	
12	$\frac{1}{4}$	
12	$\frac{1}{6}$	

19.

First Number x	Second Number y	Their Product xy
$\frac{1}{2}$	30	
$\frac{1}{5}$	30	
$\frac{1}{6}$	30	
$\frac{1}{15}$	30	

20.

First Number x	Second Number y	Their Product xy
$\frac{1}{3}$	$\frac{3}{5}$	
$\frac{3}{5}$	$\frac{5}{7}$	
$\frac{5}{7}$	$\frac{7}{9}$	
$\frac{7}{b}$	$\frac{b}{11}$	

B Multiply each of the following. Be sure all answers are written in lowest terms.

21. $\frac{9}{20} \cdot \frac{4}{3}$

22. $\frac{135}{16} \cdot \frac{2}{45}$

23. $\frac{3}{4} \cdot 12$

24. $\frac{3}{4} \cdot 20$

25. $\frac{1}{3}(3)$

26. $\frac{1}{5}(5)$

27. $\frac{2}{5} \cdot 20$

28. $\frac{3}{5} \cdot 15$

29. $\frac{72}{35} \cdot \frac{55}{108} \cdot \frac{7}{110}$

30. $\frac{32}{27} \cdot \frac{72}{49} \cdot \frac{1}{40}$

31. Find $\frac{3}{8}$ of 64.

32. Find $\frac{2}{3}$ of 18.

33. What is $\frac{1}{3}$ of the sum of 8 and 4?

34. What is $\frac{3}{5}$ of the sum of 8 and 7?

35. Find $\frac{1}{2}$ of $\frac{3}{4}$ of 24.

36. Find $\frac{3}{5}$ of $\frac{1}{3}$ of 15.

Find the mistakes in Problems 51–52. Correct the right-hand side of each one.

37. $\frac{1}{2} \cdot \frac{3}{5} = \frac{4}{10}$

38. $\frac{2}{7} \cdot \frac{3}{5} = \frac{5}{35}$

39. a. Complete the table.

b. Using the results of part a, fill in the blank in the following statement:

For numbers larger than 1, the square of the number is _____ than the number.

Number x	Square x^2
1	
2	
3	
4	
5	
6	
7	
8	

40. a. Complete the table.

b. Using the results of part a, fill in the blank in the following statement:

For numbers between 0 and 1, the square of the number is _____ than the number.

Number x	Square x^2
$\frac{1}{2}$	
$\frac{1}{3}$	
$\frac{1}{4}$	
$\frac{1}{5}$	
$\frac{1}{6}$	
$\frac{1}{7}$	
$\frac{1}{8}$	

C Apply the distributive property, then simplify.

41. $4\left(3 + \frac{1}{2}\right)$

42. $4\left(2 - \frac{3}{4}\right)$

43. $12\left(\frac{1}{2} + \frac{2}{3}\right)$

44. $12\left(\frac{3}{4} - \frac{1}{6}\right)$

45. $9\left(\frac{2}{3} - \frac{1}{9}\right)$

46. $12\left(\frac{1}{2} - \frac{1}{3}\right)$

47. $16\left(\frac{5}{8} - \frac{1}{4}\right)$

48. $24\left(\frac{2}{3} - \frac{1}{6}\right)$

Applying the Concepts

Use the information in the pie chart to answer questions 49 and 50. Round to the nearest student.

49. Reading a Pie Chart If there are approximately 15,800 students attending Cal Poly, approximately how many of them are studying agriculture?

50. Reading a Pie Chart If there are exactly 15,828 students attending Cal Poly, how many of them are studying engineering? Round to the nearest student.

Cal Poly Enrollment

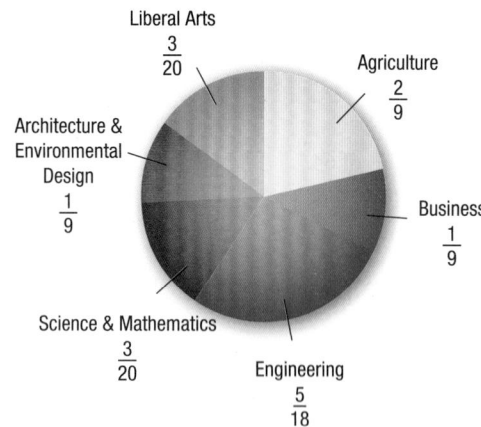

51. Hot Air Balloon Aerostar International makes a hot air balloon called the Rally 105 that has a volume of 105,400 cubic feet. Another balloon, the Rally 126, was designed with a volume that is approximately $\frac{6}{5}$ the volume of the Rally 105. Find the volume of the Rally 126 to the nearest hundred cubic feet.

52. Health Care According to the Department of Veteran's Affairs, approximately $\frac{4}{25}$ of military veterans have diabetes. If there approximately are 3.1 million veterans, how many have diabetes? Round number to the nearest ten thousand.

53. **Bicycle Safety** The National Safe Kids Campaign and Bell Sports sponsored a study that surveyed 8,159 children ages 5 to 14 who were riding bicycles. Approximately $\frac{2}{5}$ of the children were wearing helmets, and of those, only $\frac{13}{20}$ were wearing the helmets correctly. About how many of the children were wearing helmets correctly?

54. **Bicycle Safety** From the information in Problem 73, how many of the children surveyed do not wear helmets?

Geometric Sequences   Recall that a geometric sequence is a sequence in which each term comes from the previous term by multiplying by the same number each time. For example, the sequence $1, \frac{1}{2}, \frac{1}{4}, \frac{1}{8}, \ldots$ is a geometric sequence in which each term is found by multiplying the previous term by $\frac{1}{2}$. By observing this fact, we know that the next term in the sequence will be $\frac{1}{8} \cdot \frac{1}{2} = \frac{1}{16}$.

Find the next number in each of the geometric sequences below.

55. $1, \frac{1}{3}, \frac{1}{9}, \ldots$

56. $1, \frac{1}{4}, \frac{1}{16}, \ldots$

57. $\frac{3}{2}, 1, \frac{2}{3}, \frac{4}{9}, \ldots$

58. $\frac{2}{3}, 1, \frac{3}{2}, \frac{9}{4}, \ldots$

Estimating   For each problem below, mentally estimate if the answer will be closest to 0, 1, 2 or 3. Make your estimate without using pencil and paper or a calculator.

59. $\frac{11}{5} \cdot \frac{19}{20}$

60. $\frac{3}{5} \cdot \frac{1}{20}$

61. $\frac{16}{5} \cdot \frac{23}{24}$

62. $\frac{9}{8} \cdot \frac{31}{32}$

Getting Ready for the Next Section

In the next section we will do division with fractions. As you already know, division and multiplication are closely related. These review problems are intended to let you see more of the relationship between multiplication and division.

Perform the indicated operations.

63. $8 \div 4$

64. $8 \cdot \frac{1}{4}$

65. $15 \div 3$

66. $15 \cdot \frac{1}{3}$

67. $18 \div 6$

68. $18 \cdot \frac{1}{6}$

For each number below, find a number to multiply it by to obtain 1.

69. $\frac{3}{4}$

70. $\frac{9}{5}$

71. $\frac{1}{3}$

72. $\frac{1}{4}$

73. 7

74. 2

Find the Mistake

Each sentence below contains a mistake. Circle the mistake and write the correct word(s) or number(s) on the line provided.

1. To find the product of two fractions, multiply the numerators and put them over the largest denominator.

2. To multiply $\frac{6}{7}$ by $\frac{12}{9}$, find the product of the numerators and divide it by the sum of the denominators to get $\frac{72}{63}$.

2.4 Division with Fractions

Image © Ben Barczi 2010

In 2010, a Peruvian inventor won the $200,000 grand prize for a competition that requested its entrants to suggest a new and ingenious way to save the earth. To battle global warming, the inventor proposed covering 173 acres of dry rocky land in the Andes Mountains with a mixture made from egg whites, lime, and water. The mixture creates a whitewash that when spread over the rocks would reflect sunlight and ideally reduce temperatures, thus slowing the melting of the area's glaciers.

Suppose a truck transports the whitewash in a 32-gallon tank up to the mountaintop. Let's say the inventor used a bucket that only held $\frac{3}{4}$ of a gallon to pour the whitewash onto the rocks. How many times would the inventor need to fill up his bucket to empty the tank? In order to answer this question, we need to learn more about how to divide with fractions. But before we define division with fractions, we must first introduce the idea of *reciprocals*. Look at the following multiplication problems:

$$\frac{3}{4} \cdot \frac{4}{3} = \frac{12}{12} = 1 \qquad \frac{7}{8} \cdot \frac{8}{7} = \frac{56}{56} = 1$$

In each case the product is 1. Whenever the product of two numbers is 1, we say the two numbers are reciprocals.

A Dividing Fractions

DEFINITION reciprocals

Two numbers whose product is 1 are said to be **reciprocals**. In symbols, the reciprocal of $\frac{a}{b}$ is $\frac{b}{a}$, because

$$\frac{a}{b} \cdot \frac{b}{a} = \frac{a \cdot b}{b \cdot a} = \frac{a \cdot b}{a \cdot b} = 1 \qquad (a \neq 0, b \neq 0)$$

Every number has a reciprocal except 0. The reason 0 does not have a reciprocal is because the product of *any* number with 0 is 0. It can never be 1. Reciprocals of whole numbers are fractions with 1 as the numerator. For example, the reciprocal of 5 is $\frac{1}{5}$, because

$$5 \cdot \frac{1}{5} = \frac{5}{1} \cdot \frac{1}{5} = \frac{5}{5} = 1$$

Table 1 lists some numbers and their reciprocals.

Table 1

Number	Reciprocal	Reason
$\frac{3}{4}$	$\frac{4}{3}$	Because $\frac{3}{4} \cdot \frac{4}{3} = \frac{12}{12} = 1$
$\frac{9}{5}$	$\frac{5}{9}$	Because $\frac{9}{5} \cdot \frac{5}{9} = \frac{45}{45} = 1$
$\frac{1}{3}$	3	Because $\frac{1}{3} \cdot 3 = \frac{1}{3} \cdot \frac{3}{1} = \frac{3}{3} = 1$
7	$\frac{1}{7}$	Because $7 \cdot \frac{1}{7} = \frac{7}{1} \cdot \frac{1}{7} = \frac{7}{7} = 1$

Division with fractions is accomplished by using reciprocals. More specifically, we can define division by a fraction to be the same as multiplication by its reciprocal. Here is the precise definition:

DEFINITION division by a fraction

If a, b, c, and d are numbers and b, c, and d are all not equal to 0, then

$$\frac{a}{b} \div \frac{c}{d} = \frac{a}{b} \cdot \frac{d}{c}$$

This definition states that dividing by the fraction $\frac{c}{d}$ is exactly the same as multiplying by its reciprocal $\frac{d}{c}$. Because we developed the rule for multiplying fractions in the last section, we do not need a new rule for division. We simply *replace the divisor by its reciprocal* and multiply. Here are some examples to illustrate the procedure:

EXAMPLE 1 Divide: $\frac{1}{2} \div \frac{1}{4}$.

Solution The divisor is $\frac{1}{4}$, and its reciprocal is $\frac{4}{1}$. Applying the definition of division for fractions, we have

$$\frac{1}{2} \div \frac{1}{4} = \frac{1}{2} \cdot \frac{4}{1}$$
$$= \frac{1 \cdot 4}{2 \cdot 1}$$
$$= \frac{1 \cdot 2 \cdot 2}{2 \cdot 1}$$
$$= \frac{2}{1}$$
$$= 2$$

The quotient of $\frac{1}{2}$ and $\frac{1}{4}$ is 2. Or, $\frac{1}{4}$ "goes into" $\frac{1}{2}$ two times. Logically, our definition for division of fractions seems to be giving us answers that are consistent with what we know about fractions from previous experience. Because 2 times $\frac{1}{4}$ is $\frac{2}{4}$ or $\frac{1}{2}$, it seems logical that $\frac{1}{2}$ divided by $\frac{1}{4}$ should be 2.

EXAMPLE 2 Divide: $\frac{3}{8} \div \frac{9}{4}$.

Solution Dividing by $\frac{9}{4}$ is the same as multiplying by its reciprocal, which is $\frac{4}{9}$.

$$\frac{3}{8} \div \frac{9}{4} = \frac{3}{8} \cdot \frac{4}{9}$$
$$= \frac{3 \cdot 2 \cdot 2}{2 \cdot 2 \cdot 2 \cdot 3 \cdot 3}$$
$$= \frac{1}{6}$$

The quotient of $\frac{3}{8}$ and $\frac{9}{4}$ is $\frac{1}{6}$.

Note Defining division to be the same as multiplication by the reciprocal does make sense. If we divide 6 by 2, we get 3. On the other hand, if we multiply 6 by $\frac{1}{2}$ (the reciprocal of 2), we also get 3. Whether we divide by 2 or multiply by $\frac{1}{2}$, we get the same result.

Video Examples
SECTION 2.4

Practice Problems

1. Divide: $\frac{3}{4} \div \frac{1}{6}$.

2. Divide: $\frac{8}{15} \div \frac{4}{5}$.

Answers

1. $\frac{9}{2}$

2. $\frac{2}{3}$

3. Divide: $\frac{5}{6} \div 3$.

4. Divide: $4 \div \frac{2}{3}$.

5. Divide: $\frac{9}{16} \div \frac{9}{4}$.

EXAMPLE 3 Divide: $\frac{2}{3} \div 2$.

Solution The reciprocal of 2 is $\frac{1}{2}$. Applying the definition for division of fractions, we have

$$\frac{2}{3} \div 2 = \frac{2}{3} \cdot \frac{1}{2}$$

$$= \frac{2 \cdot 1}{3 \cdot 2}$$

$$= \frac{1}{3}$$

EXAMPLE 4 Divide: $2 \div \frac{1}{3}$.

Solution We replace $\frac{1}{3}$ by its reciprocal, which is 3, and multiply.

$$2 \div \frac{1}{3} = 2(3)$$

$$= 6$$

Here are some further examples of division with fractions. Notice in each case that the first step is the only new part of the process.

EXAMPLE 5 $\frac{4}{27} \div \frac{16}{9}$

Solution We replace $\frac{16}{9}$ by its reciprocal and multiply.

$$= \frac{4}{27} \cdot \frac{9}{16}$$

$$= \frac{4 \cdot 9}{3 \cdot 9 \cdot 4 \cdot 4}$$

$$= \frac{1}{12}$$

In Example 5 we did not factor the numerator and the denominator completely in order to reduce to lowest terms because, as you have probably already noticed, it is not necessary to do so. We need to factor only enough to show what numbers are common to the numerator and the denominator. If we factored completely in the second step, it would look like this:

$$= \frac{2 \cdot 2 \cdot 3 \cdot 3}{3 \cdot 3 \cdot 3 \cdot 2 \cdot 2 \cdot 2 \cdot 2}$$

$$= \frac{1}{12}$$

The result is the same in both cases. From now on, we will factor numerators and denominators only enough to show the factors we are dividing out.

EXAMPLE 6 Divide.

a. $\frac{16}{35} \div 8$ **b.** $27 \div \frac{3}{2}$

Solution

6. Divide.

  a. $\frac{15}{26} \div 5$

  b. $18 \div \frac{9}{10}$

a. $\frac{16}{35} \div 8 = \frac{16}{35} \cdot \frac{1}{8}$

$$= \frac{2 \cdot 8 \cdot 1}{35 \cdot 8}$$

$$= \frac{2}{35}$$

Answers

3. $\frac{5}{18}$

4. 6

5. $\frac{1}{4}$

6. a. $\frac{3}{26}$ **b.** 20

b. $27 \div \dfrac{3}{2} = 27 \cdot \dfrac{2}{3}$

$\qquad = \dfrac{3 \cdot 9 \cdot 2}{3}$

$\qquad = 18$

B Order of Operations

The next two examples combine what we have learned about division of fractions with the rule for order of operations.

EXAMPLE 7   The quotient of $\frac{8}{3}$ and $\frac{1}{6}$ is increased by 5. What number results?

Solution   Translating to symbols, we have

$$\frac{8}{3} \div \frac{1}{6} + 5 = \left[\frac{8}{3} \cdot \frac{6}{1} \right] + 5$$

$$= 16 + 5$$

$$= 21$$

EXAMPLE 8   A 4-H Club is making blankets to keep their lambs clean at the county fair. If each blanket requires $\frac{3}{4}$ yard of material, how many blankets can they make from 9 yards of material?

Solution   To answer this question we must divide 9 by $\frac{3}{4}$.

$$9 \div \frac{3}{4} = 9 \cdot \frac{4}{3}$$

$$= 3 \cdot 4$$

$$= 12$$

They can make 12 blankets from the 9 yards of material.

GETTING READY FOR CLASS

After reading through the preceding section, respond in your own words and in complete sentences.

A. What do we call two numbers whose product is 1?

B. True or false? The quotient of $\frac{3}{5}$ and $\frac{3}{8}$ is the same as the product of $\frac{3}{5}$ and $\frac{8}{3}$.

C. How are multiplication and division of fractions related?

D. Dividing by $\frac{19}{9}$ is the same as multiplying by what number?

7. The quotient of $\frac{2}{3}$ and $\frac{1}{6}$ is decreased by 2. What number results?

8. Repeat Example 8 if they have 16 yards of material, and each blanket requires $\frac{2}{3}$ yard of material.

Answers

7. 2

8. 24 blankets

EXERCISE SET 2.4

Vocabulary Review

Choose the correct words to fill in the blanks below.

divisor   product   fraction   reciprocal

1. Two numbers whose _____ is 1 are said to be reciprocals.

2. In symbols, the _____ of $\frac{a}{b}$ is $\frac{b}{a}$ if a and b are not equal to zero.

3. To divide by a fraction, replace the _____ by its reciprocal and multiply.

4. In symbols, division by a _____ is written as $\frac{a}{b} \div \frac{c}{d} = \frac{a}{b} \cdot \frac{d}{c}$.

Problems

A Find the quotient in each case by replacing the divisor by its reciprocal and multiplying.

1. $\frac{3}{4} \div \frac{1}{5}$ **2.** $\frac{1}{3} \div \frac{1}{2}$ **3.** $\frac{2}{3} \div \frac{1}{2}$ **4.** $\frac{5}{8} \div \frac{1}{4}$

5. $6 \div \frac{2}{3}$ **6.** $8 \div \frac{3}{4}$ **7.** $20 \div \frac{1}{10}$ **8.** $16 \div \frac{1}{8}$

9. $\frac{3}{4} \div 2$ **10.** $\frac{3}{5} \div 2$ **11.** $\frac{7}{8} \div \frac{7}{8}$ **12.** $\frac{4}{3} \div \frac{4}{3}$

13. $\frac{7}{8} \div \frac{8}{7}$ **14.** $\frac{4}{3} \div \frac{3}{4}$ **15.** $\frac{9}{16} \div \frac{3}{4}$ **16.** $\frac{25}{36} \div \frac{5}{6}$

17. $\frac{25}{46} \div \frac{40}{69}$ **18.** $\frac{25}{24} \div \frac{15}{36}$ **19.** $\frac{13}{28} \div \frac{39}{14}$ **20.** $\frac{28}{125} \div \frac{5}{2}$

21. $\frac{27}{196} \div \frac{9}{392}$ **22.** $\frac{16}{135} \div \frac{2}{45}$ **23.** $\frac{25}{18} \div 5$ **24.** $\frac{30}{27} \div 6$

25. $6 \div \frac{4}{3}$ **26.** $12 \div \frac{4}{3}$ **27.** $\frac{4}{3} \div 6$ **28.** $\frac{4}{3} \div 12$

29. $\frac{3}{4} \div \frac{1}{2} \cdot 6$ **30.** $12 \div \frac{6}{7} \cdot 7$ **31.** $\frac{2}{3} \cdot \frac{3}{4} \div \frac{5}{8}$ **32.** $4 \cdot \frac{7}{6} \div 7$

33. $\frac{35}{10} \cdot \frac{80}{63} \div \frac{16}{27}$ **34.** $\frac{20}{72} \cdot \frac{42}{18} \div \frac{20}{16}$

B Simplify each expression as much as possible using order of operations.

35. $\frac{4}{5} \div \frac{1}{10} + 5$

36. $\frac{3}{8} \div \frac{1}{16} + 4$

37. $10 + \frac{11}{12} \div \frac{11}{24}$

38. $15 + \frac{13}{14} \div \frac{13}{42}$

39. What is the quotient of $\frac{3}{8}$ and $\frac{5}{8}$?

40. Find the quotient of $\frac{4}{5}$ and $\frac{16}{25}$.

41. If the quotient of 18 and $\frac{3}{5}$ is increased by 10, what number results?

42. If the quotient of 50 and $\frac{5}{3}$ is increased by 8, what number results?

43. Show that multiplying 3 by 5 is the same as dividing 3 by $\frac{1}{5}$.

44. Show that multiplying 8 by $\frac{1}{2}$ is the same as dividing 8 by 2.

Applying the Concepts

Although many of the application problems that follow involve division with fractions, some do not. Be sure to read the problems carefully.

45. Sewing If $\frac{6}{7}$ yard of material is needed to make a blanket, how many blankets can be made from 12 yards of material?

46. Manufacturing A clothing manufacturer is making scarves that require $\frac{3}{8}$ yard of material each. How many can be made from 27 yards of material?

47. Capacity Suppose a bag of candy holds exactly $\frac{1}{4}$ pound of candy. How many of these bags can be filled from 12 pounds of candy?

48. Capacity A certain size bottle holds exactly $\frac{4}{5}$ pint of liquid. How many of these bottles can be filled from a 20-pint container?

49. Cooking Audra is making cookies from a recipe that calls for $\frac{3}{4}$ teaspoon of oil. If the only measuring spoon she can find is a $\frac{1}{8}$ teaspoon, how many of these will she have to fill with oil in order to have a total of $\frac{3}{4}$ teaspoon of oil?

50. Cooking A cake recipe calls for $\frac{1}{2}$ cup of sugar. If the only measuring cup available is a $\frac{1}{8}$ cup, how many of these will have to be filled with sugar to make a total of $\frac{1}{2}$ cup of sugar?

51. Student Population If 14 of every 32 students attending Cuesta College are female, what fraction of the students is female? (Simplify your answer.)

52. Population If 27 of every 48 residents of a small town are male, what fraction of the population is male? (Simplify your answer.)

53. Student Population If 14 of every 32 students attending Cuesta College are female, and the total number of students at the school is 4,064, how many of the students are female?

54. Population If 27 of every 48 residents of a small town are male, and the total population of the town is 17,808, how many of the residents are male?

55. Cartons of Milk If a small carton of milk holds exactly $\frac{1}{2}$ pint, how many of the $\frac{1}{2}$-pint cartons can be filled from a 14-pint container?

56. Pieces of Pipe How many pieces of pipe that are $\frac{2}{3}$ foot long must be laid together to make a pipe 16 feet long?

Find the Mistake

Each sentence below contains a mistake. Circle the mistake and write the correct word(s) or number(s) on the line provided.

1. Two numbers whose quotient is 1 are said to be reciprocals. _____

2. Dividing the fraction $\frac{12}{7}$ by $\frac{4}{9}$, is equivalent to $\frac{7}{12} \cdot \frac{9}{4}$. _____

3. To work the problem $\frac{22}{5} \div \frac{10}{3}$, multiply the first fraction by its reciprocal. _____

4. The quotient of $\frac{14}{11}$ and $\frac{32}{6}$ is $\frac{224}{33}$. _____

Supplies Needed

A Piece of graph paper
B 4 colored pens or pencils

Working With Fractions

This project will provide a visual approach for working with the multiplication and division of fractions. You will need a piece of graph paper and 4 colored pens or pencils.

1. On your graph paper, draw two squares each with a side length of 20 boxes. Fill in the boxes of your first square using your pens or pencils. You may choose any pattern as long as you use all four colors and fill in every box in your square.

2. Assign each color to a number (1-4).

   Color 1 _____

   Color 2 _____

   Color 3 _____

   Color 4 _____

3. Find the area of your first square. This will give you the total number of boxes in your square.

   Total area _____

4. Count the total number of boxes for each color. Enter these quantities in the second column of the table titled, "Number of Boxes."

Colors	Number of boxes	Fraction (not reduced)	Fraction (reduced)	Multiplied by $\frac{2}{3}$	Multiplied by $\frac{3}{4}$

5. In the third column, "Fraction (not reduced)," show the number of boxes for each color in the form of a fraction.

6. Reduce each fraction, if possible, and write the reduced fraction in the fourth column of the table.

7. Multiply each of the reduced fractions for Color 1 and Color 2 by $\frac{2}{3}$. Write these new fractions in the fifth column of the table.

8. Multiply each of the reduced fractions for Color 3 and Color 4 by $\frac{3}{4}$. Write these new fractions in the sixth column of the table.

9. Suppose the fractions in the fifth and sixth columns of your table now represent new quantities of boxes per color. Fill in your second square with these new quantities. Round to the nearest whole number. How many boxes are left over? Write this number as a fraction.

EXAMPLES

1. Each of the following is a fraction:

$$\frac{1}{2}, \quad \frac{3}{4}, \quad \frac{8}{1}, \quad \frac{7}{3}$$

2. Change $\frac{3}{4}$ to an equivalent fraction with denominator 12.

$$\frac{3}{4} = \frac{3 \cdot 3}{4 \cdot 3} = \frac{9}{12}$$

3. $\frac{5}{1} = 5, \frac{5}{5} = 1$

4. $\frac{90}{588} = \frac{2 \cdot 3 \cdot 3 \cdot 5}{2 \cdot 2 \cdot 3 \cdot 7 \cdot 7}$

$$= \frac{3 \cdot 5}{2 \cdot 7 \cdot 7}$$

$$= \frac{15}{98}$$

5. $\frac{3}{5} \cdot \frac{4}{7} = \frac{3 \cdot 4}{5 \cdot 7} = \frac{12}{35}$

6. The reciprocal of $\frac{2}{3}$ is $\frac{3}{2}$.

$$\frac{2}{3} \cdot \frac{3}{2} = 1$$

Definition of Fractions [2.1]

A fraction is any number that can be written in the form $\frac{a}{b}$, where a and b are numbers and b is not 0. The number a is called the *numerator*, and the number b is called the *denominator*.

Properties of Fractions [2.1]

Multiplying the numerator and the denominator of a fraction by the same nonzero number will produce an equivalent fraction. The same is true for dividing the numerator and denominator by the same nonzero number. In symbols the properties look like this:

If a, b, and c are numbers and b and c are not 0, then

$$\textit{Multiplication property for fractions} \quad \frac{a}{b} = \frac{a \cdot c}{b \cdot c}$$

$$\textit{Division property for fraction} \quad \frac{a}{b} = \frac{a \div c}{b \div c}$$

Fractions and the Number 1 [2.1]

If a represents any number, then

$$\frac{a}{1} = a \quad \text{and} \quad \frac{a}{a} = 1 \quad \text{(where } a \text{ is not 0)}$$

Reducing Fractions to Lowest Terms [2.2]

To reduce a fraction to lowest terms, factor the numerator and the denominator, and then divide both the numerator and denominator by any factors they have in common.

Multiplying Fractions [2.3]

To multiply fractions, multiply numerators and multiply denominators.

Reciprocals [2.4]

Any two numbers whose product is 1 are called *reciprocals*. The reciprocal of a is $\frac{1}{a}$ because their product is 1.

Division with Fractions [2.4]

To divide by a fraction, you must multiply by its reciprocal. That is, the quotient of two fractions is defined to be the product of the first fraction with the reciprocal of the second fraction (the divisor).

7. $\dfrac{3}{8} \div \dfrac{1}{3} = \dfrac{3}{8} \cdot \dfrac{3}{1} = \dfrac{9}{8}$

COMMON MISTAKE

1. A common mistake made with division of fractions occurs when we multiply by the reciprocal of the first fraction instead of the reciprocal of the divisor. For example,

$$\frac{2}{3} \div \frac{5}{6} \neq \frac{3}{2} \cdot \frac{5}{6}$$

Remember, we perform division by multiplying by the reciprocal of the divisor (the fraction to the right of the division symbol).

2. If the answer to a problem turns out to be a fraction, that fraction should always be written in lowest terms. It is a mistake not to reduce to lowest terms.

Reduce to lowest terms. [2.2]

1. $\dfrac{75}{105}$　　　　　**2.** $\dfrac{72}{192}$

3. $\dfrac{64}{208}$　　　　　**4.** $\dfrac{176}{330}$

15. $\dfrac{9}{16} \div \dfrac{3}{12}$　　　　**16.** $\dfrac{4}{3} \div 16$

17. $15 \div \dfrac{3}{5}$　　　　**18.** $\dfrac{24}{14} \div \dfrac{6}{7}$

Perform the indicated operations. Reduce all answers to lowest terms. [2.2, 2.3, 2.4]

5. $\dfrac{1}{3} \cdot \dfrac{6}{7}$　　　　　**6.** $\dfrac{2}{5} \cdot \dfrac{3}{8}$

7. $6 \cdot \dfrac{7}{12}$　　　　　**8.** $\dfrac{4}{15}\left(\dfrac{5}{8}\right)$

9. $\dfrac{3}{7} \cdot \dfrac{4}{9}$　　　　　**10.** $\dfrac{9}{4}\left(\dfrac{1}{3}\right)$

11. $\dfrac{7}{4} \cdot \dfrac{8}{3} \cdot \dfrac{9}{14}$　　　　**12.** $\dfrac{6}{5} \cdot \dfrac{15}{7} \cdot \dfrac{3}{9}$

13. $\dfrac{7}{9} \div \dfrac{2}{3}$　　　　　**14.** $\dfrac{8}{5} \div \dfrac{2}{3}$

Simplify each of the following as much as possible. [2.2, 2.3, 2.4]

19. $\dfrac{8}{5} \cdot \dfrac{3}{4} \div \dfrac{9}{10}$　　　　**20.** $\dfrac{12}{7} \div 3 \cdot \dfrac{5}{6}$

21. $\left(\dfrac{3}{14}\right)\left(\dfrac{4}{6}\right) \div \dfrac{1}{3}$　　　**22.** $\dfrac{4}{9} \div \dfrac{2}{7} \div \dfrac{1}{3}$

23. $\dfrac{1}{6} \div \left(\dfrac{15}{18} \cdot \dfrac{9}{25}\right)$　　**24.** $\dfrac{5}{9} \cdot \dfrac{6}{7} \div \dfrac{20}{14}$

25. $\left(\dfrac{4}{21}\right)\left(\dfrac{3}{8}\right) \div \dfrac{1}{6}$　　**26.** $\left(\dfrac{3}{7} \div \dfrac{9}{14}\right)\left(\dfrac{6}{7}\right)$

27. Sewing A dress requires $\dfrac{7}{4}$ yards of material to make. If you have 14 yards of material, how many dresses can you make? [2.4]

Simplify.

1.
$$\begin{array}{r} 362 \\ 4{,}104 \\ + \quad 89 \\ \hline \end{array}$$

2.
$$\begin{array}{r} 3{,}790 \\ \times \quad 23 \\ \hline \end{array}$$

3. $16 - (13 - 7)$

4. $4(2) - (19 - 15)$

5. $\dfrac{1}{2} \div \dfrac{1}{6}$

6. $\dfrac{4}{7} \cdot \dfrac{5}{8}$

7. $3 \div \dfrac{1}{5}$

8. $270 \div 15 \div 6$

9. $\dfrac{62}{12}$

10. $\dfrac{144}{240}$

11. $(8 - 5) - (9 - 7)$

12. $2{,}050(131)$

13. $\dfrac{4}{16} \div \dfrac{12}{18}$

14. $15 \cdot \dfrac{2}{3}$

15. $4{,}936 - 691$

16. $\left(\dfrac{7}{14}\right)\left(\dfrac{8}{16}\right)\left(\dfrac{4}{5}\right)$

17. $\left(\dfrac{2}{3}\right)\left(\dfrac{6}{16}\right) \div \dfrac{2}{3}$

18. Round the following numbers to the nearest ten, then add.
$$\begin{array}{r} 649 \\ 394 \\ + \quad 132 \\ \hline \end{array}$$

19. Find the product of $\dfrac{3}{5}$, $\dfrac{7}{15}$, and $\dfrac{5}{9}$.

20. Write the fraction $\dfrac{3}{7}$ as an equivalent fraction with a denominator of $28x$.

21. Reduce $\dfrac{15}{40}$ to lowest terms.

22. What is the quotient of $\dfrac{4}{5}$ and the product of $\dfrac{2}{3}$ and $\dfrac{6}{7}$

23. **Neptune's Diameter** The planet Neptune has an equatorial diameter of about 30,760 miles. What is the place value of the 3 in 30,760?

The chart shows the number of viewers for ABC's top primetime shows.

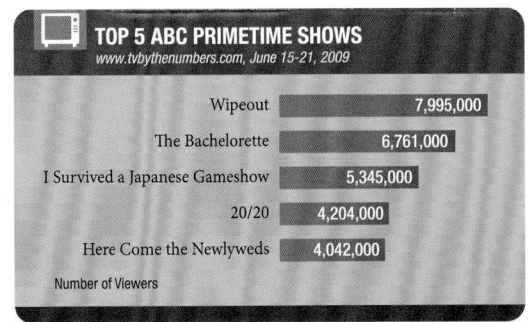

TOP 5 ABC PRIMETIME SHOWS
www.tvbythenumbers.com, June 15-21, 2009

	Number of Viewers
Wipeout	7,995,000
The Bachelorette	6,761,000
I Survived a Japanese Gameshow	5,345,000
20/20	4,204,000
Here Come the Newlyweds	4,042,000

24. **TV Shows** How many viewers watched The Bachelorette and 20/20?

Reduce to lowest terms. [2.2]

1. $\dfrac{25}{125}$

2. $\dfrac{32}{128}$

3. $\dfrac{15}{70}$

4. $\dfrac{255}{340}$

Perform the indicated operations. Reduce all answers to lowest terms. [2.2, 2.3, 2.4]

5. $\dfrac{1}{4} \cdot \dfrac{3}{5}$

6. $\dfrac{2}{3} \cdot \dfrac{5}{7}$

7. $3 \cdot \dfrac{5}{8}$

8. $\dfrac{3}{16}\left(\dfrac{8}{9}\right)$

9. $\dfrac{3}{8} \cdot \dfrac{12}{15}$

10. $\dfrac{7}{5}\left(\dfrac{1}{14}\right)$

11. $\dfrac{1}{2} \cdot \dfrac{3}{8} \cdot \dfrac{4}{5}$

12. $\dfrac{7}{5} \cdot \dfrac{12}{7} \cdot \dfrac{1}{3}$

13. $\dfrac{8}{5} \div \dfrac{2}{5}$

14. $\dfrac{3}{8} \div \dfrac{4}{5}$

15. $\dfrac{8}{15} \div \dfrac{2}{3}$

16. $\dfrac{3}{5} \div 9$

17. $16 \div \dfrac{8}{3}$

18. $\dfrac{36}{18} \div \dfrac{9}{2}$

Simplify each of the following as much as possible. [2.2, 2.3, 2.4]

19. $\dfrac{2}{3} \cdot \dfrac{1}{2} \div \dfrac{5}{6}$

20. $\dfrac{10}{7} \div 5 \cdot \dfrac{3}{4}$

21. $\left(\dfrac{4}{11}\right)\left(\dfrac{5}{8}\right) \div \dfrac{1}{4}$

22. $\dfrac{6}{11} \div \dfrac{3}{5} \div \dfrac{1}{2}$

23. $\dfrac{1}{5} \div \left(\dfrac{2}{3} \cdot \dfrac{4}{5}\right)$

24. $\dfrac{3}{8} \cdot \dfrac{5}{9} \div \dfrac{5}{12}$

25. $\left(\dfrac{5}{18}\right)\left(\dfrac{4}{5}\right) \div \dfrac{10}{9}$

26. $\left(\dfrac{6}{5} \div \dfrac{9}{8}\right)\left(\dfrac{5}{8}\right)$

27. Sewing A dress requires $\dfrac{6}{5}$ yards of material to make. If you have 12 yards of material, how many dresses can you make? [2.4]

The illustration shows what new iPhone buyers had as their previous phone.

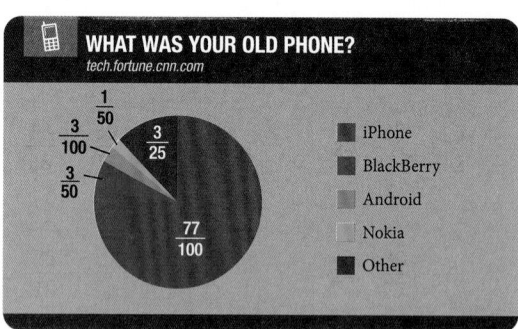

28. Write the fraction of iPhone buyers who had a Blackberry as their previous phone as an equivalent fraction with a denominator of 100.

29. Write the fraction of iPhone buyers who previously had a Nokia phone as an equivalent fraction with a denominator of 200.

Addition and Subtraction of Fractions, Mixed Numbers

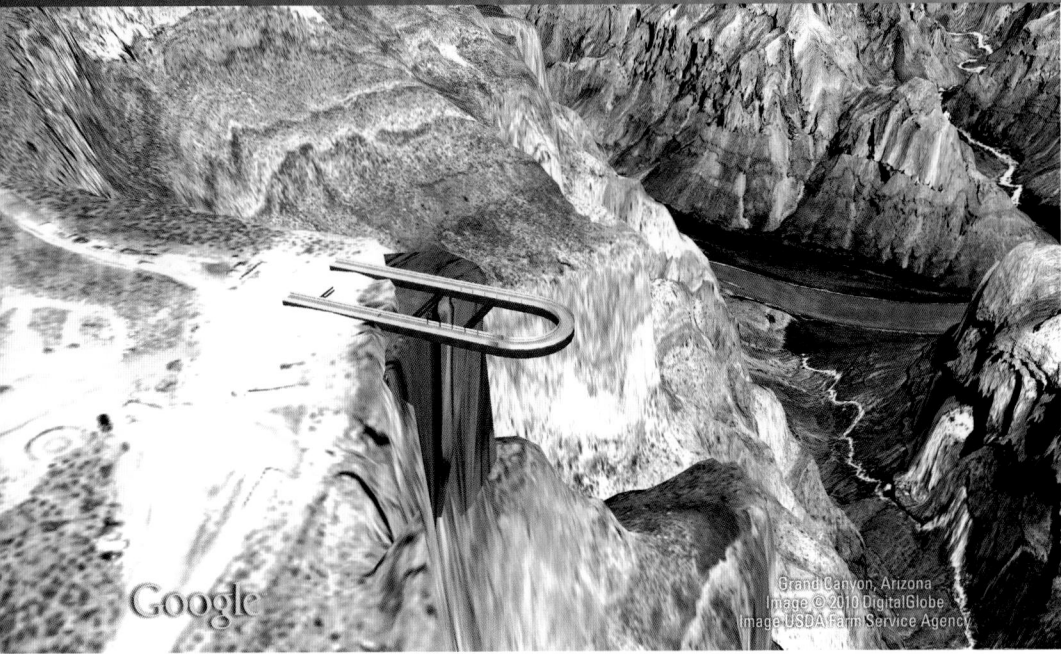

Grand Canyon, Arizona
Image © 2010 DigitalGlobe
Image USDA Farm Service Agency
Google

3

The Grand Canyon in Arizona has some of the most breathtaking views in the world. Carved by the Colorado River over millions of years, the Grand Canyon now measures 277 miles in length. If you travel to the canyon's western rim, the Grand Canyon Skywalk is not to be missed. The U-shaped observation deck has a glass bottom and allows visitors to "walk the sky" some 4,000 feet above the Colorado River. Weighing 1.2 million pounds, the glass is the only thing separating patrons from the deep canyon below. Built with permission from the local Hualapai, a Native American tribe, the skywalk has hosted over 2 million tourists from 50 countries since its 2007 grand opening.

					Inner Canyon Precipitation (in inches)						
Jan	Feb	Mar	April	May	June	July	Aug	Sept	Oct	Nov	Dec
$\frac{17}{25}$	$\frac{3}{4}$	$\frac{79}{100}$	$\frac{47}{100}$	$\frac{9}{25}$	$\frac{21}{25}$	$\frac{21}{25}$	$1\frac{2}{5}$	$\frac{97}{100}$	$\frac{65}{100}$	$\frac{43}{100}$	$\frac{87}{100}$

To ensure an optimal viewing experience, it is important to check the weather forecast before traveling to the Grand Canyon. The table shows the average precipitation inside the canyon. Suppose you were planning to spend the months of August and September touring the region. How much precipitation can you expect during those two months? If you want to know whether to pack an umbrella you must know how to add fractions, which is one of the topics we will cover in this chapter.

3.1 Addition and Subtraction with Fractions

In Las Vegas, the Stratosphere's hotel and casino has opened another attraction for thrill-seekers. SkyJump is a death-defying controlled free-fall from the 108th floor of the hotel to the ground. Jump Package 1 includes the jump cost plus a DVD of the jump for $114.99. A jump without the DVD costs $99.99. Suppose you are part of a group of people that schedules an appointment for the SkyJump. $\frac{2}{7}$ of the group buys Jump Package 1 and $\frac{3}{7}$ buys the jump without the DVD. The remaining $\frac{1}{7}$ of the group decides not to jump and instead buys the "Chicken" shirt available for purchase at the SkyJump store. What fraction represents the amount of people in the group that actually jumped? To answer this question, we must be able to add fractions with a common denominator.

A Addition and Subtraction with Common Denominators

Adding and subtracting fractions is actually just another application of the distributive property. The distributive property looks like this:

$$a(b + c) = a(b) + a(c)$$

where a, b, and c may be whole numbers or fractions. We will want to apply this property to expressions like

$$\frac{2}{7} + \frac{3}{7}$$

But before we do, we must make one additional observation about fractions.

The fraction $\frac{2}{7}$ can be written as $2 \cdot \frac{1}{7}$, because

$$2 \cdot \frac{1}{7} = \frac{2}{1} \cdot \frac{1}{7} = \frac{2}{7}$$

Likewise, the fraction $\frac{3}{7}$ can be written as $3 \cdot \frac{1}{7}$, because

$$3 \cdot \frac{1}{7} = \frac{3}{1} \cdot \frac{1}{7} = \frac{3}{7}$$

In general, we can say that the fraction $\frac{a}{b}$ can always be written as $a \cdot \frac{1}{b}$, because

$$a \cdot \frac{1}{b} = \frac{a}{1} \cdot \frac{1}{b} = \frac{a}{b}$$

To add the fractions $\frac{2}{7}$ and $\frac{3}{7}$, we simply rewrite each of them as we have done above and apply the distributive property. Here is how it works:

$$\frac{2}{7} + \frac{3}{7} = 2 \cdot \frac{1}{7} + 3 \cdot \frac{1}{7} \quad \text{Rewrite each fraction.}$$

$$= (2 + 3) \cdot \frac{1}{7} \quad \text{Apply the distributive property.}$$

$$= 5 \cdot \frac{1}{7} \quad \text{Add 2 and 3 to get 5.}$$

$$= \frac{5}{7} \quad \text{Rewrite } 5 \cdot \frac{1}{7} \text{ as } \frac{5}{7}.$$

Note Most people who have done any work with adding fractions know that you add fractions that have the same denominator by adding their numerators, but not their denominators. However, most people don't know why this works. The reason why we add numerators but not denominators is because of the distributive property. That is what the discussion at the left is all about. If you really want to understand addition of fractions, pay close attention to this discussion.

We can visualize the process shown above by using circles that are divided into 7 equal parts.

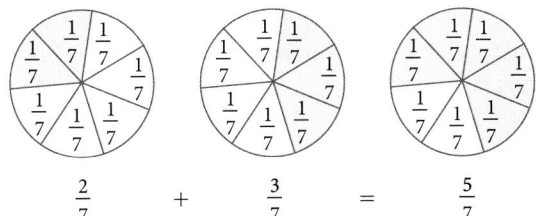

$$\frac{2}{7} \qquad + \qquad \frac{3}{7} \qquad = \qquad \frac{5}{7}$$

The fraction $\frac{5}{7}$ is the sum of $\frac{2}{7}$ and $\frac{3}{7}$. The steps and diagrams above show why we add numerators, *but do not add denominators*. Using this example as justification, we can write a rule for adding two fractions that have the same denominator.

> **RULE** Addition with Common Denominator
>
> To add two fractions that have the same denominator, we add their numerators to get the numerator of the answer. The denominator in the answer is the same denominator as in the original fractions.

What we have here is the sum of the numerators placed over the *common denominator*. In symbols, we have the following:

> **Addition and Subtraction of Fractions**
>
> If a, b, and c are numbers, and c is not equal to 0, then
> $$\frac{a}{c} + \frac{b}{c} = \frac{a+b}{c}$$
> This rule holds for subtraction as well. That is,
> $$\frac{a}{c} - \frac{b}{c} = \frac{a-b}{c}$$

EXAMPLE 1 Add or subtract.

a. $\frac{3}{8} + \frac{1}{8}$ **b.** $\frac{9}{5} - \frac{3}{5}$ **c.** $\frac{3}{7} + \frac{2}{7} + \frac{9}{7}$

Solution

a. $\frac{3}{8} + \frac{1}{8} = \frac{3+1}{8}$ Add numerators; keep the same denominator.

$\quad = \frac{4}{8}$ The sum of 3 and 1 is 4.

$\quad = \frac{1}{2}$ Reduce to lowest terms.

b. $\frac{9}{5} - \frac{3}{5} = \frac{9-3}{5}$ Subtract numerators; keep the same denominator.

$\quad = \frac{6}{5}$ The difference of 9 and 3 is 6.

c. $\frac{3}{7} + \frac{2}{7} + \frac{9}{7} = \frac{3+2+9}{7}$

$\quad = \frac{14}{7}$

$\quad = 2$

Video Examples
SECTION 3.1

Practice Problems

1. Add or subtract.

   a. $\frac{5}{12} + \frac{1}{12}$

   b. $\frac{3}{10} + \frac{7}{10}$

   c. $\frac{11}{6} - \frac{5}{6} - \frac{1}{6}$

Answers

1. **a.** $\frac{1}{2}$ **b.** 1 **c.** $\frac{5}{6}$

B Addition and Subtraction with Unlike Denominators

As Example 1 indicates, addition and subtraction are simple, straightforward processes when all the fractions have the same denominator. We will now turn our attention to the process of adding fractions that have different denominators. In order to get started, we need the following definition:

> **DEFINITION** least common denominator
>
> The *least common denominator* (LCD) for a set of denominators is the smallest number that is exactly divisible by each denominator. (Note that, in some books, the least common denominator is also called the *least common multiple*.)

In other words, all the denominators of the fractions involved in a problem must divide into the least common denominator exactly. That is, they divide it without leaving a remainder.

2. Find the LCD for the fractions $\frac{7}{15}$ and $\frac{9}{25}$.

EXAMPLE 2   Find the LCD for the fractions $\dfrac{5}{12}$ and $\dfrac{7}{18}$.

Solution   The least common denominator for the denominators 12 and 18 must be the smallest number divisible by both 12 and 18. We can factor 12 and 18 completely and then build the LCD from these factors. Factoring 12 and 18 completely gives us

$$12 = 2 \cdot 2 \cdot 3 \qquad 18 = 2 \cdot 3 \cdot 3$$

Now, if 12 is going to divide the LCD exactly, then the LCD must have factors of $2 \cdot 2 \cdot 3$. If 18 is to divide it exactly, it must have factors of $2 \cdot 3 \cdot 3$. We don't need to repeat the factors that 12 and 18 have in common.

$$\left. \begin{array}{l} 12 = 2 \cdot 2 \cdot 3 \\ 18 = 2 \cdot 3 \cdot 3 \end{array} \right\} \qquad \overset{\text{12 divides the LCD.}}{\text{LCD} = 2 \cdot 2 \cdot 3 \cdot 3 = 36} \\ {}_{\text{18 divides the LCD.}}$$

The LCD for 12 and 18 is 36. It is the smallest number that is divisible by both 12 and 18; 12 divides it exactly three times, and 18 divides it exactly two times.

Note   The ability to find least common denominators is very important in mathematics. The discussion here is a detailed explanation of how to find an LCD.

We can visualize the results in Example 2 with the diagram below. It shows that 36 is the smallest number that both 12 and 18 divide evenly. As you can see, 12 divides 36 exactly 3 times, and 18 divides 36 exactly 2 times.

12	12	12

18	18

36

3. Add: $\frac{7}{15} + \frac{9}{25}$.

EXAMPLE 3   Add: $\dfrac{5}{12} + \dfrac{7}{18}$.

Solution   We can add fractions only when they have the same denominators. In Example 2, we found the LCD for $\frac{5}{12}$ and $\frac{7}{18}$ to be 36. We change $\frac{5}{12}$ and $\frac{7}{18}$ to equivalent fractions that have 36 for a denominator by applying the multiplication property for fractions.

$$\frac{5}{12} = \frac{5 \cdot 3}{12 \cdot 3} = \frac{15}{36}$$

$$\frac{7}{18} = \frac{7 \cdot 2}{18 \cdot 2} = \frac{14}{36}$$

Answers

2. 75

3. $\frac{62}{75}$

The fraction $\frac{15}{36}$ is equivalent to $\frac{5}{12}$, because it was obtained by multiplying both the numerator and the denominator by 3. Likewise, $\frac{14}{36}$ is equivalent to $\frac{7}{18}$, because it was obtained by multiplying the numerator and the denominator by 2. All we have left to do is to add numerators.

$$\frac{15}{36} + \frac{14}{36} = \frac{29}{36}$$

The sum of $\frac{5}{12}$ and $\frac{7}{18}$ is the fraction $\frac{29}{36}$. Let's write the complete problem again step by step.

$$\frac{5}{12} + \frac{7}{18} = \frac{5 \cdot 3}{12 \cdot 3} + \frac{7 \cdot 2}{18 \cdot 2} \qquad \text{\textit{Rewrite each fraction as an equivalent fraction with denominator 36.}}$$

$$= \frac{15}{36} + \frac{14}{36}$$

$$= \frac{29}{36} \qquad \text{\textit{Add numerators; keep the common denominator.}}$$

EXAMPLE 4   Find the LCD for $\frac{3}{4}$ and $\frac{1}{6}$.

Solution   We factor 4 and 6 into products of prime factors and build the LCD from these factors.

$$\left.\begin{array}{l} 4 = 2 \cdot 2 \\ 6 = 2 \cdot 3 \end{array}\right\} \quad \text{LCD} = 2 \cdot 2 \cdot 3 = 12$$

The LCD is 12. Both denominators divide it exactly; 4 divides 12 exactly 3 times, and 6 divides 12 exactly 2 times.

EXAMPLE 5   Add: $\frac{3}{4} + \frac{1}{6}$.

Solution   In Example 4, we found that the LCD for these two fractions is 12. We begin by changing $\frac{3}{4}$ and $\frac{1}{6}$ to equivalent fractions with denominator 12.

$$\frac{3}{4} = \frac{3 \cdot 3}{4 \cdot 3} = \frac{9}{12}$$

$$\frac{1}{6} = \frac{1 \cdot 2}{6 \cdot 2} = \frac{2}{12}$$

The fraction $\frac{9}{12}$ is equal to the fraction $\frac{3}{4}$, because it was obtained by multiplying the numerator and the denominator of $\frac{3}{4}$ by 3. Likewise, $\frac{2}{12}$ is equivalent to $\frac{1}{6}$, because it was obtained by multiplying the numerator and the denominator of $\frac{1}{6}$ by 2. To complete the problem, we add numerators.

$$\frac{9}{12} + \frac{2}{12} = \frac{11}{12}$$

The sum of $\frac{3}{4}$ and $\frac{1}{6}$ is $\frac{11}{12}$. Here is how the complete problem looks:

$$\frac{3}{4} + \frac{1}{6} = \frac{3 \cdot 3}{4 \cdot 3} + \frac{1 \cdot 2}{6 \cdot 2} \qquad \text{\textit{Rewrite each fraction as an equivalent fraction with denominator 12.}}$$

$$= \frac{9}{12} + \frac{2}{12}$$

$$= \frac{11}{12} \qquad \text{\textit{Add numerators; keep the same denominator.}}$$

4. Find the LCD for $\frac{7}{12}$ and $\frac{3}{8}$.

5. Add: $\frac{7}{12} + \frac{3}{8}$.

Note   We can visualize the work in Example 5 using circles and shading.

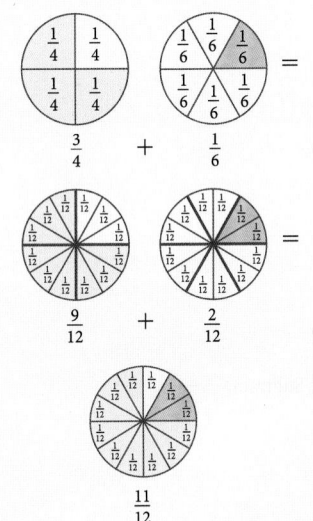

Answers

4. 24

5. $\frac{23}{24}$

6. Subtract: $\frac{3}{4} - \frac{5}{12}$.

EXAMPLE 6   Subtract: $\frac{7}{15} - \frac{3}{10}$.

Solution   Let's factor 15 and 10 completely and use these factors to build the LCD.

$$\left. \begin{array}{l} 15 = 3 \cdot 5 \\ 10 = 2 \cdot 5 \end{array} \right\} \quad \text{LCD} = 2 \cdot 3 \cdot 5 = 30$$

15 divides the LCD.

10 divides the LCD.

Changing to equivalent fractions and subtracting, we have

$$\frac{7}{15} - \frac{3}{10} = \frac{7 \cdot 2}{15 \cdot 2} - \frac{3 \cdot 3}{10 \cdot 3} \qquad \text{\textit{Rewrite as equivalent fractions with the LCD for the denominator.}}$$

$$= \frac{14}{30} - \frac{9}{30}$$

$$= \frac{5}{30} \qquad \text{\textit{Subtract numerators; keep the LCD.}}$$

$$= \frac{1}{6} \qquad \text{\textit{Reduce to lowest terms.}}$$

As a summary of what we have done so far, and as a guide to working other problems, we now list the steps involved in adding and subtracting fractions with different denominators.

> **HOW TO** **To Add or Subtract Any Two Fractions**
>
> **Step 1:** Factor each denominator completely, and use the factors to build the LCD. (Remember, the LCD is the smallest number divisible by each of the denominators in the problem.)
>
> **Step 2:** Rewrite each fraction as an equivalent fraction with the LCD. This is done by multiplying both the numerator and the denominator of the fraction in question by the appropriate whole number.
>
> **Step 3:** Add or subtract the numerators of the fractions produced in Step 2. This is the numerator of the sum or difference. The denominator of the sum or difference is the LCD.
>
> **Step 4:** Reduce the fraction produced in Step 3 to lowest terms if it is not already in lowest terms.

The idea behind adding or subtracting fractions is really very straight-forward. We can only add or subtract fractions that have the same denominators. If the fractions we are trying to add or subtract do not have the same denominators, we rewrite each of them as an equivalent fraction with the LCD for a denominator.

Here are some additional examples of sums and differences of fractions:

7. Subtract: $\frac{1}{2} - \frac{3}{10}$.

EXAMPLE 7   Subtract: $\frac{3}{5} - \frac{1}{6}$.

Solution   The LCD for 5 and 6 is their product, 30. We begin by rewriting each fraction with this common denominator.

$$\frac{3}{5} - \frac{1}{6} = \frac{3 \cdot 6}{5 \cdot 6} - \frac{1 \cdot 5}{6 \cdot 5}$$

$$= \frac{18}{30} - \frac{5}{30}$$

$$= \frac{13}{30}$$

Answers

6. $\frac{1}{3}$

7. $\frac{1}{5}$

EXAMPLE 8   Add: $\dfrac{1}{6} + \dfrac{1}{8} + \dfrac{1}{4}$.

Solution   We begin by factoring the denominators completely and building the LCD from the factors that result.

$$\left.\begin{array}{l} 6 = 2 \cdot 3 \\ 8 = 2 \cdot 2 \cdot 2 \\ 4 = 2 \cdot 2 \end{array}\right\} \quad \begin{array}{c} \text{8 divides the LCD.} \\ \text{LCD} = 2 \cdot 2 \cdot 2 \cdot 3 = 24 \\ \text{4 divides the LCD.} \quad \text{6 divides the LCD.} \end{array}$$

We then change to equivalent fractions and add as usual.

$$\frac{1}{6} + \frac{1}{8} + \frac{1}{4} = \frac{1 \cdot 4}{6 \cdot 4} + \frac{1 \cdot 3}{8 \cdot 3} + \frac{1 \cdot 6}{4 \cdot 6} = \frac{4}{24} + \frac{3}{24} + \frac{6}{24} = \frac{13}{24}$$

8. Add: $\frac{1}{3} + \frac{3}{8} + \frac{1}{4}$.

EXAMPLE 9   Subtract: $3 - \dfrac{5}{6}$.

Solution   The denominators are 1 (because $3 = \frac{3}{1}$) and 6. The smallest number divisible by both 1 and 6 is 6.

$$3 - \frac{5}{6} = \frac{3}{1} - \frac{5}{6} = \frac{3 \cdot 6}{1 \cdot 6} - \frac{5}{6} = \frac{18}{6} - \frac{5}{6} = \frac{13}{6}$$

9. Subtract: $4 - \frac{5}{7}$.

Comparing Fractions

As we have shown previously, we can compare fractions to see which is larger or smaller when they have the same denominator. Now that we know how to find the LCD for a set of fractions, we can use the LCD to write equivalent fractions with the intention of comparing them.

EXAMPLE 10   Find the LCD for the fractions below, then write each fraction as an equivalent fraction with the LCD for a denominator. Then write them in order from smallest to largest.

$$\frac{5}{8} \qquad\qquad \frac{5}{16} \qquad\qquad \frac{3}{4} \qquad\qquad \frac{1}{2}$$

10. Write the fractions from smallest to largest.
$$\frac{3}{4}, \frac{7}{12}, \frac{5}{8}, \frac{13}{16}$$

Solution   The LCD for the four fractions is 16. We begin by writing each fraction as an equivalent fraction with denominator 16.

$$\frac{5}{8} = \frac{10}{16} \qquad \frac{5}{16} = \frac{5}{16} \qquad \frac{3}{4} = \frac{12}{16} \qquad \frac{1}{2} = \frac{8}{16}$$

Now that they all have the same denominator, the smallest fraction is the one with the smallest numerator, and the largest fraction is the one with the largest numerator. Writing them in order from smallest to largest we have

$$\frac{5}{16} < \frac{8}{16} < \frac{10}{16} < \frac{12}{16}$$

$$\frac{5}{16} < \frac{1}{2} < \frac{5}{8} < \frac{3}{4}$$

After reading through the preceding section, respond in your own words and in complete sentences.

A. When adding two fractions with the same denominators, we always add their _____, but we never add their _____.

B. What does the abbreviation LCD stand for?

C. What is the first step when finding the LCD for the fractions $\frac{5}{12}$ and $\frac{7}{18}$?

D. When adding fractions, what is the last step?

Answers

8. $\frac{23}{24}$

9. $\frac{23}{7}$

10. $\frac{7}{12} < \frac{5}{8} < \frac{3}{4} < \frac{13}{16}$

Vocabulary Review

The following is a list of steps for adding and subtracting fractions. Choose the correct words to fill in the blanks below.

numerators   least common denominator   lowest terms   equivalent

Step 1: Factor each denominator completely, and use the factors to build the _____ .

Step 2: Rewrite each fraction as an _____ fraction with the LCD.

Step 3: Add or subtract the _____ of the fractions produced in Step 2.

Step 4: Reduce the fraction produced in Step 3 to _____ if it is not already.

Problems

A Find the following sums and differences, and reduce to lowest terms. (Add or subtract as indicated.)

1. $\dfrac{3}{6} + \dfrac{1}{6}$

2. $\dfrac{2}{5} + \dfrac{3}{5}$

3. $\dfrac{5}{8} - \dfrac{3}{8}$

4. $\dfrac{6}{7} - \dfrac{1}{7}$

5. $\dfrac{3}{4} - \dfrac{1}{4}$

6. $\dfrac{7}{9} - \dfrac{4}{9}$

7. $\dfrac{2}{3} - \dfrac{1}{3}$

8. $\dfrac{9}{8} - \dfrac{1}{8}$

9. $\dfrac{1}{4} + \dfrac{2}{4} + \dfrac{3}{4}$

10. $\dfrac{2}{5} + \dfrac{3}{5} + \dfrac{4}{5}$

11. $\dfrac{x+7}{2} - \dfrac{1}{2}$

12. $\dfrac{x+5}{4} - \dfrac{3}{4}$

13. $\dfrac{1}{10} + \dfrac{3}{10} + \dfrac{4}{10}$

14. $\dfrac{3}{20} + \dfrac{1}{20} + \dfrac{4}{20}$

15. $\dfrac{1}{3} + \dfrac{4}{3} + \dfrac{5}{3}$

16. $\dfrac{5}{4} + \dfrac{4}{4} + \dfrac{3}{4}$

B Complete the following tables.

17.

First Number a	Second Number b	The Sum of a and b $a + b$
$\dfrac{1}{2}$	$\dfrac{1}{3}$	
$\dfrac{1}{3}$	$\dfrac{1}{4}$	
$\dfrac{1}{4}$	$\dfrac{1}{5}$	
$\dfrac{1}{5}$	$\dfrac{1}{6}$	

18.

First Number a	Second Number b	The Sum of a and b $a + b$
1	$\dfrac{1}{2}$	
1	$\dfrac{1}{3}$	
1	$\dfrac{1}{4}$	
1	$\dfrac{1}{5}$	

19.

First Number a	Second Number b	The Sum of a and b $a + b$
$\dfrac{1}{12}$	$\dfrac{1}{2}$	
$\dfrac{1}{12}$	$\dfrac{1}{3}$	
$\dfrac{1}{12}$	$\dfrac{1}{4}$	
$\dfrac{1}{12}$	$\dfrac{1}{6}$	

20.

First Number a	Second Number b	The Sum of a and b $a + b$
$\dfrac{1}{8}$	$\dfrac{1}{2}$	
$\dfrac{1}{8}$	$\dfrac{1}{4}$	
$\dfrac{1}{8}$	$\dfrac{1}{16}$	
$\dfrac{1}{8}$	$\dfrac{1}{24}$	

Find the LCD for each of the following, then use the methods developed in this section to add or subtract as indicated.

21. $\dfrac{4}{9} + \dfrac{1}{3}$

22. $\dfrac{1}{2} + \dfrac{1}{4}$

23. $2 + \dfrac{1}{3}$

24. $3 + \dfrac{1}{2}$

25. $\dfrac{3}{4} + 1$

26. $\dfrac{3}{4} + 2$

27. $\dfrac{1}{2} + \dfrac{2}{3}$

28. $\dfrac{1}{8} + \dfrac{3}{4}$

29. $\dfrac{1}{4} + \dfrac{1}{5}$

30. $\dfrac{1}{3} + \dfrac{1}{5}$

31. $\dfrac{1}{2} + \dfrac{1}{5}$

32. $\dfrac{1}{2} - \dfrac{1}{5}$

33. $\dfrac{5}{12} + \dfrac{3}{8}$

34. $\dfrac{9}{16} + \dfrac{7}{12}$

35. $\dfrac{8}{30} - \dfrac{1}{20}$

36. $\dfrac{9}{40} - \dfrac{1}{30}$

37. $\dfrac{3}{10} + \dfrac{1}{100}$

38. $\dfrac{9}{100} + \dfrac{7}{10}$

39. $\dfrac{10}{36} + \dfrac{9}{48}$

40. $\dfrac{12}{28} + \dfrac{9}{20}$

41. $\dfrac{17}{30} + \dfrac{11}{42}$

42. $\dfrac{19}{42} + \dfrac{13}{70}$

43. $\dfrac{25}{84} + \dfrac{41}{90}$

44. $\dfrac{23}{70} + \dfrac{29}{84}$

45. $\dfrac{13}{126} - \dfrac{13}{180}$

46. $\dfrac{17}{84} - \dfrac{17}{90}$

47. $\dfrac{3}{4} + \dfrac{1}{8} + \dfrac{5}{6}$

48. $\dfrac{3}{8} + \dfrac{2}{5} + \dfrac{1}{4}$

49. $\dfrac{3}{10} + \dfrac{5}{12} + \dfrac{1}{6}$

50. $\dfrac{5}{21} + \dfrac{1}{7} + \dfrac{3}{14}$

51. $\dfrac{1}{2} + \dfrac{1}{3} + \dfrac{1}{4} + \dfrac{1}{6}$

52. $\dfrac{1}{8} + \dfrac{1}{4} + \dfrac{1}{5} + \dfrac{1}{10}$

53. $10 - \dfrac{2}{9}$

54. $9 - \dfrac{3}{5}$

55. $4 - \dfrac{2}{3}$

56. $5 - \dfrac{3}{4}$

57. $\dfrac{1}{10} + \dfrac{4}{5} - \dfrac{3}{20}$

58. $\dfrac{1}{2} + \dfrac{3}{4} - \dfrac{5}{8}$

59. $\dfrac{1}{4} - \dfrac{1}{8} + \dfrac{1}{2} - \dfrac{3}{8}$

60. $\dfrac{7}{8} - \dfrac{3}{4} + \dfrac{5}{8} - \dfrac{1}{2}$

There are two ways to work the problems below. You can combine the fractions inside the parentheses first and then multiply, or you can apply the distributive property first, then add.

61. $15\left(\dfrac{2}{3} + \dfrac{3}{5}\right)$

62. $15\left(\dfrac{4}{5} - \dfrac{1}{3}\right)$

63. $4\left(\dfrac{1}{2} + \dfrac{1}{4}\right)$

64. $6\left(\dfrac{1}{3} + \dfrac{1}{2}\right)$

65. $4\left(3 - \dfrac{3}{4}\right)$

66. $6\left(5 - \dfrac{2}{3}\right)$

67. $9\left(\dfrac{1}{3} + \dfrac{1}{9}\right)$

68. $12\left(\dfrac{1}{3} + \dfrac{1}{4}\right)$

69. Write the fractions in order from smallest to largest.

$$\dfrac{3}{4} \qquad \dfrac{3}{8} \qquad \dfrac{1}{2} \qquad \dfrac{1}{4}$$

70. Write the fractions in order from smallest to largest.

$$\dfrac{1}{2} \qquad \dfrac{1}{6} \qquad \dfrac{1}{4} \qquad \dfrac{1}{3}$$

71. Find the sum of $\dfrac{3}{7}$, 2, and $\dfrac{1}{9}$.

72. Find the sum of 6, $\dfrac{6}{11}$, and 11.

73. Give the difference of $\dfrac{7}{8}$ and $\dfrac{1}{4}$.

74. Give the difference of $\dfrac{9}{10}$ and $\dfrac{1}{100}$.

Arithmetic Sequences Recall that an arithmetic sequence is a sequence in which each term comes from the previous term by adding the same number each time. For example, the sequence $1, \dfrac{3}{2}, 2, \dfrac{5}{2}, \ldots$ is an arithmetic sequence that starts with the number 1. Then each term after that is found by adding $\dfrac{1}{2}$ to the previous term. By observing this fact, we know that the next term in the sequence will be $\dfrac{5}{2} + \dfrac{1}{2} = \dfrac{6}{2} = 3$.

Find the next number in each arithmetic sequence below.

75. $1, \dfrac{4}{3}, \dfrac{5}{3}, 2, \ldots$

76. $1, \dfrac{5}{4}, \dfrac{3}{2}, \dfrac{7}{4}, \ldots$

77. $\dfrac{3}{2}, 2, \dfrac{5}{2}, \ldots$

78. $\dfrac{2}{3}, 1, \dfrac{4}{3}, \ldots$

Applying the Concepts

Some of the application problems below involve multiplication or division, while others involve addition or subtraction.

79. Capacity One carton of milk contains $\dfrac{1}{2}$ pint while another contains 4 pints. How much milk is contained in both cartons?

80. Baking A recipe calls for $\dfrac{2}{3}$ cup of flour and $\dfrac{3}{4}$ cup of sugar. What is the total amount of flour and sugar called for in the recipe?

81. Budget A family decides that they can spend $\dfrac{5}{8}$ of their monthly income on house payments. If their monthly income is $2,120, how much can they spend for house payments?

82. Savings A family saves $\dfrac{3}{16}$ of their income each month. If their monthly income is $1,264, how much do they save each month?

Reading a Pie Chart The pie chart below shows how the students at Cal Poly State University are distributed among the different schools at the university. Use the information in the pie chart to answer questions 83 and 84.

83. If the students in the Schools of Engineering and Business are combined, what fraction results?

84. What fraction of the university's students are enrolled in the Schools of Agriculture, Engineering, and Business combined?

Cal Poly Enrollment

Liberal Arts $\frac{3}{20}$

Agriculture $\frac{2}{9}$

Architecture & Environmental Design $\frac{1}{9}$

Business $\frac{1}{9}$

Science & Mathematics $\frac{3}{20}$

Engineering $\frac{5}{18}$

85. Final Exam Grades The table gives the fraction of students in a class of 40 that received grades of A, B, or C on the final exam. Fill in all the missing parts of the table.

Grade	Number of Students	Fraction of Students
A		$\frac{1}{8}$
B		$\frac{1}{5}$
C		$\frac{1}{2}$
Below C		
Total	40	1

86. Flu During a flu epidemic a company with 200 employees has $\frac{1}{10}$ of their employees call in sick on Monday and another $\frac{3}{10}$ call in sick on Tuesday. What is the total number of employees calling in sick during this 2-day period?

87. Subdivision A 6-acre piece of land is subdivided into $\frac{3}{5}$-acre lots. How many lots are there?

88. Cutting Wood A 12-foot piece of wood is cut into shelves. If each is $\frac{3}{4}$ foot in length, how many shelves are there?

Getting Ready for the Next Section

Simplify.

89. $9 \cdot 6 + 5$

90. $4 \cdot 6 + 3$

91. Write 2 as a fraction with denominator 8.

92. Write 2 as a fraction with denominator 4.

93. Write 1 as a fraction with denominator 8.

94. Write 5 as a fraction with denominator 4.

Add.

95. $\frac{8}{4} + \frac{3}{4}$

96. $\frac{16}{8} + \frac{1}{8}$

97. $2 + \frac{1}{8}$

98. $2 + \frac{3}{4}$

99. $1 + \frac{1}{8}$

100. $5 + \frac{3}{4}$

Divide.

101. $11 \div 4$ **102.** $10 \div 3$ **103.** $208 \div 24$ **104.** $207 \div 26$

Find the Mistake

Each sentence below contains a mistake. Circle the mistake and write the correct word(s) or number(s) on the line provided.

1. The fractions $\frac{a}{c}$ and $\frac{b}{c}$ can be added to become $\frac{a+b}{c}$ because they have different denominators. _____

2. Subtracting $\frac{12}{21}$ from $\frac{18}{21}$, gives us $\frac{30}{21}$. _____

3. The least common denominator for a set of denominators is the smallest number that is exactly divisible by each numerator. _____

4. The LCD for the fractions $\frac{4}{6}$, $\frac{2}{8}$ and $\frac{3}{4}$ is 12. _____

Navigation Skills: Prepare, Study, Achieve

Completing homework assignments in full is a key piece to succeeding in this class. To do this effectively, you must pay special attention to each set of instructions. When you do your homework, you usually work a number of similar problems at a time. But the problems may vary on a test. It is very important to make a habit of paying attention to the instructions to elicit correct answers on a test. Secondly, to complete an assignment efficiently, you will need to memorize various definitions, properties, and formulas. Reading the definition in the book alone is not enough. There are many techniques for successful memorization. Here are a few:

- Spend some time rereading the definition.
- Say the definition out loud.
- Explain the definition to another person.
- Write the definition down on a separate sheets of notes.
- Create a mnemonic device using key words from the definition.
- Analyze how the definition applies to your homework problems.

The above suggestions are ways to engage your senses when memorizing an abstract concept. This will help anchor it in your memory. For instance, it is easier to remember explaining to your friend a difficult math formula, than it is to simply recall it from a single read of the chapter. Lastly, once you've completed an assignment, take any extra time you've allotted for studying to work more problems, and if you feel ready, read ahead and work problems you will encounter in the next section.

3.2 Mixed-Number Notation

Pogopalooza is an annual world championship for stunt pogo stick athletes. Pogo jumpers compete in various events, such as the most or the least jumps in a minute, the highest jump, and numerous exhibitions of acrobatic stunts. Imagine you are competing in the High Jump competition. The crowd cheers as you bounce a remarkable $8\frac{1}{4}$ feet into the air! Being a skilled mathematician, you realize that your score of $8\frac{1}{4}$ feet, or eight and one-fourth feet, is actually a *mixed number*. It is the sum of a whole number and a proper fraction. With mixed-number notation, we leave out the addition sign.

Mixed-Number Notation

Here are some further examples of mixed number notation:

$$2\frac{1}{8} = 2 + \frac{1}{8}, \quad 6\frac{5}{9} = 6 + \frac{5}{9}, \quad 11\frac{2}{3} = 11 + \frac{2}{3}$$

The notation used in writing mixed numbers (writing the whole number and the proper fraction next to each other) must always be interpreted as addition. It is a mistake to read $5\frac{3}{4}$ as meaning 5 times $\frac{3}{4}$. If we want to indicate multiplication, we must use parentheses or a multiplication symbol. That is,

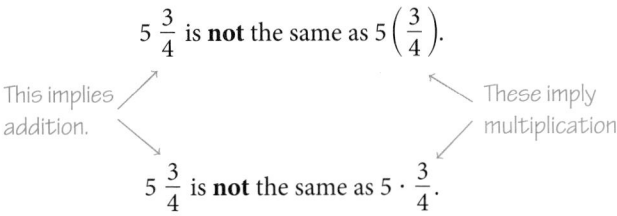

$$5\frac{3}{4} \text{ is \textbf{not} the same as } 5\left(\frac{3}{4}\right).$$

This implies addition.

These imply multiplication.

$$5\frac{3}{4} \text{ is \textbf{not} the same as } 5 \cdot \frac{3}{4}.$$

A Changing Mixed Numbers to Improper Fractions

To change a mixed number to an improper fraction, we write the mixed number with the + sign showing and then add the two numbers, as we did earlier.

EXAMPLE 1 Change $2\frac{3}{4}$ to an improper fraction.

Solution

$$2\frac{3}{4} = 2 + \frac{3}{4} \qquad \text{Write the mixed number as a sum.}$$

$$= \frac{2}{1} + \frac{3}{4} \qquad \text{Show that the denominator of 2 is 1.}$$

$$= \frac{4 \cdot 2}{4 \cdot 1} + \frac{3}{4} \qquad \text{Multiply the numerator and the denominator of } \frac{2}{1} \text{ by 4 so both fractions will have the same denominator.}$$

Video Examples
SECTION 3.2

Practice Problems

1. Change $4\frac{2}{3}$ to an improper fraction.

Answer

1. $\frac{14}{3}$

$$= \frac{8}{4} + \frac{3}{4}$$

$$= \frac{11}{4} \qquad \text{\textit{Add the numerators; keep the common denominator.}}$$

The mixed number $2\frac{3}{4}$ is equal to the improper fraction $\frac{11}{4}$. The diagram that follows further illustrates the equivalence of $2\frac{3}{4}$ and $\frac{11}{4}$.

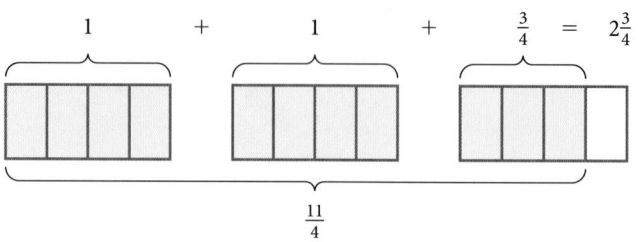

---

2. Change $3\frac{1}{5}$ to an improper fraction.

EXAMPLE 2   Change $2\frac{1}{8}$ to an improper fraction.

Solution $2\frac{1}{8} = 2 + \frac{1}{8}$ *Write as addition.*

$$= \frac{2}{1} + \frac{1}{8} \qquad \text{\textit{Write the whole number 2 as a fraction.}}$$

$$= \frac{8 \cdot 2}{8 \cdot 1} + \frac{1}{8} \qquad \text{\textit{Change } \frac{2}{1} \text{ to a fraction with denominator 8.}}$$

$$= \frac{16}{8} + \frac{1}{8}$$

$$= \frac{17}{8} \qquad \text{\textit{Add the numerators.}}$$

If we look closely at Examples 1 and 2, we can see the following shortcut that will let us change a mixed number to an improper fraction without so many steps.

   Shortcut: To change a mixed number to an improper fraction, simply multiply the whole number by the denominator of the fraction, and add the result to the numerator of the fraction. The result is the numerator of the improper fraction we are looking for. The denominator is the same as the original denominator.

3. Change $5\frac{7}{8}$ to an improper fraction.

EXAMPLE 3   Use the shortcut to change $5\frac{3}{4}$ to an improper fraction.

Solution

   1. First, we multiply 4×5 to get 20.

   2. Next, we add 20 to 3 to get 23.

   3. The improper fraction equal to $5\frac{3}{4}$ is $\frac{23}{4}$.

Here is a diagram showing what we have done:

$$
\left.
\begin{array}{l}
\textbf{Step 1} \ \text{Multiply } 4 \times 5 = 20. \\
\textbf{Step 2} \ \text{Add } 20 + 3 = 23.
\end{array}
\right\}
\begin{array}{l}
\textit{Step 2} \\
5\frac{3}{4} \\
\textit{Step 1}
\end{array}
$$

Mathematically, our shortcut is written like this:

$$5\frac{3}{4} = \frac{(4 \cdot 5) + 3}{4} = \frac{20 + 3}{4} = \frac{23}{4} \qquad \text{\textit{The result will always have the same denominator as the original mixed number.}}$$

The shortcut shown in Example 3 works because the whole-number part of a mixed number can always be written with a denominator of 1. Therefore, the LCD for a whole number and fraction will always be the denominator of the fraction. That is why we multiply the whole number by the denominator of the fraction.

$$5\frac{3}{4} = 5 + \frac{3}{4} = \frac{5}{1} + \frac{3}{4} = \frac{4 \cdot 5}{4 \cdot 1} + \frac{3}{4} = \frac{4 \cdot 5 + 3}{4} = \frac{23}{4}$$

EXAMPLE 4 Change $6\frac{5}{9}$ to an improper fraction.

Solution Using the first method, we have

$$6\frac{5}{9} = 6 + \frac{5}{9} = \frac{6}{1} + \frac{5}{9} = \frac{9 \cdot 6}{9 \cdot 1} + \frac{5}{9} = \frac{54}{9} + \frac{5}{9} = \frac{59}{9}$$

Using the shortcut method, we have

$$6\frac{5}{9} = \frac{(9 \cdot 6) + 5}{9} = \frac{54 + 5}{9} = \frac{59}{9}$$

Calculator Note The sequence of keys to press on a calculator to obtain the numerator in Example 4 looks like this:

$$9 \;\boxed{\times}\; 6 \;\boxed{+}\; 5 \;\boxed{=}$$

4. Change $8\frac{6}{7}$ to an improper fraction.

B Changing Improper Fractions to Mixed Numbers

To change an improper fraction to a mixed number, we divide the numerator by the denominator. The result is used to write the mixed number.

EXAMPLE 5 Change $\frac{11}{4}$ to a mixed number.

Solution Dividing 11 by 4 gives us

$$\begin{array}{r} 2 \\ 4{\overline{)11}} \\ -8 \\ \hline 3 \end{array}$$

We see that 4 goes into 11 two times with 3 for a remainder. We write this result as

$$\frac{11}{4} = 2 + \frac{3}{4} = 2\frac{3}{4}$$

The improper fraction $\frac{11}{4}$ is equivalent to the mixed number $2\frac{3}{4}$.

5. Change $\frac{13}{3}$ to a mixed number.

Note This division process shows us how many ones are in $\frac{11}{4}$ and, when the ones are taken out, how many fourths are left.

One easy way to visualize the results in Example 5 is to imagine running 13 laps on a $\frac{1}{4}$ mile track. Your 13 laps are equivalent to $\frac{13}{4}$ miles. In miles, your laps are equal to 3 miles plus 1 quarter-mile, or $3\frac{1}{4}$ miles.

EXAMPLE 6 Write as a mixed number.

a. $\frac{10}{3}$ **b.** $\frac{208}{24}$

Solution

a.
$$\begin{array}{r} 3 \\ 3{\overline{)10}} \\ 9 \\ \hline 1 \end{array}$$
so $\frac{10}{3} = 3 + \frac{1}{3} = 3\frac{1}{3}$

b.
$$\begin{array}{r} 8 \\ 24{\overline{)208}} \\ 192 \\ \hline 16 \end{array}$$
so $\frac{208}{24} = 8 + \frac{16}{24} = 8 + \frac{2}{3} = 8\frac{2}{3}$

$\uparrow$
Reduce to lowest terms.

6. Write as a mixed number.

a. $\frac{27}{4}$

b. $\frac{76}{8}$

Answers

4. $\frac{62}{7}$

5. $4\frac{1}{3}$

6. a. $6\frac{3}{4}$ **b.** $9\frac{1}{2}$

Long Division, Remainders, and Mixed Numbers

Mixed numbers give us another way of writing the answers to long division problems that contain remainders. Here is how we divided 1,690 by 67 in Chapter 1:

$$
\begin{array}{r}
25 \text{ R } 15 \\
67\overline{)1690} \\
134\downarrow \\
\overline{350} \\
335 \\
\overline{15}
\end{array}
$$

The answer is 25 with a remainder of 15. Using mixed numbers, we can now write the answer as $25\frac{15}{67}$. That is,

$$\frac{1,690}{67} = 25\frac{15}{67}$$

The quotient of 1,690 and 67 is $25\frac{15}{67}$.

GETTING READY FOR CLASS

After reading through the preceding section, respond in your own words and in complete sentences.

A. What is a mixed number?

B. The expression $5\frac{3}{4}$ is equivalent to what addition problem?

C. The improper fraction $\frac{11}{4}$ is equivalent to what mixed number?

D. Why is $\frac{13}{5}$ an improper fraction, but $\frac{3}{5}$ is not an improper fraction?

Vocabulary Review

Choose the correct words to fill in the blanks below.

addition   denominator   proper fraction

improper fraction   remainder   mixed number

1. A mixed number is the sum of a whole number and a _____.

2. The notation used in writing mixed numbers is always interpreted as _____.

3. We leave out the addition sign when writing a number as a _____.

4. To change a mixed number to an _____, write the mixed number with the addition sign showing and then add the two numbers.

5. To change an improper fraction to a mixed number, divide the numerator by the _____.

6. An answer to a long division problem that contains a _____ can be rewritten as a mixed number.

Problems

A Change each mixed number to an improper fraction.

1. $4\frac{2}{3}$ **2.** $3\frac{5}{8}$ **3.** $5\frac{1}{4}$ **4.** $7\frac{1}{2}$ **5.** $1\frac{5}{8}$ **6.** $1\frac{6}{7}$

7. $15\frac{2}{3}$ **8.** $17\frac{3}{4}$ **9.** $4\frac{20}{21}$ **10.** $5\frac{18}{19}$ **11.** $12\frac{31}{33}$ **12.** $14\frac{29}{31}$

B Change each improper fraction to a mixed number.

13. $\frac{9}{8}$ **14.** $\frac{10}{9}$ **15.** $\frac{19}{4}$ **16.** $\frac{23}{5}$ **17.** $\frac{29}{6}$ **18.** $\frac{7}{2}$

19. $\frac{13}{4}$ **20.** $\frac{41}{15}$ **21.** $\frac{109}{27}$ **22.** $\frac{319}{23}$ **23.** $\frac{428}{15}$ **24.** $\frac{769}{27}$

Applying the Concepts

25. iPad Applications The chart shows the number of each type of applications compatible with the iPad. Use the information to answer the following questions.

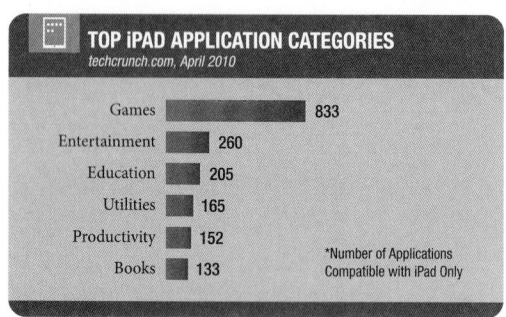

a. The number of game apps is what fraction of the education apps?

b. The number of productivity apps is what fraction of the entertainment apps?

26. NBA Finals The chart shows the number of NBA Finals appearances by several teams. Use the information to answer the following questions.

a. The number of Lakers appearances is what fraction of the Bulls appearances?

b. The number of Pistons appearances is what fraction of the Celtics appearances?

27. Stocks Suppose a stock is selling on a stock exchange for $5\frac{1}{4}$ dollars per share. If the price increases $\frac{3}{4}$ dollar per share, what is the new price of the stock?

28. Stocks Suppose a stock is selling on a stock exchange for $5\frac{1}{4}$ dollars per share. If the price increases 2 dollars per share, what is the new price of the stock?

29. Height If a man is 71 inches tall, then in feet his height is $5\frac{11}{12}$ feet. Change $5\frac{11}{12}$ to an improper fraction.

30. Height If a woman is 63 inches tall, then her height in feet is $\frac{63}{12}$. Write $\frac{63}{12}$ as a mixed number.

31. Gasoline Prices The price of unleaded gasoline is $305\frac{1}{5}$¢ per gallon. Write this number as an improper fraction.

32. Gasoline Prices Suppose the price of gasoline is $308\frac{1}{5}$¢ if purchased with a credit card, but 5¢ less if purchased with cash. What is the cash price of the gasoline?

Getting Ready for the Next Section

Change to improper fractions.

33. $2\frac{3}{4}$

34. $3\frac{1}{5}$

35. $4\frac{5}{8}$

36. $1\frac{3}{5}$

37. $2\frac{4}{5}$

38. $5\frac{9}{10}$

Find the following products. (Multiply.)

39. $\frac{3}{8} \cdot \frac{3}{5}$

40. $\frac{11}{4} \cdot \frac{16}{5}$

41. $\frac{2}{3}\left(\frac{9}{16}\right)$

42. $\frac{7}{10}\left(\frac{5}{21}\right)$

Find the quotients. (Divide.)

43. $\frac{4}{5} \div \frac{7}{8}$

44. $\frac{3}{4} \div \frac{1}{2}$

45. $\frac{8}{5} \div \frac{14}{5}$

46. $\frac{59}{10} \div 2$

Improving Your Quantitative Literacy

Starbucks Stores The chart shows the number of Starbucks stores in each state. Use the information to answer the following questions.

47. According to the chart, which of the following statements is closer to the truth?

   a. There are five times as many stores in California as there are in Illinois.

   b. There are twice as many stores in Washington as there are in New York.

48. According to the chart, which fraction best represents the fraction of stores in the chart that are described below. Choose between $\frac{1}{2}, \frac{1}{3}, \frac{1}{4}$, and $\frac{1}{5}$.

   a. Illinois as compared to California

   b. Colorado as compared to Texas

Find the Mistake

Each sentence below contains a mistake. Circle the mistake and write the correct word(s) or number(s) on the line provided.

   1. For mixed-number notation, writing the whole number next to the fraction implies multiplication.

   2. A shortcut for changing a mixed number to an improper fraction is to multiply the whole number by the numerator of the fraction, and then add the result to the denominator of the fraction.

   3. Changing $6\frac{4}{5}$ to an improper fraction gives us $\frac{29}{5}$.

   4. Writing $\frac{70}{12}$ as a mixed number gives us $6\frac{1}{6}$.

OBJECTIVES

A Multiply mixed numbers.

B Divide mixed numbers.

Video Examples

SECTION 3.3

Practice Problems

1. Multiply: $1\frac{1}{4} \cdot 2\frac{3}{5}$.

Note As you can see, once you have changed each mixed number to an improper fraction, you multiply the resulting fractions the same way you did in Section 2.3.

2. Multiply: $6 \cdot 2\frac{1}{8}$.

Answers

1. $3\frac{1}{4}$

2. $12\frac{3}{4}$

©iStockphoto.com/negaprion

Fire tornadoes are a difficult and dangerous element of firefighting. The visible part of the fire tornado is called the core, where hot ash and combustible gases ignite in flame and rise hundreds of feet to the sky. The outer layer of the tornado is the circulating air that fuels the core with fresh oxygen. As the fire tornado creeps across the land, it sets anything in its path ablaze, hurls debris into the air, and spins so fast it can knock down trees. The funnel of flames can create wind speeds of more than 100 miles per hour, which is as strong as a category 2 hurricane.

Suppose a fire tornado created a wind speed of 100 miles per hour. What if this speed was $2\frac{1}{2}$ times the wind speed outside the tornado? How fast is the wind speed outside the tornado? Recalling our work from the previous section, we know that the number $2\frac{1}{2}$ is a *mixed number*. To answer the question, we must be able to divide 100 by $2\frac{1}{2}$. Division with mixed numbers is one of the topics we will cover in this section.

A Multiplication with Mixed Numbers

EXAMPLE 1   Multiply: $2\frac{3}{4} \cdot 3\frac{1}{5}$.

Solution   We begin by changing each mixed number to an improper fraction.

$$2\frac{3}{4} = \frac{11}{4} \quad \text{and} \quad 3\frac{1}{5} = \frac{16}{5}$$

Using the resulting improper fractions, we multiply as usual. (That is, we multiply numerators and multiply denominators.)

$$\frac{11}{4} \cdot \frac{16}{5} = \frac{11 \cdot 16}{4 \cdot 5}$$

$$= \frac{11 \cdot 4 \cdot 4}{4 \cdot 5}$$

$$= \frac{44}{5} \quad \text{or} \quad 8\frac{4}{5}$$

EXAMPLE 2   Multiply: $3 \cdot 4\frac{5}{8}$.

Solution   Writing each number as an improper fraction, we have

$$3 = \frac{3}{1} \quad \text{and} \quad 4\frac{5}{8} = \frac{37}{8}$$

The complete problem looks like this:

$$3 \cdot 4\frac{5}{8} = \frac{3}{1} \cdot \frac{37}{8}$$ *Change to improper fractions.*

$$= \frac{111}{8}$$ *Multiply numerators and multiply denominators.*

$$= 13\frac{7}{8}$$ *Write the answer as a mixed number.*

B Division with Mixed Numbers

Dividing mixed numbers also requires that we change all mixed numbers to improper fractions before we actually do the division.

EXAMPLE 3   Divide: $1\frac{3}{5} \div 2\frac{4}{5}$.

Solution   We begin by rewriting each mixed number as an improper fraction.

$$1\frac{3}{5} = \frac{8}{5} \quad \text{and} \quad 2\frac{4}{5} = \frac{14}{5}$$

We then divide using the same method we used in Section 2.4. We multiply by the reciprocal of the divisor. Here is the complete problem:

$$1\frac{3}{5} \div 2\frac{4}{5} = \frac{8}{5} \div \frac{14}{5}$$ *Change to improper fractions.*

$$= \frac{8}{5} \cdot \frac{5}{14}$$ *To divide by $\frac{14}{5}$, multiply by $\frac{5}{14}$.*

$$= \frac{8 \cdot 5}{5 \cdot 14}$$ *Multiply numerators and multiply denominators.*

$$= \frac{4 \cdot 2 \cdot 5}{5 \cdot 2 \cdot 7}$$ *Divide out factors common to the numerator and denominator.*

$$= \frac{4}{7}$$ *Answer in lowest terms.*

EXAMPLE 4   Divide: $5\frac{9}{10} \div 2$.

Solution   We change to improper fractions and proceed as usual.

$$5\frac{9}{10} \div 2 = \frac{59}{10} \div \frac{2}{1}$$ *Write each number as an improper fraction.*

$$= \frac{59}{10} \cdot \frac{1}{2}$$ *Write division as multiplication by the reciprocal.*

$$= \frac{59}{20}$$ *Multiply numerators and multiply denominators.*

$$= 2\frac{19}{20}$$ *Change to a mixed number.*

3. Divide: $3\frac{3}{4} \div 2\frac{1}{4}$.

4. Divide: $8\frac{3}{4} \div 5$.

GETTING READY FOR CLASS

After reading through the preceding section, respond in your own words and in complete sentences.

A. What is the first step when multiplying or dividing mixed numbers?

B. What is the reciprocal of $2\frac{4}{5}$?

C. Dividing $5\frac{9}{10}$ by 2 is equivalent to multiplying $5\frac{9}{10}$ by what number?

D. Find $4\frac{5}{8}$ of 3.

Answers

3. $1\frac{2}{3}$

4. $1\frac{3}{4}$

Vocabulary Review

Choose the correct words to fill in the blanks below.

improper fraction   mixed number   divisor   numerators

1. To multiply mixed numbers, first change each _____ to an improper fraction.

2. To multiply improper fractions, multiply _____ and multiply denominators.

3. Division of mixed numbers requires that we change all mixed numbers to _____ before actually doing the dividing.

4. To divide improper fractions, multiply by the reciprocal of the _____ .

Problems

Write your answers as proper fractions or mixed numbers, not as improper fractions.

A Find the following products. (Multiply.)

1. $3\frac{2}{5} \cdot 1\frac{1}{2}$

2. $2\frac{1}{3} \cdot 6\frac{3}{4}$

3. $5\frac{1}{8} \cdot 2\frac{2}{3}$

4. $1\frac{5}{6} \cdot 1\frac{4}{5}$

5. $2\frac{1}{10} \cdot 3\frac{3}{10}$

6. $4\frac{7}{10} \cdot 3\frac{1}{10}$

7. $1\frac{1}{4} \cdot 4\frac{2}{3}$

8. $3\frac{1}{2} \cdot 2\frac{1}{6}$

9. $2 \cdot 4\frac{7}{8}$

10. $10 \cdot 1\frac{1}{4}$

11. $\frac{3}{5} \cdot 5\frac{1}{3}$

12. $\frac{2}{3} \cdot 4\frac{9}{10}$

13. $2\frac{1}{2} \cdot 3\frac{1}{3} \cdot 1\frac{1}{2}$

14. $3\frac{1}{5} \cdot 5\frac{1}{6} \cdot 1\frac{1}{8}$

15. $\frac{3}{4} \cdot 7 \cdot 1\frac{4}{5}$

16. $\frac{7}{8} \cdot 6 \cdot 1\frac{5}{6}$

B Find the following quotients. (Divide.)

17. $3\frac{1}{5} \div 4\frac{1}{2}$

18. $1\frac{4}{5} \div 2\frac{5}{6}$

19. $6\frac{1}{4} \div 3\frac{3}{4}$

20. $8\frac{2}{3} \div 4\frac{1}{3}$

21. $10 \div 2\frac{1}{2}$

22. $12 \div 3\frac{1}{6}$

23. $8\frac{3}{5} \div 2$

24. $12\frac{6}{7} \div 3$

25. $\left(\frac{3}{4} \div 2\frac{1}{2}\right) \div 3$

26. $\frac{7}{8} \div \left(1\frac{1}{4} \div 4\right)$

27. $\left(8 \div 1\frac{1}{4}\right) \div 2$

28. $8 \div \left(1\frac{1}{4} \div 2\right)$

29. $2\frac{1}{2} \cdot \left(3\frac{2}{5} \div 4\right)$

30. $4\frac{3}{5} \cdot \left(2\frac{1}{4} \div 5\right)$

31. Find the product of $2\frac{1}{2}$ and 3.

32. Find the product of $\frac{1}{5}$ and $3\frac{2}{3}$.

33. What is the quotient of $2\frac{3}{4}$ and $3\frac{1}{4}$?

34. What is the quotient of $1\frac{1}{5}$ and $2\frac{2}{5}$?

Applying the Concepts

35. Cooking A certain recipe calls for $2\frac{3}{4}$ cups of sugar. If the recipe is to be doubled, how much sugar should be used?

36. Cooking If a recipe calls for $3\frac{1}{2}$ cups of flour, how much flour will be needed if the recipe is tripled?

37. Cooking If a recipe calls for $2\frac{1}{2}$ cups of sugar, how much sugar is needed to make $\frac{1}{3}$ of the recipe?

38. Cooking A recipe calls for $3\frac{1}{4}$ cups of flour. If Diane is using only half the recipe, how much flour should she use?

39. Number Problem Find $\frac{3}{4}$ of $1\frac{7}{9}$. (Remember that *of* means multiply.)

40. Number Problem Find $\frac{5}{6}$ of $2\frac{4}{15}$.

41. Cost of Gasoline If a gallon of gas costs $305\frac{1}{5}$¢, how much does 8 gallons cost?

42. Cost of Gasoline If a gallon of gas costs $308\frac{1}{5}$¢, how much does $\frac{1}{2}$ gallon cost?

43. Distance Traveled If a car can travel $32\frac{3}{4}$ miles on a gallon of gas, how far will it travel on 5 gallons of gas?

44. Distance Traveled If a new car can travel $20\frac{3}{10}$ miles on 1 gallon of gas, how far can it travel on $\frac{1}{2}$ gallon of gas?

45. Sewing If it takes $1\frac{1}{2}$ yards of material to make a pillow cover, how much material will it take to make 3 pillow covers?

46. Sewing If the material for the pillow covers in Problem 45 costs $2 a yard, how much will it cost for the material for the 3 pillow covers?

Find the area of each figure.

47. Write the numbers in order from smallest to largest.

$$2\frac{1}{8} \qquad \frac{5}{4} \qquad \frac{3}{4} \qquad 1\frac{1}{2}$$

48. Write the numbers in order from smallest to largest.

$$1\frac{3}{8} \qquad \frac{7}{8} \qquad \frac{7}{4} \qquad 1\frac{11}{16}$$

Nutrition The figure below shows nutrition labels for two different cans of corn.

Can 1

Nutrition Facts

Serving Size 1 cup
Servings Per Container About 2 ½

Amount Per Serving

Calories 133   Calories from fat 15

% Daily Value*

Total Fat 3g	3%
Saturated Fat 1g	1%
Cholesterol 0mg	0%
Sodium 530mg	22%
Total Carbohydrate 30g	10%
Dietary Fiber 3g	13%
Sugars 4g	
Protein 4g	

Vitamin A 0%	•	Vitamin C 23%
Calcium 1%	•	Iron 8%

*Percent Daily Values are based on a 2,000 calorie diet

Can 2

Nutrition Facts

Serving Size 1 cup
Servings Per Container About 1 ½

Amount Per Serving

Calories 184   Calories from fat 10

% Daily Value*

Total Fat 2g	2%
Saturated Fat 1g	1%
Cholesterol 0mg	0%
Sodium 730mg	30%
Total Carbohydrate 46g	15%
Dietary Fiber 3g	12%
Sugars 6g	
Protein 4g	

Vitamin A 0%	•	Vitamin C 20%
Calcium 1%	•	Iron 5%

*Percent Daily Values are based on a 2,000 calorie diet

49. Compare the total number of calories in the two cans of corn.

50. Compare the total amount of sugar in the two cans of corn.

51. Compare the total amount of sodium in the two cans of corn.

52. Compare the total amount of protein in the two cans of corn.

Getting Ready for the Next Section

53. Write as equivalent fractions with denominator 15.

a. $\frac{2}{3}$ **b.** $\frac{1}{5}$ **c.** $\frac{3}{5}$ **d.** $\frac{1}{3}$

54. Write as equivalent fractions with denominator 12.

a. $\frac{3}{4}$ **b.** $\frac{1}{3}$ **c.** $\frac{5}{6}$ **d.** $\frac{1}{4}$

55. Write as equivalent fractions with denominator 20.

    a. $\dfrac{1}{4}$ **b.** $\dfrac{3}{5}$ **c.** $\dfrac{9}{10}$ **d.** $\dfrac{1}{10}$

56. Write as equivalent fractions with denominator 24.

    a. $\dfrac{3}{4}$ **b.** $\dfrac{7}{8}$ **c.** $\dfrac{5}{8}$ **d.** $\dfrac{3}{8}$

Add or subtract the following fractions, as indicated.

57. $\dfrac{2}{3} + \dfrac{1}{5}$
    58. $\dfrac{3}{4} + \dfrac{5}{6}$
    59. $\dfrac{2}{3} + \dfrac{8}{9}$
    60. $\dfrac{1}{4} + \dfrac{3}{5} + \dfrac{9}{10}$

61. $\dfrac{9}{10} - \dfrac{3}{10}$
    62. $\dfrac{7}{10} - \dfrac{3}{5}$
    63. $\dfrac{5}{12} - \dfrac{1}{6}$
    64. $\dfrac{2}{3} - \dfrac{1}{4} - \dfrac{1}{6}$

Find the Mistake

Each sentence below contains a mistake. Circle the mistake and write the correct word(s) or number(s) on the line provided.

1. To multiply two mixed numbers, multiply the whole numbers and multiply the fractions.

_____

2. Multiplying $4\dfrac{3}{8}$ and $9\dfrac{2}{7}$ gives us the mixed number $45\dfrac{1}{3}$. _____

3. To divide the mixed numbers $12\dfrac{2}{5}$ and $3\dfrac{12}{5}$, change the mixed numbers to improper fractions and then multiply numerators and denominators. _____

4. The answer to the division problem $3\dfrac{9}{14} \div 2$ written as a mixed number is $\dfrac{51}{28}$.

_____

Landmark Review: Checking Your Progress

Find the following sums and differences and reduce to lowest terms.

1. $\dfrac{7}{10} + \dfrac{3}{10}$

2. $\dfrac{2}{5} - \dfrac{1}{5}$

3. $\dfrac{2}{3} + \dfrac{3}{5}$

4. $\dfrac{1}{2} + \dfrac{3}{4}$

5. $\dfrac{3}{5} + \dfrac{2}{3} - \dfrac{4}{7}$

6. $\dfrac{4 + x}{3} - \dfrac{2}{3}$

7. Find the sum of $\dfrac{2}{3}$, $\dfrac{1}{5}$, and $\dfrac{1}{2}$.

8. Find the difference of $\dfrac{7}{10}$ and $\dfrac{3}{5}$.

Change each mixed number to an improper fraction.

9. $3\dfrac{5}{8}$

10. $4\dfrac{2}{3}$

11. $10\dfrac{1}{2}$

12. $1\dfrac{1}{4}$

Change each improper fraction to a mixed number.

13. $\dfrac{14}{3}$

14. $\dfrac{23}{5}$

15. $\dfrac{7}{2}$

16. $\dfrac{42}{17}$

Perform the indicated operations.

17. $4\dfrac{1}{4} \cdot 5\dfrac{1}{2}$

18. $3\dfrac{1}{3} \cdot 2\dfrac{5}{6}$

19. $5\dfrac{2}{3} \cdot 6\dfrac{5}{8}$

20. $5\dfrac{1}{4} \div 4\dfrac{3}{8}$

21. $3\dfrac{7}{10} \div 1\dfrac{3}{5}$

22. $4\dfrac{5}{8} \div 2\dfrac{2}{3}$

3.4 Addition and Subtraction with Mixed Numbers

OBJECTIVES

A Add mixed numbers.

B Subtract mixed numbers.

Dock diving is a sport where dogs compete to see who can jump the highest or the farthest off the end of a dock into a body of water. Many of the dogs' handlers use a chase object to lure the dog as far as possible off the dock. The handler commands the dog to begin a running start and then throws the chase object out over the water. The dog leaps after the object, and once he splashes into the water, an event official measures his jump distance. The official measures the dog's final distance from the end of the dock to the point where the base of the dog's tail first hit the water.

In this section, we will work addition and subtraction problems that involve mixed numbers. Let's say that the top two dogs jumped 21 feet $10\frac{1}{4}$ inches and 21 feet $11\frac{7}{8}$ inches. How much further did the latter dog jump? To solve this problem, we need to know how to subtract $10\frac{1}{4}$ from $11\frac{7}{8}$. After reading this section, you will be more comfortable working with mixed numbers such as these.

The notation we use for mixed numbers is especially useful for addition and subtraction. When adding and subtracting mixed numbers, we will assume you recall from section 3.1 how to go about finding a least common denominator (LCD).

A Addition with Mixed Numbers

EXAMPLE 1 Add: $3\frac{2}{3} + 4\frac{1}{5}$.

Solution We begin by writing each mixed number showing the + sign. We then apply the commutative and associative properties to rearrange the order and grouping.

$$3\frac{2}{3} + 4\frac{1}{5} = 3 + \frac{2}{3} + 4 + \frac{1}{5} \qquad \text{Expand each number to show the + sign.}$$

$$= 3 + 4 + \frac{2}{3} + \frac{1}{5} \qquad \text{Commutative property}$$

$$= (3 + 4) + \left(\frac{2}{3} + \frac{1}{5}\right) \qquad \text{Associative property}$$

$$= 7 + \left(\frac{5 \cdot 2}{5 \cdot 3} + \frac{3 \cdot 1}{3 \cdot 5}\right) \qquad \text{Add } 3 + 4 = 7; \text{ then multiply to get the LCD.}$$

$$= 7 + \left(\frac{10}{15} + \frac{3}{15}\right) \qquad \text{Write each fraction with the LCD.}$$

$$= 7 + \frac{13}{15} \qquad \text{Add the numerators.}$$

$$= 7\frac{13}{15} \qquad \text{Write the answer in mixed-number notation.}$$

Video Examples
SECTION 3.4

Practice Problems
1. Add: $2\frac{1}{3} + 3\frac{3}{4}$.

Answer

1. $6\frac{1}{12}$

As you can see, we obtain our result by adding the whole-number parts ($3 + 4 = 7$) and the fraction parts $\left(\frac{2}{3} + \frac{1}{5} = \frac{13}{15}\right)$ of each mixed number. Knowing this, we can save ourselves some writing by doing the same problem in columns.

$$3\frac{2}{3} = 3\frac{2 \cdot 5}{3 \cdot 5} = 3\frac{10}{15}$$

$$+ \, 4\frac{1}{5} = 4\frac{1 \cdot 3}{5 \cdot 3} = 4\frac{3}{15} \qquad \text{\textit{Write each fraction with LCD 15}}$$

$$\overline{\phantom{+ \, 4\frac{1}{5} = 4\frac{1 \cdot 3}{5 \cdot 3} = }7\frac{13}{15}} \qquad \text{\textit{Add whole numbers, then add fractions.}}$$

The second method shown above requires less writing and lends itself to mixed-number notation. We will use this method for the rest of this section.

EXAMPLE 2   Add: $5\frac{3}{4} + 9\frac{5}{6}$.

Solution   The LCD for 4 and 6 is 12. Writing the mixed numbers in a column and then adding looks like this:

$$5\frac{3}{4} = 5\frac{3 \cdot 3}{4 \cdot 3} = \;\; 5\frac{9}{12}$$

$$+ \, 9\frac{5}{6} = 9\frac{5 \cdot 2}{6 \cdot 2} = \;\; 9\frac{10}{12}$$

$$\overline{\phantom{+ \, 9\frac{5}{6} = 9\frac{5 \cdot 2}{6 \cdot 2} = }14\frac{19}{12}}$$

The fraction part of the answer is an improper fraction. We rewrite it as a whole number and a proper fraction.

$$14\frac{19}{12} = 14 + \frac{19}{12} \qquad \text{\textit{Write the mixed number with a + sign.}}$$

$$= 14 + 1\frac{7}{12} \qquad \text{\textit{Write }} \tfrac{19}{12} \text{\textit{ as a mixed number.}}$$

$$= 15\frac{7}{12} \qquad \text{\textit{Add 14 and 1.}}$$

EXAMPLE 3   Add: $5\frac{2}{3} + 6\frac{8}{9}$.

Solution

$$5\frac{2}{3} = 5\frac{2 \cdot 3}{3 \cdot 3} = \;\; 5\frac{6}{9}$$

$$+ \, 6\frac{8}{9} = 6\frac{8}{9} = \;\; 6\frac{8}{9}$$

$$\overline{\phantom{+ \, 6\frac{8}{9} = 6\frac{8}{9} = }11\frac{14}{9} = 12\frac{5}{9}}$$

The last step involves writing $\frac{14}{9}$ as $1\frac{5}{9}$ and then adding 11 and 1 to get 12.

EXAMPLE 4   Add: $3\frac{1}{4} + 2\frac{3}{5} + 1\frac{9}{10}$.

Solution   The LCD is 20. We rewrite each fraction as an equivalent fraction with denominator 20 and add.

$$3\frac{1}{4} = 3\frac{1 \cdot 5}{4 \cdot 5} = 3\frac{5}{20}$$

$$2\frac{3}{5} = 2\frac{3 \cdot 4}{5 \cdot 4} = 2\frac{12}{20}$$

$$+ \, 1\frac{9}{10} = 1\frac{9 \cdot 2}{10 \cdot 2} = 1\frac{18}{20}$$

$$\overline{\phantom{+ \, 1\frac{9}{10} = 1\frac{9 \cdot 2}{10 \cdot 2} = }6\frac{35}{20} = 7\frac{15}{20} = 7\frac{3}{4}} \qquad \text{\textit{Reduce to lowest terms.}}$$

$$\frac{35}{20} = 1\frac{15}{20} \qquad \text{\textit{Change to a mixed number.}}$$

2. Redo Practice Problem 1 using method 2.

Note   Once you see how to change from a whole number and an improper fraction to a whole number and a proper fraction, you will be able to do this step without showing any work.

3. Add: $4\frac{3}{4} + 5\frac{3}{8}$.

4. Add: $2\frac{2}{3} + 3\frac{1}{4} + 5\frac{5}{6}$.

Answers

2. $6\frac{1}{12}$

3. $10\frac{1}{8}$

4. $11\frac{3}{4}$

We should note here that we could have worked each of the first four examples in this section by first changing each mixed number to an improper fraction and then adding as we did earlier in this chapter. To illustrate, if we were to work Example 4 this way, it would look like this:

$$3\frac{1}{4} + 2\frac{3}{5} + 1\frac{9}{10} = \frac{13}{4} + \frac{13}{5} + \frac{19}{10}$$ Change to improper fractions.

$$= \frac{13 \cdot 5}{4 \cdot 5} + \frac{13 \cdot 4}{5 \cdot 4} + \frac{19 \cdot 2}{10 \cdot 2}$$ LCD is 20.

$$= \frac{65}{20} + \frac{52}{20} + \frac{38}{20}$$ Equivalent fractions

$$= \frac{155}{20}$$ Add numerators.

$$= 7\frac{15}{20} = 7\frac{3}{4}$$ Change to a mixed number, and reduce

As you can see, the result is the same as the result we obtained in Example 4.

There are advantages to both methods. The method just shown works well when the whole-number parts of the mixed numbers are small. The vertical method shown in Examples 1–4 works well when the whole-number parts of the mixed numbers are large.

B Subtraction with Mixed Numbers

Subtraction with mixed numbers is very similar to addition with mixed numbers.

EXAMPLE 5   Subtract: $3\frac{9}{10} - 1\frac{3}{10}$.

5. Subtract: $4\frac{5}{8} - 1\frac{1}{8}$.

Solution   Because the denominators are the same, we simply subtract the whole numbers and subtract the fractions.

$$\begin{array}{r} 3\frac{9}{10} \\ - 1\frac{3}{10} \\ \hline 2\frac{6}{10} = 2\frac{3}{5} \end{array}$$ Reduce to lowest terms.

An easy way to visualize the results in Example 5 is to imagine 3 dollar bills and 9 dimes in your pocket. If you spend 1 dollar and 3 dimes, you will have 2 dollars and 6 dimes left.

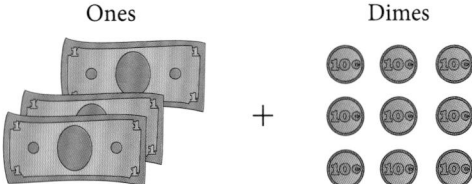

Ones   Dimes

EXAMPLE 6   Subtract: $12\frac{7}{10} - 8\frac{3}{5}$.

6. Subtract: $8\frac{1}{2} - 3\frac{1}{6}$.

Solution   The common denominator is 10. We must rewrite $8\frac{3}{5}$ as an equivalent fraction with denominator 10.

$$\begin{array}{r} 12\frac{7}{10} = 12\frac{7}{10} = 12\frac{7}{10} \\ - 8\frac{3}{5} = -8\frac{3 \cdot 2}{5 \cdot 2} = -8\frac{6}{10} \\ \hline 4\frac{1}{10} \end{array}$$

7. Subtract: $12 - 8\frac{5}{9}$.

Note Convince yourself that 10 is the same as $9\frac{7}{7}$. The reason we choose to write the 1 we borrowed as $\frac{7}{7}$ is that the fraction we eventually subtracted from $\frac{7}{7}$ was $\frac{2}{7}$. Both fractions must have the same denominator, 7, so that we can subtract.

8. Subtract: $12\frac{1}{6} - 5\frac{5}{6}$.

9. Subtract: $9\frac{1}{3} - 3\frac{3}{4}$.

EXAMPLE 7   Subtract: $10 - 5\frac{2}{7}$.

Solution   In order to have a fraction from which to subtract $\frac{2}{7}$, we borrow 1 from 10 and rewrite the 1 we borrow as $\frac{7}{7}$. The process looks like this:

$$
\begin{array}{r}
10 = \quad 9\dfrac{7}{7} \quad \longleftarrow \text{We rewrite 10 as } 9 + 1, \text{which is } 9 + \tfrac{7}{7} = 9\tfrac{7}{7}. \\[2mm]
- \ 5\dfrac{2}{7} = - 5\dfrac{2}{7} \quad \text{Then we can subtract as usual.} \\[1mm]
\hline
4\dfrac{5}{7}
\end{array}
$$

EXAMPLE 8   Subtract: $8\frac{1}{4} - 3\frac{3}{4}$.

Solution   Because $\frac{3}{4}$ is larger than $\frac{1}{4}$, we again need to borrow 1 from the whole number. The 1 that we borrow from the 8 is rewritten as $\frac{4}{4}$, because 4 is the denominator of both fractions.

$$
\begin{array}{r}
8\dfrac{1}{4} = \quad 7\dfrac{5}{4} \quad \longleftarrow \text{Borrow 1 in the form } \tfrac{4}{4}; \text{ then } \tfrac{4}{4} + \tfrac{1}{4} = \tfrac{5}{4}. \\[2mm]
- \ 3\dfrac{3}{4} = - 3\dfrac{3}{4} \\[1mm]
\hline
4\dfrac{2}{4} = 4\dfrac{1}{2} \quad \text{Reduce to lowest terms.}
\end{array}
$$

EXAMPLE 9   Subtract: $4\frac{3}{4} - 1\frac{5}{6}$.

Solution   This is about as complicated as it gets with subtraction of mixed numbers. We begin by rewriting each fraction with the common denominator 12.

$$
\begin{array}{r}
4\dfrac{3}{4} = \quad 4\dfrac{3 \cdot 3}{4 \cdot 3} = \quad 4\dfrac{9}{12} \\[2mm]
- \ 1\dfrac{5}{6} = - 1\dfrac{5 \cdot 2}{6 \cdot 2} = - 1\dfrac{10}{12}
\end{array}
$$

Because $\frac{10}{12}$ is larger than $\frac{9}{12}$, we must borrow 1 from 4 in the form $\frac{12}{12}$ before we subtract.

$$
\begin{array}{r}
4\dfrac{9}{12} = \quad 3\dfrac{21}{12} \quad \longleftarrow 4 = 3 + 1 = 3 + \dfrac{12}{12}, \text{ so } 4\dfrac{9}{12} = \left(3 + \dfrac{12}{12}\right) + \dfrac{9}{12} \\[2mm]
- \ 1\dfrac{10}{12} = - 1\dfrac{10}{12} \qquad\qquad\qquad\qquad = 3 + \left(\dfrac{12}{12} + \dfrac{9}{12}\right) \\[1mm]
\hline
2\dfrac{11}{12} \qquad\qquad\qquad\qquad\qquad = 3 + \dfrac{21}{12} \\[2mm]
= 3\dfrac{21}{12}
\end{array}
$$

GETTING READY FOR CLASS

After reading through the preceding section, respond in your own words and in complete sentences.

A. Is it necessary to "borrow" when subtracting $1\frac{3}{10}$ from $3\frac{9}{10}$?

B. To subtract $1\frac{2}{7}$ from 10, it is necessary to rewrite 10 as what mixed number?

C. To subtract $11\frac{20}{30}$ from $15\frac{3}{30}$, it is necessary to rewrite $15\frac{3}{30}$ as what mixed number?

D. Rewrite $14\frac{19}{12}$ so that the fraction part is a proper fraction instead of an improper fraction.

Answers

7. $3\frac{4}{9}$

8. $6\frac{1}{3}$

9. $5\frac{7}{12}$

Vocabulary Review

Choose the correct words to fill in the blanks below.

proper   columns   addition sign   improper   LCD   borrow

1. To add mixed numbers, rewrite each mixed number showing the _____, and then apply the commutative and associative properties.

2. Adding mixed numbers in _____ requires less writing than the method that uses the addition sign and grouping.

3. When adding mixed numbers in columns, (1) add the whole numbers, (2) write each fraction with the _____, and (3) add the fractions.

4. If your answer to a mixed-number addition problem is a(n) _____ fraction, rewrite it as a whole number and a _____ fraction.

5. When subtracting mixed numbers, if the fraction in the second mixed number is larger than the fraction in the first mixed number, _____ 1 from the whole number in the first mixed number.

Problems

A B Add and subtract the following mixed numbers as indicated.

1. $2\frac{1}{5} + 3\frac{3}{5}$

2. $8\frac{2}{9} + 1\frac{5}{9}$

3. $4\frac{3}{10} + 8\frac{1}{10}$

4. $5\frac{2}{7} + 3\frac{3}{7}$

5. $6\frac{8}{9} - 3\frac{4}{9}$

6. $12\frac{5}{12} - 7\frac{1}{12}$

7. $9\frac{1}{6} + 2\frac{5}{6}$

8. $9\frac{1}{4} + 5\frac{3}{4}$

9. $3\frac{5}{8} - 2\frac{1}{4}$

10. $7\frac{9}{10} - 6\frac{3}{5}$

11. $11\frac{1}{3} + 2\frac{5}{6}$

12. $1\frac{5}{8} + 2\frac{1}{2}$

13. $7\frac{5}{12} - 3\frac{1}{3}$

14. $7\frac{3}{4} - 3\frac{5}{12}$

15. $6\frac{1}{3} - 4\frac{1}{4}$

16. $5\frac{4}{5} - 3\frac{1}{3}$

17. $10\frac{5}{6} + 15\frac{3}{4}$

18. $11\frac{7}{8} + 9\frac{1}{6}$

19. $18\frac{1}{8} - 6\frac{3}{4}$

20. $10\frac{1}{3} - 4\frac{1}{6}$

21. $5\frac{2}{3}$
$+\ 6\frac{1}{3}$

22. $8\frac{5}{6}$
$+\ 9\frac{5}{6}$

23. $10\frac{13}{16}$
$-\ 8\frac{5}{16}$

24. $17\frac{7}{12}$
$-\ 9\frac{5}{12}$

25. $6\frac{1}{2}$
$+\ 2\frac{5}{14}$

26. $9\frac{11}{12}$
$+\ 4\frac{1}{6}$

27. $1\frac{5}{8}$
$+\ 1\frac{3}{4}$

28. $7\frac{6}{7}$
$+\ 2\frac{3}{14}$

29. $4\frac{2}{3}$
$+\ 5\frac{3}{5}$

30. $9\frac{4}{9}$
$+\ 1\frac{1}{6}$

31. $5\frac{4}{10}$
$-\ 3\frac{1}{3}$

32. $12\frac{7}{8}$
$-\ 3\frac{5}{6}$

A Find the following sums. (Add.)

33. $1\frac{1}{4} + 2\frac{3}{4} + 5$

34. $6 + 5\frac{3}{5} + 8\frac{2}{5}$

35. $7\frac{1}{10} + 8\frac{3}{10} + 2\frac{7}{10}$

36. $5\frac{2}{7} + 8\frac{1}{7} + 3\frac{5}{7}$

37. $\frac{3}{4} + 8\frac{1}{4} + 5$

38. $\frac{5}{8} + 1\frac{1}{8} + 7$

39. $3\frac{1}{2} + 8\frac{1}{3} + 5\frac{1}{6}$

40. $4\frac{1}{5} + 7\frac{1}{3} + 8\frac{1}{15}$

41. $8\frac{2}{3}$
$9\frac{1}{8}$
$+\ 6\frac{1}{4}$

42. $7\frac{3}{5}$
$8\frac{2}{3}$
$+\ 1\frac{1}{5}$

43. $6\frac{1}{7}$
$9\frac{3}{14}$
$+\ 12\frac{1}{2}$

44. $1\frac{5}{6}$
$2\frac{3}{4}$
$+\ 5\frac{1}{2}$

45. $10\frac{1}{20}$
$11\frac{4}{5}$
$+\ 15\frac{3}{10}$

46. $18\frac{7}{12}$
$19\frac{3}{16}$
$+\ 10\frac{2}{3}$

47. $10\frac{3}{4}$
$12\frac{5}{6}$
$+\ 9\frac{5}{8}$

48. $4\frac{5}{9}$
$9\frac{2}{3}$
$+\ 8\frac{5}{6}$

B The following problems all involve the concept of borrowing. Subtract in each case.

49. $8 - 1\dfrac{3}{4}$

50. $5 - 3\dfrac{1}{3}$

51. $15 - 5\dfrac{3}{10}$

52. $24 - 10\dfrac{5}{12}$

53. $8\dfrac{1}{4} - 2\dfrac{3}{4}$

54. $12\dfrac{3}{10} - 5\dfrac{7}{10}$

55. $9\dfrac{1}{3} - 8\dfrac{2}{3}$

56. $7\dfrac{1}{6} - 6\dfrac{5}{6}$

57. $4\dfrac{1}{4} - 2\dfrac{1}{3}$

58. $6\dfrac{1}{5} - 1\dfrac{2}{3}$

59. $9\dfrac{2}{3} - 5\dfrac{3}{4}$

60. $12\dfrac{5}{6} - 8\dfrac{7}{8}$

61. $16\dfrac{3}{4} - 10\dfrac{4}{5}$

62. $18\dfrac{5}{12} - 9\dfrac{3}{4}$

63. $10\dfrac{3}{10} - 4\dfrac{4}{5}$

64. $9\dfrac{4}{7} - 7\dfrac{2}{3}$

65. $13\dfrac{1}{6} - 12\dfrac{5}{8}$

66. $21\dfrac{2}{5} - 20\dfrac{5}{6}$

67. $19\dfrac{1}{4} - 8\dfrac{5}{6}$

68. $22\dfrac{7}{10} - 18\dfrac{4}{5}$

69. Find the difference between $6\dfrac{1}{5}$ and $2\dfrac{7}{10}$.

70. Give the difference between $5\dfrac{1}{3}$ and $1\dfrac{5}{6}$.

71. Find the sum of $3\dfrac{1}{8}$ and $2\dfrac{3}{5}$.

72. Find the sum of $1\dfrac{5}{6}$ and $3\dfrac{4}{9}$.

Applying the Concepts

73. Building Two pieces of molding $5\dfrac{7}{8}$ inches and $6\dfrac{3}{8}$ inches long are placed end to end. What is the total length of the two pieces of molding together?

74. Jogging A jogger runs $2\dfrac{1}{2}$ miles on Monday, $3\dfrac{1}{4}$ miles on Tuesday, and $2\dfrac{2}{5}$ miles on Wednesday. What is the jogger's total mileage for this 3-day period?

75. Horse Racing If a racehorse runs at both Churchill Downs and Keeneland racetracks, she will run $1\dfrac{3}{8}$ miles at Churchill Downs, and $1\dfrac{1}{2}$ miles at Keeneland. How much further will she run at Keeneland?

76. Triple Crown The three races that constitute the Triple Crown in horse racing are shown in the table.

   a. Write the distances in order from smallest to largest.

   b. How much longer is the Belmont Stakes race than the Preakness Stakes?

Race	Distance (miles)
Kentucky Derby	$1\dfrac{1}{4}$
Preakness Stakes	$1\dfrac{3}{16}$
Belmont Stakes	$1\dfrac{1}{2}$

Source: ESPN.com

77. Length of Jeans A pair of jeans is $32\frac{1}{2}$ inches long. How long are the jeans after they have been washed if they shrink $1\frac{1}{3}$ inches?

78. Manufacturing A clothing manufacturer has two rolls of cloth. One roll is $35\frac{1}{2}$ yards, and the other is $62\frac{5}{8}$ yards. What is the total number of yards in the two rolls?

Area and Perimeter The diagrams below show the dimensions of playing fields for the National Football League (NFL), the Canadian Football League, and arena football.

Football Fields

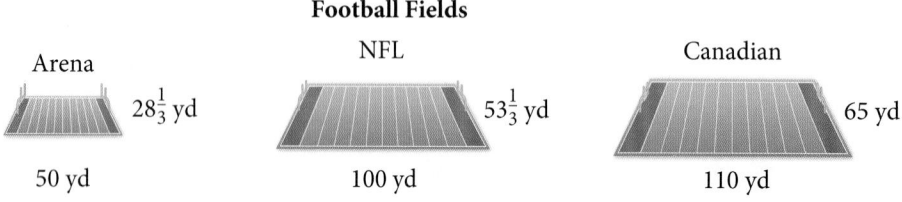

Arena   NFL   Canadian

$28\frac{1}{3}$ yd $53\frac{1}{3}$ yd   65 yd

50 yd   100 yd   110 yd

79. Find the perimeter of each football field.

80. Find the area of each football field.

Stock Prices In March 1995, rumors that Michael Jordan would return to basketball sent stock prices for the companies whose products he endorses higher. The table below gives some of the details of those increases. Use the table to work Problems 81-84.

81. a. Find the difference in the price of Nike stock between March 13 and March 8.

     b. If you owned 100 shares of Nike stock, how much more are the 100 shares worth on March 13 than on March 8?

82. a. Find the difference in price of General Mills stock between March 13 and March 8.

     b. If you owned 1,000 shares of General Mills stock on March 8, how much more would they be worth on March 13?

Stock Prices for Companies with Michael Jordan Endorsements			
Company	Product Endorsed	Stock Price (Dollars) 3/8/95	3/13/95
Nike	Air Jordans	$74\frac{7}{8}$	$77\frac{3}{8}$
Quaker Oats	Gatorade	$32\frac{1}{4}$	$32\frac{5}{8}$
General Mills	Wheaties	$60\frac{1}{2}$	$63\frac{3}{8}$
McDonald's		$32\frac{7}{8}$	$34\frac{3}{8}$

83. If you owned 200 shares of McDonald's stock on March 8, how much more would they be worth on March 13?

84. If you owned 100 shares of McDonald's stock on March 8, how much more would they be worth on March 13?

Getting Ready for the Next Section

Multiply or divide as indicated.

85. $\dfrac{11}{8} \cdot \dfrac{29}{8}$

86. $\dfrac{3}{4} \div \dfrac{5}{6}$

87. $\dfrac{7}{6} \cdot \dfrac{12}{7}$

88. $10\dfrac{1}{3} \div 8\dfrac{2}{3}$

Combine.

89. $\dfrac{3}{4} + \dfrac{5}{8}$

90. $\dfrac{1}{2} + \dfrac{2}{3}$

91. $2\dfrac{3}{8} + 1\dfrac{1}{4}$

92. $3\dfrac{2}{3} + 4\dfrac{1}{3}$

Improving Your Quantitative Literacy

93. Horse Racing A column on horse racing in the *Daily News* in Los Angeles reported that the horse Action This Day ran 3 furlongs in $35\dfrac{1}{5}$ seconds and another horse, Halfbridled, went two-fifths of a second faster. How many seconds did it take Halfbridled to run 3 furlongs?

Find the Mistake

Each sentence below contains a mistake. Circle the mistake and write the correct word(s) or number(s) on the line provided.

1. To begin adding $3\dfrac{9}{14}$ and $5\dfrac{1}{3}$, write each mixed number with the addition sign and then apply the commutative and associative properties, such that $\left(3 + \dfrac{2}{5}\right) + \left(5 + \dfrac{1}{3}\right)$. _____

2. The final answer for the problem $5\dfrac{2}{3} + 6\dfrac{7}{9}$ is $11\dfrac{13}{9}$. _____

3. The first step when subtracting $8 - 3\dfrac{2}{7} = 4\dfrac{5}{7}$, is to borrow 1 from 8 in the form of $\dfrac{8}{8}$. _____

4. The work for the subtraction problem $5\dfrac{2}{3} - 2\dfrac{4}{5}$ is shown below. Circle the mistake and write the correct work on the lines provided.

$$5\dfrac{2}{3} = 5\dfrac{2 \cdot 5}{3 \cdot 5} = 5\dfrac{10}{15} = 5\left(\dfrac{10}{15} + \dfrac{15}{15}\right) = 5\dfrac{25}{15}$$ _____

$$-\ 2\dfrac{4}{5} = 2\dfrac{4 \cdot 3}{5 \cdot 3} = 2\dfrac{12}{15} \qquad \rightarrow \qquad 2\dfrac{12}{15}$$ _____

$$\overline{ 3\dfrac{13}{15}}$$ _____

Supplies Needed

A A piece of paper

B A pen or pencil

Fractions and Word Frequency

Choose the first paragraph from one of the five sections in this chapter. Disregarding any numbers or fractions, count the total number of words in the paragraph. Now count the words grouped by the number of letters each one contains. For example, find the total number of 1-letter words in the paragraph. Do the same for 2-letter words, 3-letter words, and so on. Group any words 9 letters or greater into a single category. Create a table with this information.

Now using the information from your table, add a new column that represents each category of words as a fraction and reduce.

Answer the following questions using your reduced fractions.

1. What fraction represents the total number of words that contain two to five letters?

2. What fraction represents the total number of words that contain six to eight letters?

3. What fraction represents the difference between the category with the most words and the category with the least words?

Note: Gathering this information is a way to analyze the frequency of words in a paragraph. We will work more with frequency later in the book.

Chapter **3** Summary

Least Common Denominator (LCD) [3.1]

The *least common denominator* (LCD) for a set of denominators is the smallest number that is exactly divisible by each denominator.

Addition and Subtraction of Fractions [3.1]

To add (or subtract) two fractions with a common denominator, add (or subtract) numerators and use the common denominator. *In symbols:* If a, b, and c are numbers with c not equal to 0, then

$$\frac{a}{c} + \frac{b}{c} = \frac{a+b}{c} \quad \text{and} \quad \frac{a}{c} - \frac{b}{c} = \frac{a-b}{c}$$

EXAMPLES

1. $\dfrac{1}{8} + \dfrac{3}{8} = \dfrac{1+3}{8}$

$= \dfrac{4}{8}$

$= \dfrac{1}{2}$

Additional Facts about Fractions

1. In some books, fractions are called *rational numbers*.

2. Every whole number can be written as a fraction with a denominator of 1.

3. The commutative, associative, and distributive properties are true for fractions.

4. The word *of* as used in the expression "$\frac{2}{3}$ *of* 12" indicates that we are to multiply $\frac{2}{3}$ and 12.

5. Two fractions with the same value are called *equivalent fractions*.

Mixed-Number Notation [3.2]

A mixed number is the sum of a whole number and a fraction. The $+$ sign is not shown when we write mixed numbers; it is implied. The mixed number $4\frac{2}{3}$ is actually the sum $4 + \frac{2}{3}$.

Changing Mixed Numbers to Improper Fractions [3.2]

To change a mixed number to an improper fraction, we write the mixed number showing the $+$ sign and add as usual. The result is the same if we multiply the denominator of the fraction by the whole number and add what we get to the numerator of the fraction, putting this result over the denominator of the fraction.

2. $\underset{\uparrow}{4\frac{2}{3}} = \dfrac{3 \cdot 4 + 2}{3} = \underset{\uparrow}{\dfrac{14}{3}}$

Mixed number   Improper fraction

Changing an Improper Fraction to a Mixed Number [3.2]

To change an improper fraction to a mixed number, divide the denominator into the numerator. The quotient is the whole-number part of the mixed number. The fraction part is the remainder over the divisor.

3. Change $\dfrac{14}{3}$ to a mixed number.

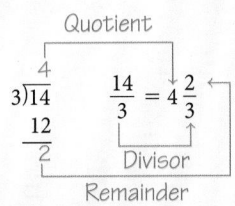

Chapter 3   Summary

4. $2\dfrac{1}{3} \cdot 1\dfrac{3}{4} = \dfrac{7}{3} \cdot \dfrac{7}{4} = \dfrac{49}{12} = 4\dfrac{1}{12}$

Multiplication and Division with Mixed Numbers [3.3]

To multiply or divide two mixed numbers, change each to an improper fraction and multiply or divide as usual.

5.
$$\begin{aligned} 3\dfrac{4}{9} &= 3\dfrac{4}{9} &= 3\dfrac{4}{9} \\ + 2\dfrac{2}{3} &= 2\dfrac{2 \cdot 3}{3 \cdot 3} &= 2\dfrac{6}{9} \\ \hline & & 5\dfrac{10}{9} = 6\dfrac{1}{9} \end{aligned}$$

Common denominator

Add fractions.

Add whole numbers.

Addition and Subtraction with Mixed Numbers [3.4]

To add or subtract two mixed numbers, add or subtract the whole-number parts and the fraction parts separately. This is best done with the numbers written in columns.

6.
$$\begin{aligned} 4\dfrac{1}{3} &= & 4\dfrac{2}{6} &= & 3\dfrac{8}{6} \\ -1\dfrac{5}{6} &= & -1\dfrac{5}{6} &= & -1\dfrac{5}{6} \\ \hline & & & & 2\dfrac{3}{6} = 2\dfrac{1}{2} \end{aligned}$$

Borrowing in Subtraction with Mixed Numbers [3.4]

It is sometimes necessary to borrow when doing subtraction with mixed numbers. We always change to a common denominator before we actually borrow.

> **COMMON MISTAKE**
>
> 1. The most common mistake when working with fractions occurs when we try to add two fractions without using a common denominator. For example,
>
> $$\dfrac{2}{3} + \dfrac{4}{5} \neq \dfrac{2+4}{3+5}$$
>
> If the two fractions we are trying to add don't have the same denominators, then we *must* rewrite each one as an equivalent fraction with a common denominator. *We never add denominators when adding fractions.*
> **Note** We do *not* need a common denominator when multiplying fractions.
>
> 2. A common mistake when working with mixed numbers is to confuse mixed-number notation for multiplication of fractions. The notation $3\dfrac{2}{5}$ does *not* mean 3 *times* $\dfrac{2}{5}$. It means 3 *plus* $\dfrac{2}{5}$.
>
> 3. Another mistake occurs when multiplying mixed numbers. The mistake occurs when we don't change the mixed number to an improper fraction before multiplying and instead try to multiply the whole numbers and fractions separately.
>
> $$2\dfrac{1}{2} \cdot 3\dfrac{1}{3} = (2 \cdot 3) + \left(\dfrac{1}{2} \cdot \dfrac{1}{3}\right) \qquad \text{Mistake}$$
>
> $$= 6 + \dfrac{1}{6}$$
>
> $$= 6\dfrac{1}{6}$$
>
> Remember, the correct way to multiply mixed numbers is to first change to improper fractions and then multiply numerators and multiply denominators. This is correct:
>
> $$2\dfrac{1}{2} \cdot 3\dfrac{1}{3} = \dfrac{5}{2} \cdot \dfrac{10}{3} = \dfrac{50}{6} = 8\dfrac{2}{6} = 8\dfrac{1}{3} \qquad \text{Correct}$$

Perform the indicated operations. Reduce all answers to lowest terms. [3.1, 3.2]

1. $\dfrac{7}{9} + \dfrac{5}{9}$

2. $\dfrac{7}{12} - \dfrac{1}{12}$

3. $4 + \dfrac{4}{5}$

4. $\dfrac{3}{8} + \dfrac{1}{4}$

5. $\dfrac{1}{2} + \dfrac{7}{12} + \dfrac{3}{20}$

6. $9\dfrac{2}{3} + 2\dfrac{3}{5}$

7. $6\dfrac{2}{5} - 4\dfrac{3}{10}$

8. $9 - \dfrac{3}{5}$

9. $\dfrac{5}{8} - \dfrac{3}{16}$

10. $\dfrac{7}{8} + \dfrac{3}{4} + 4$

11. $\dfrac{9}{24} - \dfrac{1}{8}$

12. $7\dfrac{5}{6} - 3\dfrac{1}{3}$

13. $12\dfrac{5}{7} - \dfrac{3}{14}$

14. $\dfrac{4}{9} - \dfrac{5}{18}$

15. $5\dfrac{7}{12} - 1\dfrac{3}{8}$

16. $10\dfrac{9}{16} + \dfrac{7}{8}$

17. $11\dfrac{2}{3} + 5\dfrac{5}{6}$

18. $4\dfrac{1}{4} + 3\dfrac{5}{8} - 1\dfrac{7}{12}$

19. Sewing A dress that is $24\dfrac{3}{8}$ inches long is shortened by $4\dfrac{3}{4}$ inches. What is the new length of the dress? [3.1]

Simplify each of the following as much as possible. [3.3, 3.4, 3.5]

20. $7 + 3\left(2\dfrac{4}{5}\right)$

21. $\left(5\dfrac{7}{12} - \dfrac{1}{3}\right)\left(3 - 2\dfrac{5}{8}\right)$

22. $8 - 2\left(2\dfrac{5}{8}\right)$

23. $\left(5\dfrac{3}{8} - 2\dfrac{1}{4}\right)\left(6\dfrac{7}{12} - 2\dfrac{1}{3}\right)$

24. $\left(\dfrac{2}{9}\right)\left(3\dfrac{3}{5}\right) - \dfrac{3}{10}$

The chart shows iPhone distribution around the world. Use the information to answer the following questions.

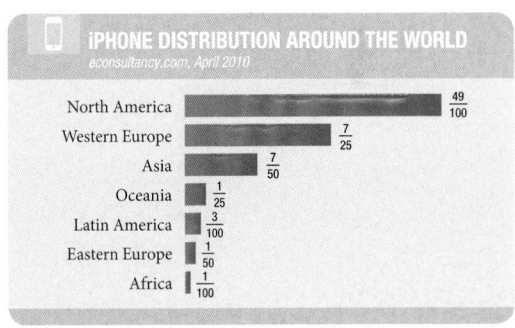

25. What is the fraction of iPhones found in Western Europe and Africa combined?

26. What is the fraction of iPhones found in Asia and Oceania combined?

Simplify.

1.
```
    394
  2,160
+    43
```

2.
```
  2,403
×    27
```

3. $\left(\dfrac{7}{12}\right)^2$

4. $24 - (18 - 9)$

5. $\dfrac{7}{12} - \dfrac{5}{12}$

6. $23\dfrac{9}{14} - 7\dfrac{13}{21}$

7. $\dfrac{4}{9} \cdot \dfrac{12}{20}$

8. $7^2 - 3^3$

9. $6 \div \dfrac{1}{2}$

10. $512 \div 16 \div 8$

11. $\dfrac{46}{13}$

12. $\dfrac{170}{306}$

13. $(9 + 13) - (8 - 4)$

14. $\dfrac{2}{5} + \dfrac{1}{3}$

15. $2,074(304)$

16. $\dfrac{4}{16} \div \dfrac{3}{8}$

17. $8 + 4^2 - 4 \cdot 5 + 7$

18. $16 \cdot \dfrac{3}{4}$

19. $7,482 - 594$

20. $\left(\dfrac{3}{8} + \dfrac{7}{24}\right) - \dfrac{13}{48}$

21. $4 + \dfrac{4}{9} \div \dfrac{2}{3}$

22. Round the following numbers to the nearest ten, then add.
```
  1,097
    563
+   216
```

23. Find the sum of $\dfrac{5}{6}$, $\dfrac{3}{4}$, and $\dfrac{1}{5}$.

24. Write the fraction $\dfrac{7}{15}$ as an equivalent fraction with a denominator of $60x$.

25. Reduce $\dfrac{39}{143}$ to lowest terms.

26. Add $\dfrac{2}{3}$ to half of $\dfrac{6}{7}$.

27. Mars' Diameter The planet Mars has an equatorial diameter of about 6,786 kilometers. Write Mars' diameter in words and expanded form.

The chart shows the number of Twitter followers for some celebrities. Use the information to answer the following questions.

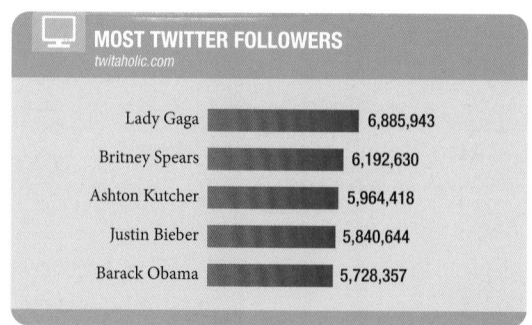

MOST TWITTER FOLLOWERS
twitaholic.com

Celebrity	Followers
Lady Gaga	6,885,943
Britney Spears	6,192,630
Ashton Kutcher	5,964,418
Justin Bieber	5,840,644
Barack Obama	5,728,357

28. How many followers do Ashton Kutcher and Lady Gaga have together?

29. How many more followers does Britney Spears have than Justin Bieber?

Perform the indicated operations. Reduce all answers to lowest terms. [3.1, 3.2]

1. $\dfrac{3}{8} + \dfrac{1}{8}$

2. $\dfrac{9}{14} - \dfrac{3}{14}$

3. $5 + \dfrac{5}{8}$

4. $\dfrac{5}{6} + \dfrac{2}{3}$

5. $\dfrac{3}{8} + \dfrac{7}{12} + \dfrac{1}{3}$

6. $5\dfrac{1}{5} + 4\dfrac{3}{4}$

7. $4\dfrac{1}{3} - 2\dfrac{7}{9}$

8. $4 - \dfrac{7}{8}$

9. $\dfrac{4}{7} - \dfrac{3}{14}$

10. $\dfrac{5}{6} + \dfrac{2}{3} + 2$

11. $\dfrac{7}{18} - \dfrac{1}{6}$

12. $4\dfrac{5}{8} - 2\dfrac{1}{4}$

13. $5\dfrac{3}{4} - \dfrac{7}{12}$

14. $\dfrac{3}{4} - \dfrac{7}{16}$

15. $3\dfrac{5}{6} - 2\dfrac{2}{3}$

16. $9\dfrac{1}{4} + \dfrac{7}{12}$

17. $9\dfrac{5}{6} + 6\dfrac{11}{18}$

18. $3\dfrac{5}{8} + 4\dfrac{1}{6} - 2\dfrac{4}{9}$

19. Sewing A dress that is $18\dfrac{5}{8}$ inches long is shortened by $2\dfrac{3}{4}$ inches. What is the new length of the dress? [3.1]

Simplify each of the following as much as possible. [3.3, 3.4, 3.5]

20. $5 + 2\left(4\dfrac{3}{4}\right)$

21. $\left(4\dfrac{3}{4} + \dfrac{1}{2}\right)\left(6\dfrac{5}{6} - 4\dfrac{1}{3}\right)$

22. $6 - 3\left(1\dfrac{4}{5}\right)$

23. $\left(7\dfrac{1}{8} - \dfrac{3}{4}\right)\left(3\dfrac{5}{6} + \dfrac{1}{3}\right)$

24. $\left(\dfrac{1}{3}\right)\left(2\dfrac{1}{4}\right) - \dfrac{3}{8}$

The chart shows the fraction of computer users who are using each platform. Use the information to answer the following questions. Write your answers as fractions and explain what the fractions mean.

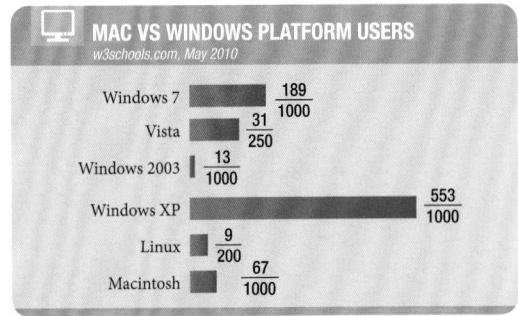

MAC VS WINDOWS PLATFORM USERS
w3schools.com, May 2010

Windows 7	$\dfrac{189}{1000}$
Vista	$\dfrac{31}{250}$
Windows 2003	$\dfrac{13}{1000}$
Windows XP	$\dfrac{553}{1000}$
Linux	$\dfrac{9}{200}$
Macintosh	$\dfrac{67}{1000}$

25. What fraction of users report using Windows 7 and Vista?

26. What fraction of users report using Macintosh and Linux platforms combined?

Decimals

El Giza, Egypt
Data SIO, NOAA, U.S. Navy, NGA, GEBCO
Image © 2010 GoeEye, Image © 2010 DigitalGlobe
© 2010 Cnes/Spot Image

The ancient Egyptian culture required that the body of a ruler be housed in a large tomb; the more impressive the structure, the smoother that ruler's journey into the afterlife would be. Thus explains the spectacular architectural wonders that are the Egyptian Pyramids. The largest of Egypt's famous pyramids, the Great Pyramid of Giza is believed to be the tomb of King Khufu and is recognized as one of the seven wonders of the ancient world. Khufu began construction on his pyramid soon after taking his throne, completing it approximately 20 years later around 2560 BC.

The current height of the Great Pyramid measures 138.8 meters. Historians believe that erosion has shortened the pyramid throughout its 4,000-year history, and that its original height was 146.5 meters. Suppose you wanted to calculate how much volume was lost due to this erosion. You would need to know that each side s of the pyramid measures 230.4 meters in length and that the area of the base B of a pyramid can be found using the formula

$$B = s \cdot s$$

You would also need to know that volume V of a pyramid can be found with the formula

$$V = \frac{1}{3} B \cdot h$$

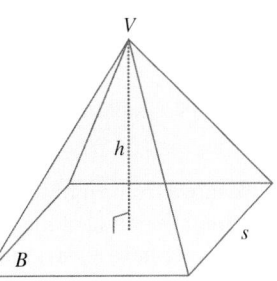

where h is the height of the pyramid at its apex. If you wanted to find the volume of the Great Pyramid when it was built and its volume now, you will need to know how to multiply and subtract numbers containing decimals. Decimal numbers are what we will explore in this chapter.

OBJECTIVES

A Write decimals in expanded form and with words or as mixed numbers.

B Round decimals to given place values.

KEY WORDS

decimals

place value

A person's handwriting is extremely difficult to mimic. To make copying signatures of the world's elite businessmen and women even more impossible, a company based in Germany has produced a pen with plant DNA embedded in the ink. Each pen sold has a distinctively different type of DNA, making words written with the pen distinguishable from words written with other pens. A forensic test is needed to view the plant DNA, but uniqueness of each pen gives peace of mind that a forgery is less likely to happen.

Each pen containing plant DNA sells for $15,850. If this pen sold in San Luis Obispo, California, the sales tax would be an additional $1,386.88. In this chapter, we will focus our attention on decimals. Anyone who has used money in the United States has worked with decimals already. For example, the sales tax on the pen contains a decimal:

$$\$1386.\underset{\underset{\text{Decimal point}}{\big|}}{88}$$

What is interesting and useful about decimals is their relationship to fractions and to powers of ten. The work we have done up to now—especially our work with fractions—can be used to develop the properties of decimal numbers.

A Decimal Notation and Place Value

In Chapter 1, we developed the idea of place value for the digits in a whole number. At that time, we gave the name and the place value of each of the first seven columns in our number system, as follows:

Millions Column	Hundred Thousands Column	Ten Thousands Column	Thousands Column	Hundreds Column	Tens Column	Ones Column
1,000,000	100,000	10,000	1,000	100	10	1

As we move from right to left, we multiply by 10 each time. The value of each column is 10 times the value of the column on its right, with the rightmost column being 1. Up until now we have always looked at place value as increasing by a factor of 10 each time we move one column to the left.

Ten Thousands	Thousands	Hundreds	Tens	Ones
10,000 ←	1,000 ←	100 ←	10 ←	1
Multiply by 10	Multiply by 10	Multiply by 10	Multiply by 10	

To understand the idea behind decimal numbers, we notice that moving in the opposite direction, from left to right, we *divide* by 10 each time.

Ten Thousands	Thousands	Hundreds	Tens	Ones
10,000	→ 1,000	→ 100	→ 10	→ 1
	Divide by 10	Divide by 10	Divide by 10	Divide by 10

If we keep going to the right, the next column will have to be

$$1 \div 10 = \frac{1}{10} \qquad \text{Tenths}$$

The next one after that will be

$$\frac{1}{10} \div 10 = \frac{1}{10} \cdot \frac{1}{10} = \frac{1}{100} \qquad \text{Hundredths}$$

After that, we have

$$\frac{1}{100} \div 10 = \frac{1}{100} \cdot \frac{1}{10} = \frac{1}{1,000} \qquad \text{Thousandths}$$

We could continue this pattern as long as we wanted. We simply divide by 10 to move one column to the right. (And remember, dividing by 10 gives the same result as multiplying by $\frac{1}{10}$.)

To show where the ones column is, we use a *decimal point* between the ones column and the tenths column.

Thousands	Hundreds	Tens	Ones		Tenths	Hundredths	Thousandths	Ten Thousandths	Hundred Thousandths
1,000	100	10	1	.	$\frac{1}{10}$	$\frac{1}{100}$	$\frac{1}{1,000}$	$\frac{1}{10,000}$	$\frac{1}{100,000}$

Decimal Point

The ones column can be thought of as the middle column, with columns larger than 1 to the left and columns smaller than 1 to the right. The first column to the right of the ones column is the tenths column, the next column to the right is the hundredths column, the next is the thousandths column, and so on. The decimal point is always written between the ones column and the tenths column.

We can use the place value of decimal fractions to write them in expanded form.

EXAMPLE 1   Write 423.576 in expanded form.

Solution $423.576 = 400 + 20 + 3 + \frac{5}{10} + \frac{7}{100} + \frac{6}{1,000}$

●

EXAMPLE 2   Write each number in words.
a. 0.4   **b.** 0.04   **c.** 0.004
Solution
a. 0.4 is "four tenths."
b. 0.04 is "four hundredths."
c. 0.004 is "four thousandths."

●

Note   Because the digits to the right of the decimal point have fractional place values, numbers with digits to the right of the decimal point are called *decimal fractions*. In this book, we will also call them *decimal numbers*, or simply *decimals* for short.

Video Examples
SECTION 4.1

Practice Problems

1. Write 18.439 in expanded form.

2. Write each number in words.
  a. 0.1
  b. 0.01
  c. 0.001

Answers

1. $10 + 8 + \frac{4}{10} + \frac{3}{100} + \frac{9}{1000}$
2. a. One tenth
   b. One hundredth
   c. One thousandth

Note   Sometimes we name decimal numbers by simply reading the digits from left to right and using the word "point" to indicate where the decimal point is. For example, using this method the number 5.04 is read "five point zero four."

When a decimal number contains digits to the left of the decimal point, we use the word "and" to indicate where the decimal point is when writing the number in words.

EXAMPLE 3   Write each number in words.

a. 5.4   **b.** 5.04   **c.** 5.004

Solution

a. 5.4 is "five and four tenths."

b. 5.04 is "five and four hundredths."

c. 5.004 is "five and four thousandths."

3. Write each number in words.
   a. 4.2
   b. 4.12
   c. 4.012

EXAMPLE 4   Write 3.64 in words.

Solution   The number 3.64 is read "three and sixty-four hundredths." The place values of the digits are as follows:

$$3 \quad . \quad 6 \quad \quad 4$$

3 ones   6 tenths   4 hundredths

4. Write 10.805 in words.

We read the decimal part as "sixty-four hundredths" because

$$6 \text{ tenths} + 4 \text{ hundredths} = \frac{6}{10} + \frac{4}{100} = \frac{60}{100} + \frac{4}{100} = \frac{64}{100}$$

EXAMPLE 5   Write 25.4936 in words.

Solution   Using the idea given in Example 4, we write 25.4936 in words as "twenty-five and four thousand, nine hundred thirty-six ten thousandths."

5. Write 14.0836 in words.

In order to understand addition and subtraction of decimals in the next section, we need to be able to convert decimal numbers to fractions or mixed numbers.

EXAMPLE 6   Write each number as a fraction or a mixed number. Do not reduce to lowest terms.

a. 0.004   **b.** 3.64   **c.** 25.4936

Solution

a. Because 0.004 is 4 thousandths, we write

$$0.004 = \frac{4}{1,000}$$

Three digits after   Three zeros
the decimal point

6. Write each number as a fraction or mixed number. Do not reduce to lowest terms.
   a. 0.08
   b. 4.206
   c. 12.5814

b. Looking over the work in Example 4, we can write

$$3.64 = 3\frac{64}{100}$$

Two digits after   Two zeros
the decimal point

c. From the way in which we wrote 25.4936 in words in Example 5, we have

$$25.4936 = 25\frac{4936}{10,000}$$

Four digits after   Four zeros
the decimal point

Answers

3. a. Four and two tenths
   b. Four and twelve hundredths
   c. Four and twelve thousandths
4. Ten and eight hundred five thousandths.
5. Fourteen and eight hundred thirty-six ten thousandths.
6. a. $\frac{8}{100}$ **b.** $4\frac{206}{1000}$ **c.** $12\frac{5814}{10,000}$

B Rounding Decimal Numbers

The rule for rounding decimal numbers is similar to the rule for rounding whole numbers. If the digit in the column to the right of the one we are rounding to is 5 or more, we add 1 to the digit in the column we are rounding to; otherwise, we leave it alone. We then replace all digits to the right of the column we are rounding to with zeros if they are to the left of the decimal point; otherwise, we simply delete them. Table 1 illustrates the procedure.

Table 1

Rounded to the Nearest

Number	Whole Number	Tenth	Hundredth
24.785	25	24.8	24.79
2.3914	2	2.4	2.39
0.98243	1	1.0	0.98
14.0942	14	14.1	14.09
0.545	1	0.5	0.55

EXAMPLE 7 Round 9,235.492 to the nearest hundred.

Solution The number next to the hundreds column is 3, which is less than 5. We change all digits to the right to 0, and we can drop all digits to the right of the decimal point, so we write

9,200

EXAMPLE 8 Round 0.00346 to the nearest ten thousandth.

Solution Because the number to the right of the ten thousandths column is more than 5, we add 1 to the 4 and get

0.0035

7. Round 8,456.085 to the nearest hundred.

8. Round 8,456.085 to the nearest hundredth.

GETTING READY FOR CLASS

After reading through the preceding section, respond in your own words and in complete sentences.

A. Write 754.326 in expanded form.

B. Write $400 + 70 + 5 + \frac{1}{10} + \frac{3}{100} + \frac{7}{1,000}$ in decimal form.

C. Write seventy-two and three tenths in decimal form.

D. How many places to the right of the decimal point is the hundredths column?

Answers
7. 8,500
8. 8,456.09

EXERCISE SET 4.1

Vocabulary Review

Choose the correct words to fill in the blanks below.

hundredths	left	decimal point	fractional
tenths	right	thousandths	place value

1. Digits to the right of a decimal point have _____ place values.

2. A _____ is used to separate the ones column and the tenths column.

3. In the decimal number 0.036, the 6 is in the _____ column.

4. In the decimal number 4.169, the 1 is in the _____ column.

5. In the decimal number 10.0977, the 9 is in the _____ column.

6. We use _____ of decimal fractions to write them in expanded form.

7. When a decimal number contains digits to the _____ of the decimal point, we use the word *and* to indicate where the decimal point is when writing the number in words.

8. When rounding decimal numbers, if the digit in the column to the _____ of the one we are rounding to is 5 or more, we add 1 to the digit in the column to which we are rounding.

Problems

A Write out the name of each number in words.

1. 0.3
2. 0.03
3. 0.015
4. 0.0015

5. 3.4
6. 2.04
7. 52.7
8. 46.8

Write each number as a fraction or a mixed number. Do not reduce your answers.

9. 405.36
10. 362.78
11. 9.009
12. 60.06

13. 1.234
14. 12.045
15. 0.00305
16. 2.00106

Give the place value of the 5 in each of the following numbers.

17. 458.327
18. 327.458
19. 29.52
20. 25.92
21. 0.00375

22. 0.00532
23. 275.01
24. 0.356
25. 539.76
26. 0.123456

Write each of the following as a decimal number.

27. Fifty-five hundredths

28. Two hundred thirty-five ten thousandths

29. Six and nine tenths

30. Forty-five thousand and six hundred twenty-one thousandths

31. Eleven and eleven hundredths

32. Twenty-six thousand, two hundred forty-five and sixteen hundredths

33. One hundred and two hundredths

34. Seventy-five and seventy-five hundred thousandths

35. Three thousand and three thousandths

36. One thousand, one hundred eleven and one hundred eleven thousandths

B Complete the following table.

	Rounded to the Nearest			
Number	Whole Number	Tenth	Hundredth	Thousandth
37. 47.5479				
38. 100.9256				
39. 0.8175				
40. 29.9876				
41. 0.1562				
42. 128.9115				
43. 2,789.3241				
44. 0.8743				
45. 99.9999				
46. 71.7634				

Applying the Concepts

47. Penny Weight If you have a penny dated anytime from 1959 through 1982, its original weight was 3.11 grams. If the penny has a date of 1983 or later, the original weight was 2.5 grams. Write the two weights in words.

48. 100 Meters The chart shows some close finishes at the 2010 Winter Olympics in Vancouver. Use the information to answer the following questions.

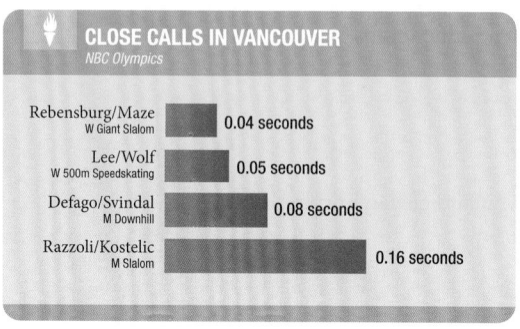

CLOSE CALLS IN VANCOUVER
NBC Olympics

Rebensburg/Maze W Giant Slalom	0.04 seconds
Lee/Wolf W 500m Speedskating	0.05 seconds
Defago/Svindal M Downhill	0.08 seconds
Razzoli/Kostelic M Slalom	0.16 seconds

a. What is the place value of the 6 in the finish of the Men's Slalom?

b. Write the the difference in times for the Defago/Svindal finish in words.

49. Speed of Light The speed of light is 186,282.3976 miles per second. Round this number to the nearest hundredth.

50. Halley's Comet Halley's comet was seen from the earth during 1986. It will be another 76.1 years before it returns. Write 76.1 in words.

51. Nutrition A 50-gram egg contains 0.15 milligram of riboflavin. Write 0.15 in words.

52. Nutrition One medium banana contains 0.64 milligram of Vitamin B6. Write 0.64 in words.

53. Gasoline Prices The bar chart below was created from a survey by the U.S. Department of Energy's Energy Information Administration during four weeks in 2011. It gives the average price of regular gasoline for the United States on each Monday throughout the four week period. Use the information in the chart to fill in the table.

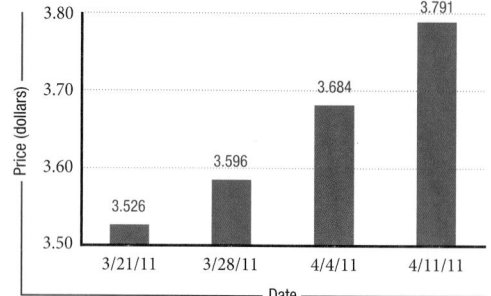

Price of 1 Gallon of Regular Gasoline	
Date	Price (Dollars)
3/21/11	
3/28/11	
4/4/11	
4/11/11	

54. Speed and Time The bar chart below was created from data given by *Car and Driver* magazine. It gives the minimum time in seconds for a Toyota Echo to reach various speeds from a complete stop. Use the information in the chart to fill in the table.

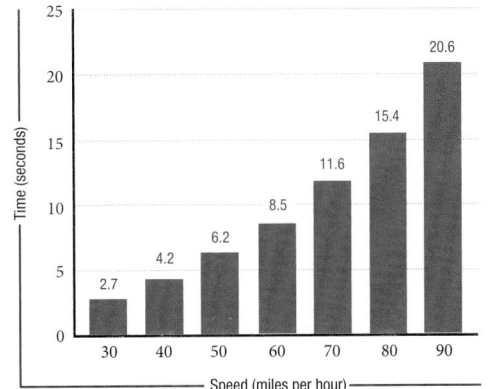

Speed (miles per hour)	Time (seconds)
30	
40	
50	
60	
70	
80	
90	

For each pair of numbers, place the correct symbol, $<$ or $>$, between the numbers.

55. a. 0.02   0.2

  b. 0.3   0.032

56. a. 0.45   0.5

  b. 0.5   0.56

57. Write the following numbers in order from smallest to largest.

0.02   0.05   0.025   0.052   0.005   0.002

58. Write the following numbers in order from smallest to largest.

0.2   0.02   0.4   0.04   0.42   0.24

59. Which of the following numbers will round to 7.5?

7.451   7.449   7.54   7.56

60. Which of the following numbers will round to 3.2?

3.14999   3.24999   3.279   3.16111

Change each decimal to a fraction, and then reduce to lowest terms.

61. 0.25

62. 0.75

63. 0.125

64. 0.375

65. 0.625

66. 0.0625

67. 0.875

68. 0.1875

Estimating   For each pair of numbers, choose the number that is closest to 10.

69. 9.9 and 9.99

70. 8.5 and 8.05

71. 10.5 and 10.05

72. 10.9 and 10.99

Estimating   For each pair of numbers, choose the number that is closest to 0.

73. 0.5 and 0.05

74. 0.10 and 0.05

75. 0.01 and 0.02

76. 0.1 and 0.01

Getting Ready for the Next Section

In the next section we will do addition and subtraction with decimals. To understand the process of addition and subtraction, we need to understand the process of addition and subtraction with mixed numbers.

Find each of the following sums and differences. (Add or subtract.)

77. $4\dfrac{3}{10} + 2\dfrac{1}{100}$

78. $5\dfrac{35}{100} + 2\dfrac{3}{10}$

79. $8\dfrac{5}{10} - 2\dfrac{4}{100}$

80. $6\dfrac{3}{100} - 2\dfrac{125}{1,000}$

81. $5\dfrac{1}{10} + 6\dfrac{2}{100} + 7\dfrac{3}{1,000}$

82. $4\dfrac{27}{100} + 6\dfrac{3}{10} + 7\dfrac{123}{1,000}$

Find the Mistake

Each sentence below contains a mistake. Circle the mistake and write the correct word(s) or number(s) on the line provided.

1. To move a place value from the tens column to the hundreds column, you must divide by ten. _____

2. The decimal 0.09 can be written as the fraction $\dfrac{9}{1,000}$. _____

3. The decimal 142.9643 written as a mixed number is $142\dfrac{9,643}{1,000}$. _____

4. Rounding the decimal 0.06479 to the nearest tenth gives us 0.065. _____

Navigation Skills: Prepare, Study, Achieve

Preparation is another key component for success in this course. What does it mean to be prepared for this class? Before you come to class, make sure to

- Complete the homework from the previous section.
- Read the upcoming section.
- Answer the Getting Ready for Class questions.
- Rework example problems.
- Work practice problems.
- Make a point to attend every class session and arrive on time.
- Prepare a list of questions to ask your instructor or fellow students that will help you work through difficult problems.
- Commit to being an engaged, attentive, and active listener while in class.
- Take notes as the instructor speaks and don't hesitate to ask questions if you need clarification.

Research note-taking techniques online if you find that you aren't quite sure how to take notes or your current method of taking notes is not helpful. You shouldn't expect to master a new topic the first time you read about it or learn about it in class. Mastering mathematics takes a lot of practice, so make the commitment to come to class prepared and practice, practice, practice.

OBJECTIVES

A Add decimals.

B Subtract decimals.

The chart shows the top finishing times for the women's 400-meter race during the 2009 World Track and Field Championship in Berlin. In order to analyze the different finishing times, it is important that you are able to add and subtract decimals, and that is what we will cover in this section.

Runner	Time (seconds)
Sanya Richards (USA)	49.00
Shericka Williams (Jamaica)	49.32
Antonia Krivoshapka (Russia)	49.71
Novlene Williams-Mills (Jamaica)	49.77

A Addition of Decimals

Suppose you are earning $8.50 an hour and you receive a raise of $1.25 an hour. Your new hourly rate of pay is

$$\begin{array}{r} \$8.50 \\ + \ \$1.25 \\ \hline \$9.75 \end{array}$$

To add the two rates of pay, we align the decimal points, and then add in columns.

To see why this is true in general, we can use mixed-number notation.

$$8.50 = 8\frac{50}{100}$$

$$+ \ 1.25 = 1\frac{25}{100}$$

$$9\frac{75}{100} = 9.75$$

We can visualize the mathematics above by thinking in terms of money.

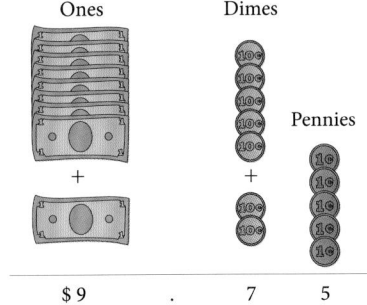

Ones   Dimes

Pennies

$9 . 7 5

Video Examples

SECTION 4.2

Practice Problems

1. Add by first changing to fractions: 16.47 + 5.9 + 45.842.

EXAMPLE 1   Add by first changing to fractions: 25.43 + 2.897 + 379.6.

Solution   We first change each decimal to a mixed number. We then write each fraction using the least common denominator and add as usual.

$$25.43 = 25\frac{43}{100} = 25\frac{430}{1{,}000}$$

$$2.897 = 2\frac{897}{1{,}000} = 2\frac{897}{1{,}000}$$

$$+\ 379.6 = 379\frac{6}{10} = 379\frac{600}{1{,}000}$$

$$406\frac{1{,}927}{1{,}000} = 407\frac{927}{1{,}000} = 407.927$$

Again, the result is the same if we just line up the decimal points and add as if we were adding whole numbers.

$$
\begin{array}{r}
25.430 \\
2.897 \\
+\ 379.600 \\
\hline
407.927 \\
\uparrow
\end{array}
$$

Notice that we can fill in zeros on the right to help keep the numbers in the correct columns. Doing this does not change the value of any of the numbers.

Note: The decimal point in the answer is directly below the decimal points in the problem.

B Subtraction of Decimals

The same thing would happen if we were to subtract two decimal numbers. We can use these facts to write a rule for addition and subtraction of decimal numbers.

> **RULE**   Addition (or Subtraction) of Decimal Numbers
>
> To add (or subtract) decimal numbers, we line up the decimal points and add (or subtract) as usual. The decimal point in the result is written directly below the decimal points in the problem.

We will use this rule for the rest of the examples in this section.

2. Subtract: 42.809 − 13.658.

EXAMPLE 2   Subtract: 39.812 − 14.236.

Solution   We write the numbers vertically, with the decimal points lined up, and subtract as usual.

$$
\begin{array}{r}
39.812 \\
-\ 14.236 \\
\hline
25.576
\end{array}
$$

3. Add: 9 + 1.05 + 8.7 + 3.86.

EXAMPLE 3   Add: 8 + 0.002 + 3.1 + 0.04.

Solution   To make sure we keep the digits in the correct columns, we can write zeros to the right of the rightmost digits.

$$
\begin{array}{l}
8 = 8.000 \\
3.1 = 3.100 \\
0.04 = 0.040
\end{array}
$$

Writing the extra zeros here is really equivalent to finding a common denominator for the fractional parts of the original four numbers—now we have a thousandths column in all the numbers.

Answers

1. $68\frac{212}{1{,}000} = 68.212$

2. 29.151

3. 22.61

This doesn't change the value of any of the numbers, and it makes our task easier. Now we have

$$
\begin{array}{r}
8.000 \\
0.002 \\
3.100 \\
+\ 0.040 \\
\hline
11.142
\end{array}
$$

EXAMPLE 4   Subtract: $5.9 - 3.0814$.

Solution   In this case, it is very helpful to write 5.9 as 5.9000, since we will have to borrow in order to subtract.

$$
\begin{array}{r}
5.9000 \\
-\ 3.0814 \\
\hline
2.8186
\end{array}
$$

EXAMPLE 5   Subtract 3.09 from the sum of 9 and 5.472.

Solution   Writing the problem in symbols, we have

$$(9 + 5.472) - 3.09 = 14.472 - 3.09$$
$$= 11.382$$

Applications

EXAMPLE 6   You stop to have lunch with a friend at a coffee shop. The bill for lunch is $15.64. You give the waitress a $20 bill. For change, you receive four $1 bills, a quarter, a nickel, and a penny. Is your change correct?

Solution   To find the total amount of money you received in change, we add.

$$
\begin{array}{lrl}
\text{Four \$1 bills} & = & \$4.00 \\
\text{One quarter} & = & 0.25 \\
\text{One nickel} & = & 0.05 \\
\text{One penny} & = & 0.01 \\
\hline
\text{Total} & = & \$4.31
\end{array}
$$

To find out if this is the correct amount, we subtract the amount of the bill from $20.00.

$$
\begin{array}{r}
\$20.00 \\
-\ 15.64 \\
\hline
\$\ 4.36
\end{array}
$$

The change was not correct. It is off by 5 cents. Instead of the nickel, you should have been given a dime.

GETTING READY FOR CLASS

After reading through the preceding section, respond in your own words and in complete sentences.

A. When adding numbers with decimals, why is it important to line up the decimal points?

B. Write 379.6 in mixed-number notation.

C. Look at Example 6 in this section of your book. If I had given the person at the cash register a $20 bill and four pennies, how much change should I then have received?

D. How many quarters does the decimal 0.75 represent?

4. Subtract: $3.7 - 1.9034$.

5. Subtract 8.92 from the sum of 12 and 5.01.

6. If a meal costs $8.37, how should the change be counted if it is paid for with a $20 bill?

Answers

4. 1.7966

5. 8.09

6. One $10 bill, one $1 bill, two quarters, one dime, three pennies

Vocabulary Review

Choose the correct words to fill in the blanks below.

decimal point columns zeros money value

1. It is helpful to think in terms of _____ to add and subtract decimal numbers.

2. To add two decimal numbers, align the decimal points and then add in _____ .

3. When adding or subtracting decimal numbers, the _____ in the answer is directly below the decimals in the problems.

4. It is important to write _____ to the right of the rightmost digits to keep the digits in the correct columns.

5. Writing zeros to the right of the rightmost digits does not change the _____ of any of the numbers.

Problems

A Find each of the following sums. (Add.)

1. $2.91 + 3.28$

2. $8.97 + 2.04$

3. $0.04 + 0.31 + 0.78$

4. $0.06 + 0.92 + 0.65$

5. $3.89 + 2.4$

6. $7.65 + 3.8$

7. $4.532 + 1.81 + 2.7$

8. $9.679 + 3.49 + 6.5$

9. $0.081 + 5 + 2.94$

10. $0.396 + 7 + 3.96$

11. $5.0003 + 6.78 + 0.004$

12. $27.0179 + 7.89 + 0.009$

13.
$$\begin{array}{r} 7.123 \\ 8.12 \\ + 9.1 \\ \hline \end{array}$$

14.
$$\begin{array}{r} 5.432 \\ 4.32 \\ + 3.2 \\ \hline \end{array}$$

15.
$$\begin{array}{r} 9.001 \\ 8.01 \\ + 7.1 \\ \hline \end{array}$$

16.
$$\begin{array}{r} 6.003 \\ 5.02 \\ + 4.1 \\ \hline \end{array}$$

17.
$$\begin{array}{r} 89.7854 \\ 3.4 \\ 65.35 \\ + 100.006 \\ \hline \end{array}$$

18.
$$\begin{array}{r} 57.4698 \\ 9.89 \\ 32.032 \\ + 572.0079 \\ \hline \end{array}$$

19.
$$\begin{array}{r} 543.21 \\ + 123.45 \\ \hline \end{array}$$

20.
$$\begin{array}{r} 987.654 \\ + 456.789 \\ \hline \end{array}$$

B Find each of the following differences. (Subtract.)

21. $99.34 - 88.23$

22. $47.69 - 36.58$

23. $5.97 - 2.4$

24. $9.87 - 1.04$

25. $6.3 - 2.08$

26. $7.5 - 3.04$

27. $149.37 - 28.96$

28. $796.45 - 32.68$

29. $45 - 0.067$

30. $48 - 0.075$

31. $8 - 0.327$

32. $12 - 0.962$

33. $765.432 - 234.567$

34. $654.321 - 123.456$

35. $100.42 - 56.87$

36. $12 - 1.93$

37. $10 - 4.082$

38. $20 - 5.86$

Subtract.

39. $\begin{array}{r} 34.07 \\ -\ 6.18 \\ \hline \end{array}$

40. $\begin{array}{r} 25.008 \\ -\ 3.119 \\ \hline \end{array}$

41. $\begin{array}{r} 40.04 \\ -\ 4.4 \\ \hline \end{array}$

42. $\begin{array}{r} 50.05 \\ -\ 5.5 \\ \hline \end{array}$

43. $\begin{array}{r} 768.436 \\ -\ 356.998 \\ \hline \end{array}$

44. $\begin{array}{r} 495.237 \\ -\ 247.668 \\ \hline \end{array}$

Add and subtract as indicated.

45. $(7.8 - 4.3) + 2.5$

46. $(8.3 - 1.2) + 3.4$

47. $7.8 - (4.3 + 2.5)$

48. $8.3 - (1.2 + 3.4)$

49. $(9.7 - 5.2) - 1.4$

50. $(7.8 - 3.2) - 1.5$

51. $9.7 - (5.2 - 1.4)$

52. $7.8 - (3.2 - 1.5)$

53. $5.9 - (4.03 - 2.3)$

54. $10 - (3 - 1.06)$

55. $12.2 - (9.1 + 0.3)$

56. $15.6 - (4.9 + 3.87)$

57. Subtract 5 from the sum of 8.2 and 0.072.

58. Subtract 8 from the sum of 9.37 and 2.5.

59. What number is added to 0.035 to obtain 4.036?

60. What number is added to 0.043 to obtain 6.054?

Applying the Concepts

61. Shopping A family buying school clothes for their two children spends $25.37 at one store, $39.41 at another, and $52.04 at a third store. What is the total amount spent at the three stores?

62. Expenses A 4-H Club member is raising a lamb to take to the county fair. If she spent $75 for the lamb, $25.60 for feed, and $35.89 for shearing tools, what was the total cost of the project?

63. Take-Home Pay A college professor making $2,105.96 per month has deducted from her check $311.93 for federal income tax, $158.21 for retirement, and $64.72 for state income tax. How much does the professor take home after the deductions have been taken from her monthly income?

64. Take-Home Pay A cook making $1,504.75 a month has deductions of $157.32 for federal income tax, $58.52 for Social Security, and $45.12 for state income tax. How much does the cook take home after the deductions have been taken from his check?

65. Rectangle The logo on a business letter is rectangular. The rectangle has a width of 0.84 inches and a length of 1.41 inches. Find the perimeter.

66. Rectangle A small sticky note is a rectangle. It has a width of 21.4 millimeters and a length of 35.8 millimeters. Find the perimeter.

67. Change A person buys $4.57 worth of candy. If he pays for the candy with a $10 bill, how much change should he receive?

68. Checking Account A checking account contains $342.38. If checks are written for $25.04, $36.71, and $210, how much money is left in the account?

Check No.	Date	Description of Transaction	Payment/Debit (-)	Deposit/Credit (+)	Balance
1630	7/3	Deposit		$342 38	$342 38
	7/5	Albertsons	$25 04		
	7/5	Rite Aid	$36 71		
	7/7	Gas Company	$210 00		?

Downhill Skiers The chart shows the times for several downhill skiers in the 2010 Vancouver Olympics. Use the information to answer the following questions.

69. How much faster was Elisabeth Goergl than Andrea Fischbacher?

70. How much faster was Lindsey Vonn than Julia Mancuso?

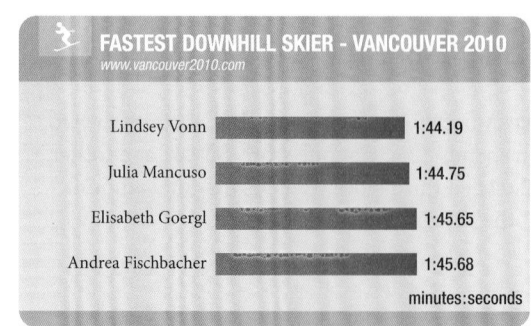

FASTEST DOWNHILL SKIER - VANCOUVER 2010
www.vancouver2010.com

Lindsey Vonn   1:44.19
Julia Mancuso   1:44.75
Elisabeth Goergl   1:45.65
Andrea Fischbacher   1:45.68

minutes:seconds

71. Mac Users The chart shows the increase in the number of Mac users each year. Use it to answer the following questions.

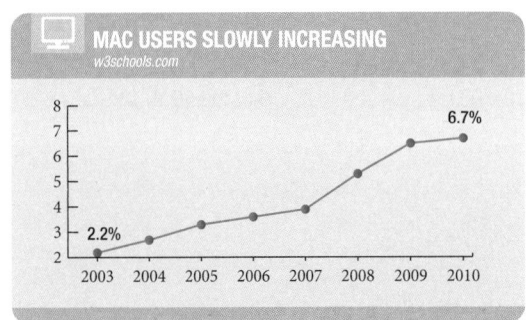

a. Was the increase in users during 2007 more or less than 5% of total users?

b. Was the increase in users during 2009 more or less than 5%?

c. Estimate the percent of total users increase from 2007 to 2009.

72. Movie Tickets The chart shows the increase in movie ticket prices. Use the information to answer the following questions.

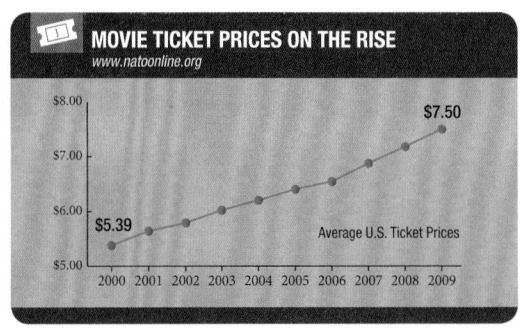

a. Were movie ticket prices above $6 in 2001?

b. Were ticket prices above $6 in 2007?

c. Were ticket prices in 2008 below $7?

73. Geometry A rectangle has a perimeter of 9.5 inches. If the length is 2.75 inches, find the width.

74. Geometry A rectangle has a perimeter of 11 inches. If the width is 2.5 inches, find the length.

75. Change Suppose you eat dinner in a restaurant and the bill comes to $16.76. If you give the cashier a $20 bill and a penny, how much change should you receive? List the bills and coins you should receive for change.

76. Change Suppose you buy some tools at the hardware store and the bill comes to $37.87. If you give the cashier two $20 bills and 2 pennies, how much change should you receive? List the bills and coins you should receive for change.

Sequences Find the next number in each sequence.

77. 2.5, 2.75, 3, . . .

78. 3.125, 3.375, 3.625, . . .

Getting Ready for the Next Section

To understand how to multiply decimals, we need to understand multiplication with whole numbers, fractions, and mixed numbers. The following problems review these concepts.

79. $\dfrac{1}{10} \cdot \dfrac{3}{10}$

80. $\dfrac{5}{10} \cdot \dfrac{6}{10}$

81. $\dfrac{3}{100} \cdot \dfrac{17}{100}$

82. $\dfrac{7}{100} \cdot \dfrac{31}{100}$

83. $5\left(\dfrac{3}{10}\right)$

84. $7 \cdot \dfrac{7}{10}$

85. $56 \cdot 25$

86. $39(48)$

87. $\dfrac{5}{10} \cdot \dfrac{3}{10}$ **88.** $\dfrac{5}{100} \cdot \dfrac{3}{1,000}$ **89.** $2\dfrac{1}{10} \cdot \dfrac{7}{100}$ **90.** $3\dfrac{5}{10} \cdot \dfrac{4}{100}$

91. 305(436)   **92.** 403(522)   **93.** 5(420 + 3)   **94.** 3(550 + 2)

Improving Your Quantitative Literacy

95. Facebook Users The chart shows the number of active Facebook users over several years. Use the information to answer the following questions.

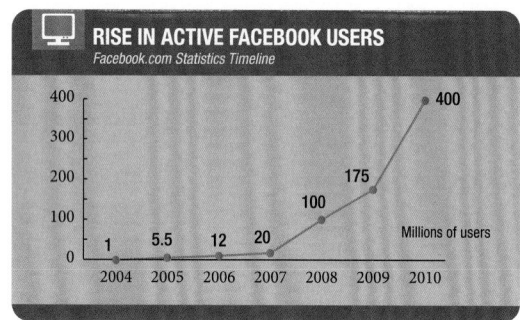

a. How many more users were there in 2007 than in 2006?

b. Between which years was the increase the most?

c. If the trend from 2009 to 2010 continues, how many users will there be in 2011?

Find the Mistake

Each sentence below contains a mistake. Circle the mistake and write the correct word(s) or number(s) on the line provided.

1. To add 32.69 and 4.837, align the rightmost digit of each number and add in columns. _____

2. To add 0.004 + 5.06 + 32 by first changing each decimal to a fraction would give us the problem $\dfrac{4}{1,000} + \dfrac{5}{600} + 32$.

_____

3. When subtracting 8.7 − 2.0163, we make sure to keep the digits in the correct columns by writing 8.7 as 8.0007.

_____

4. Subtracting 4.367 from the sum of 12.1 and 0.036 gives us 11.3333. _____

4.3 Multiplication with Decimals

OBJECTIVES

A Multiply with decimals.

B Use order of operations with decimals.

The mystery of the roving rocks in Racetrack Playa of Death Valley, California has been puzzling scientists for decades. Water from winter rains wash down the slopes of the surrounding mountains and form a small lake in the Playa. During the summer, the lake evaporates and the muddy bed dries up, cracking into a mosaic of hexagonal clay tiles. Scientists have been trying to discover what causes large stones to move across the lakebed and leave behind tracks. One hypothesis suggests that as night temperatures fall below freezing, ice forms around each tile. Frequent winds up to 90 miles per hour can move this ice, allowing for a conveyor belt of sorts to move the rocks. To date, no one has ever witnessed the rocks moving, but scientists believe they may move at half the jogging speed of a human. Let's suppose a person is jogging at 8.5 miles per hour. If a rock in Racetrack Playa was moving at half the jogger's rate, it would be moving at 4.25 miles per hour. Therefore, it must be true that

$$\frac{1}{2} \text{ of } 8.5 \text{ is } 4.25$$

But because $\frac{1}{2}$ can be written as 0.5 and *of* translates to multiply, we can write this problem again as

$$0.5 \times 8.5 = 4.25$$

If we were to ignore the decimal points in this problem and simply multiply 5 and 85, the result would be 425.

A Multiplication with Decimals

Multiplication with decimal numbers is similar to multiplication with whole numbers. The difference lies in deciding where to place the decimal point in the answer. To find out how this is done, we can use fraction notation.

EXAMPLE 1 Change each decimal to a fraction and multiply.

$$0.5 \times 0.3$$

Solution Changing each decimal to a fraction and multiplying, we have

$$0.5 \times 0.3 = \frac{5}{10} \times \frac{3}{10} \qquad \textit{Change to fractions.}$$

$$= \frac{15}{100} \qquad \textit{Multiply numerators and multiply denominators.}$$

$$= 0.15 \qquad \textit{Write the answer in decimal form.}$$

The result is 0.15, which has two digits to the right of the decimal point.

Video Examples
SECTION 4.3

Practice Problems

1. Change each decimal to a fraction and multiply.

$$0.4 \times 0.08$$

Note To indicate multiplication we are using a × sign here instead of a dot so we won't confuse the decimal points with the multiplication symbol.

Answer
1. 0.032

2. Change each decimal to a fraction and multiply.

$$0.08 \times 0.009.$$

3. Multiply: 3.2×0.09.

4. How many digits will be to the right of the decimal point in the following product?

$$4.632 \times 0.0008$$

What we want to do now is find a shortcut that will allow us to multiply decimals without first having to change each decimal number to a fraction. Let's look at another example.

EXAMPLE 2   Change each decimal to a fraction and multiply: 0.05×0.003.

Solution

$$0.05 \times 0.003 = \frac{5}{100} \times \frac{3}{1,000} \qquad \textit{Change to fractions.}$$

$$= \frac{15}{100,000} \qquad \textit{Multiply numerators and multiply denominators.}$$

$$= 0.00015 \qquad \textit{Write the answer in decimal form.}$$

The result is 0.00015, which has a total of five digits to the right of the decimal point.

Looking over these first two examples, we can see that the digits in the result are just what we would get if we simply forgot about the decimal points and multiplied; that is, $3 \times 5 = 15$. The decimal point in the result is placed so that the total number of digits to its right is the same as the total number of digits to the right of both decimal points in the original two numbers. The reason this is true becomes clear when we look at the denominators after we have changed from decimals to fractions.

EXAMPLE 3   Multiply: 2.1×0.07.

Solution

$$2.1 \times 0.07 = 2\frac{1}{10} \times \frac{7}{100} \qquad \textit{Change to fractions.}$$

$$= \frac{21}{10} \times \frac{7}{100}$$

$$= \frac{147}{1,000} \qquad \textit{Multiply numerators and multiply denominators.}$$

$$= 0.147 \qquad \textit{Write the answer as a decimal.}$$

Again, the digits in the answer come from multiplying $21 \times 7 = 147$. The decimal point is placed so that there are three digits to its right, because that is the total number of digits to the right of the decimal points in 2.1 and 0.07.

We summarize this discussion with the following rule:

> **RULE**   **Multiplication with Decimal Numbers**
>
> To multiply two decimal numbers, follow these steps:
>
> **1.** Multiply as you would if the decimal points were not there.
>
> **2.** Place the decimal point in the answer so that the number of digits to its right is equal to the total number of digits to the right of the decimal points in the original two numbers in the problem.

EXAMPLE 4   How many digits will be to the right of the decimal point in the following product?

$$2.987 \times 24.82$$

Solution   There are three digits to the right of the decimal point in 2.987 and two digits to the right in 24.82. Therefore, there will be $3 + 2 = 5$ digits to the right of the decimal point in their product.

Answers

2. 0.00072

3. 0.288

4. Seven

EXAMPLE 5 Multiply: 3.05 × 4.36.

Solution We can set this up as if it were a multiplication problem with whole numbers. We multiply and then place the decimal point in the correct position in the answer.

$$
\begin{array}{r}
3.05 \quad\longleftarrow \text{2 digits to the right of decimal point}\\
\times\ 4.36 \quad\longleftarrow \text{2 digits to the right of decimal point}\\
\hline
1830\\
915\\
+\ 12\ 20\\
\hline
13.2980\\
\end{array}
$$

The decimal point is placed so that there are 2 + 2 = 4 digits to its right.

As you can see, multiplying decimal numbers is just like multiplying whole numbers, except that we must place the decimal point in the result in the correct position.

Estimating

Look back to Example 5. We could have placed the decimal point in the answer by rounding the two numbers to the nearest whole number and then multiplying them. Because 3.05 rounds to 3 and 4.36 rounds to 4, and the product of 3 and 4 is 12, we estimate that the answer to 3.05 × 4.36 will be close to 12. Then, we place the decimal point in the product 132980 between the 3 and the 2 in order to make it into a number close to 12.

EXAMPLE 6 Estimate the answer to each of the following products.

a. 29.4 × 8.2 **b.** 68.5 × 172 **c.** $(6.32)^2$

Solution

a. Because 29.4 is approximately 30 and 8.2 is approximately 8, we estimate this product to be about 30 × 8 = 240. (If we were to multiply 29.4 and 8.2, we would find the product to be exactly 241.08.)

b. Rounding 68.5 to 70 and 172 to 170, we estimate this product to be 70 × 170 = 11,900. (The exact answer is 11,782.) Note here that we do not always round the numbers to the nearest whole number when making estimates. The idea is to round to numbers that will be easy to multiply.

c. Because 6.32 is approximately 6 and $6^2 = 36$, we estimate our answer to be close to 36. (The actual answer is 39.9424.)

B Order of Operations with Decimals

We can use the rule for order of operations to simplify expressions involving decimal numbers and addition, subtraction, and multiplication.

EXAMPLE 7 Perform the indicated operations: 0.05(4.2 + 0.03).

Solution We begin by adding inside the parentheses.

$$0.05(4.2 + 0.03) = 0.05(4.23) \quad \text{Add.}$$
$$= 0.2115 \quad \text{Multiply.}$$

Notice that we could also have used the distributive property first, and the result would be unchanged.

$$0.05(4.2 + 0.03) = 0.05(4.2) + 0.05(0.03) \quad \text{Distributive property}$$
$$= 0.210 + 0.0015 \quad \text{Multiply.}$$
$$= 0.2115 \quad \text{Add.}$$

5. Multiply: 2.16 × 3.05.

6. Estimate the answer to each of the following products.
  a. 39.6 × 9.1
  b. 58.7 × 141.3
  c. $(9.84)^2$

7. Perform the indicated operations.
  0.07 (3.9 + 6.05)

Answers
5. 6.588
6. a. 360 **b.** 8,400 **c.** 100
7. 0.6965

8. Simplify: $9.5 + 11(2.3)^2$.

EXAMPLE 8   Simplify: $4.8 + 12(3.2)^2$.

Solution   According to the rule for order of operations, we must first evaluate the number with an exponent, then multiply, and finally add.

$$4.8 + 12(3.2)^2 = 4.8 + 12(10.24) \quad (3.2)^2 = 10.24$$
$$= 4.8 + 122.88 \qquad \text{Multiply.}$$
$$= 127.68 \qquad\qquad \text{Add.}$$

Applications

9. How much will Sally from Example 9 make if she works 48 hours in one week?

EXAMPLE 9   Sally earns $6.32 for each of the first 36 hours she works in one week, and $9.48 in overtime pay for each additional hour she works in the same week. How much money will she make if she works 42 hours in one week?

Solution   The difference between 42 and 36 is 6 hours of overtime pay. The total amount of money she will make is

Note   To estimate the answer to Example 9 before doing the actual calculations, we would do the following:

$$6(40) + 9(6) = 240 + 54 = 294$$

Pay for the first   Pay for the
36 hours   next 6 hours

$$6.32(36) + 9.48(6) = 227.52 + 56.88$$
$$= 284.40$$

She will make $284.40 for working 42 hours in one week.

GETTING READY FOR CLASS

After reading through the preceding section, respond in your own words and in complete sentences.

A. If you multiply 34.76 and 0.072, how many digits will be to the right of the decimal point in your answer?

B. To simplify the expression $0.053(9) + 67.42$, what would be the first step according to the rule for order of operations?

C. What is the purpose of estimating?

D. What are some applications of decimals that we use in our everyday lives?

Vocabulary Review

Choose the correct words to fill in the blanks in the paragraph below.

answer   decimal points   multiply   digits

To multiply two decimal numbers, first _____ as you would if the decimal points were not there.
Then place the decimal point in the _____ so that the number of _____ to its
right is equal to the total number of digits to the right of the _____ in the original two numbers
in the problem.

Problems

A Find each of the following products. (Multiply.)

1.   0.7
     $\times$ 0.4

2.   0.8
     $\times$ 0.3

3.   0.07
     $\times$ 0.4

4.   0.8
     $\times$ 0.03

5.   0.03
     $\times$ 0.09

6.   0.07
     $\times$ 0.002

7. 2.6(0.3)

8. 8.9(0.2)

9.   0.9
     $\times$ 0.88

10.   0.8
      $\times$ 0.99

11.   3.12
      $\times$ 0.005

12.   4.69
      $\times$ 0.006

13.   4.003
      $\times$ 6.07

14.   7.0001
      $\times$ 3.04

15. 5(0.006)

16. 7(0.005)

17.   75.14
      $\times$ 2.5

18.   963.8
      $\times$ 0.24

19.   0.1
      $\times$ 0.02

20.   0.3
      $\times$ 0.02

21. 2.796(10)

22. 97.531(100)

23.   0.0043
      $\times$ 100

24.   12.345
      $\times$ 1,000

25.   49.94
      $\times$ 1,000

26.   157.02
      $\times$ 10,000

27.   987.654
      $\times$ 10,000

28.   1.23
      $\times$ 100,000

B Perform the following operations according to the rule for order of operations.

29. $2.1(3.5 - 2.6)$ **30.** $5.4(9.9 - 6.6)$ **31.** $0.05(0.02 + 0.03)$ **32.** $0.04(0.07 + 0.09)$

33. $2.02(0.03 + 2.5)$ **34.** $4.04(0.05 + 6.6)$ **35.** $(2.1 + 0.03)(3.4 + 0.05)$ **36.** $(9.2 + 0.01)(3.5 + 0.03)$

37. $(2.1 - 0.1)(2.1 + 0.1)$ **38.** $(9.6 - 0.5)(9.6 + 0.5)$ **39.** $3.08 - 0.2(5 + 0.03)$ **40.** $4.09 + 0.5(6 + 0.02)$

41. $4.23 - 5(0.04 + 0.09)$ **42.** $7.89 - 2(0.31 + 0.76)$ **43.** $2.5 + 10(4.3)^2$ **44.** $3.6 + 15(2.1)^2$

45. $100(1 + 0.08)^2$ **46.** $500(1 + 0.12)^2$ **47.** $(1.5)^2 + (2.5)^2 + (3.5)^2$ **48.** $(1.1)^2 + (2.1)^2 + (3.1)^2$

Applying the Concepts

Solve each of the following word problems. Note that not all of the problems are solved by simply multiplying the numbers in the problems. Many of the problems involve addition and subtraction as well as multiplication.

49. Number Problem What is the product of 6 and the sum of 0.001 and 0.02?

50. Number Problem Find the product of 8 and the sum of 0.03 and 0.002.

51. Number Problem What does multiplying a decimal number by 100 do to the decimal point?

52. Number Problem What does multiplying a decimal number by 1,000 do to the decimal point?

53. Home Mortgage On a certain home mortgage, there is a monthly payment of $9.66 for every $1,000 that is borrowed. What is the monthly payment on this type of loan if $143,000 is borrowed?

54. Caffeine Content If 1 cup of regular coffee contains 105 milligrams of caffeine, how much caffeine is contained in 3.5 cups of coffee?

55. Long-Distance Charges If a phone company charges $0.45 for the first minute and $0.35 for each additional minute for a long-distance call, how much will a 20-minute long-distance call cost?

56. Price of Gasoline If gasoline costs $3.05 per gallon when you pay with a credit card, but $0.06 per gallon less if you pay with cash, how much do you save by filling up a 12-gallon tank and paying for it with cash?

57. Car Rental Suppose it costs $15 per day and $0.12 per mile to rent a car. What is the total bill if a car is rented for 2 days and is driven 120 miles?

58. Car Rental Suppose it costs $20 per day and $0.08 per mile to rent a car. What is the total bill if the car is rented for 2 days and is driven 120 miles?

59. Wages A man earns $5.92 for each of the first 36 hours he works in one week and $8.88 in overtime pay for each additional hour he works in the same week. How much money will he make if he works 45 hours in one week?

60. Wages A student earns $8.56 for each of the first 40 hours she works in one week and $12.84 in overtime pay for each additional hour she works in the same week. How much money will she make if she works 44 hours in one week?

61. Rectangle A rectangle has a width of 33.5 millimeters and a length of 254 millimeters. Find the area.

62. Rectangle A rectangle has a width of 2.56 inches and a length of 6.14 inches. Find the area rounded to the nearest hundredth.

63. Rectangle The logo on a business letter is rectangular. The rectangle has a width of 0.84 inches and a length of 1.41 inches. Find the area rounded to the nearest hundredth.

64. Rectangle A small sticky note is a rectangle. It has a width of 21.4 millimeters and a length of 35.8 millimeters. Find the area.

Getting Ready for the Next Section

To get ready for the next section, which covers division with decimals, we will review multiplication and division with whole numbers and fractions.

Perform the following operations.

65. $3{,}758 \div 2$ **66.** $9{,}900 \div 22$ **67.** $50{,}032 \div 33$ **68.** $90{,}902 \div 5$

69. $20\overline{)5{,}960}$ **70.** $30\overline{)4{,}620}$ **71.** 4×8.7 **72.** 5×6.7

73. 27×1.848 **74.** 35×32.54 **75.** $38\overline{)31{,}350}$ **76.** $25\overline{)377{,}800}$

Find the Mistake

Each sentence below contains a mistake. Circle the mistake and write the correct word(s) or number(s) on the line provided.

1. To multiply 18.05 by 3.5, multiply as if the numbers were whole numbers and then place the decimal in the answer with two digits to its right. _____

2. To estimate the answer for 24.9×7.3, round 24.9 to 20 and 7.3 to 7. _____

3. To simplify $(8.43 + 1.002) - (0.05)(3.2)$, first subtract the product of 0.05 and 3.2 from 1.002 before adding 8.43.

_____

4. Lucy pays \$1.52 a pound for the first three pounds of candy she buys at a candy store, and pays \$3.27 for each additional pound. To find how much she will pay if she buys 5.2 pounds of candy, we must solve the problem $1.52(3) + 3.27(5.2)$.

_____

4.4 Division with Decimals

OBJECTIVES

A Divide decimal numbers with exact answers.

B Divide decimal numbers with rounded answers.

A coffee maker company announced the development of their new home espresso machine that scans your fingerprint to take an order. The new device can distinguish between six different housemates based on a scan of each fingerprint and its matching preferences (e.g., strength, froth, etc.). The current estimated selling price for the espresso machine is $3,200.

Suppose you and your three roommates have decided to purchase one of these espresso machines selling for $3,199.99. If you decide to split the bill equally, how much does each person owe? To find out, you will have to divide 3199.99 by 4. In this section, we will find out how to do division with any combination of decimal numbers.

A Dividing Decimal Numbers (Exact Answers)

EXAMPLE 1 Divide: 5,974 ÷ 20.

Solution

$$
\begin{array}{r}
298 \\
20\overline{)5974} \\
40 \\
\hline
197 \\
180 \\
\hline
174 \\
160 \\
\hline
14
\end{array}
$$

In the past, we have written this answer as $298\frac{14}{20}$ or, after reducing the fraction, $298\frac{7}{10}$. Because $\frac{7}{10}$ can be written as 0.7, we could also write our answer as 298.7. This last form of our answer is exactly the same result we obtain if we write 5,974 as 5,974.0 and continue the division until we have no remainder. Here is how it looks:

$$
\begin{array}{r}
298.7 \\
20\overline{)5974.0} \\
40 \\
\hline
197 \\
180 \\
\hline
174 \\
160 \\
\hline
140 \\
140 \\
\hline
0
\end{array}
$$

Notice that we place the decimal point in the answer directly above the decimal point in the problem.

Video Examples
SECTION 4.4

Practice Problems

1. Divide: 4,870 ÷ 50.

Note We can estimate the answer to Example 1 by rounding 5,974 to 6,000 and dividing by 20:

$$\frac{6,000}{20} = 300$$

Answer

1. 97.4

Let's try another division problem. This time one of the numbers in the problem will be a decimal.

EXAMPLE 2   Divide: 34.8 ÷ 4.

Solution   We can use the ideas from Example 1 and divide as usual. The decimal point in the answer will be placed directly above the decimal point in the problem.

$$
\begin{array}{r}
8.7 \\
4{\overline{)34.8}} \\
32 \downarrow \\
\hline
28 \\
28 \\
\hline
0
\end{array}
\qquad
\begin{array}{r}
Check: \quad 8.7 \\
\times\ 4 \\
\hline
34.8
\end{array}
$$

The answer is 8.7.

We can use these facts to write a rule for dividing decimal numbers.

> **RULE** Division with Decimal Numbers
>
> To divide a decimal by a whole number, we do the usual long division as if there were no decimal point involved. The decimal point in the answer is placed directly above the decimal point in the problem.

Here are some more examples to illustrate the procedure:

EXAMPLE 3   Divide: 49.896 ÷ 27.
Solution

$$
\begin{array}{r}
1.848 \\
27{\overline{)49.896}} \\
27 \\
\hline
228 \\
216 \\
\hline
129 \\
108 \\
\hline
216 \\
216 \\
\hline
0
\end{array}
\qquad
\begin{array}{r}
Check: \quad 1.848 \\
\times\ 27 \\
\hline
12936 \\
3696 \\
\hline
49.896
\end{array}
$$

We can write as many zeros as we choose after the rightmost digit in a decimal number without changing the value of the number. For example,

$$6.91 = 6.910 = 6.9100 = 6.91000$$

There are times when this can be very useful, as Example 4 shows.

EXAMPLE 4   Divide: 1,138.9 ÷ 35.
Solution

$$
\begin{array}{r}
32.54 \\
35{\overline{)1138.90}} \\
105 \\
\hline
88 \\
70 \\
\hline
189 \\
175 \\
\hline
140 \\
140 \\
\hline
0
\end{array}
$$

Write 0 after the 9. It doesn't change the original number, but it gives us another digit to bring down.

$$
\begin{array}{r}
Check: \quad 32.54 \\
\times\ 35 \\
\hline
16270 \\
9762 \\
\hline
1,138.90
\end{array}
$$

2. Divide: 56.9 ÷ 5.

Note We never need to make a mistake with division, because we can always check our results with multiplication.

3. Divide: 54.632 ÷ 25.

4. Divide: 1,105.8 ÷ 15.

Answers
2. 11.38
3. 2.18528
4. 73.72

Until now we have considered only division by whole numbers. Extending division to include division by decimal numbers is a matter of knowing what to do about the decimal point in the divisor.

EXAMPLE 5 Divide: $31.35 \div 3.8$.

Solution In fraction form, this problem is equivalent to

$$\frac{31.35}{3.8}$$

If we want to write the divisor as a whole number, we can multiply the numerator and the denominator of this fraction by 10:

$$\frac{31.35 \times 10}{3.8 \times 10} = \frac{313.5}{38}$$

So, since this fraction is equivalent to the original fraction, our original division problem is equivalent to

$$
\begin{array}{r}
8.25 \\
38\overline{)313.50} \\
304 \\
\hline
95 \\
76 \\
\hline
190 \\
190 \\
\hline
0
\end{array}
$$

Put 0 after the last digit.

We can summarize division with decimal numbers by listing the following points, as illustrated in the first five examples.

Summary of Division with Decimals

1. We divide decimal numbers by the same process used to divide whole numbers. The decimal point in the answer is placed directly above the decimal point in the dividend.

2. We are free to write as many zeros after the last digit in a decimal number as we need.

3. If the divisor is a decimal, we can change it to a whole number by moving the decimal point to the right as many places as necessary so long as we move the decimal point in the dividend the same number of places.

B Dividing Decimal Numbers (Rounded Answers)

EXAMPLE 6 Divide, and round the answer to the nearest hundredth.

$$0.3778 \div 0.25$$

Solution First, we move the decimal point two places to the right.

$$0.25\overline{)37.78}$$

---

5. Divide: $46.354 \div 4.9$.

Note We do not always use the rules for rounding numbers to make estimates. For example, to estimate the answer in Example 5, $31.35 \div 3.8$, we can get a rough estimate of the answer by reasoning that 3.8 is close to 4 and 31.35 is close to 32. Therefore, our answer will be approximately $32 \div 4 = 8$.

6. Divide, and round the answer to the nearest hundredth.

$$0.3849 \div 0.49$$

Note Moving the decimal point two places in both the divisor and the dividend is justified like this:

$$\frac{0.3778 \times 100}{0.25 \times 100} = \frac{37.78}{25}$$

Answers
5. 9.46
6. 0.79

Then we divide, using long division.

$$
\begin{array}{r}
1.5112 \\
25\overline{)37.7800} \\
25 \\
\hline
127 \\
125 \\
\hline
28 \\
25 \\
\hline
30 \\
25 \\
\hline
50 \\
50 \\
\hline
0
\end{array}
$$

Rounding to the nearest hundredth, we have 1.51. We actually did not need to have this many digits to round to the hundredths column. We could have stopped at the thousandths column and rounded off.

EXAMPLE 7   Divide and round to the nearest tenth: $17 \div 0.03$.

Solution   Because we are rounding to the nearest tenth, we will continue dividing until we have a digit in the hundredths column. We don't have to go any further to round to the tenths column.

$$
\begin{array}{r}
566.66 \\
0.03\overline{)17.00.00} \\
15 \\
\hline
20 \\
18 \\
\hline
20 \\
18 \\
\hline
20 \\
18 \\
\hline
20 \\
18 \\
\hline
2
\end{array}
$$

Rounding to the nearest tenth, we have 566.7.

Applications

EXAMPLE 8   If a man earning $5.26 an hour receives a paycheck for $170.95 before deductions, how many hours did he work?

Solution   To find the number of hours the man worked, we divide $170.95 by $5.26.

$$
\begin{array}{r}
32.5 \\
5.26\overline{)170.95.0} \\
1578 \\
\hline
1315 \\
1052 \\
\hline
2630 \\
2630 \\
\hline
0
\end{array}
$$

The man worked 32.5 hours.

7. Divide, and round to the nearest tenth.

$$19 \div 0.07$$

8. If you earn $8.30 per hour and receive a paycheck for $311.25 before deductions, how many hours did you work?

EXAMPLE 9 A telephone company charges $0.43 for the first minute and then $0.33 for each additional minute for a long-distance call. If a long-distance call costs $3.07, how many minutes was the call?

Solution To solve this problem we need to find the number of additional minutes for the call. To do so, we first subtract the cost of the first minute from the total cost, and then we divide the result by the cost of each additional minute. Without showing the actual arithmetic involved, the solution looks like this:

$$\text{The number of additional minutes} = \frac{\overset{\text{Total cost of the call}}{3.07} - \overset{\text{Cost of the first minute}}{0.43}}{\underset{\text{Cost of each additional minute}}{0.33}} = \frac{2.64}{0.33} = 8$$

The call was 9 minutes long. (The number 8 is the number of additional minutes past the first minute.)

EXAMPLE 10 Calculate Amy's grade point average using the previous information.

Solution We begin by creating two more columns: one for the value of each grade (4 for an A, 3 for a B, 2 for a C, 1 for a D, and 0 for an F), and another for the grade points earned for each class. To fill in the grade points column, we multiply the number of units by the value of the grade.

Class	Units	Grade	Value	Grade Points
Algebra	5	B	3	$5 \times 3 = 15$
Chemistry	4	C	2	$4 \times 2 = 8$
English	3	A	4	$3 \times 4 = 12$
History	3	B	3	$3 \times 3 = 9$
Total Units	15			Total Grade Points: 44

To find her grade point average, we divide 44 by 15 and round (if necessary) to the nearest hundredth.

$$\text{Grade point average} = \frac{44}{15} = 2.93$$

GETTING READY FOR CLASS

After reading through the preceding section, respond in your own words and in complete sentences.

A. The answer to the division problem in Example 1 is $298\frac{14}{20}$. Write this number in decimal notation.

B. In Example 4, we place a 0 at the end of a number without changing the value of the number. Why is the placement of this 0 helpful?

C. The expression $0.3778 \div 0.25$ is equivalent to the expression $37.78 \div 25$ because each number was multiplied by what?

D. Briefly explain how to divide with decimals.

9. Repeat Example 9 if the long distance call costs $13.63.

10. Calculate the grade-point average.

Class	Units	Grade
Algebra	4	A
Biology	3	B
English	3	B
History	3	C
PE	1	A

Answers
9. 41 minutes
10. 3.14

Vocabulary Review

Choose the correct words to fill in the blanks below.

divisor   above   long division   right   last

1. To divide decimal numbers, use _____ as if the decimal point was not there.

2. In a long division problem that involves a decimal point, write the decimal point in the answer directly _____ the decimal point in the problem.

3. Writing zeros after the _____ digit in a decimal number will not change the value.

4. If the _____ is a decimal, we can change it to a whole number by moving the decimal point to the _____ as many places as necessary so long as we move the decimal point in the dividend the same number of places.

Problems

A Perform each of the following divisions.

1. $394 \div 20$

2. $486 \div 30$

3. $248 \div 40$

4. $372 \div 80$

5. $5\overline{)26}$

6. $8\overline{)36}$

7. $25\overline{)276}$

8. $50\overline{)276}$

9. $28.8 \div 6$

10. $15.5 \div 5$

11. $77.6 \div 8$

12. $31.48 \div 4$

13. $35\overline{)92.05}$

14. $26\overline{)146.38}$

15. $45\overline{)190.8}$

16. $55\overline{)342.1}$

17. $86.7 \div 34$

18. $411.4 \div 44$

19. $29.7 \div 22$

20. $488.4 \div 88$

21. $4.5\overline{)29.25}$

22. $3.3\overline{)21.978}$

23. $0.11\overline{)1.089}$

24. $0.75\overline{)2.40}$

25. $2.3\overline{)0.115}$

26. $6.6\overline{)0.198}$

27. $0.012\overline{)1.068}$

28. $0.052\overline{)0.23712}$

29. $1.1\overline{)2.42}$ **30.** $2.2\overline{)7.26}$ **31.** $0.014\overline{)0.0644}$ **32.** $0.38\overline{)9.652}$

B Carry out each of the following divisions only so far as needed to round the results to the nearest hundredth.

33. $26\overline{)35}$ **34.** $18\overline{)47}$ **35.** $3.3\overline{)56}$ **36.** $4.4\overline{)75}$

37. $0.1234 \div 0.5$ **38.** $0.543 \div 2.1$ **39.** $19 \div 7$ **40.** $16 \div 6$

41. $0.059\overline{)0.69}$ **42.** $0.048\overline{)0.49}$ **43.** $1.99 \div 0.5$ **44.** $0.99 \div 0.5$

45. $2.99 \div 0.5$ **46.** $3.99 \div 0.5$ **47.** $3.82 \div 0.9$ **48.** $1.79 \div 0.08$

Applying the Concepts

49. Hot Air Balloon Since the pilot of a hot air balloon can only control the balloon's altitude, he relies on the winds for travel. To ride on the jet streams, a hot air balloon must rise as high as 12 kilometers. Convert this to miles by dividing by 1.61. Round your answer to the nearest tenth of a mile.

50. Hot Air Balloon December and January are the best times for traveling in a hot-air balloon because the jet streams in the Northern Hemisphere are the strongest. They reach speeds of 400 kilometers per hour. Convert this to miles per hour by dividing by 1.61. Round to the nearest whole number.

51. Women's Golf The table below gives the top five money earners for the Ladies' Professional Golf Association (LPGA) in 2010. Fill in the last column of the table by finding the average earning per tournament for each golfer. Round your answers to the nearest ten dollars.

Rank	Name	Number of Tournaments	Total Earnings	Average per Tournament
1.	Na Yeon Choi	23	$1,871,165.50	
2.	Jiyai Shin	19	$1,783,127.00	
3.	Cristie Kerr	21	$1,601,551.75	
4.	Yani Tseng	19	$1,573,529.00	
5.	Suzann Pettersen	19	$1,557,174.50	

52. Men's Golf The table below gives the top five earners for the men's Professional Golf Association (PGA) in 2010. Fill in the last column of the table by finding the average earnings per tournament for each golfer. Round your answers to the nearest hundred dollars.

Rank	Name	Number of Tournaments	Total Earnings	Average per Tournament
1.	Matt Kuchar	26	$4,910,477	
2.	Jim Furyk	21	$4,809,622	
3.	Ernie Els	20	$4,558,861	
4.	Dustin Johnson	23	$4,473,122	
5.	Steve Stricker	19	$4,190,235	

53. Wages If a woman earns $33.90 for working 6 hours, how much does she earn per hour?

54. Wages How many hours does a person making $6.78 per hour have to work in order to earn $257.64?

55. Gas Mileage If a car travels 336 miles on 15 gallons of gas, how far will the car travel on 1 gallon of gas?

56. Gas Mileage If a car travels 392 miles on 16 gallons of gas, how far will the car travel on 1 gallon of gas?

57. Wages Suppose a woman earns $6.78 an hour for the first 36 hours she works in a week and then $10.17 an hour in overtime pay for each additional hour she works in the same week. If she makes $294.93 in one week, how many hours did she work overtime?

58. Wages Suppose a woman makes $286.08 in one week. If she is paid $5.96 an hour for the first 36 hours she works and then $8.94 an hour in overtime pay for each additional hour she works in the same week, how many hours did she work overtime that week?

59. Phone Bill Suppose a telephone company charges $0.41 for the first minute and then $0.32 for each additional minute for a long-distance call. If a long-distance call costs $2.33, how many minutes was the call?

60. Phone Bill Suppose a telephone company charges $0.45 for each of the first three minutes and then $0.29 for each additional minute for a long-distance call. If a long-distance call costs $3.67, how many minutes was the call?

Grade Point Average The following grades were earned by Steve during his first term in college. Use these data to answer Problems 61–64.

61. Calculate Steve's GPA.

62. If his grade in chemistry had been a B instead of a C, by how much would his GPA have increased?

Class	Units	Grade
Basic mathematics	3	A
Health	2	B
History	3	B
English	3	C
Chemistry	4	C

63. If his grade in health had been a C instead of a B, by how much would his grade point average have dropped?

64. If his grades in both English and chemistry had been Bs, what would his GPA have been?

Calculator Problems   Work each of the following problems on your calculator. If rounding is necessary, round to the nearest hundred thousandth.

65. $7 \div 9$

66. $11 \div 13$

67. $243 \div 0.791$

68. $67.8 \div 37.92$

69. $0.0503 \div 0.0709$

70. $429.87 \div 16.925$

Getting Ready for the Next Section

In the next section, we will consider the relationship between fractions and decimals in more detail. The problems below review some of the material that is necessary to make a successful start in the next section.

Reduce to lowest terms.

71. $\dfrac{75}{100}$

72. $\dfrac{220}{1,000}$

73. $\dfrac{12}{18}$

74. $\dfrac{15}{30}$

75. $\dfrac{75}{200}$

76. $\dfrac{220}{2,000}$

77. $\dfrac{38}{100}$

78. $\dfrac{75}{1,000}$

Write each fraction as an equivalent fraction with denominator 100.

79. $\dfrac{3}{5}$

80. $\dfrac{1}{2}$

81. $\dfrac{5}{1}$

82. $\dfrac{17}{20}$

Write each fraction as an equivalent fraction with denominator 15.

83. $\dfrac{4}{5}$

84. $\dfrac{2}{3}$

85. $\dfrac{4}{1}$

86. $\dfrac{2}{1}$

87. $\dfrac{6}{5}$

88. $\dfrac{7}{3}$

Divide.

89. $3 \div 4$

90. $3 \div 5$

91. $7 \div 8$

92. $3 \div 8$

Find the Mistake

Each sentence below contains a mistake. Circle the mistake and write the correct word(s) or number(s) on the line provided.

1. The answer to the problem $25\overline{)70.75}$ will have a decimal point placed with four digits to its right. _____

2. To work the problem $27.468 \div 8.4$, multiply 8.4 by 10 and then divide. _____

3. To divide 0.6778 by 0.54, multiply both numbers by 10 to move the decimal point two places to the right. _____

4. Samantha earns \$10.16 an hour as a cashier. She received a paycheck for \$309.88. To find out how many hours she worked, you must solve the problem $10.16 \div 309.88$. _____

Landmark Review: Checking Your Progress

Write each of the following in words.

1. 1.15

2. 45.08

3. 0.005

4. 245.157

Write each of the following as a decimal number.

5. Sixty-seven ten thousandths

6. Five and six tenths

7. Twenty-three and fourteen thousandths

8. Two thousand thirteen and fifteen hundredths

Find each of the following sums and differences.

9. $24.13 + 4.15$

10. $6.000014 + 3.15$

11. $100.00001 + 24.1583$

12. $5.387 + 6.412$

13. $8.3 - 5.2$

14. $14.2 - 7.13$

15. $27.57 - 14.24$

16. $92.42 - 14.05$

Perform each of the following operations.

17. $4.735(10)$

18. $0.075(0.03)$

19. $1.4 \div 0.07$

20. $0.24 \div 0.6$

Perform the following operations according to the rule for order of operations.

21. $4.3(3.8 - 2.6)$

22. $(2.85 - 1.7)(5.67 + 4.2)$

23. $5.5 + 2.2(14 - 12.5)$

4.5 Fractions and Decimals

Image © sxc.hu, Thoursie, 2010

If you are shopping for clothes and a store has a sale advertising $\frac{1}{3}$ off the regular price, how much can you expect to pay for a pair of pants that normally sells for $31.95? If the sale price of the pants is $22.30, have they really been marked down by $\frac{1}{3}$? To answer questions like these, we need to know how to solve problems that involve fractions and decimals together.

We begin this section by showing how to convert back and forth between fractions and decimals.

KEY WORDS

convert

Video Examples
SECTION 4.5

A Converting Fractions to Decimals

You may recall that the notation we use for fractions can be interpreted as implying division. That is, the fraction $\frac{3}{4}$ can be thought of as meaning "3 divided by 4." We can use this idea to convert fractions to decimals.

Practice Problems

1. Write $\frac{5}{8}$ as a decimal.

EXAMPLE 1   Write $\frac{3}{4}$ as a decimal.

Solution   Dividing 3 by 4, we have

$$
\begin{array}{r}
.75 \\
4\overline{)3.00} \\
\underline{28} \\
20 \\
\underline{20} \\
0
\end{array}
$$

The fraction $\frac{3}{4}$ is equal to the decimal 0.75.

EXAMPLE 2   Write $\frac{7}{12}$ as a decimal rounded to the thousandths place.

2. Write $\frac{5}{7}$ as a decimal rounded to the thousandths place.

Solution   Because we want the decimal to be rounded to the thousandths place, we divide to the ten thousandths place and round off to the thousandths place.

$$
\begin{array}{r}
.5833 \\
12\overline{)7.0000} \\
\underline{60} \\
100 \\
\underline{96} \\
40 \\
\underline{36} \\
40 \\
\underline{36} \\
4
\end{array}
$$

Answers

1. 0.625
2. 0.714

Rounding off to the thousandths place, we have 0.583. Because $\frac{7}{12}$ is not exactly the same as 0.583, we write

$$\frac{7}{12} \approx 0.583$$

where the symbol $\approx$ is read "is approximately equal to."

If we wrote more zeros after 0.583 in Example 2, the pattern of 3s would continue for as many places as we choose to divide. When we get a sequence of digits that repeat like this, 0.58333 . . . , we can indicate the repetition by writing

$$0.58\overline{3} \qquad \textit{The bar over the 3 indicates that the 3 repeats from there on.}$$

3. Write $\frac{5}{6}$ as a decimal.

EXAMPLE 3 Write $\frac{3}{11}$ as a decimal.

Solution Dividing 3 by 11, we have

```
        .272727
   11)3.000000
      2 2
      ───
        80
        77
        ──
        30
        22
        ──
         80
         77
         ──
         30
         22
         ──
          80
          77
          ──
           3
```

No matter how long we continue the division, the remainder will never be 0, and the pattern will continue. We write the decimal form of $\frac{3}{11}$ as $0.\overline{27}$, where

$$0.\overline{27} = 0.272727 \ldots \qquad \textit{The dots mean "and so on."}$$

Note The bar over the 2 and the 7 in $0.\overline{27}$ is used to indicate that the pattern repeats itself indefinitely.

Converting Decimals to Fractions

To convert decimals to fractions, we take advantage of the place values we assigned to the digits to the right of the decimal point.

4. Write 0.76 as a fraction in lowest terms.

EXAMPLE 4 Write 0.38 as a fraction in lowest terms.

Solution 0.38 is 38 hundredths, or

$$0.38 = \frac{38}{100}$$

$$= \frac{19}{50} \qquad \textit{Divide the numerator and the denominator by 2 to reduce to lowest terms.}$$

The decimal 0.38 is equal to the fraction $\frac{19}{50}$.

We could check our work here by converting $\frac{19}{50}$ back to a decimal. We do this by dividing 19 by 50. That is,

```
        .38
   50)19.00
      15 0
      ────
        4 00
        4 00
        ────
           0
```

EXAMPLE 5   Convert 0.075 to a fraction.

Solution   We have 75 thousandths, or

$$0.075 = \frac{75}{1,000}$$

$$= \frac{3}{40} \qquad \text{\textit{Divide the numerator and the denominator by}}$$
$$\text{\textit{25 to reduce to lowest terms.}}$$

5. Convert 0.045 to a fraction.

EXAMPLE 6   Write 15.6 as a mixed number.

Solution   Converting 0.6 to a fraction, we have

$$0.6 = \frac{6}{10} = \frac{3}{5} \qquad \text{\textit{Reduce to lowest terms.}}$$

Since $0.6 = \frac{3}{5}$, we have $15.6 = 15\frac{3}{5}$.

6. Write 12.08 as a mixed number.

B Problems Containing Both Fractions and Decimals

We continue this section by working some problems that involve both fractions and decimals.

EXAMPLE 7   Simplify: $\frac{19}{50}(1.32 + 0.48)$.

Solution   In Example 4, we found that $0.38 = \frac{19}{50}$. Therefore, we can rewrite the problem as

$$\frac{19}{50}(1.32 + 0.48) = 0.38(1.32 + 0.48) \quad \text{\textit{Convert all numbers to decimals.}}$$

$$= 0.38(1.80) \qquad \text{\textit{Add: 1.32 + 0.48.}}$$
$$= 0.684 \qquad \text{\textit{Multiply: 0.38 × 1.80.}}$$

7. Simplify: $\frac{12}{25}(1.41 - 0.56)$.

EXAMPLE 8   Simplify: $\frac{1}{2} + (0.75)\left(\frac{2}{5}\right)$.

Solution   We could do this problem one of two different ways. First, we could convert all fractions to decimals and then simplify.

$$\frac{1}{2} + (0.75)\left(\frac{2}{5}\right) = 0.5 + 0.75(0.4) \qquad \text{\textit{Convert to decimals.}}$$

$$= 0.5 + 0.300 \qquad \text{\textit{Multiply: 0.75 × 0.4.}}$$
$$= 0.8 \qquad \text{\textit{Add.}}$$

Or, we could convert 0.75 to $\frac{3}{4}$ and then simplify.

$$\frac{1}{2} + (0.75)\left(\frac{2}{5}\right) = \frac{1}{2} + \frac{3}{4}\left(\frac{2}{5}\right) \qquad \text{\textit{Convert decimals to fractions.}}$$

$$= \frac{1}{2} + \frac{3}{10} \qquad \text{\textit{Multiply: } \frac{3}{4} \times \frac{2}{5}.}$$

$$= \frac{5}{10} + \frac{3}{10} \qquad \text{\textit{The common denominator is 10.}}$$

$$= \frac{8}{10} \qquad \text{\textit{Add numerators.}}$$

$$= \frac{4}{5} \qquad \text{\textit{Reduce to lowest terms.}}$$

8. Simplify: $\frac{3}{4} + \frac{2}{3}(0.66)$.

The answers are equivalent. That is, $0.8 = \frac{8}{10} = \frac{4}{5}$. Either method can be used with problems of this type.

Answers

5. $\frac{9}{200}$

6. $12\frac{2}{25}$

7. 0.408

8. 1.19

9. A pair of jeans that normally sell for $38.60 are on sale for $\frac{1}{4}$ off. What is the sale price of the jeans?

Applications

EXAMPLE 9 If a shirt that normally sells for $27.99 is on sale for $\frac{1}{3}$ off, what is the sale price of the shirt?

Solution To find out how much the shirt is marked down, we must find $\frac{1}{3}$ of 27.99. That is, we multiply $\frac{1}{3}$ and 27.99, which is the same as dividing 27.99 by 3.

$$\frac{1}{3}(27.99) = \frac{27.99}{3} = 9.33$$

The shirt is marked down $9.33. The sale price is $9.33 less than the original price.

$$\text{Sale price} = 27.99 - 9.33 = 18.66$$

The sale price is $18.66. We also could have solved this problem by simply multiplying the original price by $\frac{2}{3}$, since, if the shirt is marked $\frac{1}{3}$ off, then the sale price must be $\frac{2}{3}$ of the original price. Multiplying by $\frac{2}{3}$ is the same as dividing by 3 and then multiplying by 2. The answer would be the same.

GETTING READY FOR CLASS

After reading through the preceding section, respond in your own words and in complete sentences.

A. To convert fractions to decimals, do we multiply or divide the numerator by the denominator?

B. The decimal 0.13 is equivalent to what fraction?

C. Write 36 thousandths in decimal form and in fraction form.

D. Explain how to write the fraction $\frac{84}{1,000}$ in lowest terms.

Vocabulary Review

Choose the correct words to fill in the blanks below.

    repeats   place values   division   reduce

1. To convert a fraction to a decimal, think of the fraction in terms of _____ .

2. A bar over the right most digit(s) in a decimal number indicates that digit _____ indefinitely.

3. To convert a decimal to a fraction, use the _____ of the digits and _____ to lowest terms.

Problems

A Each circle below is divided into 8 equal parts. The number below each circle indicates what fraction of the circle is shaded. Convert each fraction to a decimal.

1.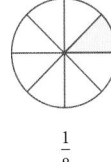

$\frac{1}{8}$

2.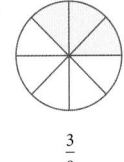

$\frac{3}{8}$

3.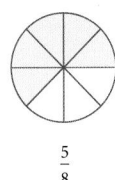

$\frac{5}{8}$

4.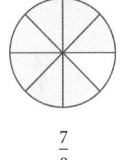

$\frac{7}{8}$

Complete the following tables by converting each fraction to a decimal.

5.

Fraction	$\frac{1}{5}$	$\frac{2}{5}$	$\frac{3}{5}$	$\frac{4}{5}$	$\frac{5}{5}$
Decimal					

6.

Fraction	$\frac{1}{6}$	$\frac{2}{6}$	$\frac{3}{6}$	$\frac{4}{6}$	$\frac{5}{6}$	$\frac{6}{6}$
Decimal						

Convert each of the following fractions to a decimal.

7. $\frac{1}{2}$

8. $\frac{12}{25}$

9. $\frac{14}{25}$

10. $\frac{14}{32}$

11. $\frac{18}{32}$

12. $\frac{9}{16}$

13. $\frac{13}{16}$

14. $\frac{13}{8}$

Write each fraction as a decimal rounded to the hundredths place.

15. $\frac{12}{13}$

16. $\frac{17}{19}$

17. $\frac{3}{11}$

18. $\frac{5}{11}$

19. $\frac{2}{23}$

20. $\frac{3}{28}$

21. $\frac{12}{43}$

22. $\frac{15}{51}$

Complete the following table by converting each decimal to a fraction.

23.

Decimal	0.125	0.250	0.375	0.500	0.625	0.750	0.875
Fraction							

24.

Decimal	0.1	0.2	0.3	0.4	0.5	0.6	0.7	0.8	0.9
Fraction									

Write each decimal as a fraction in lowest terms.

25. 0.15 **26.** 0.45 **27.** 0.08 **28.** 0.06 **29.** 0.375 **30.** 0.475

Write each decimal as a mixed number.

31. 5.6 **32.** 8.4 **33.** 5.06 **34.** 8.04 **35.** 1.22 **36.** 2.11

B Simplify each of the following as much as possible, and write all answers as decimals.

37. $\frac{1}{2}(2.3 + 2.5)$

38. $\frac{3}{4}(1.8 + 7.6)$

39. $\dfrac{1.99}{\frac{1}{2}}$

40. $\dfrac{2.99}{\frac{1}{2}}$

41. $3.4 - \frac{1}{2}(0.76)$

42. $6.7 - \frac{1}{5}(0.45)$

43. $\frac{2}{5}(0.3) + \frac{3}{5}(0.3)$

44. $\frac{1}{8}(0.7) + \frac{3}{8}(0.7)$

45. $6\left(\frac{3}{5}\right)(0.02)$

46. $8\left(\frac{4}{5}\right)(0.03)$

47. $\frac{5}{8} + 0.35\left(\frac{1}{2}\right)$

48. $\frac{7}{8} + 0.45\left(\frac{3}{4}\right)$

49. $\left(\frac{1}{3}\right)^2(5.4) + \left(\frac{1}{2}\right)^3(3.2)$

50. $\left(\frac{1}{5}\right)^2(7.5) + \left(\frac{1}{4}\right)^2(6.4)$

51. $(0.25)^2 + \left(\frac{1}{4}\right)^2(3)$

52. $(0.75)^2 + \left(\frac{1}{4}\right)^2(7)$

Applying the Concepts

53. Price of Beef If each pound of beef costs $2.59, how much does $3\frac{1}{4}$ pounds cost?

54. Price of Gasoline What does it cost to fill a $15\frac{1}{2}$-gallon gas tank if the gasoline is priced at 305.2¢ per gallon? Convert your answer to dollars.

55. Sale Price A dress that costs $57.99 is on sale for $\frac{1}{3}$ off. What is the sale price of the dress?

56. Sale Price A suit that normally sells for $121 is on sale for $\frac{1}{4}$ off. What is the sale price of the suit?

57. Average Gain in Stock Price The table below shows the amount of gain each day of one week in 2011 for the price of Verizon stock. Complete the table by converting each fraction to a decimal and rounding to the nearest hundredth if necessary.

Change in Stock Price		
Day	Gain ($)	As a Decimal ($) (to the nearest hundredth)
Monday	$\frac{3}{5}$	
Tuesday	$\frac{1}{2}$	
Wednesday	$\frac{1}{25}$	
Thursday	$\frac{1}{5}$	
Friday	$\frac{1}{10}$	

58. Average Gain in Stock Price The table below shows the amount of gain each day of one week in 2011 for the price of AT&T stock. Complete the table by converting each fraction to a decimal and rounding to the nearest hundredth, if necessary.

Change in Stock Price		
Day	Gain	As a Decimal ($) (to the nearest hundredth)
Monday	$\frac{3}{10}$	
Tuesday	$\frac{3}{50}$	
Wednesday	$\frac{2}{25}$	
Thursday	$\frac{1}{10}$	
Friday	0	

59. Nutrition If 1 ounce of ground beef contains 50.75 calories and 1 ounce of halibut contains 27.5 calories, what is the difference in calories between a $4\frac{1}{2}$-ounce serving of ground beef and a $4\frac{1}{2}$-ounce serving of halibut?

60. Nutrition If a 1-ounce serving of baked potato contains 48.3 calories and a 1-ounce serving of chicken contains 24.6 calories, how many calories are in a meal of $5\frac{1}{4}$ ounces of chicken and a $3\frac{1}{3}$-ounce baked potato?

Taxi Ride The Texas Junior College Teachers Association annual conference was held in Austin. At that time, a taxi ride in Austin was $1.25 for the first $\frac{1}{5}$ of a mile and $0.25 for each additional $\frac{1}{5}$ of a mile. The charge for a taxi to wait is $12.00 per hour. Use this information for Problems 61 through 64.

61. If the distance from one of the convention hotels to the airport is 7.5 miles, how much will it cost to take a taxi from that hotel to the airport?

62. If you were to tip the driver of the taxi in Problem 63 $1.50, how much would it cost to take a taxi from the hotel to the airport?

63. Suppose the distance from one of the hotels to one of the western dance clubs in Austin is 12.4 miles. If the fare meter in the taxi gives the charge for that trip as $16.50, is the meter working correctly?

64. Suppose that the distance from a hotel to the airport is 8.2 miles, and the ride takes 20 minutes. Is it more expensive to take a taxi to the airport or to just sit in the taxi?

Find the Mistake

Each sentence below contains a mistake. Circle the mistake and write the correct word(s) or number(s) on the line provided.

1. The correct way to write $\frac{6}{11}$ as a decimal is 0.54545454.... _____

2. Writing 14.3 as a fraction gives us $14 \cdot \frac{3}{10} = \frac{42}{10} = \frac{21}{5}$. _____

3. The simplified answer to the problem $\frac{12}{45(0.256 + 0.14)}$ contains both fractions and decimals. _____

4. Simplifying the problem $\left(\frac{3}{2}\right)(0.5) + \left(\frac{1}{2}\right)(6.7)$ by first converting all decimals to fractions gives us $\left(\frac{3}{2}\right)\left(\frac{1}{2}\right) + \left(\frac{1}{2}\right)\left(\frac{67}{100}\right)$.

_____

Chapter **4** Summary

Place Value [4.1]

The place values for the first five places to the right of the decimal point are

Decimal Point	Tenths	Hundredths	Thousandths	Ten Thousandths	Hundred Thousandths
.	$\frac{1}{10}$	$\frac{1}{100}$	$\frac{1}{1,000}$	$\frac{1}{10,000}$	$\frac{1}{100,000}$

Rounding Decimals [4.1]

If the digit in the column to the right of the one we are rounding to is 5 or more, we add 1 to the digit in the column we are rounding to; otherwise, we leave it alone. We then replace all digits to the right of the column we are rounding to with zeros if they are to the left of the decimal point; otherwise, we simply delete them.

Addition and Subtraction with Decimals [4.2]

To add (or subtract) decimal numbers, we align the decimal points and add (or subtract) as if we were adding (or subtracting) whole numbers. The decimal point in the answer goes directly below the decimal points in the problem.

Multiplication with Decimals [4.3]

To multiply two decimal numbers, we multiply as if the decimal points were not there. The decimal point in the product has as many digits to the right as there are total digits to the right of the decimal points in the two original numbers.

Division with Decimals [4.4]

To begin a division problem with decimals, we make sure that the divisor is a whole number. If it is not, we move the decimal point in the divisor to the right as many places as it takes to make it a whole number. We must then be sure to move the decimal point in the dividend the same number of places to the right. Once the divisor is a whole number, we divide as usual. The decimal point in the answer is placed directly above the decimal point in the dividend.

EXAMPLES

1. The number 4.123 in words is "four and one hundred twenty-three thousandths."

2. 357.753 rounded to the nearest
Tenth: 357.8
Ten: 360

3.
```
   3.400
  25.060
+  0.347
--------
  28.807
```

4. If we multiply 3.49 × 5.863, there will be a total of 2 + 3 = 5 digits to the right of the decimal point in the answer.

5.
```
          1.39
  2.5.)3.4.75
        2 5
        ---
          9 7
          7 5
          ---
          2 25
          2 25
          ----
             0
```

Changing Fractions to Decimals [4.5]

To change a fraction to a decimal, we divide the numerator by the denominator.

6. $\dfrac{4}{15} = 0.2\overline{6}$ because

$$
\begin{array}{r}
.266 \\
15\overline{)4.000} \\
\underline{30}\downarrow \\
100 \\
\underline{90}\downarrow \\
100 \\
\underline{90} \\
10
\end{array}
$$

Changing Decimals to Fractions [4.5]

To change a decimal to a fraction, we write the digits to the right of the decimal point over the appropriate power of 10.

7. $0.781 = \dfrac{781}{1,000}$

1. Write the decimal number 6.302 in words. [4.1]

2. Give the place value of the 6 in the number 23.4263. [4.1]

3. Write twenty-three and five thousand, six ten thousandths as a decimal number. [4.1]

4. Round 72.1950 to the nearest hundredth. [4.1]

Perform the following operations. Round to the nearest thousandth if necessary. [4.2, 4.3, 4.4]

5. $11 + 0.1 + 0.92$

6. $14.002 - 6.098$

7. $1.8(9.03)$

8. $11.913 \div 4.8$

9. $8.1 + 6.49$

10. $14.83 - 6.938$

11. $0.9(3.1)(1.1)$

12. $12.364 \div 4$

13. A person purchases $7.23 worth of goods at a drugstore. If a $10 bill is used to pay for the purchases, how much change is received? [4.2]

14. If coffee sells for $5.29 per pound, how much will 4.5 pounds of coffee cost? [4.3]

15. If a person earns $540 for working 80 hours, what is the person's hourly wage? [4.4]

16. Write $\frac{17}{20}$ as a decimal. [4.5]

17. Write 0.62 as a fraction in lowest terms. [4.5]

18. $6.8(3.9 + 0.37)$

19. $8.7 - 5(0.23)$

20. $46.918 - 6(4.92 + 0.086)$

21. $\frac{4}{3}(0.36) - \frac{7}{5}(0.3)$

22. $16.3 - 6(3.07 - 4.3)$

23. $\frac{1}{5}(0.38) + 7(9.1 - 2.7)$

The diagram shows the annual sales for different brands of cookies. Use the information to answer the following questions.

24. What are the average monthly sales for Nabisco Chips Ahoy! cookies?

25. What are the average monthly sales for Lofthouse and Nabisco Oreo Double Stuff cookies combined?

Simplify.

1. $4{,}832 + 459$

2. $620 - 476$

3. $93(190)$

4. $4.390 - 1.57$

5. $6\overline{)921.41}$

6. $\dfrac{3}{7} + \dfrac{5}{6}$

7. $9.1(11.03)$

8. $1{,}178 \div 19$

9. $\dfrac{9}{14} \div \dfrac{6}{35}$

10. Round 376,145 to the nearest million.

11. Change $\frac{81}{5}$ to a mixed number.

12. Change $3\frac{7}{8}$ to an improper fraction.

13. Find the product of $3\frac{5}{8}$ and 7.

14. Change each decimal into a fraction.

Decimal	Fraction
0.125	
0.250	
0.375	
0.500	
0.625	
0.750	
0.875	
1	

15. Give the quotient of 72 and 18.

16. Identify the property or properties used in the following:
$2(x + 3) = 6 + 2x$

17. Translate into symbols, then simplify: Seven times the sum of six and three is sixty-three.

18. Reduce $\dfrac{75}{130}$.

19. **True or False?** Adding the same number to the numerator and denominator of a fraction produces an equivalent fraction.

Simplify.

20. $\dfrac{3 + 7(5)}{10 + 9}$

21. $20\left(\dfrac{1}{4}\right) + 8\left(\dfrac{3}{8}\right)$

22. $\dfrac{3}{5}(0.65) + \dfrac{9}{10}(0.7)$

23. $\left(5\dfrac{1}{8} - \dfrac{1}{3}\right)\left(3\dfrac{1}{4} + \dfrac{7}{8}\right)$

24. **Recipe** A muffin recipe calls for $4\frac{3}{4}$ cups of flour. If the recipe is doubled, how many cups of flour will be needed?

25. **Hourly Wage** If you earn $288.75 for working 35 hours, what is your hourly wage?

The snapshot shows the number of goals scored by different countries in the FIFA World Cup. Use the information to answer the following questions. Round to the nearest hundredth if necessary.

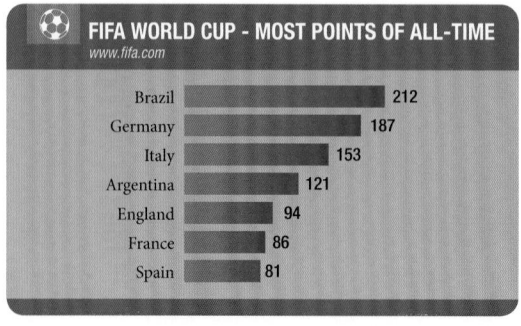

FIFA WORLD CUP - MOST POINTS OF ALL-TIME
www.fifa.com

Brazil	212
Germany	187
Italy	153
Argentina	121
England	94
France	86
Spain	81

26. If Brazil has played in all 19 World Cup tournaments, what is their average number of goals per tournament?

27. If England has played in 13 World Cup tournaments, what is their average number of goals per tournament?

1. Write the decimal number 11.819 in words. [4.1]

2. Give the place value of the 8 in the number 61.8276. [4.1]

3. Write seventy-three and forty-six ten thousandths as a decimal number. [4.1]

4. Round 100.9052 to the nearest hundredth. [4.1]

Perform the following operations. [4.2, 4.3, 4.4]

5. $6 + 0.8 + 0.22$

6. $28.332 - 16.608$

7. $6.9(2.40)$

8. $96.4768 \div 16.52$

9. $6.8 + 3.3$

10. $16.47 - 8.58$

11. $0.5(3.7)(1.8)$

12. $11.616 \div 52.8$

13. A person purchases $11.39 worth of goods at a drugstore. If a $10 bill and a $5 bill were used to pay for the purchases, how much change is received? [4.2]

14. If coffee sells for $3.29 per pound, how much will 5.5 pounds of coffee cost? [4.3]

15. If a person earns $489 for working 60 hours, what is the person's hourly wage? [4.4]

16. Write $\frac{17}{25}$ as a decimal. [4.5]

17. Write 0.38 as a fraction in lowest terms. [4.5]

18. $6.8(3.7 + 0.08)$

19. $6.1 - 4(0.93)$

20. $41.901 - 7(3.11 + 0.462)$

21. $\frac{7}{8}(0.11) + \frac{5}{6}(0.45)$

22. $23.4 - 8(6.01 - 4.2)$

23. $\frac{1}{5}(0.17) + 8(6.13 - 2.8)$

The diagram shows the annual sales for different magazines. Use the information to answer the following questions.

TOP 5 MAGAZINE SALES
The Association of Magazine Media 2009

People	$528.4M
US Weekly	$297.3M
Sports Illustrated	$280.3M
Reader's Digest	$190.6M
Time	$182.7M

24. What is the average monthly sales for People Magazine?

25. What are the average monthly sales for US Weekly and Time Magazine combined?

Ratio and Proportion

5

Los Angeles, California
© 2010 Google

The Arroyo Seco Parkway, now called the Pasadena Freeway, in Los Angeles, California is significant in the history of American transportation. It is the first limited-access freeway that utilized diamond or cloverleaf ramps, which were a big departure from the traditional easy-access parkways found in the East. The two-car family was becoming a reality in Southern California by the end of World War I, therefore, adding more traffic congestion. The new freeway became necessary to help ease this congestion. When it opened in 1940, the freeway linked downtown Los Angeles with Pasadena. Its relatively high speeds allowed more rapid commutes and made getting around in 1940s LA a much quicker process. It was also unique in that art and landscaping were incorporated into the general construction plan to enhance the driving experience.

The freeway's expansion in 1953 to what was the nation's first four-lane interchange just north of downtown Los Angeles connected the Arroyo Seco Parkway to the expanding LA freeway network. This was a big step toward the modern freeway systems found in most large cities today. It is still part of the system that allows Angelinos to travel over 300 million miles every day.

Suppose you were to use the Pasadena Freeway during a 6 hour driving trip. If you traveled 270 miles during that time, how far would you go if you drove for 10 hours? Solving problems like this requires that you know how to set up and solve proportions, which is one of the topics we will cover in this chapter.

5.1 Ratios

OBJECTIVES

A Write ratios as fractions.

KEY WORDS

ratio

If a human faced off against an elephant in a hot dog eating contest, who would win? Each July, three brave humans sign up to find out firsthand. Three elephants, Susie, Minnie, and Bunny, from Ringling Bros. and Barnum & Bailey Circus stand behind a table on which a tall pile of hot dog buns sits. A few feet away, three competitive eating contestants stand in front of their own table outfitted with stacks of buns and large cups of water in which they can dunk the buns to help their cause. When the announcer yells "Go!", the two teams begin devouring the buns. They have 6 minutes to eat as many as possible. The 2010 final tally: 41 dozen buns for the elephants, 15 dozen for the humans. In mathematical terms, the ratio of hot dog buns eaten by elephants to those eaten by humans is 41 to 15. The *ratio* of two numbers is a way of comparing them which we will discuss in this section.

A Writing Ratios as Fractions

If we say that the ratio of two numbers is 2 to 1, then the first number is twice as large as the second number. For example, if there are 10 men and 5 women enrolled in a math class, then the ratio of men to women is 10 to 5. Because 10 is twice as large as 5, we can also say that the ratio of men to women is 2 to 1.

We can define the ratio of two numbers in terms of fractions.

> **DEFINITION** ratio
>
> The *ratio* of two numbers is a fraction, where the first number in the ratio is the numerator and the second number in the ratio is the denominator.
>
> *In symbols:* If a and b are any two numbers ($b \neq 0$), then the ratio of a to b is $\frac{a}{b}$.

We handle ratios the same way we handle fractions. For example, when we said that the ratio of 10 men to 5 women was the same as the ratio 2 to 1, we were actually saying

$$\frac{10}{5} = \frac{2}{1} \qquad \textit{Reduce to lowest terms.}$$

Because we have already studied fractions in detail, much of the introductory material on ratios will seem like review.

EXAMPLE 1 Express the ratio of 16 to 48 as a fraction in lowest terms.

Solution Because the ratio is 16 to 48, the numerator of the fraction is 16 and the denominator is 48.

$$\frac{16}{48} = \frac{1}{3}$$

Notice that the first number in the ratio becomes the numerator of the fraction, and the second number in the ratio becomes the denominator.

Video Examples

SECTION 5.1

Practice Problems

1. Express the ratio of 15 to 25 as a fraction in lowest terms.

Answer

1. $\frac{3}{5}$

EXAMPLE 2 Write the ratio of $\frac{2}{3}$ to $\frac{4}{9}$ as a fraction in lowest terms.

Solution We begin by writing the ratio of $\frac{2}{3}$ to $\frac{4}{9}$ as a complex fraction. The numerator is $\frac{2}{3}$, and the denominator is $\frac{4}{9}$. Then we simplify.

$$\frac{\frac{2}{3}}{\frac{4}{9}} = \frac{2}{3} \cdot \frac{9}{4} \quad \textit{Division by } \frac{4}{9} \textit{ is the same as multiplication by } \frac{9}{4}.$$

$$= \frac{18}{12} \quad \textit{Multiply.}$$

$$= \frac{3}{2} \quad \textit{Reduce to lowest terms.}$$

EXAMPLE 3 Write the ratio of 0.08 to 0.12 as a fraction in lowest terms.

Solution When the ratio is in reduced form, it is customary to write it with whole numbers and not decimals. For this reason, we multiply the numerator and the denominator of the ratio by 100 to clear it of decimals. Then we reduce to lowest terms.

$$\frac{0.08}{0.12} = \frac{0.08 \times 100}{0.12 \times 100} \quad \textit{Multiply the numerator and the denominator by}$$
$$\textit{100 to clear the ratio of decimals.}$$

$$= \frac{8}{12} \quad \textit{Multiply.}$$

$$= \frac{2}{3} \quad \textit{Reduce to lowest terms.}$$

Table 1 shows several more ratios and their fractional equivalents. Notice that in each case the fraction has been reduced to lowest terms. Also, the ratio that contains decimals has been rewritten as a fraction that does not contain decimals.

Table 1

Ratio	Fraction		Fraction in lowest terms
25 to 35	$\frac{25}{35}$	$\frac{5}{7}$	
35 to 25	$\frac{35}{25}$	$\frac{7}{5}$	
8 to 2	$\frac{8}{2}$	$\frac{4}{1}$	We can also write this as just 4.
$\frac{1}{4}$ to $\frac{3}{4}$	$\dfrac{\frac{1}{4}}{\frac{3}{4}}$	$\frac{1}{3}$	because $\dfrac{\frac{1}{4}}{\frac{3}{4}} = \frac{1}{4} \cdot \frac{4}{3} = \frac{1}{3}$
0.6 to 1.7	$\frac{0.6}{1.7}$	$\frac{6}{17}$	because $\frac{0.6 \times 10}{1.7 \times 10} = \frac{6}{17}$

EXAMPLE 4 During a game, a basketball player makes 12 out of the 18 free throws he attempts. Write the ratio of the number of free throws he makes to the number of free throws he attempts as a fraction in lowest terms.

Solution Because he makes 12 out of 18, we want the ratio 12 to 18, or

$$\frac{12}{18} = \frac{2}{3}$$

Because the ratio is 2 to 3, we can say that, in this particular game, he made 2 out of every 3 free throws he attempted.

---

2. Write the ratio of $\frac{3}{4}$ to $\frac{5}{8}$ as a fraction in lowest terms.

3. Write the ratio of 0.16 to 0.20 as a fraction in lowest terms.

Note Another symbol used to denote ratio is the colon (:). The ratio of, say, 5 to 4 can be written as 5:4. Although we will not use it here, this notation is fairly common.

4. During a game, a baseball pitcher throws 50 strikes out of 80 pitches. Write the ratio of the strikes to total pitches as a fraction in lowest terms.

Answers

2. $\frac{6}{5}$

3. $\frac{4}{5}$

4. $\frac{5}{8}$

5. A solution of radiator fluid contains 2 pints antifreeze and 8 pints water. Find the ratio of antifreeze to water, water to antifreeze, antifreeze to total solution, and water to total solution.

EXAMPLE 5   A solution of alcohol and water contains 15 milliliters of water and 5 milliliters of alcohol. Find the ratio of alcohol to water, water to alcohol, water to total solution, and alcohol to total solution. Write each ratio as a fraction and reduce to lowest terms.

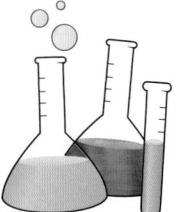

Solution   There are 5 milliliters of alcohol and 15 milliliters of water, so there are 20 milliliters of solution (alcohol + water). The ratios are as follows:

The ratio of alcohol to water is 5 to 15, or

$$\frac{5}{15} = \frac{1}{3} \qquad \text{In lowest terms}$$

The ratio of water to alcohol is 15 to 5, or

$$\frac{15}{5} = \frac{3}{1} \qquad \text{In lowest terms}$$

The ratio of water to total solution is 15 to 20, or

$$\frac{15}{20} = \frac{3}{4} \qquad \text{In lowest terms}$$

The ratio of alcohol to total solution is 5 to 20, or

$$\frac{5}{20} = \frac{1}{4} \qquad \text{In lowest terms}$$

6. Using the information from Example 6, find the ratio of the price of the medium pizza to the large pizza. Then change the ratio to a decimal rounded to the nearest hundredth.

EXAMPLE 6   Suppose a pizza restaurant advertised the following prices for their deep-dish pizza. Use the information to find the ratio of the cost of the large cheese pizza to the medium cheese pizza. Then change the ratio to a decimal rounded to the nearest tenth.

Size	Price
Medium 12" cheese	$12.00
Large 15" cheese	$16.50

Solution   The ratio of the large pizza to the medium is

$$\frac{16.5}{12.0} = \frac{16.5 \times 10}{12.0 \times 10} \qquad \textit{Multiply the numerator and denominator by 10 to clear the ratio of decimals.}$$

$$= \frac{165}{120}$$

$$= \frac{11}{8} \qquad \textit{Reduce to lowest terms.}$$

To convert to a decimal, we divide 11 by 8 and round to the nearest tenth.

$$\frac{11}{8} \approx 1.4$$

GETTING READY FOR CLASS

After reading through the preceding section, respond in your own words and in complete sentences.

A. In your own words, write a definition for the ratio of two numbers.

B. What does a ratio compare?

C. What are some different ways of using mathematics to write the ratio of *a* to *b*?

D. When will the ratio of two numbers be a complex fraction?

Answers

5. $\frac{1}{4}, \frac{4}{1}, \frac{1}{5}, \frac{4}{5}$

6. $\frac{8}{11} \approx 0.73$

Vocabulary Review

Choose the correct words to fill in the blanks below.

numerator   colon   complex   denominator   ratio   fraction

1. The ratio of two numbers is a _____, where the first number in the ratio is the numerator and second number in the ratio is the denominator.

2. When writing the ratio 6 to 8 as a fraction, 6 is the _____ and 8 is the _____.

3. If a and b are any two numbers, then the _____ of a to b is $\frac{a}{b}$.

4. A symbol used to denote a ratio is the _____.

5. The ratio of $\frac{1}{4}$ to $\frac{2}{3}$ will appear as a _____ fraction.

Problems

A Write each of the following ratios as a fraction in lowest terms. None of the answers should contain decimals.

1. 8 to 6

2. 6 to 8

3. 64 to 12

4. 12 to 64

5. 100 to 250

6. 250 to 100

7. 13 to 26

8. 36 to 18

9. $\frac{3}{4}$ to $\frac{1}{4}$

10. $\frac{5}{8}$ to $\frac{3}{8}$

11. $\frac{7}{3}$ to $\frac{6}{3}$

12. $\frac{9}{5}$ to $\frac{11}{5}$

13. $\frac{6}{5}$ to $\frac{6}{7}$

14. $\frac{5}{3}$ to $\frac{5}{8}$

15. $2\frac{1}{2}$ to $3\frac{1}{2}$

16. $5\frac{1}{4}$ to $1\frac{3}{4}$

17. $2\frac{2}{3}$ to $\frac{5}{3}$

18. $\frac{1}{2}$ to $3\frac{1}{2}$

19. 0.05 to 0.15

20. 0.21 to 0.03

21. 0.3 to 3

22. 0.5 to 10

23. 1.2 to 10

24. 6.4 to 0.8

Use the figures to answer the following questions.

25. a. What is the ratio of shaded squares to nonshaded squares?

b. What is the ratio of shaded squares to total squares?

c. What is the ratio of nonshaded squares to total squares?

26. a. What is the ratio of shaded squares to nonshaded squares?

b. What is the ratio of shaded squares to total squares?

c. What is the ratio of nonshaded squares to total squares?

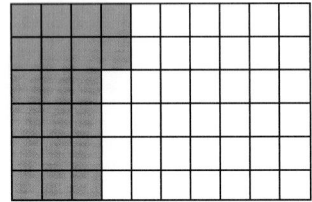

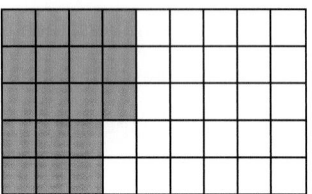

Applying the Concepts

27. Family Budget A family of four budgeted the amounts shown below for some of their monthly bills.

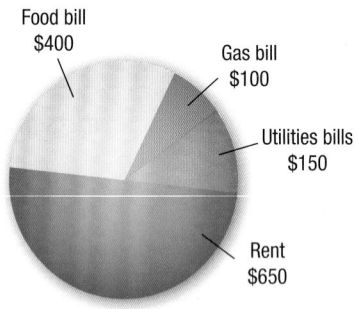

a. What is the ratio of the rent to the food bill?

b. What is the ratio of the gas bill to the food bill?

c. What is the ratio of the utilities bills to the food bill?

d. What is the ratio of the rent to the utilities bills?

28. Nutrition One cup of breakfast cereal was found to contain the nutrients shown here.

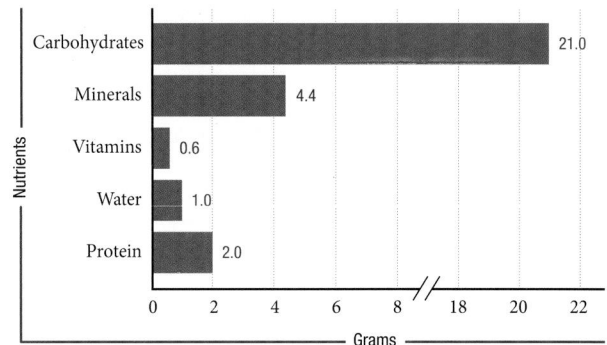

a. Find the ratio of water to protein.

b. Find the ratio of carbohydrates to protein.

c. Find the ratio of vitamins to minerals.

d. Find the ratio of protein to vitamins and minerals.

29. Pizza Prices The price of several menu items from a pizza restaurant are shown in the table. Find the ratio of the prices for the following items.

a. Large pizza to garlic bread

b. Buffalo wings to medium pizza

c. Garlic bread to buffalo wings

d. Garlic bread to medium pizza

Item	Price
Large pizza with pepperoni	$18.25
Medium pizza with pepperoni	$12.75
Buffalo wings	$6.50
Garlic Bread	$3.50

30. Profit and Revenue The following bar chart shows the profit and revenue of the Baby Steps Shoe Company each quarter for one year.

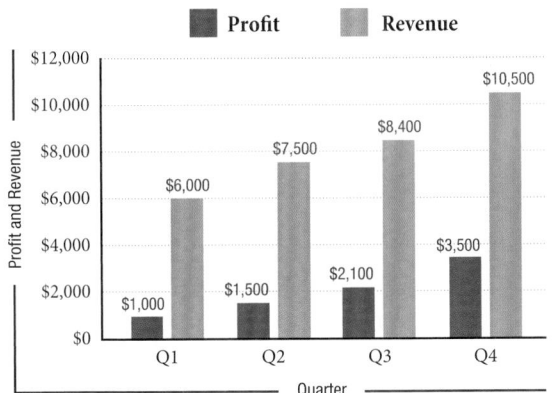

Find the ratio of revenue to profit for each of the following quarters. Write your answers in lowest terms.

a. Q1　　**b.** Q2　　**c.** Q3　　**d.** Q4

e. Find the ratio of revenue to profit for the entire year.

31. Geometry In the diagram below, AC represents the length of the line segment that starts at A and ends at C. From the diagram we see that $AC = 8$.

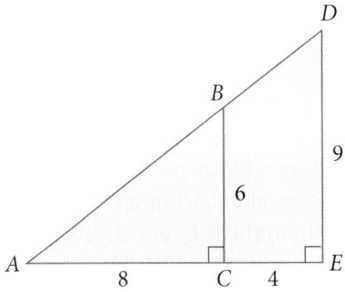

a. Find the ratio of BC to AC.

b. What is the length AE?

c. Find the ratio of DE to AE.

Calculator Problems

Write each of the following ratios as a fraction, and then use a calculator to change the fraction to a decimal. Round all decimal answers to the nearest hundredth. Do not reduce fractions.

Number of Students The total number of students attending a community college in the Midwest is 4,722. Of these students, 2,314 are male and 2,408 are female.

32. Give the ratio of males to females as a fraction and as a decimal.

33. Give the ratio of females to males as a fraction and as a decimal.

34. Give the ratio of males to total number of students as a fraction and as a decimal.

35. Give the ratio of total number of students to females as a fraction and as a decimal.

Getting Ready for the Next Section

Solve each equation by finding a number to replace n with that will make the equation a true statement.

36. $2 \cdot n = 12$　　　**37.** $3 \cdot n = 27$　　　**38.** $6 \cdot n = 24$　　　**39.** $8 \cdot n = 16$

40. $20 = 5 \cdot n$　　　**41.** $35 = 7 \cdot n$　　　**42.** $650 = 10 \cdot n$　　　**43.** $630 = 7 \cdot n$

Improving Your Quantitative Literacy

44. Stock Market One method of comparing stocks on the stock market is the price to earnings ratio, or P/E.

$$P/E = \frac{\text{Current Stock Price}}{\text{Earnings per Share}}$$

Most stocks have a P/E between 25 and 40. A stock with a P/E of less than 25 may be undervalued, while a stock with a P/E greater than 40 may be overvalued. Fill in the P/E for each stock listed in the table below. Based on your results, are any of the stocks undervalued?

Stock	Price	Earnings Per Share	P/E
IBM	146.05	$6.35	
AOL	139.69	$0.61	
DIS	30.03	$0.91	
KM	15.64	$0.68	
GE	90.75	$2.75	
TOY	19.92	$1.66	

Find the Mistake

Each sentence below contains a mistake. Circle the mistake and write the correct word(s) or number(s) on the line provided.

1. Writing the ratio of $\frac{2}{5}$ to $\frac{3}{8}$ is the same as writing $\frac{2}{5} \cdot \frac{3}{8}$.

2. The ratio of 6 to 24 expressed in lowest terms is 4.

3. To write the ratio of 0.04 to 0.20 as a fraction in lowest terms, you must first multiply 0.20 by 10.

4. A cleaning solution of bleach and water contains 100 milliliters of bleach and 150 milliliters of water. To find the ratio of water to the whole solution in lowest terms, you must write the ratio as $\frac{150}{100}$.

Navigation Skills: Prepare, Study, Achieve

Expect to encounter problems you find difficult when taking this course. Also expect to make mistakes. Mistakes highlight possible difficulties you are having and help you learn how to overcome them. We suggest making a list of problems you find difficult. As the course progresses, add new problems to the list, rework the problems on your list, and use the list to study for exams. Be aware of the mistakes you make and what you need to do to ensure you will not make that same mistake twice.

5.2 Proportions

Image © Katherine Heistand Shields, 2010

OBJECTIVES

A Solve an equation by division.

B Solve proportions.

KEY WORDS

proportion

extremes

means

In June 2010, the Children's Museum of Indianapolis had the world's largest Etch-a-Sketch on display. The large toy measured 8 feet tall, compared to the original toy's measurements of 7 inches wide by 9 inches tall. When the screen needed to be cleared, instead of shaking it like the original, the display was designed to flip upside down and then return upright again.

We can compare the measurements of the museum's Etch-a-Sketch with the original using the concept of proportions. Let's allow x to equal the width of the museum's Etch-a-Sketch. Then we can put the measurements of both toys into two ratios and set them equal to each other to solve for x.

$$\frac{x}{8} = \frac{7}{9}$$

After reading this section, you will be able to find the value for x.

A Solving Equations by Division

Earlier, we simplified expressions such as

$$\frac{2 \cdot 2 \cdot 3 \cdot 5 \cdot 7}{2 \cdot 5}$$

by dividing out any factors common to the numerator and the denominator.

$$\frac{2 \cdot 2 \cdot 3 \cdot 5 \cdot 7}{2 \cdot 5} = 2 \cdot 3 \cdot 7 = 42$$

The same process works with expressions that have variables for some of their factors. For example, the expression

$$\frac{2 \cdot n \cdot 7 \cdot 11}{n \cdot 11}$$

can be simplified by dividing out the factors common to the numerator and the denominator—namely, n and 11:

$$\frac{2 \cdot n \cdot 7 \cdot 11}{n \cdot 11} = 2 \cdot 7 = 14$$

EXAMPLE 1 Divide the expression $5 \cdot n$ by 5.

Solution Applying the method above, we have

$$5 \cdot n \text{ divided by } 5 \text{ is } \frac{5 \cdot n}{5} = n$$

Video Examples
SECTION 5.2

Practice Problems

1. Divide the expression $8 \cdot n$ by 8.

Answer

1. n

If you are having trouble understanding this process because there is a variable involved, consider what happens when we divide 6 by 2 and when we divide 6 by 3. Because $6 = 2 \cdot 3$, when we divide by 2 we get 3.

$$\frac{6}{2} = \frac{2 \cdot 3}{2} = 3$$

When we divide by 3, we get 2.

$$\frac{6}{3} = \frac{2 \cdot 3}{3} = 2$$

2. Divide $5 \cdot w$ by 5.

EXAMPLE 2   Divide $7 \cdot y$ by 7.

Solution   Dividing by 7, we have

$$7 \cdot y \text{ divided by 7 is } \frac{7 \cdot y}{7} = y$$

We can use division to solve equations such as $3 \cdot n = 12$. Notice that the left side of the equation is $3 \cdot n$. The equation is solved when we have just n, instead of $3 \cdot n$, on the left side and a number on the right side. That is, we have solved the equation when we have rewritten it as

$$n = \text{a number}$$

We can accomplish this by dividing *both* sides of the equation by 3.

$$\frac{3 \cdot n}{3} = \frac{12}{3} \qquad \textit{Divide both sides by 3.}$$

$$n = 4$$

Because 12 divided by 3 is 4, the solution to the equation is $n = 4$, which we know to be correct from our discussion at the beginning of this section. Notice that it would be incorrect to divide just the left side by 3 and not the right side also. It is important to remember that whenever we divide one side of an equation by a number, we must also divide the other side by the same number.

> *Note*   The choice of the letter we use for the variable is not important. The process works just as well with y as it does with n. The letters used for variables in equations are most often the letters a, n, x, y, or z.

> *Note*   In the last chapter of this book, we will devote a lot of time to solving equations. For now, we are concerned only with equations that can be solved by division.

3. Solve the equation $5 \cdot a = 45$ for a by dividing both sides by 5.

EXAMPLE 3   Solve the equation $7 \cdot y = 42$ for y by dividing both sides by 7.

Solution   Dividing both sides by 7, we have

$$\frac{7 \cdot y}{7} = \frac{42}{7}$$

$$y = 6$$

We can check our solution by replacing y with 6 in the original equation.

$$
\begin{array}{ll}
\text{When } \rightarrow & y = 6 \\
\text{the equation } \rightarrow & 7 \cdot y = 42 \\
\text{becomes } \rightarrow & 7 \cdot 6 = 42 \\
& 42 = 42 \qquad \textit{A true statement}
\end{array}
$$

4. Solve for b: $32 = 4 \cdot b$.

EXAMPLE 4   Solve $30 = 5 \cdot a$ for a.

Solution   Our method of solving equations by division works regardless of which side the variable is on. In this case, the right side is $5 \cdot a$, and we would like it to be just a. Dividing both sides by 5, we have

$$\frac{30}{5} = \frac{5 \cdot a}{5}$$

$$6 = a$$

The solution is $a = 6$. (If 6 is a, then a is 6.)

Answers

2. w

3. $a = 9$

4. $b = 8$

We can write our solutions as improper fractions, mixed numbers, or decimals. Let's agree to write our answers as either whole numbers, proper fractions, or mixed numbers unless otherwise stated.

B Solving Proportions Using the Fundamental Property

In this section, we will solve problems using proportions. As you will see later in this chapter, proportions can model a number of everyday applications.

> **DEFINITION** proportion
>
> A statement that two ratios are equal is called a ***proportion***. If $\frac{a}{b}$ and $\frac{c}{d}$ are two equal ratios, then the statement
>
> $$\frac{a}{b} = \frac{c}{d}$$
>
> is called a proportion.

Each of the four numbers in a proportion is called a *term* of the proportion. We number the terms of a proportion as follows:

First term $\longrightarrow \dfrac{a}{b} = \dfrac{c}{d} \longleftarrow$ Third term
Second term $\longrightarrow$ $\phantom{\dfrac{a}{b} = \dfrac{c}{d}}$ $\longleftarrow$ Fourth term

The first and fourth terms of a proportion are called the *extremes*, and the second and third terms of a proportion are called the *means*.

Means $\longrightarrow \dfrac{a}{b} = \dfrac{c}{d} \longleftarrow$ Extremes

EXAMPLE 5 In the proportion $\frac{3}{4} = \frac{6}{8}$, name the four terms, the means, and the extremes.

Solution The terms are numbered as follows:

First term = 3 $\qquad$ Third term = 6
Second term = 4 $\qquad$ Fourth term = 8

The means are 4 and 6; the extremes are 3 and 8.

The only additional thing we need to know about proportions is the following property.

> **PROPERTY** Fundamental Property of Proportions
>
> In any proportion, the product of the extremes is equal to the product of the means. In symbols, it looks like this:
>
> If $\dfrac{a}{b} = \dfrac{c}{d}$ then $ad = bc$ for $b \neq 0$ and $d \neq 0$.

Practice Problems

5. In the proportion $\frac{5}{8} = \frac{15}{24}$, name the four terms, the means, and the extremes.

Answers

5. First term = 5, second term = 8, third term = 15, fourth term = 24; means: 8 and 15; extremes: 5 and 24.

6. Verify the fundamental property of proportions for the following proportions.

   a. $\frac{9}{10} = \frac{36}{40}$

   b. $\frac{2}{3} = \frac{24}{36}$

EXAMPLE 6   Verify the fundamental property of proportions for the following proportions.

a. $\frac{3}{4} = \frac{6}{8}$ b. $\frac{17}{34} = \frac{1}{2}$

Solution   We verify the fundamental property by finding the product of the means and the product of the extremes in each case.

Proportion	Product of the Means	Product of the Extremes
a. $\frac{3}{4} = \frac{6}{8}$	$4 \cdot 6 = 24$	$3 \cdot 8 = 24$
b. $\frac{17}{34} = \frac{1}{2}$	$34 \cdot 1 = 34$	$17 \cdot 2 = 34$

For each proportion the product of the means is equal to the product of the extremes.

We can use the fundamental property of proportions, along with a property we encountered in the last section, to solve an equation that has the form of a proportion.

A Note on Multiplication   Previously, we have used a multiplication dot to indicate multiplication, both with whole numbers and with variables. A more compact form for multiplication involving variables is simply to leave out the dot.

That is, $5 \cdot y = 5y$ and $10 \cdot x \cdot y = 10xy$.

7. Solve $\frac{3}{10} = \frac{12}{x}$ for x.

Note   In some of these problems you will be able to see what the solution is just by looking the problem over. In those cases it is still best to show all the work involved in solving the proportion. It is good practice for the more difficult problems.

EXAMPLE 7   Solve for x.

$$\frac{2}{3} = \frac{4}{x}$$

Solution   Applying the fundamental property of proportions, we have

If $\frac{2}{3} = \frac{4}{x}$

then $2 \cdot x = 3 \cdot 4$ *The product of the extremes equals the product of the means.*

$2x = 12$ *Multiply.*

The result is an equation. We know that we can divide both sides of an equation by the same nonzero number to find the solution to the equation. In this case, we divide both sides by 2 to solve for x.

$$2x = 12$$

$$\frac{2x}{2} = \frac{12}{2}$$ *Divide both sides by 2.*

$$x = 6$$ *Simplify each side.*

The solution is 6. We can check our work by using the fundamental property of proportions.

$$\frac{2}{3} \times \frac{4}{6}$$

$$\underbrace{12}_{\substack{\text{Product of} \\ \text{the means}}} = \underbrace{12}_{\substack{\text{Product of} \\ \text{the extremes}}}$$

Because the product of the means and the product of the extremes are equal, our work is correct.

EXAMPLE 8 Solve $\dfrac{5}{y} = \dfrac{10}{13}$ for y.

Solution We apply the fundamental property and solve as we did in Example 3.

If $\qquad \dfrac{5}{y} = \dfrac{10}{13}$

then $\qquad 5 \cdot 13 = y \cdot 10$ *The product of the extremes equals the product of the means.*

$\qquad\qquad 65 = 10y$ *Multiply 5 · 13.*

$\qquad\qquad \dfrac{65}{10} = \dfrac{10y}{10}$ *Divide both sides by 10.*

$\qquad\qquad 6.5 = y$ *65 ÷ 10 = 6.5*

The solution is 6.5. We could check our result by substituting 6.5 for y in the original proportion and then finding the product of the means and the product of the extremes.

8. Solve $\dfrac{7}{y} = \dfrac{14}{30}$ for y.

EXAMPLE 9 Find n if $\dfrac{n}{3} = \dfrac{0.4}{8}$.

Solution We proceed as we did in the previous two examples.

If $\qquad \dfrac{n}{3} = \dfrac{0.4}{8}$

then $\qquad n \cdot 8 = 3(0.4)$ *The product of the extremes equals the product of the means.*

$\qquad\qquad 8n = 1.2$ *3(0.4) = 1.2*

$\qquad\qquad \dfrac{8n}{8} = \dfrac{1.2}{8}$ *Divide both sides by 8.*

$\qquad\qquad n = 0.15$ *1.2 ÷ 8 = 0.15*

The missing term is 0.15.

9. Find n if $\dfrac{n}{8} = \dfrac{0.5}{5}$.

EXAMPLE 10 Solve $\dfrac{\frac{2}{3}}{5} = \dfrac{x}{6}$ for x.

Solution We begin by multiplying the means and multiplying the extremes.

If $\qquad \dfrac{\frac{2}{3}}{5} = \dfrac{x}{6}$

then $\qquad \dfrac{2}{3} \cdot 6 = 5 \cdot x$ *The product of the extremes equals the product of the means.*

$\qquad\qquad 4 = 5x$ *$\frac{2}{3} \cdot 6 = 4$*

$\qquad\qquad \dfrac{4}{5} = \dfrac{5x}{5}$ *Divide both sides by 5.*

$\qquad\qquad \dfrac{4}{5} = x$

The missing term is $\dfrac{4}{5}$, or 0.8.

10. Solve $\dfrac{\frac{3}{4}}{6} = \dfrac{x}{10}$ for x.

Answers

8. $y = 15$

9. $n = 0.8$

10. $x = \dfrac{5}{4}$ or 1.25

11. Solve $\frac{a}{20} = 4$.

EXAMPLE 11   Solve $\frac{b}{15} = 2$.

Solution   Since the number 2 can be written as the ratio of 2 to 1, we can write this equation as a proportion, and then solve as we have in the examples above.

$$\frac{b}{15} = 2$$

$$\frac{b}{15} = \frac{2}{1} \qquad \text{Write 2 as a ratio.}$$

$$b \cdot 1 = 15 \cdot 2 \qquad \text{Product of the extremes equals the product of the means.}$$

$$b = 30$$

The procedure for finding a missing term in a proportion is always the same. We first apply the fundamental property of proportions to find the product of the extremes and the product of the means. Then we solve the resulting equation.

GETTING READY FOR CLASS

After reading through the preceding section, respond in your own words and in complete sentences.

A. What number results when you simplify $\frac{2 \cdot n \cdot 7 \cdot 11}{n \cdot 11}$?

B. Explain how division is used to solve the equation $30 = 5 \cdot a$.

C. In the proportion $\frac{2}{5} = \frac{4}{x}$, name the means and the extremes.

D. For the proportion $\frac{2}{5} = \frac{4}{x}$, find the product of the means and the product of the extremes.

Answer

11. $a = 80$

Vocabulary Review

Choose the correct words to fill in the blanks below.

variable   equals sign   equation   division

product   proportion   term   fundamental property of proportions

first   second   third   fourth

1. To solve an _____ , find a number with which to replace the _____
   that would make the equation a true statement.

2. Solving equations by _____ eliminates the need to guess the value that the variable
   represents.

3. We have solved an equation when the answer has a variable isolated on one side of the _____
   and a number on the other side.

4. If $\frac{a}{b}$ and $\frac{c}{d}$ are two equal ratios, then the statement $\frac{a}{b} = \frac{c}{d}$ is called a _____ .

5. Each of the four numbers in a proportion is call a _____ .

6. The _____ and _____ terms of a proportion are called the extremes.

7. The _____ and _____ terms of a proportion are called the means.

8. The fundamental property of proportions states that the _____ of the extremes is equal to
   the product of the means.

9. To find a missing term in a proportion, first apply the _____ and then solve the
   resulting equation.

Problems

A Simplify each of the following expressions by dividing out any factors common to the numerator and the denominator and
then simplifying the result.

1. $\dfrac{3 \cdot 5 \cdot 5 \cdot 7}{3 \cdot 5}$

2. $\dfrac{2 \cdot 2 \cdot 3 \cdot 5 \cdot 7}{2 \cdot 5 \cdot 7}$

3. $\dfrac{2 \cdot n \cdot 3 \cdot 3 \cdot 5}{n \cdot 5}$

4. $\dfrac{3 \cdot 5 \cdot n \cdot 7 \cdot 7}{3 \cdot n \cdot 7}$

5. $\dfrac{2 \cdot 2 \cdot n \cdot 7 \cdot 11}{2 \cdot n \cdot 11}$

6. $\dfrac{3 \cdot n \cdot 7 \cdot 13 \cdot 17}{n \cdot 13 \cdot 17}$

7. $\dfrac{9 \cdot n}{9}$

8. $\dfrac{8 \cdot a}{8}$

9. $\dfrac{4 \cdot y}{4}$

10. $\dfrac{7 \cdot x}{7}$

11. $\dfrac{12 \cdot b}{12}$

12. $\dfrac{9 \cdot w}{9}$

Solve each of the following equations by dividing both sides by the appropriate number. Be sure to show the division in each case.

13. $4 \cdot n = 8$

14. $2 \cdot n = 8$

15. $5 \cdot x = 35$

16. $7 \cdot x = 35$

17. $3 \cdot y = 21$ **18.** $7 \cdot y = 21$ **19.** $6 \cdot n = 48$ **20.** $16 \cdot n = 48$

21. $5 \cdot a = 40$ **22.** $10 \cdot a = 40$ **23.** $3 \cdot x = 6$ **24.** $8 \cdot x = 40$

25. $2 \cdot y = 2$ **26.** $2 \cdot y = 12$ **27.** $3 \cdot a = 18$ **28.** $4 \cdot a = 4$

29. $5 \cdot n = 25$ **30.** $9 \cdot n = 18$ **31.** $6 = 2 \cdot x$ **32.** $56 = 7 \cdot x$

33. $42 = 6 \cdot n$ **34.** $30 = 5 \cdot n$ **35.** $4 = 4 \cdot y$ **36.** $90 = 9 \cdot y$

37. $63 = 7 \cdot y$ **38.** $3 = 3 \cdot y$ **39.** $2 \cdot n = 7$ **40.** $4 \cdot n = 10$

41. $6 \cdot x = 21$ **42.** $7 \cdot x = 8$ **43.** $5 \cdot a = 12$ **44.** $8 \cdot a = 13$

45. $4 = 7 \cdot y$ **46.** $3 = 9 \cdot y$ **47.** $10 = 13 \cdot y$ **48.** $9 = 11 \cdot y$

49. $12 \cdot x = 30$ **50.** $16 \cdot x = 56$ **51.** $21 = 14 \cdot n$ **52.** $48 = 20 \cdot n$

B For each of the following proportions, name the means, name the extremes, and show that the product of the means is equal to the product of the extremes.

53. $\dfrac{1}{3} = \dfrac{5}{15}$ **54.** $\dfrac{6}{12} = \dfrac{1}{2}$

55. $\dfrac{10}{25} = \dfrac{2}{5}$ **56.** $\dfrac{5}{8} = \dfrac{10}{16}$

57. $\dfrac{\frac{1}{3}}{\frac{1}{2}} = \dfrac{4}{6}$

58. $\dfrac{2}{\frac{1}{4}} = \dfrac{4}{\frac{1}{2}}$

59. $\dfrac{0.5}{5} = \dfrac{1}{10}$

60. $\dfrac{0.3}{1.2} = \dfrac{1}{4}$

Find the missing term in each of the following proportions. Set up each problem like the examples in this section. For problems 30–36, write your answers in decimal form. For the other problems, write your answers as fractions in lowest terms.

61. $\dfrac{3}{5} = \dfrac{6}{x}$

62. $\dfrac{3}{8} = \dfrac{9}{x}$

63. $\dfrac{1}{y} = \dfrac{5}{12}$

64. $\dfrac{2}{y} = \dfrac{6}{10}$

65. $\dfrac{x}{4} = \dfrac{3}{8}$

66. $\dfrac{x}{5} = \dfrac{7}{10}$

67. $\dfrac{5}{9} = \dfrac{x}{2}$

68. $\dfrac{3}{7} = \dfrac{x}{3}$

69. $\dfrac{3}{7} = \dfrac{3}{x}$

70. $\dfrac{2}{9} = \dfrac{2}{x}$

71. $\dfrac{x}{2} = 7$

72. $\dfrac{x}{3} = 10$

73. $\dfrac{\frac{1}{2}}{y} = \dfrac{\frac{1}{3}}{12}$

74. $\dfrac{\frac{2}{3}}{y} = \dfrac{\frac{1}{3}}{5}$

75. $\dfrac{n}{12} = \dfrac{\frac{1}{4}}{\frac{1}{2}}$

76. $\dfrac{n}{10} = \dfrac{\frac{3}{5}}{\frac{3}{8}}$

77. $\dfrac{10}{20} = \dfrac{20}{n}$

78. $\dfrac{8}{4} = \dfrac{4}{n}$

79. $\dfrac{x}{10} = \dfrac{10}{2}$

80. $\dfrac{x}{12} = \dfrac{12}{48}$

81. $\dfrac{y}{12} = 9$

82. $\dfrac{y}{16} = 0.75$

83. $\dfrac{0.4}{1.2} = \dfrac{1}{x}$

84. $\dfrac{5}{0.5} = \dfrac{20}{x}$

85. $\dfrac{0.3}{0.18} = \dfrac{n}{0.6}$

86. $\dfrac{0.01}{0.1} = \dfrac{n}{10}$

87. $\dfrac{0.5}{x} = \dfrac{1.4}{0.7}$

88. $\dfrac{0.3}{x} = \dfrac{2.4}{0.8}$

89. $\dfrac{168}{324} = \dfrac{56}{x}$

90. $\dfrac{280}{530} = \dfrac{112}{x}$

91. $\dfrac{429}{y} = \dfrac{858}{130}$

92. $\dfrac{573}{y} = \dfrac{2{,}292}{316}$

93. $\dfrac{n}{39} = \dfrac{533}{507}$

94. $\dfrac{n}{47} = \dfrac{1{,}003}{799}$

95. $\dfrac{756}{903} = \dfrac{x}{129}$

96. $\dfrac{321}{1{,}128} = \dfrac{x}{376}$

Getting Ready for the Next Section

Divide.

97. $360 \div 18$

98. $2{,}700 \div 6$

99. $3{,}300 \div 11$

100. $1{,}440 \div 24$

Multiply.

101. $3.5(85)$

102. $4.75(105)$

103. $4.2(12)$

104. $1.25(34)$

Solve each equation.

105. $\dfrac{x}{10} = \dfrac{270}{6}$

106. $\dfrac{x}{45} = \dfrac{8}{18}$

107. $\dfrac{x}{25} = \dfrac{4}{20}$

108. $\dfrac{x}{3.5} = \dfrac{85}{1}$

Find the Mistake

Each sentence below contains a mistake. Circle the mistake and write the correct word(s) or number(s) on the line provided.

1. To simplify $\dfrac{3 \cdot a \cdot 8 \cdot 11}{a \cdot 11}$, divide out a and 11 to get $264a$. _____

2. Dividing $6 \cdot z$ by 6 gives us 1. _____

3. Solving the equation $6 \cdot a = 48$ for a gives us $a = 48$. _____

4. Solving the equation $36 = w \cdot 12$ for w gives us $w = \dfrac{12}{36} = \dfrac{1}{3}$. _____

5. A statement that two proportions are equal is called a ratio. _____

6. For the proportion $\dfrac{5}{6} = \dfrac{10}{x}$, the means are 5 and x. _____

7. To solve $\dfrac{7}{10} = \dfrac{n}{0.2}$, set the product of the first and third terms equal to the product of second and fourth terms. _____

8. Solving the proportion $\dfrac{8}{5} = \dfrac{n}{\frac{3}{10}}$ gives us $n = \dfrac{3}{16}$. _____

5.3 Applications of Proportions

OBJECTIVES

A Solve application problems using proportions.

Model railroads continue to be as popular today as they ever have been. One of the first things model railroaders ask each other is what scale they work with. The scale of a model train indicates its size relative to a full-size train. Each scale is associated with a ratio and a fraction, as shown in the table and bar chart below. An HO scale model train has a ratio of 1 to 87, meaning it is $\frac{1}{87}$ as large as an actual train.

Scale	Ratio	As a Fraction
LGB	1 to 22.5	$\frac{1}{22.5}$
#1	1 to 32	$\frac{1}{32}$
O	1 to 43.5	$\frac{1}{43.5}$
S	1 to 64	$\frac{1}{64}$
HO	1 to 87	$\frac{1}{87}$
TT	1 to 120	$\frac{1}{120}$

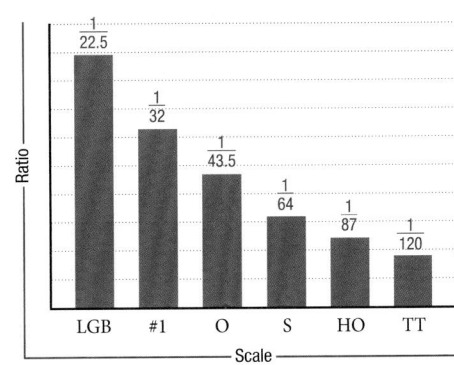

How long is an actual boxcar that has an HO scale model 5 inches long? In this section we will solve this problem using proportions.

A Solving Application Problems Using Proportions

Proportions can be used to solve a variety of word problems. The examples that follow show some of these word problems. In each case we will translate the word problem into a proportion and then solve the proportion using the methods developed in this chapter.

EXAMPLE 1 Recall the problem from the chapter opening. Suppose you drive your car 270 miles in 6 hours using the Pasadena Freeway. If you continue at the same rate, how far will you travel in 10 hours?

Solution We let x represent the distance you travel in 10 hours. Using x, we translate the problem into the following proportion:

$$\text{Miles} \longrightarrow \frac{x}{10} = \frac{270}{6} \longleftarrow \text{Miles}$$
$$\text{Hours} \longrightarrow \qquad \qquad \longleftarrow \text{Hours}$$

Video Examples
SECTION 5.3

Practice Problems

1. If you travel 310 miles in 5 hours, and continue at the same rate, how far will you travel in 12 hours?

Answer

1. 744 miles

Image © sxc.hu, bugdog, 2008

Notice that the two ratios in the proportion compare the same quantities. That is, both ratios compare miles to hours. In words, this proportion says

x miles *is to* 10 *hours as* 270 *miles is to* 6 *hours*

$$\frac{x}{10} = \frac{270}{6}$$

Next, we solve the proportion.

$$x \cdot 6 = 10 \cdot 270$$

$$x \cdot 6 = 2{,}700 \qquad 10 \cdot 270 = 2{,}700$$

$$\frac{x \cdot 6}{6} = \frac{2{,}700}{6} \qquad \text{Divide both sides by 6.}$$

$$x = 450 \text{ miles} \qquad 2{,}700 \div 6 = 450$$

If you continue at the same rate, you will travel 450 miles in 10 hours.

---

2. A baseball pitcher gives up 6 earned runs in 18 innings. If he continues at this rate, how many earned runs will he give up in 81 innings?

EXAMPLE 2   A baseball player gets 8 hits in the first 18 games of the season. If he continues at the same rate, how many hits will he get in 45 games?

Solution   We let x represent the number of hits he will get in 45 games. Then

x *is to* 45 *as* 8 *is to* 18.

$$\text{Hits} \longrightarrow \frac{x}{45} = \frac{8}{18} \longleftarrow \text{Hits}$$
$$\text{Games} \longrightarrow \qquad\qquad \longleftarrow \text{Games}$$

Notice again that the two ratios are comparing the same quantities, hits to games. We solve the proportion as follows:

$$18x = 360 \qquad 45 \cdot 8 = 360$$

$$\frac{18x}{18} = \frac{360}{18} \qquad \text{Divide both sides by 18.}$$

$$x = 20 \qquad 360 \div 18 = 20$$

If he continues to hit at the rate of 8 hits in 18 games, he will get 20 hits in 45 games.

---

3. A solution contains 3.5 g salt in 40 ml of water. If another solution is to have the same ratio of salt to water and it must contain 220 ml of water, how much salt should it contain?

EXAMPLE 3   A solution contains 4 milliliters of alcohol and 20 milliliters of water. If another solution is to have the same ratio of milliliters of alcohol to milliliters of water and must contain 25 milliliters of water, how much alcohol should it contain?

Solution   We let x represent the number of milliliters of alcohol in the second solution. The problem translates to

x milliliters *is to* 25 milliliters *as* 4 milliliters *is to* 20 milliliters.

$$\text{Alcohol} \longrightarrow \frac{x}{25} = \frac{4}{20} \longleftarrow \text{Alcohol}$$
$$\text{Water} \longrightarrow \qquad\qquad \longleftarrow \text{Water}$$

$$20x = 100 \qquad\qquad 25 \cdot 4 = 100$$

$$\frac{20x}{20} = \frac{100}{20} \qquad\qquad \text{Divide both sides by 20.}$$

$$x = 5 \text{ milliliters of alcohol} \quad 100 \div 20 = 5$$

EXAMPLE 4   The scale on a map indicates that 1 inch on the map corresponds to an actual distance of 85 miles. Two cities are 3.5 inches apart on the map. What is the actual distance between the two cities?

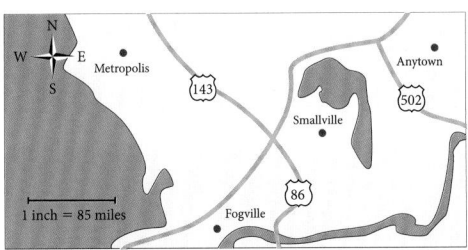

Solution   We let x represent the actual distance between the two cities. The proportion is

$$\text{Miles} \longrightarrow \frac{x}{3.5} = \frac{85}{1} \longleftarrow \text{Miles} \\ \text{Inches} \longrightarrow \qquad \qquad \longleftarrow \text{Inches}$$

$$x \cdot 1 = 3.5(85)$$

$$x = 297.5 \text{ miles}$$

EXAMPLE 5   One gallon of gasoline weighs 6.3 pounds, of which 5.5 pounds is carbon. The carbon is combined with hydrogen in gasoline. When gasoline is burned, the carbon and hydrogen separate, and the carbon recombines with two molecules of oxygen from air to form carbon dioxide. The atomic weight of carbon is 12 and the atomic weight of each molecule of oxygen is 16. Show that burning 1 gallon of gasoline produces 20.2 pounds of carbon dioxide.

Solution   First we find the ratio of the weight of carbon to the weight of the whole molecule in carbon dioxide.

Atomic weight of carbon = 12

Atomic weight of carbon dioxide = 12 + 16 + 16 = 44

Ratio of weight of carbon to weight of carbon dioxide = $\dfrac{12}{44} = \dfrac{3}{11}$

Next, since the weight of carbon in one gallon of gasoline is 5.5 pounds, if we let $x =$ the weight of carbon dioxide produced by burning one gallon of gasoline, we have

$$\text{Weight of carbon} \longrightarrow \frac{3}{11} = \frac{5.5}{x} \longleftarrow \text{Weight of carbon} \\ \text{Weight of carbon dioxide} \longrightarrow \qquad \qquad \longleftarrow \text{Weight of carbon dioxide}$$

$$3x = 11(5.5) \qquad \text{Fundamental property of proportions}$$

$$\frac{3x}{3} = \frac{11(5.5)}{3} \qquad \text{Divide both sides by 3.}$$

$$x = 20.2 \qquad \text{Round to the nearest tenth.}$$

Each gallon of gasoline burned produces 20.2 pounds of carbon dioxide.

GETTING READY FOR CLASS

After reading through the preceding section, respond in your own words and in complete sentences.

A. Give an example not found in the book of a proportion problem you may encounter.

B. Write a word problem for the proportion $\frac{2}{5} = \frac{4}{x}$.

C. What does it mean to translate a word problem into a proportion?

D. Name some jobs that may frequently require solving proportion problems.

---

4. The scale on a map indicates that $\frac{1}{2}$ inch on the map corresponds to an actual distance of 70 miles. Two cities are $3\frac{1}{4}$ inches apart on the map. What is the actual distance between the two cities?

5. Using the atomic weight information from Example 5, how many pounds of carbon dioxide are produced from burning 8 gallons of gasoline?

Answers

4. 455 miles

5. $161.\overline{33}$ pounds

Vocabulary Review

Choose the correct words to fill in the blanks below.

proportion   quantities   word problems   division

1. Proportions can be used to solve _____ .

2. When translating a word problem into a _____ , make sure the two ratios in the proportion compare the same _____ .

3. Once you translate a word problem into a proportion, use _____ to solve for the unknown term.

Problems

A Solve each of the following word problems by translating the statement into a proportion. Be sure to show the proportion used in each case.

1. **Distance** A woman drives her car 235 miles in 5 hours. At this rate how far will she travel in 7 hours?

2. **Distance** An airplane flies 1,260 miles in 3 hours. How far will it fly in 5 hours?

3. **Basketball** A basketball player scores 162 points in 9 games. At this rate how many points will he score in 20 games?

4. **Football** In the first 4 games of the season, a football team scores a total of 68 points. At this rate how many points will the team score in 11 games?

5. **Mixture** A solution contains 8 pints of antifreeze and 5 pints of water. How many pints of water must be added to 24 pints of antifreeze to get a solution with the same concentration?

6. **Nutrition** If 10 ounces of a certain breakfast cereal contains 3 ounces of sugar, how many ounces of sugar does 25 ounces of the same cereal contain?

7. **Map Reading** The scale on a map indicates that 1 inch corresponds to an actual distance of 95 miles. Two cities are 4.5 inches apart on the map. What is the actual distance between the two cities?

8. **Map Reading** A map is drawn so that every 2.5 inches on the map corresponds to an actual distance of 100 miles. If the actual distance between two cities is 350 miles, how far apart are they on the map?

9. **Farming** A farmer knows that of every 50 eggs his chickens lay, only 45 will be marketable. If his chickens lay 1,000 eggs in a week, how many of them will be marketable?

10. **Manufacturing** Of every 17 parts manufactured by a certain machine, 1 will be defective. How many parts were manufactured by the machine if 8 defective parts were found?

Model Trains In the introduction to this section, we indicated that the size of a model train relative to an actual train is referred to as its scale. Each scale is associated with a ratio as shown in the table. For example, an HO model train has a ratio of 1 to 87, meaning it is $\frac{1}{87}$ as large as an actual train.

Scale	Ratio
LGB	1 to 22.5
#1	1 to 32
O	1 to 43.5
S	1 to 64
HO	1 to 87
TT	1 to 120

11. **Boxcar** How long is an actual boxcar that has an HO scale model 5 inches long? Give your answer in inches, then divide by 12 to give the answer in feet.

12. **Length of a Flatcar** How long is an actual flatcar that has an LGB scale model 24 inches long? Give your answer in feet.

13. **Travel Expenses** A traveling salesman figures it costs 21¢ for every mile he drives his car. How much does it cost him a week to drive his car if he travels 570 miles a week?

14. **Travel Expenses** A family plans to drive their car during their annual vacation. The car can go 350 miles on a tank of gas, which is 18 gallons of gas. The vacation they have planned will cover 1,785 miles. How many gallons of gas will that take?

15. **Nutrition** A 6-ounce serving of grapefruit juice contains 159 grams of water. How many grams of water are in 10 ounces of grapefruit juice?

16. **Nutrition** If 100 grams of ice cream contains 13 grams of fat, how much fat is in 250 grams of ice cream?

17. Travel Expenses If a car travels 378.9 miles on 50 liters of gas, how many liters of gas will it take to go 692 miles if the car travels at the same rate? (Round to the nearest tenth.)

18. Nutrition If 125 grams of peas contains 26 grams of carbohydrates, how many grams of carbohydrates does 375 grams of peas contain?

19. Elections During a recent election, 47 of every 100 registered voters in a certain city voted. If there were 127,900 registered voters in that city, how many people voted?

20. Map Reading The scale on a map is drawn so that 4.5 inches corresponds to an actual distance of 250 miles. If two cities are 7.25 inches apart on the map, how many miles apart are they? (Round to the nearest tenth.)

Find the Mistake

Each sentence below contains a mistake. Circle the mistake and write the correct word(s) or number(s) on the line provided.

1. A basketball player scores 112 points in 8 games. The proportion to find how many points the player will score in 14 games is $\frac{112}{8} = \frac{14}{x}$. _____

2. The scale of a map indicates that 2 inches corresponds to 250 miles in real life. If two cities on the map are 3.5 inches apart, they are 0.028 miles apart in real life. _____

3. A jellybean company knows that for every 100 jellybeans, 4 will be misshapen. The proportion needed to find how many jelly beans were made if 36 misshapen jelly beans are found is $\frac{4}{36} = \frac{x}{100}$. _____

4. If burning 1 gallon of gasoline produces 20.2 pounds of carbon dioxide, then burning 12 gallons of gasoline produces approximately 0.59 pounds of carbon dioxide. _____

Chapter 5 Summary

Ratio [5.1]

The ratio of a to b is $\frac{a}{b}$. The ratio of two numbers is a way of comparing them using fraction notation.

EXAMPLES

1. The ratio of 6 to 8 is $\frac{6}{8}$ which can be reduced to $\frac{3}{4}$.

Solving Equations by Division [5.2]

Dividing both sides of an equation by the same number will not change the solution to the equation. For example, the equation $5 \cdot x = 40$ can be solved by dividing both sides by 5.

4. Solve: $5 \cdot x = 40$.

$$5 \cdot x = 40$$

$$\frac{5 \cdot x}{5} = \frac{40}{5} \quad \text{Divide both sides by 5.}$$

$$x = 8 \quad 40 \div 5 = 8$$

Proportion [5.2]

A proportion is an equation that indicates that two ratios are equal.
The numbers in a proportion are called *terms* and are numbered as follows:

First term $\longrightarrow \dfrac{a}{b} = \dfrac{c}{d} \longleftarrow$ Third term
Second term $\longrightarrow$ $\qquad\qquad\longleftarrow$ Fourth term

The first and fourth terms are called the *extremes*. The second and third terms are called the *means*.

Means $\longrightarrow \dfrac{a}{b} = \dfrac{c}{d} \longleftarrow$ Extremes

5. The following is a proportion:

$$\frac{6}{8} = \frac{3}{4}$$

Fundamental Property of Proportions [5.2]

In any proportion, the product of the extremes is equal to the product of the means. In symbols,

$$\text{If} \quad \frac{a}{b} = \frac{c}{d} \quad \text{then} \quad ad = bc$$

Finding an Unknown Term in a Proportion [5.2]

To find the unknown term in a proportion, we apply the fundamental property of proportions and solve the equation that results by dividing both sides by the number that is multiplied by the unknown. For instance, if we want to find the unknown in the proportion

$$\frac{2}{5} = \frac{8}{x}$$

we use the fundamental property of proportions to set the product of the extremes equal to the product of the means.

6. Find x: $\dfrac{2}{5} = \dfrac{8}{x}$.

$$2 \cdot x = 5 \cdot 8$$

$$2 \cdot x = 40$$

$$\frac{2 \cdot x}{2} = \frac{40}{2}$$

$$x = 20$$

Write each ratio as a fraction in lowest terms. [5.1]

1. 36 to 16

2. $\frac{4}{9}$ to $\frac{1}{3}$

3. 5 to $3\frac{3}{4}$

4. 0.24 to 0.14

5. $\frac{7}{12}$ to $\frac{5}{12}$

A family of three budgeted the following amounts for some of its monthly bills. Use the pie chart to solve problems 6 and 7.

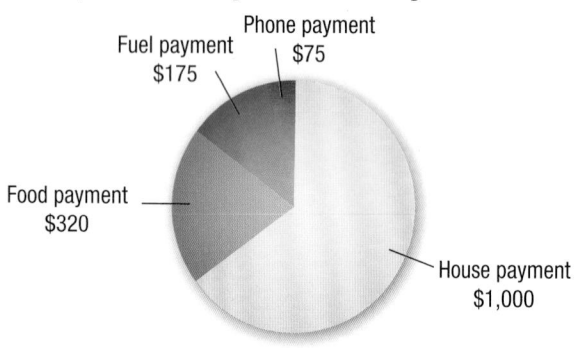

Phone payment $75

Fuel payment $175

Food payment $320

House payment $1,000

Family Budget

6. Ratio Find the ratio of phone payment to food payment. [5.1]

7. Ratio Find the ratio of house payment to fuel payment. [5.1]

Find the unknown term in each proportion. [5.2]

8. $\frac{3}{8} = \frac{21}{x}$

9. $\frac{2.25}{3} = \frac{1.5}{x}$

10. Baseball A baseball player gets 9 hits in his first 18 games of the season. If he continues at the same rate, how many hits will he get in 72 games? [5.3]

11. Map Reading The scale on a map indicates that 1 inch on the map corresponds to an actual distance of 24 miles. Two cities are $3\frac{3}{8}$ inches apart on the map. What is the actual distance between the two cities? [5.3]

Nursing Sometimes body surface area is used to calculate the necessary dosage for a patient. [5.3]

12. The dosage for a drug is 16 mg/m². If an adult has a BSA of 1.8 m², what dosage should he take?

13. Find the dosage an adult should take if her BSA is 1.6 m² and the dosage strength is 26.8 mg/m².

The diagram shows the ratio of the diameters of the planets in our solar system to Earth's diameter. Use the information to answer the following questions if the Earth's diameter is 12,742 km. Round to the nearest kilometer if necessary.

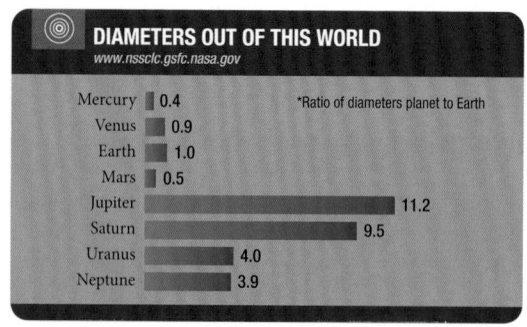

DIAMETERS OUT OF THIS WORLD
www.nssclc.gsfc.nasa.gov

Planet	Ratio
Mercury	0.4
Venus	0.9
Earth	1.0
Mars	0.5
Jupiter	11.2
Saturn	9.5
Uranus	4.0
Neptune	3.9

*Ratio of diameters planet to Earth

14. What is the diameter of Mars?

15. What is the diameter of Jupiter?

Simplify.

1. 9,341
    296
+ 3,735

2. $2,071 - 1,735$

3. $\dfrac{578}{34}$

4. $(4 \cdot 2) \cdot 6$

5. $24\overline{)12,393}$

6. $136 \div 17$

7. $63 + 28$

8. $\dfrac{81}{3}$

9. $(12 - 3) + (509 - 374)$

10. $(4.8)(6.2)$

11. $74.3 - 31.7$

12. $7.3 + 4.27 + 3.09$

13. $29.7 \div 4.5$

14. $\dfrac{3}{8} + \dfrac{5}{12}$

15. $6 \div \left(16 \div 2\dfrac{2}{3}\right)$

16. $16 - 3\dfrac{5}{7}$

Solve.

17. $\dfrac{5}{7} = \dfrac{x}{35}$

18. $\dfrac{3}{8} = \dfrac{9}{x}$

19. Ratio If the ratio of men to women in a self-defense class is 2 to 5, and there are 8 men in the class, how many women are in the class?

20. Surfboard Length A surfing company decides that a surfboard would be more efficient if its length were reduced by $1\frac{5}{8}$ inches. If the original length was 7 feet $\frac{7}{8}$ inches, what will be the new length of the board (in inches)?

21. Teaching A teacher lectures on three sections in two class periods. If she continues at the same rate, on how many sections can the teacher lecture in 46 class periods?

The snapshot shows the amount of memory available in each new generation of iPod. Use the information to answer the following questions.

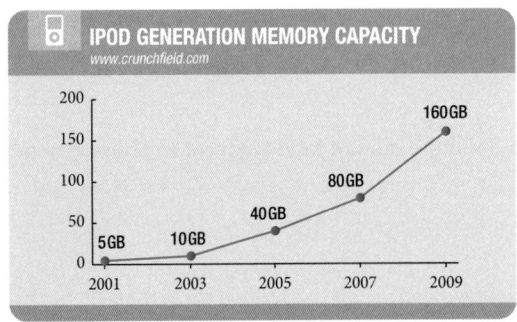

22. Ratio What is the ratio of the 2009 generation to the 2005 generation?

23. Ratio What is the ratio of the 2001 generation to the 2009 generation?

Write each ratio as a fraction in lowest terms. [5.1]

1. 48 to 18

2. $\frac{5}{8}$ to $\frac{3}{4}$

3. 6 to $2\frac{4}{7}$

4. 0.14 to 0.4

5. $\frac{7}{9}$ to $\frac{4}{9}$

A family of three budgeted the following amounts for some of its monthly bills. Use the pie chart to solve problems 6 and 7.

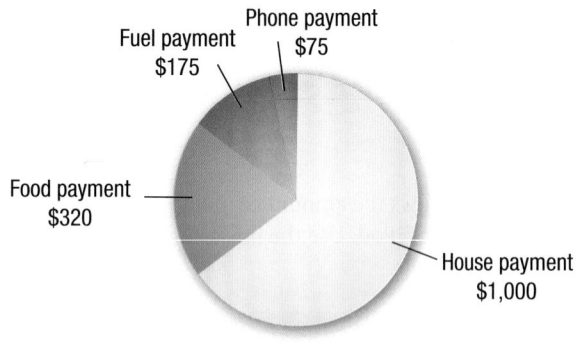

Family Budget

6. Ratio Find the ratio of food payment to phone payment. [5.1]

7. Ratio Find the ratio of house payment to food payment. [5.1]

Find the unknown term in each proportion. [5.2]

8. $\frac{4}{7} = \frac{24}{x}$

9. $\frac{2.5}{5} = \frac{1.5}{x}$

10. Baseball A baseball player gets 13 hits in his first 20 games of the season. If he continues at the same rate, how many hits will he get in 60 games? [5.3]

11. Map Reading The scale on a map indicates that 1 inch on the map corresponds to an actual distance of 15 miles. Two cities are $5\frac{1}{2}$ inches apart on the map. What is the actual distance between the two cities? [5.3]

Nursing Sometimes body surface area is used to calculate the necessary dosage for a patient. [5.3]

12. The dosage for a drug is 27 mg/m². If an adult has a BSA of 1.9 m², what dosage should he take?

13. Find the dosage an adult should take if her BSA is 1.35 m² and the dosage strength is 11.4 mg/m².

The diagram shows the number of US health club memberships in millions. Use the information to answer the following questions.

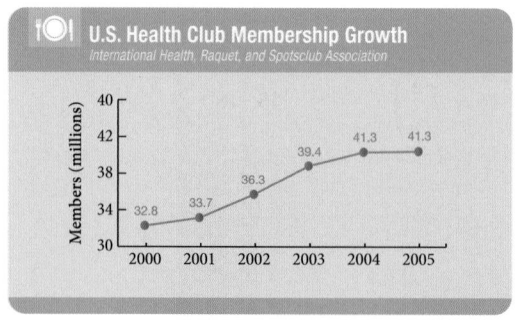

14. What is the ratio of memberships in 2000 to memberships in 2003?

15. What is the ratio of memberships in 2004 to memberships in 2005?

Percent

The largest building in the world is so big that it could hold all of the Disney Magic Kingdom theme parks inside it and still have room for twelve acres of covered parking! The Boeing facility adjacent to Paine Field in Everett, Washington has over one million light fixtures with a yearly electric bill of $18 million. The building has

the largest floor space in the world and employs 24,000 workers. It was originally opened in 1967 when the company began large-scale manufacturing of commercial aircraft. At that time, Pan American World Airways placed a $525 million order for twenty-five 747 jetliners, requiring the construction of new facilities. Over 300 employees began assembly of the first-ever jumbo jets, and on September 30, 1968, the first 747 rolled out of the factory to worldwide fanfare. Since the inaugural 747, Boeing has expanded its manufacturing programs to include the 767, the 777, and the new 787 Dreamliner.

When the 777 program was launched in 1990, the plant needed to be enlarged to accommodate the increase in production. Suppose you know that the floor space of the Boeing Plant is currently 4.3 million square feet and that the 1990 construction expanded floor space by 50%. What was the floor space of the facility prior to expansion? In order to answer this question, you will need to know how to work problems involving percent, which is one of the topics of this chapter.

OBJECTIVES

A Understand percents and change percents to decimals.

B Change decimals to percents.

C Change percents to fractions.

D Change fractions to percents.

KEY WORDS

- percent

6.1 Percents, Decimals, and Fractions

Image © sxc.hu, monmart, 2005

If you manage your own money, you know the importance of a household budget. The following pie chart represents recommended percentages for the various categories to which your money may go. The whole pie chart is represented by 100%. In general, 100% of something is the whole thing.

A Household Budget

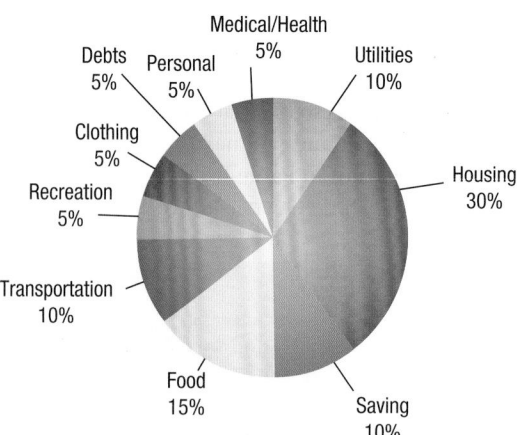

In this section, we will look at the meaning of percent. To begin, we learn to change decimals to percents and percents to decimals.

A The Meaning of Percent

Percent means "per hundred." Writing a number as a percent is a way of comparing the number with the number 100. For example, the number 42% (the % symbol is read "percent") is the same as 42 one-hundredths, that is,

$$42\% = \frac{42}{100}$$

Percents are really fractions (or ratios) with denominator 100.

Video Examples
SECTION 6.1

EXAMPLE 1 Write each percent as a fraction with a denominator of 100.

a. 33%   **b.** 6%   **c.** 160%

Solution

a. $33\% = \dfrac{33}{100}$

b. $6\% = \dfrac{6}{100}$

c. $160\% = \dfrac{160}{100}$

If you are wondering if we could reduce some of these fractions further, the answer is yes. We have not done so because the point of this example is that every percent can be written as a fraction with denominator 100.

Changing Percents to Decimals

To change a percent to a decimal number, we simply use the meaning of percent.

EXAMPLE 2 Change 35.2% to a decimal.

Solution We drop the % symbol and write 35.2 over 100.

$$35.2\% = \frac{35.2}{100} \qquad \textit{Use the meaning of percent to convert to a fraction with denominator 100.}$$

$$= 0.352 \qquad \textit{Divide 35.2 by 100.}$$

We see from Example 2 that 35.2% is the same as the decimal 0.352. The result is that the % symbol has been dropped and the decimal point has been moved two places to the *left*. Because % always means "per hundred," we will always end up moving the decimal point two places to the left when we change percents to decimals. Because of this, we can write the following rule:

> **RULE** Percent to Decimal
>
> To change a percent to a decimal, drop the % symbol and move the decimal point two places to the *left*.

EXAMPLE 3 Write each percent as a decimal.

a. 37%   **b.** 68%   **c.** 120%   **d.** 0.8%

Solution We drop the % symbol and move the decimal point to the left two places

a. 37% = 0.37

b. 68% = 0.68

Decimal point originally here   **c.** 120% = 1.20   Decimal point moved to here

d. 0.8% = 0.008

EXAMPLE 4 Suppose a cortisone cream is 0.5% hydrocortisone. Writing this number as a decimal, we have

$$0.5\% = 0.005$$

Practice Problems

1. Write each fraction with a denominator of 100.
   a. 20%
   b. 4%
   c. 230%

2. Change 23.5% to a decimal.

3. Write each percent as a decimal.
   a. 23%
   b. 72%
   c. 180%
   d. 0.03%

4. Suppose the cortisone cream in Example 4 was 1% hydrocortisone. Write this number as a decimal.

Answers

1. a. $\frac{20}{100}$ **b.** $\frac{4}{100}$ **c.** $\frac{230}{100}$

2. 0.235

3. a. 0.23   **b.** 0.72   **c.** 1.80
   d. 0.0003

4. 0.01

B Changing Decimals to Percents

Now we want to do the opposite of what we just did in Examples 2–4. We want to change decimals to percents. We know that 42% written as a decimal is 0.42, which means that in order to change 0.42 back to a percent, we must move the decimal point two places to the *right* and use the % symbol.

$$0.42 = 42\%$$

Notice that we don't show the new decimal point if it is at the end of the number.

> **RULE** Decimal to Percent
>
> To change a decimal to a percent, we move the decimal point two places to the *right* and use the % symbol.

5. Write each decimal as a percent.
   a. 0.42
   b. 3.86
   c. 0.2
   d. 0.005

EXAMPLE 5   Write each decimal as a percent.

a. 0.27   **b.** 4.89   **c.** 0.5   **d.** 0.09

Solution

a. $0.27 = 27\%$

b. $4.89 = 489\%$

c. $0.5 = 0.50 = 50\%$ *Notice here that we put a 0 after the 5 so we can move the decimal point two places to the right.*

d. $0.09 = 09\% = 9\%$ *Notice that we can drop the 0 at the left without changing the value of the number.*

6. Suppose the player in Example 6 has a batting average of 0.360. Write that number as a percent.

EXAMPLE 6   A softball player has a batting average of 0.650. As a percent, this number is $0.650 = 65.0\%$.

As you can see from these examples, percent is just a way of comparing numbers to 100. To multiply decimals by 100, we move the decimal point two places to the right. To divide by 100, we move the decimal point two places to the left. Because of this, it is a fairly simple procedure to change percents to decimals and decimals to percents.

C Changing Percents to Fractions

To change a percent to a fraction, drop the % symbol and write the original number over 100.

7. Write each percent as a fraction in lowest terms.
   a. 13%
   b. 20%
   c. 54%

EXAMPLE 7   The pie chart shows who pays for college expenses. Change each percent to a fraction.

Solution   In each case, we drop the percent symbol and write the number over 100. Then we reduce to lowest terms if possible.

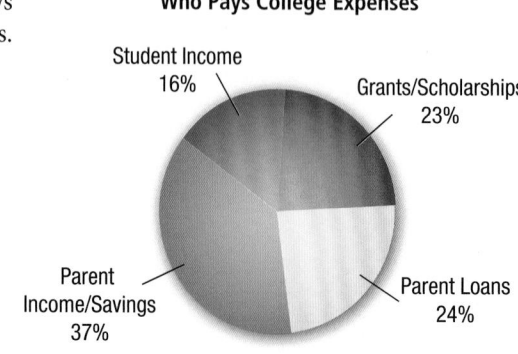

Who Pays College Expenses

Student Income 16%

Grants/Scholarships 23%

Parent Income/Savings 37%

Parent Loans 24%

$$16\% = \frac{16}{100} = \frac{4}{25} \qquad 23\% = \frac{23}{100} \qquad 24\% = \frac{24}{100} = \frac{6}{25} \qquad 37\% = \frac{37}{100}$$

EXAMPLE 8 Change 4.5% to a fraction in lowest terms.

Solution We begin by writing 4.5 over 100.

$$4.5\% = \frac{4.5}{100}$$

We now multiply the numerator and the denominator by 10 so the numerator will be a whole number.

$$\frac{4.5}{100} = \frac{4.5 \times 10}{100 \times 10} \qquad \text{Multiply the numerator and the denominator by 10.}$$

$$= \frac{45}{1,000}$$

$$= \frac{9}{200} \qquad \text{Reduce to lowest terms.}$$

EXAMPLE 9 Change $32\frac{1}{2}\%$ to a fraction in lowest terms.

Solution Writing $32\frac{1}{2}$ over 100 produces a complex fraction. We change $32\frac{1}{2}$ to an improper fraction and simplify.

$$32\frac{1}{2}\% = \frac{32\frac{1}{2}}{100}$$

$$= \frac{\frac{65}{2}}{100} \qquad \text{Change } 32\frac{1}{2} \text{ to the improper fraction } \frac{65}{2}.$$

$$= \frac{65}{2} \times \frac{1}{100} \qquad \text{Dividing by 100 is the same as multiplying by } \frac{1}{100}.$$

$$= \frac{5 \cdot 13 \cdot 1}{2 \cdot 5 \cdot 20} \qquad \text{Multiply.}$$

$$= \frac{13}{40} \qquad \text{Reduce to lowest terms.}$$

Note that we could have changed our original mixed number to a decimal first and then changed to a fraction:

$$32\frac{1}{2}\% = 32.5\% = \frac{32.5}{100} = \frac{32.5 \times 10}{100 \times 10} = \frac{325}{1000} = \frac{5 \cdot 5 \cdot 13}{5 \cdot 5 \cdot 40} = \frac{13}{40}$$

The result is the same in both cases.

D Changing Fractions to Percents

To change a fraction to a percent, we can change the fraction to a decimal and then change the decimal to a percent.

EXAMPLE 10 Suppose the price your bookstore pays for your textbook is $\frac{7}{10}$ of the price you pay for your textbook. Write $\frac{7}{10}$ as a percent.

Solution We can change $\frac{7}{10}$ to a decimal by dividing 7 by 10.

$$\begin{array}{r} 0.7 \\ 10\overline{)7.0} \\ \underline{7\ 0} \\ 0 \end{array}$$

We then change the decimal 0.7 to a percent by moving the decimal point two places to the *right* and using the % symbol.

$$0.7 = 70\%$$

8. Change 3.2% to a fraction in lowest terms.

9. Change $53\frac{1}{4}\%$ to a fraction in lowest terms.

10. Write $\frac{3}{5}$ as a percent.

Answers

8. $\frac{4}{125}$

9. $\frac{213}{400}$

10. 60%

You may have noticed that we could have saved some time by simply writing $\frac{7}{10}$ as an equivalent fraction with denominator 100; that is,

$$\frac{7}{10} = \frac{7 \cdot 10}{10 \cdot 10} = \frac{70}{100} = 70\%$$

This is a good way to convert fractions like $\frac{7}{10}$ to percents. It works well for fractions with denominators of 2, 4, 5, 10, 20, 25, and 50, because they are easy to change to fractions with denominators of 100.

11. Change $\frac{5}{8}$ to a percent.

EXAMPLE 11   Change $\frac{3}{8}$ to a percent.

Solution   We begin by dividing 3 by 8.

$$
\begin{array}{r}
.375 \\
8\overline{)3.000} \\
2\,4 \\
\hline
60 \\
56 \\
\hline
40 \\
40 \\
\hline
0
\end{array}
$$

We then change the decimal to a percent by moving the decimal point two places to the right and using the % symbol.

$$\frac{3}{8} = 0.375 = 37.5\%$$

12. Change $\frac{7}{9}$ to a percent.

EXAMPLE 12   Change $\frac{5}{12}$ to a percent.

Solution   We begin by dividing 5 by 12.

$$
\begin{array}{r}
.4166 \\
12\overline{)5.0000} \\
4\,8 \\
\hline
20 \\
12 \\
\hline
80 \\
72 \\
\hline
80 \\
72 \\
\hline
8
\end{array}
$$

Note   When rounding off, let's agree to round off to the nearest thousandth and then move the decimal point. Our answers in percent form will then be accurate to the nearest tenth of a percent, as in Example 12.

Because the 6s repeat indefinitely, we can use mixed number notation to write

$$\frac{5}{12} = 0.41\overline{6}$$

Or rounding, we can write

$$\frac{5}{12} = 41.7\%$$ *Round to the nearest tenth of a percent.*

13. Change $3\frac{1}{4}$ to a percent.

EXAMPLE 13   Change $2\frac{1}{2}$ to a percent.

Solution   We first change to a decimal and then to a percent.

$$2\frac{1}{2} = 2.5$$

$$= 250\%$$

Answers
11. 62.5%
12. 77.8%
13. 325%

Table 1 lists some of the most commonly used fractions and decimals and their equivalent percents.

Table 1

Fraction	Decimal	Percent
$\frac{1}{2}$	0.5	50%
$\frac{1}{4}$	0.25	25%
$\frac{3}{4}$	0.75	75%
$\frac{1}{3}$	$0.\overline{3}$	$33\frac{1}{3}$%
$\frac{2}{3}$	$0.\overline{6}$	$66\frac{2}{3}$%
$\frac{1}{5}$	0.2	20%
$\frac{2}{5}$	0.4	40%
$\frac{3}{5}$	0.6	60%
$\frac{4}{5}$	0.8	80%

GETTING READY FOR CLASS

After reading through the preceding section, respond in your own words and in complete sentences.

A. What is the relationship between the word *percent* and the number 100?

B. Explain in words how you would change 25% to a decimal.

C. Explain in words how you would change 25% to a fraction.

D. After reading this section you know that $\frac{1}{2}$, 0.5, and 50% are equivalent. Show mathematically why this is true.

Vocabulary Review

Choose the correct words to fill in the blanks below.

ratio   % symbol   hundred   left   decimal   right

1. The word percent means "per _____."

2. A percent is a _____ with a denominator of 100.

3. To change a percent to a decimal, drop the % symbol and move the decimal point two places to the _____.

4. To change a decimal to a percent, move the decimal point two places to the _____ and use the % symbol.

5. To change a percent to a fraction, drop the _____ and write the original number over 100.

6. To change a fraction to a percent, we can change the fraction to a _____ and then change the decimal to a percent.

Problems

A Write each percent as a fraction with denominator 100.

1. 20%   **2.** 40%   **3.** 60%   **4.** 80%

5. 24%   **6.** 48%   **7.** 65%   **8.** 35%

Change each percent to a decimal.

9. 23%   **10.** 34%   **11.** 92%   **12.** 87%

13. 9%   **14.** 7%   **15.** 3.4%   **16.** 5.8%

17. 6.34%   **18.** 7.25%   **19.** 0.9%   **20.** 0.6%

B Change each decimal to a percent.

21. 0.23   **22.** 0.34   **23.** 0.92   **24.** 0.87

25. 0.45   **26.** 0.54   **27.** 0.03   **28.** 0.04

29. 0.6   **30.** 0.9   **31.** 0.8   **32.** 0.5

33. 0.27   **34.** 0.62   **35.** 1.23   **36.** 2.34

C Change each percent to a fraction in lowest terms.

37. 60%   **38.** 40%   **39.** 75%   **40.** 25%

41. 4%   **42.** 2%   **43.** 26.5%   **44.** 34.2%

45. 71.87%   **46.** 63.6%   **47.** 0.75%   **48.** 0.45%

49. $6\frac{1}{4}\%$ **50.** $5\frac{1}{4}\%$ **51.** $33\frac{1}{3}\%$ **52.** $66\frac{2}{3}\%$

D Change each fraction or mixed number to a percent.

53. $\frac{1}{2}$ **54.** $\frac{1}{4}$ **55.** $\frac{3}{4}$ **56.** $\frac{2}{3}$

57. $\frac{1}{3}$ **58.** $\frac{1}{5}$ **59.** $\frac{4}{5}$ **60.** $\frac{1}{6}$

61. $\frac{7}{8}$ **62.** $\frac{1}{8}$ **63.** $\frac{7}{50}$ **64.** $\frac{9}{25}$

65. $3\frac{1}{4}$ **66.** $2\frac{1}{8}$ **67.** $1\frac{1}{2}$ **68.** $1\frac{3}{4}$

69. Change $\frac{21}{43}$ to a percent. Round to the nearest tenth of a percent

70. Change $\frac{36}{49}$ to a percent. Round to the nearest tenth of a percent

Applying the Concepts

71. Physiology The human body is between 50% and 75% water. Write each of these percents as a decimal.

72. Alcohol Consumption In the United States, 2.7% of those over 15 years of age drink more than 6.3 ounces of alcohol per day. In France, the same figure is 9%. Write each of these percents as a decimal.

73. iPhone The snapshot below shows what users had before their new iPhone. Use the information to answer the following questions.

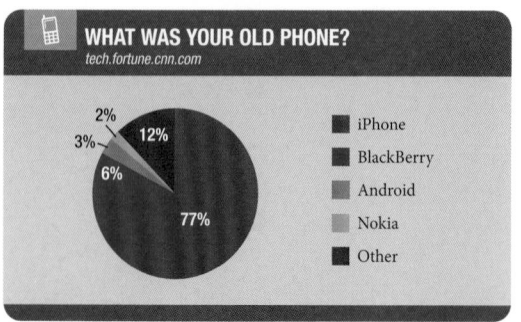

a. Convert each percent to a fraction.

b. Convert each percent to a decimal.

c. About how many times more likely are the respondents to have owned a Blackberry than an Android phone?

74. Foreign Language The chart shows the extent to which Americans say they know a foreign language. Change each percent to a fraction in lowest terms.

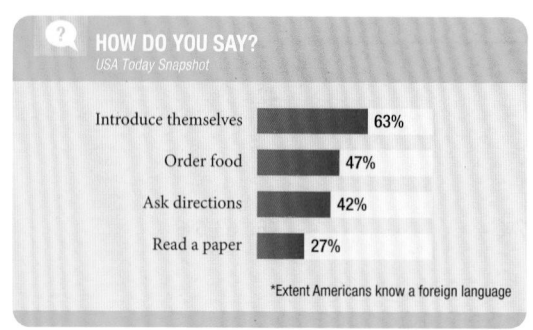

75. Nutrition Although, nutritionally, breakfast is the most important meal of the day, only $\frac{1}{5}$ of the people in the United States consistently eat breakfast. What percent of the population is this?

76. Children in School In Belgium, 96% of all children between 3 and 6 years of age go to school. In Sweden, the number is only 25%. In the United States, it is 60%. Write each of these percents as a fraction in lowest terms.

77. Student Enrollment The pie chart shows Cal Poly enrollment by college. Change each fraction to a percent.

Cal Poly Enrollment

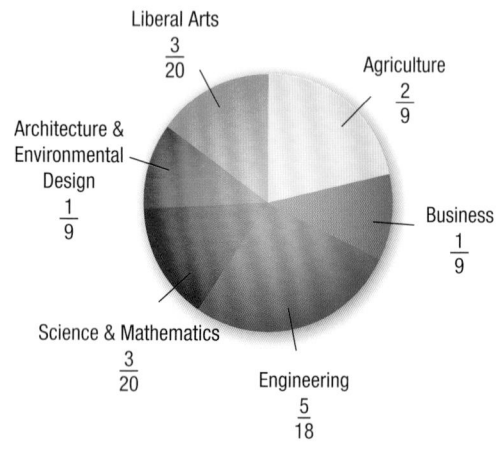

78. iPad The chart shows the percentage of the total iPad sales by state. Use the information to convert the percentage for the following states to a decimal.

a. California   **b.** Illinois   **c.** New York

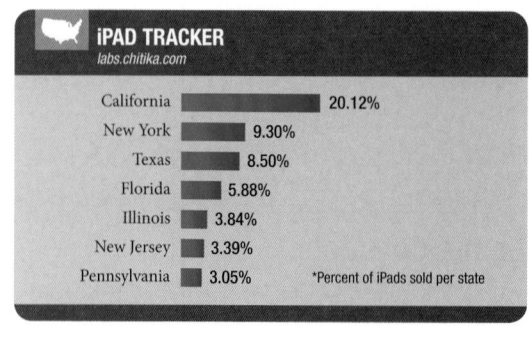

Calculator Problems

Use a calculator to write each fraction as a decimal, and then change the decimal to a percent. Round all answers to the nearest tenth of a percent.

79. $\dfrac{29}{37}$ **80.** $\dfrac{18}{83}$ **81.** $\dfrac{6}{51}$ **82.** $\dfrac{8}{95}$ **83.** $\dfrac{236}{327}$ **84.** $\dfrac{568}{732}$

85. Women in the Military During World War II, $\frac{1}{12}$ of the Soviet armed forces were women. Today only $\frac{1}{450}$ of the Russian armed forces are women. Change both fractions to percents (to the nearest tenth of a percent).

86. Number of Teachers The ratio of the number of teachers to the number of students in secondary schools in Japan is 1 to 17. In the United States, the ratio is 1 to 19. Write each of these ratios as a fraction and then as a percent. Round to the nearest tenth of a percent.

Getting Ready for the Next Section

Multiply.

87. $0.25(74)$ **88.** $0.15(63)$ **89.** $0.435(25)$ **90.** $0.635(45)$

Divide. Round the answers to the nearest thousandth, if necessary.

91. $\dfrac{21}{42}$ **92.** $\dfrac{21}{84}$ **93.** $\dfrac{25}{0.4}$ **94.** $\dfrac{31.9}{78}$

Solve for n.

95. $42n = 21$ **96.** $25 = 0.40n$

Find the Mistake

Each sentence below contains a mistake. Circle the mistake and write the correct word(s) or number(s) on the line provided.

1. Writing 0.4% as a decimal gives us 0.4. _____

2. To write 3.21 as a percent, divide the number by 100; that is, move the decimal two places to the left.

_____

3. Writing 25% as a fraction in lowest terms gives us $\frac{25}{100}$. _____

4. To change $\frac{5}{8}$ to a percent, we change $\frac{5}{8}$ to 0.625 and then move the decimal two places to the left to get 0.00625%.

_____

Navigation Skills: Prepare, Study, Achieve

Think about your current study routine. Has it been successful? There are many things that you must consider when creating a routine. One important aspect is the environment in which you choose to study. Think about the location you typically study. Are you able to focus there without distraction? Consider what things may distract you (e.g., cell phones, television, noise, friends who socialize rather than study) and find a place to study where these things are absent. Other important aspects of a productive study routine are time of day you choose to study, and sights and sounds around you during your study time. A study environment that is not distracting will help you focus and foster further success in this course.

KEY WORDS

is

of

6.2 Basic Percent Problems

Image © Richard Ling, 2005

Scientists have discovered a toxin in the spit of a sea snail that works with greater effectiveness but in smaller dosages and without the addictive risk of the painkiller morphine. The marine cone snail dwells on the ocean floor. The snail shoots its harpoon-like teeth coated in toxic saliva into its prey to poison it. Researchers have discovered how to isolate the saliva's toxin and put it into a pill for humans in pain to ingest. A patient will feel the same pain-reducing effects with 1% of a dose of a popular neuropathic painkiller prescribed in hospitals. If the prescription for an adult of the popular painkiller starts at 300 milligrams, how many milligrams of the sea snail drug would be dosed? In this section, we will work some other basic percent problems, similar to this one.

A Solving Percent Problems Using Equations

This section is concerned with three kinds of word problems that are associated with percents. Here is an example of each type:

Type A: What number is 15% of 63?

Type B: What percent of 42 is 21?

Type C: 25 is 40% of what number?

The first method we use to solve all three types of problems involves translating the sentences into equations and then solving the equations. The following translations are used to write the sentences as equations:

English	Mathematics
is	=
of	· (multiply)
a number	n
what number	n
what percent	n

The word *is* always translates to an = sign, the word *of* almost always means multiply, and the number we are looking for can be represented with a variable, such as n or x.

EXAMPLE 1 What number is 15% of 63?

Solution We translate the sentence into an equation as follows:

What number is 15% of 63?

$$n = 0.15 \cdot 63$$

Video Examples
SECTION 6.2

Practice Problems

1. What number is 20% of 70?

Answer

1. 14

To do arithmetic with percents, we have to change to decimals. That is why 15% is rewritten as 0.15. Solving the equation, we have

$$n = 0.15 \cdot 63$$

$$n = 9.45$$

Therefore, 15% of 63 is 9.45.

EXAMPLE 2   What percent of 42 is 21?

Solution   We translate the sentence as follows:

What percent of 42 is 21?
$$n \cdot 42 = 21$$

We solve for n by dividing both sides by 42.

$$\frac{n \cdot 42}{42} = \frac{21}{42}$$

$$n = \frac{21}{42}$$

$$n = 0.50$$

Because the original problem asked for a percent, we change 0.50 to a percent.

$$n = 50\%$$

Therefore, 21 is 50% of 42.

EXAMPLE 3   25 is 40% of what number?

Solution   Following the procedure from the first two examples, we have

25 is 40% of what number?
$$25 = 0.40 \cdot n$$

Again, we changed 40% to 0.40 so we can do the arithmetic involved in the problem. Dividing both sides of the equation by 0.40, we have

$$\frac{25}{0.40} = \frac{0.40 \cdot n}{0.40}$$

$$\frac{25}{0.40} = n$$

$$62.5 = n$$

Therefore, 25 is 40% of 62.5.

As you can see, all three types of percent problems are solved in a similar manner. We write *is* as $=$, *of* as $\cdot$, and *what number* as n. The resulting equation is then solved to obtain the answer to the original question. Here are some more examples:

EXAMPLE 4   What number is 43.5% of 25?
$$n = 0.435 \cdot 25$$

$$n = 10.9 \qquad \text{\textit{Round to the nearest tenth.}}$$

Therefore, 10.9 is 43.5% of 25.

2. What percent of 148 is 37?

3. 55 is 30% of what number?

4. What number is 38.2% of 45?

Answers
2. 25%
3. 183.33
4. 17.19

5. What percent of 87 is 14.8?

EXAMPLE 5   What percent of 78 is 31.9?

$$n \cdot 78 = 31.9$$

$$\frac{n \cdot 78}{78} = \frac{31.9}{78}$$

$$n = \frac{31.9}{78}$$

$$n = 0.409 \qquad \textit{Round to the nearest thousandth.}$$

$$n = 40.9\%$$

Therefore, 40.9% of 78 is 31.9.

6. 23 is 14% of what number?

EXAMPLE 6   34 is 29% of what number?

$$34 = 0.29 \cdot n$$

$$\frac{34}{0.29} = \frac{0.29 \cdot n}{0.29}$$

$$\frac{34}{0.29} = n$$

$$117.2 = n \qquad \textit{Round to the nearest tenth.}$$

Therefore, 34 is 29% of 117.2.

7. Suppose the item in Example 7 had 62 calories from fat. What percentage of the total calories would be from fat calories?

EXAMPLE 7   The American Dietetic Association recommends eating foods in which the number of calories from fat is less than 30% of the total number of calories. According to the nutrition label, what percent of the total number of calories are fat calories?

Solution   To solve this problem, we must write the question in the form of one of the three basic percent problems shown in Examples 1–6. Because there are 93 calories from fat and a total of 155 calories, we can write the question this way: 93 is what percent of 155?

Now that we have written the question in the form of one of the basic percent problems, we simply translate it into an equation. Then we solve the equation.

Nutrition Facts		
Serving Size 1 oz		
Servings Per Container About 4		
Amount Per Serving		
Calories 155		Calories from fat 93
		% Daily Value*
Total Fat 11g		**16%**
Saturated Fat 3g		**15%**
Trans Fat 0g		**0%**
Cholesterol 0mg		**0%**
Sodium 148mg		**6%**
Total Carbohydrate 14g		**5%**
Dietary Fiber 1g		**5%**
Sugars 1g		
Protein 2g		
Vitamin A 0%	•	Vitamin C 9%
Calcium 1%	•	Iron 3%
*Percent Daily Values are based on a 2,000 calorie diet		

FIGURE 1

93 *is what percent of* 155?

$$93 = n \cdot 155$$

$$\frac{93}{155} = n$$

$$n = 0.60 = 60\%$$

The number of calories from fat in this food is 60% of the total number of calories. Thus the ADA would not consider this to be a healthy food.

Answers

5. 17.01%

6. 164.29

7. 40%

B Solving Percent Problems Using Proportions

We can look at percent problems in terms of proportions also. For example, we know that 24% is the same as $\frac{24}{100}$, which reduces to $\frac{6}{25}$. That is,

$$\frac{24}{100} = \frac{6}{25}$$

$$\underbrace{24 \text{ is to } 100}_{\uparrow} \quad \text{as} \quad \underbrace{6 \text{ is to } 25}_{\uparrow}$$

We can illustrate this visually with boxes of proportional lengths.

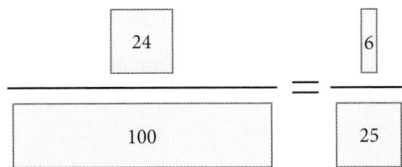

In general, we say

$$\frac{\text{Percent}}{100} = \frac{\text{Amount}}{\text{Base}}$$

$$\underbrace{\text{Percent is to } 100}_{\uparrow} \quad \text{as} \quad \underbrace{\text{amount is to base.}}_{\uparrow}$$

EXAMPLE 8 What number is 15% of 63?

Solution This is the same problem we worked in Example 1. We let n be the number in question. We reason that n will be smaller than 63 because it is only 15% of 63. The base is 63 and the amount is n. We compare n to 63 as we compare 15 to 100. Our proportion sets up as follows:

$$\underbrace{15 \text{ is to } 100}_{\downarrow} \quad \text{as} \quad \underbrace{n \text{ is to } 63}_{\downarrow}$$

$$\frac{15}{100} = \frac{n}{63}$$

Solving the proportion, we have

$15 \cdot 63 = 100n$	Fundamental property of proportions
$945 = 100n$	Simplify the left side.
$9.45 = n$	Divide each side by 100.

This gives us the same result we obtained in Example 1.

EXAMPLE 9 What percent of 42 is 21?

Solution This is the same problem we worked in Example 2. We let n be the percent in question. The amount is 21 and the base is 42. We compare n to 100 as we compare 21 to 42. Here is our reasoning and proportion:

$$\underbrace{n \text{ is to } 100}_{\downarrow} \quad \text{as} \quad \underbrace{21 \text{ is to } 42}_{\downarrow}$$

$$\frac{n}{100} = \frac{21}{42}$$

8. What number is 20% of 70?

9. What percent of 148 is 37?

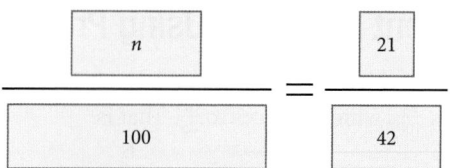

Solving the proportion, we have

$$42n = 21 \cdot 100 \qquad \text{Fundamental property of proportions}$$
$$42n = 2{,}100 \qquad \text{Simplify the right side.}$$
$$n = 50 \qquad \text{Divide each side by 42.}$$

Since n is a percent, our answer is 50%, giving us the same result we obtained in Example 2.

10. 55 is 30% of what number?

EXAMPLE 10   25 is 40% of what number?

Solution   This is the same problem we worked in Example 3. We let n be the number in question. The base is n and the amount is 25. We compare 25 to n as we compare 40 to 100. Our proportion sets up as follows:

$$\frac{40 \text{ is to } 100}{\frac{40}{100}} \quad \text{as} \quad \frac{25 \text{ is to } n}{\frac{25}{n}}$$

$$\frac{40}{100} = \frac{25}{n}$$

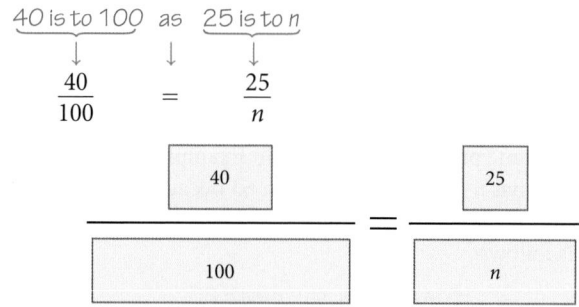

Solving the proportion, we have

$$40 \cdot n = 25 \cdot 100 \qquad \text{Fundamental property of proportions}$$
$$40 \cdot n = 2{,}500 \qquad \text{Simplify the right side.}$$
$$n = 62.5 \qquad \text{Divide each side by 40.}$$

So 25 is 40% of 62.5, which is the same result we obtained in Example 3.

Note   When you work the problems in the problem set, use whichever method you like, unless your instructor indicates that you are to use one method instead of the other.

GETTING READY FOR CLASS

After reading through the preceding section, respond in your own words and in complete sentences.

A. When we translate a sentence such as "What number is 15% of 63?" into symbols, what does each of the following translate to?

   a. is   **b.** of   **c.** what number

B. Using Example 1 in your text as a guide, answer the question below.

   The number 9.45 is what percent of 63?

C. Show that the answer to the question below is the same as the answer to the question in Example 2 of your text.

   The number 21 is what percent of 42?

D. If 21 is 50% of 42, then 21 is what percent of 84?

Answer
10. 183.33

Vocabulary Review

Choose the correct words to fill in the blanks below.

multiply   fraction   decimal   variable   equals sign

1. In a mathematical sentence, the word *is* always translates to an _____.

2. In a mathematical sentence, the word *of* almost always means _____.

3. When translating a sentence to an equation, the number we are looking for can be represented with a _____.

4. To do arithmetic with a percent, change the percent to a _____.

5. Change a percent to a _____ to help solve a percent problem using a proportion.

Problems

A B Solve each of the following problems.

1. What number is 25% of 32?

2. What number is 10% of 80?

3. What number is 20% of 120?

4. What number is 15% of 75?

5. What number is 54% of 38?

6. What number is 72% of 200?

7. What number is 11% of 67?

8. What number is 2% of 49?

9. What percent of 24 is 12?

10. What percent of 80 is 20?

11. What percent of 50 is 5?

12. What percent of 20 is 4?

13. What percent of 36 is 9?

14. What percent of 70 is 14?

15. What percent of 8 is 6?

16. What percent of 16 is 9?

17. 32 is 50% of what number?

18. 16 is 20% of what number?

19. 10 is 20% of what number?

20. 11 is 25% of what number?

21. 37 is 4% of what number?

22. 90 is 80% of what number?

23. 8 is 2% of what number?

24. 6 is 3% of what number?

The following problems can be solved by the same method you used in Problems 1–24.

25. What is 6.4% of 87?

26. What is 10% of 102?

27. 25% of what number is 30?

28. 10% of what number is 22?

29. 28% of 49 is what number?

30. 97% of 28 is what number?

31. 27 is 120% of what number?

32. 24 is 150% of what number?

33. 65 is what percent of 130?

34. 26 is what percent of 78?

35. What is 0.4% of 235,671?

36. What is 0.8% of 721,423?

37. 4.89% of 2,000 is what number?

38. 3.75% of 4,000 is what number?

39. Write a basic percent problem, the solution to which can be found by solving the equation $n = 0.25(350)$.

40. Write a basic percent problem, the solution to which can be found by solving the equation $n = 0.35(250)$.

41. Write a basic percent problem, the solution to which can be found by solving the equation $n \cdot 24 = 16$.

42. Write a basic percent problem, the solution to which can be found by solving the equation $n \cdot 16 = 24$.

43. Write a basic percent problem, the solution to which can be found by solving the equation $46 = 0.75 \cdot n$.

44. Write a basic percent problem, the solution to which can be found by solving the equation $75 = 0.46 \cdot n$.

Applying the Concepts

Nutrition For each nutrition label in Problems 45–48, find what percent of the total number of calories comes from fat calories. Then refer to Example 7 and indicate whether the label is from a food considered healthy by the American Dietetic Association. Round to the nearest tenth of a percent if necessary.

45. Pizza Dough

Nutrition Facts

Serving Size 1/6 of package (65g)
Servings Per Container: 6

Amount Per Serving

Calories 160	Calories from fat 18

	% Daily Value*
Total Fat 2g	3%
Saturated Fat 0.5g	3%
Poly unsaturated Fat 0g	
Monounsaturated Fat 0g	
Cholesterol 0mg	0%
Sodium 470mg	20%
Total Carbohydrate 31g	10%
Dietary Fiber 1g	4%
Sugars 4g	
Protein 5g	

Vitamin A 0%	•	Vitamin C 0%
Calcium 0%	•	Iron 10%

*Percent Daily Values are based on a 2,000 calorie diet

46. Cheez-It Crackers

Nutrition Facts

Serving Size 30 g. (About 27 crackers)
Servings Per Container: 9

Amount Per Serving

Calories 150	Calories from fat 70

	% Daily Value*
Total Fat 8g	12%
Saturated Fat 2g	10%
Trans Fat 0g	
Polysaturated Fat 4g	
Monounsaturated Fat 2g	
Cholesterol 0mg	0%
Sodium 230mg	10%
Total Carbohydrate 17g	6%
Dietary Fiber less than 1g	3%
Sugars 0g	
Protein 3g	

Vitamin A 2%	•	Vitamin C 0%
Calcium 4%	•	Iron 6%

*Percent Daily Values are based on a 2,000 calorie diet

47. Shredded Mozzarella Cheese

Nutrition Facts

Serving Size 1 oz (28.3g)
Servings Per Container: 12

Amount Per Serving

Calories 72	Calories from fat 41

	% Daily Value*
Total Fat 4.5g	7%
Saturated Fat 2.9g	14%
Cholesterol 18mg	6%
Sodium 175mg	7%
Total Carbohydrate 0.8g	0%
Fiber 0g	0%
Sugars 0.3g	
Protein 6.9g	

Vitamin A 3%	•	Vitamin C 0%
Calcium 22%	•	Iron 0%

*Percent Daily Values (DV) are based on a 2,000 calorie diet

48. Canned Corn

Nutrition Facts

Serving Size 1 cup
Servings Per Container About 2 ½

Amount Per Serving

Calories 133	Calories from fat 15

	% Daily Value*
Total Fat 3g	3%
Saturated Fat 1g	1%
Cholesterol 0mg	0%
Sodium 530mg	22%
Total Carbohydrate 30g	10%
Dietary Fiber 3g	13%
Sugars 4g	
Protein 4g	

Vitamin A 0%	•	Vitamin C 23%
Calcium 1%	•	Iron 8%

*Percent Daily Values are based on a 2,000 calorie diet

Getting Ready for the Next Section

Solve each equation.

49. $96 = n \cdot 120$

50. $2{,}400 = 0.48 \cdot n$

51. $114 = 150n$

52. $3{,}360 = 0.42n$

53. What number is 80% of 60?

54. What number is 25% of 300?

Improving Your Quantitative Literacy

55. Survival Rates for Sea Gulls Here is part of a report concerning the survival rates of Western Gulls that appeared on the website of Cornell University:

> *Survival of eggs to hatching is 70%–80%; of hatched chicks to fledgling 50%–70%; of fledglings to age of first breeding <50%.*

Based on this information, give an estimate of the number of gulls of breeding age that would be produced by 1,000 Western Gull eggs.

Find the Mistake

Each sentence below contains a mistake. Circle the mistake and write the correct word(s) or number(s) on the line provided.

1. The question, "What number is 28.5% of 30?" translates to $n \cdot 0.285 = 30$. _____

2. Asking "75 is 30% of what number?" gives us 0.004. _____

3. To answer the question, "What number is 45% of 90?", we can solve the proportion $\dfrac{90}{x} = \dfrac{40}{100}$. _____

4. Using a proportion to answer the question, "What percent of 65 is 26?" will give us $n = 250\%$. _____

Landmark Review: Checking Your Progress

Write each percent as a fraction with denominator 100.

1. 15%

2. 27%

3. 14%

4. 89%

Change each percent to a decimal.

5. 17%

6. 28%

7. 5%

8. 6.37%

Change each decimal to a percent.

9. 0.38

10. 0.98

11. 0.09

12. 4.87

Change each fraction or mixed number to a percent. Round to the nearest tenth of a percent if necessary

13. $\dfrac{1}{10}$

14. $\dfrac{1}{3}$

15. $\dfrac{1}{7}$

16. $3\dfrac{1}{5}$

Solve each of the following problems. Round to the nearest hundredth if necessary.

17. What number is 35% of 15?

18. What percent of 85 is 53?

19. 88 is 37% of what number?

6.3 General Applications of Percent

Scientists are blaming a long line of thunderstorms in 2005 for killing millions of trees in the Amazon. The storm winds blew as fast as 90 miles per hour and ripped trees out of the ground or snapped them in half. Some areas of the forest lost 80% of their trees. Scientists now believe that a minimum of 441 million trees were lost. According to an article on livescience.com written by the staff at OurAmazingPlanet, the storm killed upwards of 500,000 trees in Manaus, Brazil, which was 30% of the total number of trees downed by human deforestation in the same year and area. As we progress through this section, we will become more familiar with percent. Then we can work problems similar to one that may ask us to use the information about the trees in Manaus to calculate how many trees deforestation uprooted.

In this section, we continue our study of percent by doing more of the translations that were introduced in the previous section. The better you are at working those problems, the easier it will be for you to get started on the problems in this section.

A   Applications of Percent

EXAMPLE 1   On a 120-question test, a student answered 96 correctly. What percent of the problems did the student work correctly?

Solution   We have 96 correct answers out of a possible 120. The problem can be restated as

$$96 \text{ is what percent of } 120?$$

$$96 = n \cdot 120$$

$$\frac{96}{120} = \frac{n \cdot 120}{120} \qquad \text{Divide both sides by 120.}$$

$$n = \frac{96}{120} \qquad \text{Switch the left and right sides of the equation.}$$

$$n = 0.80 \qquad \text{Divide 96 by 120.}$$

$$= 80\% \qquad \text{Rewrite as a percent.}$$

When we write a test score as a percent, we are comparing the original score to an equivalent score on a 100-question test. That is, 96 correct out of 120 is the same as 80 correct out of 100.

Video Examples
SECTION 6.3

Practice Problems

1. Suppose the test in Example 1 had 130 questions. What percentage of the problems did the student work correctly?

Answer

1. 73.85%

2. How much HCl is in a 60-milliliter bottle that is marked 60% HCl?

EXAMPLE 2   How much HCl (hydrochloric acid) is in a 60-milliliter bottle that is marked 80% HCl?

Solution   If the bottle is marked 80% HCl, that means 80% of the solution is HCl and the rest is water. Because the bottle contains 60 milliliters, we can restate the question as

$$\textit{What is 80\% of 60?}$$
$$n = 0.80 \cdot 60$$

$$n = 48$$

There are 48 milliliters of HCl in 60 milliliters of 80% HCl solution.

3. If the college in Example 3 has 1,500 female students, what is the total number of students in that college?

EXAMPLE 3   If 48% of the students in a certain college are female and there are 2,400 female students, what is the total number of students in the college?

Solution   We restate the problem as

$$\textit{2,400 is 48\% of what number?}$$
$$2{,}400 = 0.48 \cdot n$$

$$\frac{2{,}400}{0.48} = \frac{0.48 \cdot n}{0.48} \qquad \textit{Divide both sides by 0.48.}$$

$$n = \frac{2{,}400}{0.48} \qquad \textit{Switch the left and right sides of the equation.}$$

$$n = 5{,}000$$

There are 5,000 students.

4. If 35% of the students in Example 4 got a B, how many students recieved a B?

EXAMPLE 4   If 25% of the students in elementary algebra courses receive a grade of A, and there are 300 students enrolled in elementary algebra this year, how many students will receive A's?

Solution   After reading the question a few times, we find that it is the same as this question:

$$\textit{What number is 25\% of 300?}$$
$$n = 0.25 \cdot 300$$

$$n = 75$$

Thus, 75 students will receive A's in elementary algebra.

Almost all application problems involving percents can be restated as one of the three basic percent problems we listed in the previous section. It takes some practice before the restating of application problems becomes automatic. You may have to review that section and Examples 1–4 above several times before you can translate word problems into mathematical expressions yourself.

> **GETTING READY FOR CLASS**
>
> *After reading through the preceding section, respond in your own words and in complete sentences.*
>
> **A.** On the test mentioned in Example 1, how many questions would the student have answered correctly if she answered 40% of the questions correctly?
>
> **B.** If the bottle in Example 2 contained 30 milliliters instead of 60, what would the answer be?
>
> **C.** In Example 3, how many of the students were male?
>
> **D.** How many of the students mentioned in Example 4 received a grade lower than an A?

Answers

2. 36 mL

3. 3,125 students

4. 105 students

Vocabulary Review

On the lines below, write the three types of problems found in applications that involve percents. (Hint: We first learned of the three types in the previous section, and then put them to use in this section.)

1. Type A: _____

2. Type B: _____

3. Type C: _____

Problems

A Solve each of the following problems by first restating it as one of the three basic percent problems from the previous section. In each case, be sure to show the equation.

1. Test Scores On a 120-question test a student answered 84 correctly. What percent of the problems did the student work correctly?

2. Test Scores An engineering student answered 81 questions correctly on a 90-question trigonometry test. What percent of the questions did she answer correctly? What percent were answered incorrectly?

3. Mixture Problem A solution of alcohol and water is 80% alcohol. The solution is found to contain 32 milliliters of alcohol. How many milliliters total (both alcohol and water) are in the solution?

4. Family Budget A family spends $450 every month on food. If the family's income each month is $1,800, what percent of the family's income is spent on food?

5. Chemistry How much HCl (hydrochloric acid) is in a 60-milliliter bottle that is marked 75% HCl?

6. Chemistry How much acetic acid is in a 5-liter container of acetic acid and water that is marked 80% acetic acid? How much is water?

7. **Farming** A farmer owns 28 acres of land. Of the 28 acres, only 65% can be farmed. How many acres are available for farming? How many are not available for farming?

8. **Number of Students** Of the 420 students enrolled in a basic math class, only 30% are first-year students. How many are first-year students? How many are not?

9. **Number of Students** If 48% of the students in a certain college are female and there are 1,440 female students, what is the total number of students in the college?

10. **Basketball** A basketball player made 63 out of 75 free throws. What percent is this?

11. **Number of Graduates** Suppose 60% of the graduating class in a certain high school goes on to college. If 240 students from this graduating class are going on to college, how many students are there in the graduating class?

12. **Defective Parts** In a shipment of airplane parts, 3% are known to be defective. If 15 parts are found to be defective, how many parts are in the shipment?

13. **Number of Students** Suppose there are 3,200 students at our school. If 52% of them are female, how many female students are there at our school?

14. **Number of Students** In a certain school, 75% of the students in first-year chemistry have had algebra. If there are 300 students in first-year chemistry, how many of them have had algebra?

15. **Population** In a city of 32,000 people, there are 10,000 people under 25 years of age. What percent of the population is under 25 years of age?

16. **Number of Students** If 45 people enrolled in a psychology course but only 35 completed it, what percent of the students completed the course? (Round to the nearest tenth of a percent.)

Calculator Problems

The following problems are similar to Problems 1–16. They should be set up the same way. Then the actual calculations should be done on a calculator.

17. Number of People Of 7,892 people attending an outdoor concert in Los Angeles, 3,972 are over 18 years of age. What percent is this? (Round to the nearest whole number percent.)

18. Manufacturing A car manufacturer estimates that 25% of the new cars sold in one city have defective engine mounts. If 2,136 new cars are sold in that city, how many will have defective engine mounts?

19. Laptops The chart shows the most popular laptops among college students surveyed. If 5,280 students were surveyed, how many preferred a Dell?

20. Video Games The chart shows the most popular video games for home gaming systems. If 12,257 people were surveyed, how many listed Pokemon Heartgold as their favorite?

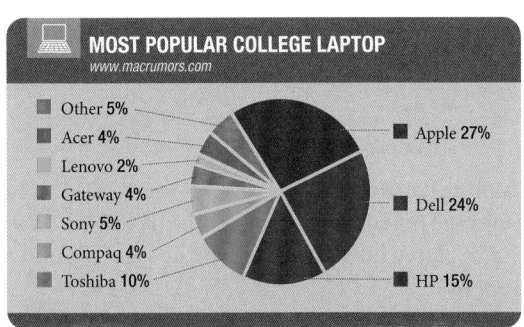

MOST POPULAR COLLEGE LAPTOP
www.macrumors.com

Other 5%
Acer 4%
Lenovo 2%
Gateway 4%
Sony 5%
Compaq 4%
Toshiba 10%
Apple 27%
Dell 24%
HP 15%

MOST POPULAR VIDEO GAMES
www.gamerankings.com

Super Mario Galaxy 2 (*WII*)	97.44%
Red Dead Redemption (*Xbox 360*)	94.88%
Pokemon HeartGold (*DS*)	87.83%
Metal Gear Solid: Peace Walker (*PSP*)	86.92%
Monster Hunter Tri (*WII*)	85.33%

Getting Ready for the Next Section

Multiply.

21. 0.06(550)

22. 0.06(625)

23. 0.03(289,500)

24. 0.03(115,900)

Divide. Write your answers as decimals.

25. 5.44 ÷ 0.04

26. 4.35 ÷ 0.03

27. 19.80 ÷ 396

28. 11.82 ÷ 197

29. $\dfrac{1,836}{0.12}$

30. $\dfrac{115}{0.1}$

31. $\dfrac{90}{600}$

32. $\dfrac{105}{750}$

One Step Further: Batting Averages

Batting averages in baseball are given as decimal numbers, rounded to the nearest thousandth. For example, at the end of the 2011 season, Miguel Cabrera had the highest batting average in the major leagues. He had 197 hits in 572 times at bat, for a batting average of .344. This average is found by dividing the number of hits by the number of times he was at bat and then rounding to the nearest thousandth.

$$\text{Batting average} = \frac{\text{Number of hits}}{\text{Number of times at bat}} = \frac{197}{572} = 0.344$$

Because we can write any decimal number as a percent, we can convert batting averages to percents and use our knowledge of percent to solve problems. Looking at Miguel Cabrera's batting average as a percent, we can say that he will get a hit 34.4% of the times he is at bat.

Each of the following problems can be solved by converting batting averages to percents and translating the problem into one of our three basic percent problems. (All numbers are from the end of the 2011 season according to espn.com.)

33. Jose Reyes had the highest batting average in the National League with 181 hits in 537 times at bat. What percent of the time Reyes is at bat can we expect him to get a hit?

34. Matt Kemp had 195 hits in 602 times at bat. What percent of the time can we expect Kemp to get a hit?

35. David Ortiz had a batting average of .309 in 2011. If his batting average remains the same and he has 550 at bats in the 2012 season, how many hits will he have? Round to the nearest hit.

36. Yadier Molina had a batting average of .305 in 2011. If his batting average remains the same and he has 500 at bats in the 2012 season, how many hits will he have? Round to the nearest hit.

37. How many hits must Miguel Cabrera have in his first 50 at bats in 2012 to maintain his average of .344?

38. How many hits must Matt Kemp have in his first 50 at bats in 2012 to maintain his average of .324?

Find the Mistake

Each sentence below contains a mistake. Circle the mistake and write the correct word(s) or number(s) on the line provided.

1. On a test with 110 questions, a student answered 98 questions correctly. The percentage of questions the student answered correctly is 112.2%. _____

2. A school track team consists of 12 boys and 10 girls. The total number of girls makes up 54.5% of the whole team. _____

3. Suppose 39 students in a college class of 130 students received a B on their tests. To find what percent of students earned a B, solve the proportion $\frac{x}{130} = \frac{39}{100}$. _____

4. Suppose a basketball player made 120 out of 150 free throws attempted. To find what percent of free throws the player made, solve the proportion $\frac{30}{150} = \frac{x}{100}$. _____

Chapter 6 Summary

The Meaning of Percent [6.1]

Percent means "per hundred." It is a way of comparing numbers to the number 100.

EXAMPLES

1. 42% means 42 per hundred or $\frac{42}{100}$.

Changing Percents to Decimals [6.1]

To change a percent to a decimal, drop the % symbol and move the decimal point two places to the *left*.

2. $75\% = 0.75$

Changing Decimals to Percents [6.1]

To change a decimal to a percent, move the decimal point two places to the *right,* and use the % symbol.

3. $0.25 = 25\%$

Changing Percents to Fractions [6.1]

To change a percent to a fraction, drop the % symbol, and use a denominator of 100. Reduce the resulting fraction to lowest terms if necessary.

4. $6\% = \frac{6}{100} = \frac{3}{50}$

Changing Fractions to Percents [6.1]

To change a fraction to a percent, either write the fraction as a decimal and then change the decimal to a percent, or write the fraction as an equivalent fraction with denominator 100, drop the 100, and use the % symbol.

5. $\frac{3}{4} = 0.75 = 75\%$

or

$\frac{9}{10} = \frac{90}{100} = 90\%$

Basic Word Problems Involving Percents [6.2]

There are three basic types of word problems:

Type A: What number is 14% of 68?

Type B: What percent of 75 is 25?

Type C: 25 is 40% of what number?

6. Translating to equations, we have:

Type A: $n = 0.14(68)$; $n = 9.52$
Type B: $75n = 25$; $n = 0.33$
Type C: $25 = 0.40n$; $n = 62.5$

COMMON MISTAKE

1. A common mistake is forgetting to change a percent to a decimal when working problems that involve percents in the calculations. We always change percents to decimals before doing any calculations.

2. Moving the decimal point in the wrong direction when converting percents to decimals or decimals to percents is another common mistake. Remember, *percent* means "per hundred." Rewriting a number expressed as a percent as a decimal will make the numerical part smaller.

   $25\% = 0.25$

Write each percent as a decimal. [6.1]

1. 56%   **2.** 3%   **3.** 0.4%

Write each decimal as a percent. [6.1]

4. 0.32   **5.** 0.7   **6.** 1.64

Write each percent as a fraction or a mixed number in lowest terms. [6.1]

7. 85%   **8.** 128%   **9.** 8.4%

Write each number as a percent. [6.1]

10. $\dfrac{13}{25}$ **11.** $\dfrac{5}{8}$ **12.** $1\dfrac{9}{20}$

13. What number is 20% of 64? [6.2]

14. What percent of 50 is 30? [6.2]

15. 64 is 80% of what number? [6.2]

16. Driver's Test On a 25-question driver's test, a student answered 21 questions correctly. What percent of the questions did the student answer correctly? [6.3]

The chart shows the distribution of iPhones throughout the world. If 190,000,000 iPhones have been sold worldwide, use the information to answer the following questions..

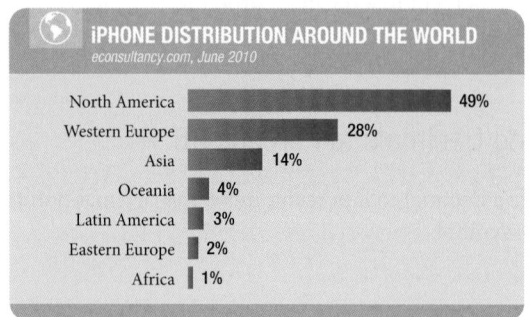

17. How many iPhones have been sold in North America?

18. How many iPhones have been sold in Eastern Europe?

Simplify.

1. 4,381
      623
    + 407

2.   3,062
      − 1,971

3. 13(613)

4. $1{,}335 \div 25$

5. $5.07\overline{)162.24}$

6. $\dfrac{6}{5} - \dfrac{2}{5}$

7. $7.462 + 2.04$

8. $3 - 2.714$

9. $3.5(0.34)$

10. $\dfrac{8}{21} \cdot \dfrac{7}{24}$

11. $\dfrac{16}{3} \div \dfrac{4}{9}$

12. $\dfrac{5}{6} + \dfrac{3}{8}$

13. $7\dfrac{2}{3} - 3\dfrac{5}{6}$

14. $4 \cdot 3\dfrac{5}{8}$

15. Subtract $2\dfrac{3}{5}$ from 8.6.

16. Find the quotient of $2\dfrac{1}{3}$ and $\dfrac{1}{6}$.

17. Translate into symbols, and then simplify: Three times the sum of 6 and 8.

18. Write the ratio of 4 to 24 as a fraction in lowest terms.

19. If 1 mile is 5,280 feet, how many feet are there in 3.6 miles?

20. If 1 square yard is 1,296 square inches, how many square inches are in $\dfrac{7}{8}$ square yard?

21. Write $\dfrac{5}{8}$ as a percent.

22. Convert 32% to a fraction.

23. Solve the equation $\dfrac{3}{x} = \dfrac{6}{7}$.

24. $2 \cdot 4^2 + 2 \cdot 3^3 - 6 \cdot 2^3$

25. What number is 13% of 30?

26. 217 is what percent of 620?

27. 26.6 is 28% of what number?

28. Unit Pricing If a six-pack of Coke costs $7.95, what is the price per can to the nearest cent?

29. Unit Pricing A quart of 2% reduced-fat milk contains four 1-cup servings. If the quart costs $3.65, find the price per serving to the nearest cent.

30. Temperature Use the formula $C = \dfrac{5(F - 32)}{9}$ to find the temperature in degrees Celsius when the Fahrenheit temperature is 95°F.

31. Percent Increase Kendra is earning $2,800 a month when she receives a raise to $3,066 a month. What is the percent increase in her monthly salary?

32. Driving Distance If Ethan drives his car 225 miles in 3 hours, how far will he drive in 5 hours if he drives at the same rate?

33. Movie Tickets A movie theater has a total of 375 seats. If they have a sellout crowd for a matinee and each ticket costs $8.50, how much money will ticket sales bring in that afternoon?

34. Hourly Pay Jean tutors in the math lab and earns $76.50 in one week. If she works 9 hours that week, what is her hourly pay?

The chart shows the minimum amount of space required for each of the sports fields or courts. Use the information to answer the following questions. Round to the nearest hundredth if necessary.

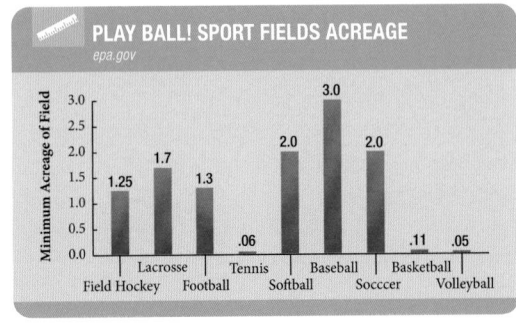

PLAY BALL! SPORT FIELDS ACREAGE *epa.gov*

35. If a school will be building 4 baseball diamonds and 7 basketball courts, what is the minimum acreage it will need?

36. If a city will be adding a field hockey facility, two soccer fields, and five volleyball courts, what is the minimum acreage necessary?

Write each percent as a decimal. [6.1]

1. 27%   **2.** 6%   **3.** 0.9%

Write each decimal as a percent. [6.1]

4. 0.64   **5.** 0.3   **6.** 1.49

Write each percent as a fraction or a mixed number in lowest terms. [6.1]

7. 45%   **8.** 136%   **9.** 7.2%

Write each number as a percent. [6.1]

10. $\dfrac{13}{20}$ **11.** $\dfrac{7}{8}$ **12.** $2\dfrac{1}{4}$

13. What number is 25% of 48? [6.2]

14. What percent of 80 is 28? [6.2]

15. 30 is 40% of what number? [6.2]

16. Driver's Test On a 25-question driver's test, a student answered 24 questions correctly. What percent of the questions did the student answer correctly? [6.3]

The diagram shows the number of finishers for the Nike Women's Marathon in San Francisco. Use the information to answer the following questions.

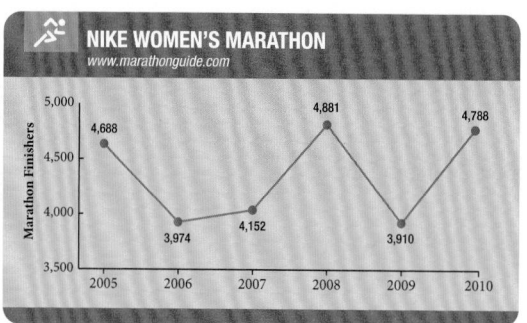

17. What is the percent increase in finishers from 2009 to 2010? Round to the nearest hundredth.

18. If the trend from 2009 to 2010 holds, how many finishers will there be in 2011? Round to the nearest person.

Measurement

Machu Picchu, Peru
Image © 2010 DigitalGlobe
Image © 2010 GeoEye
Google

The ruins of Machu Picchu stand high in the Andes mountains of Peru and are among the most beautiful and mysterious ancient building sites in the world. Most scholars believe that the Incas began construction on the site around 1400 AD. Archaeological excavations have found temples, baths, palaces, storage rooms, and 150 houses. Builders used blocks weighing up to 50 tons to create the structures. Despite the primitive technology of the time, the blocks form tight mortar-less joints that the blade of a knife cannot fit between. Alignment of some of the structures also shows remarkable knowledge of astronomy still being studied today. And the surrounding agricultural terraces and local springs are believed to have produced enough food and water to make the small city self-supporting.

The ruins are also very well preserved, adding to their archaeological value. At 2,350 meters above sea level, they sit on the edge of a sheer cliff and are invisible from the river that flows through the Urubamba Valley 600 meters below. Though the Spanish conquerors reportedly searched for the location a century after its construction, they never found it. As a result, it is one of the only Incan settlements that was not plundered by the conquering armies.

Suppose you want to convert the above heights to the more familiar units of feet and miles. You could use a table like the one shown below and a process called unit analysis, which is one of the topics of this chapter. Unit analysis can be used to compare any units of measure, such as those for length, weight, temperature, and volume. Once you have worked through this chapter, come back and convert these distances so you can begin planning your trip to Machu Picchu!

Conversion Factors Between the Metric and U.S. Systems of Measurement

Length

inches and centimeters	2.54 cm = 1 in.
feet and meters	1 m = 3.28 ft
miles and kilometers	1.61 km = 1 mi

OBJECTIVES

A Convert units of length using the metric system.

B Convert units of volume in the metric system

C Convert units of weight in the metric system.

D Convert units of length using the U.S. system of measurement.

E Convert units of volume in the U.S. system.

F Convert units of weight in the U.S. system

KEY WORDS

U.S. system of measurement

length

conversion factor

metric system of measurement

weight

volume

Video Examples
SECTION 7.1

7.1 Measurement: Metric and U.S. Systems

Image © sxc.hu, verzerk, 2005

The overall relationships in the metric system between the units of measure for length, weight and volume are all the same. The metric system has a standard way of measuring no matter what the unit. The table below is a mnemonic device for remembering some of the most common metric prefixes and their values.

Table 1

King Henry Died Drinking Chocolate Milk

Mnemonic	King	Henry	Died	Base Unit	Drinking	Chocolate	Milk
Length	Kilometer km	Hectometer hm	Decameter dam	Meter m	Decimeter dm	Centimeter cm	Millimeter mm
Volume	Kiloliter kL	Hectoliter hL	Decaliter daL	Liter L	Deciliter dL	Centiliter cL	Milliliter mL
Weight	Kilogram kg	Hectogram hg	Decagram dag	Gram g	Decigram dg	Centigram cg	Milligram mg
How many are in 1 meter/gram/liter	0.001	0.01	0.1	1	10	100	1000

A The Metric System and Length

The metric system uses prefixes to indicate what part of the basic unit of measure is being used. For example, in *milli*meter the prefix *milli* means "one thousandth" of a meter. Table 2 gives the meanings of the most common metric prefixes.

Table 2

The Meaning of Metric Prefixes

Prefix	Meaning
milli	0.001
centi	0.01
deci	0.1
deka	10
hecto	100
kilo	1,000

In the metric system, the standard unit of length is a meter. The other units of length in the metric system are written in terms of a meter.

EXAMPLE 1 Convert 5 meters to centimeters.

Solution Because 1 meter is the same length as 100 centimeters we can multiply 5 by 100 centimeters to get

$$5 \text{ meters} = 5 \times 100 \text{ centimeters}$$
$$= 500 \text{ centimeters}$$

●

This method of converting from meters to centimeters probably seems fairly simple. But as we go further in this chapter, the conversions from one kind of unit to another will become more complicated. For these more complicated problems, we need another way to show conversions so that we can be certain to end them with the correct unit of measure. For example, since 1 m = 100 cm, we can say that there are 100 cm per 1 m or 1 m per 100 cm; that is,

$$\frac{100 \text{ cm}}{1 \text{ m}} \longleftarrow \text{ Per} \quad \text{ or } \quad \frac{1 \text{ m}}{100 \text{ cm}} \longleftarrow \text{ Per}$$

We call the expressions $\frac{100 \text{ cm}}{1 \text{ m}}$ and $\frac{1 \text{ m}}{100 \text{ cm}}$ *conversion factors*. The fraction bar is read as "per." Both these conversion factors are really just the number 1. That is,

$$\frac{100 \text{ cm}}{1 \text{ m}} = \frac{100 \text{ cm}}{100 \text{ cm}} = 1$$

We already know that multiplying a number by 1 leaves the number unchanged. So, to convert from one unit to the other, we can multiply by one of the conversion factors without changing value. Both the conversion factors above say the same thing about the units meters and centimeters. They both indicate that there are 100 centimeters in every meter. The one we choose to multiply by depends on what units we are starting with and what units we want to end up with. If we start with meters and we want to end up with centimeters, we multiply by the conversion factor

$$\frac{100 \text{ cm}}{1 \text{ m}}$$

The units of meters will divide out and leave us with centimeters.

$$5 \text{ m} = 5 \text{ m} \times \frac{100 \text{ cm}}{1 \text{ m}}$$
$$= 5 \times 100 \text{ cm}$$
$$= 500 \text{ cm}$$

The key to this method of conversion lies in setting the problem up so that the correct units divide out to simplify the expression. We are treating units such as meters in the same way we treated factors when reducing fractions. If a factor is common to the numerator and the denominator, we can divide it out and simplify the fraction.

1. Convert 5 meters to millimeters.

Note We will use this method of converting from one kind of unit to another throughout the rest of this chapter. You should practice using it until you are comfortable with it and can use it correctly. However, it is not the only method of converting units. You may see shortcuts that will allow you to get results more quickly. Use shortcuts if you wish, so long as you can consistently get correct answers and are not using your shortcuts because you don't understand our method of conversion. Use the method of conversion as given here until you are good at it, and then use shortcuts if you want to.

Answer

1. 5,000 mm

Table 3

The relationship between	is	To convert from one to the other, multiply by	
millimeters (mm) and meters (m)	1,000 mm = 1 m	$\dfrac{1{,}000 \text{ mm}}{1 \text{ m}}$ or	$\dfrac{1 \text{ m}}{1{,}000 \text{ mm}}$
centimeters (cm) and meters	100 cm = 1 m	$\dfrac{100 \text{ cm}}{1 \text{ m}}$ or	$\dfrac{1 \text{ m}}{100 \text{ cm}}$
decimeters (dm) and meters	10 dm = 1 m	$\dfrac{10 \text{ dm}}{1 \text{ m}}$ or	$\dfrac{1 \text{ m}}{10 \text{ dm}}$
dekameters (dam) and meters	1 dam = 10 m	$\dfrac{10 \text{ m}}{1 \text{ dam}}$ or	$\dfrac{1 \text{ dam}}{10 \text{ m}}$
hectometers (hm) and meters	1 hm = 100 m	$\dfrac{100 \text{ m}}{1 \text{ hm}}$ or	$\dfrac{1 \text{ hm}}{100 \text{ m}}$
kilometers (km) and meters	1 km = 1,000 m	$\dfrac{1{,}000 \text{ m}}{1 \text{ km}}$ or	$\dfrac{1 \text{ km}}{1{,}000 \text{ m}}$

2. Convert 35 millimeters to meters.

EXAMPLE 2   Convert 25 millimeters to meters.

Solution   To convert from millimeters to meters, we multiply by the conversion factor $\frac{1 \text{ m}}{1{,}000 \text{ mm}}$.

$$25 \text{ mm} = 25 \text{ mm} \times \frac{1 \text{ m}}{1{,}000 \text{ mm}}$$

$$= \frac{25 \text{ m}}{1{,}000}$$

$$= 0.025 \text{ m}$$

3. Convert 50.5 centimeters to decimeters.

EXAMPLE 3   Convert 36.5 centimeters to decimeters.

Solution   We convert centimeters to meters and then meters to decimeters.

$$36.5 \text{ cm} = 36.5 \text{ cm} \times \frac{1 \text{ m}}{100 \text{ cm}} \times \frac{10 \text{ dm}}{1 \text{ m}}$$

$$= \frac{36.5 \times 10}{100} \text{ dm}$$

$$= 3.65 \text{ dm}$$

Note As you can see from the table and the discussion above, a cubic centimeter (cm³) and a milliliter (mL) are equal. Both are one thousandth of a liter. It is also common in some fields (like medicine) to abbreviate the term cubic centimeter as cc. Although we will use the notation mL when discussing volume in the metric system, you should be aware that 1 mL = 1 cm³ = 1 cc.

B Volume: The Metric System

In the metric system, the basic unit of measure for volume is the liter. A liter is the volume enclosed by a cube that is 10 cm on each edge, as shown in Figure 2. We can see that a liter is equivalent to 1,000 cm³.

The other units of volume in the metric system use the same prefixes we encountered previously. The units with prefixes centi, deci, and deka are not as common as the others, so in Table 4 we include only liters, milliliters, hectoliters, and kiloliters.

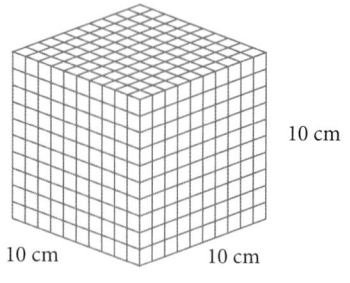

10 cm

10 cm

10 cm

1 liter = 10 cm × 10 cm × 10 cm
= 1,000 cm³

FIGURE 2

Answer

2. 0.035 m

Table 4

Metric Units of Volume

The relationship between	is	To convert from one to the other, multiply by	
milliliters (mL) and liters	1 liter (L) = 1,000 mL	$\dfrac{1{,}000 \text{ mL}}{1 \text{ liter}}$ or	$\dfrac{1 \text{ liter}}{1{,}000 \text{ mL}}$
hectoliters (hL) and liters	100 liters = 1 hL	$\dfrac{100 \text{ liters}}{1 \text{ hL}}$ or	$\dfrac{1 \text{ hL}}{100 \text{ liters}}$
kiloliters (kL) and liters	1,000 liters (L) = 1 kL	$\dfrac{1{,}000 \text{ liters}}{1 \text{ kL}}$ or	$\dfrac{1 \text{ kL}}{1{,}000 \text{ liters}}$

Here is an example of conversion from one unit of volume to another in the metric system.

EXAMPLE 4 A sports car has a 2.2-liter engine. What is the displacement (volume) of the engine in milliliters?

Solution Using the appropriate conversion factor from Table 4, we have

$$2.2 \text{ liters} = 2.2 \text{ liters} \times \frac{1{,}000 \text{ mL}}{1 \text{ liter}}$$

$$= 2.2 \times 1{,}000 \text{ mL}$$

$$= 2{,}200 \text{ mL}$$

4. A truck has a 4.9 liter engine. What is the displacement of the engine in mL?

C Weight: The Metric System

In the metric system, the basic unit of weight is a gram. We use the same prefixes we have already used to write the other units of weight in terms of grams. Table 5 lists the most common metric units of weight and their conversion factors.

Table 5

Metric Units of Weight

The relationship between	is	To convert from one to the other, multiply by	
milligrams (mg) and grams (g)	1 g = 1,000 mg	$\dfrac{1{,}000 \text{ mg}}{1 \text{ g}}$ or	$\dfrac{1 \text{ g}}{1{,}000 \text{ mg}}$
centigrams (cg) and grams	1 g = 100 cg	$\dfrac{100 \text{ cg}}{1 \text{ g}}$ or	$\dfrac{1 \text{ g}}{100 \text{ cg}}$
kilograms (kg) and grams	1,000 g = 1 kg	$\dfrac{1{,}000 \text{ g}}{1 \text{ kg}}$ or	$\dfrac{1 \text{ kg}}{1{,}000 \text{ g}}$
metric tons (t) and kilograms	1,000 kg = 1 t	$\dfrac{1{,}000 \text{ kg}}{1 \text{ t}}$ or	$\dfrac{1 \text{ t}}{1{,}000 \text{ kg}}$

Answers

3. 5.05 dm
4. 4,900 mL

5. Convert 4 metric tons to kilograms.

EXAMPLE 5 Convert 3 kilograms to centigrams.

Solution We convert kilograms to grams and then grams to centigrams.

$$3 \text{ kg} = 3 \text{ kg} \times \frac{1,000 \text{ g}}{1 \text{ kg}} \times \frac{100 \text{ cg}}{1 \text{ g}}$$

$$= 3 \times 1,000 \times 100 \text{ cg}$$

$$= 300,000 \text{ cg}$$

6. Suppose the bottle in Example 10 contained 75 tablets. How many grams of vitamin C are in the bottle?

EXAMPLE 6 A bottle of vitamin C contains 50 tablets. Each tablet contains 250 milligrams of vitamin C. What is the total number of grams of vitamin C in the bottle?

Solution We begin by finding the total number of milligrams of vitamin C in the bottle. Since there are 50 tablets, and each contains 250 mg of vitamin C, we can multiply 50 by 250 to get the total number of milligrams of vitamin C.

$$\text{Milligrams of vitamin C} = 50 \times 250 \text{ mg}$$

$$= 12,500 \text{ mg}$$

Next, we convert 12,500 mg to grams.

$$12,500 \text{ mg} = 12,500 \text{ mg} \times \frac{1 \text{ g}}{1,000 \text{ mg}}$$

$$= \frac{12,500}{1,000} \text{ g}$$

$$= 12.5 \text{ g}$$

The bottle contains 12.5 g of vitamin C.

D Length: U.S. System

Measuring the length of an object is done by assigning a number to its length. To let other people know what that number represents, we include with it a unit of measure. The most common units used to represent *length* in the U.S. system are inches, feet, yards, and miles. The basic unit of length is the foot. The other units are defined in terms of feet, as Table 6 shows.

Table 6

12 inches (in.)	=	1 foot (ft)
1 yard (yd)	=	3 feet (ft)
1 mile (mi)	=	5,280 feet (ft)

1 foot

As you can see from the table, the abbreviations for inches, feet, yards, and miles are in., ft, yd, and mi, respectively. What we haven't indicated, even though you may not have realized it, is what 1 foot represents. We have defined all our units associated with length in terms of feet, but we haven't said what a foot is.

There is a long history of the evolution of what is now called a foot. At different times in the past, a foot has represented different arbitrary lengths. Currently, a foot is defined to be exactly 0.3048 meter (the basic measure of length in the metric system), where a meter is 1,650,763.73 wavelengths of the orange-red line in the spectrum of krypton-86 in a vacuum (this doesn't mean much to me either). The reason a foot and a meter are defined this way is that we always want them to measure the same length. Because the wavelength of the orange-red line in the spectrum of krypton-86 will always remain the same, so will the length that a foot represents.

Now that we have said what we mean by 1 foot (even though we may not understand the technical definition), we can go on and look at some examples that involve converting from one kind of unit to another.

We can rewrite Table 6 so that it shows the conversion factors associated with units of length, as shown in Table 7.

Table 7

Units of Length in the U.S. System

The relationship between	is	To convert one to the other, multiply by
feet and inches	12 in. = 1 ft	$\frac{12 \text{ in.}}{1 \text{ ft}}$ or $\frac{1 \text{ ft}}{12 \text{ in.}}$
feet and yards	1 yd = 3 ft	$\frac{3 \text{ ft}}{1 \text{ yd}}$ or $\frac{1 \text{ yd}}{3 \text{ ft}}$
feet and miles	1 mi = 5,280 ft	$\frac{5,280 \text{ ft}}{1 \text{ mi}}$ or $\frac{1 \text{ mi}}{5,280 \text{ ft}}$

EXAMPLE 7   The most common ceiling height in houses is 8 feet. How many yards is this?

Solution   To convert 8 feet to yards, we multiply by the conversion factor $\frac{1 \text{ yd}}{3 \text{ ft}}$ so that feet will divide out and we will be left with yards.

$$8 \text{ ft} = 8 \text{ ft} \times \frac{1 \text{ yd}}{3 \text{ ft}} \qquad \textit{Multiply by correct conversion factor.}$$

$$= \frac{8}{3} \text{ yd} \qquad\qquad 8 \times \frac{1}{3} = \frac{8}{3}$$

$$= 2\frac{2}{3} \text{ yd} \qquad\qquad \textit{Or 2.67 yd rounded to the nearest hundredth.}$$

7. Suppose a house has high ceilings. Convert 12 feet to yards.

EXAMPLE 8   A football field is 100 yards long. How many inches long is a football field?

Solution   In this example, we must convert yards to feet and then feet to inches. We choose the conversion factors that will allow all the units except inches to divide out.

100 yd

$$100 \text{ yd} = 100 \text{ yd} \times \frac{3 \text{ ft}}{1 \text{ yd}} \times \frac{12 \text{ in.}}{1 \text{ ft}}$$

$$= 100 \times 3 \times 12 \text{ in.}$$

$$= 3,600 \text{ in.}$$

8. A football field is 53.33 yards wide. How many inches wide is a football field? Round your answer to the nearest inch.

E Volume: The U.S. System

We use the same method to convert between units in the U.S. system as we did with the metric system. We choose the conversion factor that will allow the units we start with to divide out, leaving the units we want to end up with.

Table 8 lists the units of volume in the U.S. system and their conversion factors.

Table 8	Units of Volume in the U.S. System	
The relationship between	is	To convert from one to the other, multiply by
cubic inches (in³) and cubic feet (ft³)	1 ft³ = 1,728 in³	$\frac{1{,}728\text{ in}^3}{1\text{ ft}^3}$ or $\frac{1\text{ ft}^3}{1{,}728\text{ in}^3}$
cubic feet and cubic yards (yd³)	1 yd³ = 27 ft³	$\frac{27\text{ ft}^3}{1\text{ yd}^3}$ or $\frac{1\text{ yd}^3}{27\text{ ft}^3}$
fluid ounces (fl oz) and pints (pt)	1 pt = 16 fl oz	$\frac{16\text{ fl oz}}{1\text{ pt}}$ or $\frac{1\text{ pt}}{16\text{ fl oz}}$
pints and quarts (qt)	1 qt = 2 pt	$\frac{2\text{ pt}}{1\text{ qt}}$ or $\frac{1\text{ qt}}{2\text{ pt}}$
quarts and gallons (gal)	1 gal = 4 qt	$\frac{4\text{ qt}}{1\text{ gal}}$ or $\frac{1\text{ gal}}{4\text{ qt}}$

9. How many fluid ounces are in a 1 gallon container?

EXAMPLE 9   What is the capacity (volume) in pints of a 1-gallon container of milk?

Solution   We change from gallons to quarts and then quarts to pints by multiplying by the appropriate conversion factors as given in Table 8.

$$1\text{ gal} = 1\text{ gal} \times \frac{4\text{ qt}}{1\text{ gal}} \times \frac{2\text{ pt}}{1\text{ qt}}$$

$$= 1 \times 4 \times 2 \text{ pt}$$

$$= 8 \text{ pt}$$

A 1-gallon container has the same capacity as 8 one-pint containers.

10. How many pints are produced by the dairy herd in Example 7 each day?

EXAMPLE 10   A dairy herd produces 1,800 quarts of milk each day. How many gallons is this equivalent to?

Solution   Converting 1,800 quarts to gallons, we have

$$1{,}800\text{ qt} = 1{,}800\text{ qt} \times \frac{1\text{ gal}}{4\text{ qt}}$$

$$= \frac{1{,}800}{4}\text{ gal}$$

$$= 450 \text{ gal}$$

We see that 1,800 quarts is equivalent to 450 gallons.

Answers
9. 128 fl oz
10. 3,600 pints

F Weight: The U.S. System

Pounds are a common unit of measure for weight in the U.S. system. In this section, we'll use unit analysis to work problems involving weight. The most common units of weight in the U.S. system are ounces, pounds, and tons. The relationships among these units are given in Table 9.

Table 9

Units of Weight in the U.S. System

The relationship between	is	To convert from one to the other, multiply by
ounces (oz) and pounds (lb)	1 lb = 16 oz	$\frac{16 \text{ oz}}{1 \text{ lb}}$ or $\frac{1 \text{ lb}}{16 \text{ oz}}$
pounds and tons (T)	1 T = 2,000 lb	$\frac{2,000 \text{ lb}}{1 \text{ T}}$ or $\frac{1 \text{T}}{2,000 \text{ lb}}$

EXAMPLE 11 Convert 12 pounds to ounces.

Solution Using the conversion factor from the table, and applying the method we have been using, we have

$$12 \text{ lb} = 12 \text{ lb} \times \frac{16 \text{ oz}}{1 \text{ lb}}$$

$$= 12 \times 16 \text{ oz}$$

$$= 192 \text{ oz}$$

12 pounds is equivalent to 192 ounces.

EXAMPLE 12 Convert 3 tons to pounds.

Solution We use the conversion factor from the table. We have

$$3 \text{ T} = 3 \text{ T} \times \frac{2,000 \text{ lb}}{1 \text{ T}}$$

$$= 6,000 \text{ lb}$$

6,000 pounds is the equivalent of 3 tons.

GETTING READY FOR CLASS

After reading through the preceding section, respond in your own words and in complete sentences.

A. What is a conversion factor?

B. Write the relationship between feet and miles. That is, write an equality that shows how many feet are in every mile.

C. Explain how the metric system uses prefixes to indicate units of measure.

D. List two examples of units of volume in the U.S. system and two examples of units of volume in the metric system.

11. Convert 20 pounds to ounces.

12. Convert 5 tons to pounds.

Vocabulary Review

Choose the correct words to fill in the blanks below.

conversion factor	divide	foot	unit analysis
meter	U.S. system	liter	fraction bar

1. In the U.S. system of measurement, the basic unit of length is the _____.
2. In the metric system of measurement, the basic unit of length is the _____.
3. A _____ is a way to convert one unit of measurement to another without changing the value.
4. The _____ in a conversion factor is read as "per."
5. The process of converting one unit of measurement to another is called _____.
6. For the last step of unit analysis, set up a multiplication problem so that all units except the units you want to end with will _____ out.
7. Cubic inches, pints, and gallons are units of volume in the _____.
8. In the metric system, the basic unit of measure for volume is the _____.

Problems

A Make the following conversions in the metric system by multiplying by the appropriate conversion factor. Write your answers as whole numbers or decimals.

1. 18 m to centimeters
2. 18 m to millimeters
3. 4.8 km to meters

4. 8.9 km to meters
5. 5 dm to centimeters
6. 12 dm to millimeters

7. 248 m to kilometers
8. 969 m to kilometers
9. 67 cm to millimeters

10. 67 mm to centimeters
11. 3,498 cm to meters
12. 4,388 dm to meters

13. 63.4 cm to decimeters
14. 89.5 cm to decimeters

B Make the following conversions.

15. 18 pt to quarts

16. 243 ft³ to cubic yards

17. 864 ft³ to cubic yards

18. 5 L to milliliters

19. 9.6 L to milliliters

20. 127 mL to liters

21. 93.8 mL to liters

22. 4 kL to milliliters

23. 3 kL to milliliters

24. 14.92 kL to liters

25. 4.71 kL to liters

C Make the following conversions.

26. 2 kg to centigrams

27. 5 kg to centigrams

28. 5.08 g to centigrams

29. 7.14 g to centigrams

30. 478.95 mg to centigrams

31. 659.43 mg to centigrams

32. 1,578 mg to grams

33. 1,979 mg to grams

34. 42,000 cg to kilograms

D Make the following conversions in the U.S. system by multiplying by the appropriate conversion factor. Write your answers as whole numbers or mixed numbers.

35. 5 ft to inches

36. 9 ft to inches

37. 10 ft to inches

38. 20 ft to inches

39. 2 yd to feet

40. 8 yd to feet

41. 4.5 yd to inches

42. 9.5 yd to inches

43. 27 in. to feet

44. 36 in. to feet

45. 2.5 mi to feet

46. 6.75 mi to feet

47. 48 in. to yards

48. 56 in. to yards

E Make the following conversions.

49. 3.8 yd^3 to cubic feet

50. 3 pt to fluid ounces

51. 8 pt to fluid ounces

52. 2 gal to quarts

53. 12 gal to quarts

54. 2.5 gal to pints

55. 7 gal to pints

56. 15 qt to fluid ounces

57. 5.9 qt to fluid ounces

58. 64 pt to gallons

59. 256 pt to gallons

60. 12 pt to quarts

F Use the conversion factors to make the following conversions.

61. 5 lb to ounces

62. 2 T to pounds

63. 5 T to pounds

64. 192 oz to pounds

65. 176 oz to pounds

66. 1,800 lb to tons

67. 10,200 lb to tons

68. 1 T to ounces

69. 3 T to ounces

70. 2 kg to grams

71. 5 kg to grams

Applying the Concepts

72. Softball If the distance between first and second base in softball is 60 feet, how many yards is it from first to second base?

73. Tower Height A transmitting tower is 100 feet tall. How many inches is that?

74. High Jump If a person high jumps 6 feet 8 inches, how many inches is the jump?

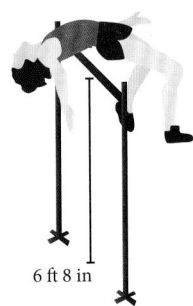

6 ft 8 in

75. Desk Width A desk is 48 inches wide. What is the width in yards?

76. Ceiling Height Suppose the ceiling of a home is 2.44 meters above the floor. Express the height of the ceiling in centimeters.

77. Notebook Width Standard-sized notebook paper is 21.6 centimeters wide. Express this width in millimeters.

78. Dollar Width A dollar bill is about 6.5 centimeters wide. Express this width in millimeters.

79. Pencil Length Most new pencils are 19 centimeters long. Express this length in meters.

80. Metric System A very small unit of measure in the metric system is the *micron* (abbreviated *μm*). There are 1,000 *μm* in 1 millimeter. How many microns are in 12 centimeters?

81. Metric System Another very small unit of measure in the metric system is the *angstrom* (abbreviated Å). There are 10,000,000 Å in 1 millimeter. How many angstroms are in 15 decimeters?

82. Horse Racing In horse racing, 1 *furlong* is 220 yards. How many feet are in 12 furlongs?

83. Sailing A *fathom* is a measurement of the depth of water and is equivalent to 6 feet. How many yards are in 19 fathoms?

84. Cell Phones The typical wavelength used by most cell phones today is between 12 and 35 centimeters. Convert these numbers to meters.

85. Credit Card A typical credit card is 85.6 millimeters long. Convert this to meters.

86. Human Brain The power used by the human brain is 16 watts. Convert this to kilowatts.

87. DNA The length of a DNA strand in the human genome is about 70.9 inches long. Convert this number to feet. Round to the nearest tenth.

88. Lung Capacity A 6-foot tall man weighing about 150 pounds has a lung capacity of 4.2 liters. Covert this volume to milliliters.

89. Heart Volume A 6-foot tall man weighing about 181 pounds has a heart with a volume of 0.2 gallons. Convert this volume to pints.

90. Red Blood Cells A 5.5-foot tall woman weighing about 130 pounds has about 1.5 liters of red blood cells. Convert this volume to milliliters.

91. Red Blood Cells A 5'3" woman weighing 124 pounds has about 214 cubic inches of blood. Convert this volume to cubic feet. Round to the nearest thousandth.

92. Filling Coffee Cups If a regular-size coffee cup holds about $\frac{1}{2}$ pint, about how many cups can be filled from a 1-gallon coffee maker?

93. Filling Glasses If a regular-size drinking glass holds about 0.25 liter of liquid, how many glasses can be filled from a 750-milliliter container?

94. Capacity of a Refrigerator A refrigerator has a capacity of 20 cubic feet. What is the capacity of the refrigerator in cubic inches?

95. Volume of a Tank The gasoline tank on a car holds 18 gallons of gas. What is the volume of the tank in quarts?

96. Filling Glasses How many 8-fluid-ounce glasses of water will it take to fill a 3-gallon aquarium?

97. Filling a Container How many 5-milliliter test tubes filled with water will it take to fill a 1-liter container?

Calculator Problems

Set up the following conversions as you have been doing. Then perform the calculations on a calculator.

98. Change 751 miles to feet.

99. Change 639.87 centimeters to meters.

100. Change 4,982 yards to inches.

101. Change 379 millimeters to kilometers.

102. Mount Whitney is the highest point in California. It is 14,494 feet above sea level. Give its height in miles to the nearest tenth.

103. The tallest mountain in the United States is Mount McKinley in Alaska. It is 20,320 feet tall. Give its height in miles to the nearest tenth.

104. California has 3,427 miles of shoreline. How many feet is this?

105. The tip of the television tower at the top of the Empire State Building in New York City is 1,472 feet above the ground. Express this height in miles to the nearest hundredth.

Set up the following problems as you have been doing. Then use a calculator to perform the actual calculations. Round all answers to two decimal places where appropriate.

106. Convert 93.4 qt to gallons.

107. Convert 7,362 fl oz to gallons.

108. How many cubic feet are contained in 796 cubic yards?

109. The engine of a car has a displacement of 440 cubic inches. What is the displacement in cubic feet?

110. Volume of Water The Grand Coulee Dam holds 10,585,000 cubic yards of water. What is the volume of water in cubic feet?

111. Volume of Water Hoover Dam was built in 1936 on the Colorado River in Nevada. It holds a volume of 4,400,000 cubic yards of water. What is this volume in cubic feet?

112. Fish Oil A bottle of fish oil contains 60 soft gels, each containing 800 mg of the omega-3 fatty acid. How many total grams of the omega-3 fatty acid are in this bottle?

113. Fish Oil A bottle of fish oil contains 50 soft gels, each containing 300 mg of the omega-6 fatty acid. How many total grams of the omega-6 fatty acid are in this bottle?

114. B-Complex A certain B-complex vitamin supplement contains 50 mg of riboflavin, or vitamin B_2. A bottle contains 80 vitamins. How many total grams of riboflavin are in this bottle?

115. B-Complex A certain B-complex vitamin supplement contains 30 mg of thiamine, or vitamin B_1. A bottle contains 80 vitamins. How many total grams of thiamine are in this bottle?

116. Aspirin A bottle of low-strength aspirin contains 120 tablets. Each tablet contains 81 mg of aspirin. How many total grams of aspirin are in this bottle?

117. Aspirin A bottle of maximum-strength aspirin contains 90 tablets. Each tablet contains 500 mg of aspirin. How many total grams of aspirin are in this bottle?

118. Dairy Cow A typical dairy cow has a mass of 0.77 tons. Convert this to pounds.

119. Snowflake The mass of a typical snowflake is 0.000003 kilograms. Convert this to milligrams.

Getting Ready for the Next Section

Perform the indicated operations.

120. 12×16

121. 15×16

122. $3 \times 2,000$

123. $5 \times 2,000$

124. $3 \times 1,000 \times 100$

125. $5 \times 1,000 \times 100$

126. 50×250

127. 75×200

128. $12,500 \times \dfrac{1}{1,000}$

129. $15,000 \times \dfrac{1}{1,000}$

Find the Mistake

Each sentence below contains a mistake. Circle the mistake and write the correct word(s) or number(s) on the line provided.

1. The average length for a house cat is roughly 18 inches. To show how many feet this is, multiply by the conversion factor $\frac{12 \text{ inches}}{1 \text{ foot}}$. _____

2. The length of a parking space is based on the average car length, which measures approximately 15 feet. This length converted to yards is 45 yards. _____

3. A cell phone measures 100 mm in length. To show how many meters this is, multiply 100 mm by the conversion factor $\frac{1 \text{ mm}}{1,000 \text{ m}}$. _____

4. A 3-quart container of ice cream can hold 1.5 pints of ice cream. _____

5. To find how many milliliters four 2-liter soda bottles can hold, you must find the product of 8 L and $\frac{1 \text{ mL}}{1,000 \text{ L}}$. _____

Navigation Skills: Prepare, Study, Achieve

Your academic self-image is how you see yourself as a student and the level of success you see yourself achieving. Do you believe you are capable of learning any subject and succeeding in any class you take? If you believe in yourself and work hard by applying the appropriate study methods, you will succeed. If you have a poor outlook for a class, most likely your performance in that class will match that outlook. Self-doubt or questioning the purpose of this course will negatively affect your focus. Furthermore, an inner dialogue of negative statements, such as "I'll never be able to learn this material" or "I'm never going to use this stuff," distract you from achieving success. Consider replacing those thoughts with three positive statements you can say when you notice your mind participating in a negative inner dialogue. Make a commitment to change your attitude for the better. Begin by thinking positively, having confidence in your abilities, and utilizing your resources if you are having difficulty. Asking for help is a sign of a successful student.

7.2 Converting Between the Two Systems, and Temperature

A Convert units of measurement between the metric system and the U.S. system.

B Solve problems involving temperature on both the Fahrenheit and the Celsius scales.

KEY WORDS

temperature

degree

©iStockphoto.com/RKSS

A Convert Between Systems

Because most of us have always used the U.S. system of measurement in our everyday lives, we are much more familiar with it on an intuitive level than we are with the metric system. We have an intuitive idea of how long feet and inches are, how much a pound weighs, and what a square yard of material looks like. The metric system is actually much easier to use than the U.S. system. The reason some of us have such a hard time with the metric system is that we don't have the feel for it that we do for the U.S. system. We have trouble visualizing how long a meter is or how much a gram weighs. The following list is intended to give you something to associate with each basic unit of measurement in the metric system.

1. A meter is just a little longer than a yard.

2. The length of the edge of a sugar cube is about 1 centimeter.

3. A liter is just a little larger than a quart.

4. A sugar cube has a volume of approximately 1 milliliter.

5. A paper clip weighs about 1 gram.

6. A 2-pound can of coffee weighs about 1 kilogram.

Table 1

Conversion Factors Between the Metric and U.S. Systems of Measurement

The relationship between	is	To convert from one to the other, multiply by	
Length			
inches and centimeters	2.54 cm = 1 in.	$\frac{2.54 \text{ cm}}{1 \text{ in.}}$	or $\frac{1 \text{ in.}}{2.54 \text{ cm}}$
feet and meters	1 m = 3.28 ft	$\frac{3.28 \text{ ft}}{1 \text{ m}}$	or $\frac{1 \text{ m}}{3.28 \text{ ft}}$
miles and kilometers	1.61 km = 1 mi	$\frac{1.61 \text{ km}}{1 \text{ mi}}$	or $\frac{1 \text{ mi}}{1.61 \text{ km}}$
Volume			
cubic inches and milliliters	16.39 mL = 1 in³	$\frac{16.39 \text{ mL}}{1 \text{ in}^3}$	or $\frac{1 \text{ in}^3}{16.39 \text{ mL}}$
liters and quarts	1.06 qt = 1 liter	$\frac{1.06 \text{ qt}}{1 \text{ liter}}$	or $\frac{1 \text{ liter}}{1.06 \text{ qt}}$
gallons and liters	3.79 liters = 1 gal	$\frac{3.79 \text{ liters}}{1 \text{ gal}}$	or $\frac{1 \text{ gal}}{3.79 \text{ liters}}$

Weight			
ounces and grams	28.3 g = 1 oz	$\dfrac{28.3 \text{ g}}{1 \text{ oz}}$ or $\dfrac{1 \text{ oz}}{28.3 \text{ g}}$	
kilograms and pounds	2.20 lb = 1 kg	$\dfrac{2.20 \text{ lb}}{1 \text{ kg}}$ or $\dfrac{1 \text{ kg}}{2.20 \text{ lb}}$	

There are many other conversion factors that we could have included in Table 1. We have listed only the most common ones. Almost all of them are approximations. That is, most of the conversion factors are decimals that have been rounded to the nearest hundredth. If we want more accuracy, we obtain a table that has more digits in the conversion factors.

EXAMPLE 1   Convert 8 inches to centimeters.

Solution   Choosing the appropriate conversion factor from Table 1, we have

$$8 \text{ in.} = 8 \text{ in.} \times \frac{2.54 \text{ cm}}{1 \text{ in.}}$$

$$= 8 \times 2.54 \text{ cm}$$

$$= 20.32 \text{ cm}$$

EXAMPLE 2   Convert 80.5 kilometers to miles.

Solution   Using the conversion factor that takes us from kilometers to miles, we have

$$80.5 \text{ km} = 80.5 \text{ km} \times \frac{1 \text{ mi}}{1.61 \text{ km}}$$

$$= \frac{80.5}{1.61} \text{ mi}$$

$$= 50 \text{ mi}$$

So 50 miles is equivalent to 80.5 kilometers. If we travel at 50 miles per hour in a car, we are moving at the rate of 80.5 kilometers per hour.

EXAMPLE 3   Convert 3 liters to pints.

Solution   Because Table 1 doesn't list a conversion factor that will take us directly from liters to pints, we first convert liters to quarts, and then convert quarts to pints.

$$3 \text{ liters} = 3 \text{ liters} \times \frac{1.06 \text{ qt}}{1 \text{ liter}} \times \frac{2 \text{ pt}}{1 \text{ qt}}$$

$$= 3 \times 1.06 \times 2 \text{ pt}$$

$$= 6.36 \text{ pt}$$

EXAMPLE 4   The engine in a car has a 2-liter displacement. What is the displacement in cubic inches?

Solution   We convert liters to milliliters and then milliliters to cubic inches.

$$2 \text{ liters} = 2 \text{ liters} \times \frac{1,000 \text{ mL}}{1 \text{ liter}} \times \frac{1 \text{ in}^3}{16.39 \text{ mL}}$$

$$= \frac{2 \times 1,000}{16.39} \text{ in}^3 \qquad \textit{This calculation should be done on a calculator.}$$

$$= 122 \text{ in}^3 \qquad \textit{Round to the nearest cubic inch.}$$

Video Examples
SECTION 7.2

Practice Problems

1. Convert 4 feet to meters.

2. Convert 400 inches to kilometers.

3. Convert 5 liters to gallons.

4. A truck engine has a 4 liter displacement. What is the displacement in quarts?

Answers

1. 1.22 meters
2. 0.01 km
3. 1.32 gallons
4. 4.24 quarts

5. What is the person's weight from Example 5 in grams?

EXAMPLE 5   If a person weighs 125 pounds, what is her weight in kilograms?

Solution   Converting from pounds to kilograms, we have

$$125 \text{ lb} = 125 \text{ lb} \times \frac{1 \text{ kg}}{2.20 \text{ lb}}$$

$$= \frac{125}{2.20} \text{ kg}$$

$$= 56.8 \text{ kg} \qquad \textit{Round to the nearest tenth.}$$

B Temperature

We end this section with a discussion of temperature in both systems of measurement.

In the U.S. system, we measure temperature on the Fahrenheit scale. On this scale, water boils at 212 degrees and freezes at 32 degrees. When we write 32 degrees measured on the Fahrenheit scale, we use the notation

32°F (read, "32 degrees Fahrenheit")

In the metric system, the scale we use to measure temperature is the Celsius scale (formerly called the centigrade scale). On this scale, water boils at 100 degrees and freezes at 0 degrees. When we write 100 degrees measured on the Celsius scale, we use the notation

100°C (read, "100 degrees Celsius")

Table 2 is intended to give you a feel for the relationship between the two temperature scales. Table 3 gives the formulas, in both symbols and words, that are used to convert between the two scales.

Table 2

Situation	Temperature Fahrenheit	Temperature Celsius
Water freezes	32°F	0°C
Room temperature	68°F	20°C
Normal body temperature	98.6°F	37°C
Water boils	212°F	100°C
Bake cookies	350°F	176.7°C
Broil meat	554°F	290°C

Table 3

To convert from	Formula In symbols	Formula In words
Fahrenheit to Celsius	$C = \dfrac{5(F - 32)}{9}$	Subtract 32, multiply by 5, and then divide by 9.
Celsius to Fahrenheit	$F = \dfrac{9}{5}C + 32$	Multiply by $\frac{9}{5}$, and then add 32.

The following examples show how we use the formulas given in Table 3.

Answers

5. 56,818 g

EXAMPLE 6   Convert 120°C to degrees Fahrenheit.

Solution   We use the formula

$$F = \frac{9}{5}C + 32$$

and replace C with 120.

When → $C = 120$

the formula → $F = \frac{9}{5}C + 32$

becomes → $F = \frac{9}{5}(120) + 32$

$$F = 216 + 32$$
$$F = 248$$

We see that 120°C is equivalent to 248°F; they both mean the same temperature.

EXAMPLE 7   A man with the flu has a temperature of 102°F. What is his temperature on the Celsius scale?

Solution

When → $F = 102$

the formula → $C = \dfrac{5(F - 32)}{9}$

becomes → $C = \dfrac{5(102 - 32)}{9}$

$$C = \frac{5(70)}{9}$$

$$C = 38.9 \qquad \textit{Round to the nearest tenth.}$$

The man's temperature, rounded to the nearest tenth, is 38.9°C on the Celsius scale.

GETTING READY FOR CLASS

After reading through the preceding section, respond in your own words and in complete sentences.

A. Write the equality that gives the relationship between centimeters and inches.

B. Write the equality that gives the relationship between grams and ounces.

C. Fill in the numerators below so that each conversion factor is equal to 1.

    a. 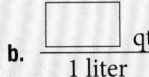   **b.** 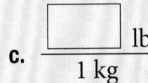   **c.** $\dfrac{\boxed{}\,\text{lb}}{1\ \text{kg}}$

D. Is it a hot day if the temperature outside is 37°C?

---

6. Convert 120°F to Celsius.

7. Convert 102°C to Fahrenheit.

Vocabulary Review

Choose the correct words to fill in the blanks below.

subtract   Celsius   multiply   Fahrenheit   centimeters   quarts

1. The relationship between _____ and inches is 2.54 cm = 1 in.
2. The relationship between _____ and liters is 1.06 qt = 1 liter.
3. To convert from Fahrenheit to Celsius, _____ 32 from the original Fahrenheit temperature, then _____ by 5, and divide by 9.
4. Use the formula $F = \frac{9}{5}C + 32$ to convert a _____ temperature to a _____ temperature.

Problems

A B Use Tables 1 and 3 to make the following conversions.

1. 6 in. to centimeters

2. 1 ft to centimeters

3. 4 m to feet

4. 2 km to feet

5. 6 m to yards

6. 15 mi to kilometers

7. 20 mi to meters (round to the nearest hundred meters)

8. 600 m to yards

9. 500 in³ to milliliters

10. 400 in³ to liters

11. 2 L to quarts

12. 15 L to quarts

13. 20 gal to liters

14. 15 gal to liters

15. 12 oz to grams

16. 1 lb to grams (round to the nearest 10 grams)

17. 15 kg to pounds

18. 10 kg to ounces (round to the nearest ounce)

19. 185°C to degrees Fahrenheit

20. 20°C to degrees Fahrenheit

21. 86°F to degrees Celsius

22. 122°F to degrees Celsius

Calculator Problems

Set up the following problems as we have set up the examples in this section. Then use a calculator for the calculations and round your answers to the nearest hundredth.

23. 10 cm to inches

24. 100 mi to kilometers

25. 25 ft to meters

26. 400 mL to cubic inches

27. 49 qt to liters

28. 65 L to gallons

29. 500 g to ounces

30. 100 lb to kilograms

31. Weight Give your weight in kilograms.

32. Height Give your height in meters and centimeters.

33. Sports The 100-yard dash is a popular race in track. How far is 100 yards in meters?

34. Engine Displacement A 351-cubic-inch engine has a displacement of how many liters?

35. Speed 55 miles per hour is equivalent to how many kilometers per hour?

36. Capacity A 1-quart container holds how many liters?

37. Sports A high jumper jumps 6 ft 8 in. How many meters is this?

38. Farming A farmer owns 57 acres of land. How many hectares is that?

39. Body Temperature A person has a temperature of 101°F. What is the person's temperature, to the nearest tenth, on the Celsius scale?

40. Air Temperature If the temperature outside is 30°C, is it a better day for water skiing or for snow skiing?

Getting Ready for the Next Section

Perform the indicated operations.

41. 15 + 60

42. 25 + 60

43.   37
        + 45

44.   37
        + 46

45. 3 + 0.25

46. 2 + 0.75

47. 82 − 60

48. 73 − 60

49.   75
        − 34

50.   85
        − 42

51. 12 × 4

52. 8 × 4

53. 3 × 60 + 15

54. 2 × 65 + 45

55. $3 + 16 \times \dfrac{1}{60}$

56. $2 + 45 \times \dfrac{1}{60}$

57. If fish costs $6.00 per pound, find the cost of 15 pounds of fish.

58. If fish costs $5.00 per pound, find the cost of 14 pounds of fish.

One Step Further

59. Caffeine Caffeine has a density of 1.23 grams per cubic centimeter. Convert this to ounces per cubic inch.

60. Caffeine A lethal dosage of caffeine is 192 milligrams per kilogram. This means a person would have to consume 192 milligrams of caffeine for every kilogram they weigh for them to get a lethal dose of caffeine. If a person weighs 150 pounds, how many grams of caffeine would they have to take for it to be lethal.

61. Ibuprofen Ibuprofen is considered toxic if a person exceeds 1,255 milligrams per kilogram. If a person weighs 120 pounds, how many grams is considered a toxic dose?

62. Molasses Molasses has a density of 1.42 grams per cubic centimeter. Convert this to pounds per cubic foot. Round to the nearest hundredth.

Find the Mistake

Each problem below contains a mistake. Circle the mistake and write the correct number(s) or word(s) on the line provided.

1. To convert 6 miles to km, divide 6 miles by $\dfrac{1.61 \text{ km}}{1 \text{ mi}}$. _____

2. Suppose a pasta recipe requires a half gallon of water, but your measuring cup only measures milliliters. To find how many milliliters are equal to a half gallon of water, multiply $\frac{1}{2}$ gal by $\dfrac{3.79 \text{ ml}}{1 \text{ gal}}$. _____

3. To convert 25° Celsius to Fahrenheit, use the formula $C = \dfrac{5(F - 32)}{9}$ to get 77° F. _____

4. A cookie recipe requires you to bake them at 325° F. This temperature in Celsius is 33° C (rounded to the nearest degree).

_____

7.3 Operations with Time, and Mixed Units

OBJECTIVES

A Solve problems involving mixed units.

Many occupations require the use of a time card. A time card records the number of hours and minutes an employee spends at work. At the end of a work week, the hours and minutes are totaled separately, and then the minutes are converted to hours.

A Time and Mixed Units

In this section, we will perform operations with mixed units of measure. For instance, mixed units are used when we use 2 hours 30 minutes, rather than 2 and a half hours, or 5 feet 9 inches, rather than five and three-quarter feet. As you will see, many of these types of problems arise in everyday life.

KEY WORDS

time

mixed units

The relationship between	is	To convert from one to the other, multiply by
minutes and seconds	1 min = 60 sec	$\frac{1 \text{ min}}{60 \text{ sec}}$ or $\frac{60 \text{ sec}}{1 \text{ min}}$
hours and minutes	1 hr = 60 min	$\frac{1 \text{ hr}}{60 \text{ min}}$ or $\frac{60 \text{ min}}{1 \text{ hr}}$

EXAMPLE 1 Convert 3 hours 15 minutes to
a. minutes. **b.** hours.

Solution

a. To convert to minutes, we multiply the hours by the conversion factor then add minutes.

$$3 \text{ hr } 15 \text{ min} = 3 \text{ hr} \times \frac{60 \text{ min}}{1 \text{ hr}} + 15 \text{ min}$$

$$= 180 \text{ min} + 15 \text{ min}$$

$$= 195 \text{ min}$$

b. To convert to hours, we multiply the minutes by the conversion factor then add hours.

$$3 \text{ hr } 15 \text{ min} = 3 \text{ hr} + 15 \text{ min} \times \frac{1 \text{ hr}}{60 \text{ min}}$$

$$= 3 \text{ hr} + 0.25 \text{ hr}$$

$$= 3.25 \text{ hr}$$

Video Examples
SECTION 7.3

Practice Problems

1. Convert 5 hours 12 minutes to
  a. minutes.
  b. hours.

Answers
1. a. 312 minutes **b.** 5.2 hours

2. Add 3 hours 45 minutes and 4 hours 20 minutes.

EXAMPLE 2   Add 5 minutes 37 seconds and 7 minutes 45 seconds.
Solution   First, we align the units properly.

$$
\begin{array}{rr}
5\ \text{min} & 37\ \text{sec} \\
+\ 7\ \text{min} & 45\ \text{sec} \\
\hline
12\ \text{min} & 82\ \text{sec}
\end{array}
$$

Since there are 60 seconds in every minute, we write 82 seconds as 1 minute 22 seconds. We have

$$
\begin{aligned}
12\ \text{min}\ 82\ \text{sec} &= 12\ \text{min} + 1\ \text{min}\ 22\ \text{sec} \\
&= 13\ \text{min}\ 22\ \text{sec}
\end{aligned}
$$

The idea of adding the units separately is similar to adding mixed numbers. That is, we align the whole numbers with the whole numbers and the fractions with the fractions.

Similarly, when we subtract units of time, we "borrow" 60 seconds from the minutes column, or 60 minutes from the hours column.

3. Subtract 43 minutes from 4 hours 10 minutes.

EXAMPLE 3   Subtract 34 minutes from 8 hours 15 minutes.
Solution   Again, we first line up the numbers in the hours column, and then the numbers in the minutes column.

$$
\begin{array}{rr}
8\ \text{hr} & 15\ \text{min} \\
- & 34\ \text{min} \\
\hline
\end{array}
$$

Since there are 60 minutes in an hour, we borrow 1 hour from the hours column and add 60 minutes to the minutes column. Then we subtract.

$$
\begin{array}{rr}
7\ \text{hr} & 75\ \text{min} \\
- & 34\ \text{min} \\
\hline
7\ \text{hr} & 41\ \text{min}
\end{array}
$$

Next we see how to multiply and divide using units of measure.

4. Suppose Jake purchased 6 of the halibut in Example 4. What is the cost?

EXAMPLE 4   Jake purchases 4 halibut. The fish cost $6.00 per pound, and each weighs 3 lb 12 oz. What is the cost of the fish?
Solution   First, we multiply each unit by 4.

$$
\begin{array}{rr}
3\ \text{lb} & 12\ \text{oz} \\
\times & 4 \\
\hline
12\ \text{lb} & 48\ \text{oz}
\end{array}
$$

To convert the 48 ounces to pounds, we multiply the ounces by the conversion factor

$$
\begin{aligned}
12\ \text{lb}\ 48\ \text{oz} &= 12\ \text{lb} + 48\ \text{oz} \times \frac{1\ \text{lb}}{16\ \text{oz}} \\
&= 12\ \text{lb} + 3\ \text{lb} \\
&= 15\ \text{lb}
\end{aligned}
$$

Finally, we multiply the 15 lb and $6.00/lb for a total price of $90.00.

GETTING READY FOR CLASS

After reading through the preceding section, respond in your own words and in complete sentences.

A. Explain the difference between saying *2 and a half hours* and saying *2 hours and 30 minutes.*

B. How are operations with mixed units of measure similar to operations with mixed numbers?

C. Why do we borrow a 1 from the hours column and add 60 to the minutes column when subtracting in Example 3?

D. Give an example of when you may have to use multiplication with mixed units of measure.

Answers

2. 8 hours 5 minutes

3. 3 hours 27 minutes

4. $135.00

Vocabulary Review

Choose the correct words to fill in the blanks below.

    columns   seconds   borrow   minutes

1. To convert from _____ to _____, multiply by the conversion factor $\frac{60 \text{ sec}}{1 \text{ min}}$.

2. Adding mixed units is similar to adding mixed numbers, such that we align the units separately in _____ and add.

3. To subtract units of time, we may need to _____ 60 seconds from the minutes column, or 60 minutes from the hours column.

Problems

A Use the tables of conversion factors given in this section and other sections in this chapter to make the following conversions. (Round your answers to the nearest hundredth if necessary.)

1. Convert 4 hours 30 minutes to
   a. minutes.

   b. hours.

2. Convert 2 hours 45 minutes to
   a. minutes.

   b. hours.

3. Convert 5 hours 20 minutes to
   a. minutes.

   b. hours.

4. Convert 4 hours 40 minutes to
   a. minutes.

   b. hours.

5. Convert 6 minutes 30 seconds to
   a. seconds.

   b. minutes.

6. Convert 8 minutes 45 seconds to
   a. seconds.

   b. minutes.

7. Convert 5 minutes 20 seconds to
   a. seconds.

   b. minutes.

8. Convert 4 minutes 40 seconds to
   a. seconds.

   b. minutes.

9. Convert 2 pounds 8 ounces to
   a. ounces.

   b. pounds.

10. Convert 3 pounds 4 ounces to
  a. ounces.

  b. pounds.

11. Convert 4 pounds 12 ounces to
  a. ounces.

  b. pounds.

12. Convert 5 pounds 16 ounces to
  a. ounces.

  b. pounds.

13. Convert 4 feet 6 inches to
  a. inches.

  b. feet.

14. Convert 3 feet 3 inches to
  a. inches.

  b. feet.

15. Convert 5 feet 9 inches to
  a. inches.

  b. feet.

16. Convert 3 feet 4 inches to
  a. inches.

  b. feet.

17. Convert 2 gallons 1 quart to
  a. quarts.

  b. gallons.

18. Convert 3 gallons 2 quarts to
  a. quarts.

  b. gallons.

Perform the indicated operation. Again, remember to use the appropriate conversion factor.

19. Add 4 hours 47 minutes and 6 hours 13 minutes.

20. Add 5 hours 39 minutes and 2 hours 21 minutes.

21. Add 8 feet 10 inches and 13 feet 6 inches.

22. Add 16 feet 7 inches and 7 feet 9 inches.

23. Add 4 pounds 12 ounces and 6 pounds 4 ounces.

24. Add 11 pounds 9 ounces and 3 pounds 7 ounces.

25. Subtract 2 hours 35 minutes from 8 hours 15 minutes.

26. Subtract 3 hours 47 minutes from 5 hours 33 minutes.

27. Subtract 3 hours 43 minutes from 7 hours 30 minutes.

28. Subtract 1 hour 44 minutes from 6 hours 22 minutes.

29. Subtract 4 hours 17 minutes from 5 hours 9 minutes.

30. Subtract 2 hours 54 minutes from 3 hours 7 minutes.

Applying the Concepts

Triathlon The Ironman Triathlon World Championship, held each October in Kona on the island of Hawaii, consists of three parts: a 2.4-mile ocean swim, a 112-mile bike race, and a 26.2-mile marathon. The table shows the results from the 2010 event. Use the table to answer Problems 31–34.

Triathlete	Swim Time (Hr:Min:Sec)	Bike Time (Hr:Min:Sec)	Run Time (Hr:Min:Sec)	Total Time (Hr:Min:Sec)
Chris McCormack	0:51:36	4:31:51	2:43:31	
Andreas Raelert	0:51:27	4:32:27	2:44:25	

31. Fill in the total time column.

32. How much faster was Chris's total time than Andreas's?

33. How much faster was Andreas's swim time than Chris's?

34. How much faster was Chris than Andreas in the run?

35. Cost of Fish Fredrick is purchasing four whole salmon. The fish cost $4.00 per pound, and each weighs 6 lb 8 oz. What is the cost of the fish?

36. Cost of Steak Mike is purchasing eight top sirloin steaks. The meat costs $4.00 per pound, and each steak weighs 1 lb 4 oz. What is the total cost of the steaks?

37. Stationary Bike Maggie rides a stationary bike for 1 hour and 15 minutes, 4 days a week. After 2 weeks, how many hours has she spent riding the stationary bike?

38. Gardening Scott works in his garden for 1 hour and 5 minutes, 3 days a week. After 4 weeks, how many hours has Scott spent gardening?

39. **Cost of Fabric** Allison is making a quilt. She buys 3 yards and 1 foot each of six different fabrics. The fabrics cost $7.50 a yard. How much will Allison spend?

40. **Cost of Lumber** Trish is building a fence. She buys six fence posts at the lumberyard, each measuring 5 ft 4 in. The lumber costs $3 per foot. How much will Trish spend?

41. **Molecular Weight** Silver nitrate has a molecular weight of 169.9 grams per mole. If you have a solution containing 2.1 moles, how many grams of silver nitrate do you have?

42. **Molecular Weight** Potassium chloride has a molecular weight of 74.6 grams per mole. How many moles do you have if you have 52.3 grams of potassium chloride? Round to the nearest tenth.

43. **Cost of Wheat** Wheat is being sold for 560 cents per bushel. If a farmer sells 5,231 bushels, how many dollars will he make?

44. **Cost of Corn** Corn is being sold for 403 cents per bushel. If a farmer sells 3,503 bushels, how many dollars will he make?

One Step Further

45. In 2010, the horse Animal Kingdom won the Kentucky Derby with a time of 2:02.04, or two minutes and 2.04 seconds. The record time for the Kentucky Derby is still held by Secretariat, who won the race with a time of 1:59.40 in 1973. How much faster did Secretariat run in 1973 than Animal Kingdom?

46. In 2010, the horse Drosselmeyer won the Belmont Stakes with a time of 2:31.57, or two minutes and 31.57 seconds. The record time for the Belmont Stakes is still held by Secretariat, who won the race with a time of 2:24.00 in 1973. How much faster did Secretariat run in 1973 than Drosselmeyer?

Find the Mistake

Each problem below contains a mistake. Circle the mistake and write the correct number(s) or word(s) on the line provided.

1. Converting 6 feet 6 inches to inches gives us 72 inches. _____

2. The correct way to write the sum of 2 hours, 55 min and 4 hours, 10 min is 6 hours and 65 minutes.

_____

3. The correct way to subtract 27 minutes from 6 hours and 12 minutes is to add 60 minutes to the 6 hours.

_____

4. Jane is buying two cups of frozen yogurt. One cup contains 3 ounces and the other contains 11.9 grams. If each ounce cost $1.50, then the total purchase price will be $4.50. _____

Conversion Factors [7.1, 7.2, 7.3]

To convert from one kind of unit to another, we choose an appropriate conversion factor from one of the tables given in this chapter. For example, if we want to convert 5 feet to inches, we look for conversion factors that give the relationship between feet and inches. There are two conversion factors for feet and inches:

$$\frac{12 \text{ in.}}{1 \text{ ft}} \quad \text{and} \quad \frac{1 \text{ ft}}{12 \text{ in.}}$$

EXAMPLES

1. Convert 5 feet to inches.

$$5 \text{ ft} = 5 \text{ ft} \times \frac{12 \text{ in.}}{1 \text{ ft}}$$
$$= 5 \times 12 \text{ in.}$$
$$= 60 \text{ in.}$$

Length [7.1]

U.S. System

The relationship between	is	To convert from one to the other, multiply by
feet and inches	12 in. = 1 ft	$\frac{12 \text{ in.}}{1 \text{ ft}}$ or $\frac{1 \text{ ft}}{12 \text{ in.}}$
feet and yards	1 yd = 3 ft	$\frac{3 \text{ ft}}{1 \text{ yd}}$ or $\frac{1 \text{ yd}}{3 \text{ ft}}$
feet and miles	1 mi = 5,280 ft	$\frac{5,280 \text{ ft}}{1 \text{ mi}}$ or $\frac{1 \text{ mi}}{5,280 \text{ ft}}$

2. Convert 8 feet to yards.

$$8 \text{ ft} = 8 \text{ ft} \times \frac{1 \text{ yd}}{3 \text{ ft}}$$
$$= \frac{8}{3} \text{ yd}$$
$$= 2\frac{2}{3} \text{ yd}$$

Metric System

The relationship between	is	To convert from one to the other, multiply by
millimeters (mm) and meters (m)	1,000 mm = 1 m	$\frac{1,000 \text{ mm}}{1 \text{ m}}$ or $\frac{1 \text{ m}}{1,000 \text{ mm}}$
centimeters (cm) and meters	100 cm = 1 m	$\frac{100 \text{ cm}}{1 \text{ m}}$ or $\frac{1 \text{ m}}{100 \text{ cm}}$
decimeters (dm) and meters	10 dm = 1 m	$\frac{10 \text{ dm}}{1 \text{ m}}$ or $\frac{1 \text{ m}}{10 \text{ dm}}$
dekameters (dam) and meters	1 dam = 10 m	$\frac{10 \text{ m}}{1 \text{ dam}}$ or $\frac{1 \text{ dam}}{10 \text{ m}}$
hectometers (hm) and meters	1 hm = 100 m	$\frac{100 \text{ m}}{1 \text{ hm}}$ or $\frac{1 \text{ hm}}{100 \text{ m}}$
kilometers (km) and meters	1 km = 1,000 m	$\frac{1,000 \text{ m}}{1 \text{ km}}$ or $\frac{1 \text{ km}}{1,000 \text{ m}}$

Volume [7.1]

U.S. System

The relationship between	is	To convert from one to the other, multiply by
cubic inches (in³) and cubic feet (ft³)	1 ft³ = 1,728 in³	$\frac{1,728 \text{ in}^3}{1 \text{ ft}^3}$ or $\frac{1 \text{ ft}^3}{1,728 \text{ in}^3}$
cubic feet and cubic yards (yd³)	1 yd³ = 27 ft³	$\frac{27 \text{ ft}^3}{1 \text{ yd}^3}$ or $\frac{1 \text{ yd}^3}{27 \text{ ft}^3}$
fluid ounces (fl oz) and pints (pt)	1 pt = 16 fl oz	$\frac{16 \text{ fl oz}}{1 \text{ pt}}$ or $\frac{1 \text{ pt}}{16 \text{ fl oz}}$
pints and quarts (qt)	1 qt = 2 pt	$\frac{2 \text{ pt}}{1 \text{ qt}}$ or $\frac{1 \text{ qt}}{2 \text{ pt}}$
quarts and gallons (gal)	1 gal = 4 qt	$\frac{4 \text{ qt}}{1 \text{ gal}}$ or $\frac{1 \text{ gal}}{4 \text{ qt}}$

3. Convert 452 hectoliters to liters.

$$452 \text{ hL} = 452 \text{ hL} \times \frac{100 \text{ L}}{1 \text{ hL}}$$
$$= 45,200 \text{ L}$$

Metric System

The relationship between	is	To convert from one to the other, multiply by
milliliters (mL) and liters	1 liter (L) = 1,000 mL	$\dfrac{1,000 \text{ mL}}{1 \text{ liter}}$ or $\dfrac{1 \text{ liter}}{1,000 \text{ mL}}$
hectoliters (hL) and liters	100 liters = 1 hL	$\dfrac{100 \text{ liters}}{1 \text{ hL}}$ or $\dfrac{1 \text{ hL}}{100 \text{ liters}}$
kiloliters (kL) and liters	1,000 liters (L) = 1 kL	$\dfrac{1,000 \text{ liters}}{1 \text{ kL}}$ or $\dfrac{1 \text{ kL}}{1,000 \text{ liters}}$

Weight [7.1]

4. Convert 12 pounds to ounces.

$$12 \text{ lb} = 12 \text{ lb} \times \frac{16 \text{ oz}}{1 \text{ lb}}$$
$$= 12 \times 16 \text{ oz}$$
$$= 192 \text{ oz}$$

U.S. System

The relationship between	is	To convert from one to the other, multiply by
ounces (oz) and pounds (lb)	1 lb = 16 oz	$\dfrac{16 \text{ oz}}{1 \text{ lb}}$ or $\dfrac{1 \text{ lb}}{16 \text{ oz}}$
pounds and tons (T)	1 T = 2,000 lb	$\dfrac{2,000 \text{ lb}}{1 \text{ T}}$ or $\dfrac{1 \text{ T}}{2,000 \text{ lb}}$

Metric System

The relationship between	is	To convert from one to the other, multiply by
milligrams (mg) and grams (g)	1 g = 1,000 mg	$\dfrac{1,000 \text{ mg}}{1 \text{ g}}$ or $\dfrac{1 \text{ g}}{1,000 \text{ mg}}$
centigrams (cg) and grams	1 g = 100 cg	$\dfrac{100 \text{ cg}}{1 \text{ g}}$ or $\dfrac{1 \text{ g}}{100 \text{ cg}}$
kilograms (kg) and grams	1,000 g = 1 kg	$\dfrac{1,000 \text{ g}}{1 \text{ kg}}$ or $\dfrac{1 \text{ kg}}{1,000 \text{ g}}$
metric tons (t) and kilograms	1,000 kg = 1 t	$\dfrac{1,000 \text{ kg}}{1 \text{ t}}$ or $\dfrac{1 \text{ t}}{1,000 \text{ kg}}$

Converting Between the Systems [7.2]

5. Convert 8 inches to centimeters.

$$8 \text{ in.} = 8 \text{ in.} \times \frac{2.54 \text{ cm}}{1 \text{ in.}}$$
$$= 8 \times 2.54 \text{ cm}$$
$$= 20.32 \text{ cm}$$

Conversion Factors

The relationship between	is	To convert from one to the other, multiply by
Length		
inches and centimeters	2.54 cm = 1 in.	$\dfrac{2.54 \text{ cm}}{1 \text{ in.}}$ or $\dfrac{1 \text{ in.}}{2.54 \text{ cm}}$
feet and meters	1 m = 3.28 ft	$\dfrac{3.28 \text{ ft}}{1 \text{ m}}$ or $\dfrac{1 \text{ m}}{3.28 \text{ ft}}$
miles and kilometers	1.61 km = 1 mi	$\dfrac{1.61 \text{ km}}{1 \text{ mi.}}$ or $\dfrac{1 \text{ mi}}{1.61 \text{ km}}$
Volume		
cubic inches and milliliters	16.39 mL = 1 in³	$\dfrac{16.39 \text{ mL}}{1 \text{ in}^3}$ or $\dfrac{1 \text{ in}^3}{16.39 \text{ mL}}$
liters and quarts	1.06 qt = 1 liter	$\dfrac{1.06 \text{ qt}}{1 \text{ liter}}$ or $\dfrac{1 \text{ liter}}{1.06 \text{ qt}}$
gallons and liters	3.79 liters = 1 gal	$\dfrac{3.79 \text{ liters}}{1 \text{ gal}}$ or $\dfrac{1 \text{ gal}}{3.79 \text{ liters}}$
Weight		
ounces and grams	28.3 g = 1 oz	$\dfrac{28.3 \text{ g}}{1 \text{ oz}}$ or $\dfrac{1 \text{ oz}}{28.3 \text{ g}}$
kilograms and pounds	2.20 lb = 1 kg	$\dfrac{2.20 \text{ lb}}{1 \text{ kg}}$ or $\dfrac{1 \text{ kg}}{2.20 \text{ lb}}$

Temperature [7.2]

To convert from	Formula in symbols	Formula in words
Fahrenheit to Celsius	$C = \dfrac{5(F - 32)}{9}$	Subtract 32, multiply by 5, and then divide by 9.
Celsius to Fahrenheit	$F = \dfrac{9}{5}C + 32$	Multiply by $\dfrac{9}{5}$, and then add 32.

Time [7.3]

The relationship between	is	To convert from one to the other, multiply by
minutes and seconds	1 min = 60 sec	$\dfrac{1 \text{ min}}{60 \text{ sec}}$ or $\dfrac{60 \text{ sec}}{1 \text{ min}}$
hours and minutes	1 hr = 60 min	$\dfrac{1 \text{ hr}}{60 \text{ min}}$ or $\dfrac{60 \text{ min}}{1 \text{ hr}}$

6. Convert 120°C to degrees Fahrenheit.

$$F = \frac{9}{5}C + 32$$

$$F = \frac{9}{5}(120) + 32$$

$$F = 216 + 32$$

$$F = 248$$

Use the tables in the chapter to make the following conversions.[7.1, 7.2]

1. 9 yd to feet

2. 570 m to kilometers

3. 16.4 L to milliliters

4. 5 mi to kilometers

5. 13 L to quarts

6. 77°F to degrees Celsius

7. 167.4 ft³ to cubic yards

8. 65°C to degrees Fahrenheit

Work the following problems. Round answers to the nearest hundredth. [7.1, 7.2]

9. How many gallons are there in a 1.5-liter bottle of cola?

10. Change 627 yd to inches.

11. A motorcycle engine has a displacement of 650 mL. What is the displacement in cubic feet?

12. Change 94 qt to liters.

13. Change 498 ft to meters.

14. How many liters are contained in a 15-quart container?

15. 37 cm to inches

16. 42 mi to kilometers

17. 57 qt to liters

18. 47 lb to kilograms

19. Change 7 hours 15 minutes to [7.3]
 a. minutes.
 b. hours.

20. Add 5 pounds 11 ounces and 10 pounds 7 ounces. [7.3]

The chart shows the annual sales for the top frozen pizza retailers in the United States. Use the information to answer the following questions.

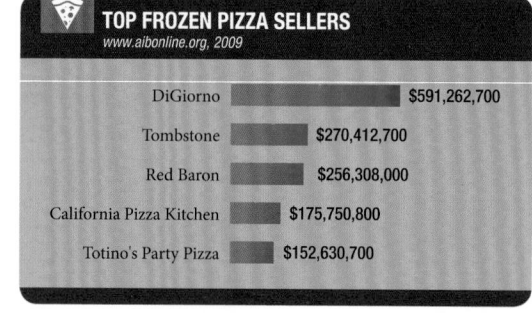

TOP FROZEN PIZZA SELLERS
www.aibonline.org, 2009

DiGiorno	$591,262,700
Tombstone	$270,412,700
Red Baron	$256,308,000
California Pizza Kitchen	$175,750,800
Totino's Party Pizza	$152,630,700

21. If there are 12.07 Mexican pesos in 1 US dollar, convert the sales of DiGiorno and Red Baron to pesos.

22. If there are 19,487.01 Vietnamese dong to 1 US dollar, convert the sales of Tombstone and Totino's to dong. You will need to use an online conversion calculator.

Simplify.

1. 3,420
  679
+ 7,524

2. 7,000
− 5,999

3. 378 ÷ 14

4. 6(3 · 9)

5. 24)8,565

6. 16 + 72 ÷ 2²

7. $\frac{468}{52}$

8. 17 + 39

9. (12 + 6) + (84 − 36)

10. $\frac{60}{4}$

11. 11.5(3.9)

12. 6.2 + 11.36 + 4.09

13. 52.6 − 3.82

14. 3.2)43.2

15. $\frac{7}{48} + \frac{5}{12}$

16. $\left(15 \div 1\frac{2}{3}\right) \div 4$

17. $13 - 4\frac{3}{4}$

18. $\frac{5}{8}(3.6) - \frac{1}{2}(0.3)$

19. $\frac{3}{8}(4.8) - \frac{1}{4}(2.9)$

20. $14 + \frac{7}{13} \div \frac{21}{26}$

Solve.

21. 4 · x = 17

22. 36 = 8 · y

23. $\frac{6}{7} = \frac{18}{x}$

24. What number is 32% of 6,450?

25. Find $\frac{3}{5}$ of the product of 15 and 6.

26. If 5,280 feet = 1 mile, convert 8,484 feet to miles. Round to the nearest tenth.

The diagram shows the number of viewers who watched the top five shows on NBC during one week. Use the information to answer the following questions. Round to the nearest hundredth if necessary.

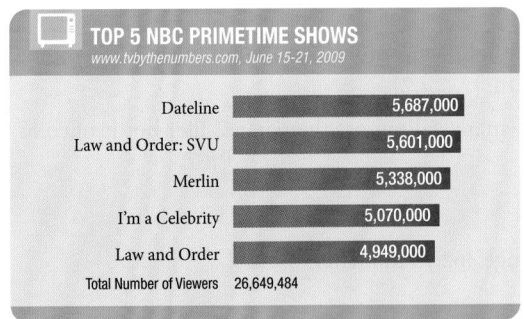

TOP 5 NBC PRIMETIME SHOWS
www.tvbythenumbers.com, June 15-21, 2009

Dateline	5,687,000
Law and Order: SVU	5,601,000
Merlin	5,338,000
I'm a Celebrity	5,070,000
Law and Order	4,949,000
Total Number of Viewers	26,649,484

27. Of the viewers who watched these shows, what percentage watched Dateline?

28. Of the viewers who watched these shows, what percentage watched the two Law and Order shows?

Use the tables in the chapter to make the following conversions. [7.1, 7.2]

1. 3 yd to feet

2. 640 m to kilometers

3. 12 L to milliliters

4. 3 mi to kilometers

5. 8 L to quarts

6. 90°F to degrees Celsius (round to the nearest tenth)

7. 116.1 ft³ to cubic yards

8. 20°C to degrees Fahrenheit

Work the following problems. Round answers to the nearest hundredth. [7.1, 7.2]

9. How many gallons are there in a 2-liter bottle of cola?

10. Change 362 yd to inches.

11. A car engine has a displacement of 376 in³. What is the displacement in cubic feet?

12. Change 65 qt to liters.

13. Change 375 ft to meters.

14. How many liters are contained in an 11-quart container?

15. 27 cm to inches

16. 9 mi to kilometers

17. 36 qt to liters

18. 23 lb to kilograms

19. Change 2 hours 45 minutes to [7.3]
   a. minutes.
   b. hours.

20. Add 4 pounds 9 ounces and 2 pounds 7 ounces. [7.3]

The chart shows the amount of caffeine in different kinds of soda, measured in milligrams. Use the information to make the following conversions.

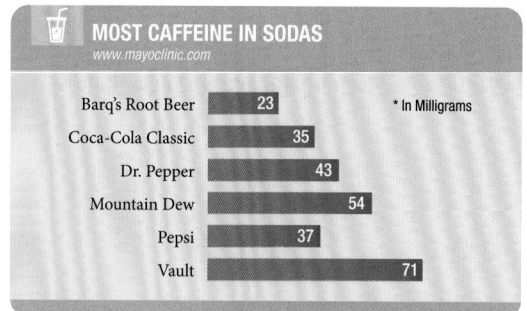

MOST CAFFEINE IN SODAS
www.mayoclinic.com

	* In Milligrams
Barq's Root Beer	23
Coca-Cola Classic	35
Dr. Pepper	43
Mountain Dew	54
Pepsi	37
Vault	71

21. Convert the amount of caffeine found in all the sodas to grams.

22. Convert the amount of caffeine found in all the sodas to ounces.

Answers to Odd-Numbered Problems

Chapter 1

Exercise Set 1.1
Vocabulary Review **1.** place value **3.** hyphen **5.** set **7.** whole
Problems **1.** 8 ones, 7 tens **3.** 5 ones, 4 tens
5. 8 ones, 4 tens, 3 hundreds **7.** 8 ones, 0 tens, 6 hundreds
9. 8 ones, 7 tens, 3 hundreds, 2 thousands **11.** 9 ones, 6 tens, 5 hundreds, 3 thousands, 7 ten thousands, 2 hundred thousands
13. Ten thousands **15.** Hundred millions **17.** Ones
19. Hundred thousands **21.** $600 + 50 + 8$ **23.** $60 + 8$
25. $4,000 + 500 + 80 + 7$ **27.** $30,000 + 2,000 + 600 + 70 + 4$
29. $3,000,000 + 400,000 + 60,000 + 2,000 + 500 + 70 + 7$
31. $400 + 7$ **33.** $30,000 + 60 + 8$ **35.** $3,000,000 + 4,000 + 8$
37. 547 **39.** 6,323 **41.** 27,035 **43.** 70,907
45. 180,643 **47.** 406,008 **49.** Twenty-nine
51. Forty **53.** Five hundred seventy-three
55. Seven hundred seven **57.** Seven hundred seventy
59. Twenty-three thousand, five hundred forty
61. Three thousand, four **63.** Three thousand, forty
65. One hundred four million, sixty-five thousand, seven hundred eighty
67. Five billion, three million, forty thousand, eight **69.** Two million, five hundred forty-six thousand, seven hundred thirty-one
71. Twenty million, four hundred thirty-two thousand **73.** 325
75. 5,432 **77.** 86,762 **79.** 2,000,200 **81.** 2,002,200
83. Thousands **85.** $100,000 + 6,000 + 700 + 20 + 1$
87. Three million, fourteen thousand, five hundred seventy-two
89. 3 inches **91.** 5 inches **93.** 6 **95.** 3 **97.** 12

Find the Mistake **1.** The place value of the 7 in the number 562,472 is tens. **3.** The number 9,023,627,003 written in words is nine billion, twenty-three million, six hundred twenty-seven thousand, three.

Exercise Set 1.2
Vocabulary Review **1.** addition **3.** carrying **5.** zero **7.** associative
Problems **1.** 15 **3.** 14 **5.** 24 **7.** 15 **9.** 20 **11.** 68
13. 98 **15.** 7,297 **17.** 6,487 **19.** 96 **21.** 7,449 **23.** 65
25. 102 **27.** 875 **29.** 829 **31.** 10,391 **33.** 16,204
35. 155,554 **37.** 111,110 **39.** 17,391 **41.** 14,892
43. 180 **45.** 2,220 **47.** 18,285 **49.** 774 **51.** 7,195
53.

First Number a	Second Number b	Their Sum a + b
61	38	99
63	36	99
65	34	99
67	32	99

55.

First Number a	Second Number b	Their Sum a + b
9	16	25
36	64	100
81	144	225
144	256	400

57. $9 + 5$ **59.** $8 + 3$ **61.** $4 + 6$ **63.** $1 + (2 + 3)$
65. $2 + (1 + 6)$ **67.** $(1 + 9) + 1$ **69.** $4 + (n + 1)$
71. 34 gallons **73.** $349

Find the Mistake **1.** To find the sum of 786 and 49, add the ones place by writing the 5 and carrying the 1.

Exercise Set 1.3
Vocabulary Review **1.** difference **3.** borrowing
Problems **1.** 32 **3.** 22 **5.** 10 **7.** 111

9. The difference of 10 and 2. **11.** The difference of a and 6.
13. The difference of 8 and 2 is 6. **15.** $8 - 3$ **17.** $y - 9$
19. $3 - 2 = 1$ **21.** 312 **23.** 403 **25.** 1,111 **27.** 4,544
29. 15 **31.** 33 **33.** 5 **35.** 33 **37.** 95 **39.** 152
41. 274 **43.** 488 **45.** 538 **47.** 163 **49.** 1,610 **51.** 46,083
53.
55.

First Number a	Second Number b	The Difference of a and b a − b	First Number a	Second Number b	The Difference of a and b a − b
25	15	10	400	256	144
24	16	8	400	144	256
23	17	6	225	144	81
22	18	4	225	81	144

57. $255 **59.** 33 feet **61.** 168 students **63.** $574
65. $350
67. a.

Year	Projected Sales (Millions)
2010	8.5
2011	19.4
2012	30.1

b. 21.6 million units

69. a.

Venue	Capacity
National Stadium	91,000
National Aquatic Center	17,000
National Indoor Stadium	18,000
Beijing Olympic Green Tennis Courts	17,400
Olympic Sports Center Stadium	38,000

b. 74,000 people

Find the Mistake **1.** Translating "The difference of 22 and 3 is 19" into symbols gives us $22 - 3 = 19$. **3.** To find the difference of 85 and 27, begin by borrowing 1 ten from the tens column and subtracting 7 from 15.

Landmark Review: 1.1–1.3
1. $500 + 40 + 9$
3. $60,000 + 200 + 40 + 3$ **5.** 18 **7.** 117
9. 103,701 **11.** 530 **13.** 17 **15.** 12

Exercise Set 1.4
Vocabulary Review **1.** round **3.** more
Problems **1.** 40 **3.** 50 **5.** 50 **7.** 80 **9.** 460 **11.** 470
13. 56,780 **15.** 4,500 **17.** 1,200 **19.** 500 **21.** 800
23. 900 **25.** 1,100 **27.** 5,000 **29.** 39,600
31. 5,000 **33.** 10,000 **35.** 1,000 **37.** 658,000
39. 608,000 **41.** 5,745,000

	Original Number	Rounded to the Nearest		
		Ten	Hundred	Thousand
43.	7,821	7,820	7,800	8,000
45.	5,999	6,000	6,000	6,000
47.	10,985	10,990	11,000	11,000
49.	99,999	100,000	100,000	100,000

51. $3,000,000 **53.** 27,380,000 views **55.** 8,500,000 viewers
57. $15,200 **59.** $31,000 **61.** 1,100 **63.** 1,900
65. 58,000 **67.** 11,900 **69.** 5,000 **71.** 96,000

Find the Mistake **1.** Rounding 12,456 to the nearest hundred gives us 12,500. **3.** To estimate the sum of 14,256 and 2,789 by rounding to the nearest hundred, add 14,300 and 2,800.

Exercise Set 1.5
Vocabulary Review **1.** addtion **3.** distributive
5. unchanged **7.** associative
Problems **1.** 300 **3.** 600 **5.** 3,000 **7.** 5,000 **9.** 21,000
11. 81,000 **13.** The product of 6 and 7 **15.** The product of 2 and n
17. The product of 9 and 7 is 63. **19.** $7 \cdot n$ **21.** $6 \cdot 7 = 42$
23. $0 \cdot 6 = 0$ **25.** Products: $9 \cdot 7$ and 63 **27.** Products: $4(4)$ and 16
29. Factors: 2, 3, and 4 **31.** Factors: 2, 2, and 3 **33.** $9(5)$
35. $7 \cdot 6$ **37.** $(2 \cdot 7) \cdot 6$ **39.** $(3 \times 9) \times 1$ **41.** $7(2) + 7(3) = 35$
43. $9(4) + 9(7) = 99$ **45.** $3(x) + 3(1) = 3x + 3$
47. $2(x) + 2(5) = 2x + 10$ **49.** 100 **51.** 228 **53.** 36
55. 1,440 **57.** 950 **59.** 1,725 **61.** 121 **63.** 1,552
65. 4,200 **67.** 66,248 **69.** 279,200 **71.** 12,321
73. 106,400 **75.** 198,592 **77.** 612,928 **79.** 333,180
81. 18,053,805 **83.** 263,646,976

85.

First Number a	Second Number b	Their product ab
11	11	121
11	22	242
22	22	484
22	44	968

87.

First Number a	Second Number b	Their product ab
25	10	250
25	100	2,500
25	1,000	25,000
25	10,000	250,000

89.

First Number a	Second Number b	Their product ab
12	20	240
36	20	720
12	40	480
36	40	1,440

91. 2,081 calories **93.** 560 calories **95.** Yes **97.** 8,000
99. 1,500,000 **101.** 1,400,000 **103.** 40 **105.** 54
Find the Mistake **1.** Factors are numbers that when multiplied together give a product. **3.** The first step when multiplying 73 and 4 is to multiply 4 and 3 by writing down the 2 and carrying the 1.

Exercise Set 1.6
Vocabulary Review **1.** quotient **3.** remainder
Problems **1.** $6 \div 3$ **3.** $45 \div 9$ **5.** $r \div s$ **7.** $20 \div 4 = 5$
9. $2 \cdot 3 = 6$ **11.** $9 \cdot 4 = 36$ **13.** $6 \cdot 8 = 48$ **15.** $7 \cdot 4 = 28$
17. 5 **19.** 8 **21.** Undefined **23.** 45 **25.** 23
27. 1,530 **29.** 1,350 **31.** 18,000 **33.** 16,680
35. 24,000 **37.** 45 **39.** 49 **41.** 432 **43.** 1,438
45. 705 **47.** 3,020 **49.** 61 R 4 **51.** 90 R 1 **53.** 13 R 7
55. 234 R 6 **57.** 402 R 4 **59.** 35 R 35
61.

First Number a	Second Number b	The Quotient of a and b $\frac{a}{b}$
100	25	4
100	26	3 R 22
100	27	3 R 19
100	28	3 R 16

63. a **65.** b **67.** 1 **69.** 2 **71.** 4 **73.** 6 **75.** $1,850
77. 16¢ **79.** 5 miles **81.** 6 glasses with 2 oz left over
83. 3 bottles **85.** $12 **87.** 665 mg **89.** 437
91. 3,247 **93.** 869 **95.** 5,684 **97.** 169 gal
Find the Mistake **1.** The division notation $\frac{10}{5}$ is equivalent to $5\overline{)10}$. **3.** To divide 1,640 by 12, first estimate the number of twelves we can subtract from 16.

Exercise Set 1.7
Vocabulary Review **1.** grouping symbols **3.** before
Problems **1.** 12 **3.** 100 **5.** 4 **7.** 43 **9.** 16
11. 84 **13.** 14 **15.** 7 **17.** 16 **19.** 84 **21.** 40
23. 41 **25.** 18 **27.** 11 **29.** 91 **31.** 7
33. $8(4 + 2) = 48$ **35.** $2(10 + 3) = 26$ **37.** $3(3 + 4) + 4 = 25$
39. $(20 \div 2) - 9 = 1$ **41.** $(8 \cdot 5) + (5 \cdot 4) = 60$ **43.** 247 calories
45. 407 calories **47.** Big Mac has 263 more calories which is more than twice the calories.
Find the Mistake **1.** Following the order of operations, work all additions and subtractions after evaluating anything inside parentheses.

Chapter 1 Review
1. Fifty thousand, six hundred thirty-one
3. $100,000 + 20,000 + 3,000 + 300 + 20 + 1$ **5.** f
7. a **9.** 16,322 **11.** 2,486 **13.** 1,096 **15.** 65
17. $3(11 + 4) = 45$ **19.** 4 **21.** $7x - 14$
23. $630,000; Six hundred thirty thousand dollars

Chapter 1 Test
1. Thirty thousand, six hundred fifty-two
3. $200,000 + 80,000 + 5,000 + 600 + 30 + 4$ **5.** g
7. b **9.** 24,603 **11.** 4,787 **13.** 810 **15.** 72
17. $2(13 + 4) = 34$ **19.** 3 **21.** $5x - 20$
23. 236,035; Two hundred thirty-six thousand, thirty-five

Chapter 2

Exercise Set 2.1
Vocabulary Review **1.** fraction **3.** proper **5.** equivalent
Problems **1.** 1 **3.** 2 **5.** 3 **7.** 127 **9.** 5 **11.** 1
13. 12
15.

Numerator	Denominator	Fraction
3	5	$\frac{3}{5}$
1	7	$\frac{1}{7}$
5	8	$\frac{5}{8}$
7	9	$\frac{7}{9}$

17. $\frac{3}{4}, \frac{1}{2}, \frac{9}{10}$
19. True
21. False

23. – 31. Answers on number line below

33. $\frac{1}{20} < \frac{4}{25} < \frac{3}{10} < \frac{2}{5}$ **35.** $\frac{4}{6}$ **37.** $\frac{5}{6}$ **39.** $\frac{8}{12}$ **41.** $\frac{8}{12}$
43. $\frac{2}{12}$ **45.** $\frac{6}{12}$ **47.** $\frac{16}{8}$ **49.** $\frac{40}{8}$ **51.** Answers will vary
53. 3 **55.** 2 **57.** 37 **59.** $\frac{3}{4}$ **61.** $\frac{43}{47}$ **63.** $\frac{4}{3}$
65. $\frac{13}{17}$ **67.** a. $\frac{1}{2}$ b. $\frac{1}{2}$ c. $\frac{1}{4}$ d. $\frac{1}{4}$

69.

How often workers send non-work-related e-mail from the office	Fraction of respondents saying yes
Never	$\frac{4}{25}$
1 to 5 times a day	$\frac{47}{100}$
5 to 10 times a day	$\frac{8}{25}$
More than 10 times a day	$\frac{1}{20}$

71. $\frac{4}{5}$ **73.** $\frac{29}{43}$ **75.** $\frac{1,121}{1,791}$

77.

Concentration Of Antidepressant

Days since discontinuing	Fraction remaining in patient's system
0	1
5	$\frac{1}{2}$
10	$\frac{1}{4}$
15	$\frac{1}{8}$
20	$\frac{1}{16}$

79. d   **81.** a   **83.** 108   **85.** 60   **87.** 4
89. 5   **91.** 7   **93.** 51   **95.** True   **97. a.** $\frac{14}{50}$ **b.** $\frac{3}{75}$
Find the Mistake   1. For the fraction $\frac{21}{7}$, the <u>denominator</u> is 7.
3. The multiplication property for fractions states that if the numerator and the denominator of a fraction are multiplied by the same nonzero number, the resulting fraction is <u>equivalent</u> to the original fraction.

Exercise Set 2.2
Vocabulary Review   1. prime   **3.** composite
Problems   1. Prime   **3.** Composite; 3, 5, and 7 are factors
5. Composite; 3 is a factor   **7.** Prime   **9.** $2^2 \cdot 3$ **11.** 3^4
13. $5 \cdot 43$ **15.** $3 \cdot 5$ **17.** $\frac{1}{2}$ **19.** $\frac{2}{3}$ **21.** $\frac{4}{5}$ **23.** $\frac{9}{5}$
25. $\frac{7}{11}$ **27.** $\frac{3}{5}$ **29.** $\frac{1}{7}$ **31.** $\frac{7}{9}$ **33.** $\frac{7}{5}$ **35.** $\frac{5}{7}$
37. $\frac{3}{5}$ **39.** $\frac{5}{3}$ **41.** $\frac{8}{9}$ **43.** $\frac{42}{55}$ **45.** $\frac{17}{19}$ **47.** $\frac{14}{33}$
49. a. $\frac{2}{17}$ **b.** $\frac{3}{26}$ **c.** $\frac{1}{9}$ **d.** $\frac{3}{28}$ **e.** $\frac{2}{19}$ **51. a.** $\frac{1}{45}$ **b.** $\frac{1}{30}$ **c.** $\frac{1}{18}$ **d.** $\frac{1}{15}$ **e.** $\frac{1}{10}$
53. a. $\frac{1}{3}$ **b.** $\frac{5}{6}$ **c.** $\frac{1}{5}$ **55.** $\frac{9}{16}$
57. – 59.

$$\frac{1}{2} = \frac{2}{4} = \frac{4}{8} = \frac{8}{16}$$

$$\frac{5}{4} = \frac{10}{8} = \frac{20}{16}$$

61. $\frac{1}{4}$ **63.** $\frac{2}{3}$ **65.** $\frac{7}{15}$ **67.** $\frac{1}{4}$ **69.** 0   **71.** 3   **73.** 45
75. 25   **77.** $2^2 \cdot 3 \cdot 5$ **79.** $2^2 \cdot 3 \cdot 5$ **81.** 9   **83.** 25   **85.** b
Find the Mistake   1. The number 30 is a <u>composite</u> number because it has 10 as a divisor.   **3.** When reducing the fraction $\frac{32}{48}$ to lowest terms, we divide out the <u>common factor 2^4</u> to get $\frac{2}{3}$.

Landmark Review: 2.1–2.2   **1.** Numerator 3; denominator 5
3. Numerator 7; denominator 15
5. $\frac{4x}{8x}$ **7.** $\frac{x}{8x}$ **9.** $\frac{1}{2}$ **11.** $\frac{3}{5}$ **13.** $\frac{17}{18}$

Exercise Set 2.3
Vocabulary Review   1. product

Problems   1. $\frac{8}{15}$ **3.** $\frac{7}{8}$ **5.** 1   **7.** $\frac{27}{4}$ **9.** 1   **11.** $\frac{1}{24}$
13. $\frac{24}{125}$ **15.** $\frac{105}{8}$

17.

First number x	Second number y	Their product xy
$\frac{1}{2}$	$\frac{2}{3}$	$\frac{1}{3}$
$\frac{2}{3}$	$\frac{3}{4}$	$\frac{1}{2}$
$\frac{3}{4}$	$\frac{4}{5}$	$\frac{3}{5}$
$\frac{5}{a}$	$\frac{a}{6}$	$\frac{5}{6}$

19.

First number x	Second number y	Their product xy
$\frac{1}{2}$	30	15
$\frac{1}{5}$	30	6
$\frac{1}{6}$	30	5
$\frac{1}{15}$	30	2

21. $\frac{3}{5}$ **23.** 9   **25.** 1   **27.** 8   **29.** $\frac{1}{15}$ **31.** 24
33. 4   **35.** 9   **37.** $\frac{3}{10}$; numerator should be 3, not 4.

39. a.

Number x	Square x^2
1	1
2	4
3	9
4	16
5	25
6	36
7	49
8	64

b. Either *larger* or *greater* will work.

41. 14   **43.** 14   **45.** 5   **47.** 6   **49.** 3,511 students
51. 126,500 ft³   **53.** About 2,121 children
55. $\frac{1}{27}$ **57.** $\frac{8}{27}$ **59.** 2   **61.** 3   **63.** 2   **65.** 5
67. 3   **69.** $\frac{4}{3}$ **71.** 3   **73.** $\frac{1}{7}$
Find the Mistake   1. To find the product of two fractions, multiply the numerators and <u>multiply the denominators.</u>

Exercise Set 2.4
Vocabulary Review   1. product   **3.** divisor
Problems   1. $\frac{15}{4}$ **3.** $\frac{4}{3}$ **5.** 9   **7.** 200   **9.** $\frac{3}{8}$ **11.** 1
13. $\frac{49}{64}$ **15.** $\frac{3}{4}$ **17.** $\frac{15}{16}$ **19.** $\frac{1}{6}$ **21.** 6   **23.** $\frac{5}{18}$
25. $\frac{9}{2}$ **27.** $\frac{2}{9}$ **29.** 9   **31.** $\frac{4}{5}$ **33.** $\frac{15}{2}$ **35.** 13   **37.** 12
39. $\frac{3}{5}$ **41.** 40   **43.** $3 \cdot 5 = 15; 3 \div \frac{1}{5} = 3 \cdot \frac{5}{1} = 15$
45. 14 blankets   **47.** 48 bags   **49.** 6   **51.** $\frac{7}{16}$
53. 1,778 students   **55.** 28 cartons
Find the Mistake   1. Two numbers whose <u>product</u> is 1 are said to be reciprocals.   **3.** To work the problem $\frac{22}{5} \div \frac{10}{3}$, multiply the first fraction by <u>the reciprocal of the second fraction.</u>

Chapter 2 Review

1. $\frac{5}{7}$ **3.** $\frac{4}{13}$ **5.** $\frac{2}{7}$ **7.** $\frac{7}{2}$ **9.** $\frac{4}{21}$ **11.** 3
13. $\frac{7}{6}$ **15.** $\frac{9}{4}$ **17.** 25 **19.** $\frac{4}{3}$ **21.** $\frac{3}{7}$ **23.** $\frac{5}{9}$
25. $\frac{3}{7}$ **27.** 8 dresses **29.** $\frac{254}{1000}$

Chapter 2 Cumulative Review

1. 4,555 **3.** 10 **5.** 3 **7.** 15 **9.** $\frac{31}{6}$ **11.** 1
13. $\frac{3}{8}$ **15.** 4,245 **17.** $\frac{3}{8}$ **19.** $\frac{7}{45}$ **21.** $\frac{3}{8}$
23. Ten thousand

Chapter 2 Test

1. $\frac{1}{5}$ **3.** $\frac{3}{14}$ **5.** $\frac{3}{20}$ **7.** $\frac{15}{8}$ **9.** $\frac{3}{10}$ **11.** $\frac{3}{20}$ **13.** 4
15. $\frac{4}{5}$ **17.** 6 **19.** $\frac{2}{5}$ **21.** $\frac{10}{11}$ **23.** $\frac{3}{8}$ **25.** $\frac{1}{5}$
27. 10 dresses **29.** $\frac{4}{200}$

Chapter 3

Exercise Set 3.1

Vocabulary Review **1.** least common denominator
3. numerators
Problems **1.** $\frac{2}{3}$ **3.** $\frac{1}{4}$ **5.** $\frac{1}{2}$ **7.** $\frac{1}{3}$ **9.** $\frac{3}{2}$ **11.** $\frac{x+6}{2}$
13. $\frac{4}{5}$ **15.** $\frac{10}{3}$ **17.**

First Number a	Second Number b	The Sum of a and b $a+b$
$\frac{1}{2}$	$\frac{1}{3}$	$\frac{5}{6}$
$\frac{1}{3}$	$\frac{1}{4}$	$\frac{7}{12}$
$\frac{1}{4}$	$\frac{1}{5}$	$\frac{9}{20}$
$\frac{1}{5}$	$\frac{1}{6}$	$\frac{11}{30}$

19.

First Number a	Second Number b	The Sum of a and b $a+b$
$\frac{1}{12}$	$\frac{1}{2}$	$\frac{7}{12}$
$\frac{1}{12}$	$\frac{1}{3}$	$\frac{5}{12}$
$\frac{1}{12}$	$\frac{1}{4}$	$\frac{1}{3}$
$\frac{1}{12}$	$\frac{1}{6}$	$\frac{1}{4}$

21. $\frac{7}{9}$ **23.** $\frac{7}{3}$ **25.** $\frac{7}{4}$ **27.** $\frac{7}{6}$ **29.** $\frac{9}{20}$ **31.** $\frac{7}{10}$
33. $\frac{19}{24}$ **35.** $\frac{13}{60}$ **37.** $\frac{31}{100}$ **39.** $\frac{67}{144}$ **41.** $\frac{29}{35}$ **43.** $\frac{949}{1,260}$
45. $\frac{13}{420}$ **47.** $\frac{41}{24}$ **49.** $\frac{53}{60}$ **51.** $\frac{5}{4}$ **53.** $\frac{88}{9}$ **55.** $\frac{10}{3}$
57. $\frac{3}{4}$ **59.** $\frac{1}{4}$ **61.** 19 **63.** 3 **65.** 9 **67.** 4
69. $\frac{1}{4} < \frac{3}{8} < \frac{1}{2} < \frac{3}{4}$ **71.** $\frac{160}{63}$ **73.** $\frac{5}{8}$ **75.** $\frac{7}{3}$ **77.** 3
79. $\frac{9}{2}$ pints **81.** $1,325 **83.** $\frac{7}{18}$

85.

Grade	Number of students	Fraction of students
A	5	$\frac{1}{8}$
B	8	$\frac{1}{5}$
C	20	$\frac{1}{2}$
Below C	7	$\frac{7}{40}$
Total	40	1

87. 10 lots
89. 59
91. $\frac{16}{8}$ **93.** $\frac{8}{8}$
95. $\frac{11}{4}$ **97.** $\frac{17}{8}$
99. $\frac{9}{8}$ **101.** 2 R 3
103. 8 R 16

Find the Mistake **1.** The fractions $\frac{a}{c}$ and $\frac{b}{c}$ can be added to become $\frac{a+b}{c}$ because they have <u>a common denominator</u>. **3.** The least common denominator for a set of denominators is the smallest number that is exactly divisible by each <u>denominator</u>.

Exercise Set 3.2

Vocabulary Review **1.** proper fraction **3.** mixed number
5. denominator
Problems **1.** $\frac{14}{3}$ **3.** $\frac{21}{4}$ **5.** $\frac{13}{8}$ **7.** $\frac{47}{3}$ **9.** $\frac{104}{21}$ **11.** $\frac{427}{33}$
13. $1\frac{1}{8}$ **15.** $4\frac{3}{4}$ **17.** $4\frac{5}{6}$ **19.** $3\frac{1}{4}$ **21.** $4\frac{1}{27}$ **23.** $28\frac{8}{15}$
25. a. $4\frac{13}{205}$ **b.** $\frac{38}{65}$ **27.** $6 **29.** $\frac{71}{12}$ **31.** $\frac{1,526}{5}$¢ **33.** $\frac{11}{4}$
35. $\frac{37}{8}$ **37.** $\frac{14}{5}$ **39.** $\frac{9}{40}$ **41.** $\frac{3}{8}$ **43.** $\frac{32}{35}$ **45.** $\frac{4}{7}$ **47.** a
Find the Mistake **1.** For mixed-number notation, writing the whole number next to the fraction implies <u>addition.</u>
3. Changing $6\frac{4}{5}$ to an improper fraction gives us $\underline{\frac{34}{5}}$.

Exercise Set 3.3

Vocabulary Review **1.** mixed number **3.** improper fractions
Problems **1.** $5\frac{1}{10}$ **3.** $13\frac{2}{3}$ **5.** $6\frac{93}{100}$ **7.** $5\frac{5}{6}$ **9.** $9\frac{3}{4}$ **11.** $3\frac{1}{5}$
13. $12\frac{1}{2}$ **15.** $9\frac{9}{20}$ **17.** $\frac{32}{45}$ **19.** $1\frac{2}{3}$ **21.** 4 **23.** $4\frac{3}{10}$
25. $\frac{1}{10}$ **27.** $3\frac{1}{5}$ **29.** $2\frac{1}{8}$ **31.** $7\frac{1}{2}$ **33.** $\frac{11}{13}$
35. $5\frac{1}{2}$ cups **37.** $\frac{5}{6}$ cup **39.** $1\frac{1}{3}$ **41.** $2,441\frac{3}{5}$ cents
43. $163\frac{3}{4}$ mi **45.** $4\frac{1}{2}$ yd **47.** $\frac{3}{4} < \frac{5}{4} < 1\frac{1}{2} < 2\frac{1}{8}$
49. Can 1 contains $332\frac{1}{2}$ calories, whereas Can 2 contains 276 calories. Can 1 contains $56\frac{1}{2}$ more calories than Can 2.
51. Can 1 contains 1,325 milligrams of sodium, whereas Can 2 contains 1,095 milligrams of sodium. Can 1 contains 230 more milligrams of sodium than Can 2.
53. a. $\frac{10}{15}$ **b.** $\frac{3}{15}$ **c.** $\frac{9}{15}$ **d.** $\frac{5}{15}$ **55. a.** $\frac{5}{20}$ **b.** $\frac{12}{20}$ **c.** $\frac{18}{20}$ **d.** $\frac{2}{20}$
57. $\frac{13}{15}$ **59.** $\frac{14}{9} = 1\frac{5}{9}$ **61.** $\frac{3}{5}$ **63.** $\frac{1}{4}$

Find the Mistake **1.** To multiply two mixed numbers, <u>change to improper fractions, then multiply numerators and multiply denominators.</u> **3.** To divide the mixed numbers $12\frac{2}{5}$ and $3\frac{12}{5}$, change the mixed numbers to improper fractions and then <u>multiply by the reciprocal of the divisor.</u>

Landmark Review: 3.1–3.3
1. 1 **3.** $\frac{19}{15}$ **5.** $\frac{73}{105}$
7. $\frac{41}{30} = 1\frac{11}{30}$ **9.** $\frac{29}{8}$ **11.** $\frac{21}{2}$ **13.** $4\frac{2}{3}$ **15.** $3\frac{1}{2}$
17. $23\frac{3}{8}$ **19.** $37\frac{13}{24}$ **21.** $2\frac{5}{16}$

Exercise Set 3.4

Vocabulary Review **1.** addition sign **3.** LCD **5.** borrow
Problems **1.** $5\frac{4}{5}$ **3.** $12\frac{2}{5}$ **5.** $3\frac{4}{9}$ **7.** 12 **9.** $1\frac{3}{8}$ **11.** $14\frac{1}{6}$
13. $4\frac{1}{12}$ **15.** $2\frac{1}{12}$ **17.** $26\frac{7}{12}$ **19.** $11\frac{3}{8}$ **21.** 12 **23.** $2\frac{1}{2}$
25. $8\frac{6}{7}$ **27.** $3\frac{3}{8}$ **29.** $10\frac{4}{15}$ **31.** $2\frac{1}{15}$ **33.** 9 **35.** $18\frac{1}{10}$
37. 14 **39.** 17 **41.** $24\frac{1}{24}$ **43.** $27\frac{6}{7}$ **45.** $37\frac{3}{20}$ **47.** $33\frac{5}{24}$
49. $6\frac{1}{4}$ **51.** $9\frac{7}{10}$ **53.** $5\frac{1}{2}$ **55.** $\frac{2}{3}$ **57.** $1\frac{11}{12}$ **59.** $3\frac{11}{12}$
61. $5\frac{19}{20}$ **63.** $5\frac{1}{2}$ **65.** $\frac{13}{24}$ **67.** $10\frac{5}{12}$ **69.** $3\frac{1}{2}$ **71.** $5\frac{29}{40}$
73. $12\frac{1}{4}$ in. **75.** $\frac{1}{8}$ mi **77.** $31\frac{1}{6}$ in. **79.** NFL: $P = 306\frac{2}{3}$ yd,
Canadian: $P = 350$ yd, Arena: $P = 156\frac{2}{3}$ yd **81. a.** $2\frac{1}{2}$ **b.** $250
83. $300 **85.** $4\frac{63}{64}$ **87.** 2 **89.** $\frac{11}{8} = 1\frac{3}{8}$ **91.** $3\frac{5}{8}$ **93.** $35\frac{3}{5}$ sec

Find the Mistake   **1.** To begin adding $3\frac{9}{14}$ and $5\frac{1}{3}$, write each mixed number with the addition sign and then apply the commutative and associative properties, such that $\left(3 + \frac{9}{14}\right) + \left(5 + \frac{1}{3}\right)$.
3. The first step when subtracting $8 - 3\frac{2}{7} = 4\frac{5}{7}$, is to borrow 1 from 8 in the form of $\frac{7}{7}$.

Chapter 3 Review

1. $\frac{4}{3}$ **3.** $\frac{24}{5} = 4\frac{4}{5}$ **5.** $\frac{37}{30} = 1\frac{7}{30}$ **7.** $2\frac{1}{10}$ **9.** $\frac{7}{16}$
11. $\frac{1}{4}$ **13.** $12\frac{1}{2}$ **15.** $4\frac{5}{24}$ **17.** $17\frac{1}{2}$ **19.** $19\frac{5}{8}$ in.
21. $1\frac{31}{32}$ **23.** $13\frac{9}{32}$ **25.** $\frac{29}{100}$

Chapter 3 Cumulative Review

1. 2,597   **3.** $\frac{49}{144}$ **5.** $\frac{1}{6}$ **7.** $\frac{4}{15}$ **9.** 12   **11.** $3\frac{7}{13}$
13. 18   **15.** 630,496   **17.** 11   **19.** 6,888   **21.** $4\frac{2}{3}$
23. $\frac{107}{60} = 1\frac{47}{60}$ **25.** $\frac{3}{11}$
27. Six thousand, seven hundred eighty-six; $6,000 + 700 + 80 + 6$
29. 351,986

Chapter 3 Test

1. $\frac{1}{2}$ **3.** $\frac{45}{8} = 5\frac{5}{8}$ **5.** $\frac{31}{24} = 1\frac{7}{24}$ **7.** $1\frac{5}{9}$ **9.** $\frac{5}{14}$ **11.** $\frac{2}{9}$
13. $5\frac{1}{6}$ **15.** $1\frac{1}{6}$ **17.** $16\frac{4}{9}$ **19.** $15\frac{7}{8}$ in.   **21.** $13\frac{1}{8}$
23. $26\frac{9}{16}$
25. $\frac{313}{1000}$; 313 out of every 1,000 users use Windows 7 or Vista

Chapter 4

Exercise Set 4.1
Vocabulary Review   **1.** fractional   **3.** thousandths
5. hundredths   **7.** left
Problems   **1.** Three tenths   **3.** Fifteen thousandths
5. Three and four tenths   **7.** Fifty-two and seven tenths
9. $405\frac{36}{100}$ **11.** $9\frac{9}{1,000}$ **13.** $1\frac{234}{1,000}$ **15.** $\frac{305}{100,000}$ **17.** Tens
19. Tenths   **21.** Hundred thousandths   **23.** Ones   **25.** Hundreds
27. 0.55   **29.** 6.9   **31.** 11.11   **33.** 100.02   **35.** 3,000.003

Rounded to the Nearest

	Number	Whole	Tenth	Hundredth	Thousandth
37.	47.5479	48	47.5	47.55	47.548
39.	0.8175	1	0.8	0.82	0.818
41.	0.1562	0	0.2	0.16	0.156
43.	2,789.3241	2,789	2,789.3	2,789.32	2,789.324
45.	99.9999	100	100.0	100.00	100.000

47. Three and eleven hundredths; two and five tenths
49. 186,282.40   **51.** Fifteen hundredths
53.

Price Of 1 Gallon Of Regular Gasoline

Date	Price (Dollars)
3/21/11	3.526
3/28/11	3.596
4/4/11	3.684
4/11/11	3.791

55. a. < **b.** >
57. 0.002   0.005   0.02   0.025   0.05   0.052
59. 7.451 and 7.54   **61.** $\frac{1}{4}$
63. $\frac{1}{8}$ **65.** $\frac{5}{8}$ **67.** $\frac{7}{8}$
69. 9.99   **71.** 10.05   **73.** 0.05   **75.** 0.01   **77.** $6\frac{31}{100}$

79. $6\frac{23}{50}$ **81.** $18\frac{123}{1,000}$
Find the Mistake   **1.** To move a place value from the tens column to the hundreds column, you must <u>multiply</u> by ten.   **3.** The decimal 142.9643 written as a mixed number is $142\frac{9,643}{10,000}$.

Exercise Set 4.2
Vocabulary Review   **1.** money   **3.** decimal point
5. value
Problems   **1.** 6.19   **3.** 1.13   **5.** 6.29   **7.** 9.042   **9.** 8.021
11. 11.7843   **13.** 24.343   **15.** 24.111   **17.** 258.5414
19. 666.66   **21.** 11.11   **23.** 3.57   **25.** 4.22   **27.** 120.41
29. 44.933   **31.** 7.673   **33.** 530.865   **35.** 43.55   **37.** 5.918
39. 27.89   **41.** 35.64   **43.** 411.438   **45.** 6   **47.** 1
49. 3.1   **51.** 5.9   **53.** 4.17   **55.** 2.8   **57.** 3.272   **59.** 4.001
61. $116.82   **63.** $1,571.10   **65.** 4.5 in.   **67.** $5.43
69. 0.03 seconds   **71. a.** Less   **b.** Less   **c.** 3%
73. 2 in.   **75.** $3.25; three $1 bills and a quarter   **77.** 3.25
79. $\frac{3}{100}$ **81.** $\frac{51}{10,000}$ **83.** $\frac{3}{2} = 1\frac{1}{2}$ **85.** 1,400   **87.** $\frac{3}{20}$
89. $\frac{147}{1,000}$ **91.** 132,980   **93.** 2,115
95. a. 8 million   **b.** Between 2009 and 2010   **c.** 625 million users
Find the Mistake   **1.** To add 32.69 and 4.837, align <u>the decimal point</u> and add in columns.   **3.** When subtracting 8.7 − 2.0163, we make sure to keep the digits in the correct columns by writing 8.7 as <u>8.7000</u>.

Exercise Set 4.3
Vocabulary Review   multiply, answer, digits, decimal points
Problems   **1.** 0.28   **3.** 0.028   **5.** 0.0027   **7.** 0.78   **9.** 0.792
11. 0.0156   **13.** 24.29821   **15.** 0.03   **17.** 187.85   **19.** 0.002
21. 27.96   **23.** 0.43   **25.** 49,940   **27.** 9,876,540   **29.** 1.89
31. 0.0025   **33.** 5.1106   **35.** 7.3485   **37.** 4.4   **39.** 2.074
41. 3.58   **43.** 187.4   **45.** 116.64   **47.** 20.75   **49.** 0.126
51. Moves it two places to the right   **53.** $1,381.38   **55.** $7.10
57. $44.40   **59.** $293.04   **61.** 8,509 mm²   **63.** 1.18 in²
65. 1,879   **67.** 1,516 R 4   **69.** 298   **71.** 34.8
73. 49.896   **75.** 825
Find the Mistake   **1.** To multiply 18.05 by 3.5, multiply as if the numbers were whole numbers and then place the decimal in the answer with <u>three</u> digits to its right.   **3.** To simplify $(8.43 + 1.002) - (0.05)(3.2)$, first <u>work the operation inside the parentheses and find the product of 0.05 and 3.2 before subtracting</u>.

Exercise Set 4.4
Vocabulary Review   **1.** long division   **3.** last
Problems   **1.** 19.7   **3.** 6.2   **5.** 5.2   **7.** 11.04   **9.** 4.8
11. 9.7   **13.** 2.63   **15.** 4.24   **17.** 2.55   **19.** 1.35
21. 6.5   **23.** 9.9   **25.** 0.05   **27.** 89   **29.** 2.2   **31.** 4.6
33. 1.35   **35.** 16.97   **37.** 0.25   **39.** 2.71   **41.** 11.69
43. 3.98   **45.** 5.98   **47.** 4.24   **49.** 7.5 mi
51.

Rank	Name	Number of Tournaments	Average per Tournament
1.	Na Yeon Choi	23	$81,360
2.	Jiyai Shin	19	$93,850
3.	Cristie Kerr	21	$76,260
4.	Yani Tseng	19	$82,820
5.	Suzann Pettersen	19	$81,960

53. $5.65/hr   **55.** 22.4 mi   **57.** 5 hr   **59.** 7 min   **61.** 2.73
63. 0.13   **65.** 0.77778   **67.** 307.20607   **69.** 0.70945   **71.** $\frac{3}{4}$
73. $\frac{2}{3}$ **75.** $\frac{3}{8}$ **77.** $\frac{19}{50}$ **79.** $\frac{60}{100}$ **81.** $\frac{500}{100}$ **83.** $\frac{12}{15}$

85. $\frac{60}{15}$ **87.** $\frac{18}{15}$ **89.** 0.75   **91.** 0.875

Find the Mistake   **1.** The answer to the problem $25\overline{)70.75}$ will have a decimal point placed with <u>two</u> digits to its right. **3.** To divide 0.6778 by 0.54, multiply both numbers by <u>100</u> to move the decimal point two places to the right.

Landmark Review: 4.1–4.4   **1.** One and fifteen hundredths
3. Five thousandths   **5.** 0.0067   **7.** 23.014   **9.** 28.28
11. 124.15831   **13.** 3.1   **15.** 13.33   **17.** 47.35   **19.** 20
21. 5.16   **23.** 8.8

Exercise Set 4.5
Vocabulary Review   **1.** division   **3.** place values, reduce
Problems   **1.** 0.125   **3.** 0.625
5.

Fraction	$\frac{1}{5}$	$\frac{2}{5}$	$\frac{3}{5}$	$\frac{4}{5}$	$\frac{5}{5}$
Decimal	0.2	0.4	0.6	0.8	1

7. 0.05   **9.** 0.56
11. 0.5625   **13.** 0.8125
15. 0.92   **17.** 0.27
19. 0.09   **21.** 0.28

23.

Decimal	0.125	0.250	0.375	0.500	0.625	0.750	0.875
Fraction	$\frac{1}{8}$	$\frac{1}{4}$	$\frac{3}{8}$	$\frac{1}{2}$	$\frac{5}{8}$	$\frac{3}{4}$	$\frac{7}{8}$

25. $\frac{3}{20}$ **27.** $\frac{2}{25}$ **29.** $\frac{3}{8}$ **31.** $5\frac{3}{5}$ **33.** $5\frac{3}{50}$ **35.** $1\frac{11}{50}$
37. 2.4   **39.** 3.98   **41.** 3.02   **43.** 0.3   **45.** 0.072   **47.** 0.8
49. 1   **51.** 0.25   **53.** $8.42   **55.** $38.66
57.

Change In Stock Price		
Date	Gain ($)	As a Decimal ($)
Monday	$\frac{3}{5}$	0.60
Tuesday	$\frac{1}{2}$	0.50
Wednesday	$\frac{1}{25}$	0.04
Thursday	$\frac{1}{5}$	0.20
Friday	$\frac{1}{10}$	0.10

59. 104.625 calories
61. $10.38
63. Yes

Find the Mistake   **1.** The correct way to write $\frac{6}{11}$ as a decimal is $0.\overline{54}$. **3.** The simplified answer to the problem $\frac{12}{45(0.256 + 0.14)}$ contains <u>only fractions or only decimals</u>.

Chapter 4 Review
1. Six and three hundred two thousandths
3. 23.5006   **5.** 12.02   **7.** 16.254   **9.** 14.59   **11.** 3.069
13. $2.77   **15.** $6.75   **17.** $\frac{31}{50}$ **19.** 7.55   **21.** 0.06
23. 44.876   25. $25,225,000 per month

Chapter 4 Cumulative Review
1. 5,291   **3.** 17,670   **5.** $153.568\overline{3}$
7. 100.373   **9.** $\frac{15}{4} = 3\frac{3}{4}$ **11.** $16\frac{1}{5}$ **13.** $25\frac{3}{8}$ **15.** 4
17. $7(6 + 3) = 63$ **19.** False   **21.** 8   **23.** $19\frac{49}{64}$
25. $8.25   **27.** 7.23 goals

Chapter 4 Test
1. Eleven and eight hundred nineteen thousandths
3. 73.0046   **5.** 7.02   **7.** 16.56   **9.** 10.1   **11.** 3.33
13. $3.61   **15.** $8.15   **17.** $\frac{19}{50}$ **19.** 2.38   **21.** 0.47125
23. 26.674   **25.** $40,000,000 per month

Chapter 5

Exercise Set 5.1
Vocabulary Review   **1.** fraction   **3.** ratio   **5.** complex
Problems   **1.** $\frac{4}{3}$ **3.** $\frac{16}{3}$ **5.** $\frac{2}{5}$ **7.** $\frac{1}{2}$ **9.** $\frac{3}{1}$ **11.** $\frac{7}{6}$ **13.** $\frac{7}{5}$
15. $\frac{5}{7}$ **17.** $\frac{8}{5}$ **19.** $\frac{1}{3}$ **21.** $\frac{1}{10}$ **23.** $\frac{3}{25}$ **25. a.** $\frac{1}{2}$ **b.** $\frac{1}{3}$ **c.** $\frac{2}{3}$
27. a. $\frac{13}{8}$ **b.** $\frac{1}{4}$ **c.** $\frac{3}{8}$ **d.** $\frac{13}{3}$ **29. a.** $\frac{73}{14}$ **b.** $\frac{26}{51}$ **c.** $\frac{7}{13}$ **d.** $\frac{14}{51}$
31. a. $\frac{3}{4}$ **b.** 12   **c.** $\frac{3}{4}$ **33.** $\frac{2,408}{2,314} \approx 1.04$ **35.** $\frac{4,722}{2,408} \approx 1.96$
37. $n = 9$ **39.** $n = 2$ **41.** $n = 5$ **43.** $n = 90$

Find the Mistake   **1.** Writing the ratio of $\frac{2}{5}$ to $\frac{3}{8}$ is the same as writing $\frac{2}{5} \cdot \frac{8}{3}$ or $\frac{\frac{2}{5}}{\frac{3}{8}}$.

3. To write the ratio of 0.04 to 0.20 as a fraction in lowest terms, you must first multiply <u>0.04 and 0.20 by 100</u> to rid the ratio of decimals.

Exercise Set 5.2
Vocabulary Review   **1.** equation, variable   **3.** equals sign
5. term   **7.** second, third   **9.** fundamental property of proportions
Problems   **1.** 35   **3.** 18   **5.** 14   **7.** n **9.** y **11.** b
13. $n = 2$ **15.** $x = 7$ **17.** $y = 7$ **19.** $n = 8$ **21.** $a = 8$
23. $x = 2$ **25.** $y = 1$ **27.** $a = 6$ **29.** $n = 5$ **31.** $x = 3$
33. $n = 7$ **35.** $y = 1$ **37.** $y = 9$ **39.** $n = \frac{7}{2} = 3\frac{1}{2}$
41. $x = \frac{7}{2} = 3\frac{1}{2}$ **43.** $a = \frac{12}{5} = 2\frac{2}{5}$ **45.** $y = \frac{4}{7}$ **47.** $y = \frac{10}{13}$
49. $x = \frac{5}{2} = 2\frac{1}{2}$ **51.** $n = \frac{3}{2} = 1\frac{1}{2}$
53. Means: 3, 5; extremes: 1, 15; products: 15
55. Means: 25, 2; extremes: 10, 5; products: 50
57. Means: $\frac{1}{2}$, 4; extremes: $\frac{1}{3}$, 6; products: 2
59. Means: 5, 1; extremes: 0.5, 10; products: 5   **61.** $x = 10$
63. $y = \frac{12}{5}$ **65.** $x = \frac{3}{2}$ **67.** $x = \frac{10}{9}$ **69.** $x = 7$ **71.** $x = 14$
73. $y = 18$ **75.** $n = 6$ **77.** $n = 40$ **79.** $x = 50$ **81.** $y = 1$
08
83. $x = 3$ **85.** $n = 1$ **87.** $x = 0.25$ **89.** $x = 108$ **91.** $y = 65$
93. $n = 41$ **95.** $x = 108$ **97.** 20   **99.** 300   **101.** 297.5
103. 50.4   **105.** $x = 450$ **107.** $x = 5$

Find the Mistake   **1.** To simplify $\frac{3 \cdot a \cdot 8 \cdot 11}{a \cdot 11}$, divide out a and 11 to get <u>24.</u>   **3.** Solving the equation $6 \cdot a = 48$ for a gives us <u>$a = 8.$</u>   **5.** A statement that two <u>ratios</u> are equal is called a <u>proportion.</u>   **7.** To solve $\frac{7}{10} = \frac{n}{0.2}$, set the <u>product of first and fourth terms equal to the product of the second and third terms.</u>

Exercise Set 5.3
Vocabulary Review   **1.** word problems   **3.** division
Problems   **1.** 329 mi   **3.** 360 points   **5.** 15 pt   **7.** 427.5 mi
9. 900 eggs   **11.** 435 in. = 36.25 ft   **13.** $119.70   **15.** 265 g
17. 91.3 liters   **19.** 60,113 people
Find the Mistake   **1.** A basketball player scores 112 points in 8 games. The proportion to find how many points the player will score in 14 games is $\frac{112}{8} = \frac{x}{14}$.   **3.** A jellybean company knows that for every 100 jellybeans, 4 will be misshapen. The proportion needed to find how many jelly beans were made if 36 misshapen jelly beans are found is $\frac{4}{100} = \frac{36}{x}$.

Chapter 5 Review
1. $\frac{9}{4}$ **3.** $\frac{4}{3}$ **5.** $\frac{7}{5}$ **7.** $\frac{40}{7}$ **9.** $x = 2$ **11.** 81 miles
13. 42.88 mg   **15.** 142,710 km

Chapter 5 Cumulative Review

1. 13,372 **3.** 17 **5.** $516\frac{3}{8}$ or 516.375 **7.** 91 **9.** 144
11. 42.6 **13.** 6.6 **15.** 1 **17.** $x = 25$ **19.** 20 women
21. 69 sections **23.** $\frac{1}{32}$

Chapter 5 Test

1. $\frac{8}{3}$ **3.** $\frac{7}{3}$ **5.** $\frac{7}{4}$ **7.** $\frac{25}{8}$ **9.** $x = 3$ **11.** 82.5 miles
13. 15.39 mg **15.** $\frac{1}{1}$

Chapter 6

Exercise Set 6.1

Vocabulary Review **1.** hundred **3.** left **5.** % symbol
Problems **1.** $\frac{20}{100}$ **3.** $\frac{60}{100}$ **5.** $\frac{24}{100}$ **7.** $\frac{65}{100}$ **9.** 0.23 **11.** 0.92
13. 0.09 **15.** 0.034 **17.** 0.0634 **19.** 0.009 **21.** 23%
23. 92% **25.** 45% **27.** 3% **29.** 60% **31.** 80%
33. 27% **35.** 123% **37.** $\frac{3}{5}$ **39.** $\frac{3}{4}$ **41.** $\frac{1}{25}$ **43.** $\frac{53}{200}$
45. $\frac{7,187}{10,000}$ **47.** $\frac{3}{400}$ **49.** $\frac{1}{16}$ **51.** $\frac{1}{3}$ **53.** 50%
55. 75% **57.** $33\frac{1}{3}$% **59.** 80% **61.** 87.5% **63.** 14%
65. 325% **67.** 150% **69.** 48.8% **71.** 0.50; 0.75
73. a. $\frac{1}{50}, \frac{3}{100}, \frac{3}{50}, \frac{3}{25}, \frac{77}{100}$ **b.** 0.02, 0.03, 0.06, 0.12, 0.77
c. About 2 times as likely. **75.** 20%
77. Liberal Arts: 15%, Science & Math: 15%, Engineering: 27.78%, Business: 11.11%, Architecture & Environmental Design: 11.11%, Agriculture: 22.22%
79. 78.4% **81.** 11.8% **83.** 72.2% **85.** 8.3%; 0.2%
87. 18.5 **89.** 10.875 **91.** 0.5 **93.** 62.5 **95.** 0.5

Find the Mistake **1.** Writing 0.4% as a decimal gives us .004.
3. Writing 25% as a fraction in lowest terms gives us $\frac{1}{4}$.

Exercise Set 6.2

Vocabulary Review **1.** equals sign **3.** variable **5.** fraction
Problems **1.** 8 **3.** 24 **5.** 20.52 **7.** 7.37 **9.** 50% **11.** 10%
13. 25% **15.** 75% **17.** 64 **19.** 50 **21.** 925 **23.** 400
25. 5.568 **27.** 120 **29.** 13.72 **31.** 22.5 **33.** 50%
35. 942.684 **37.** 97.8 **39.** What number is 25% of 350?
41. What percent of 24 is 16? **43.** 46 is 75% of what number?
45. 11.3% calories from fat; healthy **47.** 56.9% calories from fat; not healthy **49.** 0.80 **51.** 0.76 **53.** 48
55. Fewer than 175 to 280 gulls of breeding age

Find the Mistake **1.** The question, "What number is 28.5% of 30?" translates to $n = 0.285 \cdot 30$. **3.** To answer the question, "What number is 45% of 90?", we can solve the proportion $\frac{x}{90} = \frac{45}{100}$.

Landmark Review: 6.1–6.2
1. $\frac{15}{100}$ **3.** $\frac{14}{100}$
5. 0.17 **7.** 0.05 **9.** 38% **11.** 9% **13.** 10%
15. 14.3% **17.** 5.25 **19.** 237.84

Exercise Set 6.3

Vocabulary Review **1.** What number is y% of x?
3. z is y% of what number?
Problems **1.** 70% **3.** 40mL **5.** 45 mL
7. 18.2 acres for farming; 9.8 acres are not available for farming
9. 3,000 students **11.** 400 students **13.** 1,664 female students
15. 31.25% **17.** 50% **19.** 1,267 students **21.** 33 **23.** 8,685
25. 136 **27.** 0.05 **29.** 15,300 **31.** 0.15 **33.** 33.7%, to the nearest tenth of a percent **35.** 170 hits **37.** 17 hits
Find the Mistake **1.** On a test with 110 questions, a student answered 98 questions correctly. The percentage of questions the student answered correctly is 89.1%. **3.** Suppose 39 students in a college class of 130 students received a B on their tests. To find what percent of students earned a B, solve the proportion $\frac{39}{130} = \frac{x}{100}$.

Chapter 6 Review

1. 0.56 **3.** 0.004 **5.** 70% **7.** $\frac{17}{20}$ **9.** $\frac{21}{250}$ **11.** 62.5%
13. 12.8 **15.** 80 **17.** 93,100,000 iPhones

Chapter 6 Cumulative Review

1. 5,411 **3.** 7,969 **5.** 32 **7.** 9.502 **9.** 1.19 **11.** 12
13. $\frac{23}{6} = 3\frac{5}{6}$ **15.** 6 **17.** $3(6 + 8) = 42$ **19.** 19,008 feet
21. 62.5% **23.** 3.5 **25.** 3.9 **27.** 95 **29.** 91¢
31. 9.5% **33.** $3,187.50 **35.** 12.77 acres

Chapter 6 Test

1. 0.27 **3.** 0.009 **5.** 30%
7. $\frac{9}{20}$ **9.** $\frac{9}{125}$ **11.** 87.5%
13. 12 **15.** 75 **17.** 22.46%

Chapter 7

Exercise Set 7.1

Vocabulary Review **1.** foot **3.** conversion factor
5. unit analysis **7.** U.S. system
Problems **1.** 1,800 cm **3.** 4,800 m **5.** 50 cm
7. 0.248 km **9.** 670 mm **11.** 34.98 m **13.** 6.34 dm
15. 9 qt **17.** 32 yd³ **19.** 9,600 mL **21.** 0.0938 L
23. 3,000,000 mL **25.** 4,710 L **27.** 500,000 cg
29. 714 cg **31.** 65.943 cg **33.** 1.979 g **35.** 60 in.
37. 120 in. **39.** 6 ft **41.** 162 in. **43.** $2\frac{1}{4}$ ft.
45. 13,200 ft **47.** $1\frac{1}{3}$ yd **49.** 102.6 ft³ **51.** 128 fl oz
53. 48 qt **55.** 56 pt **57.** 188.8 fl oz **59.** 32 gal
61. 80 oz. **63.** 10,000 lb
65. 11 lb **67.** 5.1 T **69.** 96,000 oz **71.** 5,000 g
73. 1,200 in. **75.** $1\frac{1}{3}$ yd **77.** 216 mm
79. 0.19 m **81.** 15,000,000,000 Å **83.** 38 yd
85. 0.0856 m **87.** 5.9 ft **89.** 1.6 pints **91.** 0.124 ft³
93. 3 glasses **95.** 72 qt **97.** 200 test tubes
99. 6.3987 m **101.** 0.000379 km **103.** 3.8 mi
105. 0.28 mi **107.** 57.52 gal **109.** 0.25 ft³
111. 118,800,000 ft³ **113.** 15 g **115.** 2.4 g **117.** 45 g
119. 3 mg **121.** 240 **123.** 10,000 **125.** 500,000
127. 15,000 **129.** 15
Find the Mistake **1.** The average length for a house cat is roughly 18 inches. To show how many feet this is, multiply by the conversion factor $\frac{1 \text{ foot}}{12 \text{ inches}}$. **3.** A cell phone measures 100 mm in length. To show how many meters this is, multiply 100 mm by the conversion factor $\frac{1 \text{ m}}{1,000 \text{ mm}}$.
5. To find how many milliliters four 2-liter soda bottles can hold, you must find the product of 8 L and $\frac{1,000 \text{ mL}}{1 \text{ L}}$.

Exercise Set 7.2

Vocabulary Review **1.** centimeters **3.** subtract, multiply
Problems **1.** 15.24 cm **3.** 13.12 ft **5.** 6.56 yd **7.** 32,200 m
9. 8,195 mL **11.** 2.12 qt **13.** 75.8 L **15.** 339.6 g
17. 33 lb **19.** 365°F **21.** 30°C **23.** 3.94 in.
25. 7.62 m **27.** 46.23 L **29.** 17.67 oz
31. Answers will vary. **33.** 91.46 m **35.** 88.55 km/hr
37. 2.03 m **39.** 38.3°C **41.** 75 **43.** 82 **45.** 3.25
47. 22 **49.** 41 **51.** 48 **53.** 195 **55.** 3.27

57. $90.00   **59.** 0.71 oz/in³   **61.** 68.5 g

Find the Mistake   **1.** To convert 6 miles to km, <u>multiply</u> 6 miles by $\frac{1.61 \text{ km}}{1 \text{ mi}}$

.   **3.** To convert 25° Celsius to Fahrenheit, use the formula
$F = \frac{9}{5}C + 32$ to get 77° F.

Exercise Set 7.3
Vocabulary Review   **1.** minutes to seconds
3. borrow
Problems   **1. a.** 270 min **b.** 4.5 hr   **3. a.** 320 min **b.** 5.33 hr
5. a. 390 sec **b.** 6.5 min   **7. a.** 320 sec **b.** 5.33 min
9. a. 40 oz **b.** 2.5 lb   **11. a.** 76 oz **b.** 4.75 lb
13. a. 54 in. **b.** 4.5 ft   **15. a.** 69 in. **b.** 5.75 ft
17. a. 9 qt **b.** 2.25 gal   **19.** 11 hr   **21.** 22 ft 4 in.
23. 11 lb   **25.** 5 hr 40 min   **27.** 3 hr 47 min   **29.** 52 min
31. 8:06:58; 8:08:19   **33.** 00:00:09   **35.** $104   **37.** 10 hr
39. $150   **41.** 356.79 g   **43.** $29,293.60   **45.** 2.64 sec
Find the Mistake   **1.** Converting 6 feet 6 inches to inches gives
us <u>78 inches.</u>   **3.** The correct way to subtract 27 minutes from 6
hours and 12 minutes is to <u>borrow 60 minutes from the 6 hours to</u>
<u>get 5 hours and 45 minutes.</u>

Chapter 7 Review
1. 27 ft   **3.** 16,400 mL   **5.** 13.78 qt   **7.** 6.2 yd³
9. 0.40 gal   **11.** 0.02 ft³   **13.** 151.83 m   **15.** 14.57 in.
17. 53.77 L   **19. a.** 435 min **b.** 7.25 hr
21. DiGiorno 7,136,540,789 pesos; Red Baron 3,093,637,560 pesos

Chapter 7 Cumulative Review
1. 11,623   **3.** 27   **5.** $356\frac{7}{8} = 356.875$ **7.** 9   **9.** 66
11. 44.85   **13.** 48.78   **15.** $\frac{9}{16}$ **17.** $8\frac{1}{4}$ **19.** 1.075
21. $x = 4.25$ **23.** $x = 21$ **25.** 54   **27.** 21.34 %

Chapter 7 Test
1. 9 ft   **3.** 12,000 mL   **5.** 8.48 qt   **7.** 4.3 yd³   **9.** 0.53 gal
11. 0.22 ft³   **13.** 114.33 m   **15.** 10.63 in.   **17.** 33.96 L
19. a. 165 min **b.** 2.75 hr
21. Barq's 0.023 g; Coca-Cola Classic 0.035 g; Dr.Pepper 0.043 g;
Mountain Dew 0.054 g; Pepsi 0.037 g; Vault 0.071 g

Medical Terminology

An Illustrated Guide

8th edition

Barbara Janson Cohen, MEd

Ann DePetris, MSA, RN, CCRP

Wolters Kluwer

Philadelphia • Baltimore • New York • London
Buenos Aires • Hong Kong • Sydney • Tokyo

Contents

USER'S GUIDE

Medical Terminology: An Illustrated Guide, 8th edition, was created and developed to help you master the language of medicine. The tools and features in the text will help you work through the material presented. Please take a few moments to look through this User's Guide, which will introduce you to the features that will enhance your learning experience.

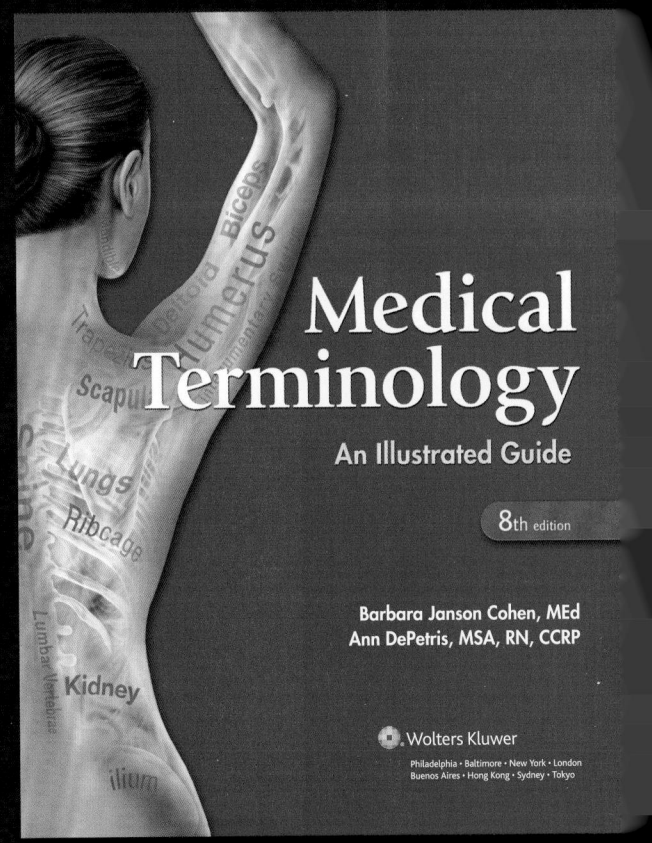

Medical Terminology
An Illustrated Guide

8th edition

Barbara Janson Cohen, MEd
Ann DePetris, MSA, RN, CCRP

Wolters Kluwer

Philadelphia · Baltimore · New York · London
Buenos Aires · Hong Kong · Sydney · Tokyo

Chapter Contents, Objectives, and Pretests

Chapter Opening Case Studies and Objectives help you identify learning goals and familiarize yourself with the materials covered in the chapter. Chapter Pretests quiz students on previous knowledge at the beginning of each chapter. Students should take each Chapter Pretest before starting the chapter and again after completing the chapter in order to measure progress.

▶ **Learning Objectives**

After study of this chapter you should be able to:

1 ▶ Describe the composition of the blood plasma. *p206*
2 ▶ Describe and give the functions of the three types of blood cells. *p206*
3 ▶ Differentiate the five different types of leukocytes. *p208*
4 ▶ Explain the basis of blood types. *p209*
5 ▶ Define immunity, and list the possible sources of immunity. *p211*
6 ▶ Identify and use roots and suffixes pertaining to the blood and immunity. *p214*

7 ▶ Identify and use roots pertaining to blood chemistry. *p216*
8 ▶ List and describe three major disorders of the blood. *p217*
9 ▶ Describe the major tests used to study blood. *pp217*
10 ▶ List and describe three major disorders of the immune system. *p221*
11 ▶ Interpret abbreviations used in blood studies. *p227*
12 ▶ Analyze medical terms in several case studies involving the blood. *pp205, 234*

Case Study: *Nurse Anesthetist M.R. with Latex Allergy*

Chief Complaint

M.R., a 36-year-old certified registered nurse anesthetist (CRNA), noticed that her hands had a red patchy rash when she removed her gloves following cases in the OR. They began to itch after a few minutes of donning the gloves, so she figured she might have developed an allergy to the latex they contained. When she began to have a runny nose and itchy swollen eyes, she was worried and sought medical advice from her primary care physician, who referred her to an allergist.

Examination
The allergist examined M.R.'s hands and observed a localized red crusty rash that stopped at the wrists. There were a few blisters spread over the hand region. Along with the examination, a history indicated M.R. had noticed the contact dermatitis for a while when she wore powdered latex gloves in the OR, and she more recently had noted generalized

allergic symptoms during surgical cases. During a recent case, she experienced some tachycardia, urticaria (hives) and rhinitis when she came in contact with latex gloves.

Clinical Course
M.R. was diagnosed with a type I hypersensitivity, IgE, T cell-mediated latex allergy, as shown by both immunologic and skin-prick tests. Although M.R. is a CRNA, she was educated on the course of latex allergies. She was reminded that there is no cure and that the only way to prevent an allergic reaction is to avoid coming into contact with latex.

This chapter describes the composition and characteristics of blood, the life-sustaining fluid that circulates throughout the body. A discussion of immunity is included because many components of the immune system are carried in the blood. M.R.'s case of allergy is an example of immunologic hyperactivity. One of the symptoms, tachycardia, was discussed in Chapter 9 and rhinitis will be introduced in the next chapter on the respiratory system.

ANCILLARIES *At-A-Glance*

Visit thePoint to access the following resources. For guidance in using the resources most effectively, see pp. ix–xvi.

Learning RESOURCES
▶ Tips for Effective Studying
▶ Web Figure: Hematopoiesis
▶ Web Chart: Childhood Immunizations
▶ Web Animation: Hemostasis
▶ Web Animation: Immune Response
▶ Audio Pronunciation Glossary

Learning ACTIVITIES
▶ Visual Activities
▶ Kinesthetic Activities
▶ Auditory Activities

Detailed Illustrations

Illustrations: Detailed, full-color drawings and photographs illuminate the chapters. These include clinical photographs and tissue micrographs. The many figures amplify and clarify the text and are particularly helpful for visual learners.

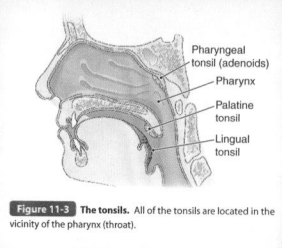

Figure 11-3 **The tonsils.** All of the tonsils are located in the vicinity of the pharynx (throat).

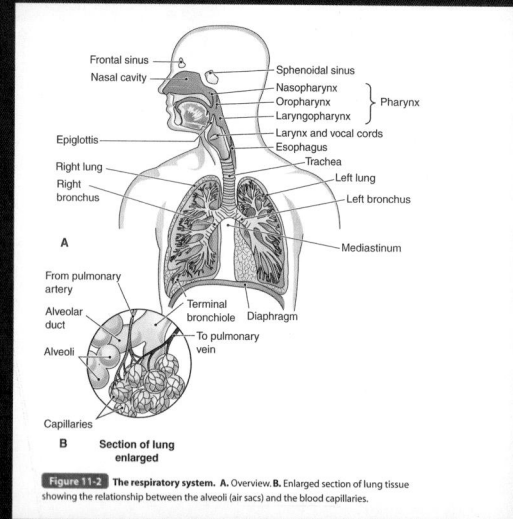

Figure 11-2 **The respiratory system. A.** Overview. **B.** Enlarged section of lung tissue showing the relationship between the alveoli (air sacs) and the blood capillaries.

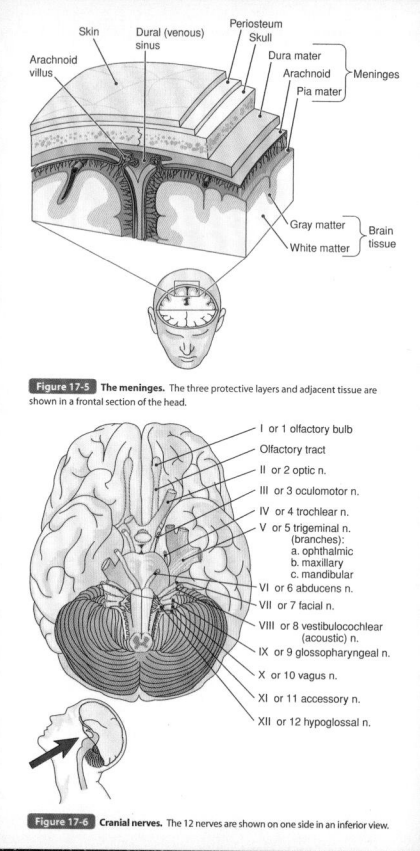

Figure 17-5 **The meninges.** The three protective layers and adjacent tissue are shown in a frontal section of the head.

Figure 17-6 **Cranial nerves.** The 12 nerves are shown on one side in an inferior view.

Feature Boxes

Feature Boxes Call Out Important Information
Focus on Words boxes provide historical or other interesting information on select terms within a chapter.

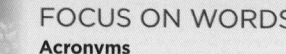

FOCUS ON WORDS
Acronyms

Box 10-2

Acronyms are abbreviations that use the first letters of the words in a name or phrase. They have become very popular because they save time and space in writing as the number and complexity of technical terms increases. Some examples that apply to studies of the blood are CBC (complete blood count) and RBC and WBC for red and white blood cells. Some other common acronyms are CNS (central nervous system or clinical nurse specialist), ECG (electrocardiogram) NIH (National Institutes of Health), and STI (sexually transmitted infection).

If the acronym has vowels and lends itself to pronunciation, it may be used as a word in itself, such as AIDS (acquired immunodeficiency syndrome); ELISA (enzyme-linked immunosorbent assay); *JAMA* (*Journal of the American Medical Association*); NSAID (nonsteroidal antiinflammatory drug), pronounced "en-sayd;" and CABG (coronary artery bypass graft), which inevitably becomes "cabbage." Few people even know that LASER is an acronym that means "light amplification by stimulated emission of radiation."

An acronym is usually introduced the first time a phrase appears in an article and is then used without explanation. If you have spent time searching back through an article in frustration for the meaning of an acronym, you probably wish, as do other readers, that all the acronyms used and their meanings would be listed at the beginning of each article.

CLINICAL PERSPECTIVES

Eye Surgery: A Glimpse of the Cutting Edge

Cataracts, glaucoma, and refractive errors are common eye disorders. In the past, cataract and glaucoma treatments concentrated on managing the diseases. Refractive errors were corrected using eyeglasses and, more recently, contact lenses. Today, using laser and microsurgical techniques, ophthalmologists can remove cataracts, reduce glaucoma, and allow people with refractive errors to put their eyeglasses and contacts away. These cutting-edge procedures include:

- LASIK (laser in situ keratomileusis) to correct refractive errors. During this procedure, a surgeon uses a laser to reshape the cornea so that it refracts light directly onto the retina, rather than in front of or behind it. A microkeratome (surgical knife) is used to cut a flap in the cornea's outer layer. A computer-controlled laser sculpts the middle layer of the cornea and then the flap is replaced. The procedure takes only a few minutes, and patients recover their vision quickly and usually with little postoperative pain.

- Phacoemulsification to remove cataracts. During this procedure, a surgeon makes a very small incision (~3 mm long) through the sclera near the cornea's outer edge. An ultrasonic probe is inserted through this opening and into the center of the lens. The probe uses sound waves to emulsify the lens's central core, which is then suctioned out. An artificial lens is then permanently implanted in the lens capsule (see **Fig. 18-15**). The procedure is typically painless, although the patient may feel some discomfort for one to two days afterward.

- Laser trabeculoplasty to treat glaucoma. This procedure uses a laser to help drain fluid from the eye and lower intraocular pressure. The laser is aimed at drainage canals located between the cornea and iris and makes several burns that are believed to open the canals and allow better fluid drainage. The procedure is typically painless and takes only a few minutes.

Clinical Perspectives boxes focus on body processing as well as techniques used in clinical settings.

HEALTH PROFESSIONS

Radiologic Technologist

Radiologic technologists help in the diagnosis of medical disorders by taking x-ray images (radiographs) of the body. They also use CT scans and other imaging technology to perform examinations on patients to aid physicians diagnosis. Following institutional safety patient mobilization procedures; they must prepare patients for radiologic examinations, place patients in appropriate positions; and then adjust equipment to the correct angles, heights, and settings for taking the x-ray or other diagnostic image. They must position the image receptors correctly and, after exposure, remove and process the images. They are also required to keep patient records and maintain equipment. Radiologic technologists must minimize radiation hazards by using protective equipment for themselves and patients and by delivering the minimum possible amount of radiation. They wear badges to monitor radiation levels and keep records of their exposure.

Radiologic technologists may specialize in a specific imaging technique such as bone densitometry, cardiovascular-

interventional radiography, computed tomography, mammography, magnetic resonance imaging, nuclear medicine, and quality management. Some of these will be described in later chapters.

The majority of radiologic technologists work in hospitals, but they may also be employed in physicians' offices, diagnostic imaging centers (e.g., doing mammograms), and outpatient care centers. Radiologic technologists must possess a minimum of an associate's degree to qualify for professional certification. A higher degree is necessary for a supervisory or teaching position. The Joint Review Committee on Education in Radiologic Technology accredits most of the education programs. The American Registry of Radiologic Technologists (ARRT) offers a national certification examination in radiography as well as in other imaging technologies (CT, MRI, nuclear medicine, etc.). ARRT certification is required for employment as a radiologic technologist in most U.S. states. Job opportunities in this field are currently good. The American Society of Radiologic Technologists has information on this career at www.asrt.org.

Health Professions boxes focus on a variety of health careers, showing how the knowledge of medical terminology is applied in real-world careers.

FOR YOUR REFERENCE

Blood Cells

Cell Type	Number Per Microliter of Blood	Description	Function
Erythrocyte (red blood cell)	5 million	Tiny (7 mcm diameter), biconcave disk without nucleus (anuclear)	Carries oxygen bound to hemoglobin; also carries some carbon dioxide and buffers blood
Leukocyte (white blood cell)	5,000 to 10,000	Larger than red cell with prominent nucleus that may be segmented (granulocyte) or unsegmented (agranulocyte); types vary in staining properties	Immunity; protects against pathogens and destroys foreign matter and debris; located in blood, tissues, and lymphatic system
Platelet (thrombocyte)	150,000 to 450,000	Fragment of large cell (megakaryocyte)	Hemostasis; forms a platelet plug and starts blood clotting (coagulation)

For Your Reference boxes provide supplemental information for terms within a chapter.

Word Part Tables

Detailed Tables

Present roots, prefixes, and suffixes covered in each chapter in an easy-to-reference format (with examples of their use in medical terminology). Word Part Knowledge aids in the learning and understanding of common terminology.

Table 21-1		Roots Pertaining to the Skin and Associated Str	
Root	**Meaning**	**Example**	**Definition of Example**
derm/o, dermat/o	skin	dermabrasion derm-ah-BRA-zhun	surgical procedure used to resu and remove imperfections
kerat/o	keratin, horny layer of the skin	keratinous keh-RAT-ih-nus	containing keratin; horny
melan/o	dark, black, melanin	melanosome MEL-ah-no-some	a small cellular body that prod
hidr/o	sweat, perspiration	anhidrosis an-hi-DRO-sis	absence of sweating
seb/o	sebum, sebaceous gland	seborrhea seb-or-E-ah	excess flow of sebum (adjective
trich/o	hair	trichomycosis trik-o-mi-KO-sis	fungal infection of the hair
onych/o	nail	onychia o-NIK-e-ah	inflammation of the nail and n -itis ending)

Exercises

Exercises are designed to tes your knowledge before you move to the next learning to that follows each table.

EXERCISE 21-1

Identify and define the roots in the following words.

	Root	Meaning of Root
1. hypodermis (*hi-po-DER-mis*)	_____	_____
2. seborrheic (*seb-o-RE-ik*)	_____	_____
3. hypermelanosis (*hi-per-mel-ah-NO-sis*)	_____	_____
4. dyskeratosis (*dis-ker-ah-TO-sis*)	_____	_____
5. hypohidrosis (*hi-po-hi-DRO-sis*)	_____	_____
6. hypertrichosis (*hi-per-trih-KO-sis*)	_____	_____
7. eponychium (*ep-o-NIK-e-um*)	_____	_____

Fill in the blanks.

8. Dermatopathology (*der-mah-to-pah-THOL-o-je*) is study of diseases of the _____.
9. Keratolysis (*ker-ah-TOL-ih-sis*) is loosening of the skin's _____.
10. A melanocyte (*MEL-ah-no-site*) is a cell that produces _____.
11. Trichoid (*TRIK-oyd*) means resembling a(n) _____.
12. Onychomycosis (*on-ih-ko-mi-KO-sis*) is a fungal infection of a(n) _____.
13. Hidradenitis (*hi-drad-eh-NI-tis*) is inflammation of a gland that produces _____.
14. A hypodermic (*hi-po-DER-mik*) injection is given under the _____.

Term Tables

Key Terms include the most commonly used terms.

Terminology	Key Terms	
glomerular capsule glo-MER-u-lar KAP-sule	The cup-shaped structure at the beginning of the nephron that surrounds the glomerulus and receives material filtered out of the blood; Bowman (BO-man) capsule
glomerular filtrate glo-MER-u-lar FIL-trate	The fluid and dissolved materials that filter out of the blood and enter the nephron through the glomerular capsule
glomerulus glo-MER-u-lus	The cluster of capillaries within the glomerular capsule (plural: glomeruli) (root: glomerul/o)
kidney KID-ne	An organ of excretion (roots: ren/o, nephr/o); the two kidneys filter the blood and form urine, which contains metabolic waste products and other substances as needed to regulate the water, electrolyte, and pH balance of body fluids
micturition mik-tu-RISH-un	The voiding of urine; urination
nephron NEF-ron	A microscopic functional unit of the kidney; working with blood vessels, the nephron filters the blood and balances the composition of urine
renal cortex RE-nal KOR-tex	The kidney's outer portion; contains portions of the nephrons
renal medulla meh-DUL-lah	The kidney's inner portion; contains portions of the nephrons and ducts that transport urine toward the renal pelvis
renal pelvis PEL-vis	The expanded upper end of the ureter that receives urine from the kidney (Greek root pyel/o means "basin")
renal pyramid PERE-ah-mid	A triangular structure in the renal medulla; composed of the nephrons' loops and collecting ducts
renin RE-nin	An enzyme produced by the kidneys that activates angiotensin in the blood
trigone TRI-gone	A triangle at the base of the bladder formed by the openings of the two ureters and the urethra (see Fig. 13-4)
tubular reabsorption TUBE-u-lar re-ab-SORP-shun	The return of substances from the glomerular filtrate to the blood through the peritubular capillaries
urea u-RE-ah	The main nitrogenous (nitrogen-containing) waste product in the urine
ureter U-re-ter	The tube that carries urine from the kidney to the bladder (root: ureter/o)
urethra u-RE-thrah	The tube that carries urine from the bladder to the outside of the body (root: urethr/o)

Supplementary Terms list more specialized terms.

Abbreviations are listed for common terms.

Chapter Review Exercises

Chapter Review Exercises are designed to test your knowledge of the chapter material and appear at the end of each chapter.

EXTERNAL SURFACE OF THE BRAIN

Write the name of each numbered part on the corresponding line.

Cerebellum   Parietal lobe
Frontal lobe   Pons
Gyri   Spinal cord
Medulla oblongata   Sulci
Occipital lobe   Temporal lobe

1. _____
2. _____
3. _____
4. _____
5. _____
6. _____
7. _____
8. _____
9. _____
10. _____

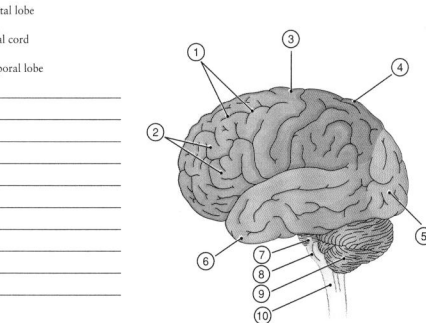

SPINAL CORD, LATERAL VIEW

Write the name of each numbered part on the corresponding line.

Brain   Lumbar enlargement
Brainstem   Lumbar nerves
Cervical enlargement Sacral nerves
Cervical nerves   Spinal cord
Coccygeal nerve   Thoracic nerves

1. _____
2. _____
3. _____
4. _____
5. _____
6. _____
7. _____
8. _____
9. _____
10. _____

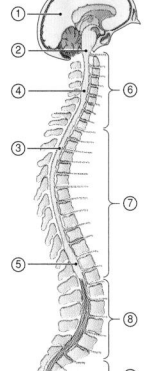

Case Studies and Case Study Questions

Case Studies and Case Study Questions at the end of every chapter present terminology in the context of a medical report. These are an excellent review tool as they test your cumulative knowledge of medical terminology and put terminology into a real-world context.

Case Study 19-2: *Osteogenesis Imperfecta*

M.H., a 3-year-old boy with osteogenesis imperfecta (OI) type III, was admitted to the pediatric orthopedic hospital for treatment of yet another fracture. Since birth he has had 15 arm and leg fractures as a result of his congenital disease. This latest fracture occurred when he twisted at the hip while standing in his wheeled walker. He has been in a research study and receives a bisphosphonate infusion every two months. He is short in stature with short limbs for his age and has bowing of both legs.

M.H. was transferred to the OR and carefully lifted to the OR table by the staff. After he was anesthetized, he was positioned with gentle manipulation, and his left hip was elevated on a small gel pillow. After skin preparation and sterile draping, a stainless steel rod was inserted into the medullary canal of his left femur to reduce and stabilize the femoral fracture. The muscle, fascia, subcutaneous tissue, and skin were sutured closed. Three nurses gently held M.H. in position on a pediatric spica box while the surgeon applied a hip spica (body cast) to stabilize the fixation, protect the leg, and maintain abduction. M.H. was transferred to the post-anesthesia care unit (PACU) for recovery. The surgeon dictated the procedure as an open reduction internal fixation (ORIF) of the left femur with intramedullary (IM) rodding and application of spica cast.

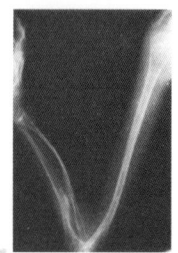

Osteogenesis imperfecta. X-ray of the upper extremity shows the thin bones and fractures that result from defective collagen production.

Case Study Questions

Multiple Choice. Select the best answer, and write the letter of your choice to the left of each number.

_____ 1. A condylectomy is
    a. removal of a joint capsule
    b. removal of a rounded bone protuberance
    c. enlargement of a cavity
    d. removal of a tumor

_____ 2. The articular surface of a bone is located
    a. under the epiphysis
    b. at a joint
    c. at a muscle attachment
    d. at a tendon attachment

_____ 3. The dissection directed anteroposteriorly was done
    a. posterior–superior
    b. circumferentially
    c. front to back
    d. top to bottom

_____ 4. Another term for bow-legged is
    a. knock-kneed
    b. adduction
    c. varus
    d. valgus

_____ 5. An IM rod is placed
    a. inferior to the femoral condyle
    b. into the acetabulum
    c. within the medullary canal
    d. lateral to the epiphysial growth plates

Student Resources and thePoint

People learn in different ways. Some students learn best by reading. Others take in new information best by listening to their instructors. You may prefer to write down notes. When you understand the way that you process information most effectively, you can choose resources that fit your learning style. ThePoint is a practical system that lets you learn faster, remember more, and achieve success.

Getting Started with the Student Resources and thePoint

Your journey begins with your textbook, *Medical Terminology: An Illustrated Guide*, 8th edition. At many points in the textbook you will find highlighted notices that guide you to resources and activities designed for your personal learning style.

Go to the pronunciation glossary on the Student Resources to hear these words pronounced.

Inside the front cover of your textbook, you will find your personal access code. Use it to log on to thePoint—the companion website for this textbook. On the website, you can access learning activities in a variety of learning styles and choose the ones that will help you

Visit thePoint.lww.com/CohenMedTerm8e
on thePoint—the companion website
for *Medical Terminology: An Illustrated
Guide*, 8th edition, which will allow you
to search and sort activities by learning
style to choose the most effective way
for you to learn the material. Resources
and activities available to students
include the following:

- **Multiple choice, true–false, and fill-in-the-blank questions**

- **Categories**

- **Listen & Label and Look & Label**

- **Word Building**

- **Zooming In**

- **Pronounce It**

- **Spell It**

- **Sound It**

- **Hangman**

- **Crossword Puzzles**

- **Quiz Show**

- **Concentration**

thePoint®

http://thePoint.lww.com

Provides flexible learning solutions and resources for students
and faculty using *Medical Terminology: An Illustrated Guide*,
Eighth Edition

Resources for students:
- More than 15 types of interactive exercises
- Image Banks
- Animations
- Audio Glossary

Resources for instructors*:
- PowerPoints
- Lesson Plans
- Test Generator

 Wolters Kluwer

PrepU: An Integrated Adaptive Learning Solution

PrepU, Lippincott's adaptive learning system, is an integral component of *Medical Terminology: An Illustrated Guide.*

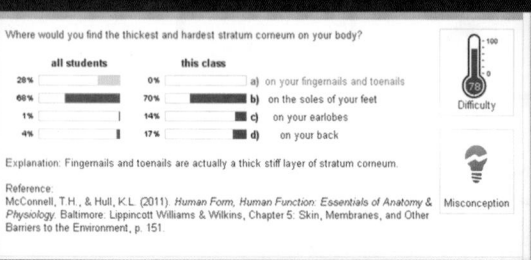

PrepU uses repetitive and adaptive quizzing to build mastery of medical terminology concepts, helping students to learn more while giving instructors the data they need to monitor each student's progress, strengths, and weaknesses. The hundreds of questions in PrepU offer students the chance to drill themselves on medical terminology and support their review and retention of the information they've learned. Each question not only provides an explanation for the correct answer, but also references the text page for the student to review the source material. PrepU for *Medical Terminology* challenges students with questions and activities that coincide with the materials they've learned in the text and gives students a proven tool to learn medical terminology more effectively. For instructors, PrepU provides tools to identify areas and topics of student misconception; instructors can use these rich course data to assess students' learning and better target their in-class activities and discussions, while collecting data that are useful for accreditation.

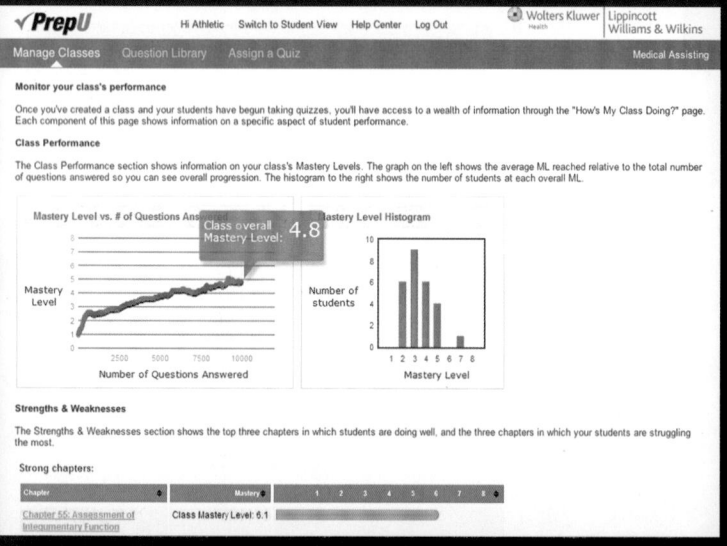

A learning experience individualized to each student. An adaptive learning engine, PrepU offers questions customized for each student's level of understanding, challenging students at an appropriate pace and difficulty level, while dispelling common misconceptions. As students review and master PrepU's questions, the system automatically increases the difficulty of questions, effectively driving student understanding of medical terminology to a mastery level. PrepU not only helps students to improve their knowledge, but also helps foster their test-taking confidence.

PrepU works! PrepU works, and not just because we say so. PrepU efficacy is backed by data:

1. In an introductory nursing course at Central Carolina Technical College, student course outcomes were positively associated with PrepU usage. The students who answered the most PrepU questions in the class also had the best overall course grades.

2. In a randomized, controlled study at UCLA, students using PrepU (for biology) achieved 62 percent higher learning gains than those who did not.

To see a video explanation of PrepU, go to http://download.lww.com/wolterskluwer_vitalstream_com/mktg/prepuvid/prepupromo01.html.

Introduction to Medical Terminology

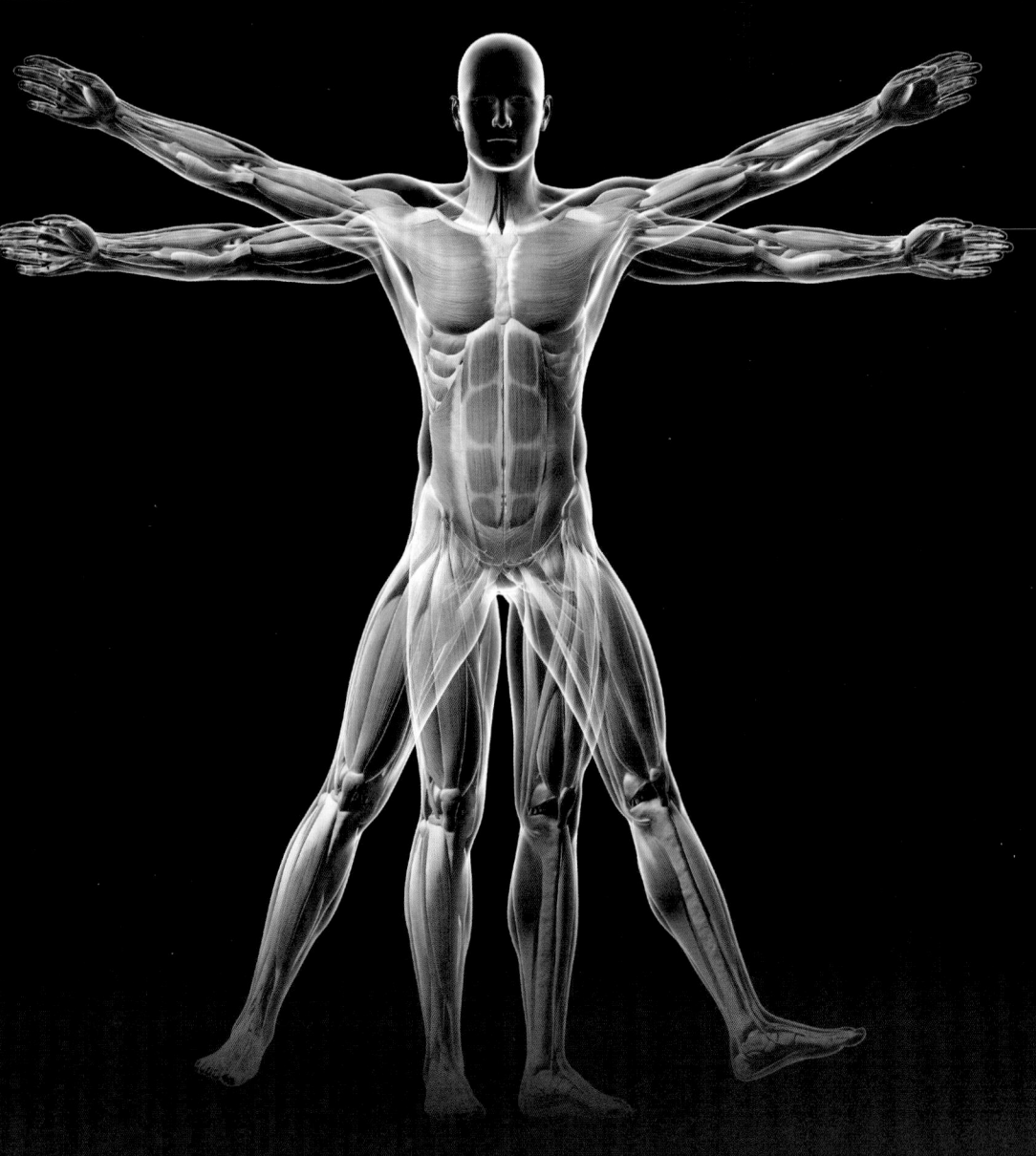

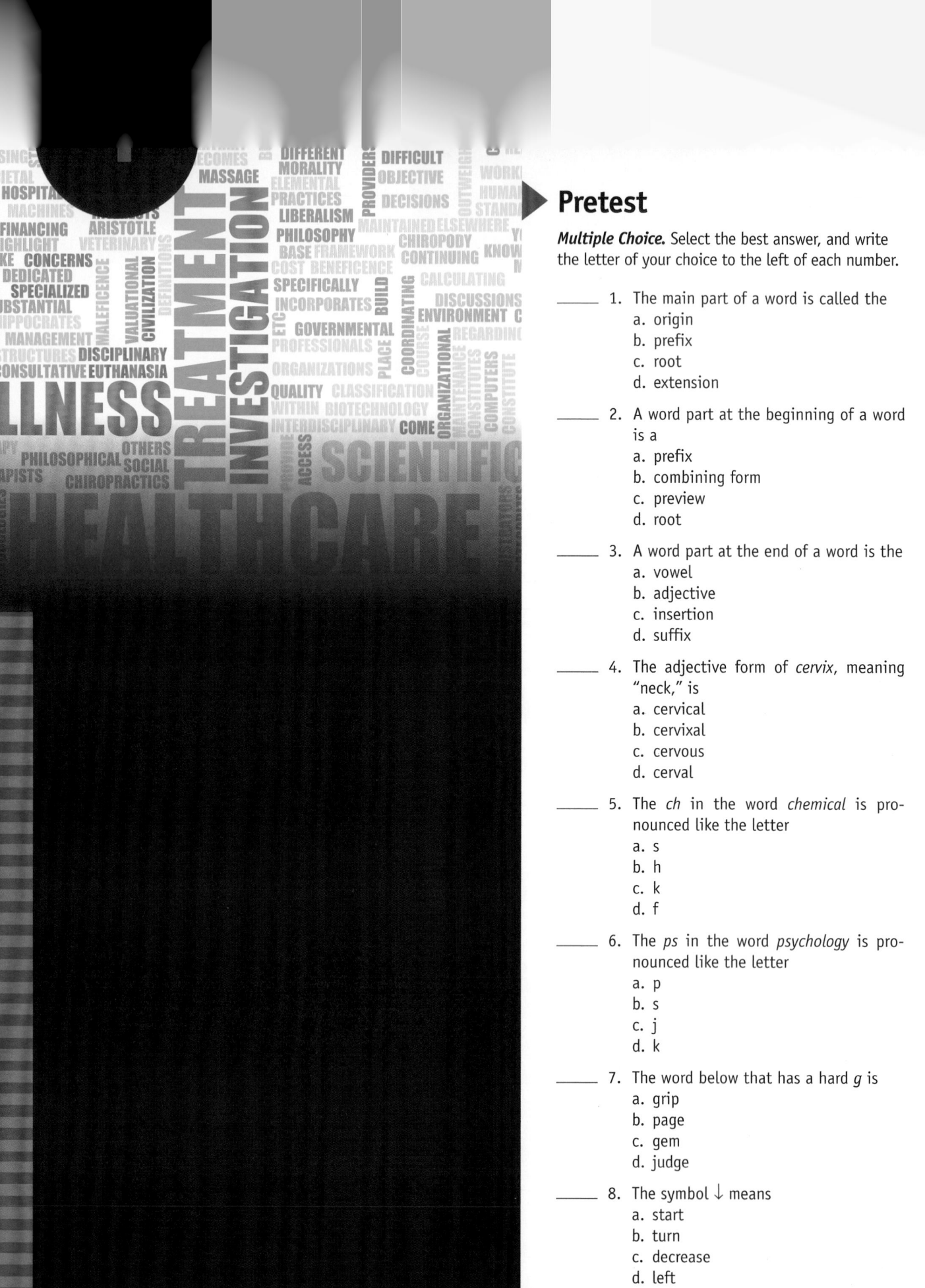

Multiple Choice. Select the best answer, and write the letter of your choice to the left of each number.

_____ 1. The main part of a word is called the
   a. origin
   b. prefix
   c. root
   d. extension

_____ 2. A word part at the beginning of a word is a
   a. prefix
   b. combining form
   c. preview
   d. root

_____ 3. A word part at the end of a word is the
   a. vowel
   b. adjective
   c. insertion
   d. suffix

_____ 4. The adjective form of *cervix*, meaning "neck," is
   a. cervical
   b. cervixal
   c. cervous
   d. cerval

_____ 5. The *ch* in the word *chemical* is pronounced like the letter
   a. s
   b. h
   c. k
   d. f

_____ 6. The *ps* in the word *psychology* is pronounced like the letter
   a. p
   b. s
   c. j
   d. k

_____ 7. The word below that has a hard *g* is
   a. grip
   b. page
   c. gem
   d. judge

_____ 8. The symbol ↓ means
   a. start
   b. turn
   c. decrease
   d. left

Learning Objectives

After study of this chapter, you should be able to:

1 ▶ Explain the purpose of medical terminology. *p4*

2 ▶ Name the languages from which most medical word parts are derived. *p4*

3 ▶ Define the terms *root, suffix,* and *prefix. p4*

4 ▶ Explain what combining forms are and why they are used. *p5*

5 ▶ Pronounce words according to the pronunciation guide used in this text. *p6*

6 ▶ List three features of medical dictionaries. *p8*

7 ▶ Identify medical words and abbreviations in case studies to review concepts of medical terminology. *pp3, 13*

Case Study: *J.V.'s Digestive Problems*

Chief Complaint

J.V., a 22-year-old (y/o) college student, visited the university health clinic and stated he had a four-month history of a burning pain in the middle of his chest. He notices it more at night and has difficulty sleeping because of the pain. He also states that the pain seems to occur more frequently following late-night college gatherings where pizza, spicy chicken wings, and beer are served.

Examination

A well-nourished 22-year-old male complaining of (c/o) epigastric (upper abdominal) pain no longer relieved by antacids; orthopnea—currently sleeping with three pillows to aid in breathing; occasional swallowing problems, or dysphagia; ETOH (alcohol) consumption is six to eight beers per week; nonsmoker; no neurologic, musculoskeletal, genitourinary, or respiratory deficits. Referred to a gastroenterologist for ↑ acid production and gastroesophageal reflux disease (GERD).

Clinical Course

The gastroenterologist saw J.V. and ordered an x-ray study of his upper gastrointestinal (GI) system. Results demonstrated reflux disease, and J.V. underwent an esophageal gastroduodenoscopy (EGD) to visually examine his digestive organs from his esophagus to his small intestine. Results showed no evidence of bleeding, ulcerations, or strictures. The student was given educational material on GERD, including dietary recommendations. He was started on Prevacid and will be reevaluated in six months.

In this chapter, you learn about how medical words are constructed and also learn about the use of abbreviations and other types of shorthand in medical writing. Later in the chapter, we revisit J.V. and see how he is progressing under treatment.

ANCILLARIES *At-A-Glance*

Visit thePoint to access the following resources. For guidance in using the resources most effectively, see pp. ix–xvi.

Learning RESOURCES

▶ Tips for Effective Studying
▶ Web Chart: "Do Not Use" Abbreviations and Symbols
▶ Audio Pronunciation Glossary

Learning ACTIVITIES

▶ Visual Activities
▶ Kinesthetic Activities
▶ Auditory Activities

Introduction

Medical terminology is a special vocabulary used by healthcare professionals for effective and accurate communication. Every health-related field requires an understanding of medical terminology, and this book highlights selected healthcare occupations in special boxes (**Box 1-1**). Because it is based mainly on Greek and Latin words, medical terminology is consistent and uniform throughout the world. It is also efficient; although some of the terms are long, they often reduce an entire phrase to a single word. The one word *gastroduoden-ostomy*, for example, means "a communication between the stomach and the first part of the small intestine" (**Fig. 1-1**). The part *gastr* means stomach; *duoden* represents the duodenum, the first part of the small intestine; and *ostomy* means a communication.

The medical vocabulary is vast, and learning it may seem like learning the entire vocabulary of a foreign language. Moreover, like the jargon that arises in all changing fields, it is always expanding. Think of the terms that have been added to our vocabulary in relation to computers, such as *software*, *search engine*, *flash drive*, *app*, and *blog*. The task may seem overwhelming, but there are methods to aid in learning and remembering words and even to help make informed guesses about unfamiliar words. Most medical terms can be divided into component parts—roots, prefixes, and suffixes—that maintain the same meaning whenever they appear. By learning these meanings, you can analyze and remember many words.

Word Parts

Word components fall into three categories:

1. The **root** is the fundamental unit of each medical word. It establishes the basic meaning of the word and is the part to which modifying word parts are added.
2. A **suffix** is a short word part or series of parts added at the end of a root to modify its meaning. This book indicates suffixes by a dash before the suffix, such as *-itis* (inflammation).

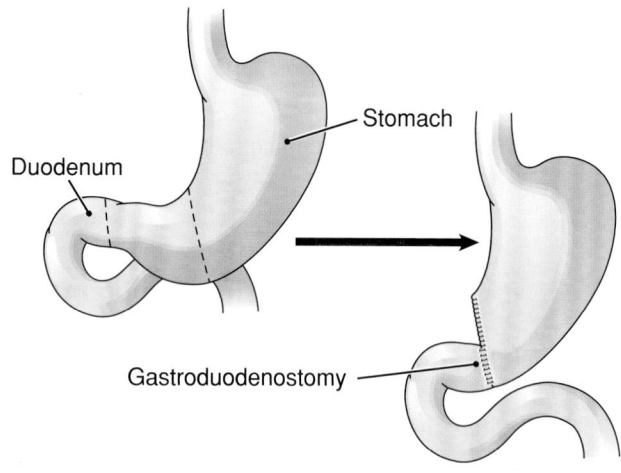

Figure 1-1   **Gastroduodenostomy.** A communication (-stomy) between the stomach (gastr) and the first part of the small intestine, or duodenum (duoden).

---

3. A **prefix** is a short word part added before a root to modify its meaning. This book indicates prefixes by a dash after the prefix, such as *pre-* (before).

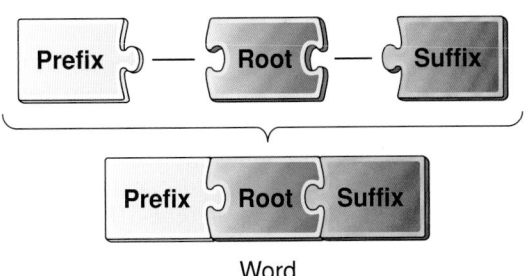

Words are formed from roots, suffixes, and prefixes.

The simple word *learn* can be used as a root to illustrate. If we add the suffix *-er* to form *learner*, we have "one who learns." If we add the prefix *re-* to form *relearn*, we have "to learn again."

Not all roots are complete words. In fact, most medical roots are derived from other languages and are meant to be used in combinations. The Greek word *kardia*, for example, meaning "heart," gives us the root *cardi*. The Latin word *pulmo*, meaning "lung," gives us the root *pulm*. In a few instances, both the Greek and Latin roots are used for the same structure. We find both the Greek root *nephr* and the Latin root *ren* used in words pertaining to the kidney (**Fig. 1-2**).

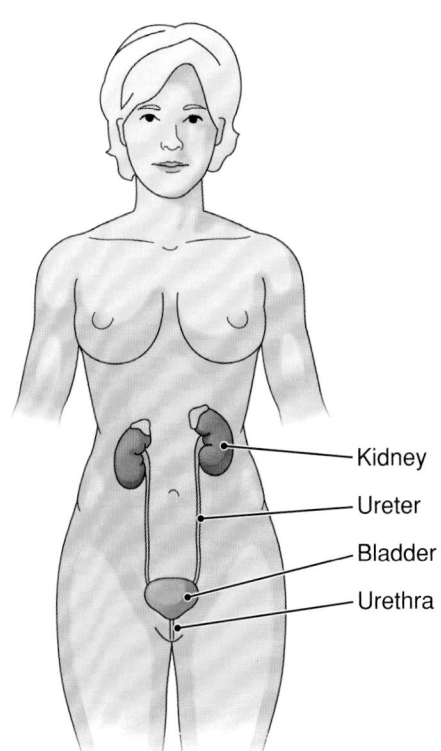

— Kidney
— Ureter
— Bladder
— Urethra

Figure 1-2 **Structures named with more than one word root.** Medical terminology uses both the Greek root *nephr* and the Latin root *ren* for the kidney, an organ of the urinary system.

Note that the same root may have different meanings in different fields of study, just as the words *web*, *spam*, *cloud*, *cookie*, and *tweet* have different meanings in common vocabulary than they do in "computerese." The root *myel* means "marrow" and may apply to either the bone marrow or the spinal cord. The root *scler* means "hard" but may also apply to the white of the eye. *Cyst* means "a filled sac or pouch" but also refers specifically to the urinary bladder. You will sometimes have to consider the context of a word before assigning its meaning. Health information technicians must be skilled in the use of medical language, as described in **Box 1-1**.

A **compound word** contains more than one root. The words *eyeball*, *bedpan*, *frostbite*, and *wheelchair* are examples. Some examples of compound medical words are *cardiovascular* (pertaining to the heart and blood vessels), *urogenital* (pertaining to the urinary and reproductive systems), and *lymphocyte* (a white blood cell found in the lymphatic system).

COMBINING FORMS

When a suffix or another root beginning with a consonant is added to a root, a vowel is inserted between the root and the next word part to aid in pronunciation. This combining vowel is usually an *o*, as seen in the previous example of gastroduodenostomy, but may occasionally be *a*, *e*, or *i*.

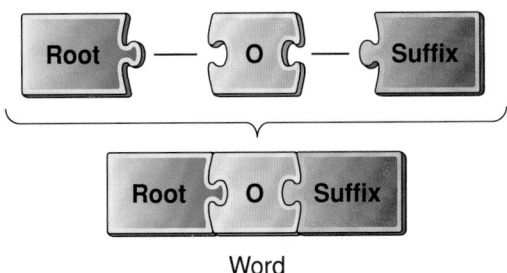

A combining vowel may be added between a root and a word part that follows.

Thus, when the suffix *-logy*, meaning "study of," is added to the root *neur*, meaning "nerve or nervous system," a combining vowel is added:

neur + o + logy = neurology (study of the nervous system)

Roots shown with a combining vowel are called **combining forms**.

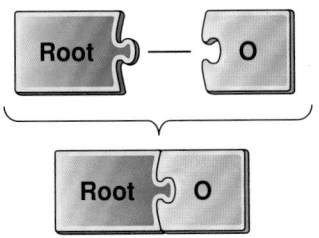

Combining form

A root with a combining vowel is called a combining form.

This text gives roots with their most common combining vowels added after a slash and refers to them simply as roots, as in *neur/o*. A combining vowel is usually not used if the ending begins with a vowel. For example, the root *neur* is combined with the suffix *-itis*, meaning "inflammation of," in this way:

neur + itis = neuritis (inflammation of a nerve)

This rule has some exceptions, particularly when they affect pronunciation or meaning, and you will observe these as you work.

Word Derivations

As mentioned, most medical word parts come from Greek (G.) and Latin (L.). The original words and their meanings are included in this text only occasionally. However, they are interesting and may aid in learning. For example, *muscle* comes from a Latin word that means "mouse" because the movement of a muscle under the skin was thought to resemble the scampering of a mouse. The coccyx, the tail end of the spine, is named for the cuckoo because it was thought to resemble the cuckoo's bill (**Fig. 1-3**). For those

interested in the derivations of medical words, a good medical dictionary will provide this information.

WORDS ENDING IN *x*

When you add a suffix to a word ending in *x*, the *x* is changed to a *g* or a *c*. If there is a consonant before the *x*, such as *yx* or *nx*, the *x* is changed to a *g*. For example, *pharynx* (throat) becomes *pharyngeal* (*fah-RIN-je-al*), to mean "pertaining to the throat;" *coccyx* (terminal portion of the spine) becomes *coccygeal* (*kok-SIJ-e-al*), to mean "pertaining to the coccyx."

If a vowel comes before the *x*, such as *ax* or *ix*, you change the *x* to a *c*. Thus, *thorax* (chest) becomes *thoracic* (*tho-RAS-ik*), to mean "pertaining to the chest;" and *cervix* (neck) becomes *cervical* (*SER-vih-kal*), to mean "pertaining to a neck."

SUFFIXES BEGINNING WITH *rh*

When you add a suffix beginning with *rh* to a root, the *r* is doubled. For example:

hem/o (blood) + -rhage (bursting forth) = hemorrhage
(a bursting forth of blood)

men/o (menses) + -rhea (flow, discharge) = menorrhea
(menstrual flow)

Pronunciation

This text provides phonetic pronunciations at every opportunity, even in the answer keys. The web resource, thePoint, has a large audio pronunciation dictionary. Take advantage of these aids. Repeat each word aloud as you learn to recognize it in print or hear it in the Student Resources.

No special marks are needed to follow the pronunciation if you keep a few simple rules in mind. Any vowel that appears at the end of a syllable gets a long pronunciation:

a as in say
e as in tea
i as in lie
o as in hose
u as in sue

Any vowel that appears within a syllable gets a short pronunciation:

a as in hat
e as in met
i as in bin
o as in not
u as in run

If a vowel is at the end of a syllable but needs a short pronunciation, an *h* is added, as in vah-nil-ah for vanilla. If a vowel within a syllable needs a long pronunciation, an *e* is added, as in re-pete for repeat. The accented syllable in each word is shown with capital letters, as in *AK-sent*.

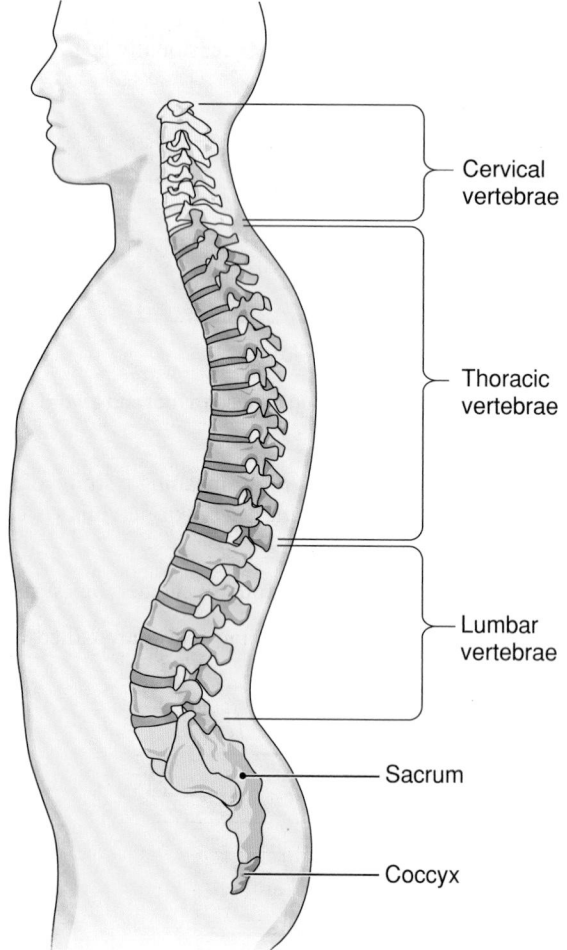

Cervical
vertebrae

Thoracic
vertebrae

Lumbar
vertebrae

Sacrum

Coccyx

Figure 1-3 **Word derivations.** The coccyx of the spine is named by its resemblance to a cuckoo's bill.

Box 1-2

FOCUS ON WORDS
Pronunciations

When pronunciations are included in a text, it is sometimes difficult for authors to know which pronunciation of a term to use. Pronunciations may vary from country to country and even in different regions of the same country. Think how easy it is to distinguish a Southern accent and one from the Midwest or Northeast United States. The general rule is to use the most common pronunciation or to list that pronunciation first if more than one is given.

The word *gynecology* is usually pronounced with a hard g in the United States, but in many areas, a soft g is used, as in *jin-eh-KOL-o-je*. Words pertaining to the cerebrum (largest part of the brain) may have an accent on different syllables.

The adjective is usually pronounced with the accent on the second syllable (*seh-RE-bral*), but in cerebrum (*SER-eh-brum*) and cerebrospinal (*ser-eh-bro-SPI-nal*), the accented syllable differs.

The name for the first part of the small intestine (duodenum) is often pronounced *du-o-DE-num*, although the pronunciation *du-OD-eh-num* is also acceptable. And the scientific term for the navel, umbilicus, is usually pronounced with the accent on the second syllable as *um-BIL-ih-kus*, but *um-bih-LI-kus* is also used. When extreme, some alternative pronunciations can sound like a foreign language. The word we pronounce as *SKEL-eh-tal* is pronounced in some other English-speaking countries as *skeh-LE-tal*.

Be aware that word parts may change in pronunciation when they are combined in different ways. Note also that accepted pronunciations may vary from place to place. Only one pronunciation for each word is given here, but be prepared for differences, as noted in **Box 1-2**.

SOFT AND HARD *c* AND *g*

- A soft *c*, as in *racer*, will be written in pronunciations as s (*RA-ser*).
- A hard *c*, as in *candy*, will be written as k (*KAN-de*).
- A soft *g*, as in *page*, will be written as j (*paje*).
- A hard *g*, as in *grow*, will be written as g (*gro*).

SILENT LETTERS AND UNUSUAL PRONUNCIATIONS

A silent letter or an unusual pronunciation can be a problem, especially if it appears at the start of a word that you are trying to look up in the dictionary. See **Box 1-3** for some examples.

The combinations in **Box 1-3** may be pronounced differently when they appear within a word, as in dia**g**nosis (*di-ag-NO-sis*), meaning determination of the cause of disease, in which the g is pronounced; a**p**nea (*AP-ne-ah*), meaning cessation of breathing, in which the *p* is pronounced; nephro**p**tosis (*nef-rop-TO-sis*), meaning dropping of the kidney, in which the *p* is pronounced.

Go to the Audio Pronunciation Glossary on the Point to hear medical terms pronounced.

LEARNING STYLES

The term *learning styles* describes how people differ in the senses on which they most depend to learn. Visual learners want to see a word in print. They like diagrams, charts, and pictures. Auditory learners need to hear words pronounced. They like to talk over what they have learned and benefit from listening again to recorded lessons. Tactile learners use touch, such as writing out answers or retyping notes. They like to follow demonstrations to learn a new skill.

Of course, we use all of our senses to some degree in learning, and the more channels we use, the more likely it is that we will absorb and remember new information. This text, in combination with the Student Resources, calls on multiple senses to aid learning: seeing new words in print, writing out answers, using flashcards, listening to pronunciations, and completing exercises on the computer. Unlike the fashion magazines that use perfumed ads to sell products, the olfactory sense has not yet been incorporated into textbooks. Perhaps someday Student Resources will have a smell feature!

Abbreviations

Shortened words or initials can save time in writing medical reports and case histories. We commonly use TV for television, Jr. for junior, F for Fahrenheit temperature readings, UV for ultraviolet, and Dr. for doctor. A few of the many medical abbreviations are mL for the metric measurement milliliter; dB for decibels, units of sound intensity; CA for cancer; hgb for hemoglobin; and ECG for electrocardiogram.

PHRASE ABBREVIATIONS

An **acronym** is an abbreviation formed from the first letter of each word in a phrase. Some everyday acronyms are ASAP (as soon as possible), ATM (automated teller machine), and a computer's RAM (random access memory). Acronyms have become popular for saving time and space in naming objects, organizations, and procedures. They abound in the names of government agencies: FDA (Food and Drug Administration), USDA (United States

FOR YOUR REFERENCE

Box 1-3

Silent Letters and Unusual Pronunciations

Letter(s)	Pronunciation	Example	Definition of Example
ch	k	chemical *KEM-ih-kal*	pertaining to the elements and their interactions (root *chem/o* means "chemical")
dys	dis	dysfunction *dis-FUNK-shun*	difficult or abnormal (dys-) function
eu	u	euphoria *u-FOR-e-ah*	exaggerated feeling of well-being (*eu-* means "true" or "good")
gn	n	gnathic *NATH-ik*	pertaining to the jaw (gnath/o)
ph	f	phantom *FAN-tom*	illusion or imaginary image
pn	n	pneumonia *nu-MO-ne-ah*	inflammation of the lungs (pneumon/o)
ps	s	pseudonym *SU-do-nim*	false name (-nym)
pt	t	ptosis *TO-sis*	dropping, downward displacement
rh	r	rhinoplasty *RI-no-plas-te*	plastic repair of the nose (rhin/o)
x	z	xiphoid *ZI-foyd*	pertaining to cartilage attached to the sternum (from Greek *xiphos*, meaning "sword")

Department of Agriculture), and NIH (National Institutes of Health). Some medical acronyms are BP for blood pressure, MRI for magnetic resonance imaging, AIDS for acquired immunodeficiency syndrome, CNS for the central nervous system, and RN for registered nurse. Acronyms and abbreviations that appear in a chapter are listed and defined at the end of that chapter. Appendix 2 is a more complete list of commonly used abbreviations and acronyms with their meanings. An abbreviation dictionary is also helpful.

SYMBOLS

Symbols are commonly used as shorthand in case histories. Some examples are Ⓛ and Ⓡ for left and right and ↑ and ↓ for increase and decrease. A list of common symbols appears in Chapter 7 and in Appendix 1.

Symbols and abbreviations can save time, but they can also cause confusion if they are not universally understood. Usage varies in different institutions, and the same abbreviation may have different meanings in different fields. For example, the acronym CRF can mean chronic renal failure or case report form, and MS can represent mitral stenosis or multiple sclerosis. Again, as with roots having multiple meanings, if the acronym is not defined, its interpretation depends on its context.

Some abbreviations and symbols are subject to error and should never be used. These appear in "Do Not Use"

lists published by organizations that promote patient safety, such as the Joint Commission on Accreditation of Healthcare Organizations (JCAHO) and the Institute for Safe Medical Practices (ISMP). Most institutions have a policy manual that details the accepted abbreviations for that facility. Only the most commonly used symbols and abbreviations are given here.

See the Student Resources on thePoint for a chart of selected "Do Not Use" abbreviations and the web addresses of organizations that publish these guidelines.

Medical Dictionaries

With few exceptions, you can do all the exercises in this book without the aid of a dictionary, but medical dictionaries are valuable references for everyone in health-related fields. These include not only complete, unabridged versions, but also easy-to-carry short versions and dictionaries of medical acronyms and abbreviations. Many of these dictionaries are also available on CD, on the internet, and also as applications for smartphones. Dictionaries give information on meanings, pronunciation, synonyms, derivations, and related terms. Those dictionaries intended for nursing and allied health professions include more complete clinical information, with notes on patient care.

Dictionaries vary in organization; in some, almost all terms are entered as nouns, such as disease, syndrome, procedure, or test. Those with a more clinical approach enter some terms according to their first word, which may be an adjective or proper name, for example, biomedical engineering, Cushing disease, and wind chill factor. This format makes it easier to look up some terms. All diction- aries have directions on how to use the book and interpret the entries, as shown in Appendix 9, taken from *Stedman's Medical Dictionary*, 28th ed.

In addition to information on individual terms and phrases, medical dictionaries have useful appendices on measurements, clinical tests, drugs, diagnosis, body struc- ture, information resources, and other topics.

Terminology Key Terms

acronym *AK-ro-nim*	An abbreviation formed from the first letter of each word in a phrase
combining forms *kom-BI-ning*	A word root combined with a vowel that links the root with another word part, such as a suffix or another root; combining forms are shown with a slash between the root and the vowel, as in *neur/o*
compound word *KOM-pownd*	A word that contains more than one root
prefix *PRE-fix*	A word part added before a root to modify its meaning
root *rute*	The fundamental unit of a word
suffix *SUH-fix*	A word part added to the end of a root to modify its meaning

Case Study Revisited

J.V.'s Case Study Follow-Up

J.V. was scheduled for an esophageal gastroduode- noscopy as an outpatient procedure. The gastroenter- ologist was able to visualize the esophagus and the inside of the stomach. The area around the esopha- geal sphincter was a normal pink in color and showed no signs of esophagitis or ulceration. J.V. was started on a proton pump inhibitor to reduce stomach acid and was advised to limit his intake of spicy foods and alcohol. At his follow-up appointment, he reported no repeat episodes of epigastric pain.

CHAPTER 1

Review

Fill in the Blanks

1. A word part that always comes after a root is a(n) _____.

2. A root with a vowel added to aid in pronunciation is called a(n) _____.

3. Combine the word parts *dia-*, meaning "through," and *-rhea*, meaning "flow," to form a word meaning "passage of fluid stool" _____.

4. The abbreviation ETOH means (refer to Appendix 2) _____.

5. Use Appendix 3 to find that the suffix in *gastroduodenoscopy*, seen in J.V.'s opening case study, means _____.

6. Combine the root *cardi*, meaning "heart," with the suffix *-logy*, meaning "study of," to form a word meaning "study of the heart" _____.

7. Use Appendix 6 at the back of the book to find that the suffix *-al*, as in *esophageal*, seen in J.V.'s case study follow-up means _____.

8. Appendix 1 shows that the symbol ↑ means _____.

MULTIPLE CHOICE

Select the best answer and write the letter of your choice to the left of each number.

_____ 9. *Epi-* in the term *epigastric* is a
   a. word root
   b. prefix
   c. suffix
   d. combining form

_____ 10. The *-oid* in the term *xiphoid* is a
   a. root
   b. prefix
   c. derivation
   d. suffix

_____ 11. The term *musculoskeletal* is a(n)
   a. abbreviation
   b. word root
   c. combining form
   d. compound word

_____ 12. The adjective for *larynx* is
   a. larynxic
   b. laryngeal
   c. larynal
   d. largeal

_____ 13. The combining form for *thorax* (chest) is
   a. thorax/o
   b. thor/o
   c. thorac/o
   d. thori/o

_____ **14.** In J.V.'s case study, the term GERD represents a(n)

    a. combining form

    b. acronym

    c. prefix

    d. suffix

_____ **15.** In the case study, the *ph* in dysphagia is pronounced as

    a. f

    b. p

    c. h

    d. s

PRONOUNCE THE FOLLOWING WORDS

16. dyslexia

17. rheumatism

18. pneumatic

19. chemist

20. pharmacy

Pronounce the following phonetic forms and write the words they represent.

21. *KAR-de-ak* _____

22. *HI-dro-jen* _____

23. *OK-u-lar* _____

24. *IN-ter-fase* _____

25. *ru-MAT-ik* _____

Word Building

Write words for the following definitions using the word parts provided. A combining vowel is included. Each word part can be used more than once.

| -itis | -logy | -ptosis | nephr | -o | -gastr | cardi | neur- |

26. Inflammation of the stomach _____

27. Study of the nervous system _____

28. Dropping of the kidney _____

29. Study of the kidney _____

30. Inflammation of a nerve _____

31. Downward displacement of the heart _____

Word Analysis

Define each of the following words, and give the meaning of the word parts in each. Use a dictionary if necessary.

32. dysmenorrhea (*dis-men-o-RE-ah*) _____

    a. dys _____

    b. men/o _____

    c. -rhea _____

33. cardiologist (*kar-de-OL-o-jist*) _____

    a. cardi/o _____

    b. -log/o _____

    c. -ist _____

34. nephritis (*nef-RI-tis*) _____

    a. nephr/o _____

    b. -itis _____

35. renogastric (*re-no-GAS-trik*) _____

    a. ren/o _____

    b. gastr/o _____

    c. -ic _____

For more learning activities, see Chapter 1 of the Student Resources on thePoint.

Additional Case Study

Case Study: D.S.'s Arthritic Knees

Chief Complaint

D.S., a 68 y/o male, presents to his family doctor c/o bilateral knee discomfort that worsens prior to a heavy rainstorm. He states that his "arthritis" is not getting any better. He has been taking NSAIDs but is not obtaining relief at this point. His family physician referred him to an orthopedic surgeon for further evaluation.

Past Medical History

D.S. was active in sports in high school and college. He tore his ACL while playing soccer during his junior year in college, at which time he retired from intercollegiate athletics. His only other physical complaint involves stiffness in his right shoulder, which he attributes to pitching while playing baseball in high school.

Current Medications

NSAIDs prn for arthritic pain; Lipitor 10 mg for mild hyperlipidemia.

X-Rays

Bilateral knee x-rays revealed moderate degenerative changes with joint space narrowing in the left knee; severe degenerative changes and joint space narrowing in the right knee.

Case Study Questions

Multiple Choice. Select the best answer, and write the letter of your choice to the left of each number.

_____ **1.** The *bi-* in the word *bilateral* is a
   a. suffix
   b. root
   c. prefix
   d. combining form

_____ **2.** The *-itis* in the word *arthritis* is a
   a. root
   b. prefix
   c. derivation
   d. suffix

_____ **3.** *Arthr/o* is a(n)
   a. combining form
   b. acronym
   c. prefix
   d. suffix

_____ **4.** The AI in the abbreviation NSAID means (see Appendix 2)
   a. antacid
   b. antiinflammatory
   c. antiinfectious
   d. after incident

Short Answer

5. Use Appendix 2 to find what the abbreviation *ACL* means.

_____

6. Use Appendix 2 to find what the abbreviation *c/o* means.

_____

7. Use Appendix 7 to find what the prefix *hyper-* means.

_____

8. Use Appendix 2 to find what the abbreviation *prn* means.

_____

9. Use Appendices 5, 6, and 7 to find what the word parts in *hyperlipidemia* mean.
   a. hyper- _____
   b. lip/o _____
   c. -emia _____

10. Use Appendix 3 to find what the word parts in *orthopedic* mean.
   a. orth/o _____
   b. ped/o _____

11. Use Appendix 7 to find what the prefix *inter-* means.

_____

▶ Pretest

Multiple Choice. Select the best answer, and write the letter of your choice to the left of each number.

_____ 1. The suffix in the word *hearing* is
   a. hear
   b. ring
   c. ing
   d. ear

_____ 2. The suffixes *-ism, -ia,* and *-ist* are found in
   a. verbs
   b. adjectives
   c. adverbs
   d. nouns

_____ 3. The suffixes *-ic, -ous, -al,* and *-oid* are found in
   a. adjectives
   b. nouns
   c. verbs
   d. roots

_____ 4. The suffix *-form* means
   a. excess
   b. origin
   c. resembling
   d. paired

_____ 5. The plural of *fungus* is
   a. fungi
   b. fungal
   c. fungae
   d. funga

_____ 6. The singular of *ova* (eggs) is
   a. ovi
   b. ovae
   c. ovum
   d. ovas

▶ Learning Objectives

After study of this chapter, you should be able to:

1 ▶ Define a suffix. *p16*

2 ▶ Give examples of how suffixes are used to convert terms into nouns, adjectives, and plurals. *p16*

3 ▶ Recognize and apply some general noun, adjective, and plural suffixes used in medical terminology. *p17*

4 ▶ Analyze the suffixes used in case studies. *pp15, 28*

Case Study: *R.F.'s Encounter with a Cerebral Aneurysm*

Chief Complaint
R.F., a 48-year-old financial analyst, has been complaining of atypical headaches for the past few weeks. With one of the headaches, she experienced vomiting that she could not attribute to the flu or something she had eaten. She does not have a history of migraines. R.F. had an appointment with a neurologist, who referred her to the neurosurgery clinic for evaluation of a possible cerebral hemorrhage.

Examination
Patient is a 48 y/o female c/o sudden and severe headaches over the past three to four weeks; one headache was accompanied with vomiting. Patient admits to recent photophobia and intermittent blurred vision. She has a history of venous thrombi (clots) following an emergency hip surgery for a fracture she suffered two years ago when she was in an automobile accident. Multiple vertebrae and her pelvis were also fractured. No other complications post-accident noted. Hypertensive with a BP of 154/86; neurologic and physical examination is otherwise normal. Diagnoses: hypertension and possible cerebral aneurysm.

Clinical Course
The neurologist ordered a CT scan that revealed a small saccular aneurysm measuring 4 mm near the cerebral arterial circle, the vascular pathway supplying the brain. R.F. was scheduled for a craniotomy and surgical insertion of a clip around the neck of the aneurysm to control bleeding and offer protection from rebleeding.

An aneurysm (*AN-yu-rizm*) is a bulge in a weakened arterial wall that can rupture and cause damage. An aneurysm is illustrated later in this chapter when we learn more about R.F.'s medical care. There is more information on aneurysms and their potential effects in Chapters 9 and 17.

ANCILLARIES *At-A-Glance*

Visit thePoint to access the following resources. For guidance in using the resources most effectively, see pp. ix–xvi.

Learning RESOURCES

▶ **Tips for Effective Studying**
▶ **Audio Pronunciation Glossary**

Learning ACTIVITIES

▶ **Visual Activities**
▶ **Kinesthetic Activities**
▶ **Auditory Activities**

Introduction

A suffix is a word ending that modifies a root. A suffix may indicate that the word is a noun or an adjective and often determines how the definition of the word will begin (**Box 2-1**). For example, using the root *myel/o*, meaning "bone marrow," the adjective ending *-oid* forms the word *myeloid*, which means "like or pertaining to bone marrow." The ending *-oma* forms *myeloma*, which is a tumor of the bone marrow. Adding another root, *gen*, which represents genesis or origin, and the adjective ending *-ous* forms the word *myelogenous*, meaning "originating in bone marrow."

The suffixes given in this chapter are general ones that are used throughout medical terminology. They include endings that form:

- Nouns: a person, place, or thing
- Adjectives: words that modify nouns
- Plurals: endings that convert single nouns to multiples

Additional suffixes will be presented in later chapters as they pertain to disease states, medical treatments, or specific body systems.

Noun Suffixes

The following general suffixes convert roots into nouns. Table 2-1 lists suffixes that represent different conditions. Note that the ending *-sis* may appear with different

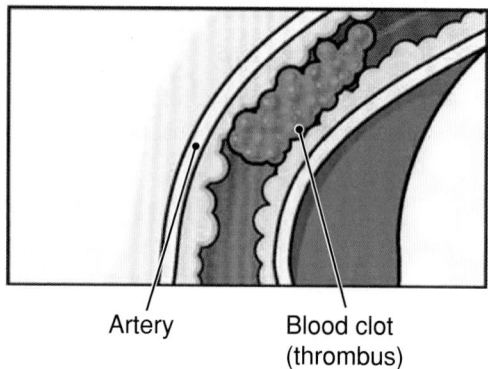

Artery — Blood clot (thrombus)

Figure 2-1 **Thrombosis.** This term refers to having a blood clot (thrombus) in a vessel. The word *thrombosis* has the noun suffix *-sis*, meaning "condition of."

FOCUS ON WORDS
Meaningful Suffixes

Box 2-1

Suffixes sometimes take on a color of their own as they are added to different words. The suffix *-thon* is taken from the name of the Greek town Marathon, from which news of a battle victory was carried by a long-distance runner. It has been attached to various words to mean a contest of great endurance. We have bike-a-thons, dance-a-thons, telethons, and even major charity fundraisers called thon-a-thons.

The adjective ending *-ish* is used, as in *boyish* or *childish*, to suggest traces of certain characteristics. People tack it onto words to indicate that they are estimates, not right on target, as in *forty-ish or blue-ish*. A vague time for a lunch appointment could be *noon-ish*.

In science and medicine, the ending *-tech* is used to imply high technology, as in the company name Genentech, and *-pure* may be added to inspire confidence, as in the naming of the Multi-Pure water filter. The ending *-mate* suggests helping, as in *helpmate*, defined in the dictionary as a helpful companion, more specifically, a wife, or sometimes, a husband. The medical device HeartMate is a pump used to assist a damaged heart.

Table 2-1   Suffixes that Mean "Condition of"

Suffix	Example	Definition of Example
-ia	dementia *de-MEN-she-ah*	loss of (de-) intellectual function (from L. *mentis*: mind)
-ism	racism *RA-sizm*	discrimination based on race
-sis	thrombosis *throm-BO-sis*	having a blood clot (thrombus) in a vessel (**Fig. 2-1**)
-y	atony *AT-o-ne*	lack (a-) of muscle tone

EXERCISE 2-1

Write the suffix that means "condition of" in the following words. Remember to use the phonetics to pronounce each word as you work through the exercises.

1. phobia (unfounded fear; from G. *phobos:* fear) _____
FO-be-ah

2. psoriasis (skin disease) _____
so-RI-ah-sis

3. egotism (exaggerated self-importance; from *ego:* self) _____
E-go-tizm

4. dystrophy (changes due to lack of nourishment; root: troph/o) _____
DIS-tro-fe

5. anesthesia (loss of sensation; root: esthesi/o) (**Fig. 2-2**) _____
an-es-THE-ze-ah

6. parasitism (infection with parasites or behaving as a parasite) _____
PAR-ah-sit-izm

7. stenosis (narrowing of a canal) _____
steh-NO-sis

8. tetany (sustained muscle contraction) _____
TET-ah-ne

9. diuresis (increased urination; root: ur/o) _____
di-u-RE-sis

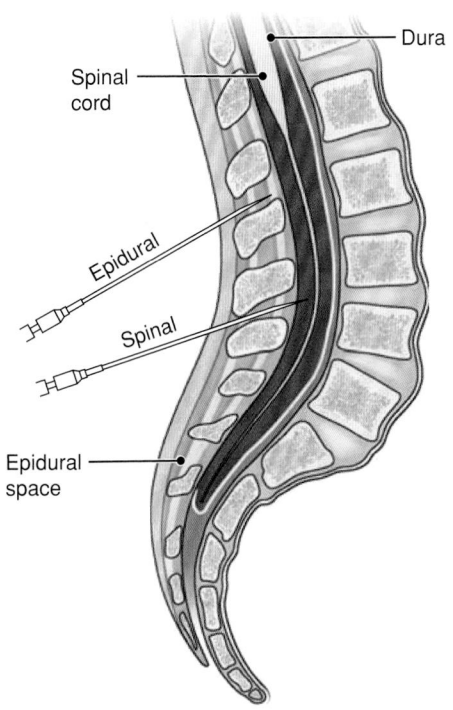

Figure 2-2 **Injection sites for anesthesia.** The word *anesthesia* uses the noun suffix *-ia,* meaning "condition of." The dura is a layer of the meninges, the membranes that cover the brain and spinal cord. One who administers anesthesia is an anesthetist or anesthesiologist.

combining vowels as *-osis*, *-iasis*, *-esis*, or *-asis*. The first two of these denote an abnormal condition.

Table 2-2 lists endings that convert roots into medical specialties or specialists. The suffix *-logy* applies to many fields other than medicine. It contains the root *log/o* taken from the Greek word *logos*, which means "word," and generally means a field of study. Some examples are biology, archeology, terminology, and technology, as in medical technology, described in **Box 2-2**. Terms with this ending are also used to identify an institutional department or a specialty, as in cardiology, dermatology, radiology, and others. The two endings *-iatrics* and *-iatry* contain the root *-iatr/o*, based on a Greek word for healing and meaning "physician" or "medical treatment."

Table 2-2	Suffixes for Medical Specialties

Suffix	Meaning	Example	Definition of Example
-ian	specialist in a field of study	physician *fih-ZISH-un*	practitioner of medicine (from root *physi/o*, meaning "nature")
-iatrics	medical specialty	pediatrics *pe-de-AT-riks*	care and treatment of children (ped/o) **(Fig. 2-3)**
-iatry	medical specialty	psychiatry *si-KI-ah-tre*	study and treatment of mental (psych/o) disorders
-ics	medical specialty	orthopedics *or-tho-PE-diks*	study and treatment of the skeleton and joints (from root *ped/o*, meaning "child," and prefix *ortho*, meaning "straight")
-ist	specialist in a field of study	podiatrist *po-DI-ah-trist*	one who studies and treats the foot (pod/o)
-logy	study of	physiology *fiz-e-OL-o-je*	study of function in a living organism (from root *physi/o*, meaning "nature")

EXERCISE 2-2

Write the suffix in the following words that means "study of," "medical specialty," or "specialist in a field of study."

1. cardiologist (specialist in the study and treatment of the heart; root: cardi/o)
kar-de-OL-o-jist   _____

2. neurology (the study of the nervous system; root: neur/o)
nu-ROL-o-je   _____

3. geriatrics (study and treatment of the aged; root: ger/e) **(Fig. 2-4)**
jer-e-AT-riks   _____

4. dermatology (study and treatment of the skin, or derma)
der-mah-TOL-o-je   _____

5. optician (one who makes and fits corrective lenses for the eyes; root: opt/o)
op-TISH-an   _____

6. anesthetist (one who administers anesthesia) (see **Fig. 2-2**)
ah-NES-theh-tist   _____

Write a word for a specialist in the following fields.

7. anatomy (study of body structure)
ah-NAT-o-me   _____

8. pediatrics (care and treatment of children; root: ped/o) (see **Fig. 2-3**)
pe-de-AT-riks   _____

9. radiology (use of radiation in diagnosis and treatment)
ra-de-OL-o-je   _____

2

10. psychology (study of the mind; root: psych/o)
    si-KOL-o-je
                                            _____

11. technology (practical application of science)
    tek-NOL-o-je
                                            _____

12. obstetrics (medical specialty concerning pregnancy and birth)
    ob-STET-riks
                                            _____

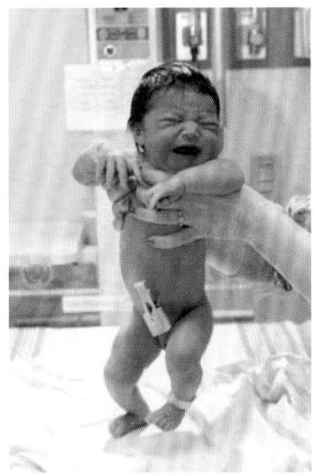

Figure 2-3   **Pediatrics is the care and treatment of children.**
The ending *-ics* indicates a medical specialty. In this photo, a pediatrician, one who practices pediatrics, is testing an infant's reflexes. The root *ped/o* means "child."

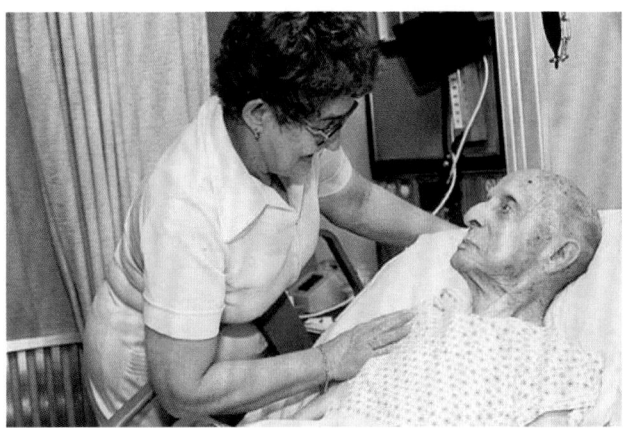

Figure 2-4   **Geriatrics is the care and treatment of the aged.**
A specialist in this field, a geriatrician, is shown.

HEALTH PROFESSIONS
Medical Laboratory Technology

Box 2-2

The field of medical laboratory technology includes a wide range of clinical sciences. The people who perform laboratory testing for the medical profession may follow either of two career paths. Clinical laboratory scientists (CLSs), also called medical technologists (MTs), require a bachelor's degree. Clinical laboratory technicians, also known as medical laboratory technicians, may practice with an associate degree. They may have more limited responsibilities and work under closer supervision than CLSs. Both training programs require internships in a laboratory following graduation.

According to the American Society of Clinical Pathology (ASCP), these healthcare professionals perform a variety of tasks from simple premarital blood tests to more complex tests for diseases, including HIV/AIDS, diabetes, and cancer. They examine specimens of human blood and tissue microscopically to look for microorganisms, such as bacteria and parasites, or cancerous cells.

They may match blood for transfusions and test blood for chemicals, drugs, and other substances. Physicians rely on the information they provide to determine a diagnosis and formulate a treatment plan for their patients. In addition, these laboratory professionals may evaluate test results; develop and modify laboratory procedures; and establish and monitor programs to ensure the accuracy of tests. They may work in several areas of the laboratory or specialize in one particular area such as immunology, microbiology, or molecular biology.

In the course of their work, they operate valuable equipment, including computers and precision instruments, such as high-powered microscopes and cell counters. Therefore, they must be proficient with instrumentation and electronic technology as well as science. Careers in medical laboratory sciences require completion of a CLS or medical technician program accredited by the National Accrediting Agency of Clinical Laboratory Science (NAA-CLS). Certification of medical laboratory technologists and technicians is required for licensure in some states and by some employers. A bachelor's degree and passing an exam may be required for licensure. For specific requirements, contact state departments of health or boards of occupational licensing.

Adjective Suffixes

The suffixes below are all adjective endings that mean "pertaining to," "like," or "resembling" (Table 2-3). There are no rules for which ending to use for a given noun. Familiarity comes with practice. When necessary, tips on proper usage are given in the text.

Note that for words ending with the suffix *-sis*, the first *s* is changed to a *t* before adding *-ic* to form the adjective, as in genetic, pertaining to genesis (origin); psychotic, pertaining to psychosis (a mental disorder); or diuretic, pertaining to diuresis (increased urination).

Table 2-3	Suffixes that Mean "Pertaining to," "Like," or "Resembling"	
Suffix	**Example**	**Definition of Example**
-ac	cardiac *KAR-de-ak*	pertaining to the heart
-al	vocal *VO-kal*	pertaining to the voice
-ar	nuclear *NU-kle-ar*	pertaining to a nucleus
-ary	salivary *SAL-ih-var-e*	pertaining to saliva
-form	muciform *MU-sih-form*	like or resembling mucus
-ic	anatomic *an-ah-TOM-ik*	pertaining to anatomy **(Fig. 2-5)**
-ical (ic + al)	electrical *e-LEK-trih-kal*	pertaining to electricity
-ile	virile *VIR-il*	pertaining to the male, masculine
-oid	lymphoid *LIM-foyd*	pertaining to the lymphatic system
-ory	circulatory *SIR-ku-lah-tor-e*	pertaining to circulation
-ous	cutaneous *ku-TA-ne-us*	pertaining to the skin (from L. *cutis*: skin)

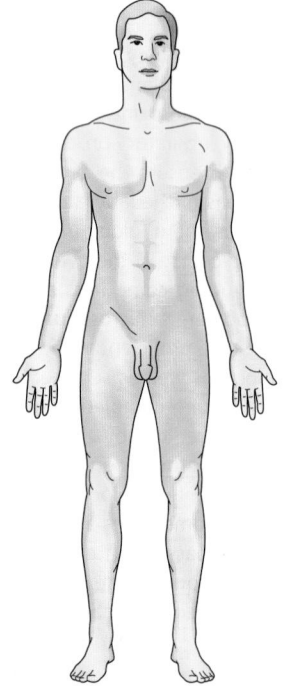

Figure 2-5 **The anatomic position.** This posture is standard in the study of anatomy. A person in this position is facing forward with arms at the side and palms forward (anterior). The adjective suffix *-ic* means "pertaining to."

EXERCISE 2-3

Identify the suffix meaning "pertaining to," "like," or "resembling" in the following words.

1. dietary (pertaining to the diet)
   DI-eh-tar-e   _____

2. neuronal (pertaining to a nerve cell, or neuron) (**Fig 2-6**)
   NU-ro-nal   _____

3. metric (pertaining to a meter or measurement; root metr/o means "measure")
   MEH-trik   _____

4. venous (pertaining to a vein; root: ven/o)
   VE-nus   _____

5. epileptiform (like or resembling epilepsy)
   ep-ih-LEP-tih-form   _____

6. toxoid (like or resembling a toxin, or poison)
   TOK-soyd   _____

7. topical (pertaining to a surface)
   TOP-ih-kal   _____

8. febrile (pertaining to fever)
   FEB-rile   _____

9. neurotic (pertaining to neurosis, a mental disorder)
   nu-ROT-ik   _____

10. surgical (pertaining to surgery)
   SUR-jih-kal   _____

11. muscular (pertaining to a muscle)
   MUS-ku-lar   _____

12. urinary (pertaining to urine; root: ur/o)
   U-rih-nar-e   _____

13. respiratory (pertaining to respiration)
   RES-pih-rah-tor-e   _____

14. pelvic (pertaining to the pelvis) (**Fig. 2-7**)
   PEL-vik   _____

15. saccular (pouch-like, resembling a small sac)
   SAK-u-lar   _____

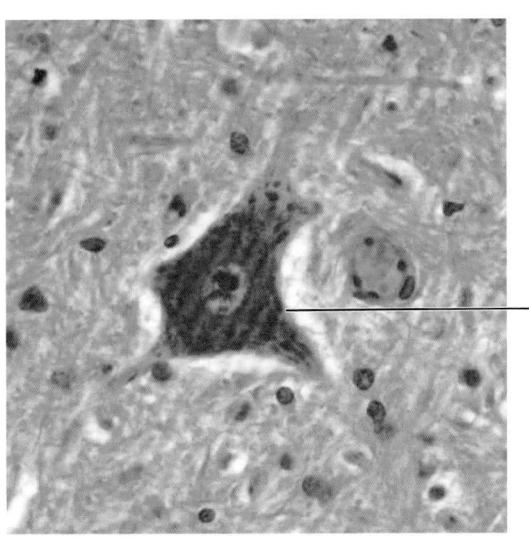 — Neuron

Figure 2-6 **A neuron is a nerve cell.**
The adjective form of *neuron* is *neuronal.*

Forming Plurals

Many medical words have special plural forms based on the ending of the word. Table 2-4 gives some general rules for the formation of plurals along with examples. The plural endings listed in the second column are substituted for the word endings in the first column. Note that both singular endings *-on* and *-um* change to *-a* for the plural. You have to learn which singular ending to use for specific words when converting a plural word ending in *-a* to the singular.

Table 2-4	Plural Endings		
Word Ending	**Plural Ending**	**Singular Example**	**Plural Example**
a	ae	vertebra (bone of the spine) *VER-teh-brah*	vertebrae (**Fig. 2-8**) *VER-teh-bre*
en	ina	lumen (central opening) *LU-men*	lumina (**Fig. 2-9**) *LU-min-ah*
ex, ix, yx	ices	matrix (background substance; mold) *MA-triks*	matrices *MA-trih-seze*
is	es	diagnosis (determination of a disease or defect) *di-ag-NO-sis*	diagnoses *di-ag-NO-seze*
ma	mata	stigma (mark or scar) *STIG-mah*	stigmata *stig-MAT-ah*
nx (anx, inx, ynx)	nges	phalanx (bone of finger or toe) *fah-LANKS*	phalanges (**Fig. 2-10**) *fah-LAN-jeze*
on	a	ganglion (mass of nervous tissue) *GANG-le-on*	ganglia *GANG-le-ah*
um	a	serum (thin fluid) *SE-rum*	sera *SE-rah*
us	i	thrombus (see **Fig. 2-1**) *THROM-bus*	thrombi *THROM-bi*

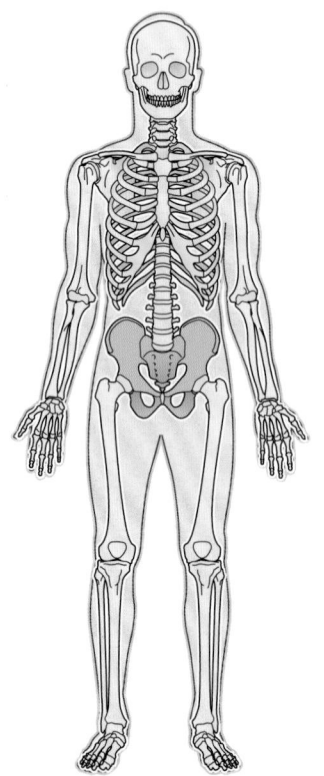

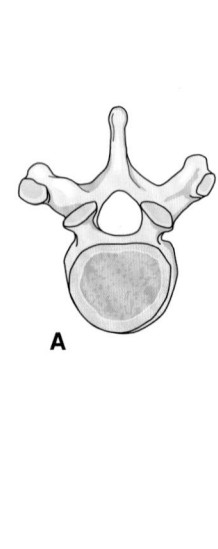

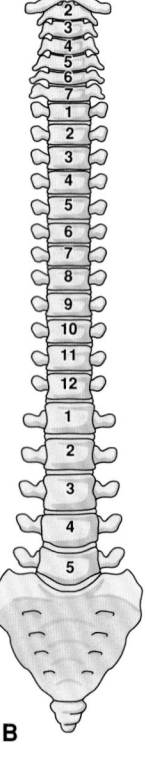

Figure 2-7   **The pelvis is the bony hip girdle.** The adjective form of pelvis is *pelvic*.

Figure 2-8   **Bones of the spine. A.** Each bone of the spine is a vertebra. **B.** The spinal column is made of 26 vertebrae.

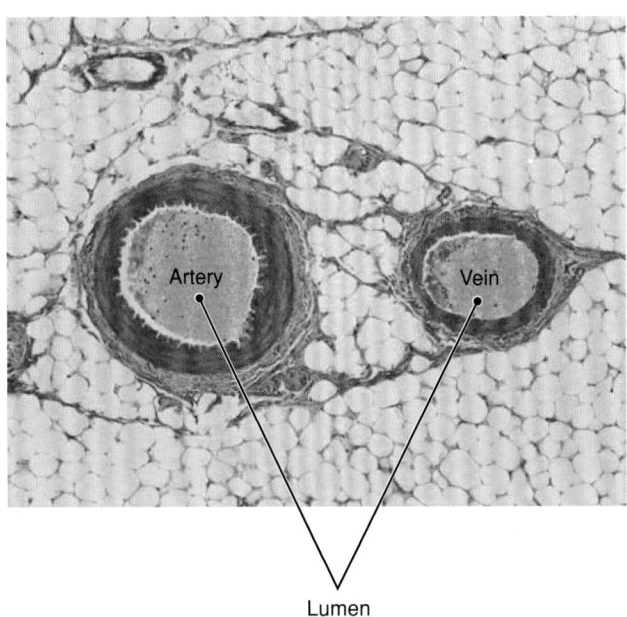

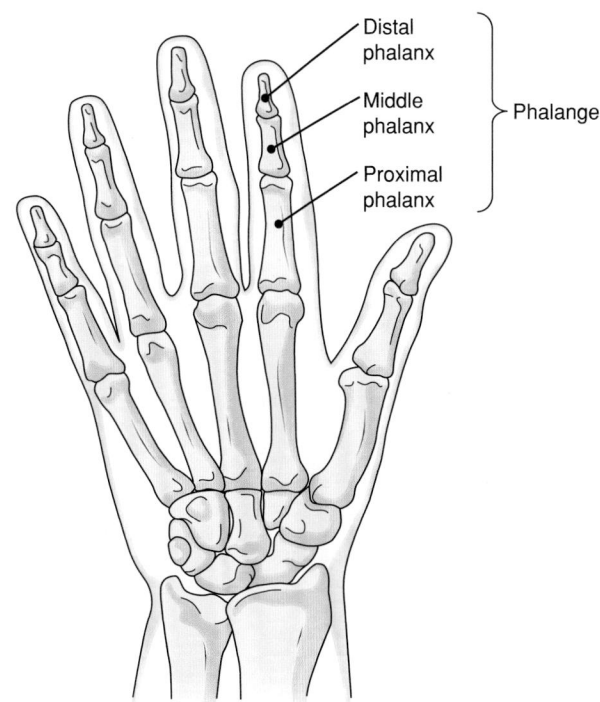

Figure 2-9 A lumen is the central opening of an organ or **vessel.** Two blood vessels are shown, an artery and a vein. The plural of lumen is *lumina*.

Figure 2-10 **Bones of the right hand (anterior view).** Each bone of a finger or toe is a phalanx. Each hand has 15 phalanges.

EXERCISE 2-4

Write the plural form of the following words. The word ending is underlined in each.

1. patell<u>a</u> (kneecap)
pah-TEL-ah

_____

2. phenomen<u>on</u> (occurrence or perception)
feh-NOM-eh-non

_____

3. oment<u>um</u> (abdominal membrane)
o-MEN-tum

_____

4. progno<u>sis</u> (prediction of disease outcome)
prog-NO-sis

_____

5. ap<u>ex</u> (tip or peak)
A-peks

_____

6. ov<u>um</u> (female reproductive cell; egg)
O-vum

_____

7. spermatozo<u>on</u> (male reproductive cell; sperm cell)
sper-mah-to-ZO-on

_____

8. meni<u>nx</u> (membrane around the brain and spinal cord)
MEH-ninks

_____

9. embol<u>us</u> (blockage in a vessel)
EM-bo-lus

_____

(continued)

EXERCISE 2-4   *(Continued)*

Write the singular form of the following words. The word ending is underlined in each.

10. protoz<u>oa</u> (single-celled animals)
pro-to-ZO-ah

_____

11. append<u>ices</u> (things added)
ah-PEN-dih-seze

_____

12. adeno<u>mata</u> (tumors of glands)
ad-eh-NO-mah-tah

_____

13. fung<u>i</u> (simple, nongreen plants)
FUN-ji

_____

14. pelv<u>es</u> (cup-shaped cavities)
PEL-veze

_____

15. foram<u>ina</u> (openings, passageways)
fo-RAM-ih-na

_____

16. curricul<u>a</u> (series of courses)
kur-RIK-u-lah

_____

17. ind<u>ices</u> (directories, lists)
IN-dih-seze

_____

18. alveol<u>i</u> (small sacs)
al-VE-o-li

_____

SOME EXCEPTIONS TO THE RULES

There are exceptions to the rules given for forming plurals, some of which will appear in later chapters. For example, the plural of *sinus* (space) is *sinuses*, the plural of *virus* is *viruses*, and *serums* (thin fluids) is sometimes used instead of *sera*. An *-es* ending may be added to words ending in *-ex* or *-ix* to form a plural, as in *appendixes*, *apexes*, and *indexes*.

Some incorrect plural forms are in common usage, for example, *stigmas* instead of *stigmata*, *referendums* instead of *referenda*, *stadiums* instead of *stadia*. Often people use *phalange* instead of *phalanx* as the singular of *phalanges*. Words ending in *-oma*, meaning "tumor," should be changed to *-omata*, but most people just add an *s* to form the plural. For example, the plural of *carcinoma* (a type of cancer) should be *carcinomata*, but *carcinomas* is commonly used.

Case Study Revisited

R.F.'s Postoperative Follow-Up

R.F. underwent a craniotomy in which a special clip was placed around the neck of the aneurysm. She was closely observed for postoperative neurologic deficits, including vascular spasm, a serious possible complication. She tolerated the procedure well with no complications.

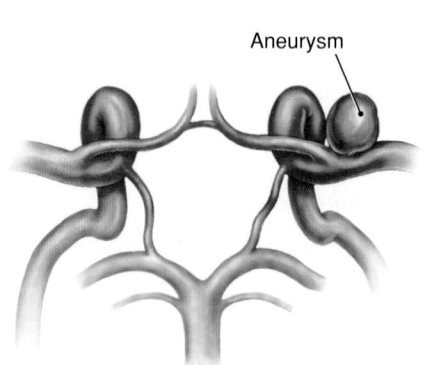

Aneurysm

Cerebral arterial circle

CHAPTER

2

Review

Identify the suffix that means "condition of" in the following words.

1. alcoholism (*AL-ko-hol-izm*) (alcohol dependence) _____

2. insomnia (*in-SOM-ne-ah*) (inability to sleep; root: somn/o) _____

3. acidosis (*as-ih-DO-sis*) (acid body condition) _____

4. dysentery (*DIS-en-ter-e*) (intestinal disorder; root: enter/o) _____

5. psychosis (*si-KO-sis*) (disorder of the mind) _____

6. anemia (*ah-NE-me-ah*) (lack of blood or hemoglobin; root: hem/o) _____

Give the suffix in the following words that means "specialty" or "specialist."

7. psychiatry (*si-KI-ah-tre*) _____

8. orthopedics (*or-tho-PE-diks*) _____

9. anesthesiologist (*an-es-the-ze-OL-o-jist*) _____

10. technician (*tek-NISH-un*) _____

11. anatomist (*ah-NAT-o-mist*) _____

12. obstetrician (*ob-steh-TRISH-un*) _____

Give the name of a specialist in the following fields.

13. dermatology (*der-mah-TOL-o-je*) _____

14. pediatrics (*pe-de-AH-triks*) _____

15. physiology (*fiz-e-OL-o-je*) _____

16. gynecology (*gi-neh-KOL-o-je*) _____

Identify the adjective suffix in the following words that means "pertaining to," "like," or "resembling."

17. basic (*BA-sik*) _____

18. oral (*OR-al*) _____

19. anxious (*ANG-shus*) _____

20. fibroid (*FI-broyd*) _____

21. circular (*SIR-ku-lar*) _____

22. arterial (*ar-TE-re-al*) _____

23. pelvic (*PEL-vik*) _____

24. binary (*BI-nar-e*) _____

25. skeletal (*SKEL-eh-tal*) _____

26. rheumatoid (*RU-mah-toyd*) _____

27. febrile (*FEB-rile*) _____

28. surgical (*SUR-jih-kal*) _____

29. vascular (*VAS-ku-lar*) _____

30. exploratory (*ek-SPLOR-ah-tor-e*) _____

Write the plural for the following words. Each word ending is underlined.

31. gingiv<u>a</u> (gums) _____

    JIN-jih-vah

32. test<u>is</u> (male reproductive organ) _____

    TEST-is

33. criter<u>ion</u> (standard) _____

    kri-TIR-e-on

34. lum<u>en</u> (central opening) _____

    LU-men

35. loc<u>us</u> (place) _____

    LO-kus

36. gangli<u>on</u> (mass of nervous tissue) _____

    GANG-le-on

37. lary<u>nx</u> (voice box) _____

    LAR-inks

38. ven<u>a</u> (vein) _____

    VE-nah

39. nucle<u>us</u> (center; core) _____

    NU-kle-us

Write the singular form for the following words. Each word ending is underlined.

40. thromb<u>i</u> (blood clots) _____

    THROM-bi

41. vertebr<u>ae</u> (bones of the spine) _____

    VER-teh-bre

42. bacteri<u>a</u> (type of microorganism) _____

    bak-TE-re-ah

43. alveol<u>i</u> (air sacs) _____

    al-VE-oli

44. ap<u>ices</u> (high points, tips) _____

    A-pih-seze

45. foram<u>ina</u> (openings) _____

    fo-RAM-ih-nah

46. diagn<u>oses</u> (identifications of disease) _____

    di-ag-NO-seze

47. carcino<u>mata</u> (cancers) _____

    kar-sih-NO-mah-tah

Word Building

Write a word for the following definitions using the word parts provided. Each may be used more than once.

> -ist   -ic   parasit   -ism   -y   log   -o-

48. pertaining to parasites   _____

49. study of parasites   _____

50. a condition of having parasites _____

51. One who studies parasites   _____

Word Analysis

Define each of the following words, and give the meaning of the word parts in each. Use a dictionary if necessary.

52. geriatrician (*jer-e-ah-TRIH-shun*) _____

    a. ger/e _____

    b. iatr/o _____

    c. -ic _____

    d. -ian _____

53. anesthesia (*an-es-THE-ze-ah*) _____

    a. an- _____

    b. esthesi/o _____

    c. -ia _____

54. photophobia (*fo-to-FO-be-ah*) _____

    a. phot/o _____

    b. phob (from Greek *phobos*) _____

    c. -ia _____

For more learning activities, see Chapter 2 of the Student Resources on thePoint.

Case Study: *C.R.'s Job-Related Breathing Problems*

Chief Complaint

C.R., a 54 y/o woman, has been having difficulty breathing (dyspnea) that was originally attributed to a left upper lobe (LUL) pneumonia. She was treated with an antibiotic, and after no improvement was noted in her breathing, C.R. had a follow-up chest x-ray that revealed a small LUL pneumothorax. She was referred to the respiratory clinic and saw Dr. Williams, a pulmonologist.

Past Medical History

C.R. has a history of smoking a pack a day for 30 years and stopped two years ago. She noticed an improvement in her breathing and tired less easily after she quit. About one month ago, she complained of general malaise, dyspnea, and a productive cough; she was expectorating pus-containing (purulent) sputum and was febrile. The chest radiograph and sputum cultures indicate that her symptoms had progressed into a bronchopneumonia with pulmonary edema complicated by a small pneumothorax in the LUL. A pea-size mass was identified in the left lobe. Also noted, C.R. is a hairstylist as well as a manicurist and recently went back to work in a beauty salon. She has complained that the fumes from the hair chemicals and nail products affect her breathing.

Clinical Course

Dr. Williams performed a bronchoscopic examination. During the examination, he took a biopsy of the mass, and the results were negative. Sputum cultures were also taken to determine the spectrum of action of an appropriate antibiotic. A respiratory therapist measured the patient's respiratory volumes and recorded any changes. The patient was told to drink plenty of liquids, get proper rest, and refrain from working for one week. She was told to wear a mask when she returned to work, avoid unventilated areas in the salon, and avoid the chemical fumes as much as possible. She is to return to the clinic in one month for follow-up.

Case Study Questions

Multiple Choice. Select the best answer, and write the letter of your choice to the left of each number.

_____ **1.** The *gh* in the terms cough and radiograph is pronounced as

    a. g

    b. h

    c. f

    d. s

_____ **2.** The *pn* in the term bronchopneumonia is pronounced as

    a. p

    b. n

    c. f

    d. s

_____ **3.** Which of the following is a compound word?

    a. pulmonary

    b. pneumothorax

    c. respiratory

    d. antibiotic

_____ **4.** The suffix that means "condition of" in *pneumonia* is

    a. -nia

    b. -monia

    c. -ia

    d. -onia

_____ **5.** The plural of *spectrum* is

    a. spectra

    b. spectria

    c. spectrina

    d. spectrums

Short Answer. Answer the following questions based on the case study of the patient C.R.

6. Find four words in the case study with a suffix that means "specialist in a field."

1. _____

2. _____

3. _____

4. _____

7. Find five words in the case study with suffixes that mean "pertaining to, like, or resembling," and write both the suffix and the word that contains it.

Suffix	Word
1. _____	_____
2. _____	_____
3. _____	_____
4. _____	_____
5. _____	_____

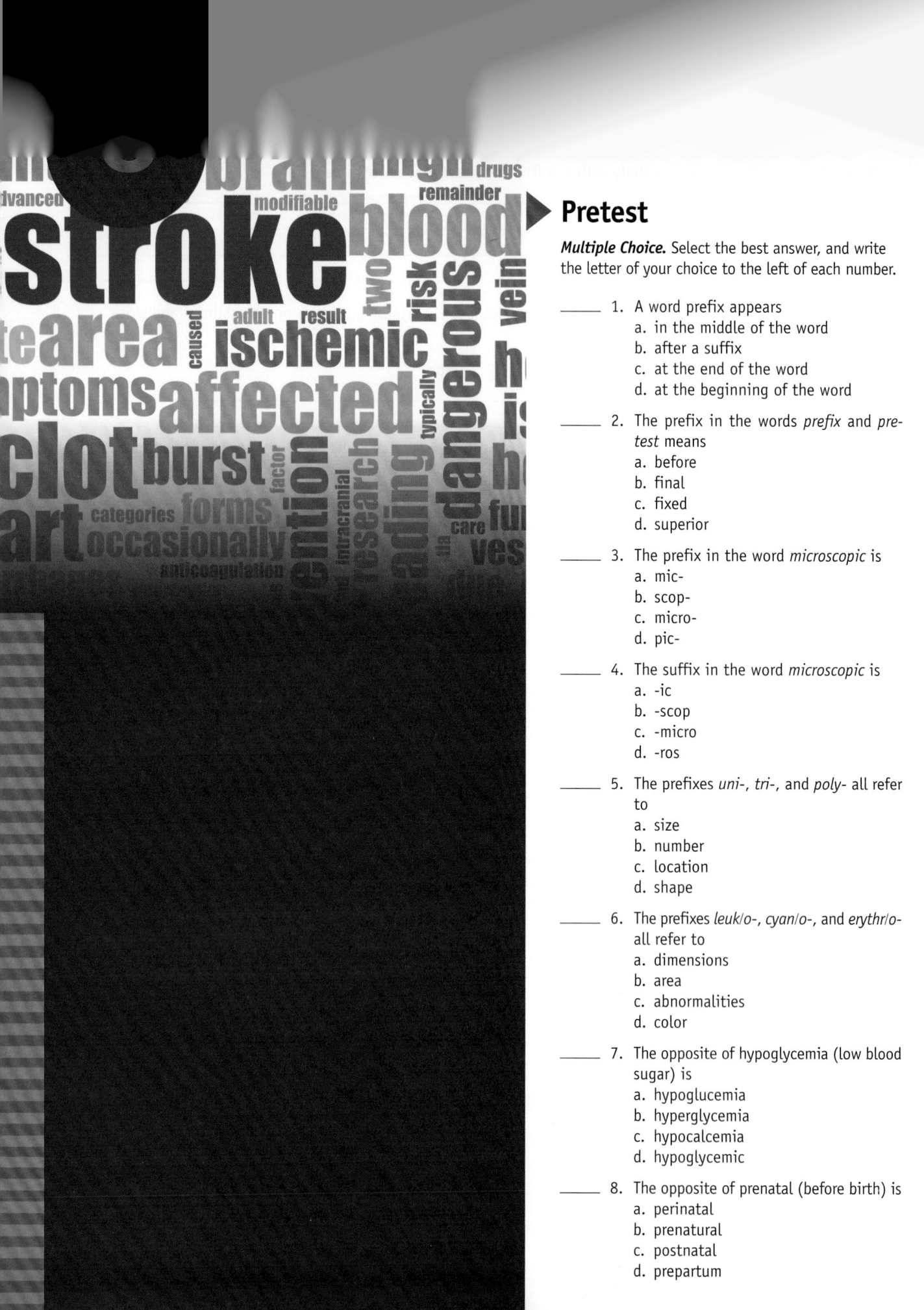

Pretest

Multiple Choice. Select the best answer, and write the letter of your choice to the left of each number.

_____ 1. A word prefix appears
   a. in the middle of the word
   b. after a suffix
   c. at the end of the word
   d. at the beginning of the word

_____ 2. The prefix in the words *prefix* and *pretest* means
   a. before
   b. final
   c. fixed
   d. superior

_____ 3. The prefix in the word *microscopic* is
   a. mic-
   b. scop-
   c. micro-
   d. pic-

_____ 4. The suffix in the word *microscopic* is
   a. -ic
   b. -scop
   c. -micro
   d. -ros

_____ 5. The prefixes *uni-*, *tri-*, and *poly-* all refer to
   a. size
   b. number
   c. location
   d. shape

_____ 6. The prefixes *leuk/o-*, *cyan/o-*, and *erythr/o-* all refer to
   a. dimensions
   b. area
   c. abnormalities
   d. color

_____ 7. The opposite of hypoglycemia (low blood sugar) is
   a. hypoglucemia
   b. hyperglycemia
   c. hypocalcemia
   d. hypoglycemic

_____ 8. The opposite of prenatal (before birth) is
   a. perinatal
   b. prenatural
   c. postnatal
   d. prepartum

▶ Learning Objectives

After study of this chapter, you should be able to:

1 ▶ Define a prefix, and explain how prefixes are used. *p32*

2 ▶ Identify and define some of the prefixes used in medical terminology. *p33*

3 ▶ Use prefixes to form words used in medical terminology. *p34*

4 ▶ Analyze the prefixes used in case studies. *pp31, 46*

Case Study: *T.S.'s Diving Accident and Spinal Cord Injury*

Chief Complaint

A 12-year-old male, T.S., was transported to the emergency room after diving into a shallow backyard cement pool. He c/o severe head and neck pain and has minimal movement of his arms. He is not able to move his legs.

Examination

A well-nourished 12-year-old male is awake and oriented, initially hypotensive and bradycardic, but vital signs are stabilizing. He reports being at a backyard pool party for his friend's birthday and remembers diving into the pool head first. The next thing he recalls is waking up on the deck of the pool with his friends standing all around him. He has a large erythematous and bruised area centered on the upper part of the forehead. T.S. has full head and neck movement with fair muscle strength. He has weak shoulder movement and is able to slightly flex his elbows and extend his wrists. His legs are areflexic and flaccid. He has no finger movement. Past medical history is noncontributory.

Clinical Course

T.S. is diagnosed with a burst or comminuted fracture of the C6 vertebra that may potentially result in quadriplegia. After surgical stabilization of the cervical fracture, T.S. was transferred to the spinal cord unit where his vital signs could be monitored closely along with frequent assessments for orthostatic hypotension and possible complications following spinal surgery. He will be moved to a rehabilitation center in about two weeks for physical and occupational therapy. His medical team consists of his primary physician (pediatrician), a neurosurgeon, a neurologist, and a physical medicine and rehabilitation (PM&R) specialist. T.S.'s condition will require a full complement of healthcare team members, including nurses, psychologists, physical and occupational therapists, pharmacists, and social workers.

A spinal cord injury can result in psychologic as well as permanent physical damage, as noted in T.S.'s follow-up study later in this chapter. There is more information on the spinal cord and behavioral disorders in Chapter 17.

ANCILLARIES *At-A-Glance*

Visit thePoint to access the following resources. For guidance in using the resources most effectively, see pp. ix–xvi.

Learning RESOURCES

▶ **Tips for Effective Studying**
▶ **Audio Pronunciation Glossary**

Learning ACTIVITIES

▶ **Visual Activities**
▶ **Kinesthetic Activities**
▶ **Auditory Activities**

Introduction

A prefix is a short word part added before a word or word root to modify its meaning. For example, the word *lateral* means "side." Adding the prefix *uni-*, meaning "one," forms *unilateral*, which means "affecting or involving one side." Adding the prefix *contra-*, meaning "against or opposite," forms *contralateral*, which refers to an opposite side. The term *equilateral* means "having equal sides." Prefixes in this book are followed by dashes to show that word parts are added to the prefix to form a word.

This chapter introduces most of the prefixes used in medical terminology in Tables 3-1 to 3-8. Although the list is long,

almost all of the prefixes you will need to work through this book are presented here. Some additional prefixes, including those related to disease, are given in several later chapters. The meanings of many of the prefixes in this chapter are familiar to you from words that are already in your vocabulary, as shown in **Box 3-1**. You may not know all the words in the exercises, but make your best guess. The words in the tables are given as examples of usage. Almost all of them reappear in other chapters. If you forget a prefix as you work, you may refer to this chapter or to the alphabetical lists of word parts and their meanings in Appendices 3 and 4. Appendix 7 lists prefixes only.

All medical personnel are familiar with these prefixes. To learn about one popular field, nursing, see **Box 3-2**.

FOCUS ON WORDS
Prefix Shorthand

Many prefixes catch on rapidly as a form of shorthand. In everyday life, the prefix *e-* for electronic has spread to words such as e-mail, e-commerce, e-zine, e-waste, and others. *X-* for extreme appears in X-games and other X-sports. The prefix *tel/e-*, meaning "far," is a shorthand indicating events occurring at a distance in words like telecommunications, telemetry, telediagnosis, and the term for extrasensory perception, telepathy.

The prefix *nan/o-* means "one billionth" but is used more generally in terms related to very small particles, such as nanotechnology. It also appears in the names of lotions and cosmetics that have ultrafine particles (nanoparticles) among their ingredients. *Steri-* implies sterility, or at least cleanliness. It

is used for naming Steri-Strip bandages and for other protective medical products and cleaning materials.

The prefix *endo-* in the names of surgical instruments signifies endoscopic instruments that are long and thin and have small working tips for use in areas where there is minimal access. Some examples are endoscissors, endosuture, endocautery, and endosnare.

Healthcare products designed for specific age groups are also encoded by prefixes. *Geri-*, pertaining to old age, as in geriatrics, appears in geri-chair, geri-pads, geri-jacket, and the patent medicine Geritol, among others. *Pedi-* or *pedia-*, meaning "child," is found in the names pedi-cath, pedi-dose, pedi-set (instruments), and Pedialyte, a product used for children to replace fluid and electrolytes.

HEALTH PROFESSIONS
Registered Nurse

Careers in nursing are the most diverse of all healthcare occupations and have the greatest number of practitioners. About 60 percent of nursing jobs are in hospitals, and other sites include offices, clinics, hospices, homes, and private companies. Within these settings, nurses may concentrate on particular specialties, such as emergency or critical care, surgery, psychiatry, and pediatric (child) or geriatric (elderly) care. Registered nurses (RNs) usually engage in direct patient contact, and they provide education; deliver health and wellness coaching; offer emotional support; maintain patient records and data registries; help with diagnostic testing; and provide follow-up and rehabilitative care. On a wider scale, they may work in industry, correctional facilities, and schools. They may also work in public health, run health screening or immunization centers, manage blood drives, or coordinate research trials.

The three possible educational pathways that lead to a nursing career are a four-year bachelor's degree (BSN), a two- to three-year associate degree (ADN) from a community or junior college, or a two- to three-year diploma from a hospital nursing program. Whereas the majority of nurses graduate from an accredited ADN or BSN program, there are still a limited number of hospital diploma programs that prepare students for a

nursing career. Courses include liberal arts, sciences, behavioral sciences, and nursing. All programs include supervised clinical training in a healthcare facility. All graduates must pass a national examination, the NCLEX-RN, to obtain a license to practice.

Some people in this field start their careers as practical nurses or nurse's aides and then return to school for an RN degree. Others may begin with an associate degree or diploma and then enroll in a bachelor's degree program while working, often receiving tuition reimbursement from their employers. There are also accelerated programs for those with degrees in other fields who wish to make a career change into nursing.

RNs who want to advance further in their careers and work more independently can train as nurse anesthetists, nurse midwives, clinical nurse specialists, or nurse practitioners (who can provide primary care and, in some states, prescribe medications). Careers as nursing educators and administrators also require advanced training. The job outlook for nursing is extremely good, especially in medically underserved areas, case management, nurse informatics, and in-home healthcare. Sources of information on nursing careers include the National League for Nursing at www.nln.org, the American Association of Colleges of Nursing at www.aacn.nche.edu, and the American Nurses Association at http://nursingworld.org.

Table 3-1 Prefixes for Numbers[a]

Prefix	Meaning	Example	Definition of Example
prim/i-	first	primary PRI-mar-e	first
mon/o-	one	monocular mon-OK-u-lar	having one eyepiece or affecting one eye
uni-	one	unite u-NITE	form into one part
hemi-	half, one side	hemisphere HEM-ih-sfere	one-half of a rounded structure (**Fig. 3-1**)
semi-	half, partial	semipermeable sem-e-PER-me-ah-bl	partially permeable (capable of being penetrated)
bi-	two, twice	binary BI-nar-e	made up of two parts
di-	two, twice	diatomic di-ah-TOM-ik	having two atoms
dipl/o-	double	diplococci dip-lo-KOK-si	round bacteria (cocci) that grow in groups of two
tri-	three	tricuspid tri-KUS-pid	having three points or cusps (**Fig. 3-2**)
quadr/i-	four	quadruplet kwah-DRUPE-let	one of four babies born together
tetra-	four	tetralogy tet-RAL-o-je	a group of four
multi-	many	multicellular mul-ti-SEL-u-lar	consisting of many cells (**Fig. 3-3**)
poly-	many, much	polymorphous pol-e-MOR-fus	having many forms (morph/o)

[a]Prefixes pertaining to the metric system are in Appendix 8-2.

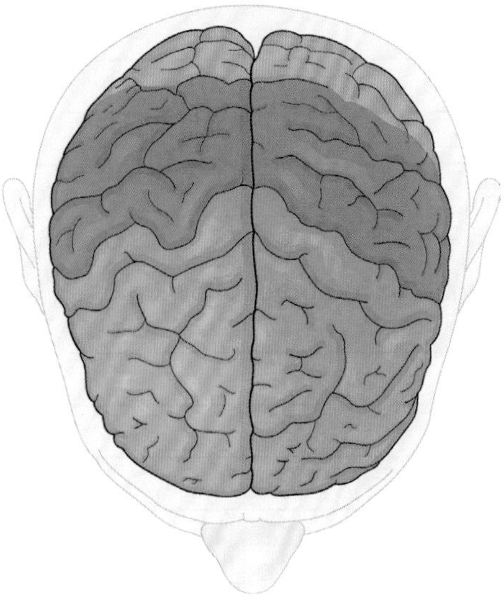

Figure 3-1 **Brain hemispheres.** Each half of the brain is a hemisphere. The prefix *hemi-* means half or one side.

POSTERIOR

Cusps of
tricuspid
valve

Cusps of
bicuspid
valve

Right

Left

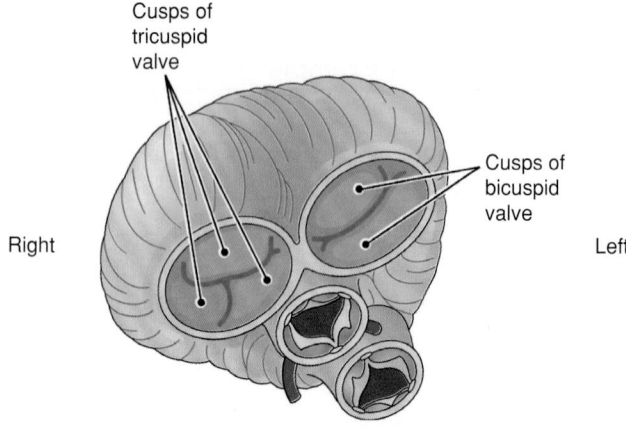

ANTERIOR

Figure 3-2 **Heart valves.** The valve on the heart's right side, the tricuspid, has three cusps (flaps); the valve on the heart's left side, the bicuspid, has two cusps. The prefixes *bi-* and *tri-* indicate number.

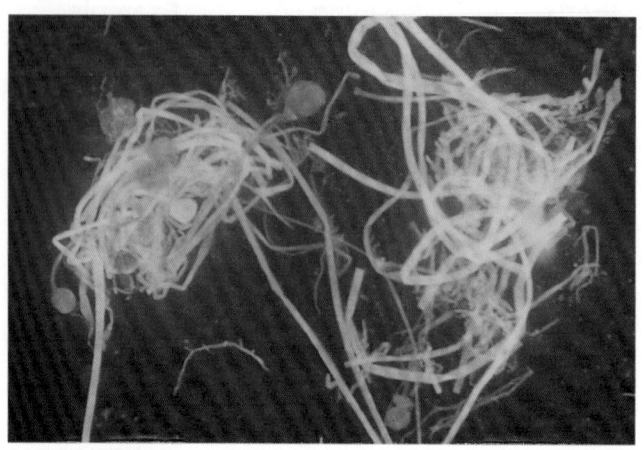

Figure 3-3 **A multicellular organism.** This fungus has more than one cell. It is a simple multicellular organism.

EXERCISE 3-1

Fill in the blanks. Use the phonetics to pronounce each word as you work through the exercises.

1. Place the following prefixes in order of increasing numbers: tri, uni-, tetra-, bi- _____

2. A binocular (*bi-NOK-u-lar*) microscope has _____ eyepieces.

3. A quadruped (*KWAD-ru-ped*) animal walks on _____ feet (ped/o).

4. The term unilateral (*u-nih-LAT-eh-ral*) refers to _____ side (later/o).

5. The term semilunar (*sem-e-LU-nar*) means shaped like a _____ moon.

6. A diploid (*DIP-loyd*) organism has _____ sets of chromosomes (-ploid).

7. A tetrad (*TET-rad*) has _____ components.

8. A tripod (*TRI-pod*) has _____ legs.

9. Monophonic (*mon-o-FON-ik*) sound has _____ channel.

Give a prefix that is similar in meaning to each of the following.

10. di- _____

11. poly- _____

12. hemi- _____

13. mon/o- _____

Table 3-2	Prefixes for Colors		
Prefix	**Meaning**	**Example**	**Definition of Example**
cyan/o-	blue	cyanosis *si-ah-NO-sis*	bluish discoloration of the skin due to lack of oxygen (**Fig. 3-4**)
erythr/o-	red	erythrocyte *eh-RITH-ro-site*	red blood cell (-cyte)
leuk/o-	white, colorless	leukemia *lu-KE-me-ah*	cancer of white blood cells
melan/o-	black, dark	melanin *MEL-ah-nin*	the dark pigment that colors the hair and skin
xanth/o-	yellow	xanthoma *zan-THO-mah*	yellow growth (-oma) on the skin

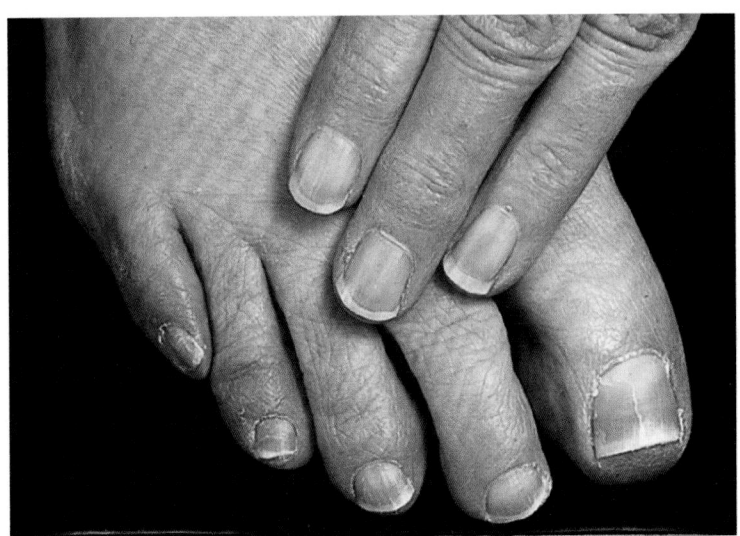

Figure 3-4 **Cyanosis, a bluish discoloration.** This abnormal coloration is seen in the toenails and toes, as compared to the normal coloration of the fingertips. The prefix *cyan/o-* means "blue."

EXERCISE 3-2

Match the following terms, and write the appropriate letter to the left of each number.

_____ **1.** melanocyte (*MEL-ah-no-site*)

_____ **2.** xanthoderma (*zan-tho-DER-mah*)

_____ **3.** cyanotic (*si-ah-NOT-ik*)

_____ **4.** erythema (*eh-RIH-the-mah*)

_____ **5.** leukocyte (*LU-ko-site*)

a. pertaining to bluish discoloration

b. redness of the skin

c. yellow coloration of the skin

d. cell that produces dark pigment

e. white blood cell

Table 3-3	Negative Prefixes		
Prefix	**Meaning**	**Example**	**Definition of Example**
a-, an-	not, without, lack of, absence	anhydrous *an-HI-drus*	lacking water (hydr/o)
anti-	against	antiseptic *an-tih-SEP-tik*	agent used to prevent infection (sepsis)
contra-	against, opposite, opposed	contraindicated *kon-trah-IN-dih-ka-ted*	against recommendations, not advisable
de-	down, without, removal, loss	decalcify *de-KAL-sih-fi*	remove calcium (calc/i) from
dis-	absence, removal, separation	dissect *dih-SEKT*	to separate tissues for anatomic study
in-[a], im- (used before b, m, p)	not	incontinent *in-KON-tih-nent*	not able to contain or control discharge of excretions
non-	not	noncontributory *non-kon-TRIB-u-tor-e*	not significant, not adding information to a medical diagnosis
un-	not	uncoordinated *un-ko-OR-dih-na-ted*	not working together, not coordinated

[a]May also mean "in" or "into" as in inject, inhale.

EXERCISE 3-3

Identify and define the prefix in the following words.

	Prefix	**Meaning of Prefix**
1. aseptic	a	not, without, lack of, absence
2. antidote	___	___
3. amnesia	___	___
4. disintegrate	___	___
5. contraception	___	___
6. inadequate	___	___
7. depilatory	___	___
8. nonconductor	___	___

Add a prefix to form the negative of the following words.

9. conscious	unconscious
10. significant	___
11. infect	___
12. usual	___
13. specific	___
14. congestant	___
15. compatible	___

Table 3-4	Prefixes for Direction		
Prefix	**Meaning**	**Example**	**Definition of Example**
ab-	away from	abduct *ab*-DUKT	to move away from the midline (see **Fig. 3-5**)
ad-	toward, near	adduct *ad*-DUKT	to move toward the midline (see **Fig. 3-5**)
dia-	through	diarrhea *di-ah*-RE-*ah*	frequent discharge of fluid fecal matter
per-	through	percutaneous *per-ku*-TA-*ne-us*	through the skin
trans-	through	transected *tran*-SEKT-*ed*	cut (sectioned) through or across

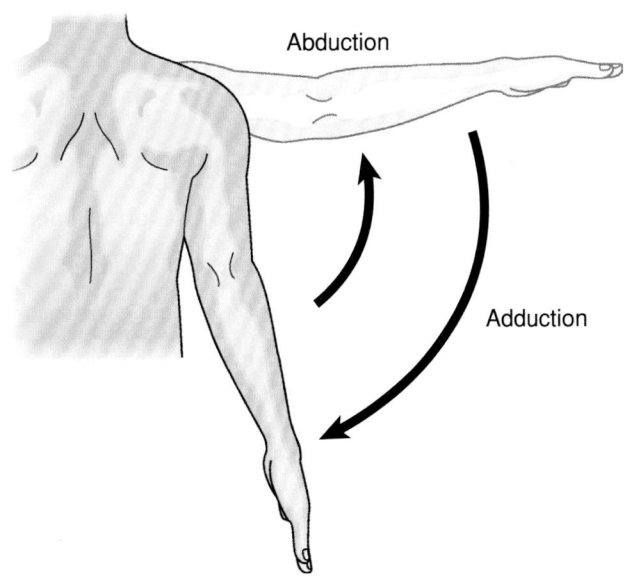

Figure 3-5 **Abduction and adduction.** The prefix *ab-* means "away from;" the arm is moved away from the body in abduction. The prefix *ad-* means "toward;" the arm is moved toward the body in adduction.

EXERCISE 3-4

Identify and define the prefix in the following words.

		Prefix	**Meaning of Prefix**
1.	dialysis	dia	through
2.	percolate		
3.	adjacent		
4.	absent		
5.	diameter		
6.	transport		

Table 3-5	Prefixes for Degree		
Prefix	**Meaning**	**Example**	**Definition of Example**
hyper-	over, excess, abnormally high, increased	hyperthermia *hi-per-THER-me-ah*	high body temperature
hypo-[a]	under, below, abnormally low, decreased	hyposecretion *hi-po-se-KRE-shun*	underproduction of a substance
olig/o-	few, scanty	oligospermia *ol-ih-go-SPER-me-ah*	abnormally low number of sperm cells in semen
pan-	all	pandemic *pan-DEM-ik*	disease affecting an entire population
super-[a]	above, excess	supernumerary *su-per-NU-mer-ar-e*	in excess number

[a]May also indicate position, as in hypodermic, superficial.

EXERCISE 3-5

Match the following terms, and write the appropriate letter to the left of each number.

_____ **1.** hypotensive (*hi-po-TEN-siv*)

_____ **2.** oligodontia (*ol-ih-go-DON-she-ah*)

_____ **3.** panplegia (*pan-PLE-je-ah*)

_____ **4.** superscript (*SU-per-skript*)

_____ **5.** hyperventilation (*hi-per-ven-tih-LA-shun*)

a. excess breathing

b. something written above

c. having low blood pressure

d. total paralysis

e. less than the normal number of teeth

Table 3-6	Prefixes for Size and Comparison		
Prefix	**Meaning**	**Example**	**Definition of Example**
equi-	equal, same	equilibrium *e-kwih-LIB-re-um*	a state of balance, state in which conditions remain the same
eu-	true, good, easy, normal	euthanasia *u-thah-NA-ze-ah*	easy or painless death (thanat/o)
hetero-	other, different, unequal	heterogeneous *het-er-o-JE-ne-us*	composed of different materials, not uniform
homo-, homeo-	same, unchanging	homograft *HO-mo-graft*	tissue transplanted to another of the same species
iso-	equal, same	isocellular *i-so-SEL-u-lar*	composed of similar cells
macro-	large, abnormally large	macroscopic *mak-ro-SKOP-ik*	large enough to be seen without a microscope

Table 3-6	Prefixes for Size and Comparison (*Continued*)		
Prefix	**Meaning**	**Example**	**Definition of Example**
mega-[a], megal/o	large, abnormally large	megacolon *meg-ah-KO-lon*	enlargement of the colon
micro-[a]	small	microcyte *MI-kro-site*	very small cell (-cyte)
neo-	new	neonate *NE-o-nate*	a newborn infant (**Fig. 3-6**)
normo-	normal	normovolemia *nor-mo-vol-E-me-ah*	normal blood volume
ortho-	straight, correct, upright	orthodontics *or-tho-DON-tiks*	branch of dentistry concerned with correction and straightening of the teeth (odont/o)
poikilo-	varied, irregular	poikilothermic *poy-kih-lo-THER-mik*	having variable body temperature (therm/o)
pseudo-	false	pseudoplegia *su-do-PLE-je-ah*	false paralysis (-plegia)
re-	again, back	reflux *RE-flux*	backward flow

[a]Mega- also means 1 million, as in megahertz. Micro- also means 1 millionth, as in microsecond.

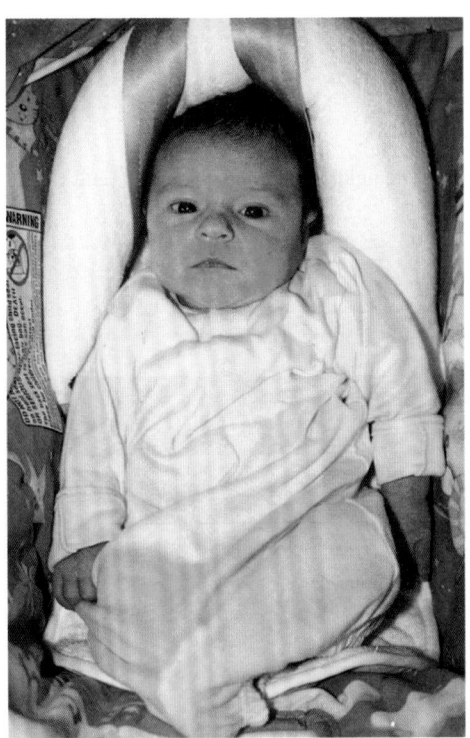

Figure 3-6 **A neonate or newborn.** The prefix *neo-* means "new."

EXERCISE 3-6

Match the following terms, and write the appropriate letter to the left of each number.

_____ **1.** isograft (*I-so-graft*)

_____ **2.** orthotic (*or-THOT-ik*)

_____ **3.** pseudoreaction (*su-do-re-AK-shun*)

_____ **4.** poikiloderma (*poy-kil-o-DER-mah*)

_____ **5.** homothermic (*ho-mo-THER-mik*)

a. having a constant body temperature

b. irregular, mottled condition of the skin

c. false response

d. tissue transplanted between identical individuals

e. straightening or correcting deformity

Identify and define the prefix in the following words.

	Prefix	Meaning of Prefix
6. homeostasis	homeo	same, unchanging
7. equivalent	_____	_____
8. orthopedics	_____	_____
9. rehabilitation	_____	_____
10. euthyroidism	_____	_____
11. neocortex	_____	_____
12. megabladder	_____	_____
13. isometric	_____	_____
14. normothermic	_____	_____

Write the opposite of the following words.

15. homogeneous (of uniform composition)   _____
    ho-mo-JE-ne-us

16. macroscopic (large enough to see with the naked eye)   _____
    mah-kro-SKOP-ik

Table 3-7   Prefixes for Time and/or Position

Prefix	Meaning	Example	Definition of Example
ante-	before	antenatal *an-te-NA-tal*	before birth (nat/i)
pre-	before, in front of	premature *pre-mah-CHUR*	occurring before the proper time
pro-	before, in front of	prodrome *PRO-drome*	symptom that precedes a disease
post-	after, behind	postnasal *post-NA-sal*	behind the nose (nas/o)

EXERCISE 3-7

Match the following terms, and write the appropriate letter to the left of each number.

_____ **1.** postmortem (*post-MOR-tem*)

_____ **2.** antedate (*AN-te-date*)

_____ **3.** progenitor (*pro-JEN-ih-tor*)

_____ **4.** prepartum (*pre-PAR-tum*)

_____ **5.** projectile (*pro-JEK-tile*)

a. to occur before another event

b. ancestor, one who comes before

c. before birth (parturition)

d. throwing or extending forward

e. occurring after death

Identify and define the prefix in the following words.

	Prefix	Meaning of Prefix
6. prediction (*pre-DIK-shun*)	pre	before, in front of
7. postmenopausal (*post-men-o-PAW-zal*)	_____	_____
8. procedure (*pro-SE-jur*)	_____	_____
9. predisposing (*pre-dis-PO-zing*)	_____	_____
10. antepartum (*an-te-PAR-tum*)	_____	_____

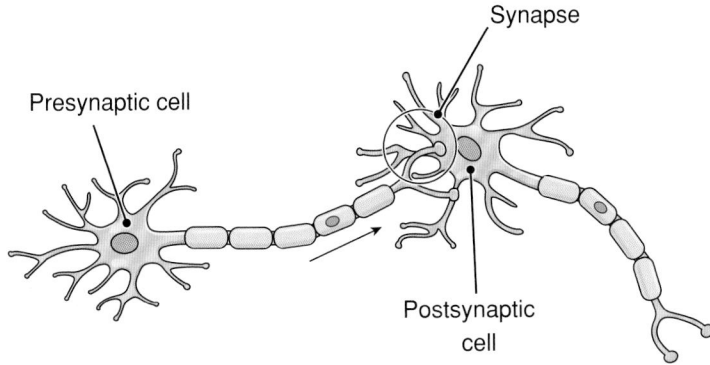

Synapse

Presynaptic cell

Postsynaptic cell

Figure 3-7 **A synapse.** Nerve cells come together at a synapse, as shown by the prefix *syn-*. The presynaptic cell is located before (prefix *pre-*) the synapse; the postsynaptic cell is located after (prefix *post-*) the synapse.

Table 3-8 · Prefixes for Position

Prefix	Meaning	Example	Definition of Example
dextr/o-	right	dextrogastria *deks-tro-GAS-tre-ah*	displacement of the stomach (gastr/o) to the right
sinistr/o-	left	sinistromanual *sin-is-tro-MAN-u-al*	left-handed
ec-, ecto-	out, outside	ectopic *ek-TOP-ik*	out of normal position
ex/o-	away from, outside	excise *ek-SIZE*	to cut out
end/o-	in, within	endoderm *EN-do-derm*	inner layer of a developing embryo
mes/o-	middle	mesencephalon *mes-en-SEF-ah-lon*	middle portion of the brain (encephalon), midbrain
syn-, sym- (used before b, m, p)	together	synapse *SIN-aps*	a junction between two nerve cells (**Fig. 3-7**)
tel/e-, tel/o-	end, far, at a distance	teletherapy *tel-eh-THER-ah-pe*	radiation therapy delivered at a distance from the body

EXERCISE 3-8

Match the following terms, and write the appropriate letter to the left of each number.

_____ **1.** mesoderm (*MES-o-derm*)

_____ **2.** symbiosis (*sim-bi-O-sis*)

_____ **3.** sinistrocardia (*sin-is-tro-KAR-de-ah*)

_____ **4.** endoscope (*EN-do-skope*)

_____ **5.** telephase (*TEL-eh-faze*)

a. displacement of the heart to the left

b. device for viewing the inside of a structure

c. two organisms living together

d. last stage of cell division (mitosis)

e. middle layer of a developing embryo

Identify and define the prefix in the following words.

	Prefix	Meaning of Prefix
6. sympathetic (*sim-pah-THET-ik*)	sym	together
7. extract (*EKS-tract*)	_____	_____
8. ectoparasite (*ek-to-PAR-ah-site*)	_____	_____
9. syndrome (*SIN-drome*)	_____	_____
10. endotoxin (*en-do-TOX-in*)	_____	_____

Write the opposite of the following words.

11. exogenous (outside the organism)
eks-OJ-eh-nus   _____

12. dextromanual (right-handed)
deks-tro-MAN-u-al   _____

13. ectoderm (outermost layer of the embryo)
EK-to-derm   _____

Case Study Revisited

T.S.'s Therapy

From the hospital, T.S. was transferred to a rehabilitation center for further evaluation and therapy. At this point in his recovery, he was unable to move his legs and had limited movement of his arms. He is participating in a plan of care with physical and occupational therapy and is working on performing basic activities of daily living. Within therapy, he is practicing wheelchair functional operations, transfers, and safe propulsions. The goal is to progress toward independence within his home lifestyle and regain status as an active member in his school and community. Despite the support and encouragement of his family and many friends, he remains depressed and anxious about his future.

Review

Match the following terms, and write the appropriate letter to the left of each number.

_____ **1.** primitive   **a.** one-half or one side of the chest

_____ **2.** biceps   **b.** having two forms

_____ **3.** unify   **c.** combine into one part

_____ **4.** dimorphous   **d.** a muscle with two parts

_____ **5.** hemithorax   **e.** occurring first in time

_____ **6.** erythematous   **a.** cell with yellow color

_____ **7.** melanoma   **b.** having a bluish discoloration

_____ **8.** xanthocyte   **c.** darkly pigmented tumor

_____ **9.** cyanotic   **d.** red in color

_____ **10.** leukocyte   **e.** white blood cell

_____ **11.** telencephalon   **a.** total paralysis

_____ **12.** mesoderm   **b.** first stage of cell division

_____ **13.** panplegia   **c.** double vision

_____ **14.** prophase   **d.** middle layer of tissue

_____ **15.** diplopia   **e.** endbrain

Match each of the following prefixes with its meaning.

_____ **16.** poikilo-   **a.** good, true, easy

_____ **17.** eu-   **b.** straight, correct

_____ **18.** ortho-   **c.** false

_____ **19.** pseudo-   **d.** few, scanty

_____ **20.** oligo-   **e.** varied, irregular

Fill in the blanks.

21. A monocle has _____ lens(es).

22. A triplet is one of _____ babies born together.

23. Sinistrad means toward the _____.

24. A disaccharide is a sugar composed of _____ subunits.

25. A contralateral structure is located on the side _____ to a given point.

26. A tetralogy is composed of _____ part(s).

27. The term in T.S.'s case study that describes his lack of reflexes is _____.

Identify and define the prefix in the following words.

	Prefix	Meaning of Prefix
28. hyperactive	_____	_____
29. transfer	_____	_____
30. distant	_____	_____
31. posttraumatic	_____	_____
32. regurgitate	_____	_____

	Prefix	Meaning of Prefix
33. extend	_____	_____
34. adhere	_____	_____
35. unusual	_____	_____
36. ectoderm	_____	_____
37. detoxify	_____	_____
38. semisolid	_____	_____
39. premenstrual	_____	_____
40. perforate	_____	_____
41. dialysis (*di-AL-ih-sis*)	_____	_____
42. antibody	_____	_____
43. microsurgery	_____	_____
44. disease	_____	_____
45. endoparasite	_____	_____
46. symbiotic (*sim-bI-OT-ik*)	_____	_____
47. prognosis (*prog-NO-sis*)	_____	_____
48. insignificant	_____	_____

True–False

Examine the following statements. If the statement is true, write T in the first blank. If the statement is false, write F in the first blank, and correct the statement by replacing the underlined word in the second blank.

	True or False	Correct Answer
49. Immune cells are primed by their <u>first</u> exposure to a disease organism.	T	_____
50. A unicellular organism is composed of <u>10</u> cells.	F	one
51. To bisect is to cut into <u>two</u> parts.	_____	_____
52. A tetrad has <u>five</u> parts.	_____	_____
53. In Latin, the oculus dexter is the <u>left</u> eye.	_____	_____
54. A triceps muscle has <u>six</u> parts.	_____	_____
55. A polygraph measures <u>many</u> physiologic responses.	_____	_____
56. In T.S.'s case study, quadriplegia refers to paralysis of <u>four</u> limbs.	_____	_____
57. T.S.'s orthostatic hypotension would occur when he is <u>upright</u>.	_____	_____

Opposites

Write a word that means the opposite of each of the following.

58. humidify _____

59. abduct _____

60. permeable _____

61. heterogeneous _____

62. exotoxin _____

63. microscopic _____

64. hyperventilation _____

65. postsynaptic _____

66. septic _____

Synonyms

Write a word that means the same as each of the following.

67. supersensitivity _____

68. megalocyte (extremely large red blood cell) _____

69. antenatal _____

70. isolateral (having equal sides) _____

Word Building

Write words for the following definitions using the word parts provided. Each may be used more than once.

| mon/o | -al | dextr/o | end/o | macro | cardi | cyt | -ic | ecto | micro | -ia |

71. Pertaining to a very small cell _____

72. A condition in which the heart is outside
its normal position _____

73. Pertaining to a cell with a single nucleus _____

74. Condition in which the heart is displaced to the right _____

75. Pertaining to the innermost layer of the heart _____

76. Pertaining to a very large cell _____

77. Condition in which the heart is extremely small _____

Word Analysis

Define each of the following words and give the meaning of the word parts in each. Use a dictionary if necessary.

78. isometric (*i-so-MET-rik*) _____

   a. iso- _____

   b. metr/o _____

   c. -ic _____

79. symbiosis (*sim-be-O-sis*) _____

   a. sym- _____

   b. bio _____

   c. -sis _____

80. monoclonal (*mon-o-KLO-nal*) _____

   a. mon/o- _____

   b. clon(e) _____

   b. -al _____

For more learning activities, see Chapter 3 of the Student Resources on thePoint.

Additional Case Studies

Case Study 3-1: *Displaced Fracture of the Femoral Neck*

While walking home from the train station, M.A., a 72 y/o woman with preexisting osteoporosis, tripped over a raised curb and fell. In the emergency department, she was assessed for severe pain, and swelling and bruising of her right thigh. A radiograph showed a fracture at the neck of the right femur (thigh bone) (**Fig. 3-8**). M.A. was prepared for surgery and given a preoperative injection of an analgesic to relieve her pain. During surgery, she was given spinal anesthesia and positioned on an operating room table, with her right hip elevated on a small pillow. Intravenous antibiotics were given before the incision was made. Her right hip was repaired with a bipolar hemiarthroplasty (joint reconstruction). Postoperative care included maintaining the right hip in abduction, fluid replacement, physical therapy, and attention to signs of tissue degeneration and possible dislocation.

Case Study 3-2: *Urinary Tract Infection*

Chief Complaint

D.S. recently noticed some blood in her urine, and at the same time, she was experiencing some pain when she urinated. She thought she might have a fever and generally felt tired. She was not sleeping well since she frequently had to get up during the night to use the bathroom. She decided to make an appointment to see her primary care physician.

Past Medical History

A 33 y/o female nonsmoker, has two children, in a monogamous relationship, is a triathlete, and is in excellent health. Has a history of occasional urinary tract infections, about one to two times a year. Presents

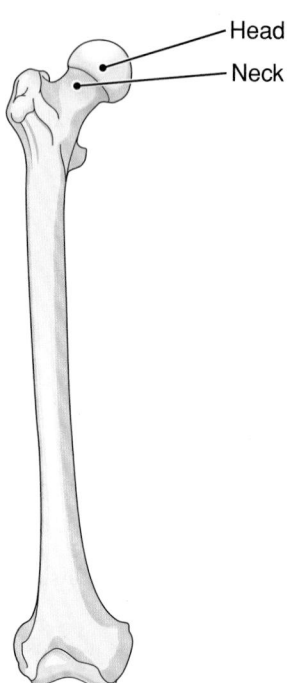

Head
Neck

Anterior view

Figure 3-8   **The right femur (thigh bone).** The femoral neck is the fracture site in Case Study 3-1.

now with dysuria (painful urination), hematuria (blood in the urine), and nocturia (nighttime urination).

Clinical Course

Urine analysis report showed cloudy urine with a large number of leukocytes and erythrocytes indicating a urinary tract infection. D.S. was given an antibiotic and told to increase her fluid intake. If symptoms persist beyond one week, D.S. is to return to the office.

Case Study Questions

Identify and define the prefixes in the following words.

		Prefix	**Meaning of Prefix**
1.	preexisting	____	_____
2.	analgesic, anesthesia	____	_____
3.	dislocation	____	_____
4.	replacement	____	_____
5.	bipolar	____	_____
6.	hemiarthroplasty	____	_____
7.	degeneration	____	_____
8.	antibiotic	____	_____
9.	erythrocyte	____	_____
10.	primary	____	_____

Fill in the blanks.

11. The suffixes in the words osteoporosis and anesthesia mean _____.

12. The suffixes in the words intravenous, femoral, and analgesic mean _____.

13. In a monogamous relationship, each person has _____ partner.

14. A triathlete competes in an event with _____ activities, such as swimming, bicycling, and running.

Find a word in the case histories that describes the following.

15. The time period before surgery _____

16. The time period after surgery _____

17. A position away from the midline of the body _____

18. Another name for a white blood cell _____

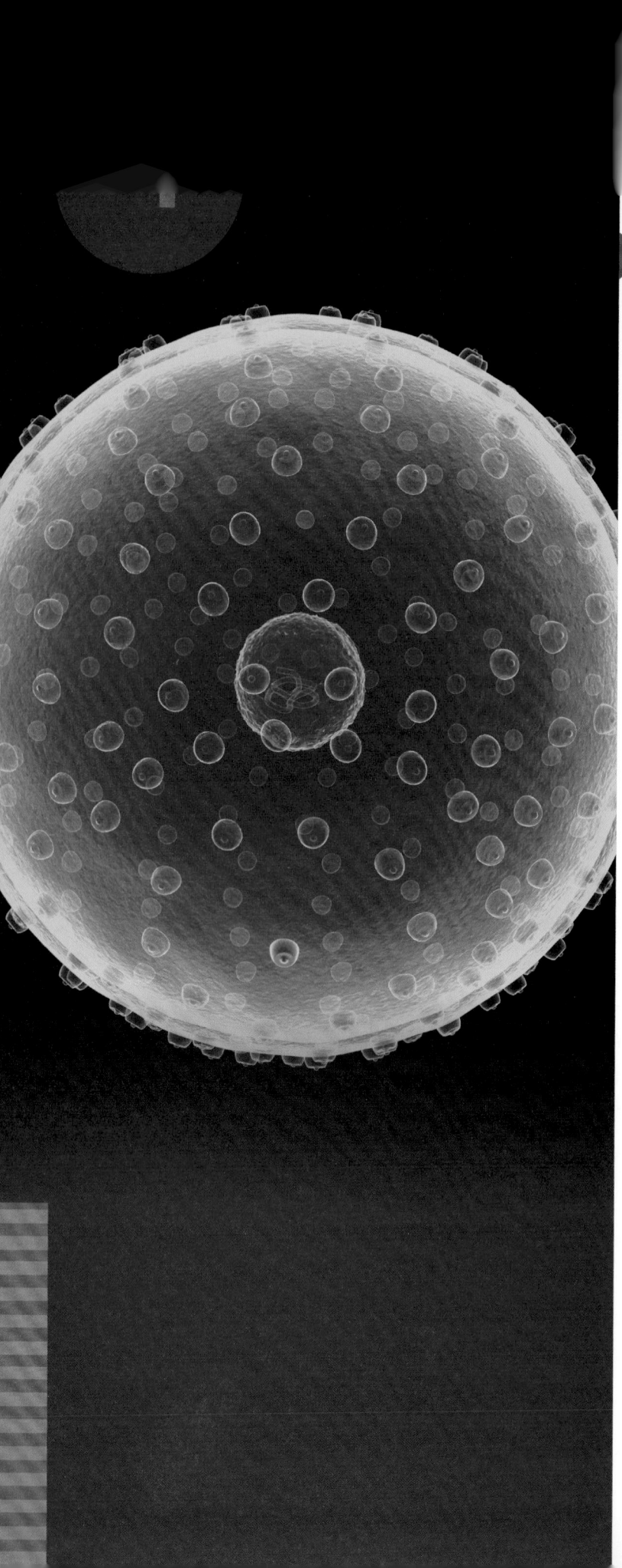

Pretest

Multiple Choice. Select the best answer, and write the letter of your choice to the left of each number.

_____ 1. The root that means "cell" is
   a. spher
   b. aden
   c. cyt
   d. gen

_____ 2. The root that means "tissue" is
   a. hist
   b. fibr
   c. plas
   d. hem

_____ 3. The control center of the cell is the
   a. membrane
   b. lysosome
   c. ribosome
   d. nucleus

_____ 4. The process of body cell division is called
   a. separation
   b. segregation
   c. mitosis
   d. gestation

_____ 5. A compound that speeds the rate of a metabolic reaction is a(n)
   a. vitamin
   b. enzyme
   c. salt
   d. lipid

_____ 6. The substance that makes up the cell's genetic material is
   a. DNA
   b. mineral
   c. base
   d. neurons

_____ 7. Chemicals: cells: tissues:_____: systems: organism. What belongs in the blank?
   a. genes
   b. enzymes
   c. nuclei
   d. organs

_____ 8. The root *morph/o* means
   a. reproduction
   b. fat
   c. form
   d. balance

▶ Learning Objectives

After study of this chapter, you should be able to:

1 ▶ List the simplest to the most complex levels of a living organism. *p50*

2 ▶ Describe and locate the main parts of a cell. *p51*

3 ▶ Name and give the functions of the four basic types of tissues in the body. *p53*

4 ▶ Define basic terms pertaining to the structure and function of body tissues. *p57*

5 ▶ Recognize and use prefixes, roots, and suffixes pertaining to cells, tissues, and organs. *p58*

6 ▶ Analyze medical words in case studies pertaining to cells, tissues, and organs. *pp49, 66*

Case Study: *R.S.'s Self-Diagnosis*

Chief Complaint

R.S. is a second-year medical student who, until recently, has done well in school. Lately, he finds that he is always tired and unable to focus in class. He decides to self-diagnose and begins with a review of systems (ROS). He notes that he is not having any cardiovascular, lymphatic, or respiratory system symptoms, such as tissue swelling, coughing, or shortness of breath. He also has not noticed any changes in urinary system functions. He realizes that he has gained some weight recently and has also been a little constipated but has no other problems with his digestive system. He rules out anything concerning his musculoskeletal system because he has no muscle cramps, joint pain, or weakness. He thinks his skin is drier than usual. He worries that this is an integumentary system sign of hypothyroidism and becomes concerned about his endocrine system function. Unable to perform any imaging studies or laboratory tests on his own, he makes an appointment to see a campus health services physician.

Examination

R.S. tells the doctor he feels he has a metabolic disorder. He thinks he might have an adenoma, a glandular tumor that is disrupting homeostasis, his normal metabolic state. The doctor takes a complete history and orders various blood tests to assist with the diagnosis. He completes a physical examination that reveals no abnormalities.

Clinical Course

The blood glucose levels, complete blood count (CBC), and thyroid function tests are all normal. Nothing in the tests indicates anything physically wrong with the patient. There is no indication that any further cytologic or histologic tests are necessary. The doctor tells R.S. that he is sleep deprived from all his studying and that his weight gain can be explained by his poor food choices in the university cafeteria. In addition, the doctor advises R.S. to schedule some exercise into his daily routine. Lastly, he reminds R.S. that although he is studying to be a doctor, self-diagnosis at this point in his career could be inaccurate and could cause undue anxiety.

ANCILLARIES *At-A-Glance*

Visit thePoint to access the following resources. For guidance in using the resources most effectively, see pp. ix–xvi.

Learning RESOURCES

▶ Tips for Effective Studying
▶ Animation: The Cell Cycle and Mitosis
▶ Audio Pronunciation Glossary

Learning ACTIVITIES

▶ Visual Activities
▶ Kinesthetic Activities
▶ Auditory Activities

Body Organization

All organisms are built from simple to more complex levels (**Fig. 4-1**). Chemicals form the materials that make up cells, which are the body's structural and functional units. Groups of cells working together make up **tissues**, which in turn make up the **organs**, which have specialized functions. Organs become components of the various systems, which together comprise the whole organism. This chapter discusses the terminology related to cells, tissues, and organs, leading to the study of all the organ systems in Part 3.

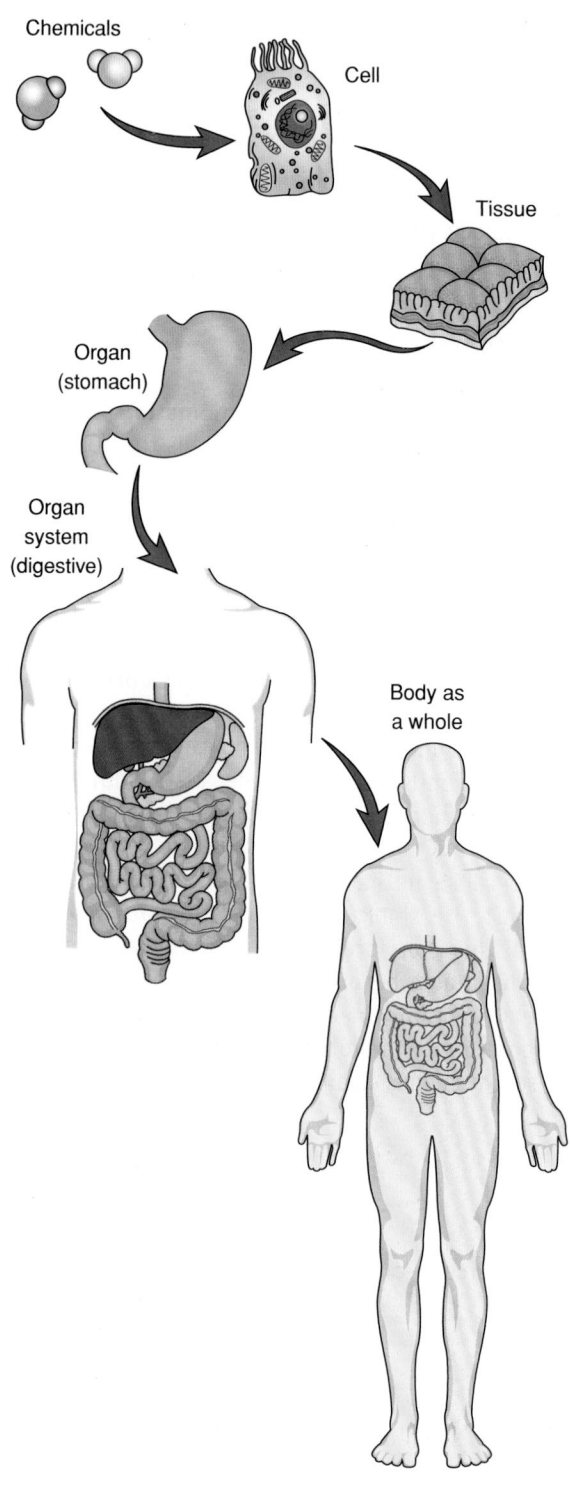

Chemicals

Cell

Tissue

Organ
(stomach)

Organ
system
(digestive)

Body as
a whole

Figure 4-1 **Levels of organization.** The body is organized from the simple level of chemicals to the most complex level of the whole organism. The organ shown is the stomach, which is part of the digestive system.

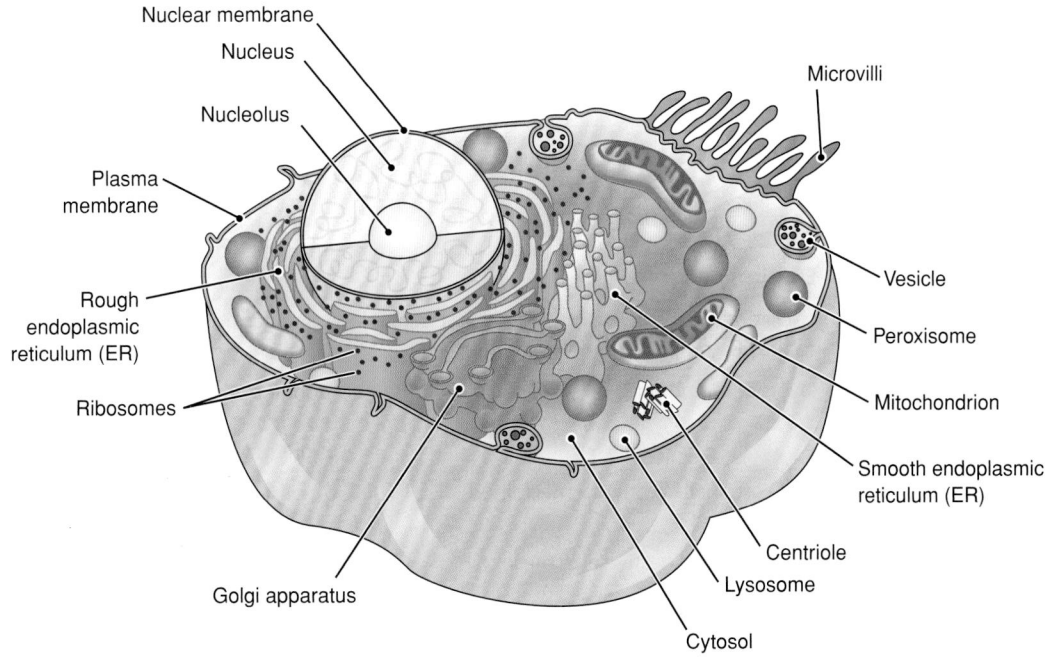

Nuclear membrane

Nucleus

Nucleolus

Microvilli

Plasma membrane

Rough endoplasmic reticulum (ER)

Ribosomes

Vesicle

Peroxisome

Mitochondrion

Smooth endoplasmic reticulum (ER)

Centriole

Lysosome

Golgi apparatus

Cytosol

Figure 4-2 **Generalized animal cell (sectional view).** The main organelles are shown.

The Cell

The **cell** is the basic unit of living organisms (**Fig. 4-2**). Cells accomplish all the activities and produce all the components of the body. They carry out **metabolism**, the sum of all the body's physical and chemical activities. They provide the energy for metabolic reactions in the form of the chemical **adenosine triphosphate (ATP)**, commonly described as the energy compound of the cell. The main categories of organic compounds contained in cells are:

- **Proteins**, which include the **enzymes**, some hormones, and structural materials.

- **Carbohydrates**, which include sugars and starches. The main carbohydrate is the sugar **glucose**, which circulates in the blood to provide energy for the cells.
- **Lipids**, which include fats. Some hormones are derived from lipids, and adipose (fat) tissue is designed to store lipids.

Within the **cytoplasm** that fills the cell are subunits called **organelles**, each with a specific function (see **Fig. 4-2**). The main cell structures are named and described in **Box 4-1**. Diseases may affect specific parts of cells. Cystic

FOR YOUR REFERENCE
Cell Structures

Box 4-1

Name	Description	Function
plasma membrane (*PLAZ-mah*)	outer layer of the cell, composed mainly of lipids and proteins	encloses the cell contents; regulates what enters and leaves the cell; participates in many activities, such as growth, reproduction, and interactions between cells
microvilli (*mi-kro-VIL-i*)	short extensions of the cell membrane	absorb materials into the cell
nucleus (*NU-kle-us*)	large, membrane-bound, dark-staining organelle near the center of the cell	contains the chromosomes, the hereditary units that direct all cellular activities
nucleolus (*nu-KLE-o-lus*)	small body in the nucleus	makes ribosomes
cytoplasm (*SI-to-plazm*)	colloidal suspension that fills the cell from the nuclear membrane to the plasma membrane	site of many cellular activities; consists of cytosol and organelles

(continued)

Cell Structures (*Continued*)

Name	Description	Function
cytosol (*SI-to-sol*)	fluid portion of the cytoplasm	surrounds the organelles
endoplasmic reticulum (ER) (*en-do-PLAZ-mik re-TIK-u-lum*)	network of membranes within the cytoplasm; rough ER has ribosomes attached to it; smooth ER does not	rough ER modifies, folds, and sorts proteins; smooth ER participates in lipid synthesis
ribosomes (*RI-bo-somz*)	small bodies free in the cytoplasm or attached to the ER, composed of RNA and protein	manufacture proteins
Golgi apparatus (*GOL-je*)	layers of membranes	modifies proteins; sorts and prepares proteins for transport to other parts of the cell or out of the cell
mitochondria (*mi-to-KON-dre-ah*)	large organelles with internal folded membranes	convert energy from nutrients into ATP
lysosomes (*LI-so-somz*)	small sacs of digestive enzymes	digest substances within the cell
peroxisomes (*per-OKS-ih-somz*)	membrane-enclosed organelles containing enzymes	break down harmful substances
vesicles (*VES-ih-klz*)	small membrane-bound sacs in the cytoplasm	store materials and move materials into or out of the cell in bulk
centrioles (*SEN-tre-olz*)	rod-shaped bodies (usually two) near the nucleus	help separate the chromosomes during cell division
surface projections	structures that extend from the cell	move the cell or the fluids around the cell
cilia (*SIL-e-ah*)	short, hair-like projections from the cell	move the fluids around the cell
flagellum (*flah-JEL-um*)	long, whip-like extension from the cell	moves the cell

fibrosis and diabetes, for example, involve the plasma membrane. Other disorders originate with mitochondria, the endoplasmic reticulum (ER), lysosomes, or peroxisomes (**Box 4-2**).

The **nucleus** is the control region of the cell. It contains the **chromosomes**, which carry genetic information (**Fig. 4-3**). Each human cell, aside from the reproductive (sex) cells, contains 46 chromosomes. These thread-like

---

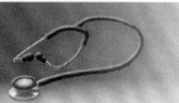

CLINICAL PERSPECTIVES

Box 4-2

Cell Organelles and Disease

Two organelles that play a vital role in cellular disposal and recycling may also be involved in disease. Lysosomes contain enzymes that break down carbohydrates, lipids, proteins, and nucleic acids to safely recycle cellular structures. Lysosomes may also digest the cell itself as a normal part of development. Cells that are no longer needed "self-destruct" by releasing lysosomal enzymes into their own cytoplasm. In Tay–Sachs disease, the lysosomes in nerve cells lack an enzyme that breaks down certain kinds of lipids. These lipids build up inside the cells, causing malfunction that leads to brain injury, blindness, and death.

Peroxisomes resemble lysosomes but contain different kinds of enzymes. They break down toxic substances that enter the cell, such as drugs and alcohol, as well as harmful

byproducts of normal metabolism. Disease may result if lysosomes or peroxisomes destroy cells in error. This may occur in cases of autoimmune diseases, in which the body develops an immune response to its own cells. The joint disease rheumatoid arthritis is one such example.

Mitochondria, because they may have been separate organisms early in evolution, have their own DNA. Mutations (changes) in their DNA or in the nuclear DNA that controls their activity can disrupt ATP production and damage organs throughout the body. These mitochondrial disorders are difficult to diagnose because they cause a variety of symptoms and have been confused with epilepsy, cerebral palsy, and multiple sclerosis.

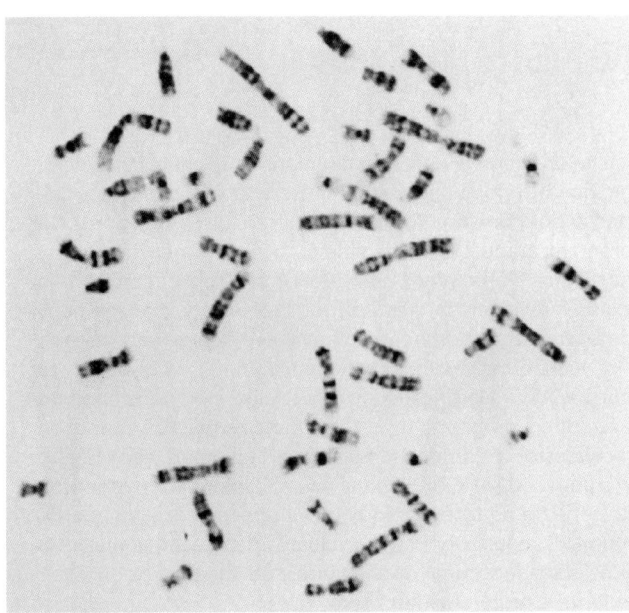

Figure 4-3 **Human chromosomes.** There are 46 chromosomes in each human cell, except the sex cells (egg and sperm).

structures are composed of a complex organic substance, **deoxyribonucleic acid (DNA)**, which is organized into separate units called **genes**. Genes control the formation of proteins, most particularly enzymes, the catalysts needed to speed the rate of metabolic reactions. To help manufacture proteins, the cells use a compound called **ribonucleic acid (RNA)**, which is chemically related to DNA. Changes (mutations) in the genes or chromosomes are the source of hereditary diseases, as described in Chapter 15.

When a body cell divides by the process of **mitosis**, the chromosomes are doubled and then equally distributed to the two daughter cells. The stages in mitosis are shown in **Figure 4-4**. When a cell is not dividing, it remains in a stage called *interphase*. In cancer, cells multiply without control causing cellular overgrowth and tumors. Reproductive cells (eggs and sperm) divide by a related process, meiosis, that halves the chromosomes in preparation for fertilization. The role of meiosis in reproduction is further explained in Chapter 14.

The study of cells is **cytology** (*si-TOL-o-je*), based on the root *cyt/o*, meaning "cell." **Box 4-3** has career information in the field of cytology.

See the animation "The Cell Cycle and Mitosis" in the Student Resources on thePoint.

Tissues

Cells are organized into four basic types of tissues that perform specific functions:

- Epithelial (*ep-ih-THE-le-al*) tissue, as shown in **Figure 4-5** covers and protects body structures and

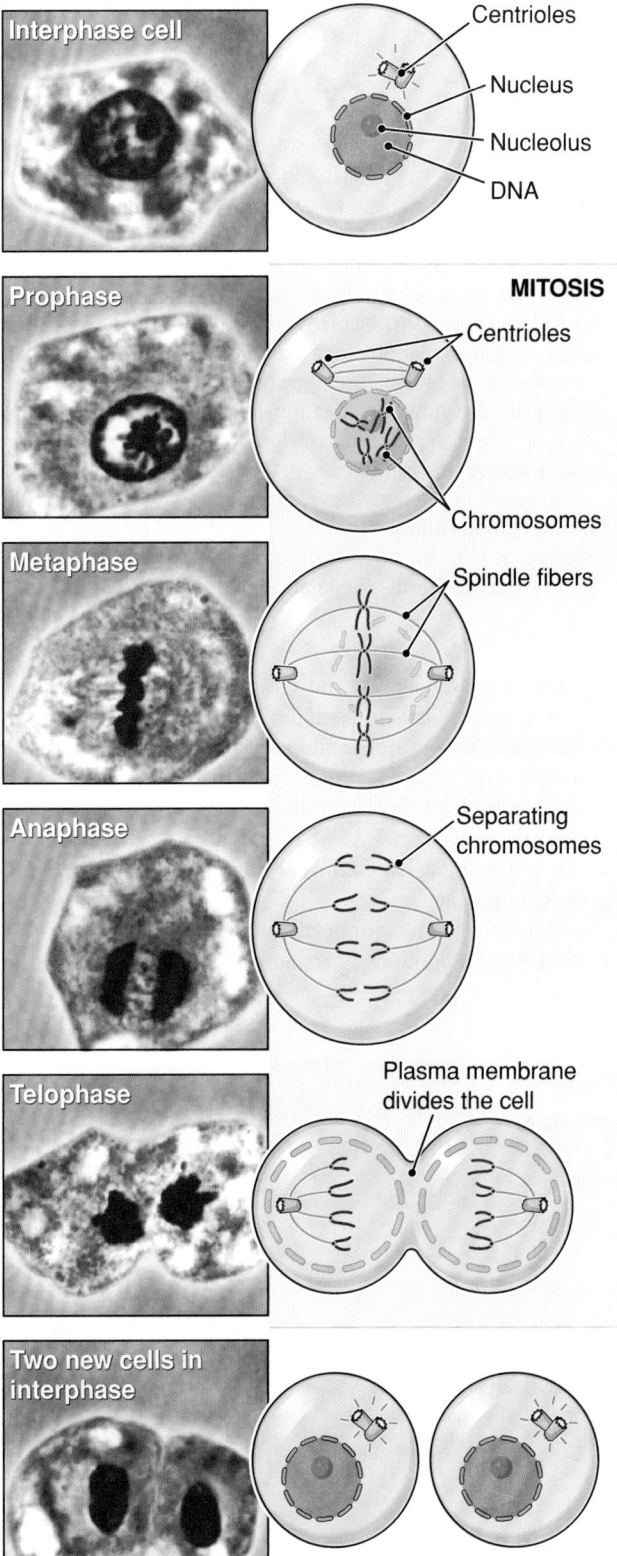

Figure 4-4 **The stages in cell division (mitosis).** When it is not undergoing mitosis, the cell is in interphase. The cell shown is for illustration only. It is not a human cell, which has 46 chromosomes.

lines organs, vessels, and cavities. Simple epithelium, composed of cells in a single layer, functions to absorb substances from one system to another, as in the respiratory and digestive tracts. Stratified epithelium, with cells in multiple layers, protects deeper tissues, as in the mouth and vagina. Most of the active cells in glands are epithelial cells. Glands are described in more detail in Chapter 16.

- Connective tissue supports and binds body structures (**Fig. 4-6**). It contains fibers and other nonliving material between the cells. Included in this category are blood (Chapter 10), adipose (fat) tissue, cartilage, and bone (Chapter 19).

- Muscle tissue (root: my/o) contracts to produce movement (**Fig. 4-7**). There are three types of muscle tissue:
  - Skeletal muscle moves the skeleton. It has visible cross-bands, or striations, that are involved in contraction. Because it is under conscious control, it is also called voluntary muscle. Skeletal muscle is discussed in greater detail in Chapter 20.
  - Cardiac muscle forms the heart. It functions without conscious control and is described as involuntary. Chapter 9 describes the heart and its actions.
  - Smooth or visceral muscle forms the walls of the abdominal organs; it is also involuntary. Many organs described in later chapters on the systems have walls made of smooth muscle. The walls of ducts and blood vessels also are composed mainly of smooth muscle.

- Nervous tissue (root: neur/o) makes up the brain, spinal cord, and nerves (**Fig. 4-8**). It coordinates and controls body responses by the transmission of electrical impulses. The basic cell in nervous tissue is the neuron, or nerve cell. The nervous system and senses are discussed in Chapters 17 and 18.

MEMBRANES

A **membrane** (*MEM-brane*) is a simple, very thin, and pliable sheet of tissue. Membranes may cover an organ, line a cavity, or separate one structure from another. Some secrete special substances. Mucous membranes secrete **mucus,** a thick fluid that lubricates surfaces and protects underlying tissue, as in the lining of the digestive tract and respiratory passages. Serous membranes, which secrete a thin, watery fluid, line body cavities and cover organs. These include the membranes around the heart and lungs. Fibrous membranes

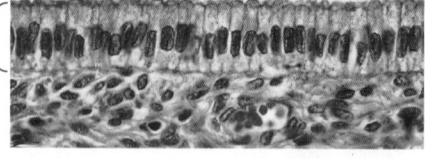

Simple epithelium

A

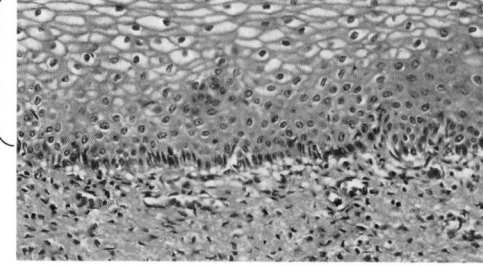

Stratified epithelium

B

Figure 4-5 **Epithelial tissue.** The cells in simple epithelium (**A**) are in a single layer and absorb materials from one system to another. The cells in stratified epithelium (**B**) are in multiple layers and protect deeper tissues.

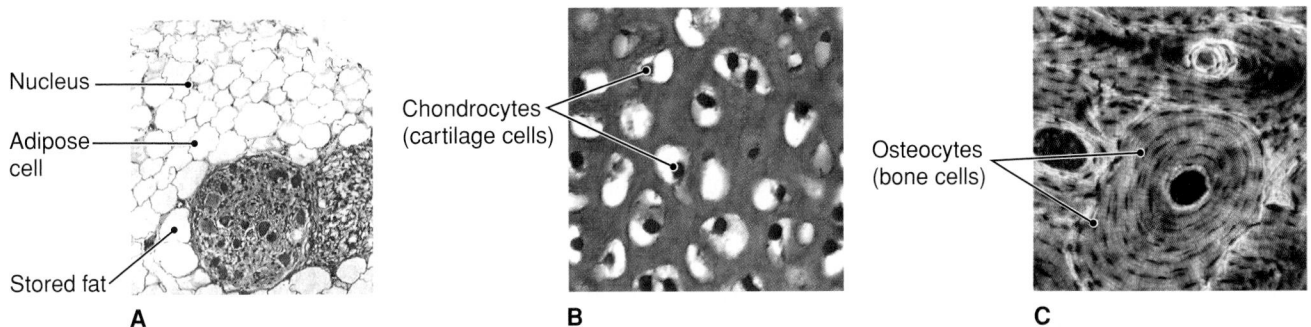

Figure 4-6 **Connective tissue.** Examples of connective tissue are adipose tissue (**A**), which stores fat; cartilage (**B**), which is used for protection and reinforcement; and bone (**C**), which makes up the skeleton.

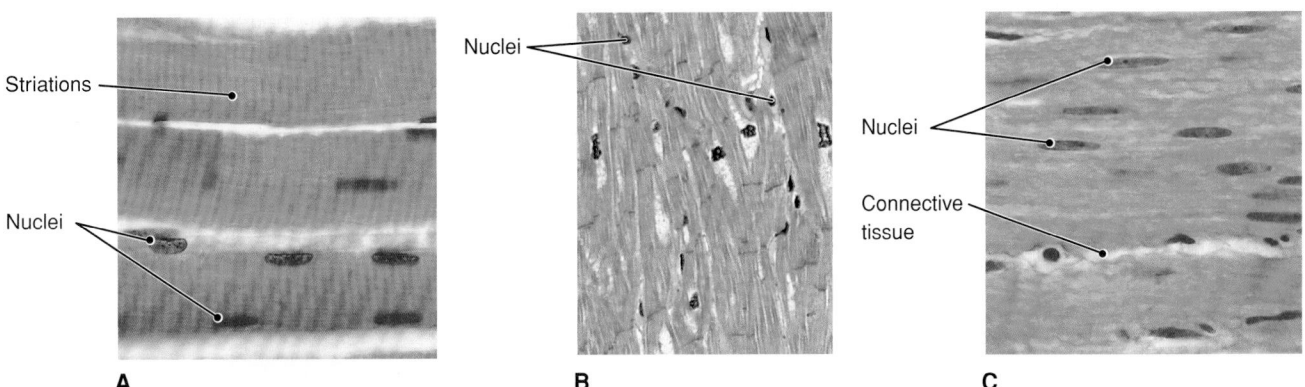

Figure 4-7 **Muscle tissue.** Skeletal muscle (**A**) moves the skeleton. It has visible bands (striations) that produce contraction. Cardiac muscle (**B**) makes up the wall of the heart. Smooth muscle (**C**) makes up the walls of hollow organs, ducts, and vessels.

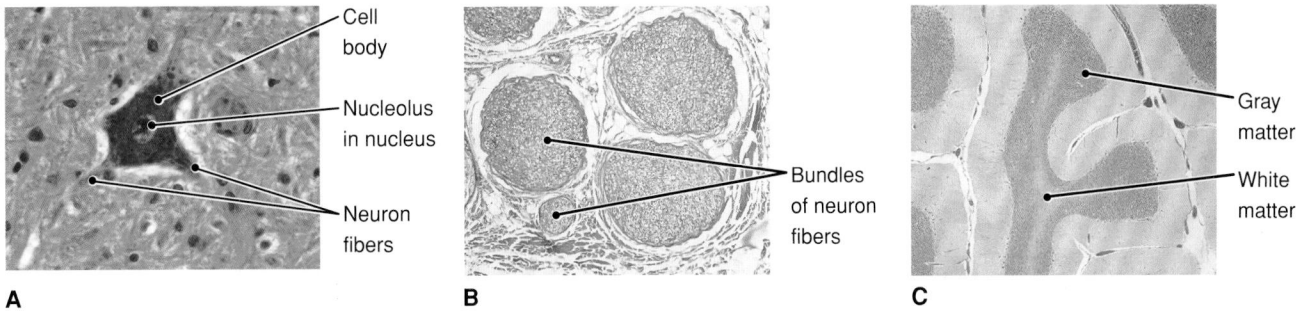

Figure 4-8 **Nervous tissue.** The functional cell of the nervous system is the neuron (**A**). Neuron fibers join to form nerves (**B**). Nervous tissue also makes up the spinal cord and brain (**C**), where it is divided into gray matter and white matter.

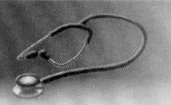

CLINICAL PERSPECTIVES

Laboratory Study of Tissues

Box 4-4

Biopsy is the removal and examination of living tissue to determine a diagnosis. The term is also applied to the specimen itself. *Biopsy* comes from the Greek word *bios*, meaning "life," plus *opsis*, meaning "vision." Together they mean the visualization of living tissue.

Some other terms that apply to cells and tissues come from Latin. *In vivo* means "in the living body," as contrasted with *in vitro*, which literally means "in glass," and refers to procedures

and experiments done in the laboratory, as compared to studies done in living organisms. *In situ* means "in its original place" and is used to refer to tumors that have not spread.

In toto means "whole" or "completely," as in referring to a structure or organ removed totally from the body. *Postmortem* literally means "after death," as in referring to an autopsy performed to determine the cause of death.

---

cover and support organs, as found around the bones, brain, and spinal cord.

The study of tissues is **histology** (*his-TOL-o-je*), based on the root *hist/o*, meaning "tissue." **Box 4-4** describes some terms used in histology.

Organs and Organ Systems

Tissues are arranged into organs, which serve specific functions, and organs, in turn, are grouped into systems. **Figure 4-9** shows the organs of the digestive system as an example. Grouped according to functions, the body systems are:

- Circulation:
  - Cardiovascular system, consisting of the heart and blood vessels.
  - Lymphatic system, organs, and vessels that aid circulation and help protect the body from foreign materials.
- Nutrition and fluid balance:
  - Respiratory system, which obtains the oxygen needed for metabolism and eliminates carbon dioxide, a byproduct of metabolism.
  - Digestive system, which takes in, breaks down, and absorbs nutrients and eliminates undigested waste.
  - Urinary system, which eliminates soluble waste and balances the volume and composition of body fluids.
- Production of offspring: The male and female reproductive systems
- Coordination and control:
  - Nervous system, consisting of the brain, spinal cord, and nerves, and including the sensory system. This system receives and processes stimuli and directs responses.
  - Endocrine system, consisting of individual glands that produce hormones.
- Body structure and movement:
  - Skeletal system, the bones and joints.
  - Muscular system, which moves the skeleton and makes up organs. The muscular system and skeleton protect vital organs.
- Body covering: The integumentary system, which includes the skin and its associated structures, such as hair,

sweat glands, and oil glands. This system functions in protection and also helps to regulate body temperature.

Each of the body systems is discussed in Part 3. However, bear in mind that the body functions as a whole; no system is independent of the others. They work together to maintain the body's state of internal stability, termed **homeostasis** (*ho-me-o-STA-sis*).

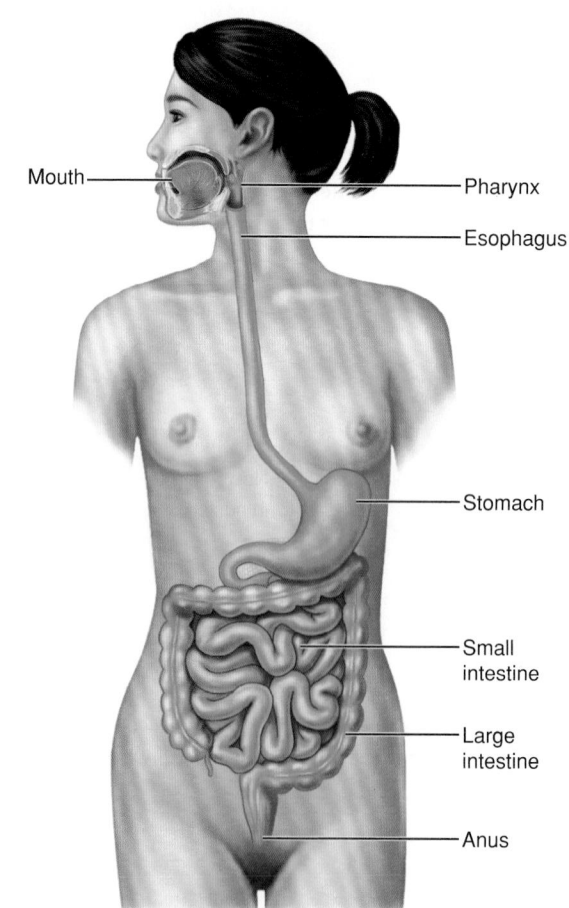

Figure 4-9 **Organs of the digestive tract.** Other organs and glands contribute to digestion, as described in Chapter 12.

Terminology | Key Terms

adenosine triphosphate (ATP) [ah-DEN-o-sene tri-FOS-fate]	The energy compound of the cell that stores energy needed for cell activities
carbohydrates kar-bo-HI-drates	The category of organic compounds that includes sugars and starches
cell sel	The basic structural and functional unit of the living organism, a microscopic unit that combines with other cells to form tissues (root: cyt/o)
chromosome KRO-mo-some	A thread-like body in a cell's nucleus that contains genetic information
cytology si-TOL-o-je	Study of cells
cytoplasm SI-to-plazm	The fluid that fills a cell and holds the organelles
deoxyribonucleic acid (DNA) [de-ok-se-ri-bo-nu-KLE-ik]	The genetic compound of the cell, makes up the genes
enzyme EN-zime	An organic substance that speeds the rate of a metabolic reaction
gene jene	A hereditary unit composed of DNA and combined with other genes to form the chromosomes
glucose GLU-kose	A simple sugar that circulates in the blood, the main energy source for metabolism (roots: gluc/o, glyc/o)
histology his-TOL-o-je	Study of tissues
homeostasis ho-me-o-STA-sis	A steady state, a condition of internal stability and constancy
lipid LIP-id	A category of organic compounds that includes fats (root: lip/o)
membrane MEM-brane	A simple, very thin, and pliable sheet of tissue that might cover an organ, line a cavity, or separate structures
metabolism meh-TAB-o-lizm	The sum of all the physical and chemical reactions that occur within an organism
mitosis mi-TO-sis	Cell division
mucus MU-kus	A thick fluid secreted by cells in membranes and glands that lubricates and protects tissues (roots: muc/o, myx/o); the adjective is *mucous*
nucleus NU-kle-us	The cell's control center; directs all cellular activities based on the information contained in its chromosomes (roots: nucle/o, kary/o)
organ OR-gan	A part of the body with a specific function, a component of a body system
organelle OR-gah-nel	A specialized structure in the cytoplasm of a cell
protein PRO-tene	A category of organic compounds that includes structural materials, enzymes, and some hormones
ribonucleic acid (RNA) [ri-bo-nu-KLE-ik]	An organic compound involved in the manufacture of proteins within cells
tissue TISH-u	A group of cells that acts together for a specific purpose (roots: hist/o, histi/o); types include epithelial tissue, connective tissue, muscle tissue, and nervous tissue

Word Parts Pertaining to Cells, Tissues, and Organs

See **Tables 4-1** to **4-3**.

Go to the audio pronunciation glossary in the Student Resources on thePoint to hear these terms pronounced.

Table 4-1	Roots for Cells and Tissues		
Root	**Meaning**	**Example**	**Definition of Example**
morph/o	form	polymorphous *pol-e-MOR-fus*	having many forms
cyt/o, -cyte	cell	cytologist *si-TOL-o-jist*	one who studies cells
nucle/o	nucleus	nuclear *NU-kle-ar*	pertaining to a nucleus
kary/o	nucleus	karyotype *KAR-e-o-tipe*	picture of a cell's chromosomes organized according to size (see **Fig. 4-10**)
hist/o, histi/o	tissue	histocompatibility *his-to-kom-pat-ih-BIL-ih-te*	tissue similarity that permits transplantation
fibr/o	fiber	fibrosis *fi-BRO-sis*	abnormal formation of fibrous tissue
reticul/o	network	reticulum *reh-TIK-u-lum*	a network
aden/o	gland	adenoma *ad-eh-NO-mah*	tumor (-oma) of a gland
papill/o	nipple	papilla *pah-PIL-ah*	projection that resembles a nipple
myx/o	mucus	myxadenitis *miks-ad-eh-NI-tis*	inflammation (-itis) of a mucus-secreting gland
muc/o	mucus, mucous membrane	mucorrhea *mu-ko-RE-ah*	increased flow (-rhea) of mucus
somat/o, -some	body, small body	chromosome *KRO-mo-some*	small body that takes up color (dye) (chrom/o)

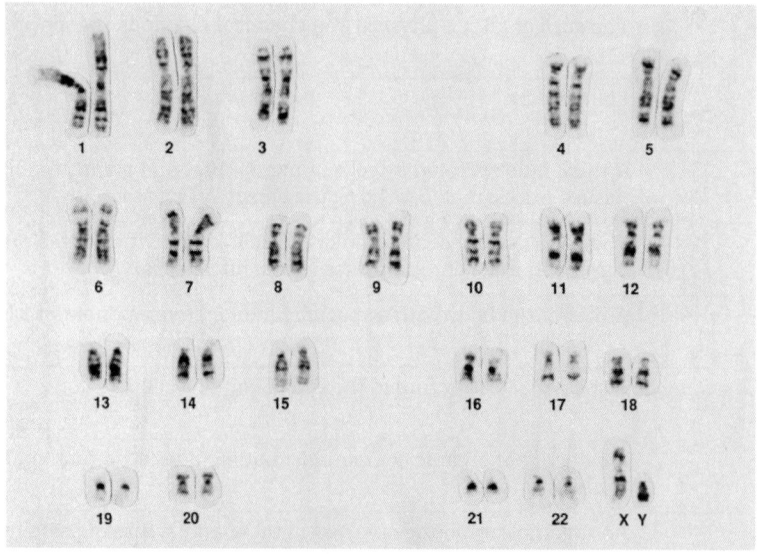

Figure 4-10 **Human karyotype.** The 46 chromosomes are in 23 pairs arranged according to size. The XY sex chromosomes, the 23rd pair at the lower right, indicate that the cell is from a male; a female cell has XX sex chromosomes.

EXERCISE 4-1

Fill in the blanks. Use the phonetics to pronounce the words in the exercises.

1. Cytogenesis (*si-to-GEN-eh-sis*) is the formation (genesis) of _____.

2. A fibril (*FI-bril*) is a small _____.

3. A histologist (*his-TOL-o-jist*) studies _____.

4. A dimorphic (*di-MOR-fik*) organism has two _____.

5. Karyomegaly (*kar-e-o-MEG-ah-le*) is enlargement (-megaly) of the _____.

6. Nucleoplasm (*NU-kle-o-plazm*) is the substance that fills the _____.

7. Adenitis (*ad-eh-NI-tis*) is inflammation (-itis) of a(n) _____.

8. A papillary (*PAP-ih-lar-e*) structure resembles a(n) _____.

9. A myxoma (*mik-SO-mah*) is a tumor of tissue that secretes _____.

10. A reticulocyte (*reh-TIK-u-lo-site*) is a cell that contains a(n) _____.

11. The term *mucosa* (*mu-KO-sah*) is used to describe a membrane that secretes _____.

12. Somatotropin (*so-mah-to-TRO-pin*), also called growth hormone, has a general stimulating effect on the
    _____.

Use the suffix -logy to build a word with each of the following meanings.

13. The study of form _____

14. The study of cells _____

15. The study of tissues _____

The roots in Table 4-2 are often combined with a simple noun suffix (*-in*, *-y*, or *-ia*) or an adjective suffix (*-ic*) and used as word endings. Such combined forms that routinely appear as word endings are simply described and used as suffixes in this book. Examples from the above list are *-trophy*, *-plasia*, *-tropin*, *-philic*, and *-genic*.

Table 4-2   Roots for Cell Activity

Root	Meaning	Example	Definition of Example
blast/o, -blast	immature cell, productive cell, embryonic cell	histioblast HIS-te-o-blast	a tissue-forming cell
gen	origin, formation	karyogenesis kar-e-o-JEN-eh-sis	formation of a nucleus
phag/o	eat, ingest	autophagy aw-TOF-ah-je	self (auto)-destruction of a cell's organelles
phil	attract, absorb	basophilic ba-so-FIL-ik	attracting basic stain
plas	formation, molding, development	hyperplasia hi-per-PLA-ze-ah	overdevelopment of an organ or tissue
trop	act on, affect	chronotropic kron-o-TROP-ik	affecting rate or timing (chron/o)
troph/o	feeding, growth, nourishment	atrophy AT-ro-fe	tissue wasting

EXERCISE 4-2

Match the following terms in the following sets, and write the appropriate letter to the left of each number.

_____ **1.** phagocyte (*FAG-o-site*)

_____ **2.** histogenesis (*his-to-JEN-eh-sis*)

_____ **3.** leukoblast (*LU-ko-blast*)

_____ **4.** genetics (*jeh-NET-iks*)

_____ **5.** hypertrophy (*hi-PER-tro-fe*)

a. overdevelopment of tissue

b. study of heredity

c. formation of tissue

d. cell that ingests waste

e. immature white blood cell

_____ **6.** neoplasia (*ne-o-PLA-ze-ah*)

_____ **7.** gonadotropin (*gon-ah-do-TRO-pin*)

_____ **8.** aplasia (*ah-PLA-ze-ah*)

_____ **9.** somatic (*so-MAT-ik*)

_____ **10.** chromophilic (*kro-mo-FIL-ik*)

a. attracting color

b. pertaining to the body

c. substance that acts on the sex glands

d. new formation of tissue

e. lack of development

Identify and define the root in the following words.

	Root	Meaning of Root
11. genesis (*JEN-eh-sis*)	gen	origin, formation
12. esophagus (*eh-SOF-ah-gus*)	_____	_____
13. normoblast (*NOR-mo-blast*)	_____	_____
14. aplastic (*ah-PLAS-tik*)	_____	_____
15. dystrophy (*DIS-tro-fe*)	_____	_____

Table 4-3   Suffixes and Roots for Body Chemistry

Word Part	Meaning	Example	Definition of Example
Suffixes			
-ase	enzyme	lipase LI-pase	enzyme that digests fat (lipid)
-ose	sugar	lactose LAK-tose	milk sugar
Roots			
hydr/o	water, fluid	hydration hi-DRA-shun	addition of water, relative amount of water present
gluc/o	glucose	glucogenesis glu-ko-JEN-eh-sis	production of glucose
glyc/o	sugar, glucose	normoglycemia nor-mo-gli-SE-me-ah	normal blood sugar level
racchar/o	sugar	polysaccharide pol-e-SAK-ah-ride	compound containing many simple sugars
amyl/o	starch	amyloid AM-ih-loyd	resembling starch
lip/o	lipid, fat	lipophilic lip-o-FIL-ik	attracting or absorbing lipids
adip/o	fat	adiposuria ad-ih-po-SUR-e-ah	presence of fat in the urine (ur/o)
steat/o	fatty	steatorrhea ste-ah-to-RE-ah	discharge (-rhea) of fatty stools
prote/o	protein	protease PRO-te-ase	enzyme that digests protein

EXERCISE 4-3

Fill in the blanks.

1. A disaccharide (*di-SAK-ah-ride*) is a compound that contains two _____.
2. The ending *-ose* indicates that fructose is a(n) _____.
3. Hydrophobia (*hi-dro-FO-be-ah*) is an aversion (-phobia) to _____.
4. Amylase (*AM-ih-lase*) is an enzyme that digests _____.
5. Liposuction (*LIP-o-suk-shun*) is the surgical removal of _____.
6. A glucocorticoid (*glu-ko-KOR-tih-koyd*) is a hormone that controls the metabolism of _____.
7. An adipocyte (*AD-ih-po-site*) is a cell that stores _____.

Identify and define the root in the following words.

		Root	Meaning of Root
8.	asteatosis (*as-te-ah-TO-sis*)	____	_____
9.	lipoma (*li-PO-mah*)	____	_____
10.	hyperglycemia (*hi-per-gli-SE-me-ah*)	____	_____
11.	glucolytic (*glu-ko-LIT-ik*)	____	_____

Terminology   Supplementary Terms

amino acids *ah-ME-no*	The nitrogen-containing compounds that make up proteins
anabolism *ah-NAB-o-lizm*	The type of metabolism in which body substances are made; the building phase of metabolism
catabolism *kah-TAB-o-lizm*	The type of metabolism in which substances are broken down for energy and simple compounds
collagen *KOL-ah-jen*	A fibrous protein found in connective tissue
cortex *KOR-tex*	The outer region of an organ
glycogen *GLI-ko-jen*	A complex sugar compound stored in liver and muscles and broken down into glucose when needed for energy
interstitial *in-ter-STISH-al*	Between parts, such as the spaces between cells in a tissue
medulla *meh-DUL-lah*	The inner region of an organ, marrow (root: medull/o)
parenchyma *par-EN-kih-mah*	The functional tissue of an organ
parietal *pah-RI-eh-tal*	Pertaining to a wall, describes a membrane that lines a body cavity
soma *SO-mah*	The body
stem cell	An immature cell that has the capacity to develop into any of a variety of different cell types, a precursor cell
visceral *VIS-er-al*	Pertaining to the internal organs; describes a membrane on the surface of an organ

Case Study Revisited

R.S.'s Return to Class Schedule

Following his appointment, R.S. decided to accept his doctor's advice. He started preparing at least two meals a day at home and often boxed a lunch to eat during the day on campus. The more nutritious meals provided him greater energy; he no longer felt sluggish. He visited the university gym to work out at least two to three times a week for 20 minutes and hoped to increase that time when his schedule permitted. He realized how important exercise is to feeling energized, upbeat, and more confident in his everyday activities. Finally, he recognized that a little knowledge is a dangerous thing and that it is not smart to try and diagnose oneself.

Labeling Exercise

DIAGRAM OF A TYPICAL ANIMAL CELL

Write the name of each numbered part on the corresponding line of the answer sheet.

Centriole	*Nucleus*
Cytosol	*Peroxisome*
Golgi apparatus	*Plasma membrane*
Lysosome	*Ribosomes*
Microvilli	*Rough ER*
Mitochondrion	*Smooth ER*
Nuclear membrane	*Vesicle*
Nucleolus	

1. _____

2. _____

3. _____

4. _____

5. _____

6. _____

7. _____

8. _____

9. _____

10. _____

11. _____

12. _____

13. _____

14. _____

15. _____

Terminology

MATCHING

Match the following terms, and write the appropriate letter to the left of each number.

_____	**1.** ATP	**a.**	small bodies that store fat
_____	**2.** DNA	**b.**	material that holds the cellular organelles
_____	**3.** nucle oplasm	**c.**	energy compound of the cells
_____	**4.** liposomes	**d.**	genetic material
_____	**5.** cytoplasm	**e.**	material that fills the nucleus

_____ **6.** blastocyte	**a.** immature cell
_____ **7.** ribosomes	**b.** organelles that produce ATP
_____ **8.** mitochondria	**c.** organelles that contain RNA
_____ **9.** mitosis	**d.** small cellular body containing digestive enzymes
_____ **10.** lysosome	**e.** cell division

_____ **11.** reticular	**a.** resembling a gland
_____ **12.** adenoid	**b.** fibrous tumor
_____ **13.** fibroma	**c.** cell with a very large nucleus
_____ **14.** megakaryocyte	**d.** pertaining to a network
_____ **15.** chromosome	**e.** structure that contains genes

_____ **16.** autotroph	**a.** resembling a nipple
_____ **17.** papilliform	**b.** having no specific form
_____ **18.** amorphous	**c.** wasting of tissue
_____ **19.** atrophy	**d.** pertaining to the body
_____ **20.** somatic	**e.** organism that can manufacture its own food

_____ **21.** fibroplasia	**a.** difficulty in eating
_____ **22.** hypoplasia	**b.** dissolving of fat
_____ **23.** dysphagia	**c.** underdevelopment of an organ or tissue
_____ **24.** cytogenesis	**d.** formation of fibrous tissue
_____ **25.** lipolysis	**e.** formation of cells

_____ **26.** adiposuria	**a.** presence of fat in the urine
_____ **27.** proteolytic	**b.** presence of glucose in the urine
_____ **28.** glucosuria	**c.** treatment using water
_____ **29.** polysaccharide	**d.** compound composed of many simple sugars
_____ **30.** hydrotherapy	**e.** destroying or dissolving protein

Supplementary Terms

_____ **31.** amino acid	**a.** pertaining to the internal organs
_____ **32.** collagen	**b.** breakdown phase of metabolism
_____ **33.** visceral	**c.** fibrous protein in connective tissue
_____ **34.** cortex	**d.** outer region of an organ
_____ **35.** catabolism	**e.** building block of protein

Fill in the blanks.

36. The study of tissues is called _____.

37. The four basic tissue types are _____.

38. All the activities of a cell make up its _____.

39. The system that includes the kidneys and bladder is the _____.

40. The systems involved in circulation are the cardiovascular system and the _____.

41. The simple sugar that is the main energy source for metabolism is _____.

42. A thick cellular secretion that lubricates and protects tissues is called _____.

43. An organic compound that speeds the rate of metabolic reactions is a(n) _____.

44. A cytotoxic substance is poisonous or damaging to _____.

45. The term _dehydration_ refers to a loss or deficiency of _____.

46. The study of form and structure is called _____.

47. A myxocyte is found in tissue that secretes _____.

True–False

Examine the following statements. If the statement is true, write T in the first blank. If the statement is false, write F in the first blank, and correct the statement by replacing the underlined word in the second blank.

	True or False	Correct Answer

48. A megakaryocyte is a cell with a large <u>nucleus</u>.

49. Hydrophobia is an aversion to <u>fats</u>.

50. An adipocyte is a cell that stores <u>glucose</u>.

51. There are <u>46</u> chromosomes in each human cell, aside from the reproductive cells.

52. A whip-like extension of a cell is a <u>flagellum</u>.

Word Building

Write a word for each of the following definitions using the word parts provided. Each may be used more than once.

-oid   amyl/o   muc/o   aden/o   -ase   lip/o   leuk/o   histi/o   blast

53. Like or resembling a gland _____

54. Immature white blood cell _____

55. Enzyme that digests fat _____

56. Resembling mucus _____

57. Cell that gives rise to tissue _____

58. Enzyme that digests starch _____

59. Resembling starch _____

Word Analysis

Define each of the following words, and give the meaning of the word parts in each. Use a dictionary if necessary.

60. homeostasis (*ho-me-o-STA-sis*) _____
   a. homeo _____
   b. stat (from Greek *states*) _____
   c. -sis _____

61. somatotropic (*so-mah-to-TROP-ik*) _____
   a. somat/o _____
   b. trop/o _____
   c. -ic _____

62. autophagy (*aw-TOF-ah-je*) _____
   a. auto _____
   b. phag/o _____
   c. -y _____

63. asteatosis (*as-te-ah-TO-sis*) _____
   a. a- _____
   b. steat/o _____
   c. -sis _____

For more learning activities, see Chapter 4 of the Student Resources on the Point.

Additional Case Studies

Case Study 4-1: *Hematology Laboratory Studies*

J.E. had a blood test as required for a preoperative anesthesia assessment in preparation for scheduled plastic surgery on her breasts. The report read as follows:

Complete blood count (CBC) and differential:
Red blood cell (RBC) count—4.5 million/mcL
Hemoglobin (Hgb)—12.6 g/dL
Hematocrit (Hct)—38 percent
White blood cell (WBC) count—8,500/mcL
Neutrophils—58 percent

Lymphocytes—34 percent
Monocytes—6 percent
Eosinophils—1.5 percent
Basophils—0.5 percent
Platelet count—200,000/mcL
Prothrombin time (PT)—11.5 seconds
Partial thromboplastin time (PTT)—65 seconds
Blood glucose—84 mg/dL

The surgeon reviewed these results and concluded that they were within normal limits (WNL).

Case Study 4-2: *Needle Aspiration of Thyroid Tumor*

Chief Complaint

D.S., a 65-year-old male, noticed a lump on the side of his neck and went to see his physician. He has a history of prostate cancer and had a prostatectomy four years ago. Bilateral lymph node dissection revealed no metastasis. His physician referred him to a surgeon for evaluation of a nodule on the thyroid gland.

Examination

Dr. Thompson, a general surgeon, examined D.S. and recommended a needle aspiration of the thyroid gland. The ultrasound-guided fine needle aspiration revealed

atypical cells with abundant cytoplasm and prominent nuclei but no metastasis. However, the nuclei showed some morphologic changes. Histologic slides of the left thyroid showed clusters of epithelial cells associated with lymphocytes suggestive of lymphocytic thyroiditis.

Clinical Course

D.S. underwent a total thyroidectomy and is healing well. A follow-up CT scan of the neck and chest showed no additional nodules or indications of metastatic disease.

Case Study Questions

Multiple Choice. Select the best answer and write the letter of your choice to the left of each number.

_____ **1.** J.E.'s blood test results were within normal limits. She could be described as being in a state of
  a. homeopathy
  b. neoplasia
  c. hematophilia
  d. homeostasis

_____ **2.** The suffix in glucose indicates that this compound is a(n)
  a. enzyme
  b. sugar
  c. protein
  d. fat

_____ **3.** The suffix in *prostatectomy* and *thyroidectomy* means
  a. removal or excision
  b. incision into
  c. inflammation
  d. resembling

_____ **4.** The singular form of *nuclei* is
  a. nucleolus
  b. nucleoli
  c. nucleum
  d. nucleus

Identify and give the meaning of the prefixes in the following words.

	Prefix	Meaning of Prefix
5. atypical	_____	_____
6. prothrombin	_____	_____
7. bilateral	_____	_____
8. monocytes	_____	_____
9. dissection	_____	_____
10. metastasis (see Appendix 7)	_____	_____

Find words in the case studies for the following.

11. Three words that contain a root that means *attract, absorb* _____

12. Two words with a root that means *formation, molding, development* _____

13. A word with a root that means *form* _____

14. A word with a root that means *tissue* _____

15. Four words that contain a root that means *cell* _____

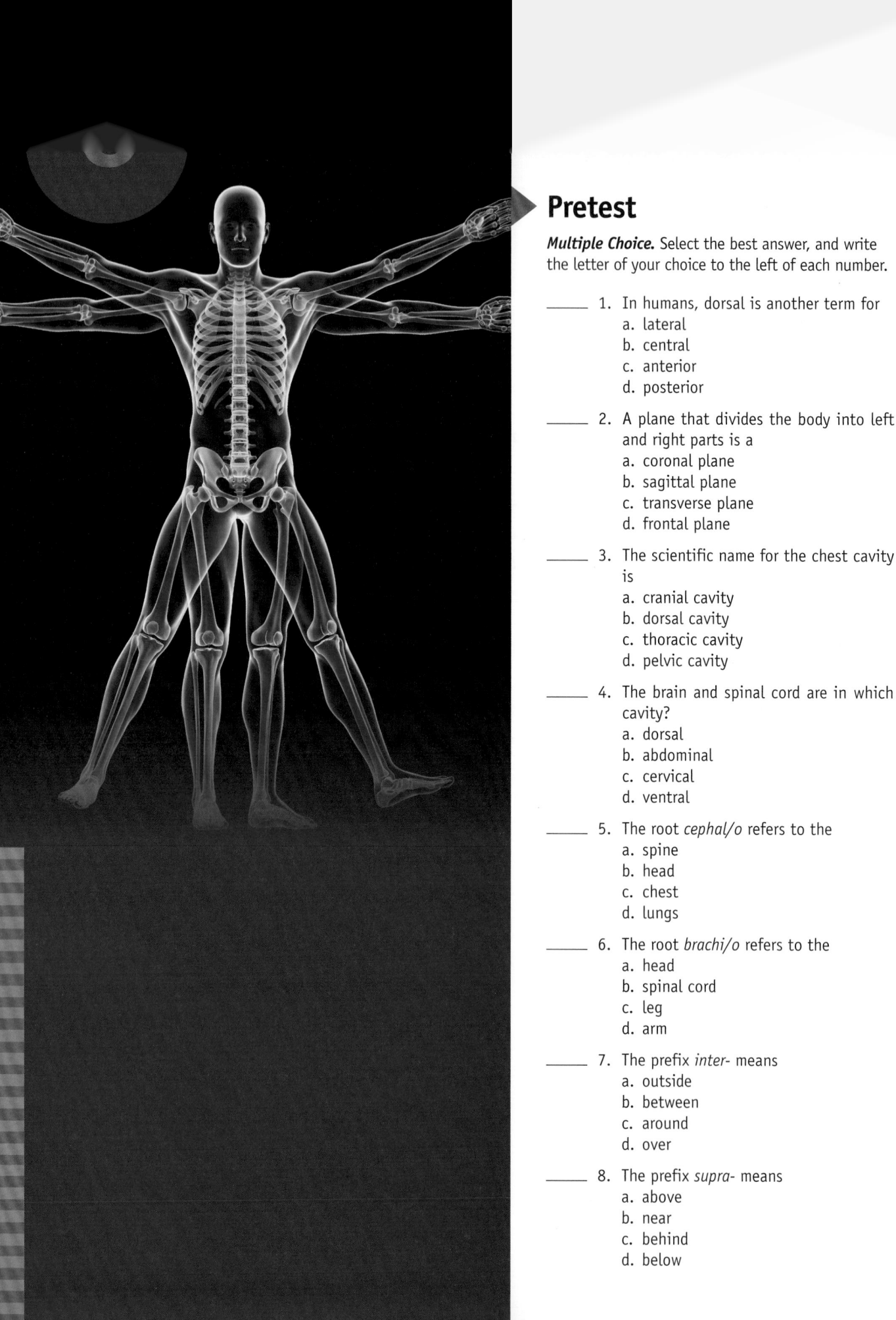

Pretest

Multiple Choice. Select the best answer, and write the letter of your choice to the left of each number.

_____ 1. In humans, dorsal is another term for
    a. lateral
    b. central
    c. anterior
    d. posterior

_____ 2. A plane that divides the body into left and right parts is a
    a. coronal plane
    b. sagittal plane
    c. transverse plane
    d. frontal plane

_____ 3. The scientific name for the chest cavity is
    a. cranial cavity
    b. dorsal cavity
    c. thoracic cavity
    d. pelvic cavity

_____ 4. The brain and spinal cord are in which cavity?
    a. dorsal
    b. abdominal
    c. cervical
    d. ventral

_____ 5. The root *cephal/o* refers to the
    a. spine
    b. head
    c. chest
    d. lungs

_____ 6. The root *brachi/o* refers to the
    a. head
    b. spinal cord
    c. leg
    d. arm

_____ 7. The prefix *inter-* means
    a. outside
    b. between
    c. around
    d. over

_____ 8. The prefix *supra-* means
    a. above
    b. near
    c. behind
    d. below

Learning Objectives

After study of this chapter, you should be able to:

1 ▶ Define the main directional terms used in anatomy. *p70*

2 ▶ Describe division of the body along three different planes. *p71*

3 ▶ Locate the dorsal and ventral body cavities. *p72*

4 ▶ Locate and name the nine divisions of the abdomen. *p72*

5 ▶ Locate and name the four quadrants of the abdomen. *p73*

6 ▶ Describe the main body positions used in medical practice. *p73*

7 ▶ Define basic terms describing body structure. *p75*

8 ▶ Recognize and use roots pertaining to body regions. *p76*

9 ▶ Recognize and use prefixes pertaining to position and direction. *p77*

10 ▶ Identify medical words and abbreviations pertaining to body structure in case studies. *pp69, 86*

Case Study: *B.K.'s Stomach Ache*

Chief Complaint

It was summer vacation, and B.K. and his older brother were hosting a lemonade stand in front of their home. Late in the afternoon, B.K., a 4-year-old male, appeared agitated and complained to his mother that he had a stomach ache. His mother recalled that she had given him a peanut butter and jelly sandwich and an apple for lunch earlier in the day. He had had no problems eating his lunch. Later in the day, she saw her son curled up on the couch crying and holding his stomach, and she decided to take him to the after-hours clinic where the child's pediatrician was on staff.

Examination

Dr. Davies, B.K.'s pediatrician, had known the boy since he was a newborn. B.K.'s parents made certain that their son had physical examinations on a regular basis. His immunizations were current, and aside from a few earaches and colds, B.K. was a healthy young boy. Upon arrival in the clinic, the office medical assistant recorded that B.K.'s vital signs were within normal limits. Dr. Davies then saw the patient and had him lie supine on the examination table. He performed a cephalocaudal assessment. The only abnormality causing concern was the abdominal pain B.K. said he was experiencing.

Dr. Davies asked B.K. to show him where it hurt the most. The boy first pointed to the left upper quadrant of his abdomen and then, somewhat confused, pointed to his right lower quadrant. The medical assistant returned and drew some blood for laboratory studies, which later showed normal results. Dr. Davies then ordered an abdominal x-ray.

Clinical Course

The x-ray revealed that B.K. had swallowed a nickel and a penny. The boy then confessed that he was trying to hide the money from his brother, so he had swallowed the coins. Dr. Davies explained to B.K. and his mother that he expected no serious complications and that the coins should be expelled in the next 24 hours or so.

In this chapter, we learn about body regions and orientations and become familiar with some of the terms healthcare professionals use to pinpoint exact locations on and within the body.

ANCILLARIES *At-A-Glance*

Visit thePoint to access the following resources. For guidance in using the resources most effectively, see pp. ix–xvi.

Learning RESOURCES

▶ Tips for Effective Studying
▶ Web Figure: Abdominal Regions
▶ Web Figure: Abdominal Quadrants
▶ Web Figure: Body Positions
▶ Web Chart: Directional Terms
▶ Web Chart: Structures in Abdominal Quadrants
▶ Audio Pronunciation Glossary

Learning ACTIVITIES

▶ Visual Activities
▶ Kinesthetic Activities
▶ Auditory Activities

Introduction

All healthcare fields require knowledge of body directions and orientations. Physicians, surgeons, nurses, occupational therapists, and physical therapists, for example, must be thoroughly familiar with the terms used to describe body locations and positions. Radiologic technologists must be able to position a person and direct x-rays to obtain suitable images for diagnosis, as noted in **Box 5-1**.

Directional Terms

In describing the location or direction of a given point in the body, it is always assumed that the subject is in the **anatomic position**, that is, upright, with face front, arms at the sides with palms forward and feet parallel. In this stance, the terms illustrated in **Figure 5-1** and listed in **Box 5-2** are used to designate relative position.

HEALTH PROFESSIONS
Radiologic Technologist

Box 5-1

Radiologic technologists help in the diagnosis of medical disorders by taking x-ray images (radiographs) of the body. They also use CT scans and other imaging technology to perform examinations on patients to aid physicians diagnosis. Following institutional safety patient mobilization procedures; they must prepare patients for radiologic examinations, place patients in appropriate positions; and then adjust equipment to the correct angles, heights, and settings for taking the x-ray or other diagnostic image. They must position the image receptors correctly and, after exposure, remove and process the images. They are also required to keep patient records and maintain equipment. Radiologic technologists must minimize radiation hazards by using protective equipment for themselves and patients and by delivering the minimum possible amount of radiation. They wear badges to monitor radiation levels and keep records of their exposure.

Radiologic technologists may specialize in a specific imaging technique such as bone densitometry, cardiovascular-interventional radiography, computed tomography, mammography, magnetic resonance imaging, nuclear medicine, and quality management. Some of these will be described in later chapters.

The majority of radiologic technologists work in hospitals, but they may also be employed in physicians' offices, diagnostic imaging centers (e.g., doing mammograms), and outpatient care centers. Radiologic technologists must possess a minimum of an associate's degree to qualify for professional certification. A higher degree is necessary for a supervisory or teaching position. The Joint Review Committee on Education in Radiologic Technology accredits most of the education programs. The American Registry of Radiologic Technologists (ARRT) offers a national certification examination in radiography as well as in other imaging technologies (CT, MRI, nuclear medicine, etc.). ARRT certification is required for employment as a radiologic technologist in most U.S. states. Job opportunities in this field are currently good. The American Society of Radiologic Technologists has information on this career at www.asrt.org.

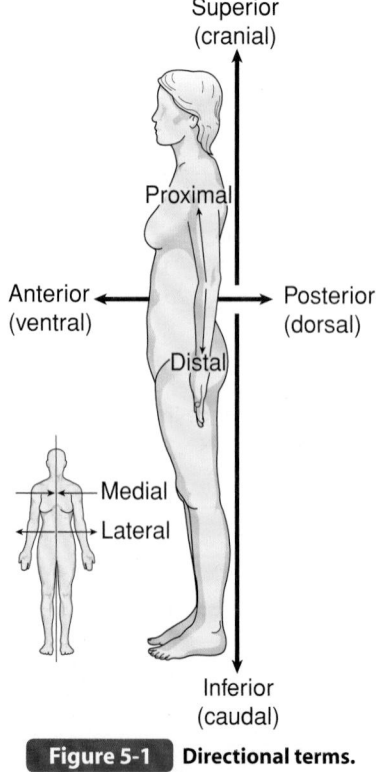

Figure 5-1   Directional terms.

FOR YOUR REFERENCE

Box 5-2

5

Anatomic Directions

Term	Definition
anterior (ventral)	toward or at the front (belly) of the body
posterior (dorsal)	toward or at the back (dorsum) of the body
medial	toward the midline of the body
lateral	toward the side of the body
proximal	nearer to the point of attachment or to a given reference point
distal	farther from the point of attachment or from a given reference point
superior	above, in a higher position
inferior	below, in a lower position
cranial (cephalad)	toward the head
caudal	toward the lower end of the spine (Latin *cauda* means "tail"); in humans, in an inferior direction
superficial (external)	closer to the surface of the body
deep (internal)	closer to the center of the body

Visit the Student Resources on the Point for an expanded list of directional terms with examples of their usage.

Figure 5-2 illustrates planes of section, that is, directions in which the body can be cut. A **frontal plane**, also called a coronal plane, is made at right angles to the midline and divides the body into anterior and posterior parts. A **sagittal** (*SAJ-ih-tal*) **plane** passes from front to back and divides the body into right and left portions. If the plane passes through the midline, it is a midsagittal or medial plane. A **transverse** (**horizontal**) **plane** passes horizontally, dividing the body into superior and inferior parts.

Frontal
(coronal)
plane

Sagittal
plane

Transverse
(horizontal)
plane

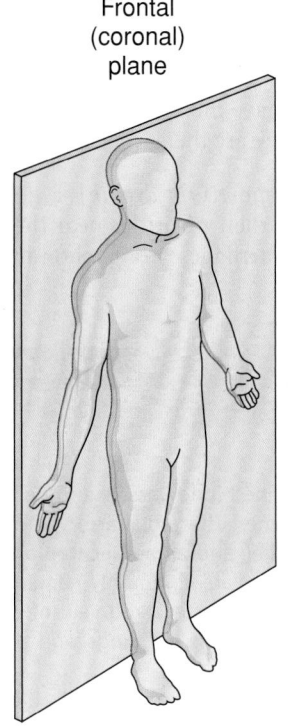

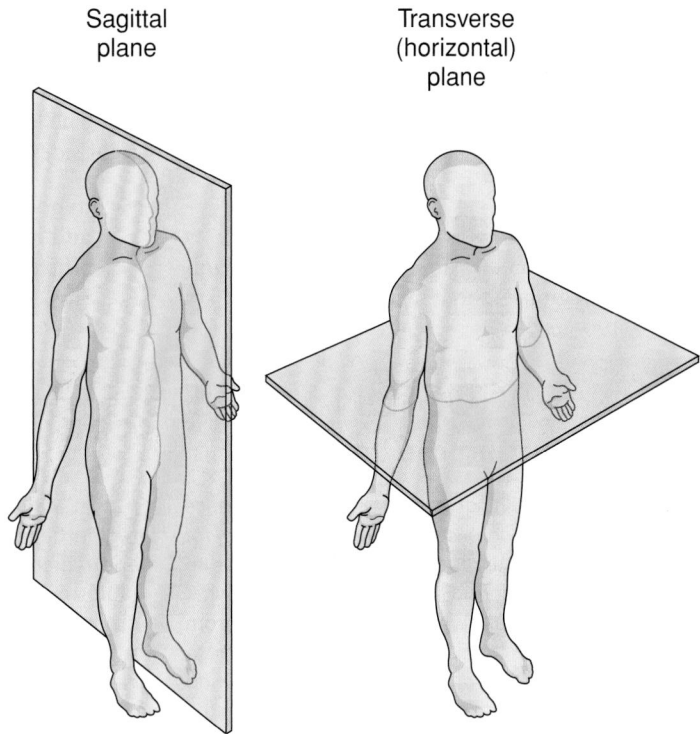

Figure 5-2   **Planes of division.**

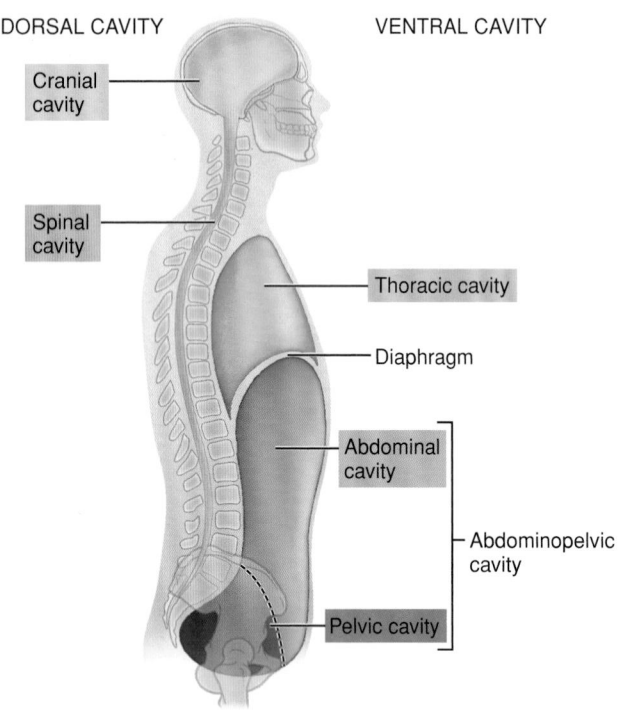

Figure 5-3 **Body cavities, lateral view.** Shown are the dorsal and ventral cavities with their subdivisions.

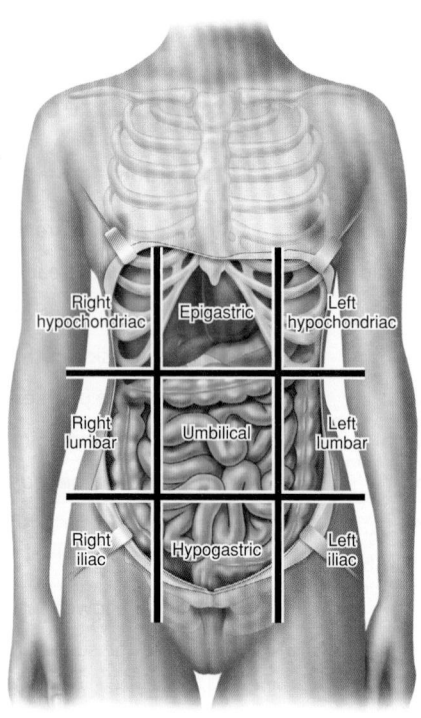

Figure 5-4 **The nine regions of the abdomen.**

Body Cavities

Internal organs are located within dorsal and ventral cavities (**Fig. 5-3**). The dorsal cavity contains the brain in the **cranial cavity** and the spinal cord in the **spinal cavity** (**canal**). The uppermost ventral space, the **thoracic cavity**, is separated from the **abdominal cavity** by the **diaphragm**, a muscle used in breathing. There is no anatomic separation between the abdominal cavity and the **pelvic cavity**, which together make up the **abdominopelvic cavity**. The large membrane that lines the abdominopelvic cavity and covers the organs within it is the **peritoneum** (*per-ih-to-NE-um*).

Abdominal Regions

For orientation, the abdomen can be divided by imaginary lines into nine regions—three medial regions and six lateral regions (**Fig. 5-4**). The sections down the midline are the:

- epigastric (*ep-ih-GAS-trik*) region, located above the stomach
- umbilical (*um-BIL-ih-kal*) region, named for the umbilicus, or navel
- hypogastric (*hi-po-GAS-trik*) region, located below the stomach

The lateral regions have the same name on the left and right sides (**Box 5-3**). They are the:

- hypochondriac (*hi-po-KON-dre-ak*) regions, right and left, named for their positions near the ribs, specifically near the cartilages (root: chondr/o) of the ribs

- lumbar (*LUM-bar*) regions, right and left, which are located near the small of the back (lumbar region of the spine)
- iliac (*IL-e-ak*) regions, right and left, named for the upper bone of the hip, the ilium; also called the inguinal (*ING-gwih-nal*) regions, with reference to the groin

More simply, but less precisely, the abdomen can be divided into four sections by a single vertical line and a single horizontal line that intersect at the umbilicus (navel) (**Fig. 5-5**). The sections are the right upper quadrant (RUQ), left upper quadrant (LUQ), right lower quadrant (RLQ), and left lower quadrant (LLQ).

Additional terms for body regions are shown in **Figures 5-6** and **5-7**. You may need to refer to these illustrations as you work through the book.

Positions

In addition to the anatomic position, there are other standard positions in which the body is placed for special purposes, such as examination, tests, surgery, or fluid drainage. The most common of these positions and some of their uses are described in **Box 5-4**.

The regions of the abdomen and some of these body positions are illustrated in the Student Resources on thePoint.

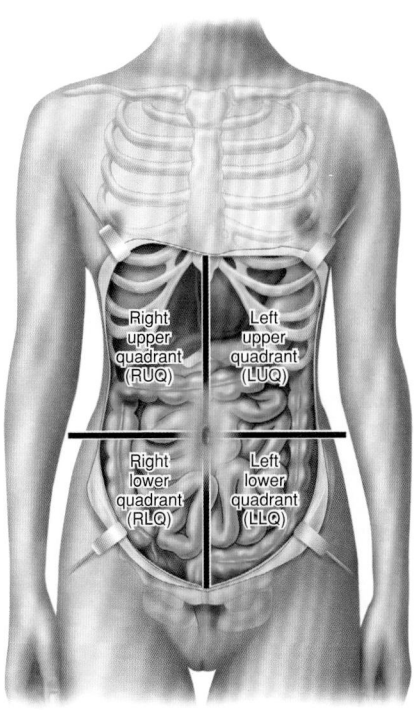

Figure 5-5 **Quadrants of the abdomen.** Some organs within the quadrants are indicated.

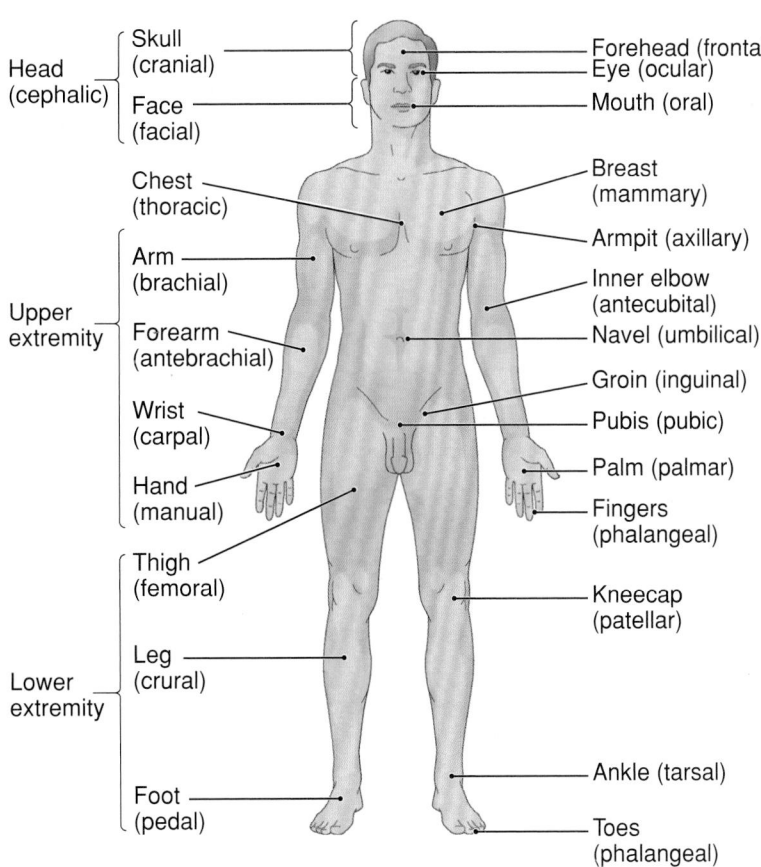

Figure 5-6 **Common terms for body regions, anterior view.** Anatomic adjectives for regions are in parentheses.

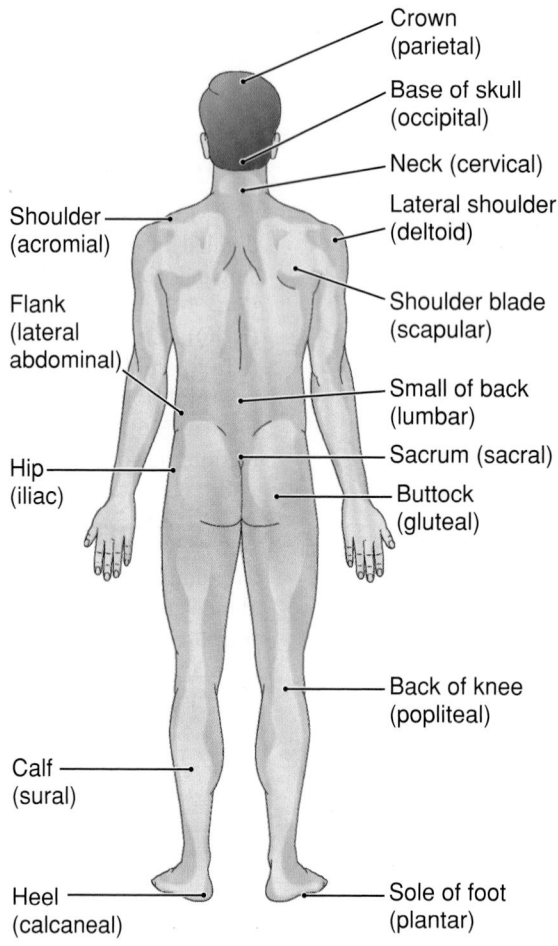

Figure 5-7   Common terms for body regions, posterior view.
Anatomic adjectives for regions are in parentheses.

FOR YOUR REFERENCE

Box 5-4

Body Positions

Position	Description
anatomic position *an-ah-TOM-ik*	standing erect, facing forward, arms at sides, palms forward, legs parallel, toes pointed forward; used for descriptions and studies of the body
decubitus position *de-KU-bih-tus*	lying down, specifically according to the part of the body resting on a flat surface, as in left or right lateral decubitus, or dorsal or ventral decubitus
dorsal recumbent position *re-KUM-bent*	on back, with legs bent and separated, feet flat; used for obstetrics and gynecology
Fowler position	on back, head of bed raised about 18 inches, knees elevated; used to ease breathing and for drainage
jackknife position *JAK-nife*	on back with shoulders elevated, legs flexed and thighs at right angles to the abdomen; used to introduce a tube into the urethra
knee–chest position	on knees, head and upper chest on table, arms crossed above head; used in gynecology and obstetrics and for flushing the intestine
lateral recumbent position	on the side with one leg flexed, arm position may vary

Body Positions (*Continued*)

Position	Description
lithotomy position *lih-THOT-o-me*	on back, legs flexed on abdomen, thighs apart; used for gynecologic and urologic surgery
prone	lying face down
Sims position	on left side, right leg drawn up high and forward, left arm along back, chest forward resting on bed; used for kidney and uterine surgery, colon examination, and enemas
supine[a] *SU-pine*	lying face up
Trendelenburg position *tren-DEL-en-berg*	on back with head lowered by tilting bed back at 45-degree angle; used for pelvic and abdominal surgery, treatment of shock

[a]To remember the difference between prone and supine, look for the word *up* in supine.

Terminology   Key Terms

abdominal cavity *ab-DOM-ih-nal*	The large ventral cavity below the diaphragm and above the pelvic cavity
abdominopelvic cavity *ab-dom-ih-no-PEL-vik*	The large ventral cavity between the diaphragm and pelvis that includes the abdominal and pelvic cavities
anatomic position *an-ah-TOM-ik*	Standard position for anatomic studies, in which the body is erect and facing forward, the arms are at the sides with palms forward, and the feet are parallel
cranial cavity *KRA-ne-al*	The dorsal cavity that contains the brain
diaphragm *DI-ah-fram*	The muscle that separates the thoracic from the abdominal cavity
frontal (coronal) plane *FRUHN-tal*	Plane of section that separates the body into anterior (front) and posterior (back) portions
pelvic cavity *PEL-vik*	The ventral cavity that is below the abdominal cavity
peritoneum *per-ih-to-NE-um*	The large serous membrane that lines the abdominopelvic cavity and covers the organs within it
sagittal plane *SAJ-ih-tal*	Plane that divides the body into right and left portions
spinal cavity (canal) *SPI-nal*	Dorsal cavity that contains the spinal cord
thoracic cavity *tho-RAS-ik*	The ventral cavity above the diaphragm, the chest cavity
transverse (horizontal) plane *trans-VERS*	Plane that divides the body into superior (upper) and inferior (lower) portions

Go to the Audio Pronunciation Glossary in the Student Resources on thePoint to hear these terms pronounced.

Word Parts Pertaining to Body Structure

Tables 5-1 to 5-3 provide word roots and prefixes pertaining to body structure.

Table 5-1	Roots for Regions of the Head and Trunk		
Root	**Meaning**	**Example**	**Definition of Example**
cephal/o	head	megacephaly *meg-ah-SEF-a-le*	abnormal largeness of the head
cervic/o	neck	cervicofacial *ser-vih-ko-FA-shal*	pertaining to the neck and face
thorac/o	chest, thorax	thoracotomy *tho-rah-KOT-o-me*	incision (-tomy) into the chest
abdomin/o	abdomen	intraabdominal *in-trah-ab-DOM-ih-nal*	within the abdomen
celi/o	abdomen	celiocentesis *se-le-o-sen-TE-sis*	surgical puncture (centesis) of the abdomen
lapar/o	abdominal wall	laparoscope *LAP-ah-ro-skope*	instrument (-scope) for viewing the peritoneal cavity through the abdominal wall
lumb/o	lumbar region, lower back	thoracolumbar *tho-rak-o-LUM-bar*	pertaining to the chest and lumbar region
periton, peritone/o	peritoneum	peritoneal *per-ih-to-NE-al*	pertaining to the peritoneum

EXERCISE 5-1

Write the adjective for each of the following definitions. The correct suffix is given in parentheses.

1. Pertaining to (-ic) the chest _____thoracic_____

2. Pertaining to (-ic) the head _____

3. Pertaining to (-al) the neck _____

4. Pertaining to (-al) the abdomen _____

5. Pertaining to (-ar) the lower back _____

Fill in the blanks.

6. Peritonitis (*per-ih-to-NI-tis*) is inflammation (-itis) of the _____.

7. The adjective celiac (*SE-le-ak*) pertains to the _____.

8. In B.K.'s opening case study, the doctor's cephalocaudal examination began at his _____.

9. In the opening study, B.K. was placed on his back in a _____ position for the doctor to examine his abdomen.

10. A laparotomy (*lap-ah-ROT-o-me*) is an incision through the _____.

Table 5-2	Roots for the Extremities		
Root	**Meaning**	**Example**	**Definition of Example**
acro	extremity, end	acrocyanosis *ak-ro-si-ah-NO-sis*	bluish discoloration of the extremities
brachi/o	arm	antebrachium *an-te-BRA-ke-um*	forearm
dactyl/o	finger, toe	polydactyly *pol-e-DAK-til-e*	having more than the normal number of fingers or toes
ped/o	foot	pedometer *pe-DOM-eh-ter*	instrument that measures footsteps
pod/o	foot	podiatric *po-de-AT-rik*	pertaining to study and treatment of the foot

EXERCISE 5-2

Fill in the blanks.

1. Acrokinesia (*ak-ro-ki-NE-se-ah*) is excess motion (-kinesia) of the _____.

2. Animals that brachiate (*BRA-ke-ate*), such as monkeys, swing from place to place using their _____.

3. A dactylospasm (*DAK-til-o-spazm*) is a spasm (cramp) of a(n) _____.

4. The term brachiocephalic (*bra-ke-o-seh-FAL-ik*) refers to the _____.

5. Sinistropedal (*sih-nis-tro-PE-dal*) refers to the use of the left _____.

Table 5-3	Prefixes for Position and Direction		
Prefix	**Meaning**	**Example**	**Definition of Example**
circum-	around	circumoral *ser-kum-OR-al*	around the mouth
peri-	around	periorbital *per-e-OR-bit-al*	around the orbit (eye socket)
intra-	in, within	intravascular *in-trah-VAS-ku-lar*	within a vessel (vascul/o)
epi-	on, over	epithelial *ep-ih-THE-le-al*	referring to epithelium, tissue that covers surfaces
extra-	outside	extrathoracic *eks-trah-tho-RAS-ik*	outside the thorax
infra-[a]	below	infrascapular *in-frah-SKAP-u-lar*	below the scapula (shoulder blade)
sub-[a]	below, under	sublingual *sub-LING-gwal*	under the tongue (lingu/o)
inter-	between	intercostal *in-ter-KOS-tal*	between the ribs (cost/o)
juxta-	near, beside	juxtaposition *juks-tah-po-ZIH-shun*	a location near or beside another structure

(continued)

Table 5-3	Prefixes for Position and Direction (*Continued*)		
Prefix	**Meaning**	**Example**	**Definition of Example**
para-	near, beside	parasagittal *par-ah-SAJ-ih-tal*	near or beside a sagittal plane
retro-	behind, backward	retrouterine *reh-tro-U-ter-in*	behind the uterus
supra-	above	suprapatellar *su-prah-pah-TEL-ar*	above the patella (kneecap)

ªAlso indicates degree.

EXERCISE 5-3

Synonyms

Write a word that means the same as each of the following.

1. perioral _____circumoral_____

2. infrascapular _____

3. perivascular _____

4. subcostal _____

5. circumorbital _____

Opposites

Write a word that means the opposite of each of the following.

6. suprapatellar _____infrapatellar_____

7. extracellular _____

8. subscapular _____

9. intrathoracic _____

Define the following words.

10. paranasal (*par-ah-NA-zal*) _____

11. retroperitoneal (*reh-tro-per-ih-to-NE-al*) _____

12. supraabdominal (*su-prah-ab-DOM-ih-nal*) _____

13. intrauterine (*in-trah-U-ter-in*) _____

Refer to Figures 5-6 and 5-7 to define the following terms.

14. periumbilical (*per-e-um-BIL-ih-kal*) _____

15. intergluteal (*in-ter-GLU-te-al*) _____

16. epitarsal (*ep-ih-TAR-sal*) _____

17. intraocular (*in-trah-OK-u-lar*) _____

18. parasacral (*par-ah-SA-kral*) _____

Terminology | Supplementary Terms

digit *DIJ-it*	A finger or toe (adjective: digital)
epigastrium *ep-ih-GAS-tre-um*	The epigastric region
fundus *FUN-dus*	The base or body of a hollow organ, the area of an organ farthest from its opening
hypochondrium *hi-po-KON-dre-um*	The hypochondriac region (left or right)
lumen *LU-men*	The central opening within a tube or hollow organ
meatus *me-A-tus*	A passage or opening
orifice *OR-ih-fis*	The opening of a cavity
os	Mouth, any body opening
septum *SEP-tum*	A wall dividing two cavities
sinus *SI-nus*	A cavity, as within a bone
sphincter *SFINK-ter*	A circular muscle that regulates an opening

Go to the Audio Pronunciation Glossary in the Student Resources on thePoint to hear these terms pronounced.

Terminology | Abbreviations

LLQ	Left lower quadrant
LUQ	Left upper quadrant
RLQ	Right lower quadrant
RUQ	Right upper quadrant

Case Study Revisited

Outcome of B.K.'s Case

Teased by his brother but reassured by the doctor, B.K. spent a quiet afternoon and evening and slept through the night. In the morning, he went into the bathroom and had a bowel movement. Examination of his stool showed that the coins had been expelled, and B.K. felt much better. Following this experience, B.K. deposited his earnings in his piggy bank.

Labeling Exercise

DIRECTIONAL TERMS

Write the name of each numbered part on the corresponding line of the answer sheet.

Anterior (ventral)   Medial
Distal   Posterior (dorsal)
Inferior (caudal)   Proximal
Lateral   Superior (cranial)

1. _____

2. _____

3. _____

4. _____

5. _____

6. _____

7. _____

8. _____

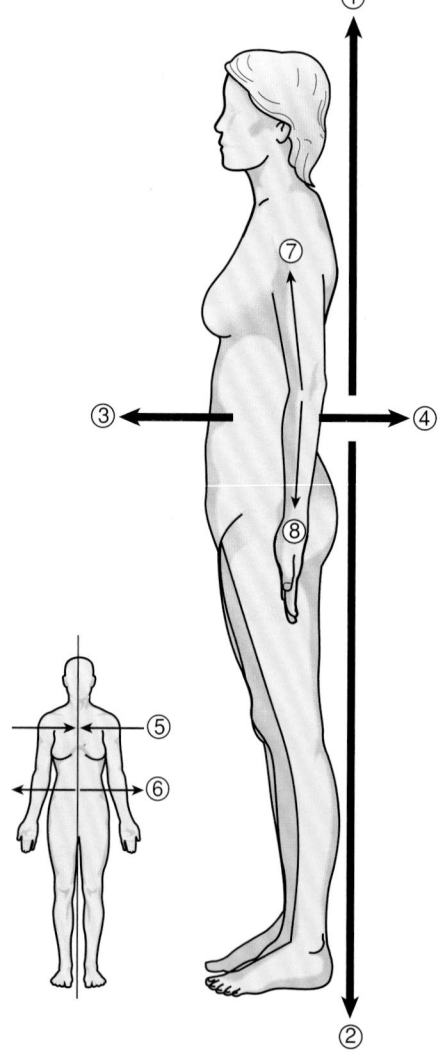

PLANES OF DIVISION

Write the name of each numbered part on the corresponding line of the answer sheet.

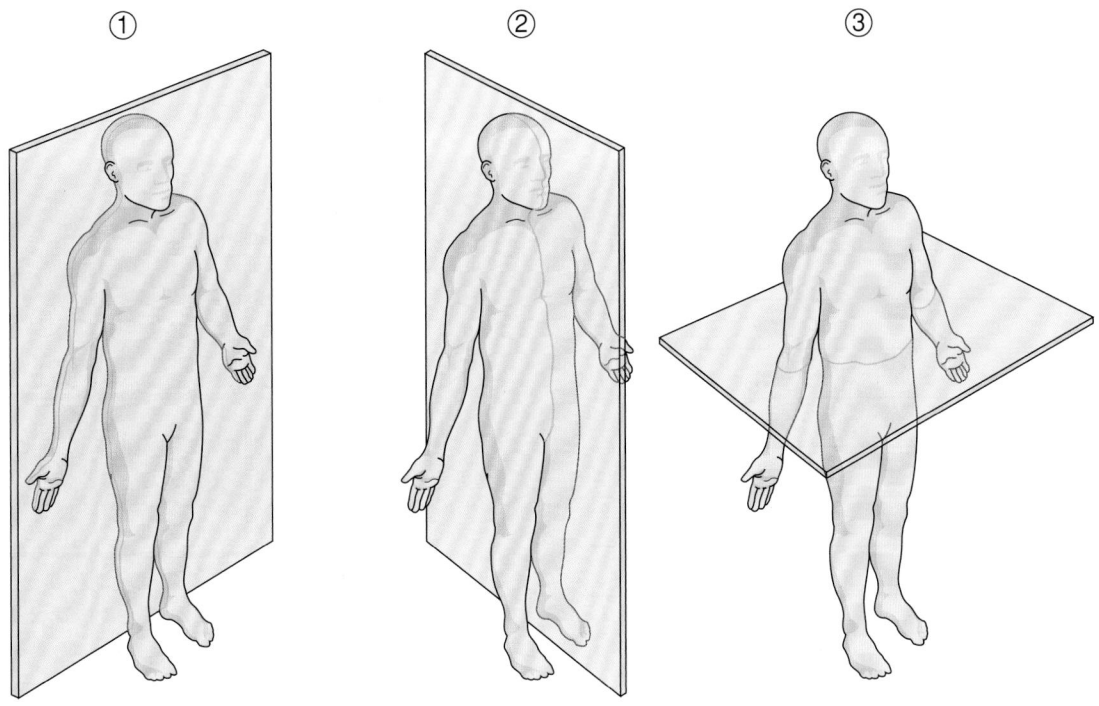

Frontal (coronal) plane   Transverse (horizontal) plane
Sagittal plane

1. _____
2. _____
3. _____

BODY CAVITIES, LATERAL VIEW

Write the name of each numbered part on the corresponding line of the answer sheet.

Abdominal cavity   Pelvic cavity
Abdominopelvic cavity   Spinal cavity (canal)
Cranial cavity   Thoracic cavity
Dorsal cavity   Ventral cavity
Diaphragm

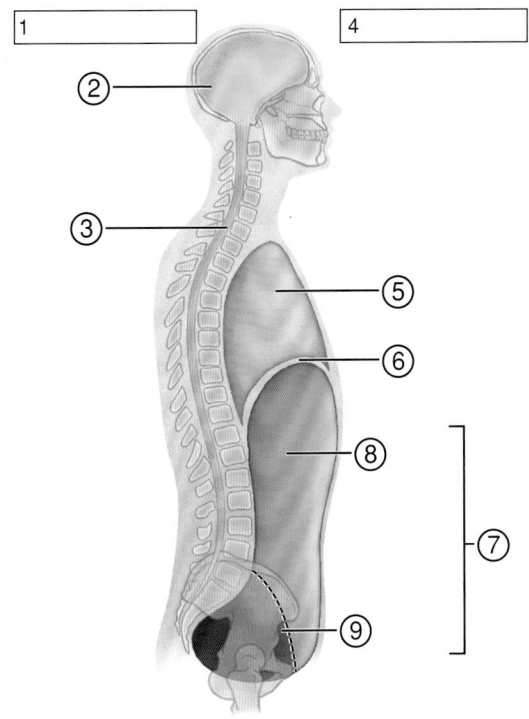

1. _____

2. _____

3. _____

4. _____

5. _____

6. _____

7. _____

8. _____

9. _____

THE NINE REGIONS OF THE ABDOMEN

Write the name of each numbered part on the corresponding line of the answer sheet.

Epigastric region
Hypogastric region
Left hypochondriac region
Left iliac (inguinal) region
Left lumbar region

Right hypochondriac region
Right iliac (inguinal) region
Right lumbar region
Umbilical region

1. _____
2. _____
3. _____
4. _____
5. _____
6. _____
7. _____
8. _____
9. _____

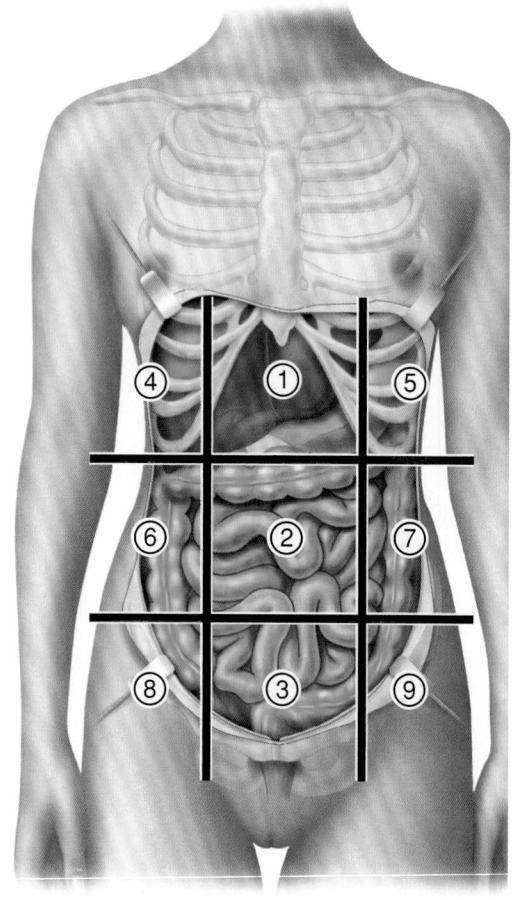

Abdominal regions

Terminology

MATCHING

Match the following terms, and write the appropriate letter to the left of each number.

_____ **1.** thoracentesis
_____ **2.** acrodermatitis
_____ **3.** laparoscopy
_____ **4.** dextropedal
_____ **5.** caudal

a. surgical puncture of the chest
b. skin inflammation of the extremities
c. pertaining to the right foot
d. examination through the abdominal wall
e. toward the tail

_____ **6.** macropodia
_____ **7.** subdermal
_____ **8.** macrocephaly
_____ **9.** celiotomy
_____ **10.** circumcision

a. circular cut
b. excessive size of the feet
c. beneath the skin
d. abnormal largeness of the head
e. incision of the abdomen

Supplementary Terms

_____ **11.** fundus
_____ **12.** meatus
_____ **13.** lumen
_____ **14.** sphincter
_____ **15.** septum

a. passage or opening
b. circular muscle that regulates an opening
c. central opening of a tube
d. base of a hollow organ
e. dividing wall

TRUE-FALSE

Examine each of the following statements. If the statement is true, write T in the first blank. If the statement is false, write F in the first blank and correct the statement by replacing the underlined word in the second blank.

	True or False	**Correct Answer**
16. The cranial and spinal cavities are the <u>ventral</u> body cavities.	F	dorsal
17. A <u>midsagittal plane</u> divides the body into equal right and left parts.		
18. The wrist is <u>proximal</u> to the elbow.		
19. A <u>transverse plane</u> divides the body into anterior and posterior parts.		
20. The abdominal cavity is <u>inferior</u> to the pelvic cavity.		
21. The hypogastric region is <u>inferior</u> to the umbilical region.		
22. When B.K. in the opening case study was lying in the supine position, he was lying <u>face down</u>.		
23. The right hypochondriac region is in the <u>RUQ</u>.		

ADJECTIVES

Name the part of the body referred to in the following adjectives.

24. celiac _____

25. phalangeal _____

26. popliteal _____

27. occipital _____

28. carpal _____

29. cervical _____

30. lumbar _____

31. brachial _____

Define the following words.

32. laparoscope _____

33. suprapubic _____

34. infraumbilical _____

35. cervicofacial _____

36. sublingual _____

37. retroperitoneal _____

38. bipedal _____

SYNONYMS

Write a word that means the same as each of the following.

39. posterior _____

40. circumocular _____

41. submammary _____

42. ventral _____

OPPOSITES

Write a word that means the opposite of each of the following.

43. microcephaly _____

44. deep _____

45. proximal _____

46. subscapular _____

47. extracellular _____

48. superior _____

ELIMINATIONS

In each of the sets below, underline the word that does not fit in with the rest and explain the reason for your choice.

49. cervic/o — dactyl/o — brachi/o — acro — pod/o _____

50. umbilical region — hypochondriac region — epigastric region — cervical region — iliac region _____

51. jackknife — supine — transverse— decubitus — prone _____

52. thoracic cavity — spinal cavity — pelvic cavity — abdominal cavity — abdominopelvic cavity _____

WORD BUILDING

Write a word for each of the following definitions using the word parts provided.

spasm	cephal	-o-	dactyl	extra-	-ic	infra-	syn-	thorac	a-	intra-	-y	poly-

53. cramp of a finger or toe _____

54. below the chest _____

55. inside the chest _____

56. condition of having extra fingers or toes _____

57. fusion of the fingers or toes _____

58. pertaining to the head and chest _____

59. absence of a finger or toe _____

60. within the head _____

61. absence of a head _____

WORD ANALYSIS

Define each of the words below, and give the meaning of the word parts in each. Use a dictionary if necessary.

62. mesocephalic (*mes-o-seh-FAL-ik*) _____

    a. mes/o _____

    b. cephal/o _____

    c. -ic _____

63. acrocyanosis (*ak-ro-si-ah-NO-sis*) _____

    a. acro _____

    b. cyan/o _____

    c. -sis _____

64. antebrachial (*an-te-BRA-ke-al*) _____

    a. ante- _____

    b. brachi/o _____

    c. -al _____

65. epigastric (*ep-ih-GAS-trik*) _____

    a. epi- _____

    b. gastr/o _____

    c. -ic _____

For more learning activities, see Chapter 5 of the Student Resources on thePoint.

Additional Case Studies

Case Study 5-1: *Emergency Care*

During a triathlon, paramedics responded to a scene with multiple patients involved in a serious bicycle accident. B.R., a 20-year-old woman, lost control of her bike while descending a hill at approximately 40 mph. As she fell, two other cyclists collided with her, sending all three crashing to the ground.

At the scene, B.R. reported pain in her head, back, chest, and leg. She also had numbness and tingling in her legs and feet. Other injuries included a cut on her face and on her right arm and an obvious deformity to both her shoulder and knee. She had slight difficulty breathing.

The paramedic did a rapid cephalocaudal assessment and immobilized B.R.'s neck in a cervical collar. She was secured on a backboard and given oxygen. After her bleeding was controlled and her injured extremities were immobilized, she was transported to the nearest emergency department.

During transport, the paramedic in charge radioed ahead to provide a prehospital report to the charge nurse. His report included the following information:

occipital and frontal head pain; laceration to right temple, superior and anterior to right ear; lumbar pain; bilateral thoracic pain on inspiration at midclavicular line on the right and midaxillary line on the left; dull aching pain of the posterior proximal right thigh; bilateral paresthesia (numbness and tingling) of distal lower legs circumferentially; varus (knock-knee) adduction deformity of left knee; and posterior displacement deformity of left shoulder.

At the hospital, the emergency department physician ordered radiographs for B.R. Before the procedure, the radiology technologist positioned a lead gonadal shield centered on the midsagittal line above B.R.'s symphysis pubis to protect her ovaries from unnecessary irradiation by the primary beam. The technologist knew that gonadal shielding is important for female patients undergoing imaging of the lumbar spine, sacroiliac joints, acetabula, pelvis, and kidneys. Shields should not be used for any examination in which an acute abdominal condition is suspected.

Case Study 5-2: *Medical Assistant in Training*

P.K. is a student in a local medical assistant training program. She was beginning her clinical rotations and was scheduled in a busy outpatient clinic. During the first week, she was assigned to follow a clinical medical assistant (CMA) who was prepping patients for examination by the physician. One of the goals for the week was to learn about body positioning for the various examinations.

The first day, P.K. assisted the CMA with a patient who came in for a gynecologic examination. After the physician completed the history, he asked P.K. and the medical assistant to help the patient into a lithotomy position.

The next morning, an elderly patient who came in with suspected pneumonia was escorted to an examination room. She was lying on her back on the examination table waiting for the physician. P.K. placed the patient into a Fowler position to aid the patient's breathing.

Later that afternoon, P.K. heard the CMA call for assistance with a patient whose blood pressure was lower than normal. P.K. walked in, and the patient had already been placed into a Trendelenburg position.

The next day, a patient came in to have some stitches or sutures removed. The patient previously had a cyst removed from his lumbar region. P.K. assisted the patient into a prone position in preparation for the nurse clinician to remove the sutures.

By the end of the week, P.K. felt comfortable with positioning patients for the various physical examinations.

Case Study Questions

Multiple Choice. Referring to Case Study 5-1, select the best answer, and write the letter of your choice to the left of each number.

_____ 1. The term for the timespan between injury and admission to the emergency department is
   a. preoperative
   b. prehospital
   c. pretrauma
   d. intrainjury

_____ 2. A cephalocaudal assessment goes from
   a. front to back
   b. head to toe
   c. side to side
   d. skin to bone

_____ 3. The victim's injured extremities were immobilized before transport. Immobilized means
   a. abducted as far as possible
   b. internally rotated and flexed
   c. adducted so that the limbs are crossed
   d. held in place to prevent movement

_____ 4. A cervical collar was placed on the victim to stabilize and immobilize the
   a. uterus
   b. shoulders
   c. neck
   d. pelvis

_____ 5. The singular form of acetabula is
   a. acetabulum
   b. acetabia
   c. acetab
   d. acetabulae

Draw or shade the appropriate area(s) on one or both diagrams for each question pertaining to case study.

6. Draw dots over the areas of the victim's occipital and frontal head pain.

7. Draw a dash (—) over the area of the right temporal laceration—superior and anterior to the right ear.

8. Crosshatch the area of lumbar pain.

9. Place an X over the area of thoracic pain at the anterior left midaxillary line.

10. Draw a star at the area of the pain on the right proximal posterior thigh.

11. Shade the area of the bilateral paresthesia of the distal lower legs, circumferentially.

12. Draw an arrow to show the direction of the varus adduction of the left knee.

13. Draw an arrow to show the direction of the posterior displacement of the left shoulder.

14. Draw a fig leaf to show the gonadal shield on the midsagittal line above the symphysis pubis.

15. Draw a circle around the area of the sacroiliac joints.

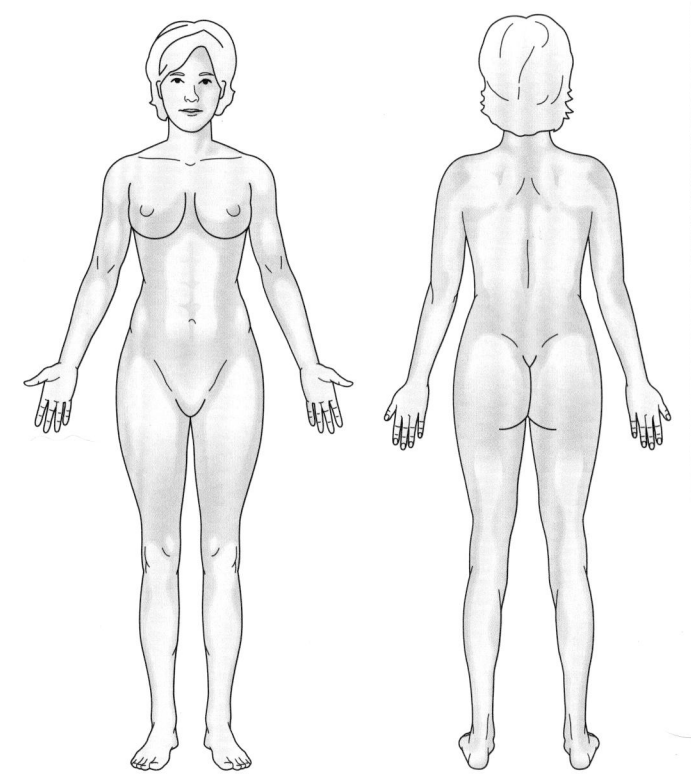

(continued)

Additional Case Studies *(Continued)*

Multiple Choice. Referring to Case Study 5-2, select the best answer, and write the letter of your choice to the left of each number.

_____**16.** The patient was placed in a Fowler position to
  a. aid breathing
  b. perform urologic surgery
  c. examine the colon
  d. palpate the vertebrae

_____**17.** The lumbar region refers to the
  a. lower abdomen
  b. chest
  c. lateral abdomen
  d. small of the back

Describe the following positions:

18. lithotomy_____

19. Trendelenburg_____

20. lateral recumbent _____

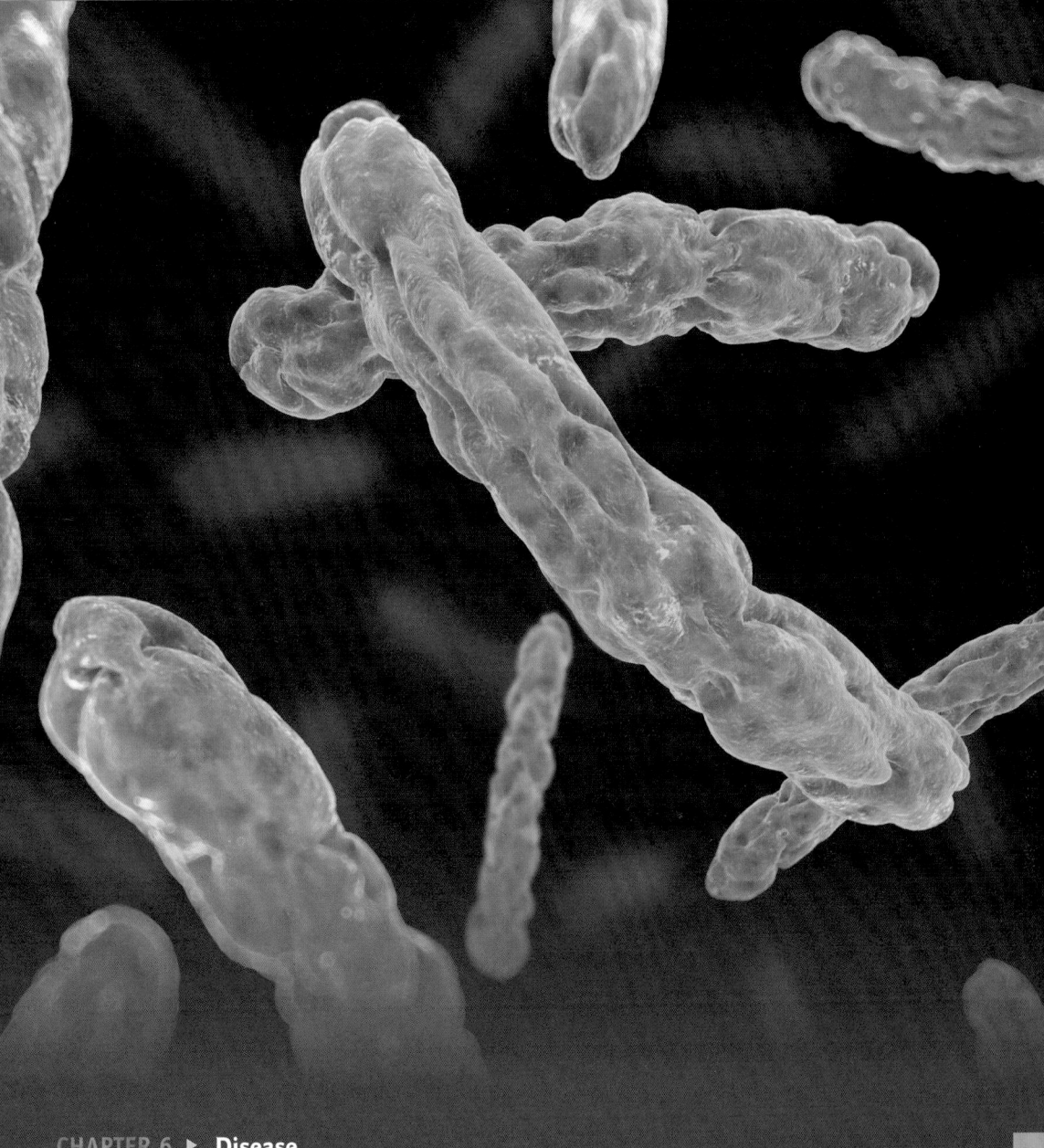

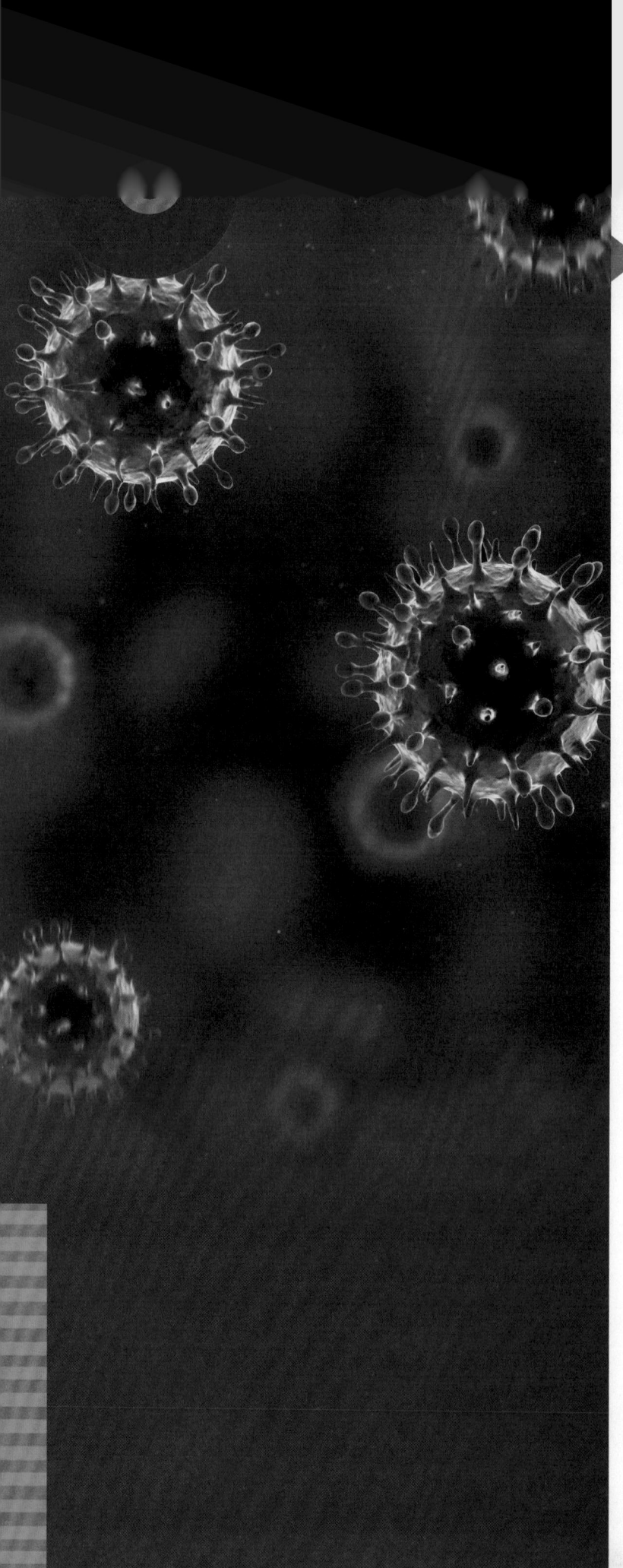

Pretest

Multiple Choice. Select the best answer, and write the letter of your choice to the left of each number.

_____ 1. Any organism so small that it can only be seen with a microscope is a
a. miniorganism
b. macroorganism
c. microcell
d. microorganism

_____ 2. A disease that has a sudden and severe onset is described as
a. chronic
b. mild
c. acute
d. infectious

_____ 3. Abnormal and uncontrolled growth of tissue is termed
a. anemia
b. neoplasia
c. parasitism
d. toxicity

_____ 4. Round bacteria are called
a. cocci
b. yeasts
c. fungi
d. bacilli

_____ 5. Single-celled animals, as a group, are called
a. algae
b. mold
c. protozoa
d. vibrios

_____ 6. Heat, pain, redness, and swelling are the characteristic signs of
a. immunity
b. fever
c. inflammation
d. healing

_____ 7. White blood cells engulf foreign organisms by the process of
a. phagocytosis
b. egestion
c. ejection
d. dysphagia

_____ 8. The sum of all body defenses against infectious disease is termed
a. pyosis
b. complementation
c. secretion
d. immunity

Learning Objectives

After study of this chapter, you should be able to:

1. ▶ List the major categories of diseases. *p92*
2. ▶ Compare the common types of infectious organisms and list some diseases caused by each. *p92*
3. ▶ Describe the common responses to disease. *p94*
4. ▶ Define and give examples of neoplasia. *p96*
5. ▶ Define the major terms pertaining to diseases. *p96*
6. ▶ Identify and use word parts pertaining to diseases. *p98*
7. ▶ Analyze the disease terminology in several case studies. *pp91, 110*

Case Study: *Infected on an African Safari*

Chief Complaint

J.N., a 56-year-old female, was on a month-long safari vacation with her husband in South Africa. During the last week of the trip, she began to experience a low-grade fever, abdominal cramping, and foul-smelling diarrhea. She returned home and promptly saw her internist.

Examination

The internist took a history, and J.N. recounted the events leading up to the acute onset of abdominal spasms and other intestinal symptoms. She explained that she and her husband went on an African safari and visited some pretty remote areas. Sanitation was a concern of hers, and she was careful to consume only bottled beverages. J.N. did admit though that she tried some of the native cuisine in the high mountain villages.

The internist ordered the following laboratory tests: complete blood count (CBC), liver enzymes, and a stool specimen. The stool specimen was checked for protozoa, helminths such as hookworm, and other parasites that may have been endemic to the region in which J.N. and her husband had traveled. The CBC showed an elevated white blood count (WBC), and the stool specimen was positive for the protozoan *Giardia lamblia*. No indications of hepatitis or any other signs of pathology were noted.

Clinical Course

J.N.'s internist explained the results of the tests and said that she most likely contracted the illness from contaminated water in the mountain villages she visited. He prescribed the drug Tindamax, also known as tinidazole, and told her to take the medicine on an empty stomach. He cautioned her about transmitting the infection. Lastly, he reinforced strict personal hygiene and instructed her to wash her hands meticulously after having a bowel movement. She was to notify the office if symptoms persisted.

In this chapter, we learn about different categories of diseases, including infectious diseases, such as the protozoal disease J.N. contracted. We also discuss how the body responds to disease and learn about word parts contained in disease terminology. Diseases often require medical intervention, such as drug treatment, as in J.N.'s case. Medical treatment in general is the subject of Chapter 7, and drugs are specifically discussed in Chapter 8.

ANCILLARIES *At-A-Glance*

Visit thePoint to access the following resources. For guidance in using the resources most effectively, see pp. ix–xvi.

Learning RESOURCES

▶ Tips for Effective Studying
▶ Web Figure: Modes of Disease Transmission
▶ Web Figure: Chain of Events in Inflammation
▶ Web Chart: Disease Terminology
▶ Web Chart: Common Routes of Disease Transmission

▶ Animation: Acute Inflammation
▶ Audio Pronunciation Glossary

Learning ACTIVITIES

▶ Visual Activities
▶ Kinesthetic Activities
▶ Auditory Activities

Types of Diseases

A disease is any disorder of normal body function. Diseases can be grouped into a number of different but often overlapping categories.

- Infectious diseases are caused by certain harmful **microorganisms** and other **parasites** that live at the expense of another organism. Any disease-causing agent is described as a **pathogen**.
- Degenerative diseases result from wear and tear, aging, or **trauma** (injury) that can lead to a **lesion** (wound) and perhaps **necrosis** (death of tissue). Common examples include arthritis, cardiovascular problems, and certain respiratory disorders such as emphysema. Structural malformations such as congenital malformations, **prolapse** (dropping), or **hernia** (rupture) may also result in degenerative changes.
- **Neoplasia** is the abnormal and uncontrolled growth of tissue.
- Immune disorders include failures of the immune system, allergies, and autoimmune diseases, in which the body makes antibodies to its own tissues. (Immune disorders receive more detailed discussion in Chapter 10.)
- Metabolic disorders result from lack of enzymes or other factors needed for cellular functions. Many hereditary disorders fall into this category. Malnutrition caused by inadequate intake of nutrients or inability of the body to absorb and use nutrients also upsets metabolism. (Metabolic disorders are discussed in more detail in Chapter 12, and hereditary disorders are discussed in Chapter 15.)
- Hormonal disorders are caused by underproduction or overproduction of hormones or by an inability of the hormones to function properly. One common example is diabetes mellitus. (Chapter 16 has more detail on hormonal disorders.)
- Mental and emotional disorders affect the mind and adaptation of an individual to his or her environment. (Chapter 17 has further discussion on behavioral disorders.)

Some methods for naming diseases are described in **Box 6-1**.

The cause of a disease is its **etiology** (*e-te-OL-o-je*), although many diseases have multiple interacting causes. An **acute** disease is sudden, severe, and of short duration. A **chronic** disease is of long duration and progresses slowly. One health profession that deals with the immediate effects of acute disease is the emergency medical technician (EMT) (**Box 6-2**).

See the Student Resources on thePoint for a complete list of disease terminology.

Infectious Diseases

Infectious diseases are caused by viruses, bacteria, fungi (yeasts and molds), protozoa (single-celled animals), and worms (helminths) (**Box 6-3**). Infecting organisms can enter the body through several routes, or portals of entry, including damaged skin, respiratory tract, digestive system, and urinary and reproductive tracts. An infected person's bodily discharges may contain organisms that spread infection through the air, food, water, or direct contact. Microorganisms often produce disease by means of the **toxins** (poisons) they release. The presence of harmful microorganisms or their toxins in the body is termed **sepsis**.

FOCUS ON WORDS
Name That Disease

Box 6-1

Diseases get their names in a variety of ways. Some are named for the places where they were first found, such as Lyme disease for Lyme, Connecticut; West Nile disease, Rift Valley fever, and Ebola for places in Africa; and hantavirus fever for a river in Korea. Others are named for the people who first described them, such as Cooley anemia; Crohn disease, an inflammatory bowel disease; and Hodgkin disease of the lymphatic system. Note, however, that the World Health Organization (WHO) is discouraging the use of people, places, and animals in naming diseases, because these names can be offensive or negative and are often inaccurate.

Many diseases are named on the basis of the symptoms they cause. Tuberculosis causes small lesions known as tubercles in the lungs and other tissues. Skin anthrax produces lesions that turn black, and its name comes from the same root as anthracite coal. In sickle cell anemia, red blood cells become distorted into a crescent shape when they give up oxygen. Having lost their smooth, round form, the cells jumble together, blocking small blood vessels and depriving tissues of oxygen.

Bubonic plague causes painful and enlarged lymph nodes called buboes. Lupus erythematosus, a systemic autoimmune disorder, is named for the Latin term for wolf, because the red rash that may form on the faces of people with this disease gives them a wolf-like appearance. Yellow fever, scarlet fever, and rubella (German measles) are named for colors associated with the pathology of these diseases.

Box 6-2

HEALTH PROFESSIONS
Emergency Medical Technicians

Emergency medical technicians (EMTs) are the first health professionals to arrive at the scene of an automobile accident, heart attack, or other emergency situation. EMTs must assess and respond rapidly to a medical crisis, taking a medical history, performing a physical examination, stabilizing the patient, and, if necessary, transporting the patient to the nearest medical facility.

To perform their lifesaving duties, EMTs need extensive training, including a thorough understanding of anatomy and physiology. EMTs must know how to use specialized equipment, such as backboards to immobilize injuries, electrocardiographs to monitor heart activity, and defibrillators to treat cardiac arrest. They must also be proficient at giving intravenous fluids, oxygen, and certain lifesaving medications. At medical facilities, EMTs work closely with physicians and nurses, reporting on histories, physical examinations, and measures taken to stabilize the patient. Most EMTs receive their training from college or technical schools and must be certified in the state where they are employed.

As the American population ages and becomes concentrated in urban centers, the rate of accidents and other emergencies is expected to rise. Thus, the need for EMTs remains high. For more information about this career, contact the National Association of Emergency Medical Technicians at http://www.naemt.org.

6

FOR YOUR REFERENCE
Common Infectious Organisms

Box 6-3

Type of Organism	Description	Examples of Diseases Caused
bacteria *bak-TE-re-ah*	simple microscopic organisms that are widespread throughout the world, some can produce disease; singular: bacterium (*bak-TE-re-um*)	
cocci *KOK-si*	round bacteria; may be in clusters (staphylococci), chains (streptococci), and other formations; singular: coccus (*KOK-us*)	pneumonia, rheumatic fever, food poisoning, septicemia, urinary tract infections, gonorrhea
bacilli *bah-SIL-i*	rod-shaped bacteria; singular: bacillus (*ba-SIL-us*)	typhoid, dysentery, salmonellosis, tuberculosis, botulism, tetanus
vibrios *VIB-re-oze*	short curved rods	cholera, gastroenteritis
spirochetes *SPI-ro-ketze*	corkscrew-shaped bacteria that move with a twisting motion	Lyme disease, syphilis, Vincent disease
chlamydia *klah-MID-e-ah*	extremely small bacteria with complex life cycles that grow in living cells but, unlike viruses, are susceptible to antibiotics	conjunctivitis, trachoma, pelvic inflammatory disease (PID), and other sexually transmitted infections (STIs)
rickettsia *rih-KET-se-ah*	extremely small bacteria that grow in living cells but are susceptible to antibiotics	typhus, Rocky Mountain spotted fever
viruses *VI-rus-es*	submicroscopic infectious agents that can live and reproduce only within living cells	colds, herpes, hepatitis, measles, varicella (chickenpox), influenza, AIDS
fungi *FUN-ji*	simple, nongreen plants, some of which are parasitic; includes yeasts and molds; singular: fungus (*FUN-gus*)	candidiasis, skin infections (tinea, ringworm), valley fever
protozoa *pro-to-ZO-ah*	single-celled animals; singular: protozoon (*pro-to-ZO-on*)	dysentery, *Trichomonas* infection, malaria
helminths *HEL-minths*	worms	trichinosis; infestations with roundworms, pinworms, hookworms

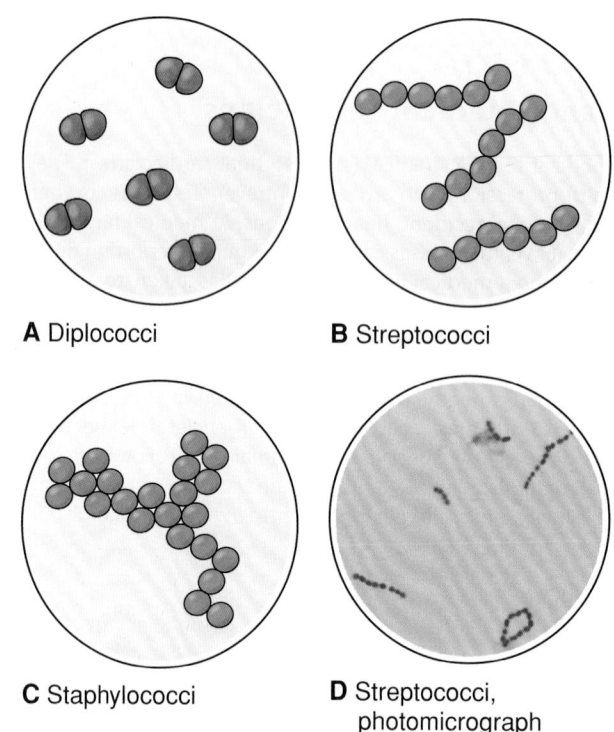

A Diplococci   **B** Streptococci

C Staphylococci   **D** Streptococci, photomicrograph

Figure 6-1 **Cocci, round bacteria, Gram stained.** **A.** Cells growing in pairs, diplococci. **B.** Cells in chains, streptococci. **C.** Cells in clusters, staphylococci. **D.** Streptococci viewed under a microscope in a photomicrograph. Gram-positive cells are purple; Gram-negative cells are red.

BACTERIA

In shape, bacteria are:

- Round, or cocci, shown in **Figure 6-1**
- Rod-shaped, or bacilli, shown in **Figure 6-2**
- Curved, including vibrios and spirochetes, shown in **Figure 6-3**

Bacteria may be named according to their shape and also by the arrangements they form (see **Fig. 6-1**). They are also described according to the dyes they take up when stained in the laboratory. The most common laboratory bacterial stain is the **Gram stain,** with which Gram-positive organisms stain purple and Gram-negative organisms stain red (see **Fig. 6-1**).

Chlamydia and rickettsia are two bacterial groups that are smaller than typical bacteria and can grow only within living host cells (**Box 6-3**).

See a figure and chart on the transmission of infectious diseases in the Student Resources on thePoint.

Responses to Disease

INFLAMMATION

A common response to infection and to other forms of disease is **inflammation**. When cells are injured, they release

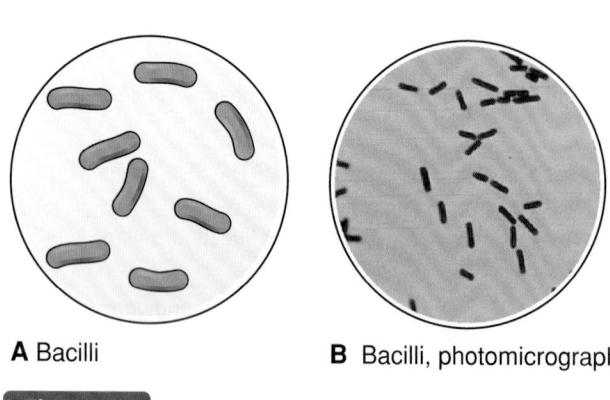

A Bacilli   **B** Bacilli, photomicrograph

Figure 6-2 **Bacilli, rod-shaped bacteria.** **A.** Drawing of bacilli. **B.** Photomicrograph of bacilli.

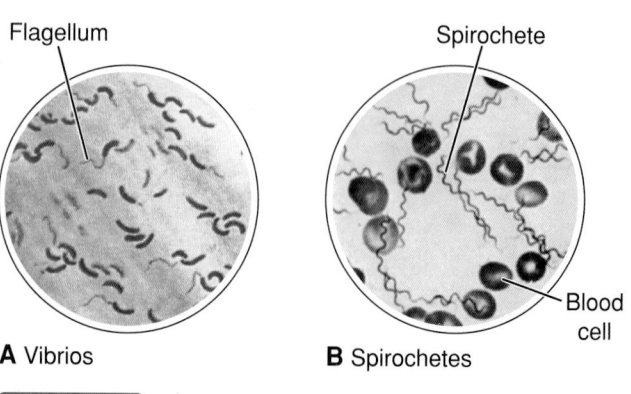

A Vibrios   **B** Spirochetes

Figure 6-3 **Curved bacteria.** **A.** Vibrios are short curved rods. **B.** Spirochetes are spiral shaped.

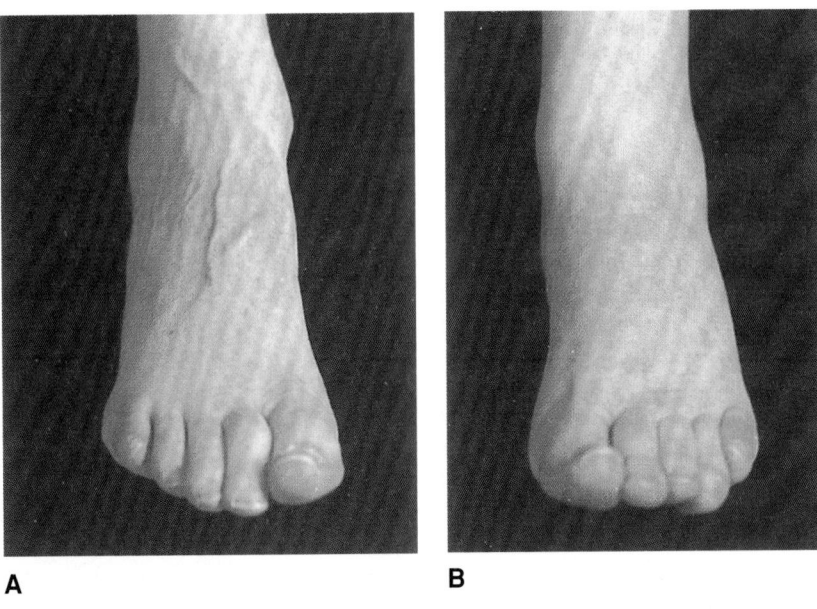

Figure 6-4 **Edema. A.** A normal foot showing veins, tendons, and bones. **B.** Edema (swelling) obscures surface features.

chemicals that allow blood cells and fluids to move into the tissues. This inflow of blood results in the four signs of inflammation:

- Heat
- Pain
- Redness
- Swelling

The suffix -*itis* indicates inflammation, as in appendicitis (inflammation of the appendix) and tonsillitis (inflammation of the tonsils).

Inflammation is one possible cause of **edema**, a swelling or accumulation of fluid in the tissues (**Fig. 6-4**). Other causes of edema include fluid blockage, heart failure, and

imbalance in body fluid composition, as described in later chapters.

See the animation "Acute Inflammation" in the Student Resources on thePoint.

PHAGOCYTOSIS

The body uses **phagocytosis** to get rid of invading microorganisms, damaged cells, and other types of harmful debris. Certain white blood cells are capable of engulfing these materials and destroying them internally (**Fig. 6-5**). Phagocytic cells are found circulating in the blood, in the tissues, and in the lymphatic system (see Chapters 9 and 10). The remains of

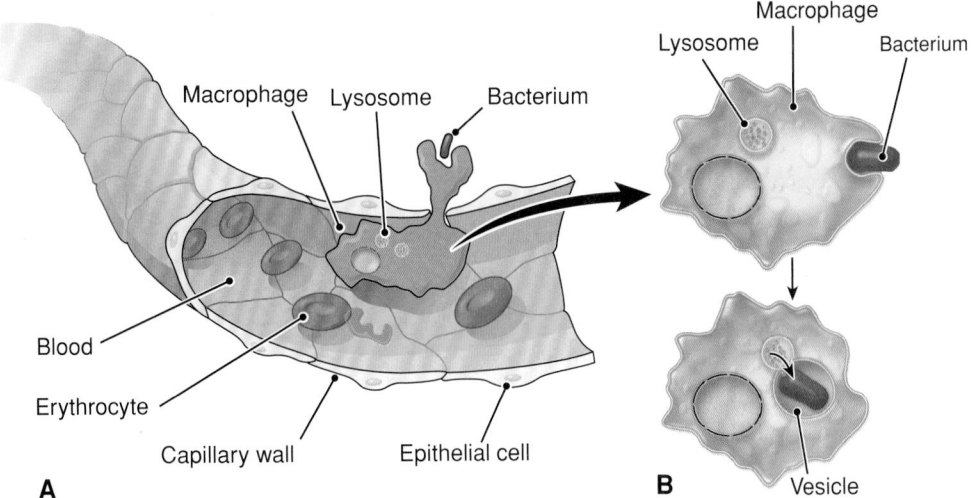

Figure 6-5 **Phagocytosis. A.** A phagocytic white blood cell squeezes through a capillary wall to engulf a bacterium. **B.** The bacterium is enclosed in a vesicle and destroyed by lysosomal enzymes.

phagocytosis consist of fluid and white blood cells, a mixture called **pus**.

IMMUNITY

Immunity refers to all our defenses against infectious disease. Inflammation and phagocytosis are examples of inborn or innate protective mechanisms, which are based on a person's genetic makeup and do not require any previous exposure to a disease organism. Other defenses that fall into this category are mechanical barriers, such as intact skin and mucous membranes, as well as body secretions, such as stomach acid and enzymes in saliva and tears.

Immunity that we develop during life from exposure to disease organisms is termed *adaptive immunity*, or acquired immunity. This type of immunity is specific for particular diseases encountered by natural exposure or by the administration of vaccines (see Chapter 10). The system responsible for adaptive immunity consists of cells in the blood, lymphatic system, and other tissues. These cells recognize different foreign invaders and get rid of them by direct attack and by producing circulating antibodies that immobilize and help destroy them. The immune system also monitors the body continuously for abnormal and malfunctioning cells, such as cancer cells. The immune system may overreact to produce allergies and may react to one's own tissues to cause autoimmune diseases.

Neoplasia

As noted earlier, a **neoplasm** is an abnormal and uncontrolled growth of tissue—a tumor or growth. A **benign** neoplasm does not spread, that is, undergo **metastasis** to other tissues, although it may cause damage at the site where it grows. An invasive neoplasm that can metastasize to other tissues is termed **malignant** and is commonly called *cancer*. A malignant tumor that involves epithelial tissue is a **carcinoma**. If the tumor arises in glandular epithelium, it is an

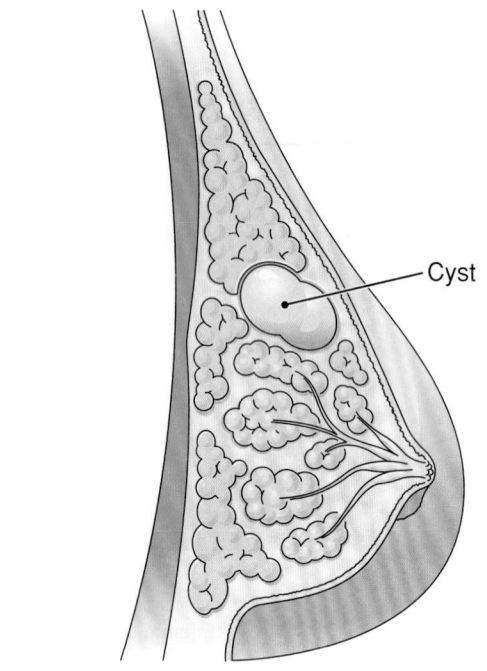

Figure 6-6   **Cyst in the breast.**

adenocarcinoma (the root *aden/o* means "gland"); a cancer of pigmented epithelial cells (melanocytes) is a melanoma. A neoplasm that involves connective tissue or muscle is a **sarcoma**. Cancers of the blood, lymphatic system, and nervous system are classified according to the cell types involved and other clinical features. Further descriptions of these cancers appear in Chapters 10 and 17.

Often mistaken for a malignancy is a **cyst**, a sac or pouch filled with fluid or semisolid material that is abnormal but not cancerous (**Fig. 6-6**). Common sites for cyst formation are the breasts, the skin's sebaceous glands, and the ovaries. Causes of cyst formation include infection or blockage of a duct.

Terminology	Key Terms
acute *ah-KUTE*	Sudden, severe; having a short course
benign *be-NINE*	Not recurrent or malignant, favorable for recovery, describing a tumor that does not spread (metastasize) to other tissues
carcinoma *kar-sih-NO-mah*	A malignant neoplasm composed of epithelial cells (from Greek root carcino, meaning "crab") (adjective: carcinomatous)
chronic *KRON-ik*	Of long duration, progressing slowly
cyst *sist*	An abnormal filled sac or pouch (see **Fig. 6-6**); used as a root meaning a normal bladder or sac, such as the urinary bladder or gallbladder (root: cyst/o)
edema *eh-DE-mah*	Accumulation of fluid in the tissues, swelling; adjective: edematous (*eh-DE-mah-tus*) (see **Fig. 6-4**)

Terminology	**Key Terms** (*Continued*)

etiology *e-te-OL-o-je*	The cause of a disease
Gram stain	A laboratory staining procedure that divides bacteria into two groups: Gram-positive, which stain purple, and Gram-negative, which stain red (see **Fig. 6-1**)
hernia *HER-ne-ah*	Protrusion of an organ through an abnormal opening; commonly called a rupture (**Fig. 6-7**)
immunity *ih-MU-nih-te*	All our defenses against infectious disease
inflammation *in-flah-MA-shun*	A localized response to tissue injury characterized by heat, pain, redness, and swelling
lesion *LE-zhun*	A distinct area of damaged tissue, an injury or wound
malignant *mah-LIG-nant*	Growing worse, harmful, tending to cause death, describing an invasive tumor that can spread (metastasize) to other tissues
metastasis *meh-TAS-tah-sis*	Spread from one part of the body to another, characteristic of cancer; verb is metastasize (*meh-TAS-tah-size*), adjective: metastatic (*met-ah-STAT-ik*); from Greek met/a (beyond, change) + stasis (stand)
microorganism *mi-kro-OR-gan-izm*	An organism too small to be seen without the aid of a microscope
necrosis *neh-KRO-sis*	Death of tissue (root necr/o means "death"); adjective: necrotic (*neh-KROT-ik*)
neoplasia *ne-o-PLA-ze-ah*	An abnormal and uncontrolled growth of tissue; from prefix neo- meaning "new" and root plasm meaning "formation"
neoplasm *NE-o-plazm*	A tumor, or abnormal growth, which may be benign or malignant (root onc/o and suffix -oma refer to neoplasms)
parasite *PAR-ah-site*	An organism that grows on or in another organism (the host), causing damage to it
pathogen *PATH-o-jen*	An organism capable of causing disease (root path/o means "disease")
phagocytosis *fag-o-si-TO-sis*	The ingestion of organisms, such as invading bacteria or small particles of waste material by a cell (root phag/o means "to eat"); the phagocytic cell, or phagocyte, then destroys the ingested material (see **Fig. 6-5**)
prolapse *PRO-laps*	A dropping or downward displacement of an organ or part, ptosis
pus	A product of inflammation consisting of fluid and white blood cells (root: py/o)
sarcoma *sar-KO-mah*	A malignant neoplasm arising from connective tissue (from Greek root sarco, meaning "flesh"); adjective: sarcomatous
sepsis *SEP-sis*	The presence of harmful microorganisms or their toxins in the blood or other tissues; adjective: septic
toxin *TOKS-in*	A poison; adjective: toxic (roots: tox/o, toxic/o)
trauma *TRAW-mah*	A physical or psychologic wound or injury

See also **Box 6-3** *on infectious organisms.*

Go to the Audio Pronunciation Glossary in the Student
Resources on thePoint to hear these terms pronounced.

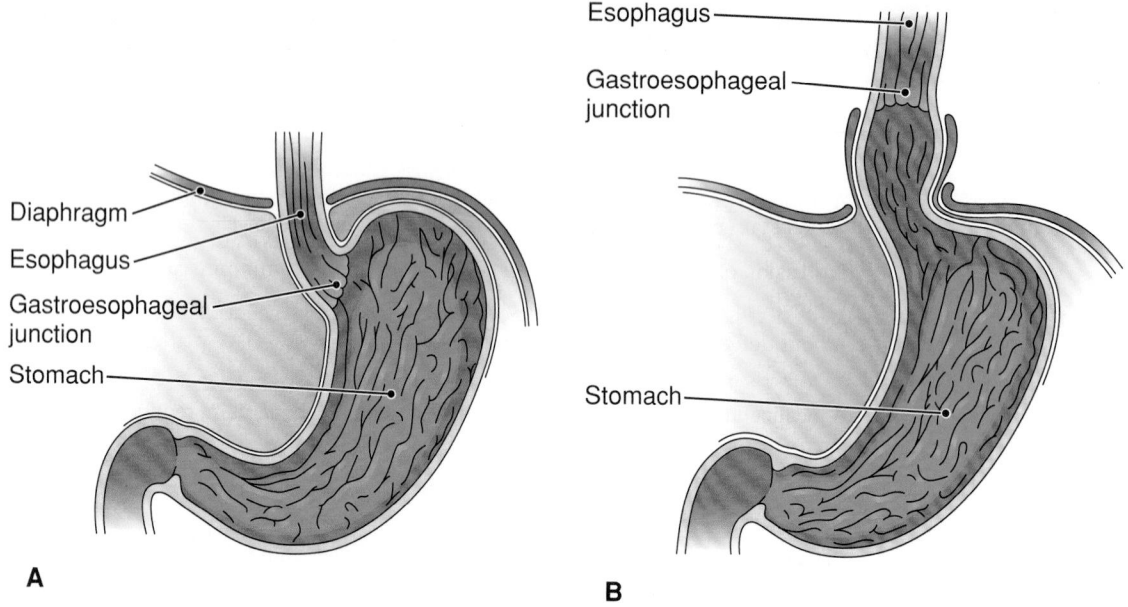

Figure 6-7 **Hernia.** **A.** Normal stomach. **B.** Hiatal hernia. The stomach protrudes through the diaphragm into the thoracic cavity, raising the level of the junction between the esophagus and the stomach.

Word Parts Pertaining to Disease

See Tables 6-1 to 6-5.

Table 6-1	Roots for Disease		
Root	**Meaning**	**Example**	**Definition of Example**
alg/o, algi/o, algesi/o	pain	algesia *al-JE-ze-ah*	condition of having pain
carcin/o	cancer, carcinoma	carcinoid *KAR-sih-noyd*	resembling a carcinoma
cyst/o	filled sac or pouch, cyst, bladder	cystic *SIS-tik*	pertaining to or having cysts
lith	calculus, stone	lithiasis *lith-I-ah-sis*	stone formation
onc/o	tumor	oncogenic *on-ko-JEN-ik*	causing a tumor
path/o	disease	pathogen *PATH-o-jen*	organism that produces disease
py/o	pus	pyocyst *PI-o-sist*	cyst filled with pus
pyr/o, pyret/o	fever, fire	pyrexia *pi-REK-se-ah*	fever
scler/o	hard	sclerosis *skle-RO-sis*	hardening of tissue
tox/o, toxic/o	poison	endotoxin *en-do-TOK-sin*	toxin within bacterial cells

EXERCISE 6-1

6

Identify and define the root in each of the following words.

	Root	Meaning of Root
1. toxicology _tok-sih-KOL-o-je_	_____	_____
2. pyorrhea _pi-o-RE-ah_	_____	_____
3. lithotomy _lih-THOT-o-me_	_____	_____
4. pathologist _pah-THOL-o-jist_	_____	_____

Fill in the blanks.

5. Arteriosclerosis (_ar-te-re-o-skleh-RO-sis_) is a(n) _____ of the arteries.

6. A urolith (_U-ro-lith_) is a(n) _____ in the urinary tract (ur/o).

7. A cystotome (_SIS-to-tome_) is an instrument for incising the _____.

8. The term pathogenic (_path-o-JEN-ik_) means producing _____.

9. A carcinogen (_kar-SIN-o-jen_) is a substance that causes _____.

10. An exotoxin (_ek-so-TOK-sin_) is a(n) _____ secreted by bacterial cells.

11. Pyoderma (_pi-o-DER-mah_) is a skin disease associated with _____.

12. An algesimeter (_al-jeh-SIM-eh-ter_) is used to measure sensitivity to _____.

13. An oncogene (_ON-ko-jene_) is a gene that causes a(n) _____.

14. A pyrogenic (_pi-ro-JEN-ik_) agent induces _____.

Table 6-2	Prefixes for Disease

Prefix	Meaning	Example	Definition of Example
brady-	slow	bradypnea _brad-ip-NE-ah_	slow breathing (-pnea) rate
dys-	abnormal, painful, difficult	dysplasia _dis-PLA-je-ah_	abnormal development (plas) of tissue
mal-	bad, poor	malabsorption _mal-ab-SORP-shun_	poor absorption of nutrients
pachy-	thick	pachycephaly _pak-ih-SEF-ah-le_	abnormal thickness of the skull
tachy-	rapid	tachycardia _tak-ih-KAR-de-ah_	rapid heart (cardi/o) rate
xero-	dry	xeroderma _ze-ro-DER-mah_	dryness of the skin

EXERCISE 6-2

Match the following terms, and write the appropriate letter to the left of each number.

_____ **1.** tachycardia (*tak-ih-KAR-de-ah*)

_____ **2.** pachydactyly (*pak-e-DAK-til-e*)

_____ **3.** bradypnea (*brad-IP-ne-ah*)

_____ **4.** dystrophy (*DIS-tro-fe*)

_____ **5.** dysphagia (*dis-FA-je-ah*)

a. abnormal thickness of the fingers

b. abnormal nourishment of tissue

c. difficulty in swallowing

d. slow breathing

e. rapid heart rate

Identify and define the prefix in each of the following words.

	Prefix	Meaning of Prefix
6. xerosis (*ze-RO-sis*)	_____	_____
7. dysentery (*DIS-en-ter-e*)	_____	_____
8. maladjustment (*mal-ad-JUST-ment*)	_____	_____

Table 6-3   Suffixes for Disease

Suffix	Meaning	Example	Definition of Example
-algia, -algesia	pain	neuralgia *nu-RAL-je-ah*	pain in a nerve (neur/o)
-cele	hernia, localized dilation	gastrocele *GAS-tro-sele*	hernia of the stomach (gastr/o)
-clasis, -clasia	breaking	karyoclasis *kar-e-OK-lah-sis*	breaking of a nucleus (kary/o)
-itis	inflammation	cystitis *sis-TI-tis*	inflammation of the urinary bladder (cyst/o)
-megaly	enlargement	hepatomegaly *hep-ah-to-MEG-ah-le*	enlargement of the liver (hepat/o)
-odynia	pain	urodynia *u-ro-DIN-e-ah*	pain on urination (ur/o)
-oma[a]	tumor	lipoma *li-PO-mah*	tumor of fat cells
-pathy	any disease of	nephropathy *nef-ROP-ah-the*	any disease of the kidney (nephr/o)
-rhage[b], -rhagia[b]	bursting forth, profuse flow, hemorrhage	hemorrhage *HEM-or-ij*	profuse flow of blood
-rhea[b]	flow, discharge	pyorrhea *pi-o-RE-ah*	discharge of pus
-rhexis[b]	rupture	amniorrhexis *am-ne-o-REK-sis*	rupture of the amniotic sac (bag of waters)
-schisis	fissure, splitting	retinoschisis *ret-ih-NOS-kih-sis*	splitting of the retina of the eye

[a]Plurals: *-omas, -omata*.

[b]Remember to double the r when adding this suffix to a root.

EXERCISE 6-3

Match the following terms, and write the appropriate letter to the left of each number.

_____ **1.** adipocele (*AD-ih-po-sele*)

_____ **2.** blastoma (*blas-TO-mah*)

_____ **3.** thoracoschisis (*tho-rah-KOS-kih-sis*)

_____ **4.** melanoma (*mel-ah-NO-mah*)

_____ **5.** osteoclasis (*os-te-OK-lah-sis*)

a. hernia containing fat

b. fissure of the chest

c. breaking of a bone

d. tumor of immature cells

e. tumor of pigmented cells

_____ **6.** gastrodynia (*gas-tro-DIN-e-ah*)

_____ **7.** menorrhagia (*men-o-RA-je-ah*)

_____ **8.** hydrocele (*HI-dro-sele*)

_____ **9.** cephalgia (*seh-FAL-je-ah*)

_____ **10.** hepatorrhexis (*hep-ah-to-REK-sis*)

a. local dilatation containing fluid

b. pain in the stomach

c. pain in the head

d. profuse menstrual flow

e. rupture of the liver

The root my/o means "muscle." Define the following terms.

11. myalgia (*mi-AL-je-ah*) _____

12. myopathy (*mi-OP-ah-the*) _____

13. myorrhexis (*mi-o-REK-sis*) _____

14. myodynia (*mi-o-DIN-e-ah*) _____

15. myoma (*mi-O-mah*) _____

Some words pertaining to disease are used as suffixes in compound words (Table 6-4). As previously noted, the term *suffix* is used in this book to mean any word part that consistently appears at the end of words. This may be a simple suffix (such as -y, -ia, -ic), a word, or a root–suffix combination, such as -megaly, -rhagia, -pathy.

Table 6-4	**Words for Disease Used as Suffixes**

Word	Meaning	Example	Definition of Example
dilation[a], dilatation[a]	expansion, widening	vasodilation *vas-o-di-LA-shun*	widening of blood vessels (vas/o)
ectasia, ectasis	dilation, dilatation, distension	gastrectasia *gas-trek-TA-se-ah*	dilatation of the stomach (gastr/o)
edema	accumulation of fluid, swelling	cephaledema *sef-al-eh-DE-mah*	swelling of the head
lysis[a]	separation, loosening, dissolving, destruction	dialysis *di-AL-ih-sis*	separation of substances by passage through (dia-) a membrane
malacia	softening	craniomalacia *kra-ne-o-mah-LA-she-ah*	softening of the skull (crani/o)
necrosis	death of tissue	osteonecrosis *os-te-o-neh-KRO-sis*	death of bone (oste/o) tissue
ptosis	dropping, downward displacement, prolapse	blepharoptosis *blef-eh-rop-TO-sis*	dropping or drooping of the eyelid (blephar/o; Fig. 6-8)

(continued)

Table 6-4	Words for Disease Used as Suffixes (*Continued*)		
Word	**Meaning**	**Example**	**Definition of Example**
sclerosis	hardening	phlebosclerosis *fleb-o-skleh-RO-sis*	hardening of veins (phleb/o)
spasm	sudden contraction, cramp	arteriospasm *ar-TERE-e-o-spazm*	spasm of an artery
stasis[a]	suppression, stoppage	menostasis *men-OS-tah-sis*	suppression of menstrual (men/o) flow
stenosis	narrowing, constriction	bronchostenosis *brong-ko-steh-NO-sis*	narrowing of a bronchus (air passageway)
toxin	poison	nephrotoxin *nef-ro-TOK-sin*	substance poisonous or harmful for the kidneys

[a]May also refer to treatment.

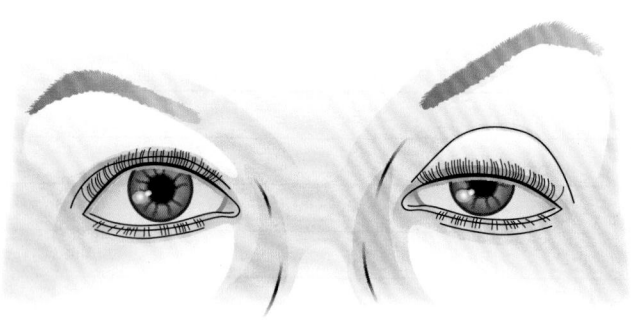

Normal lid   Drooping lid

Figure 6-8 **Blepharoptosis (dropping or drooping of the eyelid).** Ptosis means a downward displacement.

EXERCISE 6-4

Match the following terms, and write the appropriate letter to the left of each number.

_____ **1.** myolysis (*mi-OL-ih-sis*)

_____ **2.** osteomalacia (*os-te-o-mah-LA-she-ah*)

_____ **3.** cardionecrosis (*kar-de-o-neh-KRO-sis*)

_____ **4.** hemolysis (*he-MOL-ih-sis*)

_____ **5.** hemostasis (*he-mo-STA-sis*)

a. destruction of blood cells

b. death of heart tissue

c. stoppage of blood flow

d. softening of a bone

e. dissolving of muscle

The root splen/o means "spleen." Define the following words.

6. splenomalacia (*sple-no-mah-LA-she-ah*) _____

7. splenoptosis (*sple-nop-TO-sis*) _____

8. splenotoxin (*sple-no-TOK-sin*) _____

Table 6-5	Prefixes and Roots for Infectious Diseases		

Word Part	Meaning	Example	Definition of Example
Prefixes			
staphylo-	grape-like cluster	staphylococcus *staf-ih-lo-KOK-us*	a round bacterium that forms clusters
strepto-	twisted chain	streptobacillus *strep-to-bah-SIL-us*	a rod-shaped bacterium that forms chains
Roots			
bacill/i, bacill/o	bacillus	bacilluria *bas-ih-LU-re-ah*	bacilli in the urine (-uria)
bacteri/o	bacterium	bacteriostatic *bak-tere-e-o-STAT-ik*	stopping (stasis) the growth of bacteria
myc/o	fungus, mold	mycotic *mi-KOT-ik*	pertaining to a fungus
vir/o	virus	viremia *vi-RE-me-ah*	presence of viruses in the blood (-emia)

6

EXERCISE 6-5

Fill in the blanks.

1. A bactericidal (*bak-tere-ih-SI-dal*) agent kills _____.

2. A mycosis (*mi-KO-sis*) is any disease caused by a(n) _____.

3. The term bacillary (*BAS-il-ah-re*) means pertaining to _____.

4. The prefix strepto- means _____.

5. The prefix staphylo- means _____.

Use the suffix *-logy* to write a word that means the same as each of the following.

6. Study of fungi _____

7. Study of viruses _____

8. Study of bacteria _____

Terminology	Supplementary Terms

acid-fast stain	A laboratory staining procedure used mainly to identify the tuberculosis (TB) organism
communicable *ko-MUN-ih-kah-bl*	Capable of passing from one person to another, such as an infectious disease
endemic *en-DEM-ik*	Occurring at a low level but continuously in a given region, such as the common cold (from en-, meaning "in" and Greek demos, meaning "people")
epidemic *ep-ih-DEM-ik*	Affecting many people in a given region at the same time, a disease that breaks out in a large proportion of a population at a given time
exacerbation *eks-zas-er-BA-shun*	Worsening of disease, increase in severity of a disease or its symptoms

(continued)

Terminology	**Supplementary Terms** (*Continued*)

iatrogenic *i-at-ro-JEN-ik*	Caused by the effects of treatment (from Greek root iatro-, meaning "physician")
idiopathic *id-e-o-PATH-ik*	Having no known cause (root idio means "self-originating")
in situ *in SI-tu*	Localized, noninvasive (literally "in position"); said of tumors that do not spread, such as carcinoma in situ (CIS)
normal flora *FLO-rah*	The microorganisms that normally live on or in the body and are generally harmless and often beneficial but can cause disease under special circumstances, such as injury or failure of the immune system
nosocomial *nos-o-KO-me-al*	Describing an infection acquired in a hospital (root nos/o means "disease," and comial refers to a hospital), which can be a serious problem, especially if it is resistant to antibiotics, such as strains of methicillin-resistant *Staphylococcus aureus* (MRSA) and vancomycin-resistant *S. aureus* (VRSA)
opportunistic *op-por-tu-NIS-tik*	Describing an infection that occurs because of a host's poor or altered condition
pandemic *pan-DEM-ik*	Describing a disease that is prevalent throughout an entire region or the world; for example, AIDS is pandemic in certain regions of the world
remission *re-MISH-un*	A lessening of disease symptoms, the period during which such lessening occurs
septicemia *sep-tih-SE-me-ah*	Presence of pathogenic bacteria in the blood, blood poisoning
systemic *sis-TEM-ik*	Pertaining to the whole body

Manifestations of Disease

abscess *AB-ses*	A localized collection of pus
adhesion *ad-HE-zhun*	A uniting of two surfaces or parts that may normally be separated
anaplasia *ah-nah-PLA-ze-ah*	Lack of normal differentiation, as shown by cancer cells
ascites *a-SI-teze*	Accumulation of fluid in the peritoneal cavity
cellulitis *sel-u-LI-tis*	A spreading inflammation of tissue
effusion *eh-FU-zhun*	Escape of fluid into a cavity or other body part
exudate *EKS-u-date*	Material that escapes from blood vessels as a result of tissue injury
fissure *FISH-ur*	A groove or split
fistula *FIS-tu-lah*	An abnormal passage between two organs or from an organ to the surface of the body
gangrene *GANG-grene*	Death of tissue, usually caused by lack of blood supply; may be associated with bacterial infection and decomposition

Terminology | Supplementary Terms (Continued)

hyperplasia hi-per-PLA-ze-ah	Excessive growth of normal cells in normal arrangement
hypertrophy hi-PER-tro-fe	An increase in the size of an organ without increase in the number of cells; may result from an increase in activity, as in muscles
induration in-du-RA-shun	Hardening, an abnormally hard spot or place
metaplasia met-ah-PLA-ze-ah	Conversion of cells to a form that is not normal for that tissue (prefix meta- means "change")
polyp POL-ip	A tumor attached by a thin stalk
purulent PUR-u-lent	Forming or containing pus
suppuration sup-u-RA-shun	Pus formation

Go to the Audio Pronunciation Glossary in the Student Resources on thePoint to hear these terms pronounced.

Terminology | Abbreviations

AF	Acid fast		**MDR**	Multi-drug resistant
CA, Ca	Cancer		**MRSA**	Methicillin-resistant *Staphylococcus aureus*
CIS	Carcinoma in situ		**Staph**	*Staphylococcus*
FUO	Fever of unknown origin		**Strep**	*Streptococcus*
Gm+	Gram-positive		**VRSA**	Vancomycin-resistant *Staphylococcus aureus*
Gm⁻	Gram-negative			

Case Study Revisited

J.N.'s Follow-Up

J.N. took the full course of drug therapy, and her symptoms subsided. She brought in a stool specimen to her follow-up office visit. Test results were negative for the offending pathogen.

Matching

Match the following terms, and write the appropriate letter to the left of each number.

_____ **1.** cardiomegaly

_____ **2.** neuroma

_____ **3.** carcinophobia

_____ **4.** encephalitis

_____ **5.** hemorrhagic

a. pertaining to profuse flow of blood

b. fear of cancer

c. tumor of a nerve

d. enlargement of the heart

e. inflammation of the brain

_____ **6.** sclerotic

_____ **7.** oncolysis

_____ **8.** analgesia

_____ **9.** xerotic

_____ **10.** lithiasis

a. stone formation

b. dry

c. destruction of a tumor

d. absence of pain

e. hardened

_____ **11.** dysphagia

_____ **12.** apyrexia

_____ **13.** pyorrhea

_____ **14.** dactyledema

_____ **15.** pachyderma

a. swelling of the fingers or toes

b. thickness of the skin

c. discharge of pus

d. difficulty in swallowing

e. absence of fever

_____ **16.** blepharoptosis

_____ **17.** hemostasis

_____ **18.** toxoid

_____ **19.** lesion

_____ **20.** ectasia

a. local wound or injury

b. stoppage of blood flow

c. dropping of the eyelid

d. like a poison

e. dilatation

_____ **21.** spasm

_____ **22.** carcinoid

_____ **23.** venosclerosis

_____ **24.** cardiorrhexis

_____ **25.** adenopathy

a. resembling cancer

b. hardening of a vein

c. any disease of a gland

d. sudden contraction or cramp

e. rupture of the heart

Supplementary Terms

_____ **26.** nosocomial

_____ **27.** iatrogenic

_____ **28.** fistula

_____ **29.** polyp

_____ **30.** effusion

a. abnormal passageway

b. escape of fluid into a cavity

c. tumor attached by a thin stalk

d. acquired in a hospital

e. caused by effects of treatments

_____ **31.** idiopathic

_____ **32.** purulent

_____ **33.** ascites

_____ **34.** abscess

_____ **35.** exacerbation

a. localized collection of pus

b. having no known cause

c. worsening

d. fluid in the abdominal cavity

e. forming or containing pus

FILL IN THE BLANKS

36. Heat, pain, redness, and swelling are the four major signs of _____.

37. Any abnormal and uncontrolled growth of tissue, whether benign or malignant, is called a(n) _____.

38. The spreading of cancer to other parts of the body is the process of _____.

39. Protrusion of an organ through an abnormal opening is a(n) _____.

40. Toxicology is the study of _____.

41. Death of tissue is called _____.

42. An oncoprotein is a protein associated with a(n) _____.

43. Referring to J.N.'s opening case study, the suffix and its meaning in the word *diarrhea* is _____.

44. The plural of *protozoon* is _____.

45. The common name for a helminth is a(n) _____.

DEFINITIONS

Use the suffix -genesis to write words with the following meanings.

46. Formation of cancer _____

47. Origin of any disease _____

48. Formation of pus _____

49. Formation of a tumor _____

The root bronch/o pertains to a bronchus, an air passageway in the lungs. Add a suffix to this root to form words with the following meanings.

50. Excessive flow or discharge from a bronchus _____

51. Inflammation of a bronchus _____

52. Narrowing of a bronchus _____

53. Sudden contraction of a bronchus _____

Use the root oste/o, meaning "bone," to form words with the following meanings.

54. Pain in a bone _____

55. Death of bone tissue _____

56. Tumor of a bone _____

57. Breaking of a bone _____

58. Softening of a bone _____

TRUE-FALSE

Examine the following statements. If the statement is true, write T in the first blank. If the statement is false, write F in the first blank, and correct the statement by replacing the underlined word in the second blank.

	True or False	Correct Answer
59. A mycosis is an infection with a <u>protozoon</u>.	_____	_____
60. Round bacteria in chains are <u>streptococci</u>.	_____	_____
61. A sudden disease of short duration is <u>chronic</u>.	_____	_____
62. A tumor that does not metastasize is termed <u>benign</u>.	_____	_____
63. A slower than normal heart rate is <u>tachycardia</u>.	_____	_____
64. A tumor of connective tissue is classified as a <u>sarcoma</u>.	_____	_____

ELIMINATIONS

In each of the sets below, underline the word that does not fit in with the rest, and explain the reason for your choice.

65. cocci — helminths — chlamydia — bacilli — vibrios

_____

66. neoplasm — tumor — carcinoma — pathogen — oncology

_____

67. septicemic — endemic — metastatic — opportunistic — epidemic

_____

WORD BUILDING

Use the word parts given to build words for the following definitions.

tox   pyr   gen   o   py   -oma   -y   path   nephr   -logy   -ic

68. poisonous for the kidney   _____

69. producing pus   _____

70. tumor of the kidney   _____

71. study of disease   _____

72. producing fever   _____

73. study of the kidney   _____

74. producing disease   _____

75. any disease of the kidney   _____

76. producing kidney tissue   _____

WORD ANALYSIS

Define the following words, and give the meanings of the word parts in each. Use a dictionary if necessary.

77. phagocytosis (*fag-o-si-TO-sis*) _____

    a. phag/o _____

    b. cyt/o _____

    c. -sis _____

78. hypoplasia (*hi–po-PLA-ze-ah*) _____

    a. hypo- _____

    b. plas _____

    c. -ia _____

79. antipyretic (*an-te-pi-RET-ik*) _____

    a. anti- _____

    b. pyret/o _____

    c. -ic _____

80. arteriosclerosis (*ar-te-re-o-skleh-RO-sis*) _____

    a. arterio/o _____

    b. scler/o _____

    c. -sis _____

81. dysbiosis (*dis-bi-O-sis*) Imbalance in the normal flora of microorganisms _____

    a. dys- _____

    b. bio _____

    c. -sis _____

For more learning activities, see Chapter 6 of the Student Resources on thePoint.

Additional Case Studies

Case Study 6-1: *HIV Infection and Tuberculosis*

T.H., a 48-year-old man, was an admitted intravenous (IV) drug user and occasionally abused alcohol. Over four weeks, he had experienced fever, night sweats, malaise, a cough, and a 10-lb weight loss. He was also concerned about several discolored lesions that had erupted weeks before on his arms and legs.

T.H. made an appointment with a physician assistant (PA) at the neighborhood clinic. On examination, the PA noted bilateral anterior cervical and axillary lymphadenopathy and pyrexia. T.H.'s temperature was 102.2°F. The PA sent T.H. to the hospital for further studies.

T.H.'s chest radiograph (x-ray image) showed paratracheal adenopathy and bilateral interstitial infiltrates, suspicious of tuberculosis (TB). His blood study results were positive for human immunodeficiency virus (HIV) and showed a low lymphocyte count. Sputum and bronchoscopic lavage (washing) fluid were positive for an acid-fast bacillus (AFB); a PPD (purified protein derivative) skin test result was also positive. Based on these findings, T.H. was diagnosed with HIV, TB, and Kaposi sarcoma related to past IV drug abuse.

Case Study 6-2: *Endocarditis*

D.A., a 37 y/o man, sought treatment after experiencing several days of high fever and generalized weakness on return from his vacation. D.A.'s family doctor suspected cardiac involvement because of D.A.'s history of rheumatic fever. The doctor was concerned because D.A.'s brother had died of acute malignant hyperpyrexia during surgery at the age of 12. D.A. was referred to a

cardiologist, who scheduled an electrocardiogram (ECG) and a transesophageal echocardiogram (TEE).

D.A. was admitted to the hospital with subacute bacterial endocarditis (SBE) and placed on high-dose IV antibiotics and bed rest. He had also developed a heart murmur, which was diagnosed as idiopathic hypertrophic subaortic stenosis (IHSS).

Case Study Questions

Multiple Choice. Select the best answer, and write the letter of your choice to the left of each number.

_____ 1. The term *axillary* refers to the
  a. armpit
  b. groin
  c. wrist
  d. bladder

_____ 2. In referring to tissues, the term *interstitial* means
  a. around cells
  b. under cells
  c. between cells
  d. within cells

_____ 3. The cervical region is the region of the
  a. head
  b. leg
  c. heart
  d. neck

_____ 4. The term *pyrexia* refers to a
  a. fever
  b. stone
  c. tumor
  d. poison

_____ 5. Paraesophageal and paratracheal refer to a position _____ the esophagus and trachea.
  a. under
  b. near
  c. superior to
  d. in between

_____ 6. The endocardium is the tissue lining the heart's chambers. Endocarditis refers to a(n) _____ of this lining.
  a. narrowing
  b. inflammation
  c. overgrowth
  d. thinning

_____ **7.** D.A.'s heart murmur was caused by a stenosis, or _____ of the heart's aortic valve.

    a. narrowing

    b. inflammation

    c. overgrowth

    d. cancer

_____ **8.** The term for a condition or disease of
unknown etiology is

    a. hypertrophic

    b. chronic

    c. acute

    d. idiopathic

Fill in the blanks.

9. Adenopathy is any disease of a(n) _____.

10. Tuberculosis is caused by a bacterium that is rod-shaped, thus described as a(n) _____.

11. A malignant neoplasm arising from muscle or connective tissue is a(n) _____.

12. A potentially fatal disease condition characterized by a very high fever is called _____.

Give the meaning of the following abbreviations.

13. HIV _____

14. PPD _____

15. ECG _____

16. AFB _____

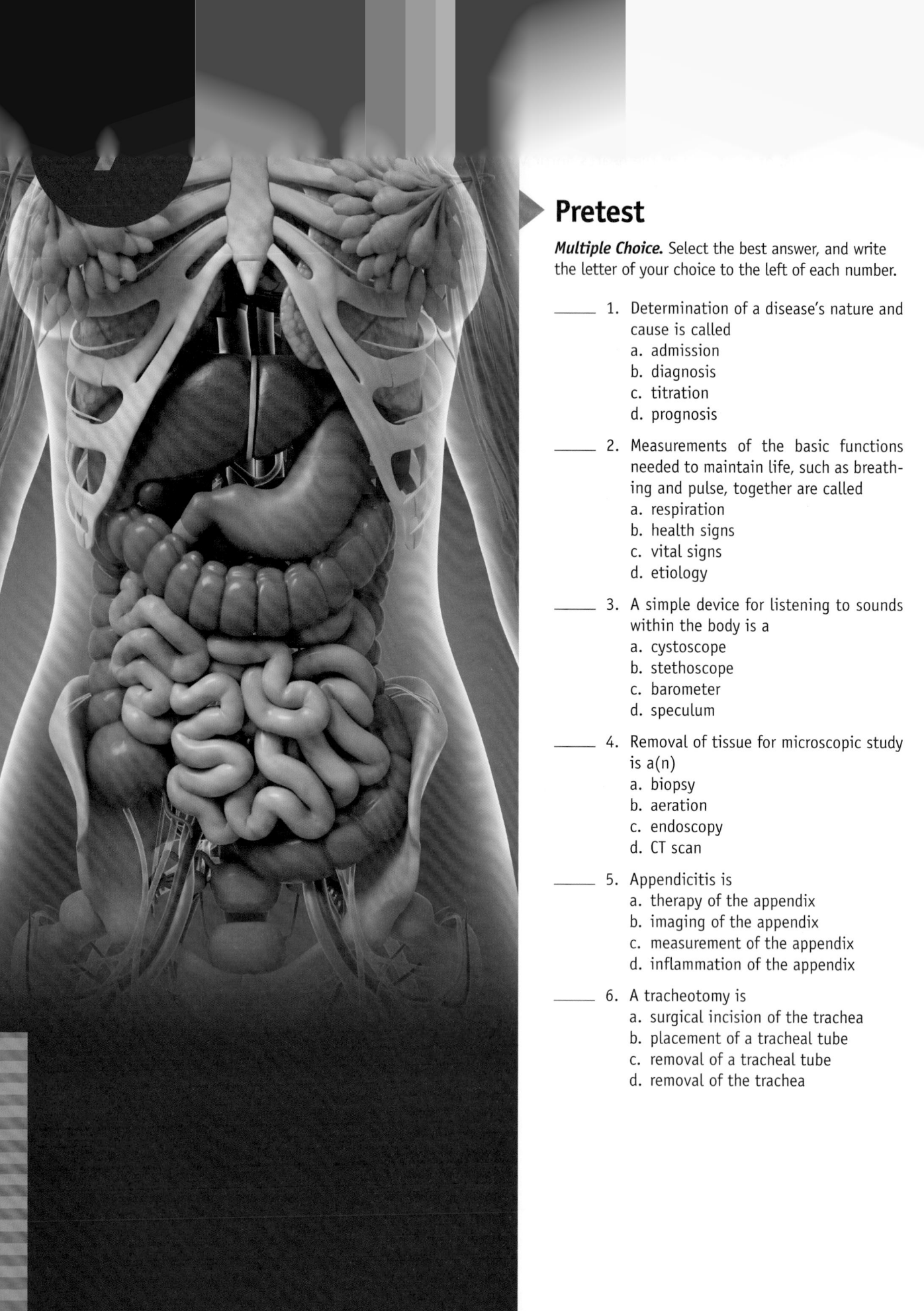

Pretest

Multiple Choice. Select the best answer, and write the letter of your choice to the left of each number.

_____ 1. Determination of a disease's nature and cause is called
   a. admission
   b. diagnosis
   c. titration
   d. prognosis

_____ 2. Measurements of the basic functions needed to maintain life, such as breathing and pulse, together are called
   a. respiration
   b. health signs
   c. vital signs
   d. etiology

_____ 3. A simple device for listening to sounds within the body is a
   a. cystoscope
   b. stethoscope
   c. barometer
   d. speculum

_____ 4. Removal of tissue for microscopic study is a(n)
   a. biopsy
   b. aeration
   c. endoscopy
   d. CT scan

_____ 5. Appendicitis is
   a. therapy of the appendix
   b. imaging of the appendix
   c. measurement of the appendix
   d. inflammation of the appendix

_____ 6. A tracheotomy is
   a. surgical incision of the trachea
   b. placement of a tracheal tube
   c. removal of a tracheal tube
   d. removal of the trachea

▶ Learning Objectives

After study of this chapter, you should be able to:

1 ▶ List the main components of a patient history. *p114*

2 ▶ Describe the main methods used in patient examination. *p114*

3 ▶ Name and describe nine imaging techniques. *p116*

4 ▶ Name possible forms of treatment. *p116*

5 ▶ Describe theories of alternative and complementary medicine and some healing practices used in these fields. *p120*

6 ▶ Describe staging and grading as they apply to cancer. *p121*

7 ▶ Define basic terms pertaining to medical examination, diagnosis, and treatment. *p121*

8 ▶ Identify and use the roots and suffixes pertaining to diagnosis and surgery. *p123*

9 ▶ Interpret symbols and abbreviations used in diagnosis and treatment. *p129*

10 ▶ Analyze medical terms related to diagnosis and treatment in case studies. *pp113, 136*

Case Study: *M.L.'s Rollerblading Mishap*

Chief Complaint

M.L., an active 59-year-old woman, was rollerblading early one morning. When attempting to avoid some loose gravel, she fell, injuring her right wrist and knee. She immediately experienced pain in her wrist and knee and noticed that her knee was swelling. She was able to use her cell phone and call her husband who came and took her to a nearby emergency room.

Examination

The physician assistant (PA) in the emergency room obtained the following history (Hx) of the incident:

M.L. was rollerblading on a path early that morning and skated into some loose gravel, causing her to fall forward. She attempted to break the fall with her arms and ended up landing with her right hand and knee bearing the impact of the fall. She was able to take off the rollerblades and, favoring her right leg, make her way over to a nearby bench, where she used her cell phone to contact her husband for help. M.L. was not wearing a helmet or any protective pads on her knees, elbows, or wrists.

The PA inspected the wrist, which was deformed and edematous. She palpated the wrist area and documented that M.L. complained of pain, weakness, and slight tingling in the fingers. There was limited range of motion (ROM) of the fingers. Next, the PA examined the knee that was now quite swollen. M.L. could not bear much weight on the right leg and complained of considerable pain. The PA explained the prognosis to M.L. and her husband and then proceeded to order some diagnostic tests.

Clinical Course

M.L. was taken to the radiology department, where an x-ray of the right wrist revealed a fracture. An MRI was ordered for the knee and showed no fractures or ligament tears. The PA explained to the patient that she might need to have an arthrocentesis, a tap to remove fluid in the knee joint, which would relieve some of the pain. She also explained that an endoscopic examination of the joint, an arthroscopy, might be required, but that the orthopedic surgeon who had already been consulted would determine whether or not this procedure was necessary.

ANCILLARIES *At-A-Glance*

Visit thePoint to access the following resources. For guidance in using the resources most effectively, see pp. ix–xvi.

Learning RESOURCES

▶ **Tips for Effective Studying**
▶ **Web Figure: Sonogram**
▶ **Web Figure: Echocardiogram**
▶ **Web Figure: Electrocardiogram**
▶ **Web Figure: Electroencephalogram**
▶ **Audio Pronunciation Glossary**

Learning ACTIVITIES

▶ **Visual Activities**
▶ **Kinesthetic Activities**
▶ **Auditory Activities**

Introduction

Medical care begins with assessing a disorder using information gathered from the patient and a variety of testing and examination methods. Based on these results, a course of treatment is recommended that may include surgery.

Diagnosis

Medical **diagnosis**, the determination of the nature and cause of an illness, begins with a patient history. This includes a history of the present illness with a description of **symptoms** (evidence of disease), a past medical history, and a family and a social history.

A physical examination, which includes a review of all systems and observation of any **signs** of illness, follows the history taking. Practitioners use the following techniques in performing physicals:

- **Inspection:** visual examination
- **Palpation:** touching the surface of the body with the hands or fingers (**Fig. 7-1**)
- **Percussion:** tapping the body to evaluate tissue according to the sounds produced (**Fig. 7-2**)
- **Auscultation:** listening to body sounds with a stethoscope (**Fig. 7-3**)

Vital signs (VS) are also recorded for comparison with normal ranges. VS are measurements that reflect basic functions necessary to maintain life and include:

- Temperature (T).
- Pulse rate, measured in beats per minute (bpm) (**Fig. 7-4**). Pulse rate normally corresponds to the heart rate (HR), the number of times the heart beats per minute.
- Respiration rate (R), measured in breaths per minute.

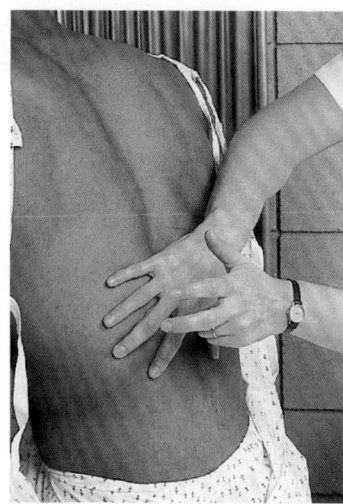

Figure 7-2 **Percussion.** The practitioner taps the body to evaluate tissues.

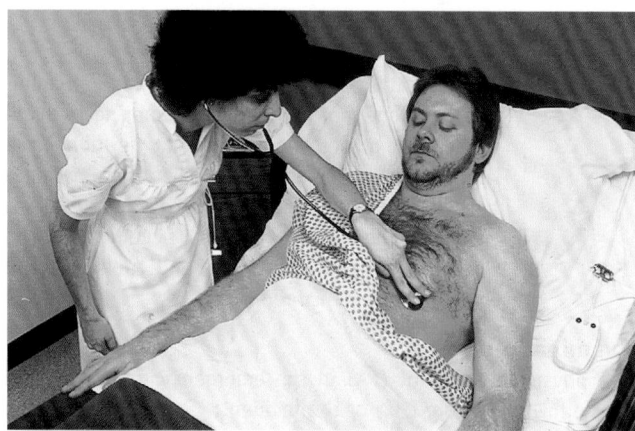

Figure 7-3 **Auscultation.** The practitioner uses a stethoscope to listen to body sounds.

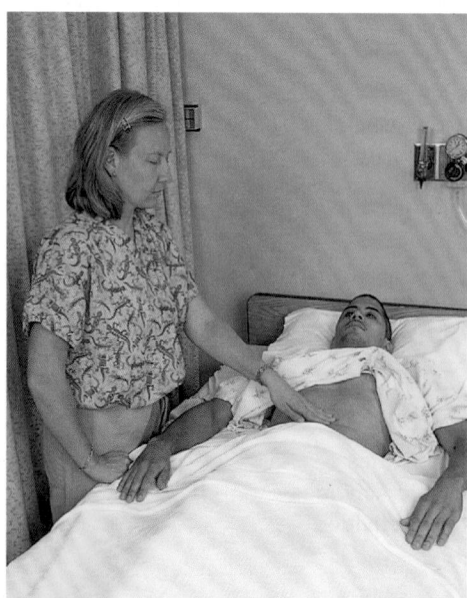

Figure 7-1 **Palpation.** The practitioner touches the body surface with the hands or fingers.

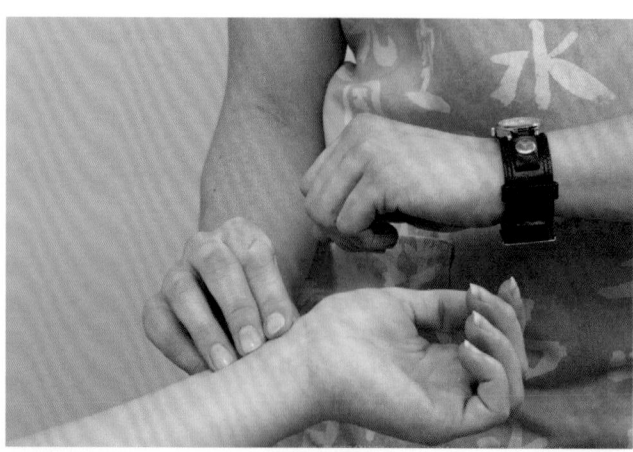

Figure 7-4 **Pulse rate.** The practitioner palpates an artery to measure pulse rate in beats per minute.

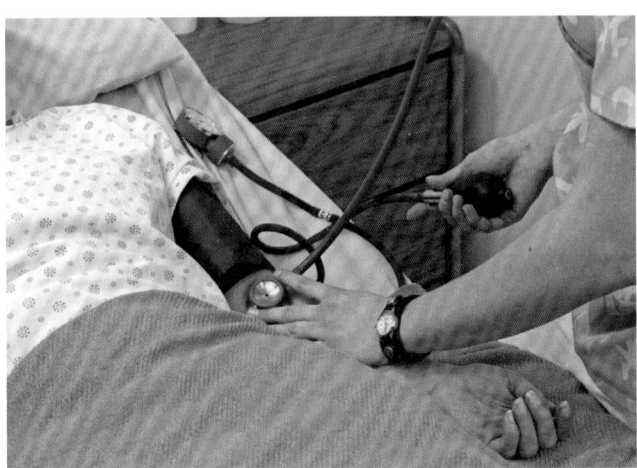

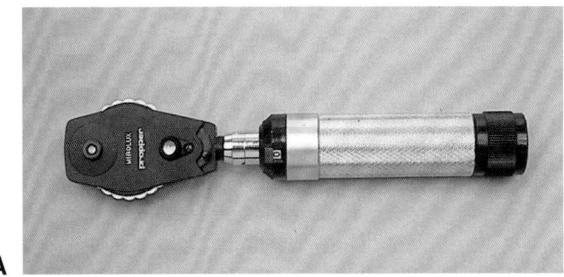

A

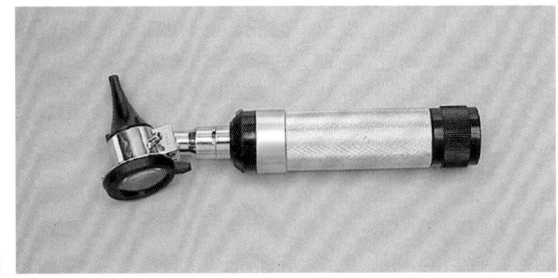

B

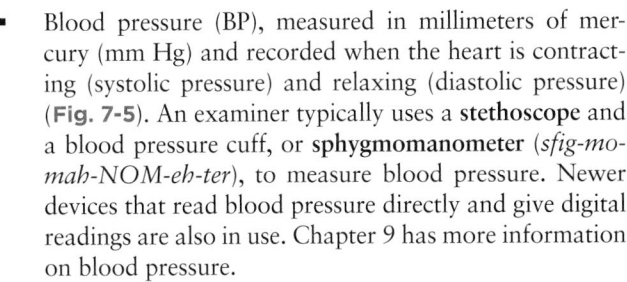

Figure 7-5   **Blood pressure.** The practitioner uses a blood pressure cuff (sphygmomanometer) and a stethoscope to measure systolic and diastolic pressures.

Figure 7-6   **Examination tools. A.** Ophthalmoscope for eye examination. **B.** Otoscope for ear examination.

- Blood pressure (BP), measured in millimeters of mercury (mm Hg) and recorded when the heart is contracting (systolic pressure) and relaxing (diastolic pressure) (**Fig. 7-5**). An examiner typically uses a **stethoscope** and a blood pressure cuff, or **sphygmomanometer** (*sfig-mo-mah-NOM-eh-ter*), to measure blood pressure. Newer devices that read blood pressure directly and give digital readings are also in use. Chapter 9 has more information on blood pressure.

Additional tools used in physical examinations include the **ophthalmoscope** (**Fig. 7-6A**), for examination of the eyes; the **otoscope** (**Fig. 7-6B**), for examination of the ears; and hammers for testing reflexes.

The skin, hair, and nails provide easily observable indications of a person's state of health. Skin features such as color, texture, thickness, and presence of lesions (local injuries) are noted throughout the course of the physical examination. Chapter 21 contains a discussion of the skin and skin diseases.

Diagnosis is further aided by laboratory test results. These may include tests on blood, urine, and other body fluids and the identification of infectious organisms. Additional tests may include study of the electrical activity of tissues such as the brain and heart, examination of body cavities by means of an **endoscope** (**Fig. 7-7**), and imaging techniques. **Biopsy** is the removal of tissue for microscopic examination. Biopsy specimens can be obtained by:

- Needle withdrawal (aspiration) of fluid, as from the chest or from a cyst

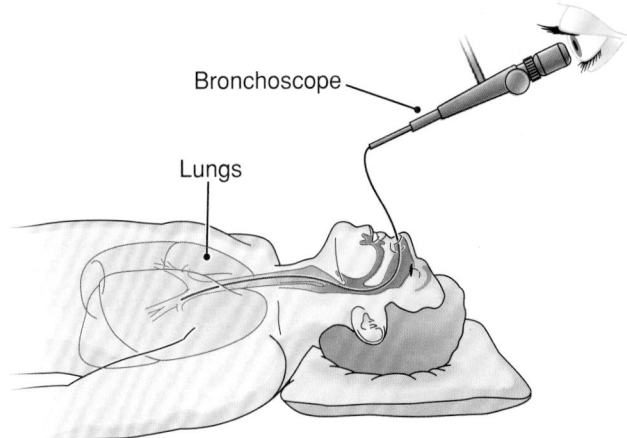

Bronchoscope

Lungs

Figure 7-7   **Endoscope.** A bronchoscope is a type of endoscope used to examine the respiratory bronchi.

Box 7-1

FOCUS ON WORDS

Terminology Evolves with Medical Science

The science of medicine never stands still, nor does its terminology. One can never say that his or her work in learning medical terminology is complete because vocabulary is constantly being added as new diagnoses, treatments, and technologies are discovered or developed.

Fifty years ago, gene therapy, genetic engineering, in vitro fertilization, cloning, and stem cell research were unknown to the public. PET scans, MRI, DNA fingerprinting, radioimmunoassay, bone density scans for identifying osteoporosis, and other diagnostic techniques were not in use. Some drug categories, such as statins for reducing cholesterol, antiviral agents, histamine antagonists for treating ulcers, ACE inhibitors and ARBs for treating hypertension, and breast cancer preventives, were undiscovered. The genes associated with certain forms of cancer and with certain hereditary abnormalities had yet to be isolated.

Each of these advances brings new terminology into use. Anyone who wants to keep current with medical terminology has a lifetime of learning ahead.

- A small punch, as of the skin
- Endoscopy, as from the respiratory or digestive tract
- Surgical removal, as of a tumor or node

In some cases, cancer can be diagnosed and its treatment monitored by a *liquid biopsy*, which relies on analysis of cancerous cells or tumor DNA in circulating blood. These samples are easier to obtain, may give a more complete picture of tumor spread than isolated tissue biopsies, and may someday be used as screening tests for hard-to-diagnose types of cancer.

When new tests appear, as in all other areas of health sciences, new terminology is added to the medical vocabulary (**Box 7-1**).

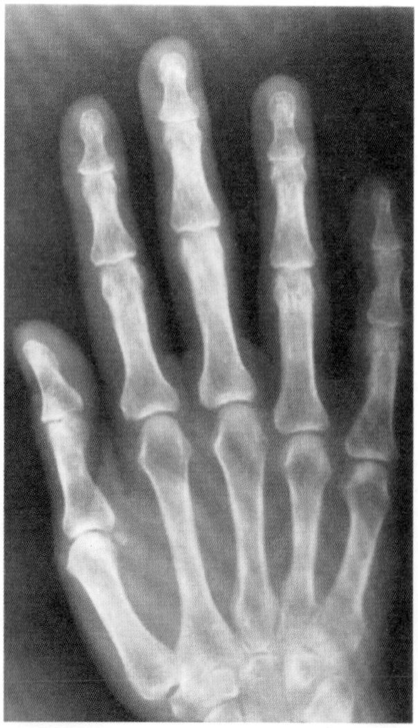

Figure 7-8 Radiography. The action of x-rays on sensitized film produced this image (radiograph) of a normal right hand.

IMAGING TECHNIQUES

Imaging techniques employ various types of energy to produce visual images of the body. The most fundamental imaging method is **radiography** (**Fig. 7-8**), which uses x-rays to produce an image (radiograph) on film or to produce a digital image that can be viewed on a monitor. Radiography is the preferred method for imaging dense tissues, such as bone. Some soft-tissue structures can be demonstrated as well, but a contrast medium, such as a barium mixture, may be needed to enhance visualization. Other forms of energy used to produce diagnostic images include sound waves, radioactive isotopes, radio waves, and magnetic fields. See **Box 7-2** for a description of the most commonly used imaging methods and **Box 7-3** for a summary of these and other imaging techniques in use.

Treatment

If diagnosis so indicates, treatment, also termed **therapy**, is begun. This may consist of counseling, drugs, surgery, radiation, physical therapy, occupational therapy, psychiatric treatment, or some combination of these. See Chapter 8 for a discussion of drugs and their actions. **Palliative therapy** is treatment that provides relief but is not intended as a cure. Terminally ill patients, for example, may receive treatment that eases pain and provides comfort but is not expected to change the outcome of the disease. During diagnosis and throughout the course of treatment, a patient is evaluated to establish a **prognosis**—that is, a prediction of the disease's outcome.

SURGERY

Surgery is a method for treating disease or injury by manual operations. Surgery may be done through an existing body opening,

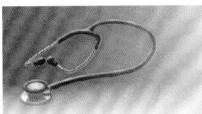

CLINICAL PERSPECTIVES
Medical Imaging

Box 7-2

Three imaging techniques that have revolutionized medicine are radiography, computed tomography (CT), and magnetic resonance imaging (MRI). With them, physicians today can "see" inside the body without making a single cut.

The oldest technique is radiography (*ra-de-OG-rah-fe*), in which a machine beams x-rays (a form of radiation) through the body onto a piece of film. The resulting image is called a radiograph. Dark areas indicate where the beam passed through the body and exposed the film, whereas light areas show where the beam did not pass through. Dense tissues (bone, teeth) absorb most of the x-rays, preventing them from exposing the film. For this reason, radiography is commonly used to visualize bone fractures and tooth decay as well as abnormally dense tissues like tumors. Radiography does not provide clear images of soft tissues because most of the beam passes through and exposes the film, but contrast media can help make structures like blood vessels and hollow organs more visible. For example, barium sulfate (which absorbs x-rays) coats the digestive tract when ingested.

During a CT scan, a machine revolves around the patient, beaming x-rays through the body onto a detector. The detector takes numerous images of the beam and a computer assembles them into transverse sections, or "slices." Unlike conventional radiography, CT produces clear images of soft structures such as the brain, liver, and lungs. It is commonly used to visualize brain injuries and tumors and even blood vessels when used with contrast media.

MRI uses a strong magnetic field and radio waves. The patient undergoing MRI lies inside a chamber within a very powerful magnet. The molecules in the patient's soft tissues align with the magnetic field inside the chamber. When radio waves hit the soft tissue, the aligned molecules emit energy that the MRI machine detects, and a computer converts these signals into an image. MRI produces even clearer images of soft tissue than does CT and can create detailed views of blood vessels without contrast media. MRI can visualize brain injuries and tumors that might be missed using CT.

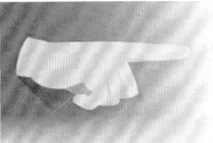

FOR YOUR REFERENCE
Imaging Techniques

Box 7-3

Method	Description
cineradiography *sin-eh-ra-de-OG-rah-fe*	making of a motion picture of successive images appearing on a fluoroscopic screen
computed tomography (CT, CT scan) *to-MOG-rah-fe*	use of a computer to generate an image from a large number of x-rays passed at different angles through the body; a three-dimensional image of a cross-section of the body is obtained; reveals more about soft tissues than does simple radiography (**Fig. 7-9A**)
fluoroscopy *flor-OS-ko-pe*	use of x-rays to examine deep structures; the shadows cast by x-rays passed through the body are observed on a fluorescent screen; the device used is called a fluoroscope
magnetic resonance imaging (MRI)	production of images through the use of a magnetic field and radio waves; the characteristics of soft tissue are revealed by differences in molecular properties; eliminates the need for x-rays and contrast media (see **Fig. 7-9B**)
positron emission tomography (PET)	production of sectional body images by administration of a natural substance, such as glucose, labeled with a positron-emitting isotope; the rays subsequently emitted are interpreted by a computer to show the internal distribution of the substance administered; PET has been used to follow blood flow through an organ and to measure metabolic activity within an organ, such as the brain, under different conditions
radiography *ra-de-OG-rah-fe*	use of x-rays passed through the body to make a visual record (radiograph) of internal structures either on specially sensitized film or digitally; also called roentgenography (*rent-geh-NOG-rah-fe*) after the developer of the technique
scintigraphy *sin-TIG-rah-fe*	imaging the radioactivity distribution in tissues after internal administration of a radioactive substance (radionuclide); the images are obtained with a scintillation camera; the record produced is a scintiscan (*SIN-tih-skan*) and usually specifies the part examined or the isotope used for the test, as in bone scan, gallium scan
single-photon emission computed tomography (SPECT)	scintigraphic technique that permits visualization of a radioisotope's cross-sectional distribution
ultrasonography *ul-trah-son-OG-rah-fe*	generation of a visual image from the echoes of high-frequency sound waves traveling back from different tissues; also called sonography (*so-NOG-rah-fe*) and echography (*ek-OG-rah-fe*) (**Fig. 7-10**)

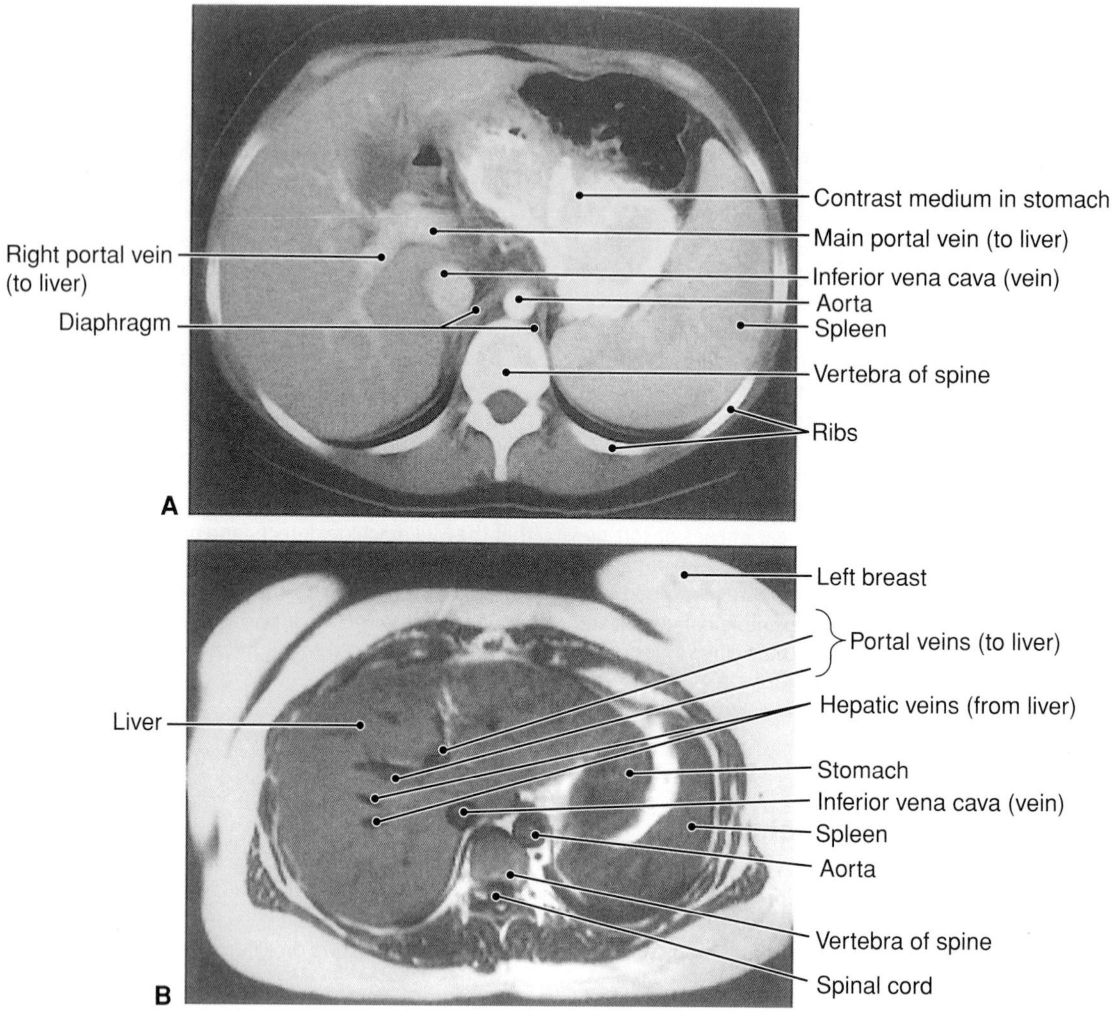

Right portal vein
(to liver)

Diaphragm

Contrast medium in stomach

Main portal vein (to liver)

Inferior vena cava (vein)

Aorta

Spleen

Vertebra of spine

Ribs

A

Liver

Left breast

Portal veins (to liver)

Hepatic veins (from liver)

Stomach

Inferior vena cava (vein)

Spleen

Aorta

Vertebra of spine

Spinal cord

B

Figure 7-9 **Imaging techniques.** Shown are cross-sections through the liver and spleen. **A.** Computed tomography (CT). **B.** Magnetic resonance imaging (MRI).

but usually it involves cutting or puncturing tissue with a sharp instrument in the process of **incision**. See **Box 7-4** for descriptions of surgical instruments and **Figure 7-11** for pictures of surgical instruments. Surgery usually requires some form of **anesthesia** to dull or eliminate pain. After surgery, incisions must be closed for proper healing. Traditionally, surgeons have used stitches or **sutures** to close wounds, but today they also use adhesive strips, staples, and skin glue.

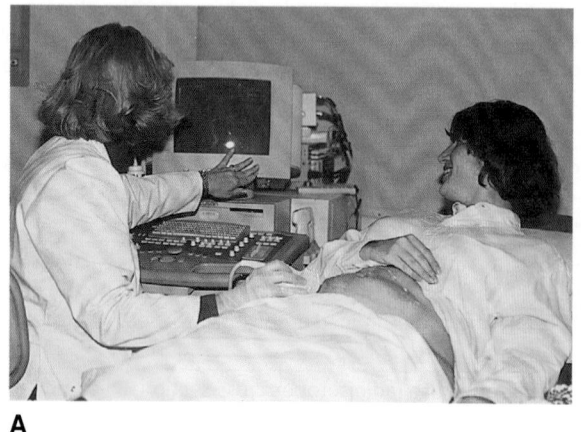

A

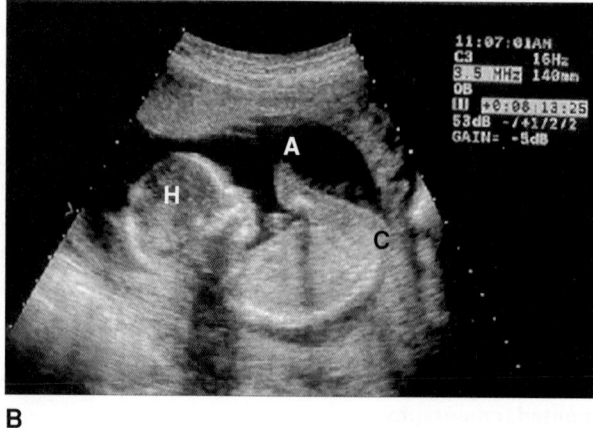

B

Figure 7-10 **Ultrasonography. A.** The practitioner is using ultrasound to monitor pregnancy. **B.** Sonogram of a pregnant uterus at 10 to 11 weeks showing the amniotic cavity (A) filled with amniotic fluid. The fetus is seen in longitudinal section showing the head (H) and coccyx (C).

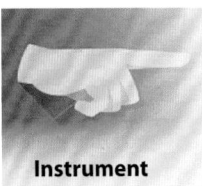

FOR YOUR REFERENCE

Box 7-4

Surgical Instruments

Instrument	Description
bougie *BOO-zhe*	slender, flexible instrument for exploring and dilating tubes
cannula *KAN-u-lah*	tube enclosing a trocar (see below) that allows escape of fluid or air after removal of the trocar
clamp	instrument used to compress tissue
curet (curette) *KU-ret*	spoon-shaped instrument for removing material from the wall of a cavity or other surface (**Fig. 7-11**)
elevator *EL-eh-va-tor*	instrument for lifting tissue or bone
forceps *FOR-seps*	instrument for holding or extracting (see **Fig. 7-11**)
Gigli saw *JE-yle*	flexible wire saw
hemostat *HE-mo-stat*	small clamp for stopping blood flow from a vessel (**Fig. 7-11**)
rasp	surgical file
retractor *re-TRAK-tor*	instrument used to maintain exposure by separating a wound and holding back organs or tissues (**Fig. 7-11**)
rongeur *ron-ZHUR*	gouge forceps
scalpel *SKAL-pel*	surgical knife with a sharp blade (**Fig. 7-11**)
scissors *SIZ-ors*	a cutting instrument with two opposing blades
sound *sownd*	instrument for exploring a cavity or canal (**Fig. 7-11**)
trocar *TRO-kar*	sharp pointed instrument contained in a cannula used to puncture a cavity

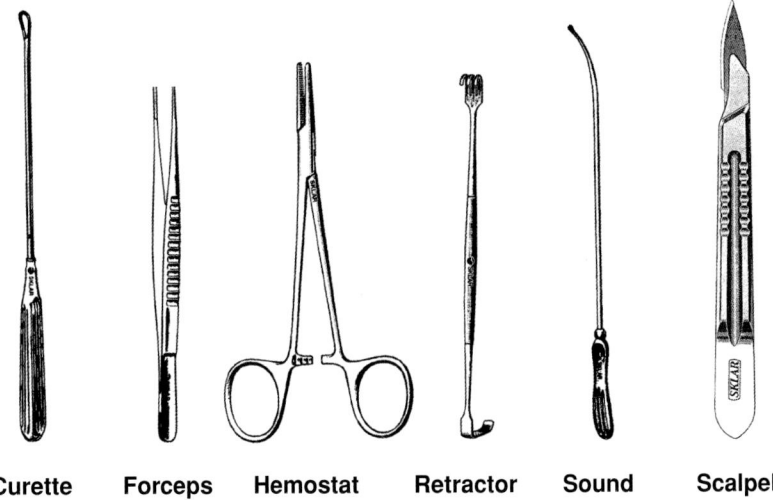

Curette   Forceps   Hemostat   Retractor   Sound   Scalpel

Figure 7-11   Surgical instruments.

Many types of operations are now performed with a **laser**, an intense beam of light. Some procedures require destruction of tissue by a harmful agent, such as by heat or a chemical, in the process of **cautery** or cauterization. Surgeons are now increasingly using computer-assisted robotic surgery for certain procedures. In this type of operation, the surgeon uses robotic instruments manipulated remotely or by a computer. These operations can be less invasive than standard surgeries and result in less bleeding. The method has been used mainly for urogenital procedures, some joint replacement, correction of certain heart abnormalities, and gallbladder removal.

Some of the purposes of surgery include:

- Treatment: For **excision** (cutting out) of diseased or abnormal tissue, such as a tumor or an inflamed appendix. Surgical methods are also used to repair wounds or injuries, as in skin grafting for burns or for realigning broken bones. Surgical methods are used to correct circulatory problems and to return structures to their normal positions, as in raising a prolapsed organ, such as the urinary bladder, in a surgical **fixation** procedure.
- Diagnosis: To remove tissue for laboratory study in a biopsy, as previously described. Exploratory surgery to investigate the cause of symptoms is performed less frequently now because of advances in noninvasive diagnostic and imaging techniques.
- Restoration: Surgery may compensate for lost function, as when a section of the intestine is redirected in a colostomy, a tube is inserted to allow breathing in a tracheostomy, a feeding tube is inserted, or an organ is transplanted. Surgeons may perform plastic or reconstructive surgery to accommodate a prosthesis (substitute part), to restore proper appearance, or for cosmetic reasons.
- Relief: Palliative surgery relieves pain or discomfort, as by cutting the nerve supply to an organ or reducing the size of a tumor to relieve pressure.

Surgery may be done in an emergency or urgent situation under conditions of acute danger, as in traumatic injury or severe blockage. Other procedures, such as cataract removal from the eye, may be planned when convenient. Elective or optional surgery would not cause serious consequences if delayed or not done.

Over time, surgery has extended beyond the classic operating room of a hospital to other hospital areas and to private surgical facilities where people can be treated within one day as outpatients. Preoperative care is given before surgery and includes examination, obtaining the patient's informed consent for the procedure, and preadmission testing. Postoperative care includes recovery from anesthesia, follow-up evaluations, and instructions for home care.

Box 7-5 describes some aspects of careers in surgical technology.

Alternative and Complementary Medicine

During the past century, the leading causes of death in industrialized countries have gradually shifted from infectious diseases to chronic diseases of the cardiovascular and respiratory systems and cancer. In addition to advancing age, life habits and the environment greatly influence these conditions. As a result, many people have begun to consider healing practices from other philosophies and cultures as alternatives and complements to conventional Western medicine. Some of these philosophies include **osteopathy**, **naturopathy**, **homeopathy**, and **chiropractic**. Techniques of **acupuncture**, **biofeedback**, **massage**, and **meditation** may also be used, as well as herbal remedies (see Chapter 8) and nutritional counseling on diet, vitamins, and minerals. Complementary and alternative therapies emphasize maintaining health rather than treating disease and allowing the body opportunity to heal itself. These ideas fit into the concept of **holistic healthcare**, which promotes treating an individual as a whole with emotional, social, and spiritual needs in addition to physical needs and encouraging people to be involved in their own health maintenance.

HEALTH PROFESSIONS   Box 7-5
Surgical Technology

Surgical technologists, also known as operating room technicians, prepare for and assist with surgical procedures under the supervision of surgeons and nurses. They prepare the operating room, surgical instruments, and equipment. They help the surgical team to scrub and put on gowns, gloves, and masks. They also prepare patients for surgery, helping to position them on the table and draping them with sterile linens. During an operation, surgical technologists hand instruments and other materials to the surgeon, maintain supplies, and operate special equipment. Finally, they help count materials to be sure that all have been removed from the patient at the conclusion of surgery, and they assist in suturing. They also take responsibility for specimens removed for laboratory testing. The job requires stamina, manual dexterity, and quick reaction time.

A career in surgical technology requires training in a surgical technology program and certification. Preparation for this training should include courses in basic sciences, math, and computer applications. The Association of Surgical Technologists at www.ast.org has additional information on this career.

The U.S. government has established the National Center for Complementary and Alternative Medicine (NCCAM) within the National Institutes of Health (NIH) to study these therapies.

Cancer

Methods used in the diagnosis of cancer include physical examination, biopsy, imaging techniques, and laboratory tests for abnormalities, or "markers," associated with specific types of malignancies. Some cancer markers are byproducts, such as enzymes, hormones, and cellular proteins, that are abnormal or are produced in abnormal amounts. Researchers have also linked specific genetic mutations to certain forms of cancer.

Oncologists (cancer specialists) use two methods, **grading** and **staging**, to classify cancers, select and evaluate therapy, and estimate disease outcome. Grading is based on histologic (tissue) changes observed in tumor cells when they are examined microscopically. Grades increase from I to IV with increasing cellular abnormality.

Staging is a procedure for establishing the clinical extent of tumor spread, both at the original site and in other parts of the body (metastases). The TNM system is commonly used. These letters stand for primary tumor (T), regional lymph nodes (N), and distant metastases (M). Evaluation in these categories varies for each type of tumor. Based on TNM results, a stage ranging in severity from I to IV is assigned. Cancers of the blood, lymphatic system, and nervous system are evaluated by different standards.

The most widely used methods for treatment of cancer are surgery, radiation therapy, and **chemotherapy** (treatment with chemicals). Newer methods of **immunotherapy** use substances that stimulate the immune system as a whole or vaccines prepared specifically against a tumor. Hormone therapy may also be effective against certain types of tumors. When no active signs of the disease remain, the cancer is said to be in **remission**.

Terminology | Key Terms

anesthesia *an-es-THE-ze-ah*	Loss of the ability to feel pain, as by administration of a drug
auscultation *aws-kul-TA-shun*	Listening for sounds within the body, usually within the chest or abdomen (see **Fig. 7-3**)
biopsy *BI-op-se*	Removal of a small amount of tissue for microscopic examination
cautery *KAW-ter-e*	Destruction of tissue by a damaging agent, such as a harmful chemical, heat, or electric current (electrocautery); cauterization
chemotherapy *ke-mo-THER-ah-pe*	Use of chemicals to treat disease; the term is often applied specifically to the treatment of cancer with chemicals
diagnosis *di-ag-NO-sis*	The process of determining the cause and nature of an illness
endoscope *EN-do-skope*	An instrument for examining the inside of an organ or cavity through a body opening or small incision; most endoscopes use fiberoptics for viewing (see **Fig. 7-7**)
excision *ek-SIZH-un*	Removal by cutting (suffix: -ectomy)
fixation *fik-SA-shun*	Holding or fastening a structure in a firm position (suffix: -pexy)
grading *GRA-ding*	A method for evaluating a tumor based on microscopic examination of the cells
immunotherapy *im-u-no-THER-ah-pe*	Treatment that involves stimulation or suppression of the immune system, either specifically or nonspecifically
incision *in-SIZH-un*	A cut, as for surgery; also the act of cutting (suffix: -tomy)
inspection *in-SPEK-shun*	Visual examination of the body

(continued)

laser LA-zer	A device that transforms light into a beam of intense heat and power; used for surgery and diagnosis
ophthalmoscope of-THAL-mo-skope	An instrument for examining the interior of the eye (see **Fig. 7-6A**)
otoscope O-to-skope	Instrument used to examine the ears (see **Fig. 7-6B**)
palliative therapy PAL-e-ah-tiv	Providing relief but not cure; a treatment that provides such relief
palpation pal-PA-shun	Examining by placing the hands or fingers on the surface of the body to determine characteristics such as texture, temperature, movement, and consistency (see **Fig. 7-1**)
percussion per-KUSH-un	Tapping the body lightly but sharply to assess the condition of the underlying tissue by the sounds obtained (see **Fig. 7-2**)
prognosis prog-NO-sis	Prediction of a disease's course and outcome
radiography ra-de-OG-rah-fe	Use of x-rays passed through the body to make a visual record (radiograph) of internal structures either on specially sensitized film or digitally; roentgenography (rent-geh-NOG-rah-fe)
remission re-MISH-un	Lessening of disease symptoms; the period during which this decrease occurs or the period when no sign of a disease exists
sign sine	Objective evidence of disease that can be observed or tested; examples are fever, rash, high blood pressure, and blood or urine abnormalities; an objective symptom
sphygmomanometer sfig-mo-mah-NOM-eh-ter	Blood pressure apparatus or blood pressure cuff; pressure is read in millimeters of mercury (mm Hg) when the heart is contracting (systolic pressure) and when the heart is relaxing (diastolic pressure) and is reported as systolic/diastolic (see **Fig. 7-5**)
staging STA-jing	The process of classifying malignant tumors for diagnosis, treatment, and prognosis
stethoscope STETH-o-skope	An instrument used for listening to sounds produced within the body (from the Greek root steth/o, meaning "chest") (see **Fig. 7-3**)
surgery SUR-jer-e	A method for treating disease or injury by manual operations
suture SU-chur	To unite parts by stitching them together; also the thread or other material used in that process or the seam formed by surgical stitching (suffix: -rhaphy)
symptom SIMP-tum	Any evidence of disease; sometimes limited to subjective evidence of disease as experienced by the individual, such as pain, dizziness, and weakness
therapy THER-ah-pe	Treatment, intervention
vital signs VI-tal	Measurements that reflect basic functions necessary to maintain life

Alternative and Complementary Medicine

acupuncture AK-u-punk-chur	An ancient Chinese method of inserting thin needles into the body at specific points to relieve pain, induce anesthesia, or promote healing; similar effects can be obtained by using firm finger pressure at the surface of the body in the technique of *acupressure*
biofeedback bi-o-FEDE-bak	A method for learning control of involuntary physiologic responses by using electronic devices to monitor bodily changes and feeding this information back to a person

Terminology	Key Terms *(Continued)*

chiropractic ki-ro-PRAK-tik	A science that stresses the condition of the nervous system in diagnosis and treatment of disease; often, the spine is manipulated to correct misalignment; most patients consult for musculoskeletal pain and headaches (from Greek *cheir*, meaning "hand")
holistic healthcare ho-LIS-tik	Practice of treating a person as a whole entity with physical, emotional, social, and spiritual needs; it stresses comprehensive care, involvement in one's own care, and the maintenance of good health rather than the treatment of disease
homeopathy ho-me-OP-ah-the	A philosophy of treating disease by administering drugs in highly diluted form along with promoting healthy life habits and a healthy environment (from *home/o*, meaning "same," and *path/o*, meaning "disease")
massage ma-SAHJ	Manipulation of the body or portion of the body to calm, relieve tension, increase circulation, and stimulate muscles
meditation med-ih-TA-shun	Process of clearing the mind by concentrating on the inner self while controlling breathing and perhaps repeating a word or phrase (mantra)
naturopathy na-chur-OP-ah-the	A therapeutic philosophy of helping people heal themselves by developing healthy lifestyles; naturopaths may use some of the methods of conventional medicine (from *nature* and *path/o*, meaning "disease")
osteopathy os-te-OP-ah-the	A system of therapy based on the theory that the body can overcome disease when it has normal structure, a favorable environment, and proper nutrition; osteopaths use standard medical practices for diagnosis and treatment but stress the identification and correction of faulty body structure (from *oste/o*, meaning "bone," and *path/o*, meaning "disease")

Go to the Audio Pronunciation Glossary in the Student Resources on the Point to hear these terms pronounced.

Word Parts Pertaining to Diagnosis and Treatment

See Tables 7-1 to 7-3.

Table 7-1	Roots for Physical Forces

Root	Meaning	Example	Definition of Example
aer/o	air, gas	aerobic air-O-bik	pertaining to or requiring air (oxygen)
bar/o	pressure	barometer bah-ROM-eh-ter	instrument used to measure pressure
chrom/o, chromat/o	color, stain	chromatic kro-MAT-ik	having color
chron/o	time	chronologic kron-o-LOJ-ik	arranged according to the time of occurrence
cry/o	cold	cryoprobe KRI-o-probe	instrument used to apply extreme cold
electr/o	electricity	electrolysis e-lek-TROL-ih-sis	decomposition of a substance by means of electric current

(continued)

| Table 7-1 | Roots for Physical Forces (*Continued*) | | |

Root	Meaning	Example	Definition of Example
erg/o	work	synergistic sin-er-JIS-tik	working together with increased effect, such as certain drugs in combination
phon/o	sound, voice	phonograph FO-no-graf	instrument used to reproduce sound
phot/o	light	photoreaction fo-to-re-AK-shun	response to light
radi/o	radiation, x-ray	radiology ra-de-OL-o-je	study and use of radiation
son/o	sound	sonogram SON-o-gram	record obtained by use of ultrasound
therm/o	heat, temperature	hypothermia hi-po-THER-me-ah	abnormally low body temperature

EXERCISE 7-1

Match the following terms, and write the appropriate letter to the left of each number.

_____ **1.** hyperthermia (*hi-per-THER-me-ah*)

_____ **2.** hyperbaric (*hi-per-BAR-ik*)

_____ **3.** synchrony (*SIN-kro-ne*)

_____ **4.** radioactive (*ra-de-o-AK-tiv*)

_____ **5.** chromocyte (*kro-mo-site*)

a. abnormally high body temperature

b. any pigmented cell

c. pertaining to increased pressure

d. occurrence at the same time

e. giving off radiation

Identify and define the root in each of the following words.

	Root	Meaning of Root
6. sonographer (*so-NOG-rah-fer*)	_____	_____
7. chronic (*KRON-ik*)	_____	_____
8. homeothermic (*ho-me-o-THER-mik*)	_____	_____
9. exergonic (*eks-er-GON-ik*)	_____	_____
10. anaerobic (*an-er-O-bik*)	_____	_____
11. achromatic (*ak-ro-MAT-ik*)	_____	_____

Fill in the blanks.

12. The term electroconvulsive (*e-lek-tro-con-VUL-siv*) means causing convulsions by means of _____.

13. A photograph (*FO-to-graf*) is an image produced by means of _____.

14. Cryotherapy (*kri-o-THER-ah-pe*) is treatment using _____.

15. Barotrauma (*bah-ro-TRAW-mah*) is injury caused by _____.

16. Phonetics (*fo-NET-iks*) is the study of _____.

Table 7-2   Suffixes for Diagnosis

Suffix	Meaning	Example	Definition of Example
-graph	instrument for recording data	polygraph POL-e-graf	instrument used to record many physiologic responses simultaneously; lie detector
-graphy	act of recording data[a]	echography ek-OG-rah-fe	recording data obtained by ultrasound
-gram[b]	a record of data	electrocardiogram eh-lek-tro-KAR-de-o-gram	record of the heart's electrical activity
-meter	instrument for measuring	calorimeter kal-o-RIM-eh-ter	instrument for measuring the caloric energy of food
-metry	measurement of	audiometry aw-de-OM-eh-tre	measurement of hearing (audi/o); root metr/o means "measure"
-scope	instrument for viewing or examining	bronchoscope BRONG-ko-skope	instrument for examining the bronchi (breathing passages) (see Fig. 7-7)
-scopy	examination of	celioscopy se-le-OS-ko-pe	examination of the abdominal cavity (celi/o)

[a]This ending is often used to mean not only the recording of data but also the evaluation and interpretation of the data.

[b]An image prepared simply using x-rays is called a radiograph. When special techniques are used to image an organ or region with x-rays, the ending -gram is used with the root for that area, as in urogram (urinary tract), angiogram (blood vessels), and mammogram (breast).

EXERCISE 7-2

Match the following terms, and write the appropriate letter to the left of each number.

_____ **1.** microscope (MI-kro-skope)

_____ **2.** ergometry (er-GOM-eh-tre)

_____ **3.** thermometer (ther-MOM-eh-ter)

_____ **4.** laparoscopy (lap-ah-ROS-ko-pe)

_____ **5.** sonogram (SON-o-gram)

a. examination of the abdomen

b. a record of sound

c. measurement of work done

d. instrument for measuring temperature

e. instrument for examining very small objects

_____ **6.** endoscope (EN-do-skope)

_____ **7.** electroencephalograph
(e-lek-tro-en-SEF-ah-lo-graf)

_____ **8.** audiometer (aw-de-OM-eh-ter)

_____ **9.** phonogram (FO-no-gram)

_____ **10.** chronometer (kron-OM-eh-ter)

a. a record of sound

b. instrument for measuring time

c. instrument for viewing the inside of a cavity or organ

d. instrument used to measure hearing

e. instrument used to record the brain's electrical activity

See examples of diagnostic records in the Student Resources on thePoint.

Table 7-3	Suffixes for Surgery		

Suffix	Meaning	Example	Definition of Example
-centesis	puncture, tap	thoracentesis *thor-ah-sen-TE-sis*	puncture of the chest (thorac/o)
-desis	binding, fusion	pleurodesis *plu-ROD-eh-sis*	binding of the pleura (membranes around the lungs)
-ectomy	excision, surgical removal	hepatectomy *hep-ah-TEK-to-me*	excision of liver tissue (hepat/o)
-pexy	surgical fixation	hysteropexy *HIS-ter-o-pek-se*	surgical fixation of the uterus (hyster/o)
-plasty	plastic repair, plastic surgery, reconstruction	rhinoplasty *RI-no-plas-te*	plastic surgery of the nose (rhin/o)
-rhaphy	surgical repair, suture	herniorrhaphy *her-ne-OR-ah-fe*	surgical repair of a hernia (herni/o)
-stomy	surgical creation of an opening	tracheostomy *tra-ke-OS-to-me*	creation of an opening into the trachea (trache/o)
-tome	instrument for incising (cutting)	microtome *MI-kro-tome*	instrument for cutting thin sections of tissue for microscopic study
-tomy	incision, cutting	laparotomy *lap-ah-ROT-o-me*	surgical incision of the abdomen (lapar/o)
-tripsy	crushing	neurotripsy *nu-ro-TRIP-se*	crushing of a nerve (neur/o)

EXERCISE 7-3

Match the following terms, and write the appropriate letter to the left of each number.

_____ **1.** nephropexy (*nef-ro-PEK-se*)

_____ **2.** rhinoplasty (*RI-no-plas-te*)

_____ **3.** lithotripsy (*LITH-o-trip-se*)

_____ **4.** adenectomy (*ad-eh-NEK-to-me*)

_____ **5.** celiocentesis (*se-le-o-sen-TE-sis*)

a. crushing of a stone

b. surgical fixation of the kidney

c. puncture of the abdomen

d. excision of a gland

e. plastic surgery of the nose

The root *cyst/o* means "urinary bladder." Use this root to write a word that means each of the following.

6. Incision into the bladder _____

7. Surgical fixation of the bladder_____

8. Plastic repair of the bladder_____

9. Surgical repair of the bladder _____

10. Creation of an opening into the bladder _____

The root *arthr/o* means "joint." Use this root to write a word that means each of the following.

11. Plastic repair of a joint _____

12. Instrument for incising a joint_____

EXERCISE 7-3 (Continued)

13. Incision of a joint _____

14. Puncture of a joint _____

15. Fusion of a joint _____

Write a word for each of the following definitions using the roots given.

16. Incision into the trachea (trache/o) _____

17. Surgical repair of the stomach (gastr/o) _____

18. Creation of an opening into the colon (col/o) _____

Terminology | Supplementary Terms

Symptoms

clubbing KLUB-ing	Enlargement of the ends of the fingers and toes because of soft-tissue growth of the nails; seen in a variety of diseases, especially lung and heart diseases (**Fig. 7-12**)
colic KOL-ik	Acute abdominal pain associated with smooth muscle spasms
cyanosis si-ah-NO-sis	Bluish discoloration of the skin due to lack of oxygen
diaphoresis di-ah-fo-RE-sis	Profuse sweating
malaise mah-LAZE	A feeling of discomfort or uneasiness, often indicative of infection or other disease (from French, meaning "discomfort," using the prefix mal-, meaning "bad")
nocturnal nok-TUR-nal	Pertaining to or occurring at night (roots noct/i and nyct/o mean "night")
pallor PAL-or	Paleness, lack of color
prodrome PRO-drome	A symptom indicating an approaching disease
sequela seh-KWEL-ah	A lasting effect of a disease (plural: sequelae)
syncope SIN-ko-pe	A temporary loss of consciousness because of inadequate blood flow to the brain, fainting

Diagnosis

alpha-fetoprotein (AFP) AL-fah-fe-to-PRO-tene	A fetal protein that appears in the blood of adults with certain types of cancer
bruit brwe	A sound, usually abnormal, heard in auscultation
facies FA-she-eze	The expression or appearance of the face

(continued)

Terminology | Supplementary Terms (Continued)

febrile *FEB-ril*	Pertaining to fever
nuclear medicine	The branch of medicine concerned with the use of radioactive substances (radionuclides) for diagnosis, therapy, and research
radiology *ra-de-OL-o-je*	The branch of medicine that uses radiation, such as x-rays, in the diagnosis and treatment of disease; a specialist in this field is a radiologist
radionuclide *ra-de-o-NU-klide*	A substance that gives off radiation; used for diagnosis and treatment; also called radioisotope or radiopharmaceutical
speculum *SPEK-u-lum*	An instrument for examining a canal (**Fig. 7-13**)
syndrome *SIN-drome*	A group of signs and symptoms that together characterize a disease condition

Treatment

catheter *KATH-eh-ter*	A thin tube that can be passed into the body; used to remove fluids from or introduce fluids into a body cavity (**Fig. 7-14**)
clysis *KLI-sis*	The introduction of fluid into the body, other than orally, as into the rectum or abdominal cavity; also refers to the solution thus used
irrigation *ir-ih-GA-shun*	Flushing of a tube, cavity, or area with a fluid (**Fig. 7-14**)
lavage *lah-VAJ*	The washing out of a cavity, irrigation
normal saline (NS) *SA-lene*	A salt (NaCl) solution compatible with living cells, also called physiologic saline solution (PSS)
paracentesis *par-ah-sen-TE-sis*	Puncture of a cavity for removal of fluid
prophylaxis *pro-fih-LAK-sis*	Prevention of disease

Surgery

drain	Device for allowing matter to escape from a wound or cavity; common types include Penrose (cigarette), T-tube, Jackson–Pratt (J-P), and Hemovac
ligature *LIG-ah-chur*	A tie or bandage, the process of binding or tying (also called ligation)
resection *re-SEK-shun*	Partial excision of a structure
stapling *STA-pling*	In surgery, the joining of tissue by using wire staples that are pushed through the tissue and then bent
surgeon *SUR-jun*	A physician who specializes in surgery

Go to the Audio Pronunciation Glossary in the Student Resources on thePoint to hear these terms pronounced.

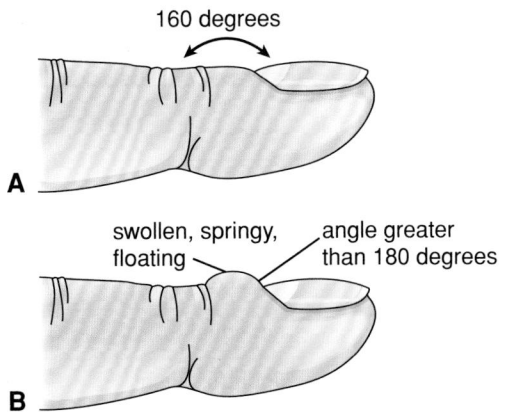

Figure 7-12 **Clubbing. A.** Normal. **B.** Clubbing; the end of the finger is enlarged because of soft-tissue growth around the nail.

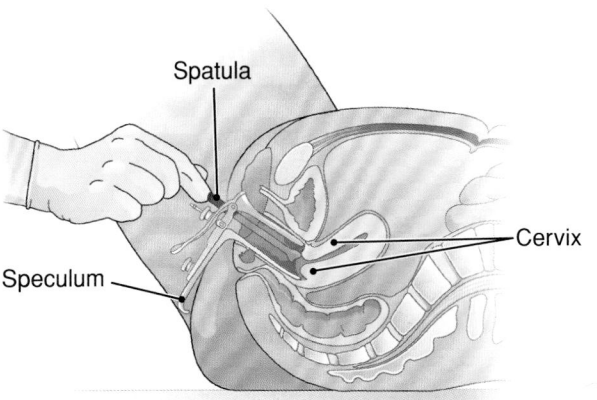

Figure 7-13 **A vaginal speculum.** This instrument is used to examine the vagina and cervix and to obtain a cervical sample for testing.

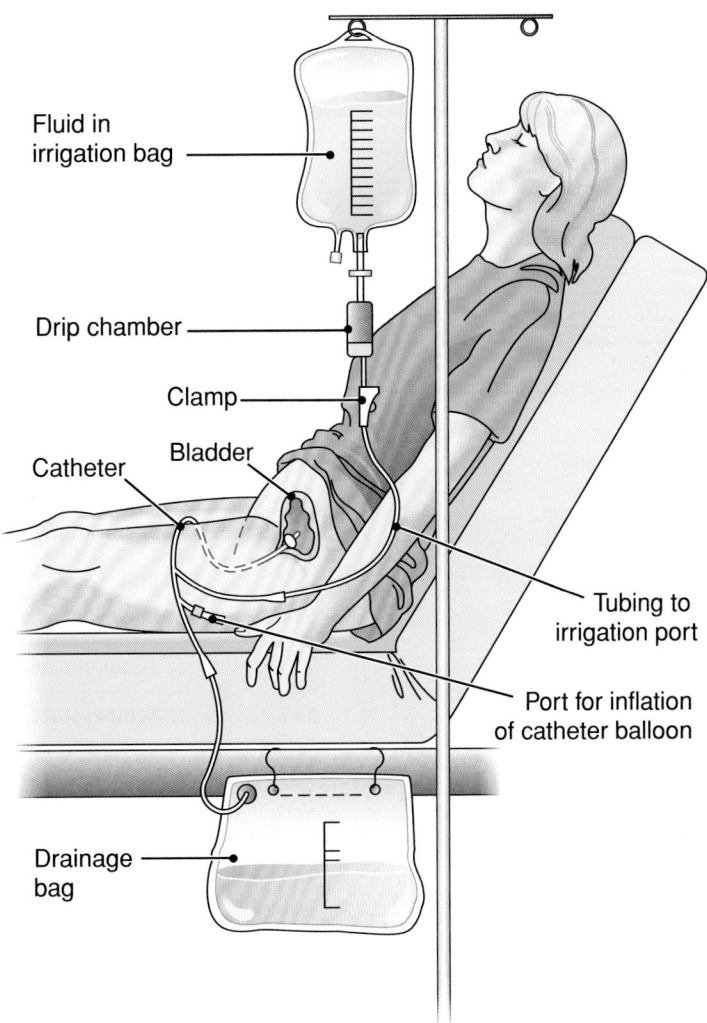

Figure 7-14 **Continuous bladder irrigation using a catheter.**

Terminology | Symbols

1°	primary	°	degree
2°	secondary (to)	∧	above
Δ	change	∨	below
Ⓛ	left	=	equal to
Ⓡ	right	≠	not equal to
↑	increase(d)	±	doubtful, slight
↓	decrease(d)	~	approximately
♂	male	×	times
♀	female	#	number, pound

Terminology | Abbreviations

History and Physical Examination

ADL	Activities of daily living
BP	Blood pressure
bpm	Beats per minute
C	Celsius (centigrade)
CC	Chief complaint
c/o, co	Complains (complaining) of
EOMI	Extraocular muscles intact
ETOH	Alcohol (ethyl alcohol)
F	Fahrenheit
HEENT	Head, eyes, ears, nose, and throat
HIPAA	Health Insurance Portability and Accountability Act
h/o	History of
H&P	History and physical
HPI	History of present illness
HR	Heart rate
Hx	History
I&O	Intake and output
IPPA	Inspection, palpation, percussion, auscultation
IVDA	Intravenous drug abuse

NAD	No apparent distress
NKDA	No known drug allergies
P	Pulse
PE	Physical examination
PE(R)RLA	Pupils equal (regular) react to light and accommodation
PMH	Past medical history
pt	Patient
R	Respiration
R/O	Rule out
ROS	Review of systems
T	Temperature
TPR	Temperature, pulse, respiration
VS	Vital signs
WD	Well developed
WNL	Within normal limits
w/o	Without
YO, y/o	Years old, year-old

Diagnosis and Treatment

ABC	Aspiration biopsy cytology
AFP	Alpha-fetoprotein
BS	Bowel sounds, breath sounds

Terminology Abbreviations *(Continued)*

bx	Biopsy
CAM	Complementary and alternative medicine
Ci	Curie (unit of radioactivity)
C&S	Culture and (drug) sensitivity (of bacteria)
CT	Computed tomography
D/C, dc	Discontinue
Dx	Diagnosis
EBL	Estimated blood loss
ICU	Intensive care unit
I&D	Incision and drainage
MET	Metastasis
MRI	Magnetic resonance imaging
NCCAM	National Center for Complementary and Alternative Medicine
NS, N/S	Normal saline
PCA	Patient-controlled analgesia
PET	Positron emission tomography
PICC	Peripherally inserted central catheter
postop	Postoperative
preop	Preoperative
PSS	Physiologic saline solution
RATx	Radiation therapy
Rx	Drug, prescription, therapy

SPECT	Single-photon emission computed tomography
TNM	(Primary) tumor, (regional lymph) nodes, (distant) metastases
UV	Ultraviolet

Views for Radiography

AP	Anteroposterior
LL	Left lateral
PA	Posteroanterior
RL	Right lateral

Orders

AMA	Against medical advice
AMB	Ambulatory
BRP	Bathroom privileges
CBR	Complete bed rest
DNR	Do not resuscitate
KVO	Keep vein open
NPO	Nothing by mouth (Latin, *non per os*)
OOB	Out of bed
QNS	Quantity not sufficient
QS	Quantity sufficient
STAT	Immediately
TKO	To keep open

Drug-related abbreviations are located in Chapter 8.

Case Study Revisited

M.L.'s Injury Follow-Up

M.L. was seen by the orthopedic surgeon, who reduced her wrist fracture and applied a short arm cast. She was scheduled for an arthrocentesis to remove fluid from the right knee. Following the procedure, M.L. was discharged and sent home with instructions to rest and to keep the right wrist and leg elevated. She was directed to take an antiinflammatory medication (NSAID) for the inflammation and pain. It was recommended that in the future M.L. wear protective padding when she rollerblades.

Matching

Match the following terms, and write the appropriate letter to the left of each number.

_____ **1.** electrolyte   **a.** substance that conducts electric current

_____ **2.** staging   **b.** evidence of disease

_____ **3.** symptom   **c.** classification of malignant tumors

_____ **4.** syndrome   **d.** a group of symptoms that characterizes a disease

_____ **5.** suture   **e.** to unite parts by stitching them together

_____ **6.** cautery   **a.** a removal of tissue for microscopic study

_____ **7.** scintiscan   **b.** pain caused by cold

_____ **8.** cryalgesia   **c.** destruction of tissue with a damaging agent

_____ **9.** vasotripsy   **d.** image obtained with a radionuclide

_____ **10.** biopsy   **e.** crushing of a vessel

_____ **11.** ergometer   **a.** instrument used to cut bone

_____ **12.** osteotome   **b.** organism that produces color

_____ **13.** acupuncture   **c.** instrument to measure work output

_____ **14.** biofeedback   **d.** method for controlling involuntary responses

_____ **15.** chromogen   **e.** treatment by insertion of thin needles

Supplementary Terms

_____ **16.** sequelae   **a.** partial excision

_____ **17.** prophylaxis   **b.** prevention of disease

_____ **18.** clubbing   **c.** symptom indicating an approaching disease

_____ **19.** prodrome   **d.** lasting effects of disease

_____ **20.** resection   **e.** enlargement of the ends of the fingers and toes

_____ **21.** catheter   **a.** thin tube

_____ **22.** colic   **b.** feeling of discomfort

_____ **23.** diaphoresis   **c.** acute abdominal pain

_____ **24.** malaise   **d.** washing out of a cavity

_____ **25.** lavage   **e.** profuse sweating

WORD ROOTS

Identify and define the root in each of the following words.

	Root	Meaning of Root
26. chromocyte	_____	_____
27. anaerobic	_____	_____
28. radiodense	_____	_____
29. thermalgia	_____	_____

	Root	Meaning of Root
30. chronology	_____	_____
31. allergy	_____	_____
32. ultrasonic	_____	_____

FILL IN THE BLANKS

33. The PA in M.L.'s case evaluated her wrist by touching it. The term for this examination technique is _____.

34. Following her examination, the PA predicted the outcome of M.L.'s injuries; that is, she gave a(n) _____.

35. Referring to M.L.'s opening case study, the adjective form of *diagnosis* is _____.

36. In the same case study, the adjective form of *edema* is _____.

37. Another word for *treatment* is _____.

38. Photochromic eyeglass lenses change color in response to _____.

39. Plastic repair of the stomach is called _____.

40. Fusion of a joint is _____.

41. Surgical creation of an opening in the colon is a(n) _____.

Use the root -hepat/o, meaning "liver," to write a word for each of the following.

42. Incision of the liver _____

43. Excision of liver tissue _____

44. Surgical fixation of the liver _____

45. Surgical repair of the liver _____

TRUE-FALSE

Examine the following statements. If the statement is true, write T in the first blank. If the statement is false, write F in the first blank, and correct the statement by replacing the underlined word in the second blank.

	True or False	Correct Answer
46. Nephrectomy is surgical removal of a <u>gland</u>.	_____	_____
47. A baroreceptor is sensitive to <u>temperature</u>.	_____	_____
48. An otoscope is used to examine the <u>eye</u>.	_____	_____
49. An image produced by x-rays is a <u>radiogram</u>.	_____	_____
50. An echogram is produced by <u>ultrasound</u>.	_____	_____
51. Arthroscopy is endoscopic examination of a <u>joint</u>.	_____	_____

ELIMINATIONS

In each of the sets below, underline the word that does not fit in with the rest, and explain the reason for your choice.

52. percussion — inspection — palpation — remission — auscultation

_____

53. ophthalmoscope — sphygmomanometer — stethoscope — syncope — endoscope

_____

54. curette — forceps — speculum — scalpel — hemostat

_____

55. TNM — MRI — PET — CT — SPECT

_____

ABBREVIATIONS

Write the meaning of the following abbreviations used in M.L.'s opening case study.

56. PA _____

57. MRI _____

58. Hx _____

59. ROM _____

60. NSAID _____

WORD BUILDING

Write words for the following definitions using the word parts provided.

lith/o	-rhaphy	neur/o	-tripsy	-tome	r	-pexy	-scopy	cyst/o

61. Crushing of a nerve   _____

62. Surgical repair of the bladder   _____

63. Surgical fixation of the bladder   _____

64. Surgical repair of a nerve   _____

65. Crushing of a stone   _____

66. Bladder stone   _____

67. Endoscopic examination of the bladder   _____

68. Instrument used to incise a nerve   _____

69. Instrument used to incise the bladder   _____

WORD ANALYSIS

Define each of the following words, and give the meanings of the word parts in each. Use a dictionary if necessary.

70. isochromatophilic (*i-so-kro-mat-o-FIL-ik*) _____

    a. iso- _____

    b. chromat/o _____

    c. phil _____

    d. -ic _____

71. synchronous (*SIN-kro-nus*) _____

    a. syn- _____

    b. chron/o _____

    c. -ous _____

72. asymmetric (*a-sim-ET-rik*) _____

    a. a- _____

    b. sym- _____

    c. metr/o _____

    d. -ic _____

73. chromogenesis (*kro-mo-JEN-eh-sis*) _____

    a. chrom/o _____

    b. gen/e _____

    c. -sis _____

For more learning activities, see Chapter 7 of the Student Resources on the Point.

Additional Case Studies

Case Study 7-1: *Comprehensive History and Physical*

C.F., a 46 YO married Asian woman, works as an office manager for an insurance company. This morning, she had a follow-up visit with her oncologist and was sent to the hospital for immediate admission for possible recurrence or sequelae of her ovarian cancer. She is alert, articulate, and a reliable reporter.

CC: C.F. presents with mild, low, aching pelvic pain and low abdominal fullness. She states, "I feel like I have cramps and am bloated. Sometimes I'm so tired I cannot do my work without a short nap."

HPI: C.F. has been in remission for 14 months from aggressively treated ovarian carcinoma. She presents with mild abdominal distention and tenderness on deep palpation of the lower pelvis. C.F. claims a feeling of fullness in the lower abdomen, loss of appetite, and inability to sleep through the night. She is afraid that her cancer was not cured. Sometimes her heart races and she cannot catch her breath, but with two children in college, she cannot afford to miss work.

MEDS: Therapeutic vitamin × 1/day. Valium 5 mg every six hours (q6h) as needed (prn) for anxiety. Benadryl 25 mg at bedtime (hs) prn for insomnia. Echinacea tea 3 cups/day to prevent colds or flu. Ginkgo biloba tea 3 cups/day for energy.

ALLERGIES: NKDA, no food allergies

PMH: C.F. was diagnosed with ovarian CA four years ago and treated with surgery, radiation, and chemotherapy. A total abdominal hysterectomy (removal of the uterus) with bilateral removal of the oviducts and ovaries was performed. At the time of surgery, the pelvic lymph nodes tested negative for disease. Chemotherapy and radiation therapy occurred after surgical recovery. C.F. has been well and capable of full ADL until four weeks ago. Childhood history is unremarkable, with normal childhood diseases, including measles, mumps, and chicken pox. C.F. was born and raised in this country. She has no other adult diseases, surgery, or injuries.

CURRENT HEALTH Hx: Denies tobacco, ETOH, or recreational drugs or substances. She exercises three to five times per week with aerobic exercise class and treadmill. She is a vegetarian and drinks one to five cups of green tea per day. Immunizations are up to date, unsure of last tetanus booster. Recent negative mammogram and negative TB test (PPD).

FAMILY Hx: Both parents alive and well. Maternal aunt died of "stomach tumor" at age 37.

TPR & BP & PAIN: 37C-96–22, 126/72, in no acute distress.

HEENT: WNL. Mesocephalic; fundi benign; PERRLA; uncorrected 20/20 vision; mouth clear; good dental health; neck supple w/o rigidity, thyromegaly, or cervical lymphadenopathy; trachea midline. No carotid bruits.

LUNGS: All lobes clear to auscultation and percussion.

HEART: Rate 96 bpm, regular; no murmurs, gallops, or rubs.

BREASTS: Symmetrical, w/o masses or discharge.

ABDOMEN: Skin intact with healed suprapubic midline surgical incision and a symmetrical area of discoloration and dermal thickness from radiation therapy. Bowel sounds active and normal. Suprapubic tenderness on palpation. No hepatosplenomegaly. Absence of inguinal lymph nodes on palpation. Kidneys palpable. Rectal examination WNL. Hemoccult test (stool test for blood) result negative.

GU: Unremarkable. Surgical menopause.

MUSCULOSKELETAL: WNL. No weakness, limitation of mobility, joint pain, stiffness, or edema.

NEUROLOGIC: All reflexes intact. No syncope, paralysis, numbness.

DIAGNOSTIC IMPRESSION: Possible recurrence of ovarian CA, ascites.

TREATMENT PLAN: Send blood for CA-125 (genetic marker for ovarian cancer). Schedule abdominal paracentesis and second-look diagnostic laparoscopy with biopsy and tissue staging. D/C all herbal supplements.

(continued)

Additional Case Studies (*Continued*)

Case Study 7-2: *Diagnostic Laparoscopy*

For a laparoscopy, C.F. was given general anesthesia and her trachea was intubated. She was placed in lithotomy position with arms abducted. Her abdomen was insufflated with carbon dioxide (CO_2) through a thin needle placed below the umbilicus. Three trocar punctures were made to insert the telescope with camera and the cutting and grasping instruments. Biopsies were taken of several pelvic lymph nodes and sent to the pathology laboratory. There were many adhesions from prior surgery, which were lysed to mobilize her organs and enhance visualization. A loop of small bowel, which had adhered to the anterior abdominal wall, had been punctured when the trocar was introduced. The surgeon repaired the defect with an endoscopic stapler and irrigated the abdomen with 3 L of NS mixed with antibiotic solution.

Case Study Questions

Write the word from the case study that completes each of the following statements.

1. Secondary conditions, complications, or lasting effects of C.F.'s cancer would be called _____.

2. Examination by listening to body sounds with a stethoscope is called _____.

3. The size and shape of C.F.'s head was described as _____.

4. A collection of abdominal fluid (ascites) is drained by a cavity puncture and drainage procedure called a(n) _____.

5. Removal of tissue for microscopic examination is _____.

6. A surgical procedure in which an endoscope is inserted through the abdominal wall to visualize the abdominal cavity and determine the cause of a disorder is a(n) _____.

7. For her examination, C.F. was placed in a supine position with knees bent. This position is used for gynecologic and urologic surgery and is called the _____.

Multiple Choice. Select the best answer, and write the letter of your choice to the left of each number.

_____ 8. C.F.'s cancer was in a state of apparent cure with no active signs of disease. This state is called
   a. tumor staging
   b. syndrome
   c. remission
   d. sequelae

_____ 9. The abbreviation NKDA refers to allergies to
   a. dust
   b. wheat
   c. eggs
   d. drugs

_____ 10. C.F. claimed that her heart races and she cannot catch her breath. The terms for these conditions are, respectively,
   a. tachypnea and dyspnea
   b. tachycardia and dyspnea
   c. dyspnea and tachycardia
   d. tachycardia and bradypnea

_____ 11. Syncope is
   a. fainting
   b. nosebleed
   c. palpitations
   d. anxiety

_____**12.** Hepatosplenomegaly means
  a. removal of the liver and spleen
  b. prolapse of the heart and spleen
  c. hemorrhage of the liver and spleen
  d. enlargement of the liver and spleen

_____**13.** C.F.'s abdominal cavity and organs were bound with fibrous tissue bands, which had to be lysed during surgery. These attachments are called
  a. sequelae
  b. adhesions
  c. ascites
  d. fibroids

_____**14.** The accidental puncture of the intestine was not an expected outcome of surgery. It was an incident that occurred despite attempts to protect C.F. from harm. The term for this type of disorder is (see Chapter 6)
  a. iatrogenic
  b. nosocomial
  c. idiopathic
  d. etiologic

Give the meaning of each of the following abbreviations.

15. HPI _____

16. CA _____

17. TPR _____

18. ADL _____

19. bpm _____

20. WNL _____

21. D/C _____

22. NS _____

7

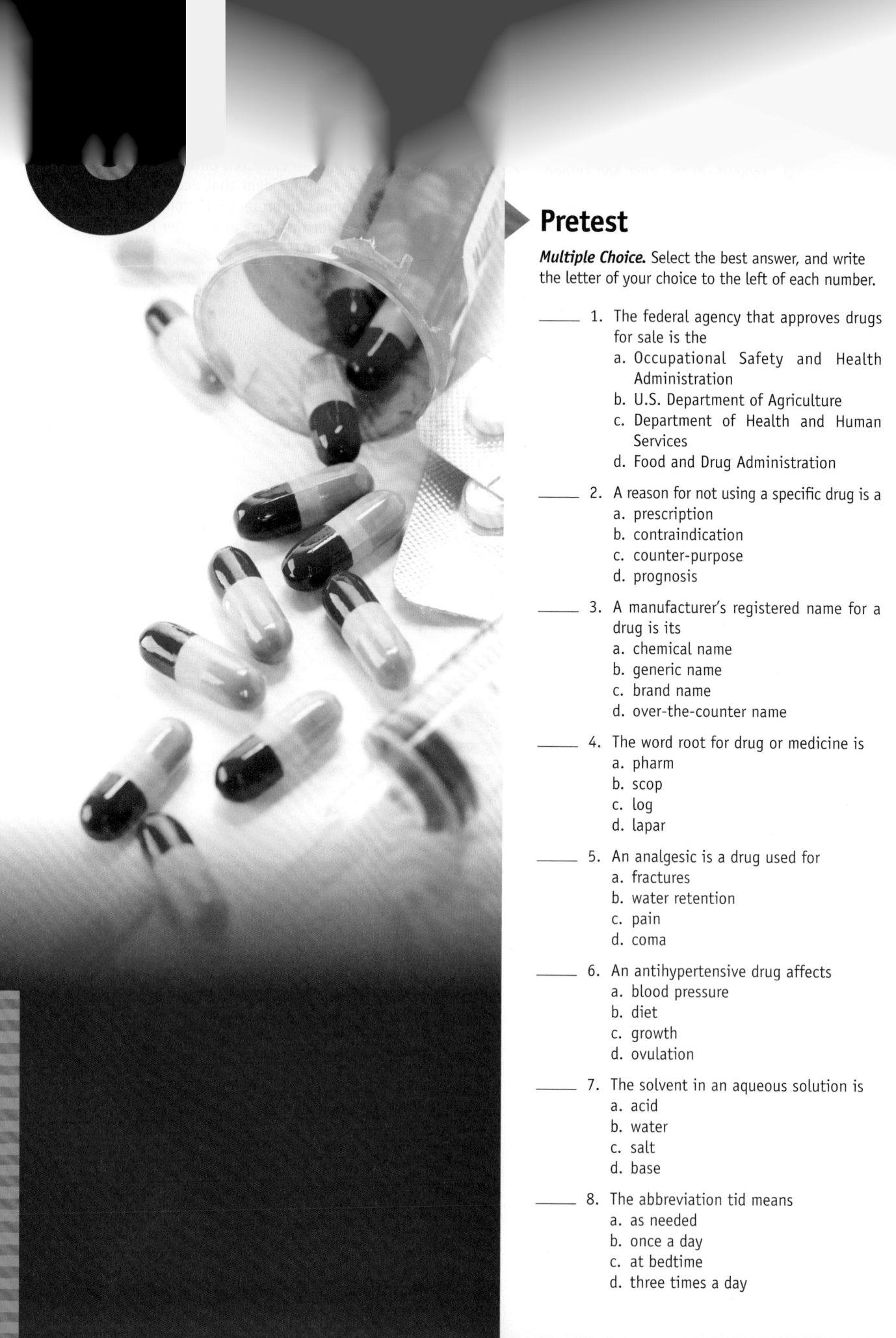

Pretest

Multiple Choice. Select the best answer, and write the letter of your choice to the left of each number.

_____ 1. The federal agency that approves drugs for sale is the
   a. Occupational Safety and Health Administration
   b. U.S. Department of Agriculture
   c. Department of Health and Human Services
   d. Food and Drug Administration

_____ 2. A reason for not using a specific drug is a
   a. prescription
   b. contraindication
   c. counter-purpose
   d. prognosis

_____ 3. A manufacturer's registered name for a drug is its
   a. chemical name
   b. generic name
   c. brand name
   d. over-the-counter name

_____ 4. The word root for drug or medicine is
   a. pharm
   b. scop
   c. log
   d. lapar

_____ 5. An analgesic is a drug used for
   a. fractures
   b. water retention
   c. pain
   d. coma

_____ 6. An antihypertensive drug affects
   a. blood pressure
   b. diet
   c. growth
   d. ovulation

_____ 7. The solvent in an aqueous solution is
   a. acid
   b. water
   c. salt
   d. base

_____ 8. The abbreviation tid means
   a. as needed
   b. once a day
   c. at bedtime
   d. three times a day

▶ Learning Objectives

After study of this chapter, you should be able to:

1 ▶ Explain the difference between over-the-counter and prescription drugs. *p140*

2 ▶ List three potential adverse side effects of drugs. *p140*

3 ▶ Explain two ways in which drugs can interact. *p140*

4 ▶ Explain the difference between the generic name and the brand name of a drug. *p140*

5 ▶ List three types of drug references. *p140*

6 ▶ Describe five safety issues related to the use of herbal medicines. *p141*

7 ▶ Define basic terms related to drugs and their actions. *p141*

8 ▶ Identify and use word parts pertaining to drugs. *p142*

9 ▶ Define abbreviations related to drugs and their uses. *p144*

10 ▶ Recognize the major categories of drugs and how they act. *p145*

11 ▶ List some common herbal medicines and how they act. *p149*

12 ▶ List common routes for drug administration. *p150*

13 ▶ List standard forms in which liquid and solid drugs are prepared. *p151*

14 ▶ Analyze the terminology related to drugs in several case studies. *pp139, 159*

Case Study: *P.L.'s Cardiac Disease and Crisis*

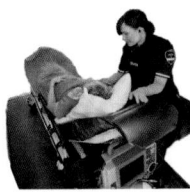

Chief Complaint

P.L. was having chest pain and had taken two nitroglycerin tablets without relief. Her family called an ambulance, and she was brought to the emergency room with chest pain that radiated down her arm, dyspnea, and syncope.

Examination

While P.L. was being admitted to the emergency room, her family provided a history to the triage nurse. They related that P.L. had a four-year history of heart disease. Her routine medications included Lanoxin to slow and strengthen her heartbeat, Inderal to support her heart rhythm, Lipitor to decrease her cholesterol, Catapres to lower her hypertension, nitroglycerin prn for chest pain, HydroDIURIL to eliminate fluid and decrease the heart's workload, Diabinese for her diabetes, and Coumadin to prevent blood clots. She also took Tagamet for her stomach ulcer and several OTC preparations, including an herbal sleeping formulation that she mixed in tea and Metamucil mixed in orange juice every morning for her bowels. Her family indicated that P.L. also took a number of other herbal and OTC medications, but they were unable to recall their names.

While P.L. was having a 12-lead ECG, her blood pressure dropped, and her heart rate deteriorated into a full cardiac arrest.

Clinical Course

Immediate resuscitation was instituted with cardiopulmonary resuscitation (CPR), defibrillation, and a bolus of IV epinephrine. Between shocks, she was given a bolus of lidocaine and a bolus of diltiazem plus repeated doses of epinephrine every five minutes. P.L. did not respond to resuscitation, and she was pronounced dead 55 minutes after arrival to the emergency room.

ANCILLARIES *At-A-Glance*

Visit thePoint to access the following resources. For guidance in using the resources most effectively, see pp. ix–xvi.

Learning RESOURCES

▶ **Tips for Effective Studying**
▶ **Web Figure: Sublingual Absorption of Drugs**
▶ **Web Figure: Intradermal Injection Sites**
▶ **Web Figure: Subcutaneous Injection Sites**
▶ **Web Figure: Intramuscular Injection Sites**
▶ **Audio Pronunciation Glossary**

Learning ACTIVITIES

▶ **Visual Activities**
▶ **Kinesthetic Activities**
▶ **Auditory Activities**

Drugs

A **drug** is a substance that alters body function. Traditionally, drugs have been derived from natural plant, animal, and mineral sources. Today, most are manufactured synthetically by pharmaceutical companies. A few, such as certain hormones and enzymes, have been produced by genetic engineering.

Many drugs, described as over-the-counter (OTC) drugs, are available without a signed order, or **prescription (Rx)**. Others require a healthcare provider's prescription for use.

Responsibility for the safety and **efficacy** (effectiveness) of all drugs sold in the United States lies with the Federal Food and Drug Administration (FDA), which must approve all drugs before they are sold.

ADVERSE DRUG EFFECTS

An unintended effect of a drug or any other form of treatment is a **side effect**. Most drugs have potential adverse side effects that must be evaluated before they are prescribed. In addition, there may be **contraindications**, or reasons not to use a particular drug for a specific individual based on the person's medical conditions, current medications, sensitivity, or family history. While a patient is under treatment, it is important to be alert for signs of adverse effects such as digestive upset, changes in the blood, or signs of allergy, such as hives or skin rashes. **Anaphylaxis** is an immediate and severe allergic reaction that may be caused by a drug. It can lead to life-threatening respiratory distress and circulatory collapse.

Because drugs given in combination may interact, the prescriber must know of any drugs the patient is taking before prescribing another. In some cases, a combination may result in **synergy** or **potentiation**, meaning that the drugs together have a greater effect than either of the drugs acting alone. In other cases, one drug may act as an **antagonist** of another, interfering with its action. Drugs may also react adversely with certain foods or substances used socially, such as alcohol and tobacco.

Drugs that act on the central nervous system may lead to psychologic or physical **substance dependence**, in which a person has a chronic or compulsive need for a drug regardless of its bad effects. With repeated use, a drug **tolerance** may develop, whereby a constant dose has less effect, and the dose must be increased to produce the original response. Cessation of the drug then leads to symptoms of substance **withdrawal**, a state that results from a drug's removal or dose reduction. Certain symptoms are associated with withdrawal from specific drugs.

DRUG NAMES

Drugs may be cited by either their generic or **brand names**. (**Box 8-1** has information on drug naming.) The **generic name** is usually a simple version of the chemical name for the drug and is not capitalized. The brand name (trade name, proprietary name) is a registered trademark of the manufacturer and is written with an initial capital letter. For example, Tylenol is the brand name for the analgesic compound acetaminophen; the antidepressant Prozac is fluoxetine. A brand name is protected by a patent; only the company that holds the patent can produce and sell that drug under its brand name until the patent expires. **Box 8-3**, which appears later in this chapter, has many more examples of generic and brand names. Note that the same drug may be marketed by different companies under different brand names. Both Motrin and Advil, for example, are the generic antiinflammatory agent ibuprofen.

DRUG INFORMATION

In the United States, the standard for drug information is the *United States Pharmacopeia* (USP). This reference is published by a national committee of pharmacologists and other scientists. It contains formulas for drugs sold in the United States; standards for testing the strength, quality, and purity of drugs; and standards for the preparation and dispensing of drugs. The American Society of Health System Pharmacists (ASHP) publishes extensive drug information, and the *Physicians' Desk Reference*, published yearly by Thomson Healthcare, contains information supplied by drug

---

FOCUS ON WORDS
Where Do Drugs Get Their Names?

Box 8-1

Drug names are derived in a variety of ways. Some are named for their origins. Adrenaline, for example, is named for its source, the adrenal gland. Even its generic name, epinephrine, informs us that it comes from the gland that is above (epi-) the kidney (nephr/o). Pitocin, a drug used to induce labor, is named for its source, the pituitary gland, combined with the chemical name of the hormone it mimics, oxytocin. Botox, currently injected into the skin for cosmetic removal of wrinkles, is the toxin from the organism that causes botulism, a type of food poisoning. Aspirin (an antiinflammatory agent), Taxol (an antitumor agent), digitalis (used to treat heart failure), and atropine (a smooth-muscle relaxant) are all named for the plants from which they come. For example, aspirin is named for the blossoms of Spiraea, from which it is derived. Taxol comes from a yew (evergreen) of the genus *Taxus*. Digitalis is from purple foxglove, genus *Digitalis*. Atropine comes from the plant *Atropa belladonna*.

Some names tell us about the drug or its actions. The name for Humulin, a form of insulin made by genetic engineering, points out that this is human insulin and not a hormone from animal sources. Lomotil reduces intestinal motility and is used to treat diarrhea. The names of new drugs that treat cancer by boosting a person's own immune system end in mab (e.g. nivolumab), because they are monoclonal antibodies, pure antibodies produced in a laboratory. The name *Belladonna* is from Italian and means "fair lady," because this drug dilates the pupils of the eyes, thereby making women appear more beautiful.

manufacturers. An enormous amount of drug information is available online through the websites for these publications and others. Another excellent source of up-to-date information on drugs is a community or hospital pharmacist. See **Box 8-2** for information on careers in pharmacy.

Herbal Medicines

For hundreds of years, people have used plants to treat diseases, a practice described as herbal medicine or **phyto-medicine**. Many people in industrialized countries are now turning to herbal products as alternatives or complements to conventional medicines. Although plants are the source of many conventional drugs, pharmaceutical companies usually purify, measure, and often modify or synthesize the active ingredients in these plants rather than presenting them in their natural states.

Some issues have arisen with the increased use of herbal medicines and nutritional supplements, including questions about their purity, safety, concentration, and efficacy. Another issue is drug interactions. Healthcare providers should ask about the use of herbal remedies when taking a patient's drug history, and patients should report any herbal medicines they take when under treatment. The FDA does not test or verify herbal medicines, and there are no requirements to report adverse effects. There are, however, restrictions on the health claims that can be made by the manufacturers of herbal medicines. The U.S. government has established the Office of Dietary Supplements (ODS) to support and coordinate research in this field.

8

HEALTH PROFESSIONS   Box 8-2

Pharmacists and Pharmacy Technicians

Medications are chemicals designed to treat illness and improve quality of life. The role of pharmacists and pharmacy technicians is to ensure that patients receive the correct medications and the education they need to use them effectively and derive their intended health benefits.

As key members of the healthcare team, pharmacists need strong clinical backgrounds with a thorough understanding of chemistry, anatomy, and physiology. Some pharmacists work in a community or retail environment; others are employed in hospitals. Different positions require different responsibilities. All pharmacists dispense prescription medications, monitor patients' responses to them, and also educate patients about their appropriate use. Hospital pharmacists also accompany physicians on their rounds and manage drug therapies by ordering and monitoring labora-tory results and adjusting medication dosages as needed. Pharmacists share their expertise with other health professionals and may participate in clinical research on drugs and their effects.

Pharmacy technicians assist pharmacists with their duties. Their training also requires a thorough background in basic sciences. State rules and regulations vary, but pharmacy technicians may perform many of the tasks related to dispensing medications, such as preparing drugs and packaging them with appropriate labels and instructions for use.

Job prospects for pharmacists and pharmacy technicians are promising because of the growing need for healthcare. In fact, pharmacy is projected to be one of the fastest growing careers in the United States. For more information about careers in pharmacy, contact the American Association of Colleges of Pharmacy at www.aacp.org.

Terminology   Key Terms

anaphylaxis *an-ah-fih-LAK-sis*	An extreme allergic reaction that can lead to respiratory distress, circulatory collapse, and death
antagonist *an-TAG-o-nist*	A substance that interferes with or opposes the action of a drug
brand name	The trade or proprietary name of a drug, a registered trademark of the manufacturer; written with an initial capital letter
contraindication *kon-trah-in-dih-KA-shun*	A factor that makes the use of a drug undesirable or dangerous
drug	A substance that alters body function
efficacy *EF-ih-kah-se*	The power to produce a specific result; effectiveness
generic name *jeh-NER-ik*	The nonproprietary name of a drug; that is, a name that is not privately owned or trademarked; usually a simplified version of the chemical name; not capitalized

(continued)

Terminology	Key Terms *(Continued)*
phytomedicine *fi-to-MED-ih-sin*	Another name for herbal medicine (root *phyt/o* meaning "plant")
potentiation *po-ten-she-A-shun*	Increased potency created by two drugs acting together
prescription (Rx) *pre-SKRIP-shun*	Written and signed order for a drug with directions for its administration
side effect	A result of drug therapy or other therapy that is unrelated to or an extension of its intended effect; usually applies to an undesirable effect of treatment
substance dependence	A condition that may result from chronic use of a drug, in which a person has a chronic or compulsive need for a drug regardless of its adverse effects; dependence may be psychologic or physical
synergy *SIN-er-je*	Combined action of two or more drugs working together to produce an effect greater than any of the drugs could produce when acting alone; also called synergism (*SIN-er-jizm*); adjective: synergistic (*sin-er-JIS-tik*)
tolerance	A condition in which chronic use of a drug results in loss of effectiveness and the dose must be increased to produce the original response
withdrawal	A condition that results from abrupt cessation or reduction of a drug that has been used regularly

Go to the Audio Pronunciation Glossary in the Student Resources on the Point to hear these terms pronounced.

Word Parts Pertaining to Drugs

Table 8-1 lists word parts pertaining to drugs.

Table 8-1	Word Parts Pertaining to Drugs		
	Meaning	**Example**	**Definition of Example**
Suffixes			
-lytic (adjective of lysis)	dissolving, reducing, loosening	thrombolytic *throm-bo-LIT-ik*	agent that dissolves a blood clot (thrombus)
-mimetic	mimicking, simulating	sympathomimetic *sim-pah-tho-mih-MET-ik*	mimicking the effects of the sympathetic nervous system
-tropic	acting on	psychotropic *si-ko-TROP-ik*	acting on the mind (psych/o)
Prefixes			
anti-	against	antiemetic *an-te-eh-MET-ik*	drug that prevents vomiting (emesis)
contra-	against, opposite, opposed	contraceptive *kon-trah-SEP-tiv*	preventing conception
counter-	against, opposed	countertransport *kown-ter-TRANS-port*	movement in an opposite direction
Roots			
alg/o, algi/o, algesi/o	pain	algesia *al-JE-ze-ah*	sense of pain
chem/o	chemical	chemotherapy *ke-mo-THER-ah-pe*	treatment with drugs

Table 8-1	Word Parts Pertaining to Drugs (*Continued*)

	Meaning	Example	Definition of Example
hypn/o	sleep	hypnosis *hip-NO-sis*	induced state of sleep
narc/o	stupor	narcotic *nar-KOT-ik*	agent that induces a state of stupor with decreased sensation
pharm, pharmac/o	drug, medicine	pharmacy *FAR-mah-se*	the science of preparing and dispensing drugs, or the place where these activities occur
pyr/o, pyret/o	fever	antipyretic *an-te-pi-RET-ik*	counteracting fever
tox/o, toxic/o	poison, toxin	toxicity *tok-SIS-ih-te*	state of being poisonous
vas/o	vessel	vasodilation *vas-o-di-LA-shun*	widening of a vessel

EXERCISE 8-1

Identify and define the suffix in each of the following words.

	Suffix	Meaning of Suffix
1. hemolytic (*he-mo-LIT-ik*)	_____	_____
2. hydrotropic (*hi-dro-TROP-ik*)	_____	_____
3. parasympathomimetic (*par-ah-sim-pah-tho-mih-MET-ik*)	_____	_____

Using the prefixes listed in Table 8-1, write the opposite of each of the following words.

4. bacterial _____

5. lateral _____

6. septic _____

7. act _____

8. emetic _____

9. pyretic _____

Identify and define the root in each of the following words.

	Root	Meaning of Root
10. narcosis (*nar-KO-sis*)	_____	_____
11. chemistry (*KEM-is-tre*)	_____	_____
12. analgesia (*an-al-JE-ze-ah*)	_____	_____
13. toxicology (*tok-sih-KOL-o-je*)	_____	_____
14. hypnotic (*hip-NOT-ik*)	_____	_____

Define each of the following words.

15. vasodilation (*va-so-di-LA–shun*)_____

16. pharmacology (*far-mah-KOL-o-je*) _____

17. mucolytic (*mu-ko-LIT-ik*) _____

18. gonadotropic (*go-nad-o-TROP-ik*)_____

Terminology   Abbreviations

Drugs and Drug Formulations

APAP	Acetaminophen
ASA	Acetylsalicylic acid (aspirin)
ASHP	American Society of Health System Pharmacists
cap	Capsule
elix	Elixir
FDA	Food and Drug Administration
INH	Isoniazid (antituberculosis drug)
MED(s)	Medicine(s), medication(s)
NSAID(s)	Nonsteroidal antiinflammatory drug(s)
ODS	Office of Dietary Supplements
OTC	Over-the-counter
PDR	*Physicians' Desk Reference*
Rx	Prescription
supp	Suppository
susp	Suspension
tab	Tablet
tinct	Tincture
ung	Ointment
USP	*United States Pharmacopeia*

Dosages and Directions

ā	Before (Latin, *ante*)
āā	Of each (Greek, *ana*)
ac	Before meals (Latin, *ante cibum*)
ad lib	As desired (Latin, *ad libitum*)
aq	Water (Latin, *aqua*)
bid, b.i.d.	Twice a day (Latin, *bis in die*)
c̄	With (Latin, *cum*)
DAW	Dispense as written

D/C, dc	Discontinue
DS	Double strength
hs	At bedtime (Latin, *hora somni*)
ID	Intradermal(ly)
IM	Intramuscular(ly)
IU	International unit
IV	Intravenous(ly)
LA	Long-acting
mcg	Microgram
mg	Milligram
mL	Milliliter
p	After, post
pc	After meals (Latin, *post cibum*)
po, PO	By mouth (Latin, *per os*)
pp	Postprandial (after a meal)
prn	As needed (Latin, *pro re nata*)
qam	Every morning (Latin, *quaque ante meridiem*)
qh	Every hour (Latin, *quaque hora*)
q __ h	Every _____ hours
qid, q.i.d.	Four times a day (Latin, *quater in die*)
s̄	Without (Latin, *sine*)
SA	Sustained action
SC, SQ, subcut	Subcutaneous(ly)
SL	sublingual(ly)
SR	Sustained release
s̄s̄	Half (Latin, *semis*)
tid, t.i.d.	Three times per day (Latin, *ter in die*)
U	Unit(s)
x	Times

Drug Reference Information

So far, this chapter has been an overview of drugs and the terminology for drugs and drug usage. The next section of the chapter contains informational boxes that you can examine now and refer to again as you work through Part 3 of the text. **Box 8-3** outlines the major categories of drugs and cites examples by both generic and brand names. **Box 8-4** lists some common herbal medicines and their uses. **Boxes 8-5** to **8-7** have information on routes of administration, drug preparations, and injectable drugs (**Figs. 8-1** to **8-6**).

8

FOR YOUR REFERENCE
Common Drugs and Their Actions

Box 8-3

Category	Actions; Applications	Generic Name	Brand Name(s)
adrenergics *ad-ren-ER-jiks* (sympathomimetics [*sim-pah-tho-mih-MET-iks*])	Mimic the action of the sympathetic nervous system, which responds to stress; used to treat bronchospasms, allergic reactions, hypotension	epinephrine phenylephrine pseudoephedrine dopamine	Bronkaid Neo-Synephrine Sudafed Intropin
analgesics *an-al-JE-siks*	Alleviate pain		
narcotics *nar-KOH-tiks*	Decrease pain sensation in central nervous system; chronic use may lead to physical dependence	codeine morphine meperidine oxycodone hydrocodone	Demerol OxyContin, Percocet Vicodin, Lortab
nonnarcotics *non-nar-KOH-tiks*	Act peripherally to inhibit prostaglandins (local hormones); they may also be antiinflammatory and antipyretic (reduce fever); Cox-2 inhibitors limit an enzyme that causes inflammation without affecting a related enzyme that protects the stomach lining	aspirin (acetylsalicylic acid; ASA) acetaminophen (APAP) ibuprofen celecoxib (Cox-2 inhibitor)	Tylenol Motrin, Advil Celebrex

anesthetics
an-es-THET-iks
	Reduce or eliminate sensation (esthesi/o)	local:
		  lidocaine
		  bupivacaine
		general:
		  nitrous oxide
		  midazolam
		  thiopental
			Xylocaine
			Marcaine
			
			Versed
			Pentothal

anticoagulants *an-te-ko-AG-u-lants*	Prevent coagulation and formation of blood clots	heparin warfarin apixaban	Coumadin Eliquis
anticonvulsants *an-te-kon-VUL-sants*	Suppress or reduce the number and/or intensity of seizures	phenobarbital phenytoin carbamazepine valproic acid	Dilantin Tegretol Depakene
antidiabetics *an-te-di-ah-BET-iks*	Prevent or alleviate diabetes	insulin glyburide linagliptin glipizide metformin	Humulin (injected) Diabeta Tradjenta Glucotrol Glucophage

(continued)

Common Drugs and Their Actions (*Continued*)

Category	Actions; Applications	Generic Name	Brand Name(s)
antiemetics *an-te-eh-MET-iks*	Relieve symptoms of nausea and prevent vomiting (emesis)	ondansetron dimenhydrinate prochlorperazine scopolamine promethazine	Zofran Dramamine Compazine TRANSDERM-SCOP Phenergan
antihistamines *an-te-HIS-tah-menes*	Prevent responses mediated by histamine: allergic and inflammatory reactions	diphenhydramine fexofenadine loratadine cetirizine	Benadryl Allegra Claritin Zyrtec
antihypertensives *an-te-hi-per-TEN-sivs*	Lower blood pressure by reducing cardiac output, dilating vessels, or promoting excretion of water by the kidneys. ACE inhibitors block production of a substance that raises blood pressure; ARBs interfere with the action of that substance. See also calcium-channel blockers and beta-blockers under cardiac drugs; diuretics	amlodipine atenolol clonidine prazosin minoxidil captopril enalapril lisinopril losartan valsartan	Norvasc Tenormin Catapres Minipress Loniten Capoten Vasotec Zestril, Prinivil Cozaar Diovan
antiinflammatory drugs *an-te-in-FLAM-ah-to-re*	Counteract inflammation and swelling		
corticosteroids *kor-tih-ko-STER-oyds*	Hormones from the cortex of the adrenal gland; used for allergy, respiratory and blood diseases, injury, and malignancy; suppress the immune system	dexamethasone cortisone prednisone hydrocortisone fluticasone	Decadron Cortone Deltasone Hydrocortone, Cortef, Solu-cortef Flonase
nonsteroidal antiinflammatory drugs (NSAIDs) *non-ster-OYD-al*	Reduce inflammation and pain by interfering with synthesis of prostaglandins; also antipyretic	aspirin ibuprofen indomethacin naproxen celecoxib	 Motrin, Advil Indocin Naprosyn, Aleve Celebrex
antiinfective agents *an-te-in-FEK-tiv*	Kill or prevent the growth of infectious organisms		
antibacterials; *an-te-bak-TE-re-als* antibiotics *an-te-bi-OT-iks*	Effective against bacteria	amoxicillin penicillin V erythromycin vancomycin gentamicin cephalexin tetracycline ciprofloxacin (for ulcer-causing *Helicobacter pylori*) isoniazid (INH) (tuberculosis)	Polymox Pen-Vee K Erythrocin Vancocin Garamycin Keflex Achromycin Cipro
antifungals *an-te-FUNG-gals*	Effective against fungi	amphotericin B miconazole nystatin	Fungizone Monistat Nilstat

Common Drugs and Their Actions (*Continued*)

Category	Actions; Applications	Generic Name	Brand Name(s)
antiparasitics *an-te-par-ah-SIT-iks*	Effective against parasites—protozoa, worms	iodoquinol (amebae) quinacrine	Yodoxin Atabrine
antivirals *an-te-VI-rals*	Effective against viruses	acyclovir zanamivir (influenza) zidovudine (HIV) indinavir (HIV protease inhibitor)	Zovirax Relenza Retrovir Crixivan
antineoplastics *an-te-ne-o-PLAS-tiks*	Destroy cancer cells; they are toxic for all cells but have greater effect on cells that are actively growing and dividing; hormones and hormone inhibitors also are used to slow tumor growth	cyclophosphamide doxorubicin methotrexate vincristine tamoxifen (estrogen inhibitor)	Cytoxan Adriamycin Oncovin Nolvadex
cardiac drugs *KAR-de-ak*	Act on the heart		
antiarrhythmics *an-te-ah-RITH-miks*	Correct or prevent abnormalities of heart rhythm	quinidine lidocaine digoxin	Quinidex Xylocaine Lanoxin
beta-adrenergic blockers (beta-blockers) *ba-tah-ad-ren-ER-jik*	Inhibit sympathetic nervous system; reduce rate and force of heart contractions	propranolol metoprolol atenolol	Inderal Toprol-XL Tenormin
calcium-channel blockers *KAL-se-um*	Dilate coronary arteries, slow heart rate, reduce contractions	diltiazem nifedipine verapamil	Cardizem Procardia Veralan, Calan
hypolipidemics *hi-po-lip-ih-DE-miks*	Lower cholesterol in patients with high serum levels that cannot be controlled with diet alone; hypocholesterolemics, statins	lovastatin pravastatin atorvastatin simvastatin	Mevacor Pravachol Lipitor Zocor
nitrates; *NI-trates* antianginal agents *an-tih-AN-ji-nal*	Dilate coronary arteries and reduce heart's workload by lowering blood pressure and reducing venous return	nitroglycerin isosorbide	Nitrostat Isordil

CNS stimulants	Stimulate the central nervous system	methylphenidate
		amphetamine (chronic
		   use may lead to
		   drug dependence)
			Ritalin
			Adderall,
			Dexedrine

diuretics *di-u-RET-iks*	Promote excretion of water, sodium, and other electrolytes by the kidneys; used to reduce edema and blood pressure; loop diuretics act on the kidney tubules (see Chapters 9 and 13)	furosemide ethacrynic acid mannitol hydrochlorothiazide (HCTZ) triamterene + HCTZ	Lasix Edecrin Osmitrol HydroDIURIL Dyazide
gastrointestinal drugs *gas-tro-in-TES-tin-al*	Act on the digestive tract		
antidiarrheals *an-te-di-ah-RE-als*	Treat or prevent diarrhea by reducing intestinal motility or absorbing irritants and soothing the intestinal lining	diphenoxylate+ atropine loperamide attapulgite	Lomotil Imodium Kaopectate

(continued)

Common Drugs and Their Actions (*Continued*)

Category	Actions; Applications	Generic Name	Brand Name(s)
histamine H₂ antagonists *HIS-tah-mene*	Decrease stomach acid secretion by interfering with the action of histamine at H₂ receptors; used to treat ulcers and other gastrointestinal problems	famotidine ranitidine	Pepcid Zantac

laxatives
LAK-sah-tivs
	Promote elimination from the large intestine; types include:
	    stimulants
	    hyperosmotics (retain water)
	    stool softeners
	    bulk-forming agents
		
		bisacodyl
		lactulose
		docusate
		psyllium
			
			Dulcolax
			Constilac, Chronulac
			Colace, Surfak
			Metamucil

proton pump inhibitors *PRO-ton*	Reduce stomach acidity by blocking transport of hydrogen ions (protons) into the stomach	esomeprazole lansoprazole omeprazole	Nexium Prevacid Prilosec
muscle relaxants *re-LAK-sants*	Depress nervous system stimulation of skeletal muscles; used to control muscle spasms and pain	baclofen carisoprodol methocarbamol	Lioresal Soma Robaxin
psychotropics *si-ko-TROP-iks*	Affect the mind, altering mental activity, mental state, or behavior		
antianxiety agents *an-te-ang-ZI-eh-te*	Reduce or dispel anxiety; tranquilizers; anxiolytic agents	lorazepam chlordiazepoxide diazepam hydroxyzine alprazolam buspirone	Ativan Librium Valium Atarax Xanax BuSpar
antidepressants *an-te-de-PRES-sants*	Relieve depression by raising brain levels of neurotransmitters (chemicals active in the nervous system)	amitriptyline imipramine fluoxetine paroxetine sertraline	Elavil Tofranil Prozac Paxil Zoloft
antipsychotics *an-te-si-KOT-iks*	Act on nervous system to relieve symptoms of psychoses	chlorpromazine haloperidol risperidone olanzapine	Thorazine Haldol Risperdal Zyprexa
respiratory drugs	Act on the respiratory system		
antitussives *an-te-TUS-sivs*	Suppress coughing	dextromethorphan	Benylin DM
asthma maintenance drugs; bronchodilators *brong-ko-di-LA-tors*	Used for prevention of asthma attacks and chronic treatment of asthma; prevent or eliminate spasm of the bronchi (breathing tubes) by relaxing bronchial smooth muscle; used to treat asthma attacks and bronchitis	fluticasone montelukast albuterol metaproterenol tiotropium	Flovent Singulair Proventil Alupent Spiriva
expectorants *ek-SPEK-to-rants*	Induce productive coughing to eliminate respiratory secretions	guaifenesin	Robitussin
mucolytics *mu-ko-LIT-iks*	Loosen mucus to promote its elimination	acetylcysteine	Mucomyst
sedatives/hypnotics *SED-ah-tivs/hip-NOT-iks*	Induce relaxation and sleep; lower (sedative) doses promote relaxation leading to sleep; higher (hypnotic) doses induce sleep; antianxiety agents also used	phenobarbital zolpidem	 Ambien

Box 8-4

FOR YOUR REFERENCE
Therapeutic Uses of Herbal Medicines

8

Name	Part Used	Therapeutic Uses
aloe *AL-o*	leaf	treatment of burns and minor skin irritations
black cohosh *KO-hosh*	root	reduction of menopausal hot flashes
chamomile *KAM-o-mile*	flower	antiinflammatory, gastrointestinal antispasmodic, sedative
echinacea *eh-kih-NA-she-ah*	all	may reduce severity and duration of colds, may stimulate the immune system, used topically for wound healing
evening primrose oil *PRIM-roze*	seed	source of essential fatty acids important for the health of the cardiovascular system; treatment of premenstrual syndrome (PMS), rheumatoid arthritis, skin disorders
flax	seed	source of fatty acids important in maintaining proper lipids (e.g., cholesterol) in the blood
ginger *JIN-jer*	root	relief of nausea and motion sickness, treatment of colds and sore throat
ginkgo *GING-ko*	leaf	improves blood circulation in and function of the brain, improves memory, used to treat dementia, antianxiety agent, protects the nervous system
ginseng *JIN-seng*	root	stress reduction, lowers blood cholesterol and blood sugar
green tea	leaf	antioxidant, acts against cancer of the gastrointestinal tract and skin, oral antimicrobial agent, reduces dental caries
kava *KAH-vah*	root	antianxiety agent, sedative
milk thistle *thisl*	seeds	protects the liver against toxins, antioxidant
saw palmetto *pal-MET-o*	berries	used to treat benign prostatic hyperplasia (BPH)
slippery elm	bark	as lozenge for throat irritation, for gastrointestinal irritation and upset, protects irritated skin
soy	bean	rich source of nutrients; protective estrogenic effects in menopausal symptoms, osteoporosis, cardiovascular disease, cancer prevention
St. John's wort	flower	treatment of anxiety and depression, has antibacterial and antiviral properties (note: this product can interact with a variety of drugs)
tea tree oil	leaf	antimicrobial; used to heal cuts, skin infections, burns
valerian *vah-LE-re-an*	root	sedative, sleep aid

FOR YOUR REFERENCE
Routes of Drug Administration

Box 8-5

Route	Description
BY ABSORPTION	
absorption *ab-SORP-shun*	drug taken into the circulation through the digestive tract or by transfer across another membrane
inhalation *in-hah-LA-shun*	administration through the respiratory system, as by breathing in an aerosol or nebulizer spray (**Fig. 8-1**)
instillation *in-stil-LA-shun*	liquid is dropped or poured slowly into a body cavity or on the surface of the body, such as into the ear or onto the conjunctiva of the eye (**Fig. 8-2**)
oral *OR-al*	given by mouth; per os (po)
rectal *REK-tal*	administered by rectal suppository or enema
sublingual (SL) *sub-LING-gwal*	administered under the tongue
topical *TOP-ih-kal*	applied to the surface of the skin
transdermal *trans-DER-mal*	absorbed through the skin, as from a patch placed on the surface of the skin
BY INJECTION	
injection *in-JEK-shun*	administered by a needle and syringe (**Fig. 8-3**); described as parenteral (*pah-REN-ter-al*) routes of administration
epidural *ep-ih-DUR-al*	injected into the space between the meninges (membranes around the spinal cord) and the spine
hypodermoclysis *hi-po-der-MOK-lih-sis*	administration of a solution by subcutaneous infusion; useful for fluid delivery as an alternative for intravenous infusion
intradermal (ID) *in-trah-DER-mal*	injected into the skin
intramuscular (IM) *in-trah-MUS-ku-lar*	injected into a muscle
intravenous (IV) *in-trah-VE-nus*	injected into a vein
spinal (intrathecal) *in-trah-THE-kal*	injected through the meninges into the spinal fluid
subcutaneous (SC) *sub-ku-TA-ne-us*	injected beneath the skin; hypodermic

See illustrations of various drug administration routes in the Student Resources on thePoint.

8

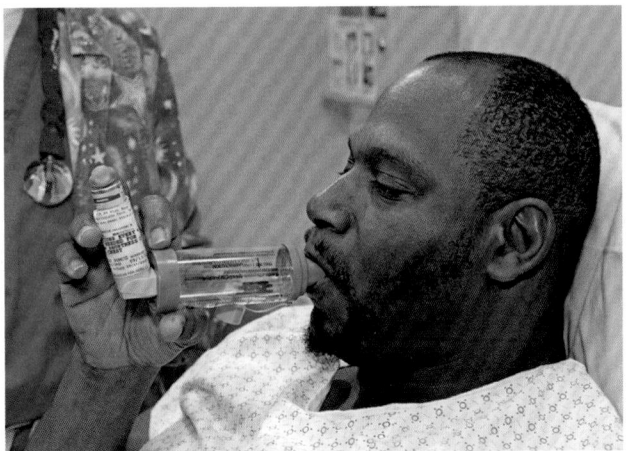

Figure 8-1 **Inhalation of a drug.** The patient is using a metered-dose inhaler for drug administration.

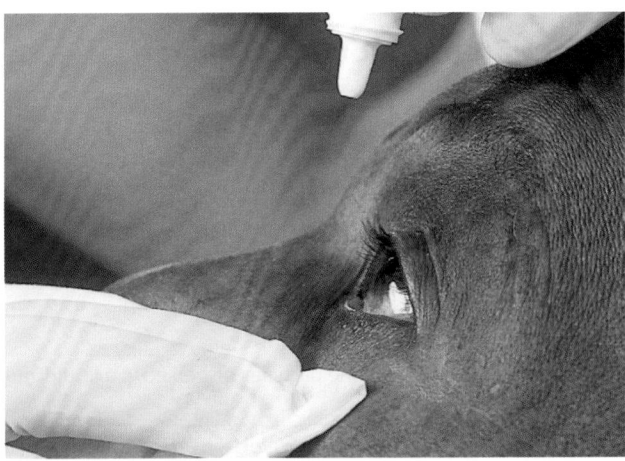

Figure 8-2 **Instillation of a drug.** A practitioner pulls down the lower lid to administer eye drops into the lower conjunctival sac.

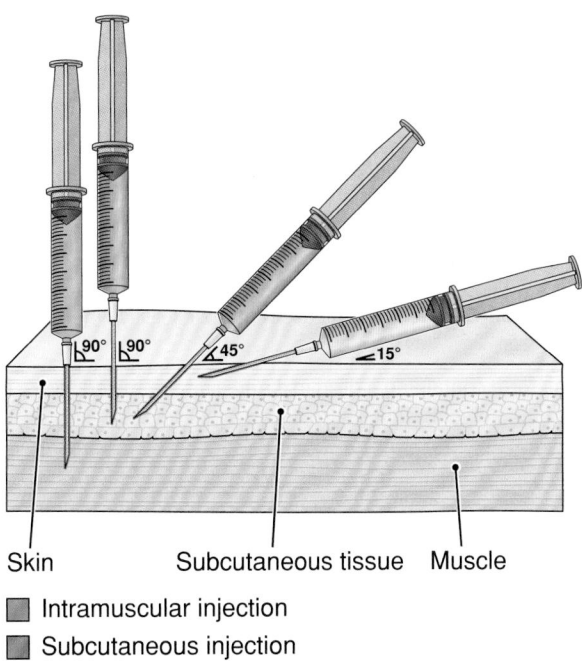

Skin   Subcutaneous tissue   Muscle

🟪 Intramuscular injection
🟦 Subcutaneous injection
⬜ Intradermal injection

Figure 8-3 **Injection.** Comparison of the angles of insertion for intramuscular, subcutaneous, and intradermal injections.

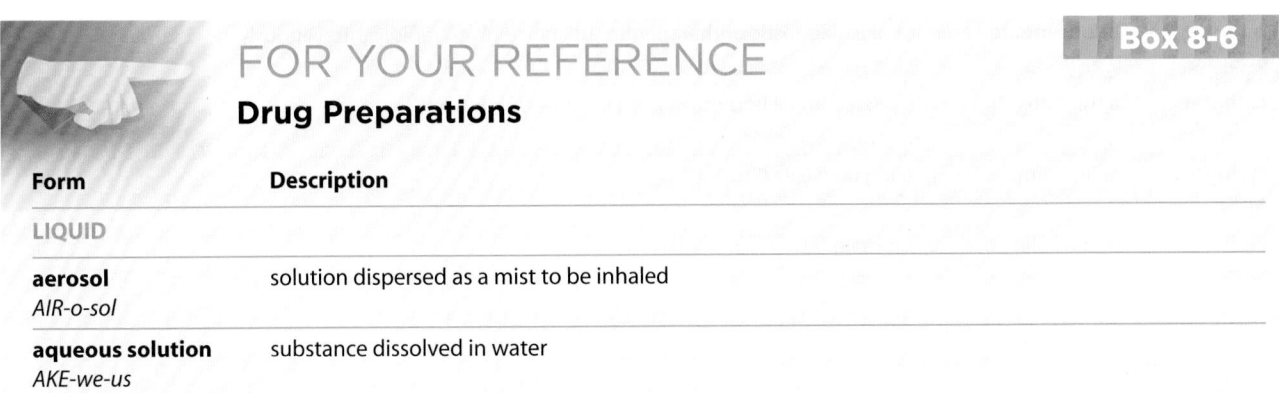

FOR YOUR REFERENCE

Box 8-6

Drug Preparations

Form	Description
LIQUID	
aerosol *AIR-o-sol*	solution dispersed as a mist to be inhaled
aqueous solution *AKE-we-us*	substance dissolved in water

(continued)

Drug Preparations (*Continued*)

Form	Description
elixir (elix) *e-LIK-sar*	a clear, pleasantly flavored and sweetened hydroalcoholic liquid intended for oral use
emulsion *e-MUL-shun*	a mixture in which one liquid is dispersed but not dissolved in another liquid
lotion *LO-shun*	solution prepared for topical use
suspension (susp) *sus-PEN-shun*	fine particles dispersed in a liquid, must be shaken before use
tincture (tinct) *TINK-chur*	substance dissolved in an alcoholic solution
SEMISOLID	
cream *kreme*	a semisolid emulsion used topically
ointment (ung) *OYNT-ment*	drug in a base that keeps it in contact with the skin
SOLID	
capsule (cap) *KAP-sule*	material in a gelatin container that dissolves easily in the stomach
lozenge *LOZ-enj*	a pleasant-tasting medicated tablet or disk to be dissolved in the mouth, such as a cough drop
suppository (supp) *su-POZ-ih-tor-e*	substance mixed and molded with a base that melts easily when inserted into a body opening
tablet (tab) *TAB-let*	a solid dosage form containing a drug in a pure state or mixed with a nonactive ingredient and prepared by compression or molding, also called a pill

---

FOR YOUR REFERENCE
Terms Pertaining to Injectable Drugs

Box 8-7

Term	Meaning
ampule *AM-pule*	a small sealed glass or plastic container used for sterile intravenous solutions (**Fig. 8-4**)
bolus *BO-lus*	a concentrated amount of a diagnostic or therapeutic substance given rapidly intravenously
catheter *KATH-eh-ter*	a thin tube that can be passed into a body cavity, organ, or vessel (**Fig. 8-5**)
syringe *sir-INJ*	an instrument for injecting fluid (see **Fig. 8-4**)
vial *VI-al*	a small glass or plastic container (see **Fig. 8-4A**)

8

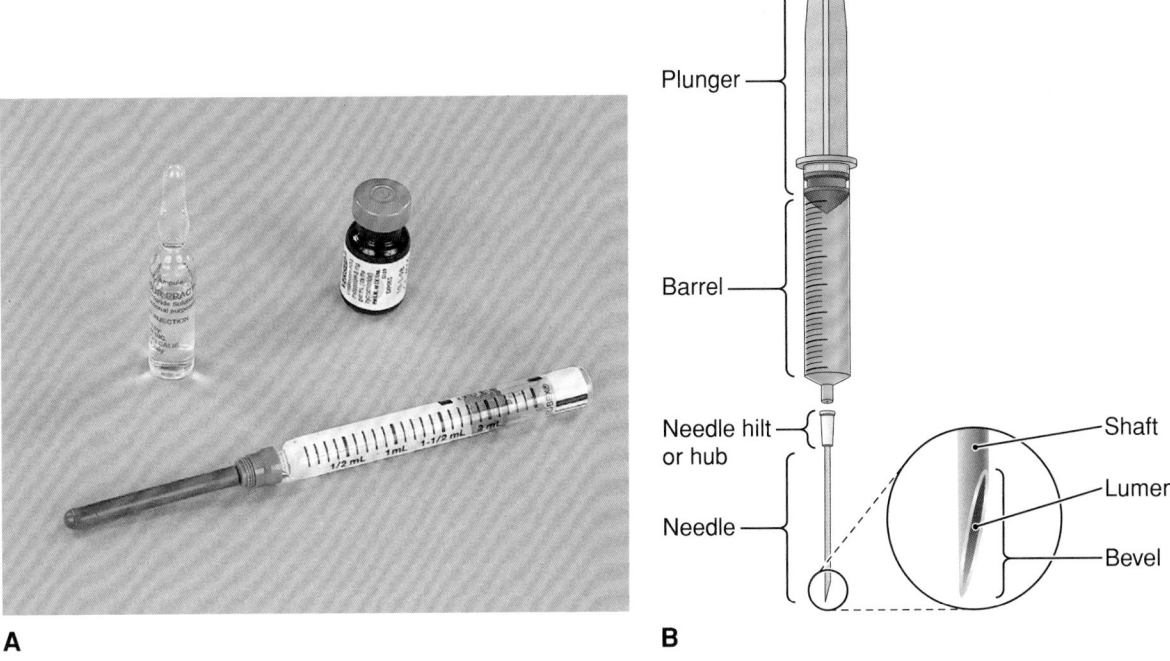

A

B

Figure 8-4 **Injectable drug materials. A.** Injectable drug containers. An ampule (*top left*), a vial (*top right*), and a syringe (*bottom*) are shown. **B.** Parts of a needle and syringe.

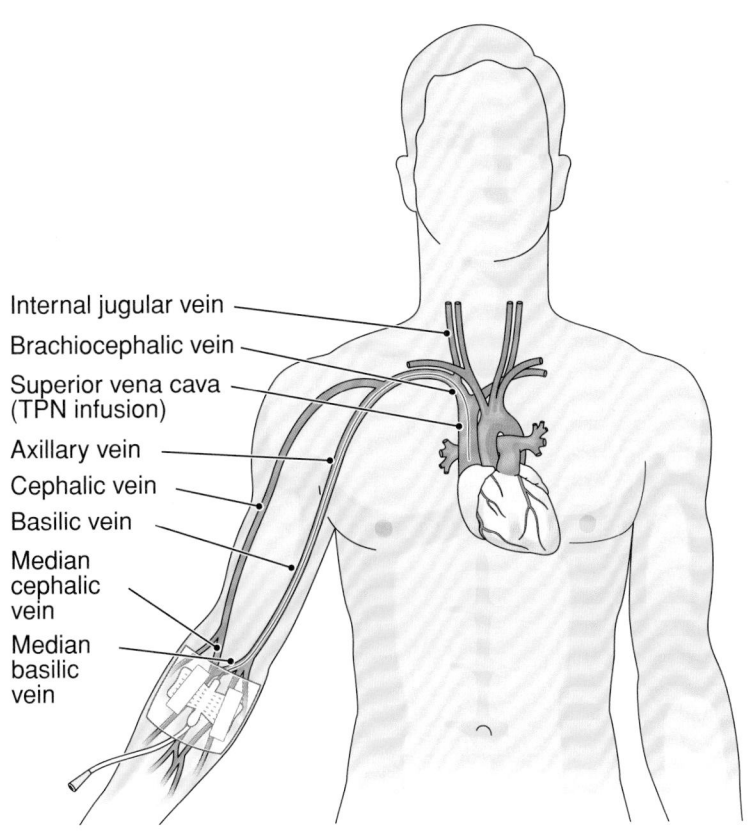

Internal jugular vein

Brachiocephalic vein

Superior vena cava (TPN infusion)

Axillary vein

Cephalic vein

Basilic vein

Median cephalic vein

Median basilic vein

—— Peripherally inserted central catheter (PICC)

Figure 8-5 **Catheter.** Shown is placement of a peripherally inserted central catheter (PICC).

Case Study Revisited

Following Up on P.L.'s Death

As the emergency room physician was documenting the course of events in P.L.'s death, he reviewed the patient's history and details provided by the family. He wondered if the patient routinely consumed any other OTC and herbal medications and thought about what potentiating effects the various drug combinations may have had. On the death certificate, her primary cause of death was listed as cardiac arrest. Multiple secondary diagnoses were listed, including polypharmacy.

Matching

Match the following terms, and write the appropriate letter to the left of each number.

_____ **1.** hyperpyrexia   **a.** abnormally high body temperature

_____ **2.** diuretic   **b.** combined drug action to greater effect

_____ **3.** potentiation   **c.** agent that prevents vomiting

_____ **4.** antiemetic   **d.** flowing in an opposite direction

_____ **5.** countercurrent   **e.** promoting excretion of water

_____ **6.** chronotropic   **a.** sympathomimetic

_____ **7.** vasomotor   **b.** affecting timing

_____ **8.** adrenergic   **c.** extreme allergic reaction

_____ **9.** anaphylaxis   **d.** effectiveness

_____ **10.** efficacy   **e.** pertaining to vessel movement

_____ **11.** ASA   **a.** aspirin

_____ **12.** bid   **b.** without

_____ **13.** aq   **c.** as needed

_____ **14.** s̄   **d.** twice a day

_____ **15.** prn   **e.** water

_____ **16.** valerian   **a.** sedative

_____ **17.** aloe   **b.** source of fatty acids

_____ **18.** ginger root   **c.** antimicrobial

_____ **19.** tea tree oil   **d.** used to treat burns, irritation

_____ **20.** flax seed   **e.** relieves nausea

Multiple Choice

Select the best answer, and write the letter of your choice to the left of each number.

_____ **21.** NSAIDs are used to treat

    a. inflammation

    b. convulsions

    c. nausea

    d. hypertension

_____ **22.** A hypolipidemic drug

    a. lowers cholesterol

    b. increases urination

    c. diminishes sensation

    d. reduces inflammation

_____ **23.** Proton pump inhibitors

    a. are used to treat asthma

    b. relax muscle spasms

    c. reduce stomach acidity

    d. are used to administer drugs

_____ **24.** An ampule is a

    a. concentrated amount given rapidly

    b. mist to be inhaled

    c. tablet to dissolve in the mouth

    d. small sealed container

_____ **25.** A drug that is administered topically is

  a. swallowed

  b. injected

  c. applied to the skin

  d. placed under the tongue

_____ **26.** Another term for hypodermic is

  a. intrathecal

  b. spinal

  c. epidural

  d. subcutaneous

_____ **27.** Another term for brand name is

  a. indicated name

  b. generic name

  c. trade name

  d. chemical name

_____ **28.** Drug administration by injection is described as

  a. instilled

  b. parenteral

  c. encapsulated

  d. nebulized

_____ **29.** P.L.'s nitroglycerine in the opening case study is ordered as prn SL. This means

  a. as needed, under the tongue

  b. at bedtime, under the tongue

  c. as needed, on the skin

  d. before meals, on the skin

_____ **30.** P.L. took several OTC preparations. OTC means

  a. on-the-cutaneous

  b. off-the-cuff

  c. over-the-counter

  d. requires a prescription

_____ **31.** During P.L.'s resuscitation, epinephrine was given in an IV bolus. This means it was administered

  a. intrathecally in a rapid concentrated dose

  b. parenterally as a topical solution

  c. intravenously in a continuous drip

  d. intravenously in a rapid concentrated dose

_____ **32.** P.L.'s herbal sleeping formulation was mixed into tea and taken at bedtime. The dissolved mixture is called a(n) _____ and is taken at _____.

  a. elixir, QAM

  b. emulsion, bid

  c. suspension, hs

  d. aqueous solution, hs

_____ **33.** P.L. had a secondary diagnosis of polypharmacy. This means that she

  a. used more than one drug store

  b. had polyps

  c. used more prescription than OTC drugs

  d. used many different drugs

FILL IN THE BLANKS

34. The study of drugs and their actions is called _____.

35. A toxicologist is one who studies _____.

36. A transdermal route of administration is through the_____.

37. Phytomedicine is the practice of treating with _____.

38. When a drug has lost its effect at a constant dose, the patient has developed _____.

39. An analgesic is used to treat _____.

40. An intravenous injection is given into a(n) _____.

41. An antipyretic drug counteracts _____.

42. With reference to drug interactions, another term for synergy is _____.

ELIMINATIONS

In each of the sets below, underline the word that does not fit in with the rest and explain the reason for your choice.

43. anesthetic — analgesic — narcotic — adrenergic — sedative

_____

44. solution — elixir — tincture — emulsion — tablet

_____

45. antineoplastics — nitrates — antiarrhythmics — calcium-channel blockers — beta-blockers

_____

46. antitussive — histamine H$_2$ antagonist — expectorant — mucolytic — bronchodilator

_____

DEFINITIONS

Define each of the following words.

47. hemolytic _____.

48. psychotropic _____.

49. bronchoconstriction _____.

OPPOSITES

Write a word that means the opposite of each of the following.

50. emetic _____.

51. vasodilation _____.

52. balance _____.

53. bacterial _____.

54. indicated _____.

55. neoplastic _____.

ABBREVIATIONS

Define each of the following abbreviations.

56. FDA _____

57. DAW _____

58. Rx _____

59. USP _____

60. D/C _____

WORD BUILDING

Write a word for each of the following definitions using the word parts given.

| narc/o | -lytic | thromb/o | muc/o | toxic/o | -sis | anxi/o | hypn/o |

61. an induced sleep-like state _____

62. reducing anxiety _____

63. condition caused by poisoning _____

64. dissolving a blood clot _____

65. condition of having a blood clot _____

66. a state of stupor _____

67. dissolving mucus _____

WORD ANALYSIS

Define each of the following words, and give the meaning of the word parts in each. Use a dictionary if necessary.

68. anaphylaxis (*an-ah-fih-LAK-sis*) _____

    a. ana- _____

    b. phylaxis _____

69. pharmacokinetic (*far-mah-ko-kih-NET-ik*) _____

    a. pharmac/o _____

    b. kinet/o _____

    c. -ic _____

70. adrenergic (*ad-ren-ER-jik*) _____

    a. adren/o _____

    b. erg/o _____

    c. -ic _____

71. hypodermoclysis (*hi-po-der-MOK-lih-sis*) _____

    a. hypo- _____

    b. derm/o _____

    c. clysis _____

For more learning activities, see Chapter 8 of the Student Resources on thePoint.

Additional Case Studies

Case Study 8-1: *Inflammatory Bowel Disease*

A.E., a 19-year-old college student, was diagnosed at the age of 13 with Crohn disease, a chronic inflammatory disease that can affect the entire gastrointestinal tract from mouth to anus. A.E.'s disease is limited to his large bowel. During a nine-month period of disease exacerbation characterized by severe cramping and bloody stools, he took oral corticosteroids (prednisone) to reduce the inflammatory response. He experienced many of the drug's side effects, but has been in remission for four years. Currently, A.E.'s condition is managed on drugs that reduce inflamma-tion by suppressing the immune response. He takes Pentasa (mesalamine) 250 mg 4 caps po bid. Pentasa is of the 5-ASA (acetylsalicylic acid or aspirin) group of antiinflammatory agents, which work topically on the inner surface of the bowel. It has an enteric coating, which dissolves in the bowel environment. He also takes 6-mercaptopurine (Purinethol) 75 mg PO daily and a therapeutic vitamin with breakfast. A.E. may take acetaminophen for pain but must avoid NSAIDs, which will irritate the intestinal mucosa (inner lining) and cause a flare-up of the disease.

Case Study 8-2: *Asthma*

E.N., a 20 YO woman with asthma, visited the preadmis-sion testing unit one week before her cosmetic surgery to meet with the nurse and anesthesiologist. Her cur-rent meds included several bronchodilators, which she takes by mouth and by inhalation, and a tranquilizer that she takes when needed for nervousness. She some-times receives inhalation treatments with Mucomyst, a mucolytic agent. On E.N.'s preoperative note, the nurse wrote:

> Theo-Dur 1 cap 200 mg tid
> Flovent inhaler 1 spray (50 mcg each nostril b.i.d.)
> Ativan (lorazepam) 1 mg po bid
> Albuterol metered-dose inhaler 2 puffs (180 mcg) prn
> q4–6h for bronchospasm and before exercise

E.N. stated that she has difficulty with her asthma when she is anxious and when she exercises. She also admitted to occasional use of marijuana and ecstasy, a hallucinogen and mood-altering illegal recreational drug. The anesthesiologist wrote an order for loraz-epam 4 mg IV one hour preop. The plastic surgeon recommended several supplements to complement her surgery and her recovery. He ordered a high-potency vitamin, 1 tab with breakfast and dinner, to support tissue health and healing. He also prescribed brome-lain, an enzyme from pineapple, to decrease inflamma-tion, one 500 mg cap po qid three days before surgery and postoperatively for two weeks. Arnica montana was prescribed to decrease discomfort, swelling, and bruising; three tabs sublingual tid the evening after surgery and for the following 10 days.

Case Study Questions

Multiple Choice. Select the best answer, and write the letter of your choice to the left of each number.

_____ **1.** A.E. takes several drugs to prevent or act against his inflammatory response. These agents are described as

 a. contrainflammatory

 b. counterinflammatory

 c. antiinflammatory

 d. proinflammatory

_____ **2.** A.E. presented with several untoward results or risks from the corticosteroid therapy. These sequelae are called

 a. contraindications

 b. side effects

 c. antagonistic effects

 d. exacerbations

(continued)

Additional Case Studies (Continued)

_____ **3.** A.E. takes four 250-mg capsules of Pentasa po bid. How many capsules does he take in one day?

    a. 2,000

    b. 1,000

    c. 4

    d. 8

_____ **4.** A.E. must avoid NSAIDs because in cases of inflammatory bowel disease, these drugs are

    a. contraindicated

    b. indicated

    c. prescriptive

    d. synergistic

_____ **5.** E.N. used a mucolytic drug when needed. This drug's action is to

    a. increase mucus secretion

    b. decrease spasms

    c. calm anxiety

    d. eliminate mucus

_____ **6.** E.N.'s Flovent inhaler is indicated as 1 spray of 50 mcg in each nostril bid. How many micrograms (mcg) does she get in one day?

    a. 100 mcg

    b. 200 mcg

    c. 250 mcg

    d. 500 mcg

_____ **7.** The Ativan that E.N. takes for nervousness is a(n) _____ drug.

    a. anxiolytic

    b. antiemetic

    c. analgesic

    d. bronchodilator

_____ **8.** The anesthesiologist ordered lorazepam (Ativan) to be given IV preop to decrease anxiety and to smooth E.N.'s anesthesia induction. The complementary way that lorazepam and anesthesia work together is called

    a. antagonistic

    b. complementary medicine

    c. synergy

    d. tolerance

_____ **9.** Bromelain and Arnica montana are supplements that can be described as all of the following except

    a. phytopharmaceutical

    b. alternative

    c. chronotropic

    d. complementary

_____ **10.** Arnica montana was prescribed three tabs SL tid. How many tablets would E.N. take in one day?

    a. 6

    b. 33

    c. 12

    d. 9

_____ **11.** Flovent is administered as an inhalant. The form in which the drug is prepared is called a(n)

    a. aerosol

    b. elixir

    c. unguent

    d. emulsion

Define each of the following abbreviations.

12. po _____

13. mg _____

14. NSAIDs _____

15. mcg _____

16. IV _____

PART

III

Body Systems

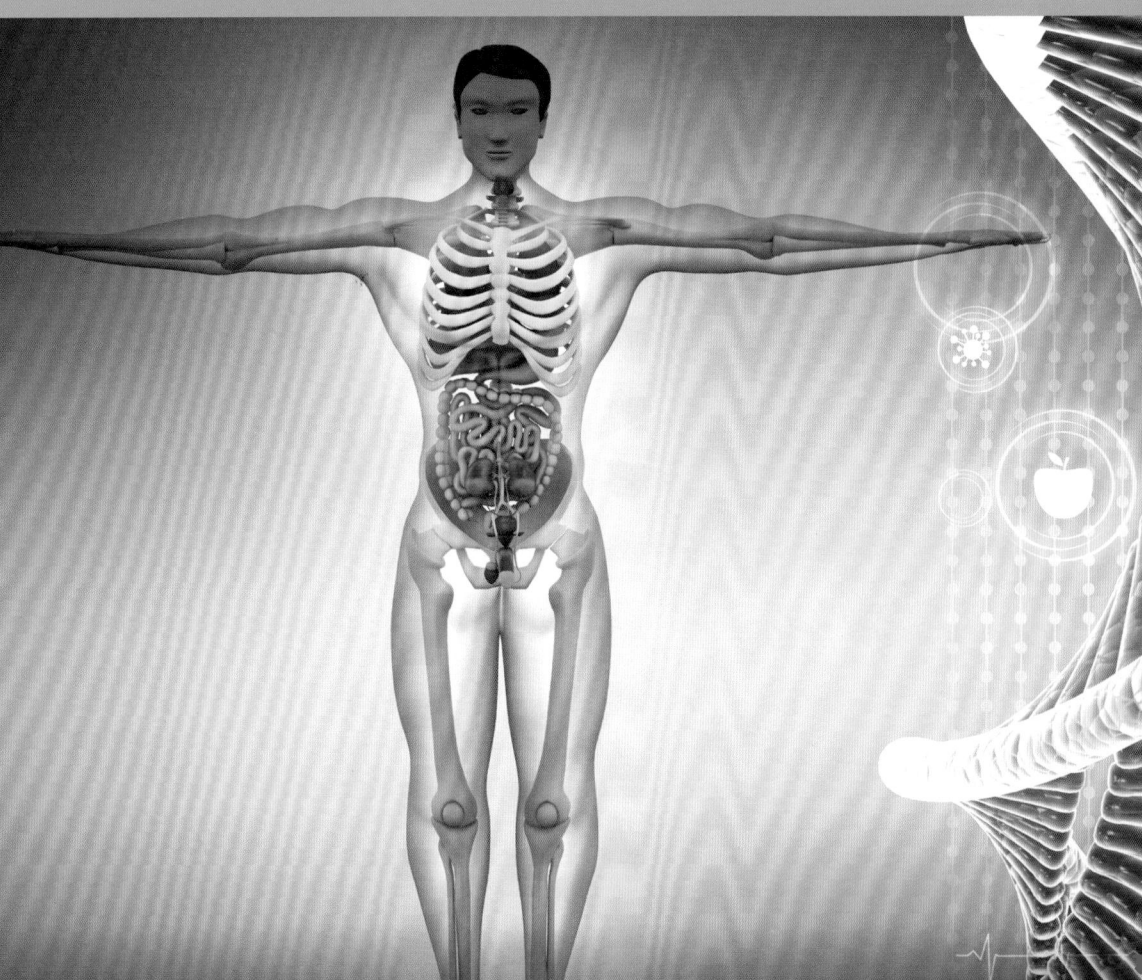

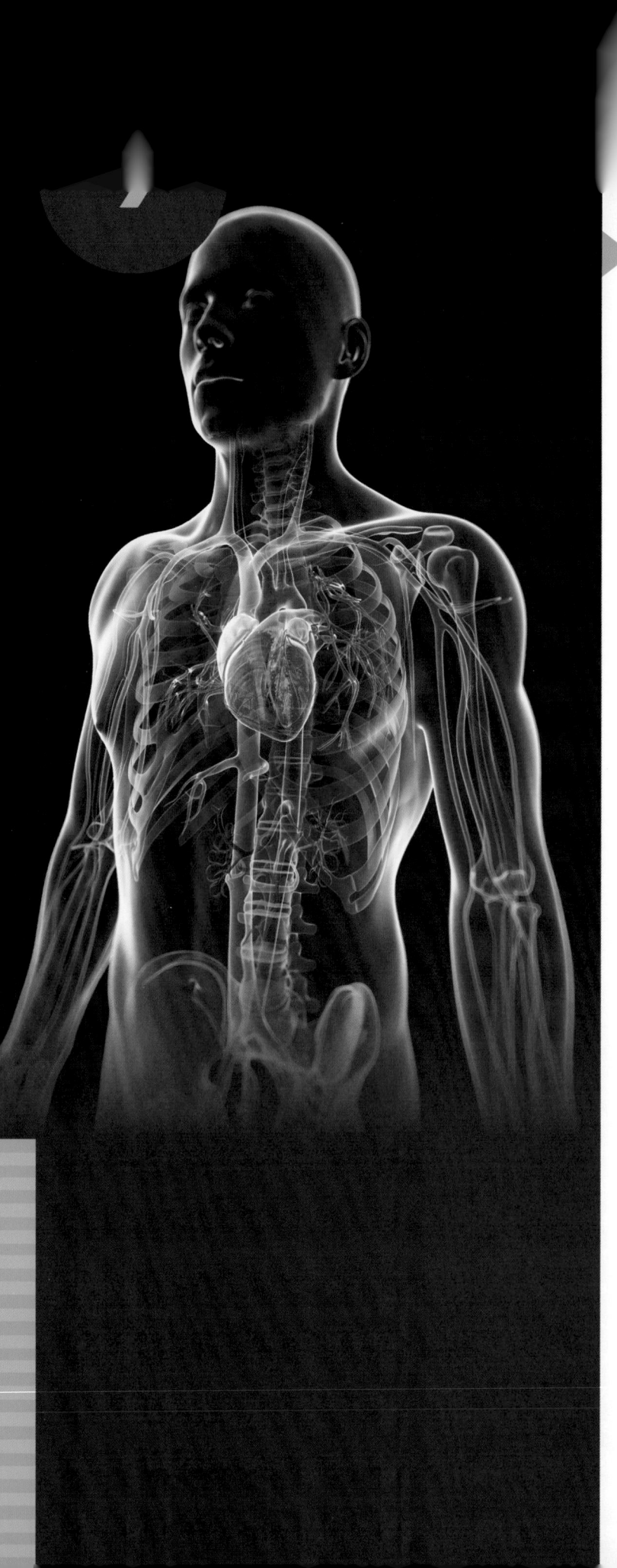

Pretest

Multiple Choice. Select the best answer, and write the letter of your choice to the left of each number.

_____ 1. The cardiovascular system includes the heart and
   a. lungs
   b. digestive organs
   c. blood vessels
   d. endocrine system

_____ 2. The thick, muscular layer of the heart wall is the
   a. endocardium
   b. valve
   c. myocardium
   d. apex

_____ 3. An upper chamber of the heart is a(n)
   a. ventricle
   b. atrium
   c. base
   d. systole

_____ 4. A vessel that carries blood away from the heart is a(n)
   a. vein
   b. chamber
   c. lymph node
   d. artery

_____ 5. The tonsils, spleen, and thymus are part of the
   a. digestive system
   b. endocrine system
   c. epicardium
   d. lymphatic system

_____ 6. The medical term for a "heart attack" is
   a. cerebrovascular accident
   b. myocardial infarction
   c. aneurysm
   d. pneumonia

_____ 7. The accumulation of fatty deposits in the lining of a vessel is called
   a. obesity
   b. stent
   c. atherosclerosis
   d. angiogenesis

_____ 8. Phlebitis is inflammation of a
   a. vein
   b. heart
   c. blood cell
   d. nerve

Learning Objectives

After study of this chapter you should be able to:

1 ▶ Describe the structure of the heart. *p164*

2 ▶ Trace the path of blood flow through the heart. *p164*

3 ▶ Trace the path of electrical conduction through the heart. *p166*

4 ▶ Identify the components of an electrocardiogram. *p166*

5 ▶ Differentiate among arteries, arterioles, capillaries, venules, and veins. *p168*

6 ▶ Explain blood pressure and describe how blood pressure is measured. *p168*

7 ▶ Identify and use the roots pertaining to the cardiovascular and lymphatic systems. *pp173, 187*

8 ▶ Describe the main disorders that affect the cardiovascular and lymphatic systems. *pp175, 188*

9 ▶ Define medical terms pertaining to the cardiovascular and lymphatic systems. *pp181, 189*

10 ▶ List the functions and components of the lymphatic system. *p184*

11 ▶ Interpret medical abbreviations referring to circulation. *p193*

12 ▶ Analyze medical terms in case studies involving circulation. *pp163, 202*

Case Study: *C.L.'s Arrhythmia during Army Boot Camp*

Chief Complaint

C.L., a 19-year-old man recently enlisted into the army, successfully passed the army physicals and reported to Fort Knox for basic training. The first two weeks were uneventful as C.L. became acclimated to the vigorous daily schedules of army life. As the physical training progressed, the platoon would go on long runs in full gear. C.L. passed out during two of these runs. The first time he was taken to the infirmary, where he was examined, cleared, and returned to duty. With the second incident, he was put on a sick leave and sent home for additional follow-up.

Examination

When C.L. came home, his family took him to see his primary care physician, who referred him to a cardiologist. C.L. explained to the physician that on some of the long, rigorous runs with full gear he would become short of breath and feel his heart start to race. He would then become dizzy and pass out. When he woke up, he would be lying on the ground with his sergeant standing over him.

The physician ordered some laboratory tests and also a Holter monitor that C.L. was to wear for a month. He explained to C.L. and his family that he suspected an abnormal heartbeat had caused the fainting spells. The monitor would record any arrhythmias that occurred during the month. He told C.L. to maintain normal activities, and the monitor would detect any abnormalities that might occur.

Clinical Course

At the conclusion of the month, C.L. saw the cardiologist again. The results of the Holter monitor indicated that he had an abnormal heart rhythm known as atrial fibrillation. The physician explained the two methods of treatment for the condition: a medical approach using anticoagulants to prevent blood clots and medication to slow the heart rate, and a surgical procedure called an ablation. It was decided after reviewing the test results and discussion with family on the pros and cons of the various treatment options that a pulmonary vein catheter ablation was the treatment of choice for C.L.

ANCILLARIES *At-A-Glance*

Visit thePoint to access the following resources. For guidance in using the resources most effectively, see pp. ix–xvi.

Learning **RESOURCES**

▶ **Tips for Effective Studying**
▶ **Web Figure: Pathway of Blood through the Heart**
▶ **Web Figure: Evolution of Atherosclerosis**
▶ **Web Figure: Clinical Picture of Acute Myocardial Infarction**
▶ **Web Chart: Lymphoid Tissue**
▶ **Animation: Blood Circulation**

▶ **Animation: Cardiac Cycle**
▶ **Animation: Hypertension**
▶ **Animation: Heart Failure**
▶ **Audio Pronunciation Glossary**

Learning **ACTIVITIES**

▶ **Visual Activities**
▶ **Kinesthetic Activities**
▶ **Auditory Activities**

Introduction

Blood circulates throughout the body in the **cardiovascular system**, which consists of the **heart** and the blood **vessels** (**Fig. 9-1**). This system forms a continuous circuit that delivers oxygen and nutrients to all cells and carries away waste products. The lymphatic system also functions in circulation. Its vessels drain fluid and proteins left in the tissues and return them to the bloodstream. The lymphatic system plays a part in immunity and in the digestive process as well, as explained in Chapters 10 and 12. This chapter discusses the circulatory system in detail, in both its normal and clinical aspects, and then proceeds to study the lymphatic system.

The Heart

The heart is located between the lungs, with its point, or **apex**, directed toward the inferior and left (**Fig. 9-2**). The wall of the heart consists of three layers, all named with the root *cardi*, meaning "heart." Moving from the innermost to the outermost layer, these are the:

1. **Endocardium**—a thin membrane that lines the chambers and valves (the prefix *endo-* means "within").
2. **Myocardium**—a thick muscle layer that makes up most of the heart wall (the root *my/o* means "muscle").
3. **Epicardium**—a thin membrane that covers the heart (the prefix *epi-* means "on").

A fibrous sac, the **pericardium**, contains the heart and anchors it to surrounding structures, such as the sternum (breastbone) and diaphragm (the prefix *peri-* means "around").

Each of the heart's upper receiving chambers is an **atrium** (plural: atria). Each of the lower pumping chambers is a **ventricle** (plural: ventricles). The chambers of the heart are divided by walls, each of which is called a **septum**. The interventricular septum separates the two ventricles; the interatrial septum divides the two atria. There is also a septum between the atrium and ventricle on each side.

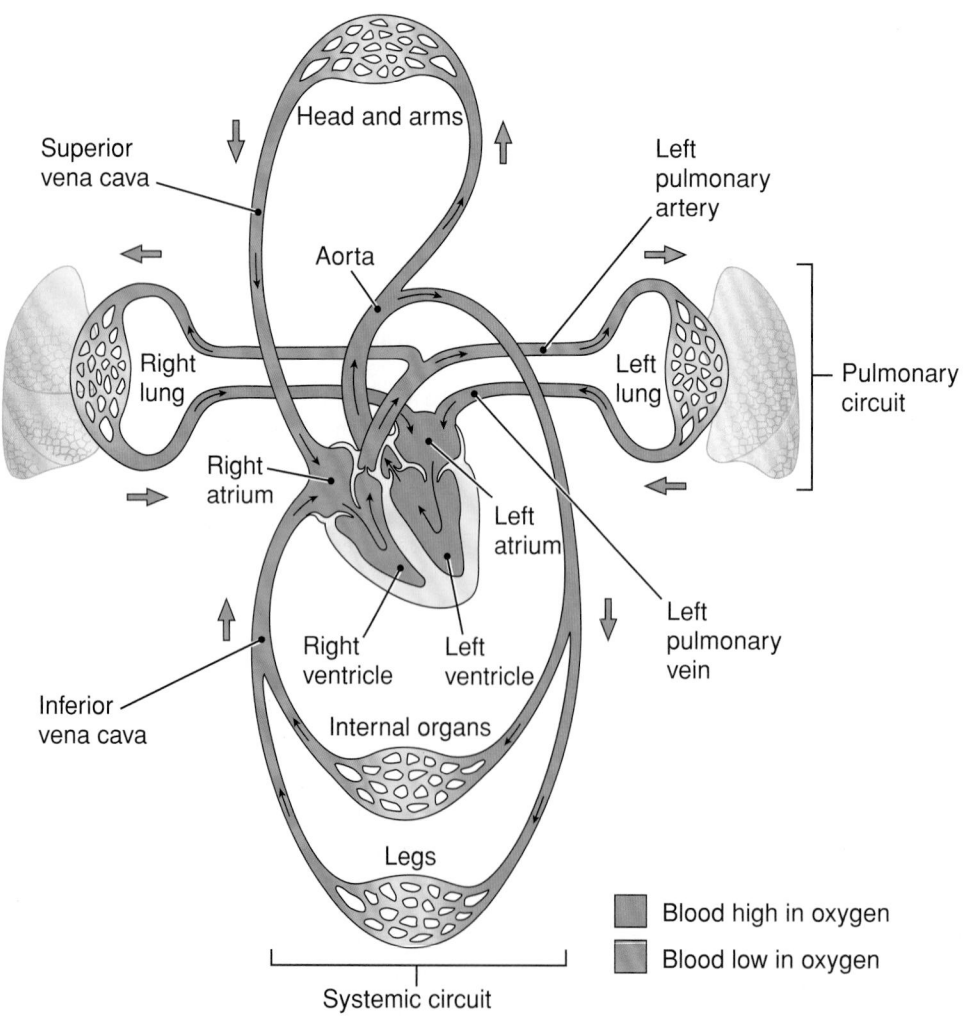

Figure 9-1 **The cardiovascular system.** The pulmonary circuit carries blood to and from the lungs; the systemic circuit carries blood to and from all other parts of the body.

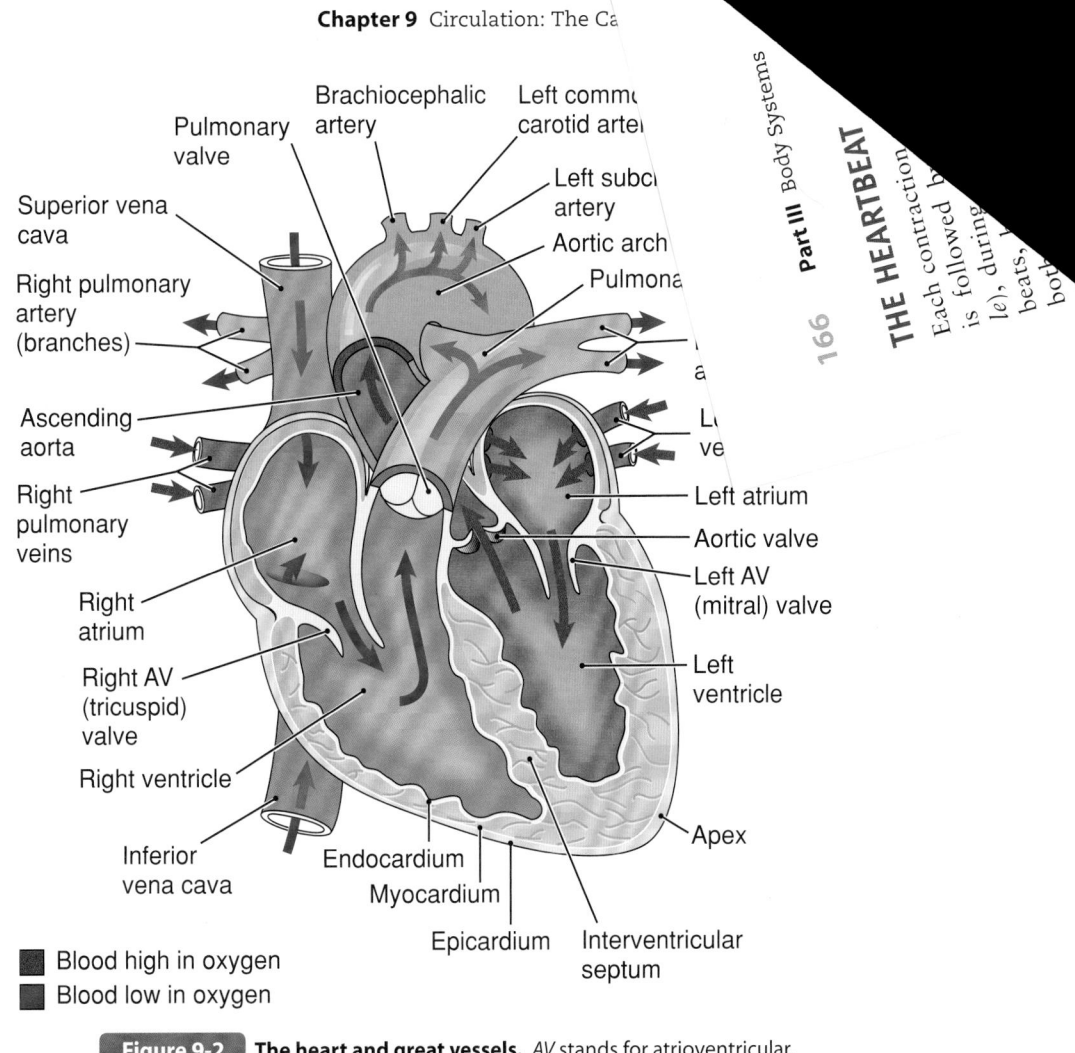

Part III Body Systems

166

THE HEARTBEAT

Each contraction
is followed b
le), during
beats,
bob

9

Figure 9-2 **The heart and great vessels.** *AV* stands for atrioventricular.

The heart pumps blood through two circuits. The right side pumps blood to the lungs to be oxygenated through the **pulmonary circuit**. The left side pumps to the remainder of the body through the **systemic circuit** (see **Fig. 9-1**).

BLOOD FLOW THROUGH THE HEART

The pathway of blood through the heart is shown by the arrows in **Figure 9-2**. The sequence is as follows.

1. The right atrium receives blood low in oxygen from all body tissues through the **superior vena cava** and the **inferior vena cava**.
2. The blood then enters the right ventricle and is pumped to the lungs through the **pulmonary artery**.
3. Blood returns from the lungs high in oxygen and enters the left atrium through the **pulmonary veins**.
4. Blood enters the left ventricle and is forcefully pumped into the **aorta** to be distributed to all tissues.

One-way **valves** in the heart keep blood moving in a forward direction. The valves between the atrium and ventricle on each side are the **atrioventricular** (AV) **valves** (see **Fig. 9-2**). The valve between the right atrium and ventricle is the **right AV valve**, also known as the tricuspid valve because it has three cusps (flaps). The valve between

the left atrium and ventricle is the **left AV valve**, which is a bicuspid valve with two cusps; it is often called the **mitral valve** (so named because it resembles a bishop's miter).

The valves leading into the pulmonary artery and the aorta have three cusps. Each cusp is shaped like a half-moon, so these valves are described as *semilunar valves* (*lunar* refers to the moon). The valve at the entrance to the pulmonary artery is specifically named the **pulmonary valve**; the valve at the entrance to the aorta is the **aortic valve**.

See the Student Resources on the Point for a figure on the pathway of blood through the heart and the animations "Blood Circulation" and "Cardiac Cycle."

Heart sounds are produced as the heart functions. The loudest of these, the familiar "lub" and "dup" that can be heard through the chest wall, are produced by alternate closings of the valves. The first heart sound (S_1) is heard when the valves between the chambers close. The second heart sound (S_2) is produced when the valves leading into the aorta and pulmonary artery close. Any sound made as the heart functions normally is termed a **functional murmur**. (The word *murmur* used alone with regard to the heart describes an abnormal sound.)

of the heart, termed **systole** (*SIS-to-le*), [followed b]y a relaxation phase, **diastole** (*di-AS-to-*[le]), [in] which the chambers fill. Each time the heart [beats, b]oth atria contract, and immediately thereafter [the] ventricles contract. The number of times the heart contracts per minute is the **heart rate**. The wave of increased pressure produced in the vessels each time the ventricles contract is the **pulse**. Pulse rate is usually counted by palpating a peripheral artery, such as the radial artery at the wrist or the carotid artery in the neck (see **Fig. 7-4**).

Cardiac contractions are stimulated by a built-in system that regularly transmits electrical impulses through the heart. The components of this conduction system are shown in **Figure 9-3**. In the sequence of action, they include the:

1. **Sinoatrial (SA) node**, located in the upper right atrium and called the *pacemaker* because it sets the rate of the heartbeat.
2. **Atrioventricular (AV) node**, located at the bottom of the right atrium near the ventricle. Internodal fibers between the SA and AV nodes carry stimulation throughout both atria.
3. **AV bundle** (bundle of His) at the top of the interventricular septum.
4. Left and right **bundle branches**, which travel along the left and right sides of the septum.

5. **Purkinje** (*pur-KIN-je*) **fibers**, which carry stimulation throughout the walls of the ventricles (see information on naming in **Box 9-1**).

Although the heart itself generates the heartbeat, factors such as nervous system stimulation, hormones, and drugs can influence the rate and the force of contractions.

Electrocardiography

Electrocardiography (**ECG**) measures the heart's electrical activity as it functions (**Fig. 9-4**). Electrodes (leads) placed on the body's surface detect the electrical signals, which are then amplified and recorded as a tracing. A normal, or **sinus rhythm**, which originates at the SA node, is shown in **Figure 9-4A**. **Figure 9-4B** shows the letters assigned to individual components of one complete cycle:

1. The P wave represents electrical change, or **depolarization**, of the atrial muscles.
2. The QRS component shows depolarization of the ventricles.
3. The T wave shows return, or **repolarization**, of the ventricles to their resting state. Atrial repolarization is hidden by the QRS wave.
4. The small U wave, if present, follows the T wave. It is of uncertain origin.

An *interval* measures the distance from one wave to the next; a *segment* is a smaller component of the tracing. Many heart disorders, some of which are described later in the chapter, appear as abnormalities in ECG components.

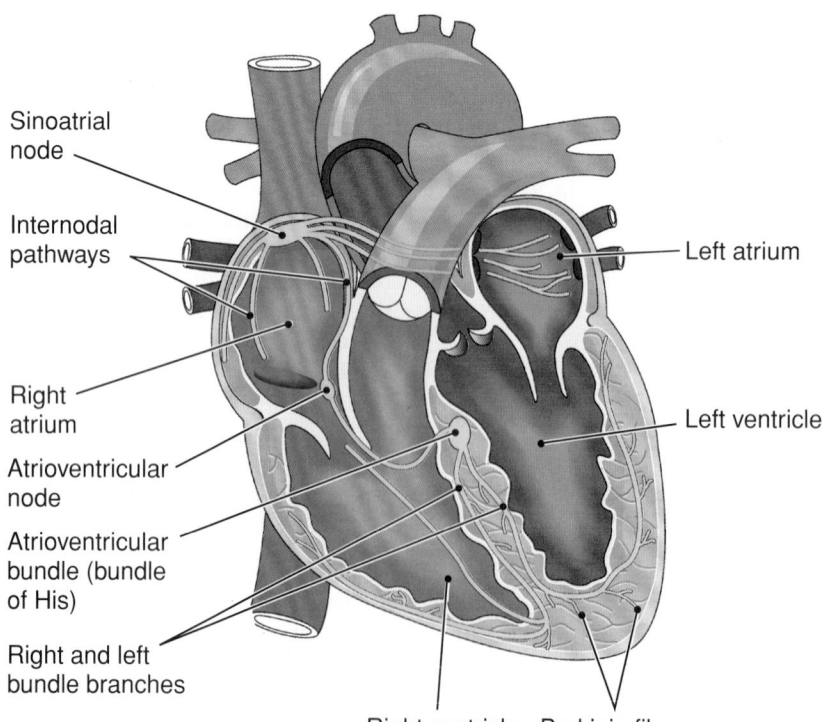

Sinoatrial node

Internodal pathways

Right atrium

Atrioventricular node

Atrioventricular bundle (bundle of His)

Right and left bundle branches

Left atrium

Left ventricle

Right ventricle Purkinje fibers

Figure 9-3 **The heart's electrical conduction system.** Impulses travel from the sinoatrial (SA) node to the atrioventricular (AV) node, then to the atrioventricular bundle, bundle branches, and Purkinje fibers. Internodal pathways carry impulses throughout the atria.

FOCUS ON WORDS
Name That Structure

Box 9-1

An eponym (*EP-o-nim*) is a name that is based on the name of a person, usually the one who discovered a particular structure, disease, principle, or procedure. Everyday examples are graham cracker, Ferris wheel, and boycott. In the heart, the bundle of His and Purkinje fibers are part of that organ's electrical conduction system. Korotkoff sounds are heard in the vessels when taking blood pressure. Cardiovascular disorders named for people include the tetralogy of Fallot, a combination of four congenital heart defects; Raynaud disease of small vessels; and the cardiac arrhythmia known as Wolff–Parkinson–White syndrome. In treatment, Doppler echocardiography is named for a physicist of the 19th century. The Holter monitor and the Swan–Ganz catheter give honors to their developers.

In other systems, the islets of Langerhans are cell clusters in the pancreas that secrete insulin. The graafian follicle in the ovary surrounds a mature egg cell. The eustachian tube connects the middle ear to the throat.

Many disease names are eponymic: Parkinson and Alzheimer, which affect the brain; Graves, a disorder of the thyroid; Addison and Cushing, involving the adrenal cortex; and Down syndrome, a hereditary disorder. The genus and species names of microorganisms often are based on the names of their discoverers: *Escherichia, Salmonella, Pasteurella,* and *Rickettsia* to name a few.

Many reagents, instruments, and procedures are named for their developers too. The original name for a radiograph was roentgenograph (*RENT-jen-o-graf*), named for Wilhelm Roentgen, discoverer of x-rays. A curie is a measure of radiation, derived from the name of Marie Curie, a co-discoverer of radioactivity.

Although eponyms give honor to physicians and scientists of the past, they do not convey any information and may be more difficult to learn. There is a trend to replace these names with more descriptive ones; for example, auditory tube instead of eustachian tube, mature ovarian follicle for graafian follicle, pancreatic islets for islets of Langerhans, and trisomy 21 for Down syndrome.

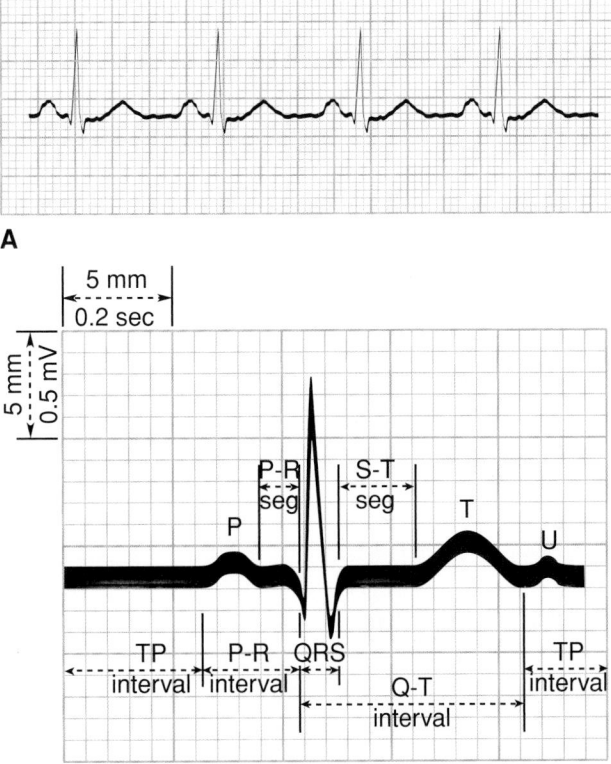

A

B

Figure 9-4 **Electrocardiography (ECG).** **A.** ECG tracing showing a normal sinus rhythm. **B.** Components of a normal ECG tracing. Shown are the P, QRS, T, and U waves, which represent electrical activity in different parts of the heart. Intervals measure from one wave to the next; segments are smaller components of the tracing.

The Vascular System

The vascular system consists of:

1. **Arteries** that carry blood away from the heart (**Fig. 9-5**)
2. **Arterioles**, vessels smaller than arteries that lead into the capillaries
3. **Capillaries**, the smallest vessels, through which exchanges take place between the blood and the tissues
4. **Venules**, small vessels that receive blood from the capillaries and drain into the veins
5. **Veins** that carry blood back to the heart (**Fig. 9-6**)

All arteries, except the pulmonary artery (and the umbilical artery in the fetus), carry highly oxygenated blood. They are thick-walled, elastic vessels that carry blood under high pressure. All veins, except the pulmonary vein (and the umbilical vein in the fetus), carry blood low in oxygen. Veins have thinner, less elastic walls and tend to give way under pressure. Like the heart, veins have one-way valves that keep blood flowing forward. Veins are classified as superficial or deep. The deep veins usually parallel arteries and carry the same names (see **Fig. 9-6**).

Nervous system stimulation can cause the diameter of a vessel to increase (vasodilation) or decrease (vasoconstriction). These changes alter blood flow to the tissues and affect blood pressure.

BLOOD PRESSURE

Blood pressure (BP) is the force exerted by blood against the wall of a blood vessel. It falls as the blood travels away from the heart and is influenced by a variety of factors, including cardiac output, vessel diameters, and total blood volume. Vasoconstriction increases BP in a vessel; vasodilation decreases pressure.

BP is commonly measured in a large artery with an inflatable cuff (**Fig. 9-7**) known as a BP cuff or BP apparatus but technically called a **sphygmomanometer**. The

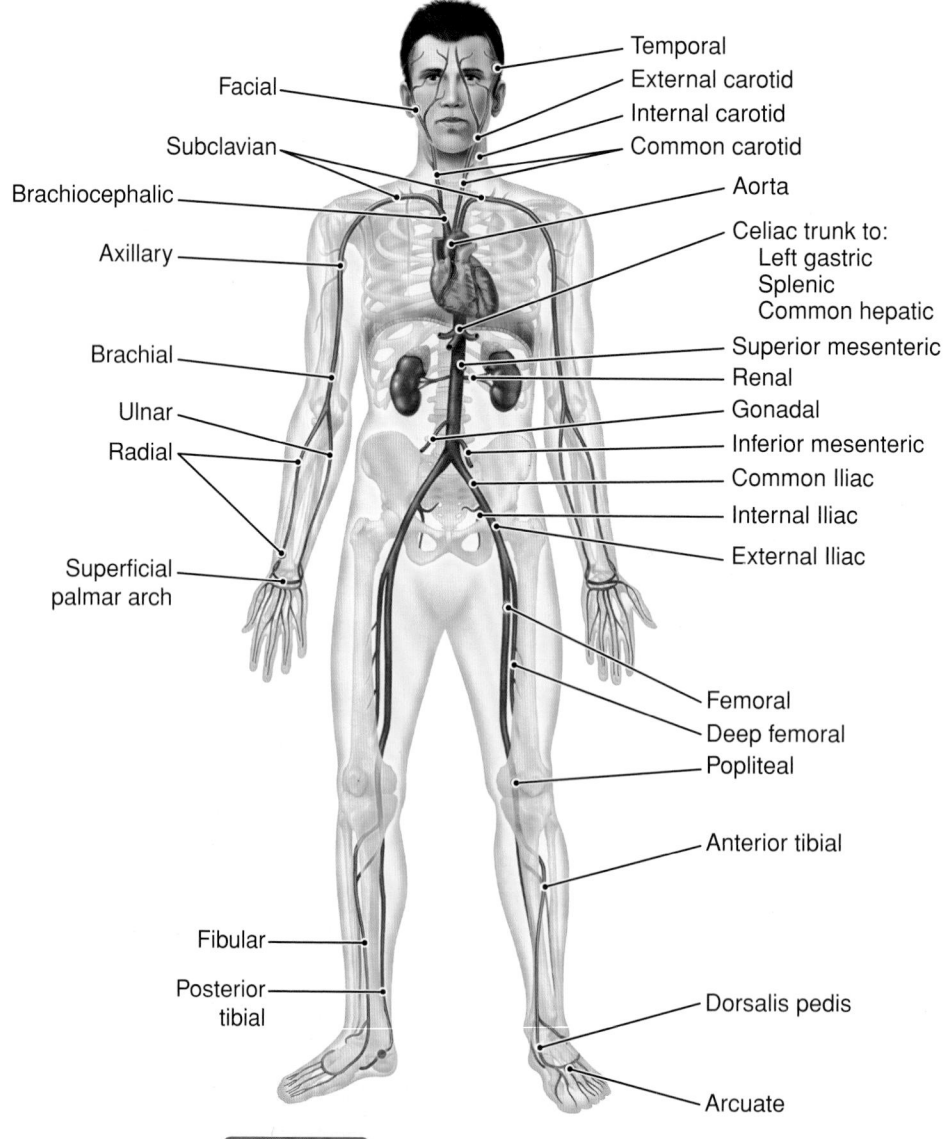

Figure 9-5   **Principal systemic arteries.**

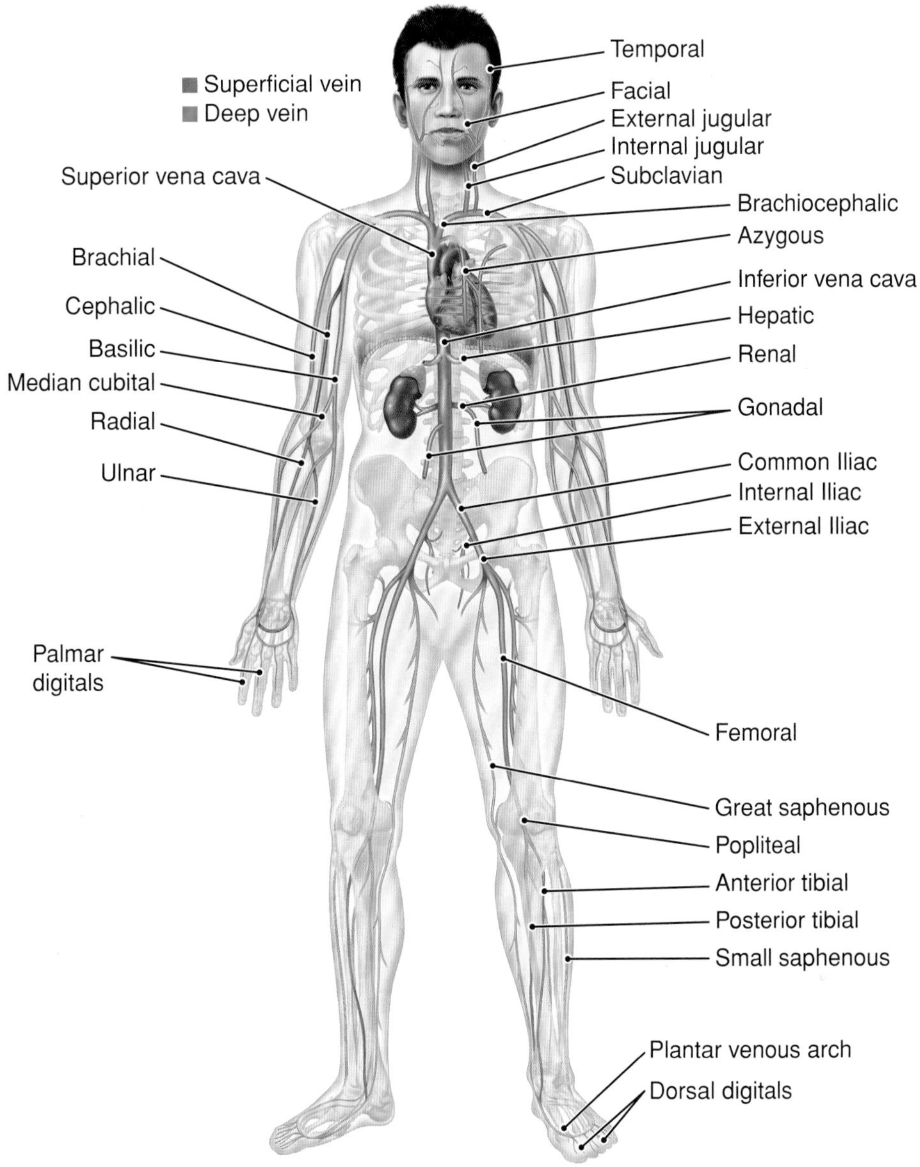

■ Superficial vein
■ Deep vein

Temporal
Facial
External jugular
Internal jugular
Subclavian
Brachiocephalic
Azygous
Inferior vena cava
Hepatic
Renal
Gonadal
Common Iliac
Internal Iliac
External Iliac

Superior vena cava
Brachial
Cephalic
Basilic
Median cubital
Radial
Ulnar
Palmar digitals

Femoral
Great saphenous
Popliteal
Anterior tibial
Posterior tibial
Small saphenous
Plantar venous arch
Dorsal digitals

Figure 9-6 **Principal systemic veins.**

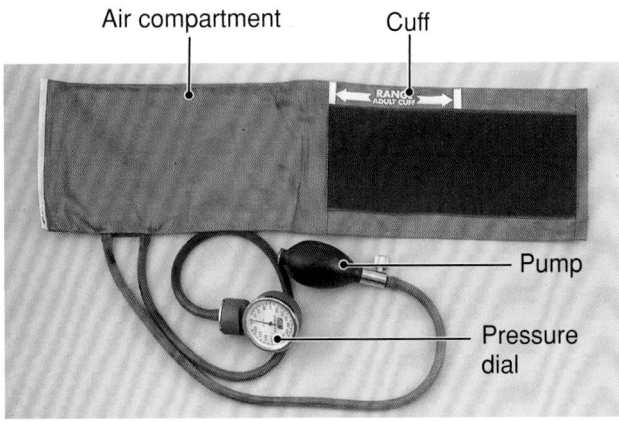

Air compartment
Cuff
Pump
Pressure dial

Figure 9-7 **Blood pressure cuff (sphygmomanometer).** Shown are the cuff, the pump for inflating the cuff, and the manometer for measuring pressure.

9

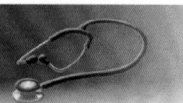

CLINICAL PERSPECTIVES

Box 9-2

Hemodynamic Monitoring: Measuring Blood Pressure from Within

Because arterial blood pressure decreases as blood flows farther away from the heart, measurement of blood pressure with a simple inflatable cuff around the arm is only a reflection of the pressure in the heart and pulmonary arteries. Precise measurement of pressure in these parts of the cardiovascular system is useful in diagnosing certain cardiac and pulmonary disorders.

More accurate readings can be obtained using a catheter (thin tube) inserted directly into the heart and large vessels. One type commonly used is the pulmonary artery catheter (also known as the Swan–Ganz catheter), which has an inflatable balloon at the tip. This device is threaded into the right side of the heart through a large vein. Typically, the right internal jugular vein is used because it is the shortest

and most direct route to the heart, but the subclavian and femoral veins may also be used. The catheter's position in the heart is confirmed by a chest x-ray, and when appropriately positioned, the atrial and ventricular blood pressures are recorded. As the catheter continues into the pulmonary artery, pressure in this vessel is readable. When the balloon is inflated, the catheter becomes wedged in a branch of the pulmonary artery, blocking blood flow. The reading obtained is called the pulmonary capillary wedge pressure (PCWP). It gives information on pressure in the heart's left side and on resistance in the lungs. Combined with other tests, hemodynamic monitoring with a Swan-Ganz catheter can be used to diagnose cardiac and pulmonary disorders such as shock, pericarditis, congenital heart disease, and heart failure.

examiner inflates the cuff to stop blood flow in a vessel. He or she then uses a stethoscope to listen for blood flow in the vessel as the pressure is slowly released (see **Fig. 7-5**). The BP reading includes both systolic pressure, measured while the heart is contracting, and diastolic pressure, measured when the heart relaxes. These are reported as systolic

then diastolic separated by a slash, such as 120/80. Pressure is expressed as millimeters of mercury (mm Hg), that is, the height to which the pressure can push a column of mercury in a tube. BP is a valuable diagnostic measurement that is easily obtained. (See **Box 9-2** for more information on blood pressure measurement.)

Terminology	**Key Terms**

Cardiovascular System

Normal Structure and Function

aorta a-OR-tah	The largest artery; it receives blood from the left ventricle and branches to all parts of the body (root: aort/o)
aortic valve a-OR-tik	The valve at the entrance to the aorta
apex A-peks	The point of a cone-shaped structure (adjective: apical); the apex of the heart is formed by the left ventricle and is pointed toward the inferior and left
artery AR-teh-re	A vessel that carries blood away from the heart; all except the pulmonary and umbilical arteries carry oxygenated blood (roots: arter, arteri/o)
arteriole ar-TE-re-ole	A small vessel that carries blood from the arteries into the capillaries (root: arteriol/o)
atrioventricular (AV) node a-tre-o-ven-TRIK-u-lar	A small mass in the lower septum of the right atrium that passes impulses from the sinoatrial (SA) node toward the ventricles
atrioventricular (AV) valve	A valve between the atrium and ventricle on the right and left sides of the heart; the right AV valve is the tricuspid valve; the left is the mitral valve
atrium A-tre-um	An entrance chamber, one of the two upper receiving chambers of the heart (root: atri/o)

| Terminology | Key Terms *(Continued)* |

AV bundle	A band of fibers that transmits impulses from the atrioventricular (AV) node to the top of the interventricular septum; it divides into the right and left bundle branches, which descend along the two sides of the septum; the bundle of His
blood pressure	The force exerted by blood against the wall of a vessel
bundle branches	Branches of the AV bundle that divide to the right and left sides of the interventricular septum
capillary KAP-ih-lar-e	A microscopic blood vessel through which materials are exchanged between the blood and the tissues
cardiovascular system kar-de-o-VAS-ku-lar	The part of the circulatory system that consists of the heart and the blood vessels
depolarization de-po-lar-ih-ZA-shun	A change in electrical charge from the resting state in nerves or muscles
diastole di-AS-to-le	The relaxation phase of the heartbeat cycle (adjective: diastolic)
electrocardiography (ECG) e-lek-tro-kar-de-OG-rah-fe	Study of the electrical activity of the heart as detected by electrodes (leads) placed on the surface of the body; also abbreviated EKG from the German electrocardiography
endocardium en-do-KAR-de-um	The thin membrane that lines the chambers of the heart and covers the valves
epicardium ep-ih-KAR-de-um	The thin outermost layer of the heart wall
functional murmur	Any sound produced as the heart functions normally
heart hart	The muscular organ with four chambers that contracts rhythmically to propel blood through vessels to all parts of the body (root: cardi/o)
heart rate	The number of times the heart contracts per minute; recorded as beats per minute (bpm)
heart sounds	Sounds produced as the heart functions: the two loudest sounds are produced by alternate closing of the valves and are designated S_1 and S_2
inferior vena cava VE-nah KA-vah	The large inferior vein that brings blood low in oxygen back to the right atrium of the heart from the lower body
left AV valve	The valve between the left atrium and the left ventricle; the mitral valve or bicuspid valve
mitral valve MI-tral	The valve between the left atrium and the left ventricle; the left AV valve or bicuspid valve
myocardium mi-o-KAR-de-um	The thick middle layer of the heart wall composed of cardiac muscle
pericardium per-ih-KAR-de-um	The fibrous sac that surrounds the heart
pulmonary artery PUL-mo-nar-e	The vessel that carries blood from the right side of the heart to the lungs
pulmonary circuit SER-kit	The system of vessels that carries blood from the right side of the heart to the lungs to be oxygenated and then back to the left side of the heart

(continued)

Terminology   Key Terms *(Continued)*

pulmonary veins	The vessels that carry blood from the lungs to the left side of the heart
pulmonary valve	The valve at the entrance to the pulmonary artery
pulse *puls*	The wave of increased pressure produced in the vessels each time the ventricles contract
Purkinje fibers *pur-KIN-je*	The terminal fibers of the cardiac conducting system; they carry impulses through the walls of the ventricles
repolarization *re-po-lar-ih-ZA-shun*	A return of electrical charge to the resting state in nerves or muscles
right AV valve	The valve between the right atrium and right ventricle; the tricuspid valve
septum *SEP-tum*	A wall dividing two cavities, such as two chambers of the heart
sinus rhythm *SI-nus RITH-um*	Normal heart rhythm
sinoatrial (SA) node *si-no-A-tre-al*	A small mass in the upper part of the right atrium that initiates the impulse for each heartbeat; the pacemaker
sphygmomanometer *sfig-mo-man-OM-eh-ter*	An instrument for determining arterial blood pressure (root sphygm/o means "pulse"); blood pressure apparatus or cuff
superior vena cava *VE-nah KA-vah*	The large superior vein that brings blood low in oxygen back to the right atrium from the upper body
systemic circuit *sis-TEM-ik SER-kit*	The system of vessels that carries oxygenated blood from the left side of the heart to all tissues except the lungs and returns deoxygenated blood to the right side of the heart
systole *SIS-to-le*	The contraction phase of the heartbeat cycle (adjective: systolic)
valve *valv*	A structure that keeps fluid flowing in a forward direction (roots: valv/o, valvul/o)
vein *vane*	A vessel that carries blood back to the heart. All except the pulmonary and umbilical veins carry blood low in oxygen (roots: ven/o, phleb/o)
ventricle *VEN-trik-l*	A small cavity. One of the two lower pumping chambers of the heart (root: ventricul/o)
venule *VEN-ule*	A small vessel that carries blood from the capillaries to the veins
vessel *VES-el*	A tube or duct to transport fluid (roots: angi/o, vas/o, vascul/o)

Go to the Audio Pronunciation Glossary in the Student Resources on thePoint to hear these terms pronounced.

Roots Pertaining to the Cardiovascular System

See Tables 9-1 and 9-2.

Table 9-1	Roots for the Heart		
Root	**Meaning**	**Example**	**Definition of Example**
cardi/o	heart	cardiomyopathy[a] *kar-de-o-mi-OP-ah-the*	any disease of the heart muscle
atri/o	atrium	atriotomy *a-tre-OT-o-me*	surgical incision of an atrium
ventricul/o	cavity, ventricle	supraventricular *su-prah-ven-TRIK-u-lar*	above a ventricle
valv/o, valvul/o	valve	valvulotome *VAL-vu-lo-tome*	instrument for incising a valve

[a]Preferred over myocardiopathy.

EXERCISE 9-1

Fill in the blanks.

1. A valvuloplasty (*val-vu-lo-PLAS-te*) is plastic repair of a(n) _____.

2. Atriotomy (*a-tre-OT-to-me*) means surgical incision of a(n) _____.

3. Interventricular (*in-ter-ven-TRIK-u-lar*) means between the _____.

4. The word *cardiomegaly* (*kar-de-o-MEG-ah-le*) means enlargement of the _____.

Write the adjective for the following definitions. The proper suffix is given for each.

5. Pertaining to an atrium (-al)   _____

6. Pertaining to the myocardium (-al; ending differs from adjective ending for the heart)   _____

7. Pertaining to the heart (-ac)   _____

8. Pertaining to a valve (-ar)   _____

9. Pertaining to a ventricle (-ar)   _____

10. Pertaining to the pericardium (-al)   _____

Following the example, write a word for the following definitions pertaining to the tissues of the heart.

11. Inflammation of the fibrous sac around the heart   _____ pericarditis _____

12. Inflammation of the heart's lining (usually at a valve)   _____

13. Inflammation of the heart muscle   _____

(continued)

EXERCISE 9-1   *(Continued)*

Write a word for the following definitions.

14. Originating (-genic) in the heart   _____

15. Surgical incision of a valve   _____

16. Pertaining to an atrium and a ventricle   _____

17. Between (inter) the atria   _____

18. Study (-logy) of the heart   _____

Table 9-2   **Roots for the Blood Vessels**

Root	Meaning	Example	Definition of Example
angi/o[a]	vessel	angiography *an-je-OG-rah-fe*	x-ray imaging of a vessel
vas/o, vascul/o	vessel, duct	vasospasm *VA-so-spazm*	sudden contraction of a vessel
arter/o, arteri/o	artery	endarterial *end-ar-TE-re-al*	within an artery
arteriol/o	arteriole	arteriolar *ar-te-re-O-lar*	pertaining to an arteriole
aort/o	aorta	aortoptosis *a-or-top-TO-sis*	downward displacement of the aorta
ven/o, ven/i	vein	venous *VE-nus*	pertaining to a vein
phleb/o	vein	phlebotomy *fleh-BOT-o-me*	incision of a vein to withdraw blood

[a]The root *angi/o* usually refers to a blood vessel but is used for other types of vessels as well. *Hemangi/o* refers specifically to a blood vessel.

EXERCISE 9-2

Fill in the blank.

1. Angioedema (*an-je-o-eh-DE-mah*) is localized swelling caused by changes in _____.

2. Vasodilation (*vas-o-DI-la-shun*) means dilation of a(n) _____.

3. Aortostenosis (*a-or-to-steh-NO-sis*) is narrowing of _____.

4. Endarterectomy (*end-ar-ter-EK-to-me*) is removal of the inner lining of a(n)_____.

5. Arteriolitis (*ar-te-re-o-LI-tis*) is inflammation of a(n) _____.

6. Phlebectasia (*fleh-ek-TA-ze-ah*) is dilatation of a(n) _____.

7. The term *microvascular* (*mi-kro-VAS-ku-lar*) means pertaining to small _____.

EXERCISE 9-2   *(Continued)*

Define the following words.

8. arteriorrhexis (*ar-te-re-o-REK-sis*) _____

9. intraaortic (*in-trah-a-OR-tik*) _____

10. angiitis (*an-je-I-tis*) (note spelling); also angitis or vasculitis _____

11. phlebitis (*fleb-I-tis*) _____

12. cardiovascular (*kar-de-o-VAS-ku-lar*) _____

Use the ending *-gram* to form a word for a radiograph of the following.

13. vessels (use angi/o) _____

14. aorta _____

15. veins _____

Use the root *angi/o* to write words with the following meanings.

16. Plastic repair (-plasty) of a vessel _____

17. Any disease (-pathy) of a vessel _____

18. Dilatation (-ectasis) of a vessel _____

19. Formation (-genesis) of a vessel _____

Use the appropriate root to write words with the following meanings.

20. Excision of a vein _____

21. Hardening (-sclerosis) of the aorta _____

22. Within (intra-) a vein _____

23. Incision of an artery _____

Clinical Aspects of the Cardiovascular System

ATHEROSCLEROSIS

The accumulation of fatty deposits within the lining of an artery is termed **atherosclerosis** (**Fig. 9-8**). This type of deposit, called **plaque** (*plak*), begins to form when a vessel receives tiny injuries, usually at a point of branching. Plaques gradually thicken and harden with fibrous material, cells, and other deposits, restricting the vessel's lumen (opening) and reducing blood flow to the tissues, a condition known as **ischemia** (*is-KE-me-ah*). A major risk factor for the development of atherosclerosis is **dyslipidemia**, abnormally high levels or imbalance in **lipoproteins** that are carried in the blood, especially high levels of cholesterol-containing, low-density lipoproteins (LDLs). Other risk factors for atherosclerosis include smoking, high blood pressure, poor diet, inactivity, stress, and a family history of the disorder. Atherosclerosis may involve any arteries, but most of its effects are seen in the coronary vessels of the heart, the aorta, the carotid arteries in the neck, and vessels in the brain. The techniques described later for treating coronary artery disease (CAD) are used for these other vessels as well.

Atherosclerosis is the most common form of a more general condition known as **arteriosclerosis** in which vessel walls harden from any cause. In addition to plaque, calcium salts and scar tissue may contribute to arterial wall thickening, with a narrowing of the lumen and loss of elasticity.

THROMBOSIS AND EMBOLISM

Atherosclerosis predisposes a person to **thrombosis**, the formation of a blood clot within a vessel (see **Fig. 9-8**). The clot, called a **thrombus**, interrupts blood flow to the tissues supplied by that vessel, resulting in necrosis (tissue death). Blockage of a vessel by a thrombus or other mass carried in the bloodstream is **embolism**, and the mass itself is called an **embolus**. Usually, the mass is a blood clot that breaks loose from a vessel's wall, but it may also

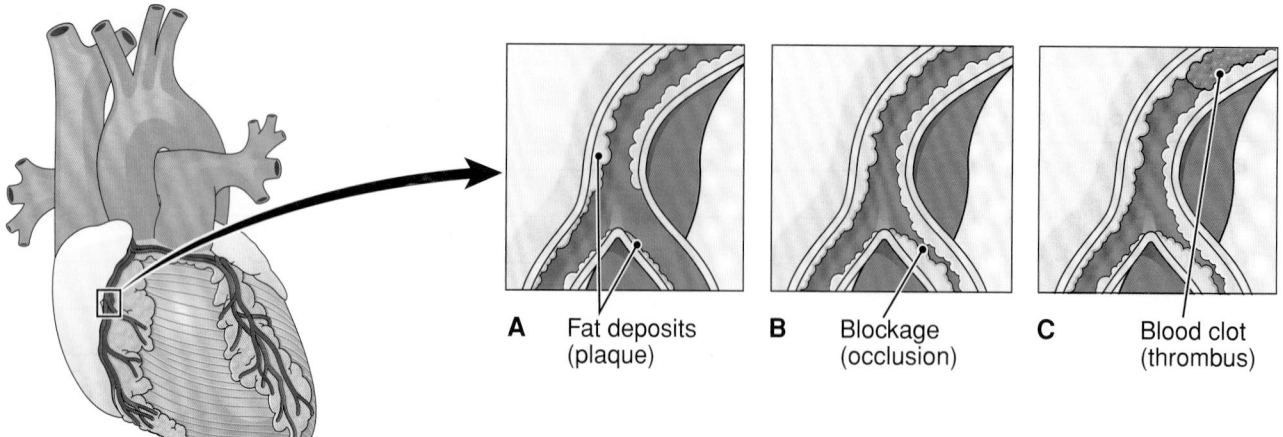

Figure 9-8 **Coronary atherosclerosis. A.** Fat deposits (plaque) narrow an artery, leading to ischemia (lack of blood supply). **B.** Plaque causes blockage (occlusion) of a vessel. **C.** Formation of a blood clot (thrombus) in a vessel leads to myocardial infarction (MI).

be air (as from injection or trauma), fat (as from marrow released after a bone break), bacteria, or other solid materials. Often a venous thrombus will travel through the heart and then lodge in an artery of the lungs, resulting in a life-threatening pulmonary embolism. An embolus from a carotid artery often blocks a cerebral vessel, causing a **cerebrovascular accident (CVA)**, commonly called **stroke** (see Chapter 17).

ANEURYSM

An arterial wall weakened by atherosclerosis, malformation, injury, or other changes may balloon out, forming an **aneurysm**. If an aneurysm ruptures, hemorrhage results. Rupture of a cerebral artery is another cause of stroke. The abdominal aorta and carotid arteries are also common aneurysm sites. In a **dissecting aneurysm** (**Fig. 9-9**), blood hemorrhages into the arterial wall's thick middle layer, separating the muscle as it spreads and sometimes rupturing the vessel. The aorta is most commonly involved. It may be possible to repair a dissecting aneurysm surgically with a graft.

HYPERTENSION

High blood pressure, or **hypertension** (HTN), is a contributing factor in all of the conditions described above. In simple terms, HTN is defined as a systolic pressure greater than 140 mm Hg or a diastolic pressure greater than 90 mm Hg. HTN causes the left ventricle to enlarge (hypertrophy) as a result of increased work. Some cases of HTN are secondary to other disorders, such as kidney malfunction or endocrine disturbance, but most of the time, the causes are unknown, a condition described as primary, or essential, HTN.

Changes in diet and life habits are the first line of defense in controlling HTN. Drugs that are used include diuretics to eliminate fluids, vasodilators to relax the blood vessels, and drugs that prevent the formation or action of

angiotensin, a substance in the blood that normally acts to increase blood pressure (see Chapter 13).

> See the Student Resources on the Point for a figure on the evolution of atherosclerosis and to view the animation "Hypertension."

HEART DISEASE

Coronary Artery Disease

Coronary artery disease (CAD) results from atherosclerosis in the vessels that supply blood to the heart muscle. It is a leading cause of death in industrialized countries (see **Fig. 9-8**).

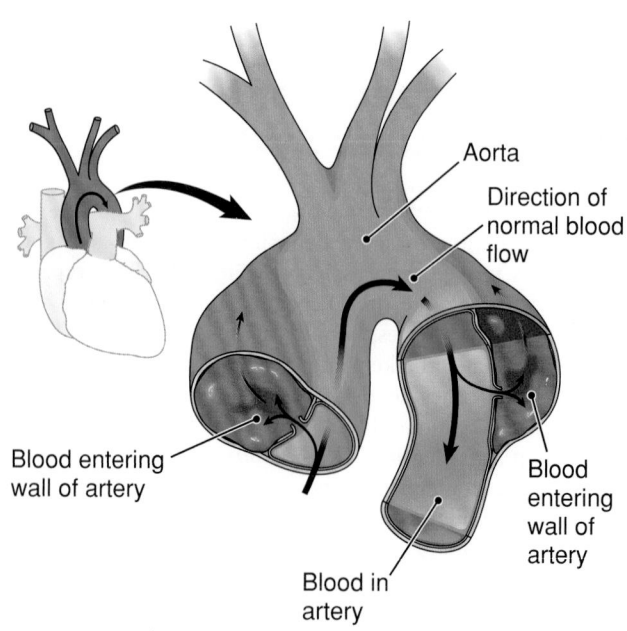

Figure 9-9 **Dissecting aortic aneurysm.** Blood separates the layers of the arterial wall.

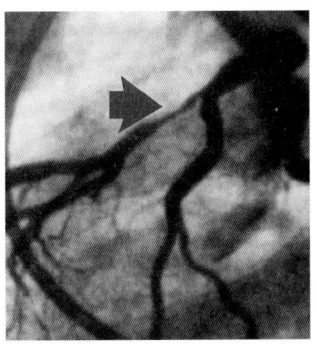 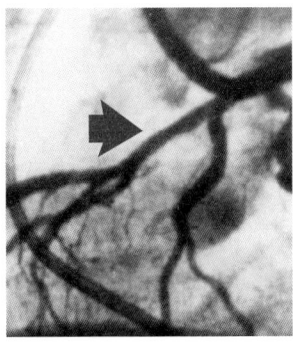

A **B**

Figure 9-10 **Coronary angiography.** Coronary vessels are imaged after administration of a dye during cardiac catheterization. **A.** Angiography shows narrowing in the mid-left anterior descending (LAD) artery (*arrow*). **B.** The same vessel after angioplasty, a procedure to distend narrowed vessels. Note the improved blood flow through the artery distal to the repair.

An early sign of CAD is the type of chest pain known as **angina pectoris**. This is a feeling of constriction around the heart or pain that may radiate to the left arm or shoulder, usually brought on by exertion. Often there is anxiety, **diaphoresis** (profuse sweating), and **dyspnea** (difficulty in breathing). CAD is diagnosed by ECG, **stress tests**, **echocardiography**, and **coronary angiography**. This invasive

x-ray imaging method requires injection of a dye into the coronary arteries by means of a catheter threaded through blood vessels into the heart (**Fig. 9-10**). Coronary **CT angiography** (CTA) is a noninvasive procedure that can be used in the diagnosis of heart disease. It employs computed tomography scans following injection of a small amount of dye into the arm. A **coronary calcium scan** (heart scan) reveals vessel-narrowing calcium deposits in the coronary arterial walls. Researchers have also found that a substance called **C-reactive protein** (CRP) is associated with poor cardiovascular health. This protein is produced during systemic inflammation, which may contribute to atherosclerosis. CRP levels can indicate cardiovascular disease and predict its outcome (prognosis). A more specific test for heart attack risk is the more accurate hs-CRP (high-sensitivity CRP) test.

CAD is treated by control of exercise and diet and by drug therapy and surgical intervention when appropriate. Drugs, such as nitroglycerin, may be used to dilate coronary vessels. Other drugs may be used to regulate the heartbeat, strengthen the force of heart contraction, lower cholesterol, or prevent blood clot formation.

Patients with severe CAD may be candidates for **angioplasty**, surgical dilatation of the blocked vessel by means of a balloon catheter, a procedure technically called **percutaneous transluminal coronary angioplasty** (PTCA) (**Figs. 9-10** and **9-11**). Angioplasty may include placement of a **stent**, a

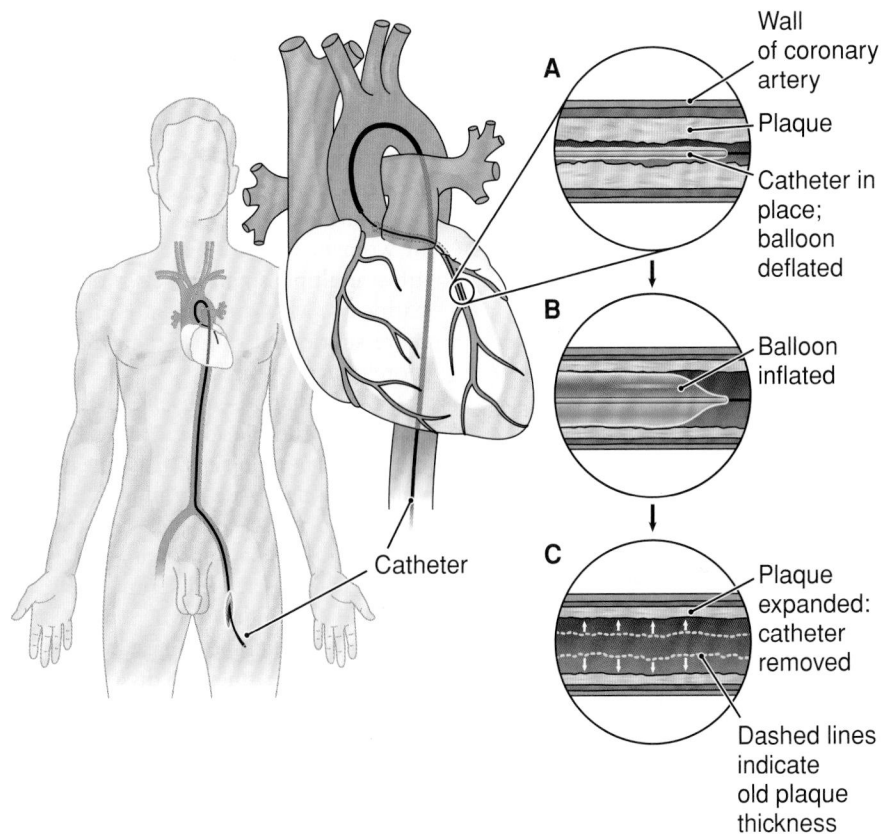

Figure 9-11 **Coronary angioplasty (PTCA). A.** A guide catheter is threaded into the coronary artery. **B.** A balloon catheter is inserted through the occlusion. **C.** The balloon is inflated and deflated until plaque is flattened and the vessel is opened.

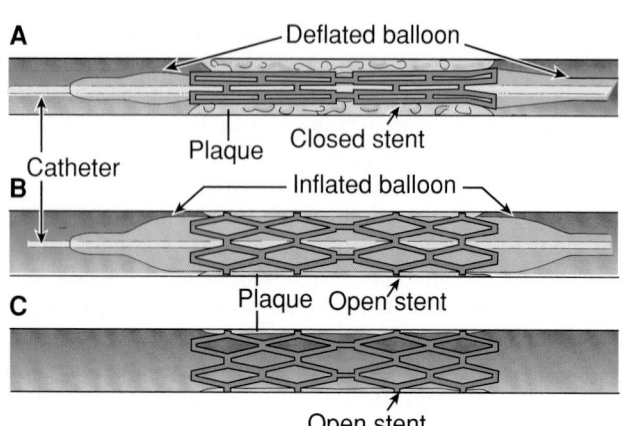

Figure 9-12 **Arterial stent. A.** Stent closed, before balloon infla-tion. **B.** Stent open, balloon inflated; stent will remain expanded after balloon is deflated and removed. **C.** Stent open, balloon removed.

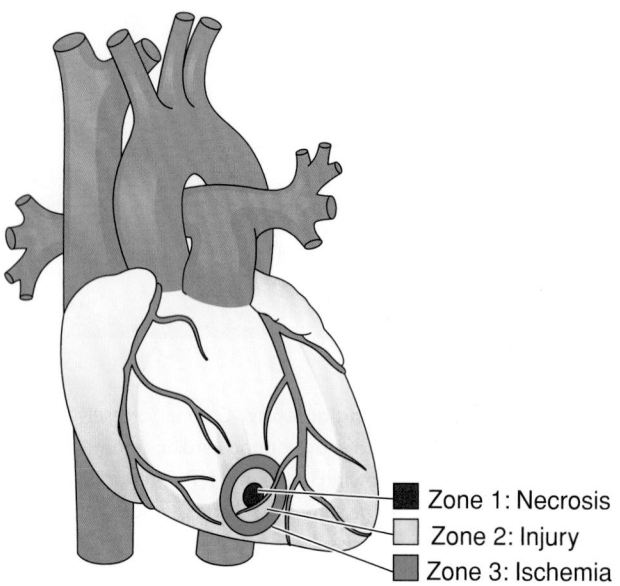

Figure 9-14 **Myocardial infarction (MI).** A blood clot (throm-bus) causes a zone of necrosis (tissue death). Surrounding tissue suf-fers from lack of blood supply (ischemia).

small mesh tube, to keep the vessel open (**Fig. 9-12**). Stents prevent recoil of the vessel and are available in different ver-sions. The basic type is the bare metal stent; another is the drug-eluting stent, which releases drugs to prevent vascular restenosis. The newest form of stent is a completely bioab-sorbable device that is gradually metabolized and absorbed into the body.

If further intervention is required, surgeons can bypass the blocked vessel or vessels with a vascular graft (**Fig. 9-13**). In this procedure, known as a **coronary artery bypass graft** (CABG), another vessel or a piece of another vessel, usually the left internal mammary artery or part of the leg's saphe-nous vein, is grafted to carry blood from the aorta to a point past the coronary vessel obstruction.

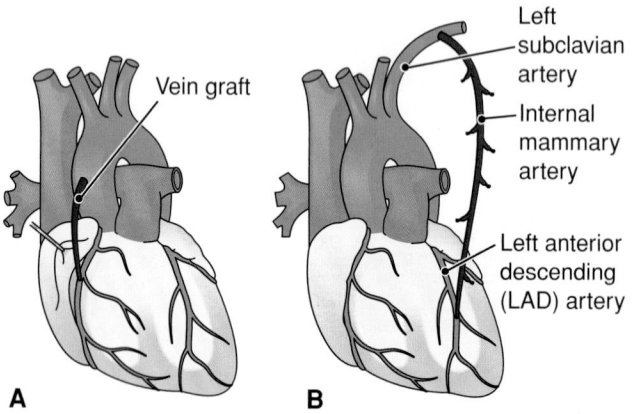

Figure 9-13 **Coronary artery bypass graft (CABG). A.** A seg-ment of the saphenous vein carries blood from the aorta to a part of the right coronary artery that is distal to an occlusion. **B.** The mammary artery is used to bypass an obstruction in the left anterior descending (LAD) coronary artery.

Myocardial Infarction

Degenerative changes in the arteries predispose a person to thrombosis and sudden coronary artery **occlusion** (obstruc-tion). The resultant area of myocardial necrosis is termed an **infarct** (**Fig. 9-14**), and the process is known as **myocardial infarction** (MI), the "heart attack" that may cause sudden death. Symptoms of MI include pain over the heart (pre-cordial pain) or upper part of the abdomen (epigastric pain) that may extend to the jaw or arms, pallor (paleness), dia-phoresis, nausea, fatigue, anxiety, and dyspnea. There may be a burning sensation similar to indigestion or heartburn. In women, because degenerative changes more commonly affect multiple small vessels rather than the major coronary pathways, MI symptoms are often more long-term and are more subtle and diffuse than the intense chest pain that is more typical in men.

MI is diagnosed by ECG and assays for specific sub-stances in the blood. Creatine kinase (CK) is an enzyme normal to muscle cells. It is released in increased amounts when muscle tissue is injured. The form of CK specific to cardiac muscle cells is **creatine kinase MB** (CK-MB). **Troponin** (Tn) is a protein that regulates contraction in muscle cells. Increased serum levels, particularly the forms TnT and TnI, indicate MI.

Patient outcome is based on the degree of damage and the speed of treatment to dissolve the clot and to reestablish normal blood flow and heart rhythm.

Arrhythmia

Arrhythmia is any irregularity of heart rhythm, such as an altered heart rate, extra beats, or a change in the pattern of the beat. **Bradycardia** is a slower-than-average rate, and **tachycardia** is a higher-than-average rate.

Damage to cardiac tissue, as by MI, may result in **heart block**, an interruption in the heart's electrical conduction

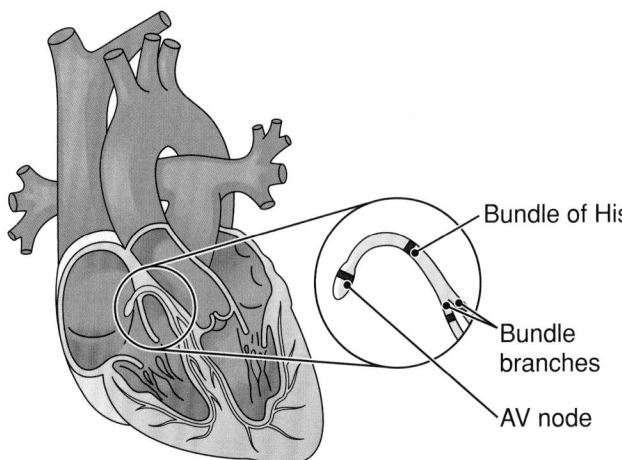

Figure 9-15 Potential sites for heart block in the atrioventricular (AV) portion of the heart's conduction system.

system resulting in arrhythmia (**Fig. 9-15**). Heart block is classified in order of increasing severity as first-, second-, or third-degree heart block. Block in a bundle branch is designated as a left or right bundle branch block (BBB).

If, for any reason, the SA node is not generating a normal heartbeat or there is heart block, an **artificial pacemaker** may be implanted to regulate the beat (**Fig. 9-16**). Usually, the pacemaker is inserted under the skin below the clavicle, and leads are threaded through veins into one or

both of the right chambers. Some pacemakers act only when the heart is not functioning on its own, and others adjust to the need for a change in heart rate based on activity.

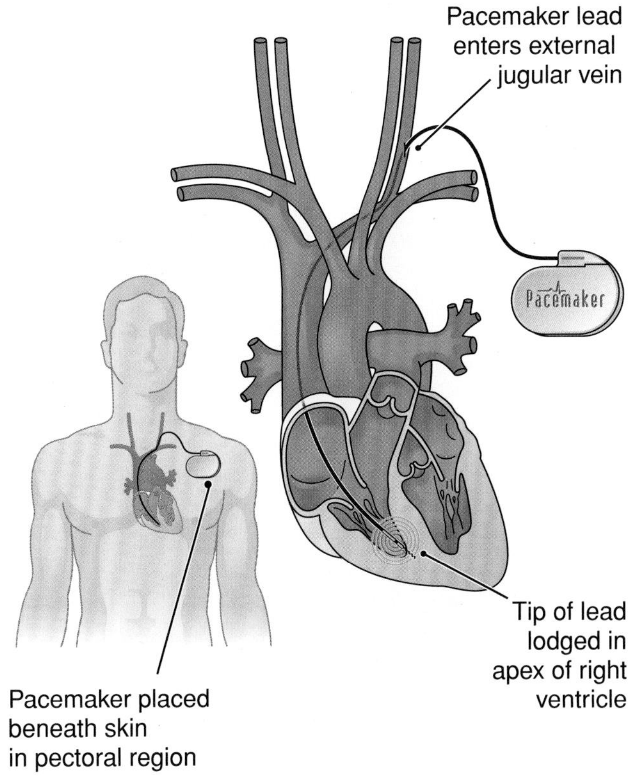

MI is also a common cause of **fibrillation**, an extremely rapid, ineffective heartbeat, especially dangerous when it affects the ventricles. (C.L. in the opening case study had atrial fibrillation.) **Cardioversion** is the general term for restoration of a normal heart rhythm, either by drugs or application of electric current. Hospital personnel use external chest "paddles" for emergency electrical **defibrillation**. In addition to **cardiopulmonary resuscitation** (CPR), automated external defibrillators (AEDs) can help save lives when available for high-risk patients or in public places, such as malls, schools, churches, aircrafts, and sports venues. The AED detects fatal arrhythmia and automatically delivers a correct preprogrammed shock. An implantable cardioverter defibrillator (ICD), applied much like a pacemaker, detects potential fibrillation and automatically shocks the heart to restore normal rhythm.

A newer approach to the treatment of heart rhythm irregularities is cardiac **ablation**, destruction of that portion of the conduction pathway that is involved in the arrhythmia. Electrode catheter ablation uses high-frequency sound waves, freezing (cryoablation), or electrical energy delivered through an intravascular catheter to ablate a defect in the conduction pathway.

Heart Failure

The general term **heart failure** refers to any condition in which the heart fails to empty effectively. The resulting increased pressure in the venous system leads to **edema**, justifying the description *congestive heart failure* (CHF). Left-side failure results in pulmonary edema with breathing difficulties (dyspnea); right-side failure causes peripheral edema with tissue swelling, especially in the legs, along with weight gain from fluid retention. Other symptoms of CHF are **cyanosis** and **syncope** (fainting).

Heart failure is treated with rest, drugs to strengthen heart contractions, diuretics to eliminate fluid, and restriction of salt in the diet.

> See the Student Resources on thePoint for a clinical picture of acute myocardial infarction and to view the animation "Heart Failure."

Heart failure is one cause of **shock**, a severe disturbance in the circulatory system resulting in inadequate blood delivery to the tissues. Shock is classified according to cause as:

- Cardiogenic shock, caused by heart failure
- Hypovolemic shock, caused by loss of blood volume
- Septic shock, caused by bacterial infection
- Anaphylactic shock, caused by severe allergic reaction

Congenital Heart Disease

A congenital defect is any defect that is present at birth. The most common type of congenital heart defect is a **septal defect**, a hole in the septum (wall) that separates the

Figure 9-16 Placement of a pacemaker. The lead is placed in an atrium or ventricle, usually on the right side. A dual-chamber pacemaker has leads in both chambers.

Pacemaker lead enters external jugular vein

Pacemaker

Tip of lead lodged in apex of right ventricle

Pacemaker placed beneath skin in pectoral region

Bundle of His

Bundle branches

AV node

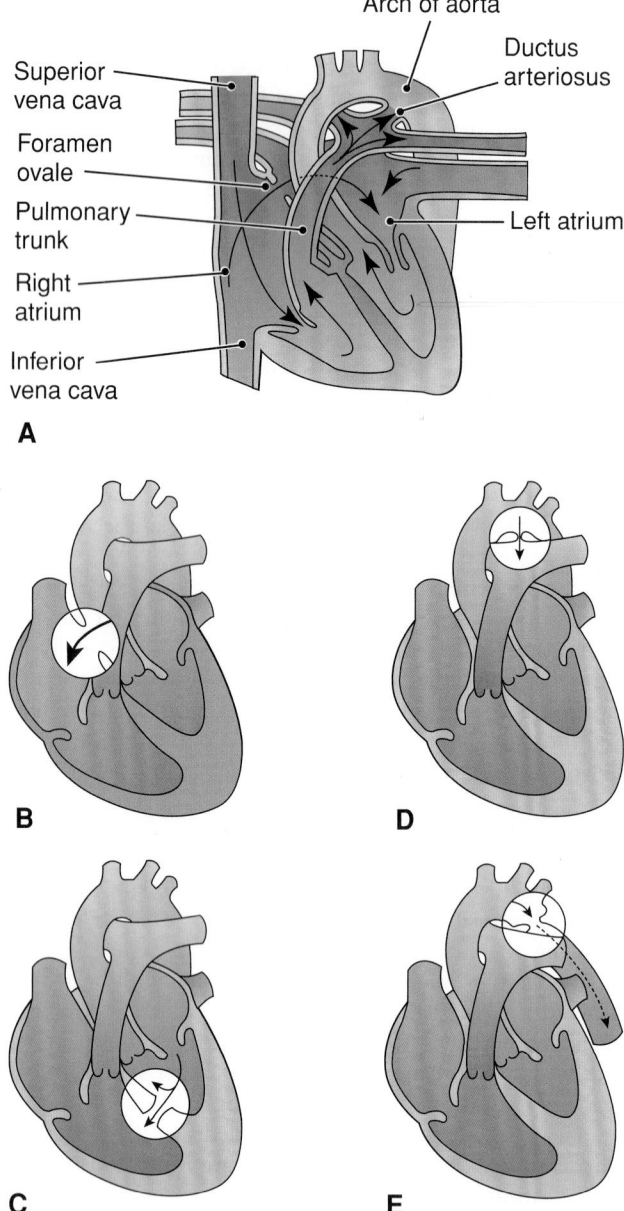

Figure 9-17 **Congenital heart defects. A.** Normal fetal heart showing the foramen ovale and ductus arteriosus. **B.** Persistence of the foramen ovale results in an atrial septal defect. **C.** A ventricular septal defect. **D.** Persistence of the ductus arteriosus (patent ductus arteriosus) forces blood back into the pulmonary artery. **E.** Coarctation of the aorta restricts outward blood flow in the aorta.

atria or the septum that separates the ventricles (**Fig. 9-17**). An atrial septal defect often results from persistence of an opening, the foramen ovale, that allows blood to bypass the lungs in fetal circulation. A septal defect permits blood to shunt from the left to the right side of the heart and return to the lungs instead of flowing out to the body. The heart has to work harder to meet the tissue's oxygen needs. Symptoms of septal defect include cyanosis (leading to the description "blue baby"), syncope, and **clubbing** of the fingers.

Another congenital defect that results from persistence of a fetal modification is **patent ductus arteriosus** (see **Fig. 9-17D**). In this case, a small bypass between the pulmonary artery and the aorta fails to close at birth. Blood then can flow from the aorta to the pulmonary artery and return to the lungs.

Heart valve malformation is another type of congenital heart defect. Failure of a valve to open or close properly is evidenced by a **murmur,** an abnormal sound heard as the heart cycles. A localized aortic narrowing, or **coarctation of the aorta,** is a congenital defect that restricts blood flow through that vessel (see **Fig. 9-17E**). Most of the congenital defects described can be corrected surgically.

Rheumatic Heart Disease

In **rheumatic heart disease,** infection with a specific type of *Streptococcus* sets up an immune reaction that ultimately damages the heart valves. The infection usually begins as a "strep throat," and most often the mitral valve is involved. Scar tissue fuses the valve's leaflets, causing a narrowing or **stenosis** that interferes with proper function. People with rheumatic heart disease are subject to repeated valvular infections and may need to take antibiotics prophylactically (preventively) before invasive medical or dental procedures. Severe cases of rheumatic heart disease may require surgical correction or even valve replacement. The incidence of rheumatic heart disease has declined with the use of antibiotics.

DISORDERS OF THE VEINS

A breakdown in the valves of the veins in combination with a chronic dilatation of these vessels results in **varicose veins** (**Fig. 9-18**). These appear twisted and swollen under the skin, most commonly in the legs. Contributing factors include heredity, obesity, prolonged standing, and

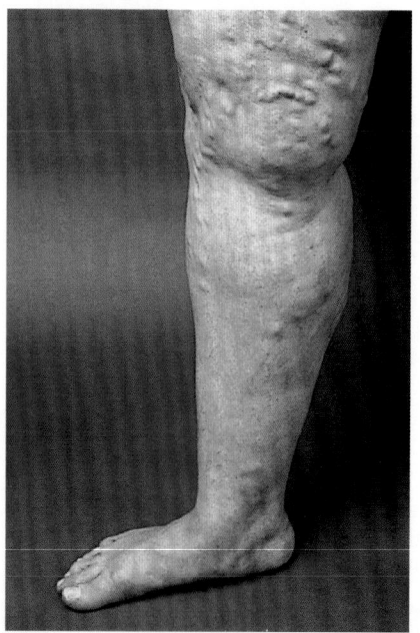

Figure 9-18 **Varicose veins.**

pregnancy, which increase pressure in the pelvic veins. Varicosities can impede blood flow and lead to edema, thrombosis, hemorrhage, or ulceration. Treatment includes the wearing of elastic stockings and, in some cases, surgical removal of the varicose veins, after which collateral circulation is naturally established. A varicose vein in the rectum or anal canal is referred to as a **hemorrhoid**.

Phlebitis is any inflammation of the veins and may be caused by infection, injury, poor circulation, or damage to valves in the veins. Such inflammation typically initiates blood clot formation, resulting in **thrombophlebitis**. Any veins are subject to thrombophlebitis, but the more serious condition involves the deep veins as opposed to the superficial veins, in the condition termed **deep vein thrombosis (DVT)**. The most common sites for DVT are the deep leg veins, causing serious reduction in venous drainage from these areas.

Vascular technologists obtain information on the blood vessels and circulation to aid in diagnosis. See **Box 9-3** for information on this career.

HEALTH PROFESSIONS   Box 9-3

Vascular Technologists

Vascular technologists perform noninvasive diagnostic studies to evaluate the blood vessels (arteries and veins) in the head, neck, extremities, and abdomen to help physicians diagnose vascular disorders. Vascular technologists obtain two-dimensional images of the blood vessels using ultrasound and measure the velocity and direction of blood flow using Doppler ultrasound. They use other instrumentation to measure blood pressure, changes in blood volume, and the blood's oxygen saturation.

Most vascular technologists work in hospitals, where they prepare patients for tests, take clinical histories, perform limited physical examinations, carry out diagnostic tests, and report results. They may also work in offices, clinics, or laboratories. Although most of their patients are elderly, vascular studies may be required on patients of any age.

Unlike early workers in this field who were often trained on the job, vascular technologists today complete a two- or four-year educational program accredited by the Commission on Accreditation of Allied Health Education Programs (CAAHEP). Certification specific to vascular technology is available from the American Registry for Diagnostic Medical Sonography at www.ardms.org and from other organizations. Certification requires appropriate education, clinical experience, examination, and continuing education. Certification will be a requirement of all vascular technologists working in IAC (Intersocietal Accreditation Commission) accredited vascular laboratories beginning in 2017. Additional information on this career is available from the Society for Vascular Ultrasound at www.svunet.org.

Terminology   Key Terms

Cardiovascular Disorders

aneurysm AN-u-rizm	A localized abnormal dilation of a blood vessel, usually an artery, caused by weakness of the vessel wall; may eventually burst
angina pectoris an-JI-nah PEK-to-ris	A feeling of constriction around the heart or pain that may radiate to the left arm or shoulder, usually brought on by exertion; caused by insufficient blood supply to the heart
arrhythmia ah-RITH-me-ah	Any abnormality in the rate or rhythm of the heartbeat (literally "without rhythm;" note doubled r); also called dysrhythmia
arteriosclerosis ar-tere-e-o-skler-O-sis	Hardening (sclerosis) of the arteries, with loss of capacity and loss of elasticity, as from fatty deposits (plaque), deposit of calcium salts, or scar tissue formation
atherosclerosis ath-er-o-skler-O-sis	The development of fatty, fibrous patches (plaques) in the lining of arteries, causing narrowing of the lumen and hardening of the vessel wall; the most common form of arteriosclerosis (hardening of the arteries) (root ather/o means "porridge" or "gruel")
bradycardia brad-e-KAR-de-ah	A slow heart rate of less than 60 bpm
cerebrovascular accident (CVA) ser-eh-bro-VAS-ku-lar	Sudden damage to the brain resulting from reduction of blood flow; causes include atherosclerosis, embolism, thrombosis, or hemorrhage from a ruptured aneurysm; commonly called stroke

(continued)

Terminology | Key Terms (*Continued*)

clubbing KLUB-*ing*	Enlargement of the ends of the fingers and toes caused by growth of the soft tissue around the nails (see **Fig. 7-12**); seen in a variety of diseases in which there is poor peripheral circulation
coarctation of the aorta ko-ark-TA-shun	Localized narrowing of the aorta with restriction of blood flow (see **Fig. 9-17E**)
C-reactive protein (CRP)	Protein produced during systemic inflammation, which may contribute to atherosclerosis; high CRP levels can indicate cardiovascular disease and its prognosis
cyanosis si-ah-NO-sis	Bluish discoloration of the skin caused by lack of oxygen (see **Fig. 3-4**)
deep vein thrombosis (DVT)	Thrombophlebitis involving the deep veins
diaphoresis di-ah-fo-RE-sis	Profuse sweating
dissecting aneurysm	An aneurysm in which blood enters the arterial wall and separates the layers; usually involves the aorta (see **Fig. 9-9**)
dyslipidemia dis-lip-ih-DE-me-ah	Disorder in serum lipid levels, which is an important factor in development of atherosclerosis; includes hyperlipidemia (high lipids), hypercholesterolemia (high cholesterol), and hypertriglyceridemia (high triglycerides)
dyspnea DISP-ne-ah	Difficult or labored breathing (-pnea)
edema eh-DE-mah	Swelling of body tissues caused by the presence of excess fluid (see **Fig. 6-4**); causes include cardiovascular disturbances, kidney failure, inflammation, and malnutrition
embolism EM-bo-lizm	Obstruction of a blood vessel by a blood clot or other matter carried in the circulation
embolus EM-bo-lus	A mass carried in the circulation; usually a blood clot, but also may be air, fat, bacteria, or other solid matter from within or from outside the body
fibrillation fih-brih-LA-shun	Spontaneous, quivering, and ineffectual contraction of muscle fibers, as in the atria or the ventricles
heart block	An interference in the electrical conduction system of the heart resulting in arrhythmia (see **Fig. 9-15**)
heart failure	A condition caused by the inability of the heart to maintain adequate blood circulation
hemorrhoid HEM-o-royd	A varicose vein in the rectum
hypertension hi-per-TEN-shun	A condition of higher-than-normal blood pressure; essential (primary, idiopathic) hypertension has no known cause
infarct in-FARKT	An area of localized tissue necrosis (death) resulting from a blockage or a narrowing of the artery that supplies the area
ischemia is-KE-me-ah	Local deficiency of blood supply caused by circulatory obstruction (root: hem/o)
murmur	An abnormal heart sound
myocardial infarction (MI) mi-o-KAR-de-al in-FARK-shun	Localized necrosis (death) of cardiac muscle tissue resulting from blockage or narrowing of the coronary artery that supplies that area; myocardial infarction is usually caused by formation of a thrombus (clot) in a vessel (see **Fig. 9-14**)

Terminology | Key Terms (*Continued*)

occlusion *o-KLU-zhun*	A closing off or obstruction, as of a vessel
patent ductus arteriosus *PA-tent DUK-tus ar-tere-e-O-sus*	Persistence of the ductus arteriosus after birth; the ductus arteriosus is a vessel that connects the pulmonary artery to the descending aorta in the fetus to bypass the lungs (see **Fig. 9-17D**)
phlebitis *fleh-BI-tis*	Inflammation of a vein
plaque *plak*	A patch; with regard to the cardiovascular system, a deposit of fatty material and other substances on a vessel wall that impedes blood flow and may block the vessel; atheromatous plaque
rheumatic heart disease *ru-MAT-ik*	Damage to heart valves after infection with a type of *Streptococcus* (group A hemolytic *Streptococcus*); the antibodies produced in response to the infection produce valvular scarring usually involving the mitral valve
septal defect *SEP-tal*	An opening in the septum between the atria or ventricles; a common cause is persistence of the foramen ovale (*for-A-men o-VAL-e*), an opening between the atria that bypasses the lungs in fetal circulation (see **Fig. 9-17B,C**)
shock	Circulatory failure resulting in an inadequate blood supply to the tissues; cardiogenic shock is caused by heart failure; hypovolemic shock is caused by a loss of blood volume; septic shock is caused by bacterial infection
stenosis *steh-NO-sis*	Constriction or narrowing of an opening
stroke	See cerebrovascular accident
syncope *SIN-ko-pe*	A temporary loss of consciousness caused by inadequate blood flow to the brain; fainting
tachycardia *tak-ih-KAR-de-ah*	An abnormally rapid heart rate, usually over 100 bpm
thrombophlebitis *throm-bo-fleh-BI-tis*	Inflammation of a vein associated with formation of a blood clot
thrombosis *throm-BO-sis*	Development of a blood clot within a vessel
thrombus *THROM-bus*	A blood clot that forms within a blood vessel (root: thromb/o)
varicose vein *VAR-ih-kose*	A twisted and swollen vein resulting from breakdown of the valves, pooling of blood, and chronic dilatation of the vessel (root: varic/o); also called varix (VAR-iks) or varicosity (*var-ih-KOS-ih-te*) (see **Fig. 9-18**)

Diagnosis and Treatment

ablation *ab-LA-shun*	Removal or destruction. In cardiac ablation, a catheter is used to destroy a portion of the heart's conduction pathway to correct an arrhythmia
angioplasty *AN-je-o-plas-te*	A procedure that reopens a narrowed vessel and restores blood flow; commonly accomplished by surgically removing plaque, inflating a balloon within the vessel, or installing a device (stent) to keep the vessel open (see **Figs. 9-10** to **9-12**)
artificial pacemaker	A battery-operated device that generates electrical impulses to regulate the heartbeat; it may be external or implanted, may be designed to respond to need, and may have the capacity to prevent tachycardia (see **Fig. 9-16**)

(continued)

Terminology	Key Terms *(Continued)*

cardiopulmonary resuscitation (CPR) *re-sus-ih-TA-shun*	Restoration of cardiac output and pulmonary ventilation after cardiac arrest using artificial respiration and chest compression or cardiac massage
cardioversion *KAR-de-o-ver-zhun*	Correction of an abnormal cardiac rhythm; may be accomplished pharmacologically, with antiarrhythmic drugs, or by application of electric current (see defibrillation)
coronary angiography *an-je-OG-rah-fe*	Radiographic study of the coronary arteries after introduction of an opaque dye by means of a catheter threaded through blood vessels into the heart (see **Fig. 9-10**)
coronary artery bypass graft (CABG)	Surgical creation of a shunt to bypass a blocked coronary artery; the aorta is connected to a point past the obstruction with another vessel or a piece of another vessel, usually the left internal mammary artery or part of the leg's saphenous vein (see **Fig. 9-13**)
coronary calcium scan	Method for visualizing vessel-narrowing calcium deposits in coronary arteries; useful for diagnosing coronary artery disease in people at moderate risk or those who have undiagnosed chest pain; also known as a heart scan
creatine kinase MB (CK-MB) *KRE-ah-tin KI-naze*	Enzyme released in increased amounts from cardiac muscle cells following myocardial infarction (MI); serum assays help diagnose MI and determine the extent of muscle damage
CT angiography (CTA)	Computed tomography scan used to visualize vessels in the heart and other organs; requires only a small amount of dye injected into the arm; can rule out blocked coronary arteries that may cause a myocardial infarction (heart attack) in people with chest pain or abnormal stress tests
defibrillation *de-fib-rih-LA-shun*	Use of an electronic device (defibrillator) to stop fibrillation by delivering a brief electric shock to the heart; the shock may be delivered to the surface of the chest, as by an automated external defibrillator (AED), or directly into the heart through wire leads, using an implantable cardioverter defibrillator (ICD)
echocardiography *ek-o-kar-de-OG-rah-fe*	A noninvasive method that uses ultrasound to visualize internal cardiac structures
lipoprotein *lip-o-PRO-tene*	A compound of protein with lipid; lipoproteins are classified according to density as very low-density (VLDL), low-density (LDL), and high-density (HDL); relatively higher levels of HDLs have been correlated with cardiovascular health
percutaneous transluminal coronary angioplasty (PTCA)	Dilatation of a sclerotic blood vessel by means of a balloon catheter inserted into the vessel and then inflated to flatten plaque against the arterial wall (see **Fig. 9-11**)
stent	A small metal device in the shape of a coil or slotted tube that is placed inside an artery to keep the vessel open after balloon angioplasty (see **Fig. 9-12**)
stress test	Evaluation of physical fitness by continuous ECG monitoring during exercise; in a thallium stress test, a radioactive isotope of thallium is administered to trace blood flow through the heart during exercise
troponin (Tn) *tro-PO-nin*	A protein in muscle cells that regulates contraction; increased serum levels, primarily in the forms TnT and TnI, indicate recent myocardial infarction (MI)

The Lymphatic System

The **lymphatic system** is a widely distributed system with multiple functions (**Fig. 9-19**). Its role in circulation is to return excess fluid and proteins from the tissues to the bloodstream. Blind-ended lymphatic capillaries pick up these materials in the tissues and carry them into larger vessels (**Fig. 9-20**). The fluid carried in the lymphatic system is called **lymph**. Lymph drains from the lower part of the body and the upper left side into the **thoracic duct** (left lymphatic duct), which travels upward through the chest and empties into the left subclavian vein near the heart (see **Fig. 9-19**). The **right lymphatic duct** drains the body's upper right side and empties into the right subclavian vein.

Another major function of the lymphatic system is to protect the body from impurities and invading microorganisms (see discussion of immunity in Chapter 10).

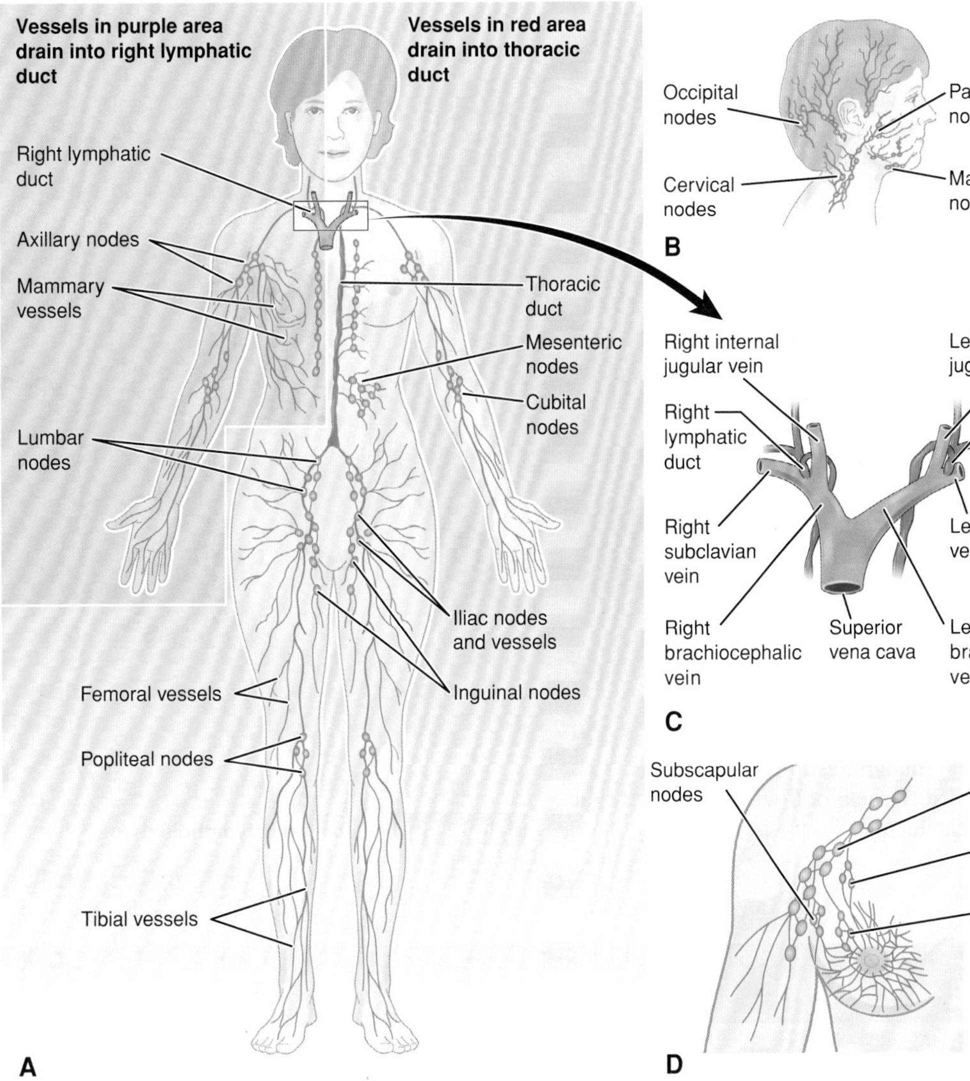

Vessels in purple area drain into right lymphatic duct

Vessels in red area drain into thoracic duct

Right lymphatic duct

Axillary nodes

Mammary vessels

Thoracic duct

Mesenteric nodes

Cubital nodes

Lumbar nodes

Iliac nodes and vessels

Inguinal nodes

Femoral vessels

Popliteal nodes

Tibial vessels

A

Occipital nodes

Parotid nodes

Cervical nodes

Mandibular nodes

B

Right internal jugular vein

Left internal jugular vein

Right lymphatic duct

Thoracic duct

Right subclavian vein

Left subclavian vein

Right brachiocephalic vein

Superior vena cava

Left brachiocephalic vein

C

Subscapular nodes

Axillary nodes

Interpectoral nodes

Mammary nodes

D

Figure 9-19 **Lymphatic system. A.** Lymphatic vessels drain almost every area of the body. Lymph nodes are distributed along the path of the vessels. Areas draining into the right lymphatic duct are shown in *purple*; areas draining into the thoracic duct are shown in *red*. **B.** Lymph nodes and vessels of the head. **C.** Drainage of the right lymphatic duct and thoracic duct into the subclavian veins. **D.** Lymph nodes and vessels of the breast, mammary glands, and surrounding areas.

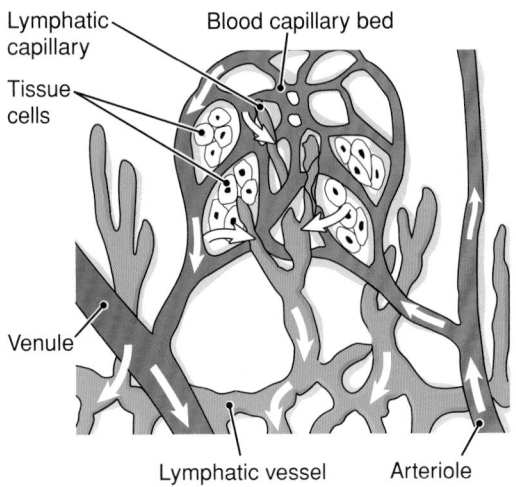

Lymphatic capillary

Blood capillary bed

Tissue cells

Venule

Lymphatic vessel

Arteriole

Figure 9-20 **Lymphatic drainage in the tissues.** Lymphatic capillaries pick up fluid and proteins left in the tissues and carry them back to the bloodstream.

Along the path of the lymphatic vessels are small masses of lymphoid tissue, the **lymph nodes** (**Fig. 9-21**). Their function is to filter the lymph as it passes through. They are concentrated in the cervical (neck), axillary (armpit), mediastinal (chest), and inguinal (groin) regions. Other protective organs and tissues of the lymphatic system include the following:

- **Tonsils,** located in the throat (pharynx). They filter inhaled or swallowed materials and aid in immunity early in life. The tonsils are further discussed in Chapter 11.
- **Thymus,** in the chest, above the heart. It processes and stimulates lymphocytes active in immunity.
- **Spleen,** in the upper left region of the abdomen. It filters blood and destroys old red blood cells.
- **Appendix,** attached to the large intestine. It may aid in the development of immunity.
- **Peyer patches,** in the lining of the intestine. They help protect against invading microorganisms.

See the Student Resources on thePoint for a chart summarizing lymphoid tissue.

A final function of the lymphatic system is to absorb digested fats from the small intestine (see Chapter 12). These fats are then added to the blood with the lymph that drains from the thoracic duct.

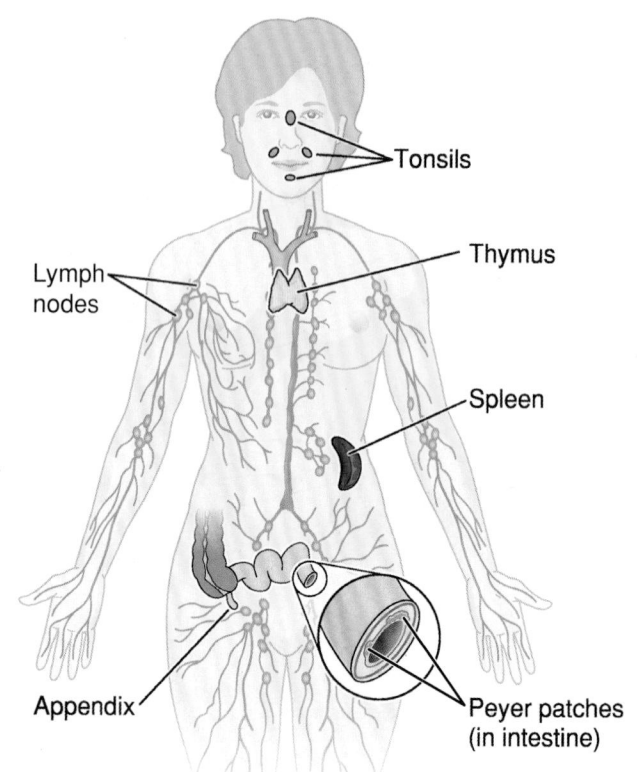

Figure 9-21   **Location of lymphoid tissue.**

Terminology | Key Terms

Lymphatic System
Normal Structure and Function

appendix *ah-PEN-diks*	A small, finger-like mass of lymphoid tissue attached to the first part of the large intestine
lymph *limf*	The thin, plasma-like fluid that drains from the tissues and is transported in lymphatic vessels (root: lymph/o)
lymph node	A small mass of lymphoid tissue along the path of a lymphatic vessel that filters lymph (root: lymphaden/o)
lymphatic system *lim-FAT-ik*	The system that drains fluid and proteins from the tissues and returns them to the bloodstream; this system also participates in immunity and aids in absorption of fats from the digestive tract
Peyer patches *PI-er*	Aggregates of lymphoid tissue in the lining of the intestine
right lymphatic duct	The lymphatic duct that drains fluid from the body's upper right side
spleen	A large reddish-brown organ in the upper left region of the abdomen; it filters blood and destroys old red blood cells (root: splen/o)
thoracic duct	The lymphatic duct that drains fluid from the upper left side of the body and all of the lower body; left lymphatic duct

Terminology	Key Terms (*Continued*)

thymus THI-mus	A lymphoid organ in the upper part of the chest beneath the sternum; it functions in immunity (root: thym/o)
tonsil TON-sil	Small mass of lymphoid tissue located in region of the throat (pharynx)

> Go to the Audio Pronunciation Glossary in the Student Resources on thePoint to hear these terms pronounced.

Roots Pertaining to the Lymphatic System

See Table 9-3.

Table 9-3	Roots for the Lymphatic System

Root	Meaning	Example	Definition of Example
lymph/o	lymph, lymphatic system	lymphoid LIM-foyd	resembling lymph or lymphatic tissue
lymphaden/o	lymph node	lymphadenitis lim-fad-eh-NI-tis	inflammation of a lymph node
lymphangi/o	lymphatic vessel	lymphangiogram lim-FAN-je-o-gram	x-ray image of lymphatic vessels
splen/o	spleen	splenalgia sple-NAL-je-ah	pain in the spleen
thym/o	thymus	athymia ah-THI-me-ah	absence of the thymus
tonsil/o	tonsil	tonsillar TON-sil-ar	pertaining to a tonsil

EXERCISE 9-3

Fill in the blanks.

1. Tonsillectomy (*ton-sil-EK-to-me*) is surgical removal of a(n) _____.

2. Thymopathy (*thi-MOP-ah-the*) is any disease of the _____.

3. Lymphadenectomy (*lim-fad-eh-NEK-to-me*) is surgical removal of a(n) _____.

4. Lymphedema (*limf-eh-DE-mah*) means swelling caused by obstruction of the flow of _____.

5. A lymphangioma (*lim-fan-je-O-mah*) is a tumor of _____.

6. Splenic (*SPLEN-ik*) means pertaining to the _____.

(continued)

EXERCISE 9-3   *(Continued)*

Identify and define the root in the following words.

	Root	Meaning of Root
7. lymphangial (*lim-FAN-je-al*)	_____	_____
8. perisplenitis (*per-e-sple-NI-tis*)	_____	_____
9. lymphadenography (*lim-fad-eh-NOG-rah-fe*)	_____	_____
10. tonsillectomy (*ton-sil-EK-to-me*)	_____	_____
11. hypothymism (*hi-po-THI-mizm*)	_____	_____

Use the appropriate root to write words with the following meanings.

12. Enlargement (-megaly) of the spleen	_____	_____
13. Inflammation of a tonsil	_____	_____
14. Any disease (-pathy) of the lymph nodes	_____	_____
15. Inflammation of lymphatic vessels	_____	_____
16. Pertaining to (-ic) the thymus	_____	_____
17. A tumor (-oma) of lymphatic tissue	_____	_____

Clinical Aspects of the Lymphatic System

Changes in the lymphatic system are often related to infection and may consist of inflammation and enlargement of the nodes, called **lymphadenitis**, or inflammation of the vessels, called **lymphangitis**. Obstruction of lymphatic vessels because of surgical excision or infection results in tissue swelling, or **lymphedema** (**Box 9-4**). Any neoplastic disease involving lymph nodes is termed **lymphoma**. These neoplastic disorders affect the white blood cells found in the lymphatic system, and they are discussed more fully in Chapter 10.

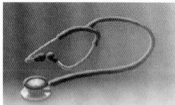

CLINICAL PERSPECTIVES

Box 9-4

Lymphedema: When Lymph Stops Flowing

Fluid balance in the body requires appropriate distribution of fluid among the cardiovascular system, lymphatic system, and the tissues. Edema occurs when the balance is tipped toward excess fluid in the tissues. Often, edema is due to heart failure. However, blockage of lymphatic vessels (with resulting fluid accumulation in the tissues) can cause another form of edema, called lymphedema. The clinical hallmark of lymphedema is chronic swelling of an arm or leg, whereas heart failure usually causes swelling of both legs.

Lymphedema may be either primary or secondary. Primary lymphedema is a rare congenital condition caused by abnormal development of lymphatic vessels. Secondary lymphedema, or acquired lymphedema, can develop as a result of trauma to a limb, surgery, radiation therapy, or infection of the lymphatic vessels (lymphangitis). One of the most common causes of lymphedema is the removal of axillary lymph nodes during mastectomy, which disrupts lymph flow from the adjacent arm. Lymphedema may also occur following prostate surgery.

Therapies that encourage the flow of fluid through the lymphatic vessels are useful in treating lymphedema. These therapies may include elevation of the affected limb, manual lymphatic drainage through massage, light exercise, and firm wrapping of the limb to apply compression. In addition, changes in daily habits can lessen the effects of lymphedema. For example, further blockage of lymph drainage can be prevented by wearing loose clothing and jewelry, carrying a purse or handbag on the unaffected arm, and not crossing the legs when sitting. Lymphangitis requires the use of appropriate antibiotics. Prompt treatment is necessary because in addition to swelling, other complications include poor wound healing, skin ulcers, and increased risk of infection.

Terminology   Key Clinical Terms

Lymphatic Disorders

lymphadenitis lim-fad-eh-NI-tis	Inflammation and enlargement of lymph nodes, usually as a result of infection
lymphangitis lim-fan-JI-tis	Inflammation of lymphatic vessels as a result of bacterial infection; appears as painful red streaks under the skin (**Fig. 9-22**)
lymphedema lim-feh-DE-mah	Swelling of tissues with lymph caused by obstruction or excision of lymphatic vessels (**Fig. 9-22B** and **Box 9-4**)
lymphoma lim-FO-mah	Any neoplastic disease of lymphoid tissue

9

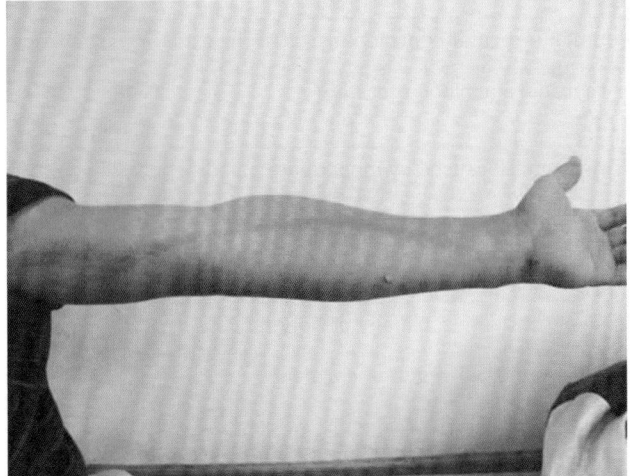
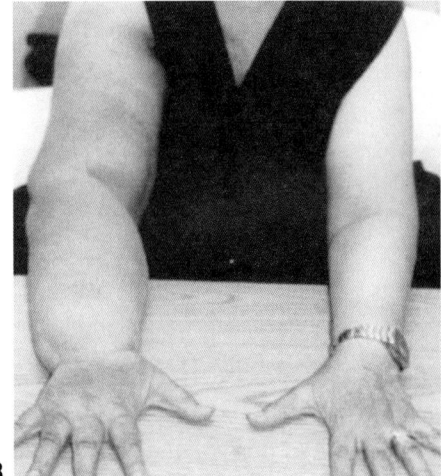

A   B

Figure 9-22 **Lymphatic disorders. A.** Lymphangitis is inflammation of lymphatic vessels. Note the linear red streak proximal to a skin infection. **B.** Lymphedema of the upper right extremity following removal of axillary lymph nodes and blockage of lymph flow.

Terminology   Supplementary Terms

Normal Structure and Function

apical pulse AP-ih-kal	Pulse felt or heard over the heart's apex; it is measured in the fifth left intercostal space (between the ribs) about 8 to 9 cm from the midline
cardiac output	The amount of blood pumped from the right or left ventricle per minute
Korotkoff sounds ko-ROT-kof	Arterial sounds heard with a stethoscope during determination of blood pressure with a cuff
perfusion per-FU-zhun	The passage of fluid, such as blood, through an organ or tissue
precordium pre-KOR-de-um	The anterior region over the heart and the lower part of the thorax; adjective: precordial
pulse pressure	The difference between systolic and diastolic pressure
stroke volume	The amount of blood ejected by the left ventricle with each beat

(continued)

Terminology   Supplementary Terms *(Continued)*

Valsalva maneuver *val-SAL-vah*	Bearing down, as in childbirth or defecation, by attempting to exhale forcefully with the nose and throat closed; this action has an effect on the cardiovascular system

Symptoms and Conditions

bruit *brwe*	An abnormal sound heard in auscultation
cardiac tamponade *tam-pon-ADE*	Pathologic accumulation of fluid in the pericardial sac; may result from pericarditis or injury to the heart or great vessels
ectopic beat *ek-TOP-ik*	A heartbeat that originates from some part of the heart other than the SA node
extrasystole *eks-trah-SIS-to-le*	Premature heart contraction that occurs separately from the normal beat and originates from a part of the heart other than the SA node
flutter	Very rapid (200–300 bpm) but regular contractions, as in the atria or the ventricles
hypotension *hi-po-TEN-shun*	A condition of lower-than-normal blood pressure
intermittent claudication *claw-dih-KA-shun*	Pain in a muscle during exercise caused by inadequate blood supply; the pain disappears with rest
mitral valve prolapse *PRO-laps*	Movement of the mitral valve cusps into the left atrium when the ventricles contract
occlusive vascular disease	Arteriosclerotic disease of the vessels, usually peripheral vessels
palpitation *pal-pih-TA-shun*	A sensation of abnormally rapid or irregular heartbeat
pitting edema	Edema that retains the impression of a finger pressed firmly into the skin (**Fig. 9-23**)

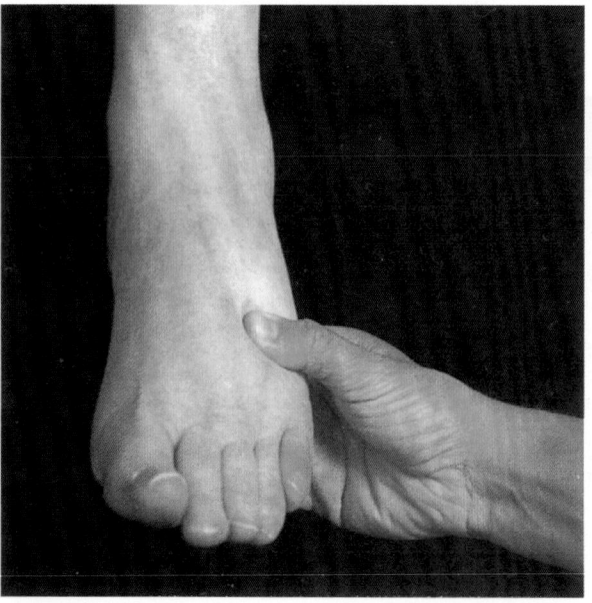 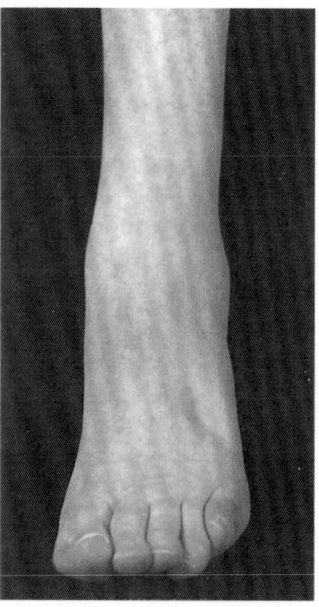

A   B

Figure 9-23   **Pitting edema.** When the skin is pressed firmly with the finger (**A**), a pit remains after the finger is removed (**B**).

Terminology	Supplementary Terms (Continued)

polyarteritis nodosa *no-DO-sah*	Potentially fatal collagen disease causing inflammation of small visceral arteries; symptoms depend on the organ affected
Raynaud disease *ra-NO*	A disorder characterized by abnormal constriction of peripheral vessels in the arms and legs on exposure to cold
regurgitation *re-gur-jih-TA-shun*	A backward flow, such as the backflow of blood through a defective valve
stasis *STA-sis*	Stoppage of normal flow, as of blood or urine; blood stasis may lead to dermatitis and ulcer formation
subacute bacterial endocarditis (SBE)	Bacterial growth in a heart or valves previously damaged by rheumatic fever
tetralogy of Fallot *fal-O*	A combination of four congenital heart abnormalities: pulmonary artery stenosis, interventricular septal defect, displacement of the aorta to the right, and right ventricular hypertrophy
thromboangiitis obliterans	Inflammation and thrombus formation resulting in occlusion of small vessels, especially in the legs; most common in young men and correlated with heavy smoking; thrombotic occlusion of leg vessels may lead to gangrene of the feet; patients show a hypersensitivity to tobacco; also called Buerger disease
vegetation	Irregular bacterial outgrowths on the heart valves; associated with rheumatic fever
Wolff–Parkinson–White syndrome (WPW)	A cardiac arrhythmia consisting of tachycardia and a premature ventricular beat caused by an alternative conduction pathway

Diagnosis

cardiac catheterization	Passage of a catheter into the heart through a vessel to inject a contrast medium for imaging, diagnosis, obtaining samples, or measuring pressure
central venous pressure (CVP)	Pressure in the superior vena cava
cineangiocardiography *sin-eh-an-je-o-kar-de-OG-rah-fe*	The photographic recording of fluoroscopic images of the heart and large vessels using motion picture techniques
Doppler echocardiography	An imaging method used to study the rate and pattern of blood flow
Holter monitor	A portable device that can record from 24 hours to one month of an individual's ECG readings during normal activity
homocysteine *ho-mo-SIS-te-ene*	An amino acid in the blood that at higher-than-normal levels is associated with increased risk of cardiovascular disease
phlebotomist *fleh-BOT-o-mist*	Technician who specializes in drawing blood
phonocardiography *fo-no-kar-de-OG-rah-fe*	Electronic recording of heart sounds
plethysmography *pleh-thiz-MOG-rah-fe*	Measurement of changes in the size of a part based on the amount of blood contained in or passing through it; impedance plethysmography measures changes in electrical resistance and is used in the diagnosis of deep vein thrombosis
pulmonary capillary wedge pressure (PCWP)	Pressure measured by a catheter in a branch of the pulmonary artery. It is an indirect measure of pressure in the left atrium (see **Box 9-2**)
radionuclide heart scan	Imaging of the heart after injection of a radioactive isotope; the PYP (pyrophosphate) scan using technetium-99 m (^{99m}Tc) is used to test for myocardial infarction because the isotope is taken up by damaged tissue; the MUGA (multigated acquisition) scan gives information on heart function

(continued)

Terminology	Supplementary Terms *(Continued)*
Swan–Ganz catheter	A cardiac catheter with a balloon at the tip that is used to measure pulmonary arterial pressure; it is flow guided through a vein into the right side of the heart and then into the pulmonary artery
transesophageal echocardiography (TEE)	Use of an ultrasound transducer placed endoscopically into the esophagus to obtain images of the heart
triglyceride *tri-GLIS-er-ide*	Simple fat that circulates in the bloodstream
ventriculography *ven-trik-u-LOG-rah-fe*	X-ray study of the heart's ventricles after introduction of an opaque dye by means of a catheter

Treatment and Surgical Procedures

atherectomy *ath-er-EK-to-me*	Removal of atheromatous plaque from the lining of a vessel; may be done by open surgery or through the vessel's lumen
commissurotomy *kom-ih-shur-OT-o-me*	Surgical incision of a scarred mitral valve to increase the size of the valvular opening
embolectomy *em-bo-LEK-to-me*	Surgical removal of an embolus
intraaortic balloon pump (IABP)	A mechanical assist device that consists of an inflatable balloon pump inserted through the femoral artery into the thoracic aorta; it inflates during diastole to improve coronary circulation and deflates before systole to allow blood ejection from the heart
ventricular assist device (VAD)	A pump that takes over a ventricle's function in delivering blood into the pulmonary or systemic circuit; these devices are used to assist patients awaiting heart transplantation or those who are recovering from heart failure; most common is a left ventricular assist device (LVAD)

Drugs

angiotensin-converting enzyme (ACE) inhibitor	A drug that lowers blood pressure by blocking the formation of angiotensin II, a substance that normally acts to increase blood pressure
angiotensin receptor blocker (ARB)	A drug that blocks tissue receptors for angiotensin II; angiotensin II receptor antagonist
antiarrhythmic agent	A drug that regulates the rate and rhythm of the heartbeat
beta-adrenergic blocking agent	Drug that decreases the rate and strength of heart contractions; beta-blocker
calcium-channel blocker	Drug that controls the rate and force of heart contraction by regulating calcium entrance into the cells
digitalis *dij-ih-TAL-is*	A drug that slows and strengthens heart muscle contractions
diuretic *di-u-RET-ik*	Drug that eliminates fluid by increasing the kidney's output of urine; lowered blood volume decreases the heart's workload
hypolipidemic agent *hi-po-lip-ih-DE-mik*	Drug that lowers serum cholesterol
lidocaine *LI-do-kane*	A local anesthetic that is used intravenously to treat cardiac arrhythmias

Terminology	Supplementary Terms *(Continued)*
loop diuretic	Drug that increases urine output by inhibiting electrolyte reabsorption in the kidney nephrons (loops) (see Chapter 13)
nitroglycerin *ni-tro-GLIS-er-in*	A drug used in the treatment of angina pectoris to dilate coronary vessels
statins	Drugs that act to lower lipids in the blood; the drug names end with -*statin*, such as lovastatin, pravastatin, and atorvastatin
streptokinase (SK) *strep-to-KI-nase*	An enzyme used to dissolve blood clots
tissue plasminogen activator (tPA)	A drug used to dissolve blood clots; it activates production of a substance (plasmin) in the blood that normally dissolves clots
vasodilator *vas-o-di-LA-tor*	A drug that widens blood vessels and improves blood flow

9

Terminology	Abbreviations

ACE	Angiotensin-converting enzyme	**CHD**	Coronary heart disease
AED	Automated external defibrillator	**CHF**	Congestive heart failure
AF	Atrial fibrillation	**CK-MB**	Creatine kinase MB
AMI	Acute myocardial infarction	**CPR**	Cardiopulmonary resuscitation
APC	Atrial premature complex	**CRP**	C-reactive protein
AR	Aortic regurgitation	**CTA**	Computed tomography angiography
ARB	Angiotensin receptor blocker	**CVA**	Cerebrovascular accident
AS	Aortic stenosis; arteriosclerosis	**CVD**	Cardiovascular disease
ASCVD	Arteriosclerotic cardiovascular disease	**CVI**	Chronic venous insufficiency
ASD	Atrial septal defect	**CVP**	Central venous pressure
ASHD	Arteriosclerotic heart disease	**DOE**	Dyspnea on exertion
AT	Atrial tachycardia	**DVT**	Deep vein thrombosis
AV	Atrioventricular	**ECG (EKG)**	Electrocardiogram, electrocardiography
BBB	Bundle branch block (left or right)	**HDL**	High-density lipoprotein
BP	Blood pressure	**hs-CRP**	High-sensitivity C-reactive protein (test)
bpm	Beats per minute	**HTN**	Hypertension
CABG	Coronary artery bypass graft	**IABP**	Intraaortic balloon pump
CAD	Coronary artery disease	**ICD**	Implantable cardioverter defibrillator
CCU	Coronary/cardiac care unit	**IVCD**	Intraventricular conduction delay

(continued)

Terminology   Abbreviations (Continued)

JVP	Jugular venous pulse		PTCA	Percutaneous transluminal coronary angioplasty
LAD	Left anterior descending (coronary artery)		PVC	Premature ventricular contraction
LAHB	Left anterior hemiblock		PVD	Peripheral vascular disease
LDL	Low-density lipoprotein		PYP	Pyrophosphate (scan)
LV	Left ventricle		S_1	First heart sound
LVAD	Left ventricular assist device		S_2	Second heart sound
LVEDP	Left ventricular end-diastolic pressure		SA	Sinoatrial
LVH	Left ventricular hypertrophy		SBE	Subacute bacterial endocarditis
MI	Myocardial infarction		SK	Streptokinase
mm Hg	Millimeters of mercury		SVT	Supraventricular tachycardia
MR	Mitral regurgitation, reflux		^{99m}Tc	Technetium-99 m
MS	Mitral stenosis		TEE	Transesophageal echocardiography
MUGA	Multigated acquisition (scan)		Tn	Troponin
MVP	Mitral valve prolapse		tPA	Tissue plasminogen activator
MVR	Mitral valve replacement		VAD	Ventricular assist device
NSR	Normal sinus rhythm		VF, v fib	Ventricular fibrillation
P	Pulse		VLDL	Very-low-density lipoprotein
PAC	Premature atrial contraction		VPC	Ventricular premature complex
PAP	Pulmonary arterial pressure		VSD	Ventricular septal defect
PCI	Percutaneous coronary intervention		VT	Ventricular tachycardia
PCWP	Pulmonary capillary wedge pressure		VTE	Venous thromboembolism
PMI	Point of maximal impulse		WPW	Wolff–Parkinson–White syndrome
PSVT	Paroxysmal supraventricular tachycardia			

Case Study Revisited

C.L.'s Follow-Up

C.L. underwent a successful ablation procedure without any complications, and he has not had a recurrence of the atrial fibrillation. C.L.'s preexisting heart condition prohibited him from performing required duties in the army, so he was not able to return to boot camp. He was released from the service and returned to civilian life.

Labeling Exercise

THE CARDIOVASCULAR SYSTEM

Write the name of each numbered part on the corresponding line of the answer sheet.

Aorta
Head and arms
Inferior vena cava
Internal organs
Left atrium
Left lung
Left pulmonary artery

Left pulmonary vein
Left ventricle
Legs
Right atrium
Right lung
Right ventricle
Superior vena cava

1. _____

2. _____

3. _____

4. _____

5. _____

6. _____

7. _____

8. _____

9. _____

10. _____

11. _____

12. _____

13. _____

14. _____

■ Blood high in oxygen
■ Blood low in oxygen

THE HEART AND GREAT VESSELS

Write the name of each numbered part on the corresponding line of the answer sheet.

Aortic arch
Aortic valve
Apex
Ascending aorta
Brachiocephalic artery
Endocardium
Epicardium
Inferior vena cava
Interventricular septum
Left atrium
Left AV (mitral) valve
Left common carotid artery
Left pulmonary artery
  (branches)

Left pulmonary veins
Left subclavian artery
Left ventricle
Myocardium
Pulmonary artery
Pulmonary valve
Right atrium
Right AV (tricuspid) valve
Right pulmonary artery
  (branches)
Right pulmonary veins
Right ventricle
Superior vena cava

■ Blood high in oxygen
■ Blood low in oxygen

1. _____
2. _____
3. _____
4. _____
5. _____
6. _____
7. _____
8. _____
9. _____
10. _____
11. _____
12. _____
13. _____
14. _____
15. _____
16. _____
17. _____

18. _____
19. _____
20. _____
21. _____
22. _____
23. _____
24. _____
25. _____

LOCATION OF LYMPHOID TISSUE

Write the name of each numbered part on the corresponding line of the answer sheet.

Appendix   Spleen
Lymph nodes   Thymus
Peyer patches (in intestine) Tonsils

1. _____

2. _____

3. _____

4. _____

5. _____

6. _____

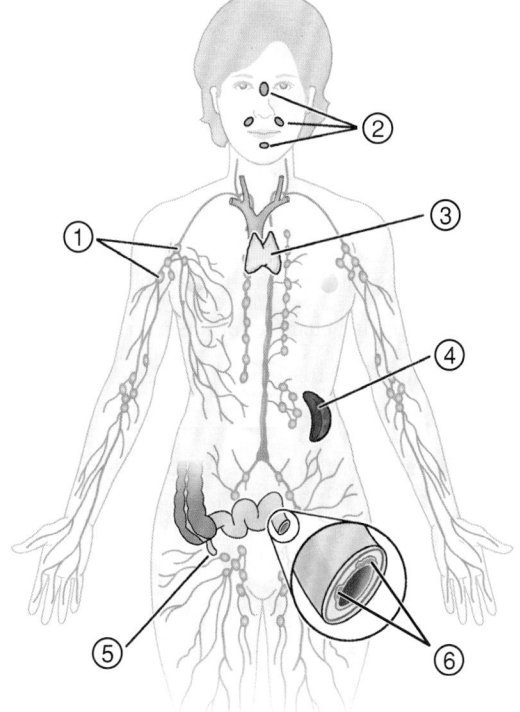

Terminology

MATCHING

Match the following terms, and write the appropriate letter to the left of each number.

_____	**1.** atherosclerosis	**a.** twisted and swollen vessel
_____	**2.** varix	**b.** blockage
_____	**3.** occlusion	**c.** absence of a heartbeat
_____	**4.** aneurysm	**d.** localized dilatation of a vessel
_____	**5.** asystole	**e.** accumulation of fatty deposits

_____	**6.** thrombosis	**a.** ineffective quivering of muscle
_____	**7.** myocarditis	**b.** formation of a blood clot in a vessel
_____	**8.** infarction	**c.** inflammation of the heart muscle
_____	**9.** fibrillation	**d.** local deficiency of blood
_____	**10.** ischemia	**e.** local death of tissue

_____	**11.** lumen	**a.** vessel that empties into the right atrium
_____	**12.** pericardium	**b.** fibrous sac around the heart
_____	**13.** apex	**c.** structure that keeps fluid moving forward
_____	**14.** vena cava	**d.** central opening of a vessel
_____	**15.** valve	**e.** lower, pointed region of the heart

_____	**16.** HDL	**a.** stroke
_____	**17.** HTN	**b.** a type of blood lipid
_____	**18.** VT	**c.** rapid beat in the heart's lower chambers
_____	**19.** CVA	**d.** high blood pressure
_____	**20.** CABG	**e.** surgery to bypass a blocked vessel

Supplementary Terms

_____ **21.** diuretic

_____ **22.** regurgitation

_____ **23.** streptokinase

_____ **24.** atherectomy

_____ **25.** extrasystole

a. removal of plaque

b. drug that increases urinary output

c. premature contraction

d. drug used to dissolve blood clots

e. backward flow

FILL IN THE BLANKS

26. The heart muscle is the _____.

27. A microscopic vessel through which materials are exchanged between the blood and the tissues is a(n) _____.

28. Each upper receiving chamber of the heart is a(n) _____.

29. A sinus rhythm originates in the _____.

30. The largest artery is the _____.

31. A phlebotomist (*fleh-BOT-o-mist*) is one who drains blood from a(n) _____.

32. The term *varicoid* pertains to a(n) _____.

33. The lymphoid organ in the chest is the _____.

34. Blood returning to the heart from the systemic circuit enters the chamber called the _____.

35. At its termination in the abdomen, the aorta divides into the right and left (see **Fig. 9-5**) _____.

36. The large artery in the neck that supplies blood to the brain is the (see **Fig. 9-5**) _____.

37. The large vein that drains the lower body and empties into the heart is the (see **Fig. 9-6**) _____.

38. The right lymphatic duct and the thoracic duct drain into vessels called the (see **Fig. 9-19**) _____.

39. In C.L.'s case study, the device he wore to record his heart rhythm is called a(n) _____.

40. The abnormal heart rhythm that prevented C.L. from completing basic training is termed _____.

41. The catheterization technique used to correct C.L.'s arrhythmia is termed cardiac _____.

TRUE–FALSE

Examine the following statements. If the statement is true, write T in the first blank. If the statement is false, write F in the first blank, and correct the statement by replacing the underlined word in the second blank.

	True or False	Correct Answer
42. The left AV valve is the <u>aortic</u> valve.	_____	_____
43. The pulmonary vein carries blood to the <u>lungs</u>.	_____	_____
44. The brachial artery supplies blood to the <u>leg</u>.	_____	_____
45. <u>Diastole</u> is the relaxation phase of the heart cycle.	_____	_____
46. The <u>left ventricle</u> pumps blood into the aorta.	_____	_____
47. Blood returning from the lungs to the heart enters the <u>left atrium</u>.	_____	_____
48. The <u>systemic circuit</u> pumps blood to the lungs.	_____	_____
49. An <u>artery</u> is a vessel that carries blood back to the heart.	_____	_____
50. Peyer patches are in the <u>intestine</u>.	_____	_____
51. <u>Bradycardia</u> is a lower-than-average heart rate.	_____	_____
52. A beta-adrenergic blocking agent <u>slows</u> the heart rate.	_____	_____

ELIMINATIONS

In each of the sets below, underline the word that does not fit in with the rest and explain the reason for your choice.

53. SA node — Purkinje fibers — apex — AV node — AV bundle

_____

54. murmur — systolic — sphygmomanometer — mm Hg — diastolic

_____

55. U — S_1 — QRS — T — P

_____

56. thymus — spleen — cusp — tonsil — Peyer patches

_____

DEFINITIONS

Define the following terms.

57. avascular (*a-VAS-ku-lar*) _____.

58. atriotomy (*a-tre-OT-o-me*) _____.

59. splenectomy (*sple-NEK-to-me*) _____.

60. supraventricular (*su-prah-ven-TRIK-u-lar*) _____.

61. phlebectasis (*fleb-EK-tah-sis*) _____.

Write words for the following definitions.

62. An instrument (-tome) for incising a valve _____.

63. Suture (-rhaphy) of the aorta _____.

64. Excision of a lymph node _____.

65. Physician who specializes in study and treatment
of the heart _____.

66. Stoppage (-stasis) of lymph flow _____.

67. Surgical fixation (-pexy) of the spleen _____.

Use the root aort/o to write words with the following meanings.

68. Narrowing (-stenosis) of the aorta _____

69. Downward displacement (-ptosis) of the aorta _____

70. Radiograph (-gram) of the aorta _____

71. Before or in front of (pre-) the aorta _____

ADJECTIVES

Write the adjective form of the following words.

72. ventricle _____

73. septum _____

74. valve _____

75. thymus _____

76. sclerosis _____

77. spleen _____

PLURALS

Write the plural form of the following words.

78. thrombus _____

79. varix _____

80. stenosis _____

81. septum _____

ABBREVIATIONS

Write the meaning of the following abbreviations as they apply to the cardiovascular system.

82. AED _____

83. LVAD _____

84. DVT _____

85. VF _____

86. BBB _____

87. PTCA _____

WORD BUILDING

Write words for the following definitions using the word parts given.

| -pathy   phleb   lymph/o   -oma   angi/o   -itis   aden/o   -plasty |

88. inflammation of a vein _____

89. any disease of a lymph node _____

90. neoplasm involving the lymphatic system _____

91. plastic repair of any vessel _____

92. inflammation of a lymphatic vessel _____

93. any disease of a vessel _____

94. inflammation of a lymph node _____

95. plastic repair of a vein _____

96. neoplasm of a lymph node _____

97. tumor involving any vessels _____

WORD ANALYSIS

Define the following words and give the meaning of the word parts in each. Use a dictionary if necessary.

98. Phonocardiography (*fo-no-kar-de-OG-rah-fe*) _____

   a. phon/o _____

   b. cardi/o _____

   c. -graphy _____

99. Endarterectomy (*end-ar-ter-EK-to-me*) _____

    a. end/o _____

    b. arteri/o _____

    c. ecto- _____

    d. -tomy _____

100. Telangiectasia (*tel-an-je-ek-TA-ze-ah*) _____

    a. tel- _____

    b. angi/o _____

    c. -ectasia _____

101. Lymphangiophlebitis (*lim-fan-je-o-fleh-BI-tis*) _____

    a. lymph/o _____

    b. angi/o _____

    c. phleb/o _____

    d. -itis _____

For more learning activities, see Chapter 9 of the Student Resources on thePoint.

Additional Case Studies

Case Study 9-1: *PTCA and Echocardiogram*

A.L., a 68-year-old woman, was admitted to the CCU with chest pain, dyspnea, diaphoresis, syncope, and nausea. She had taken three sublingual doses of nitroglycerin tablets within a 10-minute time span without relief before dialing 911. A previous stress test and thallium uptake scan suggested cardiac disease.

Her family history was significant for cardiovascular disease. Her father died at the age of 62 of an acute myocardial infarction. Her mother had bilateral carotid endarterectomies and a femoral popliteal bypass procedure and died at the age of 72 of congestive heart failure. A.L.'s elder sister died from a ruptured aortic aneurysm at the age of 65. A.L.'s ECG on admission showed tachycardia with a rate of 126 bpm with inverted T waves. A murmur was heard at S_1. Her skin color was dusky to cyanotic on her lips and fingertips. Her admitting diagnosis was possible coronary artery disease, acute myocardial infarction, and valvular disease.

Cardiac catheterization with balloon angioplasty (PTCA) was performed the next day. Significant stenosis of the left anterior descending coronary artery was shown and treated with angioplasty and stent placement. Left ventricular function was normal.

Echocardiography, two days later, showed normal-sized left and enlarged right ventricular cavities. The mitral valve had normal amplitude of motion. The anterior and posterior leaflets moved in opposite directions during diastole. There was a late systolic prolapse of the mitral leaflet at rest. The left atrium was enlarged. The impression of the study was mitral prolapse with regurgitation. Surgery was recommended.

Case Study 9-2: *Mitral Valve Replacement Operative Report*

A.L. was transferred to the operating room, placed in a supine position, and given general endotracheal anesthesia. The surgeon entered her pericardium longitudinally through a median sternotomy and found that her heart was enlarged, with a dilated right ventricle. The left atrium was dilated. Preoperative transesophageal echocardiography revealed severe mitral regurgitation with severe posterior and anterior prolapse. Extracorporeal circulation was established. The aorta was cross-clamped, and cardioplegic solution (to stop the heartbeat) was given into the aortic root intermittently for myocardial protection.

The left atrium was entered via the interatrial groove on the right, exposing the mitral valve. The middle scallop of the posterior leaflet was resected. The remaining leaflets were removed to the areas of the commissures and preserved for the sliding plasty. The elongated chordae were shortened to better anchor the valve cusps. The surgeon slid the posterior leaflet across the midline and sutured it in place. A No. 30 annuloplasty ring was sutured in place with interrupted No. 2–0 Dacron suture. The valve was tested by inflating the ventricle with NSS and proved to be competent. The left atrium was closed with continuous No. 4–0 Prolene suture. Air was removed from the heart. The cross-clamp was removed. Cardiac action resumed with normal sinus rhythm. After a period of cardiac recovery and attainment of normothermia, cardiopulmonary bypass was discontinued.

Protamine was given to counteract the heparin. Pacer wires were placed in the right atrium and ventricle. Silicone catheters were placed in the pleural and substernal spaces. The sternum and soft tissue wound was closed. A.L. recovered from her surgery and was discharged six days later.

Case Study Questions

Write the word or phrase from the case studies that means each of the following:

1. Shortness of breath _____

2. An abnormal heart sound _____

3. Test of cardiac function during physical exertion _____

4. Pertaining to both the heart and blood vessels _____

5. Excision of the inner lining along with atherosclerotic plaque from an artery (plural) _____

6. Under the tongue _____

7. Bluish discoloration of the skin due to lack of oxygen _____

8. The state of profuse perspiration _____

9. Between the atria _____

10. Below the sternum _____

Multiple Choice. Select the best answer, and write the letter of your choice to the left of each number.

_____ **11.** The word transluminal means
  a. across a wall
  b. between branches
  c. through a valve
  d. through a central opening

_____ **12.** The term that means backflow, as of blood, is
  a. infarction
  b. regurgitation
  c. amplitude
  d. prolapse

_____ **13.** The term for a narrowing of the bicuspid valve is
  a. atrial stenosis
  b. tricuspid prolapse
  c. mitral stenosis
  d. pulmonic prolapse

_____ **14.** Blowout of a dilated segment of the main artery is
  a. peritoneal infarction
  b. coarctation of the aorta
  c. cardiac tamponade
  d. ruptured aortic aneurysm

_____ **15.** Sternotomy is
  a. incision into the sternum
  b. removal of the sternum
  c. narrowing of the sternum
  d. surgical fixation of the sternum

_____ **16.** Extracorporeal circulation occurs
  a. within the brain
  b. within the pericardium
  c. outside the body
  d. in the legs

_____ **17.** Protamine was given to counteract the action of the heparin. This drug action is described as
  a. antagonistic
  b. synergy
  c. potentiating
  d. simulation

Abbreviations. Define the following abbreviations.

18. ECG _____

19. AMI _____

20. CAD _____

21. LAD _____

22. CHF _____

23. TEE _____

24. MVR _____

25. CCU _____

9

Blood and Immunity

Pretest

Multiple Choice. Select the best answer, and write the letter of your choice to the left of each number.

_____ 1. Erythrocyte is the scientific name for a
   a. white blood cell
   b. lymphocyte
   c. red blood cell
   d. muscle cell

_____ 2. Platelets, or thrombocytes, are involved in
   a. digestion
   b. inflammation
   c. immunity
   d. blood clotting

_____ 3. The white blood cells active in immunity are the
   a. chondrocytes
   b. lymphocytes
   c. adipose cells
   d. hematids

_____ 4. Substances produced by immune cells that counteract microorganisms and other foreign materials are called
   a. antigens
   b. antibodies
   c. anticoagulants
   d. Rh factors

_____ 5. A deficiency of hemoglobin results in the disorder called
   a. hypertension
   b. chromatosis
   c. anemia
   d. hemophilia

_____ 6. A neoplastic overgrowth of white blood cells is called
   a. leukemia
   b. anemia
   c. fibrosis
   d. cystitis

Learning Objectives

After study of this chapter you should be able to:

1 ▸ Describe the composition of the blood plasma. *p206*

2 ▸ Describe and give the functions of the three types of blood cells. *p206*

3 ▸ Differentiate the five different types of leukocytes. *p208*

4 ▸ Explain the basis of blood types. *p209*

5 ▸ Define immunity, and list the possible sources of immunity. *p211*

6 ▸ Identify and use roots and suffixes pertaining to the blood and immunity. *p214*

7 ▸ Identify and use roots pertaining to blood chemistry. *p216*

8 ▸ List and describe three major disorders of the blood. *p217*

9 ▸ Describe the major tests used to study blood. *pp217*

10 ▸ List and describe three major disorders of the immune system. *p221*

11 ▸ Interpret abbreviations used in blood studies. *p227*

12 ▸ Analyze medical terms in several case studies involving the blood. *pp205, 234*

Case Study: *Nurse Anesthetist M.R. with Latex Allergy*

Chief Complaint
M.R., a 36-year-old certified registered nurse anesthetist (CRNA), noticed that her hands had a red patchy rash when she removed her gloves following cases in the OR. They began to itch after a few minutes of donning the gloves, so she figured she might have developed an allergy to the latex they contained. When she began to have a runny nose and itchy swollen eyes, she was worried and sought medical advice from her primary care physician, who referred her to an allergist.

Examination
The allergist examined M.R.'s hands and observed a localized red crusty rash that stopped at the wrists. There were a few blisters spread over the hand region. Along with the examination, a history indicated M.R. had noticed the contact dermatitis for a while when she wore powdered latex gloves in the OR, and she more recently had noted generalized allergic symptoms during surgical cases. During a recent case, she experienced some tachycardia, urticaria (hives) and rhinitis when she came in contact with latex gloves.

Clinical Course
M.R. was diagnosed with a type I hypersensitivity, IgE, T cell-mediated latex allergy, as shown by both immunologic and skin-prick tests. Although M.R. is a CRNA, she was educated on the course of latex allergies. She was reminded that there is no cure and that the only way to prevent an allergic reaction is to avoid coming into contact with latex.

This chapter describes the composition and characteristics of blood, the life-sustaining fluid that circulates throughout the body. A discussion of immunity is included because many components of the immune system are carried in the blood. M.R.'s case of allergy is an example of immunologic hyperactivity. One of the symptoms, tachycardia, was discussed in Chapter 9 and rhinitis will be introduced in the next chapter on the respiratory system.

ANCILLARIES *At-A-Glance*

Visit thePoint to access the following resources. For guidance in using the resources most effectively, see pp. ix–xvi.

Learning RESOURCES

▸ **Tips for Effective Studying**
▸ **Web Figure: Hematopoiesis**
▸ **Web Chart: Childhood Immunizations**
▸ **Web Animation: Hemostasis**
▸ **Web Animation: Immune Response**
▸ **Audio Pronunciation Glossary**

Learning ACTIVITIES

▸ **Visual Activities**
▸ **Kinesthetic Activities**
▸ **Auditory Activities**

Introduction

Blood is the fluid that circulates through the vessels, bringing oxygen and nourishment to all cells and carrying away carbon dioxide and other waste products. The blood also distributes body heat and carries special substances, such as antibodies and hormones. Certain blood cells are a major component of the immune system, which protects against disease. This chapter thus includes a discussion of the immune system.

Blood

The total adult blood volume is about 5 L (5.2 qt). Whole blood can be divided into two main components: the liquid portion, or **plasma** (55 percent), and **formed elements**, more commonly known as blood cells (45 percent) (**Fig. 10-1**).

BLOOD PLASMA

Plasma is about 90 percent water. The remaining 10 percent contains nutrients, **electrolytes** (dissolved salts), gases, **albumin** (a protein), clotting factors, antibodies, wastes, enzymes, and hormones. Laboratories test for a multitude of these substances in blood chemistry tests. The pH (relative acidity) of the plasma remains steady at about 7.4.

BLOOD CELLS

The blood cells (**Fig. 10-2**) include **erythrocytes**, or red blood cells (RBCs); **leukocytes**, or white blood cells (WBCs); and **platelets**, also called **thrombocytes**. All blood cells are produced in red bone marrow. Some WBCs multiply in lymphoid tissue as well. For Your Reference **Box 10-1** summarizes the different types of blood cells; **Box 10-2** discusses time-saving acronyms, such as RBC and WBC.

Erythrocytes

The major function of erythrocytes is to carry oxygen to cells. This oxygen is bound to an iron-containing pigment in the cells called **hemoglobin**. Erythrocytes are small, disk-shaped cells with no nuclei (**Fig. 10-3**). Their concentration of about 5 million per microliter (mcL) of blood makes them by far the most numerous of the blood cells. The hemoglobin that they carry averages 15 g/dL (100 mL) of blood. An RBC gradually wears out and dies in about 120 days, so these cells must be constantly replaced. Production of red cells in the bone marrow is regulated by the hormone **erythropoietin** (EPO), which is made in the kidneys.

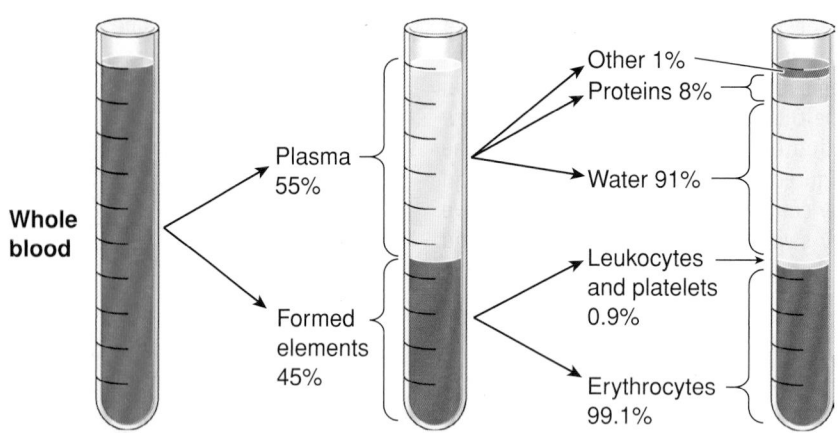

Figure 10-1 **Composition of whole blood.** Percentages show the relative proportions of the different components of plasma and formed elements.

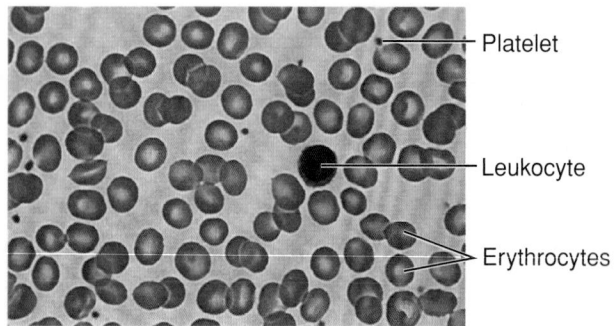

Figure 10-2 **Blood cells.** When viewed under a microscope, all three types of formed elements are visible.

FOR YOUR REFERENCE
Blood Cells

Cell Type	Number Per Microliter of Blood	Description	Function
Erythrocyte (red blood cell)	5 million	Tiny (7 mcm diameter), biconcave disk without nucleus (anuclear)	Carries oxygen bound to hemoglobin; also carries some carbon dioxide and buffers blood
Leukocyte (white blood cell)	5,000 to 10,000	Larger than red cell with prominent nucleus that may be segmented (granulocyte) or unsegmented (agranulocyte); types vary in staining properties	Immunity; protects against pathogens and destroys foreign matter and debris; located in blood, tissues, and lymphatic system
Platelet (thrombocyte)	150,000 to 450,000	Fragment of large cell (megakaryocyte)	Hemostasis; forms a platelet plug and starts blood clotting (coagulation)

Box 10-2

FOCUS ON WORDS
Acronyms

Acronyms are abbreviations that use the first letters of the words in a name or phrase. They have become very popular because they save time and space in writing as the number and complexity of technical terms increases. Some examples that apply to studies of the blood are CBC (complete blood count) and RBC and WBC for red and white blood cells. Some other common acronyms are CNS (central nervous system or clinical nurse specialist), ECG (electrocardiogram) NIH (National Institutes of Health), and STI (sexually transmitted infection).

If the acronym has vowels and lends itself to pronunciation, it may be used as a word in itself, such as AIDS (acquired immunodeficiency syndrome); ELISA (enzyme-linked immunosorbent assay); *JAMA* (*Journal of the American Medical Association*); NSAID (nonsteroidal antiinflammatory drug), pronounced "en-sayd;" and CABG (coronary artery bypass graft), which inevitably becomes "cabbage." Few people even know that LASER is an acronym that means "light amplification by stimulated emission of radiation."

An acronym is usually introduced the first time a phrase appears in an article and is then used without explanation. If you have spent time searching back through an article in frustration for the meaning of an acronym, you probably wish, as do other readers, that all the acronyms used and their meanings would be listed at the beginning of each article.

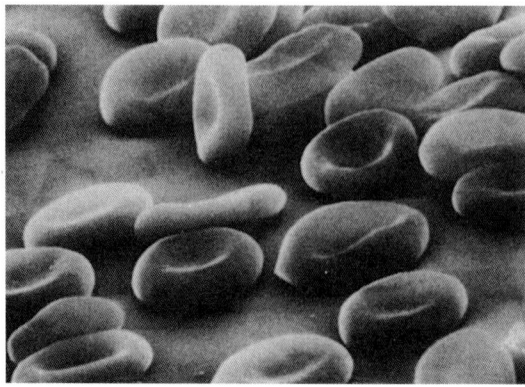

Figure 10-3 **Erythrocytes (red blood cells).** The cells are seen under a scanning electron microscope, which gives a three-dimensional view.

Box 10-3

FOR YOUR REFERENCE
Leukocytes (White Blood Cells)

Cell Type	Relative Percentage (Adult)	Function
GRANULOCYTE		
neutrophil *NU-tro-fil*	54 to 62 percent	phagocytosis
eosinophil *e-o-SIN-o-fil*	1 to 3 percent	allergic reactions; defense against parasites
basophil *BA-so-fil*	less than 1 percent	allergic reactions
AGRANULOCYTE		
lymphocyte *LIM-fo-site*	25 to 38 percent	immunity (T cells and B cells)
monocyte *MON-o-site*	3 to 7 percent	phagocytosis

Leukocytes

All WBCs show prominent nuclei when stained. They total about 5,000 to 10,000/mcL, but their number may increase during infection. There are five types of leukocytes that vary in their relative percentages and their functions. The different types are identified by the size and appearance of the nucleus, by their staining properties, and by whether or not they show visible granules in the cytoplasm when stained. The five types are illustrated and compared in **Box 10-3**. Classified as granulocytes or agranulocytes, they are as follows:

- Granulocytes, or granular leukocytes, have visible granules in the cytoplasm when stained. A granulocyte has a segmented nucleus. There are three types of granulocytes, named for the kind of stain (dye) the granules take up:
  - **Neutrophils** stain weakly with both acidic and basic dyes.
  - **Eosinophils** stain strongly with acidic dyes.
  - **Basophils** stain strongly with basic dyes.
- Agranulocytes do not show visible granules when stained. An agranulocyte's nucleus is large and either round or curved. There are two types of agranulocytes:
  - **Lymphocytes** are the smaller agranulocytes.
  - **Monocytes** are the largest of all the WBCs.

WBCs protect against foreign substances. Some engulf foreign material by the process of **phagocytosis** (**Fig. 6-5**); others have different functions in the immune system. In diagnosis, it is important to know not only the total number of leukocytes but also the relative number of each type, because these numbers can change in different disease conditions. Laboratories report these numbers as a differential count (Diff), which is part of a complete blood count (CBC).

The most numerous WBCs, neutrophils, are called *polymorphs* because of the various shapes of their nuclei. They are also referred to as *segs*, *polys*, or *PMNs* (*polymorphonuclear* leukocytes). A **band cell**, also called a *stab cell*, is an immature neutrophil with a solid curved nucleus (**Fig. 10-4**). Large numbers of band cells in the blood indicate an active infection.

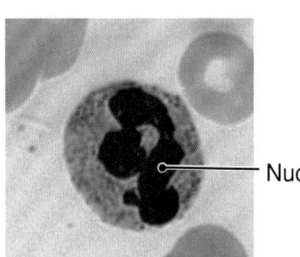

A Mature neutrophil

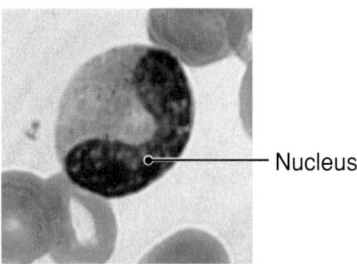

B Band cell (immature neutrophil)

Figure 10-4 **Band cell. A.** A mature neutrophil. **B.** A band cell, or stab cell, is an immature neutrophil with a thick curved nucleus.

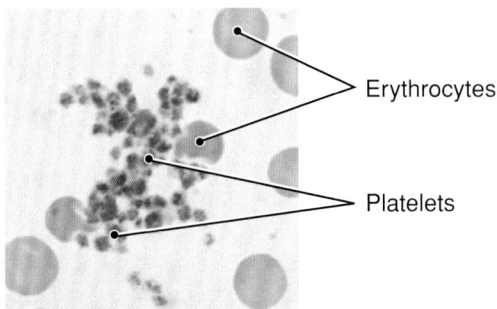

A Platelets

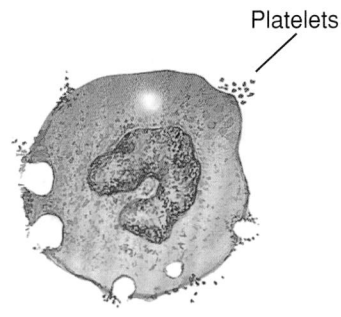

B Megakaryocyte

Figure 10-5 **Platelets (thrombocytes). A.** Platelets seen in a blood smear under the microscope. **B.** A megakaryocyte releases platelets.

Platelets

The blood platelets (thrombocytes) are not complete cells, but fragments of large cells named **megakaryocytes**, which form in bone marrow (**Fig. 10-5**). They number from 200,000 to 400,000/mcL of blood. Platelets are important in **hemostasis**, the prevention of blood loss, which includes the process of blood clotting, or **coagulation**.

See the figure on hematopoiesis (formation of blood cells) and the animation "Hemostasis" in the Student Resources on thePoint.

When a vessel is injured, platelets stick together to form a plug at the site. Substances released from the platelets and from damaged tissue then interact with clotting factors in the plasma to produce a wound-sealing clot. Clotting factors are inactive in the blood until an injury occurs. To protect against unwanted clot formation, 12 factors must interact before blood coagulates. The final reaction is the conversion of **fibrinogen** to threads of **fibrin** that trap blood cells and plasma to produce the clot (**Fig. 10-6**). The plasma that remains after blood coagulates is **serum**.

BLOOD TYPES

Genetically inherited proteins on the surface of RBCs determine blood type. More than 20 groups of these proteins

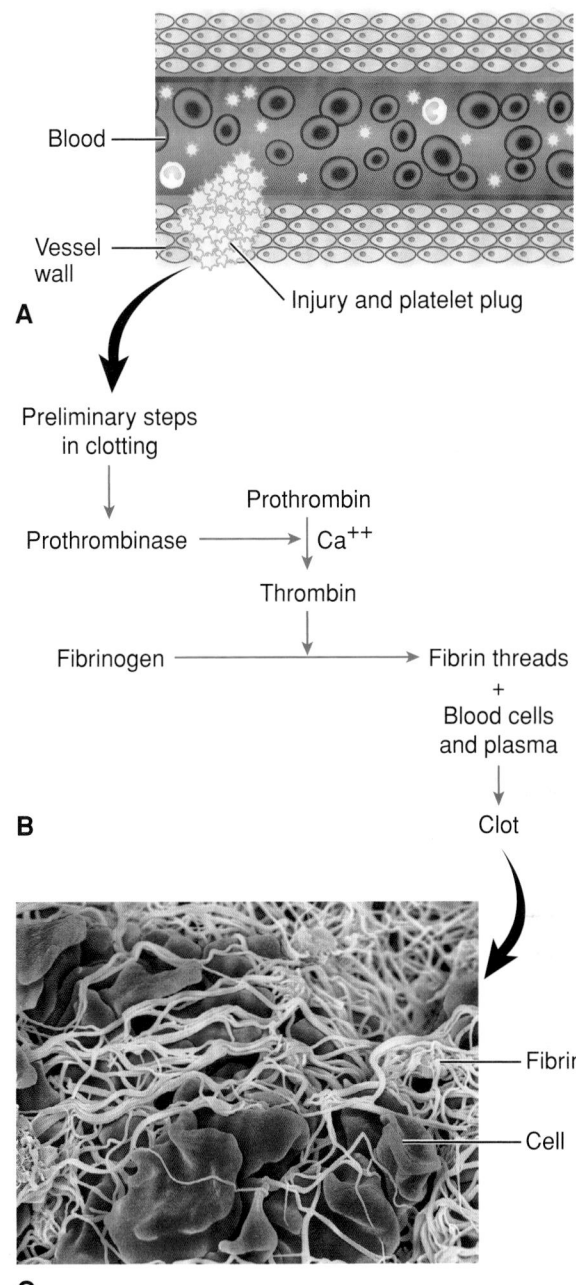

Figure 10-6 **Blood clotting (coagulation).** Blood coagulation involves a complex series of reactions that leads to formation of fibrin threads. The fibrin traps blood cells to form a clot. **A.** Substances released from damaged tissue start the clotting process. **B.** The final steps in formation of fibrin. One of these steps requires calcium (Ca^{2+}). **C.** Microscopic view of blood cells trapped in fibrin.

have now been identified, but the most familiar are the ABO and Rh blood groups. The ABO system includes types A, B, AB, and O. The Rh types are Rh⁻ positive (Rh⁺) and Rh⁻ negative (Rh⁻). Blood is typed by mixing samples separately with different prepared antisera. Red cells in the sample will agglutinate (clump) with the antiserum that corresponds

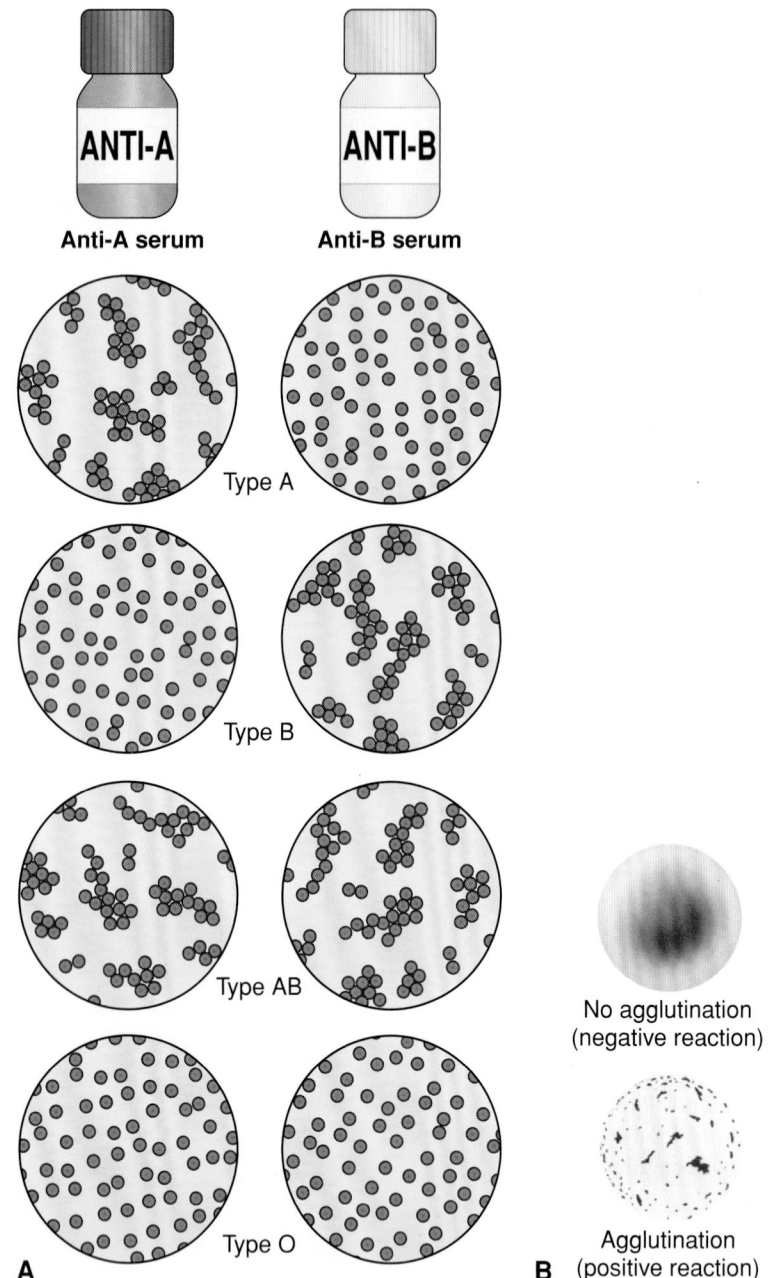

Figure 10-7 **Blood typing.** Blood type is determined by mixing samples separately with antisera prepared against the different red cell antigens. Clumping (agglutination) with an antiserum indicates the presence of the corresponding antigen. **A.** Labels at the top of each column denote the kind of antiserum added to the blood samples. Anti-A serum agglutinates red cells in type A blood, but anti-B serum does not. Anti-B serum agglutinates red cells in type B blood, but anti-A serum does not. Both sera agglutinate type AB blood cells, and neither serum agglutinates type O blood. **B.** Photographs of blood typing reactions.

to the blood type, as shown in **Figure 10-7** for the ABO system.

In giving blood transfusions, it is important to use blood that is the same type as the recipient's blood or a type to which the recipient will not have an immune reaction. In an emergency, type O, Rh-negative blood can be used because these red cells will not induce an immune response. When there is time, laboratories perform more complete tests for compatibility that take additional blood proteins into account. In this process of **cross-matching**, donor red cells are mixed with recipient serum to test for a reaction.

Whole blood may be used to replace a large volume of blood lost, but in most cases requiring blood transfusion, a blood fraction, such as packed red cells, platelets, plasma, or specific clotting factors, is administered.

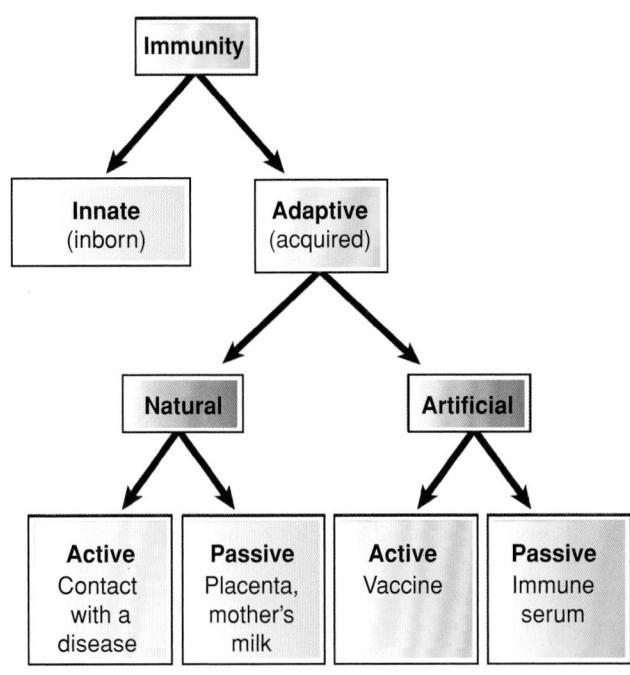

Figure 10-8 Types of immunity.

Immunity

Immunity is protection against disease. It includes defenses against harmful microorganisms, their products, or any other foreign substance. These defenses may be inborn or acquired during life (**Fig. 10-8**).

INNATE IMMUNITY

Innate defense mechanisms protect against any invading organism or harmful foreign substance, not any particular one. Thus, they are described as *nonspecific*. These defenses are inborn and are based on an individual's inherited genetic makeup. Most of these protections are physical barriers or chemical defenses and include the following:

- Unbroken skin, which acts as a barrier
- Cilia, tiny cell projections that sweep impurities out of the body, as in the respiratory tract
- Mucus that traps foreign material
- Bactericidal body secretions, as found in tears, skin, digestive tract, and reproductive tract
- Reflexes, such as coughing and sneezing, which expel impurities
- Lymphoid tissue, which filters impurities from blood and lymph, as described in Chapter 9
- Phagocytes, cells that attack, ingest, and destroy foreign organisms

ADAPTIVE IMMUNITY

Adaptive immunity is acquired during life and is *specific*, that is, directed toward a particular disease organism or other foreign substance. Protection against measles, for example, will not protect against chickenpox or any other disease.

The adaptive immune response involves complex interactions between components of the lymphatic system and the blood. Any foreign particle, but mainly proteins, may act as an **antigen**, a substance that provokes an immune response. This response comes from two types of lymphocytes that circulate in the blood and lymphatic system:

- **T cells** (T lymphocytes) mature in the thymus. They are capable of attacking a foreign cell directly, producing *cell-mediated immunity*. Immune cells known as **antigen-presenting cells** (**APCs**), which take in and process foreign antigens, are important to T cell function. A T cell is activated when it contacts an antigen on an APC's surface in combination with some of the body's own proteins. Examples of APCs are dendritic cells and macrophages, which are descendants of monocytes.
- **B cells** (B lymphocytes) mature in bone marrow. When they meet a foreign antigen, they multiply rapidly and mature into **plasma cells**. These cells produce **antibodies**, also called **immunoglobulins** (**Ig**), that inactivate antigens (**Fig. 10-9**). Antibodies remain in the blood, often providing long-term immunity to the specific organism against which

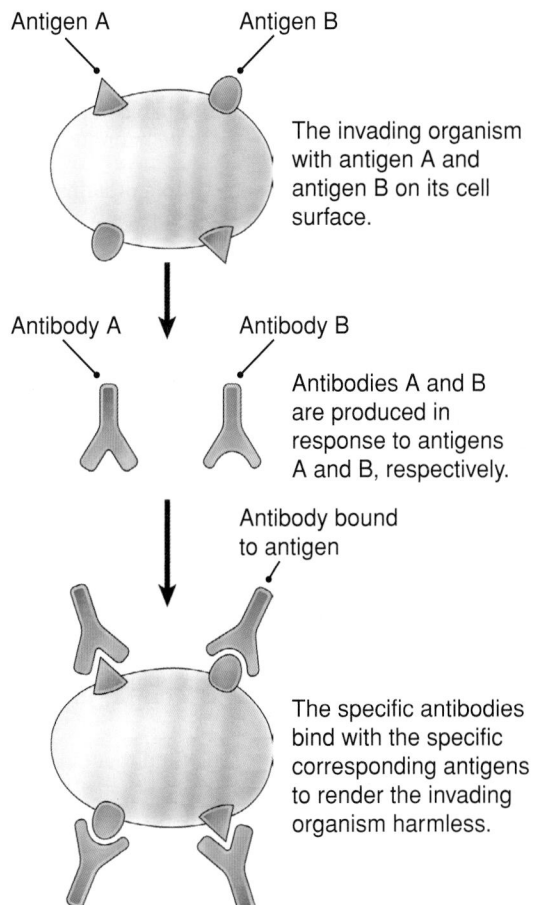

Figure 10-9 **The antigen–antibody reaction.** Antibodies produced by immune cells bind with specific antigens to aid in their inactivation and elimination.

they were formed. Antibody-based immunity is referred to as *humoral immunity*.

TYPES OF ADAPTIVE IMMUNITY

Adaptive immunity may be acquired either naturally or artificially (**Fig. 10-8**). In addition, each avenue for acquiring such immunity may be either active or passive. In active immunity, a person makes his or her own antibodies in response to contact with an antigen. In passive immunity, an antibody, known as an immune serum, is transferred from an outside source. Immune sera may come from other people or from immunized animals. The portion of the blood plasma that contains antibodies is the **gamma globulin** fraction. The types of adaptive immunity are:

- Natural adaptive immunity
  - Active—from contact with a disease organism or other foreign antigen
  - Passive—by transfer of antibodies from a mother to her fetus through the placenta or through the mother's milk

- Artificial adaptive immunity
  - Active—by administration of a vaccine, which may be a killed or weakened organism, part of an organism, or an altered toxin (toxoid)
  - Passive—by administration of an immune serum obtained from other people or animals

See the chart on childhood immunizations and the animation "Immune Response" in the Student Resources on thePoint.

Immunology has long been a very active area of research. The above description is only the barest outline of the events that are known to occur in the immune response, and there is still much to be discovered. Some of the areas of research include autoimmune diseases, in which an individual produces antibodies to his or her own body tissues; hereditary and acquired immunodeficiency diseases; the relationship between cancer and immunity; and the development of techniques for avoiding rejection of transplanted tissue.

Terminology | Key Terms

Normal Structure and Function

agranulocyte A-gran-u-lo-site	A white blood cell that does not have visible granules in its cytoplasm; agranulocytes include lymphocytes and monocytes (see **Box 10-3**)
albumin al-BU-min	A simple protein found in blood plasma
antibody AN-tih-bod-e	A protein produced in response to and interacting specifically with an antigen
antigen AN-tih-jen	A substance that induces the formation of an antibody
antigen-presenting cell (APC)	Immune cell that takes in a foreign antigen, processes it, and presents it on the cell surface in combination with the body's own proteins, thus activating a T cell; examples are dendritic cells and macrophages, which are descendants of monocytes
B cell	A lymphocyte that matures in bone marrow and is active in producing antibodies; B lymphocyte (LIM-fo-site)
band cell	An immature neutrophil with a nucleus in the shape of a band; also called a stab cell; band cell counts are used to trace infections and other diseases (see **Fig. 10-4**)
basophil BA-so-fil	A granular leukocyte that stains strongly with basic dyes; active in allergic reactions
blood blud	The fluid that circulates in the cardiovascular system (roots: hem/o, hemat/o)
coagulation ko-ag-u-LA-shun	Blood clotting
cross-matching	Testing the compatibility of donor and recipient blood in preparation for a transfusion; donor red cells are mixed with recipient serum to look for an immunologic reaction; similar tests are done on tissues before transplantation

Terminology	**Key Terms** *(Continued)*

electrolyte *e-LEK-tro-lite*	A substance that separates into charged particles (ions) in solution; a salt; term also applied to ions in body fluids
eosinophil *e-o-SIN-o-fil*	A granular leukocyte that stains strongly with acidic dyes; active in allergic reactions and defense against parasites
erythrocyte *eh-RITH-ro-site*	A red blood cell (roots: erythr/o, erythrocyt/o) **(Figs. 10-2** and **10-3)**
erythropoietin (EPO) *eh-rith-ro-POY-eh-tin*	A hormone produced in the kidneys that stimulates red blood cell production in the bone marrow; this hormone is now made by genetic engineering for clinical use
fibrin *FI-brin*	The protein that forms a clot in the blood coagulation process
fibrinogen *fi-BRIN-o-jen*	The inactive precursor of fibrin
formed elements	The cellular components of blood
gamma globulin *GLOB-u-lin*	The fraction of the blood plasma that contains antibodies; given for passive transfer of immunity
granulocyte *GRAN-u-lo-site*	A white blood cell that has visible granules in its cytoplasm; granulocytes include neutrophils, basophils, and eosinophils (see **Box 10-3**)
hemoglobin (Hb, Hgb) *HE-mo-glo-bin*	The iron-containing pigment in red blood cells that transports oxygen
hemostasis *he-mo-STA-sis*	The stoppage of bleeding
immunity *ih-MU-nih-te*	The state of being protected against a disease (root: immun/o)
immunoglobulin (Ig) *im-u-no-GLOB-u-lin*	An antibody; immunoglobulins fall into five classes, each abbreviated with a capital letter: IgG, IgM, IgA, IgD, IgE
leukocyte *LU-ko-site*	A white blood cell (roots: leuk/o, leukocyt/o)
lymphocyte *LIM-fo-site*	An agranular leukocyte active in immunity (T and B cells); found in both the blood and in lymphoid tissue (roots: lymph/o, lymphocyt/o)
megakaryocyte *meg-ah-KAR-e-o-site*	A large bone marrow cell that fragments to release platelets
monocyte *MON-o-site*	An agranular phagocytic leukocyte
neutrophil *NU-tro-fil*	A granular leukocyte that stains weakly with both acidic and basic dyes; the most numerous of the white blood cells; a type of phagocyte
phagocytosis *fag-o-si-TO-sis*	The engulfing of foreign material by white blood cells
plasma *PLAZ-mah*	The liquid portion of the blood
plasma cell	A mature form of a B cell that produces antibodies
platelet *PLATE-let*	A formed element of the blood that is active in hemostasis; a thrombocyte (root: thrombocyt/o)

(continued)

Terminology	Key Terms (*Continued*)
serum SERE-*um*	The fraction of the plasma that remains after blood coagulation; it is the equivalent of plasma without its clotting factors (plural: sera, serums)
T cell	A lymphocyte that matures in the thymus and attacks foreign cells directly; T lymphocyte
thrombocyte THROM-*bo-site*	A blood platelet (root: thrombocyt/o)

Go to the Audio Pronunciation Glossary in the Student Resources on thePoint to hear these terms pronounced.

Word Parts Pertaining to Blood and Immunity

See Tables 10-1 to 10-3.

Table 10-1	Suffixes for Blood

Suffix	Meaning	Example	Definition of Example
-emia,[a] -hemia	condition of blood	polycythemia *pol-e-si-THE-me-ah*	increase of cells (cyt) in the blood
-penia	decrease in, deficiency of	cytopenia *si-to-PE-ne-ah*	deficiency of cells
-poiesis	formation, production	hemopoiesis *he-mo-poy-E-sis*	production of blood cells

[a]A shortened form of the root hem plus the suffix -*ia.*

EXERCISE 10-1

Define the following terms.

1. thrombocytopenia (*throm-bo-si-to-PE-ne-ah*) _____

2. bacteremia (*bak-ter-E-me-ah*) _____

3. leukocytopenia (*lu-ko-si-to-PE-ne-ah*) _____

4. erythropoiesis (*eh-rith-ro-poy-E-sis*) _____

5. toxemia (*tok-SE-me-ah*) _____

6. hypoproteinemia (*hi-po-pro-tene-E-me-ah*) _____

7. hyperalbuminemia (*hi-per-al-bu-mih-NE-me-ah*) _____

Use the suffix -*emia* to write words for the following definitions.

8. Presence of viruses in the blood _____

9. Presence of excess white cells (leuk/o) in the blood _____

10. Presence of pus in the blood _____

Many of the words relating to blood cells can be formed either with or without including the root *cyt/o*, as in erythropenia or erythrocytopenia, leukopoiesis or leukocytopoiesis. The remaining types of blood cells are designated by easily recognized roots such as *agranulocyt/o*, *monocyt/o*, *granul/o*, and so on (Table 10-2).

Table 10-2	**Roots for Blood and Immunity**		
Root	**Meaning**	**Example**	**Definition of Example**
myel/o	bone marrow	myelogenous mi-eh-LOJ-eh-nus	originating in bone marrow
hem/o, hemat/o	blood	hemopathy he-MOP-ah-the	any disorder of blood
erythr/o, erythrocyt/o	red blood cell	erythroblast eh-RITH-ro-blast	immature red blood cell
leuk/o, leukocyt/o	white blood cell	leukocytosis lu-ko-si-TO-sis	increase in the number of leukocytes in the blood
lymph/o, lymphocyt/o	lymphocyte	lymphocytic lim-fo-SIT-ik	pertaining to lymphocytes
thromb/o	blood clot	thrombolytic throm-bo-LIT-ik	dissolving a blood clot
thrombocyt/o	platelet, thrombocyte	thrombopoiesis throm-bo-poy-E-sis	formation of platelets
immun/o	immunity, immune system	immunization im-u-nih-ZA-shun	production of immunity

10

EXERCISE 10-2

Identify and define the root in the following words.

	Root	**Meaning of Root**
1. leukocytosis (*lu-ko-si-TO-sis*)	_____	_____
2. ischemia (*is-KE-me-ah*)	_____	_____
3. preimmunization (*pre-im-u-nih-ZA-shun*)	_____	_____
4. hematology (*he-mah-TOL-o-je*)	_____	_____
5. prothrombin (*pro-THROM-bin*)	_____	_____
6. panmyeloid (*pan-MI-eh-loyd*)	_____	_____

Fill in the blanks.

7. Lymphokines (*LIM-fo-kines*) are chemicals active in immunity that are produced by _____.

8. A hematoma (*he-mah-TO-mah*) is a swelling caused by collection of _____.

9. Hemorrhage (*HEM-or-ij*) is a profuse flow (-rhage) of _____.

10. Myelofibrosis (*mi-eh-lo-fi-BRO-sis*) is formation of fibrous tissue in _____.

11. Erythroclasis (*er-ih-THROK-lah-sis*) is the breaking (-clasis) of _____.

12. An immunocyte (*im-u-no-SITE*) is a cell active in _____.

13. The term thrombocythemia (*throm-bo-si-THE-me-ah*) refers to a blood increase in the number of _____.

14. Leukopoiesis (*lu-ko-poy-E-sis*) refers to the production of _____.

(continued)

EXERCISE 10-2   *(Continued)*

Write a word for the following definitions.

15. Decrease in white blood cells _____

16. Tumor of bone marrow _____

17. Immature lymphocyte _____

18. Dissolving (-lysis) of a blood clot _____

19. Formation (-poiesis) of bone marrow _____

The suffix *-osis* added to a root for a type of cell means an increase in that type of cell in the blood. Use this suffix to write a word that means each of the following.

20. Increase in granulocytes in the blood _____

21. Increase in lymphocytes in the blood _____

22. Increase in red blood cells _____

23. Increase in monocytes in the blood _____

24. Increase in platelets in the blood _____

Table 10-3   Roots for Blood Chemistry

Root	Meaning	Example	Definition of Example
azot/o	nitrogenous compounds	azoturia *aze-o-TU-re-ah*	increased nitrogenous compounds in the urine (-uria)
calc/i	calcium (symbol Ca)	calcification *kal-sih-fih-KA-shun*	deposition of calcium salts
ferr/o, ferr/i	iron (symbol Fe)	ferrous *FER-ous*	pertaining to or containing iron
sider/o	iron	sideroderma *sid-er-o-DER-mah*	deposition of iron into the skin
kali	potassium (symbol K)	hyperkalemia[a] *hi-per-kah-LE-me-ah*	excess of potassium in the blood
natri	sodium (symbol Na)	natriuresis *na-tre-u-RE-sis*	excretion of sodium in the urine (ur/o)
ox/y	oxygen (symbol O)	hypoxia *hi-POK-se-ah*	deficiency of oxygen in the tissues

[a]The i in the root is dropped.

EXERCISE 10-3

Fill in the blanks.

1. A sideroblast (*SID-er-o-blast*) is an immature cell containing _____.

2. The term hypokalemia (*hi-po-kah-LE-me-ah*) refers to a blood deficiency of _____.

3. The bacterial species *Azotobacter* is named for its ability to metabolize _____.

4. Hypoxemia (*hi-pok-SE-me-ah*) is a blood deficiency of _____.

5. Ferritin (*FER-ih-tin*) is a compound that contains _____.

6. A calcareous (*kal-KAR-e-us*) substance contains _____.

Use the suffix *-emia* to form words with the following meanings.

7. Presence of sodium in the blood _____

8. Presence of nitrogenous compounds in the blood _____

9. Presence of potassium in the blood _____

10. Presence of calcium in the blood _____

Clinical Aspects of Blood

ANEMIA

Anemia is defined as an abnormally low amount of hemoglobin in the blood. Anemia may result from too few RBCs or from cells that are too small (microcytic) or have too little hemoglobin (hypochromic). Key tests in diagnosing anemia are blood counts, mean corpuscular volume (MCV), and mean corpuscular hemoglobin concentration (MCHC). **Box 10-4** describes these and other blood tests. **Box 10-5** has information on careers in hematology.

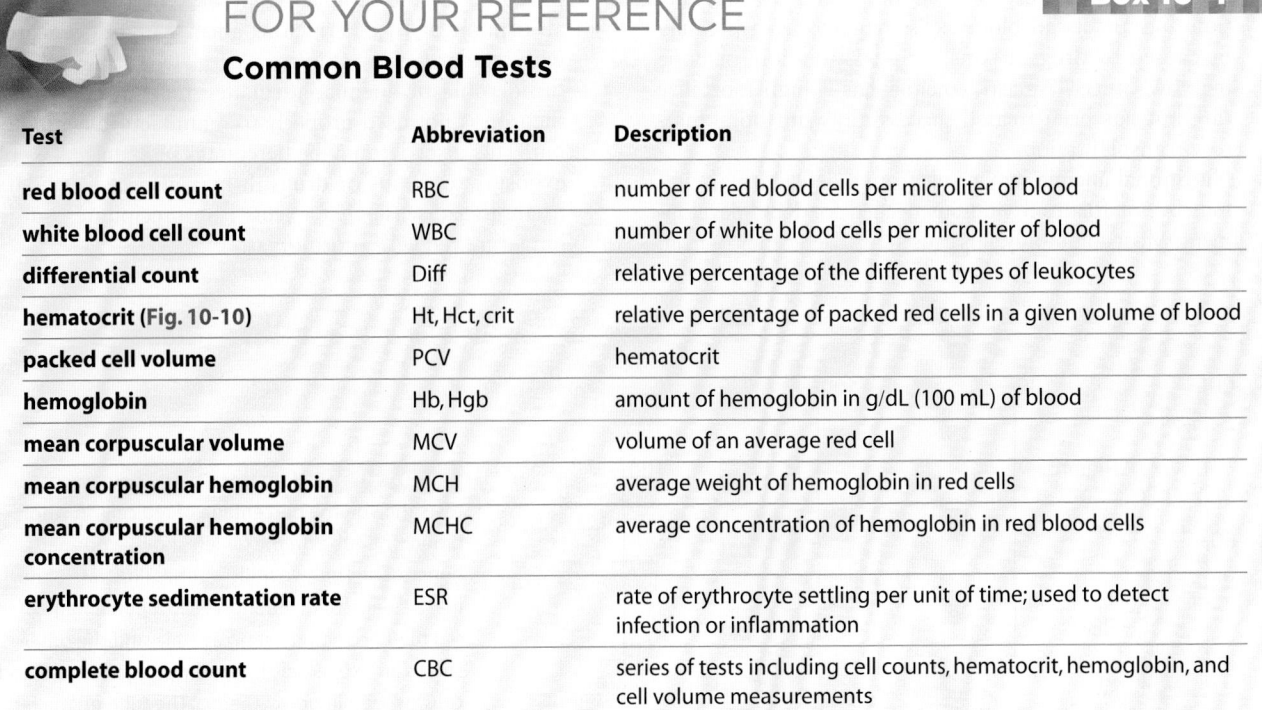

FOR YOUR REFERENCE

Box 10-4

Common Blood Tests

Test	Abbreviation	Description
red blood cell count	RBC	number of red blood cells per microliter of blood
white blood cell count	WBC	number of white blood cells per microliter of blood
differential count	Diff	relative percentage of the different types of leukocytes
hematocrit (Fig. 10-10)	Ht, Hct, crit	relative percentage of packed red cells in a given volume of blood
packed cell volume	PCV	hematocrit
hemoglobin	Hb, Hgb	amount of hemoglobin in g/dL (100 mL) of blood
mean corpuscular volume	MCV	volume of an average red cell
mean corpuscular hemoglobin	MCH	average weight of hemoglobin in red cells
mean corpuscular hemoglobin concentration	MCHC	average concentration of hemoglobin in red blood cells
erythrocyte sedimentation rate	ESR	rate of erythrocyte settling per unit of time; used to detect infection or inflammation
complete blood count	CBC	series of tests including cell counts, hematocrit, hemoglobin, and cell volume measurements

The general symptoms of anemia include fatigue, shortness of breath, heart palpitations, pallor, and irritability. There are many different types of anemia, some of which are caused by faulty production of red cells and others by loss or destruction of red cells.

Anemia due to Impaired Production of Red Cells

- **Aplastic anemia** results from bone marrow destruction and affects all blood cells (pancytopenia). It may be caused by drugs, toxins, viruses, radiation, or bone marrow cancer. Aplastic anemia has a high mortality rate but has been treated successfully with bone marrow transplantation.
- **Nutritional anemia** may result from a deficiency of vitamin B_{12} or folate, B vitamins needed for RBC development. Most commonly, it is caused by a deficiency of iron, needed to make hemoglobin (**Fig. 10-11**). Folate deficiency commonly appears in those with poor diet, in pregnant and lactating women, and in those who abuse alcohol. Iron deficiency anemia results from poor diet, poor iron absorption, or blood loss. Both folate deficiency and iron deficiency respond to dietary supplementation.
- **Pernicious anemia** is a specific form of B_{12} deficiency. It results from the lack of **intrinsic factor** (IF), a substance produced in the stomach that aids in the intestinal absorption of B_{12}. Pernicious anemia must be treated with regular B_{12} injections.
- In **sideroblastic anemia**, adequate iron is available, but the iron is not used properly to manufacture hemoglobin. This disorder may be hereditary or acquired, as by exposure to toxins or drugs. It may also be secondary to another disease. The excess iron precipitates out in immature red cells (normoblasts).

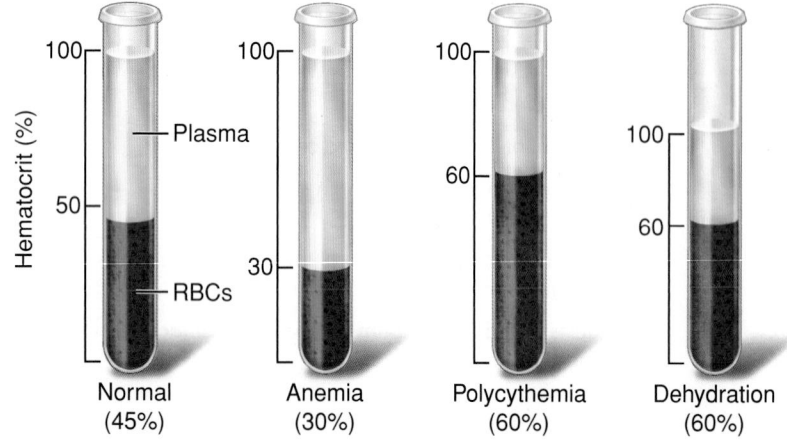

Figure 10-10 **Hematocrit.** The hematocrit tests the volume percentage of red cells in whole blood. The tube on the far left shows a normal hematocrit. The two middle tubes illustrate abnormal hematocrits. One shows a low percentage of red blood cells, indicating anemia, and the other shows an excessively high percentage of red blood cells, as seen in polycythemia. The tube on the far right shows a relatively high percentage of red cells due to dehydration.

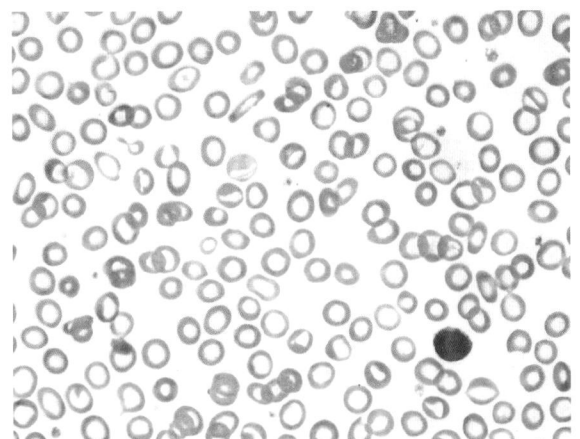

Figure 10-11 **Iron deficiency anemia.** Red cells are small (microcytic) and are lacking in hemoglobin (hypochromic).

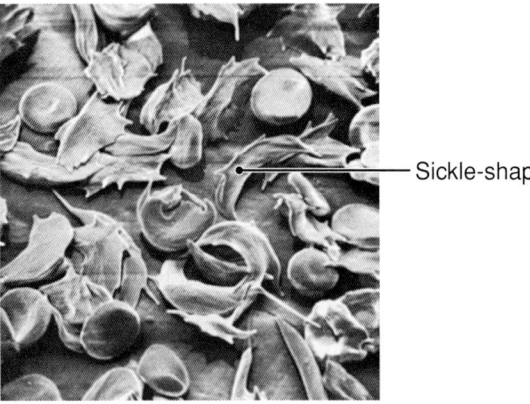

— Sickle-shaped cell

Figure 10-12 **A blood smear in sickle cell anemia.** Abnormal cells take on a crescent (sickle) shape when they give up oxygen.

Anemia due to Loss or Destruction of Red Cells

- **Hemorrhagic anemia** results from blood loss. This may be a sudden loss, as from injury, or loss from chronic internal bleeding, as from the digestive tract in cases of ulcers or cancer.
- **Thalassemia** is a hereditary disease that appears mostly in Mediterranean populations. A genetic mutation causes abnormal hemoglobin production and **hemolysis** (destruction) of red cells. Thalassemia is designated as α (alpha) or β (beta), according to the part of the hemoglobin molecule affected. Severe β thalassemia is also called **Cooley anemia** or *thalassemia major*.
- In **sickle cell anemia**, a mutation alters the hemoglobin molecule so that it precipitates (settles out) when it gives up oxygen, distorting the RBCs into a crescent shape (**Fig. 10-12**). The altered cells block small blood vessels and deprive tissues of oxygen, an episode termed

sickle cell crisis. The misshapen cells are also readily destroyed (hemolyzed). The disease predominates in black populations. Genetic carriers of the defect, those with one normal and one abnormal gene, show *sickle cell trait*. They usually have no symptoms, except when oxygen is low, such as at high altitudes. They can, however, pass the defective gene to offspring. Sickle cell anemia, as well as many other genetic diseases, can be diagnosed in carriers and in a fetus before birth.

Reticulocyte counts are useful in diagnosing the causes of anemia. Reticulocytes are immature RBCs that normally appear as a small percentage of the total erythrocytes. An increase in the reticulocyte count indicates increased red cell formation, as in response to hemorrhage or cell destruction. A decrease in reticulocytes indicates a failure in red cell production, as caused by nutritional deficiency or aplastic anemia (**Box 10-6**).

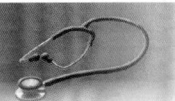

CLINICAL PERSPECTIVES

Box 10-6

Use of Reticulocytes in Diagnosis

As erythrocytes mature in the red bone marrow, they go through a series of stages in which they lose their nuclei and most other organelles, maximizing the space available for hemoglobin. In one of the last stages of development, small numbers of ribosomes and some rough endoplasmic reticulum remain in the cell and appear as a network, or reticulum, when stained. Cells at this stage are called reticulocytes. Reticulocytes leave the red bone marrow and enter the bloodstream, where they become fully mature erythrocytes in about 24 to 48 hours. The average number of red cells maturing through the reticulocyte stage at any given time is about 1 to 2 percent. Changes in these numbers can be used in diagnosing certain blood disorders.

When erythrocytes are lost or destroyed, as from chronic bleeding or some form of hemolytic anemia, red cell production is "stepped up" to compensate for the loss. Greater numbers of reticulocytes are then released into the blood before reaching full maturity, and counts increase to above normal. On the other hand, a decrease in the number of circulating reticulocytes

suggests a problem with red cell production, as in cases of deficiency anemias or suppression of bone marrow activity.

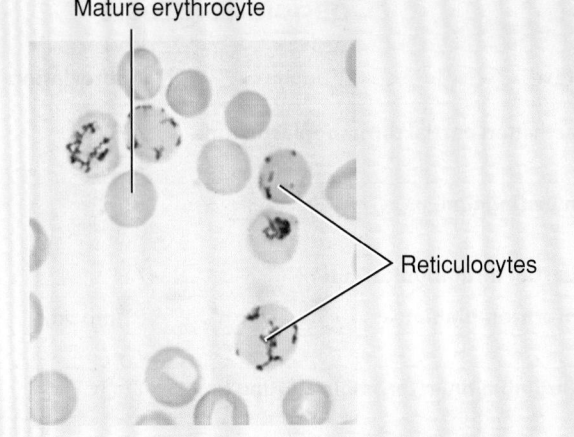

Mature erythrocyte

Reticulocytes

COAGULATION DISORDERS

The most common cause of coagulation problems is a deficiency in the number of circulating platelets, a condition termed **thrombocytopenia**. Possible causes include aplastic anemia, infections, bone marrow cancer, and agents that destroy bone marrow, such as x-rays or certain drugs. This disorder results in bleeding into the skin and mucous membranes, variously described as **petechiae** (pinpoint spots), **ecchymoses** (bruises), and **purpura** (purple lesions).

In **disseminated intravascular coagulation (DIC)**, widespread clotting in the vessels obstructs circulation to the tissues. This is followed by diffuse hemorrhages as clotting factors are removed and the coagulation process is impaired. DIC may result from a variety of causes, including infection, cancer, hemorrhage, injury, and **allergy**.

Hemophilia is a hereditary deficiency of a specific clotting factor. It is a genetically sex-linked disease that is passed from mother to son. There is bleeding into the tissues, especially into the joints (hemarthrosis). Hemophilia must be treated with transfusions of the necessary clotting factor.

Box 10-7 lists tests done for these and other coagulation disorders.

NEOPLASMS

Leukemia is a neoplasm of WBCs. The rapidly dividing but incompetent white cells accumulate in the tissues and crowd out the other blood cells. The symptoms of leukemia include anemia, fatigue, easy bleeding, **splenomegaly**, and sometimes hepatomegaly (enlargement of the liver). The causes of leukemia are unknown but may include exposure to radiation or harmful chemicals, hereditary factors, and perhaps viral infection.

The two main categories of leukemia are determined by origin and the cells involved:

- Myelogenous leukemia originates in the bone marrow and involves mainly the granular leukocytes.

- Lymphocytic leukemia affects B cells and the lymphatic system, causing **lymphadenopathy** (lymph node disease) and adverse effects on the immune system.

Leukemias are further differentiated as acute or chronic based on clinical progress. Acute leukemia is the most common form of cancer in young children. The acute forms are:

- Acute myeloblastic (myelogenous) leukemia (AML). The prognosis in AML is poor for both children and adults.
- Acute lymphoblastic (lymphocytic) leukemia (ALL). With treatment, the ALL remission rate is high.

The chronic forms of leukemia are:

- Chronic myelogenous leukemia, also called chronic granulocytic leukemia, affects young to middle-aged adults (**Fig 10-13A**). Most cases show the **Philadelphia chromosome (Ph)**, an inherited anomaly in which part of chromosome 22 shifts to chromosome 9.
- Chronic lymphocytic leukemia (CLL) appears mostly in the elderly and is the most slowly growing form of the disease (**Fig. 10-13B**).

Leukemia treatment includes chemotherapy, radiation therapy, and bone marrow transplantation. One advance in transplantation is the use of umbilical cord blood to replace blood-forming cells in bone marrow. This blood is more readily available than bone marrow and does not have to match as closely to avoid rejection.

Hodgkin disease is a disease of the lymphatic system that may spread to other tissues. It begins with enlarged but painless lymph nodes in the cervical (neck) region and then progresses to other nodes. A feature of Hodgkin disease is giant cells in the lymph nodes called **Reed–Sternberg cells** (**Fig. 10-14**). Symptoms include fever, night sweats, weight loss, and skin itching (pruritus). Persons of any age may be affected, but the disease predominates in young adults and those over 50 years. Most cases can be cured with radiation and chemotherapy.

FOR YOUR REFERENCE
Coagulation Tests

Box 10-7

Test	Abbreviation	Description
activated partial thromboplastin time	APTT	Measures time required for clot formation; used to evaluate clotting factors and monitor heparin therapy
bleeding time	BT	Measures capacity of platelets to stop bleeding after a standard skin incision
partial thromboplastin time	PTT	Evaluates clotting factors; similar to APTT, but less sensitive
prothrombin time	PT, pro time	Indirectly measures prothrombin; used to monitor anticoagulant therapy; also called Quick test
thrombin time (thrombin clotting time)	TT (TCT)	Measures how quickly a clot forms

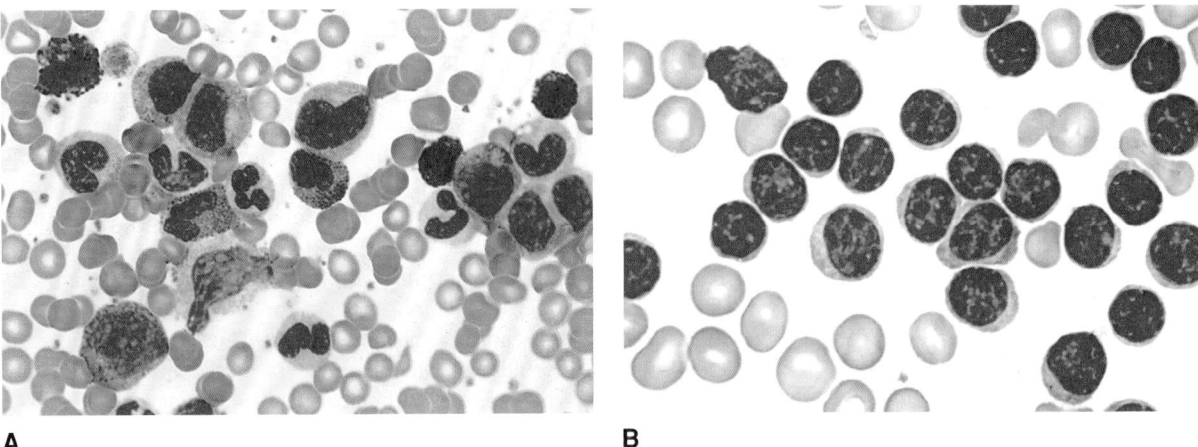

A   **B**

Figure 10-13 **Leukemia.** Leukemia is a malignant overgrowth of white cells originating in the bone marrow (myelogenous) or lymphatic system (lymphocytic). **A.** Chronic myelogenous leukemia showing overproduction of all categories of white cells. **B.** Chronic lymphocytic leukemia showing numerous lymphocytes.

Non-Hodgkin lymphoma (NHL) is also a malignant enlargement of lymph nodes but does not show Reed–Sternberg cells. It is more common than Hodgkin disease and has a higher mortality rate. Cases vary in severity and prognosis. It is most prevalent in the older adult population and in those with AIDS and other forms of immunodeficiency. NHL involves the T or B lymphocytes, and some cases may be related to infection with certain viruses. It requires systemic chemotherapy and sometimes bone marrow transplantation.

Multiple myeloma is a cancer of the blood-forming cells in bone marrow, mainly the plasma cells that produce antibodies. The disease causes anemia, bone pain, and bone weakening. Patients have a greater susceptibility to infection because of immunodeficiency. Abnormally high levels of calcium and protein in the blood often lead to kidney failure. Multiple myeloma is treated with radiation and chemotherapy, but the prognosis is generally poor.

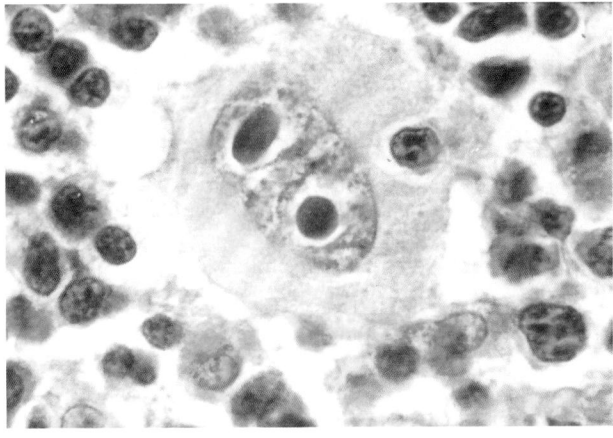

Figure 10-14 **Reed–Sternberg cell.** These cells are typical of Hodgkin disease.

Clinical Aspects of Immunity

HYPERSENSITIVITY

Hypersensitivity is a harmful overreaction of the immune system, commonly known as allergy. In cases of allergy, a person is more sensitive to a particular antigen than the average individual. Common **allergens** are pollen, animal dander, dust, and foods, but there are many more. A seasonal allergy to inhaled pollens is commonly called "hay fever." Responses may include itching, redness, or tearing of the eyes (conjunctivitis), skin rash, asthma, runny nose (rhinitis), sneezing, **urticaria** (hives), and **angioedema**, a reaction similar to hives but involving deeper layers of tissue.

An **anaphylactic reaction** is a severe generalized allergic response that can rapidly lead to death as a result of shock and respiratory distress. It must be treated by immediate administration of **epinephrine (adrenaline)** and maintenance of open airways. Oxygen, antihistamines, and corticosteroids may also be given. Common causes of anaphylaxis are drugs, especially penicillin and other antibiotics, vaccines, diagnostic chemicals, foods, and insect venom.

A **delayed hypersensitivity reaction** involves T cells and takes at least 12 hours to develop. A common example is the reaction to contact with plant irritants such as those of poison ivy and poison oak.

IMMUNODEFICIENCY

The term **immunodeficiency** refers to any failure in the immune system. This may be congenital (present at birth) or acquired and may involve any components of the system. The deficiency may vary in severity but is always evidenced by an increased susceptibility to disease.

Acquired immunodeficiency syndrome (AIDS) is acquired by infection with **human immunodeficiency virus (HIV)**, which attacks certain T cells. These cells have a specific surface attachment site, the CD4 receptor, for the virus. HIV is spread by sexual contact, use of contaminated needles, blood transfusions, and passage from an infected mother to her fetus. It leaves the host susceptible to opportunistic infections such as pneumonia caused by the fungus *Pneumocystis jirovecii*; thrush, an oral fungal infection caused by *Candida albicans*; and infection with *Cryptosporidium*, a protozoon that causes cramps and diarrhea. It also predisposes the patient to **Kaposi sarcoma**, a once-rare form of skin cancer. AIDS may also induce autoimmunity or attack the nervous system.

AIDS is diagnosed and monitored by **CD4+ T lymphocyte counts**, a measure of cells with the HIV receptor. A count of less than 200/mcL of blood signifies severe immunodeficiency. HIV antibody levels and direct viral blood counts are also used to track the disease's course. At present there is no vaccine or cure for AIDS, but drugs can delay its progress.

AUTOIMMUNE DISEASES

A disorder that results from an immune response to one's own tissues is classified as an **autoimmune disease**. The cause may be a failure in the immune system or a reaction to body cells that have been slightly altered by mutation or disease. The list of diseases that are believed to be caused, at least in part, by autoimmunity is long. Some, such as **systemic lupus erythematosus** (SLE), **systemic sclerosis** (scleroderma), and **Sjögren syndrome**, affect tissues in multiple systems. Others target more specific organs or systems. Examples are pernicious anemia, rheumatoid arthritis, Graves disease (of the thyroid), myasthenia gravis (a muscle disease), fibromyalgia syndrome (a musculoskeletal disorder), rheumatic heart disease, and glomerulonephritis (a kidney disease). These diseases are discussed in more detail in other chapters.

Terminology   Key Terms

Disorders

acquired immunodeficiency syndrome (AIDS)	Immune system failure caused by infection with HIV (human immunodeficiency virus); the virus infects certain T cells and thus interferes with immunity
allergen *AL-er-jen*	A substance that causes an allergic response
allergy *AL-er-je*	Hypersensitivity
anaphylactic reaction *an-ah-fih-LAK-tik*	An exaggerated allergic reaction to a foreign substance; it may lead to death caused by circulatory collapse and respiratory distress if untreated; also called anaphylaxis (from Greek *phylaxis*, meaning "protection")
anemia *ah-NE-me-ah*	A deficiency in the amount of hemoglobin in the blood; may result from blood loss, malnutrition, a hereditary defect, environmental factors, and other causes (**Figs. 10-11** and **10-12**)
angioedema *an-je-o-eh-DE-mah*	A localized edema with large hives (wheals) similar to urticaria but involving deeper layers of the skin and subcutaneous tissue
aplastic anemia *a-PLAS-tik*	Anemia caused by bone marrow failure resulting in deficient blood cell production, especially of red cells; pancytopenia
autoimmune disease *aw-to-ih-MUNE*	A condition in which the immune system produces antibodies against an individual's own tissues (prefix *auto* means "self")
Cooley anemia	A form of thalassemia (hereditary anemia) that affects production of the β (beta) hemoglobin chain; thalassemia major
delayed hypersensitivity reaction	An allergic reaction involving T cells that takes at least 12 hours to develop; examples are various types of contact dermatitis, such as poison ivy or poison oak; the tuberculin reaction (test for TB); and rejections of transplanted tissue
disseminated intravascular coagulation (DIC)	Widespread clot formation in the microscopic vessels; may be followed by bleeding caused by depletion of clotting factors
ecchymosis *ek-ih-MO-sis*	A collection of blood under the skin caused by leakage from small vessels (root *chym* means "juice")
hemolysis *he-MOL-ih-sis*	The rupture of red blood cells and the release of hemoglobin (adjective: hemolytic)

hemophilia *he-mo-FIL-e-ah*	A hereditary blood disease caused by lack of a clotting factor resulting in abnormal bleeding
hemorrhagic anemia *hem-o-RAJ-ik*	Anemia that results from blood loss, as from an injury or internal bleeding
human immunodeficiency virus (HIV)	The virus that causes AIDS
Hodgkin disease	A neoplastic disease of unknown cause that involves the lymph nodes, spleen, liver, and other tissues; characterized by the presence of giant Reed–Sternberg cells (**Fig. 10-14**)
hypersensitivity	An immunologic reaction to a substance that is harmless to most people; allergy
immunodeficiency *im-u-no-de-FISH-en-se*	A congenital or acquired failure of the immune system to protect against disease
intrinsic factor	A substance produced in the stomach that aids in the intestinal absorption of vitamin B_{12}, necessary for the manufacture of red blood cells; lack of intrinsic factor causes pernicious anemia
Kaposi sarcoma *KAP-o-se*	Cancerous lesion of the skin and other tissues, seen most often in patients with AIDS
leukemia *lu-KE-me-ah*	Malignant overgrowth of immature white blood cells; may be chronic or acute; may affect bone marrow (myelogenous leukemia) or lymphoid tissue (lymphocytic leukemia)
lymphadenopathy *lim-fad-eh-NOP-ah-the*	Any disease of the lymph nodes
multiple myeloma *mi-eh-LO-mah*	A tumor of the blood-forming tissue in bone marrow
non-Hodgkin lymphoma (NHL)	A widespread malignant disease of lymph nodes that involves lymphocytes; it differs from Hodgkin disease in that giant Reed–Sternberg cells are absent
nutritional anemia *nu-TRISH-un-al*	Anemia resulting from a dietary deficiency, usually of iron, vitamin B_{12}, or folate
Philadelphia chromosome (Ph)	An abnormal chromosome found in the cells of most individuals with chronic granulocytic (myelogenous) leukemia
pernicious anemia *per-NISH-us*	Anemia caused by failure of the stomach to produce intrinsic factor, a substance needed for the absorption of vitamin B_{12}; this vitamin is required for the formation of erythrocytes
petechiae *pe-E-ke-e*	Pinpoint, flat, purplish-red spots caused by bleeding within the skin or mucous membrane (singular: petechia)
purpura *PUR-pu-rah*	A condition characterized by hemorrhages into the skin, mucous membranes, internal organs, and other tissues (from Greek word meaning "purple"); thrombocytopenic purpura is caused by a deficiency of platelets
sickle cell anemia *SIK-l*	A hereditary anemia caused by the presence of abnormal hemoglobin; red blood cells become sickle-shaped when they give up oxygen and interfere with normal blood flow to the tissues (**Fig. 10-12**); most common in black populations of West African descent
sideroblastic anemia *sid-eh-ro-BLAS-tik*	Anemia caused by inability to use available iron to manufacture hemoglobin; the excess iron precipitates in normoblasts (developing red blood cells)
Sjögren syndrome *SHO-gren*	An autoimmune disease involving dysfunction of the exocrine glands and affecting secretion of tears, saliva, and other body fluids; deficiency leads to dry mouth, tooth decay, corneal damage, eye infections, and difficulty in swallowing

(continued)

Terminology | Key Terms (Continued)

splenomegaly *sple-no-MEG-ah-le*	Enlargement of the spleen
systemic lupus erythematosus *LU-pus er-ih-the-mah-TO-sus*	Inflammatory connective tissue disease affecting the skin and multiple organs; patients are sensitive to light and may have a red butterfly-shaped rash over the nose and cheeks
systemic sclerosis	A diffuse connective tissue disease that may involve any system causing inflammation, degeneration, and fibrosis; also called scleroderma because it causes thickening of the skin
thalassemia *thal-ah-SE-me-ah*	A group of hereditary anemias mostly found in populations of Mediterranean descent (the name comes from the Greek word for "sea")
thrombocytopenia *throm-bo-si-to-PE-ne-ah*	A deficiency of thrombocytes (platelets) in the blood
urticaria *ur-tih-KAR-e-ah*	A skin reaction consisting of round, raised eruptions (wheals) with itching; hives

Diagnosis and Treatment

adrenaline *ah-DREN-ah-lin*	See epinephrine
CD4+ T lymphocyte count	A count of the T cells that have the CD4 receptors for the AIDS virus (HIV); a count of less than 200/mcL of blood signifies severe immunodeficiency
epinephrine *ep-ih-NEF-rin*	A powerful stimulant produced by the adrenal gland and sympathetic nervous system; activates the cardiovascular, respiratory, and other systems needed to meet stress; used as a drug to treat severe allergic reactions and shock; also called adrenaline
reticulocyte counts *re-TIK-u-lo-site*	Blood counts of reticulocytes, a type of immature red blood cell; reticulocyte counts are useful in diagnosis to indicate the rate of erythrocyte formation (**Box 10-6**)
Reed–Sternberg cells *rede SHTERN-berg*	Giant cells that are characteristic of Hodgkin disease; they usually have two large nuclei and are surrounded by a halo (**Fig. 10-14**)

Terminology | Supplementary Terms

Normal Structure and Function

agglutination *ah-glu-tih-NA-shun*	The clumping of cells or particles in the presence of specific antibodies
bilirubin *bil-ih-RU-bin*	A pigment derived from the breakdown of hemoglobin and eliminated by the liver in bile
complement *COM-pleh-ment*	A group of plasma enzymes that interacts with antibodies
corpuscle *KOR-pus-l*	A small mass or body; a blood corpuscle is a blood cell
hemopoietic stem cell *he-mo-poy-EH-tik*	A primitive bone marrow cell that gives rise to all varieties of blood cells
heparin *HEP-ah-rin*	A substance found throughout the body that inhibits blood coagulation; an anticoagulant

Terminology | Supplementary Terms *(Continued)*

plasmin *PLAZ-min*	An enzyme that dissolves clots; also called fibrinolysin
thrombin *THROM-bin*	The enzyme derived from prothrombin that converts fibrinogen to fibrin

Symptoms and Conditions

agranulocytosis *a-gran-u-lo-si-TO-sis*	A condition involving a decrease in the number of granulocytes in the blood; also called granulocytopenia
erythrocytosis *eh-rith-ro-si-TO-sis*	Increase in the number of red cells in the blood; may be normal, such as to compensate for life at high altitudes, or abnormal, such as in cases of pulmonary or cardiac disease
Fanconi syndrome *fan-KO-ne*	Congenital aplastic anemia that appears between birth and 10 years of age; may be hereditary or caused by damage before birth, as by a virus
graft versus host reaction (GVHR)	An immunologic reaction of transplanted lymphocytes against tissues of the host; a common complication of bone marrow transplantation
hairy cell leukemia	A form of leukemia in which cells have filaments, making them look hairy
hematoma *he-mah-TO-mah*	A localized collection of blood, usually clotted, caused by a break in a blood vessel
hemolytic disease of the newborn (HDN)	Disease that results from incompatibility between the blood of a mother and her fetus, usually involving Rh factor; an Rh-negative mother produces antibody to an Rh-positive fetus that, in later pregnancies, will destroy the red cells of an Rh-positive fetus; the problem is usually avoided by treating the mother with antibodies to remove the Rh antigen; also called erythroblastosis fetalis
hemosiderosis *he-mo-sid-er-O-sis*	A condition involving the deposition of an iron-containing pigment (hemosiderin) mainly in the liver and the spleen; the pigment comes from hemoglobin released from disintegrated red blood cells
idiopathic thrombocytopenic purpura (ITP)	A clotting disorder caused by destruction of platelets that usually follows a viral illness; causes petechiae and hemorrhages into the skin and mucous membranes
infectious mononucleosis *mon-o-nu-kle-O-sis*	An acute infectious disease caused by Epstein–Barr virus (EBV); characterized by fever, weakness, lymphadenopathy, hepatosplenomegaly, and atypical lymphocytes (resembling monocytes) **(Fig. 10-15)**

(continued)

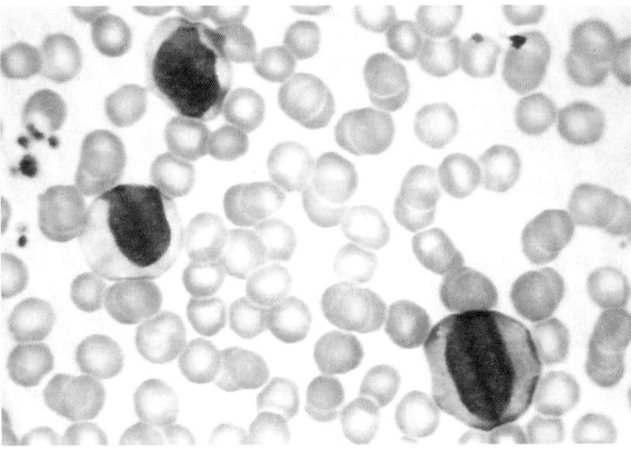

Figure 10-15 **Infectious mononucleosis.** Atypical lymphocytes characterize this viral disease.

Terminology Supplementary Terms (Continued)

lymphocytosis *lim-fo-si-TO-sis*	An increase in the number of circulating lymphocytes
myelodysplastic syndrome *mi-eh-lo-dis-PLAS-tik*	Bone marrow dysfunction resulting in anemia and deficiency of neutrophils and platelets; may develop in time into leukemia; preleukemia
myelofibrosis *mi-eh-lo-fi-BRO-sis*	Condition in which bone marrow is replaced with fibrous tissue
neutropenia *nu-tro-PE-ne-ah*	A decrease in the number of neutrophils with increased susceptibility to infection; causes include drugs, irradiation, and infection; may be a side effect of treatment for malignancy
pancytopenia *pan-si-to-PE-ne-ah*	A decrease in all cells of the blood, as in aplastic anemia
polycythemia *pol-e-si-THE-me-ah*	Any condition in which there is a relative increase in the percent of red blood cells in whole blood; may result from excessive production of red cells because of oxygen lack, as caused by high altitudes, breathing obstruction, heart failure, or certain forms of poisoning. Apparent polycythemia results from concentration of the blood, as by dehydration (see **Fig. 10-10**)
polycythemia vera *pol-e-si-THE-me-ah VE-rah*	A condition in which overactive bone marrow produces too many red blood cells (see **Fig 10-10**) that interfere with circulation and promote thrombosis and hemorrhage; treated by blood removal; also called erythremia and Vaquez–Osler disease
septicemia *sep-tih-SE-me-ah*	Presence of microorganisms in the blood
spherocytic anemia *sfer-o-SIT-ik*	Hereditary anemia in which red blood cells are round instead of disk shaped and rupture (hemolyze) excessively
thrombotic thrombocytopenic purpura (TTP)	An often fatal disorder in which multiple clots form in blood vessels
von Willebrand disease	A hereditary bleeding disease caused by lack of von Willebrand factor, a substance necessary for blood clotting

Diagnosis (see also Boxes 10-4 and 10-7)

Bence Jones protein	A protein that appears in the urine of patients with multiple myeloma
Coombs test	A test for detection of antibodies to red blood cells, such as those appearing in cases of autoimmune hemolytic anemias
electrophoresis *e-lek-tro-fo-RE-sis*	Separation of particles in a liquid by application of an electrical field; used to separate components of blood
ELISA	Enzyme-linked immunosorbent assay; a highly sensitive immunologic test used to diagnose HIV infection, hepatitis, and Lyme disease, among others
monoclonal antibody *mon-o-KLO-nal*	A pure antibody produced in the laboratory; used for diagnosis and treatment
pH	A scale that measures the relative acidity or alkalinity of a solution; represents the amount of hydrogen ion in the solution
Schilling test *SHIL-ing*	Test used to determine absorption of vitamin B_{12} by measuring excretion of radioactive B_{12} in the urine; used to distinguish pernicious from nutritional anemia
seroconversion *se-ro-con-VER-zhun*	The appearance of antibodies in the serum in response to a disease or an immunization

Terminology   Supplementary Terms *(Continued)*

Western blot assay	A very sensitive test used to detect small amounts of antibodies in the blood
Wright stain	A commonly used blood stain; **Figure 10-2** shows blood cells stained with Wright stain

Treatment

anticoagulant *an-ti-ko-AG-u-lant*	An agent that prevents or delays blood coagulation
antihistamine *an-tih-HIS-tah-meme*	A drug that counteracts the effects of histamine and is used to treat allergic reactions
apheresis *af-eh-RE-sis*	A procedure in which blood is withdrawn, a portion is separated and retained, and the remainder is returned to the donor; apheresis may be used as a suffix with a root meaning the fraction retained, such as plasmapheresis, leukapheresis
autologous blood *aw-TOL-o-gus*	A person's own blood; may be donated in advance of surgery and transfused if needed
cryoprecipitate *kri-o-pre-SIP-ih-tate*	A sediment obtained by cooling; the fraction obtained by freezing blood plasma contains clotting factors
desensitization *de-sen-sih-tih-ZA-shun*	Treatment of allergy by small injections of the offending allergen, causing an increase of antibody to destroy the antigen rapidly on contact
homologous blood *ho-MOL-o-gus*	Blood from animals of the same species, such as human blood used for transfusion from one person to another; blood used for transfusions must be compatible with the recipient's blood
immunosuppression *im-u-no-su-PRESH-un*	Depression of the immune response; may be correlated with disease but also may be induced therapeutically to prevent rejection in cases of tissue transplantation
protease inhibitor *PRO-te-ase*	An anti-HIV drug that acts by inhibiting an enzyme the virus needs to multiply

Go to the Audio Pronunciation Glossary in the Student Resources on thePoint to hear these terms pronounced.

Terminology   Abbreviations

Ab	Antibody	**CLL**	Chronic lymphocytic leukemia
Ag	Antigen, also silver	**CML**	Chronic myelogenous leukemia
AIDS	Acquired immunodeficiency syndrome	**crit**	Hematocrit
ALL	Acute lymphoblastic (lymphocytic) leukemia	**DIC**	Disseminated intravascular coagulation
AML	Acute myeloblastic (myelogenous) leukemia	**Diff**	Differential count
APC	Antigen-presenting cell	**EBV**	Epstein–Barr virus
APTT	Activated partial thromboplastin time	**ELISA**	Enzyme-linked immunosorbent assay
BT	Bleeding time	**EPO, EP**	Erythropoietin
CBC	Complete blood count	**ESR**	Erythrocyte sedimentation rate
CGL	Chronic granulocytic leukemia	**FFP**	Fresh frozen plasma

(continued)

Terminology   Abbreviations (Continued)

Hb, Hgb	Hemoglobin		PCV	Packed cell volume
Hct, Ht	Hematocrit		pH	Scale for measuring hydrogen ion concentration (acidity or alkalinity)
HDN	Hemolytic disease of the newborn		Ph	Philadelphia chromosome
HIV	Human immunodeficiency virus		PMN	Polymorphonuclear (neutrophil)
IF	Intrinsic factor		poly	Neutrophil
Ig	Immunoglobulin		polymorph	Neutrophil
ITP	Idiopathic thrombocytopenic purpura		PT	Prothrombin time; pro time
lytes	Electrolytes		PTT	Partial thromboplastin time
MCH	Mean corpuscular hemoglobin		RBC	Red blood cell; red blood (cell) count
MCHC	Mean corpuscular hemoglobin concentration		seg	Neutrophil
mcL	Microliter		SLE	Systemic lupus erythematosus
mcm	Micrometer		T(C)T	Thrombin (clotting) time
MCV	Mean corpuscular volume		TTP	Thrombotic thrombocytopenic purpura
MDS	Myelodysplastic syndrome		vWF	von Willebrand factor
mEq	Milliequivalent		WBC	White blood cell; white blood (cell) count
NHL	Non-Hodgkin lymphoma			

Case Study Revisited

M.R.'s Case Study Follow-Up

M.R. avoids all contact with any natural rubber latex in her home and at work. She can work only in a pediatric OR, as they are latex-free, because many children with congenital disorders are allergic to latex. She wears a medical alert bracelet, uses a bronchodilator inhaler at the first symptom of bronchospasm, and carries a syringe of epinephrine at all times.

CHAPTER 10 **Review**

Labeling Exercise

BLOOD CELLS

Write the name of each numbered part on the corresponding line of the answer sheet.

Erythrocyte

Leukocyte

Platelet

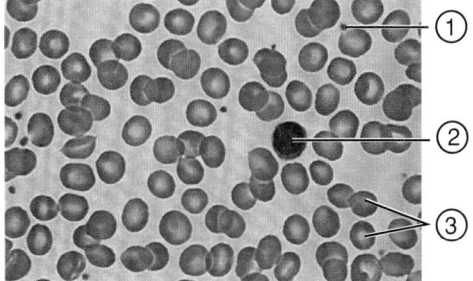

1. _____

2. _____

3. _____

LEUKOCYTES (WHITE BLOOD CELLS)

Write the name of each numbered part on the corresponding line of the answer sheet.

Basophil

Eosinophil

Lymphocyte

Monocyte

Neutrophil

Leukocytes (white blood cells)

1. _____

2. _____

3. _____

4. _____

5. _____

Terminology

MATCHING

Match the following terms, and write the appropriate letter to the left of each number.

_____ **1.** anemia

_____ **2.** thrombolytic

_____ **3.** antibody

_____ **4.** megakaryocyte

_____ **5.** prothrombin

a. substance active in blood clotting

b. cell that produces platelets

c. deficiency in the amount of hemoglobin in the blood

d. able to dissolve a blood clot

e. substance active in an immune response

_____ **6.** hypokalemia

_____ **7.** natriuresis

_____ **8.** ferric

_____ **9.** siderosis

_____ **10.** azoturia

a. condition involving iron deposits

b. deficiency of potassium in the blood

c. urinary excretion of sodium

d. urinary excretion of nitrogenous compounds

e. pertaining to iron

_____ **11.** hemophilia

_____ **12.** hemostasis

_____ **13.** hypersensitivity

_____ **14.** thalassemia

_____ **15.** purpura

a. allergy

b. hereditary form of anemia

c. stoppage of blood flow

d. hereditary clotting disorder

e. bleeding into the tissues

_____ **16.** pH

_____ **17.** HIV

_____ **18.** ALL

_____ **19.** PCV

_____ **20.** CBC

a. laboratory test of blood

b. a form of leukemia

c. hematocrit

d. virus that causes an immunodeficiency disease

e. scale for measuring acidity or alkalinity

Supplementary Terms

_____ **21.** erythrocytosis

_____ **22.** heparin

_____ **23.** apheresis

_____ **24.** ELISA

_____ **25.** electrophoresis

a. separation of blood and use of components

b. increase in the number of RBCs in the blood

c. anticoagulant

d. method for separating components of a solution

e. sensitive immunologic test

FILL IN THE BLANKS

26. The engulfing of foreign material by white cells is called _____.

27. The iron-containing pigment in red blood cells that carries oxygen is called _____.

28. A substance that separates into ions in solution is a(n) _____.

29. The cell fragments active in blood clotting are the _____.

30. A hemocytometer is used to count _____.

31. Oxyhemoglobin is hemoglobin combined with _____.

32. A hematoma is a localized collection of _____.

33. A disorder involving lack of hemoglobin in the blood is _____.

34. A myeloma is a neoplasm that involves the _____.

35. The abbreviation Ig means _____.

MULTIPLE CHOICE

Referring to M.R.'s opening case study, select the best answer, and write the letter of your choice to the left of each number.

_____ 36. Anaphylaxis, a life-threatening physiologic response, is an extreme form of

  a. remission

  b. hemostasis

  c. hypersensitivity

  d. homeostasis

_____ 37. Urticaria is commonly called

  a. hives

  b. dermatitis

  c. rhinitis

  d. congenital

_____ 38. The cells involved in a T cell-mediated allergic response are

  a. basophils

  b. monocytes

  c. lymphocytes

  d. B cells

_____ 39. The natural latex protein in latex gloves may act as a(n)

  a. antibody

  b. allergen

  c. purpura

  d. immunocyte

_____ 40. The common name for epinephrine is

  a. cortisone

  b. adrenaline

  c. heparin

  d. antihistamine

TRUE-FALSE

Examine the following statements. If the statement is true, write T in the first blank. If the statement is false, write F in the first blank, and correct the statement by replacing the underlined word in the second blank.

	True or False	Correct Answer
41. A leukocyte is also called a <u>platelet</u>.	_____	_____
42. A plasma cell produces <u>antibodies</u>.	_____	_____
43. The liquid that remains after blood coagulates is called <u>serum</u>.	_____	_____
44. Blood that does not react with either A or B antiserum is <u>type O</u>.	_____	_____
45. A band cell is an immature <u>monocyte</u>.	_____	_____
46. The root kali- pertains to <u>potassium</u>.	_____	_____

DEFINITIONS

The suffixes -ia, -osis, and -hemia all denote an increase in the type of cell indicated by the word root. Define the following terms.

47. leukocytosis (*lu-ko-si-TO-sis*) _____

48. eosinophilia (*e-o-sin-o-FIL-e-ah*) _____

49. erythrocytosis (*eh-rith-ro-si-TO-sis*)_____

50. thrombocythemia (*throm-bo-si-THE-me-ah*) _____

51. neutrophilia (*nu-tro-FIL-e-ah*) _____

52. monocytosis (*mon-o-si-TO-sis*)_____

Write a word for each of the following.

53. An immature red blood cell _____

54. A decrease in the number of platelets (thrombocytes) in the blood _____

55. Presence of pus in the blood _____

56. Specialist in the study of immunity _____

57. Profuse flow of blood _____

Define each of the following.

58. hemolysis _____

59. neutropenia _____

60. myelotoxin _____

61. autoimmunity _____

62. viremia _____

ADJECTIVES

Use the ending -ic to write the adjective form of the following words.

63. hemolysis _____

64. leukemia _____

65. basophil _____

66. septicemia _____

67. thrombosis _____

68. lymphocyte _____

ELIMINATIONS

In each of the sets below, underline the word that does not fit in with the rest and explain the reason for your choice.

69. fibrin — thrombin — thrombolysis — prothrombin — fibrinogen

_____

70. Diff — Hct — MCV — EPO — MCH

_____

71. eosinophil — reticulocyte — monocyte — basophil — lymphocyte

_____

72. allergy — hypersensitivity — gamma globulin — urticaria — anaphylaxis

_____

WORD BUILDING

Write a word for the following definitions using the word parts given.

-penia   -blast   leuk/o   -oid   -poiesis   myel/o   gen-   -emia   erythr/o   -ic   -oma   cyt/o

73. pertaining to a red blood cell _____

74. an immature white blood cell _____

75. pertaining to bone marrow _____

76. originating in bone marrow _____

77. an immature bone marrow cell _____

78. neoplastic overgrowth of white cells in the blood _____

79. deficiency of white cells in the blood _____

80. cancer of bone marrow _____

81. formation of red blood cells _____

82. pertaining to bone marrow cells _____

WORD ANALYSIS

Define the following words, and give the meaning of the word parts in each. Use a dictionary if necessary.

83. Pancytopenia (*pan-si-to-PE-ne-ah*) _____

    a. pan- _____

    b. cyt/o _____

    c. -penia _____

84. Polycythemia (*pol-e-si-THE-me-ah*) _____

    a. poly- _____

    b. cyt/o _____

    c. hem/o _____

    d. -ia _____

85. Anisochromia (*an-i-so-KRO-me-ah*) _____

    a. an- _____

    b. iso- _____

    c. chrom/o _____

    d. -ia _____

86. Myelodysplastic (*mi-eh-lo-dis-PLAS-tic*) _____

    a. myel/o _____

    b. dys- _____

    c. plast(y) _____

    d. -ic _____

For more learning activities, see Chapter 10 of the Student Resources on thePoint.

Additional Case Studies

Case Study 10-1: *Blood Replacement*

C.L., a 16-year-old girl, sustained a ruptured liver when she hit a tree while sledding. Emergency surgery was needed to stop the internal bleeding. During surgery, the ruptured segment of the liver was removed, and the laceration was sutured with a heavy, absorbable suture on a large smooth needle. Before surgery, her hemoglobin was 10.2 g/dL, but the reading decreased to 7.6 g/dL before hemostasis was attained. Cell salvage, or autotransfusion, was set up. In this procedure, the free blood was suctioned from her abdomen and mixed with an anticoagulant (heparin). The RBCs were washed in a sterile centrifuge with NS and transfused back to her through tubing fitted with a filter. She also received six units of homologous,

leukocyte-reduced whole blood, five units of fresh frozen plasma, and two units of platelets. During the surgery, the CRNA repeatedly tested her Hgb and Hct as well as prothrombin time and partial thromboplastin time to monitor her clotting mechanisms.

C.L. is B-positive. Fortunately, there was enough B-positive blood in the hospital blood bank for her surgery. The laboratory informed her surgeon that they had two units of B-negative and six units of O-negative blood, which she could have received safely if she needed more blood during the night. However, her hemoglobin level increased to 12 g/dL, and she was stable during her recovery. She was monitored for DIC and pulmonary emboli.

Case Study 10-2: *Myelofibrosis*

A.Y., a 52-year-old kindergarten teacher, had myelofibrosis that had been in remission for 25 years. She had seen her hematologist regularly and had had routine blood testing since the age of 27. After several weeks of fatigue, idiopathic joint and muscle aching, weakness, and a frightening episode of syncope, she saw her hematologist for evaluation. Her hemoglobin was 9.0 g/dL and her hematocrit was 29 percent. Concerned that she was having an exacerbation, her doctor scheduled a bone marrow aspiration, and the results were positive for myelofibrosis.

A.Y. went through a six-month therapy regimen of iron supplements in the form of ferrous sulfate tablets and received weekly vitamin B_{12} injections. Interferon was given every other week in addition to erythropoiesis therapy, which was unsuccessful. She

was treated for presumed aplastic anemia. During treatment, splenomegaly developed, which compromised her abdominal organs and pulmonary function. She continued to lose weight, and her hemoglobin dropped as low as 6.0 g/dL. Weekly transfusions of packed RBCs did not improve her hemoglobin and hematocrit.

After a regimen of high-dose chemotherapy to shrink the fibers in her bone marrow and a splenectomy, A.Y. received a stem cell transplant. The stem cells were obtained from blood donated by her brother, who was a perfect immunologic match. After a six-month period of recovery in a protected environment, required because of her immunocompromised state, A.Y. returned home and has been free of disease symptoms for over one year.

Case Study Questions

Multiple Choice. Select the best answer, and write the letter of your choice to the left of each number.

_____ **1.** The unit for hemoglobin measurement (g/dL) means
    a. grams in decimal point
    b. grains in a deciliter
    c. drops in 50 mL
    d. grams in 100 mL

_____ **2.** Heparin, an anticoagulant, is a drug that
    a. increases the rate of blood clotting
    b. takes the place of fibrin
    c. makes blood thinner than water
    d. interferes with blood clotting

_____ **3.** The RBCs were washed with NS. This means the _____ were washed with _____.

   a. reticulocytes, heparin

   b. red blood cells, nutritional solution

   c. erythrocytes, normal saline

   d. red blood cells, heparin

_____ **4.** Autotransfusion is transfusion of autologous blood, that is, the patient's own blood. Homologous blood is taken from

   a. another human

   b. synthetic chemicals

   c. plasma with clotting factors

   d. IV fluid with electrolytes

_____ **5.** Patients who lose significant amounts of blood may lose clotting ability. Effective therapy in such cases would be replacement of

   a. IV solution with electrolytes

   b. packed RBCs

   c. platelets

   d. heparin

_____ **6.** C.L.'s blood type is B-positive. The best blood for her to receive is

   a. A-negative

   b. AB-positive

   c. B-negative

   d. B-positive

_____ **7.** Myelofibrosis, like aplastic anemia, is a disease in which there is

   a. overgrowth of RBCs

   b. destruction of the bone marrow

   c. dangerously high hemoglobin and hematocrit

   d. absence of bone marrow

_____ **8.** Erythropoiesis is

   a. production of blood

   b. production of red cells

   c. destruction of platelets

   d. destruction of white cells

_____ **9.** The "ferrous" in ferrous sulfate represents

   a. electrolytes

   b. B vitamins

   c. iron

   d. oxygen

_____ **10.** Hemoglobin and hematocrit values pertain to

   a. leukocytes

   b. fibrinogen

   c. granulocytes

   d. red blood cells

_____ **11.** Splenomegaly is

   a. prolapse of the spleen

   b. movement of the spleen

   c. enlargement of the lymph glands

   d. enlargement of the spleen

_____ **12.** The stem cells A.Y. received were expected to develop into new

   a. spleen cells

   b. bone marrow cells

   c. hemoglobin

   d. cartilage

_____ **13.** A.Y.'s health was compromised because the high-dose chemotherapy caused

   a. immunodeficiency

   b. electrolyte imbalance

   c. anoxia

   d. autoimmunity

Define the following abbreviations.

14. PT _____

15. PTT _____

16. FFP _____

17. Hgb _____

18. Hct _____

19. DIC _____

The Respiratory System

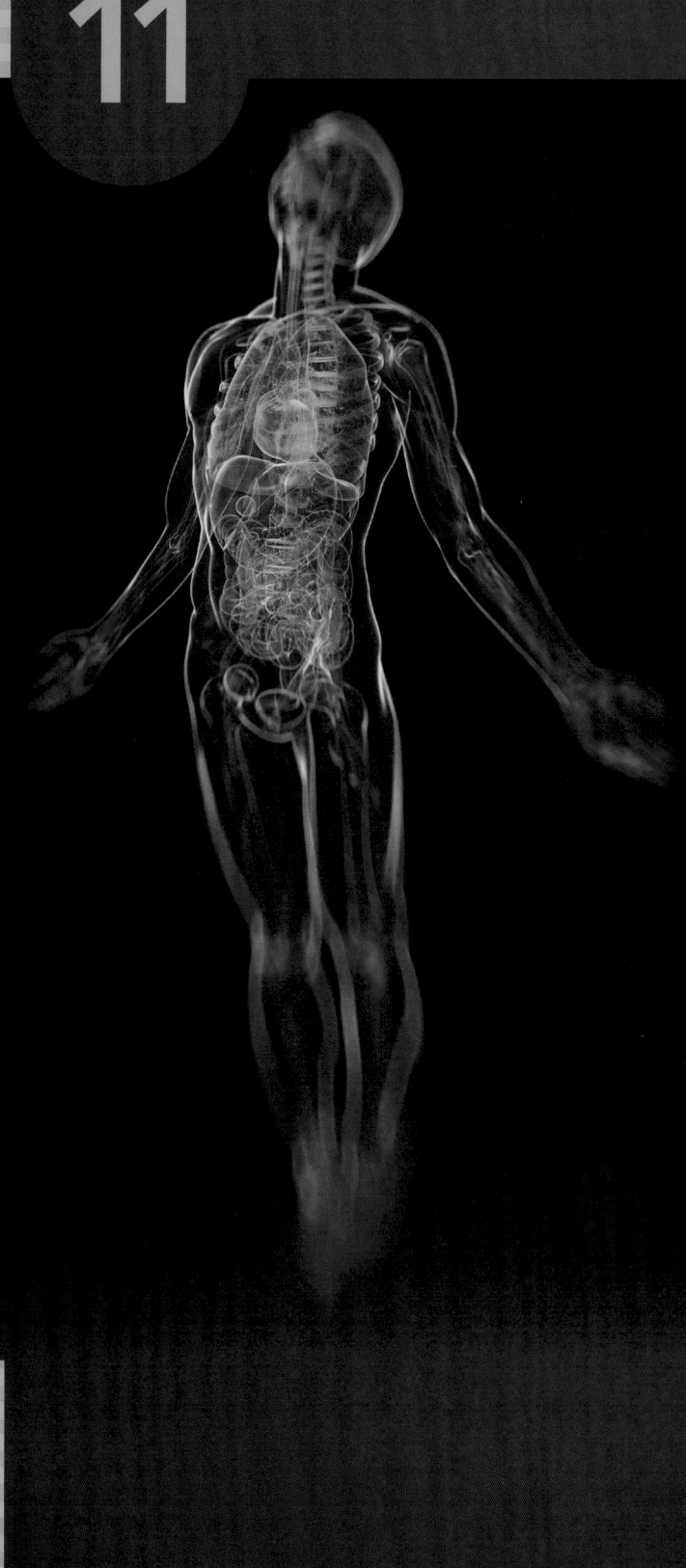

Pretest

Multiple Choice. Select the best answer, and write the letter of your choice to the left of each number.

_____ 1. The gas that is supplied to tissues by the respiratory system is
   a. sulfur
   b. neon
   c. oxygen
   d. carbon dioxide

_____ 2. The gas that is eliminated by the respiratory system is
   a. chlorine
   b. carbon dioxide
   c. hydrogen
   d. fluoride

_____ 3. The air sacs through which gases are exchanged in the lungs are the
   a. trachea
   b. bronchi
   c. bursae
   d. alveoli

_____ 4. The structure that holds the vocal folds is the
   a. larynx
   b. tongue
   c. uvula
   d. tonsils

_____ 5. The tubes that carry air from the trachea into the lungs are the
   a. arteries
   b. nares
   c. veins
   d. bronchi

_____ 6. The dome-shaped muscle under the lungs is the
   a. palate
   b. hiatus
   c. diaphragm
   d. esophagus

_____ 7. The membrane around the lungs is the
   a. peritoneum
   b. mucosa
   c. pleura
   d. mediastinum

_____ 8. A term for inflammation of the lungs is
   a. bronchitis
   b. pneumonia
   c. pleurisy
   d. laryngitis

Learning Objectives

After study of this chapter you should be able to:

1 ▶ Compare external and internal gas exchange. *p238*

2 ▶ Describe and give the functions of the structures in the respiratory tract. *p238*

3 ▶ Describe the mechanism of breathing, including the roles of the diaphragm and phrenic nerve. *p241*

4 ▶ Explain how oxygen and carbon dioxide are carried in the blood. *p242*

5 ▶ Identify and use word parts pertaining to the respiratory system. *p244*

6 ▶ Discuss nine disorders of the respiratory system. *p247*

7 ▶ Name three types of organisms that can infect the respiratory system and give examples of each. *p247*

8 ▶ List and define 10 volumes and capacities commonly used to measure pulmonary function. *p253*

9 ▶ Interpret abbreviations commonly used with reference to the respiratory system. *p260*

10 ▶ Analyze medical terms in case studies pertaining to respiration. *pp237, 268*

Case Study: *Preoperative Respiratory Testing for A.D., a Young Girl with Asthma*

Chief Complaint

A.D., a 13-year-old girl, was seen in the pre-admission testing unit in preparation for her elective spinal surgery for scoliosis. She has a history of mild asthma since age 4 with at least one attack a week. In an acute attack, she will have mild dyspnea, diffuse wheezing, yet an adequate air exchange that responds to bronchodilators. She was sent to pulmonary health services for a consult with a pulmonologist and pulmonary function studies to clear her for the upcoming spinal surgery.

Examination

Her physical examination was unremarkable except for her respiratory status. Her prebronchodilator spirometry showed a mild reduction in vital capacity but with a moderate to severe decrease in FEV_1 and FEV_1/FVC ratio. After bronchodilator administration, there was a mild but insignificant improvement in FEV_1. The postbronchodilator FEV_1 was 55 percent of predicted value and was considered moderately abnormal. The flow volume loops and spirographic curves were consistent with airflow obstruction.

Clinical Course

The anesthesiologist reviewed the pulmonologist's report. A.D.'s respiratory status was compromised for the surgical procedure and would require medical intervention prior to going to the OR. When the FEV_1 was acceptable, he spoke with A.D. and the family and explained that her respiratory status would be closely monitored during and after surgery. Additional medications would be needed to maintain optimal airflow and oxygenation.

ANCILLARIES *At-A-Glance*

Visit thePoint to access the following resources. For guidance in using the resources most effectively, see pp. ix–xvi.

Learning RESOURCES

▶ **Tips for Effective Studying**
▶ **Web Figure: Principal Muscles of Breathing and Lateral Chest**
▶ **Web Figure: Respiratory Infections**
▶ **Web Figure: Effects of Smoking**
▶ **Animation: Pulmonary Ventilation**
▶ **Animation: Oxygen Transport**

▶ **Animation: Carbon Dioxide Exchange**
▶ **Animation: Asthma**
▶ **Audio Pronunciation Glossary**

Learning ACTIVITIES

▶ **Visual Activities**
▶ **Kinesthetic Activities**
▶ **Auditory Activities**

Introduction

The main function of the respiratory system is to provide oxygen to body cells for energy metabolism and to eliminate **carbon dioxide**, a byproduct of metabolism. Because these gases must be carried to and from the cells in the blood, the respiratory system works closely with the cardiovascular system to accomplish gas exchange (**Fig. 11-1**). This activity has two phases:

- External gas exchange occurs between the outside atmosphere and the blood.
- Internal gas exchange occurs between the blood and the tissues.

External exchange takes place in the **lungs**, located in the thoracic cavity. The remainder of the respiratory tract consists of a series of passageways that conduct air to and from the lungs. No gas exchange occurs in these regions. Refer to **Figure 11-2** as you read the following description of the respiratory tract.

Upper Respiratory Passageways

The upper respiratory passageways consist of the **nose** and **pharynx** (throat). Air can also be exchanged through the mouth, but there are fewer mechanisms for cleansing the air taken in by this route.

THE NOSE

Air enters through the nose, where it is warmed, filtered, and moistened as it passes over the hair-covered mucous membranes of the nasal cavity. Cilia—microscopic hair-like projections from the cells that line the nasal passageways—sweep dirt and foreign material toward the throat for elimination. Material that is eliminated from the respiratory tract by coughing or clearing the throat is called **sputum**. Receptors for the sense of smell are located within bony side projections of the nasal cavity called **turbinate bones** or conchae.

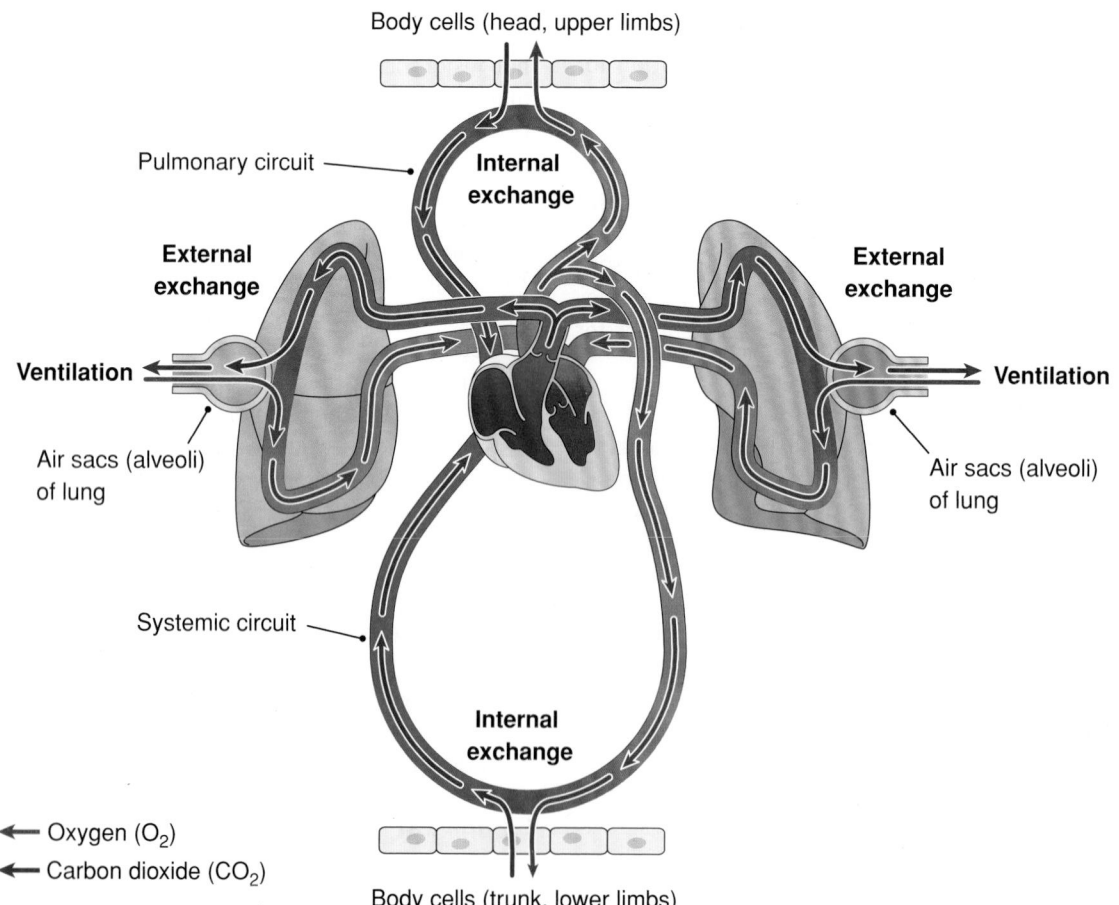

Figure 11-1   **Respiration.** In ventilation, gases are moved into and out of the lungs. In external exchange, gases move between the air sacs (alveoli) of the lungs and the blood. In internal exchange, gases move between the blood and body cells. The circulation transports gases in the blood.

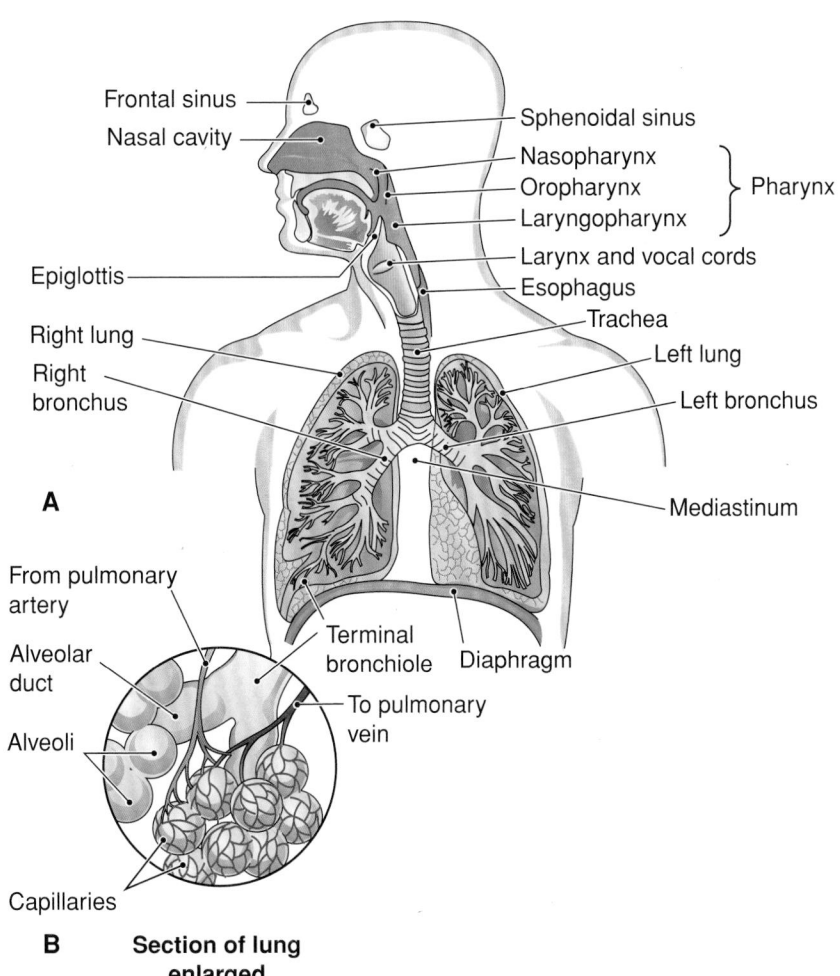

Frontal sinus

Nasal cavity

Sphenoidal sinus

Nasopharynx

Oropharynx } Pharynx

Laryngopharynx

Larynx and vocal cords

Epiglottis

Esophagus

Right lung

Trachea

Right bronchus

Left lung

Left bronchus

A

Mediastinum

From pulmonary artery

Alveolar duct

Terminal bronchiole

Diaphragm

Alveoli

To pulmonary vein

Capillaries

B **Section of lung enlarged**

Figure 11-2 **The respiratory system. A.** Overview. **B.** Enlarged section of lung tissue showing the relationship between the alveoli (air sacs) and the blood capillaries.

In the bones of the skull and face near the nose are air-filled cavities lined with a mucous membrane that drain into the nasal cavity. These chambers lighten the bones and provide resonance for speech production. These cavities, called **sinuses**, are named specifically for the bones in which they are located, such as the frontal, sphenoidal, ethmoidal, and maxillary sinuses. Together, because they are near the nose, these cavities are referred to as the paranasal sinuses. **Figure 11-2** shows the location of the frontal and sphenoidal sinuses.

THE PHARYNX

Inhaled air passes into the throat, or pharynx, where it mixes with air that enters through the mouth and also with food destined for the digestive tract. The pharynx is divided into three regions, which are shown in **Figure 11-2**:

- The nasopharynx is the superior portion located behind the nasal cavity.
- The oropharynx is the middle portion located behind the mouth.
- The laryngopharynx is the inferior portion located behind the **larynx**.

The tonsils, lymphoid tissue described in Chapter 9, are in the region of the pharynx (**Fig. 11-3**):

- The **palatine tonsils** are on either side of the soft palate in the oropharynx.

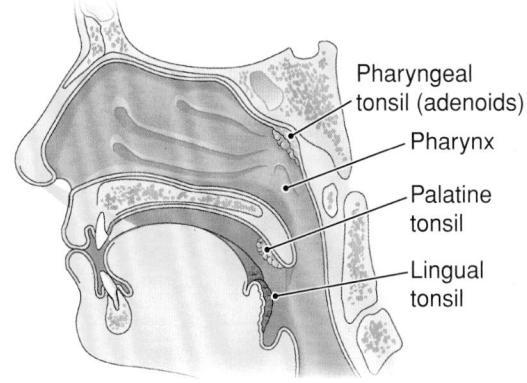

Pharyngeal tonsil (adenoids)

Pharynx

Palatine tonsil

Lingual tonsil

Figure 11-3 **The tonsils.** All of the tonsils are located in the vicinity of the pharynx (throat).

CLINICAL PERSPECTIVES

Box 11-1

Tonsillectomy: A Procedure Reconsidered

Tonsillitis, a bacterial infection of the tonsils, is a common childhood illness. In past years, surgical removal of the infected tonsils was a standard procedure, as tonsillectomy was thought to prevent severe infections like strep throat. Because tonsils were thought to have little function, surgeons often removed infected tonsils—even healthy tonsils, in order to prevent tonsillitis later. With the discovery that tonsils play an important immune function, the number of tonsillectomies performed in the United States dropped dramatically, reaching an all-time low in the 1980s.

Today, although many cases of tonsillitis are successfully treated with appropriate antibiotics, tonsillectomy is becoming more frequent; in fact, it is the second most common surgical procedure among American children. Surgery is considered if an infection recurs or if enlarged tonsils make swallowing

or breathing difficult. Many tonsillectomies are performed in children to treat obstructive sleep apnea, a condition in which the child stops breathing for a few seconds at a time during sleep. Recent studies suggest that tonsillectomy may also be beneficial for children suffering from otitis media (middle ear infection), because bacteria infecting the tonsils may travel to this region of the ear.

Most tonsillectomies are performed by electrocautery, a technique that uses an electrical current to burn the tonsils away from the throat. Now that this operation is becoming more common, surgeons are developing new techniques. For example, coblation tonsillectomy uses radio waves to break down tonsillar tissue. Studies suggest that this procedure results in a faster recovery, fewer complications, and decreased postoperative pain compared with electrocautery.

- The single pharyngeal tonsil, commonly known as the **adenoids**, is in the nasopharynx.
- The **lingual tonsils** are small mounds of lymphoid tissue at the posterior of the tongue.

Opinions on the advisability of removing the tonsils have changed over time, as described in **Box 11-1**.

Lower Respiratory Passageways and Lungs

Air moves from the pharynx into the larynx, commonly called the voice box, because it contains the **vocal folds**, or cords. The larynx is at the top of the **trachea**, commonly called the windpipe, which conducts air into the bronchial system toward the lungs.

THE LARYNX

The larynx is shaped by nine cartilages, the most prominent of which is the anterior thyroid cartilage that forms the "Adam's apple" (**Fig. 11-4**). The small leaf-shaped cartilage at the top of the larynx is the **epiglottis**. When one swallows, the epiglottis covers the opening of the larynx and helps to prevent food from entering the respiratory tract.

The larynx contains the vocal folds, bands of tissue that are important in speech production (**Fig. 11-5**). Vibrations produced by air passing over the vocal folds form the basis for voice production, although portions of the throat and mouth are needed for proper speech articulation. The opening between the vocal folds is the **glottis** (the epiglottis is above the glottis).

Epiglottis

Hyoid bone

Thyroid cartilage

Cricoid cartilage

Trachea

Figure 11-4 The larynx, anterior view.

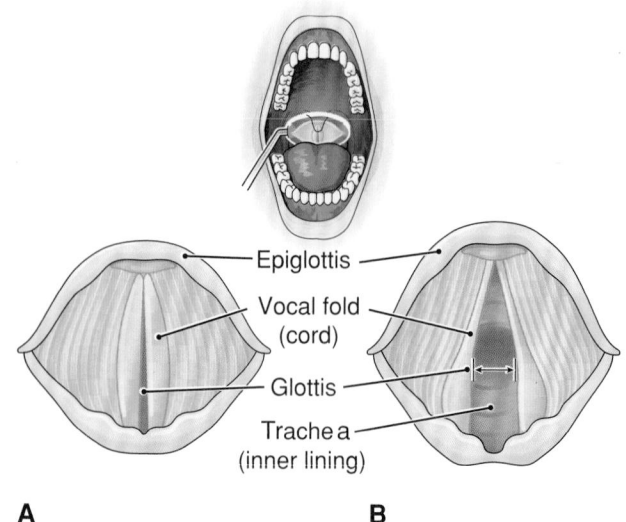

Epiglottis

Vocal fold (cord)

Glottis

Trachea (inner lining)

A   **B**

Figure 11-5 The vocal folds, superior view. **A.** The glottis in closed position. **B.** The glottis in open position.

THE TRACHEA

The trachea is a tube reinforced with C-shaped rings of cartilage to prevent its collapse (you can feel these rings if you press your fingers gently against the front of your throat). Cilia in the trachea's lining move impurities up toward the throat, where they can be eliminated by swallowing or by **expectoration**, coughing them up.

The trachea is contained in a region known as the **mediastinum**, which consists of the space between the lungs together with the organs contained in this space (see **Fig. 11-2**). In addition to the trachea, the mediastinum contains the heart, esophagus, large vessels, and other tissues.

THE BRONCHIAL SYSTEM

At its lower end, the trachea divides into a right and a left primary **bronchus**, which enter the lungs. The right bronchus is shorter and wider; it divides into three secondary bronchi in the right lung. The left bronchus divides into two branches that supply the left lung. Further divisions produce an increasing number of smaller tubes that supply air to smaller subdivisions of lung tissue. As the air passageways progress through the lungs, the cartilage in the walls gradually disappears and is replaced by smooth (involuntary) muscle.

The smallest of the conducting tubes, the **bronchioles**, carry air into the microscopic air sacs, the **alveoli**, through which gases are exchanged between the lungs and the blood. It is through the ultrathin walls of the alveoli and their surrounding capillaries that **oxygen (O_2)** diffuses into the blood and carbon dioxide diffuses out of the blood for elimination (see **Fig. 11-2**).

THE LUNGS

The cone-shaped lungs occupy the major portion of the thoracic cavity. The right lung is larger and divided into three lobes. The left lung, which is smaller to accommodate the heart, is divided into two lobes. The lobes are further subdivided to correspond to divisions of the bronchial network.

A double membrane, the **pleura**, covers the lungs and lines the thoracic cavity (**Fig. 11-6**). There are two pleural layers:

- The parietal pleura, the outer layer, is attached to the wall of the thoracic cavity.
- The visceral pleura, the inner layer, is attached to the surface of the lungs.

The very narrow, fluid-filled space between the two layers is the **pleural space**. The moist pleural membranes slide easily over each other within the chest cavity, allowing the lungs to expand during breathing.

Breathing

Air is moved into and out of the lungs by the process of breathing, technically called **pulmonary ventilation**. This consists of a steady cycle of **inspiration** (inhalation) and **expiration** (exhalation), separated by a period of rest. Breathing is normally regulated unconsciously by centers in the brainstem. These centers adjust the rate and rhythm of breathing according to changes in the blood composition, especially the concentration of carbon dioxide.

> See the figure on the principal muscles of breathing and the animation "Pulmonary Ventilation" in the Student Resources on thePoint.

INSPIRATION

The breathing cycle begins when the **phrenic nerve** stimulates the **diaphragm** to contract and flatten, enlarging the

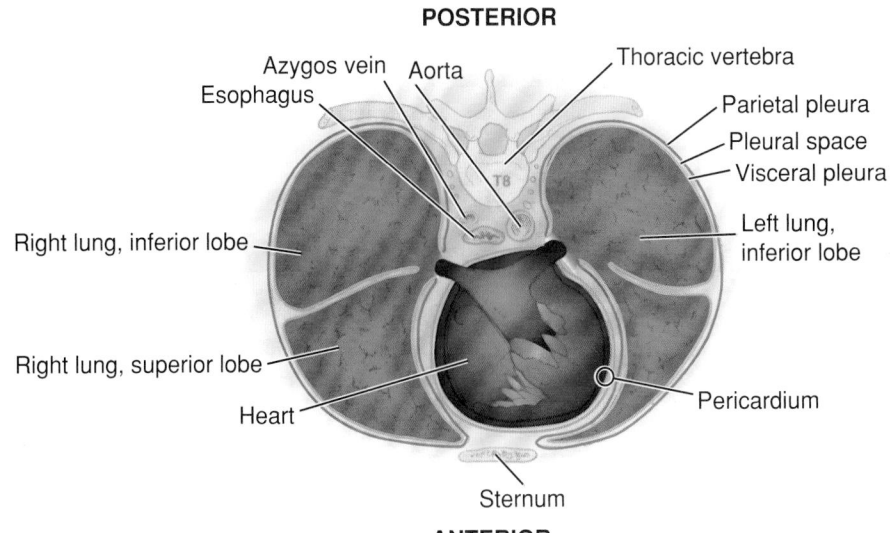

POSTERIOR

Azygos vein   Aorta

Esophagus

Thoracic vertebra

Parietal pleura

Pleural space

Visceral pleura

Left lung, inferior lobe

Right lung, inferior lobe

T8

Right lung, superior lobe

Heart

Pericardium

Sternum

ANTERIOR

Figure 11-6 **The pleura.** A transverse section through the lungs shows the parietal and visceral layers of the pleura as well as structures in the mediastinum.

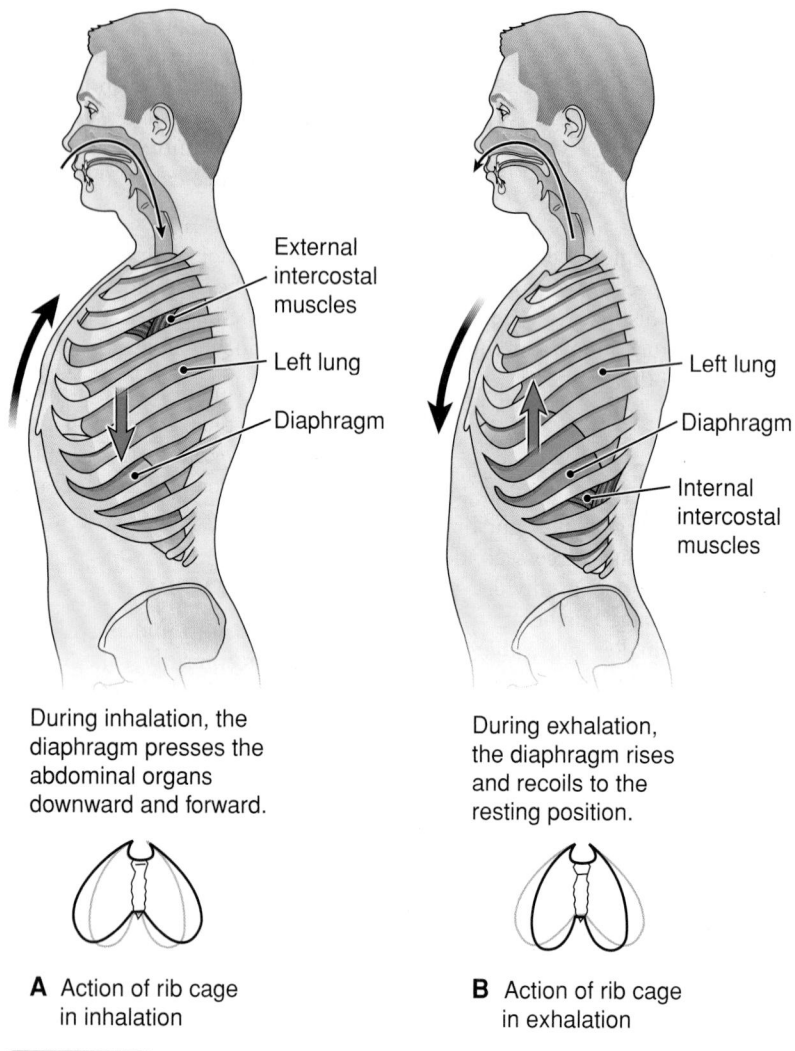

A Action of rib cage
in inhalation

B Action of rib cage
in exhalation

During inhalation, the
diaphragm presses the
abdominal organs
downward and forward.

During exhalation,
the diaphragm rises
and recoils to the
resting position.

External
intercostal
muscles

Left lung

Diaphragm

Left lung

Diaphragm

Internal
intercostal
muscles

Figure 11-7 **Pulmonary ventilation. A.** In inhalation, the diaphragm lowers, and the external intercostals elevate the rib cage. **B.** In exhalation, the breathing muscles relax, the diaphragm rises, and the lungs spring back to their original size. The internal intercostals draw the ribs downward in forceful exhalation.

chest cavity. At the same time, external intercostal muscles between the ribs elevate and expand the rib cage. A resulting decrease in pressure within the thorax causes air to flow into the lungs (**Fig. 11-7**). Muscles of the neck and thorax are used in addition for forceful inhalation.

The measure of how easily the lungs expand under pressure is **compliance**. Fluid produced in the lungs, known as **surfactant**, aids in compliance by reducing surface tension within the alveoli.

EXPIRATION

Expiration occurs as the breathing muscles relax and the elastic lungs spring back to their original size. Increased pressure in the smaller thorax forces air out of the lungs. In forceful exhalation, the internal intercostal muscles contract to lower the rib cage, and the abdominal muscles

contract, pressing internal organs upward against the diaphragm.

Gas Transport

Oxygen is carried in the blood bound to **hemoglobin** in red blood cells. The oxygen is released to the cells as needed. Carbon dioxide is carried in several ways but is mostly converted to **carbonic acid**. The amount of carbon dioxide that is exhaled is important in regulating the blood's acidity or alkalinity, based on the amount of carbonic acid that is formed. Dangerous shifts in blood pH can result from exhalation of too much or too little carbon dioxide.

See the animations "Oxygen Transport" and "Carbon Dioxide Exchange" in the Student Resources on thePoint.

Terminology   Key Terms

Normal Structure and Function

adenoids *AD-eh-noyds*	Lymphoid tissue located in the nasopharynx; the pharyngeal tonsils
alveoli *al-VE-o-li*	The tiny air sacs in the lungs through which gases are exchanged between the atmosphere and the blood in respiration (singular: alveolus); an alveolus, in general, is a small hollow or cavity; the term also applies to the bony socket for a tooth
bronchiole *BRONG-ke-ole*	One of the smaller subdivisions of the bronchial tubes (root: bronchiol/o)
bronchus *BRONG-kus*	One of the larger air passageways in the lungs; the bronchi begin as two branches of the trachea and then subdivide within the lungs (plural: bronchi) (root: bronch/o)
carbon dioxide (CO$_2$)	A gas produced by energy metabolism in cells and eliminated through the lungs
carbonic acid *kar-BON-ik*	An acid formed when carbon dioxide dissolves in water; H$_2$CO$_3$
compliance *kom-PLI-ans*	A measure of how easily the lungs expand under pressure; compliance is reduced in many types of respiratory disorders
diaphragm *DI-ah-fram*	The dome-shaped muscle under the lungs that flattens during inspiration (root: phren/o)
epiglottis *ep-ih-GLOT-is*	A leaf-shaped cartilage that covers the larynx during swallowing to prevent food from entering the trachea
expectoration *ek-spek-to-RA-shun*	The act of coughing up material from the respiratory tract; also the material thus released; sputum
expiration *ek-spih-RA-shun*	The act of breathing out or expelling air from the lungs; exhalation
glottis *GLOT-is*	The opening between the vocal folds
hemoglobin *HE-mo-glo-bin*	The iron-containing pigment in red blood cells that transports oxygen
inspiration *in-spih-RA-shun*	The act of drawing air into the lungs; inhalation
larynx *LAR-inks*	The enlarged, superior portion of the trachea that contains the vocal folds (root: laryng/o)
lingual tonsils	Small mounds of lymphoid tissue at the posterior of the tongue
lung	A cone-shaped, spongy respiratory organ contained within the thorax (roots: pneum/o, pulm/o)
mediastinum *me-de-as-TI-num*	The space between the lungs together with the organs contained in this space
nose	The organ of the face used for breathing and housing receptors for the sense of smell; includes an external portion and an internal nasal cavity (roots: nas/o, rhin/o)
oxygen (O$_2$) *OK-sih-jen*	The gas needed by cells to release energy from food during metabolism
palatine tonsils *PAL-ah-tine*	The paired masses of lymphoid tissue located on either side of the oropharynx; usually meant when the term tonsils is used alone

11

(continued)

Terminology	Key Terms *(Continued)*
pharynx *FAR-inks*	The throat; a common passageway for food entering the esophagus and air entering the larynx (root: pharyng/o)
phrenic nerve *FREN-ik*	The nerve that activates the diaphragm (root: phrenic/o)
pleura *PLURE-ah*	A double-layered membrane that lines the thoracic cavity (parietal pleura) and covers the lungs (visceral pleura) (root: pleur/o)
pleural space	The thin, fluid-filled space between the two layers of the pleura; pleural cavity
pulmonary ventilation *PUL-mo-nare-e ven-tih-LA-shun*	The movement of air into and out of the lungs
sinus *SI-nus*	A cavity or channel; the paranasal sinuses are located near the nose and drain into the nasal cavity
sputum *SPU-tum*	The substance released by coughing or clearing the throat; expectoration; it may contain a variety of materials from the respiratory tract
surfactant *sur-FAK-tant*	A substance that decreases surface tension within the alveoli and eases lung expansion
trachea *TRA-ke-ah*	The air passageway that extends from the larynx to the bronchi (root: trache/o)
turbinate bones *TUR-bih-nate*	The bony projections in the nasal cavity that contain receptors for the sense of smell; also called conchae (*KON-ke*) (singular: concha [*KON-kah*])
vocal folds *VO-kal*	Membranous folds on either side of the larynx that are important in speech production; also called vocal cords

Go to the Audio Pronunciation Glossary in the Student Resources on thePoint to hear these terms pronounced.

Word Parts Pertaining to the Respiratory System

See **Tables 11-1** to **11-3**.

Table 11-1	Suffixes for Respiration

Suffix	Meaning	Example	Definition of Example
-pnea	breathing	dyspnea *disp-NE-ah*	shortness of breath; painful or difficult breathing
-oxia[a]	level of oxygen	hypoxia *hi-POK-se-ah*	decreased amount of oxygen in the tissues
-capnia[a]	level of carbon dioxide	hypocapnia *hi-po-KAP-ne-ah*	decreased carbon dioxide in the tissues
-phonia	voice	aphonia *ah-FO-ne-ah*	loss of voice

[a]When referring to levels of oxygen and carbon dioxide in the blood, the suffix *-emia* is used as in hypoxemia, hypercapnemia.

EXERCISE 11-1

Use the suffix *-pnea* to form words with the following meanings.

1. breathing difficulty that is relieved by assuming an upright position (ortho) _____

2. slow (brady-) rate of breathing _____

3. easy, normal (eu-) breathing _____

4. painful or difficult breathing _____

Use the ending *-pneic* to write the adjective form of the above words.

5. _____

6. _____

7. _____

8. _____

Use the suffixes in Table 11-1 to write a word for each of the following definitions.

9. difficulty speaking _____

10. decreased carbon dioxide in the tissues _____

11. lack of (an-) oxygen in the tissues _____

12. increased levels of carbon dioxide in the tissues _____

11

Table 11-2	Roots for the Respiratory Passageways		
Root	**Meaning**	**Example**	**Definition of Example**
nas/o	nose	intranasal in-trah-NA-zal	within the nose
rhin/o	nose	rhinoplasty RI-no-plas-te	plastic repair of the nose
pharyng/o[a]	pharynx	pharyngeal fah-RIN-je-al	pertaining to the pharynx
laryng/o[a]	larynx	laryngospasm lah-RIN-go-spazm	spasm (sudden contraction) of the larynx
trache/o	trachea	tracheotome TRA-ke-o-tome	instrument used to incise the trachea
bronch/o, bronch/i	bronchus	bronchogenic brong-ko-GEN-ik	originating in a bronchus
bronchiol	bronchiole	bronchiolectasis brong-ke-o-LEK-tah-sis	dilatation of the bronchioles

[a]An e is added to the root before the adjective ending -al.

EXERCISE 11-2

Write words for the following definitions.

1. discharge from the nose   _____

2. pertaining to the larynx (see *pharynx* in **Table 11-2**)   _____

3. inflammation of the bronchi   _____

4. endoscopic examination of the pharynx   _____

5. plastic repair of the larynx   _____

6. surgical incision of the trachea   _____

7. narrowing of a trachea   _____

8. inflammation of the bronchioles   _____

Define the following words (note the adjectival endings).

9. bronchiolar (*brong-KE-o-lar*)   _____

10. paranasal (*par-ah-NA-zal*)   _____

11. peribronchial (*per-ih-BRONG-ke-al*)   _____

12. endotracheal (*en-do-TRA-ke-al*)   _____

13. nasopharyngeal (*na-zo-fah-RIN-je-al*)   _____

14. bronchiectasis (*brong-ke-EK-tah-sis*)   _____

Table 11-3   Roots for the Lungs and Breathing

Root	Meaning	Example	Definition of Example
phren/o	diaphragm	phrenic FREN-ik	pertaining to the diaphragm
phrenic/o	phrenic nerve	phrenicectomy fren-ih-SEK-to-me	partial excision of the phrenic nerve
pleur/o	pleura	pleurodesis plu-ROD-eh-sis	fusion of the pleura
pulm/o, pulmon/o	lung	extrapulmonary EKS-trah-pul-mo-nar-e	outside the lungs
pneumon/o	lung	pneumonitis nu-mo-NI-tis	inflammation of the lung; pneumonia
pneum/o, pneumat/o	air, gas; also respiration, lung	pneumothorax nu-mo-THO-raks	presence of air in the thorax (pleural space)
spir/o	breathing	spirometer spi-ROM-eh-ter	instrument for measuring breathing volumes

EXERCISE 11-3

Define the following words.

1. pleuralgia (*plu-RAL-je-ah*)   _____

2. intrapulmonary (*in-trah-PUL-mo-ner-e*)   _____

3. pneumonectomy (*nu-mo-NEK-to-me*)   _____

4. pneumoplasty (*NU-mo-plas-te*)   _____

5. pulmonology (*pul-mo-NOL-o-je*)   _____

6. apneumia (*ap-NU-me-ah*)   _____

7. phrenicotomy (*fren-ih-KOT-o-me*)   _____

Write words for the following definitions.

8. within the pleura   _____

9. above the diaphragm   _____

10. surgical puncture of the pleural space   _____

11. any disease of the lungs (pneumon/o)   _____

12. crushing of the phrenic nerve   _____

13. record of breathing volumes   _____

11

Clinical Aspects of the Respiratory System

Any disorder that causes resistance to airflow through the respiratory tract or that limits chest expansion will affect pulmonary function. These disorders may involve the respiratory system directly, such as infection, injury, allergy, **aspiration** (inhalation) of foreign bodies, or cancer; they may also originate in other systems, such as in the skeletal, muscular, cardiovascular, or nervous systems.

As noted above, changes in ventilation can affect the blood's pH (acidity or alkalinity). If too much carbon dioxide is exhaled by **hyperventilation**, the blood tends to become too alkaline, a condition termed **alkalosis**. If too little carbon dioxide is exhaled as a result of **hypoventilation**, the blood tends to become too acidic, a condition termed **acidosis**.

INFECTIONS

A variety of organisms infect the respiratory system. For your reference, some of these organisms are listed along with the diseases they cause in **Box 11-2**. Childhood immunizations have dramatically reduced the incidence of some

Box 11-2

FOR YOUR REFERENCE
Organisms That Infect the Respiratory System

Organism	Disease
BACTERIA	
Streptococcus pneumoniae *strep-to-KOK-us nu-MO-ne-e*	Most common cause of pneumonia; streptococcal pneumonia
Haemophilus influenzae *he-MOF-ih-lus in-flu-EN-ze*	Pneumonia, especially in debilitated patients
Klebsiella pneumoniae *kleb-se-EL-ah nu-MO-ne-e*	Pneumonia in elderly and debilitated patients

(continued)

Organisms That Infect the Respiratory System (*Continued*)

Organism	Disease
Mycoplasma pneumoniae *mi-ko-PLAZ-mah nu-MO-ne-e*	Mild pneumonia, usually in young adults and children; "walking pneumonia"
Legionella pneumophila *le-juh-NEL-lah nu-MOH-fih-lah*	Legionellosis (Legionnaire disease); respiratory disease spread through water sources, such as air conditioners, pools, humidifiers
Chlamydia psittaci *klah-MID-e-ah SIH-tah-se*	Psittacosis (ornithosis); carried by birds
Streptococcus pyogenes *strep-to-KOK-us pi-OJ-eh-neze*	"Strep throat," scarlet fever
Mycobacterium tuberculosis *mi-ko-bak-TE-re-e-um tu-ber-ku-LO-sis*	Tuberculosis
Bordetella pertussis *bor-deh-TEL-ah per-TUS-sis*	Pertussis (whooping cough)
Corynebacterium diphtheriae *ko-RI-ne-bak-te-re-e-um dif-THE-re-e*	Diphtheria
VIRUSES	
Rhinoviruses *RI-no-vi-rus-es*	Major cause of common cold; also caused by coronaviruses, adenoviruses, and others
Influenzavirus *in-flu-EN-zah-vi-rus*	Influenza
Respiratory syncytial virus (RSV) *sin-SISH-al*	Common cause of respiratory disease in infants
SARS coronavirus *ko-RO-nah-vi-rus*	Severe acute respiratory syndrome; highly infectious disease that appeared in 2003 and spreads from small mammals to humans
Hantavirus *HAN-tah-vi-rus*	Hantavirus pulmonary syndrome (HPS); spread by inhalation of virus released from dried rodent droppings
FUNGI	
Histoplasma capsulatum *his-to-PLAS-mah kap-su-LATE-um*	Histoplasmosis; spread by airborne spores
Coccidioides immitis *kok-sid-e-OY-deze IM-ih-tis*	Coccidioidomycosis (valley fever, San Joaquin fever); found in dry, alkaline soils
Blastomyces dermatitidis *blas-to-MI-seze der-mah-TIT-ih-dis*	Blastomycosis; rare but often fatal fungal disease
Pneumocystis jirovecii (formerly carinii) *nu-mo-SIS-tis jir-o-VEH-se*	*Pneumocystis* pneumonia (PCP); seen in immunocompromised hosts

infectious respiratory diseases, such as **diphtheria** and **pertussis** (the "D" and "P" in the DTaP vaccine; the "T" is for tetanus). Selected infectious diseases are described in greater detail below.

See the figure on respiratory infections in the Student Resources on thePoint.

Pneumonia

Pneumonia is caused by many different microorganisms, usually bacteria or viruses. Bacterial agents are most commonly *Streptococcus pneumoniae* and *Klebsiella pneumoniae*. Viral

pneumonia is more diffuse and is commonly caused by influenza virus, adenovirus, and in young children, respiratory syncytial virus (RSV). There are two forms of pneumonia (**Fig. 11-8**):

- Lobar pneumonia, an acute disease, involves one or more lobes of the lung.
- Bronchopneumonia (bronchial pneumonia) occurs throughout the lung. It begins in terminal bronchioles that become clogged with exudate and form consolidated (solidified) patches.

Pneumonia can usually be treated successfully in otherwise healthy people, but in debilitated patients, it is a

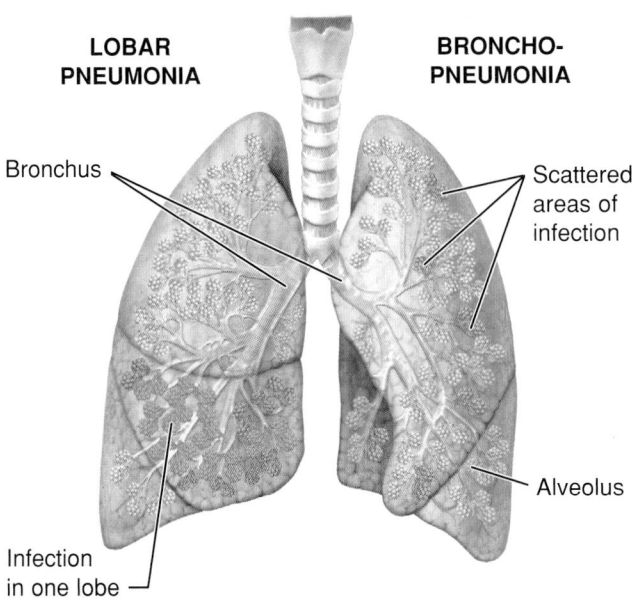

LOBAR PNEUMONIA

Bronchus

Infection in one lobe

BRONCHO-PNEUMONIA

Scattered areas of infection

Alveolus

Figure 11-8 **Pneumonia.** In lobar pneumonia (left lung), an entire lobe is consolidated. In bronchopneumonia (right lung), patchy areas of consolidation occur throughout the lung.

leading cause of death. Immunocompromised patients, such as those with AIDS, are often subject to a form of fungal pneumonia called *Pneumocystis* pneumonia (PCP).

The term *pneumonia* is also applied to noninfectious lung inflammation, such as that caused by asthma, allergy, or inhalation of irritants. In these cases, however, the more general term **pneumonitis** is often used.

Tuberculosis

The incidence of **tuberculosis** (**TB**) has increased in recent years, along with the increase of AIDS and the appearance of antibiotic resistance in the causative organism, *Mycobacterium tuberculosis* (MTB). (This organism, because of its staining properties, is also referred to as AFB, meaning *acid-fast bacillus*.) The name *tuberculosis* comes from the small lesions, or tubercles, that characterize the infection. The tubercles can liquefy in the center and then rupture to release bacteria into the bloodstream. Generalized TB is known as *miliary tuberculosis* because of the many tubercles that are the size of millet seeds in infected tissue (**Fig. 11-9**).

TB symptoms include fever, weight loss, weakness, cough, and **hemoptysis**, the coughing up of blood-containing sputum. Accumulation of exudate in the alveoli may result in consolidation of lung tissue. Active TB is diagnosed by chest x-ray and laboratory culture of sputum samples to isolate, stain, and identify any causative organisms. If found, the organisms can be tested for drug susceptibility. These laboratory studies can take up to eight weeks, as the TB organism is very slow-growing, so clinicians also use several quick tests to identify tuberculosis infections. These include:

- The **tuberculin test**, a skin test, also known as a Mantoux (*man-TOO*) test. The test material, tuberculin, is made from byproducts of the tuberculosis organism. PPD (purified protein derivative) is the form of tuberculin commonly used. In 48 to 72 hours after tuberculin is injected below the skin, a hard, raised lump appears if a person has been infected with the TB organism. This test does not distinguish active from inactive cases.
- IGRA, a rapid blood test to diagnose TB. This is an immunologic test with the full name interferon-gamma release assay. It is used to confirm results of a negative skin test in people at high risk of having TB.
- NAA, a sputum test that can confirm a positive TB diagnosis within 24 hours. The full name is nucleic acid amplification test.

BCG vaccine is used worldwide to help to prevent TB; it is not used routinely in the United States because the incidence of TB in this country is relatively low and also because it invalidates the tuberculin test. The bacillus (B) used for the vaccine is named for Calmette (C) and Guérin (G), discoverers of this avirulent mycobacterium strain.

Influenza

Influenza ("flu") is a viral respiratory disease associated with chills, fever, headaches, muscular aches, and cold-like symptoms. It usually resolves in several days, but severe forms of influenza have caused fatal pandemics, most recently in 1918, 1957, and 1968. The virus can mutate readily and spread among animals, such as birds or pigs, and humans.

Because influenza viruses change so rapidly, scientists must prepare vaccines against the strains most likely to cause an epidemic in any given year. The virus strains are grouped into categories A to C, with A the most severe and C the least. They are further designated H and N with numbers, such as H3N2 and H5N1. The "H" and "N" represent surface proteins that the virus uses to infect a host.

Medical personnel combat influenza with vaccines, isolation of infected populations, destruction of infected animals, and antiviral medications.

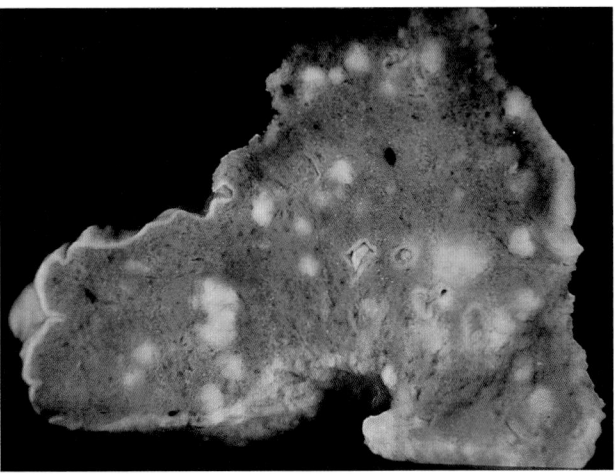

Figure 11-9 **Tuberculosis.** The cut surface of the lung reveals numerous white nodules in miliary (generalized) tuberculosis.

11

FOCUS ON WORDS
Don't Breathe a Word

Box 11-3

Some lay terms for respiratory symptoms and conditions are so old-fashioned and quaint that you might see them today only in Victorian novels. Catarrh (*kah-TAR*) is an old word for an upper respiratory infection with much mucus production. Quinsy (*KWIN-ze*) referred to a sore throat or tonsillar abscess. Consumption was tuberculosis, and dropsy referred to generalized edema. The grippe (*grip*) meant influenza, which we more often abbreviate as "flu."

Some unscientific words are still in use. These include whooping cough for pertussis, croup for laryngeal spasm, cold sore or fever blister for a herpes lesion, and phlegm for sputum.

Many people use informal terms instead of scientific words to describe their symptoms. Health professionals should be familiar with the slang or colloquialisms that patients might use so that they can better communicate with them.

Common Cold

More than 200 viruses are known to cause the common cold. About one-half of these are rhinoviruses, and the others include adenoviruses and coronaviruses. The symptoms, known to all, are sneezing; **acute rhinitis**, which is inflammation of the nasal passageways with copious secretion of watery mucus; tearing of the eyes; and congestion. The infection may spread from the nose and throat to the sinuses, middle ear, and lower respiratory tract.

Cold viruses are mostly spread by airborne virus-filled droplets released by an infected person's coughs and sneezes. Frequent hand washing and not touching one's hands to any part of the face are good preventive measures.

The disorder usually resolves in about a week. Because colds are caused by viruses, antibiotics do not cure them. Rest, fluid intake, symptomatic treatment, and time work best. The large variety of cold viruses and their frequent mutation have prevented the development of an effective vaccine.

Box 11-3 has some history on terminology related to respiratory infections and other disorders.

EMPHYSEMA

Emphysema is a chronic disease associated with overexpansion and destruction of the alveoli (**Fig. 11-10A**). Common causes are exposure to cigarette smoke and other forms of pollution as well as chronic infection. Emphysema is the main disorder included under the heading of **chronic obstructive pulmonary disease** (COPD). Other conditions included in this category are **asthma, bronchiectasis,** and chronic **bronchitis** (**Fig. 11-10B**).

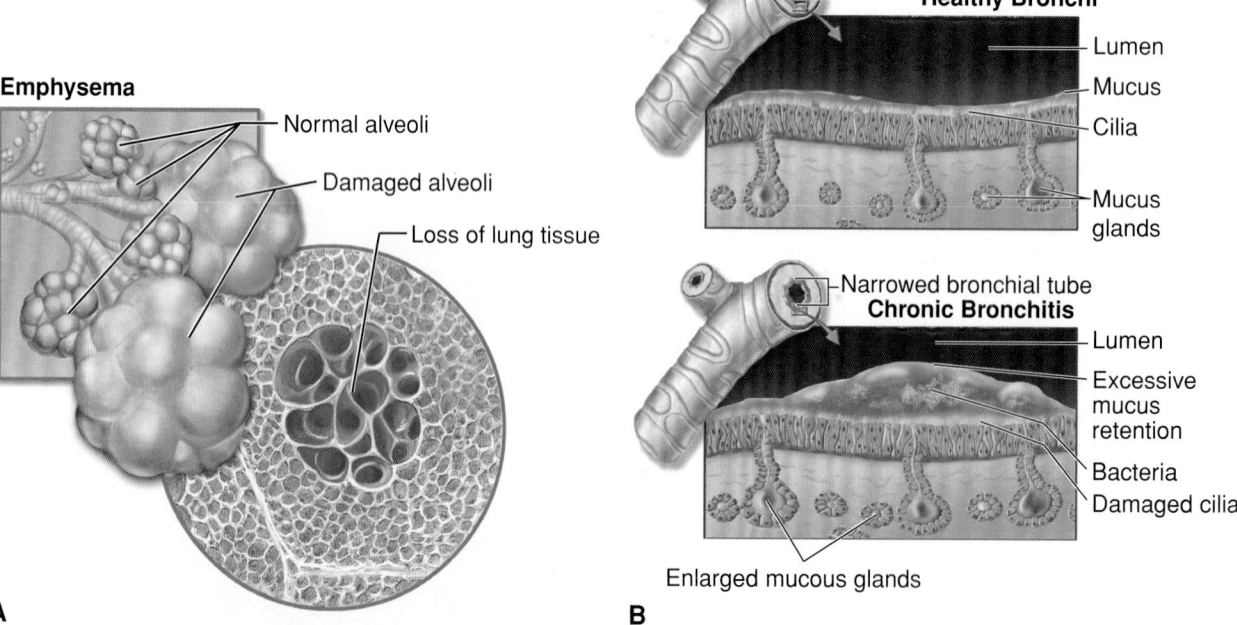

Emphysema
- Normal alveoli
- Damaged alveoli
- Loss of lung tissue

Chronic Bronchitis
- Normal bronchial tube
- **Healthy Bronchi**
- Lumen
- Mucus
- Cilia
- Mucus glands

- Narrowed bronchial tube
- **Chronic Bronchitis**
- Lumen
- Excessive mucus retention
- Bacteria
- Damaged cilia
- Enlarged mucous glands

A   **B**

Figure 11-10 **Types of chronic obstructive pulmonary disease (COPD). A.** Emphysema results in dilation and destruction of alveoli. **B.** Chronic bronchitis involves airway inflammation, damage to cilia, and excess mucus secretion.

ASTHMA

Asthma attacks result from narrowing of the bronchial tubes. This constriction, along with edema (swelling) of the bronchial linings, inflammation, and mucus accumulation, results in wheezing, extreme **dyspnea** (difficulty in breathing), and **cyanosis**.

Asthma is most common in children. Although its causes are uncertain, a main factor is irritation caused by allergy. Heredity may also play a role. Treatment of asthma includes:

- removal of allergens
- administration of bronchodilators to widen the airways
- administration of corticosteroids to reduce inflammation

See the figure on the effects of smoking and the animation "Asthma" in the Student Resources on thePoint.

PNEUMOCONIOSIS

Chronic irritation and inflammation caused by dust inhalation is termed **pneumoconiosis**. This is an occupational hazard seen mainly in people working in mining and stoneworking industries. Different forms of pneumoconiosis are named for the specific type of dust inhaled: silicosis (silica or quartz), anthracosis (coal dust), asbestosis (asbestos fibers).

Although the term *pneumoconiosis* is limited to conditions caused by inhalation of inorganic dust, lung irritation may also result from inhalation of organic dusts, such as textile or grain dusts.

LUNG CANCER

Lung cancer is the leading cause of cancer-related deaths in both men and women. The incidence of lung cancer has increased steadily over the past 50 years, especially in women. Cigarette smoking is a major risk factor in this as well as other types of cancer. The most common form of lung cancer is squamous carcinoma, originating in the lining of the bronchi (bronchogenic). Lung cancer usually cannot be detected early, and it metastasizes rapidly. The overall long-term survival rate is low.

Methods used to diagnose lung cancer include radiographic studies, computed tomography (CT) scans, and sputum examination for cancer cells. Physicians can use a **bronchoscope** to examine the airways and to collect tissue samples for study. They may also take samples by surgical or needle biopsies.

RESPIRATORY DISTRESS SYNDROME

Respiratory distress syndrome (RDS) of the newborn occurs in premature infants and is the most common cause of death in this group. It results from a lack of lung surfactant, which reduces compliance. **Acute respiratory distress syndrome (ARDS)**, also known as *shock lung*, may result

from trauma, allergic reactions, infection, and other causes. It involves edema that can lead to respiratory failure and death if untreated.

CYSTIC FIBROSIS

Cystic fibrosis (CF) is the most common fatal hereditary disease among white children. The flawed gene that causes CF affects glandular secretions by altering chloride transport across cell membranes. Thickening of bronchial secretions leads to infection and other respiratory disorders. Other mucus-secreting glands, sweat glands, and the pancreas are also involved, causing electrolyte imbalance and digestive disturbances.

CF is diagnosed by the increased amounts of sodium and chloride in the sweat. Geneticists also can identify the gene that causes CF by DNA analysis. There is no cure at present for CF. Patients are treated to relieve their symptoms, as by postural drainage, aerosol mists, bronchodilators, antibiotics, and mucolytic (mucus-dissolving) agents.

SUDDEN INFANT DEATH SYNDROME

Sudden infant death syndrome (SIDS), also called "crib death," is the unexplained death of a seemingly healthy infant under one year of age. Death usually occurs during sleep, leaving no signs of its cause. Neither autopsy nor careful investigation of family history and circumstances of death provides any clues.

Certain maternal conditions during pregnancy are associated with an increased risk of SIDS, although none is a sure predictor. These include cigarette smoking, age under 20, low weight gain, anemia, illegal drug use, and reproductive or urinary tract infections.

Some practices that have reduced the incidence of SIDS are:

- Place the baby on his or her back (supine) for sleep ("back to sleep").
- Keep the baby in a smoke-free environment.
- Use a firm, flat baby mattress.
- Don't overheat the baby.

PLEURAL DISORDERS

Pleurisy, also called pleuritis, is an inflammation of the pleura, usually associated with infection. Pain is the common symptom of pleurisy. Because this pain is intensified by breathing or coughing as the inflamed membranes move, breathing becomes rapid and shallow. Analgesics and antiinflammatory drugs are used to treat the symptoms of pleurisy.

As a result of injury, infection, or weakness in the pleural membrane, substances may accumulate between the layers of the pleura. When air or gas collects in this space, the condition is termed **pneumothorax** (**Fig. 11-11**). Compression may cause collapse of the lung, termed **atelectasis**.

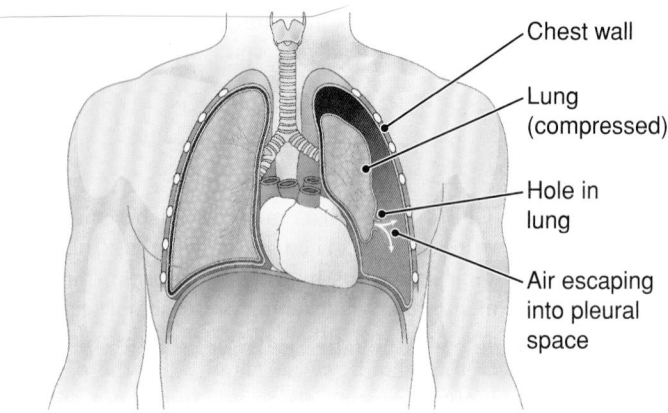

Figure 11-11 **Pneumothorax.** Injury to lung tissue allows air to leak into the pleural space and put pressure on the lung.

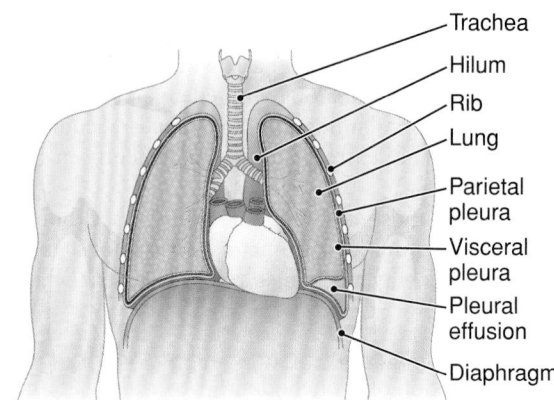

Figure 11-12 **Pleural effusion.** An abnormal volume of fluid collects in the pleural space.

In **pleural effusion**, other materials accumulate in the pleural space (**Fig. 11-12**). Depending on the substance involved, these are described as **empyema** (pus), also termed **pyothorax; hemothorax** (blood); or **hydrothorax** (fluid). Causes of these conditions include injury, infection, heart failure, and pulmonary embolism. **Thoracentesis**, needle puncture of the chest to remove fluids (**Fig. 11-13**), or fusion of the pleural membranes (pleurodesis) may be required. A chest tube may be inserted to remove air and fluid from the pleural space.

DIAGNOSIS OF RESPIRATORY DISORDERS

In addition to chest radiographs, CT scans, and magnetic resonance imaging (MRI) scans, methods for diagnosing respiratory disorders include **lung scans**, bronchoscopy, and tests of pleural fluid removed by thoracentesis. **Arterial blood gases (ABGs)** are used to evaluate gas exchange in the lungs by measuring carbon dioxide, oxygen, bicarbonate, and pH in an arterial blood sample. **Pulse oximetry** is routinely used to measure the oxygen saturation of arterial blood by means of an oximeter, a simple device placed on a thin part of the body, usually the finger or the ear (**Fig. 11-14**).

Pulmonary function tests are used to assess breathing, usually by means of a **spirometer**. They measure the volumes of air that can be moved into or out of the lungs with different degrees of effort. Often used to monitor treatment in cases of allergy, asthma, emphysema, and other respiratory conditions, they are also used to measure progress in smoking cessation. The main volumes and capacities measured in these tests are summarized in **Box 11-4** and illustrated in **Figure 11-15**. A capacity is the sum of two or more volumes.

See **Box 11-5** for information on respiratory therapists, who perform many of these tests.

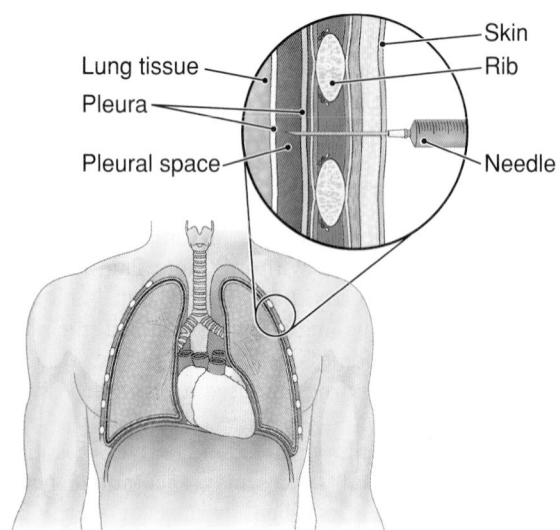

Figure 11-13 **Thoracentesis.** A needle is inserted into the pleural space.

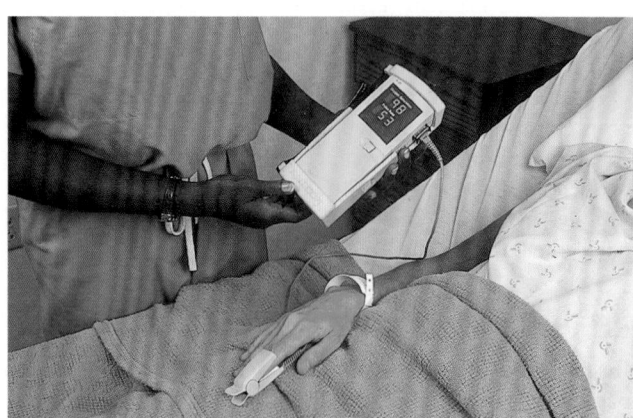

Figure 11-14 **Pulse oximetry.** The oximeter measures the oxygen saturation of arterial blood.

FOR YOUR REFERENCE

Box 11-4

Volumes and Capacities (Sums of Volumes) Used in Pulmonary Function Tests

Volume or Capacity	Definition
tidal volume (TV)	amount of air breathed into or out of the lungs in quiet, relaxed breathing
residual volume (RV)	amount of air that remains in the lungs after maximum exhalation
expiratory reserve volume (ERV)	amount of air that can be exhaled after a normal exhalation
inspiratory reserve volume (IRV)	amount of air that can be inhaled above a normal inspiration
total lung capacity (TLC)	total amount of air that can be contained in the lungs after maximum inhalation
inspiratory capacity (IC)	amount of air that can be inhaled after normal exhalation
vital capacity (VC)	amount of air that can be expelled from the lungs by maximum exhalation after maximum inhalation
functional residual capacity (FRC)	amount of air remaining in the lungs after normal exhalation
forced expiratory volume (FEV)	volume of gas exhaled with maximum force within a given interval of time; the time interval is shown as a subscript, such as FEV_1 (one second) and FEV_3 (three seconds)
forced vital capacity (FVC)	the volume of gas exhaled as rapidly and completely as possible after a complete inhalation

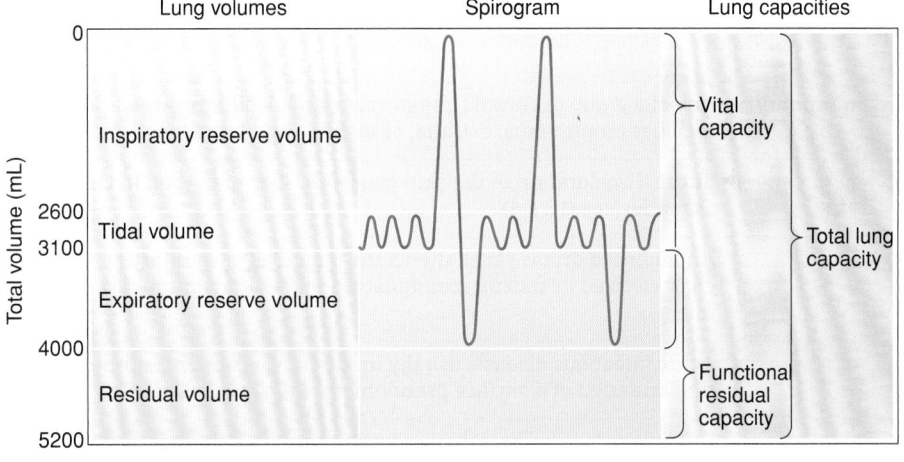

Figure 11-15 **A spirogram.** A spirometer produces a tracing of lung volumes and capacities (sums of volumes).

HEALTH PROFESSIONS

Box 11-5

Careers in Respiratory Therapy

Respiratory therapists and respiratory therapy technicians specialize in evaluating and treating breathing disorders. Respiratory therapists evaluate the severity of their patients' conditions by taking complete histories and testing respiratory function with specialized equipment. Based on their findings, and in consultation with a physician, therapists design and implement individualized treatment plans, which may include oxygen therapy and chest physiotherapy. They also educate patients on the use of ventilators and other medical devices. Respiratory therapy technicians assist in carrying out evaluations and treatments.

To perform their duties, both types of practitioners need a thorough scientific background. Most respiratory therapists in the United States receive their training from an accredited college or university and take a national licensing exam. Respiratory therapists and technicians work in a variety of settings, such as hospitals, nursing-care facilities, and private clinics. For additional information about careers in respiratory therapy, visit the American Association for Respiratory Care at www.aarc.org.

Terminology   Key Terms

Disorders

acidosis *as-ih-DO-sis*	Abnormal acidity of body fluids; respiratory acidosis is caused by abnormally high carbon dioxide levels
acute respiratory distress syndrome (ARDS)	Pulmonary edema that can lead rapidly to fatal respiratory failure; causes include trauma, aspiration into the lungs, viral pneumonia, and drug reactions; shock lung
acute rhinitis *ri-NI-tis*	Inflammation of the nasal mucosa with sneezing, tearing, and profuse secretion of watery mucus, as seen in the common cold
alkalosis *al-kah-LO-sis*	Abnormal alkalinity of body fluids; respiratory alkalosis is caused by abnormally low carbon dioxide levels
aspiration *as-pih-RA-shun*	The accidental inhalation of food or other foreign material into the lungs; also means the withdrawal of fluid from a cavity by suction
asthma *AZ-mah*	A disease characterized by dyspnea and wheezing caused by spasm of the bronchial tubes or swelling of their mucous membranes
atelectasis *at-eh-LEK-tah-sis*	Incomplete expansion of a lung or part of a lung; lung collapse; may be present at birth (as in respiratory distress syndrome) or be caused by bronchial obstruction or compression of lung tissue (prefix atel/o means "imperfect")
bronchiectasis *brong-ke-EK-tah-sis*	Chronic dilatation of a bronchus or bronchi
bronchitis *brong-KI-tis*	Inflammation of a bronchus
chronic obstructive pulmonary disease (COPD)	Any of a group of chronic, progressive, and debilitating respiratory diseases, which includes emphysema, asthma, bronchitis, and bronchiectasis (see **Fig. 11-10**)
cyanosis *si-ah-NO-sis*	Bluish discoloration of the skin caused by lack of oxygen in the blood (adjective: cyanotic) (see **Fig. 3-4**)
cystic fibrosis (CF) *SIS-tik fi-BRO-sis*	An inherited disease that affects the pancreas, respiratory system, and sweat glands; characterized by mucus accumulation in the bronchi causing obstruction and leading to infection
diphtheria *dif-THERE-e-ah*	Acute infectious disease, usually limited to the upper respiratory tract, characterized by the formation of a surface pseudomembrane composed of cells and coagulated material
dyspnea *disp-NE-ah*	Difficult or labored breathing, sometimes with pain; "air hunger"
emphysema *em-fih-SE-mah*	A chronic pulmonary disease characterized by enlargement and destruction of the alveoli
empyema *em-pi-E-mah*	Accumulation of pus in a body cavity, especially the pleural space; pyothorax
hemoptysis *he-MOP-tih-sis*	The spitting of blood from the mouth or respiratory tract (ptysis means "spitting")
hemothorax *he-mo-THOR-aks*	Presence of blood in the pleural space
hydrothorax *hi-dro-THOR-aks*	Presence of fluid in the pleural space
hyperventilation *hi-per-ven-tih-LA-shun*	Increase in the rate and depth of breathing to above optimal levels, with blood carbon dioxide decreasing to levels below normal

Terminology	Key Terms *(Continued)*
hypoventilation hi-po-ven-tih-LA-shun	Condition in which the amount of air entering the alveoli is insufficient to meet metabolic needs and blood carbon dioxide increases to levels above normal
influenza in-flu-EN-zah	An acute, contagious respiratory infection causing fever, chills, headache, and muscle pain; "flu"
pertussis per-TUS-is	An acute, infectious disease characterized by a cough ending in a whooping inspiration; whooping cough
pleural effusion PLURE-al eh-FU-zhun	Accumulation of fluid in the pleural space; the fluid may contain blood (hemothorax) or pus (pyothorax or empyema) (see **Fig. 11-12**)
pleurisy PLURE-ih-se	Inflammation of the pleura; pleuritis; a symptom of pleurisy is sharp pain on breathing
pneumoconiosis nu-mo-ko-ne-O-sis	Disease of the respiratory tract caused by inhalation of dust particles; named more specifically by the type of dust inhaled, such as silicosis, anthracosis, asbestosis
pneumonia nu-MO-ne-ah	Inflammation of the lungs generally caused by infection; may involve the bronchioles and alveoli (bronchopneumonia) or one or more lobes of the lung (lobar pneumonia) (see **Fig. 11-8**)
pneumonitis nu-mo-NI-tis	Inflammation of the lungs; may be caused by infection, asthma, allergy, or inhalation of irritants
pneumothorax nu-mo-THOR-aks	Accumulation of air or gas in the pleural space; may result from injury or disease or may be produced artificially to collapse a lung (see **Fig. 11-11**)
pyothorax pi-o-THOR-aks	Accumulation of pus in the pleural space; empyema
respiratory distress syndrome (RDS)	A respiratory disorder that affects premature infants born without enough surfactant in the lungs; it is treated with respiratory support and surfactant administration
sudden infant death syndrome (SIDS)	The sudden and unexplained death of an apparently healthy infant; crib death
tuberculosis tu-ber-ku-LO-sis	An infectious disease caused by the tubercle bacillus, *Mycobacterium tuberculosis*; often involves the lungs but may involve other parts of the body as well; miliary (MIL-e-ar-e) tuberculosis is an acute generalized form of the disease with formation of minute tubercles that resemble millet seeds (see **Fig. 11-9**)

Diagnosis

arterial blood gases (ABGs)	The concentrations of gases, specifically oxygen and carbon dioxide, in arterial blood; reported as the partial pressure (P) of the gas in arterial (a) blood, such as PaO_2 or $PaCO_2$; these measurements are important in measuring acid–base balance
bronchoscope BRONG-ko-skope	An endoscope used to examine the tracheobronchial passageways. Also allows access for tissue biopsy or removal of a foreign object (**Fig. 11-16**)
lung scan	Study based on the accumulation of radioactive isotopes in lung tissue; a ventilation scan measures ventilation after inhalation of radioactive material; a perfusion scan measures blood supply to the lungs after injection of radioactive material; also called a pulmonary scintiscan
pulse oximetry ok-SIM-eh-tre	Determination of the oxygen saturation of arterial blood by means of a photoelectric apparatus (oximeter), usually placed on the finger or the ear; reported as SpO_2 in percent (see **Fig. 11-14**)
pulmonary function tests	Tests done to assess breathing, usually by spirometry

(continued)

Terminology	Key Terms *(Continued)*

spirometer *spi-ROM-eh-ter*	An apparatus used to measure breathing volumes and capacities; record of test is a spirogram (see **Fig. 11-15**)
thoracentesis *thor-ah-sen-TE-sis*	Surgical puncture of the chest for removal of air or fluids, such as may accumulate after surgery or as a result of injury, infection, or cardiovascular problems; also called thoracocentesis (see **Fig. 11-13**)
tuberculin test *tu-BER-ku-lin*	A skin test for tuberculosis; tuberculin (PPD), the test material made from products of the tuberculosis organism, is injected below the skin; a hard, raised lump appearing within 48 to 72 hours indicates an active or inactive TB infection; also called the Mantoux (*man-TOO*) test

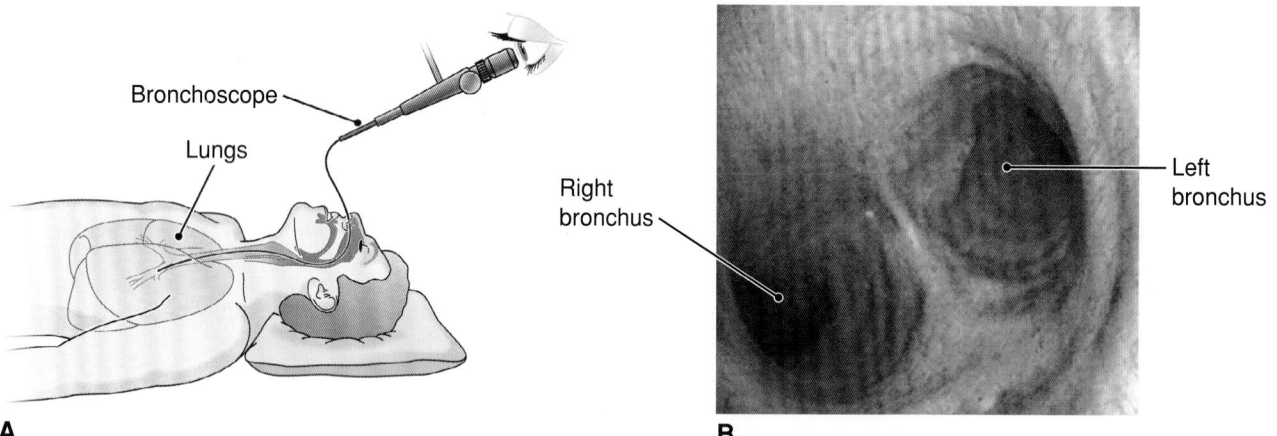

Figure 11-16 **Use of a bronchoscope. A.** A bronchoscope is a lighted tube used to inspect the bronchi, remove specimens, and remove foreign objects. **B.** View of the bronchial openings through a bronchoscope. Note the larger right bronchus.

Terminology	Supplementary Terms

Normal Structure and Function

carina *kah-RI-nah*	A projection of the lowest tracheal cartilage that forms a ridge between the two bronchi; used as a landmark for endoscopy; any ridge or ridge-like structure (from a Latin word that means "keel")
hyperpnea *hi-PERP-ne-ah*	Increase in the depth and rate of breathing to meet the body's needs, as in exercise
hypopnea *hi-POP-ne-ah*	Decrease in the rate and depth of breathing
hilum *HI-lum*	An anatomic depression in an organ where vessels and nerves enter
nares *NA-reze*	The external openings of the nose; the nostrils (singular: naris)
nasal septum	The partition that divides the nasal cavity into two parts (root sept/o means "septum")

Terminology	**Supplementary Terms** (*Continued*)	

tachypnea *tak-IP-ne-ah*	Excessive rate of breathing, which may be normal, as in exercise

Symptoms and Conditions

anoxia *an-OK-se-ah*	Lack or absence of oxygen in the tissues; often used incorrectly to mean hypoxia
asphyxia *as-FIK-se-ah*	Condition caused by inadequate intake of oxygen; suffocation (literally "lack of pulse")
Biot respirations *be-O*	Deep, fast breathing interrupted by sudden pauses; seen in spinal meningitis and other central nervous system disorders
bradypnea *brad-IP-ne-ah*	Abnormally slow rate of breathing
bronchospasm *BRONG-ko-spazm*	Narrowing of the bronchi caused by smooth muscle spasms; common in cases of asthma and bronchitis
Cheyne–Stokes respiration *chane stokes*	A repeating cycle of gradually increased and then decreased respiration followed by a period of apnea; caused by depression of the breathing centers in the brainstem; seen in cases of coma and in terminally ill patients
cor pulmonale *kor pul-mo-NA-le*	Enlargement of the heart's right ventricle caused by disease of the lungs or pulmonary blood vessels
coryza *ko-RI-zah*	Acute inflammation of the nasal passages with profuse nasal discharge; acute rhinitis
croup *Krupe*	A childhood disease usually caused by a viral infection that involves upper airway inflammation and obstruction; croup is characterized by a barking cough, difficulty breathing, and laryngeal spasm
deviated septum	A shifted nasal septum; may require surgical correction
epiglottitis *ep-ih-gloh-TI-tis*	Inflammation of the epiglottis that may lead to upper airway obstruction; commonly seen in croup (also spelled epiglottiditis)
epistaxis *ep-ih-STAK-sis*	Hemorrhage from the nose; nosebleed (Greek: staxis means "dripping")
fremitus *FREM-ih-tus*	A vibration, especially as felt through the chest wall on palpation
Kussmaul respiration *KOOS-mawl*	Rapid and deep gasping respiration without pause; characteristic of severe acidosis
pleural friction rub	A sound heard on auscultation that is produced by the rubbing together of the two pleural layers; a common sign of pleurisy
rales *rahlz*	Abnormal chest sounds heard when air enters small airways or alveoli containing fluid; usually heard during inspiration (singular: rale [*rahl*]); also called crackles
rhonchi *RONG-ki*	Abnormal chest sounds produced in airways with accumulated fluids; more noticeable during expiration (singular: rhonchus)
stridor *STRI-dor*	A harsh, high-pitched sound caused by obstruction of an upper air passageway

(continued)

11

Terminology Supplementary Terms (Continued)

tussis *TUS-is*	A cough; an antitussive drug is one that relieves or prevents coughing
wheeze	A whistling or sighing sound caused by narrowing of a respiratory passageway

Disorders

byssinosis *bis-ih-NO-sis*	Obstructive airway disease caused by reaction to the dust in unprocessed plant fibers
sleep apnea *AP-ne-ah*	Intermittent periods of breathing cessation during sleep; central sleep apnea arises from failure of the brainstem to stimulate breathing; obstructive sleep apnea results from airway obstruction during deep sleep, as from obesity or enlarged tonsils
small cell carcinoma	A highly malignant type of bronchial tumor involving small, undifferentiated cells; "oat cell" carcinoma

Diagnosis

mediastinoscopy *me-de-as-tih-NOS-ko-pe*	Examination of the mediastinum by means of an endoscope inserted through an incision above the sternum
plethysmograph *pleh-THIZ-mo-graf*	An instrument that measures changes in gas volume and pressure during respiration
pneumotachometer *nu-mo-tak-OM-eh-ter*	A device for measuring air flow
thoracoscopy *thor-ah-KOS-ko-pe*	Examination of the pleural cavity through an endoscope; pleuroscopy

Treatment

aerosol therapy	Treatment by inhalation of a drug or water in spray form
continuous positive airway pressure (CPAP)	Use of a mechanical respirator to maintain pressure throughout the respiratory cycle in a patient who is breathing spontaneously
extubation	Removal of a previously inserted tube
intermittent positive pressure breathing (IPPB)	Use of a ventilator to inflate the lungs at intervals under positive pressure during inhalation
intermittent positive pressure ventilation (IPPV)	Use of a mechanical ventilator to force air into the lungs while allowing for passive exhalation
nasal cannula *KAN-u-lah*	A two-pronged plastic device inserted into the nostrils for delivery of oxygen (**Fig. 11-17**)
orthopneic position *or-thop-NE-ik*	An upright or semi-upright position that aids breathing
positive end-expiratory pressure (PEEP)	Use of a mechanical ventilator to increase the volume of gas in the lungs at the end of exhalation, thus improving gas exchange
postural drainage *POS-tu-ral*	Use of body position to drain secretions from the lungs by gravity; the patient is placed so that secretions will move passively into the larger airways for elimination
thoracic gas volume (TGV, V_{TG})	The volume of gas in the thoracic cavity calculated from measurements made with a body plethysmograph

Terminology	**Supplementary Terms** *(Continued)*

Surgery

adenoidectomy *ad-eh-noyd-EK-to-me*	Surgical removal of the adenoids
intubation *in-tu-BA-shun*	Insertion of a tube into a hollow organ, such as into the larynx or trachea for entrance of air (**Fig. 11-18**); patients may be intubated during surgery for administration of anesthesia or to maintain an airway; endotracheal intubation may be used as an emergency measure when airways are blocked
lobectomy *lo-BEK-to-me*	Surgical removal of a lobe of the lung or of another organ
pneumoplasty *NU-mo-plas-te*	Plastic surgery of the lung; in reduction pneumoplasty, nonfunctional portions of the lung are removed, as in cases of advanced emphysema
tracheotomy *tra-ke-OT-o-me*	Incision of the trachea through the neck, usually to establish an airway in cases of tracheal obstruction
tracheostomy *tra-ke-OS-to-me*	Surgical creation of an opening into the trachea to form an airway or to prepare for the insertion of a tube for ventilation (**Fig. 11-19**); also the opening thus created

Drugs

antihistamine *an-te-HIS-tah-mene*	Agent that prevents responses mediated by histamine, such as allergic and inflammatory reactions
antitussive *an-te-TUS-iv*	Drug that prevents or relieves coughing
asthma maintenance drug	Agent used to prevent asthma attacks and for chronic treatment of asthma
bronchodilator *brong-ko-DI-la-tor*	Drug that relieves bronchial spasm and widens the bronchi
corticosteroid *kor-tih-ko-STARE-oyd*	Hormone from the adrenal cortex; used to reduce inflammation
decongestant *de-kon-JES-tant*	Agent that reduces congestion or swelling
expectorant *ek-SPEK-to-rant*	Agent that aids in removal of bronchopulmonary secretions
isoniazid (INH) *i-so-NI-ah-zid*	Drug used to treat tuberculosis
leukotriene antagonist *lu-ko-TRI-ene*	Drug that prevents or reduces inflammation by inhibiting leukotrienes, substances made in white blood cells that promote inflammation, constrict the bronchi, and increase mucus production; used in asthma treatment
mucolytic *mu-ko-LIT-ik*	Agent that loosens mucus to aid in its removal
rifampin (rifampicin) *RIF-am-pin*	Drug used to treat tuberculosis

Go to the Audio Pronunciation Glossary in the Student Resources on thePoint to hear these terms pronounced.

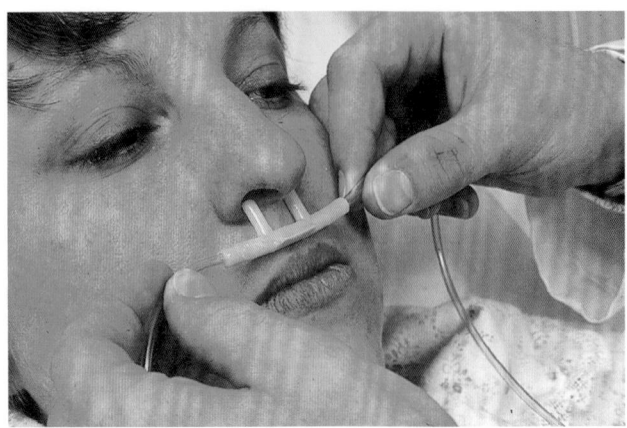

Figure 11-17 A nasal cannula.

Intranasal intubation

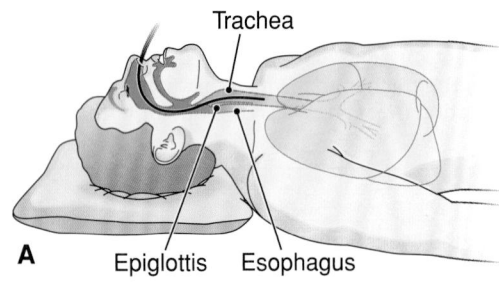

A

Oral intubation

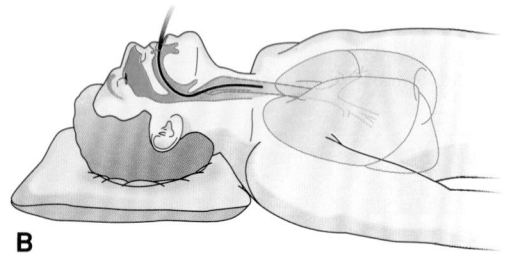

B

Figure 11-18 **Endotracheal intubation. A.** Nasal endotracheal catheter in proper position. **B.** Oral endotracheal intubation.

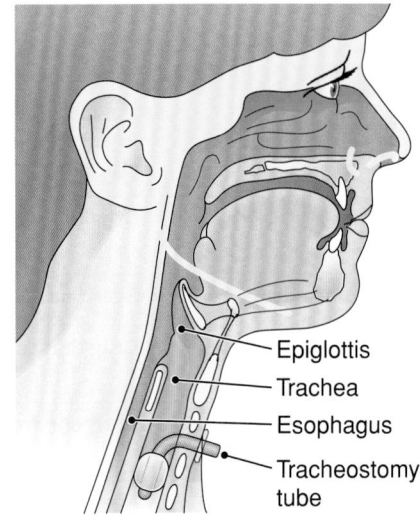

Figure 11-19 **A tracheostomy tube in place.**

Terminology Abbreviations

ABG(s)	Arterial blood gas(es)		**CF**	Cystic fibrosis
AFB	Acid-fast bacillus (usually *Mycobacterium tuberculosis*)		**CO₂**	Carbon dioxide
			COPD	Chronic obstructive pulmonary disease
ARDS	Acute respiratory distress syndrome; shock lung		**CPAP**	Continuous positive airway pressure
ARF	Acute respiratory failure		**CXR**	Chest radiograph, chest x-ray
BCG	Bacillus Calmette–Guérin (tuberculosis vaccine)		**DTaP**	Diphtheria, tetanus, pertussis (vaccine)
BS	Breath sounds		**ERV**	Expiratory reserve volume
C	Compliance			

Terminology   Abbreviations (Continued)

FEV	Forced expiratory volume		**PIP**	Peak inspiratory pressure
FRC	Functional residual capacity		**PND**	Paroxysmal nocturnal dyspnea
FVC	Forced vital capacity		**PPD**	Purified protein derivative (tuberculin)
HPS	*Hantavirus* pulmonary syndrome		**R**	Respiration
IC	Inspiratory capacity		**RDS**	Respiratory distress syndrome
IGRA	Interferon-gamma release assay (test for TB)		**RLL**	Right lower lobe (of lung)
INH	Isoniazid		**RML**	Right middle lobe (of lung)
IPPB	Intermittent positive pressure breathing		**RSV**	Respiratory syncytial virus
IPPV	Intermittent positive pressure ventilation		**RUL**	Right upper lobe (of lung)
IRV	Inspiratory reserve volume		**RV**	Residual volume
LLL	Left lower lobe (of lung)		**SARS**	Severe acute respiratory syndrome
LUL	Left upper lobe (of lung)		**SIDS**	Sudden infant death syndrome
MEFR	Maximal expiratory flow rate		**SpO$_2$**	Oxygen percent saturation
MMFR	Maximum midexpiratory flow rate		**T & A**	Tonsils and adenoids; tonsillectomy and adenoidectomy
NAA	Nucleic acid amplification (test) (for TB)		**TB**	Tuberculosis
O$_2$	Oxygen		**TGV**	Thoracic gas volume
PaCO$_2$	Arterial partial pressure of carbon dioxide		**TLC**	Total lung capacity
PaO$_2$	Arterial partial pressure of oxygen		**TV**	Tidal volume
PCP	*Pneumocystis* pneumonia		**URI**	Upper respiratory infection
PEEP	Positive end-expiratory pressure		**VC**	Vital capacity
PEFR	Peak expiratory flow rate		**V$_{TG}$**	Thoracic gas volume
PFT	Pulmonary function test(s)			

Case Study Revisited

A.D.'s Follow-Up to Surgery

A.D.'s surgery went well and there were no complications. The anesthesiologist closely monitored her respiratory status to make certain it was not compromised. He administered additional medications to maintain optimal airflow. Postoperatively, A.D.'s asthma was kept under control. The postoperative spirometry was adequate. Her discharge instructions were to resume preoperative medications and to follow up with her pulmonologist if there were any problems.

CHAPTER
11 **Review**

Labeling Exercise

THE RESPIRATORY SYSTEM

Write the name of each numbered part on the corresponding line of the answer sheet.

Alveolar duct   Left lung
Alveoli   Mediastinum
Capillaries   Nasal cavity
Diaphragm   Nasopharynx
Epiglottis   Oropharynx
Esophagus   Right bronchus
Frontal sinus   Right lung
Laryngopharynx   Sphenoidal sinus
Larynx and vocal folds   Terminal bronchiole
Left bronchus   Trachea

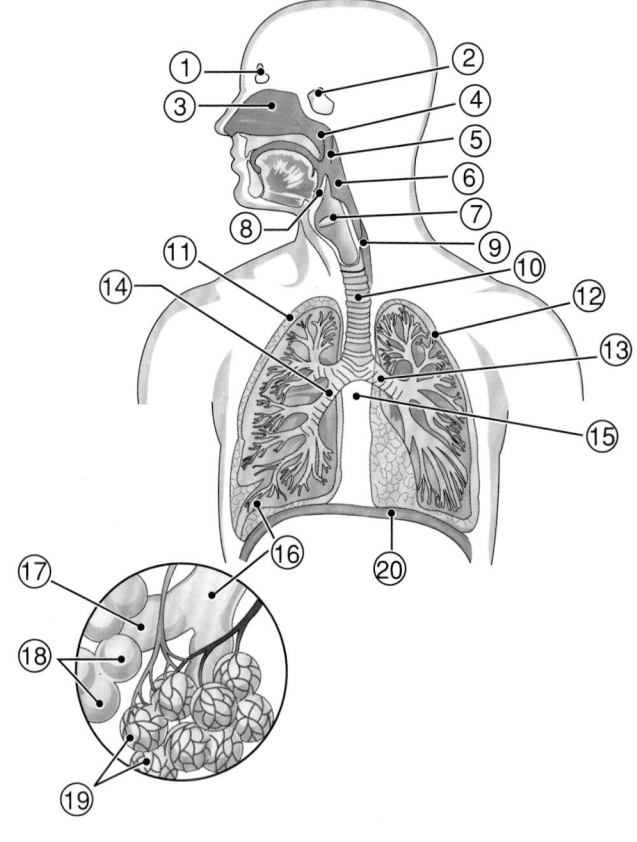

1. _____

2. _____

3. _____

4. _____

5. _____

6. _____

7. _____

8. _____

9. _____

10. _____

11. _____

12. _____

13. _____

14. _____

15. _____

16. _____

17. _____

18. _____

19. _____

20. _____

Terminology

MATCHING

Match the following terms, and write the appropriate letter to the left of each number.

_____ **1.** atelectasis   **a.** pulmonary disease with destruction of alveoli

_____ **2.** emphysema   **b.** increased carbon dioxide in the blood

_____ **3.** hypercapnemia   **c.** decreased rate and depth of breathing

_____ **4.** hypopnea   **d.** whooping cough

_____ **5.** pertussis   **e.** incomplete expansion of lung tissue

_____ **6.** mediastinum   **a.** accidental inhalation of foreign material into the lungs

_____ **7.** aspiration   **b.** space between the lungs

_____ **8.** sputum   **c.** substance that reduces surface tension

_____ **9.** surfactant   **d.** a measure of how easily the lungs expand

_____ **10.** compliance   **e.** expectoration

_____ **11.** PCP   **a.** childhood vaccine

_____ **12.** DTaP   **b.** tuberculosis vaccine

_____ **13.** CF   **c.** hereditary disease that affects respiration

_____ **14.** IPPB   **d.** pneumonia seen in compromised patients

_____ **15.** BCG   **e.** a form of respiratory treatment

Supplementary Terms

_____ **16.** epistaxis   **a.** suffocation

_____ **17.** intubation   **b.** nosebleed

_____ **18.** asphyxia   **c.** insertion of a tube into a hollow organ

_____ **19.** stridor   **d.** harsh, high-pitched respiratory sound

_____ **20.** expectorant   **e.** agent that helps remove bronchial secretions

_____ **21.** mucolytic   **a.** irregular respiration seen in terminally ill patients

_____ **22.** Cheyne–Stokes   **b.** agent that loosens mucus to aid in its removal

_____ **23.** rales   **c.** acute rhinitis

_____ **24.** orthopneic   **d.** pertaining to an upright position

_____ **25.** coryza   **e.** abnormal chest sounds

FILL IN THE BLANKS

26. The trachea divides into a right and a left primary _____.

27. The phrenic nerve activates the _____.

28. The gas produced in the tissues and exhaled in respiration is _____.

29. The double membrane that covers the lungs and lines the thoracic cavity is the _____.

30. The small air sacs in the lungs through which gases are exchanged between the atmosphere and the blood are the

_____.

31. The turbinate bones contain receptors for the sense of _____.

32. A pneumotropic virus is one that invades the _____ .

33. The term *acid-fast bacillus* (AFB) is commonly applied to the organism that causes _____ .

34. The apparatus used to measure A.D.'s breathing volumes in the opening case study is called a(n) _____ .

35. The amount of air that A.D. could expel from her lungs by maximum exhalation after maximum inhalation is termed the

_____ .

Supplementary Terms

36. A thoracoscopy is an examination of the _____ through an endoscope.

37. An antitussive agent prevents _____ .

38. A mucolytic agent dissolves _____ .

39. Intermittent periods of not breathing during sleep are termed sleep _____ .

40. A.D. was given a drug to widen the bronchi. This type of drug is called a(n) _____ .

TRUE-FALSE

Examine the following statements. If the statement is true, write T in the first blank. If the statement is false, write F in the first blank, and correct the statement by replacing the underlined word in the second blank.

	True or False	**Correct Answer**
41. The pharynx is the <u>throat</u>.	_____	_____
42. The diaphragm flattens during <u>exhalation</u>.	_____	_____
43. The vocal folds are located in the <u>pharynx</u>.	_____	_____
44. The right lung has <u>three</u> lobes.	_____	_____
45. The opening between the vocal folds is the <u>glottis</u>.	_____	_____
46. The adenoids are in the <u>nasopharynx</u>.	_____	_____

DEFINITIONS

Write words for the following definitions.

47. incision of the phrenic nerve _____

48. decrease in rate and depth of breathing _____

49. inflammation of the throat _____

50. inflammation of the bronchioles _____

51. creation of an opening into the trachea _____

The word thorax (chest) is used as an ending in compound words that mean the accumulation of substances in the pleural space. Define the following terms.

52. pneumothorax _____

53. hydrothorax _____

54. pyothorax _____

55. hemothorax _____

Define the following words.

56. tracheostenosis _____

57. hemoptysis _____

58. hypoxia _____

59. pneumonopathy _____

60. tachypnea _____

61. bronchiectasis _____

62. rhinoplasty _____

63. pleurodynia _____

Identify and define the root in the following words.

	Root	Meaning of Root
64. rhinoplasty	____	_____
65. pulmonologist	____	_____
66. respiration	____	_____
67. phrenicotomy	____	_____
68. pneumatic	____	_____

OPPOSITES

Write a word that means the opposite of the following.

69. bradypnea _____

70. hypocapnia _____

71. expiration _____

72. extrapulmonary _____

73. extubation _____

ADJECTIVES

Write the adjective form of the following words.

74. larynx _____

75. alveolus _____

76. nose _____

77. trachea _____

78. pleura _____

79. bronchus _____

PLURALS

Write the plural form of the following words.

80. naris _____

81. pleura _____

82. alveolus _____

83. concha _____

84. bronchus _____

ELIMINATIONS

In each of the sets below, underline the word that does not fit in with the rest and explain the reason for your choice.

85. turbinates — septum — nares — tonsil — conchae

_____

86. sinus — thyroid cartilage — epiglottis — cricoid cartilage — vocal folds

_____

87. diphtheria — tuberculosis — asthma — common cold — influenza

_____

88. RUL — URI — LUL — LLL — RML

_____

89. TLC — FRC — FEV — TV — RDS

_____

WORD BUILDING

Write words for the following definitions using the word parts given.

| -pnea   -ia   ox/i   a-   -metry   phon/o   hyper-   dys-   capn/o   hypo-   eu-   tachy- |

90. loss of voice _____

91. increased levels of carbon dioxide _____

92. difficulty in speaking _____

93. increased rate and depth of breathing _____

94. measurement of oxygen levels _____

95. difficulty in breathing _____

96. low levels of oxygen in the tissues _____

97. normal, regular breathing _____

98. rapid breathing _____

99. excessive voice production _____

WORD ANALYSIS

Define the following words and give the meaning of the word parts in each. Use a dictionary if necessary.

100. pneumotachometer (*nu-mo-tak-OM-eh-ter*) _____

    a. pneum/o _____

    b. tach/o _____

    c. -meter _____

101. atelectasis (*at-eh-LEK-tah-sis*) _____

    a. atel/o- _____

    b. -ectasis _____

102. pneumatocardia (*nu-mah-to-KAR-de-ah*) _____

    a. pneumat/o _____

    b. cardi _____

    c. -ia _____

103. pneumoconiosis (*nu-mo-ko-ne-O-sis*) _____

    a. pneum/o _____

    b. coni/o _____

    c. -sis _____

For more learning activities, see Chapter 11 of the Student Resources on thePoint.

Additional Case Studies

Case Study 11-1: *Giant Cell Sarcoma of the Lung*

L.E., a 68 y/o man, was admitted to the pulmonary unit with chest pain on inspiration, dyspnea, and diaphoresis. He had smoked one and a half packs of cigarettes per day for 52 years and had quit three months ago. L.E. was retired from the advertising industry and admitted to occasional alcohol use. He was treated for primary giant cell sarcoma of the left lung three years ago with a lobectomy of the left lung followed by radiation and chemotherapy.

Physical examination was unremarkable except for a thoracotomy scar in the left hemithorax, decreased breath sounds, and dullness to percussion of the left base. There was no hemoptysis. Chest and upper abdomen CT scan showed findings compatible with recurrent sarcoma of the left hemithorax. Abnormal mediastinal nodes were evident. A thoracentesis was attempted but did not yield fluid. L.E. was scheduled for a left thoracoscopy, mediastinoscopy, and biopsy.

Case Study 11-2: *Terminal Dyspnea*

N.A., a 76-year-old woman, was in the ICU in the terminal stage of multisystem organ failure. She had been admitted to the hospital for bacterial pneumonia, which had not resolved with antibiotic therapy. She had a 20-year history of COPD. She was not conscious and was unable to breathe on her own. Her ABGs were abnormal, and she was diagnosed with refractory ARDS. The decision was made to support her breathing with endotracheal intubation and mechanical ventilation. After one week and several unsuccessful attempts to wean her from the ventilator, the pulmonologist suggested a permanent tracheostomy and discussed with the family the options of continuing or withdrawing life support.

Her physiologic status met the criteria of remote or no chance for recovery.

N.A.'s family discussed her condition and decided not to pursue aggressive life-sustaining therapies. N.A. was assigned DNR status. After the written orders were read and signed by the family, the endotracheal tube, feeding tube, pulse oximeter, and ECG electrodes were removed, and a morphine IV drip was started with prn boluses ordered to promote comfort and relieve pain. The family sat with her for many hours, providing comfort and support. After a while, they noticed that her breathing had become shallow with Cheyne–Stokes respirations. N.A. died quietly in the presence of her family and the hospital chaplain.

Case Study Questions

Multiple Choice. Select the best answer, and write the letter of your choice to the left of each number.

_____ **1.** The root *pulmon*, as in *pulmonary*, means
   a. chest
   b. air
   c. lung
   d. breath sound

_____ **2.** Hemoptysis is
   a. drooping eyelids
   b. discoloration of skin
   c. blue nail beds
   d. spitting of blood

_____ **3.** Dyspnea could NOT be described as
   a. difficulty breathing
   b. eupnea
   c. air hunger
   d. Cheyne–Stokes respirations

_____ **4.** Pulse oximetry is used to measure
   a. forced expiratory volume
   b. tidal volume
   c. positive end-expiratory pressure
   d. oxygen saturation of blood

_____ **5.** An endotracheal tube is placed
   a. within the trachea
   b. beyond the carina
   c. within the bronchus
   d. under the trachea

Write words from the case studies with the following meanings.

6. Removal of a lobe _____

7. Profuse sweating _____

8. Surgical incision of the chest _____

9. Endoscopic examination of the chest cavity _____

10. Half of the chest _____

11. Endoscopic examination of the space between the lungs _____

12. Movement of air into and out of the lungs _____

Abbreviations. Define the following abbreviations.

13. COPD _____

14. ABG _____

15. ARDS _____

16. DNR _____

17. BS _____

11

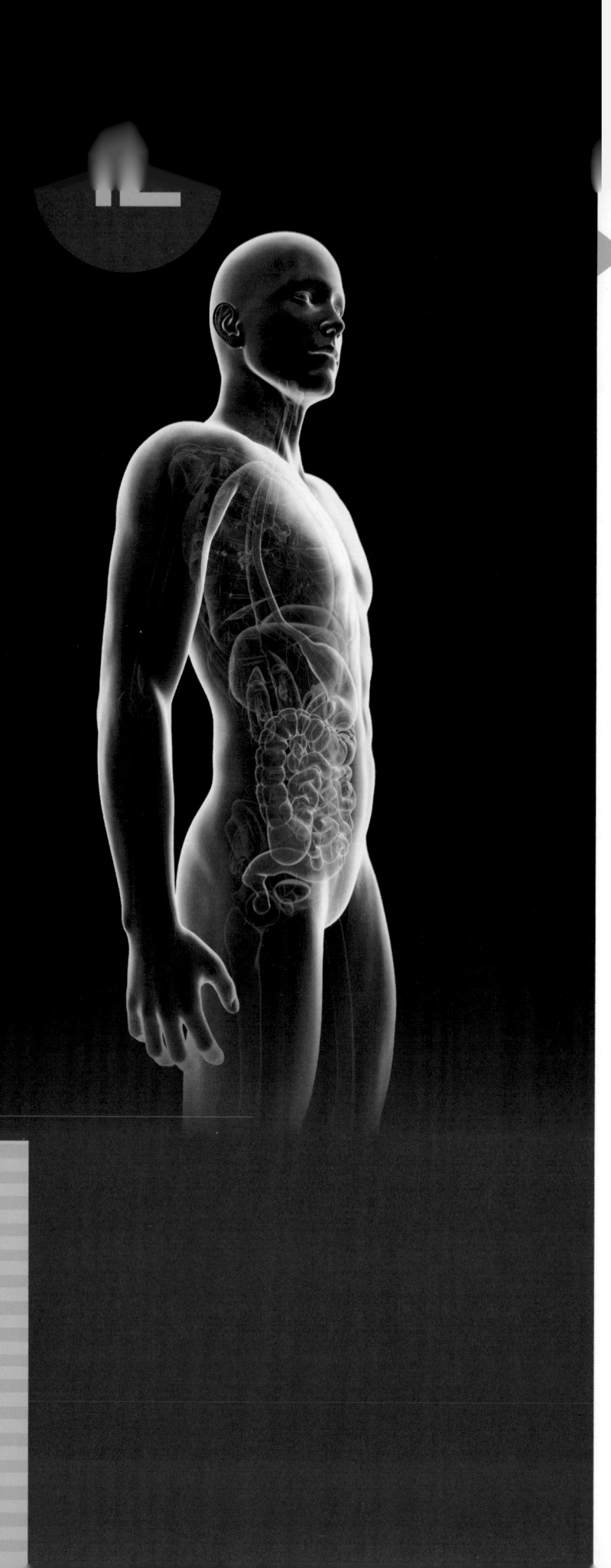

Pretest

Multiple Choice. Select the best answer, and write the letter of your choice to the left of each number.

_____ 1. An organic catalyst is a(n)
   a. enzyme
   b. sugar
   c. nucleic acid
   d. saliva

_____ 2. The organ that carries food from the pharynx to the stomach is the
   a. trachea
   b. larynx
   c. esophagus
   d. intestine

_____ 3. The word root for the stomach is
   a. hepat/o
   b. ren/o
   c. gastr/o
   d. cardi/o

_____ 4. The word root *enter/o* refers to the
   a. gallbladder
   b. intestine
   c. kidney
   d. heart

_____ 5. The wave-like action that moves substances through an organ is called
   a. pulmonary
   b. peristalsis
   c. parotid
   d. mastication

_____ 6. The process of moving digested nutrients from the intestine into the circulation is called
   a. lymphedema
   b. digestion
   c. egestion
   d. absorption

_____ 7. The organ that secretes bile is the
   a. kidney
   b. spleen
   c. liver
   d. stomach

_____ 8. Cholecystitis is inflammation of the
   a. gallbladder
   b. throat
   c. diaphragm
   d. small intestine

▶ Learning Objectives

After study of this chapter you should be able to:

1 ▶ Describe the organs of the digestive tract, and give the function of each. *p272*

2 ▶ Describe the accessory organs and explain the role of each in digestion. *p275*

3 ▶ Identify and use the roots pertaining to the digestive system and accessory organs. *p278*

4 ▶ Describe the major disorders of the digestive system. *p282*

5 ▶ Define medical terms used in reference to the digestive system. *p288*

6 ▶ Interpret abbreviations used in referring to the gastrointestinal system. *p296*

7 ▶ Analyze the medical terms in case studies related to the digestive system. *pp271, 302*

Case Study: *B.F.'s Gastroesophageal Reflux Disease (GERD) and Erosive Esophagitis*

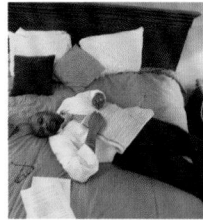

Chief Complaint

B.F. is a 51-year-old African American businessman with complaints of epigastric pain. He has a 10-year history of heartburn that he notes has become worse over the last year. The heartburn occurs both after meals and at bedtime. His sleep has been interrupted by nighttime symptoms, and he feels generally fatigued. Intermittently he says he feels that things come back up into his throat, but he lacks clear signs of aspiration into the respiratory tract. He is aware that gastroesophageal reflux disease (GERD) is a chronic condition and may be associated with a risk for complications that include serious morbidity and mortality. Due to his required travel for business, he has put off making a doctor's appointment but realizes he needs to see his physician. The heartburn has increased in frequency (daily now) and severity, so he finally schedules an office visit.

Examination

B.F. is seen by his primary care physician and describes his daily episodes of discomfort. B.F. is 6-foot-1-inch and weighs 230 pounds. The physician reviews a colonoscopy from last year with him that was normal. His blood pressure and other physical examination findings at this visit are within normal ranges. Results of a complete blood count, chemistry profile, and lipid profile are all within normal limits. He describes his self-medication by taking over-the-counter (OTC) drugs including antacids, histamine-2 receptor antagonists (H2 blockers), and the OTC proton pump inhibitor (PPI) omeprazole. He notes the latter helped "a little bit," but he discontinued use after two weeks, as noted in the packaging instructions. He has no history of smoking or alcohol abuse. He has an unremarkable past medical and family history.

Clinical Course

The physician explained to B.F. that he is experiencing classic esophageal symptoms that are highly specific to GERD, heartburn, and regurgitation. The physician also informed him that GERD might be associated with erosive esophagitis, which is best diagnosed on endoscopy via esophagogastroduodenoscopy (EGD). Because B.F. is 51 and has been experiencing heartburn for more than 10 years with daily symptoms for the past year, he should be evaluated by endoscopy. He has been referred for the procedure, but the appointment is not for seven weeks. He is prescribed a PPI and is instructed to return to the office in approximately four weeks while still on therapy for assessment of symptoms prior to his appointment.

ANCILLARIES *At-A-Glance*

Visit thePoint to access the following resources. For guidance in using the resources most effectively, see pp. ix–xvi.

Learning RESOURCES

▶ **Tips for Effective Studying**
▶ **Web Figure: The Peritoneum**
▶ **Web Figure: The Salivary Glands and Ducts**
▶ **Web Figure: Pyloric Stenosis**
▶ **Web Figure: Complications of Ulcerative Colitis**
▶ **Web Figure: Diverticulosis and Diverticulitis**
▶ **Web Figure: Clinical Features of Cirrhosis**
▶ **Web Figure: Portal Hypertension**

▶ **Animation: Enzymes**
▶ **Animation: Digestion**
▶ **Animation: The Liver in Health and Disease**
▶ **Audio Pronunciation Glossary**

Learning ACTIVITIES

▶ **Visual Activities**
▶ **Kinesthetic Activities**
▶ **Auditory Activities**

Introduction

The function of the digestive system is to prepare food for intake by body cells. Nutrients must be broken down by mechanical and chemical means into molecules that are small enough to be absorbed into circulation. Within cells, the nutrients are used for energy and for rebuilding vital cell components. The digestive system also stores undigested waste materials and then eliminates them from the body.

Digestion

Digestion takes place in the digestive tract proper, which extends from the **mouth** to the **anus** (**Fig. 12-1**). **Peristalsis**, wave-like contractions of the organ walls, moves food through the digestive tract and also moves undigested waste material out of the body. Also contributing to digestion are several accessory organs that release secretions into the digestive tract.

Enzymes are needed throughout the digestive process. These compounds are organic catalysts that speed the rate of food's chemical breakdown. The names of most enzymes can be recognized by the ending *-ase*.

The Digestive Tract

The digestive tract, also known as the alimentary canal or gastrointestinal (GI) tract, is essentially a long tube modified into separate organs with special functions (see **Fig. 12-1**). **Box 12-1** summarizes the activities of the digestive organs described below. A large serous membrane, the **peritoneum** (*per-ih-to-NE-um*), covers the organs in the abdominal cavity, supporting and separating them.

> See the animations "Enzymes" and "Digestion" and a figure on the peritoneum in the Student Resources on thePoint.

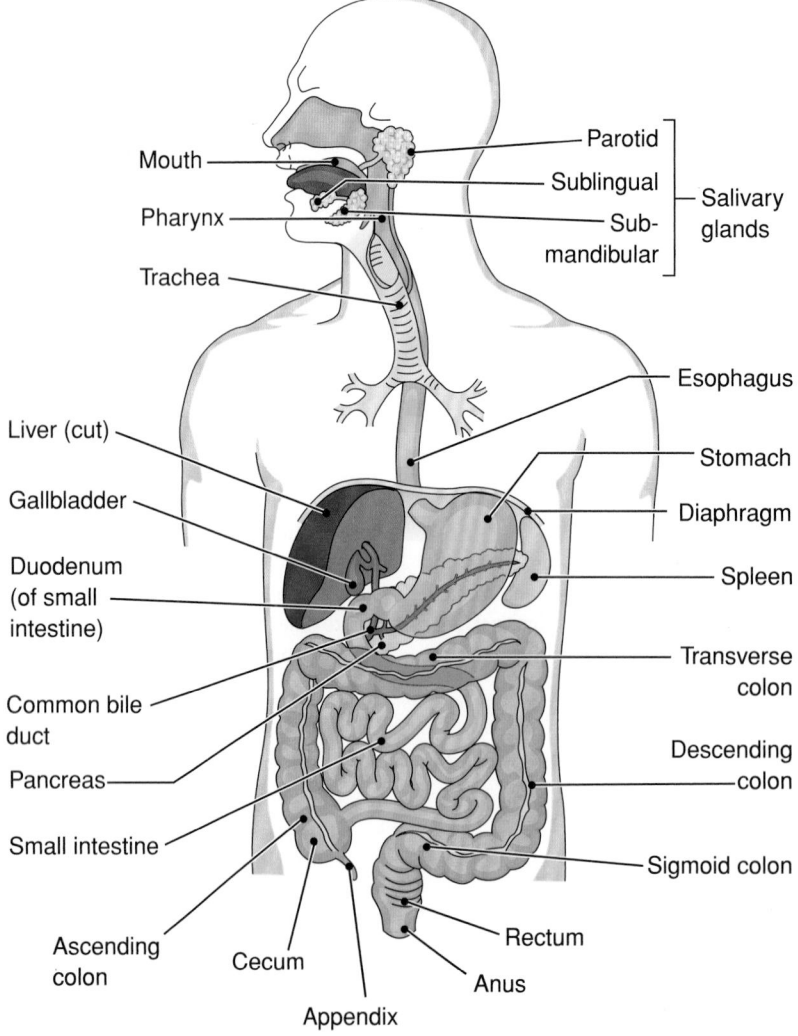

Figure 12-1 **Digestive system.** Some divisions of the small and large intestine are shown. The accessory organs are the salivary glands, liver, gallbladder, and pancreas. The trachea, diaphragm, and spleen are shown for reference.

Box 12-1

FOR YOUR REFERENCE
Organs of the Digestive Tract

Organ	Digestive Actions
mouth	Used to bite and chew food. Mixes food with saliva, which contains salivary amylase, an enzyme that begins the digestion of starch. Shapes food into small portions, which the tongue pushes into the pharynx.
pharynx	Swallows food by reflex action and moves it into the esophagus.
esophagus	Moves food into the stomach by peristalsis.
stomach	Stores food; churns to mix food with water and digestive juices. Secretes protein-digesting hydrochloric acid (HCl) and the enzyme pepsin.
small intestine	Secretes enzymes. Receives secretions from the accessory organs, which digest and neutralize food. Site of most digestion and absorption of nutrients into the circulation.
large intestine	Forms, stores, and eliminates undigested waste material.

12

THE MOUTH TO THE STOMACH

Digestion begins in the mouth (**Fig. 12-2**), also called the oral cavity. Here, food is chewed into small bits by the teeth. There are 32 teeth in a complete adult set, including incisors and canines to bite food and molars for grinding. The structural features of a molar tooth and its surrounding tissue are shown in **Figure 12-3**. The **palate** is the roof of the mouth; the anterior portion (hard palate) is formed by bone, and the posterior part (soft palate) is made of soft tissue. The fleshy **uvula**, used in speech production, hangs from the soft palate. Dental hygienists help in care of the mouth and teeth. **Box 12-2** has information on careers in dental hygiene.

In the process of chewing, or **mastication**, the tongue, lips, cheeks, and palate also help to break up food and mix it with **saliva**, a secretion that moistens the food and begins starch digestion. The salivary glands (see **Fig. 12-1**) secrete

saliva into the mouth and are considered to be accessory digestive organs.

> For a more detailed picture of the salivary glands and ducts, visit the Student Resources on thePoint.

Portions of moistened food are moved toward the **pharynx** (throat), where swallowing reflexes push them into the **esophagus**. Peristalsis moves the food through the esophagus and into the stomach. At its distal end, where it joins the **stomach**, the esophagus has muscle tissue that contracts to keep stomach contents from refluxing (flowing backward). This **lower esophageal sphincter (LES)** is also called the "cardiac sphincter" because it lies above the cardia of the stomach, the region around its upper opening.

In the stomach, food is further broken down as it is churned and mixed with secretions containing the enzyme

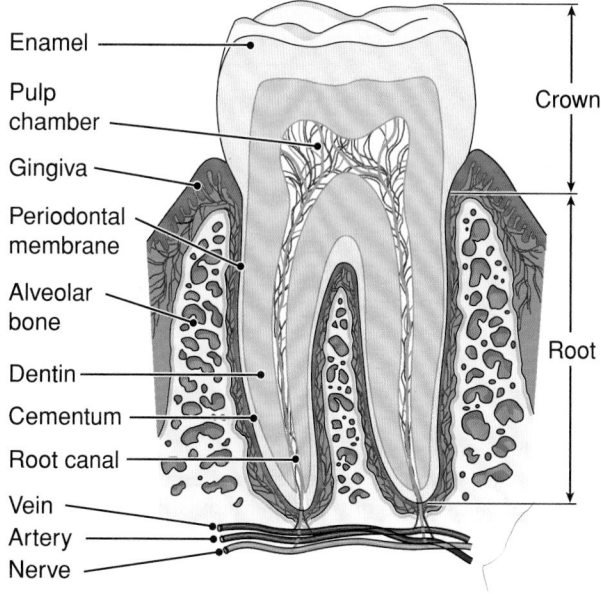

Figure 12-2   The mouth. The teeth, pharynx, tonsils, and other structures in the oral cavity are shown.

Figure 12-3   A molar tooth. The bony socket, gingiva, blood vessels, and nerve supply are shown as well as portions of the tooth.

HEALTH PROFESSIONS
Dental Hygienist

Dental hygienists focus primarily on dental health maintenance and preventive dental care. They examine patients' dentition and periodontium (supporting structures of the teeth); take radiographic images; and perform oral prophylaxis using hand and ultrasonic instruments to remove deposits, such as calculus, stains, and plaque. They may also apply fluorides to prevent caries. They work independently or along with a dentist to administer local anesthesia and nitrous oxide sedation and to do oral screenings, polish restorations, remove sutures, apply dental sealants, and perform periodontal procedures. Dental hygienists must be knowledgeable about safety concerning x-ray equipment, anesthesia, and infectious diseases. They wear safety glasses, surgical masks, and gloves to protect themselves and their patients. A major component of the dental hygienist's work is patient education for maintenance of good oral health. They may give instruction on nutrition and proper oral care, such as brushing, flossing, and the use of antimicrobial rinses.

Most dental hygiene programs award an associate degree; some offer bachelor's or master's degrees. The higher degrees are required for research, teaching, or practice in public or school health facilities. The professional program requires one year of college-level prerequisite courses. The curriculum includes courses in radiography, dental anatomy, pharmacology, head and neck anatomy, and other health- and dental-related sciences. Additional material on the legal and ethical aspects of dental hygiene practice and extensive clinical training are included in the program. After graduation, dental hygienists must be licensed in their states by passing clinical and written examinations administered by the American Dental Association's (ADA) Joint Commission on National Dental Examinations.

Almost all hygienists work in dental offices. One advantage of this field is scheduling flexibility and the opportunity for part-time work. Job prospects are good; dental hygiene is among the fastest growing occupations. Benefits vary with place of employment. For additional information, contact the American Dental Hygienists' Association at www.adha.org.

---

pepsin and powerful hydrochloric acid (HCl), both of which break down proteins. The partially digested food then passes through the stomach's lower portion, the **pylorus,** into the **intestine.**

THE SMALL INTESTINE

Food leaving the stomach enters the **duodenum,** the first portion of the **small intestine.** As the food continues through the **jejunum** and **ileum,** the small intestine's remaining sections, digestion is completed. (Ileum sounds like ilium, a large bone of the pelvis. For information on these and other homonyms, see **Box 12-3.**) The digestive substances active in the small intestine include enzymes from the intestine itself and products from accessory organs that secrete into the duodenum.

The digested nutrients, including water, minerals, and vitamins, are absorbed into the circulation, aided by small

---

FOCUS ON WORDS
Homonyms

Homonyms are words that sound alike but have different meanings. One must know the context in which they are used in order to understand the intended meaning. For example, the ilium is the upper portion of the pelvis, but the ileum is the last portion of the small intestine. Different adjectives are preferred for each—iliac for the first and ileal for the second. The word *meiosis* refers to the type of cell division that halves the chromosomes to form the gametes, but *miosis* means abnormal contraction of the pupil. Both words come from the Greek word that means a decrease.

Similar-sounding names lead to some funny misspellings. The large bone of the upper arm is the humerus, but this bone is often written as "humorous." The vagus nerve (cranial nerve X) is named with a root that means "wander," as in the words vague and vagabond, because this nerve branches to many of the internal organs. Students often write the name as if it had some relation to the famous gambling city in Nevada.

Homonyms may have a more serious side as well. Drug names may sound or look so similar that clinicians could confuse them, leading to dangerous, potentially fatal, complications. For example, a 50-year-old woman was hospitalized after she took Flomax, which is used to treat symptoms for an enlarged prostate instead of Volmax, which is used to relieve bronchospasm. Another example involved two drugs used to treat schizophrenia, clozapine and olanzapine; a young man was given the wrong drug and suffered severe complications. The FDA and the United States Adopted Names Council regulate sound-alike or look-alike drug names. The World Health Organization (WHO) has rejected many proposed names, and has even changed drug names after they have been marketed, when they have led to medication errors.

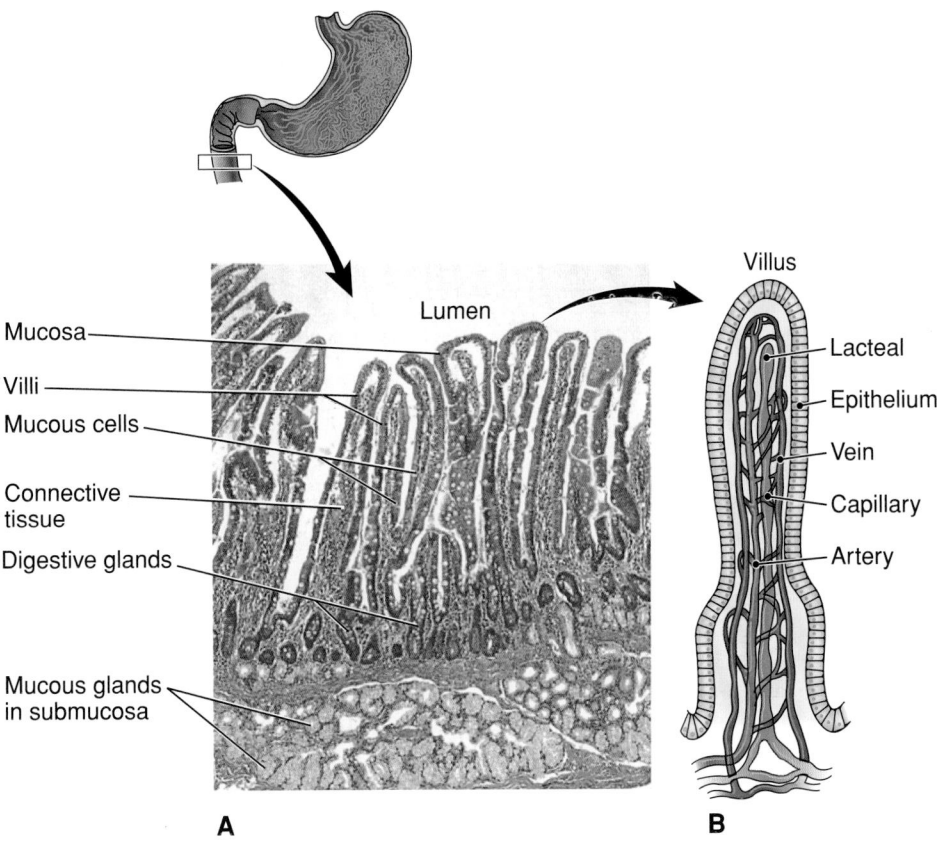

Figure 12-4 **Intestinal villi. A.** Microscopic view of the small intestine's lining showing villi and glands that secrete mucus and digestive juices. The lumen is the central opening. **B.** An intestinal villus. Each villus has blood vessels and a lacteal (lymphatic capillary) for nutrient absorption.

projections in the intestinal lining called **villi** (**Fig. 12-4**). Each villus has blood capillaries to absorb nutrients into the bloodstream and lymphatic capillaries, or **lacteals**, to absorb small molecules of digested fats into the lymph. These fats join the blood when lymph flows into the bloodstream near the heart.

THE LARGE INTESTINE

Any food that has not been digested, along with water and digestive juices, passes into the **large intestine**. This part of the digestive tract begins in the lower right region of the abdomen with a small pouch, the **cecum**, to which the **appendix** is attached. (The appendix does not aid in digestion, but contains lymphatic tissue and may function in immunity.) The large intestine continues as the **colon**, a name that is often used alone to mean the large intestine, because the colon constitutes such a large portion of that organ. The colon travels upward along the right side of the abdomen as the ascending colon, crosses below the stomach as the transverse colon, and then continues down the left side of the abdomen as the descending colon. As food is pushed through the colon, water is reabsorbed, and stool or **feces** is formed. This waste material passes into the S-shaped **sigmoid colon** and is stored in the **rectum** until eliminated through the anus.

The Accessory Organs

The salivary glands, which secrete into the mouth, are the first accessory organs to act on food. They secrete an enzyme (salivary amylase) that begins starch digestion. The remaining accessory organs are in the abdomen and secrete into the duodenum (**Fig. 12-5**). The **liver** is a large

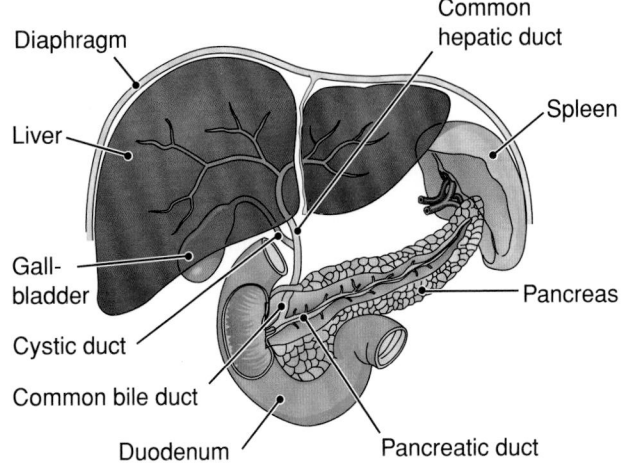

Figure 12-5 **Accessory organs of digestion.** The organs and ducts are shown. The diaphragm and spleen are shown for reference.

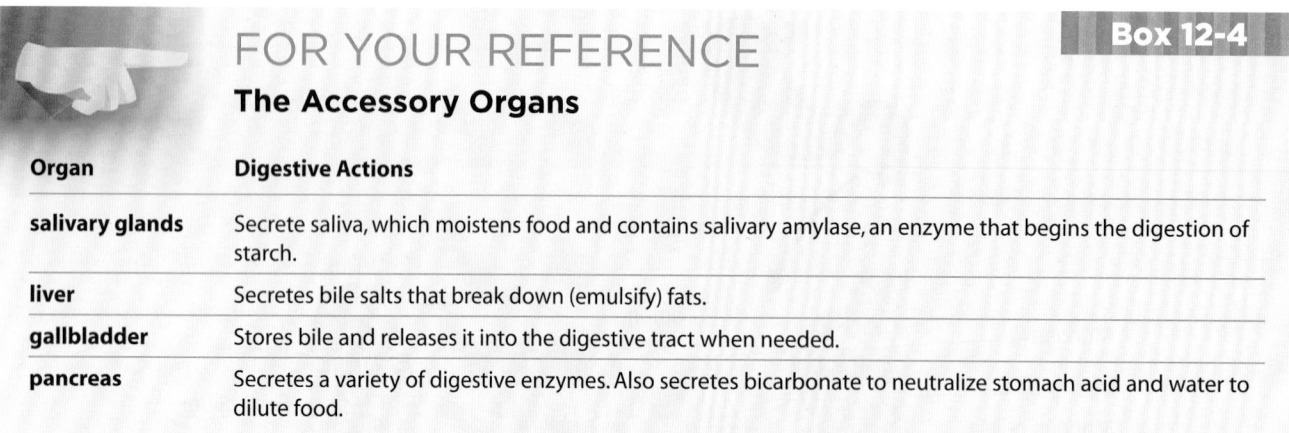

FOR YOUR REFERENCE
The Accessory Organs

Box 12-4

Organ	Digestive Actions
salivary glands	Secrete saliva, which moistens food and contains salivary amylase, an enzyme that begins the digestion of starch.
liver	Secretes bile salts that break down (emulsify) fats.
gallbladder	Stores bile and releases it into the digestive tract when needed.
pancreas	Secretes a variety of digestive enzymes. Also secretes bicarbonate to neutralize stomach acid and water to dilute food.

gland with many functions. A major activity is to process blood, removing toxins and converting nutrients into new compounds. A special circulatory pathway, the **hepatic portal system**, carries blood to the liver from the other abdominal organs. The liver functions in digestion by secreting **bile**, which emulsifies fats, that is, breaks them down into smaller units. The **gallbladder** stores bile until it is needed in digestion. The common hepatic duct from

the liver and the cystic duct from the gallbladder merge to form the **common bile duct**, which empties into the duodenum.

The **pancreas** produces a mixture of digestive enzymes that is delivered into the duodenum through the pancreatic duct. It also secretes large amounts of bicarbonate, which neutralizes the strong stomach acid. **Box 12-4** summarizes the functions of the accessory organs.

Terminology   Key Terms

Normal Structure and Function

anus A-nus	The distal opening of the digestive tract (root: an/o)
appendix ah-PEN-diks	An appendage; usually means the narrow tube of lymphatic tissue attached to the cecum, the vermiform (worm-like) appendix
bile	The fluid secreted by the liver that emulsifies fats and aids in their absorption (roots: chol/e, bili)
cecum SE-kum	A blind pouch at the beginning of the large intestine (root: cec/o)
colon KO-lon	The major portion of the large intestine; extends from the cecum to the rectum and is formed by ascending, transverse, and descending portions (roots: col/o, colon/o)
common bile duct	The duct that carries bile into the duodenum; formed by the union of the cystic duct and the common hepatic duct (root: choledoch/o)
duodenum du-o-DE-num	The first portion of the small intestine (root: duoden/o); also pronounced du-OD-eh-num
enzyme EN-zime	An organic catalyst; speeds the rate of chemical reactions
esophagus e-SOF-ah-gus	The muscular tube that carries food from the pharynx to the stomach
feces FE-seze	The waste material eliminated from the intestine (adjective: fecal); stool
gallbladder	A sac on the undersurface of the liver that stores bile (root: cholecyst/o)

Terminology	**Key Terms** *(Continued)*

hepatic portal system	A special circulatory pathway that brings blood directly from the abdominal organs to the liver for processing (also called simply the portal system); the vessel that enters the liver is the hepatic portal vein (portal vein)
ileum *IL-e-um*	The terminal portion of the small intestine (root: ile/o)
intestine *in-TES-tin*	The portion of the digestive tract between the stomach and the anus; it consists of the small and large intestines; it functions in digestion, absorption, and elimination of waste (root: enter/o); the bowel (*BOW-el*)
jejunum *jeh-JU-num*	The middle portion of the small intestine (root: jejun/o)
lacteal *lak-TELE*	A lymphatic capillary in a villus of the small intestine; lacteals absorb digested fats into the lymph
large intestine	The terminal portion of the digestive tract, consisting of the cecum, colon, rectum, and anus; it stores and eliminates undigested waste material (feces)
liver *LIV-er*	The large gland in the upper right abdomen; in addition to many other functions, it secretes bile needed for digestion and absorption of fats (root: hepat/o)
lower esophageal sphincter (LES) *e-sof-ah-JE-al SFINK-ter*	Muscle tissue at the distal end of the esophagus (gastroesophageal junction) that prevents stomach contents from refluxing into the esophagus; also called the cardiac sphincter
mastication *mas-tih-KA-shun*	Chewing
mouth	The oral cavity; contains the tongue and teeth; used to take in and chew food, mix it with saliva, and move it toward the throat to be swallowed
palate *PAL-at*	The roof of the mouth; the partition between the mouth and nasal cavity; consists of an anterior portion formed by bone, the hard palate, and a posterior portion formed of tissue, the soft palate (root: palat/o)
pancreas *PAN-kre-as*	A large, elongated gland posterior to the stomach; it produces hormones that regulate sugar metabolism and also produces digestive enzymes (root: pancreat/o)
peristalsis *per-ih-STAL-sis*	Wave-like contractions of an organ's walls; moves material through an organ or duct
peritoneum *per-ih-to-NE-um*	The large serous membrane that lines the abdominal cavity and supports the abdominal organs
pharynx *FAR-inks*	The throat; a common passageway for food entering the esophagus and air entering the larynx (root: pharyng/o)
pylorus *pi-LOR-us*	The stomach's distal opening into the duodenum (root: pylor/o); the opening is controlled by a ring of muscle, the pyloric sphincter
rectum *REK-tum*	The distal portion of the large intestine; it stores and eliminates undigested waste (roots: rect/o, proct/o)
saliva *sah-LI-vah*	The clear secretion released into the mouth that moistens food and contains a starch-digesting enzyme (root: sial/o); saliva is produced by three pairs of glands: the parotid, submandibular, and sublingual glands (see **Fig. 12-1**)
sigmoid colon	Distal S-shaped portion of the large intestine located between the descending colon and the rectum

(continued)

Terminology	Key Terms *(Continued)*
small intestine	The portion of the intestine between the stomach and the large intestine; comprised of the duodenum, jejunum, and ileum; accessory organs secrete into the small intestine, and almost all digestion and absorption occur there
stomach STUM-ak	A muscular sac-like organ below the diaphragm that stores food and secretes juices that digest proteins (root: gastr/o)
uvula U-vu-lah	The fleshy mass that hangs from the soft palate; aids in speech production (literally "little grape") (root: uvul/o)
villi VIL-i	Tiny projections in the lining of the small intestine that absorb digested foods into the circulation (singular: villus)

> Go to the Audio Pronunciation Glossary in the Student Resources on thePoint to hear these words pronounced.

Roots Pertaining to the Digestive System

See **Tables 12-1** to **12-3**.

Table 12-1	Roots for the Mouth		
Root	**Meaning**	**Example**	**Definition of Example**
bucc/o	cheek	buccoversion buk-ko-VER-zhun	turning toward the cheek
dent/o, dent/i	tooth, teeth	edentulous e-DEN-tu-lus	without teeth
odont/o	tooth, teeth	periodontics per-e-o-DON-tiks	dental specialty that deals with the study and treatment of the tissues around the teeth
gingiv/o	gum (gingiva)	gingivectomy jin-jih-VEK-to-me	excision of gum tissue
gloss/o	tongue	glossoplegia glos-o-PLE-je-ah	paralysis (-plegia) of the tongue
lingu/o	tongue	orolingual or-o-LING-gwal	pertaining to the mouth and tongue
gnath/o	jaw	prognathous PROG-nah-thus	having a projecting jaw
labi/o	lip	labium LA-be-um	lip or lip-like structure
or/o	mouth	circumoral sir-kum-OR-al	around the mouth
stoma, stomat/o	mouth	xerostomia ze-ro-STO-me-ah	dryness (xero-) of the mouth
palat/o	palate	palatine PAL-ah-tine	pertaining to the palate (also palatal)
sial/o	saliva, salivary gland, salivary duct	sialogram si-AL-o-gram	radiograph of the salivary glands and ducts
uvul/o	uvula	uvulotome U-vu-lo-tome	instrument (-tome) for incising the uvula

EXERCISE 12-1

Use the adjective suffix -al to write a word that has the same meaning as the following.

1. pertaining to the gums _____gingival_____
2. pertaining to the tongue _____
3. pertaining to the teeth _____
4. pertaining to the cheek _____
5. pertaining to the lip _____
6. pertaining to the mouth _____

Fill in the blanks.

7. Dentistry (*DEN*-tis-tre) is the profession that studies, diagnoses, and treats the _____.
8. Micrognathia (*mi-krog-NATH-e-ah*) is excessive smallness of the _____.
9. An orthodontist (*or-tho-DON-tist*) specializes in straightening (ortho-) of the _____.
10. The oropharynx is the part of the pharynx that is located behind _____.
11. Stomatoplasty (*STO-mah-to-plas-te*) is any plastic repair of the _____.
12. Hemiglossal (*hem-e-GLOS-al*) means pertaining to one half of the _____.
13. A sialolith (*si-AL-o-lith*) is a stone formed in a(n) _____ gland or duct.

Define the following words.

14. buccopharyngeal (*BUK-oh-far-in-je-al*) _____
15. gingivoplasty (*jin-jih-vo-PLAS-te*) _____
16. sublingual (*sub-LING-gwal*) _____
17. labiodental (*la-be-o-DEN-tal*) _____
18. uvuloptosis (*u-vu-lop-TO-sis*) _____
19. hypoglossal (*hi-po-GLOS-al*) _____
20. palatorrhaphy (*pal-at-OR-ah-fe*) _____

Table 12-2   Roots for the Digestive Tract (Except the Mouth)

Root	Meaning	Example	Definition of Example
esophag/o	esophagus	esophageal[a] e-sof-ah-JE-al	pertaining to the esophagus
gastr/o	stomach	gastroparesis gas-tro-pah-RE-sis	partial paralysis (paresis) of the stomach
pylor/o	pylorus	pyloroplasty pi-LOR-o-plas-te	plastic repair of the pylorus
enter/o	intestine	dysentery DIS-en-tare-e	infectious disease of the intestine
duoden/o	duodenum	duodenostomy du-o-deh-NOS-to-me	surgical creation of an opening into the duodenum

(continued)

Table 12-2	Roots for the Digestive Tract (Except the Mouth) *(Continued)*		

Root	Meaning	Example	Definition of Example
jejun/o	jejunum	jejunectomy *jeh-ju-NEK-to-me*	excision of the jejunum
ile/o	ileum	ileitis *il-e-I-tis*	inflammation of the ileum
cec/o	cecum	cecoptosis *se-kop-TO-sis*	downward displacement of the cecum
col/o, colon/o	colon	coloclysis *ko-lo-KLI-sis*	irrigation (-clysis) of the colon
sigmoid/o	sigmoid colon	sigmoidoscope *sig-MOY-do-skope*	an endoscope for examining the sigmoid colon
rect/o	rectum	rectocele *REK-to-sele*	hernia of the rectum
proct/o	rectum	proctopexy *PROK-to-pek-se*	surgical fixation of the rectum
an/o	anus	perianal *per-e-A-nal*	around the anus

^aNote addition of e before -al.

EXERCISE 12-2

Use the adjective suffix *-ic* to write a word for the following definitions.

1. pertaining to the pylorus   _____

2. pertaining to the colon   _____

3. pertaining to the stomach   _____

4. pertaining to the intestine   _____

Use the adjective suffix *-al* to write a word for the following definitions.

5. pertaining to the rectum   _____

6. pertaining to the jejunum   _____

7. pertaining to the ileum   _____

8. pertaining to the cecum   _____

9. pertaining to the anus   _____

Write a word for the following definitions.

10. pertaining to the stomach and duodenum   _____

11. inflammation of the esophagus   _____

12. surgical creation of an opening in the intestine   _____

13. study of the stomach and intestines   _____

14. endoscopic examination of the stomach   _____

15. downward displacement of the pylorus   _____

EXERCISE 12-2   *(Continued)*

16. inflammation of the jejunum and ileum _____

17. excision of the ileum _____

18. pertaining to the anus and rectum _____

Use the root *col/o* to write a word for the following definitions.

19. inflammation of the colon _____

20. surgical creation of an opening into the colon _____

21. surgical fixation of the colon _____

22. surgical puncture of the colon _____

Use the root *colon/o* to write a word for the following definitions.

23. any disease of the colon _____

24. endoscopic examination of the colon _____

Two organs of the digestive tract or even two parts of the same organ may be surgically connected by a passage (anastomosis) after removal of damaged tissue. Such a procedure is named for the connected organs plus the ending *-stomy*. Use two roots plus the suffix *-stomy* to write a word for the following definitions.

25. surgical creation of a passage between the esophagus and stomach _____esophagogastrostomy_____

26. surgical creation of a passage between the stomach and intestine _____

27. surgical creation of a passage between two portions of the jejunum _____

28. surgical creation of a passage between the duodenum and the ileum _____

29. surgical creation of a passage between the sigmoid colon and the rectum (proct/o) _____

Table 12-3	Roots for the Accessory Organs		
Root	**Meaning**	**Example**	**Definition of Example**
hepat/o	liver	hepatocyte *HEP-ah-to-site*	a liver cell
bili	bile	biliary *BIL-e-ar-e*	pertaining to the bile or bile ducts
chol/e, chol/o	bile, gall	cholestasis *ko-le-STA-sis*	stoppage of bile flow
cholecyst/o	gallbladder	cholecystogram *ko-le-SIS-to-gram*	radiograph of the gallbladder
cholangi/o	bile duct	cholangioma *ko-lan-je-O-mah*	cancer of the bile ducts
choledoch/o	common bile duct	choledochal *KO-le-dok-al*	pertaining to the common bile duct
pancreat/o	pancreas	pancreatotropic *pan-kre-at-o-TROP-ik*	acting on the pancreas

EXERCISE 12-3

Use the suffix *-ic* to write a word for the following definitions.

1. pertaining to the liver   _____

2. pertaining to the gallbladder   _____

3. pertaining to the pancreas   _____

Use the suffix *-graphy* to write a word for the following definitions.

4. radiographic study of the liver   _____

5. radiographic study of the gallbladder   _____

6. radiographic study of the bile ducts   _____

7. radiographic study of the pancreas   _____

Use the suffix *-lithiasis* to write a word for the following definitions.

8. condition of having a stone in the common bile duct   _____

9. condition of having a stone in the pancreas   _____

Fill in the blanks.

10. Inflammation of the liver is called _____.

11. The word biligenesis (*bil-ih-JEN-eh-sis*) means the formation of _____.

12. A cholelith (*KO-le-lith*) is a(n) _____.

13. Choledochotomy (*ko-led-o-KOT-o-me*) is incision of the _____.

14. Cholecystectomy (*ko-le-sis-TEK-to-me*) is removal of the _____.

15. Hepatomegaly (*hep-ah-to-MEG-ah-le*) is enlargement of the _____.

16. Cholangitis (*ko-lan-JI-tis*) is inflammation of a(n) _____.

17. Pancreatolysis (*pan-kre-ah-TOL-ih-sis*) is dissolving of the _____.

Clinical Aspects of the Digestive System

DIGESTIVE TRACT

Infection

A variety of organisms can infect the GI tract, from viruses and bacteria to protozoa and worms. In the mouth, bacterial infection contributes to tooth decay or **caries**. It may cause a mild gum infection (gingivitis) or more extensive involvement of the deeper tissues and bony support around the tooth (periodontitis). Infections of the stomach or intestine may produce short-lived upsets with **gastroenteritis**, **nausea**, **diarrhea**, and **emesis** (vomiting). Other infectious diseases of the GI tract, such as typhoid, cholera, and dysentery, are more serious, even fatal.

Appendicitis results from infection of the appendix, often secondary to its obstruction. Surgery is necessary to avoid rupture and **peritonitis**, infection of the peritoneal cavity.

Ulcers

An ulcer is a lesion of the skin or a mucous membrane marked by inflammation and tissue damage. Ulcers caused by the damaging action of gastric juices, also called peptic juices, on the lining of the GI tract are termed **peptic ulcers**. Most peptic ulcers appear in the first portion of the duodenum. The origins of such ulcers are not completely known, although infection with a bacterium, *Helicobacter pylori*, has been identified as a major cause. Heredity and stress may be factors, as well as chronic inflammation and exposure to damaging drugs, such as aspirin and other NSAIDs, or to irritants in food and drink.

Current ulcer treatment includes the administration of antibiotics to eliminate *H. pylori* infection and use of drugs that inhibit gastric acid secretion. Ulcers may lead

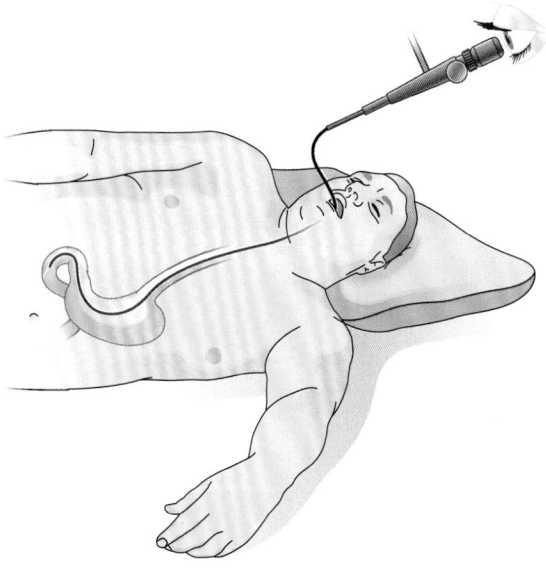

Figure 12-6 **Endoscopy.** A patient undergoing gastroscopy is shown.

to hemorrhage or to perforation of the digestive tract wall.

Ulcers can be diagnosed by **endoscopy** (**Fig. 12-6, Box 12-5**) and by radiographic study of the GI tract using a contrast medium, usually barium sulfate. A **barium study** can reveal a variety of GI disorders in addition to ulcers, including tumors and obstructions. A barium swallow is used for the study of the pharynx and esophagus; an upper GI series examines the esophagus, stomach, and small intestine.

Cancer

Cancer of the mouth generally involves the lips or tongue. Smoking is a major risk factor in these cases. **Leukoplakia,** white patches on mucous membranes, often results from smoking or other irritants and is an early sign of cancer in up

to 25 percent of cases. The most common sites for GI tract cancer are the colon and rectum. Together, these colorectal cancers rank among the most frequent causes of cancer deaths in the United States in both men and women. A diet low in fiber and calcium and high in fat is a major risk factor in colorectal cancer. Heredity is also a factor, as is chronic inflammation of the colon (colitis). **Polyps** (growths) in the intestine often become cancerous and should be removed. Polyps can be identified and even removed by endoscopy.

One sign of colorectal cancer is bleeding into the intestine, which can be detected by testing the stool for blood. Because this blood may be present in very small amounts, it is described as **occult** ("hidden") **blood.** Colorectal cancers are staged according to **Dukes classification,** ranging from A to C according to severity.

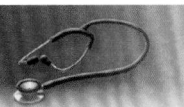

CLINICAL PERSPECTIVES

Endoscopy

Box 12-5

Modern medicine has made great strides toward looking into the body without resorting to surgery. The endoscope, an instrument that is inserted through a body opening or small incision, has allowed the noninvasive examination of passageways, hollow organs, and body cavities. The first endoscopes were rigid, lighted telescopes that could be inserted only a short distance into the body. Today, physicians can navigate the twists and turns of the digestive tract using long fiberoptic endoscopes composed of flexible, light-transmitting bundles of glass or plastic.

Physicians can endoscopically detect structural abnormalities, ulcers, inflammation, and tumors in the GI tract. In addition, they use endoscopes to remove fluid or tissue samples for testing. Some surgery can even be done with an

endoscope, such as polyp removal from the colon or sphincter expansion. Endoscopy can also be used to examine and operate on joints (arthroscopy), the bladder (cystoscopy), respiratory passages (bronchoscopy), and the abdominal cavity (laparoscopy).

A "virtual colonoscopy" uses computerized x-rays to generate detailed images of the colon. This method can provide an adequate screening for most people, although a small percentage might then need a standard colonoscopy for further assessment or surgery. Capsular endoscopy, a recent technologic advance, has made examination of the GI tract even easier. It uses a pill-sized camera that a patient can swallow! As the camera moves through the digestive tract, it transmits video images to a data recorder worn on the patient's belt.

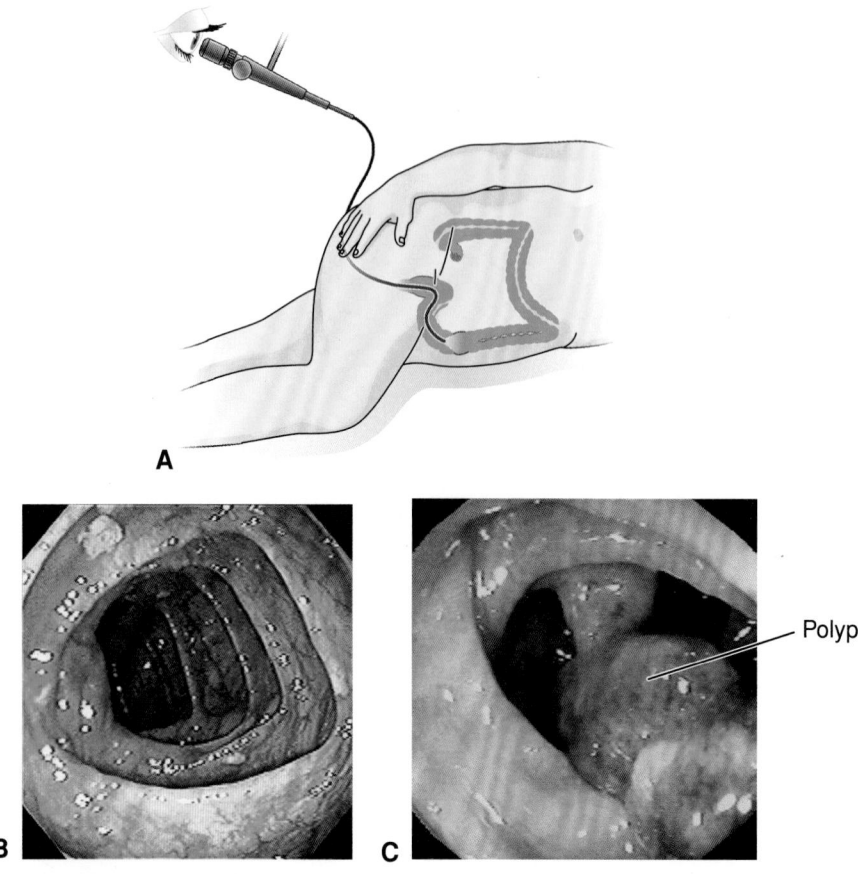

Figure 12-7 **Colonoscopy.** **A.** Sigmoidoscopy. The flexible fiberoptic endoscope is advanced past the proximal sigmoid colon and then into the descending colon. **B.** Endoscopic image of the cecum, the first portion of the large intestine. **C.** Endoscopic image of a colonic polyp.

Examiners can observe the intestine's interior with various endoscopes named for the specific area in which they are used, such as proctoscope (rectum), sigmoidoscope (sigmoid colon), and colonoscope (colon) (**Fig. 12-7**).

In some cases of cancer, and for other reasons as well, it may be necessary to surgically remove a portion of the GI tract and create a **stoma** (opening) on the abdominal wall for elimination of waste. Such **ostomy** surgery (**Fig. 12-8**)

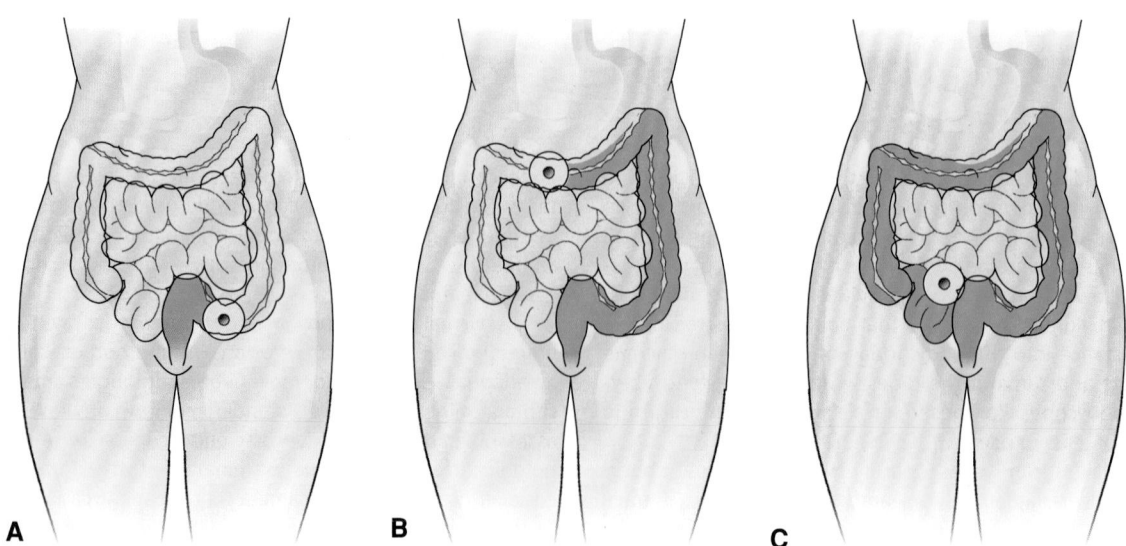

Figure 12-8 **Ostomy surgery.** Various locations are shown. The shaded portions represent the bowel sections that have been removed or are inactive. **A.** Sigmoid colostomy. **B.** Transverse colostomy. **C.** Ileostomy.

is named for the organ involved, such as ileostomy (ileum) or colostomy (colon). When an **anastomosis** (connection) is formed between two organs of the tract, both organs are included in naming, such as gastroduodenostomy (stomach and duodenum) or coloproctostomy (colon and rectum).

Obstructions

A hernia is the protrusion of an organ through an abnormal opening. The most common type is an inguinal hernia, described in Chapter 14 (see **Fig. 14-7**). In a **hiatal hernia**, part of the stomach moves upward into the chest cavity through the space (hiatus) in the diaphragm through which the esophagus passes (see **Fig. 6-7**). Often this condition produces no symptoms, but it may result in chest pain, **dysphagia** (difficulty in swallowing), or reflux (backflow) of stomach contents into the esophagus.

In **pyloric stenosis**, the opening between the stomach and small intestine is too narrow. This usually occurs in infants and in boys more often than in girls. A sign of pyloric stenosis is projectile vomiting. Surgery may be needed to correct it.

Other types of obstruction include **intussusception** (**Fig. 12-9**), slipping of an intestinal segment into a part below it; **volvulus**, twisting of the intestine (see **Fig. 12-9B**); and **ileus**, intestinal obstruction often caused by lack of peristalsis.

See the figure on pyloric stenosis in the Student Resources on thePoint.

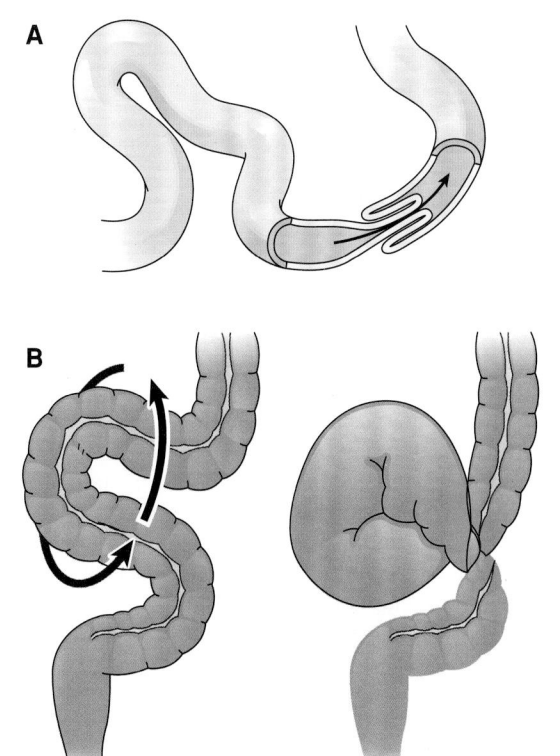

Figure 12-9 **Intestinal obstruction. A.** Intussusception. **B.** Volvulus, showing counterclockwise twist.

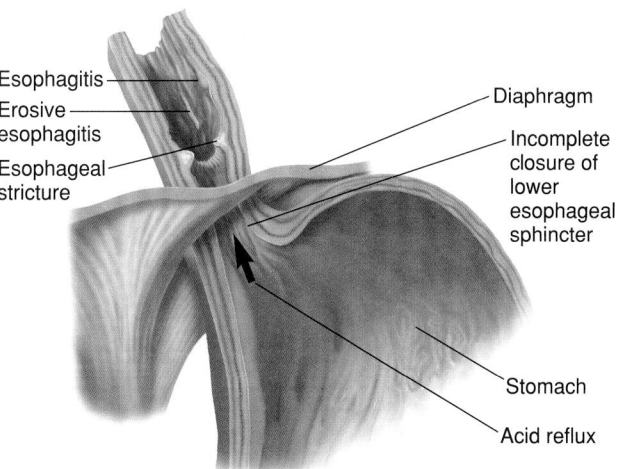

Figure 12-10 **Gastroesophageal reflux disease (GERD).** A weak LES allows acidic stomach contents to flow backward into the lower portion of the esophagus causing pain and irritation.

Hemorrhoids are varicose veins in the rectum associated with pain, bleeding, and, in some cases, rectal prolapse.

Gastroesophageal Reflux Disease

Gastroesophageal reflux disease (GERD) refers to reflux of gastric juices into the esophagus due to weakness at the gastroesophageal junction, specifically the LES (lower esophageal sphincter) (**Fig. 12-10**). These acidic secretions irritate the lining of the esophagus and even the throat and mouth if propelled upward by **regurgitation**. A GERD symptom commonly known as **heartburn**, an upward-radiating burning sensation behind the sternum, does not involve the heart, but is experienced in the area near the heart (see B.F.'s opening case study).

GERD symptoms are more likely to occur when there is increased pressure in the stomach, such as after meals when the stomach is full, when one is lying or bending down, and with obesity and pregnancy. Hiatal hernia can also lead to GERD. Treatment includes weight reduction if needed, elevating the head of the bed 4 to 6 in, avoidance of irritating foods, and drugs to reduce gastric acid secretion. Surgery to repair an incompetent LES might be needed.

Persistent reflux esophagitis may cause injury to the esophageal lining leading to **Barrett syndrome** or *Barrett esophagus*. In this condition, the esophageal mucosa is gradually replaced with epithelium resembling that of the stomach or intestines. Barrett esophagus frequently has no early symptoms, but possible complications include esophageal spasms, formation of scar tissue, esophageal strictures, and increased risk of cancer.

Inflammatory Intestinal Disease

Two similar diseases are included under the heading of inflammatory bowel disease (IBD):

- **Crohn disease** is a chronic inflammation of the intestinal wall, usually in the ileum and colon, causing pain, diarrhea, abscess, and often formation of an abnormal passageway, or **fistula**.

- **Ulcerative colitis** involves a continuous inflammation of the colon's lining that begins in the rectum and extends proximally (**Fig. 12-11**).

Both forms of IBD occur mainly in adolescents and young adults and show a hereditary pattern. They originate with an abnormal immunologic response, perhaps to the normal intestinal flora, along with autoimmunity. Treatment is with antiinflammatory agents, immunosuppressants, and frequently surgery to remove damaged portions of the colon.

Celiac disease is characterized by the inability to absorb foods containing gluten, a protein found in wheat and some other grains. It affects the upper part of the small intestine and originates with an excess immune response to gluten. Mucosal inflammation diminishes the intestinal villi and interferes with absorption. Celiac disease is treated with a gluten-free diet.

Diverticulitis most commonly affects the colon. Diverticula are small pouches in the intestinal wall that commonly appear with age. The presence of these pouches is termed **diverticulosis**, which has been attributed to a diet low in fiber. Collection of waste and bacteria in these sacs leads to diverticulitis, which is accompanied by pain and sometimes bleeding. Diverticula can be seen by radiographic studies of the lower GI tract using barium as a contrast medium, a so-called barium enema (**Fig. 12-12**). Although there is no cure, diverticulitis is treated with a high-fiber diet, stool softeners, and drugs (antispasmodics) to reduce motility. Diverticular infections are treated with antibiotics.

See figures on the complications of ulcerative colitis and on diverticulosis and diverticulitis in the Student Resources on thePoint.

Figure 12-11 **Ulcerative colitis.** Prominent erythema and ulceration of the colon begin in the ascending colon and are most severe in the rectosigmoid area.

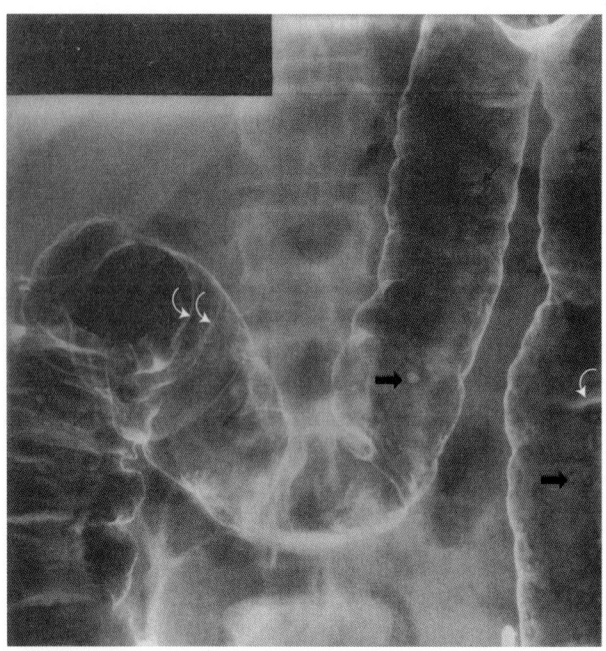

Figure 12-12 **Lower gastrointestinal (GI) series.** Barium enema shows lesions of enteritis (*straight arrows*) and thickened mucosa (*curved arrows*).

ACCESSORY ORGANS

Hepatitis

In the United States and other industrialized countries, **hepatitis** is most often caused by viral infection. More than five types of hepatitis viruses have now been identified. Vaccines are available for hepatitis A and hepatitis B.

- Hepatitis A virus (HAV) is the most common hepatitis virus. It is spread by fecal–oral contamination, often by food handlers, and in crowded, unsanitary conditions. It may also be acquired by eating contaminated food, especially seafood.
- Hepatitis B virus (HBV) is spread by blood and other body fluids. It may be transmitted sexually, by sharing injection needles, and by close interpersonal contact. Infected individuals may become carriers of the disease. Most patients recover, but the disease may be serious, even fatal, and may lead to liver cancer.
- Hepatitis C is spread through blood and blood products or by close contact with an infected person.
- Hepatitis D, the delta virus, is highly pathogenic but infects only those already infected with hepatitis B.
- Hepatitis E, like HAV, is spread by contaminated food and water. It has caused epidemics in Asia, Africa, and Mexico.

The name *hepatitis* simply means "inflammation of the liver," but this disease also causes necrosis (death) of liver cells. Other infections as well as drugs and toxins may also cause hepatitis. Liver function tests performed on blood serum are important in diagnosis.

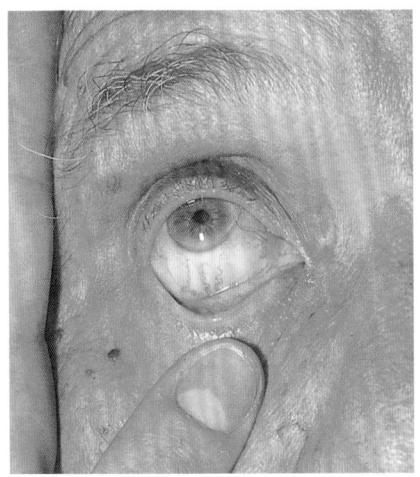

Figure 12-13 **Jaundice.** Yellowish discoloration due to bile pigments in the blood is seen in the eye.

Jaundice, or **icterus**, is a symptom of hepatitis and other diseases of the liver and biliary system (**Fig. 12-13**). It appears as yellowness of the skin, whites of the eyes, and mucous membranes due to the presence of bile pigments, mainly **bilirubin**, in the blood.

Cirrhosis

Cirrhosis is a chronic liver disease characterized by **hepatomegaly**, edema, **ascites** (fluid in the abdomen), and jaundice. Disease progression leads to internal bleeding and brain damage caused by changes in the blood's composition. One complication of cirrhosis is **portal hypertension**, increased pressure in the hepatic portal system, the vessels that carry blood from the other abdominal organs to the liver. Portal hypertension causes **splenomegaly** and the

formation of varices (varicose veins) in the distal esophagus with possible hemorrhage. The main cause of cirrhosis is the excess consumption of alcohol.

See the animation "The Liver in Health and Disease" and figures on the clinical features of cirrhosis and on portal hypertension in the Student Resources on thePoint.

Gallstones

Cholelithiasis refers to the presence of stones in the gallbladder (**Fig. 12-14**) or bile ducts, which is usually associated with **cholecystitis**, inflammation of the gallbladder. Cholelithiasis is characterized by **biliary colic** (pain) in the right upper quadrant (RUQ), nausea, and vomiting.

Most gallstones are composed of cholesterol, an ingredient of bile. They form more commonly in women than in men and are promoted by conditions that increase estrogen, as this hormone raises the cholesterol level in bile. These predisposing conditions include pregnancy, use of oral contraceptives, and obesity. Oddly, the rapid weight loss that follows stomach reduction surgery to treat morbid obesity commonly leads to gallstones because of changes in bile production and cholesterol precipitation in the bile. Drugs may dissolve gallstones, but often the cure is removal of the gallbladder in a **cholecystectomy**. Originally, this procedure required an extensive incision, but now the gallbladder is almost always removed laparoscopically through a small abdominal slit. Following gallbladder removal, bile flows directly into the duodenum through the common bile duct.

Ultrasonography, radiography, and magnetic resonance imaging are used to diagnose gallstones (see **Fig. 12-14**). **Endoscopic retrograde cholangiopancreatography (ERCP)**

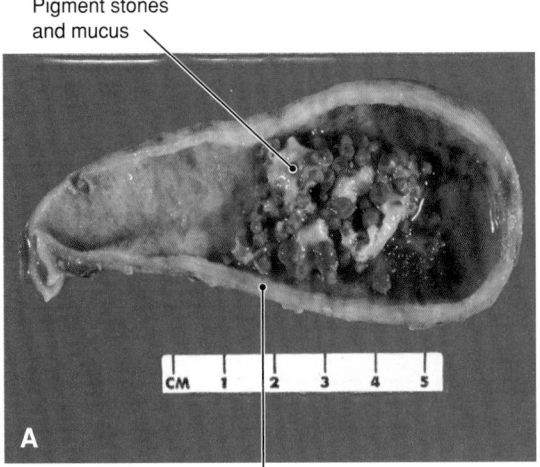
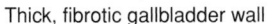
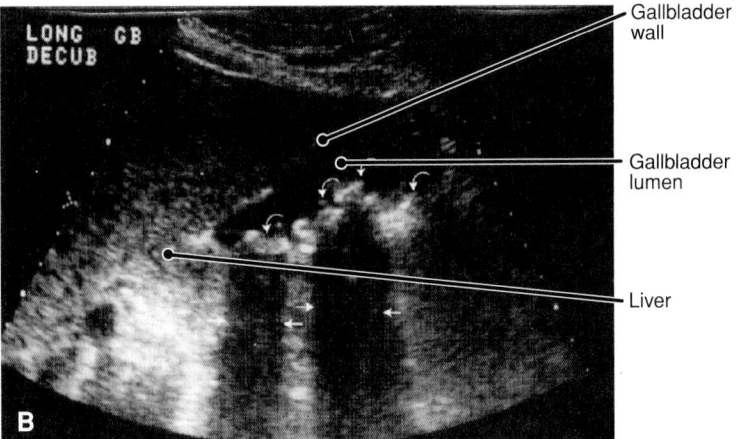

Figure 12-14 **Cholelithiasis (gallstones).** **A.** Formation of gallstones (cholelithiasis) causes gallbladder inflammation (cholecystitis) and bile obstruction. Numerous gallstones and a thickened gallbladder wall caused by chronic inflammation are evident in this figure. **B.** Sonogram shows dense gallstones (*curved arrows*). Shadows appear (between the *straight arrows*) because the sound waves cannot penetrate the stones (calculi).

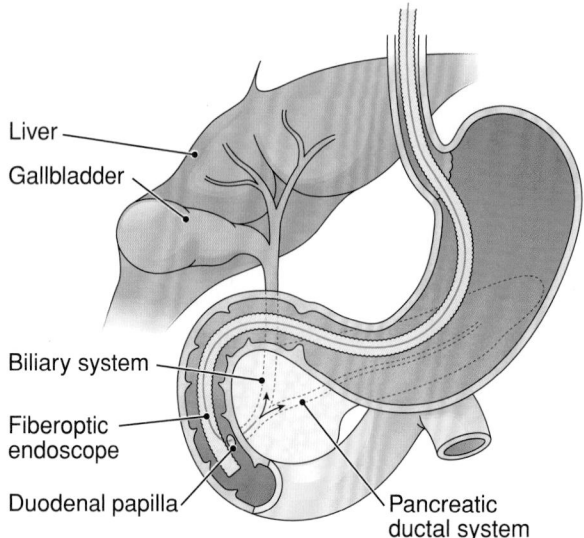

Liver

Gallbladder

Biliary system

Fiberoptic endoscope

Duodenal papilla

Pancreatic ductal system

Figure 12-15 **Endoscopic retrograde cholangiopancreatography (ERCP).** A contrast medium is injected into the pancreatic and bile ducts in preparation for radiography.

(**Fig. 12-15**) is a technique for viewing the pancreatic and bile ducts and for performing certain techniques to relieve obstructions. Contrast medium is injected into the biliary system from the duodenum before imaging.

See the figure on gallstones in the Student Resources on thePoint.

Pancreatitis

Pancreatitis, or inflammation of the pancreas, may result from alcohol abuse, drug toxicity, bile obstruction, infections, and other causes. Blood tests in acute pancreatitis show increased levels of the enzymes amylase and lipase. Glucose and bilirubin levels may also be elevated. Often the disease subsides with only symptomatic treatment.

Terminology | Key Terms

Disorders

appendicitis *ah-pen-dih-SI-tis*	Inflammation of the appendix
ascites *ah-SI-teze*	Accumulation of fluid in the abdominal cavity; a form of edema; may be caused by heart disease, lymphatic or venous obstruction, cirrhosis, or changes in blood plasma composition
Barrett syndrome *BAH-ret*	Condition resulting from chronic esophagitis, as caused by gastroesophageal reflux disease; inflammatory injury can lead to esophageal spasms, scarring, strictures, and increased risk of cancer; also called Barrett esophagus
biliary colic *BIL-e-ar-e KOL-ik*	Acute abdominal pain caused by gallstones in the bile ducts
bilirubin *bil-ih-RU-bin*	A pigment released in the breakdown of hemoglobin from red blood cells; mainly excreted by the liver in bile
caries *KAR-eze*	Tooth decay
celiac disease *SE-le-ak*	Inability to absorb foods containing gluten, a protein found in wheat and some other grains; caused by an excess immune response to gluten
cholecystitis *ko-le-sis-TI-tis*	Inflammation of the gallbladder

Terminology	Key Terms *(Continued)*

cholelithiasis *ko-le-lih-THI-ah-sis*	The condition of having stones in the gallbladder; also used to refer to stones in the common bile duct
cirrhosis *sir-RO-sis*	Chronic liver disease with degeneration of liver tissue
Crohn disease *krone*	A chronic inflammatory disease of the gastrointestinal tract usually involving the ileum and colon
diarrhea *di-ah-RE-ah*	The frequent passage of watery bowel movements
diverticulitis *di-ver-tik-u-LI-tis*	Inflammation of diverticula (small pouches) in the wall of the digestive tract, especially in the colon
diverticulosis *di-ver-tik-u-LO-sis*	The presence of diverticula, especially in the colon
dysphagia *dis-FA-je-ah*	Difficulty in swallowing
emesis *EM-eh-sis*	Vomiting
fistula *FIS-tu-lah*	An abnormal passageway between two organs such as between the rectum and anus (anorectal fistula), or from an organ to the body surface
gastroenteritis *gas-tro-en-ter-I-tis*	Inflammation of the stomach and intestine
gastroesophageal reflux disease (GERD) *gas-tro-e-sof-ah-JE-al*	Condition caused by reflux of gastric juices into the esophagus resulting in heartburn, regurgitation, inflammation, and possible damage to the esophagus; caused by weakness of the lower esophageal sphincter (LES) (see **Fig. 12-10**)
heartburn *HART-bern*	A warm or burning sensation felt behind the sternum and radiating upward; commonly associated with gastroesophageal reflux; medical name is pyrosis (pyr/o means "heat")
hemorrhoids *HEM-o-roydz*	Varicose veins in the rectum associated with pain, bleeding, and sometimes rectal prolapse; piles
hepatitis *hep-ah-TI-tis*	Inflammation of the liver; commonly caused by a viral infection
hepatomegaly *hep-ah-to-MEG-ah-le*	Enlargement of the liver
hiatal hernia *hi-A-tal*	A protrusion of the stomach through the opening (hiatus) in the diaphragm through which the esophagus passes (see **Fig. 6-7**)
icterus *IK-ter-us*	Jaundice
ileus *IL-e-us*	Intestinal obstruction; may be caused by lack of peristalsis (adynamic, paralytic ileus) or by contraction (dynamic ileus); intestinal matter and gas may be relieved by insertion of a drainage tube
intussusception *in-tuh-suh-SEP-shun*	Slipping of one intestinal segment into another part below it; occurs mainly in male infants in the ileocecal region (see **Fig. 12-9A**); may be fatal if untreated for more than one day
jaundice *JAWN-dis*	A yellowish color of the skin, mucous membranes, and whites of the eye caused by bile pigments in the blood (from French *jaune* meaning "yellow"); the main pigment is bilirubin, a byproduct of erythrocyte destruction (see **Fig. 12-13**)

(continued)

Terminology   Key Terms *(Continued)*

leukoplakia *lu-ko-PLA-ke-ah*	White patches on mucous membranes, as on the tongue or cheeks, often resulting from smoking or other irritants; may be precancerous
nausea *NAW-zhah*	An unpleasant sensation in the upper abdomen that often precedes vomiting; typically occurs in digestive upset, motion sickness, and sometimes early pregnancy
occult blood *o-KULT*	Blood present in such small amounts that it can be detected only microscopically or chemically; in the feces, a sign of intestinal bleeding (*occult* means "hidden")
pancreatitis *pan-kre-ah-TI-tis*	Inflammation of the pancreas
peptic ulcer *PEP-tik UL-ser*	A lesion in the mucous membrane of the esophagus, stomach, or duodenum caused by the action of gastric juice
peritonitis *per-ih-to-NI-tis*	Inflammation of the peritoneum, the membrane that lines the abdominal cavity and covers the abdominal organs; may result from perforation of an ulcer, ruptured appendix, or reproductive tract infection, among other causes
polyp *POL-ip*	A tumor that grows on a stalk and bleeds easily
portal hypertension	An abnormal pressure increase in the hepatic portal system; may be caused by cirrhosis, infection, thrombosis, or a tumor
pyloric stenosis *pi-LOR-ik*	Narrowing of the opening between the stomach and the duodenum; pylorostenosis
regurgitation *re-gur-jih-TA-shun*	A backward flowing, such as the backflow of undigested food
splenomegaly *sple-no-MEG-ah-le*	Enlargement of the spleen
ulcerative colitis *UL-ser-ah-tiv ko-LI-tis*	Chronic ulceration of the rectum and colon; the cause is unknown, but may involve autoimmunity
volvulus *VOL-vu-lus*	Twisting of the intestine resulting in obstruction; usually involves the sigmoid colon and occurs most often in children and in the elderly; may be caused by congenital malformation, a foreign body, or adhesion; failure to treat immediately may result in death (see **Fig. 12-9B**)

Diagnosis and Treatment

anastomosis *ah-nas-to-MO-sis*	A passage or communication between two vessels or organs; may be normal or pathologic or may be created surgically
barium study	Use of barium sulfate as a liquid contrast medium for fluoroscopic or radiographic study of the digestive tract; can show obstruction, tumors, ulcers, hiatal hernia, and motility disorders, among other conditions
cholecystectomy *ko-le-sis-TEK-to-me*	Surgical removal of the gallbladder
Dukes classification	A system for staging colorectal cancer based on degree of bowel wall penetration and lymph node involvement; severity is graded from A to C
endoscopic retrograde cholangiopancreatography (ERCP)	A technique for viewing the pancreatic and bile ducts and for performing certain techniques to relieve obstructions; contrast medium is injected into the biliary system from the duodenum before radiographs are taken (see **Fig. 12-15**)
endoscopy *en-DOS-ko-pe*	Use of a fiberoptic endoscope for direct visual examination; GI studies include esophagogastroduodenoscopy, proctosigmoidoscopy (rectum and distal colon), and colonoscopy (all regions of the colon) (see **Figs. 12-6** and **12-7**)

Terminology Key Terms *(Continued)*

ostomy OS-to-me	An opening into the body; generally refers to an opening created for elimination of body waste; also refers to the operation done to create such an opening (see stoma)
stoma STO-mah	A surgically created opening to the body surface or between two organs (literally "mouth") (see **Fig. 12-8**)

Go to the Audio Pronunciation Glossary in the Student Resources on thePoint to hear these terms pronounced.

12

Terminology Supplementary Terms

Normal Structure and Function

bolus BO-lus	A mass, such as the rounded mass of food that is swallowed
cardia KAR-de-ah	The part of the stomach near the esophagus, named for its closeness to the heart
chyme kime	The semiliquid partially digested food that moves from the stomach into the small intestine
defecation def-eh-KA-shun	The evacuation of feces from the rectum
deglutition deg-lu-TISH-un	Swallowing
duodenal bulb du-o-DE-nal	The part of the duodenum near the pylorus; the first bend (flexure) of the duodenum
duodenal papilla du-o-DE-nal pah-PIL-lah	The raised area where the common bile duct and pancreatic duct enter the duodenum (see **Fig. 12-15**); papilla of Vater (FAH-ter)
greater omentum o-MEN-tum	A fold of the peritoneum that extends from the stomach over the abdominal organs
hepatic flexure heh-PAT-ik FLEK-shur	The right bend of the colon, forming the junction between the ascending colon and the transverse colon (see **Fig. 12-1**)
ileocecal valve il-e-o-SE-kal	A valve-like structure between the ileum of the small intestine and the cecum of the large intestine
mesentery MES-en-ter-e	The portion of the peritoneum that folds over and supports the intestine
mesocolon mes-o-KO-lon	The portion of the peritoneum that folds over and supports the colon
papilla of Vater	See duodenal papilla
rugae RU-je	The large folds in the stomach's lining seen when the stomach is empty
sphincter of Oddi OD-e	The muscular ring at the opening of the common bile duct into the duodenum
splenic flexure SPLEN-ik FLEK-shur	The left bend of the colon, forming the junction between the transverse colon and the descending colon (see **Fig. 12-1**)

(continued)

Terminology   Supplementary Terms *(Continued)*

Disorders

achalasia *ak-ah-LA-ze-ah*	Failure of a smooth muscle to relax, especially the lower esophageal sphincter, so that food is retained in the esophagus
achlorhydria *a-klor-HI-dre-ah*	Lack of hydrochloric acid in the stomach; opposite is hyperchlorhydria
anorexia *an-o-REK-se-ah*	Loss of appetite; anorexia nervosa is a psychologically induced refusal or inability to eat (adjectives: anorectic, anorexic)
aphagia *ah-FA-je-ah*	Inability to swallow or difficulty in swallowing; refusal or inability to eat
aphthous ulcer *AF-thus*	An ulcer in a mucous membrane, as in the mouth
bruxism *BRUK-sizm*	Clenching and grinding of the teeth, usually during sleep
bulimia *bu-LEME-e-ah*	Excessive, insatiable appetite; a disorder characterized by overeating followed by induced vomiting, diarrhea, or fasting
cachexia *kah-KEK-se-ah*	Profound ill health, malnutrition, and wasting
cheilosis *ki-LO-sis*	Cracking at the corners of the mouth, often caused by B vitamin deficiency (root cheil/o means "lip")
cholestasis *ko-le-STA-sis*	Stoppage of bile flow; also pronounced *ko-LES-tah-sis*
constipation *con-stih-PA-shun*	Infrequency or difficulty in defecation and the passage of hard, dry feces
dyspepsia *dis-PEP-se-ah*	Poor or painful digestion
eructation *eh-ruk-TA-shun*	Belching
familial adenomatous polyposis (FAP) *fah-MIL-e-al ad-eh-NO-mah-tus pol-ih-PO-sis*	A hereditary condition in which multiple polyps form in the colon and rectum, predisposing one to colorectal cancer
flatulence *FLAT-u-lens*	Condition of having gas or air in the GI tract
flatus *FLA-tus*	Gas or air in the gastrointestinal tract; gas or air expelled through the anus
hematemesis *he-mah-TEM-eh-sis*	Vomiting of blood
irritable bowel syndrome (IBS)	A chronic stress-related disease characterized by diarrhea, constipation, and pain associated with rhythmic intestinal contractions; mucous colitis; spastic colon
megacolon *meg-ah-KO-lon*	An extremely dilated colon; usually congenital but may occur in acute ulcerative colitis
melena *MEL-e-nah*	Black tarry feces resulting from blood in the intestines; common in newborns; may also be a sign of gastrointestinal bleeding

| Terminology | Supplementary Terms *(Continued)* |

obstipation *ob-stih-PA-shun*	Extreme constipation
pernicious anemia *per-NISH-us*	A form of anemia caused by the stomach's failure to secrete intrinsic factor, a substance needed for the absorption of vitamin B_{12}
pilonidal cyst *pi-lo-NI-dal*	A dermal cyst in the sacral region, usually at the top of the cleft between the buttocks; may become infected and begin to drain
thrush	Fungal infection of the mouth and/or throat caused by *Candida*; appears as mucosal white patches or ulcers
Vincent disease *VIN-sent*	Severe gingivitis with necrosis associated with the bacterium *Treponema vincentii*; necrotizing ulcerative gingivitis; trench mouth

Diagnosis and Treatment

appendectomy *ap-en-DEK-to-me*	Surgical removal of the appendix
bariatrics *bar-e-AT-riks*	The branch of medicine concerned with prevention and control of obesity and associated diseases (from Greek *baros*, meaning "weight")
bariatric surgery	Surgery to reduce the size of the stomach and reduce nutrient absorption in the treatment of morbid obesity; most common is gastric bypass surgery, which involves division of the stomach and anastomosis of its upper part to the small intestine (jejunum) **(Fig. 12-16)**; other methods are gastric stapling, partitioning of the stomach with rows of staples, and gastric banding, which involves laparoscopic placement of an adjustable loop (Lap-Band) that reduces stomach capacity
Billroth operations	Gastrectomy with anastomosis of the stomach to the duodenum (Billroth I) or to the jejunum (Billroth II) **(Fig. 12-17)**
gavage *gah-VAHZH*	Process of feeding through a nasogastric tube into the stomach
lavage *lah-VAJ*	Washing out of a cavity; irrigation
manometry *man-OM-eh-tre*	Measurement of pressure; pertaining to the GI tract, measurement of pressure in the portal system as a sign of obstruction
Murphy sign	Inability to take a deep breath when fingers are pressed firmly below the right arch of the ribs (below the liver); signifies gallbladder disease
nasogastric (NG) tube *na-zo-GAS-trik*	Tube that is passed through the nose into the stomach **(Fig. 12-18)**; may be used for emptying the stomach, administering medication, giving liquids, or sampling stomach contents
parenteral hyperalimentation *pah-REN-ter-al*	Complete intravenous feeding for one who cannot take in food; total parenteral nutrition (TPN)
percutaneous endoscopic gastrostomy (PEG) tube	Tube inserted into the stomach for long-term feeding **(Fig. 12-19)**
vagotomy *va-GOT-o-me*	Interruption of vagal nerve impulses to reduce stomach secretions in the treatment of a gastric ulcer; originally done surgically but may also be done with drugs

Drugs

antacid *ant-AS-id*	Agent that counteracts acidity, usually gastric acidity
antidiarrheal *an-te-di-ah-RE-al*	Drug that treats or prevents diarrhea by reducing intestinal motility or absorbing irritants and soothing the intestinal lining

(continued)

| Terminology | **Supplementary Terms** (*Continued*) |

antiemetic *an-te-eh-MET-ik*	Agent that relieves or prevents nausea and vomiting
antiflatulent *an-te-FLAT-u-lent*	Agent that prevents or relieves flatulence
antispasmodic *an-te-spas-MOD-ik*	Agent that relieves spasm, usually of smooth muscle
emetic *eh-MET-ik*	An agent that causes vomiting
histamine H$_2$ antagonist	Drug that decreases secretion of stomach acid by interfering with the action of histamine at H$_2$ receptors; used to treat ulcers and other gastrointestinal problems; H$_2$-receptor-blocking agent
laxative *LAK-sah-tiv*	Agent that promotes elimination from the large intestine; types include stimulants, substances that retain water (hyperosmotics), stool softeners, and bulk-forming agents
proton pump inhibitor (PPI)	Agent that inhibits gastric acid secretion by blocking the transport of hydrogen ions (protons) into the stomach

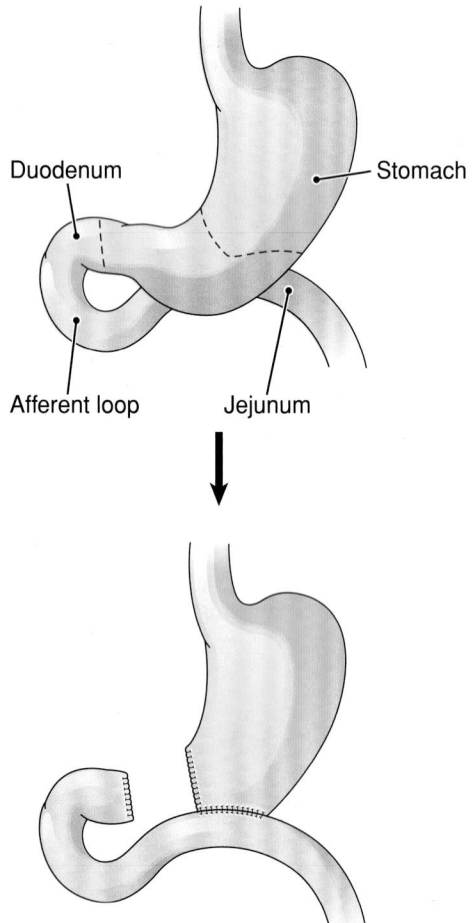

Figure 12-16 **Gastric bypass.** For treatment of morbid obesity, a small pouch is created in the stomach to limit food intake. The pouch is attached to the jejunum in a gastrojejunostomy to bypass the stomach and reduce nutrient absorption.

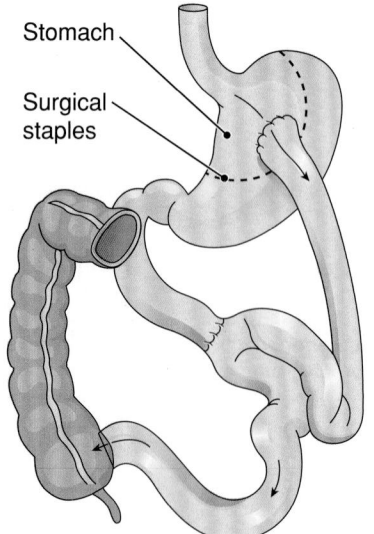

Figure 12-17 **Gastrojejunostomy (Billroth II operation).** The dotted lines show the portion removed.

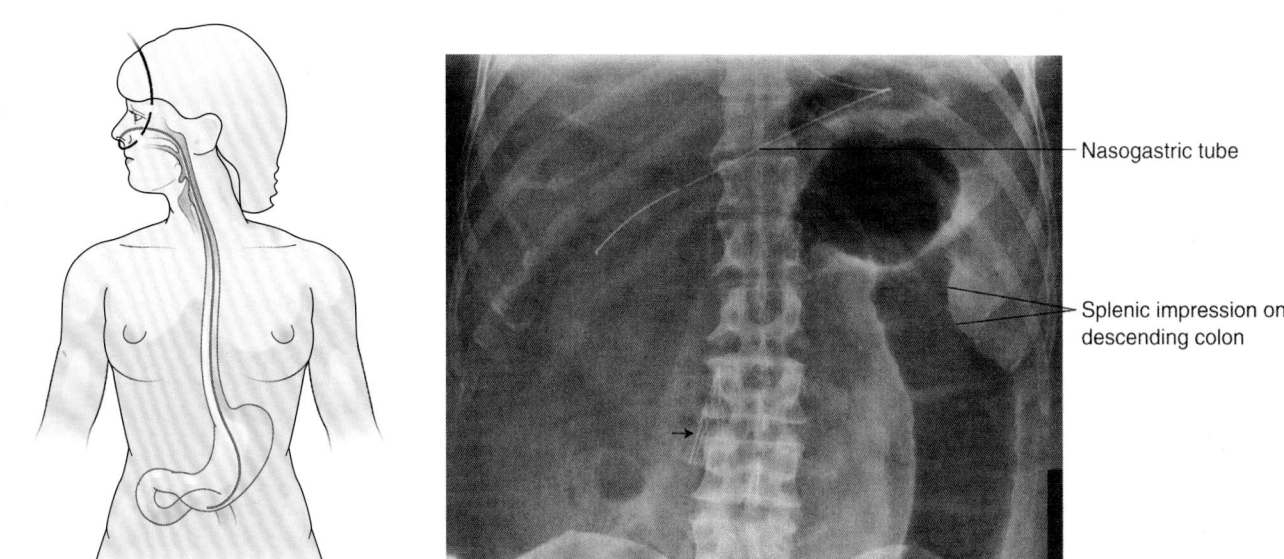

Figure 12-18 **A nasogastric (NG) tube. A.** Diagram showing an NG tube in place. **B.** Abdominal radiograph showing an NG tube. The filter (*arrow*) shown in the inferior vena cava is meant to trap emboli that might originate in the lower extremities and pelvis.

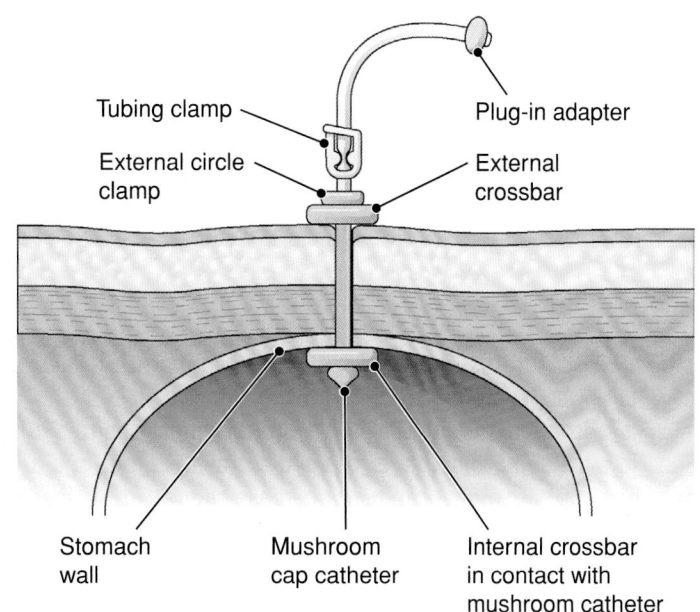

Figure 12-19 **Percutaneous endoscopic gastrostomy (PEG) tube.** The tube is shown in place in the stomach.

Terminology | Abbreviations

BE	Barium enema (for radiographic study of the colon)	HEV	Hepatitis E virus
BM	Bowel movement	HCl	Hydrochloric acid
CBD	Common bile duct	IBD	Inflammatory bowel disease
EGD	Esophagogastroduodenoscopy	IBS	Irritable bowel syndrome
ERCP	Endoscopic retrograde cholangiopancreatography	LES	Lower esophageal sphincter
FAP	Familial adenomatous polyposis	NG	Nasogastric (tube)
GERD	Gastroesophageal reflux disease	N&V	Nausea and vomiting
GI	Gastrointestinal	N/V/D	Nausea, vomiting, and diarrhea
HAV	Hepatitis A virus	PONV	Postoperative nausea and vomiting
HBV	Hepatitis B virus	PPI	Proton pump inhibitor
HCV	Hepatitis C virus	TPN	Total parenteral nutrition
HDV	Hepatitis D virus	UGI	Upper gastrointestinal (radiograph series)

Case Study Revisited

B.F.'s Follow-Up Study

When B.F. returns after four weeks for his follow-up appointment in primary care, he explains that he started feeling better, so he stopped taking the medicine after three weeks. Now his symptoms have returned. They are waking him up at night, and he also now reports experiencing mild dysphagia. The physician explained that he must remain on his medication and emphasized the importance of going to his endoscopy appointment. Results from this study indicate that B.F. does indeed have moderate erosive esophagitis. There is a small hiatal hernia present as well.

B.F. is prescribed a PPI, 40 mg/day and encouraged to take it on a regular basis. He is counseled to decrease the fat in his meals, avoid lying down for at least two hours after meals, and limit alcohol intake. He returns six weeks later with marked improvement in compliance and total control of his symptoms. He is instructed to continue the PPI and to return in six months for reassessment.

Labeling Exercise

THE DIGESTIVE SYSTEM

Write the name of each numbered part on the corresponding line of the answer sheet.

Anus
Ascending colon
Cecum
Descending colon
Duodenum (of small intestine)
Esophagus
Gallbladder
Liver
Mouth
Pancreas

Parotid salivary gland
Pharynx
Rectum
Sigmoid colon
Small intestine
Stomach
Sublingual salivary gland
Submandibular salivary gland
Transverse colon

1. _____
2. _____
3. _____
4. _____
5. _____
6. _____
7. _____
8. _____
9. _____
10. _____
11. _____
12. _____
13. _____
14. _____
15. _____
16. _____
17. _____
18. _____
19. _____

ACCESSORY ORGANS OF DIGESTION

Write the name of each numbered part on the corresponding line of the answer sheet.

Common bile duct   Gallbladder
Common hepatic duct   Liver
Cystic duct   Pancreas
Diaphragm   Pancreatic duct
Duodenum   Spleen

1. _____
2. _____
3. _____
4. _____
5. _____
6. _____
7. _____
8. _____
9. _____
10. _____

Terminology

MATCHING

Match the following terms, and write the appropriate letter to the left of each number.

_____ **1.** sublingual   **a.** pertaining to the cheek

_____ **2.** emetic   **b.** pertaining to the gum

_____ **3.** gingival   **c.** substance that induces vomiting

_____ **4.** agnathia   **d.** hypoglossal

_____ **5.** buccal   **e.** absence of the jaw

_____ **6.** enzyme   **a.** tooth decay

_____ **7.** caries   **b.** wave-like muscular contractions

_____ **8.** ileum   **c.** organic catalyst

_____ **9.** peristalsis   **d.** terminal portion of the small intestine

_____ **10.** icterus   **e.** jaundice

_____ **11.** choledochal   **a.** a type of liver disease

_____ **12.** cholelithotripsy   **b.** pertaining to the common bile duct

_____ **13.** cholangiectasis   **c.** crushing of a biliary calculus

_____ **14.** leukoplakia   **d.** dilatation of a bile duct

_____ **15.** cirrhosis   **e.** white patches on a mucous membrane

Supplementary Terms

_____ **16.** eructation   **a.** part of the stomach near the esophagus

_____ **17.** cardia   **b.** chewing

_____ **18.** achlorhydria   **c.** belching

_____ **19.** bolus   **d.** lack of hydrochloric acid in the stomach

_____ **20.** mastication   **e.** a mass, as of food

_____ **21.** gavage   **a.** swallowing

_____ **22.** bruxism   **b.** tooth grinding

_____ **23.** deglutition   **c.** malnutrition and wasting

_____ **24.** cachexia   **d.** feeding through a tube

_____ **25.** chyme   **e.** partially digested food

_____ **26.** antiflatulent   **a.** agent that controls loose watery stools

_____ **27.** antidiarrheal   **b.** agent that relieves heartburn, counteracts acidity

_____ **28.** antiemetic   **c.** agent that relieves or prevents gas

_____ **29.** antacid   **d.** agent that relieves spasm

_____ **30.** antispasmodic   **e.** agent that relieves or prevents nausea and vomiting

FILL IN THE BLANKS

31. Any surgical procedure to reduce the size of the stomach in the treatment of obesity is described as _____.

32. The blind pouch at the beginning of the colon is the _____.

33. The hepatic portal system carries blood to the _____.

34. The organ that stores bile is the _____.

35. The large serous membrane that lines the abdominal cavity and supports the abdominal organs is _____.

36. Glossorrhaphy is suture of the _____.

37. The palatine tonsils are located on either side of the _____.

38. Dentin is the main substance of a(n) _____.

39. From its name you might guess that the buccinator muscle is in the _____.

40. An enterovirus is a virus that infects the _____.

41. The anticoagulant heparin is found throughout the body, but it is named for its presence in the _____.

42. The substance cholesterol is named for its chemical composition (sterol) and for its presence in _____.

Referring to B.F.'s opening case study.

43. Protrusion of the stomach through an opening in the diaphragm is termed a(n) _____.

44. Difficulty in swallowing is technically called _____.

45. The histamine-2 receptor antagonist used to treat B.F. reduces secretion of (see Chapter 8) _____.

DEFINITIONS

Write a word for the following definitions.

46. liver enlargement _____

47. a dentist who specializes in treating the tissues around the teeth _____

48. surgical excision of the stomach _____

49. surgical repair of the palate _____

50. narrowing of the pylorus _____

51. inflammation of the pancreas _____

52. medical specialist who treats diseases of the stomach and intestine _____

53. surgical creation of an opening into the colon _____

54. surgical creation of a passage between the stomach and the duodenum _____

55. within (intra-) the liver _____

PLURALS

Write the plural form of the following words.

56. diverticulum _____

57. gingiva _____

58. calculus _____

59. anastomosis _____

SPELL CHECK

Write the correct spelling on the line to the right of the term.

60. hietal hernia _____

61. dypepsia _____

62. inginal herna _____

63. ikterus _____

64. pyeloric stenoses _____

65. diarryhea _____

TRUE-FALSE

Examine the following statements. If the statement is true, write T in the first blank. If the statement is false, write F in the first blank, and correct the statement by replacing the underlined word in the second blank.

	True or False	Correct Answer
66. In the opening case study, B.F. is experiencing his epigastric pain in the region <u>below</u> the stomach.	_____	_____
67. The middle portion of the small intestine is the <u>duodenum</u>.	_____	_____
68. Polysialia is the excess secretion of <u>bile</u>.	_____	_____
69. The cystic duct carries bile to and from the <u>gallbladder</u>.	_____	_____
70. The appendix is attached to the <u>cecum</u>.	_____	_____
71. The common hepatic duct and the cystic duct merge to form the <u>common bile duct</u>.	_____	_____
72. An emetic is an agent that promotes <u>diarrhea</u>.	_____	_____
73. A <u>lavage</u> is an irrigation of a cavity.	_____	_____

ELIMINATIONS

In each of the sets below, underline the word that does not fit in with the rest, and explain the reason for your choice.

74. gingiva — villus — palate — uvula — incisor

_____

75. spleen — cecum — colon — rectum — anus

_____

76. pancreas — gallbladder — liver — pylorus — salivary glands

_____

77. diarrhea — emesis — nausea — regurgitation — amylase

_____

ABBREVIATIONS

Write the meaning of the following abbreviations.

78. N&V _____

79. NG _____

80. TPN _____

81. GERD _____

82. EGD _____

83. GI _____

84. HCl _____

85. PPI _____

86. PEG (tube) _____

87. HAV _____

WORD BUILDING

Write a word for the following definitions using the word parts provided.

> -al   cec/o   r   -pexy   -cele   proct/o   -itis   -rhaphy   ile/o

88. inflammation of the cecum _____

89. suture of the rectum _____

90. fixation of the cecum _____

91. hernia of the rectum _____

92. pertaining to the ileum and cecum _____

93. fixation of the ileum _____

94. inflammation of the rectum _____

95. suture of the cecum _____

96. inflammation of the ileum _____

WORD ANALYSIS

Define each of the following words and give the meaning of the word parts in each. Use a dictionary if necessary.

97. myenteric (*mi-en-TER-ik*) _____

   a. my/o _____

   b. enter/o _____

   c. -ic _____

98. cholescintigraphy (*ko-le-sin-TIG-rah-fe*) _____

   a. chole _____

   b. scinti _____ spark (radiation) _____

   c. -graphy _____

99. parenteral (*pah-REN-ter-al*) _____

   a. par(a) _____

   b. enter/o _____

   c. -al _____

100. nasogastric _____

   a. nas/o _____

   b. gastr/o _____

   c. -ic _____

101. xerostomia _____

   a. xero- _____

   b. stoma _____

   c. -ia _____

Additional Case Studies

Case Study 12-1: *Cholecystectomy*

G.L., a 42-year-old obese Caucasian woman, entered the hospital with nausea and vomiting, flatulence and eructation, a fever of 100.5°F, and continuous right upper quadrant (RUQ) and subscapular pain. Examination on admission showed rebound tenderness in the RUQ with a positive Murphy sign. Her skin, nails, and conjunctivae were yellowish, and she reported frequent clay-colored stools. Her leukocyte count was 16,000. An ERCP and ultrasound of the abdomen suggested many small stones in her gallbladder and possibly in the common bile duct. Her diagnosis was cholecystitis with cholelithiasis.

A laparoscopic cholecystectomy was attempted with an intraoperative cholangiogram and common bile duct exploration. Because of G.L.'s size and some unexpected bleeding, visualization was difficult, and the procedure was converted to an open approach. Small stones and granular sludge were irrigated from her common duct, and the gallbladder was removed. She had a T-tube inserted into the duct for bile drainage; this tube was removed on the second postoperative day. An NG tube in place before and during the surgery was also removed on Day 2. She was discharged on the fifth postoperative day with a prescription for prn pain medication.

Case Study 12-2: *Colonoscopy with Biopsy*

S.M., a 24 YO man, had a recent history of lower abdominal pain with frequent loose mucoid stools. He described symptoms of occasional dysphagia, dyspepsia, nausea, and aphthous ulcers of his tongue and buccal mucosa. A previous barium enema examination showed some irregularities in the sigmoid and rectal segments of his large bowel. Stool samples for culture, ova, and parasites were negative. His tentative diagnosis was irritable bowel syndrome. He followed a lactose-free, low-residue diet and took Imodium to reduce intestinal motility. His gastroenterologist recommended a colonoscopy. After a two-day regimen of a soft to clear liquid diet, laxatives, and an enema, the morning of the procedure, he reported to the endoscopy unit. He was transported to the procedure room. ECG electrodes, a pulse oximeter sensor, and a blood pressure cuff were applied for monitoring, and an IV was inserted in S.M.'s right arm. An IV bolus of propofol was given, and S.M. was positioned on his left side. The colonoscope was gently inserted through the anal sphincter and advanced proximally.

The physician was able to advance past the ileocecal valve, examining the entire length of the colon. Ulcerated granulomatous lesions were seen throughout the colon with a concentration in the sigmoid segment. Many biopsy specimens were taken. The mucosa of the distal ileum was normal. Pathology examination of the biopsy samples was expected to establish a diagnosis of IBD.

Case Study Questions

Multiple Choice. Select the best answer, and write the letter of your choice to the left of each number.

_____ **1.** Flatulence and eructation represent
  a. regurgitation of chyme
  b. sounds heard only by abdominal auscultation
  c. passage of gas or air from the GI tract
  d. muscular movement of the alimentary tract

_____ **2.** Subscapular pain is experienced (see **Fig. 5-7**)
  a. above the navel
  b. below the shoulder blade
  c. below the sternum
  d. beside the shoulder blade

_____ **3.** Yellowish conjunctivae indicate
  a. emesis
  b. jaundice
  c. inflammation
  d. ptosis

_____ **4.** The common duct is more properly called the
  a. common bile duct
  b. common duodenal duct
  c. unified cystic duct
  d. joined bile duct

_____ **5.** The Murphy sign is a test for pain
   a. under the ribs on the left
   b. near the spleen
   c. in the lower right abdomen
   d. under the ribs on the right

_____ **6.** The NG tube is inserted through the
   _____ and terminates in the _____.
   a. nose, stomach
   b. nostril, gallbladder
   c. glottis, nephron
   d. anus, cecum

_____ **7.** Dysphagia and dyspepsia are difficulty or pain with
   a. chewing and intestinal motility
   b. swallowing and digestion
   c. breathing and absorption
   d. swallowing and nutrition

_____ **8.** The buccal mucosa is in the
   a. nostril, medial side
   b. mouth, inside of the cheek
   c. greater curvature of the stomach
   d. base of the tongue

_____ **9.** A gastroenterologist is a physician who specializes in study of
   a. mouth and teeth
   b. stomach, intestines, and related structures
   c. musculoskeletal system
   d. nutritional and weight loss diets

_____ **10.** The splenic and hepatic flexures are bends in the colon near the
   a. liver and splanchnic vein
   b. common bile duct and biliary tree
   c. spleen and appendix
   d. spleen and liver

_____ **11.** Intestinal motility refers to
   a. peristalsis
   b. chewing
   c. absorption
   d. ascites

_____ **12.** A colonoscopy is
   a. a radiograph of the small intestine
   b. an endoscopic study of the esophagus
   c. an upper endoscopy with biopsy
   d. an endoscopic examination of the large bowel

_____ **13.** The ileocecal valve is
   a. part of a colonoscope
   b. at the distal ileum
   c. in the pylorus
   d. at the proximal ileum

Write the meaning of each of the following abbreviations.

14. ERCP _____

15. RUQ _____

16. NG _____

17. IBD _____

Give the word or words in the case studies with each of the following meanings.

18. presence of stones in the gallbladder _____

19. endoscopic surgery of the gallbladder _____

20. inflammation of the gallbladder _____

21. radiographic study of the gallbladder and biliary system _____

22. ring of muscle that regulates the distal opening of the colon _____

23. surgical excision of tissue for pathology examination _____

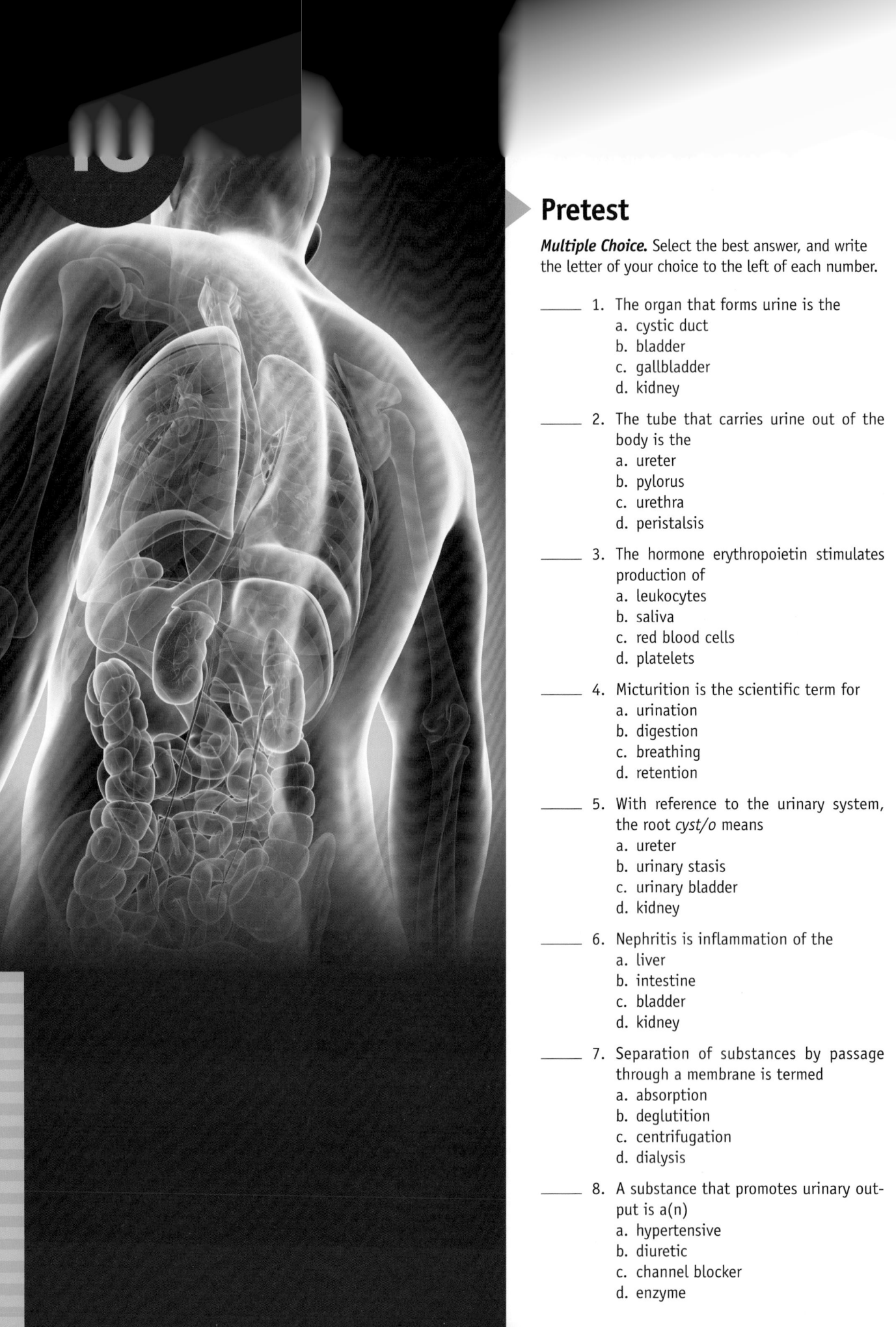

Pretest

Multiple Choice. Select the best answer, and write the letter of your choice to the left of each number.

_____ 1. The organ that forms urine is the
   a. cystic duct
   b. bladder
   c. gallbladder
   d. kidney

_____ 2. The tube that carries urine out of the body is the
   a. ureter
   b. pylorus
   c. urethra
   d. peristalsis

_____ 3. The hormone erythropoietin stimulates production of
   a. leukocytes
   b. saliva
   c. red blood cells
   d. platelets

_____ 4. Micturition is the scientific term for
   a. urination
   b. digestion
   c. breathing
   d. retention

_____ 5. With reference to the urinary system, the root *cyst/o* means
   a. ureter
   b. urinary stasis
   c. urinary bladder
   d. kidney

_____ 6. Nephritis is inflammation of the
   a. liver
   b. intestine
   c. bladder
   d. kidney

_____ 7. Separation of substances by passage through a membrane is termed
   a. absorption
   b. deglutition
   c. centrifugation
   d. dialysis

_____ 8. A substance that promotes urinary output is a(n)
   a. hypertensive
   b. diuretic
   c. channel blocker
   d. enzyme

Learning Objectives

After the study of this chapter, you should be able to:

1 ▶ Describe the functions of the urinary system. **p306**

2 ▶ Name and describe the organs of the urinary tract, and cite the functions of each. **p306**

3 ▶ Identify the portions of the nephron. **p306**

4 ▶ Explain the relationship between the kidney and the blood circulation. **p306**

5 ▶ Describe the processes involved in urine formation. **p307**

6 ▶ Explain how urine is transported and released from the body. **p308**

7 ▶ Identify and use the roots pertaining to the urinary system. **p310**

8 ▶ Describe six major disorders of the urinary system. **p312**

9 ▶ Interpret abbreviations used in reference to the urinary system. **p322**

10 ▶ Analyze medical terms in case studies pertaining to the urinary system. **pp305, 330**

Case Study: *E.O.'s Stress Incontinence*

Chief Complaint

E.O. is a 52-year-old Asian female with a history of stress incontinence. The condition has affected her quality of life, as she is not able to be active in athletics without worrying about urinary leakage under physical strain. E.O. has cut back on her sports participation and currently is involved in only two golf leagues. Although the incontinence continues to be a problem, she does not want to take medication or have corrective surgery. E.O. heard about a minimally invasive research protocol that could potentially address the incontinence. She decided to investigate to see if she would be a candidate for the study.

Examination

E.O. met with the research nurse who explained the study to her. She was told the study hoped to achieve around 75 percent improvement, which E.O. found acceptable. A urologic history was taken involving questions relating to urinary frequency, urgency, and nocturia (nighttime urination). A few procedures were required at the beginning of the study that would determine

eligibility. E.O. was required to provide a clean-catch specimen and underwent a cystometrography (CMG) and a cystoscopy. The results indicated that she would be a good candidate for the research trial. She was required to maintain a urinary diary for two weeks and record when the stress incontinence and urgency occurred. E.O. proceeded with the study.

Clinical Course

The clinical study involved taking muscle cells from E.O.'s thigh, growing them in a laboratory, and then reinserting cultured stem cells (myoblasts) into the area surrounding the urethra. Theoretically, these actively growing cells would promote sphincter muscle development and provide greater control of urination. The urologist took a punch biopsy from E.O.'s thigh muscle to obtain the necessary cells. After laboratory processing, the active cells were injected into place. They were allowed to settle and grow for three months, at which time another CMG and cystoscopy were performed. A comparison was made with the original test results to see if there was any improvement in the stress incontinence. All procedures were conducted in the office with minimal discomfort.

ANCILLARIES *At-A-Glance*

Visit thePoint to access the following resources. For guidance in using the resources most effectively, see pp. ix–xvi.

Learning RESOURCES

▶ **Tips for Effective Studying**
▶ **E-book: Chapter 13**
▶ **Web Figure: Urinary Obstruction, Reflux, and Infection**
▶ **Web Figure: Acute Pyelonephritis**
▶ **Web Figure: Hydronephrosis**
▶ **Web Chart: Role of Hormones in Electrolyte Balance**

▶ **Animation: Renal Function**
▶ **Audio Pronunciation Glossary**

Learning ACTIVITIES

▶ **Visual Activities**
▶ **Kinesthetic Activities**
▶ **Auditory Activities**

Introduction

The urinary system excretes metabolic waste. In forming and eliminating urine, it also regulates the composition, volume, and acid–base balance (pH) of body fluids. In several ways, kidney activity affects the circulation. The urinary system is thus of critical importance in maintaining homeostasis, the state of internal balance. As shown in **Figure 13-1**, the urinary system consists of:

- Two kidneys, the organs that form urine
- Two ureters, which transport urine from the kidneys to the bladder
- The urinary bladder, which stores and eliminates urine
- The urethra, which carries urine out of the body

Inferior vena cava

Aorta

Renal artery

Renal vein

Diaphragm

Adrenal gland

Kidney

Ureter

Urinary bladder

Urethra

Figure 13-1 **The urinary system.** This system consists of the kidneys, ureters, urinary bladder, and urethra. It is shown here along with the diaphragm, nearby blood vessels, and the adrenal glands.

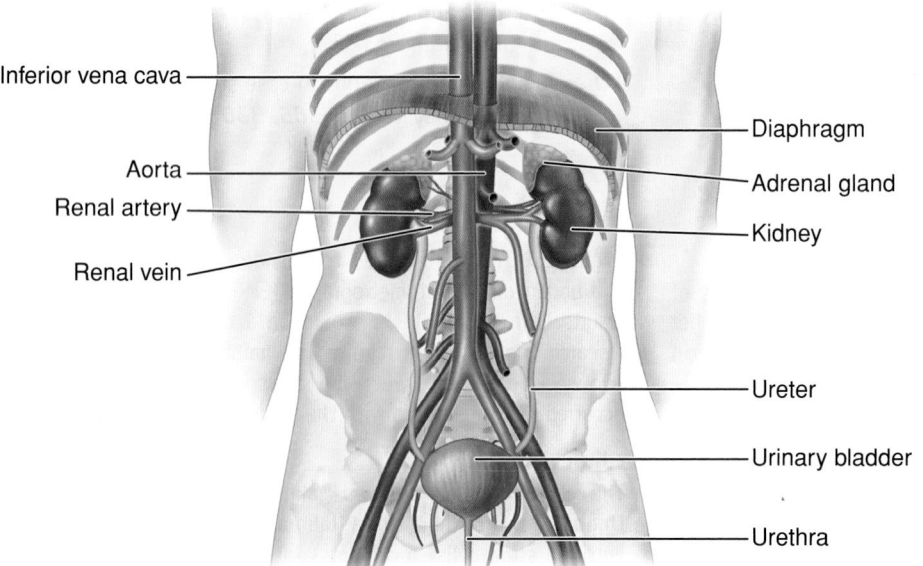

Nephrons

Calyx

Hilum

Renal pelvis

Ureter

Renal cortex

Renal medulla

Pyramids of medulla

Renal capsule

Figure 13-2 **The kidney.** A longitudinal section (*left*) through the kidney shows its internal structure. The hilum is the point where blood vessels and ducts connect with the kidney. An enlarged diagram of nephrons. Each kidney contains more than 1 million nephrons (*right*).

The Kidneys

The kidneys are the organs that form **urine** from substances filtered out of the blood. In addition to metabolic wastes, urine contains water and ions, so its formation is important in regulating the blood's volume and composition. In addition, the kidneys produce two substances that act on the circulatory system:

- **Erythropoietin (EPO)**, a hormone that stimulates red blood cell production in the bone marrow.
- **Renin**, an enzyme that functions to raise blood pressure. It activates a blood component called **angiotensin**, which causes constriction of the blood vessels. The drugs known as ACE inhibitors (angiotensin-converting enzyme inhibitors) lower blood pressure by interfering with the production of angiotensin.

KIDNEY LOCATION AND STRUCTURE

The **kidneys** are located behind the peritoneum in the lumbar region. On the top of each kidney rests an adrenal gland. The kidney is encased in a capsule of fibrous connective tissue overlaid with fat. An outermost layer of connective tissue supports the kidney and anchors it to the body wall.

If you look inside the kidney (**Fig. 13-2**), you will see that it has an outer region, the **renal cortex**, and an inner region, the **renal medulla** (**Box 13-1**). The medulla is divided into triangular sections, the **renal pyramids**. These pyramids have a lined appearance because they are made up of the loops and collecting tubules of the **nephrons**, the kidney's functional units. Each collecting tubule empties into a urine-collecting area called a **calyx** (from the Latin word meaning "cup"). Several of the smaller minor calices merge to form a major calyx. The major calices then unite to form the **renal pelvis**, the upper funnel-shaped portion of the **ureter**.

THE NEPHRONS

The tiny working units of the kidneys are the nephrons (**Fig. 13-3**). Each of these microscopic structures is basically a single

FOCUS ON WORDS
Words That Serve Double Duty

Box 13-1

Some words appear in more than one body system to represent different structures. The medulla of the kidney is the inner portion of the organ. Other organs, such as the adrenal gland, ovary, and lymph nodes, may also be divided into a central medulla and outer cortex. But *medulla* means "marrow," and this term also applies to the bone marrow, to the spinal cord, and to the part of the brain that connects with the spinal cord, the medulla oblongata.

A ventricle is a chamber. There are ventricles in the brain and in the heart. The word *fundus* means the back part or base of an organ. The uterus has a fundus, the upper rounded portion farthest from the cervix, as does the stomach. The fundus of the eye, examined for signs of diabetes and glaucoma, is the innermost layer, where the retina is located. A macula is a spot. There is a macula in the eye, which is the point of sharpest vision. There is also a macula in the ear, which contains receptors for equilibrium.

In interpreting medical terminology, it is often important to know the context in which a word is used.

tubule coiled and folded into various shapes. The tubule begins with a cup-shaped **glomerular** (Bowman) **capsule**, which is part of the nephron's blood-filtering device. The tubule then folds into the proximal tubule, straightens out to form the nephron loop (loop of Henle), coils again into

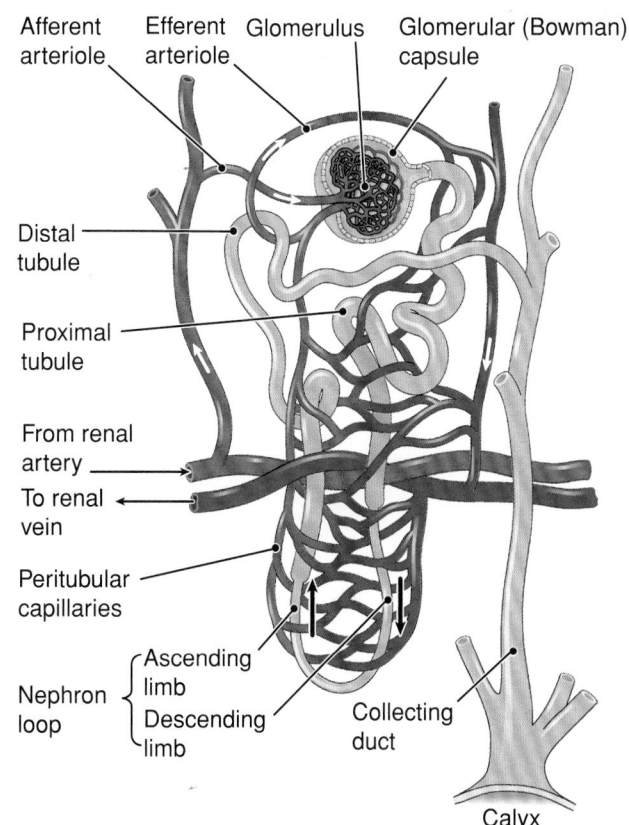

Figure 13-3 **A nephron and its blood supply.** The nephron regulates the proportion of water, waste, and other materials in urine according to the body's constantly changing needs. A nephron consists of a glomerular capsule, convoluted tubules, the nephron loop (loop of Henle), and a collecting duct. Blood filtration occurs through the glomerulus in the glomerular capsule. Materials that enter the nephron can be returned to the blood through the surrounding peritubular capillaries.

the distal tubule, and then finally straightens out to form a collecting duct.

BLOOD SUPPLY TO THE KIDNEY

Blood enters the kidney through a renal artery, a short branch of the abdominal aorta. This vessel subdivides into smaller vessels as it branches throughout the kidney tissue, until finally blood is brought into the glomerular capsule and circulated through a cluster of capillaries, called a **glomerulus**, within the capsule.

Blood leaves the kidney by a series of vessels that finally merge to form the renal vein, which empties into the inferior vena cava.

Urine Formation

As blood flows through the glomerulus, blood pressure forces materials through the glomerular wall and through the wall of the glomerular capsule into the nephron. The fluid that enters the nephron, the **glomerular filtrate**, consists mainly of water, electrolytes, soluble wastes, nutrients, and toxins. The main waste material is **urea**, the nitrogenous (nitrogen-containing) byproduct of protein metabolism. The filtrate should not contain any cells or proteins, such as albumin.

The waste material and the toxins must be eliminated, but most of the water, electrolytes, and nutrients must be returned to the blood, or we would rapidly starve and dehydrate. This return process, termed **tubular reabsorption**, occurs through the peritubular capillaries that surround the nephron.

As the filtrate flows through the nephron, other processes further regulate its composition and pH. The filtrate's concentration is also adjusted under the effects of a pituitary hormone. **Antidiuretic hormone** (ADH) promotes reabsorption of water, thus concentrating the filtrate. The final filtrate, now called urine, flows into the collecting ducts to be eliminated. A **diuretic** is a substance that promotes increased urinary output or **diuresis**. Diuretic drugs are used in treating hypertension and heart failure to decrease fluid volume and reduce the heart's workload (see Chapter 9).

See the animation "Renal Function" and a chart on the role of hormones in electrolyte balance in the Student Resources on thePoint.

TRANSPORT AND REMOVAL OF URINE

Urine is drained from the renal pelvis and carried by the left and right ureters to the **urinary bladder** (**Fig. 13-4**), where it is stored. The bladder is located posterior to the pubic bone and below the peritoneum. As the bladder fills, it expands upward from a stable triangle at its base. This triangle, the **trigone**, is marked by the ureteral openings and the urethral opening below (**Fig. 13-4**). The trigone's stability prevents urine from refluxing into the ureters.

Fullness stimulates a reflex contraction of the bladder muscle and expulsion of urine through the **urethra**. The female urethra is short (4 cm [1.5 in]) and carries only urine. The male urethra is longer (20 cm [8 in]) and carries both urine and semen.

The voiding (release) of urine, called **urination** or more technically, **micturition**, is regulated by two sphincters (circular muscles) that surround the urethra. The superior muscle, the internal urethral sphincter, is around the entrance to the urethra and functions involuntarily; the inferior muscle, the external urethral sphincter, is under conscious control. An inability to retain urine is termed *urinary incontinence*.

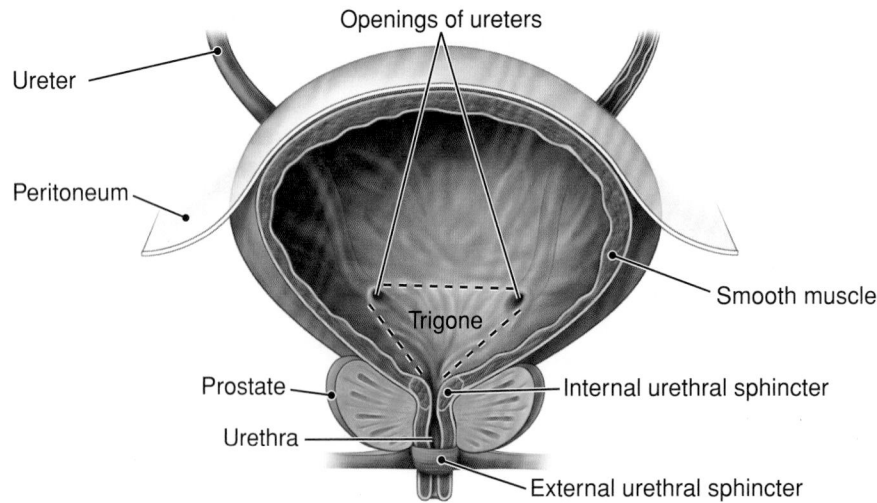

Figure 13-4 **The urinary bladder.** The interior of the male bladder is shown. The trigone is a triangular region in the bladder floor marked by the openings of the ureters and the urethra. The urethra travels through the prostate gland in the male.

Terminology	Key Terms

Normal Structure and Function

antidiuretic hormone (ADH) *an-te-di-u-RET-ik*	A hormone released from the pituitary gland that causes water reabsorption in the kidneys, thus concentrating the urine
angiotensin *an-je-o-TEN-sin*	A substance that increases blood pressure; activated in the blood by renin, an enzyme produced by the kidneys
calyx *KA-liks*	A cup-like cavity in the pelvis of the kidney; also calix (plural: calices) (roots: cali/o, calic/o)
diuresis *di-u-RE-sis*	Excretion of urine; usually meaning increased urinary excretion
diuretic *di-u-RET-ik*	A substance that increases the excretion of urine; pertaining to diuresis
erythropoietin (EPO) *eh-rith-ro-POY-eh-tin*	A hormone produced by the kidneys that stimulates red blood cell production in the bone marrow

Terminology	Key Terms *(Continued)*

glomerular capsule *glo-MER-u-lar KAP-sule*	The cup-shaped structure at the beginning of the nephron that surrounds the glomerulus and receives material filtered out of the blood; Bowman (*BO-man*) capsule
glomerular filtrate *glo-MER-u-lar FIL-trate*	The fluid and dissolved materials that filter out of the blood and enter the nephron through the glomerular capsule
glomerulus *glo-MER-u-lus*	The cluster of capillaries within the glomerular capsule (plural: glomeruli) (root: glomerul/o)
kidney *KID-ne*	An organ of excretion (roots: ren/o, nephr/o); the two kidneys filter the blood and form urine, which contains metabolic waste products and other substances as needed to regulate the water, electrolyte, and pH balance of body fluids
micturition *mik-tu-RISH-un*	The voiding of urine; urination
nephron *NEF-ron*	A microscopic functional unit of the kidney; working with blood vessels, the nephron filters the blood and balances the composition of urine
renal cortex *RE-nal KOR-tex*	The kidney's outer portion; contains portions of the nephrons
renal medulla *meh-DUL-lah*	The kidney's inner portion; contains portions of the nephrons and ducts that transport urine toward the renal pelvis
renal pelvis *PEL-vis*	The expanded upper end of the ureter that receives urine from the kidney (Greek root *pyel/o* means "basin")
renal pyramid *PERE-ah-mid*	A triangular structure in the renal medulla; composed of the nephrons' loops and collecting ducts
renin *RE-nin*	An enzyme produced by the kidneys that activates angiotensin in the blood
trigone *TRI-gone*	A triangle at the base of the bladder formed by the openings of the two ureters and the urethra (see **Fig. 13-4**)
tubular reabsorption *TUBE-u-lar re-ab-SORP-shun*	The return of substances from the glomerular filtrate to the blood through the peritubular capillaries
urea *u-RE-ah*	The main nitrogenous (nitrogen-containing) waste product in the urine
ureter *U-re-ter*	The tube that carries urine from the kidney to the bladder (root: ureter/o)
urethra *u-RE-thrah*	The tube that carries urine from the bladder to the outside of the body (root: urethr/o)
urinary bladder *u-rih-NAR-e BLAD-der*	The organ that stores and eliminates urine excreted by the kidneys (roots: cyst/o, vesic/o)
urination *u-rih-NA-shun*	The voiding of urine; micturition
urine *U-rin*	The fluid excreted by the kidneys; it consists of water, electrolytes, urea, other metabolic wastes, and pigments; a variety of other substances may appear in urine in cases of disease (root: ur/o)

Go to the Audio Pronunciation Glossary in the Student Resources on thePoint to hear these terms pronounced.

Roots Pertaining to the Urinary System

See **Tables 13-1** and **13-2**.

Table 13-1	Roots for the Kidney		
Root	**Meaning**	**Example**	**Definition of Example**
ren/o	kidney	suprarenal *su-prah-RE-nal*	above the kidney
nephr/o	kidney	nephrosis *nef-RO-sis*	any noninflammatory disease condition of the kidney
glomerul/o	glomerulus	juxtaglomerular *juks-tah-glo-MER-u-lar*	near the glomerulus
pyel/o	renal pelvis	pyelectasis *pi-eh-LEK-tah-sis*	dilatation of the renal pelvis
cali/o, calic/o	calyx	caliceal *kal-ih-SE-al*	pertaining to a renal calyx (note addition of *e*); also spelled calyceal

EXERCISE 13-1

Use the root *ren/o* to write a word for the following.

1. before or in front of (pre-) the kidney _____

2. behind (post-) the kidney _____

3. above the kidneys _____

4. around the kidneys _____

Use the root *nephr/o* to write a word for the following.

5. the medical specialist who studies the kidney _____

6. any disease of the kidney _____

7. poisonous or toxic to the kidney _____

8. softening of the kidney _____

9. enlargement of the kidney _____

Use the appropriate root to write a word for the following.

10. incision into the kidney _____

11. inflammation of the renal pelvis and kidney _____

12. plastic repair of the renal pelvis _____

13. radiograph of the renal pelvis _____

14. inflammation of a glomerulus _____

15. incision of a renal calyx _____

16. hardening of a glomerulus _____

17. dilatation of a renal calyx _____

Table 13-2	Roots for the Urinary Tract (Except the Kidney)

Root	Meaning	Example	Definition of Example
ur/o	urine, urinary tract	urosepsis *u-ro-SEP-sis*	generalized infection that originates in the urinary tract
urin/o	urine	nocturia *nok-TU-re-ah*	urination during the night (noct/i)
ureter/o	ureter	ureterostenosis *u-re-ter-o-steh-NO-sis*	narrowing of the ureter
cyst/o	urinary bladder	cystocele *SIS-to-sele*	hernia of the urinary bladder
vesic/o	urinary bladder	intravesical *in-trah-VES-ih-kal*	within the urinary bladder
urethr/o	urethra	urethrotome *u-RE-thro-tome*	instrument for incising the urethra

13

EXERCISE 13-2

Use the root *ur/o* to write a word for the following.

1. any disease of the urinary tract   _____

2. radiography of the urinary tract   _____

3. a urinary calculus (stone)   _____

4. presence of urinary waste products in the blood   _____

The root *ur/o-* is used in the suffix *-uria*, which means "condition of urine or of urination." Use *-uria* to write a word for the following.

5. lack of urine   _____

6. presence of pus in the urine   _____

7. urination at night   _____

8. painful or difficult urination   _____

9. presence of blood (hemat/o) in the urine   _____

The suffix *-uresis* means "urination." Use *-uresis* to write a word for the following.

10. increased excretion of urine   _____

11. lack of urination   _____

12. excretion of sodium (natri-) in the urine   _____

13. excretion of potassium (kali-) in the urine   _____

The adjective ending for the above words is *-uretic*, as in diuretic (pertaining to diuresis) and natriuretic (pertaining to the excretion of sodium in the urine). Use the appropriate root to write a word for the following.

14. surgical fixation of the urethra   _____

15. surgical creation of an opening in the ureter   _____

16. suture of the urethra   _____

17. endoscopic examination of the urethra   _____

18. herniation of the ureter   _____

(continued)

EXERCISE 13-2	*(Continued)*

Use the root *cyst/o* to write a word for the following.

19. inflammation of the urinary bladder   _____

20. radiography of the urinary bladder   _____

21. an instrument for examining the interior of the bladder   _____

22. incision of the bladder   _____

23. discharge from the bladder   _____

Use the root *vesic/o* to write a word for the following.

24. above the urinary bladder   _____

25. pertaining to the urethra and bladder   _____

Define the following terms.

26. cystalgia (*sis-TAL-je-ah*)   _____

27. ureterotomy (*u-re-ter-OT-o-me*)   _____

28. transurethral (*trans-u-RE-thral*)   _____

29. uropoiesis (*u-ro-poy-E-sis*)   _____

Clinical Aspects of the Urinary System

INFECTIONS

Organisms that infect the urinary tract generally enter through the urethra and ascend toward the bladder, producing **cystitis**. Untreated, the infection can ascend even further into the urinary tract. The infecting organisms are usually colon bacteria carried in feces, particularly *Escherichia coli*. Although urinary tract infections (UTIs) do occur in men, they appear more commonly in women because the female urethra is shorter than the male urethra and its opening is closer to the anus. Poor toilet habits and **urinary stasis** are contributing factors. In hospitals, UTIs may result from procedures involving the urinary system, especially **catheterization**, in which a tube is inserted into the bladder to withdraw urine (**Fig. 13-5**). Less frequently, UTIs originate in the blood and descend through the urinary system.

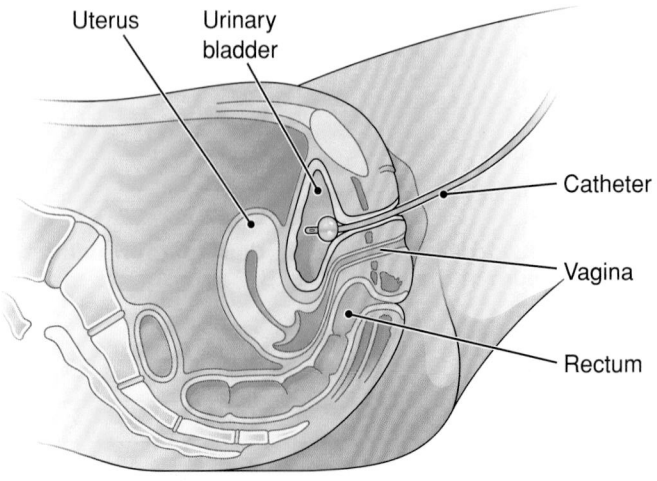

Figure 13-5   **An indwelling (Foley) catheter.** The catheter is shown in place in the female bladder.

An infection that involves the kidney and renal pelvis is termed **pyelonephritis**. As in cystitis, signs of this condition include **dysuria**, painful or difficult urination, and the presence of bacteria and pus in the urine, **bacteriuria** and **pyuria**, respectively.

Urethritis is inflammation of the urethra, generally associated with sexually transmitted infections such as gonorrhea and chlamydial infections (see Chapter 14).

> See the chart on urinary obstruction, reflux, and infection and the figure on acute pyelonephritis in the Student Resources on thePoint.

GLOMERULONEPHRITIS

Although the name simply means inflammation of the glomeruli and kidney, **glomerulonephritis** is a specific disorder that follows an immunologic reaction. It is usually a response to infection in another system, commonly a streptococcal infection of the respiratory tract or a skin infection. It may also accompany autoimmune diseases such as lupus erythematosus. The symptoms are hypertension, edema, and **oliguria**, the passage of small amounts of urine. This urine is highly concentrated. Because of damage to kidney tissue, blood and proteins escape into the nephrons, causing **hematuria**, blood in the urine, and **proteinuria**, protein in the urine. Blood cells may also form into small molds of the kidney tubule, called **casts**, which can be found in the urine. Most patients fully recover from glomerulonephritis, but in some cases, especially among the elderly, the disorder may lead to chronic renal failure (CRF) or end-stage renal disease (ESRD). In such cases, urea and other nitrogenous compounds accumulate in the blood, a condition termed **uremia**. These compounds affect the central nervous system, causing irritability, loss of appetite, stupor, and other symptoms. There is also electrolyte imbalance and **acidosis**.

NEPHROTIC SYNDROME

Glomerulonephritis is one cause of **nephrotic syndrome**, a disease in which the glomeruli become overly permeable and allow the loss of proteins. Other possible causes of nephrotic syndrome are renal vein thrombosis, diabetes, systemic lupus erythematosus, toxins, or any other condition that damages the glomeruli.

Nephrotic syndrome is marked by proteinuria and **hypoproteinemia**, low blood protein. The low plasma protein level affects capillary exchange and results in edema. There is also an increase in blood lipids, as the liver compensates for lost protein by releasing lipoproteins.

ACUTE RENAL FAILURE

Injury, shock, exposure to toxins, infections, and other renal disorders may cause damage to the nephrons, resulting in **acute renal failure** (ARF). There is rapid loss of kidney function with oliguria and accumulation of nitrogenous wastes in the blood. Failure of the kidneys to eliminate potassium leads to hyperkalemia, along with other electrolyte imbalances and acidosis (**Box 13-2**). When destruction (necrosis) of kidney tubules is involved, the condition may be referred to as *acute tubular necrosis (ATN)*.

Renal failure may lead to a need for kidney **dialysis** or, ultimately, **renal transplantation**. Dialysis refers to the movement of substances across a semipermeable membrane; it is a method used to eliminate harmful or unnecessary substances from the body when the kidneys are impaired or have been removed (**Fig. 13-6**). Two approaches are used:

- In **hemodialysis**, blood is cleansed by passage over a membrane surrounded by fluid (dialysate) that draws out unwanted substances. Most people on hemodialysis are treated for four hours three times a week in a dialysis center. Some patients are able to use simpler

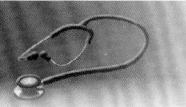

CLINICAL PERSPECTIVES   **Box 13-2**

Sodium and Potassium: Causes and Consequences of Imbalance

Sodium and potassium concentrations in body fluids are important measures of water and electrolyte balance. An excess of sodium in body fluids is termed **hypernatremia**, taken from the Latin name for sodium, *natrium*. This condition accompanies dehydration and severe vomiting and may cause hypertension, edema, convulsions, and coma. **Hyponatremia**, a sodium deficiency in body fluids, can come from water intoxication (overhydration), heart failure, kidney failure, cirrhosis of the liver, pH imbalance, or endocrine disorders. It can cause muscle weakness, hypotension, confusion, shock, convulsions, and coma.

The term **hyperkalemia** is taken from the Latin name for potassium, *kalium*. It refers to excess potassium in body fluids, which may result from kidney failure, dehydration, and other causes. Its signs and symptoms include nausea, vomiting, muscular weakness, and severe cardiac arrhythmias. **Hypokalemia**, or low potassium in body fluids, may result from taking diuretics that cause potassium to be lost along with water. It may also result from pH imbalance or secretion of too much aldosterone from the adrenal cortex, resulting in potassium excretion. Hypokalemia causes muscle fatigue, paralysis, confusion, hypoventilation, and cardiac arrhythmias.

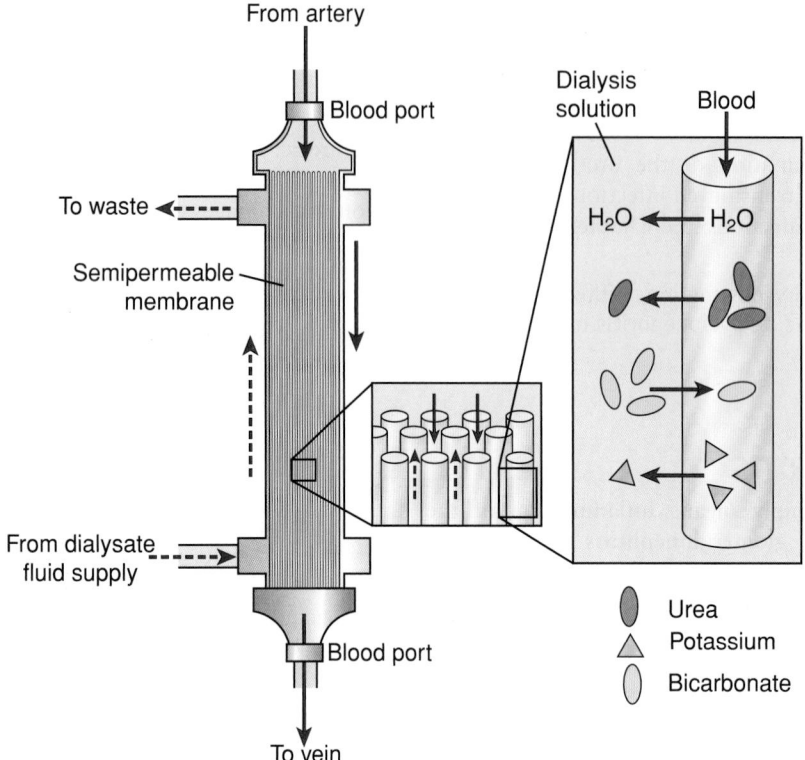

Figure 13-6 **Hemodialysis.** A semipermeable membrane separates the patient's blood from the dialysis solution. This membrane allows all the blood constituents except plasma proteins and blood cells to diffuse between the two compartments. Water, electrolytes, and other dissolved substances move from higher to lower concentration, removing waste materials, and restoring the blood's proper composition.

machines at home for daily dialysis. **Box 13-3** has information on careers in hemodialysis treatment.

- In **peritoneal dialysis,** fluid is introduced into the peritoneal cavity. The fluid, along with waste products, is periodically withdrawn and replaced (**Fig. 13-7**). Fluid may be exchanged at intervals throughout the day in continuous ambulatory peritoneal dialysis (CAPD) or during the night in continuous cyclic peritoneal dialysis (CCPD).

URINARY STONES

Urinary lithiasis (presence of stones) may be related to infection, irritation, diet, or hormone imbalances that lead to increased calcium in the blood. Most urinary calculi (stones) are made up of calcium salts, but they may be composed of other materials as well. Causes of stone formation include dehydration, infection, abnormal pH of urine, urinary stasis, and metabolic imbalances. The stones generally form in

HEALTH PROFESSIONS

Box 13-3

Hemodialysis Technician

A hemodialysis technician, also called a renal technician or a nephrology technician, specializes in the safe and effective delivery of renal dialysis therapy to patients suffering from kidney failure. Before treatment begins, the technician prepares the dialysis solutions and ensures that the dialysis machine is clean, sterile, and in proper working order. The technician measures and records the patient's weight, temperature, and vital signs; inserts a catheter into the patient's arm; and connects the dialysis machine to it. During dialysis, the technician monitors the patient for adverse reactions and guards against any equipment malfunction. After the treatment is completed,

the technician again measures and records the patient's weight, temperature, and vital signs. To perform these duties, hemodialysis technicians need thorough scientific and clinical training. Most technicians in the United States receive their training from colleges or technical schools, and many states require that the technician be certified.

Hemodialysis technicians work in a variety of settings, such as hospitals, clinics, and patients' homes. As populations age, the incidence of kidney disease is expected to rise, as will the need for hemodialysis. For more information about this career, contact the National Association of Nephrology Technicians at www.dialysistech.net.

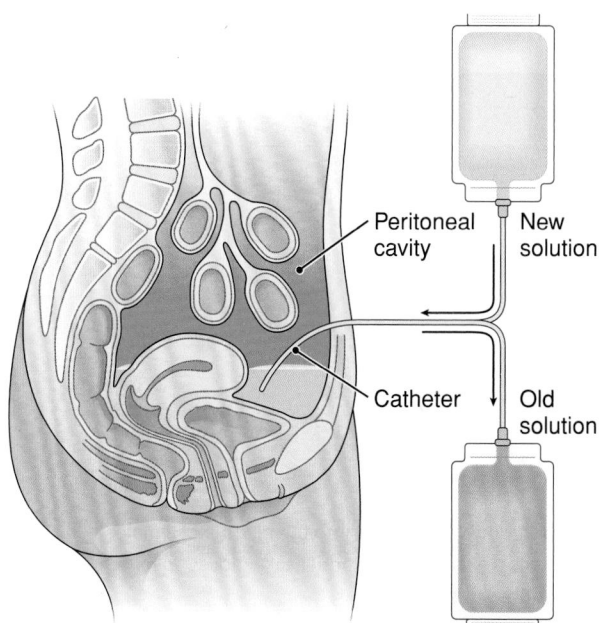

Figure 13-7 **Peritoneal dialysis.** The peritoneum, a semipermeable membrane richly supplied with small blood vessels, lines the peritoneal cavity. Waste products diffuse from the network of blood vessels into the dialysate in the peritoneal cavity.

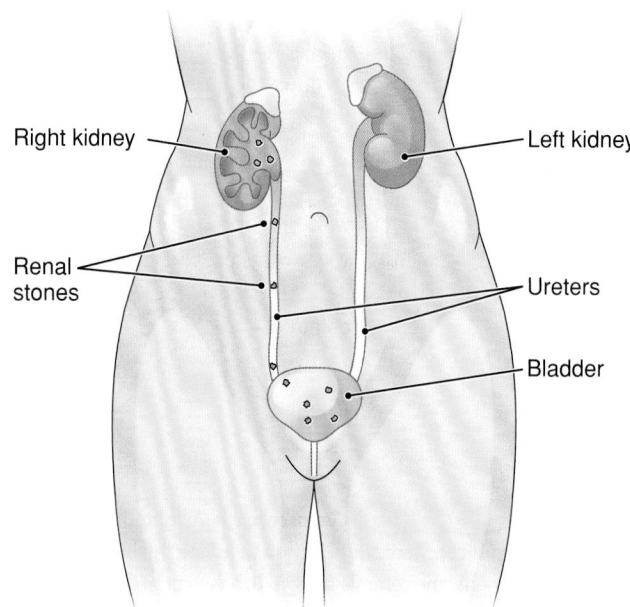

Figure 13-8 **Calculus formation in the urinary tract.** Various possible sites of calculus (stone) formation are shown.

13

the kidney and may move to the bladder (**Fig. 13-8**). This results in great pain, termed **renal colic**, and obstruction that can promote infection and cause **hydronephrosis**, collection of urine in the renal pelvis.

See the figure on hydronephrosis in the Student Resources on thePoint.

Because they are radiopaque, stones can usually be seen on simple radiographs of the abdomen. Stones may dissolve and pass out of the body on their own. If not, they

may be removed surgically, in a **lithotomy**, or by endoscopy. External shock waves are used to crush stones in the urinary tract in a procedure called extracorporeal (outside the body) shock-wave **lithotripsy** (crushing of stones) (**Fig. 13-9**).

CANCER

Carcinoma of the bladder has been linked to occupational exposure to chemicals, parasitic infections, and cigarette smoking. A key symptom is sudden, painless hematuria. Often, the cancer can be seen by viewing the bladder lining

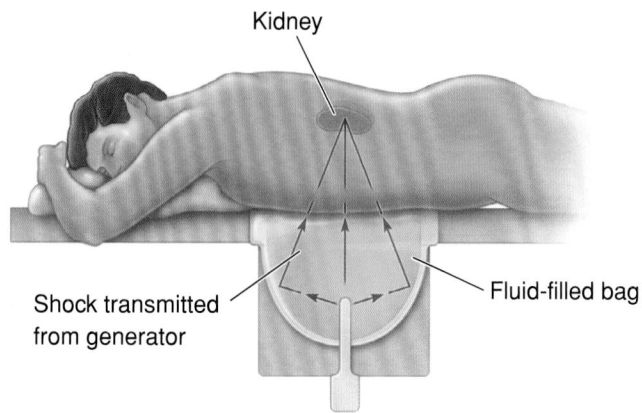

Figure 13-9 **Lithotripsy.** Shock waves are used to break kidney stones and allow for their passage. The procedure is called extracorporeal shock-wave lithotripsy (ESWL).

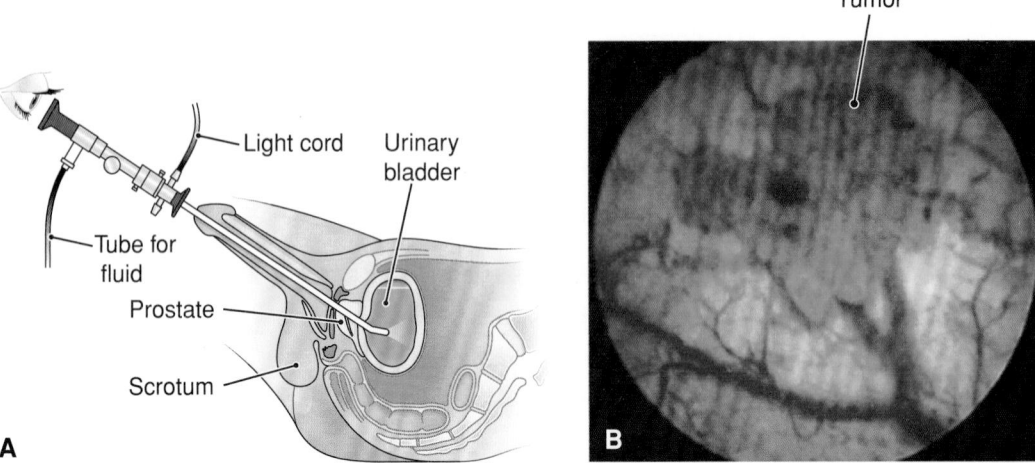

Figure 13-10 **Cystoscopy. A.** A lighted cystoscope is introduced through the urethra into the bladder of a male subject. Sterile fluid is used to inflate the bladder. Cystoscopes are used to examine the bladder, take biopsy specimens, and remove tumors. **B.** A cancer of the bladder, as viewed through a cystoscope.

with a **cystoscope** (**Fig. 13-10**). This instrument can also be used to biopsy tissue for study.

If treatment is not effective in permanently removing the tumor, a **cystectomy** (removal of the bladder) may be necessary. In this case, the ureters must be vented elsewhere, such as directly to the body surface through the ileum in an **ileal conduit** (**Fig. 13-11**), or to some other portion of the intestine.

Cancer may also involve the kidney and renal pelvis. Additional means for diagnosing cancer and other urinary tract disorders include ultrasound, computed tomography scans, and radiographic studies such as **intravenous urography (IVU)** (**Fig. 13-12**), also called **intravenous pyelography (IVP)**, and **retrograde pyelography**.

URINALYSIS

Urinalysis (UA) is a simple and widely used method for diagnosing urinary tract disorders. It may also reveal disturbances in other systems when abnormal byproducts are eliminated in the urine. In a routine UA, the urine is grossly examined for color and turbidity (a sign that bacteria are present); **specific gravity (SG)** (a measure of concentration) and pH are recorded; tests are performed for chemical components such as glucose, ketones, and hemoglobin; and the urine is examined microscopically for cells, crystals, and casts. In more detailed tests, drugs, enzymes, hormones, and other metabolites may be analyzed, and bacterial cultures may be performed.

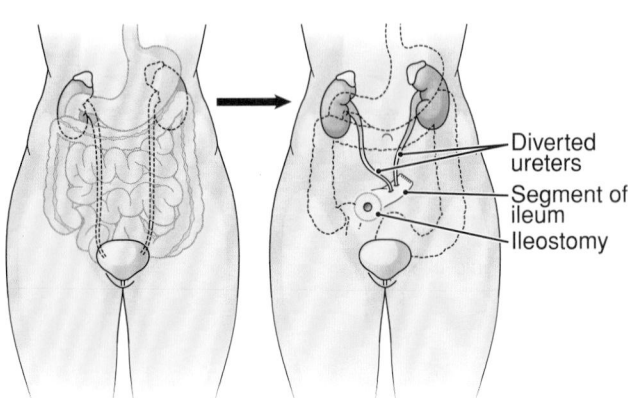

Figure 13-11 **Ileal conduit.** In this surgery, the ureters are vented to the body surface through the ileum when the bladder is removed or nonfunctional.

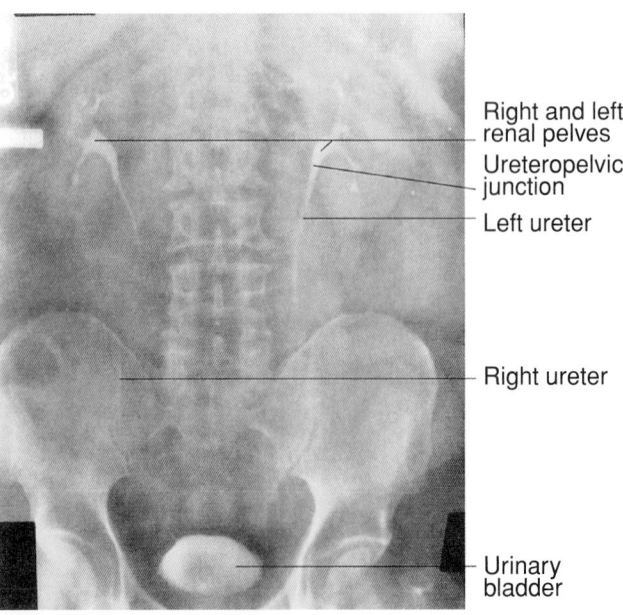

Figure 13-12 **Intravenous urogram.** The image shows the renal pelvis, ureters, and urinary bladder.

| Terminology | Key Terms |

Disorders

acidosis *as-ih-DO-sis*	Excessive acidity of body fluids
acute renal failure	Loss of kidney function resulting from damage to the nephrons; causes may be injury, shock, toxins, or infections, among others
bacteriuria *bak-te-re-U-re-ah*	Presence of bacteria in the urine
cast	A solid mold of a renal tubule found in the urine
cystitis *sis-TI-tis*	Inflammation of the urinary bladder, usually as a result of infection
dysuria *dis-U-re-ah*	Painful or difficult urination
glomerulonephritis *glo-mer-u-lo-nef-RI-tis*	Inflammation of the kidney, primarily involving the glomeruli; the acute form usually occurs after an infection elsewhere in the body; the chronic form varies in cause and usually leads to renal failure
hematuria *he-mat-U-re-ah*	Presence of blood in the urine
hydronephrosis *hi-dro-nef-RO-sis*	Collection of urine in the renal pelvis caused by obstruction; results in distention and renal atrophy
hypokalemia *hi-po-kah-LE-me-ah*	Deficiency of potassium in the blood
hyponatremia *hi-po-nah-TRE-me-ah*	Deficiency of sodium in the blood
hypoproteinemia *hi-po-pro-te-NE-me-ah*	Decreased amount of protein in the blood; may be caused by kidney damage resulting in protein loss
hyperkalemia *hi-per-kah-LE-me-ah*	Excess amount of potassium in the blood
hypernatremia *hi-per-nah-TRE-me-ah*	Excess amount of sodium in the blood
nephrotic syndrome *nef-ROT-ik*	Condition that results from glomerular damage leading to loss of protein in the urine (proteinuria); there is low plasma protein (hypoproteinemia), edema, and increased blood lipids as the liver releases lipoproteins; also called nephrosis
oliguria *ol-ig-U-re-ah*	Elimination of small amounts of urine
proteinuria *pro-te-NU-re-ah*	Presence of protein, mainly albumin, in the urine
pyelonephritis *pi-eh-lo-neh-FRI-tis*	Inflammation of the renal pelvis and kidney, usually caused by infection
pyuria *pi-U-re-ah*	Presence of pus in the urine
renal colic *KOL-ik*	Radiating pain in the region of the kidney associated with the passage of a stone
uremia *u-RE-me-ah*	Presence of toxic levels of urea and other nitrogenous substances in the blood as a result of renal insufficiency

(continued)

Terminology   Key Terms *(Continued)*

urethritis *u-re-THRI-tis*	Inflammation of the urethra, usually due to infection
urinary stasis *STA-sis*	Stoppage of urine flow; urinary stagnation

Diagnosis and Treatment

catheterization *kath-eh-ter-ih-ZA-shun*	Introduction of a tube into a passage, such as through the urethra into the bladder for withdrawal of urine (see **Fig. 13-5**)
cystoscope *SIS-to-skope*	An instrument for examining the interior of the urinary bladder; also used for removing foreign objects, for surgery, and for other forms of treatment
dialysis *di-AL-ih-sis*	Separation of substances by passage through a semipermeable membrane; dialysis is used to rid the body of unwanted substances when the kidneys are impaired or missing; the two forms of dialysis are hemodialysis and peritoneal dialysis
hemodialysis *he-mo-di-AL-ih-sis*	Removal of unwanted substances from the blood by passage through a semipermeable membrane (see **Fig. 13-6**)
intravenous pyelography (IVP) *pi-eh-LOG-rah-fe*	Intravenous urography (see **Fig. 13-12**)
intravenous urography (IVU) *u-ROG-rah-fe*	Radiographic visualization of the urinary tract after intravenous administration of a contrast medium that is excreted in the urine; also called excretory urography or intravenous pyelography, although the latter is less accurate because the procedure shows more than just the renal pelvis
lithotripsy *LITH-o-trip-se*	Crushing of a stone (see **Fig. 13-9**)
peritoneal dialysis *per-ih-to-NE-al di-AL-ih-sis*	Removal of unwanted substances from the body by introduction of a dialyzing fluid into the peritoneal cavity followed by removal of the fluid (see **Fig. 13-7**)
retrograde pyelography *RET-ro-grade pi-eh-LOG-rah-fe*	Pyelography in which the contrast medium is injected into the kidneys from below by way of the ureters
specific gravity (SG)	The weight of a substance compared with the weight of an equal volume of water; the specific gravity of normal urine ranges from 1.015 to 1.025; this value may increase or decrease in disease
urinalysis (UA) *u-rih-NAL-ih-sis*	Laboratory study of the urine; physical and chemical properties and microscopic appearance are included

Surgery

cystectomy *sis-TEK-to-me*	Surgical removal of all or part of the urinary bladder
ileal conduit *IL-e-al KON-du-it*	Diversion of urine by connection of the ureters to an isolated segment of the ileum; one end of the segment is sealed, and the other drains through an opening in the abdominal wall (see **Fig. 13-11**); a procedure used when the bladder is removed or nonfunctional; also called ileal bladder
lithotomy *lith-OT-o-me*	Incision of an organ to remove a stone (calculus)
renal transplantation	Surgical implantation of a donor kidney into a patient

Go to the Audio Pronunciation Glossary in the Student Resources on thePoint to hear these words pronounced.

| Terminology | **Supplementary Terms** |

Normal Structure and Function

aldosterone *al-DOS-ter-one*	A hormone secreted by the adrenal gland that regulates electrolyte excretion by the kidneys
clearance	The volume of plasma that the kidneys can clear of a substance per unit of time; renal plasma clearance
creatinine *kre-AT-in-in*	A nitrogenous byproduct of muscle metabolism; an increase in blood creatinine is a sign of renal failure
detrusor muscle *de-TRU-sor*	The muscle in the bladder wall
glomerular filtration rate (GFR)	The amount of filtrate formed per minute by both kidneys
maximal transport capacity (Tm)	The maximum rate at which a given substance can be transported across the renal tubule; tubular maximum
renal corpuscle *KOR-pus-l*	The glomerular capsule and the glomerulus considered as a unit; the filtration device of the kidney

Symptoms and Conditions

anuresis *an-u-RE-sis*	Lack of urination
anuria *an-U-re-ah*	Lack of urine formation
azotemia *az-o-TE-me-ah*	Presence of increased nitrogenous waste, especially urea, in the blood
azoturia *az-o-TU-re-ah*	Presence of increased nitrogenous compounds, especially urea, in the urine
cystocele *SIS-to-sele*	Herniation of the bladder into the vagina (see **Fig. 15-12**); vesicocele
dehydration *de-hi-DRA-shun*	Excessive loss of body fluids
diabetes insipidus *di-ah-BE-teze in-SIP-id-us*	A condition caused by inadequate production of antidiuretic hormone, resulting in excessive excretion of dilute urine and extreme thirst
enuresis *en-u-RE-sis*	Involuntary urination, usually at night; bed-wetting
epispadias *ep-ih-SPA-de-as*	A congenital condition in which the urethra opens on the dorsal surface of the penis as a groove or cleft; anaspadias
glycosuria *gli-ko-SU-re-ah*	Presence of glucose in the urine, as in cases of diabetes mellitus
horseshoe kidney	A congenital union of the lower poles of the kidneys, resulting in a horseshoe-shaped organ (**Fig. 13-13**)
hydroureter *hi-dro-u-RE-ter*	Distention of the ureter with urine due to obstruction
hypospadias *hi-po-SPA-de-as*	A congenital condition in which the urethra opens on the undersurface of the penis or into the vagina (**Fig. 13-14**)

(continued)

Terminology | Supplementary Terms (*Continued*)

hypovolemia *hi-po-vo-LE-me-ah*	A decrease in blood volume
neurogenic bladder *nu-ro-JEN-ik*	Any bladder dysfunction that results from a central nervous system lesion
nocturia *nok-TU-re-ah*	Excessive urination at night (root: noct/o means "night")
polycystic kidney disease *pol-e-SIS-tik*	A hereditary condition in which the kidneys are enlarged and contain many cysts (**Fig. 13-15**)
polydipsia *pol-e-DIP-se-ah*	Excessive thirst
polyuria *pol-e-U-re-ah*	Elimination of large amounts of urine, as in diabetes mellitus
retention of urine	Accumulation of urine in the bladder because of an inability to urinate
staghorn calculus	A kidney stone that fills the renal pelvis and calices to give a "staghorn" appearance (**Fig. 13-16**)
ureterocele *u-RE-ter-o-sele*	A cyst-like dilation of the ureter near its opening into the bladder; usually results from a congenital narrowing of the ureteral opening (**Fig. 13-17**)
urinary frequency	A need to urinate often without an increase in average output
urinary incontinence *in-KON-tin-ens*	Inability to retain urine; may originate with a neurologic disorder, trauma to the spinal cord, weakness of the pelvic muscles, urinary retention, or impaired bladder function; in urgency incontinence, an urge causes sudden urination before one has enough time to reach a bathroom; in stress incontinence, urine leaks during a forceful activity such as coughing, sneezing, or exercise
urinary urgency	Sudden need to urinate
water intoxication *in-tok-sih-KA-shun*	Excess intake or retention of water with decrease in sodium concentration; may result from excess drinking, excess ADH, or replacement of a large amount of body fluid with pure water; causes an imbalance in the cellular environment, with edema and other disturbances; also called hyponatremia
Wilms tumor	A malignant kidney tumor that usually appears in children before the age of 5 years

Diagnosis

anion gap *AN-i-on*	A measure of electrolyte imbalance
blood urea nitrogen (BUN)	Nitrogen in the blood in the form of urea; an increase in BUN indicates an increase in nitrogenous waste products in the blood and renal failure
clean-catch specimen	A urine sample obtained after thorough cleansing of the urethral opening and collection in midstream to minimize the chance of contamination
cystometrography *sis-to-meh-TROG-rah-fe*	A study of bladder function in which the bladder is filled with fluid or air and the pressure exerted by the bladder muscle at varying degrees of filling is measured; the tracing recorded is a cystometrogram
protein electrophoresis (PEP)	Laboratory study of urinary proteins; used to diagnose multiple myeloma, systemic lupus erythematosus, and lymphoid tumor
urinometer *u-rih-NOM-eh-ter*	Device for measuring the specific gravity of urine

| Terminology | **Supplementary Terms** (*Continued*) |

Treatment

| indwelling Foley catheter | A urinary tract catheter with a balloon at one end that prevents the catheter from leaving the bladder (see **Fig. 13-5**) |
| lithotrite
LITH-o-trite | Instrument for crushing a bladder stone |

Go to the Audio Pronunciation Glossary in the Student Resources on thePoint to hear these words pronounced.

13

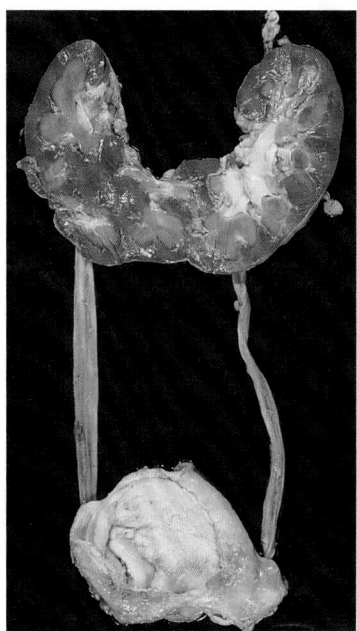

Figure 13-13 **Horseshoe kidney.** The photograph shows the kidneys fused at the poles.

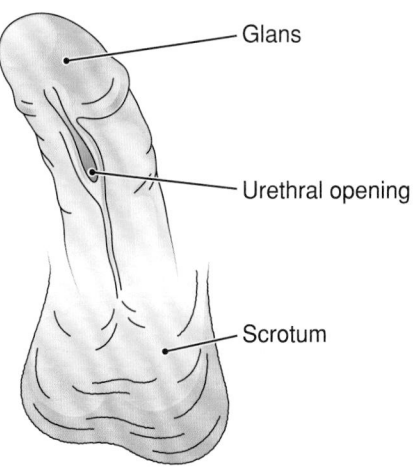

Glans

Urethral opening

Scrotum

Figure 13-14 **Hypospadias.** The urethra is shown opening on the ventral surface of the penis.

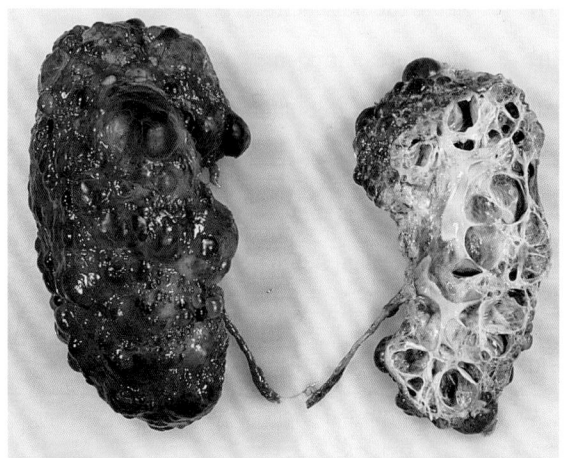

Figure 13-15 **Adult polycystic disease.** The kidney is enlarged, and the active tissue is almost entirely replaced by cysts of varying size. (*Left*) Surface view. (*Right*) Longitudinal section.

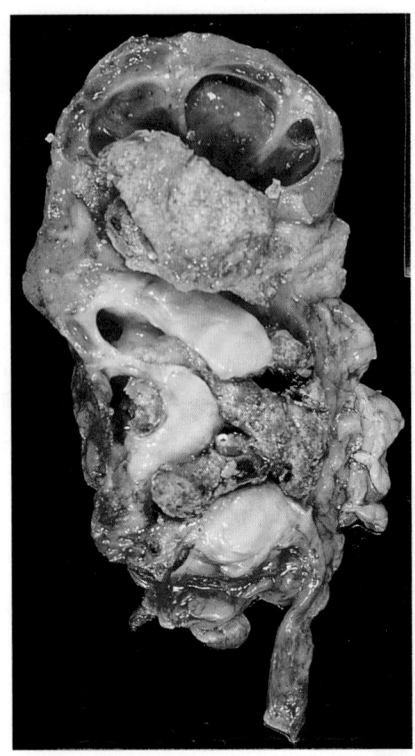

Figure 13-16 **Staghorn calculus.** The kidney shows hydro-nephrosis and stones that are casts of the dilated calices.

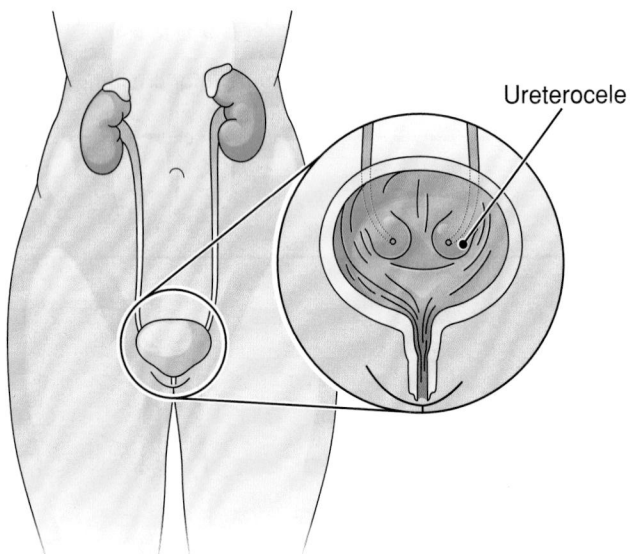

Ureterocele

Figure 13-17 **Ureterocele.** The ureter bulges into the bladder. The resulting obstruction causes urine to reflux into the ureter (hydroureter) and renal pelvis (hydronephrosis).

Terminology   Abbreviations

ACE	Angiotensin-converting enzyme		GFR	Glomerular filtration rate
ADH	Antidiuretic hormone		GU	Genitourinary
ARF	Acute renal failure		IVP	Intravenous pyelography
ATN	Acute tubular necrosis		IVU	Intravenous urography
BUN	Blood urea nitrogen		K	Potassium
CAPD	Continuous ambulatory peritoneal dialysis		KUB	Kidney-ureter-bladder (radiography)
CCPD	Continuous cyclic peritoneal dialysis		Na	Sodium
CMG	Cystometrography; cystometrogram		PEP	Protein electrophoresis
CRF	Chronic renal failure		SG	Specific gravity
EPO	Erythropoietin		Tm	Maximal transport capacity
ESRD	End-stage renal disease		UA	Urinalysis
ESWL	Extracorporeal shock-wave lithotripsy		UTI	Urinary tract infection

Case Study Revisited

E.O.'s Follow-Up Study

E.O. had excellent results from the implanted autograft of muscle cells. There was no retention of urine, and the incontinence and urgency had all but disappeared.

After a year, E.O. continued to experience about a 95 percent success rate from her stress incontinence and had a much improved quality of life score.

13

CHAPTER

13 Review

Labeling Exercise

URINARY SYSTEM

Write the name of each numbered part on the corresponding line.

Adrenal gland Renal artery
Aorta   Renal vein
Diaphragm   Ureter
Inferior vena cava Urethra
Kidney   Urinary bladder

1. _____

2. _____

3. _____

4. _____

5. _____

6. _____

7. _____

8. _____

9. _____

10. _____

THE KIDNEY

Write the name of each numbered part on the corresponding line.

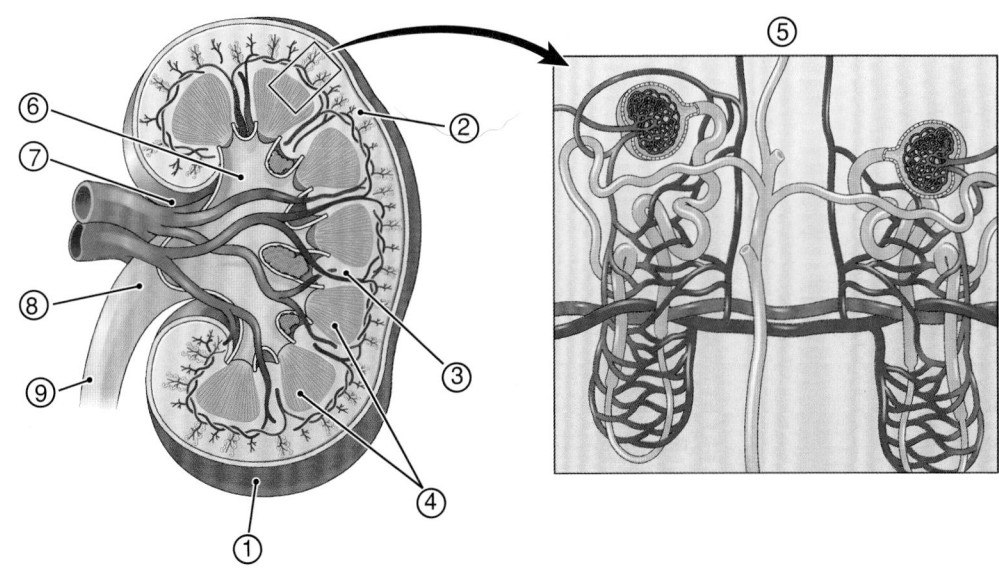

Calyx
Hilum
Nephrons
Pyramids of medulla
Renal capsule

Renal medulla
Renal pelvis
Renal cortex
Ureter

1. _____
2. _____
3. _____
4. _____
5. _____

6. _____
7. _____
8. _____
9. _____

THE URINARY BLADDER

Write the name of each numbered part on the corresponding line.

External urethral sphincter
Internal urethral sphincter
Openings of ureters
Peritoneum
Prostate

Smooth muscle
Trigone
Ureter
Urethra

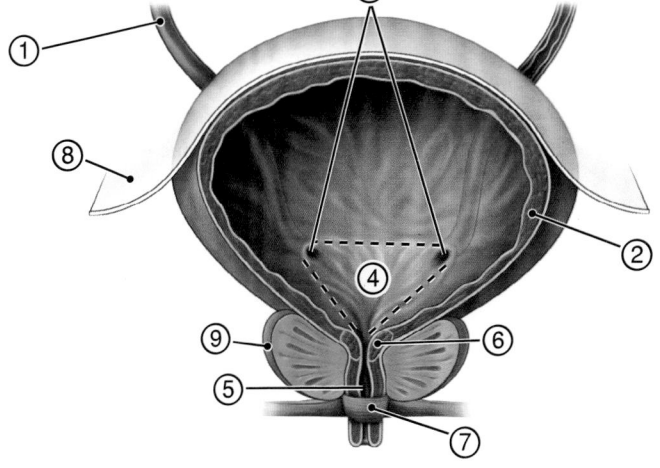

1. _____
2. _____
3. _____
4. _____
5. _____
6. _____
7. _____
8. _____
9. _____

Terminology

MATCHING

Match the following terms, and write the appropriate letter to the left of each number.

_____	**1.** hematuria	**a.**	blood in the urine
_____	**2.** oliguria	**b.**	proteinuria
_____	**3.** chromaturia	**c.**	elimination of small amounts of urine
_____	**4.** albuminuria	**d.**	abnormal color of urine
_____	**5.** pyuria	**e.**	pus in the urine

_____	**6.** renal cortex	**a.**	absence of a bladder
_____	**7.** nephron	**b.**	stagnation, as of urine
_____	**8.** stasis	**c.**	deficiency of urine
_____	**9.** acystia	**d.**	kidney's outer portion
_____	**10.** uropenia	**e.**	microscopic functional unit of the kidney

Supplementary Terms

_____	**11.** aldosterone	**a.**	amount of filtrate formed per minute by the kidney
_____	**12.** diabetes insipidus	**b.**	condition caused by lack of ADH
_____	**13.** incontinence	**c.**	nitrogenous metabolic waste
_____	**14.** glomerular filtration rate	**d.**	hormone that regulates electrolytes
_____	**15.** creatinine	**e.**	inability to retain urine

_____	**16.** polydipsia	**a.**	excessive thirst
_____	**17.** enuresis	**b.**	bed-wetting
_____	**18.** azoturia	**c.**	presence of excess nitrogenous waste in the urine
_____	**19.** anuresis	**d.**	congenital misplacement of the ureteral opening
_____	**20.** hypospadias	**e.**	lack of urination

FILL IN THE BLANKS

21. Collection of urine in the renal pelvis is a result of obstruction _____ .

22. The cluster of capillaries within the glomerular capsule is the _____ .

23. An enzyme released by the kidneys that acts to increase blood pressure is _____ .

24. Micturition is the scientific term for _____ .

25. Laboratory study of the urine is a(n) _____ .

26. The main nitrogenous waste product in urine is _____ .

Refer to E.O.'s opening case study.

27. E.O.'s inability to retain urine is termed urinary _____ .

28. A midstream urine sample collected after thorough cleansing of the urethral opening is called a(n) _____ .

29. Endoscopic examination of the urinary bladder is termed _____ .

SPELL CHECK

Write the correct spelling on the line to the right of the term.

30. cathater _____

31. uretha _____

32. dysurea _____

33. calysx _____

34. cystoceal _____

35. hypercalemia _____

36. intravesicle _____

TRUE–FALSE

Examine the following statements. If the statement is true, write T in the first blank. If the statement is false, write F in the first blank, and correct the statement by replacing the underlined word in the second blank.

	True or False	**Correct Answer**
37. A reniform structure is shaped like the <u>bladder</u>.	_____	_____
38. Pyelitis is inflammation of the <u>renal pelvis</u>.	_____	_____
39. A nephrotropic substance acts on the <u>kidney</u>.	_____	_____
40. The inner portion of the kidney is the <u>cortex</u>.	_____	_____
41. The tube that carries urine out of the body is the <u>ureter</u>.	_____	_____
42. EPO stimulates the production of <u>red blood cells</u>.	_____	_____
43. A lithotomy is an incision to remove a <u>calculus</u>.	_____	_____
44. Natriuresis refers to the excretion of <u>potassium</u> in the urine.	_____	_____

DEFINITIONS

Define the following words.

45. urethrostenosis (*u-re-thro-steh-NO-sis*) _____

46. polyuria (*pol-e-U-re-ah*) _____

47. nephrotoxic (*nef-ro-TOK-sik*) _____

48. juxtaglomerular (*juks-tah-glo-MER-u-lar*) _____

49. calicectomy (*kal-ih-SEK-to-me*) _____

50. pararenal (*par-ah-RE-nal*) _____

Write a word for the following definitions.

51. Physician who specializes in the kidney (nephr/o) _____

52. Dilatation of the renal pelvis and calices _____

53. Softening of a kidney (nephr/o) _____

54. Incision of the bladder (cyst/o) _____

55. Any disease of the kidney (nephr/o) _____

56. Radiograph of the bladder (cyst/o) and urethra _____

57. Plastic repair of a ureter and renal pelvis _____

58. Inflammation of the renal pelvis and the kidney _____

59. Surgical creation of an opening between a ureter and the sigmoid colon _____

ELIMINATIONS

In each of the sets below, underline the word that does not fit in with the rest and explain the reason for your choice.

60. capsule — cast — pyramid — nephron — cortex

_____

61. nephron loop — distal convoluted tubule — glomerular capsule — calyx — proximal convoluted tubule

_____

62. ileal conduit — specific gravity — dialysis — cystoscopy — lithotripsy

_____

OPPOSITES

Write a word that means the opposite of the following.

63. dehydration   _____

64. hypovolemia   _____

65. diuretic   _____

66. hyponatremia   _____

67. uresis   _____

ADJECTIVES

Write the adjective form of the following.

68. ureter   _____

69. nephrology   _____

70. uremia   _____

71. diuresis   _____

72. nephrosis   _____

73. calyx   _____

74. urethra   _____

PLURALS

Write the plural form of the following.

75. pelvis   _____

76. calyx   _____

77. glomerulus   _____

FOLLOW THE FLOW

Describing the pathway of urine flow, put the following steps in the correct order by placing the letters "A" through "G" in the space provided.

_____ **78.** Fluid or glomerular filtrate enters the nephron

_____ **79.** Urine flows into the collecting ducts to be eliminated

_____ **80.** Urine flows from the ureters to the bladder

_____ **81.** Tubular reabsorption, or return process of nutrients, water, and electrolytes, occurs

_____ **82.** Blood flows through the glomerulus

_____ **83.** Urine is drained from the renal pelvis to the ureters

_____ **84.** Urine flows from the bladder to the urethra

WORD BUILDING

Write a word for the following definitions using the word parts given.

| graph- | ren/o | -al | intra- | vesic/o | -y | ur/o | inter- | lith | log | supra- |

85. radiographic study of the urinary tract _____

86. pertaining to the kidney _____

87. within the kidney _____

88. radiographic study of the kidney _____

89. within the bladder _____

90. above the kidney _____

91. study of the urinary tract _____

92. between the kidneys _____

93. pertaining to the bladder _____

94. a urinary tract stone _____

ABBREVIATIONS

Write the meaning of the following abbreviations.

95. SG _____

96. ADH _____

97. EPO _____

98. IVP _____

99. Na _____

100. GFR _____

101. UA _____

WORD ANALYSIS

Define the following words, and give the meaning of the word parts in each. Use a dictionary if necessary.

102. hemodialysis (*he-mo-di-AL-ih-sis*) _____

    a. hem/o _____

    b. dia- _____

    c. lysis _____

103. cystometrography (*sis-to-meh-TROG-rah-fe*) _____

    a. cyst/o _____

    b. metr/o _____

    c. -graphy _____

104. ureteroneocystostomy (*u-re-ter-o-ne-o-sis-TOS-to-me*) _____

    a. ureter/o _____

    b. neo- _____

    c. cyst/o _____

    d. -stomy _____

For more learning activities, see Chapter 13 of the Student Resources on thePoint.

Additional Case Studies

Case Study 13-1: *Renal Calculi*

A.A., a 48-year-old woman, was admitted to the inpatient unit from the ER with severe right flank pain unresponsive to analgesics. Her pain did not decrease with administration of 100 mg of IV meperidine. She had a three-month history of chronic UTI. Six months ago, she had been prescribed calcium supplements for low bone density. Her gynecologist warned her that calcium could be a problem for people who are "stone formers." A.A. was unaware that she might be at risk. An IV urogram showed a right staghorn calculus. The diagnosis was further confirmed by a renal ultrasound. A renal flow scan showed normal perfusion and no obstruction. Kidney function was 37 percent on the right and 63 percent on the left. The pain became intermittent, and A.A. had no hematuria, dysuria, frequency, urgency, or nocturia. Urinalysis revealed no albumin, glucose, bacteria, or blood; there was evidence of cells, crystals, and casts.

A.A. was transferred to surgery for a cystoscopic ureteral laser lithotripsy, insertion of a right retrograde ureteral catheter, and right percutaneous nephrolithotomy. A ureteral calculus was fragmented with a pulsed-dye laser. Most of the staghorn was removed from the renal pelvis with no remaining stone in the renal calices. She was discharged two days later and ordered to strain her urine for the next week for evidence of stones.

Case Study 13-2: *End-Stage Renal Disease*

M.C., a 20 YO part-time college student, has had chronic glomerulonephritis since age 7. He has been treated at home with CAPD for the past 16 months as he awaits kidney transplantation. His doctor advised him to go immediately to the ER when he reported chest pain, shortness of breath, and oliguria. On admission, M.C. was placed on oxygen and given a panel of blood tests and an ECG to rule out an acute cardiac episode. His hemoglobin was 8.2, and his hematocrit was 26 percent. He had bilateral lung rales. ABGs were: pH, 7.0; Pa_{CO_2}, 28; Pa_{O_2}, 50; HCO_3, 21. His BUN, serum creatinine, and BUN/creatinine ratio were abnormally high. His ECG and liver enzyme studies were normal. His admission diagnosis was ESRD, fluid overload, and metabolic acidosis. He was typed and crossed for blood; tested for HIV, hepatitis B antigen, and sexually transmitted disease; and sent to hemodialysis. A bed was reserved for him on the transplant unit.

Case Study Questions

Multiple Choice. Select the best answer, and write the letter of your choice to the left of each number.

_____ **1.** The term *perfusion* means
  a. metabolism
  b. size
  c. passage of fluid
  d. surrounding tissue

_____ **2.** The term *percutaneous* means
  a. under the skin
  b. on the surface
  c. with a catheter
  d. through the skin

_____ **3.** M.C.'s chronic glomerulonephritis means that he has had
  a. long-term kidney stones
  b. an acute bout of kidney infection
  c. short-term bladder inflammation
  d. a long-term kidney infection

_____ **4.** Renal dialysis can be performed by shunting venous blood through a dialysis machine and returning the blood to the patient's arterial system. This procedure is called
  a. hemodialysis
  b. arteriovenous transplant
  c. CAPD
  d. glomerular filtration rate

Write a term from the case studies with the following meanings.

5. Intravenous injection of contrast dye and radiographic study of the urinary tract _____

6. Presence of blood in the urine _____

7. Referring to endoscopy of the urinary bladder _____

8. Surgical incision for removal of a kidney stone _____

9. Production of a reduced amount of urine _____

10. Getting up to go to the bathroom at night _____

11. Crushing a stone _____

12. Kidney replacement _____

Abbreviations. Define the following abbreviations.

13. UTI _____

14. CAPD _____

15. BUN _____

16. ESRD _____

17. HIV _____

13

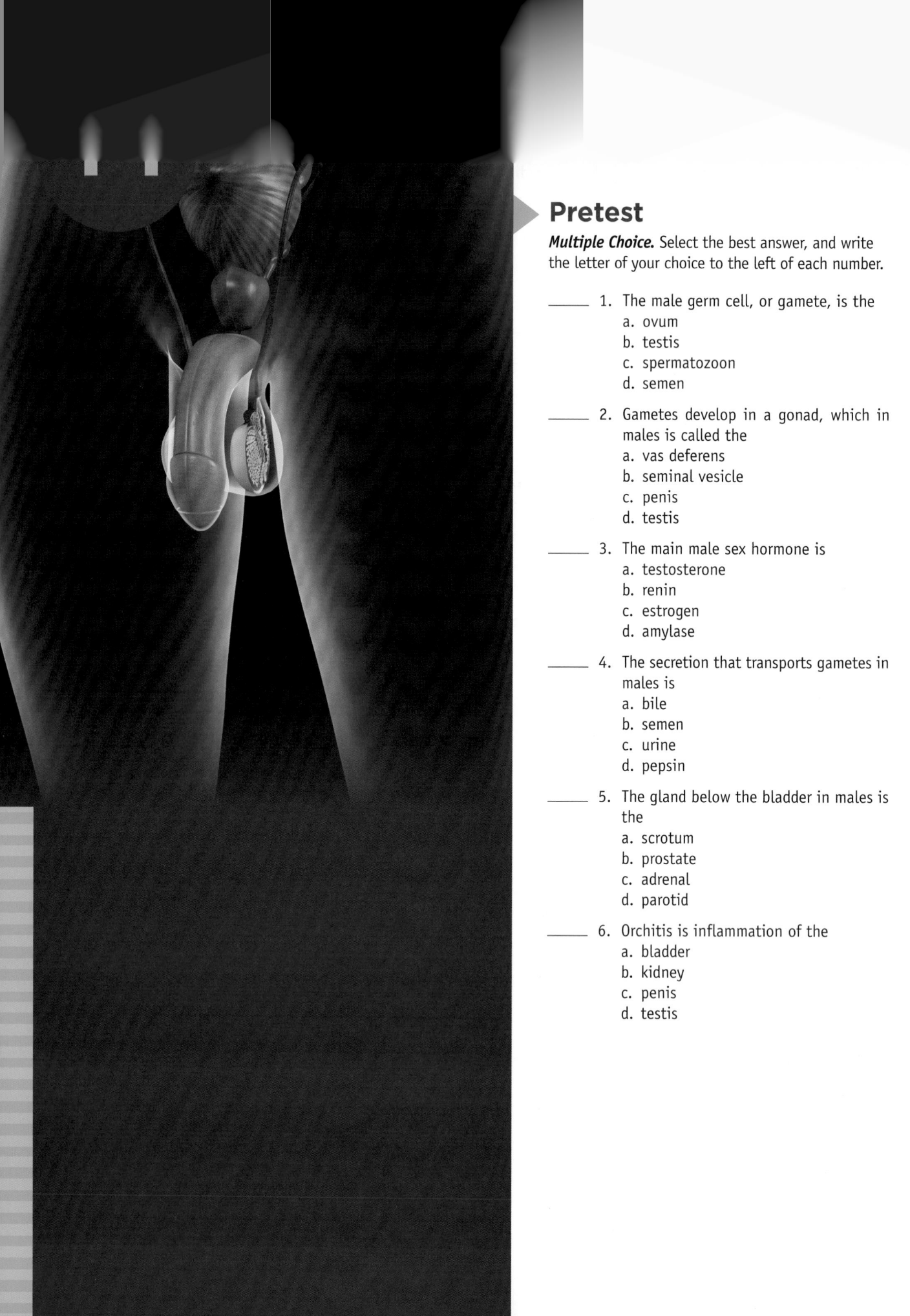

Pretest

Multiple Choice. Select the best answer, and write the letter of your choice to the left of each number.

_____ 1. The male germ cell, or gamete, is the
  a. ovum
  b. testis
  c. spermatozoon
  d. semen

_____ 2. Gametes develop in a gonad, which in males is called the
  a. vas deferens
  b. seminal vesicle
  c. penis
  d. testis

_____ 3. The main male sex hormone is
  a. testosterone
  b. renin
  c. estrogen
  d. amylase

_____ 4. The secretion that transports gametes in males is
  a. bile
  b. semen
  c. urine
  d. pepsin

_____ 5. The gland below the bladder in males is the
  a. scrotum
  b. prostate
  c. adrenal
  d. parotid

_____ 6. Orchitis is inflammation of the
  a. bladder
  b. kidney
  c. penis
  d. testis

Learning Objectives

After study of this chapter, you should be able to:

1 ▶ Describe the organs of the male reproductive tract, and give the function of each part. *p334*

2 ▶ Follow spermatozoa from their development in the testis to their release. *p334*

3 ▶ Describe the contents and functions of semen. *p336*

4 ▶ Identify and use roots pertaining to the male reproductive system. *p338*

5 ▶ Describe six main disorders of the male reproductive system. *p340*

6 ▶ Interpret abbreviations used in referring to the male reproductive system. *p346*

7 ▶ Analyze medical terms in several case studies concerning the male reproductive system. *pp333, 352*

Case Study: *C.S.'s Benign Prostatic Hyperplasia and TURP*

Chief Complaint

C.S., a 60-year-old teacher, was having a decreased force of his urine stream and ejaculation, hesitancy, and sensation of incomplete bladder emptying. He had tried using prostate-health herbal supplements without any real benefit for two years. He decided to make an appointment with a urologist.

Examination

The urologist took a history and examined the patient. C.S. reported no dysuria, hematuria, or flank pain. He had no history of UTI, epididymitis, prostatitis, renal disease, or renal calculi. His medical history was otherwise not significant to his urologic complaint.

Rectal examination revealed a 50-g prostate with slight firmness in the right prostatic lobe. The physician ordered a bladder ultrasound, which was performed later that week. The results indicated no intravesical lesions or prostate protrusion into the bladder base.

A transabdominal ultrasound was ordered and showed a residual urine volume of 120 mL. A urinalysis revealed normal values except for the following: WBC = 8; RBC = 10; bacteria = trace.

C.S. was diagnosed with benign prostatic hyperplasia (BPH) with bladder neck obstruction and was scheduled for a transurethral resection of the prostate (TURP). His urologist explained the procedure and what to expect pre- and postoperatively. The office staff notified the hospital to schedule the surgery. The next day, the hospital admissions department called C.S., went through normal admissions procedures, and scheduled a surgery date.

Clinical Course

C.S. was NPO the night before the surgery. He was taken to the operating room and was given a spinal anesthetic for the procedure. It had already been explained to him that the surgery would take about an hour and that he would be awake during the procedure but would not feel any pain. A resectoscope was used to trim the enlarged prostatic tissue. At the end of the surgery, a Foley catheter was inserted into the bladder and left in place to drain the urine and permit irrigation of the bladder to remove any clots. C.S. tolerated the procedure well and was transferred to the recovery room and later to his hospital room. He was encouraged to drink plenty of fluids postoperatively.

ANCILLARIES *At-A-Glance*

Visit thePoint to access the following resources. For guidance in using the resources most effectively, see pp. ix–xvi.

Learning RESOURCES

▶ **Tips for Effective Studying**
▶ **Web Figure: Microscopic View of the Testis**
▶ **Web Chart: Reproductive Hormones**
▶ **Audio Pronunciation Glossary**

Learning ACTIVITIES

▶ **Visual Activities**
▶ **Kinesthetic Activities**
▶ **Auditory Activities**

Introduction

The function of the **gonads** (sex glands) in both males and females is to produce the reproductive cells, the **gametes**, and to produce hormones. The gametes are generated by **meiosis**, a process of cell division that halves the chromosome number from 46 to 23. When male and female gametes unite in fertilization, the original chromosome number is restored.

Sex hormones aid in the manufacture of gametes, function in pregnancy and lactation, and also produce the secondary sex characteristics such as the typical size, shape, body hair, and voice that we associate with the male and female genders.

The reproductive tract develops in close association with the urinary tract. In females, the two systems become completely separate, whereas the male reproductive and urinary tracts share a common passage, the **urethra**. Thus, the two systems are referred together as the genitourinary (GU) or urogenital (UG) tract, and urologists are called on to treat disorders of the male reproductive system as well as those of the urinary system.

The Testes

The male germ cells, the sperm cells or **spermatozoa** (singular: spermatozoon), are produced in the paired **testes** (singular: testis) that are suspended outside of the body in the **scrotum** (**Fig. 14-1**). Although the testes develop in the abdominal cavity, they normally descend through the **inguinal canal** into the scrotum before birth or shortly thereafter (**Fig. 14-2**).

From the start of sexual maturation, or **puberty**, spermatozoa form continuously within the testes in coiled seminiferous tubules (**Fig. 14-3**). Their development requires the aid of special **Sertoli cells** and male sex hormones, or **androgens**, mainly **testosterone**. These hormones are manufactured in **interstitial cells** located between the tubules. In both males and females, the gonads are stimulated by **follicle-stimulating hormone (FSH)** and **luteinizing hormone (LH)**, released from the anterior **pituitary gland** beneath the brain. These hormones are chemically the same in males and females, although they are named for their actions in female reproduction. In males, FSH stimulates the Sertoli cells and promotes the formation of spermatozoa. LH stimulates the interstitial cells to produce testosterone.

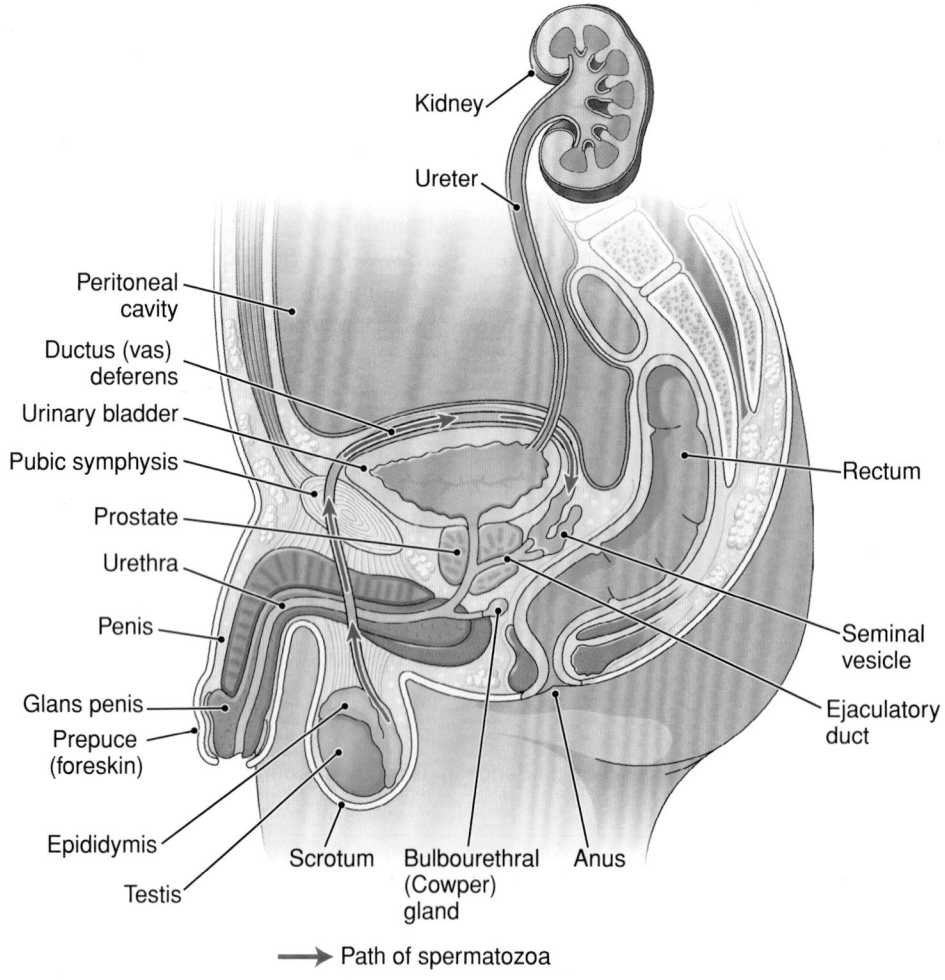

→ Path of spermatozoa

Figure 14-1 **Male reproductive system.** Parts of the urinary system and digestive system are also shown.

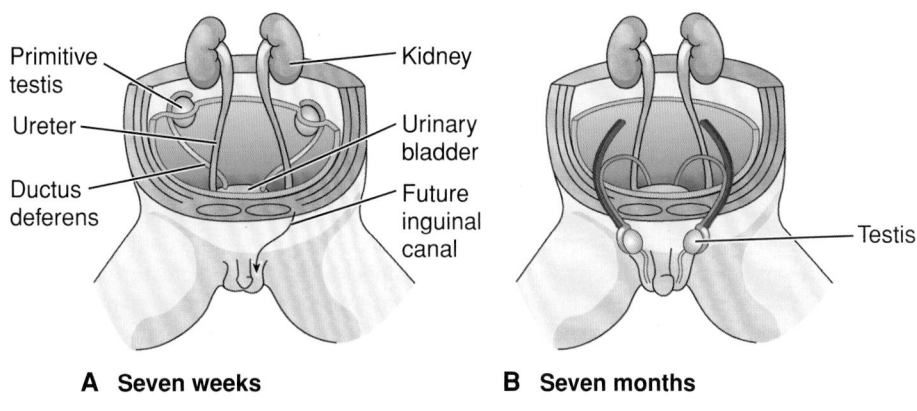

A Seven weeks

B Seven months

C Nine months

Figure 14-2 **Descent of the testes.** Drawings show formation of the inguinal canals and descent of the testes at three different times during fetal development. **A.** At 7 weeks, the testis is in the dorsal abdominal wall. **B.** At 7 months, the testis is passing through the inguinal canal. **C.** At 9 months, the testis is in the scrotum, suspended by the spermatic cord.

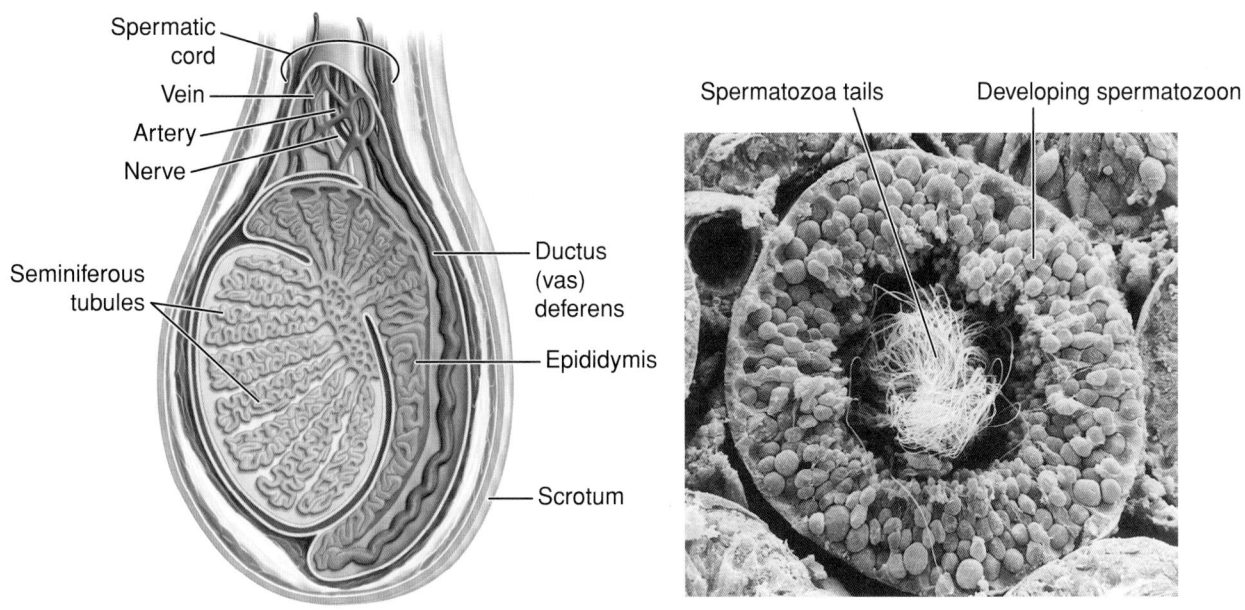

A The testes and scrotal sac

B Micrograph of seminiferous tubule

Figure 14-3 **The testis.** **A.** The testis in position in the scrotum showing the structure of the seminiferous tubules. The epididymis and spermatic cord are also shown. **B.** Spermatozoa develop within the seminiferous tubules in the testis.

14

Some of the work of learning medical terminology is made more difficult by the fact that many structures and processes are known by two or even more names. This duplication may occur because different names have been assigned at different times or places or because the name is in a state of transition to another name, and the new one has not been universally accepted.

The tube that leads from the testis to the urethra in males was originally called the vas deferens, *vas* being a general term for *vessel*. To distinguish this tube from a blood vessel, efforts have been made to change the name to ductus deferens. However, the original name has lingered because the surgical procedure used to sterilize a man is still called a vasectomy and not a "ductusectomy."

Similar inconsistencies appear in other systems. Dorsal is also posterior; ventral could be anterior. Human growth hormone is also called somatotropin. ADH, a hormone that increases blood pressure, is also known as vasopressin.

In the nervous system, the little swellings at the ends of axons that contain neurotransmitters are variously called end-feet, end-bulbs, terminal knobs, terminal feet, and even other names. In a woman, the tube that carries the ovum from the ovary to the uterus is referred to as the uterine tube, or maybe the Fallopian tube...or the oviduct...or...

See the microscopic view of the testis and the chart on reproductive hormones in the Student Resources on thePoint.

Transport of Spermatozoa

After their manufacture, sperm cells are stored in a much-coiled tube on the surface of each testis, the **epididymis** (see **Figs. 14-1** and **14-3**). Here, they remain until **ejaculation** propels them into a series of ducts that lead out of the body. The first of these is the **ductus (vas) deferens**, which is contained in the **spermatic cord** along with nerves and blood vessels that supply the testis (see **Figs. 14-2** and **14-3**). The spermatic cord ascends through the inguinal canal into the abdominal cavity, where the ductus deferens leaves the cord and travels behind the bladder. (See **Box 14-1**, which discusses how alternative names can be a challenge to learning medical terminology.)

A short continuation of the ductus deferens, the **ejaculatory duct**, delivers spermatozoa to the urethra as it passes through the **prostate gland** below the bladder. Finally, the cells, now mixed with other secretions, travel in the urethra through the penis to be released (see **Fig. 14-1**).

The Penis

The penile urethra transports both urine and **semen**. The **penis** is the male organ of sexual intercourse, or **coitus**. It is composed of three segments of spongy tissue, which become engorged with blood to produce an **erection**, a stiffening of the penis. As shown in **Figure 14-4**, the two corpora cavernosa are lateral bodies; the corpus spongiosum, through which the urethra travels, is in the center. The corpus spongiosum enlarges at the tip to form the **glans penis**, which is covered by loose skin—the **prepuce**, or foreskin. Surgery to remove the foreskin is **circumcision**. This may be performed for medical reasons but is most often performed electively in male infants for reasons of hygiene, cultural preferences, or religion.

Formation of Semen

Semen is the thick, whitish fluid that transports spermatozoa. It contains, in addition to sperm cells, secretions from three types of accessory glands (see **Fig. 14-1**). Following the sequence of sperm transport, these are:

1. The paired **seminal vesicles**, which release their secretions into the ejaculatory duct on each side.
2. The **prostate gland**, which secretes into the first part of the urethra beneath the bladder. As men age, prostatic enlargement may compress the urethra and cause urinary problems.
3. The two **bulbourethral** (Cowper) **glands**, which secrete into the urethra just below the prostate gland.

Together, these glands produce a slightly alkaline mixture that nourishes and transports the sperm cells and also protects them by neutralizing the acidity of the female vaginal tract.

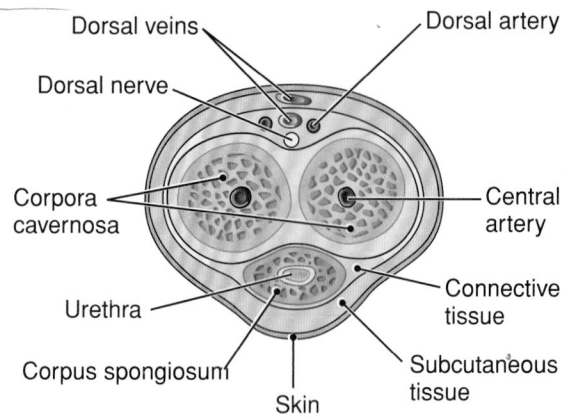

Dorsal veins — Dorsal artery
Dorsal nerve
Corpora cavernosa — Central artery
Urethra
Corpus spongiosum
Skin
Connective tissue
Subcutaneous tissue

Figure 14-4 **The penis.** This cross section shows the erectile bodies of the penis (corpora cavernosa and corpus spongiosum), the centrally located urethra, as well as blood vessels and a nerve.

Terminology	Key Terms

androgen AN-dro-jen	Any hormone that produces male characteristics (root andr/o means "male")
bulbourethral gland bul-bo-u-RE-thral	A small gland beside the urethra below the prostate that secretes part of the seminal fluid; also called Cowper gland
circumcision ser-kum-SIH-zhun	Surgical removal of the end of the prepuce (foreskin)
coitus KO-ih-tus	Sexual intercourse
ductus deferens DUK-tus DEF-er-enz	The duct that conveys spermatozoa from the epididymis to the ejaculatory duct; also called vas deferens
ejaculation e-jak-u-LA-shun	Ejection of semen from the male urethra
ejaculatory duct e-JAK-u-lah-tor-e	The duct formed by union of the ductus deferens and the duct of the seminal vesicle; it carries spermatozoa and seminal fluid into the urethra
epididymis ep-ih-DID-ih-mis	A coiled tube on the surface of the testis that stores sperm until ejaculation (root: epididym/o)
erection e-REK-shun	The stiffening or hardening of the penis or the clitoris, usually because of sexual excitement
follicle-stimulating hormone (FSH)	A hormone secreted by the anterior pituitary that acts on the gonads; in males, FSH stimulates Sertoli cells and promotes sperm cell development
gamete GAM-ete	A mature reproductive cell, the spermatozoon in the male and the ovum in the female
glans penis glanz PE-nis	The bulbous end of the penis
gonad GO-nad	A sex gland; testis or ovary
inguinal canal ING-gwin-al	The channel through which the testis descends into the scrotum in the male
interstitial cells in-ter-STISH-al	Cells located between the seminiferous tubules of the testes that produce hormones, mainly testosterone; also called cells of Leydig (LI-dig)
luteinizing hormone (LH) LU-te-in-i-zing	A hormone secreted by the anterior pituitary that acts on the gonads; in males, it stimulates the interstitial cells to produce testosterone
meiosis mi-O-sis	The type of cell division that forms the gametes; it results in cells with 23 chromosomes, half the number found in other body cells (from the Greek word meiosis meaning "diminution")
penis PE-nis	The male organ of copulation and urination (adjective: penile)
pituitary gland pih-TU-ih-tar-e	An endocrine gland at the base of the brain
prepuce PRE-pus	The fold of skin over the glans penis; the foreskin
prostate gland PROS-tate	A gland that surrounds the urethra below the bladder in males and contributes secretions to the semen (root: prostat/o)
puberty PU-ber-te	Period during which the ability for sexual reproduction is attained and secondary sex characteristics begin to develop
scrotum SKRO-tum	A double pouch that contains the testes (root: osche/o)

(contin

Terminology	**Key Terms** (*Continued*)

semen	The thick secretion that transports spermatozoa (roots: semin, sperm/i, spermat/o)
seminal vesicle *SEM-ih-nal VES-ih-kl*	A sac-like gland behind the bladder that contributes secretions to the semen (root: vesicul/o)
Sertoli cell *ser-TO-le*	Cell in a seminiferous tubule that aids in the development of spermatozoa; sustentacular (*sus-ten-TAK-u-lar*) cell
spermatic cord *sper-MAT-ik*	Cord attached to the testis that contains the ductus deferens, blood vessels, and nerves enclosed within a fibrous sheath (see **Fig. 14-3**)
spermatozoon *sper-mah-to-ZO-on*	Mature male sex cell (plural: spermatozoa) (roots: sperm/i, spermat/o)
testis *TES-tis*	The male reproductive gland (roots: test/o, orchi/o, orchid/o); plural is testes (*TES-teze*); also called testicle
testosterone *tes-TOS-ter-one*	The main male sex hormone
urethra *u-RE-thrah*	The duct that carries urine out of the body and also transports semen in the male
vas deferens *DEF-er-enz*	The duct that conveys spermatozoa from the epididymis to the ejaculatory duct; also called ductus deferens

Go to the Audio Pronunciation Glossary in the Student Resources on thePoint to hear these terms pronounced.

Roots Pertaining to Male Reproduction

See Table 14-1.

Table 14-1	**Roots for Male Reproduction**

Root	Meaning	Example	Definition of Example
test/o	testis, testicle	testosterone *tes-TOS-teh-rone*	hormone produced in the testis
orchi/o, orchid/o	testis	anorchism *an-OR-kizm*	absence of a testis
osche/o	scrotum	oscheal *OS-ke-al*	pertaining to the scrotum
semin	semen	inseminate *in-SEM-ih-nate*	to introduce semen into a vagina
sperm/i, spermat/o	semen, spermatozoa	polyspermia *pol-e-SPER-me-ah*	secretion of excess semen
epididym/o	epididymis	epididymitis *ep-ih-did-ih-MI-tis*	inflammation of the epididymis
vas/o	vas deferens, ductus deferens; also vessel	vasostomy *vas-OS-to-me*	surgical creation of an opening in the ductus deferens
vesicul/o	seminal vesicle	vesiculogram *veh-SIK-u-lo-gram*	radiograph of a seminal vesicle
prostat/o	prostate	prostatometer *pros-tah-TOM-eh-ter*	instrument for measuring the prostate

EXERCISE 14-1

Define the following words.

1. spermatogenesis (*sper-mah-to-JEN-eh-sis*) _____

2. prostatodynia (*pros-tah-to-DIN-e-ah*) _____

3. oscheoplasty (*os-ke-o-PLAS-te*) _____

4. epididymectomy (*ep-ih-did-ih-MEK-to-me*) _____

5. orchialgia (*or-ke-AL-je-ah*) _____

6. testopathy (*tes-TOP-ah-the*) _____

7. orchiepididymitis (*or-ke-ep-ih-did-ih-MI-tis*) _____

Use the root *orchi/o* to write a word for the following definitions. Each is also written with the root *orchid/o*.

8. surgical fixation of a testis _____

9. plastic repair of a testis _____

10. surgical removal of a testis _____

Use the root *spermat/o* to write a word for the following definitions.

11. Condition of having sperm in the urine (-uria) _____

12. Destruction (-lysis) of sperm _____

13. Excessive discharge (-rhea) of semen _____

14. Subnormal concentration of sperm in semen _____

15. A sperm-forming cell _____

The ending *-spermia* means "condition of sperm or semen." Add a prefix to *-spermia* to form a word for the following definitions.

16. presence of blood in the semen _____

17. lack of semen _____

18. secretion of excess (poly/o) semen _____

19. presence of pus in the semen _____

Write a word for the following definitions.

20. excision of the ductus deferens _____

21. tumor of the scrotum _____

22. suture of the vas deferens _____

23. excision of the prostate gland _____

24. radiographic study of a seminal vesicle _____

25. inflammation of a seminal vesicle _____

26. incision of the epididymis _____

Clinical Aspects of the Male Reproductive System

INFECTION

Most infections of the male reproductive tract are **sexually transmitted infections (STIs)**, listed in **Box 14-2**. The most common STI in the United States is caused by the bacterium *Chlamydia trachomatis*, which mainly causes **urethritis** in males. This same organism also causes lymphogranuloma venereum, an STI associated with lymphadenopathy, which occurs most commonly in tropical regions. Both forms of these chlamydial infections respond to treatment with antibiotics.

Gonorrhea is caused by *Neisseria gonorrhoeae*, the gonococcus (GC). Infection usually centers in the urethra, causing urethritis with burning, a purulent discharge, and dysuria. Untreated, the disease can spread through the reproductive system. Gonorrhea is treated with antibiotics, but gonococci can rapidly develop resistance to these drugs.

Another common STI is herpes infection, caused by a virus. Other STIs are discussed in Chapter 15.

Mumps is a nonsexually transmitted viral disease that can infect the testes and lead to **sterility**. Other microorganisms can infect the reproductive tract as well, causing urethritis, **prostatitis**, **orchitis**, or **epididymitis**.

BENIGN PROSTATIC HYPERPLASIA

As men age, the prostate gland commonly enlarges, a condition known as **benign prostatic hyperplasia (BPH)**, as noted in C.S.'s opening case study. Although not cancerous, this overgrown tissue can press on the urethra near the bladder and interfere with urination. Urinary retention, infection,

---

FOR YOUR REFERENCE — Box 14-2

Sexually Transmitted Infections

Disease	Organism	Description
BACTERIAL		
chlamydial infection	*Chlamydia trachomatis* types D to K	Ascending infection of reproductive and urinary tracts; may spread to pelvis in women, causing pelvic inflammatory disease (PID)
lymphogranuloma venereum	*Chlamydia trachomatis* type L	General infection with swelling of inguinal lymph nodes; scarring of genital tissue
gonorrhea	*Neisseria gonorrhoeae*; gonococcus (GC)	Inflammation of reproductive and urinary tracts; urethritis in men; vaginal discharge and cervical inflammation (cervicitis) in women, leading to pelvic inflammatory disease (PID); possible systemic infection; may spread to newborns; treated with antibiotics
bacterial vaginosis	*Gardnerella vaginalis*	Vaginal infection with foul-smelling discharge
syphilis	*Treponema pallidum* (a spirochete)	Primary stage: chancre (lesion); secondary stage: systemic infection and syphilitic warts; tertiary stage: degeneration of other systems; cause of spontaneous abortions, stillbirths, and fetal deformities; treated with antibiotics
VIRAL		
AIDS (acquired immunodeficiency syndrome)	HIV (human immunodeficiency virus)	A disease that infects T cells of the immune system, weakening the host and leading to other diseases: usually fatal if untreated
genital herpes	herpes simplex virus (HSV)	Painful genital lesions; in women, may be a risk factor in cervical carcinoma; often fatal infections of newborns; no cure at present
hepatitis B	hepatitis B virus (HBV)	Causes liver inflammation, which may be acute or may develop into a chronic carrier state; linked to liver cancer
condyloma acuminatum (genital warts)	human papillomavirus (HPV)	Benign genital warts; in women, predisposes to cervical dysplasia and carcinoma; a vaccine against the most prevalent strains is available
PROTOZOAL		
trichomoniasis	*Trichomonas vaginalis*	Vaginitis; green, frothy discharge with itching, pain on intercourse (dyspareunia), and painful urination (dysuria)

and other complications may follow if an obstruction is not corrected.

Medications to relax smooth muscle in the prostate and bladder neck are used to treat the symptoms of BPH. Alpha-adrenergic blocking agents interfere with sympathetic nervous stimulation in these regions to improve urinary flow rate. One example is tamsulosin (Flomax). Because testosterone stimulates enlargement of the prostate, drugs that interfere with prostatic testosterone activity may slow the disorder's progress. One example is finasteride (Proscar). An herbal remedy that seems to act in this same manner is an extract of the berries of the saw palmetto, a low-growing palm tree. Saw palmetto has been found to delay the need for surgery in some cases of BPH.

In advanced cases of BPH, removal of the prostate, or **prostatectomy**, may be required. When this is performed through the urethra, the procedure is called a transurethral resection of the prostate (TURP) (**Fig. 14-5A**). The prostate may also be cut in a transurethral incision of the prostate (TUIP) to reduce pressure on the urethra (**Fig. 14-5B**). Surgeons also use a laser beam or heat to destroy prostatic tissue. BPH is diagnosed by digital rectal examination (DRE) or imaging studies.

CANCER

Cancer of the Prostate

Prostatic cancer is the most common malignancy among men in the United States. Only lung cancer and colon cancer cause more cancer-related deaths in men who are past middle age. Physicians can often detect prostatic cancer by

DRE. Blood tests for prostate-specific antigen (PSA) may also help in early detection. This protein is produced in increased amounts in cases of prostatic cancer, although it may increase in other prostatic disorders as well.

The TNM system for staging prostate cancer includes the following categories:

- T_1: tumor not palpable by rectal examination; detected by biopsy or abnormal PSA
- T_2: tumor palpable and confined to the prostate
- T_3: tumor has spread locally beyond the prostate
- M: distant metastases

Treatment methods include surgery (prostatectomy); radiation; inhibition of male hormones (androgens), which stimulate prostatic growth; and chemotherapy. Radiation is usually delivered by implantation of radioactive seeds. Another approach is termed "watchful waiting" or deferred therapy, which consists of monitoring without therapy. Choice of this option is based on a man's age, tumor invasiveness, and the probability that an untreated tumor will result in harm to a patient during his lifetime.

Testicular Cancer

Cancer of the testis represents less than 1 percent of cancer in adult males. It usually appears between the ages of 25 and 45 years and shows no sign of genetic inheritance. This cancer typically originates in germ cells and can spread to abdominal lymph nodes. More than half of testicular tumors release markers that can be detected in the blood. Treatment may include removal of the testis (orchiectomy), radiation, and chemotherapy.

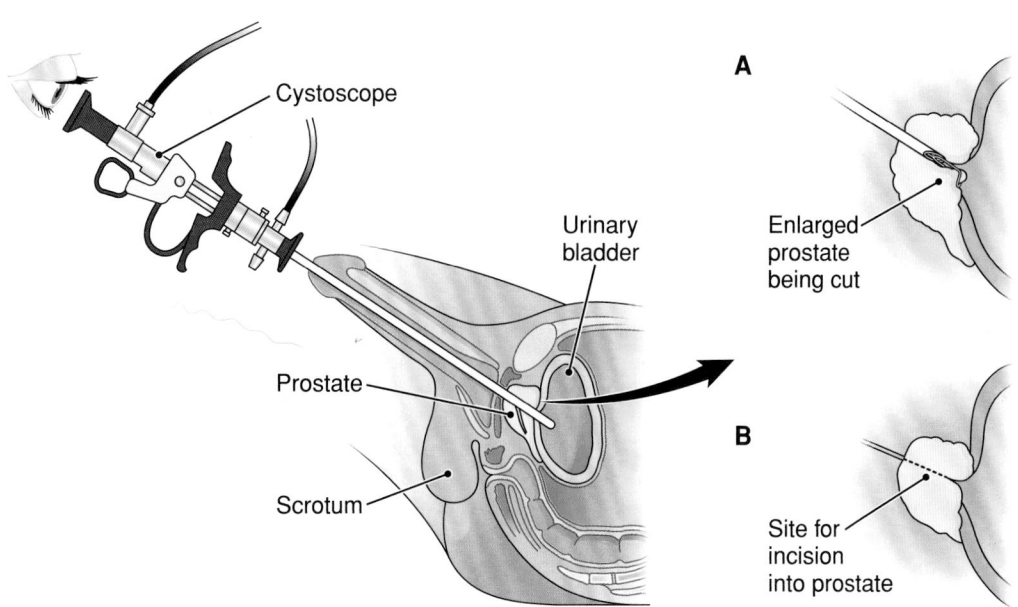

Figure 14-5 **Prostate surgery procedures. A.** Transurethral resection of the prostate (TURP). Portions of the prostate are removed at the bladder opening. **B.** Transurethral incision of the prostate (TUIP). One or two incisions are made in the prostate to reduce pressure on the urethra.

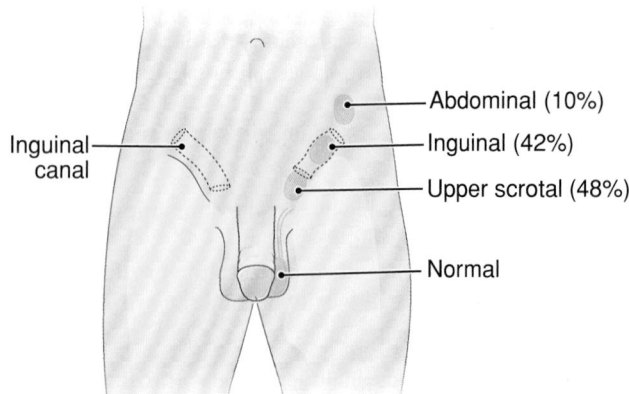

Figure 14-6 **Cryptorchidism.** The testis fails to descend into the scrotum. In most cases, the testis is retained in the upper part of the scrotal sac or in the inguinal canal. The percentages of different locations are shown.

CRYPTORCHIDISM

It is fairly common that one or both testes will fail to descend into the scrotum by the time of birth (**Fig. 14-6**). This condition is termed **cryptorchidism**, literally hidden (crypt/o) testis (orchid/o). The condition usually corrects itself within the first year of life. If not, it must be corrected surgically to avoid sterility and an increased risk of cancer.

INFERTILITY

An inability or a diminished ability to reproduce is termed **infertility**. Its causes may be hereditary, hormonal, disease-related, or the result of exposure to chemical or physical agents. The most common causes of infertility are STIs. A total inability to produce offspring may be termed sterility. Men may be voluntarily sterilized by cutting and sealing the vas deferens on both sides in a **vasectomy** (**Fig. 15-5**).

Erectile Dysfunction

Erectile dysfunction (ED), also called **impotence**, is the inability of the male to perform intercourse because of failure to initiate or maintain an erection until ejaculation. About 10 to 20 percent of such cases are psychogenic, that is, caused by emotional factors, such as stress, depression, or emotional trauma. More often, ED has a physical cause, which may be:

- A vascular disorder such as arteriosclerosis, varicose veins, or damage caused by diabetes.
- A neurologic problem, as caused by a tumor, trauma, the effects of diabetes, or damage caused by radiation or surgery.
- A side effect of a drug, such as an antihypertensive agent, antiulcer medication, or appetite suppressant.

Drugs that are used to treat ED work by dilating arteries in the penis to increase blood flow to that organ. Nondrug approaches include corrective surgery; vacuum pumps to draw blood into the penis; penile injections to dilate blood vessels; and penile prostheses. **Box 14-3** has more information on ED.

Physician assistants aid in patient examination and care in urology and many other medical and surgical fields. **Box 14-4** describes careers in this specialty.

INGUINAL HERNIA

The inguinal canal, through which the testis descends, may constitute a weakness in the abdominal wall that can lead to a hernia. In the most common form of **inguinal hernia** (**Fig. 14-7**), an abdominal organ, usually the intestine, enters the inguinal canal and may extend into the scrotum. This is an indirect, or external, inguinal hernia. In a direct, or internal, inguinal hernia, the organ protrudes through the abdominal wall into the scrotum. If blood supply to the organ is cut off, the hernia is said to be *strangulated*. Surgery to correct a hernia is a **herniorrhaphy**.

CLINICAL PERSPECTIVES

Box 14-3

Treating Erectile Dysfunction

Approximately 25 million American men and their partners are affected by ED, the inability to achieve or maintain an erection. Although ED is more common in men over the age of 65, it can occur at any age and can have many causes.

Erection results from an interaction between the autonomic nervous system and penile blood vessels. Sexual arousal stimulates parasympathetic nerves in the penis to release a compound called nitric oxide (NO). This substance activates an enzyme in vascular smooth muscle that promotes vasodilation, increasing blood flow into the penis and causing erection. Physical factors that cause ED prevent these physiologic changes.

Drugs that target the physiologic mechanisms of erection are helping men who suffer from ED. These include sildenafil (trade name, Viagra), vardenafil (Levitra), and tadalafil (Cialis). These drugs prevent the breakdown of vasodilators, thus prolonging the effects of NO. Although effective in about 80 percent of ED cases, these drugs can cause some relatively minor side effects, including headache, nasal congestion, stomach upset, and blue-tinged vision. They should never be used by men who are taking nitrate drugs to treat angina. Because nitrates elevate NO levels, taking them with drugs for ED and prolonging the effects of NO can cause life-threatening hypotension. They are also contraindicated in men with low blood pressure and heart failure.

HEALTH PROFESSIONS
Physician Assistant

Physician assistants (PAs) practice medicine under the supervision of physicians and surgeons. They are trained in diagnosis, therapy, and preventive healthcare. They are also licensed to treat minor injuries. In almost all states, they are permitted to prescribe medications. Depending on the work setting, they may also manage a practice and supervise other medical personnel. In medically underserved areas, they may work under their own direction and confer with physicians as needed. Many PAs work in general, pediatric, or family medicine practices. If they specialize in surgery, they may provide patient care before and after an operation or assist in surgery.

A PA must complete a formal six-year educational program, four years of undergraduate work, and a two-year master's degree. The majority of PA programs require candidates to enter with a bachelor's degree, core science courses, and clinical experience either in the military or some other allied health field. After successful completion of a didactic year and a year of clinical rotations, PAs must be licensed by passing a national exam. They may also become certified (PA-C) through the National Commission on Certification of Physician Assistants (NCCPA) and maintain that certification by continuing education. The job outlook is very good, especially as hospitals are required to compensate for shorter medical residents' shifts by increasing staffing with PAs. Also, medical personnel can consult with ease via telecommunication, allowing for physical independence at certain practices. For additional information, contact the American Academy of Physician Assistants at www.aapa.org.

14

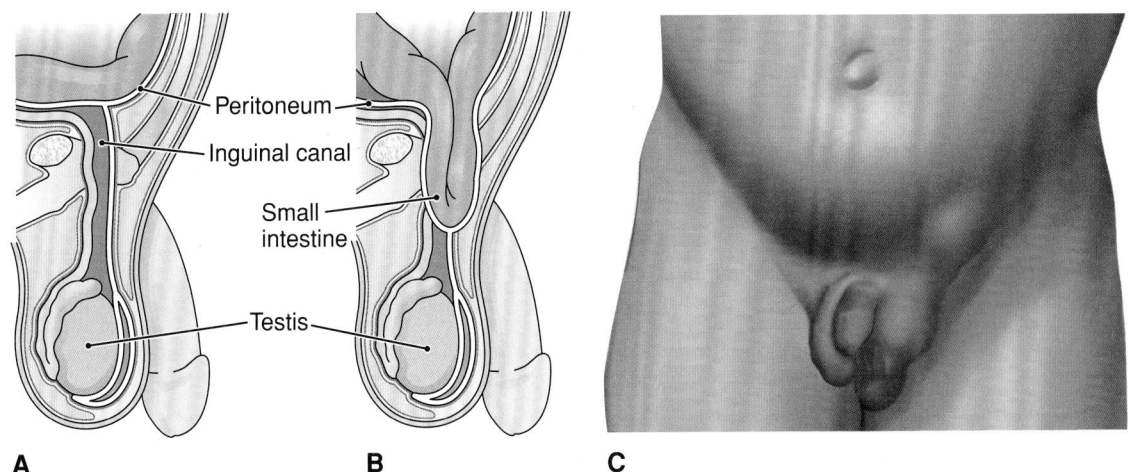

A   **B**   **C**

Figure 14-7 **Inguinal hernia. A.** Normal. **B.** Weakness in the abdominal wall allows the intestine or other abdominal contents to protrude into the inguinal canal. The hernial sac is a continuation of the peritoneum. **C.** An inguinal hernia can cause a visible bulge in the inguinal area and scrotum.

Terminology Key Terms

Disorders

benign prostatic hyperplasia (BPH)	Nonmalignant enlargement of the prostate; frequently develops with age; also called benign prostatic hypertrophy
cryptorchidism *krip-TOR-kid-izm*	Failure of the testis to descend into the scrotum (see **Fig. 14-6**)
epididymitis *ep-ih-did-ih-MI-tis*	Inflammation of the epididymis; common causes are UTIs and STIs
erectile dysfunction (ED) *eh-REK-tile dis-FUNK-shun*	Inability of the male to perform intercourse because of failure to initiate or maintain an erection until ejaculation; impotence

(continued)

Terminology | Key Terms (Continued)

impotence IM-po-tens	Erectile dysfunction
infertility in-fer-TIL-ih-te	Decreased capacity to produce offspring
inguinal hernia ING-gwin-al	Protrusion of the intestine or other abdominal organ through the inguinal canal (see **Fig. 14-7**) or through the wall of the abdomen into the scrotum
orchitis or-KI-tis	Inflammation of a testis; may be caused by injury, mumps virus, or other infections
prostatitis pros-tah-TI-tis	Inflammation of the prostate gland; often appears with UTI, STI, and a variety of other stresses
sexually transmitted infection (STI)	Infection spread through sexual activity (see **Box 14-2**); also called sexually transmitted disease (STD) and formerly venereal (veh-NE-re-al) disease (VD) (from Venus, the goddess of love)
sterility steh-RIL-ih-te	Complete inability to produce offspring
urethritis u-re-THRI-tis	Inflammation of the urethra; often caused by gonorrhea and chlamydia infections

Surgery

herniorrhaphy her-ne-OR-ah-fe	Surgical repair of a hernia
prostatectomy pros-tah-TEK-to-me	Surgical removal of the prostate
vasectomy vah-SEK-to-me	Excision of the vas deferens; usually done bilaterally to produce sterility (see **Fig. 15-5**); may be accomplished through the urethra (transurethral resection)

Terminology | Supplementary Terms

Normal Structure and Function

emission e-MISH-un	The discharge of semen
genitalia jen-ih-TA-le-ah	The organs concerned with reproduction, divided into internal and external components
insemination in-sem-ih-NA-shun	Introduction of semen into a woman's vagina
orgasm OR-gazm	A state of physical and emotional excitement, especially that which occurs at the climax of sexual intercourse
phallus FAL-us	The penis (adjective: phallic)

Disorders

balanitis bal-ah-NI-tis	Inflammation of the glans penis and mucous membrane beneath it (root balan/o means "glans penis")

Terminology   Supplementary Terms *(Continued)*

bladder neck obstruction (BNO)	Blockage of urine flow at the outlet of the bladder; the common cause is benign prostatic hyperplasia
hydrocele *HI-dro-sele*	The accumulation of fluid in a sac-like cavity, especially within the covering of the testis or spermatic cord (**Fig. 14-8**)
phimosis *fi-MO-sis*	Narrowing of the prepuce's opening so that the foreskin cannot be pushed back over the glans penis
priapism *PRI-ah-pizm*	Abnormal, painful, continuous erection of the penis, as may be caused by drugs or specific damage to the spinal cord
seminoma *sem-ih-NO-mah*	A tumor of the testis
spermatocele *SPER-mah-to-sele*	An epididymal cyst containing spermatozoa (see **Fig. 14-8**)
varicocele *VAR-ih-ko-sele*	Enlargement of the veins of the spermatic cord (see **Fig. 14-8**)

Diagnosis and Treatment

brachytherapy *brak-e-THER-ah-pe*	Radiation therapy by placement of encapsulated radiation sources, such as seeds, directly into a tumor or nearby tissue (from Greek *brachy*, meaning "short")
castration *kas-TRA-shun*	Surgical removal of the testes or ovaries; hormones and drugs can inhibit the gonads to produce functional castration
Gleason tumor grade *GLE-son*	A system for assessing the severity of cancerous changes in the prostate; reported as a Gleason score
resectoscope *re-SEK-to-skope*	Endoscopic instrument for transurethral removal of tissue from the urinary bladder, prostate gland, uterus, or urethra
Whitmore–Jewett staging *WIT-more JEW-et*	A method for staging prostatic tumors; an alternate to TNM staging

Go to the Audio Pronunciation Glossary in the Student Resources on thePoint to hear these terms pronounced.

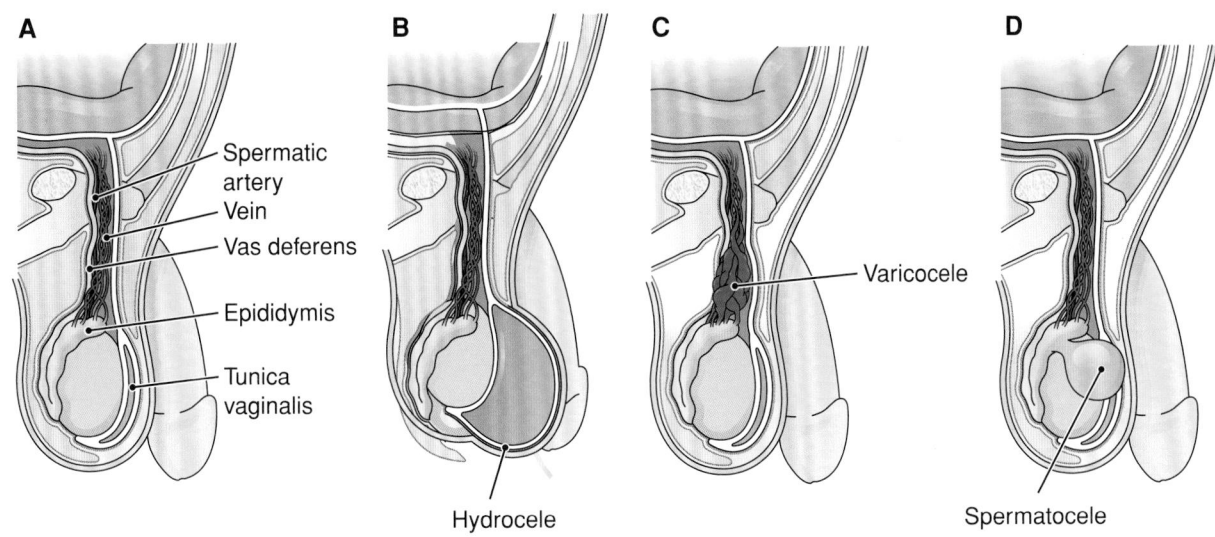

Figure 14-8   **Scrotal abnormalities. A.** Normal. **B.** Hydrocele. **C.** Varicocele. **D.** Spermatocele.

Terminology | Abbreviations

AIDS	Acquired immunodeficiency syndrome	**PSA**	Prostate-specific antigen
BNO	Bladder neck obstruction	**STD**	Sexually transmitted disease
BPH	Benign prostatic hyperplasia (hypertrophy)	**STI**	Sexually transmitted infection
DRE	Digital rectal examination	**TPUR**	Transperineal urethral resection
ED	Erectile dysfunction	**TSE**	Testicular self-examination
FSH	Follicle-stimulating hormone	**TUIP**	Transurethral incision of prostate
GC	Gonococcus	**TURP**	Transurethral resection of prostate
GU	Genitourinary	**UG**	Urogenital
HBV	Hepatitis B virus	**UTI**	Urinary tract infection
HIV	Human immunodeficiency virus	**VD**	Venereal disease (sexually transmitted infection)
HSV	Herpes simplex virus	**VDRL**	Venereal Disease Research Laboratory (test for syphilis)
LH	Luteinizing hormone		
NGU	Nongonococcal urethritis		

Case Study Revisited

C.S.'s Follow-Up

On the morning of the second postoperative day, the Foley catheter was removed, and C.S. was able to void on his own. He experienced dysuria and some burning when urinating, but otherwise did not have any postoperative complications.

He was aware that the painful urination might persist for a few weeks. He remained in the hospital through the second day and then was discharged home with specific instructions. He was to follow up with his urologist in a week.

Labeling Exercise

MALE REPRODUCTIVE SYSTEM

Write the name of each numbered part on the corresponding line.

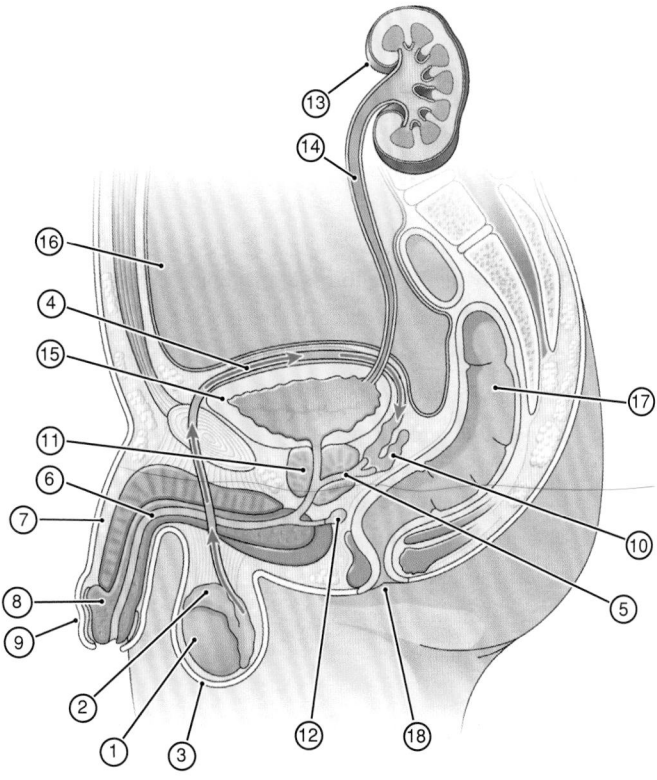

Anus	Kidney	Scrotum
Bulbourethral (Cowper) gland	Penis	Seminal vesicle
Ductus (vas) deferens	Peritoneal cavity	Testis
Ejaculatory duct	Prepuce (foreskin)	Ureter
Epididymis	Prostate	Urethra
Glans penis	Rectum	Urinary bladder

1. _____

2. _____

3. _____

4. _____

5. _____

6. _____

7. _____

8. _____

9. _____

10. _____

11. _____

12. _____

13. _____

14. _____

15. _____

16. _____

17. _____

18. _____

Terminology

MATCHING

Match the following terms, and write the appropriate letter to the left of each number.

_____ **1.** gamete

_____ **2.** androgen

_____ **3.** gonad

_____ **4.** puberty

_____ **5.** meiosis

a. reproductive cell

b. start of sexual maturity

c. hormone that produces male characteristics

d. cell division that forms the gametes

e. sex gland

_____ **6.** vasectomy

_____ **7.** circumcision

_____ **8.** impotence

_____ **9.** glans

_____ **10.** coitus

a. excision of the ductus deferens

b. erectile dysfunction

c. surgical removal of the foreskin

d. end of the penis

e. sexual intercourse

Supplementary Terms

_____ **11.** priapism

_____ **12.** phallic

_____ **13.** genitalia

_____ **14.** phimosis

_____ **15.** seminoma

a. narrowing of the foreskin opening

b. prolonged erection of the penis

c. tumor of the testis

d. reproductive organs

e. pertaining to the penis

_____ **16.** spermatocele

_____ **17.** balanitis

_____ **18.** castration

_____ **19.** emission

_____ **20.** brachytherapy

a. inflammation of the glans penis

b. a form of radiation treatment

c. discharge of semen

d. removal of the testes

e. epididymal cyst

FILL IN THE BLANKS

21. The main male sex hormone is _____ .

22. The two glands that secrete into the urethra just below the prostate gland are the_____ .

23. The thick fluid that transports spermatozoa is _____ .

24. The male gonad is the_____ .

25. The channel through which the testis descends is the _____ .

26. The sac that holds the testis is the_____ .

DEFINITIONS

Define the following terms.

27. vasorrhaphy (*vas-OR-ah-fe*) _____

28. anorchism (*an-OR-kizm*)_____

29. oscheoma (*os-ke-O-mah*)_____

30. vesiculography (*veh-sik-u-LOG-rah-fe*)_____

31. prostatometer (*pros-tah-TOM-eh-ter*) _____

32. hemospermia (*he-mo-SPER-me-ah*) _____

Write a word for the following definitions.

33. surgical fixation of the testis _____

34. stone in the scrotum _____

35. surgical incision of the epididymis _____

36. plastic repair of the scrotum _____

37. surgical creation of an opening between two parts of a cut ductus deferens (done to reverse a vasectomy) _____

Find a word in C.S.'s opening case study for each of the following definitions (see also Chapter 13).

38. blood in the urine _____

39. painful urination _____

40. within the urinary bladder _____

41. overdevelopment of tissue _____

42. instrument for excising tissue _____

SPELL CHECK

Write the correct spelling on the line to the right of the term.

43. testostirone _____

44. semin _____

45. prostrate _____

46. epididimis _____

47. hyospadias _____

TRUE-FALSE

Examine the following statements. If the statement is true, write T in the first blank. If the statement is false, write F in the first blank, and correct the statement by replacing the underlined word in the second blank.

	True or False	Correct Answer
48. Any male sex hormone is an <u>androgen</u>.	_____	_____
49. The adjective *seminal* refers to the <u>seminal vesicle</u>.	_____	_____
50. The spirochete *Treponema pallidum* causes <u>syphilis</u>.	_____	_____
51. Herpes simplex is a <u>virus</u>.	_____	_____
52. The <u>ureter</u> carries both urine and semen in males.	_____	_____
53. FSH and LH are produced by the <u>pituitary gland</u>.	_____	_____
54. Spermatogenesis begins at <u>puberty</u>.	_____	_____

ELIMINATIONS

In each of the sets below, underline the word that does not fit in with the rest, and explain the reason for your choice.

55. bulbourethral gland — prostate — testis — spermatic cord — seminal vesicle

_____

56. FSH — semen — testosterone — androgen — LH

_____

57. condyloma acuminatum — gonorrhea — hernia — AIDS — herpes

_____

ADJECTIVES

Write the adjective form of the following words.

58. semen _____

59. prostate _____

60. penis _____

61. urethra _____

62. scrotum _____

ABBREVIATIONS

Write the meaning of the following abbreviations.

63. BPH _____

64. STI _____

65. ED _____

66. GC _____

67. PSA _____

68. GU _____

69. TURP _____

FOLLOW THE FLOW

Describing the pathway of semen flow, put the following steps in the correct order by placing the letters "A" through "F" in the spaces provided.

_____ **70.** ejaculatory duct delivers sperm to the urethra

_____ **71.** sperm cells, mixed with other secretions, travel through the prostate gland

_____ **72.** sperm cells mix with secretions from the seminal vesicle

_____ **73.** sperm is propelled through ductus deferens

_____ **74.** sperm cells are manufactured and stored in the epididymis

_____ **75.** cells travel in the urethra through the penis to be released

WORD BUILDING

Write a word for the following definitions using the word parts provided.

-ar	-tomy	-graphy	-genesis	spermat/o	vas/o	-plasty	-itis	-ic	-cyte	-lysis	vesicul/o

76. plastic repair of the ductus deferens _____

77. destruction of sperm cells _____

78. pertaining to the seminal vesicle _____

79. x-ray study of the vas deferens _____

80. inflammation of the seminal vesicle _____

81. pertaining to spermatozoa _____

82. cell that develops into a sperm cell _____

83. incision of the ductus deferens _____

84. formation of spermatozoa _____

85. radiographic study of the seminal vesicle _____

WORD ANALYSIS

Define the following words, and give the meaning of the word parts in each. Use a dictionary if necessary.

86. hydrocelectomy (*hi-dro-se-LEK-to-me*) _____

    a. hydr/o _____

    b. -cele _____

    c. ecto- _____

    d. tom/o _____

    e. -y _____

87. spermicidal (*sper-mih-SI-dal*) _____

    a. sperm/i _____

    b. -cide _____

    c. -al _____

88. cryptorchidism (*krip-TOR-kid-izm*) _____

    a. crypt- _____

    b. orchid/o _____

    c. -ism _____

89. vasovesiculitis (*vas-o-veh-sik-u-LI-tis*) _____

    a. vas/o _____

    b. vesicul/o _____

    c. -itis _____

90. polyspermia _____

    a. poly- _____

    b. sperm/o _____

    c. -ia _____

For more learning activities, see Chapter 14 of the Student Resources on thePoint.

Additional Case Studies

Case Study 14-1: *Herniorrhaphy and Vasectomy*

L.D., a 48-year-old married dock worker with three children, had inguinal bulging and pain on exertion when he lifted heavy objects. An occupational health service advised a surgical referral. The surgeon diagnosed L.D. with bilateral direct inguinal hernias and suggested that he not delay surgery, although he was not at high risk for a strangulated hernia. L.D. asked the surgeon if he could also be sterilized at the same time. He was scheduled for bilateral inguinal herniorrhaphy and elective vasectomy.

During the herniorrhaphy procedure, an oblique incision was made in each groin. The incision continued through the muscle layers by either resecting or splitting the muscle fibers. The spermatic vessels and vas deferens were identified, separated, and gently retracted. The spermatic cord was examined for an indirect hernia. Repair began with suturing the defect in the rectus abdominis muscles, transverse fascia, cremaster muscle, external oblique aponeurosis, and Scarpa fascia with heavy-gauge synthetic nonabsorbable suture material.

The vasectomy began with the identification of the vas deferens through the scrotal skin. An incision was made, and the vas was gently dissected and retracted through the opening. Each vas was clamped with a small hemostat, and a 1-cm length was resected. Both cut ends were coagulated with electrosurgery and tied independently with a fine-gauge absorbable suture material. The testicles were examined, and the scrotal incision was closed with an absorbable suture material.

Case Study 14-2: *Erectile Dysfunction*

R.G., a 67-year-old attorney, was at his annual appointment with his internist when he decided to discuss what he considered an embarrassing subject, erectile dysfunction (ED). R.G. was happily married with four grown children and had continued to enjoy an active sexual relationship with his wife, until recently. He was having difficulty sustaining an erection. He had seen so much media publicity on this subject that he decided to bring it up with his physician. At the conclusion of the appointment, the internist ruled out any psychogenic causes or adverse effects of medications, such as an antidepressant or an antihypertensive, that could predispose to ED. He recommended that R.G. schedule a follow-up visit to his urologist to make certain there were no underlying physical factors that would contribute to his impotence.

R.G. made an appointment with the urologist whom he had seen about 10 years ago when he was diagnosed with BPH. At that time, the physician had reviewed various therapies with R.G., so R.G. felt comfortable discussing his present concerns.

The urologist's examination ruled out trauma, vascular disorders, or tumors. It was decided to have R.G. try an ED medication. The physician explained that the impotence agents work by targeting the physiologic mechanisms of erection. They promote vasodilation to increase blood flow to the penis. Side effects of the medications were also discussed. R.G was relieved that he had no tumor or other disease condition. He understood the therapy plan and left with follow-up instructions.

Case Study Questions

Multiple Choice. Select the best answer, and write the letter of your choice to the left of each number.

_____ **1.** The term for male sterilization surgery is
  a. herniorrhaphy
  b. circumcision
  c. vagotomy
  d. vasectomy

_____ **2.** An oblique surgical incision follows which direction?
  a. slanted or angled
  b. superior to inferior
  c. lateral
  d. circumferential

_____ **3.** When the ends of the vas were coagulated with electrosurgery, they were

    a. dilated

    b. sealed

    c. sutured

    d. clamped

_____ **4.** A urologist is a physician who treats health and disease conditions of the

    a. male reproductive system

    b. urinary system

    c. digestive system

    d. a and b

_____ **5.** Impotence is a condition that

    a. precedes a vasectomy

    b. is synonymous with ED

    c. refers to the inability to maintain penile erection

    d. b and c

_____ **6.** BPH is a condition of the prostate gland that

    a. is cancerous

    b. causes impotence

    c. requires vasodilation agents as treatment

    d. may cause urinary retention and infection

_____ **7.** The ED drugs Viagra and Cialis target the physiologic mechanisms of erection by

    a. increasing urinary and semen flow

    b. dilating arteries in the penis to increase blood flow

    c. increasing neurotransmitters to treat underlying psychogenic causes

    d. b and c

14

Write a term from the case studies with the following meanings.

8. surgical repair of a weak abdominal muscle in the groin area on both sides _____

9. entrapment of a bowel loop in a hernia _____

10. inflammation of the glans penis _____

11. narrowing of the distal opening of the foreskin _____

12. originating in the mind _____

13. widening of blood vessels _____

14. drug for treatment of high blood pressure _____

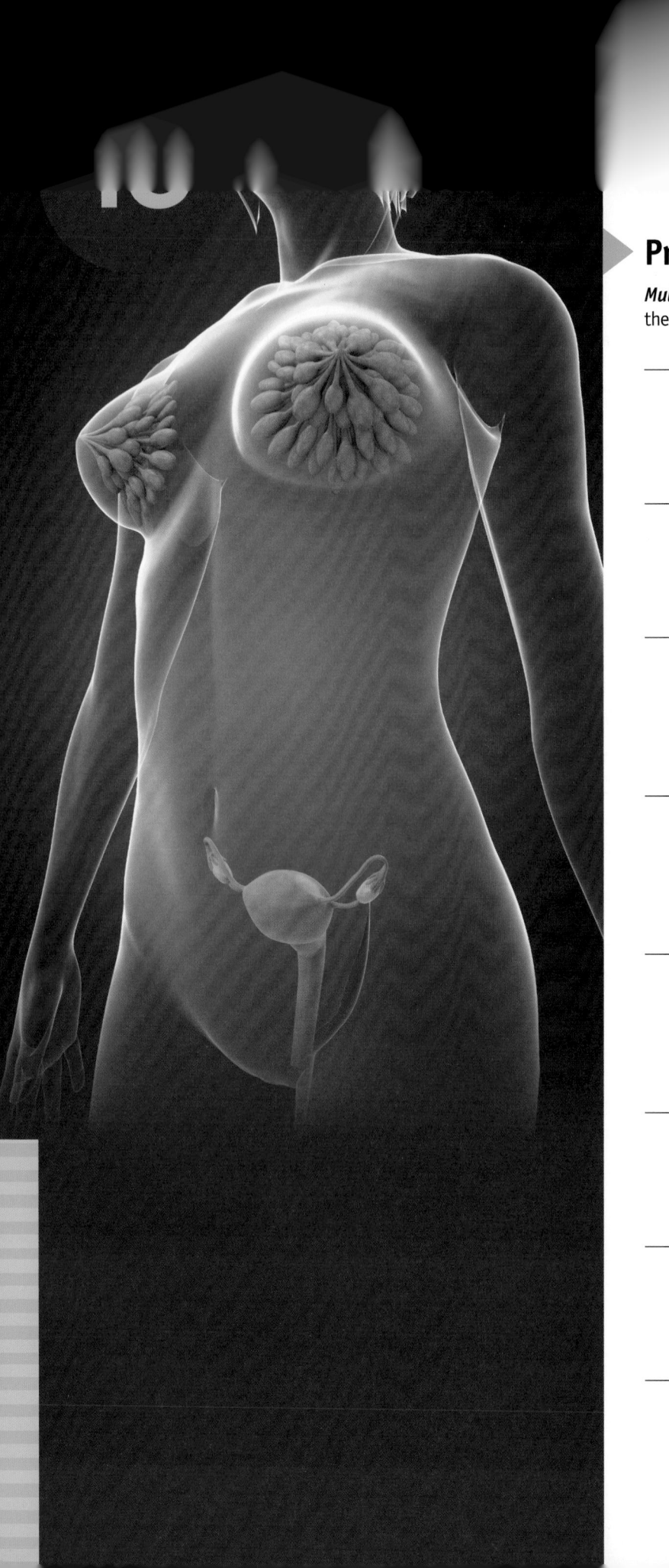

Pretest

Multiple Choice. Select the best answer, and write the letter of your choice to the left of each number.

_____ 1. The female gonad is the
    a. uterus
    b. cervix
    c. ovary
    d. testis

_____ 2. The two ovarian hormones are
    a. testosterone and estrogen
    b. estrogen and progesterone
    c. thyroxine and progesterone
    d. progesterone and testosterone

_____ 3. Use of artificial methods to prevent fertilization is termed
    a. antiception
    b. coitus
    c. contraception
    d. gestation

_____ 4. During the first two months of growth, the developing offspring is called a(n)
    a. neonate
    b. embryo
    c. zygote
    d. fetus

_____ 5. The structure that nourishes the developing fetus is the
    a. mammary gland
    b. cervix
    c. placenta
    d. follicle

_____ 6. Production of milk is technically called
    a. ovulation
    b. lactation
    c. corpus luteum
    d. parturition

_____ 7. The roots *metr/o* and *hyster/o* mean
    a. uterus
    b. vagina
    c. follicle
    d. ovary

_____ 8. Any disorder present at birth is described as
    a. hereditary
    b. genetic
    c. congenital
    d. familial

Learning Objectives

After study of this chapter you should be able to:

1 ▸ Describe the female reproductive tract, and give the function of each part. *p356*

2 ▸ Describe the structure and function of the mammary glands. *p357*

3 ▸ Outline the events in the menstrual cycle. *p357*

4 ▸ List four types of contraception with examples of each. *p358*

5 ▸ Describe seven disorders of the female reproductive system. *p365*

6 ▸ Outline the major events that occur in the first two months after fertilization. *p372*

7 ▸ Describe the structure and function of the placenta. *p372*

8 ▸ Describe two adaptations in fetal circulation, and cite their purposes. *p374*

9 ▸ Describe the three stages of childbirth. *p375*

10 ▸ List the hormonal and nervous controls over lactation. *p376*

11 ▸ Identify and use roots pertaining to the female reproductive system, pregnancy, and birth. *pp362, 377*

12 ▸ Describe six disorders of pregnancy and birth. *p378*

13 ▸ Define two types of congenital disorders and give examples each. *p380*

14 ▸ Interpret abbreviations used in referring to reproduction. *pp372, 386*

15 ▸ Analyze the medical terms in several case studies concerning the female reproductive system, pregnancy, and birth. *pp355, 394*

Case Study: *A.Y.'s Cesarean Section*

Chief Complaint

A.Y. is a 29-year-old gravida 2, para 1, at 39 weeks of gestation. Her first pregnancy resulted in a cesarean section. She had had an uneventful pregnancy with good health, moderate weight gain, good fetal heart sounds, and no signs or symptoms of pregnancy-induced hypertension. A.Y. went to the hospital when she realized she was going into labor.

Examination

A.Y. had been in active labor for several hours, fully effaced and dilated, yet unable to progress. Her obstetrician ordered an x-ray pelvimetry test that revealed CPD (cephalopelvic disproportion) with the fetus in the right occiput posterior position. Changes in fetal heart rate indicated fetal distress. A.Y. was transported to the OR for an emergency C-section under spinal anesthesia.

Clinical Course

After being placed in the supine position, A.Y. had a urethral catheter inserted, and her abdomen was prepped with antimicrobial solution. After draping, a transverse suprapubic incision was made. Dissection was continued through the muscle layers to the uterus, with care not to nick the bladder. The uterus was incised through the lower segment, 2 cm from the bladder. The fetal head was gently elevated through the incision while the assistant put gentle pressure on the fundus. The baby's mouth and nose were suctioned with a bulb syringe, and the umbilical cord was clamped and cut. The baby was handed off to an attending pediatrician and OB nurse and placed in a radiant neonate warmer bed. The Apgar score was 9/9. The placenta was gently delivered from the uterus, and the scrub nurse checked for three vessels and filled two sterile test tubes with cord blood for laboratory analysis. A.Y. was given an injection of Pitocin to stimulate uterine contraction. The uterus and abdomen were closed, and A.Y. was transported to the PACU (postanesthesia care unit).

ANCILLARIES *At-A-Glance*

Visit thePoint to access the following resources. For guidance in using the resources most effectively, see pp. ix–xvi.

Learning RESOURCES

▸ Tips for Effective Studying
▸ Web Figure: Microscopic View of the Ovary
▸ Web Figure: Microscopic View of the Uterus
▸ Web Figure: The Stages of Labor
▸ Web Figure: The Apgar Scoring System
▸ Web Figure: Placental Abnormalities
▸ Web Chart: The Main Methods of Birth Control
▸ Web Chart: Placental Hormones

▸ Web Chart: Genetic Diseases
▸ Animation: Ovulation and Fertilization
▸ Animation: Fetal Circulation
▸ Audio Pronunciation Glossary

Learning ACTIVITIES

▸ Visual Activities
▸ Kinesthetic Activities
▸ Auditory Activities

Introduction

As in males, the female reproductive tract consists of internal organs and external genitalia. The breasts, or mammary glands, although not part of the reproductive system, are usually included with a discussion of this system, as their purpose is to nourish an infant.

In contrast to the continuous gametogenesis in males, formation of the female gamete is cyclic, with an egg released midway in the menstrual cycle. Each month, the **uterus** is prepared to receive a fertilized egg. If fertilization occurs, the developing offspring is nourished and protected by the placenta and surrounding fluids until birth. If the released egg is not fertilized, the lining of the uterus is sloughed off in menstruation.

The Female Reproductive System

THE OVARIES

The female gonads are the paired **ovaries** (singular: ovary) that are held by ligaments in the pelvic cavity on either side of the uterus (**Fig. 15-1**). It is within the ovaries that the female gametes, the eggs or **ova** (singular: ovum), develop.

Every month, several ova ripen, each within a cluster of cells called an **ovarian follicle**. At the time of **ovulation**, usually only one ovum is released from an ovary, and the remainder of the ripening ova degenerate. The follicle remains behind and continues to function for about two weeks if the ovum is not fertilized and for about two months if the ovum is fertilized.

THE UTERINE TUBES, UTERUS, AND VAGINA

After ovulation, the ovum travels into a **uterine tube**, also called the **fallopian tube**, attached to the upper lateral portion of the uterus (see **Fig. 15-1**). This tube arches above the ovary and has finger-like projections called **fimbriae** that sweep the released ovum into the uterine tube. If fertilization takes place, it typically occurs in a uterine tube.

The uterus is the organ that nourishes the developing offspring. It is pear-shaped, with an upper rounded fundus, a triangular cavity, and a lower narrow **cervix** that projects into the **vagina**. The recess around the cervix in the superior vagina is the **fornix**. At the posterior cervix, the peritoneum dips downward to form a blind pouch, or **cul-de-sac** (from French, meaning "bottom of the bag"), the lowest point of the peritoneal cavity. This region is also called the *rectouterine pouch*.

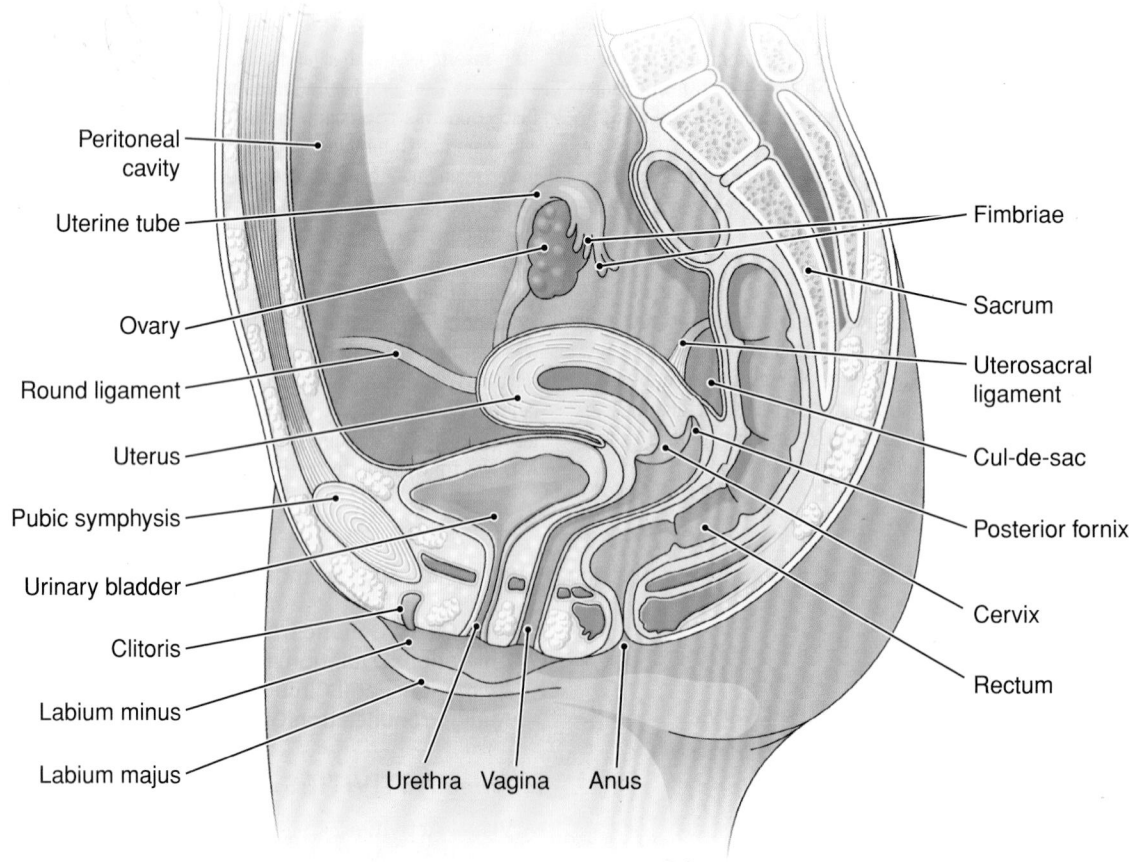

Figure 15-1 **Female reproductive system.** The system is seen in a sagittal section along with some adjacent structures.

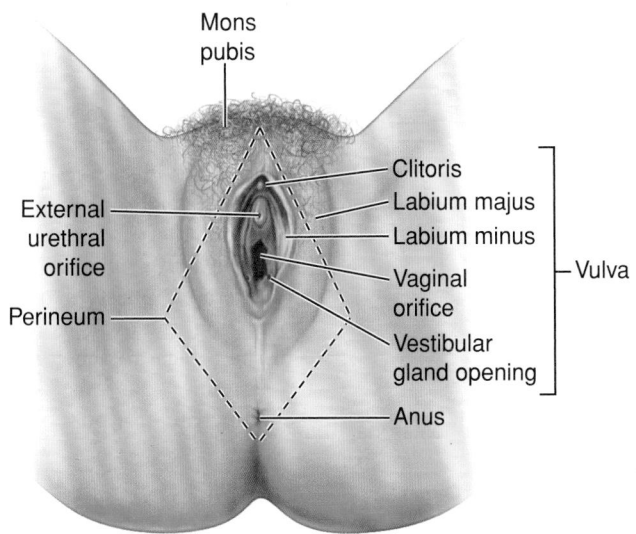

Figure 15-2 **The external female genitalia.** The vulva is shown along with nearby structures and the outlines of the perineum. The obstetrical perineum extends from the vagina to the anus.

The innermost layer of the uterine wall, the **endometrium**, has a rich blood supply. It receives the fertilized ovum and becomes part of the placenta during pregnancy. The endometrium is shed during the menstrual period if no fertilization occurs. The muscle layer of the uterine wall is the **myometrium**.

The vagina is a muscular tube that receives the penis during intercourse, functions as a birth canal, and transports the menstrual flow out of the body (see **Fig. 15-1**).

See the animation "Ovulation and Fertilization" and microscopic views of the ovary and uterus showing changes during the menstrual cycle in the Student Resources on thePoint.

THE EXTERNAL GENITAL ORGANS

All of the external female genitalia together are called the **vulva** (**Fig. 15-2**). This includes the large outer **labia majora** (singular: labium majus) and small inner **labia minora** (singular: labium minus) that enclose the vaginal and urethral openings. The **clitoris**, anterior to the urethral opening, is similar in developmental origin to the penis and responds to sexual stimulation. The vulva also includes the openings of ducts from two small glands on either side of the vagina that secrete mucus for lubrication during intercourse. These are the **greater vestibular glands** or *Bartholin glands*.

In both males and females, the region between the thighs from the external genital organs to the anus is the **perineum**. During childbirth, an incision may be made between the vagina and the anus to facilitate birth and prevent the tearing of tissue, a procedure called an *episiotomy*. (This procedure is actually a perineotomy, as the root episi/o means "vulva.")

The Mammary Glands

The **mammary glands**, or breasts, are composed mainly of glandular tissue and fat (**Fig. 15-3**). Their purpose is to provide nourishment for the newborn. The milk secreted by the glands is carried in ducts to the nipple.

The Menstrual Cycle

Female reproductive activity normally begins during puberty with **menarche**, the first menstrual period. Each month, the menstrual cycle is controlled, as is male reproductive activity, by hormones from the anterior pituitary gland.

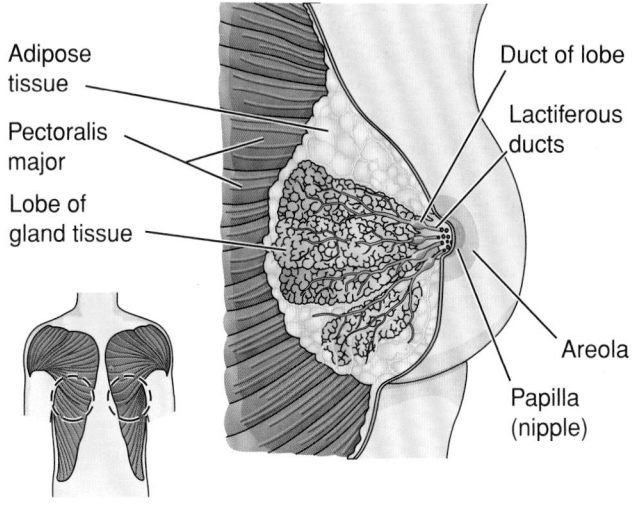

Figure 15-3 **Section of the breast.**

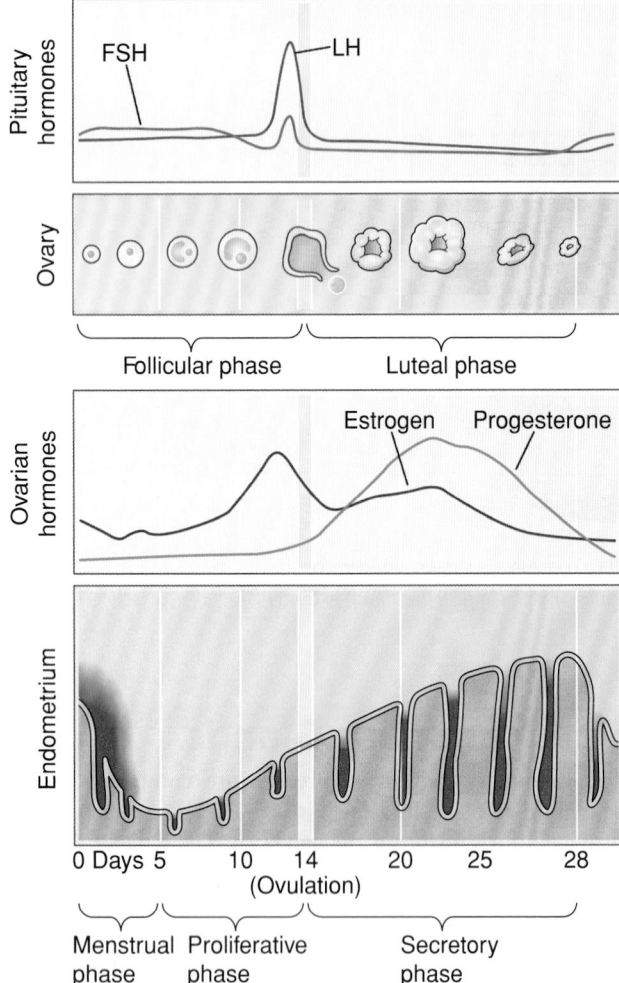

Figure 15-4 **The menstrual cycle.** Changes in pituitary and ovarian hormones, the ovary, and the uterus are shown during an average 28-day menstrual cycle with ovulation on day 14. Phases in the ovary are named for follicular development and formation of the corpus luteum. Phases in the uterus are named for changes in the endometrium.

Follicle-stimulating hormone (FSH) begins the cycle by causing the ovum to ripen in the ovarian follicle (**Fig. 15-4**). The follicle secretes **estrogen,** a hormone that starts endometrial development in preparation for the fertilized egg.

A second pituitary hormone, **luteinizing hormone (LH),** triggers ovulation and conversion of the follicle to the **corpus luteum.** This structure, left behind in the ovary, secretes **progesterone** and estrogen, which further the endometrial growth. If no fertilization occurs, hormone levels decline, and the endometrium sloughs off in the process of **menstruation.**

The average menstrual cycle lasts 28 days, with the first day of menstruation taken as day 1 and ovulation typically occurring on about day 14. Throughout the cycle, estrogen and progesterone feed back to the pituitary to regulate the production of FSH and LH. Hormonal birth control methods act by supplying estrogen and progesterone, which inhibit FSH and LH release from the pituitary and prevent ovulation while not interfering with menstruation. The

menstrual period that follows withdrawal of the hormones is anovulatory (*an-OV-u-lah-tor-e*); that is, it is not preceded by ovulation.

Figure 15-4 shows changes occurring simultaneously in the ovary and uterus during the course of one menstrual cycle under the effects of pituitary and ovarian hormones. The time before ovulation is described as the follicular phase in the ovary, because it encompasses development of the ovarian follicle. The uterus during this time is in the proliferative phase, marked by endometrial growth. After ovulation, the ovary is in the luteal phase with conversion of the follicle to the corpus luteum. The uterus is then in a secretory phase, as its glands are actively preparing the endometrium for possible implantation of a fertilized egg.

MENOPAUSE

Menopause is the cessation of monthly menstrual cycles. This change generally occurs between the ages of 45 and 55 years. Reproductive hormone levels decline, and ovarian ova gradually degenerate. Some women experience unpleasant symptoms, such as hot flashes, headaches, insomnia, mood swings, and urinary problems. There is also some atrophy of the reproductive tract with vaginal dryness. Most importantly, the decline in estrogen levels is associated with bone weakening (osteoporosis).

Physicians may prescribe hormone replacement therapy (HRT) to alleviate menopausal symptoms. This treatment, also called menopausal hormone therapy (MHT), usually consists of administering estrogen in combination with progestin (*pro-JES-tin*), a synthetic progesterone, given to minimize the risk of endometrial cancer. Estrogen replacement reduces bone loss associated with aging. However, concerns about HRT safety have caused reconsideration of this therapy beyond the early postmenopausal years. Studies with the most widely used form of HRT showed an increased risk of endometrial cancer and breast cancer and an increased risk of thrombosis and embolism, especially in women who smoke. All these risks increase with the duration of therapy, so HRT should be given at the lowest effective dose for the shortest possible time. Women with a history or a family history of breast cancer or circulatory problems should not take HRT. Studies are ongoing on HRT safety and the use of estrogen alone for women who have no uterus.

Aside from HRT, antidepressants and vitamin E may help to relieve menopausal symptoms; locally applied estrogen and moisturizers relieve vaginal dryness. Nonhormonal drugs that increase bone density are also available if needed. As always, exercise and a balanced diet with adequate calcium are important in maintaining health throughout life.

Contraception

Contraception is the use of artificial methods to prevent fertilization of the ovum or its implantation in the uterus. Temporary methods of birth control function to:

- Block sperm penetration of the uterus (e.g., condom, diaphragm).

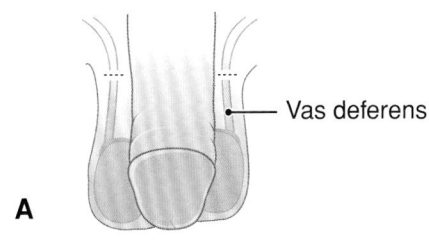

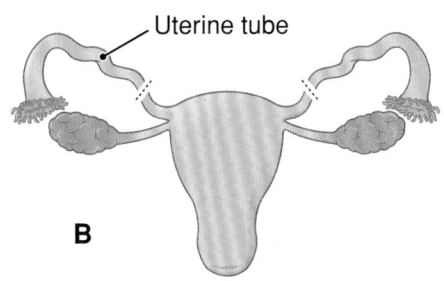

Figure 15-5 **Sterilization. A.** Vasectomy. **B.** Tubal ligation.

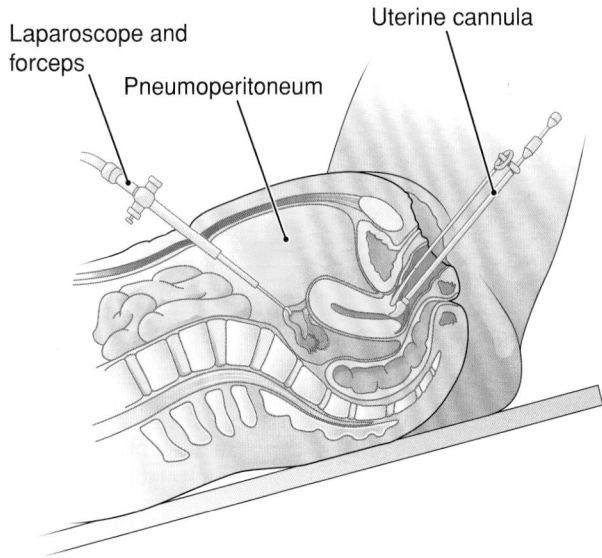

Figure 15-6 **Laparoscopic sterilization.** The peritoneal cavity is inflated (pneumoperitoneum), and the uterine tubes are cut laparoscopically through a small incision.

- Prevent implantation of the fertilized egg (e.g., intrauterine device or IUD).
- Prevent ovulation (e.g., hormones). Hormonal methods differ in dosage and route of delivery, such as oral intake (the birth control pill), injection, skin patch, and vaginal ring.

The so-called morning-after pill is intended for emergency contraception. It considerably reduces the chance of pregnancy if taken within 72 hours after unprotected sexual intercourse. One such product, Plan B, consists of two progestin doses taken 12 hours apart.

Surgical sterilization provides the most effective and usually permanent contraception. In males, this procedure is a vasectomy; in females, surgical sterilization is a **tubal ligation**, in which uterine tubes are cut and tied on both sides (**Fig. 15-5**). Laparoscopic surgery through the abdominal wall is the preferred method for performing the procedure (**Fig. 15-6**).

RU486 (mifepristone) is more widely used for birth control in other countries than in the United States. It terminates an early pregnancy by blocking progesterone, causing the endometrium to break down. Technically, RU486 is an abortion-causing agent (abortifacient), not a contraceptive.

Box 15-1 describes the main contraceptive methods currently in use. Each has advantages and disadvantages over other methods, but they are listed roughly in order of decreasing effectiveness. Note that only male and female condoms protect against the spread of STIs.

A more complete list of the main methods of birth control along with the advantages and disadvantages of each is in the Student Resources on thePoint.

FOR YOUR REFERENCE   **Box 15-1**

Main Methods of Birth Control Currently in Use

Method	Description
SURGICAL	
vasectomy/tubal ligation	cutting and tying the tubes that carry the gametes
HORMONAL	
birth control pills	estrogen and progestin or progestin alone taken orally to prevent ovulation
birth control shot	injection of synthetic progesterone every three months to prevent ovulation
birth control patch	adhesive patch placed on body that administers estrogen and progestin through the skin; left on for three weeks and removed for a fourth week

(continued)

Main Methods of Birth Control Currently in Use (*Continued*)

Method	Description
birth control ring	flexible ring inserted into vagina that releases hormones internally; left in place for three weeks and removed for a fourth week
BARRIER	
condom	sheath that prevents sperm cells from contacting an ovum; a male condom fits over an erect penis; a female condom fits into the vagina and covers the cervix
diaphragm (with spermicide)	rubber cap that fits over cervix and prevents sperm entrance
contraceptive sponge (with spermicide)	soft, disposable foam disk containing spermicide, which is moistened with water and inserted into vagina
intrauterine device (IUD)	metal or plastic device inserted into uterus through vagina; prevents fertilization and implantation by release of copper or birth control hormones
OTHER	
spermicide	chemicals used to kill sperm; best when used in combination with a barrier method
fertility awareness	abstinence during fertile part of cycle as determined by menstrual history, basal body temperature, or quality of cervical mucus

Terminology Key Terms

Female Reproductive System

Normal Structure and Function

cervix SER-viks	Neck; usually means the lower narrow portion (neck) of the uterus (root: cervic/o); also called the cervix uteri (U-ter-i)
clitoris KLIT-o-ris	A small erectile body anterior to the urethral opening that is similar in developmental origin to the penis (roots: clitor/o, clitorid/o)
contraception kon-trah-SEP-shun	The prevention of pregnancy
corpus luteum KOR-pus LU-te-um	The small yellow structure that develops from the ovarian follicle after ovulation and secretes progesterone and estrogen
cul-de-sac kul-dih-SAK	A blind pouch, such as the recess between the rectum and the uterus; the rectouterine pouch or pouch of Douglas (see **Fig. 15-1**)
endometrium en-do-ME-tre-um	The inner lining of the uterus
estrogen ES-tro-jen	A group of hormones that produce female characteristics and prepare the uterus for the fertilized egg; the most active of these is estradiol
fallopian tube fah-LO-pe-an	See uterine tube
fimbriae FIM-bre-e	The long finger-like extensions of the uterine tube that wave to capture the released ovum (see **Fig. 15-1**) (singular: fimbria)
follicle-stimulating hormone (FSH)	A hormone secreted by the anterior pituitary that acts on the gonads; in the female, it stimulates ripening of ova in the ovary
fornix FOR-niks	An arch-like space, such as the space between the uppermost wall of the vagina and the cervix (see **Fig. 15-1**); from Latin meaning "arch"

Terminology	**Key Terms** (Continued)

greater vestibular gland *ves-TIB-u-lar*	A small gland that secretes mucus through a duct that opens near the vaginal orifice; also called Bartholin (*BAR-to-lin*) gland (see **Fig. 15-2**)
labia majora *LA-be-ah mah-JOR-ah*	The two large folds of skin that form the sides of the vulva (root labi/o means "lip") (singular: labium majus)
labia minora *LA-be-ah mi-NOR-ah*	The two small folds of skin within the labia majora (singular: labium minus)
luteinizing hormone (LH) *LU-te-in-i-zing*	A hormone secreted by the anterior pituitary that acts on the gonads; in the female, it stimulates ovulation and corpus luteum formation
mammary gland *MAM-ah-re*	A specialized gland capable of secreting milk in the female (roots: mamm/o, mast/o); the breast
menarche *men-AR-ke*	The first menstrual period, which normally occurs during puberty
menopause *MEN-o-pawz*	Cessation of menstrual cycles in the female
menstruation *men-stru-A-shun*	The cyclic discharge of blood and mucosal tissues from the lining of the nonpregnant uterus (roots: men/o, mens); menstrual period, menses (*MEN-seze*)
myometrium *mi-o-ME-tre-um*	The muscular wall of the uterus
ovarian follicle *o-VAR-e-an FOL-ih-kl*	The cluster of cells in which the ovum ripens in the ovary
ovary *O-vah-re*	A female gonad (roots: ovari/o, oophor/o)
ovulation *ov-u-LA-shun*	The release of a mature ovum from the ovary (from *ovule*, meaning "little egg")
ovum *O-vum*	The female gamete or reproductive cell (roots: oo, ov/o) (plural: ova)
perineum *per-ih-NE-um*	The region between the thighs from the external genitalia to the anus (root: perine/o)
progesterone *pro-JES-ter-one*	A hormone produced by the corpus luteum and the placenta that maintains the endometrium for pregnancy
tubal ligation *li-GA-shun*	Surgical constriction of the uterine tubes to produce sterilization (see **Figs. 15-5** and **15-6**)
uterine tube *U-ter-in*	A tube extending from the upper lateral portion of the uterus that carries the ovum to the uterus (root: salping/o); also called fallopian (*fah-LO-pe-an*) tube
uterus *U-ter-us*	The organ that receives the fertilized egg and maintains the developing offspring during pregnancy (roots: uter/o, metr, hyster/o) (see **Box 15-2**)
vagina *vah-JI-nah*	The muscular tube between the cervix and the vulva (roots: vagin/o, colp/o)
vulva *VUL-va*	The external female genital organs (roots: vulv/o, episi/o)

15

Go to the Audio Pronunciation Glossary in the Student Resources on thePoint to hear these terms pronounced.

FOCUS ON WORDS
Crazy Ideas

Most women would be surprised to learn the origin of the root hyster/o, used for the uterus. It comes from the same root as the words hysterical and hysterics and was based on the very old belief that the womb was the source of mental disturbances in women.

A similar history lies at the origin of the word hypochondriac, a term for someone who has imaginary illnesses. The hypochondriac regions are in the upper portions of the abdomen, an area that the ancients believed was the seat of mental disorders.

Roots Pertaining to the Female Reproductive System

See **Tables 15-1** to **15-3**.

Table 15-1   Roots for Female Reproduction and the Ovaries

Root	Meaning	Example	Definition of Example
gyn/o, gynec/o[a]	woman	gynecology *gi-neh-KOL-o-je*	study of women's diseases
men/o, mens	month, menstruation	premenstrual *pre-MEN-stru-al*	before a menstrual period
oo	ovum, egg cell	oocyte *O-o-site*	cell that gives rise to an ovum
ov/o, ovul/o	ovum, egg cell	anovulatory *an-OV-u-lah-tore-e*	absence of egg ripening or of ovulation
ovari/o	ovary	ovariopexy *o-var-e-o-PEK-se*	surgical fixation of an ovary
oophor/o	ovary	oophorectomy *o-of-o-REK-to-me*	excision of an ovary

[a]Although the correct pronunciation of this root is *jine* (with a soft g and long i), it is commonly pronounced with a hard g as in *gine* and may also have a short i, as in *jin* or *gin*.

EXERCISE 15-1

Define the following words.

1. gynecopathy (*gi-neh-KOP-ah-the*) _____

2. intermenstrual (*in-ter-MEN-stru-al*) _____

3. oogenesis (*o-o-JEN-eh-sis*) _____

4. ovulation (*ov-u-LA-shun*) _____

5. ovarian (*o-VAR-e-an*) _____

6. oophoritis (*o-of-o-RI-tis*) _____

Write a word for the following definitions.

7. rupture (-rhexis) of an ovary _____

8. pertaining to ovulation _____

9. profuse bleeding (-hagia) at the time of menstruation _____

EXERCISE 15-1   *(Continued)*

The word menorrhea means "menstruation." Add a prefix to menorrhea to form words for the following definitions.

10. scanty menstrual flow _____

11. absence of menstruation _____

12. painful or difficult menstruation _____

Use the root *ovari/o* to write words for the following.

13. incision into an ovary _____

14. surgical puncture of an ovary _____

15. hernia of an ovary _____

Use the root *oophor/o* to write words for the following.

16. surgical repair of an ovary _____

17. malignant tumor of the ovary _____

15

Table 15-2	**Roots for the Uterine Tubes, Uterus, and Vagina**

Root	Meaning	Example	Definition of Example
salping/o	uterine tube, tube	salpingoplasty *sal-PING-o-plas-te*	plastic repair of a uterine tube
uter/o	uterus	intrauterine *in-trah-U-ter-in*	within the uterus
metr/o, metr/i	uterus	metrorrhea *me-tro-RE-ah*	abnormal uterine discharge
hyster/o	uterus	hysterotomy *his-ter-OT-o-me*	incision of the uterus
cervic/o	cervix, neck	endocervical *en-do-SER-vih-kal*	pertaining to the lining of the cervix
vagin/o	vagina	vaginometer *vaj-ih-NOM-eh-ter*	instrument for measuring the vagina
colp/o	vagina	colpostenosis *kol-po-sten-O-sis*	narrowing of the vagina

EXERCISE 15-2

Define the following terms.

1. hysterography (*his-ter-OG-rah-fe*) _____

2. metromalacia (*me-tro-mah-LA-she-ah*) _____

3. vaginoplasty (*vaj-ih-no-PLAS-te*) _____

4. colpodynia (*kol-po-DIN-e-ah*) _____

5. salpingectomy (*sal-pin-JEK-to-me*) _____

(continued)

EXERCISE 15-2   *(Continued)*

6. uterovesical (*u-ter-o-VES-ih-kal*) _____

7. intracervical (*in-trah-SER-vih-kal*) _____

Write words for the following.

8. surgical fixation of a uterine tube _____

9. radiographic study of the uterine tube _____

The root *salping/o* is taken from the word salpinx, which means "tube." Add a prefix to salpinx to write a word for the following.

10. collection of fluid in a uterine tube _____

11. presence of pus in a uterine tube _____

Note how the roots *salping/o* and *oophor/o* are combined to form salpingo-oophoritis (inflammation of a uterine tube and ovary). Write a word for the following.

12. surgical removal of a uterine tube and ovary _____

Use the roots indicated to write words for the following.

13. surgical fixation of the uterus (hyster/o) _____

14. pertaining to the uterus (uter/o) _____

15. narrowing of the uterus (metr/o) _____

16. radiograph of the uterus (hyster/o) and uterine tubes _____

17. through the cervix _____

18. prolapse of the uterus (metr/o) _____

19. hernia of the vagina (colp/o) _____

20. inflammation of the vagina (vagin/o) _____

Table 15-3	Roots for the Female Accessory Structures		
Root	**Meaning**	**Example**	**Definition of Example**
vulv/o	vulva	vulvar *VUL-var*	pertaining to the vulva
episi/o	vulva	episiotomy *eh-piz-e-OT-o-me*	incision of the vulva
perine/o	perineum	perineal *per-ih-NE-al*	pertaining to the perineum
clitor/o, clitorid/o	clitoris	clitorectomy *klih-to-REK-to-me*	excision of the clitoris
mamm/o	breast, mammary gland	mammoplasty *mam-o-PLAS-te*	plastic surgery of the breast
mast/o	breast, mammary gland	amastia *ah-MAS-te-ah*	absence of the breasts

15

Write a word for the following.

1. excision of the vulva (vulv/o) _____

2. suture of the vulva (episi/o) _____

3. pertaining to the vagina (vagin/o) and perineum _____

4. enlargement of the clitoris _____

5. radiographic record of the breast (mamm/o) _____

6. inflammation of the breast (mast/o) _____

7. excision of the breast _____

Clinical Aspects of Female Reproduction

INFECTION

The major organisms that cause sexually transmitted infections in both men and women are given in **Box 14-2**.

Genital herpes is a presently incurable viral infection that affects over 25 percent of adults in the United States. Once infection occurs, the virus lives in the nervous system, causing intermittent outbreaks that may include genital sores, itching, burning, and urinary problems. The virus is easily spread to sexual partners even if there are no active signs of the disease. Pregnant women can pass the virus to their babies during delivery, resulting in possible disabilities and even death. Some basic hygiene measures and condom use can reduce viral spread.

A fungus that infects the vulva and vagina is *Candida albicans*, causing **candidiasis**. The resultant **vaginitis**, inflammation of the vagina, causes itching and release of a thick, white, cheesy discharge. Pregnancy, diabetes mellitus, and use of antibiotics, steroids, or birth control pills predispose to this infection. Antifungal agents (mycostatics) are used in treatment.

Pelvic inflammatory disease (PID) is the spread of infection from the reproductive organs into the pelvic cavity. It is most often caused by the gonorrhea organism or by *Chlamydia*, although bacteria normally living in the reproductive tract may also be responsible when conditions allow. PID is a serious disorder that may result in septicemia or shock. Inflammation of the uterine tubes, called **salpingitis**, may close off these tubes and cause infertility.

FIBROIDS

A **fibroid** is a benign smooth muscle tumor usually occurring in the uterine wall, the myometrium (**Fig. 15-7**). This type of growth, technically called a **leiomyoma**, is one of the most common uterine disorders, but it usually causes no symptoms and requires no treatment. However, fibroids may cause heavy menstrual bleeding (menorrhagia) and rectal or bladder pressure. Treatments include:

- Suppression of hormones that stimulate fibroid growth.
- Surgical removal of the fibroids (myomectomy).
- Surgical removal of the uterus, or **hysterectomy**.

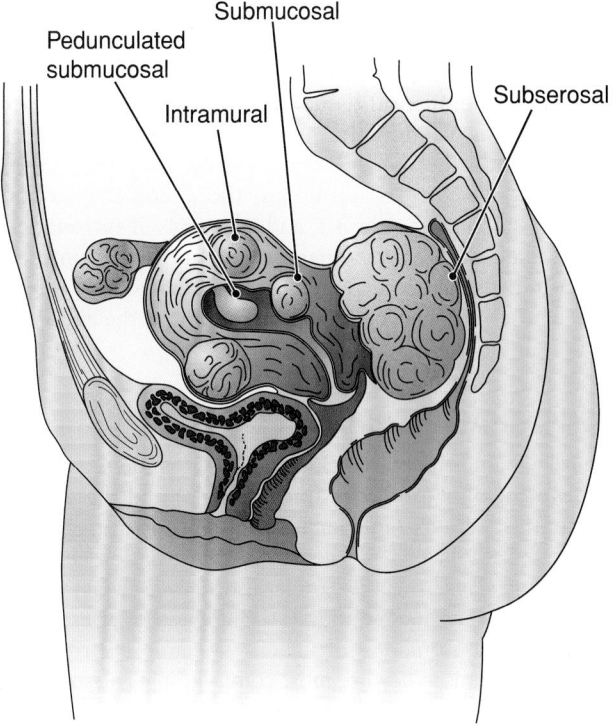

Figure 15-7 **Uterine leiomyomas (fibroids).** Various possible locations are shown. They may be within the uterine wall (intramural), below the mucous membrane (submucosal), on a stalk (pedunculated), or below the outer serous membrane (subserosal). One tumor is shown compressing the urinary bladder and another the rectum.

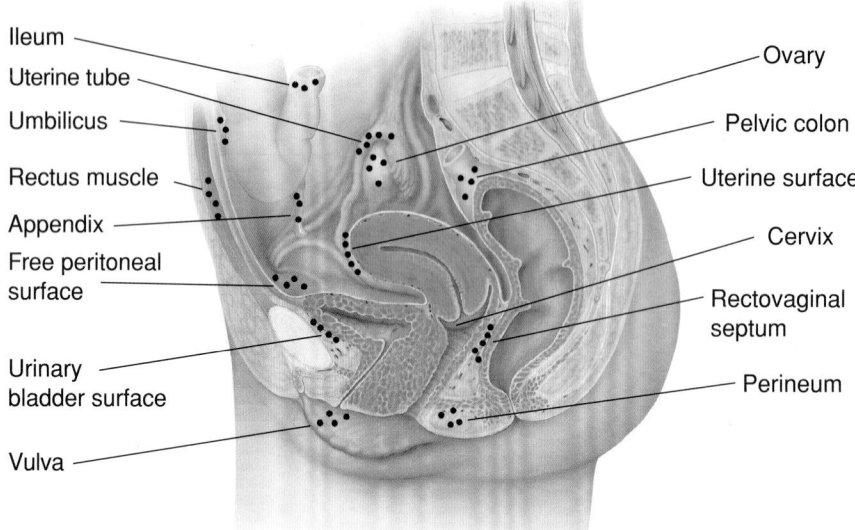

Ileum
Uterine tube
Umbilicus
Rectus muscle
Appendix
Free peritoneal surface
Urinary bladder surface
Vulva
Ovary
Pelvic colon
Uterine surface
Cervix
Rectovaginal septum
Perineum

Figure 15-8 **Endometriosis.** Endometrial tissue can grow outside the uterus almost anywhere in the peritoneal cavity, causing inflammation and other complications.

- Uterine fibroid embolization (UFE), a method that has reduced the need for hysterectomies. A specially trained radiologist uses a catheter to inject small synthetic particles into a uterine artery. These particles then block blood supply to the fibroid, causing it to shrink.

ENDOMETRIOSIS

Growth of endometrial tissue outside the uterus is termed **endometriosis**. Commonly, the ovaries, uterine tubes, peritoneum, and other pelvic organs are involved (**Fig. 15-8**). Stimulated by normal hormones, the endometrial tissue causes inflammation, fibrosis, and adhesions in surrounding areas. The results may be pain, **dysmenorrhea** (painful or difficult menstruation), and infertility. Laparoscopy is used to diagnose endometriosis and also to remove the abnormal tissue.

MENSTRUAL DISORDERS

Menstrual abnormalities include flow that is too scanty (oligomenorrhea) or too heavy (menorrhagia) and the absence of monthly periods (amenorrhea). Dysmenorrhea, when it occurs, usually begins at the start of menstruation and lasts one to two days. Together, these disorders are classified as dysfunctional uterine bleeding (DUB). These responses may be caused by hormone imbalances, systemic disorders, or uterine problems. They are most common in adolescence or near menopause. At other times, they are often related to life changes and emotional upset.

Premenstrual syndrome (PMS) describes symptoms that appear during the menstrual cycle's second half and includes emotional changes, fatigue, bloating, headaches, and appetite changes. Possible causes of PMS have been under study. Symptoms may be relieved by hormone therapy, antidepressants, or antianxiety medications. Exercise,

dietary control, rest, and relaxation strategies may also be helpful. Avoiding caffeine and taking vitamin E supplements may relieve breast tenderness; one should also drink adequate water and limit salt intake.

POLYCYSTIC OVARIAN SYNDROME

Polycystic ovarian syndrome (PCOS) is discussed here because the first-described symptoms of this disorder were enlarged ovaries with multiple cysts. These signs are not always present in PCOS, although the ovaries do show abnormalities. PCOS is an endocrine disorder involving increased androgen and estrogen secretion that interferes with normal secretion of pituitary FSH and LH. Some effects include:

- Anovulation and infertility
- Scant or absent menses (oligomenorrhea or amenorrhea)
- Excessive hair growth (hirsutism), caused by excess androgen (male hormone)
- Resistance to insulin, a hormone that lowers blood sugar, resulting in symptoms of diabetes mellitus
- Obesity

PCOS is treated with hormones to regulate hormonal imbalance, drugs to increase responsiveness to insulin, weight reduction (estrogen is produced in adipose tissue), and sometimes partial removal of the ovaries.

CANCER OF THE FEMALE REPRODUCTIVE TRACT

Endometrial Cancer

Cancer of the endometrium is the most common cancer of the female reproductive tract. Women at risk should have biopsies taken regularly because endometrial cancer is not always detected by **Pap** (Papanicolaou) **smear**, a simple

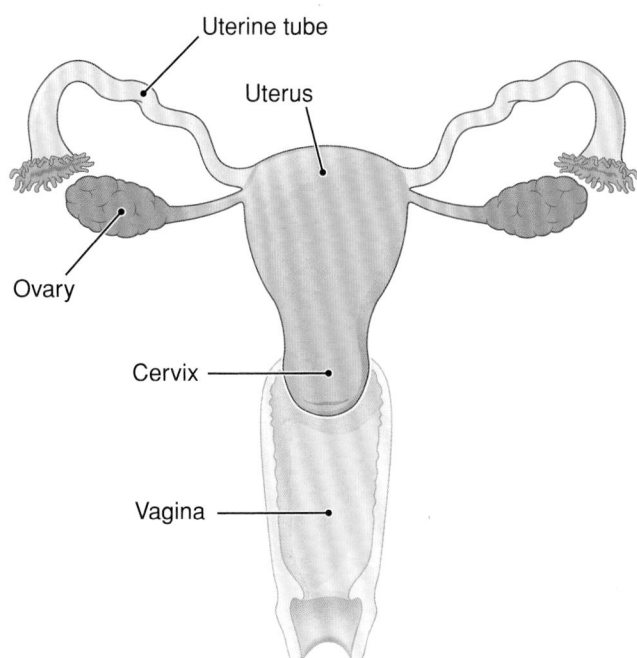

Figure 15-9 Uterine tube / Uterus / Ovary / Cervix / Vagina

Figure 15-9 **Reproductive surgery.** A hysterectomy is surgical removal of the uterus. Removal of the ovary (oophorectomy) and uterine tube (salpingectomy) may also be required either unilaterally or bilaterally.

histologic test. Treatment consists of hysterectomy (removal of the uterus) (**Fig. 15-9**) and sometimes radiation therapy. A small percentage of cases occur after endometrial overgrowth (hyperplasia). This tissue can be removed by **dilation and curettage (D&C)**, in which the cervix is widened and the lining of the uterus is scraped with a curette.

Cervical Cancer

Almost all patients with cervical cancer have been infected with human papillomavirus (HPV), a virus that causes genital warts. Incidence is also related to high sexual activity and other sexually transmitted viral infections, such as herpes. A vaccine against the most prevalent HPV strains is available and is recommended for females at 11 to 12 years of age.

In the 1940s and 1950s, the synthetic steroid DES (diethylstilbestrol) was given to prevent miscarriages. A small percentage of daughters born to women treated with this drug have shown an increased risk for cancer of the cervix and vagina. These women need to be examined regularly.

Cervical carcinoma is often preceded by abnormal growth (dysplasia) of the epithelial cells lining the cervix. Growth is graded as CIN I, II, or III, depending on the depth of tissue involved. CIN stands for cervical intraepithelial neoplasia. Diagnosis of cervical cancer is by a Pap smear, examination with a **colposcope**, and biopsy. In a **cone biopsy** (**Fig. 15-10**), a cone-shaped piece of tissue is removed from the lining of the cervix for study. Often in the procedure, all of the abnormal cells are removed as well. A newer procedure that can supplement or replace

the Pap smear involves testing a cervical cell sample for the DNA of cancer-causing HPV strains.

Ovarian Cancer

Cancer of the ovary has a high mortality rate because it usually causes no distinct early symptoms and there is no accurate routine screening test yet available. Women may overlook the vague possible signs of ovarian cancer, such as bloating, change in bowel habits, backache, urinary changes, abnormal bleeding, weight loss, and fatigue. Often by the time of diagnosis, the tumor has invaded the pelvis and abdomen. Removal of the ovaries, an **oophorectomy**, and uterine tubes, a **salpingectomy**, along with the uterus is required (**Fig. 15-9**), in addition to chemotherapy and radiation therapy.

BREAST CANCER

Carcinoma of the breast is second only to lung cancer in causing cancer-related deaths among women in the United States. This cancer metastasizes readily through the lymph nodes and blood to other sites such as the lung, liver, bones, and ovaries.

Diagnosis

Palpation is a simple first step in breast cancer diagnosis. Regular breast self-examination (BSE) is of utmost importance, because many breast cancers are discovered by women themselves.

Mammography, which provides two-dimensional x-ray images of the breast, is still the standard diagnostic

15

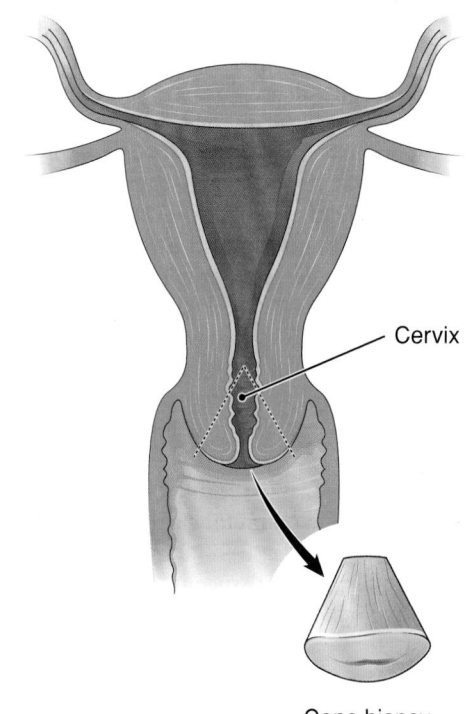

Cervix

Cone biopsy

Figure 15-10 **Cone biopsy of the uterine cervix.**

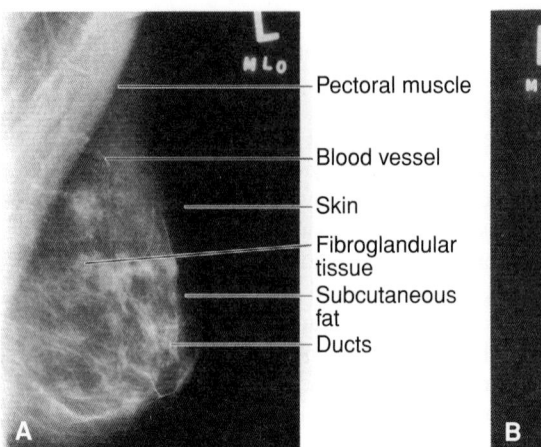

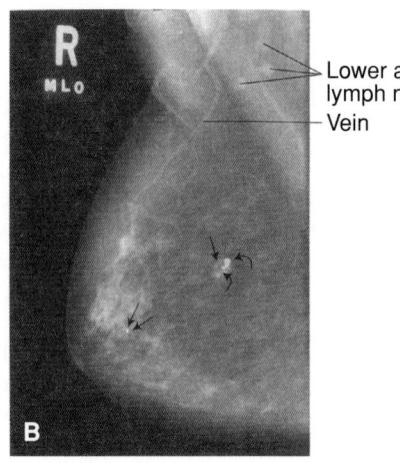

- Pectoral muscle
- Blood vessel
- Skin
- Fibroglandular tissue
- Subcutaneous fat
- Ducts

- Lower auxillary lymph nodes
- Vein

Figure 15-11 **Mammograms. A.** Normal mammogram, left breast. **B.** Mammogram of right breast showing lesions (*arrows*). In mammograms, fat tissue appears gray; breast tissue, calcium deposits, and benign or cancerous tumors appear white.

procedure for breast cancer (**Fig. 15-11**). Some health organizations recommend annual mammograms after the age of 40 years. Other health professionals recommend waiting until age 50 unless a woman is in a high-risk group, such as having a family history of breast cancer. In digital mammography, x-ray images are stored on computers instead of on film. These images can be manipulated electronically to aid interpretation. They are more easily stored and retrieved or sent to other medical facilities.

While mammography remains the most commonly recommended choice in breast cancer screening, medical researchers are currently testing new technologies. These are aimed at addressing one of the major weaknesses of mammography, which is the detection of cancer in women with radiographically dense breasts. Current procedures in these women result in many false positives and frequent recalls for additional imaging. Improvements in screening have been recognized with the three-dimensional technique called digital **tomosynthesis**. This procedure is approved by the U.S. Food and Drug Administration to be used in conjunction with mammography but is not yet considered the standard of care for breast cancer screening.

Ultrasound and MRI studies are adjuncts to mammography. Ultrasound can show whether a lump seen on mammography is simply a benign cyst. MRI with a contrast medium can show abnormal blood vessel formation signifying a tumor.

Any suspicious breast tissue must be biopsied by needle aspiration or surgical excision for further study. In a **stereotactic biopsy**, a physician uses a computer-guided imaging system to locate suspicious tissue and remove samples with a needle. This method is less invasive than surgical biopsy.

Ductal carcinoma in situ (DCIS) is an abnormality of breast tissue that arises from an overgrowth of the cells lining a milk duct. It is initially confined to the duct, that is, it does not invade nearby tissue or metastasize, and it can usually be detected by mammography in its early stages. DCIS may unpredictably become metastatic, and treatment depends on tumor pathology as well as a patient's age and family history.

Treatment

Treatment of breast cancer is usually some form of **mastectomy**, or removal of breast tissue:

- In a radical mastectomy, the entire breast is removed. Underlying muscle and axillary lymph nodes (in the armpit) are also removed.
- In a modified radical mastectomy, the breast and lymph nodes are removed, but muscles are left in place.
- In a segmental mastectomy, or "lumpectomy," just the tumor itself is removed. When the tumor is small and surgery is followed by additional treatment, this procedure gives survival rates as high as those with more radical surgeries.

Surgeons can assess the extent of tumor spread and conserve lymphatic tissue using a **sentinel node biopsy**. A dye or radioactive tracer identifies the first lymph nodes that receive lymph from a tumor. Study of possible tumor spread to these "sentinel nodes" guides further treatment.

Often after breast surgery, a patient receives chemotherapy and/or radiation therapy. It is now possible in some cases to deliver radiation to just the tumor area (brachytherapy) instead of irradiating the whole breast. A radiation source is delivered through catheters or implanted in the breast tissue for a short time.

Progress in breast cancer treatment involves genetic studies and tumor analysis that allows therapy more specific to each particular case. About 8 percent of these cancers are linked to a defective gene (*BRCA1* or *BRCA2*) that is transmitted within families. Women with these genetic predispositions can be screened more carefully or treated prophylactically.

Some types of specific drug treatments for breast cancer, which may be given in combination, are:

- Drugs that block estrogen production or block estrogen receptors in breast tissue if a tumor responds to this hormone
- Drugs that inhibit tumor growth factors
- Drugs that inhibit growth of blood vessels that supply the tumor (antiangiogenesis agents)

These and other anticancer drugs are described in more detail in the list of supplementary terms.

Terminology **Key Terms**

Female Reproductive System

Disorders

candidiasis *kan-dih-DI-ah-sis*	Infection with the fungus *Candida*, a common cause of vaginitis
dysmenorrhea *DIS-men-o-re-ah*	Painful or difficult menstruation; a common disorder that may be caused by infection, use of an intrauterine device, endometriosis, overproduction of prostaglandins, or other factors
endometriosis *en-do-me-tre-O-sis*	Growth of endometrial tissue outside the uterus, usually in the pelvic cavity (see **Fig. 15-8**)
fibroid *FI-broyd*	Benign tumor of smooth muscle (see leiomyoma)
leiomyoma *li-o-mi-O-mah*	Benign tumor of smooth muscle, usually in the uterine wall (myometrium); in the uterus, may cause bleeding and pressure on the bladder or rectum; also called fibroid or myoma (see **Fig. 15-7**)
pelvic inflammatory disease (PID)	Condition caused by the spread of infection from the reproductive tract into the pelvic cavity; commonly caused by sexually transmitted gonorrhea and *Chlamydia* infections
salpingitis *sal-pin-JI-tis*	Inflammation of a uterine tube, typically caused by urinary tract infection or sexually transmitted infection; chronic salpingitis may lead to infertility or ectopic pregnancy (development of the fertilized egg outside of the uterus)
vaginitis *vaj-ih-NI-tis*	Inflammation of the vagina

Diagnosis and Treatment

colposcope *KOL-po-skope*	Instrument for examining the vagina and cervix
cone biopsy	Removal of a cone of tissue from the cervical lining for cytologic examination; also called conization (see **Fig. 15-10**)
dilation and curettage (D&C) *ku-reh-TAJ*	Procedure in which the cervix is dilated (widened) and the uterine lining is scraped with a curette
hysterectomy *his-ter-EK-to-me*	Surgical removal of the uterus; most commonly done because of tumors; often the uterine tubes and ovaries are removed as well (see **Fig. 15-9**)
mammography *mam-OG-rah-fe*	Radiographic study of the breast for the detection of breast cancer; the image obtained is a mammogram (see **Fig. 15-11**)
mastectomy *mas-TEK-to-me*	Excision of breast tissue to eliminate malignancy
oophorectomy *o-of-o-REK-to-me*	Excision of an ovary (see **Fig. 15-9**)
Pap smear	Study of cells collected from the cervix and vagina for early detection of cancer; also called Papanicolaou smear or Pap test
salpingectomy *sal-pin-JEK-to-e*	Surgical removal of the uterine tube (see **Fig. 15-9**)
sentinel node biopsy *SEN-tih-nel*	Biopsy of the first lymph nodes to receive drainage from a tumor; used to determine spread of cancer in planning treatment
stereotactic biopsy *ster-e-o-TAK-tik*	Needle biopsy using a computer-guided imaging system to locate suspicious tissue and remove samples for study
tomosynthesis *toh-mo-SIN-theh-sis*	Three-dimensional x-ray imaging technique for detection of breast cancer; digital tomosythesis

| Terminology | **Supplementary Terms** |

Female Reproductive System

Normal Structure and Function

adnexa *ad-NEK-sah*	Appendages, such as the adnexa uteri—the ovaries, uterine tubes, and uterine ligaments
areola *ah-RE-o-lah*	A pigmented ring, such as the dark area around the nipple of the breast
Graafian follicle *GRAF-e-an*	A mature ovarian follicle
hymen *HI-men*	A fold of mucous membrane that partially covers the entrance of the vagina
mons pubis *monz PU-bis*	The rounded, fleshy elevation anterior to the pubic joint that is covered with hair after puberty
oocyte *O-o-site*	An immature ovum
perimenopause *per-ih-MEN-o-pawz*	The period immediately before menopause; begins at the time of irregular menstrual cycles and ends one year after the last menstrual period; averages three to four years
vestibule *VES-tih-bule*	The space between the labia minora that contains the openings of the urethra, vagina, and ducts of the greater vestibular glands

Disorders

cystocele *SIS-to-sele*	Herniation of the urinary bladder into the wall of the vagina (**Fig. 15-12**)
dyspareunia *dis-par-U-ne-ah*	Pain during sexual intercourse
fibrocystic disease of the breast *fi-bro-SIS-tik*	A condition in which there are palpable lumps in the breasts, usually associated with pain and tenderness; these lumps or "thickenings" change with the menstrual cycle and must be distinguished from malignant tumors by diagnostic methods
hirsutism *HIR-su-tizm*	Excess hair growth
leukorrhea *lu-ko-RE-ah*	White or yellowish discharge from the vagina; infection and other disorders may change the amount, color, or odor of the discharge
microcalcification *mi-kro-kal-sih-fih-KA-shun*	Small deposit of calcium that appears as a white spot on mammograms; most microcalcifications are harmless, but some might indicate breast cancer
prolapse of the uterus	Downward displacement of the uterus with the cervix sometimes protruding from the vagina
rectocele *REK-to-sele*	Herniation of the rectum into the wall of the vagina; also called proctocele (see **Fig. 15-12**)

Diagnosis and Treatment

culdocentesis *kul-do-sen-TE-sis*	Puncture of the vaginal wall to sample fluid from the rectouterine space for diagnosis
episiorrhaphy *eh-pis-e-OR-ah-fe*	Suture of the vulva or suture of the perineum cut in an episiotomy (incision to ease childbirth)
laparoscopy *lap-ah-ROS-ko-pe*	Endoscopic examination of the abdomen; may include surgical procedures, such as tubal ligation (see **Fig. 15-6**)

Terminology	**Supplementary Terms** *(Continued)*

myomectomy *mi-o-MEK-to-me*	Surgical removal of a uterine leiomyoma (fibroid, myoma)
speculum *SPEK-u-lum*	An instrument used to enlarge the opening of a passage or cavity to allow examination (see **Fig. 7-13**)
teletherapy *tel-eh-THER-ah-pe*	Delivery of radiation to a tumor from an external beam source, as compared to implantation of radioactive material (brachytherapy) or systemic administration of radionuclide

Drugs

aromatase inhibitor (AI) *ah-RO-mah-tase*	Agent that inhibits estrogen production; used for postmenopausal treatment of breast cancers that respond to estrogen; examples are exemestane (Aromasin), anastrozole (Arimidex), and letrozole (Femara)
bisphosphonate *bis-FOS-fo-nate*	Agent used to prevent and treat osteoporosis; increases bone mass by decreasing bone turnover; examples are alendronate (Fosamax) and risedronate (Actonel)
HER2 inhibitor	Drug used to treat breast cancers that show excess receptors (HER2) for human epidermal growth factor; example is trastuzumab (Herceptin)
paclitaxel *pak-lih-TAKS-el*	Antineoplastic agent derived from yew trees used mainly in treatment of breast and ovarian cancer; Taxol
selective estrogen receptor modulator (SERM)	Drug that acts on estrogen receptors; examples are tamoxifen (Nolvadex) and raloxifene (Evista), which is also used to prevent bone loss after menopause

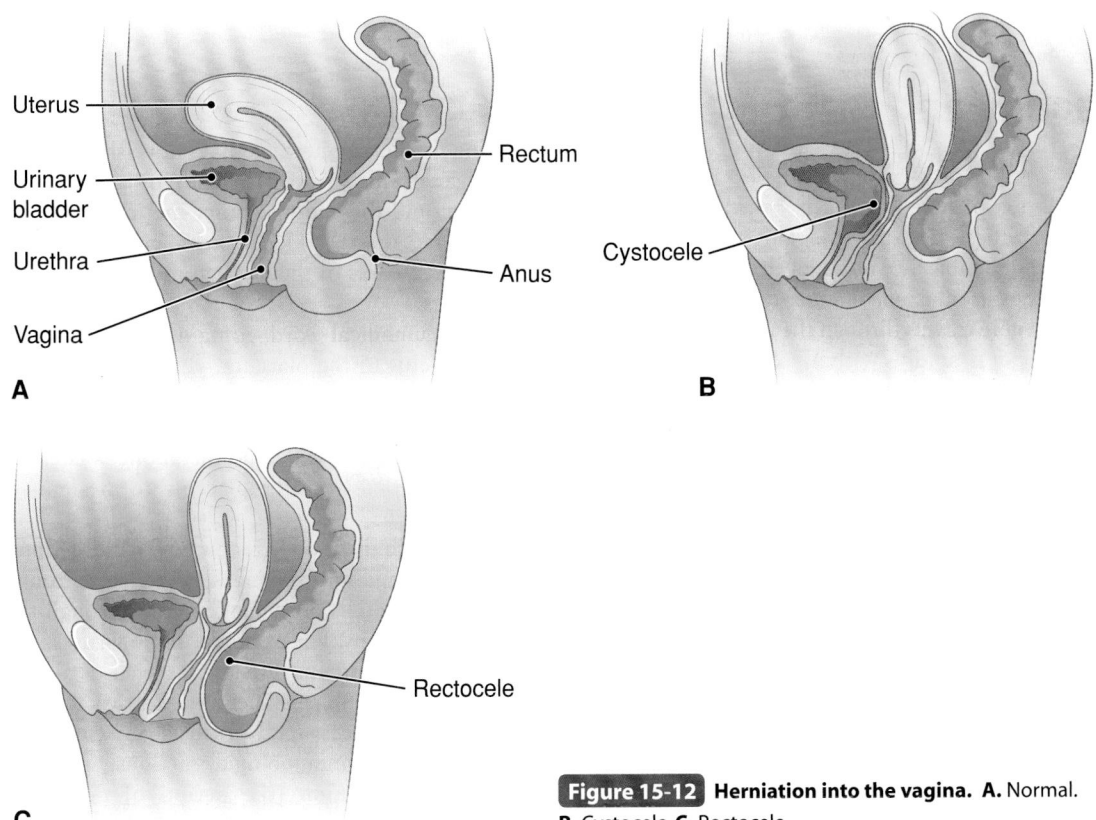

Figure 15-12 **Herniation into the vagina. A.** Normal. **B.** Cystocele. **C.** Rectocele.

AI	Aromatase inhibitor	HRT	Hormone replacement therapy
BRCA1	Breast cancer gene 1	IUD	Intrauterine device
BRCA2	Breast cancer gene 2	LH	Luteinizing hormone
BSE	Breast self-examination	MHT	Menopausal hormone therapy
BSO	Bilateral salpingo-oophorectomy	NGU	Nongonococcal urethritis
BV	Bacterial vaginosis	PCOS	Polycystic ovarian syndrome
CIN	Cervical intraepithelial neoplasia	PID	Pelvic inflammatory disease
D&C	Dilation and curettage	PMS	Premenstrual syndrome
DCIS	Ductal carcinoma in situ	SERM	Selective estrogen receptor modulator
DES	Diethylstilbestrol	STD	Sexually transmitted disease
DUB	Dysfunctional uterine bleeding	STI	Sexually transmitted infection
FSH	Follicle-stimulating hormone	TAH	Total abdominal hysterectomy
GC	Gonococcus (cause of gonorrhea)	TSS	Toxic shock syndrome
GYN	Gynecology	UFE	Uterine fibroid embolization
HPV	Human papillomavirus	VD	Venereal disease (sexually transmitted disease)

Pregnancy and Birth

FERTILIZATION AND EARLY DEVELOPMENT

Penetration of an ovulated egg cell by a spermatozoon results in **fertilization** (**Fig. 15-13**). This union normally occurs in the uterine tube. The nuclei of the sperm and ovum fuse, restoring the chromosome number to 46 and forming a **zygote**. As the zygote travels through the uterine tube toward the uterus, it divides rapidly. Within six to seven days, the fertilized egg reaches the uterus and implants into the endometrium, and the **embryo** begins to develop.

During the first eight weeks of growth, all of the major body systems are established. Embryonic tissue produces **human chorionic gonadotropin (hCG)**, a hormone that keeps the corpus luteum functional in the ovary to maintain the endometrium. (The presence of hCG in urine is the basis for the most commonly used tests for pregnancy.) After two months, placental hormones take over this function, and the corpus luteum degenerates. At this time, the embryo becomes a **fetus** (**Fig. 15-14**).

See the animation "Ovulation and Fertilization" in the Student Resources on thePoint.

THE PLACENTA

During development, the fetus is nourished by the **placenta**, an organ formed from the embryo's outermost layer, the **chorion**, and the endometrium, the innermost layer of the uterus (**Fig. 15-15**). Here, exchanges take place between the bloodstreams of the mother and the fetus through fetal capillaries.

The **umbilical cord** contains the blood vessels that link the fetus to the placenta. Fetal blood is carried to the placenta in two umbilical arteries. While traveling through the placenta, the blood picks up nutrients and oxygen and gives up carbon dioxide and metabolic waste. Replenished blood is carried from the placenta to the fetus in a single umbilical vein.

Although the bloodstreams of the mother and the fetus do not mix and all exchanges take place through capillaries, some materials do manage to get through the placenta in both directions. For example, some viruses, such as HIV and rubella (German measles), as well as drugs, alcohol, and other harmful substances are known to pass from the mother to the fetus; fetal proteins can enter the mother's blood and cause immunologic reactions.

During **gestation** (the period of development), the fetus is cushioned and protected by fluid contained in the

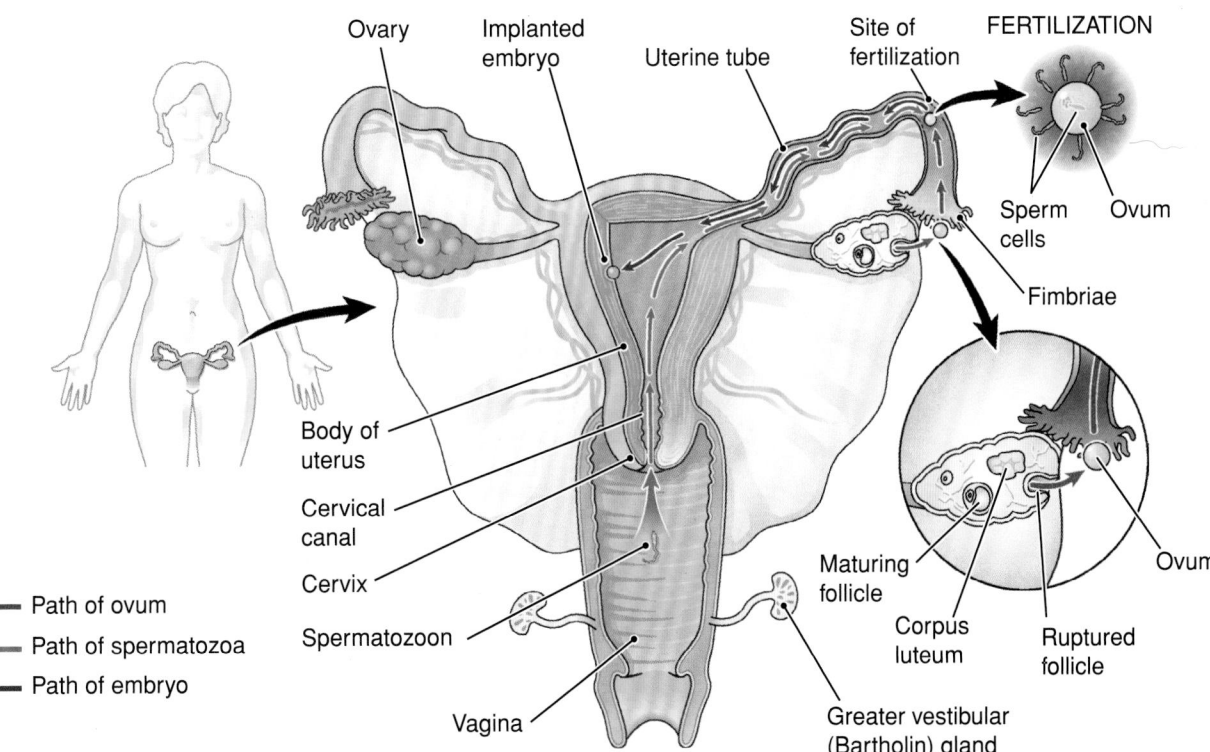

Figure 15-13 **Ovulation and fertilization.** *Arrows* show the pathway of spermatozoa and ovum. Fertilization occurs in the uterine tube, after which the zygote implants in the uterine lining.

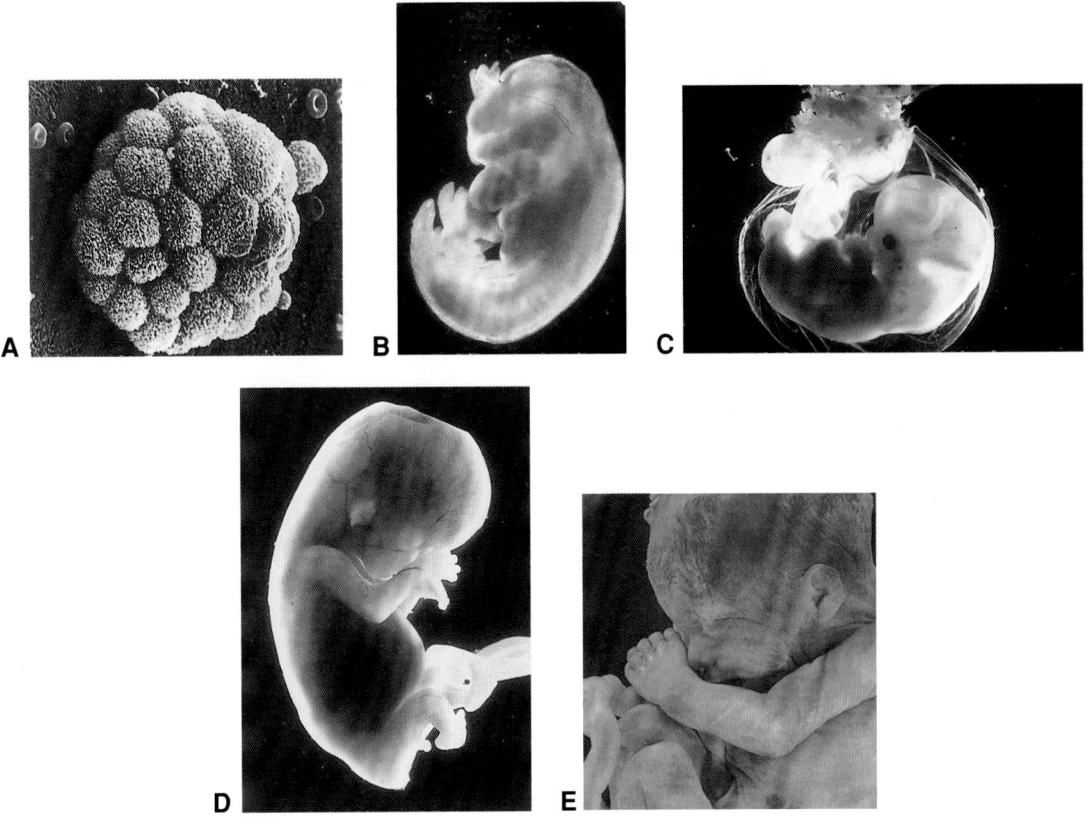

Figure 15-14 **Human development.** Human embryos and an early fetus are shown. **A.** Implantation in the uterus seven to eight days after conception. **B.** Embryo at 32 days. **C.** At 37 days. **D.** At 41 days. **E.** Fetus at 12 to 15 weeks.

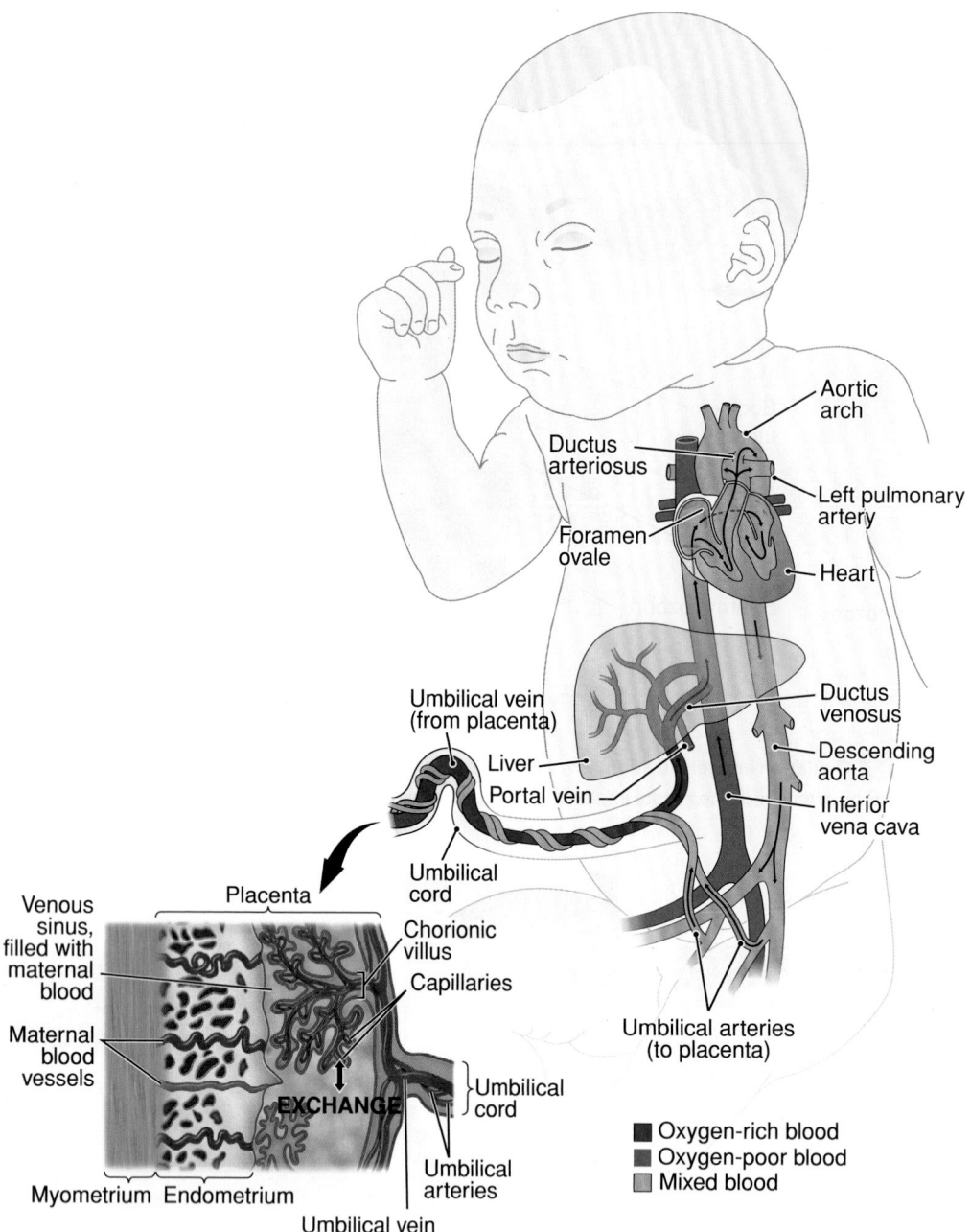

Oxygen-rich blood
Oxygen-poor blood
Mixed blood

Figure 15-15 **Fetal circulation.** Colors show relative oxygen content of blood in the various vessels. Gases, waste products, and nutrients are exchanged between the fetus and the mother through capillaries in the placenta.

amniotic sac (amnion) (**Fig. 15-16**), commonly called the "bag of waters." This sac ruptures at birth.

FETAL CIRCULATION

The fetus has several adaptations that serve to bypass the lungs, which are not needed to oxygenate the blood. When blood coming from the placenta enters the right atrium, the **foramen ovale**, a small hole in the septum between the atria, allows some of the blood to go directly into the left atrium, thus bypassing the pulmonary artery. Further,

blood pumped out of the right ventricle can shunt directly into the aorta through a short vessel, the **ductus arteriosus**, which connects the pulmonary artery with the descending aorta (see **Fig. 15-15**). Both of these passages close off at birth when the pulmonary circuit is established. Their failure to close taxes the heart and may require medical attention.

See the animation "Fetal Circulation" in the Student Resources on thePoint.

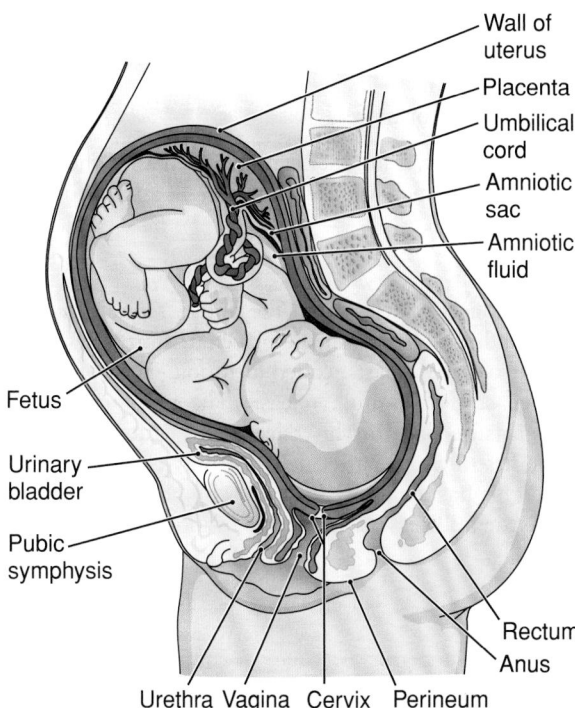

Wall of uterus
Placenta
Umbilical cord
Amniotic sac
Amniotic fluid
Fetus
Urinary bladder
Pubic symphysis
Rectum
Anus
Urethra Vagina Cervix Perineum

Figure 15-16 **Midsagittal section of a pregnant uterus with intact fetus.**

CHILDBIRTH

The length of pregnancy, from fertilization of the ovum to birth, is about 38 weeks, or 266 days. In practice, it is calculated as approximately 280 days or 40 weeks from the first day of the last menstrual period (LMP). For study purposes, pregnancy is divided into three-month periods (trimesters), during which defined changes can be observed in the fetus.

Childbirth, or **parturition**, occurs in three stages:

1. Onset of regular uterine contractions and dilation of the cervix
2. Expulsion of the fetus
3. Delivery of the placenta and fetal membranes

The third stage of childbirth is followed by contraction of the uterus and control of bleeding. The factors that start labor are not completely understood, but it is clear that the hormone **oxytocin** from the posterior pituitary gland and other hormones called **prostaglandins** are involved. **Box 15-3** has career information on midwives and other birth assistants.

Hospitals use the **Apgar score** to assess a newborn's health. Five features—heart rate, respiration, muscle tone, reaction to a nasal catheter, and skin color—are rated as 0, 1, or 2 at one minute and five minutes after birth. The

15

HEALTH PROFESSIONS   Box 15-3
Nurse-Midwives and Doulas

There are various titles associated with the term *midwife*, each having different academic preparation and certification. The name *midwife* literally means "with woman," and the practice is termed midwifery (*mid-WIF-re* or *mid-WIF-er-e*). The role of a midwife in the United States varies based on education, credentials, and licensure.

A certified nurse-midwife (CNM) is educated in the disciplines of both nursing and midwifery. A certified midwife (CM) is educated solely in the discipline of midwifery. A master's degree is required for both titles in order to take the American Midwifery Certification Board (AMCB) exam. Recertification is required every five years. CNMs and CMs provide primary healthcare to women from adolescence to beyond menopause. This includes routine gynecologic and reproductive healthcare, pregnancy, birth, and postpartum care, as well as perimenopause and menopause management. CNMs are licensed in all 50 U.S. states, Washington, D.C., and U.S. territories, and they have prescriptive authority in all U.S. jurisdictions. CMs are licensed in New York, New Jersey, and Rhode Island, and they may practice in Delaware and Missouri. They have prescriptive authority in New York. Most private insurances and Medicaid reimburse for CNM/CM services. The majority of CNM/CMs attend births in hospitals, but they may also attend home births and work in birth centers, clinics, and health departments. The American College of Nurse-Midwives at www.acnm.org has information on these careers.

A Certified Professional Midwife (CPM) is an independent midwifery provider who has met the standards for certification set by the North American Registry of Midwives (NARM). No college degree is required for this specialty. CPMs are regulated in 26 states, which vary in certification, licensure, and registration requirements. CPMs have no prescriptive authority. Private insurance in some states and Medicaid in 10 states reimburse CPMs for home and birth center births. CPMs provide care for women during pregnancy, birth, and the postpartum period and also provide newborn care. The professional associations for CPMs are the Midwives Alliance of North America (MANA) and National Association of Certified Professional Midwives (NACPM). Information is available at www.mana.org.

A doula (birth assistant) is someone who works with families during pregnancy, through labor, and after childbirth. Doulas provide emotional and physical support and education. They may help with prenatal preparation and early labor at home and continue with support throughout the hospital stay. Some doulas are trained in postpartum care and can give the family support at home after the birth. The name *doula* comes from Greek and refers to the most important female servant in the household, who probably assisted the lady of the house in childbearing. Doulas have a professional association that sets standards for training and certification. For more information visit www.dona.org.

maximum score in the test is 10. Infants with low scores require medical attention.

> See the chart on placental hormones and figures on the stages of labor and the Apgar score in the Student Resources on thePoint.

The term **gravida** refers to a pregnant woman. The term **para** refers to a woman who has given birth. This means the production of a viable infant (500 g or more or over 20 weeks gestation) regardless of whether the infant is alive at birth or whether the birth is single or multiple. Prefixes are added to both terms to indicate the number of pregnancies or births, such as:

- nulli—none
- primi—one
- secondi—two
- tri or terti—three
- quadri—four
- multi—two or more

Alternatively, a number can be added after the term to indicate events, such as gravida 1, para 3, and so forth.

LACTATION

The hormone prolactin from the anterior pituitary gland, as well as hormones from the placenta, start the secretion of milk from the breasts, called **lactation**. The baby's suckling then stimulates milk release. The pituitary hormone oxytocin is needed for this release or "letdown" of milk. For the first few days after delivery, only **colostrum** is produced. This has a slightly different composition than milk, but like the milk, it has protective antibodies.

Terminology	Key Terms

Pregnancy and Birth

Normal Structure and Function

amniotic sac am-ne-OT-ik	The membranous sac filled with fluid that holds the fetus; also called amnion (root: amnio)
Apgar score AP-gar	A system of rating an infant's physical condition immediately after birth; five features are rated as 0, 1, or 2 at one and five minutes after delivery and sometimes thereafter; the maximum possible score at each test interval is 10; infants with low scores require medical attention
chorion KOR-e-on	The outermost layer of the embryo that, with the endometrium, forms the placenta (adjective: chorionic)
colostrum ko-LOS-trum	Breast fluid that is secreted in the first few days after giving birth before milk is produced
ductus arteriosus DUK-tus ar-tere-e-O-sus	A fetal blood vessel that connects the pulmonary artery with the descending aorta, thus allowing blood to bypass the lungs
embryo EM-bre-o	The stage in development between the zygote and the fetus, extending from the second through the eighth week of growth in the uterus (root: embry/o) (adjective: embryonic)
fertilization fer-tih-lih-ZA-shun	The union of an ovum and a spermatozoon
fetus FE-tus	The developing child in the uterus from the third month to birth (root: fet/o) (adjective: fetal)
foramen ovale fo-RA-men o-VA-le	A small hole in the interatrial septum in the fetal heart that allows blood to pass directly from the right to the left side of the heart
gestation jes-TA-shun	The period of development from conception to birth
gravida GRAV-ih-da	Pregnant woman

Terminology	Key Terms *(Continued)*

human chorionic gonadotropin (hCG) *kor-e-ON-ik GO-nah-do-tro-pin*	A hormone secreted by the embryo early in pregnancy that maintains the corpus luteum so that it will continue to secrete hormones
lactation *lak-TA-shun*	The secretion of milk from the mammary glands
oxytocin *ok-se-TO-sin*	A pituitary hormone that stimulates contractions of the uterus; it also stimulates release ("letdown") of milk from the breasts
para	Woman who has produced a viable infant; multiple births are considered as single pregnancies
parturition *par-tu-RIH-shun*	Childbirth (root: nat/i); labor (root: toc/o)
placenta *plah-SEN-tah*	The organ composed of fetal and maternal tissues that nourishes and maintains the developing fetus
prostaglandins *PROS-tah-glan-dinz*	A group of hormones with varied effects, including the stimulation of uterine contractions
umbilical cord *um-BIL-ih-kal*	The structure that connects the fetus to the placenta; it contains vessels that carry blood between the mother and the fetus
zygote *ZI-gote*	The fertilized ovum

Roots Pertaining to Pregnancy and Birth

See Table 15-4.

Table 15-4	Roots for Pregnancy and Birth

Root	Meaning	Example	Definition of Example
amnio	amnion, amniotic sac	diamniotic *di-am-ne-OT-ik*	showing two amniotic sacs
embry/o	embryo	embryonic *em-bre-ON-ik*	pertaining to the embryo
fet/o	fetus	fetometry *fe-TOM-eh-tre*	measurement of a fetus
toc/o	labor	dystocia *dis-TO-se-ah*	difficult labor
nat/i	birth	neonate *NE o-nate*	newborn
lact/o	milk	lactose *LAK-tose*	sugar (-ose) found in milk
galact/o	milk	galactogogue *gah-LAK-to-gog*	agent that promotes (-agogue) the flow of milk
gravida	pregnant woman	nulligravida *nul-ih-GRAV-ih-dah*	woman who has never (nulli-) been pregnant
para	woman who has given birth	multipara *mul-TIP-ah-rah*	woman who has given birth two or more times

EXERCISE 15-4

Define the following words.

1. prenatal (*pre-NA-tal*) _____

2. embryogenesis (*em-bre-o-JEN-eh-sis*) _____

3. neonatal (*ne-o-NA-tal*) _____

4. fetoscopy (*fe-TOS-ko-pe*) _____

5. monoamniotic (*mon-o-am-ne-OT-ik*) _____

6. agalactia (*a-gah-LAK-she-ah*) _____

7. hypolactation (*hi-po-lak-TA-shun*) _____

Use the appropriate roots to write words for the following.

8. study of an embryo _____

9. after birth _____

10. incision of the amnion (to induce labor) _____

11. cell (-cyte) found in amniotic fluid _____

12. any disease of an embryo _____

13. instrument for endoscopic examination of the fetus _____

14. rupture of the amniotic sac _____

15. study of the newborn _____

16. woman who is pregnant for the first time _____

17. woman who has been pregnant two or more times _____

18. woman who has never given birth _____

19. woman who has given birth to one child _____

Use the suffix *-tocia*, meaning "condition of labor," to write words for the following.

20. dry labor _____

21. slow labor _____

Use the root *galact/o* to write words for the following.

22. discharge of milk _____

23. cystic enlargement (-cele) of a milk duct _____

Clinical Aspects of Pregnancy and Birth

INFERTILITY

About 10 to 15 percent of couples who want children are unable to conceive or to sustain a pregnancy. Some of the possible causes of infertility are discussed in Chapter 14 and in this section. In men, these causes include low sperm count, low sperm motility, blockage of the ducts that transport the sperm cells, and erectile dysfunction. In women they include:

- Lack of ovulation
- Blockage in the uterine tubes, as caused by infection or excess growth of tissue
- Uterine problems, such as tumors or abnormal growth of endometrial tissue
- Cervical scarring or infection
- Excess vaginal acidity, which harms spermatozoa, or antibodies to sperm cells

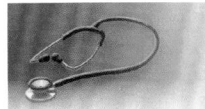

CLINICAL PERSPECTIVES

Box 15-4

Assisted Reproductive Technology: The "Art" of Conception

At least one in 10 American couples is affected by infertility. Assisted reproductive technologies such as in vitro fertilization (IVF), gamete intrafallopian transfer (GIFT), and zygote intrafallopian transfer (ZIFT) can help these couples have children.

In vitro fertilization refers to fertilization of an egg outside the mother's body in a laboratory dish, and it is often used when a woman's fallopian tubes are blocked or when a man has a low sperm count. The woman participating in IVF is given hormones to cause ovulation of several eggs. These are then withdrawn with a needle and fertilized with the father's sperm. After a few divisions, some of the fertilized eggs are placed in the uterus, thus bypassing the fallopian tubes. Additional fertilized eggs can be frozen to repeat the procedure in case of failure or for later pregnancies.

GIFT can be used when the woman has at least one normal fallopian tube and the man has an adequate sperm count.

As in IVF, the woman is given hormones to cause ovulation of several eggs, which are collected. Then, the eggs and the father's sperm are placed into the fallopian tube using a catheter. Thus, in GIFT, fertilization occurs inside the woman, not in a laboratory dish.

ZIFT is a combination of IVF and GIFT. Fertilization takes place in a laboratory dish, and then the zygote is placed into the fallopian tube.

Because of a lack of guidelines or restrictions in the United States in the field of assisted reproductive technology, some problems have arisen. These issues concern the use of stored embryos and gametes, use of embryos without consent, and improper screening for disease among donors. In addition, the implantation of more than one fertilized egg has resulted in a high incidence of multiple births, even up to seven or eight offspring in a single pregnancy, a situation that imperils the survival and health of the babies.

- Drugs, including temporary or permanent infertility following cessation of birth control pills

Box 15-4 describes some clinical approaches to helping infertile couples have children when all other diagnostic and therapeutic methods have failed.

ECTOPIC PREGNANCY

Development of a fertilized egg outside of its normal position in the uterine cavity is termed an **ectopic pregnancy** (**Fig. 15-17**). Although it may occur elsewhere in the abdominal cavity, an ectopic pregnancy usually occurs in the uterine tube, resulting in a tubal pregnancy. Salpingitis, endometriosis, and PID may lead to ectopic pregnancy by blocking the ovum's passage into the uterus. Continued growth will rupture the tube, causing dangerous hemorrhage. Symptoms of ectopic pregnancy are pain, tenderness, swelling, and shock. Diagnosis is by measurement of the hormone hCG and **ultrasonography**, confirmed by laparoscopic examination. Prompt surgery is required, sometimes including removal of the tube.

PREGNANCY-INDUCED HYPERTENSION

Pregnancy-induced hypertension (PIH), also referred to as preeclampsia or toxemia of pregnancy, is a state of hypertension during pregnancy in association with oliguria, proteinuria, and edema. The cause is a hormone imbalance that results in constriction of blood vessels. If untreated, PIH may lead to **eclampsia**, with seizures, coma, and possible death.

ABORTION

For a variety of reasons, a pregnancy may terminate before the fetus is capable of surviving outside the uterus. An **abortion** is

loss of an embryo or fetus before the 20th week of pregnancy or before a weight of 500 g (1.1 lb). When this occurs spontaneously, it is commonly referred to as a miscarriage. Most spontaneous abortions occur within the first three months of pregnancy. Causes include poor maternal health, hormonal imbalance, cervical incompetence (weakness), immune

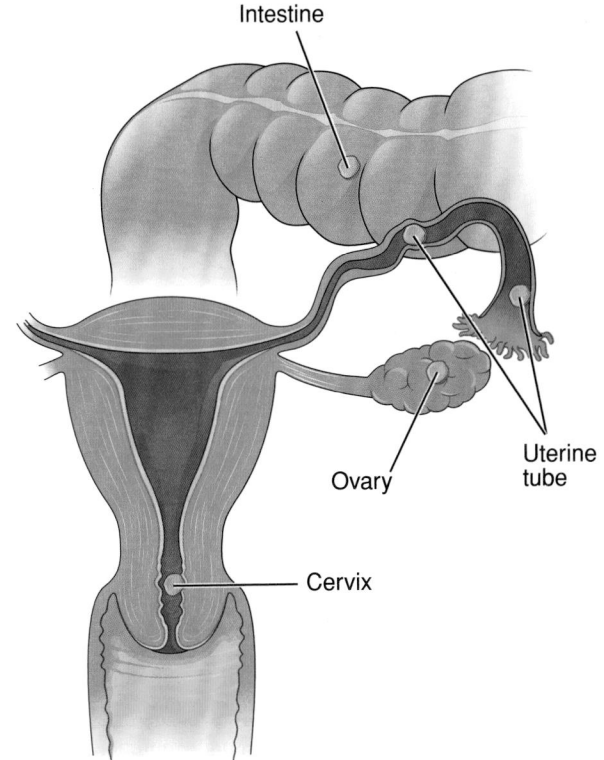

Figure 15-17 Ectopic pregnancy. Possible sites where a fertilized ovum might develop outside the body of the uterus.

reactions, tumors, and, most commonly, fetal abnormalities. If all gestational tissues are not eliminated, the abortion is described as incomplete, and a physician must remove the remaining tissue.

An induced abortion is the intentional termination of a pregnancy. A common method for inducing an abortion is **dilatation and evacuation (D&E)**, in which the cervix is dilated and the fetal tissue is removed by suction.

Rh INCOMPATIBILITY

Incompatibility between the blood of a mother and her fetus is a problem in certain pregnancies. If a mother lacks the Rh blood antigen (see Chapter 10) and her baby is positive for that factor (inherited from the father), the mother's body may make Rh antibodies as her baby's blood crosses the placenta during pregnancy or enters the maternal bloodstream during childbirth. In a subsequent pregnancy with an Rh-positive fetus, the antibodies may enter the fetus and destroy its red cells. **Hemolytic disease of the newborn (HDN)** is prevented by giving the mother preformed Rh antibodies during pregnancy and shortly after delivery to remove these proteins from her blood.

PLACENTAL ABNORMALITIES

If the placenta attaches near or over the cervix instead of in the upper portion of the uterus, the condition is termed **placenta previa**. This disorder may cause bleeding later in the pregnancy. If bleeding is heavy, it may be necessary to terminate the pregnancy.

Placental abruption (abruptio placentae) describes premature separation of the placenta from its point of attachment. The separation causes hemorrhage, which, if extensive, may result in fetal or maternal death or a need to end the pregnancy. Causative factors include injury, maternal hypertension, and advanced maternal age.

See the figure on placental abnormalities in the Student Resources on the Point.

MASTITIS

Inflammation of the breast, or **mastitis**, may occur at any time but usually occurs in the early weeks of breast-feeding. It is commonly caused by staphylococcal or streptococcal bacteria that enter through cracks in the nipple. The breast becomes red, swollen, and tender, and the patient may experience chills, fever, and general discomfort.

Congenital Disorders

Congenital disorders are those present at birth (birth defects). They fall into two categories:

- Developmental disorders that occur during fetal growth
- Hereditary (familial) disorders that can be passed from parents to children through the germ cells

A genetic disorder is caused by a **mutation** (change) in the genes or chromosomes of cells. Mutations may involve changes in the number or structure of the chromosomes or changes in single or multiple genes. The appearance and severity of genetic disorders may also involve abnormal genes interacting with environmental factors. Examples are the diseases that "run in families," such as diabetes mellitus, heart disease, hypertension, and certain forms of cancer. **Box 15-5** describes some of the most common genetic disorders.

See a more complete chart of genetic diseases in the Student Resources on the Point.

FOR YOUR REFERENCE

Box 15-5

Genetic Disorders[a]

Disease	Cause	Description
albinism AL-bih-nizm	recessive gene mutation	lack of pigmentation
cystic fibrosis sis-tik fi-BRO-sis	recessive gene mutation	affects respiratory system, pancreas, and sweat glands; most common hereditary disease in white populations (see Chapter 11)
Down syndrome	extra chromosome 21	slanted eyes, short stature, mental retardation, and others (**Fig. 15-18**); incidence increases with increasing maternal age; trisomy 21 syndrome
fragile X chromosome	defect in an X (sex-determining) chromosome	reduced intellectual abilities, autism, hyperactivity; enlarged head and ears; passed from mothers to sons with the X chromosome (sex-linked)
hemophilia he-mo-FIL-e-ah	recessive gene mutation on the X chromosome	bleeding disease inherited with an X chromosome and usually passed from mothers to sons
Huntington disease	dominant gene mutation	altered metabolism destroys specific nerve cells; appears in adulthood and is fatal within about 10 years; causes motor and mental disorders

Genetic Disorders (*Continued*)

Disease	Cause	Description
Klinefelter syndrome	extra X chromosome	lack of sexual development, lowered intelligence
Marfan syndrome	dominant gene mutation	disease of connective tissue with weakness of the aorta
neurofibromatosis *nu-ro-fi-bro-mah-TO-sis*	dominant gene mutation	multiple skin tumors containing nerve tissue
phenylketonuria (PKU) *fen-il-ke-to-NU-re-ah*	recessive gene mutation	lack of enzyme to metabolize an amino acid (phenylalanine); neurologic signs, mental retardation, lack of pigment; tested for at birth; special diet can prevent retardation
sickle cell anemia	recessive gene mutation	abnormally shaped red cells block blood vessels; mainly affects black populations
Tay–Sachs disease *ta-saks*	recessive gene mutation	an enzyme deficiency causes lipid to accumulate in nerve cells and other tissues; causes death in early childhood; carried in eastern European Jewish populations
Turner syndrome	single X chromosome	sexual immaturity, short stature, possible lowered intelligence

*ᵃ*A dominant gene is one for a trait that always appears if the gene is present; that is, it will affect the offspring even if inherited from only one parent. A recessive gene is one for a trait that will appear only if the gene is inherited from both parents.

15

A **carrier** of a genetic disorder is an individual who has a genetic defect that does not appear but that can be passed to offspring. Laboratory tests can identify carriers of some genetic disorders.

Teratogens are factors that cause malformations in the developing fetus. These include infections—such as rubella, herpes simplex, and syphilis—alcohol, drugs, chemicals, and radiation. The fetus is most susceptible to teratogenic effects during the first three months of pregnancy.

Examples of developmental disorders are **atresia** (absence or closure of a normal body opening), **anencephaly** (absence of a brain), **cleft lip**, **cleft palate**, and congenital heart disease. **Spina bifida** is incomplete closure of the spine, through which the spinal cord and its membranes may project (**Fig. 15-19**). This usually occurs in the lumbar region. If there is no herniation of tissue, the condition is spina bifida occulta. Protrusion of the meninges through

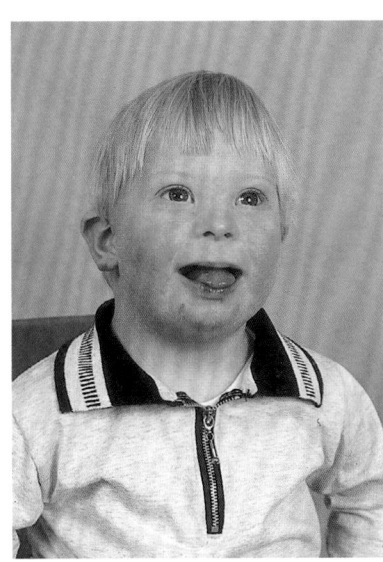

Figure 15-18 **Child with Down syndrome (trisomy 21).** The typical facial features are visible in this photo.

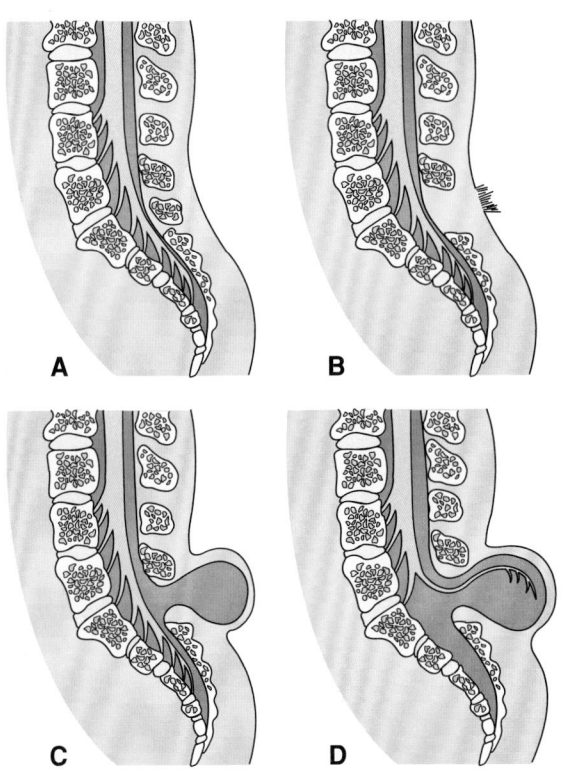

Figure 15-19 **Spinal defects. A.** Normal spinal cord. **B.** Spina bifida occulta. **C.** Meningocele. **D.** Myelomeningocele.

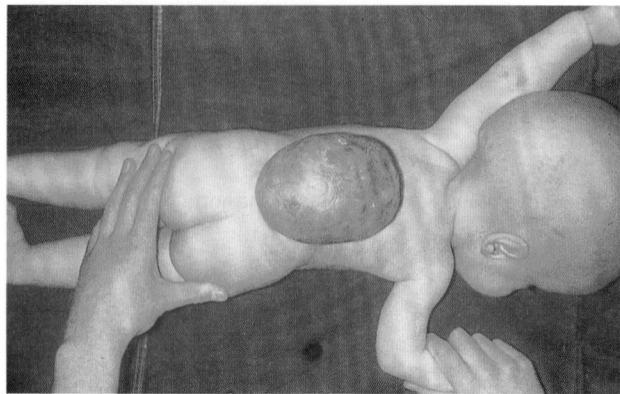

Figure 15-20 A myelomeningocele.

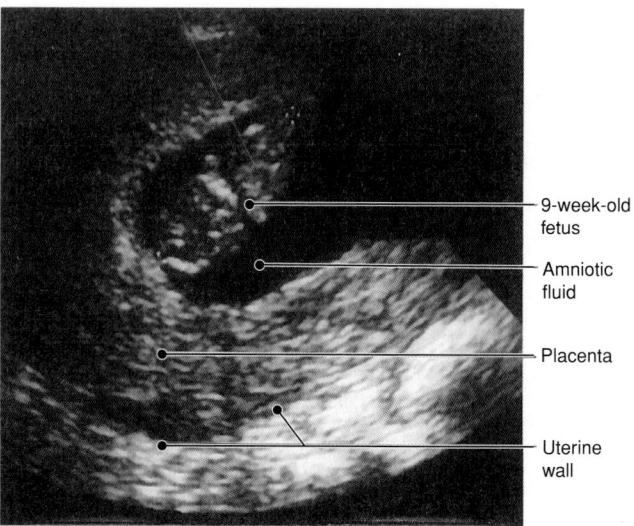

9-week-old fetus

Amniotic fluid

Placenta

Uterine wall

Figure 15-21 **Sonogram.** This transvaginal sonogram shows a 9-week-old fetus.

the opening is a meningocele; in a myelomeningocele, both the spinal cord and membranes herniate through the defect, as seen in **Figures 15-19D** and **15-20**. Note that folic acid or folate, a B vitamin, can prevent embryonic spinal malformations, known as neural tube defects. This vitamin is found in vegetables, liver, legumes, and seeds, but it is now added to some commercial foods, including cereals and breads, to provide young women with this vitamin early on in case they become pregnant.

DIAGNOSIS OF CONGENITAL DISORDERS

Many congenital disorders can now be detected before birth. Ultrasonography (**Fig. 15-21**), in addition to its use for monitoring pregnancies and determining fetal sex, can

also reveal certain fetal abnormalities. In **amniocentesis** (**Fig. 15-22**), a sample is withdrawn from the amniotic cavity with a needle. The fluid obtained is analyzed for chemical abnormalities. The cells are grown in the laboratory and tested for biochemical disorders. A **karyotype** is prepared to study the genetic material (see **Fig. 4-10**).

In **chorionic villus sampling** (**CVS**), small amounts of the membrane around the fetus are obtained through the cervix for analysis. This can be done at eight to 10 weeks of pregnancy, in comparison with 14 to 16 weeks for amniocentesis.

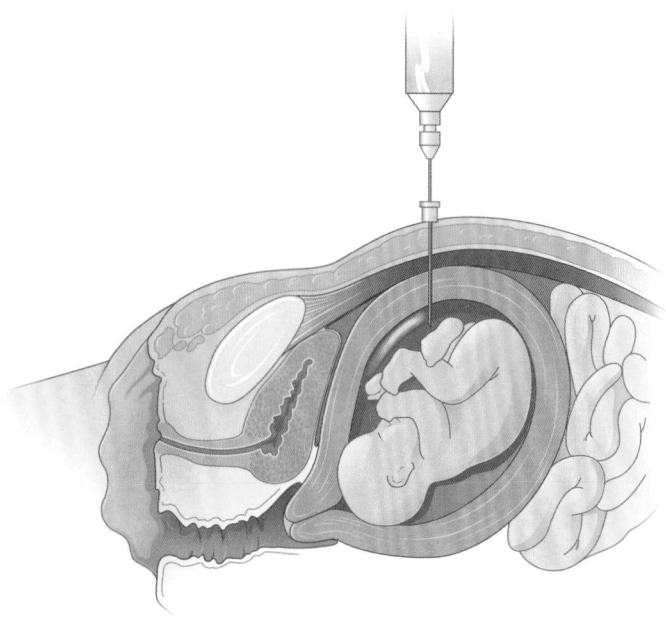

Figure 15-22 **Amniocentesis.** A sample is removed from the amniotic sac. Cells and fluid are tested for fetal abnormalities.

| Terminology | Key Terms |

Pregnancy and Birth

Disorders

abortion *ah-BOR-shun*	Termination of a pregnancy before the fetus is capable of surviving outside the uterus, usually at 20 weeks or 500 g; may be spontaneous or induced; a spontaneous abortion is commonly called a miscarriage
anencephaly *an-en-SEF-ah-le*	Congenital absence of a brain
atresia *ah-TRE-ze-ah*	Congenital absence or closure of a normal body opening
carrier	An individual who has an unexpressed genetic defect that can be passed to his or her children
cleft lip	A congenital separation of the upper lip
cleft palate	A congenital split in the roof of the mouth
congenital disorder *kon-JEN-ih-tal*	A disorder that is present at birth; may be developmental or hereditary (familial)
eclampsia *eh-KLAMP-se-ah*	Convulsions and coma occurring during pregnancy or after delivery and associated with the conditions of pregnancy-induced hypertension (see below) (adjective: eclamptic)
ectopic pregnancy *ek-TOP-ik*	Development of the fertilized ovum outside the body of the uterus; usually occurs in the uterine tube (tubal pregnancy) but may occur in other parts of the reproductive tract or abdominal cavity (see **Fig. 15-17**)
hemolytic disease of the newborn (HDN)	Disease that results from Rh incompatibility between the blood of a mother and her fetus; an Rh-negative mother produces antibody to Rh-positive fetal red cells that enter her circulation; these antibodies can destroy Rh-positive fetal red cells in a later pregnancy unless the mother is treated with antibodies to remove the Rh antigen; formerly called erythroblastosis fetalis
mastitis *mas-TI-tis*	Inflammation of the breast, usually associated with the early weeks of breast-feeding
mutation *mu-TA-shun*	A change in the genetic material of the cell; most mutations are harmful; if the change appears in the sex cells, it can be passed to future generations
placental abruption *ab-RUP-shun*	Premature separation of the placenta; abruptio placentae
placenta previa *PRE-ve-ah*	Placental attachment in the lower portion of the uterus instead of the upper portion, as is normal; may result in hemorrhage late in pregnancy
pregnancy-induced hypertension (PIH)	A toxic condition of late pregnancy associated with hypertension, edema, and proteinuria that, if untreated, may lead to eclampsia; also called preeclampsia (*pre-eh-KLAMP-se-ah*) and toxemia of pregnancy
spina bifida *SPI-nah BIF-ih-dah*	A congenital defect in the closure of the spinal column through which the spinal cord and its membranes may project (see **Figs. 15-19** and **15-20**)
teratogen *ter-AT-o-jen*	A factor that causes developmental abnormalities in the fetus (root terat/o means "malformed fetus") (adjective: teratogenic)

Diagnosis and Treatment

amniocentesis *am-ne-o-sen-TE-sis*	Transabdominal puncture of the amniotic sac to remove amniotic fluid for testing; tests on the cells and fluid obtained can reveal congenital abnormalities, blood incompatibility, and sex of the fetus (see **Fig. 15-22**)

(continued)

Terminology | Key Terms (*Continued*)

chorionic villus sampling (CVS)	Removal of chorionic cells through the cervix for prenatal testing; can be done earlier in pregnancy than amniocentesis
dilatation and evacuation (D&E)	Widening of the cervix and removal of conception products by suction
karyotype *KAR-e-o-tipe*	A picture of cellular chromosomes arranged in order of decreasing size; can reveal abnormalities in the chromosomes themselves or in their number or arrangement (root kary/o means "nucleus") (see **Fig. 4-10**)
ultrasonography *ul-trah-so-NOG-rah-fe*	The use of high-frequency sound waves to produce a photograph of an organ or tissue (see **Fig. 15-21**); used in obstetrics to diagnose pregnancy, multiple births, and abnormalities and also to study and measure the fetus; the image obtained is a sonogram or ultrasonogram

Terminology | Supplementary Terms

Pregnancy and Birth

Normal Structure and Function

afterbirth	The placenta and membranes delivered after birth of a child
antepartum *an-te-PAR-tum*	Before childbirth, with reference to the mother
Braxton Hicks contractions	Light uterine contractions that occur during pregnancy and increase in frequency and intensity during the third trimester; they strengthen the uterus for delivery
chloasma *klo-AZ-mah*	Brownish pigmentation that appears on the face during pregnancy; melasma
fontanel *fon-tan-EL*	A membrane-covered space between cranial bones in the fetus that later becomes ossified; a soft spot; also spelled fontanelle
intrapartum *in-trah-PAR-tum*	Occurring during childbirth
linea nigra *LIN-e-ah NI-grah*	A dark line on the abdomen from the umbilicus to the pubic region that may appear late in pregnancy
lochia *LO-ke-ah*	The mixture of blood, mucus, and tissue discharged from the uterus after childbirth
meconium *meh-KO-ne-um*	The first feces of the newborn
peripartum *per-ih-PAR-tum*	Occurring during the end of pregnancy or the first few months after delivery, with reference to the mother
postpartum	After childbirth, with reference to the mother
premature	Describing an infant born before the organ systems are fully developed; immature
preterm	Occurring before the 37th week of gestation; describing an infant born before the 37th week of gestation
puerperium *pu-er-PERE-e-um*	The first 42 days after childbirth, during which the mother's reproductive organs usually return to normal (root puer means "child")

Terminology	**Supplementary Terms** (*Continued*)

striae atrophicae *STRI-e ah-TRO-fih-ke*	Pinkish or gray lines that appear where skin has been stretched, as in pregnancy; stretch marks, striae gravidarum
umbilicus *um-bih-LI-kus*	The scar in the middle of the abdomen that marks the attachment point of the umbilical cord to the fetus; the navel; also pronounced *um-BIL-ih-kus*
vernix caseosa *VER-niks ka-se-O-sah*	The cheese-like deposit that covers and protects the fetus (literally "cheesy varnish")

Disorders

cephalopelvic disproportion *sef-ah-lo-PEL-vik*	The condition in which the head of the fetus is larger than the mother's pelvic outlet; also called fetopelvic disproportion
choriocarcinoma *kor-e-o-kar-sih-NO-mah*	A rare malignant neoplasm composed of placental tissue
galactorrhea *gah-lak-to-RE-ah*	Excessive secretion of milk or continued milk production after breast-feeding has ceased; often results from excess prolactin secretion and may signal a pituitary tumor
hydatidiform mole *hi-dah-TID-ih-form*	A benign overgrowth of placental tissue; the placenta dilates and resembles grape-like cysts; the neoplasm may invade the uterine wall, causing rupture; also called hydatid mole
hydramnios *hi-DRAM-ne-os*	An excess of amniotic fluid; also called polyhydramnios
oligohydramnios *ol-ih-go-hi-DRAM-ne-os*	A deficiency of amniotic fluid
patent ductus arteriosus (PDA) *PA-tent DUK-tus ar-te-re-O-sus*	Persistence of the ductus arteriosus after birth so that blood continues to shunt from the pulmonary artery to the aorta
puerperal infection *pu-ER-per-al*	Infection of the genital tract after delivery

Diagnosis and Treatment

abortifacient *a-bor-tih-FA-shent*	Agent that induces abortion
alpha-fetoprotein (AFP) *AL-fah-fe-to-PRO-tene*	A fetal protein that may be elevated in amniotic fluid and maternal serum in cases of certain fetal disorders
artificial insemination (AI)	Placement of active semen into the vagina or cervix for the purpose of impregnation; the semen can be from a husband, partner, or donor
cesarean section *seh-ZAR-e-an*	Incision of the abdominal wall and uterus for delivery of a fetus; also called cesarean birth
endometrial ablation *ab-LA-shun*	Selective destruction of the endometrium for therapeutic purpose; done to relieve excessive menstrual bleeding (menorrhagia)
extracorporeal membrane oxygenation (ECMO) *eks-trah-kor-PO-re-al*	A technique for pulmonary bypass in which deoxygenated blood is removed, passed through a circuit that oxygenates the blood, and then returned; used for selected newborn and pediatric patients in respiratory failure with an otherwise good prognosis
in vitro fertilization (IVF)	Clinical procedure for achieving fertilization when it cannot be accomplished naturally; an oocyte (immature ovum) is removed, fertilized in the laboratory, and placed as a zygote into the uterus or fallopian tube (ZIFT, zygote intrafallopian transfer); alternatively, an ovum can be removed and placed along with sperm cells into the fallopian tube (GIFT, gamete intrafallopian transfer) (see **Box 15-4**)

(*continued*)

Terminology | Supplementary Terms (*Continued*)

obstetrics *ob-STET-riks*	The branch of medicine that treats women during pregnancy, childbirth, and the puerperium; usually combined with the practice of gynecology
pediatrics *pe-de-AT-riks*	The branch of medicine that treats children and diseases of children (root ped/o means "child")
pelvimetry *pel-VIM-eh-tre*	Measurement of the pelvis by manual examination or radiographic study to determine whether delivery of a fetus through the vagina will be possible
Pitocin *pih-TO-sin*	Trade name for oxytocin; used to induce and hasten labor
presentation	Term describing the part of the fetus that can be felt by vaginal or rectal examination; normally the head presents first (vertex presentation), but sometimes the buttocks (breech presentation), face, or other part presents first
RhoGAM *RO-gam*	Trade name for a preparation of antibody to the Rh(D) antigen; used to prevent hemolytic disease of the newborn in cases of Rh incompatibility

Terminology | Abbreviations

Pregnancy and Birth

AB	Abortion		**GIFT**	Gamete intrafallopian transfer
AFP	Alpha-fetoprotein		**hCG**	Human chorionic gonadotropin
AGA	Appropriate for gestational age		**HDN**	Hemolytic disease of the newborn
AI	Artificial insemination		**IVF**	In vitro fertilization
ART	Assisted reproductive technology		**LMP**	Last menstrual period
C-section	Cesarean section		**NB**	Newborn
CPD	Cephalopelvic disproportion		**NICU**	Neonatal intensive care unit
CVS	Chorionic villus sampling		**OB**	Obstetrics, obstetrician
D&E	Dilatation and evacuation		**PDA**	Patent ductus arteriosus
ECMO	Extracorporeal membrane oxygenation		**PIH**	Pregnancy-induced hypertension
EDC	Estimated date of confinement		**PKU**	Phenylketonuria
FHR	Fetal heart rate		**SVD**	Spontaneous vaginal delivery
FHT	Fetal heart tone		**UC**	Uterine contractions
FTND	Full-term normal delivery		**UTP**	Uterine term pregnancy
FTP	Full-term pregnancy		**VBAC**	Vaginal birth after cesarean section
GA	Gestational age		**ZIFT**	Zygote intrafallopian transfer

Case Study Revisited

A.Y.'s Follow-Up Study

A.Y. was encouraged to get up and walk the next day. Her incision was healing well, and there were no signs of infection. She was able to tolerate a regular diet and required minimal medication for pain. A.Y. experienced minor discomfort with breast-feeding initially, but she and the baby began to get into a routine, and the feeding progressed well. A.Y.'s husband offered needed support and encouragement and was very helpful with their 3-year-old son, who missed his mom. Both baby and mom were doing well and were discharged home. A.Y.'s mother was stopping by every day to take care of the "big brother," help with meals, and do some light housekeeping so A.Y. could get some important rest.

CHAPTER

15 Review

Labeling Exercise

FEMALE REPRODUCTIVE SYSTEM

Write the name of each numbered part on the corresponding line.

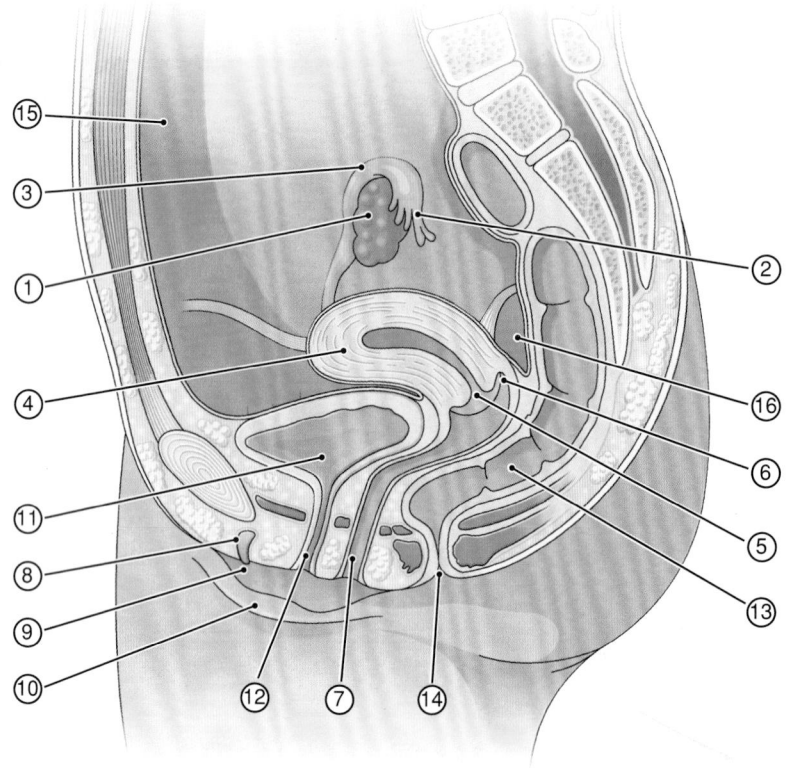

Anus

Cervix

Clitoris

Cul-de-sac

Fimbriae

Labium majus

Labium minus

Ovary

Uterine tube

Peritoneal cavity

Posterior fornix

Rectum

Urethra

Urinary bladder

Uterus

Vagina

1. _____

2. _____

3. _____

4. _____

5. _____

6. _____

7. _____

8. _____

9. _____

10. _____

11. _____

12. _____

13. _____

14. _____

15. _____

16. _____

OVULATION AND FERTILIZATION

Write the name of each numbered part on the corresponding line.

Cervix
Body of uterus
Fimbriae
Greater vestibular (Bartholin)
     gland
Implanted embryo

Ovary
Ovum
Sperm cells (spermatozoa)
Uterine tube
Vagina

1. _____
2. _____
3. _____
4. _____
5. _____
6. _____
7. _____
8. _____
9. _____
10. _____

Terminology

MATCHING

Match the following terms, and write the appropriate letter to the left of each number.

_____ **1.** vulva	**a.** fertilized egg
_____ **2.** gestation	**b.** female erectile tissue
_____ **3.** oxytocin	**c.** external female genitalia
_____ **4.** zygote	**d.** period of development in the uterus
_____ **5.** clitoris	**e.** hormone that stimulates labor

_____ **6.** menostasis	**a.** first menstrual period
_____ **7.** metrorrhagia	**b.** excess uterine bleeding
_____ **8.** menarche	**c.** suppression of menstruation
_____ **9.** gynecogenic	**d.** wasting of uterine tissue
_____ **10.** metratrophia	**e.** producing female characteristics

_____ **11.** eclampsia	**a.** fibroid
_____ **12.** mutation	**b.** absence of a normal body opening
_____ **13.** teratogen	**c.** genetic change
_____ **14.** atresia	**d.** convulsions and coma occurring during pregnancy
_____ **15.** leiomyoma	**e.** cause of fetal abnormality

Supplementary Terms

_____	**16.** puerperium	**a.** uterine discharge after childbirth
_____	**17.** linea nigra	**b.** period after childbirth
_____	**18.** meconium	**c.** first feces of the newborn
_____	**19.** hymen	**d.** membrane that covers the vaginal opening
_____	**20.** lochia	**e.** dark line on the abdomen from umbilicus to pubic region

_____	**21.** hirsutism	**a.** excess of amniotic fluid
_____	**22.** dyspareunia	**b.** pain during intercourse
_____	**23.** vernix caseosa	**c.** whitish vaginal discharge
_____	**24.** leukorrhea	**d.** excess hair growth
_____	**25.** polyhydramnios	**e.** fetal protective covering

FILL IN THE BLANKS

26. The instrument for examining the vagina and cervix is the _____.

27. The female gonad is the _____.

28. The herniation of the rectum into the vaginal wall is called _____.

29. The ovarian follicle encloses a developing _____.

30. The organ that nourishes and maintains the developing fetus is the _____.

31. The secretion of milk from the mammary glands is called _____.

32. Loss of an embryo or fetus before 20 weeks or 500 g is termed a(n) _____.

33. Parametritis (*par-ah-me-TRI-tis*) means inflammation of the tissue near the _____.

34. Polymastia (*pol-e-MAS-te-ah*) means the presence of more than one pair of _____.

SPELL CHECK

Write the correct spelling on the line to the right of the term.

35. oopherectomy _____

36. premenstral _____

37. salpinjectomy _____

38. dysmennarrhea _____

39. clef palate _____

TRUE–FALSE

Examine the following statements. If the statement is true, write T in the first blank. If the statement is false, write F in the first blank, and correct the statement by replacing the underlined word in the second blank.

	True or False	Correct Answer
40. Agalactia is the lack of <u>milk</u> production.	_____	_____
41. For the first two months, the developing offspring is called a <u>fetus</u>.	_____	_____
42. The muscular wall of the uterus is the <u>endometrium</u>.	_____	_____
43. After ovulation, the ovarian follicle becomes a <u>fimbriae</u>.	_____	_____
44. Fertilization of an ovum occurs in the <u>uterus</u>.	_____	_____
45. The Pap smear is a test for <u>cervical</u> cancer.	_____	_____
46. Parturition is <u>childbirth</u>.	_____	_____

	True or False	Correct Answer
47. The fallopian tube is the <u>uterine tube</u>.	_____	_____
48. A fontanel is the soft spot between the <u>cranial bones</u>.	_____	_____

DEFINITIONS

Define the following terms.

49. retrouterine (*reh-tro-U-ter-in*) _____

50. hysteropathy (*his-teh-ROP-ah-the*) _____

51. metromalacia (*me-tro-mah-LA-she-ah*) _____

52. pyosalpinx (*pi-o-SAL-pinx*) _____

53. colpostenosis (*kol-po-steh-NO-sis*) _____

54. vulvodynia (*vul-vo-DIN-e-ah*) _____

55. postnatal (*post-NA-tal*) _____

56. inframammary (*in-frah-MAM-ah-re*) _____

57. extraembryonic (*eks-trah-em-bre-ON-ik*) _____

58. tripara (*TRIP-ah-rah*) _____

59. teratogenic (*TER-at-o-jen-ik*) _____

Write words for the following.

60. hernia of a uterine tube _____

61. suture of the vulva (episi/o) _____

62. narrowing of the uterus (metr/o) _____

63. surgical removal of the uterus (hyster/o) and uterine tubes _____

64. radiograph of the breast (mamm/o) _____

65. abnormal or difficult labor _____

66. rupture of the amniotic sac _____

67. study of the embryo _____

68. measurement of a fetus _____

In A.Y.'s opening case study, find words for the following.

69. term that refers to a pregnant woman _____

70. upper rounded portion of the uterus _____

71. measurement of the pelvis _____

72. above the pubic bone _____

73. test to measure the health of a newborn _____

74. newborn _____

OPPOSITES

Write a word that means the opposite of the following.

75. oligohydramnios _____

76. postnatal _____

77. dystocia _____

78. ovulatory _____

79. extrauterine _____

ADJECTIVES

Write the adjective form of the following.

80. cervix _____
81. uterus _____
82. perineum _____
83. vagina _____
84. embryo _____
85. amnion _____

PLURALS

Write the plural form of the following.

86. ovum _____
87. cervix _____
88. fimbria _____
89. labium _____

ELIMINATIONS

In each of the sets below, underline the word that does not fit in with the rest, and explain the reason for your choice.

90. amniocentesis — chorionic villus sampling — karyotype — ultrasonography — candidiasis
_____

91. hemophilia — albinism — measles — PKU — cystic fibrosis
_____

92. colostrum — progesterone — LH — estrogen — FSH
_____

93. umbilical cord — labia majora — amniotic fluid — chorion — placenta
_____

94. placental abruption — spina bifida — pregnancy-induced hypertension — placenta previa — eclampsia
_____

FOLLOW THE PATH

Follow the path of an ovum from production to implantation. Place the letters "A" through "D" next to the terms on the space provided to put the terms in proper order.

_____ 95. uterine tube
_____ 96. fimbriae
_____ 97. ovary
_____ 98. uterus

WORD BUILDING

Write a word for the following definitions using the word parts provided.

| -graphy   episi/o   -plasty   intra-   cervic/o   mamm/o   -itis   -al   -tomy   trans- |

99. plastic repair of the vulva _____
100. inflammation of the cervix _____
101. radiographic study of the breast _____
102. plastic repair of the breast _____
103. radiographic study of the cervix _____

104. incision of the vulva _____

105. within the cervix _____

106. plastic repair of the cervix _____

107. incision of the cervix _____

108. through the cervix _____

ABBREVIATIONS

Write the meaning of the following abbreviations.

109. hCG _____

110. DUB _____

111. LMP _____

112. FHR _____

113. GA _____

114. VBAC _____

WORD ANALYSIS

Define the following words, and give the meaning of the word parts in each. Use a dictionary if necessary.

115. antiangiogenesis (*an-te-an-je-o-JEN-eh-sis*) _____

   a. anti- _____

   b. angi/o _____

   c. gen _____

   d. e/sis _____

116. gynecomastia (*gi-neh-ko-MAS-te-ah*) _____

   a. gynec/o _____

   b. mast/o _____

   c. -ia _____

117. oxytocia (*ok-se-TO-se-ah*) _____

   a. oxy _____

   b. toc _____

   c. -ia _____

118. oligohydramnios (*ol-ih-go-hi-DRAM-ne-os*) _____

   a. oligo- _____

   b. hydr/o _____

   c. amnio(s) _____

119. galactorrhea (*gah-LAK-tor-e-ah*) _____

   a. galact/o _____

   b. (r)rhea _____

120. anencephaly (*an-en-SEF-ah-le*) _____

   a. an- _____

   b. encephal/o _____

   c. -y _____

For more learning activities, see Chapter 15 of the Student Resources on thePoint.

Additional Case Studies

Case Study 15-1: *Total Abdominal Hysterectomy with Bilateral Salpingo-oophorectomy*

M.T., a 60-year-old gravida 2, para 2, had spent three months under the care of her gynecologist for treatment of postmenopausal bleeding and cervical dysplasia. She had had several vaginal examinations with Pap smears, a uterine ultrasound, colposcopy with endocervical biopsies, and a D&C with cone biopsy. She wanted to take hormone replacement therapy, but her doctor thought she was at too much risk with the abnormal cells on her cervix and the excessive bleeding.

She had a TAH and BSO under general anesthesia with no complications and an uneventful recovery. Her uterus had been prolapsed on abdominal examination, but there was no sign of malignancy or PID. The pathology report revealed several uterine leiomyomas and stenosis of the right uterine tube. She was discharged on the second postoperative day with few activity restrictions.

Case Study 15-2: *In Vitro Fertilization*

C.A. had worked as a technologist in the IVF laboratory at University Medical Center for four years. Her department was the advanced reproductive technology program. Although her work was primarily in the laboratory, she followed each patient through all five phases of the IVF and embryo transfer treatment cycle: follicular development, aspiration of the preovulatory follicles, sperm preparation, IVF, and embryo transfer. Her department does both GIFT and ZIFT.

While the female patient is in surgery having an ultrasound-guided transvaginal oocyte retrieval, C.A. examines the recently donated sperm for motility and quantity. She prepares to inoculate the sample into the cytoplasm of the ova as soon as she receives the cells from the OR. After inoculation, she places the sterile petri dish with the fertilized oocytes into an incubator until they are ready to be introduced into the female patient.

Case Study Questions

Multiple Choice. Select the best answer, and write the letter of your choice to the left of each number.

_____ **1.** M.T. is a gravida 2, para 2. This means
  a. she has four children from two pregnancies
  b. she has had two pregnancies and two births
  c. she has had four pregnancies and two births
  d. she has one set of twins

_____ **2.** An endocervical biopsy is
  a. a cone-shaped tissue sample from the uterine fundus
  b. a tissue sample from within the neck
  c. a tissue sample from the lining of the cervix
  d. a scraping of tissue cells from the vaginal wall

_____ **3.** A curettage is a(n)
  a. suturing
  b. scraping
  c. incision
  d. examination

_____ **4.** A colposcopy is an endoscopic examination of the
  a. vagina
  b. fundus
  c. intraperitoneal pelvic floor
  d. uterus and uterine tubes

_____ **5.** Another name for a leiomyoma is a(n)

    a. ectopic pregnancy

    b. uterine fibroid

    c. myoma

    d. b and c

_____ **6.** Pregnancy-induced hypertension is also called

    a. placenta previa

    b. congenital mutation

    c. ectopic pregnancy

    d. preeclampsia

Write a term from the case studies with each of the following meanings.

7. displaced downward _____

8. cell produced by fertilization _____

9. an immature egg cell _____

10. pertaining to the structure in which an egg ripens _____

Define each of the following abbreviations.

11. D&C _____

12. BSO _____

13. HRT _____

14. TAH _____

15. IVF _____

16. GYN _____

17. ZIFT _____

15

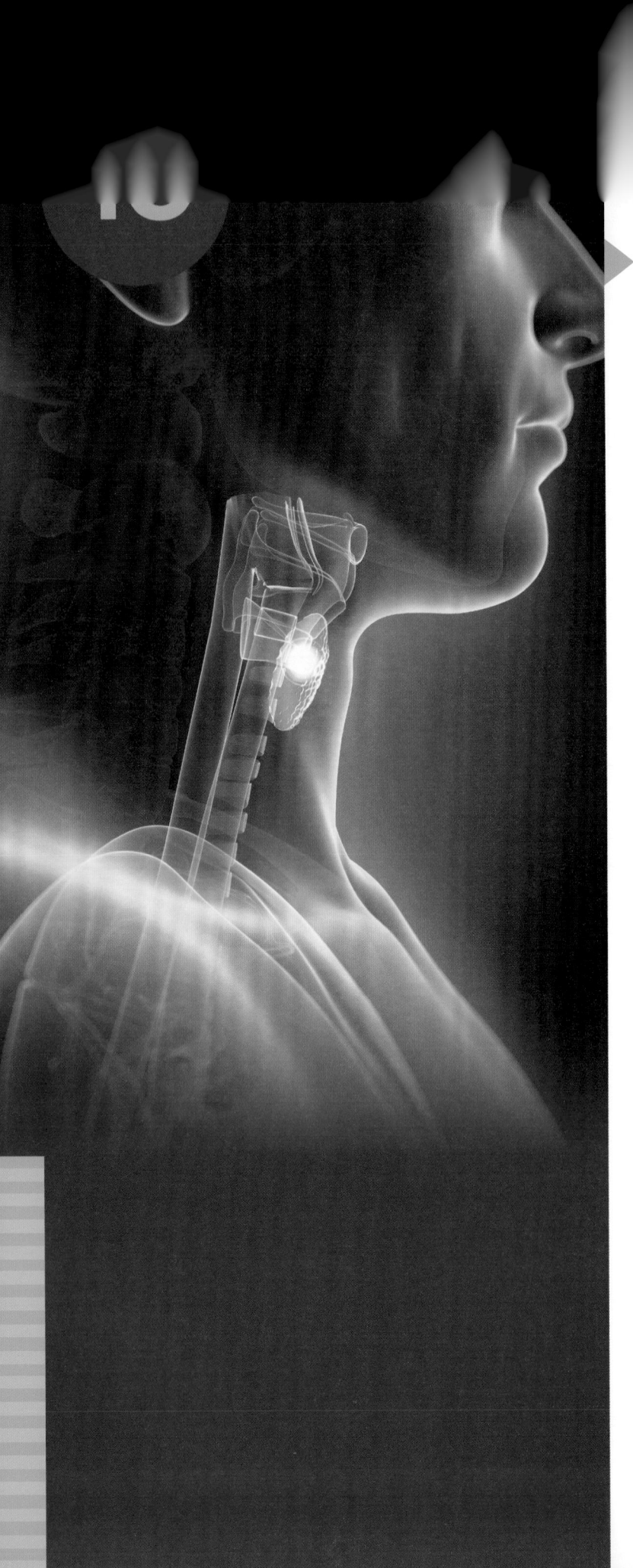

Pretest

Multiple Choice. Select the best answer, and write the letter of your choice to the left of each number.

_____ 1. The secretions of the endocrine glands are called
   a. enzymes
   b. sera
   c. lymph
   d. hormones

_____ 2. The small gland in the brain that controls other glands is the
   a. thymus
   b. pituitary
   c. appendix
   d. corpus luteum

_____ 3. The glands that are located above the kidneys are the
   a. adrenals
   b. thyroid
   c. follicles
   d. fimbriae

_____ 4. Gigantism results from overproduction of
   a. erythropoietin
   b. oxytocin
   c. growth hormone
   d. prolactin

_____ 5. Diabetes mellitus involves the hormone insulin, which is made in the
   a. kidney
   b. seminal vesicle
   c. thymus
   d. pancreas

_____ 6. A goiter involves the
   a. zygote
   b. calyx
   c. adrenal
   d. thyroid

Learning Objectives

After study of this chapter you should be able to:

1. ▶ Define hormones. *p398*
2. ▶ Compare steroid and amino acid hormones. *p398*
3. ▶ Give the location and structure of the endocrine glands. *p398*
4. ▶ Name the hormones produced by the endocrine glands, and briefly describe the function of each. *p399*
5. ▶ Identify and use roots pertaining to the endocrine system. *p403*
6. ▶ Describe the main disorders of the endocrine system. *p404*
7. ▶ Interpret abbreviations used in endocrinology. *p411*
8. ▶ Analyze medical terms in several case studies concerning the endocrine system. *pp397, 416*

Case Study: *J.D.'s Graves Disease*

Chief Complaint

J.D. is a 35-year-old second grade teacher. Her husband has been noticing that she has been very energetic over the past few months, more so than usual. She is constantly working or cleaning, and she is up during the night, unable to sleep. J.D. says that she has felt nervous and jittery for the past few months. Her husband encouraged her to make an appointment with her physician.

Examination

J.D.'s internist, Dr. Gilbert, was able to make a few observations when he walked into the examination room. J.D. had lost weight since her last appointment, and her eyes were protruding. Normally a quiet and happy person, she appeared irritable and abrupt. She complained about her edginess, dry eyes, and inability to sleep. She also mentioned that she can't tolerate the heat and frequently perspires. She said she just hasn't been "feeling herself" as of late. Dr. Gilbert examined her, and when palpating her neck, he noted an enlarged thyroid. He also noted a dermopathy on her shins where the skin had thickened and had red patches. Her vital signs were pretty consistent with previous examinations, except that she was a bit tachycardic. Dr. Gilbert suspected hyperthyroidism. He ordered some blood work to check her thyroid levels and confirm his diagnosis.

Clinical Course

Results of the laboratory work verified Dr. Gilbert's suspicion. He discussed the diagnosis of the autoimmune disorder of hyperthyroidism, also known as Graves disease or diffuse toxic goiter, with J.D. and her husband. He provided them the results of the T3 and T4 laboratory work and explained that the high levels meant her thyroid was overactive. He explained the treatment options, including antithyroid medication, partial or total thyroidectomy, or radiation therapy. Dr. Gilbert felt that a medical regime would be appropriate for J.D. and ordered the antithyroid drug Tapazole. He also ordered eye drops for the exophthalmos.

ANCILLARIES *At-A-Glance*

Visit thePoint to access the following resources. For guidance in using the resources most effectively, see pp. ix–xvi.

Learning RESOURCES

- ▶ Tips for Effective Studying
- ▶ Web Figure: Clinical Manifestations of Acromegaly
- ▶ Web Figure: Hypothyroidism and Hyperthyroidism Compared
- ▶ Web Figure: Clinical Manifestations of Hyperparathyroidism
- ▶ Web Figure: Clinical Manifestations of Addison Disease
- ▶ Web Figure: Clinical Manifestations of Cushing Syndrome
- ▶ Web Figure: Metabolic Syndrome
- ▶ Animation: Hormonal Control of Glucose
- ▶ Animation: Diabetes
- ▶ Audio Pronunciation Glossary

Learning ACTIVITIES

- ▶ Visual Activities
- ▶ Kinesthetic Activities
- ▶ Auditory Activities

Introduction

The body's main controlling systems are the endocrine system and the nervous system (discussed in this chapter and Chapter 17, respectively). The endocrine system consists of a widely distributed group of glands that secrete regulatory substances called **hormones**. Because hormones are released into the blood, the **endocrine** glands are known as the *ductless glands*, as compared to exocrine glands, such as sweat glands and digestive glands, that secrete through ducts to the outside. Despite the fact that hormones circulating in the blood reach all parts of the body, only certain tissues respond to a specific hormone. The tissue that is influenced by a specific hormone is called the **target tissue**. The cells in a target tissue have specific **receptors** on their membranes or within the cell to which the hormone attaches, enabling it to act.

Hormones

Hormones are produced in extremely small amounts and are highly potent. By means of their actions on various target tissues, they affect growth, metabolism, reproductive activity, and behavior. (**Box 16-1** describes some old ideas about the effects of substances circulating in the blood.)

Chemically, hormones fall into two categories:

- **Steroid hormones**, which are made from lipids. Steroids are produced by the sex glands (gonads) and the outer region (cortex) of the **adrenal glands**.
- Hormones are made of amino acids, which include proteins and protein-like compounds. All of the endocrine glands aside from the gonads and adrenal cortex produce amino acid hormones.

The production of hormones is controlled mainly by negative feedback—that is, the hormone itself, or some product of hormone activity, acts as a control over further manufacture of the hormone—a self-regulating system. Hormone production may also be controlled by the nervous system or by other hormones.

The Endocrine Glands

Refer to **Figure 16-1** to locate the endocrine glands described below. **Box 16-2** lists the endocrine glands, along with the hormones they secrete and their functions.

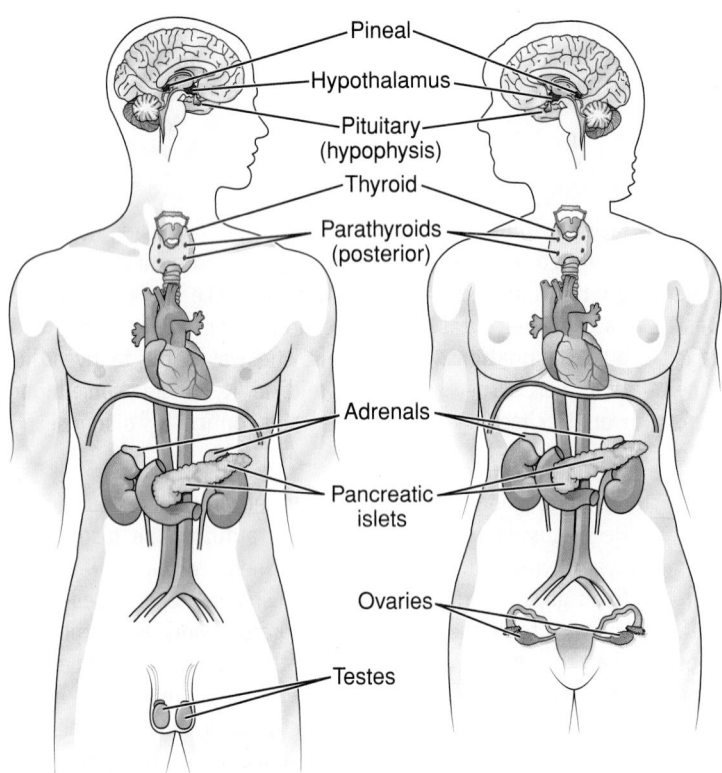

Figure 16-1 **The endocrine glands.**

Labels: Pineal, Hypothalamus, Pituitary (hypophysis), Thyroid, Parathyroids (posterior), Adrenals, Pancreatic islets, Ovaries, Testes

---

FOCUS ON WORDS
Are You in a Good Humor?

Box 16-1

In ancient times, people accepted the theory that a person's state of health depended on the balance of four body fluids. These fluids, called "humors," were yellow bile, black bile, phlegm, and blood. A predominance of any one of these humors would determine a person's mood or temperament. Yellow bile caused anger; black bile caused depression; phlegm (mucus) made a person sluggish; blood resulted in cheerfulness and optimism.

Although we no longer believe in humoralism, we still have adjectives in our vocabulary that reflect these early beliefs. Choleric describes a person under the influence of yellow bile; melancholic describes the effects of black bile (melan/o- means black or dark); a phlegmatic person is slow to respond; a sanguine individual "goes with the flow." (*Sanguine* is derived from the Greek word for blood.)

The humors persist today in the adjective *humoral*, which describes substances carried in the blood or other body fluids. The term applies to hormones and other circulating materials that influence body responses. Humoral immunity is immunity based on antibodies carried in the bloodstream.

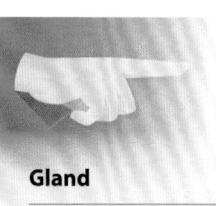

FOR YOUR REFERENCE

Box 16-2

Endocrine Glands and Their Hormones

16

Gland	Hormone	Principal Functions
anterior pituitary *pih-TU-ih-tar-e*	GH (growth hormone), also called somatotropin (*so-mah-to-TRO-pin*)	Promotes growth of all body tissues
	TSH (thyroid-stimulating hormone)	Stimulates thyroid gland to produce thyroid hormones
	ACTH (adrenocorticotropic hormone) (*ah-dre-no-kor-tih-ko-TRO-pik*)	Stimulates adrenal cortex to produce cortical hormones; aids in protecting body in stress situations (injury, pain)
	FSH (follicle-stimulating hormone)	Stimulates growth and hormonal activity of ovarian follicles; stimulates growth of testes; promotes sperm cell development
	LH (luteinizing hormone) (*LU-te-in-i-zing*)	Causes development of corpus luteum at site of ruptured ovarian follicle in female; stimulates testosterone secretion in male
	PRL (prolactin) (*pro-LAK-tin*)	Stimulates milk secretion by mammary glands
posterior pituitary	ADH (antidiuretic hormone; vasopressin) (*an-te-di-u-RET-ik; va-so-PRES-in*)	Promotes water reabsorption in kidney tubules; causes blood vessels to constrict
	oxytocin (*ok-se-TO-sin*)	Causes uterine contraction; causes milk ejection from mammary glands
thyroid	thyroxine or tetraiodothyronine (T_4) and triiodothyronine (T_3) (*thi-ROK-sin; tri-i-o-do-THI-ro-nene*)	Increase metabolic rate and heat production, influencing both physical and mental activities; required for normal growth
parathyroid	parathyroid hormone (PTH) (*par-ah-THI-royd*)	Regulates calcium exchange between blood and bones; increases blood calcium level
adrenal cortex	cortisol (hydrocortisone) (*KOR-tih-sol*)	Aids in metabolism of carbohydrates, proteins, and fats; active during stress
	aldosterone (*al-DOS-ter-one*)	Aids in regulating electrolytes and water balance
	sex hormones	May influence secondary sexual characteristics
adrenal medulla	epinephrine (*adrenaline*) (*ep-ih-NEF-rin; ah-DREN-ah-lin*)	Response to stress; increases respiration, blood pressure, and heart rate
pancreatic islet	insulin (*IN-su-lin*)	Aids glucose transport into cells; required for cellular metabolism of nutrients, especially glucose; decreases blood glucose levels
	glucagon (*GLU-kah-gon*)	Stimulates liver to release glucose, thereby increasing blood glucose levels
pineal	melatonin (*mel-ah-TONE-in*)	Regulates mood, sexual development, and daily cycles in response to environmental light
testis	testosterone (*tes-TOS-teh-rone*)	Stimulates growth and development of sexual organs plus development of secondary sexual characteristics; stimulates maturation of sperm cells
ovary	estrogen (*ES-tro-jen*)	Stimulates growth of primary sexual organs and development of secondary sexual characteristics
	progesterone (*pro-JES-ter-one*)	Prepares uterine lining for implantation of fertilized ovum; aids in maintaining pregnancy; stimulates development of mammary glands' secretory tissue

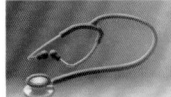

CLINICAL PERSPECTIVES

Box 16-3

Growth Hormone: Its Clinical Use Is Growing

Growth hormone (GH) is produced by the anterior pituitary. It is released mainly at the beginning of deep sleep, so the old belief that you grow while you sleep has some basis in fact. Although GH primarily affects bone and muscle development during early growth, it has a general stimulating effect on most other tissues throughout life. Its alternative name, somatotropin, comes from *soma* meaning "body" and *tropin* meaning "acting on." GH is released during times of stress to boost the liver's output of energy-rich fatty acids when blood glucose levels drop. A lack of GH in childhood results in dwarfism, and the hormone was initially prescribed only for children with a GH deficiency. Now it has also been approved for children who are in the lowest percentile of height for their age. If a child is still growing, as shown by x-rays of the hand and wrist, GH will lead to some ultimate increase in height. Because GH increases lean muscle mass, it is also touted as a bodybuilding and antiaging medication. However, it may have some side effects, and its long-term effects are not known. GH for clinical use was initially obtained from cadaver pituitaries, but it is now made by genetic engineering.

PITUITARY

The **pituitary gland,** or **hypophysis,** is a small gland beneath the brain. It is divided into an anterior lobe (adenohypophysis) and a posterior lobe (neurohypophysis). The **hypothalamus,** a part of the brain that regulates homeostasis, is connected to and controls both lobes. Because the hypothalamus secretes hormones and is active in controlling the pituitary gland, it is considered to be part of the endocrine system as well as the nervous system.

The anterior pituitary produces six hormones. One of these is growth hormone (somatotropin), which stimulates bone growth and acts on other tissues as well (**Box 16-3**). The remainder of the pituitary hormones regulate other glands, including the thyroid, adrenals, gonads, and mammary glands (see **Box 16-2**). The ending *-tropin,* as in *gonadotropin,* indicates a hormone that acts on another gland. The adjective ending is *-tropic,* as in *adrenocorticotropic.*

The posterior pituitary releases two hormones that are actually produced in the hypothalamus. These hormones are stored in the posterior pituitary until they are needed:

- Antidiuretic hormone (ADH) acts on the kidneys to conserve water and also promotes constriction of blood vessels. Both of these actions increase blood pressure.
- Oxytocin stimulates uterine contractions and promotes milk "letdown" in the breasts during lactation.

THYROID AND PARATHYROIDS

The **thyroid gland** consists of two lobes on either side of the larynx and upper trachea. The lobes are connected by a narrow band (isthmus) (**Fig. 16-2**). The thyroid secretes a mixture of hormones, mainly thyroxine (T$_4$) and

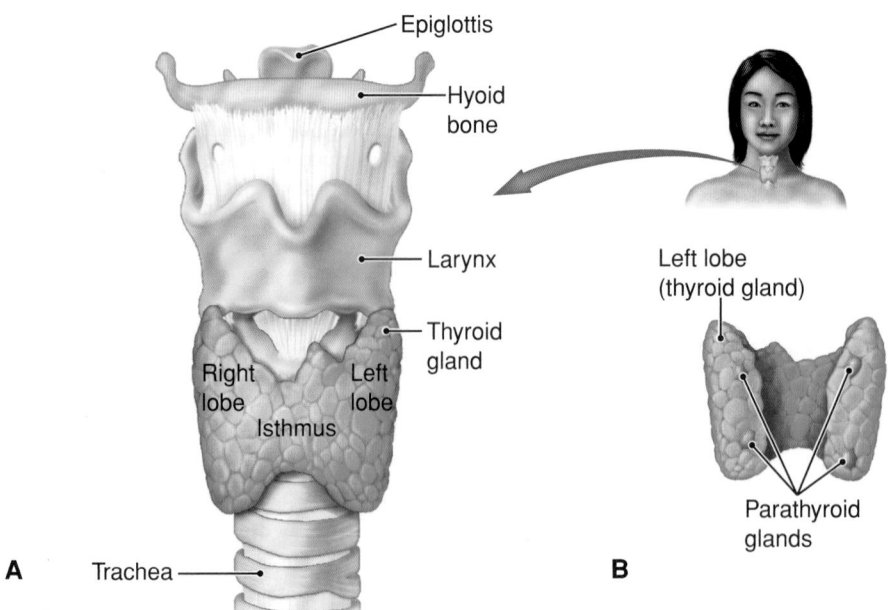

Figure 16-2 **The thyroid and parathyroid glands. A.** The thyroid has two lobes connected by an isthmus. This anterior view shows the gland in relation to other structures in the throat. **B.** The parathyroid glands are embedded in the posterior portion of the thyroid.

triiodothyronine (T$_3$). Because thyroid hormones contain iodine, laboratories can measure these hormones and study thyroid gland activity by following iodine levels. Most thyroid hormone in the blood is bound to protein, primarily thyroxine-binding globulin (TBG).

On the posterior surface of the thyroid are four to six tiny **parathyroid glands** that affect calcium metabolism (see **Fig. 16-2**). Parathyroid hormone (PTH) regulates calcium exchange between the blood and bones. It increases the blood level of calcium when needed.

ADRENALS

The adrenal glands, located atop the kidneys, are divided into two distinct regions: an outer cortex and an inner medulla (**Fig. 16-3**). The hormones produced by this gland are involved in the body's response to stress. The cortex produces steroid hormones:

- Cortisol (hydrocortisone) mobilizes fat and carbohydrate reserves to increase these nutrients in the blood. It

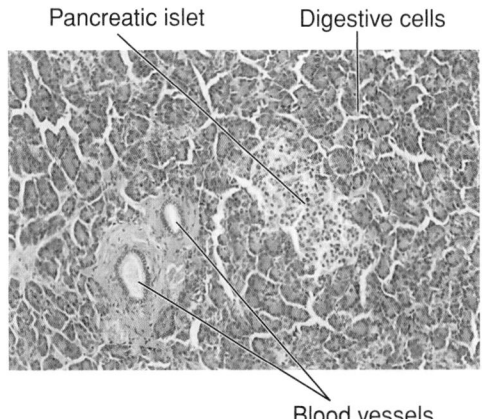

Figure 16-4 **Pancreatic cells, microscopic view.** Light-staining islet cells are seen among the cell clusters that produce digestive juices.

also reduces inflammation and is used clinically for this purpose.
- Aldosterone causes the kidneys to conserve sodium and water while eliminating potassium.
- Sex hormones, mainly testosterone, are also produced in small amounts, but their importance is not well understood. Some athletes, illegally and dangerously, take testosterone-like steroids to increase muscle size, strength, and endurance (see **Box 20-1**).

The medulla of the adrenal gland produces the hormone epinephrine (adrenaline) in response to stress. Epinephrine works with the nervous system to help the body meet physical and emotional challenges.

PANCREAS

The endocrine portions of the pancreas are the **pancreatic islets**, small cell clusters within the pancreatic tissue. The term *islet*, meaning "small island," is used because these cells look like little islands in the midst of the many pancreatic cells that secrete digestive juices (**Fig. 16-4**). The islet cells produce two hormones, insulin and glucagon, that regulate glucose metabolism. Insulin increases cellular use of glucose, thus decreasing blood glucose levels. Glucagon has the opposite effect, increasing blood glucose levels.

Other Endocrine Tissues

There are three additional types of glands that secrete hormones:

- The **pineal gland** is a small gland in the brain (see **Fig. 16-1**). It regulates mood, daily rhythms, and sexual development in response to environmental light. Its hormone is melatonin, which some people take to help regulate sleep–wake cycles when they travel between time zones.
- The thymus, described in Chapter 9, secretes the hormone thymosin that aids in the development of the immune system's T cells. The thymus lies in the upper

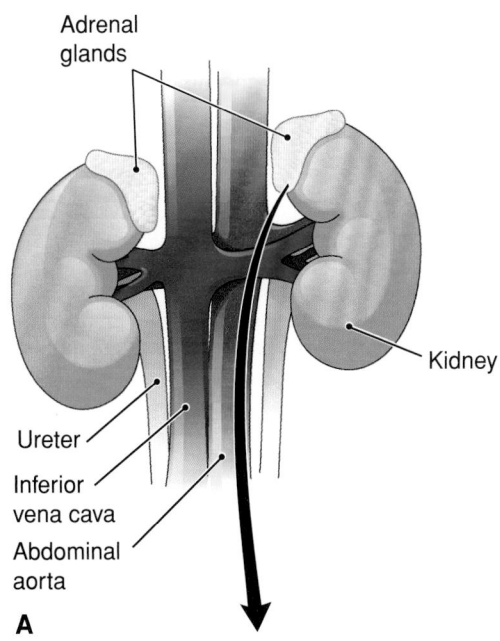

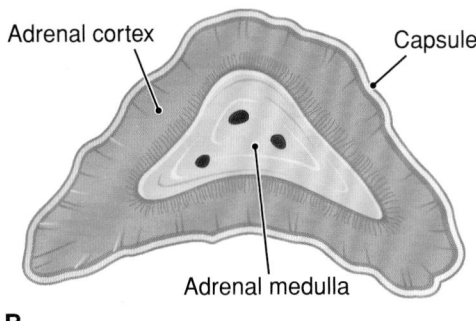

Figure 16-3 **Adrenal glands. A.** The adrenal glands shown on top of the kidneys. **B.** The adrenal gland is divided into a medulla and cortex, each secreting different hormones.

chest above the heart. It is important in early years but shrinks and becomes less important in adults.

- The gonads, testes, and ovaries, described in Chapters 14 and 15, are also included because they secrete hormones in addition to producing the sex cells.

Other organs, including the stomach, kidney, heart, and small intestine, also produce hormones. However, they have other major functions and are discussed with the systems to which they belong.

Finally, **prostaglandins** are a group of hormones produced by many cells. They have a variety of effects, including stimulation of uterine contractions, promotion of inflammation, and vasomotor activities. They are called prostaglandins because they were first discovered in the prostate gland.

Terminology   Key Terms

Normal Structure and Function

adrenal gland *ah-DRE-nal*	A gland on the superior surface of the kidney; the outer region (cortex) secretes steroid hormones; the inner region (medulla) secretes epinephrine (adrenaline) in response to stress (root: adren/o)
endocrine *EN-do-krin*	Pertaining to a ductless gland that secretes hormones into the blood
hormone *HOR-mone*	A secretion of an endocrine gland; a substance that travels in the blood and has a regulatory effect on tissues, organs, or glands
hypophysis *hi-POF-ih-sis*	The pituitary gland; named from *hypo*, meaning "below," and *physis*, meaning "growing," because the gland develops below the hypothalamus (root: hypophysi/o)
hypothalamus *hi-po-THAL-ah-mus*	A portion of the brain that controls the pituitary gland, produces hormones, and is active in maintaining homeostasis
pancreatic islet *I-let*	Cluster of endocrine cells in the pancreas that secretes hormones to regulate glucose metabolism; also called islet of Langerhans or islet cells (root insul/o means "island")
parathyroid gland *par-ah-THI-royd*	A small endocrine gland on the posterior thyroid that acts to increase blood calcium levels; there are usually four to six parathyroid glands (roots: parathyr/o, parathyroid/o); the name literally means "near the thyroid"
pineal gland *PIN-e-al*	A small gland in the brain (see **Fig. 16-1**); appears to regulate mood, daily rhythms, and sexual development in response to environmental light; secretes the hormone melatonin
pituitary gland *pih-TU-ih-tar-e*	A small endocrine gland at the base of the brain; the anterior lobe secretes growth hormone and hormones that stimulate other glands; the posterior lobe releases ADH and oxytocin manufactured in the hypothalamus (root: pituitar/i); hypophysis
prostaglandins *pros-tah-GLAN-dinz*	A group of hormones produced throughout the body that have a variety of effects, including stimulation of uterine contractions and regulation of blood pressure, blood clotting, and inflammation
receptor *re-SEP-tor*	A site on the cell membrane or within the cell to which a substance, such as a hormone, attaches
steroid hormone *STER-oyd*	A hormone made from lipids; includes the sex hormones and the hormones of the adrenal cortex
target tissue	The specific tissue on which a hormone acts; may also be called the target organ
thyroid gland *THI-royd*	An endocrine gland on either side of the larynx and upper trachea; it secretes hormones that affect metabolism and growth (roots: thyr/o, thyroid/o)

Go to the Audio Pronunciation Glossary in the Student Resources on thePoint to hear these terms pronounced.

Roots Pertaining to the Endocrine System

See **Table 16-1**.

Table 16-1	Roots Pertaining to the Endocrine System		
Root	**Meaning**	**Example**	**Definition of Example**
endocrin/o	endocrine glands or system	endocrinopathy en-do-krih-NOP-ah-the	any disease of the endocrine glands
pituitar/i	pituitary gland, hypophysis	pituitarism pih-TU-ih-tah-rizm	condition caused by any disorder of pituitary function
hypophysi/o	pituitary gland, hypophysis	hypophysial hi-po-FIZ-e-al (also spelled hypophyseal)	pertaining to the pituitary gland
thyr/o, thyroid/o	thyroid gland	thyrolytic thi-ro-LIT-ik	destroying the thyroid gland
parathyr/o, parathyroid/o	parathyroid gland	hyperparathyroidism hi-per-par-ah-THI-royd-izm	overactivity of a parathyroid gland
adren/o, adrenal/o	adrenal gland, epinephrine	adrenergic ad-ren-ER-jik	activated (erg) by or related to epinephrine (adrenaline)
adrenocortic/o	adrenal cortex	adrenocorticotropic ah-dre-no-kor-tih-ko-TRO-pik	acting on the adrenal cortex
insul/o	pancreatic islets	insular IN-su-lar	pertaining to islet cells

16

EXERCISE 16-1

Define the following words.

1. hypoadrenalism (*hi-po-ah-DRE-nal-izm*) _____

2. thyrotropic (*thi-ro-TROP-ik*) _____

3. hypophysectomy (*hi-pof-ih-SEK-to-me*) _____

4. endocrinology (*en-do-krin-OL-o-je*) _____

5. insuloma (*in-su-LO-mah*) _____

Words for conditions resulting from endocrine dysfunctions are formed by adding the suffix *-ism* to the name of the gland or its root and adding the prefix *hyper-* or *hypo-* for overactivity or underactivity of the gland. Use the full name of the gland to form words with the following definitions.

6. condition of overactivity of the thyroid gland, as seen in J.D.'s opening case study _____

7. condition of underactivity of the parathyroid gland _____

8. condition of overactivity of the adrenal gland _____

Use the word root for the gland to form words with the following definitions.

9. condition of overactivity of the adrenal cortex _____

10. condition of underactivity of the pituitary gland (use pituitar/i) _____

(continued)

EXERCISE 16-1   *(Continued)*

Write a word for the following definitions.

11. enlargement of the adrenal gland _____

12. excision of the thyroid gland, as mentioned in J.D.'s opening case study _____

13. any disease of the adrenal gland _____

14. physician who specializes in study of the endocrine system _____

15. inflammation of the pancreatic islets _____

Clinical Aspects of the Endocrine System

Endocrine diseases usually result from the overproduction (hypersecretion) or underproduction (hyposecretion) of hormones. They may also result from secretion at the wrong time or from an inadequate target tissue response. The causes of abnormal secretion may originate in the gland itself or may result from failure of the hypothalamus or the pituitary to release the proper amount of stimulating hormones. Some of the common endocrine disorders are described below. Conditions resulting from hypersecretion or hyposecretion of hormones are summarized in **Box 16-4**.

PITUITARY

A pituitary **adenoma** (glandular tumor) usually increases secretion of growth hormone or adrenocorticotropic hormone (ACTH). Less commonly, a tumor affects the secretion of prolactin. An excess of growth hormone in children causes **gigantism**. In adults it causes **acromegaly**, characterized by enlargement of the hands, feet, jaw, and facial features. Treatment is by surgery to remove the tumor (adenomectomy) or by drugs to reduce the blood levels of growth hormone. Excess ACTH overstimulates the adrenal cortex, resulting in Cushing disease. Increased prolactin causes milk secretion (galactorrhea) in both males and females. Radiographic studies in cases of pituitary adenoma usually show enlargement of the bony socket (sella turcica) that contains the pituitary.

Pituitary hypofunction, as caused by tumor or interruption of blood supply to the gland, may involve a single hormone but usually affects all functions and is referred to as **panhypopituitarism**. This condition's widespread effects include dwarfism (from lack of growth hormone), lack of sexual development and sexual function, fatigue, and weakness.

A specific lack of ADH from the posterior pituitary results in **diabetes insipidus** in which the kidneys have a decreased ability to conserve water. Symptoms are polyuria (excessive urination) and polydipsia (excessive thirst). Diabetes insipidus should not be confused with **diabetes mellitus (DM)**, a disorder of glucose metabolism described later. The two diseases share the symptoms of polyuria and polydipsia but have entirely different causes. DM is the more common disorder, and when the term *diabetes* is used

FOR YOUR REFERENCE   **Box 16-4**
Disorders Associated with Endocrine Dysfunction[a]

Hormone	Hypersecretion	Hyposecretion
growth hormone	gigantism (children), acromegaly (adults)	dwarfism (children)
antidiuretic hormone	syndrome of inappropriate ADH (SIADH)	diabetes insipidus
aldosterone	aldosteronism	Addison disease
cortisol	Cushing syndrome	Addison disease
thyroid hormone	Graves disease, thyrotoxicosis	congenital and adult hypothyroidism
insulin	hypoglycemia	diabetes mellitus
parathyroid hormone	bone degeneration	tetany (muscle spasms)

[a]Refer to key terms for pronunciations and descriptions.

alone, it generally refers to DM. The word *diabetes* is from the Greek meaning "siphon," referring to the large urinary output in both forms of diabetes.

See the figure on the clinical manifestations of acromegaly in the Student Resources on thePoint.

THYROID

Because thyroid hormone affects the growth and function of many tissues, a deficiency of this hormone in infancy causes physical and mental retardation as well as other symptoms that together constitute **congenital hypothyroidism**, also called *infantile hypothyroidism*. If not diagnosed at birth and treated, hypothyroidism will lead to mental retardation within six months. The United States and other developed countries now require testing of all newborns for hypothyroidism.

In adults, thyroid deficiency causes weight gain; lethargy; rough, dry skin; hair loss; and facial swelling. There may be reproductive problems and muscular weakness, pain, and stiffness. A common cause of **adult hypothyroidism** is autoimmune destruction of the thyroid. Hypothyroidism in both children and adults is easily treated with thyroid hormone.

The most common form of hyperthyroidism is **Graves disease**, also called *diffuse toxic goiter*. This is an autoimmune disorder in which antibodies stimulate an increased production of thyroid hormone. There is weight loss, irritability, hand tremor, and rapid heart rate (tachycardia). A most distinctive sign is bulging eyeballs, termed **exophthalmos**, caused by swelling of the tissues behind the eyes (**Fig. 16-5**). Treatment for Graves disease may include antithyroid drugs, surgical removal of all or part of the thyroid, or radiation delivered in the form of radioactive iodine.

A common sign in thyroid disease is an enlarged thyroid, or **goiter**. However, a goiter is not necessarily accompanied by thyroid malfunction. A simple or nontoxic goiter is caused by a dietary iodine deficiency. Such cases are rare in industrialized countries because of iodine addition to salt and other commercial foods.

Thyroid function is commonly tested by measuring the gland's radioactive iodine uptake (RAIU). Laboratories use radioimmunoassays to measure blood levels of pituitary thyroid-stimulating hormone (TSH), which varies with changing levels of thyroid hormones. Total and free thyroxine (T_4) and triiodothyronine (T_3) are also measured, as are the levels of TBG, a blood protein that binds to thyroid hormones. Thyroid scans following administration of radioactive iodine are also used to study this gland's activity.

See the figure comparing hypothyroidism and hyperthyroidism in the Student Resources on thePoint.

PARATHYROIDS

Overactivity of the parathyroid glands, usually from a tumor, causes a high level of calcium in the blood. Because this calcium is obtained from the bones, there is also skeletal degeneration and bone pain. A common side effect is the development of kidney stones from the high levels of circulating calcium.

Damage to the parathyroids or their surgical removal, as during thyroid surgery, results in a decrease in blood

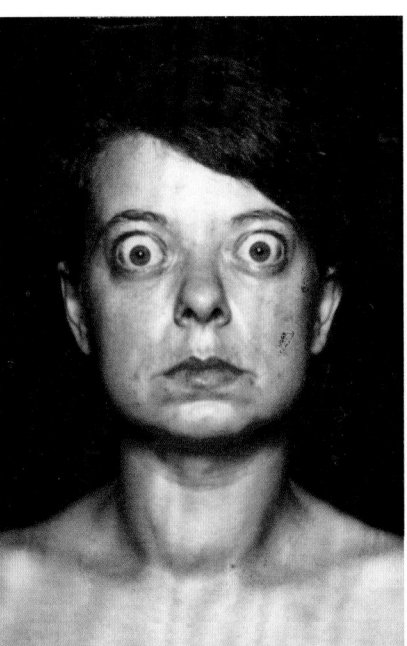

Figure 16-5 **Graves disease.** A young woman with hyperthyroidism showing a mass in the neck and exophthalmos.

calcium levels. This causes numbness and tingling in the arms and legs and around the mouth (perioral), as well as **tetany** (muscle spasms). Treatment consists of supplying calcium.

See the figure on clinical manifestations of hyperparathyroidism in the Student Resources on thePoint.

ADRENALS

Hypofunction of the adrenal cortex, or **Addison disease**, is usually caused by autoimmune destruction of the gland. It may also result from a deficiency of pituitary ACTH. The lack of aldosterone results in water loss, low blood pressure, and electrolyte imbalance. There is also weakness and nausea and an increase in brown pigmentation. This last symptom is caused by release of a pituitary hormone that stimulates the skin's pigment cells (melanocytes). Once diagnosed, Addison disease is treated with replacement of cortical hormones.

An excess of adrenal cortical hormones results in **Cushing syndrome**. Patients with this syndrome have moon-shaped faces, obesity localized in the torso, weakness, excess hair growth (hirsutism), and fluid retention (**Fig. 16-6**). The most common cause of Cushing syndrome is the therapeutic administration of steroid hormones. An adrenal tumor is another possible cause. If the disorder is caused by a pituitary tumor that increases ACTH production, it is referred to as **Cushing disease**.

See the figures on the clinical manifestation of Addison disease and Cushing syndrome in the Student Resources on thePoint.

THE PANCREAS AND DIABETES

The most common endocrine disorder, and a serious public health problem, is diabetes mellitus (DM), a failure of the body cells to use glucose effectively. The excess glucose accumulates in the blood, causing **hyperglycemia**. Increased urination (polyuria) marks the effort to eliminate the excess glucose in the urine, a condition termed **glycosuria**. The result is dehydration and excessive thirst (polydipsia). There is also weakness, weight loss, and extreme hunger (polyphagia). Unable to use carbohydrates, the body burns more fat. This leads to accumulation of ketone bodies in the blood and a shift toward acidosis, a condition termed **ketoacidosis**. If untreated, diabetes will lead to starvation of the central nervous system and coma. Diabetic patients are prone to cardiovascular, neurologic, and visual problems; infections; and renal failure.

Types of Diabetes Mellitus

There are two main types of DM:

- Type 1 diabetes mellitus (T1DM) is caused by autoimmune destruction of pancreatic islet cells and failure of the pancreas to produce insulin. It has an abrupt onset and usually appears in children and teenagers. Because insulin levels are very low or absent, patients need careful monitoring and regular administration of this hormone.

- Type 2 diabetes mellitus (T2DM) accounts for about 90 percent of diabetes cases. Heredity plays a much greater role in this form of diabetes than in type 1. Type 2 diabetes is initiated by cellular resistance to insulin. Feedback stimulation of the pancreatic islets leads to insulin overproduction followed by a failure of the overworked cells to produce enough insulin. Most cases of type 2 diabetes are linked to obesity, especially upper-body obesity. Although seen mostly in older people, the incidence of type 2 diabetes is increasing among younger generations, presumably because of increased obesity, poor diet, and sedentary habits.

Metabolic syndrome, also called *syndrome X* or *insulin resistance syndrome*, is related to T2DM and describes a state of hyperglycemia caused by insulin resistance in association with some metabolic disorders, including high

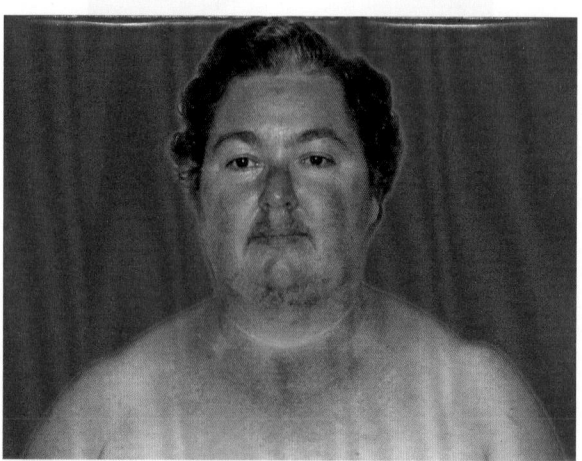

Figure 16-6   **Cushing syndrome.** The woman has a moon face, buffalo hump, increased facial hair, and thinning of the scalp hair.

levels of plasma triglycerides (fats), low levels of high-density lipoproteins (HDLs), hypertension, and coronary heart disease.

Gestational diabetes mellitus (GDM) refers to glucose intolerance during pregnancy. This imbalance usually appears in women with family histories of diabetes and in those who are obese. Women, especially those with predisposing factors, must be monitored during pregnancy for signs of DM because this condition can cause complications for both the mother and the fetus. Gestational diabetes usually disappears after childbirth, but it may be a sign that diabetes will develop later in life. As with other forms of diabetes, a proper diet is the first step to management, with insulin treatment if needed.

DM may also follow other endocrine disorders or treatment with corticosteroids and may be caused by a genetic disorder of the pancreatic islets.

Diagnosis

Diabetes is diagnosed by measuring glucose levels in blood plasma with or without fasting. The standard for diagnosis of diabetes in a random test is greater than 200 mg/dL and for a fasting plasma glucose (FPG) greater than 126 mg/dL. Measuring blood glucose levels after oral administration of glucose is an oral glucose tolerance test (OGTT). Categories of impaired fasting blood glucose (IFG) and impaired glucose tolerance (IGT) are intermediate stages between a normal response to glucose and confirmed diabetes.

Treatment

People with T1DM must monitor blood glucose levels four to eight times a day. Traditionally, this is done with blood obtained by a finger stick, but new methods of monitoring glucose through the skin are available. Systems for continuous monitoring are also available, and these can alert patients to high and low blood glucose levels. Insulin may be given in divided doses by injection or by means of an insulin pump that delivers the hormone around the clock as continuous subcutaneous insulin infusion (CSII). Newer computerized pumps monitor glucose levels and adjust insulin dosage automatically. Diet must be carefully regulated to keep glucose levels steady.

While managing diabetes, patients monitor their own glucose levels on a daily basis. Every few months, physicians obtain more precise indications of long-term glucose control with a **glycated hemoglobin (HbA1c) test**. This test is based on glucose uptake by red blood cells and reflects the average blood glucose levels for two to three months before the test.

Exercise and weight loss for those who are overweight are the first approaches to treating type 2 diabetes, and these measures often lead to management of the disorder. Drugs for increasing insulin production or improving cellular responses to insulin may also be prescribed, with insulin treatment given if necessary.

Insulin is now made by genetic engineering. There are various forms with different action times that can be alternated to achieve glucose regulation. Excess insulin may result from a pancreatic tumor, but more often it occurs after administration of too much hormone to a diabetic patient. The resultant **hypoglycemia** leads to **insulin shock**, which is treated by the administration of glucose.

Methods of administering insulin in pills or capsules, inhaler spray, or skin patches are under study. Researchers are also studying the possibility of transplanting healthy islet cells to compensate for failed cells. Another area of research is the use of immunosuppression to halt T1DM.

Also used to diagnose endocrine disorders are imaging techniques; other measurements of hormones or their metabolites in plasma and urine; and studies involving hormone stimulation or suppression.

Box 16-5 has information on dieticians and nutritionists. These healthcare professionals work with people, including those with diabetes and other metabolic disorders, to plan healthful diets.

See the animations "Hormonal Control of Glucose" and "Diabetes" and the figure on metabolic syndrome in the Student Resources on thePoint.

HEALTH PROFESSIONS

Box 16-5

Dietitians and Nutritionists

Dietitians and nutritionists specialize in planning and supervising food programs for institutions, such as hospitals, schools, and nursing care facilities, and for individuals with specific disease states, such as diabetes, renal disease, or heart disease. They assess their clients' nutritional needs and design individualized meal plans. Dietitians and nutritionists also work in community settings, educating the public about disease prevention through healthy eating. Increased public awareness about food and nutrition has also led to new opportunities in the food manufacturing industry. To perform their duties, dietitians and nutritionists need a thorough scientific and clinical background. Most dietitians and nutritionists in the United States receive their training from colleges or universities, complete internships, and take licensing or registration exams.

Job prospects for dietitians and nutritionists are good. As the American population continues to age, the need for nutritional planning in hospital and nursing care settings is expected to rise. In addition, many people now place an emphasis on healthy eating and may consult nutritionists privately. The Academy of Nutrition and Dietetics at www.eatright.org has information about these careers.

Terminology   Key Terms

Disorders

~~acromegaly~~ *ak-ro-MEG-ah-le*	Overgrowth of bone and soft tissue, especially in the hands, feet, and face, caused by excess growth hormone in an adult; the name comes from acro meaning "extremity" and megal/o meaning "enlargement"
Addison disease	A disease resulting from deficiency of adrenocortical hormones; it is marked by darkening of the skin, weakness, and alterations in salt and water balance
adenoma *ad-eh-NO-mah*	A neoplasm of a gland
adult hypothyroidism *hi-po-THI-royd-izm*	A condition caused by hypothyroidism in an adult; there is dry, waxy swelling, most notable in the face; formerly called myxedema (*miks-eh-DE-mah*)
congenital hypothyroidism *kon-JEN-ih-tal hi-po-THI-royd-izm*	A condition caused by lack of thyroid secretion during development and marked by arrested physical and mental growth; also called infantile hypothyroidism
Cushing disease	Overactivity of the adrenal cortex resulting from excess production of ACTH by the pituitary
Cushing syndrome	A condition resulting from an excess of hormones from the adrenal cortex; it is associated with obesity, weakness, hyperglycemia, hypertension, and hirsutism (excess hair growth)
diabetes insipidus *di-ah-BE-teze in-SIP-ih-dus*	A disorder caused by insufficient release of ADH from the posterior pituitary; it results in excessive thirst and production of large amounts of very dilute urine; *insipidus* means "tasteless," referring to the dilution of the urine
diabetes mellitus (DM) *MEL-ih-tus*	A disorder of glucose metabolism caused by deficiency of insulin production or inadequate tissue response to insulin; type 1 results from autoimmune destruction of pancreatic islet cells; it generally appears in children and requires insulin administration; type 2 generally occurs in obese adults; it is treated with diet, exercise, and drugs to improve insulin production or activity, and sometimes insulin; *mellitus* comes from the Latin root for honey, referring to the urine's glucose content
exophthalmos *ek-sof-THAL-mos*	Protrusion of the eyeballs, as seen in Graves disease
gigantism *JI-gan-tizm*	Overgrowth caused by excess growth hormone from the pituitary during childhood; also called gigantism
glycated hemoglobin (HbA1c) test *GLI-ka-ted*	A test that measures the binding of glucose to hemoglobin during the lifespan of a red blood cell; it reflects the average blood glucose level over two to three months and is useful in evaluating long-term therapy for diabetes mellitus; also called A1c test
glycosuria *gli-ko-SU-re-ah*	Excess glucose in the urine
goiter *GOY-ter*	Enlargement of the thyroid gland; a simple (nontoxic) goiter is caused by iodine deficiency
Graves disease	An autoimmune disease resulting in hyperthyroidism; a prominent symptom is exophthalmos (protrusion of the eyeballs); also called diffuse toxic goiter
hyperglycemia *hi-per-gli-SE-me-ah*	Excess glucose in the blood
hypoglycemia *hi-po-gli-SE-me-ah*	Abnormally low level of glucose in the blood
insulin shock	A condition resulting from an overdose of insulin, causing hypoglycemia

Terminology	**Key Terms** (*Continued*)

ketoacidosis ke-to-as-ih-DO-sis	Acidosis (increased acidity of body fluids) caused by excess ketone bodies, as in diabetes mellitus; diabetic acidosis
metabolic syndrome	A state of hyperglycemia caused by cellular resistance to insulin, as seen in type 2 diabetes, in association with other metabolic disorders; also called syndrome X or insulin resistance syndrome
panhypopituitarism pan-hi-po-pih-TU-ih-tah-rism	Underactivity of the entire pituitary gland
tetany TET-ah-ne	Irritability and spasms of muscles; may be caused by low blood calcium and other factors

Terminology	**Supplementary Terms**

Normal Structure and Function

sella turcica SEL-ah TUR-sih-kah	A saddle-shaped depression in the sphenoid bone that contains the pituitary gland (literally means "Turkish saddle")
sphenoid bone SFE-noyd	A bone at the base of the skull that houses the pituitary gland

Symptoms and Conditions

adrenogenital syndrome ad-re-no-JEN-ih-tal	Condition caused by overproduction of androgens from the adrenal cortex, resulting in masculinization; may be congenital or acquired, usually as a result of an adrenal tumor
Conn syndrome	Hyperaldosteronism caused by an adrenal tumor
craniopharyngioma kra-ne-o-far-in-je-O-mah	A benign tumor of the pituitary gland
Hashimoto disease hah-she-MO-to	A chronic thyroiditis of autoimmune origin
impaired glucose tolerance (IGT)	High blood glucose levels after glucose intake that may signal borderline diabetes mellitus
ketosis ke-TO-sis	Accumulation of ketone bodies, such as acetone, in the body; usually results from deficiency or faulty metabolism of carbohydrates, as in cases of diabetes mellitus and starvation
multiple endocrine neoplasia (MEN)	A hereditary disorder that causes tumors in several endocrine glands; classified according to the combination of glands involved
pheochromocytoma fe-o-kro-mo-si-TO-mah	A usually benign tumor of the adrenal medulla or other structures containing chromaffin cells (cells that stain with chromium salts) (phe/o means "brown" or "dusky"); the adrenal tumor causes increased production of epinephrine
pituitary apoplexy AP-o-plek-se	Sudden massive hemorrhage and degeneration of the pituitary gland associated with a pituitary tumor; common symptoms include severe headache, visual problems, and loss of consciousness
seasonal affective disorder (SAD)	A mood disorder with lethargy, depression, excessive need for sleep, and overeating that generally occurs in winter; thought to be related to melatonin levels as influenced by environmental light (**Box 16-6**)

(continued)

Simmonds disease	Hypofunction of the anterior pituitary (panhypopituitarism), usually because of an infarction; pituitary cachexia (*ka-KEK-se-a*)
thyroid storm	A sudden onset of thyrotoxicosis symptoms occurring in patients with hyperthyroidism who are untreated or poorly treated; may be brought on by illness or trauma; also called thyroid crisis
thyrotoxicosis *thi-ro-tok-sih-KO-sis*	Condition resulting from overactivity of the thyroid gland; symptoms include anxiety, irritability, weight loss, and sweating; the main example of thyrotoxicosis is Graves disease
von Recklinghausen disease *REK-ling-how-zen*	Bone degeneration caused by excess production of parathyroid hormone; also called Recklinghausen disease of bone

Diagnosis and Treatment

fasting plasma glucose (FPG)	Measurement of blood glucose after a fast of at least eight hours; a reading equal to or greater than 126 mg/dL indicates diabetes; also called fasting blood glucose (FBG) or fasting blood sugar (FBS)
free thyroxine index (FTI, T_7)	Calculation based on the amount of T_4 present and T_3 uptake, used to diagnose thyroid dysfunction
oral glucose tolerance test (OGTT)	Measurement of glucose levels in blood plasma after administration of a challenge dose of glucose to a fasting patient; used to measure patient's ability to metabolize glucose; a value equal to or greater than 200 mg/dL in the two-hour sample indicates diabetes
radioactive iodine uptake test (RAIU)	A test that measures thyroid uptake of radioactive iodine as an evaluation of thyroid function
radioimmunoassay (RIA)	A method of measuring very small amounts of a substance, especially hormones, in blood plasma using radioactively labeled hormones and specific antibodies
thyroid scan	Visualization of the thyroid gland after administration of radioactive iodine
thyroxine-binding globulin (TBG) test	Test that measures the main protein that binds T_4 in the blood
transsphenoidal adenomectomy *trans-sfe-NOY-dal ad-eh-no-MEK-to-me*	Removal of a pituitary tumor through the sphenoid sinus (space in the sphenoid bone)

Go to the Audio Pronunciation Glossary in the Student Resources on thePoint to hear these terms pronounced.

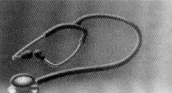

CLINICAL PERSPECTIVES   Box 16-6

Seasonal Affective Disorder: Some Light on the Subject

We all sense that long dark days make us blue and sap our motivation. Are these learned responses, or is there a physical basis for them? Studies have shown that the amount of light in the environment does have a physical effect on behavior. Evidence that light alters mood comes from people who are intensely affected by the dark days of winter—people who suffer from *seasonal affective disorder*, aptly abbreviated SAD. When days shorten, these people feel sleepy, depressed, and anxious. They tend to overeat, especially carbohydrates.

As light strikes the retina of the eye, it starts nerve impulses that decrease the amount of melatonin produced by the pineal gland in the brain. Because melatonin depresses mood, the final effect of light is to elevate mood. Daily exposure to bright lights has been found to improve the mood of most people with SAD. Exposure for 15 minutes after rising in the morning may be enough, but some people require longer sessions both morning and evening. Other aids include aerobic exercise, stress management techniques, and antidepressant medications.

Terminology Abbreviations

A1c	Glycated hemoglobin (test)		**LH**	Luteinizing hormone
ACTH	Adrenocorticotropic hormone		**MEN**	Multiple endocrine neoplasia
ADH	Antidiuretic hormone		**NPH**	Neutral protamine Hagedorn (insulin)
BS	Blood sugar		**OGTT**	Oral glucose tolerance test
CSII	Continuous subcutaneous insulin infusion		**PRL**	Prolactin
DM	Diabetes mellitus		**PTH**	Parathyroid hormone
FBG	Fasting blood glucose		**RAIU**	Radioactive iodine uptake
FBS	Fasting blood sugar		**RIA**	Radioimmunoassay
FPG	Fasting plasma glucose		**SIADH**	Syndrome of inappropriate antidiuretic hormone (secretion)
FSH	Follicle-stimulating hormone		**T1DM**	Type 1 diabetes mellitus
FTI	Free thyroxine index		**T2DM**	Type 2 diabetes mellitus
GDM	Gestational diabetes mellitus		T_3	Triiodothyronine
GH	Growth hormone		T_4	Thyroxine; tetraiodothyronine
HbA1c	Hemoglobin A1 c; glycated hemoglobin		T_7	Free thyroxine index
^{131}I	Iodine-131 (radioactive iodine)		**TBG**	Thyroxine-binding globulin
IFG	Impaired fasting blood glucose		**TSH**	Thyroid-stimulating hormone
IGT	Impaired glucose tolerance			

16

Case Study Revisited

J.D.'s Follow-Up

J.D. began her antithyroid medication therapy and began to feel better. She was able to concentrate more at work and found she was not as irritable with the children in school. She was sleeping better and began to add a few of the pounds she had previously lost. Her husband also noted the difference and mentioned this to Dr. Gilbert at the follow-up appointment four weeks later.

CHAPTER
16   **Review**

Labeling Exercise

GLANDS OF THE ENDOCRINE SYSTEM

Write the name of each numbered part on the corresponding line.

Adrenals   Pineal
Hypothalamus   Pituitary (hypophysis)
Ovaries   Testes
Pancreatic islets   Thyroid
Parathyroids

1. _____
2. _____
3. _____
4. _____
5. _____
6. _____
7. _____
8. _____
9. _____

TERMINOLOGY

Match the following terms, and write the appropriate letter to the left of each number.

_____ **1.** parathyroid   **a.** gland that is regulated by light
_____ **2.** posterior pituitary   **b.** small gland that acts to increase blood calcium levels
_____ **3.** hypothalamus   **c.** part of the brain that controls the pituitary
_____ **4.** anterior pituitary   **d.** gland that secretes ACTH
_____ **5.** pineal   **e.** gland that releases oxytocin

_____ **6.** epinephrine   **a.** hormone produced by the adrenal cortex
_____ **7.** growth hormone   **b.** somatotropin
_____ **8.** cortisol   **c.** pancreatic hormone that regulates glucose metabolism
_____ **9.** glucagon   **d.** hormone produced by the adrenal medulla
_____ **10.** melatonin   **e.** hormone from the pineal gland

_____ **11.** ADH   **a.** substance used to monitor blood glucose levels
_____ **12.** T_4 **b.** pituitary hormone that regulates water balance
_____ **13.** ACTH   **c.** a form of diabetes
_____ **14.** T2DM   **d.** thyroxine
_____ **15.** HbA1c   **e.** hormone that stimulates the adrenal cortex

_____ **16.** ketoacidosis

_____ **17.** adenoma

_____ **18.** Cushing syndrome

_____ **19.** acromegaly

_____ **20.** diabetes insipidus

a. disorder that results from excess growth hormone

b. disorder caused by insufficient release of ADH

c. a result of uncontrolled diabetes

d. disorder caused by overactivity of the adrenal cortex

e. neoplasm of a gland

Supplementary Terms

_____ **21.** craniopharyngioma

_____ **22.** Simmonds disease

_____ **23.** pheochromocytoma

_____ **24.** Hashimoto disease

_____ **25.** sella turcica

a. panhypopituitarism

b. tumor of the pituitary gland

c. chronic thyroiditis

d. bony depression that holds the pituitary

e. tumor of the adrenal medulla

FILL IN THE BLANKS

26. The gland under the brain that controls other glands is the _____.

27. The gland in the neck that affects metabolic rate is the _____.

28. The endocrine glands located above the kidneys are the _____.

29. The most common endocrine disorder is _____.

30. Excess glucose in the blood is called _____.

DEFINITIONS

Define the following words.

31. thyrotomy (*thi-ROT-o-me*) _____

32. hypopituitarism (*hi-po-pih-TU-ih-tah-rizm*) _____

33. hypophysiotropic (*hi-po-fiz-e-o-TROP-ik*) _____

34. adrenopathy (*ah-dre-NOP-ah-the*) _____

35. adrenomegaly (*ah-dre-no-MEG-ah-le*) _____

36. endocrinologist (*en-do-krih-NOL-o-jist*) _____

Write words for the following definitions.

37. tumor of the pancreatic islets _____

38. destroying the thyroid gland _____

39. pertaining to the adrenal cortex _____

Use the full name of the gland as the root to write words for the following definitions.

40. inflammation of the thyroid gland _____

41. removal of one half (hemi-) of the thyroid gland _____

42. surgical removal of parathyroid gland _____

43. overactivity of the adrenal gland _____

Use the root thyr/o to write words for the following definitions.

44. acting on the thyroid gland _____

45. downward displacement of the thyroid gland _____

46. any disease of the thyroid gland _____

TRUE-FALSE

Examine the following statements. If the statement is true, write T in the first blank. If the statement is false, write F in the first blank, and correct the statement by replacing the underlined word in the second blank.

	True or False	Correct Answer
47. Diabetes insipidus is caused by a lack of <u>thymosin</u>.	_____	_____
48. The hypophysis is the <u>pituitary</u> gland.	_____	_____
49. The outer region of an organ is the <u>medulla</u>.	_____	_____
50. The parathyroids regulate the element <u>sodium</u>.	_____	_____
51. Goiter is an enlargement of the <u>pineal</u> gland.	_____	_____
52. <u>Type 1</u> diabetes mellitus always requires insulin.	_____	_____
53. Thyroid hormones contain the element <u>iodine</u>.	_____	_____
54. The adrenal cortex produces <u>steroid</u> hormones.	_____	_____
55. Exophthalmos is protrusion of the <u>eyes</u>.	_____	_____
56. <u>Melatonin</u> regulates mood and daily cycles.	_____	_____

ELIMINATIONS

In each of the sets below, underline the term that does not fit in with the rest, and explain the reason for your choice.

57. GH — TSH — FSH — PTH — ACTH

_____

58. Cushing syndrome — gigantism — dwarfism — acromegaly — thyrotoxicosis

_____

59. TBG — GDM — FPG — IGT — IFG

_____

60. testis — spleen — adrenals — parathyroids — pituitary

_____

WORD BUILDING

Write words for the following definitions using the word parts provided.

| -ar   adren/o   -megal/o   -oma   thyr/o   -ic   -al   trop   -y   insul/o   path/o   -lytic |

61. any disease of the thyroid gland   _____

62. acting on the adrenal gland   _____

63. enlargement of the thyroid gland   _____

64. pertaining to the gland above the kidney   _____

65. enlargement of the adrenal gland   _____

66. tumor of islet cells   _____

67. destructive of thyroid tissue   _____

68. any disease of the adrenal gland   _____

69. acting on the thyroid gland   _____

70. pertaining to pancreatic islet cells   _____

WORD ANALYSIS

Define each of the following words, and give the meaning of the word parts in each. Use a dictionary if necessary.

71. craniopharyngioma (*kra-ne-o-fah-rin-je-O-mah*) _____

    a. crani/o _____

    b. pharyng/i _____

    c. -oma _____

72. panhypopituitarism (*pan-hi-po-pih-TU-ih-tah-rism*) _____

    a. pan- _____

    b. hypo- _____

    c. pituitar _____

    d. -ism _____

73. pheochromocytoma (*fe-o-kro-mo-si-TO-mah*) _____

    a. phe/o _____

    b. chrom/o _____

    c. cyt/o _____

    d. -oma _____

74. thyrotoxicosis (*thi-ro-tok-sih-KO-sis*) _____

    a. thyr/o _____

    b. toxic/o _____

    c. -sis _____

75. acromegaly _____

    a. acr/o _____

    b. megal/o _____

    c. y _____

NAME THE GLAND

Identify the gland associated with the following conditions.

76. diabetes mellitus _____

77. Addison disease _____

78. Graves disease _____

79. tetany _____

80. Simmonds disease _____

For more learning activities, see Chapter 16 of the Student Resources on thePoint.

Additional Case Studies

Case Study 16-1: *Hyperparathyroidism*

B.E., a 58 y/o woman with a history of hypertension, had a partial nephrectomy four years ago for renal calculi. During a routine physical examination, her total serum calcium level was 10.8 mg/dL. Her parathyroid hormone level was WNL; she was in no apparent distress, and the remainder of her physical examination and laboratory data were noncontributory.

B.E. underwent exploratory surgery for an enlarged right superior parathyroid gland. The remaining three glands appeared normal. The enlarged gland was excised, and a biopsy was performed on the remaining glands. The pathology report showed an adenoma of the abnormal gland. On her first postoperative day, she reported perioral numbness and tingling. She had no other symptoms, but her serum calcium level was subnormal. She was given one ampule of calcium gluconate. Within two days, her calcium level had improved, and she was discharged.

Case Study 16-2: *Diabetes Treatment with an Insulin Pump*

M.G., a 32-year-old marketing executive, was diagnosed with type 1 diabetes at the age of 3. She vividly remembers her mother taking her to the doctor because she had an illness that caused her to feel extremely tired and very thirsty and hungry. She also had begun to wet her bed and had a cut on her knee that would not heal. Her mother had had gestational diabetes during her pregnancy with M.G., and at birth, M.G. was described as having "macrosomia" because she weighed 10 lb.

M.G. has managed her disease with meticulous attention to her diet, exercise, preventive healthcare, regular blood glucose monitoring, and twice-daily injections of regular and NPH insulin, which she rotates among her upper arms, thighs, and abdomen. She continues in a smoking cessation program supported by weekly acupuncture treatments. She maintains good control of her disease in spite of the inconvenience and time it consumes each day. She will be married next summer and would like to start a family. M.G.'s doctor suggested she try an insulin pump to give her more freedom and enhance her quality of life. After intensive training, she has received her pump. It is about the size of a deck of cards with a thin catheter that she introduces through a needle into her abdominal subcutaneous tissue. She can administer her insulin in a continuous subcutaneous insulin infusion (CSII) and in calculated meal bolus doses. She still has to test her blood for hyperglycemia and hypoglycemia and her urine for ketones when her blood glucose is too high. She hopes one day to have an islet transplantation.

Case Study Questions

Multiple Choice. Select the best answer, and write the letter of your choice to the left of each number.

_____ **1.** Renal calculi are
   a. kidney stones
   b. gallstones
   c. stomach ulcers
   d. bile obstructions

_____ **2.** B.E.'s serum calcium was 10.8 mg/dL, which is
   a. 5.4 mcg of calcium in her serous fluid
   b. 10.8 g of electrolytes in parathyroid hormone
   c. 10.8 mg of calcium in 100 mL of blood
   d. 21.6 L of calcium in 100 g of serum

_____ **3.** B.E. had perioral numbness and tingling. Perioral is
   a. peripheral to any orifice
   b. lateral to the eye
   c. within the buccal mucosa
   d. around the mouth

_____ **4.** Gestational diabetes occurs
   a. in a pregnant woman
   b. to any large fetus
   c. during menopause
   d. in a large baby with high blood glucose

_____ **5.** The term macrosomia describes
   a. excessive weight gain during pregnancy
   b. a large body
   c. an excessive amount of sleep
   d. inability to sleep during pregnancy

_____ **6.** M.G. injected the insulin into the subcutaneous tissue, which is
   a. present only in the abdomen, thighs, and upper arms
   b. a topical application
   c. below the skin
   d. above the pubic bone

_____ **7.** An islet transplantation refers to
   a. transfer of insulin-secreting cells into a pancreas
   b. transfer of parathyroid cells to the liver
   c. surgical insertion of an insulin pump into the abdomen
   d. a total pancreas and kidney transplantation

16

Write the terms from the Case Studies with the following meanings.

8. surgical excision of a kidney _____

9. tumor of a gland _____

10. single-use glass injectable medication container _____

11. high serum glucose _____

12. a large dose of a therapeutic agent _____

Abbreviations. Define the following abbreviations.

13. WNL _____

14. NPH _____

15. CSII _____

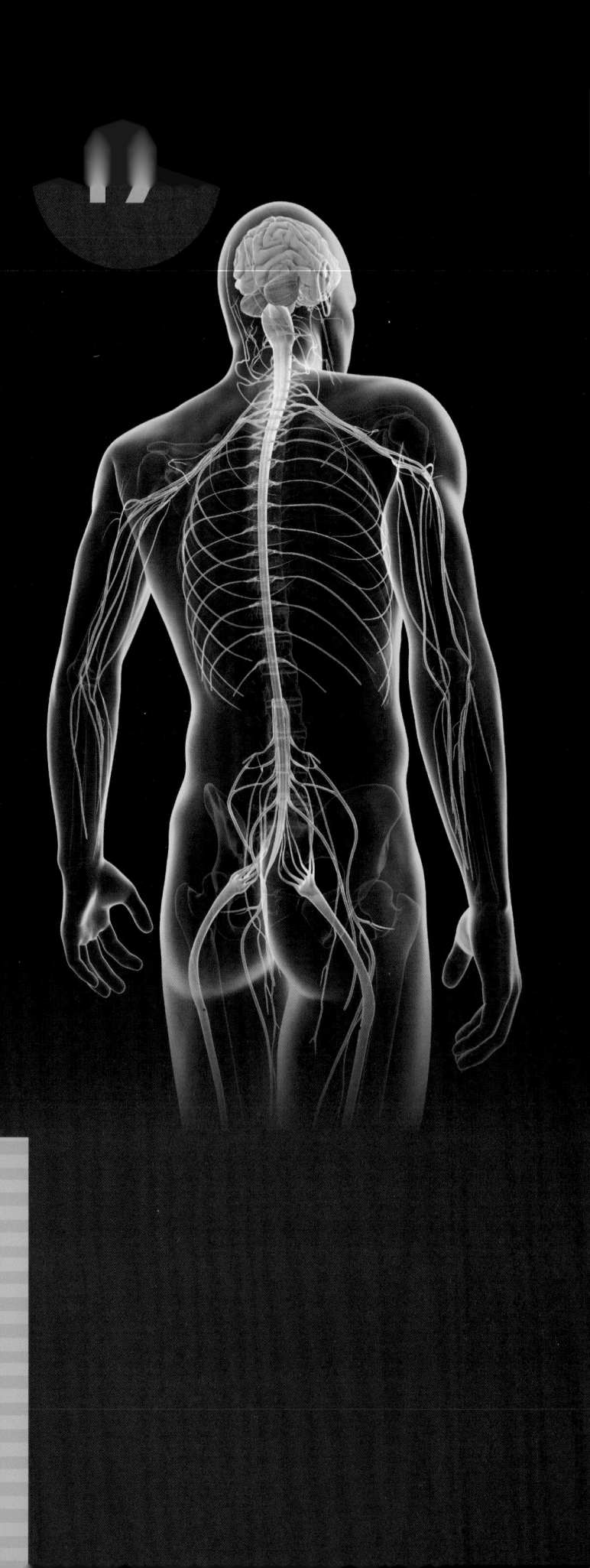

Pretest

Multiple Choice. Select the best answer, and write the letter of your choice to the left of each number.

_____ 1. The basic cell of the nervous system is a(n)
    a. myofiber
    b. neuron
    c. osteoblast
    d. chondrocyte

_____ 2. The largest part of the brain is the
    a. cerebrum
    b. adrenal
    c. cortex
    d. pituitary

_____ 3. The midbrain, pons, and medulla oblongata make up the
    a. ventricle
    b. spinal cord
    c. cerebellum
    d. brainstem

_____ 4. Involuntary responses are controlled by the
    a. somatic nervous system
    b. voluntary nervous system
    c. autonomic nervous system
    d. diaphragm

_____ 5. A simple response that requires few cells is a
    a. reflex
    b. mutation
    c. sensation
    d. stimulus

_____ 6. A disorder, often of unknown cause, characterized by seizures is called
    a. cystic fibrosis
    b. spina bifida
    c. epilepsy
    d. thyrotoxicosis

_____ 7. An instrument used to study the electric activity of the brain is the
    a. electrocardiograph
    b. electroencephalograph
    c. CT scanner
    d. sonograph

_____ 8. An extreme, persistent fear is a(n)
    a. palliative
    b. prognosis
    c. analgesic
    d. phobia

Learning Objectives

After study of this chapter, you should be able to:

1 ▶ Describe the components of the nervous system. **p420**

2 ▶ Describe the structure of a neuron. **p420**

3 ▶ Briefly describe the regions of the brain and their functions. **p422**

4 ▶ Describe how the central nervous system is protected. **p422**

5 ▶ Describe the structure of the spinal cord. **p424**

6 ▶ Name the components of a simple reflex. **p424**

7 ▶ Compare the sympathetic and parasympathetic systems. **p426**

8 ▶ Identify and use word parts pertaining to the nervous system. **p429**

9 ▶ Describe eight major types of disorders affecting the nervous system. **p433**

10 ▶ Describe five major categories of behavioral disorders. **p437**

11 ▶ Define abbreviations used in neurology. **p448**

12 ▶ Analyze medical terms in several case studies involving the nervous system. **pp419, 458**

Case Study: *B.C.'s Pediatric Brain Tumor*

Chief Complaint

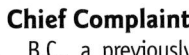

B.C., a previously healthy and active 6-year-old, woke up one morning complaining that his head hurt. He had a few episodes of vomiting early in the morning, and he was not able to walk straight when he got out of bed. His parents took him to the pediatrician, who, after noting the headache, morning emesis, and progressive loss of muscle coordination (ataxia), conducted a brief examination and then made an immediate referral to a neurologist.

Examination

Before talking with the patient, the neurologist spoke with B.C.'s parents to obtain a prior medical history. They stated that he had a healthy childhood thus far with normal illnesses such as earaches, a few colds, and sore throats. The parents indicated that B.C. is a first grader and attends a public elementary school. They said he loves school and baseball. The latter is his favorite extracurricular activity.

The neurologist spoke with B.C. and explained what he was going to do. Next he performed a thorough neurologic examination. Then he offered to B.C. a simple explanation of the tests he was going to order. Finally he answered all of the patient's and parents' questions.

Clinical Course

B.C.'s parents took him to the radiology department of the hospital for a scheduled MRI. The radiologist reported the scan revealed some dense tissue indicating a suspicious mass. A lumbar puncture (LP) was performed, which revealed some suspicious cells in the cerebrospinal fluid (CSF).

B.C. had a craniotomy with tumor resection five days later. The cerebellar tumor was found to be noninfiltrating and was enclosed within a cyst, which was totally removed. B.C. spent two days in the neurologic intensive care unit (NICU) because he was on seizure precautions and monitoring for increased intracranial pressure (ICP). A regimen of focal radiation followed after recovery from surgery. His spine was also treated because of the potential spread of tumor cells in the CSF. B.C. did not have chemotherapy because of the danger that hydrocephalus might develop, which generally requires a ventriculoperitoneal (VP) shunt.

ANCILLARIES *At-A-Glance*

Visit thePoint to access the following resources. For guidance in using the resources most effectively, see pp. ix–xvi.

Learning RESOURCES

▶ **Tips for Effective Studying**
▶ **Web Chart: Neuroglia**
▶ **Animation: The Myelin Sheath**
▶ **Animation: The Synapse and the Nerve Impulse**
▶ **Animation: The Reflex Arc**

▶ **Animation: Stroke**
▶ **Audio Pronunciation Glossary**

Learning ACTIVITIES

▶ **Visual Activities**
▶ **Kinesthetic Activities**
▶ **Auditory Activities**

Introduction

The nervous system and the endocrine system coordinate and control the body. Together they regulate our responses to the environment and maintain homeostasis. Whereas the endocrine system functions by means of circulating hormones, the nervous system functions by means of electric impulses and locally released chemicals called neurotransmitters.

Organization of the Nervous System

For study purposes, the nervous system may be divided structurally into two parts:

- The **central nervous system (CNS)**, consisting of the **brain** and **spinal cord** (**Fig.17-1**)
- The **peripheral nervous system (PNS)**, consisting of all nervous tissue outside the brain and spinal cord

Functionally, the nervous system can be divided into the:

- **Somatic nervous system**, which controls skeletal muscles
- **Autonomic nervous system (ANS)**, or **visceral nervous system**, which controls smooth muscle, cardiac muscle, and glands; regulates responses to stress; and helps to maintain homeostasis

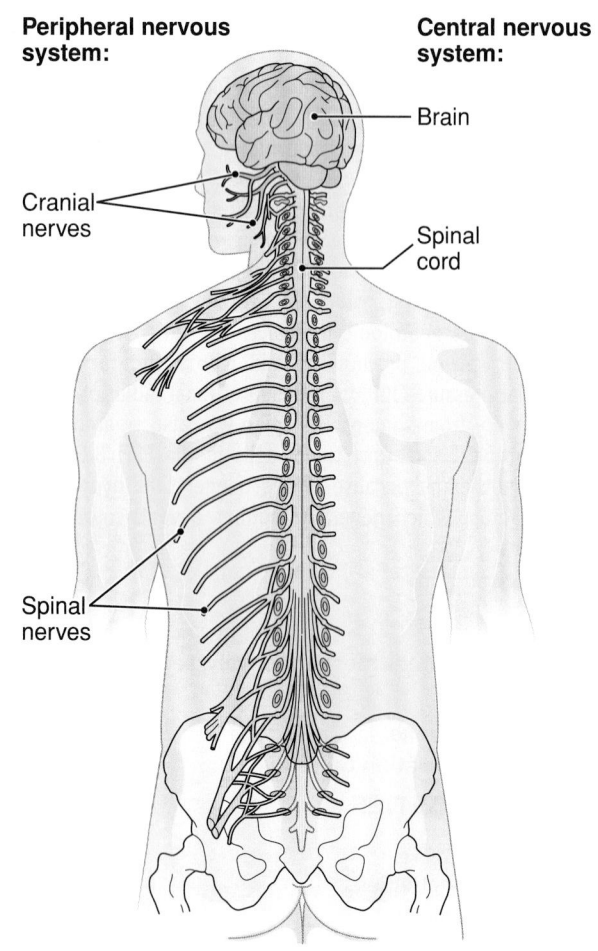

Peripheral nervous system:

- Cranial nerves
- Spinal nerves

Central nervous system:

- Brain
- Spinal cord

Figure 17-1   **Anatomic divisions of the nervous system.**

Two types of cells are found in the nervous system. **Neurons**, or nerve cells, make up the conducting tissue of the nervous system. **Neuroglia** are the cells that support and protect nervous tissue.

> See the chart on neuroglia in the Student Resources on thePoint.

The Neuron

The neuron is the nervous system's basic functional unit (**Fig. 17-2**). Each neuron has two types of fibers extending from the cell body:

- A **dendrite** carries impulses toward the cell body.
- An **axon** carries impulses away from the cell body.

Some axons are covered with **myelin**, a whitish, fatty material that insulates and protects the axon and speeds electric conduction. Axons so covered are described as *myelinated*, and they make up the **white matter** of the nervous system. Unmyelinated tissue makes up the nervous system's **gray matter**. The myelin sheath consists of individual cells that wrap around the axon. The spaces between these cells are called *nodes*. Myelinated axons conduct nerve impulses more rapidly than unmyelinated axons because the electric impulse can skip from node to node.

Each neuron is part of a pathway that carries information through the nervous system. A neuron that transmits impulses toward the CNS is a **sensory**, or **afferent**, neuron; a neuron that transmits impulses away from the CNS is a **motor**, or **efferent**, neuron. There are also connecting cells within the CNS called **interneurons**.

A **synapse** is the point of contact between two neurons. At the synapse, energy is passed from one cell to another, usually by means of a **neurotransmitter** and sometimes by direct transfer of electric current.

> See the animations "The Myelin Sheath" and "The Synapse and the Nerve Impulse" in the Student Resources on thePoint.

NERVES

Individual neuron fibers are held together in bundles like wires in a cable. If this bundle is part of the PNS, it is called a **nerve**. A collection of cell bodies along the pathway of a nerve is a **ganglion**. A few nerves (sensory nerves) contain only sensory neurons, and a few (motor nerves) contain only motor neurons, but most contain both types of fibers and are described as *mixed nerves*.

The Brain

The brain is nervous tissue contained within the cranium. It consists of the **cerebrum, diencephalon, brainstem,** and **cerebellum.** The cerebrum is the largest part of the brain (**Fig. 17-3**); it is composed largely of white matter with a thin outer layer of gray matter, the **cerebral cortex.** It is within the cortex that the higher brain functions

17

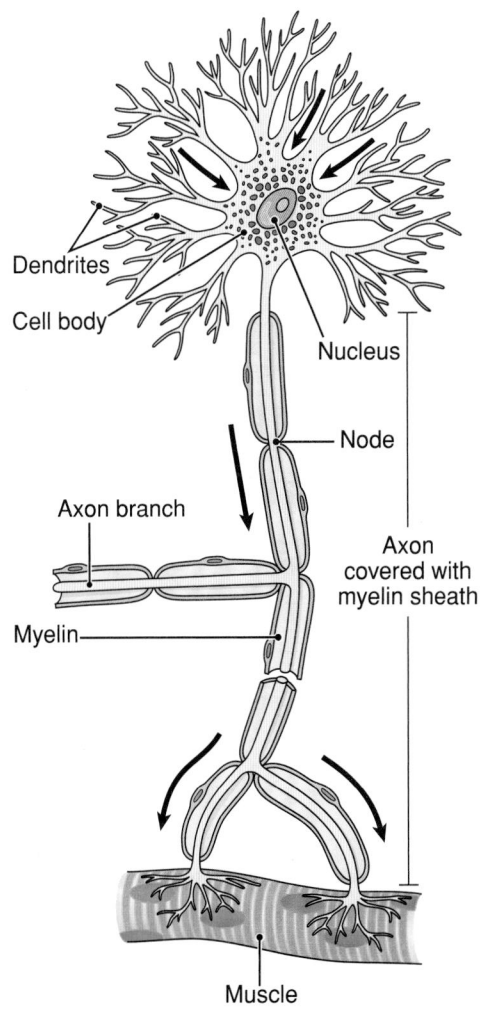

Dendrites

Cell body

Nucleus

Node

Axon branch

Axon
covered with
myelin sheath

Myelin

Muscle

Figure 17-2 **A motor neuron.** The break in the axon denotes length. The *arrows* show the direction of the nerve impulse.

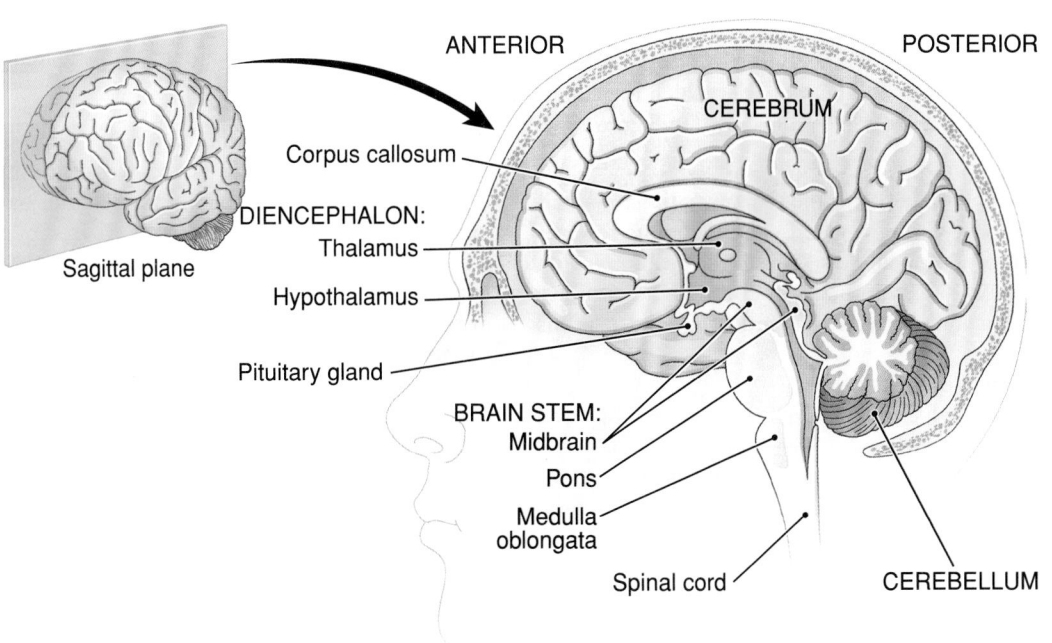

ANTERIOR

POSTERIOR

CEREBRUM

Corpus callosum

DIENCEPHALON:
Thalamus

Hypothalamus

Pituitary gland

BRAIN STEM:
Midbrain

Pons

Medulla
oblongata

Spinal cord

CEREBELLUM

Sagittal plane

Figure 17-3 **Brain, sagittal section.** The main divisions are shown.

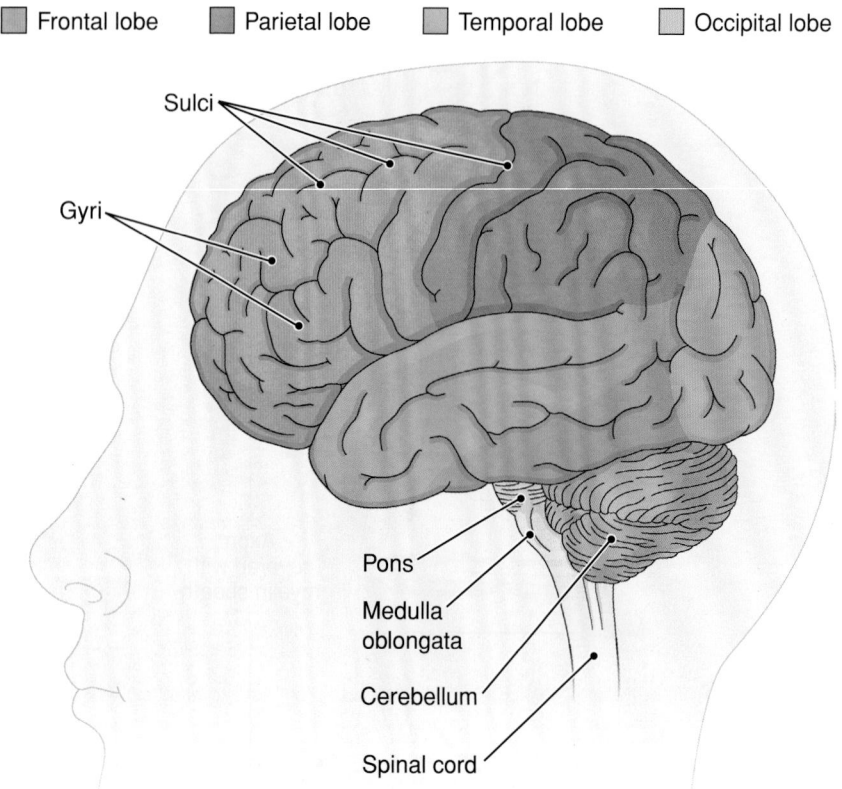

☐ Frontal lobe   ☐ Parietal lobe   ☐ Temporal lobe   ☐ Occipital lobe

Sulci

Gyri

Pons

Medulla oblongata

Cerebellum

Spinal cord

Figure 17-4 **External surface of the brain, lateral view.** The lobes and surface features of the cerebrum are shown as well as other divisions of the brain and the spinal cord.

of memory, reasoning, and abstract thought occur. The cerebrum's distinct surface is formed by grooves, or **sulci** (singular: sulcus), and raised areas, or **gyri** (singular: gyrus), that provide additional surface area (**Fig. 17-4**). The cerebrum is divided into two hemispheres by a deep groove, the longitudinal fissure. Each hemisphere is further divided into lobes with specialized functions (see **Fig. 17-4**). The lobes are named for the skull bones under which they lie.

The remaining parts of the brain, shown in Figure 17-3, are as follows:

- The diencephalon contains the **thalamus**, the **hypothalamus**, and the pituitary gland. The thalamus receives sensory information and directs it to the proper portion of the cortex. The hypothalamus controls the pituitary and forms a link between the endocrine and nervous systems.
- The brainstem consists of the:
  - **Midbrain**, which contains reflex centers for improved vision and hearing.
  - **Pons**, which forms a bulge on the anterior surface of the brainstem. It contains fibers that connect the brain's different regions.
  - **Medulla oblongata**, which connects the brain with the spinal cord. All impulses passing to and from the brain travel through this region. The medulla also has vital centers for control of heart rate, respiration, and blood pressure.

- The cerebellum is under the cerebrum and dorsal to the pons and medulla. Like the cerebrum, it is divided into two hemispheres. The cerebellum helps to control voluntary muscle movements and to maintain posture, coordination, and balance.

PROTECTING THE BRAIN

Within the brain are four **ventricles** (cavities) in which **cerebrospinal fluid** (CSF) is formed. This fluid circulates around the brain and spinal cord, acting as a protective cushion for these tissues.

Covering the brain and the spinal cord are three protective layers, together called the **meninges** (**Fig. 17-5**). All are named with the Latin word *mater*, meaning "mother," to indicate their protective function. They are the:

- **Dura mater**, the outermost and toughest of the three. *Dura* means "hard."
- **Arachnoid mater**, the thin, web-like middle layer. It is named for the Latin word for spider, because it resembles a spider web.
- **Pia mater**, the thin, vascular inner layer, attached directly to the tissue of the brain and spinal cord. *Pia* means "tender."

Twelve pairs of **cranial nerves** connect with the brain (**Fig. 17-6**). These nerves are identified by Roman numerals

17

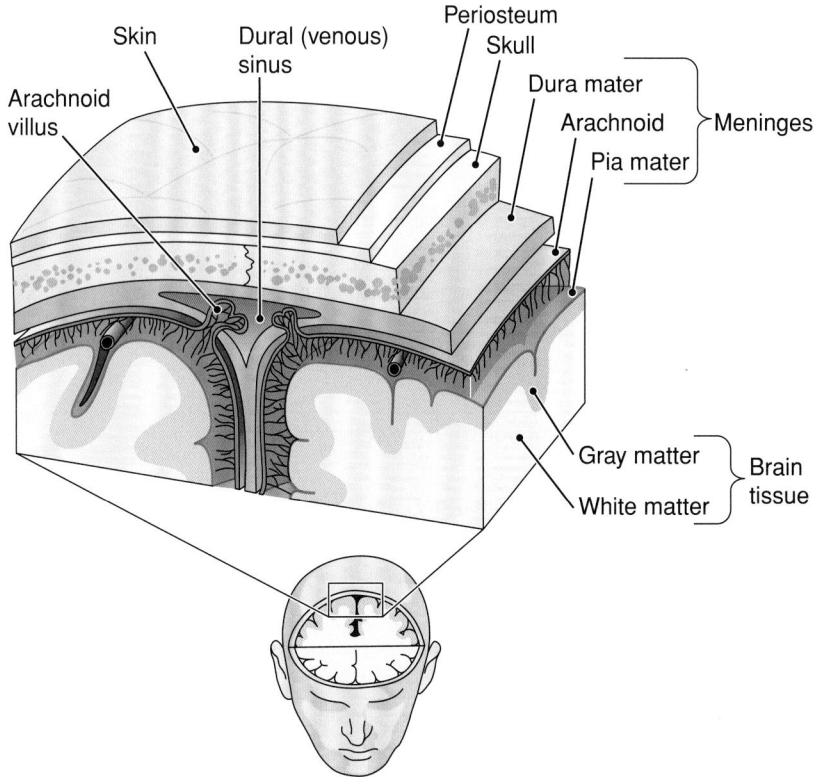

Figure 17-5 **The meninges.** The three protective layers and adjacent tissue are shown in a frontal section of the head.

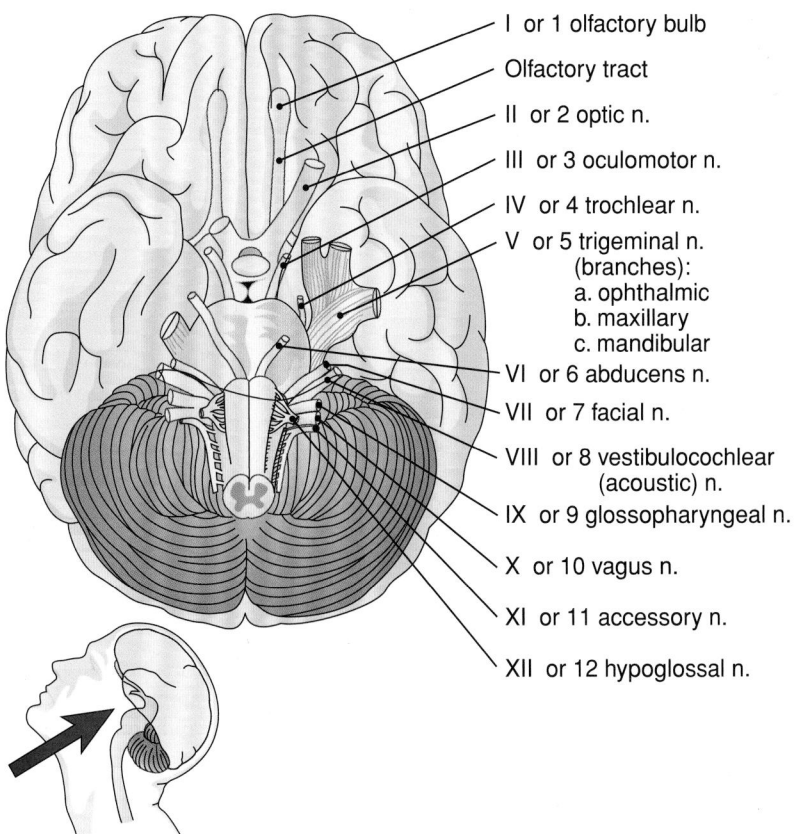

- I or 1 olfactory bulb
- Olfactory tract
- II or 2 optic n.
- III or 3 oculomotor n.
- IV or 4 trochlear n.
- V or 5 trigeminal n.
  (branches):
  a. ophthalmic
  b. maxillary
  c. mandibular
- VI or 6 abducens n.
- VII or 7 facial n.
- VIII or 8 vestibulocochlear
  (acoustic) n.
- IX or 9 glossopharyngeal n.
- X or 10 vagus n.
- XI or 11 accessory n.
- XII or 12 hypoglossal n.

Figure 17-6 **Cranial nerves.** The 12 nerves are shown on one side in an inferior view.

FOR YOUR REFERENCE
The Cranial Nerves

Box 17-1

Number	Name	Function
I	**olfactory** *ol-FAK-to-re*	carries impulses for the sense of smell
II	**optic** *OP-tik*	carries impulses for the sense of vision
III	**oculomotor** *ok-u-lo-MO-tor*	controls movement of eye muscles
IV	**trochlear** *TROK-le-ar*	controls a muscle of the eyeball
V	**trigeminal** *tri-JEM-ih-nal*	carries sensory impulses from the face; controls chewing muscles
VI	**abducens** *ab-DU-sens*	controls a muscle of the eyeball
VII	**facial** *FA-shal*	controls muscles of facial expression, salivary glands, and tear glands; conducts some impulses for taste
VIII	**vestibulocochlear** *ves-tib-u-lo-KOK-le-ar*	conducts impulses for hearing and equilibrium; also called auditory or acoustic nerve
IX	**glossopharyngeal** *glos-o-fah-RIN-je-al*	conducts sensory impulses from tongue and pharynx; stimulates parotid salivary gland and partly controls swallowing
X	**vagus** *VA-gus*	supplies most organs of thorax and abdomen; controls digestive secretions
XI	**spinal accessory** *ak-SES-o-re*	controls muscles of the neck
XII	**hypoglossal** *hi-po-GLOS-al*	controls muscles of the tongue

and also by name. **Box 17-1** is a summary chart of the cranial nerves.

The Spinal Cord

The spinal cord begins at the medulla oblongata and tapers to an end between the first and second lumbar vertebrae (**Fig. 17-7**). It has enlargements in the cervical and lumbar regions, where nerves for the arms and legs join the cord. Seen in cross-section (**Fig. 17-8**), the spinal cord has a central area of gray matter surrounded by white matter. The gray matter projects toward the posterior and the anterior as the dorsal and ventral horns. The white matter contains the ascending and descending **tracts** (fiber bundles) that carry impulses to and from the brain. A central canal contains CSF.

THE SPINAL NERVES

Thirty-one pairs of **spinal nerves** connect with the spinal cord (see **Fig. 17-7**). These nerves are grouped in the segments of the cord as follows:

- Cervical: 8
- Thoracic: 12
- Lumbar: 5
- Sacral: 5
- Coccygeal: 1

Each nerve joins the cord by two **roots** (see **Fig. 17-8**). The dorsal, or posterior, root carries sensory impulses into the cord; the ventral, or anterior, root carries motor impulses away from the cord and out toward a muscle or gland. An enlargement on the dorsal root, the dorsal root ganglion, has the cell bodies of sensory neurons carrying impulses toward the CNS.

REFLEXES

A simple response that requires few neurons is a **reflex** (**Fig.17-9**). In a spinal reflex, impulses travel through the spinal cord only and do not reach the brain. An example of this type of response is the knee-jerk reflex used in physical examinations. However, most neurologic responses involve complex interactions among multiple neurons in the CNS.

See the animation "The Reflex Arc" in the Student Resources on thePoint.

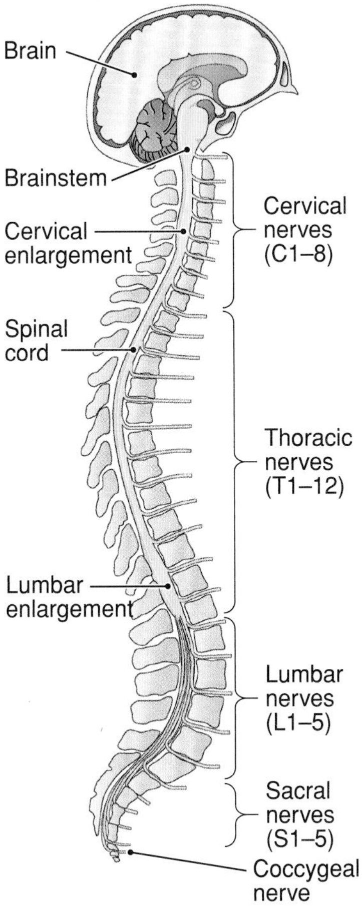

17

Brain

Brainstem

Cervical enlargement

Spinal cord

Lumbar enlargement

Cervical nerves (C1–8)

Thoracic nerves (T1–12)

Lumbar nerves (L1–5)

Sacral nerves (S1–5)

Coccygeal nerve

Figure 17-7 **Spinal cord, lateral view.** The divisions of the spinal nerves are shown.

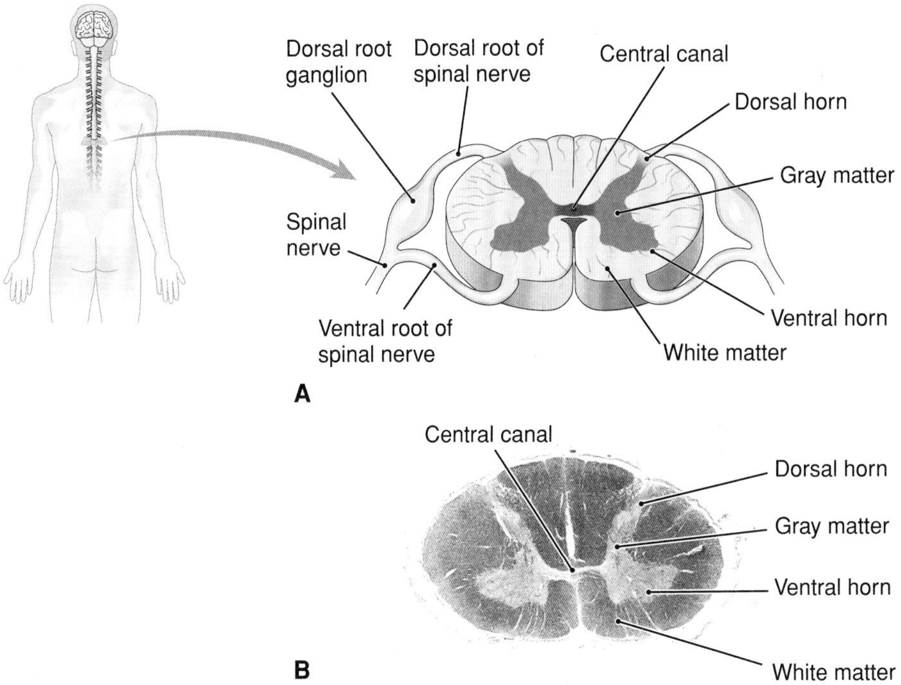

Dorsal root ganglion

Dorsal root of spinal nerve

Central canal

Dorsal horn

Gray matter

Ventral horn

White matter

Spinal nerve

Ventral root of spinal nerve

A

Central canal

Dorsal horn

Gray matter

Ventral horn

White matter

B

Figure 17-8 **Spinal cord, cross-section. A.** Diagram shows the organization of gray and white matter and the roots of the spinal nerves. **B.** Microscopic view of the spinal cord in cross-section (magnification 5×).

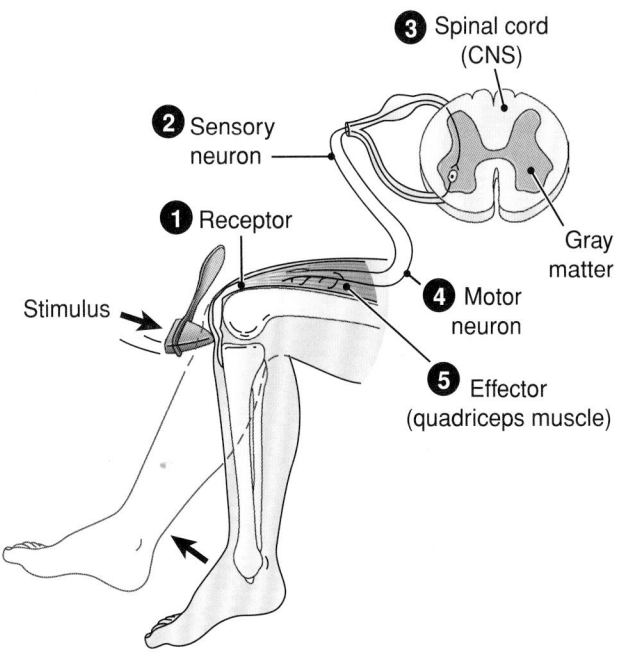

❸ Spinal cord (CNS)

❷ Sensory neuron

❶ Receptor

Stimulus

Gray matter

❹ Motor neuron

❺ Effector (quadriceps muscle)

Figure 17-9 **A reflex pathway (arc).** The patellar (knee-jerk) reflex is shown, with numbers indicating the sequence of impulses.

The Autonomic Nervous System

The ANS is the division of the nervous system that controls the involuntary actions of muscles and glands (**Fig. 17-10**). The ANS itself has two divisions:

- The **sympathetic nervous system** motivates our response to stress, the so-called fight-or-flight response.

It increases heart rate and respiration rate, stimulates the adrenal gland, and delivers more blood to skeletal muscles.

- The **parasympathetic nervous system** returns the body to a steady state and stimulates maintenance activities, such as digestion of food. Most organs are controlled by both systems, and in general, the two systems have opposite effects on a given organ.

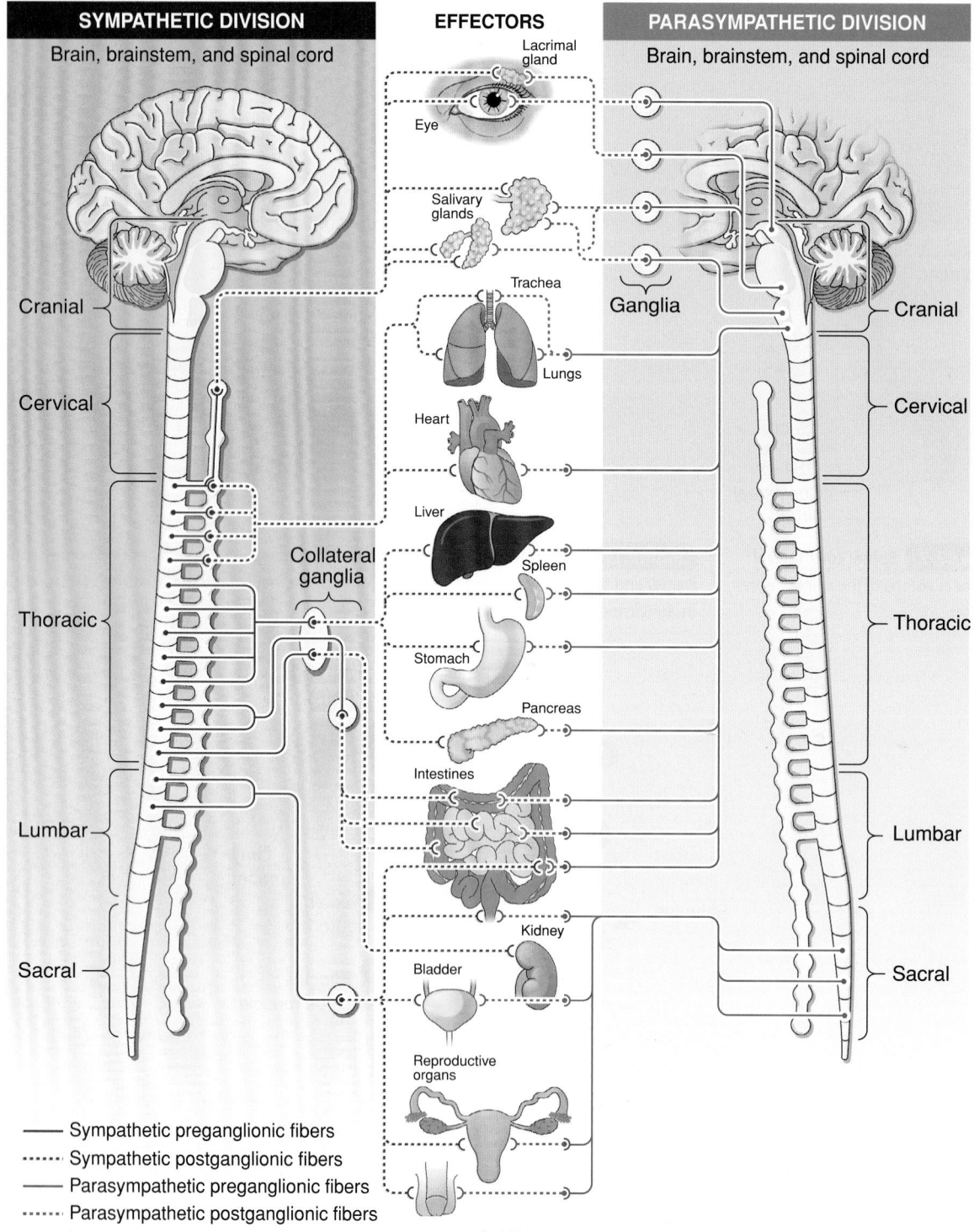

Figure 17-10 **Autonomic nervous system.** Each ANS pathway has two neurons, as shown by the *solid* and *dashed lines.* The diagram shows only one side of the body for each division (sympathetic and parasympathetic).

Terminology | Key Terms

Normal Structure and Function

afferent *AF-er-ent*	Carrying toward a given point, such as the sensory neurons and nerves that carry impulses toward the CNS (root *fer* means "to carry")
arachnoid mater *ah-RAK-noyd*	The middle layer of the meninges (from the Greek word for spider, because this tissue resembles a spider web)
autonomic nervous system (ANS) *aw-to-NOM-ik*	The division of the nervous system that regulates involuntary activities, controlling smooth muscles, cardiac muscle, and glands; the visceral nervous system
axon *AK-son*	The fiber of a neuron that conducts impulses away from the cell body
brain	The nervous tissue contained within the cranium; consists of the cerebrum, diencephalon, brainstem, and cerebellum (root: encephal/o)
brainstem	The part of the brain that consists of the midbrain, pons, and medulla oblongata
central nervous system (CNS)	The brain and spinal cord
cerebellum *ser-eh-BEL-um*	The posterior portion of the brain dorsal to the pons and medulla; helps to coordinate movement and to maintain balance and posture (cerebellum means "little brain") (root: cerebell/o)
cerebral cortex *SER-eh-bral*	The cerebrum's thin surface layer of gray matter (the cortex is the outer region of an organ) (root: cortic/o)
cerebrum *SER-eh-brum*	The large upper portion of the brain; it is divided into two hemispheres by the longitudinal fissure (root: cerebr/o)
cerebrospinal fluid (CSF) *ser-eh-bro-SPI-nal*	The watery fluid that circulates in and around the brain and spinal cord for protection
cranial nerves	The 12 pairs of nerves that are connected to the brain
dendrite *DEN-drite*	A fiber of a neuron that conducts impulses toward the cell body
diencephalon *di-en-SEF-ah-lon*	The part of the brain that contains the thalamus, hypothalamus, and pituitary gland; located between the cerebrum and the brainstem
dura mater *DU-rah MA-ter*	The strong, fibrous outermost layer of the meninges
efferent *EF-er-ent*	Carrying away from a given point, such as the motor neurons and nerves that carry impulses away from the CNS (root *fer* means "to carry")
ganglion *GANG-gle-on*	A collection of neuron cell bodies outside the CNS (plural: ganglia) (roots: gangli/o, ganglion/o)
gray matter	Unmyelinated tissue of the nervous system
gyrus *JI-rus*	A raised convolution of the surface of the cerebrum (see **Fig. 17-4**) (plural: gyri)
hypothalamus *hi-po-THAL-ah-mus*	The part of the brain that controls the pituitary gland and maintains homeostasis
interneuron *in-ter-NU-ron*	Any neuron located between a sensory and a motor neuron in a neural pathway, such as the neurons that transmit impulses within the CNS

(continued)

Terminology	Key Terms *(Continued)*
medulla oblongata *meh-DUL-lah ob-long-GAH-tah*	The portion of the brain that connects with the spinal cord; it has vital centers for control of respiration, heart rate, and blood pressure (root: medull/o); often called simply medulla
meninges *men-IN-jeze*	The three membranes that cover the brain and spinal cord (see **Fig. 17-5**) (singular: meninx) (roots: mening/o, meninge/o)
midbrain	The part of the brainstem between the diencephalon and the pons; contains centers for coordination of reflexes for vision and hearing
motor	Producing movement; describes efferent neurons and nerves that carry impulses away from the CNS
myelin *MI-eh-lin*	A whitish, fatty substance that surrounds certain axons of the nervous system
neuroglia *nu-ROG-le-ah*	The support cells of the nervous system; also called glial cells (from glia meaning "glue") (root: gli/o)
neuron *NU-ron*	The basic unit of the nervous system; a nerve cell
neurotransmitter *nu-ro-TRANS-mit-er*	A chemical that transmits energy across a synapse; examples are norepinephrine (*nor-ep-ih-NEF-rin*), acetylcholine (*ah-se-til-KO-lene*), serotonin (*ser-o-TO-nin*), and dopamine (*DO-pah-mene*)
nerve	A bundle of neuron fibers outside the CNS (root: neur/o)
parasympathetic nervous system	The part of the autonomic nervous system that reverses the response to stress and restores homeostasis; it slows heart rate and respiration rate and stimulates digestive, urinary, and reproductive activities
peripheral nervous system (PNS) *per-IF-er-al*	The portion of the nervous system outside the CNS
pia mater *PE-ah MA-ter*	The innermost layer of the meninges
pons *ponz*	A rounded area on the ventral surface of the brainstem; contains fibers that connect brain regions (adjective: pontine [*PON-tene*])
reflex *RE-fleks*	A simple, rapid, and automatic response to a stimulus
root	A branch of a spinal nerve that connects with the spinal cord; the dorsal (posterior) root joins the spinal cord's dorsal gray horn; the ventral (anterior) root joins the spinal cord's ventral gray horn (root: radicul/o)
sensory *SEN-so-re*	Pertaining to the senses or sensation; describing afferent neurons and nerves that carry impulses toward the CNS
somatic nervous system	The division of the nervous system that controls skeletal (voluntary) muscles
spinal cord	The nervous tissue contained within the spinal column; extends from the medulla oblongata to the second lumbar vertebra (root: myel/o)
spinal nerves	The 31 pairs of nerves that connect with the spinal cord
sulcus *SUL-kus*	A shallow furrow or groove, as on the surface of the cerebrum (see **Fig. 17-4**) (plural: sulci)
sympathetic nervous system	The part of the autonomic nervous system that mobilizes a response to stress, increases heart rate and respiration rate, and delivers more blood to skeletal muscles

Terminology	Key Terms *(Continued)*

synapse SIN-aps	The junction between two neurons; also the junction between a motor neuron and a muscle or gland
thalamus THAL-ah-mus	The part of the brain that receives all sensory impulses, except those for the sense of smell, and directs them to the proper portion of the cerebral cortex (root: thalam/o)
tract trakt	A bundle of neuron fibers within the CNS
ventricle VEN-trik-l	A small cavity, such as one of the cavities in the brain in which CSF is formed (root: ventricul/o)
visceral nervous system	The autonomic nervous system
white matter	Myelinated tissue of the nervous system

Go to the Audio Pronunciation Glossary in the Student Resources on thePoint to hear these terms pronounced.

Word Parts Pertaining to the Nervous System

See Tables 17-1 to 17-3

Table 17-1	Roots for the Nervous System and the Spinal Cord

Root	Meaning	Example	Definition of Example
neur/o, neur/i	nervous system, nervous tissue, nerve	neurotrophin nu-ro-TRO-fin	factor that promotes nerve growth (troph/o means "nourish")
gli/o	neuroglia	glial GLI-al	pertaining to neuroglia
gangli/o, ganglion/o	ganglion	ganglioma gang-gle-O-mah	tumor of a ganglion
mening/o, meninge/o	meninges	meningocele meh-NING-go-sele	hernia of the meninges
myel/o	spinal cord (also bone marrow)	hematomyelia he-mah-to-mi-E-le-ah	hemorrhage into the spinal cord
radicul/o	spinal nerve root	radiculopathy rah-dik-u-LOP-ah-the	any disease of a spinal nerve root

EXERCISE 17-1

Define the following adjectives.

1. neural (*NU-ral*) pertaining to a nerve or the nervous system _____
2. neuroglial (*nu-ROG-le-al*) _____
3. radicular (*rah-DIK-u-lar*) _____
4. meningeal (*meh-NIN-je-al*) _____
5. ganglionic (*gang-gle-ON-ik*) _____

(continued)

EXERCISE 17-1   *(Continued)*

Fill in the blanks.

6. A meningioma (*meh-nin-je-O-mah*) is a tumor affecting the _____.

7. A neurotropic (*nu-ro-TROP-ik*) dye has an affinity for the _____.

8. Meningococci (*meh-ning-go-KOK-si*) are bacteria (cocci) that infect the _____.

9. Myelodysplasia (*mi-eh-lo-dis-PLA-se-ah*) is abnormal development of the _____.

Define the following terms.

10. ganglionectomy (*gang-gle-o-NEK-to-me*) _____

11. polyradiculitis (*pol-e-rah-dik-u-LI-tis*) _____

12. neurolysis (*nu-ROL-ih-sis*) _____

13. radiculalgia (*rah-dik-u-LAL-je-ah*) _____

14. myelography (*mi-eh-LOG-rah-fe*) _____

Write words for the following definitions.

15. tumor of glial cells _____

16. x-ray image of the spinal cord _____

17. pain in a nerve _____

18. inflammation of the spinal cord _____

19. any disease of the nervous system _____

Table 17-2   Roots for the Brain

Root	Meaning	Example	Definition of Example
encephal/o	brain	anencephaly *an-en-SEF-ah-le*	absence of a brain
cerebr/o	cerebrum (loosely, brain)	infracerebral *in-frah-SER-eh-bral*	below the cerebrum
cortic/o	cerebral cortex, outer portion	corticospinal *kor-tih-ko-SPI-nal*	pertaining to the cerebral cortex and spinal cord
cerebell/o	cerebellum	supracerebellar *su-prah-ser-eh-BEL-ar*	above the cerebellum
thalam/o	thalamus	thalamotomy *thal-ah-MOT-o-me*	incision of the thalamus
ventricul/o	cavity, ventricle	intraventricular *in-trah-ven-TRIK-u-lar*	within a ventricle
medull/o	medulla oblongata (also spinal cord)	medullary *MED-u-lar-e*	pertaining to the medulla
psych/o	mind	psychogenic *si-ko-JEN-ik*	originating in the mind
narc/o	stupor, unconsciousness	narcosis *nar-KO-sis*	state of stupor induced by drugs
somn/o, somn/i	sleep	somnolence *SOM-no-lens*	sleepiness

EXERCISE 17-2

Fill in the blanks.

1. Somnambulism (*som-NAM-bu-lizm*) means walking during _____.

2. The term decerebrate (*de-SER-eh-brate*) refers to functional loss in the _____.

3. The hypothalamus (*hi-po-THAL-ah-mus*) is below the _____.

4. A psychoactive (*si-ko-AK-tiv*) drug has an effect on the _____.

5. A narcotic (*nar-KOT-ik*) is a drug that causes _____.

6. An electroencephalogram (*e-lek-tro-en-SEF-ah-lo-gram*) (EEG) is a record of the electric activity of the

    _____.

7. The term cerebrovascular (*ser-e-bro-VAS-ku-lar*) refers to blood vessels in the _____.

Write an adjective for the following definitions. Note the endings.

8. pertaining to (-ic) the mind   _____

9. pertaining to (-al) the cerebral cortex   _____

10. pertaining to (-ic) the thalamus   _____

11. pertaining to (-al) the cerebrum   _____

12. pertaining to (-ar) a ventricle   _____

Define the following words.

13. encephalopathy (*en-sef-ah-LOP-ah-the*) _____

14. insomnia (*in-SOM-ne-ah*) _____

15. psychology (*si-KOL-o-je*) _____

16. cerebrospinal (*ser-eh-bro-SPI-nal*) _____

17. extramedullary (*eks-trah-MED-u-lar-e*) _____

18. ventriculotomy (*ven-trik-u-LOT-o-me*) _____

Write words for the following definitions.

19. radiograph of a ventricle   _____

20. pertaining to the cerebral cortex and the thalamus   _____

21. within the cerebellum   _____

22. inflammation of the brain   _____

23. above the cerebrum   _____

Table 17-3	Suffixes for the Nervous System		

Suffix	Meaning	Example	Definition of Example
-phasia	speech	heterophasia *het-er-o-FA-ze-ah*	uttering words that are different from those intended
-lalia	speech, babble	coprolalia *kop-ro-LA-le-ah*	compulsive use of obscene words (copro- means "feces")
-lexia	reading	bradylexia *brad-e-LEK-se-ha*	slowness in reading
-plegia	paralysis	tetraplegia *tet-rah-PLE-je-ah*	paralysis of all four limbs
-paresis[a]	partial paralysis, weakness	hemiparesis *hem-e-pah-RE-sis*	partial paralysis of one side of the body
-lepsy	seizure	narcolepsy *NAR-ko-lep-se*	condition marked by sudden episodes of sleep
-phobia[a]	persistent, irrational fear	agoraphobia *ag-o-rah-FO-be-ah*	fear of being in a public place (from Greek *agora*, meaning "marketplace")
-mania[a]	excited state, obsession	megalomania *meg-ah-lo-MA-ne-ah*	exaggerated self-importance; "delusions of grandeur"

[a]May be used alone as a word.

EXERCISE 17-3

Fill in the blanks.

1. Epilepsy (*EP-ih-lep-se*) is a disease characterized by _____.

2. A person with alexia (*ah-LEK-se-ah*) lacks the ability to _____.

3. Echolalia (*ek-o-LA-le-ah*) refers to repetitive _____.

4. Another term for quadriplegia (*kwah-drih-PLE-je-ah*) is _____.

5. In myoparesis (*mi-o-pah-RE-sis*), a muscle shows _____.

Define the following words.

6. cardioplegia (*kar-de-o-PLE-je-ah*) _____

7. aphasia (*ah-FA-ze-ah*) _____

8. alexia (*ah-LEK-se-ah*) _____

9. pyromania (*pi-ro-MA-ne-ah*) _____

10. gynephobia (*gi-neh-FO-be-ah*) _____

11. quadriparesis (*kwah-drih-pah-RE-sis*) _____

Write words for the following definitions.

12. fear of (or abnormal sensitivity to) light   _____

13. fear of night and darkness   _____

14. paralysis of one side (hemi-) of the body   _____

15. slowness in speech (-lalia)   _____

Clinical Aspects of the Nervous System

VASCULAR DISORDERS

The term **cerebrovascular accident (CVA)**, or **stroke**, applies to any occurrence that deprives brain tissue of oxygen. These events include blockage in a vessel that supplies the brain, a ruptured blood vessel, or some other damage that leads to hemorrhage within the brain. Stroke is the fourth leading cause of death in developed countries and is a leading cause of **paralysis** and other neurologic disabilities. Risk factors for a stroke include hypertension, atherosclerosis, heart disease, diabetes mellitus, and cigarette smoking. Heredity is also a factor.

See the animation "Stroke" in the Student Resources on thePoint.

Thrombosis

Thrombosis is the formation of a blood clot in a vessel. Often, in cases of CVA, thrombosis occurs in the carotid artery, the large vessel in the neck that supplies the brain. Sudden blockage by an obstruction traveling from another part of the body is described as an **embolism**. In cases of stroke, the embolus usually originates in the heart.

These obstructions can be diagnosed by **cerebral angiography** with radiopaque dye, computed tomographic (CT) scans, and other radiographic techniques. In cases of thrombosis, surgeons can remove the blocked section of a vessel and insert a graft. If the carotid artery leading to the brain is involved, a **carotid endarterectomy** may be performed to open the vessel. Thrombolytic drugs for dissolving ("busting") such clots are also available.

Aneurysm

An **aneurysm** (**Fig. 17-11**) is a localized dilation of a vessel that may rupture and cause hemorrhage. An aneurysm may be congenital or may arise from other causes, especially atherosclerosis, which weakens the vessel wall. Hypertension then contributes to its rupture.

The effects of cerebral hemorrhage vary from massive functional loss to mild sensory or motor impairment depending on the degree of damage. **Aphasia**, loss or impairment of speech communication, is a common aftereffect. **Hemiplegia** (paralysis of one side of the body) on the side opposite the damage is also seen. It has been found in cases of hemorrhage, as in other forms of brain injury, that immediate retraining therapy may help to restore lost function.

TRAUMA

A **cerebral contusion** is a bruise to the brain's surface, usually caused by a blow to the head. Blood escapes from local vessels, but the injury is not deep.

A more serious injury may cause bleeding into or around the meninges, resulting in a hematoma, a localized collection of clotted blood. Damage to an artery from a skull fracture, usually on the side of the head, may be the cause of an **epidural hematoma** (**Fig. 17-12**), which appears between the dura mater and the skull bone. The rapidly accumulating blood puts pressure on local vessels and interrupts blood flow to the brain. There may be headache, loss of consciousness, or **hemiparesis** (partial paralysis) on the side opposite the blow. Diagnosis is made by CT scan

17

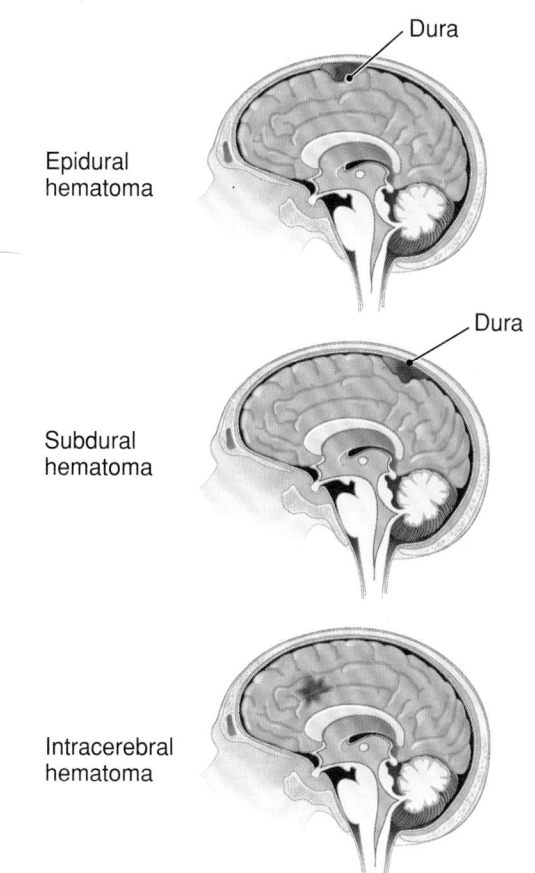

Dura

Epidural hematoma

Dura

Subdural hematoma

Intracerebral hematoma

Figure 17-12 **Cranial hematomas.** Location of epidural, subdural, and intracerebral hematomas are shown.

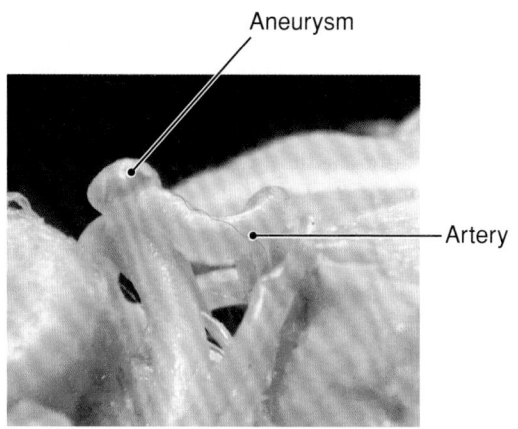

Aneurysm

Artery

Figure 17-11 **Aneurysm.** A thin-walled aneurysm protrudes from an artery.

or magnetic resonance imaging (MRI). If pressure is not relieved within one or two days, death results.

A **subdural hematoma** (see **Fig.17-12**) often results from a blow to the front or back of the head, as when the moving head hits a stationary object. The force of the blow separates the dura from the underlying arachnoid. Blood from a damaged vessel, usually a vein, slowly enters this space. The gradual blood accumulation puts pressure on the brain, causing headache, weakness, and **dementia**, loss of intellectual function. If there is continued bleeding, death results. **Figure 17-12** also shows a site of bleeding into the brain tissue itself, forming an intracerebral hematoma.

A cerebral **concussion** results from a blow to the head or from a fall and is usually followed by temporary loss of consciousness and a short period of amnesia. Aftereffects of a concussion may include headache, dizziness, vomiting, fatigue, and even paralysis, among other symptoms. Damage that occurs on the side of the brain opposite a blow as the brain is thrown against the skull is described as a **contrecoup** (*kon-treh-KU*) **injury** (from French, meaning "counterblow").

Other injuries may damage the brain directly. Injury to the base of the brain may involve vital centers in the medulla and interfere with respiration and cardiac functions.

CONFUSION AND COMA

Confusion is a state of reduced comprehension, coherence, and reasoning ability resulting in inappropriate responses to environmental stimuli. Confusion may worsen to include loss of language ability, memory loss, reduced alertness, and emotional changes. This condition may accompany a head injury, drug toxicity, extensive surgery, organ failure, infection, or degenerative disease.

Coma is a state of unconsciousness from which one cannot be aroused. Causes of coma include brain injury, **epilepsy**, toxins, metabolic imbalance (such as the ketoacidosis or glucose imbalances associated with diabetes mellitus), and respiratory, hepatic, or renal failure.

Healthcare professionals use various responses to evaluate coma, for example, reflex behavior and responses to touch, pressure, and mild pain, as from a light pin prick. Laboratory tests, **electroencephalography** (**EEG**), and sometimes CT and MRI scans help to identify the causes of coma.

INFECTION

Inflammation of the meninges, or **meningitis**, is usually caused by bacteria that enter through the ear, nose, or throat or are carried by the blood. One of these organisms, the meningococcus (*Neisseria meningitidis*), is responsible for meningitis epidemics among individuals living in close quarters. Other bacteria implicated in cases of meningitis include *Haemophilus influenzae*, *Streptococcus pneumoniae*, and *Escherichia coli*. A stiff neck is a common symptom. The presence of pus or lymphocytes in spinal fluid is also characteristic.

Physicians can withdraw fluid for diagnosis by a **lumbar puncture** (**Fig 17-13**), using a needle to remove

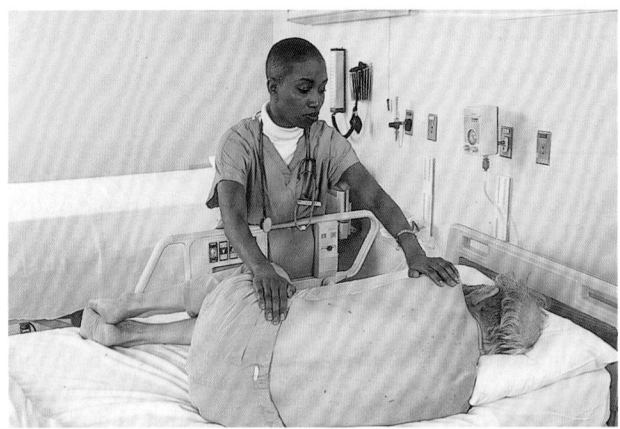

A

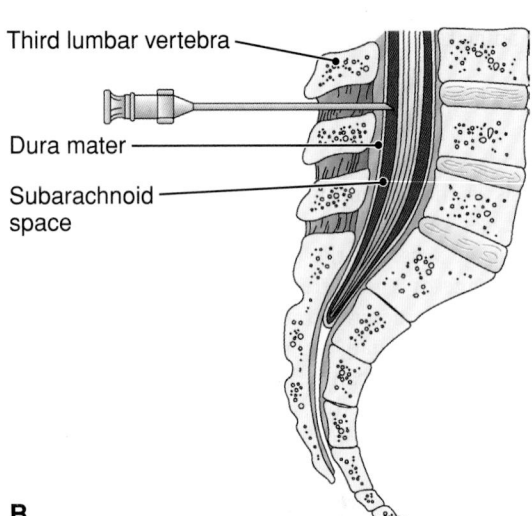

Third lumbar vertebra

Dura mater

Subarachnoid space

B

Figure 17-13 **Lumbar puncture.** **A.** Position of the patient for a lumbar puncture. **B.** CSF is withdrawn from the subarachnoid space between the third and fourth or fourth and fifth lumbar vertebrae.

CSF from the meninges in the lumbar region of the spine. A laboratory can examine this fluid for white blood cells and bacteria in the case of meningitis; for red blood cells in the case of brain injury; or for tumor cells. The fluid can also be analyzed chemically. Normally, spinal fluid is clear, with glucose and chlorides present but no protein and very few cells.

Other conditions that can cause meningitis and **encephalitis** (inflammation of the brain) include viral infections, tuberculosis, and syphilis. Viruses that can involve the CNS include the poliovirus; rabies virus; herpes virus; HIV (human immunodeficiency virus); tick- and mosquito-borne viruses, such as West Nile virus; and rarely, viruses that ordinarily cause relatively mild diseases, such as measles and chickenpox. Aseptic meningitis is a benign, nonbacterial form of the disease caused by a virus.

Varicella-zoster virus, which causes chickenpox, is also responsible for **shingles**, a nerve infection. If someone had chickenpox as a child, the latent virus can become reactivated later in life and spread along peripheral nerves,

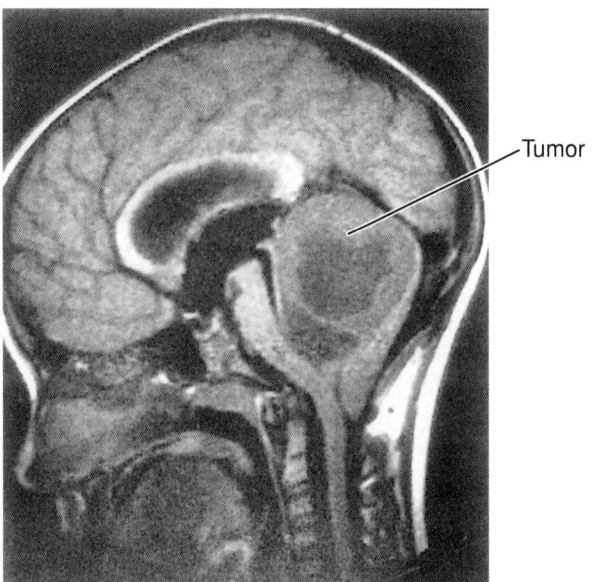

Figure 17-14 **Brain tumor.** MRI shows a large tumor that arises from the cerebellum and pushes the brainstem forward.

causing an itching, blistering rash. The name *shingles* comes from the Latin word for belt, as the shingles rash is often near or around the waist. A vaccine is now available for people over 60.

NEOPLASMS

Almost all tumors that originate in the nervous system are tumors of nonconducting support cells, the neuroglia. These growths are termed **gliomas** and may be named for the specific cell type involved, such as **astrocytoma**, a tumor of astrocytes, or **neurilemmoma** (schwannoma), a tumor of the cells that make the myelin sheath. Because they tend not to metastasize, these tumors may be described as benign. However, they do harm by compressing brain tissue (**Fig. 17-14**). The symptoms they cause depend on their size and location. There may be **seizures**, headache, vomiting, muscle weakness, or interference with a special sense, such as vision or hearing. If present, edema and **hydrocephalus**, accumulation of excess CSF in the ventricles, add to the tumor's effects (**Fig. 17-15**).

A **meningioma** is a tumor of the meninges. Because a meningioma does not spread and is localized at the surface, a surgeon can usually remove it completely.

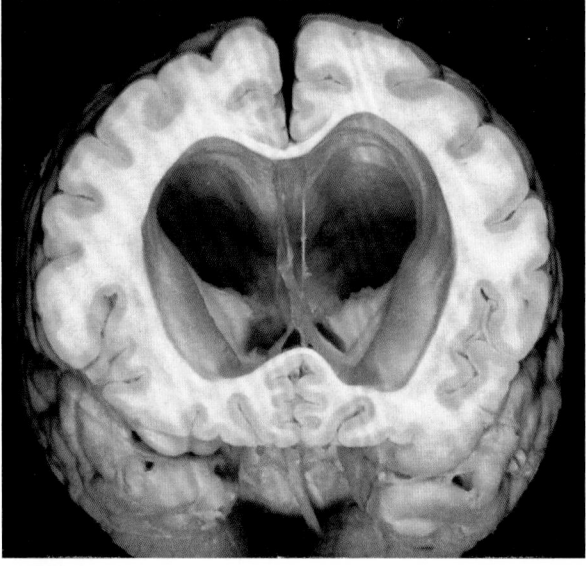

Figure 17-15 **Hydrocephalus.** Coronal section of the brain showing marked enlargement of the ventricles caused by a tumor that obstructed the flow of CSF.

Tumors of nervous tissue generally occur in childhood and may even originate before birth, when this tissue is actively multiplying. Also, cancer may metastasize to the brain from elsewhere in the body. For unknown reasons, certain forms of cancer, especially melanoma, breast cancer, and lung cancer, tend to spread to the brain.

DEGENERATIVE DISEASES

Multiple sclerosis (MS) commonly attacks people in their 20s or 30s and progresses at intervals and at varying rates. It involves patchy loss of myelin with hardening (sclerosis) of tissue in the CNS. The symptoms include vision problems, tingling or numbness in the arms and legs, urinary incontinence, **tremor** (shaking), and stiff gait. MS is thought to be an autoimmune disorder, but the exact cause is not known.

Parkinsonism occurs when, for unknown reasons, certain neurons in the midbrain fail to secrete the neurotransmitter dopamine. This leads to tremors, muscle rigidity, flexion at the joints, akinesia (loss of movement), and emotional problems. Parkinsonism is treated with daily administration of the drug L-**dopa** (levodopa), a form of dopamine that the circulation can carry into the brain.

Alzheimer disease (AD) results from unexplained degeneration of neurons and atrophy of the cerebral cortex (**Fig. 17-16**). These changes cause progressive loss of recent memory, confusion, and mood changes. Dangers associated with AD are injury, infection, malnutrition, and aspiration of food or fluids into the lungs. Originally called *presenile dementia* and used only to describe cases in patients about 50 years of age, the term is now applied to these same changes when they occur in elderly patients.

AD is diagnosed by CT or MRI scans and confirmed at autopsy. Histologic (tissue) studies show deposits of a substance called **amyloid** in the tissues. The disease may be hereditary. AD commonly develops in people with Down syndrome after age 40, indicating that AD is associated with abnormality on chromosome 21, the same chromosome that is involved in Down syndrome.

Multi-infarct dementia (MID) resembles AD in that it is a progressive cognitive impairment associated with loss of memory, loss of judgment, aphasia, altered motor and sensory function, repetitive behavior, and loss of social skills. The disorder is caused by multiple small strokes that interrupt blood flow to brain tissue and deprive areas of oxygen.

EPILEPSY

A prime characteristic of epilepsy is recurrent seizures brought on by abnormal electric activity of the brain. These attacks may vary from brief and mild episodes known as absence (petit mal) seizures to major tonic–clonic (grand mal) seizures with loss of consciousness, **convulsion** (intervals of violent involuntary muscle contractions), and sensory disturbances. In other cases (psychomotor seizures), there is a one- to two-minute period of disorientation. Epilepsy may be the result of a tumor, injury, or neurologic disease, but in most cases, the cause is unknown.

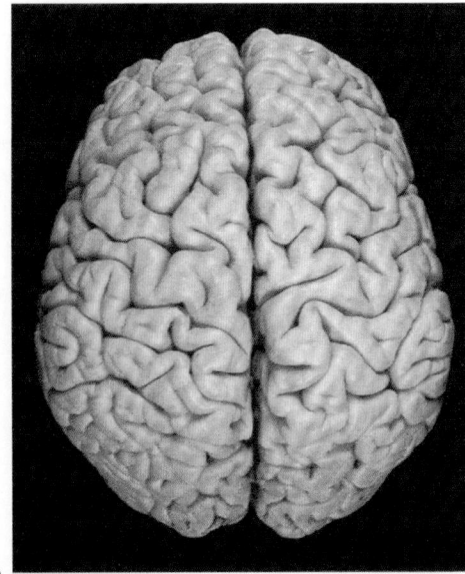

A

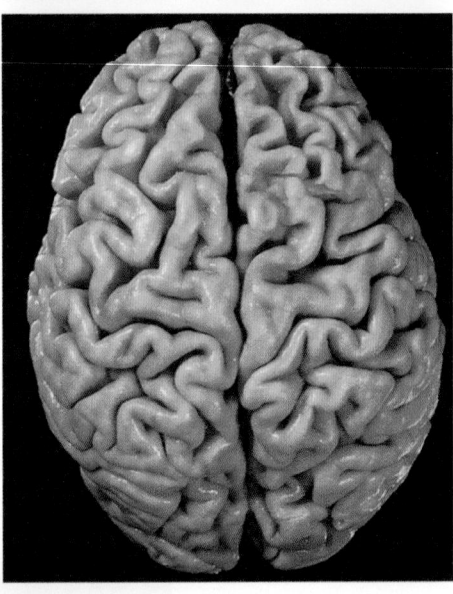

B

Figure 17-16 **Effects of Alzheimer disease. A.** Normal brain. **B.** Brain of a patient with Alzheimer disease, showing atrophy of the cortex with narrow gyri and enlarged sulci.

EEG reveals abnormalities in brain activity and can be used in the diagnosis and treatment of epilepsy. The disorder is treated with antiepileptic and anticonvulsive drugs to control seizures, and sometimes surgery is of help. If seizures cannot be controlled, the individual with epilepsy may have to avoid certain activities that can lead to harm.

SLEEP DISTURBANCES

The general term *dyssomnia* includes a variety of possible disorders that result in excessive sleepiness or difficulty in beginning or maintaining sleep. Simple causes for such disorders include schedule changes or travel to different time zones (jet lag). **Insomnia** refers to insufficient or

Box 17-2

HEALTH PROFESSIONS
Careers in Occupational Therapy

Occupational therapy (OT) helps people with physical or mental disability achieve independence at home and at work by teaching them "skills for living." Many people can benefit, including those:

- Recovering from traumas such as fractures, amputations, burns, spinal cord injury, stroke, and heart attack
- With chronic conditions such as arthritis, multiple sclerosis, Alzheimer disease, and schizophrenia
- With developmental disabilities such as Down syndrome, cerebral palsy, spina bifida, muscular dystrophy, and autism

OTs work as part of multidisciplinary teams, which include but are not limited to physicians, nurses, physical therapists, speech pathologists, and social workers. OTs also work closely with families to educate and instruct them on how to assist in the client's progress. They assess their clients' capabilities and develop individualized treatment programs that help them recover from injury or compensate for permanent disability. Treatment may include teaching activities ranging from work tasks to dressing, cooking, and eating, and using adaptive equipment such as wheelchairs and computers.

OT assistants implement treatment plans developed by an occupational therapist and regularly consult with the occupational therapist on progress and possible reassessment of goals. To perform their duties, OTs and assistants need a thorough scientific education and clinical background. A current practicing OT in the United States has either a bachelor's or master's degree. As of 2007, OTs must earn a master's degree in occupational therapy in order to practice. After graduation, they must pass a national certification exam and, where necessary, be licensed by the state to practice. Assistants typically train in two-year programs and also take a certification exam.

OTs and their assistants work in hospitals, clinics, and nursing care facilities, and also visit homes and schools. As the population continues to age and the need for rehabilitative therapy increases, job prospects remain good. The American Occupational Therapy Association at www.aota.org has more information on OT careers.

---

nonrestorative sleep despite ample opportunity to sleep. There may be physical causes for insomnia, but often it is related to emotional upset caused by stressful events. **Narcolepsy** is characterized by brief, uncontrollable attacks of sleep during the day. The disorder is treated with stimulants, regulation of sleep habits, and short daytime naps.

Sleep apnea refers to failure to breathe for brief periods during sleep. It usually results from upper airway obstruction, often associated with obesity, alcohol consumption, or weakened throat muscles, and is usually accompanied by loud snoring with brief periods of silence. Dental appliances that move the tongue and jaw forward may help to prevent sleep apnea. Other options are surgery to correct an obstruction or positive air pressure delivered through a mask.

Sleep disorders are diagnosed by physical examination, a sleep history, and a log of sleep habits, including details of the sleep environment and note of any substances consumed that may interfere with sleep. Study in a sleep laboratory with a variety of electric and other studies, constituting **polysomnography**, may also be needed.

Sleep studies identify two components of normal sleep, each showing a specific EEG pattern. Nonrapid eye movement (NREM) sleep has four stages, which take a person progressively into the deepest level of sleep. If sleepwalking (somnambulism) occurs, it occurs during this stage. NREM sleep is interrupted about every 1.5 hours by episodes of rapid eye movement (REM) sleep, during which the eyes move rapidly, although they are closed. Dreaming occurs during REM sleep and muscles lose tone, while heart rate, blood pressure, and brain activity increase.

OTHERS

Many hereditary diseases affect the nervous system. Some of these are described in Chapter 15. Hormonal imbalances that involve the nervous system are described in Chapter 16. Finally, drugs, alcohol, toxins, and nutritional deficiencies may act on the nervous system in a variety of ways.

Box 17-2 has information on occupational therapists, who are often involved in treating people with neurologic disturbances.

Behavioral Disorders

This section is an introduction to some of the behavioral disorders that involve the nervous system. Criteria for clinical diagnosis of these and other behavioral and mental disorders are set forth in the *Diagnostic and Statistical Manual of Mental Disorders* (DSM) published by the American Psychiatric Association.

ANXIETY DISORDERS

Anxiety is a feeling of fear, worry, uneasiness, or dread. It may be associated with physical problems or drugs and is often prompted by feelings of helplessness or loss of self-esteem. Generalized anxiety disorder (GAD) is characterized by chronic excessive and uncontrollable worry about various life circumstances, often with no basis. It may be accompanied by muscle tensing, restlessness, dyspnea, palpitations, insomnia, irritability, or fatigue.

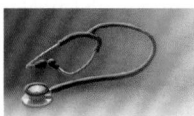

FOCUS ON WORDS
Phobias and Manias

Box 17-3

Some of the terms for phobias and manias are just as strange and interesting as the behaviors themselves.

Agoraphobia is fear of being in a public place. The agora in ancient Greece was the marketplace. Xenophobia is an irrational fear of strangers, taken from the Greek root *xen/o*, which means strange or foreign. Acrophobia, a fear of heights, is taken from the root *acro-*, meaning terminal, highest, or topmost. In most medical terms, this root is used to mean extremity, as in *acrocyanosis*. Hydrophobia is a fear of or aversion to water (*hydr/o*). The term was used as an alternative name for rabies, because people infected with this paralytic disease had difficulty swallowing water and other liquids.

Trichotillomania is the odd practice of compulsively pulling out one's hair in response to stress. The word comes from the root for hair (*trich/o*) plus a Greek word that means "to pull." Kleptomania, also spelled cleptomania, is from the Greek word for thief and describes an irresistible urge to steal in the absence of need.

Panic disorder is a form of anxiety disorder marked by episodes of intense fear. A person with panic disorder may isolate himself or herself or avoid social situations for fear of having a panic attack or in response to attacks.

A **phobia** is an extreme, persistent fear of a specific object or situation (**Box 17-3**). It may center on social situations, particular objects, such as animals or blood, or activities, such as flying or driving through tunnels.

Obsessive–compulsive disorder (OCD) is a condition marked by disturbing thoughts or images that are persistent and intrusive. To relieve anxiety about these thoughts or images, the person with OCD engages in repetitive behavior that interferes with normal daily activities, although he or she knows that such behavior is unreasonable. These patterns include repeated washing; performing rituals; arranging, touching, or counting objects; and repeating words or phrases. OCD is associated with perfectionism and rigidity in behavior. Some specialists believe that OCD is related to low levels of the neurotransmitter serotonin in the brain. Treatment is with behavioral therapy and antidepressant drugs that increase the brain's serotonin levels (**Box 17-4**).

When a highly stressful, catastrophic event results in persistent emotional difficulties, the condition is described as **posttraumatic stress disorder (PTSD)**. People who are abused, have their lives threatened, witness a crime, experience a natural disaster, and combat veterans are subject to PTSD. Responses include anger, fear, sleep disturbances, and physical symptoms, including changes in brain chemistry and hormone imbalances. PTSD is often associated with other emotional problems such as depression, withdrawal, substance abuse, and impaired social and family

---

CLINICAL PERSPECTIVES
Psychoactive Drugs: Adjusting Neurotransmitters to Alter Mood

Box 17-4

Many psychoactive drugs used today operate by affecting levels and activities of neurotransmitters, such as serotonin, norepinephrine, and dopamine, in the brain. Examples are fluoxetine (Prozac) and related compounds, which are prescribed to alter mood.

Prozac increases serotonin's activity by blocking its reuptake—that is, it blocks transporters that carry serotonin back into the secreting cell at the synapse. Like other selective serotonin reuptake inhibitors (SSRIs), Prozac prolongs the neurotransmitter's activity at the synapse, producing a mood-elevating effect. Prozac is used to treat depression, anxiety, and symptoms of obsessive–compulsive disorder.

Other psychoactive drugs are less selective than Prozac. Venlafaxine (Effexor) blocks reuptake of serotonin and norepinephrine and is used to treat depression and generalized anxiety disorder. Bupropion (Zyban) inhibits reuptake of nor- epinephrine and dopamine and is prescribed for depression and smoking cessation. Another class of antidepressants, the monoamine oxidase inhibitors (MAOIs), prevents an enzyme from breaking down serotonin in the synapse. Like SSRIs, MAOIs increase the amount of serotonin available in the synapse. Examples are phenelzine (Nardil) and tranylcypromine (Parnate).

Some herbal remedies are also used to treat depression. St. John's wort contains the active ingredient hypericin, which appears to both nonselectively inhibit serotonin reuptake and block norepinephrine and dopamine reuptake. As with any drug, care must be taken when using St. John's wort, especially if it is combined with other antidepressant medications, and healthcare providers should always be informed of any drugs, including herbal preparations, that a person is taking.

relationships. Patients need early treatment with emotional support, protection, psychotherapy, and drugs to treat depression and anxiety.

MOOD DISORDERS

Depression is a mental state characterized by profound feelings of sadness, emptiness, hopelessness, inability to concentrate, and lack of interest or pleasure in activities. Depression is often accompanied by insomnia, loss of appetite, and suicidal tendencies, and it frequently coexists with other physical or emotional conditions.

Dysthymia is a chronic mood disorder that lasts for several months to years and is often triggered by a serious event. Depression is a common symptom, as well as eating disorders, sleep disturbances, fatigue, lack of concentration, indecision, and feelings of hopelessness.

In **bipolar disorder** (formerly called manic–depressive illness), normal moods alternate with episodes of depression and **mania**, a state of elation that may include agitation, hyperexcitability, or hyperactivity. Treatment for bipolar disorder may differ from therapy for depression alone and includes mood-stabilizing drugs and professional mental health therapy.

Most of the drugs used to treat mood disorders affect the level of neurotransmitters in the brain, such as the selective serotonin reuptake inhibitors (SSRIs), which prolong the action of serotonin.

PSYCHOSIS

Psychosis is a mental state in which there is gross misperception of reality. This loss of touch with reality may be evidenced by **delusions** (false beliefs), including **paranoia**, delusions of persecution or threat, or **hallucinations**, imagined sensory experiences. Although the patient's condition makes it impossible for him or her to cope with the ordinary demands of life, there is lack of awareness that this behavior is inappropriate.

Schizophrenia is a form of chronic psychosis that may include bizarre behavior, paranoia, anxiety, delusions, withdrawal, and suicidal tendencies. The diagnosis of schizophrenia encompasses a broad category of disorders with many subtypes. The causes of schizophrenia are unknown, but there is evidence of hereditary factors and imbalance in brain chemistry.

ATTENTION DEFICIT HYPERACTIVITY DISORDER

Attention deficit hyperactivity disorder (ADHD) is difficult to diagnose because many of its symptoms overlap or coexist with other behavioral disorders. Although inattention and hyperactivity usually appear together in these cases, one component may predominate. ADHD commonly begins in childhood and is characterized by attention problems, easy boredom, impatience, and impulsive behavior. Associated hyperactivity may be manifested by fidgeting, squirming, rapid motion, or excessive talking. In adults, the signs of ADHD may be confused with other disorders, such as mood disturbances, substance abuse, and endocrine problems.

ADHD has been correlated with alterations in brain structure and metabolism. Treatment is with psychotherapy or behavioral therapy and certain drugs. A stimulant, methylphenidate (Ritalin) has traditionally been prescribed for children with ADHD, but more recently, the antidepressant atomoxetine (Strattera) has given positive results.

AUTISM SPECTRUM DISORDER

The term autism spectrum disorder (ASD) applies to a range of impairments that appear early in life and affect social interactions and communication skills. Despite their limitations, a person with ASD may be of normal or above average intelligence, and even brilliant. Each individual with ASD is unique and has his or her own specific needs. All of these conditions fall into a continuum that ranges from classic **autism**, at its most severe, to milder conditions known as high functioning autism, previously called Asperger syndrome, or other forms of developmental disorders.

Autism is a complex disorder of unknown cause that usually appears between the ages of 2 and 6 years as a child fails to reach appropriate developmental signposts. It is marked by self-absorption and lack of response to social contact and affection. Autistic children may have low intelligence and poor language skills. They often appear to be disconnected and out of place. They may overrespond to stimuli and may show self-destructive behavior. There may also be stereotyped (repetitive) behavior, preoccupations, mood swings, and resistance to change. Autism may be accompanied by neurologic problems and problems with sleeping and eating. Those with autism may need the help of mental health specialists; social workers; and occupational, physical, and speech therapists. Levels of autism are determined by the extent of disability and need for support services.

People with less extreme forms of autism are often highly intelligent and verbal, but have trouble with social interactions and understanding others' behaviors. Thus, as children, they are often isolated and bullied. Repetitive behaviors may develop. These children also may develop a strong interest in specific topics. They need help in learning to interpret social cues but often can apply their talents in satisfying occupations.

DRUGS USED IN TREATMENT

A psychotropic or psychoactive drug is one that acts on the mental state. This category of drugs includes antianxiety drugs or anxiolytics, mood stabilizers, antidepressants, and antipsychotics, also called *neuroleptics*. Many of these drugs work by increasing the brain's levels of neurotransmitters. Note that psychoactive drugs do not work in the same way for everyone. It is often necessary to try different therapies until the right drug is found. Also, it may take several weeks for a drug to become effective. For more information, see descriptions and examples of specific types of psychoactive drugs in the supplementary terms.

17

| Terminology | Key Terms |

Neurologic Disorders

Alzheimer disease (AD) *ALTS-hi-mer*	A form of dementia caused by atrophy of the cerebral cortex; presenile dementia (see **Fig. 17-16**)
amyloid *AM-ih-loyd*	A starch-like substance of unknown composition that accumulates in the brain in Alzheimer and other diseases
aneurysm *AN-u-rizm*	A localized abnormal dilation of a blood vessel that results from weakness of the vessel wall (see **Fig. 17-11**); an aneurysm may eventually burst
aphasia *ah-FA-ze-ah*	Specifically, loss or defect in speech communication (from Greek *phasis*, meaning "speech"); in practice, the term is applied more broadly to a range of language disorders, both spoken and written, that may affect the ability to understand speech (receptive aphasia) or the ability to produce speech (expressive aphasia); both forms are combined in global aphasia
astrocytoma *as-tro-si-TO-mah*	A neuroglial tumor composed of astrocytes
cerebral contusion *kon-TU-zhun*	A bruise to the surface of the brain following a blow to the head
cerebrovascular accident (CVA)	Sudden damage to the brain resulting from reduction of cerebral blood flow; possible causes are atherosclerosis, thrombosis, or a ruptured aneurysm; commonly called stroke
coma *KO-mah*	State of deep unconsciousness from which one cannot be roused
concussion *kon-KUSH-un*	Injury resulting from a violent blow or shock; a brain concussion usually results in loss of consciousness
confusion *kon-FU-zhun*	A state of reduced comprehension, coherence, and reasoning ability resulting in inappropriate responses to environmental stimuli
contrecoup injury *kon-treh-KU*	Damage to the brain on the side opposite the point of a blow as a result of the brain hitting the skull (from French, meaning "counterblow")
convulsion *kon-VUL-shun*	A series of violent, involuntary muscle contractions; a tonic convulsion involves prolonged muscle contraction; in a clonic convulsion, there is alternation of contraction and relaxation; both forms appear in grand mal epilepsy
dementia *de-MEN-she-ah*	A gradual and usually irreversible loss of intellectual function
embolism *EM-bo-lizm*	Obstruction of a blood vessel by a blood clot or other material carried in the circulation
encephalitis *en-sef-ah-LI-tis*	Inflammation of the brain
epidural hematoma	Accumulation of blood in the epidural space (between the dura mater and the skull) (see **Fig. 17-12**)
epilepsy *EP-ih-lep-se*	A chronic disease involving periodic sudden bursts of electric activity from the brain, resulting in seizures
glioma *gli-O-mah*	A tumor of neuroglial cells
hemiparesis *hem-ih-pah-RE-sis*	Partial paralysis or weakness of one side of the body

Terminology Key Terms (Continued)

hemiplegia *hem-ih-PLE-je-ah*	Paralysis of one side of the body
hydrocephalus *hi-dro-SEF-ah-lus*	Increased accumulation of CSF in or around the brain as a result of obstructed flow; may be caused by tumor, inflammation, hemorrhage, or congenital abnormality (see **Fig. 17-15**)
insomnia *in-SOM-nee-ah*	Insufficient or nonrestorative sleep despite ample opportunity to sleep
meningioma *men-nin-je-O-mah*	Tumor of the meninges
meningitis *men-in-JI-tis*	Inflammation of the meninges
multi-infarct dementia (MID)	Dementia caused by chronic cerebral ischemia (lack of blood supply) as a result of multiple small strokes; there is progressive loss of cognitive function, memory, and judgment as well as altered motor and sensory function
multiple sclerosis (MS)	A chronic, progressive disease involving loss of myelin in the CNS
narcolepsy *NAR-ko-lep-se*	Brief, uncontrollable episodes of sleep during the day
neurilemmoma *nu-rih-lem-O-mah*	A tumor of a peripheral nerve sheath (neurilemma); schwannoma
paralysis *pah-RAL-ih-sis*	Temporary or permanent loss of function; flaccid paralysis involves loss of muscle tone and reflexes and muscular degeneration; spastic paralysis involves excess muscle tone and reflexes but no degeneration
parkinsonism	A disorder originating in the brain's basal ganglia (nuclei) and characterized by slow movements, tremor, rigidity, and mask-like face; also called Parkinson disease
seizure *SE-zhur*	A sudden attack, as seen in epilepsy; the most common forms of seizure are tonic–clonic, or grand mal (*gran mal*) (from French, meaning "great illness"); absence seizure, or petit mal (*pet-E mal*), meaning "small illness;" and psychomotor seizure
shingles	An acute viral infection that follows nerve pathways causing small lesions on the skin; caused by reactivation of the virus that also causes chickenpox (varicella-zoster virus); also called herpes zoster (*HER-peze ZOS-ter*)
sleep apnea *ap-NE-ah*	Brief periods of breathing cessation during sleep
stroke	Sudden interference with blood flow in one or more cerebral vessels leading to oxygen deprivation and necrosis of brain tissue; caused by a blood clot in a vessel (ischemic stroke) or rupture of a vessel (hemorrhagic stroke); cerebrovascular accident (CVA)
subdural hematoma	Accumulation of blood beneath the dura mater (see **Fig. 17-12**)
thrombosis *throm-BO-sis*	Development of a blood clot within a vessel
tremor *TREM-or*	A shaking or involuntary movement

Diagnosis and Treatment

carotid endarterectomy *end-ar-ter-EK-to-me*	Surgical removal of the lining of the carotid artery, the large artery in the neck that supplies blood to the brain

(continued)

Terminology   Key Terms (Continued)

cerebral angiography	Radiographic study of the brain's blood vessels after injection of a contrast medium
electroencephalography (EEG) e-lek-tro-en-sef-ah-LOG-rah-fe	Amplification, recording, and interpretation of the brain's electric activity
L-dopa DO-pah	A drug used in the treatment of parkinsonism; levodopa
lumbar puncture	Puncture of the subarachnoid space in the lumbar region of the spinal cord to remove spinal fluid for diagnosis or to inject anesthesia (see **Fig. 17-13**); spinal tap
polysomnography pol-e-som-NOG-rah-fe	Simultaneous monitoring of a variety of physiologic functions during sleep to diagnose sleep disorders

Behavioral Disorders

anxiety ang-ZI-eh-te	A feeling of fear, worry, uneasiness, or dread
attention deficit hyperactivity disorder (ADHD)	A condition that begins in childhood and is characterized by attention problems, easy boredom, impulsive behavior, and hyperactivity
autism AW-tizm	A disorder of unknown cause consisting of self-absorption, lack of response to social contact and affection, preoccupations, stereotyped behavior, and resistance to change (from auto-, "self," and -ism, "condition of")
autism spectrum disorder (ASD)	A disability that falls within a range of neurodevelopmental impairments that appears early in life and affects social interactions and communications skills
bipolar disorder bi-PO-lar	A form of depression with episodes of mania (a state of elation); manic depressive illness
delusion de-LU-zhun	A false belief inconsistent with knowledge and experience
depression de-PRESH-un	A mental state characterized by profound feelings of sadness, emptiness, hopelessness, and lack of interest or pleasure in activities
dysthymia dis-THI-me-ah	A mild form of depression that usually develops in response to a serious life event (from dys- and Greek *thymos*, meaning "mind, emotion")
hallucination hah-lu-sih-NA-shun	A false perception unrelated to reality or external stimuli
mania MA-ne-ah	A state of elation, which may include agitation, hyperexcitability, or hyperactivity (adjective: manic)
obsessive–compulsive disorder (OCD)	A condition associated with recurrent and intrusive thoughts, images, and repetitive behaviors performed to relieve anxiety
panic disorder	A form of anxiety disorder marked by episodes of intense fear
paranoia par-ah-NOY-ah	A mental state characterized by jealousy, delusions of persecution, or perceptions of threat or harm
phobia FO-be-ah	An extreme, persistent fear of a specific object or situation
posttraumatic stress disorder (PTSD)	Persistent emotional disturbances that follow exposure to life-threatening, catastrophic events, such as trauma, abuse, natural disasters, and warfare
psychosis si-KO-sis	A mental disorder extreme enough to cause gross misperception of reality with delusions and hallucinations

Terminology	Key Terms (*Continued*)	

| schizophrenia
skiz-o-FRE-ne-ah | A poorly understood group of severe mental disorders with features of psychosis, delusions, hallucinations, and withdrawn or bizarre behavior (schizo means "split," and phren/o means "mind") |

Terminology	Supplementary Terms

Normal Structure and Function

acetylcholine (ACh) *as-e-til-KO-lene*	A neurotransmitter; activity involving acetylcholine is described as cholinergic
basal ganglia	Four masses of gray matter in the cerebrum and upper brainstem that are involved in movement and coordination; basal nuclei
blood–brain barrier	A special membrane between circulating blood and the brain that prevents certain damaging substances from reaching brain tissue
Broca area *BRO-kah*	An area in the left frontal lobe of the cerebrum that controls speech production
cerebral arterial circle	An interconnection (anastomosis) of several arteries supplying the brain; located at the base of the cerebrum; circle of Willis
contralateral *kon-trah-LAT-er-al*	Affecting the opposite side of the body
corpus callosum *KOR-pus kah-LO-sum*	A large band of connecting fibers between the cerebral hemispheres
dermatome *DER-mah-tome*	The area of the skin supplied by a spinal nerve; term also refers to an instrument used to cut skin for grafting (see Chapter 21)
ipsilateral *ip-sih-LAT-er-al*	On the same side; unilateral
leptomeninges *lep-to-men-IN-jeze*	The pia mater and arachnoid together
norepinephrine *nor-ep-ih-NEF-rin*	A neurotransmitter very similar in chemical composition and function to the hormone epinephrine; also called noradrenaline
nucleus *NU-kle-us*	A collection of nerve cells within the central nervous system
plexus *PLEKS-us*	A network, as of nerves or blood vessels
pyramidal tracts *pih-RAM-ih-dal*	A group of motor tracts involved in fine coordination; most of the fibers in these tracts cross in the medulla to the opposite side of the spinal cord and affect the opposite side of the body; fibers not included in the pyramidal tracts are described as extrapyramidal
reticular activating system (RAS) *reh-TIK-u-lar*	A widespread system in the brain that maintains wakefulness
Schwann cells *shvon*	Cells that produce the myelin sheath around peripheral axons

(continued)

Terminology	**Supplementary Terms** (*Continued*)

| Wernicke area
VER-nih-ke | An area in the temporal lobe concerned with speech comprehension |

Symptoms and Conditions

amyotrophic lateral sclerosis (ALS) *ah-mi-o-TROF-ik*	A disorder marked by muscular weakness, spasticity, and exaggerated reflexes caused by degeneration of motor neurons; Lou Gehrig disease
amnesia *am-NE-ze-ah*	Loss of memory (from Greek word *mneme* meaning "memory" and the negative prefix *a-*)
apraxia *ah-PRAK-se-ah*	Inability to move with purpose or to use objects properly
ataxia *ah-TAK-se-ah*	Lack of muscle coordination; dyssynergia
athetosis *ath-eh-TO-sis*	Involuntary, slow, twisting movements in the arms, especially the hands and fingers
Bell palsy *PAWL-ze*	Paralysis of the facial nerve
berry aneurysm *AN-u-rizm*	A small sac-like aneurysm of a cerebral artery
catatonia *kat-ah-TO-ne-ah*	A phase of schizophrenia in which the patient is unresponsive; there is a tendency to remain in a fixed position without moving or talking
cerebral palsy *SER-eh-bral PAWL-ze*	A nonprogressive neuromuscular disorder usually caused by damage to the CNS near the time of birth; may include spasticity, involuntary movements, or ataxia
chorea *KOR-e-ah*	A nervous condition marked by involuntary twitching of the limbs or facial muscles
claustrophobia *claws-tro-FO-be-ah*	Fear of being shut in or enclosed (from Latin *claudere*, "to shut")
compulsion *kom-PUL-shun*	A repetitive, stereotyped act performed to relieve tension
Creutzfeldt–Jakob disease (CJD) *KROITS-felt YAH-kob*	A slow-growing degenerative brain disease caused by a prion (*PRI-on*), an infectious protein; related to bovine spongiform encephalopathy (BSE, "mad cow disease") in cattle
delirium *de-LIR-e-um*	A sudden and temporary state of confusion marked by excitement, physical restlessness, and incoherence
dysarthria *dis-AR-thre-ah*	Defect in speech articulation caused by lack of control over the required muscles
dysmetria *dis-ME-tre-ah*	Disturbance in the path or placement of a limb during active movement; in hypometria, the limb falls short; in hypermetria, the limb extends beyond the target
euphoria *u-FOR-e-ah*	An exaggerated feeling of well-being; elation
glioblastoma *gli-o-blas-TO-mah*	A malignant astrocytoma
Guillain–Barré syndrome *ge-YAN bar-RA*	An acute polyneuritis with progressive muscular weakness that usually occurs after a viral infection; in most cases recovery is complete, but it may take several months to years

| Terminology | Supplementary Terms (*Continued*) |

hematomyelia *he-mah-to-mi-E-le-ah*	Hemorrhage of blood into the spinal cord, as from an injury
hemiballism *hem-e-BAL-izm*	Jerking, twitching movements of one side of the body
Huntington disease	A hereditary disease of the CNS that usually appears between ages 30 and 50; the patient shows progressive dementia and chorea, and death occurs within 10 to 15 years
hypochondriasis *hi-po-kon-DRI-ah-sis*	Abnormal anxiety about one's health
ictus *IK-tus*	A blow or sudden attack, such as an epileptic seizure
lethargy *LETH-ar-je*	A state of sluggishness or stupor
migraine *MI-grane*	Chronic intense, throbbing headache that may result from vascular changes in cerebral arteries; possible causes include genetic factors, stress, trauma, and hormonal fluctuations; headache might be signaled by visual disturbances, nausea, photophobia, and tingling sensations
neurofibromatosis *nu-ro-fi-bro-mah-TO-sis*	A condition involving multiple tumors of peripheral nerves
neurosis *nu-RO-sis*	An emotional disorder caused by unresolved conflicts, with anxiety as a main characteristic
paraplegia *par-ah-PLE-je-ah*	Paralysis of the legs and lower part of the body
parasomnia *par-ah-SOM-ne-ah*	Condition of having undesirable phenomena, such as nightmares, occur during sleep or become worse during sleep
quadriplegia *kwah-drih-PLE-je-ah*	Paralysis of all four limbs; tetraplegia
Reye syndrome *ri*	A rare acute encephalopathy occurring in children after viral infections; the liver, kidney, and heart may be involved; linked to administration of aspirin during a viral illness
sciatica *si-AT-ih-kah*	Neuritis characterized by severe pain along the sciatic nerve and its branches
somatoform disorders *so-MAH-to-form*	Conditions associated with symptoms of physical disease, such as pain, hypertension, or chronic fatigue, with no physical basis
somnambulism *som-NAM-bu-lizm*	Walking or performing other motor functions while asleep and out of bed; sleepwalking
stupor *STU-por*	A state of unconsciousness or lethargy with loss of responsiveness
syringomyelia *sir-in-go-mi-E-le-ah*	A progressive disease marked by formation of fluid-filled cavities in the spinal cord
tic *tik*	Involuntary, spasmodic, recurrent, and purposeless motor movements or vocalizations
tic douloureux *tik du-lu-RU*	Episodes of extreme pain in the area supplied by the trigeminal nerve; also called trigeminal neuralgia

(continued)

Terminology	**Supplementary Terms** (*Continued*)
tabes dorsalis *TA-beze dor-SAL-is*	Destruction of the dorsal (posterior) portion of the spinal cord with loss of sensation and awareness of body position, as seen in advanced cases of syphilis
Tourette syndrome *tu-RET*	A tic disorder with intermittent motor and vocal manifestations that begins in childhood; there also may be obsessive and compulsive behavior, hyperactivity, and distractibility
transient ischemic attack (TIA) *is-KE-mik*	A sudden, brief, and temporary cerebral dysfunction usually caused by interruption of blood flow to the brain
Wallerian degeneration *wahl-LE-re-an*	Degeneration of a nerve distal to an injury
whiplash	Cervical injury caused by rapid acceleration and deceleration, resulting in damage to muscles, ligaments, disks, and nerves

Additional terms related to neurologic symptoms can be found in Chapters 18 (on the sensory system) and 20 (on the muscular system).

Diagnosis and Treatment

Babinski reflex *bah-BIN-ske*	A spreading of the outer toes and extension of the big toe over the others when the sole of the foot is stroked; this response is normal in infants but indicates a lesion of specific motor tracts in adults (**Fig. 17-17**)
evoked potentials	Record of the brain's electric activity after sensory stimulation; included are visual evoked potentials (VEPs), brainstem auditory evoked potentials (BAEPs), and somatosensory evoked potentials (SSEPs), obtained by stimulating the hand or leg; these tests are used to evaluate CNS function
Glasgow Coma Scale	A system for assessing level of consciousness by assigning a score to each of three responses: eye opening, motor responses, and verbal responses
positron emission tomography (PET)	Use of radioactive glucose or other metabolically active substance to produce images of biochemical activity in tissues; used for study of the living brain, both healthy and diseased, and also in cardiology; **Figure 17-18** compares brain CT, MRI, and PET scans
Romberg sign	Inability to maintain balance when the eyes are shut and the feet are close together
sympathectomy *sim-pah-THEK-to-me*	Interruption of sympathetic nerve transmission either surgically or chemically
trephination *tref-ih-NA-shun*	Cutting a piece of bone out of the skull; the instrument used is a trepan (*tre-PAN*) or trephine (*tre-FIN*)

Psychoactive Drugs

antianxiety agent *an-te-ang-ZI-eh-te*	Relieves anxiety by means of a calming, sedative effect on the CNS; examples are chlordiazepoxide (Librium), diazepam (Valium), alprazolam (Xanax); anxiolytic
antidepressant (other than those listed in separate categories below)	Blocks the reuptake of neurotransmitters such as serotonin, norepinephrine, and dopamine, alone or in combination; examples are bupropion (Wellbutrin, Zyban), mirtazapine (Remeron), nefazodone (Serzone), venlafaxine (Effexor XR), atomoxetine (Strattera)
monoamine oxidase inhibitor (MAOI) *mo-no-AH-mene OK-sih-dase*	Blocks an enzyme that breaks down norepinephrine and serotonin, thus prolonging their action; examples are phenelzine (Nardil), tranylcypromine (Parnate), isocarboxazid (Marplan)
neuroleptic *nu-ro-LEP-tik*	Drug used to treat psychosis, including schizophrenia; examples are clozapine (Clozaril), haloperidol (Haldol), risperidone (Risperdal), olanzapine (Zyprexa); antipsychotic; action mechanism unknown, but may interfere with neurotransmitters
selective serotonin reuptake inhibitor (SSRI) *ser-o-TO-nin*	Blocks the reuptake of serotonin in the brain, thus increasing levels; examples are fluoxetine (Prozac), citalopram (Celexa), paroxetine (Paxil), sertraline (Zoloft)

Terminology	**Supplementary Terms** (*Continued*)
stimulant *STIM-u-lant*	Promotes activity and a sense of well-being; examples are methylphenidate (Ritalin), dextroamphetamine (Dexedrine), amphetamine + dextroamphetamine (Adderall)
tricyclic antidepressant (TCA) *tri-SI-klik*	Blocks the reuptake of norepinephrine, serotonin, or both; examples are amitriptyline (Elavil), clomipramine (Anafranil), imipramine (Tofranil), doxepin (Sinequan), trimipramine (Surmontil)

Go to the Audio Pronunciation Glossary in the Student Resources on thePoint to hear these words pronounced.

17

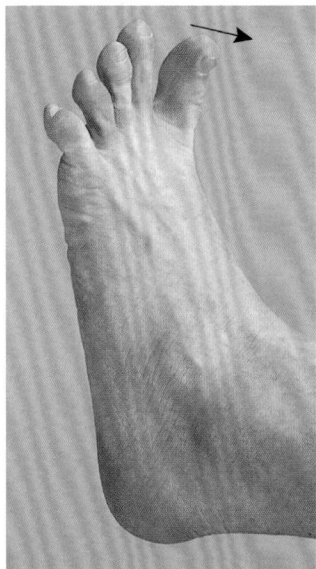

Figure 17-17 **Babinski reflex.** The big toe bends backward and the other toes spread out when the sole of the foot is stroked. This response is normal in infants but indicates a motor lesion in adults.

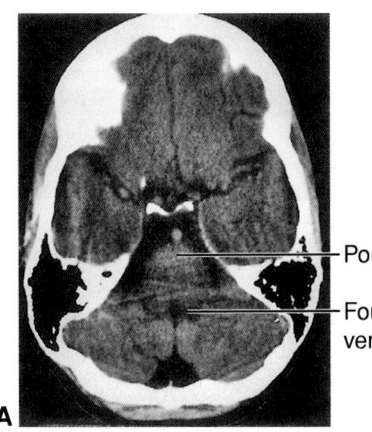
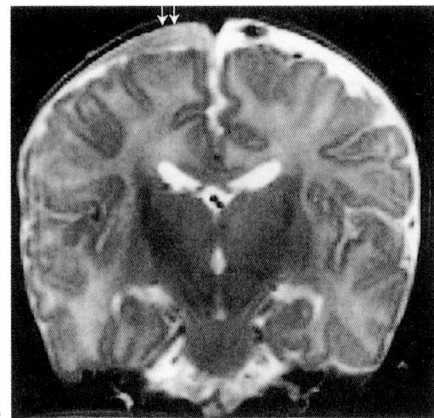
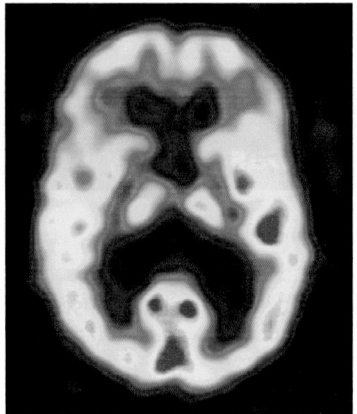

Pons

Fourth ventricle

A

B

C

Figure 17-18 **Brain images.** **A.** CT scan of a normal adult brain. **B.** MRI of the brain showing a subdural hematoma (*arrows*). **C.** PET scan showing regions of different metabolic activity.

Terminology | Abbreviations

Ach	Acetylcholine	LP	Lumbar puncture
AD	Alzheimer disease	MAOI	Monoamine oxidase inhibitor
ADHD	Attention deficit hyperactivity disorder	MID	Multi-infarct dementia
ALS	Amyotrophic lateral sclerosis	MS	Multiple sclerosis
ANS	Autonomic nervous system	NICU	Neurologic intensive care unit; also neonatal intensive care unit
ASD	Autism spectrum disorder	NPH	Normal pressure hydrocephalus
BAEP	Brainstem auditory evoked potentials	NREM	Nonrapid eye movement (sleep)
CBF	Cerebral blood flow	OCD	Obsessive–compulsive disorder
CJD	Creutzfeldt-Jakob disease	PDD	Pervasive developmental disorder
CNS	Central nervous system	PET	Positron emission tomography
CP	Cerebral palsy	PNS	Peripheral nervous system
CSF	Cerebrospinal fluid	PTSD	Posttraumatic stress disorder
CTE	Chronic traumatic encephalopathy	RAS	Reticular activating system
CVA	Cerebrovascular accident	REM	Rapid eye movement (sleep)
CVD	Cerebrovascular disease; also cardiovascular disease	SSEP	Somatosensory evoked potentials
DSM	Diagnostic and Statistical Manual of Mental Disorders	SSRI	Selective serotonin reuptake inhibitor
DTR	Deep tendon reflexes	TBI	Traumatic brain injury, thrombotic brain infarction
EEG	Electroencephalogram; electroencephalograph(y)	TCAV	Tricyclic antidepressant
GAD	Generalized anxiety disorder	TIA	Transient ischemic attack
ICP	Intracranial pressure	UMN	Upper motor neuron
LMN	Lower motor neuron	VEP	Visual evoked potentials
LOC	Level of consciousness		

Case Study Revisited

B.C.'s Follow-Up

B.C. was discharged six days after his surgery with mild hemiparesis, which was expected to resolve within the next few weeks. He was scheduled for six weeks of outpatient rehabilitation, and his prognosis was good. The pediatric physical and occupational therapists were able to motivate B.C. by playing therapeutic games with him, including using a baseball and having him "walk and run the bases." B.C. was looking forward to rejoining his baseball team next season.

CHAPTER 17 **Review**

Labeling Exercise

ANATOMIC DIVISIONS OF THE NERVOUS SYSTEM

Write the name of each numbered part on the corresponding line.

Brain   Peripheral nervous system
Central nervous system   Spinal cord
Cranial nerves   Spinal nerves

1. _____

2. _____

3. _____

4. _____

5. _____

6. _____

MOTOR NEURON

Write the name of each numbered part on the corresponding line.

Axon branch   Muscle
Axon covered with myelin sheath   Myelin
Cell body   Node
Dendrites   Nucleus

1. _____

2. _____

3. _____

4. _____

5. _____

6. _____

7. _____

8. _____

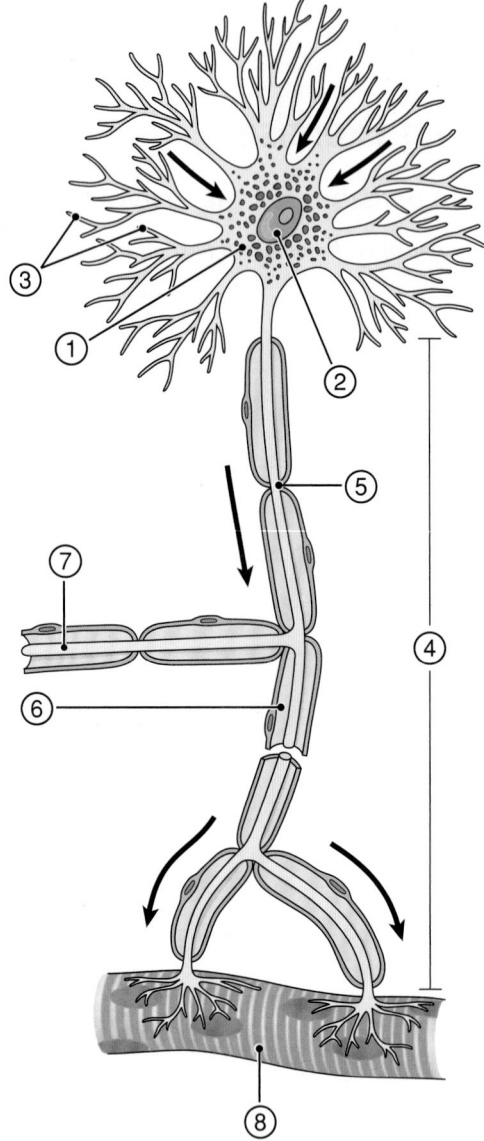

EXTERNAL SURFACE OF THE BRAIN

Write the name of each numbered part on the corresponding line.

Cerebellum   Parietal lobe
Frontal lobe   Pons
Gyri   Spinal cord
Medulla oblongata   Sulci
Occipital lobe   Temporal lobe

1. _____

2. _____

3. _____

4. _____

5. _____

6. _____

7. _____

8. _____

9. _____

10. _____

SPINAL CORD, LATERAL VIEW

Write the name of each numbered part on the corresponding line.

Brain   Lumbar enlargement
Brainstem   Lumbar nerves
Cervical enlargement Sacral nerves
Cervical nerves   Spinal cord
Coccygeal nerve   Thoracic nerves

1. _____

2. _____

3. _____

4. _____

5. _____

6. _____

7. _____

8. _____

9. _____

10. _____

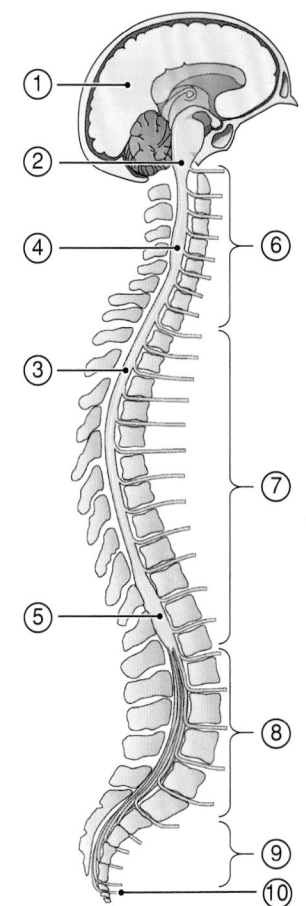

SPINAL CORD, CROSS-SECTION

Write the name of each numbered part on the corresponding line.

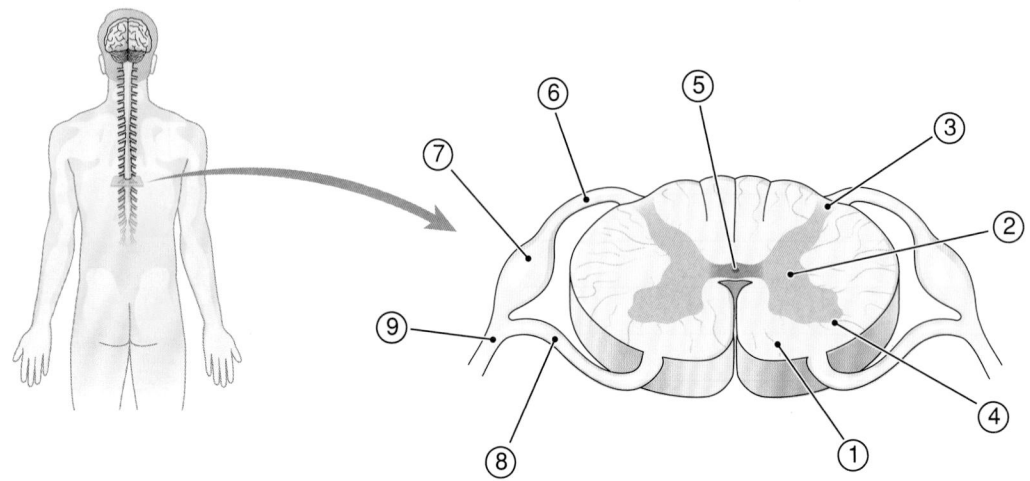

Central canal
Dorsal horn
Dorsal root ganglion
Dorsal root of spinal nerve
Gray matter

Spinal nerve
Ventral horn
Ventral root of spinal nerve
White matter

1. _____

2. _____

3. _____

4. _____

5. _____

6. _____

7. _____

8. _____

9. _____

REFLEX PATHWAY

Write the name of each numbered part on the corresponding line.

Effector
Motor neuron
Receptor

Sensory neuron
Spinal cord (CNS)

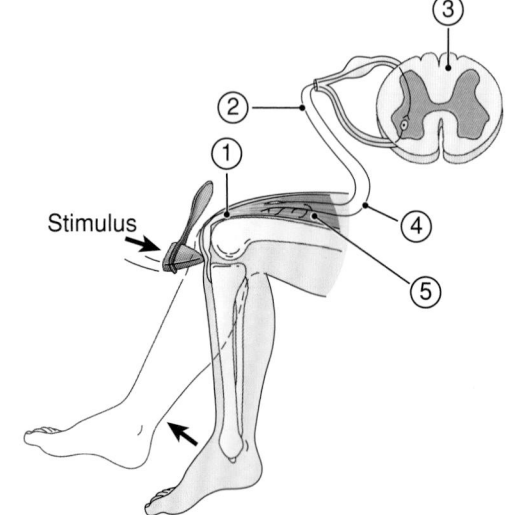

Stimulus

1. _____

2. _____

3. _____

4. _____

5. _____

Terminology

MATCHING

Match the following terms, and write the appropriate letter to the left of each number.

_____ **1.** dendrite

_____ **2.** medulla oblongata

_____ **3.** pons

_____ **4.** myelin

_____ **5.** diencephalon

a. region that connects the brain and spinal cord

b. part of the brain that contains the thalamus and pituitary

c. whitish material that covers some axons

d. rounded area on the ventral surface of the brainstem

e. fiber of a neuron that conducts impulses toward the cell body

_____ **6.** contrecoup injury

_____ **7.** aphasia

_____ **8.** hydrocephalus

_____ **9.** paranoia

_____ **10.** odynophobia

a. mental disorder associated with delusions of persecution

b. excessive fear of pain

c. loss of speech communication

d. accumulation of CSF in the brain

e. damage to the brain on the side opposite the point of a blow

_____ **11.** cystoplegia

_____ **12.** paresis

_____ **13.** meningomyelocele

_____ **14.** convulsion

_____ **15.** aneurysm

a. partial paralysis or weakness

b. paralysis of the bladder

c. series of violent, involuntary muscle contractions

d. localized dilation of a blood vessel

e. hernia of the meninges and spinal cord

Supplementary Terms

_____ **16.** plexus

_____ **17.** ipsilateral

_____ **18.** dermatome

_____ **19.** acetylcholine

_____ **20.** ictus

a. a sudden blow or attack

b. a neurotransmitter

c. area of skin supplied by a spinal nerve

d. on the same side; unilateral

e. network

_____ **21.** amnesia

_____ **22.** euphoria

_____ **23.** claustrophobia

_____ **24.** ataxia

_____ **25.** lethargy

a. fear of being enclosed

b. state of sluggishness

c. loss of memory

d. lack of muscle coordination

e. sense of elation

_____ **26.** REM

_____ **27.** SSRI

_____ **28.** DSM

_____ **29.** PTSD

_____ **30.** LP

a. type of psychoactive drug

b. eye movement during sleep

c. mental disturbances that follow trauma

d. procedure to remove fluid from the spinal column

e. reference for diagnosis of mental disorders

FILL IN THE BLANKS

31. The largest part of the brain is the _____.

32. The fluid that circulates around the central nervous system is _____.

33. The support cells of the nervous system are the _____.

34. The junction between two nerve cells is a(n) _____.

35. The scientific name for a nerve cell is _____.

36. The membranes that cover the brain and spinal cord are the _____.

37. A simple, rapid, automatic response to a stimulus is a(n) _____.

38. The sympathetic and parasympathetic systems make up the _____.

39. A chemical that acts at a synapse is a(n) _____.

40. The posterior portion of the brain that coordinates muscle movement is the _____.

41. The strong, fibrous, outermost cover of the brain and spinal cord is the _____.

DEFINITIONS

Define the following words.

42. corticothalamic (*kor-tih-ko-thah-LAM-ik*) _____

43. polyneuritis (*pol-e-nu-RI-tis*) _____

44. anencephaly (*an-en-SEF-ah-le*) _____

45. hemiparesis (*hem-e-pah-RE-sis*) _____

46. radicular (*rah-DIK-u-lar*) _____

47. psychotherapy (*si-ko-THER-ah-pe*) _____

48. panplegia (*pan-PLE-je-ah*) _____

49. encephalomalacia (*en-sef-ah-lo-mah-LA-she-ah*) _____

50. dyssomnia (*dis-SOM-ne-ah*) _____

Write words for the following definitions.

51. study of the nervous system _____

52. inflammation of the spinal cord and meninges _____

53. excision of a ganglion _____

54. any disease of the nervous system _____

55. creation of an opening into a brain ventricle _____

56. paralysis of one side of the body _____

57. within the cerebellum _____

58. difficulty in reading _____

59. fear of water _____

60. paralysis of one limb _____

SPELL CHECK

Write the correct spelling on the line to the right of the term.

61. cerebim _____

62. neuroglea _____

63. ventracle _____

64. narcksis _____

65. thalmas _____

TRUE–FALSE

Examine the following statements. If the statement is true, write T in the first blank. If the statement is false, write F in the first blank, and correct the statement by replacing the underlined word in the second blank.

	True or False	**Correct Answer**
66. <u>Sensory</u> fibers conduct impulses toward the CNS.	_____	_____
67. The spinal nerves are part of the <u>central</u> nervous system.	_____	_____
68. The cervical nerves are in the region of the <u>neck</u>.	_____	_____
69. Myelinated neurons make up the <u>gray</u> matter of the CNS.	_____	_____
70. CSF forms in the <u>ventricles</u> of the brain.	_____	_____
71. The fiber that carries impulses toward the neuron cell body is the <u>axon</u>.	_____	_____
72. There are <u>12</u> pairs of cranial nerves.	_____	_____
73. The innermost layer of the meninges is the <u>pia</u> mater.	_____	_____
74. Hyperlexia refers to increased skill in <u>reading</u>.	_____	_____

OPPOSITES

Write a word that means the opposite of the following words.

75. extramedullary _____

76. ipsilateral _____

77. postganglionic _____

78. tachylalia _____

79. motor _____

80. dorsal _____

81. afferent _____

ADJECTIVES

Write the adjective form of the following words.

82. ganglion _____

83. thalamus _____

84. dura _____

85. meninges _____

86. psychosis _____

PLURALS

Write the plural form of the following words.

87. ganglion _____

88. ventricle _____

89. meninx _____

90. embolus _____

ELIMINATIONS

In each of the sets below, underline the word that does not fit in with the rest, and explain the reason for your choice.

91. CVA — lumbar puncture — embolism — thrombus — TIA

_____

92. glioma — astrocytoma — meningioma — hematoma — neurilemmoma

_____

93. gyri — sulci — mania — ventricles — lobes

_____

94. MID — CNS — ADHD — OCD — GAD

_____

WORD BUILDING

Write a word for the following definitions using the word parts provided.

| -plegia   myel/o   -a-   -itis   dys-   brady-   my/o   tetra-   -paresis   -phasia   gangli/o   hemi- |

95. paralysis of the spinal cord _____

96. lack of speech _____

97. partial paralysis of one side of the body _____

98. muscle weakness _____

99. abnormal or difficult speech production _____

100. paralysis of a ganglion _____

101. paralysis of all four limbs _____

102. inflammation of the spinal cord _____

103. slowness of speech _____

104. paralysis of one side of the body _____

105. inflammation of a ganglion _____

WORD ANALYSIS

Define each of the following words, and give the meaning of the word parts in each. Use a dictionary if necessary.

106. hematomyelia (*he-mah-to-mi-E-le-ah*) _____

    a. hemat/o _____

    b. myel/o _____

    c. -ia _____

107. myelodysplasia (*mi-eh-lo-dis-PLA-se-ah*) _____

    a. myel/o _____

    b. dys- _____

    c. plas _____

    d. -ia _____

108. polyneuroradiculitis (*pol-e-nu-ro-rah-dik-u-LI-tis*) _____

    a. poly- _____

    b. neur/o _____

    c. radicul/o _____

    d. -itis _____

109. dyssynergia (*dis-sin-ER-je-ah*) _____

    a. dys- _____

    b. syn- _____

    c. erg _____

    d. -ia _____

For more learning activities, see Chapter 17 of the Student Resources on the Point.

Additional Case Studies

Case Study 17-1: *Cerebrovascular Accident (CVA)*

A.R., a 62 y/o man, was admitted to the ER with right hemiplegia and aphasia. He had a history of hypertension and recent transient ischemic attacks (TIAs), yet was in good health when he experienced a sudden onset of right-sided weakness. He arrived in the ER via ambulance within 15 minutes of onset and was received by a member of the hospital's stroke team. He had a rapid general assessment and neuro examination including a Glasgow Coma Scale (GCS) rating to determine his candidacy for fibrinolytic (clot-dissolving) therapy.

He was sent for a noncontrast CT scan to look for evidence of either hemorrhagic or ischemic stroke, postcardiac arrest ischemia, hypertensive encephalopathy, craniocerebral or cervical trauma, meningitis, encephalitis, brain abscess, tumor, and subdural or epidural hematoma. The CT scan, read by the radiologist, did not show intracerebral or subarachnoid hemorrhage. A.R. was diagnosed with probable acute ischemic stroke within one hour of the onset of symptoms and was cleared as a candidate for immediate fibrinolytic treatment.

He was admitted to the NICU for 48-hour observation to monitor his neuro status and vital signs. He was discharged after three days with a prognosis of full recovery.

Case Study 17-2: *Neuroleptic Malignant Syndrome*

J.N., a 21-year-old woman with chronic paranoid schizophrenia, was admitted to the hospital with a diagnosis of pneumonia. She was brought to the ER by her mother, who said J.N. had been very lethargic, had a temperature of 104°F, and had had muscular rigidity for three days. Her daily medications included Haldol (haloperidol) and Cogentin (benztropine mesylate). Her mother stated that J.N.'s psychiatrist had changed her neuroleptic medication the week before. Her secondary diagnosis was stated as neuroleptic malignant syndrome, a rare and life-threatening disorder associated with the use of antipsychotic medications. This drug-induced condition is usually characterized by alterations in mental status, temperature regulation, and autonomic and extrapyramidal functions.

J.N. was monitored for potential hypotension, tachycardia, diaphoresis, dyspnea, dysphagia, and changes in her level of consciousness (LOC). Her medications were discontinued, she was hydrated with IV fluids, and her body temperature was monitored for fluctuations. She was treated with bromocriptine, a dopamine antagonist, and dantrolene, a muscle relaxant and antispasmodic.

After five days, J.N. was transferred to a mental health facility and restarted on low-dose neuroleptics. She was monitored to prevent a recurrence of the syndrome. Both J.N. and her family were educated about neuroleptic malignant syndrome in preparation for her discharge back home in two weeks.

Case Study Questions

Multiple Choice. Select the best answer, and write the letter of your choice to the left of each number.

_____ **1.** Ischemic stroke is generally caused by
  a. hemorrhage
  b. hematoma
  c. thrombosis
  d. hemangioma

_____ **2.** Fibrinolytic therapy is directed toward
  a. stabilizing blood cells
  b. destroying RBCs
  c. triggering blood clotting
  d. dissolving a blood clot

_____ **3.** A general term for any disorder or alteration of brain tissue is

    a. encephalopathy

    b. neurocytoma

    c. dysencephaloma

    d. psychosomatic

_____ **4.** J.N. had disease manifestations related to involuntary functions and to movement controlled by motor fibers outside the pyramidal tracts. These functions are

    a. autonomic and neuroleptic

    b. autonomic and voluntary

    c. extrapyramidal and pyramidal

    d. autonomic and extrapyramidal

Write terms from the Case Studies with the following meanings.

5. physician who treats psychiatric disorders _____

6. antipsychotic medications _____

7. pertaining to a lack of blood supply _____

8. inflammation of the meninges _____

9. collection of blood below the dura mater _____

10. pertaining to a perceived feeling of threat or harm _____

11. drug that relieves muscle spasms _____

12. inability to speak or understand speech _____

13. partial paralysis on one side _____

Define the following abbreviations.

14. GCS _____

15. CT _____

16. NICU _____

17. CVA _____

18. TIA _____

19. LOC _____

17

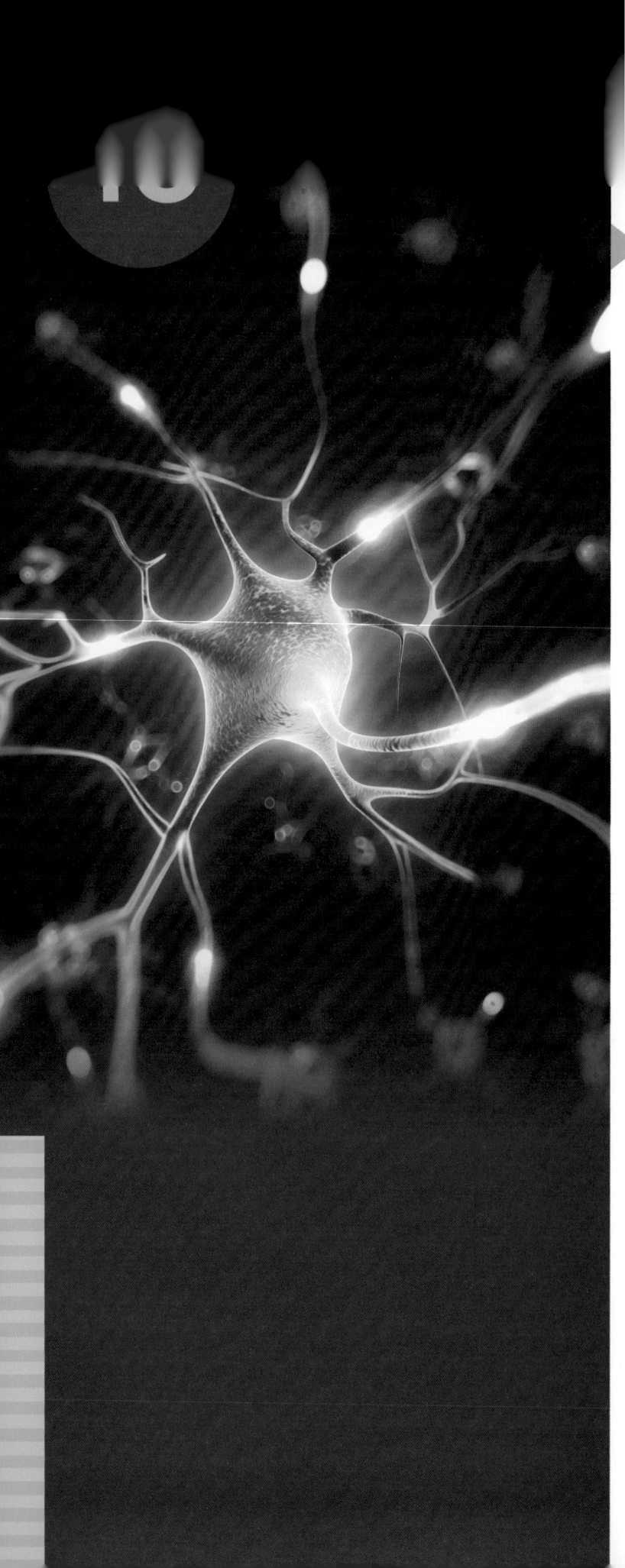

Pretest

Multiple Choice. Select the best answer, and write the letter of your choice to the left of each number.

_____ 1. The scientific name for the sense of smell is
   a. osmosis
   b. olfaction
   c. gustation
   d. dialysis

_____ 2. The term *tactile* refers to the sense of
   a. touch
   b. taste
   c. pain
   d. temperature

_____ 3. The two senses located in the ear are
   a. hearing and pressure
   b. vision and hearing
   c. balance and taste
   d. hearing and equilibrium

_____ 4. The receptor layer of the eye is the
   a. lens
   b. cornea
   c. retina
   d. pinna

_____ 5. The scientific name for the white of the eye is
   a. pupil
   b. vitreous body
   c. sclera
   d. conjunctiva

_____ 6. Clouding of the lens is termed
   a. vertigo
   b. cataract
   c. tinnitus
   d. glaucoma

► Learning Objectives

After study of this chapter, you should be able to:

1 ► Explain the role of the sensory system. *p462*

2 ► List the parts of the ear and the eye, and briefly describe the function of each structure. *pp464, 472*

3 ► Describe the pathway of nerve impulses from the ear to the brain. *p465*

4 ► Describe the roles of the retina and the optic nerve in vision. *p472*

5 ► Identify and use word parts pertaining to the senses. *pp463, 467, 476*

6 ► Describe the main disorders pertaining to the ear and the eye. *pp468, 479*

7 ► Interpret abbreviations used in the study of the ear and the eye. *pp471, 485*

8 ► Analyze medical terms in several case studies pertaining to hearing or vision. *pp461, 492*

Case Study: *K.L.'s Amblyopia*

Chief Complaint

K.L., a recently adopted 7-year-old female, was seeing a pediatrician, Dr. McLaren, for the first time. Her new family was concerned that K.L. might have visual problems resulting in self-image and schoolwork issues as one of her eyes appeared to deviate inward. Her physical examination was unremarkable except for the eye examination. Dr. McLaren explained to the parents that K.L. had a condition known as strabismic amblyopia, or a "lazy eye," and made a referral to an ophthalmologist.

Examination

Upon examining K.L., the ophthalmologist noted that the left eye deviated toward the medial canthus (angle). A complete visual examination was conducted, and the diagnosis was confirmed. K.L. did have amblyopia, in which one eye has lower visual acuity and is used less than the other eye. She also had slight hyperopia, commonly known as farsightedness. A treatment plan was devised and directed toward the development of normal visual acuity. It was discussed with the parents, who decided to move forward with the therapy.

Clinical Course

The ophthalmologist explained to K.L. that they wanted to make her weak eye stronger so she would see much better. This would be accomplished by putting a patch over the strong eye, which should correct the deviation. She would need to wear the patch for a prescribed number of hours each day, and she would also need to wear glasses. She would need to return to see the ophthalmologist so progress could be measured. While K.L. was not sure of the patch, she was excited about wearing glasses since her new mom and sister also wore glasses. She was fitted for glasses and provided with the "bandaid" type of patch to apply over her right eye.

ANCILLARIES *At-A-Glance*

Visit thePoint to access the following resources. For guidance in using the resources most effectively, see pp. ix–xvi.

Learning RESOURCES

► Tips for Effective Studying
► Web Figure: The Steps in Hearing
► Web Figure: The External Eye Muscles
► Web Figure: Trachoma
► Web Figure: Diabetic Retinopathy
► Animation: The Retina
► Audio Pronunciation Glossary

Learning ACTIVITIES

► Visual Activities
► Kinesthetic Activities
► Auditory Activities

Introduction

The sensory system is our network for detecting stimuli from the internal and external environments. It is needed to maintain homeostasis, provide us with pleasure, and protect us from harm. Pain, for example, is an important warning sign of tissue damage. The signals generated in the various **sensory receptors** must be transmitted to the central nervous system for interpretation.

The Senses

The senses are divided according to whether they are widely distributed or localized in special sense organs. The receptors for the general senses are found throughout the body. Many are located in the skin (**Fig. 18-1**). These senses include the following:

- Pain. These receptors are found in the skin and also in muscles, joints, and internal organs.
- Touch, the **tactile** sense, located in the skin. Sensitivity to touch depends on the concentration of these receptors in different areas—high on the fingers, lips, and tongue, for example, but low at the back of the neck or back of the hand.

- Pressure, or deep touch, located beneath the skin and in deeper tissues.
- Temperature. Receptors for heat and cold are located in the skin and also in the hypothalamus, which regulates body temperature.
- **Proprioception**, the awareness of body position. Receptors in muscles, tendons, and joints help to judge body position and coordinate muscle activity. They also help to maintain muscle tone.

The special senses are localized within complex sense organs in the head. These include the following:

- **Gustation** (taste) is located in receptors in taste buds on the tongue. These receptors basically detect only sweet, sour, bitter, salty, and umami (*oo-MOM-e*), a savory flavor triggered by certain amino acids and found in proteins and the flavor enhancer MSG. Researchers have also identified receptors for alkali (bases) and metallic tastes. The senses of smell and taste are chemical senses, that is, they respond to chemicals in solution.
- **Olfaction** (smell) is located in receptors in the nose. Many more chemicals can be discriminated by smell than by taste. Both senses are important in stimulating appetite and warning of harmful substances.

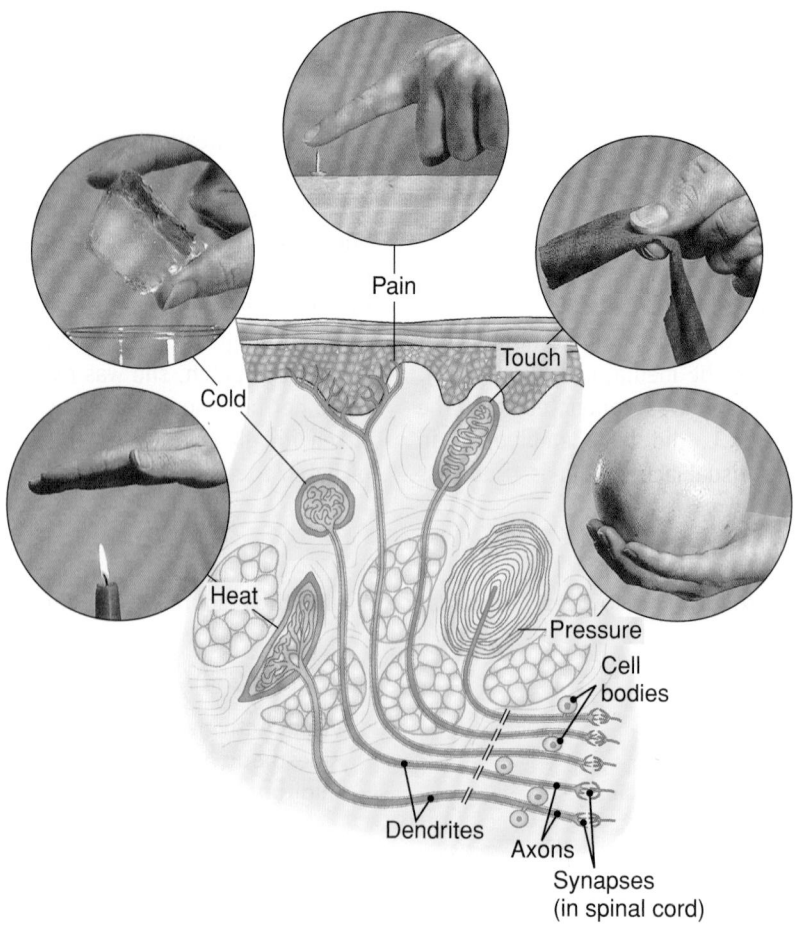

Figure 18-1 **Receptors for general senses in the skin.** Synapses for these pathways are in the spinal cord.

- **Hearing** receptors are located in the ear. These receptors respond to movement created by sound waves as they travel through the ear.
- **Equilibrium** receptors are also located in the ear. These receptors are activated by changes in the position of cells in the inner ear as we move.
- **Vision** receptors are light-sensitive and located deep within the eye, protected by surrounding bone and other support structures. The coordinated actions of external and internal eye muscles help in the formation of a clear image.

Suffixes pertaining to the senses are listed in **Table 18-1**. The remainder of this chapter concentrates on hearing and vision, the senses that have received the most clinical attention.

Go to the Audio Pronunciation Glossary in the Student Resources on thePoint to hear these terms pronounced.

18

Terminology | Key Terms

Senses

Normal Structure and Function

equilibrium *e-kwih-LIB-re-um*	The sense of balance
gustation *gus-TA-shun*	The sense of taste (Latin *geusis* means "taste")
hearing *HERE-ing*	The sense or perception of sound
olfaction *ol-FAK-shun*	The sense of smell (root *osm/o* means "smell")
proprioception *pro-pre-o-SEP-shun*	The awareness of posture, movement, and changes in equilibrium; receptors are located in muscles, tendons, and joints
sensory receptor *re-SEP-tor*	A sensory nerve ending or a specialized structure associated with a sensory nerve that responds to a stimulus
tactile *TAK-til*	Pertaining to the sense of touch
vision *VIZH-un*	The sense by which the shape, size, and color of objects are perceived by means of the light they give off

Table 18-1 | Suffixes Pertaining to the Senses

Suffix	Meaning	Example	Definition of Example
-esthesia	sensation	cryesthesia *kri-es-THE-ze-ah*	sensitivity to cold
-algesia	pain	hypalgesia[a] *hi-pal-JE-ze-ah*	decreased sensitivity to pain
-osmia	sense of smell	pseudosmia *su-DOS-me-ah*	false sense of smell
-geusia	sense of taste	parageusia *par-ah-GU-ze-ah*	abnormal (para-) sense of taste

[a]Prefix hyp/o.

EXERCISE 18-1

Define the following words.

1. analgesia (*an-al-JE-ze-ah*) _____

2. parosmia (*par-OZ-me-ah*) _____

3. ageusia (*ah-GU-ze-ah*) _____

Write words for the following definitions.

4. muscular (my/o-) sensation _____

5. false sense of taste _____

6. sensitivity to temperature _____

7. excess sensitivity to pain _____

8. abnormal (dys-) sense of taste _____

9. lack (an-) of sensation _____

The Ear

The ear has the receptors for both hearing and equilibrium. For study purposes, it may be divided into three parts: the outer, middle, and inner ear (**Fig. 18-2**).

The outer ear consists of the projecting **pinna** (auricle) and the **external auditory canal** (meatus). This canal ends at the **tympanic membrane**, or eardrum, which transmits sound waves to the middle ear. Glands in the external canal produce a waxy material, **cerumen**, which protects the ear and helps to prevent infection.

Spanning the middle ear cavity are three **ossicles** (small bones), each named for its shape: the **malleus** (hammer), **incus** (anvil), and **stapes** (stirrup) (**Fig. 18-3**). Sound waves

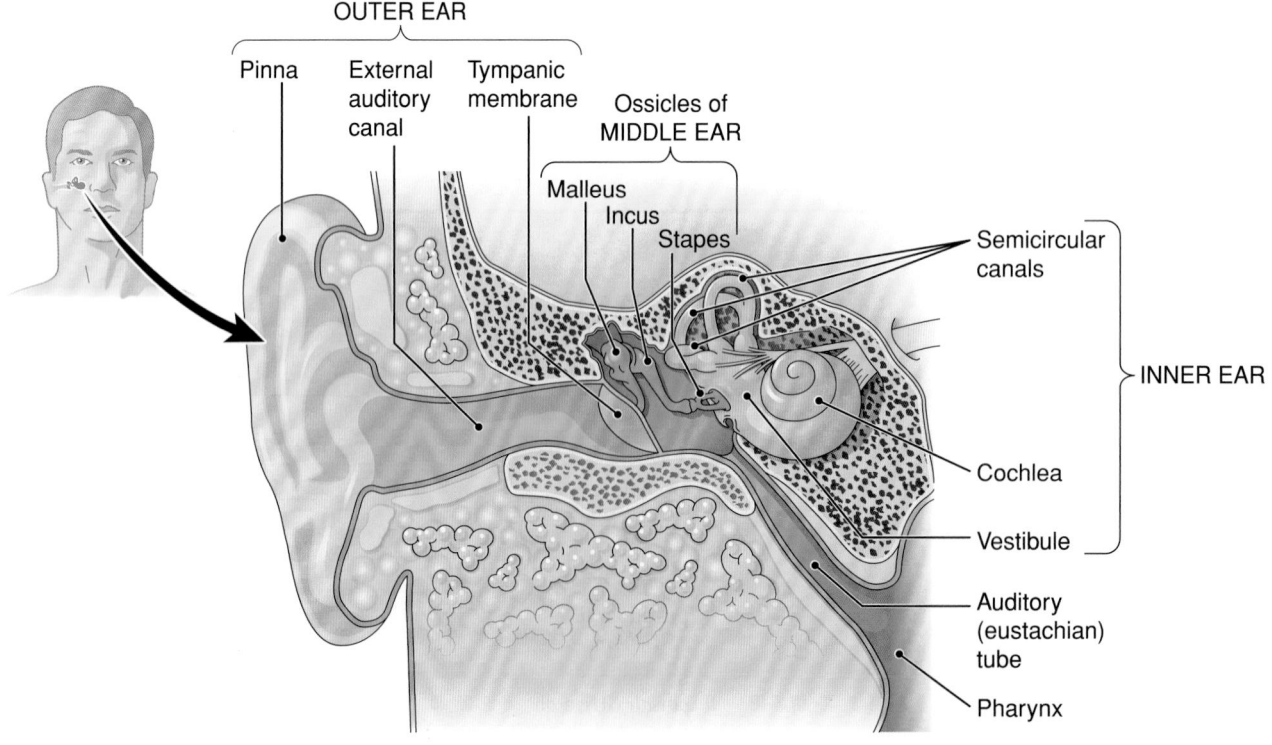

Figure 18-2 **The ear.** Structures in the outer, middle, and inner divisions are shown.

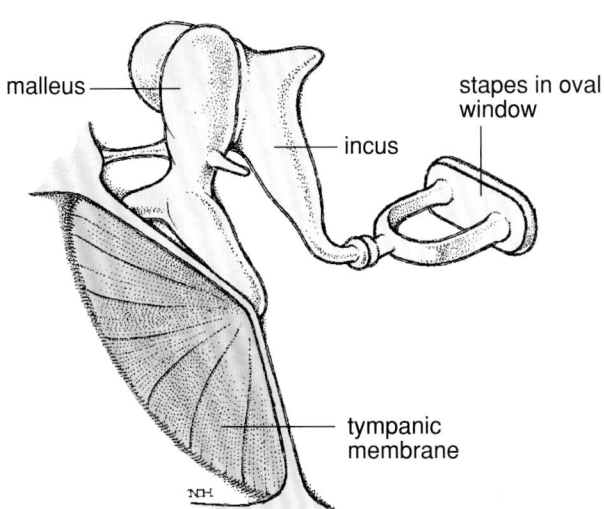

Figure 18-3 **The ossicles of the middle ear.** The malleus is in contact with the tympanic membrane. The base of the stapes is in contact with the oval window of the inner ear.

traveling over the ossicles are transmitted from the footplate of the stapes to the inner ear. The **auditory tube**, also called the *eustachian tube*, connects the middle ear with the nasopharynx and serves to equalize pressure between the outer ear and the middle ear.

The inner ear, because of its complex shape, is described as a **labyrinth**, which means "maze" (**Fig. 18-4**).

It consists of an outer bony framework containing a similarly shaped membranous channel. The entire labyrinth is filled with fluid.

The **cochlea**, shaped like a snail's shell, has the specialized **spiral organ** (organ of Corti), which is concerned with hearing. Cells in this receptor organ respond to sound waves traveling through the cochlea's fluid-filled ducts. Sound waves enter the cochlea from the base of the stapes through an opening, the oval window, and leave through another opening, the round window (see **Fig. 18-4**).

The sense of equilibrium is localized in the **vestibular apparatus**. This structure consists of the chamber-like **vestibule** and three projecting **semicircular canals**. Special cells within the vestibular apparatus respond to movement. (The senses of vision and proprioception are also important in maintaining balance.)

Nerve impulses are transmitted from the ear to the brain by way of the **vestibulocochlear nerve**, the eighth cranial nerve, also called the acoustic or auditory nerve. The cochlear branch of this nerve transmits impulses for hearing from the cochlea; the vestibular branch transmits impulses concerned with equilibrium from the vestibular apparatus (see **Fig. 18-4**). Roots pertaining to the ear and hearing are in Table 18-2.

See the figure "The Steps in Hearing" in the Student Resources on thePoint.

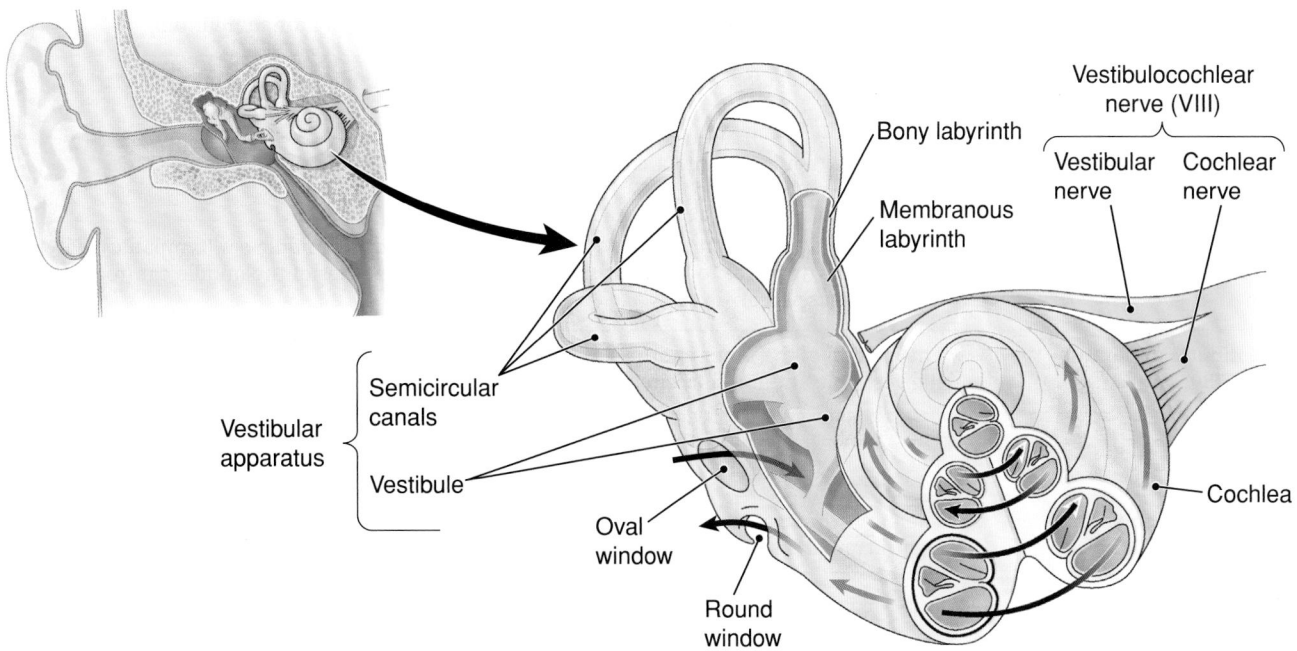

Figure 18-4 **The inner ear.** The outer bony labyrinth contains the membranous labyrinth. Receptors for equilibrium are in the vestibule and the semicircular canals. The cochlea contains the hearing receptor, the spiral organ. Sound waves enter the cochlea through the oval window, travel through the cochlea, and exit through the round window. The inner ear transmits impulses to the brain in the vestibulocochlear nerve (eighth cranial nerve).

Terminology   Key Terms

The Ear

Normal Structure and Function

auditory tube *aw-dih-TO-re*	The tube that connects the middle ear with the nasopharynx and serves to equalize pressure between the outer and middle ear (root: salping/o); pharyngotympanic tube; originally called the eustachian (*u-STA-shen*) tube
cerumen *seh-RU-men*	The brownish, wax-like secretion formed in the external ear canal to protect the ear and prevent infection (adjective: ceruminous [*seh-RU-mih-nus*])
cochlea *KOK-le-ah*	The coiled portion of the inner ear that contains the receptors for hearing (root: cochle/o)
external auditory canal	Tube that extends from the pinna of the ear to the tympanic membrane; external auditory meatus
incus *ING-kus*	The middle ossicle of the ear
labyrinth *LAB-ih-rinth*	The inner ear, named for its complex structure, which resembles a maze
malleus *MAL-e-us*	The ossicle of the middle ear that is in contact with the tympanic membrane and the incus
ossicles *OS-ih-klz*	The small bones of the middle ear; the malleus, incus, and stapes
pinna *PIN-ah*	The projecting part of the outer ear; auricle (*AW-ri-kl*)
semicircular canals	The three curved channels of the inner ear that hold receptors for equilibrium
spiral organ *SPI-ral*	The hearing receptor, which is located in the cochlea of the inner ear; organ of Corti (*KOR-te*)
stapes *STA-peze*	The ossicle that is in contact with the inner ear (roots: staped/o, stapedi/o)
tympanic membrane *tim-PAN-ik*	The membrane between the external auditory canal and the middle ear (tympanic cavity); the eardrum; it serves to transmit sound waves to the ossicles of the middle ear (roots: myring/o, tympan/o)
vestibular apparatus *ves-TIB-u-lar*	The portion of the inner ear that is concerned with the sense of equilibrium; it consists of the vestibule and the semicircular canals (root: vestibul/o)
vestibule *VES-tih-bule*	The chamber in the inner ear that holds some of the receptors for equilibrium
vestibulocochlear nerve *ves-tib-u-lo-KOK-le-ar*	The nerve that transmits impulses for hearing and equilibrium from the ear to the brain; eighth cranial nerve; auditory or acoustic nerve

Go to the Audio Pronunciation Glossary in the Student Resources on thePoint to hear these terms pronounced.

Table 18-2	Roots Pertaining to the Ear and Hearing		
Root	**Meaning**	**Example**	**Definition of Example**
audi/o	hearing	audiology *aw-de-OL-o-je*	the study of hearing
acous, acus, cus	sound, hearing	acoustic *ah-KU-stik*	pertaining to sound or hearing
ot/o	ear	ototoxic *o-to-TOKS-ik*	poisonous or harmful to the ear
myring/o	tympanic membrane	myringotome *mih-RING-go-tome*	knife used for surgery on the eardrum
tympan/o	tympanic cavity (middle ear), tympanic membrane	tympanometry *tim-pah-NOM-eh-tre*	measurement of transmission through the tympanic membrane and middle ear
salping/o	tube, auditory tube	salpingoscopy *sal-ping-GOS-ko-pe*	endoscopic examination of the auditory tube
staped/o, stapedi/o	stapes	stapedoplasty *sta-pe-do-PLAS-te*	plastic repair of the stapes
labyrinth/o	labyrinth (inner ear)	labyrinthitis *lab-ih-rin-THI-tis*	inflammation of the inner ear (labyrinth)
vestibul/o	vestibule, vestibular apparatus	vestibulotomy *ves-tib-u-LOT-o-me*	incision of the vestibule of the inner ear
cochle/o	cochlea (of inner ear)	retrocochlear *ret-ro-KOK-le-ar*	behind the cochlea

18

EXERCISE 18-2

Fill in the blanks.

1. Audition (*aw-DISH-un*) is the act of _____.

2. Hyperacusis (*hi-per-ah-KU-sis*) is abnormally high sensitivity to _____.

3. Otopathy (*o-TOP-ah-the*) means any disease of the _____.

Define the following adjectives.

4. stapedial (*sta-PE-de-al*) _____

5. cochlear (*KOK-le-ar*) _____

6. vestibular (*ves-TIB-u-lar*) _____

7. auditory (*AW-dih-tor-e*) _____

8. labyrinthine (*lab-ih-RIN-thene*) _____

9. otic (*O-tik*) _____

Write words for the following definitions.

10. pain in the ear _____

11. incision of the labyrinth _____

12. endoscope for examining the auditory tube _____

(continued)

EXERCISE 18-2   *(Continued)*

13. instrument used to examine the ear   _____

14. within the cochlea   _____

15. pertaining to the vestibular apparatus and cochlea   _____

16. measurement of hearing (audi/o-)   _____

17. plastic repair of the middle ear   _____

18. excision of the stapes   _____

Define the following words.

19. tympanitis (*tim-pah-NI-tis*)   _____

20. audiometer (*aw-de-OM-eh-ter*)   _____

21. vestibulopathy (*ves-tib-u-LOP-ah-the*)   _____

22. salpingopharyngeal (*sal-ping-go-fah-RIN-je-al*)   _____

23. myringostapediopexy (*mih-RING-go-sta-pe-de-o-PEK-se*)   _____

Clinical Aspects of Hearing

HEARING LOSS

Hearing impairment may result from disease, injury, or developmental problems that affect the ear itself or any nervous pathways concerned with the sense of hearing.

Sensorineural hearing loss results from damage to the inner ear, the eighth cranial nerve, or central auditory pathways. Heredity, toxins, exposure to loud noises, and the aging process are possible causes for this type of hearing loss. It may range from inability to hear certain sound frequencies to a complete loss of hearing (deafness). People with extreme hearing loss that originates in the inner ear may benefit from a cochlear implant. This prosthesis stimulates the cochlear nerve directly, bypassing the receptor cells of the inner ear, and may allow the recipient to hear medium to loud sounds.

Conductive hearing loss results from blockage in sound transmission to the inner ear. Causes include obstruction, severe infection, or fixation of the middle ear ossicles. Often, physicians can successfully treat the conditions that cause conductive hearing loss.

Box 18-1 has information on careers in audiology, the study, and treatment of hearing disorders.

OTITIS

Otitis is any inflammation of the ear. **Otitis media** refers to an infection that leads to fluid accumulation in the middle ear cavity. One cause is malfunction or obstruction of the

---

HEALTH PROFESSIONS   **Box 18-1**

Audiologists

Audiologists specialize in preventing, diagnosing, and treating hearing disorders that may be caused by injury, infection, birth defects, noise, or aging. They take a complete patient history to diagnose hearing disorders and use specialized equipment to measure hearing acuity. Audiologists design and implement individualized treatment plans, which may include fitting clients with assistive listening devices, such as hearing aids, or teaching alternative communication skills, such as lip reading. Audiologists also measure workplace and community noise levels and teach the public how to prevent hearing loss. Whereas in the past, audiologists had to have a master's degree, a doctoral degree is becoming more commonly the entry degree required for licensure in the United States. All 50 states require practicing audiologists to pass a national licensing exam and be registered or licensed. In some states, audiologists who dispense hearing aids must have a hearing aid dispenser license, which is separate from their license to practice audiology.

Audiologists work in a variety of settings, such as hospitals, nursing care facilities, schools, clinics, and industry. Job prospects are good, as the need for audiologists' specialized skills will increase as populations age. The American Academy of Audiology at www.audiology.org has more information on this career.

auditory tube, as by allergy, enlarged adenoids, injury, or congenital abnormalities. Another cause is infection that spreads to the middle ear, most commonly from the upper respiratory tract. Continued infection may lead to accumulation of pus and perforation of the eardrum. Otitis media usually affects children under 5 years of age and may result in hearing loss. If not treated with antibiotics, the infection may spread to other regions of the ear and head. An incision, a **myringotomy**, and placement of a tube in the tympanic membrane helps to ventilate and drain the middle ear cavity in cases of otitis media.

Otitis externa is inflammation of the external auditory canal caused by repeated fungal or bacterial infections. It is most common among those living in hot climates and among swimmers, leading to the alternative name, "swimmer's ear."

OTOSCLEROSIS

In **otosclerosis**, the bony structure of the inner ear deteriorates and then reforms into spongy bone tissue that may eventually harden. Most commonly, the stapes becomes fixed against the inner ear and is unable to vibrate, resulting in conductive hearing loss. The cause of otosclerosis is unknown, but some cases are hereditary. Surgeons usually can remove the damaged bone. In a **stapedectomy**, the stapes is removed, and a prosthetic bone is inserted.

MÉNIÈRE DISEASE

Ménière disease is a disorder that affects the inner ear. It seems to involve production and circulation of the fluid that fills the inner ear, but the cause is unknown. The symptoms include **vertigo** (dizziness), hearing loss, **tinnitus** (ringing in the ears), and a feeling of pressure in the ear. The course of the disease is uneven, and symptoms may become less severe with time. Ménière disease is treated with drugs to control nausea and dizziness, such as those used to treat motion sickness. In severe cases, the inner ear or part of the eighth cranial nerve may be surgically destroyed.

ACOUSTIC NEUROMA

An **acoustic neuroma** (also called schwannoma or neurilemmoma) is a tumor that arises from the neurilemma (sheath) of the eighth cranial nerve. As the tumor enlarges, it presses on surrounding nerves and interferes with blood supply. This leads to tinnitus, dizziness, and progressive hearing loss. Other symptoms develop as the tumor presses on the brainstem and other cranial nerves. Usually, it is necessary to remove the tumor surgically.

Terminology	Key Terms

The Ear

Disorders

acoustic neuroma *ah-KU-stik nu-RO-mah*	A tumor of the eighth cranial nerve sheath; although benign, it can press on surrounding tissue and produce symptoms; also called an acoustic or vestibular schwannoma or acoustic neurilemmoma
conductive hearing loss	Hearing impairment that results from blockage of sound transmission to the inner ear
Ménière disease *men-NYARE*	A disease associated with increased fluid pressure in the inner ear and characterized by hearing loss, vertigo, and tinnitus
otitis externa *o-TI-tis ex-TER-nah*	Inflammation of the external auditory canal; swimmer's ear
otitis media *o-TI-tis ME-de-ah*	Inflammation of the middle ear with accumulation of serous (watery) or mucoid fluid
otosclerosis *o-to-skleh-RO-sis*	Formation of abnormal and sometimes hardened bony tissue in the ear; it usually occurs around the oval window and the footplate (base) of the stapes, causing immobilization of the stapes and progressive hearing loss
sensorineural hearing loss *sen-so-re-NU-ral*	Hearing impairment that results from damage to the inner ear, eighth cranial nerve, or auditory pathways in the brain
tinnitus *TIN-ih-tus*	A sensation of noises, such as ringing or tinkling, in the ear; also pronounced *tih-NI-tus*
vertigo *VER-tih-go*	An illusion of movement, as of the body moving in space or the environment moving about the body; usually caused by disturbances in the vestibular apparatus; used loosely to mean dizziness or lightheadedness

(continued)

Terminology   Key Terms (*Continued*)

Treatment

myringotomy mir-in-GOT-o-me	Surgical incision of the tympanic membrane; performed to drain the middle ear cavity or to insert a tube into the tympanic membrane for drainage
stapedectomy sta-pe-DEK-to-me	Surgical removal of the stapes; it may be combined with insertion of a prosthesis to correct otosclerosis

Terminology   Supplementary Terms

Normal Structure and Function

aural AW-ral	Pertaining to or perceived by the ear
decibel (dB) DES-ih-bel	A unit for measuring the relative intensity of sound
hertz (Hz)	A unit for measuring the frequency (pitch) of sound
mastoid process	A small projection of the temporal bone behind the external auditory canal; it consists of loosely arranged bony material and small, air-filled cavities
stapedius sta-PE-de-us	A small muscle attached to the stapes; it contracts in the presence of a loud sound, producing the acoustic reflex

Symptoms and Conditions

cholesteatoma ko-les-te-ah-TO-mah	A cyst-like mass containing cholesterol that is most common in the middle ear and mastoid region; a possible complication of chronic middle ear infection
labyrinthitis lab-ih-rin-THI-tis	Inflammation of the ear's labyrinth (inner ear); otitis interna
mastoiditis mas-toyd-I-tis	Inflammation of the air cells of the mastoid process
presbycusis prez-be-KU-sis	Loss of hearing caused by aging presbyacusis

Diagnosis and Treatment

audiometry aw-de-OM-eh-tre	Measurement of hearing
electronystagmography (ENG) e-lek-tro-nis-tag-MOG-rah-fe	A method for recording eye movements by means of electrical responses; such movements may reflect vestibular dysfunction
otorhinolaryngology (ORL) o-to-ri-no-lar-in-GOL-o-je	The branch of medicine that deals with diseases of the ear(s), nose, and throat (ENT); also called otolaryngology (OL)
otoscope O-to-skope	Instrument for examining the ear (see **Fig. 7-6**)
Rinne test RIN-ne	Test that measures hearing by comparing results of bone conduction and air conduction (**Fig. 18-5**); bone conduction is tested through the mastoid process behind the ear
spondee spon-de	A two-syllable word with equal stress on each syllable; used in hearing tests; examples are toothbrush, baseball, cowboy, pancake

Terminology | Supplementary Terms *(Continued)*

Weber test	Test for hearing loss that uses a vibrating tuning fork placed at the center of the head (Fig. 18-6)

Go the Audio Pronunciation Glossary in the Student Resources on thePoint to hear these terms pronounced.

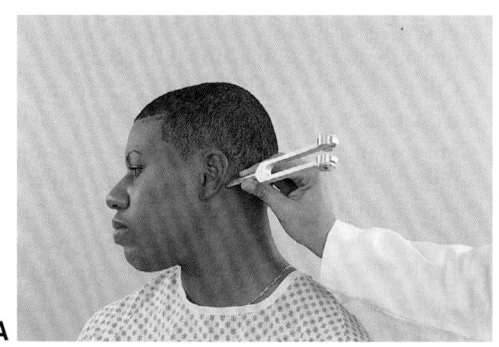

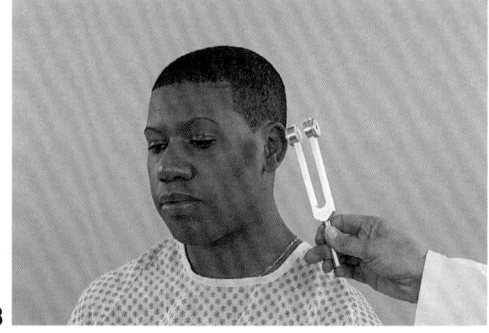

Figure 18-5 **The Rinne test.** This test assesses both bone and air conduction of sound. **A.** Test of bone conduction through the mastoid process behind the ear. **B.** Test of air conduction.

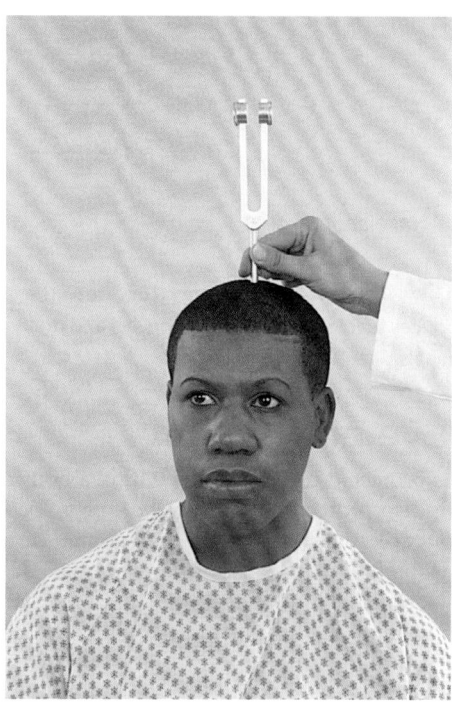

Figure 18-6 **The Weber test.** This test assesses bone conduction of sound.

Terminology | Abbreviations

The Ear

ABR	Auditory brainstem response	**Hz**	Hertz
AC	Air conduction	**OL**	Otolaryngology
BAEP	Brainstem auditory evoked potentials	**OM**	Otitis media
BC	Bone conduction	**ORL**	Otorhinolaryngology
dB	Decibel	**ST**	Speech threshold
ENG	Electronystagmography	**TM**	Tympanic membrane
ENT	Ear(s), nose, and throat	**TTS**	Temporary threshold shift
HL	Hearing level		

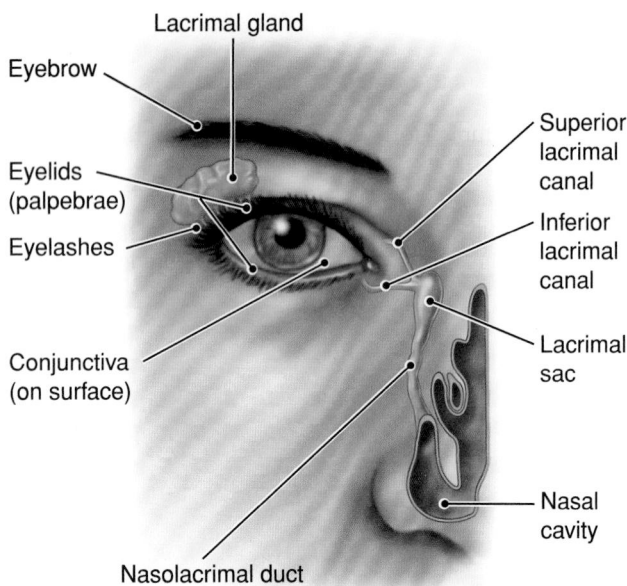

Figure 18-7 **The eye's protective structures.** The lacrimal gland produces tears that flow across the eye and drain into the lacrimal canals.

The Eye and Vision

The eye is protected by its position within a bony socket or **orbit**. It is also protected by the eyelids, or **palpebrae;** eyebrows; and eyelashes (**Fig. 18-7**). The **lacrimal (tear) glands** constantly bathe and cleanse the eyes with a lubricating fluid that drains into the nose. The protective **conjunctiva** is a thin membrane that lines the eyelids and covers the

anterior portion of the eye. This membrane folds back to form a narrow space between the eyeball and the eyelids. Medications, such as eye drops and eye ointments, can be instilled into this conjunctival sac.

The wall of the eye is composed of three layers (**Fig. 18-8**). Named from outermost to innermost, they are as follows:

1. The **sclera**, commonly called the *white of the eye*, is the tough surface protective layer. The sclera extends over the eye's anterior portion as the transparent **cornea**.
2. The **uvea** is the middle layer, which consists of the:
   - **Choroid**, a vascular and pigmented layer located in the posterior portion of the eyeball. The choroid provides nourishment for the retina.
   - **Ciliary body**, which contains a muscle that controls the shape of the **lens** to allow for near and far vision, a process known as **accommodation** (**Fig. 18-9**). The lens must become more rounded for viewing close objects.
   - **Iris**, a muscular ring that controls the size of the **pupil**, thus regulating the amount of light that enters the eye (**Fig. 18-10**). The genetically controlled pigments of the iris determine eye color.
3. The **retina** is the innermost layer and the actual visual receptor. It consists of two types of specialized cells that respond to light:
   - The **rods** function in dim light, provide low **visual acuity** (sharpness), and do not respond to color.
   - The **cones** are active in bright light, have high visual acuity, and respond to color.

Proper vision requires the **refraction** (bending) of light rays as they pass through the eye to focus on a specific

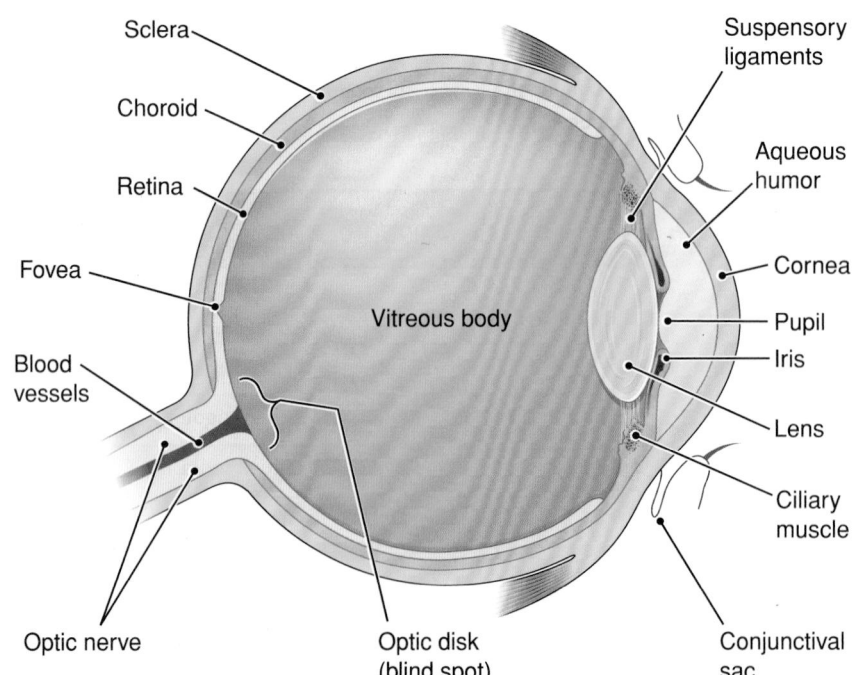

Figure 18-8 **The eye.** The three layers of the eyeball are shown along with other structures involved in vision.

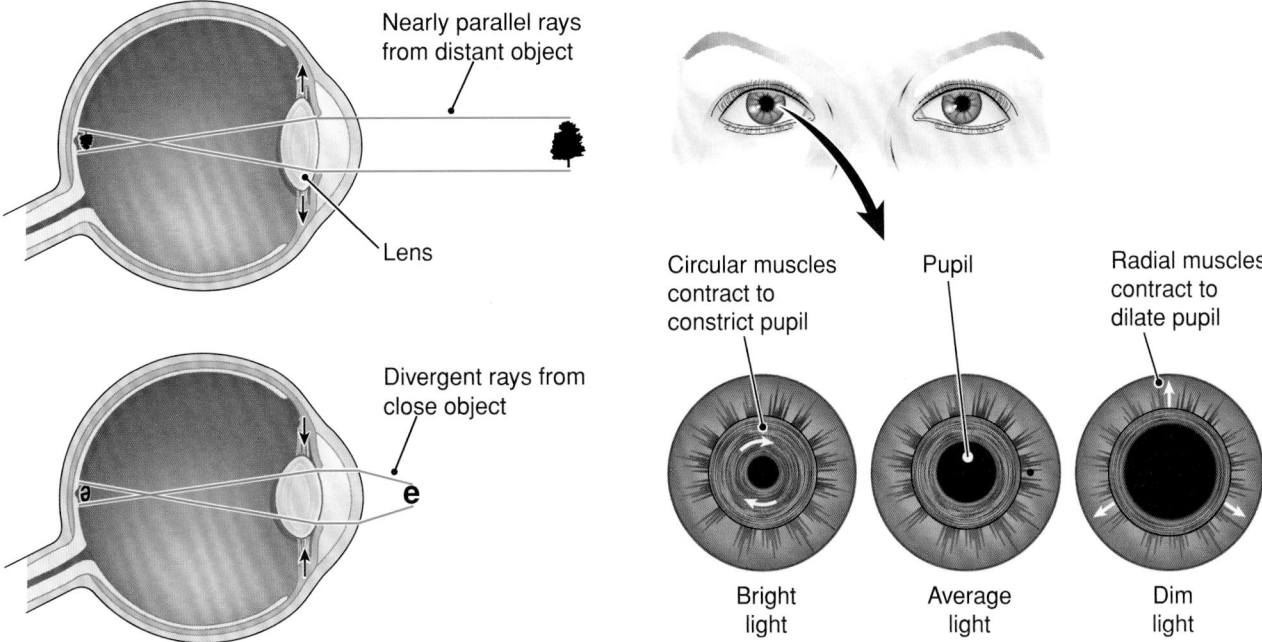

Figure 18-9 **Accommodation for near vision.** When viewing a close object, the lens must become more rounded to focus light rays on the retina.

Figure 18-10 **Function of the iris.** In bright light, muscles in the iris constrict the pupil, limiting the light that enters the eye. In dim light, the iris dilates the pupil to allow more light to enter the eye.

point on the retina. The impulses generated within the rods and cones are transmitted to the brain by way of the optic nerve (second cranial nerve). Where the optic nerve connects to the retina, there are no rods or cones. This point, at which there is no visual perception, is called the **optic disk**, or *blind spot* (see **Fig. 18-8**). The **fovea** is a tiny depression in the retina near the optic nerve that has a high concentration of cones and is the point of greatest visual acuity. The fovea is surrounded by a yellowish spot called the **macula** (**Fig. 18-11**).

The eyeball is filled with a jelly-like **vitreous body** (see **Fig. 18-9**), which helps maintain the shape of the eye and also refracts light. The **aqueous humor** is the fluid that fills the eye anterior to the lens, maintaining the cor-

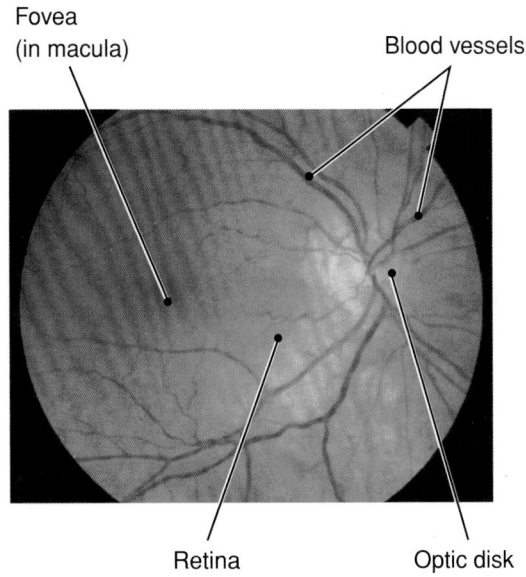

Figure 18-11 **The fundus (back) of the eye as seen through an ophthalmoscope.** The optic disk (blind spot) is shown as well as the fovea, the point of sharpest vision, in the retina.

FOCUS ON WORDS
The Greek Influence

Box 18-2

Some of our most beautiful (and difficult to spell and pronounce) words come from Greek. *Esthesi/o* means "sensation." It appears in the word *anesthesia*, a state in which there is lack of sensation, particularly pain. It is found in the word *esthetics* (also spelled aesthetics), which pertains to beauty, artistry, and appearance. The prefix *presby*, in the terms *presbycusis* and *presbyopia*, means "old," and these conditions appear with aging. The root *cycl/o*, pertaining to the ring-like ciliary body of the eye, is from the Greek word for circle or wheel. The same root appears in the words *bicycle* and *tricycle*. Also pertaining to the eye, the term *iris* means "rainbow" in Greek, and the iris is the colored part of the eye.

The root *-sthen/o* means "strength" and occurs in the words *asthenia*, meaning lack of strength, or weakness, and *neurasthenia*, an old term for vague "nervous exhaustion" now applied to conditions involving chronic symptoms of generalized fatigue, anxiety, and pain. The root also appears in the word *calisthenics* in combination with the root *cali-*, meaning "beauty." So the rhythmic strengthening and conditioning exercises that are done in calisthenics literally give us beauty through strength.

The Greek root *steth/o* means "chest," although a stethoscope is used to listen to sounds in other parts of the body as well as the chest.

Asphyxia is derived from the Greek root *sphygm/o* meaning "pulse." The word is literally "stoppage of the pulse," which is exactly what happens when one suffocates. This same root is found in *sphygmomanometer*, the apparatus used to measure blood pressure. One look at the word and one attempt to pronounce it makes it clear why most people call the device a blood pressure cuff!

nea's shape and refracting light. This fluid is constantly produced and drained from the eye.

Six muscles attached to the outside of each eye coordinate eye movements to achieve **convergence**, that is, coordinated movement of the eyes so that they both are fixed on the same point.

Box 18-2 explores the Greek origins of some medical words, including some pertaining to the eye.

See the figure on the external eye muscles and the animation "The Retina" in the Student Resources on the Point.

Terminology	Key Terms

The Eye

Normal Structure and Function

accommodation *ah-kom-o-DA-shun*	Adjustment of the lens's curvature to allow for vision at various distances
aqueous humor *AK-we-us*	Fluid that fills the eye anterior to the lens
choroid *KOR-oyd*	The dark, vascular, middle layer of the eye (roots: chori/o, choroid/o); part of the uvea (see below)
ciliary body *SIL-e-ar-e*	The muscular portion of the uvea that surrounds the lens and adjusts its shape for near and far vision (root: cycl/o)
cone	A specialized cell in the retina that responds to light; cones have high visual acuity, function in bright light, and respond to colors
conjunctiva *kon-junk-TI-vah*	The mucous membrane that lines the eyelids and covers the eyeball's anterior surface

Terminology	**Key Terms** *(Continued)*

convergence	Coordinated movement of the eyes toward fixation on the same point
kon-VER-jens	
cornea	The clear, anterior portion of the sclera (roots: corne/o, kerat/o)
KOR-ne-ah	
fovea	The tiny depression in the retina that is the point of sharpest vision; fovea centralis, central
FO-ve-ah	fovea
iris	The muscular colored ring between the lens and the cornea; regulates the amount of light
I-ris	that enters the eye by altering the size of the pupil at its center (roots: ir, irid/o, irit/o) (plural:
	irides [IR-ih-deze])
lacrimal gland	A gland above the eye that produces tears (roots: lacrim/o, dacry/o)
LAK-rih-mal	
lens	The transparent, biconvex structure in the anterior portion of the eye that refracts light and
lenz	functions in accommodation (roots: lent/i, phak/o)
macula	A small spot or colored area; used alone to mean the yellowish spot in the retina that contains
MAK-u-lah	the fovea
optic disk	The point where the optic nerve joins the retina; at this point, there are no rods or cones; also
	called the blind spot or optic papilla
orbit	The bony cavity that contains the eyeball
OR-bit	
palpebra	An eyelid; a protective fold (upper or lower) that closes over the anterior surface of the eye
PAL-peh-brah	(roots: palpebr/o, blephar/o) (adjective: palpebral) (plural: palpebrae [pal-PE-bre])
pupil	The opening at the center of the iris (root: pupil/o)
PU-pil	
refraction	The bending of light rays as they pass through the eye to focus on a specific point on the
re-FRAK-shun	retina; also the determination and correction of ocular refractive errors
retina	The innermost, light-sensitive layer of the eye; contains the rods and cones, the specialized
RET-ih-nah	receptor cells for vision (root: retin/o)
rod	A specialized cell in the retina that responds to light; rods have low visual acuity, function in
	dim light, and do not respond to color
sclera	The tough, white, fibrous outermost layer of the eye; the white of the eye (root: scler/o)
SKLERE-ah	
uvea	The middle, vascular layer of the eye (root: uve/o); consists of the choroid, ciliary body, and iris
U-ve-ah	
visual acuity	Sharpness of vision
ah-KU-ih-te	
vitreous body	The transparent jelly-like mass that fills the eyeball's main cavity; also called vitreous humor
VIT-re-us	

Go to the Audio Pronunciation Glossary in the Student
Resources on thePoint to hear these terms pronounced.

Word Parts Pertaining to the Eye and Vision

See Tables 18-3 to 18-5.

Table 18-3	Roots for External Eye Structures		
Root	**Meaning**	**Example**	**Definition of Example**
blephar/o	eyelid	symblepharon *sim-BLEF-ah-ron*	adhesion of the eyelid to the eyeball (sym- means "together")
palpebr/o	eyelid	palpebral *PAL-peh-bral*	pertaining to an eyelid
dacry/o	tear, lacrimal apparatus	dacryorrhea *dak-re-o-RE-ah*	discharge from the lacrimal apparatus
dacryocyst/o	lacrimal sac	dacryocystocele *dak-re-o-SIS-to-sele*	hernia of the lacrimal sac
lacrim/o	tear, lacrimal apparatus	lacrimation *lak-rih-MA-shun*	secretion of tears

EXERCISE 18-3

Define the following words.

1. nasolacrimal (*na-zo-LAK-rih-mal*) _____

2. interpalpebral (*in-ter-PAL-peh-bral*) _____

3. blepharoplasty (*blef-ah-ro-PLAS-te*) _____

4. dacryocystectomy (*dak-re-o-sis-TEK-to-me*) _____

Use the roots indicated to write words that mean the following.

5. paralysis of the eyelid (blephar/o) _____

6. stone in the lacrimal apparatus (dacry/o) _____

7. inflammation of a lacrimal sac _____

Table 18-4	Roots for the Eye and Vision		
Root	**Meaning**	**Example**	**Definition of Example**
opt/o	eye, vision	optometer *op-TOM-eh-ter*	instrument for measuring the refractive power of the eye
ocul/o	eye	sinistrocular *sih-nis-TROK-u-lar*	pertaining to the left eye
ophthalm/o	eye	exophthalmos *eks-of-THAL-mos*	protrusion of the eyeball
scler/o	sclera	episcleritis *ep-ih-skle-RI-tis*	inflammation of the tissue on the surface of the sclera

Table 18-4	Roots for the Eye and Vision (*Continued*)		
Root	**Meaning**	**Example**	**Definition of Example**
corne/o	cornea	circumcorneal *sir-kum-KOR-ne-al*	around the cornea
kerat/o	cornea	keratoplasty *KER-ah-to-plas-te*	plastic repair of the cornea; corneal transplant
lent/i	lens	lentiform *LEN-tih-form*	resembling a lens
phak/o, phac/o	lens	aphakia *ah-FA-ke-ah*	absence of a lens
uve/o	uvea	uveal *U-ve-al*	pertaining to the uvea
chori/o, choroid/o	choroid	subchoroidal *sub-kor-OYD-al*	below the choroid
cycl/o	ciliary body, ciliary muscle	cycloplegic *si-klo-PLE-jik*	pertaining to or causing paralysis of the ciliary muscle
ir, irit/o, irid/o	iris	iridoschisis *ir-ih-DOS-kih-sis*	splitting of the iris
pupill/o	pupil	iridopupillary *ir-ih-do-PU-pih-lar-e*	pertaining to the iris and the pupil
retin/o	retina	retinoscopy *ret-in-OS-ko-pe*	examination of the retina

18

EXERCISE 18-4

Fill in the blanks.

1. In the opening case study, the medical specialist K.L. saw for her vision problems was a(n) _____.

2. Lenticonus is conical protrusion of the _____.

3. The oculomotor (*ok-u-lo-MO-tor*) nerve controls movements of the _____.

4. The science of orthoptics (*or-THOP-tiks*) deals with correcting defects in _____.

5. The term *phacolysis* (*fah-KOL-ih-sis*) means destruction of the _____.

6. A keratometer (*ker-ah-TOM-eh-ter*) is an instrument for measuring the curves of the _____.

Identify and define the roots pertaining to the eye in the following words.

	Root	**Meaning of Root**
7. optometrist (*op-TOM-eh-trist*)	_____	_____
8. microphthalmos (*mi-krof-THAL-mus*)	_____	_____
9. interpupillary (*in-ter-PU-pih-ler-e*)	_____	_____
10. retrolental (*ret-ro-LEN-tal*)	_____	_____
11. iridodilator (*ir-id-o-DI-la-tor*)	_____	_____
12. uveitis (*u-ve-I-tis*)	_____	_____
13. phacotoxic (*fak-o-TOK-sik*)	_____	_____

(continued)

EXERCISE 18-4   *(Continued)*

Write words for the following definitions.

14. inflammation of the uvea and sclera   _____

15. hardening of the lens (use phac/o)   _____

16. pertaining to the cornea   _____

17. surgical fixation of the retina   _____

18. inflammation of the ciliary body   _____

Use the root *ophthalm/o* to write words for the following definitions.

19. an instrument used to examine the eye   _____

20. the medical specialty that deals with the eye and diseases of the eye   _____

Use the root *irid/o* to write words for the following definitions.

21. surgical removal of (part of) the iris   _____

22. paralysis of the iris   _____

Define the following words.

23. dextrocular (*deks-TROK-u-lar*)   _____

24. lenticular (*len-TIK-u-lar*)   _____

25. iridocyclitis (*ir-ih-do-si-KLI-tis*)   _____

26. chorioretinal (*kor-e-o-RET-ih-nal*)   _____

27. keratitis (*ker-ah-TI-tis*)   _____

28. cyclotomy (*si-KLOT-o-me*)   _____

29. optical (*OP-tih-kal*)   _____

30. sclerotome (*SKLERE-o-tome*)   _____

31. retinoschisis (*ret-ih-NOS-kih-sis*)   _____

Table 18-5   **Suffixes for the Eye and Vision**[a]

Suffix	Meaning	Example	Definition of Example
-opsia	condition of vision	heteropsia *het-er-OP-se-ah*	unequal vision in the two eyes
-opia	condition of the eye, vision	hemianopia *hem-e-an-O-pe-ah*	blindness in half the visual field

[a]Compounds of -ops (eye) + -ia.

EXERCISE 18-5

Use the suffix *-opsia* to write words for the following definitions.

1. a visual defect in which objects seem larger (macr/o) than they are _____

2. lack of (a-) color (chromat/o) vision (complete color blindness)_____

Use the suffix *-opia* to write words for the following definitions.

3. double vision _____

4. changes in vision due to old age (use the prefix presby- meaning "old") _____

5. In the opening case study, K.L. was diagnosed with "lazy eye," technically known as

_____.

The suffix *-opia* is added to the root *metr/o* (measure) to form words pertaining to the refractive power of the eye. Add a prefix to *-metropia* to form words for the following.

6. a lack of refractive power in the eye _____

7. unequal refractive powers in the two eyes _____

18

Clinical Aspects of Vision

ERRORS OF REFRACTION

If the eyeball is too long, images will form in front of the retina. To focus clearly, one must bring an object closer to the eye. This condition of *nearsightedness* is technically called **myopia** (**Fig. 18-12**). The opposite condition is **hyperopia**, or *farsightedness*, in which the eyeball is too short and images form behind the retina. One must move an object away from the eye for clear focus. The same effect is produced by **presbyopia**, which accompanies aging. The lens loses elasticity and can no longer accommodate for near vision, so a person gradually becomes farsighted.

Astigmatism is an irregularity in the curve of the cornea or lens that distorts light entering the eye and blurs vision.

Glasses can compensate for most of these refractive impairments, as shown for nearsightedness and farsightedness

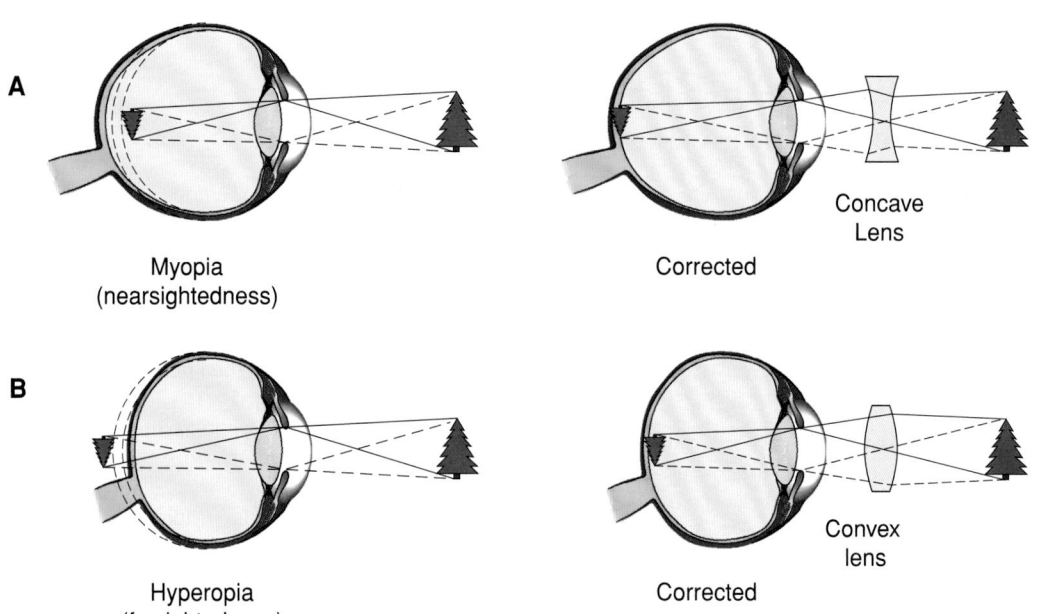

A Myopia (nearsightedness)   Concave Lens — Corrected

B Hyperopia (farsightedness)   Convex lens — Corrected

Figure 18-12 **Errors of refraction. A.** Myopia (nearsightedness). **B.** Hyperopia (farsightedness). A concave (inwardly curved) lens corrects for myopia; a convex (outwardly curved) lens corrects for hyperopia.

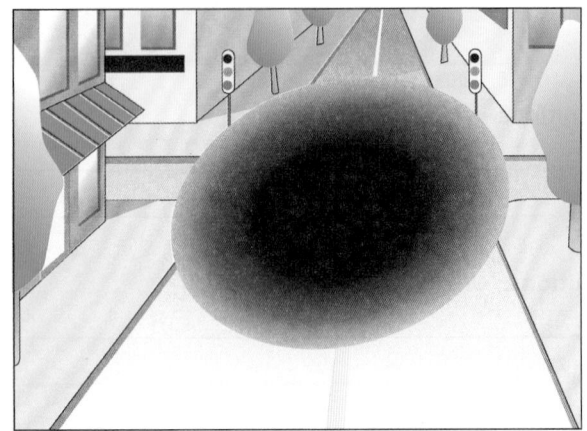

Figure 18-13 Retinal detachment.

in **Figure 18-12**. See also **Box 18-3** for information on a surgical technique to correct refractive errors.

INFECTION

Several microorganisms can cause **conjunctivitis** (inflammation of the conjunctiva). This is a highly infectious disease commonly called "pink eye."

The bacterium *Chlamydia trachomatis* causes **trachoma**, inflammation of the cornea and conjunctiva that results in scarring. This disease is rare in the United States and other industrialized countries but is a common cause of blindness in underdeveloped countries, although it is easily cured with sulfa drugs and antibiotics.

Gonorrhea is the usual cause of an acute conjunctivitis in newborns called **ophthalmia neonatorum**. An antibiotic

ointment is routinely used to prevent such eye infections in newborns.

See the figure on trachoma in the Student Resources on thePoint.

DISORDERS OF THE RETINA

Retinal detachment, separation of the retina from the underlying layer of the eye (the choroid), may be caused by a tumor, hemorrhage, or injury to the eye (**Fig. 18-13**). This condition interferes with vision and is commonly repaired with laser surgery.

Degeneration of the macula, the point of sharpest vision, is a common cause of visual problems in the elderly. When associated with aging, this deterioration is described as **age-related macular degeneration (AMD)**. In nonexudative ("dry") macular degeneration, material accumulates on the retina. Vitamins C and E, beta carotene, and zinc supplements may delay this process. In neovascular ("wet") AMD, abnormal blood vessels grow under the retina, causing it to detach. Laser surgery may stop the growth of these vessels and delay vision loss. More recently, ophthalmologists have had success in delaying the progress of wet AMD with regular intraocular injections of a drug (e.g., Lucentis) that inhibits blood vessel formation. Macular degeneration typically affects central vision but not peripheral vision (**Fig. 18-14B**). Other causes of macular degeneration are drug toxicity and hereditary diseases.

Circulatory problems associated with diabetes mellitus eventually cause changes in the retina referred to as **diabetic retinopathy**. In addition to vascular damage, there is a yellowish, waxy exudate high in lipoproteins. With time, new blood vessels form and penetrate the vitreous humor,

---

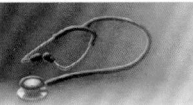

CLINICAL PERSPECTIVES

Eye Surgery: A Glimpse of the Cutting Edge

Box 18-3

Cataracts, glaucoma, and refractive errors are common eye disorders. In the past, cataract and glaucoma treatments concentrated on managing the diseases. Refractive errors were corrected using eyeglasses and, more recently, contact lenses. Today, using laser and microsurgical techniques, ophthalmologists can remove cataracts, reduce glaucoma, and allow people with refractive errors to put their eyeglasses and contacts away. These cutting-edge procedures include:

- LASIK (laser in situ keratomileusis) to correct refractive errors. During this procedure, a surgeon uses a laser to reshape the cornea so that it refracts light directly onto the retina, rather than in front of or behind it. A microkeratome (surgical knife) is used to cut a flap in the cornea's outer layer. A computer-controlled laser sculpts the middle layer of the cornea and then the flap is replaced. The procedure takes only a few minutes, and patients recover their vision quickly and usually with little postoperative pain.

- Phacoemulsification to remove cataracts. During this procedure, a surgeon makes a very small incision (~3 mm long) through the sclera near the cornea's outer edge. An ultrasonic probe is inserted through this opening and into the center of the lens. The probe uses sound waves to emulsify the lens's central core, which is then suctioned out. An artificial lens is then permanently implanted in the lens capsule (see **Fig. 18-15**). The procedure is typically painless, although the patient may feel some discomfort for one to two days afterward.

- Laser trabeculoplasty to treat glaucoma. This procedure uses a laser to help drain fluid from the eye and lower intraocular pressure. The laser is aimed at drainage canals located between the cornea and iris and makes several burns that are believed to open the canals and allow better fluid drainage. The procedure is typically painless and takes only a few minutes.

18

Figure 18-14 **Visual disorders.**

causing hemorrhage, detachment of the retina, and blindness. The visual effects of diabetic retinopathy can be seen in **Figure 18-14C**.

See the figure on diabetic retinopathy in the Student Resources on thePoint.

CATARACT

A **cataract** is an opacity (cloudiness) of the lens that blurs vision (see **Fig. 18-14D**). Causes of cataract include disease,

injury, chemicals, and exposure to physical forces, especially the ultraviolet radiation in sunlight. The cataracts that frequently appear with age may result from exposure to environmental factors in combination with degeneration attributable to aging.

To prevent blindness, an ophthalmologist must remove the cloudy lens surgically. Commonly, the lens's anterior capsule is removed along with the cataract, leaving the posterior capsule in place (**Fig. 18-15**). In **phacoemulsification**, the lens is fragmented with high-frequency ultrasound and extracted through a small incision (**Box 18-3**). After cataract removal, an artificial intraocular lens (IOL) is

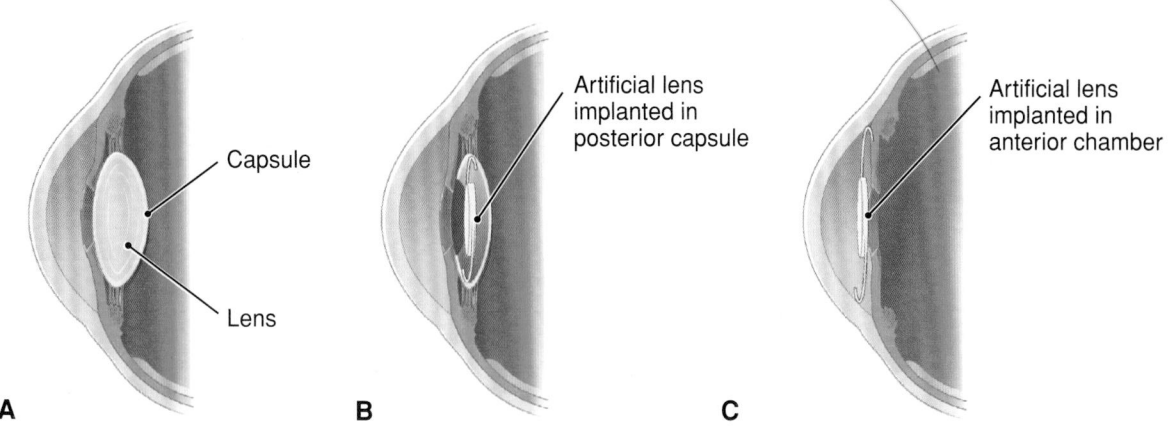

Figure 18-15 **Cataract extraction surgeries. A.** Cross-section of normal eye anatomy. **B.** Extracapsular lens extraction involves removing the lens but leaving the posterior capsule intact to receive a synthetic intraocular lens. **C.** Intracapsular lens extraction involves removing the lens and lens capsule and implanting a synthetic intraocular lens in the anterior chamber.

usually implanted to compensate for the missing lens. The original type of implant provides vision only within a fixed distance; newer implants are designed to allow for near and far accommodation. Alternatively, a person can wear a contact lens or special glasses.

GLAUCOMA

Glaucoma is an abnormal increase in pressure within the eyeball. It occurs when more aqueous humor is produced than can be drained away from the eye. There is pressure on blood vessels in the eye and on the optic nerve, leading to blindness. There are many causes of glaucoma, and screening for this disorder should be a part of every routine eye examination. Fetal infection with rubella (German measles) early in pregnancy can cause glaucoma, as well as cataracts and hearing impairment. Glaucoma is usually treated with medication to reduce pressure in the eye and occasionally is treated with surgery (**Box 18-3**).

Terminology	Key Terms

The Eye

Disorders

age-related macular degeneration (AMD)	Deterioration of the macula associated with aging; macular degeneration impairs central vision
astigmatism ah-STIG-mah-tizm	An error of refraction caused by irregularity in the curvature of the cornea or lens
cataract KAT-ah-rakt	Opacity of the lens of the eye
conjunctivitis kon-junk-tih-VI-tis	Inflammation of the conjunctiva; pink eye
diabetic retinopathy ret-ih-NOP-ah-the	Degenerative changes in the retina associated with diabetes mellitus
glaucoma glaw-KO-mah	An eye disease caused by increased intraocular pressure that damages the optic disk and causes vision loss; usually results from faulty fluid drainage from the anterior eye
hyperopia hi-per-O-pe-ah	A refractive error in which light rays focus behind the retina and objects can be seen clearly only when far from the eye; farsightedness; also called hypermetropia
myopia mi-O-pe-ah	A refractive error in which light rays focus in front of the retina and objects can be seen clearly only when very close to the eye; nearsightedness
ophthalmia neonatorum of-THAL-me-ah ne-o-na-TOR-um	Severe conjunctivitis usually caused by infection with gonococcus during birth
phacoemulsification fak-o-e-MUL-sih-fih-ka-shun	Removal of a cataract by ultrasonic destruction and extraction of the lens
presbyopia prez-be-O-pe-ah	Changes in the eye that occur with age; the lens loses elasticity and the ability to accommodate for near vision
retinal detachment	Separation of the retina from its underlying layer
trachoma trah-KO-mah	An infection caused by *Chlamydia trachomatis* leading to inflammation and scarring of the cornea and conjunctiva; a common cause of blindness in underdeveloped countries

| Terminology | **Supplementary Terms** |

The Eye

Normal Structure and Function

canthus *KAN-thus*	The angle at either end of the slit between the eyelids
diopter *DI-op-ter*	A measurement unit for the refractive power of a lens
emmetropia *em-eh-TRO-pe-ah*	The normal condition of the eye in refraction, in which parallel light rays focus exactly on the retina
fundus *FUN-dus*	A bottom or base; the region farthest from the opening of a structure; the eye's fundus is the posterior portion of the interior eyeball as seen with an ophthalmoscope
meibomian gland *mi-BO-me-an*	A sebaceous gland in the eyelid
tarsus *TAR-sus*	The framework of dense connective tissue that gives shape to the eyelid; tarsal plate
zonule *ZONE-ule*	A system of fibers that holds the lens in place; also called suspensory ligaments

Symptoms and Conditions

amblyopia *am-ble-O-pe-ah*	A condition that occurs when visual acuity is not the same in the two eyes in children (prefix ambly means "dim"); disuse of the poorer eye will result in blindness if not corrected; also called "lazy eye;" see K.L.'s opening case study on amblyopia
anisocoria *an-i-so-KO-re-ah*	Condition in which the two pupils (root: cor/o) are not of equal size
blepharoptosis *blef-ah-rop-TO-sis*	Drooping of the eyelid
chalazion *kah-LA-ze-on*	A small mass on the eyelid resulting from inflammation and blockage of a meibomian gland
drusen *DRU-zen*	Small growths that appear as tiny yellowish spots beneath the retina of the eye; typically occur with age but also occur in certain abnormal conditions
floater *FLO-ter*	A small moving object in the field of vision that originates in the vitreous body; floaters appear as spots or threads and are caused by benign degenerative or embryonic deposits in the vitreous body that cast a shadow on the retina
hordeolum *hor-DE-o-lum*	Inflammation of a sebaceous gland of the eyelid; a sty
keratoconus *ker-ah-to-KO-nus*	Conical protrusion of the corneal center
miosis *mi-O-sis*	Abnormal contraction of the pupils (from Greek *meiosis* meaning "diminution")
mydriasis *mih-DRI-ah-sis*	Pronounced or abnormal dilation of the pupil
nyctalopia *nik-tah-LO-pe-ah*	Night blindness; inability to see well in dim light or at night (root: nyct/o); often due to lack of vitamin A, which is used to make the pigment needed for vision in dim light

(continued)

Terminology | Supplementary Terms (Continued)

nystagmus *nis-TAG-mus*	Rapid, involuntary, rhythmic movements of the eyeball; may occur in neurologic diseases or disorders of the inner ear's vestibular apparatus
papilledema *pap-il-eh-DE-mah*	Swelling of the optic disk (papilla); choked disk
phlyctenule *FLIK-ten-ule*	A small blister or nodule on the cornea or conjunctiva
pseudophakia *su-do-FA-ke-ah*	A condition in which a cataractous lens has been removed and replaced with a plastic lens implant
retinitis *ret-in-I-tis*	Inflammation of the retina; causes include systemic disease, infection, hemorrhage, exposure to light
retinitis pigmentosa *ret-in-I-tis pig-men-TO-sah*	A hereditary chronic degenerative disease of the retina that begins in early childhood; there is atrophy of the optic nerve and clumping of pigment in the retina
retinoblastoma *ret-in-o-blas-TO-mah*	A malignant glioma of the retina; usually appears in early childhood and is sometimes hereditary; fatal if untreated, but current cure rates are high
scotoma *sko-TO-mah*	An area of diminished vision within the visual field
strabismus *strah-BIZ-mus*	A deviation of the eye in which the visual lines of each eye are not directed to the same object at the same time; also called heterotropia or squint; the various forms are referred to as -tropias, with the direction of turning (trop/o) indicated by a prefix, such as esotropia (inward), exotropia (outward), hypertropia (upward), and hypotropia (downward); the suffix -phoria is also used, as in esophoria
synechia *sin-EK-e-ah*	Adhesion of parts, especially adhesion of the iris to the lens and cornea (plural: synechiae)
xanthoma *zan-THO-mah*	A soft, slightly raised, yellowish patch or nodule usually on the eyelids; occurs in the elderly; also called xanthelasma

Diagnosis and Treatment

canthotomy *kan-THOT-o-me*	Surgical division of a canthus
cystotome *SIS-tih-tome*	Instrument for incising the lens capsule
electroretinography (ERG) *e-lek-tro-ret-ih-NOG-rah-fe*	Study of the retina's electrical response to light stimulation
enucleation *e-nu-kle-A-shun*	Surgical removal of the eyeball
gonioscopy *go-ne-OS-ko-pe*	Examination of the angle between the cornea and the iris (anterior chamber angle) in which fluids drain out of the eye (root *goni/o* means "angle")
keratometer *ker-ah-TOM-eh-ter*	An instrument for measuring the curvature of the cornea
mydriatic *mid-re-AT-ik*	A drug that causes dilation of the pupil
phorometer *fo-ROM-eh-ter*	An instrument for determining the degree and kind of strabismus

| Terminology | **Supplementary Terms** (*Continued*) |

retinoscope *RET-in-o-skope*	An instrument used to determine refractive errors of the eye; also called a skiascope (*SKI-ah-skope*)
slit-lamp biomicroscope	An instrument for examining the eye under magnification
Snellen chart *SNEL-en*	A chart printed with letters of decreasing size used to test visual acuity when viewed from a set distance; results reported as a fraction giving a subject's vision compared with normal vision at a distance of 20 feet
tarsorrhaphy *tar-SOR-ah-fe*	Suturing together of all or part of the upper and lower eyelids
tonometer *to-NOM-eh-ter*	An instrument used to measure fluid pressure in the eye

18

Go to the Audio Pronunciation Glossary in the Student Resources on thePoint to hear these terms pronounced.

| Terminology | **Abbreviations** |

The Eye

A, Acc	Accommodation		**HM**	Hand movements
AMD	Age-related macular degeneration		**IOL**	Intraocular lens
ARC	Abnormal retinal correspondence		**IOP**	Intraocular pressure
As, AST	Astigmatism		**NRC**	Normal retinal correspondence
cc	With correction		**NV**	Near vision
Em	Emmetropia		**sc**	Without correction
EOM	Extraocular movement, muscles		**VA**	Visual acuity
ERG	Electroretinography		**VF**	Visual field
ET	Esotropia		**XT**	Exotropia
FC	Finger counting			

Case Study Revisited

K.L.'s Follow-Up

K.L. started wearing the patch on her right eye during waking hours. She progressed to wearing it four to five hours a day as ordered by the ophthalmologist. The glasses she obtained from the optician were help-ing her to focus, and she was able to read her school-work. She had adjusted well to the treatment plan and showed improved vision. The family was satisfied with results from the therapeutic plan.

Labeling Exercise

THE EAR

Write the name of each numbered part on the corresponding line.

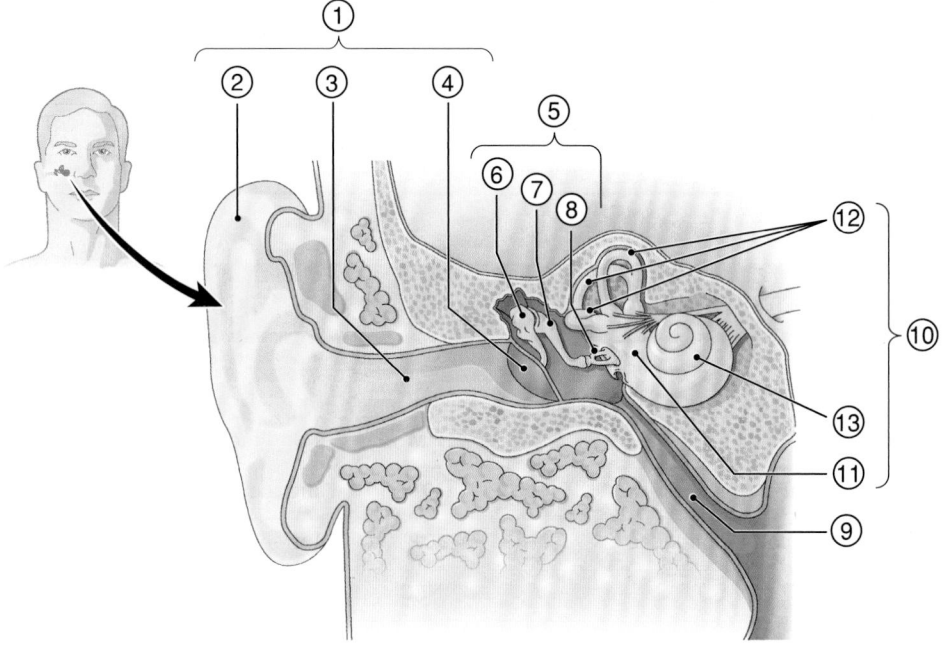

Cochlea	Outer ear
Auditory (Eustachian) tube	Pinna
External auditory canal	Semicircular canals
Incus	Stapes
Inner ear	Tympanic membrane
Malleus	Vestibule
Ossicles (of middle ear)	

1. _____

2. _____

3. _____

4. _____

5. _____

6. _____

7. _____

8. _____

9. _____

10. _____

11. _____

12. _____

13. _____

THE EYE

Write the name of each numbered part on the corresponding line.

Aqueous humor Lens
Choroid Optic disk (blind spot)
Ciliary muscle Optic nerve
Conjunctival sac Pupil
Cornea Retina
Fovea Sclera
Iris Vitreous body

1. _____

2. _____

3. _____

4. _____

5. _____

6. _____

7. _____

8. _____

9. _____

10. _____

11. _____

12. _____

13. _____

14. _____

Terminology

MATCHING

Match the following terms, and write the appropriate letter to the left of each number.

_____ **1.** palpebra

_____ **2.** ossicle

_____ **3.** rods and cones

_____ **4.** vestibular apparatus

_____ **5.** lens

a. small bone

b. structure that changes shape for near and far vision

c. an eyelid

d. location of equilibrium receptors

e. vision receptors

_____ **6.** tactile

_____ **7.** tinnitus

_____ **8.** hyperesthesia

_____ **9.** fovea

_____ **10.** hemianopia

a. increased sensation

b. blindness in half the visual field

c. point of sharpest vision

d. pertaining to touch

e. sensation of noises in the ear

_____ **11.** anacusis

_____ **12.** ophthalmoplegia

_____ **13.** phacomalacia

_____ **14.** parosmia

_____ **15.** keratoplasty

a. corneal transplant

b. abnormal smell perception

c. paralysis of an eye muscle

d. softening of the lens

e. total loss of hearing

Supplementary Terms

_____ **16.** diopter

a. angle between the eyelids

_____ **17.** mastoid process

b. small muscle attached to an ear ossicle

_____ **18.** stapedius

c. projection of the temporal bone

_____ **19.** canthus

d. unit of sound intensity

_____ **20.** decibel

e. unit for measuring the refractive power of the lens

_____ **21.** emmetropia

a. abnormal dilation of the pupil

_____ **22.** nystagmus

b. small growths beneath the retina

_____ **23.** mydriasis

c. rapid, involuntary eye movements

_____ **24.** drusen

d. normal refraction of the eye

_____ **25.** amblyopia

e. commonly called "lazy eye"

_____ **26.** AMD

a. irregularity in the curve of the eye

_____ **27.** Hz

b. an implanted lens

_____ **28.** AST

c. otorhinolaryngology

_____ **29.** ENT

d. eye disorder associated with aging

_____ **30.** IOL

e. a unit for measuring pitch of sound

FILL IN THE BLANKS

31. The scientific name for the eardrum is _____.

32. The type of hearing loss resulting from damage to the eighth cranial nerve is described as _____.

33. The ossicle that is in contact with the inner ear is the _____.

34. The outermost layer of the eye wall is the _____.

35. The bending of light rays as they pass through the eye is _____.

36. The innermost layer of the eye that contains the receptors for vision is the _____.

37. The transparent extension of the sclera that covers the front of the eye is the _____.

38. The sense of awareness of body position is _____.

DEFINITIONS

Define the following words.

39. audiologist (*aw-de-OL-o-jist*) _____

40. ophthalmometer (*of-thal-MOM-eh-ter*) _____

41. aphakia (*ah-FA-ke-ah*) _____

42. subscleral (*sub-skle-ral*) _____

43. iridotomy (*ir-ih-DOT-o-me*) _____

44. myringoscope (*mih-RING-go-skope*) _____

45. perilental (*per-e-LEN-til*) _____

46. dacryorrhea (*dak-re-o-RE-ah*) _____

47. presbycusis (*pres-be-KU-sis*) _____

48. keratoiritis (*ker-ah-to-i-RI-tis*) _____

Write words for the following definitions.

49. softening of the lens _____

50. measurement of the pupil _____

51. surgical removal of the stapes _____

52. drooping of the eyelid _____

53. plastic repair of the ear _____

54. pertaining to the vestibular apparatus and cochlea _____

55. any disease of the retina _____

56. absence of pain _____

57. pertaining to tears _____

58. excision of (part of) the ciliary body _____

59. endoscopic examination of the auditory tube _____

60. technical name for farsightedness _____

ADJECTIVES

Write the adjective form of the following words.

61. cochlea _____

62. palpebra _____

63. choroid _____

64. uvea _____

65. cornea _____

66. sclera _____

67. pupil _____

OPPOSITES

Write words that mean the opposite of the following.

68. hyperesthesia _____

69. hypalgesia _____

70. cc _____

71. hyperopia _____

72. mydriasis _____

73. esotropia _____

WORD BUILDING

Write words for the following definitions using the word parts provided.

| -pexy | -ia | osm/o | kerat/o | -al | -schisis | -scopy | pseud/o- | retin/o | an- | -plasty | salping/o | sub | -myring/o |

74. false sense of smell _____

75. plastic repair of the tympanic membrane _____

76. examination of the retina _____

77. examination of the auditory tube _____

78. absence of the sense of smell _____

79. splitting of the retina _____

80. examination of the tympanic membrane _____

81. beneath the retina _____

82. surgical fixation of the retina _____

83. examination of the cornea _____

TRUE-FALSE

Examine the following statements. If the statement is true, write T in the first blank. If the statement is false, write F in the first blank, and correct the statement by replacing the underlined word in the second blank.

	True or False	**Correct Answer**
84. The spiral organ is located in the <u>vestibule</u> of the inner ear.	_____	_____
85. An osmoceptor is a receptor for the sense of <u>smell</u>.	_____	_____
86. The malleus is located in the <u>middle ear</u>.	_____	_____
87. Gustation is the sense of <u>taste</u>.	_____	_____
88. Hypergeusia is an abnormal increase in the sense of <u>touch</u>.	_____	_____
89. In bright light the pupils <u>dilate</u>.	_____	_____
90. A myringotomy is incision of the <u>stapes</u>.	_____	_____
91. The lacrimal gland produces <u>aqueous humor</u>.	_____	_____

ELIMINATION

In each of the sets below, underline the word that does not fit in with the rest, and explain the reason for your choice.

92. pressure — temperature — smell — touch — pain

_____

93. cochlea — pinna — vestibule — oval window — semicircular canals

_____

94. incus — lacrimal gland — eyelash — conjunctiva — palpebra

_____

95. glaucoma — myopia — cataract — macular degeneration — presbycusis

_____

WORD ANALYSIS

Define the following words, and give the meaning of the word parts in each. Use a dictionary if necessary.

96. asthenopia (*as-the-NO-pe-ah*) _____

    a. a- _____

    b. sthen/o _____

    c. -op(s) _____

    d. -ia _____

97. pseudophakia (*su-do-FA-ke-ah*) _____

    a. pseudo _____

    b. phak/o _____

    c. -ia _____

98. cholesteatoma (*ko-les-te-ah-TO-mah*) _____

    a. chol/e _____

    b. steat/o _____

    c. -oma _____

99. exotropia (*ek-so-TRO-pe-ah*) _____

    a. ex/o- _____

    b. trop/o _____

    c. -ia _____

100. anisometropia (*an-i-so-meh-TRO-pe-ah*) _____

    a. an- _____

    b. iso- _____

    c. metr/o _____

    d. op(s) _____

    e. -ia _____

For more learning activities, see Chapter 18 of the Student Resources on thePoint.

Additional Case Studies

Case Study 18-1: *Audiology Report*

S.R., a 55 year-old man, reported decreased hearing sensitivity in his left ear for the past three years. In addition to hearing loss, he was experiencing tinnitus and aural fullness. Pure-tone test results revealed normal hearing sensitivity for the right ear and a moderate sensorineural hearing loss in the left ear. Speech thresholds were appropriate for the degree of hearing loss noted. Word recognition was excellent for the right ear and poor for the left ear when the signal was present at a suprathreshold level. Tympanograms were characterized by normal shape, amplitude, and peak pressure points bilaterally. The contralateral acoustic reflex was normal for the right ear but absent for the left ear at the frequencies tested (500 to 4,000 Hz). The ipsilateral acoustic reflex was present with the probe in the right ear and absent with the probe in the left ear. Brainstem auditory evoked potentials (BAEPs) were within normal range for the right ear. No repeatable response was observed from the left ear. A subsequent MRI showed a 1-cm acoustic neuroma.

Case Study 18-2: *Phacoemulsification with Intraocular Lens Implant*

W.S., a 68 y/o, was scheduled for surgery for a cataract and relief from "floaters," which she had noticed in her visual field since her surgery for a retinal detachment the previous year. She reported to the ambulatory surgery center an hour before her scheduled procedure. Before transfer to the operating room, she spoke with her ophthalmologist, who reviewed the surgical plan. Her right eye was identified as the operative eye, and it was marked with a "yes" and the surgeon's initials on the lid. She was given anesthetic drops in the right eye and an intravenous bolus of 2 mg of midazolam (Versed).

In the OR, W.S. and her operative eye were again identified by the surgeon, anesthetist, and nurses. After anesthesia and akinesia were achieved, the eye area was prepped and draped in sterile sheets. An operating microscope with video system was positioned over her eye. A 5-0 silk suture was placed through the superior rectus muscle to retract the eye. A lid speculum was placed to open the eye. A minimal conjunctival peritomy was performed, and hemostasis was achieved with wet-field cautery. The anterior chamber was entered at the 10:30 o'clock position. A capsulotomy was performed after Healon was placed in the anterior chamber. Phacoemulsification was carried out without difficulty. The remaining cortex was removed by irrigation and aspiration.

An intraocular lens (IOL) was placed into the posterior chamber. Miochol was injected to achieve papillary miosis, and the wound was closed with one 10-0 suture. Subconjunctival Celestone and Garamycin were injected. The lid speculum and retraction suture were removed. After application of Eserine and Bacitracin ointments, the eye was patched, and a shield was applied. W.S. left the OR in good condition and was discharged to home for four hours later.

Case Study Questions

Multiple Choice. Select the best answer, and write the letter of your choice to the left of each number.

_____ **1.** The study of hearing is termed
     a. acousticology
     b. radio frequency
     c. audiology
     d. otology

_____ **2.** Sensorineural hearing loss may result from
     a. damage to the second cranial nerve
     b. damage to the eighth cranial nerve
     c. otosclerosis
     d. otitis media

_____ **3.** The term that means "on the same side" is
     a. contralateral
     b. bilateral
     c. distal
     d. ipsilateral

_____ **4.** Another name for an acoustic neuroma is
     a. macular degeneration
     b. acoustic neurilemmoma
     c. auditory otosclerosis
     d. acoustic glaucoma

_____ **5.** Ultrasound destruction and aspiration of the lens is called
   a. catarectomy
   b. phacoemulsification
   c. stapedectomy
   d. radial keratotomy

_____ **6.** The term akinesia means
   a. movement
   b. lack of sensation
   c. washing
   d. lack of movement

Write terms from the case studies with the following meanings.

7. above a minimum level _____

8. pertaining to or perceived by the ear _____

9. record obtained by tympanometry _____

10. pertaining to sound or hearing _____

11. physician who specializes in conditions of the eye _____

12. perception of sounds, such as ringing or tinkling in the ear _____

13. a circular incision through the conjunctiva _____

14. within the eye _____

15. abnormal contraction of the pupil _____

16. below the conjunctiva _____

Define the following abbreviations:

17. Hz _____

18. BAEP _____

19. IOL _____

18

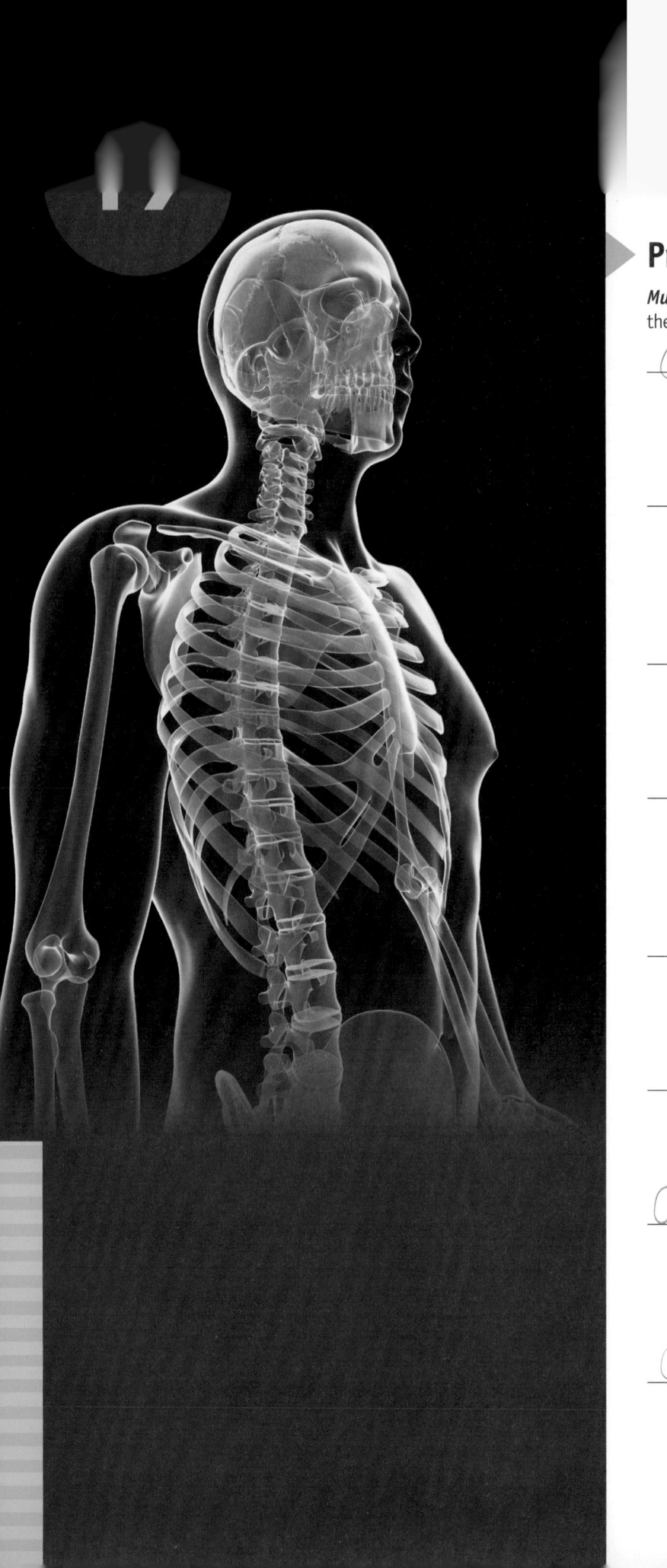

Pretest

Multiple Choice. Select the best answer, and write the letter of your choice to the left of each number.

___d___ 1. The root *oste/o* means
   a. cartilage
   b. fat
   c. heart
   d. bone

_____ 2. The root *myel/o* refers to the spinal cord. Used in reference to bones it means
   a. bone marrow
   b. joint
   c. bone shaft
   d. membrane

_____ 3. A bone of the spinal column is a
   a. ventricle
   b. cortex
   c. labyrinth
   d. vertebra

_____ 4. The large, flared superior bone of the pelvis is the
   a. phalange
   b. ilium
   c. thorax
   d. duodenum

_____ 5. The bones of the wrist are the
   a. digits
   b. cervices
   c. carpals
   d. ribs

_____ 6. The bone of the thigh is the
   a. patella
   b. cranium
   c. umbilicus
   d. femur

___a___ 7. A general term for inflammation of a joint is
   a. arthritis
   b. conjunctivitis
   c. epididymitis
   d. myocarditis

___c___ 8. Chondrosarcoma is a tumor that originates in
   a. adipose tissue
   b. bone
   c. cartilage
   d. muscle

Learning Objectives

After study of this chapter, you should be able to:

1 ▷ Compare the axial skeleton and the appendicular skeleton. *p496*

2 ▷ Briefly describe the formation of bone tissue. *p499*

3 ▷ Describe the structure of a long bone. *p499*

4 ▷ Compare a suture, a symphysis, and a synovial joint. *p499*

5 ▷ Describe the structure of a synovial joint. *p500*

6 ▷ Identify and use roots pertaining to the skeleton. *p502*

7 ▷ Describe six disorders that affect the skeleton and joints. *p504*

8 ▷ Interpret abbreviations used in relation to the skeleton. *p519*

9 ▷ Analyze medical terms in case studies related to the skeleton. *pp495, 528*

Case Study: *L.R.'s Idiopathic Adolescent Scoliosis*

Chief Complaint

Four years ago, L.R., a 15-year-old female, had a posterior spinal fusion (PSF) for correction of idiopathic adolescent scoliosis in a pediatric orthopedic hospital in another state. L.R. is a gifted musician, and her favorite pastime is playing the piano, guitar, and other musical instruments. Lately she has experienced considerable back pain that she attributed to long hours at the piano or playing the guitar. It was time for her routine follow-up orthopedic visit, and now she presents with a significant prominence of the right scapula and back pain in the mid- and lower back.

Examination

A history was taken and medical records were reviewed followed by a physical examination. The medical records indicated that the patient's spinal curvature had been surgically corrected with the insertion of bilateral laminar and pedicle hooks and two 3/16-inch rods. A bone autograft was taken from L.R.'s right posterior superior ilium and applied along the lateral processes of T4 to L2 to complete the fusion. The physical examination was normal except for surgical scarring along the spine, a projecting right scapula, and asymmetry of the rib cage. During the history, L.R. denied numbness or tingling of the lower extremities, bowel or bladder problems, chest pain, or shortness of breath. The physician ordered a CT scan to determine if there had been continued growth on the anterior portion of the spine following the posterior fusion.

Clinical Course

The results of the CT scan of the upper thoracic spine showed a prominent rotatory scoliosis deformity of the right posterior thorax with acute angulation of the ribs. L.R.'s deformity is a common consequence of overcorrection of prior spinal fusion surgery, called crankshaft phenomenon.

L.R. was referred to the chief spinal surgeon of a local pediatric orthopedic hospital for removal of the spinal instrumentation, posterior spinal osteotomies from T4 to L2, insertion of replacement hooks and rods, bilateral rib resections, autograft bone from the resected ribs, partial scapulectomy and possible bone allograft, and bilateral chest tube placement. The surgical plan was explained to her and her mother, and consent was obtained and signed. The surgical procedure and the potential benefits versus risks were discussed. L.R. and her parents stated that they fully understood and provided consent to proceed with the plan for surgery.

ANCILLARIES *At-A-Glance*

Visit thePoint to access the following resources. For guidance in using the resources most effectively, see pp. ix–xvi.

Learning RESOURCES

▷ Tips for Effective Studying
▷ Web Figure: Comparison of Male and Female Pelves
▷ Web Figure: Bone Markings and Formations
▷ Web Chart: Bones of the Skull
▷ Web Chart: Joints

▷ Animation: Bone Growth
▷ Audio Pronunciation Glossary

Learning ACTIVITIES

▷ Visual Activities
▷ Kinesthetic Activities
▷ Auditory Activities

Introduction

The **skeleton** forms the framework of the body, protects vital organs, and works with the muscular system to produce movement at the **joints**. The human adult skeleton is composed of 206 **bones**, which are organized for study into two divisions.

Divisions of the Skeleton

The axial skeleton forms the central core or "axis" of the body's bony framework (**Fig. 19-1**). It consists of:

- The skull, made up of eight cranial bones and 14 bones of the face (**Fig. 19-2**). The skull bones are joined by immovable joints (sutures), except for the joint between the lower jaw (mandible) and the temporal bone of the cranium, the temporomandibular joint (TMJ).

- The spinal column (**Fig. 19-3**) consisting of 26 vertebrae. Between the vertebrae are disks of cartilage that add strength and flexibility to the spine. The five groups of vertebrae, listed from superior to inferior with the number of bones in each group are:

1. Cervical (7), designated C1 to C7. The first and second cervical vertebrae also have specific names, the **atlas** and the **axis**, respectively (see **Fig 19-3**).
2. Thoracic (12), designated T1 to T12
3. Lumbar (5), designated L1 to L5
4. The sacrum (S), composed of five fused bones
5. The coccyx (Co), composed of four to five fused bones

- The **thorax**, consisting of 12 pairs of ribs joined by cartilage to the sternum (breastbone). The rib cage encloses and protects the thoracic organs.

Cranium

Facial bones

Mandible

Sternum

Costal cartilage

Vertebral column

Ilium (of pelvis)

Pelvis

Sacrum

Calcaneus

Clavicle

Scapula

Humerus

Ribs

Radius

Carpals

Ulna

Meta-carpals

Phalanges

Femur

Patella

Fibula

Tibia

Tarsals

Metatarsals   Phalanges

Figure 19-1 **The skeleton.** The axial skeleton is shown in yellow; the appendicular in blue.

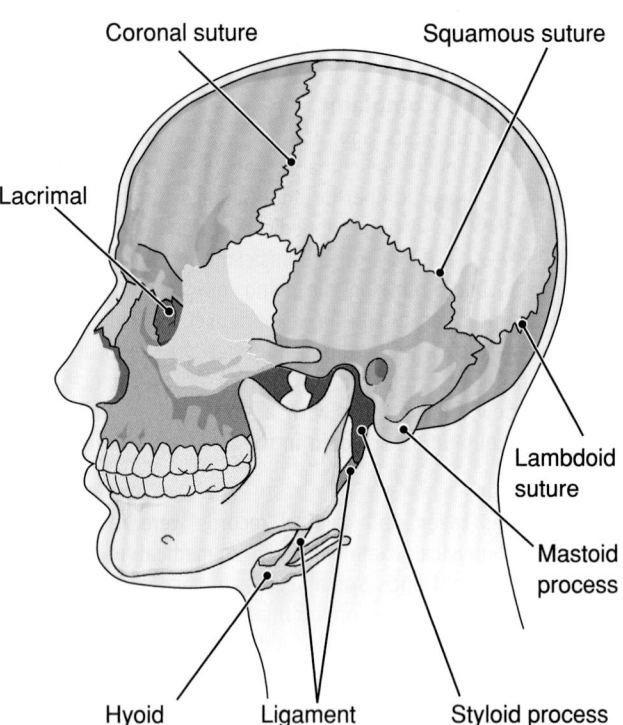

Coronal suture   Squamous suture

Lacrimal

Lambdoid suture

Mastoid process

Hyoid   Ligament   Styloid process

Bones of the skull:

☐	Frontal	☐	Maxilla
☐	Parietal	☐	Occiptial
☐	Sphenoid	☐	Zygomatic
☐	Temporal	☐	Mandible
☐	Nasal		

Figure 19-2 **The skull from the left.** An additional cranial bone, the ethmoid (*ETH-moyd*), is visible mainly from the interior of the skull. The hyoid is considered part of the axial skeleton but is not attached to any other bones. The tongue and other muscles are attached to the hyoid.

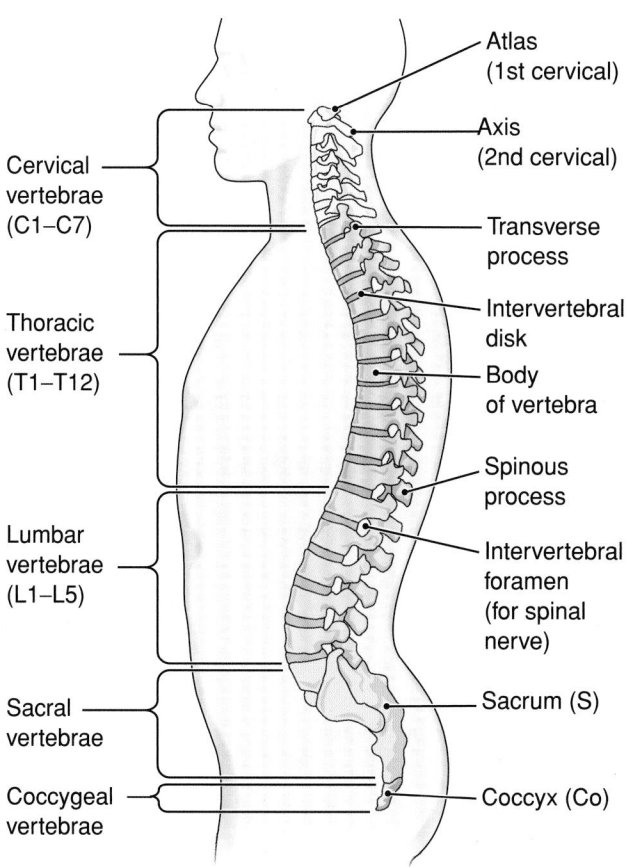

19

The appendicular skeleton is attached or "appended" to the axial skeleton (see **Fig. 19-1**). The upper division includes:

- The bones of the shoulder girdle, the clavicle (collar bone), and scapula (shoulder blade)
- The bones of the upper extremities (arms), the humerus, radius, ulna, carpals (wrist bones), metacarpals (bones of the palm), and phalanges (finger bones)

The lower division includes:

- The pelvic bones, two large bones that join the sacrum and coccyx to form the bony **pelvis**. Each pelvic or hip bone (os coxae) is formed by three fused bones: the large, flared **ilium**; the ischium; and the pubis (**Fig. 19-4**). The deep socket in the hip bone that holds the head of the femur is the **acetabulum**. The female pelvis is wider than the male pelvis and has other differences to accommodate childbirth.
- The bones of the lower extremities (legs), the femur, patella (kneecap), tibia, fibula, tarsals (ankle bones), metatarsals (bones of the instep), and phalanges (toe bones). The large tarsal bone that forms the heel is the calcaneus (*kal-KA-ne-us*), shown in **Figure 19-1**.

All of these bone groups, and also the hyoid under the jaw and the ear ossicles, are listed with phonetic pronunciations and described in **Box 19-1**.

Figure 19-3 **Vertebral column, left lateral view.** The number of vertebrae in each group and the abbreviations for each are shown. The sacrum and coccyx are formed from fused bones.

See a chart on bones of the skull and a figure comparing the male and female pelves in the Student Resources on thePoint.

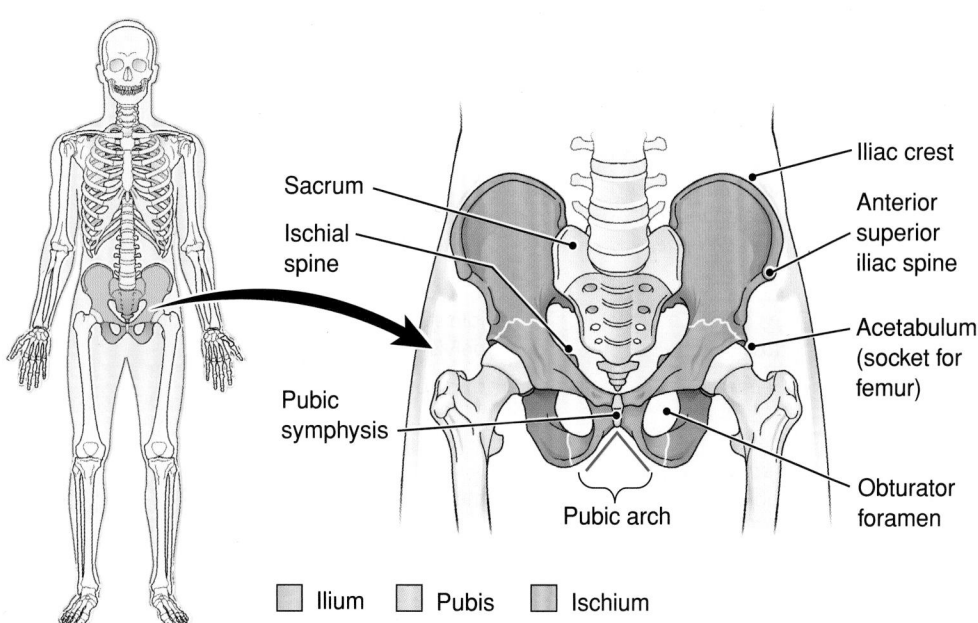

Ilium   Pubis   Ischium

Figure 19-4 **The pelvic bones.** Each pelvic or hip bone is formed from three fused bones, the ilium, ischium, and pubis. Together with the sacrum and coccyx, they form the bony pelvis. The acetabulum is the socket for the femur.

FOR YOUR REFERENCE

Box 19-1

Bones of the Skeleton

Region	Bones	Description
AXIAL SKELETON *(AK-se-al)*		
SKULL		
cranium *(KRA-ne-um)*	cranial bones (8)	form the chamber enclosing the brain; house the ear and form part of the eye socket
facial portion *(FA-shal)*	facial bones (14)	form the face and chambers for sensory organs
hyoid *(HI-oyd)*		U-shaped bone under mandible (lower jaw); used for muscle attachments
ossicles *(OS-ih-klz)*	ear bones (3)	transmit sound waves through middle ear
TRUNK		
vertebral column *(VER-teh-bral)*	vertebrae (26) *(VER-teh-bre)*	enclose the spinal cord
thorax *(THO-raks)*	sternum *(STER-num)* ribs (12 pairs)	anterior bone of the thorax enclose the organs of the thorax
APPENDICULAR SKELETON *(ap-en-DIK-u-lar)*		
UPPER DIVISION		
shoulder girdle	clavicle *(KLAV-ih-kel)*	anterior, between sternum and scapula
	scapula *(SKAP-u-lah)*	posterior, anchors muscles that move arm
upper extremity	humerus *(HU-mer-us)*	proximal arm bone
	ulna *(UL-nah)*	medial bone of forearm
	radius *(RA-de-us)*	lateral bone of forearm
	carpals (8) *(KAR-palz)*	wrist bones
	metacarpals (5) *(met-ah-KAR-palz)*	bones of palm
	phalanges (14) *(fah-LAN-jeze)*	bones of fingers
LOWER DIVISION		
pelvic bones *(PEL-vic)*	os coxae (2) *(os KOK-se)*	join sacrum and coccyx of vertebral column to form the bony pelvis
lower extremity	femur *(FE-mur)*	thigh bone
	patella *(pah-TEL-ah)*	kneecap
	tibia *(TIB-e-ah)*	medial bone of leg
	fibula *(FIB-u-lah)*	lateral bone of leg
	tarsal bones (7) *(TAR-sal)*	ankle bones; the large heel bone is the calcaneus *(kal-KA-ne-us)*
	metatarsals (5) *(met-ah-TAR-salz)*	bones of instep
	phalanges (14) *(fah-LAN-jeze)*	bones of toes

Bone Formation

Bone is formed by the gradual addition of calcium and phosphorus salts to *cartilage*, a type of dense connective tissue. This process of **ossification** begins before birth and continues to adulthood. Although bone appears to be inert, it is actually living tissue that is constantly being replaced and remodeled throughout life. Three types of cells are involved in these changes:

- **Osteoblasts**, the cells that produce bone
- **Osteocytes**, mature bone cells that help to maintain bone tissue
- **Osteoclasts**, involved in the breakdown of bone tissue to release needed minerals or to allow for reshaping and repair

The process of destroying bone so that its components can be taken into the circulation is called **resorption**. This activity occurs continuously and is normally in balance with bone formation. In disease states, resorption may occur more rapidly or more slowly than bone production.

See the animation "Bone Growth" in the Student Resources on thePoint.

Structure of a Long Bone

A typical long bone (**Fig. 19-5**) has a shaft or **diaphysis** composed of compact bone tissue. Within the shaft is a medullary cavity containing the yellow form of **bone marrow**, which is high in fat. The irregular **epiphysis** at either end is made of a less dense, spongy (cancellous) bone tissue (**Fig. 19-6**).

The spaces in spongy bone contain the blood-forming red bone marrow. A layer of cartilage covers the epiphysis to protect the bone surface at a joint. The thin layer of fibrous tissue, or **periosteum**, that covers the bone's outer surface nourishes and protects the bone and also generates new bone cells for growth and repair.

Between the diaphysis and the epiphysis at each end, in a region called the **metaphysis**, is the growth region or **epiphyseal plate**. Long bones continue to grow in length at these regions throughout childhood and into early adulthood. When the bone stops elongating, this area becomes fully calcified but remains visible as the epiphyseal line (**Fig. 19-5**).

Long bones are found in the arms, legs, hands, and feet. Other bones are described as:

- Flat (e.g., cranial bones, ribs, scapulae)
- Short (e.g., wrist and ankle bones)
- Irregular (e.g., facial bones, vertebrae)

Joints

The joints, or articulations, are classified according to the degree of movement they allow:

- A **suture** is an immovable joint held together by fibrous connective tissue, as is found between the bones of the skull (see **Fig. 19-2**).

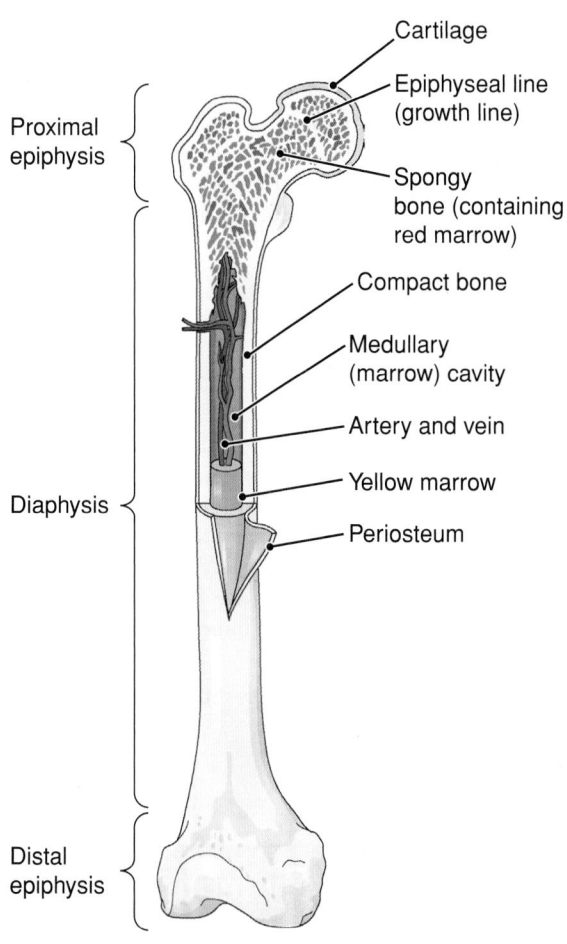

Figure 19-5 Structure of a long bone.

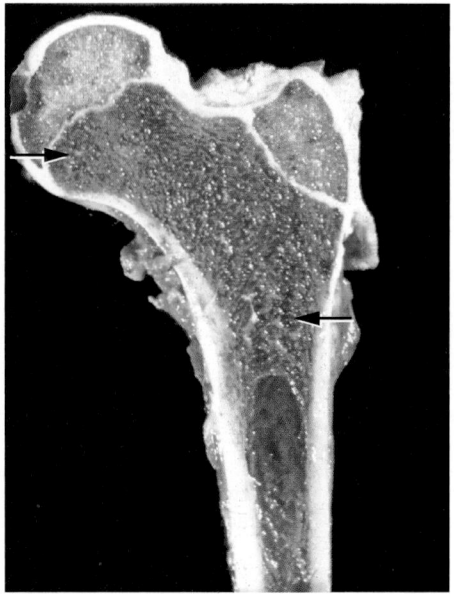

Figure 19-6 Bone tissue, longitudinal section. The epiphysis (end) of this long bone has an outer layer of compact bone. The remainder of the tissue is spongy (cancellous) bone, shown by the *arrows*. Transverse growth lines are also visible.

- A **symphysis** is a slightly movable joint connected by fibrous cartilage. Examples are the joints between the bodies of the vertebrae (see **Fig. 19-3**) and the joint between the pubic bones (see **Fig. 19-4**).
- A **synovial joint**, or **diarthrosis**, is a freely movable joint. Such joints allow for a wide range of movements, as described in Chapter 20. **Tendons** attach muscles to bones to produce movement at the joints.

Freely movable joints are subject to wear and tear, and they therefore have some protective features (**Fig. 19-7**). The cavity of a diarthrotic joint contains **synovial fluid**, which cushions and lubricates the joint. This fluid is produced by the synovial membrane that lines the joint cavity. The ends of the articulating bones are cushioned and protected by cartilage. A fibrous capsule, continuous with the periosteum, encloses the joint. Synovial joints are stabilized and strengthened by **ligaments**, which connect the articulating bones. A **bursa** is a small sac of synovial fluid that cushions the area around a joint. Bursae are found at stress points between tendons, ligaments, and bones (see **Fig. 19-7**).

See the chart on joints in the Student Resources on thePoint.

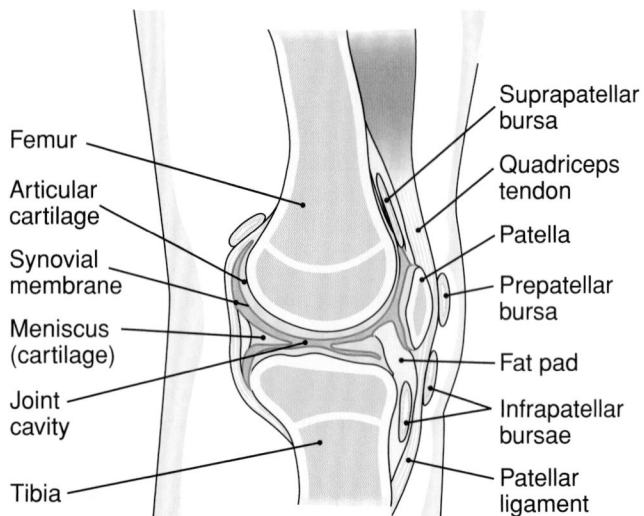

Figure 19-7 **The knee joint, sagittal section.** The knee joint is an example of a freely movable, synovial joint, also called a diarthrosis. Synovial fluid fills the joint cavity. Other protective structures such as the cartilage, joint capsule, ligaments, and bursae are also shown.

| Terminology | Key Terms |

Normal Structure and Function

acetabulum *as-eh-TAB-u-lum*	The bony socket in the hip bone that holds the head of the femur (from the Latin word for vinegar because it resembles the base of a vinegar cruet) (see **Fig 19-4**)
articulation *ar-tik-u-LA-shun*	A joint (adjective: articular)
atlas *AT-las*	The first cervical vertebra (see **Fig. 19-3**) (root: atlant/o)
axis *AK-sis*	The second cervical vertebra (see **Fig. 19-3**)
bone	A calcified form of dense connective tissue; osseous tissue; also an individual unit of the skeleton made of such tissue (root: oste/o)
bone marrow	The soft material that fills bone cavities; yellow marrow fills the central cavity of the long bones; blood cells are formed in red bone marrow, which is located in spongy bone tissue (root: myel/o)
bursa *BUR-sah*	A fluid-filled sac that reduces friction near a joint (root: burs/o)
cartilage *KAR-tih-lij*	A type of dense connective tissue that is found in the skeleton, larynx, trachea, and bronchi; it is the precursor to most bone tissue (root: chondr/o)
diarthrosis *di-ar-THRO-sis*	A freely movable joint; also called a synovial joint (adjective: diarthrotic)
diaphysis *di-AF-ih-sis*	The shaft of a long bone

Terminology	Key Terms *(Continued)*

epiphyseal plate *ep-ih-FIZ-e-al*	The growth region of a long bone; located in the metaphysis, between the diaphysis and epiphysis; when bone growth ceases, this area appears as the epiphyseal line; also spelled epiphysial
epiphysis *eh-PIF-ih-sis*	The irregularly shaped end of a long bone
ilium *IL-e-um*	The large, flared, superior portion of the pelvic bone (root: ili/o) (adjective: iliac)
joint	The junction between two bones; articulation (root: arthr/o)
ligament *LIG-ah-ment*	A strong band of connective tissue that joins one bone to another
metaphysis *meh-TAF-ih-sis*	The region of a long bone between the diaphysis (shaft) and epiphysis (end); during development, the growing region of a long bone
ossification *os-ih-fih-KA-shun*	The formation of bone tissue (from Latin *os*, meaning "bone")
osteoblast *OS-te-o-blast*	A cell that produces bone tissue
osteoclast *OS-te-o-clast*	A cell that destroys bone tissue
osteocyte *OS-te-o-site*	A mature bone cell that nourishes and maintains bone tissue
pelvis *(PEL-vis)*	The large ring of bone at the inferior trunk formed of the two hip bones (ossa coxae) joined to the sacrum and coccyx; each os coxae is formed of three bones: the superior, flared ilium (*IL-e-um*); ischium (*IS-ke-um*); and pubis (*PU-bis*) (plural: pelves [*PEL-veze*])
periosteum *per-e-OS-te-um*	The fibrous membrane that covers a bone's surface
resorption *re-SORP-shun*	Removal of bone by breakdown and absorption into the circulation
skeleton *SKEL-eh-ton*	The body's bony framework, consisting of 206 bones; the axial portion (80 bones) is composed of the skull, spinal column, ribs, and sternum; the appendicular skeleton (126 bones) contains the bones of the arms and legs, shoulder girdle, and pelvis (root: skelet/o)
suture *SU-chur*	An immovable joint, such as the joints between the skull bones
symphysis *SIM-fih-sis*	A slightly movable joint
synovial fluid *sih-NO-ve-al*	The fluid contained in a freely movable (diarthrotic) joint; synovia (root: synov/i)
synovial joint	A freely movable joint; has a joint cavity containing synovial fluid; a diarthrosis
tendon *TEN-don*	A fibrous band of connective tissue that attaches a muscle to a bone
thorax *THO-raks*	The upper part of the trunk between the neck and the abdomen; formed by the 12 pairs of ribs and sternum

Go to the Audio Pronunciation Glossary in the Student Resources on thePoint to hear these terms pronounced.

Roots Pertaining to the Skeleton, Bones, and Joints

See Tables 19-1 and 19-2.

Table 19-1	Roots for Bones and Joints		
Root	**Meaning**	**Example**	**Definition of Example**
oste/o	bone	osteopenia *os-te-o-PE-ne-ah*	deficiency of bone tissue
myel/o	bone marrow; also, spinal cord	myeloid *MI-eh-loyd*	pertaining to or resembling bone marrow
chondr/o	cartilage	chondroblast *KON-dro-blast*	a cartilage-forming cell
arthr/o	joint	arthrosis *ar-THRO-sis*	joint; condition affecting a joint
synov/i	synovial fluid, joint, or membrane	asynovia *ah-sin-O-ve-ah*	lack of synovial fluid
burs/o	bursa	peribursal *per-ih-BER-sal*	around a bursa

EXERCISE 19-1

Fill in the blanks.

1. Arthrodesis (*ar-THROD-eh-sis*) is fusion of a(n) _____.

2. Myelogenous (*mi-eh-LOJ-eh-nus*) means originating in _____.

3. Osteolysis (*os-te-OL-ih-sis*) is destruction of _____.

4. A chondrocyte (*KON-dro-site*) is a cell found in _____.

5. A bursolith (*BUR-so-lith*) is a stone in a(n) _____.

Define the following words.

6. arthrocentesis (*ar-thro-sen-TE-sis*) _____

7. myelopoiesis (*mi-eh-lo-poy-E-sis*) _____

8. chondrodynia (*kon-dro-dih-ne-ah*) _____

9. osteoid (*OS-te-oyd*) _____

10. bursitis (*bur-SI-tis*) _____

11. synovial (*sih-NO-ve-al*) _____

Write words for the following definitions.

12. inflammation of bone and bone marrow   _____

13. a bone-forming cell   _____

14. pertaining to or resembling cartilage   _____

15. any disease of a joint   _____

16. inflammation of a synovial membrane   _____

EXERCISE 19-1 *(Continued)*

17. radiography of the spinal cord _____

18. incision of a bursa _____

19. tumor of bone marrow _____

20. instrument for examining the interior of a joint _____

The word ostosis means "bone growth." Use this as a suffix for the following two words.

21. excess growth of bone _____

22. abnormal growth of bone _____

Table 19-2	Roots for the Skeleton		
Root	**Meaning**	**Example**	**Definition of Example**
crani/o	skull, cranium	craniometry *kra-ne-OM-eh-tre*	measurement of the cranium
spondyl/o	vertebra	spondylolysis *spon-dih-LOL-ih-sis*	destruction and separation of a vertebra
vertebr/o	vertebra, spinal column	paravertebral *pah-rah-VER-te-bral*	near the vertebrae or spinal column
rachi/o	spine	rachischisis *ra-KIS-kih-sis*	fissure (-schisis) of the spine; spina bifida
cost/o	rib	costochondral *kos-to-KON-dral*	pertaining to a rib and its cartilage
sacr/o	sacrum	presacral *pre-SA-kral*	in front of the sacrum
coccy, coccyg/o	coccyx	coccygeal[a] *kok-SIJ-e-al*	pertaining to the coccyx
pelvi/o	pelvis	pelviscope *PEL-vih-skope*	endoscope for examining the pelvis
ili/o	ilium	iliopelvic *il-e-o-PEL-vik*	pertaining to the ilium and pelvis

[a]Note spelling.

EXERCISE 19-2

Write adjectives for the following definitions.

1. pertaining to (-al) the skull _____

2. pertaining to (-al) a rib _____

3. pertaining to (-ic) the pelvis _____

4. pertaining to (-ac) the ilium _____

5. pertaining to (-al) the spinal column _____

6. pertaining to (-al) the sacrum _____

(continued)

EXERCISE 19-2   *(Continued)*

Define the following terms.

7. craniotomy (*kra-ne-OT-o-me*) _____

8. prevertebral (*pre-VER-teh-bral*) _____

9. spondylodynia (*spon-dih-lo-DIN-e-ah*) _____

10. pelvimetry (*pel-VIM-eh-tre*) _____

Write words for the following definitions.

11. fissure of the skull _____

12. above the pelvis _____

13. pertaining to the cranium and sacrum _____

14. pertaining to the sacrum and ilium _____

15. surgical puncture of the spine; spinal tap _____

16. surgical excision of a rib _____

17. plastic repair of a vertebra (use vertebr/o) _____

18. inflammation of the vertebrae (use spondyl/o) _____

19. around the sacrum _____

20. below the ribs _____

21. pertaining to the ilium and coccyx _____

22. excision of the coccyx _____

Clinical Aspects of the Skeleton

Disorders of the skeleton often involve surrounding tissues—ligaments, tendons, and muscles—and may be studied together as diseases of the musculoskeletal system. (The muscular system is described in Chapter 20.) The medical specialty that concentrates on diseases of the skeletal and muscular systems is **orthopedics**. Physical therapists and occupational therapists must also understand these systems (**Box 19-2**). (Some colorful terms used to describe musculoskeletal abnormalities are given in **Box 19-3**.)

Most abnormalities of the bones and joints appear on simple radiographs (see **Fig. 19-8** for a radiograph of

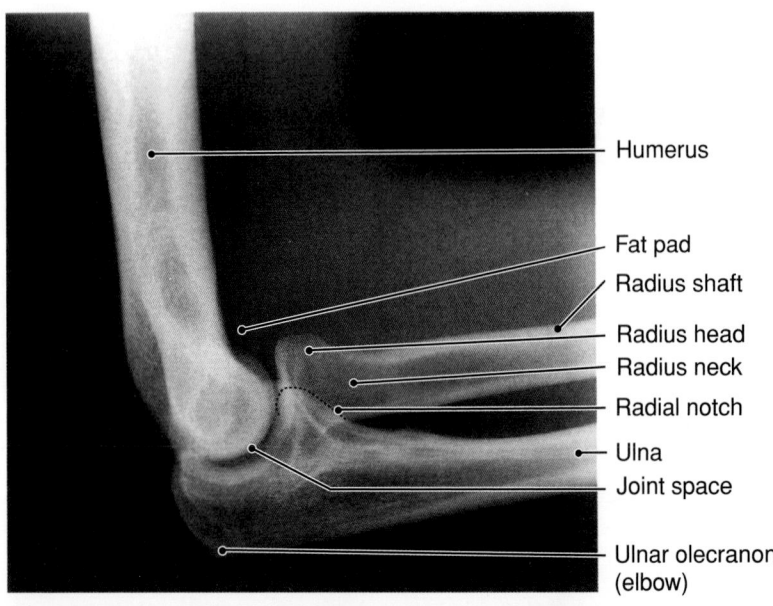

Humerus

Fat pad

Radius shaft

Radius head

Radius neck

Radial notch

Ulna

Joint space

Ulnar olecranon (elbow)

Figure 19-8 **Radiograph of a normal left elbow joint, lateral view.** The olecranon (*o-LEK-rah-non*) is the proximal ulnar enlargement that forms the prominent bone of the elbow.

Box 19-2

HEALTH PROFESSIONS
Careers in Physical Therapy

Physical therapy restores mobility and relieves pain in cases of arthritis or musculoskeletal injuries. Individuals who are recovering from neuromuscular, cardiovascular, pulmonary, and integumentary events are also candidates for physical therapy. Some examples include traumatic brain injury (TBI), myocardial infarction (MI), chronic obstructive pulmonary disease (COPD), and burns, respectively.

Physical therapists (PTs) work closely with physicians, nurses, occupational therapists, and other allied healthcare professionals. Some treat a wide range of ailments, whereas others focus on a particular age group, medical field, or sports medicine. Regardless of specialty, PTs are responsible for examining their patients and developing individualized treatment programs. The examination includes a medical history and tests measuring strength, mobility, balance, coordination, and endurance. The treatment plan may include stretching and exercise to improve mobility; hot packs, cold compresses, and massage to reduce pain; and the use of crutches, prostheses, and wheelchairs. Physical therapy assistants (PTAs) work directly under the supervision of a physical therapist. PTAs are responsible for implementing a preestablished treatment plan, teaching patients exercises and equipment use, and reporting results back to the physical therapist.

Whereas many practicing physical therapists in the United States have bachelor's or master's degrees, most accredited physical therapy schools now offer doctoral programs requiring three years of postgraduate education. PTAs in the United States usually graduate with an associate degree from a community college and must pass a licensing exam. PTs and PTAs practice in hospitals and clinics and may also visit homes and schools. As the U.S. population continues to age and the need for rehabilitative therapy increases, job prospects are good. For more information about careers in physical therapy, contact the American Physical Therapy Association at www.apta.org.

19

a normal joint). Radioactive bone scans, computed tomography (CT), and magnetic resonance imaging (MRI) scans are used as well. Also indicative of disorders are changes in blood levels of calcium and **alkaline phosphatase**, an enzyme needed for bone calcification.

INFECTION

Osteomyelitis is an inflammation of bone caused by pus-forming bacteria that enter through a wound or are carried by the blood. Often the blood-rich ends of the long bones are invaded, and the infection then spreads to other regions, such as the bone marrow and even the joints. The use of antibiotics has greatly reduced the threat of osteomyelitis.

Tuberculosis may spread to bone, especially the long bones of the arms and legs and the bones of the wrist and ankle. Tuberculosis of the spine is **Pott disease**. Infected vertebrae are weakened and may collapse, causing pain, deformity, and pressure on the spinal cord. Antibiotics can control tuberculosis as long as the strains are not resistant to these drugs and the host is not weakened by other diseases.

FRACTURES

A **fracture** is a break in a bone, usually caused by trauma. The effects of a fracture depend on the break's location and severity; the amount of associated injury; possible complications, such as infections; and success of healing, which may

Box 19-3

FOCUS ON WORDS
Names That Are Like Pictures

Some conditions are named by terms that are very descriptive. In orthopedics, several names for types of bursitis are based on the repetitive stress that leads to the irritation. For example, "tailor's bottom" involves the ischial ("sit") bones of the pelvis, as might be irritated by sitting tailor-fashion to sew. "Housemaid's knee" comes from the days of scrubbing floors on hands and knees, and "tennis elbow" is named for the sport that is its most common cause. "Student's elbow" results from leaning to pore over books while studying, although today a student is more likely to have neck and wrist problems from working at a computer.

The term *knock-knee* describes genu valgum, in which the knees are abnormally close and the space between the ankles is wide. The opposite is genu varum, in which the knees are far apart and the bottom of the legs are close together, giving rise to the term *bowleg*. A dowager's hump appears dorsally between the shoulders as a result of osteoporosis and is most commonly seen in elderly women.

Injury to the roots of nerves that supply the arm may cause the arm to abduct slightly and rotate medially with the wrist flexed and the fingers pointing backward, a condition colorfully named "waiter's tip position." "Popeye's shoulder" is a sign of a separation or tear at the head of the biceps tendon. The affected arm, when abducted with the elbow flexed, reveals a bulge on the upper arm—just like Popeye's!

Fracture	Description
closed	a simple fracture with no open wound
Colles *KOL-eze*	fracture of the distal end of the radius with backward displacement of the hand
comminuted *COM-ih-nu-ted*	fracture in which the bone is splintered or crushed
compression	fracture caused by force from both ends, as to a vertebra
greenstick	one side of the bone is broken and the other side is bent
impacted	one fragment is driven into the other
oblique	break occurs at an angle across the bone; usually one fragment slips by the other
open	fracture is associated with an open wound, or broken bone protrudes through the skin
Pott	fracture of the distal end of the fibula with injury to the tibial joint
spiral	fracture is in a spiral or S shape; usually caused by twisting injuries
transverse	a break at right angles to the long axis of a bone

take months. In a closed or simple fracture, the skin is not broken. If the fracture is accompanied by a wound in the skin, it is described as an open fracture. Various types of fractures are listed in **Box 19-4** and illustrated in **Figure 19-9**.

Reduction of a fracture refers to realignment of the broken bone. If no surgery is required, the reduction is described as closed; an open reduction is one that requires surgery to place the bone in proper position.

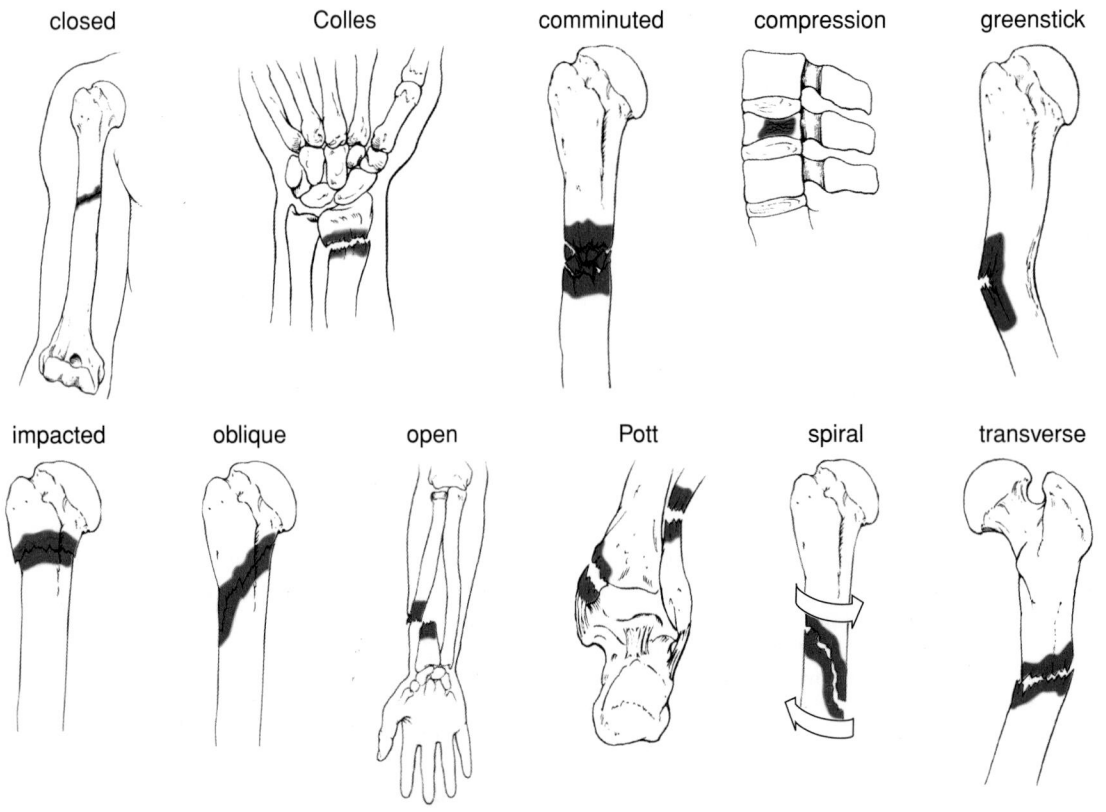

Figure 19-9 **Types of fractures.**

Figure 19-10 **Osteoporosis.** Femoral head showing osteoporosis (*right*) compared with a normal control (*left*).

Rods, plates, or screws might be needed to ensure proper healing. A splint or cast is often needed during the healing phase to immobilize the bone. **Traction** refers to using pulleys and weights to maintain alignment of a fractured bone during healing. A traction device may be attached to the skin or attached to the bone itself by means of a pin or wire.

METABOLIC BONE DISEASES

Osteoporosis is a loss of bone mass that results in bone weakening (**Fig. 19-10**). A decrease in estrogens after menopause makes women over age 50 most susceptible to the effects of this disorder. Efforts to prevent osteoporosis include a healthful diet, adequate intake of calcium and vitamin D, and engaging in regular weight-bearing exercises, such as walking, running, aerobics, and weight training. These exercises stimulate bone growth and also contribute to the balance and muscle strength needed

to prevent falls. Perimenopausal hormone replacement therapy (HRT) prevents bone loss, but because of safety concerns, this treatment is still being reevaluated. Some drugs are available for reducing bone resorption and increasing bone density. These include the **bisphosphonates** and **selective estrogen receptor modulators (SERMs)** described in Chapter 15. Bisphosphonates are used with caution, as they have been associated with unexplained bone fractures, necrosis of the jaw, and damage to the digestive tract.

Osteoporosis is diagnosed and monitored using a DEXA (dual-energy x-ray absorptiometry) scan, an imaging technique that measures bone mineral density (BMD). The diagnostic term **osteopenia** refers to a lower-than-average bone density, which is not considered to be abnormal. Osteopenia may progress to osteoporosis, but does not necessarily need treatment.

Other conditions that can lead to bone loss include nutritional deficiencies; disuse, as in paralysis or immobilization in a cast; and excess adrenocortical steroids. Overactivity of the parathyroid glands also leads to osteoporosis because parathyroid hormone causes calcium release from bones to raise blood calcium levels. Certain drugs, smoking, lack of exercise, and high intake of alcohol, caffeine, and proteins may also contribute to the development of osteoporosis.

In **osteomalacia** there is a softening of bone tissue because of diminished calcium salt formation. Possible causes include deficiency of vitamin D, needed to absorb calcium and phosphorus from the intestine; renal disorders; liver disease; and certain intestinal disorders. When osteomalacia occurs in children, the disease is called **rickets** (**Fig. 19-11**). Rickets is usually caused by a vitamin D deficiency.

Paget disease (osteitis deformans) is a disorder of aging in which bones become overgrown and thicker but

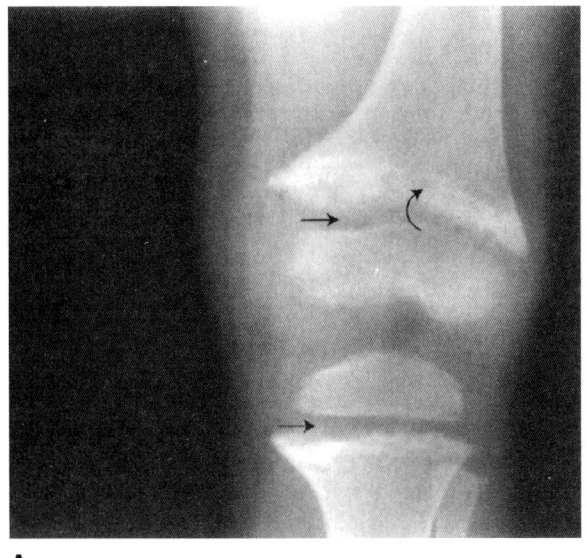
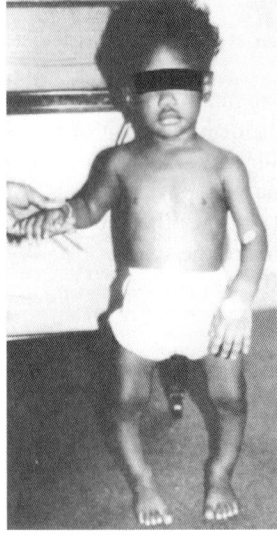

A   B

Figure 19-11 **Rickets.** **A.** Radiograph of the left knee joint showing widening of the growth regions of the bones (*arrows*). **B.** Young child showing rickets.

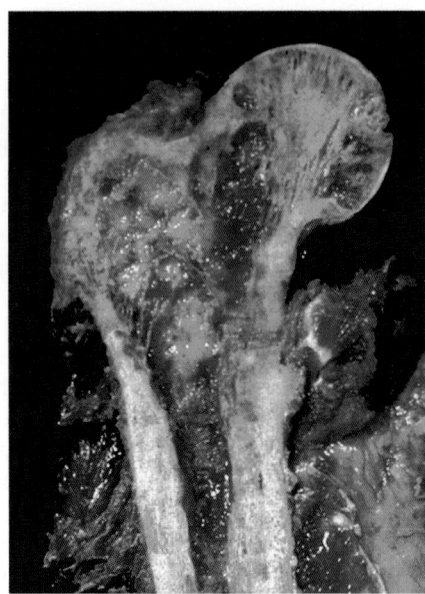

Figure 19-12 **Paget disease.** A section of the femur shows bone overgrowth in the diaphysis.

deformed (**Fig. 19-12**). The disease results in bowing of the long bones and distortion of the flat bones, such as the skull bones. Paget disease usually involves the bones of the axial skeleton, causing pain, fractures, and hearing loss. With time, there may be neurologic signs, heart failure, and predisposition to bone cancer.

NEOPLASMS

Osteogenic sarcoma (osteosarcoma) most commonly occurs in a bone's growing region, especially around the knee. This is a highly malignant tumor that often requires amputation. It most commonly metastasizes to the lungs.

Chondrosarcoma usually appears in midlife. As the name implies, this tumor arises in cartilage. It may require amputation and most frequently metastasizes to the lungs.

In cases of malignant bone tumors, early surgical removal is important for prevention of metastasis. Signs of bone tumors are pain, easy fracture, and increases in serum calcium and alkaline phosphatase levels. Aside from primary tumors, neoplasms at other sites often metastasize to bone, most commonly to the spine.

JOINT DISORDERS

Some sources of joint problems include congenital malformations; infectious disease of the joint or adjacent bones; injury leading to degeneration; and necrosis resulting from loss of blood supply. **Arthritis** is a term broadly used to mean any inflammation of a joint. Based on the cause, several types are recognized.

Arthritis

The most common form of arthritis is **osteoarthritis (OA)** or **degenerative joint disease (DJD)** (**Fig. 19-13**). This involves

a gradual degeneration of articular (joint) cartilage as a result of wear and tear. Predisposing factors for OA are age, heredity, injury, congenital skeletal abnormalities, and endocrine disorders. OA usually appears at midlife and beyond and involves the weight-bearing joints, such as the knees,

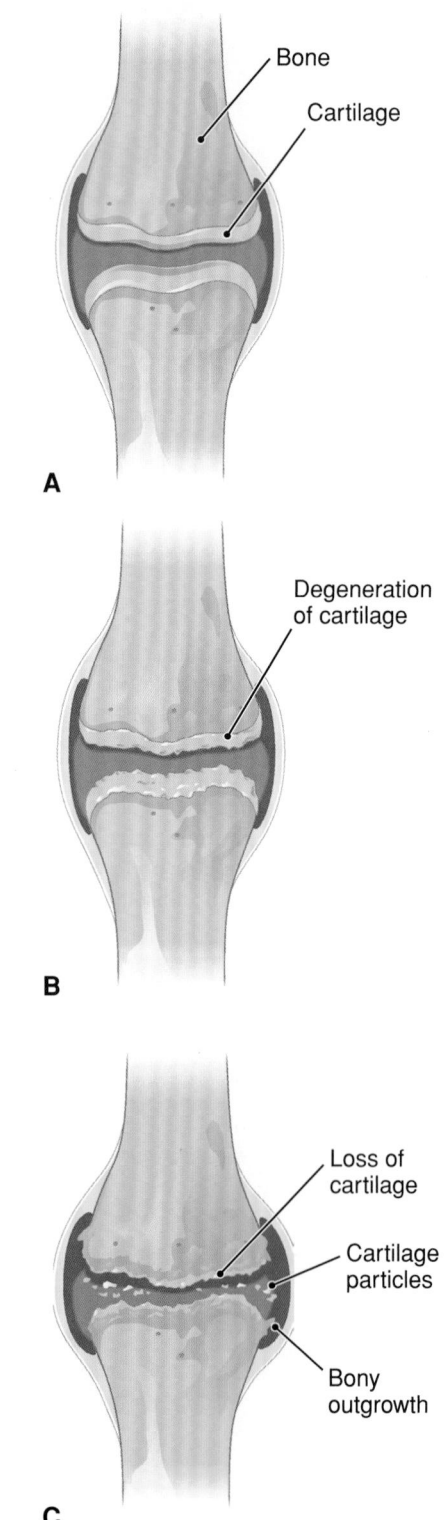

Figure 19-13 **Osteoarthritis. A.** Normal joint. **B.** Early stage of osteoarthritis. **C.** Late stage of the disease.

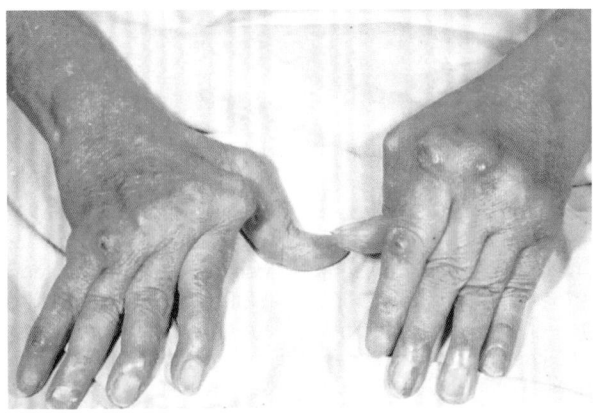

Figure 19-14 **Advanced rheumatoid arthritis.** The hands show swelling of the joints and deviation of the fingers.

hips, and finger joints. Radiographs show a narrowing of the joint cavity and bone thickening. Cartilage may crack and break loose, causing inflammation in the joint and exposing the underlying bone.

OA is treated with analgesics to relieve pain; **antiinflammatory agents**, such as corticosteroids; **nonsteroidal antiinflammatory drugs** (**NSAIDs**); and physical therapy. Steroids can be injected directly into an arthritic joint, but because they may ultimately cause cartilage damage, only a few injections can be given within a year at intervals of several months. Treatment may include drainage of excess fluid from the joint in an **arthrocentesis**. Application of ice, elevation, and acupuncture may also help to relieve pain in cases of joint inflammation.

Rheumatoid arthritis (**RA**) is a systemic inflammatory joint disease that commonly appears in young adult women. Its exact causes are unknown, but it may involve immunologic reactions. A group of antibodies called **rheumatoid factor** often appears in the blood, but it is not always specific for RA as it may occur in other systemic diseases as well. There is an overgrowth of the synovial membrane that lines the joint cavity. As this membrane covers and destroys the joint cartilage, synovial fluid accumulates, causing joint swelling (**Fig. 19-14**). There is degeneration of the underlying bones, eventually causing fusion, or **ankylosis**. Treatment includes rest, physical therapy, analgesics, and antiinflammatory drugs.

Gout is caused by an increased level of uric acid in the blood, salts of which are deposited in the joints. It mostly occurs in middle-aged men and almost always involves pain at the base of the great toe. Gout may result from a primary metabolic disturbance or may be a secondary effect of another disease, as of the kidneys. It is treated with drugs to suppress formation of uric acid or to increase its elimination (uricosuric agent).

Joint Repair

In **arthroscopy**, orthopedic surgeons use a type of endoscope called an arthroscope to examine a joint's interior and perform surgical repairs if needed (**Fig. 19-15**). With an arthroscope, it is possible to remove or reshape articular cartilage and repair or replace ligaments.

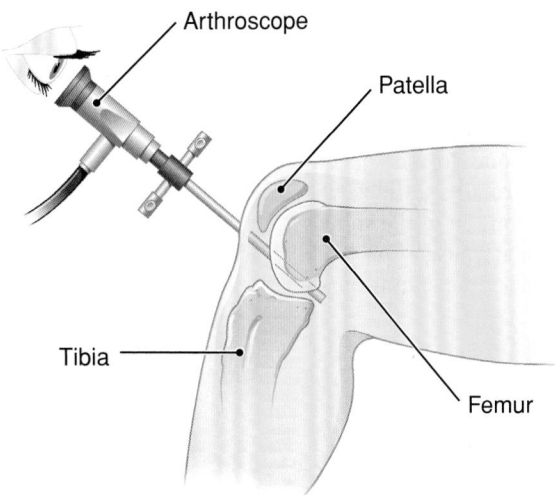

Figure 19-15 **Arthroscopic examination of the knee.** An arthroscope (a type of endoscope) is inserted between projections at the end of the femur to view the posterior of the knee.

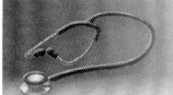

CLINICAL PERSPECTIVES

Box 19-5

Arthroplasty: Bionic Parts for a Better Life

Since the first total hip replacement in the early 1960s, millions of joint replacements, called arthroplasties, have been performed successfully. Most are done to decrease joint pain in older people with osteoarthritis and other chronic degenerative bone diseases after other treatments such as weight loss, physical therapy, and medication have been tried. Hips and knees are most commonly restored, with over 300,000 hip arthroplasties and more than 700,000 knee replacements performed each year in the United States. Orthopedic surgeons can also replace shoulder, elbow, wrist, hand, ankle, and foot joints.

Artificial, or *prosthetic*, joints are engineered to be strong, nontoxic, corrosion-resistant, and firmly bondable to the patient. Computer-controlled machines now produce individualized joints in less time and at less cost than in the past. Ball-and-socket joint prostheses, like those used in total hip replacement, consist of a cup, ball, and stem. The cup replaces

the hip socket (acetabulum) and is bonded to the pelvis using screws or glue. The cup is usually plastic but may also be made of longer-lasting ceramic or metal. The ball, made of metal or ceramic, replaces the femoral head and is attached to the stem, which is implanted into the femoral shaft. Stems are made of various metal alloys such as cobalt and titanium and are often glued into place. Stems designed to promote bone growth into them are commonly used in younger, more active patients because it is believed that they will remain firmly attached for a longer time.

Until recently, arthroplasty was rarely performed on young people because prostheses had life spans of only about 10 years. Today's materials and surgical techniques could increase this time to 20 years or more, and young people who undergo arthroplasty will require fewer replacements later on. This improvement is important because the incidence of sports-related joint injuries in young adults is increasing.

If more conservative treatments do not bring relief, orthopedists may recommend an **arthroplasty**. This term generally means any joint reconstruction but usually applies to a total or partial joint replacement. Hips, knees, shoulders, and other joints can be replaced with prostheses to eliminate pain and restore mobility, as explained in **Box 19-5**.

A final alternative to relieve pain and provide stability at a joint is fusion, or **arthrodesis**, which results in total loss of joint mobility. Surgeons use pins or bone grafts to stabilize the joint and allow bone surfaces to adhere.

DISORDERS OF THE SPINE

Ankylosing spondylitis is a disease of the spine that appears mainly in males. Joint cartilage is destroyed; eventually, the disks between the vertebrae calcify and there is ankylosis (fusion) of the bones (**Fig. 19-16**). Changes begin low in the spine and progress upward, limiting mobility.

Spondylolisthesis is a forward sliding of a vertebra over the vertebra below (-listhesis means "a slipping") (**Fig. 19-17**). The condition follows **spondylolysis**, degeneration of the joint structures that normally stabilize the vertebrae. Spondylolisthesis is most common in the spine's weight-bearing lumbar region, where it causes low back pain and sometimes leg pain resulting from irritation of spinal nerve roots.

Herniated Disk

In cases of a **herniated disk** (**Fig. 19-18**), the central mass (nucleus pulposus) of an intervertebral disk protrudes through the disk's weakened outer ring (annulus fibrosus) into the spinal canal. This commonly occurs in the spine's lumbosacral or cervical regions as a result of injury or heavy lifting. The herniated or "slipped" disk puts pressure on the spinal cord or spinal nerves, often causing **sciatica**,

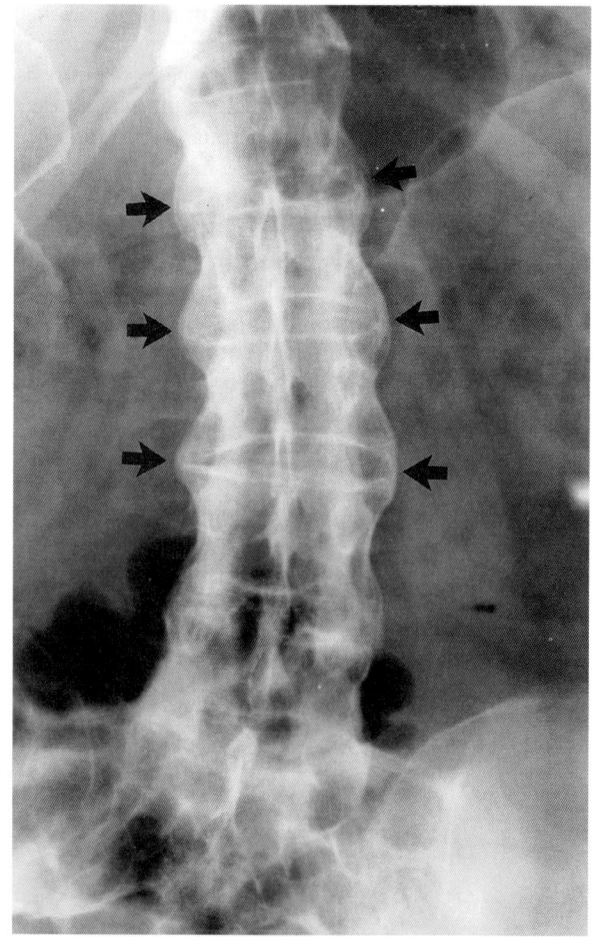

Figure 19-16 **Ankylosing spondylitis.** A frontal lumbar radiograph showing bone formation bridging the intervertebral disk spaces (*arrows*) and fusing the vertebrae.

19

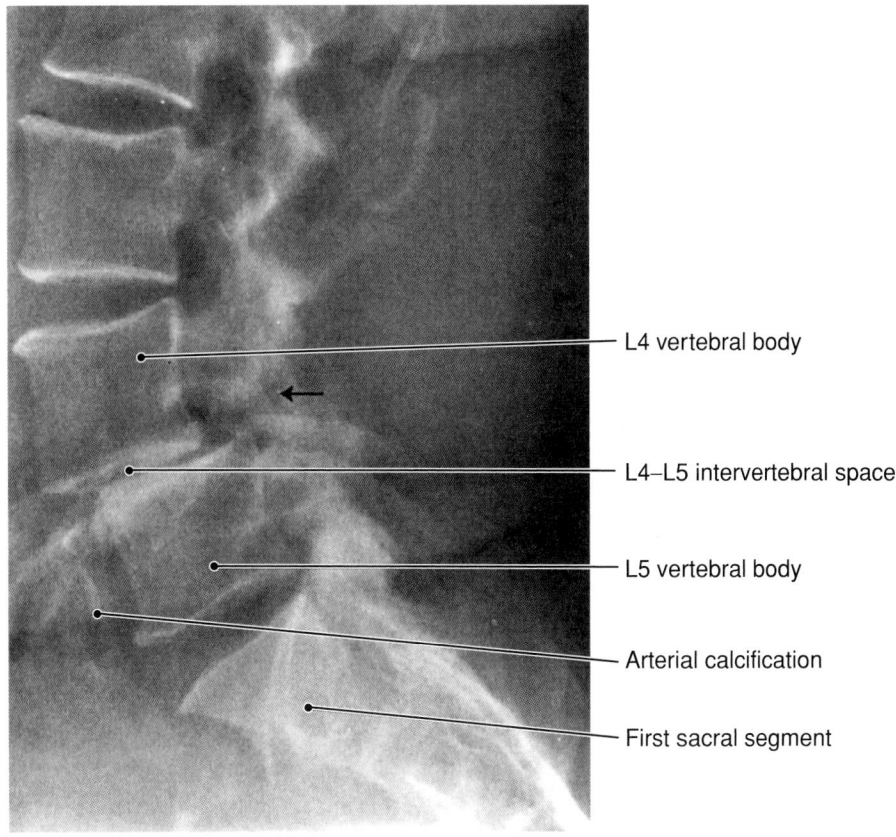

Figure 19-17 **Spondylolisthesis.** The L4 vertebral body has slid forward over L5, and there is marked narrowing of the L4–L5 intervertebral disk space.

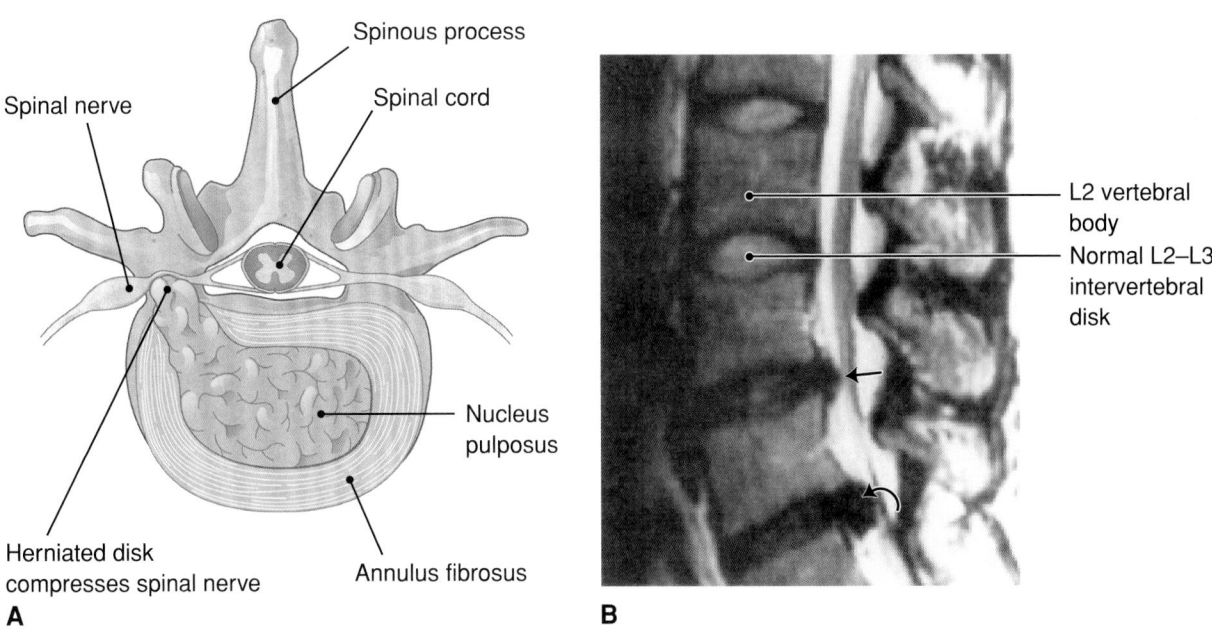

Figure 19-18 **Herniated disk.** **A.** The central mass of the disk protrudes into the spinal canal, putting pressure on the spinal nerve. **B.** Magnetic resonance image (MRI) of the lumbar spine, sagittal section, showing herniated disks at multiple levels. There is a bulging L3–L4 disk (*straight arrow*) and an extruded L4–L5 lumbar disk (*curved arrow*).

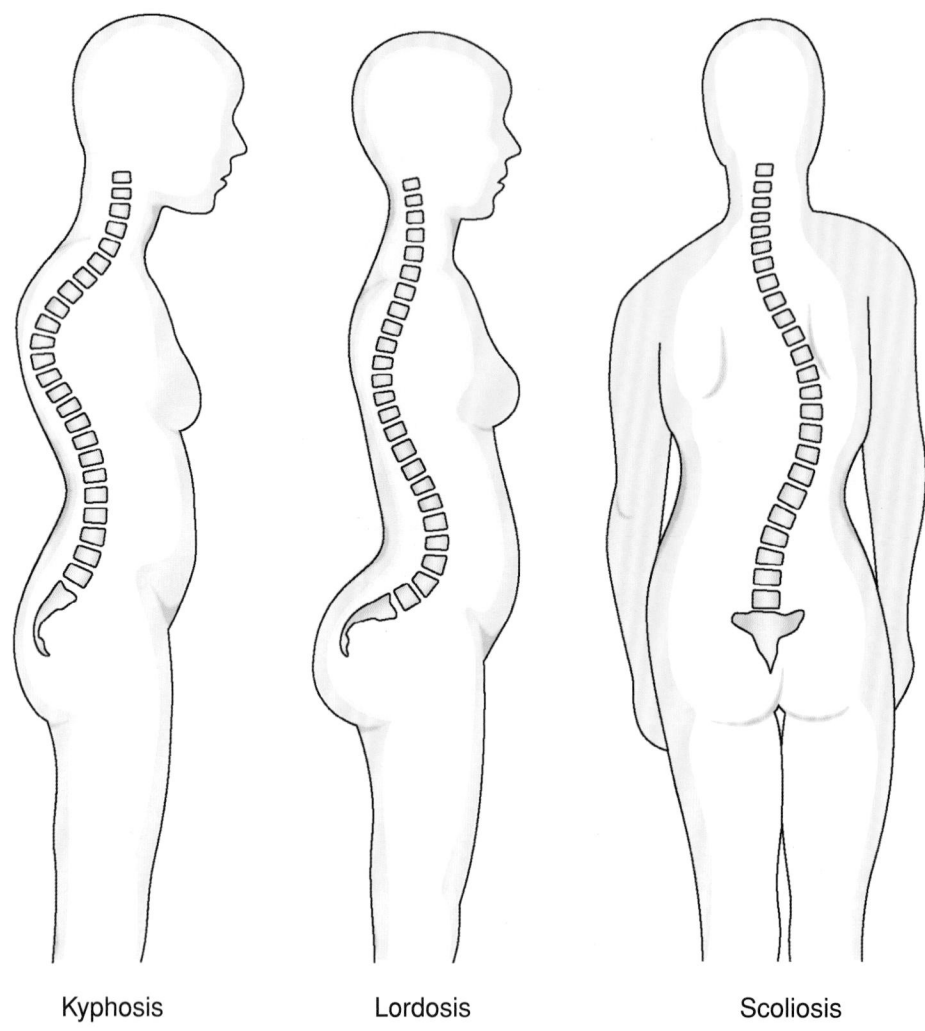

Kyphosis   Lordosis   Scoliosis

Figure 19-19 **Curvatures of the spine.** Kyphosis is an exaggerated thoracic curve; lordosis is an exaggerated lumbar curve; scoliosis is a sideways curve in any region.

which is pain along the sciatic nerve in the thigh. There may be spasms of the back muscles, leading to disability.

A herniated disk is diagnosed by myelography, CT scan, MRI, and neuromuscular tests. Treatment is bed rest and drugs to reduce pain, muscle spasms, and inflammation followed by an exercise program to strengthen core and associated muscles. In severe cases, it may be necessary to remove the disk surgically in a **diskectomy**, sometimes followed by vertebral fusion with a bone graft to stabilize the spine. Using techniques of microsurgery (surgery done under magnification through a small incision), it is now possible to remove an exact amount of extruded disk tissue instead of the entire disk.

Curvatures of the Spine

The spine has four normal curves—two directed toward the anterior in the cervical and lumbar regions and two directed toward the posterior in the thoracic and sacral regions (**Fig. 19-3**). Any exaggeration or deviation of these curves is described as **curvature of the spine**. Three common

types of spinal curvatures are shown in **Figure 19-19** and described as follows:

- **Kyphosis** is an exaggerated curve in the thoracic region, popularly known as "hunchback."
- **Lordosis** is an exaggerated curve in the lumber region, popularly known as "swayback."
- **Scoliosis** is a sideways curvature of the spine in any region. (A case of scoliosis is described in L.R.'s opening case study.)

Spinal curvatures may be congenital or may result from muscle weakness or paralysis, poor posture, joint problems, disk degeneration, extreme obesity, or disease, such as spinal tuberculosis, rickets, or osteoporosis. Extreme cases may cause pain, breathing problems, or degenerative changes.

Bracing the spine during childhood may help to correct a curvature. If surgery is needed, vertebrae are fused and bone grafts and implants are used to stabilize the spine. It is now sometimes possible for surgeons to make these corrections endoscopically.

Terminology | **Key Terms**

Disorders

ankylosing spondylitis *ang-kih-LO-sing spon-dih-LI-tis*	A chronic, progressive inflammatory disease involving the spinal joints and surrounding soft tissue, most common in young males; also called rheumatoid spondylitis
ankylosis *ang-kih-LO-sis*	Immobility and fixation of a joint
arthritis *ar-THRI-tis*	Inflammation of a joint
chondrosarcoma *kon-dro-sar-KO-mah*	A malignant tumor of cartilage
curvature of the spine *KER-vah-chure*	An exaggerated spinal curve, such as scoliosis, lordosis, or kyphosis (see **Fig. 19-19**)
degenerative joint disease (DJD)	Osteoarthritis (see below)
fracture *FRAK-chure*	A break in a bone; in a closed or simple fracture, the broken bone does not penetrate the skin; in an open fracture, there is an accompanying wound in the skin (see **Fig. 19-9**)
gout *gowt*	A form of acute arthritis, usually beginning in the knee or foot, caused by deposit of uric acid salts in the joints
herniated disk *HER-ne-a-ted*	Protrusion of the center (nucleus pulposus) of an intervertebral disk into the spinal canal; ruptured or "slipped" disk
kyphosis *ki-FO-sis*	An exaggerated curve of the spine in the thoracic region; hunchback, humpback (see **Fig. 19-19**)
lordosis *lor-DO-sis*	An exaggerated curve of the spine in the lumbar region; swayback (see **Fig. 19-19**)
osteoarthritis (OA) *os-te-o-ar-THRI-tis*	Progressive deterioration of joint cartilage with growth of new bone and soft tissue in and around the joint; the most common form of arthritis; results from wear and tear, injury, or disease; also called degenerative joint disease (DJD)
osteogenic sarcoma *os-te-o-JEN-ik*	A malignant bone tumor; osteosarcoma
osteomalacia *os-te-o-mah-LA-she-ah*	A softening and weakening of the bones due to vitamin D deficiency or other disease
osteomyelitis *os-te-o-mi-eh-LI-tis*	Inflammation of bone and bone marrow caused by infection, usually bacterial
osteopenia *os-te-o-PE-ne-ah*	A lower-than-average bone density, which may foreshadow osteoporosis
osteoporosis *os-te-o-po-RO-sis*	A condition characterized by reduction in bone density, most common in white women past menopause; predisposing factors include poor diet, inactivity, and low estrogen levels
Paget disease *PAJ-et*	Skeletal disease of the elderly characterized by bone thickening and distortion with bowing of long bones; osteitis deformans
Pott disease	Inflammation of the vertebrae, usually caused by tuberculosis
rheumatoid arthritis (RA) *RU-mah-toyd*	A chronic autoimmune disease of unknown origin resulting in inflammation of peripheral joints and related structures; more common in women than in men

19

(continued)

Terminology	Key Terms *(Continued)*

rheumatoid factor	A group of antibodies found in the blood in cases of rheumatoid arthritis and other systemic diseases
rickets *RIK-ets*	Faulty bone formation in children, usually caused by a deficiency of vitamin D
sciatica *si-AT-ih-kah*	Severe pain in the leg along the course of the sciatic nerve, usually related to spinal nerve root irritation
scoliosis *sko-le-O-sis*	A sideways curvature of the spine in any region (see **Fig. 19-19**)
spondylolisthesis *spon-dih-lo-lis-THE-sis*	A forward displacement of one vertebra over another (-listhesis means "a slipping"); also pronounced *spon-dih-lo-LIS-theh-sis*
spondylolysis *spon-dih-LOL-ih-sis*	Degeneration of the articulating portions of a vertebra allowing for spinal distortion, specifically in the lumbar region

Treatment

alkaline phosphatase *AL-kah-lin FOS-fah-tase*	An enzyme needed in the formation of bone; serum activity of this enzyme is useful in diagnosis
arthrocentesis *ar-thro-sen-TE-sis*	Aspiration of fluid from a joint by needle puncture
arthrodesis *ar-THROD-eh-sis*	Surgical immobilization (fusion) of a joint; artificial ankylosis
arthroplasty *AR-thro-plas-te*	Partial or total replacement of a joint with a prosthesis
arthroscopy *ar-THROS-ko-pe*	Use of an endoscope to examine the interior of a joint or to perform surgery on the joint (see **Fig. 19-14**); the instrument used is an arthroscope
diskectomy *dis-KEK-to-me*	Surgical removal of a herniated intervertebral disk; also spelled discectomy
orthopedics	The study and treatment of disorders of the skeleton, muscles, and associated structures; literally "straight" (ortho) "child" (ped); also spelled orthopaedics
reduction of a fracture	Return of a fractured bone to a normal position; may be closed (not requiring surgery) or open (requiring surgery)
traction *TRAK-shun*	The process of drawing or pulling, such as traction of the head in the treatment of injuries to the cervical vertebrae

Drugs

antiinflammatory agent	Drug that reduces inflammation; includes steroids, such as hydrocortisone, and nonsteroidal antiinflammatory drugs (NSAIDs)
bisphosphonate *bis-FOS-fo-nate*	Agent used to prevent and treat osteoporosis; increases bone mass by decreasing bone turnover; examples are alendronate (Fosamax), risedronate (Actonel), and ibandronate (Boniva)
nonsteroidal antiinflammatory drug (NSAID)	Drug that reduces inflammation but is not a steroid; examples include aspirin and ibuprofen and other inhibitors of prostaglandins, naturally produced substances that promote inflammation
selective estrogen receptor modulator (SERM)	Drug that acts on estrogen receptors; raloxifene (Evista) is used to prevent bone loss after menopause; other SERMs are used to prevent and treat estrogen-sensitive breast cancer

Terminology	**Supplementary Terms**

Normal Structure and Function[a]

annulus fibrosus *AN-u-lus fi-BRO-sus*	Outer ring-like portion of an intervertebral disk (see **Fig. 19-17**)
calvaria *kal-VAR-e-ah*	The dome-like upper portion of the skull
coxa *KOK-sa*	Hip
cruciate ligaments *KRU-she-ate*	Ligaments that cross in the knee joint to connect the tibia and fibula; they are the anterior cruciate ligament (ACL) and the posterior cruciate ligament (PCL); *cruciate* means "shaped like a cross"
genu *JE-nu*	The knee
glenoid cavity *GLEN-oyd*	The bony socket in the scapula that articulates with the head of the humerus
hallux *HAL-uks*	The great toe
malleolus *mah-LE-o-lus*	The projection of the tibia or fibula on either side of the ankle
meniscus *meh-NIS-kus*	Crescent-shaped disk of cartilage found in certain joints, such as the knee joint; in the knee, the medial meniscus and the lateral meniscus separate the tibia and femur; *meniscus* means "crescent;" (plural: menisci [*meh-NIS-ki*])
nucleus pulposus *NU-kle-us pul-PO-sus*	The central mass of an intervertebral disk (see **Fig. 19-17**)
olecranon *o-LEK-rah-non*	The process of the ulna that forms the elbow
os	Bone (plural: ossa)
osseous *OS-e-us*	Pertaining to bone
symphysis pubis *SIM-fih-sis*	The anterior pelvic joint, formed by the union of the two pubic bones (see **Fig. 19-4**); also called pubic symphysis

[a]See **Box 19-6** for a list of bone markings.

Symptoms and Conditions

achondroplasia *ah-kon-dro-PLA-ze-ah*	Decreased growth of cartilage in the growth plate of long bones resulting in dwarfism; a genetic disorder
Baker cyst	Mass formed at the knee joint by distention of a bursa with excess synovial fluid resulting from chronic irritation
bunion *BUN-yun*	Inflammation and enlargement of the metatarsal joint of the great toe, usually with displacement of the great toe toward the other toes
bursitis *bur-SI-tis*	Inflammation of a bursa, a small fluid-filled sac near a joint; causes include injury, irritation, and joint disease; the shoulder, hip, elbow, and knee are common sites
carpal tunnel syndrome	Numbness and weakness of the hand caused by pressure on the median nerve as it passes through a channel formed by carpal bones

(continued)

Terminology   Supplementary Terms (*Continued*)

chondroma kon-DRO-mah	A benign tumor of cartilage
Ewing tumor YU-ing	A bone tumor that usually appears in children 5 to 15 years of age; it begins in the shaft of a bone and spreads readily to other bones; it may respond to radiation therapy but then returns; also called Ewing sarcoma
exostosis eks-os-TO-sis	A bony outgrowth from the surface of a bone
giant cell tumor	A bone tumor that usually appears in children and young adults; the ends of the bones are destroyed, commonly at the knee, by a large mass that does not metastasize
hammertoe	Change in position of the toe joints so that the toe takes on a claw-like appearance and the first joint protrudes upward, causing irritation and pain on walking
hallux valgus	Painful condition involving lateral displacement of the great toe at the metatarsal joint; there is also enlargement of the metatarsal head and bunion formation
Heberden nodes HE-ber-den	Small, hard nodules formed in the cartilage of the distal finger joints in osteoarthritis
hemarthrosis heme-ar-THRO-sis	Bleeding into a joint cavity
Legg–Calvé–Perthes disease leg kahl-VA PER-tez	Degeneration (osteochondrosis) of the femur's proximal growth center; the bone is eventually restored, but there may be deformity and weakness; most common in young boys; also called coxa plana
multiple myeloma mi-eh-LO-mah	A cancer of blood-forming cells in bone marrow (see Chapter 10)
neurogenic arthropathy nu-ro-JEN-ik ar-THROP-ah-the	Degenerative joint disease caused by impaired nervous stimulation; most common cause is diabetes mellitus; Charcot (shar-KO) arthropathy
Osgood-Schlatter disease OZ-good SHLAHT-er	Degeneration (osteochondrosis) of the tibia's proximal growth center causing pain and tendinitis at the knee
osteochondroma os-te-o-kon-DRO-mah	A benign tumor consisting of cartilage and bone
osteochondrosis os-te-o-kon-DRO-sis	Disease of a bone's growth center in children; tissue degeneration is followed by recalcification
osteodystrophy os-te-o-DIS-tro-fe	Abnormal bone development
osteogenesis imperfecta (OI) os-te-o-JEN-eh-sis im-per-FEK-tah	A hereditary disease resulting in the formation of brittle bones that fracture easily; there is faulty synthesis of collagen, the main structural protein in connective tissue
osteoma os-te-O-mah	A benign bone tumor that usually remains small and localized
Reiter syndrome RI-ter	Chronic polyarthritis that usually affects young men; occurs after a bacterial infection and is common in those infected with HIV; may also involve the eyes and genitourinary tract
spondylosis spon-dih-LO-sis	Degeneration and ankylosis of the vertebrae resulting in pressure on the spinal cord and spinal nerve roots; often applied to any degenerative lesion of the spine
subluxation sub-luk-SA-shun	A partial dislocation

Terminology	**Supplementary Terms** (*Continued*)

talipes *TAL-ih-peze*	A deformity of the foot, especially one occurring congenitally; clubfoot
valgus *VAL-gus*	Bent outward
varus *VAR-us*	Bent inward
von Recklinghausen disease *fon REK-ling-how-zen*	Loss of bone tissue caused by increased parathyroid hormone; bones become decalcified and deformed and fracture easily

Diagnosis and Treatment

allograft *AL-o-graft*	Graft of tissue between individuals of the same species but different genetic makeup; homograft, allogeneic graft (see autograft)
arthroclasia *ar-thro-KLA-ze-ah*	Surgical breaking of an ankylosed joint to provide movement
aspiration *as-pih-RA-shun*	Removal by suction, as removal of fluid from a body cavity; also inhalation, such as accidental inhalation of material into the respiratory tract
autograft *AW-to-graft*	Graft of tissue taken from a site on or in the body of the person receiving the graft; autologous graft (see allograft)
chondroitin *kon-DRO-ih-tin*	A complex polysaccharide found in connective tissue; used as a dietary supplement, usually with glucosamine, for treatment of joint pain
glucosamine *glu-KOS-ah-mene*	A dietary supplement used in the treatment of joint pain
goniometer *go-ne-OM-eh-ter*	A device used to measure joint angles and movements (root goni/o means "angle")
iontophoresis *i-on-to-for-E-sis*	Introduction into the tissue by means of electric current, using the ions of a given drug; used in the treatment of musculoskeletal disorders
laminectomy *lam-ih-NEK-to-me*	Excision of the posterior arch (lamina) of a vertebra
meniscectomy *men-ih-SEK-to-me*	Removal of the crescent-shaped cartilage (meniscus) of the knee joint
myelogram *MI-eh-lo-gram*	Radiograph of the spinal canal after injection of a radiopaque dye; used to evaluate a herniated disk
osteoplasty *OS-te-o-plas-te*	Scraping and removal of damaged bone from a joint
prosthesis *PROS-the-sis*	An artificial organ or part, such as an artificial limb

See a figure on bone markings and formations in the Student Resources on the Point.

FOR YOUR REFERENCE
Bone Markings

Box 19-6

Marking	Description
condyle *KON-dile*	smooth, rounded protuberance at a joint
crest	raised, narrow ridge (see iliac crest in **Fig. 19-4**)
epicondyle *ep-ih-KON-dile*	projection above a condyle
facet *FAS-et*	small, flattened surface
foramen *for-A-men*	rounded opening (see foramen for spinal nerve in **Fig. 19-3**)
fossa *FOS-ah*	hollow cavity
meatus *me-A-tus*	passage or channel, such as a long channel within a bone; also the external opening of a canal, such as the urinary meatus
process	projection (see mastoid process and styloid process in **Fig. 19-2**)
sinus *SI-nus*	a space or channel, such as the air-filled spaces in certain skull bones (**Fig. 19-20**)
spine	sharp projection (see ischial spine in **Fig. 19-4**)
trochanter *tro-KAN-ter*	large, blunt projection as at the top of the femur
tubercle *TU-ber-kl*	small, rounded projection
tuberosity *tu-ber-OS-ih-te*	large, rounded projection

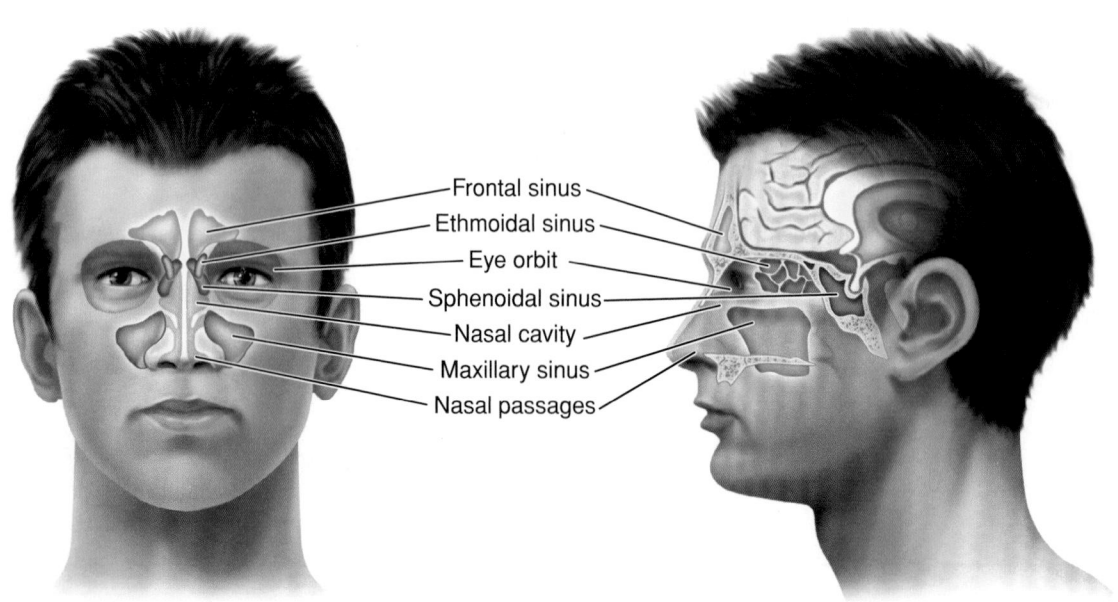

A Frontal View   **B** Lateral View

Figure 19-20 **Sinuses.** A sinus is a cavity or hollow space, such as the air-filled chambers in certain skull bones that lighten the skull's weight. **A.** Frontal view of the head showing sinuses. **B.** Lateral view.

Terminology   Abbreviations

ACL	Anterior cruciate ligament		NSAID(s)	Nonsteroidal antiinflammatory drug(s)
AE	Above the elbow		OA	Osteoarthritis
AK	Above the knee		OI	Osteogenesis imperfecta
ASF	Anterior spinal fusion		ORIF	Open reduction internal fixation
BE	Below the elbow, also barium enema		ortho, ORTH	Orthopedics
BK	Below the knee		PCL	Posterior cruciate ligament
BMD	Bone mineral density		PIP	Proximal interphalangeal (joint)
C	Cervical vertebra; numbered C1 to C7		PSF	Posterior spinal fusion
Co	Coccyx; coccygeal		RA	Rheumatoid arthritis
DEXA	Dual-energy x-ray absorptiometry (scan)		S	Sacrum; sacral
DIP	Distal interphalangeal (joint)		SERM	Selective estrogen receptor modulator
DJD	Degenerative joint disease		T	Thoracic vertebra; numbered T1 to T12
Fx	Fracture		THA	Total hip arthroplasty
HNP	Herniated nucleus pulposus		THP	Total hip precautions
IM	Intramedullary, also intramuscular		THR	Total hip replacement
L	Lumbar vertebra; numbered L1 to L5		TKA	Total knee arthroplasty
MCP	Metacarpophalangeal (joint)		TMJ	Temporomandibular joint
MTP	Metatarsophalangeal (joint)		Tx	Traction

19

Case Study Revisited

L.R.'s Follow-Up

L.R. underwent a successful surgical procedure and was transferred to the pediatric ICU. Her postoperative course progressed well. She was discharged with orders for continued physical therapy and follow-up visits to the see the surgeon. L.R. had excellent compliance with all postoperative instructions and was able to resume her musical activities sooner than expected.

CHAPTER
19 **Review**

Labeling Exercise

THE SKELETON

Write the name of each numbered part on the corresponding line.

Calcaneus   Patella
Carpals   Pelvis
Clavicle   Phalanges
Cranium   Radius
Facial bones   Ribs
Femur   Sacrum
Fibula   Scapula
Humerus   Sternum
Ilium   Tarsals
Mandible   Tibia
Metacarpals   Ulna
Metatarsals   Vertebral column

1. _____
2. _____
3. _____
4. _____
5. _____
6. _____
7. _____
8. _____
9. _____
10. _____
11. _____
12. _____
13. _____
14. _____
15. _____
16. _____
17. _____
18. _____
19. _____
20. _____
21. _____

22. _____
23. _____
24. _____

SKULL FROM THE LEFT

Write the name of each numbered part on the corresponding line.

Frontal
Hyoid
Lacrimal
Mandible
Maxilla
Nasal

Occipital
Parietal
Sphenoid
Temporal
Zygomatic

1. _____
2. _____
3. _____
4. _____
5. _____
6. _____
7. _____
8. _____
9. _____
10. _____
11. _____

VERTEBRAL COLUMN

Write the name of each numbered part on the corresponding line.

Body of vertebra
Cervical vertebrae
Coccyx
Intervertebral disk

Lumbar vertebrae
Sacrum
Thoracic vertebrae

1. _____
2. _____
3. _____
4. _____
5. _____
6. _____
7. _____

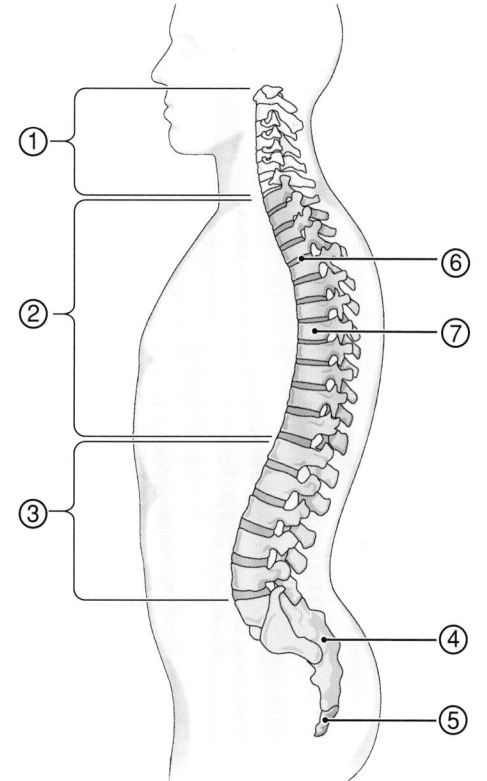

THE PELVIC BONES

Write the name of each numbered part on the corresponding line.

Ilium	Pubic symphysis
Ischium	Acetabulum
Pubis	Sacrum

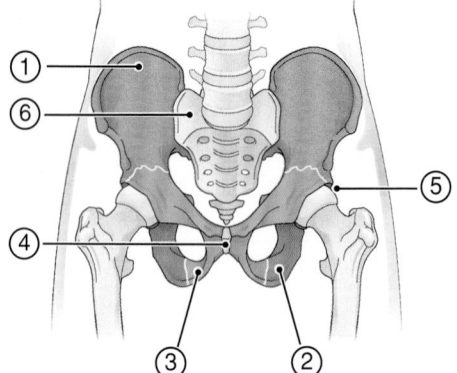

1. _____

2. _____

3. _____

4. _____

5. _____

6. _____

STRUCTURE OF A LONG BONE

Write the name of each numbered part on the corresponding line.

Artery and vein	Medullary cavity
Cartilage	Periosteum
Compact bone	Proximal epiphysis
Diaphysis	Spongy bone (containing
Distal epiphysis	red marrow)
Epiphyseal line (growth line)	Yellow marrow

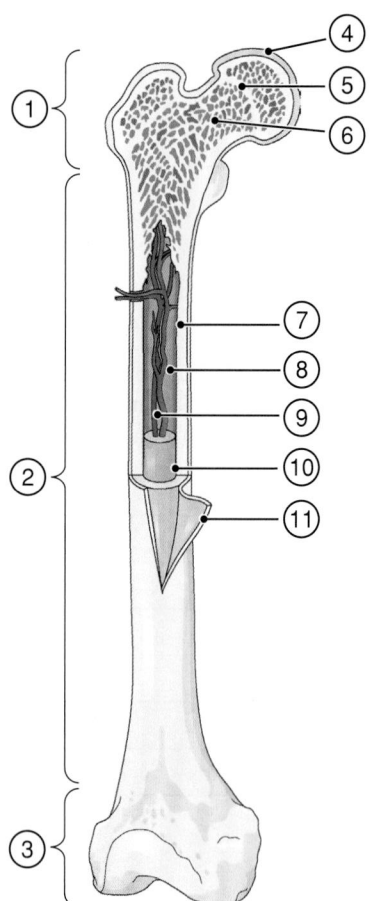

1. _____

2. _____

3. _____

4. _____

5. _____

6. _____

7. _____

8. _____

9. _____

10. _____

11. _____

Terminology

MATCHING

Match the following terms, and write the appropriate letter to the left of each number.

_____ **1.** periosteum

_____ **2.** epiphysis

_____ **3.** suture

_____ **4.** osteoclast

_____ **5.** resorption

a. an immovable joint

b. breakdown and removal of tissue

c. cell that breaks down bone

d. membrane that covers a bone

e. end of a long bone

_____ **6.** osteopenia

_____ **7.** ankylosis

_____ **8.** kyphosis

_____ **9.** spondylolisthesis

_____ **10.** rachiocentesis

a. immobility of a joint

b. spinal tap

c. displacement of a vertebra

d. exaggerated curve of the thoracic spine

e. deficiency of bone tissue

Supplementary Terms

_____ **11.** laminectomy

_____ **12.** chondroitin

_____ **13.** subluxation

_____ **14.** hallux

_____ **15.** olecranon

a. great toe

b. dietary supplement for treatment of joint pain

c. excision of part of a vertebra

d. part of the ulna that forms the elbow

e. partial dislocation

_____ **16.** meniscus

_____ **17.** goniometer

_____ **18.** arthroclasia

_____ **19.** genu

_____ **20.** prosthesis

a. breaking of a joint

b. device used to measure joint angles

c. knee

d. crescent-shaped cartilage

e. artificial part

FILL IN THE BLANKS

21. A fibrous band of connective tissue that connects a muscle to a bone is a(n) _____.

22. The type of tissue that covers the ends of the bones at the joints is _____.

23. The study and treatment of disorders of the skeleton, muscles, and associated structures is _____.

24. The part of the vertebral column that articulates with the ilium is the _____.

25. Chondrosarcoma is a malignant tumor of _____.

26. The fluid that fills a freely movable joint is _____.

27. A fluid-filled sac near a joint is a(n) _____.

28. Myelogenesis is the formation of _____.

29. Hemarthrosis is bleeding into a(n) _____.

30. Spondylarthritis (*spon-dil-ar-THRI-tis*) is arthritis of the _____.

31. Rachischisis (*ra-KIS-kih-sis*) is fissure of the _____.

DEFINITIONS

Define the following words.

32. myelitis (*mi-eh-LI-tis*) _____

33. ossification (*os-sih-fih-KA-shun*) _____

34. arthrodesis (*ar-THROD-eh-sis*) _____

35. synovectomy (*sin-o-VEK-to-me*) _____

36. chondrocyte (*KON-dro-site*) _____

37. subcostal (*sub-KOS-tal*) _____

38. coccydynia (*kok-se-DIN-e-ah*) _____

39. spondylitis (*spon-dih-LI-tis*) _____

40. polyarticular (*pol-e-ar-TIK-u-lar*) _____

41. intraosteal (*in-trah-OS-te-al*) _____

42. peribursal (*per-ih-BER-sal*) _____

Write words for the following definitions.

43. formation of cartilage _____

44. surgical immobilization of a joint _____

45. measurement of the pelvis _____

46. tumor of bone and cartilage _____

47. narrowing of a joint _____

48. death (-necrosis) of bone tissue _____

49. stone in a bursa _____

50. incision into the cranium _____

51. near the sacrum _____

52. pertaining to the sacrum and ilium _____

53. surgical excision of the coccyx _____

54. endoscopic examination of a joint _____

Find a word in L.R.'s opening case study for each of the following.

55. describing a disease with no known cause _____

56. a bone of the shoulder girdle _____

57. a bone of the pelvis _____

58. the area where T4 is located _____

59. incisions into bones _____

60. sideways curvature of the spine _____

ADJECTIVES

Write the adjective form of the following words.

61. sacrum _____

62. vertebra _____

63. coccyx _____

64. pelvis _____

65. ilium _____

TRUE–FALSE

Examine each of the following statements. If the statement is true, write T in the first blank. If the statement is false, write F in the first blank, and correct the statement by replacing the underlined word in the second blank.

	True or False	**Correct Answer**
66. The growth region of a long bone is in the <u>diaphysis</u>.	_____	_____
67. The tarsal bones are found in the <u>ankle</u>.	_____	_____
68. A slightly moveable joint is a <u>symphysis</u>.	_____	_____
69. The femur is part of the <u>axial</u> skeleton.	_____	_____
70. The <u>cervical</u> vertebrae are located in the neck.	_____	_____
71. The cells that produce cartilage are <u>chondroblasts</u>.	_____	_____
72. Blood cells are formed in <u>yellow</u> bone marrow.	_____	_____
73. An exaggerated lumbar curve of the spine is <u>scoliosis</u>.	_____	_____
74. The term *varus* means bent <u>inward</u>.	_____	_____

ELIMINATIONS

In each of the sets below, underline the word that does not fit in with the rest, and explain the reason for your choice.

75. trochanter — process — hyoid — meatus — condyle

_____

76. lambdoid — occipital — parietal — frontal — sphenoid

_____

77. sacr/o — rachi/o — spondyl/o — vertebr/o — cost/o

_____

78. Pott — sciatic — impacted — comminuted — greenstick

_____

79. T — C — L — Co — OA

_____

WORD BUILDING

Write words for the following definitions using the word parts provided.

> spondyl/o   -plasty   arthr/o   -lysis   -odynia   oste/o   -tome

80. pain in a joint _____

81. destruction of a vertebra _____

82. pain in a vertebra _____

83. loosening or separation of a joint _____

84. instrument for cutting bone tissue _____

85. plastic repair of a joint _____

86. pain in a bone _____

87. instrument for incising a joint _____

88. destruction of bone tissue _____

89. plastic repair of a bone _____

WORD ANALYSIS

Define the following words, and give the meaning of the word parts in each. Use a dictionary if necessary.

90. osteochondrosis (*os-te-o-kon-DRO-sis*) _____

    a. oste/o _____

    b. chondr/o _____

    c. -sis _____

91. spondylosyndesis (*spon-dih-lo-SIN-deh-sis*) _____

    a. spondyl/o _____

    b. syn- _____

    c. -desis _____

92. exostosis (*eks-os-TO-sis*) _____

    a. ex/o _____

    b. ost(e)/o _____

    c. -sis _____

93. achondroplasia (*ah-kon-dro-PLA-ze-ah*) _____

    a. a- _____

    b. chondr/o _____

    c. plas _____

    d. -ia _____

94. osteoporosis (*os-te-o-po-RO-sis*) _____

    a. osteo- _____

    b. poro- _____

    c. -sis _____

For more learning activities, see Chapter 19 of the Student Resources on thePoint.

Additional Case Studies

Case Study 19-1: *Arthroplasty of the Right TMJ*

S.A., a 38 YO teacher, was admitted for surgery for degenerative joint disease (DJD) of her right temporomandibular joint (TMJ). She has experienced chronic pain in her right jaw, neck, and ear since her automobile accident the previous year. S.A.'s diagnosis was confirmed by CT scan and was followed up with conservative therapy, which included a bite plate, NSAIDs, and steroid injections. She had also tried hypnosis in an attempt to manage her pain but was not able to gain relief. Her doctor referred her to an oral surgeon who specializes in TMJ disorders. S.A. was scheduled for an arthroplasty of the right TMJ to remove diseased bone on the articular surface of the right mandibular condyle.

On the following day, she was transported to the OR for surgery. She was given general endotracheal anesthesia, and a vertical incision was made from the superior aspect of the right ear down to the base of the attachment of the right earlobe. After appropriate dissection and retraction, the posterior–superior aspect of the right zygomatic arch was bluntly dissected anteroposteriorly. With a nerve stimulator, the zygomatic branch of the facial nerve was identified and retracted from the surgical field with a vessel loop. The periosteum was then incised along the superior aspect of the arch. An inferior dissection was then made along the capsular ligament and retracted posteriorly. With a Freer elevator, the meniscus was freed, and a horizontal incision was made to the condyle. With a Hall drill and saline coolant, a high condylectomy of approximately 3 mm of bone was removed while conserving function of the external pterygoid muscle. The stump of the condyle was filed smooth and irrigated copiously with NS. The lateral capsule, periosteum, subcutaneous tissue, and skin were then closed with sutures. The facial nerve was tested before closing and confirmed to be intact. A pressure pack and Barton bandage were applied. The sponge, needle, and instrument counts were correct. Estimated blood loss (EBL) was approximately 50 mL.

S.A. was discharged on the second postoperative day with instructions for a soft diet, daily mouth-opening exercises, an antibiotic (Keflex 500 mg po q6h), Tylenol no. 3 po q4h PRN for pain, and four weekly postoperative appointments.

Case Study 19-2: *Osteogenesis Imperfecta*

M.H., a 3-year-old boy with osteogenesis imperfecta (OI) type III, was admitted to the pediatric orthopedic hospital for treatment of yet another fracture. Since birth he has had 15 arm and leg fractures as a result of his congenital disease. This latest fracture occurred when he twisted at the hip while standing in his wheeled walker. He has been in a research study and receives a bisphosphonate infusion every two months. He is short in stature with short limbs for his age and has bowing of both legs.

M.H. was transferred to the OR and carefully lifted to the OR table by the staff. After he was anesthetized, he was positioned with gentle manipulation, and his left hip was elevated on a small gel pillow. After skin preparation and sterile draping, a stainless steel rod was inserted into the medullary canal of his left femur to reduce and stabilize the femoral fracture. The muscle, fascia, subcutaneous tissue, and skin were sutured closed. Three nurses gently held M.H. in position on a pediatric spica box while the surgeon applied a hip spica (body cast) to stabilize the fixation, protect the leg, and maintain abduction. M.H. was transferred to the post-anesthesia care unit (PACU) for recovery. The surgeon dictated the procedure as an open reduction internal fixation (ORIF) of the left femur with intramedullary (IM) rodding and application of spica cast.

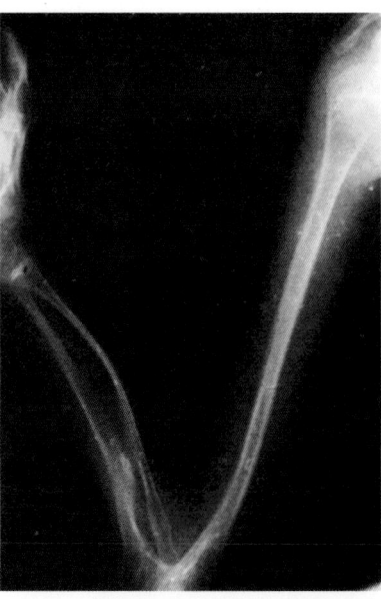

Osteogenesis imperfecta. X-ray of the upper extremity shows the thin bones and fractures that result from defective collagen production.

Case Study Questions

Multiple Choice. Select the best answer, and write the letter of your choice to the left of each number.

_____ **1.** A condylectomy is
   a. removal of a joint capsule
   b. removal of a rounded bone protuberance
   c. enlargement of a cavity
   d. removal of a tumor

_____ **2.** The articular surface of a bone is located
   a. under the epiphysis
   b. at a joint
   c. at a muscle attachment
   d. at a tendon attachment

_____ **3.** The dissection directed anteroposteriorly was done
   a. posterior–superior
   b. circumferentially
   c. front to back
   d. top to bottom

_____ **4.** Another term for bow-legged is
   a. knock-kneed
   b. adduction
   c. varus
   d. valgus

_____ **5.** An IM rod is placed
   a. inferior to the femoral condyle
   b. into the acetabulum
   c. within the medullary canal
   d. lateral to the epiphysial growth plates

Write terms from the Case Studies that mean the following.

6. pertaining to the cheek bone _____

7. the membrane around a bone _____

8. a crescent-shaped cartilage in a joint _____

9. plastic repair of a joint _____

10. formation of bone tissue _____

11. a break in a bone _____

12. present at birth _____

13. the thigh bone _____

Define the following abbreviations.

14. DJD _____

15. NS _____

16. TMJ _____

17. OI _____

18. ORIF _____

19. EBL _____

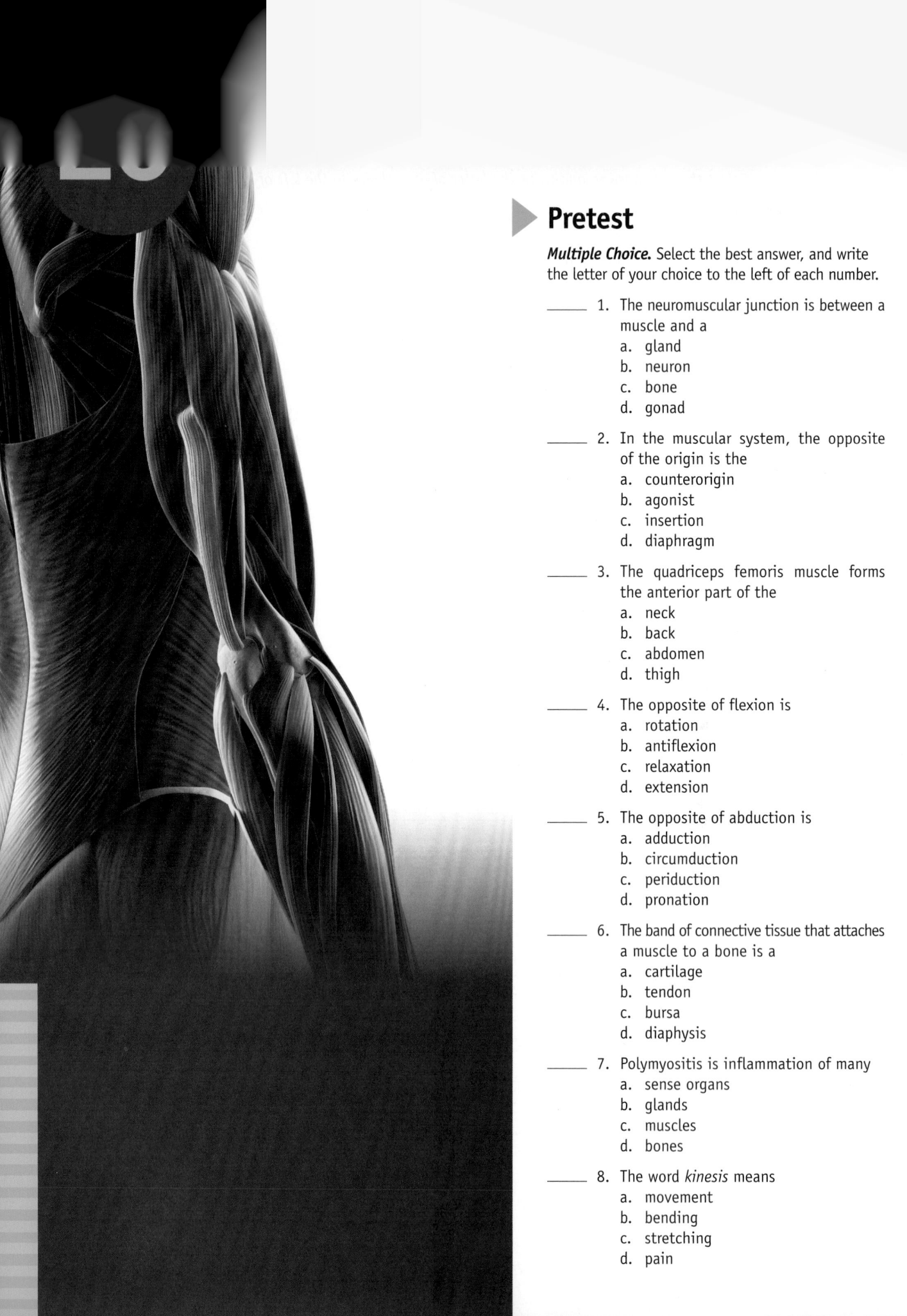

▶ Pretest

Multiple Choice. Select the best answer, and write the letter of your choice to the left of each number.

_____ 1. The neuromuscular junction is between a muscle and a
   a. gland
   b. neuron
   c. bone
   d. gonad

_____ 2. In the muscular system, the opposite of the origin is the
   a. counterorigin
   b. agonist
   c. insertion
   d. diaphragm

_____ 3. The quadriceps femoris muscle forms the anterior part of the
   a. neck
   b. back
   c. abdomen
   d. thigh

_____ 4. The opposite of flexion is
   a. rotation
   b. antiflexion
   c. relaxation
   d. extension

_____ 5. The opposite of abduction is
   a. adduction
   b. circumduction
   c. periduction
   d. pronation

_____ 6. The band of connective tissue that attaches a muscle to a bone is a
   a. cartilage
   b. tendon
   c. bursa
   d. diaphysis

_____ 7. Polymyositis is inflammation of many
   a. sense organs
   b. glands
   c. muscles
   d. bones

_____ 8. The word *kinesis* means
   a. movement
   b. bending
   c. stretching
   d. pain

Learning Objectives

After study of this chapter, you should be able to:

1 ▸ Compare the location and function of smooth, cardiac, and skeletal muscles. *p532*

2 ▸ Describe the typical structure of a skeletal muscle. *p532*

3 ▸ Briefly describe the mechanism of muscle contraction. *p532*

4 ▸ Explain how muscles work together to produce movement. *p533*

5 ▸ Describe the main types of movements produced by muscles. *p534*

6 ▸ List some of the criteria for naming muscles, and give examples of each. *p534*

7 ▸ Identify and use the roots pertaining to the muscular system. *p539*

8 ▸ Describe at least seven disorders that affect muscles. *p540*

9 ▸ Interpret abbreviations pertaining to muscles. *p546*

10 ▸ Analyze several case studies involving muscles. *pp531, 553*

Case Study: *T.D.'s Brachial Plexus Injury*

Chief Complaint

T.D., a 16-year-old high school student, had a severe lacrosse accident that resulted in a flail arm. He had sustained right brachial plexus injury and had no recovery. He has continued to take medication for neurologic pain. He was scheduled to see his orthopedic surgeon for a possible brachial plexus exploration.

Examination

The orthopedic surgeon examined T.D. and noted that there had not been any change in his condition since the previous visit. T.D. still had no feeling or motion in his right shoulder or arm. He had atrophy over the supraspinatus and infraspinatus muscles and also subluxation of his shoulder and deltoid atrophy. He had no active motion of the right upper extremity and no sensation. The rest of his orthopedic exam showed full ROM of his hips, knees, and ankles with intact sensation and palpable distal pulses as well as normal motor function.

He was diagnosed with a possible middle trunk brachial plexus injury from C7.

Clinical Course

T.D. and his parents had previous discussions with the surgeon and were aware of the prognosis and treatment plan. With middle trunk brachial plexus injury, damage to the subscapular nerve will interrupt conduction to the subscapularis and teres major muscles. Damage to the long thoracic nerve prevents conduction to the serratus anterior muscles. Injury to the pectoral nerves affects the pectoralis major and minor muscles.

T.D. was scheduled for an EMG, nerve conduction studies, and somatosensory evoked potentials (SSEPs). His diaphragm was examined under fluoroscopy to R/O phrenic nerve injury. The results of the diagnostic studies indicated that T.D. had most likely sustained a middle trunk brachial plexus injury. T.D. was scheduled for a brachial plexus exploration with possible nerve graft, nerve transfer, bilateral sural (calf) nerve harvest, or gracilis muscle graft from his right thigh.

ANCILLARIES At-A-Glance

Visit thePoint to access the following resources. For guidance in using the resources most effectively, see pp. ix–xvi.

Learning RESOURCES

▸ **Tips for Effective Studying**
▸ **Web Figure: Muscular Dystrophy**
▸ **Animation: The Neuromuscular Junction**
▸ **Audio Pronunciation Glossary**

Learning ACTIVITIES

▸ **Visual Activities**
▸ **Kinesthetic Activities**
▸ **Auditory Activities**

Introduction

The main characteristic of **muscle** tissue is its ability to contract. When stimulated, muscles shorten to produce movement of the skeleton, vessel walls, or internal organs. Muscles may also remain partially contracted to maintain posture. In addition, the heat generated by muscle contraction is the main source of body heat.

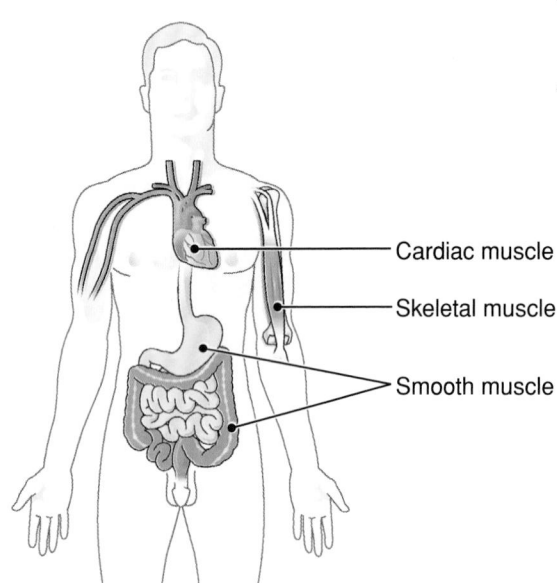

Figure 20-1   **Muscle types.** Smooth muscle makes up the walls of ducts and hollow organs, such as the stomach and intestine; cardiac muscle makes up the heart wall; skeletal muscle is attached to bones.

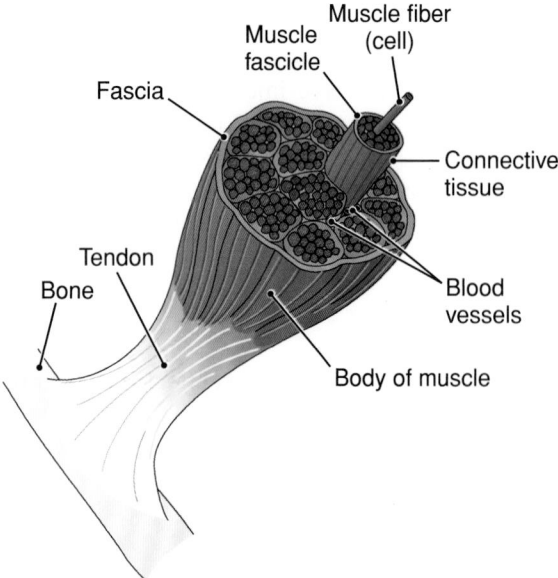

Figure 20-2   **Structure of a skeletal muscle.** Connective tissue coverings are shown as is the tendon that attaches the muscle to a bone.

Types of Muscles

There are three types of muscle tissue in the body (**Fig. 20-1**):

- **Smooth** (visceral) **muscle** makes up the walls of the hollow organs, such as the stomach, intestines, and uterus, and the walls of ducts, such as the blood vessels and bronchioles. Smooth muscle operates involuntarily and is responsible for peristalsis, the wave-like movements that propel materials through the systems.
- **Cardiac muscle** makes up the myocardium of the heart wall. It functions involuntarily and is responsible for the heart's pumping action.
- **Skeletal muscle** is attached to bones and is responsible for voluntary movement. It also maintains posture and generates a large proportion of body heat. All of these voluntary muscles together make up the muscular system.

Skeletal Muscle

The discussion that follows describes the characteristics of skeletal muscle, which has been the most extensively studied of the three muscle types.

MUSCLE STRUCTURE

Muscles are composed of individual cells, often referred to as fibers because they are so long and thread-like. These cells are held together in **fascicles** (bundles) by connective tissue (**Fig. 20-2**). Covering each muscle is a sheath of connective tissue or **fascia**. These supporting tissues merge to form the **tendons** that attach the muscle to bones.

MUSCLE ACTION

Skeletal muscles are stimulated to contract by motor neurons of the nervous system (**Fig. 20-3**). At the **neuromuscular junction (NMJ)**, the synapse (junction) where a branch of a neuron meets a muscle cell, the neurotransmitter **acetylcholine (ACh)** is released from small vesicles (sacs) in an axon branch. ACh interacts with the muscle cell membrane to prompt cellular contraction. Two special protein filaments in muscle cells, **actin** and **myosin**, interact to produce the contraction. ATP (the cell's energy compound) and calcium are needed for this response. **Box 20-1** discusses the use of steroids to increase muscle development and strength.

Most skeletal muscles contract rapidly to produce movement and then relax rapidly unless stimulation continues. Sometimes muscles are kept in a steady

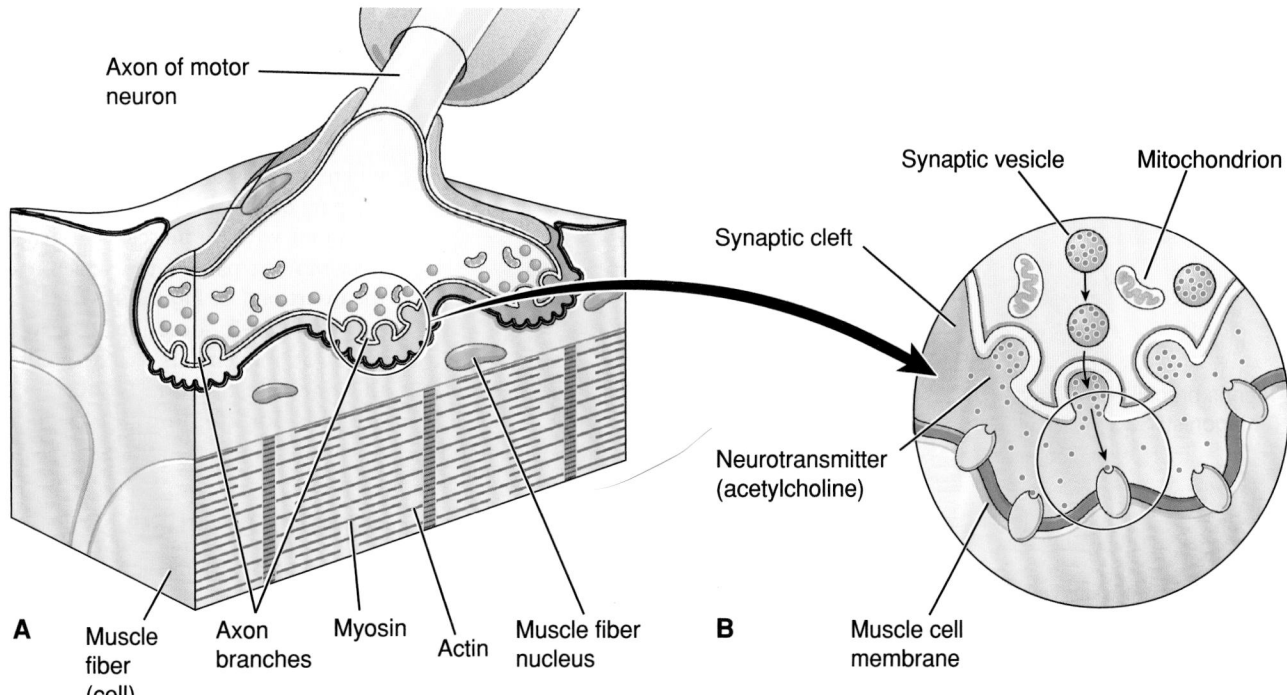

Axon of motor neuron

Synaptic cleft

Synaptic vesicle   Mitochondrion

Neurotransmitter (acetylcholine)

A   Muscle fiber (cell)   Axon branches   Myosin   Actin   Muscle fiber nucleus

B   Muscle cell membrane

Figure 20-3 **Neuromuscular junction (NMJ). A.** The branched end of a motor neuron makes contact with the membrane of a muscle fiber (cell). **B.** Enlarged view of the NMJ showing release of neurotransmitter (acetylcholine) from a neuron and its attachment to a muscle cell membrane. Mitochondria generate ATP, the cells' energy compound.

partially contracted state, to maintain posture, for example. This state of firmness is called **tonus**, or *muscle tone*.

See the animation "The Neuromuscular Junction" in the Student Resources on thePoint.

Muscles work in pairs to produce movement at the joints. Any muscle that produces a given movement is described as an **agonist**. If a group of muscles is involved in the action, the main one is called the **prime mover**. When an agonist contracts, an opposing muscle, the **antagonist**, must relax. For example, when the brachialis muscle on the anterior surface of the upper arm contracts as the prime mover to flex the arm, the triceps brachii on the posterior surface must relax (**Fig. 20-4**). When the arm is extended, these actions are reversed; the triceps brachii contracts, and the brachialis must relax. Any muscle that assists the prime mover to produce an action is called a **synergist**. For example, the biceps

CLINICAL PERSPECTIVES

Box 20-1

Anabolic Steroids: Winning at All Costs?

Anabolic steroids mimic the effects of the male sex hormone testosterone by promoting metabolism and stimulating growth. These drugs are legally prescribed to promote muscle regeneration and prevent atrophy from disuse after surgery. However, athletes also purchase them illegally, using them to increase muscle size and strength and improve endurance.

When steroids are used illegally to enhance athletic performance, the doses needed are large enough to cause serious side effects. They increase blood cholesterol levels, which may lead to atherosclerosis, heart disease, kidney failure, and stroke. Steroids damage the liver, making it more

susceptible to disease and cancer, and they suppress the immune system, increasing the risk of infection and cancer. In men, steroids cause impotence, testicular atrophy, low sperm count, infertility, and the development of female sex characteristics such as breasts (gynecomastia). In women, steroids disrupt ovulation and menstruation and produce male sex characteristics such as breast atrophy, clitoral enlargement, increased body hair, and deepening of the voice. In both sexes, steroids increase the risk for baldness, and especially in men, they cause mood swings, depression, and violence.

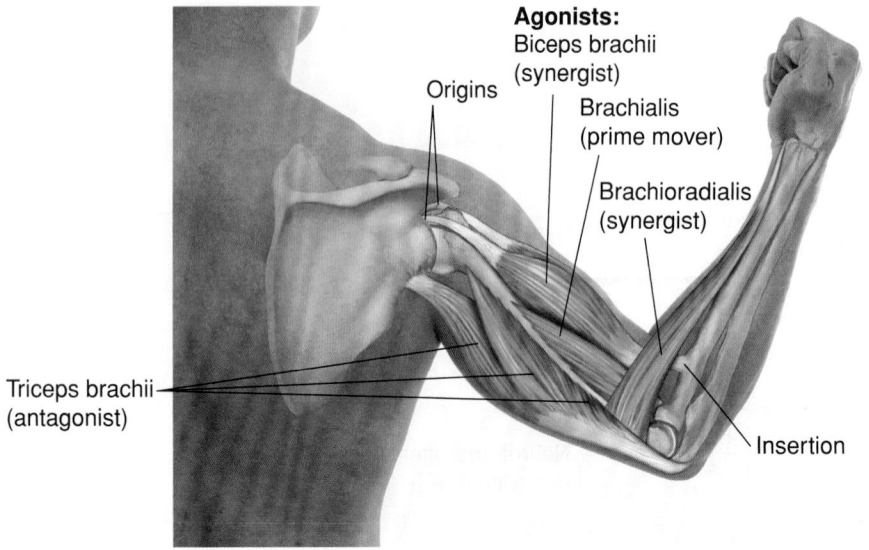

Agonists:
Biceps brachii (synergist)
Brachialis (prime mover)
Brachioradialis (synergist)

Origins

Triceps brachii (antagonist)

Insertion

Figure 20-4 **Muscles work together.** When the brachialis, the agonistic prime mover, flexes the arm, the triceps brachii, the antagonist, must relax. Synergists, the biceps brachii and the brachioradialis, assist in this action. When the arm is extended, these muscle actions are reversed. This figure also shows three attachments of the biceps brachii, two origins and one insertion.

brachii (most visible on the anterior surface when the arm is flexed) and the brachioradialis assist the brachialis to flex the arm.

In a given movement, the point where the muscle is attached to a stable part of the skeleton is the **origin**; the point where a muscle is attached to a moving part of the skeleton is the **insertion** (see **Fig. 20-4**).

Box 20-2 describes various types of movements at the joints; these are illustrated in **Figure 20-5**. See also **Box 20-3** for a description of careers in physical fitness.

NAMING OF MUSCLES

A muscle can be named by its location (e.g., near a bone), by the direction of its fibers, or by its size, shape, or number of attachment points (heads), as indicated by the suffix *-ceps*

FOR YOUR REFERENCE
Types of Movement

Box 20-2

Movement	Definition	Example
flexion FLEK-shun	closing the angle at a joint	bending at the knee or elbow
extension eks-TEN-shun	opening the angle at a joint	straightening at the knee or elbow
abduction ab-DUK-shun	movement away from the midline of the body	outward movement of the arm at the shoulder
adduction ah-DUK-shun	movement toward the midline of the body	return of lifted arm to the body
rotation ro-TA-shun	turning of a body part on its own axis	turning of the forearm from the elbow
circumduction ser-kum-DUK-shun	circular movement from a central point	tracing a circle with an outstretched arm
pronation pro-NA-shun	turning downward	turning the palm of the hand downward
supination su-pin-A-shun	turning upward	turning the palm of the hand upward
eversion e-VER-zhun	turning outward	turning the sole of the foot outward
inversion in-VER-zhun	turning inward	turning the sole of the foot inward
dorsiflexion dor-shi-FLEK-shun	bending backward	moving the foot so that the toes point upward, away from the sole of the foot
plantar flexion	bending the sole of the foot	pointing the toes downward

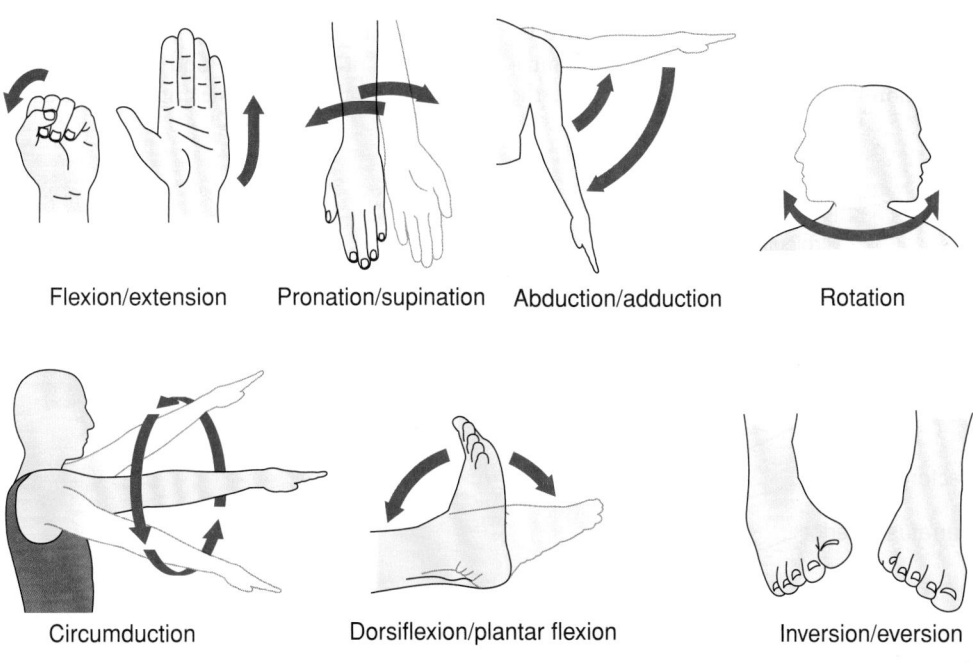

Flexion/extension Pronation/supination Abduction/adduction Rotation

Circumduction Dorsiflexion/plantar flexion Inversion/eversion

Figure 20-5 **Types of movement.** Muscle contraction produces movement at the joints. Some muscles are named for the type of movement they produce, such as flexor, extensor, and adductor.

HEALTH PROFESSIONS

Box 20-3

Careers in Exercise and Fitness

Several related careers are concerned with the management of exercise programs for therapy, health maintenance, and recreation. The American College of Sports Medicine (ACSM) at www.acsm.org has information on these fields and some certification programs.

■ Exercise physiologists study the mechanisms involved in physical exercise and the body's physiologic responses to exercise. They design programs for general health, athletics, and rehabilitation for disability or disease, such as cardiovascular and respiratory diseases. They may work in clinical settings in cooperation with physicians, in private industry, in health clubs, or in teaching. Most exercise physiologists (EPs) have master's degrees, but some jobs may require only a bachelor's degree. A PhD is needed for teaching or research. EPs may be certified through ACSM or the Center for Exercise Physiology (CEP). The American Society of Exercise Physiologists at www.asep.org has information about this profession.

■ Athletic trainers specialize in the prevention and treatment of musculoskeletal injuries. They advise clients on the proper use of exercise equipment and devices, such as braces, that help prevent injuries. They work in cooperation with physicians in private establishments, in healthcare facilities, and with athletes and sports teams. An athletic trainer's job may have a set schedule, but if the job is for a sports team, it may require long and irregular hours. A majority of athletic trainers have master's degrees or higher. Employment opportunities in healthcare and teaching are expected to be good, although jobs with sports teams are limited. The National Athletic Trainers' Association at www.nata.org has more information on this career.

■ Fitness workers make up a category that includes a variety of career activities, such as personal trainers and group fitness, yoga, and Pilates instructors. These professionals lead, instruct, and motivate individuals or groups in all types of exercise activities. Traditionally, they have worked in studios, health clubs, or private homes, but they are increasingly found in the workplace, where they organize and direct fitness programs for employees. Their jobs may involve administrative duties as well. Personal trainers must be certified, and certification is encouraged for other fitness professionals. Candidates must have a high school diploma and certification in CPR, and must pass a written exam and sometimes a practical exam as well. Increasingly, a bachelor's degree is required, and those who wish to progress to management jobs may need a higher degree. Instructors who specialize in a particular exercise method, such as Pilates or yoga, must pass their own training standards. Job opportunities in these fields are expected to increase with an aging population and increasing concern for good health and physical fitness. The National Commission for Certifying Agencies at www.credentialingexcellence.org can help locate accredited fitness certification programs.

(see **Fig. 20-4**). It may also be named for its action, adding the suffix -*or* to the root for the action. For example, a muscle that produces flexion at a joint is a flexor. Examine the muscle diagrams in **Figures 20-6** and **20-7**. See how many of these criteria you can find in the muscle names. Note that sometimes more than one criterion is used in the name.

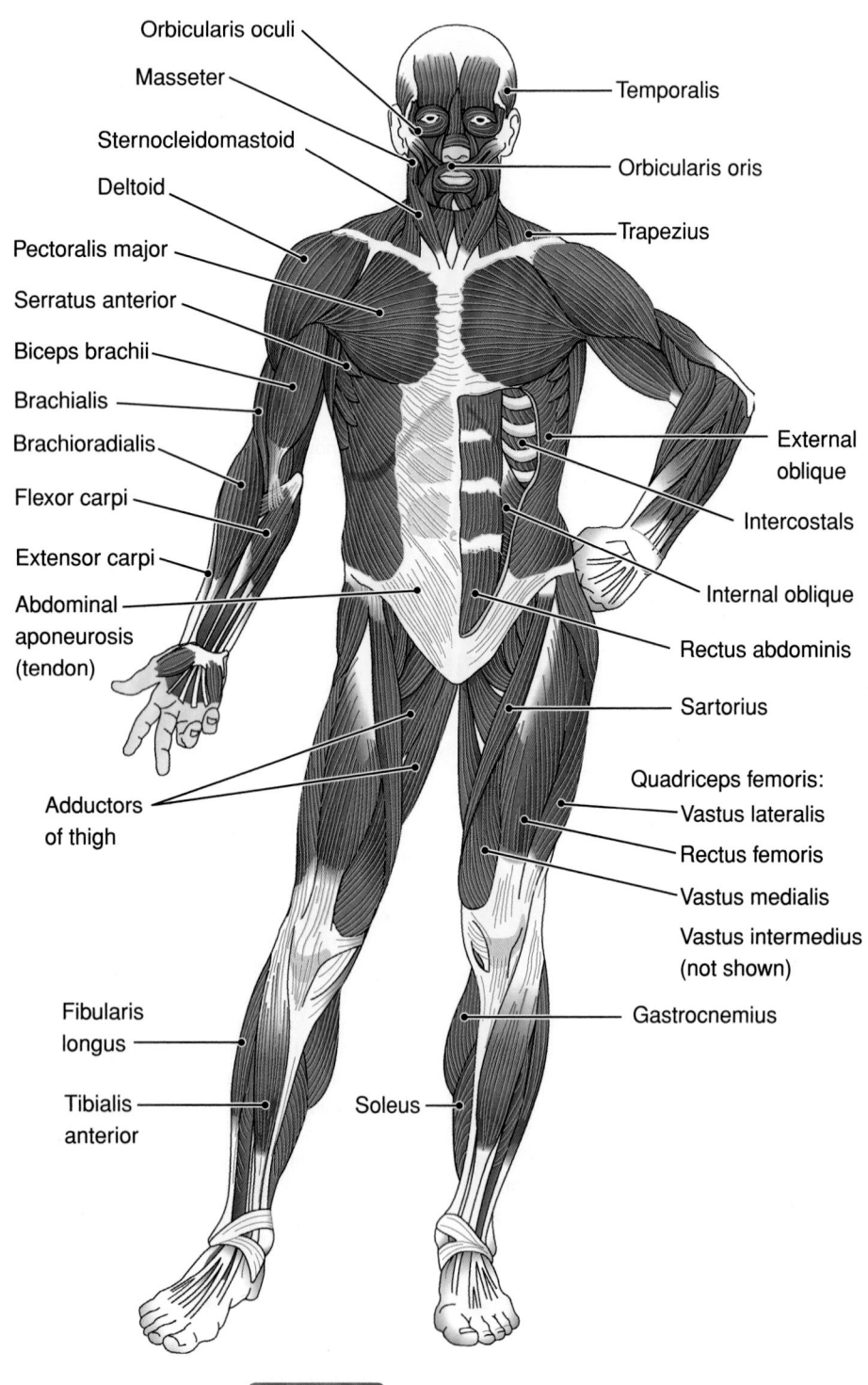

Orbicularis oculi

Masseter

Sternocleidomastoid

Deltoid

Pectoralis major

Serratus anterior

Biceps brachii

Brachialis

Brachioradialis

Flexor carpi

Extensor carpi

Abdominal aponeurosis (tendon)

Adductors of thigh

Fibularis longus

Tibialis anterior

Temporalis

Orbicularis oris

Trapezius

External oblique

Intercostals

Internal oblique

Rectus abdominis

Sartorius

Quadriceps femoris:

Vastus lateralis

Rectus femoris

Vastus medialis

Vastus intermedius (not shown)

Gastrocnemius

Soleus

Figure 20-6 **Superficial muscles, anterior view.**

20

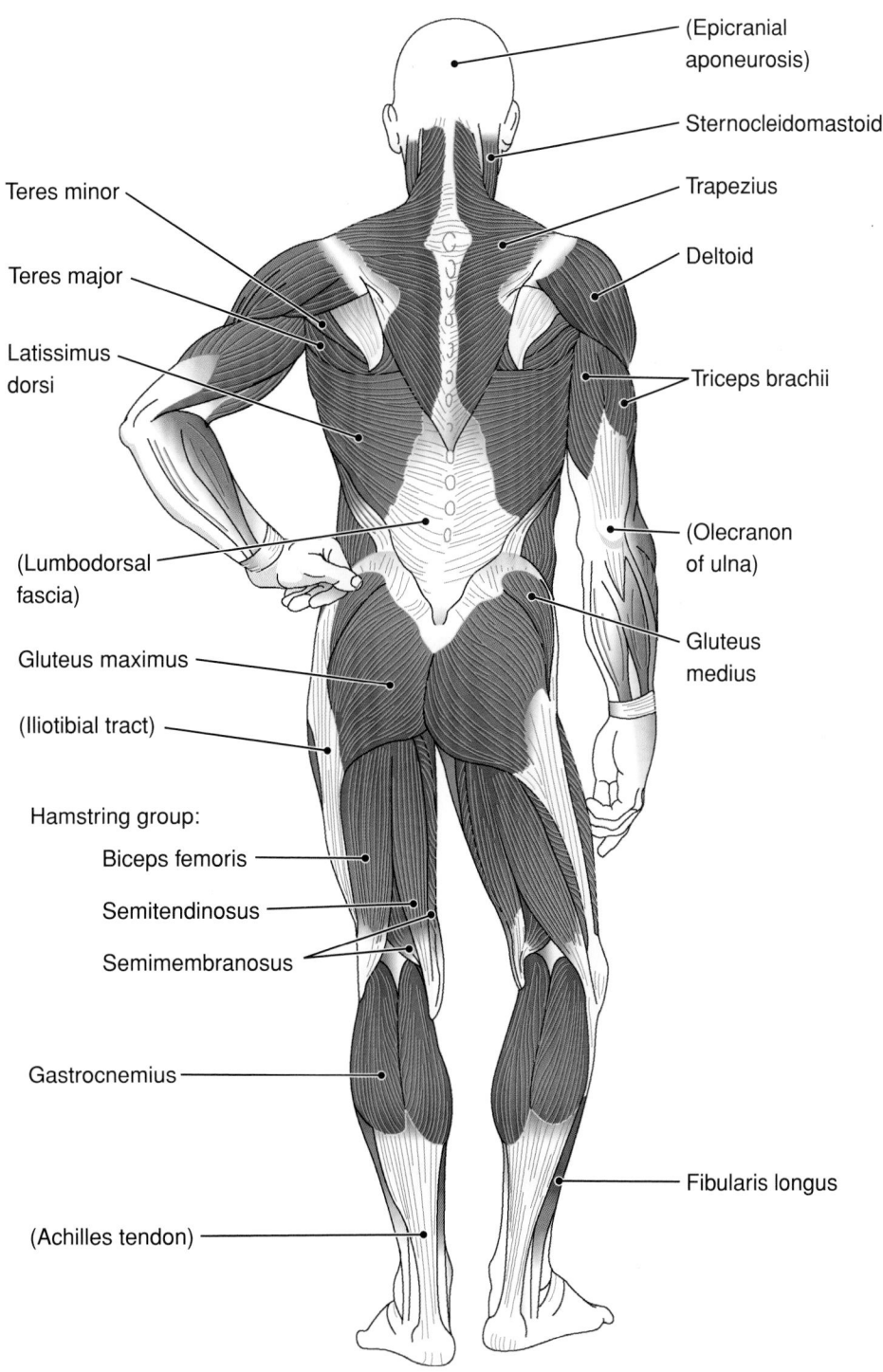

Teres minor

Teres major

Latissimus dorsi

(Lumbodorsal fascia)

Gluteus maximus

(Iliotibial tract)

Hamstring group:

Biceps femoris

Semitendinosus

Semimembranosus

Gastrocnemius

(Achilles tendon)

(Epicranial aponeurosis)

Sternocleidomastoid

Trapezius

Deltoid

Triceps brachii

(Olecranon of ulna)

Gluteus medius

Fibularis longus

Figure 20-7 **Superficial muscles, posterior view.** Associated structures are labeled in parentheses.

Terminology   Key Terms

Normal Structure and Function

acetylcholine (ACh) *as-eh-til-KO-lene*	A neurotransmitter that stimulates contraction of skeletal muscles
actin *AK-tin*	One of the two contractile proteins in muscle cells; the other is myosin
agonist *AG-on-ist*	A muscle that carries out a given movement (from Greek *agon* meaning "contest," "struggle")
antagonist *an-TAG-o-nist*	The muscle that opposes an agonist; it must relax when the agonist contracts
cardiac muscle *KAR-de-ak*	Involuntary muscle that makes up the heart wall
fascia *FASH-e-ah*	The fibrous sheath of connective tissue that covers a muscle; called deep fascia to differentiate it from the superficial fascia that underlies the skin (root: fasci/o) (plural: fasciae)
fascicle *FAS-ih-kl*	A small bundle, as of muscle or nerve fibers
insertion *in-SER-shun*	In a given movement, the point where a muscle is attached to a moving part of the skeleton
muscle *MUS-el*	An organ that produces movement by contracting; also the tissue that composes such organs (roots: my/o, muscul/o)
myosin *MI-o-sin*	One of the two contractile proteins in muscle cells; the other is actin
neuromuscular junction (NMJ) *nu-ro-MUS-ku-lar JUNK-shun*	The point of contact, or synapse, between a branch of a motor neuron and a muscle cell
origin *OR-ih-jin*	In a given movement, the point where a muscle is attached to a stable part of the skeleton
prime mover	The main muscle involved in a given movement
skeletal muscle *SKEL-eh-tal*	Voluntary muscle that moves the skeleton and maintains posture
smooth muscle	Involuntary muscle that makes up the wall of hollow organs, vessels, and ducts; visceral muscle
synergist *SIN-er-jist*	A muscle that assists a prime mover to produce a given movement
tendon *TEN-dun*	A fibrous band of connective tissue that attaches a muscle to a bone (roots: ten/o, tendin/o)
tonus *TO-nus*	A state of steady, partial muscle contraction that maintains firmness; muscle tone (root: ton/o)

Go to the Audio Pronunciation Glossary in the Student Resources on thePoint to hear these terms pronounced.

Roots Pertaining to Muscles

See Table 20-1.

Table 20-1	Roots Pertaining to Muscles		
Root	**Meaning**	**Example**	**Definition of Example**
my/o	muscle	myositis[a] *mi-o-SI-tis*	inflammation of muscle
muscul/o	muscle	musculature *MUS-kyu-lah-chur*	muscle arrangement in a part or the whole body
in/o	fiber	inotropic *in-o-TROP-ik*	acting on (muscle) fibers
fasci/o	fascia	fasciodesis *fash-e-OD-eh-sis*	binding (suture) of a fascia to a tendon or other fascia
ten/o, tendin/o	tendon	tenostosis *ten-os-TO-sis*	ossification of a tendon
ton/o	tone	cardiotonic *kar-de-o-TON-ik*	having a strengthening action on the heart muscle
erg/o	work	ergonomics *er-go-NOM-iks*	study of the efficient use of energy during work
kin/o-, kine, kinesi/o, kinet/o	movement	kinesis *ki-NE-sis*	movement (adjective: kinetic)

[a]Note addition of s to this root before the suffix -itis.

EXERCISE 20-1

Define the following adjectives.

1. muscular _____

2. fascial _____

3. kinetic _____

4. tendinous _____

5. tonic _____

Write words for the following definitions.

6. incision into a muscle _____

7. inflammation of a muscle with its tendon _____

8. study of movement _____

9. excision of fascia _____

10. pain in a tendon _____

Fill in the blanks.

11. Myoglobin (*mi-o-GLO-bin*) is a type of protein (globin) found in _____.

12. Inosclerosis (*in-o-skle-RO-sis*) is hardening of tissue from an increase in _____.

13. Fasciitis (*fash-e-I-tis*) is inflammation of _____.

14. Dystonia (*dis-TO-ne-ah*) is abnormal muscle _____.

(continued)

EXERCISE 20-1   *(Continued)*

15. An ergograph (*ER-go-graf*) is an instrument for recording muscle _____.

16. Kinesia (*ki-NE-se-ah*) is a term for sickness caused by _____.

17. Myofibrils (*mi-o-FI-brils*) are small fibers found in _____.

18. The muscularis layer in the wall of a hollow organ or duct is composed of _____.

Define the following terms.

19. hypermyotonia (*hi-per-mi-o-TO-ne-ah*) _____

20. fasciorrhaphy (*fash-e-OR-ah-fe*) _____

21. tendinitis (*ten-dih-NI-tis*), also tendonitis (*ten-don-I-tis*) _____

22. musculotendinous (*mus-ku-lo-TEN-dih-nus*) _____

23. tenodesis (*ten-OD-eh-sis*) _____

24. myalgia (*mi-AL-je-ah*) _____

25. kinesitherapy (*ki-ne-sih-THER-ah-pe*) _____

26. dyskinesia (*dis-ki-NE-se-ah*) _____

27. atony (*AT-o-ne*) _____

28. ergogenic (*er-go-JEN-ik*) _____

29. myofascial (*mi-o-FASH-e-al*) _____

30. myotenositis (*mi-o-ten-o-SI-tis*) _____

Clinical Aspects of the Muscular System

Muscle function may be affected by disorders elsewhere, particularly in the nervous system and connective tissue. The conditions described below affect the muscular system directly or involve the muscles but have not been described in other chapters. Any disorder of muscles is described as a myopathy.

Techniques for diagnosing muscle disorders include electrical studies of muscle in action, **electromyography (EMG)**, and serum assay of enzymes released in increased amounts from damaged muscles, mainly **creatine kinase (CK)**.

MUSCULAR DYSTROPHY

Muscular dystrophy refers to a group of hereditary diseases involving progressive, noninflammatory muscular degeneration. There is weakness and wasting of muscle tissue with its gradual replacement by connective tissue and fat. There may also be cardiomyopathy (cardiac muscle disease) and mental impairment.

The most common form is Duchenne muscular dystrophy, a sex-linked disease passed from mother to son. This appears at 3 to 4 years of age, and patients are incapacitated by age 10 to 15. Death is commonly caused by respiratory failure or infection.

See the figure on muscular dystrophy in the Student Resources on thePoint.

MULTIPLE-SYSTEM DISORDERS INVOLVING MUSCLES

Polymyositis

Polymyositis is inflammation of skeletal muscle leading to weakness, frequently associated with dysphagia (difficulty in swallowing) or cardiac problems. The cause is unknown and may be related to viral infection or autoimmunity. Often the disorder is associated with some other systemic disease such as rheumatoid arthritis or lupus erythematosus.

When the skin is involved, the condition is termed **dermatomyositis**. In this case, there is erythema (redness of the skin), dermatitis (inflammation of the skin), and a typical lilac-colored rash, predominantly on the face. In addition to enzyme studies and EMG, clinicians use muscle biopsy in diagnosis.

Fibromyalgia Syndrome

Fibromyalgia syndrome (FMS) is a difficult-to-diagnose condition involving the muscles. It is associated with widespread muscle aches, tenderness, and stiffness, along with fatigue and sleep disorders in the absence of neurologic abnormalities or any other known cause. The disorder may coexist with other chronic diseases, may follow a viral infection, and may involve immune system dysfunction. A current theory is that FMS results from hormonal or neurotransmitter imbalances that increase sensitivity to pain. Treatments for FMS include a carefully planned exercise program and medication with pain relievers, muscle relaxants, or antidepressants.

FOCUS ON WORDS
Some Colorful Musculoskeletal Terms

Box 20-4

Some common terms for musculoskeletal disorders have interesting origins. A charley horse describes muscular strain and soreness, especially in the legs. The term comes from common use of the name Charley for old lame horses that were kept around for family use when they could no longer be used for hard work. Wryneck, technically torticollis, uses the word *wry*, meaning twisted or turned, as in the word awry (*ah-RI*), meaning amiss or out of position.

A bunion, technically called hallux valgus, is an enlargement of the first joint of the great toe with bursitis at the joint. It probably comes from the word bony, changed to bunny, and used to mean a bump on the head and then a swelling on a joint. A clavus is commonly called a corn because it is a hardened or horny thickening of the skin in an area of friction or pressure.

Chronic Fatigue Syndrome

Chronic fatigue syndrome (CFS) involves persistent fatigue of no known cause that may be associated with impaired memory, sore throat, painful lymph nodes, muscle and joint pain, headaches, sleep problems, and immune disorders. The condition often occurs after a viral infection. Epstein-Barr virus (the cause of mononucleosis), herpesvirus, and other viruses have been suggested as possible causes of CFS. No traditional or alternative therapies have been consistently successful in treating CFS.

Myasthenia Gravis

Myasthenia gravis (MG) is an acquired autoimmune disease in which antibodies interfere with muscle stimulation at the neuromuscular junction. There is a progressive loss of muscle power, especially in the external eye muscles and facial muscles.

Amyotrophic Lateral Sclerosis

Also named *Lou Gehrig disease* after a famous baseball player who died of the disorder, **amyotrophic lateral sclerosis (ALS)** is a progressive degeneration of motor neurons that leads to muscle atrophy (amyotrophy). Early signs are weakness, cramping, and muscle twitching. The facial or respiratory muscles may be affected early depending on the site of degeneration. Mental function, sensory perception, and bowel and bladder function usually remain intact. The disease progresses and eventually leads to death from respiratory muscle paralysis in three to five years.

STRESS INJURIES

Not as grave as the above diseases perhaps, but much more common, are musculoskeletal disorders caused by physical stress. These include accidental injuries and work- or sports-related damage caused by overexertion or repetitive motion, so-called **repetitive strain injury (RSI)**. Damages to soft tissues include **sprain**, injury to a ligament caused by abnormal or excessive force at a joint but without bone dislocation or fracture; muscle **strain**, inflammation or tearing of ligaments and tendons; and bursitis. **Tenosynovitis**, commonly called **tendinitis**, is inflammation of a tendon, tendon sheath, and the synovial membrane at a joint. The signs of these injuries are pain, fatigue, weakness, stiffness, numbness, and reduced range of motion (ROM). (The origins of some colorful terms for such conditions are given in **Box 20-4**.)

Stress injuries may involve any muscles or joints, but some common upper extremity conditions are:

- Rotator cuff (RTC) injury—The RTC, which strengthens the shoulder joint, is formed by four muscles, the supraspinatus, infraspinatus, teres minor, and subscapularis, the "SITS" muscles (**Fig. 20-8**). Inflammation or

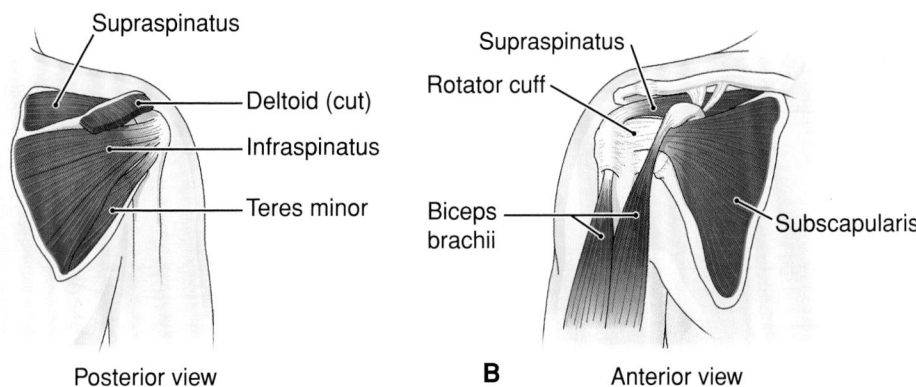

Figure 20-8 **Anatomy of the rotator cuff.** Four muscles contribute to the rotator cuff that strengthens the shoulder. They are the supraspinatus, infraspinatus, teres minor, and subscapularis. Two adjacent muscles are also shown, the deltoid and biceps brachii. **A.** Posterior. **B.** Anterior.

tearing of the RTC can occur in people who repeatedly perform overhead activities, such as swimming, painting, or pitching.

- Epicondylitis—The medial and lateral epicondyles (projections) of the distal humerus are attachment points for muscles that flex and extend the wrist and fingers. Inflammation of these tendons of origin causes pain at the elbow and forearm on lifting, carrying, squeezing, or typing. These stress injuries are often sports-related, leading to the terms "golfer's elbow" and "tennis elbow" for medial and lateral epicondylitis, respectively. A brace worn below the elbow to distribute stress on the joint may be helpful.

- Carpal tunnel syndrome (CTS)—CTS involves the tendons of the finger flexor muscles and the nerves that supply the hand and fingers (**Fig. 20-9**). Hand numbness and weakness are caused by pressure on the median nerve as it passes through a channel formed by the carpal (wrist) bones. CTS commonly appears in people who use their hands and fingers strenuously, such as musicians and keyboarders.

- Trigger finger—This is a painful snapping, triggering, or locking of a finger as it is moved. It is caused by inflammation and swelling of the flexor tendon sheath at the metacarpophalangeal joint that prevents the tendon from sliding back and forth.

Some stress injuries that involve the lower extremities are:

- Hamstring strain—The hamstring is a large muscle group in the posterior thigh that extends from the hip to the knee and flexes the knee (**Fig. 20-7**). A "pulled hamstring" is common in athletes who stop and start running suddenly. It is treated with stretching and strengthening activities.

- Shin-splint—This is pain in the leg's anterior tibial region from running on hard surfaces or overuse of the foot flexors, as in athletes and dancers. Help comes from good shoes with adequate support and avoidance of hard surfaces for exercise.

- Achilles tendinitis—The Achilles (*a-KIL-eze*) tendon is a large tendon that attaches the calf muscles to the heel and is used to plantar flex the foot at the ankle (see **Figs. 20-5** and **20-7**). Damage to the Achilles tendon hampers or prevents walking and running.

Treatment

Orthopedists diagnose musculoskeletal disorders by MRI and other imaging techniques, ROM measurements, and strength testing. Treatment of stress injuries usually begins conservatively with rest, elevation, ice packs, bracing, and medications, such as analgesics, antiinflammatory agents, and muscle relaxants. (The acronym RICE represents this simple approach—rest, ice, compression, elevation.) Treatment may progress to steroid injections, ultrasound therapy for deep heat, strengthening exercises, or even surgery.

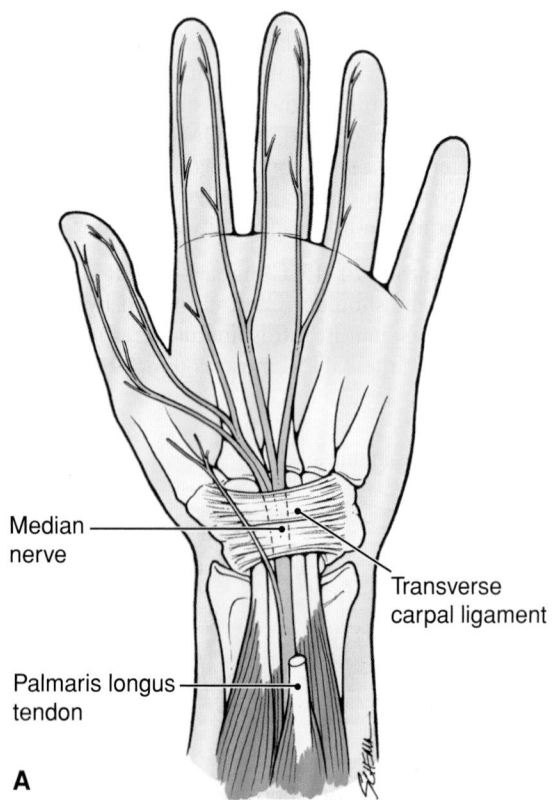

Median nerve

Transverse carpal ligament

Palmaris longus tendon

A

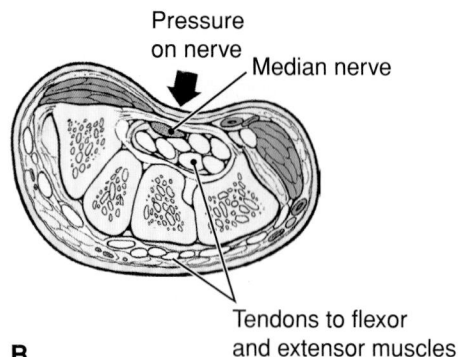

Pressure on nerve

Median nerve

Tendons to flexor and extensor muscles

B

Figure 20-9 Carpal tunnel syndrome. A. Pressure on the median nerve as it passes through the carpal (wrist) bones causes numbness and weakness in the areas of the hand supplied by the nerve. **B.** Cross-section of the wrist showing compression of the median nerve.

Terminology | Key Terms

Disorders

amyotrophic lateral sclerosis (ALS) *ah-mi-o-TROF-ik*	A disease caused by motor neuron degeneration resulting in muscular weakness and atrophy; Lou Gehrig disease
chronic fatigue syndrome (CFS)	A disease of unknown cause that involves persistent fatigue along with muscle and joint pain and other symptoms; may be virally induced
dermatomyositis *der-mah-to-mi-o-SI-tis*	A disease of unknown origin involving muscular inflammation as well as dermatitis and skin rashes
fibromyalgia syndrome (FMS) *fi-bro-mi-AL-je-ah*	A disorder associated with widespread muscular aches and stiffness and having no known cause
muscular dystrophy *DIS-tro-fe*	A group of hereditary muscular disorders marked by progressive weakness and muscular atrophy
myasthenia gravis (MG) *mi-as-THE-ne-ah GRAH-vis*	A disease characterized by progressive muscular weakness; an autoimmune disease affecting the neuromuscular junction
polymyositis *pol-e-mi-o-SI-tis*	A disease of unknown cause involving muscular inflammation and weakness
repetitive strain injury (RSI)	Tissue damage caused by repeated motion, usually overuse of the arm or hand in occupational activities such as writing, typing, painting, or using hand tools; also called repetitive motion injury, cumulative trauma injury, overuse syndrome
sprain *sprane*	Injury to a ligament caused by abnormal or excessive force at a joint, but without bone dislocation or fracture
strain *strane*	Trauma to a muscle because of overuse or excessive stretch; if severe, may involve muscular tearing, bleeding, separation of a muscle from its tendon, or tendon separation from a bone
tendinitis *ten-dih-NI-tis*	Inflammation of a tendon, usually caused by injury or overuse; the shoulder, elbow, and hip are common sites; also spelled tendonitis
tenosynovitis *ten-o-sin-o-VI-tis*	Inflammation of a tendon and its sheath

Diagnosis

creatine kinase (CK) *KRE-ah-tin KI-nase*	An enzyme found in muscle tissue; the serum CK level increases in cases of muscle damage; creatine phosphokinase (CPK)
electromyography (EMG) *e-lek-tro-mi-OG-rah-fe*	Study of the electrical activity of muscles during contraction

Go to the Audio Pronunciation Glossary in the Student Resources on thePoint to hear these terms pronounced.

20

Terminology | Supplementary Terms

Normal Structure and Function

aponeurosis *ap-o-nu-RO-sis*	A flat, white, sheet-like tendon that connects a muscle with the part that it moves (see abdominal aponeurosis, **Fig. 20-6**)
creatine *KRE-ah-tin*	A substance in muscle cells that stores energy for contraction
glycogen *GLI-ko-jen*	A complex sugar that is stored for energy in muscles and in the liver
isometric *i-so-MET-rik*	Pertaining to a muscle action in which the muscle tenses but does not shorten (literally: same measurement)
isotonic *i-so-TON-ik*	Pertaining to a muscle action in which the muscle shortens to accomplish movement (literally: same tone)
kinesthesia *kin-es-THE-ze-ah*	Awareness of movement; perception of the weight, direction, and degree of movement (-esthesia means "sensation")
lactic acid *LAK-tik*	An acid that accumulates in muscle cells functioning without enough oxygen (anaerobically), as in times of great physical exertion
motor unit	A single motor neuron and all of the muscle cells that its branches stimulate
myoglobin *mi-o-GLO-bin*	A protein similar to hemoglobin that stores oxygen in muscle cells

Symptoms and Conditions

asterixis *as-ter-IK-sis*	Rapid, jerky movements, especially in the hands, caused by intermittent loss of muscle tone
asthenia *as-THE-ne-ah*	Weakness (prefix a- meaning "without" with root sthen/o meaning "strength")
ataxia *ah-TAK-se-ah*	Lack of muscle coordination (from root *tax/o* meaning "order, arrangement") (adjective: ataxic)
athetosis *ath-eh-TO-sis*	A condition marked by slow, irregular, twisting movements, especially in the hands and fingers (adjective: athetotic)
atrophy *AT-ro-fe*	A wasting away; a decrease in the size of a tissue or organ, such as muscular wasting from disuse
avulsion *ah-VUL-shun*	Forcible tearing away of a part
clonus *KLO-nus*	Alternating spasmodic contraction and relaxation in a muscle (adjective: clonic)
contracture *kon-TRAK-chur*	Permanent contraction of a muscle
fasciculation *fah-sik-u-LA-shun*	Involuntary small contractions or twitching of muscle fiber groups (fasciculi)
fibromyositis *fi-bro-mi-o-SI-tis*	A nonspecific term for pain, tenderness, and stiffness in muscles and joints
fibrositis *fi-bro-SI-tis*	Inflammation of fibrous connective tissue, especially the muscle fasciae; marked by pain and stiffness
restless legs syndrome (RLS)	Uneasiness, twitching, or restlessness in the legs that occurs after going to bed and often leading to insomnia; may be caused by poor circulation or drug side effects
rhabdomyolysis *rab-do-mi-OL-ih-sis*	An acute disease involving diffuse destruction of skeletal muscle cells (root *rhabd/o* means "rod," referring to the long, rod-like muscle cells)

| Terminology | **Supplementary Terms** (*Continued*) |

20

rhabdomyoma *rab-do-mi-O-mah*	A benign tumor of skeletal muscle
rhabdomyosarcoma *rab-do-mi-o-sar-KO-mah*	A highly malignant tumor of skeletal muscle
rheumatism *RU-mah-tizm*	A general term for inflammation, soreness, and stiffness of muscles associated with joint pain (adjectives: rheumatic, rheumatoid)
spasm *spazm*	A sudden, involuntary muscle contraction; may be clonic (contraction alternating with relaxation) or tonic (sustained); a strong and painful spasm may be called a cramp (adjectives: spastic, spasmodic)
spasticity *spas-TIS-ih-te*	Increased tone or contractions of muscles causing stiff and awkward movements
tetanus *TET-ah-nus*	An acute infectious disease caused by the anaerobic bacillus *Clostridium tetani*; marked by persistent painful spasms of voluntary muscles; lockjaw
tetany *TET-ah-ne*	A condition marked by spasms, cramps, and muscle twitching caused by a metabolic imbalance, such as low blood calcium resulting from underactivity of the parathyroid glands
torticollis *tor-tih-KOL-is*	Spasmodic contraction of the neck muscles causing stiffness and twisting of the neck; wryneck

Diagnosis and Treatment

Chvostek sign *VOS-tek*	Spasm of facial muscles after a tap over the facial nerve; evidence of tetany
dynamometer *di-nah-MOM-eh-ter*	Instrument for measuring degree of muscle power; from root dynam/o meaning "force, energy;" also called ergometer
occupational therapy (OT)	Health profession concerned with increasing function and preventing disability through work and play activities; the goal of occupational therapy is to increase the patient's independence and quality of daily life (see **Box 17–2**)
physical therapy (PT)	Health profession concerned with physical rehabilitation and prevention of disability; exercise, massage, and other therapeutic methods are used to restore proper movement (see **Box 19–2**)
rheumatology *ru-mah-TOL-o-je*	The study and treatment of rheumatic diseases
Trousseau sign *tru-SO*	Spasmodic contractions caused by pressing the nerve supplying a muscle; seen in tetany

Drugs

antiinflammatory agent	Drug that reduces inflammation; includes steroids, such as cortisol, and nonsteroidal antiinflammatory drugs
COX-2 inhibitor	Nonsteroidal antiinflammatory drug that does not cause the stomach problems associated with other NSAIDs; inhibits the cyclooxygenase (COX)-2 enzyme without affecting the COX-1 enzyme, a lack of which can cause stomach ulcers; example is celecoxib (Celebrex); some of these drugs have been withdrawn from the market because of cardiac risk
muscle relaxant *re-LAX-ant*	A drug that reduces muscle tension; different forms may be used to relax muscles during surgery, to control spasticity, or to relieve musculoskeletal pain
nonsteroidal antiinflammatory drug (NSAID)	Drug that reduces inflammation but is not a steroid; examples include aspirin, ibuprofen, naproxen, and other inhibitors of prostaglandins, naturally produced substances that promote inflammation

Terminology Abbreviations

ACh	Acetylcholine	NMJ	Neuromuscular junction
ALS	Amyotrophic lateral sclerosis	OT	Occupational therapy/therapist
CFS	Chronic fatigue syndrome	PT	Physical therapy/therapist
C(P)K	Creatine (phospho)kinase	RICE	Rest, ice, compression, elevation
CTS	Carpal tunnel syndrome	RLE	Right lower extremity
EMG	Electromyography, electromyogram	RLS	Restless legs syndrome
FMS	Fibromyalgia syndrome	ROM	Range of motion
LLE	Left lower extremity	RSI	Repetitive strain injury
LUE	Left upper extremity	RTC	Rotator cuff
MG	Myasthenia gravis	RUE	Right upper extremity
MMT	Manual muscle test(ing)	SITS	Supraspinatus, infraspinatus, teres minor, subscapularis (muscles)

Case Study Revisited

T.D.'s Follow-Up

The exploratory surgery confirmed the brachial plexus injury, and T.D. underwent the nerve graft with muscle taken from his right thigh. After six days, he was discharged home with his right arm in a shoulder immobilizer. He received instructions on activities and was told to see the surgeon in one week and again three weeks later. Physical therapy was ordered to prevent further atrophy and to begin rebuilding the arm muscles. T.D. was frustrated with the slow progress, but the orthopedic surgeon had said that in time, he should regain full use of his right arm and normal activities of daily living should be restored.

Labeling Exercise

SUPERFICIAL MUSCLES, ANTERIOR VIEW

Write the name of each numbered part on the corresponding line.

Adductors of thigh	Gastrocnemius	Sartorius
Biceps brachii	Intercostals	Serratus anterior
Brachialis	Internal oblique	Soleus
Brachioradialis	Masseter	Sternocleidomastoid
Deltoid	Orbicularis oculi	Temporalis
Extensor carpi	Orbicularis oris	Tibialis anterior
External oblique	Pectoralis major	Trapezius
Fibularis longus	Quadriceps femoris	
Flexor carpi	Rectus abdominis	

1. _____

2. _____

3. _____

4. _____

5. _____

6. _____

7. _____

8. _____

9. _____

10. _____

11. _____

12. _____

13. _____

14. _____

15. _____

16. _____

17. _____

18. _____

19. _____

20. _____

21. _____

22. _____

23. _____

24. _____

25. _____

Anterior view

SUPERFICIAL MUSCLES, POSTERIOR VIEW

Write the name of each numbered part on the corresponding line.

Deltoid   Latissimus dorsi
Fibularis longus   Sternocleidomastoid
Gastrocnemius   Teres major
Gluteus maximus   Teres minor
Gluteus medius   Trapezius
Hamstring group   Triceps brachii

1. _____

2. _____

3. _____

4. _____

5. _____

6. _____

7. _____

8. _____

9. _____

10. _____

11. _____

12. _____

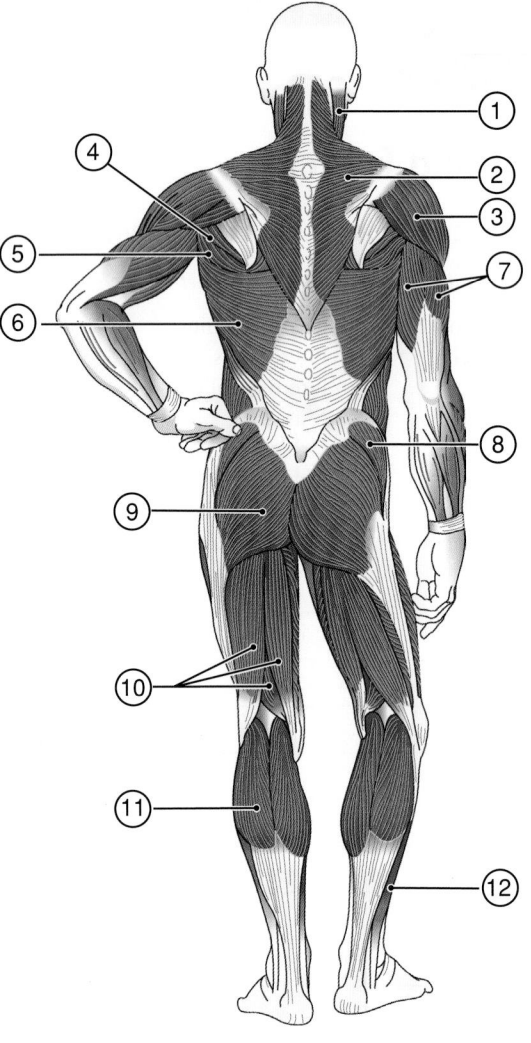

Posterior view

Terminology

MATCHING

Match the following terms, and write the appropriate letter to the left of each number.

_____ **1.** masseter   **a.** muscle used in chewing; jaw muscle

_____ **2.** quadriceps femoris   **b.** large muscle of the upper chest

_____ **3.** pectoralis major   **c.** a group of four muscles in the thigh

_____ **4.** gastrocnemius   **d.** main muscle of the calf

_____ **5.** trapezius   **e.** muscle of the upper back and neck

_____ **6.** akinesia   **a.** instrument for measuring muscle work

_____ **7.** fascicle   **b.** absence of movement

_____ **8.** inotropic   **c.** a small bundle of fibers

_____ **9.** dystonia   **d.** acting on muscle fibers

_____ **10.** ergometer   **e.** abnormal muscle tone

Supplementary Terms

_____ **11.** lactic acid	**a.** protein that stores oxygen in muscle cells
_____ **12.** aponeurosis	**b.** flat, white, sheet-like tendon
_____ **13.** tetany	**c.** muscular spasms and cramps
_____ **14.** myoglobin	**d.** complex sugar stored in muscles
_____ **15.** glycogen	**e.** byproduct of anaerobic muscle contractions

_____ **16.** asterixis	**a.** awareness of movement
_____ **17.** ataxia	**b.** weakness
_____ **18.** torticollis	**c.** rapid, jerky movements, especially of the hands
_____ **19.** asthenia	**d.** wryneck
_____ **20.** kinesthesia	**e.** lack of muscle coordination

_____ **21.** athetosis	**a.** forcible tearing away of a part
_____ **22.** clonus	**b.** acute infectious disease that affects muscles
_____ **23.** spasm	**c.** intermittent muscle contractions
_____ **24.** avulsion	**d.** sudden involuntary muscle contraction
_____ **25.** tetanus	**e.** condition marked by slow, twisting movements

REFERRING TO T.D.'S CASE HISTORY

_____ **26.** deltoid	**a.** partial dislocation
_____ **27.** atrophy	**b.** shoulder muscle
_____ **28.** subluxation	**c.** network
_____ **29.** plexus	**d.** pertaining to the diaphragm
_____ **30.** phrenic	**e.** tissue wasting

FILL IN THE BLANKS

31. A band of connective tissue that attaches a muscle to a bone is a(n) _____.

32. A musculotropic substance acts on _____.

33. The number of origins (heads) in the triceps brachii muscle is _____.

34. A muscle that produces extension at a joint is called a(n) _____.

35. The neurotransmitter released at the neuromuscular junction is _____.

36. The strong, cord-like tendon that attaches the calf muscle to the heel is the _____.

37. Movement toward the midline of the body is termed _____.

38. The sheath of connective tissue that covers a muscle is called _____.

REFERRING TO T.D.'S CASE STUDY

39. The nerves of the brachial plexus supply the _____.

40. The muscle above the spine of the scapula is the _____.

41. The vertebra C7 is in the region of the _____.

DEFINITIONS

Define the following words.

42. myofascial (*mi-o-FASH-e-al*) _____.

43. tendinoplasty (*TEN-din-o-plas-te*) _____.

44. hypotonia (*hi-po-TO-ne-ah*) _____.

45. hyperkinesia (*hi-per-ki-NE-se-ah*) _____

46. inotropic (*in-o-TROP-ik*) _____

47. myositis (*mi-o-SI-tis*) _____

Write words for the following definitions.

48. suture of fascia _____

49. death of muscle tissue _____

50. study of movement _____

51. absence of muscle tone _____

52. surgical incision of a tendon (use ten/o-) _____

53. study of muscles _____

54. excision of fascia _____

55. pertaining to a tendon _____

OPPOSITES

Write a word that means the opposite of the following terms as they pertain to muscles.

56. agonist _____

57. origin _____

58. abduction _____

59. pronation _____

60. extension _____

ADJECTIVES

From the supplementary terms, write the adjective form of the following words.

61. ataxia _____

62. athetosis _____

63. spasm _____

64. clonus _____

TRUE–FALSE

Examine the following statements. If the statement is true, write T in the first blank. If the statement is false, write F in the first blank, and correct the statement by replacing the underlined word in the second blank.

	True or False	**Correct Answer**
65. The part of a neuron that contacts a muscle cell is the <u>dendrite</u>.	_____	_____
66. Skeletal muscle is <u>involuntary</u>.	_____	_____
67. The quadriceps muscle has <u>three</u> components.	_____	_____
68. <u>Pronation</u> means turning downward.	_____	_____
69. The hamstring group is in the <u>anterior</u> thigh.	_____	_____
70. Smooth muscle is also called <u>visceral</u> muscle.	_____	_____
71. The <u>origin</u> of a muscle is attached to a moving part.	_____	_____
72. In an <u>isotonic</u> contraction, a muscle shortens.	_____	_____

ELIMINATIONS

In each of the sets below, underline the word that does not fit in with the rest, and explain the reason for your choice.

73. fascicle — fiber — tendon — osteoblast — fascia

_____

74. soleus — flexor carpi — biceps brachii — brachioradialis — extensor carpi

_____

75. vastus intermedius — intercostals — vastus lateralis — vastus medialis — rectus femoris

_____

76. circumduction — inversion — actin — dorsiflexion — rotation

_____

77. EMG — ALS — FMS — CFS — MG

_____

ABBREVIATIONS

Write the meaning of each of the following.

78. RICE _____

79. RTC _____

80. CTS _____

81. NMJ _____

82. EMG _____

WORD BUILDING

Write a word for the following definitions using the word parts provided.

| -ia   ten/o   -al   alg/o   -itis   -desis   -blast   -lysis   fasci/o   my/o |

83. inflammation of fascia _____

84. binding of a tendon _____

85. pain in a tendon _____

86. destruction of muscle tissue _____

87. binding of a fascia _____

88. an immature muscle cell _____

89. separation of a tendon _____

90. pertaining to fascia _____

91. pain in a muscle _____

WORD ANALYSIS

Define each of the following words, and give the meaning of the word parts in each. Use a dictionary if necessary.

92. fibromyositis (*fi-bro-mi-o-SI-tis*) _____

    a. fibr/o _____

    b. my/o(s) _____

    c. -itis _____

93. myasthenia (*mi-as-THE-ne-ah*) _____

   a. my/o _____

   b. a- _____

   c. sthen/o _____

   d. -ia _____

94. dyssynergia (*dis-in-ER-je-ah*) _____

   a. dys- _____

   b. syn- _____

   c. erg/o _____

   d. -ia _____

95. amyotrophic (*ah-mi-o-TRO-fik*) _____

   a. a- _____

   b. my/o _____

   c. troph/o _____

   d. -ic _____

For more learning activities, see Chapter 20 of the Student Resources on thePoint.

Additional Case Studies

Case Study 20-1: *Rotator Cuff Tear*

M.L., a 56-year-old business executive and former college football player, was referred to an orthopedic surgeon for recurrent shoulder pain. M.L. was unable to abduct his right arm without pain even after six months of physical therapy and NSAIDs. In addition, he had taken supplements of glucosamine, chondroitin, and *S*-adenosylmethionine for several months in an effort to protect the flexibility of his shoulder joint. M.L. recalled a shoulder dislocation resulting from a football injury 35 years earlier. An MRI scan confirmed a complete rotator cuff tear. The surgeon recommended the Bankart procedure for M.L.'s injury to restore his joint stability, alleviate his pain, and permit him to return to his former normal activities, including golf.

After anesthesia induction and positioning in a semisitting (beach chair) position, the surgeon made an anterosuperior deltoid incision (the standard del-topectoral approach) and divided the coracoacromial ligament at the acromial attachment. The rotator cuff was identified after the deltoid was retracted and the clavipectoral fascia was incised. The subscapularis tendon was incised proximal to its insertion. After capsular incision, inspection showed a large pouch inferiorly in the capsule, consistent with laxity (instability). The capsule's torn edges were anchored to the rim of the glenoid fossa with heavy nonabsorbable sutures. A flap from the subscapularis tendon was transposed and sutured to the supraspinatus and infraspinatus muscles to bridge the gap. An intraoperative ROM examination showed that the external rotation could be performed past neutral and that the shoulder did not dislocate. The wound was closed, and a shoulder immobilizer sling was applied. M.L. was referred to PT to begin therapy in three weeks and was assured he would be able to play golf in six months.

Case Study 20-2: *"Wake-Up" Test during Spinal Fusion Surgery*

L.N.'s somatosensory evoked potentials (SSEPs) were monitored throughout her spinal fusion surgery to provide continuous information on the functional state of her sensory pathways from the median and posterior tibial nerves through the dorsal column to the primary somatosensory cortex. Before surgery, needle electrodes were inserted into L.N.'s right and left quadriceps muscles to determine nerve conduction through L2 to L4, into the anterior tibialis muscles to measure passage through L5, and into the gastrocnemius muscles to measure S1 to S2. Electrodes were placed in her rectus abdominis to monitor S1 to S2. All electrodes were taped in place, and the wires were plugged into a transformer box with feedback to a computer. A neuromonitoring technologist placed the electrodes and attended the computer monitor throughout the case. During the procedure, selected muscle groups were stimulated with 15 to 40 milliamperes (mA) of current to test the nerves and muscles. Data fed back into the computer confirmed the neuromuscular integrity and status of the spinal fixation, the instrumentation, and implants.

After the pedicle screws, hooks, and wires were in place and the spinal rods were cinched down to straighten the spine, L.N. was permitted to emerge temporarily from anesthesia and muscle paralysis medication to a lightly sedated but pain-free state. She was given commands to move her feet, straighten her legs, and wiggle her toes to test all neuromuscular groups that could be affected by misplaced or compressed spinal fixation devices. Her feet were watched, and movement was announced to the team. Dorsiflexion cleared the tibialis anterior muscles; plantar flexion cleared the gastrocnemius muscles. Knee flexion cleared the hamstring muscle group, and knee extension determined function of the quadriceps group. L.N. had a successful "wake-up" test. She was put back into deep anesthesia, and her incision was closed. A postoperative "wake-up" test was repeated after she was moved to her bed. The surgical instruments and tables were kept sterile until after all of the monitored muscle groups were tested and showed voluntary movement. The electrodes were removed, and she was taken to the postanesthesia care unit (PACU) for recovery.

(continued)

Additional Case Studies *(Continued)*

Case Study Questions

Multiple Choice. Select the best answer, and write the letter of your choice to the left of each number.

_____ 1. The insertion of the muscle is
- **a.** the thick middle portion
- **b.** the point of attachment to a moving bone
- **c.** the point of attachment to a stable bone
- **d.** the fibrous sheath

_____ 2. M.L. was unable to abduct his affected arm. This motion is
- **a.** toward the midline
- **b.** circumferential
- **c.** away from the midline
- **d.** a position with the palm facing upward

_____ 3. An anterosuperior deltoid incision would be made
- **a.** perpendicular to the muscle fibers
- **b.** below the fascial sheath
- **c.** behind the glenoid fossa
- **d.** at the top and to the front of the deltoid muscle

_____ 4. The subscapularis tendon arises from the subscapularis
- **a.** fascia
- **b.** nerve
- **c.** bone
- **d.** flexor

_____ 5. The intraoperative ROM examination was performed
- **a.** in the OR corridor
- **b.** during surgery
- **c.** before surgery
- **d.** after surgery

_____ 6. M.L.'s arm and shoulder were placed in a sling after surgery to
- **a.** encourage movement beyond the point of pain
- **b.** minimize rapid ROM
- **c.** maintain adduction and external rotation
- **d.** prevent movement

_____ 7. The quadriceps muscle group is made up of
- **a.** smooth and cardiac muscle fibers
- **b.** four muscles in the thigh
- **c.** three muscles in the leg and one in the foot
- **d.** fascia and tendon sheaths

_____ 8. The anterior tibialis muscle is in the
- **a.** thigh
- **b.** spine
- **c.** foot
- **d.** leg

_____ 9. The nerve supply for the rectus abdominis muscle runs through S1 to S2. This anatomic region is
- **a.** the first and second sural sheath
- **b.** subluxation and suppuration
- **c.** sacral disk space 1 and 2
- **d.** sacral disk space 3

_____ 10. The movement of elevating the toes toward the anterior ankle is
- **a.** supination
- **b.** pronation
- **c.** dorsiflexion
- **d.** plantar flexion

_____ 11. Knee extension results in
- **a.** a bent knee
- **b.** a ballet position with the toes turned out
- **c.** bilateral abduction
- **d.** a straight leg

Write terms from the Case Studies with the following meanings.

12. pertaining to treatment of skeletal and muscular disorders _____

13. bending at a joint _____

14. to point the toes downward _____

Define the following abbreviations.

15. PT _____

16. ROM _____

17. SSEP _____

18. PACU _____

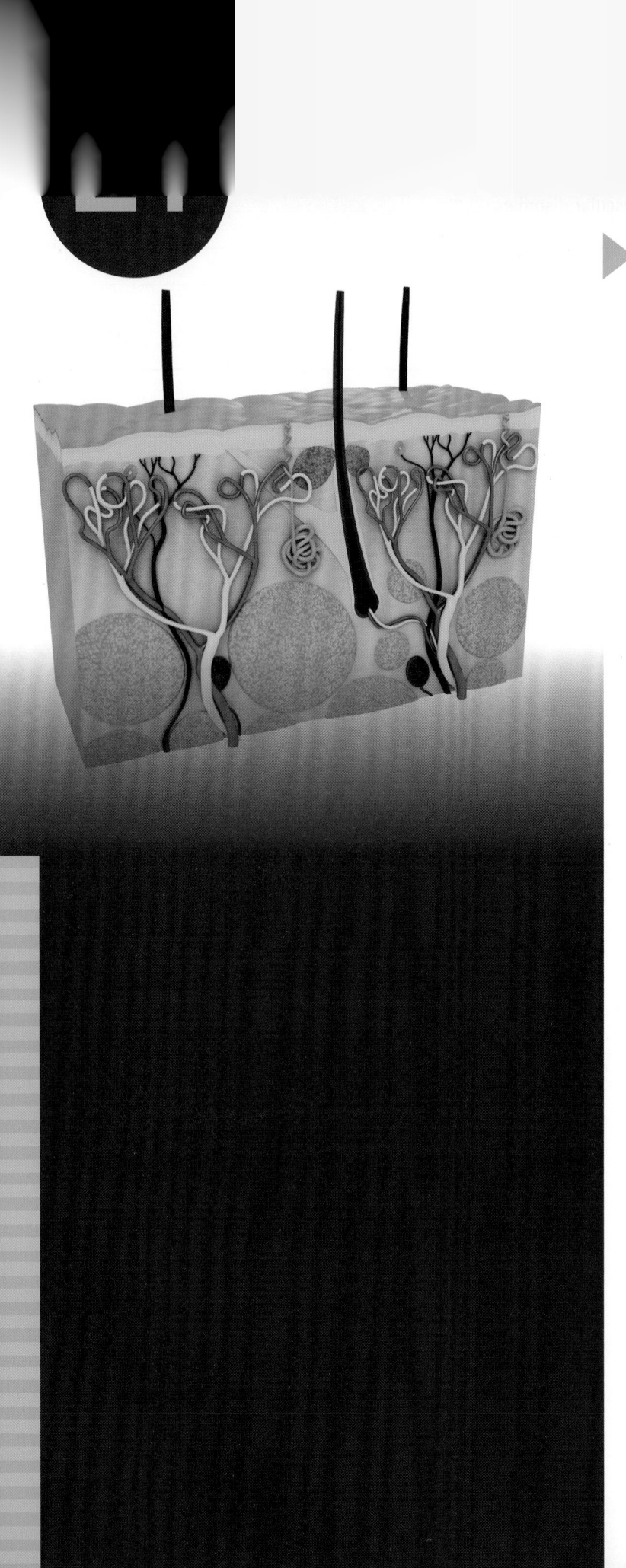

Pretest

Multiple Choice. Select the best answer, and write the letter of your choice to the left of each number.

_C_ 1. The uppermost portion of the skin is called the
   a. fossa
   b. cuticle
   c. epidermis
   d. epiphysis

_b_ 2. The glands that secrete an oily substance that lubricates the skin are the
   a. mammary glands
   b. sebaceous glands
   c. sweat glands
   d. ceruminous glands

_____ 3. The rule of nines is a system used to evaluate
   a. burns
   b. fever
   c. immunity
   d. inflammation

_b_ 4. A pigmented skin tumor is a(n)
   a. chondrosarcoma
   b. melanoma
   c. lymphoma
   d. adenoma

_____ 5. The root *hidr/o* pertains to
   a. saliva
   b. tears
   c. mucus
   d. sweat

_____ 6. Onychomycosis is a fungal infection of a(n)
   a. eyelid
   b. hair
   c. nail
   d. bone

Learning Objectives

After study of this chapter, you should be able to:

1. ▷ Define and list the functions of the integumentary system. *p558*

2. ▷ Compare the locations and structures of the epidermis, dermis, and subcutaneous tissues. *p558*

3. ▷ Describe the roles of keratin and melanin in the skin. *p558*

4. ▷ Name and describe the glands in the skin. *p558*

5. ▷ Describe the structure of hair and nails. *p558*

6. ▷ Identify and use roots pertaining to the skin. *p561*

7. ▷ Describe the main disorders that affect the skin. *p562*

8. ▷ Interpret abbreviations used in the study and treatment of the skin. *p573*

9. ▷ Analyze medical terms in several case studies involving the skin. *pp557, 579*

Case Study: *C.M.'s Pressure Ulcer*

Chief Complaint

C.M., an elderly woman in failing health, had recently moved in with her daughter after her hospitalization for a stroke. The daughter reported to the home care nurse that her mother had minimal appetite and was confused and disoriented and that a blister had developed on her lower back since she had been confined to bed.

Examination

During the biweekly visit, the home care nurse spoke with the daughter and then went in to see the mother. On her initial assessment, the nurse noted that C.M. had lost weight since her last visit and that her skin was dry, with poor skin turgor. She also observed that the mother was wearing an "adult diaper," which was wet. The nurse took the mother's BP, HR, and R, which were normal. She assessed the mother's mental status and then proceeded to a skin assessment paying special attention to the bony prominences. After examining C.M.'s sacrum, the nurse noted a nickel-sized open area, 2 cm in diameter and 1 cm in depth (stage II pressure ulcer), with a 0.5-cm reddened surrounding area with no drainage. C.M. moaned when the nurse palpated the lesion. The nurse also noted reddened areas on C.M.'s elbows and heels. The remainder of the examination saw no change from the previous visit.

Clinical Course

The nurse provided C.M.'s daughter with instructions for proper skin care, incontinence management, enhanced nutrition, and frequent repositioning to prevent pressure ischemia to the prominent body areas. However, six months later, C.M.'s pressure ulcer had deteriorated to class III. She was hospitalized under the care of a plastic surgeon and wound care nurse. Surgery was scheduled for debridement of the sacral wound and closure with a full-thickness skin graft taken from her thigh. C.M. was discharged eight days later to a long-term care facility with orders for an alternating pressure mattress, position change every two hours, supplemental nutrition, and meticulous wound care.

ANCILLARIES *At-A-Glance*

Visit thePoint to access the following resources. For guidance in using the resources most effectively, see pp. ix–xvi.

Learning RESOURCES

▷ Tips for Effective Studying
▷ Web Figure: Clinical Findings in Systemic Lupus Erythematosus
▷ Web Figure: Malar "Butterfly" Rash of Systemic Lupus Erythematosus
▷ Web Chart: Skin Structure
▷ Web Chart: Accessory Skin Structures

▷ Animation: Wound Healing
▷ Audio Pronunciation Glossary

Learning ACTIVITIES

▷ Visual Activities
▷ Kinesthetic Activities
▷ Auditory Activities

Introduction

The **skin** and its associated structures make up the **integumentary system.** This body-covering system protects against infection, dehydration, ultraviolet radiation, and injury. Extensive damage to the skin, such as by burns, can result in a host of dangerous complications.

The skin helps to regulate temperature by evaporation of sweat and by changes in the diameter of surface blood vessels, which control how much heat is lost to the environment. The skin also contains receptors for the sensory perceptions of touch, temperature, pressure, and pain. Medication can be delivered through the skin from patches, as explained in **Box 21-1.**

The word **derma** (from Greek) means "skin" and is used as an ending in words pertaining to the skin, such as xeroderma (dryness of the skin) and scleroderma (hardening of the skin). The adjective **cutaneous** refers to the skin and is from the Latin word *cutis* for skin. Like the eyes, the skin is a readily visible reflection of one's health. Its color, texture, and resilience reveal much, as does the condition of the hair and nails.

Anatomy of the Skin

The skin's outermost portion is the **epidermis,** consisting of four to five layers (strata) of epithelial cells (**Fig. 21-1**). The deepest epidermal layer, the stratum basale, or basal layer, produces new cells. As these cells gradually rise toward the surface, they die and become filled with **keratin,** a protein that thickens and toughens the skin. The outermost epidermal layer, the stratum corneum or horny layer, is composed of flat, dead, protective cells that are constantly being shed and replaced. Some of the cells in the epidermis produce **melanin,** a pigment that gives the skin color and protects against sunlight.

The **dermis** is beneath the epidermis. It contains connective tissue, nerves, blood vessels, lymphatics, and sensory receptors. This layer supplies nourishment and support for the skin. The **subcutaneous layer** beneath the dermis is composed mainly of connective tissue and fat.

Associated Skin Structures

Specialized structures within the skin are part of the integumentary system:

- The **sudoriferous** (sweat) **glands** act mainly in temperature regulation by releasing a watery fluid that evaporates to cool the body.
- The **sebaceous glands** release an oily fluid, **sebum,** that lubricates the hair and skin and prevents drying.
- **Hair** is widely distributed over the body. Each hair develops within a sheath or **hair follicle** and grows from its base within the skin's deep layers. A small muscle (arrector pili) attached to the follicle raises the hair to produce "goosebumps" when one is frightened or cold (see **Fig. 21-1**). In animals this is a warning sign and a means of insulation.
- **Nails** develop from a growing region at the proximal end (**Fig. 21-2**). The cuticle, technically named the

---

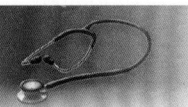

CLINICAL PERSPECTIVES

Box 21-1

Medication Patches: No Bitter Pill to Swallow

For most people, pills are a convenient way to take medication, but for some, they have drawbacks. Pills must be taken at regular intervals to ensure consistent dosing, and they must be digested and absorbed into the bloodstream before they can begin to work. For those who have difficulty swallowing or digesting pills, transdermal (TD) patches offer an effective alternative to oral medications.

TD patches deliver a consistent dose of medication that diffuses at a constant rate through the skin into the bloodstream. There is no daily schedule to follow, nothing to swallow, and no stomach upset. TD patches can also deliver medication to unconscious patients, who would otherwise require intravenous drug delivery. TD patches are used in hormone replacement therapy, to treat heart disease, to manage pain, and to suppress motion sickness. Nicotine patches are also used as part of programs to quit smoking.

TD patches must be used carefully. Drug diffusion through the skin takes time, so it is important to know how long the patch must be in place before it is effective. It is also important to know when the medication's effects disappear after the patch is removed. Because the body continues to absorb what has already diffused into the skin, removing the patch does not entirely remove the medicine. There is also a danger that patches may become unsafe when heated, as by exercise, high fever, or a hot environment, such as a hot tub, heating pad, or sauna. When heat dilates the capillaries in the skin, a dangerous increase in dosage may result as more medication enters the blood.

A recent advance in TD drug delivery is iontophoresis. Based on the principle that like charges repel each other, this method uses a mild electrical current to move ionic drugs through the skin. A small electrical device attached to the patch uses positive current to "push" positively charged drug molecules through the skin and a negative current to push negatively charged ones. Even though very low levels of electricity are used, people with pacemakers should not use iontophoretic patches. Another disadvantage of these patches is that they can move only ionic drugs through the skin.

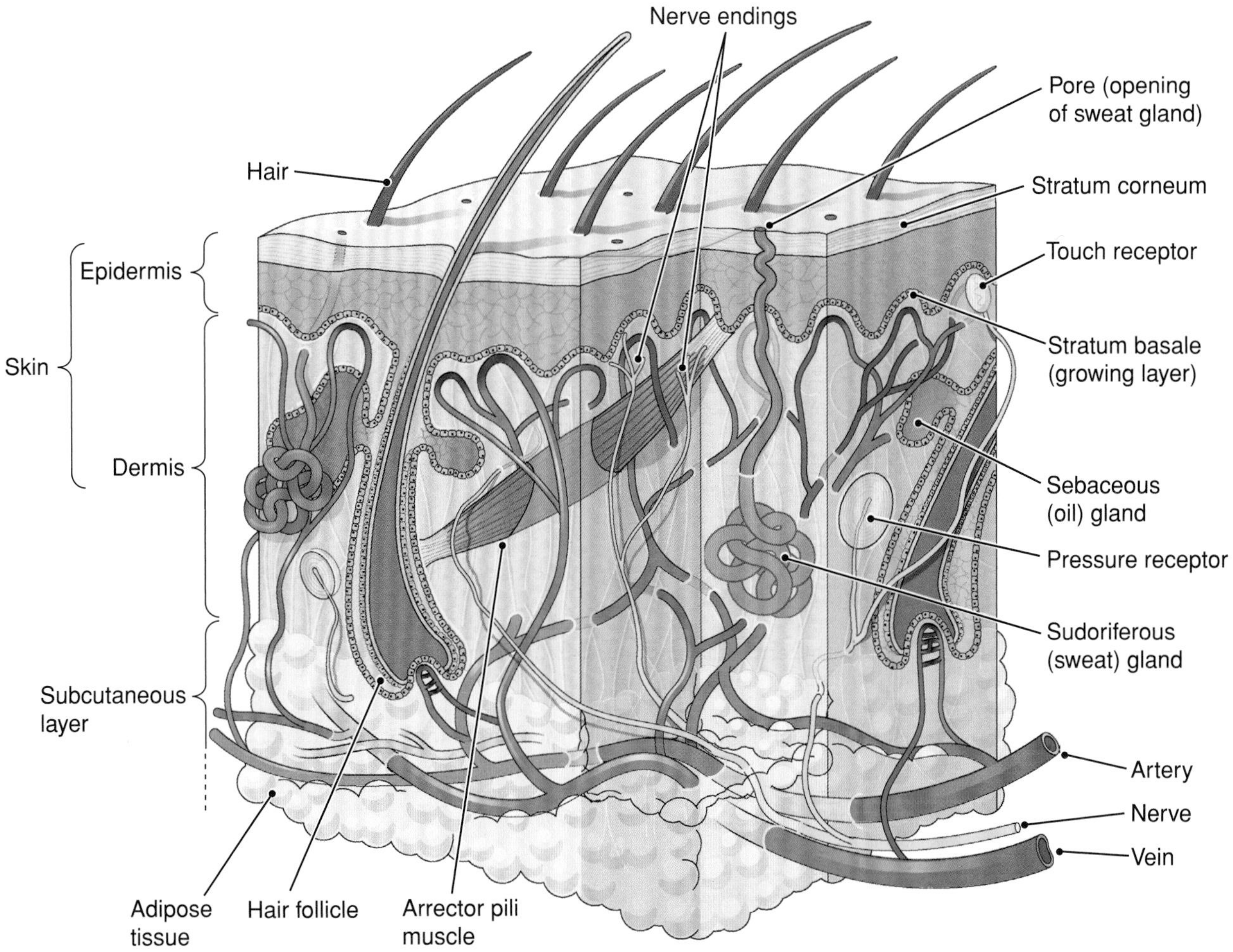

21

Nerve endings

Hair

Epidermis

Skin

Dermis

Subcutaneous
layer

Pore (opening
of sweat gland)

Stratum corneum

Touch receptor

Stratum basale
(growing layer)

Sebaceous
(oil) gland

Pressure receptor

Sudoriferous
(sweat) gland

Artery

Nerve

Vein

Adipose
tissue

Hair follicle

Arrector pili
muscle

Figure 21-1   **Cross-section of the skin.** The skin layers and associated structures are shown.

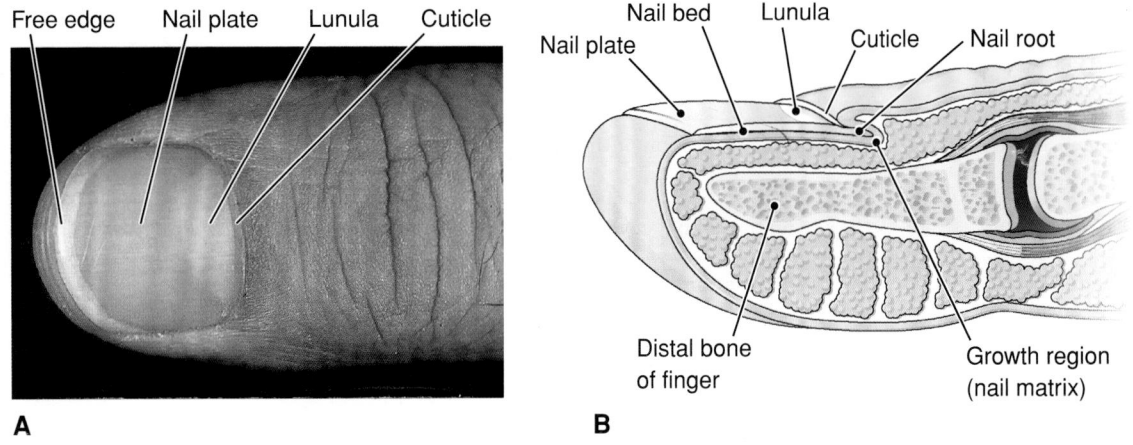

Free edge   Nail plate   Lunula   Cuticle

Nail bed   Lunula

Nail plate   Cuticle   Nail root

Distal bone
of finger

Growth region
(nail matrix)

A

B

Figure 21-2   **Nail structure. A.** Photograph of a nail, superior view. **B.** Midsagittal
section of a fingertip showing the growth region and tissue surrounding the nail plate.

eponychium (*ep-o-NIK-e-um*), is an extension of the epidermis onto the surface of the nail plate. A lighter region distal to the cuticle is called the lunula because it looks like a half moon. Here the underlying skin is thicker, and blood does not show as much through the nail.

Hair and nails are composed of nonliving material consisting mainly of keratin. Both function in protection.

See charts on skin structure and accessory skin structures in the Student Resources on thePoint.

Terminology | Key Terms

Normal Structure and Function

cutaneous *ku-TA-ne-us*	Pertaining to the skin (from Latin *cutis*, meaning "skin")
derma *DER-mah*	Skin (from Greek)
dermis *DER-mis*	The layer of the skin between the epidermis and the subcutaneous tissue; the true skin or corium
epidermis *ep-ih-DER-mis*	The outermost layer of the skin (from epi-, meaning "upon or over" and derm, meaning "skin")
hair *har*	A thread-like keratinized outgrowth from the skin (root: trich/o)
hair follicle *FOL-ih-kl*	The sheath in which a hair develops
integumentary system *in-teg-u-MEN-tah-re*	The skin and its associated glands, hair, and nails
keratin *KER-ah-tin*	A protein that thickens and toughens the skin and makes up hair and nails (root: kerat/o)
melanin *MEL-ah-nin*	A dark pigment that gives color to the hair and skin and protects the skin against the sun's radiation (root: melan/o)
nail *nale*	A plate-like keratinized outgrowth of the skin that covers the dorsal surface of the terminal phalanges (root: onych/o)
sebaceous gland *se-BA-shus*	A gland that produces sebum; usually associated with a hair follicle (root: seb/o)
sebum *SE-bum*	A fatty secretion of the sebaceous glands that lubricates the hair and skin (root: seb/o)
skin	The tissue that covers the body; the integument (roots: derm/o, dermat/o)
subcutaneous layer *sub-ku-TA-ne-us*	The layer of tissue beneath the skin; also called the hypodermis
sudoriferous gland *su-dor-IF-er-us*	A sweat gland (root: hidr/o)

Go to the Audio Pronunciation Glossary in the Student Resources on thePoint to hear these terms pronounced.

Roots Pertaining to the Integumentary System

See Table 21-1.

Table 21-1	Roots Pertaining to the Skin and Associated Structures		
Root	**Meaning**	**Example**	**Definition of Example**
derm/o, dermat/o	skin	dermabrasion *derm-ah-BRA-zhun*	surgical procedure used to resurface the skin and remove imperfections
kerat/o	keratin, horny layer of the skin	keratinous *keh-RAT-ih-nus*	containing keratin; horny
melan/o	dark, black, melanin	melanosome *MEL-ah-no-some*	a small cellular body that produces melanin
hidr/o	sweat, perspiration	anhidrosis *an-hi-DRO-sis*	absence of sweating
seb/o	sebum, sebaceous gland	seborrhea *seb-or-E-ah*	excess flow of sebum (adjective: seborrheic)
trich/o	hair	trichomycosis *trik-o-mi-KO-sis*	fungal infection of the hair
onych/o	nail	onychia *o-NIK-e-ah*	inflammation of the nail and nail bed (not an -itis ending)

21

EXERCISE 21-1

Identify and define the roots in the following words.

	Root	**Meaning of Root**
1. hypodermis (*hi-po-DER-mis*)	_____	_____
2. seborrheic (*seb-o-RE-ik*)	_____	_____
3. hypermelanosis (*hi-per-mel-ah-NO-sis*)	_____	_____
4. dyskeratosis (*dis-ker-ah-TO-sis*)	_____	_____
5. hypohidrosis (*hi-po-hi-DRO-sis*)	_____	_____
6. hypertrichosis (*hi-per-trih-KO-sis*)	_____	_____
7. eponychium (*ep-o-NIK-e-um*)	_____	_____

Fill in the blanks.

8. Dermatopathology (*der-mah-to-pah-THOL-o-je*) is study of diseases of the _____.

9. Keratolysis (*ker-ah-TOL-ih-sis*) is loosening of the skin's _____.

10. A melanocyte (*MEL-ah-no-site*) is a cell that produces _____.

11. Trichoid (*TRIK-oyd*) means resembling a(n) _____.

12. Onychomycosis (*on-ih-ko-mi-KO-sis*) is a fungal infection of a(n) _____.

13. Hidradenitis (*hi-drad-eh-NI-tis*) is inflammation of a gland that produces _____.

14. A hypodermic (*hi-po-DER-mik*) injection is given under the _____.

(continued)

EXERCISE 21-1   *(Continued)*

Write words for the following definitions.

15. loosening or separation of the skin   _____

16. study of the skin and skin diseases   _____

17. softening of a nail   _____

18. excess production of sweat   _____

19. study of the hair   _____

20. instrument for cutting the skin   _____

21. formation (-genesis) of keratin   _____

22. a tumor containing melanin   _____

Use *-derma* as a suffix meaning "skin" to write words for the following.

23. hardening of the skin   _____

24. presence of pus in the skin   _____

Clinical Aspects of the Skin

Many diseases are manifested by changes in the quality of the skin or by specific lesions. Some types of skin lesions are described and illustrated in **Box 21-2** and appear later in photographs of specific skin disorders. The study of the skin and skin diseases is **dermatology**, but careful observation of the skin, hair, and nails should be part of every physical examination. The skin should be examined for color, unusual pigmentation, and lesions. It should be

FOR YOUR REFERENCE   Box 21-2

Types of Skin Lesions

Lesion	Description
bulla BUL-ah	raised, fluid-filled lesion larger than a vesicle (plural: bullae) (see **Figs. 21-5** and **21-7**)
fissure FISH-ure	crack or break in the skin
macule MAK-ule	flat, colored spot (see **Fig. 21-19**)
nodule NOD-ule	solid, raised lesion larger than a papule; often indicative of systemic disease (see **Fig. 21-9**)
papule PAP-ule	small, circular, raised lesion at the surface of the skin
plaque plak	superficial, flat, or slightly raised differentiated patch more than 1 cm in diameter (see **Fig. 21-6**)
pustule PUS-tule	raised lesion containing pus; often in a hair follicle or sweat pore (see **Fig. 21-13**)
ulcer UL-ser	lesion resulting from destruction of the skin and perhaps subcutaneous tissue (see **Fig. 21-18**)
vesicle VES-ih-kl	small, fluid-filled, raised lesion; a blister or bleb
wheal wele	smooth, rounded, slightly raised area often associated with itching; seen in urticaria (hives), such as that resulting from allergy (see **Fig. 21-17**)

HEALTH PROFESSIONS

Box 21-3

Nurse Practitioners

A nurse practitioner (NP) is a nurse with a professional degree beyond registered nurse (RN) who provides healthcare services similar to those of a physician. All NPs have a master's degree in nursing and postmaster's, or doctoral education. They can specialize in areas such as acute care, family health, neonatology, or gerontology and medical specialties such as oncology or psychiatry. Their advanced education allows them to independently diagnose and treat patients, order testing, perform minor surgeries, and often prescribe medications. Some NPs practice autonomously, but many work in collaboration with physicians.

They focus not only on treatment of disease but also on disease prevention, patient education, and counseling. Such early intervention and education can lower overall healthcare costs.

NPs are licensed to practice in all U.S. states and must follow the rules and regulations of the state in which they are licensed. In most states, they are able to dispense and prescribe medications without a physician's cosignature, and they may bill insurance agencies for services. Their professional organizations include the American Academy of Nurse Practitioners at www.aanp.org and the American College of Nurse Practitioners at www.acnpweb.org.

palpated to evaluate its texture, temperature, moisture, firmness, and any tenderness. See **Box 21-3** on nurse practitioners, who, like other healthcare professionals, observe the skin when performing physical examinations.

WOUNDS

Wounds are caused by trauma, as in cases of accidents or attacks, or by surgery and other therapeutic or diagnostic procedures. Wounds may affect not only the injured area but also other body systems. Infection and hemorrhage may complicate wounds, as do **dehiscence**, disruption of the wound layers, and **evisceration**, protrusion of internal organs through the lesion.

As a wound heals, fluid and cells drain from the damaged tissue. This drainage, called **exudate**, may be clear, bloody (sanguinous), or pus-containing (purulent). Tubes may be used to remove exudate from the site of a wound.

Proper wound healing depends on cleanliness and care of the lesion and also on proper circulation, good general health, and good nutrition. The edges of a deep wound should be joined by sutures, either stitches or, for simple cuts in areas that can be kept dry and immobilized, with a tissue adhesive (glue). Healing is accompanied by scar formation or **cicatrization** (an alternative name for a scar is a cicatrix). Permanent scarring is lessened by appropriate wound care, but some people, especially those of African or Asian descent, may tend to form **keloids** because of excess collagen formation during healing (**Fig. 21-3**). Plastic surgery can often improve keloids and other unsightly scars.

Various types of dressings are used to protect wounded areas and promote healing. Vacuum-assisted closure (VAC) uses negative pressure to close the tissues and begin the healing process. Healing may be promoted by **debridement**, the removal of dead or damaged tissue from a wound.

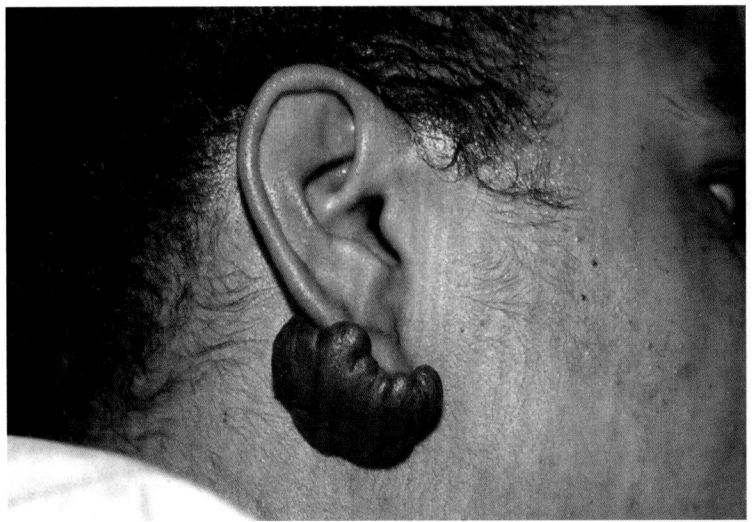

Figure 21-3 **Keloid.** Marked overgrowth of scar tissue following earlobe piercing.

Box 21-4 mentions the origin of the word debridement and gives the meaning of other medical terms taken from French. Debridement may be accomplished by cutting or scrubbing away the dead tissue or by means of enzymes. A thick, dark crust or scab (eschar) may be removed in an **escharotomy**.

Deep wounds may require skin grafting for proper healing. Grafts may be a full-thickness skin graft (FTSG), which consists of the epidermis and dermis, or a split-thickness skin graft (STSG), consisting of the epidermis only. Skin is cut for grafting with a **dermatome**.

See the animation "Wound Healing" in the Student Resources on thePoint.

Burns

Most burns are caused by hot objects, explosions, or scalding with hot liquids. They may also be caused by electricity, contact with harmful chemicals, or abrasion. Sunlight can also cause severe burns that may result in serious illness. Burns are assessed in terms of the depth of damage and the percentage of body surface area (BSA) involved. Depth of tissue destruction is categorized as follows:

1. *Superficial*—involves the epidermis only. The skin is red and dry; there is minimal pain. Typical causes are mild sunburn and very short heat exposure. This type of burn is also called a first-degree burn.

2. *Superficial partial thickness*—involves the epidermis and a portion of the dermis. The tissue reddens and blisters and is painful, as in cases of severe sunburn or scalding.

3. *Deep partial thickness*—involves the epidermis and the dermis. The tissue may be blistered with a weeping surface or dry because of sweat gland damage. These burns may be less painful than superficial burns because of nerve damage. Causes include scalding and exposure to flame or hot grease. Superficial and deep partial thickness burns are also classified as second-degree burns.

4. *Full thickness*—involves the full skin and sometimes subcutaneous tissue and underlying tissues as well. The tissue is broken, dry and pale, or charred. These injuries may require skin grafting and may result in loss of digits or limbs. Full-thickness burns are also classified as third-degree burns.

The amount of BSA involved in a burn may be estimated by using the **rule of nines**, in which areas of body surface are assigned percentages in multiples of nine (**Fig. 21-4**). The more accurate Lund and Browder method divides the body into small areas and estimates the proportion of BSA contributed by each.

Infection is a common complication of burns because a person's major defense against bacterial invasion is damaged. Respiratory complications and shock may also occur.

Treatment of burns includes respiratory care, administration of fluids, wound care, and pain control. Monitoring for cardiovascular complications, infections, and signs of posttraumatic stress is also important.

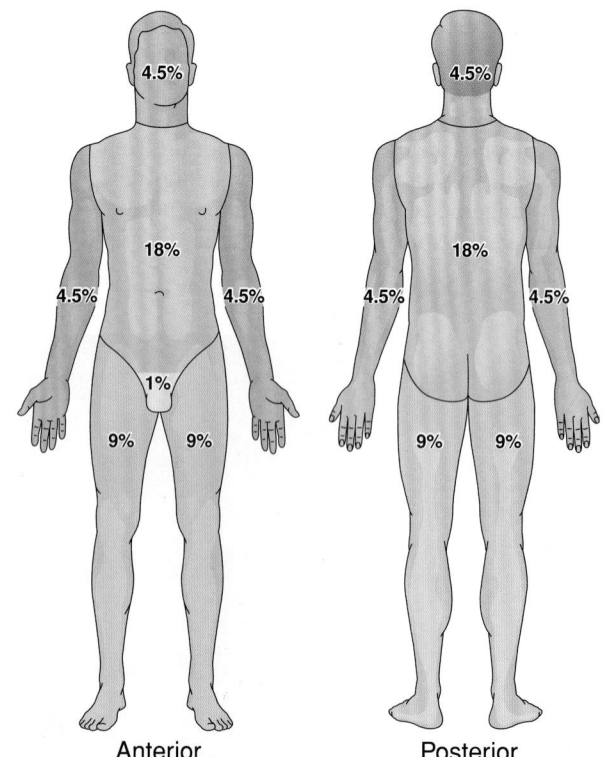

Anterior   **Posterior**

Figure 21-4 **The rule of nines.** Percentage of body surface area (BSA) in the adult is estimated by sectioning the body surface into areas with numerical values related to nine. This method is used to evaluate the extent of skin burns.

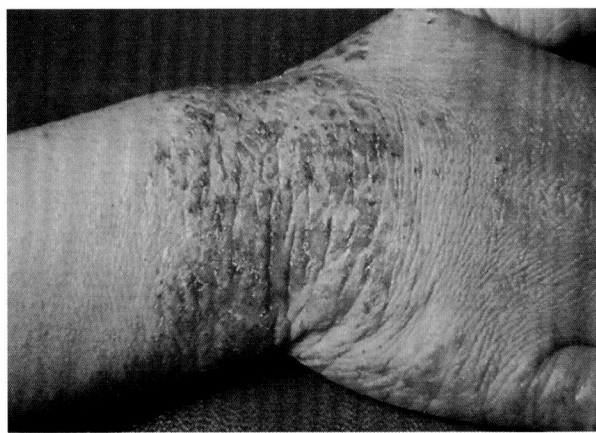

A

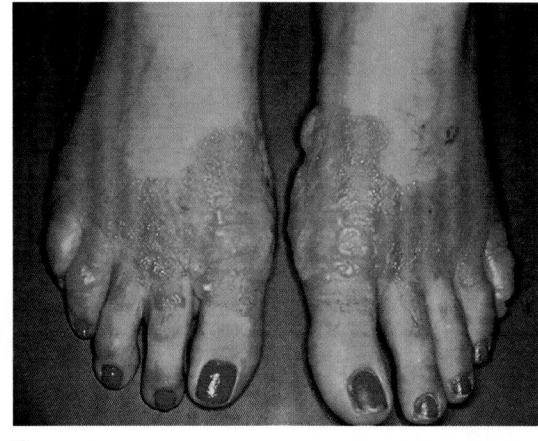

B

Figure 21-5 **Dermatitis.** **A.** Atopic dermatitis (eczema) on an infant's wrist. **B.** Contact dermatitis from shoe material. Note several fluid-filled bullae (see **Box 21-2**).

Pressure Ulcers

Pressure ulcers are necrotic skin lesions that appear where the body rests on skin that covers bony projections, such as the sacrum, heel, elbow, ischial bone of the pelvis, or greater trochanter of the femur (see *ulcer*, **Box 21-2**, and C.M.'s opening case study). The pressure interrupts circulation, leading to thrombosis, ulceration, and tissue death (necrosis). Poor general health, malnutrition, age, obesity, and infection contribute to the development of pressure ulcers.

Pressure ulcer lesions first appear as redness of the skin. If ignored, they may penetrate the skin and underlying muscle, extending even to bone, and may require months to heal.

Pads or mattresses to relieve pressure, regular cleansing and drying of the skin, frequent change in position, and good nutrition help to prevent pressure ulcers. Other terms for pressure ulcers are *decubitus ulcer* and *bedsore*. Both of these terms refer to lying down in bed, although pressure ulcers may appear in anyone with limited movement, not only those who are confined to bed.

DERMATITIS

Dermatitis is a general term for inflammation of the skin, which may be acute or chronic. Mild forms show **erythema** (redness) and edema and sometimes **pruritus** (itching), but the condition may worsen to include deeper lesions and secondary bacterial infections. A chronic allergic form of this disorder that appears early in childhood is called **atopic dermatitis** or **eczema** (**Fig. 21-5**). Although its exact cause is unknown, atopic dermatitis is made worse by allergies, infection, temperature extremes, and skin irritants.

Other forms of dermatitis include contact dermatitis, caused by allergens or chemical irritants (see **Fig. 21-5B**); seborrheic dermatitis, which involves areas with many sebaceous glands, such as the scalp and face; and stasis dermatitis, caused by poor circulation.

PSORIASIS

Psoriasis is a chronic overgrowth (hyperplasia) of the epidermis, producing large, erythematous (red) plaques with silvery scales (**Fig. 21-6**; see also *plaques*, **Box 21-2**). The cause is unknown, but there is sometimes a hereditary pattern, and autoimmunity may be involved.

Dermatologists treat psoriasis in the following ways depending on severity:

1. Topical agents, including corticosteroids, immunosuppressants, vitamins A and D
2. Phototherapy—exposure to ultraviolet B (UVB) light; administration of the drug psoralen (P) to increase skin sensitivity to light followed by exposure to ultraviolet A (UVA) light; laser treatment
3. Systemic suppression of the immune system

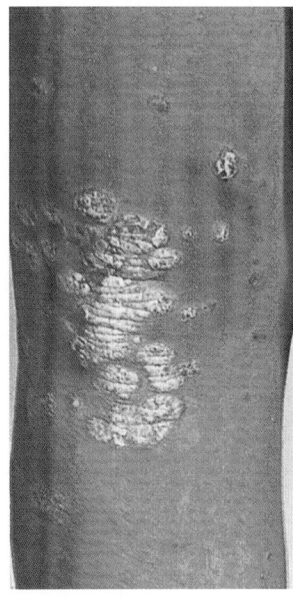

Figure 21-6 **Psoriasis.** Plaques with scales seen at the front of the knee (see *plaque*, **Box 21-2**).

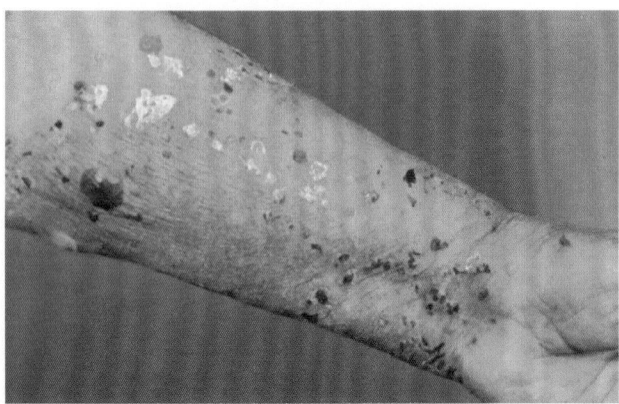

Figure 21-7 **Pemphigus.** Blisters (bullae) are seen on the forearm (see *bulla*, **Box 21-2**).

AUTOIMMUNE DISORDERS

The diseases discussed below are caused, at least in part, by autoimmune reactions. They are diagnosed by biopsy of lesions and by antibody studies.

Pemphigus is characterized by the formation of bullae (blisters) in the skin and mucous membranes caused by a separation of epidermal cells from underlying layers (**Fig. 21-7**; see also *bulla*, **Box 21-2**). Rupture of these lesions leaves deeper skin areas unprotected from infection and fluid loss, much as in cases of burns. The cause is an autoimmune reaction to epithelial cells. Pemphigus is fatal unless treated by suppressing the immune system.

Lupus erythematosus (LE) is a chronic inflammatory autoimmune disease of connective tissue. The more widespread form of the disease, systemic lupus erythematosus (SLE), involves the skin and other organs. SLE is more prevalent in women than in men and has a higher incidence among Asians and blacks than among other populations.

The discoid form (DLE) involves only the skin. It is seen as rough, raised, erythematous papules that are worsened by exposure to the ultraviolet radiation in sunlight (**Fig. 21-8**). Lupus skin lesions are confined to the face and scalp and may form a typical butterfly-shaped rash across the nose and cheeks.

See figures on clinical findings and the malar "butterfly" rash in systemic lupus erythematosus in the Student Resources on thePoint.

Scleroderma is a disease of unknown cause that involves thickening and tightening of the skin. There is gradual fibrosis of the dermis because of collagen overproduction. Sweat glands and hair follicles are also involved. A very early sign of scleroderma is Raynaud disease, in which blood vessels in the fingers and toes constrict in the cold, causing numbness, pain, coldness, and tingling. Skin symptoms first appear on the forearms and around the mouth. Internal organs become involved in a diffuse form of scleroderma called progressive systemic sclerosis (PSS).

SKIN CANCER

Skin cancer is the most common type of human cancer. Its incidence has been increasing in recent years, mainly because of the mutation-causing effects of sunlight's ultraviolet rays. **Squamous cell carcinoma** and **basal cell carcinoma** are both cancers of epithelial cells. Both appear in areas exposed to sunlight, such as the face and hands. Basal cell carcinoma constitutes more than 75 percent of all skin cancers. It usually appears as a smooth, pearly papule (**Fig. 21-9**; see also *papules*, **Box 21-2**). Because these cancers are easily seen and do not metastasize, the cure rate after excision is greater than 95 percent.

Squamous cell carcinoma appears as a painless, firm, red nodule or plaque that may develop surface scales, ulceration, or crusting (**Fig. 21-10**; see also **Box 21-2**). This cancer may invade underlying tissue but tends not to

Figure 21-8 **Discoid (cutaneous) lupus erythematosus.** Erythematous papules and plaques in a typical sun-exposed distribution on the chest.

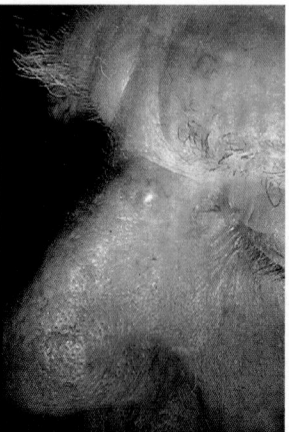

Figure 21-9 **Basal cell carcinoma.** An initial translucent nodule has spread, leaving a depressed center and a firm, elevated border (see *nodule*, **Box 21-2**).

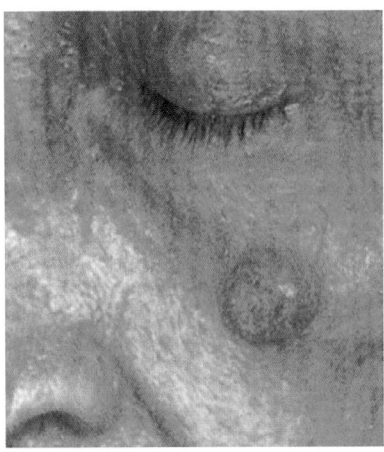 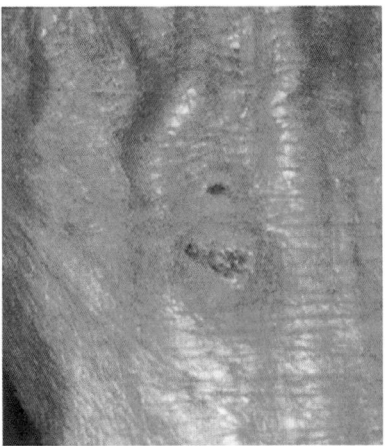

Figure 21-10 **Squamous cell carcinoma.** Lesions are shown on the face and the back of the hand, sun-exposed areas that are commonly affected.

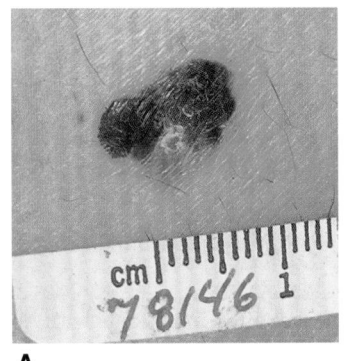 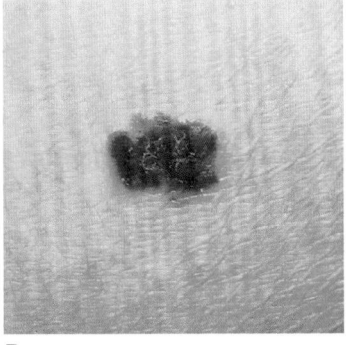 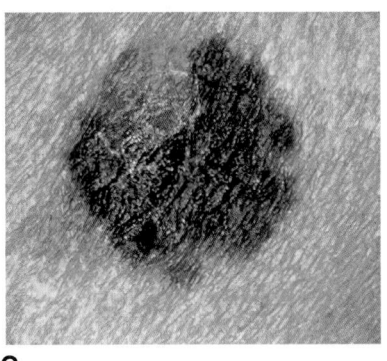

A **B** **C**

Figure 21-11 **Malignant melanoma.** Several characteristics are shown. **A.** Asymmetry. **B.** Irregular borders. **C.** Variation in color, a diameter greater than 6 mm, and elevation.

metastasize. It is treated by surgical removal and sometimes with x-irradiation or chemotherapy.

Malignant melanoma results from an overgrowth of melanocytes, the pigment-producing cells in the epidermis. It is the most dangerous form of skin cancer because of its tendency to metastasize. This cancer appears as a lesion that is variable in color with an irregular border (**Fig. 21-11**). It may spread superficially for up to one or two years before it begins to invade the deeper skin tissues and to metastasize through blood and lymph. The prognosis for cure is good if the lesion is recognized and removed surgically before it enters this invasive stage.

Kaposi sarcoma, once considered rare, is now seen frequently in association with AIDS. It usually appears as distinct brownish areas on the legs. These plaques become raised and firm as the tumor progresses. In those with weakened immune systems, such as patients with AIDS, the cancer can metastasize.

Terminology	Key Terms
atopic dermatitis *ah-TOP-ik der-mah-TI-tis*	Hereditary, allergic, chronic skin inflammation with pruritus (itching); eczema
basal cell carcinoma *BA-sal*	An epithelial tumor that rarely metastasizes and has a high cure rate with surgical removal
cicatrization *sik-ah-trih-ZA-shun*	The process of scar formation; a scar is a cicatrix (*SIK-ah-triks*)

(continued)

Terminology	Key Terms *(Continued)*
debridement *da-brede-MON*	Removal of dead or damaged tissue, as from a wound
dehiscence *de-HIS-ens*	Splitting or bursting, as when the layers of a wound separate
dermatitis *der-mah-TI-tis*	Inflammation of the skin, often associated with redness and itching; may be caused by allergy, irritants (contact dermatitis), or a variety of diseases
dermatology *der-mah-TOL-o-je*	Study of the skin and diseases of the skin
dermatome *DER-mah-tome*	Instrument for cutting thin skin sections for grafting
eczema *EK-ze-mah*	A general term for skin inflammation with redness, lesions, and itching; atopic dermatitis
erythema *er-ih-THE-mah*	Diffuse redness of the skin
escharotomy *es-kar-OT-o-me*	Removal of scab tissue resulting from burns or other skin injuries; a scab or crust is an eschar (ES-kar)
evisceration *e-vis-er-A-shun*	Protrusion of internal organs (viscera) through an opening, as through a wound
exudate *EKS-u-date*	Material, which may include fluid, cells, pus, or blood, that escapes from damaged tissue
Kaposi sarcoma *KAP-o-se*	Cancerous lesion of the skin and other tissues seen most often in patients with AIDS
keloid *KE-loyd*	A raised, thickened scar caused by tissue overgrowth during scar formation
lupus erythematosus (LE) *LU-pus er-ih-the-mah-TO-sis*	A chronic, inflammatory, autoimmune disease of connective tissue that often involves the skin; types include the more widespread systemic lupus erythematosus (SLE) and a discoid form (DLE) that involves only the skin
malignant melanoma *mah-LIG-nant mel-ah-NO-mah*	A metastasizing pigmented skin tumor
pemphigus *PEM-fih-gus*	An autoimmune disease of the skin characterized by sudden, intermittent formation of bullae (blisters); may be fatal if untreated
pressure ulcer	An ulcer caused by pressure to an area of the body, as from a bed or chair; decubitus (de-KU-bih-tus) ulcer, bedsore, pressure sore
pruritus *pru-RI-tus*	Severe itching
psoriasis *so-RI-ah-sis*	A chronic hereditary dermatitis with red lesions covered by silvery scales
rule of nines	A method for estimating the extent of body surface area involved in a burn by assigning percentages in multiples of nine to various body regions
scleroderma *sklere-o-DER-mah*	A chronic disease that is characterized by thickening and tightening of the skin and that often involves internal organs in a form called progressive systemic sclerosis (PSS)
squamous cell carcinoma *SKWA-mus*	An epidermal cancer that may invade deeper tissues but tends not to metastasize

Terminology **Supplementary Terms**

Symptoms and Conditions

acne AK-ne	An inflammatory disease of the sebaceous glands and hair follicles usually associated with excess sebum secretion; acne vulgaris
actinic ak-TIN-ik	Pertaining to the effects of radiant energy, such as sunlight, ultraviolet light, and x-rays
albinism AL-bin-izm	A hereditary lack of pigment in the skin, hair, and eyes
alopecia al-o-PE-she-ah	Absence or loss of hair; baldness
Beau lines bo	White lines across the fingernails; usually a sign of systemic disease or injury (**Fig. 21-12**)
bromhidrosis brom-hi-DRO-sis	Sweat that has a foul odor because of bacterial decomposition; also spelled bromidrosis (bro-mih-DRO-sis)
carbuncle CAR-bung-kl	A localized infection of the skin and subcutaneous tissue, usually caused by staphylococcus, and associated with pain and discharge of pus
comedo KOM-eh-do	A plug of sebum, often containing bacteria, in a hair follicle; a blackhead (plural: comedones)
dermatophytosis der-mah-to-fi-TO-sis	Fungal infection of the skin, especially between the toes; athlete's foot (root *phyt/o* means "plant")
diaphoresis di-ah-fo-RE-sis	Profuse sweating
dyskeratosis dis-ker-ah-TO-sis	Any abnormality in keratin formation in epithelial cells
ecchymosis ek-ih-MO-sis	A collection of blood under the skin caused by leakage from small vessels
erysipelas er-ih-SIP-eh-las	An acute infectious skin disease with localized redness and swelling and systemic symptoms
erythema nodosum no-DO-sum	Inflammation of subcutaneous tissues resulting in tender, erythematous nodules; may be an abnormal immune response to a systemic disease, an infection, or a drug

(continued)

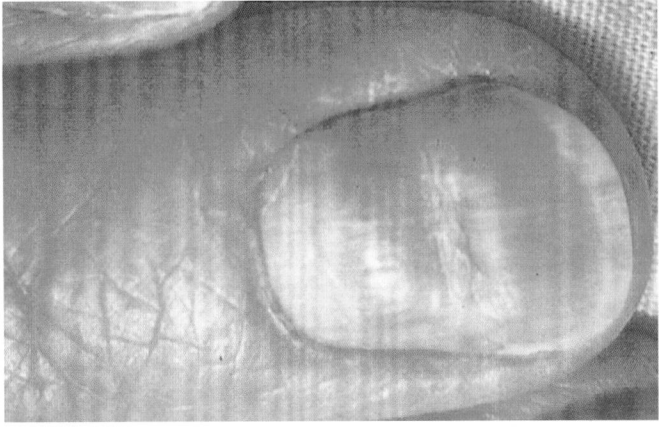

Figure 21-12 **Beau lines.** These transverse depressions in the nails are associated with acute severe illness.

Terminology   Supplementary Terms *(Continued)*

exanthema *ek-zan-THE-mah*	Any cutaneous eruption that accompanies a disease, such as measles; a rash
excoriation *eks-ko-re-A-shun*	Lesion caused by scratching or abrasion
folliculitis *fo-lik-u-LI-tis*	Inflammation of a hair follicle
furuncle *FU-rung-kl*	A painful skin nodule caused by staphylococci that enter through a hair follicle; a boil
hemangioma *he-man-je-O-mah*	A benign tumor of blood vessels; in the skin, called birthmarks or port wine stains
herpes simplex *HER-peze SIM-pleks*	A group of acute infections caused by herpes simplex virus; type I herpes simplex virus produces fluid-filled vesicles, usually on the lips, after fever, sun exposure, injury, or stress, also called cold sore or fever blister; type II infections usually involve the genital organs
hirsutism *HIR-su-tizm*	Excessive growth of hair
ichthyosis *ik-the-O-sis*	A dry, scaly condition of the skin (from the root *ichthy/o*, meaning "fish")
impetigo *im-peh-TI-go*	A bacterial skin infection with pustules that rupture and form crusts; most commonly seen in children, usually on the face (**Fig. 21-13**; see also *pustules*, **Box 21-2**)
keratosis *ker-ah-TO-sis*	Any skin condition marked by thickened or horny growth; seborrheic keratosis is a benign tumor, yellow or light brown in color, that appears in the elderly; actinic keratosis is caused by exposure to sunlight and may lead to squamous cell carcinoma
lichenification *li-ken-ih-fih-KA-shun*	Thickened marks caused by chronic rubbing, as seen in atopic dermatitis (a lichen is a flat, branching type of plant that grows on rocks and bark) (**Fig. 21-14**)
mycosis fungoides *mi-KO-sis fun-GOY-deze*	A rare malignant disease that originates in the skin and involves the internal organs and lymph nodes; there are large, painful, ulcerating tumors

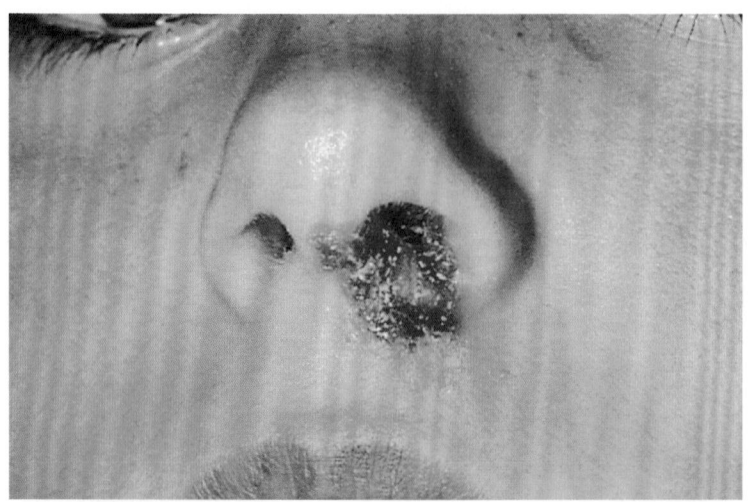

Figure 21-13 **Impetigo.** This bacterial skin infection, seen here on the nostril, causes pustules that rupture and form crusts (see *pustule*, **Box 21-2**).

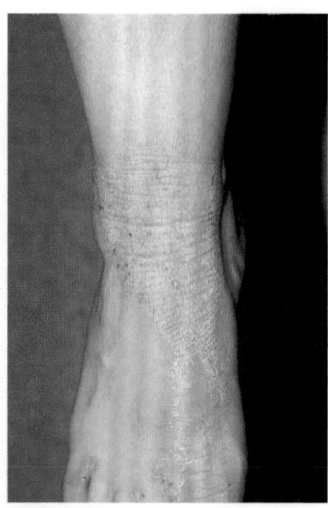

Figure 21-14 **Lichenification.** Skin shows thickened areas from chronic rubbing, as seen in atopic dermatitis.

Terminology | Supplementary Terms *(Continued)*

nevus *NE-vus*	A defined discoloration of the skin; a congenital vascular skin tumor; a mole, birthmark
paronychia *par-o-NIK-e-ah*	Infection around a nail (**Fig. 21-15**) caused by bacteria or fungi; may affect multiple nails
pediculosis *peh-dik-u-LO-sis*	Infestation with lice
petechiae *pe-TE-ke-e*	Flat, pinpoint, purplish-red spots caused by bleeding within the skin or mucous membrane (singular: petechia)
photosensitization *fo-to-sen-sih-tih-ZA-shun*	Sensitization of the skin to light, usually from the action of drugs, plant products, or other substances
purpura *PUR-pu-rah*	A condition characterized by hemorrhages into the skin and other tissues
rosacea *ro-ZA-she-ah*	A condition of unknown cause involving redness of the skin, pustules, and overactivity of sebaceous glands, mainly on the face
scabies *SKA-beze*	A highly contagious skin disease caused by a mite
senile lentigines *len-TIJ-ih-neze*	Brown macules that appear on sun-exposed skin in adults; liver spots
shingles	An acute eruption of vesicles along the path of a nerve; herpes zoster (*HER-peze ZOS-ter*); caused by the same virus that causes chickenpox
tinea *TIN-e-ah*	A fungal skin infection; ringworm (**Fig. 21-16**)
tinea versicolor *VER-sih-kol-or*	Superficial chronic fungal infection that causes varied skin pigmentation

(continued)

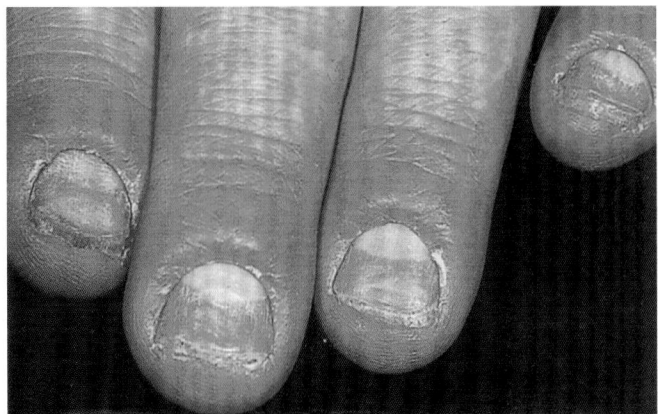

Figure 21-15 **Paronychia.** Infection and inflammation of the proximal and lateral nail folds is shown.

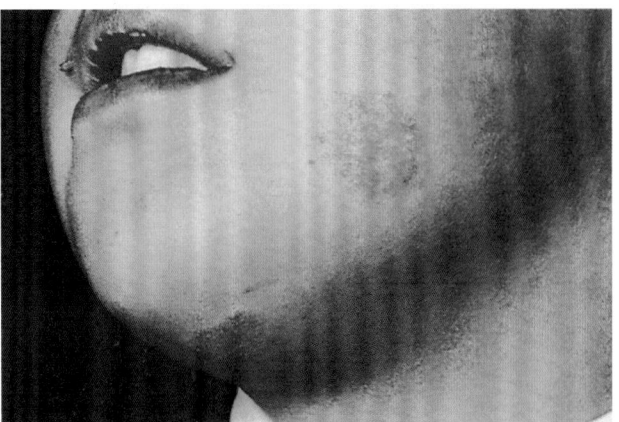

Figure 21-16 **Tinea corporis (ringworm).** This fungal infection is shown on the face.

Terminology	Supplementary Terms (*Continued*)
urticaria *ur-tih-KAR-e-ah*	A skin reaction marked by temporary, smooth, raised areas (wheals) associated with itching; hives (**Fig. 21-17**; see also *wheals*, **Box 21-2**)
venous stasis ulcer	Ulcer caused by venous insufficiency and stasis of venous blood; usually forms near the ankle (**Fig. 21-18**; see also *ulcer*, **Box 21-2**)
verruca *ver-RU-kah*	An epidermal tumor; a wart
vitiligo *vit-ih-LI-go*	Patchy disappearance of pigment in the skin; leukoderma (**Fig. 21-19**)
xeroderma pigmentosum *ze-ro-DER-mah pig-men-TO-sum*	A fatal hereditary disease that begins in childhood with skin discolorations and ulcers and muscle atrophy; there is increased sensitivity to the sun and increased susceptibility to cancer

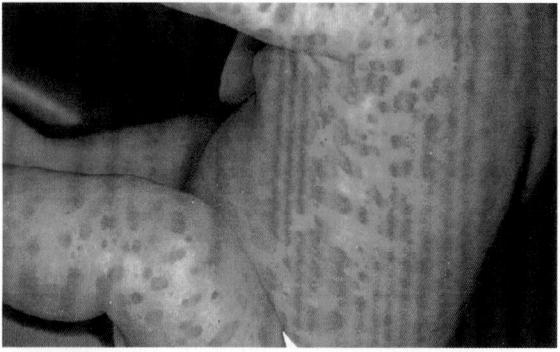

Figure 21-17 **Urticaria (hives).** Wheals associated with drug allergy are shown in an infant (see *wheal*, **Box 21-2**).

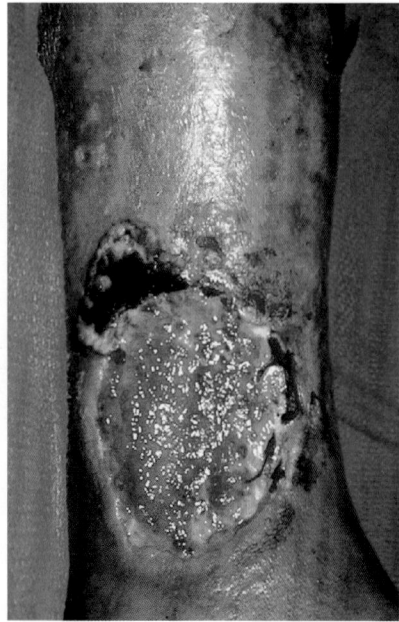

Figure 21-18 **Venous stasis ulcer.** Lesion on the ankle caused by venous insufficiency and blood stasis (see *ulcer*, **Box 21-2**).

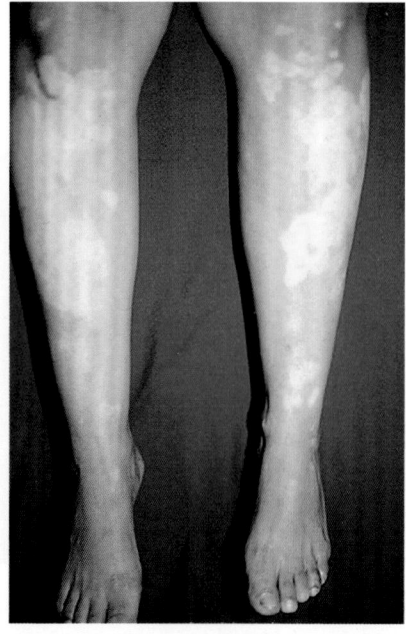

Figure 21-19 **Vitiligo.** Depigmented macules appear on the skin and may merge into large areas that lack melanin (see *macule*, **Box 21-2**). The brown pigment seen in the illustration is the person's normal skin color; the pale areas are caused by vitiligo.

Terminology Supplementary Terms *(Continued)*

Diagnosis and Treatment

aloe *AH-lo*	A gel from leaves of the plant *Aloe vera* that is used in treatment of burns and minor skin irritations
antipruritic *an-te-pru-RIT-ik*	Agent that prevents or relieves itching
cautery *KAW-ter-e*	Destruction of tissue by physical or chemical means; cauterization; also the instrument or chemical used for this purpose
dermabrasion *DERM-ah-bra-zhun*	A plastic surgical procedure for removing scars or birthmarks by chemical or mechanical destruction of epidermal tissue
dermatoplasty *DER-mah-to-plas-te*	Transplantation of human skin; skin grafting
diascopy *di-AS-ko-pe*	Examination of skin lesions by pressing a glass plate against the skin
fulguration *ful-gu-RA-shun*	Destruction of tissue by high-frequency electric sparks
skin turgor *TUR-gor*	Resistance of the skin to deformation; evidenced by the ability of the skin to return to position when pinched; skin turgor is a measure of the skin's elasticity and state of hydration; typically declines with age and when decreased may also be a sign of poor nutrition
Wood lamp	An ultraviolet light used to diagnose fungal infections

Go to the Audio Pronunciation Glossary in the Student Resources on thePoint to hear these terms pronounced.

Terminology Abbreviations

BSA	Body surface area		**SLE**	Systemic lupus erythematosus
DLE	Discoid lupus erythematosus		**SPF**	Sun protection factor
FTSG	Full-thickness skin graft		**STSG**	Split-thickness skin graft
LE	Lupus erythematosus		**UV**	Ultraviolet
PSS	Progressive systemic sclerosis		**UVA**	Ultraviolet A
PUVA	Psoralen ultraviolet A		**UVB**	Ultraviolet B
SCLE	Subacute cutaneous lupus erythematosus		**VAC**	Vacuum-assisted closure

Case Study Revisited

C.M.'s Follow-Up

C.M. made progress while in the long-term facility. She also worked with a PT and OT and began performing simple ADL. The therapists performed ROM on a regular schedule to both the stroke-affected and unaffected sides. With the increase in activity and improved nutrition, C.M.'s circulation and skin condition improved.

She also showed less confusion. C.M.'s daughter was able to observe and assist with her mother's activities and receive instruction firsthand. Goals were set, and discharge plans were made to have C.M. return home with her daughter.

Labeling Exercise

CROSS-SECTION OF THE SKIN

Write the name of each numbered part on the corresponding line of the answer sheet.

Adipose tissue
Arrector pili muscle
Artery
Dermis
Epidermis
Hair
Hair follicle
Nerve
Nerve endings
Pore (opening of sweat gland)

Pressure receptor
Sebaceous (oil) gland
Skin
Stratum basale (growing
    layer)
Stratum corneum
Subcutaneous layer
Sudoriferous (sweat) gland
Touch receptor
Vein

1. _____

2. _____

3. _____

4. _____

5. _____

6. _____

7. _____

8. _____

9. _____

10. _____

11. _____

12. _____

13. _____

14. _____

15. _____

16. _____

17. _____

18. _____

19. _____

Terminology

MATCHING

_____ **1.** cicatrization

_____ **2.** erythema

_____ **3.** eczema

_____ **4.** pruritus

_____ **5.** exudate

a. redness of the skin

b. severe itching

c. material that escapes from damaged tissue

d. atopic dermatitis

e. scar formation

_____ **6.** stratum basale   **a.** oily skin secretion

_____ **7.** hypodermis   **b.** sheath that contains a hair

_____ **8.** sebum   **c.** subcutaneous layer

_____ **9.** stratum corneum   **d.** growing layer of the epidermis

_____ **10.** follicle   **e.** thickened layer of the epidermis

Supplementary Terms

_____ **11.** alopecia   **a.** profuse sweating

_____ **12.** excoriation   **b.** lesion caused by scratching or abrasion

_____ **13.** nevus   **c.** mole or birthmark

_____ **14.** diaphoresis   **d.** blackhead

_____ **15.** comedo   **e.** baldness

_____ **16.** rosacea   **a.** condition causing redness and pustules, mainly on the face

_____ **17.** tinea   **b.** fungal skin infection

_____ **18.** bromhidrosis   **c.** infection around a nail

_____ **19.** albinism   **d.** lack of skin pigmentation

_____ **20.** paronychia   **e.** sweat with a foul odor

FILL IN THE BLANKS

21. The main pigment in skin is _____.

22. The oil-producing glands of the skin are the _____.

23. A sudoriferous gland produces _____.

24. The adjective *cutaneous* refers to the _____.

25. Dermabrasion (*der-mah-BRA-zhun*) is surface scraping of the _____.

26. The protein that thickens the skin and makes up hair and nails is _____.

27. Schizonychia (*skiz-o-NIK-e-ah*) is splitting of a(n) _____.

REFERRING TO C.M.'S OPENING CASE STUDY

28. Two other terms for a pressure ulcer are _____.

29. When the nurse palpated C.M.'s lesion, she used her sense of _____.

30. Part of C.M.'s treatment was removal of dead skin from her lesion. This process is called _____.

31. The abbreviation FTSG refers to a(n) _____.

32. A term for lack of oxygen to tissue is _____.

33. The medical specialist who treated C.M.'s deteriorating pressure ulcer was a(n) _____.

DEFINITIONS

Define the following words.

34. xeroderma (*ze-ro-DER-mah*) _____

35. dyskeratosis (*dis-ker-ah-TO-sis*) _____

36. seborrhea (*seb-or-E-ah*) _____

37. pachyderma (*pak-e-DER-mah*) _____

38. onychia (*o-NIK-e-ah*) _____

39. hypermelanosis (*hi-per-mel-ah-NO-sis*) _____

40. percutaneous (*per-ku-TA-ne-us*) _____

41. keratogenic (*ker-ah-to-JEN-ik*) _____

Write words for the following definitions.

42. pertaining to discharge of sebum _____

43. excess production of keratin _____

44. instrument for cutting the skin _____

45. tumor containing melanin _____

46. cell that produces melanin _____

47. hardening of the skin _____

Use the word hidrosis (sweating) as an ending for words with the following meanings.

48. absence of sweating _____

49. excess sweating _____

50. excretion of colored (chrom/o) sweat _____

PLURALS

Give the plural form for the following key and supplementary terms.

51. bulla _____

52. ecchymosis _____

53. fungus _____

54. comedo _____

55. staphylococcus _____

TRUE–FALSE

Examine the following statements. If the statement is true, write T in the first blank. If the statement is false, write F in the first blank, and correct the statement by replacing the underlined word in the second blank.

	True or False	**Correct Answer**
56. The skin and its associated structures make up the <u>integumentary system</u>.	_____	_____
57. The root trich/o refers to <u>hair</u>.	_____	_____
58. The <u>dermis</u> is between the epidermis and the subcutaneous layer.	_____	_____
59. A <u>cicatrix</u> is a scar.	_____	_____
60. Hirsutism is excess growth of <u>nails</u>.	_____	_____

WORD BUILDING

Write a word for the following definitions using the word parts provided.

-lysis   onych/o   -sis   myc/o   path/o   dermat/o   -y   log/o   -oid   trich/o

61. loosening or separation of the skin _____

62. fungal infection of a nail _____

63. resembling a hair _____

64. study of hair _____

65. loosening of a nail _____

66. like or resembling skin _____

67. any disease of a nail _____

68. fungal infection of the hair _____

69. any disease of the skin _____

70. study and treatment of the skin _____

ELIMINATIONS

In each of the sets below, underline the word that does not fit in with the rest, and explain the reason for your choice.

71. nodule — vesicle — keloid — macule — papule

_____

72. impetigo — escharotomy — psoriasis — dermatitis — pemphigus

_____

73. SLE — PSS — SCLE — BSA — DLE

_____

WORD ANALYSIS

Define the following words, and give the meaning of the word parts in each. Use a dictionary if necessary.

74. dermatophytosis (*der-mah-to-fi-TO-sis*) _____

    a. dermat/o _____

    b. phyt/o _____

    c. -sis _____

75. hidradenoma (*hi-drad-eh-NO-mah*) _____

    a. hidr/o _____

    b. aden/o _____

    c. -oma _____

76. onychocryptosis (*on-ih-ko-krip-TO-sis*) _____

    a. onych/o _____

    b. crypt/o _____

    c. -sis _____

77. achromotrichia (*ah-kro-mo-TRIK-e-ah*) _____

    a. a- _____

    b. chrom/o _____

    c. trich/o _____

    d. -ia _____

For more learning activities, see Chapter 21 of the Student Resources on thePoint.

Additional Case Studies

Case Study 21-1: *Basal Cell Carcinoma*

K.B., a 32-year-old fitness instructor, had noticed a "tiny hard lump" at the base of her left nostril while cleansing her face. The lesion had been present for about two months when she consulted a dermatologist. She had recently moved north from Florida, where she had worked as a lifeguard. She thought the lump might have been triggered by the regular tanning salon sessions she had used to retain her tan because it did not resemble the acne pustules, blackheads, or resulting scars of her adolescent years. Although dermabrasion had removed the obvious acne scars and left several areas of dense skin, this lump was brown-pigmented and different. K.B. was afraid it might be a malignant melanoma. On examination, the dermatologist noted a small pearly-white nodule at the lower portion of the left ala (outer flared portion of the nostril). There were no other lesions on her face or neck.

A plastic surgeon excised the lesion and was able to reapproximate the wound edges without a full-thickness skin graft. The pathology report identified the lesion as a basal cell carcinoma with clean margins of normal skin and subcutaneous tissue and stated that the entire lesion had been excised. K.B. was advised to wear SPF 30 sun protection on her face at all times and to avoid excessive sun exposure and tanning salons.

Case Study 21-2: *Cutaneous Lymphoma*

L.C., a 52-year-old female research chemist, has had a history of T cell lymphoma for eight years. She was initially treated with systemic chemotherapy with methotrexate, until she contracted stomatitis. Continued therapy with topical chemotherapeutic agents brought measurable improvement. She also had a history of hidradenitis.

A recent physical examination showed diffuse erythroderma with scaling and hyperkeratosis, plus alopecia. She had painful leukoplakia and ulcerations of the mouth and tongue. L.C. was hospitalized and given two courses of topical chemotherapy. She was referred to dental medicine for treatment of the oral lesions and was discharged in stable condition with an appointment for follow-up in four weeks. Her discharge medications included the application of 2 percent hydrocortisone ointment to the affected lesions qhs, Keralyt gel bid for the hyperkeratosis, and Dyclone and Benadryl for her mouth ulcers prn.

Case Study Questions

Multiple Choice. Select the best answer, and write the letter of your choice to the left of each number.

_____ 1. K.B.'s basal cell carcinoma may have been caused by chronic exposure to the sun and use of an ultraviolet tanning bed. The scientific explanation for this is the
   a. autoimmune response
   b. actinic effect
   c. allergic reaction
   d. sunblock tanning lotion theory

_____ 2. The characteristic pimples of adolescent acne are whiteheads and blackheads. The medical terms for these lesions are
   a. vesicles and macules
   b. pustules and blisters
   c. pustules and comedones
   d. furuncles and sebaceous cysts

_____ 3. Which skin cancer is an overgrowth of pigment-producing epidermal cells?
   a. basal cell carcinoma
   b. Kaposi sarcoma
   c. cutaneous lymphoma
   d. melanoma

_____ 4. Basal cell carcinoma involves
   a. subcutaneous tissue
   b. hair follicles
   c. connective tissue
   d. epithelial cells

(continued)

Additional Case Studies *(Continued)*

_____ **5.** Hidradenitis is inflammation of a
   a. sweat gland
   b. salivary gland
   c. sebaceous gland
   d. meibomian gland

_____ **6.** Leukoplakia is
   a. baldness
   b. ulceration
   c. formation of white patches in the mouth
   d. formation of yellow patches on the skin

_____ **7.** Hydrocortisone is a(n)
   a. vitamin
   b. steroid
   c. analgesic
   d. diuretic

_____ **8.** An example of a topical drug is a
   a. systemic chemotherapeutic agent
   b. drug derived from rainforest plants
   c. skin ointment
   d. Benadryl capsule, 25 mg

_____ **9.** Stomatitis, a common side effect of systemic chemotherapy, is an inflammatory condition of the
   a. mouth
   b. stomach
   c. teeth and hair
   d. debridement

Write terms from the case studies with the following meanings.

10. skin sanding procedure _____

11. a solid raised lesion larger than a papule _____

12. physician who cares for patients with skin diseases _____

13. layer of connective tissue and fat beneath the dermis _____

14. diffuse redness of the skin _____

15. increased production of keratin in the skin _____

Define the following abbreviations.

16. FTSG _____

17. SPF _____

18. hs _____

19. bid _____

20. prn _____

▶ Appendix 1

Commonly Used Symbols

Symbol	Meaning	Chapter
1°	primary	7
2°	secondary (to)	7
Δ	change (Greek delta)	7
Ⓛ	left	7
Ⓡ	right	7
↑	increase(d)	7
↓	decrease(d)	7
♂	male	7
♀	female	7
°	degree	7
∧	above	7
∨	below	7
=	equal to	7
≠	not equal to	7
±	doubtful, slight	7
~	approximately	7
×	times	7
#	number, pound	7

▶ Appendix 2

Abbreviations and Their Meanings

Abbreviation	Meaning	Chapter	Abbreviation	Meaning	Chapter
ā	before	8	AK	above the knee	19
A, Acc	accommodation	18	ALL	acute lymphoblastic (lymphocytic) leukemia	10
āā	of each	8			
A1c	glycated hemoglobin	16	ALS	amyotrophic lateral sclerosis	17, 20
Ab	antibody	10			
AB	abortion	15	AMA	against medical advice	7
ABC	aspiration biopsy cytology	7	AMB	ambulatory	7
			AMD	age-related macular degeneration	18
ABG(s)	arterial blood gas(es)	11			
ABR	auditory brainstem response	18	AMI	acute myocardial infarction	9
ac	before meals	8	AML	acute myeloblastic (myelogenous) leukemia	10
AC	air conduction	18			
ACE	angiotensin-converting enzyme	9	ANS	autonomic nervous system	17
ACh	acetylcholine	17, 20	AP	anteroposterior	7
ACL	anterior cruciate ligament	19	APAP	acetaminophen	8
ACTH	adrenocorticotropic hormone	16	APC	atrial premature complex; antigen-presenting cell	9, 10
ad lib	as desired	8	APTT	activated partial thromboplastin time	10
AD	Alzheimer disease	17			
ADH	antidiuretic hormone	13	aq	water, aqueous	8
ADHD	attention-deficit/hyperactivity disorder	17	AR	aortic regurgitation	9
			ARB	angiotensin receptor blocker	9
ADL	activities of daily living	7	ARC	abnormal retinal correspondence	18
AE	above the elbow	19	ARDS	acute respiratory distress syndrome	11
AED	automated external defibrillator	9	ARF	acute respiratory failure; acute renal failure	11, 13
AF	atrial fibrillation	9			
AFB	acid-fast bacillus	11	ART	assisted reproductive technology	15
AFP	alpha-fetoprotein	7, 15			
Ag	antigen; also silver	10	ASA	acetylsalicylic acid (aspirin)	8
AGA	appropriate for gestational age	15	As, Ast	astigmatism	18
AI	artificial insemination; aromatase inhibitor	15	AS	atrial stenosis; arteriosclerosis	9
AIDS	acquired immunodeficiency syndrome	10, 14	ASCVD	arteriosclerotic cardiovascular disease	9

Abbreviations and Their Meanings (*Continued*)

Abbreviation	Meaning	Chapter	Abbreviation	Meaning	Chapter
ASD	atrial septal defect	9	CA, Ca	cancer	6
ASF	anterior spinal fusion	19	CABG	coronary artery bypass graft	9
ASHD	arteriosclerotic heart disease	9	CAD	coronary artery disease	9
ASHP	American Society of Health System Pharmacists	8	CAM	complementary and alternative medicine	7
AT	atrial tachycardia	9	cap	capsule	8
ATN	acute tubular necrosis	13	CAPD	continuous ambulatory peritoneal dialysis	13
AV	atrioventricular	9			
BAEP	brainstem auditory evoked potentials	17, 18	CBC	complete blood count	10
BBB	bundle branch block	9	CBD	common bile duct	12
BC	bone conduction	18	CBF	cerebral blood flow	17
BCG	bacille Calmette–Guérin (tuberculosis vaccine)	11	CBR	complete bed rest	7
			cc	with correction	18
			CC	chief complaint	7
BE	barium enema; below the elbow	12, 19	CCPD	continuous cyclic peritoneal dialysis	13
bid, b.i.d.	twice per day	8	CCU	coronary care unit; cardiac care unit	9
BK	below the knee	19	CF	cystic fibrosis	11
BM	bowel movement	12	CFS	chronic fatigue syndrome	20
BMD	bone mineral density	19			
BNO	bladder neck obstruction	14	CGL	chronic granulocytic leukemia	10
BP	blood pressure	7, 9	CHD	coronary heart disease	9
BPH	benign prostatic hyperplasia (hypertrophy)	14	CHF	congestive heart failure	9
bpm	beats per minute	7, 9	Ci	Curie	7
BRCA1	breast cancer gene 1	15	CIN	cervical intraepithelial neoplasia	15
BRCA2	breast cancer gene 2	15			
BRP	bathroom privileges	7	CIS	carcinoma in situ	6
BS	bowel sounds; breath sounds; blood sugar	7, 11, 16	CJD	Creutzfeldt–Jakob disease	17
BSA	body surface area	21	CK	creatine kinase	20
BSE	breast self-examination	15	CK-MB	creatine kinase MB	9
BSO	bilateral salpingo-oophorectomy	15	CLL	chronic lymphocytic leukemia	10
BT	bleeding time	10	cm	centimeter	Appendix 8
BUN	blood urea nitrogen	13	CMG	cystometrography, cystometrogram	13
BV	bacterial vaginosis	15			
bx	biopsy	7	CML	chronic myelogenous leukemia	10
c̄	with	8			
C	Celsius (centigrade); compliance; cervical vertebra	7, 11, 19	CNS	central nervous system; clinical nurse specialist	17
C-section	cesarean section	15	c/o, CO	complains (complaining) of	7

(continued)

Abbreviations and Their Meanings (Continued)

Abbreviation	Meaning	Chapter	Abbreviation	Meaning	Chapter
Co	coccyx; coccygeal	19	DEXA	dual-energy x-ray absorptiometry (scan)	19
CO₂	carbon dioxide	11	DIC	disseminated intravascular coagulation	10
COPD	chronic obstructive pulmonary disease	11			
CP	cerebral palsy	17	DIFF	differential count	10
CPAP	continuous positive airway pressure	11	DIP	distal interphalangeal	19
			DJD	degenerative joint disease	19
CPD	cephalopelvic disproportion	15	dL	deciliter	Appendix 8
C(P)K	creatine (phospho)kinase	20	DLE	discoid lupus erythematosus	21
CPR	cardiopulmonary resuscitation	9	DM	diabetes mellitus	16
CRF	chronic renal failure	13	DNR	do not resuscitate	7
crit	hematocrit	10	DOE	dyspnea on exertion	9
CRP	C-reactive protein	9	DTaP	diphtheria, tetanus, acellular pertussis (vaccine)	11
C&S	culture and sensitivity	7			
CSF	cerebrospinal fluid	17	DRE	digital rectal examination	14
CSII	continuous subcutaneous insulin infusion	16	DS	double strength	8
			DSM	*Diagnostic and Statistical Manual of Mental Disorders*	17
CT	computed tomography	7			
CTA	computed tomography angiography	9	DTR	deep tendon reflex(es)	17
CTE	chronic traumatic encephalopathy	17	DUB	dysfunctional uterine bleeding	15
CTS	carpal tunnel syndrome	20	DVT	deep vein thrombosis	9
CVA	cerebrovascular accident	9, 17	Dx	diagnosis	7
CVD	cardiovascular disease; cerebrovascular disease	9, 17	EBL	estimated blood loss	7
			EBV	Epstein–Barr virus	10
			ECG (EKG)	electrocardiogram, electrocardiography	9
CVI	chronic venous insufficiency	9	ECMO	extracorporeal membrane oxygenation	15
CVP	central venous pressure	9			
CVS	chorionic villus sampling	15	ED	erectile dysfunction	14
			EDC	estimated date of confinement	15
CXR	chest x-ray	11	EEG	electroencephalogram; electroencephalograph(y)	17
D&C	dilatation and curettage	15			
DAW	dispense as written	8	EGD	esophagogastroduodenoscopy	12
dB	decibel	18			
dc, D/C	discontinue	7, 8	ELISA	enzyme-linked immunosorbent assay	10
DCIS	ductal carcinoma in situ	15			
D&E	dilation and evacuation	15	elix	elixir	8
			EM	emmetropia	18
DES	diethylstilbestrol	15	EMG	electromyography, electromyogram	20

Abbreviations and Their Meanings (*Continued*)

Abbreviation	Meaning	Chapter	Abbreviation	Meaning	Chapter
ENG	electronystagmography	18	FVC	forced vital capacity	11
			Fx	fracture	19
ENT	ear(s), nose, and throat	18	g	gram	Appendix 8
EOM	extraocular movement, muscles	18	GA	gestational age	15
			GAD	generalized anxiety disorder	17
EOMI	extraocular muscles intact	7	GC	gonococcus	14, 15
EPO, EP	erythropoietin	10, 13	GDM	gestational diabetes mellitus	16
ERCP	endoscopic retrograde cholangiopancreatography	12	GERD	gastroesophageal reflux disease	12
ERG	electroretinography	18	GFR	glomerular filtration rate	13
ERV	expiratory reserve volume	11	GH	growth hormone	16
ESR	erythrocyte sedimentation rate	10	GI	gastrointestinal	12
			GIFT	gamete intrafallopian transfer	15
ESRD	end-stage renal disease	13	GTT	glucose tolerance test	16
ESWL	extracorporeal shock wave lithotripsy	13	GU	genitourinary	13, 14
ET	esotropia	18	GYN	gynecology	15
ETOH	alcohol, ethyl alcohol	7	H&P	history and physical examination	7
F	Fahrenheit	7	HAV	hepatitis A virus	12
FAP	familial adenomatous polyposis	12	Hb, Hgb	hemoglobin	10
FBG	fasting blood glucose	16	HbA1c	hemoglobin A1c; glycated hemoglobin	16
FBS	fasting blood sugar	16	HBV	hepatitis B virus	12, 14
FC	finger counting	18	hCG	human chorionic gonadotropin	15
FDA	Food and Drug Administration	8	HCl	hydrochloric acid	12
FEV	forced expiratory volume	11	Hct, Ht	hematocrit	10
FFP	fresh frozen plasma	10	HCV	hepatitis C virus	12
FHR	fetal heart rate	15	HDL	high-density lipoprotein	9
FHT	fetal heart tone	15	HDN	hemolytic disease of the newborn	10, 15
FMS	fibromyalgia syndrome	20	HDV	hepatitis D virus	12
FPG	fasting plasma glucose	16	HEV	hepatitis E virus	12
FRC	functional residual capacity	11	HEENT	head, eyes, ears, nose, and throat	7
FSH	follicle-stimulating hormone	14, 15, 16	HIPAA	Health Insurance Portability and Accountability Act	7
FTI	free thyroxine index	16	HIV	human immunodeficiency virus	10, 14
FTND	full-term normal delivery	15			
FTP	full-term pregnancy	15	HL	hearing level	18
FTSG	full-thickness skin graft	21	HM	hand movements	18
FUO	fever of unknown origin	6	HNP	herniated nucleus pulposus	19

(continued)

Abbreviations and Their Meanings (*Continued*)

Abbreviation	Meaning	Chapter	Abbreviation	Meaning	Chapter
h/o	history of	7	IPPA	inspection, palpation, percussion, auscultation	7
HPI	history of present illness	7	IPPB	intermittent positive pressure breathing	11
HPS	*Hantavirus* pulmonary syndrome	11	IPPV	intermittent positive pressure ventilation	11
HPV	human papillomavirus	15	IRV	inspiratory reserve volume	11
HR	heart rate	7	ITP	idiopathic thrombocytopenic purpura	10
HRT	hormone replacement therapy	15			
hs	at bedtime	8	IU	international unit	8
hs-crp	high sensitivity C-reactive protein (test)	9	IUD	intrauterine device	15
			IV	intravenous(ly)	8
HSV	herpes simplex virus	14, 15	IVC	intravenous cholangiogram	12
Ht, Hct	hematocrit	10	IVCD	intraventricular conduction delay	9
HTN	hypertension	9			
Hx	history	7	IVDA	intravenous drug abuse	7
Hz	Hertz	18			
¹³¹I	iodine-131	16	IVF	in vitro fertilization	15
I&D	incision and drainage	7	IVP	intravenous pyelography	13
I&O	intake and output	7			
IABP	intra-aortic balloon pump	9	IVPB	intravenous piggyback	7
IBD	inflammatory bowel disease	12	IVU	intravenous urography	13
IBS	irritable bowel syndrome	12	JVP	jugular venous pulse	9
			K	potassium	13
IC	inspiratory capacity	11	kg	kilogram	Appendix 8
ICD	implantable cardioverter-defibrillator	9	km	kilometer	Appendix 8
			KUB	kidney-ureter-bladder	13
ICP	intracranial pressure	17	KVO	keep vein open	7
ICU	intensive care unit	7	L	lumbar vertebra; liter	19, Appendix 8
ID	intradermal	8	LA	long-acting	8
IF	intrinsic factor	10	LAD	left anterior descending (coronary artery)	9
IFG	impaired fasting blood glucose	16			
Ig	immunoglobulin	10	LAHB	left anterior hemiblock	9
IGRA	interferon gamma release assay (test for TB)	11	LDL	low-density lipoprotein	9
			LE	lupus erythematosus	21
IGT	impaired glucose tolerance	16	LES	lower esophageal sphincter	12
IM	intramuscular(ly); intramedullary	8, 19	LH	luteinizing hormone	14, 15, 16
			LL	left lateral	7
INH	isoniazid	8, 11	LLE	left lower extremity	20
IOL	intraocular lens	18	LLL	left lower lobe (of lung)	11
IOP	intraocular pressure	18			

Abbreviations and Their Meanings (Continued)

Abbreviation	Meaning	Chapter	Abbreviation	Meaning	Chapter
LLQ	left lower quadrant	5	mm	millimeter	Appendix 8
LMN	lower motor neuron	17	MMFR	maximum midexpiratory flow rate	11
LMP	last menstrual period	15			
LOC	level of consciousness	17	mm Hg	millimeters of mercury	9
LP	lumbar puncture	17	MMT	manual muscle test(ing)	20
LUE	left upper extremity	20			
LUL	left upper lobe (of lung)	11	MN	myoneural	20
			MR	mitral regurgitation, reflux	9
LUQ	left upper quadrant	5			
LV	left ventricle	9	MRI	magnetic resonance imaging	7
LVAD	left ventricular assist device	9			
			MRSA	methicillin-resistant *Staphylococcus aureus*	6
LVEDP	left ventricular end-diastolic pressure	9			
			MS	mitral stenosis; multiple sclerosis	9, 17
LVH	left ventricular hypertrophy	9			
lytes	electrolytes	10	MTP	metatarsophalangeal	19
m	meter	Appendix 8	MUGA	multigated acquisition (scan)	9
MAOI	monoamine oxidase inhibitor	17			
			MVP	mitral valve prolapse	9
mcg	microgram	8, Appendix 8	MVR	mitral valve replacement	9
MCH	mean corpuscular hemoglobin	10			
			Na	sodium	13
MCHC	mean corpuscular hemoglobin concentration	10	NAA	nucleic acid amplification (test) (for TB)	11
mcL	microliter	10, Appendix 8	NAD	no apparent distress	7
mcm	micrometer	10, Appendix 8	NB	newborn	15
MCP	metacarpophalangeal	19	NCCAM	National Center for Complementary and Alternative Medicine	7
MCV	mean corpuscular volume	10			
MDR	multi-drug resistant	6	NG	nasogastric	12
MDS	myelodysplastic syndrome	10	NGU	nongonococcal urethritis	14, 15
MED(s)	medicine(s), medication(s)	8	NHL	non-Hodgkin lymphoma	10
MEFR	maximal expiratory flow rate	11	NICU	neonatal intensive care unit; neurologic intensive care unit	15, 17
MEN	multiple endocrine neoplasia	16			
mEq	milliequivalent	10	NKDA	no known drug allergies	7
MET	metastasis	7			
mg	milligram	8, Appendix 8	NMJ	neuromuscular junction	20
MG	myasthenia gravis	20			
MHT	menopausal hormone therapy	15	NPH	neutral protamine Hagedorn (insulin)	16
MI	myocardial infarction	9	NPH	normal pressure hydrocephalus	17
MID	multi-infarct dementia	17	NPO	nothing by mouth	7
mL	milliliter	Appendix 8	NRC	normal retinal correspondence	18

(continued)

Abbreviations and Their Meanings (*Continued*)

Abbreviation	Meaning	Chapter	Abbreviation	Meaning	Chapter
NREM	nonrapid eye movement (sleep)	17	PCL	posterior cruciate ligament	19
NS, N/S	normal saline	7	PCOS	polycystic ovarian syndrome	15
NSAID(s)	nonsteroidal anti-inflammatory drug(s)	8, 19	PCP	*Pneumocystis* pneumonia	10, 11
NSR	normal sinus rhythm	9	PCV	packed cell volume	10
NV	near vision	18	PCWP	pulmonary capillary wedge pressure	9
N/V, N&V, n&v	nausea and vomiting	12	PDA	patent ductus arteriosus	15
N/V/D	nausea, vomiting, diarrhea	12	PDD	pervasive developmental disorder	17
O_2	oxygen	11			
OA	osteoarthritis	19	PDR	*Physicians' Desk Reference*	8
OB	obstetrics, obstetrician	15	PE	physical examination	7
OCD	obsessive-compulsive disorder	17	PEEP	positive end-expiratory pressure	11
ODS	Office of Dietary Supplements	8	PEFR	peak expiratory flow rate	11
OGTT	oral glucose-tolerance test	16	PEG	percutaneous endoscopic gastrostomy (tube)	12
OI	osteogenesis imperfecta	19			
OL	otolaryngology	18	PEP	protein electrophoresis	13
OOB	out of bed	7	PE(R)RLA	pupils equal, (regular) react to light and accommodation	7
OM	otitis media	18			
ORIF	open reduction internal fixation	19			
ORL	otorhinolaryngology	18	PET	positron emission tomography	7, 17
ortho, ORTH	orthopedics	19	PFT	pulmonary function test(s)	11
OT	occupational therapy	20			
OTC	over-the-counter	8	pH	scale for measuring hydrogen ion concentration (acidity or alkalinity)	10
p̄	after, post	8			
P	pulse	7, 9			
PA	posteroanterior; physician assistant	7	Ph	Philadelphia chromosome	10
PAC	premature atrial contraction	9	PICC	peripherally inserted central catheter	7
$PaCO_2$	arterial partial pressure of carbon dioxide	11	PID	pelvic inflammatory disease	15
PACU	postanesthesia care unit	19, 20	PIH	pregnancy-induced hypertension	15
PaO_2	arterial partial pressure of oxygen	11	PIP	peak inspiratory pressure	11
PAP	pulmonary arterial pressure	9	PIP	proximal interphalangeal	19
pc	after meals	8	PKU	phenylketonuria	15
PCA	patient-controlled analgesia	7	PMH	past medical history	7
PCI	percutaneous coronary intervention	9	PMI	point of maximal impulse	9

Abbreviations and Their Meanings (Continued)

Abbreviation	Meaning	Chapter	Abbreviation	Meaning	Chapter
PMN	polymorphonuclear (neutrophil)	10	PYP	pyrophosphate	9
			qam	every morning	8
PMS	premenstrual syndrome	15	qh	every hour	8
PND	paroxysmal nocturnal dyspnea	11	q __ h	every __ hours	8
			qid, q.i.d.	four times per day	8
PNS	peripheral nervous system	17	QNS	quantity not sufficient	7
po, PO	by mouth, orally	8	QS	quantity sufficient	7
poly, polymorph	neutrophil	10	R	respiration	7, 11
PONV	postoperative nausea and vomiting	12	RA	rheumatoid arthritis	19
			RAIU	radioactive iodine uptake	16
postop, post-op	postoperative	7	RAS	reticular activating system	17
pp	postprandial (after a meal)	8	RATx	radiation therapy	7
PPD	purified protein derivative (tuberculin)	11	RBC	red blood cell; red blood (cell) count	10
PPI	proton pump inhibitor	12	RDS	respiratory distress syndrome	11
preop, pre-op	preoperative	7	REM	rapid eye movement (sleep)	17
PRL	prolactin	16	RIA	radioimmunoassay	16
prn	as needed	8	RICE	rest, ice, compression, elevation	20
PSA	prostate-specific antigen	14			
PSF	posterior spinal fusion	19	RL	right lateral	7
			RLE	right lower extremity	20
PSS	physiologic saline solution; progressive systemic sclerosis	7, 21	RLL	right lower lobe (of lung)	11
			RLQ	right lower quadrant	5
PSVT	paroxysmal supraventricular tachycardia	9	RLS	restless legs syndrome	20
			RML	right middle lobe (of lung)	11
pt	patient	7	R/O	rule out	7
PT	physical therapy/ therapist	20	ROM	range of motion	20
PT, ProTime	prothrombin time	10	ROS	review of systems	7
PTCA	percutaneous transluminal coronary angioplasty	9	RSI	repetitive strain injury	20
			RSV	respiratory syncytial virus	11
PTH	parathyroid hormone	16	RTC	rotator cuff	20
PTSD	posttraumatic stress disorder	17	RUE	right upper extremity	20
PTT	partial thromboplastin time	10	RUL	right upper lobe (of lung)	11
			RUQ	right upper quadrant	5
PUVA	psoralen ultraviolet A	21	RV	residual volume	11
PVC	premature ventricular contraction	9	Rx	drug, prescription, therapy	7, 8
PVD	peripheral vascular disease	9	s̄	without	8
			S	sacrum; sacral	19

(continued)

Abbreviations and Their Meanings *(Continued)*

Abbreviation	Meaning	Chapter	Abbreviation	Meaning	Chapter
S_1	first heart sound	9	strep	streptococcus	6
S_2	second heart sound	9	STSG	split-thickness skin graft	21
SA	sustained action; sinoatrial	8, 9	supp	suppository	8
SARS	severe acute respiratory syndrome	11	susp	suspension	8
			SVD	spontaneous vaginal delivery	15
SBE	subacute bacterial endocarditis	9	SVT	supraventricular tachycardia	9
sc	without correction	18	T	temperature; thoracic vertebra	7, 19
SC, SQ, subcut.	subcutaneous(ly)	8	T1DM	type 1 diabetes mellitus	16
SCLE	subacute cutaneous lupus erythematosus	21	T2DM	type 2 diabetes mellitus	16
seg	neutrophil	10	T_3	triiodothyronine	16
SERM	selective estrogen receptor modulator	15, 19	T_4	thyroxine; tetraiodothyronine	16
SG	specific gravity	13	T_7	free thyroxine index	16
SIADH	syndrome of inappropriate antidiuretic hormone	16	T&A	tonsils and adenoids, tonsillectomy and adenoidectomy	11
SIDS	sudden infant death syndrome	11	tab	tablet	8
SITS	supraspinatus, infraspinatus, teres minor, subscapularis (muscles)	20	TAH	total abdominal hysterectomy	15
			TB	tuberculosis	11
			TBG	thyroxine-binding globulin	16
SK	streptokinase	9	TBI	traumatic brain injury; thrombolytic brain infarction	17
SL	sublingual	8			
SLE	systemic lupus erythematosus	10, 21	^{99m}Tc	technetium-99m	9
SPECT	single photon emission computed tomography	7	TCA	tricyclic antidepressant	17
			TEE	transesophageal echocardiography	9
SPF	sun protection factor	21	TGV	thoracic gas volume	11
SpO2	oxygen percent saturation	11	THA	total hip arthroplasty	19
SR	sustained release	8	THP	total hip precautions	19
$\overline{ss}$	half	8	THR	total hip replacement	19
SSEP	somatosensory evoked potentials	17	TIA	transient ischemic attack	17
SSRI	selective serotonin reuptake inhibitor	17	tid, t.i.d.	three times per day	8
ST	speech threshold	18	tinct	tincture	8
staph	staphylococcus	6	TKA	total knee arthroplasty	19
STAT	immediately	7	TKO	to keep open	7
STD	sexually transmitted disease	14, 15	TLC	total lung capacity	11
STI	sexually transmitted infection	14, 15	Tm	maximal transport capacity; tubular maximum	13

Abbreviations and Their Meanings (*Continued*)

Abbreviation	Meaning	Chapter	Abbreviation	Meaning	Chapter
TM	tympanic membrane	18	UV	ultraviolet	7, 21
Tn	troponin	9	UVA	ultraviolet A	21
TNM	(primary) tumor, (regional lymph) nodes, (distant) metastases	7	UVB	ultraviolet B	21
			VA	visual acuity	18
TMJ	temporomandibular joint	19	VAC	vacuum-assisted closure	21
tPA	tissue plasminogen activator	9	VAD	ventricular assist device	9
TPN	total parenteral nutrition	12	VBAC	vaginal birth after cesarean section	15
TPR	temperature, pulse, respiration	7	VC	vital capacity	11
			VD	venereal disease	14, 15
TPUR	transperineal urethral resection	14	VDRL	Venereal Disease Research Laboratory	14
TSE	testicular self-examination	14	VEP	visual evoked potentials	17
TSH	thyroid-stimulating hormone	16	VF	ventricular fibrillation; visual field	9, 18
TSS	toxic shock syndrome	15	v fib	ventricular fibrillation	9
T(C)T	thrombin (clotting) time	10	VLDL	very low density lipoprotein	9
TTP	thrombotic thrombocytopenic purpura	10	VPC	ventricular premature complex	9
TTS	temporary threshold shift	18	VRSA	vancomycin-resistant *Staphylococcus aureus*	6
TUIP	transurethral incision of prostate	14	VS	vital signs	7
TURP	transurethral resection of prostate	14	VSD	ventricular septal defect	9
TV	tidal volume	11	VT	ventricular tachycardia	9
Tx	traction	19	VTE	venous thromboembolism	9
U	units	8			
UA	urinalysis	13	V_{TG}	thoracic gas volume	11
UC	uterine contractions	15	vWF	von Willebrand factor	10
UFE	uterine fibroid embolization	15	WBC	white blood cell; white blood (cell) count	10
UG	urogenital	14	WD	well developed	7
UGI	upper gastrointestinal	12	WNL	within normal limits	7
UMN	upper motor neuron	17	w/o	without	7
ung	ointment	8	WPW	Wolff–Parkinson–White syndrome	9
URI	upper respiratory infection	11	x	times	8
USP	*United States Pharmacopeia*	8	XT	exotropia	18
UTI	urinary tract infection	13, 14	YO, y/o	years old, year-old	7
UTP	uterine term pregnancy	15	ZIFT	zygote intrafallopian transfer	15

Word Parts and Their Meanings

Word Part	Meaning	Reference Page	Word Part	Meaning	Reference Page
a-	not, without, lack of, absence	36	atri/o	atrium	173
			audi/o	hearing	467
ab-	away from	37	auto-	self	442
abdomin/o	abdomen	76	azot/o	nitrogenous compounds	216
-ac	pertaining to	20	bacill/i, bacill/o	bacillus	103
acous, acus	sound, hearing	467	bacteri/o	bacterium	103
acro-	extremity, end	77	balan/o	glans penis	345
ad-	toward, near	37	bar/o	pressure	123
aden/o	gland	58	bi-	two, twice	33
adip/o	fat	60	bili	bile	276
adren/o	adrenal gland, epinephrine	403	bio	life	56
			blast/o, -blast	immature cell, productive cell, embryonic cell	59
adrenal/o	adrenal gland	403			
adrenocortic/o	adrenal cortex	403			
aer/o	air, gas	123	blephar/o	eyelid	476
-agogue	promoter, stimulator	377	brachi/o	arm	77
-al	pertaining to	20	brachy-	short	345
alg/o, algi/o, algesi/o	pain	98, 142	brady-	slow	99
			bronch/o, bronch/i	bronchus	245
-algesia	pain	100, 463			
-algia	pain	100	bronchiol	bronchiole	245
ambly-	dim	502	bucc/o	cheek	278
amnio	amnion	377	burs/o	bursa	502
amyl/o	starch	60	calc/i	calcium	216
an-	not, without, lack of, absence	36	cali/o, calic/o	calyx	310
			-capnia	carbon dioxide (level of)	244
andr/o	male	337	carcin/o	cancer, carcinoma	98
angi/o	vessel	172	cardi/o	heart	173
an/o	anus	276	cec/o	cecum	280
ante-	before	41	-cele	hernia, localized dilation	100
anti-	against	36, 142			
aort/o	aorta	170	celi/o	abdomen	76
-ar	pertaining to	20	centesis	puncture, tap	126
arter/o, arteri/o	artery	174	cephal/o	head	76
arteriol/o	arteriole	174	cerebell/o	cerebellum	430
arthr/o	joint	502	cerebr/o	cerebrum	430
-ary	pertaining to	20	cervic/o	neck, cervix	76, 363
-ase	enzyme	60	chem/o	chemical	142
atel/o	imperfect	254	cheil/o	lip	292
atlant/o	atlas	500	chir/o	hand	131

Word Parts and Their Meanings (*Continued*)

Word Part	Meaning	Reference Page	Word Part	Meaning	Reference Page
cholangi/o	bile duct	281	-desis	binding, fusion	126
chol/e, chol/o	bile, gall	281	dextr/o-	right	41
cholecyst/o	gallbladder	281	di-	two, twice	33
choledoch/o	common bile duct	281	dia-	through	37
chondr/o	cartilage	502	dilation, dilatation	expansion, widening	101
chori/o, choroid/o	choroid	477	dipl/o-	double	33
chrom/o, chromat/o	color, stain	123	dis-	absence, removal, separation	36
chron/o	time	123	duoden/o	duodenum	279
circum-	around	77	dynam/o	force, energy	545
clasis, -clasia	breaking	100	dys-	abnormal, painful, difficult	99
clitor/o, clitorid/o	clitoris	364	ec-	out, outside	41
coccy, coccyg/o	coccyx	503	ectasia, ectasis	dilation, dilatation, distention	101
cochle/o	cochlea (of inner ear)	467	ecto-	out, outside	41
col/o, colon/o	colon	280	-ectomy	excision, surgical removal	126
colp/o	vagina	363	edema	accumulation of fluid, swelling	101
contra-	against, opposite, opposed	36, 142	electr/o	electricity	123
copro	feces	432	embry/o	embryo	377
cor/o, cor/e	pupil	502	emesis	vomiting	289
corne/o	cornea	477	-emia	condition of blood	214
cortic/o	outer portion, cerebral cortex	430	encephal/o	brain	430
cost/o	rib	503	end/o-	in, within	41
counter-	against, opposite, opposed	142	endocrin/o	endocrine	403
crani/o	skull, cranium	503	enter/o	intestine	279
cry/o	cold	123	epi-	on, over	77
crypt/o	hidden	356	epididym/o	epididymis	338
cus	sound, hearing	467	episi/o	vulva	364
cyan/o-	blue	35	equi-	equal, same	38
cycl/o	ciliary body, ciliary muscle (of eye)	477	erg/o	work	124, 539
cyst/o	filled sac or pouch, cyst, bladder, urinary bladder	98	erythr/o-	red, red blood cell	35
			erythrocyt/o	red blood cell	215
			esophag/o	esophagus	279
-cyte, cyt/o	cell	63	-esthesia, -esthesi/o	sensation	463
dacry/o	tear, lacrimal apparatus	476			
dacryocyst/o	lacrimal sac	476	eu-	true, good, easy, normal	38
dactyl/o	finger, toe	77	ex/o-	away from, outside	42
de-	down, without, removal, loss	39	extra-	outside	77
			fasci/o	fascia	539
dent/o, dent/i	tooth, teeth	278	fer	to carry	427
derm/o, dermat/o	skin	561	ferr/i, ferr/o	iron	216
			fet/o	fetus	377

(continued)

Word Parts and Their Meanings (Continued)

Word Part	Meaning	Reference Page	Word Part	Meaning	Reference Page
fibr/o	fiber	58	-ic	pertaining to	20
-form	like, resembling	20	-ical	pertaining to	20
galact/o	milk	377	-ics	medical specialty	18
gangli/o, ganglion/o	ganglion	429	-ile	pertaining to	20
			ile/o	ileum	280
gastr/o	stomach	279	ili/o	ilium	503
gen, genesis	origin, formation	59	im-	not	36
ger/e, ger/o	old age	35	immun/o	immunity, immune system	215
-geusia	sense of taste	463			
gingiv/o	gum, gingiva	278	in-	not	36
gli/o	neuroglia	429	infra-	below	77
glomerul/o	glomerulus	310	in/o	fiber, muscle fiber	539
gloss/o	tongue	278	insul/o	pancreatic islets	403
gluc/o	glucose	60	inter-	between	77
glyc/o	sugar, glucose	60	intra-	in, within	77
gnath/o	jaw	278	ir, irit/o, irid/o	iris	477
goni/o	angle	484, 517	-ism	condition of	16
-gram	record of data	125	iso-	equal, same	38
-graph	instrument for recording data	125	-ist	specialist	18
			-itis	inflammation	100
-graphy	act of recording data	125	jejun/o	jejunum	280
gravida	pregnant woman	377	juxta-	near, beside	77
gyn/o, gynec/o	woman	362	kali	potassium	216
hem/o, hemat/o	blood	215	kary/o	nucleus	58
hemi-	half, one side	33	kerat/o	cornea, keratin, horny layer of skin	477, 561
-hemia	condition of blood	214			
hepat/o	liver	281	kin/o, kine, kinesi/o, kinet/o	movement	539
hetero-	other, different, unequal	39			
hidr/o	sweat, perspiration	561			
hist/o, histi/o	tissue	58	labi/o	lip	278
homo-, homeo-	same, unchanging	38	labyrinth/o	labyrinth (inner ear)	467
hydr/o	water, fluid	60	lacrim/o	tear, lacrimal apparatus	476
hyper-	over, excess, increased, abnormally high	38	lact/o	milk	377
			-lalia	speech, babble	432
hypn/o	sleep	143	lapar/o	abdominal wall	76
hypo-	under, below, decreased, abnormally low	38	laryng/o	larynx	245
			lent/i	lens	477
hypophysi/o	pituitary, hypophysis	403	-lepsy	seizure	432
hyster/o	uterus	363	leuk/o-	white, colorless, white blood cell	215
-ia	condition of	17			
-ian	specialist	18	leukocyt/o	white blood cell	215
-ia/sis	condition of	17	-lexia	reading	432
-iatrics	medical specialty	18	lingu/o	tongue	278
-iatr/o	physician	18	lip/o	fat, lipid	60
-iatry	medical specialty	18	-listhesis	slipping	514

Word Parts and Their Meanings (Continued)

Word Part	Meaning	Reference Page	Word Part	Meaning	Reference Page
lith	calculus, stone	98	my/o	muscle	539
-logy	study of	18	myring/o	tympanic membrane	467
lumb/o	lumbar region, lower back	76	myx/o	mucus	58
			narc/o	stupor, unconsciousness	143, 430
lymphaden/o	lymph node	187	nas/o	nose	245
lymphangi/o	lymphatic vessel	187	nat/i	birth	377
lymph/o	lymph, lymphatic system, lymphocyte	187	natri	sodium	216
			necrosis	death of tissue	101
lymphocyt/o	lymphocyte	215	neo-	new	39
-lysis	separation, loosening, dissolving, destruction	101	nephr/o	kidney	310
			neur/o, neur/i	nervous system, nerve	429
-lytic	dissolving, reducing, loosening	142	noct/i	night	127
			non-	not	36
macro-	large, abnormally large	38	normo-	normal	39
mal-	bad, poor	99	nucle/o	nucleus	58
malacia	softening	101	nulli-	never	376
mamm/o	breast, mammary gland	364	nyct/o	night, darkness	127
-mania	excited state, obsession	432	ocul/o	eye	476
mast/o	breast, mammary gland	364	odont/o	tooth, teeth	278
medull/o	inner part, medulla oblongata, spinal cord	431	-odynia	pain	100
			-oid	like, resembling	20
mega-, megal/o-	large, abnormally large	39	olig/o-	few, scanty, deficiency of	38
-megaly	enlargement	100	-oma	tumor	100
melan/o-	black, dark, melanin	35	onc/o	tumor	98
mening/o, meninge/o	meninges	429	onych/o	nail	561
			oo	ovum	362
men/o, mens	month, menstruation	362	oophor/o	ovary	362
mes/o-	middle	41	ophthalm/o	eye	476
met/a	change, after, beyond	97	-opia	condition of the eye, vision	478
-meter	instrument for measuring	125	-opsia	condition of vision	478
metr/o	measure	125, 363	opt/o	eye, vision	476
metr/o, metr/i	uterus	363	orchid/o, orchi/o	testis	338
-metry	measurement of	125			
micro-	small, one millionth	39	or/o	mouth	278
-mimetic	mimicking, simulating	142	ortho-	straight, correct, upright	39
mon/o-	one	33	-ory	pertaining to	20
morph/o	form, structure	58	osche/o	scrotum	338
muc/o	mucus, mucous membrane	58	-ose	sugar	60
multi-	many	33	-o/sis	condition of	17
muscul/o	muscle	539	osm/o	smell	463
myc/o	fungus, mold	103	-osmia	sense of smell	463
myel/o	bone marrow, spinal cord	215, 429, 502	oste/o	bone	502
			ot/o	ear	467

(continued)

Word Parts and Their Meanings (Continued)

Word Part	Meaning	Reference Page	Word Part	Meaning	Reference Page
-ous	pertaining to	20	-plasty	plastic repair, plastic surgery, reconstruction	126
ovari/o	ovary	362	-plegia	paralysis	432
ov/o, ovul/o	ovum	362	pleur/o	pleura	246
-oxia	oxygen (level of)	244	-pnea	breathing	244
ox/y	oxygen, sharp, acute	216	pneum/o, pneumat/o	air, gas, lung, respiration	246
pachy-	thick	99	pneumon/o	lung	246
palat/o	palate	278	pod/o	foot	77
palpebr/o	eyelid	476	-poiesis	formation, production	214
pan-	all	38	poikilo-	varied, irregular	39
pancreat/o	pancreas	281	poly-	many, much	33
papill/o	nipple	58	post-	after, behind	40
para-	near, beside, abnormal	78	pre-	before, in front of	40
para	woman who has given birth	377	presby-	old	479
parathyr/o, parathyroid/o	parathyroid	403	prim/i-	first	33
-paresis	partial paralysis, weakness	432	pro-	before, in front of	40
path/o, -pathy	disease, any disease of	100	proct/o	rectum	280
ped/o	foot, child	77	prostat/o	prostate	338
pelvi/o	pelvis	503	prote/o	protein	60
-penia	decrease in, deficiency of	214	pseudo-	false	39
per-	through	37	psych/o	mind	431
peri-	around	77	ptosis	dropping, downward displacement, prolapse	101
perine/o	perineum	364	ptysis	spitting	254
periton, peritone/o	peritoneum	76	puer	child	384
-pexy	surgical fixation	126	pulm/o, pulmon/o	lung	246
phac/o, phak/o	lens	477	pupill/o	pupil	477
phag/o	eat, ingest	59	pyel/o	renal pelvis	310
pharm, pharmac/o	drug, medicine	143	pylor/o	pylorus	280
pharyng/o	pharynx	245	py/o	pus	98
-phasia	speech	432	pyr/o, pyret/o	fever, fire	98
phil, -philic	attracting, absorbing	59	quadr/i-	four	33
phleb/o	vein	184	rachi/o	spine	77
-phobia	fear	432	radicul/o	root of spinal nerve	429
phon/o	sound, voice	124	radi/o	radiation, x-ray	124
-phonia	voice	244	re-	again, back	39
phot/o	light	124	rect/o	rectum	280
phren/o	diaphragm	246	ren/o	kidney	310
phrenic/o	phrenic nerve	246	reticul/o	network	58
phyt/o	plant	142, 569	retin/o	retina	477
pituitar/i	pituitary, hypophysis	403	retro-	behind, backward	78
plas, -plasia	formation, molding, development	59	rhabd/o	rod, muscle cell	544

Word Parts and Their Meanings (Continued)

Word Part	Meaning	Reference Page	Word Part	Meaning	Reference Page
-rhage, -rhagia	bursting forth, profuse flow, hemorrhage	100	steat/o	fatty	60
			stenosis	narrowing, constriction	102
-rhaphy	surgical repair, suture	126	steth/o	chest	122
-rhea	flow, discharge	100	sthen/o	strength	544
-rhexis	rupture	100	stoma, stomat/o	mouth	278
rhin/o	nose	245			
sacchar/o	sugar	60	-stomy	surgical creation of an opening	126
sacr/o	sacrum	503			
salping/o	tube, uterine tube, auditory (eustachian) tube	363, 467	strept/o-	twisted chain, Streptococcus	103
			sub-	below, under	77
-schisis	fissure, splitting	100	super-	above, excess	38
scler/o	hard, sclera (of eye)	98, 476	supra-	above	78
sclerosis	hardening	102	syn-, sym-	together	41
-scope	instrument for viewing or examining	125	synov/i	synovial joint, synovial membrane	502
-scopy	examination of	125	tachy-	rapid	99
seb/o	sebum, sebaceous gland	561	tax/o	order, arrangement	544
semi-	half, partial	33	tel/e-, tel/o-	end, far, at a distance	41
semin	semen	338	ten/o, tendin/o	tendon	539
sept/o	septum, dividing wall, partition	256	terat/o	malformed fetus	383
			test/o	testis, testicle	338
sial/o	saliva, salivary gland, salivary duct	278	tetra-	four	33
			thalam/o	thalamus	430
sider/o	iron	216	therm/o	heat, temperature	124
sigmoid/o	sigmoid colon	280	thorac/o	chest, thorax	76
sinistr/o	left	41	thromb/o	blood clot	215
-sis	condition of	17	thrombocyt/o	platelet, thrombocyte	215
skelet/o	skeleton	501	thym/o	thymus gland	187
somat/o	body	58	thyr/o, thyroid/o	thyroid	403
-some	body, small body	58			
somn/i, somn/o	sleep	430	toc/o	labor	377
son/o	sound, ultrasound	124	-tome	instrument for incising (cutting)	126
spasm	sudden contraction, cramp	102	-tomy	incision, cutting	126
sperm/i	semen, spermatozoa	338	ton/o	tone	539
spermat/o	semen, spermatozoa	338	tonsil/o	tonsil	187
-spermia	condition of semen	338	tox/o, toxic/o	poison, toxin	98, 143
sphygm/o	pulse	172	toxin	poison	102
spir/o	breathing	246	trache/o	trachea	245
splen/o	spleen	187	trans-	through	37
spondyl/o	vertebra	503	tri-	three	33
staped/o, stapedi/o	stapes	467	trich/o	hair	561
			-tripsy	crushing	126
staphyl/o	grape-like cluster, Staphylococcus	103	trop/o	turning	484
stasis	suppression, stoppage	102	trop, -tropic	act(ing) on, affect(ing)	142

(continued)

Word Parts and Their Meanings (*Continued*)

Word Part	Meaning	Reference Page	Word Part	Meaning	Reference Page
troph/o, -trophy, -trophia	feeding, growth, nourishment	59	**valv/o, valvul/o**	valve	173
			varic/o	twisted and swollen vein, varix	183
tympan/o	tympanic cavity (middle ear), tympanic membrane	467	**vascul/o**	vessel	174
			vas/o	vessel, duct, vas deferens	143, 183, 338
un-	not	36	**ven/o, ven/i**	vein	174
uni-	one	33	**ventricul/o**	cavity, ventricle	173, 430
-uresis	urination	311	**vertebr/o**	vertebra, spinal column	503
ureter/o	ureter	311	**vesic/o**	urinary bladder	311
urethr/o	urethra	311	**vesicul/o**	seminal vesicle	338
-uria	condition of urine, urination	311	**vestibul/o**	vestibule, vestibular apparatus (of ear)	467
ur/o	urine, urinary tract	311	**vir/o**	virus	103
urin/o	urine	311	**vulv/o**	vulva	364
uter/o	uterus	363	**xanth/o-**	yellow	35
uve/o	uvea (of eye)	477	**xen/o**	foreign, strange	457
uvul/o	uvula	278	**xer/o-**	dry	99
vagin/o	sheath, vagina	363	**-y**	condition of	17

▶ Appendix 4

Meanings and Their Corresponding Word Parts

Meaning	Word Part(s)	Reference Page	Meaning	Word Part(s)	Reference Page
abdomen	abdomin/o, celi/o	76	atlas	atlant/o	500
abdominal wall	lapar/o	76	atrium	atri/o	170
abnormal	dys-, para-	78	attract(ing)	phil, -philic	59
abnormally high	hyper-	38	auditory (eustachian) tube	salping/o	363, 467
abnormally large	macro-, mega-, megal/o-	38			
abnormally low	hypo-	38	away from	ab-, ex/o-	37, 41
above	super-, supra-	38, 78	babble	-lalia	432
absence	a-, an-, dis-	36	bacillus	bacill/i, bacill/o	103
absorb(ing)	phil, -philic	59	back	re-	39
accumulation of fluid	edema	101	backward	retro-	78
			bacterium	bacteri/o	103
act of recording data	-graphy	125	bad	mal-	99
			before	ante-, pre-, pro-	40
act(ing) on	trop, -tropic	142	behind	post-, retro-	40, 78
acute	ox/y	216	below	hypo-, infra-, sub-	38, 77
adrenal gland	adren/o, adrenal/o	403	beside	para-, juxta-	77, 78
adrenaline	adren/o	403	between	inter-	77
adrenal	adren/o	403	beyond	met/a	97
adrenal cortex	adrenocortic/o	403	bile	bili, chol/e, chol/o	276
affect(ing)	trop, -tropic	142	bile duct	cholangi/o	281
after	post-, met/a	40, 97	binding	-desis	126
again	re-	39	birth	nat/i	377
against	anti-, contra-, counter-	142	black	melan/o-	35
			bladder	cyst/o	98
air	aer/o, pneumat/o	123, 246	bladder (urinary)	cyst/o, vesic/o	98, 324
all	pan-	38	blood	hem/o, hemat/o	215
amnion, amniotic sac	amnio	377	blood (condition of)	-emia, -hemia	214
angle	goni/o	484	blood clot	thromb/o	215
anus	an/o	280	blue	cyan/o-	35
any disease of	-pathy	100	body	somat/o, -some	58
aorta	aort/o	174	bone	oste/o	502
arm	brachi/o	77	bone marrow	myel/o	215, 429, 502
around	circum-, peri-	77	brain	encephal/o	430
arrangement	tax/o	544	breaking	-clasis, -clasia	100
arteriole	arteriol/o	174	breast	mamm/o, mast/o	364
artery	arter/o, arteri/o	174	breathing	-pnea, spir/o	244, 246
at a distance	tel/e, tel/o	41			

(continued)

Meanings and Their Corresponding Word Parts (Continued)

Meaning	Word Part(s)	Reference Page	Meaning	Word Part(s)	Reference Page
bronchiole	bronchiol	245	condition of semen	-spermia	339
bronchus	bronch/i, bronch/o	245	constriction	stenosis	102
bursa	burs/o	502	contraction (sudden)	spasm	102
bursting forth	-rhage, -rhagia	100			
calcium	calc/i	216	cornea	corne/o, kerat/o	477
calculus	lith	98	correct	ortho-	39
calyx	cali/o, calic/o	310	cramp	spasm	102
cancer	carcin/o	98	cranium	crani/o	503
carbon dioxide	-capnia	244	crushing	-tripsy	126
carcinoma	carcin/o	98	cutting	-tomy	126
carry	fer	427	cutting instrument	-tome	126
cartilage	chondr/o	502			
cavity	ventricul/o	173, 430	cyst	cyst/o	98
cecum	cec/o	280	dark	melan/o-	35
cell	-cyte, cyt/o	58	darkness	nyct/o	127
cerebellum	cerebell/o	430	data	-gram	125
cerebral cortex	cortic/o	430	death of tissue	necrosis	101
cerebrum	cerebr/o	430	decreased, decrease in	hypo-, -penia	38, 214
cervix	cervic/o	363			
chain (twisted)	strept/o	103	deficiency of	oligo-, -penia	214
change	met/a	97	destruction	lysis	101
cheek	bucc/o	278	development	plas, -plasia	59
chemical	chem/o	142	diaphragm	phren/o	246
chest	thorac/o, steth/o	76, 122	different	hetero-	39
child	ped/o, puer	384	difficult	dys-	99
choroid	chori/o, choroid/o	477	dilatation, dilation	ectasia, ectasis	101
ciliary body	cycl/o	477			
ciliary muscle	cycl/o	477	distention	ectasia, ectasis	101
clitoris	clitor/o, clitorid/o	364	dim	ambly-	483
clot	thromb/o	215	discharge	-rhea	100
coccyx	coccy, coccyg/o	503	disease	path/o, -pathy	100
cochlea	cochle/o	467	dissolving	lysis, -lytic	101, 142
cold	cry/o	123	distance (at a)	tel/e, tel/o	41
colon	col/o, colon/o	280	distention	ectasia, ectasis	101
color	chrom/o, chromat/o	123	double	dipl/o-	33
colorless	leuk/o-	35	down	de-	36
common bile duct	choledoch/o	281	dropping, downward displacement	ptosis	101
condition of	-ia, -ia/sis, -ism, -o/sis, -sis, -y	17			
condition of blood	-emia, -hemia	214	drug	pharm, pharmac/o	143
condition of the eye	-opia	478	dry	xer/o-	99
			duct	vas/o	174
condition of urine, urination	-uria	598	ductus deferens	vas/o	338
			duodenum	duoden/o	279
condition of vision	-opia, -opsia	478	ear	ot/o	467

Meanings and Their Corresponding Word Parts (*Continued*)

Meaning	Word Part(s)	Reference Page	Meaning	Word Part(s)	Reference Page
easy	eu-	38	fire	pyr/o, pyret/o	98
eat	phag/o	59	first	prim/i-	33
egg cell	oo, ov/o, ovul/o	362	fissure	-schisis	100
electricity	electr/o	123	fixation (surgical)	-pexy	126
embryo	embry/o	377	flow	-rhea	100
embryonic cell	-blast, blast/o	59	fluid	hydr/o	60
end	tel/e, tel/o, acro	41, 77	foot	ped/o, pod/o	77
endocrine	endocrin/o	403	foreign	xen/o	438
energy	dynam/o	545	form	morph/o	58
enlargement	-megaly, megal/o	100	formation	gen, genesis, plas, -plasia, -poiesis	59, 214
enzyme	-ase	60	force	dynam/o	545
epididymis	epididym/o	338	four	quadr/i, tetra-	33
epinephrine	adren/o	403	fungus	myc/o	103
equal	iso-, equi-	38	fusion	-desis	126
erythrocyte	erythr/o, erythrocyt/o	215	gall	chol/e, chol/o	281
esophagus	esophag/o	279	gallbladder	cholecyst/o	281
eustachian (auditory) tube	salping/o	363, 467	ganglion	gangli/o, ganglion/o	429
examination of	-scopy	125	gas	aer/o, pneum/o, pneumon/o, pneumat/o	123, 246
excess	hyper-, super-	38	gingiva (gum)	gingiv/o	278
excision	-ectomy	125	gland	aden/o	58
excited state	mania	432	glans penis	balan/o	345
expansion	dilation, dilatation, ectasia, ectasis	101	glomerulus	glomerul/o	310
extremity	acro	77	glucose	gluc/o, glyc/o	60
eye	ocul/o, ophthalm/o, opt/o, -opia	476, 478	good	eu-	38
eyelid	blephar/o, palpebr/o	476	grape-like cluster	staphyl/o	103
fallopian tube	salping/o	363, 467	growth	troph/o, -trophy, -trophia	59
false	pseudo-	39	gum, gingiva	gingiv/o	278
far	tel/e, tel/o	41	hair	trich/o	561
fascia	fasci/o	539	half	hemi-, semi-	33
fat	adip/o, lip/o	60	hand	chir/o	123
fatty	steat/o	60	hard	scler/o	98
fear	-phobia	432	hardening	sclerosis	102
feces	copro	432	head	cephal/o	76
feeding	troph/o, -trophy, -trophia	59	hearing	acous, acus, audi/o, cus	467
fetus	fet/o	377	heart	cardi/o	173
fetus (malformed)	terat/o	383	heat	therm/o	124
fever	pyr/o, pyret/o	98, 143	hemorrhage	-rhage, -rhagia	100
few	oligo-	38	hernia	-cele	100
fiber	fibr/o, in/o	58, 539	hidden	crypt/o	342
filled sac or pouch	cyst/o	98	horny layer of skin	kerat/o	477
finger	dactyl/o	77			

(continued)

Meanings and Their Corresponding Word Parts (Continued)

Meaning	Word Part(s)	Reference Page	Meaning	Word Part(s)	Reference Page
hypophysis	hypophysi/o, pituitar/i	403	level of carbon dioxide	-capnia	244
islets (pancreatic)	insul/o	403	level of oxygen	-oxia	244
ileum	ile/o	280	life	bio	56
ilium	ili/o	501	light	phot/o	124
immature cell	blast/o, -blast	59	like	-form, -oid	20
immune system	immun/o	215	lip	labi/o, cheil/o	278, 292
immunity	immun/o	215	lipid	lip/o	60
imperfect	atel/o	254	liver	hepat/o	281
in	end/o-, intra-	41, 77	localized dilation	-cele	100
in front of	pre-, pro-	40	loosening	lysis, -lytic	101, 142
incision of	-tomy	126	loss	de-	36
increased	hyper-	38	lumbar region, lower back	lumb/o	76
inflammation	-itis	100	lung, lungs	pneum/o, pneumat/o, pneumon/o, pulm/o, pulmon/o	246
ingest	phag/o	59			
inner ear	labyrinth/o	467			
instrument for incising (cutting)	-tome	126	lymph, lymphatic system	lymph/o	187
instrument for measuring	-meter	125	lymph node	lymphaden/o	187
instrument for recording data	-graph	125	lymphatic vessel	lymphangi/o	187
			lymphocyte	lymph/o, lymphocyt/o	215
instrument for viewing or examining	-scope	125	male	andr/o	337
			malformed fetus	terat/o	383
intestine	enter/o	280	mammary gland	mamm/o, mast/o	364
iris	ir, irid/o, irit/o	477	many	multi-, poly-	33
iron	ferr/i, ferr/o, sider/o	216	marrow	myel/o	215, 429, 515
irregular	poikilo-	39	measure	metr/o	125, 363
jaw	gnath/o	278	measuring instrument	-meter	125
jejunum	jejun/o	280			
joint	arthr/o	502	measurement of	-metry	125
keratin	kerat/o	477	medical specialty	-ics, -iatrics, iatry	18
kidney	nephr/o, ren/o	310	medicine	pharm, pharmac/o	143
labor	toc/o	377	medulla oblongata	medull/o	431
labyrinth	labyrinth/o	467			
lack of	a-, an-	36	melanin	melan/o	35
lacrimal apparatus	dacry/o, lacrim/o	476	meninges	mening/o, meninge/o	429
			menstruation	men/o, mens	362
lacrimal sac	dacryocyst/o	476	middle	meso-	41
large	macro-, mega-, megal/o-	39	middle ear	tympan/o	467
			milk	galact/o, lact/o	377
larynx	laryng/o	245	mimicking	-mimetic	142
left	sinistr/o	41	mind	psych/o	431
lens	lent/i, phac/o, phak/o	477	mold	myc/o	103
			molding	plas, -plasia	59
leukocyte	leuk/o, leukocyt/o	215	month	men/o, mens	362

Meanings and Their Corresponding Word Parts (*Continued*)

Meaning	Word Part(s)	Reference Page	Meaning	Word Part(s)	Reference Page
mouth	or/o, stoma, stomat/o	278	ovary	ovari/o, oophor/o	362
movement	kin/o, kine, -kinesi/o, kinet/o	539	over	hyper-, epi-	38, 77
			ovum	oo, ov/o, ovul/o	362
much	poly-	33	oxygen	ox/y, -oxia	216, 244
mucus	muc/o, myx/o	58	pain	-algia, -odynia	100
mucous membrane	muc/o	58	pain	-algesia, alg/o, algi/o, algesi/o	98, 142
muscle	my/o, muscul/o	539	painful	dys-	99
muscle cell	rhabd/o	545	palate	palat/o	278
muscle fiber	in/o	539	pancreas	pancreat/o	281
nail	onych/o	561	pancreatic islets	insul/o	403
narrowing	stenosis	102	paralysis	-plegia	432
near	ad-, juxta-, para-	77, 78	paralysis (partial)	-paresis	432
neck	cervic/o	76, 363	parathyroid	parathyr/o, parathyroid/o	403
nerve, nervous system, nervous tissue	neur/o, neur/i	429	partial	semi-	33
			partial paralysis	-paresis	432
network	reticul/o	58	partition	sept/o	256
neuroglia	gli/o	429	pelvis	pelvi/o	503
never	nulli-	376	perineum	perine/o	364
new	neo-	39	peritoneum	periton, peritone/o	76
night	noct/i, nyct/o	127	perspiration	hidr/o	561
nipple	papill/o	58	pertaining to	-ac, -al, -ar, -ary, -ic, -ical, -ile, -ory, -ous	20
nitrogenous compounds	azot/o	216	pharynx	pharyng/o	245
normal	eu-, normo-	38, 39	phrenic nerve	phrenic/o	246
nose	nas/o, rhin/o	245	physician	iatr/o	18
not	a-, an-, in-, im-, non-, un-	36	pituitary	pituitar/i, hypophysi/o	403
nourishment	troph/o, -trophy, -trophia	59	plant	phyt/o	142, 569
nucleus	kary/o, nucle/o	58	plastic repair, plastic surgery	-plasty	126
obsession	mania	432	platelet	thrombocyt/o	215
old	presby-	479	pleura	pleur/o	246
old age	ger/e, ger/o	35	poison	tox/o, toxic/o, toxin	98, 143
on	epi-	77	poor	mal-	99
one	mon/o-, uni-	33	potassium	kali	216
one side	hemi-	33	pouch (filled)	cyst/o, cyst/i	98
opening (created surgically)	-stomy	126	pregnant woman	gravida	377
opposed	contra-, counter	142	pressure	bar/o	123
opposite	contra-, counter-	142	production	-poiesis	214
order	tax/o	544	productive cell	blast/o, -blast	59
origin	gen, genesis	59	profuse flow	-rhage, -rhagia	100
other	hetero-	38	prolapse	ptosis	101
out, outside	ec-, ecto-, ex/o, extra-	41, 77	promotor	-agogue	377
outer portion	cortic/o	430	prostate	prostat/o	338
			protein	prote/o	60

(continued)

Meanings and Their Corresponding Word Parts (Continued)

Meaning	Word Part(s)	Reference Page	Meaning	Word Part(s)	Reference Page
pulse	sphygm/o	172	semen, condition of	-spermia	339
puncture	centesis	126	seminal vesicle	vesicul/o	338
pupil	pupill/o, cor/o, cor/e	477	sensation	-esthesia, esthesi/o	463
pus	py/o	98	sense of smell	-osmia	463
pylorus	pylor/o	280	sense of taste	-geusia	463
radiation	radi/o	124	separation	dis-, -lysis	36, 101
rapid	tachy-	99	septum	sept/o	256
reading	-lexia	432	sharp	ox/y	216
reconstruction	-plasty	126	short	brachy-	345
record of data	-gram	125	sigmoid colon	sigmoid/o	280
recording data (act of)	-graphy	125	simulating	-mimetic	142
rectum	rect/o, proct/o	280	skeleton	skelet/o	501
red	erythr/o-	35	skin	derm/o, dermat/o	561
red blood cell	erythr/o, erythrocyt/o	215	skull	crani/o	503
reducing	-lytic	142	sleep	hypn/o, somn/o, somn/i	143, 430
removal	de-, dis-	36	slipping	-listhesis	514
removal (surgical)	-ectomy	126	slow	brady-	99
renal pelvis	pyel/o	310	small	micro-	39
repair (plastic)	-plasty	126	small body	-some	58
repair (surgical)	-rhaphy	126	smell	osm/o	463
respiration	pneum/o, pneumat/o	246	smell (sense of)	-osmia	463
resembling	-form, -oid	20	sodium	natri	216
retina	retin/o	477	softening	malacia	101
rib	cost/o	503	sound	phon/o, son/o, acous, acus, cus	124, 467
right	dextr/o-	41	specialist	-ian, -ist, -logist	18
rod	rhabd/o	545	specialty	-ics, -iatrics, -iatry	18
root of spinal nerve	radicul/o	429	speech	-phasia, -lalia	432
rupture	-rhexis	100	sperm, spermatozoa	sperm/i, spermat/o	338
sac (filled)	cyst/o, cyst/i	98	spinal column	vertebr/o	503
sacrum	sacr/o	503	spinal cord	myel/o, medull/o	215, 429, 515
saliva, salivary gland, salivary duct	sial/o	278	spinal nerve root	radicul/o	429
same	equi-, homo-, homeo-, iso-	38	spine	rachi/o	77
			spitting	-ptysis	254
sclera (of eye)	scler/o	476	spleen	splen/o	187
scanty	oligo-	38	splitting	-schisis	100
scrotum	osche/o	338	stain	chrom/o, chromat/o	123
sebum, sebaceous gland	seb/o	561	stapes	staped/o, stapedi/o	467
			staphylococcus	staphyl/o	103
seizure	-lepsy	432	starch	amyl/o	60
self	auto-	442	stimulator	-agogue	377
semen	semin, sperm/i, spermat/o	338	stomach	gastr/o	279

Meanings and Their Corresponding Word Parts *(Continued)*

Meaning	Word Part(s)	Reference Page	Meaning	Word Part(s)	Reference Page
stone	lith	98	toe	dactyl/o	77
stoppage	stasis	102	together	syn-, sym-	41
straight	ortho-	39	tone	ton/o	539
strange	xen/o	438	tongue	gloss/o, lingu/o	278
strength	sthen/o	544	tonsil	tonsil/o	187
Streptococcus	strept/o	103	tooth	-dent/o, dent/i, odont/o	278
structure	morph/o	58			
study of	-logy	18	toward	ad-	37
stupor	narc/o	143, 430	toxin	tox/o, toxic/o	98, 143
sugar	glyc/o, sacchar/o, -ose	60	trachea	trache/o	245
sudden contraction	spasm	102	true	eu-	38
			tube	salping/o	361, 467
suppression	stasis	102	tumor	onc/o, -oma	98, 100
surgery (plastic)	-plasty	126	turning	trop/o	484
surgical creation of an opening	-stomy	126	twice	bi-, di-	33
			twisted chain	strept/o	103
surgical fixation	-pexy	126	twisted and swollen vein	varic/o	183
surgical removal	-ectomy	126			
surgical repair	-rhaphy	126	two	bi-, di-, dipl/o-	33
suture	-rhaphy	126	tympanic cavity	tympan/o	467
sweat	hidr/o	561	tympanic membrane	myring/o, tympan/o	467
swelling	edema	101			
synovial fluid, joint, membrane	synov/i	502	ultrasound	son/o	124
			unchanging	homo-, homeo-	38
			unconsciousness	narc/o	430
tap	centesis	126	under	hypo-, sub-	38, 77
taste (sense of)	-geusia	463	unequal	hetero-	38
tear	dacry/o, lacrim/o	476	upright	ortho-	39
teeth	dent/o, dent/i, odont/o	278	ureter	ureter/o	311
temperature	therm/o	124	urethra	urethr/o	311
tendon	ten/o, tendin/o	539	urinary bladder	cyst/o, vesic/o	311
testicle	test/o	338	urination	-uresis	311
testis	test/o, orchid/o, orchi/o	338	urine, urinary tract, urination	ur/o, -uria	311
thalamus	thalam/o	430	urine	urin/o	311
thick	pachy-	99	uterine tube	salping/o	361, 467
thorax	thorac/o	76	uterus	hyster/o, metr/o, metr/i, uter/o	363
three	tri-	33			
thrombocyte	thrombocyt/o	215	uvea	uve/o	477
through	dia-, per-, trans-	37	uvula	uvul/o	278
thymus gland	thym/o	187	vagina	colp/o, vagin/o	363
thyroid	thyr/o, thyroid/o	403	valve	valv/o, valvul/o	173
time	chron/o	123	varicose vein, varix	varic/o	183
tissue	hist/o, histi/o	58			
tissue death	necrosis	101	varied	poikilo-	39

(continued)

Meanings and Their Corresponding Word Parts (*Continued*)

Meaning	Word Part(s)	Reference Page	Meaning	Word Part(s)	Reference Page
vas deferens	vas/o	143	wall, dividing wall	sept/o	256
vein	ven/o, ven/i, phleb/o	174	water	hydr/o	60
vein (twisted, swollen)	varic/o	183	weakness	paresis	432
ventricle	ventricul/o	173, 430	white	leuk/o-	35
vertebra	spondyl/o, vertebr/o	503	white blood cell	leuk/o, leukocyt/o	215
vessel	angi/o, vas/o, vascul/o	143, 174	widening	ectasia, ectasis, dilation, dilatation	101
vestibular apparatus, vestibule	vestibul/o	467	within	end/o-, intra-	41, 77
			without	a-, an-, de-	36
virus	vir/o	103	woman	gyn/o, gynec/o	362
vision	opt/o, -opia, -opsia	476, 478	woman who has given birth	para	377
voice	phon/o, -phonia	124, 244	work	erg/o	124, 539
vomiting	emesis	289	x-ray	radi/o	124
vulva	episi/o, vulv/o	364	yellow	xanth/o-	35

▶ Appendix 5

Word Roots

Root	Meaning	Reference Page	Root	Meaning	Reference Page
abdomin/o	abdomen	76	burs/o	bursa	502
acous, acus	sound, hearing	467	calc/i	calcium	216
acro	extremity, end	77	cali/o, calic/o	calyx	310
aden/o	gland	58	carcin/o	cancer, carcinoma	98
adip/o	fat	60	cardi/o	heart	173
adren/o	adrenal gland, epinephrine	403	cec/o	cecum	280
			celi/o	abdomen	76
adrenal/o	adrenal gland	403	centesis	puncture, tap	126
adrenocortic/o	adrenal cortex	403	cephal/o	head	76
aer/o	air, gas	123	cerebell/o	cerebellum	430
alg/o, algi/o, algesi/o	pain	98, 142	cerebr/o	cerebrum	430
amnio	amnion	377	cervic/o	neck, cervix	76, 363
amyl/o	starch	60	cheil/o	lip	292
andr/o	male	337	chem/o	chemical	142
angi/o	vessel	174	chir/o	hand	123
an/o	anus	280	cholangi/o	bile duct	281
aort/o	aorta	174	chol/e, chol/o	bile, gall	281
arter/o, arteri/o	artery	174	cholecyst/o	gallbladder	281
arteriol/o	arteriole	174	choledoch/o	common bile duct	281
arthr/o	joint	502	chondr/o	cartilage	502
atel/o	incomplete, imperfect	254	chori/o, choroid/o	choroid	477
atlant/o	atlas	500	chrom/o, chromat/o	color, stain	123
atri/o	atrium	173	chron/o	time	123
audi/o	hearing	467	clasis	breaking	100
azot/o	nitrogenous compounds	216	clitor/o, clitorid/o	clitoris	364
			coccy, coccyg/o	coccyx	503
bacill/i, bacill/o	bacillus	103	cochle/o	cochlea (of inner ear)	467
bacteri/o	bacterium	103			
balan/o	glans penis	345	col/o, colon/o	colon	280
bar/o	pressure	123	colp/o	vagina	363
bili	bile	276	copro	feces	432
bio	life	56	cor/o, cor/e	pupil	483
blast/o	immature cell, productive cell, embryonic cell	59	corne/o	cornea	477
			cortic/o	outer portion, cerebral cortex	430
blephar/o	eyelid	476	cost/o	rib	503
brachi/o	arm	77	crani/o	skull, cranium	503
bronch/i, bronch/o	bronchus	245	cry/o	cold	123
bronchiol	bronchiole	245	crypt/o	hidden	342
bucc/o	cheek	278			

(continued)

Word Roots (Continued)

Root	Meaning	Reference Page	Root	Meaning	Reference Page
cus	sound, hearing	467	gloss/o	tongue	278
cycl/o	ciliary body, ciliary muscle (of eye)	477	gluc/o	glucose	60
			glyc/o	sugar, glucose	60
cyst/o	filled sac or pouch, cyst, bladder, urinary bladder	98, 311	gnath/o	jaw	278
			goni/o	angle	484, 517
cyt/o	cell	58	gravida	pregnant woman	377
dacry/o	tear, lacrimal apparatus	476	gyn/o, gynec/o	woman	362
			hem/o, hemat/o	blood	215
dacryocyst/o	lacrimal sac	476	hepat/o	liver	281
dactyl/o	finger, toe	77	hidr/o	sweat, perspiration	561
dent/o, dent/i	tooth, teeth	278	hist/o, histi/o	tissue	58
derm/o, dermat/o	skin	561	hydr/o	water, fluid	60
dilation, dilatation	expansion, widening	101	hypn/o	sleep	143
duoden/o	duodenum	279	hypophysi/o	pituitary, hypophysis	403
dynam/o	force, energy	545	hyster/o	uterus	363
ectasia, ectasis	dilation, dilatation, distention	101	iatr/o	physician	18
			ile/o	ileum	280
edema	accumulation of fluid, swelling	101	ili/o	ilium	501
electr/o	electricity	123	immun/o	immunity, immune system	215
embry/o	embryo	377	in/o	fiber, muscle fiber	539
emesis	vomiting	289	insul/o	pancreatic islets	403
encephal/o	brain	430	ir, irit/o, irid/o	iris	477
endocrin/o	endocrine	403	jejun/o	jejunum	280
enter/o	intestine	280	kali	potassium	216
epididym/o	epididymis	338	kary/o	nucleus	58
episi/o	vulva	364	kerat/o	cornea, keratin, horny layer of skin	477, 561
erg/o	work	124, 539			
erythr/o-	red, red blood cell	35	kin/o, kine, kinesi/o, kinet/o	movement	539
erythrocyt/o	red blood cell	215			
esophag/o	esophagus	279	labi/o	lip	278
fasci/o	fascia	539	labyrinth/o	labyrinth (inner ear)	467
fer	carry	427	lacrim/o	tear, lacrimal apparatus	476
ferr/i, ferr/o	iron	216			
fet/o	fetus	377	lact/o	milk	377
fibr/o	fiber	58	lapar/o	abdominal wall	76
galact/o	milk	377	laryng/o	larynx	245
gangli/o, ganglion/o	ganglion	429	lent/i	lens	477
gastr/o	stomach	279	leuk/o	white, colorless, white blood cell	35
gen	origin, formation	59			
ger/e, ger/o	old age	35	leukocyt/o	white blood cell	215
gingiv/o	gum, gingiva	278	lingu/o	tongue	278
gli/o	neuroglia	429	lip/o	fat, lipid	60
glomerul/o	glomerulus	310	listhesis	slipping	514

Word Roots (*Continued*)

Root	Meaning	Reference Page	Root	Meaning	Reference Page
lith	calculus, stone	98	neur/o, neur/i	nervous system, nerve	429
lumb/o	lumbar region, lower back	76	noct/i	night	127
lymphaden/o	lymph node	187	nucle/o	nucleus	58
lymphangi/o	lymphatic vessel	187	nyct/o	night, darkness	127
lymph/o	lymph, lymphatic system, lymphocyte	187	ocul/o	eye	476
			odont/o	tooth, teeth	278
			onc/o	tumor	98
lymph/o, lymphocyt/o	lymphocyte	215	onych/o	nail	561
lysis	separation, loosening, dissolving, destruction	101	oo	ovum	362
			oophor/o	ovary	362
			ophthalm/o	eye	476
			opt/o	eye, vision	476
malacia	softening	101	orchid/o, orchi/o	testis	338
mamm/o	breast, mammary gland	364	or/o	mouth	278
mania	excited state, obsession	432	osche/o	scrotum	338
			osm/o	smell	463
mast/o	breast, mammary gland	364	oste/o	bone	502
			ot/o	ear	467
medull/o	inner part, medulla oblongata, spinal cord	431	ovari/o	ovary	362
			ov/o, ovul/o	ovum	362
melan/o	dark, black, melanin	35	ox/y	oxygen, sharp, acute	216
mening/o, meninge/o	meninges	429	palat/o	palate	278
			palpebr/o	eyelid	476
men/o, mens	month, menstruation	362	pancreat/o	pancreas	281
metr/o	measure	125, 363	papill/o	nipple	58
metr/o, metr/i	uterus	363	para	woman who has given birth	377
morph/o	form, structure	58	parathyr/o, parathyroid/o	parathyroid	403
muc/o	mucus, mucous membrane	58			
muscul/o	muscle	539	paresis	partial paralysis, weakness	432
myc/o	fungus, mold	103			
myel/o	bone marrow, spinal cord	215, 429, 515	path/o	disease, any disease of	98
my/o	muscle	539	ped/o	foot, child	77
myring/o	tympanic membrane	467	pelvi/o	pelvis	503
			perine/o	perineum	364
myx/o	mucus	58	periton, peritone/o	peritoneum	76
narc/o	stupor, unconsciousness	143, 430	phac/o, phak/o	lens	477
			phag/o	eat, ingest	59
nas/o	nose	245	pharm, pharmac/o	drug, medicine	143
nat/i	birth	377	pharyng/o	pharynx	245
natri	sodium	216	phil	attracting, absorbing	59
necrosis	death of tissue	101			
nephr/o	kidney	310	phleb/o	vein	174

(continued)

Word Roots (Continued)

Root	Meaning	Reference Page	Root	Meaning	Reference Page
phobia	fear	432	schisis	fissure	100
phon/o	sound, voice	124	scler/o	hard, sclera (of eye)	98, 476
phot/o	light	124	sclerosis	hardening	102
phren/o	diaphragm	246	seb/o	sebum, sebaceous gland	561
phrenic/o	phrenic nerve	246	semin	semen	338
phyt/o	plant	142, 569	sept/o	septum, partition, dividing wall	256
pituitar/i	pituitary, hypophysis	403	sial/o	saliva, salivary gland, salivary duct	278
plas	formation, molding, development	59	sider/o	iron	216
pleur/o	pleura	246	sigmoid/o	sigmoid colon	280
pneum/o, pneumat/o	air, gas, lung, respiration	246	skelet/o	skeleton	501
pneumon/o	lung	246	somat/o	body	58
pod/o	foot	77	somn/i, somn/o	sleep	430
proct/o	rectum	280	son/o	sound, ultrasound	124
prostat/o	prostate	338	spasm	sudden contraction, cramp	102
prote/o	protein	60	sperm/i	semen, spermatozoa	338
psych/o	mind	431	spermat/o	semen, spermatozoa	338
ptosis	dropping, downward displacement, prolapse	101	sphygm/o	pulse	172
ptysis	spitting	254	spir/o	breathing	246
puer	child	384	splen/o	spleen	187
pulm/o, pulmon/o	lung	246	spondyl/o	vertebra	503
pupill/o	pupil	477	staped/o, stapedi/o	stapes	467
pyel/o	renal pelvis	310	stasis	suppression, stoppage	102
pylor/o	pylorus	280	steat/o	fatty	60
py/o	pus	98	stenosis	narrowing, constriction	102
pyr/o, pyret/o	fever, fire	98	steth/o	chest	122
rachi/o	spine	77	sthen/o	strength	544
radicul/o	root of spinal nerve	429	stoma, stomat/o	mouth	278
radi/o	radiation, x-ray	124	synov/i	synovial joint, synovial membrane	502
rect/o	rectum	280	tax/o	order, arrangement	544
ren/o	kidney	310	ten/o, tendin/o	tendon	539
reticul/o	network	58	terat/o	malformed fetus	383
retin/o	retina	477	test/o	testis, testicle	338
rhabd/o	rod, muscle cell	545	thalam/o	thalamus	430
rhin/o	nose	245	therm/o	heat, temperature	124
racchar/o	sugar	60			
sacchar/o	sugar	60			
sacr/o	sacrum	503			
salping/o	tube, uterine tube, auditory (eustachian) tube	363, 467			

Word Roots (Continued)

Root	Meaning	Reference Page	Root	Meaning	Reference Page
thorac/o	chest, thorax	76	urin/o	urine	311
thromb/o	blood clot	215	uter/o	uterus	363
thrombocyt/o	platelet, thrombocyte	215	uve/o	uvea (of eye)	477
			uvul/o	uvula	278
thym/o	thymus gland	187	vagin/o	sheath, vagina	363
thyr/o, thyroid/o	thyroid	403	valv/o, valvul/o	valve	173
toc/o	labor	377	varic/o	twisted and swollen vein, varix	183
ton/o	tone	539			
tonsil/o	tonsil	187	vascul/o	vessel	174
tox/o, toxic/o	poison, toxin	98, 143	vas/o	vessel, duct, vas deferens	174, 143
trache/o	trachea	245			
trich/o	hair	561	ven/o, ven/i	vein	174
trop/o	turning	484	ventricul/o	cavity, ventricle	173, 430
trop	act(ing) on, affect(ing)	59	vertebr/o	vertebra, spinal column	503
troph/o	feeding, growth, nourishment	59	vesic/o	urinary bladder	311
			vesicul/o	seminal vesicle	338
tympan/o	tympanic cavity (middle ear), tympanic membrane	467	vestibul/o	vestibule, vestibular apparatus (of ear)	467
			vir/o	virus	103
ureter/o	ureter	311	vulv/o	vulva	364
urethr/o	urethra	311	xen/o	foreign, strange	438
ur/o	urine, urinary tract	311			

▶ Appendix 6

Suffixes

Suffix	Meaning	Reference Page	Suffix	Meaning	Reference Page
-ac	pertaining to	20	-ia/sis	condition of	17
-agogue	promoter, stimulator	377	-iatrics	medical specialty	18
-al	pertaining to	20	-iatry	medical specialty	18
-algesia	pain	98, 142	-ic	pertaining to	20
-algia	pain	98	-ical	pertaining to	20
-ar	pertaining to	20	-ics	medical specialty	18
-ary	pertaining to	20	-ile	pertaining to	20
-ase	enzyme	60	-ism	condition of	17
-blast	immature cell, productive cell, embryonic cell	59	-ist	specialist	18
			-itis	inflammation	100
-capnia	carbon dioxide (level of)	244	-lalia	speech, babble	432
			-lepsy	seizure	432
-cele	hernia, localized dilation	100	-lexia	reading	432
			-listhesis	slipping	514
-centesis	puncture, tap	126	-logy	study of	18
-clasis, -clasia	breaking	100	-lysis	separation, loosening, dissolving, destruction	101
-cyte	cell	58			
-desis	binding, fusion	126			
-dilation, -dilatation	expansion, widening	101	-lytic	dissolving, reducing, loosening	142
-ectasia, -ectasis	dilation, dilatation, distention	101	-malacia	softening	101
-ectomy	excision, surgical removal	126	-mania	excited state, obsession	432
-edema	accumulation of fluid, swelling	101	-megaly	enlargement	100
			-meter	instrument for measuring	125
-emia	condition of blood	214	-metry	measurement of	125
-esthesia, -esthesi/o	sensation	463	-mimetic	mimicking, simulating	142
-form	like, resembling	20	-necrosis	death of tissue	101
-gen, -genesis	origin, formation	59	-odynia	pain	100
-geusia	sense of taste	463	-oid	like, resembling	20
-gram	record of data	125	-oma	tumor	100
-graph	instrument for recording data	125	-opia	condition of the eye, vision	478
-graphy	act of recording data	125	-opsia	condition of vision	478
-hemi	half, one side	33	-ory	pertaining to	20
-hemia	condition of blood	214	-ose	sugar	60
-ia	condition of	17	-o/sis	condition of	17
-ian	specialist	18	-osmia	sense of smell	463

Suffixes (*Continued*)

Suffix	Meaning	Reference Page	Suffix	Meaning	Reference Page
-ous	pertaining to	20	-rhexis	rupture	100
-oxia	oxygen (level of)	244	-schisis	fissure, splitting	100
-paresis	partial paralysis, weakness	432	-sclerosis	hardening	102
-pathy	disease, any disease of	100	-scope	instrument for viewing or examining	125
-penia	decrease in, deficiency of	214	-scopy	examination of	125
-pexy	surgical fixation	126	-sis	condition of	17
-phasia	speech	432	-some	body, small body	58
-philic	attracting, absorbing	59	-spasm	sudden contraction, cramp	102
-phobia	fear	432	-stasis	suppression, stoppage	102
-phonia	voice	244			
-plasia	formation, molding, development	59	-spermia	condition of semen	339
-plasty	plastic repair, plastic surgery, reconstruction	126	-stenosis	narrowing, constriction	102
			-stomy	surgical creation of an opening	126
-plegia	paralysis	432	-tome	instrument for incising (cutting)	126
-pnea	breathing	244			
-poiesis	formation, production	214	-tomy	incision, cutting	126
			-toxin	poison	102
-ptosis	dropping, downward displacement, prolapse	101	-tripsy	crushing	126
			-tropic	act(ing) on, affect(ing)	142
-rhage, -rhagia	bursting forth, profuse flow, hemorrhage	100	-trophy, -trophia	feeding, growth, nourishment	59
			-uresis	urination	311
-rhaphy	surgical repair, suture	126	-uria	condition of urine, urination	598
-rhea	flow, discharge	100	-y	condition of	17

▶ Appendix 7

Prefixes

Prefix	Meaning	Reference Page	Prefix	Meaning	Reference Page
a-	not, without, lack of, absence	36	extra-	outside	77
ab-	away from	37	hemi-	half, one side	33
acro-	extremity, end	77	hetero-	other, different, unequal	38
ad-	toward, near	37	homo-, homeo-	same, unchanging	38
ambly-	dim	483	hyper-	over, excess, increased, abnormally high	38
an-	not, without, lack of, absence	36			
ante-	before	40	hypo-	under, below, decreased, abnormally low	38
anti-	against	36, 142			
atel/o-	incomplete	254	im-	not	36
auto-	self	442	in-	not	36
bi-	two, twice	33	infra-	below	77
brachy-	short	345	inter-	between	77
brady-	slow	99	intra-	in, within	77
circum-	around	77	iso-	equal, same	38
contra-	against, opposite, opposed	142	juxta-	near, beside	77
counter-	against, opposite, opposed	142	leuk/o-	white, colorless, white blood cell	35
cyan/o-	blue	35	macro-	large, abnormally large	38
de-	down, without, removal, loss	36	mal-	bad, poor	99
dextr/o-	right	41	mega-, megal/o-	large, abnormally large	38
di-	two, twice	33	melan/o-	black, dark, melanin	35
dia-	through	37			
dipl/o-	double	33	mes/o-	middle	41
dis-	absence, removal, separation	36	met/a-	change, after, beyond	97
dys-	abnormal, painful, difficult	99	micro-	small, one millionth	39
ec-	out, outside	41	mon/o-	one	33
ecto-	out, outside	41	multi-	many	33
end/o-	in, within	41	neo-	new	39
epi-	on, over	77	non-	not	36
equi-	equal, same	38	normo-	normal	39
erythr/o-	red	35	nulli-	never	376
eu-	true, good, easy, normal	38	olig/o-	few, scanty, deficiency of	38
ex/o-	away from, outside	41	ortho-	straight, correct, upright	39

Prefixes *(Continued)*

Prefix	Meaning	Reference Page	Prefix	Meaning	Reference Page
pachy-	thick	99	sinistr/o-	left	41
pan-	all	38	staphyl/o-	grape-like cluster, staphylococcus	103
para-	near, beside, abnormal	78	strept/o-	twisted chain, streptococcus	103
per-	through	37	sub-	below, under	77
peri-	around	77	super-	above, excess	38
poikilo-	varied, irregular	39	supra-	above	78
poly-	many, much	33	syn-, sym-	together	41
post-	after, behind	41	tachy-	rapid	99
pre-	before, in front of	40	tel/e-, tel/o-	end, far, at a distance	41
presby-	old	479			
prim/i-	first	33	tetra-	four	33
pro-	before, in front of	41	trans-	through	37
pseudo-	false	39	tri-	three	33
quadr/i-	four	33	un-	not	36
re-	again, back	39	uni-	one	33
retro-	behind, backward	78	xanth/o-	yellow	35
semi-	half, partial	33	xer/o-	dry	99

▶ Appendix 8

Appendix 8.1 Metric Measurements

Unit	Abbreviation	Metric Equivalent	U.S. Equivalent
Units of Length			
kilometer	km	1,000 m	0.62 mi; 1.6 km/mi
meter*	m	100 cm; 1,000 mm	39.4 in; 1.1 yards
centimeter	cm	1/100 m; 0.01 m	0.39 in; 2.5 cm/in.
millimeter	mm	1/1,000 m; 0.001 m	0.039 in; 25 mm/in.
micrometer	mcm	1/1,000 mm; 0.001 mm	
Units of Weight			
kilogram	kg	1,000 g	2.2 lb
gram*	g	1,000 mg	0.035 oz; 28.5 g/oz
milligram	mg	1/1,000 g; 0.001 g	
microgram	mcg	1/1,000 mg; 0.001 mg	
Units of Volume			
liter*	L	1,000 mL	1.06 qt
deciliter	dL	1/10 L; 0.1 L	
milliliter	mL	1/1,000 L; 0.001 L	0.034 oz; 29.4 mL/oz
microliter	mcL	1/1,000 mL; 0.001 mL	

*Basic unit.

Appendix 8.2 Metric Prefixes

Prefix	Meaning of Prefix
kilo-	1,000
deci-	1/10; one tenth
centi-	1/100; one hundredth
milli-	1/1,000; one thousandth
micro-	1/1,000,000; one millionth

▶ Āppendix 9

Stedman's Medical Dictionary at a Glance

an·ti·bod·y (an′tē-bod′e) *Avoid the jargonsitic use of the plural antibodies when the reference is to a single antibody species.* An immunoglobulin molecule produced by B-lymphoid cells that combine specifically with an immunogen or antigen. A.'s may be present naturally, their specificity is determined through gene rearrangement or somatic replacement or may be synthesized in response to stimulus provided by the introduction of an antigen; a.'s are found in the blood and body fluids, although the basic structure of the molecule consists of two light and two heavy chains, a.'s may also be found as dimers, trimers, or pentamers. After binding antigen, some a.'s may fix, complement, bind to surface receptors on immune cells, and in some cases may neutralize microorganisms, SEE ALSO immunoglobulin. SYN immune protein, protective protein, sensitizer (2).

> **Usage notes appear in italics before definition**

> **Pronunciation**

> **Main entry**

ANTIGEN

an·ti·gen (Ag) (an′ti-jen). Any substance that, as a result of coming in contact with appropriate cells, induces a state of sensitivity or immune responsiveness and that reacts in a demonstrable way with antibodies or immune cells of the sensitized subject in vivo or in vitro. Modern usage tends to retain the broad meaning of a., employing the terms "antigenic determinant" or "determinant group" for the particular chemical group of a molecule that confers antigenic specificity. SEE ALSO hapten, SYN immunogen. [anti-body) + G, -gen, producing.]

> **Large header for entries with numerous subentries**

> **Indicates term is illustrated**

> **Subentry**

> **Etymologies appear in brackets**

Australia a. [MIM*209800], an a. so called because first recognized in an Australian aborigine, but now known to be a subunit of the hepatitis B virus surface antigen. SYN Au a. (2), Aus a.

> **Abbreviation**

carcinoembryonic a. (CEA), a glycoprotein constituent of the glycocalyx of embryonic endodermal epithelium, which may be elevated in the serum of some patients with colon cancer and certain other cancers and in serum of long-term tobacco smokers.

> **Main word is abbreviated in subentries**

conjugated a., SYN conjugated *hapten.*

> **Cross references in blue indicate where to find the defined / preferred term. In multi-word terms, the italicized term indicates the main entry under which the term can be found.**

prostate-specific a. (PSA), a single-chain, 31-kD glycoprotein with 240 amino acid residues and 4 carbohydrate side-chains; a kallikrein protease produced by prostatic epithelial cells and normally found in seminal fluid and circulating blood. Elevations of serum PSA are highly organ-specific but occur in both cancer (adenocarcinoma) and benign disease (e.g., benign prostatic hyperplasia, prostatitis). A significant number of patients with organ-confined cancer have normal PSA values. SEE carcinoma of the prostate. SYN human glandular kallikrein 3.

> **High profile terms (entries) with broad significance to the practice of medicine and to the world appear in blue boxes**

> **Cross references**

KEY

♻	Combining Forms
🄸	Indicates term is illustrated, *see Illustration Index*
SYN	Synonym
Cf.	Compare
[NA]	Nomina Anatomica
[TA]	Terminologia Anatomica
★	Official alternate Terminologia Anatomica term
[MIM]	Mendelian Inheritance in Man
C.I.	*Color Index*

▶ Index of Boxes

▶ Index

Note: Page numbers followed by f indicate figures, t indicate tables, and b indicate boxes, respectively.

INTRODUCTION TO HEALTH CARE & CAREERS

Roxann DeLaet, RN, MS
Professor of Nursing
Sinclair Community College
Dayton, Ohio

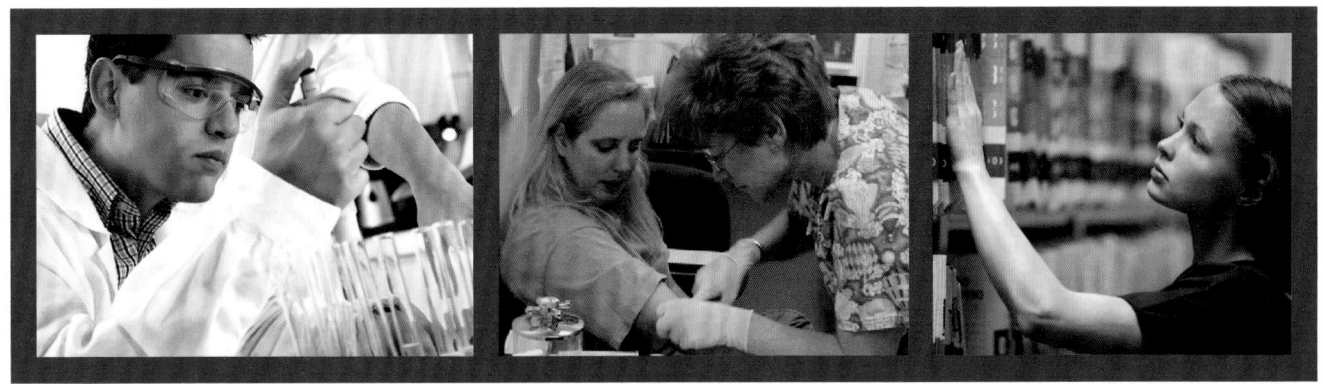

Wolters Kluwer

Philadelphia · Baltimore · New York · London
Buenos Aires · Hong Kong · Sydney · Tokyo

Contents

NOTE: Some chapters are intentionally missing, as their content was not applicable to the course objectives. This will also affect the ordering of some part and page numbers.

User's Guide

Chapter Opening Features

The Body as a Whole

25 CHAPTER

CHAPTER OBJECTIVES

After careful study of this chapter, you should be able to:

* Define *anatomy* and *physiology*.
* Name the body's levels of organization.
* Describe cells, tissues, organs, and body systems.
* Identify essential functions of the human body.
* Define *homeostasis* and give examples of feedback.
* Describe the anatomical position.
* List and define the body's three planes of division.
* List and define the main directional terms for the body.

* Identify body cavities and regions.
* List the skin's main functions.
* Name and describe the skin's layers.
* State the location and function of the skin's accessory structures.
* Explain how aging affects the skin.
* Identify common diseases and conditions of the skin.

KEY TERMS

abdomen
abdominal cavity
abdominopelvic (ab-dom-ih-no-PEL-vik) cavity
anatomical position
anatomy (ah-NAT-o-me)
anterior (ventral)
cell
cranial cavity
dermis
distal
dorsal cavity

epidermis (ep-ih-DER-mis)
feedback
frontal plane
homeostasis (ho-me-o-STA-sis)
inferior
lateral
lower extremities
medial
midsagittal (mid-SAJ-ih-tal) plane
organ

organism
pelvic cavity
physiology (fiz-e-OL-o-je)
posterior (dorsal)
proximal
sagittal (SAJ-ih-tal) plane
sebaceous (se-BA-shus) glands
sebum
spinal cavity
subcutaneous layer
sudoriferous (su-do-RIF-er-us) glands

superior
system
thoracic (tho-RAS-ik) cavity
thorax
tissue
transverse plane
trunk (torso)
upper extremities
ventral cavity

The opening page of each chapter offers multiple entry points into the material ahead and a variety of effective methods for review of that information. For example, Chapter Overviews briefly introduce the chapter to come and provide a synopsis of its contents. These jumping-off points are opportunities to spark lively and provocative classroom discussion as well as individual deliberation. Also kicking off each chapter are the following features:

* **Chapter Objectives** list key learning goals for the chapter. This useful feature has a triple function: First, review these objectives at the beginning of the chapter to familiarize yourself with what you need to take away from the chapter. Second, when you have finished the chapter and its accompanying exercises, revisit the objectives to assess your level of mastery. Third, refer back to objectives lists to provide an effective framework for test prep.
* **Key Terms** alphabetized lists present need-to-know terms for the specific chapter content covered. For your convenience, each term appears in boldface at its first use in the chapter. These lists structure each chapter and offer an alternate means of chapter review and study.

Each chapter offers a variety of fun features to complement and enliven the narrative text. Immerse yourself in these features to savor each chapter to the fullest.

Intrachapter Features

✓ CHECK POINT

1 List major factors causing a rise in health care costs.

2 What are some major differences among the three types of health care institutions (voluntary nonprofit, proprietary, and government) found in the U.S.?

CheckPoints interspersed throughout chapters pose 1 or 2 short-answer, recall questions for you to answer based on what you have read so far. They also provide interludes for you to pause and reflect on what you have learned. Complete each CheckPoint to steadily build your knowledge and reinforce learning before continuing on to the next section. Answers to CheckPoints are found with your bonus material located at the Point.

Newsreel features brief "articles" on current trends and research information. Keeping you informed in the constantly growing and developing field of health care, this feature is your very own medical "journal," conveniently located right inside your textbook!

NEWSREEL

Oral Pathology

Every dental checkup includes a thorough examination of the mouth for evidence of disease. Dentists and dental hygienists are trained to detect not just common problems like tooth decay or gum disease, but a wide range of diseases that affect the mouth and other parts of the body. The first signs of some medical problems—osteoporosis or AIDS, for example—can appear in the mouth.

In oral pathology classes, dental professionals learn to identify diseases, or narrow the possibilities, from signs such as the appearance of a lesion or ulcer or a characteristic swelling or inflammation. General dentists treat some diseases themselves; for others, they refer the patient to a specialist. Diseases that affect the teeth,

tongue, gums, jaw, and lining of the mouth may be referred to an oral and maxillofacial pathologist for final diagnosis and treatment.

Examples of oral diseases include stomatitis, a viral illness; burning mouth or burning tongue syndrome; a yeast infection known as oral candidiasis; recurrent canker sores; and various bone diseases.

The ADA recently concluded a three-year public awareness program on oral cancer. Although the number of new cases and deaths among the general public has been falling slowly for many years, the number of new cases among adults under age 40 has been rising significantly. The goals of the campaign were to boost public awareness of oral cancer and to highlight the dentist's role in identifying the disease.

Extra! Extra! boxes feature pertinent and fascinating facts about the human body. Use these boxes to expand your knowledge of topics related to key concepts such as blood facts. You'll be amazed at what your body can do— and inspired to contribute to the world of heath care!

EXTRA! EXTRA! WHITE COAT HYPERTENSION

Some patients suffer from a condition known as "white coat hypertension." For these individuals, the stress of seeing a health care professional is enough to raise their otherwise normal blood pressure. Simply leaving the health care setting allows their blood pressure to return to normal. This phenomenon is one reason why hypertension should not be diagnosed based on a limited number of blood pressure readings.

ZOOM IN

The Computer Explosion

Just a few decades ago, computers were the size of a large room. These early computers were costly to build, difficult to run, and expensive to maintain. As a result, the use of computers was limited to universities, large corporations, and governments.

In the 1980s, however, personal computers became affordable and popular. Now computers touch nearly every facet of life. While processing power and complexity increased, size and cost significantly decreased. Today, smart phones, roughly the size of a credit card, have thousands times more computing power than the machines that helped put the first man on the moon.

The use of computers in health care has paralleled the use of computers in the world in general. Initially, computers were used only in large research hospitals or institutions with vast amounts of funding. Today, however, even a small doctor's office likely maintains patient records electronically. Many health care professionals use tablet PCs as they examine patients to record temperature and other vital statistics directly into patient medical records.

Zoom In features offer useful facts and tips about patient care and other on-the-job practices. Get an inside look into working in health care with these snapshots of key day-to-day aspects of the job. Use this sneak peek to help you make the jump from classroom to job.

End-of-Chapter Features

Chapter Wrap-Up

Don't forget to visit thePoint companion website for additional study resources!

CHAPTER HIGHLIGHTS

- Personal qualities and skills that are important for any successful health care professional include enthusiasm, optimism, self-esteem, honesty, patience, cooperation, organization, responsibility, flexibility, and sociability.

REVIEW QUESTIONS

Matching

1. _____ A belief about the worth or importance of something that acts as a standard to guide one's behavior.

2. _____ Ability to act and make decisions without the help or advice of others.

Multiple Choice

6. Important personal skills for those entering a health care profession include
   - a. organization
   - b. flexibility
   - c. sociability
   - d. all of the above

Completion

11. _____ may be caused by any number of physical, chemical, or emotional factors and can produce both physical and emotional tension.

12. A common stimulant that can stay in a person's system from 6–12 hours is _____.

Short Answer

16. Why are enthusiasm and optimism important qualities for health care workers?

_____

_____

INVESTIGATE IT

1. What are your strongest personal qualities? Which qualities do you feel are your weakest? Use the Internet to search for information on personality assessment resources, such as the Myers-Briggs Type Indicator and StrengthsFinder. In addition, you can also assess your learning style (visual, auditory, or kinesthetic) by using the *MyPowerLearning* diagnostic tool provided with this text. See the inside front cover for details on how to access all the student resources that accompany this text.

RECOMMENDED READING

Eade, Diane M. *Motivational Management; Developing Leadership Skills.* Available at: http://www.adv-leadership-grp.com/Motivational_Article.html.

Heroux, Neomi. *Nutrition and Diet; Clean Living Could Reduce Your Cancer Risk.* Available at: http://www.healthnews.com/nutrition-diet/clean-living-could-reduce-your-cancer-risk-2706.html.

Chapter Wrap-Ups end each chapter on a high note. Providing the triple benefit of review, self-assessment, and suggestions for further exploration, these features are your chapter support network, assuring that you have mastered the chapter content. Well-placed, timely suggestions to visit thePoint are also included here to alert you to even more available resources relevant to the chapter you just finished. In Chapter Wrap-Ups you will find:

- **Chapter Highlights** that provide you with a summary of the chapter in easy-to-skim and remember bullet points. Make sure you take away the chapter's most significant concepts by reviewing this list. Also use Chapter Highlights to study for tests and quizzes.

- **Review Questions** help you check your learning and prepare for exams. A variety of the most effective question formats are given at the end of each chapter to keep you on your toes and engaged. They are organized into groups by type:
  - *Matching, Multiple Choice, and True/False* questions check your retention of the facts you learned in the chapter.
  - *Short Answer and Open-Ended* questions require you to apply your learning of facts and concepts to show that you have not only remembered information but also have a good grasp of its significance for health care.

Answers to the Review Questions are available on the text's companion website http://thePoint.lww.com/DeLaet so that you can check your progress and understanding.

- **Investigate It** activities invite you to take your health care knowledge outside of the classroom into the world at large to develop a fuller understanding of your chosen career. Complete these active learning exercises to connect your education with your future and begin to explore the professional sphere.

- **Recommended Reading** lists offer you suggestions for independent exploration of key chapter topics. Use these well-researched resources to learn more about the aspects of health care that intrigue and excite *you*.

- **Websites for Selected Professional Organizations** lists are your very own library of resources in a convenient and easy-to-locate spot. Visit these websites to obtain additional information about topics covered in the particular chapter, to learn more about a particular organization, and to determine whether one might be right for you to one day join.

Electronic Student Resources

Carefully designed online ancillaries available at www.thepoint.lww.com/DeLaet will offer still more opportunity to reinforce and retain skills and concepts learned from the text. In this blockbuster package, students are given free access to a host of captivating tools and exercises. Get a learning advantage with these exciting *Bonus Features:*

- Interactive question bank
- Skills assessment worksheets
- Spanish English audio glossary
- Heart and breath sounds audio
- Online activities
- Videos and animations
- Free Study Guide
- Answers to the Checkpoint and Chapter Wrap-Up questions

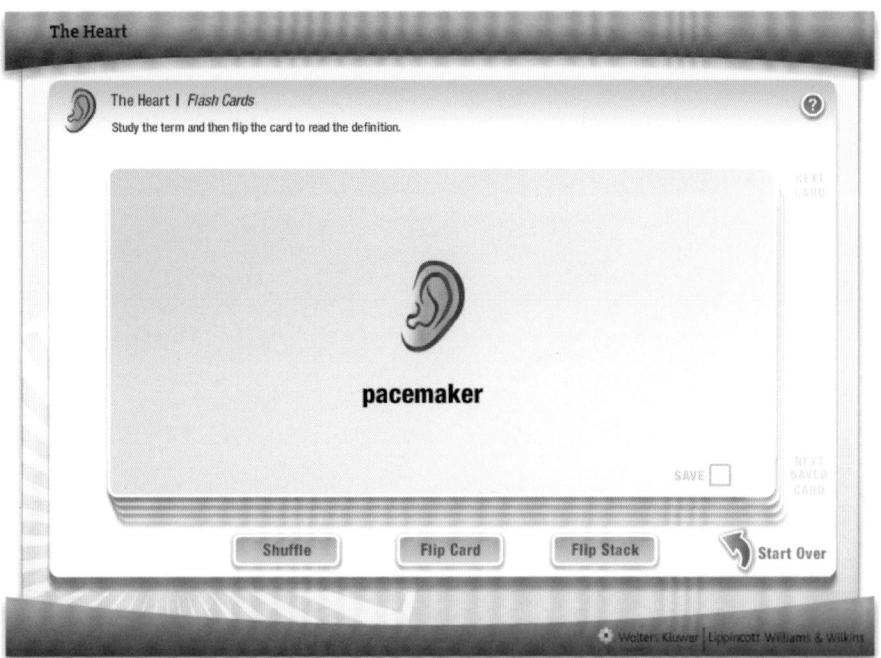

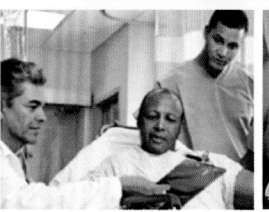
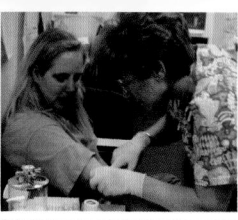

ESSENTIALS OF HUMAN ANATOMY AND PHYSIOLOGY

PART V

PART V introduces human anatomy and physiology, beginning with cells, the smallest units of life. Similar cells are grouped together as tissues, which form organs. Organs, in turn, work together in the body's systems, which together meet the entire body's needs.

CHAPTER 25 outlines the body's general overall structure and organization and introduces terms medical professionals use to describe and reference it. The chapter concludes with a study of the skin, which is the body's first line of defense. The following chapters describe the other body systems and how they fulfill essential functions.

CHAPTER 26 describes the muscular and skeletal systems, which work together to produce movement and to protect and support body structures.

CHAPTER 27 turns to the systems that coordinate and control all others, the nervous and endocrine systems.

The nervous system detects internal and external changes through the senses and makes adjustments so that body conditions stay normal.

CHAPTER 28 discusses the cardiovascular and lymphatic systems, which deliver oxygen and nutrients to all cells and carry away waste. The blood and lymphatic system also play key roles in body defenses.

CHAPTER 29 profiles systems that work together to give body cells the raw materials needed to make energy. The respiratory system supplies oxygen and eliminates carbon dioxide, while the digestive system extracts nutrients from food. The urinary system eliminates waste products and is vital in maintaining normal body conditions.

CHAPTER 30 highlights the reproductive system, which enables the body to reproduce, and processes of growth and development, which occur throughout life.

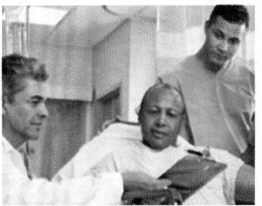
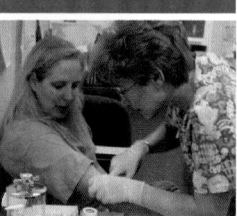

The Body as a Whole

25 CHAPTER

CHAPTER OBJECTIVES

After careful study of this chapter, you should be able to:

✳ Define *anatomy* and *physiology*.

✳ Name the body's levels of organization.

✳ Describe cells, tissues, organs, and body systems.

✳ Identify essential functions of the human body.

✳ Define *homeostasis* and give examples of feedback.

✳ Describe the anatomical position.

✳ List and define the body's three planes of division.

✳ List and define the main directional terms for the body.

✳ Identify body cavities and regions.

✳ List the skin's main functions.

✳ Name and describe the skin's layers.

✳ State the location and function of the skin's accessory structures.

✳ Explain how aging affects the skin.

✳ Identify common diseases and conditions of the skin.

KEY TERMS

abdomen
abdominal cavity
abdominopelvic (ab-dom-ih-no-PEL-vik) cavity
anatomical position
anatomy (ah-NAT-o-me)
anterior (ventral)
cell
cranial cavity
dermis
distal
dorsal cavity

epidermis (ep-ih-DER-mis)
feedback
frontal plane
homeostasis (ho-me-o-STA-sis)
inferior
lateral
lower extremities
medial
midsagittal (mid-SAJ-ih-tal) plane
organ

organism
pelvic cavity
physiology (fiz-e-OL-o-je)
posterior (dorsal)
proximal
sagittal (SAJ-ih-tal) plane
sebaceous (se-BA-shus) glands
sebum
spinal cavity
subcutaneous layer
sudoriferous (su-do-RIF-er-us) glands

superior
system
thoracic (tho-RAS-ik) cavity
thorax
tissue
transverse plane
trunk (torso)
upper extremities
ventral cavity

Anyone planning a career in health care needs to understand the body's structure and functions. Only by knowing what's normal can one understand what goes wrong in cases of disease or injury. This knowledge also helps people appreciate just how well the body's design and activities fulfill its needs.

The scientific term for the study of body structure is **anatomy**. **Physiology** is the study of how the body functions. Anatomy (structure) and physiology (function) are closely related. The stomach, for example, is shaped like a pouch to store food for digestion. The cells in the lining of the stomach are tightly packed to keep strong digestive juices from leaking out and harming body tissue.

LEVELS OF STRUCTURE AND ORGANIZATION

All **organisms**, or living things, are organized from simple to very complex levels.

- **Cells**, formed from chemicals like proteins and amino acids, are the basic units of life.
- **Tissues** consist of groups of similar cells working together.
- Tissues, in turn, make up **organs**, such as the heart, lungs, and kidneys.
- Organs working together for the same general purpose make up the body **systems**, which carry out its major functions—digesting food, eliminating waste, and so on. All the systems work together to maintain the body.

✔ **CHECK POINT**

1 What is the word for the study of the body's structure? For the study of its function?

2 How are cells, tissues, organs, and body systems related?

Cells

The cell is the basic unit of life. It is the simplest structure that, on its own, carries out activities that set living things apart. Cells grow and develop. They respond to changes in their environment. They reproduce, and they can repair themselves. And they carry on chemical reactions that make these activities possible. All the activities of the human body, which is composed of trillions of cells, result from the activities of individual cells.

Cells vary widely in size, shape, and composition according to their function. For instance, a neuron (nerve cell) has long fibers that transmit electrical energy. Red blood cells are small and round, which lets them slide through tiny blood vessels. They also have a thin outer membrane to allow for passage of gases into and out of the cell.

For cells to fulfill their role in the human body, they must multiply. Cells do this by dividing. The cells that form the sex cells (egg and sperm) divide by *meiosis* (mi-O-sis). In this process, the number of chromosomes

(structures that carry the cell's genetic information) is cut in half, so that when the egg and sperm come together, the fertilized egg will have the right number of chromosomes.

All other body cells divide by *mitosis* (mi-TO-sis). In this process, each original parent cell becomes two identical daughter cells. But first, the chromosomes in the parent cell are doubled, so that each new daughter cell will have a complete set.

Tissues

Tissues are groups of cells with a similar structure, arranged in a characteristic pattern, and specialized to perform certain tasks. There are four main tissue groups:

- *Epithelial* (ep-ih-THE-le-al) *tissue* forms a protective covering for the body. It is the main tissue of the skin's outer layer. It also lines the body's cavities, as well as some of its organs. Glands are made of epithelial tissue.
- *Connective tissue* supports and forms the body's framework. Bones and cartilage are made of connective tissue. So are the tendons that connect muscles to bones and the ligaments that connect one bone to another.
- *Muscle tissue* produces movement. When muscles contract, the body moves. Skeletal muscle (like the biceps) is the most familiar muscle tissue, but the body also contains two other types: cardiac and smooth. Cardiac muscle creates heartbeats. Smooth muscle, which makes up the walls of some organs, vessels, and passageways, moves substances through body systems.
- *Nervous tissue* makes up the brain, spinal cord, and nerves that coordinate and control the body's functions. Messages from every part of the body, in the form of electrical impulses, are carried to the brain and back again by neurons, or nerve cells.

✔ **CHECK POINT**

3 Are all cells the same? Explain.

4 What are the four main tissue groups?

Organs

Tissues are arranged into organs. Each organ has a specific function. The heart, for example, pumps blood. The lungs take in oxygen and expel carbon dioxide. These are examples of organs:

- heart
- brain
- lungs

- stomach
- liver
- small intestine
- kidneys
- large intestine

Body Systems

The body's systems, described briefly below, carry out its major functions. Each system has one or more specialized functions.

- **Integumentary system.** The integumentary (in-teg-u-MEN-tar-e) system includes the skin, hair, nails, and sweat and oil glands. The skin protects the body, helps regulate its temperature, and gathers sensory information.
- **Skeletal system.** The skeleton, a system of 206 bones and the joints between them, provides the body's framework. It supports and protects vital organs and works with the muscular system to produce movement.
- **Muscular system.** Muscles, attached to bones, move the skeleton. Skeletal muscles also give the body structure, protect organs, and maintain posture. Besides skeletal muscle, this system includes cardiac and smooth muscle.
- **Nervous system.** The brain, spinal cord, and nerves make up the nervous system, which controls and coordinates body functions. Memory, reasoning, and other higher functions take place in the brain.
- **Endocrine** (EN-do-krin) **system.** While the organs known as endocrine glands are scattered throughout the body, they are considered a single system because they share a similar function: They produce hormones that regulate body activities. Examples of endocrine glands are the thyroid, pituitary, and adrenal glands.
- **Cardiovascular system.** This system consists of the heart and blood vessels. The cardiovascular system pumps blood, containing nutrients, oxygen, and other needed substances, to the body's tissues and organs and carries away waste materials for elimination.
- **Lymphatic system.** The lymphatic system brings excess fluids and protein from the tissues back to the blood and filters out harmful substances. The lymphatic and cardiovascular systems together make up the circulatory system.
- **Respiratory system.** This system includes the lungs and the passages leading to and from them. It takes and transports air to the lungs, where oxygen passes from the air into the blood and carbon dioxide, carried from the tissues, passes into the air.
- **Digestive system.** This system consists of all the organs involved in taking in nutrients, converting them to

a form body cells can use, and absorbing them into the circulation. Digestive system organs include the mouth, esophagus, stomach, intestine, liver, and pancreas.

- **Urinary system.** The urinary system rids the body of waste products and excess water. It also returns water and other needed substances to the bloodstream. Its main components are the kidneys, ureters, bladder, and urethra.
- **Reproductive system.** This system includes the sex organs and related structures. Its function is to produce offspring.

CHECK POINT

5 Give two examples of organs.

6 Give an example of a body system and explain its function.

WHOLE BODY FUNCTIONS

Certain functions, like eating and breathing, are essential for humans to survive and thrive. Cells, tissues, organs, and body systems work in different, yet interconnected, ways to help fulfill these functions.

Essential Functions

Essential functions, and how the body systems support them, are described briefly below. They will be discussed in more detail in later chapters.

Protection, Movement, and Support

The skeletal and muscular systems work together to execute movement and to support and protect vital organs. The skin protects the body against infection and dehydration (loss of body fluid) and helps regulate its temperature.

Coordination and Control

Conditions both inside and outside the body are constantly changing. The nervous system detects and responds to these changes so the body can adapt. The endocrine and nervous systems work together to control and coordinate the other body systems.

Circulation and Body Defense

For the body to function, materials must be moved through it, bringing nutrients, oxygen, and other vital materials to cells and carrying waste away. The blood, circulating through the cardiovascular system, is the main method of transport, aided by the lymphatic system, which brings substances from the tissues back to the heart.

The body also requires defenses against disease and blood loss. The blood carries special cells and antibodies that protect against disease-causing organisms, as well as substances needed for blood clotting. In the lymphatic system, white blood cells multiply, attack foreign invaders, and destroy them. Lymphoid tissue scattered throughout the body filters out organisms that cause disease.

Energy Supply and Use

For all the activities of the body, cells require energy. To make energy, they need oxygen and nutrients. The respiratory and digestive systems meet these demands, obtaining oxygen and breaking down food into a form the cells can use.

The body also needs to dispose of materials that aren't needed. The urinary system and the intestine remove waste products and excess water.

Reproduction and Development

Reproduction is one of the basic characteristics of life. All organisms have the ability to reproduce. In humans, the male and female reproductive systems fulfill this function. During pregnancy, a single fertilized cell develops into a human child with genetic traits, such as skin, hair, and eye color, inherited through the chromosomes it received from its parents.

Homeostasis

Cells, tissues, organs, and body systems work constantly to maintain a state of balance in the body. Temperature, body fluid balances, heart and respiration rates, blood pressure, and other conditions must be kept within set limits to maintain health. This steady state within the body is called **homeostasis**, which literally means "staying (stasis) the same (homeo)." It's an important characteristic of all living things.

The chief method for maintaining homeostasis is **feedback**, a control system based on information returning to a source. A familiar example of feedback is the thermostat in a home. When the air temperature falls, the thermostat triggers the furnace to turn on. When the temperature reaches an upper limit, the furnace is shut off. In the body, most feedback systems keep conditions within a set normal range by reversing any shift up or down. For instance, a center in the brain, detecting a change in body temperature from the normal 97.8 to 99 degrees, starts mechanisms for cooling

or warming. Similarly, if the body's oxygen level drops, respirations will increase.

Interdependency of Body Systems

The essential body functions described above, and the body systems that help provide them, are discussed in the following chapters. Remember that while each system has a separate purpose, the body functions as a whole. No system is independent of the others. The cardiovascular and respiratory systems, for example, work together to provide oxygenated blood to the whole body. Without the combined efforts of the skeletal and muscular systems, movement wouldn't be possible. The systems work together to maintain homeostasis and the body's health.

When a person is ill or injured, the interdependency of body systems can have negative effects, however. For instance, if the brain's respiratory center is depressed, the lungs can't do their part in oxygenating the blood. During a heart attack, the heart may not be able to pump blood efficiently to other organs such as the kidneys, which can result in decreased urinary output.

✔ **CHECK POINT**

7 Name two essential functions of the body.

8 What is homeostasis?

BODY PLANES AND DIRECTIONS

Over the centuries, doctors and scientists have developed special terms to designate position and directions in the body. These terms enable medical personnel to describe or refer to physical conditions in a precise way. Think, for example, of being asked to bandage "the middle" of a patient's arm. Would that refer to the elbow, the forearm, the biceps muscle, or what? To prevent confusion or vagueness, special terms are used universally by health care professionals today.

Describing the Body

For consistency, all descriptions assume that the body is in the **anatomical position**. In this posture, the person stands upright with face front, arms at the sides with palms forward, and feet parallel, as shown in Figure 25-1. The anatomical position is the basis for all descriptions of body planes and directions. When we say "on the left," for example, it is the patient's left side in the anatomical position.

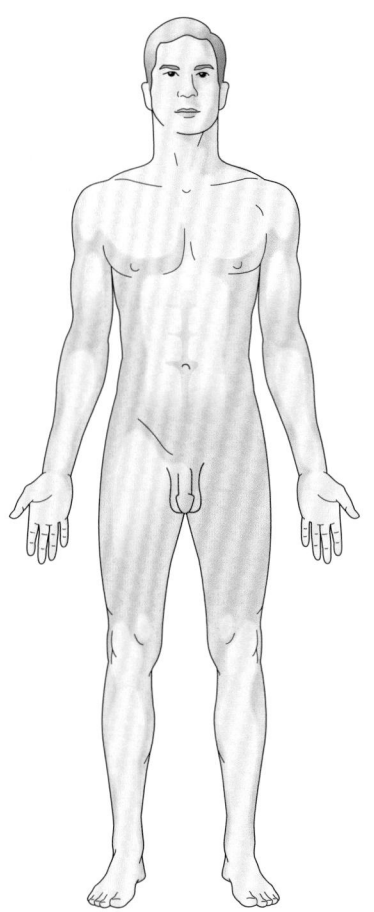

Figure 25-1 The anatomical position.

Divisional Planes

For the various structures in the body to be visualized in relation to each other, the body can be divided along three imaginary planes. Each is a cut through the body in a different direction (Figure 25-2).

- The **frontal plane**. If the cut were made in line with the ears and then down the middle of the body, the result would be a front section and a back section. Another name for this plane is the *coronal plane*.
- The **sagittal plane**. If the body were cut in two from front to back, separating it into right and left portions, the resulting two sections would be sagittal sections. A cut exactly down the midline of the body, separating it into equal right and left halves, is a **midsagittal plane**.
- The **transverse plane**. If the cut were made horizontally, across the other two planes, it would divide the body into an upper part and a lower part. There could be many such cross sections, each of which would be on a transverse plane, also called a *horizontal plane*.

Some additional terms are used to describe sections (cuts) of tissues, as used to prepare them for study under a microscope.

- A cross section is a cut made perpendicular to the long axis of an organ, such as a cut made across a banana to give a small, round slice.

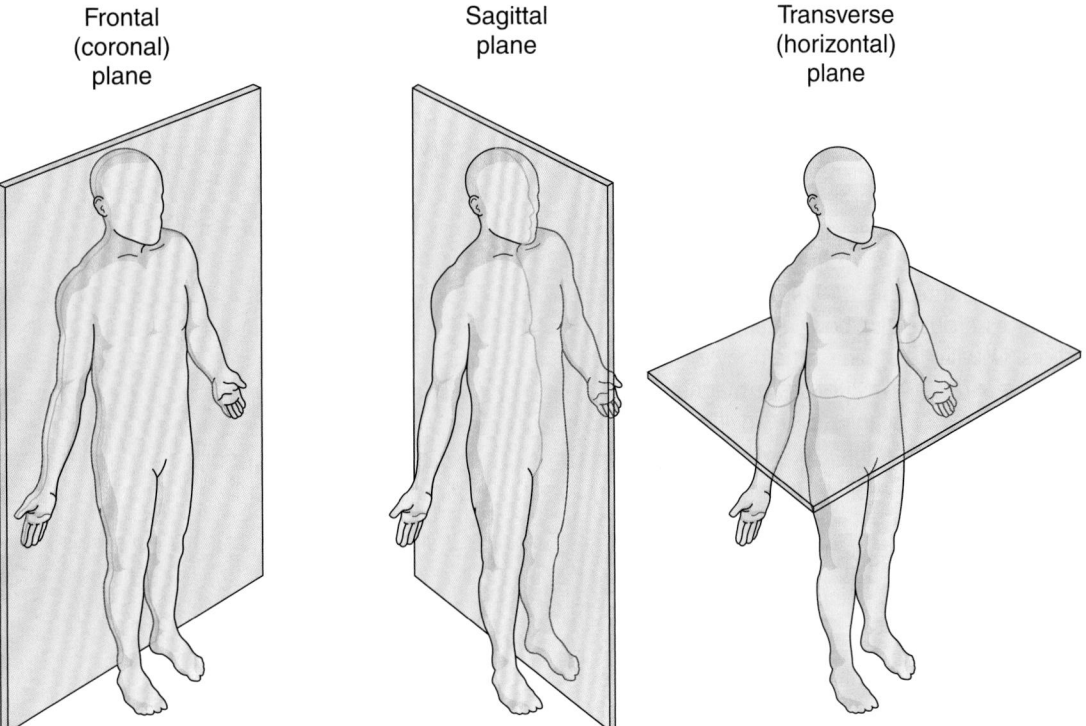

| Frontal (coronal) plane | Sagittal plane | Transverse (horizontal) plane |

Figure 25-2 Planes of division.

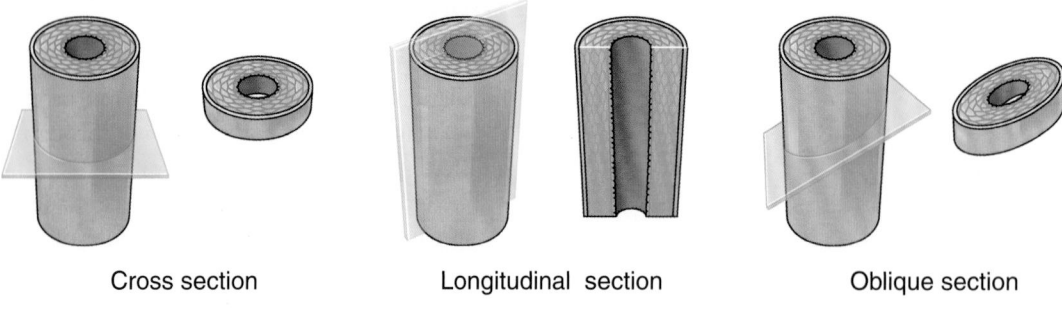

Cross section   Longitudinal section   Oblique section

Tissue sections.

• A longitudinal section is made parallel to the long axis, as in cutting a banana from tip to tip to make a slice for a banana split.

• An oblique section is made at an angle. The type of section used determines what is seen under the microscope, as shown with a blood vessel in the pictures on the right.

The same terms are used for images taken by computerized tomography (CT scan), magnetic resonance imaging (MRI), or similar techniques. Here, *cross section* is used more generally to mean any two-dimensional view.

ZOOM IN

Medical Imaging

Techniques for medical imaging (producing pictures of internal body structures or body functions) have revolutionized medicine. With them, physicians can see inside the body without making an incision. Three common techniques for viewing sections are computerized tomography (CT), magnetic resonance imaging (MRI), and positron emission tomography (PET).

The scanner that produces these images is a large machine with a tunnel through it. The patient lies on a table that moves into this tunnel. A ring inside the machine revolves around the body, scanning it in sections, or slices. Usually, just part of the body is scanned. A CT scan uses x-rays. An MRI uses a magnetic field and radio waves. A PET scan uses a small amount of radioactive material that is inhaled, swallowed, or injected into a vein. This material is designed to concentrate in a particular area of the body. The scanner sends the information to a computer, which assembles it into cross-sectional "slices" of the parts of the body being scanned.

MRI and CT are used to examine structure. PET scans are used to reveal function. Increasingly, PET scans are combined with CT scans or MRIs to yield both kinds of information.

Directional Terms

The main terms for describing directions in the body are as follows (Figure 25-3):

• **Superior** means above, or in a higher position. Its opposite, **inferior**, means below, or lower. The heart, for example, is superior to the intestine.

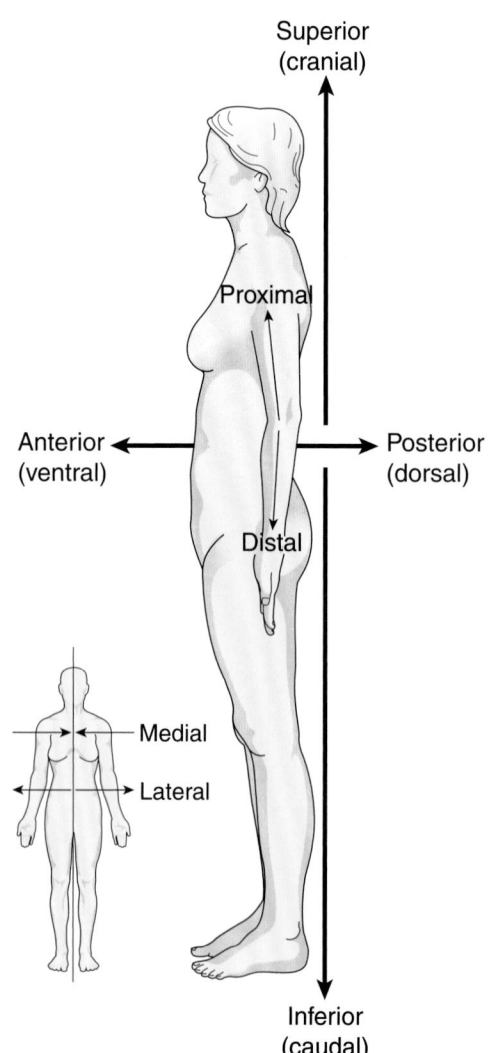

Figure 25-3 Directional terms.

- **Anterior (ventral)** is the front of the body. Its opposite is **posterior (dorsal)**, referring to the back. An anterior view would show the body from the front; a posterior view would show it from the back.
- **Medial** means nearer to an imaginary plane that passes through the midline of the body, dividing it into left and right portions. **Lateral**, its opposite, means farther away from the midline, toward the side. The spine is medial, and the arms are lateral.
- **Proximal** means nearer to the point of attachment of a structure or given reference point; **distal**, farther from that point. For example, the part of your thumb where it joins your hand is its proximal region; the tip of the thumb is its distal region.

✓ **CHECK POINT**

9 What are the three planes along which the body can be divided?

10 What kind of plane divides the body into two equal halves?

BODY CAVITIES AND REGIONS

Just as there are terms for describing position and directions, there are also terms for the internal spaces of the body. Another set of terms is used for the body's regions or areas.

Body Cavities

Internally, the body is divided into a few large spaces, or *cavities*, which contain the organs. The two main cavities are the **dorsal cavity** and the **ventral cavity** (Figure 25-4).

The dorsal cavity has two main parts: the **cranial cavity**, which contains the brain, and the **spinal cavity (canal)**, which encloses the spinal cord. These two areas form one continuous space.

The ventral cavity is much larger than the dorsal cavity. It also has two main parts, separated by the *diaphragm* (DI-ah-fram), a muscle used in breathing. The part superior to (above) the diaphragm is the **thoracic cavity**. Its contents include the heart, the lungs, and the large blood vessels that join the heart. The part inferior to (below) the diaphragm is the **abdominopelvic cavity**. It is divided into two regions:

- The superior portion, the **abdominal cavity**, contains the stomach, most of the intestine, and the liver, gallbladder, pancreas, and spleen.
- The inferior portion, set off by an imaginary line across the top of the hipbones, is the **pelvic cavity**. It houses the urinary bladder, rectum, and internal parts of the reproductive system.

✓ **CHECK POINT**

11 There are two main body cavities, one posterior and one anterior. Name these two cavities.

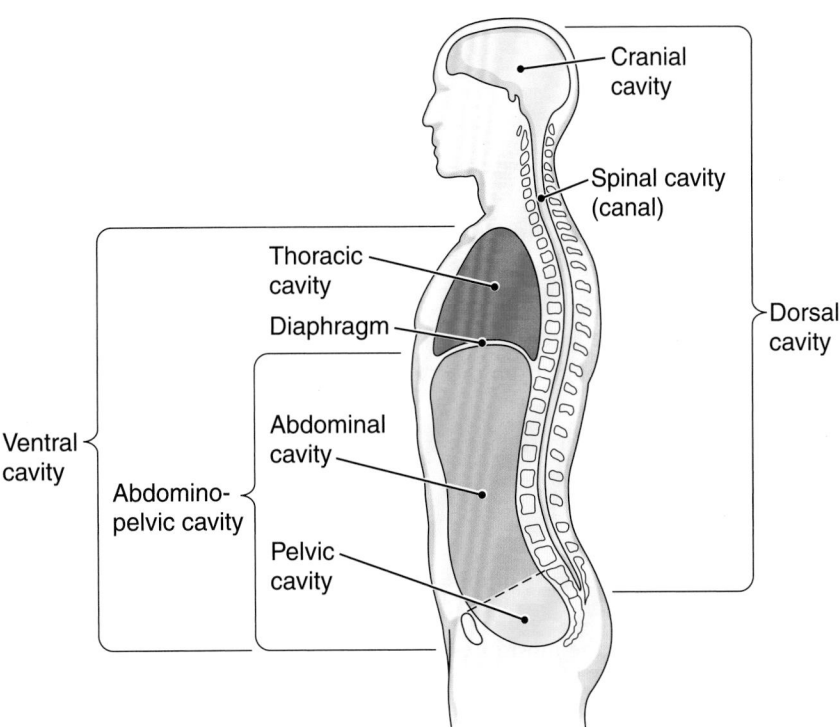

Figure 25-4 Body cavities, lateral view. The dorsal and ventral cavities with their subdivisions are shown.

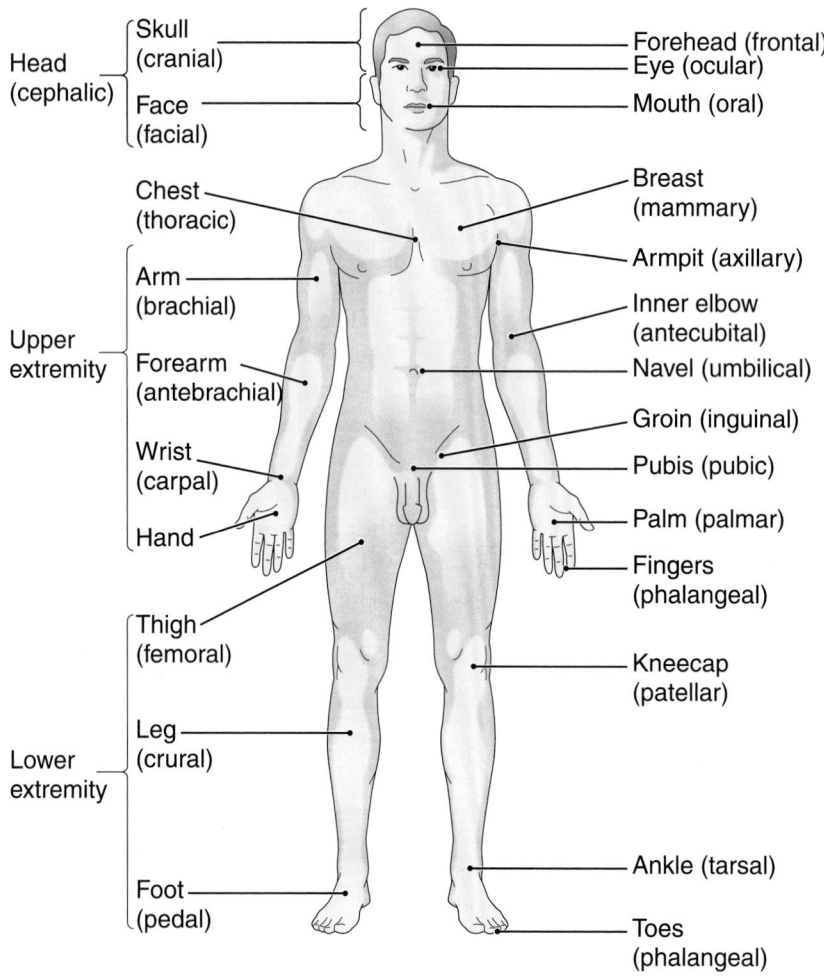

Head (cephalic) — Skull (cranial), Face (facial)

Forehead (frontal)
Eye (ocular)
Mouth (oral)

Chest (thoracic)

Breast (mammary)
Armpit (axillary)

Upper extremity — Arm (brachial)

Inner elbow (antecubital)
Navel (umbilical)

Forearm (antebrachial)

Groin (inguinal)
Pubis (pubic)

Wrist (carpal)

Palm (palmar)

Hand

Fingers (phalangeal)

Thigh (femoral)

Kneecap (patellar)

Leg (crural)

Lower extremity

Ankle (tarsal)

Foot (pedal)

Toes (phalangeal)

Figure 25-5 Major body regions.

Body Regions

The major body regions are the head, trunk, upper extremities, and lower extremities (Figure 25-5).

The head is divided into two regions: the cranium (top and back of the head) and the face. The **trunk** (or **torso**), the central part of the body, has two parts. The upper part, the **thorax** (chest), extends from the neck to the diaphragm. The lower part, the **abdomen**, extends from the diaphragm to the legs.

The abdomen is divided into nine regions (Figure 25-6). The three central regions, from superior to inferior, are:
- The *epigastric region*, located just inferior to the breastbone
- The *umbilical* (um-BIL-ih-kal) *region* around the umbilicus (um-BIL-ih-kus), or navel
- The *hypogastric* (hi-po-GAS-trik) *region*, the most inferior of all the midline regions

The regions on the right and left, from superior to inferior, are:
- The *hypochondriac* (hi-po-KON-dre-ak) *regions*, just inferior to the ribs

- The *lumbar regions*, which are on a level with the lumbar regions of the spine (the part between the ribs and the hipbones)
- The *iliac*, or *inguinal* (IN-gwhi-nal), *regions*, named for the top of the hipbone and the groin region, respectively.

A simpler but less precise division into four quadrants is sometimes used (Figure 25-7). These regions are the right upper quadrant (RUQ), left upper quadrant (LUQ), right lower quadrant (RLQ), and left lower quadrant (LLQ).

The extremities are the body's limbs (the arms and legs). The **upper extremities** (arms) can be divided into four regions: arm, forearm, wrist, and hand. The **lower extremities** (legs) also can be divided into four regions: thigh, knee, leg, and foot.

✔ **CHECK POINT**

12 What are the four major body regions?

13 Name the three central regions and the three left and right lateral regions of the abdomen.

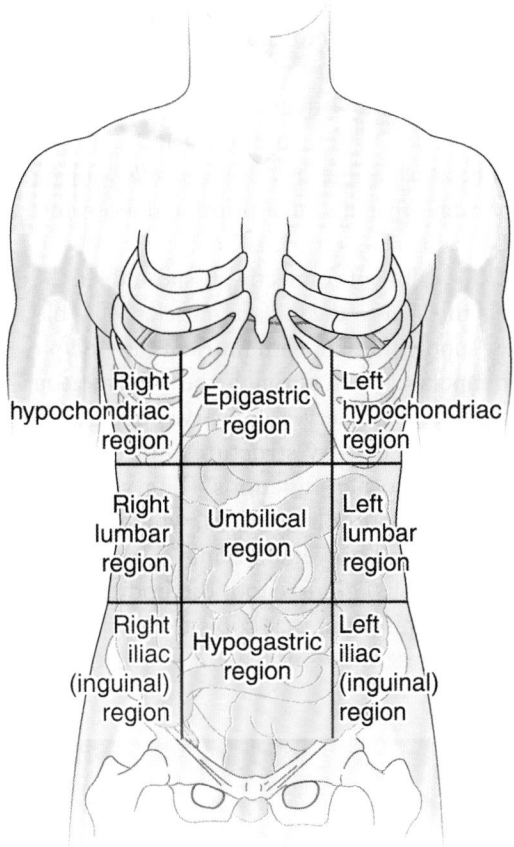

Figure 25-6 The nine regions of the abdomen.

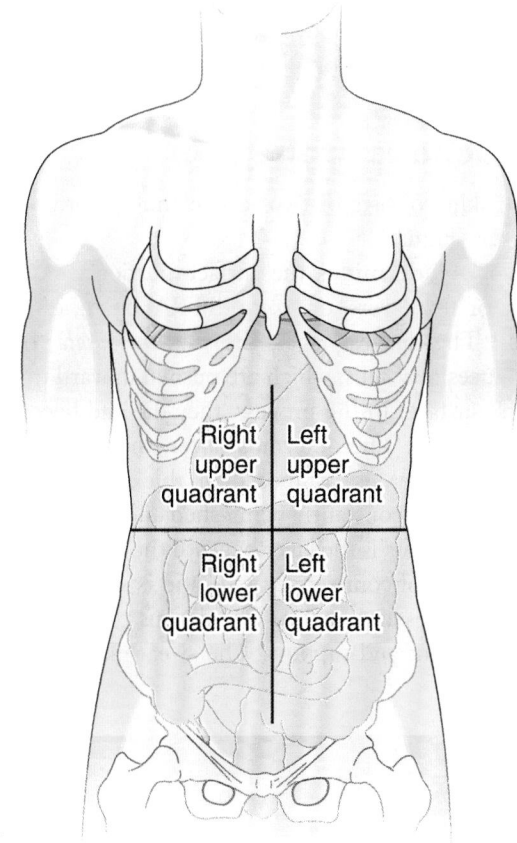

Figure 25-7 Quadrants of the abdomen.

THE INTEGUMENTARY SYSTEM

The skin is an organ, the largest in the human body. The structures that develop from it, including glands, hair, and nails, are known as *accessory structures*. Together with blood vessels, nerves, and sensory organs, the skin and its accessory structures form the integumentary system.

The skin has many functions. The following are its four major functions.

- **Protection against infection and the environment.** The skin is the body's first line of defense, a barrier against disease-causing organisms. Damage to the skin, from a serious burn, for example, can have dangerous consequences for the body as a whole or for its systems. The skin also protects against ultraviolet radiation, bacteria, and other environmental hazards.

- **Protection against dehydration.** The surface of the skin is filled with *keratin*, a protein that thickens and protects it. Lubrication is provided by an oily fluid called **sebum**. Together, these two substances help to waterproof the skin and prevent water loss by evaporation.

- **Regulation of body temperature.** The skin helps to regulate temperature by evaporation of sweat and by changes in the diameter of surface blood vessels,

which control how much heat is lost to the environment. The skin also serves as a large surface for radiating body heat to the surrounding air.

- **Collection of sensory information.** Because of its many nerve endings and special receptors, the skin is one of the body's chief sensory organs. Some nerve endings detect pain and changes in temperature. Other receptors respond to light touch or deep pressure. Many of the reflexes that make it possible for humans to adjust to the environment begin as sensory impulses from the skin. For example, when the skin senses the cold, the brain signals to constrict skin blood vessels so that

 **HEALTH CARE SPECIALTY**

Dermatologist

A dermatologist is a physician who specializes in treating skin diseases. To diagnose many skin disorders, a dermatologist obtains a skin biopsy. A clinical laboratory technologist or technician does clinical laboratory testing on the biopsy. The dermatologist interprets the results to diagnose a skin disease.

heat carried in the blood is not lost out the skin. As elsewhere in the body, the skin works with the brain and spinal cord to accomplish these functions.

Structures of the Skin

The skin consists of two layers: the epidermis and the dermis (Figure 25-8).

The **epidermis** is the surface portion. It consists of four or five layers, or *strata* (STRAH-tah), of epithelial cells. The deepest layer, the *stratum basale* (bas-A-le), produces new cells, which are pushed upward toward the skin's surface. In the process, they die and become filled with keratin. The outermost layer, the *stratum corneum* (KOR-ne-um), is composed of thick, dead, protective cells that are constantly being shed and replaced.

The **dermis** is the layer beneath the epidermis. It has a framework of connective tissue and is well supplied with blood vessels and nerves. The dermis provides the skin's nourishment and support. The sweat glands, oil glands, hair, and other accessory structures are located in the dermis and may extend into the subcutaneous layer under the skin.

Parts of the dermis extend up into the epidermis, allowing blood vessels to get closer to surface cells to nourish them. These extensions, or *dermal papillae*, form the patterns of ridges that are fingerprints and footprints.

The dermis rests on the **subcutaneous layer**, which is made up mainly of connective tissue and fat. This layer connects the skin to the surface muscles. The blood vessels that supply the skin with nutrients and help regulate body temperature run through the subcutaneous layer. The tissue is rich in nerves and nerve endings.

The skin's accessory structures not only protect it but also serve other functions. The **sebaceous** (se-BA-shus) **glands** produce sebum, which lubricates the skin and hair and prevents drying. The **sudoriferous** (su-do-RIF-er-us) **glands** cool the body. They release sweat, or perspiration, that cools the skin as the moisture evaporates at the surface.

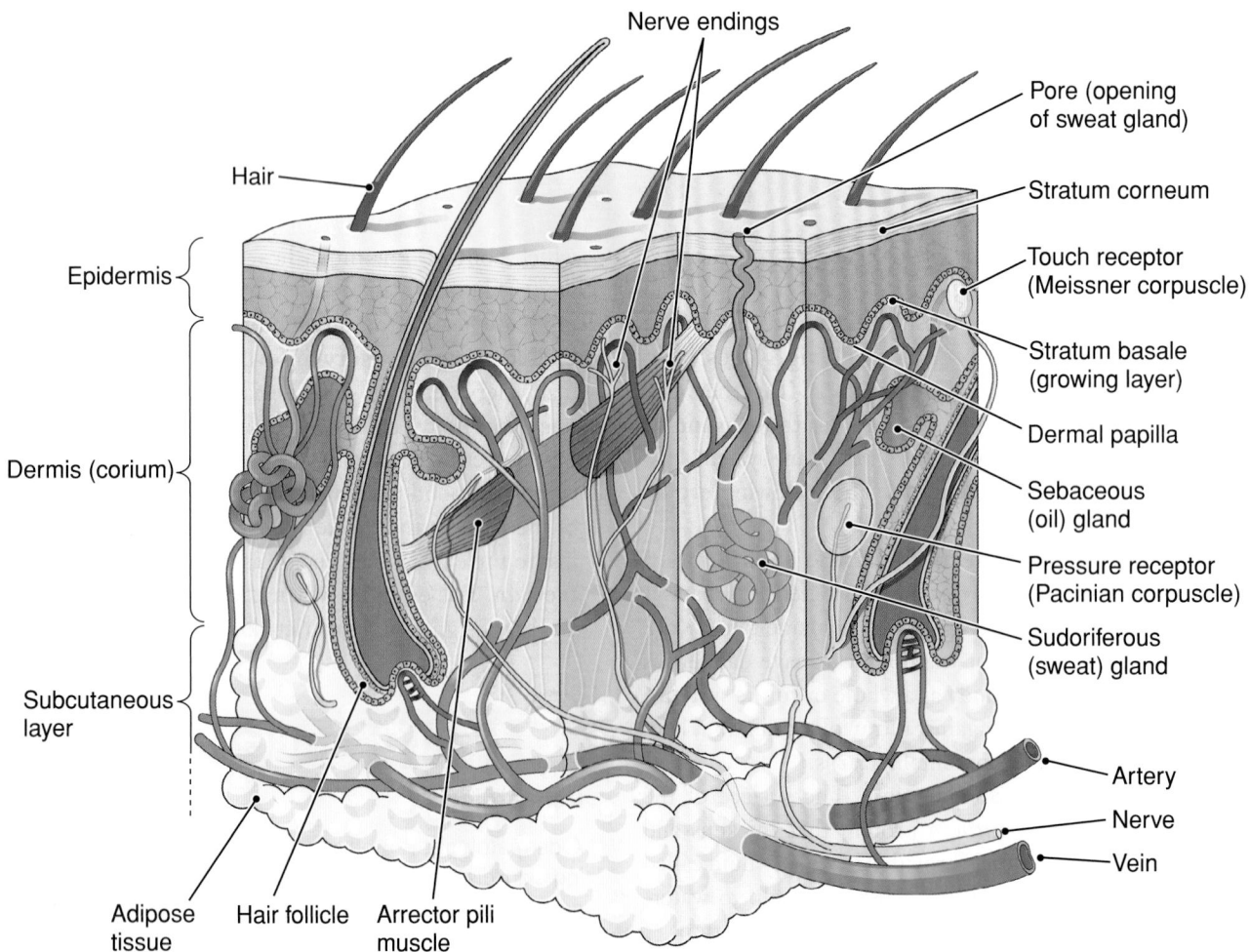

Figure 25-8 Cross section of the skin.

Nearly all the skin's surface is covered with hair, which insulates and protects it. Each hair develops within a sheath, or hair follicle.

Nails protect the fingers and toes and help in grasping small objects. New nail cells form continuously in a growth region under the half-moon area above the cuticle. Nails, like hair, are made of nonliving material, mostly keratin.

Effects of Aging

Like other body systems, the integumentary system is affected by aging. Decreased production of *melanin*, a pigment that colors the skin and hair and protects the skin against the sun's radiation, leads to gray or white hair. The skin becomes drier as sebum production decreases. There may be areas of extra pigmentation in the skin, or brown spots, especially on areas exposed to the sun, like the back of the hands. Wrinkles, or crow's feet, develop around the eyes and mouth due to loss of fat and collagen in the underlying tissues. Older adults often are more sensitive to cold because of less fat in the skin and less effective circulation.

✓ CHECK POINT

14 Name the four major functions of the skin.

15 The skin itself is composed of two layers. What is the name of the outermost layer? The layer beneath it?

Common Diseases and Conditions of the Skin

Common diseases and conditions of the skin range from simply minor and bothersome to serious and life-threatening. Some common skin diseases and conditions are described below.

Warts

Warts (also known as *verruca*, ver-RU-ka) are infections caused by viruses. The virus causes an overgrowth of epidermal cells, forming a rough, raised lesion (an area of damaged tissue) with a pitted surface. Warts occur singly or in groups and appear mostly on the fingers, hands, and feet. They are often treated with over-the-counter medications.

Type 1 Herpes Simplex

Type 1 herpes simplex is a viral infection caused by the Type 1 herpes virus. It produces cold sores, or fever blisters, on the lips, face, or nose, or in the mouth. When the blisters subside, the virus remains, residing in the skin's nerve cells. Fever, colds, stress, and other conditions can trigger a recurrence. Cold sores usually clear up on their own. For frequent or severe outbreaks, doctors may prescribe an antiviral medication such as acyclovir.

Acne

Acne is an inflammatory disease of the sebaceous glands and hair follicles. It occurs most often during adolescence as a result of increased hormone production. Too much sebum is produced, blocking hair follicles. Bacteria multiply, and then white blood cells, forming elevated skin lesions. Acne usually affects the face, back, chest, and shoulders. It is treated with over-the-counter or prescription drugs.

Dermatitis

Dermatitis is a general term for inflammation of the skin, which may be acute or chronic. It can have many different causes. Two examples are contact dermatitis, caused by allergens or chemical irritants, and seborrheic dermatitis, which involves areas with large numbers of sebaceous glands. Symptoms of mild forms of dermatitis are redness, swelling, and sometimes itching. The condition may worsen to include deeper lesions and secondary bacterial infections. Treatment depends on the cause and symptoms.

Skin Cancer

Basal cell cancer, squamous cell cancer, and melanomas are all forms of skin cancer. Skin cancer is the most common type of cancer in the U.S., due to excessive exposure to the sun. A melanoma, which results from an overgrowth of pigment-producing cells in the epidermis, is the most aggressive type of skin cancer. The other two types are highly curable if detected early. The most common symptom of skin cancer is a change in the skin's appearance: a new growth, a sore that doesn't heal, or a change in an old growth. Skin cancer is usually treated with surgery.

Chapter Wrap-Up

Don't forget to visit the Point. companion website for additional study resources!

CHAPTER HIGHLIGHTS

- All living things are organized from simple to very complex levels: cells→tissues→ organs→body systems.
- Certain functions are essential for an organism to survive and thrive: protection, movement, and support; coordination and control; circulation and body defense; energy supply and use; and reproduction and development.
- Special terms are used in the medical professions to designate positions and directions in the body.
- The integumentary system consists of the skin and accessory structures, which include the sebaceous and sudoriferous glands, hair, and nails. Its major functions are to protect against infection and the environment, to protect against dehydration, to help regulate body temperature, and to collect sensory information.
- Like other body systems, the integumentary system is affected by aging. Gray or white hair, brown spots, wrinkles, and poor circulation are some effects. Common diseases and conditions of the skin include warts, Type 1 herpes simplex, acne, dermatitis, and skin cancer. A dermatologist is a physician who specializes in treating skin diseases.

REVIEW QUESTIONS

Matching

1. _____ This system filters out harmful substances.
2. _____ This system brings needed substances to body tissues.
3. _____ This system converts food into a form body cells can use.
4. _____ Glands that produce hormones are part of this system.
5. _____ The skin and its accessory structures form this system.

   a. lymphatic system   **b.** digestive system   **c.** integumentary system
   d. cardiovascular system   **e.** endocrine system

Multiple Choice

6. Which is an effect of loss of fat in the skin as a person ages?
   - **a.** brown spots
   - **b.** wrinkles
   - **c.** sensitivity to cold
   - **d.** Both b and c are correct.

7. Which divisional plane is described by a cut through the body in line with the ears and then down the middle?
   - **a.** the frontal plane
   - **b.** the sagittal plane
   - **c.** the transverse plane
   - **d.** the cross-sectional plane

8. The two main body cavities are the dorsal cavity and the ventral cavity. Which of the following cavities is part of the dorsal cavity?
   - **a.** the abdominal cavity
   - **b.** the pelvic cavity
   - **c.** the cranial cavity
   - **d.** the thoracic cavity

9. What are the major body regions?
   - **a.** the epigastric, umbilical, and hypogastric regions
   - **b.** the hypochondriac, lumbar, and iliac regions

c. the right upper quadrant, left upper quadrant, right lower quadrant, and left lower quadrant

d. the head, trunk, upper extremities, and lower extremities

10. Which common disease or condition is caused by a virus?
   a. acne
   b. Type 1 herpes simplex
   c. skin cancer
   d. contact dermatitis

Completion

11. The most aggressive type of skin cancer is a/an _____.

12. The opposite of *medial* is _____.

13. A _____ is a physician who specializes in treating skin diseases.

14. _____ means nearer to the point of attachment of a structure or given reference point; _____ means farther from that point.

15. The type of muscle tissue that people move voluntarily is _____.

Short Answer

16. Compare and contrast the studies of anatomy and physiology. Would it be wise to study one without the other?

17. List in sequence the levels of organization in the body from simplest to most complex. Give an example for each level.

18. Explain how an internal state of balance is maintained in the body.

19. Describe two effects of aging on the integumentary system.

20. What is acne, and what causes it?

INVESTIGATE IT

1. The main parts of a cell are the plasma membrane, nucleus, cytoplasm, endoplasmic reticulum, ribosomes, mitochondria, Golgi apparatus, and lysosomes. Research the function of each part. Draw a picture of a cell with the parts labeled. Use the search words *parts of a cell* to begin your Internet search.

2. Choose one of the medical imaging techniques described in this chapter's Zoom In feature and read more about it. What is the science of this technique? How does it work? Why is it used in health care? Find an image produced from that type of scan. A good online resource is RadiologyInfo, a web site produced by the Radiological Society of North America (http://www.radiologyinfo.org).

3. Sketch the human body showing both anterior and posterior views. What are some common terms for body regions in the posterior view? Label them on your drawing. What smaller body regions (such as the forehead and eye) could be added? Add some labels to each view. For additional terms, use an anatomy text or search the Internet using the search words *body regions*. Try an image search engine or a search engine with an image feature.

4. Skin cancer is the most common type of cancer in the U.S. What are the symptoms of skin cancer? How is it diagnosed, and how is it treated? What can people do to reduce their risk of developing skin cancer? A good starting point for answering these questions is the web site of the Skin Cancer Foundation (http://www.skincancer.org).

RECOMMENDED READING

Daniels PS, Stein L, Gura T, Restak R. *Body: The Complete Human.* Margate, FL: National Geographic; 2009.

"Guided Tour of the Visible Human: Planes of Section." MadSci Network. Available at http://www.madsci.org/~lynn/VH/planes.html.

Innerbody: Your Guide to Human Anatomy Online. Available at http://www.innerbody.com/htm/body.html.

Jablonski NG. *Skin: A Natural History.* Berkeley and Los Angeles: University of California; 2008.

"MedlinePlus: Interactive Health Tutorials." U.S. National Library of Medicine and National Institutes of Health." Available at http://www.nlm.nih.gov/medlineplus/tutorials.html.

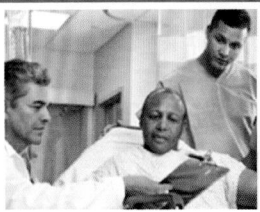
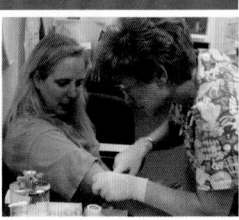

Protection, Movement, and Support

CHAPTER OBJECTIVES

After careful study of this chapter, you should be able to:

* List the main functions of muscle.
* Compare and contrast the three types of muscle tissue.
* Describe how skeletal muscles contract and work in pairs to produce movement.
* Recognize the effects of exercise on muscles.
* List the functions of bones.

* Describe the structure of a long bone.
* Name the three types of joints.
* Give six examples of synovial joints and demonstrate the six types of movement that occur at these joints.
* Explain how aging affects the muscles and bones.
* Identify common diseases and conditions of the muscular and skeletal systems.

KEY TERMS

abduction (ab-DUK-shun)
adduction
antagonist
appendicular skeleton
axial skeleton
bone marrow
cartilage
circumduction (ser-kum-DUK-shun)

diaphysis (di-AF-ih-sis)
dorsiflexion (dor-sih-FLEK-shun)
epiphyses (eh-PIF-ih-sēz) (*sing.* epiphysis)
eversion (e-VER-zhun)
extension
flexion (FLEK-shun)
insertion

inversion (in-VER-zhun)
long bone
motor unit
origin
plantar flexion
prime mover
pronation (pro-NA-shun)
rotation
skeleton

supination (su-pin-A-shun)
synovial (sin-O-ve-al) joint

The muscular and skeletal systems work together to execute movement and to support and protect vital organs. Bones and joints give form to the body and serve as the levers and fulcrums that play important roles in movement. Movement results from a skeletal muscle contracting and exerting force on a tendon, which, in turn, pulls on a bone to cause movement at a joint. Together, these two systems are sometimes referred to as the musculoskeletal system.

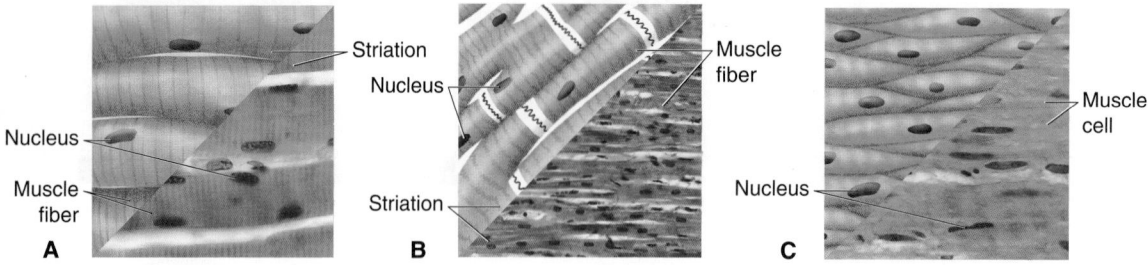

Figure 26-1 The three types of muscle tissue: A) skeletal, B) cardiac, and C) smooth.

THE MUSCULAR SYSTEM

The main characteristic of muscle tissue is its ability to contract. When stimulated, muscles shorten to produce movement of the skeleton, vessels, or internal organs. A person can't breathe, blink, eat, walk, or run without muscles. The heart can't beat, and food can't make its way through the digestive system without them.

Chapter 25, "The Body as a Whole," introduced the three kinds of muscle tissue: smooth, cardiac, and skeletal (Figure 26-1). Each type has one or more main functions. The main function of smooth muscle is to move substances, like food, through the body. It does this with smooth, wave-like movements called *peristalsis*. Cardiac muscle is responsible for the heart's pumping action. Skeletal muscle works with tendons and bones to move the body. It is voluntary muscle because it can contract with conscious thought.

Types of Muscle

The three types of muscle tissue have some similarities in design. They all contract, of course. But they are also specialized to perform particular functions (Table 26-1).

Smooth Muscle

Smooth muscle makes up the walls of hollow organs like the stomach, blood vessels, and respiratory passageways. As Figure 26-1 shows, the cells look smooth under a microscope because they don't have the bands, or striations, seen in the other types of muscle cells. Smooth muscle moves involuntarily, or without a person's conscious intent. Nerve impulses, hormones, stretching, and other stimuli cause it to contract. This type of muscle contracts and relaxes slowly and can stay contracted for a long time.

Cardiac Muscle

Cardiac muscle, which also moves involuntarily, makes up the heart's wall. The cells of cardiac muscle are striated (Figure 26-1). The membranes between these cells are specialized to allow electrical impulses to travel rapidly through them, so contractions can be better coordinated. The muscle itself generates the electrical impulses that make cardiac muscle contract, but the nervous system and hormones can modify those impulses.

Skeletal Muscle

Skeletal muscle makes up the largest amount of the body's muscle tissue and about 40 percent of total body weight. The skeletal muscular system is composed of more than 600 individual muscles. These muscle cells are long, cylindrical, and heavily striated (Figure 26-1). They are often referred to as fibers because they are so long and threadlike. During development, the nuclei of these cells

Table 26-1 Comparison of the Different Types of Muscle			
	Smooth	**Cardiac**	**Skeletal**
Location	Wall of hollow organs, vessels, respiratory passageways	Wall of heart	Attached to bones
Cell characteristics	Tapered at each end, branching networks, nonstriated	Branching networks, special membranes (intercalated disks) between cells; single nucleus; lightly striated	Long and cylindrical; multinucleated; heavily striated
Control	Involuntary	Involuntary	Voluntary
Action	Produces peristalsis; contracts and relaxes slowly; may sustain contraction	Pumps blood out of heart; self-excitatory but influenced by nervous system and hormones	Produces movement at joints; stimulated by nervous system; contracts and relaxes rapidly

divide repeatedly by mitosis, but the cell contents are not divided. The result is a large cell with multiple nuclei. Such cells can contract as a large unit when stimulated.

The nervous system stimulates skeletal muscles to contract. Most skeletal muscles contract rapidly to produce movement and then relax rapidly unless stimulation continues. While some skeletal muscle contractions can be involuntary—such as in a reflex action—people can contract their skeletal muscles voluntarily.

Figures 26-2 and 26-3 (following page) show the body's superficial muscles (muscles close to the surface of the skin) from the anterior and posterior views.

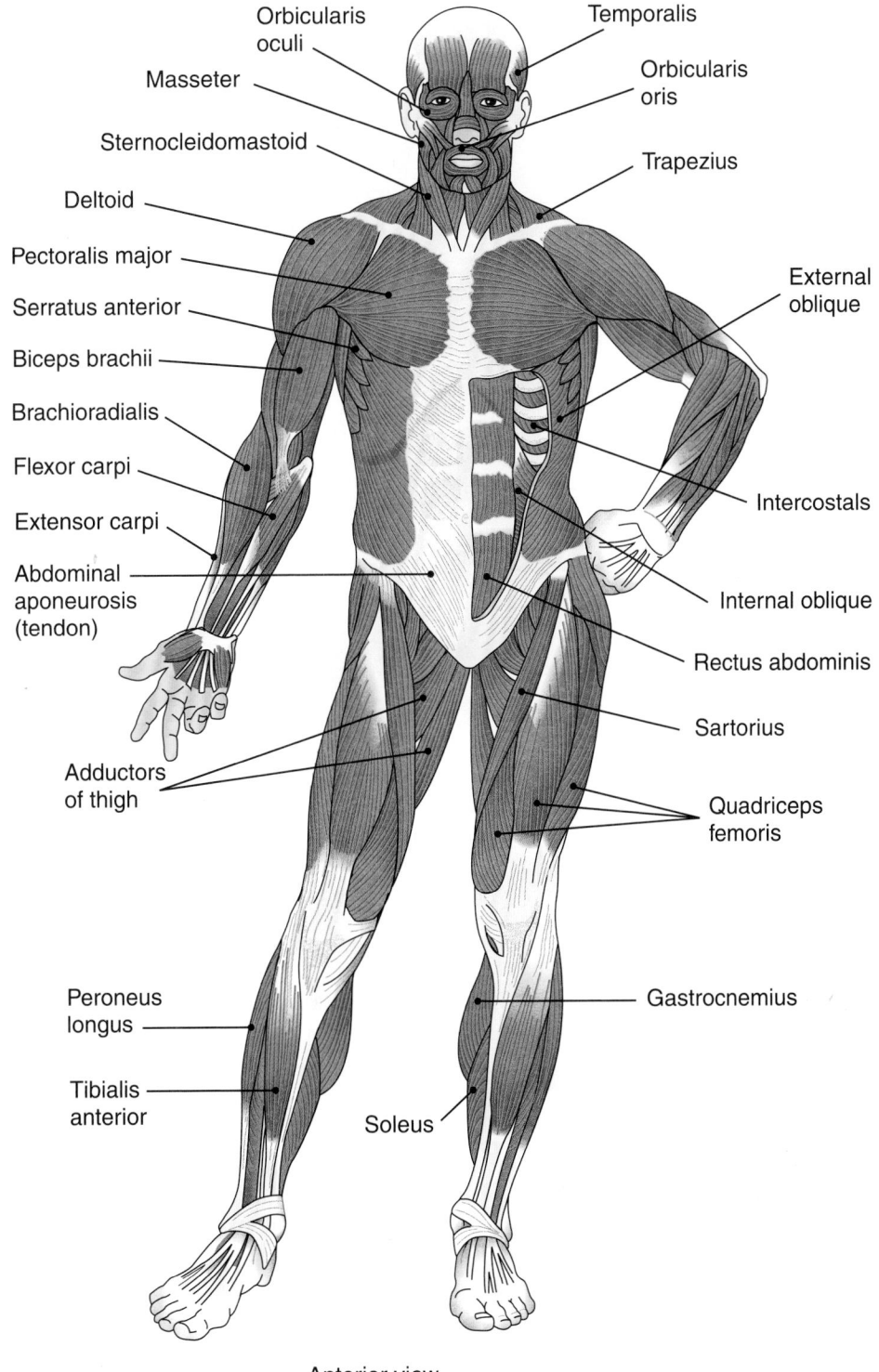

Anterior view

Figure 26-2   Superficial muscles, anterior view.

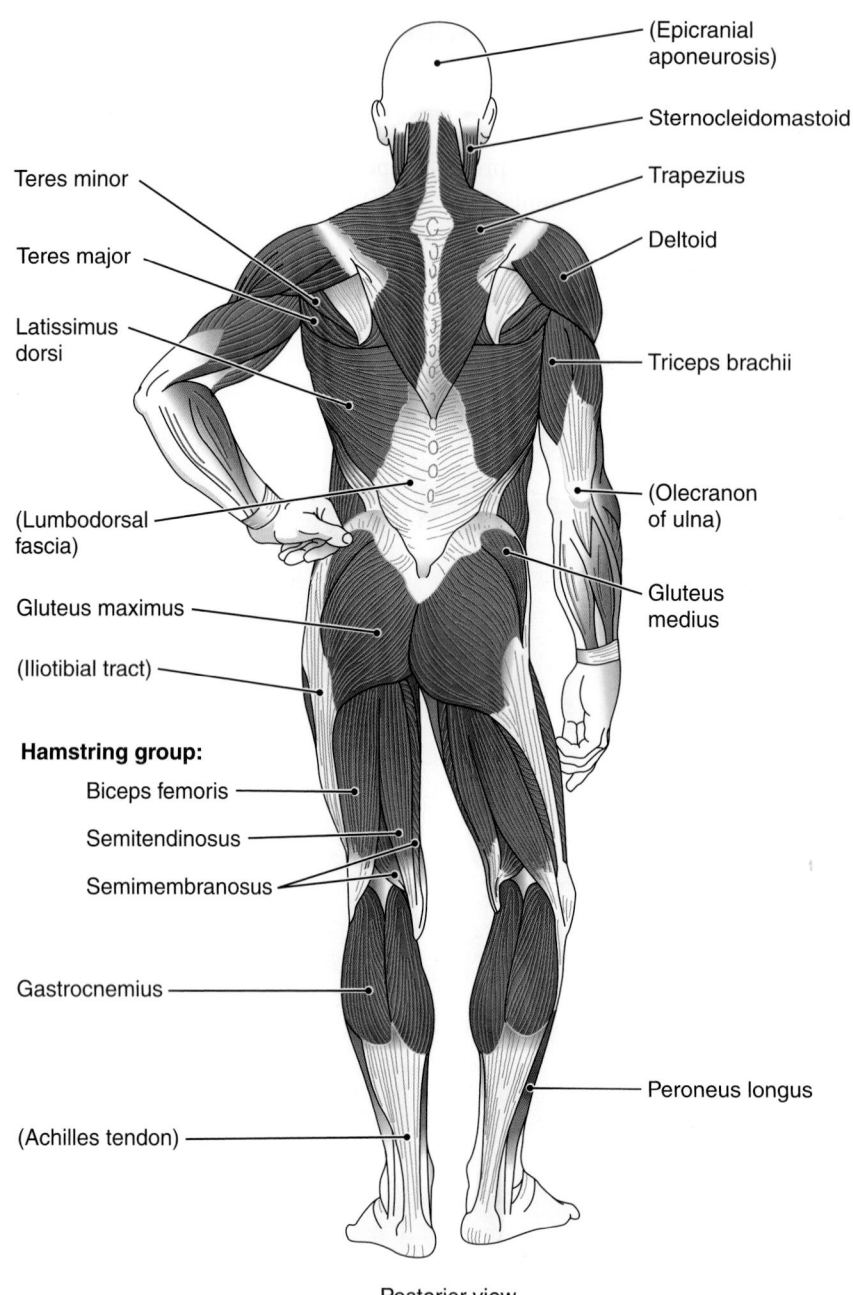

Posterior view

Figure 26-3 Superficial muscles, posterior view.

✓ **CHECK POINT**

1 What are the three types of muscle?

Muscle Function

The means by which muscles contract and then keep working during exertion involve several body systems and chemicals, as well as mechanical action.

How Skeletal Muscle Cells Work

Each skeletal muscle contains alternating bundles of thin and thick filaments. The thin filaments are made of a pro-

tein called *actin*. The thick filaments are made of another protein called *myosin*. These alternating bands of filaments give skeletal muscle its striated appearance.

The actin and myosin filaments overlap where they meet, just as your fingers overlap when your hands are folded together. A band of myosin filaments and the actin filaments on either side of it work as a unit to contract. This unit is called a *sarcomere* (SAR-ko-mere). The myosin filaments have paddle-like extensions called *myosin heads*, which they use to latch on to the actin filaments, forming attachments known as *cross-bridges*. Like oars moving water, the myosin heads pull the actin filaments closer together. As the overlapping filaments slide together, the muscle fiber contracts, becoming shorter and thicker.

Once the cross-bridges have been formed, the myosin heads move the actin filaments forward. Then they detach and move back to position for another "power stroke." As the cell contracts, the filaments overlap more and more.

During contraction, each sarcomere becomes shorter, but the individual filaments don't change in length. It's like shuffling a deck of cards. As the cards are pushed together, the deck becomes smaller, but the length of individual cards doesn't change.

Contraction

Muscles contract in response to stimulation delivered by nerve impulses from the brain and spinal cord. At the point of contact with a muscle, a neuron's axon (the conducting arm of the nerve cell) branches to individual muscle cells. Each neuron can reach from a few muscle cells to hundreds and in some cases more than a thousand. A single neuron and all the muscle fibers it stimulates make up a **motor unit**. Small motor units are used for fine motor skills such as eye movements. Large motor units are used to maintain posture or for broader movements, like walking or swinging a tennis racquet.

The point at which a neuron branch meets a muscle cell is called a *neuromuscular junction*. To stimulate the muscle fiber to contract, the neuron releases a chemical called *acetylcholine* (as-e-til-KO-lene), or ACh. The ACh crosses the small gap, or *synaptic cleft*, between the nerve and the muscle cell and attaches itself to proteins in the membrane of the muscle cell. An electrical impulse is generated that spreads rapidly along the membrane. This spreading wave of electrical current is called the *action potential* because it calls the muscle cell into action.

The muscle cell responds by releasing calcium. When muscles are at rest, two proteins block the sites on actin filaments where cross-bridges can form. Calcium forces these proteins aside. The myosin heads bind to actin, and the contraction proceeds as described above. The repeated movements of the myosin heads are powered by *adenosine triphosphate* (ah-DEN-o-sene tri-FOS-fate), or *ATP*, a compound that stores energy for cell activities. When the stimulation ends, the muscle relaxes, and the calcium is pumped back into the cell for storage. This all happens in a fraction of second.

✔ CHECK POINT

2 Muscles are activated by the nervous system. What is the name of the point of contact between a nerve cell and a muscle cell?

3 What two filaments interact to produce muscle contraction?

Muscles Work Together

Most skeletal muscles are attached to the skeleton at two or more points. Each end of a muscle is attached to a bone by a cordlike extension called a tendon. All the connective tissue within and around the muscle merges to form the tendon. In some instances, a broad sheet of connective tissue called an *aponeurosis* (ap-o-nu-RO-sis) attaches muscles to bones or other muscles.

One end of a muscle is attached to a more movable part of the skeleton, and the other end is attached to a more stable part. The point where the muscle is attached to a stable part of the skeleton is the **origin**. The other point, attached to the moving part of the skeleton, is the **insertion**. Between these two points is the fleshy "belly" of the muscle. When a muscle contracts, it pulls on both attachment points, bringing the more movable insertion point on one bone closer to the origin point on the other bone; that action makes the body part move.

Muscles work in pairs to produce movement at the joints. As one muscle, the **prime mover**, contracts, an opposing muscle, the **antagonist**, must relax, or stretch out. For example, when the biceps brachii at the front of the arm contracts to flex the arm, the triceps brachii at the back of the arm must relax. When the arm is extended, these actions are reversed.

Energy Sources

Muscle contraction requires energy, in the form of ATP. To make ATP, muscle cells need oxygen and a nutrient like glucose. The blood delivers enough of these substances for most daily activities. Muscle cells also store a small reserve supply.

During strenuous activity, a person may not be able to breathe in oxygen rapidly enough to meet the muscles' need for oxygen. Reserve supplies, while they last, meet the increased demand. After that, glucose is used without oxygen. This method generates ATP rapidly and allows more strenuous activity, such as sprinting instead of jogging. However, it doesn't produce as much ATP as when oxygen is used, and a by-product called *lactic acid* can build up and lead to muscle fatigue.

Until recently, lactic acid was thought to be merely a waste product. But research has shown that muscles also burn this by-product to produce even more energy. Exercise that builds endurance teaches muscles to use lactic acid efficiently.

Muscles operating without enough oxygen are in *oxygen debt*. After people stop exercising, they must continue to take in oxygen by breathing rapidly (panting) until the debt is paid. Enough oxygen must be taken in to convert the lactic acid to other substances, and the reserve supplies must be replenished.

HEALTH CARE SPECIALTIES

Specialties Involving the Musculoskeletal System

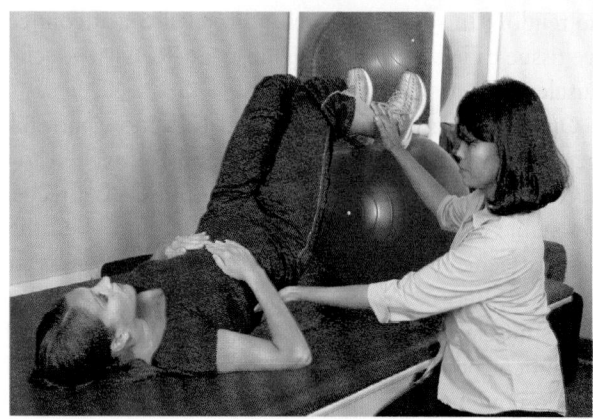

Therapy is often part of orthopedic rehabilitation.

Orthopedic Surgeon

When an injury or disease involving the bones, muscles, or other supporting structures causes a loss of function, an orthopedic surgeon may operate to restore that function. However, the American Academy of Orthopaedic Surgeons reports that up to half of a typical orthopedic surgeon's practice doesn't involve surgery. Orthopedic surgeons also manage musculoskeletal disorders through rehabilitation and other means. They also serve as consultants and play a key role in emergency care as part of trauma teams.

Radiologic Technologist

To diagnose injuries and diseases that affect bones and joints, x-rays and other types of imaging tests may be needed. Radiologic technologists perform these tests. They work in one of four practice areas: radiography (x-rays), sonography (ultrasound), nuclear medicine, or radiation therapy, and they may specialize in CT scans, MRIs, or other types of imaging.

Physical Therapist and Physical Therapist Assistant

Physical therapy restores or improves mobility after joint and muscle injuries and helps relieve back pain or arthritis. It also may prevent or limit the effects of a physical disability. Physical therapists evaluate a patient and design a treatment plan. Some work with a wide range of ailments, while others specialize in pediatrics, geriatrics, orthopedics, sports medicine, or other areas. Physical therapist assistants are responsible for implementing the treatment plan.

Effects of Exercise

Regular exercise causes a number of changes in muscle tissue. When muscles are stretched, they contract more forcefully, because the filaments can interact over a greater length. Stretching also helps with balance and joint flexibility. *Aerobic exercise* (exercise that increases oxygen consumption) leads to improved endurance. *Resistance training* increases the size of muscle cells, making muscles bigger. Some of the changes in muscle tissue that lead to improved endurance and strength include:

● an increased number of capillaries, the smallest blood vessels, which brings more blood to the cells
● more *mitochondria* (the "power plants" of a cell), which increases ATP production
● bigger energy reserves

Effects of Aging

After about age 40, people begin to lose muscle cells gradually, and muscles get smaller. With less muscle, people burn fewer calories. They may gain weight, and "bad" cholesterol levels may increase. There is also a loss of power, notably in the extensor muscles, which causes the bent-over appearance observed in many older adults. Sometimes, there is a tendency to bend (flex) the hips and knees while standing. These effects on the extensor muscles can decrease an older person's height.

Activity and exercise throughout life delay and decrease these and other undesirable effects of aging. Even for older adults, resistance exercise is valuable, as it increases muscle strength and function. Other benefits include weight and cholesterol control and reduction of arthritis pain.

Common Diseases and Conditions of the Muscles

Some musculoskeletal disorders are caused by physical stress. These include accidental injuries and work- or sports-related damage caused by overexertion or repetitive motion.

Strains

Many people have experienced the sudden pain associated with a strain from lifting a box the wrong way or running to hit a tennis ball. A *strain* is an injury to a muscle and

ZOOM IN

Exercise for Everyone

It's no secret that exercise is good for muscles. Muscles benefit the most from an exercise routine that includes the following three types of exercise:

- **Stretching** makes muscles contract more forcefully. It helps with balance, flexibility, and protection against injury.
- **Aerobic exercise**, like running, biking, or swimming, increases oxygen consumption and leads to improved endurance and improved cardiovascular fitness.
- **Resistance training**, such as weight lifting, makes muscles larger. It strengthens muscles and improves their function.

Exercise, of course, not only benefits the muscles, but is important for total body health. It helps people of all ages to:

- relax
- reduce stress
- lift their mood
- control weight
- sleep better
- improve their self-esteem
- have more energy
- prevent and manage heart disease, diabetes, osteoporosis, high blood pressure, and other diseases
- increase the likelihood of living longer

An exercise program should include stretching, aerobic exercise, and resistance training, with periods of warm-up and cool-down before and after working out. The Centers for Disease Control and Prevention recommend a weekly mix of aerobic exercise and muscle-strengthening activities that work all major muscle groups to strengthen muscles and improve health.

---

its surrounding tendons. Symptoms include pain, limited motion, muscle spasms or weakness, and inflammation. Mild strains can be treated with RICE—rest, ice, compression (bandage), and elevation.

Carpal Tunnel Syndrome

Carpal tunnel syndrome (CTS) is numbness and weakness of the hand caused by pressure on the median nerve as it passes through a tunnel formed by the carpal (wrist) bones. The pressure (from swelled tissues) causes numbness, weakness, and pain in the areas of the hand supplied by the nerve. CTS commonly appears in people who use their hands and fingers strenuously, such as some musicians and people who spend much of their time working on keyboards. Treatments include over-the-counter pain relievers, exercise, and surgery.

CHECK POINT

4 Muscles are attached to bones by tendons, with one end attached to a less movable part of the skeleton and the other end attached to a more movable part. What are the names of these two attachment points?

5 What effects does exercise have on muscles?

THE SKELETAL SYSTEM

The **skeleton** is the strong, bony framework on which the body is constructed. Like the frame of a building, the skeleton must be strong enough to support and protect all the body structures. The bones and joints, together with supporting connective tissue, form the skeletal system. The bones have five main functions:

- to serve as a framework for the body
- to protect the brain, spinal cord, and other delicate structures
- to work with muscles to produce movement
- to store calcium
- to produce blood cells

The skeleton is made up of 206 bones and has two main parts:

- a central part, called the **axial skeleton** (the central core or *axis* of the body's framework)
- the extremities, which are known as the **appendicular skeleton** (attached or *appended* to the axial skeleton)

In Figure 26-4 (on the following page), the axial skeleton is shown in yellow. The appendicular skeleton is shown in blue. Table 26-2 (on the following page) details the bones of the skeleton.

Bones

Bones have different shapes. They may be flat (ribs, cranium), short (wrist and ankle bones), or irregular (vertebrae, facial bones). The most familiar shape, however, is the **long bone,** the type of bone that makes up the arms and legs.

Long Bones

Each long bone (Figure 26-5, following page) has a long, narrow shaft called the **diaphysis**. At the center of the

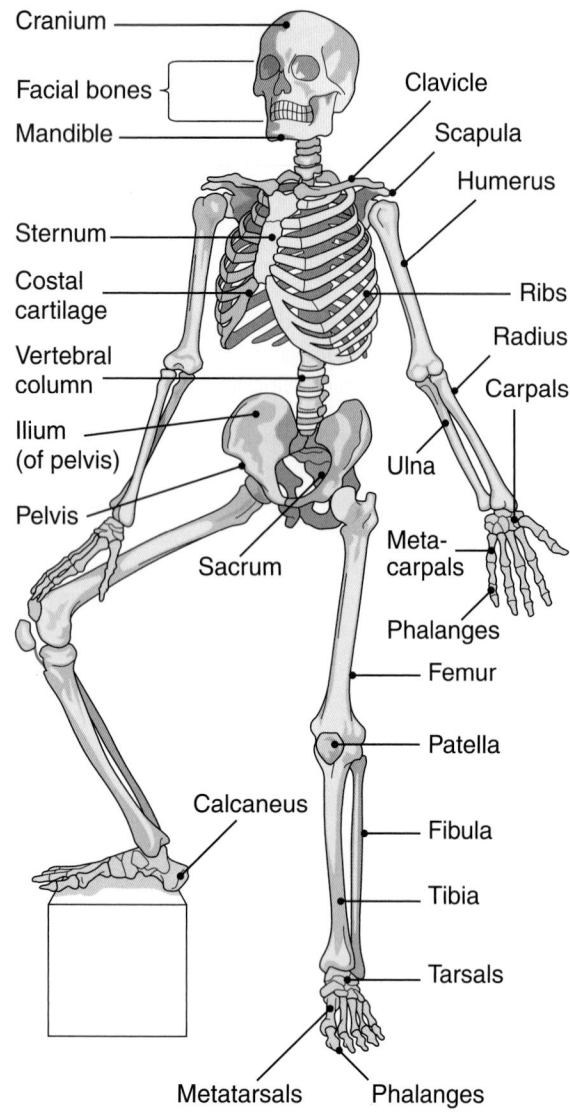

Figure 26-4 The skeleton.

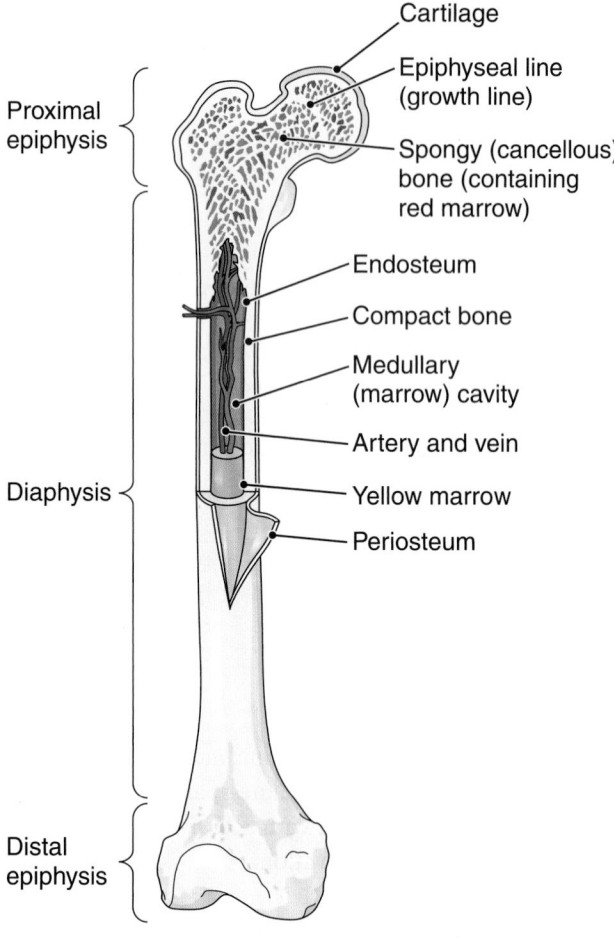

Figure 26-5 The structure of a long bone.

diaphysis is the medullary (MED-u-lar-e) cavity, which contains **bone marrow**. The two irregular ends of a long bone are the proximal and distal **epiphyses** (*sing.* epiphysis).

A thin layer of tissue called the *periosteum* (per-e-OS-te-um) covers the bone's outer surface. The periosteum nourishes and protects the bone. It also makes new bone cells for growth and repair. A layer of tissue called **cartilage** covers the epiphysis to protect the bone surface at a joint.

Tissue and Marrow

Bones are not lifeless. Although the spaces between bone tissue cells are filled with deposits of calcium, the cells themselves are very much alive. Bones are organs, with their own system of blood vessels, lymphatic vessels, and nerves.

Bone tissue is the densest form of connective tissue. There are two types. *Compact bone* is hard and dense. It

makes up the main shaft of long bones and the outer layer of other bones. The second type, *spongy* or *cancellous bone*, consists of a mesh of small, bony plates filled with red marrow. Spongy bone is found at the epiphyses of the long bones and the center of other bones.

Bones contain two kinds of marrow. Red marrow, which makes blood cells, is found at the ends of the long bones and at the center of other bones. Yellow marrow, mostly fat, is found mainly in the central cavities of the long bones.

✓ CHECK POINT

6 What are the five functions of the bones?

7 What are the scientific names for the shaft and ends of a long bone?

Joints

A joint, or *articulation*, is the junction between two or more bones. The bones don't actually touch. Ligaments, strong bands of connective tissue, join one bone to another. They stabilize a joint and control its range of motion.

Table 26-2 Bones of the Skeleton

Region	Bones	Description
		AXIAL SKELETON
Skull		
Cranium	Cranial bones (8)	Chamber enclosing the brain; houses the ear and forms of the eye socket
Facial portion	Facial bones (14)	Form the face and chambers for sensory organs
Hyoid		U-shapes bone under lower jaw; used for muscle attachments
Ossicles	Ear bones (3)	Transmit sound waves in inner ear
Trunk		
Vertebral column	Vertebrae (26)	Enclose the spinal cord
Thorax	Sternum ribs (12 pair)	Anterior bone of the thorax
Appendicular Skeleton		Enclose the organs of the thorax
Upper division		
Shoulder girdle	Clavicle	Anterior; between sternum and scapula
	Scapula	Posterior; anchors muscles that move arm
Upper extremity	Humerus	Proximal arm bone
	Ulna	Medial bone of forearm
	Radius	Lateral bone of forearm
	Carpals (8)	Wrist bones
	Metacarpals (5)	Bones of palm
	Phalanges (14)	Bones of fingers
Lower division		
Pelvis	Os coxae	Join sacrum and coccyx of vertebral column to form the bony pelvis
Lower extremity	Femur	Thigh bone
	Patella	Kneecap
	Tibia	Medial bone of leg
	Fibula	Lateral bone of leg
	Tarsal bones (7)	Ankle bones
	Metatarsals (5)	Bones of instep
	Phalanges (14)	Bones of toes

Types of Joints

Joints are classified in two ways: by the material between the adjoining bones and by the degree of movement they allow (Table 26-3).

- *Fibrous joints* are held together by connective tissue made of fibers. This type of joint doesn't move. The joints of the skull are a good example.

- *Cartilaginous joints* are connected by cartilage. This type of joint moves a little. For example, the joints of the vertebrae are cartilaginous joints.

- *Synovial joints* have a space called the joint cavity that contains a lubricant called synovial fluid. This type of joint moves freely. Most joints, including the hip joint, are synovial.

Table 26-3 Joints

Type	Movement	Material Between the Bones	Examples
Fibrous	Immovable	No joint cavity; fibrous connective tissue between the bones	Sutures (immovable joints) between skull bones
Cartilaginous	Slightly movable	No joint cavity; cartilage between bones	Joints between vertebral bodies
Synovial	Freely movable	Joint cavity containing synovial fluid	Gliding, hinge, pivot, condyloid, saddle, ball-and-socket joints

Table 26-4 Synovial Joints

Type of Joint	Type of Movement	Examples
Gliding joint	Bone surfaces slide over one another	Joints in the wrist and ankles
Hinge joint	Allows movement in one direction, changing the angle of the bones at the joint	Elbow joint; joints between phalanges of fingers
Pivot joint	Allows rotation around the length of the bone	Joint between the first and second cervical vertebrae; joint at proximal ends of the radius and ulna
Condyloid joint	Allows movement in two directions	Joint between the metacarpal and the first phalanx of the finger (knuckle); joint between the occipital bone of the skull and the first cervical vertebra (atlas)
Saddle joint	Like a condyloid joint, but with deeper articulating surfaces, except that the surfaces where bones meet are deeper	Joint between the wrist and the metacarpal bone of the thumb
Ball-and-socket joint	Allows movement in many directions around a central point; gives the greatest freedom of movement	Shoulder joint and hip joint

Synovial Joint Movement

Synovial joints allow for changes of position and, therefore, for motion. They are classified according to the types of movement they allow (Table 26-4). A gliding joint, for example, allows bone surfaces to glide or slide over one another. Listed in order of increasing range of motion, the synovial joints are:

- gliding joint
- hinge joint
- pivot joint
- condyloid joint
- saddle joint
- ball-and-socket joint

A second set of terms describes the changes in position of body parts that result from movement at synovial joints (Figure 26-6). For example, four kinds of movements change the angles between bones:

- **Flexion** is a bending motion that decreases the angle between bones, as in bending the fingers to make a fist.
- **Extension** is a straightening motion that increases the angle between bones, as in straightening the fingers to open the hand.
- **Abduction** is movement away from the midline of the body, as in moving an arm straight out to the side.
- **Adduction** is movement toward the midline of the body, as in bringing an extended arm back beside the body.

These movements can be combined into a **circumduction**. To perform this movement, a person stands with arms outstretched and hands open, and then draws large, imaginary circles in the air.

Rotation refers to a twisting or turning of a bone on its own axis, as in turning the head from side to side to say "no," or rotating the forearm to turn the palm up or down.

The forearm and ankle have special sets of movements:
- **Supination** means turning the palm up. **Pronation** means turning it down.
- **Inversion** means turning the sole inward, so it faces the opposite foot. **Eversion** means turning it outward, away from the body.
- In **dorsiflexion**, the foot is bent upward at the ankle. In **plantar flexion**, the toes point downward, flexing the arch of the foot, as when dancing on tiptoe.

Effects of Aging

Aging causes significant changes in all connective tissues, including bone. The process of breakdown and buildup of bone tissue, which occurs throughout life, slows in older adults, especially women. As a result, bones become weaker and more fragile. This age-related, slowed buildup is one of several causes, not completely understood, of the extreme loss of bone mass known as *osteoporosis*. Older people also have a decreased ability to form proteins on which calcium is deposited, which causes fractures to heal more slowly. Finally, older people experience a reduction of collagen (a protein that makes connective tissue strong and resilient) in tendons, ligaments, and skin, contributing to the stiffness many people experience.

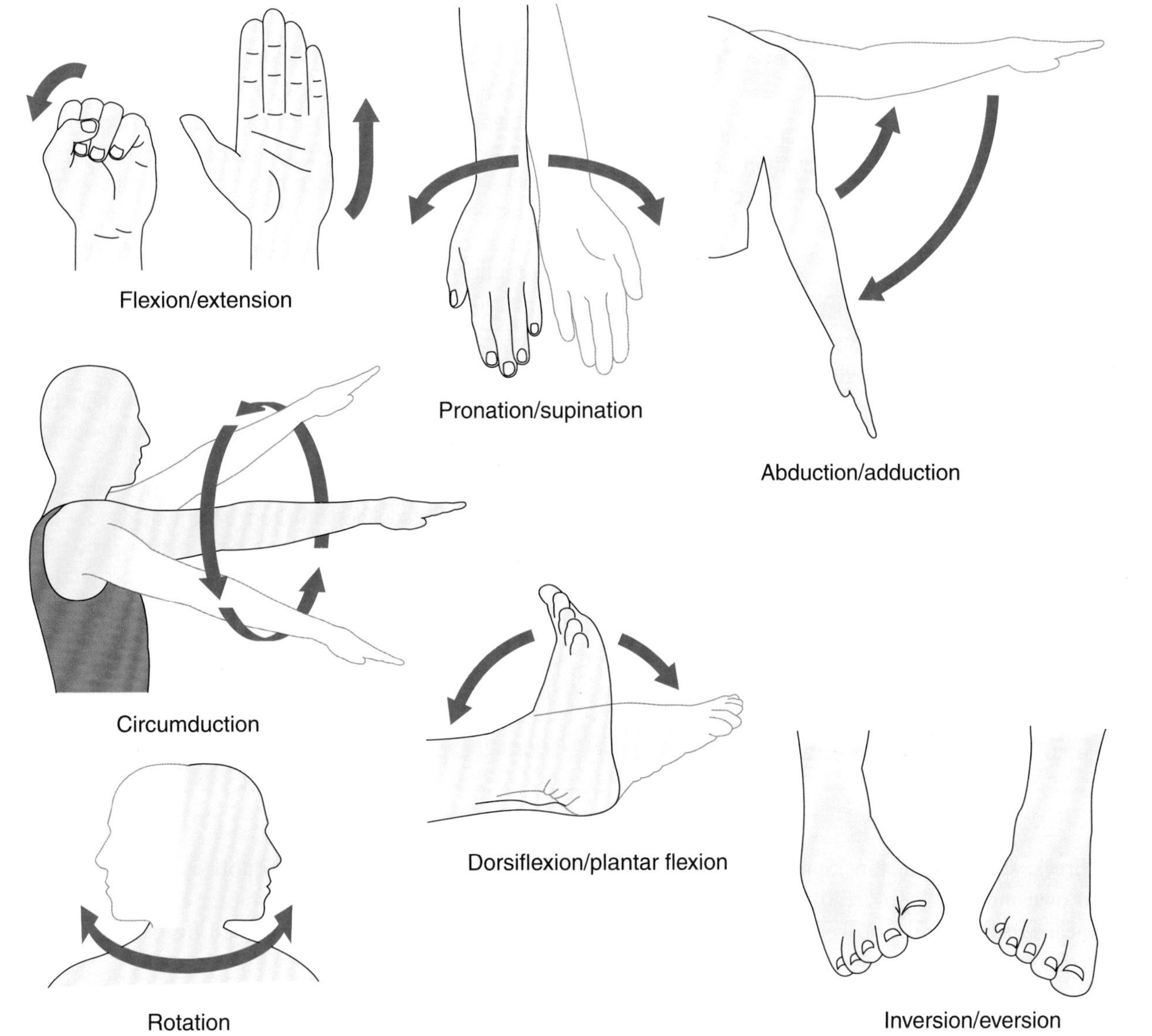

Flexion/extension

Pronation/supination

Abduction/adduction

Circumduction

Dorsiflexion/plantar flexion

Rotation

Inversion/eversion

Figure 26-6 Movements at synovial joints.

Exercise can help combat the effects of aging.

Another change associated with aging is loss of height. Beginning at about age 40, people lose roughly 1.2 cm (0.5 in) of their height every 20 years. This is due mostly to a thinning of the disks between the bodies of the vertebrae.

Common Diseases and Conditions of the Skeletal System

Common diseases and conditions of the skeletal system range from mild sprains or fractures to progressive deteriorating diseases.

Fracture

A *fracture* is a break in a bone, usually caused by an injury. The effects depend on the fracture's location, the severity

Preventing Bone Loss

According to the National Institutes of Health, 44 million Americans suffer from osteoporosis, and an additional 34 million are at risk of developing the disease. Fifty percent of women and twenty-five percent of men age 50 and over will have an osteoporosis-related fracture during their lifetime.

Efforts to prevent osteoporosis include eating a healthy diet, getting enough calcium and vitamin D (which helps the body absorb calcium), and engaging in regular weight-bearing exercise, like walking, running, aerobics, and weight training. These types of exercise stimulate bone growth and also contribute to muscle strength and balance, which helps prevent falls.

Doctors currently prescribe several different drugs to prevent or treat osteoporosis:

- *Bisphosphonates* (bis-FOS-fo-nates) decrease the breakdown of bone tissue.
- *Hormone replacement therapy* in women raises the level of estrogen hormones in the body, slowing bone thinning and increasing bone mass. This approach is used less often now because of safety concerns.

Studies continue to assess how it should be used. In men, testosterone replacement may be used.

- *Selective estrogen receptor modulators* (SERMS) work like estrogen to reduce bone tissue breakdown and increase bone density.
- *Calcitonin*, a naturally occurring hormone that helps regulate calcium levels, can be given to slow the rate of bone loss.
- *Teriparitide*, a form of human parathyroid hormone, helps to build bone.

Over-the-counter calcium supplements also have proven effective in helping to prevent and treat osteoporosis, but they alone may not be enough.

In 2008, the American College of Physicians (ACP) issued new guidelines on drug treatment of low bone density and osteoporosis to prevent fractures. The group evaluated research on the benefits, risk factors, and side effects of these osteoporosis drugs. They found that no one drug had proven better than the others. ACP recommends that doctors and patients work together to select a drug based on the patient's risk factors and preferences.

A promising avenue for current research is a protein called Notch that plays an important role in bone formation.

---

of the break, and other factors. Some fractures may heal on their own and don't need treatment. For others, treatment means realigning the broken bone, which is known as *reduction* of the fracture.

Sprain

A *sprain* is an injury to a joint involving the ligaments. It occurs when a joint is forced out of its normal position, causing ligaments around the joint to stretch and tear. A sprained ankle is the most common type. Like strains, a mild sprain can be treated with RICE.

Osteoporosis

Osteoporosis is a loss of bone mass that weakens the bones, increasing the risk of fractures. A decrease in estrogen hormones after menopause makes women over 50 the most susceptible to this disease. People are often unaware that they have osteoporosis. The first symptom may be a

bone that breaks easily. Osteoporosis is treated with prescription drugs or over-the-counter calcium supplements (see "Newsreel: Preventing Bone Loss").

Osteoarthritis

The most common form of arthritis, *osteoarthritis* is a progressive deterioration of joint cartilage, with growth of new bone and soft tissue in and around the joint. It can be caused by wear and tear, injury, or disease. Symptoms include joint pain and stiffness. Osteoarthritis typically affects joints in the knees, hips, fingers, and spine. Treatment options include analgesics to relieve pain, antiinflammatory agents like corticosteroids, and physical therapy.

✔ CHECK POINT

8 What is a fracture, and what causes it?

9 What is the most freely movable type of joint?

Don't forget to visit the Point companion website for additional study resources!

CHAPTER HIGHLIGHTS

- The muscular and skeletal systems work together to execute movement and to support and protect vital organs.
- The means by which muscles contract and then keep working during exertion involve several body systems and chemicals, as well as mechanical action.
- Health care specialties involving the musculoskeletal system include orthopedic surgeon, radiological technologist, physical therapist, and physical therapist assistant.
- The bones, joints, and supporting connective tissue form the skeletal system. In addition to serving as a framework for the body and playing a role in movement, bones protect delicate structures, store calcium, and make red blood cells.
- There are several types of joints, some of which do not allow movement. Motion occurs at the synovial joints, which are classified according to the types of movement they allow. A second set of terms describes the resulting changes in body part position.
- As people age, muscle size and power decrease, and bones become weaker and more fragile. Less collagen in tendons, ligaments, and skin contributes to the stiffness older people often experience. As people age, they also lose height. Activity and exercise throughout life delay and decrease many undesirable effects of aging.
- Common diseases and conditions of the muscular system include strains and carpal tunnel syndrome. Common diseases and conditions of the skeletal system include fractures, sprains, osteoporosis, and osteoarthritis.

REVIEW QUESTIONS

Matching

1. _____ Connects a muscle to a bone
2. _____ Connects a bone to a bone
3. _____ The point where a muscle is attached to a more movable part of the skeleton
4. _____ The point where a muscle is attached to a more stable part of the skeleton
5. _____ Movement toward the midline of the body

   a. origin   **b.** adduction   **c.** ligament   **d.** tendon   **e.** insertion

Multiple Choice

6. Which is NOT a function of skeletal muscles?
   - **a.** To move bones
   - **b.** To move substances through the body
   - **c.** To maintain posture
   - **d.** To generate heat

7. How does exercise benefit the muscles?
   - **a.** It increases the number of muscles.
   - **b.** It makes muscles bigger and stronger.
   - **c.** It uses up ATP.
   - **d.** It helps people relax.

8. Which type of joint allows movement in two directions?
   - **a.** hinge joint
   - **b.** fibrous joint
   - **c.** condyloid joint
   - **d.** pivot joint

9. Which word is used to describe a bending motion that decreases the angle between bones?
   - **a.** flexion
   - **b.** extension
   - **c.** supination
   - **d.** eversion

10. For which problem might calcium supplements be an appropriate treatment?
    - **a.** carpal tunnel syndrome
    - **b.** oxygen debt
    - **c.** a fracture
    - **d.** osteoporosis

Completion

11. _____ take x-rays and perform other types of imaging tests.

12. The type of bone that makes up the arms and legs is the _____.

13. _____ increases oxygen consumption and leads to improved endurance and improved cardiovascular fitness.

14. Red bone marrow manufactures _____.

15. The type of joint that moves freely is a/an _____.

Short Answer

16. What is the difference in terms of job responsibilities between a physical therapist and a physical therapist assistant?

    _____

    _____

17. Explain how muscles work in pairs, using the biceps brachii and the triceps brachii as an example.

    _____

    _____

18. Sue has multiple sclerosis. Her disorder prevents nerve impulses from arriving at neuromuscular junctions. Based on your understanding of how muscles function, explain why one of her symptoms is muscle atrophy, a wasting or decrease in muscle size.

    _____

    _____

19. List the five main functions of bones.

    _____

    _____

20. Explain the differences between the terms in each of the following pairs:
    - **a.** sprain and strain
    - **b.** epiphysis and diaphysis
    - **c.** axial skeleton and appendicular skeleton

    _____

    _____

INVESTIGATE IT

1. Most body structures lie beneath the skin. A technique called *landmarking* allows health care providers to locate many internal body structures more easily. Bony prominences, or landmarks, can be palpated (felt) beneath the skin to serve as reference points for locating other internal structures. Landmarking is used during physical examinations and surgeries, when

giving injections, and for other clinical procedures. Practice landmarking on yourself by feeling for these bony prominences:

- Feel for the joint between the mandible and the temporal bone of the skull (the temporomandibular joint, or TMJ) anterior to the ear canal as you move your lower jaw up and down.
- Feel for the notch in the sternum (breast bone) between the clavicles (collar bones). Approximately 4 cm (1.5 inches) below this notch you will feel a bump called the sternal angle. This prominence is an important landmark because its location marks where the trachea splits to deliver air to both lungs. Move your fingers lateral to the sternal angle to palpate the second ribs, important landmarks for locating the heart and lungs.
- Feel for the most lateral bony prominence of the shoulder, called the acromion process of the scapula (shoulder blade). Two to three fingerbreadths down from this point is the correct injection site into the deltoid muscle of the shoulder.
- Place your hands on your hips and palpate the iliac crest of the hip bone. Move your hands forward until you reach the anterior end of the crest, called the anterior superior iliac spine (ASIS). Feel for the part of the bony pelvis that you sit on. This is the ischial tuberosity. It and the ASIS are important landmarks for locating safe injection sites in the gluteal region.

2. Many people exercise regularly. Still, there's often room for improvement. Use the Internet or library resources to evaluate the exercise you get. Are you exercising enough? Does your routine include aerobic, muscle-strengthening, and flexibility exercise? Design a better exercise routine for yourself. A good place to start is http://www.healthierus.gov/exercise.html.

3. Anabolic steroids are prescribed legally to help muscles regenerate and to prevent atrophy from disuse after surgery. However, some athletes also purchase them illegally, using them to increase muscle size and strength and improve endurance. How do anabolic steroids work? What are the positive and negative effects of using them? Two web sites that may be helpful are listed below.
http://www.nlm.nih.gov/medlineplus/anabolicsteroids.html
http://www.usatoday.com/news/graphics/steroids/flash.htm

RECOMMENDED READING

Centers for Disease Control and Prevention. Physical Activity. Available at: http://www.cdc.gov/physicalactivity.

Loyola University Medical Education Network. Master Muscle List. Available at: http://www.meddean.luc.edu/lumen/MedEd/GrossAnatomy/dissector/mml/mmlregn.htm.

MyHealthScore.Com. Skeletal System (Front View). Human Anatomy Online. Available at: http://www.innerbody.com/image/skelfov.html.

NOVA. *NOVA: The Universe Within.* Boston: WGBH Boston; 2004.

San Diego State University College of Sciences. Actin Myosin Crossbridge 3D Animation. Available at: http://www.sci.sdsu.edu/movies/actin_myosin.html.

U.S. National Library of Medicine and National Institutes of Health. Muscles. Available at: http://www.nlm.nih.gov/medlineplus/tutorials/muscles/htm/index.htm.

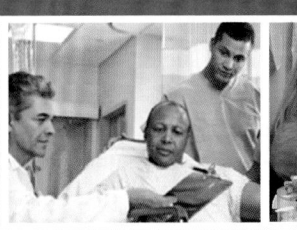
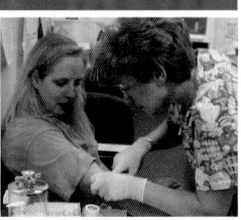

Coordination and Control

27 CHAPTER

CHAPTER OBJECTIVES

After careful study of this chapter, you should be able to:

* Describe the organization of the nervous system.
* Name the four main divisions of the brain.
* Identify four lobes of the brain and cite one function of the cerebral cortex in each.
* Describe the function of the sensory system.
* Differentiate between the special and general senses and give examples of each.
* List and describe the structures of the eye and structures that protect the eye.
* Describe the three divisions of the ear.

* Compare the effects of the nervous system and the endocrine system in controlling the body.
* Describe the functions of hormones.
* Identify the endocrine glands on a diagram.
* List the hormones produced by each endocrine gland and describe their effects on the body.
* Explain how aging affects the nervous, sensory, and endocrine systems.
* Identify common diseases and conditions of the nervous system, special senses, and the endocrine system.

KEY TERMS

aqueous (A-kwe-us) humor
autonomic nervous system
axon
central nervous system
cerebral cortex
cerebrum (SER-e-brum)
choroid (KO-royd)
cochlea (KOK-le-ah)

cornea (KOR-ne-ah)
endocrine glands
Eustachian (u-STA-shun) tube
external auditory canal
hormone
hypothalamus
iris (I-ris)
lacrimal (LAK-rih-mal) glands

lens
neurotransmitter
ossicles (OS-ih-klz)
parasympathetic nervous system
peripheral nervous system
pinna
pituitary (pih-TU-ih-tar-e) gland
pupil

receptor
retina (RET-ih-nah)
sclera (SKLE-rah)
semicircular canals
somatic nervous system
sympathetic nervous system
tympanic (tim-PAN-ik) membrane
vitreous (VIT-re-us) body

The nervous system and the endocrine system coordinate and control all other body systems. Together, they regulate responses to the environment and maintain homeostasis. As you learned in Chapter 25, "The Body as a Whole," homeostasis is a steady state, the normal operating conditions that organisms strive to maintain in order to function well.

The nervous system controls actions such as muscle movement and intestinal activity. It does this rapidly by means of electric impulses and locally released chemicals called **neurotransmitters** The effects of the endocrine system occur more slowly and over a longer period. This system acts by circulating hormones, chemical messengers that have widespread effects on the body.

The sensory system, which is part of the nervous system, is the body's network for detecting external and some internal stimuli. This system helps maintain homeostasis, provides pleasure, and helps protect the body from harm. Pain, for example, is an important warning sign of tissue damage. The sensory system includes the organs of special sense and other sensory receptors. The signals generated in these receptors are transmitted to the central nervous system for interpretation.

THE NERVOUS SYSTEM

None of the body's systems can function alone. They all depend on one another, and they work together to maintain homeostasis. Conditions inside and outside the body are constantly changing. The nervous system must detect and respond to these changes (*stimuli*) so the body can adapt to new conditions.

The nervous system is the chief coordinating agency for all body systems. Its components function like the parts of a large corporation. Market researchers (sensory receptors) send information to middle management (the spinal cord), which transmits it to the chief executive officer, or CEO (brain). The CEO organizes and interprets the information and sends directions to workers (*effectors*—muscles or glands) that carry out appropriate actions for the good of the company. In the process, emails and memos, like the nerves, carry information throughout the system.

Organization of the Nervous System

The nervous system has two anatomic, or structural, divisions (Figure 27-1):
- The **central nervous system** (CNS) includes the brain and spinal cord.
- The **peripheral nervous system** (PNS) is made up of all the nerves and nervous tissue outside the CNS. It includes all the cranial nerves that carry impulses to and from the brain and all the spinal nerves that carry messages to and from the spinal cord.

The CNS and PNS together include all the nervous tissue in the body.

Functionally, the nervous system can be divided into two parts:
- The **somatic nervous system** controls skeletal muscles (described in Chapter 26, "Protection, Movement, and Support"). This system is under a person's voluntary control.
- The **autonomic nervous system** (ANS) controls glands, the smooth muscles of hollow organs and vessels, and the heart muscle. It regulates responses to stress and helps to maintain homeostasis. When a change occurs that calls for a regulatory adjustment, the ANS makes it without a person being aware of it.

The ANS itself has two divisions:
- The **sympathetic nervous system** controls the body's response to stress, the so-called fight-or-flight response. In the face of danger, or excitement, it increases the heart and respiration rates, stimulates the adrenal gland, and delivers more blood to skeletal muscles.
- The **parasympathetic nervous system** returns the body to a steady state and stimulates maintenance activities, like digesting food.

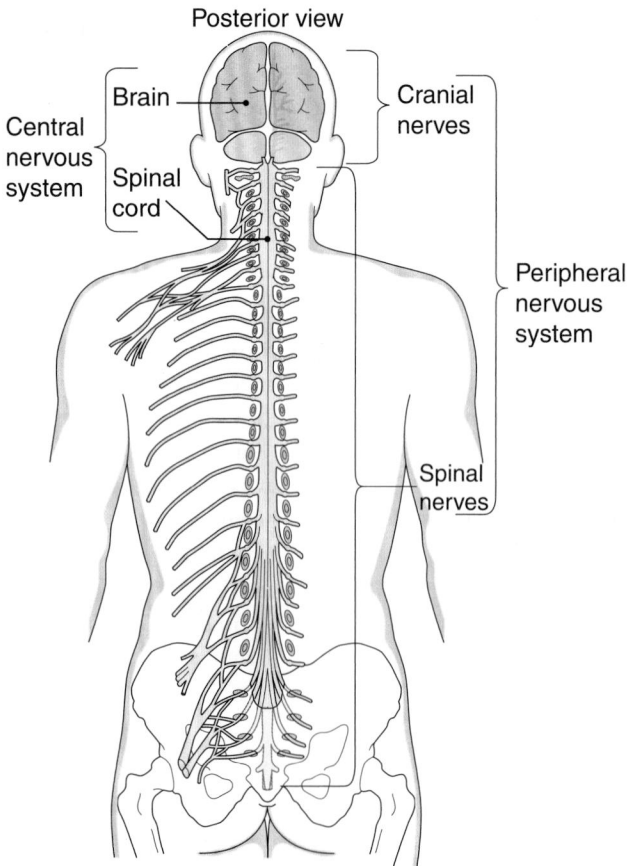

Figure 27-1 Anatomic divisions of the nervous system.

Most organs are controlled by both the sympathetic and parasympathetic systems. Generally, the two systems have opposite effects on a given organ.

The division of the nervous system into somatic and autonomic parts is useful for study and reference. Still, the differences aren't as clear-cut as they appear. For example, the diaphragm, a skeletal muscle that is under the control of the somatic nervous system, can function in breathing without a person's conscious effort.

The Spinal Cord

The spinal cord is the link between many parts of the peripheral nervous system and the brain. It also helps to coordinate impulses within the CNS. The spinal cord is contained in and protected by the vertebrae, which fit together to form a continuous tube extending from the occipital bone (at the base of the skull) to the coccyx, or tailbone. (The spinal cord itself does not extend all the way down to the coccyx.)

The Brain

The brain is the nervous tissue contained within the cranial cavity. It is covered and protected by membranes, fluid, and the skull bones. The brain has four main parts: the *cerebrum*, *diencephalon* (di-en-SEF-ah-lon), *brainstem*, and *cerebellum* (ser-eh-BEL-um).

The largest part is the **cerebrum**. It is divided into two hemispheres, each of which is further subdivided into lobes. The thin outer layer of the cerebrum is the cerebral cortex. The **cerebral cortex** is where conscious thought, memory, reasoning, and abstract thought take place; where voluntary actions arise; and where information from the senses is processed and interpreted.

NEWSREEL

Regrowing Nerves

According to a study completed in 2009 by the University of New Mexico's Center for Development and Disability, nearly 1.3 million Americans live with spinal cord injuries. A typical spinal cord injury damages the vertebrae, which crush and destroy **axons,** the long fibers that conduct impulses away from a neuron's body. Additional harm, including destruction of neurons, results from the body's reaction. Spinal cord injuries almost always result in a loss of sensory function, motor function, or both. Some, like that sustained by *Superman* actor Christopher Reeve when he fell from a horse in 1995, leave large parts of the body paralyzed.

Because neurons have little or no capacity to repair themselves, therapy has focused on managing spinal cord injuries rather than curing them. Current research raises exciting possibilities for treating spinal cord injuries by stimulating nerves to regrow. Several different directions are being taken in research.

Using nerve growth factor to induce repair. Some nervous system cells produce chemicals that aid in nerve cell repair. In experiments, delivering these chemicals to injured neurons causes them to generate new axons.

"Turning off" chemicals that keep axons from growing. In the adult CNS, certain proteins block axon growth. The purpose seems to be to safeguard the system and to prevent existing axons from growing inappropriately. Current research explores ways of blocking or removing these proteins or changing the way the growing axon responds to them.

Drawing on genes that other animals use to regenerate. Another approach looks at animals that are capable of regenerating nerve cells to isolate the genes that trigger that action. In a study reported in 2009, University of Utah scientists identified genes in worms that are necessary for damaged nerve cells to regenerate. They used one of these genes to speed regrowth of nerve cells. Humans possess this same gene.

Producing neurons and repairer cells from stem cells. Stem cells have the capacity to develop into any of a variety of different cell types. Adult and fetal stem cells can evolve into a limited number of cell types, while embryonic stem cells can evolve into any type of cell. In 2009, the Food and Drug Administration approved the first human clinical trial using embryonic stem cells as a therapy for spinal cord injuries.

Growing neurons face several obstacles. Axons need guidance to grow along the proper pathways and make the right connections. A multidisciplinary team in Canada is attempting to develop a microchip to perform this function. A second problem is scar tissue that can block the way of new or regenerating axons. A recent experiment successfully used bacterial enzymes to clear a path through scar tissue. Another experiment used a gel to create a scaffold for axons to use to climb across an injury. When researchers injected this gel into the spinal cord of injured mice, the axons grew all the way across a spinal cord injury.

The lobes of the brain are named for the skull bones under which they lie. Although the different areas of the brain act in a coordinated way to produce behavior, the cerebral cortex area of each lobe is responsible for specific functions. Some of these are described below.

- The *frontal lobe* contains the primary motor area, which allows people to control their skeletal muscles. It also has two areas for speech.
- The *parietal lobe* contains the primary sensory area, where impulses from the skin, like touch, pain, and temperature, are interpreted. The estimation of distances, sizes, and shapes also takes place here.
- The *temporal lobe* contains the auditory area for receiving and interpreting impulses from the ear, as well as the olfactory area, concerned with smell.
- The *occipital lobe* has a visual area for receiving and interpreting impulses from the retina of the eye.

Effects of Aging

Natural changes occur in the nervous system as people age. The brain decreases in size and weight due to loss of cells. Information is processed less rapidly, and movements are slowed. There is also a slowing of thought and memory. For each person, the degree of these changes, and the parts of the nervous system that are affected, can vary significantly. The nervous system has vast reserves, and most older adults are able to cope with life's demands.

Common Diseases and Conditions of the Nervous System

Disorders of the nervous system range from minor inconveniences to lethal diseases. Three of the most common are stroke, seizures, and Alzheimer's disease.

Stroke

A *stroke* is any occurrence that deprives brain tissue of oxygen. Such events include blockage in a vessel that supplies the brain, a ruptured blood vessel, or some other damage that leads to hemorrhage in the brain. Symptoms, which occur suddenly, may include numbness or weakness, particularly on one side of the body, confusion, difficulty speaking or understanding, vision problems in one or both eyes, difficulty walking, dizziness, loss of balance or coordination, and a severe headache.

When a stroke results from a blood clot or hemorrhage, doctors may try to halt the stroke in progress by dissolving the clot or stopping the bleeding. Post-stroke treatment is aimed at helping people overcome the dis-

abilities that the stroke causes. The most common treatment is medication or drug therapy. Rehabilitation may be needed to help stroke victims recover some or all of their previous capabilities. Strokes and other cerebrovascular diseases are the second leading cause of death in developed countries. They also are a leading cause of paralysis and other neurological disabilities.

Seizures

Seizures are sudden attacks that result from an abnormal firing of nerve impulses in the brain. Most people associate seizures with twitching, losing muscle control, falling, and losing consciousness. But symptoms can vary widely, depending on the part of the brain affected. In most cases, seizures are mild and very brief and may include the following symptoms:

- Not being able to remember a period of time
- Experiencing sudden, unexplained panic or fear
- Seeing flashing lights

Seizures can have many causes, including head injuries, infections, epilepsy, and alcohol or drug withdrawal. Recurrent seizures are generally treated with anti-seizure medications.

Alzheimer's Disease

Alzheimer's disease results from an unexplained deterioration of neurons and atrophy (wasting) of the cerebral cortex. These changes, which usually appear after age 60, cause progressive loss of recent memory, confusion, changes in mood and behavior, and an eventual inability to carry out the tasks of daily life.

The causes of Alzheimer's disease are not yet fully understood. But they probably include genetic, lifestyle, and environmental factors. Doctors are not yet able to

HEALTH CARE SPECIALTY

Electroneurodiagnostic (END) Technologist

When an injury or suspected disease affects the brain, a physician often orders an *electroencephalogram* (e-lek-tro-en-SEF-ah-lo-gram), or EEG. This test records the brain's electrical activity. The person who performs it is an electroneurodiagnostic (END) technologist. EEGs and related procedures range from all-night studies for sleep disorders to monitoring brain activity during surgery. END technologists need initiative, good judgment, and reasoning skills.

cure the disease or stop its progress, but there are drugs for treating symptoms. An estimated 2.4 to 4.5 million Americans have Alzheimer's disease. That number is expected to grow as the number of older people rises.

1 The nervous system can be divided functionally into two divisions. Which division is under a person's control and controls skeletal muscle, and which division is involuntary and controls involuntary muscles and glands?

2 What are the two divisions of the nervous system based on structure?

THE SENSORY SYSTEM

The sensory system protects a person by detecting changes in the environment. An environmental change becomes a stimulus when it initiates a nerve impulse, which travels to the central nervous system (CNS) by way of a nerve. A stimulus becomes a sensation—something we experience—only when a specialized area of the cerebral cortex interprets the nerve impulse received. Many stimuli arrive from the external environment and are detected at or near the body surface. Others originate internally and help the body maintain homeostasis.

There are many different senses in the body. They can be classified according to the distribution of their **receptors**, specialized cells or nerve endings that can be excited by a stimulus. Special senses are localized in special organs; general senses are distributed widely throughout the body.

● **Special senses**
  • Vision from receptors in the eye
  • Hearing from receptors in the inner ear
  • Equilibrium from receptors in the inner ear
  • Taste from receptors in the tongue
  • Smell from receptors in the upper nasal cavity
● **General senses**
  • Pressure, temperature, pain, and touch from receptors in the skin and internal organs
  • Sense of position from receptors in the muscles, tendons, and joints

Vision

The sensory organ with receptors for vision is the eye. Like other sensory organs, the eye is protected by several structures. The bones that form the eye's cavity protect the posterior part of the eyeball. The eyelashes, eyebrow, and eyelids keep out harmful materials. The **lacrimal glands** produce tears, which lubricate the eye and contain an enzyme that protects against infection.

Figure 27-2 shows the parts of the eye. The wall of the eye is composed of three layers. From outermost to innermost, they are as follows:
● The **sclera**, or white of the eye, is made of tough connective tissue. It extends over the eye's anterior

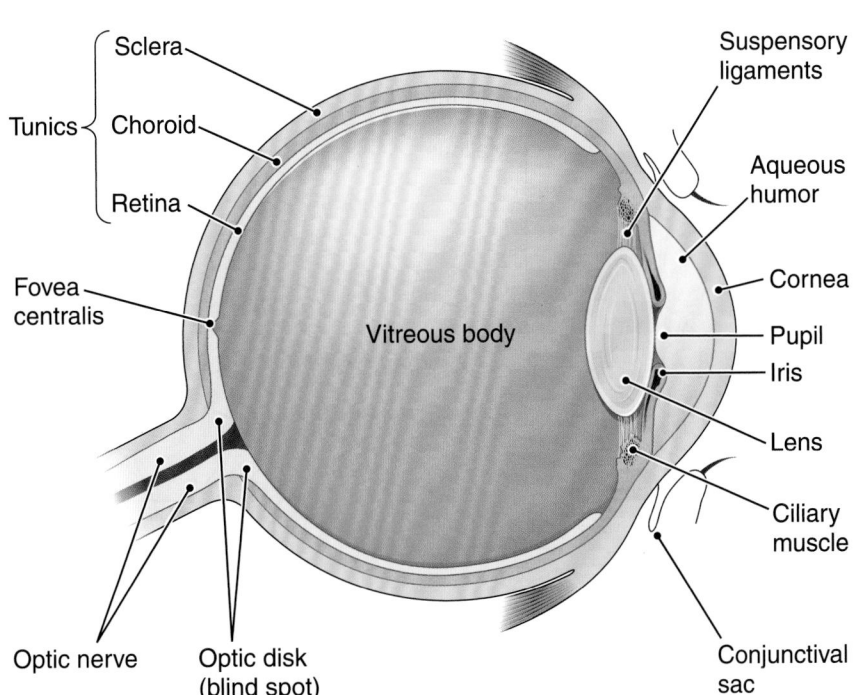

Figure 27-2 The eye.

portion as the transparent **cornea**, often referred to as the window of the eye.

- The **choroid**, the middle layer, provides nourishment for the retina.
- The **retina** is the innermost layer and the actual visual receptor. It contains two types of specialized cells, *rods* and *cones*, which respond to light. Proper vision requires the *refraction* (bending) of light rays as they pass through parts of the eye to focus on a specific point in the retina. Impulses generated within the rods and cones are transmitted to the brain by the *optic nerve*.

The **iris** is a muscular ring that controls the size of the **pupil** (the circular opening in the center of the eye), thereby regulating the amount of light that enters the eye. The genetically controlled pigments of the iris determine eye color.

The **lens**, which is located behind the iris, is a clear structure with two bulging surfaces. It refracts light and focuses it for near or far vision. The **aqueous humor** is a fluid that fills the eye anterior to the lens, maintaining the shape of the cornea and refracting light. The eyeball is filled with a jellylike **vitreous body** that helps maintain the eye's shape and helps refract light.

Six muscles attached to the outside of each eye coordinate eye movements to achieve *convergence*—coordinated movement of the eyes so they are both fixed on the same point.

Hearing and Equilibrium

The sense organ for both hearing and equilibrium, or balance, is the ear (Figure 27-3). It has three main sections:

- The *outer ear*, with the outer projection and canal
- The *middle ear*, which contains three small bones and a tube
- The *inner ear*, which has the sensory receptors for hearing and equilibrium

The outer ear consists of the projecting **pinna** and the **external auditory canal**. This canal ends at the **tympanic membrane**, or eardrum, which transmits sound waves to the middle ear.

Spanning the middle ear cavity are three **ossicles** (small bones). They are joined in such a way that they amplify the sound waves received from the eardrum as they transmit those sounds to the inner ear. The **Eustachian tube** connects the middle ear with the throat, or *pharynx* (FAR-inks). It equalizes pressure between the outer and middle ear.

The inner ear consists of an outer bony framework containing a channel filled with fluid. The **cochlea** contains the actual organ of hearing, the *organ of Corti* (KOR-te). The hearing receptors in this organ respond to sound waves traveling through the fluid-filled ducts of the cochlea. The resulting impulses travel to the brain via the *vestibulocochlear nerve*.

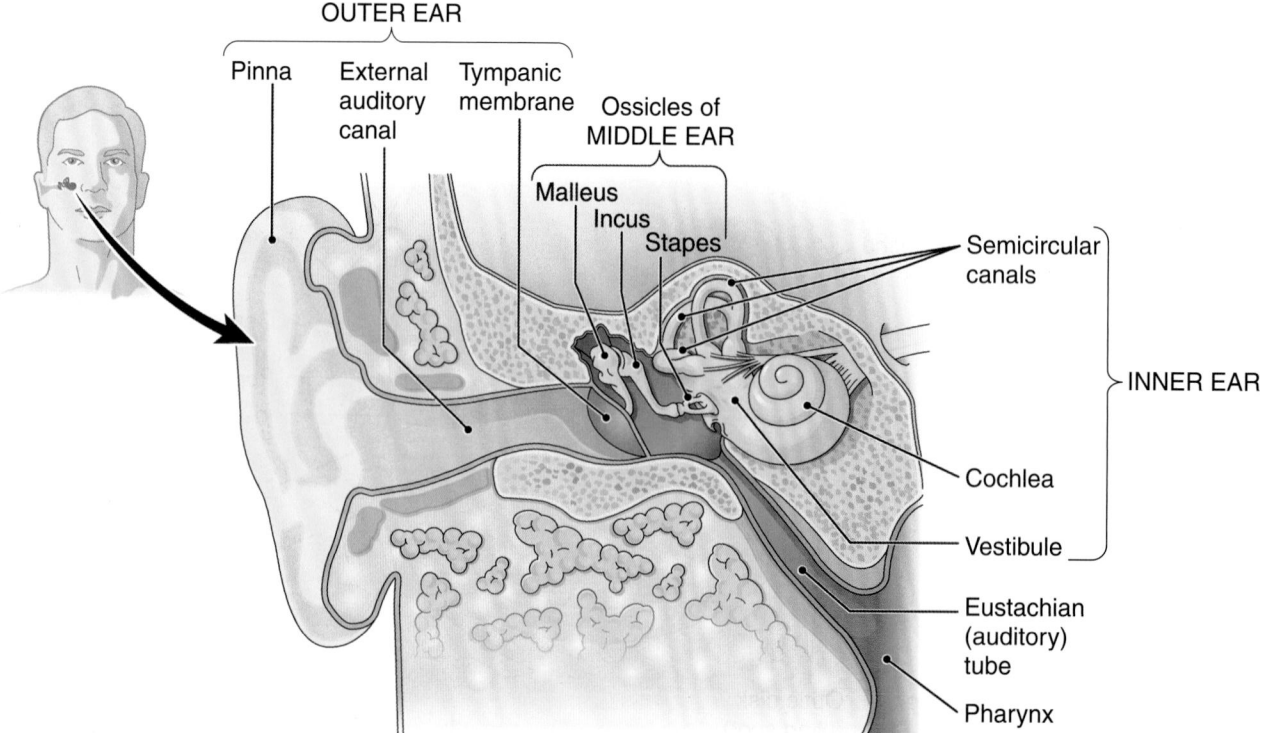

Figure 27-3 The ear.

The sense of equilibrium is located in the *vestibule* and three projecting **semicircular canals**. Special receptors in this area respond to movement. They transmit signals to the brain through the vestibulocochlear nerve.

Taste

Taste, or *gustation* (gus-TA-shun), involves receptors in the tongue known as taste buds. These receptors detect sweet, salty, sour, and bitter tastes. Researchers have recently identified receptors for a few other tastes, including water. The sense organs of taste and smell are designed to respond to chemical stimuli. Both senses are important in stimulating appetite and warning of harmful substances.

Smell

Receptors for the sense of smell, or *olfaction* (ol-FAK-shun), are located in the epithelium of the nasal cavity's superior region. Because these receptors are high in the nasal cavity, a person must sniff to bring odors upward in the nose. Like the sense of taste, the sense of smell is designed to respond to chemical stimuli (different odors) in a way that protects or assists the body.

General Senses

The receptors for the general senses are found throughout the body. These include receptors for pressure, heat, cold, pain, touch, and position. These receptors transmit information either to the brain or to the spinal cord, where they may trigger automatic, or reflex, responses. An example is the reflex that causes you to jerk back your hand if you touch a hot stove.

Pressure

Even when the skin is anesthetized, it can still respond to pressure stimuli. The receptors for deep touch are located in the subcutaneous tissues beneath the skin and near joints, muscles, and other deep tissues.

Temperature

Temperature receptors are widely distributed in the skin. There are separate receptors for heat and cold.

Pain

Pain is the most important protective sense. The receptors for pain are found in the skin, muscles, and joints and, to a lesser extent, in most internal organs.

Touch

Touch receptors are found mostly in the dermis of the skin and around hair follicles. Touch sensitivity varies with the number of touch receptors in different areas.

Position

Receptors in muscles, tendons, and joints relay impulses that aid in judging one's position and changes in the location of body parts in relation to each other. They also inform the brain of the amount of muscle contraction and tendon tension. This information is needed to coordinate muscles and is important for walking, running, and many more complicated skills, like playing a musical instrument. It also helps in assessing the weight of an object that a person wants to lift so the right amount of force is used.

Effects of Aging

Aging is accompanied by many changes in the senses. The olfactory receptors deteriorate with age, and the sense of taste may decrease. Consequently, food may become less appealing. Additionally, temperature control and perception of pain and pressure become less efficient.

As people grow older, the structures of the eye change. The lens loses elasticity, so that focusing clearly on close objects becomes difficult. This is a common vision problem associated with aging that can be corrected with glasses. Older people may also be more sensitive to glare and less able to adjust to darkness, and they may have decreased depth perception. Cataracts (KAT-a-rakts) occur frequently with age (see "Common Diseases and Conditions of the Special Senses").

Many older adults have some hearing loss. Hearing may, for example, become less sharp, and it may become more difficult to hear when there is background noise, as in a busy restaurant. Exposure to loud noises through one's life can produce persistent ringing or other noises in the ears, known as *tinnitus* (tin-I-tus). Some people lose their hearing gradually as they get older. While the exact cause is unknown, this type of hearing loss appears to run in families. Older adults may also have difficulty with balance, coordination, fine movements, and spatial orientation, resulting in an increased risk for falls.

Common Diseases and Conditions of the Special Senses

Problems with the special senses are usually treatable and not life-threatening. Four of the most common are cataracts, glaucoma, otitis media, and vertigo. Cataracts and glaucoma occur often in older people. Otitis media affects mostly young children. Vertigo can affect adults of all ages.

Cataract

A *cataract* is an opacity (cloudiness) of the eye's lens. Common symptoms of cataracts are blurry vision, fading of colors, difficulty seeing at night, double vision in one eye, frequent eyeglass prescription changes, and problems with glare. Causes include disease, injury, chemicals, and environmental factors, especially the ultraviolet radiation in sunlight. In older people, cataracts may result from exposure to environmental factors combined with age-related degeneration.

Some cataracts can lead to blindness. In such cases, an ophthalmologist must remove the cloudy lens surgically. An artificial lens is usually implanted.

Glaucoma

Glaucoma is an abnormal increase in pressure within the eyeball. It occurs when more aqueous humor is produced than can be drained away. The increased amount of fluid puts pressure on blood vessels in the eye and on the optic nerve, leading to blindness. Glaucoma can have many causes.

Glaucoma often has no early symptoms. It can be detected in a thorough eye exam, however, so a glaucoma screening should be part of every routine eye exam. Glaucoma is usually treated with medication to reduce pressure in the eye and sometimes with surgery.

Otitis Media

Otitis media (o-TI-tis ME-de-a) is an inflammation of the middle ear with a buildup of fluid in the middle ear cavity. It may begin with an infection that spreads to the middle ear, most often from the upper respiratory tract. Among young children, symptoms include tugging at the ears and crying more than usual. Other symptoms are drainage from the ear and trouble sleeping, hearing, or maintaining balance. This disorder can result in hearing loss. If not treated with antibiotics, the infection may spread to other regions of the ear and head. For persistent cases, inserting a tube in the tympanic membrane helps to ventilate and drain the middle ear cavity, preventing infection from recurring.

Vertigo

Vertigo is an illusion of movement, such as the body moving in space or the environment moving about the body. The word is used loosely to mean dizziness or lightheadedness, but true vertigo includes a false sense of movement.

HEALTH CARE SPECIALTIES

Audiologist, Audiometric Technician, and Ophthalmologist

Audiologists specialize in preventing, diagnosing, and treating hearing disorders that may be caused by injury, infection, birth defects, noise, or aging. Most audiologists have a master's degree. The *Occupational Outlook Handbook* reports that a doctoral degree is becoming more common for individuals newly entering this career. *U.S. News and World Report* named audiologist as one of its 30 best careers of 2009.

Audiometry testing is often done when a hearing loss is reported or suspected. An audiometer (device used to test hearing) emits different tones. Patients, wearing headphones, signal when they hear a tone. An audiometric technician may perform this work. This career is profiled briefly in Chapter 17, "Overview of Health Care Careers."

An ophthalmologist is a physician who specializes in eye and vision care. Ophthalmologists conduct vision examinations and diagnose and treat eye diseases and injuries. They prescribe glasses and contact lenses, and they also perform eye surgery. After graduating from medical school, ophthalmologists must undergo four years of residency to train in their specialty.

Vertigo can have many causes. The most common are benign postural vertigo, caused by a disturbance in the inner ear, and labyrinthitis, caused by a viral infection of the inner ear following a cold or flu. Treatments vary depending on the cause. Two options are medications from a doctor and physical therapy.

✔ CHECK POINT

3 What are the names of the layers of the eye?

4 What are the ossicles of the ear, and what do they do?

THE ENDOCRINE SYSTEM

The endocrine system works with the nervous system to help regulate the body's activities. It consists of a widely distributed group of glands (Figure 27-4) that produce hormones. Because the hormones are released directly into surrounding tissue fluids, the **endocrine glands** are known as ductless glands, as compared to glands that secrete through ducts, like sweat glands and digestive glands. From the tissue fluids, most hormones diffuse into the bloodstream, which carries them throughout the

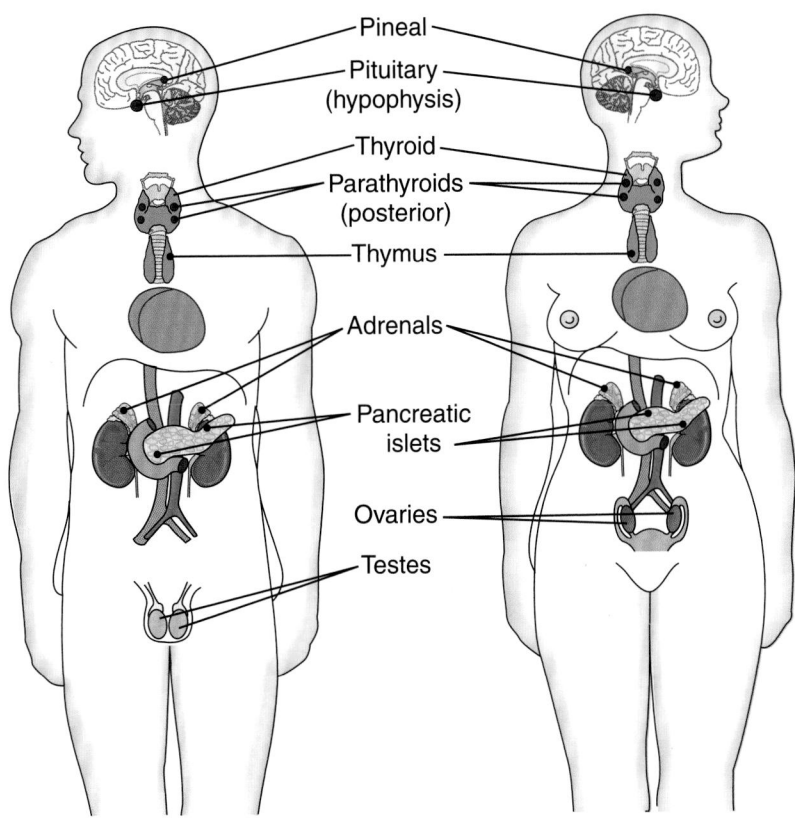

Pineal
Pituitary (hypophysis)
Thyroid
Parathyroids (posterior)
Thymus
Adrenals
Pancreatic islets
Ovaries
Testes

Figure 27-4   The endocrine glands.

body. These hormones affect *metabolism* (all the physical and chemical reactions that occur within an organism), growth, and development.

Hormones

Hormones are chemical messengers that have specific regulatory effects on certain cells or organs. Although hormones circulating in the blood are carried to all parts of the body, only certain tissues respond to a specific hormone. The tissue that is influenced by a particular hormone is the *target tissue*. The cells in a target tissue have specific receptors on their membranes or within the cell to which the hormone attaches, enabling its effects.

Endocrine Glands

The endocrine glands make nearly two dozen hormones. Production is controlled mainly by negative feedback. That is, the hormone itself, or a product of its activity, acts to control further manufacture of the hormone. Table 27-1 (following page) lists the endocrine glands, along with the hormones they secrete and their functions. Figure 27-4 shows their locations.

The **pituitary gland** is often called the master gland because it releases hormones that affect the working of other glands. The pituitary gland is controlled by the part of the brain called the **hypothalamus**. The hypothalamus forms a link between the endocrine and nervous systems and helps maintain homeostasis.

HEALTH CARE SPECIALTIES

Medical Assistant and Licensed Practical Nurse

Two occupations that provide care for patients are medical assistant and licensed practical nurse, or LPN. Medical assistants combine administrative functions with basic clinical tasks to keep a doctor's office running smoothly. LPNs perform many routine nursing duties under the direction of a doctor or registered nurse. For example, a medical assistant or LPN may test a patient's blood sugar with a glucose meter. The meter lets the physician know the blood glucose level of the patient, which is important if the patient has diabetes.

A New "Epidemic"

The word *epidemic* brings to mind communicable diseases like cholera, polio, or plague. The latest addition to that sinister list is diabetes. Diabetes is a disorder in which the pancreas makes too little insulin or none at all, or the body's cells aren't able to use properly the insulin produced by the body. Insulin is a hormone needed to move glucose, the body's main source of fuel, from the blood into the cells and to help process it. Diabetes can cause serious health problems.

In 2007, an estimated 23.6 million Americans—7.8 percent of the population—had diabetes, and the number of new cases is rising rapidly. From 1997 to 2003, it increased by 41 percent. The drastic rise in the number of diabetes diagnoses has led people to call it an "epidemic," though that term is technically not correct, because diabetes is not a communicable disease.

One of the factors driving this increase is the increasing number of older Americans. As a group, older people have a higher risk of developing Type 2 diabetes, by far

the most common type. A recent study by Duke University Medical Center found that over a period of about eight years, the number of Americans older than 65 who were diagnosed with diabetes increased 23 percent.

A second key factor is the rise in obesity (having too much body fat). Obesity is another high-risk factor for diabetes. In the 1960s, obesity occurred in 13 percent of American adults. Recent statistics from the federal government show that more than 34 percent of American adults are now obese.

Diabetes is a leading cause of death and disability among Americans. The Centers for Disease Control and Prevention predict that if current trends continue, 1 in 3 Americans will develop diabetes in their lifetime, and those with diabetes will lose, on average, 10 to 15 years of life.

In 2007, diabetes cost the U.S. $174 billion. The increasing number of patients; newer, more expensive drugs; and a trend toward using multiple medications to manage the disease resulted in a near-doubling of costs over six years. Prevention of diabetes is becoming a national priority.

Effects of Aging

Aging has many effects on the endocrine system, including a decrease in hormone production and secretion and an alteration in hormone metabolism. Many older adults develop Type 2 diabetes as a result of decreased insulin secretion, which is made worse by poor diet, inactivity, and increased body fat. Some older people also show effects of decreased thyroid hormone production, such as fatigue, dry skin, and forgetfulness.

Common Diseases and Conditions of the Endocrine System

Endocrine diseases usually result from the overproduction or underproduction of hormones. They also may result from secretion at the wrong time or from failure of the target tissue to respond.

Diabetes Mellitus

Diabetes mellitus is a disorder in which glucose accumulates in the blood because of a deficiency of insulin production or failure of the tissues to respond to insulin. The body attempts to expel the excess glucose through increased urination, causing dehydration and excessive thirst. A person with diabetes also may experience weakness, weight loss, and extreme hunger. If

untreated, diabetes will lead to starvation of the CNS and coma. Diabetic patients are prone to cardiovascular, neurologic, and visual problems; as well as infections and kidney failure.

There are two main types of diabetes mellitus. Type 1 is an *autoimmune disease*—a disease in which the body's system for fighting infections turns against the body. It has an abrupt onset and usually appears in children and teenagers. Type 2 is far more common, accounting for 90 to 95 percent of all diabetes cases. Most Type 2 cases are linked to obesity, especially upper-body obesity. Although seen mostly in older people, the incidence of Type 2 diabetes is increasing among younger generations, presumably because of increased obesity, poor diet, and sedentary habits (see "Newsreel: A New Epidemic"). Type 1 is managed through blood sugar monitoring and doses of insulin. Type 2 often can be managed through exercise and weight loss. Drugs for increasing insulin production or improving cellular responses to insulin may also be prescribed, with insulin treatment given if necessary.

Hypothyroidism

Hypothyroidism results from too little secretion of the thyroid hormone, which affects the growth and function of many tissues. This condition can be *congenital* (present at birth) or acquired. Infants with congenital

Table 27-1 The Endocrine Glands and Their Hormones

Gland	Hormones	Main Functions
anterior pituitary	GH (growth hormone)	Promotes growth of all body tissues
	TSH (thyroid-stimulating hormone)	Stimulates thyroid gland to produce thyroid hormones
	ACTH (adrenocorticotropic hormone) (ad-re-no-kor-tih-ko-TRO-pik)	Stimulates cortex of adrenal glands to produce hormones; helps protect body in stress situations (injury, pain)
	FSH (follicle-stimulating hormone)	Stimulates development of eggs in ovaries and sperm cells in testes
	LH (luteinizing hormone) (LU-te-in-i-zing)	Causes ovulation in females and sex hormone secretion in both males and females
	PRL (prolactin) (pro-LAK-tin)	Stimulates milk production in the breasts
posterior pituitary	ADH (antidiuretic hormone) (an-ti-di-u-RET-ik)	Acts on kidneys to conserve water; stimulates blood vessels to constrict
	oxytocin (ok-se-TO-sin)	Makes uterus contract; promotes milk "letdown" in breasts
thyroid	thyroxine (T_4) and triiodothyronine (T_3) (thi-ROK-sin, tri-i-o-do-THI-ro-nene)	Increase metabolic rate in cells; required for normal growth
	calcitonin (kal-sih-TO-nin)	Decreases calcium level in blood
parathyroids	parathyroid hormone	Regulates exchange of calcium between blood and bones; increases calcium level in blood
adrenal medulla	epinephrine and norepinephrine	Active in response to stress; increase respiration, blood pressure, and heart rate
adrenal cortex	cortisol	Raises levels of nutrients in blood; active during stress; reduces inflammation
	aldosterone (al-DOS-te-rone)	Makes kidneys conserve sodium and water while eliminating potassium
	sex hormones	May influence secondary sexual characteristics, like facial hair in males and wider hips in females
pancreatic islets	insulin (IN-su-lin)	Aids transport of glucose into cells; required for cells to process foods, especially glucose; decreases blood sugar levels
	glucagon (GLU-kah-gon)	Increases blood sugar levels
testes	testosterone (tes-TOS-te-rone)	Stimulates growth and development of sexual organs plus development of secondary sexual characteristics; stimulates maturation of sperm cells
ovaries	estrogens (ES-tro-jens)	Stimulate growth of primary sexual organs and development of secondary sexual characteristics
	progesterone (pro-JES-ter-one)	Assists in normal development of pregnancy
thymus	thymosin (THI-mo-sin))	Promotes growth of T cells needed for immunity
pineal	melatonin (mel-ah-TO-nin)	Regulates mood, sexual development, and daily sleep-wake cycles in response to environmental light

hypothyroidism are usually diagnosed at birth and treated. If not, hypothyroidism can lead to mental retardation within six months.

In adults, thyroid deficiency causes myxedema, a condition characterized by weight gain, lethargy, rough, dry skin, hair loss, and facial swelling. The person may have reproductive problems and muscular weakness, pain, and stiffness. A common cause of hypothyroidism in adults is autoimmune destruction of the thyroid. Hypothyroidism is easily treated with thyroid hormone.

Hyperthyroidism

Hyperthyroidism occurs when the thyroid gland makes more thyroid hormone than the body needs. The most common form is Graves disease, an autoimmune disorder. Symptoms include weight loss, irritability, hand tremors, and rapid heart rate. A distinctive sign is a bulging of the eyeballs caused by swelling of tissues behind the eyes. Treatment for Graves disease may include drugs, surgery, or radiation delivered in the form of radioactive iodine.

✔ **CHECK POINT**

5 What is the effect of thyroid hormones on cells?

6 What two hormones produced by the islets of the pancreas act to regulate glucose levels in the blood?

ZOOM IN

Home Glucose Monitors

People with diabetes need to check their blood glucose levels frequently. If the levels rise too high, a person can become ill. A basic tool for managing diabetes is the home glucose monitor. The person pricks a finger with a small needle called a lancet, puts a drop of blood on a test strip, and then puts the strip on a meter that displays the blood sugar level. The person can use the results of the test to make decisions about food, medicine, and physical activity.

Don't forget to visit the Point. companion website for additional study resources!

CHAPTER HIGHLIGHTS

- The nervous and endocrine systems coordinate and control all other body systems. Together, they regulate responses to the environment and maintain homeostasis.
- The nervous system controls actions like muscle movement and intestinal activity, using electric impulses and locally released neurotransmitters. The effects of the endocrine system occur more slowly and over a longer period via circulating hormones with widespread effects on the body.
- The nervous system detects and responds to stimuli from both inside and outside the body. Sensory data travel via the spinal cord and cranial nerves to the brain for processing. The brain organizes and interprets them and sends "directions" via the nerves to the muscles or glands to respond.
- The sensory system is a part of the nervous system that detects stimuli. It consists of the special senses (vision, hearing, equilibrium, taste, and smell), which are localized in special organs, and the general senses (pressure, temperature, pain, touch, and sense of position), which are found throughout the body.
- The endocrine system consists of a widely distributed group of glands that produce hormones, released mostly into the bloodstream. These hormones have specific regulatory effects on certain cells or organs, influencing metabolism, growth, and development.
- Health care specialties involving the nervous and endocrine systems include END technologist, audiologist, auditory technician, ophthalmologist, medical assistant, and LPN.
- The nervous and endocrine systems are affected by aging. Natural changes in the brain slow thought processes and memory, but most older adults can cope. Sensory changes often include some hearing loss. Problems with near vision, correctable with glasses, are also common. Many older adults develop Type 2 diabetes, due partly to decreased insulin secretion.
- Common diseases and conditions of the nervous system include stroke, seizures, and Alzheimer's disease. Common diseases and conditions of the special senses include cataracts, glaucoma, otitis media, and vertigo. Common diseases and conditions of the endocrine system include diabetes mellitus, hypothyroidism, and hyperthyroidism.

REVIEW QUESTIONS

Matching

1. _____ Links the peripheral nervous system and the brain
2. _____ Receptor cells of the retina
3. _____ Eardrum
4. _____ Links the endocrine and nervous systems
5. _____ Nerve cell fibers

   a. tympanic membrane   **b.** axons   **c.** spinal cord   **d.** rods and cones   **e.** hypothalamus

Multiple Choice

6. Skeletal muscles are voluntarily controlled by the
   - **a.** central nervous system
   - **b.** somatic nervous system
   - **c.** parasympathetic nervous system
   - **d.** sympathetic nervous system

7. The fight-or-flight response is promoted by the
   a. sympathetic nervous system
   b. parasympathetic nervous system
   c. somatic nervous system
   d. frontal lobe

8. All of the following are special senses EXCEPT
   a. smell
   b. taste
   c. equilibrium
   d. pain

9. Which health care specialist may take part in all-night studies for sleep disorders?
   a. LPN
   b. medical assistant
   c. END technologist
   d. audiologist

10. Which disease or condition is common among older adults?
    a. Type 1 diabetes
    b. cataract
    c. vertigo
    d. otitis media

Completion

11. The brain and spinal cord make up the _____.

12. Higher functions of the brain occur in the _____.

13. A/an _____ is any occurrence that deprives brain tissue of oxygen.

14. A/an _____ is a physician who specializes in eye and vision care.

15. Chemical messengers carried by the blood are called _____.

Short Answer

16. Compare and contrast the sympathetic and parasympathetic divisions of the autonomic nervous system in terms of their functions.

    _____

    _____

17. Why has diabetes become an epidemic?

    _____

    _____

18. Explain the differences between the terms in each of the following pairs:
    a. special sense and general sense
    b. aqueous humor and vitreous body
    c. insulin and glucagon
    d. testosterone and estrogen

    _____

    _____

19. What are the main differences between how the nervous system and the endocrine system regulate body functions?

    _____

    _____

20. Describe two effects of aging on the sensory system.

    _____

    _____

INVESTIGATE IT

1. Through biofeedback, people can be trained to control consciously certain functions that are normally controlled by the body automatically. This 40-year-old technique is enjoying new popularity as a treatment for conditions such as migraines, high blood pressure, hypertension, and stress. There are even pocket-size gadgets that people can use to teach themselves. Find and read a news article about biofeedback.

2. The brain stores information, much of which can be recalled on demand through memory. What do scientists know about memory? How does it work? Investigate one of the topics below. Two web sites that may be helpful follow the list of topics.
   * How memories are recorded
   * What parts of the brain are involved
   * Sensory memory
   * Short-term memory—how much can be stored and how long it lasts
   * Why some memories are stronger or more easily recalled than others
   * Why people forget
   * How memories are recalled
   * How memory can be improved
   * Current research

   "The Brain from Top to Bottom" (choose "Memory and the Brain")
   http://thebrain.mcgill.ca/flash/index_d.html
   "How Human Memory Works"
   http://health.howstuffworks.com/human-memory1.htm

3. Some hormones are used for medical treatment. They may be extracted from animal tissues or manufactured in commercial laboratories. A few are produced by the genetic engineering technique of recombinant DNA. Choose two hormones from the following list. Compare and contrast their roles in the body with their use in medicine. To find information about medical uses, do a search on the Internet using the name of the hormone and the word *treatment*.
   * growth hormone
   * insulin
   * adrenal steroids
   * epinephrine
   * thyroid hormones
   * oxytocin
   * androgens
   * estrogen and progesterone

RECOMMENDED READING

Aamodt, S., and S. Wang. *Welcome to Your Brain: Why You Lose Your Car Keys but Never Forget How to Drive and Other Puzzles of Everyday Life*. New York: Bloomsbury USA, 2008.

Howard Hughes Medical Institute. Seeing, Hearing, and Smelling the World. Available at: http://www.hhmi.org/senses.

MyHealthScore.Com. Endocrine System. Human Anatomy Online. Available at: http://www.innerbody.com/image/endoov.html.

MyHealthScore.Com. Nervous System. Human Anatomy Online. Available at: http://www.innerbody.com/image/nervov.html.

Neuroscience for Kids. (Interesting for adults, too.) Available at: http://faculty.washington.edu/chudler/introb.html#bb.

NOVA. Obesity. NOVA: Science Now. Available at: http://www.pbs.org/wgbh/nova/sciencenow/3313/03.html.

Tenenbaum, D.J. Disgusting—but Cool Science! The Why Files. February 26, 2009. Available at: http://whyfiles.org/shorties/278disgust.

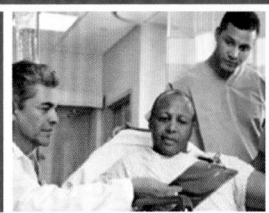
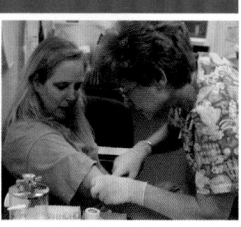

Circulation and Body Defense

28 CHAPTER

CHAPTER OBJECTIVES

After careful study of this chapter, you should be able to:

* List the functions of the circulatory system.
* Compare the functions of the right and left sides of the heart.
* Name the four chambers of the heart and compare their functions.
* Briefly describe the cardiac cycle.
* Name the valves at the entrance and exit of each ventricle and explain their function.
* Name and locate the components of the heart's conduction system.
* Explain how aging affects the heart.
* List the functions of blood.
* Identify the main ingredients in plasma.
* Name and describe the three types of formed elements in the blood and state the function of each.

* Define *blood type* and explain the relation between blood type and transfusions.
* List the five types of blood vessels and their functions.
* Explain the forces that affect exchange across the capillary wall.
* Explain how blood pressure is commonly measured.
* List the functions of the lymphatic system.
* Explain how lymphatic capillaries differ from blood capillaries.
* List the major structures of the lymphatic system and give the location and functions of each.
* Identify common diseases and conditions of the heart and lymphatic system.

KEY TERMS

antibody
antigen (AN-ti-jen)
arteriole
artery
atrium (pl. atria) (A-tre-um, A-tre-ah)
capillary
cardiac cycle
coagulation

diastole (di-AS-to-le)
erythrocyte (eh-RITH-ro-site)
formed elements
hematocrit (he-MAT-o-krit)
hemoglobin (he-mo-GLO-bin)
immunity
leukocyte (LU-ko-site)

lymph (limf)
lymph node
lymphocyte
phagocytosis (fag-o-si-TO-sis)
plasma
platelet (thrombocyte) (THROM-bo-site)
serum

sinus rhythm
spleen
systole (SIS-to-le)
thymus (THI-mus) gland
tonsil
vein
ventricle (VEN-trih-kle)
venule (VEN-ule)

everal systems are involved in the movement of materials through the body. The blood is the main transport medium. It circulates through the cardiovascular system, which consists of the heart and blood vessels.

The lymphatic system helps to balance body fluids by bringing substances from the tissues back to the blood. Both the blood and lymphatic systems also play key roles in the body's defenses against disease and are critical to the survival of tissues and cells.

THE CIRCULATORY SYSTEM

The circulatory system, which is made up of the cardiovascular and lymphatic systems, is the body's system for transportation. It might be compared to a city's bus system. Buses travel around the city, picking up and delivering passengers at each stop on their route. Similarly, as blood flows through the lungs, it picks up oxygen and unloads carbon dioxide. It carries that oxygen throughout the body, where it unloads that gas to tissues that need it and picks up carbon dioxide and other substances. The cardiovascular system (the blood vessels and heart) forms a continuous circuit in which blood is carried to and from the tissues.

The other part of the circulatory system, the lymphatic system, is like a special one-way bus route. It picks up passengers only—excess fluids and proteins in the body tissues—and carries them to the veins, where they join the bloodstream.

The circulatory system transports these substances:

- **Oxygen and nutrients.** Oxygen from inhaled air passes into the blood through thin membranes in the lungs. Then it is carried by the blood to all body tissues. The blood also transports nutrients and other needed substances, like electrolytes (salts) and vitamins, to the cells. These materials enter the blood from the digestive system or are released into the blood from the body's reserves.
- **Carbon dioxide and other waste products.** Carbon dioxide, a waste product of cell metabolism, is carried by the blood from the tissues to the lungs, where it is exhaled. The circulatory system also transports waste products like excess fluids, acid, and hormones from the cells to special structures for removal.
- **Hormones and antibodies.** The blood carries hormones from their sites of origin to the organs they affect. It also carries **antibodies**, infection-fighting cells that give long-term **immunity**, or protection, against some diseases.

THE HEART

The heart (Figure 28-1) is the prime mover, the force that propels blood throughout the body. It is enclosed in the thoracic cavity for protection. The heart is a double-sided, hollow muscular pump with four chambers.

Chambers of the Heart

Health care professionals often refer to the *right heart* and the *left heart*, because the human heart is really a double pump. The right side pumps blood low in oxygen to the lungs. The left side pumps oxygenated blood to the remainder of the body. Each side has two chambers. Each upper chamber, called an **atrium** (plural *atria*), is mainly a blood-receiving chamber. The lower chambers, called the **ventricles**, are forceful pumps. Table 28-1 describes the location of the chambers and how blood flows through the heart.

✓ CHECK POINT

1 What is the function of the circulatory system? Of the heart?

2 The heart is divided into four chambers. What is the upper receiving chamber on each side called? What is the lower pumping chamber called?

The Cardiac Cycle

A heartbeat begins with the contraction of both atria, which forces blood into the ventricles. Immediately after the atria contract, both ventricles contract, pumping blood out of the heart.

While the atria contract, the ventricles relax. This phase is known as **diastole**. While the ventricles contract, the atria relax. This phase is known as **systole**. After the ventricles have contracted, all chambers are relaxed for a short period as the atria fill with blood. Then the heart beats again.

One complete sequence of heart contraction and relaxation is called the **cardiac cycle** (Figure 28-2, page 4). Each cardiac cycle represents a single heartbeat. At rest, one cycle takes an average of 0.8 seconds.

Heart Valves

One-way valves in the heart keep blood moving in a forward direction. The atrioventricular (a-tre-o-ven-TRIK-u-lar) (AV) valves are located at the entrance of each ventricle, between the atria and the ventricles. The semilunar (sem-e-LU-nar) valves are located at the exit of each ventricle, leading into the pulmonary artery and aorta. Table 28-2 (page 4) describes the location, structure, and function of these four valves, which are illustrated in Figure 28-1.

✓ CHECK POINT

3 The cardiac cycle consists of an alternating pattern of contraction and relaxation. What name is given to the contraction phase of the ventricles? What name is given to the relaxation phase of the ventricles?

4 What is the purpose of valves in the heart?

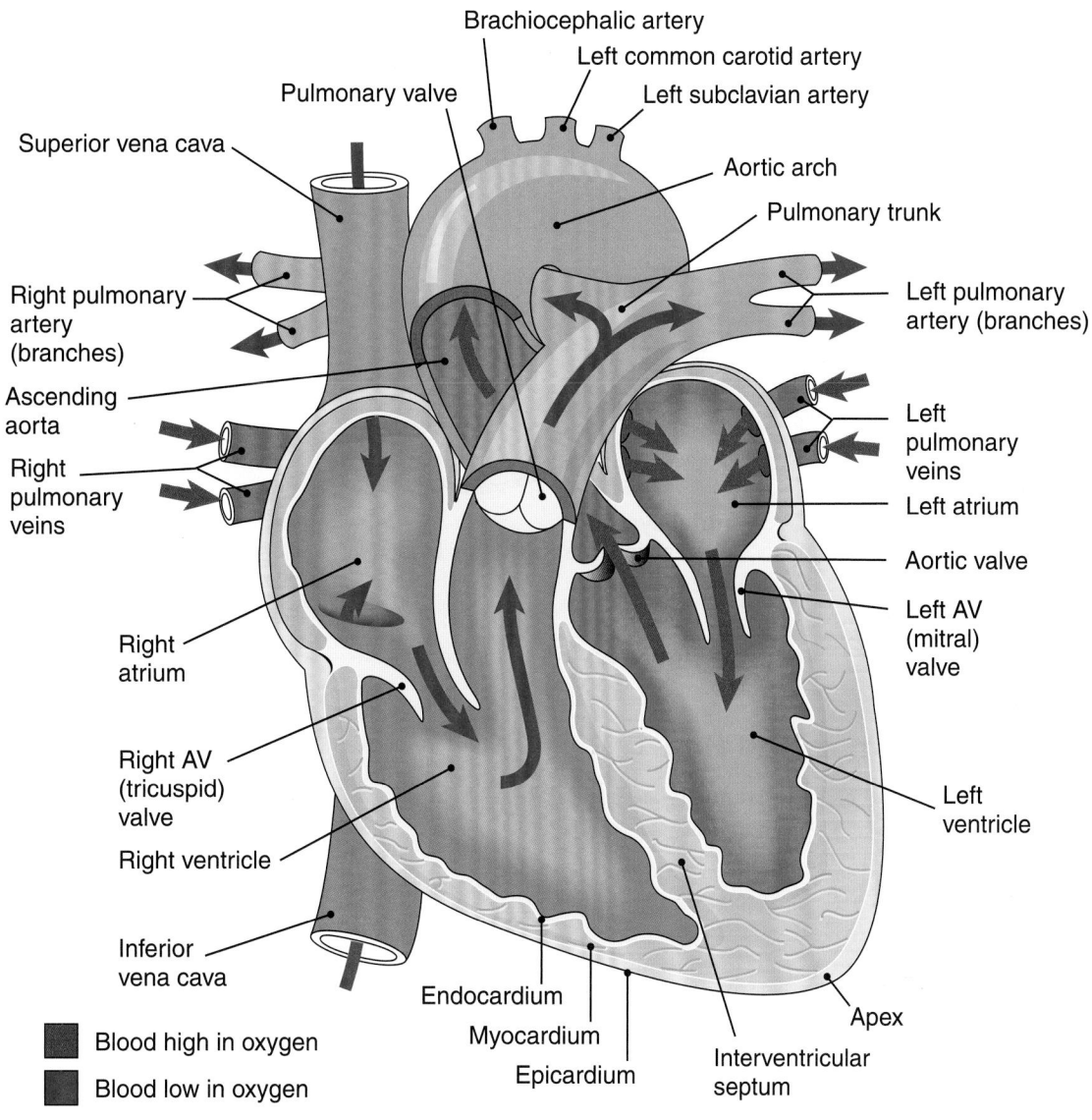

Figure 28-1 The heart and great vessels.

Table 28-1 Chambers of the Heart		
Chamber	**Location**	**Blood Flow**
Right atrium	Upper right	1. The right atrium receives blood low in oxygen from all body tissues through the superior vena cava (VE-nah KA-vah) and the inferior vena cava. Blood moves from it to the right ventricle.
Right ventricle	Lower right	2. The right ventricle pumps blood to the lungs through the pulmonary artery.
Left atrium	Upper left	3. Blood high in oxygen returns from the lungs through the pulmonary veins and enters the left atrium. From there, it flows to the left ventricle.
Left ventricle	Lower left	4. The left ventricle forcefully pumps the oxygenated blood into the aorta to be distributed to all the tissues.

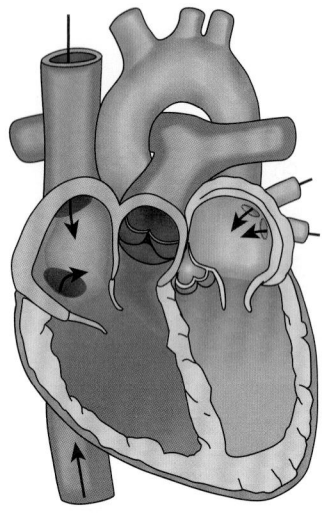 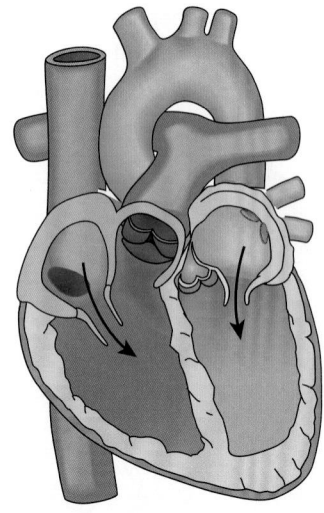 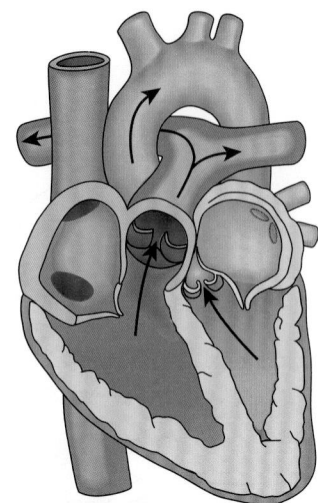

Diastole
Atria fill with blood, which begins to flow into ventricles as soon as their walls relax.

Atrial systole
Contraction of atria pumps blood into the ventricles.

Ventricular systole
Contraction of ventricles pumps blood into aorta and pulmonary arteries.

Figure 28-2 The cardiac cycle.

Conduction System of the Heart

Like other muscles, the heart muscle is stimulated to contract by a wave of electrical energy (an action potential) that passes along its cells. The conduction system of the heart is illustrated in Figure 28-3. The sequence of events that make up a heartbeat is as follows:

1. The *sinoatrial (SA) node* generates the electrical impulse that begins the heartbeat. The SA node is commonly called the pacemaker because it sets the rate of heart contractions.

2. The excitation wave travels throughout the muscle of each atrium, causing the atria to contract. At the same time, impulses travel to the *atrioventricular (AV) node*.

3. The AV node is stimulated. A slower rate of conduction through this node allows time for the atria to contract and fill the ventricles before the ventricles contract.

4. The excitation wave travels rapidly through the *atrioventricular (AV) bundle (bundle of His)* and then throughout the ventricular walls by means of the *right and left bundle branches* and the *Purkinje* (pur-KIN-je) *fibers*, causing the ventricles to contract.

Heart Rate

A normal heart rate originating at the SA node is called a **sinus rhythm**. For an adult, when the body is at rest, an average normal heart rate ranges from 60 to 100 beats per minute. It can be as low as 30 in athletes and much higher

Table 28-2 Valves of the Heart			
Valve	**Location**	**Description**	**Function**
Right AV (tricuspid) valve	Between the right atrium and right ventricle	Valve with three cusps (flaps)	Prevents blood from flowing back up into the right atrium when the right ventricle contracts (systole)
Left AV (mitral or bicuspid) valve	Between the left atrium and left ventricle	Valve with two cusps	Prevents blood from flowing back up into the left atrium when the left ventricle contracts (systole)
Pulmonary semilunar valve	At the entrance to the pulmonary artery	Valve with three cusps shaped like half-moons	Prevents blood from flowing back into the right ventricle when the right ventricle relaxes (diastole)
Aortic semilunar valve	At the entrance to the aorta	Valve with three cusps shaped like half-moons	Prevents blood from flowing back into the left ventricle when the left ventricle relaxes (diastole)

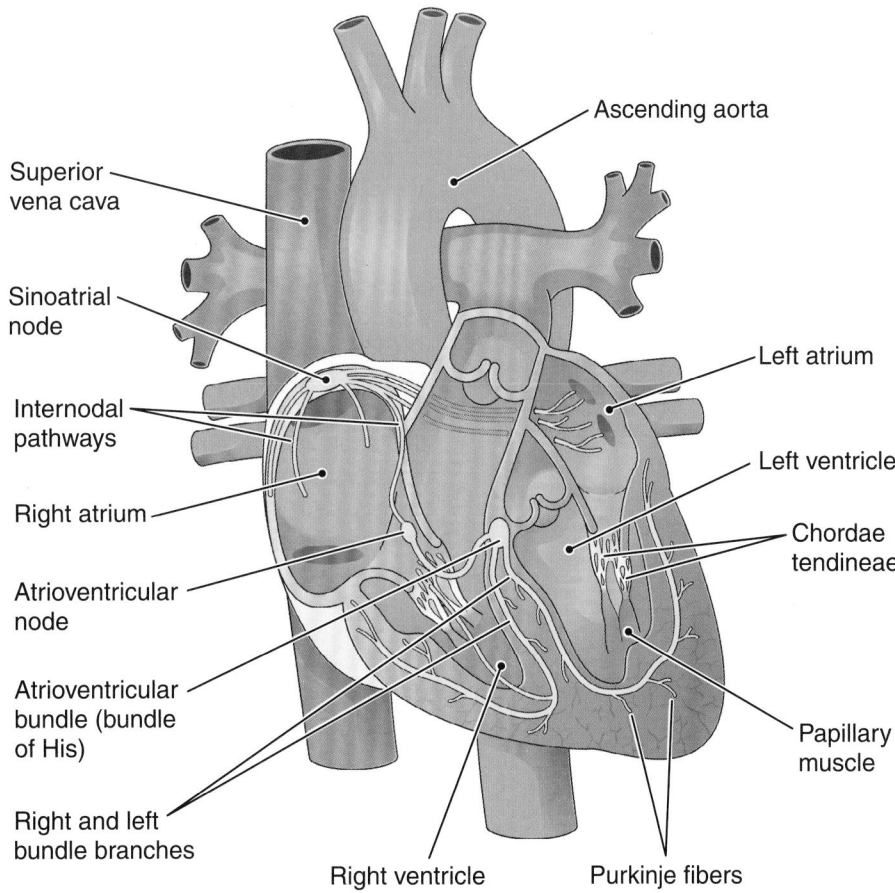

Superior vena cava

Ascending aorta

Sinoatrial node

Left atrium

Internodal pathways

Right atrium

Left ventricle

Atrioventricular node

Chordae tendineae

Atrioventricular bundle (bundle of His)

Right and left bundle branches

Papillary muscle

Right ventricle

Purkinje fibers

Figure 28-3 Conduction system of the heart.

in young children and still be normal. Though the heart's fundamental beat originates within the heart itself, it can be influenced by the nervous system, hormones, and other factors. The autonomic nervous system plays a major role in modifying the heart rate in response to increased activity or other needs.

Bradycardia is a slower-than-average heart rate, the kind of rate that might occur during rest and sleep. Tachycardia is a higher-than-average rate, normal during exercise or stress. But bradycardia or tachycardia can also indicate a medical problem.

Effects of Aging

How the heart ages varies widely, depending on heredity, environmental factors, diseases, and personal habits. Generally, it gradually loses muscle fiber and elasticity, and calcium builds up on heart valves. As a result, contractions aren't as strong, and the valves become less flexible, so they may not close completely. Valves not closing completely can produce an abnormal sound (a heart *murmur*) that can be heard with a stethoscope. The murmur may or may not require treatment, depending on which valve is leaking and how much. Additionally, the heart often

has less reserve strength with age, limiting an older person's ability to respond to physical or emotional stress.

 HEALTH CARE SPECIALTIES

Cardiovascular Technologist and Cardiovascular Technician

Cardiovascular technologists and technicians perform tests that aid in diagnosing cardiovascular disease. Cardiovascular technicians perform EKGs. Cardiovascular technologists carry out ultrasound scans of the heart and blood vessels. They also assist in invasive testing and treatment procedures. For example, a cardiologist may suspect that a person is having blood flow problems to the heart after a heart attack or another heart-related problem. To assess blood flow within the heart muscle, the cardiologist may perform a cardiac catheterization, a procedure that involves threading a small tube through a blood vessel and guiding it toward the heart (see "Zoom In: Cardiac Catheterization"). Cardiovascular technologists assist during the procedure by monitoring blood pressure and heart rate, as well as performing other tasks.

CPR and AED

Each year, millions of people are trained by the American Heart Association (AHA) and others in cardiopulmonary resuscitation, or CPR. CPR is a technique used to temporarily circulate blood through the body when the heart has stopped. Conventional CPR has two components: rescue breathing and chest compressions. In 2009, AHA introduced hands-only CPR, a simplified technique consisting only of chest compressions. According to AHA, effective CPR done by a bystander can double a victim's chance of surviving a heart attack.

Defibrillation is the process of using electric shock to restore normal heart rhythm, as is often needed after a heart attack. Once, only trained medical professionals could use this technique. But in recent years, automated external defibrillator (AED) devices, small, portable, and easy to use, have cropped up in offices, hospitals, schools, and many other places, from amusement parks to shopping malls. The devices recognize when a shock is needed and guide the rescuer through the steps, using voice cues, lights, and text messages.

CPR and AED require only a few hours of training. AHA's CPR Anytime program takes 22 minutes. Certification in CPR and AED is required for health care professionals. People in many other occupations, such as lifeguards, rescue workers, daycare providers, coaches, and physical trainers, usually need to know CPR. Often, people who've had the training say they never thought they'd need to use it—and then, they save somebody's life.

Common Diseases and Conditions of the Heart

Heart disease is the leading cause of death in the U.S., accounting for more than one in four deaths each year. The good news is that nearly everyone can take steps to lower the risk of heart disease. Some common heart conditions are described below.

Myocardial Infarction

A *myocardial infarction* (MI), or heart attack, occurs when one or more of the coronary arteries become partially or totally blocked. This usually results from *arteriosclerosis*, the buildup, over the years, of fatty material in an artery wall, which causes a blood clot to form. The clot reduces or blocks blood flow to the heart, and heart tissue begins to die from lack of oxygen. Symptoms of MI include pain over the heart or upper abdomen that may extend to the jaw or arms. Other symptoms include paleness, profuse sweating, nausea, and difficulty breathing. The possibility of surviving an MI depends on the degree of damage and the speed of treatment to dissolve the clot and to reestablish normal blood flow and rhythm.

Congestive Heart Failure

Congestive heart failure (CHF) is a condition in which the heart does not pump effectively. CHF can affect either side of the heart—or, most often, both sides. Right-side heart failure makes it harder for the heart to pump blood to the lungs to get oxygen. It can cause swelling in the lower extremities. Left-side failure affects the pumping of blood to body tissues. It can cause breathing difficulties. Other symptoms of CHF include fatigue, a bluish discoloration of the skin caused by lack of oxygen, and fainting.

The most common causes of CHF are coronary artery disease, high blood pressure, and diabetes. There is no cure; treatment is aimed at relieving symptoms and preventing permanent damage. CHF is treated with rest, drugs to strengthen heart contractions and eliminate fluid, and restriction of salt in the diet.

Angina Pectoris

Angina pectoris is a condition marked by a feeling of tightness around the heart or pain that may radiate to the left arm or shoulder. It can also feel like indigestion. Angina pectoris is often accompanied by anxiety, sweating, and difficulty breathing. It occurs when the heart muscle doesn't get enough blood and is usually brought on by exertion. Treatment includes drugs and medical procedures to treat underlying heart disease, as well as lifestyle changes such as losing weight and stopping smoking.

Arrhythmia

Arrhythmia is any irregularity of heart rhythm, such as tachycardia, bradycardia, extra beats, or an alteration in the beat's pattern. Most arrhythmias are harmless. But some can be fatal if they're not treated at once. Others aren't immediately dangerous but can become more serious over time, because an arrhythmia can impair the heart's ability to pump blood throughout the body. Arrhythmias can have many causes, including high blood pressure, heart disease, smoking, too much caffeine or

Cardiac Catheterization

Cardiac catheterization is a common procedure used to diagnose and treat certain heart disorders. A physician (usually a cardiologist) inserts a flexible tube called a catheter into a blood vessel in the patient's arm, groin, or neck and guides the tube gently toward the heart. Once the catheter is in place, the physician injects a special dye to show blood flow. A C-shaped x-ray unit moves around the chest, taking radiographs from different angles. The physician can see how effectively blood is flowing and whether there's a buildup of fatty material in any of the vessels. The catheter also may be used to measure pressure in the heart's chambers and pulmonary artery, to take samples of blood or heart muscle, or to perform minor surgery, such as a balloon angioplasty (described in Chapter 22, "Diagnostic and Imaging Services").

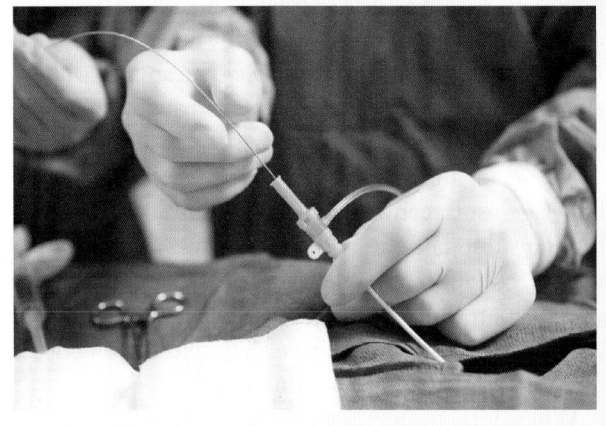

Catheter insertion.

alcohol, drug abuse, and stress. Serious arrhythmias are usually treated with drugs or medical procedures.

5 What is a heart murmur?

6 The heartbeat is started by a small mass of tissue in the upper right atrium. This structure is commonly called the pacemaker. What is its scientific name?

BLOOD AND BLOOD VESSELS

Blood is essential in maintaining homeostasis. This life-giving fluid brings nutrients, oxygen, and other needed substances to the cells and carries waste away. Circulating blood serves the body in three ways: transportation, regulation, and protection.

- **Transportation.** Blood is the body's main method of transport. Circulating through the blood vessels, it brings oxygen and nourishment to every cell and takes carbon dioxide and other waste products away for disposal.
- **Regulation.** Chemicals in the blood called *buffers* help keep the acid/base balance (pH) of body fluids steady at about 7.4. (The actual range of blood pH is 7.35 to 7.45.) The blood also regulates the amount of fluid in the tissues through proteins and other substances. Finally, the blood transports heat generated in the muscles to other parts of the body, helping to regulate body temperature.
- **Protection.** Blood plays a key role in defending the body against disease. It carries the cells and antibodies of the immune system that protect against disease-causing

organisms. The blood also contains cell fragments and proteins called clotting factors that play a key role in clotting, or **coagulation**, which stops bleeding.

Constituents of the Blood

The blood has two main components: the liquid portion, or **plasma** (55 percent), and **formed elements**, which include blood cells and cell fragments (45 percent).

Plasma

Plasma is about 91 percent water. Many different substances, dissolved or suspended in the water, make up the other 9 percent. These substances are nutrients, electrolytes (dissolved salts), gases (mostly oxygen and carbon dioxide), albumin (a protein), clotting factors, antibodies, enzymes that work with antibodies, wastes, and hormones. Blood chemistry tests check for many of these substances.

Formed Elements

The cells and cell fragments that make up the blood's formed elements are erythrocytes, leukocytes, and platelets. They are all produced in the red bone marrow. Some leukocytes also multiply in lymphoid tissue. Most blood cells live only a short time, so they must be replaced constantly.

- **Erythrocytes**, from the Latin *erythro*, meaning "red," are the red blood cells. They are small, disk-shaped cells and are by far the most numerous of the blood cells.

  The main function of erythrocytes is to carry oxygen to cells. The oxygen is bound to **hemoglobin**, a protein containing iron. It is hemoglobin, combined with oxygen, that makes blood red. The hemoglobin in red blood cells has two additional functions. It acts as a buffer, playing an important role in acid-base balance. It also carries some carbon dioxide from the tissues to the lungs.

- **Leukocytes,** from the Latin *leuko,* meaning "white," are the white blood cells. They are round, colorless, and larger than red blood cells.

  The main function of leukocytes is to protect the body against infection by destroying invaders. When a foreign substance enters the tissues, such as through a wound, certain types of leukocytes are attracted to the area. In a process called **phagocytosis,** they engulf and digest the invaders. Leukocytes also clear the body of foreign material and cellular debris.

  When foreign organisms invade, the bone marrow and lymphoid tissue go into emergency production of white blood cells, and their numbers increase enormously. One type of white blood cell makes the circulating antibodies needed for immunity.

- **Platelets,** also called **thrombocytes,** are the smallest of the formed elements. They are not complete cells, but cell fragments.

  Platelets help prevent blood loss. When a vessel is injured, platelets stick together to form a plug at the site. Substances released from the platelets and from damaged tissue interact with clotting factors in the plasma to produce a wound-sealing clot. Clotting factors are inactive in the blood until an injury occurs.

Hematocrit

The **hematocrit** is the volume percentage of red blood cells in whole blood. A hematocrit of 40 percent, for example, indicates that 40 percent of the total blood volume consists of red blood cells. The remaining 60 percent is plasma, white blood cells, and platelets. For adult men, the normal range is 42 percent to 54 percent. For adult women, it is 36 percent to 46 percent.

The hematocrit is determined by spinning a blood sample in a high-speed centrifuge for 3 to 5 minutes to separate the formed elements from the plasma. This test is used to diagnose anemia, leukemia, and other medical conditions (see "Common Diseases of the Blood").

✔ CHECK POINT

7 Why is hemoglobin an important part of red blood cells?

8 What is the hematocrit, and what can it show?

Blood Types

Genetically inherited proteins on the surface of red blood cells determine a person's blood type. The blood types

HEALTH CARE SPECIALTY

Clinical Laboratory Technologist

Blood tests are ordered to screen for or diagnose medical problems and to monitor their progress. The person who performs these tests is often a clinical laboratory technologist. These health care professionals also analyze the results of tests and communicate them to the physician. They may determine values and monitor treatment, such as drug levels, to verify that a patient is adhering to a prescribed drug regimen or to provide a physician with feedback on the effect a treatment is having. Tests might be performed for early disease detection or to assess a patient's health status, such as with cholesterol measurements.

are named for these proteins. More than 20 groups of proteins have been identified, but the most familiar are the ABO and Rh blood groups.

These genetically inherited proteins are **antigens,** substances that provoke the formation of antibodies, an immune response. In giving blood transfusions, it is important to use blood that is the same type as the recipient's blood or a type to which the recipient will not have an immune reaction. Otherwise, the patient's immune system may produce antibodies that will attack the donated red blood cells.

ABO Blood Type Group

The ABO group includes types A, B, AB, and O (Table 28-3). If only the A antigen is present, the person has type A blood. If only the B antigen is present, the person has type B blood. Type AB red cells have both antigens, and type O cells have neither.

Blood **serum** (plasma minus the clotting factors) containing antibodies to the A or B antigens is used to test for blood type. Blood serum with antibodies that can destroy red cells with A antigen is called anti-A serum. Blood serum with antibodies that can destroy red cells with B antigen is called anti-B serum. Type A blood reacts with anti-A serum only. Type B reacts with anti-B serum only. Type AB blood, since it has both A and B antigens, reacts with both anti-A and anti-B serum. Type O blood, which has neither A nor B antigens, reacts with neither anti-A nor anti-B serum.

Rh Factor

More than 85 percent of the U.S. population has another red cell antigen group called the *Rh factor,* named for

Table 28-3 The ABO Blood Group System

Blood Type	Red Blood Cell Antigen	Plasma Antibodies Present	Serum Reacts With	Can Receive Blood From	Can Donate Blood To
A	A	Anti-B	Anti-A	A, O	A, AB
B	B	Anti-A	Anti-B	B, O	B, AB
AB	A, B	None	Anti-A, Anti-B	AB, A, B, O	AB
O	None	Anti-A, Anti-B	None	O	O, A, B, AB

*rh*esus monkeys, in which it was first found. People with this antigen are said to be Rh positive. Those who lack it are said to be Rh negative. If Rh-positive blood is given to an Rh-negative person, he or she may produce antibodies to the "foreign" Rh antigens. The blood of this Rh-sensitized person will then destroy any Rh-positive cells received in a later transfusion.

CHECK POINT

9 What are the four ABO blood type groups?

Common Diseases of the Blood

Common diseases of the blood affect red blood cells and white blood cells, altering their makeup, shape, number, or ability to do their work. Some of these common blood diseases are described below.

Anemia

Anemia is an abnormally low amount of hemoglobin in the blood. With too little hemoglobin, the blood cannot bring enough oxygen to all parts of the body, so organs and tissues do not function as well as they should. Symptoms may include fatigue, shortness of breath, heart palpitations, paleness, and irritability.

The most common type of anemia is iron-deficiency anemia, or IDA. If the body doesn't get enough iron, it makes fewer red blood cells, and those cells carry less hemoglobin than normal. IDA most often affects women, young children, and adults who have internal bleeding, such as from an ulcer. It is caused by blood loss, failure to get enough iron in the diet, or problems absorbing iron because of surgery or an underlying disease. Treatment depends on the cause and severity. It may include changing one's diet, taking supplements, having surgery, or taking medicines.

Sickle Cell Anemia

In *sickle cell anemia*, an inherited gene causes the body to make an abnormal form of hemoglobin that distorts red blood cells into a crescent shape. The cells don't live very long, and the bone marrow can't make new ones fast enough, so anemia results, causing fatigue, shortness of breath, and other typical anemia symptoms. Another common symptom of sickle cell anemia is pain, caused by the altered cells blocking small blood vessels and depriving tissues of oxygen. This "sickle cell crisis" can lead to infections and organ damage. Treatment focuses on relieving pain and treating infections and other complications. In the U.S., sickle cell anemia most often affects African Americans, occurring in about 1 of every 500 births.

Leukemia

Leukemia is a form of cancer in which the body makes abnormal white blood cells. These cells multiply rapidly and crowd out other blood cells. Symptoms include anemia, fatigue, a tendency to bleed easily, and enlargement of the spleen and liver. Causes are unknown but may include exposure to radiation or harmful chemicals, hereditary factors, and viruses. Leukemia may be acute (worsening quickly) or chronic (progressing slowly). Treatment can include chemotherapy, radiation therapy, and bone marrow transplants.

Arteries

Arteries carry blood from the heart to all body tissues. The largest artery is the aorta. The aorta receives blood from the left ventricle. Arteries branching from the aorta travel upward toward the head and arms or downward through the body to all organs. Small subdivisions of the arteries, called **arterioles**, carry blood into the capillaries. Figure 28-4 (following page) shows the main systemic arteries, the arteries that serve all areas of the body except the lungs.

All arteries, except the pulmonary arteries from the heart to the lungs, carry blood that is high in oxygen. The arteries have thick walls because they carry blood pumped under pressure from the heart's ventricles.

The heart's ventricles pump blood into the arteries about 60 to 100 times a minute. The force of ventricular

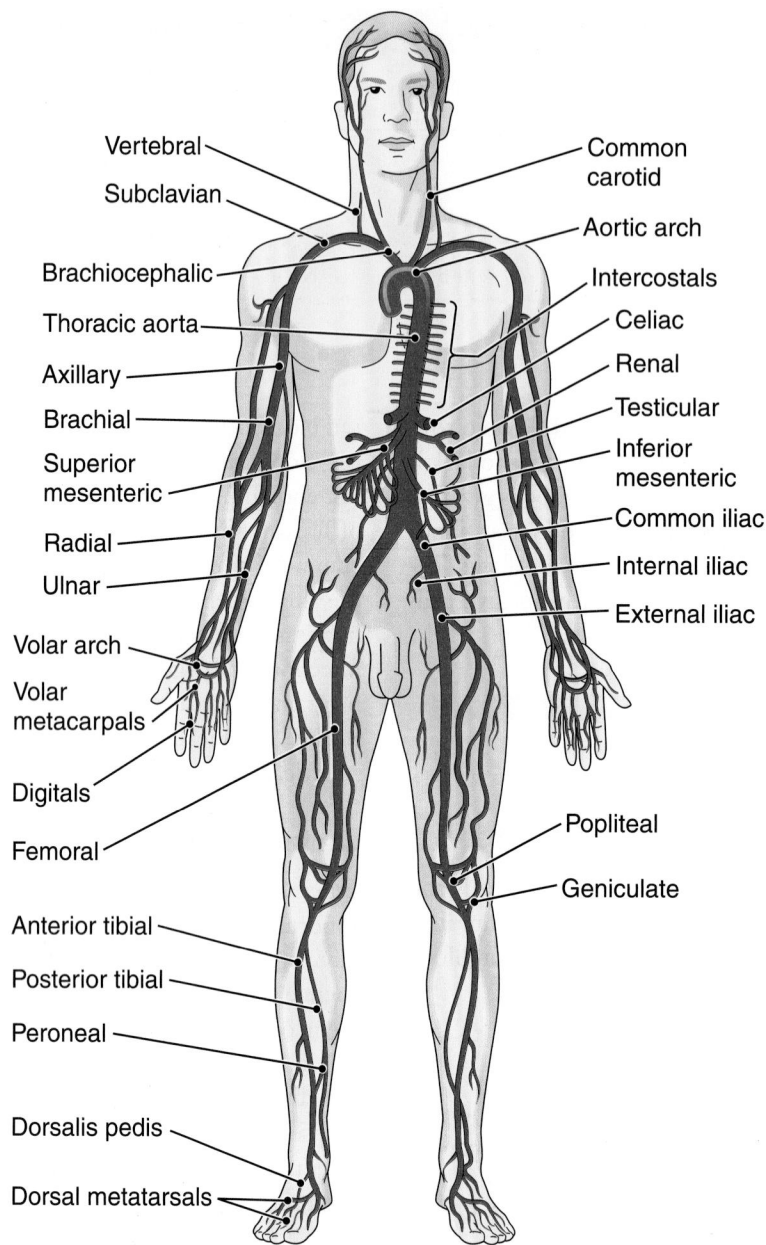

Figure 28-4 Principal systemic arteries.

contraction starts a wave of increased pressure that begins at the heart and travels along the arteries. The arteries' walls expand in response to the rush of blood and then return to their resting size.

Blood pressure is the force exerted by blood against the wall of a blood vessel. It falls as the blood travels away from the heart and is influenced by a variety of factors, two of which are vessel diameter and total blood volume.

Blood pressure is commonly measured in a large artery, typically one in the arm, with an inflatable cuff. The cuff is inflated to stop the blood flow in the vessel temporarily. A stethoscope is used to listen for renewed blood flow in the vessel as the cuff pressure is then slowly released. The

blood pressure measurement includes both systolic pressure, measured while the heart is contracting, and diastolic pressure, measured when the heart relaxes. The results are reported as systolic and then diastolic, separated by a slash, such as 120/80. Pressure is expressed as millimeters of mercury (mm Hg)—that is, the height to which the pressure can push a column of mercury in a tube.

Veins

Veins carry blood back to the heart. They are formed by the merger of **venules**, small vessels that receive blood from the capillaries and begin its transport back toward the heart.

While most arteries are located in protected and deep areas of the body, many of the principal systemic veins are found near the surface (Figure 28-5). The veins at the front of the elbow are often used for drawing blood for tests. The deep veins tend to parallel arteries and usually have the same names as the corresponding arteries.

Two large veins receive blood from the systemic vessels and empty directly into the heart's right atrium: the *superior vena cava*, which drains the head, neck, upper extremities, and chest wall, and the *inferior vena cava*, which returns blood from areas below the diaphragm. All veins carry blood that is low in oxygen, except the four pulmonary veins that carry blood from the lungs to the heart.

Veins have thinner, less elastic walls than arteries because blood in veins is under much lower pressure than blood in arteries. Because of their thinner walls, the veins are easily collapsed. Only slight pressure on a vein, such as the pressure of a tumor, may interfere with return blood flow.

Blood flows in a closed system and must continually move forward as the heart contracts. But by the time blood arrives in the veins, little force remains from the heart's pumping action. In addition, gravity works against the upward flow of blood from parts of the body below the heart.

Several mechanisms help to overcome these forces and keep blood moving toward the heart. In fact, the blood even picks up some speed along the way.

● As skeletal muscles contract, they compress the veins and squeeze blood forward.

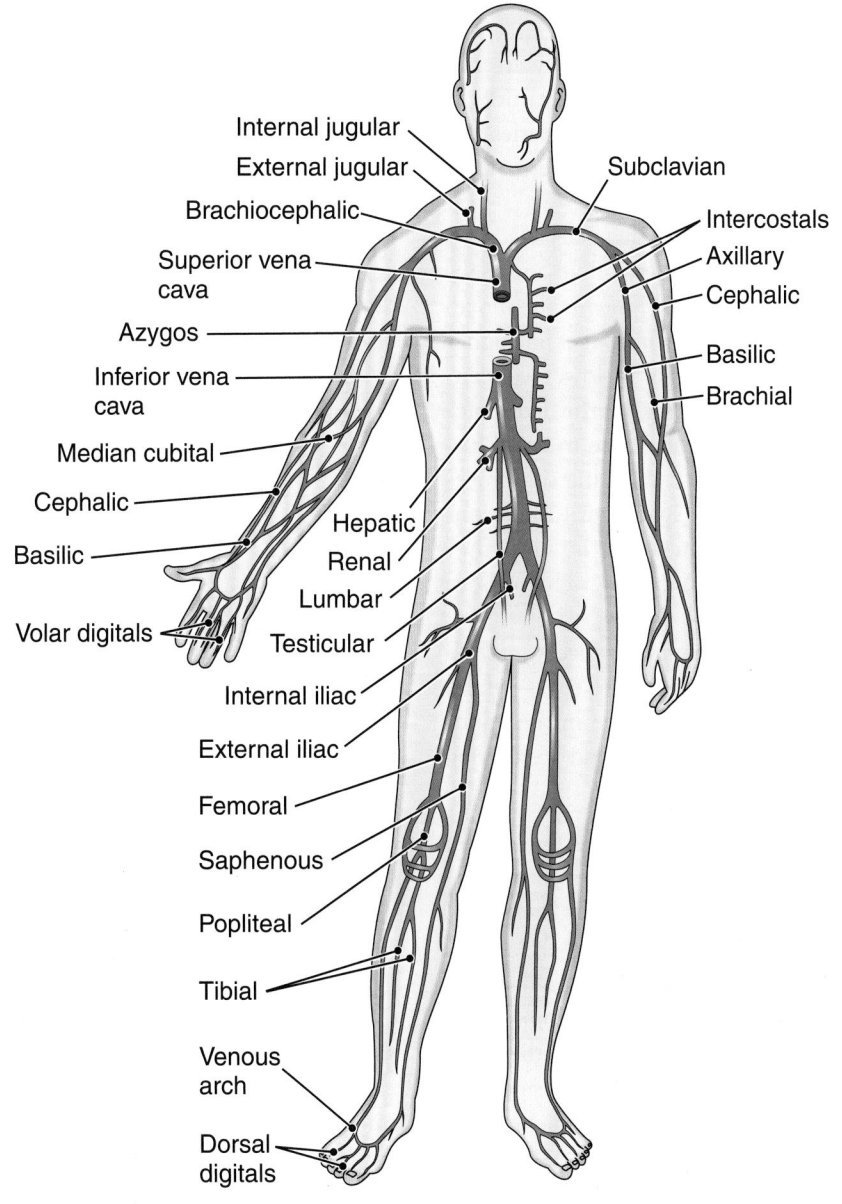

Figure 28-5 Principal systemic veins.

- Valves in the veins prevent backflow and keep blood flowing toward the heart.
- As a person inhales, the diaphragm flattens and puts pressure on the large abdominal veins. At the same time, chest expansion causes pressure to drop in the thorax. Together, these actions serve both to push and to pull blood through these cavities and return it to the heart.

Capillaries

Capillaries are the smallest and most numerous of all the vessels. Capillaries also have the thinnest walls, consisting of a single cell layer. This large surface area and the thinness of capillary walls allow for the efficient exchange of oxygen, carbon dioxide, and other substances between blood and tissues.

In Figures 28-4 and 28-5, notice how closely arteries and veins run to one another. *Capillary beds* (networks of capillaries, embedded in tissues) connect the arteries and veins, through arterioles and venules. It is here that the exchange of gases and substances takes place.

Water, oxygen, and other materials that cells need pass through the capillary walls into the tissue fluid and make their way by diffusion to the cells. *Diffusion* is the movement of a substance from an area where it is in higher concentration to an area where it is in lower concentration. Think about how couples on a crowded dance floor spread out into all the available space to avoid hitting other dancers. In the same way, diffusing substances spread throughout their available space until their concentration everywhere is the same—that is, until they reach equilibrium. This diffusion causes rich loads of oxygen in capillaries to diffuse into tissues.

At the same time and by the same process, carbon dioxide and other waste products leave the cells—where they are in high concentration—and move in the opposite direction. They enter the capillaries and are carried away in the bloodstream for elimination.

Common Diseases of the Blood Vessels

Hypertension and arteriosclerosis, two common diseases, can develop gradually, with no signs or symptoms. Both can have serious consequences. Eating a healthy diet, getting regular exercise, controlling weight, not smoking, and not drinking excessive amounts of alcohol can help prevent these diseases. The American Heart Association recommends that people with normal blood pressure have it checked at least once every two years.

BLOOD FACTS

- It takes only about 20 seconds for blood to circulate through the entire body.
- In a day, blood travels about 19,000 kilometers (12,000 miles)—four times the distance across the U.S.
- The body's system of blood vessels is more than 96,500 kilometers (60,000 miles) long—long enough to circle the globe more than twice.
- In a day, the adult heart pumps about 2,000 gallons of blood and beats about 100,000 times.
- During an average lifetime, the heart will beat 2.5 billion times. It will pump enough blood to fill more than three supertankers.

Hypertension

Hypertension is a condition of higher-than-normal blood pressure. It's defined as a systolic pressure greater than 140 mm Hg or a diastolic pressure greater than 90 mm Hg. Usually, there are no symptoms. Most of the time, the exact cause of hypertension can't be identified. Hypertension can lead to serious medical problems such as cardiovascular disease and stroke. Changes in diet and life habits are the first line of defense in controlling this disorder.

Arteriosclerosis

Arteriosclerosis is a condition in which artery walls thicken and harden and the artery opening narrows, due to a buildup of fatty deposits or calcium or as a result of the formation of scar tissue. Typically, people experience no symptoms until the artery is totally or almost completely blocked, a condition that can produce a heart attack or stroke. Treatment may include lifestyle changes, drugs to dilate the blood vessels or to prevent blood clots from forming, and surgical procedures, such as angioplasty.

✓ CHECK POINT

10 What are the five types of blood vessels?

11 What two components of blood pressure are measured? What measures constitute hypertension, or high blood pressure?

THE LYMPHATIC SYSTEM

Another part of the circulatory system, the lymphatic system, is a widespread system of tissues and vessels. Its organs are scattered throughout the body. This system serves almost the entire body. Lymphatic vessels pick up excess fluids and protein from tissues and return them to the bloodstream. The lymphoid organs also contribute to the immune system by destroying harmful microorganisms.

The functions of the lymphatic system fall into three categories:

- **Fluid balance.** As materials move from the tissues to the capillaries, a little fluid is always left behind. In addition, some proteins escape from the capillaries into the tissues. The lymphatic system helps clean up by returning excess fluid and proteins from the tissues to the bloodstream (Figure 28-6).

- **Protection from infection.** The lymphatic system is an important part of the immune system. One group of white blood cells, the **lymphocytes**, can live and multiply in the lymphatic system. When foreign organisms enter the body, lymphocytes attack and destroy them. Lymphoid tissue throughout the body filters foreign matter and cellular debris from body fluids.

- **Absorption of fats.** After food is broken down in the digestive tract, most nutrients are absorbed into the blood through intestinal capillaries. Many digested fats, however, are too large to enter these capillaries and are

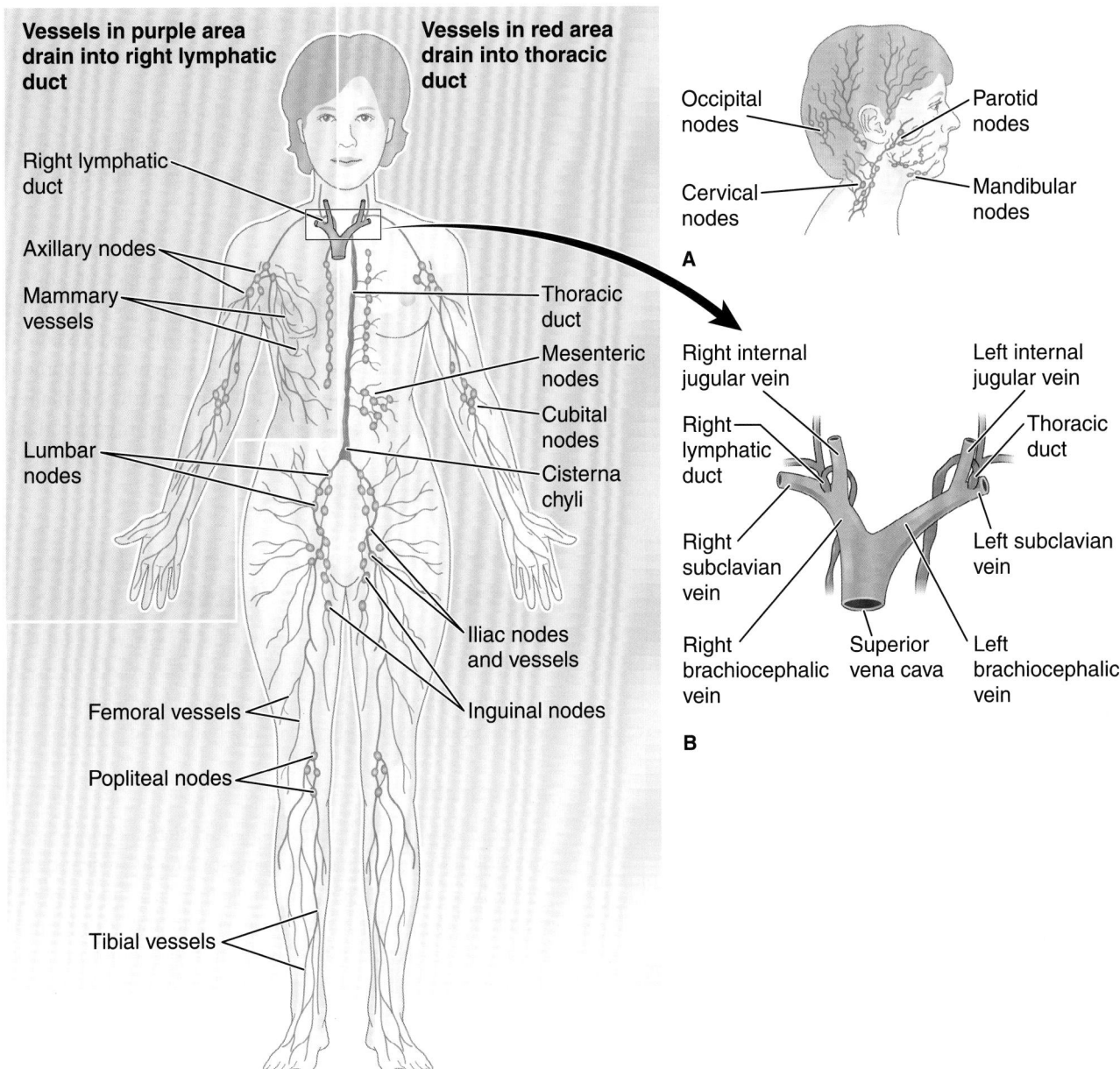

Figure 28-6 Vessels and nodes of the lymphatic system. A) Lymph nodes and vessels of the head. B) Drainage of the right lymphatic duct and thoracic duct into subclavian veins.

instead absorbed into lymphatic capillaries. These fats are added to the blood when **lymph** (the fluid that circulates in the lymphatic system) joins the bloodstream.

Lymphatic Vessels

Lymph travels through a network of vessels that are somewhat similar to blood vessels. Unlike the cardiovascular system, however, the lymphatic system is a one-way system that begins in the tissues and ends when the lymph joins the blood.

Like the blood capillaries, the lymphatic capillaries have walls that are a single cell thick, allowing for the passage of fluids. The gaps between the cells are bigger than those of the blood capillaries, so large protein molecules move through more easily. And the cells overlap slightly, so the proteins can't back out.

The larger lymphatic vessels often lie near veins. They are named for their location. For example, those in the thigh are called femoral lymphatic vessels. These vessels have valves, like those in some veins, that prevent backflow.

At certain points, lymphatic vessels drain through lymph nodes, small masses of lymphatic tissue that filter the lymph. The nodes are in groups that serve a particular region. Lymphatic vessels eventually drain into the right lymphatic duct or the thoracic duct, both of which empty into the bloodstream.

Lymph is moved by several different means. The segments of lymphatic vessels located between the valves contract rhythmically, propelling the lymph forward. Lymph is also moved by the same mechanisms that promote the return of blood through the veins to the heart. As skeletal muscles contract during movement, they compress the lymphatic vessels and drive lymph forward. Breathing produces changes in pressure that help move lymph through the abdominal and thoracic cavities.

Lymph Nodes

Lymph nodes are bean-shaped masses of tissue scattered throughout the body along lymphatic vessels. They filter harmful bacteria and other foreign substances from the lymph, trapping them in a mesh-like fiber so they can be destroyed. The body has about 600 lymph nodes. They are concentrated in the cervical (neck), axillary (armpit), chest, and groin regions.

Lymphoid Organs and Tissues

Other protective organs and tissues of the lymphatic system include the tonsils, spleen, and thymus gland.

Tonsils

The **tonsils** are in the throat (pharynx). They filter inhaled or swallowed materials, removing contaminants that lymphocytes then destroy. The tonsils also aid in immunity early in life. They may become so loaded with bacteria that they become reservoirs for repeated infections. If that happens, the tonsils are usually removed.

Spleen

The **spleen** is an organ that contains lymphoid tissue designed to filter blood. It is located in the upper left quadrant of the abdomen. The spleen contains white blood cells that are active in immunity. It carries out several functions in addition to those in the lymphatic system:

- Cleansing the blood of impurities and cellular debris by filtration and phagocytosis
- Destroying old, worn-out red blood cells
- Serving as a reservoir for blood, which can be returned to the bloodstream in case of hemorrhage or emergency

Thymus Gland

The **thymus gland** is located in the superior thorax beneath the sternum. Recent studies suggest that it has a much wider function than other lymphoid tissue. It appears to play a key role in immune system development before birth and during the first few months of infancy. Certain lymphocytes must mature in the thymus gland before they can perform their functions. The thymus is most active during early life.

Common Diseases and Conditions of the Lymphatic System

Changes in the lymphatic system are often related to infection. Any disease with uncontrolled growth of tissue involving lymph nodes is termed *lymphoma*. Lymphomas affect the white blood cells in the lymphatic system.

Lymphedema

In *lymphedema*, lymph accumulates in the tissues and causes swelling. Lymphedema occurs most often in an arm or leg when lymphatic vessels are blocked. It can develop as a result of trauma to a limb, surgery, radiation therapy, or lymphatic vessel infection. One of the most common causes is the removal of axillary lymph nodes during mastectomy, which disrupts lymph flow from the adjacent arm.

Lymphadenopathy

Lymphadenopathy is any disease process affecting one or more lymph nodes. The term is commonly used to refer to swollen lymph nodes. Although lymphadenopathy can indicate a serious disease, like cancer or AIDS, it most often signals an infection like a cold, measles, or strep throat. During an infection, white blood cells and fluids build up, causing the lymph nodes to swell.

The site of the swollen nodes can point to the source of an infection. For example, the cervical nodes often become enlarged during an upper respiratory infection. Swollen nodes in different parts of the body may indicate a viral infection. Treatment may include antibiotics to treat the underlying infection.

Autoimmune Diseases

A disorder that results from an immune response to one's own tissues is classified as an *autoimmune disease*. The cause may be a failure in the immune system or a reaction to body cells that have been slightly altered by mutation or disease. The list of diseases that are believed to be caused, at least in part, by autoimmunity is long. Examples are pernicious anemia, rheumatoid arthritis, Graves disease, myasthenia gravis, and rheumatic heart disease.

AIDS

AIDS (acquired immunodeficiency syndrome) results from infection with HIV (human immunodeficiency virus), which attacks certain T cells (a type of lymphocyte). HIV is spread by sexual contact, use of contaminated needles, blood transfusions, and passage from an infected mother to a fetus. It leaves the host susceptible to infections like pneumonia and to Kaposi sarcoma, a once-rare form of skin cancer. AIDS also may cause the immune system to attack the body's own tissues, or it may attack the nervous system. At present, there is no cure for AIDS, but some drugs can delay its progress, and research toward developing a vaccine has had promising results.

Hodgkin's Disease

Hodgkin's disease is a cancer of the lymphatic system that may spread to other tissues. The first symptom is enlarged but painless lymph nodes in the neck. The disease then progresses to other nodes. Symptoms include fever, night sweats, weight loss, and itching. The exact cause of Hodgkin's disease is unknown. The disease occurs most often in young adults and those over age 50. Most cases can be cured with radiation and chemotherapy.

Tonsillitis

Tonsillitis, a bacterial infection of the tonsils, is a common childhood illness. Many cases are treated successfully with antibiotics, but some patients need a *tonsillectomy*—having their tonsils removed. Tonsillectomy is one of the most common surgical procedures for American children. Surgery is considered if there are frequent infections or if enlarged tonsils make swallowing or breathing difficult. Recent studies suggest that tonsillectomy also may be beneficial for children suffering from otitis media, because bacteria infecting the tonsils may travel to the middle ear.

✓ CHECK POINT

12 What are the three functions of the lymphatic system?

13 What is filtered by the spleen?

Chapter Wrap-Up

Don't forget to visit the Point₊ companion website for additional study resources!

CHAPTER HIGHLIGHTS

- The circulatory system, which consists of the cardiovascular and lymphatic systems, is the body's transportation system. It delivers oxygen, nutrients, and other vital substances to all the body's cells and carries waste products away.
- The heart, a part of the cardiovascular system, is a powerful muscle that pumps blood throughout the body.
- How the heart ages varies widely, depending on heredity, environmental factors, diseases, and personal habits. Generally, as a person ages, contractions aren't as strong, and the heart often has less reserve strength, limiting an older person's ability to respond to physical or emotional stress.
- Blood has three functions. It brings nutrients, oxygen, and other needed substances to cells and carries waste products away. It also regulates the amount of fluid in the tissues and helps keep body temperature and the acid-base balance of body fluids steady. And it plays a key role in defending the body against disease.
- Blood consists of plasma, which is mostly water, and three types of cells or cell fragments: red blood cells, which carry oxygen to the cells; white blood cells, which protect against infection; and platelets, which help with clotting. The five types of blood vessels are arteries, veins, capillaries, arterioles, and venules.
- The lymphatic system is a widely distributed system of tissues and vessels. It helps to balance body fluids by returning excess fluid and proteins from the tissues to the bloodstream. It protects the body from impurities and invading microorganisms by producing lymphocytes and filtering body fluids. It also transports digested fats that are too large to enter the capillaries from the digestive system to the blood.
- Health care specialties involving the heart include cardiovascular technologist and cardiovascular technician. A health care specialty involving the blood is clinical laboratory technologist.
- Common diseases and conditions of the heart include myocardial infarction, congestive heart failure, angina pectoris, and arrhythmia. Common diseases and conditions of the lymphatic system include lymphedema, lymphadenopathy, autoimmune diseases, AIDS, Hodgkin's disease, and tonsillitis.

REVIEW QUESTIONS

Matching

1. _____ cardiovascular technologist

2. _____ cardiovascular technician

3. _____ clinical laboratory technologist

4. _____ health care professional

5. _____ cardiologist

   a. professional who performs EKGs   **b.** professional who must know CPR   **c.** professional who performs ultrasound scans of the heart and blood vessels   **d.** professional who performs blood tests   **e.** professional who performs cardiac catheterization

Multiple Choice

6. One complete sequence of heart contraction and relaxation is called
   a. systole
   b. diastole
   c. the cardiac cycle
   d. cardiac output

7. The medical term for a heart attack is
   a. myocardial infarction
   b. congestive heart failure
   c. angina pectoris
   d. arrhythmia

8. Red blood cells transport oxygen that is bound to
   a. antigens
   b. albumin
   c. hemoglobin
   d. enzymes

9. Which is NOT a function of the lymphatic system?
   a. fluid balance
   b. growth of body tissues
   c. protection from infections
   d. absorption of fats

10. Which structure of the lymphatic system filters lymph?
    a. lymph nodes
    b. tonsils
    c. spleen
    d. thymus gland

Completion

11. The _____ is the body's system of transportation.

12. One-way _____ in the heart keep blood moving in a forward direction.

13. The process by which leukocytes engulf and digest foreign organisms is called _____.

14. _____ are a group of white blood cells in the lymphatic system that attack and destroy foreign invaders.

15. A disorder that results from an immune response to one's own tissues is a/an _____
    _____.

Short Answer

16. Describe the flow of blood through the chambers of the heart.

    _____

    _____

17. Describe the effects of aging on the heart.

    _____

    _____

18. Compare and contrast the following:
    a. formed elements and plasma
    b. erythrocyte and leukocyte
    c. artery and vein
    d. arteriole and venule

    _____

    _____

19. Describe three mechanisms that promote the return of blood to the heart.

    _____

    _____

20. Explain the absence of arteries in the lymphatic circulatory system.

INVESTIGATE IT

1. Naomi is a 22-year-old woman. Heart disease runs in both sides of her family, and on her mother's side, high cholesterol does too. Naomi wants to make some decisions about her life that will reduce her risk of developing heart disease. Use the Internet to identify risk factors for heart disease and steps for prevention. Look also at what Naomi can do to control her cholesterol. Make a list of steps she can take. These web sites are good resources:
"Heart Disease Risk Factors"
http://www.cdc.gov/heartdisease/risk_factors.htm
"Heart Disease Prevention: What You Can Do"
http://www.cdc.gov/heartdisease/prevention.htm
"Cholesterol"
http://www.cdc.gov/cholesterol

2. Many kinds of studies can be done on blood. Besides the hematocrit, what are some other common blood tests? What are they used for? Use the search words *blood tests* for your Internet search.

3. According to the Red Cross, someone in the U.S. needs blood every two seconds. Find out more about blood transfusions. Explore one or two of these topics:
   - The history of blood transfusions
   - Examples of situations in which blood transfusions are needed
   - Who can donate blood
   - Where donated blood comes from in the U.S.
   - The use of blood components
   - How quickly the body replaces the plasma and red blood cells that are donated
   - The safety of donated blood

   These sites may be helpful:

   The American Red Cross
   http://www.redcross.org
   "Blood Transfusion and Donation"
   Medline Plus (U.S. National Library of Medicine/U.S. National Institutes of Health)
   http://www.nlm.nih.gov/medlineplus/bloodtransfusionanddonation.html
   "Red Gold: The Epic Story of Blood"
   Frontline
   http://www.pbs.org/wnet/redgold/index.html

4. Immunity is the body's final line of defense against disease. Answer two of these questions about immunity.
   - What are innate and adaptive immunity?
   - What are natural and acquired immunity?
   - What is the difference between passive and active immunity?
   - Why do we take vaccines? What are their effects?

   Use the terms in the questions for your Internet search (*innate immunity*, *vaccines*, etc.), or try a web site like one of these:
   "The Immune System"
   http://www3.niaid.nih.gov/topics/immuneSystem
   "Immune System"
   http://kidshealth.org/parent/general/body_basics/immune.html

RECOMMENDED READING

Boston Scientific. Heart and Blood Vessel Basics. Available at: http://www.bostonscientific.com/templatedata/imports/HTML/CRM/heart/index.html.

Brown, P. Lymphatic system: unlocking the drains. *Nature* 2005, vol. 436, pp. 456–458.

Clark, W.R. *In Defense of Self: How the Immune System Really Works.* New York: Oxford University Press, 2008.

Cold Spring Harbor Laboratory. Cell Signals (blood clotting). Available at: http://www.dnalc.org/resources/3d/cellsignals.html.

MyHealthScore.Com. Cardiovascular System. Human Anatomy Online. Available at: http://www.innerbody.com/image/cardov.html.

MyHealthScore.Com. Lymphatic System. Human Anatomy Online. Available at: http://www.innerbody.com/image/lympov.html.

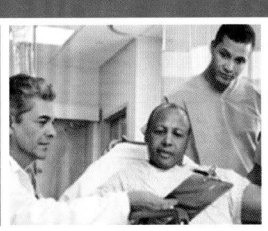
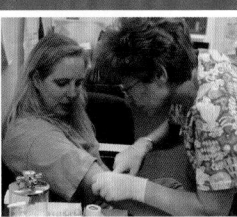
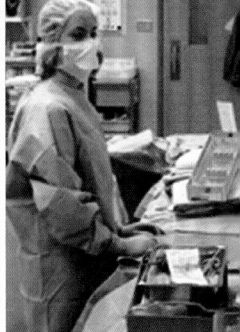

Energy Supply and Use

29 CHAPTER

CHAPTER OBJECTIVES

After careful study of this chapter, you should be able to:

✳ Define *respiration* and describe its three phases.

✳ Name and describe the chief structures of the respiratory system.

✳ Explain pulmonary ventilation and the external exchange of gases.

✳ Name the three main functions of the digestive system.

✳ List the organs of the digestive tract and describe their functions.

✳ Describe how waste is eliminated from the large intestine.

✳ List the accessory organs of digestion and describe their functions.

✳ Define absorption and describe how it occurs.

✳ Compare the energy contents of fats, proteins, and carbohydrates and list recommended percentages for the diet.

✳ Explain the roles of minerals and vitamins in nutrition and give examples.

✳ List the parts of the urinary system and describe their functions.

✳ Explain how the kidneys filter blood.

✳ Name three substances normally found in urine.

✳ Explain how aging affects the respiratory, digestive, and urinary systems, as well as metabolism and nutrition.

✳ Identify common diseases and conditions of the respiratory, digestive, and urinary systems and those related to metabolism and nutrition.

KEY TERMS

absorption
alveoli (al-VE-o-li)
bolus
bronchiole (BRONG-ke-ole)
bronchus (pl., bronchi) (BRONG-ki)
diaphragm (DI-ah-fram)
digestion

duodenum (du-o-DE-num)
elimination
epiglottis (ep-ih-GLOT-is)
esophagus (eh-SOF-ah-gus)
gallbladder (GAWL-blad-er)
ileum (IL-e-um)
jejunum (je-JU-num)

kidney
large intestine
larynx (LAR-inks)
liver (LIV-er)
metabolism
nephron (NEF-ron)
pancreas (PAN-kre-as)
peristalsis (per-ih-STAL-sis)

pharynx (FAR-inks)
small intestine
trachea (TRA-ke-ah)
ureter (U-re-ter)
urethra (u-RE-thrah)
urinary bladder
ventilation

■he human body needs energy to function. Three body systems work together to supply energy for use within the body and to process the results of the consumption of that energy: the respiratory, digestive, and urinary systems.

The respiratory system supplies cells with oxygen from the air and eliminates carbon dioxide, while the digestive system extracts nutrients from food. Through the body's metabolism, energy is consumed, cells function and grow, and waste products are generated. To complete the cycle of energy use, the digestive and urinary systems eliminate the waste products, and the urinary system helps maintain homeostasis.

THE RESPIRATORY SYSTEM

The main functions of the respiratory system are to provide oxygen to body cells so they can make energy and to eliminate carbon dioxide, a byproduct of this energy-making process. These gases are carried to and from the cells in the blood. The respiratory system works closely with the cardiovascular system to accomplish gas exchange and carries out the external phases of respiration.

Phases of Respiration

Most people think of respiration as simply moving air in and out of the lungs, or breathing. In scientific terms, respiration is the process by which oxygen is obtained from the environment and delivered to the cells. Carbon dioxide is transported to the outside in a reverse pathway. Respiration has three phases (Figure 29-1):

- Pulmonary ventilation, which is the exchange of air between the atmosphere and the air sacs of the lungs
- External exchange of gases, which occurs in the lungs as oxygen diffuses from the air sacs into the blood and carbon dioxide diffuses out of the blood into the air sacs to be eliminated from the body
- Internal exchange of gases, which occurs in the body's tissues as oxygen diffuses from the blood to the cells and carbon dioxide passes from the cells into the blood

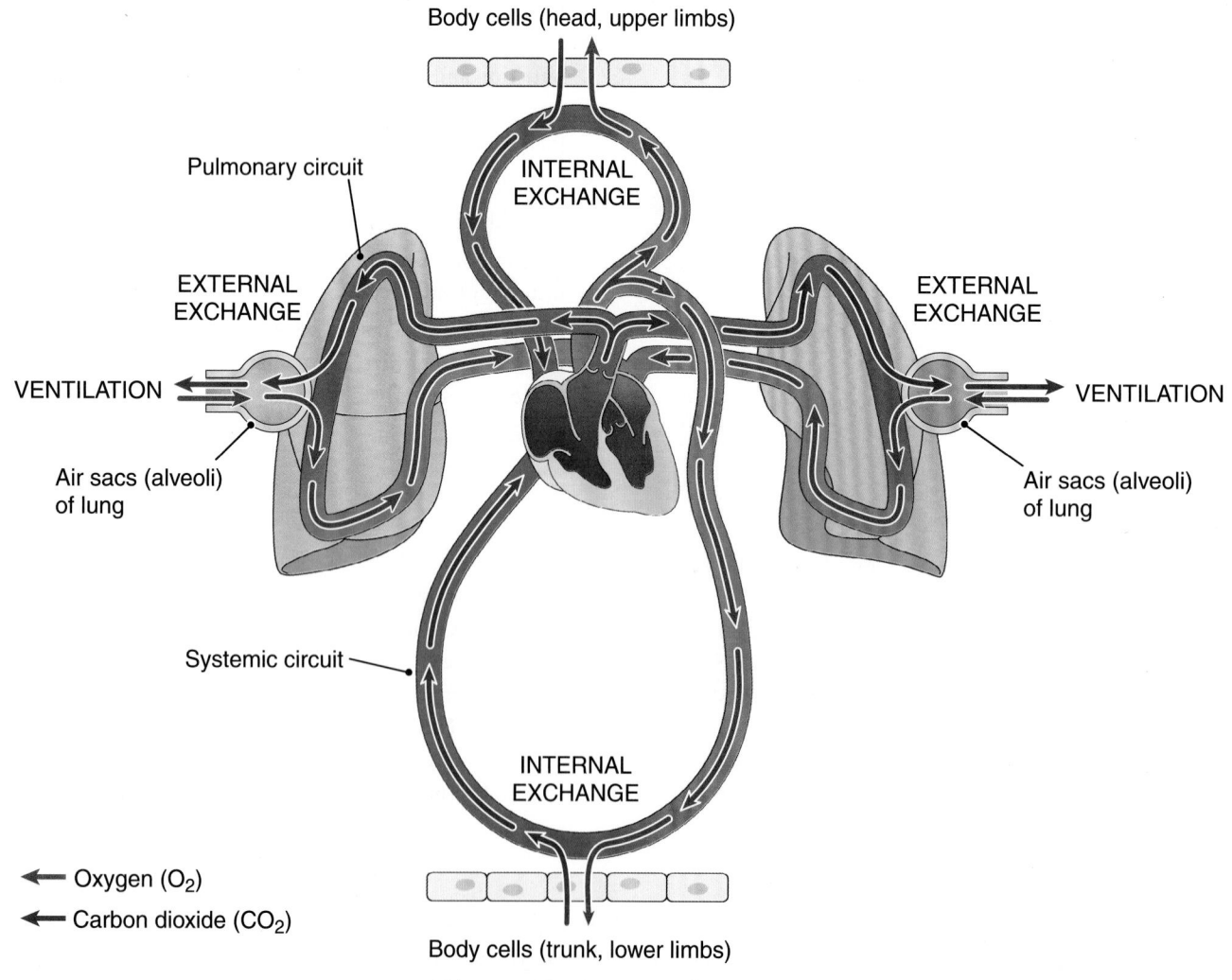

Figure 29-1 Overview of respiration.

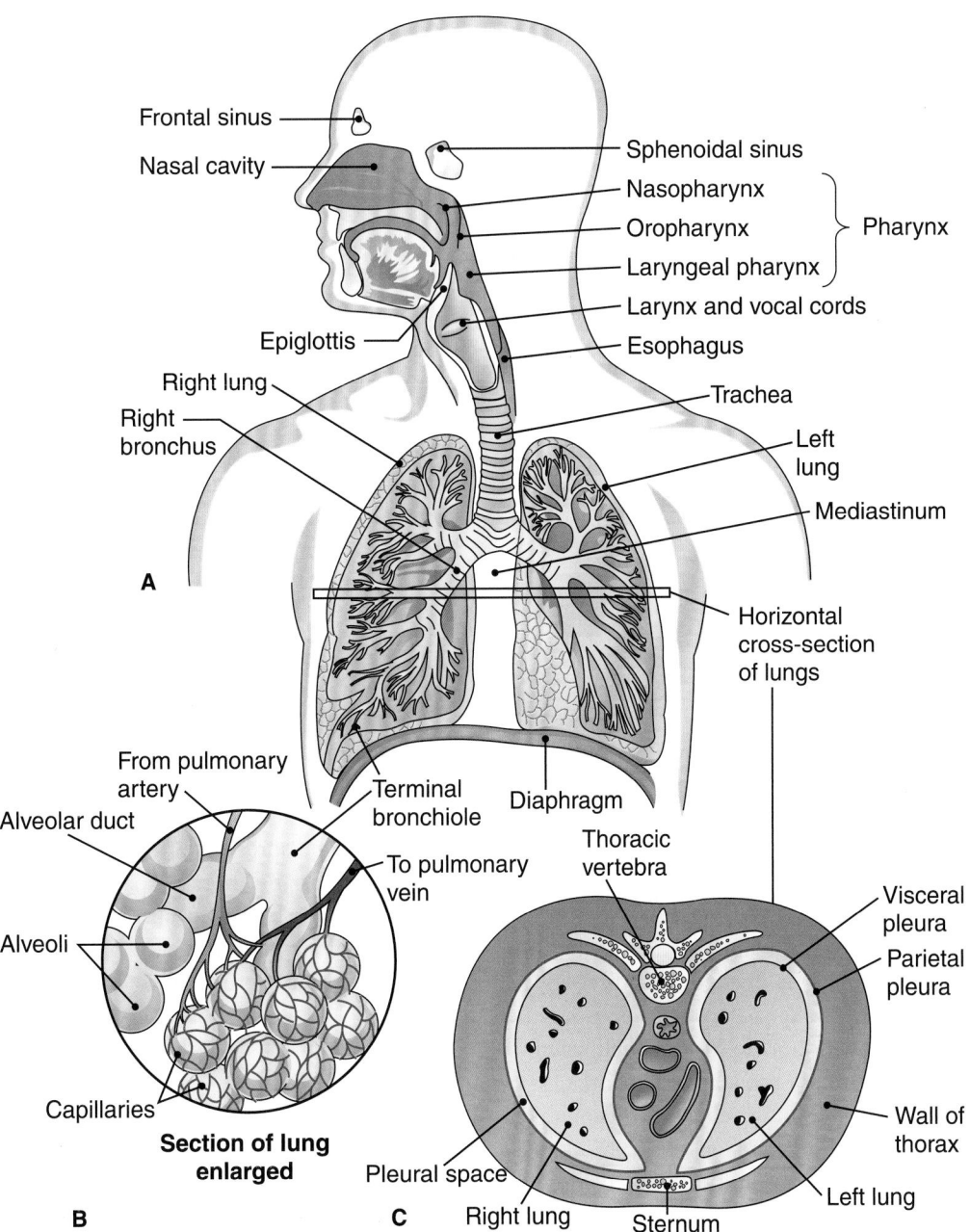

Figure 29-2 The respiratory system.

Structures of the Respiratory System

The respiratory system (Figure 29-2) has an intricate arrangement of spaces and passageways. Think of it as a pathway for air between the atmosphere and the blood.

The Upper Airway

In the upper airway, air moves from the nasal cavities to the pharynx (throat). Air can also enter through the mouth, but more filtering takes place when air enters through the nostrils. From the pharynx, air passes to the larynx and then to the trachea.

Nasal Cavities. Air enters the body through the nostrils and is filtered, moistened, and warmed as it passes through the nasal cavities. The job of filtering is carried out by *cilia*—tiny, hairlike projections from the cavities' lining—and *mucus*, a thick, sticky substance that coats the lining of the nasal cavities. Cilia sweep dirt and foreign material toward the throat, where they can be swallowed or eliminated by coughing, sneezing, or blowing one's nose. Cilia line all the passageways of the respiratory system. Other particles are trapped and destroyed by mucus, which also moistens the air. The many blood vessels in the lining of the nasal cavities deliver heat that warms the air entering the body.

Pharynx. Air passes from the nasal cavities (and mouth) into the throat, or pharynx. The pharynx also carries food that's been swallowed toward the digestive system.

Larynx. Commonly called the voice box, the larynx contains the vocal cords, which vibrate as air from the lungs flows over them, creating sound. A leaf-shaped cartilage called the epiglottis covers the larynx when food is swallowed to prevent food and liquids from entering the rest of the respiratory tract.

Trachea. The trachea, or windpipe, conducts air from the larynx into the lungs.

The Lower Airway

The lower airway consists of the bronchi and lungs.

Bronchi. At its inferior (lower) end, the trachea divides into two bronchi, each of which enters one lung. Further divisions produce an increasing number of smaller tubes that supply air to smaller subdivisions of lung tissue.

Lungs. The lungs occupy the major portion of the thoracic cavity. The right lung is divided into three lobes. The left lung, which is smaller to provide space for the heart, has two lobes. The lobes are further subdivided to correspond to divisions of the bronchiole network.

The lungs are the organs in which gas diffusion takes place. The smallest of the bronchial tubes, the bronchioles, carry air into millions and millions of tiny air sacs, the alveoli. It is through the ultra-thin walls of the alveoli and their surrounding capillaries that oxygen diffuses into the blood and carbon dioxide diffuses out of it.

✔ **CHECK POINT**

1 What are the three phases of respiration?

2 Name the four structures of the upper airway and the two structures of the lower airway in the order in which air passes through them.

Ventilation

Pulmonary ventilation or simply ventilation, the first phase of respiration, is the movement of air into and out of the lungs. It is normally accomplished by breathing. The normal breathing rate for adults varies from 12 to 20 breaths per minute. Ventilation has two phases:

- *Inhalation*, or inspiration, is the drawing of air into the lungs.
- *Exhalation*, or expiration, is the expulsion of air from the lungs.

Normally, the autonomic nervous system regulates breathing automatically. It adjusts the rate and rhythm according to changes in the blood, especially the concentration of carbon dioxide. For example, when you exercise or otherwise exert yourself physically, the action of your muscles automatically makes more carbon dioxide than when you were at rest, so you breathe harder and faster to rid your body of that carbon dioxide.

Inspiration

The breathing cycle begins when a nerve stimulates the diaphragm, a strong, dome-shaped muscle under the lungs, to contract and flatten. This enlarges the chest cavity considerably. At the same time, muscles between the ribs elevate and spread the rib cage. Pressure in the chest cavity drops as the thorax expands. When the pressure drops to slightly below the air pressure outside the lungs, air is pulled in. The measure of how easily the lungs expand under pressure is called *compliance*.

Expiration

Expiration occurs as the diaphragm relaxes and the lungs spring back to their original size. Increased pressure in the now smaller thorax forces air out of the lungs.

EXTRA! EXTRA! **RESPIRATORY FACTS**

- The respiratory system has almost 932 kilometers (1,500 miles) of airways.
- People breathe in about 6.15 liters (13 pints) of air each minute.
- The fastest sneeze ever recorded expelled air at 165 kilometers (103 miles) per hour.
- The lungs contain about 300 million alveoli. The resulting surface area for gas exchange is equivalent to a classroom that is 7 by 7 meters (24 by 24 feet).
- The lungs have about 1,600 kilometers (994 miles) of capillaries.

Gas Exchange

External exchange, the second phase of respiration, is the movement of gases between the alveoli and the capillary blood in the lungs. The alveolar wall and the capillary wall form a membrane through which the gases pass by diffusion. Remember that diffusion refers to the movement of molecules from an area where they're in high concentration to an area where they're in lower concentration. Therefore, the concentrations of a gas on the two sides of a membrane determine the direction of diffusion.

Normally, inhaled air contains about 21 percent oxygen. Oxygen diffuses from the area of higher concentration (the alveoli) to the area of lower concentration (the blood). Similarly, carbon dioxide diffuses from the area of higher concentration (the blood) to the area of lower concentration (the alveoli).

The third phase of respiration, internal exchange, is the exchange of gases between the blood and the tissues. This phase is discussed in Chapter 28, "Circulation and Body Defense."

Effects of Aging

With age, the tissues of the respiratory tract lose elasticity. For example, the chest wall may become more rigid. When combined with arthritis and loss of strength in breathing muscles, this rigidity can cause an overall decrease in compliance. Age-related reductions in the protective mechanisms of the lungs can make a person more susceptible to infection. Lung disorders increase with age and are hastened by cigarette smoking and exposure to other environmental irritants.

Common Diseases and Conditions of the Respiratory System

Lung function is affected by conditions that cause resistance to air flow through the respiratory tract or that limit chest expansion. Some of these conditions affect the respiratory system directly; others result from disturbances in other body systems.

Asthma

Attacks of *asthma* are caused by a narrowing of the bronchial tubes. This, along with edema (swelling) of the bronchial linings, inflammation, and accumulation of mucus, results in the wheezing and difficulty breathing that characterize this disease.

Asthma is most common in children. Although its causes are uncertain, a main factor is irritation caused by allergies. Heredity also may play a role. Treatment now generally involves regular doses of medications to keep the airways open and prevent the shortness of breath that may occur. Sometimes, though, acute attacks can happen, and fast-acting medications are needed to alleviate symptoms and help return the patient to normal lung function.

Bronchitis

Bronchitis is an inflammation of the bronchial tubes caused by an infection or irritation. A common symptom is a cough that produces mucus. Treatment for acute bronchitis generally includes an antibiotic for bacterial infections, rest, increased fluids, and not smoking. For chronic bronchitis, bronchodilators and corticosteroids may be used to open airways and clear away mucus.

Emphysema

Emphysema is a chronic disease in which alveoli are destroyed. Common causes are exposure to cigarette smoke and other forms of pollution, as well as chronic infection. Emphysema is the main type of chronic obstructive pulmonary disease (COPD). Two other types of COPD are asthma and chronic bronchitis. Symptoms of emphysema include a cough that doesn't go away, shortness of breath, tightness in the chest, and wheezing. Treatment focuses on managing symptoms, slowing the disease's progress, and preventing and treating complications.

 HEALTH CARE SPECIALTY

Respiratory Therapist

Respiratory therapists evaluate and treat breathing disorders. They perform breathing, blood, and exercise tests, assess the results, help design treatment plans, and implement those plans. They are also educators, teaching people about the importance of not smoking, giving advice on how to stop smoking, and conducting rehabilitation classes for people with chronic lung problems.

While they work under a doctor's direction, respiratory therapists have primary responsibility for respiratory care diagnostic procedures and therapeutic treatments. Their work requires a high degree of independent judgment. Specialties in respiratory therapy include continuing and long-term care, critical care, diagnostics, disease management, home care, pediatrics, and pulmonary rehabilitation. This career is profiled in Chapter 23, "Therapy and Rehabilitation."

Lung Cancer

Lung cancer is the leading cause of cancer-related deaths in both men and women. The incidence of lung cancer has increased steadily over the past 50 years, especially in women. Cigarette smoking is a major risk factor for this type of cancer, as well as for other types. The most common form of lung cancer, *squamous carcinoma*, starts in the lining of the bronchi. Lung cancer usually cannot be detected early, and it spreads rapidly. Symptoms include shortness of breath, a persistent cough, a change in the nature of a cough, weight loss, and chest pain. Lung cancer is treated with surgery, chemotherapy, and radiation.

Pneumonia

Pneumonia is an infection in one or both lungs, most often caused by bacteria or viruses. A buildup of fluid and congestion in the alveoli as a result of this infection prevents effective gas exchange. Symptoms vary but can include fever, a cough (often with mucus), severe chills, chest pain when coughing or breathing, and shortness of breath. Pneumonia usually can be treated successfully in otherwise healthy people. In patients who are in poor health, it is a leading cause of death. People with weakened immune systems, like those with AIDS, are subject to a form of pneumonia called *Pneumocystis jiroveci pneumonia* (PCP), which is caused by a fungus.

Tuberculosis

Tuberculosis (TB) is an infectious disease caused by bacteria and spread through the air. Its incidence has increased dramatically worldwide since the mid-1980s, mostly because of AIDS. Many people carry TB bacteria without becoming sick, but because of their weakened immune systems, people with AIDS are at a greatly increased risk of developing the disease. Antibiotic resistance in the organism that causes TB has also contributed to the increased incidence of this disease.

Symptoms of TB include fever, weight loss, weakness, a cough, and the coughing up of sputum with blood, resulting from damage to pulmonary vessels. Tuberculosis is usually treated with a lengthy course of antibiotics.

Rhinitis

Rhinitis is an inflammation of the nasal passageways; symptoms include excessive mucus, a runny nose, and itching in the eyes or nose. *Allergic rhinitis* results when the body mistakenly identifies a harmless substance like dust, mold, or animal dander as an attacker and mounts an immune reaction to it. The body releases histamine and other chemicals that produce the symptoms. *Hay fever* is allergic rhinitis caused by the pollen from plants. Nonallergic rhinitis can be triggered by several causes, including changes in the weather, infections, and certain medications. People who are prone to rhinitis should avoid the substances or conditions that trigger the rhinitis, when possible. Rhinitis may be treated with over-the-counter or prescription medications. Allergy shots can bring relief to those with severe allergic rhinitis.

Sinusitis

Sinusitis is an infection or inflammation of the sinuses, small cavities near the nose that lessen the skull's weight and give the voice depth or tone. One of the most common symptoms is pain in the area of the affected sinuses—in the ears or neck, for example. Other frequent symptoms are thick nasal secretions, a stuffy nose, and a feeling of fullness over the face. Treatment may include antibiotics, if there's an infection, decongestants, and pain relievers.

Upper Respiratory Infections (URIs)

More than 200 viruses are known to cause an *upper respiratory infection* (URI)—also known as the common cold. The symptoms, known to all, are sneezing, acute rhinitis, watery eyes, and congestion. The infection may spread from the nose and throat to the sinuses, middle ear, and lower respiratory tract. Cold viruses are spread mostly by airborne, virus-filled droplets released when an infected person coughs and sneezes. Frequent hand washing and not touching one's face are good preventive measures.

A URI usually lasts about a week. Because it is caused by viruses, antibiotics do not cure it. Rest, fluid intake, treatment of symptoms, and time work best. The existence of so many types of cold viruses and their frequent mutation has prevented the development of an effective vaccine.

Influenza

Influenza (flu) is a viral disease of the respiratory tract associated with chills, fever, headaches, muscular aches, and cold-like symptoms. It usually resolves in several days. Severe forms of influenza have caused fatal pandemics, most recently in 1918, 1957, 1968, and 2009. For that most recent outbreak, see "Newsreel: Novel Influenza A (H1N1) Flu (Swine Flu)."

Because an influenza virus changes so rapidly, scientists must prepare vaccines against the strains most likely to cause an epidemic in any given year. Medical personnel combat influenza with vaccines, isolation and treatment of infected people with antiviral medications, and destruction of any infected animals.

NEWSREEL

Novel Influenza A (H1N1) (Swine Flu)

In late February 2009, in the village of La Gloria in the Mexican state of Veracruz, people starting getting severe colds. A month later, health officials came and took saliva samples. About 450 townspeople were diagnosed with acute respiratory infections. By early April, the Veracruz government had alerted the Mexican government of a possible flu outbreak in La Gloria. April 13 saw the first death from this virus. On April 14, the first U.S. case was confirmed, and the disease had a name: Influenza A (H1N1), or swine flu. In less than three weeks, it spread to 20 American states. By June, the World Health Organization (WHO) reported more than 17,400 cases and declared the first *pandemic* (worldwide epidemic) in 41 years.

H1N1 is a type of swine flu virus—a flu that's common in pigs. Among pigs, it usually causes a high incidence of illness but a low rate of deaths. Like all viruses, swine flu virus changes constantly. The H1N1 strain, which was identified in 1930, is a mix of pig, avian (bird), and human flu. However, scientists quickly determined that the 2009 H1N1 was a new strain with two genes from flu viruses common among pigs in Europe and Asia, as well as avian and human genes.

The severity of the outbreak in Mexico and the flu's rapid spread raised worldwide alarm, as did the incidence of severe flu among young people and older adults. (Usually, flu strikes hardest in the very young, very old, and chronically ill). A vaccine was developed and became available in early October. Supplies were initially limited due to an unexpectedly slow growth rate for the virus and other factors. The vaccine was distributed to state health departments, with state and local health officials deciding who would receive it. The U.S. Centers for Disease Control and Prevention (CDC) recommended giving priority to pregnant women, people who live with or care for children less than 6 months old, health-care and emergency medical services personnel, children and young adults ages 6 months to 24 years, and people ages 25 to 64 with health conditions that the flu could exacerbate.

In the past, the CDC received reports of about one swine flu infection in the U.S. every 1 to 2 years. Within seven months of H1N1's appearance in the U.S., the CDC estimated that 50,000,000 Americans, one-sixth of the population, had caught the disease and that almost 10,000 people had died of it, including 1,100 children and 7,500 younger adults. According to the WHO, as of December 4, 2009, more than 207 countries and overseas territories or communities had H1N1 cases.

✓ CHECK POINT

3 What is the normal breathing rate for adults?

4 Gases move between the alveoli and the blood by the process of diffusion. What is the definition of diffusion?

THE DIGESTIVE SYSTEM

The digestive system prepares food for intake by body cells. It fulfills this function by extracting nutrients from food and breaking them down into particles small enough to enter the circulatory system and eventually pass through cell walls. Cells need a constant supply of nutrients for energy and for building and maintaining vital cell components.

The digestive system has three main functions:

- **Digestion**—the process of breaking down food
- **Absorption**—the transfer of nutrients into the circulation
- **Elimination**—the removal of undigested waste material

Organs of the Digestive System

The digestive tract (Figure 29-3) is a long, muscular tube that extends through the body. It is also referred to as the *alimentary* or *gastrointestinal (GI) tract*.

Mouth

Digestion begins in the mouth, or oral cavity. The mouth receives food (*ingestion*) and breaks it into small portions, mainly through chewing, or *mastication*. Chewing involves not just the teeth but the tongue, cheeks, lips, and *palate* (roof of the mouth). An adult has 32 teeth, including incisors and canines for biting and molars for grinding.

As it's chewed, food is mixed with saliva, which moistens it and makes chewing and swallowing easier. Saliva contains an enzyme called *salivary amylase* that begins digesting the starch in food. In the process, the food is formed into a soft mass small enough to be swallowed, known as a **bolus**. The mouth moves the moistened food toward the throat to be swallowed. The scientific word for swallowing is *deglutition* (deg-lu-TISH-un).

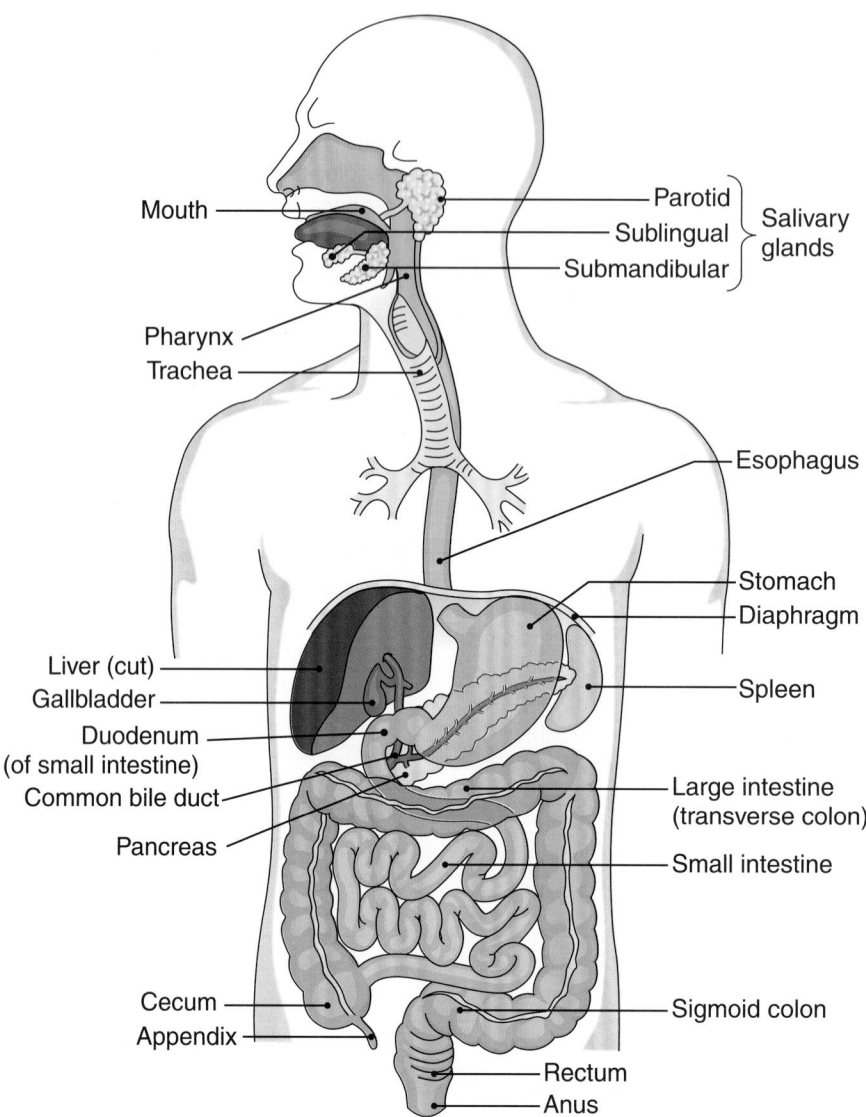

Figure 29-3 The digestive system.

The tongue, a muscular organ, aids in chewing and swallowing. As explained in Chapter 27, "Coordination and Control," its surface receptors, the taste buds, detect mostly bitter, sweet, sour, or salty tastes. The tongue is also one of the principal organs of speech.

Pharynx

The tongue pushes each bolus of food into the pharynx, where it is swallowed and moved into the esophagus. Although swallowing begins voluntarily, once it's started, it becomes involuntary and is controlled by the nerves.

The pharynx has several protections to prevent food from returning to the mouth or entering the nose or larynx. During swallowing, the *soft palate*, a tissue that forms the posterior roof of the oral cavity, and the *uvula*, a soft, fleshy, V-shaped mass that hangs from the soft palate, are raised to keep food out of the nasal cavity. The tongue is raised to seal the back of the oral cavity, and the larynx is covered by the epiglottis.

Esophagus

The **esophagus** is about 25 centimeters (10 inches) long. Here, food is lubricated with mucus and moved into the stomach. Movement through the esophagus is accomplished by **peristalsis**, wavelike movements produced by contractions of smooth muscle. No additional digestion occurs in this area.

Stomach

The stomach is a J-shaped organ that serves as a storage pouch, digestive organ, and mixer. When it receives food,

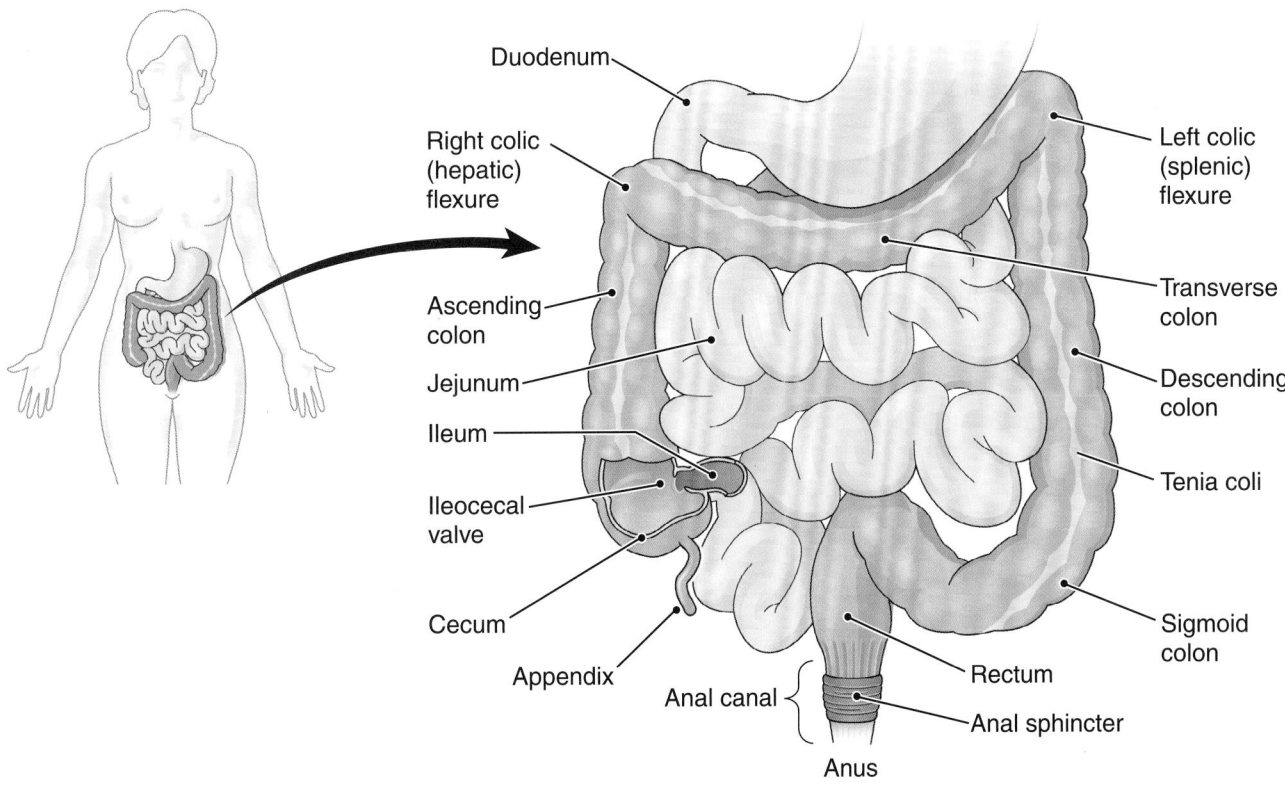

Figure 29-4 The small and large intestines.

it balloons out, stretching to accommodate as much as half a gallon. Special cells in the stomach's lining secrete hydrochloric acid, which helps break down proteins and destroys foreign organisms. They also give off *pepsin*, a protein-digesting enzyme. Through muscle action, the stomach mixes these substances with the food, breaking it down. The partially digested food, called *chime* (kime), then passes slowly into the small intestine.

Small Intestine

The **small intestine** (Figure 29-4), the longest part of the digestive tract, is 3 meters (10 feet) long. It is here that most digestion takes place. Food leaving the stomach enters the first part of the small intestine, the **duodenum**. Enzymes digest proteins and carbohydrates, and digestive juices from the liver break down carbohydrates, fats, proteins, and enzymes. Peristalsis moves the contents along and helps to mix them.

The food then passes through the **jejunum** and **ileum**, the remaining sections of the small intestine. Most absorption of digested food occurs in these sections. Nutrients are absorbed into the circulation through the walls of the small intestine. The lining of the small intestine contains folds covered with small projections called *villi*. The villi have microscopic projections called *microvilli*. Together,

these structures create a vast surface area for absorption. Each villus has blood capillaries to absorb nutrients into the bloodstream and lymphatic capillaries to absorb fat into the lymph.

Large Intestine

Any food that hasn't been digested, along with water and digestive juices, passes into the **large intestine** (Figure 29-4). The large intestine is about 1.5 meters (5 feet) long. It consists of the cecum, ascending colon, transverse colon, descending colon, sigmoid colon, rectum, and anus.

Food is not digested in the large intestine. But some water is reabsorbed, and undigested food is stored and formed into solid waste material (feces, or stool). As in the small intestine, material moves through the large intestine by peristalsis. Heavy secretions of mucus help move things along. While the stomach is emptied in a few hours, it takes days for material to make its way through the large intestine.

Feces are stored in the rectum and eliminated by *defecation* (def-e-KA-shun) through the anus. Stretching of the rectum stimulates contraction of smooth muscle in the rectal wall. Aided by voluntary contractions of the diaphragm and the abdominal muscles, feces are eliminated from the body. An anal sphincter—a circular muscle—provides voluntary control over defecation.

Bacteria living in the colon act on food residue to produce vitamin K and some of the B-complex vitamins. They also help protect against infection. Prolonged antibiotic therapy may destroy these helpful bacteria and leave the patient more vulnerable to *clostridium difficile* (klo-STRID-ee-um dif-uh-SEEL), a bacterial infection that can cause diarrhea and other more serious effects.

✓ CHECK POINT

5 How does the small intestine function in the digestive process?

6 What are the functions of the large intestine?

Accessory Digestive Organs

Accessory organs such as the salivary glands, liver, gallbladder, and pancreas also play an important role in digestion. These organs release secretions through ducts into the digestive tract. The salivary glands release their secretions into the mouth. All the other accessory organs secrete into the duodenum.

Salivary Glands

Saliva is produced by three pairs of glands, which empty through ducts into the oral cavity. Besides beginning to break down food, saliva helps keep the teeth and mouth clean. And it contains antibodies and an enzyme (lysozyme) that help reduce bacterial growth.

Liver

The **liver** is the body's largest glandular organ. It has many functions that affect digestion, metabolism, blood content, and elimination of waste. These are some of its major activities:

- Production of bile, which is needed to digest fats.
- Storage of glucose as glycogen. When the blood sugar level falls below normal, liver cells convert glycogen to glucose and release it into the blood to restore the normal blood sugar concentration.
- Modification of fats so they can be used more efficiently by cells all over the body.
- Storage of vitamins and iron.
- Formation of blood plasma proteins, like albumin and clotting factors.
- Destruction of old red blood cells and recycling or elimination of their parts.
- Manufacture of urea, a waste product of protein metabolism.

- *Detoxification* (removal of poisonous properties) of harmful substances, like alcohol and certain drugs.

Gallbladder

The **gallbladder** is a muscular sac that stores bile. Although the liver makes bile continuously, the body needs it only a few times a day. When food enters the duodenum, the gallbladder contracts and delivers the bile.

Pancreas

The **pancreas** makes enzymes that digest fats, proteins, carbohydrates, and nucleic acids. It also releases large amounts of sodium bicarbonate, which neutralizes acid in the duodenum, protecting the duodenum's lining. In addition, the pancreas produces the hormones insulin and glucagon that regulate blood sugar levels (see Chapter 27, "Coordination and Control," on the endocrine system).

Effects of Aging

As people grow older, receptors for taste and smell deteriorate, leading to a loss of appetite and decreased enjoyment of food. A decrease in saliva and poor gag reflex make swallowing more difficult. Tooth loss or poorly fitting dentures may make chewing food harder. The activity of the digestive organs also decreases, which can lead to poor absorption of certain vitamins and poor protein digestion. In the large intestine, peristalsis can slow, leading to constipation.

Common Diseases and Conditions of the Digestive System

Common diseases and conditions of the digestive system have a variety of causes. They include infection, gastric juices that end up in the wrong place, and diet. For some, the cause isn't known. Eating a well-balanced diet makes the digestive system healthier and prevents or eases some of these problems.

Appendicitis

Appendicitis is an inflammation of the appendix resulting from an infection, often caused by a blockage of stool or other material. The main symptom is abdominal pain. Usually, the appendix is removed immediately because it could rupture and spill bacteria into the abdominal cavity. This could lead to a serious infection called peritonitis, discussed under the following heading. Surgery can sometimes be done laparoscopically—with a camera on a small tube placed in the abdomen. This type of surgery

Camera in a Capsule

For nearly ten years, capsule endoscopy has been an alternative to traditional endoscopy for seeing the small intestine from the inside. The patient swallows a capsule containing a tiny camera, which makes its way, as food does, through the digestive tract, taking hundreds of pictures in the process. The images are transmitted to a data recorder worn on the patient's belt. Eventually, the camera is eliminated in the stool. The test involves less discomfort than a traditional endoscopy and takes photos of areas of the small intestine that a manual endoscope can't reach.

According to the American Society for Gastrointestinal Endoscopy, capsule endoscopy is most commonly used to look for the cause of bleeding in the small intestine, and it may also be useful for detecting inflammatory bowel disease and ulcers. Technical problems have limited widespread use of this tool, however. For instance, the camera may move through the system so rapidly that some areas are missed or so slowly that the battery fails before the transit is complete. Another problem is that the procedure isn't always covered by insurance.

Scientists continue to explore ways to use capsule technology to diagnose and treat digestive system disease.

These three devices, for example, are currently being developed or tested:

- A camera pill for the esophagus. The traditional camera pill passes through the esophagus in just three or four seconds, so only a few pictures are taken. This new camera is magnetically controlled; a doctor can hold a device roughly the size of a candy bar over the patient's body and, by moving it, move the camera.
- The intelligent pill (iPill), developed by Philips Research in 2008, which will deliver drugs electronically, traveling directly to the site of a disease. As it moves along, it measures pH, which is different in different parts of the digestive tract. Combined with the iPill's travel time, doctors can use these pH measurements to determine the iPill's location and to know when to release the drugs. The iPill may allow the use of lower doses of drugs and may reduce side effects.
- Pills with an array of tools and sensors that will travel through the digestive tract, searching for diseased cells. Unlike traditional camera pills, these pills would be controlled by a doctor or computer system, and they could be stopped or backed up when something unusual is spotted. Besides having ultrasound and other diagnostic tools, the pills could take tissue samples.

uses smaller incisions, has fewer complications, and leads to a quicker recovery than traditional abdominal surgery.

Peritonitis

Peritonitis is an inflammation of the *peritoneum*, the membrane that lines the abdominal cavity and covers the abdominal organs. It results from a perforated ulcer (an ulcer that pierces the wall of an organ), a ruptured appendix, an infection of the reproductive tract, or other causes. Symptoms include fever, a swollen abdomen, and abdominal pain. Peritonitis can be life-threatening and must be treated swiftly. Treatments include antibiotics and surgery.

Gastroesophageal Reflux Disease (GERD)

Gastroesophageal reflux disease (GERD) is a condition caused by the backward flow of acidic gastric juices from the stomach into the esophagus. It occurs when the *lower esophageal sphincter* (LES), a muscle that acts as a valve between the esophagus and the stomach, fails to close properly. The gastric juices irritate the esophagus's lining. A symptom of GERD, which is commonly known as heartburn, is an upward-radiating burning sensation near the heart. This type of heartburn is both frequent and persistent.

Treatment includes losing weight, if that's needed; elevating the head of the bed; avoiding irritating foods; eating smaller amounts of food, more slowly; and taking drugs to reduce secretion of stomach acid. Some patients require surgery to repair the LES.

Inflammatory Bowel Disease (IBD)

Two similar diseases are included under the heading of *inflammatory bowel disease* (IBD). *Crohn's disease* is a chronic inflammation of parts of the intestinal wall, usually in the ileum and colon. *Ulcerative colitis* involves a continuous inflammation of the colon lining that begins in the rectum and extends proximally. Both diseases can have periods of inactivity. Symptoms of active disease include abdominal cramping, frequent diarrhea, and unexplained weight loss.

Both forms of IBD occur mainly in adolescents and young adults and show a hereditary pattern. They start with an abnormal response by the immune system, perhaps to bacteria that normally live in the intestine, which doesn't "shut off" but attacks the body itself. Treatment is with anti-inflammatory drugs, drugs that suppress the immune system, and sometimes surgery.

Ulcer

An *ulcer* is a sore, marked by inflammation and tissue damage, on the skin or tissues lining some organs and cavities. Ulcers caused by the damaging action of gastric, or peptic, juices on the lining of the GI tract are called *peptic ulcers*. Peptic ulcers usually appear in the first portion of the duodenum. The most common symptom is a dull or burning pain felt at night and when the stomach is empty. The pain lasts for minutes to hours and goes away briefly with the use of antacids.

A major cause of peptic ulcers is bacterial infection. Some are caused by long-term use of nonsteroidal anti-inflammatory drugs (NSAIDs), like aspirin and ibuprofen. The bacteria or NSAID weakens the GI tract lining, so gastric juices reach the wall. Stress or eating spicy foods doesn't cause ulcers, as often supposed, but they can make ulcers worse. Treatment of ulcers includes antibiotics to eliminate a bacterial infection and drugs that inhibit the secretion of gastric acid. Ulcers may lead to hemorrhage or perforation of the digestive tract wall.

Cirrhosis

Cirrhosis (sih-RO-sis) is a chronic disease that destroys liver tissue. It is characterized by enlargement of the liver, fluid in the abdomen, and jaundice. In the early stages of cirrhosis, there are no symptoms. Later symptoms include fatigue, weakness, loss of appetite, vomiting, and weight loss. Progression of the disease leads to internal bleeding and brain damage caused by changes in the blood's composition. The main cause of cirrhosis is excessive consumption of alcohol.

To help slow tissue destruction, doctors recommend that people with cirrhosis consume a healthy, low-sodium diet and avoid alcohol and other substances that can affect liver function. Medications may be prescribed to manage symptoms and to prevent or treat complications.

Hepatitis

Hepatitis is an inflammation of the liver commonly caused by a virus. Symptoms include jaundice, fever, nausea, diarrhea, and a general feeling of being unwell. More than six hepatitis viruses have been identified. Vaccines are available for two of them, Hepatitis A and Hepatitis B.

Hepatitis A, the most common hepatitis virus, is spread by fecal-oral contamination, often by food handlers, and in crowded, unsanitary conditions. It also may be acquired by eating contaminated food, especially seafood. The disease usually resolves on its own after several weeks.

Of special concern to health-care workers is Hepatitis B, which is spread by blood and other body fluids. Infected individuals may become carriers of the disease. Most patients recover, but the disease may be serious, even fatal. In some cases, it leads to liver cancer. CDC recommends the Hepatitis B vaccine for infants, previously unvaccinated children and adolescents through age 18, and adults at increased risk of contracting the disease, including health-care workers.

Constipation

Constipation is infrequency or difficulty in defecation and the passing of hard, dry feces. It is a symptom, not a disease, experienced by almost everyone sometime during life. Constipation is usually caused by a poor diet. Most constipation is temporary and not serious. Constipation can be treated and prevented by eating high-fiber foods, drinking 8 to 10 glasses of water daily, and exercise.

Diarrhea

Diarrhea is the frequent passage of watery bowel movements. It is a protective response to irritants in the intestinal tract. Diarrhea is a common problem that usually lasts a day or two and goes away on its own. Diarrhea that lasts longer than two days can cause dehydration and may be a sign of a more serious problem. Treatment for diarrhea depends on the cause. In most cases, drinking fluids to prevent dehydration is the only treatment needed. If the diarrhea is the result of a bacterial infection, antibiotics may be prescribed. Over-the-counter medications that stop diarrhea are generally not recommended, because they keep the body from eliminating the cause of the diarrhea.

Gastritis

Gastritis is the name for a group of conditions that inflame the stomach lining. Causes include bacterial infections, too much alcohol, or prolonged use of NSAIDs. The symptoms most people experience are abdominal upset and pain. Gastritis is typically treated with drugs to reduce stomach acid and antibiotics if the gastritis was caused by a bacterial infection.

Colon Cancer

Colon cancer forms in the tissues of the colon. The exact cause isn't known. Some risk factors are age (over 50), *polyps* (growths) on the inner wall of the colon, IBD, and a family history of this type of cancer. No conclusive evidence has been found linking dietary factors to this disease. A change in bowel habits can be a sign of colon cancer. Doctors encourage regular screening for people at an increased risk for colon cancer, because treatment is more effective when started early and removing polyps may prevent the cancer. Colon cancer is usually treated with surgery, along with chemotherapy or radiation therapy, or both.

Diverticulitis

Diverticulitis is an inflammation of *diverticula*, small pouches in the wall of the digestive tract, especially in the colon. Many people develop the pouches, but they occur most often in older people. The exact cause of diverticulitis isn't certain, but it may begin with collection of waste and bacteria in these sacs. Diverticulitis is accompanied by pain and sometimes bleeding. It can't be cured but is treated with diet, stool softeners, and drugs that ease smooth muscle contraction and pain.

HEALTH CARE SPECIALTY

Gastroenterologist

A gastroenterologist is a physician who specializes in digestive and intestinal disorders. One of the most common tests performed by gastroenterologists is a colonoscopy. In a colonoscopy, a lighted scope is used to see inside the lower gastrointestinal tract. Doctors recommend regular colonoscopies after age 50 to screen for a variety of digestive system diseases and conditions.

View of the inside of the colon.

Cholecystitis

Cholecystitis is an inflammation of the gallbladder. It is almost always caused by *gallstones*, clusters of solid material in the gallbladder. The most common symptom is abdominal pain. People with cholecystitis may be treated with intravenous fluids and antibiotics. Cholecystitis may be relieved with dietary changes, but the gallbladder may need to be removed.

Hemorrhoids

Hemorrhoids are *varicose veins* (twisted and swollen veins) in the rectum or anal canal. Straining during a bowel movement can produce hemorrhoids. Chronic constipation or diarrhea, pregnancy, aging, and anal intercourse can be contributing causes. Common symptoms of hemorrhoids are bleeding during bowel movements, itching, and rectal pain. Most symptoms subside on their own in a few days. The steps for treating and preventing constipation are effective against hemorrhoids as well.

CHECK POINT

7 What is the role of the gallbladder?

8 What is the role of bile in digestion?

METABOLISM AND NUTRITION

Nutrients absorbed from the digestive tract are used for all the body's cellular activities, which together make up **metabolism**. Metabolism consists of thousands of coordinated, carefully regulated chemical reactions that sustain life. Metabolic activities fall into two categories, or phases, in which the body either breaks down complex substances into simpler ones or builds simple compounds into needed materials:

- *Catabolism* (kah-TAB-o-lizm), the breakdown phase of metabolism, includes the digestion of food into small molecules and the release of energy from those molecules within the cell. Much of the energy is used to form ATP, which stores the energy needed to power all cellular activities. Some of the energy is released as heat, which is used to maintain body temperature.

- In *anabolism* (ah-NAB-o-lizm), the building phase of metabolism, simple compounds are used to manufacture materials needed for cellular activities and for the growth, function, and repair of tissues. The body can synthesize some of these materials, but others must be obtained from food.

Through the steps of catabolism and anabolism, there is a constant turnover of body materials as energy is consumed, cells function and grow, and waste products are generated.

Nutrients for Energy

With a typical diet, the body gets most of its energy from carbohydrates, some from fats, and a little from proteins. The relative amounts of these types of food that should be in the daily diet vary somewhat with the individual. Typical recommendations for the percentage of calories derived each day from each type are as follows:

- Carbohydrates: 55 to 60 percent
- Fats: 30 percent or less
- Proteins: 15 to 20 percent

Carbohydrates

Glucose is the body's main energy source. Most carbohydrates in the diet are converted to glucose and stored in the liver and muscle cells as glycogen. When glucose is needed for energy, glycogen is broken down to yield glucose.

There are two types of carbohydrates. *Simple carbohydrates*, also known as simple sugars, are found in table sugar and products like cookies that contain sugar. They also occur naturally in foods like fruit and milk. *Complex carbohydrates*, which include starches and fibers, can be natural (found in vegetables, fruit, whole grains, and legumes like peas and beans) or refined (found in processed foods).

Most carbohydrates in the diet should be complex, natural carbohydrates. Complex carbohydrates help maintain steady blood glucose levels. Fiber helps in weight and cholesterol control; the elimination of toxins and waste; and the prevention of diabetes, hemorrhoids, colon cancer, and other disorders. Starches are also rich in vitamins and minerals.

Fats

Once the body has burned up its stores of carbohydrates, which occurs after about 20 minutes of exercise, it turns for energy to fats. Fats belong to a group of substances called *lipids*. During digestion, they are broken down into glycerol, an energy source, and fatty acids, which are *essential* nutrients, meaning that they can't be made in the body but must be taken in as food.

Fats yield more than twice as much energy as protein and carbohydrates. They are digested slowly, and it takes time for stored fats to be broken down and made available as energy. But because fats are such an efficient source of energy, they are the main form in which energy is stored. When a person takes in more calories than are needed, the excess is stored as fat.

Fats are divided into saturated and unsaturated based on their chemical structure. *Unsaturated fats* come from plants and are generally referred to as oils, like corn, olive, and canola oil. Most *saturated fats* come from animal sources. An example is butter.

Saturated fats should make up less than a third of the fat in the diet and less than 10 percent of total calories. Diets high in saturated fats are associated with a higher-than-normal incidence of cancer, heart disease, and cardiovascular problems.

Many commercial products contain fats that are artificially saturated. These *partially hydrogenated* (HI-dro-jen-a-ted) vegetable oils are found in baked goods, processed peanut butter, vegetable shortening, and solid margarine. Evidence shows that components of hydrogenated fats, known as trans-fatty acids, may be just as harmful as natural saturated fats, if not more so, and therefore should be avoided.

Proteins

Proteins serve as both an energy source and the body's structural materials, found in muscles, bones, and connective tissue. They are composed of building blocks called *amino acids*.

The body breaks down proteins in food into amino acids. It then puts together amino acids to build the particular proteins it needs. The body can make 11 of the 20 amino acids needed to build proteins, but the other nine have to come from the diet. These nine are called the *essential amino acids*.

The body doesn't store protein reserves as it does reserves of carbohydrates and fats. People need to consume the right amount of protein on a regular basis so the body doesn't draw it from body substances, like muscle tissue or plasma proteins, to make the protein it requires. Fats and carbohydrates are described as "protein sparing," because they are used for energy before proteins are and thus spare proteins for use in making necessary body components.

Foods with significant amounts of protein include beef, poultry, fish, beans, eggs, cheese, nuts, and milk. Most animal proteins supply all the essential amino acids. Most vegetables are lacking in one or more of the essential amino acids. People on strict vegetarian diets must combine foods, such as legumes with grains, to obtain all the essential amino acids.

✓ CHECK POINT

9 What are the two phases of metabolism?

10 What is the main energy source for cells?

Vitamins and Minerals

In addition to fats, proteins, and carbohydrates for energy, the body requires vitamins and minerals.

- Vitamins are complex *organic compounds*, or chemical compounds characteristically found in living things. Vitamins are parts of enzymes or other substances essential for metabolism. (Enzymes increase the speed of chemical reactions. Without them, metabolism would not occur at a fast enough rate to sustain life.) Vitamin deficiencies lead to a variety of nutritional diseases.

Table 29-1 lists the essential vitamins, their functions, good sources of them, and the problems that arise from deficiencies.

- Minerals are *inorganic* chemical substances that are needed for the formation of bones and teeth, fluid balance, and activities such as muscle contraction, nerve impulse conduction, and blood clotting. Table 29-2 lists the main minerals needed in a proper diet, their functions and sources, and the problems that result if they are not consumed in sufficient supply.

Table 29-1 Vitamins

Vitamin	Functions	Sources	Results of Deficiency
A (retinol)	Required for healthy epithelial tissue and for eye pigments; involved in reproduction and immunity	Orange fruits and vegetables, liver, eggs, dairy products, dark green vegetables	Night blindness; dry, scaly skin; decreased immunity
B_1 (thiamin)	Energy metabolism; important in heart, nervous system, and muscle function	Cereals, grains, meats, legumes, nuts	Beriberi
B_2 (riboflavin)	Energy metabolism; important for growth and red blood cell production	Milk; eggs; liver; green, leafy vegetables; grains	Skin and tongue disorders
B_3 (niacin, nicotinic acid)	Energy metabolism; proper function of nervous and digestive systems, muscles, and skin	Yeast, meat, grains, legumes, nuts	Pellagra with dermatitis, diarrhea, mental disorders
B_6 (pyridoxine)	Amino acid and fatty acid metabolism; formation of niacin; manufacture of red blood cells	Meat, fish, poultry, fruit, grains, legumes, vegetables	Anemia, irritability, convulsions, muscle twitching, skin disorders
Pantothenic acid	Essential for normal growth; energy metabolism	Yeast, liver, eggs, many other foods	Sleep disturbances, digestive upset
B_{12} (cyanocobalamin)	Production of cells; maintenance of nerve cells; fatty acid and amino acid metabolism	Animal products	Pernicious anemia
Biotin (a B vitamin)	Involved in fat and glycogen formation, amino acid metabolism	Peanuts, liver, tomatoes, eggs, oatmeal, soy, many other foods	Lack of coordination, dermatitis, fatigue
Folate (folic acid, a B vitamin)	Required for amino acid metabolism, DNA synthesis, production of red blood cells	Vegetables, liver, legumes, seeds	Anemia, digestive disorders, neural tube defects in embryo
C (ascorbic acid)	Maintains healthy skin and linings of body cavities and passageways; helps make collagen, which makes connective tissue strong; protects against free radicals that can injure cells	Citrus fruits, green vegetables, potatoes, orange fruits	Scurvy, poor wound healing, anemia, weak bones
D (calciferol)	Aids in absorption of calcium and phosphorus	Fatty fish, liver, eggs, fortified milk	Rickets, bone deformities
E (tocopherol)	Protects cell membranes; protects against free radicals	Seeds, green vegetables, nuts, grains, oils	Anemia, muscle and liver degeneration, pain
K	Synthesis of clotting factors; bone formation	Bacteria in digestive tract, liver, cabbage, leafy green vegetables	Hemorrhage

Table 29-2 Minerals

Mineral	Functions	Sources	Results of Deficiency
Calcium (Ca)	Formation of bones and teeth, blood clotting, nerve conduction, muscle contraction	Dairy products, eggs, green vegetables, legumes	Rickets, tetany, osteoporosis
Phosphorus (P)	Formation of bones and teeth; found in ATP, nucleic acids	Meat, fish, poultry, egg yolks, dairy products	Osteoporosis, abnormal metabolism
Sodium (Na)	Fluid balance, nerve impulse conduction, muscle contraction	Most foods, especially processed foods; table salt	Weakness, cramps, diarrhea, dehydration
Potassium (K)	Fluid balance, nerve and muscle activity	Fruits, meat, seafood, milk, vegetables, grains	Muscular and neurological disorders
Chloride (Cl)	Fluid balance, hydrochloric acid in stomach	Meat, milk, eggs, processed foods, table salt	Rarely occurs
Iron (Fe)	Oxygen transport (hemoglobin, myoglobin)	Meat, eggs, fortified cereals, legumes, dried fruit	Anemia, dry skin, indigestion
Iodine (I)	Thyroid hormones	Seafood, iodized salt	Hypothyroidism, goiter
Magnesium (Mg)	Chemical reactions, carbohydrate metabolism	Green vegetables, grains, nuts, legumes	Spasticity, arrhythmia, vasodilation
Manganese (Mg)	Part of several enzymes; activates others	Many foods	Possible reproductive disorders
Copper (Cu)	Necessary for absorption and use of iron in forming hemoglobin; part of some enzymes	Meat, water	Anemia
Chromium (Cr)	Works with insulin to regulate blood glucose levels	Meat, unrefined foods, fats and oils	Inability to use glucose
Cobalt (Co)	Part of vitamin B_{12}	Animal products	Pernicious anemia
Zinc (Zn)	Promotes carbon dioxide transport and energy metabolism; found in enzymes	Meat, fish, poultry, grains, vegetables	Alopecia (baldness); may be related to diabetes
Fluoride (F)	Prevents tooth decay	Fluoridated water, tea, seafood	Cavities

A Healthy Diet

The U.S. Department of Agriculture (USDA) publishes the *Dietary Guidelines for Americans*, a set of science-based guidelines for eating and physical activity designed to promote and improve health, combat overweight and obesity, and reduce the risk of developing major chronic diseases, such as cardiac disease and Type 2 diabetes. The 2005 guidelines (the most recent at the time of this writing) define a healthy diet as one that:

- Emphasizes fruits, vegetables, whole grains, and fat-free or low-fat milk and milk products
- Includes lean meats, poultry, fish, beans, eggs, and nuts
- Is low in saturated fats, trans fats, cholesterol, salt (sodium), and added sugars

Since 1992, the USDA has produced a food pyramid (Figure 29-5) to help people make healthy food choices. The pyramid incorporates the principles of the guidelines

Figure 29-5 USDA MyPyramid showing basic dietary guidelines. (U.S. Department of Agriculture/Center for Nutrition Policy and Promotion)

ZOOM IN

Dieticians

Dietitians plan food and nutrition programs. They prevent and treat illnesses by promoting healthy eating habits and recommending changes in diet. Many work directly with patients, assessing nutritional needs, developing and implementing nutrition programs, and evaluating the results. They help people control cholesterol; reduce the need for medications; manage medical problems like diabetes, heart disease, and high blood pressure; lessen their risk of developing diseases; and increase their chances of living a long, healthy life.

Dieticians are managers as well. Many run the food service department at hospitals, schools, and other institutions. Dieticians oversee meal planning and preparation; hire, train, and supervise staff; budget for and buy food, equipment, and supplies; and enforce sanitary and safety regulations.

Some dieticians answer questions and dispense advice by phone and on web sites, including HealthCastle.com, the biggest nutrition site on the Internet run by registered dieticians. Others provide these services while working for food processing companies, handling questions from customers about the nutritional benefits of the foods and ways of preparing them.

Dieticians often work in hospitals, doctors' offices, public health clinics, home health agencies, and health maintenance organizations. They also work for wellness programs, sports teams, and supermarkets. Some are consultants, performing nutrition screenings or dispensing advice on sanitation, safety procedures, or menu development. Dieticians work in food manufacturing, advertising, and marketing, where they analyze foods, write materials related to nutrition and diet for consumers, and report on issues like fiber, vitamin supplements, or recipes' nutritional content.

Becoming a dietician requires a bachelor's degree and, in nearly every state, a license or certification. Dieticians also may obtain the American Dietetic Association's (ADA's) Registered Dietician credential. Job opportunities are good and predicted to stay that way, as a result of increased public interest in nutrition and a growing body of research that shows how intimately diet is linked to disease and good health.

and other nutritional standards. The colored bands show five different categories of foods in widths that indicate how much should be chosen from each group daily. The narrow yellow band between fruits and milk represents oils. The pyramid and guidelines stress:

- Variety in the diet. Foods in all the groups are needed every day for good health.
- Moderation. A single serving or portion is smaller than most people think.
- Eating fruits and vegetables. Most people need more of these in their diets.
- Choosing "nutrient-dense" foods that are rich in nutrients compared to their calorie content. This helps people get all needed nutrients without the excess calories that lead to weight gain, a risk factor for many diseases. This recommendation also includes eating unrefined foods, such as whole grains, and unprocessed foods.
- The importance of exercise, as represented by the climbing figure on the side of the pyramid. Exercise, like good nutrition, promotes good health.

Nutrition and Aging

People sometimes find it difficult to maintain a balanced diet as they age. Because of changes in the sensory system, food may be less appealing. Medications may interfere with appetite and the absorption and use of some nutrients. Because metabolism generally slows and less food is required to meet energy needs, an older person eating the same amount of food as in earlier years may gain weight. Nutritional deficiencies may also develop; therefore, it's important for older people to seek out foods that are nutrient-dense to avoid becoming full on empty calories. Exercise may help boost appetite in older adults.

Common Diseases and Conditions of Metabolism and Nutrition

Common diseases and conditions of metabolism and nutrition include eating disorders and obesity.

Eating Disorders

According to the National Institute of Mental Health, eating disorders have complex psychological and medical causes that are not fully understood. They may be accompanied by depression, anxiety disorders, substance abuse, or other psychiatric disorders. Eating disorders can cause serious health problems, including heart and kidney damage, and they can be fatal. There are three main eating disorders:

- **Anorexia nervosa.** A person with *anorexia* (a-neh-RECK-see-ah) *nervosa* is extremely fearful of gaining weight. Many people with this disorder see themselves as overweight even when they are obviously malnourished or starved. People with anorexia may diet or exercise too much, make themselves vomit, or take laxatives and other drugs to speed food through the body.

- **Bulimia.** *Bulimia* (buh-LEE-me-ah) is characterized by overeating followed by efforts to purge the body, using many of the same methods as in anorexia nervosa. Most people with bulimia and anorexia nervosa are women.

- **Binge eating.** *Binge eating disorder*, the most common eating disorder, is consuming unusually large amounts of food in a short period of time and feeling unable to control one's eating in the process. An estimated 35 percent of people with this disorder are men. Unlike bulimia, binge eating isn't followed by attempts to purge the body, so people with this disorder are frequently overweight or obese.

Treatment for eating disorders involves getting the person back to a healthy weight, treating the psychological issues that led to the disorder, and trying to prevent relapses. Depending on the disorder, antidepressants and other drugs may be prescribed.

Obesity

Obesity is having too much body fat. It is determined from a person's body mass index (BMI), which is calculated using height and weight. As Table 29-3 shows, an adult with a BMI of 30 or more is considered obese. In children, the measure is more complex because age and sex are considered. According to the CDC, more than 34 percent of American adults and 16 percent of American children are obese.

HEALTH CARE SPECIALTY

Dietetic Technician

Dietetic technicians often assist dieticians and nutritionists, although they also work independently. At hospitals, they help plan meals for patients. At schools and businesses, they develop cafeteria food selections. Dietary technicians teach people about diet and gather information from patients for doctors, dieticians, and nutritionists. Nursing homes, long-term care facilities, daycare centers, and weight management clinics are some of the many organizations that employ dietary technicians. ADA offers a credential for this career. This career is profiled in Chapter 17, "Overview of Health Care Careers."

Obesity has increased dramatically in the past 30 years, mostly because of changes in lifestyle. Key contributing factors are lower levels of physical activity; larger portions in meals; and higher consumption of prepared foods and restaurant meals, which are often higher in fat and calories than food prepared at home from raw ingredients.

According to the National Heart Lung and Blood Institute, obese children and adults have an increased risk of developing Type 2 diabetes. Obesity in adults is associated with an increased risk of developing many other diseases, including heart disease, high blood pressure, stroke, osteoarthritis, and certain cancers. Obesity is usually treated with diet and exercise.

✓ CHECK POINT

11 Both vitamins and minerals are needed in metabolism. What is the difference between vitamins and minerals?

12 What are the typical recommendations for the percentage of calories derived each day from carbohydrates, fats, and proteins in the diet?

THE URINARY SYSTEM

The urinary system is also called the *excretory system* because one of its main functions is *excretion*, the removal and elimination of the waste products of metabolism from the blood. This system is also critically important for maintaining homeostasis.

The urinary system is involved in the following processes:

- **Excretion of waste products.** The main waste material is *urea*. After being formed in the liver, urea is transported in the blood to the kidneys for elimination.

- **Fluid balance.** Although the amount of water gained and lost in a day can vary tremendously, the kidneys can adapt to these variations so that the volume of water in the body remains relatively stable.

- **Acid-base balance.** Metabolism produces acids, certain foods can yield acids or bases, and people may also take antacids—all of which affect the pH balance of body fluids. The urinary system helps maintain the normal pH of body fluids.

- **Blood pressure regulation.** The kidneys, which are part of the urinary system, depend on blood pressure to filter the blood. If blood pressure falls too low, the kidneys release an enzyme that causes it to rise.

- **Regulation of red blood cell production.** When the kidneys don't get enough oxygen, they produce a hormone that stimulates red cell production in the bone marrow.

Table 29-3 Normal, Overweight, and Obese Body Mass Index

BMI	Normal											Overweight							Obese												
	19	20	21	22	23	24	25	26	27	28	29	30	31	32	33	34	35	36	37	38	39
Height (inches)												Body Weight (pounds)										
58	91	96	100	105	110	115	119	124	129	134	138	143	148	153	158	162	167	172	177	181	186
59	94	99	104	109	114	119	124	128	133	138	143	148	153	158	163	168	173	178	183	188	193
60	97	102	107	112	118	123	128	133	138	143	148	153	158	163	168	174	179	184	189	194	199
61	100	106	111	116	122	127	132	137	143	148	153	158	164	169	174	180	185	190	195	201	206
62	104	109	115	120	126	131	136	142	147	153	158	164	169	175	180	186	191	196	202	207	213
63	107	113	118	124	130	135	141	146	152	158	163	169	175	180	186	191	197	203	208	214	220
64	110	116	122	128	134	140	145	151	157	163	169	174	180	186	192	197	204	209	215	221	227
65	114	120	126	132	138	144	150	156	162	168	174	180	186	192	198	204	210	216	222	228	234
66	118	124	130	136	142	148	155	161	167	173	179	186	192	198	204	210	216	223	229	235	241
67	121	127	134	140	146	153	159	166	172	178	185	191	198	204	211	217	223	230	236	242	249
68	125	131	138	144	151	158	164	171	177	184	190	197	203	210	216	223	230	236	243	249	256
69	128	135	142	149	155	162	169	176	182	189	196	203	209	216	223	230	236	243	250	257	263
70	132	139	146	153	160	167	174	181	188	195	202	209	216	222	229	236	243	250	257	264	271
71	136	143	150	157	165	172	179	186	193	200	208	215	222	229	236	243	250	257	265	272	279
72	140	147	154	162	169	177	184	191	199	206	213	221	228	235	242	250	258	265	272	279	287
73	144	151	159	166	174	182	189	197	204	212	219	227	235	242	250	257	265	272	280	288	295
74	148	155	163	171	179	186	194	202	210	218	225	233	241	249	256	264	272	280	287	295	303
75	152	160	168	176	184	192	200	208	216	224	232	240	248	256	264	272	279	287	295	303	311
76	156	164	172	180	189	197	205	213	221	230	238	246	254	263	271	279	287	295	304	312	320

Table 29-3 Extremely Obese Body Mass Index *(continued)*

BMI	40	41	42	43	44	45	46	47	48	49	50	51	52	53	54
Height (inches)	Body Weight (pounds)														
58	191	196	201	205	210	215	220	224	229	234	239	244	248	253	258
59	198	203	208	212	217	222	227	232	237	242	247	252	257	262	267
60	204	209	215	220	225	230	265	240	245	250	255	261	266	271	276
61	211	217	222	227	232	238	243	248	254	259	264	269	275	280	285
62	218	224	229	265	240	246	251	256	262	267	273	278	284	289	295
63	225	231	237	242	248	254	259	265	270	278	282	287	293	299	304
64	232	238	244	250	256	262	267	273	279	285	291	296	302	308	314
65	240	246	252	258	264	270	276	282	288	294	300	306	312	318	324
66	247	253	260	266	272	278	284	291	297	303	309	315	322	328	334
67	255	261	268	274	280	287	293	299	306	312	319	325	331	338	344
68	262	269	276	282	289	295	302	308	315	322	328	335	341	348	354
69	270	277	284	291	297	304	311	318	324	331	338	345	351	358	365
70	278	285	292	299	306	313	320	327	334	341	348	355	362	369	376
71	286	293	301	308	315	322	329	338	343	351	358	365	372	379	386
72	294	302	309	316	324	331	338	346	353	361	368	375	383	390	397
73	302	310	318	325	333	340	348	355	363	371	378	386	393	401	408
74	311	319	326	334	342	350	358	365	373	381	389	396	404	412	420
75	319	327	335	343	351	359	367	375	383	391	399	407	415	423	431
76	328	336	344	353	361	369	377	385	394	402	410	418	426	435	443

Organs of the Urinary System

The main parts of the urinary system (Figure 29-6) are as follows:

Kidneys

The two **kidneys** lie against the back muscles in the upper abdomen. These organs extract wastes from the blood by filtering it (discussed below), balance body fluids, and form urine.

Ureters

The two **ureters** are long, slender, muscular tubes that transport urine from the kidneys to the urinary bladder. Urine is moved through the ureters by gravity and peristalsis.

Urinary Bladder

The **urinary bladder** is a temporary reservoir for urine. A moderately full bladder holds about 470 milliliters (1 pint).

Urethra

The **urethra** is a tube that carries urine from the bladder to the outside of the body. The urethra differs in males and females. In males, the urethra is part of both the reproductive and the urinary systems, and it is much longer than the female urethra.

✔ **CHECK POINT**

13 What are the functions of the urinary system?

14 What is the name of the tubes that carry urine from the kidney to the bladder?

Kidney Function

The basic working units of the kidneys are the **nephrons**, which total about 1 million. If laid out end to end, a person's nephrons would span 120 kilometers (75 miles)! Refer to Figure 29-7 (following page) in the following discussion of how nephrons function.

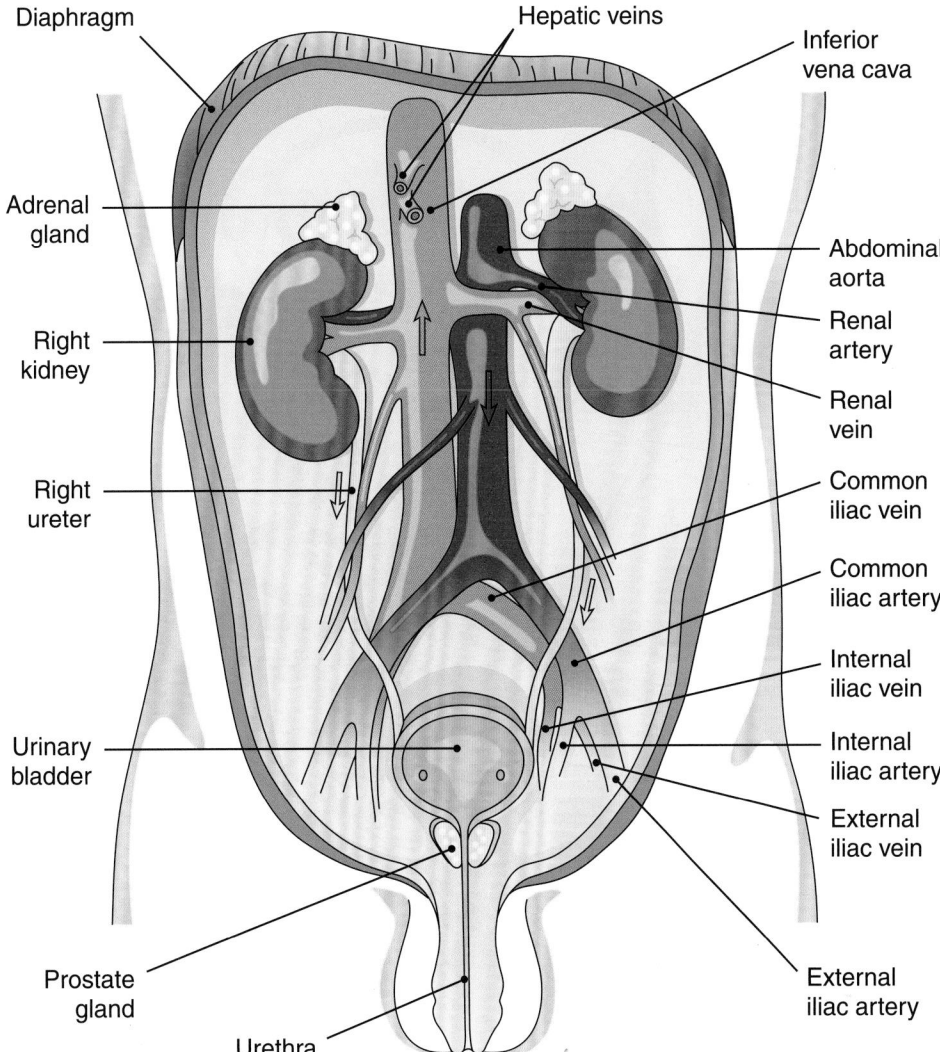

Figure 29-6 Male urinary system.

A nephron is basically a tiny coiled tube with a bulb at one end. This bulb, known as the *glomerular (Bowman) capsule*, surrounds a cluster of capillaries called the *glomerulus*. Blood pressure forces certain materials from the blood through the walls of these capillaries into the Bowman capsule and through the wall of the Bowman capsule into the tube part of the nephron. Blood cells and large protein molecules do not pass through.

The materials forced into the nephron are mainly water, electrolytes (salts), wastes, nutrients, and toxins. The wastes and toxins must be eliminated, but most of the water, electrolytes, and nutrients must be returned to the blood or a person would quickly starve or dehydrate.

This return process occurs through the peritubular capillaries that surround the nephron. Other processes further regulate the fluid's composition, concentration, and pH. As fluid travels slowly through the nephrons'

twists and turns, there is ample time for exchanges (by osmosis, diffusion, and cell energy) to take place. These processes together allow the kidney to fine-tune body fluids.

Urine

When all useful materials have been filtered back into the blood, the end product that the kidneys produce is *urine*. It is a yellowish liquid that's about 95 percent water and 5 percent dissolved solids and gases. The dissolved substances normally found in the urine include:

● Certain waste products, including urea, produced when protein-containing foods are broken down; *uric acid*, produced from the breakdown of purine, a substance found in many foods; and *creatinine* (kre-AT-ih-nin), a byproduct of muscle activity.

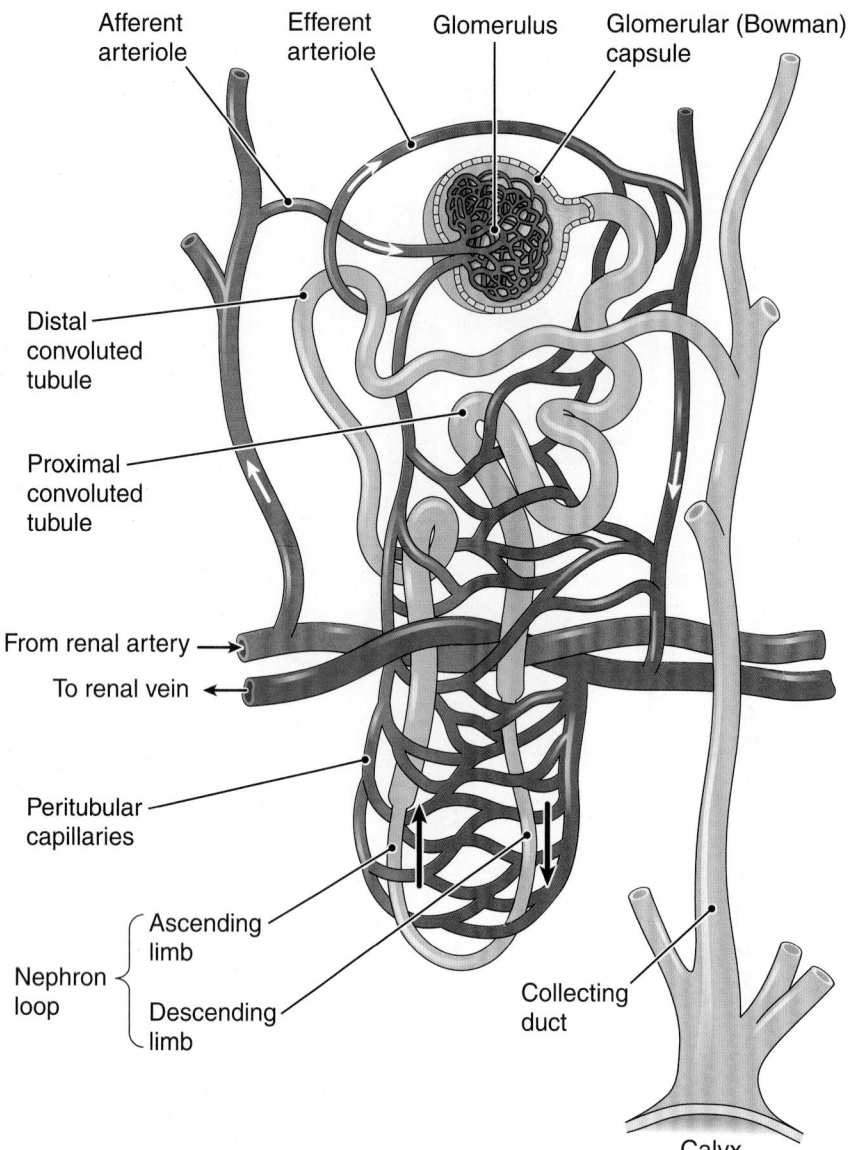

Figure 29-7   A nephron and its blood supply.

- Electrolytes, which are excreted in appropriate amounts to keep their blood concentration constant.
- Pigment, mainly yellow pigment from bile. Pigments from foods and drugs also may appear in the urine.

Urinalysis, or laboratory study of the urine, is a simple and widely used method for diagnosing urinary tract disorders. It may also reveal disturbances in other systems when abnormal byproducts are eliminated in the urine. During a routine urinalysis:

- The urine is examined for color and clarity. (Cloudiness is a sign of bacteria).
- Specific gravity (a measure of concentration) and pH are recorded.
- Tests are performed for chemical components such as glucose, ketones, and hemoglobin.

- The urine is examined microscopically for cells, crystals, and casts (tube-shaped particles made of blood cells or kidney cells).

In more detailed tests, drugs, enzymes, hormones, and other products of metabolism may be analyzed, and bacterial cultures performed.

Effects of Aging

Aging causes the kidneys to lose some of their ability to concentrate urine. More and more water is needed to excrete the same amount of waste. Older people find it necessary to drink more water than young people, and they eliminate more urine, even at night. Older adults are also more susceptible to urinary system infections.

Enlargement of the prostate, common in older men, may cause obstruction and pressure in the ureters and kidneys. If this condition isn't treated, it causes permanent kidney damage. Other changes with age include decreased bladder capacity and decreased muscle tone in the bladder, which may lead to incontinence.

Common Diseases and Conditions of the Urinary System

Common medical problems in the urinary system are caused by illness, aging, or injury.

Urinary Tract Infections (UTIs)

Organisms that infect the urinary tract generally enter the body through the urethra. They are generally colon bacteria carried in feces. Urinary tract infections (UTIs) occur more commonly in women because the female urethra is shorter and the opening is closer to the anus. Common symptoms are an urge to urinate frequently and a painful or burning sensation when urinating. Antibiotics are given to kill the bacteria that cause the infection.

Pyelonephritis

Inflammation of the kidney and renal pelvis, usually as a result of infection, is called *pyelonephritis*. The infection is most often caused by bacteria that have spread from the bladder. Symptoms include painful or difficult urination and the presence of bacteria and pus in the urine. Pyelonephritis is treated with antibiotics.

Kidney Stones

Kidney stones (also known as *urinary tract calculi*) develop from crystals in the urine. Normally, chemicals in the urine keep crystals from forming, but in some people, these chemicals don't seem to work. Often, kidney stones don't cause any symptoms. When they do, the first symptom is usually pain. Most kidney stones pass out of the body on their own, but patients may be advised to drink a lot of water to help keep the stone moving. If a kidney stone is too large to pass on its own, surgery may be needed, or the stone may be broken into smaller pieces using shock waves. Because kidney stones are likely to recur, doctors may recommend lifestyle changes, such as drinking more liquids, or prescribe drugs to help keep crystals from forming.

Kidney Failure

Kidney failure is the inability of the kidneys to perform their functions. It may occur suddenly, as a result of injury, shock, exposure to toxins, infections, and other kidney disorders, or it may occur gradually over a number of years, due to high blood pressure or diabetes. Symptoms vary widely. Early symptoms may include fatigue and a general feeling of illness. Examples of later symptoms are sleep problems and swelling of the feet and hands. Sudden kidney failure may resolve after the cause is identified and treated. During this time, the patient may need to follow a carefully regulated diet. A person with gradual kidney failure may eventually need dialysis or a kidney transplant.

 HEALTH CARE SPECIALTY

Dialysis Nurse

Patients with kidney failure may require dialysis. Dialysis treatments cleanse the patient's blood of the by-products that are normally filtered by the kidneys but that can't be filtered that way because of the kidneys' impaired function. Dialysis nurses care for patients who are undergoing dialysis at home, in a dialysis center, or during travel—even on cruises. Their responsibilities include operating dialysis equipment, teaching patients to do dialysis at home, assessing the response to treatment, checking medications and lab work, and performing general tasks related to nursing and managing care.

✓ CHECK POINT

15 What is the functional unit of the kidney called?

16 What is the glomerulus, and what is its function?

Chapter Wrap-Up

Don't forget to visit the Point companion website for additional study resources!

CHAPTER HIGHLIGHTS

- The main functions of the respiratory system are to provide oxygen to body cells and to eliminate carbon dioxide. Respiration has three phases: pulmonary ventilation, external exchange of gases, and internal exchange of gases.
- Air enters the body through the nasal cavities (or mouth) and passes through the rest of the upper airway—pharynx, larynx, and trachea—before entering the lower airway—the bronchi and lungs. The smallest bronchial tubes, the bronchioles, carry air into the alveoli, where oxygen and carbon dioxide are exchanged with capillaries.
- The digestive system has three chief functions: digestion, absorption, and elimination.
- The digestive tract is a long, muscular tube that consists of the mouth, pharynx, esophagus, stomach, small intestine, and large intestine. Accessory organs include the salivary glands, liver, gallbladder, and pancreas.
- Nutrients power all the bodies' cellular activities, which together make up metabolism. The body gets its energy from carbohydrates, fats, and proteins. It also needs certain minerals for the formation of bones and teeth, fluid balance, and activities like contracting muscles, conducting nerve impulses, and clotting. Vitamins are essential for metabolism and many other activities.
- The USDA's food guide pyramid summarizes healthy eating choices. Following these guidelines provides the needed nutrients in the necessary amounts.
- The urinary system excretes waste products, helps maintain the body's fluid and acid-base balances, and helps regulate blood pressure and red blood cell production. The main parts of the urinary system are the kidneys, ureters, urinary bladder, and urethra.
- The respiratory, digestive, and urinary systems and metabolism work less effectively with age, resulting in increased lung disorders and urinary system infections, decreased bladder capacity, nutritional deficiencies, constipation, incontinence, and other problems.
- A health care specialty involving the respiratory system is respiratory therapist. A health care specialty involving the digestive system is gastroenterologist. Health care specialties involving nutrition include dietician and dietetic technician. A health care specialty involving the urinary system is dialysis nurse.
- Common diseases and conditions of the respiratory system include asthma, bronchitis, emphysema, lung cancer, pneumonia, tuberculosis, rhinitis, sinusitis, upper respiratory infections, and influenza.
- Common diseases and conditions of the digestive system include appendicitis, peritonitis, gastroesophageal reflux disease, inflammatory bowel disease, ulcer, cirrhosis, hepatitis, constipation, diarrhea, gastritis, colon cancer, diverticulitis, cholecystitis, and hemorrhoids.
- Common diseases and conditions of metabolism and nutrition include anorexia nervosa, bulimia, binge eating, and obesity.
- Common diseases and conditions of the urinary system include urinary tract infections, pyelonephritis, kidney stones, and kidney failure.

REVIEW QUESTIONS

Matching

1. _____ Main energy source for the body

2. _____ Inorganic chemical substance required for normal body function.

3. _____ Complex organic compound required for normal body function

4. _____ Lipid that comes mostly from animal sources

5. _____ Lipid that comes from plants

    a. saturated fat   **b.** vitamin   **c.** mineral   **d.** unsaturated fat   **e.** glucose

Multiple Choice

6. Chronic obstructive pulmonary disease (COPD) includes all of the following diseases EXCEPT
    a. emphysema   **c.** pneumonia
    b. asthma   **d.** chronic bronchitis

7. Hydrochloric acid and pepsin are secreted by the
    a. salivary glands   **c.** pancreas
    b. stomach   **d.** liver

8. The health care specialty that performs colonoscopies is
    a. gastroenterologist   **c.** respiratory therapist
    b. dietetic technician   **d.** dialysis nurse

9. Which disease is commonly known as heartburn?
    a. angina pectoris   **c.** ulcer
    b. appendicitis   **d.** GERD

10. The functional unit of the kidney is the
    a. ureter   **c.** glomerulus
    b. nephron   **d.** bladder

Completion

11. The exchange of air between the atmosphere and the lungs is called _____ _____.

12. _____ help plan meals for patients and develop cafeteria food selections at schools and businesses.

13. A soft mass of food small enough to be swallowed is called a/an _____.

14. The _____ is a temporary reservoir for urine.

15. The tube that carries urine outside the body is the _____.

Short Answer

16. Trace the path of air from the nostrils to the lung capillaries.

_____

_____

17. Describe how aging affects nutrition.

_____

_____

18. Where does most absorption occur in the digestive tract, and what structures are needed for absorption? What materials are absorbed into the blood? Into the lymph?

19. List the main parts of the urinary system and explain the function of each of them.

20. Catherine, an older woman, mentions to her doctor that she is always thirsty and that she needs to get up at night to urinate. What age-related changes in the urinary system might be causing these symptoms?

INVESTIGATE IT

1. Why do we yawn? Why do we sneeze? What causes hiccups? Find the answer to one of these questions. If you use the Internet, search phrases like these will yield helpful results:

   why people yawn
   why people sneeze
   what causes hiccups

   Two web sites you might consult are these:
   http://www.howstuffworks.com/
   http://kidshealth.org/kid/

2. Use the food pyramid and other resources to develop a healthy diet for yourself. What types of foods should it include? How many portions of each type of food would be needed each day? What's the right portion size? How many calories would be provided by each meal? Make use of any interactive tools that the USDA (http://mypyramid.gov) or other web sites offer.

3. Alcohol interferes with metabolism and contributes to a variety of disorders. Find out how alcohol acts in the body. What is alcoholism, and what effects can it have on a person's health? Use search terms like *alcohol* and *alcoholism* in your Internet search.

4. Make a list of five or six facts about smoking. Include items like these:

   - Where smoking stands in the list of preventable causes of death in the U.S.
   - The percentage of adults in the U.S. who smoke
   - How many deaths smoking causes each year
   - How much earlier smokers die than nonsmokers
   - How much smoking costs the nation annually

   Two good resources are given below. The CDC will likely have more recent statistics.

   Centers for Disease Control and Prevention: http://www.cdc.gov/tobacco/data_statistics/fact_sheets/index.htm

   The Health Museum: http://www.mhms.org/uploads/Respiratory%20Cart%20Activities%20-%20Details.pdf

5. Read about one of the major flu pandemics of the twentieth century (1918, 1957, 1968, or 2009). What kind of virus was involved? How did the epidemic start? How did it spread? How many people died? How long did it last? If you use the Internet, search for *flu pandemic* followed by one of the years given above.

RECOMMENDED READING

Duyff, R.L. *American Dietetic Association Complete Food and Nutrition Guide.* Hoboken, NJ: John Wiley & Sons; 2006.

Kidney Structure and Function. Biology Mad. Available at: http://www.biologymad.com/resources/kidney.swf.

MyHealthScore.Com. Digestive System. Available at: http://www.innerbody.com/image/digeov.html.

MyHealthScore.Com. Urinary System. Available at: http://www.innerbody.com/image/cardov.html.

What We Know About Gas Exchange in the Lungs. Partnership for Environmental Education and Rural Health Curriculum. Texas A&M University. Available at: http://peer.tamu.edu/curriculum_modules/OrganSystems/module_4/whatweknow_lungs.htm.

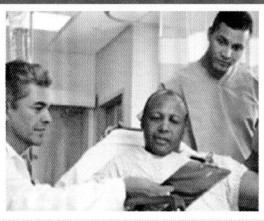
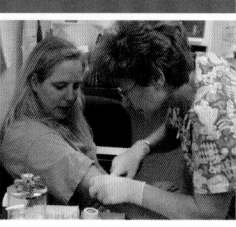
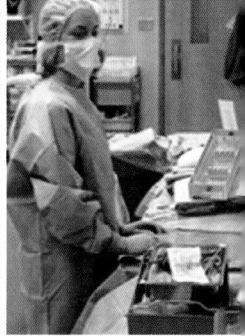

Reproduction and Development

CHAPTER OBJECTIVES

After careful study of this chapter, you should be able to:

* Name the male and female gonads and describe the function of each.
* List the accessory organs of the male and female reproductive systems and describe the function of each.
* Describe ovulation and menstruation.
* Explain how aging affects the reproductive system.
* Identify common diseases and conditions of the male and female reproductive systems.

* List factors influencing growth and development.
* Name major developments for each stage of life.
* Describe Kübler-Ross's stages of grief.
* Discuss the developmental theories of Erikson, Havighurst, and Freud.
* Describe each level of Maslow's hierarchy of basic human needs.

KEY TERMS

breasts
cervix (SER-viks)
development
embryo (EM-bre-o)
endometrium (en-do-ME-tre-um)
estrogen
fallopian (fah-LO-pe-an) tubes
fetus (FE-tus)

gestation (jes-TA-shun)
labia (LA-be-ah)
menopause (MEN-o-pawz)
menstrual cycle
menstruation (men-stru-A-shun)
ova (s., ovum) (O-vah)
ovary (pl., ovaries) (O-vah-re)

ovulation (ov-u-LA-shun)
penis (PE-nis)
perineum (per-ih-NE-um)
progesterone
prostate gland
scrotum (SKRO-tum)
secondary sex characteristics
semen (SE-men)

spermatozoa (sper-mah-to-ZO-ah)
testes (s., testis) (TES-teze)
testosterone (tes-TOS-ter-one)
uterus (U-ter-us)
vagina (vah-JI-nah)
vulva (VUL-vah)

The reproductive system isn't necessary for the continuation of the life of the individual. Rather, it's needed for the continuation of the human species. Human development begins at conception and continues throughout life.

THE MALE AND FEMALE REPRODUCTIVE SYSTEMS

In humans, as with most other animals, reproduction is sexual. This means there are two kinds of individuals, males and females, each of which produces cells designed specifically for the perpetuation of the species. In men, those specialized reproduction cells are called **spermatozoa,** or sperm cells. In women, they're called **ova,** or egg cells.

The Male Reproductive System

The male reproductive system (Figure 30-1) has two groups of structures: primary organs and accessory structures. The primary organs are the *gonads*, or sex glands.

- In males, the gonads are the **testes**, which produce both sperm cells and hormones.
- The accessory structures include a series of ducts that transport sperm cells, as well as various *exocrine*

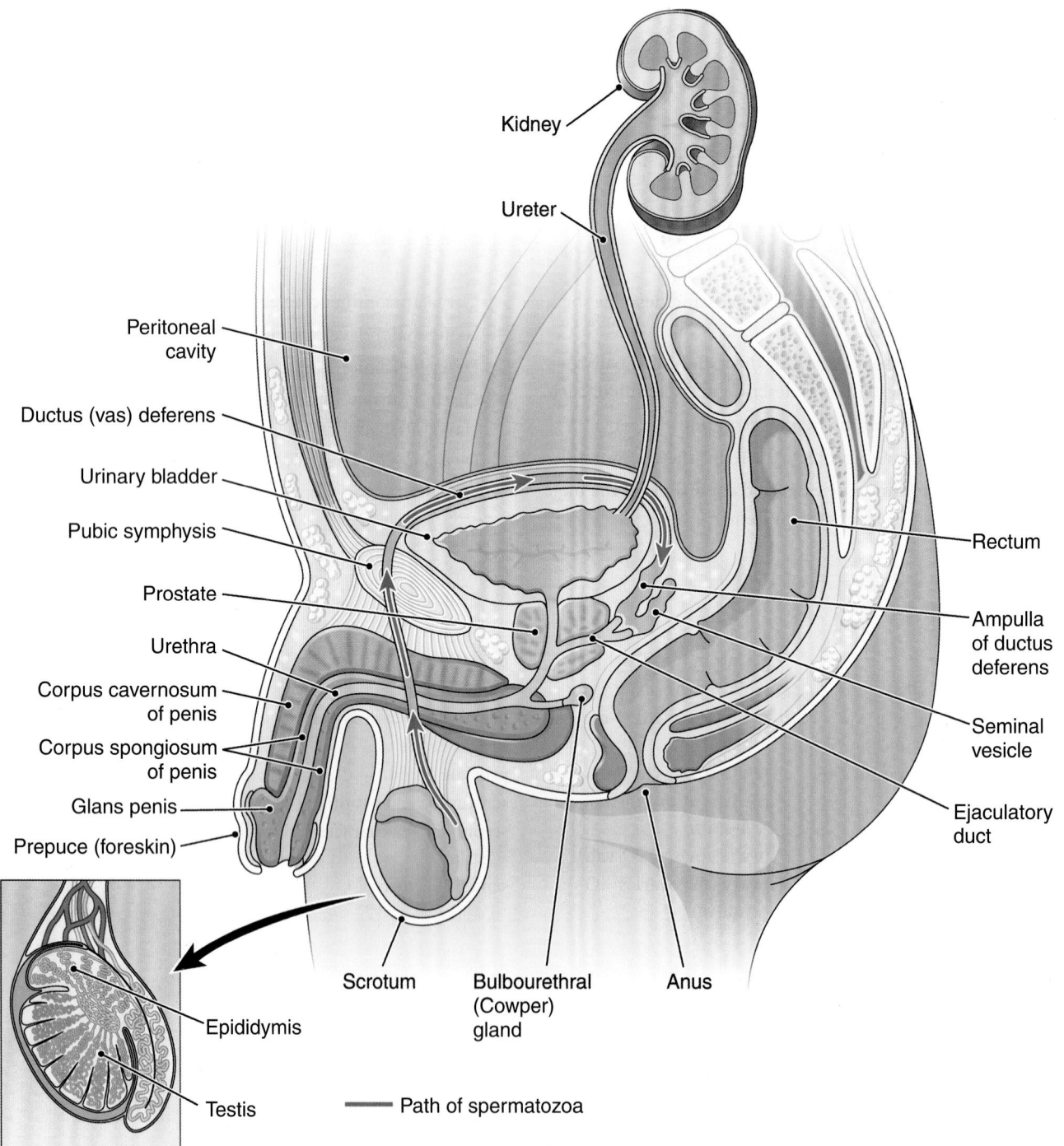

Figure 30-1 Male reproductive system.

(EK-so-krin) *glands*. Unlike endocrine glands (which are described in Chapter 27, "Coordination and Control"), these glands have ducts or tubes that carry secretions away from the gland.

The Testes

The testes are located outside the body, midline below the torso, suspended in a sac called the **scrotum**. They are oval-shaped. Each testis is suspended by a spermatic cord containing blood vessels, lymphatic vessels, and nerves that supply the testis and the tube through which sperm travel during an ejaculation.

Testosterone. **Testosterone** is the main male sex hormone. It diffuses from the testes into surrounding fluid and is then absorbed into the bloodstream. Testosterone has three functions:

- Developing and maintaining the reproductive structures.
- Developing sperm cells.
- Developing **secondary sex characteristics**. In males, these traits include a deeper voice, broader shoulders, narrower hips, a greater percentage of muscle tissue, and more body hair than in females.

Spermatozoa. Spermatozoa are tiny individual cells. The average ejaculation contains at least 200 million spermatozoa, but only one sperm will fertilize an egg cell. After puberty, sperm cells are manufactured continuously in the seminiferous (seh-mih-NIF-er-us) tubules of the testes (Figure 30-2).

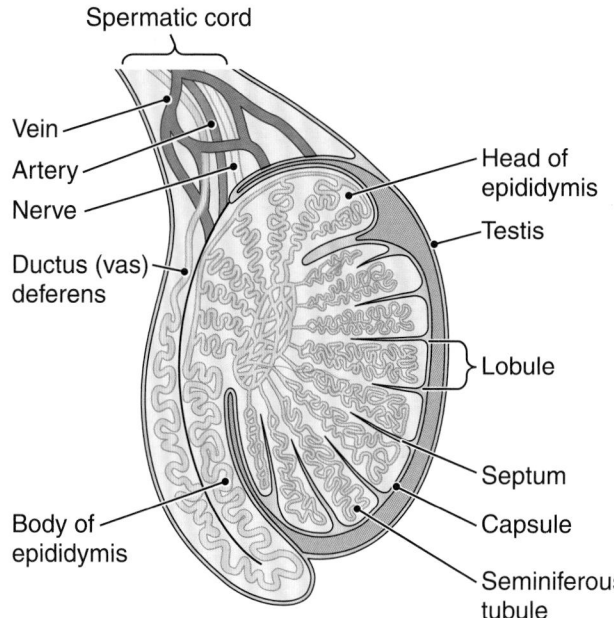

Figure 30-2 Structure of the testis.

The sperm cell has an oval head that is mostly a nucleus containing chromosomes. The acrosome (AK-ro-some), which covers the head like a cap, contains enzymes that help the sperm cell to penetrate the ovum. Whiplike movements of the tail propel the sperm through the female reproductive system to reach the ovum.

Accessory Structures

The system of ducts that transports the sperm cells from the body begins with the testis. Sperm cells are stored in a much-coiled tube on the surface of each testis called the *epididymis* (ep-ih-DID-ih-mus). They remain there until ejaculation propels them into a series of ducts that lead out of the body.

The first of these, the vas deferens (DEF-er-enz), is in the spermatic cord. The spermatic cord ascends through the inguinal (ING-gwih-nal) canal (the channel through which the testis descends into the scrotum) and into the abdominal cavity.

In the abdominal cavity, the vas deferens separates from the rest of the spermatic cord and curves behind the urinary bladder. A short continuation of the vas deferens, the ejaculatory duct, delivers the sperm cells to the urethra as it passes through the **prostate gland** below the bladder. Finally, the cells, now mixed with other secretions, travel in the urethra through the **penis** to be released.

Semen

Semen is a mixture of sperm cells and secretions from the seminal vesicles (VES-ih-kls), prostate gland, and bulbourethral (bul-bo-u-RE-thral) glands that is expelled from the body in an ejaculation. The secretions in semen serve several functions:

- Nourishing the sperm cells
- Transporting them
- Neutralizing the acidity of the male urethra and the female vaginal tract
- Lubricating the female reproductive tract during sexual intercourse
- Preventing infection by using antibacterial enzymes and antibodies

The Urethra and Penis

The male urethra transports both urine and semen. The ejection of semen is made possible by *erection*, the stiffening and enlargement of the penis.

The penis is made of spongy tissue that becomes engorged with blood to produce an erection. Ejaculation is initiated by reflex centers in the spinal cord that stimulate smooth muscle contraction in the prostate. This is followed by contraction of skeletal muscle in the pelvic floor, which provides the force needed for expulsion of semen. The penis and scrotum together make up the male external genitalia (jen-ih-TA-le-ah).

Common Diseases and Conditions of the Male Reproductive System

Several common diseases and conditions are unique to the male reproductive system. Prostate cancer and testicular cancer are two of these. Others include an enlarged prostate, orchitis, cryptorchidism, and epididymitis.

Enlarged Prostate

As men age, the prostate gland commonly enlarges, a condition known as *benign prostatic hyperplasia*, or BPH. The exact cause of BPH isn't known. Although not cancerous, the overgrown tissue can press on the urethra near the bladder and interfere with urination. If an obstruction occurs and is not corrected, urinary retention, infection, and other complications may follow.

Common symptoms of BPH are problems urinating and the need to urinate more frequently, especially at night. Depending on the severity of the symptoms, BPH may not need to be treated. Medications to relax the smooth muscle in the prostate and bladder neck can alleviate symptoms, while other drugs may slow the progress of the disorder. In advanced cases, the prostate may need to be removed.

Prostate Cancer

Prostate cancer is the second most common form of cancer in men in the U.S. It is typically a slowly growing form of cancer that most often affects older men. The cause isn't known. Like most cancers, prostate cancer has no symptoms in the early stages. Treatment options include radiation (usually by implanting radioactive seeds), hormones, chemotherapy, and surgery. Sometimes the decision is "watchful waiting," or monitoring without therapy.

Treatment for prostate cancer has improved in recent years. The number of deaths has been declining since the early 1990s.

Testicular Cancer

According to the National Cancer Institute, testicular cancer is the most common type of cancer among men ages 20 to 35. What causes this cancer isn't known. Symptoms include a painless lump or swelling in a testicle or a change in how the testicle feels. Most testicular cancer is found by the patient himself, either accidentally or by self-examination. Standard treatments are surgery to remove the testicle, radiation, and chemotherapy.

Orchitis

Orchitis is inflammation of one or both testicles. It may be caused by injury or infections, such as mumps. Treatment may include antibiotics (for bacterial infections), pain relievers, rest, ice packs, and elevation.

Cryptorchidism

Sometimes one or both testes will fail to descend into the scrotum by the time of birth. This condition is called *cryptorchidism*. It usually corrects itself within the first year of life. If not, it is usually corrected surgically to avoid sterility and an increased risk of cancer.

Epididymitis

Epididymitis is inflammation of the epididymis. Common causes are urinary tract infections and sexually transmitted infections. Symptoms include chills, fever, blood in the semen, and swelling or pain in the scrotum. Epididymitis can become chronic if not treated. The infection is managed with medications; symptoms are treated in various ways.

✔ **CHECK POINT**

1 What are the three functions of testosterone?

2 What is the order of the tubes and ducts through which sperm cells travel?

The Female Reproductive System

Like the male reproductive system, the female reproductive system (Figures 30-3 and 30-4, pages 511–512) has primary and accessory structures.

- The female gonads are the paired **ovaries** where the egg cells are formed.
- The accessory structures consist of the uterus, which holds and nourishes a developing infant; various passageways; the Bartholin glands; the external genitalia; and the breasts.

The Ovaries

The outer layer of an ovary is made of a single layer of epithelium. Beneath this layer, egg cells are produced. Each month during the reproductive years, several ova ripen, but usually only one is released.

An ovum ripens in a cluster of cells called an *ovarian follicle*. The follicle also secretes the hormone **estrogen**, which starts development of the **endometrium**, the uterine lining, in preparation for the fertilized egg. The hormone **progesterone** furthers this process. **Ovulation** occurs when an ovarian follicle ruptures and discharges a ripened egg from the ovary's surface. Any developing egg cells that aren't released degenerate.

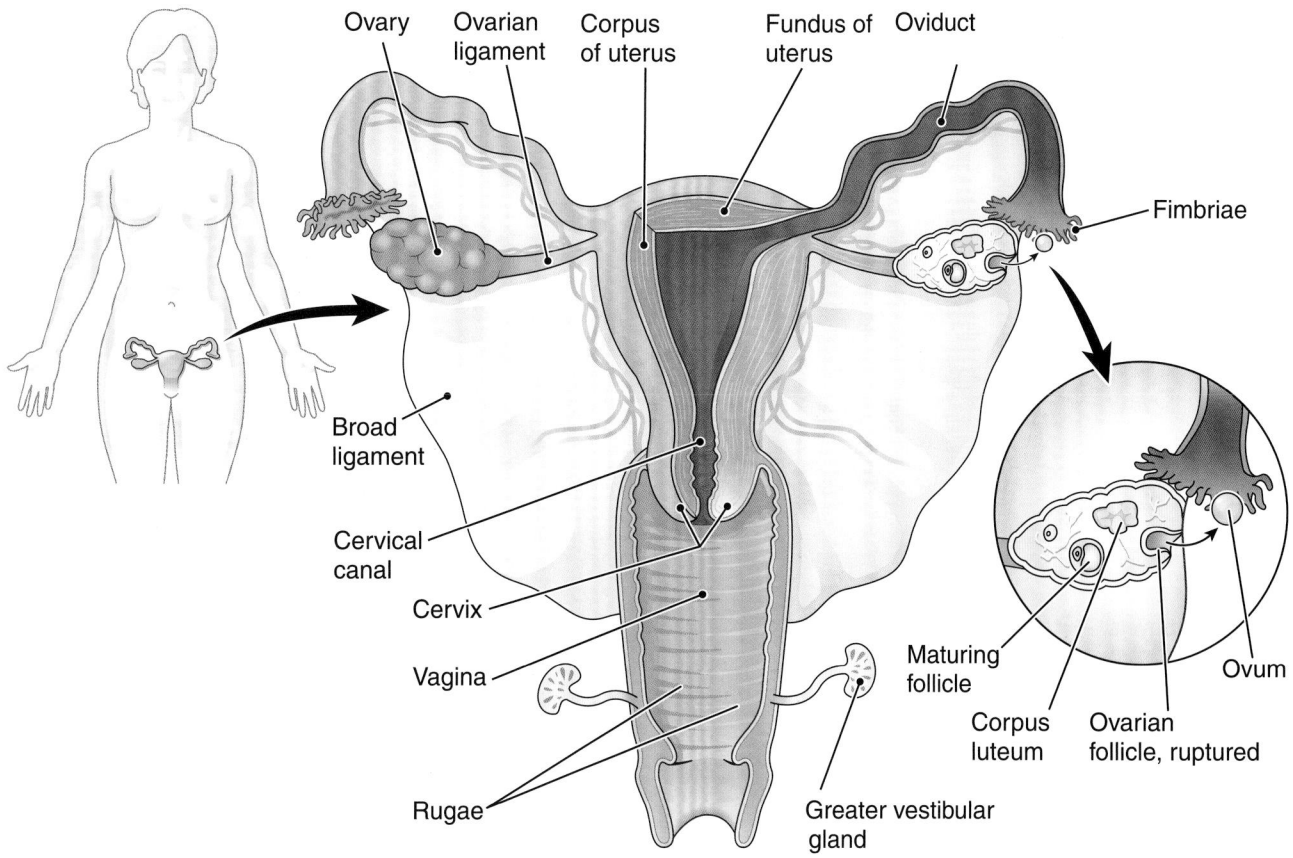

Figure 30-3 Female reproductive system.

If the ripened egg isn't fertilized, the endometrium sloughs off, and the egg is expelled from the body in the process of **menstruation**. The average menstrual cycle lasts 28 days, with ovulation occurring at about day 14.

Accessory Structures

The accessory structures in the female are the fallopian tubes, uterus, vagina, Bartholin glands, vulva, perineum, and breasts.

REPRODUCTIVE FACTS

- An average man produces about 525 billion sperm cells over a lifetime.
- Women are born with an average of 2 million egg follicles.
- The epididymis of a testis is 6 meters (20 feet) long.
- There are 125 million multiples (twins, triplets, etc.) in the world.
- Within 45 hours of birth, a baby knows his or her mother by smell.

The Fallopian Tubes. After its release, an egg cell is swept into the nearest of the two **fallopian tubes,** small, muscular structures that arch over the ovaries and lead to the uterus. If fertilization occurs, it usually takes place in a fallopian tube.

Unlike a sperm cell, an ovum can't move by itself. It depends on the sweeping action of cilia in the lining of the fallopian tubes and on peristalsis of the tube to be moved to the uterus, a process that takes about five days.

The Uterus. The **uterus** is the organ in which a fetus develops to maturity. It's a pear-shaped, muscular organ with an upper rounded fundus, a triangular cavity, and a lower narrow **cervix** that projects into the vagina. The uterine cavity changes shape and expands as a fetus develops. The endometrium, which lines the uterus, has a rich blood supply. It receives a fertilized ovum and becomes part of the placenta during pregnancy. Through the placenta, the developing fetus receives nutrients and oxygen from the mother's body.

The Vagina. The cervix leads to the **vagina,** the distal part of the birth canal, which opens to the outside of the body. The vagina has a wrinkled lining that permits enlargement so that childbirth usually doesn't tear the lining.

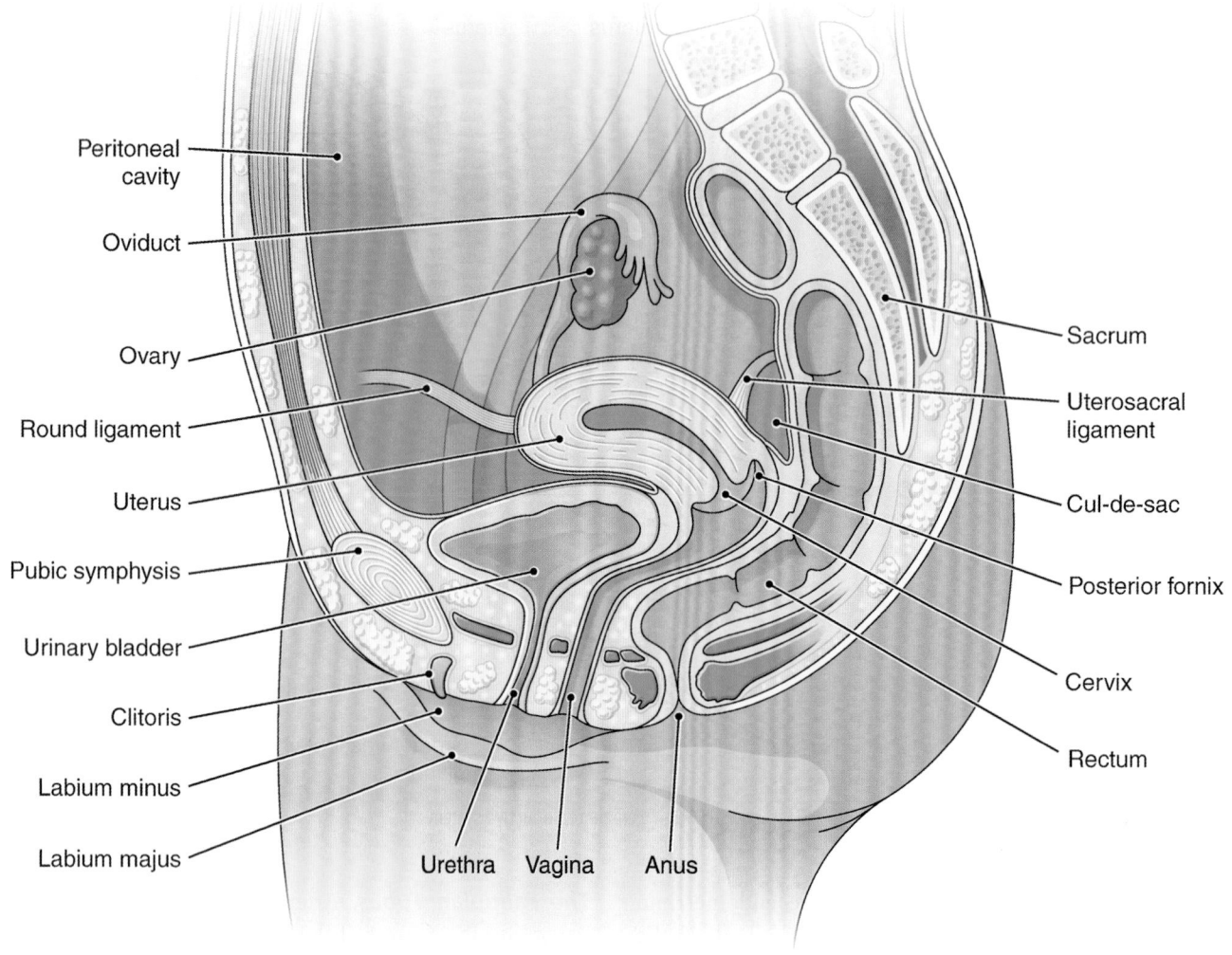

Peritoneal cavity

Oviduct

Ovary

Round ligament

Uterus

Pubic symphysis

Urinary bladder

Clitoris

Labium minus

Labium majus

Urethra Vagina Anus

Sacrum

Uterosacral ligament

Cul-de-sac

Posterior fornix

Cervix

Rectum

Figure 30-4   Female reproductive system (sagittal view).

The Bartholin Glands. Just superior and lateral to the vaginal opening are the two mucus-producing Bartholin glands. These glands provide lubrication during intercourse.

The Vulva and Perineum. The external genitalia of the female are the **vulva**, which includes two pairs of **labia**, or lips, and the clitoris, a small organ of great sensitivity. The pelvic floor is called the **perineum**.

The Breasts. The **breasts**, or mammary glands, are the organs of milk production. They are composed mainly of glandular tissue and fat. Milk production is functional in the female only after birth of a child.

The Menstrual Cycle

Reproductive activity in the female normally begins during puberty with the first menstrual period. In the U.S., the average age at which a female begins menstruating is 12. The **menstrual cycle** is the process that prepares a female's body for pregnancy. During the menstrual cycle, an egg ripens and is released, and the endometrium is prepared. If fertilization does not occur, the levels of estrogen and progesterone decrease and a bloody discharge known as menstrual flow, or *menses*, occurs. Bits of endometrium break away and accompany the blood flow during this period. The average duration of menstruation is two to six days. The first day of menstrual flow is the first day of the menstrual cycle.

Common Diseases and Conditions of the Female Reproductive System

Several common medical problems are unique to the female reproductive system. They include some cancers (cervical, uterine, or breast) and tumors (ovarian or fibroid). Pelvic inflammatory disease, endometriosis, menstrual disorders, and yeast infections are other commonly occurring problems.

HEALTH CARE SPECIALTIES

Gynecologist and Diagnostic Medical Sonographer

A gynecologist is a physician who cares for a woman's reproductive and sexual health. Many gynecologists are also obstetricians, who care for pregnant women and deliver babies.

A common test performed during pregnancy is an ultrasound to assess the fetus's condition. The health-care professional who performs this test is a diagnostic medical sonographer. This career is profiled in Chapter 22, "Diagnostic and Imaging Services."

Cervical Cancer

Almost all patients with cervical cancer have been infected with human papillomavirus (HPV), which is discussed later in the chapter. However, most people infected with the virus don't develop cancer, so the cause of cervical cancer isn't known. Risk factors include having multiple partners and smoking. Women can decrease the odds of developing this cancer by getting regular Pap smears. Pap tests look for abnormal cells that could become cancerous if not treated. Early cervical cancer usually doesn't produce symptoms. Later, the woman may notice abnormal vaginal bleeding and increased vaginal discharge. Cervical cancer is treated with surgery, chemotherapy, radiation therapy, or a combination of treatments.

Women can lower their risk of cervical cancer by being vaccinated and by using condoms. Two vaccines, available for females ages 9 to 26, have proven extremely effective in preventing persistent infections with the two HPVs that cause most cervical cancers. Research shows that condom use is also linked to lower rates of cervical cancer.

Ovarian Tumors

There are many different types of ovarian tumors. The most common arise from an ovary's surface. Ovarian tumors differ from cysts in that they are solid, not filled with fluid. The cause of ovarian cancer isn't known. Usually, it produces no distinct early symptoms. Possible signs include bloating, change in bowel habits, backache, urinary changes, abnormal bleeding, weight loss, and fatigue. Benign ovarian tumors may be watched or removed. Malignant tumors are treated with chemotherapy, radiation, and surgery.

Pelvic Inflammatory Disease

Pelvic inflammatory disease (PID) is the spread of infection from the reproductive organs into the pelvic cavity.

It is caused most often by the chlamydia or gonorrhea bacterium. PID is a serious disorder that can cause *septicemia* (bacteria in the blood, or blood poisoning) or shock. Women with PID may have no symptoms or symptoms that range from mild to severe. A common symptom is lower abdominal pain. PID can be cured with antibiotics.

Uterine Cancer

There are several types of uterine cancer. The most common begins in the tissue lining of the uterus and usually affects women after menopause. The cause isn't certain. Two risk factors for this type of cancer are obesity and hormone replacement therapy with estrogen only. The most common symptom is vaginal bleeding.

Uterine cancer often is detected early, when it is easiest to treat. At this stage, removing the uterus often eliminates the cancer.

Breast Cancer

Among women in the U.S., breast cancer is the most common type of cancer and is second only to lung cancer in causing cancer-related deaths. Breast cancer spreads readily through the lymph nodes and blood to other sites, such as the lung, liver, bones, and ovaries. Its causes aren't known. Symptoms include a lump or thick or firm tissue in or near a breast or under an arm; a change in the size or shape of the breast; nipple discharge; or changes to the nipple or breast skin. Risk factors for breast cancer include a family history of the disease; being Caucasian, or white; having a first menstrual period before age 12; and increased alcohol consumption. (The more alcohol a woman drinks, the greater the risk). Breast cancer also may occur in men, although it is much less common in men than in women.

The most common treatment for breast cancer is surgery. Other treatments include radiation therapy, hormone therapy, chemotherapy, and targeted therapy, which uses drugs that block the growth of breast cancer cells.

Mammography, which provides two-dimensional X-ray images of the breast, is the standard diagnostic procedure for breast cancer. The U.S. Preventive Services Task Force, a government-appointed panel of experts that reviews scientific data regarding the effectiveness of many preventive services, recommends that women ages 50 to 74 receive mammograms every other year. It also recommends that when women reach age 40, they consult with their doctors to determine when to start biannual mammograms. Some physicians also recommend monthly breast self-examination (BSE), in which women check for lumps and other changes in their own breasts.

Endometriosis

Endometriosis is a growth of the tissue that usually lines the uterus in abnormal locations. Common locations include the ovaries, behind the uterus, on the tissues that hold the uterus in place, and on the bowels or bladder. The results may include pain, painful or difficult menstruation, and infertility. The cause of endometriosis is unknown. One option for diagnosing endometriosis and removing the abnormal tissue is to conduct a *laparoscopy*, in which a tiny camera in a thin tube is inserted into the body through a small incision. In addition to detecting the endometrial tissue, the tube can be fitted with equipment that can be used to destroy the endometriosis.

Fibroid Tumors

Fibroid tumors are benign (noncancerous) tumors occurring in the wall of the uterus. What causes them isn't known. These tumors usually cause no symptoms and require no treatment. However, they may produce heavy menstrual bleeding and rectal or bladder pressure. Treatments include drugs to suppress hormones that stimulate fibroid growth, surgical removal of the tumor or uterus, and *uterine artery embolization* (UAE). In this procedure, a specially trained radiologist uses a catheter to inject particles into uterine arteries, blocking blood supply to the fibroid and causing it to shrink.

Menstrual Disorders

Menstrual disorders include flow that is too scanty (*oligomenorrhea*) or too heavy (*menorrhagia*); the absence of monthly periods (*amenorrhea*); and painful or difficult menstruation (*dysmenorrhea*). These disorders may be caused by hormone imbalances, systemic disorders, or uterine problems. They are most common in adolescence or near menopause. At other times, they often are related to life changes and emotional upset.

Premenstrual syndrome (PMS) is a group of symptoms that appear during the second half of the menstrual cycle. They include emotional changes, fatigue, bloating, headaches, and appetite changes. What causes PMS isn't clear. Symptoms may be relieved by hormone therapy, antidepressants, or antianxiety medications. Exercise, dietary control, rest, and relaxation strategies also may be helpful. Vitamin E supplements and avoiding caffeine may relieve breast tenderness. Drinking adequate water and limiting salt intake also help.

Yeast Infection

A *yeast infection* is an irritation of the vagina and surrounding area. The yeast that causes the infection normally lives in the vagina. When too much yeast grows, an infection can result. The most common symptom is extreme itchiness. Some symptoms are similar to those of sexually transmitted diseases (STDs), which are discussed below. Because untreated STDs can seriously affect one's health, people who suspect they have an infection should see a health care provider for a test. Yeast infections can be treated with prescription or over-the-counter medicines.

Effects of Aging

Both the male and the female reproductive systems change during aging. As men get older, production of testosterone gradually decreases. Women undergo **menopause**, the period in which menstruation gradually ceases. Menopause is caused by a normal decline in ovarian function.

Common Diseases and Conditions of Both the Male and Female Reproductive Systems

Both men and women may contract *sexually transmitted diseases*, or STDs. Chlamydia, gonorrhea, and syphilis are all STDs caused by bacteria. If they aren't treated, they can cause serious health problems. Several STDs are viral, including herpes and human papillomavirus. Like STDs, pubic lice can be spread by sexual contact. Infertility is another condition that can affect both men and women.

Chlamydia

Chlamydia is an infection of the reproductive and urinary tracts. It often has no symptoms. The CDC recommends yearly testing for all sexually active women age 25 and under, older women with risk factors, and pregnant women. Chlamydia can be cured with antibiotics. If not treated early, it may spread to the pelvis in women, causing PID.

Gonorrhea

Gonorrhea is an inflammation of the reproductive and urinary tracts. Most women infected with gonorrhea have no symptoms. Men may have no symptoms, or they may experience a burning sensation when urinating, discharge from the penis, or painful or swollen testicles. Gonorrhea usually can be cured with antibiotics. Like chlamydia, it may lead to PID in women if not treated early.

Syphilis

Syphilis can infect the genital area, lips, mouth, and anus. Many people infected with syphilis have no symptoms for many years. In its early stages, this disease can be cured easily with antibiotics. Left untreated, syphilis can have very grave consequences, including infection of a fetus during pregnancy, an increased risk of acquiring and transmitting HIV, damage to internal organs, gradual blindness, and dementia.

Genital Herpes

Genital herpes, another STD, is caused by the herpes simplex viruses, usually Type 2. Most people infected with this virus experience no symptoms. Complications range from mild to severe. Herpes can cause fatal infections of newborns; it may be a risk factor in cervical cancer; and it can make people more susceptible to HIV infection. (To learn about that infection, see Chapter 28, "Circulation and Body Defense.") Herpes cannot be cured, but antiviral medications can ease symptoms, shorten outbreaks, reduce recurrences, and lessen the chance of transmitting the disease to a partner.

Human Papillomavirus (HPV)

Human papillomavirus (HPV) infection is an STD that can be caused by more than 40 different strains of the HPV virus. In most people, an infection produces no symptoms, and in 90 percent of cases, the immune system destroys the virus. Some strains of HPV can cause genital warts, which may go away on their own. The warts can

also be treated with medication, or a doctor can remove them. As discussed earlier in the chapter, two strains of HPV can cause cervical cancer and other types of cancer. A vaccine against these strains is available for girls and young women and is recommended by the CDC.

Pubic Lice

Pubic lice are very small insects with a crablike appearance that feed on human blood. They're usually found attached to pubic hair and are spread by sexual contact. Intense itching is a common symptom. Infestations can be treated with prescription or over-the-counter medications.

Infertility

Infertility is usually defined as not being able to become pregnant after a year of trying. About a third of the time, the problem is due to women; a third of the time to men; and a third due to both partners or an unknown cause. The causes of infertility may be hereditary, hormonal, disease-related, or the result of exposure to chemical or physical agents. The most common causes are STDs. Infertility may be treated with medicine, surgery, *artificial insemination* (injecting sperm into a woman's reproductive tract), and assisted reproductive technologies. (See "Newsreel: Assisted Reproductive Technologies.").

NEWSREEL

Assisted Reproductive Technologies

About 10 to 15 percent of couples who want children are unable to conceive or to sustain a pregnancy. The American Society for Reproductive Medicine reports that in 85 to 90 percent of these cases, infertility can be treated with surgery or drug therapy. But in a small percentage (less than 3 percent), people turn to assisted reproductive technologies for help.

In vitro fertilization (IVF) is the fertilization of an ovum in a laboratory dish followed by implantation in the uterus. It is often used when a woman's fallopian tubes are blocked or when a man has a low sperm count. The woman is given hormones so that she'll produce more than the usual one egg per month. The eggs are withdrawn with a needle and placed in the dish. Sperm from the father are added, and soon they begin to penetrate the eggs and fertilize them. Some of the fertilized eggs are placed in the uterus, bypassing the fallopian tubes.

A variation of IVF is *gamete intrafallopian transfer* (GIFT), used when the woman has at least one normal fallopian tube and the man has an adequate sperm count. The egg and sperm are placed in the fallopian tube using a catheter, so fertilization occurs inside the woman.

Zygote intrafallopian transfer (ZIFT) combines features of both IVF and GIFT. Fertilization takes place in a laboratory dish. Then the fertilized egg is inserted into the fallopian tube.

Sometimes the shell of the embryo is thick, making it difficult for the embryo to implant in the lining of the uterus. In a process called *assisted hatching*, the shell is thinned using various techniques, the most common of which is a diluted acid solution.

Intracytoplasmic sperm injection (ICSI) involves injecting a single sperm directly into an egg in a laboratory dish.

In related procedures, sperm are extracted from different parts of a man's reproductive tract, such as the epididymis or testis. All these procedures are used in conjunction with IVF.

✓ CHECK POINT

3 Where are the female ova formed?

4 What is the process of releasing an egg cell from an ovary called?

GROWTH AND DEVELOPMENT

Growth and development occur throughout the life span. *Growth* is an increase in body size or changes in body cell structure, function, and complexity. **Development** is an orderly pattern of changes in structure, thoughts, feelings, or behaviors resulting from maturation, life experiences, and learning. Growth and development result from the interrelated effects of heredity and environment.

Factors Influencing Growth and Development

Many factors influence both growth and development. An individual's growth and development might be facilitated or delayed by these factors:

- Heredity
- Prenatal factors, like the mother's age or health during pregnancy
- Caregiver factors, like mental illness
- Individual differences, such as vision and hearing impairments
- Health or illness
- Environment, including culture
- Nutrition

Because of a variety of factors and the complex ways in which they interact, each person's growth and development is unique within general patterns.

Stages of Growth and Development

Human development takes place in two overall periods, childhood and adulthood, each of which has several specific stages. Childhood includes these stages: **embryo** (the developing offspring during the first 8 weeks of life), **fetus** (the developing offspring from the beginning of the third month until birth), *neonate* (the child from birth to 28 days), infant, toddler, preschooler, school-aged child, and adolescent. The three remaining stages of growth and development are young adult, middle-aged adult, and older adult.

Embryo and Fetus

Pregnancy begins with fertilization of an ovum and ends with delivery of the fetus. During this approximately 38-week period of development, known as **gestation**, all fetal tissues develop from a single fertilized egg. Along the way, many changes occur. During the two stages of embryo and fetus, the following changes take place:

- All body organ systems grow and develop.
- By birth, the average infant weighs 7.5 pounds and is 20 inches long.

📷 ZOOM IN

Genes, Environment, and Individual Differences

We're accustomed to being told that we look like someone in our family—that we have our grandmother's hair, for example, or our mother's eyes. Heredity determines many of a person's physical characteristics, and it influences many others, such as weight, body build, life span, and susceptibility to disease. But what about nonphysical traits? Can a person inherit a tendency toward calmness or an optimistic attitude, for instance?

A good way to study questions like these is to look at twins. *Identical twins* develop from a single egg cell fertilized by a single sperm cell that splits after fertilization to produce two distinct but genetically identical embryos. If heredity determined everything about us, identical twins would be the same in every way. In fact, identical twins have many similarities, but they're also different. They have different personalities and different likes and dislikes.

In an ongoing landmark project, researchers at the University of Minnesota have studied more than 10,000 twins. They've looked at identical twins, *fraternal twins* (twins that develop from different eggs fertilized by different sperm), and *virtual twins*—children the same age, reared in the same household, but not sharing genetic similarities, such as a natural and an adopted child.

Researchers have concluded that identical twins are much more alike than fraternal twins, even when they don't grow up together. Fraternal twins are much more alike than virtual twins. This similarity holds true for a wide range of characteristics, including personality traits like being introverted or extroverted and decision making.

Genetics may influence more of our personality and behavior than we might think, but environment plays an important part, too. For example, we inherit a potential for a given size, but our actual size is also influenced by nutrition, development, and general health. Scientists are still discovering how intimately related heredity and environment—nature and nurture—can be.

Neonate

At birth, the neonate must adapt to extrauterine life (life outside the uterus) through several significant physiologic adjustments. The most important occur in the respiratory and circulatory systems as the neonate begins breathing and becomes independent of the umbilical cord.

- The neonate displays certain reflexes, including sucking, swallowing, blinking, sneezing, and yawning.
- Body temperature responds quickly to environmental temperature.
- Senses are used to respond to the environment, see color and form, hear and turn toward sound, smell and taste, and feel touch and pain.
- Stool and urine are eliminated from the body.
- Both an active crying state and a quiet alert state are exhibited.

Infant

The infant stage lasts from 1 month to 1 year. Growth and development are extremely rapid at this stage.

- The brain grows to about half the adult size, and the heart doubles in weight.
- Height increases by 50 percent, and birth weight usually triples.
- At 4 to 6 months, teething begins.
- The infant learns to crawl, walk, and use building blocks and attempts to feed himself or herself.
- By 12 months of age, the infant can convey wishes through a few key words.
- Attachments and bonds to people are formed.
- The infant begins to discover his or her environment and to learn how to control it through play. Social play, like rolling a ball to someone, is motivated by a desire for pleasure and relationships with others. Cognitive play, like assembling a puzzle, is motivated by the desire to learn.

Toddler

From 1 to 3 years of age, a child is considered a toddler. Growth and development continue steadily but more slowly than in infancy.

- The brain grows rapidly.
- The arms and legs grow, and so do the muscles.
- The toddler learns to pick up small objects, walk forward and backward, run, kick, climb stairs, ride a tricycle, drink from a cup, use a spoon, turn pages, and draw stick people.
- By 2½ to 3 years of age, a toddler has bladder control during the day and sometimes during the night.
- By age 2, the toddler begins to use short sentences.
- The toddler has a sense of self and of gender identity.
- Increased independence from the mother begins.

Preschool Child

This stage is from 3 to 6. Growth and development are slower but still steady.

- By age 6, the head is close to adult size.
- The body is less chubby and becomes leaner and more coordinated.
- Baby teeth begin to fall out and are replaced by permanent teeth.
- The preschool child learns to skip, throw and catch a ball, copy figures, and print.
- Socialization with other children increases.
- Curiosity results in frequent questions and improved reasoning ability.

School-Aged Child

School-aged children, from 6 to 12 years, are typically sturdy and strong. Physical growth is relatively slow but continues steadily.

- The brain reaches 90 to 95 percent of adult size, and the nervous system is almost completely matured.
- Height increases by 2 to 3 inches, and weight by 5 to 7 pounds, per year.
- By age 12, a child has nearly all permanent teeth.
- The school-aged child thinks logically and uses inductive reasoning to solve new problems.
- Peer relationships become the major means of determining status, skill, and likeability.

Adolescent

Adolescence begins with puberty. It generally extends from 12 to 18 years of age, but this time period varies greatly with the individual. Adolescence is a period of rapid growth and development. Changes in the adolescent's body transform him or her in appearance from a child to an adult.

- The feet, hands, arms, and legs grow rapidly, accompanied by an increase in muscle mass.
- The genital organs mature, and secondary sex characteristics emerge, like breast development and menstruation in girls and facial hair growth and voice changes in boys.
- *Puberty* (the time when a person becomes able to reproduce) usually begins at 9 to 13 years in girls, with menstruation usually starting between 10 and 14. In boys, puberty usually begins at 11 to 14 years.

- The adolescent uses deductive, reflective, and hypothetical reasoning and abstract concepts.
- A characteristic of this stage is self-centeredness. Imaginary audiences and daydreaming are common.

Young Adult

Early adulthood extends from age 18 to about age 40. Full growth and development is complete by the mid-20s, and most body systems are functioning at maximum levels. Changes in weight and muscle mass result mostly from diet and exercise. As the young adult years progress, hair begins to thin and turn gray, and skin develops wrinkles. Young adults, compared to adolescents, are more creative in thought, more objective and realistic, and less self-centered. Major developments are choosing a vocation and establishing a family.

Middle-Aged Adult

Middle adulthood spans the ages of 40 to 65. The adult usually enters this phase of life functioning at near-peak efficiency. Middle adulthood is a period of gradual and individualized change. Some physical changes are a continuation of changes that began at the end of the young adult period. Women undergo menopause. Other changes, such as a gradual loss of hearing, described in the "Effects of Aging" sections of Chapters 25–29, generally start in middle age.

The middle adult years are often a time of increased personal freedom, economic stability, and social relationships. Other characteristic changes at this stage are increased responsibility and an awareness of one's own mortality.

Older Adult

Older adulthood usually begins at about age 65. Normal aging involves a decline in various functions, which is usually gradual unless it is impacted by illness. The "Effects of Aging" discussions in this and earlier chapters describe such changes. An older adult who has a strong sense of self-identity and who has successfully met challenges earlier in life will probably continue to do so. However, depending on the person's outlook on life and past ability to cope, events such as retirement, loss of health or income, and isolation can be devastating.

Death and Dying

Elisabeth Kübler-Ross studied people's emotional responses to death and dying in depth, and health care providers have used her findings extensively. Kübler-Ross identified these five stages of grief that people go through when they learn that they are going to die:

1. **Denial.** The person denies that he or she will die and may isolate himself or herself from reality. The person may think the physician made a mistake with the diagnosis.
2. **Anger.** The person expresses rage and hostility and adopts a "why me?" attitude.
3. **Bargaining.** The person tries to barter for more time: "If I can just make it to my son's graduation, I'll be satisfied."
4. **Depression.** The person goes through a period of grief before death, often characterized by crying and not speaking much.
5. **Acceptance.** When this stage is reached, the person feels tranquil. He or she has accepted death and is prepared to die.

The stages may overlap. In addition, any stage may last from as little as a few hours to as long as months. The process varies from person to person.

✔ CHECK POINT

5 What are the stages of childhood?

6 What are the major developments of the young adult years?

Theories of Development

Human development and behavior have been studied from many different perspectives. Psychologists and other experts have developed theories that explain human responses that might be expected at certain ages.

Erik Erikson

Psychologist Erik Erikson believed that development is a continuous process made up of distinct stages. Each stage is characterized by the achievement (or failure to achieve) certain developmental goals. The goals are affected by one's social environment and significant others. Erickson's eight stages are outlined in Table 30-1.

Robert J. Havighurst

Psychologist Robert J. Havighurst believed that living and growing are based on learning and that a person must learn continuously to adjust to changing societal conditions. He described learned behaviors as developmental tasks that occur at certain periods in life. Table 30-2 lists two examples of developmental tasks identified by Havighurst for each age group.

Table 30-1 Erikson's Eight Stages of Development

Stage	Developmental Task or Crisis	Indicators of Positive or Negative Resolution
Infancy	Trust vs. Mistrust	Learns to rely on caregivers to meet basic needs. Mistrust results from inconsistent, inadequate, or unsafe care.
Toddler	Autonomy vs. Shame and Doubt	Gains independence through encouragement from caregivers. If caregivers are overprotective or have expectations that are too high, shame and doubt might develop.
Preschool	Initiative vs. Guilt	Actively seeks out new experiences and explores the how and why of activities. If the child is restricted or reprimanded for seeking new experiences and learning, guilt might result, and he or she might hesitate to attempt more challenging skills.
School-Aged Child	Industry vs. Inferiority	Gains pleasure from finishing projects and being recognized for accomplishments. If the child is not accepted by peers or cannot meet parental expectations, feelings of inferiority and lack of self-worth might develop.
Adolescence	Identity vs. Role Confusion	Acquires a sense of self and decides what direction to take in life. Role confusion occurs when the adolescent is unable to establish identity and a sense of direction.
Young Adulthood	Intimacy vs. Isolation	Unites self-identity with identities of friends and makes commitments to others. Fear of such commitments results in isolation and loneliness.
Middle Adulthood	Generativity vs. Stagnation	Wants to contribute to the world. If this task is not met, stagnation might result. The person might become self-absorbed or regress to an earlier level of coping.
Later Adulthood	Ego Integrity vs. Despair	Thinking about life events provides a sense of fulfillment and purpose. If one believes that one's life has been a series of failures or missed directions, despair might prevail.

Table 30-2 Havighurst's Developmental Tasks

Age	Examples of Developmental Tasks
Infancy and Early Childhood	• Learning to walk and talk • Learning to relate emotionally to parents, siblings, and other people
Middle Childhood	• Learning to get along with children who are the same age • Developing basic skills in reading, writing, and mathematics
Adolescence	• Achieving a masculine or feminine gender role • Achieving emotional independence from parents or other adults
Young Adulthood	• Starting a family and rearing children • Getting started in an occupation
Middle Adulthood	• Accepting and adjusting to physical changes • Attaining and maintaining satisfactory occupational performance
Later Maturity	• Adjusting to decreasing physical strength and health • Adjusting to retirement and reduced income

Table 30-3 Freud's Stages of Development

Stage	Description
Oral (0–18 months)	The mouth (eating, biting, chewing, and sucking) is the main source of pleasure and exploration. The greatest need is security. Weaning causes a major conflict.
Anal (18 months– 3 years)	Toilet training is an important issue, requiring delayed gratification.
Phallic (3–7 years)	The child has increased interest in gender differences. There is conflict and resolution of that conflict with the parent of the same sex, based on feelings of sexual possessiveness for the parent of the opposite sex. Curiosity about the genital organs and masturbation increase.
Latency (7–12 years)	In this stage, the child increasingly identifies with the parent of the same sex, which prepares him or her for adult roles and relationships.
Genital (12–20 years)	Sexual interest can be expressed in overt sexual relationships. Sexual pressures and conflicts typically cause turmoil as the adolescent makes adjustments in relationships.

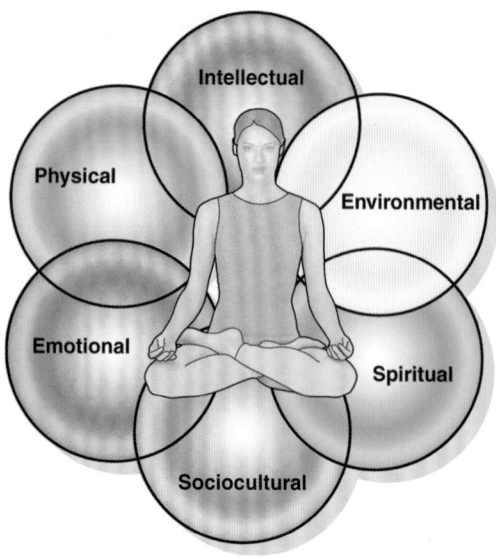

Figure 30-5   Maslow's hierarchy of basic human needs.

Sigmund Freud

Freud's theory emphasizes the effect of instinctual human drives on behavior. Freud identified the underlying stimulus for human behavior as sexuality, which he called libido. *Libido* is defined as general pleasure-seeking instincts rather than purely genital gratification. Freud described a series of developmental stages, based on sexual motivation, through which all people must pass. Freud's theory is outlined in Table 30-3.

Maslow's Hierarchy of Basic Human Needs

Psychologist Abraham Maslow developed a hierarchy of basic human needs (Figure 30-5). Certain needs are more basic than others and must be met, at least minimally, before other needs can be considered. The five levels of needs are as follows:

Level 1: Physiologic needs. Examples of these needs are oxygen, water, food, elimination, sexuality, and physical activity. They must be met, at least minimally, to maintain life. Because physiologic needs are the most basic and the most essential to life, they have the highest priority.

Level 2: Safety and security needs. Safety and security needs come next. These needs are both physical and emotional. Physical safety and security means being protected from potential or actual harm. Emotional safety and security involves trusting others and being free of fear, anxiety, and apprehension.

Level 3: Love and belonging needs. All humans have a basic need for love and belonging. These needs are the next priority. They include the understanding and acceptance of others in both giving and receiving love and the feeling of belonging to families, peers, friends, a neighborhood, and a community.

Level 4: Self-esteem needs. The next priority is self-esteem needs, which include the need to feel good about oneself, to feel pride and a sense of accomplishment, and to believe that others also respect and appreciate one's accomplishments.

Level 5: Self-actualization needs. The highest level of Maslow's hierarchy is self-actualization needs, which include the need for individuals to reach their full potential through development of their unique capabilities.

✔ **CHECK POINT**

7 What are the eight developmental tasks or crises in Erik Erikson's theory of development?

8 What are the five levels in Maslow's hierarchy of basic human needs?

Don't forget to visit thePoint companion website for additional study resources!

CHAPTER HIGHLIGHTS

- Males and females have cells designed specifically for sexual reproduction: spermatozoa (sperm cells) and ova (egg cells).
- The male reproductive system consists of the testes and secondary structures (ducts that transport sperm cells and various exocrine glands). The female reproductive system consists of the ovaries and accessory structures (the fallopian tubes, uterus, vagina, Bartholin glands, vulva, perineum, and breasts).
- As men age, the production of testosterone gradually decreases. Common diseases and conditions of the male reproductive system include an enlarged prostate, prostate cancer, testicular cancer, orchitis, cryptorchidism, and epididymitis.
- As women age, they undergo menopause. Common diseases and conditions of the female reproductive system include cervical cancer, ovarian tumors, pelvic inflammatory disease, uterine cancer, breast cancer, endometriosis, fibroid tumors, menstrual disorders, and yeast infections.
- Health care specialties involving the female reproductive system include gynecologist and diagnostic medical sonographer.
- Common diseases and conditions of both the male and female reproductive systems include chlamydia, gonorrhea, syphilis, human papillomavirus, pubic lice, and infertility.
- Growth and development occur throughout life. They may be facilitated or delayed by heredity, prenatal factors, individual differences, caregiver factors, environment, and nutrition. Other factors that influence growth and development are health or illness and culture. Because of these interdependent factors, each person's growth and development are individual.
- Developmental theories attempt to explain human responses that might be expected at certain ages during life. Three important theories of human development were established by Erik Erikson, Robert Havighurst, and Sigmund Freud. Elisabeth Kübler-Ross identified five stages of grief, and Abraham Maslow developed a hierarchy of basic human needs.

REVIEW QUESTIONS

Matching

1. _____ This stage usually involves a gradual decline of function.
2. _____ At this stage, most body systems function at maximum levels.
3. _____ Menopause occurs at this stage.
4. _____ At this stage, the brain reaches 90 to 95 percent of adult size.
5. _____ At this stage, genital organs mature, and secondary sex characteristics develop.

   a. school-aged child **b.** adolescent **c.** young adult **d.** middle-aged adult **e.** older adult

Multiple Choice

6. The male gonads are the
   - **a.** exocrine glands
   - **b.** spermatozoa
   - **c.** testes
   - **d.** seminal vesicles

7. Which health-care professional performs ultrasound scans to assess a fetus's condition?
   a. diagnostic medical sonographer
   b. obstetrician
   c. radiologist
   d. clinical laboratory technologist

8. Which is a primary organ of the female reproductive system?
   a. perineum
   b. vagina
   c. breast
   d. ovary

9. Which of the following is NOT a sexually transmitted disease?
   a. chlamydia
   b. yeast infection
   c. genital herpes
   d. HPV infection

10. Which of the following is a factor that might facilitate or delay growth and development?
    a. heredity
    b. environment
    c. nutrition
    d. all of the above

Completion

11. The health-care specialist who is responsible for a woman's reproductive and sexual health is a/an _____.

12. The main male sex hormone is _____.

13. The process of releasing an ovum from the ovary is called _____.

14. _____ is the time when the ability to reproduce begins.

15. _____ is an orderly pattern of changes in structure, thoughts, feelings, or behaviors resulting from maturation, experiences, and learning.

Short Answer

16. Describe the effects of aging on the male and female reproductive systems.

_____

_____

17. In the U.S., what is the most common type of cancer among men ages 20 to 35? What is the second most common type of cancer among all men in the U.S.? What is the most common type of cancer among women in the U.S.?

_____

_____

18. Compare and contrast Erikson's and Havighurst's theories of development at the level of young adulthood. Do you agree or disagree with their concepts? Explain your views.

_____

_____

19. Describe the five stages of grief, according to Elisabeth Kübler-Ross.

_____

_____

20. Describe the five levels in Maslow's hierarchy of basic human needs.

_____

_____

INVESTIGATE IT

1. Skin, eye, and hair color are examples of hereditary traits. What are some others? Use the Internet to find five to ten additional examples of hereditary traits. (Use the search phrase *hereditary traits*.) Make a list of these traits. Write a paragraph that explains what traits are and how they are inherited. Write another paragraph that identifies the traits you think you have inherited and from whom.

2. In 2003, scientists completed the mapping of the human genome. What are some implications for health care of genome research and discoveries? Read a news article on one of the following topics or a related topic:
    *   The Human Genome Project
    *   Epigenetics
    *   Individual genetic profiles
    *   Genetic testing
    *   Use of genetic information by insurance companies or others
    *   Privacy and confidentiality of genetic information
    *   Selection of embryos based on desirable genetic characteristics

3. Identify significant developmental changes for five of your family members or friends who are at different ages across the life span. (For example, you might note that your preschool nephew is interacting increasingly with other children.)

4. Think of a health-care profession that interests you and that deals with patients of varying ages. What differences could you expect to encounter when working with adults and children as patients because of developmental differences?

RECOMMENDED READING

Berk, L. *Development Through the Life Span*, 4th ed. Boston: Allyn and Bacon, 2007.

Genetic Science Learning Center. Heredity and Traits. Last updated December 4, 2009. Available at: http://learn.genetics.utah.edu/content/begin/traits.

MSNBC. The Menstrual Cycle. Available at: http://msnbcmedia.msn.com/i/msnbc/Components/Interactives/Health/WomensHealth/zFlashAssets/menstrual_cycle_dw2%5B1%5D.swf.

MyHealthScore.Com. Female Reproductive System. Human Anatomy Online. Available at: http://www.innerbody.com/image/repfov.html.

MyHealthScore.Com. Male Reproductive System. Human Anatomy Online. Available at: http://www.innerbody.com/image/repmov.html.

NOVA. Life's Greatest Miracle. Available at: http://www.pbs.org/wgbh/nova/miracle/program.html.

WebMD. Conception Slideshow: From Egg to Embryo. Available at: http://www.webmd.com/baby/slideshow-conception.

Index

Note: Page numbers followed by *f* indicate figures; those followed by a *t* indicate tables and those followed by a *b* indicate a box.